CASES AND MATERIALS

EVIDENCE

NINTH EDITION

by

JACK B. WEINSTEIN
Adjunct Professor of Law
Columbia University

JOHN H. MANSFIELD
John H. Watson, Jr. Professor of Law
Harvard University

NORMAN ABRAMS
Vice Chancellor, Academic Personnel and Professor of Law
University of California, Los Angeles

MARGARET A. BERGER
Suzanne J. and Norman Miles Professor of Law
Brooklyn Law School

NEW YORK, NEW YORK
FOUNDATION PRESS
1997

COPYRIGHT © 1934, 1942, 1951, 1957, 1965, 1973, 1983, 1988 FOUNDATION PRESS

COPYRIGHT © 1997 By FOUNDATION PRESS
         395 Hudson Street
         New York, NY 10014
         Phone Toll Free 1–877–888–1330
         Fax (212) 367–6799
         fdpress.com

ISBN 1–56662–474–6

TEXT IS PRINTED ON 10% POST
CONSUMER RECYCLED PAPER

3rd Reprint—2003

PREFACE

I

This edition of our casebook traces its lineage back to James Bradley Thayer's Select Cases on Evidence at the Common Law, with notes, published in 1892. In 1900 came the second edition of his casebook, which had such vitality that it was still used by teachers in 1924–1925 and later.

In 1925 Professor John M. Maguire, by special arrangement with the Thayer family, published a revision of the 1900 casebook. In 1934 Professor Edmund M. Morgan, together with Maguire, took over leadership of the series with what was referred to as the first edition; they also were authors of the second and third editions. The fourth edition was by Morgan, Maguire and Jack B. Weinstein. The fifth and sixth were by Maguire, Weinstein, James H. Chadbourn and John H. Mansfield. The seventh and eighth editions were by the present authors. Since Morgan, Maguire and Chadbourn are deceased, we have not placed their names on the title page together with Thayer's. Responsibility for this edition is wholly our own.

II

The present edition is a thorough revision and updating of the 1988 edition. It takes into account important intervening changes in the law by statute, judicial decision and, most important, by application of the Federal Rules of Evidence and variations in the states. A glance at almost any section of this volume will reveal a wealth of new cases and secondary materials and notes that have been expanded and enriched.

The ninth edition has not been shortened for a number of reasons. In some instances a more extended discussion is required because the cases and analyses have grown quite complex, reflecting the greater complexity of scientific, economic, social and political underpinnings of litigation. The commercial advantages of a simple, short book have not convinced us that the richness of the subject and related procedural, substantive, tactical, psychological and sociological aspects should be slighted. Instructor and student are left free to explore in detail those matters of most concern to them. The book will accommodate a three to six point course and advanced seminar and serve as a basic treatise for the student turned practitioner.

Experience with the Federal Rules, and many cases construing them, have clarified some of the issues of concern in the last edition. This has permitted, for example, a reduction of the discussion of the best evidence rule.

Credibility issues, especially with respect to bad acts and convictions, remain as difficult as ever under the Federal Rules, as does substantive use of other crimes evidence. Privileges, too, constitute a constantly changing phenomenon, requiring longer treatment.

We have set the notes in the same size type as the main cases and materials. We have found in the past that some students tended to skip important notes because of the physical difficulty in reading them.

We have avoided extensive cutting of some cases, particularly those involving Supreme Court decisions in such areas as burdens of proof, presumptions and constitutional rights, in order to avoid oversimplifying the problem and so that the student might better see the complexities and the inter–relationships of the cases. We have indicated omissions in text as well as citations; the student will better appreciate the fact that the entire case has not been reproduced so that if he or she wishes to study the matter in more detail, the original publication should be checked.

It is expected that the teacher will require the student to obtain a statutory and rule supplement, such as the one by the editors of this volume, which contains the California and federal codifications, the Uniform Rules, and excerpts from the Model Rules of Professional Conduct. This combination of casebook and supplementary pamphlet has the following advantages: 1) It enables the student to refer to the provisions without the inconvenience of constantly turning to the back of the book to consult an appendix. 2) Each of these important bodies of rules should be studied as a whole, for the purpose of understanding its organization and connecting principles; having the codification in one place, as well as the California Code, the Federal Rules and the Uniform Rules guides the student to interesting comparisons and by this means to an throughout the book, facilitates such study. 3) Juxtaposing the California Code helps understanding of basic policy conflicts. Including in the course some examination of the American Bar Association's Model Rules of Professional Conduct allows attention to professional issues: Ethics, procedure and substance frequently meet in the field of evidence.

III

The organization of topics in the casebook has been changed in certain respects from the 1988 edition. Expert testimony, formerly dealt with in the chapter on Testimonial Evidence, has been given a chapter of its own and placed after discussion of the hearsay rule and circumstantial evidence. This change has been made because of the ever–increasing importance of the subject and the need for a thorough understanding of other issues before it is tackled. In addition, past recollection recorded and rehabilitation by prior consistent statement have been moved from their former location, also in the chapter on Testimonial Evidence, to the chapter on Hearsay, where they can be more carefully evaluated. Apart from these changes, the organization of topics in the casebook is basically that of the 1988 edition. No clear case has been made for a pedagogically sounder arrangement. Although the present organization suits the tastes and teaching techniques of the editors as well as any could, many instructors will find it desirable to use the materials in accordance with a teaching sequence of their own.

The trends reflected in the eighth edition have been carried forward into the ninth. Only the highlights are mentioned here.

Chapter One collects a variety of materials dealing with relevancy. This material is basic to an understanding of any case since it provides the framework of any rational system of proof. The method of diagramming reflected in the analysis of the Adamson case in this first chapter can readily be utilized in connection with many other cases in the book. The chapter also stresses problems of probability that underlie trials. Additional references are made to the interesting research in how people think and decide issues of fact. The discussion of spoliation, using the term in its most general sense, is important since so much of inference and evaluation of credibility depends upon what the trier expects the litigant to produce. Negative inferences based on disbelief of testimony have also been retained in this first chapter since many cases require an understanding of this concept. Material on the basis for appealability is also developed in this Chapter.

In these introductory Chapter One materials, we have included discussion of statistical and mathematical issues that underlie much modern litigation. Discussion of probability and mathematics requires a close analysis of how the trier thinks and integrates his or her own experience, information derived from experts, detailed information on the events in question and a variety of databases.

In Chapter Three on Testimonial Evidence, we have retained the introductory materials on the nature and weakness of testimonial proof. Psychological research on this subject has been canvassed and a distillation of the results, together with illustrative extracts, presented in a way that it is hoped will make clear the usefulness and the limits on usefulness of this sort of research for the law. The relation between the results of this research and the Supreme Court's Lineup decisions is discussed, as well as the admissibility of expert evidence relating to the reliability of eyewitness testimony.

In regard to the competency of witnesses, new material has been added on the perplexing requirement of "personal knowledge" (Fed.R.Evid. 602). Likewise a more ample discussion of accrediting witnesses is included, a matter that has only gradually emerged as a topic needing discussion. Most important, the subject of character evidence bearing on witness credibility, whether in the form of evidence of convictions, bad acts, reputation or opinion, is dealt with more fully than in the prior edition in an effort to clarify the nature of this evidence.

A criminal defendant's right to present evidence, in particular testimonial evidence, under the Compulsory Process Clause of the Sixth Amendment is given attention at the beginning of the section on the competency of witnesses. Decisions attempting to deal with the conflict between this right and exclusionary rules and privileges are discussed. At the beginning of the section on cross–examination, the focus is on the criminal defendant's right under the Confrontation Clause to test the evidence introduced against him, and note is taken of the problem presented by the relation between the Compulsory Process and Confrontation Clauses. The Confrontation Clause is further examined in the chapter on Hearsay.

The section on Preparation of Witnesses is enlarged so as to provide the student with the necessary understanding of the ethical considerations involved. This is in accord with the increased concern of the profession with these matters.

Aside from obvious updating, an introduction has been added to the Hearsay chapter that explores the policies underlying the hearsay doctrine and provides a guide to the materials that follow. Material has been added on empirical studies that analyze how the courts are handling some of the exceptions, and a new section is devoted to the proposed amendment that would admit statements by a declarant whose unavailability as a witness was procured by the defendant. Most of the constitutional materials are integrated with the specific hearsay exceptions to which they relate, but a final new section returns to the Confrontation Clause and examines a variety of proposals for how the clause should be interpreted. Treatment has been expanded of those exceptions which have been troublesome for the courts under the Federal Rules, i.e., inculpatory declarations against interest, the investigatory report, and residual exceptions. The conspirators' exception is utilized to illustrate the power of the judge to pass on preliminary questions of fact. The existence of the Federal Rules and notes in the pamphlet permit elimination of detailed treatment of a number of exceptions.

The chapter on Circumstantial Evidence continues exploration of problems to which the student was introduced in Chapters One and Two. Here will be found revised and updated materials on the much–litigated subject of character evidence, introduced for substantive purposes rather than for its bearing on credibility. Evidence of convictions, bad acts, reputation and opinion of character are all explored. New Fed.R.Evid. 413–15, dealing with a defendant's prior acts in sexual cases, as well as Fed.R.Evid. 412, the rape shield provision, are discussed. The debate over the admissibility of evidence of subsequent repairs in product liability cases and its resolution in amended Fed.R.Evid. 407 is noted.

As stated earlier, a new chapter on Expert Evidence has been created. Although material from the prior edition is included, new material has been added relating to the Daubert decision and the on–going debate over scientific evidence. The closely connected problem concerning the basis for expert opinion testimony (Fed.R.Evid. 703) is carefully examined. The chapter ends with new materials on court–appointed experts, special masters and technical advisors, as well as material showing how expertise is employed in the Civil Law system.

The chapters on Burden of Proof and Presumptions and Judicial Notice have not been changed from the prior edition. In the area of judicial notice there is a discussion of the limits of judicial factfinding in the legislative area as a basis for discussions in constitutional and jurisprudential courses. Restrictions of the judicial role may respond in part to theoretical and in part to practical limitations on the ability of judges to make findings of fact necessary for responsible legislative judgments. From a pedagogical point of view, we find it useful to put this material late in the course, because much of it is quite sophisticated and requires an understanding of the problems and limitations of proof through ordinary techniques. The material on judicial notice of law is limited, but sufficient so that the topic can be covered in this course if it is not taken up in courses in Civil Procedure or Conflicts.

The material on Privileges has been brought up–to–date with many new cases utilized. This chapter develops fully five privileges—the privilege against self incrimination; the attorney–client privilege; the spousal privileges (adverse spousal testimony and confidential communications between spouses); and doctor–patient or psychotherapist–patient privileges.

Other privileges—both recognized and developing—are covered more briefly. Relationship privileges including clergy–penitent; various professional–client; and privileges applicable to journalists and scholars; and parent–child; as well as peer review and critical self–analysis, are treated through extended notes and some limited case material.

The material on state secrets and official information is also treated in summary fashion. Although, for example, United States v. Nixon is an extremely important case on Presidential privilege, it seems more appropriately handled in depth in the course on Constitutional Law.

The section on the privilege against self–incrimination traces in detail the doctrines governing the claim of the privilege by a witness or one against whom a subpoena duces tecum has been issued. This section also deals with the privilege of the criminal defendant but does not directly address the privilege of the criminal suspect outside of a courtroom setting. Thus Miranda v. Arizona and its progeny are not treated here, except in limited contexts such as in connection with admissions by silence after warnings. The assumption is that the Miranda doctrine is being given detailed coverage in the Criminal Procedure course. Although the same might be said about all of the Fifth Amendment issues, the fact that many of those issues can be profitably viewed from a different perspective and in more detail in the Evidence course merits their development here.

There is much on the substantial interrelationships among the privileges. Material is provided on the relationship between the attorney–client privilege and the Sixth Amendment. Questions relating to the privilege against self–incrimination applied to documents and physical evidence, including the collective entity and required records doctrines, are fully explored.

The impact on the attorney–client privilege and the relationship between client and lawyer of recurring prosecutorial attempts, sometimes acting under the authority of federal statutes, to obtain client–related information from attorneys, to trace criminal proceeds, and forfeit attorney fee moneys are covered in considerable detail. There is also coverage derived from the Model Rules of Professional Responsibility in various versions that addresses ethical as well as evidentiary attorney–client issues, particularly with regard to client misconduct.

We have introduced considerable material on rape and other sex crimes and abuse of children. This subject is presently receiving a great deal of attention from the courts and legislatures. It cuts across almost every area of the law of evidence, but it particularly illustrates critical problems in such areas as expert witnesses and the right of confrontation. A problem based upon alleged sexual abuse of a stepdaughter that may be made the basis for a discussion throughout the course is used by some of the editors. It will be made available to any teacher upon request. It is helpful in illustrating how the rules as well as ethical and practical considerations affect the structure of a case before and during trials.

JACK B. WEINSTEIN
JOHN H. MANSFIELD
NORMAN ABRAMS
MARGARET A. BERGER

May, 1997

SUMMARY OF CONTENTS

TABLE OF CONTENTS

CHAPTER 5   Circumstantial Proof: Further Problems ------ 808

TABLE OF CASES

Principal cases are in bold type. Non-principal cases are in roman type. References are to Pages.

TABLE OF FEDERAL RULES OF EVIDENCE

CHAPTER 1

RELEVANCY AND RELATED PROBLEMS

1. Introduction

SELECT CASES ON EVIDENCE AT THE COMMON LAW, JAMES BRADLEY THAYER (1892)

What is our law of evidence? It is a set of rules which has to do with judicial investigations into questions of fact.... These rules relate to the mode of ascertaining an unknown, and generally a disputed, matter of fact, in courts of justice. But they do not regulate the process of reasoning and argument. This may go on after all the "evidence" is in, or when all the facts are admitted except such as are deducible by reasoning from these admitted facts.... But when one offers "evidence," in the sense of the word which is now under consideration, he offers to prove, otherwise than by mere reasoning from what is already known, a matter of fact to be used as a basis of inference to another matter of fact; as when I offer the testimony of A. to prove the fact in issue,—for even direct testimony, to be believed or disbelieved, according as we trust the witness, is but a basis of inference,—or to prove an evidential fact from which, by a process of reasoning, the fact in issue may be made out; and as when I present to the senses of the tribunal a visible object which may furnish a ground of inference. In giving evidence we are furnishing to a tribunal a new basis for reasoning. This is not saying that we do not have to reason in order to ascertain this basis; it is merely saying that reasoning alone will not, or at least does not, supply it. The new element which is added is what we call the evidence.

A. RELEVANCY

The concept of relevancy is basic to the law of evidence. It provides the framework on which any rational system of proof is constructed. This is reflected in the two most important provisions of the Federal Rules of Evidence, set out here because they are the capstones of the Rules.

Rule 401

DEFINITION OF "RELEVANT EVIDENCE"

"Relevant evidence" means evidence having any tendency to make the existence of any fact that is of consequence to the determination of the action more probable or less probable than it would be without the evidence.

Rule 402

RELEVANT EVIDENCE GENERALLY ADMISSIBLE; IRRELEVANT EVIDENCE INADMISSIBLE

All relevant evidence is admissible, except as otherwise provided by the Constitution of the United States, by Act of Congress, by these rules, or by other rules prescribed by the Supreme Court pursuant to statutory authority. Evidence which is not relevant is not admissible.

Stated another way, the basic rule of relevancy is that anything proffered to the senses of the trier that may change his or her evaluation of the probabilities that a "fact that is of consequence to the determination of the action" is true, is relevant and admissible unless excluded under the many rules studied in this course. Even the most superficial reading of Rule 401 and the above restatement of it suggests the critical importance in litigation of determining the meaning of the phrase "fact that is of consequence to the determination of the action." See also, e.g., Cal.Evid.Code §§ 140, 190, 210, 235, 350, 351. Equivalent phrases used with the same meaning are "ultimate facts," "operative facts" and "material propositions of fact." In the notes in this section we will generally use the last phrase, which is somewhat more precise.

Any judicial trial is controlled by the questions of fact made material by the applicable rule of substantive law. The trier must determine, for the purposes of the litigation, whether these material propositions of fact have been established with the requisite degree of probability—e.g., (1) the defendant killed X and (2) intended to do so; the defendant (1) issued a prospectus and (2) knew it contained false statements; Y was (1) driving at 60 miles per hour when (2) his car hit the plaintiff; (1) the substance carried by defendant (2) was cocaine, (3) was known by him to be cocaine and (4) was intended by him to be distributed; or the food (1) sold by defendant to plaintiff (2) caused the plaintiff to (3) become ill. These examples are obviously simplifications of an enormous amount of complex substantive law.

If all the material propositions of fact required to be found in order to bring into play a rule of law are established, then certain legal consequences will follow—e.g., a defendant may be subject to certain criminal penalties or to damages in tort. As will become more apparent from the materials which follow, what will be relevant may well depend upon how the rule of law is formulated—i.e., what is the precise material proposition of fact.

Since a trial is a practical enterprise, more than mere logical relevancy may determine admissibility. For example, the other central provision of the Federal Rules of Evidence reads:

Rule 403

EXCLUSION OF RELEVANT EVIDENCE ON GROUNDS OF PREJUDICE, CONFUSION, OR WASTE OF TIME

Although relevant, evidence may be excluded if its probative value is substantially outweighed by the danger of unfair prejudice, confusion of the issues, or misleading the jury, or by considerations of undue delay, waste of time, or needless presentation of cumulative evidence.

Thus, in determining admissibility, trial judges must weigh shrewdly the propriety of admitting much evidence offered to build the bases for inferences designed to convince the trier that a material proposition of fact is probably true or untrue. To some extent the judges are guided by rules resulting from frequent recurrence of particular problems. To a large extent, however, they do not have these guides and must resort to practical common sense and their understanding of how the world inside and outside the courtroom operates.

Determinative factors may be suggested in a series of questions: (1) Is the offered evidence logically relevant? (2) Will its presentation consume much time? (3) Will it befog the trier by confusing the issues? (4) Will it unfairly surprise the opponent? (5) Will it tend to excite the emotions of the trier to the undue prejudice of the opponent? (6) Are there considerations of so-called public policy which reception of the evidence would offend or tend to offend? (7) Is the value of the evidence upon any issue of the case sufficient to substantially outweigh disadvantages perceived under questions (2)–(6) inclusive?

The last question as to relative help and hindrance cannot be answered well without exact scrutiny of the process of inference. Whenever an item of evidence is offered as tending circumstantially—that is, inferentially—to establish a proposition the truth of which is at issue in a case, it is essential to articulate honestly and fully the inference or series of inferences invited. Each specific step of reasoning must invariably match a premise, usually unarticulated, which the judge judicially notices. Thus where the contested proposition is whether D is the person who killed H, and the evidence is a love letter from D to W, H's wife, the inferential series runs from (1) the expression in the letter to (2) D's love of W to (3) D's desire for exclusive possession of W to (4) D's wish to get rid of H to (5) D's plan to get rid of H to (6) D's execution of the plan by killing H. The unarticulated major premises, evidential hypotheses, conjoined with and supposed to justify the inferential steps are:

(1–2) A man who writes a love letter to a woman probably does love her. (The term "probably" as used here means that the proposition of fact is more probably or likely true as to this man than an identical proposition as to a person of whom nothing is known.)

(2–3) A man who loves a woman probably desires her for himself alone.

(3–4) A man who loves a married woman probably wishes to get rid of her husband.

(4–5) A man who wishes to get rid of the husband of the woman he loves probably plans to do so.

(5–6) A man who plans to get rid of the husband of the woman he loves probably kills him.

Obviously the value of item (1) as probative of conclusion (6) varies inversely with the number and dubiousness of the intervening inferences. Application of premise (1–2) to item (1) cannot produce more than fractional certitude of intermediate conclusion (2)—the qualifying term "probably" which had to be inserted in (1–2) shows that. And so on down the line. This type of reasoning is progressively attenuative. Here it fractionizes at five successive points.

The probability that the killing was done by the man who wrote the letter, determined from this line of proof alone, is the product of multiplying the probability of each step of the line of proof.

Despite this attenuation of probabilities, and of resulting probative force, the judge often concludes that the initial item of evidence should be admitted. Relevance is present and there is enough weight to justify consideration by the trier. At the same time, though, he may also be forced to conclude, if he conscientiously follows through the attenuation, that the item of evidence standing alone would not sustain a finding of the ultimate conclusion desired. When this is so, and the burden of persuasion is upon the party offering the evidence, that party must undertake an accumulative process by collecting and presenting other items of evidence tending toward the conclusion through other supporting lines of proof. In the case imagined such other items might be (a) threats by D against H's life; (b) purchase of a pistol and ammunition by D; (c) procurement by D of a key to the front door of H's house; (d) D's presence in the neighborhood of the house shortly before and after the killing; and (e) the finding of D's hat in the house immediately after the killing. See discussion and illustrations in O'Hara and Osterburg, An Introduction to Criminalistics **666–79** (1949).

The greater the number of independent lines of proof pointing toward a common conclusion, the greater the confidence in that conclusion, but no matter how many the circumstantial items may be, they can never produce absolute certainty. Nor will they, under the assumption above as to placement of burden of persuasion, even make the ultimate proposition or conclusion a question for the trier of fact unless the judge believes that their total effect would justify reasonable people in deciding that the conclusion is more likely true than not in a civil case or beyond a reasonable doubt in a criminal case.

Plainly enough it is the presence of more or less incalculable human factors which makes particularly substantial the lack of certitude in the hypothetical situations mentioned above. Human beings may resist temptation instead of yielding to it, may speak or write jocosely although with the appearance of seriousness, or may have interests, intentions, or motives not readily perceptible to others. Higher degrees of certitude are readily and properly obtainable when the variability of human impulse and action is removed. Thus if reliable observers of the commission of a crime agree that the guilty person was baldheaded, one-eyed, lacking two fingers on his right hand, swarthy of complexion, club-footed, and afflicted with a nervous tick and an impediment of speech, the police may feel just confidence of having the right man if they pick up near the time and place of the crime a person with this entire distinctive collection of characteristics. And, to prove presence at some time of a particular person in a room, the finding on walls and furniture of finger prints exactly agreeing with his may be even more convincing. See, generally, James, Relevancy, Probability and the Law, 29 Calif.L.Rev. 689 (1941).

The concept of Conditional Relevancy—a phrase criticized in Ball, The Myth of Conditional Relevancy, 14 Georgia L.Rev. 435 (1980)—is embodied in Federal Rule 104(b). It was designed to deal with the division of function between judge and jury infra, rather than the logical relation between evidence and material propositions and the assessment of the probable truth of the latter that constitutes the subject of this chapter.

The question of what role the judge plays with respect to juries in deciding questions of admissibility and other matters is pervasive in the materials which follow. See, e.g., discussion of Articles IX and X of the Federal Rules of Evidence dealing with documentary evidence in chapter 2, infra and Rule 104 of the Federal Rules of Evidence. See, e.g., Maguire & Epstein, Preliminary Questions of Fact in Determining the Admissibility of Evidence, 40 Harv.L.Rev. 392 (1927); Morgan, Functions of Judge and Jury in the Determination of Preliminary Questions of Fact, 43 Harv.L.Rev. 165 (1929); Saltzberg, Standards of Proof and Preliminary Questions of Fact, 27 Stan.L.Rev. 271 (1975); Laughlin, Preliminary Questions of Fact: A New Theory, 31 Wash. & Lee L.Rev. 285 (1974); J.B. Weinstein & M. Berger, Weinstein's Evidence Manual, Chapter 3 (1987); Norman M. Garland and Jay A. Schmitz, Of Judges and Juries: A Proposed Revision of Federal Rule of Evidence 104, 23 U.C. Davis L. Rev. 77 85–86 (1987).

Professors Garland and Schmitz propose that Congress amend Rule 104 to read (23 U.C. Davis L. Rev. at 85–86, footnotes omitted):

Rule 104: Preliminary Questions: Functions of Judge and Jury

(a) The court shall commit a preliminary question upon which the admissibility of an item of evidence depends to the jury for determination if the following conditions are met:

(1) The preliminary question is one of fact; and

(2) The proponent introduces evidence sufficient to support a jury finding that the preliminary fact exists; and

(3) A reasonable juror

(A) would consider and resolve the preliminary factual question if the juror makes any use of the evidence; and

(B) would necessarily resolve the preliminary factual question before making any inference based on the evidence as to the existence or nonexistence of a fact of consequence to the determination of the action; and

(C) would completely disregard the evidence if the juror found the preliminary fact not to exist.

(b) The court shall determine all other preliminary questions, whether of fact or otherwise, which affect the admissibility of evidence. Rules of evidence other than those based on privilege do not bind the court in making its determination.

Do you agree with this change? Would it, in operation, complicate or simplify pretrial determinations, trial determinations? Would it increase or decrease the ability of the jury to nullify instructions on the law? How would problems arising under Rule 403 be handled? Would special findings be required for appeal and would it decrease or increase the possibility of reversals? By letter dated June 17, 1995 from the chair of the Federal Advisory Committee on Evidence Rules to the Chair of the Federal Standing Committee on Rules of Practice and Procedure, the Advisory Committee noted that it had "tentatively" decided not to propose amendments to Rule 103 (a), (b), (c), (d) (Rulings on Evidence) and Rule 104 (Preliminary Questions). Do you agree with this decision? As you study these materials decide what rules you think should be amended, added or dropped and why.

The opportunity of the jury to fail to apply the law by misinterpretation of the evidence in the light of juror predilections and social and cultural backgrounds and norms can be minimized by good advocacy. But see Jack B. Weinstein, Considering Jury "Nullification": When May and Should a Jury Reject the Law to Do Justice, 30 Am. Crim. L. Rev. 239 (1993).

The relation between trial judge and appellate court is partly explicated in Federal Rule 103. See J.B. Weinstein & M. Berger, Weinstein's Evidence Manual 2–18 ff. (1987). David P. Leonard, Appellate Review of Evidentiary Rulings, 70 N.C.L. Rev. 1155 (1992) (appellate courts have essentially granted unreviewable power to trial courts in evidentiary matters). Have appellate courts been so deferential? Why? On what kinds of questions? In answering this question note that only a minute percentage of evidentiary rulings are discussed in printed appellate decisions. Can you expect the same deference in a capital crime with the death penalty imposed as in a single credit card fraud case with probation imposed? See Rule 103 which makes no distinction among types of cases and with whether they are tried by bench or jury.

For a description of the history of the development of the Federal Rules and the wide discretion afforded trial courts see United States v. Shonubi, 895 F.Supp. 460, 494 ff. (E.D.N.Y.1995) (contrast between Wigmore's detailed proposed code with Thayer's rejection of "mechanistic systems of evidence in favor of broad principles of relevancy."), rev'd on other g'ds, 103 F.3d 1085 (2d Cir.1977). Whose view prevailed? Why? Note the Continental system's approach. See United States v. Jurado–Rodriguez, 907 F.Supp. 568, 575 (E.D.N.Y. 1995) ("no rules of evidence as we know them in Anglo–American law exist. Judges base their decisions on personal conviction arrived at after weighing all available information.") Why do you think this difference exists? Is the difference as great as it once was?

A detailed consideration of examples of circumstantial proof will be found in Chapter 5, infra.

People v. Adamson

Supreme Court of California, 1946.
27 Cal.2d 478, 165 P.2d 3, aff'd, 332 U.S. 46 (1947).

■ TRAYNOR, JUSTICE.

The body of Stella Blauvelt, a widow 64 years of age, was found on the floor of her Los Angeles apartment on July 25, 1944. The evidence indicated that she died on the afternoon of the preceding day. The body was found with the face upward covered with two bloodstained pillows. A lamp cord was wrapped tightly around the neck three times and tied in a knot. The medical testimony was that death was caused by strangulation. Bruises on the face and hands indicated that the deceased had been severely beaten before her death.

The defendant does not contend that the evidence does not justify a finding that murder in the first degree had been committed. Pen.Code, § 189. The sole contention of fact that he makes is that the evidence is not sufficient to identify him as the perpetrator. The strongest circumstance tending to so identify the defendant was the finding of six fingerprints, each identified by expert testimony as that of the defendant, spread over the surface of the inner door to the garbage compartment of the kitchen of the deceased's apartment. See Wigmore, Evidence, 3d Ed., 389. After the murder, this door was found unhinged, leaning against the kitchen sink. Counsel for defendant questioned witnesses as to the possibility of defendant's fingerprints being forged, but the record does not indicate that any evidence to that effect was uncovered. The theory of the prosecution was that the murderer gained his entrance through the garbage compartment, found the inner door thereof latched from the kitchen side, and forced the door from its hinges. It was established that defendant could have entered through the garbage compartment by having a man about his size do so. The fact that the key to the apartment could not be found after search and the testimony of a neighboring tenant as to sounds heard indicate that the murderer left the apartment through the door thereof and made his exit from the building down a rear stairway.

The tops of three women's stockings identified as having been taken from defendant's room were admitted in evidence. One of the stocking tops was found on a dresser, the other two in a drawer of the dresser among other articles of apparel. The stocking parts were not all of the same color. At the end of each part, away from what was formerly the top of the stocking, a knot or knots were tied. When the body of the deceased was found, it did not have on any shoes or stockings. There was evidence that on the day of the murder deceased had been wearing stockings. The lower part of a silk stocking with the top part torn off was found lying on the floor under the body. No part of the other stocking was found. There were other stockings in the apartment, some hanging in the kitchen and some in drawers in a dressing alcove, but no other parts of stockings were found. None of the stocking tops from defendant's room matched with the bottom part of the stocking found under the body.

In reply to questions by the police, defendant denied that he resided or had ever been at the apartment house identified by testimony as his residence. At different times he gave two other addresses as his residence. When shown a picture of the murdered victim, he refused to look at it, stating that he did not like to look at dead people.

The theory of the prosecution was that the motive of the murder was burglary. Testimony revealed that the deceased was in the habit of wearing rings with large-sized diamonds and that she was wearing them on the day of the murder. The rings were not on the body and search has failed to uncover them. A witness, positively identifying the defendant, testified that at some time between the 10th and 14th of August, 1944, she overheard defendant ask an unidentified person whether he was interested in buying a diamond ring.

From the foregoing evidence a reasonable jury could conclude that beyond a reasonable doubt defendant committed the murder and burglary. See People v. Ramirez, 113 Cal.App. 204, 298 P. 60; 2 Wigmore, supra, 389. Testimony that the screws were still in the hinges of the door when it was found and that fragments of wood that appeared to have come from the screw holes were clinging to them, indicating a forced removal, served to discount the possibilities that at some previous date the door had been taken from the apartment for some unknown reason and at that time handled by the defendant, or that defendant had handled the door during some earlier visit to the deceased's apartment. Testimony to the effect that the garbage pail was not in its customary place when found after the murder further tended to substantiate the prosecution's theory as to time and mode of entrance.

Defendant contends that error was committed in the admission of the testimony of part of a conversation in which he asked an unidentified person whether the latter was interested in purchasing a diamond ring. Conceding that this evidence, though hearsay, was admissible in so far as the hearsay rule is concerned as an admission ... defendant contends that it was irrelevant. The rule is well settled that a witness may testify to part of a conversation if that is all that he heard and it appears to be intelligible....

People v. Rabalete, 28 Cal.App.2d 480, 485, 82 P.2d 707, 709, is not contrary to this rule. The fragment of the sentence there held inadmissible, "242 to show," was held to create merely a suspicion of the meaning of the entire sentence. People v. Jacquaino, 63 Cal.App.2d 390, 393, 394, 146 P.2d 697. The part of the conversation here admitted, however, in view of the evidence indicating that the motive of the murderer was the theft of diamonds, tended to identify defendant as the perpetrator.

To be admissible, evidence must tend to prove a material issue in the light of human experience. See 1 Wigmore, 407 [(3rd ed.)]. The stocking tops found in defendant's room were relevant to identify defendant because their presence on his dresser and in a drawer thereof among other articles of wearing apparel with a knot or knots tied in the end away from what was formerly the top of the stocking indicates that defendant had some use for women's stocking tops. This interest in women's stocking tops is a circumstance that tends to identify defendant as the person who removed the stockings from the victim and took away the top of one and the whole of the other. Although the presence of the stocking tops in defendant's room was not by itself sufficient to identify defendant as the criminal, it constituted a logical link in the chain of evidence.... Evidence that tends to throw light on a fact in dispute may be admitted. The weight to be given such evidence will be determined by the jury.... Codification of this rule as applied to demonstrative evidence is found in section 1954 of the Code of Civil Procedure: "Whenever an object, cognizable by the senses, has such a relation to the fact in dispute as to afford reasonable grounds of belief respecting it, or to make an item in the sum of the evidence, such object may be exhibited to the jury.... The admission of such evidence must be regulated by the sound discretion of the court."

It is contended that the admission of the stocking tops deprived defendant of a fair trial and therefore denied him due process of law. Defendant states that their admission could serve no purpose except to create prejudice against him as a Negro by the implication of a fetish or sexual degeneracy. No implication of either was made by the prosecutor in his brief treatment of the evidence in oral argument. Moreover, except in rare cases of abuse, demonstrative evidence that tends to prove a material issue or clarify the circumstances of the crime is admissible despite its prejudicial tendency....

The prosecuting attorney commented repeatedly on the failure of the defendant to take the stand. [The analysis approving these comments is omitted. On this point the case has been overruled. See, e.g., Carter v. Kentucky, 450 U.S. 288 (1981).]

There has been much criticism of the present state of the law, which places a defendant who has been convicted of prior crimes in the dilemma of having to choose between not taking the stand to explain or deny the evidence against him thereby risking unfavorable inferences, and taking the stand and having his prior crimes disclosed to the jury on cross-examination.... In the present case defendant admitted two prior felony convictions for which he served terms of imprisonment in the Missouri state prison. The fact of the commission of these crimes was not offered or introduced into evidence and would have been inadmissible under the general rule with respect to prior crimes.... Had defendant taken the stand, however, the commission of these crimes could have been revealed to the jury on cross-examination to impeach his testimony.... Since fear of this result is a plausible explanation of his failure to take the stand to deny or explain evidence against him ... the inference of the credibility and unfavorable tenor of such evidence that arises from this failure is definitely weakened by this rule of impeachment. This weakness, however, could not be revealed to the jury by counsel or court without prejudicing the defendant through the revelation of past crimes.

A major part of the testimony and of the prosecutor's oral argument concerned the presence of six of defendant's fingerprints on the garbage compartment door. Fingerprints are the strongest evidence of identity of a person and under the circumstances of the present case they were alone sufficient to identify the defendant as the criminal....

The judgments and the order denying a new trial are affirmed.

NOTES

1. Assume that one possible meaning of the presumption of innocence is that the trial starts with an assumption that there is an almost zero probability that defendant in the main case committed the crime charged. How would your assessment of probabilities be changed by considering individually and collectively proof respecting the silence of defendant, his attempt, if that is what it was, to sell jewelry belonging to the deceased, the stockings evidence, the fingerprint evidence, his criminal record, and other evidence?

What assumptions are you making in coming to these conclusions and how much of your private individually acquired knowledge are you using? Is your analysis affected by the knowledge that in some areas of the country it was rather common for dockworkers and some kinds of laborers to wear women's stocking tops over their hair? Probably most middle class persons likely to be on a jury would not be aware of this fact. Should this fact affect admissibility? Are experts useful in this connection?

Since so much of the evaluation of evidence depends upon varying hypotheses applied by triers with different backgrounds and views of life, fact finding differences among jurors and between judge and jury are to be expected. The court's function is, in the usual simple case, only to decide whether a reasonable person might have his or her assessment of the probabilities of a material proposition changed by the piece of evidence sought to be admitted. If it may affect that evaluation it is relevant and, subject to certain other rules, admissible. See United States v. Schipani, 293 F.Supp. 156 (E.D.N.Y.1968), aff'd, 414 F.2d 1262 (2d Cir.1969), cert. denied, 397 U.S. 922, 90 S.Ct. 902, 25 L.Ed.2d 102 (1970). Cf. Trautman, Logical or Legal Relevancy—A Conflict of Theory, 5 Vand.L.Rev. 385, 390 (1951). See also People v. Thompson, 300 N.W.2d 645, 646 (Mich.App.1980):

> Defendant ... submits that it was error for the trial court to allow the prosecutor, over objection, to question him concerning his use of aliases. One panel of this Court has characterized the use of an alias as "highly probative" of a witness's credibility.... We disagree. The utilization of assumed names is very common among certain cultures in American society. While there are undoubtedly instances where aliases are used to deceive, it is also likely that an assumed name is being used for entirely innocent reasons and therefore should not be deemed especially probative of a person's credibility. Furthermore, a defendant may be highly prejudiced by the jury's learning that he has used aliases. This could be a particular problem in cases where the defendant and the jurors come from different cultures. If the utilization of assumed names is unknown among the jurors' backgrounds, they may place undue emphasis on defendant's employment of an alias.

Note the large degree of judicial "knowledge" about how people act inside and outside the courtroom involved in cases such as this. See the discussion of judicial notice, chapter 8, infra.

Compare with Thompson, People v. Dietrich, 274 N.W.2d 472, 481–482 (Mich.App.1978). In a first degree murder case the defendant took the stand and was cross-examined on the use of aliases before and after the crime. Collecting supporting cases, the court held:

> We think that the witness's use of an alias is highly probative of the witness's credibility. In this case, the introduction into evidence of defendant's use of aliases was not highly inflammatory or prejudicial to the defendant.... The trial judge did not err in allowing this testimony into evidence for impeachment purposes.

How is this evidence relevant to whether he is telling the truth on the witness stand? Would knowledge of the general practice in the defendant's environment be helpful? Would the "prejudices" or "assumptions" of a middle class jury or panel of judges be significant? How could counsel for defendant "neutralize" this evidence or convince the judge to exclude, perhaps under Rule 403?

Is the fact-finding skill of the court trying a case without a jury, or ruling on admissibility, or deciding the facts necessary to application of the Sentencing Guidelines greater than that of juries? Why? See, e.g. United States v. Shonubi, 895 F.Supp. 460 (E.D.N.Y.1995), reversed in the light of greater "quality" of evidence required in guideline sentencing, 103 F.3d 1085 (2d Cir.1997), where the trial court relied on the court's experience in trying many drug cases to conclude that a smuggler who conceals drugs in his intestines will tend to swallow as much as possible. How can that judgment be confirmed or disputed? In Shonubi the court utilized its own knowledge of the drug trade, demeanor of the defendant, and inferences from discussion as to character, assumptions about criminals' behaviors generally, expert testimony and statistical analysis of other smugglers' activities. Id. at 523–524. The factual findings of the court resulted in a sentence many years longer than would have resulted had the court failed to make these findings. Under these circumstances is it fair to apply in sentencing, as many courts do, a burden of proof of a mere preponderance rather than a beyond a reasonable doubt standard? See Id. at 470–472. In United States v. Watts, 117 S.Ct. 633 (1997), the Supreme Court acknowledged "a divergence of opinion among the Circuits as to whether, in extreme circumstances, relevant conduct that would dramatically increase the sentence must be based on clear and convincing evidence." What is the role of the appellate court? The Second Circuit provides protection against the Guidelines hard rules enhancing imprisonment for unconvicted relevant conduct by increasing burdens of proof. See United States v. Gigante, 94 F.3d 53, 56–57 (2d Cir.1996). It also requires "specific evidence"—drug records, admissions or live testimony of drug quantities. United States v. Shonubi, 103 F.3d 1085 (2d Cir.1997). See note immediately before the main case, supra. Is manipulation of the fact finding process to circumvent "bad" substantive law of sentencing appropriate? See the criticism of the Second Circuit standard in United States v. Shonubi, ___ F.Supp. ___ (E.D.N.Y.1997) (on second remand).

Compare with the reference in the main case to the "interest of the defendant in stocking tops," United States v. Truong Dinh Hung, 629 F.2d 908 (4th Cir.1980), cert. denied, 454 U.S. 1144 (1982) (an espionage prosecution where defendant was accused of transmitting classified information to the North Vietnamese during the 1977 Paris negotiations. Defendant claimed he merely had a benign scholarly interest in the classified cables he had obtained. There was no error in admitting several items found in defendant's apartment such as classification codes, lists of "spooks" in the state department and handwritten notes on espionage and counter-espionage).

In United States v. Zimeri–Safie, 585 F.2d 1318, 1321–22 (5th Cir.1978), defendant was charged with knowingly receiving and possessing a firearm while being an alien illegally or unlawfully in the United States, and knowingly making a false statement as to the legality of his alien status with the intent to deceive a firearms dealer. After defendant's visa had expired, the Bureau of Alcohol, Tobacco and Firearms searched defendant's apartment and seized from the apartment a book entitled "The Paper Trap" which described methods of acquiring false identification, one of those ways being the use of names taken from tombstones. At the same time, the agent also seized defendant's address book which contained the names of persons buried in a local cemetery. In upholding the lower court's admission of the evidence the court said:

> Zimeri's possession of the manual on deception and a notebook indicating he had taken the first step to make use of the manual's information, though falling short of proving he had a knowing intent to deceive one year earlier, does similarly tend to make it more probable that Zimeri realized at the time of his firearm purchases that he was an illegal alien.

2. What foundation should be laid before the evidence described in the main case is introduced? For example, what would be needed to introduce the stocking tops and bottom? Would the proof needed to place this evidence before the jury have probabilities of truth associated with it? Would it enhance or attenuate the probabilities you assigned in answering questions posed in the previous note?

3. In United States v. Bear Ribs, 722 F.2d 420 (8th Cir.1983), the defendant was convicted of assault with intent to commit rape. The victim was found unclothed. Defendant denied having taken off her clothes as part of his assault. The Eighth Circuit held that the trial judge properly excluded evidence that the victim, when intoxicated, routinely undressed and publicly exposed herself since no one testified to seeing the victim in a nude or semi-nude condition prior to the incident.

Compare Wood v. Alaska, 957 F.2d 1544 (9th Cir.1992). Defendant was convicted of sexual assault. The victim was a former Penthouse Pet and pornographic movie actress, and defendant had sought to admit evidence that she showed nude photographs and described her pornographic acting experiences to him to establish that they had a prior sexual relationship. Affirming, the Ninth Circuit allowed that the evidence was probative, but exclusion was not an abuse of discretion because of the possibility that a jury might be improperly swayed against her on grounds of "perceived immorality."

Note that subsequent to Wood, in the "Violent Crime Control and Law Enforcement Act of 1994," P.L. No. 103–322, Rule 412 of the Federal Rules of Evidence was amended by Congress, according to the Committee Notes, "to expand the protection afforded alleged victims of sexual misconduct.

Would this amendment leave changed the trial court's power or decision in Wood? How? Should it have? See Rule 403.

In State v. Bray, 278 S.W.2d 49, 56–57 (Mo.App.1955), the defendant was charged with the theft of a red dress from a women's wear store. Police arrested the defendant while she was driving in her car, and found the dress and various items of men's and boys' clothing, some with price tags still attached. All of this clothing was put in evidence. Introduction of everything except the red dress was held to be prejudicial error:

> There was no proof whatever that these garments were stolen.... Yet these other garments were described and displayed to the jury for the obvious purpose of suggesting that same had been stolen, in order to make more certain the inference that the red dress had been stolen.... We do not rule upon the question of whether "the other garments" would be admissible in evidence, if proof had shown that they were stolen....

For cases dealing with the possession of burglar's tools, see Annot., Admissibility, in prosecution for burglary, of evidence that defendant, after alleged burglary, was in possession of burglarious tools and implements, 143 A.L.R. 1199 (1943). What does the admission of such tools and instruments prove? See State v. Toney, 537 S.W.2d 586 (Mo.App.1976) (holding that, where .38 caliber weapon had been used in crime, admission of bandoliers carrying the same caliber ammunition, found in defendant's apartment, was admissible even though bandoliers had not been worn during the crime).

4. In analyzing relevancy, probative force, probabilities and prejudice, some scholars have found the terminology of Professor Jerome Michael useful in differentiating between the real world where events actually occurred or did not occur and the world of the courtroom where we deal in propositions of fact about the real world and probabilities that these propositions represent the truth. Using the terminology set out below and the analysis it suggests, diagram the various steps and lines of proof leading to the material propositions in People v. Adamson.

Proposition   —Declarative sentence used to express our actual or potential knowledge about a thing or event.

Material proposition	—Statement about a matter of fact which is a specific example falling within the general class which is one of the elements of the applicable rule of law.
Immediate proposition	—Statement of knowledge of things and events as they appear to our senses.
Demonstrable proposition	—Statement of knowledge achieved inferentially.
Evidence	—Perceptive objects—e.g., persons, things and events presented to the senses of the tribunal; all evidence must be perceived through senses.
probandum; probanda (pl.)	—Proposition being proved; if ultimate, a material proposition.
probans; probantia (pl.)	—Proposition being used to prove another; if ultimate it is an immediate proposition (i.e., based on sense impression with minimal inference).
evidential or evidentiary proposition	—Elementary proposition employed as a probans; it may be simple or compound.
evidentiary hypothesis	—General proposition employed as a probans.
Step of proof	—A syllogism containing a probandum, an evidential hypothesis and a probans.
Line of proof	—Series of steps of proof beginning in an immediate proposition and ending in a material proposition.
syllogism conclusion	—probandum
major premise	—general proposition—evidential hypothesis
minor premise	—probans

See Michael & Adler, The Nature of Judicial Proof (1931); Michael & Adler, The Trial of An Issue Of Fact, 34 Colum.L.Rev. 1224, 1252 (1934).

The diagram method is utilized extensively in J.H. Wigmore, The Science of Judicial Proof (3rd ed.1937), but it has been suggested that his system of charts with its complex system of symbols has been one of the factors that resulted in that work being given less weight than it should have received. W. Twining, Theories of Evidence: Bentham and Wigmore, 11–12 (1985). A more modern attempt to use diagrams to assist in analysis is the helpful work of Professor Friedman—e.g., Diagrammatic Approach to Evidence, 66 Boston U.L. Rev. 571 (1986); A Close Look at Probative Value, 66 Boston U.L.Rev. 733 (1986); Route Analysis of Credibility and Hearsay, 96 Yale L.J. 667 (1987).

In United States v. Shonubi, 895 F.Supp. 460 (E.D.N.Y.1995), rev'd, 103 F.3d 1085 (2d Cir.1997), the court estimated drugs smuggled in prior trips of the accused utilizing the classical step-by-step approach of Professor Michael (Id. at 483), statistical and Bayesian analysis (Id. at 484), set out its perceived biases (Id. at 486), used a "storytelling" technique (Id. at 487) and relied upon experts including statisticians employed by the government, the defendant, and a panel appointed by the court pursuant to Rule 706 of the Federal Rules of Evidence. Id. at 499 ff.

In Adamson assume, in a slight but significant variation from the actual evidence, that the state's Exhibit 1, for identification, was a few pieces of jewelry; the police found the jewelry in defendant's possession a day after the killing; a neighbor saw the deceased wearing "something that looked just like that jewelry" the day before the killing, June 7, 1981, a day she remembers because she went to a friend's wedding.

LINE 1 — JEWELRY FOUND ON DEFENDANT

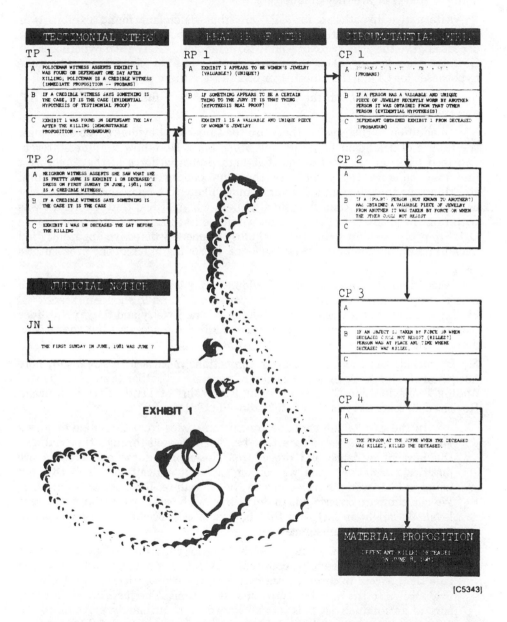

EXHIBIT 1

[C5343]

In the above diagram, the credibility of the witnesses and thus the probability of their statements being true will depend on their (1) ability to have made the observation, (2) to have remembered it accurately, (3) to want to tell truthfully what was remembered, and (4) to communicate effectively with the tribunal.

Admissibility of the real proof, in addition to the need for authentication (supplied by TP1 and TP2 and JN1), will depend on relative prejudicial aspects (Federal Rules of Evidence Rule 403), extrinsic policies such as Fourth Amendment protections, and the ability of the trier to determine from observation such matters as whether it is jewelry normally worn by a woman, its value, and how commonly available it is to the public, e.g., do these pieces have particular dents or marks or are they unique?

Alternative hypotheses for CP1 are that defendant found exhibit 1 or obtained it from an intermediary. Alternate hypotheses for CP2 are that deceased gave the jewelry to, or sold it to, defendant. Alternative hypotheses for CP3 are that it was taken some time before or after the killing. Alternate hypotheses for CP4 is that another or others were there at the time.

In each step of proof, the minor premise is "A," the major premise "B," and the conclusion "C."

In addition to the jewelry, there are the fingerprint evidence, the stockings, the failure of defendant to testify and other lines. Note how the lines interact and feed back on one another so that high probative force of the fingerprint line may enhance the probability that the policeman who says he found stocking tops in defendant's drawer is more likely to be perceived by the trier as a credible witness; contrariwise, a witness who testified that defendant was with him the entire day of the murder would be less likely to be believed. In the O.J. Simpson case destroying the credibility of one key detective apparently fed back to an evaluation of the other evidence, poisoning much of the prosecutor's case.

Also note how the same piece of evidence may tend to prove more than one material proposition. The use of a lamp cord would tend to show an intentional killing and also that it was not in self-defense. The jewelry and fingerprint lines would tend to show not only that defendant killed the deceased but that it was done in the course of a felony.

5. In considering the issue of prior convictions discussed in Adamson, note how the rules for trials may be based on "normative" rather than pure "truth-finding" considerations. See Bankowski, The Value of Truth: Fact Skepticism Revisited, 1 Legal Studies (Eng.) 257, 265–66 (1981):

In the case of the trial the conclusion comes from the judge or jury's view of a complex set of data that has been filtered through the trial and the laws of evidence and procedure. These procedures and criteria are justified normatively and we cannot say that a result obtained through using one is wrong by reference to the procedure and criteria of another. We can compare criteria but in doing that we have to operate at a different level. We might in fact find that both sets of procedures are appropriate but in different circumstances.

Let us take an example: according to our rules of evidence past convictions are not be to be counted as evidence of present guilt. Thus the rule that, except in certain circumstances, the prosecution cannot [rely on] evidence as to the accused's previous convictions. The justification for this sort of anti-inductivist bias is well known and ultimately pertains to the moral basis of the system: the presumption of innocence and the burden of proof. The procedure for the police, however, does not employ this anti-inductivist criteria and indeed the police would be in dereliction of their duty if they did so. If a crime has been committed we expect the police, within limits, not to ignore their knowledge of known malefactors on the assumption that all past evidence is to be ignored. This knowledge ought to influence the police inquiries and procedures just as it ought not so to influence the courts'. We expect of the police, then, a laxer criterion than we do of the courts. We should, therefore, not be surprised if the police make more arrests than there are convictions. This is one of the ways that the system should work. The 'he did it' of the police is different and ought to be so from the 'he did it' of the jury.

If we accept all this then we can see the problems of asking, in the [Jerome] Frank tradition, whether and can the jury get it right. The only way we can answer that question is by seeing whether the criteria in the trial have been followed: to use any other criteria would be judging it by reference to another truth-certifying procedure. This is why jury verdicts are so difficult to overturn except if the jury perversely does not decide according to the evidence. It is not a question of whether the jury, in some absolute way, get it right but whether they fulfill their allotted role in the system.

In Kaplan, Decision Theory and the Factfinding Process, 20 Stanford L.Rev. 1065, 1074 (1968), Professor Kaplan puts the prior conviction issue in a slightly different way:

Not only may such evidence [of previous convictions] lead the jurors to the wholly rational conclusion that if the defendant has committed previous crimes he is more likely to be guilty of this one; it may also lead them to the perhaps rational but clearly undesirable conclusion that because of his earlier convictions, ... the disutility of convicting the defendant should he be innocent, is minimal. Obviously, in a system of justice that regards it as crucial that the defendant be found guilty only of the crime specifically charged, we cannot permit a mistaken factual judgment to be made either on the theory that even if the defendant did not commit the crime charged he probably committed others, or on the theory that since the defendant has been convicted several times before it is not very important to him or to society that he is convicted one more time.

See the discussion of use of other crimes, infra.

6. Does the Continental system of free evaluation require the same methods of analysis set forth in United States v. Shonubi, 895 F.Supp. 460 (E.D.N.Y. 1995), rev'd103 F.3d 1085 (2d Cir.1997), supra? Cf. United States v. Jurado–Rodriguez, 907 F.Supp. 568 (E.D.N.Y.1995), a prosecution for dealing in drugs after extradition from Luxembourg, where defendant had been convicted of, and served a prison term for money laundering. The principles of international law, the doctrine of specialty, and the rule of non bis in dem (double jeopardy) precluded prosecution for the same crime in the United States. Decision of a motion to dismiss the indictment for drug conspiracy in the United States depended in large part on the meaning of "faits" in the extradition decree. The court, citing Michael and Adler, held that "faits" meant material propositions of fact and not evidence. It permitted the case to proceed in the United States after dismissing a money laundering count. A negotiated plea avoided trial and appeal.

B.   RELEVANCE AND PREJUDICE

Robbins v. Whelan

United States Court of Appeals, First Circuit, 1981.
653 F.2d 47, cert. denied, 454 U.S. 1123 (1981).

■ COFFIN, CHIEF JUDGE. This appeal stems from an automobile accident involving a 1971 Mercedes car driven by the defendant-appellee, Robert Whelan, and a second car in which the two plaintiffs-appellants were passengers. The driver of the second car, Curtis Frye, is not a party to this suit. The accident took place as the Mercedes was traveling east on a four lane undivided highway and the Frye car was exiting a rest area, abutting the southern edge of that same highway. The plaintiffs assert that the Mercedes was first noticed some 700 feet away at the time Frye first approached the highway. Before entering the highway Frye looked in both directions. Upon entering he again looked in the direction of the Mercedes, and this time noticed that it was only 300 feet away and approaching at a speed of about 70 miles per hour. At this point Frye attempted to reenter the rest area. As the resulting collision attests, he was unsuccessful.

The defendant's version claims that he was traveling at about 40 to 48 miles per hour when the Frye car was first noticed some 750–900 feet away advancing in the rest area in the opposite direction. The defendant says he maintained his speed up to a point where the Frye car entered the highway in a "sudden swerve" which left little time for any reaction. After a bifurcated trial the jury decided the issue of liability in favor of the defendant.

Appellants' first claim of error is that the trial court should have admitted into evidence a copy of a Department of Transportation National Highway Safety Bureau report entitled "Performance Data for New 1971 Passenger Cars and Motorcycles." This report contains information on the maximum stopping distances for all automobiles manufactured in a certain year. Specifically, the plaintiffs sought to introduce into evidence that part of these tables stating that the particular type of automobile driven by the defendant had, when traveling at a speed of 60 miles per hour, a maximum stopping distance of 160 feet with a light load and 169 feet with a heavy load. The defendant objected to this document on the grounds that it was not relevant. The district court agreed.

We think the evidence was relevant.[1] A Massachusetts State Police Trooper previously had testified that the defendant's car, which he thought had been traveling faster than 50 miles per hour, had left 160 feet of skid marks. The braking performance report stated the new cars of the defendant's model required at most 169 feet to stop under the test conditions of 60 miles per hour. If factors other than speed were common to both the test and the accident, the report would have supported an inference that the defendant—who presumably was trying to stop as fast as possible—was in fact driving faster than his claimed 40 to 48 miles per hour.

The factors other than speed prevailing both during the test and at the accident were sufficiently similar to allow the jury to hear this evidence. In general, because "perfect identity between experimental or actual conditions is

---

1. We pause to note an anomaly that not infrequently attends the review of trials—the extensive discussion in the appellate court opinion directed to an incident at trial that received only fleeting attention. Here, for example, appellant called an official of the Registry of Motor Vehicles to testify regarding information from the National Highway Safety Bureau report. Defendant immediately objected that "because there is some agency in Washington that compiles a book of information with respect to various cars and what they might do or will not do under the circumstances, I don't think that has any relevancy, materiality or admissibility in this case."

When read in retrospect, the subsequent colloquy reveals that appellant was referring, none too succinctly, to use of the report as an indirect means of calculating the Mercedes' speed prior to braking. It appears that the court was considering only the relevance of the report as bearing on inadequate brakes, a factor that was not in issue. Nevertheless, we cannot say that the record is so confused that the point as to relevance was not sufficiently made. That point being preserved, we cannot avoid the analysis that follows. [Footnotes by the court].

neither attainable nor required ... [,] [d]issimilarities affect the weight of the evidence, not admissibility." Ramseyer v. General Motors Corporation, 417 F.2d 859, 864 (8th Cir.1969) (citations omitted).[2] Each case must be judged under its own particular facts taking into account the specific purposes for which this type of evidence is submitted.[3] In this particular case, although the tests were performed under specific controlled conditions, see 49 CFR § 575.101(d) and (e) (1980),[4] the defendant has not attempted to demonstrate to us any differences existing at the time of the accident that were significant, except perhaps for the skill of the driver. The evidence that was presented at trial had otherwise established a dry road, no abnormal weather conditions, and a relatively new car in "A–1" condition. On this record the matchup of conditions was sufficient to allow the data to be presented to the jury. It is for the defendant to attack the weight to be accorded such evidence by presenting contrary evidence about how the variance between the test and actual conditions—for instance, as when one car stops with skidmarks and the other without—might affect the inferences that the plaintiff urges be drawn.

[Discussion of hearsay problems under Fed.R.Evid. 803(8)(C) omitted.]

We ... conclude that the trial court's exclusion of the performance report was more than harmless error. Fed.R.Evid. 103(a); Fed.R.Civ.Proc. 61; 28 U.S.C. § 2111. This case turned in great measure on the critical element of speed. In making this factual determination the jury essentially had before it only the conflicting versions of the two drivers and the defendant's expert witness who testified to the effect that plaintiff's car was traveling at the faster speed at the time of the collision, and that the skid marks on the road were not made by defendant's car. There was no other evidence presented at trial that could serve the same purpose of establishing a relationship between the skid marks and probable speed. See de Mars v. The Equitable Life Assurance Society, 610 F.2d 55, 61–62 (1st Cir.1979) (harmless error when the excluded evidence is cumulative, repetitious, or ambiguous); see also Garbincius v. Boston Edison Company, 621 F.2d 1171, 1175 (1st Cir.1980).

On this close question of negligence it is obvious that plaintiffs' case was made considerably weaker by the error. Because we cannot say with reasonable assurance that the jury, had it been given the opportunity to consider the data, would still have found in favor of the defendant we find no alternative but to remand for a new trial....

The case is remanded for a new trial.

■ CAMPBELL, CIRCUIT JUDGE (Dissenting).

... I believe the court fails to give adequate attention to the fact that the trial judge excluded the data ... for lack of relevance, *and* that appellant never correctly stated the purpose for which the evidence was being offered. Before a party may claim error on appeal in the exclusion of evidence, he must have told

---

2. Cf. Winekoff v. Pospisil, 384 Mich. 260, 181 N.W.2d 897, 898 (1970) ("our steady experience with automobile negligence cases suggests that these widely published and pretty well understood stopping distances have some value as evidence, provided the proof preceding their admission discloses a fair and relevant reason for submitting them to the jury as an aid to the solution of the everpresent issues of due care and causation").

3. The fact that the detailed conditions under which the tests for individual models

were performed may be easily verified helps distinguish the report in this case from those in which the opaque averaging of generalized results masked variation in the underlying data and created uncertainty about testing conditions.

4. The testing conditions and procedures used to compile the information in the 1970 Report have changed very little in 10 years. They are nearly identical to those listed at 49 CFR Part 575 (1980).

the court not only what he intended to prove but *for what purpose.* McCormick, Evidence § 51, at 110–11 (2d ed. 1972), and cases at n. 12, and 1978 Supp. at 16, n. 12; see also Weinstein's Evidence § 103[03], at 103–27, and cases at n. 3; 1 Wigmore, Evidence § 17, at 319–20 and 1980 Supp., cases at p. 97–98; Fed.R.Evid. 103(a)(2); Fed.R.Civ.P. 46. This rule serves important ends. Backlogged courts should not be required to repeat trials (especially civil trials) because the trial judge has excluded evidence for lack of a clear understanding of the proponent's purpose in offering it. Here, plaintiffs' counsel never explained, as he could easily have done, that his purpose was not to show stopping distance at 60 m.p.h. as such, but rather to give rise to the inference, based on a disputed skid mark, that the car was speeding. It seems clear from the judge's remarks that she did not understand that the evidence was being offered for the latter purpose. The document was thereupon excluded for lack of relevance (the hearsay issue was never reached). All this occurred at the end of a week long trial, in a context where the judge could reasonably have felt that matters were being unduly prolonged.

This court skirts the issue in footnote 1. It says that "read in retrospect," the colloquy between court and counsel "reveals that appellant was referring, none too succinctly, to use of the report as an indirect means of calculating the Mercedes' speed prior to the braking." For this reason, "we cannot say . . . that the point as to relevance was not sufficiently made." The rule, however, is not served by looking at the record retrospectively. The reason a party must communicate the purpose for offering evidence is to put the trial judge on notice while there is still time to save the situation. A trial judge is only human; he may not have perfect recall of earlier testimony; it is counsel's duty, not the court's, to articulate the purpose for which evidence is being offered. Nowhere in this record did counsel say something like, "Judge, I am offering this because we earlier had evidence of 160 foot skid marks and this exhibit will show that if it took the car 160 feet to stop, it must have been going faster than 60 m.p.h." Had this been stated, a different ruling might have been rendered.

To be sure, this court may not mean that counsel here actually *stated* the purpose for the evidence, but only that the purpose was so obvious that counsel was excused from stating it. See McCormick, Evidence § 51, at 111. Defendant's speed was already in issue, and the judge arguably should have realized how the performance data report, taken with the other evidence, would relate to the question of speed. But I do not think the indirect relationship between speed and skid marks was so obvious that counsel was excused from stating it. It was clear from the judge's comments that she was laboring under the misimpression that the evidence was being offered merely to show when the brakes had been applied. If the point was that obvious, one would have expected the judge to perceive it; the whole object of the rule is to require counsel to articulate the purpose when the judge is likely otherwise to misunderstand. At the end of the colloquy, counsel stated his intention to prove that the Mercedes going 60 m.p.h. could stop in 160 feet; but that was to state matters backwards. He never once stated the data was offered for the purpose of showing that the 160 foot skid marks means the Mercedes was going faster than 60.

If I saw evidence of injustice, I might be more tempted to stretch the rule, but I see no such evidence here. Plaintiffs presented their own driver, who testified that the defendant was going 70 m.p.h. or more, as well as the state trooper who testified to his opinion, based on the skid marks, that defendant was going faster than 50—so the excluded evidence would not have established a new point that was not otherwise made. To be sure, the performance data might have corroborated these witnesses, if the jury believed the skid marks came from the Mercedes, which was put in doubt by one of the plaintiffs' own witnesses as well as by defendant's expert. Even so, the test data was refutable by arguments that it applied only to new, mechanically perfect cars driven by professional drivers who did not lock the wheels and skid. (The tests were expressly said to have been conducted without locked wheels; thus for all we know the stopping distances were quite different from those of a skidding car.) If it could conceivably have tipped the scales in a close case, this case does not seem to have been close—the jury was out for only an hour. I think that plaintiffs had their day in court, before a jury and a judge who was fair. I do not think plaintiffs should receive a second trial.

NOTE

State of Arizona v. Atwood, 832 P.2d 593, 656–657 (Ariz.1992) (en banc) (a gruesome kidnapping and child sex-murder case of wide notoriety):

Defendant next asserts that he was prejudiced by the trial court's refusal to allow his trial counsel fully to cross-examine James Corby, the FBI agent who analyzed the paint transfers between defendant's car and the victim's bike. Particularly, he argues that his attorney was unfairly precluded from questioning Corby about areas in which Corby's test results varied from the results obtained in similar tests run by Tim Carlson, the state's first paint expert who died prior to trial. As noted, Carlson's testimony was not preserved before his death.

Our review of the record, however, does not reveal the defense counsel ever actually objected to the court's prohibition against the use of Carlson's conclusions and opinions as an impeachment tool. A lengthy discussion ensued after the prosecution objected to the defense's attempt to use the Carlson material. The prosecution argued that the defense was improperly attempting to bring in Carlson's inadmissible opinions via Corby's cross-examination. The transcript of the discussion reveals considerable confusion among the trial judge, prosecutor, and defense counsel concerning which aspects of the Carlson materials the defense was attempting to use (i.e., the charts, graphs, and other findings generated by the Carlson experiments as opposed to the actual conclusions Carlson reached from those materials). The trial court eventually concluded, based on its understanding of defense counsel's argument, that the defense was seeking only to introduce Carlson's graphs and charts to impeach Corby's testimony. Because the court believed that the materials were "charts and items upon which Mr. Corby and Mr. Carlson and other of their colleagues would normally rely in the preparing of their conclusions and opinions," it determined that the items could be employed by the defense pursuant to rule 703 ("If of a type reasonably relied upon by experts in the particular field in forming opinions or inferences upon the subject, the facts or data need not be admissible in evidence."). In response to this ruling, defense counsel stated:

I have nothing to add. That's what I was trying to argue yesterday, and I guess I misunderstood Your Honor's ruling.

Thus, our reading of the record indicates that the defense received exactly what it requested.

Assuming, however, that the defense in fact desired to use Carlson's opinions for impeachment purposes, the record does not reflect that, once the trial court's ruling was clear, defense counsel objected to the limitation placed upon his cross-examination of Corby, nor does it reflect that he made an offer of proof demonstrating the admissibility of Carlson's opinions.... We recognize that an offer of proof may not be necessary if "the purpose and purport of the testimony expected to be elicited is obvious.".... We do not believe, however, that the "purpose and purport" of using the Carlson materials was "obvious" to the trial court in this case. Indeed, the only obvious aspects of the defense's attempt to use Carlson's material were defense counsel's miscommunication and the trial court's confusion as to the defense's intent. Accordingly, we find no basis for considering on appeal whether the defense was unfairly limited in cross-examining Corby.

State v. Poe

Supreme Court of Utah, 1968.
21 Utah 2d 113, 441 P.2d 512, appeal after remand, 471 P.2d 870 (Utah 1970).

■ CALLISTER, JUSTICE. Defendant, Roy Lee Poe, was convicted of the first degree murder of Kenneth Hall. The murder occurred in St. George, Utah (population about 5,130), and the trial was held there. The deceased had been a lifelong resident of the community, whereas the defendant was a comparative newcomer. The jury, in returning its verdict of guilty, did not recommend life imprisonment. Whereupon, the court pronounced the death penalty....

[D]efendant contends that he was denied a fair trial because of "the community pattern of thought as expressed by potential jurors and (because) of the proximity of relationships which existed between members of the jury and witnesses for the prosecution, the victim, the prosecutors, and the defendant." It cannot be disputed that a large majority of the prospective jurors were aware of the crime and some of its purported facts. This could hardly be otherwise in a sparsely populated community (Washington County, of which St. George is the county seat, has a population of 10,271). However, the trial judge carefully and exhaustively examined the panel and the prospective jurors. There was selected a jury of 12 who had neither formed an opinion or, if they had, it would not prevent them from basing their verdict solely upon the evidence. We cannot say that it was biased or prejudiced. Furthermore, the jury panel was passed for cause by the defendant.

Nor is it strange that members of the jury were acquainted with the sheriff, some of the witnesses for the prosecution,[1] the victim, the defendant, and the prosecutors. However, we are unable to find in the record wherein these acquaintanceships were prejudicial to the defendant....

Finally, defendant contends the trial court abused its discretion in admitting some colored slides into evidence and permitting them to be displayed to the jury by means of a slide projector and screen. With this contention, we are in agreement.

To begin with, the identity of the deceased, his death and its cause had already been established. Black and white photographs had been introduced showing the victim lying in his bed, in a sleeping position, with two bullet holes in his head. The colored slides were made during the course of an autopsy. To describe them as being gruesome would be a gross understatement. One of them, for example, depicted the deceased's head, showing the base of the skull after the skull cap and brain had been removed by the pathologist. The skin is

---

1. Most members of the jury were also acquainted with one or both of defendant's counsel. [Some footnotes have been omitted; this one is renumbered; footnote by the court.]

peeled over the edge of the skull showing the empty brain cavity. Another is a top view of the empty cavity. They would have been gruesome in black and white but the color accentuates the gruesomeness.

Initially, it is within the sound discretion of the trial court to determine whether the inflammatory nature of such slides is outweighed by their probative value with respect to a fact in issue. If the latter they may be admitted even though gruesome. In the instant case they had no probative value. All the material facts which could conceivably have been adduced from a viewing of the slides had been established by uncontradicted lay and medical testimony. The only purpose served was to inflame and arouse the jury.

It must be remembered that the jury in this case not only determined the question of guilt but also fixed the punishment itself. The only use of the slides from the prosecution's standpoint was to arouse the emotions of the jury so that they would not recommend life imprisonment. It could very well be that the jury would have returned the same verdict absent its view of the slides. However, with the defendant's life at stake, this court should not hazard a guess. The slides could very well have tipped the scales in favor of the death penalty.

The counsel for defendant did not make the proper objection to the admission of the slides. However, this court will not allow such a technicality to influence its decision in a case such as this.

Because the trial court abused its discretion in permitting the slides into evidence and because of the other doubtful aspects of the trial, this case is reversed and remanded for a new trial.

■ CROCKETT, C.J., and HENRIOD, J., concur.

■ ELLETT, JUSTICE (dissenting).

I dissent from that part of the main opinion holding that the trial court abused its discretion in admitting colored slides into evidence. In the first place, colored pictures should be dealt with exactly the same as black and white pictures. All pictures are admissible in evidence if they tend to prove a matter which would be relevant for a witness to testify to orally. 23 C.J.S. Criminal Law § 852(1)a. When pictures are thus competent there cannot be any proper objection made to them on the ground that they may prejudice the jury. All evidence given tends to prejudice the jury, and pictures are no exception. Just why anyone should ever have supposed a colored picture should be rejected because it shows a true likeness of any given scene escapes me. One would think that of two pictures, the one more accurately portraying the scene would be the proper one to place in evidence....

It is true that the pictures taken of the deceased before he had been removed from his bed showed a considerable amount of blood on his face and on the bedding. He was lying with his arms folded across his chest exactly as if he were asleep. He had two holes in his face, and one could not tell by looking at the holes what had caused them.

.   .   .

The cause of death had to be proved, and so there was an autopsy on the body. The doctor testified as to two metallic substances he found inside the cranium of the deceased and traced the course from the holes in the head with a metal probe which he placed through the holes to the place where the metallic substances were found. It was relevant and proper for the State to show that the deceased was shot while asleep in bed, and these metallic probes in the head were photographed to show the course of the bullet....

Before allowing the pictures to be seen by the jury in this case, the court on its own motion excused the jury and had the pictures projected onto a screen, "so that counsel for the defendant may have an opportunity to object to them, if they desire after seeing them.... I am going to ask that they be shown on the screen and out of the presence of the jury so that counsel may voice an objection if they have any objection."

The pictures were shown out of the presence of the jury, and the only objection made by counsel for the defendant was that the pathologist did not know the deceased personally and, therefore, the pictures were not properly identified as being those of Kenneth Hall, the deceased. The identity of the body was otherwise established. The trial court did not abuse its discretion in admitting into evidence these pictures, especially when no objection was suggested by counsel on the ground that there was anything gruesome or inflammatory about them....

Had defendant wished to avoid having the jury see the pictures, he could have stipulated that Kenneth Hall died as a result of being shot in the face while he was lying in bed. This would have been no admission that he was the one who fired the shots. He didn't have to do this, but he ought not now complain because the State proved those elements of the crime of murder in the first degree which were put in issue by his plea of not guilty....

Since most cases involving gruesome pictures are concerned with conditions created by the defendant, the jury is much more apt to be affected against the defendant than it would be when the condition is caused by a surgeon in the quest for truth. The pictures so vividly described in the prevailing opinion were no more gruesome than was the open heart surgery portrayed on television a few nights ago.

The evidence given to the jury in this case would warrant a finding that the defendant was a guest in the home of the deceased; that while the deceased slept, the defendant shot him twice with a .22 caliber rifle; that defendant immediately sold the murder weapon and deceased's high-powered rifle; and that defendant stole the deceased's station wagon and was intending to get to Old Mexico down the back roads from Las Vegas, Nevada, where he was arrested. The verdict of murder in the first degree without recommendation was warranted by the evidence. The defendant had a fair trial before an unbiased jury, and I think this conviction should be affirmed.

■ TUCKETT, J., concurs in the dissenting opinion of ELLETT, J.

NOTES

1. The danger of such evidence is the possibility of its prejudicial effect outweighing its probative value. Otherwise, "if the mere gruesomeness of the evidence were ground for its exclusion, then it would have to be said that the more gruesome the crime, the greater the difficulty of the prosecution in proving its case." Rivers v. United States, 270 F.2d 435, 438 (9th Cir.1959), cert. denied, 362 U.S. 920 (1960).

Courts use the power to exclude prejudicial evidence with caution. United States v. Pirolli, 673 F.2d 1200 (11th Cir.), cert. denied, 459 U.S. 871 (1982). See, e.g., United States v. White, 23 M.J. 84, 22 Fed. R. Evid. Serv. 29 (C.M.App.1986) (disturbing pictures showing injuries and signs of prior injuries to child admitted when relied upon by experts testifying as to "battered child syndrome").

Should expert's reliance on such physical proof be treated in the same way as evidence of children's mental impressions related to investigators or recall of former abuses under hypnosis in prosecutions for sex abuse or assaults during "satanic" orgies? Can prior physical abuse of a mate as revealed by pictures showing prior injuries be relied on in a murder prosecution of the alleged abuser who shot and killed his wife after allegedly beating her on prior occasions? In United States v. Naranjo, 710 F.2d 1465, 1467 (10th Cir.1983), the court held that "The evidence of defendant's previous batteries of the victim becomes admissible when defendant took the stand and testified that the shooting was accidental." What if defendant had not taken the stand? Is a history of wife abuse relevant? See The Nat. L.J. Dec. 25, 1995, p. C3, trial of O.J. Simpson, defense counsel named lawyer of the year, Id. p. 1.

2. Russell v. Coffman, 376 S.W.2d 269 (Ark.1964), approved use by a surgeon of the preserved knee cap of the plaintiff to demonstrate to the jury the nature of plaintiff's injuries and the reason his knee cap had to be removed. Defendant had argued that the X ray plates, pictures of the knee cap, exhibition of plaintiff's knee and the expert evidence of the surgeon, which included use of a plastic model, should have sufficed. Compare Rost v. The Brooklyn Heights Railroad Co., 41 N.Y.S. 1069 (N.Y.A.D. 2d Dept.1896), reversing after introduction of a child's foot preserved in alcohol to show her size and thus her age.

In Marsee v. United States Tobacco Company, 866 F.2d 319 (10th Cir. 1989), a products liability action against a snuff manufacturer, a videotaped deposition of a severely disfigured postsurgical oral cancer patient was excluded even though he was similar in age, background use habits and extent of illness to plaintiff's decedent. The probative value on causation of decedent's cancer was low where there was no solid proof that the deponent's cancer resulted from snuff use. The disease is widespread and has many causes, the court pointed out, citing In re "Agent Orange" Product Liability Litigation, 611 F.Supp. 1223, 1252–53 (E.D.N.Y.1985) (evidence that 17 of 7500 with Hodgkin's disease were exposed to Agent Orange was not sufficiently probative on issue of whether exposure to Agent Orange caused Hodgkin's disease).

In Harper v. Bolton, 124 S.E.2d 54, 55 (S.C.1962), it was conceded that plaintiff had lost her eye in an automobile accident and the court held it reversible error to introduce "a small glass vial containing the removed eye." The dissent felt that the concession was not sufficiently clear. Compare Allen v. Seacoast Products, Inc., 623 F.2d 355, 365 n. 23 (5th Cir.1980) (plaintiff demonstrated the removal and replacement of glass eye before the jury, leading to what defendant claims was an excessive verdict; no abuse of discretion in showing the daily regimen that plaintiff must endure).

In re Richardson–Merrell, Inc. Benedectin Prods., 624 F.Supp. 1212 (S.D.Ohio 1985), the court held that children allegedly crippled at birth by defendant's drug were properly excluded from the courtroom during the liability phase of a product liability action. The court explained that:

> the presence ... of children suffering from severe birth defects is inherently prejudicial. There is no more protected and beloved member of human society than a helpless newborn infant. Conversely, it has become fashionable to castigate and punish that depersonalized segment of society identified variously as "big business," "soulless corporations," or "industrial complex." If the battle is emotional alone, between newborn infants and big business, there can be but one winner. Emotional battles, however, should not be staged in the federal courtroom. We deal in liability imposed not by emotion but by law.

624 F.Supp. at 1224. This decision is quite unusual.

Normally a party, no matter how deformed, has a right to be present. But cf., excluding the plaintiff, a severely injured seven-year old quadriplegic at the liability stage. Gage v. Bozarth, 505 N.E.2d 64 (Ind.App.1987). See also Helminski v. Ayerst Lab., 766 F.2d 208, 213 (6th Cir.1985). What of a party who brings spouse and children, father and mother and others to show support and engender sympathy? Should they be excluded?

3. Should gruesome photographs be allowed when other proof describing the details depicted in the photographs has already been admitted? In Baggett v. Ashland Oil & Refining Co., 236 N.E.2d 243, 250 (Ill.App.1968), photographs of plaintiff's extensive burns were admitted over defendant's objection that they were merely cumulative to the medical testimony and would be used only to evoke sympathy from the jury. In Burns v. State, 388 S.W.2d 690, 693–699 (Tex.Cr.App.1965), six different photographs, one of which showed the victim in color lying on his back in a pool of blood with his throat cut from ear to ear, were admitted after testimony to the same effect. The court held them admissible as tending to solve a disputed fact issue. The dissent found them too prejudicial. In Martin v. State, 475 S.W.2d 265 (Tex.Crim.App.1972), the test applied in Burns for the admissibility of photographs was overruled. The court formulated a new test:

> We hold that if a photograph is competent, material and relevant to the issue on trial, it is not rendered inadmissible merely because it is gruesome or might tend to arouse the passions of the jury, unless it is offered solely to inflame the minds of the jury. If a verbal description of the body and the scene would be admissible, a photograph depicting the same is admissible.

Id. at 267 (footnotes omitted).

Are color rather than black-and-white photographs more likely to be prejudicial? People v. Mathis, 406 P.2d 65, 69–70, cert. denied, 385 U.S. 857 (1966): Color photographs of the victim showing blood and brain matter around the victim's head were admitted in a murder prosecution. The defendant conceded the probative value of the photographs to discredit his self-defense theory but had objected to the use of color when black-and-white photographs were available.

4. State v. Blakely, 445 S.W.2d 280 (Mo.1969): a photograph of the defendant with a mustache, a beard, long hair, and a T-shirt was admitted. The defendant had objected because the photograph had prejudicially portrayed him as a "hippie" or "Zippie."

Radosh v. Shipstad, 230 N.Y.S.2d 295 (N.Y.A.D. 2d Dep't 1962), required reversal, apparently on the ground that the evidence was too appealing rather than too gruesome. In a breach of contract action the defense claimed that plaintiff, a professional skater, had weighed too much. The court felt that the jury was distracted from the issue of her prior weight by having the plaintiff appear in court in her skating costume.

5. In Douglass v. Hustler Magazine, Inc., 769 F.2d 1128 (7th Cir.1985), cert. denied, 475 U.S. 1094 (1986), a suit for invasion of privacy, the court held that the trial judge improperly admitted a slide show containing 128 of the vilest photographs and cartoons published by the defendant over the years. The court explained that "the prejudicial effect of the parade of filth in the slide show so clearly outweighed its probative value as to require exclusion under Rule 403.... " 769 F.2d at 1142.

6. People v. Salemi, New York L.J., April 28, 1955, p. 8, col. 4 (Gen.Sess.). On a motion for a new trial, the defendant claimed that newly discovered evidence indicated that the victim's injuries were such that he could not have spoken at all and thus could not, before he died, have named the defendant as his killer. Diametrically opposed medical testimony as to what were the victim's injuries was introduced at the hearing of this motion. The court ordered the victim's body exhumed, and observed a reexamination of the corpse. On the basis of this observation, the court found that the victim could have spoken, and denied plaintiff's motion. The Court of Appeals affirmed at 128 N.E.2d 377 (N.Y.C.A. 1955). If the issue had been presented at the original trial, should the court have permitted the jury to attend the exhumation and subsequent examination of the corpse?

7. In United States v. Layton, 767 F.2d 549 (9th Cir.1985), the defendant was charged with the murder of Congressman Leo Ryan in connection with the Jonestown massacre in Guyana. At trial, the government sought to introduce the so-called "Last Hour Tape" made while the mass suicide was in progress to establish a conspiratorial link between Jim Jones and the defendant. The Ninth Circuit upheld the trial court's decision to exclude the tape, concluding that the probative value of the tape was weak and that other evidence already admitted established the conspiratorial link. The court also emphasized the prejudicial effect of the tape:

> It would be virtually impossible for a jury to listen to this tape and ignore the sounds of innocent infants crying (and presumably dying) in the background. The discussion of the impending mass suicide set against the background cacophony of innocent children who have apparently already been given poison would distract even the most conscientious juror from the real issues in the case.

767 F.2d at 556.

8. People v. Cavanaugh, 282 P.2d 53, 64 (Cal.1955), a murder prosecution, affirmed a conviction when there had been introduced three amputated fingers of the deceased, blood-stained seat covers from the car, a tooth, and pictures of the badly decomposed body crawling with maggots. Dissenting, Justice Traynor noted: "The majority opinion concedes that unnecessary but highly inflammatory evidence and evidence of other crimes was erroneously admitted, and it is apparent from the record that the prosecutor deliberately presented his case with the purpose of inflaming the jury. I cannot say that he did not succeed in this purpose or that a different verdict would have been improbable had the evidence been excluded." Is there a difference in the role of the trial and appellate judges in evaluating probative force and prejudice under rule 403 of the Federal Rules of Evidence?

Compare the habeas corpus problem in Kealohapauole v. Shimoda, 800 F.2d 1463 (9th Cir.1986), refusing to find a violation of the Constitution where conviction in a state court for murder depended in part on a forty-five minute video presentation of the autopsy (black and white without sound track) while the pathologist described what was going on. The body was decomposed and the defendant refused to stipulate that the cause of death was blows to the victim's head.

9. To what extent can a party avoid adverse prejudice by stipulating to the reasonable inferences that may be drawn from gruesome or otherwise prejudicial evidence? See, e.g., Fortune, Judicial Admissions in Criminal Cases: Blocking the Introduction of Prejudicial Evidence, 17 Criminal Law Bulletin 101, 104–05 (1981):

> A distinction should be drawn between admissions of *ultimate facts* and admissions of *evidentiary facts*. When a jury is presented with a

judicial admission of an ultimate fact it has no function as regards that fact. The jury is told, in effect, not to concern itself with debating the fact but to pass to matters in dispute. In such a case, there is no reason to permit proof of that which is admitted. On the other hand, when the admission is as to an evidentiary fact the jury has a function; it must decide whether to infer from the evidentiary fact an ultimate fact in issue. It is then reasonable to permit the proponent to prove the evidentiary fact by evidence best calculated to persuade the jury to make the desired inference. To limit the proponent to a judicial admission of the evidentiary fact may rob the evidentiary fact of its probative value. Whether the proponent should be precluded from proving an admitted evidentiary fact should be determined by the principles codified in Rule 403 of the Federal Rules of Evidence—balancing the additional probative value of the proof (over the probative value of the judicial admission) against the prejudice to the other party.

The Court may utilize a combination of stipulations and conditions to minimize prejudice. See, e.g., United States v. Jackson, 405 F.Supp. 938 (E.D.N.Y.1975). Defendant was accused of robbing a bank in New York on August 23, 1971. On November 7 of that year, he was stopped in Georgia by a policeman and arrested for driving without a license. He was using a false name and guns were found in the car. Subsequently, the defendant escaped from the local jail. The court held the defendant's arrest and subsequent escape inadmissible, provided the defendant entered into a stipulation that he was in Georgia shortly after the robbery and that while there he used a false name. In addition to the principal case which follows, see, e.g., James Joseph Duane, "Right" to Prove Undisputed Facts, 168 F.R.D. 405 (1997).

10. Admission of prejudicial evidence may be proper even though the party against whom it is offered would be willing to stipulate to the proposition for which it is offered since the stipulation may not provide a jury with a basis for evaluating probative force. For example, in United States v. Bowers, 660 F.2d 527 (5th Cir.1981), a prosecution for child abuse, the court admitted a photograph of a child's lacerated heart even though the defendant was willing to stipulate the cause of the child's death. The court deemed the evidence essential to show that the defendant used cruel and excessive physical force on the child. See also United States v. Gantzer, 810 F.2d 349 (2d Cir.1987), a prosecution for sending obscene matter through the mail where defendant offered to stipulate that the pictures were obscene:

> We have long recognized that the decision whether to admit potentially prejudicial evidence is entrusted to the sound discretion of the district judge and will not be disturbed absent an abuse of discretion. . . . [He] acted well within his discretion in admitting the photographs for which Gantzer was indicted, Gantzer's concession of obscenity notwithstanding. A party is not obliged to accept an adversary's "judicial admission" in lieu of proving the fact, ... particularly in the context of a criminal prosecution where the accused seeks to stipulate to an element of the crime charged.

Do you agree?

If the crime itself requires proof of prejudicial matter as an element of the offense there is almost no way to avoid the evidence. In United States v. Petrov, 747 F.2d 824 (2d Cir.1984), for example, a prosecution for mailing obscene material by a commercial developer was based on pictures showing human sexual relations with animals and naked children. The majority dismissed some of the counts as not proven as to a commercial photoprocessor such as the defendant. It found "spillover prejudice" to those counts where even such a photoprocessor could be convicted. The trial court's exclusion of defendant's evidence to show community standards without explanation of how he applied Rule 403 was criticized. The dissent would have declared the statute not applicable to photoprocessors, who cannot be expected to make a judgment on films sent by clients for processing. The case with three opinions from the panel of three suggests the close relationship between substantive and evidentiary law.

Old Chief v. United States

Supreme Court of United States, 1997.
___ U.S. ___, 117 S.Ct. 644, 136 L.Ed.2d 574.

■ JUSTICE SOUTER delivered the opinion of the Court.

Subject to certain limitations, 18 U.S.C. § 922(g)(1) prohibits possession of a firearm by anyone with a prior felony conviction, which the government can prove by introducing a record of judgment or similar evidence identifying the previous offense. Fearing prejudice if the jury learns the nature of the earlier crime, defendants sometimes seek to avoid such an informative disclosure by offering to concede the fact of the prior conviction. The issue here is whether a district court abuses its discretion if it spurns such an offer and admits the full record of a prior judgment, when the name or nature of the prior offense raises the risk of a verdict tainted by improper considerations, and when the purpose of the evidence is solely to prove the element of prior conviction. We hold that it does.

I

In 1993, petitioner, Old Chief, was arrested after a fracas involving at least one gunshot. The ensuing federal charges included not only assault with a dangerous weapon and using a firearm in relation to a crime of violence but violation of 18 U.S.C. § 922(g)(1). This statute makes it unlawful for anyone "who has been convicted in any court of, a crime punishable by imprisonment for a term exceeding one year" to "possess in or affecting commerce, any firearm...." "[A] crime punishable by imprisonment for a term exceeding one year" is defined to exclude "any Federal or State offenses pertaining to antitrust violations, unfair trade practices, restraints of trade, or other similar offenses relating to the regulation of business practices" and "any State offense classified by the laws of the State as a misdemeanor and punishable by a term of imprisonment of two years or less." 18 U.S.C. § 921(a)(20).

The earlier crime charged in the indictment against Old Chief was assault causing serious bodily injury. Before trial, he moved for an order requiring the government "to refrain from mentioning—by reading the Indictment, during jury selection, in opening statement, or closing argument—and to refrain from offering into evidence or soliciting any testimony from any witness regarding the prior criminal convictions of the Defendant, except to state that the Defendant has been convicted of a crime punishable by imprisonment exceeding one (1) year." App. 6. He said that revealing the name and nature of his prior assault conviction would unfairly tax the jury's capacity to hold the Government to its burden of proof beyond a reasonable doubt on current charges of assault, possession, and violence with a firearm, and he offered to "solve the problem here by stipulating, agreeing and requesting the Court to instruct the jury that he has been convicted of a crime punishable by imprisonment exceeding one (1) year[ ]." App. 7. He argued that the offer to stipulate to the fact of the prior conviction rendered evidence of the name and nature of the offense inadmissible under Rule 403 of the Federal Rules of Evidence, the danger being that unfair prejudice from that evidence would substantially outweigh its probative value. He also proposed this jury instruction:

> "The phrase 'crime punishable by imprisonment for a term exceeding one year' generally means a crime which is a felony. The phrase does not include any state offense classified by the laws of that state as a misdemeanor and punishable by a term of imprisonment of two years or less and certain crimes concerning the regulation of business practices.

> "[I] hereby instruct you that Defendant JOHNNY LYNN OLD CHIEF has been convicted of a crime punishable by imprisonment for a term exceeding one year."

The Assistant United States Attorney refused to join in a stipulation, insisting on his right to prove his case his own way, and the District Court agreed, ruling orally that, "If he doesn't want to stipulate, he doesn't have to." App. 15–16. At trial, over renewed objection, the Government introduced the order of judgment and commitment for Old Chief's prior conviction. This document disclosed that on December 18, 1988, he "did knowingly and unlawfully assault Rory Dean Fenner, said assault resulting in serious bodily injury," for which Old Chief was sentenced to five years' imprisonment. App. 18–19. The jury found Old Chief guilty on all counts, and he appealed.

II

A

As a threshold matter, there is Old Chief's erroneous argument that the name of his prior offense as contained in the record of conviction is irrelevant to the prior-conviction element, and for that reason inadmissible under Rule 402 of the Federal Rules of Evidence. Rule 401 defines relevant evidence as having "any tendency to make the existence of any fact that is of consequence to the determination of the action more probable or less probable than it would be without the evidence." Fed. Rule Evid. 401. To be sure, the fact that Old Chief's prior conviction was for assault resulting in serious bodily injury rather than, say, for theft was not itself an ultimate fact, as if the statute had specifically required proof of injurious assault. But its demonstration was a step on one evidentiary route to the ultimate fact, since it served to place Old Chief within a particular sub-class of offenders for whom firearms possession is outlawed by § 922(g)(1). A documentary record of the conviction for that named offense was thus relevant evidence in making Old Chief's § 922(g)(1) status more probable than it would have been without the evidence.

Nor was its evidentiary relevance under Rule 401 affected by the availability of alternative proofs of the element to which it went, such as an admission by Old Chief that he had been convicted of a crime "punishable by imprisonment for a term exceeding one year" within the meaning of the statute. The 1972 Advisory Committee Notes to Rule 401 make this point directly:

> "The fact to which the evidence is directed need not be in dispute. While situations will arise which call for the exclusion of evidence offered to prove a point conceded by the opponent, the ruling should be made on the basis of such considerations as waste of time and undue prejudice (see Rule 403), rather than under any general requirement that evidence is admissible only if directed to matters in dispute." Advisory Committee's Notes on Fed. Rule Evid. 401, 28 U.S.C.App., p. 859.

If, then, relevant evidence is inadmissible in the presence of other evidence related to it, its exclusion must rest not on the ground that the other evidence has rendered it "irrelevant," but on its character as unfairly prejudicial, cumulative or the like, its relevance notwithstanding.

B

The principal issue is the scope of a trial judge's discretion under Rule 403, which authorizes exclusion of relevant evidence when its "probative value is substantially outweighed by the danger of unfair prejudice, confusion of the issues, or misleading the jury, or by considerations of undue delay, waste of time, or needless presentation of cumulative evidence." Fed. Rule Evid. 403. Old Chief relies on the danger of unfair prejudice.

1

The term "unfair prejudice," as to a criminal defendant, speaks to the capacity of some concededly relevant evidence to lure the factfinder into declaring guilt on a ground different from proof specific to the offense charged. See generally 1 J. Weinstein, M. Berger, & J. McLaughlin, Weinstein's Evidence, ¶ 403[03] (1996) (discussing the meaning of "unfair prejudice" under Rule 403). So, the Committee Notes to Rule 403 explain, " 'Unfair prejudice' within its context means an undue tendency to suggest decision on an improper basis, commonly, though not necessarily, an emotional one." Advisory Committee's Notes on Fed. Rule Evid. 403, 28 U.S.C.App., p. 860.

Such improper grounds certainly include the one that Old Chief points to here: generalizing a defendant's earlier bad act into bad character and taking that as raising the odds that he did the later bad act now charged (or, worse, as calling for preventive conviction even if he should happen to be innocent momentarily). As then-Judge Breyer put it, "Although ... 'propensity evidence' is relevant, the risk that a jury will convict for crimes other than those charged—or that, uncertain of guilt, it will convict anyway because a bad person deserves punishment—creates a prejudicial effect that outweighs ordinary relevance." United States v. Moccia, 681 F.2d 61, 63 (C.A.1 1982). Justice Jackson described how the law has handled this risk:

> "Courts that follow the common-law tradition almost unanimously have come to disallow resort by the prosecution to any kind of evidence of a defendant's evil character to establish a probability of his guilt. Not that the law invests the defendant with a presumption of good character, Greer v. United States, 245 U.S. 559, 38 S.Ct. 209, 62 L.Ed. 469, but it simply closes the whole matter of character, disposition and reputation on the prosecution's case-in-chief. The state may not show defendant's prior trouble with the law, specific criminal acts, or ill name among his neighbors, even though such facts might logically be persuasive that he is by propensity a probable perpetrator o the crime. The inquiry is not rejected because character is irrelevant; on the contrary, it is said to weigh too much with the jury and to so overpersuade them as to prejudge one with a bad general record and deny him a fair opportunity to defend against a particular charge. The overriding policy of excluding such evidence, despite its admitted probative value, is the practical experience that its disallowance tends to prevent confusion of issues, unfair surprise and undue prejudice." Michelson v. United States, 335 U.S. 469, 475–476, 69 S.Ct. 213, 218–219, 93 L.Ed. 168 (1948) (footnotes omitted).

Rule of Evidence 404(b) reflects this common law tradition by addressing propensity reasoning directly: "Evidence of other crimes, wrongs, or acts is not admissible to prove the character of a person in order to show action in conformity therewith." Fed. Rule Evid. 404(b). There is, accordingly, no question that propensity would be an "improper basis" for conviction and that evidence of a prior conviction is subject to analysis under Rule 403 for relative probative value and for prejudicial risk of misuse as propensity evidence. Cf. 1 J. Strong, McCormick on Evidence 780 (4th ed. 1992) (hereinafter McCormick) (Rule 403 prejudice may occur, for example, when "evidence of convictions for prior, unrelated crimes may lead a juror to think that since the defendant already has a criminal record, an erroneous conviction would not be quite as serious as would otherwise be the case").

As for the analytical method to be used in Rule 403 balancing, two basic possibilities present themselves. An item of evidence might be viewed as an island, with estimates of its own probative value and unfairly prejudicial risk the sole reference points in deciding whether the danger substantially outweighs the value and whether the evidence ought to be excluded. Or the question of admissibility might be seen as inviting further comparisons to take account of the full evidentiary context of the case as the court understands it when the ruling must be made. This second approach would start out like the first but be ready to go further. On objection, the court would decide whether a particular item of evidence raised a danger of unfair prejudice. If it did, the judge would go on to evaluate the degrees of probative value and unfair prejudice not only for the item in question but for any actually available substitutes as well. If an alternative were found to have substantially the same or greater probative value but a lower danger of unfair prejudice, sound judicial discretion would discount the value of the item first offered and exclude it if its discounted probative value were substantially outweighed by unfairly prejudicial risk. As we will explain later on, the judge would have to make these calculations with an appreciation of the offering party's need for evidentiary richness and narrative integrity in presenting a case, and the mere fact that two pieces of evidence might go to the same point would not, of course, necessarily mean that only one of them might come in. It would only mean that a judge applying Rule 403 could reasonably apply some discount to the probative value of an item of evidence when faced with less risky alternative proof going to the same point. Even under this second approach, as we explain below, a defendant's Rule 403 objection offering to concede a point generally cannot prevail over the Government's choice to offer evidence showing guilt and all the circumstances surrounding the offense.

The first understanding of the rule is open to a very telling objection. That reading would leave the party offering evidence with the option to structure a trial in whatever way would produce the maximum unfair prejudice consistent with relevance. He could choose the available alternative carrying the greatest threat of improper influence, despite the availability of less prejudicial but equally probative evidence. The worst he would have to fear would be a ruling sustaining a Rule 403 objection, and if that occurred, he could simply fall back to offering substitute evidence. This would be a strange rule. It would be very odd for the law of evidence to recognize the danger of unfair prejudice only to confer such a degree of autonomy on the party subject to temptation, and the Rules of Evidence are not so odd.

Rather, a reading of the companions to Rule 403, and of the commentaries that went with them to Congress, makes it clear that what counts as the Rule 403 "probative value" of an item of evidence, as distinct from its Rule 401 "relevance," may be calculated by comparing evidentiary alternatives. The Committee Notes to Rule 401 explicitly say that a party's concession is pertinent to the court's discretion to exclude evidence on the point conceded. Such a concession, according to the Notes, will sometimes "call for the exclusion of evidence offered to prove [the] point conceded by the opponent. . . ." Advisory Committee's Notes on Fed. Rule Evid. 401, 28 U.S.C.App., p. 859. As already mentioned, the Notes make it clear that such rulings should be made not on the basis of Rule 401 relevance but on "such considerations as waste of time and undue prejudice (see Rule 403). . . ." Ibid. The Notes to Rule 403 then take up the point by stating that when a court considers "whether to exclude on grounds of unfair prejudice," the "availability of other means of proof may . . . be an appropriate factor." Advisory Committee's Notes on Fed. Rule Evid. 403, 28 U.S.C.App., p. 860. The point gets a reprise in the Notes to Rule 404(b), dealing with admissibility when a given evidentiary item has the dual nature of legitimate evidence of an element and illegitimate evidence of character: "No mechanical solution is offered. The determination must be made whether the danger of undue prejudice outweighs the probative value of the evidence in view of the availability of other means of proof and other facts appropriate for making decision of this kind under 403." Advisory Committee's Notes on Fed. Rule Evid. 404, 28 U.S.C.App., p. 861. Thus the notes leave no question that when Rule 403 confers discretion by providing that evidence "may" be excluded, the discretionary judgment may be informed not only by assessing an evidentiary item's twin tendencies, but by placing the result of that assessment alongside similar assessments of evidentiary alternatives. See McCormick 782, and n. 41 (suggesting that Rule 403's "probative value" signifies the "marginal probative value" of the evidence relative to the other evidence in the case); 22 C. Wright & K. Graham, Federal Practice and Procedure § 5250, pp. 546–547 (1978) ("The probative worth of any particular bit of evidence is obviously affected by the scarcity or abundance of other evidence on the same point").

2

In dealing with the specific problem raised by § 922(g)(1) and its prior-conviction element, there can be no question that evidence of the name or nature of the prior offense generally carries a risk of unfair prejudice to the defendant. That risk will vary from case to case, for the reasons already given, but will be substantial whenever the official record offered by the government would be arresting enough to lure a juror into a sequence of bad character reasoning. Where a prior conviction was for a gun crime or one similar to other charges in a pending case the risk of unfair prejudice would be especially obvious, and Old Chief sensibly worried that the prejudicial effect of his prior assault conviction, significant enough with respect to the current gun charges alone, would take on added weight from the related assault charge against him.

The District Court was also presented with alternative, relevant, admissible evidence of the prior conviction by Old Chief's offer to stipulate, evidence necessarily subject to the District Court's consideration on the motion to exclude the record offered by the Government. Although Old Chief's formal offer to stipulate was, strictly, to enter a formal agreement with the Government to be given to the jury, even without the Government's acceptance his proposal amounted to an offer to admit that the prior-conviction element was satisfied, and a defendant's admission is, of course, good evidence. See Fed. Rule Evid. 801(d)(2)(A).

Old Chief's proffered admission would, in fact, have been not merely relevant but seemingly conclusive evidence of the element. The statutory language in which the prior-conviction requirement is couched shows no congressional concern with the specific name or nature of the prior offense beyond what is necessary to place it within the broad category of qualifying felonies, and Old Chief clearly meant to admit that his felony did qualify, by stipulating "that the Government has proven one of the essential elements of the offense." App. 7. As a consequence, although the name of the prior offense may have been technically relevant, it addressed no detail in the definition of the prior-conviction element that would not have been covered by the stipulation or admission. Logic, then, seems to side with Old Chief.

3

There is, however, one more question to be considered before deciding whether Old Chief's offer was to supply evidentiary value at least equivalent to what the Government's own evidence carried. In arguing that the stipulation or admission would not have carried equivalent value, the Government invokes the familiar, standard rule that the prosecution is entitled to prove its case by evidence of its own choice, or, more exactly, that a criminal defendant may not stipulate or admit his way out of the full evidentiary force of the case as the government chooses to present it. . . .

This is unquestionably true as a general matter. The "fair and legitimate weight" of conventional evidence showing individual thoughts and acts amounting to a crime reflects the fact that making a case with testimony and tangible things not only satisfies the formal definition of an offense, but tells a colorful story with descriptive richness. Unlike an abstract premise, whose force depends on going precisely to a particular step in a course of reasoning, a piece of evidence may address any number of separate elements, striking hard just because it shows so much at once; the account of a shooting that establishes capacity and causation may tell just as much about the triggerman's motive and intent. Evidence thus has force beyond any linear scheme of reasoning, and as its pieces come together a narrative gains momentum, with power not only to support conclusions but to sustain the willingness of jurors to draw the inferences, whatever they may be, necessary to reach an honest verdict. This persuasive power of the concrete and particular is often essential to the capacity of jurors to satisfy the obligations that the law places on them. Jury duty is usually unsought and sometimes resisted, and it may be as difficult for one juror suddenly to face the findings that can send another human being to prison, as it is for another to hold out conscientiously for acquittal. When a juror's duty does seem hard, the evidentiary account of what a defendant has thought and done can accomplish what no set of abstract statements ever could, not just to prove a fact but to establish its human significance, and so to implicate the law's moral underpinnings and a juror's obligation to sit in judgment. Thus, the prosecution may fairly seek to place its evidence before the jurors, as much to tell a story of guiltiness as to support an inference of guilt, to convince the jurors that a guilty verdict would be morally reasonable as much as to point to the discrete elements of a defendant's legal fault. Cf. United States v. Gilliam, 994 F.2d 97, 100–102 (CA2), cert. denied, 510 U.S. 927, 114 S.Ct. 335, 126 L.Ed.2d 280 (1993).

But there is something even more to the prosecution's interest in resisting efforts to replace the evidence of its choice with admissions and stipulations, for beyond the power of conventional evidence to support allegations and give life to the moral underpinnings of law's claims, there lies the need for evidence in all its particularity to satisfy the jurors' expectations about what proper proof should be. Some such demands they bring with them to the courthouse, assuming, for example, that a charge of using a firearm to commit an offense will be proven by introducing a gun in evidence. A prosecutor who fails to produce one, or some good reason for his failure, has something to be concerned about. "If [jurors'] expectations are not satisfied, triers of fact may penalize the party who disappoints them by drawing a negative inference against that party." Saltzburg, A Special Aspect of Relevance: Countering Negative Inferences Associated with the Absence of Evidence, 66 Calif. L.Rev. 1011, 1019 (1978) (footnotes omitted). Expectations may also arise in jurors' minds simply from the experience of a trial itself. The use of witnesses to describe a train of events naturally related can raise the prospect of learning about every ingredient of that natural sequence the same way. If suddenly the prosecution presents some occurrence in the series differently, as by announcing a stipulation or admission, the effect may be like saying, "never mind what's behind the door," and jurors may well wonder what they are being kept from knowing. A party seemingly responsible for cloaking something has reason for apprehension, and the prosecution with its burden of proof may prudently demur at a defense request to interrupt the flow of evidence telling the story in the usual way.

In sum, the accepted rule that the prosecution is entitled to prove its case free from any defendant's option to stipulate the evidence away rests on good sense. A syllogism is not a story, and a naked proposition in a courtroom may be no match for the robust evidence that would be used to prove it. People who hear a story interrupted by gaps of abstraction may be puzzled at the missing chapters, and jurors asked to rest a momentous decision on the story's truth can feel put upon at being asked to take responsibility knowing that more could be said than they have heard. A convincing tale can be told with economy, but when economy becomes a break in the natural sequence of narrative evidence, an assurance that the missing link is really there is never more than second best.

4

This recognition that the prosecution with its burden of persuasion needs evidentiary depth to tell a continuous story has, however, virtually no application when the point at issue is a defendant's legal status, dependent on some judgment rendered wholly independently of the concrete events of later criminal behavior charged against him. As in this case, the choice of evidence for such an element is usually not between eventful narrative and abstract proposition, but between propositions of slightly varying abstraction, either a record saying that conviction for some crime occurred at a certain time or a statement admitting the same thing without naming the particular offense. The issue of substituting one statement for the other normally arises only when the record of conviction would not be admissible for any purpose beyond proving status, so that excluding it would not deprive the prosecution of evidence with multiple utility; if, indeed, there were a justification for receiving evidence of the nature of prior acts on some issue other than status (i.e., to prove "motive, opportunity, intent, preparation, plan, knowledge, identity, or absence of mistake or accident," Fed. Rule Evid. 404(b)), Rule 404(b) guarantees the opportunity to seek its admission. Nor can it be argued that the events behind the prior conviction are proper nourishment for the jurors' sense of obligation to vindicate the public interest. The issue is not whether concrete details of the prior crime should come to the jurors' attention but whether the name or general character of that crime is to be disclosed. Congress, however, has made it plain that distinctions among generic felonies do not count for this purpose; the fact of the qualifying conviction is alone what matters under the statute. "A defendant falls within the category simply by virtue of past conviction for any [qualifying] crime ranging from possession of short lobsters, see 16 U.S.C. § 3372, to the most aggravated murder." Tavares, 21 F.3d, at 4. The most the jury needs to know is that the conviction admitted by the defendant falls within the class of crimes that Congress thought should bar a convict from possessing a gun, and this point may be made readily in a defendant's admission and underscored in the court's jury instructions. Finally, the most obvious reason that the general presumption that the prosecution may choose its evidence is so remote from application here is that proof of the defendant's status goes to an element entirely outside the natural sequence of what the defendant is charged with thinking and doing to commit the current offense. Proving status without telling exactly why that status was imposed leaves no gap in the story of a defendant's subsequent criminality, and its demonstration by stipulation or admission neither displaces a chapter from a continuous sequence of conventional evidence nor comes across as an officious substitution, to confuse or offend or provoke reproach.

Given these peculiarities of the element of felony-convict status and of admissions and the like when used to prove it, there is no cognizable difference between the evidentiary significance of an admission and of the legitimately probative component of the official record the prosecution would prefer to place in evidence. For purposes of the Rule 403 weighing of the probative against the prejudicial, the functions of the competing evidence are distinguishable only by the risk inherent in the one and wholly absent from the other. In this case, as in any other in which the prior conviction is for an offense likely to support conviction on some improper ground, the only reasonable conclusion was that the risk of unfair prejudice did substantially outweigh the discounted probative value of the record of conviction, and it was an abuse of discretion to admit the record when an admission was available. [A redacted judgment is an alternative.] What we have said shows why this will be the general rule when proof of convict status is at issue, just as the prosecutor's choice will generally survive a Rule 403 analysis when a defendant seeks to force the substitution of an admission for evidence creating a coherent narrative of his thoughts and actions in perpetrating the offense for which he is being tried.

The judgment is reversed, and the case is remanded to the Ninth Circuit for further proceedings consistent with this opinion.

It is so ordered.

■ Justice O'Connor, with whom The Chief Justice, Justice Scalia, and Justice Thomas join, dissenting.

The Court today announces a rule that misapplies Federal Rule of Evidence 403 and upsets, without explanation, longstanding precedent regarding criminal prosecutions. I do not agree that the Government's introduction of evidence that reveals the name and basic nature of a defendant's prior felony conviction in a prosecution brought under 18 U.S.C. § 922(g)(1) "unfairly" prejudices the defendant within the meaning of Rule 403. Nor do I agree with the Court's newly minted rule that a defendant charged with violating § 922(g)(1) can force the Government to accept his concession to the prior conviction element of that offense, thereby precluding the Government from offering evidence on this point. I therefore dissent. . . .

The principle is illustrated by the evidence that was admitted at petitioner's trial to prove the other element of the § 922(g)(1) offense—possession of a "firearm." The Government submitted evidence showing that petitioner possessed a 9mm semiautomatic pistol. Although petitioner's possession of any number of weapons would have satisfied the requirements of § 922(g)(1), obviously the Government was entitled to prove with specific evidence that petitioner possessed the weapon he did. In the same vein, consider a murder case. Surely the Government can submit proof establishing the victim's identity, even though, strictly speaking, the jury has no "need" to know the victim's name, and even though the victim might be a particularly well loved public figure. The same logic should govern proof of the prior conviction element of the § 922(g)(1) offense. That is, the Government ought to be able to prove, with specific evidence, that petitioner committed a crime that came within § 922(g)(1)'s coverage....

Any incremental harm resulting from proving the name or basic nature of the prior felony can be properly mitigated by limiting jury instructions. Federal Rule of Evidence 105 provides that when evidence is admissible for one purpose, but not another, "the court, upon request, shall restrict the evidence to its proper scope and instruct the jury accordingly." Indeed, on petitioner's own motion in this case, the District Court instructed the jury that it was not to " 'consider a prior conviction as evidence of guilt of the crime for which the defendant is now on trial.' " Brief for United States 32. The jury is presumed to have followed this cautionary instruction, see Shannon v. United States, 512 U.S. 573, ___, 114 S.Ct. 2419, 129 L.Ed.2d 459 (1994), and the instruction offset whatever prejudice might have arisen from the introduction of petitioner's prior conviction....

The Court manufactures a new rule that, in a § 922(g)(1) case, a defendant can force the Government to accept his admission to the prior felony conviction element of the offense, thereby precluding the Government from offering evidence to directly prove a necessary element of its case. I cannot agree that it "unfairly" prejudices a defendant for the Government to prove his prior conviction with evidence that reveals the name or basic nature of his past crime. Like it or not, Congress chose to make a defendant's prior criminal conviction one of the two elements of the § 922(g)(1) offense. Moreover, crimes have names; a defendant is not convicted of some indeterminate, unspecified "crime." Nor do I think that Federal Rule of Evidence 403 can be read to obviate the well accepted principle, grounded in both the Constitution and in our precedent, that the Government may not be forced to accept a defendant's concession to an element of a charged offense as proof of that element. I respectfully dissent.

C.   SUFFICIENCY AND CIRCUMSTANTIAL EVIDENCE

Regina v. Onufrejczyk

Court of Criminal Appeals of England, 1955.
[1955] 1 All E.R. 247.

■ LORD GODDARD, C.J. The appellant, a Pole, who has been in this country since 1947, was convicted before Oliver J. at the last assizes for Swansea of the murder of his partner, another Pole, named Sykut. The trial lasted for some 12 days and was summed up with meticulous care by the judge, who analyzed the evidence in what I think I might describe as a masterly fashion, and the principal question argued on this appeal is whether there was proof of what the law calls a corpus delicti. For the remarkable fact about this case—and it has remained remarkable and unexplained—is that the body of Sykut who was last seen, so far as anybody knows, on December 14, 1953, has completely disappeared, and there is no trace whatever either of him or his clothes or his ashes. [The court held that the law did not require that the deceased's body or parts of it be located.]

The case against the prisoner was this: He and Sykut had a farm. The farm was a failure, and the appellant had come to the end of his resources. He was in dire need of money; of that there cannot be any doubt, for his own letters show it. He was trying to borrow money from this person and that, that relation and near friend; and he failed every time. He had actually got to the point when he was obviously considering fraud, for he was hoping to find a valuer who would overvalue the farm so that he might be able to raise more money on mortgage from his bank. Meanwhile, Sykut wanted to break off his association with the appellant. There was a suggestion that he should be paid out. Sykut had invested his money in the farm and was willing to sell his share in it for £700 if he could get it from the appellant; otherwise, Sykut had said, the farm must be put up for sale. They had been to Mr. Roberts, a solicitor of Llandilo, and their difficulties had been discussed before him. There was evidence—though for myself I do not think it was anything like so strong or convincing, as was much of the other evidence, as to point towards murder—that the men had quarreled; but by December 14 nothing had happened for any conclusion to be reached between the two men about the sale of the farm. Whether or not the appellant had at that time any money beyond perhaps a few shillings or a few pounds it seems clear that he had nothing at all to enable him to buy out his partner. He, the appellant, was very anxious to avoid the sale by auction and wanted to get the whole farm, because presumably he thought that if he had the whole of it he could make a satisfactory business out of it.

On December 14 Sykut disappeared, not only from Carmarthenshire, not only from England but, so far as is known, from the face of the earth. Letters came from Poland from his wife after his complete disappearance when there would have been ample time for him to have got back to Poland and to have got into touch with his friends, which would seem to show that he had not gone back to Poland; and the last person who is known to have seen Sykut is the appellant.

The appellant's activities after December 14 were certainly very remarkable. There was evidence, and very strong evidence, that the appellant must have posted a letter to a Polish woman living not very far away not later than a quarter to five, or possibly five o'clock on December 18. In that letter he said: "My case is already completed, but I must if only for a few hours pop in to London to take from my acquaintances money. I gave my partner the gross of the money"—I suppose that means the larger part of the money—"because I borrowed for a few weeks, only I must sell what is possible. So beg you very much to help me in this matter and I will be very grateful, at the moment this is all for now, the rest we talk over when Mrs. comes over. Beg you to inquire whether it is possible to sell the poultry alive before the holidays, as I must have at least part of the money to begin something and may be some of the cattle. Hand kisses, expecting as soon as possible to see you because my partner is leaving for 14 days and might change his mind. Please don't wait a moment because it might be too late." There he is saying that he has fixed up matters with his partner, that he has paid him most of the money and that he is expecting him to go away for a few days. What we know is that the appellant went to London and that he was trying by every means in his power to borrow money from relatives there to enable him to pay off his partner. He was getting a woman, who gave evidence and who evidently impressed the judge, to forge—there is no other word for it, though she may not have known that she was forging—documents purporting to be agreements, and then adding a signature to them which purported to be the signature of Sykut, and he was giving all sorts of contradictory accounts. When he was required to give an account of how his partner disappeared, he told the sort of story that might well be found in a magazine or a detective story, or a story by the late Phillips Oppenheim, as to how a large, dark car, sometimes described as black and sometimes as green, had arrived at this lonely farm at 7:30 at night, finding its way up a dreadful rocky path; that there were three men, one of whom had had a revolver; and that the unfortunate Sykut was put into the car at the point of the revolver and driven away. That was the kind of story that was told; and yet, remarkably enough, on December 18, when a sheriff's officer had gone to the farm before 7 p.m. to levy an execution against the appellant alone and in order to ensure that he was not levying on partnership property the officer had asked: "Where is Mr. Sykut?" he was told: "Oh, Sykut has gone to a doctor at Llandilo." According to the evidence that was given he never went to a doctor at Llandilo, but at 7:30 that night he was supposed to have been kidnapped and taken to London. The appellant said in his evidence that he was expecting his partner back at the farm, and yet all the letters which he wrote at that time seem to say that his partner had gone to Poland and that he would not see him back; his letters can only be explained on the footing that he knew perfectly well that his partner could never appear again.

It seems to me that one of the matters of the greatest possible importance is that when the appellant was in London, telling all sorts of contradictory stories to the people from whom he was trying to borrow money, he made two remarkable proposals. First, he asked Mrs. Pokora, with whom he was evidently on terms of close friendship, to send him sham registered letters, that is to say, to get registered envelopes, put sheets of paper in them, and send them to him, purporting to send him a couple of hundred pounds. Another more remarkable proposal was that he actually asked Mrs. Pokora's husband should go with him to see a solicitor at Llandilo and impersonate his partner. Could he have done that—would he have dared to do that, if he had thought that there was the smallest chance of this man appearing again? Yet he said in his evidence that he did expect Sykut to come back again. Sykut had new clothes and other property, and yet, if the appellant's story is true, he went off with these people, whether to Poland or somewhere else, leaving his clothes and everything behind and never came back or made any attempt to come back. Indeed, the appellant said that he knew one of the men, Jablonski—which I daresay is as good as any other name if one is using a Polish name—and that Mr. Jablonski had arranged to meet his partner at Paddington Station at 3 o'clock, on which day does not matter; that he went there and waited till 3 o'clock and that nobody came. Later, he said that he met Jablonski and Sykut at a Polish club and that there a document was signed; and that the signature said by the prosecution to be a forgery was affixed by Sykut in the presence of Jablonski and another gentleman; but nobody was called from the Polish club to say that these people ever existed at all.

I do not propose to go all through the evidence called, but one very remarkable piece of evidence cannot possibly be accounted for in any way other than that the appellant was deliberately trying to manufacture evidence with regard to the life of Sykut. That was the evidence of the local blacksmith. On December 14, the last day on which anyone saw Sykut alive, the appellant had taken a horse from the farm to the blacksmith for shoeing; the horse had been fetched away from the forge by Sykut, and the blacksmith had charged 17s. 6d. for shoeing the horse. The blacksmith's evidence was perfectly clear about that. He said that there was no doubt in his mind at all about it. Whether he referred to his books or not I do not know, but I think that he did; and it was on December 14 that Sykut came and took away the horse. Later in the month, at the end of December, when the police were beginning to make inquiries, the appellant visited the blacksmith and paid him the money, and he then tried to persuade the blacksmith to say that it was on December 17 that Sykut had gone there to take the horse away. The case for the prosecution was that Sykut was dead by the 17th, having been killed either on or immediately after the 14th. December 14 was the last day on which anybody had seen that unhappy man alive. Yet here was the appellant, at the end of December, when the police had begun to make inquiries, trying to get a man whose evidence on one point was vital, to give untrue evidence as to the date on which Sykut had fetched the horse. There can be no doubt about it; the blacksmith's evidence was either true or untrue. If it was true, the appellant was trying to get him to say something untrue.

Those are all matters which were pointed out to the jury by the judge, matters on which they had the advantage of hearing counsel on both sides. It is perfectly true that the judge did not point out to the jury all the matters. A judge does very often say to a jury: "It is very remarkable that such a point has not been proved, and if it could be, it ought to have been proved." The case for the prosecution was: this man has disappeared; he has completely gone from the ken of mankind; it is impossible to believe that he is alive now. I suppose that it would have been possible for him to have got out of the country and become immured behind what is sometimes called the "iron curtain"; but here there are facts which point inevitably, as it is said irresistibly, towards the appellant being the person who knows what happened to the missing man and who disposed of that man in one way or another. It may be that it would have been desirable to emphasize to the jury that the first thing to which they must apply their minds was whether a murder had been committed; but, speaking for myself, I think that the way the judge put it in the two passages which I have read did sufficiently direct the attention of the jury to the fact that they had to be satisfied of that, and that if they were satisfied of the death, the violent death, of this man, they need not go any further. It is no doubt true that the prosecution relied considerably on certain minute spots in the kitchen—a minute quantity on the wall and a minute quantity on the ceiling—which were found to be blood when scientifically examined; spots so small that they might easily have escaped the attention of somebody who was trying to wash or wipe up blood. The appellant did not deny that the blood which was found was that of his partner. He said that it was due to the fact that his partner had cut his hand in the field, on one of the tractors, and that on coming in he must have shaken his hand and shaken off some blood. That, of course, was a possibility, and it was put to the jury. It was also a possibility that Sykut was disposed of in the kitchen; but there is no evidence that he was; indeed as Mr. Elwyn Jones has very properly stressed, there is no evidence at all as to how the man met his death. But this court is of opinion that there was evidence on which the jury could infer that he did meet his death, and that he was dead; and if he was dead, the circumstances of the case point to the fact that his death was not a natural one. If that establishes, as it would, a corpus delicti, the evidence was such that the jury were entitled to find that the appellant murdered his partner.

For these reasons, we have been unable to find any misdirection by the judge, or anything in the summing up which would justify us in saying that the case was not properly presented to the jury. We have come to the conclusion that there was evidence on which the jury were entitled to find that the appellant's partner was murdered and that the appellant was the murderer, and accordingly this appeal is dismissed.

Appeal dismissed.

NOTES

1. 33 Can.B.Rev. 603 (1955) criticizes the main case. See also Morris, Corpus Delicti and Circumstantial Evidence, 68 L.Q.Rev. 391 (1952), discussing Rex v. Horry. An aspect of this striking case that merits discussion is the question of the proper charge to a jury in a circumstantial case. While Lord Goddard objects to the use of "epithets" to enhance the value of evidence, many American jurisdictions require a special charge in a circumstantial case. The circumstantial evidence charge in criminal cases is sometimes put in these terms: "where the evidence is circumstantial it must be such as to exclude every reasonable hypothesis other than that of guilt" or even "to exclude to a moral certainty every other inference except guilt." But compare the essentially identical provisions of the New York Pattern Jury Instructions for civil cases (1971 revision):

PJI 1:70. GENERAL INSTRUCTION—CIRCUMSTANTIAL EVIDENCE

Facts may be proved by circumstantial evidence. In order to prove a fact by circumstances, there must be positive proof of some fact which, though true, does not itself directly establish the fact in dispute but affords a reasonable inference of its existence. The fact or facts upon which it is sought to base an inference must be proved and not left to rest in conjecture, and when proved it must appear that the inference drawn is the only one that can fairly and reasonably be drawn from the facts and that any other explanation is fairly and reasonably excluded. If the fact or facts proved permit you to draw two inferences, one of which supports (negligence, freedom from contributory negligence) and the other (non-negligence, contributory negligence), you are required to draw the one which accords with (non-negligence, contributory negligence).

See also, In re Winship, 397 U.S. 358, 369–372, (1970) (Harlan J., concurring).

In People v. Morris, 347 N.Y.S.2d 975, 977 (N.Y.A.D.1973), aff'd, 334 N.E.2d 10 (N.Y.C.A.1975), a criminal case where the defendant's guilt was based entirely on circumstantial evidence, it was held that "the trial court should have charged the jury that the evidence must point logically to defendant's guilt so as to exclude to a moral certainty every other reasonable hypothesis."

The concurring opinion in Vargas v. Keane, 86 F.3d 1273, 1281 (2d Cir.1996) describes the results of a questionnaire to jurors testing their reaction to various forms of instruction. At least one form of the moral certainty charge provided less protection to defendants than standard forms. The conclusion of the concurring judge was that the less said about defining reasonable doubt, the better.

Professor Shapiro, in "To a Moral Certainty": Theories of Knowledge and Anglo–American Juries, 1600–1850, 38 Hastings L.J. 153 (1986), concludes that the phrase "moral certainty" once had the meaning of highest degree of probability. Influenced by contemporary philosophical thought, it began to be used to mean "satisfied conscience," as free evaluation of probative force to form a satisfied belief began to supplant the more mechanical evaluation of witnesses under medieval practice.

Early in the seventeenth century the concern for evaluating evidence was encapsulated in "satisfied conscience" or "satisfied belief" formulas that resonated to the moral and religious obligations of jurors serving under oath. During the seventeenth and eighteenth centuries, the concepts of probability, degrees of certainty, and moral certainty were poured into the old formulas so that they emerged at the end of the eighteenth century as the secular moral standard of "beyond reasonable doubt."

.... The earliest standards we have identified were "satisfied belief" and "satisfied conscience." They were succeeded by "satisfied mind" or "satisfied understanding," or something closely approximating them. Gradually this language, too, was replaced by the concept of "moral certainty" and "beyond reasonable doubt."

Throughout this development two ideas to be conveyed to the jury have remained central. The first idea is that there are two realms of human knowledge. In one it is possible to obtain the absolute certainty of mathematical demonstration, as when we say that the square of the hypotenuse of a right triangle is equal to the sum of the squares of the other two sides. In the other, which is the empirical realm of events, absolute certainty of this kind is not possible. The second idea is that, in this realm of events, just because absolute certainty is not possible, we ought not to treat everything as merely a guess or a matter of opinion. Instead, in this realm there are levels of certainty, and we reach higher levels of certainty as the quantity and quality of the evidence available to us increases. The highest level of certainty in this realm in which no absolute certainty is possible is what traditionally has been called moral certainty.

There is little doubt that "moral certainty" no longer conveys these two ideas, but it may be worthwhile to continue to convey them. To further that task I present the following proposed jury instruction as a supplement to a revised reasonable court instruction that omits "moral certainty":

We can be absolutely certain that two plus two equals four. In the real world of human actions we can never be absolutely certain of anything. When we say that the prosecution must prove the defendant's guilt beyond a reasonable doubt, we do not mean that you, the jury, must be absolutely certain of the defendant's guilt before finding the defendant guilty. Instead, we mean that you should not find the defendant guilty unless you have reached the highest level of certainty of the defendant's guilt that it is possible to have about things that happen in the real world and that you must learn about by evidence presented in the courtroom.

Id. at 192–93.

The California Jury Instructions, Criminal (CALJIC) (4th ed.) No. 2.01 (1979 revision) provided:

However, a finding of guilt as to any crime may not be based on circumstantial evidence unless the proved circumstances are not only (1) consistent with the theory that the defendant is guilty of the crime, but (2) cannot be reconciled with any other rational conclusion.

Further, each fact which is essential to complete a set of circumstances necessary to establish the defendant's guilt must be proved beyond a reasonable doubt. In other words, before an inference essential to establish guilt may be found to have been proved beyond a reasonable doubt, each fact or circumstance upon which such inference necessarily rests must be proved beyond a reasonable doubt.

Also, if the circumstantial evidence [as to any particular count] is susceptible of two reasonable interpretations, one of which points to the defendant's guilt and the other to his innocence, it is your duty to adopt that interpretation which points to the defendant's innocence, and reject that interpretation which points to his guilt.

If, on the other hand, one interpretation of such evidence appears to you to be reasonable and the other interpretation to be unreasonable, it would be your duty to accept the reasonable interpretation and to reject the unreasonable.

A different approach is taken in the federal courts. In Holland v. United States, 348 U.S. 121, 139–40 (1954), the Supreme Court concluded that "the better rule is that where the jury is properly instructed on the standards for reasonable doubt, such an additional instruction on circumstantial evidence is confusing and incorrect," for the reason that "circumstantial evidence in this respect is intrinsically no different from testimonial evidence." Notes, 55 Col.L.Rev. 549, 558 (1955), and 38 Geo.L.Rev. (1950) approve this position. The present rule of law in England rejects the use of additional instructions on circumstantial evidence. In McGreevy v. Director of Public Prosecutors (1973) 1 All E.R. 503, the court held there is no rule that, where the prosecutor's case is based entirely on circumstantial evidence, the judge must as a matter of law give an instruction that the jury must not convict unless it is satisfied that the facts proved are not only consistent with the guilt of the defendant, but also such as to be inconsistent with any other conclusion.

Considering the multiple inferential assessments of error, veracity, bias, and so on, necessary to sustain testimonial proof, is there any substantial difference between a case like Onufrejczyk and a "pure" testimonial case?

2. Another problem suggested by the Onufrejczyk case is that of appellate review of convictions. Curley v. United States, 160 F.2d 229, 232–33 (App.D.C. 1947) (Prettyman, J.):

> The true rule ... is that a trial judge, in passing upon a motion for directed verdict of acquittal, must determine whether upon the evidence, giving full play to the right of the jury to determine credibility, weigh the evidence, and draw justifiable inferences of fact, a reasonable mind might fairly conclude guilt beyond a reasonable doubt. If he concludes that upon the evidence there must be such a doubt in a reasonable mind, he must grant the motion; or, to state it another way, if there is no evidence, upon which a reasonable mind might fairly conclude guilt beyond reasonable doubt, the motion must be granted. If he concludes that either of the two results, a reasonable doubt or no reasonable doubt, is fairly possible, he must let the jury decide the matter. In a given case, particularly one of circumstantial evidence, that determination may depend upon the difference between pure speculation and legitimate inference from proven facts. The task of the judge in such case is not easy, for the rule of reason is frequently difficult to apply, but we know of no way to avoid that difficulty....

> If the judge were to direct acquittal whenever in his opinion the evidence failed to exclude every hypothesis but that of guilt, he would preempt the functions of the jury. Under such rule, the judge would have to be convinced of guilt beyond peradventure of doubt before the jury would be permitted to consider the case. That is not the place of the jury in criminal procedure. They are the judges of the facts and of guilt or innocence, not merely a device for checking upon the conclusions of the judge.

See generally, discussion of burden of production, infra.

3. A case similar to Regina v. Onufrejczyk is People v. Scott, 1 Cal.Rptr. 600 (Cal.App.1959), appeal dismissed and cert. denied, 364 U.S. 471 (1960); 61 Colum.L.Rev. 740 (1960). In People v. Manson, 139 Cal.Rptr. 275, cert. denied, 435 U.S. 953 (1978), the death of the alleged victim—one of two elements of the corpus delicti—was proven by circumstantial evidence. See also, Perkins, The Corpus Delicti of Murder, 48 Va.L.Rev. 173, 184 (1962).

4. In American Communications Association, CIO v. Douds, 339 U.S. 382, 411 (1950), the court pointed out:

> To state the difference, however, is but to recognize that while objective facts may be proved directly, the state of a man's mind must be inferred from the things he says or does. Of course we agree that the courts cannot "ascertain the thought that has had no outward manifestation." But courts and juries every day pass upon knowledge, belief and intent—the state of men's minds—having before them no more than evidence of their words and conduct, from which, in ordinary human experience, mental condition may be inferred. See 2 Wigmore, Evidence (3d ed.) §§ 244, 256 et seq. False swearing in signing the affidavit must, as in other cases where mental state is in issue, be proved by the outward manifestations of state of mind. In the absence of such manifestations, which are as much "overt acts" as the act of joining the Communist Party, there can be no successful prosecution for false swearing.

5. Statements can be found in the cases that in a circumstantial evidence case no inference may be based upon an inference. See Waldman v. Shipyard Marina, 230 A.2d 841, 845–46 (R.I.1967), where an action for negligence was brought to recover damages to a motorboat resulting from a fire that occurred while the boat was berthed at the defendant's marina. The court, in holding that one could not properly infer that defendant's actions proximately caused the accident based on the facts produced at trial said:

> The facts established by the direct evidence ... are simply that the Muehlberg boat was fueled by the dockmaster; that the dockmaster without taking any prior precautions to ventilate the vessel, attempted to start the engine; and that a fire occurred. To establish a causal connection between the omissions of the dockmaster to take precautions after fueling and the fire, the trial justice inferred the gasoline fumes had collected either in the engine room or in the bilges of the Muehlberg boat. From this inferential fact he then inferred that these fumes were ignited when the dockmaster attempted to start the engine.

> It is clear from our prior discussion that the second inference can be accepted as being of probative force only if the inference upon which it rests, that is, that the fumes accumulated in the engine room or bilges, necessarily excludes the drawing of any other reasonable inference from the fact that the fueling operation had been carried out. We are unable to agree that such is the only reasonable inference that can be drawn from the carrying out of the fueling operation. That degree of probability necessary to exclude other reasonable or contrary inferences does not inhere in the basic inference. . . .

> It may well be that the inference that fumes accumulated as a result of the fueling operation would possess such a degree of probability as to exclude other reasonable inferences had it been established that there was some defect in the fuel tank or gasoline line or some spillage during the fueling operation.

How would you have analyzed the case for the plaintiff? What other proof could you have supplied to buttress your argument?

Wigmore's criticism of the no inference on an inference rule seems unanswerable.

> There is no such orthodox rule; nor can there be. If there were, hardly a single trial could be adequately prosecuted. [Footnote omitted.] For example, on a charge of murder, the defendant's gun is found discharged;

from this we infer that he discharged it; and from this we infer that it was his bullet which struck and killed the deceased. Or, the defendant is shown to have been sharpening a knife; from this we argue that he had a design to use it upon the deceased; and from this we argue that the fatal stab was the result of this design. In these and innumerable daily instances we build up inference upon inference, and yet no court (until in very modern times) ever thought of forbidding it. All departments of reasoning, all scientific work, every day's life and every day's trial, proceed upon such data.

1 Wigmore § 41, at 435–36 (3d ed.).

In spite of such criticism (and see Jennings, Probative Value of an Inference Drawn Upon an Inference, 22 U.Cin.L.Rev. 39 (1953)), the no inference on an inference rule continues to put in an appearance when courts seek to exercise control they believe necessary. It would seem that adequate control can be maintained through enforcement of sound notions, consonant with ordinary reasoning, concerning the exclusion of evidence of excessive remoteness and insignificant probative value.

Note the criticism in United States v. Shonubi, 895 F.Supp. 460, 475–478 (E.D.N.Y.1995), rev'd. on this ground, 103 F.3d 1085 (2d Cir.1997), of the court of appeals ruling that estimation of drug quantity must be based upon "specific evidence." See Id. at 478:

> Perhaps the appellate court, embarrassed either by the Guidelines' excessive reliance on quantity as a surrogate for culpability or by the low burden of proof required at sentencing, believes that a specific or direct evidence requirement offers defendants some necessary protection.... If so, it has taken a road that leads to less accurate fact-finding with haphazard over- and under-"protection" of defendants. The "specific evidence" rule does not guard against injustice. Instead, it introduces—in the language of the court of appeals—a "baffling" distinction.

In Shonubi, the court of appeals insisted that "specific evidence" was required to provide adequate protection to defendants in guideline sentencing. What is "specific evidence"? Would increasing the burden of proof provide better protection? See, criticizing the court of appeals decision as based on medieval concepts of evidence, United States v. Shonubi, __ F. Supp. __ (E.D.N.Y.1997).

Interlake Iron Corp. v. N.L.R.B., 131 F.2d 129, 133 (7th Cir.1942):

> [I]nferences alone may, if reasonable, provide a link in the chain of evidence and constitute in that regard substantial evidence. But an inference cannot be piled upon an inference, and then another inference upon that, as such inferences are unreasonable and cannot be considered as substantial evidence. Such a method could be extended indefinitely until there would be no more substance to it than the soup Lincoln talked about that was "made by boiling the shadow of a pigeon that had starved to death."

United States v. Medico, 557 F.2d 309, 317–18 (2d Cir.1977): The defendant was convicted of armed robbery. At trial, an F.B.I. agent identified a pair of red pants which he had taken from the defendant's apartment. The pants contained numerous holes in them that the agent testified appeared to be "pellet holes possibly from a shotgun." He also identified various caliber shells as objects taken from defendant's apartment.

The probative value of the trousers and the pellets in identifying the appellant as one of the bank robbers rested on the jury's drawing two inferences from this evidence. The first inference involved the appellant's possession of the weapons used to discharge the pellets into the wall and trousers at the time of the robbery. The second inference would have been that one or more of these weapons was used in the robbery....

One bank employee testified that one of the robbers carried a rifle and the other carried a shotgun....

There was, concededly, no evidence linking the shotgun used in the robbery to the shotgun fired in Medico's apartment. Absent additional factors, this court has indicated that the mere similarity of the weapons would be an insufficient ground for admission.... The inferences required to be drawn by the jury—that at the time of the crime, appellant had access to weapons, at least one of which was used in the robbery—without more would be too weak.

The court upheld the admission of the evidence stating:

Where, however, direct and circumstantial evidence independent of the defendant's possession of guns exists to link him to the crime, the basis for those inferences is strengthened, ... and admission of such evidence is less questionable. Two eyewitnesses to the crime identified Medico in court as one of the perpetrators, ... [and t]here was also testimony that before the robbery Medico had been seen driving the car used for the getaway.

In Goodwin v. Misticos, 42 So.2d 397, 401 (Miss.1949) the court held that a widow should have had the presence of mind to keep a sample of her dying husband's regurgitations as proof of the source of his food poisoning.

The second admonition is that, in allowing inference upon inference, we should do so no further than the reasonable necessities of the case, in the interest of justice, require. Fortunately, in nearly all cases, particularly in civil cases, the necessities of the case do not require that the chain of inferences shall be lengthened, one link to another, through such an extent as to present as a practical question the problem whether the chain of inferences has become too long and therefore too weak to hold; for in nearly every case it will be found that one or more of the essential facts sought to be established by inference is or are capable of proof by direct, positive, or by demonstrative evidence, and thereupon there comes into play the rule that, where a party, who has the burden of proof, has the power to produce evidence of a more explicit, direct, and satisfactory character than that which he does introduce and relies on, he must introduce that more explicit, direct, and satisfactory proof, or else suffer the presumption that, if the more satisfactory evidence had been given, it would have been detrimental to him and would have laid open deficiencies in, and objections to, his case, which the more obscure and uncertain evidence did not disclose.

See Annot., "Modern Status of the Rules Against Basing an Inference upon an Inference or a Presumption upon a Presumption", 5 A.L.R.3d 100 (1966).

Most courts by now accept the need to base an inference upon an inference. For example, in Cora Pub, Inc. v. Continental Casualty Co., 619 F.2d 482, 486 (5th Cir.1980), the court explained that "[t]he important question is whether the inference is reasonably well supported by the evidence. We must judge the inference as we would any other, taking into consideration that its probability may be attenuated by each underlying inference." See also Daniels v. Twin Oaks Nursing Home, 692 F.2d 1321 (11th Cir.1982); Fenner v. General Motors Corp., 657 F.2d 647 (5th Cir.1981), cert. denied, 455 U.S. 942 (1982). Is a contrary rule merely a shorthand expression for judicial distrust of strained reasoning or of reliance upon remote or unfounded inferences or conclusions?

State v. Brewer

Supreme Judicial Court of Maine, 1985.
505 A.2d 774.

■ GLASSMAN, JUSTICE.

Ricky Brewer appeals from a judgment of the Superior Court, Androscoggin County, affirming the judgment of the District Court, Livermore Falls, finding him guilty of operating a motor vehicle while under the influence of intoxicating liquor ... and operating a motor vehicle while his license to operate had been suspended ...

I

Virginia Curtis advised the sheriff's department by telephone that there was an accident on the Line Road in Leeds. The accident had occurred within approximately 20 minutes after she had traveled that road to reach her home. Within 5 minutes of the telephone call she went to the scene where she observed the defendant sitting alone behind the wheel in a pick-up truck. The motor was not running. When assured by the defendant that he was all right, she returned to her home to report this to the sheriff's office and was advised that a Maine State Police officer was on the way to the scene. Shortly after this telephone call the defendant came into the Curtis home.

On arrival at the scene, the trooper found the truck a few feet from the Line Road lodged too close to a tree to permit the left door to open. The trooper observed tracks on the right side of the truck near the door. There was no one in the truck when the trooper arrived, and the trooper was unable to determine how many people had been in the truck when the accident occurred. In the trooper's opinion someone could have left the truck by the passenger door, reached the road and left the scene of the accident. The only evidence as to the direction of the footprints was the trooper's testimony "there weren't any leading off into the woods." The trooper also observed a star-shaped crack high on the windshield to the left of the driver's seat and fragments of glass from the shattered sunroof on both the driver's and passenger's seats. From the registration in the vehicle, the trooper determined that Andrew Pratt was the owner.

At the Curtis home the trooper observed that the defendant had a cut under his chin and scratches on his face. His breath smelled of alcohol, and his eyes were red and glassy with the eyelids drooping. The defendant insisted he had not been driving the truck. A breath test was administered that gave a blood-alcohol level of 0.212 percent of weight.

In response to the question—"You didn't contact Andrew Pratt, to see whether he had been using the [truck] that night, did you?"—the trooper testified that when Pratt came to "pick up" the defendant, he stated he had not been using the truck, but had gone to bed and left the keys on the table in the apartment that he and the defendant shared.

At trial in the District Court the defendant freely admitted his intoxication and the suspension of his license, but denied driving the truck. The defendant testified that he and Pratt had been drinking together at a bar in Lewiston. They left together and got into Pratt's truck. Pratt was driving, and the defendant had gone to sleep and did not awaken until after the accident. At that time he was alone in the truck.

Neither party called Pratt as a witness. In his closing argument the prosecutor asked the court to draw an inference adverse to the defendant based on the defendant's failure to call Pratt. In making findings of fact the court stated:

> [T]he defendant, while on the stand, admitted that he was under the influence of alcohol or intoxicating liquor.... But the question ... revolves around the issue of operation.... The Court does have the right to infer, that if someone else was operating this car, as the defendant contends, then that someone, Mr. Pratt, is the party who would be his— Brewer's best alibi witness. He's not here today, ... obviously he's the witness who might clear him of this charge.

The court found the defendant guilty as charged, and the defendant appeals. The defendant contends on appeal, *inter alia,* that the evidence is insufficient to support the conviction and that the inference drawn by the trial court is improper.

II

When, as here, a defendant challenges the sufficiency of the evidence, we will set the conviction aside only if no trier of fact rationally could have found the elements of the crime beyond a reasonable doubt.... A conviction based on circumstantial evidence is not for that reason any less conclusive.... While the element of operation is a close question in this case, we cannot say on the facts presented that no trier of fact rationally could have found the elements of the crime beyond a reasonable doubt.

III

The defendant contends that it was improper for the trial court to draw any inference of the defendant's guilt by reason of the defendant's failure to call Pratt as a witness. We agree ...

Any inference as to the content of testimony not given presents grave dangers of speculation and conjecture. See McCormick, Law of Evidence § 272 at 657 (E. Cleary ed. 1972). Accordingly, even when we have permitted the inference, we cautioned that it can involve serious risks of unfairness to the accused.... We have held the drawing of an inference improper when neither party can be said to have greater power to produce the witness....

The promulgation of the Maine Rules of Evidence removed any logical basis for the missing-witness inference by abolishing the practice of vouching. Rule 607 provides: "The credibility of a witness may be attacked by any party, including the party calling him." Under Rule 607 a party may call a witness, elicit the witness's testimony, and then freely attack the witness's credibility if the testimony proves to be adverse. See M.R.Evid. 607 Advisers' Note, reprinted in R. Field & P. Murray, supra, at 136; State v. Price, 275 N.W.2d 82, 90 (Neb.1979) (the identical Nebraska Rule 607 represents a repudiation "of the ancient and universally criticized rule that a party 'vouches' for the credibility of his own witnesses and may not impeach them"). Since neither party vouches for any witness's credibility, the failure of a party to call a witness cannot be treated as an evidentiary fact that permits any inference as to the content of the testimony of that witness.

Also, the availability of modern discovery procedures sharply undercuts whatever utility the inference might once have possessed in compelling a reluctant party to identify witnesses who might be expected to testify to relevant evidence. If a party violates his discovery obligation, the trial court has available to it a variety of sanctions.

To allow the missing-witness inference in a criminal case is particularly inappropriate since it distorts the allocation of the burden of proving the defendant's guilt. The defendant is not obligated to present evidence on his own behalf. The inference may have the effect of requiring the defendant to produce evidence to rebut the inference. If he fails to do so, the missing-witness inference allows the state to create "evidence" from the defendant's failure to produce evidence. Such a result is impermissible. . . . See also State v. **Cavness,** 381 P.2d 685, 686–87 (Haw.1963) (inference improper, when the missing witness is an accomplice or codefendant); accord Christensen v. State, 333 A.2d 45, 49 (Md.1975); Schrameck v. State, 595 P.2d 799 (Okla.Crim.App.1979) (per curiam).

The facts of the instant case amply illustrate the impropriety of the missing-witness inference in a criminal case. The defendant testified that Pratt had been drinking for a couple hours and then drove the truck. If Pratt had testified to corroborate the defendant's story, Pratt might have subjected himself to criminal liability on charges of operating under the influence of intoxicating liquor, 29 M.R.S.A. § 1312–B (Supp.1984–1985) and leaving the scene of an accident, id. §§ 893–894 (1978). Thus the defendant's failure to call Pratt might as strongly suggest that Pratt's testimony would have been favorable to the defendant as it would suggest unfavorable testimony, but either inference would be speculative.

We hold, therefore, that in a criminal case the failure of a party to call a witness does not permit the opposing party to argue, or the factfinder to draw, any inference as to whether the witness's testimony would be favorable or unfavorable to either party. We overrule any prior decisions to the extent that they permitted such an inference.

Accordingly, we hold that the trial court erred in drawing an inference of the defendant's guilt from the defendant's failure to call Pratt as a witness. [Remanded for a new trial.]

NOTES

1. The Brewer case is discussed in detail in John H. Mansfield, Evidential Use of Litigation Activity of the Parties, 43 Syracuse L.Rev. 695, 730 ff. (1992) (effect of not introducing evidence).

2. A usual charge includes the sentence: "Reasonable doubt may be based upon the evidence or the lack of evidence." After Brewer could a defendant argue: "Where is the key witness? Might she not have raised a doubt?" or, "Why was no picture taken?" or "Why did not the police investigate by _____?" Should the same rule apply to both defence and prosecution? If the government does not call a key witness, should the judge? See also the discussion of grants of immunity by the prosecutor and refusal to do so on demand of defendant, infra.

3. In State v. Cloutier, 628 A.2d 1047, 1049 (Me.1993), the court found objectionable the state's informing the jury that after its chemist tested blood samples, it gave samples to defendant's chemist for testing. The latter's tests were never submitted to the jury. The court feared "creat[ing] a missing-test-result inference similar to the missing-witness inference created in Brewer." Can and should the defendant always have the opportunity to test DNA? What might be the effect of a rigid rule?

4. In Lewis v. State, 862 P.2d 181, 191 (Alaska App.1993), the court refused to reverse a conviction after the state argued to the jurors that defendant had failed to call key defense witnesses. After describing variants of the rule, of which Brewer was the strictest, the court apparently applied a soft version, refusing to reverse since the jury knew the state had the burden of proof and the trial court "had broad discretion to determine the need for a mistrial."

NOTES ON SPOLIATION

In its most general sense, spoliation covers a broad category of situations where a litigant destroys evidence, induces witnesses not to testify, relies upon a variety of privileges to prevent evidence from being adduced or fails to answer questions or call witnesses who might be expected to give favorable testimony or is otherwise not forthcoming with the tribunal. Some of the ethical obligations of the attorney, which raise related but quite distinct sets of problems, are discussed in Chapter 3, infra, under Preparation of Witnesses and in Chapter 8 on Privileges under Attorney–Client Privileges.

In McQueeney v. Wilmington Trust Co., 779 F.2d 916 (3d Cir.1985), the court held that the trial judge improperly excluded evidence suggesting that the plaintiff had suborned perjury. The court explained that:

> [t]he intuitive appeal of defendants' proffer is immediate. One who believes his own case to be weak is more likely to suborn perjury than one who thinks he has a strong case, and a party knows better than anyone else the truth about his own case. Thus, subornation of perjury by a party is strong evidence that the party's case is weak. Admittedly the conclusion is not inescapable: parties may be mistaken about the merits or force of their own cases. But evidence need not lead inescapably towards a single conclusion to be relevant, it need only make certain facts more probable than not. The evidence of subornation here does cast into doubt the merits of McQueeney's claims, even if it does not extinguish them.

779 F.2d at 921. As to tampering with witnesses, see United States v. Bongard, 713 F.2d 419 (8th Cir.1983) (per curiam) (government may offer evidence of defendant's attempts to influence testimony to show defendant's consciousness of guilt); United States v. Qamar, 671 F.2d 732 (2d Cir.1982) (trial judge properly admitted evidence that the defendant issued death threats against a witness and his family).

In United States v. Obayagbona, 627 F.Supp. 329 (E.D.N.Y.1985), the court refused to charge the jury that the prosecution's failure to call a confidential informant as a witness gave rise to an inference that the testimony would be unfavorable since the witness had been available to the defense throughout the trial. The court explained that:

> [t]he missing witness rule charges should almost never be given unless a party has procured the witness' unavailability. Where this occurs, the missing witness argument is insignificant as compared to the much more powerful inference of guilty mind through spoliation. Counsel are quite capable of dealing with the probative force of such lines of proof without having the court single them out for special emphasis.

627 F.Supp. at 344–45.

Along this same line, one commentator has argued that the attempt to sort and balance the relative disadvantages of particular testimony to each side for the sole purpose of identifying an inference of weakness through absence of a witness is largely a waste of judicial resources. Stier, Revisiting the Missing

Witness Inference—Quieting the Loud Voice from the Empty Chair, 44 Md. L.Rev. 137 (1985).

The spoliation doctrine only applies to the conduct of the parties to a lawsuit. Thus, the spoliation inference is inapplicable where a *witness,* independently of a party, destroys evidence. United States v. Esposito, 771 F.2d 283 (7th Cir.1985), cert. denied, 475 U.S. 1011 (1986). But cf. Penfield v. Venuti, 589 F.Supp. 250 (D.Conn.1984) (reliance on vehicle owner's son's refusal to answer at deposition on Fifth Amendment grounds usable against father).

On the issue of the use of false testimony, see United States v. Agurs, 427 U.S. 97, 103 (1976). The Federal Sentencing Guidelines provide for an increased sentence for perjury by the defendant at his trial. United States v. Shonubi, 998 F.2d 84 (2d Cir.1993), criticized on remand, 895 F.Supp. 460, 524–28 (E.D.N.Y. 1995). See also on the government's withholding of exculpatory evidence, Brady v. Maryland, 373 U.S. 83 (1963); United States v. Bagley, 473 U.S. 667 (1985).

Some courts recognize a civil cause of action for spoliation of evidence. See Smith v. Superior Court, 198 Cal.Rptr. 829 (Cal.App.1984) (recognizing a cause of action for intentional spoliation of evidence); Bondu v. Gurvich, 473 So.2d 1307 (Fla.App.1984) (recognizing a cause of action for negligent spoliation of evidence). For a general discussion of this issue, see Note, Spoliation: Civil Liability for Destruction of Evidence, 20 U.Rich.L.Rev. 191 (1985). Sanctions may be imposed for intentional destruction of evidence; what are the permissible forms? See United States v. Sommer, 815 F.2d 15 (2d Cir.1987), and cases cited.

In National Life & Accident Insurance Co. v. Eddings, 221 S.W.2d 695 (Tenn.1949), the plaintiff, suing to recover benefits on account of illness on an industrial insurance policy, effectively blocked the insurance company from proving he had lied on his application when he said he had no prior serious illnesses. Plaintiff refused to waive his physician-patient privilege to permit examination of certain hospital records. The court concluded that this exercise of the privilege was not affirmative proof of the defense. It declared:

> The inference to be drawn from such conduct may well be a persuasive factor in the process of weighing and interpreting the testimony offered by the party who can produce evidence and fails to do so, but it cannot be treated as affirmative evidence of a fact otherwise unproved. Logic and precedent combine to establish this conclusion.

221 S.W.2d at 698. Do you agree with the "logic" of this conclusion? Is it consistent with the Onufrejczyk case? See comment in Chapter 8, dealing with the privilege against self-incrimination and inferences to be drawn.

Contrast with the Eddings opinion, cases such as United States v. Monahan, 633 F.2d 984 (1st Cir.1980), where defendant's conviction for threats to witnesses in the case being tried were admitted on a theory of consciousness of guilt. The court impliedly recognized the strong probative force of such evidence, suggesting that only if the threat is "inflammatory or macabre in content," would it be "excluded under Rule 403." Id. at 985.

In Parker v. Southern Railway, 134 F.Supp. 185, 190 (E.D.S.C.1955), the trial judge directed a verdict for the defendant-railroad. On motion for a new trial plaintiff argued that the failure of the railroad to call the crew of the train gave rise to an inference that their testimony would have been unfavorable to the railroad. The judge rejected this contention, saying that defendant was not obliged to do anything until plaintiff made out a prima facie case, which, he held, had not been done.

Suppose each side has made out a prima facie case and thus the court must instruct the jury on the nature of the inference arising from failure to call a witness, or, in a non-jury case, must draw the inference itself. Pacific–Atlantic S.S. Co. v. United States, 175 F.2d 632, 636 (4th Cir.), cert. denied, 338 U.S. 868 (1949), involved a collision at sea. The respondent produced a number of eye-witnesses but failed to produce three others who saw the event. Libellant vigorously attacked the credibility of respondent's witnesses and asked the court to assume that if the three missing witnesses had been called their testimony would have been damaging to respondent and would have contradicted the testimony of respondent's witnesses. The court ruled that a trier of fact can draw the inference that the testimony of uncalled witnesses would be unfavorable. But, said the court, there is no principle that when there are twelve witnesses to an event and two are not called the trier must discredit the testimony of the other ten. What should the court do if the witnesses are equally available to both sides?

The statement in the Pacific–Atlantic S.S. Co. case that failure to call a witness gives rise to an inference that his testimony would be unfavorable, is criticized in 34 Corn.L.Q. 637 (1949). It is there argued that the trier should only construe the evidence in the case most strongly against the party who would be expected to call the witness. The New York rule is in accord with this position. See The Eraser Co. v. Kaufman, 138 N.Y.S.2d 743 (1955). Hofstadter & Richter, Effect of Failure to Call a Witness—New Rule Proposed, New York L.J., June 4–7, 1956, argues that the trier should be permitted to draw whatever inference it feels justified in the particular case from failure to call a witness. See 5 A.L.R.2d 893 (1949).

Pennewell v. United States, 353 F.2d 870 (D.C.App.1965): Error for prosecutor to refer to defendant's failure to call a witness who under the prosecution theory was defendant's front man and under defendant's theory committed the crime himself; it could not reasonably be supposed that the missing witness would support the defendant's story. See also Morrison v. United States, 365 F.2d 521 (D.C.App.1966): When a witness' claim of privilege against self-incrimination is sustained and the prosecution refuses to grant immunity, the defendant should not be allowed to make a "missing witness" argument, emphasizing the peculiar availability of the witness to the prosecution. "The large number of considerations which enter into the relatively rare use of immunity grants indicates that government reluctance to use this power cannot reasonably be equated to the failure of a litigant to produce an otherwise available witness." See Comment, Judicial Response to Governmental Loss or Destruction of Evidence, 39 U.Chi.L.Rev. 542 (1972); Orena v. United States, 956 F.Supp. 1071 (E.D.N.Y.1997) (effect of claiming privilege by witness in a habeas corpus case who is later granted immunity and testifies).

In a prosecution for abortion, may the defendant testify that when the police searched her house, where the prosecuting witness testified the abortion took place, they found no abortion paraphernalia? See State v. Harling, 170 N.W.2d 720, 725–26 (Wis.1969).

Many of the cases in this area raise interrelated questions of ambiguity of inference and privilege: The prosecution in a narcotics case fails to put on the stand an informer. Defendant contends an inference results that the informer's testimony would be unfavorable to the prosecution, and therefore there was not sufficient evidence to find defendant guilty beyond reasonable doubt. People v. Lewis, 198 N.E.2d 812 (Ill.1964). May not the prosecution have preferred to hide the identity of the informer so that he might be used again, or to protect him from criminal vengeance?

In a felony murder case, there were repeated references to defendant's refusal to take a lie detector test, evidence of the conclusions drawn from which would have been inadmissible. State v. Driver, 183 A.2d 655, 657–61 (N.J.1962), overruled on other grounds, State v. McDavitt, 297 A.2d 849 (N.J.1972). Assuming the test to be unreliable as a demonstrator of guilt or innocence, why did defendant refuse? Because he was conscious of guilt and erroneously believed the test infallible; or because he believed the test unreliable; or for some other reason? Contrast refusal to submit to ultra-violet ray test for presence of fluorescent powder on hands or clothing, People v. Gallagher, 336 P.2d 259, 265–66 (Cal.App.1959), and refusal to speak for purposes of voice identification, State v. Cary, 230 A.2d 384, 389 (N.J.1967).

In a murder prosecution, part of the prosecution's theory of defendant's motive for killing her husband related to the financial situation of the family. Was it objectionable for the prosecutor to introduce the testimony of an accountant, employed by defendant and her husband, that he was contacted by defendant's attorneys the day after the husband died and asked to hand over records relating to the family's affairs? People v. Miller, 53 Cal.Rptr. 720, 736 (1966), cert. dismissed, 392 U.S. 616 (1968).

There is a tendency in some jurisdictions to punish a party who destroyed or hid evidence by shifting the burden of proof on that issue to that party. See, e.g., Public Health Trust of Dade County v. Valcin, 507 So.2d 596 (Fla.1987); Thor v. Boska, 113 Cal.Rptr. 296 (1974); See Telectron, Inc. v. Overhead Door Corp., 116 F.R.D. 107 (S.D.Fla.1987).

If a lawyer working for a corporation refuses to destroy documents needed in a litigation, can he or she block discharge for disobedience of orders? Suggesting that the answer is no are Herbster v. North American Co., 501 N.E.2d 343 (Ill.App.1986); Willy v. The Coastal Corporation, 647 F.Supp. 116 (S.D.Tex.1986). What if the lawyer were working for outside counsel? What remedies apart from an action for reinstatement might exist? What if the lawyer were working for the government and there was a whistle blowing statute? See generally, Closen & Wojck, Lawyers Out in the Cold, ABAJ Nov. 1, 1987, p. 94.

On the ethics of counsel or client suppressing documents see, e.g., Jack B. Weinstein, Individual Justice in Mass Tort Litigation, 66 ff. (1995). Consider also the possibility of utilizing Rule 11 of the Federal Rules of Civil Procedure, various tort law damage theories and disciplinary proceedings.

D.   PROBABILITY AND STATISTICAL EVIDENCE IN DECISIONMAKING

Smith v. Rapid Transit, Inc.

Supreme Judicial Court of Massachusetts, 1945.
58 N.E.2d 754.

Action by Betty Smith against Rapid Transit, Inc., for personal injuries sustained by plaintiff as the result of negligent operation of a bus claimed to belong to defendant.

■ SPALDING, JUSTICE. The decisive question in this case is whether there was evidence for the jury that the plaintiff was injured by a bus of the defendant that was operated by one of its employees in the course of his employment. If there was, the defendant concedes that the evidence warranted the submission to the jury of the question of the operator's negligence in the management of the bus. The case is here on the plaintiff's exception to the direction of a verdict for the defendant.

These facts could have been found: While the plaintiff at about 1:00 A.M. on February 6, 1941, was driving an automobile on Main Street, Winthrop, in an easterly direction toward Winthrop Highlands, she observed a bus coming toward her which she described as a "great big, long, wide affair." The bus, which was proceeding at about forty miles an hour, "forced her to turn to the right," and her automobile collided with a "parked car." The plaintiff was coming from Dorchester. The department of public utilities had issued a certificate of public convenience or necessity to the defendant for three routes in Winthrop, one of which included Main Street [at the point where the accident occurred], and this was in effect in February, 1941. "There was another bus line in operation in Winthrop at that time but not on Main Street." According to the defendant's time-table, buses were scheduled to leave Winthrop Highlands for Maverick Square via Main Street at 12:10 A.M., 12:45 A.M., 1:15 A.M., and 2:15 A.M. The running time for this trip at that time of night was thirty minutes.

The direction of a verdict for the defendant was right. The ownership of the bus was a matter of conjecture. While the defendant had the sole franchise for operating a bus line on Main Street, Winthrop, this did not preclude private or chartered buses from using this street; the bus in question could very well have been one operated by someone other than the defendant. It was said in Sargent v. Massachusetts Accident Co., 307 Mass. 246, at page 250, 29 N.E.2d 825, at page 827, that it is "not enough that mathematically the chances somewhat favor a proposition to be proved; for example, the fact that colored automobiles made in the current year outnumber black ones would not warrant a finding that an undescribed automobile of the current year is colored and not black, nor would the fact that only a minority of men die of cancer warrant a finding that a particular man did not die of cancer." The most that can be said of the evidence in the instant case is that perhaps the mathematical chances somewhat favor the proposition that a bus of the defendant caused the accident. This was not enough. A "proposition is proved by a preponderance of the evidence if it is made to appear more likely or probable in the sense that actual belief in its truth, derived from the evidence, exists in the mind or minds of the tribunal notwithstanding any doubts that may still linger there." Sargent v. Massachusetts Accident Co., 307 Mass. 246, at page 250, 29 N.E.2d 825, at page 827.

In cases where it has been held that a vehicle was sufficiently identified so as to warrant a finding that it was owned by the defendant, the evidence was considerably stronger than that in the case at bar.

The evidence in the instant case is no stronger for the plaintiff than that in Atlas v. Silsbury–Gamble Motors Co., 278 Mass. 279, 180 N.E. 127, or in Cochrane v. Great Atlantic & Pacific Tea Co., 281 Mass. 386, 183 N.E. 757, where it was held that a finding that the vehicle in question was owned by the defendant was not warranted.

Exceptions overruled.

NOTES

1. Application of Kaufman, 143 N.Y.S.2d 853 (1955). Plaintiff was struck by a taxicab, but did not know the identity of its owner and driver. An agent of a liability insurance company "investigated the accident and made some effort to adjust it." This company did not deny that it had pertinent information.

Plaintiff sought to take the deposition of the claims manager of the company under New York Civ.Prac.Act § 295, which permits the taking of a deposition before action is commenced for the purpose of ascertaining the identity of prospective defendants. The court ordered the examination "as to the identity of the taxicab striking the plaintiff or coming upon the sidewalk at the time when and the place mentioned where the applicant was injured including its license number, and as to name and residence and P.O. addresses of owner and driver thereof."

What other information could the jury have expected the plaintiff to produce in Smith? Was it proper to consider the possible availability of other evidence in determining whether plaintiff had made out a prima facie case?

2. If understood as insisting on a numerically higher showing—an "extra margin" of probability above, say, .55—then the decision in Smith would make no sense, at least if the court's objective were the minimization of the total number of judicial errors in situations of this kind, an objective essentially implicit in the adoption of a "preponderance of the evidence" standard. See Ball, The Moment of Truth: Probability Theory and Standards of Proof, 14 Vand.L.Rev. 807 (1961). But cases like Smith are entirely sensible if understood instead as insisting on the presentation of some nonstatistical and individualized proof of identity before compelling a party to pay damages, and even before compelling him to come forward with defensive evidence, absent an adequate explanation of the failure to present such individualized proof. Tribe, Trial by Mathematics: Precision and Ritual in the Legal Process, 84 Harv.L.Rev. 1329, 1341 n. 37 (1971). This article is one of a series of thrusts and parries encouraged by People v. Collins, 68 Cal.2d 319, 66 Cal.Rptr. 497, 438 P.2d 33, 36 A.L.R.3d 1176 (1968), noted following State v. Rolls, infra. See also in the series Finkelstein and Fairley, A Bayesian Approach to Identification Evidence, 83 Harv.L.Rev. 489 (1970); Finkelstein and Fairley, A Comment on "Trial by Mathematics," 84 Harv.L.Rev. 1801 (1971); and Tribe, a Further Critique of Mathematical Proof, 84 Harv.L.Rev. 1810 (1971).

M.O. Finkelstein does not object to applying a "spoliation" view to naked statistical evidence as a policy matter to encourage the production of more particular evidence. In his book, Quantitative Methods in Law, 76–78 (1978), he suggests that pure statistical evidence is regarded as inadequate in most situations (except where overwhelming) because decisions based solely on statistics would tilt the balance of errors too much one way (in the examples he gives, toward plaintiffs). Professor Kaye believes a .50 + subjective probability should be used to minimize total errors. Kaye, Naked Statistical Evidence, 89 Yale L.J. 601 (1980) (in most cases the naked aspect of the statistical evidence "spoils" the numerical showing, making the subjective probability drop below one-half).

3. See United States v. Shonubi, 895 F. Supp. 460, 512–518 (E.D.N.Y.1995), rev'd on other grounds, 103 F.3d 1085 (2d Cir.1997). grounds for reversal criticized on remand, __ F. Supp. __ (E.D.N.Y.1997) omissions not indicated).

Law Applicable to Statistical and Other Information

A. Admissibility of probabilistic evidence

As Jeremy Bentham observed:

Certainty, absolute certainty, is a satisfaction which on every ground of inquiry we are continually grasping at, but which the inexorable nature of things has placed forever out of reach. Practical certainty, a degree of assurance sufficient for practice, is a blessing, the attainment of which, as often as it lies in our way to attain it, may be sufficient to console us under the want of any such superfluous and unattainable acquisitions.

5 Jeremy Bentham, Rationale of Judicial Evidence 351 (J.S. Mill ed. 1827).

As already noted, Rules 401 and 402 of the Federal Rules of Evidence provide for the admissibility of any evidence which can logically influence the trier's assessment of the probability of a material fact. From these rules "one might infer that the court wishes and expects to have its judgments about facts at issue ... expressed in terms of probabilities." The Evolving Role of Statistical Assessments as Evidence in the Courts 193 (Report of the Panel on Statistical Assessments as Evidence in the Courts) (Stephen E. Fienberg ed., 1989) [hereinafter Evolving Role].

The value of statistical evidence has been recognized, at least in theory, for several hundred years. See Peter Tillers, Intellectual History, Probability, and the Law of Evidence, 91 Mich.L.Rev. 1465, 1473–74 (1991) (reviewing Barbara J. Shapiro, "Beyond Reasonable Doubt" and "Probable Cause": Historical Perspective on the Anglo–American Law of Evidence (1991)) (describing 17th–19th century mathematical approaches to problems of proof).

Today, complex statistical evidence is being introduced in American courts in a wide variety of both civil and criminal matters. Evolving Role, supra, at 7–9; see also Cimino v. Raymark Indus., 751 F.Supp. 649, 661 (E.D.Tex.1990) ("Acceptance of statistical evidence is now commonplace in the courts."); id. (listing wide variety of cases in which statistical evidence has been accepted); David W. Barnes & John M. Conley, Statistical Evidence in Litigation 13 (1986) ("There is at present virtually no area of the law in which properly conceived and executed statistical proof cannot be admitted."). As one measure of the rise of statistical proof in litigation, a LEXIS search of district court opinions using the words "statistic," "statistics," or "statistical" turned up 608 examples in the years 1960 to 1969; 2,786 cases from 1970 to 1979; 4,364 cases from 1980 to 1989; and 3,015 from 1990 thru July 31, 1995. A similar search on Westlaw turned up nearly identical numbers. In fact, with the rise of "public law" litigation involving discrimination and mass torts, statistical and epidemiological evidence have become essential to legal fact-finding. At the same time, the adoption of the Federal Rules of Evidence permits judges to exercise broad discretion in admitting useful statistical evidence. See, e.g., Fed.R.Evid. 102, 401, 402, 403, 702–706, 803(18).

A few commentators have argued that triers need to curtail evidentiary uses of statistics. See Laurence Tribe, Trial By Mathematics: Precision and Ritual in the Legal Process, 84 Harv.L.Rev. 1329 (1971); Charles Nesson, The Evidence or the Event? On Judicial Proof and the Accessibility of Verdicts, 98 Harv.L.Rev. 1357 (1985). This thesis has been rejected both by judges and academicians. As Professor Rosenberg has pointed out, the exclusion of probabilistic evidence is impossible, because all evidence is probabilistic:

The entire notion that "particularistic" evidence differs in some significant qualitative way from statistical evidence must be questioned. The concept of "particularistic" evidence suggests that there exists a form of proof that can provide direct and actual knowledge of [the parties' conduct]. "Particularistic" evidence, however, is in fact no less probabilistic than is the statistical evidence that courts purport to sun.... "Particularistic" evidence offers nothing more than a basis for conclusions about a perceived balance of probabilities.

David Rosenberg, The Causal Connection in Mass Exposure Cases: A "Public Law" Vision of the Tort System, 97 Harv.L.Rev. 849, 870 (1984) (footnotes omitted), quoted in In re "Agent Orange" Prod. Liab. Litig., 597 F.Supp. 740, 835–36 (E.D.N.Y.1984); id., 597 F. Supp. at 836 (even with seemingly non-probabilistic evidence, "issues of credibility and varying inferences drawn by the trier based upon varying assessment of probative force may cause reasonable people to assess these percentages in a range"). See also, e.g., Michael J. Saks & Robert F. Kidd, Human Information Processing and Adjudication: Trial by Heuristics, 15 Law & Soc'y Rev. 123, 151 (1980–1981) ("Much of the testimony that is commonly thought of as particularistic only seems so. It is far more probabilistic than we normally allow jurors (or judges) to realize.") (citations omitted); cf. Evolving Role 78–79 (noting the contradiction between the court's insistence on evidence that seems certain, and such "probabilistic" institutions as plea bargaining, in which decisions are made on the basis of "probable" outcome).

Nevertheless, some scholars fear that the seeming precision of numerical evidence tends to overshadow evidence not expressed in quantitative form. See, e.g., Laurence Tribe, Trial by Mathematics, 84 Harv. L. Rev. 1329, 1330 n. 2 (1971) (arguing for exclusion of statistics despite acknowledgement that "all factual evidence is ultimately statistical, and all legal proof ultimately probabilistic") (emphasis in original). These scholars argue that

> [t]he apparent precision of statistical evidence often stands in marked contrast to the uncertainties of other testimony.... The danger is that such evidence will overshadow equally probative but admittedly unscientific and anecdotal nonstatistical evidence.

Evolving Role, supra, at 150 (citations omitted).

This limited view of the intellectual powers of judges and jurors when properly advised by experts and counsel has been rebutted. In one of the leading analyses of how decision-makers process information, Professors Saks and Kidd noted that triers are more likely to underestimate than overestimate the probative force of statistical analysis and quantitative proof. They wrote:

> Research demonstrates ... that people ... cannot integrate ... statistical and anecdotal evidence and consequently tend to ignore that statistical information. Intuitive, heuristic, human decision makers must dispense with certain information, and that tends strongly to be the quantitative information. While commentators' arguments have been that the [statistical] data are inordinately persuasive, the evidence says that the reverse is true.

Saks & Kidd, supra, at 149 (emphasis omitted). The Committee on Statistical Assessments as Evidence in the Courts, in a report written at the request of the National Science Foundation, reached a similar conclusion:

> When statistical evidence conflicts with anecdotal evidence that bears on the same issue, highly probative statistical data may be rejected in favor of a less probative but more striking anecdotal instance.... [A]necdotal evidence is vivid and reaches us in a way that ... statistical information cannot.

Evolving Role, supra, at 153–54.

As Professors Kaye and Koehler suggest, research is not decisive on this point. See generally D.H. Kaye & Jonathan J. Koehler, Can Jurors Understand Probabilistic Evidence?, supra; see also Edward J. Imwinkelried, The Next Step After Daubert: Developing a Similarly Epistemological Approach to Ensuring the Reliability of Nonscientific Expert Testimony, 15 Cardozo L. Rev. 2271,

2286 (1994) ("[G]iven the research data currently available, it would be dishonest to make any purportedly scientific claim about the impact of scientific or nonscientific testimony on lay jurors"). But cf. Evolving Role, supra, at 154 (citing R. Nisbett & L. Ross, Human Inference: Strategies and Shortcomings of Social Judgment (1980)); R.M. Reyes et al., Judgmental Biases Resulting from Different Availabilities of Arguments, 2 J. Personality & Soc. Psych. 39 (1980); see also United States v. Starzecpyzel, 880 F.Supp. 1027, 1048–49 (S.D.N.Y.1995) (urging triers "not to overreact" to supposed dangers of scientific proof); Edward J. Imwinkelried, The Standard for Admitting Scientific Evidence: A Critique from the Perspective of Juror Psychology, 28 Vill. L. Rev. 554, 566–68 (1982) (reviewing studies showing that jurors are not overly influenced by scientific proof); Michael S. Jacobs, Testing the Assumptions Underlying the Debate About Scientific Evidence: A Closer Look at Juror "Incompetence" and Scientific "Objectivity", 25 Conn. L. Rev. 1083 (1993) (reviewing recent studies that show jurors capable of decided complex cases involving scientific and technical matters); Joe S. Cecil et al., Citizen Comprehension of Difficult Issues: Lessons from Civil Jury Trials, 50 Am. U. L. Rev. 727, 764 (1991) (same); Elizabeth Loftus, Psychological Aspects of Courtroom Testimony, 347 Annals of the New York Academy of Sciences 27, 34 (1980) (jurors more willing to convict on the basis of lay testimony than on high-caliber scientific proof); see also United States v. Jakobetz, 955 F.2d 786, 797 (2d Cir.) ("[A]lthough scientific and statistical evidence may seem complicated, we do not think that a jury will be so dazzled or swayed as to ignore evidence suggesting that an experiment was improperly conducted or that testing procedures have not been established."), cert. denied, 506 U.S. 834 (1992). Studies of juror behavior, while not decisive as to judges, are probably representative of professional as well as lay decision-making.

Statistical evidence must be presented with care. See Margaret A. Berger, "Evidentiary Framework," in Federal Judicial Center, Reference Manual on Scientific Evidence 95, 97 (1994) (" '[P]rosecutor's fallacy' occurs when a prosecutor presents statistical evidence to suggest that the evidence indicates the likelihood of the defendant's guilt rather than the odds of the evidence having been found in a randomly selected sample."); William C. Thompson & Edward L. Schumann, Interpretation of Statistical Evidence in Criminal Trials: The Prosecutor's Fallacy and the Defense Attorney's Fallacy, 11 Law & Hum. Behv. 167, 181–82 (1987). Powerful tools such as DNA evidence require particular care. But to reject them is to shackle the courts in their search for the truth. See, e.g., United States v. Jakobetz, 955 F.2d 786 (2d Cir.) (approving use of DNA evidence in kidnapping trial), cert. denied, 506 U.S. 834 (1992); Eric S. Lander, DNA Fingerprinting on Trial, 339 Nature 501 (1989); National Research Council of the National Academy of Sciences, DNA Technology in Forensic Science (1992); cf. Ronald J. Allen et al., An Internet Exchange, supra (discussing error requiring reversal in State v. Skipper, 637 A.2d 1101 (Conn. 1994), but finding fault with broad negative dicta in decision). Courts which deny themselves the help of statistical tools increase the risks of incorrect conclusions. See Mirjan Damaska, "Approaches to the Evaluation of Evidence: A Comparative View," in John Henry Merryman: A Festschrift (Berlin 1988) (critiquing "atomistic" approach to admissibility in American system).

Effective techniques for developing and presenting scientific evidence to juries do exist. They will be further developed and refined in the wake of the Supreme Court's decision in Daubert [v. Merrell Dow Pharmaceuticals, Inc., 509 U.S. 579 (1993)]. See, e.g., Jack B. Weinstein, The Effect of Daubert on the Work of Federal Trial Judges, Shepard's Expert & Sci. Evidence Q., Summer

1994, at 1. Putting aside questions of cost and availability to both sides, there is no reason to deny factfinders reliable information or analytic techniques.

Once introduced, how much can statistics prove? "[T]he interrelationship between an opinion couched in probabilistic terms and the applicable burden of proof" has proved to be a "perplexing problem for the courts." Margaret A. Berger, "Evidentiary Framework," in Federal Judicial Center, Reference Manual on Scientific Evidence 95 (1994).

Law professors properly dote on hypotheticals in which triers must decide cases on the basis of statistical evidence alone. Popular examples include the "blue bus case" (percentage of blue and white buses passing a point is only evidence of which company's bus hit plaintiff) (see, e.g., Jack B. Weinstein, John H. Mansfield, Norman Abrams & Margaret A. Berger, et al., Cases and Materials on Evidence, 45–73 (8th ed. 1988) (discussing Smith v. Rapid Transit, Inc., 317 Mass. 469, 58 N.E.2d 754 (1945)); Charles Nesson, Agent Orange Meets the Blue Bus: Factfinding at the Frontiers of Knowledge, 66 B.U. L. Rev. 521 (1986)); the gatecrasher hypothetical (percentage of gatecrashers at rodeo is over 50 percent; can all be found liable?) (see, e.g., L. Cohen, The Probable and the Provable 77–81 (1977); Richard Lempert, Symposium, Probability and Inference in the Law of Evidence: I. Theories of Inference and Adjudication: The New Evidence Scholarship: Analyzing the Process of Proof, 66 B.U.L.Rev. 439, 454 (1986)); and the prison yard hypothetical (999 prisoners out of one thousand have rioted; can each be found guilty?) (see, e.g., Terence Anderson & William Twining, Analysis of Evidence 39–40 (1991); Daniel Shaviro, Statistical–Probability Evidence and the Appearance of Justice, 103 Harv. L. Rev. 530, 533–36 (1989)). As Prof. Green has noted, "[i]n the ensuing debate [on 'naked' statistical evidence], numerous blue buses have run untold numbers of nearsighted elderly ladies off the road; hundreds of alleged gatecrashers have been collared; dozens of murderous prisoners have been brought to justice, and countless articles, books, and opinions have been written on the subject." Eric D. Green, Symposium: Probability and Inference in the Law of Evidence: Foreword, 66 B.U. L. Rev. 377, 378 (1986) (footnotes omitted).

In at least two classes of cases, "naked"—or nearly naked—statistical evidence has proven essential. In mass torts, proof of causation often requires the use of statistically based epidemiological proof. See, e.g., Steve Gold, Causation in Toxic Torts: Burdens of Proof, Standards of Persuasion, and Statistical Evidence, 96 Yale L.J. 376 (1986). Given that determining the causation of many diseases—particularly those with latent effects and no "signature" relationship—is extremely difficult, plaintiffs in many mass tort cases would be unable to prove that a defendant caused an illness were it not for statistical epidemiological data. See Joseph Sanders, From Science to Evidence: The Testimony on Causation in the Bendectin Cases, 46 Stanford L. Rev. 1, 14–18 (1993) (discussing use of statistics to prove causation in mass torts). In the Agent Orange litigation, the court noted two possible responses to this problem:

> Under the "strong" version of the preponderance rule, statistical correlations alone indicating that the probability of causation exceeds fifty percent are insufficient; some "particularistic" or anecdotal evidence, that is, "proof that can provide direct and actual knowledge of the causal relationship between the defendant's tortious conduct and the plaintiff's injury is required." . . . The "weak" version of the preponderance rule would allow a verdict solely on statistical evidence. . . .

In re "Agent Orange" Prod. Liability Litig., 597 F.Supp. 740, 835 (E.D.N.Y.1984) (citations omitted). The court went on to explain its decision to reject the strong version of the preponderance rule in mass exposure cases:

> [W]here the chance that there would be particularistic evidence would be quite small, the consequence of retaining the requirement might be to allow defendants who, it is virtually certain, have injured thousands of people and caused billions of dollars in damages, to escape liability.

Id. at 836. The court concluded: "Except where it appears that the absence of anecdotal evidence may be due to spoliation, probabilities based upon quantitative analysis should support a recovery." Id. Thus, in mass tort cases the decision to rely on "naked" statistical proof if that is all that can be presented is consistent with the goal of providing the most justice for the most people. See, e.g., Deborah Hensler, Resolving Mass Toxic Torts: Myths and Realities, 1989 U. Ill. L. Rev. 89, 90 (concluding that aggregative procedures provide the best possible match between victims' losses and compensation).

"Naked" statistical evidence has also been decisive in discrimination cases. For example, under Title VII of the Civil Rights Act of 1964, a plaintiff can prove employment discrimination by introducing statistical data showing that the defendant's hiring practices had a racially disparate impact. See Griggs v. Duke Power Co., 401 U.S. 424, 429–30 (1971). But see Wards Cove Packing Co. v. Atonio, 490 U.S. 642, 660 (1989) (restricting use of disparate-impact studies in Title VII cases); see also, e.g., Castaneda v. Partida, 430 U.S. 482 (1977) (statistical evidence drawn from census data and grand jury records can establish a prima facie case of discrimination in grand jury selection); Machetti v. Linahan, 679 F.2d 236 (11th Cir.1982) (statistical evidence of disparity between percentage of females in adult population and percentage of females on jury lists sufficient to prove discrimination), cert. denied, 459 U.S. 1127 (1983); Ramona L. Paetzold, The Statistics of Discrimination: Using Statistical Evidence in Discrimination Cases (1994).

In other types of litigation, "pure" statistical cases rarely arise. Statistical evidence is almost always evaluated in the light of non-statistical proof. See In re "Agent Orange" Prod. Liability Litig., 597 F.Supp. 740, 836 (E.D.N.Y.1984) (in cases other than those involving mass torts, anecdotal "evidence is almost always available"). Courts expect parties to proffer anecdotal as well as statistical evidence. As Professor Berger has pointed out, "failure by experts to consider [individual case histories] could lead a court to conclude that the proffered opinion failed to satisfy Rule 703 [requiring a proper basis for expert testimony]." Berger, "Evidentiary Framework," supra, at 96; cf. Richard Lempert, The New Evidence Scholarship: Analyzing the Process of Proof, 66 B.U.L. Rev. 439, 450–62 (1986) (discussing spoliation inference in litigation). Thus, the issue of "naked" statistical evidence is more hypothetical than real.

3. Criminal Cases

Several commentators have expressed particular concern about the use of explicitly probabilistic evidence in criminal cases. See, e.g., Ronald Dworkin, Taking Rights Seriously 13 (1977); Andrew von Hirsch, Prediction of Criminal Conduct and Preventive Confinement of Convicted Persons, 21 Buff. L. Rev. 717, 744–50 (1972), cited in Barbara D. Underwood, Law and the Crystal Ball: Predicting Behavior with Statistical Inference and Individualized Judgement, 88 Yale L. J. 1309, 1312 (1979); Saks & Kidd, supra, at 152; Tribe, supra; Nesson, supra; L. Jonathan Cohen, Subjective Probability and the Paradox of the Gatecrasher, 1918 Ariz. St. L.J. 627, 632 (rejecting use of statistics in criminal cases); Alex Stein, On the Unbearable Lightness of "Weight" and the Refoundation of Evidence Law 48–49 (forthcoming 1995, on file in the instant case) (arguing that the problem with "naked" statistical evidence in criminal cases is not that it is unreliable, but that its "weight" is insufficient to support conviction).

The better view is that no special rule of exclusion is required in criminal cases. In criminal as in civil cases, factfinders need all available information. Significantly, the Federal Rules of Evidence do not distinguish between civil and criminal cases in their pertinent provisions. See, e.g., Rules 401 to 403, Rule 1101, and Article VII.

Protection of defendants in criminal cases warrants special concern, but burdens of proof and existing rules of evidence, as well as constitutional and statutory protections, rather than exclusions of highly probative evidence that happens to be in statistical form, are the best means of avoiding injustice. See, e.g., Daniel Shaviro, Statistical–Probability Evidence and the Appearance of Justice, 103 Harv. L. Rev. 530, 538 (1989) (possibility of unwarranted conviction "suggests raising the burden of proof for all cases. It does not support a special rule for statistical probability cases."). Rather than excluding statistics, courts should provide for defense and court-appointed experts to ensure that statistics, when available, are properly used. These devices were utilized in this case.

Even were attempts to impose blanket exclusion of statistical evidence in criminal cases not contrary to Rules 401, 402, 403, and 1101, which encourage use of all available probative evidence, the law could not afford to exclude highly probative statistical evidence and useful quantitative methods. Courts ignore whole categories of evidence only at their peril. Thus the court of appeals for this circuit has held that "doubts about whether an expert's testimony will be useful should generally be resolved in favor of admissibility unless there are strong factors such as time or surprise favoring exclusion." United States v. Jakobetz, 955 F.2d 786, 797 (2d Cir.) (citation omitted), cert. denied 506 U.S. 834 (1992).

4. Some commentators argue that so-called "naked" statistical evidence may be sufficient only in certain contexts. See Brook, The Use of Statistical Evidence of Identification in Civil Litigation: Well–Worn Hypotheticals, Real Cases, and Controversy, 29 St. Louis U.L.J. 293 (1985); Black & Lilienfield, Epidemiologic Proof in Toxic Tort Litigation, 52 Fordham L.Rev. 732 (1984); Gold, Causation in Toxic Torts: Burdens of Proof, Standards of Persuasion, and Statistical Evidence, 96 Yale L.J. 376 (1986); Rosenberg, The Causal Connection in Mass Exposure Cases: A "Public Law" Vision of the Tort System, 97 Harv.L.Rev. 851 (1984); Note, Proving Causation in Toxic Torts Litigation, 11 Hofstra L.J. 1299 (1983). See also Final Report of the Royal Commission on the Use and Effects of Chemical Agents on Australian Personnel in Vietnam (July 1985). As one student has noted:

> We can expect more situations in which there appears to be an increased incidence of a fairly widespread disease, but it is not clear which, if any, persons suffer from it as a result of exposure to a particular toxic substance, and it is also not clear which of many producers is responsible for any particular injury. This is the situation that may exist in the DES cases, in many hazardous waste injury cases and in cases where workers have moved from job to job and have been exposed to toxic substances over many years.

Weinstein, Preliminary Reflections of the Law's Reaction to Disasters, 11 Colum.J.Envtl.L. 1, 11 (1986). See also, e.g., Bethlehem Mines Corp. v. Massey, 736 F.2d 120 (4th Cir.1984); Rutledge v. Tultex Corp., 301 S.E.2d 359 (N.C. 1983); Brawn v. St. Regis Paper, 430 A.2d 843 (Me.1981); Swink v. Cone Mills,

Inc., 309 S.E.2d 271 (N.C.App.1983). But see Bazemore v. Friday, 478 U.S. 385 (1986) (regression analysis should not have been rejected even though all factors were not considered and nonstatistical information should have been admitted in employment discrimination suit).

5. Related substantive developments, put increasing pressure on experts, making the rules on the use of such witnesses more important. See Weinstein, Improving Expert Testimony, 20 U.Rich.L.Rev. 473 (1986); Weinstein, Litigation and Statistics: Obtaining Assistance Without Abuse, 1 Toxics L.Rep. (BNA) 813 (Dec. 24, 1986). Whether the substantive law needs revision in the light of evidentiary and procedural problems raised by these developments as well as social, political and technological changes remains a critical question. See generally, Jack B. Weinstein, Individual Justice in Mass Tort Litigations (1995); Kenneth R. Feinberg and Jack B. Weinstein, Mass Torts, Cases and Materials (1995).

6. For the combination of the colored bus and credibility issue, see P. Gardnerfors et al., Evidentiary Value, Philosophical, Judicial and Psychological Aspects of a Theory, 44–45 (1983) (footnotes omitted):

> (At the beginning of this dialogue on evidentiary value the conversation involves two persons: The first is Basie, a statistician, very much interested in subjective probabilities. Then working on a problem involving assessments of probabilities, he always thinks to himself: What would Bayes say in a situation like this? The second person is Lazy, an ordinary man, neither a statistician, nor a lawyer, but a representative of what the lay say.)

> *Lazy:* Look, Basie. I've just come from the Psychology Department where I participated as a subject in an experiment on probabilistic reasoning. One of the problems given to me was the following:

> > "Two cab companies operate in a given city, the Blue and the Green (according to the color of cab they run). Eighty-five per cent of the cabs in the city are Blue, and the remaining 15% are Green.

> > A cab was involved in a hit-and-run accident at night.

> > A witness later identified the cab as a Green cab.

> > The court tested the witness's ability to distinguish between Blue and Green cabs under nighttime visibility conditions. It found that the witness was able to identify each color correctly about 80% of the time, but confused it with the other color about 20% of the time. What do you think are the chances that the errant cab was indeed Green, as the witness claimed?"

> Well, I answered that the chance was 80%, because that is the probability that the witness was correct. But I smell a rat here. I am not so certain that my reasoning is valid. What do you say?

> *Basie:* It seems to me that you are the victim of a very common cognitive illusion. You fail to consider that there are many more Blue cabs than Green. In fact, it is more probable that the cab was Blue and the witness incorrectly identified it as Green than that it was Green and the witness made a correct identification. Since 85% of the cabs are Blue and the witness is wrong in 20% of the cases, the first situation should occur in $85\% \times 20\% = 17\%$ of the cases in the long run. The other situation occurs in only $15\% \times 80\% = 12\%$ of the cases. So, the probability that the cab is Green, given that the witness says it is Green, is only $0.12/(0.12 + 0.17) = 0.41$.

Lazy: I seé how you count, Basie, but where did I go wrong?

Basie: The problem is a standard case of Bayesian inference. There are two pieces of information. One is in the form of background data, often called *base-rate* information. The second, the witness report, may be called *indicator* information. In your reasoning, when you fail to consider the first piece of information, you commit what has been called the *base-rate fallacy*.

Lazy: After the experiment at the Psychology Department I was informed by the experimenter that most of the subjects gave the same answer as I did. Even lawyers seem to be reasoning in the same way.

Basie: It does not surprise me. The base-rate fallacy is a persistent illusion. It is the duty of statisticians to show people where their intuitions go wrong. One way of doing this is to point out that the probability that the cab is Green (let us denote this by G) given that the witness says green (denoted WG), i.e. $P(G/WG)$, is not the same as the probability that the witness says green given that the cab is Green, i.e. $P(WG/G)$. The latter is 0.80 ($P(WG/G)$), as was given in the problem, but the former ($P(G/WG)$), as I showed earlier, is only 0.41. . . .

Assuming Basie is correct, will the jury make the same "mistake" as Lazy if the attorneys, their experts and the court fill their roles properly? What are those roles and the techniques available?

State v. Rolls

Supreme Court of Maine, 1978.
389 A.2d 824.

■ Before POMEROY, ARCHIBALD, DELAHANTY, GODFREY and NICHOLS, JJ.

■ NICHOLS, JUSTICE.

The Defendant, Raymond C. Rolls, waived prosecution by indictment and was charged in a four-count information with burglary with a firearm, gross sexual misconduct, rape, and possession of a firearm by a felon. He was tried by jury in Superior Court in Cumberland County, and was found guilty on each charge. He brings this appeal from the judgment of conviction entered on the verdicts.

We deny the appeal.

The three issues which merit discussion are whether the court erred in admitting a prior consistent statement of the victim; whether the court erred in allowing expert testimony about the percentage of the population possessing a certain combination of blood grouping characteristics; and whether the evidence was sufficient to permit the jury to find beyond a reasonable doubt that it was the Defendant who committed the crimes. These issues arise in the following factual context:

On the night of June 11–12, 1976, a thirteen-year-old girl was awakened by an intruder in her bedroom in her parent's home in Portland's West End. After removing her underwear, the intruder bent over the bed and picked her up. An object, described at trial as an Iver–Johnson .32 caliber five-shot revolver, fell on the bed and was later recovered.[1]

---

1. The Defendant asserts that there was insufficient evidence to support a finding that this "object" was in fact a firearm as defined in 17A M.R.S.A. § 2(12 A). This point is without merit. Not only was there testimony which would support such a finding, but the revolver itself was admitted into evidence and became subject to examination by the

The victim was carried by the intruder downstairs to a back hall, where the act forming the basis for the charge of gross sexual misconduct was committed under threat of harm to her family. Subsequently, the intruder took the girl outside to an area behind the house. There she was sexually assaulted. Although she did not then know it, she received a laceration in her vaginal area which bled a noticeable amount.

Altogether she was with the intruder for approximately fifty minutes. After he departed, the victim ran upstairs and awoke her parents. They immediately called the police, who arrived within minutes.

The lighting was poor, and she was without her glasses. Her impression of the assailant was, in her word, "blurry." Because of allergies, she was unable to detect any particular odor, such as alcohol, about the person of her assailant. Nevertheless, she was able to describe him as being approximately in his twenties, with long hair, thin, about 5′9″ or 5′10″ in height, wearing a denim jacket and dark-colored pants which may have been green. This description was immediately broadcast over the police radio. The time was approximately 2:20 a.m.

Approximately one-half hour after the assailant left his victim a Portland police officer in a cruiser observed the Defendant traveling on foot along a street some four to five blocks (approximately ½ mile) from the site of the assault. The Defendant was the only person the officer observed on the street. Since the Defendant appeared to fit the general description broadcast over the radio, the officer asked him to stop and talk, which he did. He was wearing a denim jacket, blue jeans, and western-style boots. It was later shown that his height was about 5′10½″ or 5′11″, and that he was in his mid-thirties.[2]

The officer noticed that the knees of the Defendant's pants and the tips of his boots were wet, and there was a noticeable odor of alcohol about his person. At the officer's request, the Defendant agreed to accompany the officer to the crime scene. There, he stood under a street light where the victim viewed him from inside the house. She was unable to say any more than that he could have been her assailant.

Although told he was not under arrest, the Defendant was taken to the police station to verify his identity. At the station, the officer first noticed some red stains on the upper right leg of the Defendant's jeans near the zipper. While this particular officer did not touch the pants to determine whether the stains were wet, the police evidence technician testified that the stains were still wet some time later.

It was after the red stains were noticed that the Defendant was formally arrested. He was subjected to a strip search, which revealed he was wearing no underwear. The police were unable to detect anything resembling blood on his person despite a close examination. Nevertheless, the jeans were seized for evidentiary purposes.

The jeans were later sent for analysis of the stains to the F.B.I. laboratory in Washington, where they were examined by Special Agent Robert Spalding.

jury. United States v. Samson, 533 F.2d 721 (1st Cir.) cert. den., 429 U.S. 845, 97 S.Ct. 126, 50 L.Ed.2d 116 (1976). [Footnotes by the court].

2. The jury was able to observe the degree to which the Defendant's other characteristics matched the description given by

At trial, after establishing his qualifications as a forensic serologist,[3] Agent Spalding testified about his examination of the Defendant's jeans.

After first receiving the pants in June, 1976, Agent Spalding tested them for purposes of determining the presence of blood or semen. These tests were inconclusive on the presence of semen, but did disclose the presence of human blood, which was determined to be of type A_1 in the well-known ABO blood-type classification system.

About two months later, a second series of tests was performed on these pants by Agent Spalding. The ABO classification test was repeated to verify the results of the earlier tests, and as a check for any indication of deterioration. A test attempting to classify the stain under the RH system was unsuccessful because of the passage of time. However, Agent Spalding testified that he was able to type the stain according to both the EAP and PGM classification systems.

The erythrocyte acid phosphatase (EAP) and phosphoglucomutage (PGM) blood classifications are based on the presence of enzymes in the blood. These systems are genetically controlled, as in the ABO classification system, and all three are independently inherited, such that the blood type in one system does not depend upon the type in either of the others.

The theory of the PGM system is that there are slight differences between enzyme molecules in the blood. Under certain conditions, these different molecules separate and migrate and can be visually classified by the formation of "banding patterns" in reaction to charging by an electric field (electrophoresis) in a starch gel solution.

The theory of the EAP system is similar except that it involves the use of ultraviolet light rather than an electrical charge. The end result which is subject to typing is again a banding pattern.

In the PGM system, there are three classifications which are normally used: 1–1, 2–1, and 2–2. In the EAP system, there are six classifications. A, B, AB, C, AC, and CB. Agent Spalding testified that type "C" is very rare, and that the letter classifications used in the EAP system are unrelated to those of the ABO system.

From testing the stain on the pants, Agent Spalding determined that the blood was of type 2–1 in the PGM system and BA in the EAP system, in addition to the type A_1 in the ABO system noted earlier.

Agent Spalding also performed similar tests on blood samples taken directly from the victim and from the Defendant. The results of the tests performed upon the stains on the pants and the blood from the victim and the Defendant may be summarized as follows:

	ABO	EAP	PGM
Pants	A_1	BA	2–1
Victim	A_1	BA	2–1
Defendant	A_1	A	1–1

Thus, on the basis of these tests, it is evident that the stains on the pants could have been the victim's blood and could not have been the Defendant's.

Agent Spalding was also permitted to testify, without objection, that approximately 35% of the Caucasian population of the United States possess

the victim, although such was not articulated in the record.

3. According to the testimony, a forensic serologist works with criminal evidence where blood and body fluids are involved.

type A$_1$ blood in the ABO classification, that studies done by Scotland Yard reported that approximately 37% of those studied possessed type 2–1 in the PGM group and that research done at the F.B.I. laboratory showed that approximately 39% of the population possess the EAP characteristic BA. He was then asked about how he would, from these three independently obtained figures, determine the percentage of the population that possessed all three of them in their blood. He responded that he would multiply the three figures together to obtain a compound probability.

He was then asked to state the calculation he had performed with the three figures given above. Over objection, and after extensive *voir dire,* the witness was permitted to testify that approximately 5% of the population, or one person in twenty, would possess all three blood characteristics which the victim possessed and which were present in the bloodstain on the Defendant's pants.

When the State had rested the Defendant testified on his own behalf. He denied any involvement in the crimes. He related that he had been present at a party in his apartment in Portland that evening, where he had consumed large quantities of alcoholic beverages. At about 11:30 p.m., he said he had escorted one of the guests home and then had escorted her baby-sitter to her home. The two other witnesses presented by the Defendant corroborated his activities up until that time. He related that, at that point, he did not feel like returning home, so he hitchhiked to Saco where he attempted to work on a car he owned, which was located in Saco. After discovering that he was unable to perform the intended work, he said he hitch-hiked back to Portland and was going home when stopped by the police.

Regarding the blood on his pants, he stated that some of it may have been from cuts he received while working on his car, but that the majority of it was from an occasion sometime in April or May when his girlfriend's daughter cut herself in his presence.

The Defendant admitted he knew blood analysis would be an issue in the trial, but he stated that it had not occurred to him to have the girl's blood analyzed.

I.

During cross-examination of the victim, counsel for the Defendant elicited testimony that her parents had hired an attorney to "go over" her testimony, and to "reassure" her about it.

[Discussion of M.R.Evid. 801(d)(1) is omitted.]

II.

Prior to the adoption of the Maine Rules of Evidence, there was authority in Maine for the proposition that an expert opinion based on hearsay was as objectionable as hearsay itself. Brouillette v. Weymouth Shoe Co., 157 Me. 143, 170 A.2d 412 (1961). Relying upon this case, the Defendant argues that it was error to permit Agent Spalding to give his opinion that 5% of the population possessed the combination of three blood characteristics possessed by the victim, and found in the bloodstain on the Defendant's pants. The Defendant argues that there was an insufficient foundation to support admission of this testimony because the witness based his opinion on hearsay about the percentage of the population possessing each of the three blood grouping characteristics in issue.

. . .

The Defendant's objection to this testimony was more properly directed to its weight rather than its admissibility.[4]

III.

The defendant's final claim of error is that the presiding justice erred in denying his motion for a judgment of acquittal, made at the conclusion of all the evidence, and again after the jury reached its verdict. The sole issue for our review is whether, in view of all the evidence in the case, including reasonable inferences to be drawn therefrom, the jury was warranted in believing beyond a reasonable doubt that the accused was guilty. E.g., State v. O'Clair, Me., 292 A.2d 186, 196 (1972). Our limited role in determining the sufficiency of the evidence is essentially the same where the evidence is largely circumstantial in nature. See State v. Luce, Me., 384 A.2d 50 (1978).

Here the only question is whether the evidence was sufficient to permit the jury to conclude beyond a reasonable doubt that it was this Defendant who committed the crimes. We conclude that it was.

Despite some relatively minor inaccuracies, the Defendant matched the victim's memory of her assailant very closely. The Defendant was stopped within a half mile of the assault not long after it occurred, in the early morning hours when few persons were out and about. He had what proved to be a bloodstain on his pants, which was damp to the touch some time later. The blood on the stain could not have been the Defendant's, and could have been the victim's, and was of a type possessed by approximately 5% to 10% of the population.

The jury was not required to give the Defendant's own story any probative force. His alibi, that he was in Saco, was entirely uncorroborated. While one of his other witnesses did corroborate the Defendant's explanation of the bloodstain, the jury could have fairly concluded that the bloodstain on the Defendant's pants, which was later tested, could not have come from the incident to which the Defendant attributed it, since the alleged incident occurred sometime in April or May. It could hardly have been still damp some time after June 12.

In sum, the evidence, although circumstantial, was sufficient to support the jury's finding that it was the Defendant who committed the crimes.

Judgment affirmed.

NOTES

1. Much of the blood analyzed in the main case would now turn on DNA samples. See discussion of DNA, infra; see, e.g., Harlan Levy, And the Blood

---

4. We have examined the record as a whole to determine whether utilization of this evidence was unfair to the Defendant. By order of court, counsel for the Defendant was permitted to propound interrogatories to Agent Spalding concerning the tests he had performed. These interrogatories specifically included a question about the probabilities of two named samples coming from the same person. Thus, the Defendant was in no way surprised by this testimony. Secondly, counsel for the Defendant, in the interrogatories he submitted, as well as at trial, demonstrated considerable fluency in the techniques and theory of blood grouping. The defense, therefore, had adequate ability and opportunity to rebut any possible inaccuracies or inconsistencies in the testimony. Finally, it was at no time suggested to the jury that the 5% figure, or those figures from which it was drawn were ironclad. Indeed, there was testimony that if each of the underlying figures were off by a factor of ten percentage points, and thus were 45%, 49% and 47% respectively, then about one in ten, or 10% of the population, would possess all three of the characteristics present in the victim's blood and on the Defendant's pants. Therefore, despite the crucial nature of this testimony, the chances that the jury would take it entirely out of perspective were lessened. [Footnote renumbered.]

Cried Out (1996). Nevertheless, the relevancy discussion in the main case is still useful. Were the data bases in Rolls appropriate for the population of the area of the crime? Cf. Zegura, Blood Test, Natural History, July 1987, p. 6 (frequency of blood types varies geographically and may be used to trace ancient migrations).

2. Courts now generally agree in holding that a blood test excluding paternity is conclusive. In State ex rel. Steiger v. Gray, 145 N.E.2d 162, 168 (Ohio Juv.1957), the court stated:

> In accordance with enlightened judicial acceptance of the high value of blood-grouping tests properly conducted, I hold that in the absence of any competent proof that blood-grouping tests establishing non-paternity were not properly made, the results of such tests, scientifically conducted and objectively made by doctors expert in such field should be given such great weight by the court that the exclusion of the defendant as the father of the child follows irresistibly.

See Uniform Act on Paternity, § 7–10. Contra: Berry v. Chaplin, 169 P.2d 442, 451 (Cal.App.1946) ("When scientific testimony and evidence as to facts conflict the jury or the trial court must determine the relative weight of the evidence . . . the law makes no distinction between expert evidence and that of any other character"). The Berry case has met with almost universal criticism from commentators. See Britt, Blood Grouping Tests and More Cultural Lag, 22 Minn.L.Rev. 836 (1938). Note, 19 Rocky Mt.L.Rev. 169 (1947).

The results of the "Human Leukocyte Antigen" blood tissue test (HLA) have been admitted for the purpose of affirmatively proving paternity. See, e.g., Matter of Jane L., 438 N.Y.S.2d 726 (N.Y.Fam.Ct.1981) admitting HLA test results pursuant to 1981 N.Y.Laws ch. 9:

> In contrast to previous test methods, which afforded only a 75 percent possibility of excluding a falsely accused man, the HLA and adjunct blood grouping tests establish, according to unanimous expert opinion, a 91 to 98 percent probability that a man who tests as a possible father is in fact the father (the difference in percentage depending on how many related blood group systems are used besides HLA itself). See Joint AMA–ABA Guidelines: Present Status of Serologic Testing in Problems of Disputed Parentage, 10 Family L.Q. 247, 257 (1976). As the highest court of Washington said in upholding the constitutionality of an order for an HLA test: "No other evidence that is at all comparable in effectiveness is available . . . to prove paternity." [State v.] Meacham, 612 P.2d [795 (Wn.1980)] at p. 797. . . . State v. Hanson, 277 N.W.2d 205, 206–207 (Minn.1979); Cramer v. Morrison, 88 Cal.App.3d 873, 884–885, 153 Cal.Rptr. 865, 871–872 (1979) [98% probability of paternity].

See also Hennepin County Welfare Board v. Ayers, 304 N.W.2d 879 (Minn. 1981) (proof of intercourse plus tests showing 99.9% probability that defendant was father admissible, without prejudice to defendant's right to challenge reliability and to have other tests taken). Cf. Simons v. Jorg, 384 So.2d 1362 (Fla.App.1980) (on discovery motion in paternity suit defendant ordered to submit to HLA test).

When a court terms blood test evidence as "conclusive," is it using judicial notice to create a rule of substantive or of procedural law? In a jury case is there then any issue to submit for its consideration? Does the conclusive nature of a blood test overcome a presumption of legitimacy? Is a court well-suited to decide this question? What underlying policies are involved? What effect should be given a blood test excluding the husband as the father in a criminal trial of the wife for adultery?

Does adoption of the Federal or Uniform Rule of Evidence 402, supersede a bastardy statute which permits blood type evidence only to exclude the putative father, but not as affirmative proof that he was the father? Giving a negative answer is, e.g., Winston v. Robinson, 606 S.W.2d 757, 760–61 (Ark.1980); Cardenas v. Chavez, 103 Mich.App. 646, 303 N.W.2d 3 (1980). Should a bastardy statute designed to liberalize admissibility of scientific evidence become a barrier to new kinds of evidence available as scientific knowledge expands? Could defendant, particularly in a criminal case, make a due process argument if he sought to use this kind of evidence as exculpatory? Cf. People v. Allen, 304 N.W.2d 483 (Mich.App.1981) (Blood type A on defendant's shoe matched deceased's but not defendant's, admissible); Lincoln, Blood Group Evidence for the Defense, 20 Med.Sci.Law 239 (1980).

3. Note the extreme care that is required to ensure that blood sampling and testing are accurate. Cf. Saks & Kidd, Human Information Processing in Adjudication: Trial by Heuristics, 15 Law & Society Rev. 123, 155 (1980) (high proportion of police laboratories misidentifying blood and other samples). A continuing problem is the lack of reliability of laboratory work. One group has advocated the creation of central laboratories that are capable of doing the testing accurately. Joint AMA–ABA Guidelines: Present Status of Serologic Testing in Problems of Disputed Parentage, 10 Family L.Q. 247 (1976). For a more general discussion, see Jonakait, When Blood is Their Argument: Probabilities in Criminal Cases, Genetic Markers, and, Once Again, Bayes' Theorem, 1983 Ill.L.Rev. 309 (questioning use of blood test evidence without precautionary steps).

4. Sophisticated genetic testing may prove even more useful than blood tests heretofore used. It does not, however, eliminate the need for reliable statistical bases of relative frequency in the subject populations. In Argentina genetic tracing was used to locate children of murdered parents and to prove they were closely related to their still living grandparents. See Film by WGBH Boston, Nova, The Search for the Disappeared (1986). Cf. United States v. Massey, 594 F.2d 676 (8th Cir.1979) (hair on ski mask used to identify defendant; error in reference to mathematical probabilities of guilt).

5. In People v. Collins, 438 P.2d 33, 36 A.L.R.3rd 1176 (Cal.1968), eyewitnesses testified that a Caucasian woman with blond hair and a ponytail ran from the scene of the assault and entered a yellow automobile driven by a male Negro with a mustache and beard. At the trial of a couple fitting this description, a college mathematics instructor testified to the "product rule" of elementary probability theory: the probability of the joint occurrence of a number of mutually independent events equals the product of their individual probabilities. The witness was asked to assume the following individual probabilities:

Yellow automobile	$\frac{1}{10}$
Man with mustache	$\frac{1}{4}$
Girl with ponytail	$\frac{1}{10}$
Girl with blond hair	$\frac{1}{3}$
Negro man with beard	$\frac{1}{10}$
Interracial couple in car	$\frac{1}{1000}$

Applying the product rule to the assumed values, the prosecutor concluded that the chance that a couple chosen at random would possess all the incriminating characteristics was one in twelve million. The jury convicted; but the Supreme

Court of California reversed, holding that the evidence concerning probability theory had been improperly admitted.

The court voiced several objections: on its own terms the theory had been misapplied; the assumed probabilities lacked any evidential foundation; the six characteristics were not shown to be independent; and the whole procedure tended to embarrass jurors and opposing counsel unused to thinking in mathematical terms. See M.O. Finkelstein, Quantitative Methods in Law, 78 ff. (1978), approving the appellate result but not its entire reasoning and indicating how quantitative analysis combined with intuitive assessment of probabilities may be useful if a Bayesian technique is utilized. See also Fairley and Mosteller, A Conversation About Collins, 41 Univ.Chi.L.Rev. 242 (1974) (includes a discussion on whether dependent or independent probabilities were the basis for the prosecutor's arguments in Collins and offers an interpretation more favorable to the prosecution than usually given); Charrow and Smith, A Conversation About "A Conversation About Collins", 64 Geo.L.J. 669 (1976); Brown & Kelly, Playing the Percentages and the Law of Evidence, 1970 Law Forum 23, 41–46 (a balanced analysis concluding that probability statements in litigation will be infrequent but should not be foreclosed). But see Braun, Quantitative Analysis and the Law: Probability Theory as a Tool of Evidence in Criminal Trials, 1982 Utah L.Rev. 41 (rejecting use of Bayesian technique but advocating increased use of frequency and classical probability theory in criminal trials); Eggleston, The Probability Debate, 1980 Crim.L.Rev. 678 (defending use of classical probability theory).

6. Compare with Collins, Rowan v. Owens, 752 F.2d 1186, 1188 (7th Cir. 1984), (Posner, J.), on claim that no reasonable jury could have found voluntary manslaughter:

> True, there is less than complete certainty that Rowan was the assailant. He points out that each piece of evidence—the fingerprint, the comb, the hair, the car keys—that placed him in Miss Ayer's home is inconclusive, but he ignores the fact that the probability that all four pieces of evidence falsely point to him as the assailant is very small. Suppose that the probability that the fingerprint was not his (or, as he argues, was put on the can months earlier when he was shopping in the store where it was bought) is .01 (a generous estimate); the probability the comb was not his is .50; the probability that the hair was not his is .30; and the probability that someone else discarded Miss Ayer's car keys near his mother's house is .05. Then, assuming these probabilities are independent of each other, the probability that Rowan was not in Miss Ayer's house at a time near when she died is only .000075 (.01 X .50 X .30 X .05), which is less than one-hundredth of one percent. (This is the "product rule," lucidly discussed in McCormick's Handbook of the Law of Evidence 492–99 (2d ed., Cleary, 1972).) True, it would not follow that he had killed her; someone else might have entered the house before or after him, and done the deed. But that is exceedingly unlikely (especially in light of a statement he made to the police) ... and does not cast substantial doubt on his guilt. And true, the numbers in our example are arbitrary; but they bring out the point that it is wrong to view items of evidence in isolation when they point in the same direction. The jury was not irrational....

Are Rowan and Collins distinguishable? How? Does judicial notice, stereotyping or other bases for evidential hypotheses or the roles of attorney, jury, judge or appellate court affect your answer? Is there a different standard before or after trial? See Backes v. Valspar Corp., 783 F.2d 77 (7th Cir.1986).

7. In their 1996 paper, United States v. Shonubi, and the Use of Statistics in Court, Johan Bring of Uppsala University, Sweden and Colin Aitken of the University of Edinburgh, write (pp. 5–6):

> Statistical theory can also be helpful in the determination of the combined value of several pieces of evidence. The value of several pieces of evidence is combined by use of the odds version of Bayes theorem. The basic form in the context of our discussion is

$$\frac{P(H_g \,|\, e)}{P(H_i \,|\, e)} = \frac{P(e \,|\, H_g)}{P(e \,|\, H_i)} * \frac{P(H_g)}{P(H_i)}$$

> The probabilities of guilt (g) and innocence (i) prior to the presentation of evidence e are denoted $P(H_g)$ and $P(H_i)$ and known as prior probabilities. Their ratio is known as the prior odds in favour of guilt. The left hand side of the equation is the posterior odds for guilt, i.e. odds in favour of guilt after, or posterior to the presentation of the evidence e. When new evidence, f say, is presented this posterior odds serves as the prior odds for the new piece of evidence.... Generalisation to more than two pieces of evidence follows in an intuitively straightforward manner. Schum [Evidential Foundations of Probabilistic Reasoning] (1994) gives a thorough analysis of how to apply Bayes theorem in different situations and for different kinds of evidence. Thus, Bayes theorem can be seen as a formal method for continuously updating our beliefs about a person's guilt. Note here the use of probability as a measure of the strength of personal belief in a hypothesis. The use of the Bayesian framework in the law has been advocated for a long time (Lempert, [Modelling Relevance, 89 Mich. L. Rev. 1021] 1977). However, it has not yet gained general acceptance in the courtrooms. It remains to be seen if this is because of practical problems which are currently insurmountable or perhaps because of a lack of education. A good introductory discussion of the application of Bayes theorem in a court case can be found in the interesting discussion in Allen et al. [Probability and Proof in State v. Skipper, 35 Jurimetrics J. 277] (1995). Another useful source for the uses and limitations of Bayesian ideas is Tillers and Green, [Probability and Inferences in the Law of Evidence: The Use and Limits of Bayesianism] (1988).

The authors conclude that the technique used in Shonubi was essentially intuitive rather than statistical, though statistics and a "semi-Bayesian approach" were relied upon. See generally S.E. Fienberg and M.O. Finkelstein, Bayesian Statistics and the Law, 130–146, in J.M. Bernardo, J.O. Berger, A.P. David & A.F.M. Smith, Bayesian Statistics (1996), for another formulae for application of Bayesian analysis.

8. Students who are interested in the mathematical analysis will find extensive bibliographical references to the use of the Bayes and other formulae to aid triers in assessing statistical evidence in Kaye, The Laws of Probability and the Law of the Land, 47 U. of Chi.L.Rev. 34 (1979). The Table of Posterior Probability, below, is from M.O. Finkelstein, Quantitative Methods in Law, 90 (1978); the table does not, of course, take account of such attenuation of posterior probabilities that will be assigned subjectively by the trier because of belief in such factors as poor statistical bases, mistakes of testing or other credibility problems with experts, or of police misconduct.

Finkelstein and Fairley, A Bayesian Approach to Identification Evidence, 83 Harv.L.Rev. 489 (1970), suggest the use of Bayes's formula to convey to the jurors the probative force of the quantitative evidence. They illustrate their proposal by a graphic example. Suppose a woman's body is found in a ditch. There is evidence that the deceased had a violent quarrel with her boyfriend the night before. He is known to have struck her on other occasions. Investigators find the murder weapon, a knife, whose handle bears a latent palm print similar to the defendant's. The information on the print is limited so that an expert can say only that such prints appear in no more than one case in a thousand. Finkelstein and Fairley believe that the jurors will be aided in accurately assessing the total probative value of the evidence if they are first shown a chart depicting, in numerical terms, how much the probability that the defendant wielded the murder weapon is enhanced by the discovery of the prints. The chart they use is set forth below. The mathematical tool for devising such a chart is the Bayes formula. Finkelstein and Fairley suggest using the Bayesian chart as a pedagogical device, which would give the jurors some guidance in assessing the significance of the statistical evidence.

Table of Posterior Probabilities

Frequency of Characteristic in Suspect Population	Prior Probability				
	.01	.1	.25	.50	.75
.50	.019	.181	.400	.666	.857
.25	.038	.307	.571	.800	.923
.1	.091	.526	.769	.909	.967
.01	.502	.917	.970	.990	.996
.001	.909	.991	.997	.999	.999

Among those critical of the above approach relying on mathematical analysis to assist in evaluating probabilities are Tribe, Trial by Mathematics: Precision and Ritual in Legal Process, 84 Harv.L.Rev. 1329 (1971); Brilmayer & Kornhauser, Review: Quantitative Methods and Legal Decisions, 46 U.Chi. L.Rev. 116 (1978). Many are merely dubious. See, e.g., Kaplan, Decision Theory and the Fact Finding Process, 20 Stanford L.Rev. 1065, 1083 ff. (1968).

Even such a strong proponent of proper use of statistics and mathematical analysis as Professor Kaye warns of dangers in the Admissibility of "Probability Evidence" in Criminal Trials—Part I, 26 Jurimetrics J. 343 (1986), describing instances where dubious probability evidence was used. In Part II of this article, 27 Id. 160 (1987), he maintains:

(1) that reasonable estimates of pertinent population proportions should be admissible, (2) that argument on the part of counsel as to corresponding estimates of the probability of a coincidental misidentification should be permitted, and (3) that neither expert opinions as to whether the defendant left the trace evidence nor displays of the posterior probability that defendant did so should be admissible.

Minnesota, following Professor Tribe's warning against reliance on statistical proof, in Minnesota v. Boyd, 331 N.W.2d 480 (Minn.1983), held blood test results to show the defendant fathered the child were allowed, but the expert was only permitted to say that "the test results [are] consistent with" the view that defendant is the father of the baby. This was a rather pallid statement compared to the expert's opinion (expressed outside the jury's presence) that "1121 unrelated men would have to be randomly selected from the general population of men before another man would be found with all the appropriate genes to have fathered the child in question."

9. The "paradox of the gatecrasher", originally posed by Jonathan Cohen, an English philosopher of science, presents interesting problems in applying probability theory to the process of legal proof:

Consider a case in which it is common ground that 499 people paid for admission to a rodeo, and that 1,000 are counted on the seats, of whom A is one. Suppose no tickets were issued and there can be no testimony as to whether A paid for admission or climbed over the fence. So there is a .501 probability, on the admitted facts, that he did not pay. The conventionally accepted theory of probability would apparently imply that in such circumstances the rodeo organizers are entitled to judgment against A for the admission money, since the balance of the probability would lie in their favor. But it seems manifestly unjust that A should lose when there is an agreed probability of as high as .499 that he in fact paid for admission.

Indeed, if the organizers were really entitled to judgment against A, they would be entitled to judgment against each person in the same position as A. So they might conceivably be entitled to recover 1,000 admission prices when it was admitted that 499 had actually been paid. The absurd injustice of this suffices to show that there is something wrong somewhere. But where?

Kaye, The Paradox of the Gatecrasher and Other Stories, 1979 Ariz.St.L.J. 101, quoting the paradox almost verbatim from L. Cohen: The Probable and the Provable 75 (1977). For the two authors' particular resolutions of the paradox see Kaye, supra, at 104–108, Cohen, supra, at 270. See also the response of Cohen, Subjective Probability and the Paradox of the Gatecrasher, 1981 Ariz. L.J. 627, and Professor Kaye's surrebuttal, Paradoxes, Gedanken Experiments and the Burden of Proof: A Response to Dr. Cohen's Reply. Id. at 635. See generally, Eggleston, The Probability Debate, 1980 Crim.L.Rev. 678, 681 ("[I]f one accepts that the figures postulated make it more probable then not that a person chosen at random from the group of spectators did not pay, I do not see why that evidence would not be admissible, and being admitted make a prima facie case."); Williams, The Mathematics of Proof—I, 1979 Crim.L.Rev. 297, 304 (Even if only fifty spectators paid for their seats, "[i]t would still be wrong to give judgment against A."). To what extent does an unimaginably high a priori probability deflect inquiry from the special facts of the case at hand? Compare the effect of statutory presumptions; if 98% of all heroin in the United States is illegally imported, should the factfinder be allowed to infer importation from the single fact of possession? See discussion of constitutionality of presumptions, in Chapter 6, infra.

10. A great deal of basic research on how people think, remember, reason and come to conclusions has been followed with fascination by lawyers, students and judges, who have tended to ignore intradisciplinary debates such as those of the cognitive and behaviorist psychologists. See Introduction: Nature of Testimonial Proof, Chapter 3, infra. Some of that research has been applied to such matters as Jury Instructions. See e.g., M.F. Kaplan, The Impact of Social Psychologist of Procedural Justice 44 (1986). Other data have been used in such matters as determining the proper scope of expect testimony in assisting the trier to assess eyewitness testimony, Id. at 109, or in jury selection. Id. at 167. Some of this material finds its way into practical guides for lawyers. See, e.g., D.E. Vinson, Jury Trials: The Psychololgy of Winning Strategy, xiii (1986):

It has been said that there are key moments in every trial. These are the voir dire, the opening statement, the presentation of certain critical visual communications, and the testimony of key witnesses. Critical issues for jurors in any trial are relatively small numbers of anchoring ideas which they use to form their own understanding of a case. These ideas can be legal points, but they are often psychological or emotional issues which may not be immediately evident from a legal standpoint. An important part of psychological strategy in any trial is aimed at uncovering these key issues.

In the courtroom, the emotional and stereotypical feelings of triers, witnesses and lawyers need to be recognized. See, e.g., Goleman, "Useful" Modes of Thinking Contribute to the Power of Prejudice; Studies of strong stereotypes also point to the primacy of feelings over rational thought, N.Y. Times, May 12, 1987, p. c. 1 (cognitive role of categorizing and stereotyping essential to living). They also affect judgments in setting policy and risk analysis in regulation and product development. See, e.g., Slovic, Perception of Risk, 236 Science 280 (April 1987):

> The elusive and hard to manage qualities of today's hazards have forced the creation of a new intellectual discipline called risk assessment, designed to aid in identifying, characterizing and quantifying risk.... Whereas technologically sophisticated analysts employ side assessment to evaluate hazards, the majority of citizens rely on intuitive risk judgments, typically called 'risk perceptions'. For these people experience with hazards tends to come from the news media, which rather thoroughly document mishaps and threats occurring throughout the world. The dominant perception for most Americans (and one that contrasts sharply with the views of professional risk assessors) is that they face more risk today than in the past and that future risks will be even greater than today's.

See also specific perceptions on toxic substances and cancer under judicial notice, Chapter 7, infra.

How will such perceptions, stereotypes, prejudices and psychological and social psychological information be obtained by the lawyer? How will it affect what happens in the courtroom? How can or should the rules of court procedure and evidence be affected by this information? See, e.g., Gold, Causation in Toxic Torts: Burdens of Proof, Standards of Persuasion, and Statistical Evidence, 96 Yale L.J. 376 (1986); National Research Council, Proceedings of Conference on Valuing Health Risks, Costs, and Benefits for Environmental Policy Making (June 23–24, 1987) and particularly M.J. Machine, The Economic Theory of Choice under Uncertainty at 30 ("alternative means of representing or 'framing' probabilistically equivalent choice problems will lead to systematic differences in choice."). The problems of risk analysis for substantive purposes is analogous. See, e.g., Stephen Breyer, Breaking the Vicious Circle: Toward Effective Risk Management (1993). See also introduction to Witnesses, Chapter 3, infra. Systematic errors in assessing probabilistic information and in misleading heuristics throw serious doubt on the ability of triers to formulate probabilities correctly. Id. Are these conclusions, reached largely on the basis of laboratory studies, valid in the courtroom?

Does "jury science" utilized to advise litigants on how jurors of certain backgrounds may react to a case and how the evidence and arguments can deal with specific jurors offer help in rationalizing trials? See, e.g., Jeremy W. Barber, The Jury is Still Out: The Role of Jury Science in the Modern American Courtroom, 31 Am. Crim. L. Rev. 1225 (1994) (suggesting, among other devices for dealing with this matter, equal access to data, state funding for indigent defendants, abolishing peremptory challenges, and conducting the voir dire only by the court). See, e.g., the kinds of research available from commercial firms, Donald E. Vinson (of Decision Quest, Inc.), The O.J. Simpson Trial: A Lesson in Persuasion (1996) (referring not only to selection of jurors and persuasion in court, but to a calculated pretrial effort to deal with the media and, through it, potential jurors). Ethnic and gender backgrounds had an impact on reaction to the O.J. Simpson verdict. Post-verdict surveys showed 42% of "blacks" thought Simpson not guilty, compared to 16% of whites. Surprisingly, 23% of "black" males thought him guilty, but only 7% of "black" females were of this opinion. In view of this analysis is this a case fairly characterized as demonstrating jury nullification? See Jack B. Weinstein, Considering Jury "Nullification": When May and Should a Jury Reject The Law to Do Justice, 30 Am. Crim. L. Rev. 239 (1993).

Should behavioral research be conducted to identify conditions that might cause a trier of fact to misinterpret such evidence as DNA profiling and how well various ways of presenting expert evidence on DNA can reduce such misunderstandings? How might such research affect jury selection as well as methods of presenting evidence?

To what extent can these problems be dealt with by the voir dire in jury selection or by instruction by the court. See Mansfield, Jury Notice, 74 Georgetown L.J. 395 (1985). To what extent are all of the lawyer's tactical decisions at the trial affected by such considerations. See D.E. Vinson, Jury Trials: The Psychology of Winning Strategy, xiii (1986). Critical of the Vinson approach is Gold, Psychological Manipulation in the Courtroom, 66 Neb.L.Rev. 562 (1987); 65 N.C.L.Rev. 481 (1987).

11. Whether or not various mathematical models and statistical tools are explicitly brought to the attention of jurors through experts, arguments of counsel or judicial notice, an attempt to understand them has an important bearing on the practitioner's approach to preparation for trial and trial itself. Moreover, since the lawyer is often a factfinder himself in nonlitigation setting such as advising a client whether there is sufficient risk of harm to consumer or environment to warrant production of a product or whether to report a matter to the S.E.C. pr police or change employment techniques to avoid discrimination litigation, he or she must attempt to understand how people arrive at decisions and how the process may be improved.

A particularly useful article is Saks & Kidd's, Human Information Processing and Adjudication: Trial by Heuristics, 15 Law & Society Review 123 (1980) (relying on behavioral decision theory and research particularly of Professor Tversky, and extensive bibliography in the article, with emphasis on the problem of squaring individual triers' intuitive assumptions of base rates and empirical observation of such rates when they must integrate this information with case-specific information). Illustrative of how people use simplifying mental operations, called "heuristics" to reduce the complexity of information and to integrate it with other knowledge in making decisions, is the following example from Saks and Kidd at 127–129:

> The following description is of a man selected at random from a group composed of 70 lawyers and 30 engineers. "John is a 39–year–old man. He is married and has two children. He is active in local politics. The hobby that he most enjoys is rare book collecting. He is competitive, argumentative, and articulate." A large group of respondents was asked to estimate the probability that John is a lawyer rather than an engineer. Their median probability estimate was .95. Another group of respondents was asked the same question, except that they were first told that the group from which John was selected consisted of 30 lawyers and 70 engineers. The second group's median estimate of the likelihood that John is a lawyer was also .95. Information about the composition of the group from which John was selected logically should have affected the estimated probability, but it had no effect at all on the decision makers' judgment. (This problem is taken from Kahneman and Tversky, 1973 ["On the Psychology of

Predictions," 80 Psychological Review 237].) Only at the extremes of the distributions, where the group approaches 100 lawyers and 0 engineers (or the converse) do the decision makers become sensitive to the information about group composition....

The ... example illustrates how human decision making tends to be insensitive to base rates when case-specific information is available. Given only the group base rates—30 lawyers: 70 engineers—people rely heavily on this information to make their judgments. They correctly say the probability is .30 that the person selected is a lawyer. When descriptive case-specific information is added, they tend to ignore the numerical base rate and rely instead on the degree to which the description of John is representative of their stereotype of lawyers. Subjects base their estimate of the probability that John is a lawyer on the degree of correspondence between his description and their stereotype of lawyers as argumentative, competitive, and politically aware. Given the base-rate data in this example, it is 5.44 times as likely that John is a lawyer when the group is composed of 70 lawyers and 30 engineers than when the opposite membership distribution holds.

See also, e.g., Lempert, Modeling Relevance, 75 Mich.L.Rev. 1021 (1977); R. Nisbett & L. Ross, Human Inference (1980), reviewed by Spitzer, 9 Hofstra L.Rev. 1621 (1981); Loftus and Beach, Human Inference and Judgment, Is the Glass Half Empty or Half Full?, 34 Stanf.L.Rev. 939 (1982), reviewing R. Nisbett and R. Beach, Human Inference: Strategies and Shortcomings of Social Judgment (1980). Cullison, Probability Analysis of Judicial Fact Finding: A Preliminary Outline of the Subjective Approach, 1969 Toledo L.Rev. 538; Jackson, Probability and Mathematics in Court Fact–Finding, 31 Northern Ireland Legal Quarterly 239 (1980) (referring to both Commonwealth and American literature).

It may well be that newer information on trier's reasoning can be utilized most effectively at this stage in our development in fact finding situations outside the courtroom. Often, however, the "factual" and "normative" decisions in such situations are mingled, making it difficult sometimes to distinguish between a scientific or managerial fact consensus and a negotiated agreement where policy such as corporate or governmental image and risks are at stake. See, e.g., Center for Public Resources, Dispute Management, A Manual of Innovative Corporate Strategies for the Avoidance and Resolution of Legal Disputes (1980); M.R. Wessel, Science and Conscience, xii–xiv (1980) ("Socioscientific disputes have a number of important special characteristics which distinguish them from older, more traditional disputes;" adversarialism leads to increased public acrimony; a "scientific consensus finding conference" might avoid such difficulties; a "rule of reason" requiring much more candor is recommended). The process may even be designed to avoid fact finding that pins the parties down to an outcome based upon assessment of real world events. See, e.g., R. Fisher & W. Vry, Getting to Yes, Negotiating Agreement Without Giving In (1980) (fact finding, except in a reference to use of "phony facts" among "tricky tactics," p. 138, is not mentioned). Compare the "give" in court fact finding permitted by the rules of burdens of proof and degree of probability required.

12. Research and writing on the theory of decision making in courts, other adjudicative bodies and rule making fora was reflected in the rich symposium published in 66 Boston University Law Review 377 (1986). The primary issue as stated by Professor Twining was "what constitutes valid cogent, and appropriate modes of reasoning about disputed questions of fact in adjudication." Id. at 391. See also the symposium contributions by Professors Green, Tillers, Allen, Lempert, Zuckerman, Friedman, Nesson, Cohn, Edwards, Shafer, Feinberg, Kaye, Brilmayer, Martin, Schervish, Shafer, Schum, Edwards, Ashford, and Nance. Gardenfas et al., Evidential Value: Philosophical Judicial and Psychological Aspects of a Theory (1983); Cohen, Confidence in Probability: Burdens of Persuasion in a World of Imperfect Knowledge, 60 N.Y.U.L.Rev. 385 (1985); Pennington and Hastie, Evidence Evaluation in Complex Decision-making, 51 J. of Personality and Social Psychology 242 (1986); Pennington and Hastie, Juror Decision–Making models: Use Generalization Gap, 89 Psychological Bulletin 246 (1981) (in their later unpublished writings the authors have developed a "story model" for juror decision making). See generally, Richard D. Friedman, Assessing Evidence, 94 Mich. L.Rev. 1810, reviewing C.G.G. Aitken, Statistics and the Evaluation of Evidence for Forensic Scientists (1995); Bernard Robertson and G.A. Vignaux, Interpreting Evidence: Evaluating Forensic Science in the Courtroom (1995); David A. Schum, Evidential Foundations of Probabilistic Reasoning (1994).

In a sense, the burgeoning of theoretical discussion of the theory of proof and of inference and decisionmaking is a response to a whole host of new economic, scientific, social and political problems placing our regulatory and judicial system under increasing strain. We expect more precision and certainty from our scientists and our courts than they can often deliver. See e.g., Jack B. Weinstein Individual Justice in Mass Tort Litigation, 115 (1995) ("We tend to exaggerate the purity of scientists and their ability to provide precise answers when needed."). Should a judicial system in a democracy such as ours try to find the best answers to issues of fact and face up to the unreliability and lack of precision of much of our fact finding? What values favor disguising lack of certainty in fact finding, treating our triers as infallible and their judgments as if they were in fact, indubitably accurate? How can lawyers, judges and juries use new forms of evidence and more sophisticated reasoning effectively?

13. Should there be any difference in the reasoning techniques used depending on the degrees of risk involved? See Chapter 7, infra, on burdens of proof. Kaplan, Decision Theory and the Factfinding Process, 20 Stanford L.Rev. 1065, 1073–74 (1968):

> Probably the most important reason why we do not attempt to express reasonable doubt in terms of quantitative odds, however, is that in any rational system the utilities (or disutilities) that determine the necessary probability of guilt will vary with the crime for which the defendant is being tried, and indeed with the particular defendant. In a criminal trial, as in any decision process, we must consider the utilities associated with differing decisions of the particular case at issue—not just the average utilities over many disparate types of criminal cases. Thus the rational factfinder should consider the disadvantages of convicting this defendant of this crime if he is innocent as compared with those of acquitting him if he is guilty. It is obviously far less serious to society, for instance, to acquit an embezzler, who, in any event, may find it very difficult to be placed again in a position of trust, than it would be to acquit a child molester, since the latter crime is one that tends to be repeated. The utilities ... will vary then, not only with the seriousness of the offense, but with the danger of its repetition.

Speaking of the problem of the officer in the street making the decision to stop and frisk a passerby, the Supreme Court noted, United States v. Cortez, 449 U.S. 411 (1981):

The process does not deal with hard certainties, but with probabilities. Long before the law of probabilities was articulated as such, practical people formulated certain common sense conclusions about human behavior; jurors as factfinders are permitted to do the same—and so are law enforcement officers. Finally, the evidence thus collected must be seen and weighed not in terms of library analysis by scholars, but as understood by those versed in the field of law enforcement.

14. On the importance of statistical proof see, e.g., Stephen E. Feinberg, Samuel H. Krislov, Miron L. Straf, Understanding and Evaluating Statistical Evidence in Litigation, 36 Jurimetrics 1 (1995). Compare with Collins, supra, cases utilizing "trait evidence" for the purpose of identification in both civil and criminal cases. See, e.g., United States v. Massey, 594 F.2d 676 (8th Cir.1979) (a conviction for bank robbery was reversed where crucial evidence against defendant consisted of an analysis comparing hair samples found at the scene of the crime with those found in a ski mask resembling that used in commission of the crime; it was held that the prosecutors remarks suggesting the expert's analysis of the hair samples was 99.4% foolproof "confused the probability of concurrence of identifying marks with probability of mistaken identification," thus having the effect of making the uncertain seem all but proven; reversible error); State v. Carlson, 267 N.W.2d 170 (Minn.1978) (expert testimony that there was only a 1–in–800 chance that foreign pubic hairs found on victim did not come from defendant and 1–in–400 chance that head hairs found in victim's hand did not belong to defendant was improperly received since such statistical probability testimony could suggest by qualification, guilt beyond a reasonable doubt). See also, Kaye, The Laws of Probability and the Law of the Land, 47 Univ.Chi.L.Rev. 34 (1979); Charrow and Smith, Upper and Lower Bounds for Probability of Guilt Based on Circumstantial Evidence, 70 J.Am.Stat.Ass'n 555 (1975) (the authors develop a mathematical model for use in determining the probability that the suspect and the perpetrator are one and the same based solely on the circumstantial evidence, i.e., matching traits, with a key assumption that the underlying events were independent or any dependence is de minimis; they suggest such independence occurs in cases involving typewriter identification, fingerprint identification, or in a scenario where a perpetrator with facial scars and a blue overcoat is seen fleeing the scene in a Chevrolet pickup); Gaudette and Keeping, An Attempt at Determining Probabilities in Human Scalp Hair Comparison, 19 J.For.Sci. 599, 605 (1974). Cf. Lincoln, Blood Group Evidence for the Defense, 20 Med.Sci.Law 239 (1980). Note the method of offering blood evidence by affidavit in California Evidence Code § 712.

See United States v. Shonubi, 103 F.3d 1085 (2d Cir.1997), reversing 895 F.Supp. 460 (E.D.N.Y.1995), criticized in ___ F.Supp. ___ (E.D.N.Y.1977) on the ground that statistical evidence was not "specific evidence" required in the context of sentencing guidelines. Is this a distortion of Rules 401 and 402?

15. Many of the scientific proof avenues are limited by extrinsic policies. See the discussion in Chapter 8, infra. For example, a suspect may be ordered to give a blood sample if there is a clear indication of need and the method of intrusion into the suspect is safe and reliable. In re Abe A., 452 N.Y.S.2d 6, 437 N.E.2d 265 (N.Y.1982). What inference can be drawn from a suspect's refusal to cooperate? What constitutional issues are implicated? See Id. 452 N.Y.S.2d at 10, 437 N.E.2d at 268:

[I]n Cupp v. Murphy, 412 U.S. 291 [removal of fingernail scrapings] and in Schmerber v. California, 384 U.S. 757 [testing for alcohol in blood], the Supreme Court, while in each case excusing the absence of a warrant because of "the ready destructibility of the evidence," emphasized that the police had the requisite probable cause (Cupp v. Murphy, supra, at pp. 294–296; Schmerber v. California, supra, at pp. 770–771).... [W]hen the physical evidence whose possession is the raison d'etre for detaining a person cannot be altered or destroyed, as in the case of the type of blood integral to one's body (Graves v. Beto, 301 F.Supp. 264, 265, affd. 424 F.2d 524), by definition there can be no exigency to justify exemption from the warrant standard of probable cause....

How would you treat an operation to obtain a bullet from defendant's body to compare its rifling marks with the bullets fired from the victim's gun in order to show that the defendant was the person the deceased fired at and therefore more probably the person who shot at the deceased?

16. The use of statistics and explicit reference to probability theory and mathematics in the courtroom has increased enormously in recent years. A number of factors explain this increased use. First, the loosening of the rules of evidence governing experts has made it easier to use statistics. Second, the substantive law is increasingly based on social and economic changes which require statistics as proof—e.g., discrimination, antitrust or carcinogen-based environmental damages cases. Third, technological developments such as computers and large available data bases make statistical proof easier. Fourth, expanding government regulation has presented factual issues and administrative staff inviting the use of statistical argument. Fifth, the more positive attitude of the legal profession and education of young lawyers favors this kind of proof.

17. While courts are reluctant to replace traditional adjudicative methods with more complex forms of mathematical analysis, intuitive appraisals of statistics frequently underlie racial discrimination cases. See, e.g., Texas Department of Community Affairs v. Burdine, 450 U.S. 248 (1981); D.C. Baldus & J.W.I. Cole, Statistical Proof of Discrimination (1979); discussion of Burdens of Proof Chapter 7, infra. See also Keyes v. School District Number 1, 413 U.S. 189 (1973) (school desegregation); Swain v. Alabama, 380 U.S. 202 (1965) (court viewed statistical evidence as showing that few African–Americans have been selected to serve on juries); United States v. Jenkins, 496 F.2d 57 (2d Cir.), cert. denied, 420 U.S. 925 (1975) (jury selection); Hawkins v. Town of Shaw, 437 F.2d 1286 (5th Cir.1971) (municipal improvements); See also, Note, 89 Harv.L.Rev. 387 (1975). "Scientifically designed samples and polls, meeting the tests of necessity and trustworthiness, are useful adjuncts to conventional methods of proof and may contribute materially to shortening the trial of the complex case." Federal Judicial Center, Manual for Complex and Multidistrict Litigation, 2.612. See Rosado v. Wyman, 322 F.Supp. 1173, 1180–1181 (E.D.N.Y.), aff'd 437 F.2d 619 (2d Cir.1970) (citing considerable authority):

> Such mathematical and statistical methods are well recognized by the courts as reliable and acceptable in determining adjudicative facts. [Extensive citations omitted.] It was a principal recommendation of the prestigious committee which wrote the Manual for Complex and Multidistrict Litigation that "[s]cientifically designed samples ... meeting the tests of necessity and trustworthiness ... [be used to] contribute materially to shortening the trial of the complex case." Manual for Complex and Multidistrict Litigation, supra, at 2.612.
>
> Statisticians can tell us with some assurance what the reliability factors and probabilities are. Only the law can decide, as a matter of procedural and substantive policy, what probabilities will be required before the courts will change the status quo by granting a remedy.

See also South Dakota Pub. Util. Comm'n v. FERC, 643 F.2d 504 (8th Cir.1981) (use of statistical models to determine propriety of accelerated depreciation of public utility's gas pipeline); Contemporary Mission Inc. v. Famous Music Corp., 557 F.2d 918 (2d Cir.1977) (a statistical analysis of record industry sales figures offered by the plaintiff to prove how successful its record might have been if defendant had not breached his contract); American Brands, Inc. v. R.J. Reynolds Tobacco Co., 413 F.Supp. 1352 (S.D.N.Y.1976) (poll used in a false advertising case to determine consumer's reaction to the advertisement): United States v. Lopez, 328 F.Supp. 1077 (S.D.N.Y.1971) (probable cause to search airline passengers based on statistical "profile" of recurring characteristics in hijackers); Boucher v. Bomhoff, 495 P.2d 77 (Alaska 1972) (at issue was whether prefatory language of the constitutional referendum ballot suggested that a constitutional convention had to be held; lower court admitting the results of a survey conducted to determine if the prefatory language had a bias towards an affirmative vote was proper, concurring opinion per J. Erwin); United States v. Twitty, 72 F.3d 228 (1st Cir.1995) (statistics about guns retrieved by the police to show unlawful sale).

18.   Sometimes the statistical analysis becomes the basis for what is in effect a substantive rule of law. See, for example, the two-or-three-standard deviation rule for assessing significance in a jury discrimination case. While the Court spoke of a prima facie case and shifting burdens, was it really creating a rule of substantive law that could be easily applied in Castaneda v. Partida, 430 U.S. 482, 497 n. 17 (1977) when it wrote:

> If the jurors were drawn randomly from the general population, then the number of Mexican–Americans in the sample could be modeled by a binomial distribution. See Finkelstein, The Application of Statistical Decision Theory to the Jury Discrimination Cases, 80 Harv.L.Rev. 338, 353–356 (1966). See generally P. Hoel, Introduction to Mathematical Statistics 58–61, 79–86 (4th ed. 1971); F. Mosteller, R. Rourke, & G. Thomas, Probability with Statistical Applications 130–146, 270–291 (2d ed. 1970). Given that 79.1% of the population is Mexican–American, the expected number of Mexican–Americans among the 870 persons summoned to serve as grand jurors over the 11–year period is approximately 688. The observed number is 339. Of course, in any given drawing some fluctuation from the expected number is predicted. The important point however, is that the statistical model shows that the results of a random drawing are likely to fall in the vicinity of the expected value. See F. Mosteller, R. Rourke, & G. Thomas, supra, at 270–290. The measure of the predicted fluctuations from the expected value is the standard deviation, defined for the binomial distribution as the square root of the product of the total number in the sample (here 870) times the probability of selecting a Mexican–American (0.791) times the probability of selecting a non-Mexican–American (0.209). Id., at 213. Thus, in this case the standard deviation is approximately 12. *As a general rule for such large samples, if the difference between the expected value and the observed number is greater than two or three standard deviations, then the hypothesis that the jury drawing was random would be suspect to a social scientist.* The 11–year data here reflect a difference between the expected and observed number of Mexican–Americans of approximately 29 standard deviations. A detailed calculation reveals that the likelihood that such a substantial departure from the expected value would occur by chance is less than 1 in 10.

> The data for the 2½–year period during which the State District Judge supervised the selection process similarly support the inference that the exclusion of Mexican–Americans did not occur by chance. Of 220 persons

called to serve as grand jurors, only 100 were Mexican–Americans. The expected Mexican–American representation is approximately 174 and the standard deviation, as calculated from the binomial model, is approximately six. The discrepancy between the expected and observed values is more than 12 standard deviations. Again, a detailed calculation shows that the likelihood of drawing not more than 100 Mexican–Americans by chance is negligible, being less than 1 in 10. (Emphasis supplied; footnotes omitted.)

Compare Kaye, The Numbers Game: Statistical Inference in Discrimination Cases, 80 Mich.L.Rev. 833, 840 (1984), criticizing two standard deviation rule as requiring higher than a more probable than not standard, with particular objection to the application in Hazelwood School District v. United States, 433 U.S. 299 (1977). See also Kaye, Is Proof of Statistical Significance Relevant, 61 Washington L.Rev. 1333 (1986).

Proper use of statistical evidence requires extensive early planning, often with the assistance of the court to obtain data bases both sides can use and to narrow differences among the experts. See, e.g., Trout v. Hidalgo, 517 F.Supp. 873, 877 n. 4 (D.C.D.C.1981):

> The data used by both parties' experts for statistical analysis consisted of a computer tape and a computer printout furnished to plaintiffs by defendants in response to an interrogatory. The tape included eighteen recent job actions taken with respect to each employee from 1970 to 1979, as well as the employee's age, sex, date of entry in federal service, date of hire by, and departure from, NARDAC, and the prior employing agency. The printout included age, sex, educational level, date of entry in federal service, date of hire by NAVCOSSACT, and all job actions between 1972 and 1977. These data, from which all subsequent analyses were derived, were first requested by plaintiffs on May 9, 1980, five weeks before the trial began. Some of the deficiencies in the parties' statistical analysis can be traced directly to certain gaps in these two sources of data. Had either party focused its attention earlier on the critical role statistical analysis would play in the proof of this case, it might have been possible to obtain and analyze the personnel records themselves as a basis for more accurate determinations.

NOTES ON NEGATIVE INFERENCES BASED ON DISBELIEF OF TESTIMONY

The trier of fact may disbelieve the testimony of a witness even though that testimony is uncontradicted. Does the rejection of the witness' testimony warrant a negative inference, that the opposite of what he says is true? Thus, if the defendant testifies that he has paid a debt and he is not believed, should the jury—on this testimony alone—be permitted to conclude that he has not paid the debt?

Appellate courts have generally announced the rule that disbelief of testimony is not the equivalent of proof of facts contrary to that testimony. E.g., Hudiburgh v. Palvic, 274 S.W.2d 94, 99 (Tex.Civ.App.1954); Maniscalco v. Director, 97 N.E.2d 639, 642 (Mass.1951) (review of an administrative decision); Boice–Perrine Co. v. Kelley, 137 N.E. 731, 733 (Mass.1923); Wallace v. Berdell, 97 N.Y. 13, 21 (1884); see 6 Jones, Evidence § 2468 (2d ed. 1926). But see Duffy v. National Janitorial Services, Inc., 240 A.2d 527 (Pa.1968). Judge Hand in Pariso v. Towse, 45 F.2d 962, 964 (2d Cir.1930), recognized the theoretical unsoundness of this position: "Upon such an issue as that at bar it might indeed be possible to argue that the owner's denial could be used in positive support of his consent. He has personal acquaintance with the fact, and the jury is certainly free to find affirmatively that his denial is untrue. Moreover, to find the denial false of something necessarily known to the witness, ought to result in finding true the proposition denied. That, however, would, at least if generalized, carry matters too far. An executor could not, for example, prove a contract with his testator by calling the promisor, and demanding a verdict because his denial was patently untrue. The law does not ordinarily cut so fine; a party must produce affirmative proof." See also Orena v. United States, ___ F.Supp. ___, 1997 WL 109000 (E.D.N.Y.1997). Similar reasoning was used in Kirby v. President, Etc., Delaware & H. Canal Co., 46 N.Y.S. 777, 780 (N.Y.A.D. 3d Dept.1897): The proponent of a fact "cannot call his adversary as a witness as to that fact, elicit testimony from him to the effect that such alleged fact has no existence, and then call upon the jury to discredit the evidence of such adversary simply because he is interested as a party, and to base upon the assumed falsity of his evidence an affirmative finding of the existence of such alleged fact, without any other evidence of its existence, or from which it may be inferred." Is this reasoning implicitly based on a sporting theory of justice—i.e., each side ought to obtain its proof without the aid of the other? Is there more reason to apply the rule in criminal than in civil cases? Would it tend to discourage a defendant from taking the witness stand whenever his attorney had a serious doubt about whether the plaintiff had proved a prima facie case? If no such rule existed would the power of the courts to control juries be reduced?

Consider the following situations:

1. Defendant moves for summary judgment and plaintiff's affidavit presents no evidence but merely urges the possibility of cross-examining the defendant or his witnesses. In Dyer v. MacDougall, 201 F.2d 265 (2d Cir.1952), plaintiff's complaint alleged that defendant slandered him in plaintiff's absence, but in the presence of two witnesses. Defendant's motion for summary judgment was supported by his own affidavit and those of the alleged witnesses, all denying that the slander had been committed. The trial judge summarily dismissed the complaint and the second circuit affirmed. Judge Hand recognized that the jury might rationally be convinced by the demeanor of the defendant on the witness stand that the truth was the opposite of what he said it was. Nevertheless, he voted to affirm: "This is owing to the fact that otherwise in such cases there could not be an effective appeal from the judge's disposition of a motion for a directed verdict. He, who has seen and heard the 'demeanor' evidence, may have been right or wrong in thinking that it gave rational support to a verdict; yet, since that evidence has disappeared, it will be impossible for an appellate court to say which he was." (Footnote omitted.)

Judge Frank disagreed with Judge Hand's reasoning, although voting to affirm on other grounds. First he pointed out that the problem bothering Judge Hand is equally pressing in any case in which oral testimony plays a significant role; then Judge Frank disposed of the issue by noting that on a motion for a directed verdict the trial judge does not weigh the evidence, including the credibility of witnesses, but assumes that the jury will believe all the evidence, including demeanor evidence, favorable to the adverse party. "The rule that a trial judge ... may not legitimately consider demeanor in considering directed verdict motions means that his orders on such motions are readily reviewable." See N.L.R.B. v. Walton Manufacturing Co., 369 U.S. 404, 408, 417–421 (1962), for a sharp difference among the members of the Court as to practical significance and application of the principles put forward in Dyer v. MacDougall.

Subin v. Goldsmith, 224 F.2d 753, 757 (2d Cir.), cert. denied, 350 U.S. 883 (1955), saw Judge Frank prevail. This was a stockholders' derivative action in which the court reversed a summary judgment for the defendant. Judge Frank, writing for the majority, said: "We shall assume, arguendo, that Feinberg's affidavit, if taken as true, completely controverted the allegations of Count V. But we have held that, in such derivative stockholder's suit—especially as to facts peculiarly within the knowledge of the defendants—plaintiff is entitled to a trial at which he may cross-examine the defendants and at which the trial judge can observe their demeanor in order, thereby, to evaluate their credibility." In his dissenting opinion Judge Medina said, at p. 776: "Perhaps the most significant feature of the papers submitted in support of and in opposition to the motion for summary judgment is the complete failure of plaintiff to present any proofs whatever to establish his charges. The affidavit of counsel is no more than an argumentative memorandum. And so the proofs submitted in support of the motion remain unanswered." It is now generally conceded that Judge Medina was right, the opponent cannot simply sit back and depend upon a possible negative evaluation of adverse witnesses with knowledge to supply gaps in the proponent's proof. See, e.g., Celotex v. Catrett, 477 U.S. 317 (1986); Anderson v. Liberty Lobby, Inc., 477 U.S. 242 (1986); Charles Alan Wright, Law of Federal Courts, § 99 (1994).

Does the result in the Subin case depend on the fact that it is a shareholders' derivative action? If so, what characteristics does such an action have that are lacking in the slander action involved in Dyer? Cf. Paul E. Hawkinson Co. v. Dennis, 166 F.2d 61 (5th Cir.1948) (patent infringement).

2. Are courts permitting negative inferences when they hold that false or contradictory extra-judicial statements are indicative of consciousness of guilt sufficient to satisfy the requirement that the testimony of an accomplice be corroborated by independent evidence? See People v. Coakley, 238 P.2d 633, 636 (Cal.App.1951) ("Such contradictions by one accused or his silence or his lies are independent corroborative evidence."). See also People v. Sandelin, 233 P.2d 147 (Cal. App. 1951); People v. Willmurth, 176 P. 2d 102 (Cal. App. 1947). Contra: State v. Elsberg, 295 N.W. 91 (Minn.1941). In each of these cases there appears to have been sufficient corroborative evidence apart from the false or contradictory statements.

What is the bearing on this problem of the rule that an accusation and reply are admissible as proof of guilt if the defendant does not remain silent in the face of a charge but equivocally denies or makes false, evasive, or contradictory statements? The theory is that such an equivocal response gives rise to an inference of acquiescence in the truth of the accusation or that such a response is evidence of a consciousness of guilt. E.g., People v. Carmelo, 210 P.2d 538 (Cal.App.1949); People v. McKnight, 196 P.2d 104 (Cal.App.1948); People v. Popilsky, 8 N.E.2d 640 (Ill.1937); Commonwealth v. Hebert, 163 N.E. 189 (Mass.1928); Commonwealth v. Spiropoulos, 94 N.E. 451 (Mass.1911). Does it make any difference that these cases are not based on the principle that disbelief of a statement raises the inference that the opposite of that statement is true, but rather on the principle that a man's conduct may be affirmative evidence of his guilt? In this connection, note that where there is an unequivocal denial of guilt, testimony as to the accusatory statement or the defendant's response is excluded. 4 Wigmore, Evidence § 1072(5) (3d ed. 1940).

3. In an action for fraudulently inducing plaintiff to enter into a bilateral contract, plaintiff must prove, among other things, that the defendant promised to do something and that at the time he made his promise he had no intention of keeping it. Plaintiff offers testimony which, if believed, proves that the promise was made and never carried out. Defendant testifies that he never made the promise. If the jury believes that the promise was made, may it conclude that at the time it was made defendant did not intend to keep it? See, e.g., McCreight v. Davey Tree Expert Co., 254 N.W. 623, 625 (Minn.1934); cf. Kley v. Healy, 44 N.E. 150, 152 (N.Y.C.A. 1896).

4. Would it help the opponent if the judge charged: "If you believe a witness lied to you, you may not assume that the opposite of what the witness said is true?" Apart from the logical difficulties with this task, is this charge—and many charges directing a jury to ignore something, counterproductive. See, e.g., Wegner, Schneider, Carter and White, Paradoxical Effects of Thought Suppression, 53 J. of Personality and Social Psychology 5 (1987) (asking a subject not to think of something increases the likelihood that the thought will not be suppressed).

E.   PRESERVATION OF ISSUES FOR APPEAL

The Brewer case, set out below, may be easier to understand after differences between substantive and impeachment use and character rules have been studied. The Wilson case in Note 6, infra, presents the preservation issue more simply.

United States v. Brewer

Court of Appeals, Fourth Circuit, 1993.
1 F.3d 1430.

■ PHILLIPS, CIRCUIT JUDGE:

Appellant Dennis Brewer challenges his convictions on eight counts of possession with intent to distribute cocaine. . . .

Brewer first contends that the district court erred in admitting the testimony of his fiancee, Waquesha Scott, because she was called solely to provide improper character evidence "for the purpose of proving action in conformity therewith on a particular occasion," evidence generally forbidden by Fed. R. Evid. 404 (a). The government argues (1) that Brewer failed to preserve this error and (2) that Scott was called to provide testimony that she'd told federal marshals Brewer was a "drug dealer," which the government claims constituted evidence of "of other crimes, wrongs, or acts" admissible under Rule 404(b) to show Brewer's intent to distribute and knowing possession. Both intent and knowledge are elements of the indicted offense put in issue by Brewer's "not guilty" plea. See United States v. Sparks, 560 F. 2d 1173, 1175 (4th Cir.1977).

We agree with the government that Brewer failed to preserve this error. Before Scott took the stand, Brewer's counsel objected to the government's request to treat Scott as a hostile witness. The district court sustained that objection, requiring the government to demonstrate adversity before it could treat Scott as hostile. Immediately thereafter followed this frequently interrupted examination of Scott by the government:

Q. Were you interviewed by United States Marshals about Mr. Brewer?

A. Yes, I was.

Q. And did you tell the marshals—

[Brewer's counsel]: Objection, Your Honor.

[United States]: I'll rephrase the question . . .

[District Court]: All right.

Q. Does Dennis Brewer deal drugs?

A. No.

[Brewer's counsel]: Objection.

[District Court]: Overruled.

A. No, he does not. They tried to make me say he did.

Q. Has he ever dealt drugs?

A. No, he has not.

Q. Have you ever seen him with drugs?

A. No . . .

Q. Do you remember when you were interviewed by the marshals?

A. . . . I remember . . .

Q. And isn't it true that you told the marshals at that time that—

[Brewer's counsel]: Objection, Your Honor.

[District Court]: Stand up and tell me what the objection is.

[Brewer's counsel]: It's his witness.

[District Court]: Overruled. You [the United States] may now lead [the witness].

J.A. at 262–63. While the transcript excerpt reveals that Brewer's counsel objected to the question "Does Dennis Brewer deal drugs?" (after Scott had already answered it), he stated no basis for his objection. To preserve an objection to admissibility for appeal, Fed. R. Evid. 103(a) requires such a statement unless the specific ground was "apparent from the context." The convoluted nature of the above questioning, in which Brewer's counsel apparently focused on the form of the government's questions rather than their content, reveals that was not the case.

Where counsel fails adequately to present and preserve an objection on the record, we review the admission of evidence solely for plain error. Fed. R. Evid. 103(a) (1), 103 (d); Fed. R. Crim. P. 52(b). The Supreme Court's recent decision in United States v. Olano, 113 S. Ct. 1770 (1993), clarifies the role of appellate courts undertaking plain error review. To reverse for plain error the reviewing court must (1) identify an error, 113 S. Ct. at 1777, (2) which is plain, id., (3) which affects substantial rights, 113 S. Ct. at 1777–78, and (4) which "seriously affect[s] the fairness, integrity or public reputation of judicial proceedings." 113 S. Ct. at 1779 (quoting United States v. Atkinson, 297 U.S. 157, 160, 56 S. Ct. 391, 392, 80 L. Ed. 555 (1936)).

It's not clear whether the admission of this testimony was proper; we have some doubt whether evidence of an occupation or status like "drug dealer" falls within the realm of "other crimes, wrongs, or acts" admissible to show knowledge or intent under Rule 404(b). See United States v. Reed, 647 F. 2d 678, 686 (6th Cir.) (Rule 404(b) doesn't justify elicitation of testimony that defendants are known burglars or fences in trial on charges of receiving stolen goods.), cert. denied, 454 U.S. 837, 1037, 102 S. Ct. 142, 580, 70 L. Ed. 2d 118, 483 (1981). On the surface, at least, it more closely resembles the forbidden character evidence suggested by Brewer.

Law on the latter question remains unsettled, however, see Charles A. Wright and Kenneth W. Graham, Jr., 22 Federal Practice and Procedure

§ 5233 n. 50 and accompanying text (1978 & 1992 Supp.) (identifying the problem), and we needn't address this difficulty, because the claimed error certainly wasn't "plain" by Olano's standards. " '[P]lain' is synonymous with 'clear' or, equivalently, 'obvious.' . . . At a minimum, the Court of Appeals cannot correct an error pursuant to Rule 52(b) unless the error is clear under current law." Olano, 113 S. Ct. at 1779 (emphasis added). That's not so here. Accordingly, we find no plain error in the district court's admission of the challenged evidence.

B

When Scott denied that Brewer was a drug dealer, then parried the government's attempt to impeach her by denying that she told federal marshals he was, the government called Marshal Flynn to rebut her testimony, and Flynn did. Brewer now argues that the district court erred in failing to instruct the jury that Flynn's testimony was admissible only to impeach Scott and not for its substance. Although Brewer was entitled to such an instruction at trial "upon request," Fed. R. Evid. 105, he didn't make such a request, and again we review for plain error. Fed. R. Crim. P. 30, 52(b).

Applying Olano's test for plain error to another case of forfeited rights, it's once again clear that no plain error occurred. While our cases suggest that a limited purpose instruction need be given only upon request, United States v. Mark, 943 F. 2d 444, 449 (4th Cir.1991); United States v. Echeverri–Jaramillo, 777 F. 2d 933, 937 (4th Cir.1985), cert. denied, 475 U.S. 1031, 106 S. Ct. 1237, 89 L. Ed. 2d 345 (1986), they leave upon the possibility that the district court must provide one sua sponte in some circumstances. Id. (relying on both failure to request and nature of evidence admitted in declining to reverse). As the issue remains unsettled, however, Brewer's claim once again founders on the second of Olano's requirements, that a legal error be clear at least by the time of appellate review. Olano, 113 S. Ct. at 1779. . . .

AFFIRMED.

■ WIDENER, CIRCUIT JUDGE, dissenting:

. . . . Because I believe that the error was preserved and that the prosecution attempted to set up its own witness as a straw man whom it could impeach by the use of inadmissible hearsay, I would reverse the conviction and remand for a new trial. I respectfully dissent.

I

The majority finds that the defense did not preserve its error because its objection was not clear from the context or otherwise. However, the defense's objections were made each time the prosecution attempted either to question Miss Scott about her hearsay statement to the United States Marshal or to have her comment on whether Brewer was a drug dealer. In fact, the transcript the majority quotes makes clear that the government did not begin by asking her whether Brewer was a drug dealer and then proceed to question her about the statement, but instead began its questioning by asking about what she had told the marshal. Op. at 1434. The prosecutor also knew that Miss Scott would deny that her fiance, Brewer, was [a] drug dealer. This is shown from the fact that the government asked to treat Miss Scott as a hostile witness, which the majority notes in its opinion. Op. at 1434. There is no doubt that the prosecutor wanted the statement admitted, and this was the prosecutor's intent from the outset.

Of relevance both to the merits of this case and as to whether the objection was clear is our decision in United States v. Morlang, 531 F. 2d 183 (4th Cir.1975), in which we stated that "it has never been the rule that a party may call a witness where his testimony is known to be adverse for the purpose of impeaching him. To so hold would permit the government, in the name of impeachment, to present testimony to the jury by indirection which would not otherwise be admissible." 531 F. 2d at 189. We further stated, "Despite the fact that impeachment of one's own witness may be permitted, this does not go so far as to permit the use of the rule as a subterfuge to get to the jury evidence otherwise inadmissible." 531 F. 2d at 190. The government engaged in such subterfuge in this case. Miss Scott's testimony was of no value other than the attempt to get into evidence her prior hearsay statement that Brewer's occupation was drug dealing, which as the majority notes, was testimony of doubtful admissibility under Rule 404(b) in the first place. Op. at 1435. The government knew she would deny her statement, which is evident from its asking at the outset for permission to treat her as a hostile witness. Thus, we have exactly the situation in Morlang, and I would hold that the error was preserved. The government has known, at least since our decision in 1975, that such tactics are impermissible, and the rule is so well-settled that it can be said without hesitation that the objection was clear from the context.

II

Because I believe the error was preserved, I also would reach the issue of whether the error was prejudicial to Brewer. I would find that it was prejudicial to admit Marshal Flynn's testimony and reverse for a new trial.

Flynn's testimony about Miss Scott's statement was rank hearsay and should not have been admitted. The fact that the testimony was offered to impeach Miss Scott does not, under the facts of this case, exempt the statement from the usual rule that the prior unsworn statement of a witness cannot be admitted. See Morlang, 531 F. 2d at 190 (noting, under similar facts, that juries often cannot distinguish between impeachment and substantive evidence and that such evidence therefore should be excluded); see also Martin v. United States, 528 F. 2d 1157 (4th Cir.1975) (finding that prior statements used for impeachment purposes may not be used as substantive evidence).

The substance of the impeaching testimony was that Miss Scott had told the marshal that Brewer was a drug dealer. It clearly was offered to prove the truth of the matter asserted, and as such, may only create the impression that the government's charges must, of course, be correct. Cf. Fed. R. Evid. 404 (b) (prohibiting character evidence used to show that accused acted in conformity therewith on occasion in question). I see no reason to distinguish the impeachment evidence offered here from the evidence offered in Morlang. In Morlang the witness had given a statement to one Raymond Crist that implicated the defendant in the crime being tried, but he denied the defendant's involvement in interviews with the government and on the witness stand. The government apparently knew he would deny the defendant's involvement on the stand and had Crist standing ready to offer the impeaching statement. Even though the jury was given a limiting instruction, we reversed, based upon the government's apparent subterfuge in calling the first witness solely for the purpose of having the witness's otherwise inadmissible statement admitted as impeachment evidence. In finding that the statement was damaging, we reasoned: "To permit the government in this case to supply testimony which was a naked conclusion as to [the defendant's] guilt in the name of impeachment would be tantamount to permitting the use of hearsay and would seriously undermine the important policies underlying Justice Douglas' opinion in Bridges [v. Wixon, 326 U.S. 135, 65 S. Ct. 1443, 89 L. Ed. 2103 (1945)]." 531 F. 2d at 190.

I would find that Flynn's testimony about Miss Scott's prior statement was just as damaging to Brewer as Crist's was to the defendant in Morlang. Although Miss Scott's statement may not have expressly referred to the guilt of Brewer in the particular drug transactions with which Brewer was charged, the jury obviously would have believed that if his fiancee said he was a drug dealer, it must be so. This adds the additional concern that he was being convicted of being a drug dealer without regard to whether he committed the offenses charged. I think there is ample prejudice here.

III

The government simply should not be allowed to employ tactics of overkill that fly in the face of direct circuit precedent that has been established for more than fifteen years. Accordingly, I would reverse and remand for a new trial.

NOTES

The rules of evidence manifest themselves in a trial through offers of, and objections to, evidence. Many aspects of making such offers and objections have to do with tactics, trial technique and advocacy, matters treated in depth in other courses. There are certain basic issues relating to this subject that merit brief treatment here. The issues will be brought up over and over again in connection with almost every appellate case in the text.

1. Rules governing offers of and objections to evidence have three dimensions. They are directed to the parties, placing a responsibility on each side to make clear what is being offered and what is being objected to and the grounds of objection so that errors can be corrected, if possible, at the trial level. They are aimed at the trial court. The making of specific objections and adequate offers of proof supported by specific grounds for admitting or excluding are designed to enable the trial judge to rule intelligently and quickly. They are also designed to provide an adequate basis for appeal with enough material in the record so that the appellate court can intelligently decide whether the error, if any, merits reversal. Overall, they should serve the goal of reducing the necessity for retrials which, of course, involve costs for the parties and the administration of justice.

Rule 103 of the Federal Rules captures the essential thrust of these policies. It places the initiative on the party for raising and preserving the issue in connection with a ruling on the admission or exclusion of evidence. Although the court has a role, it is the party's primary responsibility. It also makes clear that an evidentiary ruling will not be a basis for reversal unless it affects the substantial rights of the parties.

2. In considering the following materials, keep in mind the following:

It must be remembered in reading evidence cases that the evidence point is often but a peg to hang a reversal on where the court, for some articulated or unexpressed reason, feels an injustice has been done. Predicting reversals or affirmances on errors in evidence rulings is therefore difficult and the precedential value of most such decisions is weak. Since almost no trial is completely error free, the process increases appellate discretion to prevent what the bench may conceive to be a miscarriage of justice though it may lack such undifferentiated power.

J.B. Weinstein and M.A. Berger, Weinstein's Evidence ¶ 103(02) at 103–24.

3. Generally, the approach taken today is to pay less attention to strictly technical requirements. It is less common nowadays, for instance, to require the formal taking of an "exception", as well as the making of an objection, to save rights regarding an adverse evidential ruling. Where a full trial record is kept stenographically or otherwise there is far less need for use of a magic technical vocabulary. See 1 Wigmore, Evidence § 20 (Rev. P. Tillers, 1983). Statutes and court rules exert a large force here; it is essential to know them well. Id.

4. An objection to the introduction of evidence must be timely. 1 Wigmore, Evidence § 18 (Rev. by P. Tillers, 1983) (as soon as it is known or reasonably could be known unless there are special circumstances). See also Isaacs v. United States, 301 F.2d 706 (8th Cir.), cert. denied, 371 U.S. 818 (1962).

Failure to object promptly to an item of evidence will normally result in waiver. As Wigmore said, "A rule of Evidence not invoked is waived." 1 Wigmore, Evidence § 18 at 790 (Rev. by P. Tillers, 1983) (emphasis on *waived* in original in 1940 edition, but not 1983 edition). The reasons for requiring prompt objection on pain of loss of the opportunity to raise the issue are multiple: It promotes finality and economy in litigation. It makes possible clarification of the facts relating to an issue at the time it is raised. It speeds up the tempo of the trial by permitting it to forge ahead without backtracking. It avoids the often futile direction to the jury to ignore what it has already heard. It permits correction by the party and a ruling by the trial court.

"If testimony, even though improper, is introduced into evidence without objection it becomes part of the record and is available to be considered for its probative value by the trier of fact." United States v. Jamerson, 549 F.2d 1263, 1267 (9th Cir.1977) (unobjected-to hearsay may be considered by the trier of fact). A limitation on the notion of waiver is the obvious logical one that a court may not rely on irrelevant evidence even if received without objection. Waiver may be implied even where objection has been made to the evidence, if the objecting party refers to or relies upon the erroneously admitted evidence or introduces like evidence that tends to prove the same facts.

5. Rules of evidence may be explicitly waived. Caranta v. Pioneer Home Improvements, Inc., 467 P.2d 719 (N.M.1970) ("Where documentary evidence is admitted by stipulation, hearsay statements contained therein become competent evidence."). But the stipulation cannot violate some rule of "public policy." DeCarbo v. Borough of Ellwood City, 284 A.2d 342 (Pa.1971) (stipulation cannot enlarge or limit jurisdiction); State v. Chavez, 461 P.2d 919 (N.M.App.1969) (whether or not stipulating to the admittance of results of a polygraph test is against state policy).

The rules can also be bypassed by stipulating facts which could only be proved by inadmissible evidence. Normally, these stipulations concern facts about which there can be little doubt. They are binding on the court and parties. For a general discussion of stipulations see Note, Judicial Admissions, 64 Colum.L.Rev. 1121 (1964). See also notes 7 and 10 following State v. Poe, supra. Compare Old Chief v. United States, 117 S.Ct. 644 (1997), supra.

Attorneys have broad power to bind their clients. Once made, the parties are bound by the stipulation, unless they mutually ignore it as by trying the issue. Stipulations are judicial admissions which cannot be contradicted by evidence and are to be distinguished from extra-judicial admissions, i.e., hearsay.

With the present state of overcrowded calendars, many courts have added their own pressures to sound professional practice of stipulating where there is no real dispute. Where requests to stipulate are made in open court, there is also a natural reluctance to appear obstructive. On the other hand, clients emotionally involved in a litigation may insist that it be made as expensive as possible for the other side. There is, too, the loss of color and ability of the trier to evaluate credibility where parties stipulate that witnesses would say so and so, were they called, or that an expert is "qualified" without specifying his background. Courts and attorneys, therefore, sometimes discourage this practice.

May stipulations be bargained for? State v. Ruud, 491 P.2d 1351, 1355 n. 5 (Wash.App.1971) (record suggests that defendant's counsel gave a stipulation in exchange for a stipulation that the question of the death penalty not be submitted to the jury). Should evidence be offered when the attorney knows that it is inadmissible?

6. Normally the ground for an objection to the admission of evidence must be specified. See Federal Rule of Evidence 103(a)(1). Generally, stating the grounds as "incompetent, irrelevant and immaterial" is not sufficiently specific although it has been suggested that if the basis for the objection is relevancy, then that wording may be sufficient. J.B. Weinstein and M.A. Berger, Weinstein's Evidence ¶ 103(02) at n. 30, citing Ladd, Objections, Motions and Foundation Testimony, 43 Cornell L.Q. 543, 546 (1958).

Suppose an objection is made in general terms without specifying the grounds and the trial judge sustains it. On appeal what should the appellate court do, assuming that there are valid grounds for the objection? See id. at 548–549.

Suppose an objection is made in general terms without specifying the grounds, and the objection is overruled. On appeal, should the court consider the proper specific objection? In Een v. Consolidated Freightways, 220 F.2d 82, 88 (8th Cir.1955) the court declined to do so. See also United States v. Long, 574 F.2d 761 (3d Cir.1978) where a non-specific objection was made to other crime evidence which the appellate court characterized as "[c]haritably" adding up to a relevancy objection under Fed.R.Evid. 404(b) and which the court proceeded to consider. Since the concurring judge on appeal also addressed the Federal Rule 403 issue not explicitly raised below, the majority did too, indicating that the balancing required under that provision was "subsumed" in the trial judge's ruling.

Suppose a specific objection is made, but on the wrong grounds and it is overruled. May the correct grounds be specified on appeal? See Huff v. White Motor Corp., 609 F.2d 286, 290, n. 2 (7th Cir.1979).

United States v. Holland, 880 F.2d 1091, 1094–95 (9th Cir.1989):

The tape records a casual, rambling conversation more than 90 minutes in length. Although portions of the conversation were admissible under Fed. R. Evid. 804(b)(3), much of the tape was irrelevant. . . .

Although Holland objected to the admission of the tape as a whole, the record reflects no objection sufficient to inform the district court that Holland also objected to failure to redact the tape.

Holland's blanket objection to the admission of the tape does not preserve an objection to failure to redact the tape. See Fed. R. Evid. 103(a)(1). . . .

Reversal for plain error would not be appropriate. "Reversal of a criminal conviction on the basis of plain error is an exceptional remedy, which we invoke only when it appears necessary to prevent a miscarriage of justice or to preserve the integrity and reputation of the judicial process." United States v. Bordallo, 857 F.2d 519, 527 (9th Cir.1988) (internal quotation omitted). In light of the copious evidence of Holland's guilt, and the relatively small part of the statement Holland identifies as improperly admitted, we conclude there was no "miscarriage of justice" which alone would justify relief.

United States v. Wilson, 966 F.2d 243, 245–246 (7th Cir.1992):

In his appeal, Wilson invokes Fed. R. Evid. 403 which provides that "although relevant, evidence may be excluded if its probative value is substantially outweighed by the danger of unfair prejudice. . . ." Wilson concedes on appeal that guns are relevant to show that a defendant knowingly and intentionally possessed drugs. However, Wilson points out that he had already been convicted of possession with intent to distribute in November 1989 and could not contest that issue at his May 1990 conspiracy trial. Since knowledge and intent to possess were not at issue, Wilson argues that the gun had little probative value with respect to the issue of his conspiracy while it had substantial prejudicial effect. Wilson maintains that after determining that the gun was relevant, the district court should have engaged in Rule 403 balancing.

Although Wilson objected to the admission of the gun both before and at trial, he did not raise Rule 403 or even mention the prejudicial effect of the gun before the district court. When the government proffered testimony about the gun, Wilson stated that the gun had "no relevance to today's charge [conspiracy]" without mentioning the gun's prejudicial effect. (Tr. at 86). Later, at a side bar conference, the district court justified its ruling on the record by explaining that this court's decisions in United States v. Alvarez, 860 F.2d 801 (7th Cir.1988), cert. denied, 490 U.S. 1051 (1989) and United States v. Rush, 890 F.2d 45 (7th Cir.1989) held that guns are "tools of the [drug] trade" and are relevant when found in close proximity with the drugs. (Tr. at 135). Once again, Wilson did not raise the gun's prejudicial effect.

The government argues that by not raising the prejudicial effect of the gun or Rule 403 before the district court, Wilson waived the issue on appeal. We agree. An objection based on "relevance" does not preserve an error based on Rule 403. . . . Under Fed. R. Evid. 103 (a) (1) error may not be predicated upon a ruling that admits evidence unless a timely objection appears on the record "stating the specific ground of objection, if the specific ground was not apparent from the context." Fed. R. Evid. 103 (a) (1). Providing specific grounds for an objection alerts the district judge to the asserted nature of the error and enables opposing counsel to take proper corrective action. Fed. R. Evid. 103 Advisory Committee Notes. Wilson's objection based on "relevance" alerted the court to consider two rules of evidence: Rule 401, which defines relevant evidence, and Rule 402, which provides that relevant evidence is generally admissible, but irrelevant evidence is not. Wilson implicitly asked the court to exclude the gun under Rule 402 because it did not fit the definition in Rule 401. Rule 403, on which Wilson now relies, however, constitutes one of the exceptions to

Rule 402. It provides that even if the evidence is "relevant" the court may exclude it because of its extensive prejudicial effect. Wilson's objection was not specific enough to alert the district court to Wilson's concerns about the prejudicial effect of the gun, and therefore Wilson did not properly preserve for appeal any error based on Rule 403. See Mejia, 909 F. 2d at 247 (defendant cannot complain about Rule 403 balancing on appeal since he never gave the district court the opportunity to balance probative value against prejudice); United States v. Chaidez, 919 F.2d 1193, 1202–1203 (7th Cir.1990), cert. denied sub nom. Chavira v. United States, 501 U.S. 1234 (1991) (defendant's assertion that drug records were irrelevant was insufficient to preserve on appeal his argument based on Rule 403); also see C. McCormick, McCormick on Evidence § 52 at 130 (E. Cleary, 3d ed. 1984) (in principle, a relevance objection does not raise Rule 403 considerations).

Wilson argues that once a court embarks on a relevance inquiry it must also consider the evidence's probative value compared to its prejudicial effect. However, to reach his conclusion, Wilson reads too much into this court's decision in Alvarez. In Alvarez, the defendants, who had been convicted of narcotics distribution conspiracy and operation of racketeering enterprise, argued that the district court should have excluded a pistol from evidence either because the pistol was irrelevant or because its prejudicial effect outweighed its probative value. Alvarez, 860 F. 2d at 829. The court joined the "overwhelming majority of courts of appeal" and held that the pistol was relevant as a "tool of the trade." Id. at 829–30. The opinion continued:

> However, our analysis does not stop here. We must determine if the pistol should not have been admitted because it unduly prejudiced the appellant. See Fed. R. Evid. 403 [footnote omitted].

Id. at 830. Wilson argues that under Alvarez a court must consider not only relevance but "must determine whether to exclude the evidence because the danger of unfair prejudice outweighs its probative value." (Appellant's Brief at 17) (emphasis added). Wilson is wrong. Nothing in Alvarez indicates that a court must apply Rule 403 even if the defendant did not raise the issue of unfair prejudice at trial. Alvarez simply does not address the issue of waiver.

Suppose a specific objection is made to evidence and it is excluded but the ground relied upon was incorrect although a correct reason for exclusion could have been offered. Should the appellate court reverse? Wigmore concluded no. 1 Wigmore, Evidence § 18 (P. Tillers Rev.1983). Morgan argued, however, that if the defect in the evidence was curable, the proponent is prejudiced by the giving of the wrong reason for exclusion. "It would be improper for him to reframe his question or to lay a foundation in order to make other objections inapplicable so long as the judge's ruling on the specified matter stands." Morgan, Basic Problems of Evidence 47–49 (5th ed. by J.B. Weinstein). For a case applying the Morgan approach, see Bloodgood v. Lynch, 56 N.E.2d 718 (N.Y.1944).

A judge should inform the parties of the grounds he or she is relying on to sustain a general objection—if he is willing to entertain one—or on which of several urged specific grounds he is sustaining a specific objection, so that the proponent of the evidence can reframe his proffer to meet the ruling. If the judge does not do so, the burden is on the proponent to request a ruling.

A motion to strike out testimony will of course be appropriate when a witness makes an unresponsive and inadmissible answer to a proper question as well as when evidence is admitted conditionally and the proponent ultimately fails to satisfy the condition. Such a motion should be made with all possible dispatch. An instruction to the jury to disregard the expunged evidence should be requested in supplementation, even though the efficacy of such instructions is questionable.

7. Counsel examining on direct and encountering objection must be prepared to make an "offer of proof," a statement for the record of what he intends to prove. See Rule 103(a)(2) Fed.Rules Evid. In the absence of a record the reviewing court will be unable to ascertain whether an error occurred. Counsel may, however, be spared actual explanation and offer of proof when the purpose is obvious.

What attitude should be taken with respect to requiring offers of proof on cross-examination? Assuming that the examiner is not pursuing the dangerous practice of fishing blindly, should he be required to disclose in advance his line of attack? See Note, Excluded Evidence on Cross–Examination—Preservation for Appeal, 33 N.C.L.Rev. 476 (1955).

8. Some objections must be raised before trial—e.g., a motion to suppress evidence obtained by illegal search and seizure. See Rule 12(b)(3), Fed.R.Cr.Pr. Regarding government appeals from pretrial evidentiary rulings, see note 9 below.

General policies relevant to the question of whether advance rulings should be issued have been described as follows:

> The general rule permitting the district judge to delay evidentiary rulings is designed to prevent unnecessary and unwarranted advisory opinions. It is sometimes unwise to decide whether to admit evidence before it is actually presented. If no advance ruling is made, the parties may decide to abandon their positions for reasons unrelated to the anticipated ruling of the court. A refusal to rule may thus promote judicial economy. In other situations, a delayed ruling is advisable because the facts as they develop during the course of the proceeding may affect the determination of admissibility. United States v. Burkhead, 646 F.2d 1283, 1286 (8th Cir.1981).

Some courts have indicated a favorable attitude toward advance rulings on the admissibility of prior convictions for impeachment. In United States v. Oakes, 565 F.2d 170, 171 (1st Cir.1977), for example, the court stated:

> [W]hile we emphasize that the timing is discretionary, we think a court should, when feasible, make reasonable efforts to accommodate a defendant by ruling in advance on the admissibility of a criminal record so that he can make an informed decision whether or not to testify.

> The balancing problems faced by the court can be minimized by attempting to ascertain in advance what it needs to know about defendant's likely testimony and other relevant information. Defendant could be asked to state the substance of his testimony in advance. Indeed a court's advance ruling might ... still be helpful even if made expressly provisional, allowing the court greater leeway to change it in light of later events and testimony.

Later, in its opinion, however, the court referred to the fact that "many judges may feel [i]t is impossible to accomplish [the balancing required under Rule 609(a)] conscientiously without hearing defendant's actual testimony." Id. at 173. As to the need of the defendant to take the stand after an in limine adverse ruling on a Rule 607(a) issue, see Luce v. United States, 469 U.S. 38 (1984), infra.

9. Intertwined with the subject of advance rulings is the question whether appellate review of an evidentiary ruling can be obtained immediately or must await final judgment in the matter. The subject is complex; only a few highlights will be mentioned here. 18 U.S.C. § 3731 provides for appeals by the government in criminal cases from a district court decision "suppressing or excluding evidence ... not made after the defendant has been put in jeopardy and before the verdict or finding ... if the United States Attorney certifies ... that the appeal is not taken for purpose of delay and that the evidence is a substantial proof of a fact material in the proceeding."

United States v. Barletta, 644 F.2d 50 (1st Cir.1981) after tracing the intricate relationship between § 3731, supra and Rule 12(e) of the Federal Rules of Criminal Procedure, concluded that the government may appeal from a pretrial evidentiary ruling (whether resulting from the granting of defendant's motion to suppress or exclude evidence or from the denial of the government's motion to admit evidence). The court also concluded that absent "good cause" to defer a ruling, the government could compel the trial court to rule in advance on the admissibility of evidence only in one "limited class of cases," namely where the issue is "entirely segregable from the evidence to be presented at trial," i.e. not involving "the presentation of any significant quantity of evidence relevant to the question of guilt or innocence." As illustrative of such issues, the court mentioned, "the existence of an attorney-client privilege or the satisfaction of a hearsay exception." See also United States v. Horwitz, 622 F.2d 1101 (2d Cir.1980).

Collins v. Wayne Corp., 621 F.2d 777, 784 (5th Cir.1980) stands for the proposition that in a civil case the overruling of a motion *in limine* does not preserve error for appeal; that such motions are frequently made in the abstract and in anticipation of some hypothetical situations that may not develop at trial; that when a motion *in limine* is overruled, the party must renew his objection when the evidence is offered at trial.

10. There are three categories of error well recognized in statutory law and judicial opinion. "Harmless error" is that raised at trial but found not to affect substantial rights. Rule 103(a) of the Federal Rules of Evidence has the effect of establishing a harmless error rule for reviewing evidentiary rulings. "Reversible error" is that raised at trial which is found to affect substantial rights. "Plain error" is that not raised at trial but nevertheless considered by a reviewing court because it is found to affect substantial rights. The plain error doctrine thus acts as a general limitation on the notion of waiver. The distinction between harmless and plain error turns on whether the particular error in the case excuses the party's failure to bring it properly to the trial court's attention. In United States v. Dixon, 562 F.2d 1138, 1143 (9th Cir. 1977), the court compared the standard to be applied for determining plain error with that for harmless error. As to plain error "we would reverse only if it were *highly* probable that the error materially affected the jury's verdict." As to harmless error, "we will ... affirm only if it is more probable than not that the error did not materially affect the verdict." See also United States v. Valle-Valdez, 554 F.2d 911, 915 (9th Cir.1977). Compare, however, Government of the Virgin Islands v. Toto, 529 F.2d 278 (3d Cir.1976) where applying a harmless error approach the court reversed the conviction because it could not say that it was highly probable that the improperly admitted evidence did not prejudice the defendant. If the error would have been easily correctable at trial, it will not be deemed plain error on appeal. See United States v. Richardson, 562 F.2d 476, 478 (7th Cir.1977), cert. denied, 434 U.S. 1072 (1978).

11.   Is error which adversely affects a party's constitutional right always reversible or plain error? See Chapman v. California, 386 U.S. 18, 21–24 (1967) (error affecting some constitutional rights may sometimes be harmless). The problem of "harmless error" in cases involving collateral attacks on a criminal judgment for government's failing to reveal information helpful to defendant in violation of the constitution and on the basis of newly discovered evidence is discussed in Kyles v. Whitley, 514 U.S. 419 (1995). See also Orena v. United States,__ F.Supp. __, 1997 WL 109000 (E.D.N.Y.1997).

12.   Should the lawyer's strategy at trial affect an appellate court's assessment of errors in the admission of evidence when there was no objection? See Marshall v. United States, 409 F.2d 925, 927 (9th Cir.1969) (defendant asserted for the first time on appeal that the testimony of a government agent should have been excluded as a product of an unlawful search and seizure; the record suggested that the defendant's counsel deliberately chose not to object in order to attempt to use the agent's testimony to the advantage of the defendant).

13.   In utilizing the harmless error rule, to what extent should appellate courts consider the personalities and setting at trial? Judge Traynor in his discussion of the harmless error rule recognized such factors but rejects the possibility of an appellate court taking them into account. "The appellate court is limited to the mute record made below. Many factors may affect the probative value of testimony, such as age, sex, intelligence, experience, occupation, demeanor, or temperament of the witnesses. A trial court or jury before whom witnesses appear is at least in a position to take note of such factors. An appellate court has no way of doing so. It cannot know whether a witness answered some questions forthrightly but evaded others.... A clumsy sentence in the record may not convey the ring of truth that attended it when the witness groped his way to its articulation.... an appellate court can never conjure up the impact of live confrontation." Traynor, The Riddle of Harmless Error 20–21 (1970). Most appellate lawyers, however, assume that the appellate court's knowledge of the personality of the judge and trial attorney has some impact.

A possible technique would be for the trial judge to state on the record why he thought some errors were or were not prejudicial. Rule 33 of the Federal Rules of Criminal Procedure, Rule 59 of the Rules of Civil Procedure, and the post-trial motion practice provide an opportunity for the trial court to evaluate claimed error, permitting him to make his or her views known to the appellate tribunal.

14.   Many determinations of the trial judge are practically unreviewable because of wide discretion. For example, see scope of cross-examination and order of witnesses, discussed in Chapter 3, infra.

CHAPTER 2

REAL PROOF

PUERTO RICO RULES OF EVIDENCE (1980)

Demonstrative and Scientific Evidence

Rule 80

OBJECTS COGNIZABLE BY THE SENSES

Whenever an object, cognizable by the senses, is pertinent pursuant to the provisions of Rule 18 [Federal Rules 401 and 402], such object, after previous identification or authentication, is admissible in evidence, subject to the discretion of the court pursuant to the factors or criteria set forth in Rule 19 [Federal Rule 403].

4 WIGMORE, EVIDENCE, § 1150 (Chadbourn Rev. 1972)

If, for example, it is desired to ascertain whether the accused has lost his right hand and wears an iron hook in place of it, one source of belief on the subject would be the testimony of a witness who had seen the arm.... A second source of belief would be the mark left on some substance grasped or carried by the accused.... A third source of belief remains, namely, *the inspection by the tribunal of the accused's arm.*

In an action for annulment of marriage based on fraud where defendant "induced plaintiff to marry him, by falsely representing to her that he would cohabit with her and perform the customary duties of the married state," the question of whether the marriage was consummated was sharply contested. De Baillet–Latour v. De Baillet–Latour, 94 N.E.2d 715 (N.Y.C.A.1950). The New York Statute required "other satisfactory evidence of the facts" in addition to admissions of the defendant. The court noted:

> ... The "other proof" pointed to by plaintiff consisted of this: defendant, who insisted that he had had normal physical relations with his wife on many occasions, was asked whether she had any conspicuous scars on her body, which he denied. The existence of such scars was then demonstrated. That, of course, was not proof of defendant's fraudulent intent. It did no more than impugn defendant's truthfulness, without in itself proving or disproving his asserted cohabitation with his wife. However, it seems to us, that it was, in the meaning of section 1143 "other satisfactory evidence of the facts." That language must be construed according to its purpose and, so construed, it requires only that there be in the record, in addition to "declarations" or "confessions" of the parties, other material from other sources, substantial and reliable enough to satisfy the conscience of the trier of the facts (see Winston v. Winston, 165 N.Y. 553, 556, 557, 59 N.E. 273, affd. 189 U.S. 506, 23 S.Ct. 852). It follows that the requirements of the second sentence of section 1143 were met by the proofs offered by plaintiff on the trial of this case.

The record on appeal indicates that the demonstration took place in the following manner (Record on Appeal 2251–4):

Now, Dr. Peters and Dr. Richards, will you retire to the adjoining room and examine the plaintiff.

(At this point Dr. Johannes T. Peters and Dr. John H. Richards retired to the adjoining room.)

(After a lapse of some minutes, the door to the adjoining room was opened, and some colloquy ensued between the Court and the doctors and then the following statement was made by the plaintiff:)

The Plaintiff: I demand that Justice Pecora be present at this examination. I have traveled 180 miles to come down here to do this and I wish him to be present here.

The Court: All right. What do you say, counsel?

Mr. Rosenblatt: I think the Court should take enlightenment from any source it sees fit and make any normal observations necessary.

Mr. Bauman: I think that this whole procedure as now conducted is entirely irregular . . .

The Court: Well, I think, I will comply with the request.

Mr. Rosenblatt: Please do so.

The Court: Yes. Are you ready, madam?

The Plaintiff: Yes. Thank you very much.

(At this point the Court retired to the adjoining room, in the presence of the plaintiff and Drs. Peters and Richards. . . .)

NOTES

1. Attempts are made to distinguish between certain types of real, or demonstrative evidence, and the weight to be given to them at trial. What useful purposes do they serve? Should the jury be told of them? If so, how? If not, what difference does it make whether "demeanor," for example, is defined as "evidence" if the jury in fact considers everything made available to its senses in arriving at a conclusion? See, e.g., Smith v. Ohio Oil Co., 134 N.E.2d 526, 530 (Ill.App.1956), where the court permitted the doctor to use a plastic skeleton "to assist the explanations." Approving this exercise of the trial court's discretion, the appellate court wrote: "Real evidence involves the production of some object which had a direct part in the incident, and includes the exhibition of injured parts of the body. . . . [T]he courts weigh the explanatory value of an object against its possible emotional effect with no flat rule that a gruesome object cannot be used. Demonstrative evidence (a model, map, photograph, X-ray, etc.) is distinguished from real evidence in that it has no probative value itself, but serves merely as a visual aid to the jury in comprehending the verbal testimony of a witness. . . . The limitations are: that the evidence must be relevant and the use of the object actually explanatory. Articles by law professors and trial attorneys in various law reviews have pointed out that . . . people learn and understand better with the eyes than with the ears. . . ." But see People v. Diaz, 111 Misc.2d 1083, 1084, 445 N.Y.S.2d 888, 889 (1981) ("Some treatises draw a distinction between real and demonstrative evidence. . . . The distinction seems unnecessary. The jury, in all cases, will make its own judgment as to the weight accorded the object."; the court allowed "introduction" of another "suspect" for comparison with defendant and described perpetrator).

2. United States v. Shonubi, 895 F.Supp. 460, 479–481 (E.D.N.Y.1995), rev'd., 103 F.3d 1085 (2d Cir.1997):

C. Demeanor

"The tongue of the witness," it has been said, "is not the only organ for conveying testimony." Jerome Frank, Law and the Modern Mind 109 (1931). Given this obvious truth, jury instructions routinely state that consideration of demeanor is not merely permitted, but expected. Cf. Henriod v. Henriod, 198 Wash. 519, 524–25, 89 P.2d 222, 225 (1938) (to watch attitude and demeanor "is not only the right but also the duty of the trier of facts"); 3A Wigmore on Evidence § 946, at 783 (James H. Chadbourn rev. ed. 1970) (demeanor, "without any definite rules as to its significance, is always assumed to be in evidence"); Fed.R.Evid., art. VIII, Advisory Committee's introductory note (hearsay rule) ("The demeanor of the witness traditionally has been believed to furnish trier ... with valuable clues."); NLRB v. Dinion Coil Co., 201 F.2d 484, 487–90 (2d Cir.1952) (Frank, J.) (recounting the history of "demeanor evidence" from Roman times); Olin Guy Wellborn, Demeanor, 76 Cornell L.Rev. 1075 (1991) (summarizing social science data relating to potential uses of demeanor).

Demeanor includes facial expressions, body language, and such matters as a defendant's forcefulness in consulting with an attorney during court proceedings. See, e.g., United States v. Schipani, 293 F.Supp. 156 (E.D.N.Y.1968) (judge, at a bench trial, confirmed conclusions about susceptibility to coercion by observing and assessing demeanor), aff'd, 414 F.2d 1262 (2d Cir.1969), cert. denied, 397 U.S. 922, 90 S.Ct. 902, 25 L.Ed.2d 102 (1970). Triers must decide cases on the basis of evidence, which is on the record, interpreted in light of demeanor, which is not.

A judge may consider the demeanor and actions of a person even when that person is not testifying. In Schipani, the defendant whose demeanor influenced the trial judge's conclusions never took the stand. 293 F.Supp. at 163. The court of appeals agreed with the district court that "[t]he trier's observation of the non-witness defendant's demeanor and general appearance may be—and almost invariably is—considered by him in evaluating evidence introduced at the trial." Schipani, 414 F.2d at 1268. The Supreme Court has also implicitly recognized that triers can rely on non-witness demeanor. See Stein, 346 U.S. at 181, 73 S.Ct. at 1091 (noting advantages of "observing the witnesses and parties") (emphasis added); United States v. Grayson, 438 U.S. 41, 50, 98 S.Ct. 2610, 2615–16, 57 L.Ed.2d 582 (1978) ("[O]ne serious study has concluded that the trial judge's 'opportunity to observe the defendant, particularly if he chose to take the stand in his defense, can often provide useful insights into an appropriate disposition.'" (quoting ABA Project on Standards for Criminal Justice, Sentencing Alternatives and Procedures § 5.1, at 32 (App. Draft 1968))). See also Michael & Adler, Real Proof, supra, at 365 ("Demeanor, whether that of a witness while testifying or of a person who is not giving testimony, is ... a kind of event ... which occurs in the presence of a jury and is sensibly apparent to it. Consequently, such an event need not be offered and cannot be excluded."). Cf. United States v. Nichols, 56 F.3d 403, 412–13 (2d Cir.1995) ("We must ... defer to the judgment of the district court, which had the benefit of examining [the defendant] that [the defendant had] ... the ability to assist his lawyer in mounting his defense.").

1. How judges use demeanor

Gauging credibility is the best known application of demeanor. Ironically, this may be one of its least effective uses. See, e.g., Victor Barall, Book Review, Thanks for the Memories: Criminal Law and the Psychology of Memory, 59 Brook.L.Rev. 1473, 1482 (1994) ("[T]he proverbial sweaty palms and averted gaze may be more indicative of language difficulties, cultural differences in etiquette or stowage than of fabrication."); Jeremy A. Blumenthal, A Wipe of the Hands, A Lick of the Lips: The Validity of Demeanor Evidence in Assessing Witness Credibility, 78 Neb.L.Rev. 1157 (1993) (similar). Cf. Quercia v. United States, 289 U.S. 466, 53 S.Ct. 698, 77 L.Ed. 1321 (1933) (reversible error for trial judge to tell jury that wiping hands during testimony "is almost always an indication of lying").

Other applications of demeanor may produce more reliable results. In Stein, supra, the issue before the trial court was whether the defendants' confessions had been coerced. Demeanor was relevant to the susceptibility of the defendants to coercion. Likewise, in an action for an order of physical protection, no judge would ignore a threatening gesture made by the respondent on his way out of the courtroom. In such situations, behavior in the courtroom properly supports inferences about behavior out of court.

2.   Demeanor and appellate review

As Professors Michael and Adler have observed:

In observing ... demeanor and in coming to a conclusion on that demeanor a judge does not use any approved formulas; nor does he practice any art; nor does he proceed in any scientific way. So there is no terminology that he may employ to explain to an appellate court what has taken place.

Michael & Adler, Real Proof, supra, at 102. Thus, while demeanor evidence must be used by the trier in evaluating evidence, it is generally unavailable to the court of appeals in reviewing that evaluation. The trial court cannot "transmit" demeanor to the court of appeals. At most, it can attempt to briefly describe that demeanor, and assume that the court of appeals will give its judgments adequate deference. It is desirable at times, for purposes of assisting appellate review, for the judge to describe demeanor that departs from that suggested by the transcript.

The opportunity, which exists in the trial court alone, to observe and assess credibility explains in part the reluctance of appellate courts to overturn findings of fact. See Olin Guy Wellborn, Demeanor, 76 Cornell L.Rev. 1075, 1077 (1991) ("The opportunity of the trier to observe the demeanor of the witnesses is a principal basis for the deference accorded by reviewing courts to factual determinations of trial courts...."); see also United States v. Pfeiffer, No. 94–1331, at 2, 50 F.3d 3 (2d Cir.1995) (unpublished) ("[D]eference is owed to the district court's determinations with respect to competence when they are based on observation of the defendant during the proceedings."). Since appellate courts cannot with-hold "permission" to consider demeanor, they must allow for the existence of factors not discernible from the written record.

For further discussion of demeanor off the witness stand see infra.

SECTION 1.   CONDITIONS OF ADMISSIBILITY
A.   ABILITY OF TRIER TO ACQUIRE KNOWLEDGE

McAndrews v. Leonard
Supreme Court of Vermont, 1926.
99 Vt. 512, 134 A. 710.

STATEMENT BY REPORTER. This is an action of tort to recover for personal injuries received by plaintiff in an automobile accident....

■ Watson, C.J. ... It appeared that as a result of the accident there was a depressed fracture of the plaintiff's skull, causing pressure on the brain, by reason of which a surgical operation technically known as trepanning, was necessarily performed, removing a portion of the bone to relieve the brain from pressure. It further appeared that in performing this operation a circular piece of bone, probably half an inch in diameter, was cut out of the top of the skull on the left side, making and leaving a hole through the bone and over the brain of that size. Dr. Ray E. Smith, a physician and surgeon, was called by plaintiff as an expert witness, and testified that he examined the plaintiff on March 23 (about a week before testifying), giving her a general examination and more in particular relative to her skull and her mental condition. He testified to finding cracks in and some through the skull itself, extending somewhere about the point of the trepanning operation; that the cracks were filled in, not with bone which is a hard rather unyielding substance, but with fibrous tissue which is soft and stringy, never becoming bone; that the fibrous tissue filled in the hole and covered it up.

Defendant called as an expert witness Dr. Alberic H. Bellerose, a practicing physician in Rutland, who testified that he and Dr. Hammond had recently (March 29) examined the plaintiff, making a general physical examination that would have any special relation to her injury, and also examined the skull; that they first made an examination by their hands of the depression in the skull, and in that examination found that the hole, made by the trepanning, had filled in with something which, in this opinion, was "callus," describing callus as the next thing that forms in fractures, a bony substance that repairs the bone; that he felt there for the purpose of finding out whether there was any pulsation, but found none, which meant to him that there was solid covering over the hole. In cross-examination the witness said that primary callus was soft, and permanent callus was hard, sometimes harder than bone itself; that the callus examined by him on the plaintiff's head, the day named, was hard, and in his opinion had become a bony substance. "Q. Well, then, doctor, you go by experience, that nine months have elapsed since this injury, that it must be, if nature has performed its function, it must be as hard as the bones around it, is that what you mean? A. That is solid enough, yes, that is what my opinion, that is my opinion."

In view of the foregoing testimony given by Dr. Bellerose with reference to the examination he made of the plaintiff at the point where the bone was taken out of her skull, and his statement that callus had formed there, that was as hard as the bone surrounding it, the plaintiff, through her counsel, asked in rebuttal that the court, in its discretion, permit the witness, Dr. Smith, to demonstrate to the jury the plaintiff's head, by having the jurors themselves make examination by the touch of the finger on that part of her skull where the bone was taken out, and compare it in hardness with that part of the skull which remains. Defendant objected to such examination by the jurors, for that the question is one of fact requiring expert testimony, and not one that laymen can determine by the sense of touch; that the jury must determine it upon all the evidence, giving such weight as they think proper to the testimony of the experts on the subject.

The court inquired of Dr. Smith whether it was a matter that could be ascertained by a layman by feeling of the skull. To this question the doctor answered that he thought it could be. Thereupon, subject to exception by defendant, the court ruled permitting such examination, saying "the doctor can point out the spot, where it is." Counsel for defendant, Mr. Webber, said he understood that all the doctor was to do was "to point out the place and let the jurymen feel of it." The court said, "Yes." Webber, "I suppose Dr. Smith understands all he is to point out?" To this the doctor said he was "simply pointing to the firm portion of the skull, then the depressed portion in the back."

While the record does not state that such examination was in fact made by the jurors, we think it is fairly inferable from what is there said, and we so treat it in deciding the question presented by the exception.

It should be borne in mind that the particular examination the jurors were thus permitted to make was not technical in nature, nor was it one requiring special knowledge or skill. It was not for the purpose of ascertaining the kind of substance that had filled into the hole in the skull, made by the trepanning operation, that is, whether it was fibrous tissue as the evidence on the part of the plaintiff tended to show, or callus as the evidence on the part of the defendant tended to show; but it was to examine by the touch of the finger, the substance so filled in, the spot to be pointed out to them by plaintiff's expert witness, Dr. Smith, to see whether the substance with which the hole had become filled, was as hard as the surrounding bone or was softer. Its quality in this respect was an important question; for the harder the substance was, until it equalled in such respect the normality of the surrounding bone, the greater was the resulting protection to the part of the brain covered by it.

The verdict, however, could not be based exclusively on the knowledge so acquired. But the jury had a right to base their verdict upon such examination together with all the evidence in the case.... The exception is without force....

Judgment affirmed.

NOTES

1. For a comprehensive analysis of the theoretical bases underlying the admissibility of real proof, see Michael & Adler, Real Proof, 5 Vand.L.Rev. 344 (1952).

Real proof can appeal to any of the senses. Taste: Martin v. Shell Petroleum Corp., 299 P. 261 (Kan.1931) (salt water); Smell: Enyart v. People, 201 P. 564 (Colo.1921) (liquor); Western Cottonoil Co. v. Pinkston, 279 S.W.2d 150 (Tex.Civ.App.1955); Touch: McAndrews v. Leonard, p. 97, supra; Hearing: Robinson v. State, 593 P.2d 621 (Alaska 1979) (admission into evidence of tape recordings of conversations between informer and defendant at defendant's trial for sale of cocaine and herion); People v. Young, 36 Cal.Rptr.672 (Cal.App.1964) (recording of conversation of driver, allegedly drunk, including slurring and foul language); Sight: Wheeler v. Helterbrand, 358 S.W.2d 501 (Ky.1962).

2. For what purpose or purposes was the real evidence used by the trial court in the main case? Was it used for the same purposes by the appellate court? See also, Harper v. Bolton, 124 S.E.2d 54 (S.C.1962) (the appellate court deemed it error that the trial court had admitted before a jury a glass vial containing an eye which the plaintiff had lost in an automobile accident; defendant had admitted that the eye was removed necessarily because of injuries sustained in a motor vehicular accident, and the exhibition of the removed eye to the jurors did not tend to throw any light upon any disputed or controverted fact in issue before them).

3. Must each member of the jury make the particular examination? See Curry v. American Enka, Inc., 452 F.Supp. 178, 182 (E.D.Tenn.1977) (dictum) (if motion to allow jurors to touch plaintiff's burnt hand is granted, any manual touching of plaintiff's hands would be confined to those jurors who indicated "a belief that such touching may enable them to understand and apply the evidence introduced in the ordinary manner."). See Gray v. L–M Chevrolet Co., 368 S.W.2d 861, 865 (Tex.Civ.App.1963) (request by jury to have female juror feel the purportedly injured back muscles of the lady plaintiff "would have been a 'demonstration', and was objectionable."). Normally every member of a jury looks at, touches or smells each piece of evidence proffered.

Almeida v. Correa

Supreme Court of Hawai'i, 1970.
51 Haw. 594, 465 P.2d 564.

■ Before RICHARDSON, C.J., and MARUMOTO, ABE, LEVINSON, and KOBAYASHI, JJ.

■ RICHARDSON, CHIEF JUSTICE, and LEVINSON, JUSTICE. The petitioner-appellee, pursuant to HRS § 579–1, petitioned the family court (1) for an adjudication of paternity against the defendant-appellant, (2) for an order of reimbursement of expenses incurred because of the pregnancy of the petitioner and the birth of her alleged illegitimate son, and (3) for an order to pay for the support, maintenance and education of the child until he reaches the age of 20 years. The defendant appeals from an adverse judgment following a jury trial.

Prior to the close of the petitioner's case-in-chief and over the defendant's objection, the court permitted the mother to carry the baby, then aged nine months, through the courtroom and in front of the jury for approximately 30 seconds. The defendant objected to the exhibition for the following reasons: (1) that the presence of the child would create sympathy in favor of the petitioner, (2) that the exhibition of the child for the purpose of showing some physical resemblance to the defendant is "contrary to the facts of life," and (3) that the exhibition "does not and would not add to the probative evidence in the case." The court ruled that the reasons for permitting the exhibition were twofold: "to let the jurors see that there is a live baby and to *generally* appraise the physical characteristics of the baby." (Emphasis added.) The defendant specifies the exhibition of the child as error.

. . .

I.   EXHIBITION OF THE CHILD.

It is often said that "like is apt to beget like"; yet this literary epigram cannot serve as the basis for a wholesale or limited exhibition of the child to a jury in a paternity case in light of contemporary scientific knowledge. The law must rely upon hard facts rather than flaccid assumptions which have outlived their usefulness. A rule grounded in the popular beliefs of many generations may become so entrenched that its claim to authority appears absolute when in fact the reason for the rule has long been undercut by scientific knowledge. The present case requires that we question the assumption that laymen, as jurors who must determine the paternity of a child can profit from an exhibition of the child. This necessarily compels consideration of relevant scientific facts with respect to physical resemblances, especially in the fields of genetics and physical anthropology. After exhaustive research we can discern no good reason either in law or in science to warrant the exhibition of a child to a jury for the purpose of proving paternity. . . .

In sum, we agree that the specific resemblance between a child and the person alleged to be the father is a relevant issue in a paternity case but we cannot find any rule of reason, any policy of the law of evidence, or any fact of science which provides a basis for allowing the exhibition of a child to show resemblance. As we have stated, a jury gains nothing from an exhibition even when their attention is focused upon the relevant inherited traits since independent expert interpretation is required. An exhibition can only serve to expose the defendant to proven dangers. Therefore, we hold that the exhibition of a child to the finder of fact in a paternity case is not to be permitted. However, expert testimony concerning the resemblance of a child to a person alleged to be the father is admissible to prove or disprove the paternity of the child.

In the case of In re Ah Sam, 24 Haw. 591 (1918) this court held that it was not error for the trial court to permit the alleged illegitimate child to remain in the courtroom in the presence of the jury and be carried by the mother to the witness stand while testifying. That portion of Ah Sam which approves of such exposure of the child to the jury is hereby overruled....

Reversed and remanded for a new trial.

■ KOBAYASHI, JUSTICE (dissenting).

I dissent.

The majority opinion is tantamount to the Supreme Court taking judicial notice and subscribing to the absolute truth and correctness of the various scientific propositions mentioned in the majority opinion. Yet none of the relied upon scientific principles, texts and articles were admitted into evidence. The trial is barren of any testimony supporting the validity of the alleged scientific principles relied upon by the majority of the court. None of the principles, texts and articles were subjected to the fire of cross-examination in the trial court. Furthermore, the parties were never given the opportunity to brief this court in connection with any scientific principles, texts or articles that may be available.

The majority has concluded that the trial court has committed prejudicial error. Yet none of the cited scientific authorities, relied upon by the majority, deal with or resolve the following crucial questions:

1. Can a relevant inference of paternity be legitimately drawn from the child's appearance, complexion, and features?

2. If the answer is yes, is the jury capable of drawing such an inference by viewing the child?

The various jurisdictions throughout our nation are in considerable disharmony in their answers to the questions. In our jurisdiction the courts have a long history of permitting the jury to view the child. Thus, when the various jurisdictions are in such conflict and if our long-standing practice of exhibiting the child is to be reversed, a new law can better be developed if this appellate court, a court that is not a fact-finding body, provides the necessary impetus, direction, and requirement for the trial court to adduce all necessary scientific-oriented evidence and testimony to determine what are the proper and correct facts in answer to the questions above stated.

The method employed in the majority opinion endangers the proper growth of a possibly good law and also slants the course or direction taken by the law. Furthermore, the majority opinion effects a distinct and unwarranted invasion into the province of the trial court.

The majority opinion poses another question, a question which has never been resolved in an adversary hearing in this jurisdiction, to-wit: Is a scientifically trained expert the only person capable of drawing the proper inference of paternity from the child's appearance, complexion, and features?

The majority, in effect, says "yes" to that question. Here, again the majority opinion effects an unwarranted and dangerous invasion into the province of the trial court. . . .

NOTES

1. DNA and blood typing should avoid the "exhibition" problem. Should a jury be permitted to give greater weight to resemblance than to DNA?

Virtually all courts permit exhibition of the child for the purpose of showing whether or not it is of that race which would characterize the offspring of its mother and putative father. See White v. Holderby, 192 F.2d 722 (5th Cir.1951) (jury allowed to observe color and physical characteristics of children to determine whether they should attend Negro school or white school where there was issue as to whether their grandfather had been part Negro or part Indian); Peters v. Campbell, 345 P.2d 234, 241 (Wyo.1959) (testimony about "Spanish" "appearance" of putative father excluded because no evidence to show "features of the child were Spanish").

2. With respect to the propriety of exhibiting the child in order to prove physical resemblance to the putative father, the courts are divided into three general groups. Some courts hold that the child may be exhibited whenever paternity is in issue. See, e.g., Commonwealth v. Kennedy, 450 N.E.2d 167 (Mass.1983); State v. Green, 284 S.E.2d 688 (N.C.App.1981); State v. Clay, 236 S.E.2d 230 (W.Va.1977); Hunt v. State, 112 S.E.2d 817 (Ga.App.1960). Even in these jurisdictions there is no corollary that the child must be brought in to show a lack of resemblance. See, e.g., Melanson v. Rogers, 451 A.2d 825 (Conn.App.1982).

The second group permits exhibition of the child only under certain conditions. The most common of these requirements is that the child be sufficiently old to possess settled features. Some jurisdictions have a fixed age, below which a child is not considered to have settled features, State v. Harvey, 84 N.W. 535, 536 (Iowa 1900) (two years), while others require the trial judge to exercise his discretion in determining whether the child's features are settled, Hall v. Centolanza, 101 A.2d 44 (N.J. Super.1953); State ex rel. Fitch v. Powers, 62 N.W.2d 764 (S.D.1954); cf. State v. Cabrera, 478 P.2d 142, 144 (Ariz.App.1970) (age of child (3 months) goes to weight to be accorded the comparison of features rather than admissibility of exhibition); Glascock v. Anderson, 497 P.2d 727, 729, 55 A.L.R.3d 1079 (N.M.1972) (same).

Other jurisdictions permit exhibition of the child to show resemblance only of specific features. Thus the real evidence must be accompanied by testimony specifically comparing one or more features, and discussing these points of resemblance. See, e.g., Lawhead v. State, 226 P. 376, 378 (Okla.1924) (in bastardy proceeding in which the jury was allowed to compare the similar tips of the seven week old child's ears with those of the putative father); cf. Fillipone v. United States, 2 F.2d 928, 931 (D.C.Cir.1924) (recognizes propriety of exhibition in instances of "striking" resemblance or non-resemblance). Wigmore's view is that the trial judge should exercise discretion in determining whether the child should be exhibited, and a comparison of specific traits should be required. 1 Wigmore Evidence 627 (3d ed. 1940).

The last group of courts refuse to permit exhibition of the child. See, e.g., in addition to the main case, People in Interest of R.D.S., 514 P.2d 772, 775 (Colo.1973) ("exhibition of a child to jury, when offered to show paternity by way of resemblance is irrelevant as a matter of law."; testimony as to specific resemblance by expert permitted). See generally Kenny, Physical Resemblance as Evidence of Consanguinity, 39 L.Q.Rev. 297 (1923). While courts have admitted that resemblance is often exceedingly fanciful, and that what is taken as resemblance by one is not perceived by another, Kenny says that this "is merely to state (what is true in all disputes) that some are more observant than others." Kenny, supra. Is Kenny's statement correct? If not, how do you explain the fact that what is taken to be resemblance by some is not perceived by others?

3. There are collateral problems concerning exhibition of the child. In jurisdictions which prohibit or limit exhibition, the problem of whether there has been an informal exhibition of the child may arise. It is generally held that the mere presence of the child in the courtroom, or the holding of the child by the mother while she testifies, does not constitute informal exhibition. See State v. Wells, 367 S.W.2d 652 (Mo.1963). On the other hand, reference to the child in the presence of the jurors is reversible error if formal exhibition would have been improper. Cf. McLemore v. Richardson, 343 A.2d 229, 231 (Conn.Sup.App. 1975) (a jurisdiction permitting exhibitions, stating that while it was not sufficient grounds for a mistrial, the better practice is for the child not to stay in the presence of the jury for an additional period of time beyond his formal exhibition).

4. The manner in which the child is exhibited may be objected to as prejudicial. Berry v. Chaplin, 169 P.2d 442, 452 (Cal.App.1946):

> Defendant complains of the order of the court directing him to stand in front of the jury in close proximity to the mother holding her child in her arms in order that the jurors might study and compare the physical features of the infant plaintiff with those of defendant.... We are not impressed with the thought advanced by counsel for defendant that the sympathy of the jurors could have been aroused by the juxtaposition of the three parties in interest. The apprehension expressed by counsel that plaintiff in the arms of her mother caused compassionate visualization of the ancient masterpieces of "Madonna and the Child" is dispelled by the character of the evidence in the case which kept the minds of the jurors fixed on the unspiritual and terrestrial affairs of the mother and defendant.

5. Can a witness testify as to resemblance between the child and its putative father without exhibiting the child? Eddy v. Gray, 4 Allen (Mass.) 435 (1862), excluded such testimony because of the opinion rule. Compare with Eddy, the principal case requiring a qualified expert witness to make the comparison. Dubiousness of resemblance testimony suggests why eyewitness identifications have long been suspect. The "annals of criminal law are rife with instances of mistaken identification." United States v. Wade, 388 U.S. 218, 228 (1967). For discussions of psychological, legal and other reasons for judicial skepticism about eyewitness identification, see the introduction to Chapter 3. The constitutional issues related to identification are covered in the introduction to Chapter 3.

6. The suspect may be prevented from thwarting the witness's accuracy by altering his appearance before trial. United States v. Frazier, 417 F.2d 1138 (4th Cir.1969), cert. denied, 397 U.S. 1013 (1970) (defendant shaved off his beard and moustache while in jail). In such a case, the court may permit the jury to see photos of the hirsute suspect at the lineup to corroborate the witness's accuracy. United States v. Sherman, 421 F.2d 198, 200 (4th Cir.), cert. denied, 398 U.S. 914 (1970).

7. There is frequent resort to voice identification for purposes of identifying the defendant. See, e.g., United States v. Delaplane, 778 F.2d 570 (10th Cir.1985), cert. denied, 479 U.S. 827 (1986) (voice exemplar of words spoken at scene of crime); United States v. Williams, 704 F.2d 315 (6th Cir.), cert. denied, 464 U.S. 991 (1983) (live voice exemplar). In United States v. Wade, supra, there was a line-up in which each person was required to wear strips of tape on his face and to say, "Put the money in the bag." The court held that such a line-up did not violate the accused's privilege against self-incrimination, nor did it require the presence of counsel under the sixth amendment. Cf. United States v. Otero–Hernandez, 418 F.Supp. 572 (M.D.Fla.1976), holding that in a prosecution arising out of an airport bombing, a witness's in-court identification of defendant as the person who called the airport to warn of the bombing based on an out-of-court identification of defendant's voice as a result of listening to a "voice spread" (i.e., tape recording of various voices, including defendant's repeating the same words), was not rendered inadmissible on grounds that defendant's counsel was not present at the out-of-court identification; the court viewed a "voice spread" as the functional equivalent of a photo spread.

Voice identifications are best made in a manner that minimizes suggestive procedures such as previous visual identification. See, e.g., Sanchell v. Parratt, 530 F.2d 286 (8th Cir.1976) (identification testimony based partly or totally on voice of defendant tainted by suggestive visual showup procedure and thus violative of due process, where record revealed little as to the circumstances under which the witnesses heard defendant's voice so that they might compare it with voice they heard at time of the crime, where the comparisons were made with voices none of which resembled that of the perpetrator, and where two witnesses made the identification with the knowledge that the defendant had been formally charged and had been identified by others); Commonwealth v. Marini, 378 N.E.2d 51 (Mass.1978) (in-court identification of alleged rapist by victim was improper and prejudicial error where it was conducted one-on-one, with defendant in full sight of victim, where words used by criminal at scene of crime were used rather than neutral expressions, and where victim had already committed herself by having made separate positive identification). See also, Annot., 70 A.L.R.2d 995 (1960) (identification of accused by his voice). The analogous visual identification problems are treated in Chapter 3, infra.

8. Similarly, hair and handwriting exemplars may be taken for the purpose of identification. See, e.g., In re Grand Jury Proceedings, 686 F.2d 135 (3d Cir.), cert. denied sub nom. Mills v. United States, 459 U.S. 1020 (1982) (facial hair); Bouse v. Bussey, 573 F.2d 548 (9th Cir.1977) (pubic hair obtained in a humiliating way); United States v. McKeon, 558 F.Supp. 1243 (E.D.N.Y.1983) (handwriting).

Watson v. State

Supreme Court of Indiana, 1957.
236 Ind. 329, 140 N.E.2d 109.

■ ARTERBURN, JUDGE. This is an appeal by the appellant, Cecil Moss Watson, from a judgment convicting him of Armed Robbery under Acts 1929, ch. 55, § 1, p. 139, being § 10–4709, Burns' 1956 Replacement. Appellant claims errors which have been properly presented, (1) that the verdict is not sustained by sufficient evidence, and (2) the giving of the following instruction to the jury.

"One of the essential elements of the offense of armed robbery is that the person charged is over the age of sixteen years and this fact, if it be a fact, must be proven beyond a reasonable doubt by the State of Indiana the same as any other fact, and in the event you find this was not proven then you should find the defendant not guilty of armed robbery, *but you are further instructed that*

*you may observe the defendant and draw upon your observation of him in
determining whether or not the defendant was a person over sixteen years of age
at the time of the commission of the alleged offense."* (Our italics.). . . .

There was no direct testimony given at the trial concerning appellant's age.
He did not take the witness stand. The statute under which appellant was
convicted, it will be observed, unlike most definitions of a crime, sets out the
age of the offender as an element therein. . . .

The verdict of the jury, and the judgment of the court is as follows:

"We, the Jury, find the defendant guilty of Robbery while armed with
a dangerous or deadly weapon, as charged in the affidavit herein, and that
he is 38 years of age.". . . .

The essence of the question before us then is, whether or not the jury had
any evidence before it from which any inferences could be drawn as a basis for
its finding and verdict that the defendant was "38 years of age." It is conceded
that the state introduced no evidence formally and directly as to the age of the
appellant. This could have been done by a witness giving his opinion from
observation of the appellant as to his age. . . .

The most that can be said for the state's evidence on this point is that one
witness pointed out the appellant for identification, saying: "The man sitting
right there is the man that held me up." A witness also referred to appellant as
a "man" he had seen in a tavern. The defendant did not testify or take the
witness stand. May the jury observe the defendant as he sat in the court room
and therefrom determine his age or conclude from the use of the term "man"
that he was more than sixteen years of age? If the defendant had taken the
witness stand the jury would have been entitled to observe his demeanor and
other characteristics while testifying. In observing the witness the jury undoubtedly could have arrived at some conclusion as to his age. It could have
considered his proper age in weighing his testimony as to creditability. . . .

A defendant sitting in the court room may be pointed out and identified by
various witnesses while testifying, and may be asked to stand for that purpose,
if a description has been given for the jury's consideration. That is proper
testimony coming from the witness stand from persons other than the defendant, and is evidence which the court and jury may properly consider. If such
observation and identification may be made before trial, then there is no reason
why it may not be done during the trial in the court room by a witness. . . .

However, we find no such testimony presented to the jury of this character
in this case. He was merely pointed out, and nothing more, for the purpose of
identification. No physical characteristics from which a jury can draw any
inferences of age were presented. The mere pointing out by the defendant for
identification is no proof of his age in itself. As a part of the identification the
witness might have given his judgment as to age of the defendant, but that was
not done in this case. . . .

One of the purposes of the trial is to confine the evidence which a jury or
court may consider to that which meets the legal test of being material,
relevant, and otherwise competent. These rules have been developed through
centuries of experience as the best method of excluding in so far as possible
hearsay and other unreliable sources of information in an endeavor to seek the
truth. To let the bars down and turn the jury loose to seek its own information
where it cares to find it, would open a pandora's box of innumerable injustices
in verdicts rendered.

A jury looking about the court room, seeing objects brought into the court
room, has no right to consider such extrinsic material, and base their verdict

thereon, or draw inferences therefrom, without such exhibits being properly referred to for their observation as evidence in the trial. The same rule holds true as to persons within the view of the jury during the trial. The doctrine of judicial notice as to scientific, historical, or other facts of general common knowledge, may not be invoked here. . . .

Since there was no evidence presented to the jury from which it could draw any reasonable inference as to the age of the defendant, the evidence was not sufficient to sustain the verdict and likewise the giving of instruction authorizing the jury to consider matters not presented in evidence, was improper.

Judgment is reversed with directions to grant the appellant a new trial.

■ EMMERT and LANDIS, JJ., concur.

[Dissenting opinion omitted.]

NOTES

1. Courts uniformly hold that a defendant's physical appearance may be considered by the jury to determine his age. Some courts require additional proof of age in conjunction with physical appearance. See, e.g., People v. Montalvo, 482 P.2d 205, 210 (Cal.1971), a prosecution for furnishing narcotics to a minor, where it was held that since by its express terms the statute applied only to persons over twenty-one years old who distributed narcotics, the defendant's conviction could not stand where the record was barren of any evidence or even mention of defendant's age and question of age was in no way presented to or passed on by the jury. The court did, however, state:

Our holding should not be interpreted so as to require the prosecution in every instance to prove the actual age of the defendant. There will be occasions when his physical appearance will be such that the jury could not entertain a reasonable doubt that he was over the age of 21 years. "Experience teaches us that corporal appearances are approximately an index of the *age* of their bearer, particularly for the marked extremes of old age and youth. In every case such evidence should be accepted and weighed for what it may be in each case worth. In particular, the *outward physical* appearance of an alleged minor may be considered in judging of his *age;* a contrary rule would for such an inference be pedantically over-cautious." 2 Wigmore, Evidence (3d ed. 1940) § 222, pp. 5–6 (emphasis in original). . . . Similarly, a view of the defendant by the trier of fact in an appropriate case may be sufficient to support a finding that the defendant is an adult. In any event, the information or indictment must contain the necessary language as to age and in jury trials, the jury must be properly instructed as to all of the elements of the offense.

Proof may be in the form of circumstantial evidence. See, e.g., Barnett v. State, 488 So.2d 24 (Ala.Cr.App.1986) (in prosecution for rape, jury could consider defendant's physical appearance, the fact that he had been married for eight years, and had "grown-up" with one who was now 37 years old in determining that the defendant was at least 16 years old); State v. Thompson, 365 N.W.2d 40 (Iowa App.1985) (jury could consider the defendant's appearance and his admission that he had purchased beer and cigarettes in determining that he was at least 18 years old).

2. State v. Dorathy, 170 A. 506, 508 (Me.1934): There was no evidence that defendant who failed to take the stand was over 21; the indictment stated that he was 74 at the time of the felony. Verdict of guilty affirmed:

We take judicial notice that when the trial was at its beginning, respondent was informed, by statement of the Court, through its clerk, that certain persons were about to be qualified to try the case; that if he were to object to any persons called, he must do so before they were sworn. And the inference is unavoidable that every alert and intelligent juror sworn then must have seen respondent, whom probably to know aright as to age was but to see.... There is force to the claim that respondent was not compelled to produce evidence against himself. He must, however, present himself before court and jury, to secure acquittal. This he may do voluntarily, but whether voluntarily as a witness, or by force of his compelled attendance, as here, he inevitably reveals that he is a person, a male perhaps. He reveals his race, color, and, we hold, somewhat as to his age.

See Note, A Defendant's Appearance as Evidence of His Age, 15 Wash. & Lee L.Rev. 290 (1958).

3. Schnoor v. Meinecke, 40 N.W.2d 803 (N.D.1950): Plaintiff's right to maintain an action for personal injuries received while an employee, rather than seek Workmen's Compensation depended on whether or not he was 16 years old when injured. Plaintiff and his parents testified that he was under 16 at the time of the accident and introduced a certified birth certificate to that effect; defendant proved that both at the time of his employment and after he was injured plaintiff stated he was 17 years old. The jury found he was over 16 at the time of the injury. On appeal, plaintiff challenged the sufficiency of the evidence to support that finding. The court found that the statements plaintiff had made as to his age together with his physical appearance which the jury had an opportunity to observe constituted sufficient evidence to sustain the verdict.

4. People v. Kielczewski, 109 N.E. 981, 982–983 (Ill.1915): The question was whether at the time of their conviction of the crime of robbery each of the defendants had reached the age of twenty-one. One of them testified that he was then twenty-one and the other that he was then twenty-two. The jury nevertheless found that each of them was "between the ages of ten and twenty-one and ... about the age of twenty years." Each of the defendants sought to sustain this finding on the ground that "having become a witness in his own behalf, his appearance, demeanor and conduct while on the witness stand were evidence in the case, and the jury might determine that his statement was not true and fix his age from his appearance." Reversed:

> It is true that appearances approximately indicate the age of a person and as between the extremes of youth and old age are quite reliable. In any case, appearances may be accepted and weighed for what they are worth. Anyone knows, however, that there are remarkable differences in the appearances of persons of the same age, and as between twenty and twenty-one no one would accept appearances, alone, as a reliable standard. Undoubtedly, the appearance of an alleged minor may be considered in determining his age, but there must be some proper rule of evidence as to how it shall be proved.... The rule of evidence is that a witness, after describing the appearance of a person as best he can, may give an opinion of his age.... This court has applied the general rule that jurors cannot make up their verdict on any disputed fact from their own individual observation.

Cf. Rich v. State, 266 P.2d 476, 478 (Okl.Cr.1954). Can the last two note cases be reconciled? If so, what factors must be considered? Experiments have shown "age to be a particularly unreliable aspect of descriptive information," with some skilled police officers testing ten times as accurately as untrained layper-sons. A. Trankell, Reconstructing the Past, The Role of Psychologists in Criminal Trials 295 (1982).

5.   United States v. Hall, 999 F.2d 1298, 1300 (8th Cir.1993): In summation the prosecutor argued that of a male and female in the room with the deceased at the time of the killing it was more likely to have been the male because it's "in the genes."

> We construe the prosecutor's remarks as an invitation to the jury to consider the defendant's [observed] sex in deciding his guilt. The jury, of course, is entitled to notice such facts as it has acquired knowledge of in its daily experience, but we are more than a little disturbed by the prospect that a jury might be authorized to put a person's sex in the balance in deciding whether to convict him. We wonder, too, about the propriety, in some future similar case, of admitting into evidence statistics and testimo-ny about sex-based behavioral differences, including the propensity, if any, to commit certain kinds of crime. We view with special alarm the govern-ment's appeal to some alleged common knowledge about sex differences that are genetically determined.

State v. Scarlett

Supreme Court of New Hampshire, 1978.
118 N.H. 904, 395 A.2d 1244.

■ Bois, Justice.

. . . . On April 22, 1977, a six-year-old female child was lured away from her playmates by an adult male. She was beaten and sexually molested. The defendant does not dispute the fact that these acts were committed; he does dispute the State's accusation that he is the one who did them. Consequently, identity was the central issue at trial.

Substantial evidence was presented to the jury linking the defendant to the crime. Most incriminating was the testimony of the victim's young playmates who were with her when she left with her molester. Photographs of the defendant's apartment, the alleged scene of the attack, also served to connect the defendant to the crime. Most damaging of these was a photograph of an apparently blood-stained bedspread that covered the defendant's bed, the bed upon which the State contended that the attack occurred.

The incident underlying the issue that we find dispositive in the present case occurred halfway through the trial. The State, while eliciting testimony from a police officer, displayed to the jury what appeared to be a blood-stained bedspread, marked it for identification, and began an attempt to admit it into evidence.

Five months prior to the trial, the State was aware that the testimony of the chemist who had tested and analyzed the stains on the bedspread would be necessary in order to prove them to be blood. We must presume that the prosecutor, as an experienced attorney, realized that the chemist's testimony was essential in order to establish the foundation for admissibility of this incriminating item of evidence. Nevertheless, the chemist was not present at trial or even scheduled to testify on behalf of the State. Only through defense counsel oversight coupled with judicial error could the bedspread have been admitted into evidence. We hold public prosecutors to a high standard of conduct. State v. Arthur, 118 N.H. 561, 562, 391 A.2d 884, 885 (1978). The State overreached when it displayed the bedspread to the jury under these circumstances. ABA Standards Relating to the Prosecution Function § 5.6(d) (1971).

The defense counsel made timely objection to the bedspread being marked for identification. The court overruled the objection, undoubtedly assuming that proper foundation for admissibility would be forthcoming. Although the defense counsel's objections to the subsequent testimony concerning the bedspread were properly sustained, and the testimony stricken, the jury had already heard the police officer's testimony that the stains were blood, and that the sheet had been taken from the defendant's bedroom. This highly incriminating information struck a telling blow to the essence of the defendant's defense, that the State could not identify him as the molester.

At this juncture, the trial court first suspected that the proper foundation for admissibility would not be forthcoming from the State. The court inquired: "Does the State, at some point further in its case, intend to establish through some other evidence that the stains, in fact, appearing on that bedspread have been analyzed as blood?" The State replied, "No." The defense counsel immediately moved for a mistrial. The trial court took the motion under advisement, recessed the proceedings for the remainder of the day, and ordered both counsel to meet with him privately in his chambers.

The court denied the mistrial motion the next morning. It then attempted to cure the prejudice to the defendant by giving a considered and stern limiting instruction to the jury. The court ordered the jury to "disregard entirely your observations" and "disregard any testimony" concerning the bedspread. The court warned the jury that the bedspread "has no evidentiary or probative value," and advised it that "the State was in error in attempting to offer this evidence." The defendant excepted to the court's denial of his motion for a mistrial, arguing that he had been irreparably prejudiced by the improper display of the bedspread to the jury, and that no curative instruction could remedy that prejudice. We agree and sustain the defendant's exception. "Although the actions of the presiding judge were commendable as well as perceptive ... we are unable to conclude that his efforts were sufficient to purge the prejudicial questioning." Morgan v. Hall, 569 F.2d 1161, 1167 (1st Cir.1978); see United States v. Hale, 422 U.S. 171, 180–81, 95 S.Ct. 2133, 45 L.Ed.2d 99 (1975).

The State concedes that its display of the inadmissible bedspread was error, but contends that it was harmless because there was sufficient other evidence against the defendant to support a conviction. That standard for harmless error is one we have considered and specifically rejected.

The present case is technically distinguishable from State v. Ruelke because the improper evidence was never erroneously admitted, but the distinction is one without legal significance. It was error for the State to have displayed the bedspread knowing that the bedspread could not have been admitted into evidence. The burden of establishing that the error was harmless beyond a reasonable doubt rests upon the State. . . .

As an appellate court, we could never precisely determine the degree to which the jury may have been influenced by the sight of the bloodied bedspread. See State v. Labranche, 118 N.H. at 179, 385 A.2d at 110. We can confidently hold, however, that under our harmless error standard, the State has not shown "beyond a reasonable doubt that the [improper display of] inadmissible evidence did not affect the verdict." State v. Ruelke, 116 N.H. at 694, 366 A.2d at 498.

Exception sustained; remanded for a new trial.

All concurred.

NOTES

1. On remand, the court admitted the bloodstained bedspread, the prosecution having established a foundation for its introduction with the testimony of a chemist. State v. Scarlett, 426 A.2d 25, 26 (N.H.1981).

Compare the curious case of Miller v. Pate, 386 U.S. 1 (1967): Defendant had been charged with the murder of an eight-year-old girl who had died as the result of a brutal sexual attack. There were no eyewitnesses to the crime. A vital component of the case against defendant was a pair of men's shorts with reddish-brown stains that had been found one mile from the scene of the crime. The prosecutor exhibited the stained shorts to the jury, alluded to the stains as blood stains and introduced expert testimony to show that the blood type was that of the victim. The jury trial ended in a verdict of guilty and a sentence of death. Upon application for a writ of habeas corpus, the shorts were examined by a chemical microanalyst who determined that the stains were not from blood but rather were from paint. It was further established that the prosecution had full knowledge of this fact when it portrayed the stains to be from blood. The United States Supreme Court found that the conviction was in violation of the Fourteenth Amendment since it was obtained by the prosecution's knowing use of false evidence.

Responding to a request from one of the editors, counsel for defendant explained the circumstances of Miller v. Pate, supra:

> At the trial in 1956, the State produced an expert witness who testified that there was blood on the shorts. The defense made an effort to have the shorts examined by defense expert but this request was denied by the court. There the matter rested until 1963. In 1963 it occurred to us that it might be possible to determine by chemical analysis of body residues on the shorts whether or not Miller had ever worn the shorts. I was referred to a New York hematologist who informed me that in the case of some people, perspiration can be typed in much the same manner as blood. Up to this point we had no inkling that the stains were other than blood. With the court's permission, swatches were cut from the garment and sent to New York. To our great surprise, the hematologist reported that he could find no trace of blood on the shorts. Moreover, the test he contemplated for typing perspiration could not be performed because of contamination of the garment, probably soap from prior washings. By this time, the habeas corpus hearing was about ready to begin. We made a feverish search in Chicago to find somebody competent to tell us what the staining material was. We found a chemist at a laboratory who identified the stains as paint. The question then came up whether there was any blood on the shorts at all. Because of time factors, our expert was able only to perform one test for blood, or rather for hemoglobin, the presence of which can be detected long after the blood has disintegrated. The test was to spray the garment with luminal. There was no evidence of the presence of hemoglobin as a result of this test.

Letter from Willard Lassers, March 28, 1972. No response was received to a similar request from the prosecutor. In the state appellate court the main point of contention had been the voluntariness of the confession. People v. Miller, 148 N.E.2d 455 (Ill.1958).

2. People v. Gonzalez, 35 N.Y. 49, 61–62 (1866). Defendant was convicted of murder. A lay witness testified that clothes worn by Gonzalez on the night of the murder were marked with stains apparently caused by blood. In upholding the conviction, the New York Court of Appeals said that

> Stains of blood, found upon the person or clothing of the party accused, have always been recognized among the ordinary indicia of homicide.

> Blood stains on garments occur so frequently in the experience of all, from a great variety of causes, that they are easily recognized by persons of ordinary observation. We all know that, when recently made, they are as readily discernible as spots produced by paint or oil.... Matters of common observation may ordinarily be proved by those who witness them, without resorting to mechanical or scientific tests to verify them with definite precision.... The affairs of life are too pressing and manifold to have everything reduced to absolute certainty, even in the administration of justice. Some reliance must be placed in the intelligence and good faith of witnesses, and the judgment and discrimination of jurors.

3. How easily recognizable is blood to "persons of ordinary observation?" A former restaurant owner opened the door of his home one night to a stranger holding a red stained rag to his face, claiming he had just been involved in an accident. Once inside, the stranger pulled a gun and robbed him of over $5,300. The "blood" on the rag turned out to be catsup. Newsday, p. 5, Oct. 20, 1972. See Comment, Examination of Biological Fluids, FBI Law Enforcement Bulletin, June 1972, 13:

> Occasionally a contributor sends a knife or ax to the laboratory and wants the blood on it grouped for comparison with the human blood of the victims. It is not unusual to find that the "bloodstains" are actually rust. Under some conditions rust stains have an appearance similar to bloodstains and sometimes will give a weak positive result when tested with benzedrine.

4. Wimberley v. Paterson, 183 A.2d 691, 704 (N.J.Super.1962) was a wrongful death action involving a slaying by a policeman who claimed that he had only intended to fire a warning shot:

> In the case here presented the allowance in evidence of any bullet-torn or blood-stained articles of clothing could well have had a tendency to prejudice the jury against the defendants. On the other hand, the allowance into evidence of articles of outer clothing might have been helpful to the jury in determining the degree of visibility which was presented by the decedent at the time of the shooting. We are unable to find that the trial court abused its discretion in rejecting the proffered evidence.

Accord, State v. Bowman, 491 So.2d 1380 (La.App.1986) (admission of blood-stained shirt to show violent nature of killing); State v. Clark, 616 P.2d 888 (Ariz. en banc), cert. denied, 449 U.S. 1067 (1980) (admission of blood-stained shirt to link defendant to crime).

5. In State v. Bowden, 324 A.2d 631, 635 (R.I.1974), a blood-stained automobile seat and floor mat taken from an automobile in which the kidnapping and murder victim was allegedly transported were admitted as exhibits. There was testimony by an eyewitness "that some of the three persons in the Cadillac made 'punching motions' where [the victim] was sitting, but he did not see where the blows were landing." The body of the victim was later found in a river, but the "[m]edical examination showed that death was due to blunt forces applied to various parts of the body and not to drowning." While an expert could not say whether the blood traces found on the car seat were the victim's, another expert testified there was a "high degree of probability," that hairs found on the floor mat were the decedent's. The court held the two exhibits were admissible; although "probative value may not have been substantial, the exhibits furnished a link in the chain of circumstances tying defendants to the crime."

6. Compare the probative value of the clothing in Miller, Gonzalez, Wimberley and Bowden. Could testimony rather than the exhibition of the clothing have supplied the necessary proof in each of these cases? What testimony was required before the real evidence could be utilized by the trier to arrive at a rational conclusion?

7. Bruce's Juices v. United States, 194 F.2d 935, 937 (5th Cir.1952): Libel to condemn, because adulterated, shipments of cans of blended pineapple and grapefruit juice:

> The libel charged that the product was adulterated in that it was decomposed and the proof conformed to the verdict. The libellee appealed from a judgment of condemnation, entered on a verdict. "Its final complaint, that the court erred in refusing to permit the jury to subject the samples to the test of their senses of sight, smell and taste, on first and casual consideration, does seem to have merit. Wigmore on Evidence, 3rd Ed., Vol. 4, Sec. 1151; but see Sec. 1152. But the merit is only seeming, for the matter proposed to be determined by the senses of the jury, whether the article is decomposed, was not a matter cognizable by the senses, and was, therefore, not a matter for which such tests are suitable.... The issue being what it was, sampling by the jury could not have solved it."

8. Woodward & Lothrop v. Heed, 44 A.2d 369, 371 (D.C.Mun.App.1945), was an action for breach of an implied warranty that a muskrat fur coat was reasonably fit for the purpose for which it was sold. The plaintiff testified that the fur was worn off, but defendant's expert witnesses testified that the fur was only "matted down." Defendant moved for a directed verdict on the basis of plaintiff's failure to meet his expert testimony. The court held that this motion was properly denied:

> But the coat itself ... was admitted in evidence and placed before the jury for its inspection. Coats made of muskrat pelts are not uncommon or unusual. The fur is one with which the average man or woman is reasonably familiar. It is not improbable that the average juror would be able to determine by inspection, or on examination, whether the fur had worn off or was matted down, and would reject any testimony, expert or otherwise, at variance with the results of his own observations. When the issue of fact is the condition of such an article the introduction in evidence of the thing itself, to enable the jury to observe its condition, is competent and persuasive evidence.

B.   IDENTIFICATION AS A CONDITION OF RELEVANCY

HEARINGS BEFORE THE PRESIDENT'S COMMISSION ON THE ASSASSINATION OF PRESIDENT KENNEDY, 1964

Mr. THORNE. Exhibit 139.[1]

Mrs. OSWALD. This is the fateful rifle of Lee Oswald.

Mr. RANKIN. Is that the scope that it had on it, as far as you know?

---

1. Extensive references to Exhibit No. 139 will be found in the index, Vol. XV, p. 139.

Mrs. OSWALD. Yes.

Mr. RANKIN. I offer in evidence Exhibit 139.

The CHAIRMAN. It may be admitted.

(The article referred to was marked Commission Exhibit No. 139a., and received in evidence.) [Vol. 1, p. 119]

Mr. BALL. What is your specialty with the F.B.I.?

Mr. CUNNINGHAM. I am assigned to the F.B.I. laboratory in the Firearms Identification Unit.

Mr. BALL. There is a rifle here that has been identified as Commission Exhibit No. 139, it has been in your custody, hasn't it?

Mr. CUNNINGHAM. It has.

Mr. BALL. You brought it over here this morning?

Mr. CUNNINGHAM. I did. [Vol. 2, p. 252]

Mr. BALL. I show you a rifle which is Commission Exhibit 139. Can you tell us whether or not that looks like the rifle you saw on the floor that day?

Mr. BOONE. It looks like the same rifle. I have no way of being positive.

Mr. BALL. You never handled it?

Mr. BOONE. I did not touch the weapon at all. [Vol. 3, p. 294]

Mr. McCLOY. How soon after the assassination did you examine this rifle?

Mr. FRAZIER. We received the rifle the following morning.

Mr. McCLOY. Received it in Washington?

Mr. FRAZIER. Yes, sir.

Mr. McCLOY. And you immediately made your examination of it then?

Mr. FRAZIER. We made an examination of it at that time, and kept it temporarily in the laboratory.

It was then returned to the Dallas Police Department, returned again to the laboratory—the second time on November 27th, and has been either in the laboratory's possession or the Commission's possession since then. [Vol. 3, p. 395]

Mr. EISENBERG. Do you recognize Exhibit 139? Are you familiar with that?

Mr. STOMBAUGH. Yes; I am.

Mr. EISENBERG. Did you examine that in the laboratory?

Mr. STOMBAUGH. Yes; I did.

Mr. EISENBERG. Do you know when you made that examination?

Mr. STOMBAUGH. On the morning of November 23, 1963.

Mr. EISENBERG. Is your mark on it?

Mr. STOMBAUGH. Yes, sir; here is my mark.

Mr. EISENBERG. Which consists of your initials?

Mr. STOMBAUGH. My initials, and the date 11–23–63. Do you mind if I check to see if this is unloaded? [Vol. 4, p. 81]

Mr. BALL. What happened after that?

Mr. FRITZ. A few minutes later some officer called me and said they had found the rifle over near the back stairway and I told them the same thing, not to move it, not to touch it, not to move any of the boxes until we could get pictures, and as soon as Lieutenant Day could get over there he made pictures of that.

Mr. BALL. After the pictures had been taken of the rifle what happened then?

Mr. FRITZ. After the pictures had been made then I ejected a live shell, a live cartridge from the rifle. [Vol. 4, p. 205]

Mr. BALL. Did you initial the rifle?

Mr. FRITZ. The rifle; no sir.

Mr. BALL. You didn't. Who did you give the rifle to after you ejected this live cartridge?

Mr. FRITZ.... Lieutenant Day took that rifle, I believe, to the city hall, and later I asked him to bring it down—I don't believe I ever carried that rifle to city hall. I believe Lieutenant Day carried it to city hall, anyway if you will ask him he can be more positive than I. [Vol. 4, p. 206]

Mr. BELIN. Then what did you do?

Mr. DAY. I met Captain Fritz. He wanted photographs of the rifle before it was moved.

Mr. BELIN. Do you remember if Captain Fritz told you that the rifle had not been moved?

Mr. DAY. He told me he wanted photographs before it was moved, if I remember correctly. He definitely told me it had not been moved, and the reason for the photographs he wanted it photographed before it was moved.

Mr. BELIN. I am going to hand you what the reporter has marked or what has been marked as Commission Exhibit 718, and ask you to state, if you know, what this is.

Mr. DAY. This is a photograph made by me of the rifle where it was found in the northwest portion of the sixth floor, 411 Elm Street, Dallas. [Vol. 4, p. 257]

Mr. BELIN. What else did you do in connection with the rifle at that particular time?

Mr. DAY. Captain Fritz was present. After we got the photographs I asked him if he was ready for me to pick it up, and he said, yes. I picked the gun up by the wooden stock. I noted that the stock was too rough apparently to take fingerprints, so I picked it up, and Captain Fritz opened the bolt as I held the gun. A live round fell to the floor.

Mr. BELIN. Did you initial that live round at all?

Mr. DAY. Yes, sir; my name is on it. [Vol. 4, p. 258]

Mr. BELIN. I am going to hand you what has been marked Commission Exhibit 139 and ask you to state if you know what this is.

Mr. DAY. This is the rifle found on the sixth floor of the Texas Book Store at 411 Elm Street, November 23, 1963.

Mr. BELIN. What date?

Mr. DAY. November 22, 1963.

Mr. BELIN. Does it have any identification mark of yours on it?

Mr. DAY. It has my name "J.C. Day" scratched on the stock.

Mr. BELIN. And on the stock you are pointing to your name which is scratched as you would hold the rifle and rest it on the stock, approximately an inch or so from the bottom of the stock on the sling side of the stock, is that correct?

Mr. DAY. Yes, sir.

Mr. BELIN. Do you have any recollection as to what the serial number was of that?

Mr. DAY. Yes, sir; I recorded it at the time, C–2566.

Mr. BELIN. Before you say that—

Mr. DAY. C–2766, excuse me.

Mr. BELIN. Do you have any record of that with you or not?

Mr. DAY. Yes, sir; this is the record I made of the gun when I took it back to the office. Now, the gun did not leave my possession.

Mr. BELIN. From the time it was found at the School Book Depository Building?

Mr. DAY. Yes, sir; I took the gun myself and retained possession, took it to the office where I dictated—

Mr. BELIN. Could you just read into the record what you dictated.

Mr. DAY. To my secretary. She wrote on the typewriter: "4 × 18, coated, Ordinance Optics, Inc., Hollywood, California, 010 Japan. OSC inside a cloverleaf design."

Mr. BELIN. What did that have reference to?

Mr. DAY. That was stamped on the scopic sight on top of the gun. On the gun itself, "6.5 caliber C–2766, 1940 made in Italy." That was what was on the gun. [Vol. 4, pp. 259–60]

Mr. BELIN. At what time, if you know, did you release the rifle to the FBI?

Mr. DAY. 11:45 p.m. the rifle was released or picked up by them and taken from the office.

Mr. BELIN. Was that on November 22?

Mr. DAY. November 22, 1963. [Vol. 4, p. 261]

Mr. BELIN. What else did you do, or what was the next thing you did after you completed photographing and inspecting the rifle on the sixth floor of the Texas School Book Depository Building for whatever prints you could find, what did you do next?

Mr. DAY. I took the gun at the time to the office and locked it up in a box in my office at Captain Fritz' direction. [Vol. 4, p. 264]

NOTES

1. What different types of identification were used? If this were a trial rather than a hearing what differences, if any, might you expect in the transcript?

2. Would Mrs. Oswald's identification of the rifle have been sufficient at an adversarial trial? Five years after her testimony before the Warren Commission, Mrs. Oswald (now Mrs. Porter) appeared before a New Orleans court in the Kennedy murder-conspiracy trial brought by Louisiana District Attorney James Garrison. Mrs. Porter reportedly was unable to say whether the rifle shown to her resembled the weapon she said Oswald owned. "'I am not familiar with rifles,' she explained." New York Post 3, Feb. 22, 1969.

3.   Often the problem of identification arises in connection with testimonial proof as where an expert testifies with respect to a test he made out of court. See, for example, Woolley v. Hafner's Wagon Wheel, Inc., 169 N.E.2d 119 (1960), rev'd, 176 N.E.2d 757 (Ill.1961), where evidence of a blood alcohol test to prove intoxication was excluded because the court was not satisfied that the specimen tested by a laboratory was the one taken from defendant by the police. A complete and rigorously adhered to system of identification and custody of such specimens is essential where possible court testimony will be required. But see Caldwell v. State, 891 S.W.2d 42, 47 (Ark.1995) (geneticist in private laboratory sufficiently authenticated blood sample without a clear chain of custody because he kept records and gave sufficient assurance of no tampering). See also United States v. Ricco, 52 F.3d 58 (4th Cir.1995) (detective, police officer and forensic chemist utilized in establishing claim of custody of crack vials).

In Eisentrager v. State, 378 P.2d 526, 530–531 (Nev.1963), a technician, in the presence of a police officer who testified, extracted blood from the defendant and placed the blood in two vials. The technician went alone into an adjoining room with the blood samples. After "two or several minutes" he returned and gave the vials containing the blood to the officer. The samples were later sent to the FBI laboratory and introduced in evidence through the FBI agent who had made the analysis. The medical technician who drew the blood did not testify. The court rejected the defendant's contention that there was no positive proof that the blood samples which the technician took to the adjoining room were the same as those returned to the officer a few minutes later:

> The burden is upon the party relying upon expert testimony to prove the identity of the object upon which such testimony is based. However, the practicalities of proof do not require such party to negative all possibility of substitution or tampering. He need only establish that it is reasonably certain that substitution, alteration, or tampering did not occur. In the present case there is absolutely no indication that the medical technician, who had sole possession of the vials for approximately two minutes, substituted, altered, changed or tampered with their contents, nor is there the remotest suggestion that he may have been interested in doing so.

See also, United States v. Archambault, 670 F.2d 800, 802 (8th Cir.1982) ("There was ample evidence at trial to support the district court's finding that a chain of custody was established with respect to the speedometers. The supervisor of the crime laboratory who examined the speedometers testified that the speedometers were received by laboratory personnel from the officer who removed them from the cars, were recorded in the log book, and were kept locked in a storage room."); White v. State, 717 S.W.2d 784, 790 (Ark.1986) ("Minor discrepancies in the chain of custody are for the trial court to weigh."); Munnerlyn v. State, 576 S.W.2d 714, 716 (Ark.1979) ("To allow the introduction of physical evidence, it is nòt necessary that every moment from the time that the evidence comes into possession of a law enforcement agency until it is introduced at trial be accounted for by every person who could have conceivably come in contact with the evidence during that period ...; it is only necessary that the trial judge ... be satisfied that the evidence presented is genuine and, in reasonable probability, not tampered with.").

In State v. Lunsford, 204 N.W.2d 613, 617 (Iowa 1973), the defendant was convicted of selling marijuana. Junior Jones was an informant for the police who had assisted them in a narcotics "buy." After the purchase was made by Jones and the police intervened arresting the defendants, a policeman told Jones to go to the police station and ask for a support force. In the car which Jones used to go to the station was the box which allegedly contained the marijuana involved in the sale. Jones met Sergeant Hayes at the police station who, hearing Jones' story, told him to go back to the scene of the arrest. Upon Jones' return to the scene of the arrest, the box containing the marijuana was removed from the car. Later chemical analysis showed the contents to be slightly more than ten pounds of good quality marijuana. The defendant objected to the marijuana's admissibility on the ground there was a fatal gap in the chain of possession. In admitting the evidence the court stated:

> In this case there was no direct evidence of continuous custody or to negative tampering by Junior Jones during the approximately two minutes he had exclusive possession of the exhibit since he did not testify. The question becomes as a condition precedent to admissibility, whether there was sufficient circumstantial evidence to make it reasonably probable it was the substance received from the defendant.

The court concluded that there was sufficient circumstantial evidence for among other reasons: Jones was alone with the exhibit for only about two minutes, during most if not all of which time he must have been driving the car, thus making it difficult for him to substitute the marijuana and package it in the same distinctive way and a policeman saw the exhibit before and after Jones' trip and it looked the same to him. Compare, Amaro v. City of New York, 351 N.E.2d 665, 668–69 (N.Y.C.A.1976), an action by a fireman against city charging negligence for failing to maintain adequate lighting and guards at the sliding pole hole through which he had fallen. A doctor who had drawn a blood sample from the injured fireman gave it to a fire department chauffeur whose name he could not recall and who was not produced at trial. The sample was given to the chauffeur on Saturday evening and was not delivered to the laboratory until Monday morning, leaving over thirty-six hours of custody completely unaccounted for. The Court of Appeals upheld the trial court's exclusion of the evidence stating:

> [T]here can be no reasonable assurance of the unchanged condition of the blood sample. Nonetheless, it is argued that there is no indication that the sample was tampered with while it was in the chauffeur's possession and that it ought to be admitted for that reason. This claim, of course, begs the question for the driver was never produced and could not be examined regarding his care and custody of the sample.

4. In Wood v. State, 74 So.2d 851 (Miss.1954), four men tied up their victims after robbing them. The police took these pieces of rope into custody, and placed them in a labelled envelope. Subsequently the police arrested Rose, Ballow, Wood and Scott as they were riding in a car. In the car the police found a piece of rope, which they placed in a labelled envelope. The sheriff kept both envelopes until the trial of Rose, when they were introduced into evidence. The two lots of rope were handed back to the court clerk by a juror, and the clerk kept them under lock and key until the trial of Ballow, when they were again introduced into evidence and taken into the jury room. When the jury returned their verdict in the Ballow case the envelopes and labels had been removed and the two lots of rope were returned as a single lot. The clerk kept all the rope under lock and key until the trial of the present defendant, Wood. The police are no longer able to say which rope came from the victims' home and which from the car in which defendant was riding at the time of his arrest. Held: "a sufficient chain of identification was made to admit the rope in evidence." See 21 A.L.R.2d 1216 (1952).

5. In "Presumed Innocent," a novel by Scott Turow (1987), a key piece of evidence is the fingerprints of the defendant on a glass. At trial the glass is missing. Should the expert who lifted and identified the fingerprints be permitted to testify? What if he has a picture of the glass with the dusted prints clearly showing? What if the court ordered production so defendant's experts could examine the glass, but it could not be produced? See Id. at 319–324. Is authentication possible without the glass itself? See the discussion of the best evidence rule, infra.

6. Proof of identity and custody may raise difficult and diverse problems. In Wheeler v. United States, 211 F.2d 19 (D.C.App.1953), cert. denied, 347 U.S. 1019, (1954), a doctor working in the admitting office of a hospital testified that he had taken an urethral and a vaginal smear from the child involved in an alleged rape and had placed them on separate slides for delivery to the hospital laboratory technicians for microscopic analyses. Two slides were produced in court. The doctor could not specifically identify them, but did say that they were of the type used in the hospital and were labelled as the hospital labelled them. The child's last name and the date of "8/11/51" were scratched on each slide. A bacteriologist from the hospital laboratory testified that two slides bearing the child's last name and the date of "8/11" were received by the laboratory from the admitting office in accordance with established practice. He then testified as to the results of microscopic examination of those two slides, and the slides produced by the prosecution were admitted into evidence. Despite the witnesses' lack of knowledge of any of the steps from preparation of the slides to their production in court, the court held that they were hospital records, made in the regular course of business, admissible under the Federal Business Records Act. Accord, United States v. Duhart, 496 F.2d 941 (9th Cir.), cert. denied, 419 U.S. 967 (1974) (markings on specimen bottle). If this rationale is sufficient to overcome gaps in the chain of custody between the doctor and the bacteriologist, can it serve to meet the objection that the slides produced by the prosecution were not those examined by the bacteriologist? What, if anything, did introduction of the slides add to the prosecution's case? Even if the gaps between doctor and bacteriologist, and bacteriologist and prosecutor are sufficiently closed, an issue may still exist if the testimony does not show that the tissue taken from the patient was in fact taken at the time of the operation and that it was then marked for proper identity. Browne v. Browne, 259 A.2d 108 (D.C.App.1969).

7. It has been suggested that the degree of probability necessary to establish proper identification and chain of custody may be less stringent in a civil than in a criminal case. In Woolley v. Hafner's Wagon Wheel, Inc., 169 N.E.2d 119 (1960), the appellate court ruled that since the degree of proof necessary in a civil trial was not as high as that in a criminal trial, it would be improper to require the party seeking to introduce evidence of a laboratory test to bear the responsibility for a procedure over which she had no control. "In our opinion, in a civil case, the foundation laid for introduction of evidence of a blood analysis need not preclude every possibility of a doubt as to the identity of the specimen or the possibility of a change of condition of the blood." 176 N.E.2d 757, 760 (Ill.1961). Did Woolley state the proper test in criminal cases? Cf. United States v. Rizzo, 418 F.2d 71, 81 (7th Cir.1969), cert. denied sub nom. Tornabene v. United States, 397 U.S. 967 (1970) ("The failure of positive identification bears upon the weight of the evidence, not its legal sufficiency"); Cf. Fed.R.Evid. 901(a).

8. A piece of real evidence may be admissible even though no chain of custody is established, if a witness testifies that he recognizes the object sought to be introduced as the object it purports to be. See, e.g., United States v. Phillips, 640 F.2d 87, 94 (7th Cir.), cert. denied, 451 U.S. 991 (1981) (chain of custody breaks not important where witness identifies clothing as those she was wearing on day of kidnapping); Higginbotham v. State, 78 So.2d 637, 640 (Ala.1955).

Nor does his recognition have to be certain. In Isaacs v. National Bank of Commerce of Seattle, 50 Wash.2d 548, 550, 313 P.2d 684, 686 (1957), the court held the following colloquy sufficient to establish the identity of a watering hose on which the plaintiff allegedly tripped:

"Q. Did you see the same hose [exhibit no. 7] yesterday?

"A. I saw a hose I believe to be the same hose.

"Q. How long is this hose?

"A. Fifty feet, or slightly more. . . .

"Q. Do you know whether or not the hose you saw the other day was the same hose?

"A. No sir, I don't know absolutely. I believe it to be."

See also People v. Levia, 158 N.Y.S.2d 448, 450 (App.Div.1956) where the court held that "the absence of direct and positive proof (of identification) went to the weight, not to the competency."; United States v. Johnson, 637 F.2d 1224 (9th Cir.1980) (witness "pretty sure"; inability to specify particular identifying features went to weight, not admissibility).

Anderson v. Berg

Supreme Court of Kansas, 1969.
202 Kan. 659, 451 P.2d 248.

■ HATCHER, COMMISSIONER. This is an action to recover damages for alleged negligent injury. . . .

The plaintiff, Dolly Anderson, was walking down the corridor on the fourth floor of the Brotherhood Building in Kansas City, Kansas. The building is owned and operated by the defendants as an office building. Shortly before the plaintiff reached the door of her office she allegedly slipped upon a heavy accumulation of wax causing her to fall to the floor and be seriously injured.

This action was then brought by the plaintiff in which she alleged her injuries were caused by the defendants or their employees carelessly and negligently permitting the floor to become and remain slick and slippery as the result of the presence of an excessive amount of wax.

The case was tried to a jury which returned a verdict in favor of the defendant and judgment was rendered thereon. The plaintiff has appealed, raising but one issue. She claims:

"It was a manifest abuse of discretion by the trial Court to reopen the defendants' case-in-chief, after the jury had begun its deliberations, for the offering and admission into evidence of the bottle of wax.". . . .

During the course of the trial a small bottle containing a sample of the wax used on the floor was identified and the identity was admitted by plaintiff. The bottle of wax was not offered or received in evidence during the regular course of the trial. Neither does it appear that either party made any further use of it or desired it in evidence.

In due course the case was closed for the introduction of evidence, closing arguments were made and the jury retired to consider its verdict. Shortly after it had retired the jury returned and, before the trial court and counsel, requested, through their foreman, that the bottle of wax be sent to the jury room. The time for adjournment being near, the jury was excused until the following day. The matter was then considered by court and counsel. Defendants' counsel moved to reopen the case and admit the bottle of wax in evidence. Counsel for plaintiff objected to opening the case and admitting the sample as an exhibit. The trial court reopened the case, admitted the bottle of wax in evidence and gave it to the jury with instructions not to open the bottle for the purpose of experimenting with the wax. The foreman of the jury stated:

"The only thing would be so they could see how thin it was inside the bottle, and we could take it up with us."

Although the jury requested the sample, the case was reopened and the sample introduced as an exhibit at the request of the appellees. . . .

The appellant . . . contends that the reopening of the case and the admission of the bottle of wax as an exhibit constituted a clear and manifest abuse of discretion on the part of the trial court requiring a reversal.

Under the circumstances we would not interfere with the trial court's discretion if the sample of wax was otherwise admissible. However, the appellant's contention that "it was an abuse of discretion to admit into evidence the bottle of wax without the proper foundation having been laid for it," presents a much more serious question. The fact that a case is reopened for admission of additional evidence in the form of an exhibit furnishes no basis for the abandonment of the necessary preliminary proof to make it admissible.

The question which we have here is more a question of admissibility of evidence than a question of the trial court's discretion. If the evidence was not admissible it was not a discretionary matter.

Samples to be admissible as evidence must be shown to reflect the condition of the substance at the time involved in the issues. It must be shown that no substantial change has taken place in the substance to be exhibited because of lapse of time. Although we have no case in this state specifically in point the statement would appear to be the very general rule. In 32 C.J.S. Evidence § 607, page 765, we find the following:

". . . It must also be shown to the satisfaction of the court that no such substantial change in the article exhibited as to render the evidence misleading has taken place. The determination of whether there has been a change, so substantial or material, in an article or object, that it should not be admitted rests largely in the discretion of the trial court, and it is not necessary that the article be identically the same as at the time in controversy. . . ."

In 95 A.L.R.2d page 696, the general rule is stated in quite similar language:

"It has been generally held that at the time a sample is offered in evidence, it must be shown that it is in the same or substantially the same condition it was in at the time such condition became material to the issues involved; however, the fact that the offered sample has undergone some change in condition, whether occasioned by lapse of time, or otherwise, may not of itself afford sufficient grounds for excluding it. . . ."

Here there was no evidence whatsoever offered as to the condition of the four and one-half year old sample. . . .

The record discloses that the accident occurred on September 25, 1962. The sample bottle of wax was obtained in October or November, 1962. The case was tried and the sample submitted to the jury the latter part of May, 1967. The sample of wax stood in the bottle for four and one-half years before it was submitted to the jury. We are not informed as to how many times the cork was removed from the bottle or how well the cork was fitted to prevent evaporation. There are plant waxes, earth or bituminous waxes and synthetic waxes and each has a different volatile quality. . . . The waxes vary all the way from thin liquids to solids. It would be improper for us to assume that a liquid wax would remain four and one-half years in an unsealed bottle without a change in its consistency.

The only foundation laid for the admission of the bottle of wax was its source and chain of possession. We are inclined to believe that had it been intended to introduce the sample as an exhibit in the case in chief the jury would have been informed as to what happened to the sample of wax in the normal course of events while it remained in the bottle for four and one-half years. The thinness or thickness of the wax would mean nothing to the jury unless it was the same when delivered to them as at the time of the accident.

We must conclude that lacking proper preliminary proof the sample bottle of wax was improperly admitted as an exhibit.

We cannot agree with appellees' suggestion that the exhibit, even though erroneously admitted, did not affect the substantial rights of the parties. The much ado which was made about the bottle of wax must have left a rather deep impression on the members of the jury.

The judgment is reversed with instructions to grant a new trial.

Approved by the Court.

NOTES

1. The requirement of identification is not only designed to prevent the introduction of an object other than the one about which there has been testimony, but to insure that significant changes in the condition of the object have not occurred. See McElfresh v. Commonwealth, 243 S.W.2d 497 (Ky.1951). Some changes in condition are permitted. In Duke v. State, 58 So.2d 764, 769 (Ala.1952), a shell was admissible even though the sheriff scratched his initials into it for purposes of identification. The clothing worn by the deceased was introduced in Davidson v. State, 69 S.E.2d 757, 759 (Ga.1952), despite the fact that the deceased's widow had washed the clothes after having received them from the police. And in State v. Cooper, 92 A.2d 786, 798 (N.J.1952), the police dusted the murder weapon for fingerprints, found only useless fragments, and wiped the weapon clean. The weapon was held admissible. See also Brown v. State, 74 So.2d 273, 276, aff'd, 74 So.2d 277 (Ala.1954); 4 Wigmore 1154(6) (Chadbourn Rev.1972 & Supp.1980). In McElfresh v. Commonwealth, supra, each custodian but one was called as a witness. There was thus a gap in the chain of custody and no testimony that no change in condition had occurred during this interval. Each custodian who was produced testified that the object was in the same condition as when he had received it. And some of the custodians had possession before the unexplained interval while others had possession afterwards. Held: admission of the object was error. In view of the testimony presented, is this decision correct? Might your answer depend upon the purpose for which the object was admitted in evidence?

2. A bottle of cola containing a partially decomposed mouse was held admissible in Coca–Cola Bottling Co. v. Davidson, 102 S.W.2d 833, 835 (Ark.1937), even though in the interval from its purchase to its introduction at trial the color of the liquid had changed and the mouse had broken down into smaller pieces. "... [S]o long as delay, or even changed conditions by reason of delay do not destroy the evidentiary factor, ... is not improper to make it an exhibit.... [E]very one of common or ordinary intelligence must admit, the production and exhibition of the bottle was to show there was some foreign matter in it...."

3. In Franko v. State, 584 P.2d 678 (Nev.1978) the defendant was convicted of battery with intent to commit rape and robbery with use of a deadly weapon. The court held that the defendant's objection to the victim's possession of the blouse, which assertedly had been torn from her and from which buttons had been ripped at the time of the offense, and the objection to its altered conditions because the victim had attempted to mend it, went to the weight of the evidence, rather than to admissibility.

4. Where proper identification has failed, resourceful attorneys have attempted to introduce their evidence on the "replica" theory—that the object illustrates what the object looked like. Much depends upon the purpose of the proof. See Burns v. Bombard, 260 A.2d 219 (Vt.1969) (replica of dented auto fenders offered to prove extent of damage excluded because it did not show identical damage; discretion upheld); Sears Roebuck & Co. v. Daniels, 299 F.2d 154 (8th Cir.1962) (trial court had discretion to exclude a mat "similar" to one plaintiff had tripped over and to require oral descriptive testimony; appellate court indicated either decision would have been sustained).

In Young v. Price, 442 P.2d 67, 69 (Haw.1968), the trial court permitted the defendant construction company to put into evidence and stand in full sight of the jury throughout the trial a large yellow warning cone and an 18″ × 19″ red flag which stood 31″ high, although the presence of such cone and flag at the scene of the accident was hotly contested by the plaintiff. The appellate court ruled the admission of the "replica" to be an abuse of discretion by the trial court. The flag "stood like a flaming fireball ... (and) precluded any doubt in the minds of the jury as to its existence. Where there is a conflict in the testimony as to the presence of warning devices, ... the credibility of the witnesses is for the jury without an assist from the trial judge." What do you think of the appellate court's reading of the cases to conclude that, "There is an implication that demonstrative evidence must be based upon undisputed preliminary facts?" It held: "Admission ... was tantamount to the court telling the jury that there was a yellow cone and red flag to warn pedestrians and therefore defendant took the necessary and proper precautions." Is there a distinction between prejudice from introducing the objects and from allowing them to be before the jury during the entire trial?

SECTION 2.   DEMEANOR

State v. Murphy

Supreme Court of Washington, 1960.
56 Wn.2d 761, 355 P.2d 323.

■ FINLEY, JUDGE. Appellant, James Michael Murphy, was charged (by information filed by the state of Washington, respondent herein, on October 6, 1959) with the crime of murder in the first degree....

To this charge, appellant entered an oral plea of not guilty, and filed a special written plea of not guilty by reason of insanity. However, at the jury trial in King County superior court, appellant, testifying in his own behalf, freely and candidly admitted commission of the acts alleged in the information. Relying solely upon his special plea of insanity, he called upon two expert witnesses. . . .

We turn now to a consideration of appellant's third assignment of error, relating to the tranquilizing drugs. The facts regarding this aspect of the case are essentially undisputed. During the period prior to trial, at which time appellant was confined in the King County jail, he was interrogated on numerous occasions by his court-appointed counsel, Mr. Murray Guterson and Mr. Alfred Bianchi. On each of these occasions, according to the testimony of Mr. Guterson, appellant appeared to be

"... extremely nervous, extremely taut, extremely changing from a sweating condition to a very cold and clammy condition, and it made little or no difference what the topic or subject matter of our discussion concerned, we might be discussing matters entirely foreign to the actual proceedings which were to face us in April, and still his demeanor on all of these matters was such to make me feel as a layman that he was extremely nervous and taut and unable to properly express himself or to control his emotions satisfactorily. . . . "

After consultation between appellant and his counsel, it was decided that appellant should participate in the trial as a witness in his own behalf. Trial commenced on April 6, 1959. The state rested its case on the afternoon of April 7, 1959. On the morning of April 8, 1959, prior to being conducted from the county jail to the courtroom, appellant complained of a severe cold to one Robert Gibson, a fellow prisoner who was also serving as a medical trusty under the supervision of the jail physician. Gibson gave appellant a pill containing equanil, a tranquilizing drug, at about 8:30 a.m., and saw appellant take the pill. At about 9:00 a.m., Gibson gave appellant two pills containing trancopal, another tranquilizing drug, and saw him take one of them. Although appellant was told that these latter two pills were tranquilizers, he had never taken a tranquilizer before and did not know their effect.

Thereafter, appellant was conducted to the courtroom. He took his place on the witness stand at about 10:00 a.m. In response to questions posed by Mr. Guterson, he first described in some detail the events of his life leading up to the commission of the crime charged. He then candidly testified with respect to his commission of the criminal act itself.

According to the undisputed testimony of Mr. Bianchi and Mr. Guterson, appellant's appearance, demeanor, and manner of speaking while on the witness stand were markedly different from what they had been during the numerous pretrial interrogations. . . .

Mr. Guterson testified:

"Q. Did you notice any difference, in your opinion, in his demeanor or attitude or expression? A. I most certainly did. I noticed a change that was beyond comprehension in my humble opinion as a layman. It was an entirely different approach to the entire subject matter and I was at a loss to understand it."

Appellant has not claimed, either before the trial court or on this appeal, that the tranquilizing drugs affected the *content* of his testimony. He has not asserted that the fact he testified while under the influence of the drugs had any bearing upon the jury's general verdict finding him guilty of first degree murder, as charged. Rather, defense counsel's contention in the trial court and on this appeal is that, but for appellant's casual, cool, somewhat lackadaisical attitude, appearance and demeanor, induced by the tranquilizer drugs, the jury might not have imposed the death penalty. The trial judge's answer to this claim, as stated in his oral ruling denying the motion for new trial, was that

"... although I believe the tranquilizer relaxed him [the appellant], I feel that it did not affect the jury in their verdict."

The difficulty with this answer is that neither the trial judge nor the members of this court on appeal can know to what extent, if any, appellant's attitude and appearance as a witness influenced the jury with respect to the penalty to be imposed. Pursuant to RCW 9.48.030, full and absolute responsibility has been placed upon the jury to determine whether, in a first degree murder case, the death penalty shall be imposed. However, the statute does not set forth any criteria to be considered by the jury in exercising this grave responsibility. Yet, as a practical, common-sense matter, it can hardly be denied that in a case such as this, where the defendant appears as a witness and admits committing the criminal acts charged, constituting first degree murder, a significant consideration in the minds of the members of the jury respecting the penalty to be imposed may well be their evaluation of defendant's attitude in regard to the crime he has committed.

Article I, § 22 (amendment 10) of our state constitution, declares that

"In criminal prosecutions, the accused shall have the right to appear and defend in person."

Of this right, this court, in State v. Williams, 1897, 18 Wash. 47, 50 P. 580, 581, 39 L.R.A. 821, stated:

"The right here declared is to appear with the use of not only his mental but his physical faculties unfettered."

We believe that this right is of particular significance in a case such as that now before us, where the matter of the life or death of the accused may well depend upon the attitude, demeanor and appearance he presents to the members of the jury, who are the ultimate determiners of his fate. In such a case, strong and compelling reasons manifestly exist for careful judicial scrutiny of every aspect of the trial afforded to the accused to the end that a new trial be granted in the event of a showing by the accused of a reasonable possibility that his attitude, appearance, and demeanor, as observed by the jury, have been substantially influenced or affected by circumstances over which he had no real control. We are satisfied that such a showing has been made in the instant case, i.e., it reasonably appears in the instant case that the attitude, appearance, and demeanor of the accused may have been influenced by the tranquilizer drugs, administered to him under at least a semblance of authority or approval from the public officers who had custody over him, and taken by the accused apparently without awareness of their probable effect upon him.

... In any event, in the instant case, we are convinced for the reasons indicated above that a new trial should be granted. It is so ordered.

■ WEAVER, C.J., and DONWORTH, ROSELLINI, FOSTER and HUNTER, JJ., concur.

■ HILL, MALLERY and OTT, JJ., would affirm.

NOTES

1. Rhodes, A Thin Disguise, N.Y. Times Magazine, July 19, 1987, p. 62:

We all wear disguises. The simple act of dressing is a disguising. Clothes are disguises, beards, pitch of voice, what we say, what we keep secret. Costumes declare us, but disguises protect us from exposure. Wearing them, we blend in. Every salesman dressing for a client knows the drill, every young intern pulling on a white lab coat, every recent graduate struggling with an unfamiliar suit and tie.

Are there limits in the courtroom?

2. See generally on the use of psychotropic drugs, B.J. Winick, Psychotropic Medication and Competence to Stand Trial, 1977 Am.Bar Found.Research J. 769. The author indicates that generally use of these drugs will not interfere with defendant's mental processes—i.e., his competency to stand trial. But note that that problem in the main case is different. Is it ethical to give a client such a drug to calm him or her down so that demeanor will be more favorable? How can opposing counsel or the court deal with this practice? Cf. Note, The Forcible Medication of Involuntarily Committed Mental Patients with Antipsychotic Drugs—Rogers v. Okin, 15 Georgia L.Rev. 739 (1981). See Riggins v. Nevada, 504 U.S. 127 (1992) (forced administration of antipsychotic medication during trial violated defendant's rights under the Sixth and Fourteenth Amendments).

3. What are the ethical limits, if any, on an attorney's instructing his witness to dress in a certain way or react calmly rather than aggressively on cross-examination? May he suggest that an excitable witness take valium or other drug to appear calmer than he otherwise would? Cf. United States v. Thoreen, 653 F.2d 1332 (9th Cir.1981): Counsel arranged for a man resembling the defendant to sit at counsel table while the defendant sat in the audience; counsel and the look-alike consulted with each other in the jury's presence as would an attorney and client and counsel did not correct the court when it referred to the look-alike as the defendant. From the witness stand, the witnesses identified the look-alike as the person involved in the crime. Although defendant was ultimately convicted, a great deal of confusion resulted. In upholding a criminal contempt finding against the defense counsel and finding this behavior a violation of the court order to exclude witnesses from the courtroom, the court noted:

> While we agree that defense counsel should represent his client vigorously, regardless of counsel's view of guilt or innocence,.... Washington Code of Professional Responsibility (CPR), Canon 7, we conclude that Thoreen's conduct falls outside this protected behavior.
>
> Vigorous advocacy by defense counsel may properly entail impeaching or confusing a witness, even if counsel thinks the witness is truthful, and refaining from presenting evidence even if he knows the truth.... When we review this conduct and find that the line between vigorous advocacy and actual obstruction is close, our doubts should be resolved in favor of the former.
>
> The latitude allowed an attorney is not unlimited. He must represent his client within the bounds of the law. CPR Canon 7. As an officer of the court, he must "preserve and promote the efficient operation of our system of justice."
>
> Thoreen's view of appropriate cross-examination, which encompasses his substitution, crossed over the line from zealous advocacy to actual obstruction because, as we discuss later, it impeded the court's search for truth, resulted in delays, and violated a court custom and rule. Moreover,

this conduct harms rather than enhances an attorney's effectiveness as an advocate.

> It is fundamental that in relations with the court, defense counsel must be scrupulously candid and truthful in representations of any matter before the court. This is not only a basic ethical requirement, but it is essential if the lawyer is to be effective in the role of advocate, for if the lawyer's reputation for veracity is suspect, he or she will lack the confidence of the court when it is needed most to serve the client.

American Bar Association Standards for Criminal Justice, The Defense Function 4.9 (1980) (footnote omitted) (herein The Defense Function). . . .

> Making misrepresentations to the court is also inappropriate and unprofessional behavior under ethical standards that guide attorneys' conduct. These guidelines, in effect in Washington and elsewhere, decree explicitly that an attorney's participation in the presentation or preservation of false evidence is unprofessional and subjects him to discipline. See CPR DR 7–102(A)(4), (5), (6); EC 7–6, 7–26; The Defense Function 4.93.

> Substituting a person for the defendant in a criminal case without a court's knowledge has been noted as an example of unethical behavior by the ABA Committee on Professional Ethics. See Informal Opinion No. 914, 2/24/66 (decided under the former ABA Code of Professional Responsibility). . . .

> Making misrepresentations to the fact finder is inherently obstructive because it frustrates the rational search for truth. It may also delay the proceedings. In In re Dellinger, 502 F.2d 813, 816 (7th Cir.1974), cert. denied, 420 U.S. 990, 95 S.Ct. 1425, 43 L.Ed.2d 671 (1975), for example, the Seventh Circuit held that an attorney obstructed justice by putting inadmissible evidence before the jury hampering its ability to decide the case according to the legal principles provided them. A witness's sham denial of knowledge similarly obstructs justice by closing off avenues of inquiry and stifling a jury's ability to ascertain the truth. United States v. Griffin, 589 F.2d 200, 205 (5th Cir.), cert. denied, 444 U.S. 825, 100 S.Ct. 48, 62 L.Ed.2d 32 (1979).

Id. at 1338–40.

Compare United States v. Murray, 523 F.2d 489, 490, 492 (8th Cir.1975): it was not error for the prosecution to require the defendant to place a wig, similar to one found in his possession when arrested, on his head to assist the witness and jury in determining whether he was in fact the person who had been photographed wearing the wig while participating in the robbery.

4. Rains v. Rains, 8 A.2d 715, 717–718, rev'd, 12 A.2d 857 (N.J.1940): Court refused to grant an uncontested divorce because it disbelieved the testimony of the witnesses based on their demeanor when testifying:

> Multitudinous things are indicated by the word "demeanor", when the appearance of witnesses and their manner of testifying are referred to in the books. "And the courts have repeatedly declared that it is one of the most important functions of the trial judge, in determining the value and weight of the evidence, to consider the demeanor of the witness. They have called attention, as of the gravest importance, to such facts as the tone of voice in which a witness' statement is made, the hesitation or readiness with which his answers are given, the look of the witness, his carriage, his evidences of surprise, his gestures, his zeal, his bearing, his expression, his yawns, the use of his eyes, his furtive or meaning glances, or his shrugs, the pitch of his voice, his self-possession or embarrassment, his air of

candor or seeming levity." Jerome Frank, Law and the Modern Mind, 1931. Evidence of demeanor to the extent that it appears or is perceived in a trial court may be said, I think, to be "real" evidence in a very real sense.

When a judge in chancery functions at a hearing it is to be assumed that he does his duty, that is, that he observes the appearance of witnesses and their manner of testifying, in an endeavor to discover the truth; and that in so doing, that he uses his experience and every apprehending and perceiving faculty, with his judiciousness and his conscience joined in the process. And when he finds a witness to be honest or a liar, the matter is not made any clearer by calling what he has done "recognition," or "inspiration," as one prominent psychologist calls a similar process, or by calling what he has done "a hunch", as does an eminent judge. To label his finding of fact is not to tell what has taken place. In observing the demeanor of a witness and in coming to a conclusion on that demeanor a judge does not use any approved formulas; nor does he practice any art; nor does he proceed in any scientific way. So there is no terminology that he may employ to explain to an appellate court what has taken place. And, probably in most cases, he may not be able to satisfactorily declare, even to himself, the total process, to call it a process, that resulted in his being convinced. But in observing the appearance of witnesses and their manner of testifying, he has functioned as he should in properly coming to a conclusion concerning the true facts of the controversy before him for decision.

It is because of the demeanor circumstances that "can be manifest only to one who actually hears and sees the witnesses that upper courts have frequently stated that they are hesitant to overturn the decision of the trial judge in a case where the evidence has been based upon oral testimony; for the upper courts have recognized that they have before them only a stenographic or printed report of the testimony, and that such a black and white report cannot reproduce anything but the cold words of the witness. 'The tongue of the witness', it has been said, 'is not the only organ for conveying testimony'. Yet, it is only the words that can be transmitted to the reviewing court, while the story that is told by the manner, by the tone, by the eyes, must be lost to all but him who observes the witness on the stand." Jerome Frank, Law and the Modern Mind, 1931.

An appellate court can hardly set aside a dismissal of a petition for divorce on the ground that the finding of a judge in chancery is "palpably against the evidence" when the dismissal is rested upon a finding of fact based on demeanor evidence, which finding has gone to the appellate court as a fact, as established evidence, but which evidence may not, because of its nature, be examined in the appellate court. There is nothing in the appellate court as a logical or a legal base for its disestablishment. There is nothing whatever for the appellate court to lay its hands on. The demeanor evidence appeared in the trial court and it entirely disappeared there. It cannot be resurrected in any way in the appellate court. It is not communicable to the appellate court. I have called demeanor evidence "real" evidence, to emphasize what I am stating.

In reversing 12 A.2d 857, 860 (N.J.1940) the appellate court declared: "[W]here the testimony would be sufficient to establish grounds for divorce, and that testimony is unimpeached, uncontested and not inherently improbable, we do not think that a mere general observation of demeanor, unsupported by examples of action or attitude which would inspire disbelief, is sufficient to support a finding that the testimony was untrue."

5. Compare Stores v. State, 625 P.2d 820, 828–829 (Alaska 1980), where the use of video tape of deposition testimony was held to be reversible error:

> Significant differences exist between testimony by videotape and testimony face-to-face with the jury. Videotape may affect the jurors' impressions of the witness' demeanor and credibility. Such considerations are of particular importance when the demeanor and credibility of the witness are crucial to the state's case. . . .
>
> Moreover, there is a further distinction between trial testimony and videotaped testimony taken prior to trial which may have significance here. With videotape, the witness cannot be cross-examined in the context of other evidence and testimony which has been presented at trial. . . .
>
> The use of videotape in the trial process is relatively new. Its real impact remains undetermined. This is not to say that a videotaped deposition should never be used at trial; in fact, it may provide the most reliable and accurate means of preserving testimony when the witness is truly unavailable for trial. It is quite a different matter, however, to conclude that the erroneous admission of a videotaped deposition of a crucial witness, who was available to testify at trial, had no effect on the outcome of the trial.

In a footnote, the court stated:

> As one commentator has pointed out, there is a potential for distortion of a juror's perception of a witness whose testimony is presented by videotape.
>
>> "Some courts and legal commentators have assumed that evidence recorded on videotape can simply be transported from courtroom to television monitor with little or no effect upon it. In reality, however, the camera unintentionally becomes the juror's eyes, necessarily selecting and commenting upon what is seen. . . .
>>
>> "Evidence distortion is most serious when videotaping a witness because the picture conveyed may influence a juror's feelings about guilt or believability. . . . Variations in lens or angle, may result in failure to convey subtle nuances, including changes in witness demeanor such as a nervous twitch or paling and blushing in response to an important question, all of which are potentially important to jury decision making. Whether testimony is taped in black and white or in more expensive color may also be of critical importance.
>>
>> "Furthermore, the camera itself is selective of what it relates to the viewer. Transmission of valuable first impressions may be impossible, and off-camera evidence is necessarily excluded while the focus is on another part of the body or another witness." (footnote omitted).

Id., citing Note, The Criminal Videotape Trial: Serious Constitutional Questions, 55 Or.L.Rev. 567, 574–76 (1976). The dissenting judge, arguing in favor of the use of videotape testimony stated:

> A videotape records the demeanor of a witness with even more faithfulness than a sound recording. With regard to the latter, we said in McBride v. State, 368 P.2d 925, 928–29 (Alaska 1962) (footnotes omitted), cert. denied, 374 U.S. 811 (1963):

The entire direct and cross-examination were played back through a high fidelity loudspeaker mounted on the courtroom wall. The jury was able to hear the inflections of voice which are so often important. They were able to note the readiness and promptness of the witness's answers or the reverse; the distinctness of what he related or lack of it; the directness or evasiveness of his answers; the frankness or equivocation; the responsiveness or reluctance to answer questions; the silences; the explanations; the contradictions; and the apparent intelligence or lack of it. These are vital elements touching upon the witness's veracity which are available in this jurisdiction to be noted and weighed by a jury even when the witness is not present in person. To a large extent, then, demeanor evidence is available for a subsequent jury; it is no longer wholly "elusive and incommunicable" as in the case of manual reporting of former testimony.

Id. at 830. The dissent represents the view of most judges.

On November 18, 1971, a civil jury trial in Ohio was conducted by videotape. Only the opening and closing statements were "live." The entire testimony had been recorded on a master tape; after a pre-trial conference, the jury tape was prepared with all objectionable testimony edited out. The judge also recorded his charge. The trial itself thus took markedly less time, and left all participants not unexpectedly enthusiastic. See Symposium, 45 Ohio Bar 1, 25, 45 (January 3, 1972). See also de Vries, Videotapes in Depositions, 11 For The Defense 113 (Dec.1970); Merlo and Sorenson, Video Tape: The Coming Courtroom Tool, Trial, Nov. 1971, 55. What are the advantages and disadvantages of this practice?

The Supreme Court sent to Congress in 1996 an amendment to Rule 43 of the Federal Rules of Civil Procedure. The Rule, showing strike outs of matter omitted and underlining of new material, reads as follows:

(a) Form. In ~~all~~ every trial, the testimony of witness shall be taken ~~orally~~ in open court, unless ~~otherwise provided by an Act of Congress or by~~ a federal law, these rules, the Federal Rules of Evidence, or other rules adopted by the Supreme Court provide otherwise. The court may, for good cause shown in compelling circumstances and upon appropriate safeguards, permit presentation of testimony in open court by contemporaneous transmission from a different location.

Should the words "or the court for good cause shown" be added after the words "Supreme Court" in the first sentence. Would this, particularly in mass torts, permit a saving of considerable money and allow the courts to attract eminent neutral scientists pursuant to Rule 706 of the Federal Rules of Evidence. They could be appointed to a national panel, be examined and cross examined by all interested counsel and then not be called again. The rule as drafted would not permit their video testimony to be used since they are theoretically "available" under the deposition rule and the transmission is not contemporaneous. Only on a promise that they will not have to disrupt their treatment and research schedules could eminent neutral scientists be induced to testify. As Rule 43 was adopted probably only scientists whose testimony is paid for by the parties will testify repeatedly. The situation created by some of these professional testifiers has led to considerable criticism of our legal system. See e.g., Michael D. Green, *Bendectin and Birth Defects, The Challenge of Mass Toxic Substances Litigation* (U. of Pa. Press 1996); Marcia Angell, M.D., *Science on Trial, The Clash of Medical Evidence and The Law in The Breast Implant Case* (W.W. Norton & Co. 1996). See court appointed experts, infra.

Are videotaped trials sometimes too antiseptic? See, e.g., "First Taped Trial Set in Slaying Case," N.Y. Times, March 22, 1982, p. 11, col. 1:

SANDUSKY, Ohio, March 21 (AP)—When the murder trial of 19–year–old David Lange begins Monday in Erie County Common Pleas Court there will be no objections to testimony, no arguments about evidence and no lengthy conferences at the judge's bench.

All that has been edited out, in the first murder trial to be conducted on videotape....

Both Judge McCrystal and Mr. Lange's attorney, George Howells, say there is no need for a jury to watch the defendant's behavior in a trial.

"That's not evidence," Mr. Howells said. "The defendant's courtroom behavior is not to be considered by a jury. But we all know it is. This method is more 'pure' in that sense."

However, Judge McCrystal warns that there is potential for manipulating a jury's emotions through videotape.

"Any evidentiary material can be abused," he said. "But videotape can be edited before a jury ever sees it. A prejudicial question, once asked, can't be erased from a juror's mind—you can't unring a bell."

Compare People v. Diaz, 445 N.Y.S.2d 888 (N.Y.Sup.Ct.1981) (government has the right to "introduce" a person claimed by defendant to have committed crime charged: jury should be permitted to compare this person with defendant and the description furnished by witnesses). Does such a comparison violate defendant's right against self incrimination? See Chapter 8, section 2, infra. How would such a comparison be accomplished in a televised trial such as that described in this note, supra?

Distinguished videotapes of the events in question as in People v. Eisenberg, 238 N.E.2d 719 (N.Y.C.A.1968), infra, or the Abscam tapes, Application of National Broadcasting Co., Inc., 635 F.2d 945 (2d Cir.1980). What of legal arguments where the attorneys argue to a bench in a different city? See Robin Topping, Cameras in the [Appellate] Court, Newsday, April 23, 1997, p. A29 (Second Circuit Court of Appeals will hear in New York lawyers at many city's in the circuit; all lawyers and judges appear on the screen; fee is $200 per argument). Why shouldn't the public see these tapes?

6. See United States v. Salim, 664 F.Supp. 682 (E.D.N.Y.1987), where letters rogatory to take the deposition of a key witness were used against the defendant in a criminal case:

Defendant also objected to introduction of the deposition because it was not recorded on video or aural tape, as contemplated in the government's papers seeking issuance of a request for judicial assistance to the French court. This objection is directed to the jury's inability to observe the witness' demeanor while she was testifying. The only evidence of the witness' demeanor presented at trial was the testimony of the court reporter, Michael Picozzi, describing the witness and indicating that she was on the verge of tears throughout the deposition.

Demeanor of a witness, whether on or off the witness stand, may be observed by the jury both on the issue of credibility and, where relevant, as evidence-in-chief. See, e.g., United States v. Schipani, 293 F.Supp. 156, 163

(E.D.N.Y.1968), aff'd, 414 F.2d 1262 (2d Cir.1969), cert. denied, 397 U.S. 922 (1970); Georgia Home Insurance Co. v. Campbell, 29 S.E. 148, 149 (Ga.1897). Where the witness is not present, as in the case of a deposition, someone who observed the deposition may describe what occurred. Morrow v. Wyrick, 646 F.2d 1229 (8th Cir.), cert. denied, 454 U.S. 899 (1981). That description may include the setting as well as the demeanor and words of the declarant. The witness to the declaration is present at the trial and subject to cross-examination before the jury. This commonsensical result is supported by Rule 806 of the Federal Rules of Evidence. It permits evidence on "credibility of the declarant" to the same extent as "if declarant had testified as a witness."

This case is quite unlike Gill v. Stolow, 16 F.R.D. 9 (S.D.N.Y.1954). In that case the deposition was being taken before a United States Vice Consul in Germany. The Vice Consul gratuitously indicated on the record that the deponent "referred constantly to a copy of the interrogatories ... on which he had entered comments in longhand," and "referred frequently to a piece of paper on which he had jotted down certain dates and facts." 16 F.R.D. 9. In addition, the Vice Consul noted "that the witness interrupted the questioning at one point to eat hazel nuts and drink a glass of water, and that he stated it was always necessary for him to eat something when he became nervous." Id. The court properly suppressed these portions of the deposition which were hearsay. There was no opportunity to question the Vice Consul about the accuracy of his observations. In the case now before us, by contrast, the official court reporter, who observed the deponent's demeanor, was present at the trial in this court, subject to examination and cross-examination. The reporter testified to his recollection of observations he had made directly. This is not hearsay. The only reason for excluding this testimony would be lack of relevancy. This testimony was, however, highly relevant on the issue of the deponent's credibility and thus was properly admitted under Rules 401–403 of the Federal Rules of Evidence.

7.   People v. Kroeger, 390 P.2d 369, 373 (Cal. 1964):

It is contended ... that the court erred in not holding a hearing to determine her [defendant's] sanity as of the time of the trial. The lengthy trial was marked by much disruptive and erratic conduct by Iva [defendant] which started during the selection of the jury, increased in frequency as time went by, and included several hundred comments and outbursts.... Her most bizarre behavior began about a month after the trial commenced. She made statements purporting to indicate a belief that the reason she was appearing in court was to obtain custody of her "babies". Her conduct also included the singing of songs while on the witness stand and the making of repeated statements that she was the mother of God and that Ralph was her father. Uncontradicted psychiatric testimony was introduced at the guilt trial that Iva was a cunning and diabolical liar, that her conduct in court did not show insanity, and that she was feigning insanity.... Where prior to judgment a doubt arises as to the present sanity of a defendant ... a hearing must be had to determine that question, but whether the doubt exists is a matter resting within the discretion of the trial judge....

Held, no abuse of discretion. To what extent is the trial court justified in relying on his estimate of defendant's behavior in court? See People v. Merkouris, 344 P.2d 1, 4–5 (Cal.1959).

8.   Georgia Home Insurance Co. v. Campbell, 29 S.E. 148, 149 (Ga.1897):

Exception is taken to the following charge to the jury: "You are authorized to consider the manner of the witnesses on the stand, and their conduct in your presence as they gave their evidence; ... you may consider their testimony in the light of personal appearance and conduct of the witnesses." Unquestionably, the manner and conduct of witnesses on the stand are legitimate matters for consideration by the jury; and this is equally true as to the "appearance" of the witnesses, in so far as the word just quoted relates to manner or conduct, or to the way in which the witnesses gave their testimony. The expression upon the face of a witness, the look in his eyes, the intonation of his voice, the promptness or hesitancy with which he replies to questions, all these things and others indefinable in words may be considered as constituting the "appearance" of the witness; and, whether so instructed or not, any intelligent jury would necessarily be impressed favorably or unfavorably by these outward signs and manifestations.

9.   Goleman, Studies Point to Power of Nonverbal Signals, N.Y. Times, April 8, 1986, p. C1, col. 1:

The nonverbal messages people send, with a look, a gesture, a tone of voice, are far more pervasive and important in the workaday world than have been generally realized, researchers are finding. But they are concluding, too, that these messages are more complex and subtle than the popular accounts of "body language" that have appeared in recent years have indicated.

Such covert cues, the new data show, have a strong impact in key relationships such as those between judge and jury, physician and patient, or teacher and student. . . .

How a judge gives his instructions to a jury was perceived to double the likelihood that the jury would deliver a verdict of guilty or not guilty—even when on the surface the judge's demeanor seemed perfectly impartial . . .

And findings of the new research are likely to have repercussions in areas of life where it is crucial to avoid bias, even the most subtle. For example, according to some legal experts, one consequence of the study of research of judges, if it is borne out by further research, may be to provide a more precise basis for showing when a judge may have silently biased a trial. . . . One striking finding concerned trials in which the judge knew that the defendant had a record of previous felonies, a fact that a jury, by law, is not allowed to know unless the defendant takes the stand. When the judges were aware of past felonies, the Stanford study found, their final instructions to juries were lacking in warmth, tolerance, patience and competence.

The juries in these cases said they were unaware of any bias on the part of the judges, yet their verdicts were twice as likely to be "guilty" than in cases in which the charges were as serious but defendants had no record of felonies.

When videotapes were analyzed by independent raters, they found that the judges' tone of voice, rather than anything in their words or body movements, communicated the strongest, most negative messages.

"Judges can't come out and say, 'This defendant is guilty,' " said Peter Blanck, who did the study.[1] "But they may say it subtly, nonverbally—even if that message is inadvertent."

---

1. Blanck, The Appearance of Justice: Criminal Trials, 38 Stanf.L.Rev. 89 (1985). Judges' Verbal and Non Verbal Behavior in

See also P. Levi, Moments of Reprieve, 100 (1986) ("Those who bear witness by their behavior are the most valuable witnesses, because they are certainly truthful."). Compare Johnson, "Testimony of Youth that is Thrown Out," N.Y. Times, May 29, 1987, p. 1, col 2. James Ramseur, a youth shot in the subway by defendant Goetz along with three companions, refused to testify further for the prosecution and his testimony was "stricken." His tantrum was so terrifying that jurors later indicated that they were afraid the witness would attack them. Since the critical issue was whether the defendant was fearful of an attack, most observers believed this "evidence" was the most critical in this celebrated case. How could the judge have dealt with the problem? The court reportedly told the jury: "The entirety of the testimony of James Ramseur has been stricken and it is not for your consideration in this case. It is no longer any proof in this case for your consideration." Id. In sentencing the witness for contempt, however, he declared: "The jurors saw your contemptuous conduct—that they can never erase from their minds. That conduct conveyed viciousness and selfishness more eloquently than words could." Id. at p. B4, col. 3. The case also featured a view in a subway car similar to the one where the incident occurred. In the courtroom an exact diagram of the car was taped to the floor and professional actors enacted defendant's version of the incident with the help of an expert. Id.

10. State v. Clark, 58 A. 796, 797 (Vt.1904): prosecution for assault with intent to carnally know a female person under the age of sixteen years. "Counsel for the State argued to the jury regarding the girl's appearance when being examined in court, saying that 'the recollection of those terrible moments down there still brings tears of shame to her face.' This was held to be legitimate, to which the respondent excepted. The appearance of a witness on the stand may always be taken into consideration by the jury. Consequently counsel may properly argue concerning it."

Pooschke v. Union Pacific Railroad Co., 426 P.2d 866, 870 (Or.1967): defendant's motion for a mistrial "because tears came to plaintiff's eyes when plaintiff's counsel asked plaintiff how looking at his injured leg affected him," was denied.

11. Quercia v. United States, 289 U.S. 466 (1933): Petitioner was convicted of violating the Narcotic Act after a trial in which he testified in his own behalf. He sought reversal on the ground that the following instructions of the judge to the jury exceeded the bounds of fair comment and constituted prejudicial error: "And now I am going to tell you what I think of the defendant's testimony. You may have noticed, Mr. Foreman and gentlemen, that he wiped his hands during his testimony. It is rather a curious thing, but that is almost always an indication of lying. Why it should be so we don't know, but that is the fact. I think that every single word that he said, except when he agreed with the Government's testimony, was a lie. Now, that opinion is an opinion of evidence and is not binding on you, and if you don't agree with it, it is your duty to find him not guilty." Reversed. (i) In a trial by jury in a federal court the judge may by his instructions explain and comment upon the evidence and also express his opinion upon the facts, provided he makes it clear to the jury that all matters of fact are submitted to their determination. But in commenting upon testimony he may not distort it or add to it. (ii) "In the instant case, the trial judge did not analyze the evidence; he added to it, and he based his instruction upon his own addition. Dealing with a mere mannerism of the accused in giving his testimony, the judge put his own experience, with all the weight that could be attached to it, in the scale against the accused. He told the jury that 'wiping' one's hands while testifying was 'almost always an indication of lying.' Why it should be so, he was unable to say, but it was 'the fact.' He did not review the evidence to assist the jury in reaching the truth, but in a sweeping denunciation repudiated as a lie all that the accused had said in his own behalf which conflicted with the statements of the Government's witnesses. This was error and we cannot doubt that it was highly prejudicial." (iii) "Nor do we think that the error was cured by the statement of the trial judge that his opinion of the evidence was not binding on the jury and that if they did not agree with it they should find the defendant not guilty. His definite and concrete assertion of fact, which he had made with all the persuasiveness of judicial utterance, as to the basis of his opinion, was not withdrawn. His characterization of the manner and testimony of the accused was of a sort most likely to remain firmly lodged in the memory of the jury and to excite a prejudice which would preclude a fair and dispassionate consideration of the evidence."

12.   See United States v. Shonubi, 103 F.3d 1085 (2d Cir.1997). The trial court utilized, among other evidence in determining drugs smuggled on prior trips for guideline sentencing purposes, demeanor. In reversing, the court of appeals wrote:

> The demeanor evidence relates to Shonubi specifically, but, with all respect to the experienced District Judge's ability to gauge the character from defendant's demeanor, his conclusions about the defendant's "extremely low level of risk aversion and an overconfidence in his own powers," Id. [802 F.Supp. 859] at 489, are not based on "specific evidence" of the quantities carried on the prior seven trips.

NOTES ON DEMEANOR OFF THE WITNESS STAND

1.   Should there be a distinction made between the demeanor of a person testifying and of that person off the witness stand by the trier of fact? In United States v. Schipani, 293 F.Supp. 156, 163 (E.D.N.Y.1968), aff'd, 414 F.2d 1262 (2d Cir.1969), cert. denied, 397 U.S. 922 (1970), the court, in a non-jury, net worth tax fraud case, took note of the defendant's demeanor, although he did not testify. The court stated:

> In this case the conclusion that defendant was guilty beyond a reasonable doubt was reached solely on the record. Confirmation came from observation of the defendant in court.

2.   State v. McKinnon, 138 N.W. 523 (Iowa 1912), was a prosecution for "ravishing and carnally knowing" an imbecile girl of twenty, so deficient in understanding that she did not comprehend the nature of the act. "On behalf of the state, the illicit intercourse was proved by the testimony of the prosecuting witness and by corroborative evidence which was all but conclusive." The defendant was not a witness in his own behalf. "In the closing argument to the jury, the prosecuting attorney used the following language: ... 'While she is telling her story of shame and disgrace, the defendant sits here smiling, grinning at her, apparently gloating over his conquest.' This was objected to as 'improper, and as referring to something that cannot be in the record.' ... If the defendant conducted himself in the manner stated while the prosecutrix was upon the stand, he was necessarily subject to the observation of the jury, nor do we see any fair reason why reasonable comment upon such conduct might not be made in argument to the jury." Compare Morrison v. California, 291 U.S. 82, 94 (1934): In holding unconstitutional a criminal statute shifting to the defendant the burden of proving that he was not a member of various oriental races, the court reasoned that, where defendant was a full-blooded oriental, the jury will be able to determine this fact by looking at him sitting in the courtroom. Cf. Rich v. State, 266 P.2d 476, 478 (Okl.Cr.1954).

3. State v. Stacy, 160 A. 257, 267 (Vt.1932): Defendant was convicted of murder in the first degree. The victim was his wife. His

> defense was that he did not shoot his wife, but that if he did he was temporarily insane at the time and governed by an irresistible impulse, caused by information he had received concerning her improper relations with other men, and certain incidents which he had observed which corroborated that information. He took the stand and testified.... In the argument of the Attorney General, after commenting upon the examination of the respondent by Dr. O'Neil, and claiming that the former was then attempting to induce the belief that he was insane, attention was called to the fact that the respondent's counsel had been consulting with him during the trial. An exception was taken, upon the ground that such consultations were proper. Of course they were, as the court remarked at the time. But the point of the argument was that this conduct was inconsistent with the defense of insanity existing at the time of the crime; and with the erratic conduct of the respondent at Dr. O'Neil's visit to him. As we have seen, the mental condition of the respondent at the trial was material as having some bearing upon his claimed derangement on the prior date. The jury had the right to consider his appearance and actions and his apparent interest and participation in the trial, upon this question. The fact that it was not claimed that the respondent was then insane did not make the argument improper. The exception is not sustained.... The comment by the same counsel upon the inability of the respondent to meet his eye while testifying was not improper, because it was based upon his appearance upon the stand, while giving material evidence.

4. Henriod v. Henriod, 89 P.2d 222, 224–225 (Wash.1938): Plaintiff appealed from a judgment dismissing her complaint:

> Appellant contends that the court, in deciding the case ..., was controlled by matters not in issue, and in support of that contention calls to our attention the following portion of the trial judge's oral decision ...: "It seems to me from the attitude and the conduct of Mrs. Henriod on this case that she was endeavoring to recover something that she knew she wasn't entitled to. Now, may I call your attention to this fact: on the first day of the trial when she was called to the witness stand, it seemed almost impossible that she could mount that stand. She walked hesitatingly. Mr. Walker assisted her. She couldn't get up on that stand without assistance. He almost lifted her there. It was [a day or two later] when Mr. Williams called Mrs. Henriod over to the jury box there to assist him in some matters. She walked spryly as a girl across this court room. She mounted those steps over there alone without any assistance. She did that not only that time but repeatedly since. I didn't like that appearance at all. I didn't like the looks of things. That just throws some light on the case that it seems to me controls the entire testimony. I better not say any more. You may prepare your findings." ... We do not see any reflection of error in the court's statement. Considered as a whole, it only indicates that the court was observant not only of the facts testified to in the court room, but also of the attitude and conduct of the witness during the progress of the trial. To watch the attitude and demeanor of a witness testifying at a trial is not only the right but also the duty of the trier of facts.

See 2 Belli, Modern Trials 1535 (1954): "I have seen designing counsel for defendant deliberately and repeatedly engage a plaintiff in discussion during recess, laughing and smiling, to minimize complaints of serious injury. Jurors observe the demeanor of a witness in the corridor as well as on the witness stand."

5. In Conkey v. New York Central Railroad, 136 N.Y.S.2d 189, 193 (N.Y.Sup. Ct.1954), the court held that photographs showing plaintiff's injuries were properly admitted, since they no more tended to inflame the jury than the view the jury had throughout the trial of plaintiff sitting in his wheelchair.

6. Claffey v. Claffey, 64 A.2d 540, 541 (Conn.1949), sustained the trial judge in drawing inferences as to the degree of affection between a child and the child's mother and grandmother from observation of their conduct in the courtroom, where at least the mother and grandmother testified, cites earlier Connecticut decisions making rather delicate distinctions between permissible probative consequences of observations by the trier of fact respecting conduct (a) of persons who testify and (b) of persons present in the courtroom who do not testify or at least are not testifying when their conduct is observed.

7. In Stein v. New York, 346 U.S. 156, 181–183 (1953), the Supreme Court said that the trial judge and the jury have an advantage over the appellate court in determining whether a confession is coerced. For, said the Court, the trial judge and jury can observe the witnesses and parties. But note that defendants in the case at bar did not take the stand.

8. Should it make any difference whether the off-stand demeanor does or does not support the actor's position? See Stein, Process of Undercover Investigation, II, 22 Ins.Counsel J. 357, 360–64 (1955), dealing with the use of motion pictures taken by defendant of plaintiff's daily activities to show that plaintiff is not as severely injured as is alleged. Cf. Annot., Motion Pictures as Evidence, 62 A.L.R.2d 686 (1958).

9. Compare the annotation, manifestations of grief, crying and the like by victim or family of victim during criminal trial as ground for reversal, new trial or mistrial in 46 A.L.R.2d 949 (1956).

SECTION 3. VIEWS

People v. Crimmins

Court of Appeals of New York, 1970.
26 N.Y.2d 319, 310 N.Y.S.2d 300, 258 N.E.2d 708.

■ BURKE, JUDGE. Defendant was indicted for, and convicted of, killing her daughter. At the trial the People established that the child died of strangulation within two or three hours of her last meal. The body was found at about 2:00 P.M., on July 14, 1965, and an autopsy determined that death occurred approximately 8 to 24 hours prior to discovery. Two of the People's witnesses, Sophie Earomirski and Joseph Rorech, presented substantially all of the evidence which connected defendant to the crime. The former testified that at about 2:00 A.M., on July 14, 1965, she saw defendant carrying a bundle and holding the hand of a little boy; she was accompanied by a man. Defendant's companion took the bundle and threw it into an automobile, and Mrs. Earomirski, from her third floor window across the street, heard defendant say, "My God, don't do that to *her*." Mr. Rorech testified that at a subsequent time defendant admitted to him, "Joseph, please forgive me, I killed her."

Although defendant raised several alleged errors in the Appellate Division, reversal was predicated on only one—an unauthorized visit by three jurors to the neighborhood which was the subject of Mrs. Earomirski's testimony.... A hearing was held, and the juror, Samuel Ehrlich, testified that, after Mrs. Earomirski had testified, he wanted to see that area. He went there between 1:00 and 2:00 A.M. Ehrlich further testified that his visit did not influence his opinion.

Another visit was made by Ehrlich and two other jurors, Harry Tunis and Irving Furst, at about 5:30 P.M.

During the jury's deliberations the lighting in the area was discussed in "small talk" and, according to Ehrlich, someone mentioned that the area was well-lit. Another juror, Philip Seidman, testified that the subject was discussed.

During the length of the trial, the jurors were never admonished not to visit any place which had been the subject of testimony. Ironically, after Mrs. Earomirski had testified, defense counsel requested that the court arrange a controlled visit to the area. The court denied the visit as unnecessary.

In People v. De Lucia, this court held: "In this type of case, proof of the fact of the unauthorized visit is sufficient to warrant a new trial without proof of how such visit may have influenced individual jurors in their juryroom deliberations. *Such a visit, in and of itself, constitutes inherent prejudice to the defendants.*" (20 N.Y.2d 275, 280, 282 N.Y.S.2d 526, 529, 229 N.E.2d 211, 214 [emphasis supplied].) Appellant's attempt to distinguish De Lucia fails to comprehend the nature of the decision in that case. Although the affidavit averred that the jurors had re-enacted the crime, we did not predicate our decision on actual prejudice. That discussion merely demonstrates one of the manifest evils of an unauthorized visit. Since De Lucia was in the court on mere allegations, a hearing was ordered, and the afore-quoted statement indicates the quantum of proof which would mandate a new trial. The defendants were not required to establish prejudice....

The attempt to distinguish the view made herein from one of the scene of a crime is also without merit. Mrs. Earomirski's ability to see and hear the events to which she testified depended very much on the lighting in the area and the distances involved. And the credibility of her testimony is essential to the prosecution's case. The Legislature perceived the evil in such a view and directed court supervision of views of the place where the crime is alleged to have been committed or where "any material fact occurred" (Code Crim.Proc., § 411). The statutory inclusion is sound, and we ought not to make a tenuous distinction....

Order affirmed.

NOTES

1. Why do you think the trial court denied the request for a view in Crimmins? What kinds of problems do you think it was trying to avoid? Assuming that no proof of juror's visits had been adduced, could defendant have successfully argued on appeal that he was denied the right to introduce relevant evidence when his application for a view by the jury was rejected?

In People v. De Lucia, 229 N.E.2d 211 (N.Y.C.A.1967), relied on in the main case, the jury had made an unauthorized visit and partially re-enacted the alleged crime. The court reversed the conviction: "To use the reasoning of the Supreme Court in Parker v. Gladden, 385 U.S. 363, 87 S.Ct. 468, 17 L.Ed.2d 420 (1966), these jurors became unsworn witnesses against the defendants in direct contravention of their right, under the Sixth Amendment, 'to be confronted with the witnesses' against them." Cf. United States ex rel. De Lucia v.

McMann, 373 F.2d 759 (2d Cir.1967). Does this make any unauthorized view by jurors a constitutional violation?

See also People v. Brown, 399 N.E.2d 51 (N.Y.C.A.1979), where the only evidence placing defendant at the scene of a crime was testimony by a police officer that while at a stoplight in an unmarked General Motors police van, he saw defendant in an adjacent vehicle. One of the jurors conducted a "test" in her Volkswagen van to determine whether it would have been possible to see defendant from the position described by the policeman. The court impeached the resulting verdict finding that such testing constituted prejudicial jury misconduct. Suppose during deliberations the juror had merely told another, "I drive a van and I know you can see what the policeman said he saw."?

2.   Except in Texas where jury views have been said to be prohibited (see Wendorf, Some Views on Jury Views, 15 Baylor L.Rev. 379 (1963)), it is generally held that whether or not to permit the view is a matter of the court's discretion. See United States v. Jorge–Salon, 734 F.2d 789, 791 (11th Cir.), cert. denied, 469 U.S. 869 (1984) ("The district court's denial of defendants' request for a jury view of the Atlanta penitentiary was within the sound discretion of the trial judge."); United States v. Gallagher, 620 F.2d 797, 801 (10th Cir.), cert. denied, 449 U.S. 878 (1980) ("Whether the jury is permitted to view evidence outside the courtroom is a matter for the discretion of the trial court."). A statute authorizing only the viewing of premises does not alter the court's inherent power to order the viewing of any object. See State v. Coburn, 82 Idaho 437, 354 P.2d 751 (1960).

3.   Courts are divided as to whether a view constitutes independent evidence. Wigmore's position is that it does, 4 Evidence § 1168 (Chadbourn rev.1972). See also Price Bros. Co. v. Philadelphia Gear Corp., 649 F.2d 416, 419 (6th Cir.), cert. denied, 454 U.S. 1099 (1981) ("[W]here the fact finder's observations upon a view are used as evidence to determine the facts, then the procedural safeguards of a trial, including the rules of evidence and the participation of the parties must apply."). Some decisions hold that the purpose of a view is to enable the jury to better understand the evidence, but not to supply evidence. Uhrig v. Coffin, 240 P.2d 480, 481 (Idaho 1952); Jack v. Hunt, 265 P.2d 251 (Or.1954); Jacks v. Townsend, 88 S.E.2d 776, 778 (S.C.1955); Weber Basin Water Conservancy District v. Moore, 272 P.2d 176 (Utah 1954). The Ontario Court of Appeals in Chambers v. Murphy, [1953] 2 D.L.R. 705, went even further. There the trial judge, trying the case without a jury, viewed the scene of the accident. On the basis of what he saw, the judge concluded that defendant "told me what was not so," and rendered judgment for the plaintiff. The Court of Appeal said that the function of a view was to enable the judge to follow and apply the evidence, but held that the trial judge had "in reality supplied that evidence himself and erroneously acted upon it." See the excellent criticism of this case in 31 Can.B.Rev. 305 (1953). In Carpenter v. Carpenter, 101 A. 628, 631 (N.H.1917), the court said: "If the object is black when seen by the jury it would be absurd to expect them to find that it was white, in the absence of evidence indicating that they had been imposed upon."

4.   Why do some courts take the position that a view does not supply evidence but only permits the jurors to better understand the evidence? The Supreme Court of New Hampshire has said that this is "nonsense," Carpenter v. Carpenter, supra and the Supreme Court of Nebraska termed it a "psychological fiction," Carter v. Parsons, 286 N.W. 696, 698 (Neb.1939). Is it possible for the appellate court to adequately review a case in which there has been a view? Does demeanor create similar problems? In some jurisdictions the judge need not be present at the view by the jury. Shahan v. American Telephone &

Telegraph Co., 35 S.E.2d 5, 9, (Ga.App.1945); Yeary v. Holbrook, 198 S.E. 441, 446 (Va.1938). If the judge is not present, will it be possible for him to rule on a motion directed at the sufficiency of the evidence? In State v. Garden, 125 N.W.2d 591 (Minn.1963), a homicide conviction was set aside where no court reporter was present at the view. If a court reporter records his own impression does he become a witness as far as the appellate court is concerned, or does his record fulfill other functions?

5.   In Price Bros. Co. v. Philadelphia Gear Corp., 649 F.2d 416, 419 (6th Cir.), cert. denied, 454 U.S. 1099 (1981), supra, a breach of warranty action arising out of the sale of a pipe wrapping machine, the trial judge's law clerk travelled to the plaintiff's factory to observe the operation of the machine. The defendant, however, was not notified. The appellate court held that this procedure was improper, explaining:

> The view involved in this case was more than a simple observation of the place where a specified event was alleged to have occurred. The subject viewed here, the machine, was under the control of the plaintiff. The plaintiff had the opportunity to manipulate what the law clerk saw in order to present an image most favorable to the plaintiff. The defendant was not present to learn what the law clerk observed, what conversations the law clerk had with plaintiff's employees, or what impressions the law clerk conveyed to the trial judge. Obviously, the defendant could not rebut any of the off-the-record information that the trial judge received from this source. These factors created a presumption of prejudice to the defendant in the trial judge's determination of the facts that must be rebutted before his decision can stand.

649 F.2d at 420.

6.   What is the effect of a change in condition in the property or object being viewed since the time of the accident or incident? Does mere passage of time affect the right to a view? See Annot., 85 A.L.R.2d 512 (1962).

7.   Subsidiary procedural problems may arise with respect to a view. To what extent does the position on whether information obtained by the view constitutes evidence affect the answers to the following questions? Can a view be taken in a criminal case without the presence of the accused? See Snyder v. Massachusetts, 291 U.S. 97 (1934). Can a view be taken beyond the jurisdiction of the trial court? see 27 Yale L.J. 287 (1917). What is the effect of an unauthorized experiment or demonstration conducted by the jury at an authorized view? See 150 A.L.R. 958 (1944). Should it matter whether the jury's actions are classified as an experiment rather than a view?

SECTION 4.   DEMONSTRATIONS AND EXPERIMENTS

United States v. Wanoskia

United States Court of Appeals, Tenth Circuit, 1986.
800 F.2d 235.

■ LOGAN, CIRCUIT JUDGE. After examining the briefs and the appellate record, this three-judge panel has determined unanimously that oral argument would not be of material assistance in the determination of this appeal. See Fed.R.App.P. 34(a); Tenth Cir.R. 10(e). The cause is therefore ordered submitted without oral argument.

Defendant, Elward Roe Wanoskia, was convicted by a jury of second-degree murder pursuant to 18 U.S.C. §§ 1111 and 1153. The district court sentenced him to sixty years in prison. In this appeal defendant argues that: (1) the government's use of demonstrative evidence was prejudicial; and (2) his conviction violated his rights under the Equal Protection Clause because, had he not been an Indian, he would have been subjected to a lesser penalty under New Mexico state law.

On April 8, 1984, defendant's wife, Linda Martinez Wanoskia, was shot in the head and killed. The shooting occurred at approximately 1:30 a.m., after defendant, his wife, and their friend Erlinda Menarco had returned to defendant's Indian reservation home from an afternoon and evening of drinking. Both defendant and his wife were enrolled members of the Jicarilla Apache Tribe.

The government's version of how the death occurred was presented primarily through the testimony of Menarco. She stated that after returning home during the early morning of April 8, defendant began to beat his wife. Menarco tried to intervene, but defendant threw plants at her and then kicked her in the chin. Menarco testified that defendant next got his pistol and attempted to shoot Menarco, but his wife pushed his arm and the shot went through the window. After shooting at Menarco again, and again missing, defendant shot his wife in the head. Defendant then attempted again to shoot Menarco but the gun failed to fire. Then, according to Menarco, defendant threatened to kill her unless she told the police that defendant's wife shot herself. This is in fact what Menarco first told the police. Later, however, she recanted and told the police that defendant had killed his wife and that she had lied out of fear of defendant.

Defendant's version was presented primarily through his own testimony. He testified that an argument began between his wife and Menarco shortly after their return home. When he tried to stop the argument, his wife struck him and then Menarco with a frying pan. Defendant testified that his wife then took his .357 revolver from the bedroom and threatened to shoot him. A scuffle ensued between Wanoskia, his wife, and Menarco. Eventually, his wife got control of the gun and after saying, "Watch this," shot herself in the head.

I

At trial the government sought to show by expert testimony and a demonstration that defendant's wife did not shoot herself. The expert testimony related to the powder burns on the wife's face and how far away the pistol must have been when it discharged. The demonstration was to show that defendant's wife could not have held the weapon that far away from her face.

The government presented as a witness an FBI special agent with expertise in firearms identification who had performed a series of tests with defendant's revolver to determine the pattern of gunpowder particles and residue that the gun left when fired at different distances. The agent had fired the gun into sheets of cotton from varying distances; he testified to the patterns of gunpowder residue at the respective distances. The agent declined to testify as to how far the gun was from the victim when it was fired because he lacked expertise in examining gun powder residue left on human skin.

The government next presented Dr. John Smialek, chief medical investigator for the State of New Mexico in Albuquerque. Smialek, who performed the autopsy on Mrs. Wanoskia, testified that he found gun powder on the victim's face in a pattern with a nine inch diameter. Based on the earlier witness' test firings, Smialek estimated that the gun was eighteen inches from Mrs. Wanoskia when fired.

Smialek also stated that Mrs. Wanoskia weighed 171 pounds and was five feet two inches tall. He estimated the length of her arms to be between nineteen and twenty inches. He candidly admitted that he had neglected to measure her arms, but based his estimate on his experience with other women of similar weight and height and on his measurement of the arm length of two Hispanic women working in his office who were of similar weight and height. Defendant's objection to this estimate was overruled.

The government then sought to demonstrate that it was physically impossible for a woman with approximately twenty-inch arms to hold this particular gun eighteen inches from her head. The court would not allow the female assistant U.S. attorney who tried the case to perform the demonstration herself. A search began of the halls of the courthouse for a woman with twenty-inch arms. The defense attorney told the court that he had found one woman of similar height and weight to Mrs. Wanoskia, but she had twenty-four-inch arms. Eventually, a woman with twenty-four-inch arms was used as a model in the demonstration. In the first demonstration, the model held the revolver with her thumb on the trigger and pointed at her head. The distance from the muzzle to her face was twelve inches. Next, the model held the gun with her forefinger on the trigger. In this position, the distance from the muzzle of the gun to her face was roughly four inches. Finally, the model held the gun with both thumbs on the trigger. In this position, the distance from the muzzle of the gun to her face was eleven and three-quarter inches. Defendant objected to this demonstration and a similar one during the prosecution's rebuttal presentation.

Demonstrative evidence, and in particular, reenactments of events, can be highly persuasive. The opportunity for the jury to see what supposedly happened can accomplish in seconds what might otherwise take days of testimony. By conveying a visual image of what allegedly occurred, one side can imprint on the jury's mind its version of the facts.... McCormick on Evidence § 215 (3d ed. 1984). Thus the court must take special care to ensure that the demonstration fairly depicts the events at issue. Nevertheless, a trial court's decision to admit or exclude such evidence will be reversed only if the court abused its discretion.... In Jackson v. Fletcher, 647 F.2d 1020 (10th Cir.1981), we established a strict threshold requirement for the admission of experimental evidence. This standard is also appropriate for the admission of the demonstrative evidence in this case:

> "Where ... an experiment purports to simulate actual events and to show the jury what presumably occurred at the scene of the accident, the party introducing the evidence has a burden of demonstrating substantial similarity of conditions. They may not be identical but they ought to be sufficiently similar so as to provide a fair comparison."

Id. at 1027 (citations omitted); accord United States v. Hart, 729 F.2d at 669 (10th Cir.1984) (excluding admission of demonstrative hairpin absent evidence that it was comparable to hairpin actually used to open lock); see also Randall v. Warnaco, Inc., 677 F.2d 1226, 1234, 1234 n. 7 [10 Fed.Rules Evid.Serv. 638] (8th Cir.1982) (admission of experimental evidence "very close to a reenactment of the accident ... could be deemed unduly prejudicial"). Adhering to this standard in a criminal prosecution is even more important than in a civil case.

Defendant's primary challenge to the government's use of the demonstrative evidence is that there was insufficient evidence of his wife's arm length. The government and its expert medical witness clearly should have measured the victim's arms in the circumstances of this case. Nevertheless, we hold that the expert was qualified to estimate her arm length. Measurement of two women in his office was an insufficient basis for his conclusion, but, as the district court held, the witness was competent to estimate the victim's arm length based on his medical expertise as an experienced medical pathologist.

That actual measurements were not taken affects the weight of the evidence, not its admissibility. See Szeliga v. General Motors Corp., 728 F.2d 566, 567 (1st Cir.1984) ("Dissimilarities between experimental and actual conditions affect the weight of the evidence, not its admissibility."); Renfro Hosiery Mills Co. v. National Cash Register Co., 552 F.2d 1061, 1065 (4th Cir.1977) ("If there is substantial similarity, the differences between the test and the actual occurrence ordinarily are regarded as affecting the weight of the evidence rather than its admissibility."). The court properly instructed the jury to disregard the expert testimony if it believed the testimony lacked adequate foundation.

At this point it became incumbent upon the defense to rebut or impeach the expert's testimony through cross-examination or other expert testimony.... We note that defendant had available to him photographs of his wife and possibly articles of her clothing. If he seriously disputed the pathologist's estimates, he could have made his own estimates from these sources.

Defendant also challenges the relevancy of the demonstrations. We agree with the district court that they were relevant to the government's theory of how the shooting occurred. Cf. Schleunes v. American Casualty Co., 528 F.2d 634, 637 (5th Cir.1976) (evidence of how weapon was fired generally admissible in suicide cases). The government presented testimony that defendant had told the police his wife pulled the trigger with her index finger, not with her thumb as he contended at trial. With the model's finger on the trigger, the demonstration showed that a woman with twenty-four-inch arms could only hold the gun about four inches from her face. Thus, even if the pathologist's estimate of the victim's arm length was off by several inches, the demonstration showed that the victim could not have shot herself if she had her finger on the trigger.

We also note that the trial court took great care in ensuring that the demonstrations did not unduly prejudice defendant. Before permitting the demonstrations during the case-in-chief, the court viewed the demonstrations outside the presence of the jury. Only after being satisfied that these demonstrations were probative did the court permit them. In addition, the court intentionally had the demonstration performed by a woman with arms longer than the estimate of the expert witness. We find no abuse of discretion in the court's allowing the demonstrations. See Hart, 729 F.2d at 669.

Defendant also makes vague allegations that he was prejudiced because he did not have notice of the government's intent to conduct demonstrations. We find no prejudice in this respect. Defendant himself presented expert testimony concerning the distance between the gun and his wife when it was fired; he had to consider the length of his wife's arms if this evidence was to have any meaning....

Affirmed.

NOTES

1. Would you have wanted oral argument in the main case? Why?

2. Slattery v. Marra Brothers, 186 F.2d 134, 138 (2d Cir.1951): "It is sometimes said that the jury should not be allowed to see repulsive injuries since they may excite their emotions. That may at times be true; but ordinarily it would seem that the very hideousness of the deformity was a part of the suffering of the victim, and could not rationally be excluded in the assessment of his damages." See also Allen v. Seacoast Prods., Inc., 623 F.2d 355 (5th Cir.1980) (demonstration of removal and replacement of artificial eye proper to show daily regimen that the plaintiff must undergo); Brown v. Billy Marlar Chevrolet, Inc., 381 So.2d 191 (Ala.1980) (allowed demonstration of how artificial leg functioned).

Monk v. Doctors Hospital, 403 F.2d 580, 584 (D.C.Cir.1968): The showing of the effect of cosmetics on plaintiff's scar was allowed but reasonable safeguards such as the scar's appearance without cosmetic aids were required. Likewise, the plaintiff in South Highlands Infirmary v. Camp, 180 So.2d 904, 909 (Ala.1965) was allowed to appear before the jury dressed in shorts so that the scars on her thigh could be observed. Darling v. Charleston Community Memorial Hospital, 200 N.E.2d 149, 185 (Ill.App.), cert. denied 383 U.S. 946 (1966): "A personal view of the stump and artificial leg here could aid the jury in understanding the voluminous evidence and was relevant as to the nature and extent of the claimed injury and the various elements of the claimed damages. We cannot say the only purpose of the exhibition thereof was to excite the feeling of the jury. There was no abuse of discretion...."

But see Happy v. Walz, 244 S.W.2d 380, 383 (Mo.App.1951): "If such examination in the presence of the jury would expose ghastly wounds, hideous deformities, or would elicit cries of pain by the plaintiff, or induce pitiful attempts at locomotion, or otherwise would dramatize plaintiff's injuries in a manner calculated to inflame the minds of the jury, then such demonstration becomes prejudicial and improper."

3. Osborne v. Detroit, 32 Fed. 36 (C.C.E.D.Mich.1886), rev'd on other grounds, 135 U.S. 492 (1890): Personal injury action in which the jury returned a verdict for plaintiff for $10,000 and defendant moved for a new trial upon the ground, among others, that the court erred in permitting a doctor, who had not been sworn, to thrust a pin into the right side of plaintiff's face and her right arm and leg. From "the witness' failing to wince, the jury were asked to infer that there was a complete paralysis of her right side." Defendant objected to this on the ground "that the doctor was not sworn as to the instrument he was using, nor was the plaintiff sworn to behave naturally while she was being experimented upon. It is argued that both the doctor and plaintiff might have wholly deceived the court and jury without laying themselves open to a charge of perjury, and that plaintiff was not even asked to swear whether the instrument hurt her when it was used on the left side, or did not hurt when used on the right side; in short, that there was no sworn testimony or evidence in the whole performance, and no practical way of detecting any trickery which might have been practiced." Motion for new trial denied. (i) "We know ... of no oath which could be administered to the doctor or the witness touching this exhibition. So far as we are aware, the law recognizes no oaths to be administered upon the witness stand except the ordinary oath to tell the truth, or to interpret correctly from one language to another." (ii) "The pin by which the experiment was performed was exhibited to the jury. There was nothing which tended to show trickery on the part of the doctor in inserting the pin as he was requested to do, nor was there any cross-examination attempted from the witness upon this point. Counsel were certainly at liberty to examine the pin and to ascertain whether in fact it was inserted in the flesh, and, having failed to exercise this privilege, it is now too late to raise the objection that the exhibition was incompetent." (iii) "It is certainly competent for the plaintiff to appear before the jury, and, if she had lost an arm or a leg by reason of the accident, they could hardly fail to notice it. By parity of reasoning, it would seem that she was at liberty to exhibit her wounds if she chose to do so, as is frequently the case where an ankle has been sprained or broken, a wrist fractured, or any maiming has occurred. I know of no objection to her showing the extent of the paralysis which had supervened by reason of the accident, and evidence that her right side was insensible to pain certainly tended to show this paralyzed condition." (iv) But even considering "the testimony" to have been improper, it could not have prejudiced defendant. In its argument to the jury defendant "substantially admitted" that plaintiff was completely paralyzed and, "considering the physical wreck of the plaintiff," the damages awarded her were not so excessive as to justify the court in setting aside the verdict upon that ground. See Annot., Permitting demonstration to show effect of injury in action for bodily injury, 66 A.L.R.2d 1382 (1959).

Maguire, Evidence—Common Sense and Common Law 20 (1947): "... a resolute plaintiff, having the glitter of big damages before his mental vision, might steel himself to endure quite a lot of needling in nonvital areas without any manifestation of pain. So here we certainly do get a live problem of sincerity lacking any sure-fire mechanical or psychological check." See also People v. True, 407 N.E.2d 153 (Ill.App.1980) (plaintiff was denied the opportunity to demonstrate to the jury the range of motion in her injured shoulder); Lampa v. Hakola, 55 P.2d 13 (Or.1936) (action to recover damages for injuries to plaintiff's right sacral region and sacroiliac joint, sciatic nerve, and back bone; verdict for plaintiff was set aside and new trial was granted upon the ground that it was an error to permit plaintiff's medical witness to conduct a demonstration with plaintiff for the jury, showing plaintiff's pain and restricted mobility resulting from the injuries).

Clark v. Brooklyn Heights Railroad Co., 69 N.E. 647 (N.Y.1904):

> In this action, brought to recover damages for personal injuries sustained by the plaintiff, ... he was allowed to leave the witness stand assisted and ... to exhibit himself to the jury in the act of writing his name and of taking a drink of water. The record represents him, through the stenographer's notes, as taking a glass of water with both hands and as spilling the water, through the trembling of his hands, and using his handkerchief in the same manner. The point of this exhibition was to illustrate or to emphasize, his testimony that he could use his hands with difficulty, either to hold things, or to drink a glass of water.... [I]t was his claim that, about two months after the accident, he was affected by a tremor, or muscular twitching, and medical testimony was given to that effect....

While permitting the exhibition may not have been an abuse of discretion, the court noted, "it was on the borderline" of error because "as something under the sole control of the witness," it was beyond the ordinary tests of examination and because it was intended and calculated to prejudice the minds of the jurors. "The plaintiff in such cases has sufficient advantages without adding to them a spectacular illustration of his symptoms." Suppose this activity of plaintiff had taken place while he was seated at counsel table? Would the jury have seen it?

Hays v. Herman, 322 P.2d 119, 122 (Or.1958): "We cannot agree with appellant that before an emotional display can amount to misconduct sufficient to warrant a new trial it must be deliberate or falsely simulated."

The principal problem with respect to demonstrations is the voluntariness of the witness's behavior. How can this difficulty be met—by oath, expert testimony, requirement of corroborating evidence, judicial notice?

It has been held that the demonstration must take place during the trial to afford an opportunity for cross-examination. See Robinson v. Kathryn, 161 N.E.2d 477 (Ill.App.1959) (a demonstration during the closing argument by the plaintiff was improper because the defendant had no opportunity to cross-examine, defend, or reply). But what if the event was described by an expert or layman in an out of court observation? See Ishler v. Cook, 299 F.2d 507 (7th Cir.1962) (defendant's physician was allowed to measure plaintiff's legs when plaintiff's doctor had testified that one leg was ⅝ inch shorter than the other; the change had occurred after a first examination by defendant's doctor).

4. State v. Roby, 263 P.2d 273 (Wash.1953), an assault case, involved a situation in which the litigant has every motive to act efficiently, although other demonstration problems are involved. The prosecution said that defendant could not have drawn and opened his knife with one hand while holding off the complaining witness with the other. On cross-examination, at the prosecution's request, the scuffle was staged as defendant said it occurred. Defendant could not open the knife with one hand. In the colloquy between the defendant and the prosecution and defense attorneys it was brought out that, since the fight, defendant's fingernails had been rotted away by cleaning fluid and that the knife had become rusty. The appellate court said that, in view of these factors, there might be merit in defendant's assignment of error, if the objection had been properly raised. But the conviction was affirmed since the defense attorney's only objection to the demonstration was that it was "not proper cross-examination."

5. In United States v. Arthur, 949 F.2d 211 (6th Cir.1991), the defendant wanted to try on before the jury a wig and cap found in the getaway car to show that with it on he and a person he claimed to be the real criminal looked alike. It was error not to permit the demonstration on the issue of mistaken identification. Note too the failure of "the" gloves to fit over latex gloves in the O.J. Simpson case. How could this problem have been avoided?

Hall v. General Motors Corp.

United States Court of Appeals, District of Columbia, 1980.
647 F.2d 175.

■ GINSBURG, CIRCUIT JUDGE:

On a clear September afternoon in 1975, Georgia Hall had a tragic accident. Her five-month old Buick Electra left Suitland Parkway in the District of Columbia and careened across a grassy field until it collided with a tree. The accident left Mrs. Hall a quadriplegic....

I. *Facts*

On September 29, 1975, in full daylight, Georgia Hall was driving alone in her 1975 Buick, purchased some five months earlier. She was in the right-hand, eastbound lane on Suitland Parkway, maintaining a speed of 40–45 miles per hour along the dry, smooth road. As GM described the accident, the car veered to the right, crossed the shoulder into a field of grass, then traveled across an elevated exit-entrance ramp into a wooded area where it hit a tree that stood over 700 feet from the road. When the car crossed the ramp, Mrs. Hall was thrown from behind the wheel. Witnesses found her lying across the front seat with her foot "hooked up" between the accelerator and the brake pedal. She had suffered a broken neck, resulting in permanent quadriplegia.

Mrs. Hall's testimony indicated that, at the time of the accident, she was a healthy woman, who did not drink or take drugs. She was an experienced driver and, when the fateful episode occurred, she was traveling on a familiar road maintaining, according to her testimony, a moderate speed. She said she heard a loud explosion while the car was on the road, followed by vibrations and popping. As the car surged off the road, she claimed that she mashed continuously on the brakes but the car would not stop. She had lost control.

The Halls presented evidence of their multiple complaints about the car, complaints they reported repeatedly to the dealer, Larry Buick, Inc. Surging, vibrations, and other malfunctions existed, the Halls said, from the time Mrs. Hall purchased the car until the time of the accident. Despite inspections and servicing by the dealer, no correction was accomplished.

The car's drive shaft system was found after the accident to have been destroyed. At trial, the Halls attempted to show that a defect in the shaft had caused the accident. GM, on the other hand, maintained that the destroyed drive shaft was the result of the accident, not its cause. The cause, GM suggested, was Mrs. Hall's momentary inattention to the road, followed by panic, which led her to apply the accelerator instead of the brake.[1]

Expert testimony on behalf of the plaintiffs accounted for the accident roughly as follows. A defective joint in the drive shaft exploded on the highway, causing the rear of the shaft, with part of the joint still attached, to drop to the road, still spinning rapidly. The force of the contact with the road produced a forward reaction, upward and to the right, which pushed the drive shaft tube into the rear of the transmission housing with sufficient force to raise the car off its suspension and drive it from the road. This testimony also attributed the intermittent vibrations, about which the Halls had complained prior to the accident, to defects in the rear portion of the drive shaft.

GM, contrarily, presented evidence to support its contention that the drive shaft did not disintegrate until the car smashed into the ground after traversing the elevated exit-entrance ramp. In particular, GM showed that the seventeen separate parts of the shaft found after the accident were all in the immediate vicinity of the area where the violent ground impact had occurred. GM further pointed out that the police accident investigator, called to the scene immediately after the accident, found no scratches or stains on the road that could be associated with the Halls' theory of the accident. In addition, GM presented a wealth of expert testimony supporting its position that Mrs. Hall's Buick was not defective in any material respect....

Test Evidence

In an attempt to pinpoint a specific defect in Georgia Hall's Buick, the plaintiffs sought to establish that the drive shaft broke off at the constant velocity joint,[2] causing the car to surge upward and to the right, careening out of control off the road. As part of its massive effort to disprove this theory, GM conducted a series of tests. In the first test GM ran, a 1975 Buick Electra's

---

1. GM did not choose to cross-examine Mrs. Hall, however. Under the District of Columbia law applicable to this diversity action, it was GM's burden to show negligence, if any existed, on Mrs. Hall's part. Ballard v. Polly, 387 F.Supp. 895, 901 (D.D.C.1975). [Footnotes renumbered; some omitted; footnotes by the court.]

2. The drive shaft transmits the power of the engine from the transmission to the rear wheels, which propel the car. The drive-shaft tube is a hollow cast-iron cylinder. It is fitted, both front and rear, into flexible joints. The rear or "constant velocity" joint is welded to the drive-shaft tube, and the rear-most part of the joint (the rear flange yoke) is then bolted to the differential of the rear axle. See Brief of Defendant–Appellant at 6 n. 5.

drive shaft was taped, not bolted, at the rear; it was then pushed by another car until it attained a speed of 50 miles per hour, at which point the engine speed was correspondingly increased and the transmission was shifted into "drive." Supporting GM's position, the shaft eventually dropped to the road, but there was no upward or rightward pull.

At a pre-trial session, Judge Green rejected this test on the ground that it did not depict a situation sufficiently comparable to that of Mrs. Hall's vehicle at the time of the accident. Over plaintiffs' objection, however, and although the trial was to start in two weeks time, Judge Green permitted GM to pursue further testing.

GM next conducted tests with bolted rather than taped rear flange yokes. The yokes were deliberately and increasingly weakened with the aim of determining what would happen when a defective rear flange yoke breaks and the drive shaft then drops to the ground. This aim was not achieved because the shaft never came apart. Judge Green permitted GM to introduce expert testimony explaining this testing. Still photographs were admitted as well, but not motion pictures.

GM also sought to introduce testimony that a car used in the experiments, equipped with the most defective yoke, withstood a trip from Michigan to Washington, D.C., without incident. Plaintiffs' representative, who had attended the earlier testing, all of it occurring in Michigan, had returned to Washington, D.C., to prepare for trial before the road test occurred. Judge Green excluded evidence concerning this test on the ground, *inter alia*, that time for GM's experiments had run out.

Judge Green's central concern, in ruling on GM's tests, was to keep from the jury experiments conducted under conditions not sufficiently similar to the circumstances surrounding the accident. A test is not admissible unless the test conditions are "so nearly the same in substantial particulars [as those involved in the episode in litigation] as to afford a fair comparison in respect to the particular issue to which the test is directed." Illinois Central Gulf R.R. v. Ishee, 317 So.2d 923, 926 (Miss.1975), quoted with approval in Barnes v. General Motors Corp., 547 F.2d 275, 277 (5th Cir.1977). The trial judge has broad leeway in making this determination; her ruling will not be upset unless it is clearly erroneous. Derr v. Safeway Stores, Inc., 404 F.2d 634, 639 (10th Cir.1968). We cannot say that Judge Green's test evidence rulings exceeded the latitude appropriately accorded trial courts in this area.

Judge Green excluded GM's first proffered test for insufficient comparability: the drive shaft was taped, not bolted, at the rear; the test car was pushed, not driven, to a speed of 50 miles per hour. We find no abuse of discretion in her determination....

As to the second test series, Judge Green acceded to GM's proffer, except for the film. We see no clear error in her exclusion of motion pictures that "[did] not portray original facts in controversy." See McCormick, Law of Evidence § 214, at 534 (2d ed. 1972). Nor do we see error in Judge Green's exclusion of the test drive from Michigan to Washington, D.C., a test of limited probative value conducted at the eleventh hour when plaintiffs' representative was no longer in attendance....

Affirmed.

NOTES

1. Discretion of the trial court, in a case such as the principal one, is generally sustained despite minor variations in conditions. See, e.g., Four Corners Helicopters, Inc. v. Turbomeca, S.A., 979 F.2d 1434 (10th Cir.1992) (effect of loose screws on turbine helicopter engine; exclusion in court's discretion); Larson v. Meyer, 161 N.W.2d 165 (N.D.1968) (different equipment at a different location to illustrate capacity of a tractor to pull a similar load without overturning). But see Jackson v. Fletcher, 647 F.2d 1020 (10th Cir.1981) (experiment to prove truck had not stopped at intersection; weight, engine power, skid marks all different; abuse of discretion). In Jackson the experiment was conducted ex parte without notice to the opponent. Should this factor affect the court's ruling? Should the court intervene in the experiment? How?

2. The principal problem in regard to experiments is whether the conditions at the time of the experiment are substantially similar to the conditions of the actual occurrence. See Kehm v. Procter & Gamble Mfg. Co., 724 F.2d 613 (8th Cir.1983) (in product liability action against tampon manufacturer, expert permitted to testify to differences between experimental conditions and actual vaginal environment to allow jury to determine significance of experimental results).

As the court explained in Ramseyer v. General Motors Corp., 417 F.2d 859, 864 (8th Cir.1969):

> Admissibility of evidence depends upon the foundational showing of substantial similarity between the tests conducted and actual conditions [citation omitted]. Perfect identity between experimental and actual conditions is neither attainable nor required.... Dissimilarities affect the weight of the evidence and not the admissibility [citation omitted]. Finally, the decision whether to admit or exclude evidence of experiments in a particular case rests largely in the discretion of the trial judge and his decision will not be overturned on appeal absent a clear showing of an abuse of discretion.

3. For cases where the requirement of similarity has not been met, see e.g., Kent v. Knox Motor Service, Inc., 419 N.E.2d 1253 (Ill.App.1981) (automobile accident case; where type of vehicle, light conditions, and conditions of highway at time of test were not the same, nor substantially the same, evidence regarding experiment to determine driving visibility at time of accident was excluded). Pacheco v. United States, 367 F.2d 878, 881 (10th Cir.1966): Defendant attempted to discredit a police agent's testimony as to conversations heard by the agent while hidden in the trunk of an informer's automobile. The defendant and his counsel conducted an experiment by reading a transcript of the conversation while sitting in the car with a tape recorder in the trunk. The court, holding the experiment inadmissible, stated:

> The court, out of the presence of the jury, heard the testimony of the witness Pickett which was presented as an offer of proof by appellant. Although the same car was used as the one in which Jordan was located at the time of the conversation, the testimony of Pickett discloses that the experiment was at a different place; the voice was that of appellant's counsel and not that of the appellant or Aragon; the car door was closed and not open as shown by the testimony and plaintiff's counsel spoke in a volume of voice "that anybody would normally use who was keeping a kind of hush-hush conversation outside the car." The evidence does not disclose that the conversation between Aragon and appellant on September 20, 1965 was a "hush-hush" conversation.

4. Larramendy v. Myres, 272 P.2d 824 (Cal.App.1954). Defendants sold "Abbotts Pufferoo," a device designed for use in theatrical productions, which produced a puff of smoke when a switch was tripped. Plaintiff-dancer set off the device, which then emitted flame in addition to smoke, and plaintiff was severely burned. The fire chief testified that fire was produced in tests he made with the device. In these tests the fire chief did not use the powder that came with the "Pufferoo." But the chief testified that he had this powder chemically analyzed and that he used in his tests powder of the same quality. The court held that there was no competent evidence (see Ch. 6, infra on Hearsay) that the powder used by the chief was of the same quality as the powder which came with the device and that therefore the fire chief's testimony should not have been received. At the trial the "Pufferoo" was tested, the powder that came with it being used. The device produced flame. The court adverted to defendant's argument that there was no evidence that the draft conditions were the same in the courtroom as on stage at the time of the accident. But the court held that the trial judge did not abuse his discretion in permitting the experiment. See Annot., Admissibility of Experimental Evidence as to Explosion, 76 A.L.R.2d 402 (1961); Note, Experimental Evidence, 34 Ill.L.Rev. 206 (1939).

See also Ripp v. Riesland, 141 N.W.2d 840, 844–845 (Neb.1966) (testimony of an expert of an experiment by him for the stopping distance required of an automobile of the type involved on the same road under similar conditions); Norton Co. v. Harrelson, 176 So.2d 18, 21–22 (Ala.1965) (experts testified that two grinding wheels identical to the one which injured the plaintiff "developed flaws when subjected to rather simple stress testing").

Are the applicable principles the same when the court is determining the admissibility of (1) an experiment to be conducted before the jury or (2) testimony concerning an experiment performed outside the courtroom? Can the court rely on an expert's testimony evaluating the experiment as fair?

5.   United States v. Beach, 296 F.2d 153 (4th Cir.1961), held it a violation of defendant's rights to permit the jury to run an adding machine in the jury room in order to help it determine whether defendant had lied when he testified he never heard one operating in a rented room in his house. This experiment had not been conducted in court although the machine had been received in evidence and taken into the jury room.

Is it proper for the jury to duplicate an experiment in the jury room that had been performed in the courtroom? See McLane v. State, 379 S.W.2d 339 (Tex.Cr.App.1964).

Is it proper for a jury to use a magnifying glass to examine various exhibits? See Annot., Tests or Experiments in Jury Room, 95 A.L.R.2d 351 (1964).

Hughes v. General Motors Corporation, 35 F.3d 571 (9th Cir.1994), was a case arising from a rollover accident.

> The Rolled–Up Paper Demonstration—Benoy's declaration stated that one of the jurors, Earlinor Odom, performed during deliberations a demonstration which involved cutting a hole in a piece of paper, rolling it up into a cylinder, and pressing down on its top. General Motors claims that this demonstration was an impermissible juror experiment which brought extrinsic material before the jury. The district court rejected this claim, and we conclude that it did not abuse its discretion.

> Although jurors may not go beyond the record to develop their own evidence, they are entitled to evaluate the evidence presented at trial in light of their own experience. As we emphasized in Hard II, "the type of after-acquired information that potentially taints a jury verdict should be carefully distinguished from the general knowledge, opinions, feelings, and bias that every juror carries into the jury room." Hard II, 870 F.2d at 1461. See also United States v. Navarro–Garcia, 926 F.2d 818, 822 (9th Cir.1991) ("Personal experiences are relevant only for purposes of interpreting the

record evidence."). Like personal experiences, other aids in interpreting and explaining the evidence are permissible, so long as they do not introduce facts outside of the record. See, e.g., United States v. Bassler, 651 F.2d 600, 602 (8th Cir.) cert. denied, 454 U.S. 944 (1981), 454 U.S. 1151 (1982). See also United States v. Hephner, 410 F.2d 930, 936 (7th Cir.1969) ("Jurors must be given enough latitude in their deliberations to permit them to use common experience and illustrations in reaching their verdict.").

These cases draw a line between impermissible "extrinsic" influences on jury deliberations and permissible "intrinsic" influences. The district court found that Odom's actions with the rolled-up piece of paper fell on the permissible, "intrinsic" side of that line. It found that the use of the rolled-up paper was simply "graphic speech"—a "demonstration" which served to illustrate the theory Odom was advocating and to explain her point of view. We discern no error in this finding. Accordingly, we see no reason to hold an evidentiary hearing.

Since this demonstration took place during jury deliberations should inquiry have been permitted? See Federal Rules of Evidence, Rule 606(b), Inquiry into validity of verdict or indictment.

6. Courts are particularly apt to show concern about overvaluation of experiments when the jury may tend to forget the experiment is not being conducted on the articles involved in the event that is the subject of the suit. See United States v. Pjecha, 7 M.J. 455 (1979) (marijuana originally seized from accused not available; special agent produced a substance at trial and conducted Becton–Dickinson test of substance to show how he determined what had been seized was marijuana; trial court expressed concern about leaving substance unattended in courtroom; held, little relevance and highly inflammatory; conviction reversed). But cf. United States v. Cox, 633 F.2d 871 (9th Cir.1980) (expert had constructed mock-ups of pipe bombs using same kinds of remains of objects found at each site of explosion, relying heavily on his expertise on how such devices are manufactured; trial court made hypothetical nature of construction clear; taken into jury room; should have been used as "testimonial aid" for illustrative purposes only but no abuse of discretion).

7. Sometimes the court's ruling seems to be based on a misunderstanding of what is being proved. See, e.g., Thomas v. Chicago Transit Authority, 253 N.E.2d 492 (Ill.App.1969) (passenger claimed she caught her foot in door and bus started up causing injury as she was dragged; defendant claimed that the bus could not start with door held open by foot; experiment in presence of jury conducted with same bus; held error; two-and-a-half years had elapsed; injury occurred on crowded pre-Christmas shopping day when driver was harried and behind schedule). Should defendant in Thomas have made it clear that it was showing how an interlock works rather than that the interlock was working properly on the day in question?

SECTION 5. REPRODUCTIONS OF THE EVENT AND OF EVIDENCE OF THE EVENT

Knihal v. State

Supreme Court of Nebraska, 1949.
150 Neb. 771, 36 N.W.2d 109, 9 A.L.R.2d 891.

■ SIMMONS, CHIEF JUSTICE. Plaintiff in error, hereinafter referred to as defendant, was charged by information with murder in the second degree in the killing of one Martin Urn. He entered a plea of not guilty. Upon trial he was found guilty of manslaughter. Motion for new trial was made and overruled. Defendant was sentenced to imprisonment for a period of three years. Defendant brings the cause here by petition in error. We reverse the judgment of the district court, and remand the cause.

We recite the evidence only in so far as is necessary to an understanding of the assignments of error.

The state's evidence is to the effect that the defendant operated a tavern in South Omaha where beer and intoxicating liquors were served by the drink. The tavern room was 23 feet wide and 40 feet in length. It faced north. Along the west wall was a back bar. In front of that was a serving space, and then, making a solid barrier extending about 30 feet from the north wall, a cigar case, a long front bar, and a cooler. The front bar was 3½ to 4 feet in height.

During the evening of January 17, 1947, the defendant was in his place of business and tending bar. The deceased, Martin Urn, was at the bar. One Shymkawicz came into the tavern. He had been drinking, and a police officer testified that he was drunk. An argument arose between the defendant and Shymkawicz over the change of another customer who came in with Shymkawicz. Before it ended the defendant took a double-barreled shotgun from the back bar and Urn was shot. The state's witnesses do not agree as to what happened leading up to the firing of the shot. Shymkawicz testified that he entered the tavern, ordered wine, went to the lavatory, returned to the bar, and took a sip of his drink. Then the discussion over the change began. One witness denied that Shymkawicz was served. Shymkawicz said the defendant took the shotgun from a niche in the back bar, put "a shell" in it, and put it back on the back bar. Shymkawicz testified that he thought defendant was bluffing then. There were two shells, one exploded and one unexploded, in the gun after the shooting. The discussion continued. The defendant again picked up the gun, ordered Shymkawicz out and said, " 'You son-of-a-gun I will blow your head off.' " Shymkawicz ran out. The shot which killed Urn was fired. . . .

The main charge of the gun struck Mr. Urn in the head; he fell backward and was dead when the police arrived. Two pellets struck Shymkawicz and another bystander was slightly wounded in the ear. . . .

The defendant assigns as error the admission in evidence of three photographs. The testimony of the photographer was that the pictures were taken at the tavern about an hour after the shooting; that they were true reflections of the objects intended to be photographed; and that one of the pictures included the defendant. There was no further foundation evidence and no evidence related to the pictures descriptive of what they showed, other than the pictures themselves.

Exhibit 5 shows what appear to be a man in the foreground with his back to the camera, a back bar with bottles, a mirror, pictures, etc., a front bar, cigar case, cash register, and what appear to be the legs of a person on the floor. Between the bars and facing the camera is a man wearing a white jacket and holding what appears to be a shotgun in a port position.

Exhibit 6 shows what appears to be a man with his arms outstretched lying on his back on the floor. There are black blotches about the mouth and below the right ear and a large black blotch surrounding the head.

Defendant objected to the admission of exhibits 5 and 6, challenging competency, relevancy, and materiality, and for specific other reasons.

Exhibit 7 was received in evidence when first offered without objection and is here subject to the rule that "Where testimony is offered and admitted in evidence without objection being made thereto, error cannot be predicated thereon in the Supreme Court on appeal." Fisk Tire Co. v. Hastings Warehouse & Storage Co., 268 N.W. 86 (Neb.1936).

As a general rule photographs are admissible in evidence only when they are verified or authenticated by some other evidence. 20 Am.Jur., Evidence, s. 730, p. 609. Photographs are generally inadmissible as original or substantive evidence. They must be sponsored by a witness or witnesses whose testimony they serve to explain and illustrate. 32 C.J.S., Evidence, s. 709, p. 613.

Wigmore states as follows: "We are to remember, then, that a document purporting to be a map, picture, or diagram, is, for evidential purposes simply nothing, except so far as it has a human being's credit to support it. It is mere waste paper,—testimonial nonentity. It speaks to us no more than a stick or a stone. It can of itself tell us no more as to the existence of the thing portrayed upon it than can a tree or an ox. We must somehow put a testimonial human being behind it (as it were) before it can be treated as having any testimonial standing in court. It is somebody's testimony,—or it is nothing. It may, sometimes, to be sure, not be offered as a source of evidence, but only as a document whose existence and tenor are material in the substantive law applicable to the case,—as where, on a prosecution for stealing a map or in ejectment of land conveyed by deed containing a map, the map is to be used irrespective of the correctness of the drawing; here we do not believe anything because the map represents it. But whenever such a document is offered as proving a thing to be as therein represented, then it is offered testimonially, and it must be associated with a testifier." 3 Wigmore, Evidence (3d ed.), § 790, p. 174. "The use of maps, models, diagrams, and photographs as testimony to the objects represented rests fundamentally (as already noted in § 790) on the theory that they are the pictorial communications of a qualified witness who uses this method of communication instead of or in addition to some other method. It follows, then, that the map or photograph must first, to be admissible, be made a part of some qualified person's testimony. Some one must stand forth as its testimonial sponsor; in other words (as commonly said), it must be verified. There is nothing anomalous or exceptional in this requirement of verification; it is simply the exaction of those testimonial qualities which are required equally for all witnesses; the application merely takes a different form. A witness must have had observation of the data in question (ante, § 650), must recollect his observations (ante, § 725), and must correctly express his observation and recollection (ante, § 766). Here, then, is a form of expression ready prepared pictorially; he must supply the missing elements; in brief, it must appear that there is a witness who has competent knowledge, and that the picture is affirmed by him to represent it." 3 Wigmore, Evidence (3d ed.), § 793, p. 186. "A map or photograph cannot be received anonymously; it must be 'verified' by some witness." 3 Wigmore, Evidence (3d ed.), § 794, p. 186. . . .

Under the limited foundation given it is patent that these pictures became substantive evidence. They spoke for themselves. 3 Wigmore, Evidence (3d ed.), § 790, p. 174; Reed v. Davidson Dairy Co., 97 Colo. 462, 50 P.2d 532 (1935). As to who and what they showed, they did not have behind them the testimony of any witness supported by the sanctity of an oath, nor were they subject to the tests of cross-examination. The admission of exhibits 5 and 6 was error. Considering the nature of the scenes and objects portrayed, the error was prejudicial. Under these circumstances questions of admissibility which might arise after a proper foundation is laid should not now be determined. . . .

For the reasons given herein, the judgment of the district court is reversed and the cause remanded.

NOTE

All exhibits, including pictures should be marked in advance of trial and full lists exchanged by the parties with a copy to the judge so that there is a precise record of which photograph or document has been introduced. As a document is introduced its number should be checked and, if the jury calls for it during deliberations, another mark should be made next to the number so there is never any sloppiness about what was introduced and what the jury saw. See, for example, Gilliam v. Foster, 75 F.3d 881 (4th Cir.1996), a difficult double jeopardy, habeas corpus case arising from carelessness in showing a jury documents in a series that had been referred to but not fully introduced.

United States v. Alexander

United States Court of Appeals, Fifth Circuit, 1987.
816 F.2d 164.

■ JERRE S. WILLIAMS, CIRCUIT JUDGE:

A jury found Victor Alexander, a physician, guilty of the robbery of a savings & loan institution in New Orleans' central business district. Dr. Alexander is appealing his conviction, claiming that the district court erred in excluding the testimony of two expert witness[es] who were crucial to his defense of mistaken identity. These witnesses would have testified as to the difficulties and inaccuracies involved in comparing photographs of Dr. Alexander with pictures of the robber taken by the bank surveillance cameras. We reverse the conviction.

I. *Facts*

On May 21, 1985, the Central Savings & Loan Association in downtown New Orleans was robbed of approximately $2,640. Still photographs and a videotape taken by the bank surveillance cameras revealed that the robber was a tall, heavy-set man with a large nose, dark hair, a dark beard and mustache, and an olive complexion. He was wearing dark brown slacks, a tan or beige sports coat, a tie, and very dark sunglasses.

The Federal Bureau of Investigation[s] was in charge of the robbery investigation. F.B.I. agents showed the videotape of the robbery to three bank employees who verified that the man depicted on the tape was the same person who robbed the bank. Two days later, those same employees identified a photographic enlargement of a picture of the robber which had been taken by the still camera.

The agents also displayed throughout the central business district copies of the photographs which had been shown to the bank employees. An undisclosed person told the agents that the picture looked liked Victor Alexander, a physician who had an office in a building a few blocks from the bank. A black and white enlargement of Dr. Alexander's Louisiana driver license photograph, together with six black and white fill-in "mug shot" photos, were shown to the three bank employees who had previously seen the videotape of the robbery. Each employee independently identified Dr. Alexander from the photograph as the man who had robbed the bank.

On May 24, 1985, FBI agents arrested Dr. Alexander and took him to their headquarters for interrogation. Dr. Alexander cooperated fully, insisting that this was simply a case of mistaken identity. Significantly, no physical evidence was ever recovered connecting Dr. Alexander with the robbery. Although the FBI conducted a thorough search of Dr. Alexander's car, office, and home, they did not find any clothes matching those worn during the robbery, any sunglasses, the briefcase used in the robbery, or any of the money taken from the bank.[1] The only evidence linking Dr. Alexander to the robbery was the identification of his photo by the three bank employees.

The three bank employees who had made the photo identification testified at trial. The government also presented four acquaintances of Dr. Alexander who testified that they believed him to be the man in the robbery photos. Dr. Alexander, on the other hand, produced five witnesses who stated that he was not the person photographed by the bank surveillance cameras. The jury deliberated for more than eight hours before returning a verdict of "guilty as charged." The district court denied Dr. Alexander's motion for a new trial and sentenced him to five years imprisonment. Timely notice of appeal was filed. An amicus brief was filed on Dr. Alexander's behalf by the Louisiana Association of Criminal Defense Lawyers.

II. *Exclusion of Expert Testimony*

Dr. Alexander steadfastly denied that he was the person who robbed the Central Savings & Loan Association on May 21, 1985. To support his defense of mistaken identity, Dr. Alexander intended to call as expert witnesses Dr. Marshall I. Gottsegen, an orthodontist specializing in celphalometrics,[2] and Lyndal L. Shaneyfelt, a former F.B.I. agent with expertise in photographic comparisons. Both men examined the film taken during the bank robbery and concluded that it was impossible for Dr. Alexander to be the person depicted in the photographs.

This evidence was unquestionably crucial to the successful presentation of Dr. Alexander's defense. The jury, however, was not given the opportunity to hear and evaluate the testimony of either Dr. Gottsegen or Mr. Shaneyfelt. Prior to trial, the government filed two motions in limine to prohibit the expert witnesses from testifying. After listening to the arguments of counsel for both parties, the district court granted the government's motions. The court, relying upon United States v. Johnson, 575 F.2d 1347 (5th Cir.1978), cert. denied, 440 U.S. 907, 99 S.Ct. 1213, 59 L.Ed.2d 454 (1979), determined that the jury was able to make the necessary photographic comparisons without the aid of expert witnesses. *Johnson* held that "[i]f the question is one which the layman is competent to determine for himself, the opinion is excluded; if he reasonably cannot form his own conclusion without the assistance of the expert, the testimony is admissible." Id. at 1361 (citation omitted).

. . . Because of the specific nature of the proffered testimony in this case, together with the complete lack of any evidence other than the eyewitness identification connecting Dr. Alexander to the robbery, we find that the district court's exclusion of Dr. Alexander's expert witnesses was clearly erroneous.[3]

---

1. A "bait-pack" was included in the money given to the robber. This is a pack of bills with an electronic device inside of it which, when detonated, will expel dye on the money and whatever else is in contact with the pack at the time. No dye-stained money or clothing was recovered from Dr. Alexander. [Footnotes by court.]

2. Cephalometry is defined as the scientific measurement of the dimensions of the head.

3. Dr. Alexander also claims that the district court's exclusion of the expert testi-

Contrary to the conclusion of the district court, the jury was not as well-qualified as Dr. Gottsegen to determine whether Dr. Alexander was the man in the bank surveillance photographs. As Dr. Gottsegen said in his final report, Dr. Alexander and the bank robber possessed similar physical characteristics, and it would be easy for the jury to be misled by the superficial resemblance between the two men. Dr. Gottsegen's testimony, however, would have illustrated claimed specific differences in their facial features which were revealed as a result of his scientific analysis of the photographs.[4] It is unlikely that any of the jurors were sufficiently informed about cephalometry to undertake this type of comparison without expert assistance.

Expert testimony is commonly used to aid jurors in the visual comparison of objects. . . . Yet the features of a human face are much more complicated than the design on the soles of a pair of shoes. The information that Dr. Gottsegen obtained through his analysis of the photographs of Dr. Alexander and the robber constituted competent, relevant evidence of great assistance to the jury in reaching its decision. Federal Rule of Evidence 702 provides that "[i]f scientific, technical, or other specialized knowledge will assist the trier of fact to understand the evidence or to determine a fact in issue, a witness qualified as an expert by knowledge, skill, experience, training or education may testify thereto in the form of an opinion or may otherwise." Dr. Gottsegen's testimony was highly relevant and should have been admitted. . . .

We also conclude that the district court erred in barring the testimony of Mr. Shaneyfelt, the photographic comparison expert. Mr. Shaneyfelt would have presented evidence regarding the amount of distortion in the pictures taken by the bank surveillance cameras and the effect such distortion would have upon the subject of the photographs. This testimony would have aided the jury in visually comparing the photos and would not have tended just to confuse the jury, as the district court held.

Mr. Shaneyfelt also arranged for a professional photographer to take pictures of Dr. Alexander. These photos duplicated the exact distance, camera angle, and focal length of those taken at the bank. Mr. Shaneyfelt compared the two sets of photographs and concluded that it was impossible for Dr. Alexander to be the man photographed in the bank. The district court, in excluding Mr. Shaneyfelt's testimony, also prohibited Dr. Alexander from introducing in evidence the professionally posed photographs. The stated ground was that they could be misleading. The jury, therefore, was required to make a decision regarding the identification of Dr. Alexander as the bank robber without the benefit of expert assistance or even a standard basis of photographic comparison. . . .

mony denied him his constitutional right to present a full defense under the holding of Chambers v. Mississippi, 410 U.S. 284, 93 S.Ct. 1038, 35 L.Ed.2d 297 (1973). Because the exclusion of the expert testimony in this case can be decided on narrower grounds, we pretermit the constitutional issue.

4. Dr. Gottsegen compared the profiles of Dr. Alexander and the bank robber by constructing a standard reference plane for each photograph. A standard reference plane is created by drawing a straight line from the tragion, the most anterior point in the supra-tragal notch of the ear, to the tip of the nose. A mesh-type grid of a simple four-square design is then created by drawing three lines perpendicular and two lines parallel to the original line. The perpendicular lines are tangent to the back of the head, through the tragion itself and tangent to the tip of the nose. The two parallel lines are tangent to the top of the head and to the bottom of the chin. Facial landmarks and other physical features are then examined in relation to the particular quadrant of the grid in which they are located. The ratio of any portion of the face to the whole may also be determined and compared.

Although we find that the district court erred in granting the motion in limine to exclude the testimony of Dr. Alexander's expert witnesses, we do not hold that such evidence will always be admissible in every case. The particular circumstances of this situation mandate that Dr. Gottsegen and Mr. Shaneyfelt be allowed to testify. The only substantial evidence connecting Dr. Alexander to the robbery was the bank employees' identification of Dr. Alexander's driver's license photograph.[5] United States v. Moore, 786 F.2d 1308, 1313 (5th Cir.1986) recognized that "[i]n some cases, casual eyewitness testimony may make the entire difference between a finding of guilt or innocence." The entire case against Victor Alexander turned on the photographic identification, and it was clearly erroneous for the district court to exclude without good reason relevant expert testimony bearing directly on that issue.

The decision in Moore, holding that the district court did not err in excluding expert testimony on the reliability of eyewitness identification, is properly distinguishable from the present case. Moore's expert witness would have testified only about general problems with perception and memory.[6] Requiring the admission of the expert testimony proffered in Moore would have established a rule that experts testifying generally as to the value of eyewitness testimony would have to be allowed to testify in every case in which eyewitness testimony is relevant. This would constitute a gross overburdening of the trial process by testimony about matters which juries have always been deemed competent to evaluate. Dr. Alexander's witnesses, in stark contrast, would have dealt with the precise issue before the jury, comparison photo identification of Dr. Alexander as the bank robber. Exclusion of this type of testimony by the district court's granting of the motions in limine was an abuse of discretion.

Later, at the trial, the issue arose again. As part of its case-in-chief, the government introduced the testimony of four witnesses who had no connection at all with the savings and loan institution or with the robbery. They were, however, acquainted with Dr. Alexander, and they identified him as the man pictured in the bank surveillance photographs. This testimony was admitted under Rule 701 of the Federal Rules of Evidence, which provides that "[i]f a witness is not testifying as an expert, his testimony in the form of opinions or inferences is limited to those opinions or inferences which are (a) rationally based on the perception of the witness and (b) helpful to a clear understanding of his testimony or the determination of a fact in issue." In response, Dr. Alexander undertook by motion to have the court allow him to call Dr. Gottsegen and Mr. Shaneyfelt to rebut the lay opinion testimony of the government's witnesses. The district court again refused to permit the testimony. The result was that casual lay witness opinion testimony of photo identification on behalf of the government was admitted, but careful expert analytical photo identification on behalf of Dr. Alexander was excluded. We find that the district court's decision not to allow the expert rebuttal testimony on the very same facts in issue because "it would not be helpful to the jury" was clearly erroneous. . . .

Reversed.

---

5. A review of the record reveals that the prosecution's case against Dr. Alexander mainly consisted of an in-depth recitation of his sloppy bookkeeping procedures and his habit of visiting night clubs featuring exotic dancers.

6. Expert testimony on the subject of eyewitness identification may include such things as "the 'forgetting curve,' which shows that memory decreases at a geometric rather than an arithmetic rate; the 'assimilation factor,' which indicates that witnesses sometimes incorporate inaccurate post-event information into their identifications; [and] the 'feedback factor,' which demonstrates that witnesses who discuss the case with each other may unconsciously reenforce mistaken identifications." Moore, 786 F.2d at 311.

NOTES

1. See United States v. Fadayini, 28 F.3d 1236, 1241 (D.C.Cir.1994) (individuals identified from automatic teller camera pictures; the jury was capable without the aid of an expert witness of comparing the defendants with the pictures). The court of appeals held it was not an abuse of discretion to allow the expert to testify since "we cannot say it was totally unhelpful to the jury. It may have served to focus the jury on particular characteristics of the defendant (e.g. facial features, distinguishing marks), thereby aiding the jurors' independent assessment of the photographs." See also United States v. Dorsey, 45 F.3d 809 (4th Cir.1995) (no abuse of discretion under Rule 702 to exclude testimony of anthropologists offered by defendant to testify that bank robbery photographs were not of him).

In 3 Wigmore, Evidence § 790, at 220 (Chadbourn rev. 1970), it is now noted that as a result of advances in the art of photography,

> it has become clear that an additional theory of admissibility of photographs is entitled to recognition. Thus, even though no human is capable of swearing that he personally perceived what a photograph purports to portray (so that it is not possible to satisfy the requirements of the "pictorial testimony" rationale) there may nevertheless be good warrant for receiving the photograph in evidence. Given an adequate foundation assuring the accuracy of the process of producing it, the photograph should then be received as so-called silent witness or as a witness which "speaks for itself."

The older rule continues to have some vitality. See, e.g., New York Times, September 10, 1980 p. A16:

Judge Bars Videotapes At Klan–Nazi Murder Trial

> GREENSBORO, N.C., Sept. 9 (UPI)—A state judge ruled today that the prosecution could not show slow-motion videotapes of a gun battle last fall in which five Communists died at a "Death to the Klan" rally....

> Judge James Long of Superior Court watched one of the slow-motion tapes before saying it could not be presented to the jury. "As I saw it I couldn't help but see a lot of things that had not been testified about," he said.

> Under North Carolina law, videotapes and photographs can be used only to illustrate previous testimony and cannot be used by the jury as the sole basis for a verdict.

2. Hurst v. State, 397 So.2d 203, 206 (Ala.Crim.App.1981):

> As a general rule, photographs are admissible in evidence if they tend to prove or disprove some disputed or material issue, to illustrate or elucidate some other relevant fact or evidence, to corroborate or disprove some other evidence offered or to be offered, and their admission is within the sound discretion of the trial judge.... Photographs may be admitted if they tend to shed light on, strengthen, or to illustrate other testimony in the case.... The fact that a photograph is gruesome is no reason for excluding it, if relevant, even if the photograph may tend to inflame the jury.... and the fact that photographic evidence is merely cumulative of detailed oral testimony does not affect its admissibility.... The admission of cumulative evidence, even upon an undisputed fact, is not prejudicial error.

United States v. Valdes, 417 F.2d 335, 338 (2d Cir.1969), cert. denied, 399 U.S. 912 (1970), is a typical example of authentication. In support of a photograph rebutting defendant's claim of police brutality, witnesses testified to the fact that this photograph had been taken at the time of the arrest, and that it correctly pictured the defendant as they had observed him.

As Hurst suggests, a photograph may be used to counter other evidence. In United States v. Laughlin, 772 F.2d 1382 (7th Cir.1985), a prosecution for distribution of drugs, the defendant's wife testified that her husband only used drugs for recreational purposes. To rebut this claim, the government introduced photographs of the defendant smoking marijuana, standing amid marijuana plants, and in the presence of large sums of cash spread out on the floor. In approving the admission of this evidence, the court explained:

> At trial, the Government argued that the photographs were relevant because they tended to show that Laughlin was involved in the business of dealing in narcotics. Because Laughlin's wife testified that Laughlin used drugs for recreational purposes, the Government was entitled to introduce evidence to demonstrate that Laughlin did not simply use drugs but that he also dealt in narcotics for profit.

772 F.2d at 1392.

3.   Heimbach v. Peltz, 121 A.2d 114, 116–117 (Pa.1956):

> While it is properly assumed that the lens of a camera will not lie, the reliability of the resulting product, in so far as evidence in a factual controversy is concerned, depends on many factors which have little or nothing to do with the fidelity of the mechanical process.... Many questions must be answered before a photograph may be accepted as incontrovertible. When was the picture taken? Had the photographed objects been moved ...? Who took the picture? At what angle was the shot made? It is common knowledge that a given condition may be so photographed from different angles as to produce conflicting views of the situation under the camera's lens.

See Scott, Photographic Evidence (2d Ed.1969), Ch. 3; id. at §§ 977, 1475 (composite photographs); id. at § 1050 (retouching); 72 A.L.R.2d 308 (1960) (enlargements); Houts, From Evidence to Proof 173–87 (1956); Houts, Photographic Misrepresentation (1969).

4.   Color prints are admissible. People v. Talbot, 414 P.2d 633 (Cal. 1966), cert. denied, 385 U.S. 1015, (1967), overruled on other grounds, People v. Ireland, 450 P.2d 580 (Cal. 1969) (photograph of deceased on autopsy table). See Capecelatro, Color Photography—A New Technique, 24 N.Y.State Bar Bull. 372 (1952). See 53 A.L.R.2d 1102 (1957). What problems may arise regarding color photographs that do not exist if black and white pictures are used? See Faught v. Washam, 329 S.W.2d 588, 599–601 (Mo.1959); Shaffer, Bullets, Bad Florins and Old Boots: A Report of the Indiana Trial Judges Seminar on the Judge's Control over Demonstrative Evidence, 39 Notre Dame Lawyer 20, 28–29 (1963); K.B. Hughes & B.J. Cantor, Photographs in Civil Litigation (1973).

5.   New York Family Court Act Part 2, Child Protective Proceedings § 1027(g):

> In all cases involving abuse the court shall order, and in all cases involving neglect the court may order, an examination of the child pursuant to section two hundred fifty-one of this act or by a physician appointed or designated for the purpose by the court. As part of such examination, the physician shall arrange to have colored photographs taken as soon as practical of the areas of trauma visible on such child and may, if indicated, arrange to have a radiological examination performed on the child. The physician, on the completion of such examination, shall forward the results

thereof together with the color photographs to the court ordering such examination. The court may dispense with such examination in those cases which were commenced on the basis of a physical examination by a physician. Unless colored photographs have already been taken or unless there are no areas of visible trauma, the court shall arrange to have colored photographs taken even if the examination is dispensed with.

6. Even where the representation is accurate, a photograph may be inadmissible because its subject matter is irrelevant. In Evansville School Corp. v. Price, 208 N.E.2d 689 (Ind.App.1965), a wrongful death action, a photograph of the dead boy in his coffin was admitted at trial as tending to show the boy's good health and the expense incurred by his parents. The appellate court reversed on the ground of lack of legitimate relevance except to establish the fact of death, which was admitted in the pleadings. Cf. Loftin v. Howard, 82 So.2d 125, 127 (Fla.1955) in which photographs of the railroad yard where the accident occurred were held inadmissible: "It is a matter of common knowledge that a railroad yard is a working place, that the spectacle of it changes from day to day and hour to hour. Having been taken more than a year after the accident, the photographs were remote and misleading and did not depict the scene that they were intended to do." See also Liberty National Life Ins. Co. v. Kendrick, 231 So.2d 750, 753 (Ala.Civ.App.1970) (photographs offered to show road conditions): ". . . considering the length of time that had elapsed between the date of the accident and the date of the photographs, with the changes that logically could have occurred, such as grass growing on the edge of the roadway, or not growing thereon, foliage on bushes and trees, or the absence of foliage thereon, all being dependent on the seasons and the condition of the roadway itself, whether worn by traffic or weather, and its upkeep and repair; we are, therefore, unable to say that the trial judge abused his discretion in refusing to admit the photographs offered by appellant."

In Crouse v. Knights Life Insurance Co., 124 F.Supp. 668, 670 (W.D.Pa. 1954), the issue was whether decedent's death was caused by accident or suicide. Plaintiff's theory was that decedent while suspended from a tree and engaged in shooting sparrows off his roof had met death accidentally. Defense witnesses testified that this tree could not support the weight of a man. Plaintiff then introduced a photograph of the tree taken two years after decedent's death. The court held that this photograph was admissible, since the jury could determine if the tree could, two years before, have supported a man's weight.

7. Photographs, like other real evidence, may be excluded as unduly prejudicial. See Chapter 1, supra.

8. Much of the scientific evidence developed in police laboratories and by medical examiners is presented in court by means of photographs. Accepted routines provide for extensive use of photography to record original conditions and the results of tests. See generally, Scott, Photographic Evidence, chs. 6–17 (2d ed. 1969); Kennedy, Photography in Arson Investigations, 46 J.Crim.L. 726 (1956). See 26 A.L.R.2d 892 (1952) (ballistics); 28 A.L.R.2d 1115, 1141 (1953) (fingerprints); 35 A.L.R.2d 856, 874 (1954) (footprints). Photographs permitting the trier visually to check the observations related by the expert no doubt enhance the effectiveness of the expert testimony; see 77 A.L.R. 946, Expert Testimony to Interpret or Explain or Draw Conclusions from Photographs (1932).

9. 2 Wharton, Criminal Evidence 773 (11th ed. 1935), with reference to the admissibility of "posed photographs":

There is a decided conflict of authority as to whether or not photographs of an attempted reproduction of the scene of a crime showing posed persons, dummies, or other objects are admissible to illustrate the contention of the party offering them as to the relative positions of the movable objects so represented at the time and place of the crime involved in the prosecution under consideration. Some courts have looked with disfavor upon the admission of photographs of an attempted theory or contention of the party offering them, as recalled by his witnesses, of movable or moving objects. Thus, it was held error to introduce in evidence in a prosecution for murder photographic representations of tableaux vivants carefully arranged by the chief witness for the State, intended to exhibit the situations of the parties and the scene of the tragedy according to such witness's account of it.... In most jurisdictions where this question of admissibility has arisen, however, the courts have held such photographs admissible, when a proper foundation therefor has been laid by preliminary testimony showing that the objects and situations portrayed are faithfully represented as to position. The holding of these cases has been elucidated by one court, in a case in which it held admissible a photograph of the interior of a saloon in which a shooting occurred showing a group of prearranged figures to indicate the position of the principal parties at the time of the homicide as near as the witness could determine, as follows: "It has always been permissible to use diagrams in the trial of causes, both civil and criminal, and especially in the latter class to use diagrams, if shown to be correct, to illustrate the position of persons and places, and to better enable the witnesses to properly locate them. If, then, a diagram may be used for such a purpose, we can see no good reason why a photograph may not be, by which is presented to view everything within the range of the camera at the time the photograph is taken. This did not deprive the defendant of the right to cross-examine the witnesses who testified to its correctness, and as to the positions of the persons in the saloon, or its fixtures. He had the same right in this regard that he would have had, had a diagram been used instead of the photograph."

Roberts v. State, 166 P.2d 111 (Okl.Crim.App.1946) (court declared that the Oklahoma rule is that "posed photographs" are admissible, if properly identified, if they purport to represent conditions as they actually existed at some crucial time and place, but not if they are "intended only to illustrate hypothetical situations and to explain certain theories of the parties"). But see Borough v. Duluth, Missabe & Iron Range Ry. Co., 762 F.2d 66, 70 (8th Cir.1985) (questioning propriety of film "carefully staged ... for the purposes of this litigation").

NOTES ON X–RAYS AND ANALOGOUS TECHNIQUES

1. Admissibility requirements of identity, accuracy, and relevancy are no different for X-rays or electromagnetic scanning devices than for any other photographs; attesting to them is complicated, however, by the impossibility of naked-eye comparisons by a witness present when the X-ray is taken. See, generally, Scott, X-ray Pictures as Evidence, 44 Mich.L.Rev. 773 (1946); Annot., Preliminary Proof, Verification, or Authentication of X-rays Requisite to Their Introduction in Evidence in Civil Cases, 5 A.L.R.3d 303 (1966). In one case, Carlson v. Benton, 92 N.W. 600 (Neb.1902), the X-ray of a fracture was held properly authenticated by a doctor's account of his manual examination of the injury. It is also possible to show the mechanical accuracy of the equipment and the competence of the operator. See Highland Underwriters Ins. Co. v. Helm,

449 S.W.2d 548 (Tex.Civ.App.1969), where the foundation testimony came from an attending physician who observed the X-ray process. It would be unusual to have this happen in a large hospital, however; in the typical case the testifying doctor assumes that the record on the X-ray plate is correct, and no issue of authentication is raised. See Fed.R.Evid. 703.

2. In Crocker v. Lee, 74 So.2d 429, 436 (Ala.1954), the appellate court reversed the trial judge for refusing to permit professional medical witnesses to illustrate X-ray photographs through a view screen or illuminator: "There is nothing inherently improper in the use of such a device and the trial court should be careful in unreasonably restricting such use, since it would be of considerable benefit to the jury in determining the exact status of the injuries."

Beauchamp v. Davis, 217 S.W.2d 822, 824 (Ky.1948): "The evidence offered and rejected was the print of an X-ray, the negative of which disappeared during the trial of the case. The Court erred in rejecting this evidence.... The print made from the negative of the X-ray is no less authentic than a print made from the negative of any other film. It is an exact reproduction of the picture on paper, or some other material, and often, if not always, is clearer than the negative to the eye of a layman."

3. Texas Employers' Insurance Association v. Crow, 221 S.W.2d 235, 10 A.L.R.2d 913 (Tex.1949): "It has become a matter of common knowledge that X-ray pictures only reflect shadows of solid or hard substances. A nonexpert may see whatever the shadowgram reflects, the same as an expert. What is apparent to one would be apparent to the other. The science of X-ray photography has developed to the point that it is customary for dentists and doctors to make their own pictures. The things portrayed in such pictures are depicted with such clarity and definiteness that quite often no interpretation of them is needed. Certainly, the jury, having inspected X-ray photographs during the trial of the case after their proper introduction and irrespective of whether there has been an explanation of them, should be permitted to re-examine them in the jury room if in their opinion they deem it necessary." See Hall v. State, 219 S.W.2d 475 (Tex.Crim.App.1949); 10 A.L.R.2d 918 (1950).

4. In Slow Development Co. v. Coulter, 353 P.2d 890 (Ariz.1960) the court admitted colored drawings prepared by a medical artist, who did not testify, which were copied from X-rays which had also been admitted. A doctor testified that the drawings were accurate reproductions of the X-rays he had been shown.

5. Problems similar to that posed by X-rays are presented by infra-red pictures, automatic tape recordings or automatic surveillance pictures where there is no witness to testify that the recording or picture conformed to what he heard or saw. See, e.g., United States v. Clayton, 643 F.2d 1071 (5th Cir.1981) (where some frames from bank robbery pictures were authenticated and others were taken from the same roll, not all need to be authenticated by person who saw event; use of model wearing clothing of defendant with companion pictures approved). Does enhancement of photographs at various wave lengths—i.e. infra-red or radio wave—through computers present solvable issues under the rules of evidence?

Bannister v. Town of Noble, Okl.

United States Court of Appeals, Tenth Circuit, 1987.
812 F.2d 1265.

■ TACHA, CIRCUIT JUDGE.

A.

The first videotape Noble challenges is a "Day in the Life" film. Such films purport to show how an injury has affected the daily routine of its victim. Typical "Day in the Life" films show the victim in a variety of everyday situations, including getting around the home, eating meals, and interacting with family members. These films are prepared solely to be used as evidence in litigation concerning the injury. Such evidence is often desired because "films illustrate, better than words, the impact the injury had had on the plaintiff's life." Grimes v. Employers Mut. Liab. Ins. Co., 73 F.R.D. 607, 610 (D.Alaska 1977). Noble argues that Bannister's "Day in the Life" videotape was unduly prejudicial within the meaning of Fed.R.Evid. 403 and thus inadmissible.

The admission of a "Day in the Life" film as evidence in a trial raises obvious dangers of prejudice to the opposing party. In Bolstridge v. Central Maine Power Co., 621 F.Supp. 1202, 1203–04 (D.Me.1985), the court outlined several concerns which led it to conclude that the prejudicial impact of a "Day in the Life" film outweighed its probative value. We think the concerns expressed by the court in *Bolstridge* are instructive and we examine each in turn.

The first concern of the court in Bolstridge was whether the videotape fairly represented the facts with respect to the impact of the injuries on the plaintiff's day-to-day activities. 621 F.Supp. at 1203. As we have stated, "Motion pictures ... must be premised by a foundation of accuracy and fairness." Sanchez v. Denver & Rio Grande W. R.R. Co., 538 F.2d 304, 306 n. 1 (10th Cir.1976), cert. denied, 429 U.S. 1042, 97 S.Ct. 742, 50 L.Ed.2d 754 (1977). A film depicting the victim in unlikely circumstances or performing improbable tasks cannot be said to fairly portray a typical "Day in the Life" of the victim. The probative value of a film is greatest, and the possibility of prejudice lowest, when the conduct portrayed is limited to ordinary, day-to-day situations.

The second concern of the court in Bolstridge was that "the fact that a plaintiff is aware of being videotaped for [the purpose of litigation] is likely to cause self-serving behavior, consciously or otherwise." 621 F.Supp. at 1203 (citing Haley v. Byers Transp. Co., 414 S.W.2d 777, 780 (Mo.1967)). This is probably inevitable to some degree in any film that is prepared specifically for trial, and it counsels against the admission of such evidence. Particularly egregious self-serving conduct raises still greater prejudice problems. For instance, when considering a filmed reenactment of the plaintiff's injuries in Sanchez, we wrote that "had the subject motion picture portrayed the plaintiff entering his position of peril with a look of alarm on the face of his stand-in the film should be rejected as corrupt even though otherwise accurate." 538 F.2d at 306 n. 1. Exaggerated difficulty in performing ordinary tasks presents a similar danger of prejudice. Additionally, conduct that "serve[s] little purpose other than to create sympathy for the plaintiff" is highly prejudicial. Grimes, 73 F.R.D. at 610 (the prejudicial effect of scenes of the plaintiff with his quadriplegic brother outweighed their probative value).

The Bolstridge court next recognized the dominating nature of film evidence. 621 F.Supp. at 1204. See also Thomas v. C.G. Tate Constr. Co., Inc., 465 F.Supp. 566, 571 (D.S.C.1979). The concern is that a jury will better remember, and thus give greater weight to, evidence presented in a film as opposed to more conventionally elicited testimony. This, too, is a legitimate concern that must be recognized in determining the prejudicial effect of a "Day in the Life" film.

The final concern expressed by the court in Bolstridge was that a "Day in the Life" film could distract the jury because the benefit of effective cross-examination is lost. 621 F.Supp. at 1204. While it is true that opposing counsel will not be present to question the victim during the making of a film, this difficulty is lessened if the victim can be cross-examined at trial regarding the events depicted in the film. Films are frequently used at trial in conjunction with live testimony. See, e.g., Slakan v. Porter, 737 F.2d 368, 378 (4th Cir.1984) (videotape demonstrating power of water hose shown along with the expert testimony of a fireman), cert. denied, 470 U.S. 1035, 105 S.Ct. 1413, 84 L.Ed.2d 796 (1985); Szeliga v. General Motors Corp., 728 F.2d 566, 567–68 (1st Cir.1984) (videotapes demonstrating wheels crashing into cement wall shown in conjunction with expert's testimony about cause of accident). The possibility that a film will be prejudicial is significantly reduced when the subject of that film can be cross-examined at trial.

We have held that "the prejudicial effect of a videotape is to be decided on a case by case basis." Durflinger v. Artiles, 727 F.2d 888, 894 (10th Cir.1984). The district court must determine whether the probative value of a particular "Day in the Life" film outweighs the possibility of prejudice in light of the concerns outlined above. The judge should examine a film outside the presence of the jury in order to make this determination. The resulting decision regarding the prejudicial impact of showing the film to the jury is within the discretion of the trial court. Id. We will reverse that decision only if it was an abuse of discretion.

In the present case, the district court examined the film and concluded that it accurately portrayed the daily routine of the plaintiff and that it was not unduly prejudicial. We have reviewed the film as well. The film shows Bannister getting around school, getting into his car, pumping gasoline for his car, and performing several different tasks in his home. Although there are a couple of scenes that show Bannister conducting activities that he would be unlikely to do frequently, the film as a whole demonstrates Bannister's adaptation to his injury. We hold that the district court did not abuse its discretion in admitting the film depicting a "Day in the Life" of Clifford Bannister. . . .

C.

Noble also argues that the district court erred when it allowed Bannister to show a videotape to the jury during closing argument. The videotape was edited to show portions of the "Day in the Life" tape, the demonstration tape, and a portion of a taped deposition of one of Bannister's doctors. We first note that the district court has a great deal of discretion in controlling arguments of counsel. Ramsey v. Culpepper, 738 F.2d 1092, 1100 (10th Cir.1984) (quoting Ward v. H.B. Zachry Constr. Co., 570 F.2d 892, 895 (10th Cir.1978)). Furthermore, a judgment should not be set aside unless it is clear that the closing argument has unduly aroused the sympathy of the jury thereby influencing the verdict. Ramsey, 738 F.2d at 1100 (quoting Julander v. Ford Motor Co., 488 F.2d 839, 842 (10th Cir.1973)). All of the videotapes used to make the closing argument tape had been properly admitted into evidence during the course of the trial. In addition, the district court viewed the videotape prior to allowing it to be shown to the jury. We have also reviewed the tape. We find that the district court did not abuse its discretion.

Affirmed.

NOTES

1. The question of admissibility should be handled by an in limine motion to allow introduction so that the court and opposing counsel can examine the film or tape and oppose entirely or provide for redaction. See Grimes v. Employers Mutual Liability Ins. Co., 73 F.R.D. 607 (D.Alaska 1977) (discussing hearsay aspects and admitting). Do surreptitiously taken films by an opponent present the same dangers?

Compare Cisarik v. Palos Community Hospital, 193 Ill.App.3d 41, 549 N.E.2d 840 (1989) (shooting of a day-in-the-life film is not a deposition and opposing counsel had no right to be present; prior to trial opposing counsel has the right to see the film and may use any portion of the film taken and not intended to be used by the proponent). Cisarik would require retaining all film shot.

2. People v. Eisenberg, 238 N.E.2d 719 (N.Y.1968): The court admitted a television newsreel "not 'in sequence' "and which had been "cut and spliced." Although the tape depicted a version of events that conflicted with testimony, the court would not hold, as a matter of law, that the spliced and cut television tape constituted a complete refutation of testimony. But see the dissent:

> The majority has found the record in this case—containing 229 pages of conflicting and inconclusive testimony supplied by interested witnesses—sufficient to sustain the defendant's conviction. An objective account of the occurrence, supplied by the continuous filming of the events in question, flatly contradicts their determination. Stated otherwise, the evidence that was presented at the trial is, in our opinion, incredible as a matter of law, to sustain the conviction of this defendant. The film, viewed by this court, presents an accurate record of the events which, according to the majority, constitute the crime of willfully interfering with an officer in the performance of his duty. While the film and photographs are not conclusive, nevertheless, the cumulative pictorial evidence both supplies deficiencies existing in Officer Pollino's testimony and does substantial damage to it. Thus, Officer Pollino testified that he did not know how many officers were present when he was handcuffing Barkin. The film and pictures show that at least seven other officers were there at that time, who were not engaged in any discernible activity. Also, the officer testified that the defendant grabbed him and spun him around, while he was performing this act. (His information described it as a violent act on defendant's part.) There is not one photograph showing that the defendant either grabbed or spun the officer. Certain photographs do show that Officer Pollino—while applying the handcuffs—did in fact turn his head to the right on two occasions to observe the defendant. However, the only hand visible that would cause him to turn from force or pressure belonged to a fellow patrolman, as evidenced by his uniform sleeve. The film also confirms defendant's testimony. As noted above, the testimony in support of the officer was furnished by two fellow patrolmen and a civilian who admitted a dislike for the DuBois Club. In like manner, the witnesses appearing on behalf of the defendant were members of the club. For all these reasons, the only conclusion to be drawn from the record is that there was in fact no interference.

3. Increasingly, videotapes are being relied upon in both civil and criminal trials. The use of such techniques often proves highly persuasive to juries which can observe demeanor as well as hear the words—including pauses and intonations—of the actors and see the subtle body language and use of objects. Such evidence was devastating in the Abscam cases. For example, in United States v. Weisz, 718 F.2d 413, 431 (D.C.Cir.1983), cert. denied, 465 U.S. 1027 (1984), the court stated (footnotes omitted):

> The probative value of the video tape of [Congressman] Kelly's meeting with Amoroso, including the money stuffing scene, cannot be gainsaid. The meeting provided direct evidence of Kelly's relationship with Ciuzio when, during the meeting, Kelly asked to talk to Ciuzio and later requested that Amoroso "deal with Gino [Ciuzio] about" Kelly's $25,000. The video tape itself allowed the jury the unique opportunity to observe Kelly's demeanor as Amoroso explained and Kelly accepted the obviously corrupt proposal. Kelly registered no surprise or protest during Amoroso's discourse, but rather demonstrated familiarity with the proposal by revealing that he understood the purpose for the Arabs' investments in his district. When Amoroso offered the $25,000 in cash, Kelly calmly stuffed the five packets of bills into his suit, all the while continuing his conversation with Amoroso about a possible investment for the Arabs in Florida.... [T]he video tape was irrefutable evidence that Kelly had, in fact, been bribed....

Cf. Application of National Broadcasting Co., Inc., 635 F.2d 945 (2d Cir.1980). One danger of the technique is that other juries may be persuaded that failure to produce tapes or recordings or pictures creates a reasonable doubt and is evidence of a frame-up.

4. In Pritchard v. Downie, 326 F.2d 323 (8th Cir.1964), the court held that the editing of a television newsreel affected weight, not admissibility, and the fact that the film was a composite of the work of several photographers did not require exclusion, at least in a non-jury case.

5. United States v. Moran, 194 F.2d 623, 624, 626 (2d Cir.1952), cert. denied, 343 U.S. 965 (1952):

> The appellant was convicted of violating the perjury statute, 18 U.S.C.A. § 1621, in testifying falsely to a material matter before a duly created subcommittee of the United States Senate's Special Committee to Investigate Organized Crime in Interstate Commerce....
>
> During the trial the government asked to show a ten minute film, with sound track removed, of Moran testifying before the subcommittee. This film was exhibited to the jury without any opportunity by defense counsel to see it first. Such a procedure was highly irregular, but unless failure to see it in advance deprived appellant of an opportunity to make a valid objection to the exhibit he was not prejudiced. No such objection could have been made. The film was admissible to show the defendant's demeanor when testifying before the subcommittee. This was important because counsel for appellant had inferred that so much confusion existed that the defendant might well have made a misstatement in good faith. Any possible objection that the film should have shown the three hour proceeding rather than a ten minute speed-up could have been remedied by counsel's request to show the entire proceeding or at least warn the jury that they had seen a shortened version, but no such request was made.

6. In State v. Lusk, 452 S.W.2d 219 (Mo.1970), a sound videotape of the defendant making a confession to police officers was admitted. See also People v. Hayes, 71 P.2d 321 (1937); Commonwealth v. Roller, 100 Pa.Super. 125 (1930). People v. Dabb, 197 P.2d 1 (Cal.1948), involved the admission into evidence of a sound motion picture showing defendants reenacting the crime and admitting that they had committed the crime in the manner depicted. See Busch, Photographic Evidence, 4 De Paul L.Rev. 195, 199 (1954); 62 A.L.R.2d 686 (1958); Hickam and Scanlon, Preparation for Trial, 167–174 (1963).

7.   Sometimes too much is demanded of filmed evidence. In its November 26, 1966, issue, *Life* magazine made the following report on the Warren Commission investigations:

> Of all the witnesses to the tragedy, the only unimpeachable one is the 8–mm. movie camera of Abraham Zapruder, which recorded the assassination in sequence. Film passed through the camera at 18.3 frames a second, a little more than a 20th of a second (.055 seconds) for each frame. By studying individual frames one can see what happened at every instant and measure precisely the intervals between events.

The Commission used this film, together with ballistics evidence, to construct a timetable purporting to prove that the same bullet struck both the President and Governor Connally. But the necessarily subjective interpretation of the events in the film (plus the absence of accurate information about bullet wound reaction times) makes this sort of synchronization suspect. See Houts, Where Death Delights, 67–71 (1967).

United States v. Carbone

United States Court of Appeals, First Circuit, 1986.
798 F.2d 21.

■ BOWNES, CIRCUIT JUDGE. Appellant–defendant Luis Carbone was convicted by a jury on all three counts of an indictment charging: conspiracy with intent to distribute cocaine in violation of 21 U.S.C. § 246; aiding and abetting in the possession of half a kilogram of cocaine with intent to distribute it; and aiding and abetting in the distribution of half a kilogram of cocaine. The second and third counts allege violations of 21 U.S.C. § 841(a)(1) and 18 U.S.C. § 2.

Defendant raises three issues on appeal: the admission into evidence of tape recordings and the use of transcripts of the recordings; whether the evidence was sufficient to prove a conspiracy with intent to distribute; and whether the district court should have conducted a post-trial in camera hearing to determine whether a government witness had committed perjury during the trial.

I.   THE ADMISSION OF THE TAPE RECORDINGS
AND THE USE OF TRANSCRIPTS

A.   The Tape Recordings

Defendant challenges the admission of the tape recordings on the grounds that none of them were authenticated properly, that some of them were inaudible, and that one was inadmissible because it was "enhanced." The contours of the law governing the admissibility of tape recordings are well defined. The government has the duty of laying a foundation that the tape recordings accurately reproduce the conversations that took place, i.e., that they are accurate, authentic, and trustworthy. Once this is done, the party challenging the recordings bears the burden of showing that they are inaccurate. United States v. Rengifo, 789 F.2d 975, 978–79 (1st Cir.1986). "The decision to admit [tape recordings] into evidence is reversible only if the district court abused its discretion." United States v. Cortellesso, 663 F.2d 361, 364 (1st Cir.1981). . . .

This circuit has long followed the generally accepted rule that where a tape recording is challenged on the grounds of audibility the question is whether "the inaudible parts are so substantial as to make the rest more misleading than helpful" and that admissibility rests within the discretion of the trial judge. Gorin v. United States, 313 F.2d 641, 651 (1st Cir.1963); ... 1 Weinstein's Evidence, J. Weinstein & M. Berger, § 106[01] at 106–10–11 (May, 1986).

We have upheld the use of composite tapes as evidence.... As long as the tape recording is properly authenticated, we see no reason why a recording that has been enhanced to improve its audibility by filtering out background noises and improving the clarity of the voices should not also be allowed in evidence....

The preferred way of handling challenges to the accuracy and audibility of tape recordings is at a pretrial hearing. If this is not possible, we see no reason why the district court must lengthen a trial by listening to the tapes outside the presence of the jury. Some tape recording playbacks run for a considerable period of time. If the recordings are properly authenticated, the trial judge can listen to them as they are played to the jury and rule on objections when made. This is the manner in which most testimony is presented. It is within the district court's discretion to determine how evidentiary challenges shall be met. The basic question is whether the tapes were properly admitted into evidence. We find that they were.

Before the tape recordings were admitted into evidence, Edwin Hernandez, the DEA agent in charge of the investigation, explained how each recording was made. There were two types of recordings used: a body recorder, called a Nagra, used by an undercover agent to record conversations uttered at meetings; and tape recordings of telephone conversations. Hernandez described in detail how the body recorder worked and how the conversations were recorded. An expert witness, Robert Brady, also testified as to the operation of the tape recorders. The voices on each of the recordings were identified by a person present during the meeting or privy to the telephone conversation. All the conversations were in Spanish but before the tapes were played the trial judge ascertained that Spanish was the native language of all the jurors. Appellant has suggested that since the conversants used Puerto Rico "street" language the jurors would have had difficulty understanding what was said. This overlooks the fact that the jurors were natives of Puerto Rico and its street language is not foreign to them. We find that the authentication process was satisfactory.

We have played all of the tapes and find that none of them were so inaudible or unintelligible as to make them more misleading than helpful. It is true that exhibit 15, the tape of the visit of government informant Rivera (Manny on the tape) to defendant's office on September 19, 1984, had large gaps due to inaudibility caused by the overlay of background noises. This tape, however, was filtered and then enhanced into a new tape, exhibit 19, which was clear and understandable. The judge explained to the jury that exhibits 15 and 19 were recordings of the same conversations and had them both played.

Defendant objects to the admission of exhibits 15 and 19 because of the enhancement. There is no basis for finding as a matter of law that the enhancement process rendered exhibits 15 and 19 inaccurate and untrustworthy. Robert Brady, a self-employed electrical engineer specializing in developing surveillance equipment for law enforcement agencies, testified for the government. He explained the filtration and enhancement process; it was his opinion that neither process altered or distorted the words recorded. Defendant's expert, Frank M. McDermott, gave a detailed critique of the tape recordings; it was his opinion that they were not accurate. The credibility of the expert witnesses was properly left to the jury.

B. The Use of Transcripts

The trial judge permitted the jury to use transcripts to follow each recording as it was played. Each transcript had two columns: the left-hand column, entitled "Transcript," was in Spanish; the right-hand column, entitled "Translation," was in English. Copies of the transcripts had been furnished defendant prior to trial along with the tape recordings so he had ample opportunity to check their accuracy. When the government first offered a transcript for use by the jury, defendant objected to the admissibility of all the transcripts on two grounds: lack of proper authentication, and inaccuracies in both the Spanish transcripts and the English translations. Defendant requested that the judge check the transcripts against the tape for accuracy before allowing the jury to use them. The judge ruled that the transcripts would not be admitted in evidence, that the jury would be instructed that the tapes, not the transcripts, were evidence and that any differences between the two must be resolved in favor of what was heard on the recording. The motion that the judge check the transcripts against the tapes for accuracy outside the presence of the jury was denied but defense counsel was told that she could point out any inaccuracies in the transcripts "as we go along." Our reading of the record reveals that no specific inaccuracies in any of the transcripts were pointed out or made the basis of an objection as they were used during the trial. Evidently, defense counsel relied on her general objection to the use of the transcripts. The record shows that each time a transcript was furnished the jurors the judge carefully instructed them in accord with his ruling and that the transcripts were taken from the jurors as soon as the playback of each recording was finished.

The trial judge's handling of the transcripts was in accord with the law in this circuit. We have approved, as have most circuits, the use of transcripts as a jury aid in following tape recording playbacks. The trial judge's instructions that the tapes, not the transcripts, constituted the evidence and that the tapes controlled if there was any difference between them reflected accurately the rule in this circuit. . . .

Nor do we find any merit in defendant's objection to the translations. No specific objections were made during the course of the trial to the English translation transcripts, nor have any specific mistakes been pointed out to us, for whose benefit we assume the translations were made. The case was tried by a bilingual jury whose native tongue was Spanish. We can see no error in the use of the transcript translations. . . .

We think that when transcripts are offered for use, either as evidence or a jury aid, they should be authenticated in the same manner as tape recordings that are offered in evidence, i.e., by testimony as to how they were prepared, the sources used, and the qualifications of the person who prepared them. . . . Even if transcripts are not admitted in evidence, in the sense of being marked as exhibits, they are read and relied on by the jury to follow the playback. They should, therefore, be as accurate as possible, which can only be determined if they are authenticated. Authentication does not impose an undue burden either on the government or on a defendant submitting alternate transcripts. . . .

Affirmed.

NOTE

Taping of conversations and the use of transcripts often require interpretation by experts. On experts generally see chapter 3, infra. See, e.g., United States v. Nersesian, 824 F.2d 1294, 1307 (2d Cir.1987) (conversation drug related; in context words such as cheese, land, room, house, car and stick shift related to narcotics); United States v. Rosenthal, 793 F.2d 1214 (11th Cir.1986), cert. denied, 107 S.Ct. 1377 (1987) (expert on inaudibility, enhancement and accuracy of transcripts).

United States v. Sliker

United States Court of Appeals, Second Circuit, 1984.
751 F.2d 477, cert. denied, 470 U.S. 1058 (1985).

■ FRIENDLY, CIRCUIT JUDGE:

Carbone makes several arguments relating to the admission into evidence of a tape recording of a telephone conversation between him and Sliker on January 7, 1982, which the Government was allowed to play to the jury during his cross-examination. After Carbone professed an inability to recall the conversation, the prosecutor sought to refresh his recollection by having him listen to a tape of it, stating that if this should fail, he would offer the tape in evidence. After listening to the tape on an earphone, Carbone was asked whether the tape refreshed his recollection; Carbone replied: "Not too much." When asked whether he tape recorded a conversation between him and Sliker, he responded:

I refuse to answer. I'm not sure. I take the Fifth on that one.

Questioned whether he recognized his own voice, Carbone answered in the negative, adding "I never heard myself on tape." Questioned whether he recognized Sliker's voice, Carbone answered "[n]ot that much." The prosecutor then offered the tape, asking the judge if he would like to listen to it "for the voice identification." The judge did so, the prosecutor then offered the tape,[1] and Carbone's counsel objected.

At a sidebar conference the judge noted that the tape was very clear and stated that "it is clear that it is Mr. Carbone's voice." Carbone's counsel argued that "[t]he court can't be a witness against my client to authenticate—with regard to voice identification." Observing that "I am just acting as the judge," Judge Griesa overruled this objection. The tape was then played to the jury.[2] In addition to showing cordiality and continued dealings between Carbone and Sliker and thus contradicting Carbone's testimony that Sliker's conduct had outraged him and discrediting Carbone's assertion that he had threatened Sliker's life after learning of the fraud, the tape showed that both Sliker and Saluzzi were heavily indebted to Carbone, thereby providing a motive for Carbone to bring them together in an endeavor that might provide them with funds.

Carbone raises two related arguments regarding the authentication of this tape. First, he claims that the judge improperly "testified," in violation of F.R.E. 605, that it was Carbone's voice on the tape. Second, he claims that since no one ever testified before the jury that it was Carbone's voice on the

---

1. The prosecutor wavered as to whether the tape's admissibility for a purpose other than impeachment was as a prior inconsistent statement, which it clearly was not in the sense required by F.R.E. 801(d)(1) or as an admission, which it clearly was, see F.R.E. 801(d)(2). He offered it on both bases. [Footnotes are the court's; some omitted.]

2. After the tape was played, the prosecutor asked whether the "Bill" referred to on the tape was Bill Foster and Carbone answered affirmatively. An objection by Sliker's counsel that his client's voice had not been authenticated led the prosecutor to question Carbone a second time whether he recognized Sliker's voice on the tape; this time Carbone admitted that he did.

tape, no proper foundation was laid for its admission into evidence. Discussion of these objections requires some preliminary analysis.

In order for a piece of evidence to be of probative value, there must be proof that it is what its proponent says it is. The requirement of authentication is thus a condition precedent to admitting evidence. However, whether a given piece of evidence is authentic is itself a question of fact. Contrary to the first branch of Lord Coke's maxim, *ad quaestionem facti non respondent judices; ad quaestionem juris non respondent juratores* (judges don't answer questions of fact; juries don't answer questions of law), the common law rule was that the judge and not the jury should decide "any preliminary questions of fact, however intricate, the solution of which may be necessary to enable him to determine . . . the admissibility" of evidence. Thayer, Preliminary Treatise on Evidence 258 n. 3 (1898) (quoting Gorton v. Hadsell, 9 Cush. 508, 511 (Mass.1852)). The justification for this principle centered on the supposedly limited abilities of juries and on the circularity of having a jury hear evidence in order to determine whether it should hear the evidence. See Maguire & Epstein, Preliminary Questions of Fact in Determining the Admissibility of Evidence, 40 Harv.L.Rev. 392, 393–95 (1926); McCormick, supra, § 53 at 135. . . .

F.R.E. 104 retains the principles thus developed at common law. Subsection (a) provides that

> [p]reliminary questions concerning the qualification of a person to be a witness, the existence of a privilege, or the admissibility of evidence shall be determined by the court, subject to the provisions of subdivision (b).

Subdivision (b) provides:

> When the relevancy of evidence depends upon the fulfillment of a condition of fact, the court shall admit it upon, or subject to, the introduction of evidence sufficient to support a finding of the fulfillment of the condition.

Thus, subsection (a) governs questions concerning the competency of evidence, i.e., evidence which is relevant but may be subject to exclusion by virtue of some principle of the law of evidence, leaving it for the judge to resolve factual issues in connection with these principles. Cf. United States v. Eskow, 422 F.2d 1060, 1069 (2d Cir.1970) ("We have repeatedly emphasized that it is for the court to make the initial determination of a preliminary issue upon which competency of evidence depends." (citing cases)). Examples include not only those expressly stated in the rule (privileged information and witness competency), but others such as the hearsay rule, based on the policy of excluding inherently unreliable evidence; the exclusionary rule, designed to insure the observance by police of Fourth or Fifth Amendment rights; and many others. 1 Weinstein's Evidence, supra, ¶ 104[01] at 104–10; . . . . Removing factual issues related to determining whether evidence is competent from the jury is based on recognition that the typical juror is intent mainly on reaching a verdict in accord with what he believes to be true in the case he is called upon to decide, and is not concerned with the long term policies of evidence law. McCormick, supra, § 53 at 135.

Subsection (b) provides different treatment for situations in which the *relevancy* (i.e., probative value) of evidence, rather than its *competency*, depends upon the existence of a prior fact. United States v. James, 590 F.2d 575, 579 (5th Cir.), cert. denied, 442 U.S. 917, 99 S.Ct. 2836, 61 L.Ed.2d 283 (1979); 1 Weinstein's Evidence, supra, ¶¶ 104[01] at 104–9, 104[09] at 104–71; McCormick, supra, § 53 at 137–38. Judge Weinstein explains why the Federal Rules leave such issues to the jury:

> This exception to the judge's broad power under Rule 104(a) is based on the theory that these questions of conditional relevance are merely matters of probative force, rather than evidentiary policy, and that the jury is competent to receive the evidence-in-chief and still disregard it if they find the non-existence of the preliminary fact.

1 Weinstein's Evidence, supra, ¶ 104[01] at 104–10.

The requirement that a given piece of evidence be what its proponent claims does not reflect some special evidentiary policy like hearsay rules or privileges. Wigmore described the need for authentication as "an inherent logical necessity." 7 Wigmore § 2129, supra, at 703 (emphasis omitted). Authentication is perhaps the purest example of a rule respecting relevance: evidence admitted as something can have no probative value unless that is what it really is. Cf. Notes of Advisory Committee to Rule 901(a). Thus, the Notes of the Advisory Committee accompanying Rule 901 state that questions concerning authentication are governed by the procedures in Rule 104(b). . . .

Under Rule 104(b), the trial judge may make a preliminary determination as to the prior fact and admit the evidence to the jury's final determination that the prior fact exists. See O'Neal, supra, 637 F.2d at 850–51. That is what Judge Griesa did here; as he succinctly put it, he was "just acting as the judge." He listened to the tape and determined, based on his own comparison of the voices, that there was sufficient evidence of the prior fact (that the voice on the tape was Carbone's) to admit the evidence for the jury to hear. This is the course which this court has recommended. . . . although it would have been preferable for the judge to have done it in camera. . . . Carbone's first claim is thus without merit.

The judge's preliminary determination does not, however, finally establish the authenticity of the tape. As with other matters under Rule 104(b), only the jury can finally decide that issue. The judge's admission of the evidence under Rule 104(b) is conditional and "subject to the introduction of evidence sufficient to support a finding of the fulfillment of the condition." F.R.E. 104(b). We thus reach the question whether there was evidence before the jury sufficient to establish that the voice on the tape was Carbone's. Carbone claims there was not. While the Government does not squarely address the issue in its brief, its basic position must be that hearing the tape after having heard Carbone's voice when he testified provided the jury with sufficient evidence to conclude that the voice on the tape was Carbone's.

F.R.E. 901(a) requires "evidence sufficient to support a finding that the matter in question is what its proponent claims," but does not definitively establish the nature or quantum of proof that is required. Cf. F.R.E. 901(a), (b), Notes of Advisory Committee. Subsection (b) provides illustrations of what will suffice. Subsection (b)(5), dealing specifically with the question of voice identification, states that "[i]dentification of a voice, whether heard firsthand or through mechanical or electronic transmission or recording," can be established "by opinion based upon hearing the voice at any time under circumstances connecting it with the alleged speaker." Carbone argues that the opinion referred to must be that of a witness and not that of the trier of the fact, and the Notes of the Advisory Committee suggest that this is so, as does Judge Weinstein, 5 Weinstein's Evidence, supra, ¶¶ 901(b)(5)[01], [02]. However, subsection (b)(5) is only an illustration and several of the other illustrations do not require opinion testimony and leave it to the jury to make its own comparison. Subsection (b)(3), for example, states that authentication of a writing may be established by "[c]omparison by the trier of fact ... with specimens which have been authenticated." Similarly, subsection (b)(4) permits a finding of authenticity based on "distinctive characteristics, taken in conjunction with circumstances." See F.R.E. 901(b)(3), (4), Notes of Advisory Committee; see, e.g., Bagaric, supra, 706 F.2d at 67 (letter authenticated based on contents and location at which it was found). We thus see no reason in principle why, in a case like this, where the person whose voice on a tape is to be identified has testified, the jury cannot itself make the comparison. Had the judge put this question to them, that would end this matter. Cf. United States v. Rizzo, 492 F.2d 443, 448 (2d Cir.) (rejecting challenge to authentication because the "jury was properly instructed" that the Government had to prove that voice on tape was defendant's), cert. denied, 417 U.S. 944, 94 S.Ct. 3069, 41 L.Ed.2d 665 (1974); United States v. Cambindo Valencia, 609 F.2d 603, 640 (2d Cir.1979) (jury was instructed that it must judge worth of testimony of witness who heard a voice exemplar in determining if tape was authenticated), cert. denied sub nom. Prado v. United States, 446 U.S. 940, 100 S.Ct. 2163, 64 L.Ed.2d 795 (1980). Here, moreover, the Government's case was aided by Carbone's identification of the "Bill" referred to on the tape as Foster and of the other voice as Sliker's, see note 10, supra.

Such difficulty as exists comes from the fact that the question was not specifically put to the jury, which might have assumed that the judge had ruled that the voice was Carbone's, not merely preliminarily, but definitively. However, the jury knew there was an issue since it had heard Carbone disclaimability to identify the voice as his own, and the judge delivered the appropriate instruction in his general charge to the effect that the jury was the ultimate judge as to all factual issues. We understand the general rule to be that the judge is permitted but not required to deliver a specific instruction to the jury to consider particularly any preliminary question under Rule 104(b). See 1 Weinstein's Evidence, supra, ¶ 104[09] at 104–72. Particularly where, as here, counsel fails to request such an instruction, cf. F.R.E. 105, the decision whether or not to give one lies in the discretion of the trial judge. Undoubtedly it would have been better to have delivered such an instruction here. However, we see no reason why Judge Griesa was required to fear that a juror who, having just heard Carbone testify, thought that the voice on the tape was not Carbone's would have felt constrained to assume that it was. It was thus not an abuse of discretion for him to have failed to instruct the jury *sua sponte* that it must specifically decide this issue of authentication.

Carbone's remaining contentions in regard to the tape can be disposed of in short order.... Carbone claims that the Government did not adequately demonstrate the accuracy of the tapes. This point was not raised below, where it might have been resolved by the trial judge, and thus may not be raised for the first time on appeal. See United States v. Fuentes, supra, 563 F.2d at 531 (failure to object to authentication and accuracy of tape recordings). The judge correctly ruled that the tape's contents were relevant, since as we have already indicated, they tended both to impeach Carbone's testimony and to provide a motive....

The judgments of conviction are affirmed.

NOTES

1. For a case relying on the main case and criticizing the trial judge for excluding a recording of a police officer on the radio offered by defendant to show he was abused by the officer, see Ricketts v. Hartford, 74 F.3d 1397 (2d

Cir.1996). The judge did not believe the officer's voice in court and the voice on the recording came from the same person; this, the appellate court said, should have been left to the jury.

What is the level of proof required to authenticate a tape under the Federal Rules? See the discussion of burdens of proof, infra, suggesting a single standard of preponderance on all foundational issues. But cf. People v. Ely, 503 N.E.2d 88, 92 (N.Y.1986) ("Admissibility of tape-recorded conversation requires proof of the accuracy or authenticity of the tape by 'clear and convincing evidence' establishing 'that the offered evidence is genuine and that there has been no tampering with it.' ").

Did the court in United States v. Fuentes, 563 F.2d 527, 532 (2d Cir.1977), provide a higher than justifiable standard where a Nagra tape recorder was placed upon the informant and the tape was introduced although the informant was not a witness? The court rejected inflexible criteria, but required "clear and convincing evidence of authenticity and accuracy," "since recorded evidence is likely to have a strong impression upon a jury and is susceptible of alteration."

2. Redaction of objectionable material in the tape and transcript is often essential. How can that be accomplished given the Best Evidence Rule discussed, infra? See, e.g., People v. Ely, 68 N.Y.S.2d 532, 503 N.E.2d 88 (1986). Objections to audibility and accuracy of translations or to authentication must be made with specificity and if not raised before trial will be likely to get short shrift in the exercise of discretion on trial and on appeal. See United States v. Font–Ramirez, 944 F.2d 42 (1st Cir.1991).

3. The rule of completeness is usually applied to documents but it may be used with sound recordings and should be considered in connection with other forms of real proof as well as conversations and other events described by a witness. See Fed.R.Evid. 106(a). In re Air Crash Disaster at John F. Kennedy International Airport on June 24, 1975, 635 F.2d 67, 72 (2d Cir.1980):

> The Refusal of the Judge to Allow the Playing of the One Channel of the Cockpit Voice Recorder by Itself.
>
> This purported error was an action clearly within the discretion of the trial judge. He ruled, under Fed.R.Evid. 106, that the one channel of the tape was an integral part of the entire tape. The judge heard the tape five times, and then decided it must be played all at once. It was clearly not error to require the tape to be played in that manner.
>
> Federal Rule of Evidence 106 requires any other part of a writing or recorded statement to be admitted "which ought in fairness to be considered contemporaneously with" [the written or recorded statement]. F.R.Evid. 106. Rule 106 applies to tape recordings. 1. J. Weinstein, Evidence, ¶ 106[01] at 106–10. The Judge properly required that the entire tape be played, with adjustments in the volume to make the channels of the tape clearer.
>
> Fountain v. United States, 384 F.2d 624 (5th Cir.1967), cert. denied, 390 U.S. 1005, 88 S.Ct. 1246, 20 L.Ed.2d 105 (1968), does not support Eastern's position, but rather supports the ruling of the Judge. The relevant part of that case dealt with the admissibility of a noise-suppressed copy of a tape recording. The court allowed the noise-suppressed tape to be admitted. Appellant contends that, similarly, the cockpit tape should be played without the other channels. However, the only thing removed from the tape in Fountain was

> "the noise between words.... [I]f a signal is coming through and a man *stops talking* or an individual *stops talking* and there is noise in the background, it removes this noise, *but only this noise.... This at no time is affecting the original tape.*" 384 F.2d at 629 n. 4. (emphasis supplied).

See discussion of Rule 106 in Hearsay Chapter, infra.

4. See A.B.A. Standards Relating to Electronic Surveillance (1971) (the standard is based upon 18 U.S.C. § 2518(8)(a) of Chapter 119, Wire Interception and Interception of Oral Communications):

§ 5.13. Authenticity

(a) Electronic surveillance techniques employed by law enforcement officers for the recording of communications uttered in private without the consent of the parties should be so employed that a complete, accurate and intelligible record of the communication will be obtained.

(b) The contents of any wire or oral communication overheard by any means authorized by these standards should, if possible, be recorded on tape or wire or other comparable device. The recording of the contents of any wire or oral communication authorized under these standards should be done in such way as will protect the recording from editing or other alterations.

5. The use of a sound recording may raise problems of admissibility because of the constitutional prohibition against unreasonable searches and seizures; the statutory prohibition of the Federal Communications Act if the telephone is involved, Lee v. State of Florida, 392 U.S. 378 (1968); an exclusionary state statute, e.g., New York CPLR 4506, 5 Weinstein, Korn & Miller, New York Civil Practice ¶ 4506.01 et seq.; or the due process clause, Katz v. United States, 389 U.S. 347 (1967), United States v. White, 401 U.S. 745 (1971), Irvine v. California, 347 U.S. 128 (1954). See 18 U.S.C. §§ 2510–2520; A.B.A., Minimum Standards Relating to Electronic Surveillance, passim (1968). Ethical problems may also be involved. See A.B.A. Minimum Standards Relating to the Prosecution Function and the Defense Function § 3.1(b) (1968).

6. Recordings may be used to attack the credibility of a witness by showing his amenability to suggestions by the other side. Were this technique used to eavesdrop on a lawyer preparing a witness for trial, would it raise any problems of privilege? Where the recordings are introduced to corroborate a witness' testimony as to what was overheard, is there any violation of the rule against the use of prior consistent statements? See Kilpatrick v. Kilpatrick, 193 A. 765 (Conn.1937).

7. In a prosecution for treason in that defendant allegedly made recordings for radio broadcasts in Germany, the recordings were introduced in evidence. Burgman v. United States, 188 F.2d 637, 639 (D.C.Cir.1951). In rejecting the contention that their use constituted compulsory self-incrimination in violation of the Fifth Amendment, Judge Prettyman wrote:

> They were not mere testimony concerning the acts of treason; they were the physical embodiment of the very acts themselves. The fact that modern science permitted the prosecution to reproduce in the courtroom before the jury the very overt act with which appellant was charged does not lessen the propriety of the presentation....

Are these records the embodiment of the acts of treason, as the court said, or testimony concerning the acts of treason, as the court said they were not, or circumstantial evidence that the acts of treason were in fact committed, or are they something else? Compare Commonwealth v. Clark, 123 Pa.Super. 277, 187

A. 237 (1936), where a record of the attempt at bribery was introduced. Regarding the current doctrine of the privilege against self-incrimination, see chapter 7, section 2.

8. In Boyne City G. & A.R. v. Anderson, 109 N.W. 429 (Mich.1906), a proceeding to condemn land for a railroad's right of way, the court permitted the reproduction of sounds claimed to have been made by the operation of trains in proximity to defendant's hotel. Where a sound recording is used to show the extent of the noise rather than its nature, what precautions can be taken to insure that the volume of the playback device has not been increased?

In one case in the Eastern District of New York where the question involved the level of noise as jet aircraft used an airport, engineers were permitted to install elaborate equipment in a courtroom in an attempt to duplicate the noise surrounding the airport. What are the advantages and disadvantages of such a technique over a "view", over an experiment conducted during the "view"?

9. See United States v. Le Fevour, 798 F.2d 977, 981 (7th Cir.1986):

> In ruling that the rest of the tape could not be placed in evidence because it was inadmissible, the judge implicitly treated Rule 106 as merely regulating the order of proof. So the Rule is often described, see, e.g., United States v. Costner, 684 F.2d 370, 373 (6th Cir.1982); 1 Weinstein's Evidence ¶ 106[02], at p. 106–12 (1985), but the description is misleading. If otherwise inadmissible evidence is necessary to correct a misleading impression, then either it is admissible for this limited purpose by force of Rule 106, the view taken in 21 Wright & Graham, Federal Practice and Procedure § 5072, at p. 344 (1977), or, if it is inadmissible (maybe because of privilege), the misleading evidence must be excluded too. The party against whom that evidence is offered can hardly care which route is taken, provided he honestly wanted the otherwise inadmissible evidence admitted only for the purpose of pulling the sting from evidence his opponent wanted to use against him. Rule 106 was not intended to override every privilege and other exclusionary rule of evidence in the legal armamentarium, for there must be cases where if an excerpt is misleading the only cure is to exclude it rather than to put in other excerpts....

> The purpose of the "completeness" rule codified in Rule 106 is merely to make sure that a misleading impression created by taking matters out of context is corrected on the spot, because of "the inadequacy of repair work when delayed to a point later in the trial." Notes of Advisory Comm. on Proposed rule 106. An example would be accusing the Biblical David of blasphemy for saying, "There is no God," his full statement being, "The fool hath said in his heart, there is no God." Trial of Algernon Sidney, 9 Howell's State Trials 818, 868–69 (K.B.1683). We are far from that paradigmatic case here.

See also United States v. Sutton, 801 F.2d 1346 (D.C.Cir.1986) (portions of taped telephone conversation admitted; other portions admitted on motion of opponent despite claim that they constituted exculpatory inadmissible evidence; Rule 106 is not limited to order of proof). Are hearsay and other exclusionary rules overridden by Rule 106?

10. The tape is introduced in evidence. Transcripts are for the aid of the jury and they are marked for identification. Should the jury wish to see the transcript during deliberation, it must come into the courtroom to use it while listening to the tape. What result if the tape, without the transcript, is played by the jury in the jury room? Cf. United States v. Binder, 769 F.2d 595, 600 n. 1

(9th Cir.1985), where videotaped testimony of a child witness was used in lieu of a court appearance, playing back the testimony—particularly in this case where it was done in the jury room—has the impact of repeating testimony as contrasted with reading back of a transcript. In United States v. Berry, Jr., 64 F.3d 305 (7th Cir.1995), the conviction was reversed when the government prepared transcript was sent into the jury room over objection.

SECTION 6.   BLACKBOARDS, MAPS, MODELS AND THE LIKE

United States v. Brennan

United States District Court, Eastern District New York, 1986.
629 F.Supp. 283, aff'd, 798 F.2d 581 (2d Cir.1986).

■ WEINSTEIN, CHIEF JUDGE:

After an extensive jury trial the defendant, William C. Brennan, has been found guilty of soliciting and accepting a series of bribes to fix cases in his court over many years. This most serious of crimes attacks the foundation of our judicial system and the faith of citizens in its impartiality....

In May 1984 Salvatore Polisi, a career criminal, was arrested in Queens and charged in the state court with the sale of cocaine. Since he had previously been convicted of forgery, gambling, and robbery and was a known associate of the organized crime fraternity, Polisi faced a long prison term. He decided it would be in his interest to approach the Federal Bureau of Investigation and seek employment as an informant.

Polisi was aware that Justice Brennan had a reputation in the criminal community for taking bribes....

A deal was struck between the F.B.I. and Polisi to seek evidence against Bruno [the judge's bagman] and Brennan....

On February 2 Brennan arrived in Florida and told Bruno he had reviewed the Polisi court file. He gave Bruno key information from the file. Since he and his friend, the judge, were spending the day at the Gulfstream Racetrack, Bruno wrote the information on a betting slip. The slip was later retrieved and constituted an important piece of evidence since it contained information that could not have come to Bruno except from someone cognizant of the details of criminal proceedings in Queens.

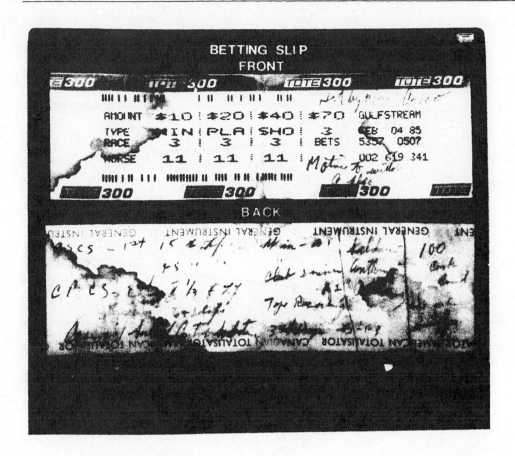

Pursuant to Brennan's instructions, Bruno informed Polisi that a $25,000 down payment was required. [A conversation and surreptitious activity of the judge and Bruno was contemporaneously observed at Lee's restaurant.]

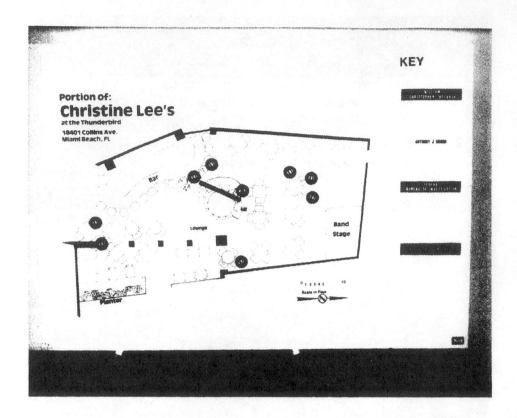

. . .

Although the defendant moved, pursuant to Rule 29 of the Rules of Criminal Procedure, to have the verdict set aside on the ground that there was insufficient evidence to support any of the counts of the indictment, it is obvious that there was no merit to this contention. To be convinced of this one need merely examine some of the charts used by the government in final arguments describing the *Polisi* case. Much of the information on the charts is based on interlocking telephone records, and wiretap and sound recordings whose authenticity could not be challenged. [One of these charts is set out below.]

PEOPLE OF THE STATE OF NEW YORK
v SALVATORE POLISI (IND NO 3738 84)

1985 (cont'd)

Feb. 9, Sat.	Bruno telephones Polisi in New York to tell him that BRENNAN will be in Florida through the following Wednesday or Thursday. Polisi says that he will not be back to Florida before Friday. Bruno tells him that he will get BRENNAN to stay longer.
Feb. 10, Sun.	BRENNAN telephones Bruno at home (at 11:36 a.m.) to confirm dinner arrangements at Christine Lee's the following night. Bruno tells BRENNAN that he has to talk with him about something and remarks that "it will work out then" when BRENNAN tells him that he plans to still be in Florida on Friday, 2/15/85.
Feb. 11, Mon.	Bruno and BRENNAN meet at Christine Lee's and discuss *Polisi* case.
Feb. 14, Thur.	Polisi returns to Florida from New York and meets with Bruno at Runway 84. Arrangements made for money to be paid to Bruno at racetrack after Polisi sees Bruno with BRENNAN.
Feb. 15, Fri.	Bruno meets BRENNAN at Diplomat Hotel and explains arrangements for payoff. BRENNAN extremely suspicious that Polisi is an informant and tells Bruno to call it off.
Feb. 15, Fri.	Bruno telephones Polisi and arranges for meeting that night to discuss a problem created by Polisi.
Feb. 15, Fri.	Bruno searches Polisi for concealed tape recorder and, finding none, arranges for money to be paid to him on 2/16 after which he will give it to BRENNAN to take back to New York.
Feb. 16, Sat.	Bruno meets BRENNAN at Gulfstream Racetrack; BRENNAN tells Bruno "...no, no, no we're not going to do it that way." Instead, he instructs Bruno to hold money and bring it to New York himself when summoned.
	Bruno telephones Polisi and instructs him to bring money to restaurant that night because BRENNAN is leaving the next day.

. . .

VI.   CONCLUSION

The defendant has betrayed the public trust and committed a long series of felonies. He is sentenced to five years in prison in addition to five years probation; denied the right to serve in a position of public office and trust; compelled to disgorge $14,000, the maximum amount recoverable as restitution and fined and assessed the maximum amount permitted by law, $210,300.

So ordered.

NOTES

1. Which of the illustrations in Brennan should have been introduced in evidence and which marked for identification and shown to the jury only in the courtroom as pedagogical devices? If introduced as evidence they can generally be used in the jury room (except for narcotics, weapons and the like) during deliberations. See United States v. Dishmey, 986 F.2d 1416 (4th Cir.1993) (map masked by witness admitted in evidence and therefore proper to send it into jury room). See companion of pedagogic devices compared to summaries in Hearsay chapter.

2. The better practice is to use a large paper pad and easel with each page being marked for reference in the record rather than a blackboard when an exhibit is created in the courtroom.

3. The National Law Journal, Dec. 2, 1985, p. S–4:

> Looking back over the years of excitement and publicity that have surrounded him, Mr. [Melvin] Belli points to one case—a 1947 trial involving an ordinary citizen doing an ordinary job—as one of the most important in his 50–year career.

> The case involved a fireman passing through an intersection on his way to a fire. At the intersection, a truck ran into the fire engine. Mr. Belli's client, Fire Capt. Fred Reckenbiel, suffered serious brain damage as a result of the accident and remains institutionalized today. Reckenbiel v. Taylor–Walcott Co., Civ. No. 14120.

> The driver of the commercial truck maintained that he had not heard the fire engine's siren, and because he had a green light at the intersection, he proceeded through. The fire truck, however, also drove through the intersection at that time, because with its sirens on it legally had the right-of-way despite any contradicting traffic signals.

> What did he do? In a tactic that may seem almost obvious today, Mr. Belli took an aerial photo of the intersection where the accident occurred and then had it blown up to a 5–foot–by–8–foot size. He brought into the courtroom the people who lived near the intersection and along the road the commercial truck followed before reaching it. As Mr. Belli brought them individually to the stand, he asked each witness where he lived and placed a piece of paper on the map in that location. Then he asked if the witness had heard the siren at an indicated time just before the accident.

> After 57 pieces of paper had been placed on the map, Mr. Belli connected them with a red crayon to show "a zone of sound" through which the commercial truck had to have traveled. The point the farthest away was more than a mile from the point of impact. "In this manner the sound was visually portrayed," explained Mr. Belli, showing that "the truck driver must have been negligent and imprudent" not to have heard the siren.

> From that trial on, the litigator continued, "we started bringing in all sorts of objects," including photographs, models, and laboratory experiments. "I think if I'm noted for anything, it's for trying cases with demonstrative evidence, for showing rather than telling, for portraying to all the senses rather than just illustrating by oral testimony," he said.

> Tierney, Demonstrative Evidence, Working with the Specialist, Trial, January 1986, p. 46:

> > For demonstrative evidence to have a dramatic impact in court, trial lawyers must work closely with a communications specialist and have a

grasp of all the media options, including video, graphic, photographic, print, tape, film, and computer simulation. But before negotiating a contract with the expert, lawyers should make certain that they understand the projected costs and that the specialist is qualified to execute the chosen option.

An unenthusiastic observer has noted:

> If you should wander into one of our courtrooms during the trial of a personal injury suit, you might well wonder if by chance you had not stepped into a display room of some medical supply house.... In the courtroom you would find strewn about the counsel table and set up on easels, pedestals, and what have you, anatomical models, charts, blown-up (and I use that word advisedly) pictures, both in gruesome color and in black and white, Thomas collars of the daytime and nighttime varieties, back braces, pelvic traction braces, corsets, girdles and a multitude of orthopedic appliances and, of course, a skeleton, and in the midst of all this equipment with a pointer is "the unsworn witness"—the plaintiff's lawyer.

Milwid, The Misuse of Demonstrative Evidence, 28 Ins.Counsel J. 435 (1961). What does Mr. Milwid mean by "the unsworn witness"?

5. While more expensive, the use of computer generated video and audio reproductions of how events did or might have occurred are of increasing importance. They involve issues of recreations, opinions, hearsay and expert evidence covered throughout the course. It is essential that they be revealed well before trial and the basis and programming be made available to all experts. Usually they will require experts on scientific evidence, see discussion of expert evidence, infra.

SECTION 7. WRITINGS AND RELATED MATTERS

A. AUTHENTICATION

The rules with respect to authentication of documents and best evidence have now been so substantially simplified and codified in many jurisdictions that knowledge of Articles IX and X of the Federal Rules of Evidence and their equivalents in many states which have codified the subjects will suffice without much reliance on caselaw. Nevertheless, the great importance of this class of evidence at trial requires full preparation and use of discovery and admission devices as well as stipulations and pretrial conferences to ensure that there is no slip-up at the time of trial. No matter how liberal the rules for the introduction of evidence, there can be no substitute for preparation and clear thinking in advance about how, practically and theoretically, documents will be introduced and used by the trier.

Keegan v. Green Giant Co.

Supreme Judicial Court of Maine, 1954.
150 Me. 283, 110 A.2d 599.

■ TAPLEY, JUSTICE. On exceptions. Action is brought by plaintiff, Carolyn Keegan, against defendant, Green Giant Company, for damages alleging that the defendant negligently prepared, manufactured, packed and distributed a can of peas which contained a sharp piece of metal concealed in the peas and that the plaintiff while eating them swallowed the piece of metal, it lodging in her throat. Plaintiff, William Keegan, husband of Carolyn Keegan, seeks recovery for expenses of his wife and loss of consortium. The cases were tried before a jury at the November Term, A.D.1953 of the Superior Court in the County of Penobscot and State of Maine.

At the close of the plaintiffs' cases, the defendant rested without submission of evidence and requested the Court to direct a verdict for the defendant in both cases.

The plaintiffs excepted to the refusal of the presiding Justice to admit certain evidence in the nature of a proposed exhibit in the form of a tin can encircled with a label, and also to the direction of the verdicts in favor of the defendant.

The record discloses that on the fourth day of February, 1953, Carolyn Keegan was living in Jonesport, Maine and working at D.O. Hall's Grocery Store and that the store purchased Green Giant Company canned peas from T.R. Savage & Company of Bangor, a distributor.

Mrs. Nettie R. Alley, mother of Carolyn, purchased a can of peas from the store in which her daughter was employed on the day that the peas from this can were served to her daughter in Mrs. Alley's home. Mrs. Alley opened the can, poured the peas into a pan, warmed them and later served a portion to her daughter Carolyn at the evening meal. Carolyn in eating the peas, along with other food, suddenly experienced a choking sensation and then dislodged a triangular piece of steel identified as "Plaintiff's Exhibit 3."

The exceptions in these cases concerning the direction of verdicts for the defendant will be determined by the disposition of those exceptions pertaining to the refusal of the presiding Justice to admit the can with the label thereon and marked "Plaintiff's Exhibit 1" (for identification).

The can is described as the usual sized tin can ordinarily used to contain green peas. It has imprinted on the bottom portion the following:

"A C f C 5"

and directly underneath these letters and number is:

"3 L Y"

The can is encircled by a label. The pertinent and important material printed thereon are the words:

"Green
Giant
Brand
Great Big
Tender
Sweet Peas.

Distributed by
Green Giant
Company
Le Sueur, Minn.

C GG Co. Reg. U.S. Pat. Off.

Packed in U.S.A.

Replacement or refund of money
*

Guaranteed by
Good Housekeeping
If not as advertised therein."

There is other printed matter on the label which is not material or germane to the issue.

The plaintiffs contend that "Plaintiff's Exhibit 1" (marked for identification), being the can with label thereon, should have been admitted as evidence for the purpose of showing that the Green Giant Company was the distributor of this can of peas and for the further purpose that the can of peas by reasonable inference was packed by the defendant, Green Giant Company, and that the jury should have had an opportunity of determining if these were the facts. The defendant contends that Plaintiff's Exhibit 1 (marked for identification) should not have been admitted without extrinsic evidence connecting the defendant with the case other than through the medium of the label on the can.

Exceptions to the refusal of the presiding Justice to admit Plaintiff's Exhibit 1 are stated in the record as follows:

"Mr. Stern: Your Honor, I would like to introduce Plaintiff's Exhibit Number One in evidence for the purpose of showing that it is self evident that the Green Giant Company was the distributor of this can of peas and also for the purpose of showing that if the jury did find that the Green Giant Company was the distributor that the jury could reasonably infer that this can of peas was also packed by the Green Giant Company.

"The Court: I will exclude it and you may have an exception."

Plaintiff's mother, Nettie R. Alley, testified that she purchased the can of peas from D.O. Hall's Grocery Store in Jonesport on the morning of the day she served them to her daughter and that Plaintiff's Exhibit 1 is the same can which contained the peas that she purchased.

The question here to be determined is whether or not Plaintiff's Exhibit 1 (marked for identification) is admissible in and of itself as evidence to prove that the defendant manufactured, packed and distributed the peas.

The plaintiffs in their brief cite a number of cases which they argue sustain their contention that this label is sufficient by itself to establish that the company whose name and other information appears upon the label is the manufacturer and packer of the contents of the can upon which it is placed. A careful analysis of the cases cited shows that in addition to the printed matter on the label, there was other evidence in connection therewith which identified the defendants with being the manufacturer, packer or distributor of the product.

There are no decisions precisely determining the question of admissibility of an exhibit under circumstances similar to those in this case. This fact requires reference to the substantive law for an answer to the problem. We are here concerned with the authorship of the printed matter on the label and are asked to approve its admissibility without proof of authorship. The admission of such material under these circumstances would violate the cardinal principle of proof of a written or printed document.

Wigmore on Evidence, Vol. VII, Sec. 2150:

"Printed matter in general bears upon itself no marks of authorship other than contents. But there is ordinarily no necessity for resting upon such evidence, since the responsibility for printed matter, under the substantive law, usually arises from the act of causing publication, and [not] merely of writing, and hence there is usually available as much evidence of the act of printing or handing to the printer as there would be of any other act, such as chopping a tree or building a fence.

"There is therefore no judicial sanction for considering the contents alone as sufficient evidence."

Sec. 2130:

". . . The general principle has been enforced that a writing purporting to be of a certain authorship cannot go to the jury as possibly genuine, merely on the strength of this purport; there must be some evidence of the genuineness (or execution) of it."

See 131 A.L.R., Page 301.

This case is devoid of any evidence connecting the defendant as the author of the printed material on the label and, further, that it was the packer, manufacturer or distributor of the contents of the can encircled by the label.

The can itself bore certain distinguishing letters and figures which might be code numbers identifying the packer but here again there is no extrinsic evidence bearing on the fact.

The presiding Justice below committed no error in excluding the exhibit.

Exceptions, in each case, overruled, to the exclusion of evidence.

Exceptions, in each case, overruled to the direction of verdicts for the defendant.

■ BELIVEAU, J., did not sit.

■ WILLIAMSON, JUSTICE (dissenting). I would sustain the exceptions. The position of the Green Giant Company as I understand it is this: A can of peas with certain letters and numbers imprinted on the bottom portion and encircled with a label bearing the defendant's registered trademark and its name as the distributor, and in no way distinguishable to the purchaser or consumer from the defendant's product, is not evidence in itself sufficient to prove that the particular can was distributed by the defendant.

Day in and day out every one of us accepts the label on canned food products as sufficient proof of the brand and the producer or distributor. How else can we identify as a practical matter types and brands of canned food products? We are urged by every method of publicity to purchase "brand" products by the label. Further, it is common knowledge that the misuse of a trademark and the misbranding of food products are serious offenses under Federal laws designed to protect all concerned from producer to consumer.

There is of course the possibility of substitution or imitation. This risk must be small indeed in a business which has gained the confidence of the consuming public through the use of distinctive labels.

Surely we may assume that the defendant does in fact distribute a product of the type described in the label. If this were not so, it could readily have disposed of the case. There is no suggestion by the defendant that such is not the fact. There are imprinted on the bottom portion of the can certain letters and numbers, e.g., "A C f C 5" "3 L Y". They have no meaning to the purchaser. A distributor can readily tell us whether they identify its own product.

Apart from the question of proof of the fact of distribution, there is no objection by the defendant to the sufficiency of the evidence on the other issues in the case. In my opinion the can and label should have been admitted in evidence and the case submitted to the jury.

NOTES

1. Assume that the Green Giant case was to be retired and that Maine continued to follow the rule of the main case but had in force the federal rules of Civil Procedure. If you were counsel for the plaintiff and were afforded a retrial, exactly how would you proceed to avoid this difficulty at the new trial? Maine has now adopted, with minor modification of no moment for the present discussion, both the Federal Rules of Evidence and the Federal Rules of Civil Procedure. Were the retrial to take place now, how would you proceed?

Note the critical commentary in 103 U.Pa.L.Rev. 1095 (pointing out that it would be a crime for someone to steal genuine Green Giant labels); 29 Temp.L.Q. 109 (1955). Cf. 7 Wigmore, Evidence § 2148 (Chadbourn Rev.1978); 131 A.L.R. 295, 301 (1941) (authentication by contents). See also Alexander & Alexander, The Authentication of Documents Requirements: Barrier to Falsehood or to Truth, 10 San Diego L.Rev. 266 (1973); Brown, Authentication and Contents of Writings, 1969 Law and the Social Order 611 (1969); Strong, Liberalizing the Authentication of Private Writings, 52 Cornell L.Q. 284 (1967). Cf. Mancari v. Frank P. Smith, Inc., 114 F.2d 834, 131 A.L.R. 295 (App.D.C. 1940): Plaintiff sued because his name was mentioned in a widely distributed printed circular which purported to be issued by a manufacturer and by defendant, a local retailer. Held: the terms of the circular did not serve to make out a prima facie case that defendant was its author; the direction of a verdict for the defendant was proper.

2. In Mohr v. Shultz, 388 P.2d 1002, 1010 (Idaho 1964) the appellate court held that the trial court should have admitted a catalogue published by a bakery equipment supply company as evidence of current market prices for bakery equipment where

> appellant identified the catalogue prior to offering it in evidence; his uncontradicted testimony showed it to be the monthly publication of Rust Sales Company ... a large bakery equipment supplier ... Appellant further testified that he had purchased baking equipment from Rust Company salesmen who carried these catalogues ... that appellant made use of these catalogues....

Did appellant's testimony establish that the particular catalogue in question was what it purported to be?

3. A person relying on an important document should not be allowed to escape authentication requirements by referring to the document without formally introducing it in evidence. See McIntyre v. McIntyre, 377 S.W.2d 421, 423 (Mo.1964):

> In fact the record is far from satisfactory as far as the appellate court is concerned. While on the witness stand, Mrs. McIntyre produced a number of savings account books and testified with respect to these and other matters. The description of the accounts as stated into the record is fragmentary and incomplete. None of the books or other records were marked as exhibits or introduced in evidence although there was a suggestion at one point that this ought to be done. The situation was undoubtedly quite clear to the trial court and counsel with the books and records before them, but the review by this court is limited by the fact that the record before us does not give the complete picture. Neither party objected to this

procedure; nevertheless, where a witness is permitted to give incomplete and fragmentary testimony as to the contents of records which are not introduced in evidence, it is impossible for an appellate court to obtain a clear understanding of the facts, and the practice should be discouraged.

4. See Teleglobe v. Telease, 78–CV–1229 (E.D.N.Y.1982) (unreported) (control box for pay TV admitted pursuant to Fed.R.Evid. 902(7) on the basis of logos stamped on metal cover). Can this theory be applied to a bus that caused an accident? Is the problem of objects and documents different?

5. Making it easier to authenticate documents tends to shift costs to the opponent—generally the defendant. Is that a reason not to allow cases like Keegan? See Swift, Abolishing the hearsay Rule, 69 California L.Rev. 495 (1981), and discussing Zenith Radio Corp. v. Matsushita Electronic Industrial Co., infra, under the concept of Burden—Shifting.

United States v. Branch

United States Court of Appeals, Fourth Circuit, 1992.
970 F.2d 1368.

■ WILKINS, CIRCUIT JUDGE:

Jonathan Branch appeals his convictions for conspiracy to distribute and distribution of heroin and cocaine, see 18 U.S.C.A. § 2 (West 1969); 21 U.S.C.A. §§ 841, 846 (West 1981 & Supp. 1992), and for attempting to evade or defeat income taxes, see 26 U.S.C.A. § 7201 (West 1989). Although Branch raises numerous allegations of error, he primarily argues that the district court erred by conducting an in camera hearing addressing the authenticity of tape recordings of conversations in which Branch and his co-conspirators participated and by not requiring the Government to offer sufficient evidence before the jury to support a finding of authenticity. Finding no error, we affirm.

I.

Branch and his co-conspirators were suspected of heroin and cocaine distribution activities in Baltimore, Maryland. The government began an investigation into these activities and, subsequently, obtained authorization to place wiretaps on certain telephone lines. Over 80 conversations relating to the conspiracy were recorded as a result of the wiretaps.

Before trial the Government requested an in camera hearing to present testimony that it proposed would establish the authenticity of these tape recordings. The district court conducted the hearing, during which the Government presented the testimony of 26 government agents who monitored the recording of the conversations. These monitors verified the proper operation of the recording devices, their own competence to operate the recorders, the accuracy of the tapes, the improbability of any additions or deletions, and the absence of any inducement by the government that would have encouraged the conversations. Branch objected to authentication of the tapes at the in camera hearing, claiming that this procedure prevented the jury from properly evaluating their accuracy and genuineness. The district court concluded that the Government presented sufficient authenticating evidence and assured Branch that, although the Government would not have to present the testimony of all of the monitors, it would require the Government to lay a proper foundation for admission of the tapes before the jury.

During the nine-day trial, the Government presented testimony from Agent Thompson, the FBI supervisor of the wiretap operations in Baltimore.

Thompson identified many of the voices in the recorded conversations and explained how he prepared extracts from the original tape recordings. Earlous Tripp, a co-conspirator who had participated in many of the conversations, also testified to the accuracy of the recordings and provided additional voice identifications. Further, Detective Walter Akers, who participated in the investigation and prepared transcripts of the tapes, identified voices on the tapes. The Government, however, did not present testimony from the monitors. The district court admitted the tapes into evidence over Branch's objection that the Government had failed to present sufficient evidence to allow the jury to find that the tapes were authentic.

II.

Branch argues that the district court conducted an in camera hearing in lieu of requiring the Government to present sufficient evidence at trial to support a finding that the tape recordings were authentic. This procedure, he contends, prevented the jury from properly assessing their authenticity. His argument misconstrues the procedure followed by the district court and evinces a misunderstanding of the showing the Government must make in order to properly authenticate tape recordings.

A.

In order to be relevant and admissible, evidence must have a "tendency to make the existence of any fact that is of consequence to the determination of the action more probable or less probable than it would be without the evidence." Fed.R.Evid. 401; see Fed.R.Evid. 402. Authentication "represent[s] a special aspect of relevancy," Fed.R.Evid. 901(a) advisory committee's note, in that evidence cannot have a tendency to make the existence of a disputed fact more or less likely if the evidence is not that which its proponent claims, United States v. Sliker, 751 F.2d 477, 497–99 (2d Cir.1984), cert. denied, 470 U.S. 1058, 105 S.Ct. 1772, 84 L.Ed.2d 832, and 471 U.S. 1137, 105 S.Ct. 2679, 86 L.Ed. 2d 697 (1985). "The requirement of authentication or identification as a condition precedent to admissibility is satisfied by evidence sufficient to support a finding that the matter in question is what its proponent claims." Fed.R.Evid. 901(a).

Resolution of whether evidence is authentic calls for a factual determination by the jury, Sliker 751 F.2d at 497–99, and admissibility, therefore, is governed by the procedure set forth in Federal Rule of Evidence 104(b) "relating to matters of conditional relevance generally." 5 Weinstein & Berger, Weinstein's Evidence ¶ 901(a)[02], at 901–26 (1991) [hereinafter Weinstein's Evidence]; see also In re Japanese Elec. Prods. Antitrust Litig., 723 F.2d 238, 284–85 (3d Cir.1983), rev'd on other grounds sub nom. Matsushita Elec. Indus. Co. v. Zenith Radio Corp., 475 U.S. 574, 106 S.Ct. 1348, 89 L.Ed.2d 538 (1986). Before admitting evidence for consideration by the jury, the district court must determine whether its proponent has offered a satisfactory foundation from which the jury could reasonably find that the evidence is authentic. See Fed.R.Evid. 104(b) advisory committee's note; see also Fed.R.Evid. 901(a) advisory committee's note; see generally 2 Saltzburg & Martin, Federal Rules of Evidence Manual 476–81 (5th ed. 1990). Although the district court is charged with making this preliminary determination, because authentication is essentially a question of conditional relevancy, the jury ultimately resolves whether evidence admitted for its consideration is that which the proponent claims. See id.

Because the ultimate resolution of authenticity is a question for the jury, in rendering its preliminary decision on whether the proponent of evidence has laid a sufficient foundation for admission, the district court must necessarily assess the adequacy of the showing made before the jury. Weinstein's Evidence ¶ 901(a)[02], at 901–27. An in camera hearing addressing authenticity does not replace the presentation of authenticating evidence before the jury; the district court must revisit this issue at trial. Thus, even though the district court may have ruled during an in camera proceeding that the proponent had presented sufficient evidence to support a finding that a tape recording was authentic, evidence that would support this same ruling must be presented again, to the jury, before the tape recording may be admitted.

This is not to say that an in camera hearing to assess the authenticity of evidence may not be appropriate. This procedure insures that the jury will not be tainted by hearing prejudicial evidence—or learning of its existence—until the proponent has demonstrated that it will be able to provide an adequate foundation for admission. Moreover, in deciding the admissibility of tape recordings district courts must consider the statutory requirements imposed by 18 U.S.C.A. §§ 2510–21 (West 1970 & Supp. 1992) and will often be required to rule on hearsay objections to co-conspirators' statements, see generally Bourjaily v. United States, 483 U.S. 171, 107 S.Ct. 2775, 97 L.Ed.2d 144 (1987). In camera consideration of the admissibility of tape recordings is particularly appropriate under these circumstances. The district court, therefore, did not err in conducting an in camera hearing to address the authenticity of the tape recordings; indeed, this practice may be preferable. . . .

B.

Having concluded that the procedure followed by the district court was proper, we next address whether the Government presented sufficient evidence before the jury to support a finding that the tape recordings were authentic. Branch argues that the foundation was insufficient because the Government failed to present evidence on each of the factors set forth in United States v. McKeever, 169 F.Supp. 426 (S.D.N.Y.1958), rev'd on other grounds, 271 F.2d 669 (2d Cir.1959).[3] We disagree. Although the presentation of evidence satisfying each of the McKeever factors generally would provide a sufficient foundation for admission of tape recordings, we have not held that such a presentation is required in every case. Rather, these factors provide guidance to the district court when called upon to make rulings on authentication issues. See United States v. Long, 651 F.2d 239 (4th Cir.), cert. denied, 454 U.S. 896, 102 S.Ct. 396, 70 L.Ed. 2d 212 (1981); United States v. Jones, 730 F.2d 593, 597 (10th Cir.1984). . . .

Applying this standard, we hold that the district court did not abuse its discretion in determining that the Government presented sufficient evidence of authentication before the jury. Agent Thompson's testimony conveyed detailed information about implementation and operation of the wiretaps. He explained how he and another agent prepared the extracted tape recordings introduced at trial. Thompson stated that he was familiar with the voices on the tapes because he talked with many of the participants and because he reviewed the original tapes and voice exemplars. He then identified various voices, including

---

3. [Footnote renumbered; some omitted.]

These criteria include proof: (1) That the recording device was capable of taking the conversation now offered in evidence. (2) That the operator of the device was competent to operate the device. (3) That the recording is authentic and correct. (4) That changes, additions or deletions have not been made in the recording. (5) That the recording has been preserved in a manner that is shown to the court. (6) That the speakers are identified. (7) That the conversation elicited was made voluntarily and in good faith, without any kind of inducement. 169 F.Supp. at 430.

Branch's, as the recordings were played to the jury. Tripp also verified the accuracy of the recorded conversations in which he participated and identified voices on the tapes, including Branch's. Finally, detective Akers testified that he was familiar with many of the voices on the tapes based on personal conversations that he had with some of the co-conspirators. This testimony was sufficient to support a finding by the jury that the tapes were what the Government claimed—accurately recorded conversations involving Branch, his co-conspirators, and others....

Affirmed.

United States v. Moore

United States Court of Appeals, First Circuit, 1991.
923 F.2d 910.

■ BREYER, Chief Judge.

A jury convicted the appellant, Iona Moore, (1) of conspiring with Priscilla Russell and Adrienne Bristol fraudulently to obtain money from the First Trade Union Savings Bank of Boston, and (2) of fraudulently obtaining $5000 from the bank on each of four separate occasions. See 18 U.S.C. § 657 (unlawful to embezzle, abstract, purloin or willfully misapply federally insured bank's money); 18 U.S.C. § 371 (conspiracy). The evidence showed that Moore (a bank teller), Russell (a bank credit-checking official), and Bristol (a bank loan-payment collector) hatched a fraudulent loan scheme that typically worked roughly as follows:

1. Russell would write up a loan application in the name of a non-existent person, usually for $5000. She would invent a social security number, a home address, and a workplace. She would pretend to her supervisor that she had checked sufficiently to warrant granting the loan.

2. The bank would approve the loan and prepare a $5000 check made out to the applicant.

3. Russell, or more often someone else pretending to be the nonexistent borrower, would pick up the check, and go to a teller (usually Moore). The person would have nothing identifying him or her as the nonexistent person. Moore would not insist upon, or check, identification. She would simply cash the check.

4. The three conspirators would divide the money. Sometimes they would make a few monthly loan payments often by presenting a money order to Moore at her teller's station. Then they would stop repayment.

5. Bristol, the loan-payment collector, would tell the bank it simply had made a bad loan, and the bank would write-off the loan as a bad debt.

Eventually, Bristol quit her job at the bank. A new loan-payment collector, trying to collect some of the old, bad loans, discovered that some of the borrowers did not exist. The FBI investigated.

The Government brought charges against all three conspirators. Russell and Bristol pleaded guilty and, in return for reduced sentence recommendations, they testified against Moore at her trial. Aside from the testimony of these two key witnesses, the Government's evidence against Moore basically consisted of fourteen sets of documents (loan application, promissory note, cashed check, and loan-repayment record), one for each of the fourteen bad loans that Russell said she had helped to engineer. Moore now appeals her conviction....

Computer Records. The government introduced into evidence fourteen computer-generated "loan histories," one for each bad loan. Each loan history consisted of a piece of paper with the borrower's name, the amount of the loan, and the date of each loan payment made, along with a notation showing whether it was made in person to a teller (and which teller) or was made by mail. The "history," in other words, is simply a piece of paper printed out by a computer that stores the relevant information. Appellant correctly points out that these histories are hearsay. She then claims that the district court could not admit them under the "business records" exception because, in her view, the Government failed to lay an adequate "foundation." In her view, the Government failed to show that this "compilation" of "data" about "events" was

> made at or near the time by, or from information transmitted by, a person with knowledge, ... kept in the course of a regularly conducted business activity, and [made as part of] ... the regular practice of that business activity ..., as shown by the testimony of the custodian or other qualified witness....

Fed.R.Evid. 803(6).

The problem for appellant is that the Government did lay an adequate foundation for the records. Its witness, Louise Slattery, testified that she was the head of the bank's consumer loan department, that the records in question were made in the "regular course" of the bank's business, that they were compiled by a "service bureau" connected by phone lines to the bank, and that she and others at the bank could retrieve, and did retrieve, that information from time to time by requesting the information from the bureau. This testimony is more than sufficient to permit the court to find that Louise Slattery was a "qualified witness" (the head of consumer loans is likely to know how loan data are compiled and kept), that the information was kept in the "regular course of business" (she said as much), that they were made on the basis of information transmitted by a person with knowledge (a "service bureau" connected by phone lines to the bank's receiving officials), and that it was the "regular practice" of the bank and bureau to keep such records (she said as much). See United States v. Catabran, 836 F.2d 453, 457 (9th Cir.1988) (computer records properly admitted as business records if "(1) made or based on information transmitted by a person with knowledge at or near the time of the transaction; (2) made in the ordinary course of business; and (3) trustworthy...."); United States v. Hayes, 861 F.2d 1225, 1228 (10th Cir.1988) (proper foundation laid for IRS computer records under Fed.R.Evid. 803(6) where IRS employees testified that "tax records were kept in the ordinary course of business and that it was the regular practice of the IRS to keep such records"). We add that it is not required that the qualified witness be a computer programmer, see United States v. Linn, 880 F.2d 209, 216 (9th Cir.1989), or that she "be the person who actually prepared the record." See Wallace Motor Sales, Inc. v. American Motors Sales Corp., 780 F.2d 1049, 1060–61 (1st Cir.1985); accord United States v. Hutson, 821 F.2d 1015, 1020 (5th Cir.1987).

Appellant goes on to argue that Fed.R.Evid. 803(6) prohibits the introduction of business records that meet the requirement just mentioned if ("unless")

> the source of information or the method or circumstances of preparation indicate lack of trustworthiness.

And, she says that the Government's foundation did not show such "trustworthiness." See, e.g., United States v. Glasser, 773 F.2d 1553, 1559 (11th Cir.1985) (computer records must be kept pursuant to some routine procedure designed to assure their accuracy). The short and conclusive answer to this argument, however, is that the ordinary business circumstances described suggest trustworthiness, see Hayes 861 F.2d at 1228–29, at least where absolutely nothing in the record in any way implies the lack thereof. If counsel had some special reason for thinking the information untrustworthy, he failed to call it to the court's attention. Indeed, he did not even mention "trustworthiness," or its lack, to the court. See United States v. Briscoe, 896 F.2d 1476, 1494–95 (7th Cir.), cert. denied, 498 U.S. 863, 111 S.Ct. 173, 112 L.Ed. 2d 137 (1990) (proper foundation established where "government provides sufficient facts to warrant a finding that the [computer] records are trustworthy and the opposing party is afforded an opportunity to inquire into the accuracy thereof and how the records were maintained and produced"); Linn, 880 F.2d at 216. Rather, the appellant objected simply by uttering the word "foundation;" this is not a sufficient objection in these circumstances. See Fed.R.Evid. 103(a)(1) (requiring that grounds of objection be specifically stated). finally, we note that it is not required that computers be tested for programming errors before computer records can be admitted under Fed.R.Evid. 803(6). See Briscoe, 896 F.2d at 1494. In sum, we can find no abuse of discretion in the district court's admission of the computer records. See United States v. Hernandez, 913 F.2d 1506, 1512–13 (10th Cir.1990) (abuse of discretion review for admission of computer records).

The judgment of the district court is

Affirmed.

United States of America v. Labovitz

United States District Court, District Massachusetts, 1996.
1996 WL 417113.

MEMORANDUM AND ORDER REGARDING GOVERNMENT'S MOTION TO CONDUCT A "PAPERLESS TRIAL"

■ Ponsor, District Judge.

The motion is hereby ALLOWED upon the following conditions:

1. The government will create images of its documentary exhibits on a computer. A copy of these images will be provided to the defendant on one or more CD–ROMs within seventy-five (75) days of this Order.

2. The Government will arrange for setting up the following equipment in the courtroom for the trial: a monitor for the court, a monitor to be shared by the clerk and court reporter, a monitor for the witness and a monitor at the witness box for use by the attorney examining the witness, a monitor for the defense table, a monitor for the prosecution table, two large monitors for the jury, an extra monitor for any juror unable clearly to see the large monitors, a computer and monitor to be used by a technician who will facilitate the projection of images onto the various monitors, a switch to control when the images are shown to the jury and, finally, a document camera or video presenter for projecting onto the monitors paper documents that have not been imaged.

3. Other than those costs which can be born by the court, the Government will pay for the installation of the system in the courtroom.

4. During the trial the defendant will have access to the system in the courtroom either by projecting images of documents through his own computer onto the courtroom's screens using his own computer operator, or by bringing CD–ROMs containing his document images into the courtroom to be displayed

through the Government's computer using the Government's computer operator.

5.   After the system is installed, the court will schedule a pretrial conference to examine the system and establish procedures for its use during the trial.

6.   The Government will provide the defendant with an index correlating Government exhibit numbers to image document numbers.

7.   The Government will disclose to the defendant within forty-five (45) days of the date of this order specific information regarding the identity of the software package to be used in the courtroom.

8.   The Government will make disclosure of Jencks material to the defendant no later than thirty (30) days prior to the commencement of the trial.

The imposition of this final condition for the "paperless trial" deserves some comment. The court recognizes that under the Jencks Act, 18 U.S.C. 3500, the court lacks the power in ordinary circumstances to require the Government to produce witness statements before the witness has completed his direct examination at trial. The Government has the option here to proceed with the traditional trial and retain its discretion regarding the disclosure of witness statements, right up to the conclusion of the witness' direct testimony.

A "paperless trial," however, presents special problems, which require the court to be alert to possible unfairness to the defendant. The defendant must be given sufficient time to prepare his case, and particularly the documents to be used in cross-examining witnesses, through the special procedures and techniques to be used in this "paperless" case. For example, documents the defense intends to use on cross-examination must be "imaged" and indexed in some manner to make them accessible to defense counsel before the trial commences. Without some opportunity to review witness statements before trial, select the documents for cross-examination and prepare them for use in the system, the "paperless" approach will place defense counsel at an unfair disadvantage. For this reason, the court has conditioned the use of the "paperless" procedure upon the disclosure by the government of Jencks materials thirty days in advance of trial. It is worth noting in this regard that the Government had already agreed to produce witness statements two weeks prior to trial, in order to avoid the delays that inevitably result from literal enforcement of the Jencks Act.

The defendant has asked for disclosure of Jencks material ninety days prior to trial. this is excessive, for several reasons. First, defense counsel already knows a great deal about the Government's case and its witnesses through the disclosures that have been made to date. The vast majority of the defense preparation, including imaging, can be accomplished long before Jencks disclosures are made. The thirty-day window provided by the court will give defense counsel ample time to refine and focus its case to the extent that such adjustments are necessitated by review of the witness statements. Moreover, if some documents are not imaged in time to be used in the system, both the Government and defense counsel will always have the option of sing the video presenter, which permits transmission of a document onto the monitors directly from the document itself without the necessity of prior imaging.

In sum, by requiring early disclosure of Jencks material as a condition of conducting the "paperless trial" the court is striking a fair balance among the competing interests of efficiency, the Government's right to retain witness statements and the defendant's legitimate need for time adequately to prepare using the innovative procedure that will be employed in this trial. . . .

It is So Ordered.

NOTES

1. New York has adopted a provision in CPLR 4539(b) conditioning admission of computer generated copies on a showing that the reproduction process does not permit changes in the underlying data unless the process leaves a record of them. There are few systems that would comply. Is the rigorousness of the standard so high that the few errors or deliberate misrepresentations that would be caught are overbalanced by interference with the ease of admissibility now taken for granted? See Thomas F. Gleason, New Law on Computer Generated Evidence: Legislature Permits Optically Imaged Proof, N.Y.L.J. May 8, 1996, p. 3:

> The genesis of these extraordinary standards is based on the new ways in which digital or computer generated reproductions are created.

> Older tools such as film photography, photocopiers or microfiche recorders store by image-to-image reproduction processes. These project and record images on media without losing the integrity of the whole image during the process. Hence, the resulting images are relatively difficult to alter without evidence of tampering in the image product itself.

> Widely available digital imaging systems, such as fax machines or document "scanners", are fundamentally different, They use storage and reconstitution mechanisms that bring about the disintegration of the original image. The image is stored by software that allows the recording by binary code: a series of zeros and ones. In black and white, the image is transformed into a grid of tiny dots. Each dot, or pixel, in the image is stored as either dark or light, reflected as a zero or a one, according to the way the particular software codes the image. Color images can be recorded and stored by a similar process.

> If enough pixels of an image are recorded and stored, a very high resolution image can be reproduced, transmitted and, at least theoretically, manipulated. The stored image is merely a string of zeros and ones, incorporated into computer software files ready to be reconstituted. Alteration of some of these zeros and ones can, in principle, leave an undetectable change in the image.

2. Jordan S. Gruber, Potential for Fabricating Recorded Evidence Grows, Technological Advances in Audio and Video Recordings may Affect Court Admissibility Standards, Nat.L.J. April 22, 1996, P. B.13:

> Given the increase in corporate monitoring of employees, video conferencing, camcorder ownership and the making of computer-based audio and video recordings of all types, the number of legal cases involving audio and video recordings can be expected to grow. As such cases have become more common, there has been a trend toward the relaxation of admissibility and foundation requirements.

> Sophisticated editing capabilities now increase the chances that recordings can be misused, manipulated or even fabricated. Such capabilities, combined with the easing of evidentiary requirements and the utter persuasiveness of such evidence, could raise some serious evidentiary concerns....

> Once an electronic recording is made, there are two types of editing that can occur: editing that physically affects and changes the source recording—the actual original recording—and editing that does not. Thus, if a portion of a video recording is erased or re-recorded over, or if the sequences of an audiotape are rearranged via splicing—relatively rare these days but not unheard of—the source recording has been changed.

Prior tests for admissibility did not consider these more sophisticated recording devices using electronic digital techniques. See, e.g., United States v. McKeever, 169 F.Supp. 426 (D.C.N.Y.1958) (7 steps); United States v. Biggins, 551 F.2d 64 (5th Cir.1977) (4 steps); Vermont v. Chenette, 560 A.2d 365 (Vt.1989) (computer summaries of patient records generally admitted). What tests should be required of digital equipment? Who should have the burden on falsification? *Compare* United States v. Faurote, 749 F.2d 40 (7th Cir.1984) *with* United States v. De La Fuente, 548 F.2d 528 (5th Cir.1977) (opponent must show falsification). For use of computer disks and tapes of Medicaid providers used in fraud prosecutions, *compare* People v. Perry, 605 N.Y.S.2d 790 (N.Y.A.D. 3d Dept. 1993) (liberal approach) *with* Ohio v. Vogelsong, 612 N.E.2d 462 (Ohio App. 10th Dist.1992) (restrictive ruling).

3. How should E Mail and related methods of communication via internets be treated? Authentication and hearsay problems are closely related. Does the approach in Rule 803(b) offer sufficient protection to the records produced in the main case as well as to other recording and storing techniques? See, e.g., Anthony J. Dreyer, When the Postman Beeps Twice: The Admissibility of Electronic Mail Under the Business Records Exception of the Federal Rules of Evidence, 64 Fordham L.Rev. 2285 (1996). See also, e.g., United States v. Polk, 56 F.3d 613 (5th Cir.1995) (broad discretion in district court to determine authentication of sound recordings). Where two or three dimension virtual reality creations, internet, cyberspace, encryption, foreign language recordings and the like are involved, can the jury or court decide authentication problems without the aid of an expert if the issue is pressed by the opponent? Even if the court decides to admit as sufficiently authenticated, the jury may have to reconsider the issue in deciding probative force. See, e.g. Bissett v. Burlington Northern R. Co. 969 F.2d 727 (8th Cir.1992) (videotaped reenactment; wide trial court discretion); Nicholas Robbins, Note, When Baby Needs a New Pair of Cybershoes: Gambling on the Internet, 2 B.U.J. Science & Tech. L. 7 (1996) (encryption problems); Religious Technology Center v. Netcom On–Line Communication Services, Inc., 907 F.Supp. 1361 (N.D.Cal.1995) (copyright infringement on internet); Marty Rimm, Marketing Pornography On the Information Superhighway, 83 Geo. L.J. 1849 (1995); Note, Updates on Science & Technology, 1 B.U.J. Sci & Tech. L. 10 (1995) (collecting cases on e-mail, interactive electronic communications and cellular telephones); Cybersex and Community Standards, 75 B.U.L. Rev. 865 (1995); Henry H. Perritt, Jr., President Clinton's National Information Initiative: Community Regained?, 69 Chi-Kent L.Rev. 991 (1994); Timothy B. Lennon, the Fourth Amendments Prohibitions on Encryption Limitation: Will 1995 be like 1984, 58 Alb. L. Rev. 467 (1994); Anne G. Bruckner–Harvey, Inadvertent Disclosure in the Age of Fax Machines, 46 Baylor L. Rev. 385 (1994); Trotter Hardy, Symposium, Electronic Communications and Legal Change: Computer Network Abuse, 6 Harv. J. Law & Tech. 213, 307 (1993); John Robinson Thomas, Legal Responses to Commercial Transactions Employing Novel Communications, 90 Mich. L. Rev. 1145 (1992).

How would you advise your corporate clients to create and maintain such records? See, e.g., Daniel R. Marcus, Hanging up on Phone Hackers, Am. Lawyer, April 1997, p. 42 (security problems with E-mail and internet use); Geanne Rosenberg, Looking for Evidence in Discarded E-Mail, N.Y. Times, March 31, 1997, p. D5 (delete key does not delete all data); Anthony J. Dreyer, Note, Electronic Mail, 64 Ford.L.R. 2285 (1996) (evidence problems).

Zenith Radio Corp. v. Matsushita Electric Industrial Co., Limited

United States District Court, Eastern District of Pennsylvania, 1980.
505 F.Supp. 1190, rev'd on related grounds, 723 F.2d 238 (3d Cir.1983), rev'd on other grounds, 475 U.S. 574, 106 S.Ct. 1348, 89 L.Ed.2d 538 (1986).

■ EDWARD R. BECKER, DISTRICT JUDGE.

II. Rulings on Contested Legal Issues Concerning Interpretation of the Federal Rules of Evidence

A. Authentication

1. The Standard for a Preliminary Ruling on Authentication Under Rule 104; Will Inadmissible Evidence Suffice?

Plaintiffs and defendants differ as to whether admissible evidence is necessary to authenticate evidence. Defendants say "yes" and plaintiffs say "no." We begin with the Advisory Committee's Note to Rule 901, which states expressly that the requirement of showing authentication falls in the category of "relevancy dependent upon fulfillment of a condition of fact," and is thus governed by the procedure set forth in Rule 104(b), and not that set forth in Rule 104(a).

The Advisory Committee Note to Rule 104(b) makes plain that preliminary questions of *conditional relevancy* are not determined solely by the judge, for to do so would greatly restrict the function of the jury as the trier of fact. If, for instance, there were serious questions in this case as to whether Mr. Yajima's diary was a forgery, it is obvious that a question of evidence so critical could not be decided solely by the court. Under the aegis of Rule 104(b), the judge makes a preliminary determination whether the foundation evidence is sufficient to permit a factfinder to conclude that the condition in question has been fulfilled. If so, according to the Advisory Committee Note:

. . . . the item is admitted. If after all of the evidence on the issue is in, pro and con, the jury could reasonably conclude that fulfillment of the condition is not established the issue is for them. If the evidence is not such as to allow a finding, the judge withdraws the matter from their consideration.

In United States v. Goichman, 547 F.2d 778, 784 (3d Cir.1976), the Court of Appeals formulated this principle as follows:

[T]he showing of authenticity is not on a par with more technical evidentiary rules, such as hearsay exceptions, governing admissibility. Rather, there need be only a prima facie showing, to the court, of authenticity, not a full argument on admissibility.

Thus, once a *prima facie* showing has been made to the court that a document is what its proponent claims, it should be admitted. At that point the burden of going forward with respect to authentication shifts to the opponent to rebut the *prima facie* showing by presenting evidence to the trier of fact which would raise questions as to the genuineness of the document. The required *prima facie* showing of authentication need not consist of a preponderance of the evidence. Rather, all that is required is substantial evidence from which the trier of fact might conclude that a document is authentic. As the court in Goichman, supra, stated:

[I]t is the jury who will ultimately determine the authenticity of the evidence, not the court. The only requirement is that there has been *substantial evidence* from which they could infer that the document was authentic.

Id. (emphasis added).

The plaintiffs contend that in determining whether an adequate *prima facie* showing has been made, the court may consider inadmissible evidence. We disagree. Under Rule 104(b), authentication must be established by the "introduction of evidence." By using this language, the Rule plainly contemplates that the jury's determination of authenticity will be made only on the basis of admissible evidence. We find nothing in either Rule 104 or the Advisory Committee Notes to suggest that the jury may consider inadmissible evidence in this regard, except to the extent that evidence may be admitted "subject to" the introduction of subsequent (admissible) evidence of its authenticity.

So then, while the court's power to "consider" inadmissible evidence under Rule 104(a) is clear, the substantive determination which the court is required to make on the issue of authentication is whether *admissible* evidence exists which is sufficient to support a jury finding of authenticity. For it would be a pointless exercise for a judge to rely upon inadmissible evidence to fulfill the substantial evidence requirement when the trier of fact can only consider *admissible* evidence that a proffered document is authentic. Accordingly, we hold that under Rule 104(a), Rule 104(b), and Goichman, our task in ruling on authenticity is limited to determining whether there is *substantial admissible evidence* to support a finding of authentication by the trier of fact.

2. The Notion of Authentication and the Scope of Rule 901(a); is Authenticity More Than Mere Genuineness?

Another important issue addressed in argument and briefs is the intended scope of Rule 901(a) and, in particular, the meaning of the last phrase which defines authentication as a finding "that the matter in question is what its proponent claims." In contrast to the position of the plaintiffs, who equate authentication with genuineness, the defendants contend that the scope of authentication is determined by the claims made by the proponent of a document and encompasses all of what the proponent "*must* claim it is in order to use it as he wishes to" (emphasis in original). They argue that the subject documents' "logical status as evidence, and hence their authenticity, could be established only by showing that they are accurate and reliable accounts . . ." (of the allegedly conspiratorial meetings reported), otherwise "they are not probative" and thus not what their proponent claims. Since authentication is but a "special aspect of relevancy," Advisory Committee Note to Rule 901(a), this is an appealing argument. After all, the plaintiffs claim that Yajima's diary should be admitted to portray the agreements made at certain meetings. What does it matter then that the diary is not a forgery, if it is not an accurate and reliable account of what transpired at the meetings Yajima purported to record?

The problem with defendants' argument is that it reads the language of 901 to subsume nearly all of the issues involved in many cases in which the issue may arise. For example, the proponent claims that many of the documents under consideration here are "business records." As the Advisory Committee Notes to 901 make clear, however, this is a completely separate determination which must be addressed outside the scope of the authentication inquiry. While the Advisory Committee Notes state specifically that authentication is an aspect of conditional relevancy, they are also quite clear that it is but one kind of conditional relevancy, and does not subsume all of the evidentiary foundation which must be established in order to show that a document is relevant evidence:

> Authentication and identification represent a *special aspect* of relevancy. Thus a telephone conversation may be irrelevant because on an

unrelated topic or because the speaker is not identified. The *latter aspect* is the one here involved.

(emphasis added) (citations omitted).

The specific illustrations under subsection (b) further support a narrow interpretation of authentication. For example, authentication can be established by expert or nonexpert opinion on handwriting, F.R.E. 901(b)(2), a method which would do nothing to establish a document as the "accurate and reliable account" that defendants claim it must be in order to authenticate it. . . .

We conclude that, notwithstanding the apparent sweep of 901, created by its use of a rather expansive locution, i.e., the prescription that authentication is satisfied by evidence sufficient to support a finding that the matter in question is "what its proponent claims," the notion of authentication is a narrow one, akin to the notion of genuineness. The other foundation requirements should not be simply subsumed under the authenticity terminology, but should remain analytically distinct. . . .

3. Methods of Authentication

Rule 901(b) lists several examples of methods of authentication which would meet the requirements of 901(a). The Advisory Committee Notes for this subsection state that these examples are not intended to exhaust all the possibilities, "but are meant to guide and suggest, leaving room for growth and development in this area of the law."

In their endeavors to authenticate the matters before us, the plaintiffs place primary emphasis on 901(b)(4), Distinctive Characteristics. They also assert, however, that the testimony and protocols from the J[apanese] FTC proceedings may provide evidence of authenticity under 901(b)(1) (Testimony of a Witness with Knowledge), and that since some of the documents fall just short of the age requirements under 901(b)(8) (Ancient Documents), this subsection in conjunction with other circumstances would be sufficient to fulfill the 901(a) requirements. Once authenticity has been established for one document, 901(b)(3) may be used to authenticate other documents of a similar type.

Rule 903 (Subscribing Witness' Testimony Unnecessary) and the illustrations given under 901(b) make it clear that *testimony* is not essential to establish authenticity, and, as McCormick states, "authentication by circumstantial evidence is uniformly recognized as permissible." [§ 222 (2d ed. 1972).] Elements which tend to establish authenticity may be found both in Rule 901 itself, in the Advisory Committee Notes, and in the cases which we will outline in the following discussion. One such element is the source of a particular document, i.e., the method or place of its discovery.

a. Source of the Document

Plaintiffs urge that the defendants' production of certain of the documents in answer to interrogatories under Rule 33(c) is itself sufficient to establish them *ipso facto* as authentic. We disagree with this reading of the Rule. Given the breadth of the discovery rules and the broad requirements for production, we feel it would undermine the liberal intent of those rules to interpret such production as an admission of authenticity in the absence of a specific assertion by the producing party regarding the nature or authorship of the documents produced. . . .

The production of the documents by the defendants may, however, provide circumstantial evidence of authenticity. McCormick notes that a *prima facie* showing of authenticity is made by the emergence of a document from public custody. He concludes that, while the circumstances of private custody are too varied to warrant an expansion of the rule in every case, "proof of private custody, together with other circumstances, is frequently, strong circumstantial evidence of authenticity." [§ 224 at p. 552]....

b.   Characteristics of the Document Itself

The characteristics of the document itself are also a basis for establishing authentication, Rule 901(b)(4). The last phrase of the rule indicates, however, that characteristics of a document must be considered "in conjunction with circumstances." Although Weinstein states that a document "can be authenticated by its contents alone," it is clear, from the examples used, that he "means in light of surrounding circumstances." ¶ 901(b)(4) [01] at 901–46. All of the characteristics mentioned in 901(b)(4) are also subject to the overriding requirement of "distinctiveness" under that example.

The first characteristic mentioned in 901(b)(4) is "appearance." Weinstein gives as examples of the types of appearance the courts may wish to consider: a postmark, a return address, a letterhead, a signature even where affixed by a rubber stamp, typing or form which corresponds to usual practice. The aspect of the document's appearance which is most relevant with respect to the JFTC documents is the fact that many of them are marked with a particular person's name in the form of a "chop," a Japanese seal which contains a stylized rendition of a person's name and is sometimes used in lieu of a signature. During the discussion of authenticity of the so-called MITI statement, proffered by defendants, they urged that the "chop" affixed to the document made it the legal equivalent of a signed document. Though this contention was resisted at that time by plaintiffs, we conclude that a "chop" should be given weight equivalent to a signature. We recognize that a "chop," like a signature, may not always be genuine. Furthermore, many people with the same surname may have a common "chop," hence the "chop" does not in every case indicate authorship. The particular use of a "chop" will be considered with respect to the individual document upon which it appears. Many of the import transaction documents also have distinguishing characteristics, particularly letterheads.

A second characteristic mentioned in 901(b)(4), again subject to the distinctiveness requirement, is the contents, or substance, of the document. Contents have been used to establish authentication in a variety of ways. In United States v. Smith, 609 F.2d 1294 (9th Cir.1979), hotel records of defendant's registration and charges incurred were introduced. Included in the evidence linking the defendant to the records were independent corroboration of his presence at meetings in the hotel, the use of names used by defendant in signing records, and the use of the address which appeared on defendant's business card. In [United States v. Natale, 526 F.2d 1160 (2d Cir.1975)], the court similarly relied upon the corroboration of the contents of the notebook involved by independent evidence. One of the entries referred to a loan made to a witness in the case, and served to authenticate the document.

In Goichman, supra, 547 F.2d at 783, an unsigned document entitled "History of Children's Assets," which listed the defendants' expenditures, had been produced as part of the docket record in a prior (domestic relations) proceeding. The contents of the document were corroborated by defendant's complaint in that proceeding, and the words "I" and "my" were used in conjunction with the first names of the defendant's three children. The Third

Circuit held that this evidence of contents was sufficient to establish a prima facie showing of authentication.

If the subject matter of a document refers to knowledge which only one individual would have had, it is sufficient to authenticate the document. 7 Wigmore on Evidence § 2148 (3d ed. 1940). Weinstein disagrees with the insistence on knowledge by only a single person, however, as he states, "the force of the inference decreases as the number of people who know the details ... increases." Weinstein, ¶ 901(b)(4) [01] at 901–46 and 47. In United States v. Wilson, 532 F.2d 641 (8th Cir.), cert. denied, 429 U.S. 846, 97 S.Ct. 128, 50 L.Ed.2d 117 (1976), the prosecution sought to introduce a notebook which contained records of drug transactions. Though it was admitted that the author was unknown, the Court of Appeals upheld the authentication of the notebook on the grounds that only those persons acquainted with the particular transactions involved could have written the entries.

Some of the documents involved are said to contain information allegedly known only to a limited number of individuals who attended various meetings. The plaintiffs' own showing demonstrates that the number was not all that limited. However, to the extent that information contained in documents is corroborated by other admissible evidence, and is known to a limited number of individuals, these factors may be considered in determining whether sufficient evidence exists to authenticate it.

c. Testimony and Interrogatory Answers

Testimony before the JFTC, to the extent that it is found admissible, may also be used to authenticate other documents. Rule 901(b)(1) specifically holds testimony sufficient to establish authenticity. Where the testimony does not deal directly with any particular document offered, it may still be helpful in proving authenticity circumstantially. Weinstein ¶ 901(b)(1) [01] at 901–22. We will have occasion below to consider JFTC testimony both as circumstantial and as direct evidence of authenticity.

The answers to interrogatories may also be considered as "testimony" where they directly identify a document's source or author, corroborate the contents of particular documents, indicate the presence of a purported author at a meeting or a meeting's limited attendance, or otherwise establish the document's authenticity. While Weinstein notes that Interrogatories, Requests for Admissions and Stipulations "should be relied upon to dispose of most authentication problems before trial," ¶ 901(b)(2) [01] at 901–23, the questions and answers in most of the interrogatories here are not specific enough to constitute a concession of authenticity.

Since we have ruled that documents must be authenticated by admissible evidence, the admissibility of former testimony and the interrogatory answers themselves is an additional issue to be determined. Since the interrogatories may not be admissible against all defendants unless the plaintiffs' conspiracy theory is accepted, this presents a particularly difficult situation. Where authentication depends on the admissibility of an interrogatory, which itself depends on the plaintiffs' establishment of a conspiracy, the documents may be admitted "subject to" such a showing.

d. Similarity to Other Authenticated Documents

The example in 901(b)(3) allows the trier of fact to compare a document to another authenticated document in order to establish its authentication. In [Alexander Dawson, Inc. v. N.L.R.B., 586 F.2d 1300 (9th Cir.1978)] the employment applications involved were "on the same form" as applications whose authenticity was conceded. This, in conjunction with the circumstances of production, was considered sufficient to establish their authenticity, 586 F.2d at 1303. Many of the documents involved here are members of "groups" of documents, sharing similar characteristics. The authentication of one such document may serve as the basis for authenticating the others in a group on the basis of comparison, initially by the court, and ultimately by the trier of fact.

e. Age of the Document

A final element to be considered in our determination of authenticity is the age of the document. Rule 901(b)(8)(C) sets twenty years as the age requirement for "Ancient Documents." None of the documents now before us is twenty years old, although some may reach that age by the time of trial. While Weinstein urges that this figure should not be regarded as an absolute necessity, it is itself ten years shorter than the period under common law. This is explained in the Advisory Committee Notes as being due to a shift in the underlying rationale for the rule from an emphasis on the unavailability of witnesses to an emphasis on the unlikeliness of a fraud over such an extended time period. While the Notes state that any time period is bound to be arbitrary, we feel that in the present case some additional indicia of authenticity are needed where all of the documents fall short of the twenty year limit.

4. Self–Authentication Under Rule 902

Rule 902 provides that certain documents are "self-authenticating" to the extent that no extrinsic evidence of authenticity is needed. Although 902(3) lists Foreign Public Documents as being of this type, the Advisory Committee Notes to 902(4) make it clear that 902(3) applies to the originals of documents and that 902(4) is the section applicable to copies. Under this section the copy must be certified as correct by either the custodian or other authorized person, and this certification must itself conform to Rule 902(3) in order to be received.

None of the documents involved here were obtained by plaintiffs from official custody or were accompanied by this type of official certification, and thus none are "self-authenticating" under Rule 902. Since the method of authentication provided in Rule 902 is not exclusive, however, plaintiffs' failure to procure certified copies does not bar authentication of the documents under Rule 901.

[Discussion of best evidence and hearsay problems in millions of documents produced in discovery omitted; extensive discussion of other evidence is omitted.]

NOTES

1. A comparison of Keegan and Zenith illustrates the different scale of the document problem in a complex and relatively simple case. How could counsel have avoided some of the problems in Zenith? Should the standards for admissibility have been strict at the pretrial stages? Why? Some trial judges refer matters such as are discussed in Zenith to a Federal Magistrate Judge or a Special Master. What are the advantages and disadvantages of this technique? Cf. United States v. Raddatz, 447 U.S. 667 (1980) (suppression motion ruled on by magistrate, limits on reference and method of appeal to district court; district court not required to rehear testimony).

2. See Warren v. United States, 447 F.2d 259 (9th Cir.1971) (defendant charged with possessing an unregistered firearm; special agent of Alcohol,

Tobacco and Firearms Division, Internal Revenue Service requested records check on gun found in possession of defendant; pursuant to request, government official conducted records check and determined that the firearm was not properly registered; document prepared by the official reporting these findings was admitted pursuant to Fed.R.Crim.Pro. 27. The alternative would have been "to require the declarant, the official conducting the records check, and perhaps every employee of the Records Division who might have received a registration for filing, to testify in person. Not only would such procedure [have] defeat[ed] the goal of administrative convenience which Rule 27 seeks to foster ..., but it would appear unnecessary since a probability of trustworthiness is found in the official's duty to maintain accurate records ...").

Authentication of certified copies of an official document involves the problem of self-authentication. The document appears and says, "Accept me as being what I purport to be. If you have any doubt about it, I will give you assurances by telling you that an official with authority to do so who had custody of my original once called me authentic." To be satisfied with this self-serving declaration, the court must accept (1) the custody and authority of the officer to certify, (2) the incumbency in office of the particular alleged certifying officer, and (3) the fact that he did certify—i.e., the genuineness of his signature or seal. Many special statutes provide for admissibility and authentication of documents. For a method of showing non-existence of a public record see Jackson v. United States, 250 F.2d 897, 900–901 (5th Cir.1958).

3. At common law the method of proving the content of a public record was by presenting a witness who had made a copy or who had compared the original with a copy, and who would swear that the copy presented was a true and correct copy of the original. Of course, it was essential to show that the original was a public record. In some American jurisdictions a duly certified copy either is required or is preferred to an examined copy. Under the English common law the official duty to keep a record did not by implication include an official duty to issue a certified copy of the record. Most American courts, however, accept the rule which prevails in the Federal courts. L. Hand, J., in Lembeck v. United States Shipping Board Emergency Fleet Corp., 9 F.2d 558, 559 (2d Cir.1925), said: "It was early established by the Supreme Court that 'on general principles,' and regardless of statutes, copies of public documents, properly certified by their custodian, were competent evidence without the production of the originals.... The rule is quite independent of any statute.... " See 70 A.L.R.2d 1227 (1960).

RULE 44(a)(2) OF THE FEDERAL RULES OF CIVIL PROCEDURE[1]

Foreign. A foreign official record, or an entry therein, when admissible for any purpose, may be evidenced by an official publication thereof; or a copy thereof, attested by a person authorized to make the attestation, and accompanied by a final certification as to the genuineness of the signature and official position (i) of the attesting person, or (ii) of any foreign official whose certificate of genuineness of signature and official position relates to the attestation or is in a chain of certificates of genuineness of signature and official position relating to the attestation. A final certification may be made by a secretary of embassy or legation, consul general, consul, vice consul, or consular agent of the United States, or a diplomatic or consular official of the foreign country assigned or accredited to the United States. If reasonable

---

1. These materials were developed collaboratively by the Commission and Advisory Committee on International Rules of Judicial Procedure, the Columbia Law School Project on International Procedure, and the Reporter to the Advisory Committee on Civil Rules.

opportunity has been given to all parties to investigate the authenticity and accuracy of the documents, the court may, for good cause shown, (i) admit an attested copy without final certification or (ii) permit the foreign official record to be evidenced by an attested summary with or without a final certification.

ADVISORY COMMITTEE'S NOTE

. . .

One of the difficulties with the certification requirement of Rule 44 has been that it requires one person, a United States foreign service officer, to certify the genuineness of the attesting person's signature, the incumbency of the office he purports to hold, and his authority to prepare and attest the copy. See Schlesinger, Comparative Law 57 (2d ed. 1959); Smit, International Aspect of Federal Civil Procedure, 61 Colum.L.Rev. 1031, 1061 (1961); 22 C.F.R. § 92.41(a)(e) (1958). This difficulty is alleviated by the elimination of the element of authority which raised issues of foreign law that, as a practical matter, were beyond the expertise of the certifying officer, and by specifically authorizing use of the chain-certification method. . . .

Although amended Rule 44 facilitates proof of foreign official records, it is recognized that in some situations the foregoing requirement may be difficult or even impossible to satisfy. The difficulty may be due to the fact that there is no American consul in the country in question; to a lack of co-operation on the part of foreign officials; or to peculiarities that presently exist or may arise in the future in the law or practice of any one or more than one hundred foreign countries and of their even more numerous states and political subdivisions. See United States v. Grabina, 119 F.2d 863 (2d Cir.1941). See generally Jones, International Judicial Assistance: Procedural Chaos and a Program for Reform, 62 Yale L.J. 515, 548–49 (1953). Therefore, the final sentence of paragraph (a)(2) provides the court with discretionary power to admit a document that is attested but uncertified, or a summary of the record rather than a copy. . . .

NOTES

1. See also Section 5.02 of the Uniform Interstate and International Procedure Act and Rule 902(3) of the Federal Rules of Evidence.

2. Compliance with Rule 902(3) of the Federal Rules of Evidence will no longer be necessary in many instances because the Senate gave its advice and consent to the ratification by the United States of the Convention Abolishing the Requirement of Legalization for Foreign Public Documents, which had been adopted at the Ninth Session of the Hague Conference on Private International Law. The Convention took effect in the United States on October 15, 1981. Under the Supremacy Clause, the Convention will be applicable in state courts and before state administrative agencies.

Each country designates those public officials by their titles, who may affix a form of certification known as the "apostille." The certificate simply states that the document was signed by an individual in his official capacity and that the seal or stamp is genuine. Public documents from countries which are parties to the Convention are to be recognized in the courts here so long as the apostille is affixed. Similarly, American documents bearing the apostille are to be recognized in foreign courts.

The treaty applies to the states and governs over more restrictive authentication methods. In the Matter of Estate of Kate McDermott, 447 N.Y.S.2d 107

(Bronx Surr.Ct.1982); Opinion of Attorney General of California, No. 81–1213 (March 19, 1982).

3. Statutes governing proof of official records of sister states or of foreign governments often require unessential details and yet are strictly construed, with the result that a litigant is deprived of the benefit of highly valuable evidence merely because he has omitted some required detail of authentication which seems to have little or no intrinsic value. In State v. Hendrix, 56 S.W.2d 76 (Mo.1932), evidence of contents of official records was excluded because of proponent's failure properly to prove (a) that the records were required by law to be kept, or (b) that the certifying officer was the keeper of the record, or because the official certified not a verbatim copy of the record but a general statement as to its contents. In Duncan v. United States, 68 F.2d 136, 138 (9th Cir.1933), a photographic copy of a record of a birth in a Rumanian municipality was certified by a person representing himself to be the mayor made before a person representing himself to be a notary public. Their signatures were authenticated by a certificate of the local prefecture, which was in turn attested by the purported signature and seal of the Minister of the Interior. The Minister's signature was certified by a United States Consul, and the Consul's certificate was certified by the Secretary of State of the United States. In addition there was a certificate purporting to be executed by the Rumanian Prefect and by a representative of the "Director", that the purported Mayor and the purported notary were actually such. With all this authentication, the court indicated that the certificate was inadmissible for lack of evidence that the record was kept in compliance with and conformity to the law of Rumania, but held that the defendant's general objection was not sufficient to make reception of the certificate erroneous. See also People v. Reese, 179 N.E. 305 (N.Y.1932), for an opinion by Cardozo, Ch. J. construing a New York statute as applicable only to certificates of domestic custodians.

NOTES ON METHODS OF PROVING AUTHENTICITY

There are several means by which the authenticity of a writing can be established. In addition to the special statutes governing public documents noted above, they can be classified as 1) admissions of authenticity, 2) testimony by the asserted writer, or 3) someone who saw him write, and 4) circumstantial evidence of authenticity.

1. The simplest practice is to obtain an admission of authenticity by, or on behalf of, the litigant against whom the document is to be offered in evidence. Stipulations in advance of trial or hearing as to the authenticity and admissibility of relevant writings are common. Ponderosa System, Inc. v. Brandt, 767 F.2d 668 (10th Cir.1985) (in action for breach of contract, complaints received by franchisee restaurant regarding meat supplied by franchiser were admissible where franchiser stipulated to authenticity of complaints). They are encouraged, sometimes to the extent of perceptible coercion, by modern legislation and rules of court. See, e.g., Fed.Rule Civ.Proc. 36; Mass.Gen.Laws Ann. c. 231, § 29 (1956) ("A signature to an instrument declared on or set forth as a cause of action or as a ground of defense or set-off shall be taken as admitted unless the party sought to be charged thereby files in court, within the same length of time after such instrument is pleaded as is allowed for an answer, a specific denial of the genuineness thereof and a demand that it shall be proved at the trial"); id. § 69 (provision laying down procedure of formal demand for admission for purposes of the immediate case "of any material fact or facts or the execution of any material paper or document which the party filing the demand intends to use at the trial" and terminating: "If the party upon whom such demand is made refuses to admit any fact or the execution of any paper or document mentioned in the demand, the reasonable expense of proving such fact or the execution of such paper or document, as determined after summary hearing by the justice presiding at the trial, shall, unless the justice certifies that the refusal to admit was reasonable, be paid by said party to the other party and the amount thereof shall be added to the taxable costs of the party in whose favor such amount is awarded or deducted from the amount of any judgment or decree against him."). Pre-trial hearings offer an excellent opportunity to clear away mock disputes respecting documentary authentication. Unfortunately this device has not been effectively used in most cases, although Federal Courts are using it effectively in antitrust and other extensive litigations which frequently involve thousands of documents. See, generally, Rosenberg, The Pretrial Conference and Effective Justice (Columbia University Press 1964).

2. The asserted writer may take the stand and testify that he did write the document. See United States v. Wright, 704 F.2d 420 (8th Cir.1983) (copies of application for search warrant and supporting affidavits properly admitted after being authenticated by police officer who prepared them); Wallace v. Lockhart, 701 F.2d 719 (8th Cir.), cert. denied, 464 U.S. 934 (1983) (copies of the victim's dental charts were properly authenticated by the testimony of the doctors who compiled the original charts).

3. While a distinction was once drawn between formal attesting witnesses and mere observers, the Federal Rules of Evidence permit any competent witness with knowledge of relevant facts to testify that a matter is what it appears to be. Fed.R.Evid. 901(b)(1). For a history of the former rule, see Fox v. Reil, 3 Johns. 477 (N.Y.1808).

4. In considering circumstantial evidence to prove authorship, the cases separate into two groups. Those in the first group deal with unsystematized situations, each resting on its own facts, and presenting an individualized challenge to the practitioner's ingenuity. See, e.g., McFarland v. McFarland, 107 A.2d 615, 616 (Pa.Super.1954) (authentication by writing style); Arens & Meadow, Psycholinguistics and the Confession Dilemma, 56 Colum.L.Rev. 19 (1956).

The second group of cases deal with regularized situations which have arisen over and over again, so that set rules have been formulated as to the kind and amount of proof necessary to justify admission of the contested writings. Set out below are materials on authentication through reliance upon proof of proper custody, opinion as to handwriting, the reply doctrine and the ancient document rule.

5. A writing that purports to be an official record and that is proved to have come from the proper public office where such papers are kept, is generally considered to be sufficiently authenticated. United States v. Rice, 652 F.2d 521, 533 (5th Cir.1981) (Goldberg, J., dissenting); United States v. Ward, 173 F.2d 628 (2d Cir.1949). The same rule applies where the public office is the depository for private papers, such as wills or income tax returns. Morgan v. United States, 149 F.2d 185 (5th Cir.1945).

Where the document is found in private custody the decisions had been more restrictive. In People v. Manganaro, 112 N.E. 436 (N.Y.1916), a letter, signed with defendant's name, was found in the defendant's room, and the contents indicated that defendant wrote it. The letter was held to be inadmissible. McCormick called the "strictness" of some of these decisions "misguided" and suggested a greater exercise of discretion in favor of admission where custody and "other attending circumstances make ... genuineness substantially probable." McCormick, Evidence 403 (1954). The courts have since adopted a more rational view:

> Since the circumstances of private custody are infinitely more varied than those of public custody, a new rule in an already rule-ridden area seems inadvisable. No such rule, in fact, is needed, provided that, in their discretion, courts recognize that proof of private custody, together with other circumstances, is frequently strong circumstantial evidence of authenticity.

McCormick, Evidence § 224, at 551–52 (Cleary, 2d ed. 1972).

6. Both lay witnesses and expert witnesses may testify to their opinions respecting authorship or genuineness of writings, subject to proof of proper qualification. See Fed.R.Evid. 901(b)(2), (3). In the case of the lay witness, reasonable familiarity with the handwriting of the person whose authorship of the contested document is required. Generally, the necessary familiarity is obtained by seeing the person write or receiving from him letters or other holographic material. See, e.g., United States v. Mauchlin, 670 F.2d 746 (7th Cir.1982) (prison official could testify that documents in prison files were written by defendant since he had seen him write on approximately six occasions); Farmers Union Oil Co. v. Wood, 301 N.W.2d 129 (N.D.1980). But the work of a bank clerk or teller may give him the requisite familiarity with the signature of a depositor, and it may safely be said that no hidebound rules cramp the scope of proof as to qualification to testify. See the compact statement in Hershberger v. Hershberger, 29 A.2d 95, 98 (Pa.1942). In Ryan v. United States, 384 F.2d 379 (1st Cir.1967), a bank treasurer testified that an allegedly forged signature had been written by someone other than the purported signer; held error (though harmless) on the ground that the witness's only special familiarity was with the signer's signature card, not her handwriting. But cf. In re Marriage of Schulz, 583 S.W.2d 735, 745 (Mo.App.1979) ("The authenticity of the signature to be employed as an exemplar for comparison with the disputed signature must be established to the satisfaction of the trial judge.").

The trial judge has considerable free discretion to admit or exclude lay handwriting testimony. He may, for instance, accept as a minimum for qualification a showing that the witness has seen the asserted author write on a single occasion although never again; or, particularly when there is other evidence bearing upon authenticity, he may insist upon a more rigorous standard for qualification. See, e.g., United States v. Pitts, 569 F.2d 343 (5th Cir.), cert. denied, 436 U.S. 959 (1978) (single opportunity to see signature; insufficient familiarity to authenticate).

Handwriting testimony involves a process of comparison. The lay witness in this field is not permitted to fortify the opinion to which he testifies by physical comparison in court of the contested writing with genuine standards. This is because he has by hypothesis no more skill for making such comparison than do the lay triers of fact, who should therefore do the comparing themselves. Cf. Bowles v. Kennemore, 139 F.2d 541, 542 (4th Cir.1944), reiterating per curiam the well established federal doctrine that a judge or jury trying the facts "may compare writings in evidence which are admitted to have been made by a person with writings that he disputes in order to determine whether all the writings were made by the same person"; and cf. Sack v. Siekman, 23 N.W.2d 706 (Neb.1946), where the judges followed expert methodology to the best of their ability. Noyes v. Noyes, supra, contains the statement: "Where undoubted standards of handwriting, as well as the questioned signature, are before the jury, there is no occasion for the testimony of one who is neither an expert nor possessed of considerable familiarity with the handwriting of the person whose [purported] signature is under examination."

What the lay opinion witness in this connection · supposedly does is to compare a mental image with the physical writing in the contested document. Normally, this mental image will have originated before the witness is confronted with the contested document, but, despite prohibition of direct comparison while testifying, it has been held that he may refresh his recollection by scrutinizing genuine standards, Thomas v. State, 2 N.E. 808, 815 (Ind.1885), and even that, in a case where the contested document was lost after the witness saw it, he may testify although he first made the acquaintance of genuine standards subsequently to the loss, Cochran v. Stein, 136 N.W. 1037, 41 L.R.A.N.S. 391 (Minn.1912). From the foregoing it will be appreciated that much lay witness handwriting testimony is highly unreliable. Inbau, Lay Witness Identification of Handwriting, 34 Ill.L.Rev. 433 (1939); A.S. Osborn, The Problem of Proof, 462–473 (2d ed. 1926).

The expert handwriting witness, on the contrary, is allowed in the course of his testimony, as well as before taking the stand, to buttress his views by comparing the disputed document with genuine standards. This his "special knowledge, skill, experience or training" justifies. See A.L.I. Code, Rule 402, from which the quoted words are taken. The expert may compare the disputed writing with photographic copies of genuine standards and he can use an enlargement of the disputed writing in order to explain his conclusion to the jury. See, e.g., Hilton, Scientific Examination of Questioned Documents (1956); A.S. & A.D. Osborn, Questioned Documents Problems (2d ed. 1946); Baker, Law of Disputed and Forged Documents (1955); Busch, Law and Tactics in Jury Trials 878–934 (1949); Appel, Advances in Analysis of Questioned Documents, 38 Geo.L.J. 385 (1950); Beacon, Modern Educational Aids for Simplified Explanations of Handwriting Comparisons, 13 J. of Forensic Sciences 509 (1968). 101 A.L.R. 767 (1936) (opinion testimony as to genuineness of signature by mark). Cf. Annot., Admissibility of Expert Evidence to Decipher Illegible Documents, 11 A.L.R.3d 1015 (1967).

Considerable distrust of expert evidence persists, which may be largely explained by the varying competency of the witnesses offered. Certainly some experts do not strengthen their testimony by declaring themselves infallible. See, e.g., the curious case of the purported autobiography of Howard Hughes and the newspaper reports of the positive, and later concededly incorrect expert handwriting opinion of Osborn Associates, well-known examiners of questioned documents. N.Y. Times, Feb. 8, 1972, p. 14, Col. 1. Note, too, the mistake conceded in a voiceprint case after a police officer had been demoted partly on the basis of this evidence. N.Y. Times, March 27, 1971, p. 57, col. 2. The document may be authenticated by a comparison of typewriting rather than handwriting. See, e.g., Forte v. Schiebe, 302 P.2d 336, 337 (Cal.App.1956); 106 A.L.R. 714, 721 (1957). Will handwriting expert testimony receive more critical analysis since Daubert v. Merrell Dow Pharmaceuticals, Inc., 509 U.S. 579 (1993) under expert evidence, infra.

7. Special authentication statutes may apply. See, e.g., 18 U.S.C. § 3505 (certification as basis for hearsay and authentication); United States v. Chan, 680 F.Supp. 521 (E.D.N.Y.1988).

University of Illinois v. Spalding

Supreme Court of New Hampshire, 1901.
71 N.H. 163, 51 A. 731, 62 L.R.A. 817.

[Debt on a bond. The defense was that, after the bond was signed and before it was delivered to the plaintiff, the name of one surety was erased and another written over it. The plaintiff claimed that the erasure was a part of the defendant's name accidentally written by him upon the line below his full signature; while defendant denied that the words erased were in his handwriting. For the purpose of comparison the defendant introduced in evidence his signature written upon stock certificates, and sworn to be genuine by him and by the treasurer of the corporation. The plaintiff excepted to the receipt of this evidence on the ground that the signatures were neither admitted to be genuine nor found in papers otherwise in the case. Verdict for defendant.]

■ REMICK, J. ... It may be safely stated as a fundamental proposition that, on the question whether a given signature is in the handwriting of a particular person, comparison of the disputed signature with other writings of that person known to be genuine is a rational method of investigation, and that similarities and dissimilarities thus disclosed are probative and as satisfactory in the instinctive search for truth as opinion formed by the unquestioned method of comparing the signature in issue with an exemplar of the person's handwriting existing in the mind and derived from direct acquaintance, however little, with the party's handwriting....

The whole doctrine of comparison presupposes the existence of genuine standards. Comparison of a disputed signature in issue with disputed specimens would not be comparison in any proper sense. When the identity of anything is fully and certainly established, you may compare other things with it which are doubtful, to ascertain whether they belong to the same class or not; but when both are doubtful and uncertain, comparison is not only useless as to any certain result, but clearly dangerous and more likely to bewilder than to instruct a jury. If disputed signatures were admissible for the purpose of comparison, a collateral inquiry would be raised as to each standard; and the proof upon this inquiry would be comparison again, which would only lead to an endless series of issues, each more unsatisfactory than the first; and the case would thus be filled with issues aside from the real question before the jury.

... The true rule is, that when a writing in issue is claimed on the one hand and denied upon the other to be the writing of a particular person, any other writing of that person's may be admitted in evidence for the mere purpose of comparison with the writing in dispute, whether the latter is susceptible of or supported by direct proof or not; but before any such writing shall be admissible for such purpose its genuineness must be found as a preliminary fact by the presiding judge, upon clear and undoubted evidence.... This involves, indeed, a marked departure from the common law. It does away with the common-law limitation of comparison to standards otherwise in the case, and hence with its exceptions and the controversy and confusion which have grown out of them.... The value of comparison as a method of proof being now generally conceded; juries being no longer too ignorant to derive benefit from that source; the danger of spurious specimens and the objections to collateral issues being fully met by requiring the genuineness of the standard to be determined as a preliminary fact by the trial judge, there remains, it would seem, no satisfactory reason for the old limitations and exceptions. And it is fair to assume that, had no statute been enacted, the common law of England, adjusting itself to changed conditions, would now accord with the rule we have announced....

Exceptions overruled.

NOTES

1. As the main case illustrates, only authenticated specimens may be used for comparison. The authentication requirements for such specimens under the

Federal Rules of Evidence are theoretically the same as those for the admission of any other writing: the proponent of the specimen must provide sufficient evidence to permit a jury to find that the specimen is what it purports to be. For an explanation of this see, Chemical Corn Exchange Bank & Trust Co. v. Frankel, 111 So.2d 99, 101, 72 A.L.R.2d 1270 (Fla.App.1959):

The genuineness of the standard to be used may be established in any one of several ways. If its genuineness is admitted by the parties, this may be accepted by the trial judge, and further proof thereof rendered unnecessary. If, however, the genuineness of the standard is not admitted, it may be used as a basis for comparison if it is in evidence before the court in the case for some other purpose, or forms a part of the pleadings in the case. Even though the standard was written after the controversy arose or the suit was instituted, its genuineness may nevertheless be established by proof that it was written in the ordinary course of business and not for the occasion of the trial or for the purpose of creating testimony. A signature or specimen writing that is made for the occasion and post litem motam may not be used for a comparison by the party making it. It is only when a writing is written, not by design, but unconstrainedly and in the natural manner of the writer so as to bear the impress of the general character of his chirography as the involuntary and unconscious result of constitution, habit, or other permanent cause that it furnishes, if otherwise admissible in evidence, any satisfactory test of genuineness.

The Federal Rules of Evidence do not differentiate between authentication of exemplars and that of any other writings. See Rules 104(b) and 901(a). Is this sound? How much discretion should the court have to set higher standards for exemplars under the Federal Rules?

2. If neither lay witnesses nor expert witnesses testify as to the authenticity of the document in dispute, may the jury compare the disputed writing with a writing admitted as authentic? Mo–Kan Teamsters Pension Fund v. Creason, 716 F.2d 772 (10th Cir.1983), cert. denied, 464 U.S. 1045 (1984) (trier of fact may authenticate writing by comparing it with authenticated specimen).

3. A variety of interlocking procedural questions append themselves to the doctrine that on issues involving identification or authentication of handwriting it is permissible to use for comparison specimens proved to be genuine, in addition to or substitution for those stipulated or admitted to be genuine. Must the proof be made primarily to the judge, rather than to the jury? If so, does the judge's duty extend only to making sure there is sufficient evidence of genuineness, to sustain a finding, or does this duty go the length of requiring the judge to find one way or the other on the issue of genuiness of the specimens? If it be held that the judge must make a finding as to genuineness is his determination final only in case he excludes the proffered specimens as not genuine, and subject to review by the jury if he finds the specimens genuine and admits them? In connection with the last two questions, has a constitutional provisions guaranteeing the inviolability of trial by jury any bearing? Is the bearing of such a provision different in civil and in criminal cases? Is a particular type of evidence—e.g. testimony by a witness that he saw the specimens made and so knew from personal observation who wrote them—essential to "proof" of genuineness? Aside from questions as to doubt, or by clear and convincing evidence, or merely by a preproderance of evidence? See 7 Wigmore, Evidence §§ 2020 et seq. (Chadbourn Rev.1978) (particularly the citations in § 2020 n. 3).

4. Are there constitutional protections against the procuring of exemplars? See chapter 8, section 2, infra.

5. Care must be taken to prevent the use of exemplars to get information before the jury that might be prejudicial. See People v. Dinkins, 52 Cal.Rptr. 134 (Cal.App.1966) (handwriting exemplar written in jail and sent to victim's former wife was intercepted by prison censor).

6. See Whelton v. Daly, 37 A.2d 1 (N.H.1944) (power of attorney authenticated by foreign notary signature and seal, postmarked envelopes and interlocking correspondence); People v. Dinkins, 52 Cal.Rptr. 134 (Cal.App.1966) (reply telegram); House Grain Co. v. Finerman & Sons, 253 P.2d 1034, 1039 (Cal.App. 1953) (involving telegram received in response to telephone call, but treated as being in reply to another telegram); People v. Dunbar Contracting Co., 109 N.E. 554 (N.Y.1915) (letter received in response to telephone call); 52 A.L.R. 580, 583 (1928) (authentication of telegrams); 7 Wigmore, Evidence § 2154 (Chadbourn Rev.1978) (reply telegram).

If the reply comes from one who purports to sign as agent for the person addressed, the authority of the agent may be assumed. Anstine v. McWilliams, 163 P.2d 816 (Wash.1945).

For an interesting case involving authentication of many radiotelegrams from a ship at sea see United States v. Reilly, 33 F.3d 1396, 1402 ff. (3d Cir.1994), relying on testimony, circumstantial evidence of interlocking materials, the reply doctrine, appearance of authenticity, and the business record of the ship's log.

7. United States v. Alessi, 638 F.2d 466 (2d Cir.1980):

Ferrara claims that the court erred in admitting against him the testimony of Milton Freedman regarding telephone conversations with a person named "Corky" in which Freedman arranged cash purchases of airline tickets at a discount. He argues that the conversations were not authenticated as prescribed by Rule 901, Fed.R.Evid. The claim is meritless.

The phone number called by Freedman was listed in the name of Ferrara's wife at their residence. At trial Freedman identified Ferrara as "Corky" and further testified to meeting Ferrara, known as "Corky," at Kennedy Airport where Freedman paid him for the tickets. Thereafter he arranged further purchases of tickets by telephone with Ferrara in the same manner, mailing money to Ferrara and receiving airline tickets in return.

This authentication of Ferrara's voice was adequate. The illustrations in Rule 901(b)(6) are just that, illustrations, and not limitations on methods of identification that may be used.

If a witness telephones X's business number, and a voice answers "This is X," the witness' testimony that the voice made an assertion is admissible to prove that X made it. Cwach v. United States, 212 F.2d 520, 524–525 (8th Cir.1954). See also United States v. Portsmouth Paving Corp., 694 F.2d 312 (4th Cir.1982) (witness' testimony that he called defendant's business office supports inference that one who answered phone was defendant's agent). Compare People v. Horace, 273 P.2d 923, 924–925 (Cal.App.1954), where the voice identifying itself as X knew the nature of the business about which the witness telephoned. In Benson v. Commonwealth, 58 S.E.2d 312, 314 (Va.1950), such testimony was held inadmissible because the witness did not obtain X's telephone number, a residence, from the directory, but from an individual. But in the Cwach and other cases, involving business telephones, the opinions do not indicate how the witness obtained the telephone number, and Horace involved a residential telephone number obtained from X. If a person telephones the witness and identifies himself as X, testimony by the witness as to an assertion made by this voice is not admissible to prove that X made the assertion where X's voice is not recognized. Should internal evidence in the conversation that it was X be permitted to establish authenticity? Cf. O'Neal v. Morgan, 637 F.2d 846 (2d Cir.1980), cert. denied sub nom. Esty v. O'Neal, 451 U.S. 972 (1981) (self-identification of the person called at a place where he could reasonably be expected to be).

8. A scientific technique that has been the source of considerable controversy is "voiceprint" identification through the use of a sound spectrograph. The spectrograph reproduces graphic impressions from tapes of human utterances. The basic principle is that whenever a sound is uttered, an energy output is required to transform it into an intelligible word. The print is a visual representation of the sound. The voiceprint can be used for comparison and identification purposes.

Is there a danger that a jury will attribute the reliability of fingerprint identification to voiceprint identification? See National Research Council, On the Theory and Practice of Voice Identification 59 (1979), rejecting this evidence as unreliable:

> Voicegrams differ from fingerprints in a fundamental way, in that different utterances of a given word by a given speaker are not acoustically invariant whereas the anatomical ridges in the skin are topologically invariant. The variability among different utterances of a given word by a given speaker, at least for most speakers, seems to be less than the variability among the utterances of a given word by different speakers. . . .

No court has taken judicial notice of the technique. However, a few courts have held the evidence admissible if a sufficient foundation is laid through the use of expert testimony. See, e.g., *admissible:* United States v. Franks, 511 F.2d 25 (6th Cir.), cert. denied, 422 U.S. 1042 (1975); United States v. Baller, 519 F.2d 463 (4th Cir.), cert. denied, 423 U.S. 1019 (1975); *inadmissible:* United States v. Addison, 498 F.2d 741 (D.C.Cir.1974); People v. Kelly, 549 P.2d 1240 (Cal. 1976); Reed v. State, 391 A.2d 364 (Md.1978) (but see dissent); People v. Tobey, 257 N.W.2d 537 (Mich.1977) (contains overview of the law as it pertains to scientific evidence); Commonwealth v. Topa, 369 A.2d 1277 (Pa.1977); Note, Voiceprints in the Courtroom, 21 Ariz.L.Rev. 1163 (1979). See also O. Tosi, Voice Identification Theory and Legal Applications (1979); Decker & Handler, Voiceprint Identification Evidence—Out of the Frye Pan and into Admissibility, 26 Am.U.L.Rev. 314 (1977); Thomas, Voiceprint—Myth or Miracle (The eyes have it), 3 U. of San Fernando V.L.Rev. 15 (1974); Greene, Voiceprint Identification: The Case in Favor of Admissibility, 13 Am.Crim.L.Rev. 171 (1975); Weissman, Voiceprints and the Defense, 10 N.Eng.L.Rev. 25 (1974); Note, A Foundational Standard for the Admission of Sound Recordings into Evidence in Criminal Trials, 4 So.Cal.L.Rev. 1273 (1979). Should the rules on expert evidence affect the result? See the discussion of the Frye doctrine and of Daubert v. Merrell Dow Pharmaceuticals, Inc., 509 U.S. 579 (1993), under expert evidence, infra.

NOTES ON ANCIENT DOCUMENTS

1. The rule was stated succinctly in Louden v. Apollo Gas Co., 417 A.2d 1185, 1187 (Pa.Super.1980):

The "Ancient Document Rule" has been uniformly interpreted to exempt from the general rule requiring documents to be authenticated by the testimony of subscribing witnesses when: the document is at least thirty years old, is free from suspicious alterations and erasures, and has been in the proper custody. . . .

The Rule creates a presumption that a document under the conditions set forth above is self-authenticating; otherwise, the antiquity of the document itself would, by definition, create great difficulty or impossibility of actual authentication.

The ancient document rule covering authentication should be distinguished from the ancient document exception to the hearsay rule. See Appeal of Jarboe, 99 A. 563 (Conn.1917).

2. The court may refuse to apply the ancient document rule because of the suspicious appearance of the document. See Stewart Oil Co. v. Sohio Petroleum Co., 202 F.Supp. 952 (E.D.Ill.1962), aff'd, 315 F.2d 759 (7th Cir.), cert. denied, 375 U.S. 828 (1963): Fed.R.Evid. 901(b)(8).

In Sinkora v. Wlach, 35 N.W.2d 40 (Iowa 1948), the ancient document rule was applied to authenticate an instrument purporting to be a passport. This case emphasizes the importance of producing the original writing when ancient document authentication is attempted. However, that method of authentication is sometimes successful despite loss of the original when testimony can be adduced as to its appearance and custody. See, e.g., Lamons v. Mathes, 232 S.W.2d 558 (Tenn.App.1950).

While the ancient document rule requires that the document be free of suspicion, that suspicion goes not to the content of the document, but rather to whether the document is what it purports to be. In United States v. Kairys, 782 F.2d 1374 (7th Cir.), cert. denied, 476 U.S. 1153 (1986), the government brought a denaturalization proceeding against an alleged Nazi concentration camp guard for concealing his World War II activities when he applied for naturalization. To prove the defendant's former identity, the government introduced his Nazi SS personnel card which was found in the archives of the Soviet Union. The trial court admitted the document under the ancient document rule.

On appeal, the defendant contended that the personnel card should not have been admitted since it contained various inaccuracies. The Seventh Circuit, however, held that the document was properly admitted. The court explained:

Although the rule requires that the document be free of suspicion, that suspicion goes not to the content of the document, but rather to whether the document is what it purports to be. . . . In other words, the issue of admissibility is whether the document is a Personalbogen from the German SS records located in the Soviet Union archives and is over 20 years old. Whether the contents of the document correctly identify the defendant goes to its weight and is a matter for the trier of fact; it is not relevant to the threshold determination of its admissibility.

782 F.2d at 1379. Does Rule 403 of the Federal Rules of Evidence permit the court to deal with an authentic but entirely unreliable document?

B. BEST EVIDENCE RULE

When a litigant has the choice of several ways to prove a proposition of fact, it is no more than simple common sense to put upon him some pressure to produce the most reliable and enlightening evidence he can get. This has been stated over and over again by cases and commentators on evidence from the most ancient to the most modern. These general statements, however, leave very obscure the nature of the pressure legally required or countenanced. In many kinds of factual contests the pressure is only persuasive. A plaintiff seeking to prove the making of a loan to the defendant may rely upon his own testimony, or the testimony of a disinterested eye-and-ear witness, or evidence of an admission by the defendant, or a regular business entry, or some combination of these. A prosecutor in a murder case may rely upon eye witness testimony, or a dying declaration of the asserted victim, or a confession, or circumstantial evidence. The pressure to make the evidential side of either of these cases strong and clear lies in the risk that natural suspicion, sharpened by adverse comment of opposing counsel, may arise from failure to adduce cogent proof which the trier believes should be available if the proponent's contention as to the facts is sound.

In one area, however, the demand for the most satisfactory proof has made itself recognized as a coercive requirement. This requirement is called the Best Evidence Rule, and is generally stated substantially as follows: For the purpose of proving the content of a writing, the original writing itself is regarded as the primary evidence, and secondary evidence is inadmissible unless failure to offer the original is satisfactorily explained. See Thayer, Evidence, 484 et seq. (1890). Cf. the somewhat broader scope of Federal Rules of Evidence 1001, 1002, and 1003.

Practical elucidation of this statement of the rule demands answers to a series of questions: (1) What are the reasons for the Best Evidence Rule? (2) What is a writing? (3) When is a litigant treated as seeking to prove the content of a writing? (4) What is the original of a writing? (5) What are accepted as satisfactory explanations for failure to offer the original? (6) What if any subordinate preferences exist among different kinds of secondary evidence of contents? (7) What relevant procedural devices are utilized in applying the Best Evidence Rule?

Questions (1) and (7) are, of course, pervasive; (1) cannot be fully answered without consideration of the material at large. For example, when a court is in the shadow of judicial, notice need it be concerned with best evidence rules? Cf. United States v. State of Louisiana, 225 F.Supp. 353, 375 (E.D.La.1963) where the court was concerned with the history of voting provisions in Louisiana to determine whether new state provisions had a discriminatory intent. "Handicapped in studying the legislative history of the Constitution of 1921 because . . . the Committee met in secrecy and no minutes were kept . . .," newspaper accounts, "the next best evidence," was relied upon. Question (7) crops up at various points.

The following material is presented in an arrangement tending to suggest answers, successively, to questions (2)–(6). Compare with the Federal Rules the California Best Evidence Rules. Cal.Evid.Code §§ 1500 et seq.

Seiler v. Lucasfilm, Ltd.

United States Court of Appeals, Ninth Circuit, 1986.
797 F.2d 1504.

■ FARRIS, CIRCUIT JUDGE. Lee Seiler, a graphic artist and creator of science fiction creatures, alleged copyright infringement by George Lucas and others who created and produced the science fiction movie "The Empire Strikes Back."

Seiler claimed that creatures known as "Imperial Walkers" which appeared in The Empire Strikes Back infringed Seiler's copyright on his own creatures called "Garthian Striders." The Empire Strikes Back appeared in 1980; Seiler did not obtain his copyright until 1981. . . .

FACTS

Seiler contends that he created and published in 1976 and 1977 science fiction creatures called Garthian Striders. In 1980, George Lucas released The Empire Strikes Back, a motion picture that contains a battle sequence depicting giant machines called Imperial Walkers. In 1981 Seiler obtained a copyright on his Striders, depositing with the Copyright Office "reconstructions" of the originals as they had appeared in 1976 and 1977.

Seiler contends that Lucas' Walkers were copied from Seiler's Striders which were allegedly published in 1976 and 1977. Lucas responds that Seiler did not obtain his copyright until one year after the release of The Empire Strikes Back and that Seiler can produce no documents that antedate The Empire Strikes Back.

Because Seiler proposed to exhibit his Striders in a blow-up comparison to Lucas' Walkers at opening statement, the district judge held an evidentiary hearing on the admissibility of the "reconstructions" of Seiler's Striders. Applying the "best evidence rule," Fed.R.Evid. 1001–1008, the district court found at the end of a seven-day hearing that Seiler lost or destroyed the originals in bad faith under Rule 1004(1) and that consequently no secondary evidence, such as the post-Empire Strikes Back reconstructions, was admissible. In its opinion the court found specifically that Seiler testified falsely, purposefully destroyed or withheld in bad faith the originals, and fabricated and misrepresented the nature of his reconstructions. The district court granted summary judgment to Lucas after the evidentiary hearing.

On appeal, Seiler contends 1) that the best evidence rule does not apply to his works, 2) that if the best evidence rule does apply, Rule 1008 requires a jury determination of the existence and authenticity of his originals, and 3) that 17 U.S.C. § 410(c) of the copyright laws overrides the Federal Rules of Evidence and mandates admission of his secondary evidence.

DISCUSSION

1.   Application of the best evidence rule.

The best evidence rule embodied in Rules 1001–1008 represented a codification of longstanding common law doctrine. Dating back to 1700, the rule requires not, as its common name implies, the best evidence in every case but rather the production of an original document instead of a copy. Many commentators refer to the rule not as the best evidence rule but as the original document rule.

Rule 1001 states: "To prove the content of a writing, recording, or photograph, the original writing, recording, or photograph is required, except as otherwise provided in these rules or by Act of Congress." Writings and recordings are defined in Rule 1001 as "letters, words, or numbers, or their equivalent, set down by handwriting, typewriting, printing, photostating, photographing, magnetic impulse, mechanical or electronic recording, or other form of data compilation."

The Advisory Committee Note supplies the following gloss:

"Traditionally the rule requiring the original centered upon accumulations of data and expressions affecting legal relations set forth in words and figures. This meant that the rule was one essentially related to writings. Present day techniques have expanded methods of storing data, yet the essential form which the information ultimately assumes for usable purposes is words and figures. Hence the considerations underlying the rule dictate its expansion to include computers, photographic systems, and other modern developments."

Some treatises, whose approach seems more historical than rigorously analytic, opine without support from any cases that the Rule is limited to words and figures. 5 Weinstein's Evidence (1983), ¶ 1001(1)[01] at 1001–11; 5 Louisell & Mueller, § 550 at 285.

We hold that Seiler's drawings were "writings" within the meaning of Rule 1001(1); they consist not of "letters, words, or numbers" but of "their equivalent." To hold otherwise would frustrate the policies underlying the Rule and introduce undesirable inconsistencies into the application of the Rule.

In the days before liberal rules of discovery and modern techniques of electronic copying, the rule guarded against incomplete or fraudulent proof. By requiring the possessor of the original to produce it, the rule prevented the introduction of altered copies and the withholding of originals. The purpose of the rule was thus long thought to be one of fraud prevention, but Wigmore pointed out that the rule operated even in cases where fraud was not at issue, such as where secondary evidence is not admitted even though its proponent acts in utmost good faith. Wigmore also noted that if prevention of fraud were the foundation of the rule, it should apply to objects as well as writings, which it does not. 4 Wigmore, Evidence § 1180 (Chadbourn rev. 1972).

The modern justification for the rule has expanded from prevention of fraud to a recognition that writings occupy a central position in the law. When the contents of a writing are at issue, oral testimony as to the terms of the writing is subject to a greater risk of error than oral testimony as to events or other situations. The human memory is not often capable of reciting the precise terms of a writing, and when the terms are in dispute only the writing itself, or a true copy, provides reliable evidence. To summarize, then, we observe that the importance of the precise terms of writings in the world of legal relations, the fallibility of the human memory as reliable evidence of the terms, and the hazards of inaccurate or incomplete duplication are the concerns addressed by the best evidence rule. See 5 Louisell & Mueller, Federal Evidence, § 550 at 283; McCormick on Evidence (3d ed. 1984) § 231 at 704; Cleary & Strong, The Best Evidence Rule: An Evaluation in Context, 51 Iowa L.Rev. 825, 828 (1966).

Viewing the dispute in the context of the concerns underlying the best evidence rule, we conclude that the rule applies. McCormick summarizes the rule as follows:

"[I]n proving the terms of a writing, where the terms are material, the original writing must be produced unless it is shown to be unavailable for some reason other than the serious fault of the proponent." McCormick on Evidence § 230, at 704.

The contents of Seiler's work are at issue. There can be no proof of "substantial similarity" and thus of copyright infringement unless Seiler's works are juxtaposed with Lucas' and their contents compared. Since the contents are material and must be proved, Seiler must either produce the original or show that it is unavailable through no fault of his own. Rule 1004(1). This he could not do.

The facts of this case implicate the very concerns that justify the best evidence rule. Seiler alleges infringement by The Empire Strikes Back, but he can produce no documentary evidence of any originals existing before the release of the movie. His secondary evidence does not consist of true copies or exact duplicates but of "reconstructions" made after The Empire Strikes Back. In short, Seiler claims that the movie infringed his originals, yet he has no proof of those originals.

The dangers of fraud in this situation are clear. The rule would ensure that proof of the infringement claim consists of the works alleged to be infringed. Otherwise, "reconstructions" which might have no resemblance to the purported original would suffice as proof for infringement of the original. Furthermore, application of the rule here defers to the rule's special concern for the contents of writings. Seiler's claim depends on the content of the originals, and the rule would exclude reconstituted proof of the originals' content. Under the circumstances here, no "reconstruction" can substitute for the original....

A creative literary work, which is artwork, and a photograph whose contents are sought to be proved, as in copyright, defamation, or invasion of privacy, are both covered by the best evidence rule. See McCormick, § 232 at 706 n. 9; Advisory Committee's Note to Rule 1002; 5 Louisell & Mueller, § 550 at 285 n. 27. We would be inconsistent to apply the rule to artwork which is literary or photographic but not to artwork of other forms. Furthermore, blueprints, engineering drawings, architectural designs may all lack words or numbers yet still be capable of copyright and susceptible to fraudulent alteration. In short, Seiler's argument would have us restrict the definitions of Rule 1001(1) to "words" and "numbers" but ignore "or their equivalent." We will not do so in the circumstances of this case.

Our holding is also supported by the policy served by the best evidence rule in protecting against faulty memory. Seiler's reconstructions were made four to seven years after the alleged originals; his memory as to specifications and dimensions may have dimmed significantly. Furthermore, reconstructions made after the release of the Empire Strikes Back may be tainted, even if unintentionally, by exposure to the movie. Our holding guards against these problems.

2. Rule 1008.

As we hold that the district court correctly concluded that the best evidence rule applies to Seiler's drawings, Seiler was required to produce his original drawings unless excused by the exceptions set forth in Rule 1004. The pertinent subsection is 1004(1), which provides:

> "The original is not required, and other evidence of the contents of a writing, recording, or photograph is admissible if—
>
> (1) Originals lost or destroyed. All originals are lost or have been destroyed, unless the proponent lost or destroyed them in bad faith; ..."

In the instant case, prior to opening statement, Seiler indicated he planned to show to the jury reconstructions of his "Garthian Striders" during the opening statement. The trial judge would not allow items to be shown to the jury until they were admitted in evidence. Seiler's counsel reiterated that he needed to show the reconstructions to the jury during his opening statement. Hence, the court excused the jury and held a seven-day hearing on their admissibility. At the conclusion of the hearing, the trial judge found that the reconstructions were inadmissible under the best evidence rule as the originals were lost or destroyed in bad faith. This finding is amply supported by the record.

Seiler argues on appeal that regardless of Rule 1004(1), Rule 1008 requires a trial because a key issue would be whether the reconstructions correctly reflect the content of the originals. Rule 1008 provides:

"When the admissibility of other evidence of contents of writings, recordings, or photographs under these rules depends upon the fulfillment of a condition of fact, the question whether the condition has been fulfilled is ordinarily for the court to determine in accordance with the provisions of rule 104. However, when an issue is raised (a) whether the asserted writing ever existed, or (b) whether another writing, recording or photograph produced at the trial is the original, or (c) whether other evidence of contents correctly reflects the contents, the issue is for the trier of facts to determine as in the case of other issues of fact."[2]

Seiler's position confuses admissibility of the reconstructions with the weight, if any, the trier of fact should give them, after the judge has ruled that they are admissible. Rule 1008 states, in essence, that when the *admissibility* of evidence other than the original depends upon the fulfillment of a condition of fact, the trial judge generally makes the determination of that condition of fact. The Notes of the Advisory Committee are consistent with this interpretation in stating: "Most preliminary questions of fact in connection with applying the rule preferring the original as evidence of contents are for the judge ... [t]hus the question of ... fulfillment of other conditions specified in Rule 1004 ... is for the judge." In the instant case, the condition of fact which Seiler needed to prove was that the originals were not lost or destroyed in bad faith. Had he been able to prove this, his reconstructions would have been admissible and then their accuracy would have been a question for the jury. In sum, since admissibility of the reconstructions was dependent upon a finding that the originals were not lost or destroyed in bad faith, the trial judge properly held the hearing to determine their admissibility.

3. Does 17 U.S.C. § 410(c) require the admissibility of the copies of Seiler's work deposited at the Copyright Office?

Since Seiler's drawings are within the best evidence rule, we must address the question whether § 410(c) of the Copyright Act mandates their admission in evidence. Section 410(c) states:

"In any judicial proceedings the certificate of a registration made before or within five years after first publication of the work shall constitute prima facie evidence of the validity of the copyright and of the facts stated in the certificate. The evidentiary weight to be accorded the certificate of a registration made thereafter shall be within the discretion of the court."

....We hold that when the deposited copies are subject to evidentiary challenge under the best evidence rule, the copies are not deemed to be incorporated into the certificate and are not therefore automatically admissible under § 410(c). This holding allows admissibility of the certificate, so that a party may present presumptive evidence of the validity of the copyright. But the deposited copies, when challenged as not the original documents or true copies, will not share this admissibility or presumption. We limit this holding to situations involving the best evidence rule, and leave for another case the decision as to whether, under other circumstances, the deposited copies may be incorporated in the certificate.

Affirmed.

---

2. Lucas conceded the originals existed and Seiler conceded the items he sought to introduce were not the originals. Hence, as subsections (a) and (b) are not in issue, Seiler is arguing that 1008(c) requires that the case be submitted to the jury.

NOTE ON WHAT IS A WRITING

1. Under the Federal Rules of Evidence, writings, recordings and photographs are subject to the best evidence rule. See Fed.R.Evid. 1002. A "writing" for purposes of the best evidence rule consists of "letters, words, or numbers, or their equivalent" that have been set down in some form of writing. Fed.R.Evid. 1001. Some courts have emphasized this latter phrase to include within the scope of the best evidence rule non-traditional materials, as in the main case.

A witness testifies that she cannot identify the defendant, who is present in the courtroom, as the man who attacked her. Can she be permitted to identify pictures of the defendant that she picked out immediately after the alleged attack? Is this a hearsay or best evidence problem? Brown v. State, 210 S.W.2d 670 (Tenn.1948). Cf. People v. Stein, 122 P.2d 932 (Cal.App.1942). See generally, J. Weinstein & M. Berger, 5 Weinstein's Evidence ¶ 1001(2)[01].

2. Kennedy v. Bay City Taxi Cab Co., 39 N.W.2d 220 (Mich.1949), required production of an X-ray picture upon examination of which an expert medical witness based his testimony of P's injuries; but from the report it appears there was "no direct evidence as to what the X-rays consisted of." This lack of even verbal description left the expert's opinion devoid of supporting foundation. Why should there be a need for the X-ray in court? Is it to permit examination by the court, jury, opposing counsel, opposing experts, or the expert testifying? See Goetsch v. State, 172 N.W.2d 688 (Wis.1969) (where not requested by defendant, "best evidence rule" does not require prosecution to introduce original tests whose value lay wholly in expert witnesses' interpretation). See also Fed.R.Evid. 703.

3. Where the content of a photograph or motion picture is at issue, the best evidence rule applies. See Walker v. Time Life Films, Inc., 784 F.2d 44 (2d Cir.), cert. denied, 476 U.S. 1159 (1986) (in action for copyright infringement against producers and screenwriter of the motion picture Fort Apache: the Bronx, released version of the film was the best evidence of substantial similarity to plaintiff's book). Thus, when a witness testifies to the content of a picture, the court must have the picture before it.

Where a sound recording is not produced, can a witness who heard it testify? May a transcript previously prepared be used?

Meyers v. United States

United States Court of Appeals, District of Columbia Circuit, 1948.
171 F.2d 800, cert. denied 336 U.S. 912 (1949).

■ Before WILBUR K. MILLER, PRETTYMAN and PROCTOR, CIRCUIT JUDGES.

■ WILBUR K. MILLER, CIRCUIT JUDGE. Bleriot H. Lamarre and the appellant, Bennett E. Meyers, were jointly indicted for violating the District of Columbia statute which denounces perjury and subornation thereof. Three counts of the indictment charged Lamarre with as many separate perjuries in his testimony before a subcommittee of a committee of the United States Senate constituted to investigate the national defense program, and three more counts accused Meyers of suborning the perjuries of his codefendant....

William P. Rogers, chief counsel to the senatorial committee, who had examined Lamarre before the subcommittee and consequently had heard all the testimony given by him before that body, was permitted to testify as to what Lamarre had sworn to the subcommittee. Later in the trial the government introduced in evidence a stenographic transcript of Lamarre's testimony at the senatorial hearing.

In his brief here the appellant characterizes this as a "bizarre procedure" but does not assign as error the reception of Rogers' testimony. The dissenting opinion, however, asserts it was reversible error to allow Rogers to testify at all as to what Lamarre had said to the subcommittee, on the theory that the transcript itself was the best evidence of Lamarre's testimony before the subcommittee.

That theory is, in our view, based upon a misconception of the best evidence rule. As applied generally in federal courts, the rule is limited to cases where the contents of a writing are to be proved. Here there was no attempt to prove the contents of a writing; the issue was what Lamarre had said, not what the transcript contained. The transcript made from shorthand notes of his testimony was, to be sure, evidence of what he had said, but it was not the only admissible evidence concerning it. Rogers' testimony was equally competent, and was admissible whether given before or after the transcript was received in evidence. Statements alleged to be perjurious may be proved by any person who heard them, as well as by a reporter who recorded them in shorthand.

A somewhat similar situation was presented in Herzig v. Swift & Co., 146 F.2d 444, decided by the United States Court of Appeals for the Second Circuit in 1945. In that case the trial court had excluded oral testimony concerning the earnings of a partnership on the ground that the books of account were the best evidence. After pointing out the real nature and scope of the best evidence rule, the court said, 146 F.2d at page 446: "... Here there was no attempt to prove the contents of a writing; the issue was the earnings of a partnership, which for convenience were recorded in books of account after the relevant facts occurred. Generally, this differentiation has been adopted by the courts. On the precise question of admitting oral testimony to prove matters that are contained in books of account, the courts have divided, some holding the oral testimony admissible, others excluding it. The federal courts have generally adopted the rationale limiting the 'best evidence rule' to cases where the contents of the writing are to be proved. We hold, therefore, that the district judge erred in excluding the oral testimony as to the earnings of the partnership."....

With the best evidence rule shown to be inapplicable, it is clearly seen that it was neither "preposterously unfair", as the appellant asserts, nor unfair at all, to permit the transcript of Lamarre's evidence to be introduced after Rogers had testified. Since both methods of proving the perjury were permissible, the prosecution could present its proof in any order it chose.

There is no substance in the criticism, voiced by the appellant and in the dissent, of the fact that Rogers testified early in the unduly protracted trial and the transcript was introduced near its close. Appellant's counsel had a copy of the transcript from the second day of the trial, and had full opportunity to study it and to cross-examine Rogers in the light of that study. The mistaken notion that, had the transcript been first put in evidence, Rogers' testimony would have been incompetent is, of course, based on the erroneous idea that the best evidence rule had application.

It is quite clear that Meyers was in no way prejudiced by the order in which the evidence against him was introduced, nor does it appear that his position before the jury would have been more favorable had the transcript been offered on an earlier day of the trial.

The matters discussed in the second division of the dissenting opinion have been covered adequately, we think, in the earlier portion of this opinion.

Since we perceive no prejudicial error in appellant's trial, the judgment entered pursuant to the jury's verdict will not be disturbed.

Affirmed.

■ PRETTYMAN, CIRCUIT JUDGE (dissenting) [omitted].

NOTES

1. Judge Prettyman, dissenting, argued that when there is a verbatim transcript, a best evidence rule should be applied preferring such evidence to oral testimony: "From the theoretical point of view, the case poses this question: given both (1) an accurate stenographic transcript of a witness' testimony during a two-day hearing and (2) the recollection of one of the complainants as to the substance of the testimony, is the latter admissible as evidence in a trial of the witness for perjury? I think not. To say that it is, is to apply a meaningless formula and ignore crystal-clear actualities. The transcript is, as a matter of simple indisputable fact, the best evidence. The principle and not the rule of law ought to be applied." Id. at 817–18.

If analytically sound, was the result in the main case unfair? Was the problem essentially one of effective cross-examination? The government was forced to produce the transcript and the defense allowed to introduce it, but counsel for the defendant was then stopped by the trial judge in his attempt to show discrepancies between the testimony of the government's witness and the transcript on the ground that the latter "speaks for itself." Would more latitude in cross-examination rather than a reinterpretation of the best evidence rule have protected the defendant? Should counsel's attack have been hampered by his failure to obtain the transcript before trial? See Fed.R.Evid. 612. In a case such as Meyers, would a trial court be justified in requiring the proponent to produce the transcript and rely on it rather than allow oral testimony? Would such a procedure reduce the confusion and wasted time associated with oral testimony? See generally, J. Weinstein & M. Berger, 5 Weinstein's Evidence ¶ 1002[03]. The A.L.R. note appended to the reprint of this case, 11 A.L.R.2d 1 (1948), covers in detail the methods of proving prior testimony in civil and criminal cases.

2. In Gray v. State, 30 A.2d 744 (Md.1943), where prosecution witnesses had testified to various admissions of the defendant, the court held that a signed confession should have been produced as best evidence because it might have contained "qualifications or explanations" of his verbal statements. Similarly, in Conti v. State, 664 S.W.2d 502 (Ark.App.1984), the trial court properly admitted a transcribed copy of the appellant's oral confession which he subsequently signed, rather than the recording of the statement. The court explained: "We do not perceive the issue here to involve the best evidence rule. What we have is a new statement, signed by appellant after he was admittedly advised of his rights." 664 S.W.2d at 503.

3. A deputy sheriff accused of conspiring to protect criminals by filing a false report sought to introduce evidence of prior oral acts showing a pure state of mind. Does the best evidence rule apply if these oral reports purported to be summaries of contemporaneous written reports not produced at the trial? See Parmenter v. United States, 2 F.2d 945 (6th Cir.1924).

4. A wife left property to her husband. Opponents claimed that the will was coerced by the husband's undue influence. The husband then attempted to prove that his wife and he got along well and that he was thus the natural object of her bounty. Testimony was introduced that husband had made a will naming his wife as beneficiary. This testimony was held properly admitted, as offered not to establish the contents of husband's will, but to show his state of mind. In re Will of Duke, 85 S.E.2d 332, 335–336 (N.C.1955). If the name of the beneficiary is viewed as part of the contents of the will, is this case sound? Should someone else who had seen the will have been permitted to testify?

5. The witness looked at copies of some 400 corporate checks to refresh his recollection before testifying. Weir v. C.I.R., 283 F.2d 675, 678–679 (6th Cir.1960):

> It is not the memorandum which is the evidence, but the testimony as to the personal recollection of the witness; and a witness may refresh his recollection by looking at any document, whether made by himself or by others, and, in the same way, his memory may be refreshed by conversations with others. None of the foregoing instances would be subject to objection as being in violation of the best evidence rule, or the hearsay rule. If any objection could be envisaged, it would go to the weight, rather than to the competency of the testimony. . . .

What protection analogous to the best evidence rule is available where recollection is refreshed by a document?

6. To prove that he had been employed by appellant on a salary arrangement, respondent produced a "voucher portion of a check." Neither payee nor payer's name appeared on the voucher but there was a typewritten notation "Salary $1500." Respondent testified that the voucher had been attached to a check he had received from appellant. It was common ground between respondent (plaintiff) and appellant (defendant) that appellant had employed respondent in connection with a lumber mill that appellant was building. The terms of the employment contract were disputed, however, Respondent contended that appellant had agreed to pay him a salary regardless of whether the mill ever actually got into operation. Appellant contended that he had agreed to pay respondent only if the mill started up. In fact the mill never opened. Should the best evidence rule have been applied to exclude the voucher? See Fish v. Fleishman, 87 Idaho 126, 391 P.2d 344 (1964).

Are the following cases sound?

P sued D on a note; D produced a cancelled check which he testified he gave and P received in part payment on the note; P held properly allowed to testify that he had owned another note of D's, since paid in full and surrendered to D, and also without producing this other note, that D's check had been received in part payment on it, rather than on the first note. Coonrod v. Madden, 25 N.E. 1102 (Ind.1890).

Oral testimony was held properly admitted to prove that a decedent had contributed to a church fund, the church records of receipts not being deemed the best evidence. Hale v. Hale, 33 S.E.2d 441 (Ga.1945). See also Jones v. Liberty Mutual Fire Insurance Co., 83 S.E.2d 837, 840 (Ga.App.1954) (oral testimony that insured reported loss to insurer admissible).

P, to prove that he had paid taxes on Blackacre, produced tax receipts and cancelled drafts and checks, and offered to testify that the payments thus evidenced had to do with taxes on Blackacre; held by a divided court that exclusion of the testimony was improper; the original tax returns and assessment records need not be produced on this issue. Peterson v. Lott, 37 S.E.2d 358, 360 (Ga.1946).

Federal Union Surety Co. v. Indiana Lumber & Manufacturing Co.

Supreme Court of Indiana, 1911.
176 Ind. 328, 95 N.E. 1104.

Action by the Indiana Lumber and Manufacturing Company against the Federal Union Surety Company and [Peter Suzio]. From a judgment for plaintiff, defendants appeal. . . .

■ MORRIS, J. . . . In November, 1903, a contract was executed by Peter Suzio, contractor, and the board of public works of the city of South Bend, by the terms of which Suzio agreed to construct a certain sewer in that city, and to pay for all "material used in said work." It was also provided in the contract that the city might reserve out of any allowance made on any estimate in favor of the contractor so much as might be necessary to pay materialmen for material furnished by them. Accompanying the contract, and attached thereto, was a bond executed by Suzio, as principal, and appellant Federal Union Surety Company as surety, in the penalty of $17,500, for the faithful performance of the contract by the principal.

The complaint was for the value of lumber furnished by appellee to Suzio, and to be used by him in constructing the sewer.

Appellee was engaged in the lumber business in South Bend. After getting the contract, Suzio informed appellee that he would need lumber to use in constructing the sewer. Appellee quoted prices, and it was agreed that it should furnish the lumber as it was needed in the work. The orders for the lumber were given by Suzio at various times, usually over the telephone. The method used by appellee in transacting the business was as follows: When one of appellee's agents received an order from the contractor, he wrote on a small order-blank the substance of the order. This slip was given to the yard clerk, who, in turn, gave it to a loader. The loader put the material on the wagon, and returned the slip to the yard clerk. Before the load was delivered, the clerk made, on a machine called an autographic register, three "original slips." These slips were on printed blanks, with appropriate headings, and when filled out showed the name of the employee who received the order, the name of the person who ordered the lumber, the name of the employee who checked the load, the name of the driver who was to deliver it, and the particular point of delivery; under a heading "Quantity," the number of pieces of lumber was stated; under the heading "Description," the kind and dimensions of the pieces were written; under a heading of "Feet," the number of feet was stated; under the heading of "Price," the price per thousand feet of each kind of lumber ordered was written; under the heading "Amount," the charge for the lumber was stated, and where more than one kind was ordered these charges were added and the total amount stated. In filling out these blanks, the machine made three exact copies by one impression, and automatically numbered them. One of these "original slips" was given to the driver, who delivered it to the contractor when he delivered the lumber. The contractor examined the slip as the lumber was unloaded. In this case there were forty-three deliveries of lumber. Appellee retained two of the three "original slips," and also the original written memorandum made by the employee receiving the order, and placed it in its files.

Over appellants' objection, the court admitted in evidence one of each of the two "original slips" retained in its office by appellee. Appellants contend that this was error, because the original written memorandum, retained by appellee, was the best evidence, and that the register slip was but a copy of the original memorandum.

This position is not tenable. The original written memorandum stood on the same footing as a shop-book entry, and would not ordinarily have been admissible, over proper objection. The register slip was admissible, however, because it, or a triplicate original thereof, was delivered to the contractor with the lumber, as a part of the same transaction, and was admissible to prove the kind and quantity of lumber delivered to the contractor. It was not necessary, in this case, to account for the slip delivered to the contractor before offering the copy thereof retained by appellee. Each of the three slips was printed by a single mechanical impression. There is a distinction between letterpress copies of writing, and triplicate writings produced as was the slip in controversy. The law does not require the doing of unnecessary things. The slip delivered to the contractor was of necessity exactly like the slip admitted and may be regarded as a triplicate original, and no useful purpose would be subserved by requiring a notice for the production of the slip delivered to the contractor. . . .

The evidence supported the decision of the court. The judgment should be, and is, affirmed.

NOTES

1. In the main case the court points out that the original written memorandum (the order blank that was filled in by a Lumber Company employee when an order was taken over the telephone) stood on the same footing as a shop-book entry, and would not ordinarily have been admissible, over proper objection. What the court is referring to here is the fact that at the time of this decision, the business records exception to the hearsay rule did not exist, or at least did not exist in its present form, so that the Lumber Company was barred from introducing into evidence documents in its files whose probative value depended upon the credibility of Lumber Company employees. The question in the case therefore, is whether there is some way to use the documents the Lumber Company offered that does not involve reliance on the credibility of Lumber Company employees who made them and that, at the same time, does not run into difficulties with the Best Evidence Rule.

There is a time-honored assertion that the requirements of the best evidence rule are satisfied when the writing produced and offered as evidence, and the writing of which the content is sought to be proved, are "duplicate originals." See, e.g., Colling v. Treweek, 6 Barn. & Cr. 394, 398 (Eng.1827). If "duplicate originals" are synonymous with "exact facsimiles having identical legal significance" the assertion is no more than a truism, since the Best Evidence Rule is plainly intended to furnish the trier of fact, so far as may be practicable, with the most direct, unquestionable, and generally satisfactory evidence of the contents of writings. Where a single transaction results in two or more "originals" not identical in content, the problems are normally substantive as much as evidentiary.

There is a judicial and legislative realization, slowly and unevenly growing and manifested, that some writings which are by nature copies and not originals at all so reliably reproduce the content of the originals that they may safely be used interchangeably with the originals for the purpose of proving content. Unfortunately it has been common to try to justify the admission of these writings by calling them "duplicate originals" and this usage has made for muddy thinking.

Federal Rules of Evidence 1001(4) and 1003 have eliminated much of the theoretical basis for discussion, with the courts giving a rather short shrift to the argument that there is "1) a genuine question . . . raised as to authenticity of the original or 2) in the circumstances it would be unfair to admit the duplicate . . ." Fed.R.Evid. 1003. See, e.g., United States v. Hausmann, 711 F.2d 615 (5th Cir.1983); United States v. Miller, 19 F.3d 1431 (4th Cir.1994) (photocopy of twenty dollar bill showing policeman's identifying marks allowed after police department had apparently spent the money; reliance on Rules 901(b) and 1003. See also United States v. Georgalis, 631 F.2d 1199, 1205 (5th Cir.1980):

> A duplicate may be admitted into evidence unless opposing counsel meets the burden of showing that there is a genuine issue as to the authenticity of the unintroduced original, or as to the trustworthiness of the duplicate, or as to the fairness of substituting the duplicate for the original. Fed.R.Evid. 1003; 11 J. Moore Federal Practice ¶ 1003.02 (2nd ed. 1976). That the government had exclusive possession of certain copies for five years raises no issue.

2. Execution by both parties signing the form contract's carbon "copy" may, of course, make it the "original" for purposes of the best evidence rule. See Greater Kansas City Laborers Pension Fund v. Thummel, 738 F.2d 926 (8th Cir.1984) (carbon copy contract admissible as an original).

If A contracts to buy a chattel on time from B, and B transfers to C his claim against A, the carbon or other document purporting to state the agreement which B leaves with A may be the original in litigation between A on one side and B and C on the other as to A's obligations; while the document delivered by B to C may be the original if C sues B for misrepresenting A's obligations. See the suggestion of this situation in Killingsworth v. General Motors Acceptance Corp., 37 S.W.2d 823 and 54 id. 266 (Tex.Civ.App.1931, 1932). In case of telegraphic communication, the original may be determined according to responsibility for initiating the use of the telegraph. How if a telegraphic message is originated by a telephone call but delivered in typed form?

3. The question of what is an original is essentially one of relevancy. If we ask, "what is the document being offered to prove?" the identity of the original often becomes apparent. If it is the terms of a contract, then the signed agreement is the contract containing its terms. If we are trying to show delivery of goods, the original is the signed receipt. If we are trying to show shipment of goods, the original may be the shipping clerk's tally sheet. If we are trying to show an offer, the original may be the signed letter received. If we are trying to show authority to make the offer, the original may be a carbon copy of the agent's letter in the principal's file.

Depending upon the issue, a document may be both a copy and an original in the same case. To show an offer, the original signed copy of a letter is the original. To show that someone knew of the offer, a carbon copy in his file would be the original. The carbon would, however, be a copy when seeking to show what was received by the offeree, and the signed letter a copy to show what was in the file.

4. The spread of photographic and microphotographic systems of record making has caused much legislation tending to allow utilization of such evidence interchangeably with literal originals. See 48 Mich.L.Rev. 489 (1950). 142 A.L.R. 1262, 1270 (1943), shows the older unfavorable judicial attitude toward this evidence.

The Photographic Copies of Business and Public Records as Evidence Act has been adopted in most American jurisdictions. See 13 Uniform Laws Ann. 350–361 (1980); Annot. Photographic Representation or Photostat of Writing as Primary or Secondary Evidence within Best Evidence Rule, 76 A.L.R.2d 1356 (1961). It provides:

> If any business, institution, member of a profession or calling, or any department or agency of government, in the regular course of business or activity has kept or recorded any memorandum, writing, entry, print, representation or combination thereof, of any act, transaction, occurrence or event, and in the regular course of business has caused any or all of the same to be recorded, copied or reproduced by any photographic, photostatic, microfilm, microcard, miniature photographic, or other process which accurately reproduces or forms a durable medium for so reproducing the original, the original may be destroyed in the regular course of business unless held in a custodial or fiduciary capacity or unless its preservation is required by law. Such reproduction, when satisfactorily identified, is as admissible in evidence as the original itself in any judicial or administrative proceeding whether the original is in existence or not and an enlargement or facsimile of such reproduction is likewise admissible in evidence if the original reproduction is in existence and available for inspection under direction of court. The introduction of a reproduced record, enlargement or facsimile, does not preclude admission of the original.

Cf. Annot., Proof of Records Kept in Computing Equipment, 11 A.L.R.3d 1377 (1967).

Photostats prepared specially for the litigation do not come within the act. See Toho Bussan Kaisha Limited v. American President Lines, Limited, 265 F.2d 418, 76 A.L.R.2d 1344 (2d Cir.1959). Compare the rule on Business Entries as an exception to the hearsay rule. Normal practice in any litigation is, however, for counsel to stipulate to substitute photostated or photostatic copies for the originals which have been made available for inspection. What would the result in Toho be under the Federal Rules of Evidence?

There was a growing tendency in the courts to treat carbon copies as the equivalent of the original, although the practice is not without dangers in view of the possibility of "corrections" which may be made on a ribbon copy. See, e.g., Hi Hat Elkhorn Coal Co. v. Kelly, 205 F.Supp. 764 (E.D.Ky.1962) (carbon copy contained clause claimed not to be in original). In Campbell v. Pure Oil Co., 88 S.E.2d 630 (Ga.App.1955), plaintiff, in order to establish an employment relationship, sought to introduce a carbon copy of a statement given to him at the time of his discharge itemizing his contributions to a retirement fund to which only employees contributed. Exclusion of this document was ground for reversal: "duplicate or triplicate originals, made with the same stroke of the pen or typewriter as the original, are admissible as primary evidence." See also Liberty Plan Co. v. Francis T. Smith Lumber Co., 360 P.2d 500 (Okl.1961) (testimony that original had been mailed and a signed receipt returned by postal authorities although the receipt was not offered; was testimony as to the signed receipt proper?); Lumber Fabricators, Inc. v. Appalachian Oak Flooring, etc., 41 Ala.App. 570, 141 So.2d 210, 213 (1962) ("carbon copies of the invoices were admissible as primary evidence, and were properly admitted as memoranda of the transactions, made at the time and in the usual course of business."); Annot., carbon copies of letters or other written instruments as evidence, 65 A.L.R.2d 342 (1959). Cf. Walker v. Lorehn, 355 S.W.2d 71 (Tex.Civ.App.1962) (permitting introduction of handwritten "work copy" where carbon copy was missing from files).

Where a carbon copy of an incriminating letter is found in defendant's file, can it be used as an admission without regard to the best evidence rule, on the theory that if the defendant did not think it accurate, he would not have retained it in his file? For an affirmative answer, see Hall v. Pierce, 307 P.2d 292, 65 A.L.R.2d 316 (Or.1957). What of a photostatic copy?

5. Under modern codes and rules, computer printouts provide no great evidentiary problems if evidence with respect to the accuracy of information fed into the memory-banks, and information on the programs to retrieve the information and to prevent tampering is made available to the court and opponents. See, e.g., Sherman & Kinnard, The Development, Discovery and Use of Computer Support Systems in Achieving Efficiency in Litigation, 79 Colum.L.Rev. 267 (1979); Tapper, Evidence From Computers, 8 Ga.L.Rev. 562 (1974); 4 Rutgers J. Computers 324 (1975); Miller, Personal Privacy in the Computer Age: The Challenge of a New Technology in an Information-Oriented Society, 67 Mich.L.Rev. 1089 (1969); Freed, Roy N., Computer Print-outs as Evidence, 16 Am.Juris., Proof of Facts 273 (1965); Roberts, A Practitioner's Primer on Computer Generated Evidence, 41 U. of Chi.L.Rev. 254 (1974); M. Berger & J.B. Weinstein, Weinstein's Evidence, ¶¶ 1001(3)[04], 1001(4)[07]; 901(b)(9)[02]; Note, Appropriate Foundation Requirements for Admitting Computer Printouts Into Evidence, 1977 Wash.U.L.Q. 59 (1977); Note, Reconsideration of the Admissibility of Computer Generated Evidence, 126 U.Pa.L.Rev. 425 (1977); Note, Computer–Nourisher Experts: An Evidentiary and Procedural Perspective, 43 B'klyn L.Rev. 119 (1977).

Issues respecting computers seldom relate to authentication or even best evidence. They are usually discussed in connection with hearsay, often under the business entry exception, infra, or as a problem of expert testimony, since, if there is a challenge, an expert, or at least some one familiar with the system will be needed to describe it and testify that it was working properly. See, e.g., United States v. Miller, 771 F.2d 1219, 1237–38 (9th Cir.1985). Testimony sometimes will be needed on the method of programming the equipment; the court will normally take judicial notice of the fact that such equipment, properly operated, can absorb, store, retrieve, reorganize and print data in a variety of forms. See, e.g., Transport Indemnity Co. v. Seib, 132 N.W.2d 871 (Neb.1965) (approving use under business entry exception to hearsay rule); King v. State ex rel. Murdock Acceptance Corp., 222 So.2d 393 (Miss.1969); Merrick v. United States Rubber Co., 440 P.2d 314 (Ariz.App.1968); United States v. Foley, 598 F.2d 1323, 1338 (4th Cir.1979) (computer print-outs of information contained on machine readable diskettes qualified as duplicates under Fed.R.Evid. 1001(4). The information contained on the diskettes was a summary of data contained on original). What of CD–ROM methods of storage?

Davenport v. Ourisman–Mandell Chevrolet, Inc.

District of Columbia Court of Appeals, 1963.
195 A.2d 743.

■ QUINN, ASSOCIATE JUDGE. This was a suit for compensatory and punitive damages resulting from fraud and misrepresentation in the sale of an automobile. The jury returned a verdict for Mrs. Davenport in the amount of $805 compensatory damages and $7,500 punitive damages. Ourisman's motion for a new trial was denied, but its motion for judgment *non obstante veredicto* was granted as to the punitive damages. Mrs. Davenport has appealed from the judgment *non obstante veredicto* and Ourisman has cross-appealed from the award of compensatory damages and the denial of its motion for a new trial.

Because we are convinced that a new trial must be granted we will limit our discussion to only one assignment of error. In brief, Mrs. Davenport claimed that she was charged the full retail price of a new car but in reality was sold a demonstrator used by Ourisman's salesmen for a period of ten months. Ourisman's defense was that Mrs. Davenport was fully aware of these facts. One of the crucial points was her claim that the car had been driven over 7,000 miles by Ourisman's salesmen. To prove this Mr. Davenport testified that shortly after delivery he discovered lubrication stickers on the inside of the car door. Counsel for Ourisman objected to this testimony in the following colloquy:

"MR. FEISSNER: We will object to the witness testifying what the mileage was on the service sticker. Counsel indicated in his opening statement he had the service stickers here.

"MR. HELLER: I have the figures down. We have the car outside. The service stickers are on the car. He has memorized them and he has them written down.

"The Court: Objection overruled."

Mr. Davenport then gave the dates of the stickers and stated they listed the mileage figures as 2,708 and 7,244, respectively. Ourisman contends that Mr. Davenport's testimony violated the best evidence rule. We agree.

In Anderson v. District of Columbia, D.C.Mun.App., 48 A.2d 710, 712 (1946), we said:

"It is an elementary principle of the law of evidence that the best evidence of which the case from its nature is susceptible must be produced, and that no evidence will be received from a party which is not the best evidence he can produce. Before he can be permitted to introduce proof which from its character presupposes greater or better evidence, he must adequately explain his inability to produce the better evidence.

"The best evidence rule is usually invoked only where the contents of a writing are to be proved. Where such writing is not produced, parol evidence is inadmissible to prove its contents unless its absence is satisfactorily explained." (Footnotes omitted.)

In the case at bar no explanation was given as to why the service stickers were not offered as evidence. No showing was made that they could not be detached from the door or otherwise reproduced. We hold that it was insufficient to say they were still on the car which was outside the courtroom, and therefore it was error to permit Mr. Davenport to testify.

Judgment . . . reversed with instructions to award a new trial.

NOTES

1. Impossibility or inconvenience of producing original writings can of course furnish satisfactory explanation of non-production and permit proof of contents by secondary evidence. One does not have to uproot a tombstone to prove in court the inscriptions which it bears, but the sound advocate, recognizing psychological factors, would produce a photograph. Distance may impede production in specie as much as ponderousness or fixity, particularly when a writing is in a foreign jurisdiction. See Fed.R.Evid. 1004(1), (2). For example, where the original has been lost or destroyed, a party is excused from producing the original. See, e.g., Neville Constr. Co. v. Cook Paint and Varnish Co.,

671 F.2d 1107 (8th Cir.1982) (in breach of warranty action, trial court did not err in permitting buyer to testify regarding contents of manufacturer's sales brochure where brochure had been destroyed by fire). Where the loss or destruction results from the bad faith of the proponent, secondary evidence of the contents of the writing is inadmissible. See, e.g., Seiler v. Lucasfilm, Ltd., 613 F.Supp. 1253 (N.D.Cal.1984), aff'd, 797 F.2d 1504 (9th Cir.1986), supra.

Similarly, production of the original is excused when it cannot be "obtained by an available judicial process or procedure." Fed.R.Evid. 1004(2). This may be the case when the writing is outside of the jurisdiction and no procedure exists to compel its production. See, e.g., United States v. Benedict, 647 F.2d 928 (9th Cir.), cert. denied, 454 U.S. 1087 (1981) (testimony by DEA agents as to business records in Thailand); United States v. Ratliff, 623 F.2d 1293 (8th Cir.), cert. denied, 449 U.S. 876 (1980) (not error for trial court to assume it had no subpoena power over documents in Germany). Note that 28 U.S.C. § 3505 permits certification of foreign document copies. See United States v. Chan, 680 F.Supp. 521 (E.D.N.Y.1988).

2. When a writing is "collateral" the courts will often not insist upon the original. See Fed.R.Evid. 1004(4). What the much abused term "collateral" means here is hard to pin down. It is often tossed into an opinion when other reasons are adequate. See Doman v. Baltimore & Ohio Railroad Co., 22 S.E.2d 703, 705 (W.Va.1942), seeming to accept a suggestion in C.J.S. Evidence, § 781, that the content of a writing "relating to a matter which does not form the foundation of the cause of action or defense" falls outside the Best Evidence Rule; but the opinion offers several other arguments for its result; the document proved by secondary evidence was a prior settlement agreement tending at most to limit plaintiff's recoverable damages; the jury gave its verdict for defendant.

In some cases "collateral" seems to connote that the party using or desiring to use secondary evidence need only prove the general purport and not the details of the writing—e.g., fact of occupancy as a tenant without respect to the terms of the lease, Minnesota Debenture Co. v. Johnson, 104 N.W. 1149 (Minn.1906); or fact of ownership of land without exact terms of deed as to area, boundaries, and the like, Farr v. Zoning Board, 95 A.2d 792, 794 (Conn.1953); or to show negotiations between the parties had taken place, Grunwaldt v. Wisconsin State Highway Commission, 124 N.W.2d 13 (Wis.1963) (failure to employ available state procedure for discovery and admissions was no reason to exclude).

Another explanation of the "collateral" label makes it usable when trouble, expense, or tediousness of adducing primary documentary evidence outbalances its significance in the case. Williams v. Selby, 24 P.2d 728 (N.M.1933), suggests this, as do some of the deed and lease cases. Finally, there is an occasional statement that when P sues D, P may orally prove the contents of a relevant written contract between P and X, because D is not a party to the contract. Carden v. McConnell, 21 S.E. 923 (N.C.1895).

3. Considerable authority supports the view that when a party desiring to prove the contents of a writing can give evidence of an adequately comprehensive admission by his opponent, he may use this evidence without troubling to produce the original writing. See, e.g., Gardner v. City of Columbia Police Department, 57 S.E.2d 308 (S.C.1950). See also Trossbach v. Trossbach, 42 A.2d 905, 907, 908 (Md.1945), where an admission obviated difficulty with the Statute of Frauds in connection with an oral agreement to convey real estate. The admissions cases import an ad hominem element not entirely harmonious with the primary explanation of the Best Evidence Rule as designed to provide the safest evidence. Cf. Fed.R.Evid. 1007.

4. When a litigant can prove that his opponent has control of a writing, he may clear the way for secondary evidence of contents by using the device of notifying the party to produce the original at trial. Should a notice to produce, rather than a subpoena duces tecum, be sufficient in this situation: X sues A and B; A has no real interest in the subject matter and fails to answer; A is called as a witness by X; A has the original of a document which B would like to introduce? See 4 Wigmore, Evidence § 1212 (Chadbourn rev. 1972); Fed. R.Evid. 1004(3).

Notices to produce must be sharply distinguished from subpoenas directed to opponents or third persons to compel production of such originals. The penalties for disobedience of a subpoena may include default of an offending defendant or dismissal of the suit of an offending plaintiff. See Bova v. Roanoke Oil Co., 23 S.E.2d 347, 144 A.L.R. 364 (Va.1942). The penalty for noncompliance with a notice to produce is normally nothing beyond permitting the notifying party to prove contents by secondary evidence—a consequence of the adversary system.

A litigant lacking satisfactory secondary evidence of contents may not rely upon a notice to produce; he must use a subpoena or other like coercive device. Then, too, the notice to produce does not meet the needs of the situation unless the desired writing is in control of the opponent with respect to whom proof of contents is to be made. If the control is in anybody else, a subpoena is appropriate.

In some jurisdictions a potential penalty attaches to the notice to produce from the notifying party's point of view. If, before or at trial, he calls upon an opponent to produce an original writing, the opponent complies, and the notifying party examines the contents of the writing, the opponent may put the writing in evidence irrespective of the hearsay rule and very likely of other exclusionary rules. The reasons for this doctrine are best stated in Leonard v. Taylor, 53 N.E.2d 705, 151 A.L.R. 1002 (Mass.1944). They grow in large part out of the old-time distaste for "fishing expeditions". This distaste has now greatly diminished, as witness Fed.Rules Civ.Proc. 26, 30, 31, 33, and 34; Fed.Rules Crim.Proc. 16 and 17(c).

Requirement of notice to produce as a condition precedent to utilization of secondary evidence is intended only to give the notified party reasonable opportunity to come forward with the original, not to allow him time to work up a counter-case to the point suggested by the giving of the notice. Hence such notices can often be very summary—e.g., oral notice during trial to produce an original present in the court room. It has been held that notice to produce is unnecessary when the opponent has possession of an original writing which is itself a notice or when from the nature of the writing in relation to the case he must know that he is charged with its possession and that its contents will be drawn into issue at the trial. Colling v. Treweek, 6 Barn. & Cr. 394 (Eng.1827); see United States v. E.I. duPont De Nemours & Co., 126 F.Supp. 27, 35–36 (N.D.Ill.1954) (semble). Peculiar problems arise when the litigant possessing the writing may claim privilege, particularly privilege against self-incrimination, with respect to production.

5. In order to save the defendant in a criminal case the embarrassment of refusing a demand in open court, the doctrine has grown up that secondary evidence of documents in his possession may be admitted. See, e.g., McKnight v. United States, 115 Fed. 972 (6th Cir.1902); People v. Gibson, 112 N.E. 730

(N.Y.1916); Lisansky v. United States, 31 F.2d 846 (4th Cir.1929); 67 A.L.R. 77 (1930).

This rule was applied to reverse a conviction in People v. Minkowitz, 115 N.E. 987 (N.Y.1917). See 67 A.L.R. 67, 77 (1930). It is perhaps not without significance that the McKnight case has been several times distinguished in later federal cases. But Powell v. Commonwealth, 189 S.E. 433, 110 A.L.R. 90 (Va.1937), reviews the authorities and adheres to the McKnight principle.

Whether or not the McKnight principle is accepted, it seems reasonable to prevent a criminal defendant from testifying orally to the contents of relevant written records which he declines to produce. Paschen v. United States, 70 F.2d 491, 501 (7th Cir.1934). Likewise when a criminal defendant denies before trial that he has or has ever had relevant documents, and the trial judge finds that these documents were sent to defendant, it seems proper to allow the prosecution to give secondary evidence of the contents of these writings without notice to produce. See, e.g., Heller v. United States, 104 F.2d 446, 448 (4th Cir.1939). If in such a case the defendant purports to produce at the trial the original documents, and the prosecution denies that the papers thus produced are in fact the originals, an exceedingly difficult procedural problem may arise. See discussion of Relationship of Judge and Jury, chapter 6, section 4, infra, and consider Welch v. New York, New Haven & Hartford Railroad Co., 64 N.E. 695 (Mass.1902), where, controversy having arisen as to true contents of an accident report by W, testimony by W as to contents was admitted after D had produced and put in evidence what was asserted to be the original.

Would a defendant be better protected if a demand had to be made, but it was required to be made outside the presence of the jury?

Amoco Production Co. v. United States

United States Court of Appeals, Tenth Circuit, 1980.
619 F.2d 1383.

■ McKAY, CIRCUIT JUDGE.

In 1942, the Federal Farm Mortgage Corporation (FFMC) conveyed by special warranty deed a fee simply [sic] interest in certain land in Summit County, Utah, to Hyrum and Florence Newton. The original deed and all copies other than a recorded version kept in the Summit County Recorder's Office are apparently no longer in existence. The parties dispute the exact contents of the original 1942 deed. Appellants claim that the deed reserved to the FFMC a one-half mineral interest in the property. As recorded, however, the deed contains no such reservation.

In 1957, the FFMC conveyed by quitclaim deed to the United States all of its mineral interest in various tracts of property, including the Newtons' property. The United States subsequently leased its claimed one-half mineral interest to the other appellants in this case.

In 1960, the Newtons conveyed their entire interest in the property to a family corporation, the Hyrum J. Newton & Sons Sheep Company (Newton Company). Beginning in 1971, this family corporation leased the entire mineral interest in the property to the appellees.

Appellees brought suit on January 21, 1976, under 28 U.S.C. § 2409a to quiet title to the disputed mineral rights....

The appellees ... moved for summary judgment. After excluding all of appellants' proffered evidence bearing on the contents of the 1942 deed, the court granted appellees' motion, quieting title in the appellees and requiring the appellants to account to the appellees for all profits realized under the claimed one-half mineral interest. . . .

II.   Exclusion of Evidence

. . . . The court selected . . . to decide first whether FFMC conveyed the disputed mineral interest to the Newtons in the 1942 deed, or whether it reserved the interest to itself.[1] If the original 1942 deed contained no mineral reservation clause, the appellants obviously have no mineral interest in the property.

Because appellees brought this quiet title action, they have the burden of establishing their title to the disputed interest. . . . By introducing the recorded version of the deed, which showed that they received the entire interest in the property, appellees established a prima facie right to relief. See Utah Code Ann. § 78-25-3 (1953). The burden then shifted to the appellants to introduce evidence of the invalidity or inaccuracy of the recorded version of the deed. In granting summary judgment, the court excluded all of the evidence proffered by appellants.

Routine Practice

The appellants offered evidence in an attempt to show that the routine practice of the FFMC was to reserve a one-half mineral interest in all property transferred during the relevant period. The court excluded this evidence on the ground that under Rule 1005 of the Federal Rules of Evidence, the availability of a properly recorded version of the 1942 deed precluded admission of any other evidence of the contents of the deed. We believe the court misinterpreted the purpose and effect of Rule 1005. . . .

Rule 1005 authorizes the admission of certified copies of records and documents filed and stored in public offices. The purpose of the rule is to eliminate the necessity of the custodian of public records producing the originals in court. This purpose is not furthered by extending the rule to encompass documents not filed and stored in public offices.

Rule 1005, by its terms, extends to "a document authorized to be recorded or filed and actually recorded or filed." This language encompasses deeds, mortgages and other documents filed in a county recorder's office. However, it is the actual record maintained by the public office which is the object of Rule 1005, not the original deed from which the record is made. If the original deed is returned to the parties after it is recorded, it is not a public record as contemplated by Rule 1005.

Applying Rule 1005 to exclude all other evidence of the contents of a deed is especially troublesome in a case such as this one. We cannot embrace an interpretation of the Rule which would exclude all evidence of the original deed other than the recorded version when the very question in controversy is whether the original deed was correctly transcribed onto the recorded version. Rule 1004(1), which authorizes the admission of other evidence of the contents of a writing if all originals are lost or destroyed, rather than Rule 1005, is applicable to the 1942 deed.[2] Accordingly, assuming it is otherwise admissible,

---

1.   The actual contents of the 1942 deed control as between the original parties and successors who are not bona fide purchasers. The recorded instrument is only prima facie evidence of the contents of the original.

[Footnote renumbered; others omitted; footnotes by the Court.]

2.   The court properly applied Rule 1005 in admitting a certified copy of the deed as recorded by the county recorder. Furthermore, because such a certified copy was avail-

evidence of a routine practice of the FFMC is relevant to prove conduct under Rule 406, and is admissible in lieu of the original under Rule 1004(1). Even if the evidence is not extremely probative, as indicated by the court, Record, vol. 2, at 431 n. 2, it is sufficient to create a question of fact and render summary judgment improper. Accordingly, the case must be remanded for the district court to consider admissibility of the evidence under a proper interpretation of Rules 1004 and 1005.

BLM File Copy

The appellants offered into evidence a photocopy of what is purportedly a conformed copy of the 1942 deed. The copy was found in a case file of the Bureau of Land Management (BLM). In excluding the file copy, the court indicated that it was "apparently incapable of being properly authenticated," and, in any event, admission would be "unfair" under Rule 1003 of the Federal Rules of Evidence. Record, vol. 2, at 428–30.

Documentary evidence introduced in federal courts must be authenticated under the provisions of Rules 901 or 902 of the Federal Rules of Evidence. Specifically, the proponent of such evidence must produce evidence "sufficient to support a finding that the matter in question is what its proponent claims." Fed.R.Evid. 901(a). The district court did not decide that the file copy could not be properly authenticated, but rather that it was "apparently incapable" of proper authentication. On remand, the appellants should be given the opportunity to properly authenticate the file copy under the provisions of Rule 901.[3]

The court also excluded the file copy on the ground that it would be "unfair to admit the duplicate in lieu of the original" under Rule 1003.[4] The trial court felt that admission of the file copy would be unfair because the most critical part of the original conformed copy (the reservation clause) is not completely reproduced in the "duplicate." We find no abuse of discretion in this holding.

In determining that admission of the file copy would be "unfair," the court was apparently considering admission for purposes of proving the contents of the original conformed copy (and ultimately, the original 1942 deed). However, the appellants also urge admissibility of the file copy for other purposes. They argue that the file copy supports their claim that the original 1942 deed was prepared on standard form 657, that it bears the same identification number as the county recorder's copy and the Federal Land Bank ledger, and that it demonstrates the physical length of the land description, supporting the theory that a flapped attachment was used on the 1942 deed. Even if admission of the file copy is unfair for the purpose of proving the contents of the original conformed copy, it may not be unfair for other purposes. Assuming the appellants can satisfactorily authenticate the file copy, on remand the district court should consider admissibility for these purposes.

able, the court should properly exclude any other proffered evidence of the contents of the recorded version of the deed. However, Rule 1005 does not preclude the admission of other evidence of the contents of the original 1942 deed. That deed is not a public record and Rule 1005 does not apply to it.

3. Appellants urge that the file copy can be authenticated as a public record under Rules 901(b)(7) or 902(4). However, the mere fact that a document is kept in a working file of a governmental agency does not automatically qualify it as a public record for purposes of authentication or hearsay. Although the recorded version of a deed is a public record, a copy of a deed deposited in a working file of the BLM is not, by that fact alone, a public record.

4. Although the BLM file copy is not a "duplicate" of the original 1942 deed, see Rule 1001(4), it is apparently a duplicate of the original conformed copy of the deed. As such, it is admissible to the same extent as the original conformed copy unless the trial court exercises its discretion under Rule 1003 to exclude it as "unfair."

BLM Plat and Index

The appellants urge that the district court improperly failed to consider an official BLM land office plat and a historical index which reflects the government's retained mineral interest. The court did not rule on this evidence, but said in a footnote:

> [D]efendants allege that certain official land office plats or indexes reflect a mineral reservation in the federal government. The court, however, has seen no evidence supporting this allegation or the inference defendants wish to be drawn therefrom.

Record, vol. 2, at 431 n. 1.

In fact, the evidence was before the court. The index and plat were submitted by some of the appellants as exhibits to a July 6, 1976, motion for summary judgment. Record, vol. 1, at 34–36. Furthermore, they were specifically mentioned in the appellants' memorandum in opposition to the appellees' motion for summary judgment. Record, vol. 2, at 317–18. Accordingly, on remand the district court should consider this evidence.[5]

Other Evidence

The appellants also offered other evidence including a blank standard deed form 657, a copy of the 1957 quitclaim deed and certain working files of the BLM. On remand, the court should consider the admissibility of such evidence. The blank standard deed form would be relevant upon sufficient showing that the 1942 deed was prepared on a similar form. The 1957 quitclaim deed is not a "nullity" as suggested by the court. Record, vol. 2, at 431 n. 1. Rather, it represents a valid transfer of all interest retained by the FFMC, if any, to the United States. However, the appellants must show that it is relevant to issues in this case and otherwise admissible. The working files of the BLM, although not necessarily admissible as public records, may be admissible to show the practice of the agency and the manner in which deeds with lengthy descriptions were constructed. . . .

Reversed and remanded.

NOTES

1.   Baroda State Bank v. Peck, 209 N.W. 827 (Mich.1926):

> The current authority in this country, as shown by the adjudications in a majority of the States, has adopted what is known as the American rule, which holds that a copy of a lost paper is the next best evidence, and if it is available, oral evidence is inadmissible.

> In this State we are committed to the English rule, which holds that there are no degrees in secondary evidence, and that a party may give oral testimony of the contents of a lost letter which is a private writing, even though he may have a copy in his possession or control.

See 38 Mich.L.Rev. 864 (1940) for a thorough study of this problem. As to the validity of assuming an "English" and an "American" rule in this connection, consult 4 Wigmore, Evidence §§ 1268–71 (Chadbourn rev. 1972). Adoption of

---

5.   Unlike the file copy which is not a public record simply by virtue of its presence in a BLM working file, the BLM land office plat and historical index appear to be official records of a governmental agency and may qualify as "public records" under the federal rules.

the Federal Rules in most states has resulted in the general absorption of the English rule.

2. A specialized problem as to preferred secondary evidence comes up in connection with the records of deeds and other conveyances in public registries. The solution reached may reasonably extend to all instances in which the government offers facilities for the recording of the contents of writings.

There is, to begin with, a question as to how far existence of an available public governmental record of a writing permits the party seeking to prove the contents of the writing to dispense with production of the original itself and rely upon the record. As to recorded conveyances, it has sometimes been reasoned that natural implications from the nature and purposes of the recording system permit unrestricted use of the record to prove contents; sometimes that the record may be freely used for this purpose except where, under local conveyancing practice, the original deed is, or is presumed to be, in the control of the party seeking to prove contents or of that party's opponent; and sometimes that the best evidence rule applies as in any normal case. See 4 Wigmore, Evidence §§ 1224–25 (Chadbourn rev.1972), for analysis and detailed presentation of common law and statutory authorities, legislation being widespread but not uniform.

Public record books cannot, except under most extraordinary circumstances, be removed from their repositories for courtroom purposes. When contents of public registry records are to be proved, there is a strong general evidentiary preference for copies, as contrasted with oral testimony, and a perceptible preference for officially certified copies, as contrasted with other copies. Fed.R.Evid. 1005.

3. Where an appellate court finds itself dissatisfied with proof that a preferred copy was not available, should the case be sent back for a new trial, or should there be an opportunity to supply the missing proof to the appellate court, or on remand? See Successions of Hilton, 165 So.2d 332 (La.App.1964), where the record showed the possibility that a copy of relevant adoption papers were still in the files of a deceased attorney and the court remanded so that "the record may be supplemented to supply the deficiency."

4. Testimony of lack of entry is receivable. But it is sometimes held that the source of testimony for this purpose should be the custodian of the record, when he is available, and not an outsider who has searched the record unavailingly. Pen–Ken Gas & Oil Corp. v. Warfield Natural Gas Co., 137 F.2d 871, 881, 887 (6th Cir.1943), cert. denied, 320 U.S. 800, and 321 U.S. 803 (1944), conceding a split of authority. Later cases rejecting this preference include International Life Insurance Co. v. Sorteberg, 216 P.2d 702, 706 (Ariz.1950), (corporation records); Irwin v. Peals, 33 So.2d 298 (Miss.1948), (marriage license records in several counties); and Clough v. North Central Gas Co., 34 N.W.2d 862, 866, 36 N.W.2d 573 (Neb. 1948, 1949) (municipal records). It is not necessary to adduce the whole original record. E.g., Peoples National Bank v. Manos Brothers, Inc., 84 S.E.2d 857, 871 (S.C.1954). But cf. In re 716 Third Avenue Holding Corp., 225 F.Supp. 268, 271–272 (S.D.N.Y.), rev'd on other grounds 340 F.2d 42 (2d Cir.1964) (court refused to receive a certificate for 25 shares of stock to prove that there was more than one shareholder in the corporation since there were no transfer stamps attached; proof of loss of the corporation's minute book, stock certificate book and stock record book were insufficient).

5. Sometimes it is sounder to view certain secondary evidence as inherently inadequate, not merely subordinated to another kind of secondary evidence. A borderline case will serve as an example. In an election contest, it was shown that the original ballots had been destroyed according to routine practice. The litigant having the risk of non-persuasion was, however, able to produce the record or tabulation resulting from a recount of votes for the contested office, which recount was not itself determinative of the issue because it had been made too late. The majority of the appellate court held that this evidence had been improperly excluded, likening it to photostatic copies of the ballots themselves. A dissenter reasoned that the analogy was unsound. The issue was what votes the ballots showed "and the tabulation did not qualify in any sense as secondary evidence of the ballots. It was at best but a computation of the number of marks appearing on the ballots opposite the respective names of the contending nominees for the office. . . . But, a ballot discloses far more essential to a recount than is shown by a tabulation of the vote for a particular office. A ballot contains the evidence of its own validity or invalidity in general." Only the ballots or facsimiles of them can show how the voters made their marks, etc. A defect not in respect of the vote for the particular office might invalidate a ballot as a whole. If photostatic copies could be had, the ballots having been lost or destroyed, "the copies would constitute secondary evidence of the ballots and, as such, be admissible in the circumstances supposed. But, figures cannot in my opinion be said to be secondary evidence of the ballots." Koch Election Contest Case, 46 A.2d 263, 268 (Pa.1946).

6.   In considering degrees of secondary evidence, the student should not lose sight of the continuing problem of authentication. See, e.g., R. v. Collins, 44 Cr.App.R. 170, 174 (1960) where the Lord Chief Justice remarked, "as presently advised, they can see no objection to a copy of a copy being produced, provided that somebody is called who can verify not only that the copy produced is a true copy of the original copy, but also that it is in the same terms as the original." Does this statement contain a redundancy?

7.   United States v. Foley, 598 F.2d 1323, 1337–38 (4th Cir.1979), cert. denied, 444 U.S. 1043 (1980):

> Defendants object to the admission of a series of charts, designated Government Exhibits Numbers 39 through 51. Numbers 39 through 50 summarized the number of listings filed by each realtor with the multiple listing service and portrayed the percentage of those listings which were at the higher, seven percent commission rate. These charts were compiled by a Justice Department economist from data obtained from the multiple listing service. Defendants were apprised that the government intended to use a compilation of such data well before trial and the documents were available for inspection at the Justice Department throughout May and June 1977. Defendants complain, however, that the charts themselves were not made available until the weekend before trial.

> Fed.R.Evid. 1006 provides: "The contents of voluminous writings . . . which cannot conveniently be examined in court may be presented in the form of a chart, summary or calculation. The originals, or duplicates, shall be made available for examination or copying, or both, by other parties at reasonable time and place." The data upon which these charts were based came from defendants' own listing service, the documents were made available to defendants at the Justice Department well before trial and the charts themselves were provided the weekend before trial. Defendants complain that the charts should have been made available longer in advance of trial, relying on the last sentence of Rule 1006. That sentence refers to making available the original documents, not the charts themselves. 5 J. Weinstein & M. Berger, Weinstein's Evidence ¶ 1006[04], at

1006–8 (1975). The charts themselves are not misleading and we cannot say Judge Blair abused his discretion in allowing their admission.

Government Exhibit No. 51 summarized the percentage of houses sold by each defendant that were purchased with loans guaranteed by the Veterans Administration or the Federal Housing Administration. Defendant Foley and his firm complain that the base data for this chart was never made available to them. The chart was compiled from data contained in machine-readable "diskettes" provided by the multiple listing service. The diskettes were not made available to defendants, but a computer print-out of the information they contained was and the diskettes themselves only contained data that was provided to defendants themselves by their multiple listing service in the normal course of business. The computer print-outs qualify as duplicates of the diskettes within the meaning of Rule 1006. Fed.R.Evid. 1001(4).

8. The originals of voluminous or multitudinous documents may often be held in reserve, available for checking by opposing litigants, with summaries of the originals introduced in the first instance on proper verification. As to the use of this technique, obviously forced upon the courts by sheer necessity in such intricate litigation as antitrust proceedings, and highly convenient in many less complicated cases, the trial judge has wide discretion. Unless the original documents are made available in the courtroom—or, preferably, during pre-trial discovery procedures—exclusion is called for. The better practice is to make both the summary and the underlying documents available prior to trial so that the court's time is not wasted while checking and preparation for cross-examination goes forward. Cf. McAllister, The Big Case: Procedural Problems in Antitrust Litigation, 64 Harv.L.Rev. 27, 32, 36, 48, 54 (1950). United States v. Stephens, 779 F.2d 232 (5th Cir.1985) (trial court properly admitted charts summarizing evidence already received since the evidence was complex and involved hundreds of exhibits); United States v. Schuster, 777 F.2d 264 (5th Cir.1985), vacated on other grounds, 778 F.2d 1132 (5th Cir.1985) (in prosecution for illegal distribution of controlled substances, district court did not err in admitting exhibits which summarized voluminous documentary evidence).

9. What should the rule be at administrative hearings? See Brown for Brown v. Bowen, 668 F.Supp. 146 (E.D.N.Y.1987), where an administrative law judge denied social security coverage to an illegitimate child on the ground that the father's written acknowledgement of paternity had not been produced. The records had been destroyed by the city as a part of its regular destruction program. Three eye witnesses testified that they saw the now deceased father sign after having the significance of the document explained to him. What should be the result on appeal to the district court?

10. What of the increasing tendency to place original material directly into computers with widespread access, continuous updating and power to amend? What are the problems for the client and the attorney? See, e.g., Fergus, Designing a Mass–Tort Case Management System, Nat.L.J. July 27, 1987, p. 24, col. 1:

Law firms are striving to integrate computers into the practice of law in order to provide better legal services to their clients. Until now, computers were used in law firms primarily for legal research and word processing, as well as document and deposition indexing in complex litigation. With the new computers that are available today, law firms can dramatically expand the use of technology to manage the legal services they provide. . . .

To date, more than 30,000 personal injury claims nationwide have been filed against former manufacturers and suppliers of asbestos-containing products.... In northern California alone, more than 6,000 cases have been filed. During the past year, more than 600 cases were set for trial in northern California in four state jurisdictions and two federal jurisdictions. Each month, hundreds of depositions are scheduled and rescheduled, thousands of documents are produced and cases are settled, tried or dismissed....

For each case, there is an electronic file that records pertinent facts, maintains the case calendar, monitors discovery in progress and serves as the working file for attorneys' notes and trial plans. The paper files are integrated with the electronic file maintained on a central computer system through the use of bar code readers similar to those used in grocery stores. The bar codes allow us to monitor the location and existence of files, pleadings, depositions and library materials for all 6,000 cases....

The first goal ... was to collect, store and retrieve case information....

The second goal was that the system had to make the firm's most expensive resources—the attorneys—more efficient and effective. This meant that the system had to be easy to use and available to all the attorneys and legal assistants interactively. In other words, when an attorney or paralegal wanted information about a particular case or wanted to record that case evaluation, the system had to have the information available immediately on the screen rather than later in the day on some written report.

CHAPTER 3

TESTIMONIAL PROOF

INTRODUCTION: NATURE OF TESTIMONIAL PROOF

Evidence almost invariably consists in part at least of the testimony of witnesses. To understand the problems involved in the use of testimonial evidence, it is necessary to be aware of the intellectual operations that the trier of fact must perform when presented with such evidence. This is important not only for an understanding of the matters discussed in the present chapter, but also in connection with the hearsay rule, which will be discussed later. In determining the effect to be given to the testimony of a witness, the trier must consider whether he, the trier, has heard correctly what the witness said and has observed accurately his actions and demeanor. Perhaps some condition in the courtroom or defect in the trier's perceptual equipment or mental processes has hindered accurate perception. In addition, the trier must consider whether he has apprehended correctly the witness's meaning. Did the witness mean to convey what would ordinarily be intended by the words used or did he intend some special meaning? If the trier has correctly heard what the witness said and correctly understood his meaning, did this meaning correspond with the witness's actual state of mind? In other words, was the witness sincere or was he misrepresenting his state of mind? Next, does the witness have a reliable memory? Whereas the witness may once have had a belief or mental image corresponding to an actual experience or perception, time or the influence of intervening events may have broken or altered the connection. Finally, if the witness's memory is reliable, was the original perception itself accurate? What the witness thought existed or happened may never have existed or happened, or at least not in the way the witness supposed. The effect the trier may properly give to the testimony of a witness should reflect a careful appraisal of all these aspects of credibility: use of language, sincerity, memory and perception. Doubt about any one of these may seriously undermine the probative value of the testimony.

Lawyers have long been aware of the difficulties inherent in our great reliance on the testimony of witnesses. See, e.g., J. Wigmore, The Science of Judicial Proof 386 et seq. (1937); F. Wellman, The Art of Cross–Examination 142 et seq. (1936). Much of the material in this chapter represents the law's attempt to devise rules of evidence that will reduce some of the dangers inherent in the use of testimonial proof without making a trial impossibly difficult and expensive. Since the end of the nineteenth century, the efforts of lawyers to understand and use properly this sort of evidence have been augmented by the research of psychologists. B. Clifford and R. Bull, The Psychology of Person Identification 3–4 (1978), contains a careful review of the history of this work. See also Wells and Loftus, Eyewitness Research: Then and Now, in Eyewitness Testimony 3–7 (G. Wells and E. Loftus eds., 1984). From the 1970's this research has developed from a trickle to a veritable flood. See E. Loftus and J. Doyle, Eyewitness Testimony, chaps. 1–4 (2d ed. 1992); Williams, Loftus and Deffenbacher, Eyewitness Evidence and Testimony, in Handbook of Psychology and Law (D. Kagehiro and W. Laufer eds. 1992); B. Cutler and S. Penrod, Mistaken Identification: The Eyewitness, Psychology, and the Law

(1995). We give here an example of the sort of study being done by psychologists that is of interest and potential value to lawyers. The passages are from J. Marshall, Law and Psychology in Conflict (1966), and Stewart, Perception, Memory and Hearsay: A Criticism of Present Law and the Proposed Federal Rules of Evidence, 1970 Utah L.Rev. 1, commenting upon Marshall's study.[1]

Stewart at p. 10:

A number of studies illustrate the point and demonstrate the substantial degree of perceptual and memory error in recounting the types of events that frequently are the subject of litigation. A recent study by Marshall illustrates the extent to which people inaccurately perceive and recall events of a nonroutine, episodic nature. Two hundred and ninety-one subjects, composed of 167 law students, 102 police trainees, and 22 people who attended a settlement house and lived in low income housing were shown a moving picture sound film of 45 seconds duration which represented a fact situation posing testimonial problems that are not atypical. The subjects were asked to assume that "they were walking around a corner and what they saw and heard was what they saw and heard in the picture."

Marshall at p. 43:

The picture which we showed had background music through most of the sequence. It opened with a boy lowering a mosquito net on a baby carriage. The boy was in his late teens or early twenties, of average build, wore a dark jacket, lighter baggy slacks, and a white shirt open at the neck. There were white buttons on the jacket and around his neck there were two strings or chains with a flute or whistle on one and a looking glass on the other. He had sideburns, curly hair. The baby was crying. At the beginning, the boy was smiling at the baby carriage. He appeared uncertain or nervous. He faced the baby carriage and touched the handle and started rocking it, then he removed his hands from the handle. The baby cried louder. The boy rocked the baby carriage back and forth, shifting his weight from foot to foot. The rocking became more violent and he pulled the carriage backward off the grass on which it had been to the driveway. A woman called out or shouted, "Mrs. Gerard, Mrs. Gerard, quick! Someone's running away with your baby." The boy turned toward the fence of the yard and then toward the house. A woman came running from the house toward the boy and the carriage. The woman was young. She wore a white smock and a darker skirt. She shouted, "You bad boy! You bad boy!", and waved her left arm as she ran. The boy hesitated, looked startled, ran through the gate and crouched in a corner by a white picket fence near a bush growing through the fence. A mailbox was above his head. At this point the picture stopped.

Stewart at pp. 11–13:

The author [Marshall] obtained two narrative reports of the film, one immediately after the showing and the second a week later. Following the second narrative report, all subjects were asked to answer a multiple choice questionnaire concerning the film. . . .

[A]ll groups reported accurately relatively few details of the incident (115 details might have been reported), thereby demonstrating that percep-

---

1. Footnotes have been omitted and there are omissions from the texts, including Marshall's supporting tables. The passages from Marshall are reprinted by permission of the Bobbs–Merrill Co., all rights reserved. A second edition of Marshall's book was published in 1980.

tion and recall are highly selective. Their mean scores ... range from fourteen to five correctly recalled items.... The ratio of inaccurate to accurate items varied from approximately 20% to 31.5%.

In addition, all subjects reported as facts a significant number of inferences which they had made about what they had seen. An inference usually reflects an attempt to give meaning or continuity to an event and is generally based on one's own past experiences, attitudes, and values. These are neither fact nor nonfact since a review of the film would not prove or disprove the inference. However, when included in a report as positive statements without factual basis, they must be classified as erroneous.... [T]he mean number of inferences and their ratio to accurately recalled items ... ranged from 51.4% to 90.5%.

Reports of things which the subjects thought they perceived and recalled but which were nonexistent (as contrasted with inaccurate statements about a fact that is clearly represented in the film) were given by all groups in approximately the same proportions.... [T]he ratio of nonfact items to correctly recalled items was approximately 4% for all groups. Of particular importance, however, is the ratio of total error (inaccurately recalled items, nonfact items, and inferences) to accurate recall. The total error to accurate fact expressed as a ratio ... shows that settlement house people made approximately five errors for every four accurate responses (126%) while the law students gave three inaccurate for every four accurate responses (76%) and the police trainees were slightly less efficient than the law students (85%). These ratios, however, should be viewed in light of the bias given the figures by the disproportionately large number of inferences compared with incorrect and nonfact items. But even excluding inferences, there is still substantial inaccuracy. [Excluding inferences] ... the ratio of the sum of incorrect plus nonfact items to correctly recalled items ranges between 24% for the law students and 34% for the settlement house people.

Compared with the conditions of perception and memory of events which witnesses are frequently called upon in court to describe, the conditions of perception and memory in the study were far more favorable. The subjects knew they were going to witness an event about which they would later be questioned; their free narrative responses were not subject to distortion produced by responding to particular questions; they were not subject to great emotional stress or excitement; there were few distracting stimuli; the memory period was short; and the subjects were not subject to the often highly suggestive influence of pretrial interviews. Nevertheless, the incidence of error, inference, and nonfact reporting was substantial.

The results of the multiple choice questionnaire administered one week following the film presentation and immediately after the second narrative report showed that the subjects accepted and reported as facts inferences and nonfacts implicitly suggested by some of the direct questions. Three questions concerned the identity of the young man in the film. His race was correctly identified by direct question and also, when mentioned, in the narrative report. A description of his jacket was not generally given in the narrative report and, when given, it was more often inaccurate than accurate. With attention directed to the issue by direct question, only one-half the subjects chose the correct answer. (Since there were three alternative answers, the probability of guessing correctly is 33%. The error, however, must be considered in light of the fact that the multiple choice questionnaire did not provide an alternative indicating uncertainty or lack of recall and hence forced a choice). In response to other questions directed to specific details, all subjects affirmed some incorrect statements. In addition, 8% of the law students, 19% of police trainees, and 5% of settlement house people agreed that they had seen the man place his hand in the carriage and take something out, a fact that did not occur. Those who gave a positive response to this question were also able to describe the item he took from the carriage and what he did with it.

Marshall at pp. 54–55, 52, 81:

An analysis of the sound items recalled is also instructive with reference to testimony. Two women's voices were heard during the picture; only one of the women could be seen. Both voices were frequently mentioned in the answers, although in a number of cases the substance of what they said was merged and they were heard as if there had been only one speaker. However, the *content* of what was said was almost uniformly *inaccurate*. This corroborates the finding discussed in Chapter I that blanks in perceptions are filled in by the witness in conformity to his expectations. As Thucydides said, in reporting speeches, it was necessary "to make the speaker say what was in my opinion demanded of them by the various occasions . . . . "

Many a case, of course, turns on the precise language used in the situation. It would seem that testimony of precise language is extremely unreliable.

An illustration of such unreliability is dramatized by replies to questions asked the subjects in a post-questionnaire after they had recorded their recall the week after they had seen the picture. In the course of the picture, a woman's voice called out, "Mrs. Gerard, Mrs. Gerard, someone's running away with your baby." A young woman then ran out of the house shouting, "You bad boy! You bad boy!" The subjects were asked whether they thought the woman was the boy's grandmother, mother, a sitter, a sister, or a neighbor and why they thought so. Seventy percent of all subjects thought she was the mother. About a quarter of this three-quarters said that they thought so because she had said, "My baby." No such words were used. Another 42% ascribed their conclusion to concern in voice, to her appearance or age. The other remaining 32% gave a variety of reasons such as "situation," and what "neighbor" said, etc.

. . .

[This study] . . . brings out in stark contrasts the high degree of erroneous "recall" by the three socio-educational groups. This would indicate that a witness may testify to a substantial proportion of "facts" which are not facts at all, and that the lower the socio-educational status of the witness the greater will be the inaccuracy of his testimony, assuming that his testimony is truthful as he perceives truth . . . .

In summary, where there is a greater verbal capacity, there is greater correct recall and there are a greater number of inferences but a lower ratio of inferences to correct recall. Within each socio-educational group, where there is high punitiveness [readiness to punish severely particular conduct, as determined by tests that Marshall administered to his subjects], there is greater recall and less where there is low punitiveness. When a status figure urges subjects to do well there is a greater number of inferences by law students and less by the police trainees than by their control groups. Among the law students, those who were told that they would be witnesses for the prosecution had greater recall than those who were told that they would be witnesses for the defendants.

Perception, Memory and Retrieval

It will be helpful to explore further the various aspects of human testimony that Marshall's study touches upon, with special attention to the work of the psychologists.

Perception: The witness's senses may be impaired in some way so that he imperfectly records what is going on. For example, he may be color blind or poor at adapting to changes in light or hard of hearing. See Bull and Clifford, Earwitness Voice Recognition Accuracy, in Eyewitness Testimony 92, 94–97 (G. Wells and E. Loftus eds., 1984). He may suffer from some mental deficiency, so that he imagines things to have occurred when they have not. Even if the witness has normal physical and mental equipment, he can, and witnesses frequently do, make mistakes in perception. The opportunity the witness had for observation may have been too brief to leave any reliable impression. See E. Loftus, Eyewitness Testimony 23 (1979); Manson v. Brathwaite, 432 U.S. 98, 129–30 (1977) (dissenting opinion). "Time to observe a critical item such as the perpetrator's face clearly is reduced by increased complexity of the scene being viewed and by the presence of a focus of attention away from the critical item, a weapon focus, for instance." Williams, Loftus and Deffenbacher, supra, at 143. The number of opportunities for observation that the witness had may be significant. E. Loftus, supra, at 24–25. So far as the identification of persons is concerned, many people think they are good at recognizing faces, but their belief is probably based upon situations in which they had an opportunity for relatively long observation or repeated observation and were not dependent upon a single fleeting look, as is often the case in criminal situations. Goldstein, The Fallibility of the Eyewitness: Psychological Evidence, in Psychology in the Legal Process 223, 227 (Sales ed., 1977). See also Manson v. Brathwaite, 432 U.S. 98, 129–30 (1977) (dissenting opinion).

Considerable research supports the view that cross-race eyewitness identifications are less accurate than same-race identifications, see Johnson, Cross–Racial Identification Errors in Criminal Cases, 69 Cornell L.Rev. 934 (1984), but a review of the literature takes the position that this conclusion is premature and oversimplified. Lindsay and Wells, What Do We Really Know About Cross–Race Eyewitness Identification?, in Evaluating Witness Evidence 219 (S. Lloyd–Bostock and B. Clifford eds., 1983).

Stress created by the phenomenon being observed, for example an automobile accident or a violent crime, may interfere with or distort seriously a witness's perception. A. Yarmey, The Psychology of Eyewitness Testimony 79 (1979); E. Loftus and J. Doyle, supra, at 24–25, 28. On the other hand, moderate stress may assist it. Levine and Tapp, The Psychology of Criminal Identification: The Gap From Wade to Kirby, 121 U. Pa. L. Rev. 1079, 1098 (1973); Goldstein, supra, at 233. "[T]he more complex the task the lower the level of stress at which the best performance is obtained. [However] because there is no way to compare the complexity of an eyewitness's 'task' to tasks for which arousal-performance functions have been obtained, and because (for obvious ethical reasons) there are no data concerning eyewitness performance under levels of stress comparable to those experienced by actual witnesses, there is no way to determine from the available data what levels of stress will lead to good eyewitness performance, and what levels will impair performance." McCloskey, Egeth and McKenna, The Experimental Psychologist in Court, 10 Law and Hum. Behav. 1, 8 (1986). See also Deffenbacher, The Influence of

Arousal on Reliability of Testimony, in Evaluating Witness Evidence 235 (S. Lloyd–Bostock and B. Clifford eds., 1983).

Selectivity by witnesses is encountered as part of the human effort to make experience manageable and useful. A witness is likely to focus on those features of a situation that are important to him and so later not be able to give a report or be able to give only an inaccurate report of other features. Levine and Tapp, supra, at 1096; E. Loftus, supra, at 35. The emotional significance of an object to the particular witness will deeply affect the manner in which he perceives it. Levine and Tapp, supra, at 1104. Expectations also can shape what a witness sees. M. Guttmacher and H. Weihofen, Psychiatry and the Law 371 (1952); H. Burtt, Legal Psychology 54–55 (1931). Recent studies emphasize that human perception is by no means analogous to the operation of a movie camera or a tape recorder, infallibly recording images or sounds, which then can be exactly reproduced. Rather, human perception is a complex process in which the witness brings to bear the thoughts and feelings that he has at the time of the particular experience. As Clifford and Bull put it, "[M]an perceives and conceives the new through the old." Supra, at 32. What the witness sees or hears is fitted into and made sense of by means of pre-existing ideas. Gaps in observation are filled from this existing stock, although to the witness what is subjective often seems to exist in actuality. As Marshall's experiment indicates, witnesses often draw inferences from what they observe, but report them as facts. Thus the process of perception is in significant measure a process of active interpretation rather than one of passive recording. Although such active interpretation may be essential for ordinary living, it is often highly unreliable as a source of evidence for use in trials.

Memory: It is artificial to separate memory from perception, for they in fact constitute different aspects of a single, integrated process, which also includes the recounting or recognition of what has been perceived. That which was perceived may be quickly forgotten or it may be "encoded" in such a way as to ensure its long endurance. Encoding essentially involves finding a meaning in what has been perceived that enables one to make sense of it in accordance with pre-existing ideas, a process that has already been referred to. The nature of what a person observes will influence how well he remembers it. Generally speaking, remembering voices is more difficult than remembering faces. Clifford, Memory for Voices: The Feasibility and Quality of Earwitness Evidence, in Evaluating Witness Evidence 189, 213 (S. Lloyd–Bostock and B. Clifford eds., 1983). See also Yarmey, Earwitness Evidence, in Adult Eyewitness Testimony 101 (D. Ross, J. Read and M. Toglia eds., 1994); Shepherd, Identification After Long Delays, in Evaluating Witness Evidence 173, 175 (S. Lloyd–Bostock and B. Clifford eds., 1983). A particular individual may have an especially good memory for faces, but a poor memory for sounds. H. Munsterberg, The Witness in Court 61–62 (1908). See also MacLeod, Frowley and Shepherd, Whole Body Information: Its Relevance to Eyewitnesses, in Adult Eyewitness Testimony 125 (D. Ross, J. Read and M. Toglia eds., 1994). A motive to remember will play a part in the way in which a perception is encoded. The duration of perception and the number of perceptions will affect the strength of a memory.

As time passes, memory falls off, sharply at first, then more slowly. Brown, Legal Psychology 88–89 (1926); E. Loftus, supra, at 53; Egan, Pittner and Goldstein, Eyewitness Identification: Photographs vs. Live Models, 1 Law and Hum. Behav. 199, 204 (1977). But there is a curious finding in regard to "photo-fit" identification (in which the witness uses alternative photographs of five facial features to reconstruct a remembered face) that the passage of time does not affect accuracy. B. Clifford and R. Bull, supra, at 103. Perhaps it is more accurate to say that memories are lost or altered not simply by the passage of time, but on account of subsequent experiences and the continuing mental process of filling gaps and reducing inconsistencies in order to make sense out of life. Woocher, Did Your Eyes Deceive You? Expert Psychological Testimony on the Unreliability of Eyewitness Identification, 29 Stan. L. Rev. 969, 983–84 (1977). Subsequent experiences, whether they be the internal intellectual or emotional experiences of the witness himself, E. Loftus, supra, at 78–80, the giving of accounts to others, id. at 84; Loftus and Ketcham, The Malleability of Eyewitness Accounts, in Evaluating Witness Evidence 159, 161 (S. Lloyd–Bostock and B. Clifford eds., 1983); Shepherd, Identification After Long Delays, in id. at 173, 181, questioning by police or lawyers, E. Loftus, supra, at 75–77 (1979); Loftus and Ketcham, supra, at 159, reading about the event in the newspapers or listening to others talk about it, Ellis, Practical Aspects of Face Memory, in Eyewitness Testimony 12, 26, 28 (G. Wells and E. Loftus eds., 1984), all can have a shaping effect on a witness's memory. See generally Hall, Loftus and Tousignant, Postevent Information and Changes in Recollection for a Natural Event, in Eyewitness Testimony 124 (G. Wells and E. Loftus eds., 1984). The witness believes himself to remember the event, but what he in fact remembers, to some extent at least, is the subsequent experience, which has overlaid and transformed the original perception. An example of how ideas that had different perceptual origins combined to produce a single memory is found in the case of the hold-up victim who identified as the robber a man he had indeed seen at the place where the hold-up occurred, but not at the time of the hold-up. E. Loftus, supra, at 142–44 (1979). The psychologists refer to this as "transference." Ellis, supra, at 31–32.

Controversy presently surrounds the question of "repressed memories," particularly of childhood sexual abuse. The suggestion has been made that certain sorts of experiences are so traumatic that their memory is barred from consciousness, sometimes for long periods of time, but that in the right circumstances the memory will emerge into consciousness and in an accurate and undistorted form. Apparently there is no substantial empirical evidence to support this idea. See Loftus, The Reality of Repressed Memories, 48 Am. Psychologist 518 (1993); Lindsay and Read, "Memory Work" and Recovered Memories of Childhood Sexual Abuse, 1 Psychology, Pub. Policy and L. 846, 886 (1995); S. Ceci and M. Bruck, Jeopardy in the Courtroom: A Scientific Analysis of Children's Testimony 187–96, 210, 232 (1995).

Retrieval: The conditions of retrieval influence the content of memory in much the same way as do other experiences subsequent to perception. For example, if the police show the witness a photo display containing a picture of the defendant that sets him off in some way from the other persons pictured, the witness may well pick out the defendant as the criminal in response to the suggestiveness of the photo display. Lineups as well as photo displays involve suggestiveness and there has been considerable study of what must be done to make them fair. See, e.g., Doob and Kirschenbaum, Bias in Police Lineups— Partial Remembering, 1 J. Pol. Sci. and Admin. 287 (1973); Wells, Leippe and Ostrom, Guidelines for Empirically Assessing the Fairness of a Lineup, 3 Law and Hum. Behav. 285 (1979); B. Cutler and S. Penrod, supra, at 115–36; Williams, Loftus and Deffenbacher, supra, at 151. The police, because they have an interest in finding the criminal, may indirectly and often unconsciously convey to the witness their idea as to who is the guilty person. The witness may see the lineup as a sort of multiple choice question, with no opportunity to pick "none of the above." After all, the witness may think, why would the authorities go to all the trouble of organizing a lineup unless they have a suspect?

The method of inquiry plays a crucial role in the accuracy of testimony. Studies show that free narrative, although it may leave many subjects uncovered, yields the most accurate results. A. Yarmey, supra, at 194; E. Loftus, supra, at 19–94. Nonsuggestive interrogation can increase coverage by focusing the witness's attention on matters in regard to which information is desired, but it does so at the cost of accuracy. Lipton, On the Psychology of Eyewitness Testimony, 62 J. Appl'd Psychology 90, 93 (1977). Leading questions or suggestive identification procedures—lineups, showups, or photo displays—run the greatest risk of inaccuracy. The suggestiveness in a question can be very subtle. Compare "How tall was the basketball player?" with "How short was the basketball player?" E. Loftus, supra, at 94. Moreover, a leading question asked at one time may influence the answer given to a nonleading question asked at a later time. Loftus, Leading Questions and the Eyewitness Report, 7 Cognitive Psychology 560 (1975). The rule against the use of leading questions on direct examination, which will be discussed infra pp. 333–39, is designed to eliminate this source of inaccuracy.

Recently there have been studies of what is called the "Cognitive Interview." "This procedure involves getting the witness to reinstate mentally the environmental and personal context prevailing at the time of the incident and to recall the event, as completely as possible from various perceptual perspectives and in a variety of orders." Williams, Loftus and Deffenbacher, supra, at 150. A revised version of this procedure produced 45% more correct facts recalled than the traditional police interview and a lesser rate of incorrect information. See also E. Loftus and J. Doyle, supra, at 81.

There has been considerable research into the question of whether there is any correlation between the confidence with which witnesses give their testimony or make their identifications and accuracy. Although some studies show a correlation, others show none at all. E. Loftus, supra, at 100–01; Buckhout et als., Determinants of Eyewitness Performance on a Lineup, 4 Bul. Psychonomic Soc. 191, 192 (1974); Woocher, supra, at 985; Wells and Murray, Eyewitness Confidence, in Eyewitness Testimony 155, 168 (G. Wells and E. Loftus eds., 1984). Finally, in considering the accuracy of human recall or recognition, it is necessary to keep in mind the presence among human beings of different "cognitive styles." For example, some people are more willing to take risks than others, and so are ready to guess when others will say that they do not know. B. Clifford and R. Bull, supra, at 180.

The possibility of a lying witness must be faced. A witness may make things up or exaggerate in order to be important to the authorities or to be part of history. A. Yarmey, supra, at 167. In a dramatic trial situation, witnesses are likely to "improve" their testimony for the stage. Recent research suggests that there is some relation between rigid posture, few gesticulations, agitated shifts of feet and legs, pitch of voice and length of eye contact and deceit. A liar, apparently, at least on the basis of this research, makes more errors in speech, talks less and at a slower rate than a truth teller. A. Yarmey, supra, at 168–71. Obviously these are generalizations and a particular witness who has all these characteristics may well be telling the truth. Jurors proceeding upon intuitions about the significance of nonverbal cues may well be mistaken.

Some research indicates that it is verbal content, not facial expressions or other nonverbal cues, that provides the most reliable guide to sincerity. A. Yarmey, supra, at 170–71. This research may call into question the appropriateness of an appellate court's deferring to the trier of fact on the matter of sincerity because it had no opportunity to observe the demeanor of a witness. Furthermore, it fits well with the suggestion of one psychologist that psychology can make an important contribution to the search for truth by "the development and description of methods which can be used for the analysis of the content and form of witness statements." A. Trankell, Reliability of Evidence 45 (1972). See also id. at 80–92, 140–46.

The pathological liar presents a particularly difficult case. His demeanor is perfect. He tells a coherent, internally consistent story. Self-interest in the conventional sense does not motivate his lies and, in fact, his story may even tend to be degrading to himself, thereby making it more believable. W. Healy & M. Healy, Pathological Lying, Accusation and Swindling 265–66 (1915); Credibility of Certain Lay Witnesses, The Psychopathic Liar on the Witness Stand, 1 Current Med. for Attorneys (No. 5) 21 (1954). Furthermore, this type of witness bears up extremely well under cross-examination, since his fertile imagination and convincing demeanor permit him to repair any flaws in his testimony that have been brought out. Credibility of Certain Lay Witnesses, The Psychopathic Liar, supra. Cf. Note, Psychiatric Challenge of Witnesses, 9 Vand. L. Rev. 860 (1956).

King and Ford in 144 Am. J. Psychiatry 920 (1987) speak of one kind of pathological lie: Pseudologia Fantastick. It is characterized by

> telling of stories without, or entirely disproportionate to, discernible motive and with such zeal that the liar may convince himself of their truth.... While a defective or incomplete distinction between fiction and reality must be present, pseudologia is distinct from delusions in that when pseudologues' attention is energetically brought to the subject, they can acknowledge, at least partly, the falseness of their utterings.

The foregoing survey has focussed on the work of psychologists, but account must also be taken of the work of neurobiologists and other scientists regarding the brain. In recent years, this work has made remarkable progress in finding out how the brain works in respect to perception and memory. See Goldman–Rakic, Working Memory and the Mind, 267 Sci. Am. 110 (1992). It has been learned, for instance, what parts of the brain are involved in long-term and in short-term memory, in "explicit memory" and in "implicit memory." See Kandel and Kandel, Flights of Memory, 15 Discover 32 (1994). Study is going forward to determine where in the brain the filling-in function is performed by virtue of which we see, at the blind spot in the eye, something that may not be there but that is consistent with the surroundings. Grady et al., The Vision Thing: Mainly in the Brain, 14 Discover 56 (1993). An area of the brain has been discovered where in-put from the eye is processed and memories combined with present scenes. See Harvard Gazette, Jan. 15, 1993, at 1,8. Recently it has become possible to determine whether what a person believes to be a memory is coming from the part of the brain where memories of actual experiences are stored or from another part of the brain. New York Times, July 7, 1996, sect. 4, at 10, col. 1. It is being increasingly understood not only where in the brain different perceptual and cognitive functions are performed, but how these areas interact and work together in systems. These advances in knowledge and many others have become possible because scientists are no longer restricted to animal studies and studies of human brains in abnormal conditions caused by disease or accident, but have the use of noninvasive techniques—notably PET (positron emission tomography)—that permit observation of normal human brains as they perform a variety of tasks. Goldman–Rakic, supra. Will it be possible someday to determine whether there are anatomical changes in the brain, which are memories, from which can be inferred that the person had a certain experience?

Note also should be taken of new knowledge of the effect of drugs on memory. It has been found, for instance, that a certain drug given to rats before a learning task substantially improves memory: the drug makes sure that the pores of the cell that contains the memory stay open longer and so are more likely to fire. See New York Times, Jan. 15, 1994, at 10, col. 4. Dopamine has been found to have an effect on working memory in aged monkeys. Goldman-Rakic, supra.

Sooner or later, perhaps, the work of neurobiologists and other scientists studying the brain will lead to knowledge about perception, memory and retrieval that is useful to the law in its attempt to assess the probative value of human testimony. Ultimately this knowledge may prove more valuable than that developed by the psychologists. As work goes forward, psychologists and neurobiologists are combining their efforts. See account of a conference of psychologists, biologists and neurologists, New York Times, May 31, 1994, sect. C, at 1, 8.

The Problem of Eyewitness Identification

Both the psychological literature cited above and actual cases in which innocent persons have been convicted have repeatedly demonstrated the unreliability of eyewitness identification. See, e.g., E. Loftus, supra, at 8–9; Manson v. Brathwaite, 432 U.S. 98, 118–36 (1977) (dissenting opinion). Other useful references are P. Wall, Eye–Witness Identification in Criminal Cases (1965); Williams and Hammelmann, Identification Parades, I and II, [1963] Crim. L.Rev. 499, 545; O'Connor, 'That's the Man': A Sobering Study of Eyewitness Identification and the Polygraph, 49 St. John's L. Rev. 1 (1974). Notwithstanding the unreliability of eyewitness identifications, juries apparently often give them considerable weight. E. Loftus, supra, at 8–12; Cunningham and Tyrrell, Eyewitness Credibility: Adjusting the Sights of the Judiciary, 37 Ala. Law. 563, 564 n. 4 (1976).

Fear of the conviction of the innocent and consciousness of the unreliability of eyewitness identification produced the Supreme Court's first Lineup decisions. In United States v. Wade, 388 U.S. 218 (1967), and Gilbert v. California, 388 U.S. 263 (1967), the Court held that an identification made at a lineup held without defendant's counsel being present must be excluded at trial. Furthermore, an in-court identification following a lineup at which counsel was not present, the Court held, was also inadmissible unless the prosecution could establish by clear and convincing evidence that the in-court identification had a source independent of the lineup. These results were reached through an interpretation of the Right to Counsel and Confrontation Clauses of the Sixth Amendment. Since a lineup identification would in all likelihood exert a powerful influence on an in-court identification, the Court reasoned, an opportunity to confront and cross-examine the witness at trial was not an adequate substitute for the presence of counsel at the lineup, itself a "critical stage" in the prosecution. The Court did not indicate what counsel could do at the lineup if he were present, nor how to deal with the difficult situation that would arise at trial if counsel took the stand to testify concerning the conditions of the lineup. See infra p. 272.

In Kirby v. Illinois, 406 U.S. 682, 689 (1972), the Court held that the right to counsel announced in Wade and Gilbert attached only to identification procedures taking place "at or after the initiation of adversary judicial criminal proceedings—whether by way of formal charge, preliminary hearing, indictment, information, or arraignment," thus, as a practical matter, greatly restricting the availability of the Wade–Gilbert right. Many commentators have criticized the restriction contained in the Kirby decision. E.g., Levine and Tapp, supra, at 1080–81 (1973); N. Sobel, Eye–Witness Identification 12 (1972). One state has managed to interpret Kirby, in the light of the state's procedural laws, to make the Wade–Gilbert right available if the defendant was in custody at the time of the lineup. Commonwealth v. Richman, 320 A.2d 351 (Pa.1974). See also United States v. Larkin, 978 F.2d 964, 969 (7th Cir.1992), cert. denied, 507 U.S. 935 (1993) (even though formal adversary proceedings have not been initiated, right to counsel at lineup attaches if the government has "crossed the constitutionally significant divide from fact-finder to adversary").

In United States v. Ash, 413 U.S. 300 (1973), the Supreme Court held that the Wade–Gilbert right did not apply to identification through photographic displays even though conducted after the initiation of adversary judicial criminal proceedings. On the other hand, in Moore v. Illinois, 434 U.S. 220 (1977), the Court held that the Wade–Gilbert right does apply to an identification at a preliminary hearing.

The Court announced in Stovall v. Denno, 388 U.S. 293 (1967), a distinct due process right to have excluded from evidence the results of an identification procedure that was "unnecessarily suggestive and conducive to irreparable mistaken identification." Id. at 301–02. This right applies even in situations that do not bring into play the Wade–Gilbert Sixth Amendment right, for instance when the identification procedure is conducted before the initiation of adversary judicial criminal proceedings. In Simmons v. United States, 390 U.S. 377 (1968), the Court found that an in-court identification that had been preceded by an identification from snapshots, which took place before the defendant was apprehended, did not violate this due process right. The court cited as reasons for its decision the value of rapid, effective police work and circumstances tending to support the correctness of the identification. In Foster v. California, 394 U.S. 440 (1969), however, the right was held to have been violated by the allowance of an in-court identification and the admission of the results of two lineups found to have been highly suggestive, as was an intervening show-up. But in Neil v. Biggers, 409 U.S. 188 (1972), the Court found that the due process right was not violated in the circumstances presented by that case by the introduction of evidence of a show-up, since although the police could have arranged a less suggestive procedure, there was no substantial likelihood of a misidentification. This was held to be the correct result, in any event, when the show-up had taken place before the Court's decision in Stovall. Manson v. Brathwaite, 432 U.S. 98 (1977), a case involving the use of a photograph for purposes of identification, made clear that the Neil v. Biggers test also applies to post-Stovall cases. See also United States v. Crews, 445 U.S. 463, 472–73 (1980) (in-court identifications independent of and uninfluenced by pretrial identifications that were the products of an arrest which violated the Fourth Amendment). Reviews of lower court decisions applying the due process right show that the Supreme Court's formulation of the right has been vague enough to permit considerable conflict and confusion in these decisions and that in practice the right seldom functions as a significant barrier to the admission of relevant identification testimony. See Rosenberg, Rethinking the Right to Due Process in Connection with Pretrial Identification Procedures, 79 Ky. L. J. 259 (1990–91); Mayer, Due Process Challenges to Eyewitness Identification Based on Pretrial Photographic Arrays, 13 Pace L. Rev. 815 (1994); Ann. Rev. Crim. Proc., 82 Geo. L. J. 597, 721–30 (1993–94).

In–Court Identifications

Whereas the Supreme Court decisions just outlined focused on the admissibility of the results of lineups or other pretrial identification procedures and in-court identifications that those procedures may have influenced, other cases have been concerned with the reliability of in-court identifications themselves, without regard to the influence of pretrial identification. The courtroom is a patently suggestive setting. With the defendant sitting at the counsel table, a witness called upon to point out the person who committed the crime undoubtedly will understand that the defendant is the person suspected by the authorities and very likely make an identification influenced by this realization. Constitutional objection to in-court identification probably will elicit the response that although courtroom conditions may be suggestive, counsel has an opportunity to emphasize this suggestiveness in cross-examination of the witness and argument to the jury. Commentators have noted, however, that cross-examination is less effective in exposing the weakness of identification testimony than other sorts of testimony. The witness tells no story that can be probed. He simply says, "that's the man." Furthermore, the witness himself is often unconscious of the elements that make eyewitness identification unreliable. Woocher, supra, at 994–95. Some lawyers confronted by these difficulties in cross-examination have been known to resort to questionable tactics. E.g., People v. Gow, 382 N.E.2d 673 (Ill.App.1978) (model with appearance altered to look like defendant sitting at counsel table); United States v. Thoreen, 653 F.2d 1332 (9th Cir.1981), cert. denied, 455 U.S. 938 (1982), stated supra p. 125.

Code v. Montgomery, 725 F.2d 1316, 1319–21 (11th Cir.1984): Prosecution for armed robbery. In-court identification of defendant as one of the robbers did not violate due process even though defendant was seated at counsel table, the prosecutor asked the witnesses such questions as "And the Sonny that you are talking about is the defendant Joseph Sonny Code?" and there had been no pretrial lineup. Two of the three victims identified defendant as one of the robbers and a person already convicted of the robbery identified defendant as an accomplice. "In sum, given the witnesses' opportunity to view the robbers, their identification carried with it no 'very substantial likelihood of misidentification.'" Id. at 1320. United States v. Domina, 784 F.2d 1361, 1367–72 (9th Cir.1986), cert. denied, 479 U.S. 1038 (1987): Under the circumstances, not abuse of discretion to admit in-court identifications of defendant as bank robber even though he was required to wear mask worn by robber and speak words spoken by robber, nor to deny request for in-court lineup. Other decisions holding it not an abuse of discretion to refuse a lineup are United States v. Estremera, 531 F.2d 1103, 1110–12 (2d Cir.), cert. denied, 425 U.S. 979 (1976); United States v. Ravich, 421 F.2d 1196, 1202–03 (2d Cir.), cert. denied, 400 U.S. 834 (1970); State v. Walls, 351 A.2d 379 (N.J.Super.Ct.App.Div.1976). See also Commonwealth v. Jones, 287 N.E.2d 599 (Mass.1972) (not abuse of discretion to refuse defendant's request to sit among spectators).

Some courts have held that in an appropriate case an in-court identification should not be permitted unless there has been a pretrial lineup, at least if the defendant has requested one. Commonwealth v. Sexton, 400 A.2d 1289 (Pa.1979); United States v. Caldwell, 481 F.2d 487 (D.C.Cir.1973); Evans v. Superior Court, 522 P.2d 681 (Cal.1974).

The Devlin Report in Great Britain recommended that "identification on parade or in some other similar way in which the witness takes the initiative in picking out the accused, should be regarded in law, as in the normal case it is already regarded in practice, as a condition precedent to identification in court, the fulfillment of the condition to be dispensed with only in exceptional circumstances." Report to the Secretary of State for the Home Department of the Departmental Committee on Evidence of Identification in Criminal Cases 101 (1976). See also Salisbury, Eyewitness Identifications: A New Perspective on Old Law, 15 Tulsa L. Rev. 38 (1979). For an account of how the recommendations of the Devlin Report have been acted upon, for the most part directly through control of police discipline, see the review of Loftus' book, supra, in Weinstein, 81 Colum. L. Rev. 441, 444, 451–52 (1981).

Corroboration and Cautionary Instructions

A requirement of corroboration has generally been rejected as a solution to the problem of the unreliability of eyewitness identification testimony, Woocher, supra, at 1001–02; The Devlin Report, supra, at 82, although some commentators endorse it. E.g., Goldstein, supra, at 237–40. See infra p. 281 on the requirement of corroboration in other contexts. Another approach is to employ special cautionary instructions. The leading case supporting this requirement is United States v. Telfaire, 469 F.2d 552 (D.C.Cir.1972) (model instruction appended to opinion). See also United States v. Greene, 591 F.2d 471 (8th Cir.1979); United States v. Anderson, 739 F.2d 1254, 1257–58 (7th Cir.1984) (court must give instruction that calls attention to factors bearing on reliability of identification, but instruction need not be as specific as that in Telfaire); People v. Wright, 755 P.2d 1049 (Cal.1988) (error, though harmless, not to give instruction, but instruction should not take position on impact of psychological factors listed). A number of courts have refused to follow the Telfaire decision and have held it a matter of discretion for the trial judge whether to give such an instruction. E.g., United States v. Luis, 835 F.2d 37 (2d Cir.1987); Hampton v. State, 285 N.W.2d 868 (Wis.1979).

The Devlin Report, supra, at 150, recommended that the trial judge be required "to direct the jury that it is not safe to convict upon eye-witness evidence unless the circumstances of the identification are exceptional or the eye-witness evidence is supported by substantial evidence of another sort; and to indicate to the jury the circumstances, if any, which they might regard as exceptional and the evidence, if any, which they might regard as supporting the identification; and if he is unable to indicate either such circumstances or such evidence, to direct the jury to return a verdict of not guilty."

Commentators have expressed skepticism about the effectiveness of instructions to bring home to the jury the unreliability of eyewitness identification testimony. Starkman, The Use of Eyewitness Identification Evidence in Criminal Trials, 21 Crim. L. Q. 361, 376–77 (1979); Buckhout, Nobody Likes a Smart Ass, 3 Soc. Action and the Law 41, 45 (1976).

Expert Testimony on the Unreliability of Eyewitness Evidence

Another suggested solution to the problem of eyewitness evidence is the introduction of expert testimony regarding its unreliability. The opinion in United States v. Collins, 395 F.Supp. 629 (M.D.Pa.) (memorandum and order denying motion for new trial), aff'd, 523 F.2d 1051 (3d Cir. 1975), indicates many of the questions that arise in connection with such testimony.[2]

> Without deciding whether the subject matter of Dr. Buckhout's testimony would have been a proper one for expert testimony, or whether Dr. Buckhout is properly qualified to testify on that subject, I conclude, as I did at trial, that the potential prejudice of his testimony outweighed its probative value. To begin with, the probative value of the expert testimony would not have been significant. It is conceded that Burkeen was stabbed by the defendant while in the stairwell, although the defendant contended that he acted in self-defense. Thus, the area of dispute is restricted to which one was the aggressor. Moreover, Dr. Buckhout would have testified about something which is generally brought out by effective cross-examination at the trial—the factors, such as undue stress on the viewer and environmental conditions, which would tend to render a given eyewitness account unreliable, and the possibility or probability that the account in

2. Footnote omitted.

question is inaccurate. Defense counsel had ample opportunity to attack the eyewitness testimony in this case, and did so by attempting to point out alleged inconsistencies in the accounts offered at trial by the three eyewitnesses. In addition, counsel argued to the jury that because of those inconsistencies and other factors the accounts of the eyewitnesses should not be believed, and the jury was charged, at the defendant's request, about the vagaries of eyewitness accounts. Dr. Buckhout's testimony would have done little more than add a scientific luster to the facts and ideas which were amply presented by cross-examination, counsel's argument to the jury and the charge of the Court.

Weighed against the limited probative value of that testimony is the substantial possibility of prejudice that it would have presented. To start with, the testimony adduced at the trial failed to reveal the existence in this record of those factors previously mentioned that usually form the basis for opinion evidence challenging the reliability of eyewitness testimony. Further, the proffered testimony would not materially assist the jury in analyzing the evidence in this case but would be directed to the expert's thesis that eyewitness accounts generally are not as reliable as one would believe. Consequently, there was a substantial risk that the credentials and persuasive powers of the expert would have had a greater influence on the jury than the evidence presented at trial, thereby interfering with the jury's special role as fact finder. Scientific or expert testimony particularly courts the substantial danger of undue prejudice or of confusing the issues or of misleading the jury because of its aura of special reliability and trustworthiness.... Therefore, considering all the circumstances of this case, I conclude that the probative value of Dr. Buckhout's testimony was outweighed by its potentially prejudicial effect and was properly excluded.

Most appellate decisions have held the exclusion of expert testimony on the unreliability of eyewitness testimony not an abuse of discretion. Commonwealth v. Francis, 453 N.E.2d 1204 (Mass.1983); State v. Reed, 601 P.2d 1125 (Kan.1979); State v. Lewisohn, 379 A.2d 1192, 1203–04 (Me.1977); United States v. Serna, 799 F.2d 842, 850 (2d Cir.1986), cert. denied, 481 U.S. 1013 (1987); United States v. Amaral, 488 F.2d 1148 (9th Cir.1973). Nevertheless, some decisions have found error in such exclusion. In United States v. Stevens, 935 F.2d 1380, 1397, 1401 (3d Cir.1991), it was held error to have excluded testimony about a low correlation between levels of confidence and identification accuracy, but not error to have excluded evidence of the suggestiveness of a photo display and that a later identification may be influenced by an earlier one. In State v. Chapple, 660 P.2d 1208, 1217–24 (Ariz.1983), a murder prosecution in which the only issue was the accuracy of eyewitness identification, the court held it error in the circumstances of the case to have excluded expert testimony offered by the defendant regarding factors present in the case that were relevant to the accuracy of identification: the effect of stress on perception, the rate of forgetting, "transference"—the tendency to believe you saw a person at a certain time and place when you actually saw him at that place at a different time or at another place—and the tendency of witnesses who have talked together to reinforce one another's identifications. People v. McDonald, 690 P.2d 709, 715–27 (Cal.1984), held that "when an eyewitness identification ... is a key element of the prosecution's case but is not substantially corroborated by evidence giving it independent reliability, and the defendant offers qualified expert testimony on specific psychological factors shown by the record that could have affected the accuracy of the identification but are not likely to be fully known to or understood by the jury, it will ordinarily be error to exclude that testimony." Id. at 727. See also United States v. Smith,

736 F.2d 1103 (6th Cir.1984) (error but harmless to exclude testimony). For a comprehensive review of the cases, see Penrod et al., Expert Psychological Testimony on Eyewitness Reliability Before and After Daubert: The State of the Law and the Science, 13 Behav. Sci. and L. 229 (1995); 46 A.L.R. 4th 1047 (1986) (state cases).

Many trial courts in fact have permitted psychologists to testify concerning the reliability of eyewitness identifications even though possibly not required to do so, see Buckhout, Nobody Likes, supra at 43 n. 13; E. Loftus, supra, at 191–200, and there are strong advocates among the psychologists for the admission of such testimony. E. Loftus, supra, at 200–01; Starkman, supra, at 386; Katz and Reid, Expert Testimony on the Fallibility of Eyewitness Identification, 1 Crim.Justice J. 177, 204–06 (1977); Buckhout, Nobody Likes, supra, at 47–48; Leippe, The Case for Expert Testimony About Eyewitness Memory, 1 Psychology, Pub. Policy and L. 909 (1995); Westling, The Case for Expert Witness Assistance to the Jury in Eyewitness Identification Cases, 71 Or. L. Rev. 93 (1992).

Testimony by psychologists on the unreliability of eyewitness testimony perhaps may be distinguished from testimony by psychiatrists or psychologists addressed to some abnormal condition in the particular witness said to affect his credibility. See Woocher, supra, at 1020 n. 235, and infra pp. 449–51.

Reasons for caution in admitting testimony on the reliability of eyewitness identifications are discussed in Wells, Applied Eyewitness Testimony Research: System Variables and Estimator Variables, 36 J. of Personality and Soc. Psychology 1546, 1551–55 (1978):[3]

> [P]erhaps estimator-variable research [research into variables that affect the reliability of eyewitness testimony but which are not under the control of the legal system] can yield *general* statements of use to the courts. For example, one might conclude that because the experimental literature shows such poor accuracy rates in general, jurors and judges must be informed of this fact by psychologists. Yet, even this trivial contribution to criminal justice involves risky suppositions. For example, it assumes that judges and jurors currently believe that witnesses are less fallible than they are. Yet *there is no empirical evidence to support the assumption that jurors and judges are overbelieving of witnesses.* Thus, where is the empirical justification for this courtroom intervention? How can we be assured that psychologists' expert testimony will not create jurors and judges who are less believing of witnesses than they should be? Perhaps even more problematic is the fact that to make a statement about the fallibility of eyewitness testimony on the basis of estimator-variable research, the expert would supposedly rely on an *average* level of accuracy, a *typical* accuracy rate, or an average accuracy rate of a "typical study." If the expert is able to do so (which is questionable) he or she is also assuming that the literature is unbiased. Yet it can be proposed that the literature is replete with potential biases. For one thing, only one eyewitness study used the concept of "volunteerism" (i.e., only those witnesses who overtly indicate that they could possibly make a positive identification are allowed to see pictures or a lineup). Thus, a study that shows 30% of the witnesses correct and 70% incorrect might find a very high accurate/inaccurate ratio if it selected witnesses as police often do (i.e., testing only

witnesses who *freely* indicate that they saw the criminal, freely indicate that they had a sufficient view, and freely volunteer their services).

Another factor that might make the accuracy rates of eyewitness research somewhat unrepresentative is that subject-witnesses almost always know that the "crime" was staged by the time they are given a recall or recognition task. This knowledge could increase the tendency of those who have limited information to go ahead and identify someone. If it were a real crime, however, a false identification would have important implications, and this possibility could reduce the percentage of witnesses who simply guess.

In addition, no research exists in which the subject-witness is also the victim, yet such situations apply to virtually all rape, robbery, and assault cases. It may be that accuracy is extremely high under these conditions, as opposed to the relatively uninvolved, passive-role conditions typical of staged crimes.[4]

There are other reasons why accuracy rates in estimator-variable research may be misleading. The current author suspects that in general, low accuracy rates may be *preferred* among researchers. Specifically, researchers may perceive it as infinitely more interesting, more publishable, and more socially important to show low eyewitness accuracy in eyewitness research than to show high accuracy. A high accuracy rate is an implicit null hypothesis that is to be rejected, and the stronger the rejection, the better. Not surprisingly, eyewitness researchers sometimes feel a greater need to dismiss high accuracy, but not low accuracy, as a research fluke. For example, Buckhout [231 Scientific American 23–31] (1974), in reporting the results of a staged crime, noted that subject-witnesses were quite accurate in estimating the "criminal's" height and concluded, "This may be because the subject was of average height. . . ." Buckhout's observation may be correct, but it introduces the possibility that researchers do not

---

4. Eds.: Very few studies exist of the accuracy of accounts of real life events, events that have not been staged. One such study is Yuille and Cutshall, A Case Study of Eyewitness Memory of a Crime, 71 J. Appl'd Psychology 291 (1986). A large number of persons saw a shoot-out on a city street. Some of them gave accounts to the police at the scene and again to researchers five months later. Due to special circumstances, the researchers were able to determine to a high degree of probability from evidence other than the witnesses' accounts what had happened, so that it was possible to reach reliable conclusions about the witnesses' accuracy. The witnesses' accounts were found to be highly accurate, both those given at the scene and those given five months later. The authors suggest among other things that "perhaps the laboratory stress on negative aspects of eyewitness performance has been aided by ignoring the effect of unique and striking events" and also that "the passivity demanded of witnesses in laboratory research has precluded examining the effect of active involvement on subsequent recall. . . ." Id. at 299. See also Malpass and Devine, Research on Suggestion in Lineups and Photospreads, in Eyewitness Testimony 81, 86 (G. Wells and E. Loftus eds. 1984):

Subjects in eyewitness identification experiments . . . probably do not anticipate facing the disfavor of either those running the lineup or the person who is identified; they do not risk making an error in the important natural environment senses of having wrongly incriminated someone or having allowed a criminal to go unidentified. They do not risk having to continue what may be perceived to be time-consuming or inconvenient participation in an investigation or trial, and they do not have to confront the question of whether or not to participate in an episode of formal and perhaps intimidating contact with the powerful institutions of authority in our society. . . . [U]ntil we know more about the degree to which simulations actually produce results that can be validly applied to genuine events in the natural environment, realism will be an important aspect of psychological research in this area, and its absence will be an important source of reservation about the applicability of the research literature.

want high accuracy or that high-accuracy data warrant discounting, whereas low-accuracy data speak for themselves.

There is yet another possible reason to question the representativeness of staged "crimes." Personal communications between the author of the current article and other eyewitness researchers suggest that criminal-confederates may be chosen by researchers on an unrepresentative basis. Eyewitness researchers often go to great lengths to insure that their criminal-confederates do not have outstanding features. It is not clear how this concern for "no outstanding features" becomes operationalized in the selection of a criminal-confederate. However, it is possible that the chosen criminal-confederates have physical features that go a long way toward being unrepresentative, and therefore, perhaps criminal-confederates are more difficult to recognize than most criminals.

. . .

How can system-variable research [research into variables that affect the reliability of eyewitness testimony and which are under the control of the legal system] be applied to the betterment of criminal justice? One possibility is to use it in the courtroom as an estimator variable. For example, an expert could suggest to the court that the conditions of the lineup, courtroom procedures, or length of time between the original event and subsequent testing is so great that the witness is quite likely to be wrong. However, any such courtroom statement, no matter how it is phrased, would imply a likelihood of accuracy with regard to the case at hand. Suppose, for example, that the expert observed a biased lineup. Can he or she say that it is likely that the witness was incorrect because past research shows strong effects for biased lineups? No. If all of the measurable and unmeasurable influencing factors for that specific case were known (lighting, exposure time, etc.) it may be that the probability of accuracy would be .95 without a biased lineup and .92 with a biased lineup. Biased lineups may have consistently debilitating effects, but likelihood of accuracy depends on too many factors in a given case for any semblance of reasonable estimation. In other words, *this* use of system-variable research entails the same problems of application as did the estimator-variable research. As discussed earlier, discounting eyewitness testimony is a practice that is based upon questionable derivations from the eyewitness literature (overinduction) and fails to provide an alternative source of evidence.

The alternative use of system-variable research is to manipulate the relevant variables so as to *reduce the inaccuracies of witnesses*. For example, system-variable research can be used to advocate short witness-testing intervals, fairer lineups, reduced use of composite drawings, and so forth. This gives the criminal justice system empirically derived tools with which to better the criminal justice process. It provides an alternative to current practices without advocating the elimination of eyewitness testimony as a rule of evidence. Using system-variable research in this manner can contribute to criminal justice without the practice of post hoc discounting of an eyewitness.

See also Elliott, Expert Testimony About Eyewitness Identification, 17 Law and Hum. Behav. 423, 424–25 (1993), questioning the support in existing studies for nearly all the generalizations psychologists have testified to regarding eyewitness identifications:

In a paradoxical way, as studies have accumulated and have included more complicated and ecologically valid designs, the ease and confidence with which we may speak to makers of law and policy have diminished.... The pressure for clear, definite, usable assertions means that the greatest temptation is to produce answers for which there is no sound body of knowledge, without making clear just how tenuous the evidentiary basis is.

See also B. Cutler and S. Penrod, supra, at 214–15 (1995); Goldstein, supra, at 241–43 (1977). E. Loftus, supra, at 200–01, criticizes Wells.

As Wells indicates, an important question is whether the results of the psychological research thus far conducted permit a psychologist to say something sufficiently addressed to the litigated case to significantly affect the probabilities for that case without at the same time excluding the proper influence of the jury's own knowledge. The problem is seen by comparing United States v. Fosher, 590 F.2d 381 (1st Cir.1979), where the exclusion of the testimony of a psychologist was justified on the ground that he failed to address himself to the circumstances of the particular case, with Hampton v. State, 285 N.W.2d 868, 870–75 (Wis.1979), where the court upheld a trial court's ruling that a psychologist could not testify about particular features of the litigated case that would have tended to make the eyewitness's testimony unreliable, but could testify to factors that influence the reliability of eyewitness testimony, on the ground that the former might cause the jury to surrender its proper function.

The question of how the findings of psychology may best be employed in improving the quality of fact-finding in the legal system must be considered a matter as yet unsettled and one for continuing debate. However, an outstanding book on this subject, written in response to a challenge to psychologists laid down in the Devlin Report, B. Clifford and R. Bull, The Psychology of Person Identification (1978), leaves no doubt that an appropriate way or ways sooner or later will be found. This book, full of stimulating insights, makes it clear that a large body of information pertinent to questions that must be decided by triers of fact has already been assembled by researchers, id. at 209–12, that this information is constantly being augmented by further research and that increasingly research is being directed to the practical needs of the legal system. At the very least, the results of this research will find their way into the consciousness of judges and jurors through a process of informal education. See id. at 212–14.

For further discussions among the psychologists about whether their testimony can aid juries in the assessment of eyewitness identifications, see Wells, How Adequate is Human Intuition for Judging Eyewitness Testimony, in Eyewitness Testimony 256 (G. Wells and E. Loftus eds., 1984); Wells, Expert Psychological Testimony, 10 Law and Hum. Behav. 83, 86–88 (1986); Egeth and McCloskey, Expert Testimony About Eyewitness Behavior: Is It Safe and Effective? in Eyewitness Testimony 283 (G. Wells and E. Loftus eds., 1984); Wells, A Reanalysis of the Expert Testimony Issue, in id. at 304 (criticizing Egeth and McCloskey).

In a later chapter the question of the standard for the admissibility of expert testimony generally will be considered. At that time it will be necessary to reconsider the admissibility of expert testimony on the reliability of eyewitness evidence. See Faigman, The Evidentiary Status of Social Science Under Daubert, 1 Psychology, Pub. Policy and L. 960 (1995). See also infra pp. 447–51 on expert testimony regarding the credibility of witnesses.

Further useful references relevant to the topic of testimonial proof: J. Adams, Human Memory (1967); Lezak, Some Psychological Limitations on

Witness Reliability, 20 Wayne L. Rev. 117 (1973); Marshall, Evidence, Psychology, and the Trial: Some Challenges to Law, 63 Colum.L.Rev. 197 (1963); Redmount, The Psychological Basis of Evidence Practices: Memory, 50 J. Crim. L. & Criminology 249 (1959); Redmount, The Psychological Basis of Evidence Practices: Intelligence, 42 Minn. L. Rev. 559 (1958); Moore, Elements of Error in Testimony, 28 Or. L. Rev. 293 (1949); Hutchins and Slesinger, Some Observations on the Law of Evidence—Memory, 41 Harv. L. Rev. 860 (1928); Hutchins and Slesinger, Some Observations on the Law of Evidence, 28 Colum. L. Rev. 432 (1928).

SECTION 1. COMPETENCY

A. DISQUALIFICATIONS UNDER THE COMMON LAW

1. IN GENERAL

Thayer, Cases on Evidence 1066 (2d ed. 1900):

> Fortescue (De Laud. c. 26), who has the earliest account (about 1470) of witnesses testifying regularly to the jury, gives no information as to any ground for challenging them. But Coke, a century and a third later, makes certain qualifications of the assertion of the older judges, that "they had not seen witnesses challenged." He mentions as grounds of exclusion, legal infamy, being an "infidel," of non-sane memory, "not of discretion," a party interested, "or the like." And he says that "it hath been resolved by the justices [in 1612] that a wife cannot be produced either against or for her husband, *quia sunt duae animae in carne una.*" He also points out that "he that challengeth a right in the thing in demand cannot be a witness."
>
> Here are the outlines of the subsequent tests for the competency of witnesses. They were much refined upon, particularly the excluding ground of interest; and great inconvenience resulted. At last in the fourth and fifth decades of the [nineteenth] century, in England, nearly all objections of competency were abolished, or turned into matters of privilege. Similar changes, a little later, were widely made in this country.

For further information on the development of rules of incompetence in the sixteenth and seventeenth centuries and their virtual abolition in the nineteenth, see 9 Holdsworth, History of English Law 185–98 (3d ed. 1944) and 15 Holdsworth, History of English Law 139 (Goodhart and Hanbury ed. 1965).

Tennessee, the last state to abolish the disqualification for conviction of crime, did not do so until 1953. Tenn.Acts, ch. 194, § 1 (1953).

Disqualification for conviction of perjury continues in some jurisdictions. E.g., Ala.Code § 12–21–162 (1995); 42 Pa. Consol. Stats. Ann. § 5922 (1982); Miss.Code Ann. § 13–1–11 (1995).

2. INTEREST

It is highly probable that a party to a civil action tried by jury was never fully competent as a witness at common law. Certainly the precedents from the time of Elizabeth onward make it clear that under ordinary circumstances a party could not testify in his own favor in the common law courts. Counterbalancing the incompetency to testify in his own behalf was the party's privilege not to testify against himself. In criminal cases, also, the common law forbade the defendant to testify, at least to testify under oath. As to persons other than parties, courts and text-writers usually drew the deduction that any person was disqualified as a witness if he had a legal, certain and immediate interest in the result of the lawsuit, or if the record might be used as evidence for or against him in any subsequent action.

However, considerations such as the following have led to the almost total abolition of disqualification of witnesses for interest. "Now, plain sense and reason would obviously suggest that any living witness who could throw light upon a fact in issue should be heard to state what he knows, subject always to such observations as may arise as to his means of knowledge or his disposition to the truth.... It is painful to contemplate the amount of injustice which must have taken place under the exclusive system of the English law, not only in cases actually brought into Court and there wrongly decided in consequence of the exclusion of evidence, but in numberless cases in which parties silently submitted to wrongs from inability to avail themselves of proof, which, though morally conclusive, was in law inadmissible." Second Report of Her Majesty's Commissioners for Inquiry into the Process, Practice and System of Pleading in Superior Courts of Common Law 10 (1853).

Rock v. Arkansas

Supreme Court of the United States, 1987.
483 U.S. 44, 107 S.Ct. 2704, 97 L.Ed.2d 37.

■ JUSTICE BLACKMUN delivered the opinion of the Court.

The issue presented in this case is whether Arkansas' evidentiary rule prohibiting the admission of hypnotically refreshed testimony violated petitioner's constitutional right to testify on her own behalf as a defendant in a criminal case.

I

Petitioner Vickie Lorene Rock was charged with manslaughter in the death of her husband, Frank Rock, on July 2, 1983. A dispute had been simmering about Frank's wish to move from the couple's small apartment adjacent to Vickie's beauty parlor to a trailer she owned outside town. That night a fight erupted when Frank refused to let petitioner eat some pizza and prevented her from leaving the apartment to get something else to eat. App. 98, 103–104. When police arrived on the scene they found Frank on the floor with a bullet wound in his chest. Petitioner urged the officers to help her husband, Tr. 230, and cried to a sergeant who took her in charge, "please save him" and "don't let him die." Id., at 268. The police removed her from the building because she was upset and because she interfered with their investigation by her repeated attempts to use the telephone to call her husband's parents. Id., at 263–264, 267–268. According to the testimony of one of the investigating officers, petitioner told him that "she stood up to leave the room and [her husband] grabbed her by the throat and choked her and threw her against the wall and ... at that time she walked over and picked up the weapon and pointed it toward the floor and he hit her again and she shot him." Id., at 281.[1]

---

1. Another officer reported a slightly different version of the events:

"She stated that she had told her husband that she was going to go outside. He refused to let her leave and grabbed her by the throat and began choking her.

They struggled for a moment and she grabbed a gun. She told him to leave her alone and he hit her at which time the gun went off. She stated that it was an accident and she didn't mean to shoot

Because petitioner could not remember the precise details of the shooting, her attorney suggested that she submit to hypnosis in order to refresh her memory. Petitioner was hypnotized twice by Doctor Betty Back, a licensed neuropsychologist with training in the field of hypnosis. Id., at 901–903. Doctor Back interviewed petitioner for an hour prior to the first hypnosis session, taking notes on petitioner's general history and her recollections of the shooting. App. 46–47.[2] Both hypnosis sessions were recorded on tape. Id., at 53. Petitioner did not relate any new information during either of the sessions, id., at 78, 83, but, after the hypnosis, she was able to remember that at the time of the incident she had her thumb on the hammer of the gun, but had not held her finger on the trigger. She also recalled that the gun had discharged when her husband grabbed her arm during the scuffle. Id., at 29, 38. As a result of the details that petitioner was able to remember about the shooting, her counsel arranged for a gun expert to examine the handgun, a single action Hawes .22 Deputy Marshal. That inspection revealed that the gun was defective and prone to fire, when hit or dropped, without the trigger's being pulled. Tr. 662–663, 711.

When the prosecutor learned of the hypnosis sessions, he filed a motion to exclude petitioner's testimony. The trial judge held a pretrial hearing on the motion and concluded that no hypnotically refreshed testimony would be admitted. The court issued an order limiting petitioner's testimony to "matters remembered and stated to the examiner prior to being placed under hypnosis." App. to Pet. for Cert. xvii.[3] At trial, petitioner introduced testimony by the gun expert, Tr. 647–712, but the court limited petitioner's own description of the

him. She said she had to get to the hospital and talk to him." Tr. 388.

See also id., at 301–304, 337–338; App. 3–10. [Footnotes are the Court's. Some have been omitted, others renumbered.]

2. Doctor Back's handwritten notes regarding petitioner's memory of the day of the shooting read as follows:

"Pt states she & husb. were discussing moving out to a trailer she had prev. owned. He was 'set on' moving out to the trailer—she felt they should discuss. She bec[ame] upset & went to another room to lay down. Bro. came & left. She came out to eat some of the pizza, he wouldn't allow her to have any. She said she would go out and get [something] to eat he wouldn't allow her—He pushed her against a wall an end table in the corner [with] a gun on it. They were the night watchmen for business that sets behind them. She picked gun up stated she didn't want him hitting her anymore. He wouldn't let her out door, slammed door & 'gun went off & he fell & he died' [pt looked misty eyed here—near tears]" (additions by Doctor Back). App. 40.

3. The full pretrial order reads as follows:

"NOW on this 26th day of November, 1984, comes on the captioned matter for pre-trial hearing, and the Court finds:

"1. On September 27 and 28, 1984, Defendant was placed under hypnotic

trance by Dr. Bettye Back, PhD, Fayetteville, Arkansas, for the express purpose of enhancing her memory of the events of July 2, 1983, involving the death of Frank Rock.

"2. Dr. Back was professionally qualified to administer hypnosis. She was objective in the application of the technique and did not suggest by leading questions the responses expected to be made by Defendant. She was employed on an independent, professional basis. She made written notes of facts related to her by Defendant during the pre-hypnotic interview. She did employ post-hypnotic suggestion with Defendant. No one else was present during any phase of the hypnosis sessions except Dr. Back and Defendant.

"3. Defendant cannot be prevented by the Court from testifying at her trial on criminal charges under the Arkansas Constitution, but testimony of matters recalled by Defendant due to hypnosis will be excluded because of inherent unreliability and the effect of hypnosis in eliminating any meaningful cross-examination on those matters. Defendant may testify to matters remembered and stated to the examiner prior to being placed under hypnosis. Testimony resulting from post-hypnotic suggestion will be excluded." App. to Pet. for Cert. xvii.

events on the day of the shooting to a reiteration of the sketchy information in Doctor Back's notes. See App. 96–104.[4] The jury convicted petitioner on the manslaughter charge and she was sentenced to 10 years imprisonment and a $10,000 fine.

On appeal, the Supreme Court of Arkansas rejected petitioner's claim that the limitations on her testimony violated her right to present her defense. The court concluded that "the dangers of admitting this kind of testimony outweigh whatever probative value it may have," and decided to follow the approach of States that have held hypnotically refreshed testimony of witnesses inadmissible *per se*. Rock v. State, 288 Ark. 566, 573, 708 S.W.2d 78, 81 (1986). Although the court acknowledged that "a defendant's right to testify is fundamental," id., at 578, 708 S.W.2d, at 84, it ruled that the exclusion of petitioner's testimony did not violate her constitutional rights. Any "prejudice or deprivation" she suffered "was minimal and resulted from her own actions and not by any erroneous ruling of the court." Id., at 580, 708 S.W.2d, at 86. We granted certiorari ... to consider the constitutionality of Arkansas' *per se* rule excluding a criminal defendant's hypnotically refreshed testimony.

II

Petitioner's claim that her testimony was impermissibly excluded is bottomed on her constitutional right to testify in her own defense. At this point in the development of our adversary system, it cannot be doubted that a defendant in a criminal case has the right to take the witness stand and to testify in his or her own defense. This, of course, is a change from the historic common-law view, which was that all parties to litigation, including criminal defendants, were disqualified from testifying because of their interest in the outcome of the trial. See generally 2 J. Wigmore, Evidence §§ 576, 579 (J. Chadbourn rev. 1979). The principal rationale for this rule was the possible untrustworthiness of a party's testimony. Under the common law, the practice did develop of permitting criminal defendants to tell their side of the story, but they were limited to making an unsworn statement that could not be elicited through direct examination by counsel and was not subject to cross-examination. Id., at § 579, p. 827.

This Court in Ferguson v. Georgia, 365 U.S. 570, 573–582, 81 S.Ct. 756, 758–763 (1961), detailed the history of the transition from a rule of a defendant's incompetency to a rule of competency. As the Court there recounted, it came to be recognized that permitting a defendant to testify advances both the " 'detection of guilt' " and " 'the protection of innocence,' " id., at 581, 81 S.Ct., at 762, quoting 1 Am.L.Rev. 396 (1867), and by the end of the second half of the 19th century,[5] all States except Georgia had enacted statutes that

---

4. When petitioner began to testify, she was repeatedly interrupted by the prosecutor, who objected that her statements fell outside the scope of the pretrial order. Each time she attempted to describe an event on the day of the shooting, she was unable to proceed for more than a few words before her testimony was ruled inadmissible. For example, she was unable to testify without objection about her husband's activities on the morning of the shooting, App. 11, about their discussion and disagreement concerning the move to her trailer, id., at 12, 14, about her husband's and his brother's replacing the shock absorbers on a van, id., at 16, and about her broth-

er-in-law's return to eat pizza, id., at 19–20. She then made a proffer, outside the hearing of the jury, of testimony about the fight in an attempt to show that she could adhere to the court's order. The prosecution objected to every detail not expressly described in Doctor Back's notes or in the testimony the doctor gave at the pretrial hearing. Id., at 32–35. The court agreed with the prosecutor's statement that "ninety-nine percent of everything [petitioner] testified to in the proffer" was inadmissible. Id., at 35.

5. The removal of the disqualifications for accused persons occurred later than the establishment of the competence to testify of

declared criminal defendants competent to testify. See id., at 577 and n. 6, 596–598, 81 S.Ct., at 760 and n. 6, 770–771.[6] Congress enacted a general competency statute in the Act of Mar. 16, 1878, 20 Stat. 30, as amended, 18 U.S.C. § 3481, and similar developments followed in other common-law countries. Thus, more than 25 years ago this Court was able to state:

> "In sum, decades ago the considered consensus of the English-speaking world came to be that there was no rational justification for prohibiting the sworn testimony of the accused, who above all others may be in a position to meet the prosecution's case." Ferguson v. Georgia, 365 U.S., at 582, 81 S.Ct., at 763.[7]

The right to testify on one's own behalf at a criminal trial has sources in several provisions of the Constitution. It is one of the rights that "are essential to due process of law in a fair adversary process." Faretta v. California, 422 U.S. 806, 819, n. 15, 95 S.Ct. 2525, 2533 n. 15 (1975). The necessary ingredients of the Fourteenth Amendment's guarantee that no one shall be deprived of liberty without due process of law include a right to be heard and to offer testimony:

> "A person's right to reasonable notice of a charge against him, and *an opportunity to be heard in his defense*—a right to his day in court—are basic in our system of jurisprudence; and these rights include, as a minimum, a right to examine the witnesses against him, to offer testimony, and to be represented by counsel." (Emphasis added.) In re Oliver, 333 U.S. 257, 273, 68 S.Ct. 499, 507, . . . (1948).[8]

See also Ferguson v. Georgia, 365 U.S., at 602, 81 S.Ct., at 773. (Clark, J., concurring) (Fourteenth Amendment secures "right of a criminal defendant to choose between silence and testifying in his own behalf").[9]

---

civil parties. 2 J. Wigmore § 579, p. 826 (J. Chadbourn rev. 1979). This was not due to concern that criminal defendants were more likely to be unreliable than other witnesses, but to a concern for the accused:

> "If, being competent, he failed to testify, that (it was believed) would damage his cause more seriously than if he were able to claim that his silence were enforced by law. Moreover, if he did testify, that (it was believed) would injure more than assist his cause, since by undergoing the ordeal of cross-examination, he would appear at a disadvantage dangerous even to an innocent man." Id., at 828.

6. The Arkansas Constitution guarantees an accused the right "to be heard by himself and his counsel." Art. 2, § 10. Rule 601 of the Arkansas Rules of Evidence provides a general rule of competency: "Every person is competent to be a witness except as otherwise provided in these rules."

7. Ferguson v. Georgia, 365 U.S. 570, 81 S.Ct. 756 (1961), struck down as unconstitutional under the Fourteenth Amendment a Georgia statute that limited a defendant's presentation at trial to an unsworn statement, insofar as it denied the accused "the right to have his counsel question him to elicit his statement." Id., at 596, 81 S.Ct., at 770. The Court declined to reach the question

of a defendant's constitutional right to testify, because the case did not involve a challenge to the particular Georgia statute that rendered a defendant incompetent to testify. Id., at 572, n. 1, 81 S.Ct., at 758 n. 1. Two Justices, however, urged that such a right be recognized explicitly. Id., at 600–601, 602, 81 S.Ct., at 772–773 (concurring opinions).

8. Before Ferguson v. Georgia, it might have been argued that a defendant's ability to present an unsworn statement would satisfy this right. Once that procedure was eliminated, however, there was no longer any doubt that the right to be heard, which is so essential to due process in an adversary system of adjudication, could be vindicated only by affording a defendant an opportunity to testify before the factfinder.

9. This right reaches beyond the criminal trial: the procedural due process constitutionally required in some extra-judicial proceedings includes the right of the affected person to testify. See, e.g., Gagnon v. Scarpelli, 411 U.S. 778, 782, 786, 93 S.Ct. 1756, 1759, 1761 (1973) (probation revocation); Morrissey v. Brewer, 408 U.S. 471, 489, 92 S.Ct. 2593, 2604 (1972) (parole revocation); Goldberg v. Kelly, 397 U.S. 254, 269, 90 S.Ct. 1011, 1021 (1970) (termination of welfare benefits).

The right to testify is also found in the Compulsory Process Clause of the Sixth Amendment, which grants a defendant the right to call "witnesses in his favor," a right that is guaranteed in the criminal courts of the States by the Fourteenth Amendment. Washington v. Texas, 388 U.S. 14, 17–19, 87 S.Ct. 1920, 1922–1923 (1967). Logically included in the accused's right to call witnesses whose testimony is "material and favorable to his defense," United States v. Valenzuela–Bernal, 458 U.S. 858, 867, 102 S.Ct. 3440, 3446 (1982), is a right to testify himself, should he decide it is in his favor to do so. In fact, the most important witness for the defense in many criminal cases is the defendant himself. There is no justification today for a rule that denies an accused the opportunity to offer his own testimony. Like the truthfulness of other witnesses, the defendant's veracity, which was the concern behind the original common-law rule, can be tested adequately by cross-examination. See generally Westen, The Compulsory Process Clause, 73 Mich.L.Rev. 71, 119–120 (1974).

Moreover, in Faretta v. California, 422 U.S., at 819, 95 S.Ct., at 2533, the Court recognized that the Sixth Amendment

"grants to the accused *personally* the right to make his defense. It is the accused, not counsel, who must be 'informed of the nature and cause of the accusation,' who must be 'confronted with the witnesses against him,' and who must be accorded 'compulsory process for obtaining witnesses in his favor.' "(Emphasis added.)

Even more fundamental to a personal defense than the right of self-representation, which was found to be "necessarily implied by the structure of the Amendment," ibid., is an accused's right to present his own version of events in his own words. A defendant's opportunity to conduct his own defense by calling witnesses is incomplete if he may not present himself as a witness.

The opportunity to testify is also a necessary corollary to the Fifth Amendment's guarantee against compelled testimony. In Harris v. New York, 401 U.S. 222, 230, 91 S.Ct. 643, 648 (1971), the Court stated: "Every criminal defendant is privileged to testify in his own defense, or to refuse to do so." Id., at 225, 91 S.Ct., at 645. Three of the dissenting Justices in that case agreed that the Fifth Amendment encompasses this right: "[The Fifth Amendment's privilege against self-incrimination] is fulfilled only when an accused is guaranteed the right 'to remain silent unless he chooses to speak in the unfettered exercise of his own will.' ... The choice of whether to testify in one's own defense ... is an exercise of the constitutional privilege." Id., at 230, 91 S.Ct., at 648, quoting Malloy v. Hogan, 378 U.S. 1, 8, 84 S.Ct. 1489, 1493 (1964). (Emphasis removed.)[10]

III

The question now before the Court is whether a criminal defendant's right to testify may be restricted by a state rule that excludes her post-hypnosis testimony. This is not the first time this Court has faced a constitutional challenge to a state rule, designed to ensure trustworthy evidence, that interfered with the ability of a defendant to offer testimony. In Washington v. Texas,

---

10. On numerous occasions the Court has proceeded on the premise that the right to testify on one's own behalf in defense to a criminal charge is a fundamental constitutional right. See, e.g., Nix v. Whiteside, 475 U.S. 157, 164, 106 S.Ct. 988, 993 (1986); id., at 186, n. 5, 106 S.Ct., at 995, n. 5 (Blackmun, J., opinion concurring in the judgment); Jones v. Barnes, 463 U.S. 745, 751, 103 S.Ct. 3308, 3312 (1983) (defendant has the "ultimate authority to make certain fundamental decisions regarding the case, as to whether to ... testify in his or her own behalf"); Brooks v. Tennessee, 406 U.S. 605, 612, 92 S.Ct. 1891, 1895 (1972) ("Whether the defendant is to testify is an important tactical decision as well as a matter of constitutional right").

388 U.S. 14, 87 S.Ct. 1920 (1967), the Court was confronted with a state statute that prevented persons charged as principals, accomplices, or accessories in the same crime from being introduced as witnesses for one another. The statute, like the original common-law prohibition on testimony by the accused, was grounded in a concern for the reliability of evidence presented by an interested party:

"It was thought that if two persons charged with the same crime were allowed to testify on behalf of each other, 'each would try to swear the other out of the charge.' This rule, as well as the other disqualifications for interest, rested on the unstated premises that the right to present witnesses was subordinate to the court's interest in preventing perjury, and that erroneous decisions were best avoided by preventing the jury from hearing any testimony that might be perjured, even if it were the only testimony available on a crucial issue." (Footnote omitted.) Id., at 21, 87 S.Ct. at 1924, quoting Benson v. United States, 146 U.S. 325, 335, 13 S.Ct. 60, 63 (1892).

As the Court recognized, the incompetency of a codefendant to testify had been rejected on nonconstitutional grounds in 1918, when the Court, refusing to be bound by "the dead hand of the common-law rule of 1789," stated:

" '[T]he conviction of our time [is] that the truth is more likely to be arrived at by hearing the testimony of all persons of competent understanding who may seem to have knowledge of the facts involved in a case, leaving the credit and weight of such testimony to be determined by the jury or by the court. . . .' " 388 U.S., at 22, 87 S.Ct., at 1924, quoting Rosen v. United States, 245 U.S. 467, 471, 38 S.Ct. 148, 150 (1918).

The Court concluded that this reasoning was compelled by the Sixth Amendment's protections for the accused. In particular, the Court reasoned that the Sixth Amendment was designed in part "to make the testimony of a defendant's witnesses admissible on his behalf in court." 388 U.S., at 22, 87 S.Ct., at 1925.

With the rationale for the common-law incompetency rule thus rejected on constitutional grounds, the Court found that the mere presence of the witness in the courtroom was not enough to satisfy the Constitution's Compulsory Process Clause. By preventing the defendant from having the benefit of his accomplice's testimony, "the State *arbitrarily* denied him the right to put on the stand a witness who was physically and mentally capable of testifying to events that he had personally observed, and whose testimony would have been relevant and material to the defense." (Emphasis added.) Id., at 23, 87 S.Ct., at 1925.

Just as a State may not apply an arbitrary rule of competence to exclude a material defense witness from taking the stand, it also may not apply a rule of evidence that permits a witness to take the stand, but arbitrarily excludes material portions of his testimony. In Chambers v. Mississippi, 410 U.S. 284, 93 S.Ct. 1038 (1973), the Court invalidated a State's hearsay rule on the ground that it abridged the defendant's right to "present witnesses in his own defense." Id., at 302, 93 S.Ct., at 1049. Chambers was tried for a murder to which another person repeatedly had confessed in the presence of acquaintances. The State's hearsay rule, coupled with a "voucher" rule that did not allow the defendant to cross-examine the confessed murderer directly, prevented Chambers from introducing testimony concerning these confessions, which were critical to his defense. This Court reversed the judgment of conviction, holding that when a state rule of evidence conflicts with the right to present witnesses, the rule may "not be applied mechanistically to defeat the ends of justice," but must meet the fundamental standards of due process. Ibid. In the Court's view, the State in Chambers did not demonstrate that the hearsay testimony in that case, which bore "assurances of trustworthiness" including corroboration by other evidence, would be unreliable, and thus the defendant should have been able to introduce the exculpatory testimony. Ibid.

Of course, the right to present relevant testimony is not without limitation. The right "may, in appropriate cases, bow to accommodate other legitimate interests in the criminal trial process." Id., at 295, 93 S.Ct., at 1046.[11] But restrictions of a defendant's right to testify may not be arbitrary or disproportionate to the purposes they are designed to serve. In applying its evidentiary rules a State must evaluate whether the interests served by a rule justify the limitation imposed on the defendant's constitutional right to testify.

IV

The Arkansas rule enunciated by the state courts does not allow a trial court to consider whether posthypnosis testimony may be admissible in a particular case; it is a *per se* rule prohibiting the admission at trial of any defendant's hypnotically refreshed testimony on the ground that such testimony is always unreliable.[12] Thus, in Arkansas, an accused's testimony is limited to matters that he or she can prove were remembered *before* hypnosis. This rule operates to the detriment of any defendant who undergoes hypnosis, without regard to the reasons for it, the circumstances under which it took place, or any independent verification of the information it produced.[13]

In this case, the application of that rule had a significant adverse effect on petitioner's ability to testify. It virtually prevented her from describing any of the events that occurred on the day of the shooting, despite corroboration of many of those events by other witnesses. Even more importantly, under the court's rule petitioner was not permitted to describe the actual shooting except in the words contained in Doctor Back's notes. The expert's description of the gun's tendency to misfire would have taken on greater significance if the jury had heard petitioner testify that she did not have her finger on the trigger and that the gun went off when her husband hit her arm.

In establishing its *per se* rule, the Arkansas Supreme Court simply followed the approach taken by a number of States that have decided that hypnotically enhanced testimony should be excluded at trial on the ground that it tends to

11. Numerous state procedural and evidentiary rules control the presentation of evidence and do not offend the defendant's right to testify. See, e.g., Chambers v. Mississippi, 410 U.S. 284, 302, 93 S.Ct. 1038, 1049 (1973) ("In the exercise of this right, the accused, as is required of the State, must comply with established rules of procedure and evidence designed to assure both fairness and reliability in the ascertainment of guilt and innocence"); Washington v. Texas, 388 U.S. 14, 23, n. 21, 87 S.Ct. 1920, 1925, n. 21 (1967) (opinion should not be construed as disapproving testimonial privileges or nonarbitrary rules that disqualify those incapable of observing events due to mental infirmity or infancy from being witnesses).

12. The rule leaves a trial judge no discretion to admit this testimony, even if the judge is persuaded of its reliability by testimony at a pretrial hearing. Tr. of Oral Arg. 36 (statement of the Attorney General of Arkansas).

13. The Arkansas Supreme Court took the position that petitioner was fully responsible for any prejudice that resulted from the restriction on her testimony because it was she who chose to resort to the technique of hypnosis. Rock v. State, 288 Ark. 566, 580, 708 S.W.2d 78, 86 (1986). The prosecution and the trial court each expressed a similar view and the theme was renewed repeatedly at trial as a justification for limiting petitioner's testimony. See App. 15, 20, 21–22, 24, 36. It should be noted, however, that Arkansas had given no previous indication that it looked with disfavor on the use of hypnosis to assist in the preparation for trial and there were no previous state-court rulings on the issue.

be unreliable. Other States that have adopted an exclusionary rule, however, have done so for the testimony of *witnesses,* not for the testimony of a *defendant.* The Arkansas Supreme Court failed to perform the constitutional analysis that is necessary when a defendant's right to testify is at stake.[14]

Although the Arkansas court concluded that any testimony that cannot be proved to be the product of prehypnosis memory is unreliable, many courts have eschewed a *per se* rule and permit the admission of hypnotically refreshed testimony.[15] Hypnosis by trained physicians or psychologists has been recognized as a valid therapeutic technique since 1958, although there is no generally accepted theory to explain the phenomenon, or even a consensus on a single definition of hypnosis. See Council on Scientific Affairs, Scientific Status of Refreshing Recollection by the Use of Hypnosis, 253 J.A.M.A. 1918, 1918–1919 (1985) (Council Report).[16] The use of hypnosis in criminal investigations, however, is controversial, and the current medical and legal view of its appropriate role is unsettled.

Responses of individuals to hypnosis vary greatly. The popular belief that hypnosis guarantees the accuracy of recall is as yet without established foundation and, in fact, hypnosis often has no effect at all on memory. The most common response to hypnosis, however, appears to be an increase in both correct and incorrect recollections.[17] Three general characteristics of hypnosis may lead to the introduction of inaccurate memories: the subject becomes "suggestible" and may try to please the hypnotist with answers the subject thinks will be met with approval; the subject is likely to "confabulate," that is, to fill in details from the imagination in order to make an answer more

---

14. The Arkansas court relied on a California case, People v. Shirley, 31 Cal.3d 18, 181 Cal.Rptr. 243, 723 P.2d 1354, cert. denied, 459 U.S. 860, 103 S.Ct. 133 (1982), for much of its reasoning as to the unreliability of hypnosis. 288 Ark., at 575–578, 708 S.W.2d, at 83–84. But while the California court adopted a far stricter general rule—barring entirely testimony by any witness who has been hypnotized—it explicitly excepted testimony by an accused:

"[W]hen it is the defendant himself—not merely a defense witness—who submits to pretrial hypnosis, the experience will not render his testimony inadmissible if he elects to take the stand. In that case, the rule we adopt herein is subject to a necessary exception to avoid impairing the fundamental right of an accused to testify in his own behalf." 31 Cal.3d, at 67, 723 P.2d, at 1384.

This case does not involve the admissibility of testimony of previously hypnotized witnesses other than criminal defendants and we express no opinion on that issue.

15. Some jurisdictions have adopted a rule that hypnosis affects the credibility, but not the admissibility, of testimony....

Other courts conduct an individualized inquiry in each case. See, e.g., McQueen v. Garrison, 814 F.2d 951, 958 (C.A.4 1987) (reliability evaluation); Wicker v. McCotter, 783 F.2d 487, 492–493 (C.A.5 1986) (probative value of the testimony weighed against

its prejudicial effect), cert. denied, 478 U.S. 1010, 106 S.Ct. 3310 (1986); State v. Iwakiri, 106 Idaho 618, 625, 682 P.2d 571, 578 (1984) (weigh "totality of circumstances").

In some jurisdictions, courts have established procedural prerequisites for admissibility in order to reduce the risks associated with hypnosis. Perhaps the leading case in this line is State v. Hurd, 86 N.J. 525, 432 A.2d 86 (1981)....

16. Hypnosis has been described as "involv[ing] the focusing of attention; increased responsiveness to suggestions; suspension of disbelief with a lowering of critical judgment; potential for altering perception, motor control, or memory in response to suggestions; and the subjective experience of responding involuntarily." Council Report, 253 J.A.M.A., at 1919.

17. "[W]hen hypnosis is used to refresh recollection, one of the following outcomes occurs: (1) hypnosis produces recollections that are not substantially different from nonhypnotic recollections; (2) it yields recollections that are more inaccurate than nonhypnotic memory; or, most frequently, (3) it results in more information being reported, but these recollections contain both accurate and inaccurate details.... There are no data to support a fourth alternative, namely, that hypnosis increases remembering of only accurate information." Id., at 1921.

coherent and complete; and, the subject experiences "memory hardening," which gives him great confidence in both true and false memories, making effective cross-examination more difficult. See generally M. Orne, et al., Hypnotically Induced Testimony, in Eyewitness Testimony: Psychological Perspectives 171 (G. Wells and E. Loftus, eds., 1985); Diamond, Inherent Problems in the Use of Pretrial Hypnosis on a Prospective Witness, 68 Calif.L.Rev. 313, 333–342 (1980). Despite the unreliability that hypnosis concededly may introduce, however, the procedure has been credited as instrumental in obtaining investigative leads or identifications that were later confirmed by independent evidence. See, e.g., People v. Hughes, 59 N.Y.2d 523, 533, 466 N.Y.S.2d 255, 453 N.E.2d 484, 488 (1983); see generally R. Udolf, Forensic Hypnosis 11–16 (1983).

The inaccuracies the process introduces can be reduced, although perhaps not eliminated, by the use of procedural safeguards. One set of suggested guidelines calls for hypnosis to be performed only by a psychologist or psychiatrist with special training in its use and who is independent of the investigation. See Orne, The Use and Misuse of Hypnosis in Court, 27 Int'l J. Clinical & Experimental Hypnosis 311, 335–336 (1979). These procedures reduce the possibility that biases will be communicated to the hypersuggestive subject by the hypnotist. Suggestion will be less likely also if the hypnosis is conducted in a neutral setting with no one present but the hypnotist and the subject. Tape or video recording of all interrogations, before, during, and after hypnosis, can help reveal if leading questions were asked. Id., at 336. Such guidelines do not guarantee the accuracy of the testimony, because they cannot control the subject's own motivations or any tendency to confabulate, but they do provide a means of controlling overt suggestions.

The more traditional means of assessing accuracy of testimony also remain applicable in the case of a previously hypnotized defendant. Certain information recalled as a result of hypnosis may be verified as highly accurate by corroborating evidence. Cross-examination, even in the face of a confident defendant, is an effective tool for revealing inconsistencies. Moreover, a jury can be educated to the risks of hypnosis through expert testimony and cautionary instructions. Indeed, it is probably to a defendant's advantage to establish carefully the extent of his memory prior to hypnosis, in order to minimize the decrease in credibility the procedure might introduce.

We are not now prepared to endorse without qualifications the use of hypnosis as an investigative tool; scientific understanding of the phenomenon and of the means to control the effects of hypnosis is still in its infancy. Arkansas, however, has not justified the exclusion of *all* of a defendant's testimony that the defendant is unable to prove to be the product of prehypnosis memory. A State's legitimate interest in barring unreliable evidence does not extend to *per se* exclusions that may be reliable in an individual case. Wholesale inadmissibility of a defendant's testimony is an arbitrary restriction on the right to testify in the absence of clear evidence by the State repudiating the validity of all posthypnosis recollections. The State would be well within its powers if it established guidelines to aid trial courts in the evaluation of posthypnosis testimony and it may be able to show that testimony in a particular case is so unreliable that exclusion is justified. But it has not shown that hypnotically enhanced testimony is always so untrustworthy and so immune to the traditional means of evaluating credibility that it should disable a defendant from presenting her version of the events for which she is on trial.

In this case, the defective condition of the gun corroborated the details petitioner remembered about the shooting. The tape recordings provided some means to evaluate the hypnosis and the trial judge concluded that Doctor Back did not suggest responses with leading questions. See n. 3, supra. Those circumstances present an argument for admissibility of petitioner's testimony in this particular case, an argument that must be considered by the trial court. Arkansas' *per se* rule excluding all posthypnosis testimony infringes impermissibly on the right of a defendant to testify on his or her own behalf.[18]

The judgment of the Supreme Court of Arkansas is vacated and the case is remanded to that court for further proceedings not inconsistent with this opinion.

It is so ordered.

■ CHIEF JUSTICE REHNQUIST, with whom JUSTICE WHITE, JUSTICE O'CONNOR, and JUSTICE SCALIA join, dissenting.

In deciding that petitioner Rock's testimony was properly limited at her trial, the Arkansas Supreme Court cited several factors that undermine the reliability of hypnotically induced testimony. Like the Court today, the Arkansas Supreme Court observed that a hypnotized individual becomes subject to suggestion, is likely to confabulate, and experiences artificially increased confidence in both true and false memories following hypnosis. No known set of procedures, both courts agree, can insure against the inherently unreliable nature of such testimony. Having acceded to the factual premises of the Arkansas Supreme Court, the Court nevertheless concludes that a state trial court must attempt to make its own scientific assessment of reliability in each case it is confronted with a request for the admission of hypnotically induced testimony. I find no justification in the Constitution for such a ruling.

In the Court's words, the decision today is "bottomed" on recognition of Rock's "constitutional right to testify in her own defense." Ante, [107 S.Ct.] at 2708. While it is true that this Court, in dictum, has recognized the existence of such a right, see, e.g., Faretta v. California, 422 U.S. 806, 819, n. 15, 95 S.Ct. 2525, 2533 n. 15, 45 L.Ed.2d 562 (1975), the principles identified by the Court as underlying this right provide little support for invalidating the evidentiary rule applied by the Arkansas Supreme Court.

As a general matter, the Court first recites, a defendant's right to testify facilitates the truth-seeking function of a criminal trial by advancing both the " 'detection of guilt' " and " 'the protection of innocence.' " Ante, at 2708, quoting Ferguson v. Georgia, 365 U.S. 570, 581, 81 S.Ct. 756, 762, 5 L.Ed.2d 783 (1961). Such reasoning is hardly controlling here, where advancement of the truth-seeking function of Rock's trial was the sole motivation behind limiting her testimony. The Court also posits, however, that "a rule that denies an accused the opportunity to offer his own testimony" cannot be upheld because, "[l]ike the truthfulness of other witnesses, the defendant's veracity . . . can be tested adequately by cross-examination." Ante, at 2709. But the Court candidly admits that the increased confidence inspired by hypnotism makes "cross-examination more difficult," ante, 2713, thereby diminishing an adverse party's ability to test the truthfulness of defendants such as Rock. Nevertheless, we are told, the exclusion of a defendant's testimony cannot be sanctioned because the defendant " 'above all others may be in a position to meet the prosecution's case.' " Ante, [107 S.Ct.] 2708, quoting Ferguson v.

---

18. This disposition makes it unnecessary to consider petitioner's claims that the trial court's order restricting her testimony was unconstitutionally broad and that the trial court's application of the order resulted in a denial of due process of law. We also need not reach petitioner's argument that Arkansas' restriction on her testimony interferes with her Sixth Amendment right to counsel. Petitioner concedes that there is a "substantial question" whether she raised this federal question on appeal to the Arkansas Supreme Court. Reply Brief for Petitioner 2.

Georgia, supra, at 582, 81 S.Ct., at 763. In relying on such reasoning, the Court apparently forgets that the issue before us arises only by virtue of Rock's memory loss, which rendered her less able "to meet the prosecution's case." Ibid.

In conjunction with its reliance on broad principles that have little relevance here, the Court barely concerns itself with the recognition, present throughout our decisions, that an individual's right to present evidence is subject always to reasonable restrictions. Indeed, the due process decisions relied on by the Court all envision that an individual's right to present evidence on his behalf is not absolute and must often times give way to countervailing considerations. See, e.g., In re Oliver, 333 U.S. 257, 273, 275, 68 S.Ct. 499 (1948); Morrissey v. Brewer, 408 U.S. 471, 481–482, 92 S.Ct. 2593, 2600–2601 (1972); Goldberg v. Kelly, 397 U.S. 254, 263, 90 S.Ct. 1011, 1018 (1970). Similarly, our Compulsory Process Clause decisions make clear that the right to present relevant testimony "may, in appropriate cases, bow to accommodate other legitimate interests in the criminal trial process." Chambers v. Mississippi, 410 U.S. 284, 295, 93 S.Ct. 1038, 1046 (1973); see Washington v. Texas, 388 U.S. 14, 22, 87 S.Ct. 1920, 1925 (1967). The Constitution does not in any way relieve a defendant from compliance with "rules of procedure and evidence designed to assure both fairness and reliability in the ascertainment of guilt and innocence." Chambers v. Mississippi, supra, at 302, 93 S.Ct., at 1049. Surely a rule designed to exclude testimony whose trustworthiness is inherently suspect cannot be said to fall outside this description.[19]

This Court has traditionally accorded the States "respect ... in the establishment and implementation of their own criminal trial rules and procedures." 410 U.S., at 302–303, 93 S.Ct., at 1049–1050; see, e.g., Marshall v. Lonberger, 459 U.S. 422, 438, n. 6, 103 S.Ct. 843, 853, n. 6 (1983) ("[T]he Due Process Clause does not permit the federal courts to engage in a finely tuned review of the wisdom of state evidentiary rules"); Patterson v. New York, 432 U.S. 197, 201, 97 S.Ct. 2319, 2322 (1977) ("[W]e should not lightly construe the Constitution so as to intrude upon the administration of justice by the individual States"). One would think that this deference would be at its highest in an area such as this, where, as the Court concedes, "scientific understanding ... is still in its infancy." Ante, [107 S.Ct.] 2714. Turning a blind eye to this concession, the Court chooses instead to restrict the ability of both state and federal courts to respond to changes in the understanding of hypnosis.

The Supreme Court of Arkansas' decision was an entirely permissible response to a novel and difficult question. See National Institute of Justice, Issues and Practices, M. Orne et al., Hypnotically Refreshed Testimony: Enhanced Memory or Tampering with Evidence? 51 (1985). As an original proposition, the solution this Court imposes upon Arkansas may be equally sensible, though requiring the matter to be considered *res nova* by every single trial judge in every single case might seem to some to pose serious administrative difficulties. But until there is a much more general consensus on the use of hypnosis than there is now, the Constitution does not warrant this Court's mandating its own view of how to deal with the issue.

---

19. The Court recognizes, as it must, that rules governing "testimonial privileges [and] nonarbitrary rules that disqualify those incapable of observing events due to mental infirmity or infancy from being witnesses" do not "offend the defendant's right to testify." Ante, [107 S.Ct. at] 2711, n. 11. I fail to discern any meaningful constitutional difference between such rules and the one at issue here.

NOTES

1. As will be noted, Rock does not settle the question of what the standard is for admissibility against a criminal defendant, rather than in his favor, of the testimony of a witness who has been hypnotized. In some states the answer is that the testimony is admissible only if based upon a prehypnotic memory. The difficulty in administering this standard is indicated in this passage from Commonwealth v. Kater, 567 N.E.2d 885, 890 (Mass.1991):

> Because another retrial will be necessary ... we take this opportunity to state again what procedures are required.... Before the next retrial the judge should hold a hearing to determine whether the proffered testimony is based on prehypnotic memory.[20] The judge may hear from the witnesses, and from police, friends and others as to what the witnesses told them.[21] From the evidence the judge should determine the substance of each witness's prehypnotic memory. After making that determination, the judge should compare it to the proffered trial testimony and decide if any part of the proffered testimony exceeds the witness's prehypnotic memory. The judge must exclude as inadmissible details about events that the witness remembers for the first time after hypnosis. The record of the witness's prehypnotic memory may contain facts that the witness no longer recalls at the time of the evidentiary hearing. If the witness recalls such facts which the judge determines to be prehypnotic memory at the time of trial, that testimony is admissible.

It has been suggested that restrictions on the admissibility of the testimony of witnesses who have been hypnotized may conflict with other values. The prevention of injury and further crime may call for rapid action by the police, employing every means, including hypnosis, in the hope that a witness will remember something useful in identifying the criminal. But such action may jeopardize the admissibility of the witness's testimony at trial. See People v. Lee, 450 N.W.2d 883, 905 (Mich.1990) (dissenting opinion). Likewise the mental health of a witness may call for psychotherapy that includes hypnosis, but this also may jeopardize admissibility.

For a review of the law in the different states relating to testimony of witnesses who have been hypnotized, see Borawick v. Shay, 68 F.3d 597 (2d Cir.1995) (adopting an approach that considers all the circumstances and weighs probative value against prejudice); Annot., 77 A.L.R.4th 927 (1995). See also Kanovitz, Hypnotic Memories and Civil Sexual Abuse Trials, 45 Vand. L.Rev. 1185 (1992).

2(a). In Brooks v. Tennessee, 406 U.S. 605 (1972), cited in the Rock decision, the Supreme Court held violative of the privilege against self-incrimination a state statute which required that a criminal defendant take the stand before any other testimony for the defense is heard or not at all.

But our adversary system reposes judgment of the credibility of all witnesses in the jury. Pressuring the defendant to take the stand, by foreclos-

---

20. This screening procedure is required only for matters which were the subject of inquiry during the hypnotic session.... Testimony concerning matters that were not discussed under hypnosis is irrelevant. [Footnotes are the court's. Some are omitted, others renumbered.]

21. Oral, written, and recorded statements or testimony from other persons who spoke to the witness before the hypnosis may suffice to establish the boundaries of the witness's prehypnotic memory. We do not think, however, that a hypnotized witness should be barred from testifying at the hearing as to his prehypnotic memory, nor is the motion judge limited to contemporaneously recorded reports of what the witness said before hypnosis.... It is for the motion judge to assess the credibility of the witnesses' testimony.

ing later testimony if he refuses, is not a constitutionally permissible means of ensuring his honesty. It fails to take into account the very real and legitimate concerns that might motivate a defendant to exercise his right of silence. And it may compel even a wholly truthful defendant, who might otherwise decline to testify for legitimate reasons, to subject himself to impeachment and cross-examination at a time when the strength of his other evidence is not yet clear. For these reasons we hold that § 40–2403 violates an accused's constitutional right to remain silent insofar as it requires him to testify first for the defense or not at all.... For closely related reasons we also regard the Tennessee rule as an infringement on the defendant's right of due process as defined in Ferguson v. Georgia.... Whether the defendant is to testify is an important tactical decision as well as a matter of constitutional right. By requiring the accused and his lawyer to make the choice without an opportunity to evaluate the actual worth of their evidence, the statute restricts the defense—particularly counsel—in the planning of its case. Furthermore, the penalty for not testifying first is to keep the defendant off the stand entirely, even though as a matter of professional judgment his lawyer might want to call him later in the trial. The accused is thereby deprived of the "guiding hand of counsel" in the timing of this critical element of his defense.... Id. at 611–13.

CHIEF JUSTICE BURGER, dissenting:

... The Court's holding that the Tennessee rule deprives the defendant of the "guiding hand of counsel" at every stage of the proceedings fares no better.... It amounts to nothing more than the assertion that counsel may not be restricted by ordinary rules of evidence and procedure in presenting an accused's defense if it might be more advantageous to present it in some other way. A rule forbidding defense counsel to ask leading questions of the defendant when he takes the stand may restrict defense counsel in his options and may in many cases bear only remote relationship to the goal of truthful testimony. Yet no one would seriously contend that such a universal rule of procedure is prohibited by the Constitution. The rule that the defendant waives the Fifth Amendment privilege as to any and all relevant matters when he decides to take the stand certainly inhibits the choices and options of counsel, yet this Court has never questioned such a rule.... Id. at 615–16.

JUSTICE REHNQUIST, dissenting:

... The state rule responds to the fear that interested parties, if allowed to present their own testimony after other disinterested witnesses have testified, may well shape their version of events in a way inconsistent with their oath as witnesses. This fear is not groundless, nor is its importance denigrated by vague generalities such as the statement that "our adversary system reposes judgment of the credibility of all witnesses in the jury." ...
Assuredly the traditional common law charge to the jury confides to that body the determination as to the truth or falsity of the testimony of each witness. But the fact that the jury is instructed to make such a determination in reaching its verdict has never been thought to militate against the desirability, to say nothing of the constitutionality, of additional inhibitions against perjury during the course of a trial. The traditional policy of sequestering nonparty witnesses, the requirement of an oath on the part of all witnesses, and the opportunity afforded for cross-examination of witnesses are but examples of such inhibitions.... Id. at 619–20.

State v. Cassidy, 672 A.2d 899 (Conn.1996): Prejudicial error, unduly burdening defendant's Confrontation Clause right to be present throughout the trial, for prosecutor to comment in closing argument that because defendant had been present and heard the other witnesses, he could doctor up his story.

Webb v. State, 766 S.W.2d 236 (Tex.Crim.App.1989): Rights to compulsory process and due process violated by exclusion of defense witness's testimony for sole reason that the witness had been present in the courtroom and heard the testimony of other witnesses in contravention of a sequestration order. Defendant and defense counsel were unaware of the witness's presence and at the time the witness was present did not know that she would have relevant testimony.

(b) United States v. Nobles, 422 U.S. 225 (1975): At defendant's trial for bank robbery, the only significant evidence linking him with the crime was the testimony of two witnesses for the government who identified defendant as one of the robbers. Defense counsel cross-examined these witnesses and later, in the defendant's own case, proposed to introduce the testimony of a defense investigator that the witnesses had made statements to him inconsistent with their trial testimony or which cast doubt upon its reliability. The trial court refused to allow this testimony unless the defendant agreed to produce for prosecution use a written report by the investigator concerning his interview of the government's witnesses. Confronted with this condition, the defendant chose not to call the investigator. Held: Thus conditioning the introduction of this evidence did not violate defendant's "Sixth Amendment rights to compulsory process and cross-examination" (citing Washington v. Texas), nor any other right including the privilege against self-incrimination and the work product privilege. For discussions of Nobles in connection with these privileges, see pp. 1391–93, 1455–56 infra.

In Taylor v. Illinois, 484 U.S. 400 (1988), the Supreme Court held it not violative of the Compulsory Process Clause to exclude testimony of a defense witness where defense counsel, in order to gain a tactical advantage, wilfully failed to comply with a statute requiring pretrial disclosure of names of witnesses the defense intended to call. See also Michigan v. Lucas, 500 U.S. 145 (1991): State court erred in supposing that in rape prosecution in which consent was the issue, Sixth Amendment would prohibit in all circumstances exclusion of evidence offered by defendant of prior sexual relations between himself and the victim, because of failure to comply with requirement that pretrial notice be given that such evidence would be introduced. In Williams v. Florida, 399 U.S. 78 (1970), the Court did not decide whether it would be permissible to exclude defendant's alibi evidence because of failure to comply with a pretrial notice requirement, but it did sustain his conviction against challenge under the Fifth Amendment when the prosecution was able to impeach a defense witness by reason of information gained from defendant's compliance with a pretrial notice requirement.

(c) People v. Leahy, 863 P.2d 635, 647–48, 652, 671–72 (Cal.1993): Exclusion of defense witness on ground that he was unworthy of belief was error under state law (although harmless), but did not violate the federal constitution. "[W]e will not lightly assume that a trial court invites federal constitutional scrutiny each and every time it decides, on the basis of particular circumstances, to exclude a defense witness as unworthy of credit." Dissent:

> From these decisions of the high court, I conclude that the Sixth Amendment's compulsory process guarantee requires that defense witnesses be permitted to testify to the jury, regardless of the trial court's apparent distrust of the proposed testimony, if the credibility question is one that the jury is reasonably well equipped to deal with. Here, the reasons for the trial court's apparent distrust of the defense witness—his

prior friendship with defendant, inconsistencies both within his testimony and between his testimony and other evidence in the case—were reasons that the trial jury was competent to assess.

See also Government of Virgin Islands v. Mills, 956 F.2d 443 (3d Cir.1992).

United States v. Scheffer, 44 M.J. 442 (C.A.A.F. 1996). cert. granted, 117 S.Ct. 1817 (1997): Application of Mil.R.Evid. 707 to exclude polygraph evidence offered by accused to rebut attack on his credibility would violate Sixth Amendment right to present a defense if evidence satisfies Daubert v. Merrell Dow Pharmaceutical, Inc., 509 U.S. 579 (1993), see infra p. 962, and Mil.R.Evid 403.

(d) In contrast to constitutional issues raised by exclusion of evidence offered by the defense, consider the problems created by the government's destruction or failure to preserve evidence that might have been useful to the defense. Arizona v. Youngblood, 488 U.S. 51 (1988) (due process not violated because police did not act in bad faith and defendant had other means to attack prosecution's case). See also California v. Trombetta, 467 U.S. 479 (1984).

United States v. Valenzuela–Bernal, 458 U.S. 858 (1982): Neither the Compulsory Process Clause nor the Due Process Clause required dismissal of an indictment for knowingly transporting illegal aliens when, shortly after defendant's arrest and without giving him an opportunity to interview them, the Government deported aliens, other than the one with whose transportation defendant was charged, who had been in the car that defendant had driven. To be entitled to a dismissal of the indictment, defendant was required to make "a plausible showing that the testimony of the deported witnesses would have been material and favorable to his defense, in ways not merely cumulative to the testimony of available witnesses." Id. at 873. The Court made reference to the policy of the Government to enforce the immigration laws by prompt deportation of illegal aliens and the problems involved in keeping in custody large numbers of material witnesses.

(e) Courts and commentators have given increasing attention to the conflict between a criminal defendant's interest in obtaining and introducing evidence and various testimonial privileges. In United States v. Roberts, 503 F.2d 598 (9th Cir.1974), cert. denied, 419 U.S. 1113 (1975), the defendant's conviction was upheld notwithstanding the trial court's refusal to allow him to call as a witness a coindictee who had indicated that he would invoke the privilege against self-incrimination; and in Valdez v. Winans, 738 F.2d 1087, 1089–90 (10th Cir.1984), the court held that the Compulsory Process Clause did not require admission of evidence protected by the lawyer-client privilege. On the other hand, in State v. Jones, 363 So.2d 455 (La.1978), a refusal to order a witness called by the defendant to testify because of the danger of reprisal was held to violate the defendant's right to compulsory process. Pennsylvania v. Ritchie, 480 U.S. 39, 55–56 (1987): In a prosecution for sexual abuse of a child, the defendant had a right under the Due Process Clause to have the trial court examine in camera a file of a state agency made confidential by statute to determine whether the file contained information material to the defendant's case, at least when the statute required the agency to disclose the file on order of a court. If the Compulsory Process Clause required anything in these circumstances, the Court said, it required no more than the Due Process Clause. See infra p. 364 on the Ritchie decision in connection with the

Confrontation Clause. See also infra pp. 895–907 on issues under the Due Process, Confrontation and Compulsory Process Clauses created by the Rape Shield statutes, which prevent a defendant under certain circumstances from introducing evidence of the prior sexual behavior of the victim.

Should a privilege be overridden and a witness compelled to testify because of a defendant's need for evidence? See In re Farber, 394 A.2d 330 (N.J.), cert. denied, 439 U.S. 997 (1978). What if the witness will not answer even when threatened with contempt? When a witness's privilege not to testify is sustained, is it sufficient help to the defendant to inform the jury why the witness is not required to testify? Should the prosecution be dismissed? If the probability that the witness would have given testimony favorable to the defendant and decisive for the case is small, this would seem to give to the defendant an unjustified benefit. Determining by an in camera hearing what testimony from the witness would be likely may be a reasonable way to proceed in the case of some privileges but not others. In some cases compelling the witness to testify even in camera will compromise the policy of the privilege. For further discussion of these problems in connection with the privilege against self-incrimination and the journalist's privilege, see infra pp. 1378–80 and p. 1538. See also Hill, Testimonial Privilege and Fair Trial, 80 Colum.L.Rev. 1173 (1980), and Westen, Reflections on Alfred Hill's "Testimonial Privilege and Fair Trial," 14 U.Mich.J.L.Ref. 371 (1981). On the question of whether immunity should ever be available for witnesses the defendant wishes to call, see infra pp. 1378–80.

For similar problems arising under the Confrontation Clause, see infra pp. 363–66, and for a careful analysis of the relation between the Compulsory Process Clause and the Confrontation Clause, see Westen, The Compulsory Process Clause, 73 Mich.L.Rev. 71 (1974); Westen, Compulsory Process II, 74 Mich.L.Rev. 191 (1975); Westen, Confrontation and Compulsory Process: A Unified Theory of Evidence for Criminal Cases, 91 Harv.L.Rev. 567 (1978).

B. REPRESENTATIVE STATUTES

FEDERAL RULES OF EVIDENCE

Rules 601, 602 and 603 [See Rules Supplement].

ALABAMA CODE (1995)

§ 12–21–162.Witness convicted of crime

(a) No objection must be allowed to the competency of a witness because of his conviction for any crime, except perjury or subornation of perjury.

(b) As affecting his credibility, a witness may be examined touching his conviction for a crime involving moral turpitude, and his answers may be contradicted by other evidence.

§ 12–21–163. Witness having interest

In civil actions and proceedings, there must be no exclusion of any witness because he is a party or interested in the issue tried. . . .

§ 12–21–165. Incompetent witnesses

(a) Persons who have not the use of reason, such as idiots, lunatics during lunacy and children who do not understand the nature of an oath, are incompetent witnesses.

(b) The court must, by examination, decide upon the capacity of one alleged to be incompetent from idiocy, lunacy, insanity, drunkenness or infancy.

CONNECTICUT GEN.STATS.ANN. (1994)

§ 52–145. Certain Witnesses Not Disqualified. Credibility

(a) A person shall not be disqualified as a witness in any action because of, (1) his interest in the outcome of the action as a party or otherwise, (2) his disbelief in the existence of a supreme being, or (3) his conviction of crime.

(b) A person's interest in the outcome of the action or his conviction of crime may be shown for the purpose of affecting his credibility.

For the rules disqualifying judges and jurors as witnesses, see Fed.R.Evid. 605 and 606 and accompanying legislative history. Rule 606(b) under some circumstances bars testimony by jurors designed to undermine the validity of verdicts. Tanner v. United States, 483 U.S. 107 (1987), interpreted 606(b) to prohibit testimony by jurors about drinking and drug-taking by jurors during the trial. See Cammack, The Jurisprudence of Jury Trials: The No Impeachment Rule and the Conditions for Legitimate Decisionmaking, 64 U.Colo.L.Rev. 57 (1993); Diehm, Impeachment of Jury Verdicts: Tanner v. United States and Beyond, 65 St. John's L.Rev. 391 (1991). For the ethical restraints on lawyers testifying as witnesses or accepting employment when there is a likelihood that they will be called to testify, see ABA Annot.Code Professional Responsibility 208–21 (1979) (DR 5–101(B), DR 5–102, EC 5–9, EC 5–10) and ABA Model Rules of Professional Conduct and Code of Judicial Conduct, Rule 3.7 (1983). For the rules relating to the competency of spouses, see infra p. 1494.

C.   The Dead Man Rule

The abolition of the disqualification of witnesses on the ground of interest cannot be considered complete. A significant number of reported cases every year show disqualification under what are commonly termed "Dead Man" laws. Legislation of this kind takes so many different forms that no single statute can be called typical, and interpretative decisions present a welter of confusion and contradiction. The editors offer a highly selective treatment suggestive merely of the general outlines of the subject.

Ladd, the Dead Man Statute: Some Further Observations and a Legislative Proposal

26 Iowa L. Rev. 207 (1941).[1]

Dead man statutes in different states continue to mystify able courts and good lawyers in their endless complexities of interpretation and application to the ever changing facts requiring proof to establish transactions and communications had with a person since deceased. Statutes vary greatly as do the interpretations of similar statutes. The basic objective of all statutes is the same. Survivors of a deceased person are looked upon with suspicion as persons ready on first opportunity to fabricate false claims against the decedent's estate because the deceased is unable to repudiate them. The right of living claimants

---

1. Copyright 1941 University of Iowa (Iowa Law Review).

to establish honest claims is sacrificed because of the danger that a substantially greater number of the survivors would take advantage of the situation and give perjured testimony for their gain. The existence of the dead man statutes represents the judgment of legislative bodies that the general honesty and truthfulness of people in modern society is at a pretty low ebb and that all it takes is the motive of interest plus a good chance created by death of one of the parties to cause the majority of people to concoct false claims to plunder the estates of deceased persons. The core of these statutes goes to the simple question of the truthfulness of people today. It must be based upon a normative standard of the people as a whole and can be justified only on the theory that dishonesty outweighs honesty so much that all people should be rendered incompetent to testify upon their claims, transactions, and communications with another member of society since deceased. Originating at the time when general disqualification of witnesses because of interest as it existed at common law was abolished, the dead man statutes reflect the doubts of that day by excepting from the qualifying statutes claimants and interested persons from testifying as to their dealings with persons since deceased. Once enacted these statutes have been slow to be changed. Even if the premise back of the statutes were accepted, the statutes would be psychologically unsound because the statutes do not render the witnesses totally incompetent but incompetent only as to certain subject matter of testimony. Consequently if the witness were prone to falsify, there is still ample opportunity to do so by testifying to matters not within range of the exclusion and still sufficient to establish a claim. This shows one of the greatest objections to the statutes, namely, that it has not prevented the dishonest from establishing false claims and yet it has prevented the truthful litigant from testifying to establish honest demands. While practically every authority has condemned the statute and urged its abolition, bad legislation is often harder to change than an objectionable judicial opinion, and it may be some time before the statute is repealed. Until this is done, lawyers and courts are going to be forced to deal with the dead man statute....

NOTES

1. The American Law Institute Model Code of Evidence, Rule 101 (1942), and the Uniform Rules of Evidence, Rule 7 (1954), rejected the Dead Man Rule. Federal Rule of Evidence 601 also rejects it, except that the way is left open for the application of state Dead Man statutes in civil cases if proffered testimony bears upon an element of a claim or defense as to which state law supplies the rule of decision. The sentence in Rule 601 saving the application of state law in regard to competence was added by Congress to the rule adopted by the Supreme Court. For the legislative history of this change, see 3 Weinstein and Berger, Evidence 601-1 to 601-14. Adoption of Rule 601 by a state will usually repeal the state Dead Man statute, see Annot., 50 A.L.R. 4th 1238 (1986), but not always. See Wis. Stat. Annot. §§ 885.16, 906.01 (West 1995).

2. For general discussions of the Dead Man statutes, see Report of Committee on Administration and Distribution of Decedents' Estates, Dead Man Statutes: Their Purposes, Effect, and Future, 7 Real Prop., Prob. & Tr.J. 343 (1972); Ray, Dead Man's Statutes, 24 Ohio St. L. J. 89 (1963); Ford, Dead-man's Statute in Auto Collision Cases, 24 Ala. Law. 138 (1963); Stout, Should The Dead Man's Statute Apply to Automobile Collisions?, 38 Tex. L. Rev. 14 (1959); Coker, Competency of a Defendant to Testify When Sued Under the Wrongful Death Statute, 29 Miss. L. J. 258 (1958); Maguire, Witnesses—Suppression of Testimony by Reason of Death, 6 Am. U. L. Rev. 1 (1957); Ray, The Dead Man's Statute—A Relic of the Past, 10 Sw. L. J. 390 (1956).

Zeigler v. Moore

Supreme Court of Nevada, 1959.
75 Nev. 91, 335 P.2d 425.

■ BADT, JUSTICE. This appeal is taken from an order and judgment of involuntary dismissal entered on defendant's motion under Rule 41(b) NRCP at the conclusion of plaintiff's case.

Plaintiff sued one Al Christ for damages alleging that her automobile was struck in the rear by a car negligently operated by Christ in August 1955 on Highway 40 about one and one-half miles west of Winnemucca, while plaintiff was driving easterly toward that city. Christ answered, denying negligence but admitting a collision between the two cars. He also pleaded plaintiff's contributory negligence. Christ died in May 1957 and Robert Moore was substituted as his administrator before trial. At the trial the court excluded under the dead man's rule certain testimony of the plaintiff and of plaintiff's witness, sheriff Delbert Moore. These and other rulings are assigned as error.

. . .

Delbert Moore, sheriff of Humboldt County, testified that Christ, after the accident, had come to the office and made an "accident report" and, in his conversation in making the report, talked to the witness "about how the accident happened." He was then asked: "What did he tell you?" Objection on the ground "that this witness is rendered incompetent by reason of § 48.010 NRS" was sustained.

The statute commonly known as the dead man's rule now appears, in pertinent part, in our codes as NRS 48.010 and 48.030, as follows:

"48.010 1. All persons, without exception, otherwise than as specified in this chapter, who, having organs of sense, can perceive, and perceiving can make known their perceptions to others, may be witnesses in any action or proceeding in any court of the state. Facts which, by the common law, would cause the exclusion of witnesses, may still be shown for the purpose of affecting their credibility. No person shall be allowed to testify:

"(a) When the other party to the transaction is dead.

"(b) When the opposite party to the action, . . . is the representative of a deceased person, when the facts to be proven transpired before the death of such deceased person; . . .

"48.030 The following persons cannot be witnesses: . . .

"3. Parties to an action . . . against an executor or administrator upon a claim or demand against the estate of a deceased person, as to any matter of fact occurring before the death of such deceased person."

. . .

The error assigned in sustaining the objection to the testimony of sheriff Delbert Moore as to statements made to him by the decedent is well taken. The statutory exclusion of the testimony of witnesses under the sections above quoted has been consistently held by this court not to apply to disinterested third persons. . . .

. . .

Appellant assigns as error the court's ruling precluding appellant from testifying *as to any fact* prior to Christ's death. The position taken by the respective parties is somewhat confusing. Respondent, in support of the court's ruling, recites the way the issue arose as follows: "At the trial appellant was called as a witness in her own behalf to testify *to the facts of the accident* "and says that the question presented is "whether the survivor of an automobile accident can give uncontradicted testimony *as to the manner in which the collision occurred* when the lips of the other party are sealed by death." However, respondent's objection as made in the trial court and the rulings which the trial court was prevailed on to make by reason of such objection were far broader than the enunciation of the proper rule sought from this court and as expressed in italics above. Plaintiff took the stand and was asked, "Will you please state your name?" Objection was made that the plaintiff "is rendered incompetent [to testify] under the so-called Nevada dead man's statute." Thereupon the jury was excused and over thirty pages of the transcript are devoted to argument, whereupon the objection was sustained. Thereupon the following took place:

"Mr. Jensen: Now, just so I understand the court's ruling, . . . that means that under the court's ruling that plaintiff cannot testify as to any fact prior to May 11th, 1957, May 11th being the death of the decedent? Right?

"Mr. Taber: Well, that is the basis of my objection, yes.

"The Court: Yes.

"Mr. Jensen: So then any fact that occurred prior to May 11, 1957, that relates to the medical bills sustained, and relates to any other facts related to the accident?

"Mr. Taber: Medical bills haven't been offered.

"Mr. Jensen: Yes. So the ruling would exclude them?

"The Court: Yes."

Appellant then proceeded to make an offer of proof including her age, place of employment, rate of employment, nature and hours of employment, her leaving of her place of employment, the route pursued by her, the nature of the road, visibility, traffic, the striking of her car from behind, her confinement in the hospital, her doctor bills, the amount of her lost wages and her pain and suffering.

She also offered to testify that, presumably at the time when defendant was close enough behind her to have observed the matters testified to and could have contradicted the same of his own knowledge, "at no time prior to the time of collision did she cause the brakes to be applied in a sudden manner, nor did she indicate that she was going to make either a left or a right turn . . . that her car was suddenly and without warning hit from the rear."

The offer of proof was objected to in its entirety and was denied in its entirety.

Appellant now contends as follows: "She is not attempting to testify that the decedent's car was driven in a reckless manner. She is not by any direct statement or inference attempting to fix blame or attach fault to any person. Stating it succinctly, she merely desires to testify that she was driving down the highway in the proper lane, at a speed reasonable under the circumstances and that thereafter her car was struck in the rear."

It will thus be seen that on the one hand respondent obtained an exclusionary ruling far broader than the one he now seeks to sustain; and on the other hand appellant sought, by her offer of proof, to testify in far wider scope than she now claims admissible.

Appellant insists first in this respect that she is not precluded from testifying under NRS 48.010(1)(a) because the decedent cannot be said to be "the other party to the transaction" inasmuch as no "transaction" was involved; that a tort action is not a transaction. There is indeed some authority to support this view. See Shaneybrook v. Blizzard, 1956, 209 Md. 304, 121 A.2d 218. In many cases this is based upon the wording of the particular state statute involved and is of no assistance here. The Maryland case just cited, for example, expresses a preference for the New York rule. The New York statute, Civil Practice Act, § 347, however, definitely fixed the exclusion as applying to testimony concerning a "personal transaction or communication" with the decedent. The overwhelming weight of authority supports the rule that the dead man's statute applies to actions ex delicto and that such actions are embraced within the statutory use of the word "transactions." 97 C.J.S. Witnesses § 133, note 92, p. 565; 58 Am.Jur. 151, Witnesses, § 223. In Warren v. DeLong, 59 Nev. 481, 97 P.2d 792, 795, this court had under consideration our statute providing that if the defendant omit to set up a counterclaim arising "out of the transaction" he could not afterward maintain an action against the plaintiff therefor. N.C.L.1929, §§ 8603, 8604. This court there held that the term "transaction" was broader than "contract" and broader than "tort" and that it might include either or both. It approved the setting up of a counterclaim for conversion under such statute.

If then we apply the statute to tort actions as well as personal transactions between the parties the testimony of the plaintiff was properly excluded under the holdings of this court in earlier cases, defining the purpose and extent of the rule with reference to those matters which the decedent could have contradicted of his own knowledge. By the same token, the appellant's testimony as to her medical bills, her pain and suffering and matters of like nature which the decedent could not have contradicted of his own knowledge, was clearly admissible and the rejection of such testimony was prejudicial error.

Those items were entirely beyond the operation of the reasons for the rule of exclusion repeatedly enunciated by this court: To prevent the living from obtaining unfair advantage because of death of the other. Maitia v. Allied Land & Live Stock Co., 49 Nev. 451, 248 P. 893. Nor shall the living be entitled to the undue advantage of giving his own uncontradicted and unexplained account of what transpired beyond possibility of contradiction by the decedent. Reinhart v. Echave, 43 Nev. 323, 185 P. 1070, rehearing denied 43 Nev. 323, 187 P. 1006. The whole object of the code provision is to place the living and dead on terms of perfect equality, and, the dead not being able to testify, the living shall not. Bright v. Virginia & Gold Hill Water Co., 9 Cir., 270 F. 410. The object of the statute is to prevent one interested party from giving testimony when the other party's lips are sealed by death. Goldsworthy v. Johnson, 45 Nev. 355, 204 P. 505. But when the above stated reasons for the rule do not appear, this court has not hesitated to admit in evidence the testimony of an interested party. Goldsworthy v. Johnson, supra; Maitia v. Allied Land & Live Stock Co., supra; Hough v. Reserve Gold Mining Co., 55 Nev. 375, 35 P.2d 742; Edmonds v. Perry, 62 Nev. 41, 140 P.2d 566. Therefore the rule would not preclude plaintiff's description of her own actions and the road conditions prior to the point when within limitations of time or space the decedent could have contradicted her testimony of his own knowledge.

The lines delimiting the actual "transaction" within the knowledge of the decedent must be drawn by the trial court. Whether these lines are drawn within limits of space or within limits of time within which matters were under the observation of the decedent, or both, must likewise be determined by the trial court.

Finally it is contended by appellant that the effect of our statute providing for the survival of tort actions against the estate of a decedent (NRS 41.110) is entirely destroyed by application of the dead man's rule in cases such as the present one where the collision occurs in the desert without witnesses other than the parties. This is not necessarily so. In virtually all cases much physical evidence is available—skid marks, tire tracks, the condition of the respective cars involved showing the nature of the collision, etc. Appellant further contends that inasmuch as the application of the dead man's rule is condemned by all writers of the law of evidence as leading to harsh and unjust results (see Wright v. Wilson, 3 Cir., 154 F.2d 616, 170 A.L.R. 1237) this court should not, in a situation that is res integra in this state, extend its application to tort actions. This, however, is a matter of public policy, in which are balanced against each other the chance of injustice in individual cases on the one hand and the protection of estates from fraudulent demands on the other. A change of policy having such far-reaching results should be a matter for consideration by the legislature rather than of the court. . . .

Reversed and remanded for new trial.

■ MERRILL, C.J., and McNAMEE, J., concur.[2]

NOTES

1. The position taken by the court in Zeigler is widely accepted. E.g., Stathas v. Wade Estate, 380 A.2d 482 (Pa.Super.1977) (auto accident case: plaintiffs' testimony regarding their losses not barred though incurred while defendant's decedent still alive); Foster v. Englewood Hospital Association, 313 N.E.2d 255, 264–67 (Ill.App.1974) (in wrongful death action widow of deceased patient not barred from testifying against estate of allegedly negligent doctor regarding her marriage to patient and births of their children).

But in Tompkins v. DeLeon, 595 P.2d 242 (Colo.1979), the Supreme Court of Colorado held that the Dead Man statute was "clear and unambiguous" in prohibiting survivors of an automobile accident from testifying to pain and suffering that they had endured prior to the decedent's death. The statute allowed testimony by a party or interested person only to "facts occurring after the death of such deceased person." The dissenting opinion observed: "The majority of this court . . . has construed the statute to exclude evidence not intended to be excluded, evidence which could not have been rebutted by the decedent had he lived, evidence of a kind not within the rationale for which the statute sanctions exclusion, evidence whose exclusion produced an injustice not intended or required by the statute. . . . Whether the legislature has power for an irrelevant reason to preclude a witness from giving material testimony in a court trial raises serious issues touching the constitutionality of the statute. . . . I cannot believe that the majority of this court would have inflicted the obvious injustice resulting from today's decision if they did not believe that the General Assembly's action compelled this result. Although I respectfully disagree with their premise that they are precedent-bound, I am hopeful that a fair-minded General Assembly will give early consideration to the problem exemplified in this case." Id. at 246, 248. The legislature responded to the dissent's hope by enacting Colo. Rev. Stat. Ann. § 13–90–102 (1989), which permits the survivor to testify to events about which the deceased could not have testified of his own knowledge.

2. In 1971 Nevada abolished its Dead Man statute. Nev. Rev. Stat. § 50.015 (1995).

Romines v. Illinois Motor Freight, Inc., 158 N.E.2d 97 (Ill.App.1959): Wrongful death action arising out of vehicular collision. Defendant truck driver attempted to testify that the day after the accident he went to the scene of the accident and observed marks on the pavement. Held: Testimony properly excluded.

2.   *Grant v. Griffin,* 390 S.W.2d 746 (Tex.1965), presented the question whether an automobile ride in which increasing intoxication and recklessness of the driver finally caused his death and injury to his passenger was a "transaction" between the two. Should it make any difference that the passenger before the catastrophe made futile efforts to part company with the driver? Cf. *Harper v. Johnson,* 345 S.W.2d 277 (Tex.1961) (automobile-truck collision between strangers not a transaction).

Germann v. Matriss, 260 A.2d 825, 833–40 (N.J.1970): Suit arising out of death of patient from tetanus poisoning following extraction of teeth by defendant dentist. Claim of negligence in failure properly to sterilize denture inserted after extraction and affirmative defense of contributory negligence in patient's failure to follow post-operative instructions. Held: The New Jersey statute, which speaks of "oral testimony of a promise, statement or act" of the decedent, does not prohibit defendant dentist's testimony about his and the patient's behavior. The statute embraces only "claims or defenses dependent upon undertakings having their origin in an express or implied relationship of a personal and mutual nature." No extension of coverage was intended by the change from earlier statutory language—"transaction with or statement . . . by the decedent."

Burns v. Caughman, 178 S.E.2d 151 (S.C.1970): Action by sister against brother's estate to recover for value of household services rendered under implied contract. Held: Sister's testimony as to services rendered barred.

Midler v. Shapiro, 364 A.2d 99, 107–09 (Md.App.1976): Action by son, personal representative of deceased mother, against niece to recover proceeds of joint bank accounts opened in the names of the mother and the niece in which the mother had deposited money. The issue was whether the niece had abused a confidential relationship with the mother in order to obtain an interest in the bank accounts. Held: Error, but harmless, to allow the niece to testify that she had nothing to do with the opening of the accounts. "[T]estimony that a party litigant did not participate in a transaction with a decedent is as much a violation of the statute as is testimony that they did participate and why they did so."

3.   *Clark v. A. Bazzoni & Co.,* 129 N.E.2d 435 (Ill.App.1955): In action for personal injuries arising out of collision between truck and bicycle against corporate owner of truck and estate of its driver, although plaintiff bicycle rider may have been barred from testifying about the accident against the driver's estate, he was not barred from testifying against the corporate defendant.

State Farm Life Ins. Co. v. Fort Wayne Nat'l Bank, 474 N.E.2d 524 (Ind.App.1985): In action by the personal representative of a decedent against an insurance company and its agents for negligent failure of the agents to warn the decedent of the tax consequences of making himself the owner of an insurance policy rather than making the beneficiary the owner, the Dead Man statute barred the agents from testifying to statements the decedent had made at the time he applied for insurance.

Bengyak v. Rosin, 437 So.2d 220, 221 (Fla.Dist.Ct.App.1983): In suit on a note, the Dead Man statute did not prevent the defendant-obligor from testifying that the agent of the obligee had released the defendant from the obligation represented by the note, even though the agent was dead at the time of trial.

Stevens v. Thompson, 184 So.2d 140 (Ala.1966): Exchange of gunfire between plaintiff and defendant's decedent resulted in wounding of plaintiff and death of decedent. Plaintiff sued for his injuries, defendant interposed a plea of recoupment for wrongful death. Held: Assuming without deciding that the Dead Man statute prevented plaintiff from testifying in support of his claim, it did not prevent him from testifying in defense to the plea of recoupment. The damages recoverable on the plea of recoupment are not assets of decedent's estate.

Lowry v. Ireland Bank, 779 P.2d 22, 25 (Idaho App.1989): In suit by widow against bank for payment of credit life insurance proceeds, Dead Man statute interpreted not to preclude bank from introducing testimony of bank manager of telephone conversation with deceased husband. "The statute does not apply to evidence used to defend against a claim. Because the evidence at issue here was used to defeat Mrs. Lowry's claim, I.R.E. 601(b) is inapposite."

4. If the survivor's testimony is excluded, does it follow that his hearsay statements should also be excluded? See Goldstein v. Sklar, 216 A.2d 298, 306–07 (Me.1966).

5. Waiver of the statute. In McGugart v. Brumback, 463 P.2d 140 (Wash. 1969), a court divided 5 to 4 overruled earlier decisions and held that the Dead Man Statute is not waived when the personal representative of the decedent submits interrogatories to the survivor and receives answers thereto and the answers are not introduced into evidence.

At a time when depositions were always taken with a view toward introducing them in evidence and broad questions for purposes of discovery were prohibited, there was reason for the rule that objections to a party's competency were waived by deposing that party—particularly when the party questioned also waived any objections not made during the taking of the deposition.

. . .

Further, the conclusion that the mere taking of a deposition constitutes a waiver is negated by CR 26(f), which reads:

A party shall not be deemed to make a person his own witness for any purpose by taking his deposition. The introduction in evidence of the deposition or any part thereof for any purpose other than that of contradicting or impeaching the deponent makes the deponent the witness of the party introducing the deposition, . . .

. . .

This mutual access to knowledge, secured by discovery, is a basic premise upon which civil litigation is now conducted and its availability should not be strictly contingent upon the rules of evidence or competency as are applied at trial.

To hold that the mere *taking* of a deposition constitutes a waiver arbitrarily forces the decedent's representative to forego either the protection of the deadman's statute or the benefit of the discovery processes. Judicial dissatisfaction with the deadman's statute as expressed by some legal writers should not be used as an excuse to deprive a personal representative of an otherwise acceptable and acknowledged benefit of a fact finding process. The wisdom of the deadman's statute is a matter which has been determined by the legislature. The prudent personal representative can hardly be expected to waive a statutory protection and thus risk an unwarranted exposure for heirs, legatees and other claimants. The result, for all practical purposes, is that an estate is deprived of the discovery machinery available to other civil litigants. Any imbalance of the relationship between a decedent's estate and a claimant against the estate is created by the deadman's statute, not by a legitimate use of discovery procedures.

HAMILTON, J., dissenting:

[It] is reasonable to conclude that the basic purpose of the first sentence of Rule 26(f), supra, is to enhance the opportunity to reveal truth and uncover falsity at the trial of a cause, by permitting a party before trial to freely seek and lay a foundation upon which to impeach or otherwise mount attacks upon the credibility of the opposing party's claim at the time of trial. Such a purpose, in my view, is inconsistent with the majority's expansion of the deadman's statute to the point where a claimant's mouth can now be forced open during pretrial discovery but may be effectively and unfairly closed at trial. Although the majority's approach may materially aid a personal representative in his pretrial search for the truth, it appears to me that it can seriously hamper a fair and equal revelation of the same truth at the time of trial.... Thus, the majority would permit the personal representative on behalf of the estate to explore by way of oral examination, depositions, written interrogatories, and requests for admission of facts every facet of the claimant's cause; extract and shrewdly utilize the favorable information while discarding the unfavorable matter; and at trial force the claimant to overcome not only the usually heavy burden of proof but also the restrictions of the deadman's statute. This, the majority contends, is essential to maintain a fair balance between the parties.... [I]n my view, our former rule provided a happy balance between the deadman's statute and pretrial discovery.

Reaching the same result as the McGugart decision are Plummer v. Ulsh, 229 N.E.2d 799 (Ind.1967), and Hortman v. Henderson, 434 F.2d 77 (7th Cir.1970). See also Bishop, Waiver of the Missouri Dead Man's Statute, 39 Mo. L. Rev. 218 (1974); Degnan, The Evidence Law of Discovery: Exclusion of Evidence Because of Fear of Perjury, 43 Tex. L. Rev. 435–44 (1965); Comment, Pre–Trial Discovery in Pennsylvania: Requiem for the Dead Man's Act?, 30 U. Pitt. L. Rev. 315 (1968); Annot., 35 A.L.R.3d 955 (1971); Annot., 23 A.L.R.3d 389 (1969).

In Johnson v. Mielke, 181 N.W.2d 503, 509 (Wis.1970), an action for an accounting against JM and others brought by an executrix, the executrix called JM as an adverse witness. By skillfully limiting examination of JM, the executrix avoided waiver of the Dead Man Statute as to critical aspects of activities and the state of mind of the decedent concerning which JM sought to testify. See Note, 45 Chi.–Kent L. Rev. 60, 61 (1968).

6. Some states have repealed their Dead Man statutes altogether. E.g., Ark. Code Ann. § 16–41–101 (Michie 1995); Ga. Code Ann. 24–9–1 (1995); Kan. Stat. Ann. § 60–407 (1995); Ky. Rev. Stat. Ann. 421.210 (Baldwin 1995); Minn. R. Evid. 617 (1996); Mont. R. Evid. 601 (1995); Nev. Rev. Stat. §§ 48.075, 50.015 (1995); Okla. Stat. Ann. tit. 12 § 2606 (West 1995).

Other states allow the survivor to testify, but only if the testimony is corroborated. E.g., Ariz. Rev. Stat. Ann. § 12–2251 (1995) (See Troutman v. Valley Nat. Bank, 826 P.2d 810 (Ariz.App.1992)); Tex. R. Civ. Evid. 601 (1995).

New Jersey, in 1960, abandoned its rule excluding the survivor's testimony and adopted instead a requirement that a claim or defense, supported by oral testimony of a promise, statement or act of a decedent, be established by "clear and convincing proof." N. J. Stat. Ann. § 2A: 81–2 (West 1995). This change is interestingly discussed in Germann v. Matriss, 260 A.2d 825 (N.J.1970).

Some states allow the survivor to testify, but at the same time allow evidence of hearsay statements by the decedent to come in. In some cases the hearsay is let in without qualification, in others only if the decedent made the hearsay statement in good faith and on his personal knowledge. E.g., Cal. Evid. Code §§ 1227, 1261 (West 1995); Conn. Gen. Stat. Ann. § 52–172 (1995); N. H. R. Evid. 864(b)(5) (1995); Ohio Rev. Code Ann., Rules of Court, Evidence Rules 601, 804(b)(5) (1995) (see Johnson v. Porter, 471 N.E.2d 484 (Ohio 1984)); S. D. Cod. L. Ann. 19–16–34 (1996) and S. D. R. Evid. 804(b)(5) (1996).

Virginia both requires corroboration of the survivor's testimony and admits hearsay statements by the decedent. Va. Code Ann. § 8.01–397 (1996). See also Wyom. Stat. § 1–12–102 (1996) and Wyom.R.Evid. 601 (1996).

J. Weinstein and M. Berger, 3 Weinstein's Evidence 601–21, point out that the effect of the second sentence in Fed.R.Evid. 601 may be in some cases where state law provides the rule of decision, to let in decedent's hearsay statements that otherwise would not be admissible under the Federal Rules of Evidence.

For a discussion of alternatives to the traditional Dead Man statute, see Comment, Illinois' Amended Dead Man's Act: A Partial Reform, 1973 Univ. Ill. L. For. 700.

It will be seen from the foregoing that the trend is running strongly against Dead Man statutes.

7. For a discussion of the battle in one state to modify the Dead Man statute and the reasons given by the bar for rejecting change, see 5 Weinstein, Korn and Miller, New York Civil Practice ¶¶ 4519.01–4510.03.

D.   CORROBORATION

If the Dead Man laws are remnants of earlier attitudes about achieving accuracy through exclusion of classes of witnesses believed to be unreliable, so also requirements of corroboration of certain kinds of evidence often find their origin in earlier systems of proof that stressed the quantity and independence of evidentiary sources, rather than simply the probative value of all the evidence introduced. But if it can be said in the case of the Dead Man laws that this survival from the past is gradually fading away, it is not clear that such a statement can be made about corroboration requirements. Although in some areas of law corroboration requirements that long obtained have recently been abandoned, in other areas corroboration requirements have recently been instituted.

A corroboration requirement is found in Article III, section 3 of the Constitution: "No Person shall be convicted of treason unless on the testimony of two Witnesses to the same overt Act, or on Confession in open Court."

In many jurisdictions, corroboration is required for a valid conviction of perjury. See, e.g., Commonwealth v. Butler, 601 A.2d 268 (Pa.1991). In reaffirming the requirement of corroboration of perjury in federal law, the Supreme Court, in Weiler v. United States, 323 U.S. 606 (1945), justified the requirement on the ground that "[the] rules of law must be so fashioned as to protect honest witnesses from hasty and spiteful retaliation in the form of unfounded perjury prosecutions." See also Model Penal Code, Comment to § 241.1 (9) (1980).

It is universally held in American jurisdictions that a defendant may not be convicted on his own confession alone, but that the confession must be corroborated by other evidence. E.g., Warszower v. United States, 312 U.S. 342 (1941); Opper v. United States, 348 U.S. 84 (1954). See Comment, 1984 Wis. L. Rev. 1121; 103 U. Pa. L. Rev. 638 (1955). The requirement usually is extended beyond formal confessions to government officials to include all admissions, at least if made after the commission of the crime. Although fear of police coercion and other improper practices has sometimes been cited as a reason for the requirement, the fact that the requirement is usually applied to all inculpatory admissions, not just to those made in custody, and that it has continued to be applied even though other mechanisms have been developed to deter these practices—e.g., Miranda v. Arizona, 384 U.S. 436 (1966)—suggests that the policy of the requirement goes beyond concern with coercion. See the reference in Government of Virgin Islands v. Harris, 938 F.2d 401, 409 (3d Cir.1991), to the observation that "physically uncoerced false confessions occur with sufficient regularity to justify prophylactic measures." It is not unusual for mentally unstable persons to confess to crimes when there has been no crime at all or if there was a crime, they did not commit it. See Comment, 1984 Wis. L. Rev. 1121, 1155–79.

The testimony of an accomplice is required to be corroborated in many jurisdictions. See 96 A.L.R.2d 1185 (1964); 53 A.L.R.2d 812, 817 (1957) (thief and receiver).

In most jurisdictions it formerly was required in prosecutions for sexual offenses, most notably rape, that the testimony of the complaining witness be corroborated. This requirement has been swept away as part of a movement that has had other consequences as well. See Fed. R. Evid. 412, limiting the admissibility in sexual misconduct cases of evidence of the alleged victim's sexual conduct or predisposition, infra p. 901. The provision of the Model Penal Code relating to sexual offenses, § 213.6(5) (1980), retains the corroboration requirement. The Comment to this provision includes this explanation:

> [Retaining the corroboration requirement is] only a particular implementation of the general policy that uncertainty should be resolved in favor of the accused. Thus, it may seem off point to conclude, as does one commentator, that "the difficulty of defending against an uncorroborated rape accusation is far less than the difficulty in prosecuting one successfully."
> ... Far from being a reason to abandon the corroboration requirement, that is precisely its objective.

§ 213.6, Comment 6, at p. 429. However, if it is judged that the burden of proof and the determination of the sufficiency of the evidence generally provide a criminal defendant with adequate protection against erroneous conviction, must it not be that an additional requirement of corroboration in sexual cases reflects a judgment of special unreliability on the testimony of complaining witnesses in those cases?

Corroboration has often been required as to the grounds for divorce. See 15 A.L.R.2d 170 (1951); De Baillet–Latour v. De Baillet–Latour, 94 N.E.2d 715 (N.Y.1950), supra p. 94.

Declarations against penal interest by third persons, offered by criminal defendants to exonerate themselves, is one of the situations referred to above in which a requirement of corroboration has recently been established. Prior to adoption of the Federal Rules of Evidence, extrajudicial declarations against penal interest by third persons, as contrasted with declarations against pecuniary or proprietary interest, were found insufficiently reliable to justify exemption from the hearsay rule. Judicial decisions manifested a fear that criminals would orchestrate the manufacture of confessions by third persons, who would then conveniently become unavailable. But in 1973, the Supreme Court in Chambers v. Mississippi, 410 U.S. 284 (1973), supra p. 261, held that a state evidence rule which prohibited a criminal defendant from introducing inculpatory statements by a third person, when accompanied by another state rule that prevented the defendant from cross-examining that very person about the inculpatory statements, in the circumstances presented by the case violated the defendant's constitutional right to present evidence. Fed. R. Evid. 804(b)(3) provides: A hearsay statement "tending to expose the declarant to criminal liability and offered to exculpate the accused is not admissible unless corroborating circumstances clearly indicate the trustworthiness of the statement." See Note, The Corroboration Requirement (or Lack Thereof) for Statements Against Penal Interest in Wisconsin: State v. Anderson, 1989 Wis. L. Rev. 403, discussing state rules of Evidence that adopted a preliminary version of the Federal Rules.

Another situation in which a corroboration requirement has emerged is in connection with hearsay statements made by children in sexual abuse cases. The path of change here has been similar to that in the case of hearsay statements against penal interest: Hearsay statements by children in sexual abuse cases generally were held inadmissible. Public concern with child sexual abuse led to permitting such statements into evidence if reliable and corroborated. See, e.g., In re Nicole V., 518 N.E.2d 914 (N.Y.1987); Stevens v. People, 796 P.2d 946 (Colo.1990): Hearsay statement of child admitted if reliable, but if child unavailable, statement must be corroborated.

It will be noted that in the preceding catalogue there are two distinct but related types of situations in which corroboration is required. In one type, what is required to be corroborated is an item of evidence that is otherwise free from objection under any exclusionary rule. Thus the testimony of a witness in a perjury prosecution regarding the falsity of what the defendant said under oath is not objectionable under any other rule of evidence; nevertheless it must be corroborated. In the other type of situation, the evidence that is required to be corroborated may be subject to objection under another exclusionary rule: extrajudicial statements against penal interest and by children in sexual abuse cases are hearsay. As a consequence, in the second type of case, questions are presented both whether the extrajudicial statement is sufficiently reliable to come within an exception to the exclusionary rule and whether the corroboration requirement is satisfied. See Stevens v. People, 796 P.2d 946, 951 (Colo. 1990) (reliability and corroboration requirements distinct).

Should the requirement of corroboration be conceived as a requirement governing the admissibility of evidence or as a requirement regarding the necessary basis for conviction? This question is asked in 1 McCormick, Evidence 561–62 (4th ed. 1992). See also Comment, 1984 Wis. L. Rev. 1121, 1136–37; Government of Virgin Islands v. Harris, 938 F.2d 401, 409 n. 6 (3d Cir.1991) (doctrine that corpus delicti must be corroborated in the case of a confession governs the admissibility of evidence, not sufficiency). Does it make any difference?

What must be the probative force of the corroborating evidence? Under the constitutional requirement of two witnesses for treason, is it enough that the testimony of one witness is barely relevant or must each witness's testimony have substantial probative value? Weiler v. United States, 323 U.S. 606, 610 (1945): Corroborating evidence in perjury prosecution must be trustworthy.

Opper v. United States, 348 U.S. 84, 92 (1954), which concerns corroboration of confessions, speaks of substantial corroborating evidence. The Wisconsin Rules of Evidence, which adopted the preliminary draft of the Federal Rules, require in the case of a declaration against penal interest simply that it be corroborated, whereas Fed. R. Evid. 804(b)(3) provides that such a declaration is not admissible "unless corroborating circumstances clearly indicate the trustworthiness of the statement."

More difficult than the question of the probative value required for corroboration is the question as to what are the permissible means by which that probative value may be achieved. This problem is raised by the following passages from two decisions concerned with the corroboration of confessions.

Opper v. United States, 348 U.S. 84, 93 (1954):

It is necessary, therefore, to require the Government to introduce substantial independent evidence which would tend to establish the trustworthiness of the statement.

Smith v. United States, 348 U.S. 147, 156 (1954):

All elements of the offense must be established by independent evidence or corroborated admissions, but one available mode of corroboration is for the independent evidence to bolster the confession itself and thereby prove the offense "through" the statements of the accused.

Wong Sun v. United States, 371 U.S. 471, 489 (1963), another confession case, speaks of "extrinsic corroboration."

Corroborating evidence may be relevant to an ultimate issue entirely independently of the item of evidence it is introduced to corroborate. Thus if two witnesses saw an accident, the testimony of either has the capacity to alter probabilities as to how the accident occurred even if the testimony of the other is not introduced. When in the Opper and Smith cases the Court speaks of "independent" evidence, does it mean corroborating evidence that is relevant in this way? See In re Nicole V., 518 N.E.2d 914, 919 (N.Y.1987) (child sexual abuse case; the extrajudicial statements of two brothers may cross-corroborate each other). On the other hand, corroborating evidence may be relevant to an ultimate issue only if it accompanies the evidence intended to be corroborated, although its relevance does not depend upon the same kind of background information that the probative value of the evidence to be corroborated depends upon. See the reference in Government of Virgin Islands v. Harris, 938 F.2d 401, 410 (3d Cir.1991), to the possibility of corroborating a confession by evidence that it contained information that only the criminal would have known; In re Nicole V., 518 N.E.2d 914 (N.Y.1987): Extrajudicial statements of children in sexual abuse case corroborated by evidence of the children's disturbed behavior and the testimony of an expert that such behavior is characteristic of sexually abused children. See also De Baillet–Latour v. De Baillet–Latour, supra p. 94. The corroborating evidence in the Smith and Opper cases appears to have been independent in this sense. Finally, the corroborating evidence may be relevant only if it accompanies the evidence to be corroborated and in addition its probative value depends upon the same kind of background information as does the probative value of the evidence to be corroborated. See Annot., 96 A.L.R.2d 1185 (1964): Testimony of accomplice may not be corroborated by real evidence that can only be authenticated by the testimony of the accomplice. Evidence of circumstances surrounding the making of a confession that make it unlikely the person who made the confession failed to consider carefully what he remembered or to speak sincerely would be corroborating evidence of this sort. Would corroborating evidence of this sort satisfy the reason for having a corroboration requirement? If corroboration of this sort is acceptable, it may be difficult to maintain a distinction between the corroboration requirement and the requirement of sufficiency. See Comment to Model Penal Code § 241.1 (6) (1980): The corroboration requirement for perjury may be "in effect only a special gloss on 'reasonable doubt.'" Compare the idea expressed in the Opper and Smith decisions that the corroborating evidence must be "independent" with the Court's insistence that in judging the reliability of an extrajudicial statement to determine its admissibility under the Confrontation Clause, it is permissible only to take into account circumstances affecting the credibility of the statement, not other evidence that may be relevant to the ultimate issue. See Idaho v. Wright, 497 U.S. 805 (1990).

Evidence relevant to which elements of an offense must be corroborated? All the elements of the offense or only some? In Smith v. United States, 348 U.S. 147, 156 (1954), in the context of confessions, the Court said that all elements of the offense must be corroborated. In the same case, however, it seemed to qualify this statement by suggesting that admissions relevant to an element of the offense might not need to be corroborated if not "basic to the Government's case." But then the Court qualified the qualification by saying: "[W]here a fact is sufficiently important that the Government adduces extrajudicial statements of the accused bearing on its existence, and then relies on its existence to sustain the defendant's conviction, there is need for corroboration." Id. at 158 n. 4. In Wong Sun v. United States, 371 U.S. 471, 490 n. 15 (1963), the Court said that when a crime involves physical damage to person or property, there need be corroboration only of the corpus delicti—the fact of damage and a criminal cause of the damage—but not that the defendant was the cause. However, when there is no tangible object involved, corroboration must implicate the accused. In perjury prosecutions, it is generally accepted that the only element of the offense that needs to be corroborated is the falsity of the statement the defendant made, not that he made it or was aware of its falsity. See Commonwealth v. Butler, 601 A.2d 268, 272, 274 (Pa.1991) (concurring and dissenting opinions); Model Penal Code, Comment to § 241.1 (6) (1980).

Finally, should the question whether the corroboration requirement has been satisfied be put to the jury? Weiler v. United States, 323 U.S. 606 (1945), says yes, at least in a perjury prosecution. See also State v. Shoop, 441 N.W.2d 475, 478–79 (Minn.1989) (accomplice). But there is a conflict of authority. See 2 McCormick, Evidence 562–63 (4th ed. 1992); 1984 Wis. L. Rev. 1121, 1137–41; Model Penal Code, Comment to § 241.1 (6) (1980). In Weiler v. United States, supra, the Court said: "[T]o permit the judge finally to pass upon this question [whether the corroboration requirement is satisfied] would enable a jury to convict on the evidence of a single witness, even though it believed, contrary to the belief of the trial judge, that the corroborative testimony was wholly untrustworthy. Such a result would defeat the very purpose of the rule, which is to bar a jury from convicting for perjury on the uncorroborated oath of a single witness." 323 U.S. at 610–11. Does this state a reason for requiring the corroboration requirement to be put to the jury or only repeat that it should be? Would a corroboration requirement administered exclusively by the judge be wholly ineffective? Is the decision whether or not to put the question to the jury influenced by whether it is viewed as a matter of admissibility or of the required evidential basis for conviction?

E. TRUTHFULNESS

United States v. Ward

United States Court of Appeals, Ninth Circuit, 1992.
989 F.2d 1015.

■ Before FLETCHER, POOLE and T.G. NELSON, CIRCUIT JUDGES.

■ FLETCHER, CIRCUIT JUDGE:[1]

Wallace Ward appeals his conviction of three counts of attempt to evade income tax in violation of 26 U.S.C. § 7201 and three counts of failure to file income taxes in violation of 26 U.S.C. § 7203. Ward argues that a new trial is necessary because the district court did not allow him to swear to an oath of his own creation, thereby precluding him from testifying in his own defense. We reverse and remand for a new trial.

. . .

Ward is the president of I & O Publishing Company, a mail-order house and publisher located in Boulder City, Nevada. The prosecution presented evidence at trial that despite having substantial income, neither I & O nor Ward filed tax returns or paid income taxes for the years 1983, 1984 and 1985.

On March 29, 1990 a grand jury indicted Ward on three counts each of tax evasion and failure to file income tax returns. Ward chose to represent himself at trial. On July 9, 1990, Ward filed a "Motion to Challenge the Oath," which proposed an alternative oath that replaced the word "truth" with the phrase "fully integrated Honesty." The oath would read, "Do you affirm to speak with fully integrated Honesty, only with fully integrated Honesty and nothing but fully integrated Honesty?" For reasons we will not attempt to explain, Ward believes that honesty is superior to truth. Magistrate Lawrence R. Leavitt ruled on August 2, 1990 that "the oath or affirmation which has been administered in courts of law throughout the United States to millions of witnesses for hundreds of years should not be required to give way to the defendant's idiosyncratic distinctions between truth and honesty." The district court over-ruled Ward's objections to the magistrate's order on August 28, 1990, and again on October 8, 1990. . . .

A three-day trial commenced on February 11, 1991. Ward made a lengthy opening statement and actively cross-examined government witnesses. At a sidebar during the second day of trial, Ward offered to take both the standard oath and his oath. The prosecutor was amenable to the compromise, but the district court refused to allow it. "This is an oath that has been used for a very long time," the district court said, "And I'm not going to establish a precedent where someone can come in and require the court to address that matter differently." . . . Ward did not testify and presented no witnesses. The jury convicted Ward of all counts after an hour's deliberation.

Ward now appeals. He argues that the district court's insistence on an oath that violated his beliefs abridged his First Amendment right to free exercise of religion and his Fifth Amendment right to testify in his own defense.

. . .

Questions of trial management are ordinarily reviewed for abuse of discretion. . . .

Ward does not describe his beliefs in terms ordinarily used in discussions of theology or cosmology (although he at one point uses the term "atheistic"), but he clearly attempts to express a moral or ethical sense of right and wrong. Ward's actions are evidence of the strength of his beliefs. He strongly professes innocence of the crimes charged, yet he preferred to risk conviction and incarceration rather than abandon his version of the oath. Compelling

---

1. Footnote omitted.

him to testify under the "truth" oath would, he says, "profoundly violate" his "freedom of belief" and run counter to the "convictions that are the central theme of all his published books and writings for the past 22 years." This is the sincerity of true religious conviction. We conclude that Ward professes beliefs that are protected by the First Amendment.

The court's interest in administering its precise form of oath must yield to Ward's First Amendment rights. To begin with, there is no constitutionally or statutorily required form of oath. Federal Rule of Evidence 603 requires only that a witness "declare that the witness will testify truthfully, by oath or affirmation administered in a form calculated to awaken the witness' conscience and impress the witness' mind with the duty to do so." The advisory committee notes to Rule 603 explain that "the rule is designed to afford the flexibility required in dealing with religious adults, atheists, conscientious objectors, mental defectives, and children. Affirmation is simply a solemn undertaking to tell the truth; no special verbal formula is required." This rule represents no break with the common law, which recognized that

> the oath's efficacy may depend upon both the general name and nature of the witness' faith and the formula of words or ceremonies which he considers as binding, i.e., as subjecting him to the risk of punishment. But it *cannot matter what tenets of theological belief or what ecclesiastical organization he adheres to, provided the above essentials are fulfilled, and it cannot matter what words or ceremonies are used* in imposing the oath, provided he recognizes them as binding by his belief.

6 Wigmore, Evidence § 1818 (Chadbourn rev. 1976) (original emphasis).

Our cases have routinely held that it is reversible error for a district court to prevent a party from testifying solely on the basis of the party's religiously-based objections to the form of the oath. In Gordon v. State of Idaho, 778 F.2d 1397 (9th Cir.1985), a plaintiff in a § 1983 action professed religious objections to oath or affirmation, offering instead to say "I understand that I must tell the truth. I agree to testify under penalty of perjury." Using First Amendment analysis requiring that government use the "least restrictive means" to its ends when free exercise is at stake, we held that it was an abuse of discretion for the district court to insist upon the standard oath and to dismiss plaintiff's case for failure to present evidence. . . .

> All that the common law requires is a form or statement which impresses upon the mind and conscience of a witness the necessity for telling the truth. Thus, defendant's privilege to testify may not be denied him solely because he would not accede to a form of oath or affirmation not required by the common law. . . . [A]ll the district judge need do is to make inquiry as to what form of oath or affirmation would not offend defendant's religious beliefs but would give rise to a duty to speak the truth.

United States v. Looper, 419 F.2d 1405, 1407 (4th Cir.1969). See also Moore v. United States, 348 U.S. 966, 99 L.Ed. 753, 75 S.Ct. 530 (1955) (per curiam) (criminal defendant with religious objections to the word "solemnly" in the oath must be allowed to testify).

Neither the magistrate nor the district court cited to any of these authorities, relying instead on their perception that the standard oath had not changed "for hundreds of years." While oaths including the familiar "truth, whole truth, and nothing but the truth" formulation date back at least to the seventeenth century, see 6 Wigmore, Evidence § 1818(2) (Chadbourn rev. 1976), the principle that the form of the oath must be crafted in a way that is meaningful to the witness also predates our constitution. In Omichund v.

Barker, 1 Atk. 22, 45 (1744), Lord Chief Judge Willes wrote, "It would be absurd for [a non-Christian witness] to swear according to the Christian oath, which he does not believe; and therefore, out of necessity, he must be allowed to swear according to his own notion of an oath." See also Atcheson v. Everitt, 1 Cowp. 382, 389 (1776) (Mansfield, L.C.J.) ("[A]s the purpose of [the oath] is to bind his conscience, every man of every religion should be bound by that form which he himself thinks will bind his own conscience most").

This case has an odd twist in that the defendant offered to take the traditional "truth" oath, but only if he were permitted to also take his "fully integrated honesty" oath. In Ward's view, as best we can state it, only his oath expressed a commitment to the abstract purity of absolute "fully integrated honesty" that must be extracted from anyone before that person's word can be relied upon. The standard "truth" oath was so much surplusage—distasteful, wrong, but not necessarily a mortal sin to take.

His own oath superimposed on the traditional one would have taken nothing away from the commitment to tell the truth under penalties of perjury and, indeed, in the defendant's mind imposed upon him a higher duty. Under these circumstances the district court clearly abused its discretion in refusing the oath and preventing the defendant's testimony. We do not have a case where the witness offers to swear only to a cleverly worded oath that creates loopholes for falsehood or attempts to create a safe harbor for perjury as in United States v. Fowler, 605 F.2d 181, 185 (5th Cir.1979), cert. denied, 445 U.S. 950 (1980), where the court properly refused testimony from a defendant who would not say so much as "I state that I will tell the truth in my testimony," and was willing to say only "I am a truthful man" or "I would not tell a lie to stay out of jail." . . .

Ward also seeks to vindicate what he perceives to be his right to have all his witnesses sworn to his oath. This he cannot do. Ward has no standing to assert the First or Fifth Amendment rights of others. . . .

REVERSED and REMANDED.

■ POOLE, CIRCUIT JUDGE, dissenting:

The majority seizes upon the defendant's semantic objection to the word "truth" and concomitant preference for the term "honesty" to reverse a conviction, but this result is not commanded by the Free Exercise Clause and runs afoul of the rule that any oath taken must convince the court that a witness is committed to truthful testimony and is aware of the cost of dishonesty on the stand. I would hold that the district court did not abuse its discretion in failing to provide a customized oath for Ward.

. . .

Even were I to give Ward the benefit of the doubt and ascribe religious significance to his "ultimate concern" with the merits of the word "honesty," I would still decline to require the district court to accommodate his objection. The district court must modify the oath to reflect genuinely held objections to it, but the court must also satisfy itself that the witness has committed himself to speak the truth. It is not enough that the witness says he knows of his obligation to do so; there must be a promise based on the awareness that failure to be honest is punishable under our law. . . . Ward's proposed alternative oath does not contain an acknowledgment of the *duty* to speak truthfully and does not ensure that the defendant is aware of the cost of dishonesty.

The majority's accommodation of Ward's "purely secular philosophical concerns," Callahan, 658 F.2d at 683, will result not in protection of a valuable Constitutional right but in numerous wasteful and time-consuming attacks on the oath mandated as a means of guaranteeing truth and of expediting the administration of justice. I dissent.

NOTES

1. Was it necessary for the court in the Ward case to reach any questions under the First Amendment? What are the implications of the Compulsory Process Clause of the Sixth Amendment for a case like Ward? See supra pp. 256–70.

2. In addition to the requirement that a witness take an oath or make an affirmation, is there a requirement that a witness have a sense of moral obligation to tell the truth? Where would such a requirement be found in the Federal Rules of Evidence? In Rule 603? Compare the Calif. Evid. Code, which in § 710 provides: "Every witness before testifying shall take an oath or make an affirmation or declaration in the form provided by law," and in § 701(a)(2): "A person is disqualified to be a witness if he or she is ... Incapable of understanding the duty of a witness to tell the truth." Is a person qualified to be a witness if he says he will tell the truth only out of fear of punishment for perjury? Is it troubling that the weight of the burden of the obligation of an oath or affirmation depends on the nature of the witness's religious or moral belief?

3. In a murder prosecution a witness responded, "I do," to the clerk's question, "You do solemnly swear that in the cause now on trial before this Court you will tell the truth, the whole truth, and nothing but the truth, so help you God?" On cross-examination the witness stated that he did not believe in God. What should the ruling be on a motion to strike the direct testimony? Flores v. State, 443 P.2d 73 (Alaska 1968). What should the ruling be on an objection to the testimony of a prosecution witness that although he is a Moslem he will only affirm and not swear on the Koran? United States v. Kalaydjian, 784 F.2d 53 (2d Cir.1986).

4. In the court martial of Captain Ernest Medina arising out of the events at My Lai during the Vietnam War, a prosecution witness was withdrawn after the following exchange took place: Q. [F. Lee Bailey, defense counsel] "Didn't you say last night, 'I don't know whether I'll tell the truth tomorrow?' "A. "I don't remember." Q. "Didn't you say you'd knowingly tell untruth to preserve a principle—namely, justice?" A. "I don't remember." Q. "Would you lie if you thought it would serve the ends of justice?" A. "Okay. In answer to your question, yes I could." Q. "When Captain Kadish asked you if you intended to exercise your prerogative today about telling or not telling the truth, did you reply: 'Be surprised,'?" A. "Yes." N.Y. Times, Aug. 26, 1971, p. 15, col. 1.

5. United States v. Thompson, 615 F.2d 329 (5th Cir.1980): Prosecution for buying votes in a federal election. W testified to the grand jury that her vote had been bought. When called as a witness at the trial, however, she omitted in her testimony any reference to cash offers for her vote. During "refreshment" of her recollection by the prosecutor outside the hearing of the jury, she acknowledged that she had admitted to the grand jury that she had taken money for her vote. When the jury returned, however, W denied ever having taken money for her vote. The trial judge then dismissed the witness from the stand as unworthy of belief, directed her to be held for perjury and ordered the jury to disregard her testimony. Held: Conviction reversed: The judge's action deprived the defendant of his constitutional right to a fair trial. But see People v. Leahy, supra p. 269. United States v. Bedonie, 913 F.2d 782, 799–801 (10th Cir.), cert. denied, 501 U.S. 1253 (1991): That the witnesses had made a great number of inconsistent statements did not render them incompetent. United States v. Smith, 592 F.Supp. 424 (E.D.Va.), vacated on other grounds, 780 F.2d 1102 (4th Cir.1985) (en banc): Doctrine of inherent incredibility may not be used to exclude defendant's testimony in criminal case.

6. Anderson v. State, 217 N.E.2d 840 (Ind.1966): Conviction of manslaughter affirmed although evidence that it was defendant who did the killing consisted entirely of the testimony of a 30–year–old woman, in whose apartment the killing took place while she was present, who had been a prostitute since she was 20, a narcotics addict since she was 18 or 19, had never had a legitimate source of livelihood, had been convicted of contributing to the delinquency of a minor, prostitution, obscene conduct and public intoxication, had been arrested for larceny and apparently had made a statement before trial inconsistent with her testimony.

7. Brown v. United States, 375 F.2d 310, 315 (D.C.Cir.1966), cert. denied, 388 U.S. 915 (1967): "It is suggested that Whitmire's testimony resulted from the pressure of the police or prosecuting officials. This was not pursued at trial on the theory his testimony was inadmissible as though it were an involuntary confession. The matter was pursued evidently to weaken or destroy Whitmire's credibility.... Although Whitmire denied any promise or inducement and none was proved, there are the known circumstances that he had not been charged as were appellants, and had not been retained in custody. Appellants' suspicion that some understanding existed that Whitmire might not be prosecuted, or that he believed he would not be, is not enough to exclude his testimony. On the contrary, we conclude with confidence that he testified as one who of his own volition desired to state what he knew. If the case is unusual Whitmire's testimony is not for that reason inadmissible." See also United States v. Insana, 423 F.2d 1165, 1168–69 (2d Cir.), cert. denied, 400 U.S. 841 (1970) (no error in the admission of testimony of prosecution witness who had pleaded guilty but whose sentencing was delayed until after defendant's trial).

Recent cases raise the question whether it violates due process to admit against the defendant in a criminal trial the testimony of an accomplice who has been promised favorable treatment contingent on how he testifies. In United States v. Dailey, 759 F.2d 192 (1st Cir.1985), there was an agreement that the prosecution would recommend a reduction in the accomplice's sentence, "depending principally upon the value to the Government of the defendant's [the accomplice's] cooperation." Id. at 194. The court held that admission of the accomplice's testimony would not violate due process because the provision quoted, taken in the context of the whole agreement, did not call for false testimony and the agreement and all the circumstances could be put before the jury. The court observed, however, in regard to a similar case in another circuit: "[W]e think it obvious that the Eighth Circuit ... served notice that benefits made contingent upon subsequent indictments or convictions skate very close to, if indeed they do not cross, the limits imposed by the due process clause." 759 F.2d at 201 n. 9. State v. Fisher, 859 P.2d 179 (Ariz.1993): Plea agreement requiring person to testify consistently with prior statements to investigators unenforceable. Implied: Testimony made under such an agreement would be inadmissible.

Golden Door Jewelry Creations, Inc. v. Lloyds Underwriters Non–Marine Ass'n, 865 F.Supp. 1516, 1526 (S.D.Fla.1994): Testimony of "fact witnesses" excluded because of ethical violation by party, acting with knowledge and assistance of counsel, in paying witnesses for the purpose of obtaining their testimony, even if only truthful testimony was sought. "That Lloyds' willingness to pay was contingent on the condition that the testimony had to be helpful to Lloyds in its defense of this civil action makes even more pronounced the subversive and egregious nature of Lloyds' and its counsel's actions."

Expert witnesses are routinely paid for testifying and are not called unless the calling party thinks there is good reason to believe they will testify in his favor.

8. The requirement of religious belief for the competency of a witness is discussed in Note, 11 S.C.L.Q. 548 (1959). See also Swancara, A Religious Fiction of the Common Law, 23 J. Crim. L. and Criminology 614 (1932); Williams, The Oath as an Aid in Securing Trustworthy Testimony, 10 Tex. L. Rev. 64 (1931); Hartogensis, Denial of Equal Rights to Religious Minorities and Non–Believers in the United States, 39 Yale L.J. 659, 666 (1930); Thayer, A Chapter of Legal History in Massachusetts, 9 Harv. L. Rev. 1 (1895); Comment, 38 N.D.Law. 95 (1962). As to exploring religious beliefs for their bearing on credibility, see infra pp. 405–06.

9. For references to the problem of children as witnesses in respect to their sense of obligation to tell the truth, see infra pp. 301–03.

F. ABILITY TO OBSERVE, REMEMBER AND RELATE

Gladden v. State

Court of Appeals of Alabama, 1951.
36 Ala.App. 197, 54 So.2d 607, cert. denied, 54 So.2d 610.

■ HARWOOD, JUDGE. This appellant's jury trial on an affidavit charging him with operating a motor vehicle on a public highway while drunk resulted in a verdict of guilty.

The evidence presented by the State consisted of the testimony of C.M. Garrett, Sheriff of Cherokee County, and C.R. Hurley, a deputy sheriff of said county.

These officers testified that as they were driving down a state highway in Cherokee County, at a speed of about forty miles per hour, they met two cars. One was driven by the appellant. This car was driven in a "wabbly" manner, and it was necessary for the Sheriff to drive his vehicle partly off the highway to avoid a collision.

The officers immediately turned their car around and pursued the two other vehicles. They stopped these cars, with their vehicle being between the two pursued automobiles.

Two boys jumped out of one of the automobiles, and the officers chased them. During this time appellant drove his car down a side road about 200 yards, got out and walked back toward the Sheriff's automobile. He was met by the officers and placed under arrest.

Both officers testified that all of the above transactions occurred within a space of from five to ten minutes.

Sheriff Garrett testified without objection that he observed the appellant as he drove the automobile and that he was drunk, and that he was drunk when he was arrested some five or ten minutes later.

Over appellant's objection that it was not a part of the res gestae Deputy Hurley was permitted to testify that the appellant was drunk at the time he was arrested.

Also, over appellant's objections, on the ground that the witness was not qualified by observation or knowledge, this witness testified that in his opinion the appellant was drunk when he saw him driving on the highway.

On cross examination Hurley testified that he saw the appellant as he approached the officers' automobile; that appellant's vehicle went from one side of the road to the other, and that the Sheriff had to drive partly off the road to avoid a collision; that while he did not recognize the appellant at the moment, he did see him, and formed his opinion as to appellant's condition at this time on the few seconds that he observed him driving.

Appellant thereupon moved to exclude Hurley's testimony as to appellant's condition at the time he was driving on the highway. This motion was denied by the court.

It appears to be the rule in this jurisdiction that where it is proper to permit nonexpert opinion evidence, the witness may state his opinion without first detailing the facts on which he bases such opinion, where the matter testified about is not of a complex nature. Intoxication is such a matter. . . .

All testimony must be based on a witness' observation of the matter about which he is testifying. Where in a proper case a nonexpert is permitted to give opinion evidence, and cross examination discloses that his opportunity for observation was insufficient to afford any reasonable basis for the conclusion expressed, his opinion testimony should be excluded on motion. Where however an opportunity for observation is shown, even though slight, a witness should be considered competent to testify as to what he did observe. Certainly we know of no way to measure a witness' capacity for observation, other than as it may be determined by a jury which hears the testimony tending to show its strength or weakness on the facts developed from examination of the witness. When such facts are shown the weight of such testimony is for the jury.

The court therefore did not err in denying the motion to exclude the testimony of the witness Hurley as to appellant's condition of sobriety at the time he observed him driving on the highway.

[Affirmed, but remanded for proper sentence.]

NOTES

1. In Burton v. Oldfield, 72 S.E.2d 357 (Va.1952), a witness was permitted to testify as to the speed of a vehicle he first saw 90 feet before the collision. In Johnson v. Cox, 262 S.W.2d 13 (Mo.1953), the testimony was permitted although the distance was only five feet. But in Jakubiec v. Hasty, 59 N.W.2d 385 (Mich.1953), the testimony was inadmissible when the witness saw the vehicle 15 feet before the crash. In Hall v. Kimber, 171 S.E.2d 99 (N.C.Ct.App. 1969), it was held not error to exclude the plaintiff's testimony that the defendant's car was travelling 80 to 90 m.p.h. in view of the fact that given the distance at which the plaintiff first saw the defendant's car, according to her own testimony, she would have had at the most only three seconds for observation if the car was going at the speed she said it was. Cf. Peake v. Omaha Cold Storage Co., 64 N.W.2d 470 (Neb.1954) (fleeting glimpse from 100–300 feet away without having speed in mind).

2. Guyette v. Schmer, 35 N.W.2d 689, 691–92 (Neb.1949): "This is an action for damage suffered by a 13–year–old girl in a collision [on a bridge] between a truck driven by the defendant and a saddle horse ridden by the girl." The judge directed a verdict for defendant at the close of plaintiff's case. On plaintiff's appeal the court reversed the judgment, saying that it did so largely because of the testimony of Strong, one of the witnesses. With respect to his testimony the court said: "Strong testifies that when he was at the point above described, a point lower than the level of the bridge, he saw the truck strike the horse, it appearing to him that the horse was turning a somersault. He testifies that the horse was on the west side of the bridge when it was struck.... We think the evidence of the witness Strong was competent. The distance from which he viewed the accident and the fact that he was below the level of the bridge go to the credibility of the witness and the weight to be given his testimony. We do not concur with the contentions advanced by the defendant that objects the size of a truck and the horse described in this record could not be observed from a distance of 1,150 feet, or that under some circumstances a witness might not be able to determine their position on the road from that distance. It becomes a question for the jury to determine the weight to be given to it."

People v. Regina, 224 N.E.2d 108, 109–12 (N.Y.1966): Prosecution of Regina and Battista for the murder of Mariani. Getch testified as follows: He was riding in an automobile with Mariani and Mangiamelli when a Chrysler pulled alongside containing Regina, Battista and a third person whom he did not recognize. Regina, who was driving, had a pistol in his right hand and started firing. Battista was in the back seat. After about two shots were fired, Getch dove under the dashboard and saw no more. The entire elapsed time from when Getch first saw the Chrysler and the firing of the first shots was about 4 or 5 seconds. At the time of the killing Getch was on parole. Twenty-seven years old, he had spent the better part of the preceding twelve years in jail. Getch and Mariani were members of the Gallo mob, Regina of the rival Profaci mob. Held: Getch's testimony was not "incredible as a matter of law."

3. When does intoxication or the influence of drugs at the time of observation render a witness incompetent? United States v. Blankenship, 923 F.2d 1110, 1116 (5th Cir.), cert. denied, 500 U.S. 954 (1991): Fact that witness was drug addict, that her drug use occasionally caused her to hallucinate and that she had taken drugs throughout the period to which she testified did not render her incompetent. Fox v. State, 491 P.2d 35 (Nev.1971): Prosecution for sale of narcotics. Not error to admit testimony of addict who took heroin at the time and place of the alleged sale and on the evening of the day before his testimony. In United States v. Strahl, 590 F.2d 10, 12 (1st Cir.1978), cert. denied, 440 U.S. 918 (1979), heavy drinking at the time of the events to which the witness testified did not render his testimony inadmissible. In Commonwealth v. Whitehead, 400 N.E.2d 821, 833–34 (Mass.1980), the victim-witness was not incompetent to testify although badly beaten in connection with the events to which she testified.

4. In United States v. Villalta, 662 F.2d 1205 (5th Cir.1981), cert. denied, 456 U.S. 916 (1982), imperfect understanding of Spanish did not render a witness incompetent to testify to his understanding of conversations in Spanish that took place in his presence.

State v. Ranieri

Supreme Court of Rhode Island, 1991.
586 A.2d 1094.

[Prosecution for burglary and assault. Someone broke into Elsie's apartment at night and brutally assaulted her. Hearing a disturbance, Picard, a neighbor, rushed into the apartment and in the course of attempting to pull the assailant away from Elsie was himself assaulted. For many months afterwards, Elsie said she could not identify the assailant. However, on the eve of trial, she said she could identify him. Before trial she picked defendant's picture out of a photo spread and also identified him at the trial.]

[Defendant] ... challenges the admission of Elsie's in and out-of-court identifications on the basis that Elsie was not a competent witness under Rule 602 of the Rhode Island Rules of Evidence ... in that she had no personal knowledge of her assailant's identity because she had an insufficient opportunity to view the assailant. We are persuaded by his second argument.

... For purposes of this appeal, we are convinced that Elsie was not competent to identify her assailant because she had no personal knowledge of her assailant's identity as required by Rule 602. We think it evident that Elsie had a preformed opinion about defendant and is now unjustifiably accusing him.

In consideration of Ranieri's challenge, we note that he has not styled his legal argument as a Rule 602 competency question. He argues that Elsie's testimony is "unreliable" and that it should be suppressed because it should be likened to an expression of an opinion by a lay witness under Rule 701 of the Rhode Island Rules of Evidence. Reading defendant's argument in its totality, we think his argument really is an objection under Rule 602.[1] ...

Under Rule 602, "A witness may not testify to a matter unless evidence is introduced sufficient to support a finding that the witness has personal knowledge of the matter. Evidence to prove personal knowledge may, but need not, consist of the testimony of the witness himself or herself." If a witness lacks such personal knowledge, then the witness is deemed to be incompetent to testify with respect to that matter. See Rule 601.

In deciding whether a witness is competent for purposes of Rule 602, the trial justice must determine whether a witness had a sufficient opportunity to perceive the subject matter about which he is testifying. See Hallquist v. Local 276, Plumbers & Pipefitters Union, 843 F.2d 18, 24 (1st Cir.1988); 3 J. Weinstein & M. Berger, Weinstein's Evidence ¶ 602[02] at 602–12 (M.B.1988). The justice is not making a credibility determination and is not judging whether the witness is accurately and truthfully relating that which he perceived. See 3 J. Weinstein & M. Berger, ¶ 602[02] at 602–10, 602–11 (citing United States v. Smith, 592 F.Supp. 424, 441 n. 22 (E.D.Va.1984), rev'd on other grounds, 780 F.2d 1102 (4th Cir. en banc 1985) (discussing distinction between F.R.E.Rule 602 and Doctrine of Inherent Incredibility)). Further, "Rule 602 ... does not require that the witness' knowledge be positive or rise to the level of absolute certainty. Evidence is inadmissible under this rule only if in the proper exercise of the trial court's discretion it finds that the witness could not have actually perceived or observed that which he testifies to." M.B.A.F.B. Federal Credit Union v. Cumis Insurance Society, Inc., 681 F.2d

---

1. We comment that Ranieri has not clearly made his legal arguments because he emphasizes that the identifications made against him are "unreliable." There is no legal objection in regard to identifications based on "unreliability" per se. Under the due process clause, if an identification procedure is suggestive and, in the totality of the circumstances, unreliable, then the identification must be suppressed. See Manson v. Brathwaite, 432 U.S. 98, 97 S.Ct. 2243 ... (1977); State v. Ivy, 558 A.2d 209, 211 (R.I. 1989). However, defendant explicitly states in his appellate brief that he is not claiming the identification procedures were suggestive.

Upon closer examination of what defendant is calling "reliability," we see that defendant is really claiming that the identification witnesses never saw the assailant because of the conditions surrounding the attack. Such a legal argument is properly called a Rhode Island Rules of Evidence Rule 602 objection for lack of personal knowledge. It unduly confuses the matter to couch a Rule 602 argument in terms of "reliability."

. . .

[Footnotes of the court, some renumbered, some omitted.]

930, 932 (4th Cir.1982).[2] In a situation in which the question of a witness's Rule 602 competency is close (that is, the jury could find that the witness perceived the matter testified to), the judge should admit the testimony since the matter then becomes one of credibility and is properly for the jury. See 3 J. Weinstein & M. Berger, ¶ 602[02] at 602–11. Further, "[i]n a criminal case where the proponent is the defense, the court should hesitate even more than in other instances in excluding testimony on Rule 602 grounds." Id. at 602–10.

. . .

On the facts of the instant case, the trial justice never made an explicit Rule 602 ruling since the parties did not frame the issue as a Rule 602 competency question. Nevertheless, we will undertake our review as if the trial justice had ruled that Elsie had personal knowledge of her assailant's identity and was thus competent under Rule 602 to so testify.

Two incidents in particular lead us to believe that Elsie is not competent under Rule 602. Elsie's uncontroverted testimony is that she believed for some time that defendant was always spying on her through the shade of her neighbor's house. She claimed that defendant had cut a hole in her neighbor's window shade in order to view her and that defendant would seal the hole back up when he was done. Assuming that there was such a hole and that there was such a person viewing her, Elsie readily admits she never saw that it was defendant who was looking at her. Yet, without any basis, Elsie still adamantly maintains that "she knew" it was Ranieri who was spying on her. She claims Ranieri watched her and always knew when she was in or out of the house.

Second, Elsie claims that prior to the present crime, defendant broke into her apartment on five different occasions. Again, Elsie has absolutely no evidence to substantiate her allegations. She readily admits she never saw Ranieri or anyone else actually enter her home. Elsie confronted defendant with her breaking and entering allegations sometime before the instant attack. It is at this prior confrontation in her back yard that he purportedly told her, "I'll get even with you."

The night of the attack, Elsie was grabbed from behind moments after she awoke at 4 a.m. Her uncontradicted testimony is that she never saw her assailant come up behind her, yet she knew it was Ranieri because he was always "watching her." Quickly the assailant threw Elsie to the floor and proceeded to strike her senselessly with a metal rod. Picard testified that after the assailant escaped, Elsie was crying, "Who was doing this to me?" Elsie never made any identification to anyone, despite repeated police urgings to give details of her attacker. She maintained for over eighteen months that she saw nothing. Even at trial she testified that she did not remember seeing Picard in her apartment the night of the attack.

Then on the eve of the trial, Elsie claimed she could make an identification. Elsie explained that she did not give a description of her assailant earlier because she was afraid of retribution from defendant or from defendant's friends in the neighborhood. She also claims that she had the opportunity to see her attacker despite the fact that she was grabbed from behind in her dark apartment.

---

2. Also, it should be noted that the justice's role in deciding a witness' Rule 602 competency is analogous to the justice's role in making an evidence Rule 104(b) ruling. See Advisory Committee Note to Rule 602 of the Rhode Island Rules of Evidence (" '[i]t will be observed that the rule [Rule 602] is in fact a specialized application of the provisions of Rule 104(b) on conditional relevancy' ").

We think it unmistakably clear that Elsie has a history of making unwarranted and unfair accusations against defendant. Elsie had absolutely no factual basis to make two prior serious allegations against defendant and we see nothing to indicate a factual basis for this third, most serious, allegation. We think Elsie's eighteen-month delay is not sufficiently explained merely by saying she was afraid. During all this time, defendant was incarcerated because of another charge or because he was unable to meet the bail set on this case. Despite this eighteen months of confinement, Elsie was never threatened by anyone. Elsie knew that defendant was in custody all during this period and that presumably he would be there for a significant period if he was convicted at a trial that was going to go forward without her assistance. During this eighteen-month period the Journal had published defendant's picture several times. We are incredulous that all these facts can be outweighed by Elsie's suddenly coming forward to make an identification, saying she knew all along that defendant was her assailant and that she was afraid to come forward.

Therefore, we rule that it was clearly erroneous for the trial justice to find that sufficient evidence was introduced that Elsie had personal knowledge of her assailant's identity. Accordingly Elsie was not competent under Rule 602 of the Rhode Island Rules of Evidence to testify as to her assailant's identity, and her out-of-court and in-court identifications should have been suppressed.

. . .

[Reversed in part and remanded for new trial.]

NOTES

1. McCrary–El v. Shaw, 992 F.2d 809, 810–11 (8th Cir.1993): In action by prisoner against prison guards for use of excessive force, not error to exclude, under Fed.R.Evid. 602, testimony of another prisoner, who occupied the cell next to the plaintiff's, that he had seen the assault through a crack in his cell door. The trial court had determined that this witness "had an inability to testify about what [was] relevant and at issue in the case." But see United States v. Hickey, 917 F.2d 901, 904–05 (6th Cir.1990): The trial court did not err in rejecting defendant's contention that prosecution witness Ventimiglia should be excluded from testifying on the ground that inconsistencies in his testimony showed he was prevented by his drug addiction from obtaining personal knowledge of the events to which he testified. "[T]he threshold of Rule 602 is low. . . . Despite the fact that Ventimiglia's testimony may have been, in large part, unbelievable to some and in spite of the possibility that his perception was sometimes impaired, a reasonable or rational juror could believe that Ventimiglia and the other prosecution witnesses perceived the course of events to which they testified. . . ."

2. Is the subject of Fed.R.Evid. 602 already covered by Rule 402, which excludes irrelevant evidence? Uniform Rule 19 (1954) also contained a "personal knowledge" requirement. The California Law Revision Commission in its study of that rule made the following observation: "[I]f a witness proposes to testify that 'D was driving 40 miles per hour,' and it appears that the witness was locked in a soundproof, windowless room at the time of the collision, but claims to be possessed of powers of extrasensory perception, the offered testimony does not meet the 'knowledge' requirement." Tentative Recommendation and a Study Relating to the Uniform Rules of Evidence (Art. VII, Expert and Other Opinion Testimony), 6 Cal.L.Revision Comm'n Rep., Rec. & Studies 929 (1964). Is there any reason to interpret Rule 602 to require of testimony more than that it be relevant so far as opportunity to observe is concerned?

3. A statement in the Advisory Committee's Note to Rule 602 suggests that the purpose of the Rule is to exclude testimony that relies upon hearsay but does not reveal that reliance on its face. "This rule does not govern the situation of a witness who testifies to the hearsay statement as such, if he has personal knowledge of the making of the statement. Rules 801 and 805 would be applicable. This rule would, however, prevent him from testifying to the subject matter of the hearsay statement, as he has no personal knowledge of it." See Phillip R. Morrow v. FBS Ins., 770 P.2d 859, 863 (Mont.1989); United States v. Stratton, 779 F.2d 820, 829–30 (2d Cir.1985); 2 Wigmore, Evidence § 657, at 894 (Chadbourn rev. 1979), and 5 Wigmore, Evidence § 1361, at 2 (Chadbourn rev. 1974). Why should not the hearsay rule itself be understood to cover both the case where the witness expressly testifies to an extrajudicial statement and the case where he testifies to another matter, but his knowledge of that matter depends upon information received from another?

4. Is the subject of Rule 602 also covered by Rule 701, the Opinion Rule? The California Law Revision Commission in the study just referred to is clear that the "personal knowledge" requirement and the Opinion Rule are not the same. "[S]uppose an eyewitness to a collision . . . is offered to testify that 'D was reckless.' The testimony offered is, of course, inadmissible. However, the vice in the offer is not the want of knowledge . . . [but] the 'opinion' rule. . . ." 6 Cal.L.Revision Comm'n Rep., Rec. & Studies 929.

5. An objection that there is no showing of personal knowledge could be an objection to the form of testimony. The testimony may be excludable for one or more of the reasons just indicated—irrelevance, hearsay, opinion—but because of the form of the testimony, it is impossible to say. Thus, if the witness testifies that the Smiths ate dinner at home on a certain evening, with his own eyes he may have seen them sitting at the dinner table eating. On the other hand, he may have no relevant knowledge whatsoever of the matter, or he may have inferred that the Smiths ate dinner at home from seeing dirty dishes in the sink, or he may believe they ate dinner at home because someone told him that they did. Objection of no personal knowledge may be an objection intended to cast upon the proponent of the evidence the burden of removing this unclarity. See 2 Wigmore, Evidence § 654, at 883–84 (Chadbourn rev. 1979). As will be seen later, the objection that testimony is opinion is sometimes employed in the same way.

State v. Singh

Missouri Court of Appeals, 1979.
586 S.W.2d 410.

[Defendant was convicted of manslaughter of his wife. He testified that in the course of an argument his wife had become violent, that she had gone to a closet and obtained a revolver, which defendant had then taken from her and put in his pocket, that she had hit him with a stick several times, that a struggle ensued first inside the house then outside, and that when his wife tried to get the revolver out of his pocket, it went off.]

■ MAUS, JUDGE.

. . .

The state presented the daughter whose testimony is summarized. She was awakened by the quarrel. She went downstairs and her mother was trying to hit the defendant who was holding her. Her mother said "[p]lease don't kill me" and Michael said "shut up". She first said she saw the gun in defendant's hand inside the house, but later said it was outside. She and her mother went out the back door and got to the corner of the house when she "looked over and he already had shot her, and I looked over and she was lying down." She first stated the decedent tried to hit the defendant with a stick of wood that night, but later said it was before that night.

. . .

The defendant first asserts the trial court erred in determining the daughter was a competent witness. She was approximately five years nine and one-half months of age at the time of the occurrence and approximately six years and eight months of age at the time of trial. By statute, § 491.060 RSMo, V.A.M.S., a child under 10 years is by a rebuttable presumption incompetent. The burden was upon the state to establish her competency. Hildreth v. Key, 341 S.W.2d 601 (Mo.App.1960).

There is no fixed age at which a child may be a competent witness. Competency is to be measured by the standard hereafter set forth under the singular facts and circumstances of each case. State v. Watson, 536 S.W.2d 59 (Mo.App.1976). Children of an age comparable to that of the daughter have been determined to be competent in a variety of situations.[1]

The competency of a child offered as a witness is to be determined by the court. The established procedure is for this determination to be made upon a voir dire examination held outside the presence of the jury. J.L.W. v. D.C.W., 519 S.W.2d 724 (Mo.App.1975).[2] Such was done in this case.

It is in connection with the voir dire examination the defendant in his pro se brief asserts that the trial court erred by conducting "extensive cross-examination" of the daughter aiding in establishing her competency. We do not agree. It is fundamental that a trial court must maintain complete fairness and impartiality. This does not mean, however, the trial judge was cast into "the position of the umpire of a game, whose duty it was to interfere only so far as needed to decide whether the rules of the game had been violated." III Wigmore, Evidence, § 784, p. 188 (Chadbourn rev. 1970). "One of the well-recognized powers of the judicial function is the right and duty of the trial judge to propound additional questions to witnesses in order to develop the truth more fully and to clarify the testimony given." State v. Grant, 394 S.W.2d 285, 287 (Mo.1965).

The conduct of the voir dire examination is within the control of the trial court. State v. Statler, 331 S.W.2d 526 (Mo.1960). J.L.W. v. D.C.W., supra. The trial court may conduct the examination, permitting subsequent questions by counsel or the trial court may permit the examination to be conducted by counsel, with such questions by the court as it determines proper. State v. Young, 477 S.W.2d 114 (Mo.1972). "The ultimate responsibility for determining the competency of a child to testify rests with the trial court who occupies the best position to judge the qualifications of the witnesses." State v. Sanders, 533 S.W.2d 632, 633 (Mo.App.1976). It is eminently proper that the trial court,

---

1. A child four years seven months old was competent as a witness to an accident, Hildreth v. Key, 341 S.W.2d 601 (Mo.App. 1960); a child of 6 concerning her rape, State v. Parton, 487 S.W.2d 523 (Mo.1972). . . . [Footnotes are those of the court. Some footnotes have been omitted and others renumbered.]

2. However, an examination before the jury was not reversible error where no objection was made and the point was not preserved in a motion for new trial. State v. Obie, 501 S.W.2d 513 (Mo.App.1973). For a case where a prosecutor for the apparent purpose of avoiding comment upon the failure of the victim's sister to testify called the child before the jury[,] established she was 7 years of age and made no attempt to qualify her, see State v. Tandy, 401 S.W.2d 409 (Mo. 1966).

within the bounds of fairness and impartiality, participate in such a voir dire examination.

In this case, the trial court permitted counsel to initially examine the daughter concerning her competency. When their extensive examinations were completed the court asked a total of thirteen questions. We have carefully examined those questions and find they were fair and impartial, designed to aid in arriving at the truth concerning the competency of the witness. No error was committed.

Turning to the merits of the daughter's competency, the standards for competency are well established.

"They are: (1) present understanding of or intelligence to understand, on instruction, an obligation to speak the truth; (2) mental capacity at the time of the occurrence in question truly to observe and to register such occurrence; (3) memory sufficient to retain an independent recollection of the observations made; and (4) capacity truly to translate into words the memory of such observation." State v. Young, 477 S.W.2d 114, 116 (Mo. 1972); State v. Watson, supra, at 60.

In the voir dire examination it was established that the prosecutor and her father had talked with the daughter about the occurrence and her testimony. At their suggestion she practiced counting and the ABC's. During her examination she did state that she would not be able to remember all that she testified to without the help of the prosecutor and that in testifying she relied on her father. On the other hand, she also stated she hadn't forgotten the events and she would have been able to remember had she not talked with them. Her answers first referred to may indicate she had permissible help in refreshing her memory. There is no basis for any intimation that she was told what to say. Nor is there any indication that she testified other than on the basis of her recollection as demonstrated by the following cross-examination:

"Q. If you said what somebody else told you to say, would that be telling the truth, because they told you that's what to say? A. You don't always have to say what they say. Q. You don't have to say what they say? A. Huh-uh. Q. Okay. A. It might not be the truth, what they say."

She clearly stated that she had an independent memory of the occurrence as demonstrated by the following:

"THE COURT: Okay. You told us earlier this morning that you remember that Michael and your mommy were fighting. THE WITNESS: Yeah. THE COURT: Do you actually remember that happening or do you just recall your daddy telling you that it did happen? THE WITNESS: I remember it happening.... THE COURT: You told us earlier this morning that your mother went outside. Do you remember telling us that? THE WITNESS: Yes. THE COURT: Did you tell us that because you heard your daddy say that's what happened or because you now remember that it did happen? THE WITNESS: I remember that it did happen."

Other factors favoring the competency of the daughter were before the trial court. In addition to her testimony upon the voir dire hearing and at the trial, her testimony at her deposition and upon an aborted trial given within six months of the occurrence was before the court. Her testimony on four separate interrogations was both forthright and unswerving. Her testimony was consistent with facts otherwise established by the evidence. State v. Young, supra; State v. Sigh, 579 S.W.2d 657 (Mo.App.1979). The death of her mother was a shocking occurrence that will undoubtedly scar her memory forever. State v. Parton, 487 S.W.2d 523 (Mo.1972); State v. Ball, 529 S.W.2d 901 (Mo.App.

1975). The time between the event and her testimony was relatively short. From the record, this child appears to have been candid, alert and intelligent. However, this factor could better be determined and weighed with what is now her printed testimony by the trial court who had the benefit of personal observation. It is the opportunity of personal observation that is the basis for the time-honored maxim that "[t]he trial court's determination that the child is qualified to give testimony will be reversed only for a clear abuse of discretion." State v. Ball, supra, at 904. Also State v. Young, supra, at 116. The trial court properly found the daughter a competent witness.

. . .

The judgment is affirmed.

■ BILLINGS, P.J., HOGAN, J., and KELSO, SPECIAL JUDGE, concur.

NOTES

1. Psychologists have carried out considerable research directed to determining the testimonial accuracy of children and how it compares with that of adults. Most of this research indicates that children are less reliable witnesses than adults and that younger children are less reliable witnesses than older children, at least so far as concerns recognition identification of persons. E. Loftus, Eyewitness Testimony 159 (1979); B. Clifford and R. Bull, The Psychology of Person Identification 164 (1978); A. Yarmey, The Psychology of Eyewitness Testimony 207, 213 (1979); Chance and Goldstein, Face–Recognition Memory: Implications for Children's Eyewitness Testimony, 40 J.Soc. Issues 69, 82 (1984) (children less accurate in laboratory studies); Johnson and Foley, Differentiating Fact from Fantasy: The Reliability of Children's Memory, 40 J. Soc. Issues 33, 45 (1984) (children recall fewer items). But see Marin et al., The Potential of Children as Eyewitnesses, 3 L. and Hum. Behav. 295 (1979), surprisingly suggesting that age makes no difference for the accuracy of recognition nor in a number of other memory tasks. Research results showing that children are less reliable witnesses than adults may be explained by the fact that they are at an earlier stage in general cognitive development. See A. Yarmey, supra, at 199, 201, summarizing the Swiss psychologist Piaget's theories. Adult superiority in certain memory tasks may be due to their greater ability to organize information. See id. at 204–05. There is some basis for believing that children have greater difficulty than adults in distinguishing what they did from what they only thought of doing, but little experimental support for believing they have greater difficulty in distinguishing what they perceived from what they only imagined. Johnson and Foley, Differentiating Fact from Fantasy: The Reliability of Children's Memory, 40 J. Soc. Issues 33, 45 (1984).

To what extent does the competency of a child depend upon his capacity at the time of the occurrence? See Rosche v. McCoy, 156 A.2d 307 (Pa.1959). See also the discussion by Professor Leo Levin in 1960 Ann. Survey Am.L. 565. Piaget suggests that a child's memory for an event will get better with development as he more clearly understands what it is that he originally perceived. See A. Yarmey, supra, at 201 (1979).

In State v. Rippy, 626 A.2d 334, 337–38 (Me.1993), it was held error to find competent a girl who was four at the time of the incident and eleven at the time of trial. "The evidence does not support a finding that Jane had a reasonable ability to recall [a requirement of Me.R.Evid. 601], in 1991, events that occurred in 1983. She was unable to recall even basic aspects of her life as it was in 1983 other than the detailed description of the events of the one day on which she was allegedly assaulted by Rippy." At the same time, it was held error to find incompetent as a matter of law witnesses who were 32 and 22 months old at the time of the incident and ten and nine years old at the time of trial. "However improbable it might seem that children under the age of three at the time of the alleged assault would be competent to testify, it is not possible to rule out this competency as a matter of law." In People v. Price, 211 Cal.Rptr. 642 (App.1985), a sex-abuse case, the prosecutor interviewed the child, a 4–year-old, and found her fidgety and with a short attention span. As a result, the prosecutor decided the child would not qualify as a witness and had the charges dismissed in order to let the child mature. About a year later, new charges were brought, and the child, now five years old, qualified as a witness.

As indicated in State v. Singh, there is considerable judicial concern with the susceptibility of children to suggestion from others. In some cases testimony has been rejected because coaching made it unlikely the child was actually remembering the event. Davis v. State, 348 So.2d 1228 (Fla.App.1977); State v. Ranger, 98 A.2d 652 (Me.1953); Cross v. Commonwealth, 77 S.E.2d 447 (Va.1953). See also Slaten v. State, 367 So.2d 562, 567–68 (Ala.Cr.App.1978), for an example of the problem of parental influence both on and off the stand. Defendant's lawyer sought to have the mother removed from the courtroom because the child kept looking at her from the stand. During the first part of direct examination by the prosecutor, the child was unresponsive in regard to the facts of the crime. However, after a recess during which she was with the prosecutor and her mother, she readily testified. Most of the psychological research confirms the popular view that children are more subject to suggestion than adults. S. Ceci and M. Bruck, Jeopardy in the Courtroom: A Scientific Analysis of Children's Testimony 233–41 (1995); E. Loftus, supra, at 162; A. Yarmey, supra, at 200, 213. But the observation is made in Loftus and Davies, Distortions in the Memory of Children, 40 J. Soc. Issues 51, 63 (1984): "Perhaps age alone is the wrong focus for these studies.... If an event is understandable and interesting to both children and adults, and if their memory for it is still equally strong, age differences in suggestibility may not be found. But if the event is not encoded well to begin with, or if a delay weakens the child's memory relative to an adult's, then age differences may emerge." And see the surprising results of the experiment reported by Marin, et al., supra, at 303. In order to obtain accurate information from young children, one must take into account both the danger of suggestion and the fact that children have greater communication difficulties than adults and are often in need of special help in this regard. See A. Yarmey, supra, at 212–13; Government of Virgin Islands v. Riley, 750 F.Supp. 727, 729 (D.V.I.1990): Four-year-old son of murder victim held incompetent to testify. "I am confident that the child is capable of receiving just impressions of fact and of relating them truly ... but I am equally certain that the child may be unable to communicate to the jury at trial, either because of generalized courtroom trauma, nervousness or excitement."

As to qualifying children in respect to the oath and a sense of obligation to tell the truth, see State in Interest of R.R., Jr., Juvenile, 398 A.2d 76, 78–85 (N.J.1979) (adjudication of delinquency of a 15–year-old for having committed the offense of private lewdness against a 4–year-old; not error to permit the 4–year-old to testify, he having said he understood that it would be bad to lie, that if he was bad he would get a beating and that he would not be bad in answering questions in court); State v. Ayers, 470 S.W.2d 534 (Mo.1971) (not abuse of discretion to allow testimony by 12–year-old who stated she had no idea of the meaning of the oath, but when asked what happens to a person who does not tell the truth said, "They will go to jail."); State v. Sims, 480 P.2d 228 (Wash.Ct.App.1971) (stressing child's ability to give examples of lying); People v. Pearson, 261 N.E.2d 519, 522 (Ill.App.1970) (10–year-old witness learned just before trial God would punish her if she lied.) In Harrold v. Schluep, 264 So.2d 431 (Fla.Dist.Ct.App.1972), the trial court had found a child incompetent to be a witness when he answered "no" to the question whether he understood what it meant to tell the truth. The appellate court held that the trial court should have made a greater effort to qualify the child. In People v. Sims, 251 N.E.2d 795 (Ill.App.1969), a determination of delinquency was reversed because of inadequate inquiry into competency of 13–year-old witness. The inquiry consisted entirely of the following questions and answers: "Q. Do you know what will happen to you if you don't tell the truth? A. No. Q. What happens to you if you tell a lie? A. I don't know. Q. [by defense counsel] What is the truth, Randolph; what does it mean, the truth? A. (No response.)" If a child cannot be punished for the crime of perjury, should that bear on the question of competency? See S. Ceci and M. Bruck, supra, at 263; Hauggard et al., Children's Definitions of the Truth and Their Competency as Witnesses in Legal Proceedings, 15 L. and Hum. Behav. 253 (1991) (study of preschool and kindergarten children suggesting they have adult-like sense of why statement by child [in a movie they were shown] was a lie); Morton, When Can Lying Start? in The Child Witness—Do Courts Abuse Children? 35 (G. Davies and J. Drinkwater eds., 1988): Lying requires ability to conceptualize the possibility of other minds representing events in a way at variance with one's own representation and the belief that one has the power to induce such different representations, and children under four do not have this ability or belief. Comment, The Competency Requirement for the Child Victim of Sexual Abuse: Must We Abandon It? 40 U. Miami L.Rev. 245, 267 n. 99 (1985).

The moral development of children, including their views on truth-telling, has been extensively studied by Lawrence Kohlberg. See, e.g., Stage and Sequence: The Cognitive–Developmental Approach to Socialization, in Handbook of Socialization Theory and Research 347 (Goslin ed., 1969). A. Yarmey, supra, at 214–17, discusses Kohlberg's theories.

Recently considerable attention has been given to the subject of children as witnesses in sex abuse cases. In some jurisdictions legislation has been enacted specifically addressed to the question of the competency of children in such cases. A Colorado statute, for example, provides:

> The following persons shall not be witnesses: . . . (b)(I) Children under ten years of age who appear incapable of receiving just impressions of the facts respecting which they are examined or of relating them truly. (II) This proscription does not apply to a child under ten years of age, in any civil or criminal proceeding for child abuse, sexual abuse, sexual assault, or incest, when the child is able to describe or relate in language appropriate for a child of that age the events or facts respecting which the child is examined.

Colo.Rev.Stat. § 13–90–106 (1995). In People v. District Court, 791 P.2d 682 (Colo.1990), this statute was interpreted to make a child competent even though he did not know the difference between telling the truth and lying. See also Mo.Ann.Stat. § 491.060 (Vernon 1987 Supp.), a similar statute, held in State v. Williams, 729 S.W.2d 197 (Mo.1987), not to violate the Due Process or Equal Protection Clauses; Comment, The Competency Requirement for the Child Victim of Sexual Abuse: Must We Abandon It? 40 U.Miami L.Rev. 245, 273–74 (1985). But see State v. Michaels, 642 A.2d 1372 (N.J.1994): Testimony of children regarding sex abuse must be excluded if interrogation was improperly suggestive or coercive and the state cannot prove by clear and convincing evidence that, notwithstanding the interrogation, the testimony retains a sufficient degree of reliability. "[We recognize that] assessing reliability as a predicate to the admission of in-court testimony is a somewhat extraordinary step. Nevertheless, it is not unprecedented," citing among other authorities United States Supreme Court decisions regarding in-court testimony following a lineup, supra p. 246, and State v. Hurd, 432 A.2d 86 (N.J.1981), regarding testimony after hypnosis. Is the Michaels decision in conflict with the trend exemplified in the Colorado and Missouri statutes cited above?

A number of states allow videotape or closed-circuit television to be used for testimony by children in sex abuse cases, and also, in certain circumstances, the introduction of hearsay statements by children. For a discussion of these developments, see infra p. 563. The admissibility of a hearsay statement by a child is sometimes made to turn upon the reliability of the statement. What is the relation between this requirement and the question of the child's competence to be a witness? Idaho v. Wright, 497 U.S. 805, 825, 110 S.Ct. 3139, 3151 (1990): That a child is found incapable of communicating to the jury and barred from testifying on that ground, although such inability might be relevant to whether a hearsay statement possessed guarantees of trustworthiness required for admission under the Confrontation Clause, would not per se exclude the hearsay statement. State v. Lanam, 459 N.W.2d 656 (Minn.1990), cert. denied, 498 U.S. 1033 (1991): Prosecution for sexual abuse of child. Admission of hearsay statements did not violate the confrontation clauses of the federal and state constitutions even though child had been held incompetent to testify. Dissent:

> That finding [of incompetence] implicitly is based on the alleged child victim's inability to understand the truthfulness of the accusation or inability to form an adequate recollection. Is it not ironical that hearsay statements made by the child at an even younger age when questioned at an earlier date by doctors, therapists, police officers, counselors, social workers, parents, and foster parents, and then when asked to understand the truthfulness and distinguish between fantasy and reality are deemed admissible because they are reliable and because the child is unavailable?

Id. at 667. As the passage indicates, the admissibility of a hearsay statement under either the hearsay rule or the Confrontation Clause sometimes depends upon the declarant being unavailable at the time of trial. Will a finding of incompetence to be a witness automatically satisfy this unavailability requirement? See State v. Ryan, 691 P.2d 197, 202–04 (Wash.1984); Comment, The Competency Requirement for the Child Victim of Sexual Abuse: Must We Abandon It? 40 U.Miami L.Rev. 245, 260–61 and n. 68 (1985).

As to the English and Canadian Practice of permitting unsworn testimony by certain children but requiring corroboration, see Gertner, The Unsworn Evidence of Children and Mutual Corroboration, 16 Osgoode Hall L.J. 495 (1978). See also N.Y.Crim.Proc.Law § 60.20 (McKinney 1981).

For other discussions of children as witnesses, see J. Myers, Child Witness Law and Practice (1987); Myers, The Testimonial Competence of Children, 25 J.Fam.L. 287 (1986–87); Goodman and Helgeson, Child Sexual Assault: Children's Memory and the Law, 40 U.Miami L.Rev. 181 (1985); Melton et al., Children's Competency to Testify, in Child Sexual Abuse and the Law 12 (J. Bulkley, ed., 1982); Stafford, The Child as a Witness, 37 Wash.L.Rev. 303 (1962); Spencer, Child Witness: A Case for Legal Reform? in The Child Witness—Do the Courts Abuse Children? (G. Davies and J. Drinkwater eds., 1988). Notes, 13 N.Ky.L.Rev. 181 (1986); 63 Wash.U.L.Q. 815 (1985).

Consideration also needs to be given to the competence of the elderly. See Williams et al., Eyewitness Evidence and Testimony, in Handbook of Psychology and Law 141, 146 (D. Kagehiro and W. Laufer eds., 1992); Lindsay, Memory Source Monitoring and Eyewitness Testimony, in Adult Eyewitness Testimony 27, 47 (D. Ross et als. eds., 1994). See also New York Times, Mar. 27, 1990, Sec. C, pp. 1, 8, reporting research showing elderly experience decline in episodic memory, but not in implicit memory (e.g., how to hit a golf ball) or semantic memory, and also tend to suffer from source amnesia (know it but cannot remember when or where they learned it).

2. In Caperna v. Williams–Bauer Corp., 53 N.Y.S.2d 295, 300 (1945), plaintiff sued for overtime compensation under Fair Labor Standards Act. Plaintiff's proof consisted solely of his recollection as to the number of hours worked, namely, never less than 72 hours per week. This work had been done between two and six years previously. Since plaintiff testified as to an unvarying routine, the court held that he was a competent witness: "It is therefore not at all incredible that he could testify solely from memory, and years later, that he never worked less than seventy-two hours per week; the existence of such a fact could, within reason, indelibly impress itself on his mind, and thus enable him to give such testimony, and this without necessarily rendering it incredible. Testimony is incredible when it is so extraordinarily in conflict with probability, or so utterly hostile to reason and intelligence, as to become so nearly impossible that it ought not to be believed by the trier of the facts.... The testimony of the plaintiff, in the circumstances shown, is not brought within that category."

In re Bragg's Estate, 76 P.2d 57, 67 (Mont.1938): "All testimony is given and received on the theory that it is given according to the best memory of the witness; more cannot be required."

State v. Johnson, 447 P.2d 10, 12–13 (Idaho 1968): Defendant was prosecuted for the burglary of a drugstore. The police found him inside the drugstore in the early hours of the morning with a window pried open. The defense was that defendant was under the influence of alcohol and drugs at the time of the incident and could not have formed the intent required for the crime. Defendant testified on direct examination that he remembered nothing concerning the period of the alleged burglary. Held: Not error to sustain prosecution objection to the question, "Did you knowingly, wilfully and intentionally burglarize the Owl drug store?"

3. It will be recalled that at the beginning of this chapter there was a discussion of the Supreme Court's Lineup Cases beginning with United States v. Wade and Gilbert v. California, supra p. 246. From this series of cases emerged two constitutional rights relating to eyewitness identification testimony: a right to counsel applicable to lineups held at or after the commencement of adversary judicial criminal proceedings and a more broadly applicable due process right to have excluded from evidence the results of identification procedures that are "unnecessarily suggestive and conducive to irreparable mistaken identification." The due process right can require the exclusion of the results of a pretrial identification procedure as well as in-court identification influenced by such a procedure. See Foster v. California, 394 U.S. 440, 89 S.Ct. 1127 (1969). Whether the due process right can be invoked to bring about the exclusion of an in-court identification under suggestive conditions at the trial itself is more doubtful. See supra p. 247. What is of interest now, however, is the relation between the due process right to have excluded evidence that is the product of an "unnecessarily suggestive" identification procedure that was "conducive to irreparable mistaken identification" and the nonconstitutional standard of competence to be a witness, particularly so far as concerns memory of the event to which the witness testifies. See United States v. Evans, 484 F.2d 1178, 1181–82 (2d Cir.1973), rejecting a contention that government witnesses who claimed they were able to identify defendant as the robber were incompetent because they had been shown surveillance films and other photos of the defendants by government agents. See also United States v. Baker, 419 F.2d 83, 90–91 (2d Cir.1969), cert. denied, 397 U.S. 976 (1970) (in-court identification of defendant as the criminal where, with the exception of two jurors, defendant was the only negro in the courtroom).

Schneiderman v. Interstate Transit Lines

Supreme Court of Illinois, 1946.
394 Ill. 569, 69 N.E.2d 293.

■ MURPHY, JUSTICE. Jack Schneiderman started this suit in the superior court of Cook county against Interstate Transit Lines, Inc., to recover damages for personal injuries sustained when the automobile he was driving collided with one of defendant's busses. A jury trial resulted in a verdict for plaintiff for $100,000. In response to a special interrogatory submitted at defendant's request, the jury found that the bus had been operated in a wilful and wanton manner. The court overruled defendant's motion for judgment notwithstanding the verdict, for a new trial, and its motion to require a remittitur and to set aside the answer to the special interrogatory. Judgment was entered on the verdict. On appeal the Appellate Court reversed the judgment without remanding the cause. We granted plaintiff's petition for leave to appeal.

The accident occurred at 5:20 on the morning of November 26, 1941, at the intersection of Oak Park avenue and Madison street in the village of Oak Park. The avenue extends north and south and Madison street east and west. Plaintiff drove his automobile south on Oak Park avenue toward and into the intersection of the two streets. Defendant's bus approached the intersection from the west. The collision occurred near the center of the intersection. Traffic at the intersection was regulated by stop-and-go lights located on each corner of the intersection.

. . .

Plaintiff's injuries affected his power to speak coherently and intelligently at all times and he could not make answer to any but simple questions. The Appellate Court held that plaintiff's mental condition was such as to render him incompetent to testify and that, therefore, none of his evidence should be considered. On the remainder of the evidence it was held that no cause of action was proved and that defendant's motion for a directed verdict, made at the close of the evidence, or its motion for judgment non obstante veredicto, should have been allowed. The questions presented here are as to plaintiff's competency to testify and whether the evidence was such as to require the allowance of defendant's motion for judgment non obstante veredicto.

The facts pertinent to the inquiry on plaintiff's competency are as follows: Plaintiff received chest and head injuries and two medical experts were called as witnesses to prove the nature and extent of such injuries. After the doctors testified, plaintiff was called as a witness by his counsel and in response to the questions propounded he gave a few, short, simple answers. He gave his name, residence, age, the day of the month and year on which the accident occurred. He was unable to state the month, but he fixed the location of the accident at the particular street intersection. He stated that there were traffic lights at the intersection, and the following questions and answers concluded his direct examination:

"Q. What street were you driving in when the accident happened? A. Oak Park and Madison Street.

"Q. Were there any traffic lights at Oak Park and Madison street? A. Yes.

"Q. What direction were you going? A. South.

"Q. Now what was the color of the light as you approached and reached the intersection? A. Green.

"Q. What happened as you were going over? Tell the jury what happened. A. Green and amber, amber and bus struck.

"Q. What happened as you were going over the crossing? A. I get hit.

"Q. You got hit? A. Yes.

"Q. By what? A. A bus.

"Q. What do you next remember after that? A. I don't remember."

At no time during the trial did defendant object to plaintiff's competency. It is for the court to decide upon the competency of the witness and for the jury to determine what credit shall be given to his testimony under the various tests recognized by the law. People v. Enright, 256 Ill. 221, 99 N.E. 936, Am.Ann. Cas. 1913E,318; Kelly v. People, 29 Ill. 287. Except for the possible future course that this case may take, the question of the competency of plaintiff might well be disposed of on the ground that the question was not raised by defendant in the trial court.

The cross-examination covers twenty pages of the record. It will be impossible to detail all the answers which reflect plaintiff's mental condition. A summary of it is that his answers to the questions that were first asked on cross-examination fixed the time when he left his home on the morning of the accident, that he went some place to eat but could not tell where, that he drove on to Oak Park avenue at Washington boulevard. Plaintiff stated that this intersection was one block north of the intersection where the collision occurred and that answer was correct. His testimony shows that there were traffic control lights at the Washington boulevard intersection, that he drove onto Oak Park avenue on the flash of the green light, that he turned south on the avenue, that he was driving 20 or 25 miles per hour. In reference to seeing the light at Madison street intersection as covered by his direct examination, it is as follows:

"Q. Now, you saw an amber light, did you? A. Yes.

"Q. And where did you see the amber light? A. Green.

"Q. No. I say, where were you when you saw the amber light? A. About half a block.

"Q. You were half a block north of the corner when you saw the amber light, were you? A. Yes.

"Q. Now, was there any other light on besides the amber light when you saw it? Wasn't there a green and amber light on together when you saw it? A. Amber.

"Q. But was there more than one color light on when you saw it? Wasn't there both green and amber lights when you saw it? A. No.

"Q. Did the green light go off when the amber light came on? A. Yes.

"Q. At the time the amber light came on you were about in the middle of the block between Washington and Madison, were you? A. Yes.

"Q. And you were going about twenty or twenty-five miles an hour then? A. Yes."

He further stated that the brakes on his automobile were good and when going at 20 to 25 miles per hour, he could stop his automobile in 3 or 4 feet. At first he stated he did not apply his brakes and when interrogated further he said, he put them on "right away." At times his answers lack consistency; that is, he would testify differently to the same question. At times his answers were incoherent and meaningless. A fair sample of such incoherent and meaningless testimony is set forth in the Appellate Court opinion. 326 Ill.App. 1, 60 N.E.2d 908[1] On the other hand, some of his answers are corroborated by other credible evidence.

Prior to the accident plaintiff was a strong, healthy, active individual, 37 years of age and had served six years on the police force of the city of Chicago. One of the physicians who cared for him immediately after the accident testified to a head injury but stated there was no skull fracture. Plaintiff was taken from the scene of the accident to an Oak Park hospital in an unconscious condition. The doctor stated that when the plaintiff arrived at the hospital he had lost his power of reason and speech and that physical restraint was necessary. He improved, and in about two weeks the doctors consented that he be removed from the hospital to his home. On being taken to his home he suffered an embolus, which the doctor testified was due to a traumatic injury of the chest, the left side of the brain became involved and there was a complete paralysis of his right limbs and side. He was taken to the Cook County Hospital, placed under the care of a neurologist and in about five weeks he was removed to the University Hospital where he remained under the care of the same specialist for more than a year. The neurologist testified that for a period

---

1. Eds. note: The appellate court opinion states: "The physician who treated him shortly after the accident and examined him several times thereafter, testified that at the time of the trial plaintiff's 'answers to questions are not dependable at all.' The other physician who examined plaintiff, for the purpose of testifying on the trial, said that plaintiff was suffering from a 'marked aphasia of a motor type, which means that he is unable to formulate words and express them, either by speech or by writing. I found that ... once his mind got in the groove, he stayed on one particular word, he kept repeating the same word, no matter what question was directed toward him'; that plaintiff 'is not able to formulate sentences to speak of at all'; that most of plaintiff's history was obtained from his brother and from material furnished to the witness; that 'his answers to questions on account of the injury he received did not permit him to say what he meant'; that 'you cannot converse with the man (plaintiff) at all.' The nature of plaintiff's testimony and the degree of his incompetency may be judged from the following excerpts from his cross-examination:

'Q. When did you go to the Cook County Hospital? Ans. Right arm and brain.

'Q. Do you remember when you went to the County Hospital? Ans. One day.'

And later:

'Q. Then after you were in the Cook County Hospital, where did you go? Ans. Five weeks, Cook County, five weeks.

'Q. Well, from Cook County Hospital, where did you go? Ans. Oak Park Hospital, thirteen days, and County Hospital five weeks.

'Q. Where did you go from County Hospital? Ans. I was going to take light, doctor, Light.

'Q. You went to Dr. Light? Ans. Yes, green.

'Q. Green light? Ans. Light.

'Q. Was that the name of your doctor at Cook County Hospital? Ans. No, no. Six days, Light.

'Q. Light for six days? Ans. Kalamazoo.' "

326 Ill.App. at 7, 60 N.E.2d at 910.

of two years following the accident there was slow but continuous improvement, but since then there had been no change in his mental condition. He stated that immediately after the accident he could not enunciate clearly, that he spoke in a jargon, but that after a lapse of time he had improved, and that it was apparent he understood the questions asked. The medical experts said that his speech was involved, his mental condition disturbed, he could not repeat simple phrases, his judgment was poor, he could not recall events or names correctly. At times he was confused on directions. He testified plaintiff could answer single word questions correctly but that on repeated questioning, he tired easily and became confused. This he said was typical of this class of cases known in the medical profession as aphasia, or the inability to coordinate thoughts and use words to express them.

The question of the competency of a witness and the credit to be attached to his testimony are closely related and should not be confused. The question of competency is for the court, and the weight to be accorded the testimony is for the jury. On the question of competency it is said in Wigmore on Evidence, 2d Ed., sec. 501: "The tendency of modern times is to abandon all attempts to distinguish between incapacity which affects only the degree of credibility and incapacity which excludes the witness entirely. The whole question is one of degree only, and the attempt to measure degrees and to define that point at which total incredibility ceases and credibility begins is an attempt to discover the intangible. The subject is not one which deserves to be brought within the realm of legal principle, and it is profitless to pretend to make it so. Here is a person on the stand; perhaps he is a total imbecile, in manner, but perhaps, also, there will be a gleam of sense here and there in his story. The jury had better be given the opportunity of disregarding the evident nonsense and of accepting such sense as may appear. There is usually abundant evidence ready at hand to discredit him when he is truly an imbecile or suffers under a dangerous delusion. It is simpler and safer to let the jury perform the process of measuring the impeached testimony and of sifting out whatever traces of truth may seem to be contained in it."

In Truttmann v. Truttmann, 328 Ill. 338, 159 N.E. 775, it was noted that there was a time when an idiot could not be sworn as a witness but that the test now is whether the derangement or feeblemindedness is such as to make the person untrustworthy as a witness. The standard by which the competency of the witness may be ascertained is to determine whether the witness has the capacity to observe, recollect and communicate. If he has, he is competent and his mental deficiency is considered only in so far as it affects the weight to be given his testimony. People v. Enright, 256 Ill. 221, 99 N.E. 936. . . .

We have referred to the record to study the exact language employed by plaintiff in making his answers and, in view of such answers and in the light of evidence of medical experts as to the character of his mental ailment and the effect it has had on his powers of speech, we conclude that he was competent to testify and that the Appellate Court erred in rejecting his testimony in toto. The discrepancies in answers given to the same or similar questions to a great measure indicate lack of control of the power of speech and under the circumstances shown it was for the jury to determine which answers would be given greater weight. The Appellate Court cited Conley v. People, 170 Ill. 587, 48 N.E. 911, and People v. Brothers, 347 Ill. 530, 180 N.E. 442, to the proposition that the incompetency of a witness entirely destroys his testimony as evidence, and counsel refer to the same cases in their briefs. The general proposition that incompetency of a witness may be such as to render him incompetent to testify is correct, but neither of the cases relied upon supports the proposition that plaintiff was incompetent. The cases cited were criminal actions and the discussions there in regard to incompetency of a witness were made in considering the question as to whether the defendant had been proved guilty beyond a reasonable doubt.

At the close of all the evidence, defendant moved for a directed verdict as to each count of the complaint. The motions made challenged the sufficiency of the evidence to establish a charge of ordinary negligence under the first count, and of wilful and wanton negligence under the second count. The answer to the special interrogatory which was to the effect that defendant's bus was operated in a wilful and wanton manner, and the general verdict in favor of plaintiff amounted to a finding that defendant was guilty of wilful and wanton negligence as charged in the second count. Defendant's motion for judgment notwithstanding the verdict therefore raises a question as to whether plaintiff proved a case of wilful and wanton negligence under the second count.

. . .

There was no error in the trial court's refusal of defendant's motion for judgment notwithstanding the verdict. The judgment of the Appellate Court is reversed, and in view of the uncertainty as to whether the Appellate Court passed upon all the other questions involved, the cause is remanded to that court with directions to consider any other questions not previously considered and to either affirm the judgment or reverse it and remand the cause for a new trial.

Reversed and remanded, with directions.

■ WILSON, J., dissenting.

People v. White

Supreme Court of Illinois, 1968.
40 Ill.2d 137, 238 N.E.2d 389.

■ HOUSE, JUSTICE. Anita White was convicted of the misdemeanor of theft of property not from the person and not exceeding $150 in value in a trial before a magistrate of the circuit court of Cook County. Defendant's application for probation was granted and she was released to a probation officer for one year on condition that she serve the first 30 days in jail. A constitutional question gives us jurisdiction.

There was no reporter present during the trial of the defendant, so no transcript of the evidence is available. There has been furnished a narrative report of proceedings under Rule 323(c), Ill.Rev.Stat.1967, c. 110A, § 323(c), from which the following facts appear.

Mrs. Idelle Broday shared a room in a nursing home with Mrs. Mickey Kallick. She was robbed of a ring which was taken from her with sufficient force to lacerate her finger. The defendant, who was employed as a nurse's aid in the nursing home the night the ring was taken, was accused of the crime. Mrs. Broday was incompetent to testify and there are grave doubts as to the competency of Mrs. Kallick, the only alleged eyewitness. The complaint was signed by Mrs. Broday's son, apparently on the word of a Mrs. Van Kirk, the head nurse at the home.

Because of the condition of Mrs. Kallick (whose doctors would not permit her to be moved) a portion of the trial was held at the nursing home. Mrs. Van Kirk testified that the eyewitness could not speak but her hearing was normal. The only way she could communicate was to raise her right knee if her answer was "yes" and to remain still if the answer was "no". The trial judge, after extensive examination, stated he thought her competent and she then testified by communicating her answers through the raising of a knee or failure to do so. Her testimony was that she was the roommate of the victim, that she had known the defendant for some time and she identified the defendant as the person who came into their room late at night and removed the ring. Aside from a daughter-in-law of the victim who described the ring and stated that it could not be removed, the only other witness was Mrs. Van Kirk.

She testified that sometime prior to the incident Mrs. Kallick had been taught to answer questions in the manner described. According to her testimony, she asked Mrs. Kallick if she knew who had taken Mrs. Broday's ring and she answered "yes" by moving her right knee. Mrs. Van Kirk then checked the employment records to determine who was employed on the night of the theft and she had each such employee come into the room. When the defendant, Anita White, came into the room Mrs. Kallick raised her knee and Mrs. Van Kirk then informed the police of her investigation.

While the record may not establish total incompetency of the eyewitness, we are of the opinion that her condition was such that defendant could not get a fair trial. The witness had no means of originally communicating an accusation. She was unable to state what she saw nor could she describe the ring or the person who took it. Cross-examination was necessarily limited and had to be conducted under circumstances which we feel violated the fundamental right of cross-examination. Not only was cross-examination unduly restricted by the condition of the witness, but identification left much to be desired. It is practically impossible to gauge the influence which Mrs. Van Kirk may have exerted upon the witness.

The conviction must be reversed and the condition of the only eyewitness is such that it would be useless to remand. Other questions are raised by the defendant, but in view of our holding it is unnecessary to discuss them.

The judgment of the circuit court of Cook County is reversed.

Judgment reversed.

NOTES

People v. Seel, 386 N.E.2d 370, 380 (Ill.App.1979), involved a prosecution witness who had been diagnosed as a schizophrenic and hospitalized four times. The witness was also deaf in one ear and had difficulty in speaking English and even Polish, apparently her native tongue, in connection with which an interpreter was used. In regard to this witness the court observed: "Rather, it is the overall confusion of testimony which merits attention. In view of Nash's various impairments, a certain degree of confusion was to be expected in her examination under the pressure of a trial. In our view, if the confusion reflected in her testimony exceeded that degree which was to be expected, it was due in large measure to defense counsel's efforts to treat her as a normal witness and engage in the same form of verbal pyrotechnics by which counsel traditionally shakes the testimony of adverse witnesses. If the fruits of these efforts were incoherent exchanges, we believe that that is due as much to the failure of counsel to adapt cross examination technique to fit the witness as to weaknesses in the witness' testimony."

A.H. Angerstein, Inc. v. Jankowski, 187 A.2d 81 (Del.1962) (workmen's compensation claimant able to say only one word, namely, "No"); Jones v. State, 275 A.2d 508 (Md.App.1971) (not error to refuse to strike testimony of 12–year-old in sodomy prosecution who experienced "emotional blockage" during cross-examination); Villarreal v. State, 576 S.W.2d 51, 57 (Tex.Crim. App.1978), cert. denied, 444 U.S. 885 (1979) (not abuse of discretion to rule competent a deaf mute with an I.Q. on the borderline of dull to normal who at trial could only testify in simple terms and through an interpreter and who relied heavily on photographic exhibits). See also Garcia v. State, 463 N.E.2d 1099 (Ind.1984) (deaf mute); Annot., Deaf Mute as Witness, 50 A.L.R.4th 1183 (1986); Dennis v. Sears, Roebuck & Co., 461 S.W.2d 325 (Mo.Ct.App.1970) (59–year-old woman with mental age of 10 or 11 competent to testify concerning fall on escalator).

United States v. Van Meerbeke, 548 F.2d 415 (2d Cir.), cert. denied, 430 U.S. 974, (1977), is an unusual case. The government's witness, while on the stand, ate small quantities of opium that he found in a suitcase, a government exhibit shown to him for purposes of identification. The opium, according to the witness, caused him to have minor hallucinations. The judge, and perhaps some of the jurors, but not counsel, saw the opium-eating incident, but the judge said nothing to counsel. Counsel did observe a second incident of opium eating by the witness on the next trial day, and the judge's earlier observation was then revealed. Held: It was not error to find the witness competent: the opium-eating incidents were fully aired before the jury. It was error, although harmless, for the judge not to have notified counsel promptly about what he had seen.

Cramer v. Tyars

Supreme Court of California, 1979.
23 Cal.3d 131, 151 Cal.Rptr. 653, 588 P.2d 793.

■ RICHARDSON, J.—May a mentally retarded person who is the subject of a petition for civil commitment to the state Department of Health pursuant to former Welfare and Institutions Code section 6502 (all further statutory references are to that code unless otherwise cited) be called as a witness at the commitment hearing? We conclude that he may.

Preliminarily, we review certain provisions of sections 6500–6512 governing the commitment proceedings in issue. Section 6502 authorizes the verified petition for commitment be filed by the following: a parent, guardian, or other person charged with the support of the mentally retarded person, any district attorney or probation officer, the Youth authority, any person so designated by the superior court in the county of the person's residence, or by the Director of Corrections. Mentally retarded persons are defined as those nonpsychotic persons "who are so mentally retarded from infancy or before reaching maturity that they are incapable of managing themselves and their affairs independently, with ordinary prudence, or of being taught to do so, and who require supervision, control, and care, for their own welfare or the welfare of others, or for the welfare of the community" (§ 6500). Only those mentally retarded persons who constitute a danger to themselves or others can be committed to the Department of Health and the commitment is for one year's duration subject to renewal by the same petition process (§ 6500.1).

Upon the filing of such petition the matter is set for hearing. The alleged mentally retarded person must be notified of the hearing, and, if the petition is filed by a probation officer, district attorney, the Youth Authority, or the Director of Corrections, the person's parent or guardian also must be given such notice as is deemed proper by the court (§ 6504). Counsel must be furnished unless the person has his own attorney (§ 6500.1). At the hearing section 6507 directs the court to inquire into the "condition or status" of the alleged mentally retarded person and authorizes the court to invoke its subpoena power to require the attendance of medical specialists who have "made a special study of mental retardation," a clinical psychologist and such other persons "as it deems advisable, to give evidence." . . .

Against this statutory background we trace appellant's history. Tyars was born on February 12, 1957. At the time of the commitment proceedings under consideration he was almost 20 years old. Before 1965 he had lived with his mother in the Los Angeles area, and from 1965 to 1971 he was in a residential center in Ontario, California. In January 1971 Tyars was placed in the Patton State Hospital in San Bernardino County because of assaultive behavior against his family. Appellant has resided at Patton since that time.

On April 12, 1976, the District Attorney of San Bernardino County filed in the superior court of that county a petition for the commitment of appellant as a mentally retarded person pursuant to section 6502. The petition duly alleged the fact of Tyars' mental retardation and that he was a danger to himself or others. The court appointed a public defender to represent appellant and the matter was set for hearing. The court also granted appellant's request for trial by jury, required that any verdict be unanimous, allowed 13 peremptory challenges, and instructed the jury that it must find in favor of Tyars unless convinced of the truth of the essential allegations of the petition beyond a reasonable doubt.

Two medical examiners at the hearing diagnosed Tyars' condition as mental retardation encephalopathy caused by a postnatal injury. The experts described further medical findings: that he suffered from seizures which were controlled by use of drugs such as dilantin, phenobarbital, and mysoline; that, depending on the measuring test used, Tyars' I.Q. was between 48 and 57, well below the average range of 90–110; and that he was incapable of functioning in a community without supervision. The examiners concluded that his mental defect is permanent and that he is a danger to himself or others. Evidence further adduced at the hearing established that appellant lacks communication skills and has a physical problem, a speech impediment diagnosed as "dysarthria," in which the muscles controlling speech do not permit the affected person to enunciate words clearly. A psychiatric technician at Patton State Hospital, describing appellant's assaultive behavior, testified that Tyars had often attacked other residents and staff members of the hospital, including the technician, using his fists, tables, cue balls, or cue sticks, causing personal injuries and property damage.

At the hearing and over the objections of his counsel appellant was called as a witness pursuant to Evidence Code section 776 which provides for the examination of an adverse party in any civil action. The customary oath was not administered to him (he sat wherever it was comfortable for him in the courtroom) but the trial judge elicited a promise from him that he would tell the truth. The court expressly found that Tyars, while incapable of understanding the oath, did understand the obligation to tell the truth.

Because of his speech handicap Tyars had difficulty in making himself understood. The trial court thereupon caused an "interpreter" who was familiar with appellant's speech to be sworn to "translate English into English," i.e., to make his answers intelligible. The court's questions posed to Tyars were not restated by the interpreter; moreover, Tyars' understandable words were not always the same as those repeated by the interpreter who would either summarize Tyars' answer or simply answer the court directly. In substance, Tyars admitted several acts of violence including the throwing of chairs, "breaking someone's head wide open," and striking a hospital technician; he also named victims of other assaults and batteries and illustrated his testimony by swinging his arms in descriptive punching motions.

After 38 minutes of deliberations the jury returned its verdict finding that appellant was a mentally retarded person who is a danger to himself and others. The court thereafter ordered that he be committed to the Department of Health for placement in a state hospital.

. . .

The principal issue raised by appellant is the propriety of calling him, over objections, as a witness in his own commitment hearing.

We stress, preliminarily, the two separate and distinct testimonial privileges here involved. In a *criminal* matter a defendant has an absolute right not to be called as a witness and not to testify. (Amend. V of the U.S. Const. and art. I, § 15, of the Cal. Const. as codified in Evid.Code, § 930.) Further, in any proceeding, *civil or criminal*, a witness has the right to decline to answer questions which may tend to incriminate him in criminal activity (Evid.Code, § 940). However, as we shall develop more fully, notwithstanding these privileges, no witness has a privilege to refuse to reveal to the trier of fact his physical or mental characteristics where they are relevant to the issues under consideration.

Several features of the applicable statutes (§§ 6500–6512) persuade us that commitment of mentally retarded persons must be deemed essentially civil in nature. . . .

. . .

It follows from the foregoing that while appellant could properly be called as a witness at his commitment proceeding, like any other individual in any proceeding, civil or criminal, he could not be required to give evidence which would tend to incriminate him in any criminal activity and which could subject him to criminal prosecution. . . . To the extent that the necessary elements of mental retardation and dangerousness may be established by evidence of criminal conduct, such evidence must, in its entirety, be elicited from sources other than the individual who is the subject of the commitment proceeding. In the matter before us the trial court, referring to Tyars, observed that "This is not a proceeding in which he could refuse to testify on the grounds that his testimony might tend to incriminate him." This was error. As we have explained, appellant could clearly have refused to testify regarding any *criminal* conduct in which he might have engaged or about any other matter which would tend to implicate him in *criminal* activity.

. . .

We are of the view, however, that the foregoing error does not require a reversal under these circumstances. There was overwhelming evidence of appellant's severe and irreversible mental retardation from both medical experts. The testimony of these two witnesses in conjunction with that of the psychiatric technician who, along with others, had been the object of appellant's repeated assaultive behavior established beyond question that he was a danger to himself and others. No contrary evidence was introduced. Given the weight and nature of the uncontradicted evidence supporting the allegations of the petition it is clear that any erroneous questioning of the appellant was harmless beyond all reasonable doubt. . . .

We conclude that, while appellant could not be questioned about matters that would tend to incriminate him, he was subject to call as a witness and could be required to respond to nonincriminatory questioning which may have revealed his mental condition to the jury, whose duty it was to determine whether he was mentally retarded. Reason and common sense suggest that it is appropriate under such circumstances that a jury be permitted fully to observe the person sought to be committed, and to hear him speak and respond in order that it may make an informed judgment as to the level of his mental and intellectual functioning. The receipt of such evidence may be analogized to the disclosure of physical as opposed to testimonial evidence and may in fact be the most reliable proof and probative indicator of the person's present mental condition. (See People v. Ellis (1966) 65 Cal.2d 529, 533–534, 55 Cal.Rptr. 385, 421 P.2d 393 [voice identification not within the privilege against self-incrimination]; People v. Arnold (1966) 243 Cal.App.2d 510, 52 Cal.Rptr. 475 [handwriting identification not within the privilege against self-incrimination].) Similarly, a defendant even in a criminal proceeding may be required to give "real or physical" evidence in contrast to "communications or testimony" in the sense of disclosing knowledge. Thus the criminal defendant may be asked to stand, wear clothing, hold items, or speak words. (People v. Ellis, supra, at pp. 533–534, 55 Cal.Rptr. at 385, 421 P.2d at 393; People v. Sims (1976) 64 Cal.App.3d 544, 552, 134 Cal.Rptr. 566.) It was proper for the jury to have the benefit of its own observations of Tyars' responses, both in manner and content, to the court's questions.

> .   .   .

Appellant now argues that he was incompetent to be a witness because of mental incapacity. His counsel, however, made no objection as to his competency as a witness at any time during the hearing and the objection must therefore be deemed waived.... Nor do we find merit in appellant's claim that his speech handicap necessarily made him an incompetent witness. As previously noted, a ward attendant who was very familiar with appellant's speech served as an "interpreter" and there was no contention made at the hearing that this arrangement was unsatisfactory.[1]

The judgment is affirmed.

■ TOBRINER, J., MOSK, J., CLARK, J., and MANUEL, J. concurred.

[The dissenting opinion of CHIEF JUSTICE BIRD, concurred in by JUSTICE NEWMAN, is omitted.]

NOTES

1. What is the relation between the testimonial-non-testimonial distinction developed for the purposes of the privilege against self-incrimination, referred to by the court in Cramer v. Tyars, and the question of competence to be a witness? Might a person be incompetent to give "testimony," but nevertheless "a jury be permitted fully to observe the person ... to hear him speak and respond in order that it may make an informed judgment as to the level of his mental and intellectual functioning"?

2. In People v. McCaughan, 317 P.2d 974, 981 (Cal.1957), a prosecution of a psychiatric technician at a mental hospital for involuntary manslaughter of a patient through spoon feeding alleged to have been done improperly, where much of the prosecution's evidence came from patients at the hospital, the court observed: "[S]ound discretion demands the exercise of great caution in

---

1. According to the dissenting opinion, the interpreter was the main witness against appellant on the issue of his dangerousness. Eds.

qualifying as competent a witness who has a history of insane delusions relating to the very subject of inquiry in a case in which the question is not simply whether or not an act was done but, rather, the manner in which it was done and in which testimony as to details may mean the difference between conviction and acquittal." Hilscher v. State, 314 N.Y.S.2d 904 (Ct.Cl.1970) (not error to allow inmate of mental hospital with I.Q. of 45–59 to testify he set fires).

3. See Weihofen, Testimonial Competence and Credibility, 34 Geo. Wash.L.Rev. 53 (1965), on expert testimony bearing on the competence of witnesses. In regard to ordering psychiatric examination of a witness, in United States v. Gutman, 725 F.2d 417, 420 (7th Cir.), cert. denied, 469 U.S. 880 (1984), it was held not error to refuse to order an examination of a prosecution witness even though there was evidence of mental illness and the witness was committed to a mental health facility shortly after the trial. Evidence of earlier psychiatric reports was put before the jury. "It is unpleasant enough to have to testify in a public trial subject to cross-examination without also being asked to submit to a psychiatric examination the results of which will be spread on the record in open court to disqualify you, or at least to spice up your cross-examination." See also State v. Lairby, 699 P.2d 1187, 1197–98 (Utah 1984) (not abuse of discretion to refuse to order examination of prosecution witness, a child, in sexual abuse case, no substantial question having been raised as to witness's suffering a "mental aberration" affecting her veracity); Government of the Virgin Islands v. Leonard, 922 F.2d 1141, 1142–44 (3d Cir.1991) (not error in rape case to refuse to order psychiatric examination of defendant's 13–year-old daughter contended to be a liar and manipulator); Government of Virgin Islands v. Scuito, 623 F.2d 869, 874–76 (3d Cir.1980) (not error to refuse to order examination in rape prosecution although affidavit supporting motion for examination alleged complainant used drugs that led to altered states of consciousness); United States v. Heinlein, 490 F.2d 725, 727–32 (D.C.Cir.1973) (not error to refuse to order examination of prosecution witness although witness was chronic alcoholic with moderate to severe memory defect and was probably drunk at time of the events to which he testified); United States v. Benn, 476 F.2d 1127 (D.C.Cir.1972) (not abuse of discretion to refuse to order examination of 18–year-old retarded prosecutrix in sexual assault case in view of her father's testimony as to her condition, the character of her testimony, the witness's interest in privacy and the importance of not deterring complaints of sexual assaults). State v. R.W., 514 A.2d 1287, 1291 (N.J.1986): Party requesting psychiatric examination to determine competency "must present evidence reasonably indicating something peculiar, unique, or abnormal about the young witness that would influence the witness's competence or the court's ability to assess that competence, or raise unusual difficulties in assessing the witness's credibility.... [A]ge per se cannot serve as a basis for ordering psychiatric testing...."

In Easterday v. State, 256 N.E.2d 901 (Ind.1970), a sodomy conviction was reversed because of refusal to order a psychiatric examination of the prosecuting witness, a 10–year-old girl who had told false stories about sexual matters before. But in Hoover v. State, 589 N.E.2d 243 (Ind.1992), a prosecution for child molestation, it was held not error to refuse defendant's motion for a psychiatric examination of child witness, the court expressing displeasure with language in Easterday to the effect that testimony of female witnesses in sex offense cases is inherently unreliable. State v. Franklin, 229 A.2d 657 (N.J. 1967) (error not to order prosecution witness to submit to psychiatric examination: she had been in mental institution and trial court's order appointing a psychiatrist showed it had doubts about her competency).

As will be noted, some of the cases include among the considerations to be taken into account in deciding whether to order a psychiatric examination, protection of privacy and not deterring complaints and law suits of certain kinds. These same considerations appear in connection with Fed.R.Evid. 412, which concerns evidence of a victim's sexual behavior or predisposition in cases involving alleged sexual misconduct. See infra p. 901.

What is the difference between requiring a witness to submit to a psychiatric examination to determine competency and requiring him to submit to interrogation by a lawyer for the same purpose?

For the admissibility of expert testimony on credibility, see infra p. 447.

4.   Eisen v. Picard, 452 F.2d 860 (1st Cir.1971), cert. denied, 406 U.S. 950 (1972), raises the question of the relation between competence to testify as a witness and certain other issues. Defendant was prosecuted for first degree murder. The only issue was his sanity at the time he killed the victims, his wife and daughter. There was evidence tending to show that he was in a psychotic state at the time he killed the victims, as a result of a suicide attempt by his wife. At trial, the prosecution was allowed to introduce evidence of extrajudicial statements made by defendant. Some of these statements were made before defendant was taken into custody, for instance statements made to hunters who found defendant wandering in the Connecticut woods in a distraught condition, and some were made while defendant was in custody. Defendant unsuccessfully attempted to have all these extrajudicial statements excluded on the ground that he was insane at the time he made them. Defendant was convicted and his conviction affirmed by the state appellate court. He prevailed, however, in a federal habeas corpus proceeding, the court of appeals holding that the state courts had not properly distinguished between the question of the "voluntariness" of the defendant's statements and his "competence" at the time he made them. In regard to in-custody statements, a finding of "voluntariness", the court held, was necessary, and "a finding of voluntariness using a test for determining competency is not adequate because it does not take account of the absence of free will." As to the defendant's "competency" at the time he made the extrajudicial statements, both those made before he was taken into custody and those made in custody, the court observed that the defendant's objection "raised an issue which should have been resolved by the trial court on grounds more substantial than the bare possibility that they [the extrajudicial statements] *might have been competent*." When the term "competence" is used in respect to an extrajudicial declarant, does it have the same meaning as when used for in-court witnesses? How is the question of the competence of an extrajudicial declarant related to the question whether his extrajudicial statement is inadmissible hearsay? Eisen v. Picard also indirectly touches upon the question of the relation between competence to be a witness and competence to stand trial and the relation between these issues and the insanity defense.

SECTION 2.   PREPARATION OF WITNESSES

People v. McGuirk

Appellate Court of Illinois.
106 Ill.App.2d 266, 245 N.E.2d 917, cert. denied, 396 U.S. 972 (1969).

[The defendant was convicted of rape and indecent liberties with a 9–year-old girl.]

■ DEMPSEY, JUSTICE.

. . .

In cross-examination, following her testimony in chief, the prosecutrix testified that the prosecutor had read something to her [a transcript of her testimony before the grand jury] and told her to say the same thing that was on the paper. She also answered "yes" to the following questions:

"And you want to do what the nice man says, do you not, honey?"

"Did he tell you that he [McGuirk] would be the only colored man that was sitting at the table?"

"And he told you to point out the colored man, did he not, is that right, honey?"

"And you would do what the man says, would you not, honey, because he is a good man?"

"Whatever he says you are to say you would say, is that not right honey?"

On re-direct examination she reaffirmed that the prosecutor had told her "some to say" and that he had said that the man she was to identify would be seated at the table.

An attorney is bound by the testimony of his witnesses and there is nothing improper in refreshing their memories before they take the stand. Reviewing their testimony before trial makes for better direct examination, facilitates the trial and lessens the possibility of irrelevant and perhaps prejudicial interpolations. It is particularly advisable in a sex case to prepare a prosecutrix for the ordeal she will face in the courtroom. A State's attorney must go over her story with her, ease her embarrassment, familiarize himself with the sexual terms she uses and perhaps suggest others. There is nothing wrong with this if the witness' essential testimony is neither altered nor colored by emphasis or suggestion.

A more serious question is raised by the testimony of the prosecutrix that the prosecutor told her "some to say" and to identify the colored man at the counsel table. It is highly improper for a prosecutor to induce a witness to say anything but the truth and it is a denial of due process for a conviction to be obtained on testimony known by the prosecution to be false. Napue v. Illinois, 360 U.S. 264, 79 S.Ct. 1173, 3 L.Ed.2d 1217 (1959). What the prosecutor told the child to say, however, is not disclosed in the record. The case was tried before the court and the court was aware of her statement and could weigh the truth of her testimony accordingly. There was ample corroboration of her testimony and no reason to suspect that the "some to say" included untruthful suggestion.

Although the prosecutor told the prosecutrix that McGuirk would be seated at the counsel table the implication that this induced his identification is not justified under the facts of this case. She was not identifying a stranger. The defendant was the janitor of the building in which she lived and they had spoken together several times before the day of the crime. Moreover, she testified that she informed the prosecutor that McGuirk had raped her and that he never used the defendant's name until she mentioned it to him.

This is not a case where the defendant's conviction rests solely upon the testimony of the complaining witness. The defendant was almost caught in the act. The corroborating evidence surrounding the commission of the crime . . .

would justify the finding of guilty even if her testimony were less convincing than it was.

. . .

Affirmed in part and reversed in part.[1]

■ SULLIVAN, P.J., and SCHWARTZ, J., concur.

Resolution Trust Corp. v. Bright

United States Court of Appeals, Fifth Circuit, 1993.
6 F.3d 336.

■ KAZEN, DISTRICT JUDGE.

This appeal arises out of a lawsuit filed in May 1992 by the Resolution Trust Corporation ("RTC") against H.R. "Bum" Bright and James B. "Boots" Reeder, based on their alleged misconduct in connection with activities at Bright Banc Savings Association, Dallas ("Bright Banc"). Approximately two months after the suit was filed, appellees moved for a protective order and sanctions against the RTC for the manner in which its attorneys, Peter F. Lovato III and Thomas D. Graber, interviewed a former Bright Banc employee. After four days of hearings on the motion for sanctions, the district court issued an oral order on October 19, 1992, finding that the attorneys, appellants herein, impermissibly attempted to persuade the witness to sign an affidavit containing statements which the witness had not previously told appellants. The order disbarred the attorneys from practicing before the district judge and disqualified the attorneys' law firm, Hopkins & Sutter, from further representing RTC in the underlying case. In a December 28, 1992 written order, the court assessed attorneys' fees against the law firm for costs incurred by appellees in prosecuting the sanctions motion. Appellants timely appealed the district court's decision. We reverse.

. . .

On May 14, 1992, the RTC filed suit in federal district court charging appellees Bright and Reeder, as shareholders, directors and officers of Bright Banc, with fraud, negligence, and breach of fiduciary and other duties owed to the bank's shareholders. As part of their pre-filing investigation of the case, attorneys Lovato and Graber conducted several interviews—all voluntary—with Barbara Erhart, formerly the Senior Vice President of Finance Support at Bright Banc. Erhart had worked closely with defendant Reeder and had contact with defendant Bright on "critical matters."

The primary focus of the Erhart interviews was the method Bright Banc used to calculate the amount of non-cash assets it had converted to cash for a December 1986 report on the bank's financial health to the Federal Home Loan Bank Board ("FHLBB"). The RTC attorneys, including Lovato and Graber, questioned Erhart extensively about who made and authorized the computations used in the report. At the conclusion of the third interview, Lovato and Graber asked Erhart to return to their office the next day—April 9, 1992—to review and sign an affidavit summarizing what she had told them in the course of the prior interviews.

1. The partial reversal was on grounds unconnected with the subject discussed in the portion of the opinion printed.

When Erhart arrived at the office of Hopkins & Sutter on April 9th, she was not immediately given the affidavit. Instead, the attorneys questioned her again about the cash conversion calculations. As Lovato and Graber spoke to Erhart, they made some last-minute changes to the draft. The changes were incorporated into a revised draft which Graber then presented to Erhart. He warned her that it "contained a couple of things [they hadn't] discussed with [her]," but which the attorneys nevertheless believed to be true. Erhart was instructed to read the affidavit "very carefully."

Erhart made several changes to the draft affidavit. Some related only to semantical differences, while others reflected Erhart's disagreement with substantive claims in the affidavit. Lovato and Graber questioned Erhart extensively about the changes she made. During this questioning, the attorneys asked Erhart whether she could reword some of her changes to emphasize that Bright and Reeder were more directly involved in the decision to use the controversial cash conversion computations. Erhart declined because she did not have personal knowledge of the statements the attorneys wanted her to include in her affidavit. With respect to some of the statements in the affidavit, the attorneys were not content to accept Erhart's initial refusal to revise her changes. In an effort to have Erhart see things their way, Lovato and Graber described their understanding of how certain events transpired at Bright Banc, presented Erhart with independent evidence to support this interpretation of events, and aggressively challenged some of Erhart's assumptions about Bright and Reeder. After making their case for further revisions, Lovato and Graber asked Erhart whether she believed them and whether she was now convinced that their version of certain events was correct. Erhart, unconvinced, declined to alter the initial changes she had made to the draft affidavit.

When it was clear to the attorneys that Erhart would not sign a statement agreeing with the attorneys' version of some of the disputed events at Bright Banc, they incorporated Erhart's handwritten changes into a new draft affidavit. Erhart read this draft and made a few changes which were then included in a third draft. Erhart read and approved this version of the affidavit, signed it and left the offices of Hopkins & Sutter.

Approximately one month later, Erhart told appellees' attorneys that she had given a statement to appellant-attorneys regarding some of the transactions at issue in the underlying law suit. Appellees' counsel then arranged for Erhart to give them an ex parte statement on June 12, 1992 about her meetings with Lovato and Graber. This statement was transcribed by the court reporter but never signed by Erhart. However, she later adopted portions of it during testimony before Judge Kendall on August 9, 1992.

In that testimony, Erhart stated, among other things, that she did not think Lovato and Graber were asking her to say something she did not believe but rather were trying to determine if she could see the case the way they did. She denied being harassed or intimidated and expressed the view that "they were doing their job, just like everybody else." The district court essentially disregarded this testimony, finding it contrary to Erhart's earlier ex parte statement given to appellees' attorneys, and concluding that the change must have been the result of "obvious job pressure." Erhart's earlier statement clearly has a different tone from her subsequent court testimony. For example, she earlier described Lovato as having been particularly aggressive in attempts to persuade her to agree with appellants' version of certain events, "almost like browbeating me." Nevertheless even in her ex parte statement, Erhart indicated that Lovato and Graber were not trying to have her change facts but rather to agree with a different "interpretation" or "slant" from the facts.

. . .

On July 15, 1992, Bright and Reeder moved for sanctions and a protective order against the RTC based on Lovato and Graber's conduct during the Erhart interviews. The motion alleged that the manner in which the RTC's attorneys interviewed Erhart violated Texas Disciplinary Rules of Professional Conduct 3.04, 4.01(a) and 4.04(a) and probably violated 18 U.S.C. §§ 1503, 1512. Appellees also called upon the court to exercise its "inherent powers" to sanction the RTC for intimidating Erhart. The motion asked the court to prevent the RTC from using any notes or statements obtained through the Erhart interviews, to order the RTC not to make any further contact with Erhart, and to award attorneys fees to Bright and Reeder for their efforts in bringing and prosecuting the motion for sanctions.

. . .

The [district] court found that Lovato and Graber "knowingly attempted to get a key witness . . . to commit to a sworn statement that they knew contained assertions of fact she had not made or told them previously in matters highly relevant to the plaintiff's civil claim." It found that the attorneys were "going to try to talk her into" those statements. The Court was particularly troubled because the draft affidavit given to Erhart added matters only in areas "that established or buttressed the [RTC's] claims." The court characterized the attorneys' actions concerning the draft affidavit as "tampering with" or attempting to "manufacture" evidence to "cause, or aid in, Defendants' downfall."

Based on its inherent power to regulate the conduct of attorneys, Judge Kendall disbarred Lovato and Graber from practicing before him. He assessed $110,000 in attorneys fees against Hopkins & Sutter for expenses incurred by Bright and Reeder in the prosecution of the sanctions motion. Pursuant to its authority under Local Rule 13.2 (N.D.Tex.),[1] the court removed Hopkins & Sutter from further representing the RTC in the underlying action. Finally, it ordered the firm not to charge the RTC for defending against the sanction motion. No sanctions were assessed against the RTC. Lovato, Graber and Hopkins & Sutter timely appealed.

. . .

Because disbarment is a quasi-criminal proceeding, any disciplinary rules used to impose this sanction on attorneys must be strictly construed, resolving ambiguities in favor of the person charged. . . . The Texas Disciplinary Rules of Professional Conduct do not expressly apply to sanctions in federal courts, but a federal court may nevertheless hold attorneys accountable to the state code of professional conduct. . . .

The district court failed to make specific findings of how appellants violated the Disciplinary Rules. In its oral findings, the court concluded that Lovato and Graber engaged in "inappropriate conduct, conduct that probably

---

1. Local Rule 13.2 of the U.S. District Court For the Northern District of Texas states, in pertinent part,

Any member of the bar of this Court . . . who proves to be incompetent to practice before this Court because of unethical behavior . . . is subject to revocation of

admission to practice in this District and to other appropriate discipline, after such hearing as the Court may direct in each particular instance.

[Footnote of the court, renumbered. Other footnotes omitted.]

violates the DRs, unethical conduct, as well as a probable violation of the obstruction of justice statutes." We shall assume that the district court's comments referred to the Disciplinary Rules invoked by Appellees in their motion for sanctions.

The sanctionable conduct found by the district court was the attorneys' inclusion of statements in draft affidavits that had not been previously discussed with Erhart, combined with the attorneys' attempts to persuade Erhart to agree with their understanding of how certain events transpired at the bank. Placing statements in a draft affidavit that have not been previously discussed with a witness does not automatically constitute bad-faith conduct. See United States v. Brand, 775 F.2d 1460, 1469 (11th Cir.1985) (giving witness affidavit with statements not previously discussed not obstruction of justice). It is one thing to ask a witness to swear to facts which are knowingly false. It is another thing, in an arms-length interview with a witness, for an attorney to attempt to persuade her, even aggressively, that her initial version of a certain fact situation is not complete or accurate. Disciplinary Rules 3.04(b) and 4.01(a) concern the former circumstance, not the latter. The district court never found that appellants asked Erhart to make statements which they knew to be false. Indeed, the district court pretermitted any consideration of the truth of the draft affidavits. Appellees nevertheless argue that because appellant attorneys attempted to persuade Erhart to adopt certain statements which she had not expressly made and which she refused to adopt, the attorneys thereby were either making or urging the making of "false" statements in violation of DRs 3.04(b) and 4.01(a). We disagree. The district court characterized the attorneys' behavior as "manufacturing" evidence, but there is no indication that the attorneys did not have a factual basis for the additional statements included in the draft affidavit. See Koller v. Richardson–Merrell, 737 F.2d 1038, 1058–59 (D.C.Cir.1984), vacated on other grounds 472 U.S. 424, 105 S.Ct. 2757, 86 L.Ed.2d 340 (1985). On the contrary, appellants have attempted to demonstrate in a detailed chart that the contested portions of the affidavit were based either on their notes of interviews with Erhart or on evidence from other sources (e.g., internal bank memorandum).

We recognize that the Texas Disciplinary Rules are not the sole authority governing a motion to disqualify in federal court; rather, such a motion must be determined by standards developed under federal law. In re Dresser Industries, Inc., 972 F.2d 540, 543 (5th Cir.1992). Our source for professional standards has been the canons of ethics developed by the American Bar Association. Id. The district court opinion, however, makes no reference to any national canons which would add to the analysis here, nor do appellees. A court obviously would be justified in disbarring an attorney for attempting to induce a witness to testify falsely under oath, see Thalheim, 853 F.2d at 390 (citing United States v. Friedland, 502 F.Supp. 611, 619 (D.N.J.1980), aff'd. 672 F.2d 905 (3d Cir.1981)), but this record does not support the conclusion that Lovato and Graber engaged in such behavior. While the attorneys were persistent and aggressive in presenting their theory of the case to Erhart, they nevertheless made sure that Erhart signed the affidavit only if she agreed with its contents. The attorneys never attempted to hide from Erhart the fact that some statements were included in draft affidavits that had not been discussed with her previously. Instead, they brought the statements to her attention and warned her to read them carefully. Additionally, Lovato and Graber never claimed to be neutral parties. Erhart knew that these attorneys were advocates for a particular position, and she was also in communication with attorneys who were advocating the contrary position. Were Erhart giving testimony at a deposition or at trial, the attorneys for either side would not be required to accept her initial testimony at face value but would be able to confront her with other information to challenge her testimony or attempt to persuade her to change it.

Appellees also alleged that RTC attorneys violated Disciplinary Rule 4.04(a), which prohibits an attorney from burdening a third party without a valid "substantial purpose" or violating a third party's legal rights. The district court findings do not reveal that Lovato and Graber committed either wrong. The attorneys' sometimes laborious interviews with Erhart were conducted with the goal of eliciting an accurate and favorable affidavit from a key witness in the underlying case. Additionally, the district court made no findings that the interviews violated Erhart's legal rights, nor does the record contain any evidence to support such a finding.

.   .   .

We conclude that the district court abused its discretion when it issued its sanctions ruling against appellants. We reverse and remand for proceedings not inconsistent with this opinion.

Opinion No. 79, Legal Ethics Committee of the District of Columbia Bar

Code of Professional Responsibility and Opinions of the District of Columbia.
Legal Ethics Committee, District of Columbia Bar 169 (1980).

We have been asked to delineate the ethical limitations upon a lawyer's participation in preparing the testimony of witnesses.

The specific inquiry before us arises out of adjudicatory hearings before a federal regulatory agency. The agency's rules of practice provide that direct testimony of witnesses is to be submitted in written form prior to the hearing session at which the testimony is offered; at that session, the witness adopts the testimony and attests that it is true and correct to the best of his or her knowledge and information and then is offered for cross-examination on the testimony thus submitted. The particular questions put by the inquirer are whether it is ethically proper for a lawyer actually to write the testimony the witness will adopt under oath; whether, if so, the lawyer may include in such testimony information that the lawyer has initially secured from sources other than the witness; and whether, after the written direct testimony has been prepared, the lawyer may engage in "practice cross-examination exercises" intended to prepare the witness for questions that may be asked at the hearing.

Although the particular questions posed by the inquiry are appropriate to the procedural background against which they arise, the issues they raise have broader significance. Submission of direct testimony in written form in advance of a hearing at which the witness is subject to questioning about the testimony is a frequent and familiar pattern, but it is by no means the only kind of setting in which lawyers are called upon to assist in the preparation of a witness's testimony. Written testimony is offered in a variety of forms and circumstances: in answers to written interrogatories, for instance; and in all sorts of affidavits. Lawyers are almost invariably involved in the preparation of the former, and frequently in the latter as well. There is also a pattern, somewhat parallel to that of the administrative agency in the present inquiry, to be found in legislative hearings, where witnesses are commonly expected to submit written statements in advance of their appearances before the legislative committees where they then elaborate upon their testimony viva voce.[1] Lawyers are frequently involved in the preparation of such legislative statements and testimony also.

In addition, lawyers commonly, and quite properly, prepare witnesses for testimony that is to be given orally in its entirety. In consequence, questions of whether a lawyer may properly suggest the language in which a witness's testimony will be cast, or suggest subjects for inclusion in testimony, do not arise solely in connection with written testimony. For this reason also, the inquirer's questions about "practice cross-examination exercises" is narrower than it needs to be: there may equally well be practice direct examination.

In sum, the ethical issues raised by the inquiry before us apply more broadly than is implied by the particular questions put by the inquirer. In order to present those issues in a more inclusive setting, the questions may usefully be rephrased as follows:

(1) What are the ethical limitations on a lawyer's suggesting the actual language in which a witness's testimony is to be presented, whether in written form or otherwise?

(2) What are the ethical limitations on a lawyer's suggesting that a witness's testimony include information that was not initially furnished to the lawyer by the witness?

(3) What are the ethical limitations on a lawyer's preparing a witness for the presentation of testimony under live examination, whether direct or cross, and whether by practice questioning or otherwise?

A single prohibitory principle governs the answer to all three of these questions: it is, simply, that a lawyer may not prepare, or assist in preparing, testimony that he or she knows, or ought to know, is false or misleading. So long as this prohibition is not transgressed, a lawyer may properly suggest language as well as the substance of testimony, and may—indeed, should—do whatever is feasible to prepare his or her witnesses for examination.

The governing ethical provisions, which are cast in quite general terms, appear to be EC 7–26 and DR 7–102(A)(4), (6) and (7). The Ethical Consideration reads as follows:

> The law and Disciplinary Rules prohibit the use of fraudulent, false, or perjured testimony or evidence. A lawyer who knowingly participates in introduction of such testimony or evidence is subject to discipline. A lawyer should, however, present any admissible evidence his client desires to have presented unless he knows, or from facts within his knowledge should know, that such testimony or evidence is false, fraudulent, or perjured.

The disciplinary provisions are these:

> DR 7–102. Representing A Client Within The Bounds of The Law.
>
> (A) In his representation of a client, a lawyer shall not:
>
> . . .
>
> (4) Knowingly use perjured testimony or false evidence.
>
> . . .

---

1. The principal difference between this pattern and that of the adjudicatory proceeding of the kind giving rise to the instant inquiry is, ordinarily, that neither the written statements nor the oral testimony are under oath. This difference is not necessarily a significant one for ethical purposes, however. [Footnotes are those of the Committee.]

(6) Participate in the creation or preservation of evidence when he knows or it is obvious that the evidence is false.

(7) Counsel or assist his client in conduct that the lawyer knows to be illegal or fraudulent.

Curiously, there appear to be no decisions of bar ethics committees directly addressing the line of demarcation between permissible and impermissible lawyer participation in the preparation of testimony from the perspective. involved in this inquiry, focusing on the lawyer's conduct rather than on the nature of the testimony; and while there is some authority from other sources, it is scant, and not brightly illuminating.[2] In any event, it seems to us clear that the proper focus is indeed on the substance of the witness's testimony which the lawyer has, in one way or another, assisted in shaping; and not on the manner of the lawyer's involvement. In this regard, the pertinent provisions of the Code, quoted above, do not call for an excessively close analysis. They employ the terms "false," "fraudulent" and "perjured," the terms "testimony" and "evidence," and the terms "illegal" and "fraudulent," in a manner that suggests, not that fine differences are intended, but that the terms are used casually and interchangeably. We think therefore, that all of these provisions, so far as here pertinent, are to the same effect: that a lawyer may not ethically participate in the preparation of testimony that he or she knows, or ought to know, is false or misleading.

It follows, therefore—to address the first question here raised—that the fact that the particular words in which testimony, whether written or oral, is cast originated with a lawyer rather than the witness whose testimony it is has no significance so long as the substance of that testimony is not, so far as the lawyer knows or ought to know, false or misleading. If the particular words suggested by the lawyer, even though not literally false, are calculated to convey a misleading impression, this would be equally impermissible from the ethical point of view. Herein, indeed, lies the principal hazard (leaving aside outright subornation of perjury) in a lawyer's suggesting particular forms of language to a witness instead of leaving the witness to articulate his or her thought wholly without prompting: there may be differences in nuance among variant phrasings of the same substantive point, which are so significant as to make one version misleading while another is not. Yet it is obvious that by the same token, choice of words may also improve the clarity and precision of a statement: even subtle changes of shading may as readily improve testimony as impair it. The fact that a lawyer suggests particular language to a witness means only that the lawyer may be affecting the testimony as respects its clarity and accuracy; and not necessarily that the effect is to debase rather than improve the testimony in these respects. It is not, we think, a matter of undue difficulty for a reasonably competent and conscientious lawyer to discern the line of impermissibility, where truth shades into untruth, and to refrain from crossing it.[3]

2. The United States Supreme Court has referred to EC 7–26 and DR 7–102 as embodying "the important ethical distinction between discussing testimony and seeking improperly to influence it," Geders v. United States, 425 U.S. 80, 90 n. 3 (1976), but the Court did not elaborate on the distinction.

3. The United States Court of Appeals for the Fourth Circuit has articulated the line of impermissibility (in the context of the sequestration of a defendant during a short recess in the course of a trial) about as clearly as it can be done:

> The danger ... is that counsel's advice may significantly shape or alter the giving of further testimony ... that will be untrue or a tailored distortion or evasion of the truth.

United States v. Allen, 542 F.2d 630, 633 (4th Cir.1976), cert. denied, 430 U.S. 908 (1977).

We note that in the particular circumstances giving rise to this inquiry, there is some built-in assurance against hazards of this kind, to be found in the fact that the testimony will be subject to cross examination—which, of course, may properly probe the extent of the lawyer's participation in the actual drafting of the direct testimony, including whether language used by the witness originated with the lawyer rather than the witness, what other language was considered but rejected, the nuances involved, and so forth. The risk of distortion, whether intentional or unintentional, is obviously greater where (as will often be the case with affidavits or written answers to interrogatories) the testimony is not going to be subject to cross examination. Nonetheless, even in that context there should be no undue difficulty for a lawyer in avoiding such distortion.

The second question raised by the inquiry—as to the propriety of a lawyer's suggesting the inclusion in a witness's testimony of information not initially secured from the witness—may, again, arise not only with respect to written testimony but with oral testimony as well. In either case, it appears to us that the governing consideration for ethical purposes is whether the substance of the testimony is something the witness can truthfully and properly testify to. If he or she is willing and (as respects his or her state of knowledge) able honestly so to testify, the fact that the inclusion of a particular point of substance was initially suggested by the lawyer rather than the witness seems to us wholly without significance. There are two principal hazards here. One hazard is the possibility of undue suggestion: that is, the risk that the witness may thoughtlessly adopt testimony offered by the lawyer simply because it is so offered, without considering whether it is testimony that he or she may appropriately give under oath. The other hazard is the possibility of a suggestion or implication in the witness's resulting testimony that the witness is testifying on a particular matter of his own knowledge when this is not in fact the case.[4] For reasons explained above, these hazards are likely to be somewhat less serious in a case like the one giving rise to the present inquiry, where cross-examination can inquire into the source of the testimony, and test its truth and genuineness, than in the numerous situations where written testimony will probably not be followed by any examination of the witness at all. Even in the latter situation, however, there should be no difficulty, for a reasonably skilled and scrupulous lawyer, in avoiding the hazards in question.

We turn, finally, to the extent of a lawyer's proper participation in preparing a witness for giving live testimony—whether the testimony is only to be under cross-examination, as in the particular circumstances giving rise to the present inquiry or, as is more usually the case, direct examination as well. Here again it appears to us that the only touchstones are the truth and genuineness of the testimony to be given. The mere fact of a lawyer's having prepared the witness for the presentation of testimony is simply irrelevant: indeed, a lawyer who did not prepare his or her witness for testimony, having had an opportunity to do so, would not be doing his or her professional job properly. This is so if the witness is also a client; but it is no less so if the witness is merely one who is offered by the lawyer on the client's behalf. See Hamdi & Ibrahim Mango Co. v. Fire Association of Philadelphia, 20 F.R.D. 181, 182–83 (S.D.N.Y.1957):

> [It] could scarcely be suggested that it would be improper for counsel who called the witness to review with him prior to the deposition the testimony to be elicited. It is usual and legitimate practice for ethical and diligent counsel to confer with a witness whom he is about to call prior to his giving

---

4. Cf. Rule 602 of the Federal Rules of Evidence....

testimony, whether the testimony is to be given on deposition or at trial. Wigmore recognizes "the absolute necessity of such a conference for legitimate purposes" as part of intelligent and thorough preparation for trial. 3 Wigmore on Evidence, (3d Edition; § 788).

In such a preliminary conference counsel will usually, in more or less general terms, ask the witness the same questions as he expects to put to him on the stand. He will also, particularly in a case involving complicated transactions and numerous documents, review with the witness the pertinent documents, both for the purpose of refreshing the witness' recollection and to familiarize him with those which are expected to be offered in evidence. This sort of preparation is essential to the proper presentation of a case and to avoid surprise.[5]

It matters not at all that the preparation of such testimony takes the form of "practice" examination or cross examination. What does matter is that whatever the mode of witness preparation chosen, the lawyer does not engage in suppressing, distorting or falsifying the testimony that the witness will give.

NOTES

1. Improper preparation of witnesses may lead to a variety of consequences. It may lead to professional discipline, the principal concern of the Legal Ethics Committee of the District of Columbia Bar and one of the means sought to be employed by the District Court in the Resolution Trust case. It may lead to sanctions such as the imposition of costs, also involved in the Resolution Trust case. It may lead to the exclusion of evidence found to have been tainted by the improper preparation. In the section of the casebook dealing with the competency of witnesses, see supra pp. 256–316, this possibility was considered. Exclusion may be on the ground that improper preparation has fatally affected the probative value of the testimony or it may be with an eye to punishment and deterrence. See on exclusion of testimony resulting from plea bargains that contain impermissible conditions, supra p. 290, exclusion of testimony that has been paid for, supra p. 290, and exclusion of post-hypnotic testimony, supra p. 267. Exclusion may be by force of the law of Evidence or by reason of a constitutional provision such as the Due Process Clause or the Confrontation Clause. Improper preparation of witnesses may lead to prosecution for suborning perjury or obstructing justice. Finally, even if improper preparation does not lead to any of the foregoing consequences, disclosure on cross-examination of the fact that it has occurred may impair the credibility of the witness.

---

5. The court in Hamdi went on to say:

There is no doubt that these practices are often abused. The line is not easily drawn between proper review of the facts and refreshment of the recollection of a witness and putting words in the mouth of the witness or ideas in his mind. The line must depend in large measure, as do so many other matters of practice, on the ethics of counsel. Id. at 183.

Although this passage might be read broadly to mean that any suggestion by the attorney of language or ideas to the witness is improper, we think it is more correctly read in the narrower sense of a lawyer's suggesting false testimony. Thus, immediately after the passage in question, the court quoted 3 Wigmore on Evidence (3d ed.) § 788:

This right may be abused, and often is; but to prevent the abuse by any definite rule seems impracticable.

It would seem, therefore, that nothing short of an actual fraudulent conference for concoction of testimony could properly be taken notice of; there is no specific rule of behavior capable of being substituted for the proof of such facts.

Hamdi & Ibrahim Mango Co. v. Fire Assn. of Philadelphia, supra, 20 F.R.D. at 183.

2. It is generally recognized that it is entirely proper and indeed necessary to prepare witnesses to testify. No sound trial lawyer would put a witness on the stand without first hearing his testimony. He interviews his client and witnesses and checks their stories for accuracy and consistency. A few weeks before trial he may stage a mock cross-examination in which he imitates opposing counsel's manner and method of questioning. Witnesses are sometimes advised what to wear, how to sit, whom to face and how to handle trick questions. Exceptionally nervous witnesses may be taken to see a trial and have the proceedings explained to them in an effort to reduce tension. One of the objectives of preparation must be to educate witnesses not to testify in a way that includes inadmissible matter. See Green, "The Whole Truth?": How Rules of Evidence Make Lawyers Deceitful, 25 Loy.L.A. L.Rev. 699, 708 (1992). However, preparation of this sort, essential as it may be to useful testimony and success at trial can pose serious ethical difficulties for a lawyer. How can a lawyer give to his client and other witnesses the sort of assistance necessary for the development of accurate and complete testimony without crossing over the line into improper manipulation and suggestion?

How would you deal with these situations if they arose in office interviews?

(a) Witness: As I stepped off the curb, a truck passed in front of me—I heard a terrific crash. X had turned the corner much too quickly—he hadn't signalled, and he hit Y.

Counsel: How could you see the entire accident if your view was blocked by a truck?

Witness: Well—the truck must have passed before the crash.

(b) Client: I stepped off the curb and the truck hit me.

Counsel: What color was the traffic light?

Client: I don't remember.

Counsel: You're sure you don't remember?

Client: Why is it important?

Counsel: If the light was green in your direction you might have a good case.

Client: I think I remember now. It was green.

Professor Monroe Freedman observes: "In interviewing ... the attorney must take into account the practical psychological realities of the situation. That means, at least at the earlier stages of eliciting the client's story, that the attorney should assume a skeptical attitude, and that the attorney should give the client legal advice that might help in drawing out useful information that the client, consciously or unconsciously, might be withholding. To that extent ... I adhere to my ... position that there are situations in which it may be proper for the attorney to give the client legal advice even though the attorney has reason to believe that the advice may induce the client to commit perjury. There does come a point, however, where nothing less than 'brute rationalization' can purport to justify a conclusion that the lawyer is seeking in good faith to elicit truth rather than actively participating in the creation of perjury." M. Freedman, Lawyers' Ethics in an Adversary System 75 (1975).

In the Resolution Trust case, what was it about the witness and her relation to the lawyers that made their way of dealing with her unobjectionable, whereas it would have been objectionable in the McGuirk case?

In State v. Earp, 571 A.2d 1227 (Md.1990), a prosecution for attempted murder, the fact that the prosecutor had shown the witness a videotape of the victim's deposition did not render the witness's testimony inadmissible. See Applegate, Witness Preparation, 68 Tex.L.Rev. 277, 304–06, 349–51 (1989), discussing whether it is permissible or desirable for a lawyer to arrange a joint meeting of witnesses to go over their testimony. See supra p. 269 on sequestration of witnesses during trial.

Landsman, Reforming Adversary Procedure: A Proposal Concerning the Psychology of Memory and the Testimony of Disinterested Witnesses, 45 U.Pitt.L.Rev. 547 (1984), makes the radical suggestion that to avoid the distorting influence of witnesses' contact with lawyers, contact should be strictly limited, opposing counsel should be present and recordings of meetings required.

3. In the opinion set forth above of the District of Columbia Legal Ethics Committee, the Committee quotes Ethical Consideration 7–26 and Disciplinary Rules 7–102(A)(4), (6) and (7) of the Code of Professional Responsibility of the American Bar Association. Ethical Considerations are "aspirational" in character, whereas Disciplinary Rules are mandatory. See ABA Annot.Code of Professional Responsibility 3 (1979). It may be helpful to set forth some additional provisions of the Code that are relevant to the responsibilities of a lawyer in the preparation of testimony and the problems he may confront when he thinks that testimony may be perjured.

EC 7–5 provides: A lawyer "... may continue in the representation of his client even though his client has elected to pursue a course of conduct contrary to the advice of the lawyer so long as he does not thereby knowingly assist the client to engage in illegal conduct.... A lawyer should never encourage or aid his client to commit criminal acts or counsel his client on how to violate the law and avoid punishment therefor."

EC 7–6 provides: "Whether the proposed action of a lawyer is within the bounds of the law may be a perplexing question when his client is contemplating a course of conduct having legal consequences that vary according to the client's intent, motive, or desires at the time of the action. Often a lawyer is asked to assist his client in developing evidence relevant to the state of mind of the client at a particular time. He may properly assist his client in the development and preservation of evidence of existing motive, intent, or desire; obviously, he may not do anything furthering the creation or preservation of false evidence. In many cases a lawyer may not be certain as to the state of mind of his client, and in those situations he should resolve reasonable doubts in favor of his client." ABA Annot.Code of Professional Responsibility 303–04 (1979).

DR 7–102(A)(8) provides: "In his representation of a client, a lawyer shall not ... [k]nowingly engage in other illegal conduct or conduct contrary to a Disciplinary Rule."

DR 7–102(B) provides: "A lawyer who receives information clearly establishing that:

> (1) His client has, in the course of the representation, perpetrated a fraud upon a person or tribunal shall promptly call upon his client to rectify the same, and if his client refuses or is unable to do so, he shall reveal the fraud to the affected person or tribunal, except when the information is protected as a privileged communication.

> (2) A person other than his client has perpetrated a fraud upon a tribunal shall promptly reveal the fraud to the tribunal."

See also DR 2–110(C)(1)(b), dealing with "withdrawal from employment," which makes permissible a withdrawal from employment if a client "[p]ersonally seeks to pursue an illegal course of conduct," DR 2–110(C)(2), which makes permissible withdrawal from employment if the lawyer's "continued employ-ment is likely to result in a violation of a Disciplinary Rule" and DR 4–101(C)(3), permitting a lawyer to reveal "[t]he intention of his client to commit a crime and the information necessary to prevent the crime." ABA Annot.Code of Professional Responsibility 306, 122, 170–71 (1979).[1]

Increasing sensitivity to the ethical problems confronting lawyers led in 1983 to the adoption by the American Bar Association of the Model Rules of Professional Conduct. ABA Annot. Model Rules of Professional Conduct (1995). As of 1995, thirty-nine jurisdictions had adopted the Model Rules, although in some cases with amendments. Set forth below are provisions of the Model Rules particularly relevant to the lawyer's role in the preparation of testimony and his duty when he has reason to think that testimony may be perjured.

RULE 1.2 SCOPE OF REPRESENTATION

. . .

(d) A lawyer shall not counsel a client to engage, or assist a client, in conduct that the lawyer knows is criminal or fraudulent, but a lawyer may discuss the legal consequences of any proposed course of conduct with a client and may counsel or assist a client to make a good faith effort to determine the validity, scope, meaning or application of the law.

(e) When a lawyer knows that a client expects assistance not permit-ted by the rules of professional conduct or other law, the lawyer shall consult with the client regarding the relevant limitations on the lawyer's conduct.

RULE 1.6 CONFIDENTIALITY OF INFORMATION

(a) A lawyer shall not reveal information relating to representation of a client unless the client consents after consultation, except for disclosures that are impliedly authorized in order to carry out the representation, and except as stated in paragraph (b).

(b) A lawyer may reveal such information to the extent the lawyer reasonably believes necessary:

(1) to prevent the client from committing a criminal act that the lawyer believes is likely to result in imminent death or substantial bodily harm. . . .

. . .

RULE 1.16 DECLINING OR TERMINATING REPRESENTATION

(a) . . . [A] lawyer shall not represent a client or, where representation has commenced, shall withdraw from the representation of a client if:

1. See also 1 ABA Standards for Crimi-nal Justice, Chapter 4, The Defense Func-tion, Standards 4–3.2, 4–3.7, 4–4.3 and 4–7.7 (2d ed. 1980). Of particular interest are the provisions in Standard 4–3.2 that "the lawyer should probe for all legally relevant informa-tion without seeking to influence the di-rection of the client's responses," and that "It is unprofessional conduct for the lawyer to instruct the client or to intimate to the client in any way that the client should not be candid in revealing facts so as to afford the lawyer free rein to take action which would be precluded by the lawyer's knowing of such facts."

(1) the representation will result in violation of the rules of professional conduct or other law;

. . .

(b) ... [A] lawyer may withdraw from representing a client if withdrawal can be accomplished without material adverse effect on the interests of the client, or if:

(1) the client persists in a course of action involving the lawyer's services that the lawyer reasonably believes is criminal or fraudulent;

(2) the client has used the lawyer's services to perpetrate a crime or fraud;

. . .

RULE 3.3 CANDOR TOWARD THE TRIBUNAL

(a) A lawyer shall not knowingly:

(1) make a false statement of material fact or law to a tribunal;

(2) fail to disclose a material fact to a tribunal when disclosure is necessary to avoid assisting a criminal or fraudulent act by the client;

. . .

(4) offer evidence that the lawyer knows to be false. If a lawyer has offered material evidence and comes to know of its falsity, the lawyer shall take reasonable remedial measures.

(b) The duties stated in paragraph (a) continue to the conclusion of the proceeding, and apply even if compliance requires disclosure of information otherwise protected by Rule 1.6.

(c) A lawyer may refuse to offer evidence that the lawyer reasonably believes is false.

. . .

RULE 3.4 FAIRNESS TO OPPOSING PARTY AND COUNSEL

A lawyer shall not:

(b) falsify evidence, counsel or assist a witness to testify falsely, or offer an inducement to a witness that is prohibited by law;

. . .

RULE 4.1 TRUTHFULNESS IN STATEMENTS TO OTHERS

In the course of representing a client a lawyer shall not knowingly:

. . .

(b) fail to disclose a material fact to a third person when disclosure is necessary to avoid assisting a criminal or fraudulent act by a client, unless disclosure is prohibited by Rule 1.6.

. . .

For reference to the Model Rules of Professional Conduct in the context of the lawyer-client privilege, see infra p. 1396.

4. A problem that has received considerable attention in recent years is what a lawyer may or must do, particularly in a criminal case, when his client proposes to take the stand and commit perjury or has committed perjury. Here

conflict is presented between loyalty to the client and preservation of his confidences and the necessity of avoiding participation in fraud. Among the solutions that have been proposed are these: First, that the lawyer after seeking to persuade his client not to commit perjury should, if the client insists upon proceeding, examine him as a witness in the usual manner. Second, that the lawyer should introduce the client as a witness and allow him to give his testimony, but refrain from questioning him. Third, the lawyer should ask the court for permission to withdraw from the case, but not reveal his reason. Fourth, the lawyer should inform the court that his client proposes to give testimony that the lawyer believes will be perjurious. The leading spokesman for the first view is Professor Monroe Freedman. M. Freedman, Lawyers' Ethics in an Adversary System 27–41 (1975); M. Freedman, Understanding Lawyers' Ethics 109–41 (1990). Others have taken positions that give somewhat more or much more weight to the importance of the lawyer's not participating in misleading the tribunal. See Pye, The Role of Counsel in the Suppression of Truth, 1978 Duke L.J. 921; Wolfram, Client Perjury, 50 S.Cal. L.Rev. 809 (1977); Polster, The Dilemma of the Perjurious Defendant, 28 Case W. Res. L. Rev. 3 (1977). See also G. Hazard, Ethics in the Practice of the Law 126–32 (1978); A. Kaufman, Problems in Professional Responsibility 223–30 (2d ed. 1984); K. Kipnis, Legal Ethics 93–94 (1986); Rieger, Client Perjury: A Proposed Resolution of the Constitutional and Ethical Issues, 70 Minn.L.Rev. 121 (1985).

Silver, Truth, Justice, and the American Way: The Case *Against* the Client Perjury Rules, 47 Vand.L.Rev. 339 (1994), advocates, because of the difficulties with any other approach, allowing or requiring the lawyer to proceed as if he believed his client were telling the truth. On what basis, the author asks, is the lawyer to judge the truthfulness of the client's testimony? Is he to rely upon his own, the lawyer's, background beliefs? Is he to take into account inadmissible evidence? To what degree of probability must the lawyer judge the witness's testimony to be false? If the client knows that the lawyer may refuse to question him as a witness, withdraw as counsel or disclose his doubts to the judge, will this not cause the client to withhold important information from the lawyer, or cause him not to testify, thus depriving the trier of fact of possibly relevant evidence? If the lawyer reveals his doubts to the judge, fails to question the client as a witness, or withdraws, his action is likely to provide relevant evidence against his client and in breach of confidence.

The Code of Professional Responsibility is not clear regarding the lawyer's obligation in this difficult situation. DR 7–102(B)(1) calls upon the lawyer to reveal the fraud if the client will not do so, "except when the information is protected as a privileged communication." DR 2–110(C) tells the lawyer that he may withdraw from employment if the client seeks to pursue an illegal course of conduct, and DR 4–101(C)(3) that he may reveal the intention of his client to commit a crime. But must the lawyer do so? What is the answer under the Model Rules of Professional Conduct? See ABA Comm. on Ethics and Professional Responsibility, Formal Op. 87–353 (1987). In Nix v. Whiteside, 475 U.S. 157, 106 S.Ct. 988 (1986), the Court held that the Sixth Amendment right to the effective assistance of counsel was not violated when a criminal defendant refrained from testifying falsely because counsel threatened that if the defendant did testify falsely, counsel would disclose the perjury. But see United States v. Long, 857 F.2d 436, 442, 448 (8th Cir.1988), cert. denied, 502 U.S. 828 (1991), discussing necessity of lawyer having "a firm factual basis" for believing client will commit perjury before taking steps that are likely to prejudice the client and conflict with the lawyer's duty of loyalty.

Fed.R.Civ.Proc. 11, as amended in 1983, requires every pleading, motion and other paper of a party represented by an attorney to be signed by an attorney of record, and provides that "[t]he signature of an attorney ... constitutes a certificate by him that he has read the pleading, motion, or other paper; that to the best of his knowledge, information, and belief formed after reasonable inquiry it is well grounded in fact. . . ." The Rule provides sanctions if a pleading, motion, or other paper is signed in violation of the Rule. Consider carefully the significance of amended Rule 11 for what is required in the preparation of witnesses, especially party witnesses.

5.   In Geders v. United States, 425 U.S. 80 (1976), cited in Opinion 79 of the District of Columbia Legal Ethics Committee, the Court held that the trial court had violated a criminal defendant's right to counsel by prohibiting him from talking to his lawyer during an overnight recess that came after his direct testimony was concluded and before cross-examination. The Court found that the importance of consultation between lawyer and client outweighed the danger of improper coaching. Improper coaching, the Court thought, could be brought to light on cross-examination. But in Perry v. Leeke, 488 U.S. 272 (1989), the Court held that it did not violate defendant's right to counsel to forbid contact with his lawyer during a brief recess called while the defendant was on the stand. Discussion during such a recess, the Court thought, would likely be directed to the defendant's testimony rather than to other trial issues, and there was no constitutional right to such guidance during testimony. Cross-examination, the Court said, will be more effective if it follows direct testimony without consultation with counsel.

6.   Gross, Expert Evidence, 1991 Wis.L.Rev. 1113, 1139:

[E]xpert witnesses are given the means to spend time working to prepare their testimony with the attorneys who call them; there is a special need to prepare carefully, since their evidence is generally complex and technical; and they have a powerful motive to do so—the desire to construct defenses against opposing lawyers and opposing experts. The result is that the preparation of expert testimony often involves extensive detailed cooperative work by the expert and the attorneys who hired her, work that is done in anticipation of battle, under threat of attack. This type of preparation, perhaps even more than the processes of choice and payment, pushes the expert to identify with the lawyers on her side and to become a partisan member of the litigation team. The expert is not merely subject to the camaraderie that grows between co-workers on a difficult project, she is dependent on the lawyer for the preparation that will make her success possible, and for protection from a dangerous enemy.

That an expert witness may be informed about the facts of the litigated case in a variety of ways, including by the lawyer who plans to call him, see infra p. 1056, affects what are permissible interactions between witness and lawyer.

7.   In Civil Law jurisdictions, the issues raised by the foregoing materials usually are not presented because investigation and fact-gathering is done primarily by the judge and not by the parties' lawyers. The lawyers generally do not have contact with the witnesses other than the client. See Langbein, The German Advantage in Civil Procedure, 52 U. Chi. L. Rev. 823 (1985). In England, on the other hand, although barristers avoid contact with witnesses before trial, solicitors do not, and are as much involved in the preparation of testimony as are lawyers in the United States. See Wydick, The Ethics of Witness Coaching, 17 Card.L.Rev. 1, 5–8 (1995).

8. In the section that follows we examine a trial rule that prohibits the use of leading questions on direct examination and rules relating to the refreshment of a witness's recollection. In appraising these rules it is important to keep in mind what takes place in preparation for trial. Does the rule against leading questions unrealistically assume that the lawyer and the witness have not already gone over the witness's testimony? If there has been careful preparation for trial, will not "refreshment of recollection" on the stand often be a meaningless charade? Perhaps it can be said, however, that the rule against leading questions and the rules relating to refreshment of recollection share with the ethical restrictions on preparation for trial the common purpose of seeking to increase the accuracy of testimony, a form of evidence that at the beginning of this chapter we saw was particularly liable to inaccuracy, especially as a consequence of suggestive influences working on a witness.

SECTION 3. FORM OF EXAMINATION

A. LEADING QUESTIONS—MISLEADING QUESTIONS—ARGUMENTATIVE QUESTIONS—NARRATIVE

Straub v. Reading Co.

United States Court of Appeals, Third Circuit, 1955.
220 F.2d 177.

■ McLAUGHLIN, CIRCUIT JUDGE. Appellant's main ground for reversal of this district court judgment in favor of appellee is that it was deprived of a fair trial by reason of the deliberate conduct of appellee's attorney throughout the trial. . . .

. . .

The proof of plaintiff's claim both as to the accident and injury was put in to an unconscionably large extent by leading questions. Little seems to have been left to a spontaneous explanatory answer. At times the witnesses seemed relatively unnecessary except as sounding boards. The defense finally stated to the court:

"Mr. McConnell:—If Your Honor please, Mr. Richter has asked quite a number of leading questions up to this point and I have not objected because to do so does our cause a greater harm in the eyes of the jury; and, as a matter of fact, I won't be able to object effectively without greater loss than gain even in the future. So I want to ask Your Honor if you won't caution him not to ask leading questions.

"The Court:—I will be glad to.

"Mr. McConnell:—Thank you very much.

"The Court:—I don't think the leading questions have been very productive in the way of leadership.

"Mr. McConnell:—But they could become so.

"The Court:—They could become so. Will you watch it please?"

Immediately thereafter the same sort of questions continued; for example to the plaintiff regarding an acute cervical sprain in his neck. "Q. Now, then, did that clear right up after that? A. Yes, sir." Objection was made to this on the ground "That is exactly what we have just discussed." The court commented "I don't think that offends" but suggested that in the future Mr. Richter phrase such questions "did it or did it not." The leading questions continued in this manner with the plaintiff replying correctly to the statements of his lawyer. Sometime thereafter in the further course of the direct examination of plaintiff as to his duties the following happened:

"Q. Does that involve the movements of men that are actually moving trains or assisting in the movements of trains, or in the furtherance of interstate commerce throughout the Reading system?

"A. Yes, sir.

"Mr. McConnell:—I object to the question.

"The Court:—What was that, Mr. McConnell?

"Mr. McConnell:—I object to that question as suggesting the answer that it requires.

"The Witness:—I check all employees.

"The Court:—Is that satisfactory to you, Mr. McConnell?

"Mr. McConnell:—Well, if the question is stricken it will be. He just practically told him what to say in it.

"Mr. Richter:—That is not so.

"The Court:—He asked what work he does and he is telling it now. If you want to go with more particularity into it—"

And on the next page of the transcript:

"Q. So that these men work in all these four states that you have just mentioned; is that correct? A. Yes.

"Q. Right on the Reading system? A. That is right.

"Q. And do you personally have to go to these different states and go in interstate commerce yourself personally? A. Yes, sir."

The testimony of Dr. John was given at least partially by affirming question statements to him by Mr. Richter. This also applied to Mr. Arinsberg, the plaintiff's witness who brought the Veterans Administration records. For example:

"Q. In other words, Mr. Arinsberg, the only thing that he came out of the war with and the government was concerned with was the question of whether there was any condition of disability due to the influenza that he had during the war. A. That is correct, anything service-connected.

"Q. And there was no service connection in any way with the back condition of any kind? A. That is correct."

The direct examination of witnesses on behalf of plaintiff was in part a systematic detailed presentation of the Straub claim on both its aspects, negligence and damages, by his attorney through leading questions. That course of conduct was grossly improper. It was objected to in timely fashion by the other side. Beyond question the court's attention had been sharply focused on the method being employed with the realistic reminder that the defense could not be constantly objecting, especially when nothing was done about it, because of the probable prejudice to its cause in the minds of the jury.

. . .

Regarding the leading questions, appellee asserts that this problem is within the control of the trial court. This may be true in an ordinary law suit.

But where that control is lost or at least palpably ignored and the conduct is a set piece running the length of the trial which produces a warped version of the issues as received by the jury, then that body never did have the opportunity to pass upon the whole case and a judgment based on that kind of a twisted trial must be set aside. . . .

. . .

The judgment of the district court will be reversed and the cause remanded for a new trial.

NOTE

At the beginning of our discussion of testimonial evidence, we considered from a particular perspective the problem to which the rule against leading questions is addressed. We examined the shaping influence of pretrial events, particularly identification procedures and questioning by police and lawyers, on a witness's memory. Research by psychologists, as we then saw, has enlarged our understanding of this phenomenon. Increased judicial awareness, as we have noted, led to the Supreme Court's Lineup decisions. The matter to which we now turn is the effect on the accuracy of testimony of conditions at the trial itself and in particular the mode of interrogation there employed.

There is no easy, foolproof test for a "leading question." A question forcing a witness to shape for himself an answer other than "yes" or "no" is less likely to be condemned as leading. Ingalls v. Holleman, 12 So.2d 751, 753 (Ala.1943): "Was she turning to the left or to the right or was she continuing straight?" But Williams v. State, 42 So.2d 500, 503 (Ala.App.), cert. denied, 42 So.2d 504 (Ala.1949), and Porter v. State, 386 So.2d 1209, 1210–11 (Fla.Dist.Ct.App. 1980), indicate disapproval of such a test. So does Foster v. Sol Greisler & Sons, Inc., 29 A.2d 103, 105–07 (Pa.Super.1942), with a series of illustrative questions. The mere insertion of "whether or not" before an objectionable question rarely will make it into an unobjectionable one. State v. Cook, 28 S.E.2d 842, 845–46 (S.C.1944). But see State v. Scott, 149 P.2d 152, 153–54 (Wash.1944), where "whether or not" seems to have been helpful to the examiner. B. Clifford & R. Bull, The Psychology of Person Identification 145–46 (1978), discusses the different forms of questions.

The essential point is whether or not the question asked suggests the answer desired. In addressing this point, it is necessary to consider many other factors in addition to the form of the question. Of importance, for example, are the tone and inflection of the questioner's voice and his emphasis upon particular words and phrases. The particular words and the nature of the topic addressed also may be important, as well as the witness's temper, bias, age, personality and condition. Many of these factors are included in lists contained in Williams v. State, 42 So.2d at 503–04, supra, and State v. Greene, 206 S.E.2d 229, 236 (N.C.1974). See also Moody v. Rowell, 34 Mass. (17 Pick.) 490, 498 (1835).

In Urbani v. Razza, 238 A.2d 383 (R.I.1968), it was held that the trial court had erroneously sustained objection to a question that merely suggested a topic for testimony rather than an answer. Accord Ealey v. State, 227 S.E.2d 902 (Ga.Ct.App.1976) (burglary prosecution; "had you given . . . [the defendant] authority to go into your house and to remove that sofa?"). Some see the distinction between improper leading and merely "suggesting a topic" as expressing a preference for "questions on the highest plane of generality which still provide sufficient direction to advance the story." Denbeaux & Risinger,

Questioning Questions: Objections to Form in the Interrogation of Witnesses, 33 Ark. L. Rev. 439, 451 (1979).

As to the importance of the particular words used, an example given earlier was "How tall was the basketball player?" compared with "How short was the basketball player?" We may add an example from the work of the psychologist Elizabeth Loftus: "How fast were the cars going when they smashed into each other?" compared with "How fast were the cars going when they hit each other?" E. Loftus, Eyewitness Testimony 77 (1979). See also B. Clifford & R. Bull, supra, at 146–47, on the importance of the particular words used.

Ogle et. al., Questions: Leading and Otherwise, 19 Judges J. 42, 45 (1980), contains some subtle suggestions regarding what may make a question leading. The authors point out, for instance, that the question "Was the car red, yellow or blue?" may suggest that the car probably was one of these colors; that a question rich in detail, such as "Was the ... car a red 1978 Firebird with whitewalls and a pair of dice hanging from the rear-view mirror," may cause the witness to think that counsel would not provide all this detail unless he had some basis for it; and that a question may influence a witness to give one answer rather than another because he can see that one answer will end questioning whereas the other will lead to further questioning, and he assumes that counsel is attempting to establish a fact as efficiently as possible.

Moody v. Rowell, 34 Mass. at 498, supra, refers to the permissibility of using leading questions with "a child of tender years, whose attention can be called to the matter required only by a pointed or leading question." In Rotolo v. United States, 404 F.2d 316 (5th Cir.1968), it was held error not to allow leading questions to a 15–year-old Mann Act victim who was reluctant and upset. See also State v. Brown, 574 A.2d 745, 748 (R.I.1990): Emotionally distraught 16–year-old; California Evid. Code § 767(b), allowing the court, in the interest of justice, to permit leading questions of a child under 10 years of age in prosecutions under specified statutes. However, account needs to be taken of the concern, mentioned earlier, supra p. 301, that children are particularly susceptible to suggestion. But see Note, Are Children Competent Witnesses?: A Psychological Perspective, 63 Wash. U. L.Q. 815, 826 (1985) (studies show children not more susceptible to suggestion from leading questions than adults).

Leading questions may be used with a witness who is reluctant or hostile to the party calling him. E.g., United States v. Brown, 603 F.2d 1022, 1025–26 (1st Cir.1979). Some jurisdictions give permission for leading questions when the witness is the opposite party. Denbeaux & Risinger, supra, at 457. See Fed.R.Evid. 611(c), providing that when a party calls a hostile witness, an adverse party, or a witness identified with an adverse party, interrogation may be by leading questions. Ellis v. City of Chicago, 667 F.2d 606, 612–13 (7th Cir.1981): In suit against city, police department and individual policeman for actions of the policeman claimed to violate plaintiffs' civil rights, error not to allow leading questions to be asked of other policemen who were present during the incident in question, because they were "identified with an adverse party."

Leading questions may be permitted when a witness has failed to include in his testimony a matter that cannot be pointed to by a general interrogatory. State v. McKinney, 917 P.2d 1214, 1222 (Ariz.1996), cert. denied, 117 S.Ct. 310: Did you see anything else in the trunk of the car? Did you see the defendant's .22 rifle? Likewise, leading questions about the nonhappening of an event or about a particular matter in regard to which the witness's memory has failed, may be acceptable. The latter use of leading questions falls under the topic "refreshment of recollection," shortly to be discussed.

Leading questions generally are allowed on cross-examination. However, there are exceptions, such as "where the witness shows a strong interest or bias in favor of the cross-examining party, and ... needs only an intimation to say whatever is most favorable to that party." Moody v. Rowell, supra, at 498. Rine v. Irisari, 420 S.E.2d 541, 551 (W.Va.1992): Leading questions usually not permitted on cross-examination where witness is party called by adverse party; Three "M" Investments, Inc. v. Ahrend Co., 827 P.2d 1324, 1328–29 (Okla. 1992): On cross-examination of party called by adverse party, leading questions allowed only when purpose is to impeach. Dissent opposed to flat rule; would allow leading questions if purpose is, e.g., to rehabilitate after hostile direct. Id. at 1381. See 38 A.L.R.2d 952 (1954) on cross-examination by leading questions of a witness friendly to the cross-examiner. It should be noted that a question asked on cross-examination that is full of detail may be designed not to lead the witness, but improperly to convey information to the trier of fact.

Should there be greater leniency for leading questions on redirect than on direct? People v. Terczak, 238 N.E.2d 626, 628–29 (Ill.Ct.App.1968): A defense alibi witness testified on direct examination that she had seen defendant at her place of employment at 7:30 p.m., which, if true, would have made it unlikely that he committed the robbery with which he was charged. On cross-examination, after being shown a time sheet which indicated that on the day in question the witness had worked only until 6:30 p.m., she stated that she could have been mistaken about the date on which she had seen defendant. Held: Not error to prohibit defense counsel from asking on redirect, "Sandy, could it have been 6:30 that you saw Dennis?"

The "misleading question" of "When did you stop beating your wife?" variety, with its tendency to trip an unwary witness into a tacit concession of something that he does not mean to concede, is likely to be treated severely. Some call these "questions with trick assumptions." Denbeaux & Risinger, supra, at 479. Such questions usually occur on cross-examination. A few illustrations are given: Life & Casualty Insurance Co. of Tennessee v. Garrett, 35 So.2d 109, 111 (Ala.1948): Action to recover accidental death benefit not payable unless the insured when killed was riding in or driving a motor vehicle; the trial judge allowed: "When you first observed the jeep in which [the insured] was riding at the time he was killed, please state whether or not the same bore any signs of external or visible injury...."; reversed. Zeleznik v. Jewish Chronic Disease Hospital, 366 N.Y.S.2d 163, 169 (App.Div.1975): Medical malpractice case in which defendant doctors were charged with negligent delay in performing certain remedial procedures; held, error to allow plaintiff to ask an expert witness: "[H]aving in mind all of the symptoms and signs I have given you, was the time delay from the time that the symptoms were first noticed until ... the time that the exploratory occurred a contributing factor towards the plaintiff's present condition?" "The question assumed the very matter in issue, whether the time lapse ... constituted a *delay,* i.e., a departure from good medical practice." Rimmer v. Chadron Printing Co., 56 N.W.2d 806, 809 (Neb.1953), required reversal because, in a libel action, defendant was required to answer a question prefaced by "Even though you knew that you had done this man a grievous wrong." 100 A.L.R. 1062, 1067 (1936), contains a selection of "misleading questions." For a psychologist's report on the influence of a question containing an assumption on the answers to later questions, see E. Loftus, supra, at 55–62, 77–78. See also B. Clifford & R. Bull, supra, at 148–52.

On the topic of leading questions and misleading questions, see Enfield, Direct Examination of Witnesses, 15 Ark.L.Rev. 32 (1960); Moss, Examination and Cross Examination of Witnesses, 5 S.Texas L.J. 83 (1959); Denroche, Leading Questions, 6 Cr.L.Q. 21 (1963).

The objection that a question is "argumentative" should be distinguished from the objection that it is leading or misleading. As already stated, the essential objection to a leading question is that it suggests the answer and to a misleading question that it tricks the witness into conceding something he does not mean to concede. Objection to a question as argumentative appears to mean, at least in some cases, that the questioner is putting impermissible pressure on the witness to change his testimony or that he is continuing to attempt to refresh the witness's recollection when it is clear that it cannot be refreshed. In most instances, however, the gist of the objection "argumentative" is that behind the appearance of questioning for the sake of information, counsel in fact is arguing to the trier about the significance of evidence already before it, an exercise that ought to be deferred until later in the trial. An objection that a question is argumentative is not the same as an objection that a question impermissibly seeks an opinion. In the latter situation the question may seek to obtain relevant information from the witness, although in an unacceptable form. The opinion objection is discussed infra p. 352.

On the subject of argumentative questions, consider these cases: People v. Colarco, 417 N.Y.S.2d 681, 684 (App.Div.1979), aff'd, 418 N.E.2d 393 (N.Y. 1980): An alibi witness for the defendant who had already stated on cross-examination that she had not gone to the police or the district attorney with her story was asked additionally, "Well, certainly you went to the Grand Jury, didn't you, the citizens who comprise that body, and asked to testify before them?" State v. Atkins, 261 S.E.2d 55, 63–64 (W.Va.1979), cert. denied, 445 U.S. 904 (1980): A defense witness who had given testimony directly conflicting with that of a prosecution witness, after being given a summary of the testimony of the prosecution witness was asked, "[Y]ou say he is not telling the truth about that?" High–Plains Cooperative v. Stevens, 284 N.W.2d 846, 849 (Neb.1979): In a suit on an open account where the issue was whether a check for $25,000 given plaintiff by defendant constituted an accord and satisfaction that discharged defendant's debt, defendant was asked on cross-examination whether he thought that an attempt to settle a debt of over $86,000 for $25,000 was unconscionable.

Whether it is permissible on direct examination for a witness to testify in the form of an uninterrupted narrative rather than by means of answers to specific questions is generally held to be within the discretion of the trial court. 3 Wigmore § 767 (Chadbourn rev. 1970); McCormick, Evidence § 5 (4th ed. 1992); People v. Belcher, 11 Cal.Rptr. 175 (App.1961). In favor of narrative is the consideration that it avoids the possible distorting influence of counsel's questions and produces a more accurate version of the facts. An uninterrupted narrative in which the witness tells the story in his own way may give the trier of fact a clearer sense of what occurred than answers to carefully elaborated questions by counsel. Furthermore, letting the witness narrate sometimes saves time and avoids misunderstanding and confusion. On the other hand, free narrative may omit important matters that can only be brought out by specific questions. Such questions may add precision at points where it is vital. As with leading questions, much necessarily turns on the character of the witness, his ability to produce unaided a coherent account of what he saw or heard and the nature of the incident testified to. Holding the interest and attention of the trier of fact must always be an important consideration for counsel; under some circumstances this is best done by narrative, under other circumstances by answers to specific questions.

A frequently expressed objection to narrative is that it deprives the other party of a fair opportunity to prevent irrelevant or incompetent matter from getting before the trier of fact. There is no question to give warning of what is to come. An order to strike that part of the narrative that recites hearsay, for example, is obviously a less effective measure than sustaining objection to a question. In deciding whether to permit narrative, the trial judge should give serious consideration to this difficulty, taking into account the risk of irrelevant or incompetent matter appearing in a narrative by the particular witness about the particular matter that he is to testify to. If "the request for narrative has not been preceded by sufficient directed questioning to establish the boundaries of what may reasonably be expected in reply," Denbeaux & Risinger, supra, at 471, narrative probably should not be permitted. One solution is to warn the witness before he commences his narrative, to stick to certain incidents and avoid relying upon certain sources of information. See Teufel v. Wienir, 411 P.2d 151 (Wash.1966) (not error to permit narrative; judge who was trier of fact would not be influenced by inadmissible matter).

Marshall et. al., Effects of Kind of Question and Atmosphere of Interrogation on Accuracy and Completeness of Testimony, 84 Harv.L.Rev. 1620 (1971), reports the results of a study of the effect on the completeness and accuracy of testimony of free narration, questions involving "high guidance," questions involving "moderate guidance," multiple choice questions and leading questions. The study shows that narration provides less complete coverage than various forms of questioning, but that narration is more accurate than testimony in response to questions. However, the difference in coverage is far greater than the difference in accuracy. Furthermore, the decrease in accuracy from "moderate guidance" through "high guidance" and multiple choice to leading questions is not as great, the authors say, as earlier studies suggest. The decrease is especially slight for testimony relating to items the authors characterize as "salient," as determined by the frequency with which they are mentioned by observers. The authors' suggestion is that courts should be less fearful of the impact on accuracy of leading questions, especially in view of their advantage in respect to completeness of coverage. They recognize, however, that the effect on accuracy of a leading question when put to a friendly witness in a courtroom setting may be quite different from the effect they found on disinterested subjects in their experiment, and also that a loss of accuracy in the testimony of a single witness may have a significance in a lawsuit that it does not have in a statistical study involving the aggregation of the results of testimony by a large number of persons. For other studies on free narration compared with questioning of different sorts, see Loftus, supra, at 91–94; Clifford & Bull, supra, at 154–160, and Lipton, On the Psychology of Eyewitness Testimony, 62 J. Appl'd Psychology 90, 93 (1977).

B. REFRESHING RECOLLECTION

"Perhaps *This* Will Refresh Your Memory"

United States v. Riccardi

United States Court of Appeals, Third Circuit, 1949.
174 F.2d 883, cert. denied, 337 U.S. 941, 69 S.Ct. 1519, 93 L.Ed. 1746.

■ KALODNER, CIRCUIT JUDGE. The defendant was indicted under 18 U.S.C. (1940 Ed.) Sections 415 and 417[1] in four counts charging him with wilfully, unlawfully and feloniously having transported or having caused to be transported in interstate commerce certain [stolen] chattels of the value of $5,000 or more. The first and third counts were dismissed, and the defendant was convicted on the second and fourth counts, from which conviction he appeals.

We are not here primarily concerned with the particular fraudulent representations which the defendant made. Rather we are called upon to decide the propriety of the method utilized at the trial to prove what chattels the defendant obtained and transported, and their value. In short, the principal question is whether the witnesses who testified to these essentials were properly permitted to refresh their memory. . . .

The chattels involved are numerous items of bric-a-brac, linens, silverware, and other household articles of quality and distinction. They were the property of Doris Farid es Sultaneh, and were kept in her home at Morristown, New Jersey, from which the defendant is alleged to have transported them to Arizona in a truck and station wagon. The defendant did not deny receiving some of the lady's chattels, but did deny both the quantity and quality alleged. Moreover, it does not appear open to doubt that the truck made but one trip, and the station wagon three, carrying the goods in controversy.

---

1. Now contained in Revised Title 18 U.S.C.A. §§ 2311 and 2314, effective September 1, 1948. [The footnotes except footnote 7 are the court's. Some footnotes have been omitted and others renumbered.]

To prove the specific chattels involved, the government relied on the testimony of Doris Farid; to prove their value, it relied on the testimony of an expert, one Leo Berlow.

Farid testified that as the chattels were being moved from the house, she made longhand notes, and that later she copied these notes on her typewriter. Only one of the original notes was produced, and became part of the evidence of the case, a search by Farid having failed to disclose the others. The government sought to have Farid testify with respect to the chattels by using the typewritten notes for the purpose of refreshing her recollection.[2] Although the defendant's objection was overruled, the government, on the next day of the trial, submitted to Farid lists of chattels taken out of a copy of the indictment, but from which had been deleted such information as dates and values.[3] With the aid of these lists, the witness testified that her recollection was refreshed[4] and that she presently recognized and could identify each item. She was then permitted to read the lists aloud, and testified that she knew that the items were loaded on the truck or station wagon, as the case was. The lists were neither offered nor received in evidence.

The expert, Berlow, testified that he had visited Doris Farid's home on numerous occasions in his professional capacity as dealer in antiques, bric-a-brac, etc.; that he was very familiar with the furnishings therein, having examined the household for the purpose of buying items from Farid or selling them for her on commission. He was shown the same lists which Farid had used to refresh her recollection, and with their aid testified that he could recall the items individually, with some exceptions; that he remembered them to the extent that he could not only describe the items, but in many instances could state where in the house he had seen them; and that he could give an opinion as to their value. This he was permitted to do.

In denying the acceptability of the evidence related, the defendant rests primarily on Putnam v. United States, 1896, 162 U.S. 687, 16 S.Ct. 923, 40 L.Ed. 1118, and refers to this Court's decision in Delaney v. United States, 3

---

2. At pages 114a–115a of Appellant's Appendix, the following appears:

"The Court: That isn't the question. When you look at that typewritten sheet, does that refresh your recollection as to the items therein mentioned?

"The Witness: It does.

"The Court: In what way?

"The Witness: Well, every item here—for instance: 2 Chinese vases octagonal shape Satsuma, light for mantel I remember.

"The Court: You remember those items individually as packed?

"The Witness: Individually, each one.

"The Court: I will allow her to refresh her recollection, but I will expect you to produce the original notes."

3. At page 136a of Appellant's Appendix it appears that government counsel began by showing to Farid a list which did not have values. At page 137a, the following appears:

"The Court: Well, I think with these evaluations cut off it is all right. This is the

same paper that was shown to the witness yesterday?

"Mr. Pearse (defendant's counsel): No, sir, this is the indictment.

"Mr. Tyne (U.S. Attorney): No, sir, this is the indictment."

Following this, at the suggestion of the trial judge, the dates on the lists, to which defendant had previously objected, were cut off. The lists were then shown to the witness.

4. For example, at page 140a of Appellant's Appendix:

"The Court: Well, Madam, as you look at that list does it refresh your recollection?

"The Witness: I lived with these things, your Honor, I know them.

"The Court: You lived with them yourself?

"The Witness: I did.

"The Court: So when you look at that paper, it does refresh your recollection?

"The Witness: Absolutely."

Cir., 1935, 77 F.2d 916. It is his position that the lists should not have been used because they were not made by the witnesses at or shortly after the time of the transaction while the facts were fresh in memory. It is further contended that the witnesses were not hostile to the government, and what Farid did, in fact, was to read off the lists as proof of the actual articles loaded on the vehicles.

The government, on the other hand, asserts that the witnesses gave their independent recollection, which is admissible, albeit refreshed, because it is the recollection and not the writing which is the evidence. It goes further, and urges that where the witness has an independent recollection, anything may be used to stimulate and vitalize that recollection without regard to source or origin.[5]

Refreshing the recollection of a witness is not an uncommon trial practice, but as a theory of evidentiary law its content and application are far from clear.... An analysis as good and trustworthy as presently exists appears in Chapter XXVIII, 3 Wigmore, Evidence (3rd ed. 1940). Professor Wigmore separated broadly, what he called "past recollection recorded" from "present recollection revived", attributing much of the confusion in the cases to a failure to make this distinction and to the use of the phrase "refreshing the recollection" for both classes of testimony. The primary difference between the two classifications is the ability of the witness to testify from present knowledge: where the witness' memory is revived, and he presently recollects the facts and swears to them, he is obviously in a different position from the witness who cannot directly state the facts from present memory and who must ask the court to accept a writing for the truth of its contents because he is willing to swear, for one reason or another, that its contents are true.

Recognition of the basic difference between the two categories of evidence referred to is explicit in the federal cases, although in some the distinction is obscured by the lack of necessity for it. In Cohen v. United States, 3 Cir., 1929, 36 F.2d 461, 462, this Court noted that the witness "testified not from her present recollection ... but rather from her past recollection recorded". And in Delaney v. United States, 3 Cir., 1935, 77 F.2d 916, we referred with approval to Jewett v. United States, 9 Cir., 1926, 15 F.2d 955, 956, wherein the Court said:

"It is one thing to awaken a slumbering recollection of an event but quite another to use a memorandum of a recollection, fresh when it was correctly recorded, but presently beyond the power of the witness so to restore that it will exist apart from the record."

The difference between present recollection revived and past recollection recorded has a demonstrable effect upon the method of proof. In the instance of past recollection recorded, the witness, by hypothesis, has no present recollection of the matter contained in the writing. Whether the record is directly admitted into evidence, or indirectly by the permissive parroting of the witness, it is nevertheless a substitute for his memory and is offered for the truth of its contents. It assumes a distinct significance as an independent probative force,

---

5. This is in paraphrase of Lord Ellenborough's statement in Henry v. Lee, 2 Chitty 124: "If upon looking at any document he can so far refresh his memory as to recollect a circumstance, it is sufficient; and it makes no difference, that the memorandum was written by himself, for it is not the memorandum that is the evidence, but the recollection of the witness." [The quotation has been

and is therefore ordinarily required to meet certain standards.[6]

. . .

In the case of present recollection revived, the witness, by hypothesis, relates his present recollection, and under oath and subject to cross-examination asserts that it is true; his capacities for memory and perception may be attacked and tested; his determination to tell the truth investigated and revealed; protestations of lack of memory, which escape criticism and indeed constitute a refuge in the situation of past recollection recorded, merely undermine the probative worth of his testimony. It is in recognition of these factors that we find:

"The law of contemporary writing or entry qualifying it as primary evidence has no application. The primary evidence here is not the writing. It was not introduced in evidence. It was not offered. The primary evidence is the oral statement of the hostile witness. It is not so important when the statement was made or by whom if it serves the purpose to refresh the mind and unfold the truth." Hoffman v. United States, 9 Cir., 1937, 87 F.2d 410, 411.

"When a party uses an earlier statement of his own witness to refresh the witness' memory, the only evidence recognized as such is the testimony so refreshed. . . . Anything may in fact revive a memory: a song, a scent, a photograph, an allusion, even a past statement known to be false.[7] When a witness declares that any of these has evoked a memory, the opposite party may show, either that it has not evoked what appears to the witness as a memory, or that, although it may so appear to him, the memory is a phantom and not a reliable record of its content. When the evoking stimulus is not itself an account of the relevant occasion, no question of its truth can arise; but when it is an account of that occasion, its falsity, if raised by the opposing party, will become a relevant issue if the witness has declared that the evoked memory accords with it. . . ." United States v. Rappy, 2 Cir., 1946, 157 F.2d 964, 967–968, certiorari denied 329 U.S. 806, 67 S.Ct. 501, 91 L.Ed. 688.

. . .

Since the purpose of the writing is to activate the memory of the witness, there is always the possibility, if not probability, that the writing will exert a strong influence upon the direction of the memory, that is, the nearer the writing to the truth, the lesser the deviation of the witness' memory from the truth. But this is not a binding reason for insistence upon establishing the reliability of the writing previous to permitting the witness to state whether his memory is refreshed. The reception of a witness' testimony does not depend upon whether it is true; truth is a matter for the trier of fact unless, of course, the evidence is so improbable that reasonable men would not differ upon it. When the witness testifies that he has a present recollection, that is the evidence in the case, and not the writing which stimulates it. If his recollection agrees with the writing, it is pointless to require proof of the accuracy of the writing, for such proof can only amount to corroborative evidence. The testimony is received for what it is worth. New York & Colorado Mining Syndicate v.

editorially corrected to accord with its original text.]

6. Generally, see 3 Wigmore, Evidence. Sections 744–755 (3d ed. 1940). . . .

7. Speed v. State, 500 N.E.2d 186, 190 (Ind.1986), held that an audio-video tape of defendant's statement to police, though of such poor quality as to be inadmissible, could nevertheless be used to refresh a policeman's recollection. Eds.

Fraser, 1889, 130 U.S. 611, 620, 9 S.Ct. 665, 32 L.Ed. 1031. And the testimony should be received if it is capable of a reasonably satisfactory evaluation. Undoubtedly, the nature of the writing which the witness says is effective to stimulate his memory plays a part in that evaluation, and the dangers from deficiencies in the witness' testimonial qualifications are not less susceptible of evaluation by the trier of fact than in the case of past perception recorded; indeed, they are more readily subject to test, for the witness, as already noted, asserts a present memory and cannot gain protection from a denial of the very memory which he claims to have.

Of course, the categories, present recollection revived and past recollection recorded, are clearest in their extremes, but they are, in practice, converging rather than parallel lines; the difference is frequently one of degree. Moreover, it is in complication thereof that a cooperative witness, yielding to suggestion, deceives himself, that a hostile witness seizes an opportunity, or that a writing is used to convey an improper suggestion. Circumstances, or the nature of the testimony, may belie an assertion of present memory; more often the credibility of the witness generally and the cross-examiner's attack upon the reliability of his memory, will decide the claim to an independent recollection.

Properly, the burden to ascertain the state of affairs, as near as may be, devolves upon the trial judge, who should in the first instance satisfy himself as to whether the witness testifies upon a record or from his own recollection. It is upon this satisfaction that the reception of the evidence depends, for if it appear to the court that the witness is wholly dependent for the fact upon the memorandum he holds in his hand, the memorandum acquires a significance which, as stated, brings into operation certain guiding rules. Similarly, the trial judge must determine whether the device of refreshing recollection is merely a subterfuge to improperly suggest to the witness the testimony expected of him. It is axiomatic, particularly with respect to the reception of evidence, that much depends upon the discretion of the trial judge. . . .

In the instant case, the learned trial judge determined that both Farid and the expert, Berlow, testified from present recollection. On the record, we cannot say that it was plainly not so. Both witnesses stated that they knew the chattels and could identify them. Farid, who testified that she was present and helped to pack them, said she could remember which were transported; Berlow said he could give an opinion of their value. On a number of occasions the trial judge investigated the foundations of their claim to present recollection and satisfied himself as to its bona fides. The case is, therefore, distinguishable from Jewett v. United States, supra, wherein it was held that the witness had no independent recollection, and from Delaney v. United States, supra, where the Court concluded that the witness did no more than read from a photostatic copy. While the defendant asserts that neither Farid nor Berlow did more, the trial judge immediately recognized that the items of property involved were so numerous that in the ordinary course of events no one would be expected to recite them without having learned a list by rote memory. On the other hand, the items were such that a person familiar with them reasonably could be expected to recognize them and tell what he knows. Under these circumstances, the District Judge might well have permitted the government, in lieu of the procedure followed, to ask Farid leading questions, directing her attention to specific items, and asking her whether she knew what happened to them. This is especially true of Berlow, who did not purport to have any knowledge of the movement of the articles. Clearly, it would have been pointless to ask him to give the value of every article he had ever seen in Farid's home. The same result could have been achieved legitimately without the use of the lists by orally directing his attention to any specific article previously identified by

Farid and asking him whether he had seen it, presently remembered it, and could give an opinion as to its value. By the use of lists, nothing more or different was accomplished.

Moreover, we think the procedure followed lay within the discretion of the trial court, and that no prejudicial error ensued. The evidence was capable of a reasonably satisfactory evaluation and was receivable for what it was worth. In the long run, the primary issue of the case was that of credibility, and it is sufficient that the jury had as sound a basis for weighing the testimony as it would in any other instance. The defense had at its disposal the customary opportunities and all the necessary material to test the witness' recollection and other testimonial qualifications, including the single original longhand list which Farid located, the typewritten lists which she said were made at the time of the events involved, and the lists the prosecution used. It might very well have put Farid through severe cross-examination with respect to each chattel she identified on direct examination, but chose instead to attack the reliability of her memory by other means.

Accordingly, it is our conclusion that the learned trial judge did not abuse his discretion, either in determining that the witnesses testified from present recollection, or in permitting the use of the lists described herein....

For the reasons stated, the judgment of the District Court will be affirmed.

NOTES

1. *Showing required as to the necessity for refreshment.* The opinion in Minneapolis v. Price, 159 N.W.2d 776 (Minn.1968), states that a memorandum should not be used to refresh until it has been ascertained that the witness cannot recall the events in question without it. See also People v. Pena, 292 N.W.2d 141 (Mich.App.1980) (witness insisted his memory did not need refreshing); Griffith v. St. Louis–San Francisco Ry., 559 S.W.2d 278, 281 (Mo.App. 1977), cert. denied, 436 U.S. 926 (1978) (witness had "already testified clearly and unhesitatingly regarding everything that was contained in the proffered statement"). In Thompson v. United States, 342 F.2d 137, 140 (5th Cir.), cert. denied, 381 U.S. 926 (1965), the court rejected a contention that it had not been shown that refreshment was necessary or that the witness's memory was in fact refreshed.

> In the present case, however, the court properly supervised the use of the statement to refresh Thorn's recollection; and, where there was an absence of the customary formalistic wording to show inability to recollect without aid and the refreshing effect of the writing, the context of the specific queries, the witness' spoken reaction and the trial judge's opportunity to observe the witness' demeanor, leave no occasion to find reversible error in his rulings on these objections.

See also Montgomery v. Tufford, 437 P.2d 36, 39–40 (Colo.1968) (allowing witness to look at memorandum without first asking if she remembered facts not error when from nature of subject unlikely she could).

2. *Whether memory has been refreshed.* State v. Gibson, 424 S.E.2d 95, 107 (N.C.1992):

> The rule in Smith [231 S.E.2d 663 (N.C.1977)] which we hold controls the resolution of this issue states, "Where the testimony of the witness purports to be from his refreshed memory but is *clearly* a mere recitation of the refreshing memorandum, such testimony is not admissible as present recollection refreshed and should be excluded by the trial judge." ...

231 S.E.2d at 671. Thus, we must determine whether the spirit of the rule of present recollection refreshed has been violated by testimony which was not the product of a refreshed memory, but clearly nothing more than a recitation of the witness' notes.

The witness was initially directed to his notes by the prosecutor. It was at that time that the witness stated that he remembered a statement defendant had made to him and that he made the notes so he "could remember exactly what happened." After further testimony the witness asked if he might look at his notes again, and following another question he said, "It's not in my notes, but it just popped into my head." The fact that the witness asked to look at his notes tends to show that prior to that moment he had not been using them. Once he looked at his notes he was apparently able to testify from his own memory. The record conclusively indicates only that the witness used his notes on more than one occasion during this portion of his testimony. After reviewing the transcript, we cannot say that the witness' testimony was clearly a mere recitation of the notes he had before him. Thus, we find no error in that the notes did nothing more than refresh the witness' memory, and the resulting testimony was therefore admissible under the doctrine of present recollection refreshed.

Compare Eastover Bank v. Hall, 587 So.2d 266, 270–71 (Miss.1991): When witness in his deposition said he could not remember, but at trial said that he could as a result of a conversation with another person, not abuse of discretion to exclude the claimed memory: The witness's testimony would have been a vehicle for circumventing the hearsay rule.

In determining whether memory has been refreshed, is the question for the court simply whether the witness's testimony is relevant? See the discussion of witness competence in respect to memory, supra p. 304.

3. *Opponent's right to inspect a memorandum used while the witness is on the stand to refresh recollection.* Inspection may be a necessary safeguard to avoid sharp practice in the form of conveying to the witness improper hints or instructions. A flagrant example would be handing a witness written instructions to answer the next four questions "No."

United States v. Socony–Vacuum Oil Co., 310 U.S. 150, 60 S.Ct. 811 (1940), says that while it is normal to permit opposing counsel to inspect the memorandum before it is shown to the witness, no iron-clad rule requires it; some other appropriate procedure to prevent improper use will suffice. In this case the trial judge had adopted the practice of inspecting the writing—a transcript of prior testimony—and reading to the witnesses appropriate passages therefrom. Held not to exceed sound discretion. On the other hand, considerable authority points in the direction of a nearly unqualified right to inspect. See People v. Gezzo, 121 N.E.2d 380, 384 (N.Y.1954) (conviction reversed after defendant denied notes used by witness because he "might have been prejudiced by this limitation on cross-examination"); Shell Oil Co. v. Pou, 204 So.2d 155 (Miss. 1967) (error not to allow inspection).

Apart from preventing the proponent from improperly using certain memoranda, what other reasons has the opponent for wanting production? What are the uses that he may make of the memorandum?

4. *Opponent's right to inspect a memorandum used before the witness takes the stand to refresh recollection.* Rose v. State, 427 S.W.2d 609 (Tex.Crim.App. 1968): A witness had a summary of facts prepared by the prosecutor in his hands while he testified. He had used this summary to refresh his recollection before taking the stand but did not refer to it while testifying. The prosecutor also had a copy of the summary in his possession. Held: Not error to refuse to allow defense counsel to inspect the document. There is a right to inspect only if the witness refers to the document on the stand or the document was "exhibited or read from or used to question the witness in the jury's presence." One judge reluctantly concurred in the result, expressing unhappiness at the distinction between refreshment before taking the stand and while testifying. He also strongly disapproved the practice of putting into the hands of a witness for refreshment purposes a statement of facts prepared by counsel. The opinions are unclear as to what is encompassed by the phrase "exhibited or read from or used to question the witness in the jury's presence." Suppose counsel holds a summary of facts in his hands and glances at it from time to time in framing questions. Must he allow opposing counsel to see it? What use may opposing counsel make of the document that justifies a right of inspection under these circumstances? Is there any theory under which opposing counsel would be allowed to inform the jury of the content of the document?

Many cases agree with the Rose decision in denying a right to inspect a document used before the witness takes the stand to refresh recollection, but there is a significant trend toward permitting inspection. Fed.R.Evid. 612 entitles the adverse party to production of a writing used by a witness "to refresh memory for the purpose of testifying, either—(1) while testifying, or (2) before testifying, if the court in its discretion determines it is necessary in the interests of justice...." See United States v. Blas, 947 F.2d 1320, 1327–28 (7th Cir.1991), cert. denied, 502 U.S. 1118 (1992) (Not abuse of discretion to refuse to require production of numerous documents witness reviewed before testifying; defendant failed to sustain burden of showing production necessary in interest of justice). Congress added the qualification regarding discretionary power to the Supreme Court's version of Rule 612. Cal. Evid. Code § 771 gives a right of inspection of writings used to refresh without any such limitation. A right to inspect writings used before a witness takes the stand to refresh recollection obviously involves problems not present when refreshment takes place on the stand. For example, suppose it is disputed whether the witness did in fact look at the document in question. Cf. United States v. Wright, 489 F.2d 1181 (D.C.Cir.1973). And what if the party calling the witness cannot produce the document that the witness saw before he took the stand, perhaps because counsel did not know that the witness had consulted it? See Note, 37 Mo.L.Rev. 571, 575–76 (1972); Cal. Evid. Code § 771(c).

Compare the right to production of pretrial refreshers with the right to production of prior statements of witnesses conferred by the Jencks Act, 18 U.S.C. § 3500, and Fed.R.Crim.Proc. 26.2. The Jencks Act and Rule 26.2 confer a right to production of certain witness statements regardless of whether they have been used for refreshment. The Jencks Act applies to statements by prosecution witnesses. Rule 26.2 applies to statements by both prosecution and defense witnesses. Cf. United States v. Nobles, 422 U.S. 225, 95 S.Ct. 2160 (1975), supra p. 269. Rule 612 contains a provision making it inapplicable "when otherwise provided in criminal proceedings" by the Jencks Act. However, see J. Weinstein and M. Berger, 3 Weinstein's Evidence § 612[02], on the possibility that Rule 26.2 has modified both the Jencks Act and Rule 612.

Discussion of the opponent's right to inspect and possibly place before the jury memoranda used before a witness takes the stand to refresh his recollection naturally leads to discussion of the opponent's right to know of other memory-influencing pretrial events and to inform the jury of them. See Eastover Bank v. Hall, 587 So.2d 266, 270–71 (Miss.1991), supra. United States v. Miller, 411 F.2d 825 (2d Cir.1969): Order denying motion for new trial reversed. In view of what transpired at the trial, the Government had a duty to disclose to the defense that a key identification witness for the Government had, before trial, been hypnotized and interrogated under hypnosis by an expert hypnotist and the Assistant United States Attorney in charge of the case. There was a significant chance that knowledge of the hypnosis would have induced a reasonable doubt in the minds of the jurors as to the credibility of the witness. On the motion for a new trial, experts for the defense contended that repetition under hypnosis of the story, which the witness had already told, could have imprinted it upon his mind in such a way as to make him impervious to defense suggestions that the facts were otherwise. The defense experts also contended that there was a possibility that when he testified at the trial, in response to questions from one of his former hypnotists—the Assistant United States Attorney—the witness was in a mild trance. The Court of Appeals expressly disavowed any view that the hypnosis disqualified the witness from testifying at a new trial. For other discussion of problems raised by the use of hypnosis, see supra p. 267. The importance of counsel knowing about pretrial events that possibly influenced testimony was also brought out in the discussion of the Supreme Court's Lineup decisions, supra p. 246.

5. *Whether the writing used to stimulate recollection may itself be admitted into evidence.* The opinion in the Riccardi case correctly implies, although it does not state with unmistakable clarity, that the litigant using the writing to refresh recollection is not as a matter of course entitled to introduce it into evidence. In Krupp v. Sataline, 200 A.2d 475 (Conn.1964), admission of the writing in evidence was held to be reversible error.

The problem should perhaps be broken down into more specific questions: Should counsel or the witness be allowed to read the document aloud to the jury? Should the jurors be allowed to read the document themselves? Should they be allowed to take the document with them into the jury room? There is considerable authority that it is error to permit the document to be read aloud. New Mexico Savings & Loan Ass'n v. United States Fidelity & Guaranty Co., 454 F.2d 328, 336–37 (10th Cir.1972) (better practice to have witness read silently, but no error under circumstances); Goings v. United States, 377 F.2d 753, 761–62 (8th Cir.1967); Gaines v. United States, 349 F.2d 190 (D.C.Cir. 1965) (error but not prejudicial); People v. Parks, 485 P.2d 257 (Cal.1971) (error but not prejudicial); Payne v. Zapp, 431 S.W.2d 890, 892 (Ky.1968). A complaint of Riccardi's counsel, not mentioned in the opinion, was that because the indictment went to the jury room and was known by the jurors to carry a replica of the material used in questioning both Farid and Berlow, the prosecution in actual effect made its memory refresher an exhibit. Although some uses that a jury might make of a document used to refresh recollection would be consistent with the theory of present recollection refreshed, others obviously would not be, and there is always the risk that limiting instructions will be ignored.

Consider United States v. Rappy, cited and quoted in United States v. Riccardi. In the Rappy case a government witness did not remember or said he did not remember whether the defendant had said to him in a telephone conversation that certain watches which the defendant was offering to sell the witness were "hot." After being shown a memorandum, the witness said that it refreshed his recollection and that he did remember that the defendant had said that the watches were "hot." A government agent had written out this memorandum while questioning the witness, purporting to make it a narrative of the witness's answers, and the witness had signed the memorandum. On cross-examination defense counsel sought at great length to get from the witness an admission that at the interview when the statement was prepared, it was the government agent who introduced the word "hot." As to this the witness's testimony was "somewhat confused." "After the cross, re-direct, and re-cross had been long directed to the preparation and execution of the statement, the prosecution offered it in evidence and the judge received it." On appeal the procedure was sustained: When a memorandum used to refresh is an account of the occasion "its falsity, if raised by the opposing party, will become a relevant issue if the witness has declared that the evoked memory accords with it. This is true because the evoked memory cannot be a truthful record when it tracks a statement shown to be false. Hence in the case at bar, when Rappy chose to attack the veracity of the statement which Moscowitz had said evoked an accordant memory, he interjected a new issue, and the prosecution was entitled to meet his attack. It was obviously proper that upon that issue the statement itself should be in evidence." 157 F.2d at 967–68. In what sense did the defendant "attack the veracity of the statement"? Is the memorandum admitted for its full evidential value or is the defendant entitled to a limiting instruction?

The opponent may ordinarily put into evidence the document that has been used to refresh. See Fed. R. Evid. 612 and Cal. Evid. Code § 771. But this right may not be absolute. See United States v. Ratliff, 623 F.2d 1293, 1297 n. 8 (8th Cir.), cert. denied, 449 U.S. 876 (1980) (not error to refuse to allow into evidence booklet in German used by expert to refresh his recollection because of considerations of "judicial economy and concern over confusing the jury," the court citing Fed. R. 403 as well as Rule 612). For what purposes may the opponent have the document admitted into evidence? The courts frequently fail to clarify this issue. E.g., United States v. Smith, 521 F.2d 957, 968–69 (D.C.Cir.1975); Borel v. Fibreboard Paper Products Corp., 493 F.2d 1076, 1102–03 (5th Cir.1973), cert. denied, 419 U.S. 869 (1974).

6. *The relation of refreshment to impeachment.* The process of refreshment of recollection obviously stands in close relation to the process of impeachment through prior inconsistent statement, discussed infra pp. 453–64. Attempted refreshment may simply be the prelude to the introduction of impeaching evidence. In many cases what goes on cannot candidly be described as attempted refreshment at all. The witness has not really forgotten. It is more a matter of intimidating him into testifying in accordance with the writing by the threat of impeachment.

7. *Refreshment and waiver of privilege.* Kerns Constr. Co. v. Super. Court for Orange County, 72 Cal.Rptr. 74 (App.1968): In a personal injury action arising out of a gas explosion, the Kerns Company, cross-defendant, requested the taking of the deposition of Reynolds, an employee of the defendant Gas Company. Reynolds had prepared reports after the accident for the Gas Company and its attorney. Shortly before his deposition was taken, Reynolds obtained the reports from the attorney for the Gas Company and used them to refresh his recollection. He also used them to refresh his recollection during the taking of the deposition, both on direct and cross-examination. Kerns requested that the reports be appended to the deposition and subsequently moved, under § 771 of the Cal. Evid. Code, for an order requiring the Gas Company to produce the reports. The motion was denied. Held: Mandamus issued ordering the lower court to grant Kerns' motion. The work product and attorney-client privileges were waived when with knowledge of their intended use the attorney for the Gas Company gave the reports to Reynolds and Reynolds testified from them. See also Doxtator v. Swarthout, 328 N.Y.S.2d 150 (App.Div.1972). On the other hand, in Sullivan v. Superior Court for San Mateo County, 105 Cal.Rptr. 241 (App.1972), prohibition issued to prevent the enforcement of an order that the transcript of a recording of a conference between an attorney and a client-witness, used by the client-witness before testifying, be produced. The court cited the unique nature of the writing involved and the importance of the attorney-client privilege and distinguished Kerns on the ground that in that case the witness had used the writing to refresh his recollection while testifying. See Comment, Evidence Code Section 771: Conflict with Privileged Communications, 6 Pac.L.J. 612 (1975).

In James Julian, Inc. v. Raytheon Co., 93 F.R.D. 138, 144–46 (D.Del.1982), discovery was ordered of binders containing documents selected by plaintiff's counsel and given to witnesses prior to their depositions.

> Without reviewing those binders defendants' counsel cannot know or inquire into the extent to which the witnesses' testimony has been shaded by counsel's presentation of the factual background. The instant request constitutes neither a fishing expedition into plaintiff's files nor an invasion of counsel's "zone of privacy." Plaintiff's counsel made a decision to educate their witnesses by supplying them with the binders, and the ... defendants are entitled to know the content of that education. Based on the foregoing the Court concludes that the binders are properly within the scope of ... [Fed.R.Evid.] 612(2) and in the interests of justice should be disclosed.

See also In re Comair Air Disaster Litigation, 100 F.R.D. 350 (D.Ky.1983), ordering production under Rule 612 of an accident report prepared by defendant's employees and submitted to and examined by defendant's expert; Wheeling–Pittsburgh Steel Corp. v. Underwriters Laboratories, Inc., 81 F.R.D. 8 (N.D.Ill.1978), ordering production of documents assumed to be covered by the lawyer-client privilege when the witness had consulted them before testifying, citing Fed. R. 612 and also stating that the lawyer-client privilege had been waived; Berkey Photo, Inc. v. Eastman Kodak Co., 74 F.R.D. 613 (S.D.N.Y. 1977), stating that work product materials shown to witnesses before they testify and that arguably have an effect on their testimony should be produced.

In Boring v. Keller, 97 F.R.D. 404 (D.Colo.1983), the court ordered production of "opinion work product" that defense counsel had given to defendant's expert and that the expert had examined. The work product rule is codified in Fed.R.Civ.Proc. 26(b)(3):

> Subject to the provisions of subdivision (b)(4) of this rule, a party may obtain discovery of documents ... otherwise discoverable ... and prepared in anticipation of litigation or for trial by or for another party or by or for that other party's representative ... only upon a showing that the party seeking discovery has substantial need of the materials in the preparation of the party's case and that the party is unable without undue hardship to obtain the substantial equivalent of the materials by other means. In ordering discovery of such materials when the required showing has been made, the court shall protect against disclosure of the mental impressions, conclusions, opinions, or legal theories of an attorney or other representative of a party concerning the litigation.

See infra p. 1454. In Boring, the court in ordering production did not rely on Fed. R. Evid. 612, but on Fed. R. Civ. Proc. 26(b)(4), which is concerned with discovery of facts known and opinions held by experts. See infra p. 1082. Rule 26(b)(4) is not limited to discovery of materials that have been used to refresh recollection.

Sporck v. Peil, 759 F.2d 312 (3d Cir.), cert. denied, 474 U.S. 903 (1985): During discovery, defendant turned over a large number of documents to plaintiff. In preparation for taking defendant Sporck's deposition, defense counsel showed Sporck a selection from these documents. At the start of the deposition, plaintiff requested identification and production of all documents examined, reviewed or referred to by Sporck in preparing for the deposition. Held: Counsel's selection of documents expressed his opinion about the facts and the law and thus fell within "the highly protected category of opinion work product." Id. at 316. Rule 612 was not applicable because plaintiff had not elicited Sporck's testimony and established that in giving it Sporck relied on or was influenced by certain documents. Thus the trial court's order to defendants to produce or identify all documents reviewed by Sporck in preparing for his deposition was improper.

See also Bogosian v. Gulf Oil Corp., 738 F.2d 587 (3d Cir.1984), reversing order of trial court that defendant identify and produce all documents, even though they contained opinion work product, seen by defendant's experts in preparing for depositions. The appellate court said that the order was based on erroneous readings of Rule 26(b)(4) and Fed. R. Evid. 612.

For further discussion of Fed. R. Evid. 612 and Fed.R.Civ.Proc. 26(b)(4) and conflict with the work product rule, see Floyd, "A Delicate and Difficult Task": Balancing the Competing Interests of Federal Rule of Evidence 612, the Work Product Doctrine, and the Attorney–Client Privilege, 44 Buff. L. Rev. 101 (1996); Note, Discovery of Attorney Work Product Reviewed by an Expert Witness, 85 Colum. L. Rev. 812 (1985); Note, Interactions Between Memory Refreshment Doctrine and Work Product Protection Under the Federal Rules, 88 Yale L.J. 390 (1978); Comment, Resolving the Conflict Between Federal Rule of Evidence 612 and the Work-Product Doctrine, 38 Kan. L. Rev. 1039 (1990) (review of recent cases requiring reasons for production).

8. *Refreshment with privileged material or material obtained illegally.* Ackerman v. Theis, 160 N.W.2d 583, 584 (Minn.1968):

During the cross-examination of the police officer, counsel for defendant asked him to check his records with respect to the distance between the accident and Highway No. 55. Thereupon, plaintiff's counsel asked the witness, "Mr. Martinson, what is it that Mr. Quinlivan has just given you?" The witness answered, "These are the accident records that were made out that night after the accident, that was sent in to the State Highway Commissioner's Office." Objection [evidently to the defendant's request that the police officer check his records] was sustained on the ground the information was privileged under Minn.St. 169.09, subd. 13. Relevant portions of that statute are as follows: "All required accident reports ... shall be for the confidential use of the department for accident prevention purposes.... No such report shall be used as evidence in any trial, civil or criminal, arising out of an accident.... Nothing herein shall be construed to prevent any person who has made a report pursuant to this chapter from testifying in any trial, civil or criminal, arising out of an accident, as to facts within his knowledge. It is intended by this subdivision to render privileged the reports required but it is not intended to prohibit proof of the facts to which such reports relate."

Although no prejudice could have resulted from this interrogation since objection to the question was sustained, we have held in a series of cases that the testimony was in fact admissible. It is proper for an officer to testify to facts which are within his knowledge.... The statute does not bar the use of those portions of a traffic accident report prepared by the officer who is testifying, if they are based on information derived from his own observations.... It is always proper to use such a report to refresh the witness' memory whether it is received in evidence or not....

See also J.H. Rutter, Rex Mfg. Co. v. NLRB, 473 F.2d 223 (5th Cir.), cert. denied, 414 U.S. 822 (1973), where the court held that a qualified privilege covering investigatory files of the Labor Board did not prevent obtaining the notes of a former employee contained in such files to refresh his recollection.

United States v. Baratta, 397 F.2d 215, 221–22 (2d Cir.), cert. denied, 393 U.S. 939 (1968): Prosecution of several defendants for unlawful sale of heroin. Baratta was the only defendant to take the stand. He testified that he was not involved in selling narcotics. He explained his presence and behavior on the night of the illegal transaction by testifying that he was destitute and was trying to borrow money from one of the other defendants. On cross-examination he denied he had ever used the name Barrone. He was then shown a paper containing a prior statement (obtained without complying with Miranda v. Arizona, 384 U.S. 436, 86 S.Ct. 1602 (1966)) in which he said that he had used the name Barrone and was asked if this refreshed his recollection. He said that it did not. The jury was not told the contents of the paper. Baratta was then shown documents reflecting the purchase of a Chris–Craft boat and an automobile by one Philip Barrone, as well as a baptismal certificate, an automobile registration, a driver's license and a check book, all in that name. He denied that he had ever seen these documents before. In rebuttal, the Government offered the testimony of a narcotics agent, who had arrested Baratta, that the documents shown to Baratta were found at the time of his arrest in the room where he was arrested and in an automobile parked in the driveway next to the house in which the arrest took place. Held: If there was error it was not prejudicial. The defendant's prior statement as such could have had no impact upon the jury and, furthermore, it was merely cumulative of the other evidence that defendant had used the name Barrone. In United States v. Ricco, 566 F.2d 433 (2d Cir.1977), cert. denied, 436 U.S. 926 (1978), the court interpreted the federal wiretap statute not to prevent use of a recording of a telephone conversation not timely sealed in accordance with the provisions of the statute to refresh recollection. In 20th Century Wear, Inc. v. Sanmark–Stardust, Inc., 747 F.2d 81, 93 n. 17 (2d Cir.1984), cert. denied, 470 U.S. 1052 (1985), the court held that a tape-recording made by an attorney in violation of professional ethics could nevertheless be used to refresh a witness's recollection.

Compare the Baratta, Ricco and 20th Century Wear cases with Harris v. New York, 401 U.S. 222, 91 S.Ct. 643 (1971), and Oregon v. Hass, 420 U.S. 714, 95 S.Ct. 1215 (1975), infra p. 463. Is the argument for refreshment use stronger or weaker than the argument for impeaching use?

9. The opinion in United States v. Riccardi distinguishes between present recollection refreshed and past recollection recorded. The latter theory of admissibility, embodied in Fed. R. Evid. 803(5), is developed in the chapter on hearsay, infra pp. 539–40.

C. LAY OPINIONS

State v. Garver

Supreme Court of Oregon, 1950.
190 Or. 291, 225 P.2d 771.

■ LUSK, CHIEF JUSTICE. The defendant, Robert Edgar Garver, has appealed from a conviction of first degree murder. The jury, by its verdict, did not recommend life imprisonment, and the death penalty followed as a matter of course.

. . .

The actual substantial controversy arises out of the defense of insanity.

. . .

As to the testimony of Mrs. Mitchell, if there was error in striking her statement that the defendant was mentally ill, it was cured when later she was permitted to give her opinion that he was insane.

Apparently, the court struck the phrases used by her, "such a terrible shape" and "physically ill", on the theory that they were the opinions or conclusions of the witness. The general rule, of course, is that a lay witness may testify only to facts and not to opinions or conclusions. But lay witnesses are frequently permitted to use so-called "short hand" descriptions, in reality opinions, in presenting to the court their impression of the general physical condition of a person. 3 Jones on Evidence (2d ed.) 2306, § 1252. This court has held it proper in a personal injury case to permit laymen, who were intimately acquainted with the plaintiff prior to her injury and observed her condition thereafter, to testify that her health and general physical condition had materially changed for the worse. Crosby v. Portland Ry. Co., 53 Or. 496, 504, 100 P. 300, 101 P. 204. . . . This seems to us to be a common sense view of the matter. It leaves the witness free to speak his ordinary language, unbewildered by admonitions from the judge to testify to facts, when all the while the witness is sure in his own mind that he is testifying to facts. The jury understands what the witness means, and the right of cross-examination removes the likelihood of harm to the other side. Too strict an adherence to the "opinion" rule is undesirable. See, 2 Wigmore on Evidence (3d ed.) 660, § 568. When a witness of less than ordinary education and powers of expression is on the stand, technical rulings not infrequently result in bickerings between counsel and vain attempts of the court to make the witness comply with its rulings; while in the end the opinion of the witness usually comes out anyway, and nothing whatever is gained.

Mrs. Mitchell was a fairly intelligent witness, but she became so confused by the objections and rulings that at one time she said to counsel for the defendant: "Mr. Johns, I don't know what you mean by—when you ask me a question and I answer it to the best of my ability; I don't know what you mean for me to answer. I just try to tell what you ask me." A little later, after another of her answers was stricken, she said: ". . . I don't know how to express it; when I say what was in my heart then it is stricken from the records."

Mrs. Mitchell related to the jury the history of her son from infancy to the day of the alleged crime—including his illnesses, both mental and physical; his hospitalizations; his moral delinquencies; and his crimes—whatever might throw light on his mental condition. She used the expression "in such a terrible shape" when trying to explain why she had not taken the defendant back to the State Hospital as she had intended to do, and immediately afterwards said: "He asked me if he could get built up a little bit before he went back up there." She testified that "he was mentally and physically ill" in answer to a question as to why the defendant did nothing when he was at home with her in December, 1948. Presumably, she knew as much about his condition of health as any lay person could. Before giving the testimony which was stricken, she had described his former physical appearance to the jury, told of his robust health, and how he had lost sixty pounds during a certain period. The ruling complained of may not have been reversible error; but the same reasons which led the court in the cases cited to approve the admission of testimony of lay witnesses that a person injured in an accident was in a worse condition of health after the accident, than before, impel us to hold that the court should have let the stricken testimony stand.

.   .   .

For the error in refusing to give the instruction on the presumption of continuing insanity, the judgment is reversed and the cause remanded for further proceedings in conformity to this opinion.

NOTES

1. L. Hand, J., in Central Railroad Co. of New Jersey v. Monahan, 11 F.2d 212, 213–14 (2d Cir.1926):

> The other rulings sustained objections to questions which called for the opinion of the witnesses. These were probably correct, according to the orthodox American canon, and in any event the substance of the evidence ruled out either got before the jury or was unimportant. But in fact the questions excluded were reasonable, and it would have been better to allow them. The truth is, as Mr. Wigmore has observed at length (§§ 1917–1929), that the exclusion of opinion evidence has been carried beyond reason in this country, and that it would be a large advance if courts were to admit it with freedom. The line between opinion and fact is at best only one of degree, and ought to depend solely upon practical considerations, as, for example, the saving of time and the mentality of the witness. It is hardly ever reversible error to admit such evidence; its foundation may generally be as conveniently left to cross-examination. Every judge of experience in the trial of causes has again and again seen the whole story garbled, because of insistence upon a form with which the witness cannot comply, since, like most men, he is unaware of the extent to which inference enters into his perceptions. He is telling the "facts" in the only way that he knows how, and the result of nagging and checking him is often to choke him altogether, which is, indeed, usually its purpose.

> It is a good rule as nearly as one can, to reproduce the scene as it was, and so to correct against the personal equations of the witnesses. But one must be careful not to miss the forest for the trees, as generally happens, unless much latitude is allowed. In the case at bar it would have been better to allow the conductor to say whether he could have felt the jerk where he was standing, and whether it was necessary for him to give a starting signal in addition to the movement of the dwarf switch. Both these perceptions could be otherwise elicited only by a disproportionate amount of nice examination, in which his real contribution to the truth was likely to be lost. In fact, they were not brought out at all, and the plaintiff, by houghing at the questions, succeeded in suppressing what he had to say in the only way he could probably have said it. But, except in extreme cases, where we can see that harm is done, all such matters are in the discretion of the trial judge.

2. Felty v. State, 816 S.W.2d 872, 875 (Ark.1991): "For example, if a witness is asked, 'What kind of day was it?' he might respond, 'Beautiful.' It would be an admissible opinion. He would not have to state it was a clear skied, sunny, 72 degree spring day with a slight breeze. The witness can respond in everyday language which includes his conclusion about the type of day."

United States v. Yazzie, 976 F.2d 1252, 1255–56 (9th Cir.1992): In prosecution for statutory rape in which an affirmative defense was that defendant reasonably believed the minor was over sixteen years of age, held, error to exclude testimony of defense witnesses that their observations of the minor had caused them to believe that she was between sixteen and twenty years old.

In the case before us, the jurors could not themselves assess how old the minor looked at the time of the incident: by the time of the trial, the minor was almost seventeen years old, and her appearance was undoubtedly substantially different than it had been on the night in question, a year and a half earlier. Thus, the jurors were wholly dependent on the testimony of witnesses. Yet the witnesses were permitted to testify only to the minor's describable features and behavior. Their testimony was no substitute for a clear and unequivocal statement of their opinions. It did not tell the jury that these witnesses believed the minor to be at least sixteen years old at the time of the incident.

Our finding that the trial judge erred in not admitting the opinions of Yazzie's witnesses as to the minor's age is supported by all of the considerations that underlie Rule 701's authorization of the use of lay opinion testimony. First, it is difficult to distinguish a fifteen-and-a-half-year-old from a sixteen-year-old, and it is still more difficult to put into words why one believes that a person is one age and not the other. There is a certain intangible element involved in one's conclusions on such a question. We form an opinion of a person's age from "a combination of circumstances and appearances which cannot be adequately described and presented with the force and clearness as they appear[ ]" to us. Skeet, 665 F.2d at 985. Mannerisms and facial features are notoriously difficult to describe accurately, and one's reasons for concluding that a person is a particular age are both too complex and too indefinable to set out fully.

In addition, a witness may not know, let alone be able to report precisely, what factors induced his or her conclusion. In such a case, the fact that the witness reached the conclusion is the important part of the testimony, not the largely undeterminable or inexplicable reasons that prompted the conclusion.

Furthermore, age is a matter on which everyone has an opinion. Knowingly or unknowingly, we all form conclusions about people's ages every day. It is therefore particularly appropriate for a lay witness to express an opinion on the subject.

Here, the witnesses' opinions were especially appropriate for another reason. The issue was whether the defendant held an opinion and if so whether that opinion was reasonable. It is relevant that others having a similar opportunity to observe the minor formed an opinion as to her age that was similar to the opinion the defendant claimed to have formed. Their testimony goes both to Yazzie's credibility and to the reasonableness of his belief. The district court's decision deprived the jury of the most direct evidence available as to the age that the minor reasonably appeared to be on the night of the incident. Thus, the judge's ruling constituted a clear abuse of discretion.

C.W. Stuart & Co. v. Smith, 204 A.2d 297 (R.I.1964): In seller's action for price of plants, not error to admit buyer's testimony that plants were dead on arrival.

But see Wilson v. Pennsylvania Railroad Co., 219 A.2d 666, 671 (Pa.1966):

Next, the plaintiff assigns as error the trial court's affirmance of defendant's ninth point for charge which instructed the jury to disregard as conclusions Joseph Byrne's testimony that the decedent's car wheels were spinning on the approach to the crossing and that the car had stalled after reaching the crossing. The testimony of Byrne, who was not qualified as an expert, was definitely a recital of his own conclusion; he admitted, on cross-examination, that he could not see the wheels spinning but rather could only hear a screeching noise and that he only surmised the car had stalled "because there was no exhaust from the tailpipe". Plaintiff submits that these conclusions are admissible as an exception to the opinion evidence rule because the facts of which Byrne had knowledge were incapable of adequate description to the jury without accompanying opinions.... However, the application of this rule lies within the trial court's discretion, and its ruling will not be reversed on appeal unless there is an abuse of discretion.... Whether Byrne's conclusions were necessary is a question upon which reasonable men could differ, and we find no abuse of discretion in the trial court's exclusion of this testimony.

In United States v. Cox, 633 F.2d 871, 875–76 (9th Cir.1980), cert. denied, 454 U.S. 844 (1981), a prosecution for possession of unregistered firearms, the question was whether the defendant was the person who had placed pipe bombs in automobiles and blown them up. It was error, the court held, but harmless, to allow a witness to whom defendant had said that he knew someone who would blow up cars for $50 and to whom defendant had shown a newspaper article concerning one of the bombing incidents, to testify that it was "my impression when we were done talking that he was involved in having blown it up."

Should a policeman be allowed to testify that the account the defendant gave him of a certain incident was different from the account the defendant had given him earlier? See State v. Houde, 596 A.2d 330, 336 (R.I.1991).

3. Salley v. State, 796 S.W.2d 335 (Ark.1990): Prosecution for attempted capital felony murder. When police officers stopped defendant and told him to move against a wall, defendant took a handgun out of his pants and fired three shots, none of which hit the policemen. Held, not error to allow the police to testify they thought defendant was trying to kill one of them when he fired the shots. United States v. Oliver, 908 F.2d 260, 263 (8th Cir.1990): Not error to permit witness who had seen defendant and another together on a number of occasions to testify that defendant knew the other person's last name. In United States v. Smith, 550 F.2d 277, 281 (5th Cir.), cert. denied, 434 U.S. 841 (1977), a prosecution for conspiracy and misapplication of federal funds, it was held not error to admit the testimony of a witness who worked with the defendant that the defendant knew and understood the requirements of the federal act under which the funds were received. John Hancock Mut. Life Ins. Co. v. Dutton, 585 F.2d 1289, 1293–94 (5th Cir.1978), was a suit on a life insurance policy in which the question was whether the insured's death was "accidental." The insured had been shot by his wife during an altercation. The substantive law permitted recovery only if the husband believed that his wife would not kill him and his belief was reasonable. The court held, construing Federal Rule of Evidence 701, that it was not error to admit testimony of the wife's daughter, who was present during the altercation, that she did not think the insured believed his wife would shoot him.

But see State v. Ellis, 619 A.2d 418, 423 (R.I.1993): Not error to prohibit defense counsel from asking a witness whether a person he had encountered had been threatened or was in court against his will.

> There is no rational basis upon which a witness can determine that another person looks as though he has been threatened or is in court against his will. There was no inhibition against defense counsel's inquiring concerning the appearance of Patrick or the witness's perceptions that

might be based upon external observations. However, it can scarcely be contended that in the ordinary course of events a lay witness is able to determine such inner feelings as might arise if a person was threatened. This is a question that a lay witness (and probably most expert witnesses) would be totally unqualified to answer.

4. Cyr v. J.I. Case Co., 652 A.2d 685, 689–91 (N.H.1994): Worker was injured when he was backed into by a bulldozer that was not equipped with a back-up alarm. In suit against the manufacturer, an issue was whether the accident would have occurred if there had been a back-up alarm.

Cyr was injured while he was checking the grade of a road and a bulldozer operator was leveling dirt and gravel. While Cyr knelt on the ground, the bulldozer moved toward him from his left, in reverse gear. Nancy Linda–Marie Veilleux Tarbox, a flagger, stood slightly behind Cyr and to his right. She was looking over his shoulder when the bulldozer hit him; neither noticed the bulldozer's approach until it was too late. At a videotaped deposition, Tarbox testified as follows on examination by Cyr's attorney:

Q. Okay. And if this bulldozer had been equipped with a back-up alarm, you would agree, would you not, that this accident likely would not have happened?

[Defendants' Counsel]: I'm going to object. That's totally speculative based on what she's testified so far. There's no foundation for that.

Q. By [Cyr's Counsel]: *Ma'am, based on your experience with back-up alarms, construction equipment, and your observations of the speed with which this bulldozer moved back and forth, you would agree, would you not, that if this bulldozer had a back-up alarm that you would have had sufficient warning before the accident happened?*

[Defendants' Counsel]: I object to that for the same reason.

A. *I—I don't know. Probably, yes.*

Q. By [Cyr's Counsel]: Okay. This is, in fact, the second time today that you've testified under oath?

A. Yes.

. . .

Q. And I asked you pretty much the same question earlier this morning, and you said, did you not, that you felt that if a back-up alarm had been equipped on this bulldozer that the accident likely would not have happened?

A. Yes.

Q. And that's still your view right now; isn't it?

A. Yes.

(Emphasis added.) At trial, the court played Tarbox's videotaped deposition for the jury but deleted the entire portion quoted above at the defendants' request. On appeal, Cyr asserts error in this exclusion.

We first address the admissibility of the highlighted portion of the quoted testimony, concerning Tarbox's opinion of her own probable reaction to a back-up alarm. Admission is governed by New Hampshire Rule [ ]of Evidence ... 701....

· · ·

Tarbox's opinion about her own probable reaction to a back-up alarm satisfies all of these evidentiary principles. First, she rationally based her opinion on her own perception and personal knowledge of the accident and surrounding circumstances. Her testimony reveals a familiarity with the work performed by Cyr and the bulldozer driver, as well as the operation of back-up alarms and the noise level of the construction site. Moreover, she vividly described the moment her attention was first drawn to the bulldozer's approach and her reaction to it. We appreciate that the usual witness can only make informed predictions as to "what might have been," but Tarbox's opinion, based on self-knowledge and a perception of her environment, is neither farfetched nor irrational. In Sullivan v. LeBlanc, 125 A.2d 652, 655–56 (N.H.1956), a case involving a two-car accident, this court upheld admission of one driver's testimony that he " 'would have slowed down and given [the other driver] the right of way' "if the other driver had signaled an intention to turn.... We conclude that Tarbox's opinion about her own probable reaction to a back-up alarm on the bulldozer satisfies ... Rule 701(a).

We also find that her testimony meets Rule 701(b)'s requirement that an opinion be "helpful to a clear understanding of the testimony or the determination of a fact in issue." Causation was one of the primary issues of the trial. The jury had to determine, as best it could, what would have happened had the bulldozer been equipped with a back-up alarm. Tarbox's opinion was plainly relevant to this issue: if a back-up alarm would have given Tarbox sufficient warning, the jury could infer that it would have given Cyr sufficient warning, too. See N.H.R.Ev. 401. Tarbox's opinion was also helpful in the literal sense because a description of the numerous facts and observations that led her to this conclusion would likely have been impractical, inefficient, and a waste of time. See G. Lilly, An Introduction to the Law of Evidence § 4.9, at 107 (1987). Moreover, Tarbox was obviously in a much better position to judge her own behavior than was the jury. Cf. Saltzman, 475 A.2d at 6 (superfluous opinions not helpful to jury).

· · ·

We now consider the admissibility of the remaining portion of the testimony quoted above, concerning Tarbox's opinion that a back-up alarm would have prevented the accident. We do not think this opinion satisfies the requirements of Rule 701(b) because it is not "helpful to a clear understanding of the testimony or the determination of a fact in issue." The questions asked of Tarbox in this part of the deposition required her to speculate about Cyr's probable response to a hypothetical situation. Although Tarbox's conclusions may have been rationally based on her perception of Cyr and her personal knowledge about him, ... 701(a), we do not believe she was in any better position to read his mind and predict his behavior than was the jury. Her opinion followed a detailed description of the events leading up to the accident and her observations of Cyr's behavior. The jury heard all of this and could draw its own conclusions. Accordingly, Tarbox's opinion was superfluous, cf. Saltzman, 475 A.2d at 6, and thus, not helpful.

5. S.E.C. v. Singer, 786 F.Supp. 1158, 1168–69 (S.D.N.Y.1992): Prosecution for use of insider information in violation of the Securities Exchange Act. The disputed issue was whether McLernon, an insider, had told the defendant, who was a close social friend and business associate, of an impending leveraged buyout. McLernon said that their relationship was so close that it was almost a stream of consciousness and that he believed he had discussed the matter with defendant, and that it was "inconceivable to me that we didn't discuss it." Held, not error under Rule 602 or Rule 701 to admit McLernon's testimony. McLernon's opinion was "rationally based on his knowledge, accumulated over a period of time, of the relationship that existed between them. McLernon's inability to provide the specific circumstances of a conversation does not render inadmissible his conclusion that the conversation did occur. As with relevancy, defects in recollection do not render testimony inadmissible as personal knowledge/opinion but rather are factors for consideration by the jury.... "

Recall Meyers v. United States, supra p. 217, in which Rogers testified to "the substance" of the defendant's testimony, rather than to particular words he had heard, perhaps because he could not remember particular words. See also Delaware v. Fensterer, 474 U.S. 15, 106 S.Ct. 292 (1985), infra p. 363.

6. Does Fed.R.Evid. 701 require more of opinion evidence than that it be relevant? If it does, how is the exclusionary principle to be stated and what policy does it enforce? The Advisory Committee's Note to Rule 701 refers to "the traditional objective of putting the trier of fact in possession of an accurate reproduction of the event." What does this mean? The Note also suggests that Rule 701(a) repeats Rule 602. If it does, why was this necessary?

7. In the earlier discussion of Fed.R.Evid. 602, it was suggested that the requirement of "personal knowledge" set forth in that rule might be invoked when the form of the testimony is such as to present the possibilities that the evidence is irrelevant, lacks required specificity (the opinion rule), rests upon hearsay or is entirely unobjectionable. Rule 602 could be read to give the opponent a right to have testimony excluded that creates such uncertainty. An objection that testimony is "opinion" is sometimes employed to achieve the same end. This is interestingly brought out in Letwin, Waiver of Objections to Former Testimony, 15 UCLA L. Rev. 118, 134–39 (1967). The author deals with the question whether an answer in the form of an opinion contained in a deposition may be excluded at the trial even though the opponent failed to object at the time the deposition was taken. Failure to object at the time the deposition was taken waives objection to admission at trial only if the objectionable feature of the testimony could have been obviated. Whether the objectionable feature "opinion" could have been obviated depends of course upon which of the three distinct objections mentioned above is intended. The necessity of carefully distinguishing among these objections will be appreciated by reflecting on the following situation: A and Proffitt are charged with robbing W1. Only A is brought to trial. W1, called as a witness by the prosecution, testifies that he was robbed by A and Proffitt. W2, a policeman, is then called by the prosecution and asked, "Where is Proffitt?" W2 answers, "Mr. Proffitt is a fugitive at this time, his whereabouts is unknown." See Potter v. State, 274 N.E.2d 699 (Ind.1971).

8. So far as concerns adequacy of opportunity for observation underlying opinion, is there any reason to require more than that the opinion be relevant? See supra p. 291 on competency of witnesses in respect to observation.

In State v. Butner, 206 P.2d 253 (Nev.1949), cert. denied, 338 U.S. 950 (1950), rehearing denied for second time by divided court, 220 P.2d 631 (Nev.1950), cert. denied, 340 U.S. 913 (1951), a taxicab driver was accidentally and at imminent peril to himself involved in defendant's fatal shooting of defendant's wife. The driver's entire contact with defendant was for a period of time from three to eight minutes during this episode. He was allowed to testify for the prosecution that in his opinion defendant was sane at the time of the shooting. Admission of this testimony was sustained over a prolonged and vigorous dissent, which considered that the driver could not possibly have assembled enough factual data to make an adequate foundation for his opinion. Bernardini v. Salas, 448 P.2d 43 (Nev.1968): Witnesses who heard jeep going down mountain road while they were lying in sleeping bags by side of the road held incompetent to testify, on the basis of sound alone, whether already awake or awakened by the sound of the jeep, that it was moving at a high rate of speed. People v. Gonzales, 439 P.2d 655, 658 (Cal. 1968), cert. denied, 393 U.S. 1055 (1969):

> There is likewise no merit to defendant's claim that the court erred in overruling an objection, based on the opinion rule, to testimony of Officer Hanks regarding the identity of the man who left the bar.... Hanks testified that in his opinion the man he saw leave the bar was defendant, that clothing and specified characteristics of the man appeared to be the same as those of defendant, but that Hanks did not see the facial characteristics of the man and could not positively identify defendant as the man. Lack of positiveness as to the man's identity went to the weight and not to the competency of the evidence.

9.   In Chapter 6, attention will be given to the difference between lay and expert testimony. A problem that will receive extensive consideration in connection with expert testimony may profitably be opened for discussion here. This is the matter of the relation between opinion testimony and legal standards.

United States v. Stamps, 430 F.2d 33 (5th Cir.1970): Officer Sayre had reason to think that defendant was in possession of stolen postal money orders. Sayre did not know defendant's name, but looking in the register of the hotel where defendant was staying found that he was registered under the name of William Saunders. Sayre approached defendant as defendant was leaving the hotel and asked him if he was William Saunders. Defendant said that he was. Sayre then asked, "May I see your identification, please?" Defendant handed him an identification that bore the name Don Stamps. Sayre asked defendant if this was his name and defendant said that it was. Sayre then arrested defendant saying, "You are under arrest for giving false information to a police officer." Sayre searched defendant and found stolen money orders in his pockets. A complaint was filed against defendant in a municipal court charging that defendant did "make a false and misleading report to a police officer of the City of Miami, which report interfered with or hindered the proper operation of the police officer's duties or his investigation." This complaint was later dismissed. A federal prosecution was commenced against defendant for possession of stolen postal money orders. Defendant moved to suppress the money orders found during the search. The motion was denied, the money orders admitted into evidence, and the defendant convicted.

ORIE L. PHILLIPS, CIRCUIT JUDGE:

> Stamps contends that there was no evidence that the false information he gave to Sayre interfered with or hindered the proper operation of Sayre's duty or investigation as a police officer, and hence the arrest was unlawful and the search of Stamps at the Detective Bureau was not incident to a valid arrest and was therefore illegal.

> If Stamps, instead of falsely stating to Sayre that his name was William Saunders, had told Sayre that his true name was Rex Don Stamps, it certainly would have simplified Sayre's investigation of Stamps as a suspect of the post office burglary. The identity of a person being investi-

gated with respect to the commission of a crime is usually important. If Stamps had used his true name in registering at the Hotel, it would have tended to allay the suspicion of him which had been engendered by the imprint of the validating stamp of the burglarized branch post office on the envelope found in his room. But if he had registered under a fictitious name, it would have greatly increased the basis for believing he was connected with such burglary. We are of the opinion that the trial court was justified in concluding from the evidence that the false statement, at the time it was made, hindered the investigation of Stamps being made by Sayre, even though it was only for a short time, and even though Sayre thereafter was able to obtain an admission from Stamps that his true name was Rex Don Stamps. We conclude the arrest was lawful.

. . .

The questions to which objections were sustained that are now urged as error, in substance were: How did Stamps's false answers as to his name "interfere with or hinder the proper operation" of Sayre's "duty or his investigation" as a police officer? Sayre fully and frankly testified as to all the pertinent and attendant facts. There was no testimony to the contrary. Since all the pertinent and attendant facts were before the court, the question as to whether those facts established that Stamps by his false answers had violated the city ordinance was one of law for the determination of the trial court and called for a legal conclusion. The trial court held that they did interfere with Sayre's investigation. A majority of this court now holds that they did so interfere. With that determination the dissenting judge agrees. We hold the questions, in effect, called for a legal conclusion by Sayre, and the objections thereto were properly sustained.

Accordingly, we affirm.

Simpson, Circuit Judge (dissenting):

. . . I disagree with the majority's statement that the excluded questions called for legal conclusions. To the contrary, the questions were an entirely legitimate endeavor to determine the grounds for Officer Sayre's belief that he had probable cause to make the arrest and subsequent search. Probable cause was, of course . . . the primary issue in the inquiry into the legality of the warrantless search.

With the majority's analysis of the issue as to interference with an officer's investigation, I express no quarrel, but I would reverse and remand for a new trial on the clearly demonstrated basis of the trial court's prejudicial limitation of examination of the witness Sayre.

In a passage from the majority opinion omitted here, some significance is attached to the fact that defendant, not the government, called Sayre to the stand and that the question about interfering with or hindering the investigation or the operation of a police officer's duty was put to Sayre on direct rather than on cross-examination.

Dallis v. Aetna Life Ins. Co., 768 F.2d 1303, 1305–06 (11th Cir.1985): Suit on health insurance policy in which the issue was whether treatment that the insured had undergone—immuno-augmentative therapy—was necessary for the treatment of her cancer. The treatment was obtained at the Immunology Research Center (IRC) in the Bahamas and had not been approved by any agency of the United States Government. Held: Not error to admit testimony by plaintiff's witnesses that they had cancer, that they had undergone treatment at IRC, and that it had improved their condition.

Was it error to prevent plaintiff's counsel, in an action for personal injuries arising out of an automobile accident, from asking defendant driver on cross-examination whether he believed in view of the nature of the road that he was travelling at an excessive speed? See Starner v. Wirth, 269 A.2d 674 (Pa.1970). In Church v. West, 452 P.2d 265, 268 (Wash.1969), where the failure of the defendant to have his lights on in a foggy area was charged as negligence, the court held it not error to allow a witness who was driving another car just behind defendant's to state that he had his lights on and felt he needed them.

Torres v. County of Oakland, 758 F.2d 147 (6th Cir.1985): In action for discrimination on ground of national origin in not appointing plaintiff to a position, held error, although harmless, to ask a witness knowledgeable of the appointment process whether she thought plaintiff had been discriminated against on the ground of national origin, but it would not have been error to ask the witness whether national origin motivated the decision.

10. Discussions of lay opinion evidence in general and with reference to specific topics include: Slovenko, The Opinion Rule and Wittgenstein's Tractatus, 14 Miami L.Rev. 1 (1959); Spies, Opinion Evidence, 15 Ark. L.Rev. 105 (1960); Parker, Opinion Evidence, 6 Cr.L.Q. 187 (1963) (intoxication); Pederson, The Opinion Evidence Rule in Oregon as It Relates to Cases Involving Medical Matters and Insanity, 33 Or.L.Rev. 243, 262–71 (1954); Construction and Application of Rule 701 of Federal Rules of Evidence, Providing for Opinion Testimony by Lay Witnesses Under Certain Circumstances, 44 A.L.R.Fed. 919 (1979).

D. CROSS-EXAMINATION

1. The profound significance of cross-examination as an evidentiary process is brought out in the discussion of hearsay, infra in Chapter 4. In an appropriate situation, failure of an opportunity for cross-examination may cause the entire testimony of a witness to be struck, even though this leads to dismissal of the suit for inadequacy of remaining evidence. See Rutger v. Walken, 143 P.2d 866 (Wash.1943) (motor vehicle case dismissed when plaintiff persistently dodged pivotal question put on cross-examination). If after giving direct testimony and before there is an opportunity for cross-examination the witness is taken ill or dies, generally the direct testimony will be struck. See Commonwealth v. Kirouac, 542 N.E.2d 270, 273 n. 5 (Mass.1989). In Smith v. Illinois, 390 U.S. 129 (1968), a conviction for the sale of narcotics was reversed because the informer who testified that the defendant had sold him narcotics was not required to divulge his name and address on cross-examination. The Court held that this limitation violated the Confrontation Clause of the Sixth Amendment. The Court pointed out that the refusal to answer the questions was not based upon the privilege against self-incrimination and that the state-law informer privilege apparently was not applicable since the informer was actually called as a witness. A concurring opinion attached significance to the fact that no claim had been made that the informer would be endangered by revealing his name and address. See State v. Mannhalt, 845 P.2d 1023, 1028–29 (Wash.Ct.App.1992), discussing personal safety exception.

2. Whether a failure of memory on cross-examination should result in the direct examination being struck is the subject of controversy. The highest court in one jurisdiction seemed to hold that when a witness testifies on direct examination about a subject and then on cross-examination says that he cannot remember about that subject, the Confrontation Clause does not require that the direct be struck, Commonwealth v. Amirault, 535 N.E.2d 193, 202 (Mass. 1989), but in a later decision, the court appeared to interpret the first decision

as holding only that the direct need not be struck when the failure of memory is not significant. Commonwealth v. Kirouac, 542 N.E.2d 270, 271–74 (Mass. 1989). In the second decision the court said that in the first case the witness had not asserted a lapse of memory as a general response to questions, whereas in the second case the witness had. In the second case the child witness had testified on direct that the defendant had done certain things to her, but on cross-examination, the next day, when asked whether she remembered what she had said the day before, kept saying no and that she was tired and wanted to go to her nanny's. Why should a distinction be drawn between a witness who cannot remember and a witness who becomes ill or dies or who simply refuses to answer? Is the predicament of the cross-examiner any different in these situations?

Delaware v. Fensterer, 474 U.S. 15 (1985): Murder case in which a prosecution expert testified that hairs found on a cat's leash claimed to have been used to strangle the victim were similar to the victim's hair and that one of the hairs on the leash had been forcibly removed from the head. The expert testified that there were three methods of determining whether a hair had been forcibly removed—one of the methods he mentioned was the presence of a "follicular tag" on the hair—but that he could not remember which method he had used in this case. A defense expert testified that the prosecution's expert had told him on the telephone that he relied on the presence of a follicular tag, but that he, the defense expert, considered this theory not to have adequate scientific support. Held: The admission of the prosecution's expert's testimony did not violate defendant's rights under the Confrontation Clause of the Sixth Amendment.

For more on the significance of loss of memory for problems under the Confrontation Clause and the hearsay rule, see infra p. 554.

3. The obstacle to cross-examination may not be loss of memory, illness or death or a simple refusal to answer, but another policy of the law: there may be conflict with a privilege. The possible solutions to this conflict are that the privilege be overridden and the witness ordered to testify, that the privilege be respected but the opponent's interest upheld by striking the direct testimony, that the direct be allowed to stand and the opponent's interest in cross-examination disregarded. A difference between this situation and those involving illness, death, failed memory or simple refusal to answer is that the barrier to cross-examination is created by law.

In Davis v. Alaska, 415 U.S. 308 (1974), there was conflict between the defendant's interest in cross-examination and a state policy of nondisclosure of juvenile offenses. The Court reversed defendant's conviction of burglary because he was prevented from bringing out on cross-examination of a prosecution witness the fact that the witness was on probation for a juvenile offense. Inquiry into this matter was forbidden by a state statute. The Court pointed out that the fact of the witness's probationary status went directly to the issue of bias: since the stolen property had been found near the witness's home, he could have been worried that the police would suspect him of having committed the crime, that his probationary status would somehow be jeopardized, or both. But see Delaware v. Van Arsdall, 475 U.S. 673 (1986) (constitutionally improper denial of opportunity to impeach for bias does not require reversal if error was harmless beyond a reasonable doubt).

In Olden v. Kentucky, 488 U.S. 227 (1988), a prosecution of a black man for raping a white woman in which the sole issue was consent, the Court held that it violated the Confrontation Clause to prohibit cross-examination of the woman as to whether at the time of the incident and the trial she was living with another black man. (She was married to a third man, a white man.) The reason for cross-examination into this matter stressed by the Court was that it might suggest the witness's interest in protecting her relationship with the man she was living with. It may also be noted that the relationship might have cast light on the witness's character and her attitude toward interracial sex. The Court mentioned in its opinion that it had not been suggested that the state rape-shield statute barred inquiry into the witness's relationship with the other black man. See infra pp. 895–907 on rape shield laws. At the same time it would seem implicit in the Court's decision that any damage or prejudice to the witness and the prosecution that might result from revealing the interracial relationship, did not justify prohibiting cross-examination about it.

Earlier, conflict between a criminal defendant's need for evidence and a privilege or other state policy was examined from the perspective of the Compulsory Process Clause. See supra p. 270. There the focus was on the defendant's interest in obtaining and introducing exculpatory evidence. The alternatives were to override the privilege and require the evidence, to dismiss the prosecution or to require the defendant to conduct his defense as best he could without the evidence. In the present context the focus is on the need of the defendant to protect himself against damage resulting from the testimony of a prosecution witness. In some cases, cross-examination of the witness will be fruitful only if it is guided by information obtained from some source other than the witness himself. As noted earlier, see supra p. 270, in Pennsylvania v. Ritchie, 480 U.S. 39 (1987), a prosecution for child sexual abuse, the Court held that the Due Process Clause conferred on the defendant a right to have the trial court examine in camera a file of a state agency made confidential by statute, to determine whether the file contained information material to the defendant's case, at least when the statute required the agency to disclose the file on order of a court. The Court also held that the Compulsory Process Clause would confer upon the defendant no greater right. So far as concerns the defendant's right under the Confrontation Clause to obtain privileged material to cross-examine a prosecution witness, however, the opinions in the Ritchie case are inconclusive. See 480 U.S. at 51, 54 (plurality opinion), id. at 63–66 (concurring opinion), id. at 66–72 (dissenting opinion). See also Commonwealth v. Stockhammer, 570 N.E.2d 992, 1000–02 (Mass.1991): Although in camera inspection may satisfy Compulsory Process Clause of the federal constitution, it does not satisfy the state Declaration of Rights: the judge is not in a position to determine what in the records would be helpful to the defendant's case. (But see Commonwealth v. Bishop, 617 N.E.2d 990, 993–98 (Mass.1993), qualifying Stockhammer and permitting the judge to determine in camera whether the privileged materials contain anything relevant, and only if he finds that they do does the defendant have a right of access to those materials for purpose of determining whether a fair trial requires that they be put before the trier of fact.) See also State v. Pierson, 514 A.2d 724, 728–34 (Conn.1986): Privilege covering communications to a psychotherapist must give way to the interest of a criminal defendant in determining whether there is substantial evidence of the mental condition of a vital prosecution witness that might reasonably affect the witness's credibility; Note, Defendant vs. Witness: Measuring Confrontation and Compulsory Process Rights Against Statutory Communications Privilege, 30 Stan.L.Rev. 935 (1978).

In Chambers v. Mississippi, 410 U.S. 284 (1973), supra p. 261 and infra p. 399, although it was the defendant who called the witness, the witness damaged him and the defendant was prevented by state rules from either impeaching the witness or introducing extrajudicial statements by the witness that inculpated the witness and exculpated the defendant. Such limitations, the Court held, deprived the defendant of due process.

4. Limitations on cross-examination by reason of a witness's invoking the privilege against self-incrimination merit separate consideration because of the possibility of protecting the policy of the privilege by immunizing the witness.

United States v. Cardillo, 316 F.2d 606, 612–13 (2d Cir.), cert. denied, 375 U.S. 857 (1963): Error not to have struck the direct testimony of a government witness when he refused to answer questions on cross-examination on the ground of self-incrimination. The prosecution was for interstate transportation and knowing receipt of stolen furs. The witness testified that one of the defendants had asked him for a loan of money to buy stolen furs and that the witness had borrowed $5000 from a friend to make the loan. On cross-examination the witness refused to say from whom he had borrowed the $5000. The court noted the importance of an answer to this question:

> Had Friedman disclosed the name of the lender, there would have been several possibilities. The lender might not have been available as a witness, he might have confirmed the loan, he might have denied making it or the defense might have been able to introduce other proof to show that the alleged lender could not possibly have made the loan. If the proof were sufficiently convincing to induce a belief that the loan had never been made, the court's reaction to all of Friedman's testimony might have been so adverse that it would have accepted no part thereof. Disclosure of a direct lie relating to the events testified to might have had far more influence on the court's ultimate decision than testimony merely establishing the unsavory character of the witness by admissions of prior crimes.

See also Turner v. Fair, 476 F.Supp. 874 (D.Mass.1979), vacated on other grounds, 617 F.2d 7 (1st Cir.1980): Prosecution for robbery of a store and murder in the course of the robbery. Prosecution witnesses who admitted that they were participants in the crime testified that they had waited in the car while the defendants went into the store. They refused on cross-examination to say whether they had robbed the same store on earlier occasions, invoking the privilege against self-incrimination. Held: The Confrontation Clause required the striking of the direct testimony.

In other cases in which the privilege against self-incrimination has been invoked, it has been held that the direct testimony need not be struck. For example, in Coil v. United States, 343 F.2d 573, 577–80 (8th Cir.), cert. denied, 382 U.S. 821 (1965), the issue was whether the defendant, a pharmacist, had made illegal sales of morphine to W, as the government contended, or whether W had stolen the morphine from defendant's pharmacy. W testified for the government that defendant had sold him the morphine. On cross-examination W admitted that he would steal or cheat to get narcotics. However, when questioned concerning specific incidents of possession of stolen narcotics and feigning illness in order to get narcotics from a doctor (neither incident involving the narcotics covered by the indictment), W refused to answer, invoking the privilege against self-incrimination. The trial court sustained the claim of privilege and also refused to strike W's direct testimony. Held: The claim of privilege was properly sustained. Furthermore, it was not error to refuse to strike the direct testimony since the information withheld on cross-examination concerned collateral matters, cumulative in nature, going only to the witness's credibility. See infra p. 429 on cross-examination of a witness regarding bad acts as to which he has not been convicted.

See Note, The Existing Conflict Between the Defendant's Right of Confrontation and the Witness's Right to Avoid Self–Incrimination, 38 Cath.U.L.Rev. 245 (1988).

If a prosecution witness's direct testimony must be struck when the witness invokes the privilege against self-incrimination on cross-examination, must a defense witness's direct testimony also be struck under the same circumstance? A criminal defendant has a Due Process or Compulsory Process right to introduce evidence favorable to himself, but the prosecution has a right to cross-examination, albeit not based upon the Constitution. Denham v. Deeds, 954 F.2d 1501 (9th Cir.1992): Compulsory Process right not violated by striking direct testimony of defense witness who invoked privilege against self-incrimination during cross-examination. United States v. Frank, 520 F.2d 1287, 1291–92 (2d Cir.1975), cert. denied, 423 U.S. 1087 (1976): In prosecution for securities fraud, a witness called by defendant X gave testimony that tended to exonerate defendant Y. This witness, when confronted on cross-examination by evidence showing that his direct testimony was probably perjured, invoked the privilege against self-incrimination. The court held that it was not error to have struck the direct testimony. "[B]y virtue of Allen's refusing to answer (for whatever reason) proper, relevant questions on cross-examination going directly to the heart of his testimony on direct examination, the direct testimony became hearsay, since not subject to cross-examination and was therefore properly struck." See also People v. Barthel, 42 Cal.Rptr. 290 (App.1965): Defendant's direct testimony struck because she invoked the privilege against self-incrimination and did not answer certain questions on cross-examination. United States v. Deutsch, 987 F.2d 878, 883–84 (2d Cir.1993): Not abuse of discretion to refuse to allow defendant to call a witness when it was clear that all the witness would do would be to invoke the privilege against self-incrimination.

But see Wisconsin ex rel. Monsoor v. Gagnon, 497 F.2d 1126 (7th Cir. 1974): Compulsory Process Clause violated by striking of direct testimony of defense witness who had invoked the privilege against self-incrimination when asked on cross-examination about certain criminal conduct: the question went to a collateral issue relating to credibility and not to the subject matter of the direct testimony.

The authorities on immunizing witnesses from whom defendant would like to obtain information are reviewed in United States v. Bahadar, 954 F.2d 821, 824–26 (2d Cir.), cert. denied, 116 S.Ct. 149 (1992). See also Ann. Rev. of Crim. Procedure, 83 Geo.L.J. 1177, 1189–90 (1995). Bahadar itself requires immunity only when "the government has engaged in a discriminatory use of immunity to gain a tactical advantage or, through its own overreaching, has forced the witness to invoke the Fifth Amendment."

5. A line of Supreme Court decisions under the Confrontation Clause has addressed the conflict between the interest in protecting a witness from injury and the defendant's interest in cross-examination and confrontation, a problem closely related to that presented by conflict between evidentiary privilege and the right of confrontation. The Court has been closely divided in these cases. Kentucky v. Stincer, 482 U.S. 730 (1987), was a prosecution for sodomy committed upon two minors. Defendant was excluded from the hearing to determine the competency of the minors to testify, although his counsel was present and allowed to participate. The Court found no violation of the Sixth Amendment because it concluded, after reviewing the nature of a competency hearing and the record of the hearing and the trial, that excluding the defendant from the hearing had not interfered with his opportunity for effec-

tive cross-examination at trial. The three dissenters objected that the text of the Sixth Amendment "plainly envisions that witnesses against the accused shall, as a rule, testify *in his presence*." They pointed out that "[p]hysical presence of the defendant enhances the reliability of the factfinding process" and "serves certain 'symbolic goals' as well" in assuring the perception of fairness. 480 U.S. at 748–50. After Stincer, in Coy v. Iowa, 487 U.S. 1012 (1988), also a child sexual abuse case, the Court held that the right to confrontation had been violated when the child witnesses were allowed to testify at the trial with a one-way screen between them and the defendant, which prevented them from seeing the defendant. This arrangement violated the Sixth Amendment, the Court held, at least in the absence of individualized findings that the witnesses needed special protection. But then in Maryland v. Craig, 497 U.S. 836 (1990), yet another child sexual abuse case, the Court held that the Confrontation Clause had not been violated when the child witnesses were allowed to testify from outside the courtroom by closed circuit television, the trial court having made individualized findings, based upon expert testimony, that testifying in the presence of the defendant would cause the witnesses such serious emotional distress that they could not reasonably communicate. Actual physical confrontation by the defendant, the Court held, was not required when the reliability of the evidence was assured and an important interest protected.

6. In a civil context, the Sixth Amendment of course does not apply. Kraut v. Morgan & Brother Manhattan Storage Co., 343 N.E.2d 744 (N.Y.App. Div.1976), was an action for damages to compensate plaintiff for a ransom paid to recover art works stolen as a result of the negligence of defendant's employees. Judgment for the plaintiff was affirmed even though on cross-examination he had refused to disclose, out of fear for his own safety and that of his family, the identity of the intermediary to whom he had paid the ransom. In Withers v. Levine, 615 F.2d 158, 163 (4th Cir.), cert. denied, 449 U.S. 849 (1980), an action for injunctive and declaratory relief to require prison officials to provide prisoners with reasonable protection from sexual assaults, prisoner-witnesses called by plaintiff to testify to the prevalence of sexual assaults in prisons were allowed to give the names of assailants to the judge in camera, who then passed them on to defense counsel without revealing which witness had identified which assailant. The court cited Federal Rule of Evidence 611(a)(3), which allows a court to protect witnesses from "harassment and undue embarrassment."

Finch v. Weiner

Supreme Court of Connecticut, 1929.
109 Conn. 616, 145 A. 31.

Action to recover damages for personal injuries, alleged to have been caused by the defendant's negligence, brought to the City Court of Meriden and tried to the jury before Aubrey, Deputy–Judge; verdict and judgment for the defendant and appeal by the plaintiff. Error and new trial ordered.

■ HINMAN, J. The plaintiff claimed and offered evidence tending to prove that a collision between a truck owned by the defendant and operated by his employee, one Skinner, and a sedan, owned by one Hoskings, in which the plaintiff was riding as a guest, was caused by negligent operation of the truck, and that the plaintiff was injured thereby. At the beginning of the presentation of evidence by the plaintiff, Skinner was called as a witness and was inquired of, only, as to whether, at the time of the collision, he was in the employ of the defendant and engaged in his business, and to identify an accident report made by the witness to the State Commissioner of Motor Vehicles. Thereupon counsel for the defendant, notwithstanding objection that it was not admissible cross-examination, was permitted to elicit from the witness his version of the details of the collision and the events preceding and following it, none of which had been touched upon in the direct examination.

After the plaintiff had rested his case, the defendant recalled the same witness who again testified, with greater particularity, to the same matters which he had related in his previous testimony. The plaintiff's objection, that the witness had already, under the guise of cross-examination, been fully examined as to the subject-matter, was overruled.

These rulings are made grounds of appeal. The record indicates that the trial court, in overruling the objection to the proposed line of "cross-examination," regarded the question presented as one of order of proof, only, as to which a liberal discretion is vested in the trial court. The exercise of such discretion ordinarily cannot be reviewed on appeal. Hurlburt v. Bussemey, 101 Conn. 406, 416, 126 A. 273; 6 Jones Commentaries on Evidence (2d Ed.) Chap. 29, p. 4950 et seq. However, the purpose of allowing discretionary variations from the logical order of proof relates largely to convenience or accommodation in forwarding the trial, usually to avoid the necessity of detaining or recalling a witness, or some similar consideration, but the discretion must be exercised with due regard to the substantial rights involved and in accord with that which is just and proper under the circumstances. Departure from the regular order should not be permitted where it will work injustice to either party. 6 Jones Commentaries on Evidence (2d Ed.) sec. 2511. The practical effect of the ruling complained of tended to give the defendant the distinct advantage of placing before the jury, at the outset of the trial, a version of the circumstances favorable to his contentions, proceeding from a witness called and in a sense vouched for by the plaintiff, and in sharp contradiction to the testimony of other witnesses called by the plaintiff, as to those facts and circumstances. A further natural and probable effect of such a course of procedure would be to create confusion in the minds of the jury and to weaken the effect of the plaintiff's evidence. Considered simply as a matter of order of proof it would seem that the evidence in question might have been admitted at that stage of the case without undue prejudice, only upon the defendant expressly making the witness his own for the purposes of the new line of inquiry, with a clear explanation in the charge of the effect thereof, neither of which conditions occur in the present case. Even with these safeguards the propriety of admitting such testimony, at the inception of the plaintiff's case, would be extremely doubtful. "It was part of the defendant's case, and the time to put that in had not arrived." Finken v. Elm City Brass Co., 73 Conn. 423, 427, 47 A. 670.

The admission of this evidence also involved a conspicuous transgression of the established and salutary general rule that cross-examination shall be limited to the subject-matter of the direct examination. Roberts v. New York, N.H. & H.R.R., 107 Conn. 681, 690, 142 A. 455; Richmond v. Norwich, 96 Conn. 582, 591, 115 A. 11; 5 Jones Commentaries on Evidence (2d Ed.) secs. 2340, 2341, 2342. Particularly where, as here, a witness is called by one party for examination as to some particular or formal point only, the adversary is not entitled to examine him generally or to draw out facts having no connection with the direct testimony and tending to establish a substantive claim or defense of the cross-examiner, but should be confined to the subject testified to in chief. In re Hotchkiss' Will, 88 Conn. 655, 663, 92 A. 419; Finken v. Elm City Brass Co., supra. In this, as in other matters pertaining to control over cross-examination, a considerable latitude of discretion is allowed. Murphy v. Murphy, 74 Conn. 198, 50 A. 394; State v. McGowan, 66 Conn. 392, 34 A. 99. But the so-called cross-examination of Skinner was so completely foreign to the subject-matter of the direct and so palpably prejudicial to the plaintiff that its admission was not within the limits of permissible exercise of the court's discretion and must be regarded as reversible error.

The testimony given by Skinner during the presentation of the defendant's case was objectionable only in being substantially an elaborated repetition of his evidence previously given as cross-examination. Standing by itself it was proper, but considered in connection with his prior testimony it enhanced the tendency of the original error to prejudice the plaintiff through reiteration of and emphasis upon a version of the circumstances which was adverse to his recovery....

There is error and a new trial is ordered.

In this opinion the other judges concurred.

NOTES

1. The opinion in Finch v. Weiner suggests various reasons for restricting cross-examination by some criterion other than simply relevance. Among the reasons suggested is that the witness is in some sense vouched for by the party who calls him. This idea is put forth in Resurrection Gold Mining v. Fortune Gold Mining, 129 F. 668, 675–76 (8th Cir.1904), where the court spoke of a party being bound by the testimony of a witness he called. If any such consequence ever attached to calling a witness, no trace of it is to be found in present law. See infra p. 395. Furthermore, even if such a consequence did attach, that fact could not function as a reason for limiting the cross-examiner to what had been gone into on direct: it simply could be determined that in regard to the new matter brought out on cross-examination, the party that called the witness would not be bound, but the cross-examiner would be. Different from the reason for limiting cross-examination that a party is bound by the testimony of a witness he calls is the idea that cross-examination ought to be limited because a party may not impeach the testimony of a witness he calls, for instance by bringing out facts suggesting bias or that the witness on an earlier occasion made a statement inconsistent with present testimony. This topic will be considered at length infra p. 390. In fact, Fed.R.Evid. 607 has abolished the prohibition against impeaching one's own witness. But even if it were retained, as in the case of the notion that a party is bound by the testimony of a witness he calls, it cannot function as a reason for limiting cross-examination: in regard to new matter brought out on cross-examination, it can be held simply that the party who called the witness may impeach him, but the cross-examiner may not.

Distinct from but related to the suggested reasons for limiting cross-examination that the party calling the witness is bound by his testimony or may not impeach him is the suggestion that if unfavorable information is brought out on cross-examination, it will count more strongly against the party who called the witness than if the same information came out when the opponent called the witness. R. Klonoff and P. Colby, Sponsorship Strategy 226–27, 231 (1990), make this suggestion. Trial lawyers disagree on the question, but even if the authors are correct about jurors' reactions, it does not necessarily follow that the party calling the witness should be protected from this effect by a rule limiting cross-examination.

The opinion in Finch v. Weiner suggests as a reason for limiting cross-examination that unless there is a restriction, the opponent will be able to put before the trier "at the outset of the trial, a version of the circumstances favorable to his contentions ... in sharp contradiction to the testimony of other witnesses called by the plaintiff...." In other words, if there is no restriction on cross-examination, the opponent will be able to disrupt the presentation that the plaintiff has carefully planned to achieve what from his point of view would be the optimal effect on the trier of facts. That such disruption will occur may be true, but that does not answer the question why it should not occur. See McCormick, Evidence § 27, at 60 (3d ed. 1984). Is there implicit in the adversary system a notion of fairness requiring that a party be allowed a time to make the presentation he wishes without excessive interruption by his opponent? A cross-examiner is not allowed to ask questions in the middle of direct examination, nor is a party allowed to call witnesses in the middle of his opponent's case.

Another reason suggested by the Finch opinion for restricting cross-examination is the avoidance of confusion. Conceding that this objective is laudable, will it be achieved by a rule such as that sought to be applied in Finch, rather than by a discretionary power to take into account the circumstances of a particular trial at a particular time? Consider for instance the following situation. The plaintiff has already injected issue A into his presentation of the case by direct examination of W1, but has avoided issue A when directly examining W2. Should defendant be prevented on cross-examination from interrogating W2 about issue A? Should the scope of cross-examination be determined by the posture of the whole case rather than by the extent of direct examination of W2 alone? Yet see such cases as Aplin v. United States, 41 F.2d 495 (9th Cir.1930); Dickson v. United States, 182 F.2d 131 (10th Cir.1950) (majority allow cross-examination but do not discuss this reason); and Panitz v. Webb, 130 A. 913, 914 (Md.1925). Further, if restricted cross-examination is intended to avoid confusion, what of the doctrine that inquiry referring to a topic opened on direct is proper although the purpose of the cross-examiner is different from that of the direct examiner? See Atlantic Greyhound Lines v. Isabelle, 157 F.2d 260, 262 (D.C.Cir.1946), where P testified on direct that in the accident which was the basis of the action he had suffered an injured right hand, which precluded his writing his own name without help; held error to prevent D on cross from eliciting testimony that P on the morning after the accident signed his name legibly and in his customary penmanship to a release, the validity of which was challenged.

The virtues of the wide-open or so-called English rule, are described by the Wisconsin Supreme Court, and the rule adopted in dictum, in Boller v. Cofrances, 166 N.W.2d 129, 134 (Wis.1969):

The rule against questioning any witness "beyond the scope of direct examination" has no intrinsic merit and does not demonstrably assist in the search for the truth. Rather, by encouraging pettifogging objections that go to form and not substance, the rule is likely to be disruptive of trial procedure and results in appeals that basically have no merit.

The only claimed virtue for the rule is that it ensures the orderly presentation of evidence, i.e., that a plaintiff's witness should not be expected to help make the defendant's case on cross-examination. But why shouldn't he? If the question is relevant and is otherwise admissible and the information solicited is within the knowledge of the witness, it should be within the sound discretion of the trial judge to determine whether or not questions on cross-examination prevent an orderly and cogent presentation of the evidence. They well might, and usually would, contribute to the intelligent search for the truth

This test, which leaves the admission or exclusion to the discretion of the trial judge, is infinitely preferable to the artificial and meaningless rule that excludes all evidence whether it should then logically come into the record or not, simply because it is "beyond the scope.".[1]

The Wisconsin Rules of Evidence, adopted in 1973, provide: "A witness may be cross-examined on any matter relevant to any issue in the case, including credibility. In the interests of justice, the judge may limit cross-examination with respect to matters not testified to on direct examination." W.S.A. § 906.11(2) (1975).

See generally Degnan, Non–Rules Evidence Law: Cross–Examination, 6 Utah L.Rev. 323, 330–38 (1959).

2. In regard to limitations on cross-examination, Dean Wigmore sought to group the jurisdictions into three categories. First, a minority embracing the doctrine that a cross-examiner may interrogate as to "the whole case"—see Moody v. Rowell, 34 Mass. (17 Pick.) 490, 499 (1835), relying upon English authorities; second, the majority, restricting cross-examination more or less tightly to matters stated in direct examination; third, a minority permitting cross-examination regarding matters that tend to modify or explain away the effect, immediate or inferential, of the direct examination. 6 Wigmore, Evidence §§ 1885–95 (Chadbourn rev. 1976).

A more elaborate classification that looks particularly to the vocabulary employed in judicial opinions, is as follows:

a. Some opinions and discussions speak of limiting the cross-examiner to "the case" of the direct examiner. See Wigmore, supra, for full statement in these terms, and the somewhat wavering language in Conley v. Mervis, 188 A. 350, 353 (Pa.1936). Such language suggests reference to probative obligations cast upon the parties by pleadings or otherwise.

b. However in the same opinion in Conley v. Mervis there is the remark: "Where testimony has been adduced relevant to a *particular issue* involved [italics supplied], cross-examination may embrace any circumstances pertaining thereto, though prejudicial to plaintiff's case and reaching beyond the direct testimony." Id. at 355.

c. Authorities that speak of "the matters inquired about" on direct examination allow the trial judge to subdivide an issue and restrict cross-examination to a fraction only of that issue. See Kline v. Kachmar, 61 A.2d 825 (Pa.1948); Grievance Committee v. Dacey, 222 A.2d 339, 349–50 (Conn.1966), appeal dismissed, 386 U.S. 683 (1967). The opinion in Conley v. Mervis, supra, contains much language about "matters testified to in chief," "new matter" and "matter germane to the direct examination."

d. The terms "fact" or "facts" elicited on direct examination presumably carries a connotation like that of "matters" or "subjects", being also used in Conley v. Mervis.

e. Compare the approach of "disprove, weaken, or modify the case against him [the cross-examiner] which the witness himself has made" in the Resurrection Gold Mining case, supra. In re Campbell's Will, 138 A. 725, 726 (Vt.1927), says, "only that which tends to limit, explain, or refute the statements of the direct examination or to modify the inferences deducible therefrom, comes within the range of proper cross-examination.... Thus far opposing counsel may go as a matter of right." See also State v. O'Brien, 412 A.2d 231 (R.I.1980); Troutman v. Erlandson, 569 P.2d 575 (Or.1977).

---

1. Footnote omitted.

Under any of the formulations set forth above, cross-examination that seeks to undermine the credibility of the witness is not precluded. See Fed. R.Evid. 611(b).

In some jurisdictions it is permissible to cross-examine more sweepingly than an ordinary witness a party who takes the stand voluntarily in his own behalf. See Knight v. Willey, 138 A.2d 596 (Vt.1958); Tolomeo v. Harmony Short Line Motor Transportation Co., 37 A.2d 511, 513 (Pa.1944); W.Va.R.Evid. 611(b)(1) (wide-open rule for parties).

3. The Federal Rules of Evidence recommended by the Advisory Committee and promulgated by the Supreme Court adopted the wide-open rule, tempered by judicial discretion to limit cross-examination in the interests of justice to matters testified to on direct. This was rejected by Congress, which instead adopted an approach falling within category c, supra: "Cross-examination should be limited to the subject matter of the direct examination and matters affecting the credibility of the witness. The court may, in the exercise of discretion, permit inquiry into additional matters as if on direct examination." The House Committee Report observed: "This traditional rule facilitates orderly presentation by each party at trial." Van Pelt, The Background of Federal Rules 611(b) and 607, 57 Neb.L.Rev. 898 (1978), discusses the opposing views within the Advisory Committee. See also Annot., Construction and Application of Provision of Rule 611(b) of Federal Rules of Evidence that Cross–Examination Should be Limited to Subject Matter of Direct Examination, 45 A.L.R.Fed. 639 (1979).

4. Fed.R.Evid. 611(b) is applied in United States v. Carter, 910 F.2d 1524, 1530 (7th Cir.1990), cert. denied, 499 U.S. 978 (1991): In a prosecution for bank robbery in which the only issue was identity, defendant called Riggins, his fiancé, as a witness. Riggins had been with defendant when he was arrested and was brought to the police station with him. Her direct testimony is not described in the appellate court's opinion, but probably it concerned events in the police station, which were relevant to the voluntariness and probative value of a confession made there by defendant.

Defendant argues that the trial court improperly allowed the government to exceed the scope of direct examination when it cross-examined Lashan Riggins.

The government did not call Riggins as a witness in its case in chief. Defendant called her as a defense witness. On cross-examination, the government exceeded the scope of direct examination by inquiring into the following subjects: (1) defendant's statement to her that he committed the robberies, made to her in the holding room at the police station after he confessed to the authorities; (2) her recollection of the clothing defendant wore when he left Indianapolis for Chicago on January 20, 1989; and (3) her recognition of the clothing discarded following the January 9 robbery as similar to clothing owned by defendant. Defendant objected to these questions at trial on the ground that they were prohibited by Fed.R.Evid. 611(b), but in each instance the trial court invoked its discretion under the rule to permit the questions.

The district court did not act improperly in so ruling. Although Fed.R.Evid. 611(b) limits cross-examination to the subject matter of direct examination, it grants the trial court discretion to "permit inquiry into additional matters as if on direct examination." A district court's evidentiary rulings are not subject to reversal unless the defendant can show a clear abuse of discretion. . . .

Despite this deferential appellate standard, defendant argues that the court's decision to allow Riggins to be questioned on such matters constitutes an abuse of discretion because it enabled the government to present evidence that it chose not to offer in its case in chief and that would not have been proper rebuttal. Although defendant is correct in these assertions, he must show more than this to establish that the trial court abused its discretion. The testimony elicited challenged some of the alibis that defendant was presenting, such as his contention that he was not at the CNA building on January 9, 1989 [the place and date of the litigated robbery] and that he was misidentified as the robber on January 20, 1989 [when another robbery of the same bank took place]. In light of the probative value of this evidence, the trial judge did not abuse his discretion by allowing the government to exceed the scope of Riggins's direct examination.

Assuming that Riggins' direct testimony was as suggested above, was it necessary to concede, as the court does, that the cross-examination exceeded the scope of the direct? Why did the prosecutor not call Riggins in its case-in-chief? If as the court says Riggins' testimony on cross-examination would not have been proper rebuttal, what justification was there for allowing the prosecution to elicit it on cross-examination? Does the court's rationale for upholding the cross-examination leave any limit to what the trial court may permit? For another decision seemingly as sweeping as Carter, see United States v. Beechum, 582 F.2d 898, 905–07 (5th Cir.1978), cert. denied, 440 U.S. 920 (1979).

With United States v. Carter compare Lis v. Robert Packer Hospital, 579 F.2d 819, 821–23 (3d Cir.), cert. denied, 439 U.S. 955 (1978). In that case the court held that it was error for the trial court to permit cross-examination beyond the scope of the direct when the reason the trial court gave was that "I have the right to permit inquiry beyond the scope of the direct, and I do it in every case unless it causes confusion." According to the appellate court, the trial court's ruling "effectuated neither the letter nor the spirit of Rule 611(b). Simply stated, the Rule does not confer upon a federal judge 'the right to permit inquiry beyond the scope of the direct ... in every case'. Rather, the general prescription is precisely the opposite. Any right to counter the stated procedure is granted to the trial court only 'in the exercise of discretion'. To follow the practice announced by the trial judge in this case is not to exercise discretion; it is to use no discretion whatever."

See also Williams v. Giant Eagle Markets, 883 F.2d 1184, 1189–90 (3d Cir.1989): Plaintiff, one of defendant's cashiers, had been present at an argument between a customer and another cashier. The store manager's effort to end the argument by silencing the other cashier led to an argument between the manager and the plaintiff. This argument in turn led to the plaintiff's being fired, she contended because of her race and sex, the defendant contended because of insubordination. Defendant sued for discrimination on grounds of race and sex. At trial, defendant called Sobocinski, another of its employees.

Williams [the plaintiff] next argues that the district court abused its discretion by limiting Johnson's [the plaintiff's lawyer's] cross-examination of ... [Sobocinski] about his acts of insubordination. Williams contends that this alleged trial error merits reversal since proof that Giant Eagle disciplined its white employees less severely for insubordination than it did its black employees was critical to her case. The district court's conduct with respect to limiting Johnson's cross-examination is governed by Fed. R.Evid. 611(b)....

In this case, Sobocinski was called to testify by Giant Eagle as to the authenticity of his signed statement taken May 6, 1984, concerning the argument he had witnessed between Williams and Lichius [the store manager]. Upon cross-examination, Johnson sought to expand the scope of the direct examination by questioning Sobocinski as to whether Giant Eagle had ever charged him with insubordination. Based upon our understanding of Rule 611(b), the district court did not act improperly in sustaining Giant Eagle's counsel's objection to such questioning on grounds of relevance. This case is at the opposite end of the spectrum from Lis v. Robert Packer Hospital, 579 F.2d 819, 822–23 (3d Cir.), cert. denied, 439 U.S. 955 ... (1978), where a district court abused its discretion by permitting cross-examination to go beyond the scope of the direct examination in every instance. Here, the trial judge rigidly confined cross-examination to the precise issues covered on direct examination.

While we agree with Williams that evidence of a white male employee being treated less severely than she for acts of insubordination would demonstrate that Giant Eagle's asserted justification for her dismissal was pretextual, the district court's action did not preclude her from calling Sobocinski to testify in her case-in-chief. We were careful in Lis "to distinguish between cross examination beyond the scope of direct examination and the act of summoning a witness for one side to become a witness for the other." 579 F.2d at 823. Williams could have sought to call Sobocinski as a witness and to question him directly about his insubordinate conduct. She chose, however, not to exercise this option.

The instant case exemplifies the broad discretion given to the trial judge. While another judge may have been less stringent in limiting counsel's cross-examination, we do not find that the trial judge's rulings in this case rise to the level of reversible error....

People v. Sallis

Colorado Court of Appeals, 1993.
857 P.2d 572.

■ Opinion by JUDGE PIERCE.

In this prosecution for sexual assault on a child, the People appeal from a ruling of the trial court limiting the scope of cross-examination of defendant, Daniel V. Sallis, II, and from a ruling concerning the procedure followed in that cross-examination. We disapprove the rulings.

Defendant, a friend of the victim's mother, was accused of sexually assaulting the victim, a young boy, after having invited him on a motorcycle ride.

At trial, as a means to assist him in deciding whether to testify in his own defense, defendant requested a ruling as to the permissible scope of the prosecutor's cross-examination. Stating that it could not issue such a ruling without first hearing defendant's testimony, the trial court ordered that, if defendant took the stand, it would excuse the jury and require the prosecutor to conduct a mock cross-examination of defendant, at which time it would rule on any objections to the prosecutor's questions.

Defendant elected to testify and was cross-examined outside the presence of the jury. Following the cross-examination, the trial court identified seven questions that it would permit the prosecutor to ask. The trial court also ruled that questions relating to all other matters were beyond the scope of direct examination and would not be permitted.

Arguing that this ruling rendered any cross-examination "completely ineffective," the prosecutor declined to cross-examine defendant, and subsequently, he was acquitted.

. . .

On appeal, the People contend that the trial court abused its discretion in limiting the scope of its cross-examination of defendant. We agree.

Although the scope and limits of cross-examination are matters committed to the sound discretion of the trial court, its decisions thereon will be reversed on appeal if that discretion is abused.... To constitute an abuse of discretion, the trial court's ruling must be arbitrary, unreasonable, or unfair....

A criminal defendant who voluntarily takes the witness stand in his or her own defense waives the Fifth Amendment protection against self-incrimination to the extent necessary to permit effective cross-examination. People v. Mozee, 723 P.2d 117 (Colo.1986). In such a case, the defendant may be cross-examined in the same manner as any other witness. See People v. Thiery, 780 P.2d 8 (Colo.App.1989).

Here, on direct examination, defendant was asked only two questions: (1) whether he had invaded "the rectum or anus of [the victim] on the date and time that he alleges" and (2) whether he had "threatened [the victim] that if he was not silent that you would harm or kill his mother." To both questions, defendant responded: "No, I did not."

During the mock cross-examination, the prosecutor sought to ask defendant how defendant came to know the victim, whether he was aware the victim was shy, whether he had dinner with the victim and his mother a week after the motorcycle ride, and other details about his motorcycle ride with the victim. The trial court sustained objections to each of these questions on the ground that they exceeded the scope of defendant's general denial of assaulting or threatening the victim. However, the prosecutor was permitted to inquire as to the date of the motorcycle ride, whether the victim had been entrusted to his care during that ride, and whether he believed that the victim loved his mother.

Under the circumstances of this case, we conclude that the trial court construed the scope of defendant's direct examination in too restrictive a manner. In ruling on defendant's objections, the trial court stated:

> that if the defendant limits the scope of the inquiry of direct examination, if the defendant does take the stand, that I would limit the district attorney to areas which are specifically within that scope of the questions that are asked.

That test is improper because it is too restrictive.

In general, cross-examination should be limited to the subject matter of the direct examination and matters affecting the credibility of the witness. CRE 611(b). However, this rule does not limit cross-examination to the same acts and facts to which a witness has testified on direct examination; rather, it must be liberally construed to permit cross-examination on any matter germane to the direct examination, qualifying or destroying it, or tending to elucidate, modify, explain, contradict, or rebut testimony given by the witness. See United States v. Varoz, 740 F.2d 772 (10th Cir.1984) (interpreting the identical Fed.R.Evid. 611(b)); Leeper v. United States, 446 F.2d 281 (10th Cir.1971). See also McCormick on Evidence § 21 at 84–85 (E. Cleary 4th ed. 1992). In addition, the prosecutor must be permitted to inquire as to the witness' motives, intentions, bias, or prejudice....

If, as here, a defendant makes a general denial of the offense charged or as to a matter of ultimate fact, the prosecutor is not limited to a mere categorical review of the evidence testified to on direct examination. Rather, the prosecutor must be permitted to examine the defendant in detail as to matters generally referred to during direct examination. See People v. Lanphear, 26 Cal.3d 814, 163 Cal.Rptr. 601, 608 P.2d 689 (1980), rev'd in part on other grounds, 28 Cal.3d 463, 171 Cal.Rptr. 505, 622 P.2d 950 (1980); State v. Lamborn, 452 S.W.2d 216 (Mo.1970).

Each of the prosecutor's proffered questions was reasonably related to the ultimate acts which defendant denied, and therefore, these questions were within the permissible scope of cross-examination. See United States v. Varoz, supra.

By limiting cross-examination to essentially a recitation of the evidence to which defendant testified on direct examination, the trial court denied the prosecutor an opportunity to develop fully the facts surrounding the incident and any inconsistencies in the defense. Without the ability to explore these issues, the function of the prosecutor's cross-examination was severely impeded. See United States v. Havens, 446 U.S. 620, 100 S.Ct. 1912, 64 L.Ed.2d 559 (1980).

Moreover, the trial court was inconsistent in ruling as to the scope of defendant's testimony on direct examination, even under the standard it chose to apply. Although it had ruled that questions concerning the circumstances leading up to and including defendant's motorcycle ride with the victim were beyond the scope of direct examination, it indicated that it would permit the prosecutor to ask questions regarding his subsequent contact with the victim, such as whether he had purchased a gift for the victim and whether he had offered to take care of the victim if his mother went to work.

Therefore, we conclude that the trial court erred in applying the rule it selected in limiting the scope of cross-examination. Because the prosecutor was thus prevented from effectively cross-examining defendant, we find sufficient prejudice to mandate disapproval....

We also agree with the People that the procedure of conducting a mock cross-examination of defendant outside the presence of the jury was improper. Having waived the protection of the Fifth Amendment, a criminal defendant should not have the benefit of procedures that are not extended to other witnesses.... He must take his chances, as any other witness, and can only expect the limitations on cross-examination which have been previously set forth in this opinion.

The imbalance of this procedure was set forth by the People in its brief when it stated:

It [the trial court] allowed the defendant the opportunity to plan the best possible responses to what it knew would be the prosecutor's questions. The interests of justice are not served through a rehearsal cross-examination when the search for truth is through effective inquiry.

In this case, defendant was permitted to place his version of the facts before the jury; however, the prosecution was not permitted to test the veracity of that testimony.

The rulings of the trial court are disapproved.

NOTES

1. Were the questions the trial court disallowed for cross-examination in People v. Sallis within the scope of the direct? Compare the appellate court's decision on this question with that of the court in Williams v. Giant Eagle Markets, Inc., supra.

2. Requiring a mock cross-examination did not give the defendant all that he wanted in Sallis. He might have thought that the trial court's ruling on the questions that the prosecutor would be permitted to ask on cross-examination was too liberal, but it would have been too late to withdraw the defendant's direct testimony. However, the defendant obtained some of the protection he sought. On the permissibility or necessity of his obtaining that much protection, see Brooks v. Tennessee, 406 U.S. 605 (1972), supra p. 267, striking down a requirement that a criminal defendant testify first in his case or not at all, and Leeke, supra p. 332, upholding prohibition of defendant's consulting with counsel during brief recess.

3. Carlson, Cross–Examination of the Accused, 52 Cornell L. Rev. 705, 708–09 n. 7 (1967):

> It should be noted that the question of the scope of cross-examination and that of the scope of waiver of the privilege are separate and distinct.... Although both may serve to limit cross-examination, the former operates by virtue of statutory or decisional authority, whereas the latter expresses a constitutional concept. The interaction of the two principles occurs when the accused takes the witness stand. If the scope of waiver is limited, i.e., if the privilege is waived only as to matters testified to on direct examination, the rule of limited cross-examination may operate as an ancillary procedural device to implement such a concept of waiver and prevent cross-examination offensive to the constitutional privilege. Of course, a jurisdiction can apply a broad waiver rule and deem the privilege destroyed as to every matter relevant to the merits, yet employ the limited cross-examination rule as a procedural device. But the converse does not appear equally true. A jurisdiction applying a narrow waiver rule may be prohibited by privilege considerations from applying a rule of wide-open cross-examination of the accused since such interrogations, exceeding the boundaries of the waiver, delve into matter respecting which the privilege has not been waived....[2]

See also Carlson, Scope of Cross Examination and the Proposed Federal Rules, 32 Fed. B. J. 244 (1973); Comment, Speak No Evil: The Impact of Rule 611(b) on the Accused's Privilege Against Self–Incrimination, 48 U.Cin.L.Rev. 842 (1979).

The Advisory Committee's Note to Rule 611(b) states that the rule does not purport to determine the extent to which an accused who elects to testify thereby waives his privilege against self-incrimination. The question is a constitutional one, rather than a mere matter of administering the trial. In its Note the Committee calls attention to the fact that in Simmons v. United States, 390 U.S. 377 (1968), it was held that no general waiver occurs when an accused testifies on such preliminary matters as the validity of a search and seizure. Following this reference, the Committee cites Federal Rule of Evidence 104(d). In McGautha v. California, 402 U.S. 183, 215 (1971), in the course of holding that the privilege against self-incrimination is not violated by confronting a defendant with the choice between giving testimony usable both on the issue of guilt and the matter of punishment in a unitary procedure, or not testifying at all, the Court observed: "It has long been held that a defendant who takes the stand in his own behalf cannot then claim the privilege against cross-examination on matters reasonably related to the subject matter of his

2. © Copyright 1967 by Cornell University.

direct examination." See also United States v. Nobles, 422 U.S. 225 (1975), supra p. 269.

United States v. Hearst, 563 F.2d 1331, 1338–41 (9th Cir.1977), cert. denied, 435 U.S. 1000 (1978). Prosecution for bank robbery. The defense was duress. Taking the stand, the accused testified regarding events immediately following her kidnapping on February 4, 1974 by the so-called Symbionese Liberation Army (SLA); how she had been compelled to participate in the bank robbery on April 15, 1974; how and why she had participated in a disturbance involving the firing of shots at a Los Angeles sporting goods store a month after the robbery (concerning which the prosecution, too, had presented evidence in its case-in-chief); and how she had travelled with the kidnappers and others across the country and back ending up in Las Vegas in September 1974. Her testimony then jumped to the time of her arrest on September 18, 1975. On cross-examination, invoking the privilege against self-incrimination 42 times, she refused to answer most questions about her activities, residences and associations with other members of the SLA between September 1974 and September 1975. Held: The trial court did not abuse its discretion in ruling that defendant's silence regarding this period was not protected by the privilege against self-incrimination and in permitting the prosecutor to question her about it. Defendant refused to answer the questions, repeatedly invoking the privilege in the presence of the jury. "Although appellant did not discuss this year [in her direct testimony], the natural inference from her other testimony, if believed, was that she had acted involuntarily during this period. Having offered selective evidence of the nature of her behavior for the whole period, appellant had no valid objection to the government's attempt to show that her conduct during the omitted year belied her story. . . . [T]he government's questions about her activities, associations, and residences during the interim year were more than 'reasonably related' to the subject matter of her prior testimony." For other discussions of this case, see supra pp. 1020, 1385.

For other cases attempting to establish the proper relationship between the rule confining cross-examination to matters opened on direct and waiver of the privilege against self-incrimination, and in addition seeking to apply correctly the rule excluding evidence of crimes other than the crimes charged in the indictment, infra p. 808, see People v. Ing, 422 P.2d 590 (Cal.1967), and People v. Perez, 422 P.2d 597 (Cal.1967).

United States v. Segal

United States Court of Appeals, Third Circuit, 1976.
534 F.2d 578.

■ Before SEITZ, CHIEF JUDGE, and VAN DUSEN and WEIS, CIRCUIT JUDGES.

OPINION OF THE COURT

■ WEIS, CIRCUIT JUDGE.

Defendants were tried jointly and convicted of conspiracy and bribery of a public official in violation of 18 U.S.C. §§ 371 and 201(b)(2), arising out of the payment of money to an Internal Revenue agent to falsify a tax liability. We reverse the convictions and remand for a new trial because the voir dire examination of the jury panel and the cross-examination of the prosecution's witnesses were improperly restricted.

Defendant Segal was a certified public accountant who represented the defendant Hurst during an audit of his tax returns by Internal Revenue Agent Edward Sigmond. During the period from June to December, 1974, Sigmond contacted Segal on a number of occasions. At their first meeting, Segal intimated that he might offer Sigmond a bribe, a matter which the agent reported to the Inspection Service. Thereafter, on visits to Segal's office, Sigmond wore a body recorder. He also recorded a number of telephone conversations with Segal and one with Hurst.

At the trial, Sigmond was the principal government witness. He testified that Segal offered to obtain $20,000.00 from Hurst, of which $15,000.00 would go to the agent in return for submitting a false audit report, and the remaining $5,000.00 would be retained by the C.P.A. In December of 1974, Sigmond received $5,000.00 from Hurst through Segal, with a promise that the remainder would follow. On January 7, 1975, Sigmond telephoned Hurst and recorded the conversation in which Hurst admitted providing the bribe and promised to pay the amount still due. Hurst was arrested the following day and gave a statement to Internal Revenue officials admitting his participation and also implicating Segal.

On appeal, both defendants claim that the voir dire of prospective jurors was unduly limited and that the cross-examination of Sigmond was improperly restricted. Hurst also contends that because a redacted version of his confession presented an erroneous view of his part in the affair, a severance was required.

[Discussion of the voir dire issue omitted.]

Since upon a retrial it is likely that the scope of cross-examination will again become an issue, we shall discuss it at this time.

Agent Sigmond testified about the several conferences and telephone conversations he had with Segal from May to December, 1974. Excerpts from some of the recordings were played for the jurors who were supplied with transcripts of these conversations for use while listening to the tapes. Since some of the recordings, particularly those of all-day conferences, were quite lengthy, some editing was necessary. Obviously, much of the material was inconsequential, and playing all of it would have unduly prolonged the trial and aided no one.

In an effort to keep the trial moving, the judge ruled that on cross-examination defense counsel would not be permitted to replay tapes which had been heard during direct examination. He directed that cross-examination be conducted by use of the transcripts. Defense counsel assert that they wished to replay portions of the tape rather than relying on the transcripts because voice inflections were important.

If in any specific instance this contention should appear to be valid, the court should consider the advisability of allowing replay. In general, however, we cannot find error in the court's suggestion that the transcript be used in reviewing material which had once been played. The court's policy offered a practical way to eliminate the delays which necessarily accompany the playing of selected excerpts from lengthy and unindexed tapes.

However, the court also prohibited defense counsel from using transcripts or playing parts of a recording which had not been heard during direct examination. This restriction was based on the premise that cross-examination should not exceed the scope of direct and that the defendants were free to present the proffered evidence in their own case. We think this limitation unduly narrowed the scope of cross-examination and hindered proper presentation of the defense case.

Federal Rule of Evidence 611(b) provides that cross-examination should be limited to the subject matter of the direct examination and matters affecting the credibility of the witness. While the trial court has wide discretion to prevent repetition, harassment of the witness or production of irrelevant material, the right of cross-examination is of constitutional dimension and may not be denied. Davis v. Alaska, 415 U.S. 308, 94 S.Ct. 1105, 39 L.Ed.2d 347 (1974). Therefore, if a matter has been raised on direct examination, generally cross-examination must be permitted. Moreover, questioning of the witness which tests his perception, memory, or otherwise tends to discredit him is proper. Davis v. Alaska, supra.

One of defendants' complaints is directed at an incident which occurred during the cross-examination of Agent Sigmond. He had testified about statements made during a conference with Segal on September 16, 1974. Although Sigmond used a body recorder on that date and a transcript had been prepared, the tape was not played to the jury during the direct examination. On cross-examination, defense counsel's attempts to use either selected portions of the tape or the transcript for that day were blocked by the court. Counsel for Segal explains in his brief:

"... the meeting of September 16, 1974 and the tape recorded conversations arising therefrom became crucial to the defense in their endeavor to show that, in fact, at no time during this meeting did the defendant attempt to or offer to Agent Sigmond a bribe in the form of money or gratuities and that rather, certain conversations recorded on that day indicated that Agent Sigmond was himself attempting to solicit a bribe from the defendant."

Since the court did permit some inquiry about that meeting and restricted counsel only on the use of the recording, it seems that the difficulty centered on the question of what constituted the scope of direct examination. In our view, the scope is to be measured by the subject matter of the direct examination rather than by specific exhibits which are introduced at that time. See Federal Rule of Evidence 611(b).

Moreover, the fact that some of the points which defendant sought to explore could have been introduced in the defense case is not determinative. That specific evidence could have been a part of the defense does not preclude its development on cross-examination if the prosecution makes the subject matter part of its direct testimony. United States v. Lewis, 447 F.2d 134 (2d Cir.1971).

The ruling of the trial court in this instance was erroneous because it unduly limited cross-examination.

. . .

The judgment of the district court will be reversed and a new trial ordered as to both defendants.[1]

NOTE

In United States v. Segal, is the court right that the question of the admissibility of the tape or transcript of the meeting of September 16 arises under Fed.R.Evid. 611(b)? If it arises under Rule 611(a), what is the answer to the question whether the tape or transcript should be admitted?

1. Footnotes omitted.

United States v. Ellison, 557 F.2d 128 (7th Cir.), cert. denied, 434 U.S. 965 (1977): Prosecution for conspiracy to distribute a controlled substance. The conspiracy alleged was between defendant, a pharmacist, and a physician. In order to prove an overt act in furtherance of the conspiracy, the government introduced telephone company records and elicited testimony from a telephone company executive to the effect that a direct private line had been installed between defendant's pharmacy and the physician's office. Held: Not an abuse of discretion to prohibit defendant on cross-examination of the executive from introducing telephone company records showing it was a common practice to install private lines between pharmacies and physicians' offices.

E. REDIRECT AND RECROSS EXAMINATION

Commonwealth v. O'Brien

Supreme Judicial Court of Massachusetts, 1995.
419 Mass. 470, 645 N.E.2d 1170.

[Prosecution for murder of an infant. It was important to the defendant's theory of how the infant's death occurred whether the infant had displayed certain symptoms before or only after a particular time. The mother of the infant, a prosecution witness, testified on direct examination that she first noticed the symptoms after that time.]

■ Before LIACOS, C.J., and WILKINS, ABRAMS, NOLAN, LYNCH, O'CONNOR and GREANEY, J.J.

■ LIACOS, CHIEF JUSTICE.

. . .

Under cross-examination, Carol Shanahan [the mother] testified, consistent with her testimony on direct examination, that she did not see Sean [the infant] on October 2, 1987, from the time she left for work in the morning until around dinner time. When she saw him, Sean appeared to have a runny nose but exhibited no other cold symptoms. Defense counsel asked Shanahan whether she remembered making a statement to the police shortly after Sean's death in which she stated that when she got home with Darlene in the afternoon the two of them looked in on Sean and that he appeared to have a cold, and that he was wheezing and gasping and sounded hoarse. Shanahan testified that, while she remembered making a statement to the police, she could not remember stating that she checked on Sean in the afternoon or that he had appeared to have had a cold at that time. On being shown her written statement to police made following Sean's death, Shanahan repeated that she could not recall stating she had checked on Sean in the afternoon.

On redirect examination, the prosecutor elicited testimony from Shanahan explaining that she was in an upset state on October 7 when she gave the statement because Sean's funeral had been the day before. On recross-examination, defense counsel attempted to ask Shanahan about a second statement she made some time after the October 7 statement, in preparation for trial. On the prosecutor's objection and the court's suggestion that the second statement was beyond the scope of redirect examination, defense counsel argued that the statement was within the scope of redirect because it impeached Shanahan's explanation as to why her October 7 statement was inconsistent with her trial testimony. The judge sustained the prosecution's objection. The judge precluded defense counsel from asking Shanahan about the contents of the second statement, which was not in evidence, ruling that it did not address a new matter raised on redirect.

The defendant argues that his right to confrontation under the Federal and Massachusetts Constitutions was violated when the judge denied his request to recross-examine Carol Shanahan regarding the second statement. We conclude that the judge acted within his sound discretion in ruling that the matter on which the defendant sought to examine Shanahan was not a new matter raised for the first time on redirect examination of the witness. Therefore, the defendant had no right to recross-examine her on the statement as it was beyond the scope of redirect examination.

The confrontation clause of the Sixth Amendment to the United States Constitution and art. 12 of the Declaration of Rights of the Massachusetts Constitution guarantee a defendant the right to cross-examine each witness against him. This right to cross-examination is an essential component to the right to a fair trial.... However, as opposed to cross-examination, a defendant has no right to recross-examination unless the examination addresses a new matter brought out for the first time on redirect examination.... If the recross-examination proposes to enter new territory not raised on redirect, the trial judge has discretion in determining whether to allow the examination....

The questions asked by the prosecutor on redirect examination regarding Shanahan's state of mind at the time she gave her October 7 statement were entirely proper in that they sought to explain the circumstances surrounding the making of a statement which had been used to impeach the witness on cross-examination. "One purpose of redirect examination is to allow a witness to 'explain, correct or modify the evidence elicited from ... [him] on cross by the defendant.' " Commonwealth v. Caine, 366 Mass. 366, 368–369, 318 N.E.2d 901 (1974), quoting Commonwealth v. Galvin, 310 Mass. 733, 747, 39 N.E.2d 656 (1942). "A witness who has been impeached by a prior inconsistent statement may explain *why* he has made inconsistent statements" (emphasis supplied). Commonwealth v. Errington, 390 Mass. 875, 880, 460 N.E.2d 598 (1984). The questions which defense counsel proposed to ask on recross-examination involved an entirely separate statement, a statement which was not brought out at any point on direct, cross, or redirect examination. He asked no question pertaining directly to her alleged state of mind. While it is true that had the defendant been permitted to recross-examine Shanahan on the second statement, her testimony might have been impeached, this possibility does not affect the outcome of this issue....

The defendant had every opportunity to examine Shanahan regarding the second statement during the original cross-examination. Counsel's conduct in not taking that opportunity may have been an unfortunate tactical decision, but such a decision cannot now be considered a constitutional error on the judge's part....

. . .

Judgment affirmed.

■ O'CONNOR, JUSTICE (dissenting, with whom WILKINS and GREANEY, JJ., join).

Darlene, a sister of the infant victim's mother, testified that, in the evening, after the mother had left the family's apartment, the infant cried and vomited on the defendant's shoulder, and that the defendant got a "mean" look on his face and threw the infant in the air. Darlene also testified that the infant hit the floor, making a "loud noise" when he landed. As the court notes ... the defendant's theory of the case at trial was that the injury occurred earlier in the day while the defendant was playing with the infant on the living room floor; that the defendant "flipped the [infant] while holding his hands and that [the infant] accidentally slipped and landed on the floor." It was important to the defense that Darlene's testimony be impeached, as it would have been if the jury had heard that the infant showed symptoms of head injury before the infant's mother left the apartment.

"The defendant claims that the 'cold' symptoms observed by [the mother] and other witnesses were actually symptoms of a head injury. Therefore, the defendant argues, the issue of when [the infant's] 'cold' symptoms appeared was crucial to the defense." ... If the symptoms appeared before the mother left the apartment in the evening, that would suggest that the fatal incident did not occur when and as described by Darlene, but that it occurred earlier in the day in conformity with the defendant's theory of the case.

As the court notes, "Under cross-examination, [the mother] testified, consistent with her testimony on direct examination, that she did not see [the infant] on October 2, 1987, from the time she left for work in the morning until around dinner time. When she saw him, [the infant] appeared to have a runny nose but exhibited no other cold symptoms. Defense counsel asked [the mother] whether she remembered making a statement to the police shortly after [the infant's] death in which she stated that when she got home with Darlene in the afternoon the two of them looked in on [the infant] and that he appeared to have a cold, and that he was wheezing and gasping and sounded hoarse. [The mother] testified that, while she remembered making a statement to the police, she could not remember stating that she checked on [the infant] in the afternoon or that he appeared to have had a cold at that time. On being shown her written statement to police made following [the infant's] death, [the mother] repeated that she could not recall stating she had checked on [the infant] in the afternoon." ...

At that juncture, the message to the jury was that the mother's testimony that she first saw the "head injury" symptoms in the evening, thus supporting the Commonwealth's case, was inconsistent with her October 7, 1987, statement to the police, when her memory was fresh and distortion of the truth was less likely. The October 7 statement tended to support the defense theory. In those circumstances, defense counsel had no need to refer to a second statement, similar to the first, which the mother gave to the police many months after the first statement was made. Counsel's point had been made. Counsel had no reason, as the defendant's representative, to explore with the mother possible explanations for her inconsistency. Furthermore, counsel was in no position to predict the explanation, if any, that would be elicited by the prosecutor's redirect examination, or to pose appropriate anticipatory questions designed to test the validity of the yet-to-be-given explanation. Counsel had a right, in my view, to assume that, if an explanation were to be presented in the course of redirect examination, his exploration of that new matter would be available by recross-examination.

Indeed, on redirect examination, an explanation was forthcoming. In response to the prosecutor's questions, the mother testified that on October 7, the day on which she gave her statement to the police, which was just one day after her baby was buried, she was upset. The obvious implication was that the statement was the product of that mental condition, that it was incorrect, and that her testimony, not the statement, should be credited by the jury. Then, for the first time, on recross-examination, defense counsel had a reason—a need— and therefore a realistic opportunity (if his questions had been allowed) to ask the witness mother whether, at a later time, when she was not upset, she gave a statement not substantially different from her statement on October 7.

. . .

In my view, it is abundantly clear that material new matters were brought out on redirect examination of the victim's mother, namely, that when she gave her statement to the police on October 7, which was inconsistent with her testimony concerning the important question as to when the infant's symptoms first appeared, she was upset by the very recent traumatic events. The implication was that the statement should be dismissed and the testimony should be credited. That mental state evidence was injected into the case for the first time on the prosecutor's redirect examination of the witness. It was critical, and the defendant was constitutionally entitled to cross-examine with respect to it.

The court states . . . "The questions which defense counsel proposed to ask on recross-examination involved an entirely separate statement, a statement which was not brought out at any point on direct, cross, or redirect examination." The court misses the point. The material new matter which was brought out for the first time on redirect examination was not the mother's second statement, but was the witness mother's upset state of mind when she gave her first statement, brought out to reduce that statement's impact. Defense counsel's questions on recross-examination, asked at the earliest opportunity, were designed to counter the thrust of the new material that had just been introduced by the prosecutor.

Efficiency and expedition in the conduct of trials is desirable—but not at the expense of truth. Recross-examination as to new material matters is essential to the truth-finding process. It was disallowed in this case. The judgment should be set aside and the case should be remanded for a new trial.

NOTES

Singletary v. United States, 383 A.2d 1064, 1073–76 (D.C.App.1978): Prosecution for robbery. On redirect examination an identification witness stated that he had a certain number of minutes for observation, that his identification was on the basis of defendants' faces and that he was uncertain whether he had seen the men who robbed him on some other occasion than the robbery and a show-up conducted by the police shortly afterwards. Held: Not error to prohibit the defendants from recross-examining the witness. The first and second topics were not new matters: direct and cross-examination had already established that the robbery lasted for a substantial period of time, giving the witness a good opportunity for observation, and that identification was based, in part at least, upon the men's faces. As to the third topic, "[the witness's] uncertainty as to whether he had ever before seen the men whom the police brought back other than at the robbery would tend to undercut rather than strengthen the trustworthiness of his identification. Accordingly, appellant's lack of opportunity for recross-examination on this testimony under the circumstances was not prejudicial and the trial court's ruling was not an abuse of discretion which would justify reversal." State v. McSloy, 261 P.2d 663, 666 (Mont.1953): Recross properly denied because no new matter brought out on redirect. "Reduced to its simplest terms, the complaint amounts to nothing more than this that they were not permitted to have the same questions answered over and over again."

United States v. Riggi, 951 F.2d 1368, 1371–76 (3d Cir.1991): Blanket prohibition on recross examination violated Confrontation Clause, at least when court had not given notice ahead of time that this would be its policy and that only acceptable response to new matter brought out on redirect was to object to it and have it excluded. United States v. Caudle, 606 F.2d 451 (4th Cir.1979): Prosecution for obtaining a government loan by making a false statement. One disputed issue was the truth of a statement that a feasibility study which accompanied the loan application had been prepared by a certain consultant. On redirect examination of the consultant, the prosecutor went through the study page by page, asking the consultant whether the contents were his original work. The witness answered in terms of whether the words, spelling and punctuation originated with him. Held: Error to prevent defendants on recross examination from also going through the study page by page with the witness, asking whether the sense originated with him. See also United States v. Baker, 10 F.3d 1374, 1404–05 (9th Cir.1993).

United States v. Rodriquez–Cardenas, 866 F.2d 390, 394–95 (11th Cir. 1989), cert. denied, 493 U.S. 1069 (1990): Not abuse of discretion to allow prosecution on redirect of its witness to introduce a tape recording of a conversation between the witness and another person to counter an impression that might have been left from answers given on cross-examination that the witness and the other person did not think of the defendant as being involved in the drug transaction. How does the question of introducing items of evidence other than the testimony of the witness differ in the case of redirect examination from that question in the case of cross-examination? See United States v. Segal, supra p. 378.

SECTION 4.   CREDIBILITY

A.   ACCREDITING

United States v. Cosentino

United States Court of Appeals, Second Circuit, 1988.
844 F.2d 30, cert. denied, 488 U.S. 923 (1988).

[Prosecution of Project Supervisor of the New York City Housing Authority for extortion and use of the mails to bribe. The prosecution witnesses were vendors who had dealt with the defendant. They testified pursuant to plea bargains. Error was claimed in the prosecutor's reference to the plea bargains in his opening statement and to the allowance in evidence of the plea bargains in connection with the direct testimony of the witnesses.]

■ Before FEINBERG, CHIEF JUDGE, and MESKILL and MAHONEY, CIRCUIT JUDGES.

■ MESKILL, CIRCUIT JUDGE:

. . .

This appeal requires us to define the circumstances in which witness cooperation agreements may properly be admitted into evidence during the direct testimony of government witnesses. The existence and contents of such agreements are inevitably of considerable interest to both prosecution and defense. They tend to support witnesses' credibility by setting out promises to testify truthfully as well as penalties for failure to do so, such as prosecution for perjury and reinstatement of any charges dropped pursuant to the deal. The agreements can impeach, however, by revealing the witnesses' criminal background. Defense counsel can also argue that such witnesses cannot be believed because they are under pressure to deliver convictions and correspondingly tempted to twist facts to do so.

Cooperation agreements accordingly demand careful treatment under principles governing attack on and rehabilitation of witnesses' credibility. It is well settled that absent an attack, no evidence may be admitted to support a witness' credibility. See generally McCormick on Evidence § 49 (E. Cleary 3d ed. 1984); 3 J. Weinstein & M. Berger, Weinstein's Evidence ¶ 608[08] (1987). We have invoked this rule in considering the admissibility of cooperation agreements because of their tendency to support or bolster credibility. See, e.g., United States v. Smith, 778 F.2d 925, 928 (2d Cir.1985); United States v. Borello, 766 F.2d 46, 56 (2d Cir.1985); United States v. Edwards, 631 F.2d 1049, 1051 (2d Cir.1980); United States v. Arroyo–Angulo, 580 F.2d 1137, 1146 (2d Cir.), cert. denied, 439 U.S. 913, 99 S.Ct. 285, 58 L.Ed.2d 260 (1978).

A witness' credibility is often tested by a sequence of attack on cross-examination followed by rehabilitation on redirect. It may sometimes be useful, however, to develop impeaching matter in direct examination of a "friendly" witness in order to deprive an adversary of the psychological advantage of revealing it to the jury for the first time during cross-examination. We have accordingly held that impeaching aspects of cooperation agreements may be brought out in the government's direct examination of a witness who testifies pursuant to such an agreement. See Borello, 766 F.2d at 57; Edwards, 631 F.2d at 1051–52. Cf. United States v. Fernandez, 829 F.2d 363, 365 (2d Cir.1987) (discussing scope of permissible reference to agreement in direct examination). Even in the absence of a prior attack on credibility, "the elicitation of the fact of the agreement and the witness' understanding of it, as a motivation for the witness to testify for the Government, should be permitted on direct examination in order to anticipate cross-examination by the defendant which might give the jury the unjustified impression that the Government was concealing this relevant fact." Edwards, 631 F.2d at 1052.

Because of the bolstering potential of cooperation agreements, however, we have permitted such agreements to be admitted in their entirety only after the credibility of the witness has been attacked. See Smith, 778 F.2d at 928. This restriction proceeds from our view that "the entire cooperation agreement bolsters more than it impeaches." Edwards, 631 F.2d at 1052; see also Borello, 766 F.2d at 56–57. Thus, although the prosecutor may inquire into impeaching aspects of cooperation agreements on direct, bolstering aspects such as promises to testify truthfully or penalties for failure to do so may only be developed to rehabilitate the witness after a defense attack on credibility.[1]

Such an attack may come in a defendant's opening statement. If the opening sufficiently implicates the credibility of a government witness, we have held that testimonial evidence of bolstering aspects of a cooperation agreement may be introduced for rehabilitative purposes during direct examination. . . . In such a situation the "rehabilitation" stage has already been reached on direct.

As a threshold matter, we must first decide whether the government's opening statement permissibly referred to the agreements in this case. Consis-

---

1. Other courts, apparently less concerned with the precise balance between impeaching and bolstering aspects, have declined to impose comparable conditions on admission of evidence of agreements that include bolstering provisions. . . . [citations showing conflict among the circuits omitted.]

Were we writing on a blank slate, we might have followed the other circuits that avoid the distinctions we have required judges and lawyers to make during the heat of trial. [Footnote by the court; another footnote omitted.]

tent with the foregoing principles, a prosecutor may refer to a witness cooperation agreement in opening only to the extent he or she could develop the same matter in direct questioning of a witness whose credibility has not been attacked. The prosecutor thus may advert to the existence of the agreement and related impeaching facts such as the witness' criminal background, but may not raise bolstering aspects of the agreement such as truth telling provisions, charge reinstatement conditions or penalties of perjury clauses. Because the witness alone can testify to his or her understanding of the agreement, the prosecutor also cannot discuss this aspect in opening. The excerpt from the record set forth above makes plain that the government in this case properly restricted its opening to appropriate matters.

It is also plain that Cosentino's counsel sufficiently raised matters of credibility in opening that the government could develop the whole cooperation agreements on direct. Cosentino's counsel made representations about reduction of charges and government intervention on behalf of the witnesses in the sentencing process, as well as the possibility of prosecution for charges dropped in exchange for testimony in the event the witnesses failed to deliver convictions. These references clearly opened the door to rehabilitation on direct by evidence of bolstering aspects of the cooperation agreements

. . .

We conclude that there was no abuse of discretion in the district court's decision to admit the entire witness cooperation agreements during the direct testimony of the government witnesses.

. . .

[C]osentino argues that a limiting instruction should have been given on the truth telling portions of the agreements. He seeks an instruction under which the jury could use the impeaching motive or bias aspects of the agreements to undercut credibility, but could not use the bolstering portions as support for credibility.

No request for such an instruction was made below, so we review only for plain error. See Fed.R.Crim.P. 30, 52(b). We discern no error of any kind in this respect. The proposed instruction would have been fundamentally at odds with the distinctions we have drawn between the impeachment and bolstering aspects of cooperation agreements. Although we have required a prior attack on credibility so that the whole agreement serves a rehabilitative function, we have never restricted use of an agreement to support credibility once that condition is satisfied. Our view presupposes that the agreement may and will be used to support credibility. The district court's treatment of the cooperation agreements was fully consistent with these principles.

. . .

For the foregoing reasons, Cosentino's conviction is affirmed.

NOTES

1. With the position taken by the Second Circuit on plea agreements to accredit, compare United States v. Spriggs, 996 F.2d 320, 323–24 (D.C.Cir. 1993), holding it not error to allow the prosecutor to bring out on direct all the terms of the agreement.

[W]e are not persuaded that evidence of the contents of a cooperation agreement unduly bolsters the credibility of a Government witness. First, insofar as the agreement provides that if the witness lies the agreement is revocable, that the witness is liable to prosecution for perjury, and that his perjurious testimony may be used against him, it adds nothing to the law— as the defense is free to bring out upon cross-examination. Therefore, the agreement provides no special incentive for the Government witness to testify truthfully; hence, the jury is not likely to place special credence in the witness merely because of the terms of the agreement. Furthermore, that the Government may (obviously) impose a sanction upon the witness if he lies does nothing to enhance the Government's ability to detect whether he is in fact lying; again, the terms of the cooperation agreement should do nothing to enhance the witness's credibility.

2. The opinion in Cosentino states it is well settled that absent an attack on a witness's credibility, no evidence may be admitted simply to support or bolster credibility. A possible reason for this prohibition is suggested by Wigmore, relied on in United States v. Price, 722 F.2d 88, 90 (5th Cir.1983), cert. denied, 473 U.S. 904 (1985), addressing the particular matter of accrediting by evidence of good character: "[T]here is no reason why time should be spent in proving that which may be assumed to exist. Every witness must be assumed to be of normal moral character for veracity, just as he is assumed to be of normal sanity.... Good character, therefore, in his support is excluded *until his character is brought into question* and it thus becomes worthwhile to deny that his character is bad."[1] 4 Wigmore, Evidence § 1104, at 233–34 (Chadbourn rev. 1972). The point would seem to be that if no discrediting evidence is introduced, the probative force of accrediting evidence, judged in the light of the background information that the trier of fact is entitled to take into account, is slight and does not justify the consumption of time and distraction that might be involved in its presentation. A corollary may be that if the accrediting evidence has more than slight probative value, it should be admitted.

Is it in compliance with or in derogation of the foregoing suggested principle that some "background" information is customarily allowed to be brought out on direct examination? It would be surprising to hear objection to questions to a witness regarding his occupation or the office that he holds or where he resides. Expert witnesses are extensively questioned on direct examination about their educational background and professional accomplishments. Often witnesses testify to details they have observed, which although not strictly relevant may make more believable what they have to say on the matter principally in dispute. All of these familiar situations appear to involve what might be characterized as accrediting. In Government of Virgin Islands v. Grant, 775 F.2d 508, 513 (3d Cir.1985), the court noted that it is customary to allow a defendant to introduce evidence concerning his background, such as information concerning his education and employment and lack of arrests. "The jurisprudence of 'background' evidence is essentially undeveloped. 'Background' or 'preliminary' evidence is not mentioned in the evidence codes, nor has it received attention in the treatises. One justification for its admission, at least in terms of the background of a witness qua witness, is that it may establish absence of bias or motive by showing the witness' relationship (or non-relationship) to the parties or to the case. It may also be said to bear on the credibility of the witness by showing the witness to be a stable person." The court held, nevertheless, in the case before it—a prosecution for assault—that it was not an abuse of discretion to prohibit the defendant from testifying that he had never been arrested.

1. Footnote omitted.

The question of whether accrediting is permissible may come up in regard to a number of different aspects of credibility. One of these is memory. If in a personal injury case the plaintiff takes the stand and testifies to facts favorable to herself but says she cannot remember a certain period of time during which events may have occurred unfavorable to her, may she introduce the testimony of a medical witness that the injuries she suffered could have caused a loss of memory as to this period? See Abramson v. Levinson, 250 N.E.2d 796, 798 (Ill.Ct.App.1969), cert. denied, 398 U.S. 950 (1970), where the question is raised but not decided. United States v. Awkard, 597 F.2d 667, 670 (9th Cir.), cert. denied, 444 U.S. 885 (1979): Error to permit prosecution witness to testify on direct examination that he had been hypnotized and to permit prosecution expert who had hypnotized the first witness to testify concerning the nature and usual effects of hypnosis and that the first witness recalled accurately as a result of the hypnosis. The fact that a witness has been hypnotized does not render his testimony inadmissible, the court noted. Furthermore, the court said, if the fact of hypnosis is brought out on cross-examination, the prosecution may introduce expert testimony regarding its nature and usual effects. But, "unless an adverse party attacks the witness's ability to recall by bringing out or exploring the fact of hypnosis, the use of expert testimony to support the efficacy of hypnosis is improper. The party calling a witness should not be permitted to inquire in any way into the witness's ability to recall, or methods of pretrial memory refreshment, until such questions have been raised by the adversary. In this case, before the introduction of Kroger's [the expert's] testimony, defense counsel indicated that they preferred not to cross-examine Hackney [the first witness] about his hypnosis.... If defendants strategically chose not to challenge the use of hypnosis, there was no purpose consistent with the Federal Rules in having the jury hear his testimony."

Examination of one's own witness in respect to bias in favor of the adverse party is ordinarily not permitted. McLaughlin v. Los Angeles R.R., 182 P. 44 (Cal.1919). This restriction is sometimes based on the rule against impeaching one's own witness. See the reference to this rule in the Cosentino opinion and infra p. 390. But in United States v. Akitoye, 923 F.2d 221, 223–25 (1st Cir.1991), where A had been a witness called by the prosecution, no error was found in allowing the prosecutor to ask the defendant on cross-examination whether he knew of any reason A would have to lie about him. Indeed, an earlier question to defendant whether A was defendant's friend passed without objection from the defendant. Keeton, Proprietorship over Deponents, 68 Harv. L.Rev. 600, 632–33 (1955), argues that accrediting in this manner should be permitted.

A prohibition against accrediting by showing good character for veracity was the particular focus of Wigmore's observation quoted above. Generally, testimony about a witness's good character is barred unless the witness's character has been attacked. See Bryant v. State, 118 N.E.2d 894 (1954). In Pointer v. State, 74 So.2d 615 (Ala.Ct.App.1954), the prosecutor in his closing argument said that if the prosecution witness had been of bad character, the defense would have introduced evidence of that fact. The court reversed the conviction, holding that since the lack of impeachment referred to prevented the prosecutor from bolstering the witness's testimony, the line of argument was prejudicial. See also Poole v. Commonwealth, 176 S.E.2d 917 (Va.1970). As to what constitutes an attack on a witness's character to open the way for rehabilitating evidence of his good character, see infra p. 465.

Federal Rule of Evidence 608 deals with evidence of character introduced for the purpose of attacking or supporting the credibility of a witness. Evidence of reputation or opinion of character for truthfulness may be introduced to attack credibility. This subject is discussed infra p. 438. It may also be introduced to support credibility, but "only after the character of the witness for truthfulness has been attacked by opinion or reputation evidence or otherwise." See Blake v. Cich, 79 F.R.D. 398, 403 (D.Minn.1978). "Rehabilitation" of this sort is discussed infra p. 465. Extrinsic evidence of specific instances of the conduct of a witness bearing on his character for truthfulness may not, under the Federal Rules, be introduced either to attack or support his credibility. Specific instances of conduct bearing on character for truthfulness may be inquired into on cross-examination in the discretion of the court. See Rule 608(b). It is reasonably clear from Rule 608(b) that specific instances of conduct tending to show a good character for truthfulness may not be inquired into on direct examination for the purpose of supporting credibility. Perhaps they may be inquired into on redirect examination if character has been attacked on cross-examination. Rule 608 does not appear to have been intended to cover the subject of accrediting or discrediting by means other than a showing of character regarding truthfulness. Can a prohibition against accrediting by other means be found elsewhere in the Federal Rules or in retained federal common law?

People v. Harris, 767 P.2d 619, 640–41 (Cal.1989), holds that a state constitutional amendment had the effect of making inapplicable § 790 of the California Evidence Code, which prohibits introduction of evidence of good character of a witness until evidence of his bad character has been introduced, with the consequence that it was not error in that case to admit evidence of past instances of an informer's reliability. State v. Frost, 577 A.2d 1282, 1287–88 (N.J.Super.), cert. denied, 604 A.2d 596 (N.J.1990), holds that an amendment to that state's evidence code had the effect of removing generally any barrier to the admission of evidence bolstering credibility.

Accrediting through evidence of prior statements by a witness consistent with present testimony raises questions not only in respect to the prohibition against accrediting before the witness has been discredited, but also under the hearsay rule. For this reason, consideration of this situation is deferred until there is an opportunity to study the topic of hearsay. See infra p. 540.

In a particular case, when considering whether offered evidence violates the prohibition against accrediting before the witness has been discredited, attention should be given to the possibility of using the evidence in some other way than merely to accredit. See, e.g., Coppolino v. State, 223 So.2d 68, 72, 75–76 (Fla.Dist.Ct.App.), appeal dismissed, 223 So.2d 68 (Fla.App.1968), cert. denied, 399 U.S. 927 (1970): Defendant was charged with the murder of his wife. The prosecutor called X as a witness. X testified the defendant told her he had committed the murder. The prosecutor asked X what her relationship with the defendant was. She answered she was his lover.

B. DISCREDITING

1. OWN WITNESS

United States v. Ince

United States Court of Appeals, Fourth Circuit, 1994.
21 F.3d 576.

■ Before MURNAGHAN and HAMILTON, CIRCUIT JUDGES, and KAUFMAN, DISTRICT JUDGE.

■ MURNAGHAN, CIRCUIT JUDGE:

Appellant Nigel D. Ince was convicted by a jury for assault with a dangerous weapon, with intent to do bodily harm. Because the United States' only apparent purpose for impeaching one of its own witnesses was to circumvent the hearsay rule and to expose the jury to otherwise inadmissible evidence of Ince's alleged confession, we reverse.

I

Late on the evening of September 4, 1992, a rap concert and dance at the Sosa Recreation Center at Fort Belvoir, Virginia ended abruptly when members of two of the bands performing there got in a scuffle. Shortly thereafter, a black male wearing an orange shirt or jacket fired a nine millimeter pistol twice at trucks leaving the Recreation Center's parking lot. Defendant-appellant Nigel Ince, Angela Neumann, and two of their friends hopped in their van and headed for Pence Gate, Fort Belvoir's nearest exit. The military police pulled the van, as well as other vehicles leaving the parking lot, over to the side of the road and asked the drivers and passengers to stand on the curb. Two men whose vehicles had also been pulled over identified Ince as the black male who had fired the shots in the parking lot, although they noted that he was no longer wearing an orange shirt. As part of the investigation that followed, Military Policeman Roger D. Stevens interviewed and took a signed, unsworn statement from Neumann. She recounted that Ince had admitted to firing the shots, but said he no longer had the gun.

The United States indicted Ince for violating 18 U.S.C. § 113(c), assault with a dangerous weapon, with intent to do bodily harm. At Ince's trial the Government called Neumann to the stand. When her memory supposedly failed her, the prosecution attempted to refresh her recollection with a copy of the signed statement that she had given Stevens on the night of the shooting. Even with her recollection refreshed, she testified that she could no longer recall the details of her conversation with Ince. Following Neumann's testimony, the Government excused her and called Stevens, who testified (over the objection of defense counsel) as to what Neumann had told him shortly after the shooting. The trial ended with a deadlocked jury.

At the second trial, the Government again called Neumann. She again acknowledged that she had given the military police a signed statement describing what Ince had told her immediately after the shooting. But she repeatedly testified that she could no longer recall the details of Ince's remarks, despite the prosecution's effort to refresh her recollection with a copy of the statement. . . .

Over defense counsel's repeated objections, the Government again called MP Stevens to the stand, supposedly to impeach Neumann as to her memory loss. He testified that, within hours of the shooting, Neumann had told him that Ince had confessed to firing the gun. The Government also called two eyewitnesses who identified Ince as the gunman.

The defense's theory of the case was mistaken identity: Frank Kelly, not Nigel Ince, had fired the shots. Kelly, also a young black male (although of somewhat different physique), attended the dance, wore a long-sleeved orange jacket, was supposedly spotted by Neumann in the parking lot holding a handgun, and was found by the FBI five days later with a nine millimeter pistol hidden in his bedroom. In an attempt to undermine the defense's theory of the case, the prosecution, in its closing argument, reminded the jurors that they had "heard testimony that Ms. Neumann made a statement to an MP [immediately following the shooting]. And she told [him] at that time that the defendant said, 'Frank didn't shoot the gun; I shot the gun.' "

The second time around, the jury convicted Ince. The district judge sentenced him to forty-one months in prison, plus two years of supervised release. Ince now appeals, requesting a reversal of his conviction and a new trial.

II

Appellant Ince argues that the testimony of MP Stevens was inadmissible hearsay because the Government offered it to prove the truth of the matter asserted in Neumann's out-of-court statement (i.e., that Ince confessed to the crime). The United States counters that Stevens's testimony was admissible because the Government offered it only to impeach Neumann's credibility. Ince responds that the prosecution, having already seen Neumann's performance on the stand at the first trial, was fully aware that she would not testify as to Ince's alleged confession at the second trial either. Nevertheless, the prosecution put her on the stand a second time to elicit testimony inconsistent with her prior statement to Stevens, so as to provide a foundation to offer Stevens's so-called "impeaching" evidence and thereby to get Ince's confession before the jury. Thus, the sole question presented on appeal is whether the admission of Stevens's testimony constituted reversible error.

A

Rule 607 of the Federal Rules of Evidence provides that "[t]he credibility of a witness may be attacked by any party, including the party calling the witness." ... One method of attacking the credibility of (i.e., impeaching) a witness is to show that he has previously made a statement that is inconsistent with his present testimony. Even if that prior inconsistent statement would otherwise be inadmissible as hearsay, it may be admissible for the limited purpose of impeaching the witness. At a criminal trial, however, there are limits on the Government's power to impeach its own witness by presenting his prior inconsistent statements. See United States v. Morlang, 531 F.2d 183 (4th Cir.1975). In Morlang, we reversed the defendant's conviction for conspiracy to bribe and bribery because the Government had employed impeachment by prior inconsistent statement "as a mere subterfuge to get before the jury evidence not otherwise admissible." Id. at 190.

At Morlang's trial the Government had called Fred Wilmoth, an original codefendant who had subsequently pleaded guilty, as its first witness despite the fact that his previous statements to the Government suggested he would be hostile. The real purpose for calling Wilmoth was apparently to elicit a denial that he had ever had a conversation with a fellow prisoner in which he had implicated Morlang. Having obtained the expected denial, the Government then called Raymond Crist, another prisoner, to impeach Wilmoth with the alleged prior inconsistent statement. As expected, Crist testified that his fellow inmate Wilmoth had made a conclusory statement from which one could only infer Morlang's guilt. As expected, the jury delivered a guilty verdict. See id. at 188–90 & 188 n. 11.

In reversing Morlang's conviction, Judge Widener explained that courts must not "permit the government, in the name of impeachment, to present testimony to the jury by indirection which would not otherwise be admissible." Id. at 189. "To permit the government in this case to supply testimony which was a naked conclusion as to Morlang's guilt in the name of impeachment," he explained, would be tantamount to convicting a defendant on the basis of hearsay:

Foremost among [the notions of fairness upon which our system is based] is the principle that men should not be allowed to be convicted on the basis of unsworn testimony....

We must be mindful of the fact that prior unsworn statements of a witness are mere hearsay and are, as such, generally inadmissible as affirmative proof. The introduction of such testimony, even where limited to impeachment, necessarily increases the possibility that a defendant may be convicted on the basis of unsworn evidence, for despite proper instructions to the jury, it is often difficult for [jurors] to distinguish between impeachment and substantive evidence.... Thus, the danger of confusion which arises from the introduction of testimony under circumstances such as are presented here is so great as to upset the balance and [to] warrant continuation of the rule of exclusion.

Id. at 190 (citations omitted).

Federal evidence law does not ask the judge, either at trial or upon appellate review, to crawl inside the prosecutor's head to divine his or her true motivation. See 3 Jack B. Weinstein & Margaret A. Berger, Weinstein's Evidence ¶ 607[01], at 607-20 (1993). Rather, in determining whether a Government witness' testimony offered as impeachment is admissible, or on the contrary is a "mere subterfuge" to get before the jury substantive evidence which is otherwise inadmissible as hearsay, a trial court must apply Federal Rule of Evidence 403 and weigh the testimony's impeachment value against its tendency to prejudice the defendant unfairly or to confuse the jury....

When the prosecution attempts to introduce a prior inconsistent statement to impeach its own witness, the statement's likely prejudicial impact often substantially outweighs its probative value for impeachment purposes because the jury may ignore the judge's limiting instructions and consider the "impeachment" testimony for substantive purposes.... That risk is multiplied when the statement offered as impeachment testimony contains the defendant's alleged admission of guilt. Thus, a trial judge should rarely, if ever, permit the Government to "impeach" its own witness by presenting what would otherwise be inadmissible hearsay if that hearsay contains an alleged confession to the crime for which the defendant is being tried....

B

In the case at bar, MP Stevens testified that Ince had admitted to firing the gun—the critical element of the crime for which he was being tried. It is hard to imagine any piece of evidence that could have had a greater prejudicial impact than such a supposed naked confession of guilt. Even if the other evidence which was properly admitted at trial had provided overwhelming proof of Ince's guilt ... and even if the judge had given the jury a clear limiting instruction—which he did not, ... Stevens's presentation of additional unsworn hearsay testimony going directly to the issue of Ince's guilt was extremely prejudicial....

Given the likely prejudicial impact of Stevens's testimony, the trial judge should have excluded it absent some extraordinary probative value. Because evidence of Neumann's prior inconsistent statement was admitted solely for purposes of impeachment, its probative value must be assessed solely in terms of its impeaching effect upon Neumann's testimony or overall credibility. Our review of the record below, however, shows that the probative value of Stevens's testimony for impeachment purposes was nil. Unlike the classic "turncoat" witness, Neumann certainly had not shocked the Government with her "loss of memory" at the second trial, as she had made it plain during the first trial that she would not readily testify to the alleged confession of her friend, Nigel Ince.[1]

Furthermore, Neumann's actual in-court testimony did not affirmatively damage the Government's case; she merely refused to give testimony that the Government had hoped she would give. Thus, the prosecution had no need to attack her credibility. Cf. 27 Charles Alan Wright & Victor James Gold, Federal Practice and Procedure: Evidence § 6093, at 515 (1990) ("If testimony does no damage, impeachment evidence has no probative value."); 27 id. § 6092, at 492 n. 31. She testified that, immediately after the shooting, as they left the scene of the crime but before the military police pulled them over, (1) Ince stated that Frank Kelly—the person whom Ince's lawyer identified at trial as the likely perpetrator of the crime—was not the person who had fired the gun, (2) Ince stated that "he didn't have [the gun] with him," and (3) Ince instructed Neumann to tell the military police that she knew nothing about the events of the evening. She presented no evidence affirming or denying Ince's alleged confession. Taken as a whole, then, Neumann's testimony probably *strengthened* the Government's case. Therefore, evidence attacking her credibility had no probative value *for impeachment purposes*.

Because Stevens's so-called "impeachment" testimony was both highly prejudicial and devoid of probative value as impeachment evidence, the trial judge should have recognized the Government's tactic for what it was—an attempt to circumvent the hearsay rule and to infect the jury with otherwise inadmissible evidence of Ince's alleged confession. Instead, the judge allowed Stevens's testimony to come before the jury in clear violation of Morlang and its progeny, notwithstanding defense counsel's proper and timely objections. As Judge Widener recently wrote, "The government simply should not be allowed to employ tactics of overkill that fly in the face of direct circuit precedent that has been established for more than fifteen years." Brewer, 1 F.3d at 1439 (Widener, J., dissenting).

. . .

[The court found that the error was not harmless.]

Reversed and Remanded.

NOTES

1. Historical explanation of the traditional rule against impeaching your own witness, said by the Advisory Committee's Note to Fed.R.Evid. 607 to be abolished by that rule, is hazy and wavering. The suggestion that the process of compurgation or winning a case with "oath helpers" lies at the base of the matter is unsubstantiated. Another possibility is that the restriction, taking definite, documented form toward the close of the 17th century, resulted from abandonment of inquisitorial trial procedures and substitution of adversary procedures; during the earlier stages of this changeover it may have been the view that use of witnesses in the modern sense of the word was a favor to the litigant both from the point of view of the court and from that of the witnesses

---

1. The prosecution claims, for the first time at oral argument on appeal, that Neumann had cooperated with the prosecution between the two trials and that it therefore had reason to believe that her testimony at the second trial would be entirely different from her testimony at the first trial. Even if we were to credit the Government's account, we would reach the same result. The prosecution's supposed uncertainty about how Neumann would testify on direct examination at the second trial does not affect whether the jury was misled, confused, or unfairly prejudiced by Stevens's subsequent testimony. [Footnote is the court's, renumbered. Other footnotes omitted.]

themselves; the litigant might not look his gift horse in the mouth. This, too, is frankly speculative. Consult the opening pages of Ladd, Impeachment of One's Own Witness—New Developments, 4 U.Chi.L.Rev. 69 (1936). See also 3A Wigmore, Evidence § 896 (Chadbourn rev. 1970).

2. The prohibition against impeaching one's own witness is to be distinguished from the notion, sometimes put forward, that a party is bound by the testimony of a witness he calls, at least if it is uncontradicted and perhaps even if it is. See, e.g., Watson v. Terminal R.R., 876 S.W.2d 722, 725 (Mo.Ct.App. 1994). If there ever was a rule with this effect, it is clear that it has long been abandoned. See Johnson v. Baltimore and O. R. Co., 208 F.2d 633 (3d Cir.1953), cert. denied, 347 U.S. 943 (1954); Becker v. Koch, 10 N.E. 701, 703–04 (N.Y.1887): "[A]ll the cases ... concur in the right of a party to contradict his own witness by calling witnesses to prove a fact (material to the issue) to be otherwise than as sworn to by him, even when the necessary effect is to impeach him." Thus the traditional rule prohibiting impeachment of one's own witness refers to impeachment by means other than simple contradiction.

3. As indicated by the Advisory Committee's Note to Rule 607, the reasons traditionally put forward to justify the rule against impeaching one's own witness have not been found persuasive by most modern observers. One of these reasons is stated in People v. Minsky, 124 N.E. 126, 128 (N.Y.1919): "A witness of bad character has enough to fear from the adverse party without being intimidated by the party calling him. The power to coerce a witness may as reasonably be expected to beget a lie as to force the truth from unwilling lips." See also State v. Bailey, 377 S.E.2d 581, 583 (S.C.1989). Does this reasoning suggest that a very great rascal should be made entirely comfortable on the stand by denying both parties opportunity to impeach him? Another suggested reason for the rule against impeaching one's own witness is that a party "vouches" for the witness he calls. But this would seem to be either simply a restatement of the rule rather than a reason for it, or a comment on some significance that the trier of fact might attach to the circumstance that a party has called a witness.

4. Even when the traditional rule has been in force, in most jurisdictions impeachment of one's own witness was permitted if the party who called the witness was surprised and damaged by the witness's testimony. What was meant by "surprise" is not entirely clear. Sullivan v. United States, 28 F.2d 147 (9th Cir.1928): Three persons who had pleaded guilty to participation in a mail robbery for which D was to be tried signed a joint statement of facts that encouraged the prosecution to bring them from the penitentiary to testify at D's trial; the first of these persons then surprised the prosecutor by giving testimony entirely exculpating D; nevertheless the prosecution put on the second and third signers of the statement, who gave like unfavorable testimony; held error to permit the prosecution to impeach the last two witnesses by proving their contradictory statements. People v. Spinosa, 252 P.2d 409 (Cal.Ct. App.1953): The witness, prior to the trial, first said that he did not commit a crime and then later said that he did. At the trial the witness testified that he did not commit the crime and the proponent sought to impeach. The adversary argued that there was no surprise, no matter which way the witness testified. But the court held that the proponent had the right to assume that the witness would testify according to his latest story, and was therefore surprised. See also Wheeler v. United States, 211 F.2d 19 (D.C.Cir.), cert. denied, 347 U.S. 1019 (1954), where the prosecution was allowed to impeach when the witness's testimony at the trial, contrary to her police report and grand jury testimony, exculpated the defendant; the defendant before trial had shown the police an exculpatory statement, purportedly signed by the witness. In Wilson v. State,

219 S.E.2d 756 (Ga.1975), the prosecutor was found sufficiently "surprised" to be allowed to introduce a prior inconsistent statement when as a result of a conversation with the witness before trial he did not know which way the witness would testify. In People v. Miller, 53 Cal.Rptr. 720, 734–35 (App.1966), cert. dismissed, 392 U.S. 616 (1968), and State v. Guy, 105 N.W.2d 892 (Minn.1960), the prosecutor was held entitled to claim surprise although he had not interviewed the witnesses before trial but relied on statements they had made to police. In Gaitan v. People, 447 P.2d 1001 (Colo.1968), it was held not error to permit the prosecutor to impeach a witness he had called even though he knew that the witness was hostile and during an in camera hearing on a related matter concerning the witness the prosecutor declined to question her for the expressed reason that if she changed her story from that given the police, he would not be able to claim surprise and impeach her.

5. In the opinion in People v. Ince, the court seems to say that Neumann's forgetfulness regarding defendant's confession did not harm the prosecution and that her testimony as a whole, if it had any effect, strengthened the prosecution's case. The evidence of Neumann's prior inconsistent statement indeed had no probative value for impeachment purposes if there was nothing to impeach. The question of whether there is something to impeach, that is whether there has been damage, is addressed in a number of cases.

People v. Le Beau, 245 P.2d 302 (Cal.1952): In a prosecution for possessing cocaine, defendant took the stand and on direct examination testified that he had never had narcotics in his possession, "wouldn't know narcotics," and had "never been in contact with any of them." On cross-examination he was asked if he had not been using narcotics for many years prior to his arrest and answered that he had not. Also on cross-examination, the defendant admitted knowing one Nancy, but denied ever telling Nancy that he used narcotics. The state then called Nancy, who said that defendant never made any such statement to her. Furthermore, Nancy denied having told the police that defendant had said to her that he used narcotics. At this point the state called a policeman; he testified that Nancy told him that defendant told her that defendant used narcotics. It was conceded that the state was surprised by Nancy's testimony. The court held that this testimony damaged the state's case because the jury might, in view of defendant's denial and Nancy's corroboration thereof, believe that the state was trying to create prejudice against the defendant. "Here we are satisfied that the witness' answer was more than a harmless refusal to testify as expected and that it prejudiced the People's case. [Nancy] was placed on the stand by the prosecution for the purpose of impeaching defendant's credibility and rebutting his testimony that he did not use narcotics. Her denial that defendant had ever told her that he used cocaine was likely to make it appear to the jury that the district attorney was harassing defendant and attempting to discredit him without any basis in fact by asking him on cross-examination if he had not told [Nancy] that he had used the drug. This impression might well have been aggravated in the jurors' minds by the fact that the subject of defendant's use of narcotics was brought into the case by defendant himself." See Falknor, Evidence, in N.Y.U. Annual Survey of American Law 723, 730–32 (1952).

Compare with People v. Le Beau the later People v. Coleman, 459 P.2d 248, 251 (Cal.1969): A murder prosecution. Defendant took the stand and denied any participation in the crime. He testified that he had sold the gun which had been used to kill the victim to Stevenson a week before the crime. On appeal from his conviction defendant contended that the trial court committed error in admitting into evidence "a hearsay statement of witness Hood that defendant had approached Hood in jail and asked him to secure Stevenson's signature on a piece of paper so that defendant could fabricate a sales slip for the murder weapon." The California Supreme Court agreed with this contention:

> Defendant testified that when he sold the murder weapon to Stevenson about a week before the crime was committed, he did not request or receive a receipt for the sale. On cross-examination he denied that he ever attempted to procure Stevenson's signature for the purpose of making a false receipt as evidence of the alleged sale of the gun. In rebuttal the prosecution called Hood, who had been an inmate in the same jail with defendant and Stevenson before defendant's trial. Hood testified that he had never seen defendant before he saw him at the trial. Hood also stated that a police officer, Inspector Hughes, had tried to get him to agree that defendant had asked him to procure Stevenson's signature but that he had told Inspector Hughes that no such request was made of him.

> Inspector Hughes was then called and testified over objection to a conversation that he had with Hood in which Hood stated that defendant had asked Hood to secure Stevenson's signature on a piece of paper that could be used to create a false sales slip for the gun to be predated before the Sulezich murder.

> . . . .

> It must also be noted that the error was not limited to the failure to restrict the jury's consideration of Hood's statement to impeachment of Hood's testimony. That statement was not admissible at all, for its probative value to impeach Hood's testimony was obviously "substantially outweighed by the probability that its admission [would] ... create substantial danger of undue prejudice." (Evid.Code, § 352.) Hood's testimony that he had not seen defendant before he saw him at the trial and that defendant had not asked him to secure Stevenson's signature detracted not at all from the prosecution's case before the jury. At most the prosecution was denied advantageous testimony that it may have hoped to elicit, even though it knew before it put Hood on the stand that he would not testify as the prosecution wished. Accordingly, proof that Hood was a liar was a benefit to the prosecution only if the jury were to believe the truth of Hood's prior statement. The prosecution, however, was not entitled to that benefit, and the risk that it might improperly secure that benefit by impeaching Hood far outweighed any legitimate interest the prosecution had in such impeachment.

See, however, United States v. Long Soldier, 562 F.2d 601, 605 (8th Cir.1977); Not error to admit evidence that a prosecution witness stated that defendant had made incriminating statements to him. "There exists a substantive difference between a witness' failure to recall an incriminating statement made by the defendant and an affirmative denial that a defendant made an admission of guilt to him. There is more than a subtle distinction here. In the first instance there is nothing harmful in evidence and any attempt to 'impeach' becomes a subterfuge.... However, where a witness affirmatively denies that the defendant made an admission of guilt to him, there is at least an exculpatory inference that something did not take place as alleged...."

Is the damage requirement satisfied in the following cases? United States v. Cunningham, 446 F.2d 194 (2d Cir.), cert. denied, 404 U.S. 950 (1971): A bank was robbed by two men on July 28, 1970. Rudolph and Cunningham were charged with the robbery. Eyewitness and photographic evidence clearly established that Rudolph was one of the robbers, but the identification of Cunningham was weaker. The prosecution called Rudolph's brother Roger as a witness and asked him how often he had seen Rudolph and Cunningham together during July. He answered, "Maybe twice. Maybe three times." The prosecutor was allowed to elicit from the witness a concession that before the grand jury he had answered the question, "Do they see each other often?" by saying, "Yes, you know, hang around." State v. Tate, 468 S.W.2d 646 (Mo.1971): Prosecution of E for murder in connection with the hold-up of a restaurant. E's defense was that although he was with the men who held up the restaurant, he tried to dissuade them from committing the crime and did not go into the restaurant. W, a prosecution witness, testified that A, B, C, D and E were present at her house while the robbery was being planned. When asked to name the persons who came to her house later, after the robbery had taken place, she listed A, B, C and D. The prosecutor was then permitted to ask W if she had not earlier told him that E had also come back to the house.

Suppose the prosecutor calls a witness who testifies that he saw the defendant commit the crime. On cross-examination the witness recants and says that he knows nothing about the matter. May the prosecutor now introduce a prior statement of the witness that he saw the defendant commit the crime? See People v. Fuller, 409 N.E.2d 834, 839–40 (N.Y.1980), holding it error to permit introduction of the prior statement on the ground that "there was no literal compliance with . . . [CPL 60.35's] requirement that the damaging statements be given 'upon examination by the party who called [her].' " However, the error was held to be harmless.

6.   Although cases interpreting Fed.R.Evid. 607 usually consider whether the witness's testimony has inflicted damage on the party who called him, they often avoid speaking of the other traditional requirement of surprise. Indeed at least one court has taken the position that surprise is no longer required. United States v. Dennis, 625 F.2d 782, 795 n. 6 (8th Cir.1980). Instead of speaking of surprise, many courts, such as the court in Ince, look to whether there has been "subterfuge" or whether the "primary purpose" of the party calling the witness was impeachment. If there was subterfuge or impeachment was the primary purpose, impeachment is not allowed, notwithstanding the seemingly absolute character of Rule 607. It has been suggested that the old surprise requirement may actually find a new home in the requirements that there be no subterfuge or that the primary purpose not be impeachment, or at least that it constitutes a part of those requirements. See Note, Impeachment with an Unsworn Prior Inconsistent Statement as Subterfuge, 28 Wm. & Mary L.Rev. 295, 325 (1987). The subterfuge and primary purpose tests, as indeed does the surprise test as well, appear to call for inquiry into the likelihood of favorable or unfavorable testimony judged from the point of view of the lawyer who called the witness, or a reasonable lawyer in his position, at the time he called the witness or opened up a particular line of inquiry. These tests do not look simply to whether there has been damage and what the risk is that the trier of fact will use impeaching evidence for an impermissible purpose. If there was reasonable notice that damage would occur, then there was subterfuge or a primary purpose of putting impeaching evidence before the trier of fact for an impermissible purpose. If there was subterfuge or such a primary purpose, the courts using these tests appear to doubt that the risk of improper use should be run to protect a party who without good reason brought the damage upon himself. The situation of a party who has been damaged by a witness he called may be compared with that of a party damaged by a witness called by his opponent. In the latter case, the injured party did not bring the injury upon himself and no question of subterfuge or improper purpose arises. The injured party may introduce impeaching evidence in an effort to undo the damage, and customarily the only protection against an impermissible use of the evidence is a limiting instruction—in the case of a prior inconsistent statement that it be used for impeachment purposes only and not for substantive purposes. When cross-examination goes beyond the scope of the direct, then in regard to the new matter, the party who called the witness is considered not to have brought the damage upon himself and so may impeach the witness in respect to the new matter. At the same time, the cross-examiner is burdened with whatever limitations exist on impeaching your own witness in respect to the new matter. See State v. Litteral, 793 P.2d 268, 273 (N.M.1990).

When impeachment of one's own witness is by prior inconsistent statement, the concern is that notwithstanding a limiting instruction, the statement will be given substantive effect by the trier of fact. When impeachment is by character evidence, there may be the possibility of a different impermissible use. See United States v. Peterman, 841 F.2d 1474, 1479–80 (10th Cir.1988), cert. denied, 488 U.S. 1004 (1989): Prosecution properly allowed to impeach its own witness with evidence of witness's conviction in earlier trial in which he and defendant were codefendants; surprise was required, but it was present. State v. Burke, 574 A.2d 1217, 1227–28 (R.I.1990): Error, although harmless, to allow prosecutor to call a witness, apparently an acquaintance of the defendant's, and then, although seemingly not surprised, to impeach the witness with evidence of his past crimes. If in a particular case there is no possible use of character evidence other than for impeachment, and yet surprise is required, must not justification for the requirement be found in one of the "false premises" (see the Advisory Committee's Note) supposedly rejected by Fed. R.Evid. 607? The same observation would apply in the case of other types of impeachment, such as by a showing of bias.

Graham, Examination of a Party's Own Witness Under the Federal Rules of Evidence: A Promise Unfulfilled, 54 Tex.L.Rev. 917, 977–95 (1976), takes the position that in regard to impeaching one's own witness, the traditional surprise and damage requirements should be found to have been retained by the Federal Rules of Evidence. He criticizes the suggestion that the limits on impeachment of one's own witness should be determined merely by weighing the factors set forth in Rule 403. Graham, The Relationship Among Federal Rules of Evidence 607, 801(d)(1)(A), and 403: A Reply to Weinstein's Evidence, 55 Tex.L.Rev. 573 (1977). The damage and surprise requirements, he believes, should apply to impeachment both by prior inconsistent statement and character impeachment. In the former case, he holds that the requirements are necessary to prevent evasion of Congress's decision, in Rule 801(d)(1)(A), to limit the use of many prior inconsistent statements to impeachment rather than to permit their full evidential use. The author would allow only limited relief from the traditional requirements. Because of the weight of the criminal defendant's interest in eliciting favorable testimony, he should be allowed to impeach his own witness even though not surprised by unfavorable testimony. See also Ordover, Surprise! That Damaging Turncoat Witness Is Still With Us: An Analysis of Federal Rules of Evidence 607, 801(d)(1)(A) and 403, 5 Hofstra L.Rev. 65 (1977). Note the Ince court's reliance on Fed.R.Evid. 403. Could a surprise or nonsubterfuge requirement be found in Rule 607 itself, notwithstanding its seemingly absolute language, or is resort to Rule 403 necessary?

7. Limitations on impeachment of one's own witness may themselves be limited by constitutional standards. In Chambers v. Mississippi, 410 U.S. 284, 93 S.Ct. 1038 (1973), the Court held that a refusal to allow defendant to cross-examine a witness he had called, together with the exclusion of certain extrajudicial statements by the witness, deprived defendant of a fair trial in violation of the Due Process Clause of the Fourteenth Amendment. Someone in

a crowd of which defendant was a member shot a policeman. Defendant was indicted for the murder. At the trial the prosecution introduced evidence tending to show that defendant was the person who shot the policeman. The prosecution did not call one McDonald as a witness. Defendant sought to prove that not he, but McDonald, had shot the policeman. Defendant called McDonald as a witness and by his testimony laid a predicate for the admission of a sworn, written confession by McDonald that he had shot the policeman. The confession was admitted into evidence. On cross-examination by the prosecution, McDonald stated that he had repudiated the confession, gave reasons why he had falsely confessed and testified that he had not been present at the time of the killing and had not shot the policeman. Defendant then sought and was denied the right "to examine McDonald as an adverse witness." Furthermore, defendant was not allowed to show that in addition to the written confession, McDonald had on several occasions stated to different persons that he had shot the policeman. The restriction on cross-examination, together with the exclusion of McDonald's extrajudicial statements, were held by the Court to have deprived defendant of a fair trial in violation of the Due Process Clause of the Fourteenth Amendment. For other discussions of this case, see supra pp. 261, 364. See also Wasko v. Singletary, 966 F.2d 1377 (11th Cir.1992) (assumed without deciding that Confrontation Clause required that defendant be allowed to ask witness called by him, originally a codefendant in the case, about details of the witness's plea bargain).

8. Calling and impeaching the other party. In Lovinger v. Anglo California National Bank, 243 P.2d 561, 574–75 (Cal.App.1952), a statute permitting a party to call his adversary as a witness provided that the proponent of such a witness would not be bound by his testimony. The court held that the proponent of the adverse party could impeach him, in this case by proof of a prior felony conviction, even though the general rule prohibited impeachment of one's own witness. However, a limitation on this doctrine was created by the court: the trial judge must be satisfied that the adverse party was not called solely to enable the proponent to impeach him. But see Love v. Baum, 806 S.W.2d 72 (Mo.Ct.App.1991): Impeachment of other party permitted seemingly without restriction: in auto accident case, plaintiff allowed to call defendant and impeach him with convictions of automobile driving offenses. In Georgia a statute permits impeachment of the other party as if the witness testified in his own behalf and were being cross-examined, but only if counsel announces in open court that the other party is put up for cross-examination. See Hicks v. State, 418 S.E.2d 794 (Ga.Ct.App.1992).

9. When a rule of law requires a litigant to call a specified witness to testify on an issue—as, for instance, an attesting witness to prove due execution in the contest of an alleged will—impeachment of credibility has long been permitted. Williams v. Walker, 14 S.C. Eq. (1846). Some cases may be read as extending this exception to litigation where peculiarities of factual situations, rather than rules of law, compel parties to resort to the testimony of witnesses whom they distrust. E.g., Fine v. Moomjian, 158 A. 241, 244 (Conn.1932). Suppose a party is not surprised by a witness's damaging testimony, but called the witness to avoid a possible adverse inference from his failure to call this witness. See State v. Brewer, supra p. 45. Should the party be allowed to impeach the witness? Cf. United States v. Gilbert, 57 F.3d 709, 710 (9th Cir.1995).

10. Impeaching a witness called by a party to undo damage inflicted by the witness on that party should be distinguished from impeaching a witness who has given favorable testimony to "minimize the sting" of the opposing party's initiating the impeachment. Such anticipatory impeachment is customarily permitted, see United States v. Ewings, 936 F.2d 903, 909 (7th Cir.1991);

United States v. Wuliger, 999 F.2d 1090, 1100 (6th Cir. 1993), cert. denied, 510 U.S. 1191 (1994), and has already been mentioned in connection with accrediting, see supra p. 386.

11. Other references on the subject of impeaching one's own witness are: McCormick, The Turncoat Witness, 25 Tex.L.Rev. 573 (1947); Bell, Impeaching Own Witness, 34 Aust.L.J. 200 (1960); Bull, The Hostile Witness, 4 Crim.L.Q. 384 (1962); Slough, Impeachment of Witnesses: Common Law Principles and Modern Trends, 34 Ind.L.J. 1, 13–14 (1958); Annot., Propriety Under Federal Rule of Evidence 607, of Impeachment of Party's Own Witness, 89 A.L.R. Fed. 13 (1988).

2.   OPPONENT'S WITNESS

Various techniques of testonial impeachment should be distinguished. In the first place, impeachment may focus upon certain matters that have been discussed already under the topic of competency. Thus an issue may be made of the witness's inability to observe, the weakness of his memory or his difficulty in communicating. Second, an effort may be made to show motive, bias, interest, subjection to influence or any other similar matter likely to affect his testimony, a line of attack that for convenience will be described by the single term "bias." Third, attack may be directed to revealing the witness's bad character insofar as that bears upon the likelihood that he will tell the truth. Here consideration must be given both to criminal conduct that has resulted in conviction and other criminal and immoral conduct, as well as to reputation and opinion evidence bearing on character. Finally, impeachment through a showing of self-contradiction is a method of persisting importance and interest.

In respect to each of these methods of impeachment, a question arises as to the form of inquiry or demonstration permitted. Will questions to the primary witness be allowed? If the primary witness's answers are unsatisfactory, may extrinsic evidence be introduced? As the materials that follow indicate, a variety of considerations determine the answers to these questions: How persuasive is the impeachment proposed? How great is the danger of being drawn into difficult and complicated inquiries not directly related to the central issues in the case? Will inquiry into impeaching matters create risks of improper use by the trier of fact of the information revealed? The problem is frequently dealt with in the cases by asking whether the matter inquired into is "collateral." The term is so commonly used that discussion must to some extent be based upon it, but at the same time it must be frankly admitted that the term is one of infuriating vagueness and instability of meaning.

In regard to impeachment by means of attack on the witness's ability to perceive, remember or communicate, the following cases are illustrative. Fitzer v. Bloom, 253 N.W.2d 395 (Minn.1977) (not error to permit examination of witness who claimed inability to remember details of accident about effects of past drinking experiences). State v. Miskell, 161 N.W.2d 732 (Iowa 1968) (permissible to ask witness if she had been adjudicated senile). Sturdevant v. State, 181 N.W.2d 523 (Wis.1970) (not error to disallow question about witness's epilepsy in absence of showing of effect on credibility). On inquiries into a witness's mental state, see infra p. 447 and Annot. 44 A.L.R. 3d 1203 (1972). On use of drugs and alcohol, see 106 A.L.R. Fed. 371 (1992) and infra p. 451. See supra p. 389 on whether witness has been hypnotized.

Green, "The Whole Truth?", How Rules of Evidence Make Lawyers Deceitful, 25 Loyola L.A. L.Rev. 699, 704 n. 25 (1992):

[M]any judges are reluctant to permit extensive cross-examination into the nature and scope of witness preparation for understandable reasons. A superficial inquiry is likely to create a perception that the attorney acted improperly—a perception that would be inappropriate because, within limits, the practice of witness preparation is an entirely acceptable and necessary aspect of advocacy. A more extensive inquiry, designed to show that in the particular instance witness preparation was excessive and resulted in inaccurate testimony, would be time-consuming, confusing and unproductive, since jurors have no understanding of what methods are and are not appropriate. . . .

Impeachment Through Contradiction

The following cases deal with what may be characterized as contradiction of a witness, a process that arguably is a form of impeachment. The focus is upon contradiction regarding matters relevant to a material issue and, in some instances, matters bearing upon the witness's ability or opportunity to observe. Whether contradiction should be allowed as to matters that do not fall under either of these heads, nor within any of the standardized techniques of impeachment discussed infra pp. 406–64, is a question that cannot be answered without consideration of particular fact situations.

The start of discussion of when contradiction is permitted is usually the opinion of Chief Baron Pollock in Attorney–General v. Hitchcock, 1 Exch. 90 (1847): "[T]he test, whether the matter is collateral or not [and so may be contradicted], is this: if the answer of a witness is a matter which you would be allowed on your part to prove in evidence—if it have such a connection with the issue, that you would be allowed to give it in evidence—then it is a matter on which you may contradict him." "It must be connected with the issue as a matter capable of distinctly being given in evidence. . . ." In the case, the witness testified on direct examination to a matter relevant to a material issue. On cross-examination he was asked if he had not said that he had been offered a bribe to testify as he did. When the witness denied that he had said any such thing, the cross-examiner sought to call another witness to contradict him about what he had said. The court held that it was not error to forbid contradiction.

State v. Oswalt, 381 P.2d 617, 618–19 (Wash.1963): Prosecution of O for robbery in Seattle, on July 14, 1961. Defense witness Ardiss, operator of a restaurant in Portland, testifies that O, a regular patron, was in his restaurant at the time of the robbery in Seattle. On cross-examination, Ardiss states that he thinks O has been in the restaurant every day for the past two months. (Apparently the witness was referring to the two months preceding July 14.) In rebuttal the prosecution offers a police officer to testify that he saw O in Seattle on June 12, 1961, and O stated to the officer that he had arrived there two days before, having come from Portland. Held, admission of the officer's testimony was error.

It is to the rebuttal testimony of the police detective that defendant assigns error. The state, in response, contends such testimony to be admissible not only because it challenges the credibility of witness Ardiss, but also establishes de^ ndant's presence in Seattle preparatory to the offense.

It is a well recognized and firmly established rule in this jurisdiction, and elsewhere, that a witness cannot be impeached upon matters collateral to the principal issues being tried. . . .

The purpose of the rule is basically twofold: (1) avoidance of undue confusion of issues, and (2) prevention of unfair advantage over a witness unprepared to answer concerning matters unrelated or remote to the issues at hand.... 3 Wigmore on Evidence (3d ed.) § 1002, p. 656.

We, in common with other jurisdictions, have stated the test of collateralness to be: Could the fact, as to which error is predicated, have been shown in evidence for any purpose independently of the contradiction? ...

So far as appears by this record, the sole issue raised by defendant's defense of alibi, through the direct testimony of witness Ardiss, was whether or not the defendant was or could have been in Seattle at the time of the offense on July 14, 1961. The defendant did not contend or seek to prove by this witness that he had not been in Seattle prior to such date. Thus, for purposes of impeaching this witness, whether the defendant was in Seattle on a given occasion one month prior to July 14th, was irrelevant and collateral. While a cross-examiner is, within the sound discretion of the trial court, permitted to inquire into collateral matters testing the credibility of a witness, he does so at the risk of being concluded by the answers given....

The state, however, contends that the quoted testimony of Ardiss, as elicited by its cross-examination, carries with it an inference that defendant could not have been in Seattle sufficiently in advance of July 14, 1961, to have participated in necessary planning of and preparation for the offense. Upon the inference so erected, the state asserts the questioned testimony becomes material and admissible independently of its contradictory nature. The state further supports this argument by testimony elicited from the police detective to the effect that defendant admitted, in the interview of June 12, 1961, that he had purchased some adhesive tape.

Admittedly, relevant and probative evidence of preparations by an accused for the commission of a crime is admissible.... Based upon the limited record before us, however, the state's argument requires us to speculate that the defendant could not readily commute between Portland and Seattle, and that his presence in Seattle and acquisition of adhesive tape, upon an isolated occasion approximately a month before the offense in question, constituted significant evidence of planning and preparation for the offense in question, the particular mechanics of which are unrevealed by the record. This we decline to do....

Upon the record before us, we must conclude it was error to admit the questioned testimony.

People v. Terczak, 238 N.E.2d 626 (Ill.Ct.App.1968): Prosecution for robbery committed on December 19. Defendant's girl friend testified that defendant was with her on a bowling date on December 19. She testified that she knew she had the right date because December 19 was a Monday and she was off work on Mondays and Fridays. In rebuttal the prosecution called the assistant manager of the shoe store where the girl friend worked. He identified time records which showed that the girl friend worked on Monday, December 19, but not on Thursday, December 22. In surrebuttal, the girl friend testified that since pay day was Thursday, her Thursday work was recorded as having been done on Monday, a practice that she said was approved by the manager of the store. The manager was not available to be called as a witness. The assistant manager said that he knew of no such practice.

People v. Pargo, 50 Cal.Rptr. 719 (App.1966): A driver of a car of a certain description stole a wristwatch from a hitchhiker on November 8th in the San Diego area. Defendant was prosecuted for the theft. Defendant took the stand, denied the theft and insisted that he was at the home of Mrs. Moss and Mrs. Lee at the relevant time on November 8th. Mrs. Moss confirmed defendant's presence at her home. Mrs. Lee owned a car that fitted the description of the car driven by the thief. She testified that she was away from home on November 8th, had the car with her, and that defendant was not with her. When defendant was arrested on November 14th, he was riding as a passenger in Mrs. Lee's car, which was driven at the time by Mrs. Lee. On cross-examination of defendant, he was asked whether on October 16th he had been given a traffic citation while driving Mrs. Lee's car. He admitted this incident. He stated (it is not clear whether on direct or cross-examination) that he had never driven Mrs. Lee's car south of National City. In rebuttal, the police officer who issued the citation testified that the incident occurred some five miles south of National City and two miles north of the Mexican border and that defendant said he was returning from Tijuana. Held: No error in the examination of the defendant or the admission of the police officer's testimony.

Stephens v. People, 19 N.Y. 549, 572 (1859): Prosecution for poisoning; proved that defendant or his brother-in-law bought arsenic shortly before the death; witnesses for defendant testified on cross-examination that this poison was used on rats in a provision cellar; prosecution gave evidence that there were no provisions in the cellar; conviction affirmed.

People v. Wilson, 62 Cal.Rptr. 240, 242–43 (App.1967): Prosecution for assault with deadly weapon—shooting G in the arm. A defense witness testified that he was sitting in his car at a location different from where prosecution evidence tended to show the assault took place, that he saw G with some persons not including defendant, that there was a sound like a shot and G grabbed his arm, that G and the others then entered a nearby house and that about 15 minutes later B drove up and entered the house. Held, proper for prosecution to call B to testify that he did not go near the house during the period in question.

East Tennessee, V. & G. Ry. Co. v. Daniel, 18 S.E. 22 (Ga.1893): Asserted witness of an accident testified on cross-examination that he saw the episode on his way home from making purchases at a certain store; testimony by the storekeeper that the witness did not come to the store excluded; reversed.

People v. Larson, 402 N.E.2d 732, 743 (Ill.App.1980): Defendants were prosecuted for stealing gems and minerals from a museum. The principal disputed issue was identity. A prosecution witness testified that a few days after the robbery, she saw defendants breaking up a rock on her patio. When asked on cross-examination about her activities that day, she testified that she had picked up her son from summer school. Held, not error to prohibit introduction of extrinsic evidence that the witness's son was not enrolled in summer school.

Bonilla v. Yamaha Motors Corp., 955 F.2d 150, 154–55 (1st Cir.1992): When a witness was directed to answer an improper question—whether he had been ticketed for speeding on other occasions, as tending to show he was speeding on the litigated occasion and that it was his speeding that caused the accident rather than a design defect—see infra p. 914 on evidence of similar acts—it was error to allow extrinsic evidence to contradict the witness's denial that he had been ticketed.

Rosario v. Kuhlman, 839 F.2d 918 (2d Cir.1988), presented the question of a right to contradict from a federal constitutional perspective. Cartegena testified he saw the defendant commit the crime. Cartegena explained his presence by saying that he was sharing a nearby apartment with Lopez and that she was with him when he witnessed the crime. Held: It violated defendant's right to a fair trial to exclude Coreano's testimony that Cartegena did not make Lopez's acquaintance until after the date of the crime.

Seidelson, Extrinsic Evidence on a Collateral Matter May Not Be Used to Impeach Credibility, 9 Rev. Litig. 203 (1990), suggests that extrinsic evidence should be allowed only if it "significantly impeaches."

California Evidence Code § 780 (West 1996): "General rule as to credibility. Except as otherwise provided by statute, the court or jury may consider in determining the credibility of a witness any matter that has any tendency in reason to prove or disprove the truthfulness of his testimony at the hearing, including but not limited to any of the following: ... (i) The existence or nonexistence of any fact testified to by him." Law Revision Commission Comment: "There is no specific limitation in the Evidence Code on the use of impeaching evidence on the ground that it is 'collateral'.... The effect of Section 780 (together with Section 351) is to eliminate this inflexible rule of exclusion. This is not to say that all evidence of a collateral nature offered to attack the credibility of a witness would be admissible. Under Section 352, the Court has substantial discretion to exclude collateral evidence. The effect of Section 780, therefore, is to change the present somewhat inflexible rule of exclusion to a rule of discretion to be exercised by the trial judge."

It is sometimes contended that when the direct examiner opens a "collateral" matter, the trial judge must or may allow the cross-examiner to pursue it further than if he had originally raised it. 1 Wash.L.Rev. 133 (1925) gives some citations and a compact suggestion of the arguments each way. People v. Wells, 202 P.2d 53, 58 (Cal.), cert. denied, 338 U.S. 836 (1949), suggests disinclination to press the distinction far, and State v. Johnson, 383 P.2d 862 (Ariz.1963), takes a firm stand against it.

Religious Belief Affecting Credibility

Mention may be made here of a prohibition against inquiring into a witness's religious beliefs for the purpose of affecting credibility. State v. Duke, 362 So.2d 559 (La.1978): Improper to cross-examine defense witnesses about church membership, church attendance, obedience to the Ten Commandments and their religious and political views. State v. Estabrook, 91 P.2d 838, 846 (Or.1939): Improper to question Christian Scientist about her religious faith and its tenets regarding sin and evil. State v. Kimbrell, 360 S.E.2d 691 (N.C.1987): Prejudicial error to ask defendant if he knew about and participated in devil worship.

Fed.R.Evid. 610 provides: "Evidence of the beliefs or opinions of a witness on matters of religion is not admissible for the purpose of showing that by reason of their nature the witness' credibility is impaired or enhanced." United States v. Kalaydjian, 784 F.2d 53 (2d Cir.1986), supra p. 289, held that Rule 610 had been properly interpreted to forbid asking a prosecution witness why he had affirmed rather than sworn on the Koran. Is Fed.R.Evid. 603, regarding oaths and affirmations, an exception to Rule 610?

The Advisory Committee's Note to Rule 610 observes that although the rule "forecloses inquiry into the religious beliefs or opinions of a witness for the purpose of showing that his character for truthfulness is affected by their nature, an inquiry for the purpose of showing interest or bias because of them is not within the prohibition." Redman v. Watch Tower Bible and Tract Soc'y, 630 N.E.2d 676 (Ohio 1994): In suit to invalidate a will leaving property to church on the ground of undue influence, permissible to question witnesses who were members of the church about their membership in the church and the work they did for it, but not permissible to admit evidence of the tenets of the church, including the alleged tenet that members should perjure themselves to protect the church. But see Malek v. Federal Ins. Co., 994 F.2d 49, 54–55 (2d Cir.1993): In action on fire insurance policy in which insureds introduced testimony of accountant as to their financial stability to negative inference that they had motive to set the fire, error to allow cross-examination of accountant as to whether he provided accounting services to Hasidic community (of which insureds were members). Dissent: "At no point was . . . [the accountant] asked about his opinions or beliefs. Nor, indeed, was he questioned about what religion he followed. He was queried solely about his livelihood, presumably to demonstrate that he earned his living by service to the Hasidic community [to which insured belonged]. . . . Nobody, in short, suggested that . . . [the accountant] was less credible because of his belief on matters of religion." Id. at 59.

Is the prohibition in Rule 610 designed to protect a privacy interest of the witness? But Rule 610 applies even when the witness is willing to testify about his religion. What other purposes does the rule serve? Is religious belief relevant to credibility?

Would it violate the religion clauses of the First Amendment to admit evidence of religious belief to affect credibility? Does it violate those clauses to prohibit the use of such evidence? State v. Hall, 215 N.W.2d 166, 170–71 (Mich.1974), held it improper under both a constitutional provision and a statute to ask a criminal defendant on cross-examination whether he believed in God. Ariz. Const. art. 2, § 12 contains a prohibition against questioning a witness on religious belief to affect the weight of his testimony.

Does the exclusion of evidence of religious belief, when offered by a criminal defendant, present a problem under the Compulsory Process or the Confrontation Clause?

Useful references are: Swancara, Impeachment of Non–Religious Witnesses, 13 Rocky Mtn.L.Rev. 336 (1941); Ariens, Evidence of Religion and the Religion of Evidence, 40 Buff.L.Rev. 65, 77–91 (1992); Annots., 27 A.L.R. 4th 1167 (1984) (religious belief), 76 A.L.R.3d 539 (1977) (same), 18 A.L.R. 5th 804 (1994) (witchcraft and Satanism).

a.   Bias, Interest and Corruption

United States v. Abel
Supreme Court of the United States, 1984.
469 U.S. 45, 105 S.Ct. 465, 83 L.Ed.2d 450.

■ JUSTICE REHNQUIST delivered the opinion of the Court.

A divided panel of the Court of Appeals for the Ninth Circuit reversed respondent's conviction for bank robbery.[1] The Court of Appeals held that the District Court improperly admitted testimony which impeached one of respondent's witnesses. We hold that the District Court did not err, and we reverse.

Respondent John Abel and two cohorts were indicted for robbing a savings and loan in Bellflower, Cal., in violation of 18 U.S.C. §§ 2113(a) and (d). The cohorts elected to plead guilty, but respondent went to trial. One of the cohorts,

---

1.   707 F.2d 1013 (9th Cir.1983). [Footnotes are the Court's. Some footnotes have been omitted.]

Kurt Ehle, agreed to testify against respondent and identify him as a participant in the robbery.

Respondent informed the District Court at a pretrial conference that he would seek to counter Ehle's testimony with that of Robert Mills. Mills was not a participant in the robbery but was friendly with respondent and with Ehle, and had spent time with both in prison. Mills planned to testify that after the robbery Ehle had admitted to Mills that Ehle intended to implicate respondent falsely, in order to receive favorable treatment from the Government. The prosecutor in turn disclosed that he intended to discredit Mills' testimony by calling Ehle back to the stand and eliciting from Ehle the fact that respondent, Mills, and Ehle were all members of the "Aryan Brotherhood," a secret prison gang that required its members always to deny the existence of the organization and to commit perjury, theft, and murder on each member's behalf.

Defense counsel objected to Ehle's proffered rebuttal testimony as too prejudicial to respondent. After a lengthy discussion in chambers the District Court decided to permit the prosecutor to cross-examine Mills about the gang, and if Mills denied knowledge of the gang, to introduce Ehle's rebuttal testimony concerning the tenets of the gang and Mills' and respondent's membership in it. The District Court held that the probative value of Ehle's rebuttal testimony outweighed its prejudicial effect, but that respondent might be entitled to a limiting instruction if his counsel would submit one to the court.

At trial Ehle implicated respondent as a participant in the robbery. Mills, called by respondent, testified that Ehle told him in prison that Ehle planned to implicate respondent falsely. When the prosecutor sought to cross-examine Mills concerning membership in the prison gang, the District Court conferred again with counsel outside of the jury's presence, and ordered the prosecutor not to use the term "Aryan Brotherhood" because it was unduly prejudicial. Accordingly, the prosecutor asked Mills if he and respondent were members of a "secret type of prison organization" which had a creed requiring members to deny its existence and lie for each other. When Mills denied knowledge of such an organization the prosecutor recalled Ehle.

Ehle testified that respondent, Mills, and he were indeed members of a secret prison organization whose tenets required its members to deny its existence and "lie, cheat, steal [and] kill" to protect each other. The District Court sustained a defense objection to a question concerning the punishment for violating the organization's rules. Ehle then further described the organization and testified that "in view of the fact of how close Abel and Mills were" it would have been "suicide" for Ehle to have told Mills what Mills attributed to him. Respondent's counsel did not request a limiting instruction and none was given.

The jury convicted respondent. On his appeal a divided panel of the Court of Appeals reversed. 707 F.2d 1013 (9th Cir.1983). The Court of Appeals held that Ehle's rebuttal testimony was admitted not just to show that respondent's and Mills' membership in the same group might cause Mills to color his testimony; the court held that the contested evidence was also admitted to show that because Mills belonged to a perjurious organization, he must be lying on the stand. This suggestion of perjury, based upon a group tenet, was impermissible. The court reasoned:

> "It is settled law that the government may not convict an individual merely for belonging to an organization that advocates illegal activity. Scales v. United States, 367 U.S. 203, 219–24 [81 S.Ct. 1469, 1481–83, 6 L.Ed.2d 782] ... ; Brandenb[u]rg v. Ohio, 395 U.S. 444 [89 S.Ct. 1827, 23

L.Ed.2d 430].... Rather, the government must show that the individual knows of and personally accepts the tenets of the organization. Neither should the government be allowed to impeach on the grounds of mere membership, since membership, without more, has no probative value. It establishes nothing about the individual's own actions, beliefs, or veracity." Id., at 1016 (citations omitted).

The court concluded that Ehle's testimony implicated respondent as a member of the gang; but since respondent did not take the stand, the testimony could not have been offered to impeach him and it prejudiced him "by mere association." Id., at 1017.

We hold that the evidence showing Mills' and respondent's membership in the prison gang was sufficiently probative of Mills' possible bias towards respondent to warrant its admission into evidence. Thus it was within the District Court's discretion to admit Ehle's testimony, and the Court of Appeals was wrong in concluding otherwise.

Both parties correctly assume, as did the District Court and the Court of Appeals, that the question is governed by the Federal Rules of Evidence. But the Rules do not by their terms deal with impeachment for "bias," although they do expressly treat impeachment by character evidence and conduct, Rule 608, by evidence of conviction of a crime, Rule 609, and by showing of religious beliefs or opinion, Rule 610. Neither party has suggested what significance we should attribute to this fact. Although we are nominally the promulgators of the Rules, and should in theory need only to consult our collective memories to analyze the situation properly, we are in truth merely a conduit when we deal with an undertaking as substantial as the preparation of the Federal Rules of Evidence. In the case of these Rules, too, it must be remembered that Congress extensively reviewed our submission, and considerably revised it. See 28 U.S.C. § 2076: 4 J. Bailey III & O. Trelles II, Federal Rules of Evidence: Legislative Histories and Related Documents (1980).

Before the present Rules were promulgated, the admissibility of evidence in the federal courts was governed in part by statutes or Rules, and in part by case law. See, e.g., Fed.Rule Civ.Proc. 43(a) (prior to 1975 amendment); Fed.Rule Crim.Proc. 26 (prior to 1975 amendment); Palmer v. Hoffman, 318 U.S. 109, 63 S.Ct. 477, 87 L.Ed. 645 (1943); Funk v. United States, 290 U.S. 371, 54 S.Ct. 212, 78 L.Ed. 369 (1933); Shepard v. United States, 290 U.S. 96, 54 S.Ct. 22, 78 L.Ed. 196 (1933). This Court had held in Alford v. United States, 282 U.S. 687, 51 S.Ct. 218, 75 L.Ed. 624 (1931), that a trial court must allow some cross-examination of a witness to show bias. This holding was in accord with the overwhelming weight of authority in the state courts as reflected in Wigmore's classic treatise on the law of evidence. See id., at 691, 54 S.Ct. at 219, citing 3 J. Wigmore, Evidence § 1368 (2d ed.1923); see also District of Columbia v. Clawans, 300 U.S. 617, 630–633, 57 S.Ct. 660, 664–666, 81 L.Ed. 843 (1937). Our decision in Davis v. Alaska, 415 U.S. 308, 94 S.Ct. 1105, 39 L.Ed.2d 347 (1974), holds that the Confrontation Clause of the Sixth Amendment requires a defendant to have some opportunity to show bias on the part of a prosecution witness.

With this state of unanimity confronting the drafters of the Federal Rules of Evidence, we think it unlikely that they intended to scuttle entirely the evidentiary availability of cross-examination for bias. One commentator, recognizing the omission of any express treatment of impeachment for bias, prejudice, or corruption, observes that the Rules "clearly contemplate the use of the above-mentioned grounds of impeachment." E. Cleary, McCormick on Evidence § 40, p. 85 (3d ed.1984). Other commentators, without mentioning the omission, treat bias as a permissible and established basis of impeachment under the Rules. 3 D. Louisell & C. Mueller, Federal Evidence § 341, p. 470 (1979); 3 J. Weinstein & M. Berger, Weinstein's Evidence ¶ 607[03] (1981).

We think this conclusion is obviously correct. Rule 401 defines as "relevant evidence" evidence having any tendency to make the existence of any fact that is of consequence to the determination of the action more probable or less probable than it would be without the evidence. Rule 402 provides that all relevant evidence is admissible, except as otherwise provided by the United States Constitution, Act of Congress, or by applicable rule. A successful showing of bias on the part of a witness would have a tendency to make the facts to which he testified less probable in the eyes of the jury than it would be without such testimony.

The correctness of the conclusion that the Rules contemplate impeachment by showing of bias is confirmed by the references to bias in the Advisory Committee Notes to Rules 608 and 610, and by the provisions allowing any party to attack credibility in Rule 607, and allowing cross-examination on "matters affecting the credibility of the witness" in Rule 611(b). The Courts of Appeals have upheld use of extrinsic evidence to show bias both before and after the adoption of the Federal Rules of Evidence....

We think the lesson to be drawn from all of this is that it is permissible to impeach a witness by showing his bias under the Federal Rules of Evidence just as it was permissible to do so before their adoption....

Ehle's testimony about the prison gang certainly made the existence of Mills' bias towards respondent more probable. Thus it was relevant to support that inference. Bias is a term used in the "common law of evidence" to describe the relationship between a party and a witness which might lead the witness to slant, unconsciously or otherwise, his testimony in favor of or against a party. Bias may be induced by a witness' like, dislike, or fear of a party, or by the witness' self-interest. Proof of bias is almost always relevant because the jury, as finder of fact and weigher of credibility, has historically been entitled to assess all evidence which might bear on the accuracy and truth of a witness' testimony. The "common law of evidence" allowed the showing of bias by extrinsic evidence, while requiring the cross-examiner to "take the answer of the witness" with respect to less favored forms of impeachment. See generally, McCormick on Evidence, supra, § 40, at 89; Hale, Bias as Affecting Credibility, 1 Hastings L.J. 1 (1949).

Mills' and respondent's membership in the Aryan Brotherhood supported the inference that Mills' testimony was slanted or perhaps fabricated in respondent's favor. A witness' and a party's common membership in an organization, even without proof that the witness or party has personally adopted its tenets, is certainly probative of bias. We do not read our holdings in Scales v. United States, 367 U.S. 203, 81 S.Ct. 1469, 6 L.Ed.2d 782 (1961), and Brandenburg v. Ohio, 395 U.S. 444, 89 S.Ct. 1827, 23 L.Ed.2d 430 (1969), to require a different conclusion. Those cases dealt with the constitutional requirements for convicting persons under the Smith Act and state syndicalism laws for belonging to organizations which espoused illegal aims and engaged in illegal conduct. Mills' and respondent's membership in the Aryan Brotherhood was not offered to convict either of a crime, but to impeach Mills' testimony. Mills was subject to no sanction other than that he might be disbelieved. Under these circumstances there is no requirement that the witness must be shown to have subscribed to all the tenets of the organization, either casually or in a manner sufficient to permit him to be convicted under laws such as those involved in Scales and Brandenburg.[2] For purposes of the law of evidence the jury may be permitted to draw an inference of subscription to the tenets of the organization from membership alone, even though such an inference would not be sufficient to convict beyond a reasonable doubt in a criminal prosecution under the Smith Act.

Respondent argues that even if the evidence of membership in the prison gang were relevant to show bias, the District Court erred in permitting a full description of the gang and its odious tenets. Respondent contends that the District Court abused its discretion under Federal Rule of Evidence 403, because the prejudicial effect of the contested evidence outweighed its probative value. In other words, testimony about the gang inflamed the jury against respondent, and the chance that he would be convicted by his mere association with the organization outweighed any probative value the testimony may have had on Mills' bias.

Respondent specifically contends that the District Court should not have permitted Ehle's precise description of the gang as a lying and murderous group. Respondent suggests that the District Court should have cut off the testimony after the prosecutor had elicited that Mills knew respondent and both may have belonged to an organization together. This argument ignores the fact that the *type* of organization in which a witness and a party share membership may be relevant to show bias. If the organization is a loosely knit group having nothing to do with the subject matter of the litigation, the inference of bias arising from common membership may be small or nonexistent. If the prosecutor had elicited that both respondent and Mills belonged to the Book of the Month Club, the jury probably would not have inferred bias even if the District Court had admitted the testimony. The attributes of the Aryan Brotherhood—a secret prison sect sworn to perjury and self-protection— bore directly not only on the *fact* of bias but also on the *source* and *strength* of Mills' bias. The tenets of this group showed that Mills had a powerful motive to slant his testimony towards respondent, or even commit perjury outright.

A district court is accorded a wide discretion in determining the admissibility of evidence under the Federal Rules. Assessing the probative value of common membership in any particular group, and weighing any factors counseling against admissibility is a matter first for the district court's sound judgment under Rules 401 and 403 and ultimately, if the evidence is admitted, for the trier of fact.

Before admitting Ehle's rebuttal testimony, the District Court gave heed to the extensive arguments of counsel, both in chambers and at the bench. In an attempt to avoid undue prejudice to respondent the court ordered that the name "Aryan Brotherhood" not be used. The court also offered to give a limiting instruction concerning the testimony, and it sustained defense objections to the prosecutor's questions concerning the punishment meted out to unfaithful members. These precautions did not prevent *all* prejudice to respondent from Ehle's testimony, but they did, in our opinion, ensure that the admission of this highly probative evidence did not *unduly* prejudice respon-

---

2. In Scales and Brandenburg we discussed the First Amendment right of association as it bore on the right of persons freely to associate in political groups, short of participating in unlawful activity. See 395 U.S., at 449, 89 S.Ct., at 1830; 367 U.S., at 229–230, 81 S.Ct., at 1486–1487. Whatever First Amendment associational rights, an inmate may have to join a prison group, see Jones v. North Carolina Prisoners' Labor Union, Inc., 433 U.S. 119, 97 S.Ct. 2532, 53 L.Ed.2d 629 (1977), those rights were not implicated by Ehle's rebuttal of Mills.

dent. We hold there was no abuse of discretion under Rule 403 in admitting Ehle's testimony as to membership and tenets.

. . .

The judgment of the Court of Appeals is reversed.

NOTES

The subject of these notes is the technique of impeachment by proof of bias. The importance of this form of impeachment has already been indicated in the discussion of the Supreme Court's decisions in Davis v. Alaska and Olden v. Kentucky, supra pp. 363–64. In those cases defendants' convictions were reversed on constitutional grounds because cross-examination of an important prosecution witness regarding matters relevant to bias was prevented. Now we explore the various mental attitudes that are grouped together under the term "bias," the importance of an opponent's interest in bringing these matters to the attention of the trier of fact, and a number of considerations that weigh against admissibility.

1. With the tenets of the Aryan Brotherhood, which the Court says in the Able case were admissible for their bearing on bias, compare the alleged tenets of the Jehovah's Witnesses, referred to in Redman v. Watch Tower Bible and Tract Soc'y, supra p. 405.

2. Gordon v. United States, 344 U.S. 414, 416–17, 421–22, 73 S.Ct. 369, 372, 374–75 (1953): Judgment reversed because the jury was kept from learning that the prosecution witness had been awaiting sentence for months and had been urged by the sentencing judge to cooperate. State v. Hector, 249 N.E.2d 912 (Ohio 1969): Error not to allow defendant to ask prosecution witness whether he was under indictment for various crimes. United States v. Anderson, 881 F.2d 1128, 1139 (D.C.Cir.1989): Confrontation Clause violated by not allowing cross-examination of prosecution witness about indictment against her that had been dismissed without prejudice: The charge "hung over the witness' head like the sword of Damocles." Merritt v. People, 842 P.2d 162 (Colo.1992): Confrontation Clause violated by not allowing defendants on cross-examination of prosecution witness to bring out that the witness had invoked the privilege against self-incrimination and at the request of the prosecution been granted use immunity.

United States v. Campbell, 426 F.2d 547 (2d Cir.1970), was a prosecution for conspiracy to bribe officers of the Internal Revenue Service and to defraud the United States of delinquent taxes owed by one Matthews. Matthews testified as a prosecution witness. Although named in the indictment as a co-conspirator, Matthews was not charged. After defendant's cross-examination of Matthews, defendant offered evidence of "fraud referrals" by the IRS agent in charge of Matthews' account and rejection of these referrals by the Intelligence Division of the IRS. Defendant also offered evidence of repeated postponements by the IRS of the "target date" for the collection of Matthews' penalty assessment account. Defendant's evidence was excluded. The Court of Appeals sustained the exclusion of the evidence, doubting it would have given the jury a significantly different basis for judging bias than it had from evidence already in the case, principally the cross-examination of Matthews. Friendly, J., dissenting:

> Our reports record countless instances where a man has been convicted principally upon the testimony of another at least as guilty, who has received a light sentence, has remained unsentenced or, as in this case, has

not even been indicted. In all likelihood there is no viable alternative to such prosecutorial discretion, although the contrary has been strongly argued.... However, when the prosecution proceeds in this manner, the defendant must be given full opportunity to bring out just what favors the witness has already received from the government and what further ones he may be expecting. The defendant is not limited to cross-examination in attempting to elicit this information and is neither required to accept the witness' statement of ignorance of how kind the government had been to him nor bound to submit other direct evidence of knowledge. Proof of what the government has done may convince the jury that the witness must have known of it, thereby casting him as a liar in his denial as well....

Id. at 553–54.

See also the discussion of plea agreements in connection with accrediting and impeaching one's own witness, supra pp. 385–88.

3. Blair v. United States, 401 F.2d 387, 389–90 (D.C.Cir.1968): Evidence of brutality of policemen toward defendant admissible to impeach them when called as witnesses by prosecution. Wynn v. United States, 397 F.2d 621, 622–23 (D.C.Cir.1967): Error to prevent defendant from testifying that several days after larceny with which defendant was charged, prosecution witness had accused defendant of another offense. Henry v. Speckard, 22 F.3d 1209 (2d Cir.), cert. denied, 115 S.Ct. 606 (1994): Error, although harmless, not to allow defendant in prosecution for sexual abuse of minor to ask minor whether she felt resentment towards defendant because he had requested her to babysit other children. United States v. Harvey, 547 F.2d 720 (2d Cir.1976): Error to exclude extrinsic evidence that prosecution witness who had identified defendant as the bank robber had said to defendant's mother that defendant was the father of the witness's child and that she would have revenge on him for not owning up to it. The hearsay problem should be noted. See infra p. 645.

United States v. Kartman, 417 F.2d 893 (9th Cir.1969): Conviction for assaulting a federal marshal at an anti-war demonstration reversed because the defendant was not allowed to cross-examine the marshal about his hostile feelings towards persons who participate in such demonstrations. People v. Taylor, 545 P.2d 703 (Colo.1976): In prosecution of police officer for assault, not error to admit evidence of racial slur by the police officer during course of arrests by him of other blacks. However, the court held that it was error to permit inquiry into the details of those arrests, including the use of excessive force. Simmons v. Collins, 655 So.2d 330 (La.1995), reversing 654 So.2d 793 (La.Ct.App.1995): In automobile accident case in which plaintiffs were black and defendants white, permissible to introduce evidence that white witness who supported the defendants' version of what happened had, ten months before the accident, assaulted a black man, called him a nigger and said he did not belong in that part of town. See also the impeachment of Detective Fuhrman in the notorious O.J. Simpson criminal prosecution. But see Outley v. City of New York, 837 F.2d 587 (2d Cir.1988): In action against city and police officers for misconduct by the officers towards plaintiff, error to disclose in argument and to bring out on cross-examination of plaintiff that he had filed numerous other law suits against police and government agencies.

4. United States v. Bratton, 875 F.2d 439 (5th Cir.1989): Not error to question wife who gave testimony exculpating defendant, her husband, whether he had physically abused her.

5. Joice v. Missouri–Kansas–Texas Railroad, 189 S.W.2d 568, 574 (Mo.1945): Questioning of defense witness involved in same accident as to his claim against and making settlement with defendant. Frierson v. Hines, 426 P.2d 362

(Okla.1967): Judgment for plaintiff bus driver against defendant truck driver reversed because defendant not allowed to interrogate plaintiff's witness, a bus passenger, who testified that plaintiff did everything he could to avoid the collision, about passenger's claim against plaintiff and its settlement.

For further discussion of the conflict between the importance of showing a witness's bias and the policy favoring settlements, see infra p. 943.

United States v. Gambler, 662 F.2d 834 (D.C.Cir.1981): In prosecution for fraud, error, although harmless, to prohibit cross-examination of the victim, called as a witness by the prosecution, concerning civil litigation between him and the defendant arising out of the same incidents that were the subject of the fraud prosecution. A careful dissent finds the error not harmless and would allow fairly extensive inquiry into the facts of the civil litigation, including the amount of the victim's claim. The dissent distinguishes different evidentiary uses of the civil litigation: the outcome of the criminal prosecution might affect the witness's interest; the civil litigation might affect the witness's feelings; the civil litigation may express the witness's feelings. See also State v. Kellogg, 350 So.2d 656 (La.1977): Error not to permit cross-examination of battery victim as to his civil suit against the defendant for his injuries. Commonwealth v. Butler, 601 A.2d 268, 271 (Pa.1991): Error to prohibit cross-examination of prosecution witness as to civil suit brought by the criminal defendant against the witness. See also Annot., 98 A.L.R. 3d 1060 (1980).

St. Louis–San Francisco Railway v. Thompson, 30 F.2d 586 (5th Cir.1929): Questioning of defense witness in negligence case as to having been charged with contributing to creation of allegedly dangerous conditions. Terminal Transport v. Foster, 164 F.2d 248, 249 (5th Cir.1947): Questioning of defense witness in motor vehicle accident case as to his being under indictment by reason of the accident.

6. Bias in expert witness: Henning v. Thomas, 366 S.E.2d 109 (Va.1988): In medical malpractice case, error not to allow cross-examination of expert as to his connection with a professional witness organization. "[P]laintiff makes this point: 'It is respectfully submitted that it was the obvious intent and sole purpose of this proposed line of questioning for the jury to draw some adverse, clandestine inference from Dr. Culley's perfectly proper association with Dr. Charow and Professional Medical Witnesses.' Our response can be summed up in one word: 'Precisely.' The trial court's ruling prevented defendants from doing precisely what defendants had a right to do. The defendant doctors were entitled to attempt to persuade the jury that Dr. Culley was a 'doctor for hire,' who was part of a nationwide group that offered themselves as witnesses, on behalf of medical malpractice plaintiffs. Once the jury was made aware of this information it was for the jury to decide what weight, if any, to give to Culley's testimony. This was a classic case of an effort to establish bias, prejudice, or relationship. The trial court went too far when it limited defendants' cross examination to the bare question whether Dr. Culley was being paid to testify." See also Annot., 39 A.L.R. 4th 742 (1985), and further discussion of bias in expert witnesses, infra p. 1064.

7. Manifested desire to sell testimony (or silence): State v. Wilson, 111 So. 484 (La.1927): Error to exclude testimony that primary witness had said to defendant he would testify favorably for defendant or change his testimony if paid to do so. Thompson v. State, 283 P. 151, 159 (Wyo.1929): Evidence admissible that primary witness wrote defendant a letter that might be interpreted as a suggestion that defendant could buy him off. United States v. Cohen, 163 F.2d 667, 668 (3d Cir.1947): Error to sustain objection to question directed to primary witness as to his having demanded $1,300 of defendants. Is the fact that a witness has sold or was willing to sell his story to the media relevant to bias? To some other ground of impeachment? In reaction to the O.J. Simpson case, California made it a crime, with certain limitations, to receive money for providing information obtained as a result of witnessing a crime. Cal. Penal Code § 132.5. See also Golden Door Jewelry Creations, Inc. v. Lloyds Underwriters Non–Marine Ass'n, supra p. 290.

8. A distinction must be drawn between proof of such misconduct as bribery or subornation of perjury to indicate bias on the part of a third party witness and proof of like acts by or on behalf of a party litigant to indicate an implied admission of a weak case. The latter has more or less direct bearing on the merits, the former normally does not. Ware v. State, 37 So.2d 18 (Miss.1948): Prosecutor cross-examined a defense character witness as to having offered money to parents of alleged victim if they would withdraw the prosecution, which offer the witness denied; prosecutor then called the victim's mother, who testified that the character witness did make the offer, stating that *he did so after having talked with defendant;* held error to admit the mother's testimony, there being no evidence aside from the italicized statement that defendant had participated. But what if the mother's testimony had omitted the italicized statement? United States v. Spagnuolo, 168 F.2d 768, 771 (2d Cir.), cert. denied, 335 U.S. 824 (1948): Evidence of talks with purported representative of defendant to show absence of bias in witness. Commonwealth v. Robinson, 60 A.2d 824, 826 (Pa.Super.1948): Evidence of importunities to show bias of those making them. Cf. Manning v. Commonwealth, 217 S.W.2d 226 (Ky.1949), where defendants gave evidence that the alleged victim of the crime tried to extract from them a money settlement, while the victim testified that the witness who gave this defense evidence left the company of defendants, approached the victim, and forthwith suggested out-of-court settlement to the victim.

9. As some of the foregoing authorities indicate, the fact that a matter sought to be opened up for purposes of impeachment has some probative value on the issue of bias does not invariably assure the right to introduce extrinsic evidence, nor for that matter even to pursue cross-examination of the primary witness. Though inquiries as to bias may have a license not granted in respect to certain other subjects, considerations of confusion, surprise, improper use of the evidence, unnecessary embarrassment of the witness and so forth receive recognition.

People v. Wilson, 62 Cal.Rptr. 240, 244 (App.1967): Prosecution for assaulting G. Defendant denied he committed the assault. Evidence tended to show that G had supplanted defendant in Y's affections. Held, not error to prohibit defendant on cross-examination of Y from inquiring into the details of her relations with G, since her feelings for G and against defendant had already been adequately brought out. Tinker v. United States, 417 F.2d 542, 544 (D.C.Cir.), cert. denied, 396 U.S. 864 (1969): Not error to prohibit evidence of homosexual behavior by O, a prosecution witness, with W, a defense witness, since evidence already admitted indicated participation by O with W and defendant in the "gay" life, and inquiry into homosexual acts would degrade and humiliate O. "Even where testimony . . . has some tendency to connote motivation, any exercise of judicial discretion worthy of the name necessitates consideration of these adverse effects."

Grudt v. City of Los Angeles, 468 P.2d 825, 831–34 (Cal.1970): Wrongful death action against police officers. Judgment for defendants reversed because of error in permitting impeachment of plaintiff's claimed eyewitnesses, Graves and Plankers. On cross-examination Graves was asked about arrests for a felony and several misdemeanors. Plankers' impeachment was by extrinsic evidence. Craig, a man who worked with Plankers, testified that Plankers had said to him that he and his family were being harassed by the police, that his son had been arrested in an auto theft ring and his wife for drunk driving, that he was going to "get even with those goddam cops." Police officers then testified that Plankers' son and wife had indeed been arrested for such offenses. Held: The only part of this evidence properly admitted was "the testimony of Leroy Craig relating to the attitude of Plankers. Testimony that Plankers had complained of harassment and had vowed to 'get even' with the police, if believed, had some tendency to indicate that Plankers was biased against the police generally and therefore may have been biased against Officers Kilgo and Rinehart [the defendants] in particular." Admission of the rest of the evidence, however, violated the policy of section 787 of the California Evidence Code, which provides that "evidence of specific instances of his conduct relevant only as tending to prove a trait of his character is inadmissible to attack or support the credibility of a witness." Furthermore,

> [t]he thread of inferences from past arrests by the police, to hostility against police in general, to a willingness to distort testimony in a civil action involving individual police officers unknown to the witness is so tenuous as to render invalid the professed purpose of the defense counsel in offering the evidence.
>
> Were we to approve the trial judge's acceptance of this impeachment evidence, we would erect an insurmountable barrier to an aggrieved citizen's ability to gain proper civil redress against errant peace officers. Parties electing to sue any policeman—for damages in tort, for contract reparations, or merely to collect a debt—would be obliged to produce witnesses willing to be subjected to the degradation of a courtroom examination of their prior arrest records and the records of all members of their families to show bias against police generally. And even if such witnesses were found, their credibility in the eyes of the jury would be seriously impaired by evidence of prior criminal arrests, not because of the likelihood of actual bias, but because of the "bad character" suggested by the mere arrests.

But see Ellis v. Capps, 500 F.2d 225 (5th Cir.1974): In action against a prison warden for overseeing the beating of the plaintiff, a prisoner, held not error to admit evidence of numerous instances of violence and misconduct by the plaintiff-witness while incarcerated in penal institutions of the state to show hatred of prison life and officialdom. The dissent observed: "[The evidence] contained such shocking accounts ... that the jury could hardly have avoided the feeling that ... [the plaintiff] should not succeed in his lawsuit, even if ... [the defendant] had assaulted him." Id. at 229.

10. There is substantial, but not unanimous authority, that if a party desires to introduce extrinsic evidence of a statement of a witness for the purpose of showing bias, he must first question the witness in a way sufficient to remind him of the making of the statement. United States v. Betts, 16 F.3d 748, 764 (7th Cir.1994): Evidence of statement by prosecution witness that he was testifying because of promise that his sentence would be reduced properly excluded because of failure to give witness opportunity to explain; opinion reviews conflicting authorities. Compare the requirement of a "foundation" or opportunity to explain in the case of extrinsic evidence of a prior statement offered to impeach a witness by a showing of self-contradiction, infra p. 460. If there are reasons for the requirement in the case of self-contradiction, do they apply in the case of bias? See United States v. Harvey, 547 F.2d 720 (2d

Cir.1976), incorrectly suggesting that the requirement is found in Fed.R.Evid. 613(b) in the case of bias. What if the impeaching party seeks to introduce evidence not of a statement by the witness, but of other conduct of the witness indicative of bias, or simply of facts that if known to the witness could have engendered certain feelings in him? Pettie v. State, 560 A.2d 577 (Md.1989): Evidence that police officer had threatened witness that he would be prosecuted if he testified contrary to his original accusation against defendant could be introduced even though the witness had not been asked about it on cross-examination. Schmertz & Czapanskiy, Bias Impeachment and the Proposed Federal Rules of Evidence, 61 Geo.L.J. 257, 265–71 (1972), proposed that a rule about bias impeachment be added to the Federal Rules of Evidence that would have included the provision: "Extrinsic evidence as to matters indicating . . . bias is not ordinarily admissible unless the witness has been afforded an opportunity to deny or explain such matters."

b.   *Prior Convictions*

United States v. Valencia

United States Court of Appeals, Eighth Circuit, 1995.
61 F.3d 616.

■ Before WOLLMAN and M. ARNOLD, CIRCUIT JUDGES, and BOGUE SENIOR DISTRICT JUDGE.

■ BOGUE, SENIOR DISTRICT JUDGE.

Otoniel Maldonado Valencia (appellant) was charged by superseding indictment with one count of conspiracy to possess with intent to distribute and to distribute cocaine HCl, three counts of distribution of cocaine HCl, and one count of money laundering. Witnesses cooperating with the government gave testimony to the effect that appellant was the California connection for various North Dakota drug dealers. A jury returned guilty verdicts on all counts and appellant was subsequently sentenced by the district court to 240 months imprisonment. For reversal he asserts error in the district court's admission of a prior conviction under Fed.R.Evid. 609, prosecutorial misconduct, and errors in calculating his sentence. Additional facts will be presented where indicated. For the reasons stated below, we affirm.

I.   Conviction

Appellant first contends the district court erred when it admitted, for impeachment purposes, a prior conviction of the appellant for unlawful possession for sale and purchase for sale of a controlled substance. Previously, in its case in chief, the government had offered the prior conviction pursuant to Fed.R.Evid. 404(b).[1] The district court denied the use of the previous conviction during the government's case in chief, finding that the balancing required under Fed.R.Evid. 403 militated against admission. Anticipating that the issue would likely arise later in the proceedings, the district court noted that

---

1. Fed.R.Evid. 404(b) provides in pertinent part:

Evidence of other crimes, wrongs, or acts is not admissible to prove the character of a person in order to show action in conformity therewith. It may, however, be admissible for other purposes, such as proof of motive, opportunity, intent, preparation, plan, knowledge, identity, or absence of mistake or accident. . . .

It is not clear what specific "other purposes" the government was asserting as a basis for admission of the prior conviction. [Footnotes by the court, renumbered. Some footnotes omitted.]

I'm going to exclude this evidence in the government's case in chief as it is observed under 404(b) and my reasoning again is under 403 and I find within my judgment and my discretion that I believe this evidence, though it may be relevant, is highly prejudicial and this unfair prejudice substantially outweighs any probative value of the evidence as it is observed. Now as I've indicated this ruling applies to the offer of the evidence under 404(b). My ruling under 609 at least as the facts of this case presently stand would be different. . . .

Later in the trial the appellant testified in his own defense. On direct examination he admitted that he had a prior conviction for the possession of a controlled substance. On cross examination, the government offered a certified copy of the appellant's prior conviction. The government believed the appellant attempted to "explain away or minimize his guilt on the prior conviction" on direct examination. Over the appellant's objection, the copy of the prior conviction was admitted under Fed.R.Evid. 609 for impeachment purposes.[2]

Whether evidence of a prior conviction should be admitted is left to the discretion of the trial court. United States v. Swanson, 9 F.3d 1354, 1356 (8th Cir.1993) (citing United States v. Reeves, 730 F.2d 1189, 1196 (8th Cir.1984)). The standard of review on appeal is an abuse of discretion standard. Swanson, 9 F.3d at 1356.

The admission of prior bad acts evidence under Rule 404(b) is restricted by Rule 403 which states that otherwise relevant evidence may be excluded if its probative value is substantially outweighed by the danger of unfair prejudice. The appellant contends that Rule 609(a)'s internalized balancing test is stricter in terms of admissibility in that a prior conviction is not admissible against the accused for impeachment purposes unless the probative value of the evidence outweighs its prejudicial effect. Appellant's argument is that after finding that the prejudice of the prior conviction *substantially* outweighed the probative value under 404(b), the district court abused its discretion in admitting the same evidence under Rule 609, where it would be excluded if the prejudice *merely* outweighed its probative effect. We disagree.

---

2. As it relates to witnesses accused of a crime, Rule 609(a) states:

For the purpose of attacking the credibility of a witness, . . . evidence that an accused has been convicted of [a felony] shall be admitted if the court determines that the probative value of admitting this evidence outweighs its prejudicial effect to the accused.

[Eds. Note: As amended in 1990 Rule 609 provides:

(a) General rule. For the purpose of attacking the credibility of a witness.

(1) evidence that a witness other than an accused has been convicted of a crime shall be admitted, subject to Rule 403, if the crime was punishable by death or imprisonment in excess of one year under the law under which the witness was convicted, and evidence that an accused has been convicted of such a crime shall be admitted if the court determines that the probative value of admitting this evidence outweighs its prejudicial effect to the accused; and

(2) evidence that any witness has been convicted of a crime shall be admitted if it involved dishonesty or false statement, regardless of the punishment.

(b) Time limit. Evidence of a conviction under this rule is not admissible if a period of more than ten years has elapsed since the date of the conviction or of the release of the witness from the confinement imposed for that conviction, whichever is the later date, unless the court determines, in the interests of justice, that the probative value of the conviction supported by specific facts and circumstances substantially outweighs its prejudicial effect. However, evidence of a conviction more than 10 years old as calculated herein, is not admissible unless the proponent gives to the adverse party sufficient written notice of intent to use such evidence to provide the adverse party with a fair opportunity to contest the use of such evidence. . . .]

First, it should be noted that we are not confronted with the district court's rulings in combination. No party has appealed the district court's Rule 404(b) decision excluding the prior conviction during the government's case in chief. Each ruling must be treated independently, divorced from prior rulings. We are faced solely with the ruling regarding whether the district court erred in admitting appellant's prior conviction for impeachment purposes under Rule 609. The appellant has offered no authority, and we have discovered none, which indicates that a ruling under 404(b) governs a decision or forecloses analysis in a later-presented Rule 609 question.

This lack of support for appellant's position is not surprising in that the respective rules operate in two completely different situations. In a criminal setting, evidence offered under Rule 404(b) is substantive evidence against the accused, i.e., it is part of the government's case offered to prove his guilt beyond a reasonable doubt. Rule 609 evidence on the other hand has to do with the accused's ability to tell the truth when testifying on his or her own behalf. While both rules speak of "probative value" and "prejudice," it is critical to note that evidence offered under the respective rules is probative as to different matters. The probative character of evidence under Rule 609 has to do with credibility of a witness, while 404(b) "probativeness" essentially goes to the question of whether or not the accused committed the crime charged. Any similarity or overlap in the standards of admissibility under the respective rules is irrelevant because the rules apply to completely distinct situations.

Having found the district court's earlier ruling under Rule 404(b) irrelevant in terms of the subsequent ruling under Rule 609, we turn to the specific ruling appealed. When he testified on direct examination, the appellant admitted that he had a prior conviction for possession of cocaine, but attempted to minimize his guilt regarding the prior conviction.[3] The government thereafter properly cross-examined the appellant in an effort to clarify the facts of the prior conviction and impeach his direct testimony. This cross-examination included the offer and receipt into evidence of a certified copy of the appellant's prior conviction. The appellant in effect opened the door for the government's cross-examination by attempting to explain away or minimize his guilt. Swanson, 9 F.3d at 1357 (citing United States v. Amahia, 825 F.2d 177, 180 (8th Cir.1987)). Viewing the entire record before us, we cannot say that the prior conviction had no bearing on the case or that the district court abused its discretion in admitting the same. United States v. Sykes, 977 F.2d 1242, 1246 (8th Cir.1992).[4]

.   .   .

Accordingly, we affirm the appellant's conviction and sentence.

NOTES

1. On the probative value of different kinds of offenses to credibility, see Ely, J., concurring in Burg v. United States, 406 F.2d 235, 238 (9th Cir.1969): "It is fiction, if not hypocrisy, to say, for example, that proof that a man has been

---

3. Appellant testified to the effect that he was arrested and pled guilty to the possession charge, but the cocaine actually belonged to someone else.

4. This conclusion is strengthened by the fact that the district court gave the jury a clear cautionary instruction that it could not consider the evidence of the prior conviction in determining whether the defendant committed the act charged in the indictment. The court instructed that the jury may only use the evidence of the prior conviction "to help you decide whether to believe his testimony and how much weight to give it."

convicted of drunk driving 'affects his credibility' if he should be on trial for a crime such as the use of the mails to defraud. One might be convicted of a felony for failing to support an undeserving wife. Would proof of this fact 'affect his credibility' in a subsequent prosecution for violating the Selective Service Act or provisions of federal laws regulating the sale of securities? It would not, in my judgment, but it surely might prejudice him in the eyes of a juror who had been aggrieved by a neglectful husband." McIntosh v. Pittsburgh Ry., 247 A.2d 467, 468 (Pa.1968): Judgment for defendant in collision case reversed: "We are hard put to understand what relevance appellant's twelve year old pandering conviction could have in helping a jury ascertain whether his description of a trolley collision was true. After being released from prison appellant for eight years had apparently led an exemplary life. It seems unfair to plague appellant with his prior misdeeds in any way at all at this point. Certainly it is unfair to handicap him in an attempt to make a damage recovery which might properly be due him."

2. Has the court in United States v. Valencia correctly interpreted and applied Fed.R.Evid. 609(a) as it read at the time of the defendant's trial? The court observes: "Viewing the entire record before us, we cannot say that the prior conviction had no bearing on the case or that the district court abused its discretion in admitting the same." Would the decision be correct under Rule 609(a) as amended in 1990? See Gold, Impeachment by Conviction Evidence: Judicial Discretion and the Politics of Rule 609, 15 Card.L.Rev. 2295, 2322–23 (1994), remarking that many courts in applying Rule 609(a) fail to give serious attention to the potential for prejudice.

3. At a later time, thorough consideration will be given to Fed.R.Evid. 404, referred to in the Valencia decision, and the "substantive" use of evidence of other crimes. See infra pp. 808–75. For the moment attention is directed to the relationship between Fed.R.Evid. 609 and Fed.R.Evid. 404 and the adequacy of the Valencia court's discussion of that relationship. Suppose at an in limine hearing the trial court is called upon to consider the admissibility of evidence of a conviction for both substantive and impeachment purposes. In assessing the probative value of the evidence, should not the court take into account both its probative value as impeaching evidence and its probative value on the issue of whether the defendant committed the crime with which he is charged? Probative value for each use may be different, but probative value for the combined uses is likely to be greater than for either alone. The prejudice against which probative value is to be weighed could be seen as the danger that the jury, learning of the prior conviction, will decide to punish the defendant for the other crime rather than determine whether he committed the crime with which he is charged, or decide that the defendant should be put away because the evidence has revealed him to be generally a bad man. The combined probative value for substantive and impeachment uses of the conviction might or might not justify running the risk of this prejudice.

However, a criminal defendant is not required to introduce evidence until the prosecution has made out a prima facie case against him. As to his own testimony, as we have seen, supra p. 267, he is entitled to postpone decision whether to testify until the end of his case. Thus in an in limine hearing, if the court is called upon to decide whether the prosecutor may introduce evidence of a conviction in its case in chief, it must proceed on the assumption that the defendant will not take the stand. The probative value of the conviction for purposes of impeachment will have to be left out of account. However, if the defendant in fact does take the stand, it would seem that the ruling on substantive use could then be reconsidered. Thus, in Valencia, the court having excluded, in limine, the conviction evidence under 404, but the defendant having decided to take the stand, possibly a request should have been made for reconsideration of the original ruling.

It has just been suggested that the prejudice that probative value is to be weighed against is the danger that the jury will lose interest in deciding whether beyond a reasonable doubt the defendant committed the crime with which he is charged and decide instead that he should be punished for the other offense or because he is a bad man. If on a consideration of probative value for both substantive and impeaching uses it is decided that the risk of such prejudice should be run and the evidence admitted, then the only instruction to be given to the jury is that they should not rest their verdict upon one of these impermissible bases: no instruction should be given forbidding them from making evidentiary use of the prior conviction by way of inference through a bad character thus revealed. But objection is commonly voiced to the view of prejudice just suggested, and it is often insisted that prejudice lies both in a decision to punish the defendant because he committed the other offense or is a bad man, and in the substantive use of the conviction as character evidence. Whether the narrower or broader view of prejudice is adopted will affect both the outcome of balancing—if the narrower view is taken, there will be less in the prejudice pan of the scale—and what the court should say to the jury if the evidence is admitted.

It is to be noted that if the conditions for admissibility in Rule 609 are met, that rule permits the use of character evidence for impeaching purposes. If this is permitted, is there any reason to prohibit such use for substantive purposes?

Consider whether the foregoing observations are in harmony with the court's discussion in State v. Brown, 782 P.2d 1013, 1019–21 (Wash.1989): The defendant was prosecuted for theft. The prosecution evidence tended to show that defendant had offered to sell the victim a TV set at a very low price, had the victim drive to a certain part of town, took the victim's money saying he would be right back with the merchandise and then never returned. The prosecution offered evidence of two prior convictions of the defendant for thefts in which the same modus operandi was employed. The trial court admitted these convictions both for substantive and impeachment purposes.

> We said in Laureano, 682 P.2d 889, that "when a prior conviction has been admitted as substantive evidence under ER 404(b), that same conviction is admissible as a matter of course for impeachment purposes under ER 609(a)." Upon reflection, we conclude that this statement is incorrect. We have said that if evidence is admitted under ER 404(b), the trial court should explain to the jury the purpose for which the evidence is admitted, and should give a cautionary instruction that the evidence is to be considered for no other purpose.... Similarly, where evidence of prior crimes is admitted under ER 609(a) for the purpose of impeaching a witness' credibility, an instruction should be given that the conviction is admissible only on the issue of the witness' credibility, and, where the defendant is the witness impeached, may not be considered on the issue of guilt.... Due to the potentially prejudicial nature of prior conviction evidence, these limiting instructions are of critical importance. Therefore, where evidence of a defendant's prior conviction is admitted for a substantive purpose under ER 404(b) and the evidence is also ruled admissible for impeachment purposes, the jury should be given limiting instructions as to each purpose for which it may consider the evidence.

> From this premise, the specific requirements of ER 609, and our cases interpreting ER 609, it follows that not all convictions admissible under ER 404(b) are also automatically admissible under ER 609....

Where a prior conviction was not punishable by death or imprisonment in excess of 1 year, and was not a crime involving dishonesty or false statement, it is not admissible under ER 609 regardless of its admissibility under ER 404(b). The State is therefore not always entitled to an instruction that the conviction evidence may be considered by the jury for the purpose of weighing the defendant's credibility merely because the evidence is admissible under ER 404(b). "Simply because a defendant has committed a crime in the past does not mean the defendant will lie when testifying." State v. Jones, 101 Wash.2d 113, 119, 677 P.2d 131 (1984). A defendant's credibility, key to the believability of his testimony, is quite a different matter from the purposes for which evidence is admitted under ER 404(b).

Where a jury is instructed that the prior crime may be considered on the question of the defendant's credibility as well as on the issue of identity, the reasonable assumption is that the jury will place even greater weight on that prior conviction than it would if the jury were instructed to consider the evidence only for identity purposes. Therefore, where the prior crime does not meet ER 609's requirements independently of admissibility under ER 404(b), the defendant could be exposed to particularly prejudicial evidence to which the jury may ascribe undue weight under a rule that any crime admissible under ER 404(b) is automatically admissible under ER 609.

Of course, ER 609(a)(1) requires the trial judge to balance probative evidence against prejudicial effect before admitting crimes punishable by death or imprisonment in excess of 1 year which do not involve dishonesty or false statement, and ER 404(b) also requires the trial court to balance probative value against prejudicial effect. On the one hand, because the trial court has already engaged in this balancing for ER 404(b) purposes and the evidence is admitted substantively in the State's case in chief, it seems little additional prejudice to the defendant would result from admitting the evidence for impeachment purposes as well.... Moreover, a major factor to be considered in the balancing procedure under ER 609(a)(1) is a comparison of the importance of the jury hearing the defendant's account of events with the importance that it know of his prior convictions.... A defendant faced with impeachment evidence of convictions may elect not to testify.... Where the evidence has already been admitted for ER 404(b) purposes, however, there is little additional effect on the defendant's decision to testify which would result from the evidence being admitted for impeachment purposes.

On the other hand, ER 609 applies by its terms only to convictions admissible "[f]or the purpose of attacking the credibility of a witness". Unlike the balancing procedure for evidence offered for a purpose under ER 404(b), the balancing process for ER 609 purposes must be made with this principle in mind.

Therefore, we conclude that once a prior conviction has been ruled admissible under ER 404(b), the trial court should consider this fact when it engages in the balancing procedure required under ER 609(a)(1). As part of the court's comparison of the importance that the jury hear the defendant's account of events with the importance that the jury know of the prior conviction ... the trial court should consider the fact that [because] the jury has already learned of the prior conviction, its admissibility for impeachment purposes is unlikely to affect the defendant's decision to take the stand, and therefore there may be little additional prejudice resulting from ruling the prior conviction admissible for impeachment purposes under ER 609(a)(1)....

Where the prior conviction is sought to be admitted under ER 609(a)(2), however, the trial court is obliged to determine its admissibility as a crime involving dishonesty or false statement independently of its decision to admit the conviction evidence under ER 404(b).[1]

4. In Valencia the conviction used to impeach was for the same crime as that with which defendant was charged—dealing in drugs. In many cases the similarity of offenses plays a prominent role in the judgment of potential prejudice: the greater the similarity, the greater the likelihood of prejudice. In State v. Brunson, 625 A.2d 1085 (N.J.1993), the court, overruling earlier decisions, held that when the conviction offered to impeach is of a similar crime, the evidence must be "sanitized" in the sense that the jury must be told only of the degree, number and date of the convictions, but not what sort of crime the defendant was convicted of. See also Commonwealth v. Richardson, 674 S.W.2d 515 (Ky.1984); State v. Rutchik, 341 N.W.2d 639, 646 (Wis.1984). Does concern with similarity imply a certain view of the nature of the prejudice to be avoided? For discussion of similarity in the context of substantive use of other crime evidence, see infra pp. 848–53.

5. In Valencia, the defendant admitted his conviction of the prior drug offense on direct examination, evidently because it was clear that the prosecutor planned to bring it out on cross examination. See Advisory Committee's Note to Rule 609 stating that this is permissible to "remove the sting." In admitting the conviction, however, the defendant added the comment that in the earlier case the cocaine in fact belonged to someone else. Could the prosecutor have objected to this exculpatory comment? When a conviction is introduced for impeachment purposes, should it be permissible to go into the facts of the crime itself, either to enhance or reduce the impeaching effect of the conviction standing alone? Concern here must be with consumption of time and distraction from central issues. The introduction of evidence in addition to the conviction can lead to an entire secondary trial. See Fed.R.Evid. 608(b), infra p. 434, on impeachment by evidence of bad acts when there has been no conviction. United States v. Robinson, 8 F.3d 398, 409–10 (7th Cir.1993): Error to permit prosecutor to go beyond the conviction to bring out details of prior criminal conduct; on direct examination defendant had admitted the conviction, but said that he was not guilty of the crime of which had been convicted.

6. Rule 609(a) distinguishes the situation of the criminal defendant as witness from other situations—the criminal defendant's witnesses other than the defendant himself, prosecution witnesses, the parties in civil cases as witnesses, other witnesses in civil cases—and creates different standards of admissibility for these two categories. Before the 1990 amendment, no consideration was paid to prejudice except in the case of the criminal defendant. What is the prejudice in the case of witnesses other than the criminal defendant? See People v. Woodard, 590 P.2d 391, 396 (Cal. 1979), where the court held, under the California Evidence Code, that the trial court must exercise its discretion to exclude unduly prejudicial convictions offered to impeach not only when the witness is a criminal defendant, but in all cases. Regarding the prejudice that may occur when the witness is not a criminal defendant, the court observed:

It may be true that a nonparty witness suffers no legally cognizable prejudice by impeachment with prior felony convictions and he may not refuse to testify on this ground. However, a *party* in a case, civil or

---

1. Footnote omitted.

criminal, may nevertheless be prejudiced by the admission of a nonparty witness' prior felony convictions. Where the resolution of a critical issue depends on whose testimony is to be believed, a jury may act arbitrarily and give little weight to the testimony of a witness whose character has been brought into question by the introduction of prior felony convictions. If the witness is called by a defendant in a criminal trial, a reasonable doubt may be resolved against the accused because he associates with felons, even though the prosecution has not proven beyond a reasonable doubt that the defendant committed the offense.... In addition, the possibility of prejudice may influence a party so that a witness, who might otherwise present relevant evidence, is not called....

7. In Luce v. United States, 469 U.S. 38, 43 (1984), the Court held that "to raise and preserve for review the claim of improper impeachment with a prior conviction, a defendant must testify." "Requiring that a defendant testify in order to preserve Rule 609(a) claims, will enable the reviewing court to determine the impact any erroneous impeachment may have had in light of the record as a whole; it will also tend to discourage making such motions solely to 'plant' reversible error in the event of conviction." See also State v. Brown, 782 P.2d 1013, 1018–25 (Wash.1989), adopting Luce as state law, although recognizing that not all states have done so; Annot. 80 A.L.R. 4th 1028 (1990).

8. Are there constitutional limits to impeaching by prior conviction? State v. Minnieweather, 781 P.2d 401 (Or.Ct.App.1989), was a prosecution for burglary in which a prior burglary conviction was admitted to impeach the defendant. The court interpreted state law—the same as Fed.R.Evid. 609—to allow admission without any consideration of prejudice. Nevertheless, the court held, use of the conviction to impeach did not violate the state or the federal constitution. Compare People v. Castro, 696 P.2d 111 (Cal.1985), where state law was interpreted to require balancing, to some extent because the opposite conclusion might result in a federal constitutional violation. State v. Santiago, 492 P.2d 657, 659–62 (Haw.1971), holds that the introduction of a criminal defendant's prior convictions for the purpose of impeachment, at least when he has not introduced evidence for the sole purpose of establishing his credibility, violates due process, specifying particularly the defendant's right to testify in his own behalf. On the other hand, Dixon v. United States, 287 A.2d 89, 92–96 (D.C.App.), cert. denied, 407 U.S. 926 (1972), rejects constitutional challenge based on the Due Process Clause and the Sixth Amendment right to trial by an impartial jury. See generally Nichol, Prior Crime Impeachment of Criminal Defendants: A Constitutional Analysis of Rule 609, 82 W.Va.L.Rev. 391 (1980).

9. Impeachment by conviction in California has a special convoluted history of its own. Starting with an Evidence Code provision that seemed flatly to admit felony convictions to impeach, the state Supreme Court found in another provision of the code authority to balance probative value against prejudice. In a long line of cases, it spelled out particular consequences of this balancing process. Then, the state constitution was amended to provide that any prior felony conviction could be used without limitation for purposes of impeachment. Notwithstanding this amendment, the state Supreme Court found in another provision of the constitutional amendment, permission to continue balancing. The story is set forth in People v. Castro, 696 P.2d 111 (Cal.1985); People v. Wheeler, 841 P.2d 938 (Cal.1992); Note, Rush to Judgment: Criminal Propensity Clothed as Credibility Evidence in the Post–Proposition 8 Era of California Criminal Law, 15 Whittier L.Rev. 241 (1994).

10. For the legislative history of Fed.R.Evid. 609, see Green v. Bock Laundry Mach. Co., 490 U.S. 504, 511–12 (1989); Gold, Impeachment by Conviction Evidence, 15 Card.L.Rev. 2295, 2298–2309 (1994).

Cree v. Hatcher

United States Court of Appeals, Third Circuit, 1992.
969 F.2d 34, cert. dismissed, 506 U.S. 1017 (1992).

■ Before STAPLETON and MANSMANN, CIRCUIT JUDGES, and POLLACK, DISTRICT JUDGE.

OPINION OF THE COURT

■ LOUIS H. POLLACK, DISTRICT JUDGE.

This diversity medical malpractice case arose in the Western District of Pennsylvania. The case comes before us on appeal of a defense verdict and the district court's subsequent denial of plaintiff's motion for a new trial. Because we conclude that the district court permitted one of plaintiff's expert witnesses to be impeached on the basis of inadmissible evidence, we will reverse and remand for a new trial.

I.

Plaintiff Patricia Cree, appellant before this court, first obtained the professional services of defendant Kim Allen Hatcher, M.D., in February 1982. On February 3, 1986, defendant performed a gynecological examination of plaintiff. At the time of the examination, plaintiff complained of discomfort, dryness, and bleeding after sexual intercourse. As part of the examination, defendant performed a Pap test, a procedure in which cells are sampled from the cervix for the purpose of laboratory examination. On February 12, 1986, plaintiff was informed that laboratory analysis had revealed her Pap smear to be Class II, indicating benign atypia. Defendant did not tell plaintiff the implications of the Class II result, but did request that plaintiff return in six months for an additional test.

In the months following the February 1986 examination, plaintiff moved; as a result, she did not return to defendant for a subsequent examination. In December 1986, however, she was examined by another physician; at that time, her Pap smear was found to be Class IV, a classification which strongly suggests the presence of cancer. Plaintiff was then referred to a specialist, who, on January 22, 1987, diagnosed plaintiff as suffering from squamous cell carcinoma of the cervix. Six days later, plaintiff underwent a radical hysterectomy, appendectomy, and pelvic lymphadenectomy.

Plaintiff initiated the present action on December 1, 1988, claiming that defendant had negligently failed to diagnose and monitor her condition. Trial began on February 7, 1991. After a five-day trial, the jury was unable to reach a verdict, and the district court declared a mistrial. A second trial commenced on May 28, 1991. At the conclusion of the six-day trial, the jury returned a verdict for defendant. Plaintiff moved for a new trial, and the district court denied the motion on July 9, 1991. The present appeal ensued.

II.

Plaintiff alleges three grounds for a new trial. First, she argues that the district court improperly permitted her expert pathologist to be impeached by evidence of a prior conviction. Second, she contends that the district court erred in refusing to permit her to rebut what she claims was surprise evidence presented by defendant in the course of the second trial. Finally, she claims that the district court improperly limited the scope of her expert's testimony. Of these three asserted grounds for a new trial, only the first need be discussed in detail.

Plaintiff's expert pathologist, Hernando Salazar, M.D., had been convicted in 1984 of the misdemeanor of willful failure to file a federal income tax return, in violation of 26 U.S.C. § 7203. Prior to calling Dr. Salazar, plaintiff filed a motion in limine to preclude defendant from introducing evidence of the conviction. After hearing argument, the court denied the motion. Plaintiff, without waiving her objection to the evidence's admissibility, then brought out the conviction on direct examination. On voir dire examination on qualifications, defendant reinforced that Dr. Salazar had pled guilty to the offense, and that he had been incarcerated for a term of six months. Defendant again referred to the conviction during closing argument. Plaintiff now contends that the denial of her motion in limine was reversible error.

... The district court premised its conclusion that the conviction was admissible on subsection (2) of [Rule 609(a)] ..., concluding that the willful failure to file a federal income tax return was a crime involving dishonesty or false statement. In so deciding, the court relied on the four reported cases addressing the admissibility of violation of section 7203 under Rule 609(a)(2). See Dean v. Trans World Airlines, Inc., 924 F.2d 805, 811 (9th Cir.1991); United States v. Gellman, 677 F.2d 65, 66 (11th Cir.1982); Zukowski v. Dunton, 650 F.2d 30, 34 (4th Cir.1981); United States v. Klein, 438 F.Supp. 485, 487 (S.D.N.Y.1977).

We disagree with the rationale of those cases, and therefore reverse. The Conference Committee that reported Rule 609(a)(2), as originally adopted, described the scope of the Rule as follows:

> By the phrase "dishonesty and false statement" the Conference means crimes such as perjury or subornation of perjury, false statement, criminal fraud, embezzlement, or false pretense, or any other offense in the nature of crimen falsi, the commission of which involves some element of deceit, untruthfulness, or falsification bearing on the accused's propensity to testify truthfully.

H.R.Conf.Rep. No. 1597, 93d Cong., 2d Sess. 9, reprinted in 1974 U.S.C.C.A.N. 7098, 7103. Unlike other crimes evidence of which is admissible for the purpose of impeachment, evidence of crimes involving dishonesty or false statement is automatically admissible; the district court is without discretion to weigh the prejudicial effect of admitting the evidence against its probative value. See United States v. Wong, 703 F.2d 65, 68 (3d Cir.), cert. denied, 464 U.S. 842, 104 S.Ct. 140, 78 L.Ed.2d 132 (1983). Because the district court lacks discretion to engage in balancing, Rule 609(a)(2) must be interpreted narrowly to apply only to those crimes that, in the words of the Conference Committee, bear on a witness's propensity to testify truthfully. See United States v. Fearwell, 595 F.2d 771, 777 (D.C.Cir.1978).

As interpreted in this Circuit, section 7203 is not such a crime. In 1980, at the time of Dr. Salazar's offense, section 7203 provided:

> Any person required under this title to pay any estimated tax or tax, or required by this title or by regulations made under authority thereof to make a return ..., keep any records, or supply any information, who willfully fails to pay such estimated tax or tax, make such return, keep such records, or supply such information, at the time or times required by law or regulations, shall, in addition to other penalties provided by law, be guilty of a misdemeanor and, upon conviction thereof, shall be fined not

more than $10,000, or imprisoned not more than 1 year, or both, together with the costs of prosecution....

26 U.S.C.A. § 7203 (West 1967) (superseded). We have previously explored the content of section 7203's willfulness requirement in United States v. Greenlee, 517 F.2d 899 (3d Cir.), cert. denied, 423 U.S. 985, 96 S.Ct. 391, 46 L.Ed.2d 301 (1975). In that case, we rejected defendant's contention that "the evil purpose requirement demands that defendant have acted with some purpose to conceal his tax liability from the government." Id. at 904. Instead, we concluded: "[T]he use of terms such as 'bad purpose' does not imply that the government must prove more than that the defendant acted with a guilty mind, i.e., voluntarily and with the deliberate intent to violate the law." Id.; see also United States v. Klee, 494 F.2d 394, 395 (9th Cir.) (concluding that in a section 7203 prosecution the government need not prove "an intent to defraud the government, or to conceal from the government facts relevant to a determination of the accused's tax liability"), cert. denied, 419 U.S. 835, 95 S.Ct. 62, 42 L.Ed.2d 61 (1974). In light of the conclusion that a section 7203 defendant need not have intended to conceal his tax liability or deceive the government, we do not believe that being convicted of violating section 7203 necessarily connotes dishonesty or a false statement within the narrow ambit of Rule 609(a)(2).[1] In so concluding, we disagree with United States v. Klein, in which the court concluded that willful failure to file a federal income tax return involved the making of a false statement and therefore fell within Rule 609(a)(2). See Klein, 438 F.Supp. at 487.

In United States v. Gellman, the Eleventh Circuit appeared to provide an alternate justification for concluding that a conviction under section 7203 falls within Rule 609(a)(2), stating that violation of the statute was "sufficiently reprehensible to meet the exception of Rule 609(a)(2)." See Gellman, 677 F.2d at 66 (quoting Zukowski v. Dunton, 650 F.2d 30, 34 (4th Cir.1981)). To the extent that the Gellman court provided a second rationale, we decline to adopt the proposed standard. The proper test for admissibility under Rule 609(a)(2) does not measure the severity or reprehensibility of the crime, but rather focuses on the witness's propensity for falsehood, deceit, or deception. To conclude that evidence of a crime was admissible under Rule 609(a)(2) simply because the crime was reprehensible would do violence to both the text of Rule 609(a)(2) and the interpretive framework suggested by the Conference Committee.[2]

We conclude that the district court erred in denying plaintiff's motion in limine and permitting the impeachment of Dr. Salazar. We further conclude that the improper impeachment of a key expert witness prejudiced plaintiff. We therefore reverse and remand for a new trial.

NOTES

1. In accord with the Cree decision, it appears generally to be held that if the conviction offered to impeach falls within Rule 609(a)(2), no balancing of

1. It is certainly possible, and perhaps even likely, that in some instances individuals who willfully fail to file federal income tax returns do so with the conscious intent to conceal their tax liability from the government. For the purposes of Rule 609(a)(2), however, the manner in which a particular defendant commits a crime is irrelevant; what matters is whether dishonesty or false statement is an element of the statutory offense. See United States v. Lewis, 626 F.2d 940, 946 (D.C.Cir.1980). [Footnotes by the court, renumbered. Some footnotes omitted.]

2. It is worth noting that because a conviction under section 7203 is not punishable by a term of imprisonment in excess of one year, a witness other than a criminal defendant who has been convicted under section 7203 may never be impeached under Rule 609(a)(1) on the basis of that conviction.

probative value against prejudice is required or permitted. This was the view taken before the 1990 amendment of Rule 609, which did not change the words of 609(a)(2). Some commentators have asked why there should not be consideration of prejudice even when the conviction falls under 602(a)(2), since in a particular case prejudice may greatly outweigh probative value. In laying down a general rule based upon the probative value of convictions involving dishonesty or false statement, the legislature could not take into account the prejudice that might exist in a particular case. In view of this fact, would it not make sense to invoke the court's excluding power under Rule 403? But this argument is harder to make since the 1990 amendment, because Congress had an opportunity to address the question directly, but did not do so. See Gold, Impeachment by Conviction Evidence, 15 Card.L.Rev. 2295, 2320 (1994).

If it is settled that there is no balancing under 609(a)(2), is a constitutional question presented? Does the fact that probative value for credibility of crimes involving dishonesty or false statement as a class is considerable allay constitutional doubts that, as indicated supra p. 423, exist in the case of impeachment by other sorts of crimes? See State v. Brown, 782 P.2d 1013, 1021 (Wash.1989), stressing that under Rule 609(a)(1), the balancing procedure must be "a meaningful one directly related to the particular circumstances of the case." See also Rock v. Arkansas, supra p. 256, striking down a per se rule excluding post-hypnotic memories.

2. Rule 609(a)(2) erects a preliminary issue controlling the admissibility of evidence, as to whether a conviction "involved dishonesty or false statement." The opinion in Cree takes the position that the question thus posed concerns only whether dishonesty or false statement is an element of the offense, not whether in the particular case the defendant committed the offense with an intent to deceive or conceal. Other courts look beyond the elements of the offense to the particular facts. See State v. Wight, 765 P.2d 12, 18 (Utah App.1988); United States v. Dorsey, 591 F.2d 922, 933–36 (D.C.Cir.1978); United States v. Hayes, 553 F.2d 824, 826–28 (2d Cir.), cert. denied, 434 U.S. 867 (1977). As indicated supra p. 422, this question also arises in connection with determining probative value under 609(a)(1). What evidence should the court consider in making the determination? If the conviction is to be admitted, what evidence may be put before the jury?

3. United States v. Wilson, 985 F.2d 348, 351 (7th Cir.1993), disagrees with the Cree decision as to whether failure to file an income tax return falls within 609(a)(2). State v. Brown, 782 P.2d 1013 (Wash.1989): Convictions for theft, including robbery, involve "dishonesty" and so fall within 609(a)(2); purely assaultive crimes do not. Logan v. Drew, 790 F.Supp. 181 (N.D.Ill.1992): Illegal use of credit card within 609(a)(2). But see United States v. Mejia-Alarcon, 995 F.2d 982, 988–90 (10th Cir.), cert. denied, 510 U.S. 927 (1993): Illegally obtaining food stamps not within 609(a)(2). United States v. Brackeen, 969 F.2d 827 (9th Cir.1992) (en banc): Bank robbery not within 609(a)(2). United States v. Fearwell, 595 F.2d 771, 777 (D.C.Cir.1978), held that a conviction for attempted petty larceny did not fall within Rule 609(a)(2): "Rule 609(a)(2) is to be construed narrowly; it is not carte blanche for admission on an undifferentiated basis of all previous convictions for purposes of impeachment; rather, precisely because it involves no discretion on the part of the trial court, in the sense that all crimes meeting its stipulation of dishonesty or false statement must be permitted to be used, for impeachment purposes, Rule 609(a)(2) must be confined ... to a 'narrow subset of crimes'—those that bear *directly* upon the accused's propensity to testify truthfully."

4. In regard to convictions more than ten years old, the subject of Rule 609(b), the cases are clear that in view of the language and legislative history of the rule, evidence of these convictions should be admitted "very rarely" and under "exceptional circumstances," and that there is a "presumption" against their use. See United States v. Cathey, 591 F.2d 268, 274–77 (5th Cir.1979) (error in income tax prosecution to admit evidence of 16–year–old military conviction for larceny); United States v. Sims, 588 F.2d 1145 (6th Cir.1978) (error to admit evidence of 21–year–old burglary conviction and 12–year–old conviction for transporting stolen vehicle). In Lenard v. Argento, 699 F.2d 874, 895 (7th Cir.), cert. denied, 464 U.S. 815 (1983), the court was able without difficulty to uphold the trial court's determination that the introduction of a civil plaintiff's 24–year-old conviction for voluntary manslaughter to impeach him "would be highly prejudicial and not in the interest of justice" and so should be prohibited. United States v. Pritchard, 973 F.2d 905 (11th Cir.1992), upholding use of thirteen-year-old conviction for burglary to impeach defendant in prosecution for bank robbery, seems wrongly decided.

5. As to impeachment when the witness has pleaded nolo, see United States v. Williams, 642 F.2d 136 (5th Cir.1981) (impeachment permissible); Singleton v. State, 622 So.2d 935 (Ala.1993) (impeachment impermissible).

6. A conviction used to impeach is hearsay under Fed.R.Evid. 801, but comes within the exception provided in 803(22). In California, the parallel hearsay exception—Cal. Evid. Code § 1300—applies only to convictions for felonies, so that a conviction for a misdemeanor is inadmissible because of the hearsay rule, even though admissible under the principles relating to impeachment by conviction. People v. Wheeler, 841 P.2d 938, 941–44 (Cal.1992), supra p. 423.

7. Consider the problem presented by State v. Ponton, 399 P.2d 30, 32 (Or.1965), cert. denied, 382 U.S. 1014 (1966):

> In the case at bar the defendant had been convicted of a felony in Nevada. During the trial the state was not in a position to prove that fact. Although it had a fragmentary record of the defendant's plea of guilty, the state had neglected to obtain an exemplified copy of the Nevada judgment in time for the trial. (The record shows that when the time came for sentencing, the proof of the Nevada conviction was in proper form.) In cross-examining the defendant, the deputy trying the case asked the defendant whether he had not been convicted of a felony, in addition to a petit larceny conviction which he had brought up in his direct examination. The defendant denied the felony conviction and his denial was challenged. The defendant's counsel immediately moved for a mistrial. The trial court properly instructed the jury that there was no proof of the former conviction, and told them to disregard the mention of it.
>
> The state cannot be charged with intentional misconduct in asking about the Nevada conviction. The district attorney's office had no reason to believe that the defendant would lie under oath and deny that he had been convicted of a felony in Nevada. When the defendant elected to deny the matter, the deputy district attorney was entitled to ask him if he was sure, and whether he was expressing himself accurately.

It is not clear that the reasoning of the Ponton decision would be universally accepted. See People v. Perez, 373 P.2d 617, 621–23 (Cal.1962); State v. Beard, 444 P.2d 651 (Wash.1968).

8. It is settled that due process is violated when impeachment is attempted by a prior conviction obtained in contravention of the defendant's right to counsel. A majority of Justices adopt this position in Loper v. Beto, 405 U.S. 473 (1972).

Before Loper, in Burgett v. Texas, 389 U.S. 109 (1967), the Court held that a conviction resulting from a trial in which defendant was deprived of counsel could not be used to enhance punishment under a recidivist statute. In Loper, Justice Stewart, writing for a plurality of Justices, indicates a distinction between Loper and two other cases. "This is not a case where the record of a prior conviction was used for the purpose of directly rebutting a specific false statement made from the witness stand.... [S]ee Harris v. New York, 401 U.S. 222 ...; Walder v. United States, 347 U.S. 62.... The previous convictions were used, rather, simply in an effort to convict Loper by blackening his character and thus damaging his general credibility in the eyes of the jury." 405 U.S. at 482 n. 11. For the holdings in Harris and Walder, see infra p. 463.

c.   *Prior Bad Acts*

People v. Sorge

Court of Appeals of New York, 1950.
301 N.Y. 198, 93 N.E.2d 637.

■ FULD, JUDGE. In this prosecution for the crime of abortion, the evidence given on behalf of the People was more than sufficient to justify the verdict of guilt— for the conflicting testimony of the victim and of the defendant but presented a question of veracity and credibility for the jury. Accordingly, an affirmance is compelled, unless prejudicial error was committed by the district attorney in conducting his cross-examination of defendant. He interrogated her about abortions which she had allegedly performed upon four other women and, after she had answered his questions in the negative, pressed her further as to whether she had not signed a statement admitting that she had aborted one of the women, as to whether that particular operation had not furnished the predicate for her plea of guilty to the crime of practicing medicine without a license, and as to whether she had not been present while a fifth abortion had been performed.

There can, of course, be no doubt as to the propriety of cross-examining a defendant concerning the commission of other specific criminal or immoral acts. A defendant, like any other witness, may be "interrogated upon cross-examination in regard to any vicious or criminal act of his life" that has a bearing on his credibility as a witness. People v. Webster, 139 N.Y. 73, 84, 34 N.E. 730, 733; see, also, People v. Jones, 297 N.Y. 459, 74 N.E.2d 173; People v. Brown, 284 N.Y. 753, 31 N.E.2d 511; People v. Johnston, 228 N.Y. 332, 340, 127 N.E. 186, 188; People v. Casey, 72 N.Y. 393, 398–399; see, also, 8 Wigmore on Evidence [3d Ed.] § 2277, p. 453. It does not matter that the offenses or the acts inquired about are similar in nature and character to the crime for which the defendant is standing trial. See People v. Jones, supra, 297 N.Y. 459, 74 N.E.2d 173; murder prosecution, defendant interrogated as to another murder.... And if the questions have basis in fact and are asked by the district attorney in good faith, they are not rendered improper merely because of their number. Entitled to delve into past misdeeds, the prosecutor may not arbitrarily be shackled by the circumstance that the defendant has pursued a specialized field of crime and has committed many offenses. See, e.g., People v. Brown, supra, 284 N.Y. 753, 31 N.E.2d 511; cf. People v. Goldstein, 295 N.Y. 61, 65, 65 N.E.2d 169, 170; People v. Thau, 219 N.Y. 39, 42, 113 N.E. 556, 557, 3 A.L.R. 1537.

Nor is it improper for a district attorney to continue his cross-examination about a specific crime after a defendant has denied committing it. As long as he acts in good faith, in the hope of inducing the witness to abandon his negative answers, the prosecutor may question further. See People v. Jones, supra, 297 N.Y. 459, 74 N.E.2d 173; People v. Weiss, 129 App.Div. 671, 676, 114 N.Y.S. 236, 240; 3 Wigmore on Evidence, op. cit. § 1023, pp. 700–701. In other words, a negative response will not fob off further interrogation of the witness himself, for, if it did, the witness would have it within his power to render futile most cross-examination. The rule is clear that while a witness' testimony regarding collateral matters may not be refuted by the calling of other witnesses or by the production of extrinsic evidence (see, e.g., People v. Perry, 277 N.Y. 460, 14 N.E.2d 793; People v. Malkin, 250 N.Y. 185, 164 N.E. 900; People v. Freeman, 203 N.Y. 267, 96 N.E. 413), there is no prohibition against examining the witness himself further on the chance that he may change his testimony or his answer.

This principle covers not only the questions put to defendant which were based upon her prior statement, see People v. Jones, supra, 297 N.Y. 459, 74 N.E.2d 173, but also the questions grounded upon her prior conviction—following her guilty plea—of practicing medicine without a license. Since a witness may be examined properly with respect to criminal acts that have escaped prosecution, there is no reason why indictment followed by conviction should proscribe inquiry as to what those acts were. See People v. Romeo, 273 App.Div. 891, 78 N.Y.S.2d 563; Ochsner v. Commonwealth, 128 Ky. 761, 764, 109 S.W. 326; State v. Rusnak, 108 N.J.L. 84, 90, 154 A. 754; State v. Brames, 154 Wash. 304, 309–311, 282 P. 48. A knowledge of those acts casts light upon the degree of turpitude involved and assists the jury in evaluating the witness' credibility—all the more so in a case such as the present where conviction of a crime such as practicing medicine without a license gives no inkling whatsoever of the acts upon which the charge and conviction against defendant had been predicated. In point of fact, the matters sought to be elicited by the cross-examination were precisely those matters that could have been established by proof of the official record of defendant's conviction—a course which the people could unquestionably have pursued under section 2444 of the Penal Law, Consol.Laws, c. 40. See State v. Brames, supra, 154 Wash. 304, 310, 282 P. 48, involving a statute identical with section 2444.

While, for the reasons outlined above, we cannot single out any questions and say that they were improper as a matter of law, there still remains the problem of whether the cumulative effect of the sustained cross-examination constituted error, despite the propriety of the individual queries. Basic in this connection is the rule that "[t]he manner and extent of the cross-examination lies largely within the discretion of the trial judge." [Citations omitted.] Accordingly, although there may be room for a difference of opinion as to the scope and extent of cross-examination, the wide latitude and the broad discretion that must be vouchsafed to the trial judge, if he is to administer a trial effectively, precludes this court, in the absence of "plain abuse and injustice", La Beau v. People, supra, 34 N.Y. 223, 230, from substituting its judgment for his and from making that difference of opinion, in the difficult and ineffable realm of discretion, a basis for reversal.

We may not here say that prejudice or "injustice" resulted from the district attorney's interrogation or that permitting the vigorous cross-examination constituted "plain abuse." The evidence against defendant was clear and, since the outcome of the case depended almost entirely upon whether the testimony of the victim or of the defendant was credited by the jury, there was good and ample reason to give both sides a relatively free hand on cross-examination in order to afford the jury full opportunity to weigh and evaluate the credibility of each witness.

The judgment should be affirmed.

■ LOUGHRAN, C.J., and LEWIS, CONWAY, DESMOND, DYE and FROESSEL, JJ., concur.

Judgment affirmed.[1]

NOTES

1. People v. Sandoval, 314 N.E.2d 413 (N.Y.1974), sets limits to the cross-examination permitted under People v. Sorge and directs the trial court to

1. The following excerpts from the trial record serve to suggest the nature of the cross-examination.

Q. During the month of January, 1947 did you perform an abortion in your home at 64 Eleanor Street on Mrs. John Peeler, of Willow Springs, North Carolina, also known as "Sandy"? A. No.

. . .

Q. During the month of January, 1947 did you perform an abortion on a Mrs. P.V. Saunders, of Willow Springs, North Carolina?

. . .

A. No.

Q. And during the month of November, 1947 did you perform an abortion on Mrs. L. Myles, of 67 Arch Street, Greenwich, Connecticut?

. . .

A. No.

Q. I ask you again: Did you on April 12, 1948, at approximately 8:30 P.M. perform an abortion on Ruth Schultz, of Jersey City?

. . .

A. No.

Q. I show you this copy of a statement and ask you if it refreshes your recollection.

A. Yes, it does.

Q. Having seen that, will you now tell us whether or not you performed an abortion on Ruth Schultz? A. No.

. . .

Q. And on November 12, 1948 did you tell Loraine Schymanski that you wouldn't perform an abortion for her, but that you had a friend by the name of Margaret in New Jersey, who would do it for $150? A. No.

Q. On November 12, 1948, at nine o'clock in the morning did you, in your automobile bearing license number 4–U–88, pick up Loraine Schymanski in front of the lunch wagon at Meyers Corners? A. No.

Q. Did you a few minutes after that, on the same day, pick up Mae Florentine at the corner of Bradley Avenue and Victory Boulevard? A. I did not, no.

. . .

Q. Did you drive Loraine Schymanski, Mae Florentine, and another girl, to the home of Henrietta Forster, at 15 Fourth Place, South Beach, on November 12th?

A. No, I did not.

. . .

Q. Were you present in the living room of Henrietta Forster at 15 Fourth Place about nine o'clock in the morning of November 12th, 1948 when Mrs. Florentine performed an abortion on Loraine Schymanski in the kitchen of Mrs. Forster's home? A. No.

. . .

Q. You told this jury that on August 20, 1948 you pleaded guilty to the practice of—to the unlawful practice of medicine, is that correct? A. That's right.

Q. And you did that in this court? A. That's right.

Q. And do you remember Judge Walsh reading to you exactly what you pleaded guilty to on that day?

. . .

A. I don't recall the words right now.

Q. Do you remember Judge Walsh sitting up in the same place where he is sitting now and asking you if you, Louise Sorge, pleaded guilty to the crime of unlawful practice of medicine, in that on April 12, 1948, in premises situate 64 Eleanor Street, Egbertville, you administered and used upon one Ruth Schultz a certain instrument, to wit, a rubber tube known as a catheter with intent thereby to procure the miscarriage of the said Ruth Schultz, the same not being necessary to preserve the life of the aforesaid Ruth Schultz or the life of the child with which she was then and there pregnant, against the form of the statute in such case made and provided, and against the peace of the People of the State of New York and their dignity?

Judge Tiernan [defense counsel]: I object to that on the ground it is incompetent, irrelevant and immaterial and that the question is framed purposely for the purpose of inflaming the minds of the jury against the defendant, and I now move for the withdrawal of a juror and the direction of a mistrial.

The Court: Objection overruled. Motion to withdraw and for the declaration of a mistrial denied.

Judge Tiernan: Exception.

The Court: She may say, "Yes, I remember," or "No, I don't."

No, I don't remember those words.

A.

Q. Well, do you remember Judge Walsh saying to you substantially the same as I have read to you? A. Yes, in different words, I remember.

prevent cross-examination into the criminal and immoral conduct of the witness if the prejudicial effect of the inquiry "far outweighs" its probative worth on the issue of credibility. People v. Ocasio, 389 N.E.2d 1101 (N.Y.1979), holds that the protection afforded by the Sandoval decision is not available when the witness is other than a criminal defendant.

2.   Fed.R.Evid. 608(b) provides:

Specific instances of the conduct of a witness, for the purpose of attacking or supporting the witness' credibility, other than conviction of crime as provided in rule 609, may not be proved by extrinsic evidence. They may, however, in the discretion of the court, if probative of truthfulness or untruthfulness, be inquired into on cross-examination of the witness (1) concerning the witness' character for truthfulness or untruthfulness....

Compare 608(b) with Rule 609, which explicitly distinguishes between types of witnesses and between types of crimes. When Rule 609 was amended in 1990, Rule 608(b) was not touched. Does Rule 608(b) permit or require the court to consider the risk of prejudice and to balance prejudice against probative value? If it does, is its standard the same or different from that of Rule 403? Compare the relationship between 609 and 403. In the Sorge opinion, the court attaches no significance to the similarity between the crime with which the defendant was charged and the bad acts used to impeach her. Should similarity figure in weighing prejudice against probative value under Rule 608? See the discussion of similarity in the context of impeachment by conviction, supra p. 422, and substantive use, infra pp. 848–53.

3.   In regard to the specific instances that may be inquired into on cross-examination, Rule 608 requires that they be "probative of truthfulness or untruthfulness" and that the cross-examination concern "character for truthfulness or untruthfulness." Must the specific instances have the same probative value for truthfulness as the convictions described in Rule 609(a)(2)? Rule 608(b) has no provision equivalent to Rule 609(a)(1), dealing with felonies. What is the justification for this difference between 608 and 609?

Recent decisions explore the meaning of "probative of truthfulness." Chnapkova v. Koh, 985 F.2d 79 (2d Cir.1993): In medical malpractice case in which plaintiff-patient's credibility as a witness was in issue, abuse of discretion and not harmless error to forbid asking the plaintiff on cross-examination about her failure to file income tax returns. See supra p. 427, dealing with this same question under Rule 609(a)(2). United States v. Ojeda, 23 F.3d 1473, 1477 (8th Cir.1994): Permissible to ask witness if he once used a false name. Compare People v. Thompson, supra p. 9. United States v. McMillon, 14 F.3d 948, 956 (4th Cir.1994): In prosecution for drug conspiracy, not error to prohibit defendant from cross-examining prosecution witness about his using drugs to manipulate people for sex.

Murphy v. Bonanno, 663 A.2d 505 (D.C.App.1995): Prior incidents in which the plaintiff-witness had filed false insurance claims, made a false statement to obtain a loan and threatened falsely to claim sexual harassment in order to compel settlement of a loan are incidents of the sort that could be inquired into on cross-examination (under D.C. Evidence law, which is not the Federal Rules of Evidence but is influenced by them). State v. Cappo, 345 So.2d 443 (La. 1977): Error not to admit evidence that prosecution witness on another occasion had falsely implicated others in effort to cover up his own crimes. Of course, a prior accusation does not undermine credibility unless it was false.

Should more be required than that there is some probability that the prior accusation was false? Roundtree v. United States, 581 A.2d 315 (D.C.App.1990): Unless "shown convincingly" to be false, Confrontation Clause does not require that inquiry into prior accusations be permitted; determination of admissibility may take into account interest in privacy and concern to avoid distraction of jury; case involved prosecution for sodomy and prior accusations related to other sexual assaults. For discussion of burden of proof in connection with substantive use of other crime evidence, see infra p. 861.

Hawkins v. District of Columbia, 203 A.2d 116, 117–18 (D.C.App.1964): Paternity proceeding in which defendant was found to be the father of A and B, children of W. Held: Trial court committed prejudicial error in excluding defendant's evidence that W had executed sworn complaints that defendant was the father of A, B and C (C being another of W's children), but that a blood grouping test had excluded him as the father of C, with the result that the government dismissed as to C.

> By its exclusion appellant lost any benefit he may have derived, for impeachment purposes, by being able to show that although the mother had originally charged him with being the father of three of her children, he had been excluded as father of one of them.

> To avoid any misconception as to the sole purpose of the testimony of Dr. Hunter, an appropriate instruction by the trial judge, to the effect that this testimony is to be considered only in assessing the credibility of the natural mother and is not probative of whether appellant is the father of the other two children, would go far in eliminating any undue prejudice to the mother and still preserve such testimony for appellant's benefit.

Are instances of sexual behavior relevant to credibility? May they be inquired into under Rule 608(b)? Kansas v. Cook, 578 P.2d 257 (Kan.1978) (irrelevant); State v. Darling, 493 P.2d 216, 223 (1972): Prosecution for abortion; the woman testified on direct that she had been pregnant; held, not error to prohibit the defendant from cross-examining her about the circumstances surrounding her pregnancy, in particular her marital status and the identity of the father. See also State v. Lampshire, 447 P.2d 727, 730 (Wash.1968), a prosecution of a woman for carnal knowledge of several males under the age of 18, where the court held it was not error to prohibit the defendant from cross-examining the males as to other acts of unchastity committed by them. Even if inquiry into sexual behavior is relevant to credibility, are there reasons for prohibiting it? For extensive discussion of this question and also the substantive use of evidence of a victim-witness's sexual behavior, especially in rape cases, and recent statutes addressed to these matters, see infra p. 895.

4. Rule 608(b) provides that specific instances of conduct probative of truthfulness may be inquired into "concerning the witness' character for truthfulness or untruthfulness...." When does the inquiry concern character for truthfulness and when does it concern something else? If it does not concern character, it does not fall under 608(b). Reread the opinion in United States v. Abel, reprinted supra p. 406. The passages reprinted there are followed by others discussing an argument made by respondent regarding Rule 608(b):

> Respondent claims that the prosecutor cross-examined Mills about the gang not to show bias but to offer Mills' membership in the gang as past conduct bearing on his veracity. This was error under Rule 608(b), respondent contends, because the mere fact of Mills' membership, without more, was not sufficiently probative of Mills' character for truthfulness. Respondent cites a second error under the same Rule, contending that Ehle's

rebuttal testimony concerning the gang was extrinsic evidence offered to impugn Mills' veracity, and extrinsic evidence is barred by Rule 608(b).

The Court of Appeals appears to have accepted respondent's argument to this effect, at least in part. It said:

> "Ehle's testimony was not simply a matter of showing that Abel's and Mills' membership in the same organization might 'cause [Mills], consciously or otherwise, to color his testimony.' ... Rather it was to show as well that because Mills and Abel were members of a gang whose members 'will lie to protect the members,' Mills must be lying on the stand." 707 F.2d, at 1016.

It seems clear to us that the proffered testimony with respect to Mills' membership in the Aryan Brotherhood sufficed to show potential bias in favor of respondent; because of the tenets of the organization described, it might also impeach his veracity directly. But there is no rule of evidence which provides that testimony admissible for one purpose and inadmissible for another purpose is thereby rendered inadmissible; quite the contrary is the case. It would be a strange rule of law which held that relevant, competent evidence which tended to show bias on the part of a witness was nonetheless inadmissible because it also tended to show that the witness was a liar.

We intimate no view as to whether the evidence of Mills' membership in an organization having the tenets ascribed to the Aryan Brotherhood would be a specific instance of Mills' conduct which could not be proved against him by extrinsic evidence except as otherwise provided in Rule 608(b). It was enough that such evidence could properly be found admissible to show bias.

469 U.S. 45, 55–56 (1984).

People v. Pearson, 261 N.E.2d 519, 524–25 (Ill.App.1970): Defendant was convicted of taking indecent liberties with two sisters, Cora and Beverly. Prosecution evidence tended to show that defendant had induced Cora, Beverly and their brother Marshall to enter his apartment and that he there engaged in the conduct charged. Beverly and Marshall were witnesses for the prosecution, Cora was in a mental institution at the time of trial. At the time of the alleged offenses, Marshall was 7 years old, Beverly 9, and Cora 11. Prosecution evidence tended to show that after the alleged incident in defendant's apartment, the children returned home and their mother called the police. The appellate court opinion does not state whether evidence of what the children told their mother when they returned home was admitted. Defendant sought to cross-examine the mother about certain trouble Cora had been in, particularly running away from home and striking a teacher at school. The appellate court sustained the trial court's disallowance of this questioning on the ground that if the credibility of Beverly and Marshall was susceptible to attack, it should have been attacked directly. Would the evidence about Cora be considered character evidence within the meaning of Rule 608(b)?

5. Inquiry under Rule 608(b) goes, of course, to the facts of the witness's conduct. The particulars of the conduct may have more or less power to impeach. In Sorge, the court states that the inquiry can be made even though the conduct in question was the predicate for a conviction. What reason could there be, the court asks, to prohibit such inquiry when there has been a conviction if it is permitted when there has not been. Yet some courts are troubled by inquiry into conduct when there has been a conviction, or at least when evidence of a conviction is introduced. It is clear that Rule 608(b) prohibits the introduction of extrinsic evidence. See, e.g., United States v. Brooke, 4 F.3d 1480 (9th Cir.1993): Extrinsic evidence that witness had falsely claimed to have cancer inadmissible. One commentator has suggested that Rules 608(b) and 609 should be read to provide that the only extrinsic evidence of misconduct admissible is evidence of a conviction, but not to impose any limit on inquiry into conduct on cross-examination. Uviller, Credence, Character, and the Rules of Evidence: Seeing Through the Liar's Tale, 42 Duke L.J. 776, 803–09 (1993). Note the question of extrinsic evidence present in People v. Pearson, supra. A witness may say something on direct examination suggesting he did not commit a bad act that may open him to impeachment by extrinsic evidence that would not otherwise be admissible. United States v. Garcia, 900 F.2d 571, 575 (2d Cir.), cert. denied, 498 U.S. 862 (1990). People v. Wheeler, 841 P.2d 938 (Cal.1992), states in dictum that the amendment to the California constitution referred to in the discussion of impeachment by conviction, supra p. 423, had the effect of sweeping away the prohibition against extrinsic evidence to show bad acts to impeach.

6. The opinion in Sorge states that the cross-examiner may ask the witness about a bad act if the question has a "basis in fact" and is asked in "good faith," and that even if the witness denies the act, the cross-examiner may persist in questioning in the hope of inducing the witness to abandon his negative answer. Administration of the good faith requirement has proved difficult. See People v. Alamo, 246 N.E.2d 496 (N.Y.), cert. denied, 396 U.S. 879 (1969): In prosecution for assaulting police officer, prosecutor had sufficient reason to ask the defendant about selling marijuana and robbing taxi drivers; dissent charged majority with failure to enforce good faith requirement of Sorge.

United States v. Blake, 941 F.2d 334, 339–44 (5th Cir.1991), cert. denied, 506 U.S. 998 (1992): Prosecution for narcotics and weapons offenses committed in the United States. In the prosecution's case, police officers testified to statements made to them by the defendant admitting the offenses. Defendant testified, denying the offenses and denying that he had told the officers he committed them. On cross-examination, the following transpired:

Q. Mr. Blake, have you ever killed anybody?

MR. GLOVER: Your Honor, we would object to that as being highly—

THE COURT: I sustain that.

MR. WEBSTER: Your Honor, could we approach the bench?

THE COURT: Yes, sir.

(Bench conference on the record.)

MR. WEBSTER: Your Honor, this is part of the statement that we did not get into on direct examination with regard to him killing ten people, two of which were police officers in Jamaica.

THE COURT: Well, does he have a statement to you to that effect?

MR. WEBSTER: He has a statement to two agents to Agent Barber to that effect that we did not get into on cross-examination because we felt—

THE COURT: You mean on direct?

MR. WEBSTER: Yes, sir, on good faith basis and all three of those individuals were willing to come up to this and state there were at least ten people in Jamaica were killed by Blake.

THE COURT: What about that?

MR. GLOVER: I assume he is going to deny it but that is pretty bizarre.

MR. WEBSTER: Bizarre is common place in this case.

MR. GLOVER: If he has denied that he did it he has denied all this other.

THE COURT: I understand. I think it is overdoing it myself but I think the question is allowable.

MR. GLOVER: Okay.

THE COURT: I will take it on your representation that you have those statements to support it.

(End of bench conference on the record.)

THE COURT: Okay, Mr. Webster.

Q. (By Mr. Webster) Mr. Blake, did you ever kill anybody before you left Jamaica?

A. No, sir.

Q. At any time did you ever tell Agent Scott Pickett in the presence of Special Agent Blake Boteler or Investigator Terry Barber that you killed at least ten people in Jamaica?

A. No, sir.

No evidence was introduced by the prosecution regarding the defendant's statement about killing people in Jamaica. The appellate court held it an abuse of discretion to permit questioning the defendant about killing people in Jamaica, but that the error was harmless. "[A]fter asking the inflammatory question and receiving the anticipated negative response, the government chose not to call rebuttal witnesses to contradict this testimony. Neither did it attempt to argue this discrepancy in closing to emphasize Blake's lack of credibility. Instead, the prosecution threw the damning questions into the jury box without the follow-up it led the court to believe would be forthcoming from its agents." Did the prosecutor lead the court to believe that a follow-up was forthcoming? Would a follow-up have been permissible?

Murphy v. Bonanno, 663 A.2d 505, 510 (D.C.App.1995): Error because "the judge did not determine ... whether ... [the defendant] had an adequate 'factual predicate' for the proffered questions, which were of a kind that, if hurled into the proceedings recklessly, could work unfair prejudice to ... [the plaintiff] despite her (expected) denial of the accusations." What is the "adequate factual predicate," or the "basis in fact", referred to in Sorge, that the cross-examiner must have in order to be justified in asking a question? Even if the cross-examiner has an "adequate factual predicate," should he be allowed to ask a question if he has no reason to believe the witness will admit the bad act? See State v. Phillips, 82 S.E.2d 762, 766–71 (N.C.1954), where a conviction was reversed because the way the questions were asked insinuated that they were based on facts for which the district attorney could vouch. Recall the requirement of surprise in the context of impeaching one's own witness, supra p. 398. There concern was with prohibited use of a prior statement of the witness.

7. United States v. Schwab, 886 F.2d 509, 511, 513 (2d Cir.1989): Error, although harmless, to ask defendant on cross-examination whether he had committed income tax fraud and perjury, when the prosecutor knew the defendant had been acquitted of these charges.

An acquittal establishes that the defendant's perpetration of the charged misconduct has not been proven beyond a reasonable doubt. It is therefore arguable that whether the misconduct occurred may be inquired about within the constraints of Rule 608(b) and Rule 403 since the reasonable doubt standard applies to the jury's ultimate determination of guilt and does not apply to its assessment of each subsidiary fact that may contribute to that determination, such as the credibility of the defendant. . . .

. . .

[W]e need not rest decision on collateral estoppel nor on more general considerations of fundamental fairness since the evidence is inadmissible under the standards of Rules 608(b) and 403. Rule 608(b) provides that specific instances of misconduct may be inquired into on cross-examination "in the discretion of the court, if probative of truthfulness or untruthfulness." Rule 403 obliges the trial judge to exclude relevant evidence "if its probative value is substantially outweighed by the danger of unfair prejudice," among other factors. Both rules thus require the exercise of discretion with respect to admission of prior acts of misconduct. Whether or not an acquittal technically stops the prosecution from eliciting the fact of prior misconduct, it will normally alter the balance between probative force and prejudice, which is already a close matter in many cases where prior misconduct of a defendant is offered. . . . Moreover, there is the blunt reality that a witness who has been acquitted will almost certainly deny the misconduct, either because he did no wrong or because he may understandably believe that when asked about it after an acquittal, he is entitled to have the law regard him as innocent. Thus, the only purpose served by permitting the inquiry is to place before the jury the allegation of misconduct contained in the prosecutor's question, an allegation the jury will be instructed has no evidentiary weight. To permit the inquiry risks unfair prejudice, which is not justified by the theoretical possibility that the witness, though acquitted, will admit to the misconduct. When the witness is the defendant, the significance of the prejudice is magnified.

In the pending case, not only had the alleged prior misconduct concerning the tax charge resulted in an acquittal, but the matter had arisen eighteen years prior to the trial at which it was sought to be probed on cross-examination. Moreover, the prosecutor had no information in his possession to indicate that Schwab was guilty of the misconduct. Under these circumstances, cross-examination concerning the tax matter was beyond the discretion confided in the trial judge by Rules 608(b) and 403.

For discussion of the effect of an acquittal in the context of substantive use of evidence of bad acts, see infra p. 867.

8. Fed.R.Evid. 806 permits the impeachment of extrajudicial declarants when their statements are admitted into evidence under exceptions to the hearsay rule. Does the prohibition against extrinsic evidence of bad acts to impeach apply in this context? Bennett, How to Administer the "Big Hurt" in a Criminal Case: The Life and Times of Federal Rule of Evidence 806, 44 Cath.U.L.Rev. 1135, 1154–56 (1995), suggests that it does not. Note the possible presence of this question in People v. Pearson, supra p. 434: The mother's testimony would have been extrinsic evidence.

9. To what extent does the privilege against self-incrimination protect a witness against cross-examination with respect to other crimes? See supra p. 365 for discussion of whether to strike direct testimony when a claim of privilege is sustained, and also infra p. 1379. See also the second paragraph of Rule 608(b). Assertion of a privilege against giving answers merely degrading is questionable. In re Vince, 67 A.2d 141, 145 (N.J.1949), discusses the matter fully and states that the latter privilege has disappeared in all save one or two states. Scrutiny of the authorities collected in 3A Wigmore, Evidence §§ 986–87 (Chadbourn rev. 1970) and Annot., 88 A.L.R.3d 304 (1978), indicates that this statement may be an oversimplification. The trial judge may in his discretion, taking into account the importance of the matter, restrict questioning that unduly disgraces, degrades, or embarrasses the witness. See Grudt v. City of Los Angeles, 468 P.2d 825, 834 (Cal.1970); United States v. Nuccio, 373 F.2d 168, 171 (2d Cir.), cert. denied, 387 U.S. 906 (1967); Fed.R.Evid. 611(a)(3).

10. For further reading see Friedman, Character Impeachment Evidence: Psycho-Bayesian [!?] Analysis and a Proposed Overhaul, 38 UCLA L.Rev. 637 (1991); Okun, Character and Credibility: A Proposal to Realign Federal Rules of Evidence 608 and 609, 37 Vill.L.Rev. 533 (1992).

d.   Reputation and Opinion of Character

State v. Ternan

Supreme Court of Washington, 1949.
32 Wash.2d 584, 203 P.2d 342.

■ GRADY, JUSTICE. The appellants were found guilty by a jury of the crime of assault in the second degree and from the judgment entered on the verdict have taken this appeal. . . .

(d) The remaining assignment of error arises out of the following situation: The appellants were called as witnesses in their own behalf and gave testimony. In rebuttal the respondent called witnesses who were asked over the objection of appellants if they knew the general reputation of appellants for truth and veracity in a certain named area or community. The witnesses answered in the affirmative, and in response to further questions stated that such reputation was bad.

The court gave the jury the following instruction:

"Evidence relative to the reputation of the defendants for truth and veracity was admitted solely for the purpose of affecting their credibility as a witness, and is to be considered by you for that purpose only, and in connection with all the other evidence in the case, in deciding how much weight or credence you will give their testimony."

Error is assigned in the giving of this instruction, but clearly it was beneficial to the appellants rather than prejudicial as it limited the jury to a consideration of the only purpose for which such testimony would be relevant and excluded from the minds of the jurors the idea that they might consider such evidence in determining whether the appellants were guilty of any offense.

The appellants in their argument and their discussion of the cases cited in support thereof, have not drawn the very important distinction existing between the character of a person and his reputation made in State v. Refsnes, 14 Wash.2d 569, 128 P.2d 773.[1] We agree with the appellants that the character of a defendant in a criminal case is not open to inquiry unless he himself puts it in issue, but when a defendant in a criminal case takes the witness stand he subjects himself to cross-examination the same as any other witness, and the

---

1. "Character is what a man is; that is, the qualities which constitute the individual. Reputation is what people say of him." 14 Wash.2d at 573, 128 P.2d at 775 (1942). Eds.

state has the right to impeach him as a witness to the extent of proving by witnesses that his general reputation for truth and veracity in the community where he resides is bad. Our statute, Rem.Rev.Stat. § 2148, provides that an accused person may offer himself as a witness in his own behalf and shall be allowed to testify as other witnesses in such case, but when he shall so testify he shall be subject to all the rules of law relating to cross-examination of other witnesses. This statute has been construed to mean that such witness may be impeached with reference to his general reputation for truth and veracity in the community where he resides. State v. Hooker, 99 Wash. 661, 170 P. 374; State v. Friedlander, 141 Wash. 1, 250 P. 453.

The appellants criticize the Friedlander case and ask us to overrule it, their argument being that it is contrary to the provisions of Rem.Rev.Stat. § 2148. If we understand the appellants correctly their contention is to the effect that it is proper to impeach a defendant who takes the witness stand in his own behalf with reference to his credibility as a witness if that can be accomplished by proper cross-examination, but he cannot be impeached by witnesses in rebuttal testifying as to his bad reputation for truth and veracity until he puts such reputation in issue. In view of such criticism and request we have made an investigation of the origin and history of the doctrine of the Friedlander case and find the greater part of any confusion or disagreement among the courts that may exist arises out of evidence adduced with reference to traits of character of an accused when he had not put them in issue rather than impeachment of an accused as a witness with reference to his general reputation for truth and veracity in the community where he resides. The great preponderance of judicial thought is in accord with that case and we do not think it should be overruled.

The judgment is affirmed.

■ JEFFERS, C.J., and ROBINSON, SIMPSON, and SCHWELLENBACH, JJ., concur.

United States v. Dotson

United States Court of Appeals, Fifth Circuit, 1986.
799 F.2d 189.

■ Before CLARK, CHIEF JUDGE, RUBIN, and GARZA, CIRCUIT JUDGES.

■ CLARK, CHIEF JUDGE:

Appellant Leon Frederick Dotson appeals his conviction on three counts of receiving firearms in violation of 18 U.S.C. §§ 922(h) and 922(a). Finding that the district court erred in allowing government agents to testify as to their opinions of the truth and veracity of Dotson and Dotson's witnesses without offering an adequate predicate upon which they based their opinions, we reverse.

I.

Dotson was convicted in 1977 and 1978 of state and federal felonies for the possession of marijuana. In 1982 he was released from federal detention and placed on parole. As a result of his status as a convicted felon on parole, federal law prohibited Dotson from knowingly receiving firearms. 18 U.S.C. § 922(h).

The three handguns that were the subject of the charges against Dotson included a Colt .38 revolver, a Colt .45 pistol, and a .9 mm Walther pistol. As part of his defense of necessity, Dotson took the stand himself and called various witnesses to explain how and why he had obtained the handguns.

The essence of Dotson's defense is his contention that he was faced with serious and repeated threats to his physical safety shortly after his release and return home. On one occasion, an Officer Charles Kirk of the Greenville, Mississippi police was called to investigate an alleged attack in which 30 bullets were fired into Dotson's house. Kirk testified at trial that he advised Dotson to obtain a weapon for protection.

Dotson testified that he had purchased the Colt .38 before his earlier convictions, and that he had left the handgun with others during his incarceration and before the attack. He testified that, after his talk with Kirk, he reclaimed the weapon for his protection. Both Dotson and his mother, Erma Dotson, testified that he had received the Colt .45 as part of his father's estate. Finally, both Dotson and his friend, Reginald Owens, testified that the .9 mm Walther was obtained in pawn for a gambling loan, and that Owens had kept the pistol until Dotson needed it for his protection. In addition, Dotson's girlfriend, Crystal Johnson, offered testimony corroborating Dotson's version of how he acquired the handguns; her testimony also bolstered Dotson's claims of serious threats, as did the testimony of Kirk, Owens, and Erma Dotson.

As part of its rebuttal to Dotson's defense of necessity, the government called four government agents to testify that, in their opinion, Dotson and one or more of his witnesses were not of truthful character and not to be believed under oath.

The government first called FBI agent John Canale, who testified as follows:

Q. Have you had occasion to conduct an investigation into the activities of the defendant, Fred Dotson, and his associates?

A. Yes, sir, I have.

Q. As a result of this investigation and what you have learned and all that you have seen in this case, have you formed an opinion as to the truthfulness of the defendant, Frederick Leon Dotson?

A. Yes, sir, I have.

Q. Is that opinion of his truthfulness good or bad?

A. Bad.

Q. Would you believe Frederick Leon Dotson under oath?

A. No, sir, I would not.

The prosecutor then asked Canale the same questions with regard to Dotson's girlfriend, Crystal Johnson. After Canale stated his opinion, defense counsel objected as follows:

If the court please, I object to that your honor. I don't believe that an adequate predicate has been laid. He knows her and general reputation in the community that he lives—The court interrupted at this point and overruled the objection.

Thereupon the prosecutor proceeded in similar fashion to elicit opinions from Canale as to Owens and Kirk. Three more government agents were called—another FBI agent, a state narcotics agent, and an Internal Revenue Services agent—to offer their opinions on the truthfulness of Dotson and his witnesses. The form of questioning and the opinions elicited did not differ materially from the example offered above, with two exceptions. The Mississippi narcotics agent testified that she had known Dotson for six or seven years and Owens "[w]ithin the last year"; otherwise, she also based her opinion of Dotson, Owens and two more of his witnesses on her investigation of this case.

The IRS agent limited his opinion testimony to the truthfulness of Erma Dotson, whom he had investigated on a separate occasion.

The jury returned verdicts of guilty on all three counts of receiving firearms. Dotson was convicted and sentenced to a total of five years.

On appeal, Dotson challenges the admission of the government agents' opinion testimony based solely on their conduct of an investigation....

II.

Federal Rule of Evidence 608(a) reads in relevant part:

> The credibility of a witness may be attacked or supported by evidence in the form of opinion or reputation ... for truthfulness or untruthfulness....

Prior to the adoption of Rule 608(a), there had been confusion and conflict among courts and commentators as to the propriety of offering opinion evidence to impeach the credibility of a witness. See McCormick, Evidence § 44, at 90–93 (2d ed. 1972); 7 Wigmore, Evidence §§ 1981–1986 (Chadbourn rev. 1978); Ladd, Techniques of Character Testimony, 24 Iowa L.Rev. 498, 509–13 (1939). It had been common practice for counsel to ask witnesses whether, based upon their knowledge of the principal witness's reputation in the community for truth and veracity, they would believe him under oath. See United States v. Walker, 313 F.2d 236, 239–41 (6th Cir.), cert. denied, 374 U.S. 807, 83 S.Ct. 1695, 10 L.Ed.2d 1031 (1963). Recognizing that "witnesses who testify to reputation often seem in fact to be giving their opinions, disguised somewhat misleadingly as reputation," Advisory Committee's Note, Fed. R.Evid. 608(a), Rule 608(a) makes clear that witnesses may state their opinions directly.

In United States v. Lollar, 606 F.2d 587 (5th Cir.1979), a case in which a challenge was made only to the impeachment of the defendant, this Circuit stated that Rule 608(a) imposes no requirement that "counsel first ask the impeaching witness about his knowledge of the defendant's reputation for truth and veracity, and whether based on that knowledge he would believe the defendant under oath...." Id. at 589. The Lollar decision quotes Judge Weinstein at length:

> [w]itnesses may now be asked directly to state their opinion of the principal witness's character for truthfulness and they may answer for example, "I think X is a liar." The rule imposes no prerequisite conditioned upon long acquaintance or recent information about the witness....

Id. (citing 3 Weinstein's Evidence ¶ 608[04], at 608–20 (1978)).

In the case before us on review, Dotson does not challenge the form of the evidence at issue. Rather he asserts that there are limits to the introduction of opinion testimony. In particular, he refers to Federal Rules of Evidence 403 and 701, which operate to exclude opinions (1) whose probative value is outweighed by the danger of confusion and prejudice and (2) that are not helpful to the trier of fact.

Federal Rule of Evidence 403 provides that relevant "evidence may be excluded if its probative value is substantially outweighed by the danger of unfair prejudice, confusion of the issues, or misleading the jury...." We do not decide here whether or not such considerations may be sufficient to exclude the impeachment testimony of government agents in certain cases. No objection was made which required a Rule 403 balancing....

Dotson's trial counsel did at one point object to the introduction of the opinion testimony. Although the objection was phrased in very general terms—"I don't believe an adequate predicate has been laid"—we deem this sufficient, in view of the court's interruption, to put the trial judge on notice that defense counsel objected to the lack of a basis upon which the opinions of the government witnesses were stated.

Although Rule 608(a) clarifies the older, more confusing approach to eliciting an impeaching witness's opinion, we do not construe it to abandon all limits on the reliability and relevance of opinion evidence. Judge Weinstein, in explaining Rule 608(a)'s liberalized approach (which Lollar quotes above) qualifies the admissibility of such testimony thus: "If the court finds the witness lacks sufficient information to have formed a reliable opinion, [the judge] can exclude relying on Rules 403 and 602." 3 Weinstein's Evidence ¶ 608 [04], at 608–20 (1985). In addition, Rule 701 explicitly limits opinion evidence:

> If the witness is not testifying as an expert, his testimony in the form of opinions or inferences is limited to those opinions or inferences which are (a) rationally based on the perception of the witness and (b) helpful to a clear understanding of . . . the determination of a fact in issue.

The Rule 701(a) limitation is characterized by the committee as the "familiar requirement of first-hand knowledge or observation," Advisory Committee's Note, Fed.R.Evid. 701(a). The second limitation, (b), requires that opinion testimony be helpful in resolving issues. The Advisory Committee warns that "[i]f . . . attempts are made to introduce meaningless assertions which amount to little more than choosing up sides, exclusion for lack of helpfulness is called for by the rule." Advisory Committee's Note, Fed.R.Evid. 701(b).

An opinion, or indeed any form of testimony, without the underlying facts, may be excluded if it amounts to no more than a conclusory observation. . . .

The only basis offered by three of the four government agents who testified at Dotson's trial that Dotson and his witnesses were not to be believed under oath was the fact that they took part in a criminal investigation of Dotson. The two FBI agents merely stated that they had taken part in an investigation of Dotson. No other testimony was elicited with respect to how long the agents had known Dotson, or in what way they had acted to form their opinions of his veracity. Each agent offered his opinion of not only Dotson's character for truthfulness, but also the veracity of his girlfriend Johnson, his friend Owens, and Officer Kirk. The state narcotics agent stated that she had known Dotson for six or seven years and had gotten to know Owens within the last year. No further basis for opinion was offered outside of the fact that she took part in an investigation. She also testified as to the character of Johnson and Kirk. On the other hand, IRS agent Alvin Patton's testimony on the truthfulness of Erma Dotson did in fact evidence a sufficient basis. For example, Patton stated that he interviewed Erma Dotson four times, that he investigated her tax returns and financial information, and that he studied her testimony before the grand jury. He also limited his opinion to Erma Dotson's truthfulness with respect to the financial aspects of her son's case. Patton was entitled to express his opinion that Erma Dotson was not to be believed under oath. Of all the agents who testified, only Patton provided a predicate upon which the court could have determined that the opinion was reliable and helpful.

In the absence of some underlying basis to demonstrate that the opinions were more than bare assertions that the defendant and his witnesses were persons not to be believed, the opinion evidence should not have been admitted.

When and by whom the basis for such opinion must be developed is a question initially committed to the sound discretion of the trial court. That court has the responsibility for determining the order of proof, but the determination should be made deliberately and in the exercise of a considered discretion. Here, no account was taken of the value to the jury of the opinion expressed or of the possible prejudice to the defendant from the brusque branding of his testimony as lies. The record should reflect some indication that the court did not merely let down the bars to the expression of any opinions the prosecutor's witnesses wanted to voice.

As Judge Weinstein has noted, cross examination is available to test opinions. 3 Weinstein's Evidence ¶ 608[04], at 608–20 (1985). In some cases, cross-examination may suffice to protect a defendant who raises no objection to an opinion witness's testimony. Where, however, the defendant in a criminal case objects to the lack of a basis for a government agent's unsupported assertion that the defendant and his witnesses are unworthy of belief, the court should require that the witness identify the basis or source of the opinion. Unless that basis or source demonstrates that the opinion is rationally based on the perception of the witness and would be helpful to the jury in determining the fact of credibility, it should not become a part of the proof in the case.

We do not hold that government agents may never testify as to the truthfulness of a defendant or defense witnesses. Nor do we hold that a government agent's opinion of a witness's character may never be based exclusively on what the agent learned on an official investigation. But the fact that one has conducted an investigation of the defendant, has known the defendant, or has had minimal contact with defendant's witnesses is not a sufficiently reliable basis under Rules 608(a) and 701 for that witness, over objection, to put before the jury the opinion that they are liars.

The vice of this procedure was heightened in the case at bar by the use made of the opinions. The prosecutor, in closing argument, referred to this opinion testimony in the following manner:

> Another fact that you can consider is what the people, the good solid people in this community; narcotics officers, police officers, the FBI, what they think about [the defendant] and his associates. His associates, such as—if you believe his defense, you have to believe Reginald Owens, Frederick Dotson, Frederick Dotson's latest girlfriend.

If this is permitted, the government's agents and attorney could move from presenting factual proof of incrimination to suggesting to the jury that the "good people" of the community ought to put the "bad people" behind bars. This is but a variation on the theme of attempts to convict, not for the criminal act charged, but by showing the defendant to be a "bad person" through proof about other crimes. See McCormick, Evidence, § 43, at 89–90 (2d ed. 1972). A prosecutor errs if he goes outside the record to express a personal opinion to the jury that the defendant's testimony is incredible. If his witnesses may state such opinions without providing basis in fact, and the prosecutor sums them up as fact, the same vice inheres.

The government observes that the agents who testified were not technically "case agents" in the case for which Dotson was on trial. This is not determinative. As we stated above, we do not hold that government agents may not ever express opinion about witnesses in their cases. They may do so on the same basis as any other witness. Indeed, we hold that admitting Patton's testimony was not error. The error as to the others lay in admitting, over objection, opinion proof without predicate facts showing its reliability and helpfulness. With the exception of Patton's testimony, the admission of the investigators' opinions was reversible error.

. . .

Because the testimony of the government agents should not have been admitted absent evidence of the underlying facts upon which it was based, the judgment of conviction is

Reversed.

NOTES

1. The use of reputation and opinion of character evidence for substantive purposes, which is adverted to in the Ternan case, is explored infra pp. 875–914. As indicated in the Ternan and Dotson cases, when such evidence is admissible substantively, it is at the initiative of the party wishing to establish good character, whereas when it is admissible for the purpose of affecting credibility, it is at the initiative of the party attacking credibility. Why should there be this difference? See supra p. 385 on accrediting.

2. Fed. R. Evid. 608(a) requires that reputation or opinion evidence refer only to character for truthfulness or untruthfulness, whereas Fed. R. Evid. 404(a)(1), which permits a criminal defendant to introduce good character evidence for substantive purposes, speaks of a "pertinent trait of character." Does it follow that evidence of character for truthfulness is not admissible for substantive purposes and evidence of character for being law-abiding is not admissible for impeachment purposes, even though each sort of evidence is relevant for both purposes?

3. Fed. R. Evid. 608(a) does not contain a provision like that found in Rule 608(b), referring to "the discretion of the court." The Dotson opinion suggests however, that evidence that falls within 608(a) may be excluded under Fed. R. Evid. 403 when there is prejudice. The prejudice the court has in mind appears to be substantive use of bad character evidence when a criminal defendant takes the stand. But the question asked earlier—see p. 419—recurs: Why if the evidence is to be put before the trier of fact for the purpose of attacking credibility should it not also be available for substantive use? Does prejudice consist in substantive use or only in the danger that the trier of fact will punish the defendant because he has committed a crime with which he is not charged or because he is a bad person?

4. As the Ternan opinion shows, formerly it was required that character for truthfulness be proved only through evidence of reputation. Some jurisdictions still adhere to this limitation. E.g., State v. Mazerolle, 614 A.2d 68, 73 (Me.1992). Traditionally, evidence of reputation in the community where the witness resides was required. More recently, in response to the realities of modern life, reputation with any group with which the witness has significant contacts is permitted. United States v. Mandel, 591 F.2d 1347, 1370 (4th Cir.1979), cert. denied, 445 U.S. 961 (1980) (reputation in law office where witness worked); Wilson v. City of Chicago, 6 F.3d 1233 (7th Cir.1993), cert. denied, 511 U.S. 1088 (1994) (people who worked with witness and members of his family). But see State v. Trosclair, 350 So.2d 1164, 1166–68 (La.1977) (reputation among owners of bars frequented by witness inadmissible).

5. Fed. R. Evid. 608(a) permits both reputation evidence and opinion of character evidence. The allowance of opinion of character evidence has led to considerable confusion, particularly in regard to the relation between Fed. R. Evid. 608(a), 404 and 405 on the one hand, and Fed. R. Evid. 701 on the other.

Fed. R. Evid. 701, the Opinion Rule, has already been discussed, supra pp. 352–62. That rule requires witnesses to state their memories with particularity, avoiding so far as reasonably possible inferences and general characterizations. The aim of Rule 701 is to reduce the risk that the trier of fact will abandon its own background beliefs for those of witnesses in areas in which such substitution is not permitted. Contrary to the suggestion in the Dotson case, Rule 701 would appear to have no application to the situation presented by that case. The witnesses whom the prosecution proffered to give their opinions of the defense witnesses' truthfulness did not base their opinions upon background beliefs of the sort that should come only from the trier of fact; to the contrary, the witnesses sought to communicate experiences and information concerning the defense witnesses that the jurors did not have. Possibly the prosecution witnesses could have expressed with specificity some of what they knew about the defense witnesses, but even if this was so, Rule 701 would not prevent them from giving their opinions of the defense witnesses' truthfulness, if there was any risk that if they were not allowed to do so, relevant information would be lost.

Rule 701 is not pertinent to the Dotson case for another reason: Rule 701 forbids opinion testimony when there can be more specific communication. Rules 404, 405 and 608(a), taken together, forbid just such specification, even when it is possible. These rules relating to character evidence not only constitute exceptions to Rule 701; they are the reverse of Rule 701: when "character" is to be proved, only opinions are permissible, not specifics, whether about the conduct of the witness to be impeached or about what others have said of him. Rule 404(a)(3) allows evidence of the character of a witness; Rule 405(a) restricts proof of character to opinion of character or reputation; Rule 608(b) permits evidence of particular acts to show character, but prohibits extrinsic evidence for such a purpose. The special nature of reputation and opinion of character evidence is discussed further in the context of the substantive use of such evidence, infra p. 875.

6. The Dotson case and other recent decisions suggest that for either reputation or opinion of character evidence to be admissible, more than relevance is required. State v. Vachon, 659 A.2d 426, 429 (N.H.1995):

[I]t must be established that the reputation witness possesses a sufficient basis of knowledge such that the reputation evidence may be considered to be reliable. For this foundational predicate we require the following: the individual's reputation must be held generally in a community of significant size; it must be developed over enough time to truly reflect character for truthfulness; and it must be based on the need of the members of the community to deal with the individual on a frequent basis. . . .

Measuring against this standard, we hold that the State failed to lay a sufficient foundation for the admissibility of the reputation evidence here. Prior to eliciting the evidence from Officer Giguere, the prosecutor asked only a few general questions that revealed that Officer Giguere had been a Milton police officer for two and a half years, that he had been involved in the community by way of interviewing people during criminal investigations, that he had come in contact with many people familiar with the defendant, and that he was familiar with the defendant's reputation for truthfulness. This testimony fails to demonstrate that a sufficient number of people in the community at large held an opinion as to the defendant's reputation for veracity. Notably, the officer only testified that his dealings with community members familiar with the defendant was in the law enforcement context, not a representative sample. . . .

See also State v. Mazerolle, 614 A.2d 68, 73 (Me.1992): Not abuse of discretion to exclude opinion of reputation for truthfulness when basis was that six persons in primary witness's town of residence said the witness was not honest; State v. Caldwell, 529 N.W.2d 282 (Iowa 1995): Proper to exclude testimony about reputation when based upon comments of a few friends of the impeaching witness, but error to exclude testimony based upon comments by numerous persons with various backgrounds and connections to the community; State v. Dutton, 896 S.W.2d 114, 118 (Tenn.1995):

> We conclude that a sufficient foundation was developed for the introduction of the victim's grandfather's testimony concerning his opinion of the victim's character for truthfulness, but it was insufficient to warrant admission of the reputation testimony. The defendant did not elicit information concerning the victim's grandfather's acquaintance with the community in which the victim lived in order to insure that the testimony adequately reflected the community's assessment. However, the grandfather's testimony that he had been around the victim on and off for a number of years on weekends did sufficiently create a foundation to support his testimony concerning his own opinion of the child's character for truthfulness.

Is there any reason to require that evidence offered under Rule 608(a) be more than relevant, at least if there is no risk of prejudice? If in order to gain admission under Rule 608(a) there must be a showing to the court of certain contacts with the witness to be impeached or with his community, as indicated in Note 5 it may not be permitted to put this information before the trier of fact.

7. Is there any reason to prevent a witness testifying under Rule 608(a), who has had long acquaintance with the primary witness and who has heard the primary witness testify in the litigated case, from stating that he has a poor opinion of the primary witness's character for truthfulness and that because of this opinion, he does not believe the primary witness's present testimony? See United States v. Akitoye, 923 F.2d 221, 223 (1st Cir.1991), suggesting that the last remark is impermissible. For further exploration of this question in connection with the topic of the permissible bases of expert testimony, see United States v. Scop, infra p. 1043.

8. Wilson v. City of Chicago, 6 F.3d 1233, 1239 (7th Cir.1993), cert. denied, 114 S.Ct. 1844 (1994), a suit against police for torturing the plaintiff, presents many of the questions touched upon in the preceding Notes. The plaintiff sought to introduce character evidence to discredit one of the defense witnesses.

> The judge excluded the testimony of a British journalist, Gregory Miskiw, that one of the defense witnesses, William Coleman, was a liar. . . . [T]he plaintiff wanted to impeach Coleman's credibility with testimony by Miskiw that Coleman had once fed him two pieces of juicy gossip, one concerning a cousin of the Queen of England, that had turned out to be false.
>
> The rules of evidence permit (with various limitations) impeaching a witness by evidence that he has a reputation for untruthfulness or even—a novelty—by *opinion* evidence that he is untruthful. Fed.R.Evid. 608(a); Note to Rule 608(a) of Advisory Comm. on 1972 Proposed Rules. The fact that Coleman had lied to Miskiw about Queen Elizabeth's cousin would not

fit the older or newer version of the rule. The telling of a lie not only cannot be equated to the possession of a *reputation* for untruthfulness, but does not by itself establish a *character* for untruthfulness, as the rule explicitly requires whether the form of the impeaching evidence is evidence of reputation or opinion evidence. Trials would be endless if a witness could be impeached by evidence that he had once told a lie or two. Which of us has never lied? ... But there is more here. Miskiw wanted to testify that Coleman had a reputation for untruthfulness among people who had worked with Coleman and members of his family, who regarded him as "the blackest of the black sheep of the family." Was this a "community" within the meaning of the rule? We suppose so. Coleman is a peripatetic felon. He is not a member of any stable community, but that is true of a lot of law-abiding people in our mobile society, and a community doesn't have to be stable in order to qualify under the rule. Cf. McCormick on Evidence § 43 at p. 159 (4th ed. 1992). It was Miskiw's job as a reporter to determine Coleman's reputation for trustworthiness in order to decide whether to place any credence in his gossip about the royal cousin. His interviews with members of Coleman's "community" enabled him to testify to Coleman's reputation in that community on the basis of personal knowledge.

Miskiw had also spent a fair amount of time with Coleman himself, in an effort to determine whether the gossip was accurate. On the basis of his personal contacts with Coleman he formed the apparently well-substantiated opinion that Coleman was "a consummate liar." This opinion was admissible wholly apart from evidence about Coleman's reputation in his own community.

9. Expert opinion evidence respecting credibility: United States v. Hiss, 88 F.Supp. 559 (S.D.N.Y.), aff'd, 185 F.2d 822 (2d Cir.1950), cert. denied, 340 U.S. 948 (1951), is said to be the first case in the federal courts admitting psychiatric testimony to impeach (not to disqualify on grounds of insanity). Comment, 59 Yale L.J. 1324 (1950), contains an extensive discussion. See also the discussion in United States v. Daileda, 229 F.Supp. 148 (M.D.Pa.1964), aff'd, 342 F.2d 218 (3d Cir.1965). Slovenko, Witnesses, Psychiatry and the Credibility of Testimony, 19 U. Fla. L. Rev. 1 (1966), contains letters of Dr. Carl Binger, the psychiatrist in the Hiss case, giving his point of view about the cross-examination to which he was subjected.

The opinion in United States v. Awkard, 597 F.2d 667, 670–71 (9th Cir.1979), presents a number of the issues that surround this subject. This was a case involving a prison stabbing. A prosecution witness testified that the defendants had participated in the stabbing. The prosecution also introduced in its case in chief the testimony of an expert in hypnosis. This witness testified that he had hypnotized the first witness and that it was only as a result of this hypnosis that the witness remembered the participation of some of the defendants in the stabbing. The expert also testified to the general nature and effects of hypnosis and that in his opinion the first witness's memory had been accurately refreshed as a result of hypnosis. The appellate court held it was error to admit this testimony.

Even had the defense challenged Hackney on cross-examination because of his hypnosis, portions of Kroger's testimony would have been inadmissible. In addition to testifying that he had hypnotized Hackney, and that hypnosis generally helps subjects to remember past events, the doctor stated his opinion that Hackney's memory had been accurately refreshed by hypnosis. While Kroger's testimony on the general nature and usual effects of hypnosis would have been proper had Hackney been challenged, Kroger's opinion of its effects on Hackney would still have been inadmissible, under Fed.R.Evid. 608(a). That rule strictly limits opinion evidence on witness credibility to "character for truthfulness or untruthfulness"; Hackney's ability to recall the stabbing, while relevant to credibility, had nothing to do with his character. Thus, even if hypnosis of the witness had been raised as a ground for discrediting his testimony, Kroger should have been permitted to testify only about the general nature and usual effects of hypnosis, and the details of his hypnosis of Hackney.

"Credibility ... is for the jury—the jury is the lie detector in the courtroom." United States v. Barnard, 490 F.2d 907, 912 (9th Cir.1973), cert. denied, 416 U.S. 959, 94 S.Ct. 1976, 40 L.Ed.2d 310 (1974). In Barnard, a case decided before the effective date of the Federal Rules, we upheld the district judge's exclusion of expert psychiatric testimony that a defendant-witness was a sociopath who would lie if it was to his advantage to do so. We held that such evidence should be received only in unusual cases. Expert medical evidence on the effect of hypnosis on a particular witness's ability to recall is inadmissible for the same reasons as those invoked in Barnard. Under the Federal Rules, opinion testimony on credibility is limited to character; all other opinions on credibility are for the jurors themselves to form.

As will be seen, the Awkard case involved some question that have already been addressed, namely, accrediting a witness whose credibility has not been attacked, supra p. 389, and discrediting one's own witness. See supra pp. 385—401. See also Rock v. Arkansas, supra p. 256, on the admissibility of post-hypnosis memories.

One issue presented by the Awkard opinion is the relation between expert testimony on credibility and Rule 608(a). The opinion suggests that if such testimony does not fit under Rule 608—if it is not "character" evidence—it is inadmissible. Some commentators dispute this analysis. E.g., Berger, United States v. Scop: The Common–Law Approach to an Expert's Opinion About a Witness's Credibility Still Does Not Work, 55 Brook. L. Rev. 559, 585 (1989): "The conclusion that 'opinion testimony on credibility is limited to character' [quoting Awkard] rests on the faulty assumption that all other types of opinion evidence are barred because they are not mentioned in Article VI [of the Federal Rules]." Recall the Able case, supra p. 406, where the result of evidence being classified as relevant to bias rather than character was not exclusion but more certain admission. Whether expert opinion on credibility is admissible as character evidence depends on what is meant by "character." United States v. Shay, 57 F.3d 126, 131 (1st Cir.1995), points out that the Advisory Committee's Note to Fed. R. Evid. 405(a), which concerns proof of character, contemplates that expert opinion testimony may be included within that rule: "If character is defined as the kind of person one is, then account must be taken of the varying ways of arriving at the estimate. These may range from the opinion of the employer who has found the man honest to the opinion of the psychiatrist based upon examination and testing." Possibly some expert testimony on credibility is "character" evidence and some is not, but is admissible nevertheless.

Another issue presented by the Awkard opinion is whether the admissibility of expert testimony regarding credibility is to be determined by the standard that controls the admissibility of expert testimony generally or by a special standard. The topic of expert testimony is addressed at length infra p. 954. For present purposes it is enough to note that two principal questions arise in connection with the topic. The first is what criterion determines the information that may be presented to the trier of fact through the process of formal proof—e.g., sworn and cross-examined witnesses—rather than through the informal process of the trier of fact's taking note of what it already knows. The second question is whether expert testimony to be admissible need only be relevant or must achieve some specified degree of probative value. See also supra p. 249 (expert testimony concerning the reliability of eye-witness testimony) and supra p. 315 (expert testimony for the purpose of determining competence).

The Awkard decision and other judicial utterances seem to suggest that there is a special need for caution in the case of expert testimony when it relates to witness credibility. State v. Batangan, 799 P.2d 48 (Hawai'i 1990) (overruling State v. Kim, 645 P.2d 1330 (Hawai'i 1982)): In child sex abuse case, error to allow expert on subject of sexually abused children to testify in a way that communicated that the child in the case was truthful in telling her story; State v. Milbradt, 756 P.2d 620 (Or.1988): Error to allow psychologist called by prosecution to testify that in his opinion prosecution witness, who was severely retarded, did not show any signs of deceptiveness and that her mental defect rendered her too unsophisticated to plan or carry through systematic deception; State v. Woodburn, 559 A.2d 343 (Me.1989): In child sex abuse case, not error to exclude testimony of psychologist, who had seen child for many sessions, that child suffered from problems that resulted in an inability to distinguish fantasy from reality, an overwhelming need to please adults, unwillingness to take personal responsibility and an absence of remorse for misconduct, including lying; People v. Alcala, 842 P.2d 1192, 1217–20 (Cal.1992), cert. denied, 510 U.S. 877 (1993): Not error to exclude testimony of psychologist, who had reviewed testimony of the primary witness at a former trial and tapes of interviews by police, that in his opinion the primary witness had been hypnotized and subjected to sophisticated methods of memory manipulation.

But see State v. Middleton, 657 P.2d 1215, 1219–20 (Or.1983), a prosecution for rape of the defendant's 14–year-old daughter. The daughter at first said the defendant had raped her, then retracted the charge, and finally, at the trial, testified that the defendant had raped her. Social workers were allowed to testify that the behavior of the daughter was typical of the behavior of juvenile sex abuse victims.

If a complaining witness in a burglary trial, after making the initial report, denied several times before testifying at trial that the crime had happened, the jury would have good reason to doubt seriously her credibility at any time. However, in this instance we are concerned with a child who states she has been the victim of sexual abuse by a member of her family. The experts testified that in this situation the young victim often feels guilty about testifying against someone she loves and wonders if she is doing the right thing in so testifying. It would be useful to the jury to know that not just this victim but many child victims are ambivalent about the forcefulness with which they want to pursue the complaint, and it is not uncommon for them to deny the act ever happened. Explaining this superficially bizarre behavior by identifying its emotional antecedents could help the jury better assess the witness's credibility.

We recognize that sexual abuse of children is a problem in our culture. Defendant does not deny that this form of behavior may exist following familial sexual abuse, or that the experts described it correctly. It is information that the jury did not have. In the present case, 18 of the prospective jurors questioned during voir dire were asked whether they knew a child victim of sexual abuse or if they had heard of any children who had been abused sexually by members of their families. Fifteen reported that they knew no one who had suffered from this sort of abuse; two others said they remembered hearing reports of such abuse. Because the jurors said they had no experience with victims of child abuse, we assume they would not have been exposed to the contention that it is common for children to report familial sexual abuse and then retract the story. Such evidence might well help a jury make a more informed decision in evaluating the credibility of a testifying child.

. . .

The dissent from the Court of Appeals stated: "The door is now open to permit an expert or other 'skilled' witness to testify that it is typical behavior for a witness, a victim or a criminal defendant to tell the truth the first time and then later to recant." State v. Middleton, 58 Or.App. 447, 456, 648 P.2d 1296 (1982). This is a legitimate concern, but our holding today does not open the door so widely. We expressly hold that in Oregon a witness, expert or otherwise, may not give an opinion on whether he believes a witness is telling the truth. We reject testimony from a witness about the credibility of another witness, although we recognize some jurisdictions accept it.

We hold that if a witness is accepted as an expert by the trial court, it is not error to allow testimony describing the reaction of the typical child victim of familial sexual abuse and whether a testifying victim impeached by her prior inconsistent statement reacted in the typical manner when she made that inconsistent statement.

Compare Commonwealth v. Dunkle, 602 A.2d 830 (Pa.1992), on facts very similar to Middleton, squarely rejecting the reasons for admissibility that the Middleton court found persuasive. See United States v. Shay, 57 F.3d 126, 131 (1st Cir.1995): When in murder case the prosecution had introduced incriminating statements by the defendant, the trial court incorrectly interpreted Fed. R. Evid. 702 to exclude testimony of psychiatrist that defendant suffered from the condition known as pseudologia fantastica, which caused him to make false statements even though in conflict with his apparent self-interest (see supra p. 245); People v. Schuemann, 548 P.2d 911 (Colo.1976): Error to exclude psychiatric testimony that prosecution witness was a delusional paranoid schizophrenic; Mosley v. Commonwealth, 420 S.W.2d 679 (Ky.1967): In rape case, error to exclude testimony of psychologist that complaining witness, who had been in mental institution, was a schizophrenic and had certain sex fantasies; State v. Petrich, 683 P.2d 173, 178–80 (Wash.1984): Proper to allow worker at sexual assault center to testify that in over 50 per cent of sexual abuse cases involving children, there is delay in reporting; the fact of delay in the litigated case had been brought out on direct examination and further inquired into on cross-examination.

See Mullane, The Truthsayer and the Court: Expert Testimony on Credibility, 43 Maine L. Rev. 53, 73, 76, 85 (1991), taking the position that there should be no special standard for the admissibility of expert testimony on credibility.

A third issue presented by the Awkard decision is whether the admissibility of expert testimony on credibility should be affected by whether the expert testifies only to principles, or to the general credibility of the primary witness, or to the credibility of the story told by the witness in the litigated case. Judicial disapproval is most often voiced to expert testimony of the third kind. E.g., State v. Batangan, 799 P.2d 48 (Hawai'i 1990): Testimony communicated opinion that child was truthful in telling her story; United States v. Azure, 801 F.2d 336, 341–42 (8th Cir.1986): In prosecution for child sex abuse, error to allow doctor with experience of such cases to testify to "the specific believability and truthfulness of … [the victim's] story," although it might have been permissible to testify generally about "patterns of consistency in stories of child sex abuse victims and comparing these patterns with patterns in … [the victim's] story." See supra p. 446, addressing the same question in regard to character witnesses not classified as experts. Mullane, The Truthsayer and the Court, supra, at 86–87, states that it should make no difference whether the expert on credibility confines himself to generalizations or gives an opinion on the truthfulness of the witness's story in the litigated case. The author also suggests that it should make no difference whether the expert addresses the question of sincerity or speaks to other aspects of credibility, such as ability to perceive, remember or communicate. Id. at 96.

See generally Conrad, Mental Examination of Witnesses, 11 Syr. L. Rev. 149 (1960); Juviler, Psychiatric Opinions as to Credibility of Witnesses: A Suggested Approach, 48 Calif. L. Rev. 648 (1960); Miller, Psychiatric Testimony to Impeach the Credibility of Witnesses, 14 N. Y. U. Intra. L. Rev. 239 (1959); Allen, Admission of Psychiatric Evidence, 8 Ariz. L. Rev 205 (1967) (dealing at 221–23 with the adequacy of courtroom observation as a basis for diagnosis); Notes, Psychiatric Impeachment Under Rule 608(a), 32 Okla. L. Rev. 401 (1979).

10. Is evidence of drug or alcohol use admissible to impeach on grounds of character? State v. Wilson, 456 S.E.2d 870 (N.C.App.1995): In child sex abuse prosecution, prejudicial error to ask defendant on cross-examination about drug use. See also People v. Smith, 231 N.E.2d 185 (Ill.1967): Prosecution for theft in which conviction was reversed because of admission of defendant's addiction to drugs to impeach his credibility. The court distinguishes the use of such evidence to attack the credibility of a criminal defendant from its use to attack the credibility of other witnesses. It also discusses the conflict in medical and legal opinion as to the effect of drug use on veracity. Compare evidence of drug or alcohol use on the question of competency, supra p. 293, and to attack credibility by showing effect on ability to perceive, remember or communicate, supra p. 401.

Newton v. State

Court of Appeals of Maryland, 1924.
147 Md. 71, 127 A. 123.

[Prosecution for criminal conspiracy to defraud by misrepresenting the financial condition of a business concern. Defendant was jointly indicted with Harold R. Dickey, Jr., and another, but tried separately. Being convicted, he appealed.]

■ OFFUTT, J., delivered the opinion of the Court....

The thirty-seventh and thirty-eighth exceptions relate to the action of the court in permitting certain questions to be asked in the cross-examination of Harold R. Dickey, Jr., a witness for the defense. After having testified at some length as to the preparation of the Gillespie audit and the result of his examination of the resources and liabilities of the trust, he was asked: "You testified concerning these transactions in the case of the State against Dickey, and the State against Gillespie, giving then the same explanations that you have given us here, did you not?" He was directed over objection to answer that question, and the following colloquy took place: "Well, I can't remember exactly all that I said in the last case. Q. Now, don't split hairs with me. Did you testify in this same way in the trial of your own case? A. I can't remember all of those things, Mr. Leach. Q. Didn't you make substantially the same explanation then that you are making here now today? By Mr. Owens: We are noting an objection and exception to all this. The Court: Yes. Q. (Question by Mr. Leach): In your own trial? A. Practically. Q. And you were convicted, were you not? Q. (Question by Mr. Leach): Go on and answer me. You were convicted in your trial before Judge Gorter and Judge Bond and Judge Stanton, were you not?" In answer to the last question the witness replied that he had been so convicted. This method of cross-examining the witness was in our opinion highly objectionable. If the purpose of the examiner was to impeach the credibility of the witness by showing that he had been convicted of crime, he should have asked him that question directly (40 Cyc. 2607), or if he had intended to show that he had in some other case sworn to statements contrary to his testimony in the instant case, he could have been asked whether he had made such conflicting statements. But these questions had no such object. In addition to intimidating the witness, their only apparent purpose was to bring to the attention of the jury the fact that he had made in his own case, when he was tried for the same crime, not a different but the same statement as that to which he testified in this case, and that the three judges before whom he was tried discredited that statement and convicted him. The obvious purpose was to induce the jury to believe that, as the testimony of the witness as given before them had already been discredited by three judges sitting in the same court in another case, that, therefore, they should discredit it in this case, a wholly unwarranted conclusion unsupported by any authority with which we are familiar. . . .

Judgment reversed and case remanded for a new trial.

■ PARKE, J., dissents.

NOTE

Would it have been permissible for the prosecution in the main case to call the judges who had presided in the earlier trial and elicit from them testimony that they had disbelieved Dickey's story? See State v. Paiz, 277 P. 966 (N.M.1929), holding it improper to allow a justice of the peace who had bound defendant over to narrate a confession made by defendant and add: "I found beyond a reasonable doubt that [defendant] was guilty." Does it make any difference that as the main case was actually conducted the impeachment was attempted by cross-examination of the primary witness, without complicating the trial by calling any impeaching witnesses?

In Green v. State, 155 A. 164, 167 (Md.1931), D was prosecuted for rape, attempted rape and assault and battery on X, P giving evidence that D and W successively ravished X. W, called by D, testified that X consented to intercourse with both D and W. On cross-examination W was compelled to answer questions eliciting testimony to the effect that W had already been convicted of rape on X during the episode. When D appealed from a conviction for assault and battery, the upper court distinguished Newton v. State and affirmed the conviction. Can the cases be justly distinguished? See also Zeller v. Mayson, 179 A. 179, 182 (Md.1935), a civil action for personal injuries, which had been preceded by a cognate criminal case; one party testified in both proceedings; it was held permissible to bring out in the civil trial that this witness had been fined in the prosecution.

The approach tried in Newton v. State is very tempting, but often rejected, as in German v. German, 3 A.2d 849, 850 (Conn.1938), involving alimony and holding improper a reference to a report in previous related action that one party had given untrue testimony. In Shewbart v. State, 32 So.2d 241, 242 (Ala.App.), cert. denied, 32 So.2d 244 (Ala.1947), it was held proper to prevent cross-examination of peace officers who apparently testified against defendant as to whether they had testified against defendant before the grand jury, the grand jury thereafter refusing to indict. In Strong v. State, 23 So.2d 750, 752 (Miss.1945), a man, M, and a woman, W, were prosecuted for unlawful cohabitation; W testified in her own behalf that she had been prosecuted previously, apparently for some phase of the same offense; on cross-examination W was forced to admit that she had been found guilty, but W managed to insert a declaration seeming to mean that the adverse verdict had been set aside; on appeal by M and W, held no error justifying reversal. Cf. disapproval in Martin v. People, 162 P.2d 597, 600 (Colo.1945), of an attempt to strengthen the testimony of a witness for the prosecution by bringing out that he had been acquitted in an earlier related prosecution instigated by the present defendant. Mack v. Commonwealth, 15 S.E.2d 62, 63, 65 (Va.1941), sustains refusal to allow a criminal defendant to attack the credibility of a third party witness by getting the witness to admit that despite his testimony against an alleged associate of defendant, the associate had been acquitted; State v. Williams, 487 P.2d 100 (Or.Ct.App.1971), cert. denied, 406 U.S. 973 (1972), holds it not error to prevent cross-examination of informer, prosecution's only witness to a marijuana sale, as to whether in other cases involving marijuana in which he had testified there had been acquittals; Brazee v. Morris, 179 P.2d 442, 444 (Ariz.1947), reverses for cross-examination of an expert witness bringing out the fact that in a prior disconnected case the verdict had been contrary to the expert's testimony relating to that case; but see United States v. Terry, 702 F.2d 299, 316 (2d Cir.), cert. denied, 461 U.S. 931 (1983), holding it not error to allow question to expert witness on cross-examination whether a judge in another case in which the expert had testified had not found that the expert had "guessed under oath"; the court relied upon Fed.R.Evid. 608(b). See 149 A.L.R. 929, 935 (1944), collecting authorities on admissibility in a civil action of evidence that a witness is under arrest on a charge growing out of the transaction in issue. Contrast Leech v. People, 146 P.2d 346, 347 (Colo.1944), a criminal case in which defendant's associate turned state's evidence; on direct examination the prosecutor elicited testimony from this associate as to his having been charged with the same crime and having pleaded guilty.

e. Prior Inconsistent Statements

Denver City Tramway Co. v. Lomovt

Supreme Court of Colorado, 1912.
53 Colo. 292, 126 P. 276.

■ Mr. Justice Hill delivered the opinion of the court:

Action for personal injuries; judgment was for the plaintiff; the defendant appeals.

The appellee (a minor about eight years of age) while attempting to cross the appellant's street car tracks at the intersection of what is known as West Cable Place and Dale Court in the city of Denver, was struck by an eastbound car, knocked under the fender or guard-rail, and partially run over, from which she received serious and permanent injuries, including the loss of one foot except the heel.

. . .

Earl Murray, a witness upon behalf of the defendant, testified that he saw the accident, was probably one hundred or one hundred twenty feet from where it occurred; that he noticed the car first about twenty feet from the point of the collision; that the little girl was running down the sidewalk near the board fence, pretty close to the track; that the car was coming towards Dale Court; that just before the collision the car was moving five or six miles an hour or a little faster than he could walk, but it appeared to slow down a little before the child was hit; that he carried the child to the drug store. On cross-examination he said that he had made no statement to the defendant or its claim-agent; that he did not talk to him about how the accident occurred; that he simply came and subpoenaed him, and said "How do you do," and went on; that he could not remember the name of the man who subpoenaed him, did not talk with him about the case; that he had never talked with anybody, nor told them what he would testify to; that he had never told a soul, neither the lawyers, the claim-agent, nor anybody else what he would testify to; that when he appeared upon the witness stand they hadn't any idea what he was going to say; that he was positive of these facts; that they brought him there without any knowledge of what his testimony would be. He was further asked and gave answers as follows. "Q. You were pretty mad at the time you picked up this little child, weren't you? A. Yes sir, I was. Q. You said this (with an oath) '. . . motorman ought to be lynched' did you not? A. No sir, I said that you people stand around here—they wouldn't give me a shawl to put around the little girl's foot. Q. Did you say that, that this motorman ought to be lynched? A. No sir. Q. You are as sure of that as you are of the rest of your testimony? A. Yes, Sir. Q. Or that the motorman ought to be lynched or killed? A. No, sir, I didn't say that to nobody." There were no objections to any of this testimony.

In rebuttal two witnesses were called by plaintiff, both of whom, over objections, testified that the witness Murray, at the time and place of the accident, said with an oath that the motorman ought to be lynched. When the objection was made, counsel for the plaintiff said that the evidence was offered solely as affecting the credibility of the witness. The court, in ruling upon the objections, said:

"I think the objections will be overruled; that is, the testimony may be received in a limited sense. Any statement made by the witness at that time, if he did make one upon the line indicated, would not be binding upon this company in any sense, and would not be received by the jury for the purpose of binding the company, or showing their responsibility, but I think I will allow it to go to the question of the credibility of the witness."

Two objections are urged to this evidence. First, that no proper foundation was laid for it at the time the witness Murray was upon the stand. Second, that had the proper foundation been laid, the statement of the witness is wholly immaterial and irrelevant; that it does not throw any light upon his credibility, and his character was not in issue; that it contained no statement of facts and that a witness cannot be impeached upon an immaterial question.

We will consider the objections in the order urged. As to the first, while each question asked the witness Murray concerning the statement purported to have been made did not specifically mention the time and place, they all referred to the time and place, when and where the accident occurred and while he was assisting in removing the child. He was being interrogated as to what he said at that time, and the questions were of such a nature that he could not have misunderstood those facts or have been misled thereby; if other proof was needed, his answers are conclusive of this fact.

In Vol. 2, Elliott on Evidence, the general rule is said to be that the proper foundation must be laid by asking the witness if he made such a statement, in order to give him full opportunity to understand all of the circumstances so as not to be taken off his guard, and his attention must be directed to the time and place when and where the statements were made. But in commenting upon this rule, in section 974, the author says:

"But this rule is to be given a practical application, and it is sufficient if the time, place, person and substance of the statement are designated with reasonable certainty, so that the witness will clearly understand the matter and not be misled.... if the attention is clearly called to the alleged conversation or statement, and circumstances are so detailed that there can be no misunderstanding, it will be sufficient, even though time, place and person are not all fully and specifically designated."

This rule was reasonably complied with; neither the witness, jury, court or counsel could have been misled for any failure to make it more specific.

The second objection presents a more serious question. It is claimed that ... the statement, if true, pertained to no fact concerning the accident; that it was entirely foreign to that issue, simply a declaration by the witness (a bystander) after the accident as to something that he thought ought to be done. This objection raises two questions: first, was the impeaching testimony improperly admitted? second, if so, was it prejudicial? ...

The questions to the witness Murray were without objection. On cross-examination in such matters a large discretion is vested in the trial court, but when it comes to contradicting the answers the discretion is not so extensive. Was this statement by the witness Murray, if made, at variance and inconsistent with his testimony? and was it pertinent to the substance of any material subject testified to by him? or did it constitute an extraordinary statement in any way conflicting, or tending to conflict with, his testimony? It will be observed that he was an eyewitness to the accident, and according to his testimony the car was running at an unusual slow rate of speed, and made a good stop. The substance of his entire testimony is that there was no negligence upon behalf of the motorman, but that the child was running down the sidewalk near the board fence, and ran upon the track where she was hit. The only rational conclusion to be drawn from his testimony is that the accident was due solely to the negligence of the child; yet, regardless of this and immediately at that time while assisting in removing the child he stated, according to the other witnesses, that the motorman ought to be lynched. The jury heard his testimony, which, as far as it went, was to exonerate the employees of the company from any negligence.

In the case of Askew v. The People, 23 Colo. 446, 48 P. 524, this court said, "The test of whether a fact inquired of in cross-examination is collateral, is this: Would the cross-examining party be entitled to prove it as a part of his case, tending to establish his plea?" Accepting this as a correct declaration of the law, when applied to this case, was not the substance of the purported statement by the witness Murray what the plaintiff had the right to prove to establish her cause of action, to wit, the wrongdoing, the negligence of the motorman in the operation of the car? The witness is purported to have said that the motorman ought to be lynched. Is not this, in substance, a statement by him that the motorman had committed a wrong, had done an injury to the child? The only way that he could have done her an injury or have committed a wrong was in his negligence in the management and operation of his car. It will be observed that the witness did not condemn the company in the appliances furnished or otherwise, nor the conductor in the discharge of his duties. This statement was purported to have been given at the time of the accident; the witness had an opportunity on the stand to explain it, but instead he denied making it.

Applying the general principles announced in the books heretofore cited to the facts here, we think this alleged statement of the witness Murray was of such a character that the jury might rightfully draw the inference that it was equivalent to a declaration that the motorman was negligent in the operation of his car, and was therefore inconsistent with his testimony at the trial, and under the circumstances of this case was proper as an inconsistent statement as affecting the credibility of his evidence. Further, some of his answers were peculiar wherein he says that he had never talked with anybody about this matter, or what he would testify to; that he had never told a soul, neither the lawyers, the claim-agent, nor anybody else; that when he appeared upon the witness stand they hadn't any idea what he was going to say; that he was positive of these facts. His testimony was very favorable to the defendant, and in conflict with that of numerous other witnesses.

From these facts, when considered with the fact that the substance and effect of this purported statement could probably be construed as in conflict with the substance of his testimony, and when considered with the further fact that the trial court, in admitting it, stated that it might be received in a limited sense only, that it would not be received by the jury for the purpose of binding the defendant, or showing their responsibility, the jury not taking it for these purposes, but only upon the question of the credibility of the witness; we conclude that the trial court was justified in thus allowing this liberal attitude as affecting the credibility of the witness. Having determined that the impeaching matter was not immaterial but in substance as coming within the rule of contradictory or inconsistent acts and statements, it is unnecessary to discuss whether its admission would have been a harmless error.

The other errors urged have been considered, but from a careful review of the entire record, we are of opinion that no error of sufficient importance is shown to justify a reversal. The judgment is affirmed....

■ MR. JUSTICE MUSSER and MR. JUSTICE GARRIGUES, concur.

NOTES

The foregoing case illustrates application of a method of witness impeachment that is extremely common and hedged in by rules frequently mentioned but not always adequately understood. The following matters, most of which the case mentions, are important:

1. If a witness on cross-examination unreservedly admits a self-contradiction, the trial judge's ruling that he should not be questioned further on the matter ordinarily will be sustained. But when such an admission is hesitant or qualified or lacking in circumstantial detail, the cross-examiner will be entitled to press his point further. If cross-examination fails to elicit a satisfactory admission of self-contradiction, the cross-examiner will be entitled to introduce extrinsic evidence to establish it, assuming other requirements for the use of such evidence are satisfied. People v. Schainuck, 36 N.E.2d 94 (N.Y.1941), mere "conclusory statement" of admission by primary witness does not bar further evidence of details of contradiction; Chicago, M. & St. P. R. Co. v. Harrelson, 14 F.2d 893, 896 (8th Cir.1926), hesitant or qualified admission; United States v.

Lashmett, 965 F.2d 179, 181–83 (7th Cir.1992), error, though harmless, not to permit introduction of extrinsic evidence of prior inconsistent statements even though witness had admitted making them. See also Bentley v. State, 397 P.2d 976, 978 (Alaska 1965):

> The jury had the duty of appraising Mrs. Fambrough's trustworthiness. Such an appraisal might have been made with far greater discernment if the jury had been permitted to hear the taped conversation rather than being limited to hearing only Mrs. Fambrough's simple, unemphatic admission that she made a statement to appellant which was inconsistent with her testimony at the trial. The jury ought to have had the opportunity to consider the circumstances in which Mrs. Fambrough conversed with appellant and to weigh what she actually said against her testimony at the trial in order, if possible, to ferret out every detail of the motive which induced her to say to appellant that she had not seen a knife and then to tell the jury that she had seen one. Such an opportunity was not available to the jury from the cross examination of Mrs. Fambrough to as great an extent as it would have been if they had been permitted to consider the tape recording. We hold that appellant was entitled to have the recording considered by the jury because it would have best informed the jury as to the recording's impeaching weight and significance.[1]

2. When is there inconsistency between testimony and prior statement? In United States v. Barrett, 539 F.2d 244, 253–54 (1st Cir.1976), the court found sufficient inconsistency to justify holding that the trial court had erred in excluding evidence of the prior statement. On direct examination a prosecution witness testified that shortly after the defendant's arrest defendant had described to the witness his involvement in the crime. The witness's prior statement was: "[I]t was a shame that Bucky [the defendant] got arrested on this matter," because he knew that "Bucky didn't have anything to do with it." "To be received as a prior inconsistent statement, the contradiction need not be 'in plain terms. It is enough if the proffered testimony, taken as a whole, either by what it says or by what it omits to say, affords some indication that the fact was different from the testimony of the witness whom it is sought to contradict.' " Id. at 254, quoting Commonwealth v. West, 45 N.E.2d 260, 262 (Mass.1942). United States v. Williams, 737 F.2d 594, 608 (7th Cir.1984), cert. denied, 470 U.S. 1003 (1985): "As long as people speak in nonmathematical languages such as English . . . it will be difficult to determine precisely whether two statements are inconsistent. But we do not read the word 'inconsistent' in [Federal] Rule [of Evidence] 801(d)(1)(A) to include only statements diametrically opposed or logically incompatible. Inconsistency 'may be found in evasive answers, . . . silence, or changes in positions.' " But see Rogall v. Kischer, 273 N.E.2d 681, 687 (Ill.App.1971): Collision between automobile and pedestrian; the court found no error in prohibiting inquiry of a witness whether he had not earlier said that he saw "three boys trying to beat the traffic across" North Avenue when he testified on direct examination that he saw children "crossing or attempting to cross" North Avenue.

Should the defendant in a bank robbery case be entitled to impeach an identification witness with the witness's prior statement to a defense investigator that "all blacks looked alike" to him? See United States v. Nobles, 422 U.S. 225, 232 (1975).

As to the plea of nolo contendere as a prior inconsistent statement, see Dunham v. Pannell, 263 F.2d 725 (5th Cir.1959).

---

1. Footnotes omitted.

If a witness testifies that he has no memory of a particular matter, is a prior statement concerning the matter inconsistent with present testimony? Is the requirement that there be inconsistency nothing more than a requirement that the evidence of the prior statement be relevant to credibility? If a witness omits in an earlier statement mention of a fact that he covers in his testimony, or has been entirely silent about the matter to which he later testifies, should the earlier omission or silence be treated as inconsistent for impeachment purposes?

United States v. Hale, 422 U.S. 171 (1975), involved the impeachment of a criminal defendant with his earlier silence. Defendant had been pointed out to the police by a robbery victim as one of the men who held him up and took $65 or $96. Defendant was arrested, taken to the police station and advised of his right to remain silent. He was searched and found in possession of $158. When a policeman asked him where he got the money, defendant made no response. At trial defendant took the stand and testified to his innocence. He explained his possession of the money by saying that his wife had cashed her welfare check that day and given him the proceeds to buy money orders. On cross-examination, the prosecutor caused the defendant to admit that he had not offered this explanation to the police at the time of his arrest. The Supreme Court, exercising its supervisory power over the lower federal courts, held the cross-examination impermissible. Under the circumstances of the case, the Court said, the probative value of defendant's silence was outweighed by its prejudicial effect. As bearing on the probative value of the defendant's silence, the Court listed these considerations: defendant had been advised that he had a right not to speak and that anything he said might be used against him; defendant might not have understood the question; the situation in which the defendant found himself was hostile and unfamiliar; the questioning took place in secret and lacked any safeguards for the defendant; given the evidence that the police had against the defendant, he had no reason to think that any explanation by him would hasten his release. The Court observed, furthermore, that the jury was likely to assign more weight to defendant's silence than was warranted. "We recognize that the question whether evidence is sufficiently inconsistent to be sent to the jury on the issue of credibility is ordinarily in the discretion of the trial court. 'But where such evidentiary matters have grave constitutional overtones . . . we feel justified in exercising this Court's supervisory control.' " Id. at 180 n. 7. For the Court's subsequent answer to the constitutional question, see Doyle v. Ohio, 426 U.S. 610, 96 S.Ct. 2240 (1976), infra p. 463.

People v. Colarco, 417 N.Y.S.2d 681 (App.Div.1979), involved an attempt to impeach by evidence of silence not the defendant, but his alibi witness. The prosecutor asked the witness when she did or did not tell her story to the prosecutor. The alibi witness was the defendant's mother-in-law; two eyewitnesses had told the prosecutor that the defendant had committed the crime. See also United States v. Carr, 584 F.2d 612, 618 (2d Cir.1978), cert. denied, 440 U.S. 935 (1979): Not error to seek to elicit from a defense witness who had testified that defendant's son rather than defendant had received certain firearms, that the witness had not volunteered this information to the authorities. United States v. Sheffield, 992 F.2d 1164, 1167–69 (11th Cir.1993): Where prosecution witness testified it was defendant who had ordered use of government facilities for private purpose, error to prevent defendant from introducing evidence that when on an earlier occasion an official had questioned the witness about the matter, the witness had not mentioned the defendant.

3. It would appear that unless a witness's testimony has damaged a party, there is no justification for impeachment either by prior inconsistent statement or otherwise, if by impeachment is meant undermining credibility for the purpose of returning probabilities to what they were before the witness testified. The requirement of damage is as applicable in the case of attacking an opponent's witness, the topic now being considered, as in the case of attacking one's own witness, a topic discussed supra p. 396. The requirement of damage is closely connected with the principle, shortly to be discussed, that a prior inconsistent statement may be used only to impeach and not for "substantive" purposes. Testimony of lack of knowledge or inability to remember ordinarily, although not invariably, as was seen in the discussion of impeaching one's own witness, supra p. 396, does not cause damage. On the other hand, if a witness testifies that he has no memory of topic A, there may be no damage on that topic, but he may have given damaging testimony on topic B. If there is inconsistency between his claimed present lack of recollection on topic A and his earlier statement about A, that inconsistency, arguably, can undermine the witness's credibility on topic B. Whether the prior inconsistent statement is admissible to impeach in this indirect fashion is addressed in the next paragraph.

4. An earlier discussion of when evidence may be introduced to contradict a witness with the testimony of another witness found a limiting principle in the opinion of Chief Baron Pollock in Attorney–General v. Hitchcock, 1 Exch. 91 (1847), supra p. 402: "[I]f the answer of a witness is a matter which you would be allowed on your part to prove in evidence—if it have such a connection with the issue, that you would be allowed to give it in evidence—then it is a matter on which you may contradict him." The opinion of Baron Rolfe in the same case applies the principle to evidence of self-contradiction by a witness. The opinion gives a hypothetical: "The witness is asked, 'Have you not received a bribe?' 'I have not.' 'Have you never said you had?' 'I never said so.' " In this hypothetical, the opinion implies, if the witness denies he said he received a bribe, evidence could be introduced to show that he had said so. It is to be noted that Baron Rolfe's hypothetical concerns a fact relevant to bias, not to a material issue in the case. If the opinions in Attorney–General v. Hitchcock are taken together, they can be read to stand for the proposition that evidence of self-contradiction on the part of a witness may be introduced about any topic in respect to which the cross-examiner would be permitted to introduce evidence independently of the self-contradiction. A topic relevant to a material issue in the case, or concerning the witness's opportunity for observation or bias, would be such topics; bad acts bearing on character for truthfulness would not be.

State v. Swartz, 126 P. 1091 (Kan.1912): The witness said he saw the defendant come home at midnight, thereby providing him with an alibi. On cross-examination, the witness denied having previously told X that he had been asleep when the defendant came home. The state was permitted to call X, who testified that the witness had made such a statement. State v. Veluzat, 578 A.2d 93, 95 (R.I.1990): Prosecution for sexual assault on Miller's daughter by defendant, a part-time resident in Miller's home. In the course of her direct examination, Miller stated that her nephew did not live in her home. On cross-examination of Miller, defendant sought to ask if in an application for public assistance, Miller had not said that the nephew lived in her home. Held: Not abuse of discretion to disallow the question.

5. The still-prevailing rule in the United States is that a prior inconsistent statement may be used only to impeach and not for "substantive" value. See Barrowman, Current and Proposed Use of Prior Inconsistent Statements in Criminal Trials, 1991 Crim. L. Q. 444, 458–62 (survey of jurisdictions). Note, 38 Vill. L. Rev. 285 (1993), tracing repudiation by Pennsylvania of orthodox rule in 1986, followed six years later by imposition of limitations; survey of jurisdictions. The explanation usually given is that to allow full evidential use would violate the policy of the hearsay rule. Judgment on this question must await full discussion of the hearsay rule and its application generally to extrajudicial statements by witnesses, infra pp. 522–63. That discussion may also provide a basis for deciding whether even mere impeaching use of a prior inconsistent statement is possible without compromising to some degree the hearsay policy. See People v. Hults, 556 N.E.2d 1077 (N.Y.1990): Defendant barred from impeaching identification witness with prior inconsistent statement because defense counsel conceded the unreliability of the statement; argument rejected that since the statement was offered only to impeach, unreliability was irrelevant. A minority of states permit full evidential use of a prior inconsistent statement by a witness who testifies and is subject to cross-examination. Fed. R. Evid. 801(d)(1)(A) permits such use if the statement was "given under oath subject to the penalty of perjury at a trial, hearing, or other proceeding. . . ." Is the inconsistency required for a statement to come within 801(d)(1)(A) the same as the inconsistency required for mere impeachment—supra p. 457—or does the function of 801(d)(1)(A) in distinguishing hearsay from nonhearsay suggest a different standard? See United States v. Williams, 737 F.2d 594, 607–08 (7th Cir.1984), cert. denied, 470 U.S. 1003 (1985).

If a prior inconsistent statement is admissible only to impeach, an instruction ordinarily will be given that the statement may be used for this purpose alone and not for full evidential value. That there is a risk the jury will not understand or will ignore this limitation ordinarily is not ground for exclusion. By contrast, when a party seeks to impeach his own witness, this danger is taken into account and inquiry is made into whether the party created the need for impeachment in order to evade the prohibition against substantive use, supra p. 398. In the context now being considered—impeachment of a witness called by the other party—the party seeking to impeach is simply trying to undo damage caused to him by his opponent.

6. The opinion in the Lomovt case discusses and applies the traditional requirement that a "foundation" must be laid during cross-examination of a witness, alerting him to the substance and circumstances of the prior inconsistent statement, before extrinsic evidence of the statement may be introduced. There has always been debate about the desirability of this requirement. Tucker v. Welsh, 17 Mass. 160, 166 (1821): "[T]he utility of such a practice is not very obvious. Witnesses about to be impeached are generally persons of a doubtful or unknown character, and the wisdom of putting them upon their guard, and enabling them to forestall an answer to [by?] the opposing witness, is not very discernible." Coles v. Harsch, 276 P. 248, 250 (1929):

> Every witness, whose testimony is shown in conflict with a previous statement made by him, is not necessarily revealed thereby as a dishonest person; the impeachment, in many instances, may uncover only a faulty memory in the discredited witness. The requirement that identifying circumstances of time, place, those present, and the statement that the witness then made shall be related to him, is founded upon the experience, which frequently presents itself in the courtroom, that a witness, who has stoutly denied having made an alleged statement, may finally blushingly and apologetically admit it, when the questioner throws into association with it identifying circumstances. It is a common observation that associated ideas, as they are related, one after another, not infrequently succeed in upturning a fact which previously had defied all efforts of recollection. And so this rule of evidence is intended to reveal not only the dishonest witness, but is also intended to afford all witnesses ample opportunity to recall a fact before they may be assailed as dishonest. The requirement also tends

to reduce to the minimum a confusion of issues by eliminating unnecessary impeachments: Wig. on Ev. (2d Ed.) § 1019.

Fed.R.Evid. 613(b) relaxes the foundation requirement to the extent that the witness need not be questioned about the inconsistent statement before extrinsic evidence is introduced. All that is required is an opportunity to explain or deny and an opportunity for the opposite party to interrogate regarding the statement at some time. See United States v. Hudson, 970 F.2d 948 (1st Cir.1992), reversing conviction because trial court excluded extrinsic evidence of prior inconsistent statement without evaluating the availability of the primary witness for recall or considering what delay or inconvenience might have been caused by defense counsel's failure to confront the witness with the prior inconsistent statement during cross-examination. The court reaffirmed the position it took in United States v. Barrett, 539 F.2d 244 (1st Cir.1976), that Rule 613(b) does not have a strict requirement that an opportunity to explain have been provided during cross-examination. But see Wammock v. Celotex Corp., 793 F.2d 1518, 1521–27 (11th Cir.1986): Cross-examining counsel knew that an expert witness's testimony was inconsistent with the general nature of the witness's testimony in prior trials, although counsel did not know the exact content of the former testimony. Nevertheless, counsel did not show surprise nor indicate, while the witness was on the stand, that he might introduce prior inconsistent statements. Instead, counsel offered evidence of the prior inconsistent statements at the end of the trial, when the witness had become unavailable. Held, not an abuse of discretion to exclude the evidence under Fed.R.Evid. 613(b). For a discussion of Rule 613(b), see Graham, Employing Inconsistent Statements for Impeachment and as Substantive Evidence: A Critical Review and Proposed Amendments of Federal Rules of Evidence 801(d)(1)(A), 613, and 607, 75 Mich.L.Rev. 1565, 1593–1610 (1977). See also Annot., 40 A.L.R.Fed. 629 (1978). United States v. Bibbs, 564 F.2d 1165 (5th Cir.1977), cert. denied, 435 U.S. 1007 (1978), points out that Rule 613 does not apply to inconsistent statements made after a witness has testified and that in that situation the trial court should fashion a fair procedure in accordance with the mandate of Fed.R.Evid. 102. In Bibbs the inconsistent statement was made after the witness had left the stand, following direct and cross-examination.

It is usually held that when the witness is a party litigant, and his extrajudicial inconsistent utterances consequently are admissions, no foundation need be laid on his examination as a prerequisite to admission of evidence of these utterances. E.g., State v. Mays, 395 P.2d 758 (Wash.1964), cert. denied, 380 U.S. 953 (1965); People v. Ashford, 71 Cal.Rptr. 619 (App.1968). See the last sentence of Fed.R.Evid. 613(b). In Moe v. Blue Springs Truck Lines, 426 S.W.2d 1 (Mo.1968), defendant testified that just before he ran into plaintiff's vehicle, the light was green, plaintiff started forward and then suddenly stopped. Held, not error to allow plaintiff on rebuttal to introduce evidence of defendant's conviction on a plea of guilty of operating a vehicle in a careless manner on the occasion in question without having inquired into the matter on cross-examination. See supra p. 415 on whether a foundation must be laid before extrinsic evidence may be introduced relevant to bias.

Fed. R. Evid. 806 provides: "Evidence of a statement or conduct by the declarant at any time, inconsistent with the declarant's hearsay statement, is not subject to any requirement that the declarant may have been afforded an opportunity to deny or explain." Frey v. Barnes Hosp., 706 S.W.2d 51 (Mo.App. 1986): Permissible to impeach deponent with an inconsistent statement contained in another deposition in another case, taken after the first deposition, because the proponent of the first deposition knew the impeachment was planned and had ample opportunity to present the deponent to explain or rebut the inconsistent statement. People v. Collup, 167 P.2d 714, 717, 719 (Cal.1946): Enforcement of foundation requirement disapproved in connection with reported testimony of absent witness. But see Gong v. Hirsch, 913 F.2d 1269, 1274 (7th Cir.1990):

> The plaintiff also sought to introduce the letter to impeach the videotaped deposition testimony of Dr. Schleinkofer. The doctor had given deposition testimony on behalf of the plaintiff in April 1988, and this videotaped deposition was played for the jury during the trial. During the defendant's videotaped cross-examination of Dr. Schleinkofer, the doctor had testified that he could not say within a reasonable degree of medical certainty that the ulcer was caused by prednisone. On redirect examination, the plaintiff's counsel had shown Dr. Schleinkofer the letter and asked him whether he authored the letter, to which the doctor responded "yes." Counsel then immediately moved on to the discussion of another topic without asking the doctor any questions about the content of the letter or the alleged inconsistency between the statement in the letter that Mr. Gong's ulcer was "due to prednisone" and the doctor's response on cross-examination that he could not say whether the ulcer was caused by prednisone.

> The videotaped deposition was shown to the jury during trial on the morning of September 14, 1988. That afternoon during trial, plaintiff's counsel sought to introduce the letter into evidence to impeach the videotaped testimony of Dr. Schleinkofer. The district court sustained an objection to admission of the letter on the ground that plaintiff's counsel had failed to lay a proper foundation for its introduction. The court explained that counsel had failed in this regard by neglecting to ask the witness any questions about the contents of the letter or to give the witness a chance to explain the circumstances in which he wrote the letter.

> Under the circumstances presented here, we do not believe that the district court abused its discretion in concluding that plaintiff's counsel did not lay a sufficient foundation for admission of the letter for purposes of impeaching Dr. Schleinkofer.... Here, counsel for the plaintiff merely elicited the witness' admission that he authored a letter and then proceeded to another topic without establishing the significance of the letter or affording the witness an opportunity to explain the alleged inconsistent statement in the letter.... Given the potential prejudicial effect of allowing the admission of the letter for impeachment purposes at a time when the witness was unavailable to explain the alleged inconsistency or to be examined by the defendant concerning the contents of the letter, the district court acted within its discretion in refusing to admit the letter.[2]

7. An earlier rule called the "Rule of the Queen's Case" required that before a witness could be cross-examined about a written prior inconsistent statement, it was necessary to show him the writing. This rule is abolished by Fed. R. Evid. 613(a).

8. As a precondition to asking a witness if he has made a prior inconsistent statement, must counsel have admissible evidence that he did so? United States v. Bohle, 445 F.2d 54, 72–76 (7th Cir.1971), says that he must. See the list of authorities to the same effect in Graham, cited in Note 6 supra, at 1599–1600 n. 104. United States v. Gholston, 10 F.3d 384, 388–89 (6th Cir.1993), cert. denied, 114 S.Ct. 2116, suggests that he need not. Is this requirement consis-

---

2.   Footnote omitted.

tent with what is required in the case of impeachment by bias, convictions, bad acts?

9. In Harris v. New York, 401 U.S. 222 (1971), the Supreme Court held that there is no constitutional violation in using a prior inconsistent statement to impeach a criminal defendant who takes the stand even though the statement was obtained by police officers without informing defendant of his right to remain silent and to counsel as required by Miranda v. Arizona, 384 U.S. 436 (1966). Impeachment use was also permitted in Oregon v. Hass, 420 U.S. 714 (1975), where Miranda warnings were given. After the warnings were given, the defendant asked to see a lawyer, but was told that he would have to wait until they reached the police station. Shortly after this the defendant made the inculpatory statement that was used to impeach him. See also Michigan v. Harvey, 494 U.S. 344 (1990): Permissible to impeach defendant with statement taken after he had been formally charged and had requested assistance of his counsel. In Mincey v. Arizona, 437 U.S. 385 (1978), however, the Court held that an involuntary statement could not be used for any purpose including impeachment. See also New Jersey v. Portash, 440 U.S. 450 (1979), prohibiting impeachment with grand jury testimony obtained under a grant of immunity.

In Doyle v. Ohio, 426 U.S. 610 (1976), the Court held that due process was violated by eliciting from the defendant on cross-examination the information that when he was under arrest and had been given Miranda warnings, he kept silent and did not give the exculpatory explanation that he gave in his direct testimony. Likewise in Wainwright v. Greenfield, 474 U.S. 284 (1986), it was held violative of due process to use a defendant's post-Miranda warnings exercise of his right to remain silent and consult with counsel to show his sanity. In Greer v. Miller, 483 U.S. 756 (1987), the prosecutor asked the defendant why he had not told the exculpatory story he testified to at the trial at the time he was arrested—at which time he had been given Miranda warnings. The trial court instructed the jury to disregard the question and there was no mention of the incident in argument. The Supreme Court held there was no Doyle violation because "the postarrest silence was not submitted to the jury" and the prosecutorial misconduct in asking the question did not so infect the trial with unfairness that the defendant's conviction was a violation of due process.

In Jenkins v. Anderson, 447 U.S. 231 (1980), the Court held it did not violate due process to impeach the defendant with prearrest silence. In that case the defendant claimed he had acted in self-defense in killing the victim, but the prosecutor brought out in cross-examination that defendant had not reported the incident to the authorities for some weeks. Finally, in Fletcher v. Weir, 455 U.S. 603 (1982), the Court held it did not violate due process to impeach the defendant with post-arrest silence when he had not been given Miranda warnings.

Walder v. United States, 347 U.S. 62 (1954), permits the use of evidence obtained through an unconstitutional search and seizure to contradict a defendant in what he asserts in his direct testimony. United States v. Havens, 446 U.S. 620 (1980), permits the use of illegally obtained evidence not only for this purpose, but also to contradict "statements made in response to proper cross-examination reasonably suggested by defendant's direct examination...." Id. at 627. But James v. Illinois, 493 U.S. 307 (1990), holds that a defendant's confession, which was the fruit of an illegal arrest, could not be used to contradict a defense witness other than the defendant.

In regard to the related subjects of using unconstitutionally obtained evidence to refresh recollection, and unconstitutionally obtained convictions to impeach, see supra p. 351 and p. 428.

C. REHABILITATION

Rodriguez v. State

Court of Criminal Appeals of Texas, 1957.
165 Tex.Crim. 179, 305 S.W.2d 350.

■ WOODLEY, J.

The offense is aggravated assault; the punishment, 9 months in jail and a fine of $750.

Appellant, aged 66 years, came to the home of Ramon Gavia on a Sunday afternoon to see Gavia.

Gavia was not at home and appellant was invited by Gavia's daughter, Cathalina, to wait for her father.

Cathalina Gavia testified that she left the room for a few minutes and upon her return appellant and her seven year old foster daughter were on the couch and appellant was holding one hand on the child's mouth and was taking her pants off, and she ran and got the child and called some friends who notified the officers.

The child was found not to be competent to testify.

Appellant testified and denied any assault was made on the child. His version was that the little girl went to the bathroom and returned with her panties down, and he called her to him to assist her in pulling them up which he was doing when Cathalina Gavia came into the room, ordered him to leave and called the officers.

Appellant further testified that on the previous day he had seen Cathalina in a car on a country road and a man was 'lying down on her legs'; that when he came to see Cathalina's father, he spoke to her about what he had seen and she denied it and got mad, and shortly thereafter charged him with assaulting the child.

Cathalina was then recalled and denied that she had been on any country road or with a man on Saturday, and further denied that appellant had spoken to her about any such incident at her home on Sunday.

The jury accepted the State's version of the matter and the testimony of Cathalina Gavia as true, and such evidence is sufficient to sustain their verdict.

. . .

After the testimony above mentioned had been given by appellant and by the State's witness Cathalina Gavia, the State was permitted over objection to prove that Cathalina's reputation in the community for truth and veracity was good.

We are cited to the rule that where there is no evidence to impeach the testimony of a witness except contradictory evidence, it is not permissible to bolster the testimony of the witness by proof of his good reputation for truth and veracity. Jones v. State, 52 Tex.Cr.R. 206, 106 S.W. 126; Zysman v. State, 42 Tex.Cr.R. 432, 60 S.W. 669.

This rule has no application here for where an attack is made upon the veracity of a witness, such as by evidence that the witness has conspired with another to falsely accuse the defendant, or where it is attempted to be shown that the witness is testifying under corrupt motives, or is fabricating testimony, it is proper to permit testimony that the witness has a good reputation for truth and veracity. Helton v. State, Tex.Cr.App., 125 S.W. 21; Thompson v. State, 74 Tex.Cr.R. 145, 167 S.W. 345; Wilkerson v. State, 60 Tex.Cr.R. 388, 131 S.W. 1108.

No reversible error appearing, the judgment is affirmed.

NOTE

Fed. R. Evid. 608(a)(2) provides: "[E]vidence of truthful character is admissible only after the character of the witness for truthfulness has been attacked by opinion or reputation evidence or otherwise." Fed. R. Evid. 608(b), as earlier noted, supra p. 432, provides that specific instances of the conduct of a witness "for the purpose of attacking or supporting the witness' credibility ... may ... be inquired into on cross-examination of the witness (1) concerning the witness' character for truthfulness or untruthfulness...." See also the discussion supra p. 388 as to when a witness may be accredited and the observations at the beginning of the discussion of Reputation and Opinion of Character Evidence concerning who may initiate an inquiry into character for substantive and impeachment purposes, supra p. 444.

The Advisory Committee's Note to Fed. R. Evid. 608(a) includes the following observation: "Opinion or reputation that the witness is untruthful specifically qualifies as an attack under the rule, and evidence of misconduct, including conviction of crime, and of corruption also fall within this category. Evidence of bias or interest does not.... Whether evidence in the form of contradiction is an attack upon the character of the witness must depend upon the circumstances.... " In the Rodriguez case was there an attack on Cathalina's character such as would justify rehabilitation under 608(a)?

United States v. Medical Therapy Sciences, Inc., 583 F.2d 36, 38–42 (2d Cir.1978), cert. denied, 439 U.S. 1130 (1979), interestingly discusses the questions addressed by the Advisory Committee. In regard to bias, the court observed: "Some types of bias, for example bias stemming from a relationship with a party, do not necessarily involve any issue relating to the moral character of the witness, but suggest only that the witness' testimony may perhaps unwittingly be slanted for reasons unrelated to general propensity for untruthfulness. As such, character evidence is not relevant to meet such an attack. On the other hand, alleged partiality based on hostility or self-interest may assume greater significance if it is sought to be proven by conduct rising to the level of corruption." Id. at 41. The court found that corruption was involved in the conduct of the witness in the case before it. In regard to contradiction, the court observed: "[H]ere the contradiction specifically implicated ... [the witness's] veracity." Id. at 41 n. 6. State v. Wells, 423 A.2d 221, 226 (Me.1980), states that the authorities are nearly unanimous that mere contradiction does not open the way to evidence of character for truthfulness. United States v. Danehy, 680 F.2d 1311, 1314 (11th Cir.1982), holds that the mere fact that the prosecutor pointed out a discrepancy between defendant's testimony and that of other witnesses did not open the way for evidence of defendant's good reputation for truthfulness. People v. Miller, 890 P.2d 84 (Colo.1995): Lower court erred in finding there was the requisite attack on credibility simply because defendant had taken the stand and his credibility was an issue in the case.

But see Sahin v. State, 653 A.2d 452, 457, 459 (Md.1995): Error not to allow defendant to introduce in his case evidence of his good reputation and opinion of character for truthfulness when the crime for which he was being prosecuted was an "impeachable offense." The prosecution was for distribution of cocaine.

> We hold that, when a defendant charged with a crime which would be an impeachable offense elects to testify, the State's evidence that the defendant committed the impeachable offense constitutes an attack sufficient to allow the defendant to present character evidence of his or her good character for truthfulness.

The 1971 Revision of the initial draft of the proposed federal rules of evidence added language which would have expressly allowed a criminal defendant who testifies to introduce evidence of good character for truthfulness. Revised Draft of Proposed Rules of Evidence for the United States Courts and Magistrates, 51 F.R.D. 315, 388–90 (March, 1971). An explanation for that proposal was:

> "In a sense a defendant is always intensely interested in the outcome of the case and is impeached by his status alone. While this change was a modification of common law theory, it followed courthouse practice in many parts of the country. Typically a character witness for the defendant is called once and asked all the questions under Rules 404(a)(1) and 404(a)(3) and 608. For example, in an assault case he is asked both about defendant's reputation for peacefulness and, when defendant will take, or has taken, the stand, about the defendant's reputation for veracity. Since character witnesses normally have other things to do and their testimony is usually brief, they are typically put on the stand as soon as they arrive in court, whether or not the defendant has already testified."[1]

Beard v. Mitchell, 604 F.2d 485, 503 (7th Cir.1979), held it was not error to permit the defendant to introduce evidence of his good reputation for truthfulness, the plaintiff having impeached him with a prior inconsistent statement.

United States v. Medical Therapy Sciences, Inc., supra, presents the question whether a party should be allowed to introduce evidence of a good reputation for truthfulness when his own direct examination of the witness first brought out the impeaching information that the reputation evidence seeks to offset. In that case, a prosecution for fraudulent Medicare claims, on direct examination of the prosecution witness, a former associate of the defendant, it was brought out that she had twice been convicted of fraud and also that the defendant had accused her of embezzling from him. On cross-examination and also by extrinsic evidence, defendant explored the matter of the witness's convictions and her alleged embezzlement. "While we do not think that Rule 608(a) should make supporting character evidence available to a party who elicits impeachment material on direct examination for impeaching purposes, we do believe that, when the tenor of the direct examination does not suggest an 'attack' on veracity, and when cross examination *can* be characterized as such an attack, the trial judge should retain the discretion to permit the use of character witnesses. His proximity to the situation allows him to make the determination of when, and by whom, an attack is made. Were the rule to be otherwise, a party would have to choose between revealing, on direct, the

---

1. Footnote omitted.

background of a witness and its right to use character evidence if the witness' veracity is subsequently impugned." Id. at 40.

State v. Webb, 828 P.2d 1351 (Mont.1992): Although prosecution may have been entitled to bring out on direct examination its witness's use of drugs in order to avoid jury surmise that it was hiding the information, when the defense did no more on cross-examination than ask a few questions about drug use, questions that were neither sharp nor accusatory, it was error to allow the prosecution to introduce opinion evidence of the witness's good character for truthfulness.

In United States v. Lechoco, 542 F.2d 84 (D.C.Cir.1976), it was held error not to allow the defendant to introduce evidence of his good reputation for veracity even though he did not take the stand as a witness. The issue was defendant's sanity and three psychiatrists testified for him that he was suffering from mental disease at the time of the acts with which he was charged. Their opinions depended substantially on interviews with the defendant. On cross-examination of the psychiatrists, questions were asked that either directly or inferentially suggested that defendant had deceived them.

Consideration of rehabilitation by prior consistent statement after impeachment by prior inconsistent statement, a topic closely involved with hearsay policy, is found infra pp. 540–52.

D. MECHANICAL AND CHEMICAL MEANS OF ASSESSING CREDIBILITY

1. THE LIE DETECTOR

Some information about how lie detectors work and important bibliographical references as contained in the court's opinion in Brown v. Darcy, 783 F.2d 1389, 1392 n. 2 (9th Cir.1986):

> Modern polygraph instruments measure blood pressure, pulse, respiration, and galvanic skin reflex. See Reid & Inbau, Truth and Deception, The Polygraph ("Lie–Detector") Technique 5–6 (2d ed. 1977); Tarlow, Admissibility of Polygraph Evidence in 1975: An Aid in Determining Credibility In a Perjury–Plagued System, 26 Hastings L.J. 917, 921–22 (1975). Polygraphy is based on the theory that the stress of lying creates physiological responses which can be detected by monitoring these four factors. Tarlow, supra, at 921–22; Skolnick, Scientific Theory and Scientific Evidence: An Analysis of Lie–Detection, 70 Yale L.J. 694, 699–703 (1961). In a zone of comparison polygraph test ... the subject is asked a "control question" designed to elicit an untruthful response. Reid & Inbau, supra at 28–30; Tarlow, supra at 921–22 & n. 35. This lie will give the examiner feedback which will be used for comparison when the subject is asked questions regarding the subject under investigation, known as "relevant questions." If the subject is telling the truth in response to the relevant questions, the physiological response should be less significant than the response measured when the control question is answered. Reid & Inbau, supra at 29.

The court's opinion in Brown v. Darcy also provides information on the accuracy of lie detector tests as determined by laboratory and field studies. 783 F.2d at 1395–96 n. 12. The court sums-up the information by saying: "Estimates on the reliability with which polygraph examinations predict whether the examiner is telling the truth range from seventy percent to ninety-five percent."

. . . Inbau & Reid, Lie Detection and Criminal Interrogation 111–12 (3d ed. 1953) (estimating 95% accuracy in 4,280 criminal investigations over five years); Holmes, The Degree of Objectivity in Chart Interpretation, reprinted in II Academy Lectures in Lie Detection, 62, 62–70 (1958) (75% accuracy estimate); Hunter & Ash, The Accuracy and Consistency of Polygraph Examiners' Diagnosis, 1 J. Pol.Sci. & Admin. 370, 372 (1973) (86% accuracy achieved by seven examiners in controlled study); Stern-bach, Gustafson, & Colier, Don't Trust the Lie Detector, 127, 130 Harv. Bus.Rev., (Nov.-Dec. 1962) (70% accuracy estimate). Accuracy is lower for individual questions than for overall conclusions regarding truthfulness. See Horvath & Reid, The Reliability of Polygraph Examiner Diagnosis of Truth and Deception, 62 J.Crim.L., C., & P.S. 276, 278–80 (1971) (overall accuracy 88% in controlled study by ten examiners; per question accuracy of 79%); Hunter & Ash, supra, at 372 (overall accuracy 86%, per question accuracy of 82%). Inexperienced examiners are less accurate in their evaluations than experienced examiners, see Horvath & Reid, supra, at 279 (examiners with less than six months experience were 12% less accurate in overall predictions of truth than experienced examiners in controlled study), and the same examiner may reach different conclusions regarding truthfulness when reviewing the same examination results on two different occasions, see Hunter & Ash, supra, at 372 (examiners achieved only 85% consistency in overall determinations of truth and deception and 80% consistency in rating individual questions with lapse of at least three months between interpretations).

These accuracy figures may be inflated. The Inbau & Reid study claiming 95% accuracy has been criticized because the determinations of accuracy was based on a comparison between polygraph results and trial outcomes or confessions. Sternbach, Gustafson & Colier, supra, at 130. Such an approach assumes the accuracy of polygraph determinations which coincide with trial outcomes. Only forty-eight percent of the cases in the Inbau & Reid study were actually verified by confession or other corroborative evidence. Id. The controlled studies inflate accuracy figures because they protect against errors in the formulation of questions and physical problems of the examinee among other variables. Even Reid & Inbau, the primary proponents of polygraphy in the United States, admit these difficulties:

> In many case investigations involving the use of the Polygraph tech-nique, the truth or falsity of the examiner's findings is never factually established by subsequent events or disclosures. Proof is often lacking, therefore, as to whether the examiner in any given case was right or wrong. Nor can the accuracy of the Polygraph technique be deter-mined in a psychology laboratory setting or by the use of fictitious crimes under other testing circumstances. This limitation prevails for the simple reason that it is practically impossible to simulate condi-tions comparable to those involved in actual case situations.

Reid & Inbau, supra . . . , at 304.

A more recent review of studies of lie detector accuracy is found in Honts and Quick, The Polygraph in 1995: Progress in Science and the Law, 71 N. D. L. Rev. 987, 993–94 (1995). The reviewers

> found eight high quality laboratory studies of the CQT [Control Question Test] and five high quality laboratory studies of the CKT [Concealed Knowledge Test]. . . . The high quality laboratory studies indicate that both the CQT and the CKT are very accurate discriminators of truthtellers and

deceivers. Over all of the studies, the CQT correctly classified about 90 percent of the subjects and produced approximately equal numbers of false positive and false negative errors. Similarly, the CKT produces overall accuracy rates that exceeded 90 percent, but the CKT clearly makes more false negative than false positive errors. . . .

[The reviewers] were able to find four field studies of the CQT and two field studies of the CKT that met the criteria for meaningful field studies of psychophysiological credibility assessment tests. . . . Overall, the independent evaluations of the field studies produce results that are quite similar to the results of the high quality laboratory studies. The average accuracy of field decisions for the CQT was 90.5 percent. However, with the field studies nearly all of the errors made by the CQT were false positive errors.

Over the two high quality field studies of the CKT the accuracy was only, 72.5 percent, with virtually all of the errors being false negative errors. The overall false negative rate of 53 percent, indicates that more than half of the guilty subjects were able to pass CKTs given in the field. Although the field false negative rate is much higher than the laboratory false negative rate, this may not be surprising since conditions for the detection of the guilty with the CKT are optimized in the laboratory while problems of memorability will be particularly acute in field settings.[1]

It will be appreciated from the foregoing that in order for polygraph results to have probative value, they must be interpreted by a qualified examiner. In the literature there is much criticism of the training and competence of examiners, see, e.g., Honts and Quick, The Polygraph in 1995, at 998, but little explanation of the principles and methods that guide interpretation.

For the most part, American courts have refused to admit polygraph results and their interpretation as evidence of the matter about which the examinee has been questioned. The reasons usually given are the unreliability of the evidence and the supposed excessive influence of the evidence upon the trier of fact. As will be appreciated, these are the same reasons given for reluctance to admit expert opinion on credibility. See supra p. 447. See also supra p. 249 on expert testimony regarding the reliability of eye-witness identifications. One court has justified the exclusion of polygraph evidence thus:

> If courts were to permit lie-detector evidence of credibility generally, we would face the intolerable effect of potentially requiring the testimony of every defendant and every witness to be bolstered or attacked with lie-detector analysis. Jurors would come to expect such tests or an explanation of why the lie detector was not used. Considerations of wastefulness of resources, potential invasion of privacy and excessive reliance on a technique easily susceptible of abuse support a strong public policy against lie-detector evidence. So, too, does the likelihood that the results would often be overvalued by the jury because of the seeming mechanical verisimilitude of these results when in fact their effective use depends upon the operator, the person taking the "test" and analysis by an expert.

United States v. Sessa, 806 F.Supp. 1063, 1069 (E.D.N.Y.1992). Are these reasons persuasive? Can the exclusion of polygraph evidence be justified under Fed. R. Evid. 403?

In a substantial number of jurisdictions, polygraph evidence is admitted if the parties have stipulated its admissibility and the court finds certain conditions to be satisfied. A very few jurisdictions allow polygraph evidence to

---

1. Footnotes omitted.

corroborate or impeach a witness's testimony. N.M. R.Evid. 11–707; United States v. Piccinonna, 885 F.2d 1529 (11th Cir.1989). Several jurisdictions allowed polygraph evidence to corroborate and impeach and then retreated from this position. Compare Commonwealth v. Juvenile (No. 1), 313 N.E.2d 120 (Mass.1974), with Commonwealth v. Mendes, 547 N.E.2d 35 (Mass.1989); United States v. Gipson, 24 M.J. 246 (C.M.A. 1987), overruled by Executive Order in 1991 promulgating Military R.Evid. 707; Witherspoon v. Superior Court, 183 Cal.Rptr. 615 (App.1982), overruled by legislation that bans the use of unstipulated polygraph evidence in criminal cases, Cal. Evid. Code § 351.1 (West 1989 & Supp. 1994).

Some uses of polygraph evidence thought not to involve the objections recited above are permitted. Thorne v. City of El Segundo, 726 F.2d 459, 469–71 (9th Cir.1983), cert. denied, 469 U.S. 979 (1984): Polygraph questions admissible in action by employee against employer and polygraph examiner for sexual discrimination in firing and in administration of polygraph; Smiddy v. Varney, 665 F.2d 261, 265 (9th Cir.1981), cert. denied, 459 U.S. 829 (1982): Polygraph evidence admissible when polygraph examination was cause of unlawful arrest of plaintiff; Rothgeb v. United States, 789 F.2d 647, 650–51 (8th Cir.1986): Not error to allow policeman to testify he was present during polygraph interrogation of defendant and that each time defendant was asked whether he had killed the victims, defendant held his breath for five to fifteen seconds, said "no," and then panted like a dog; Murphy v. Cincinnati Ins. Co., 772 F.2d 273, 277 (6th Cir.1985): In suit on an insurance policy to recover for property destroyed by fire, where the insurance company alleged that the insured had set the fire, not abuse of discretion to admit evidence of insured's willingness to take polygraph test. Even though the results of the polygraph test might be inadmissible, insured's willingness to take the test reflected on his credibility and on the insurance company's motive in refusing the claim.

In the federal courts decisions excluding polygraph evidence frequently relied on the authority of Frye v. United States, 293 Fed. 1013 (D.C.Cir.1923), a decision that announced principles controlling the admissibility of scientific evidence generally and applied these principles to exclude polygraph evidence. In 1993, the Supreme Court in Daubert v. Merrell Dow Pharmaceuticals, Inc., 509 U.S. 579, held that the test for the admissibility of scientific evidence laid down in Frye had not been adopted by the Federal Rules of Evidence. The significance of the Daubert decision will be explored at length infra p. 962. The Daubert decision has necessitated a re-examination of the admissibility of polygraph evidence by the lower federal courts. Of those that have spoken so far, most have reaffirmed the exclusion of the evidence, applying the principles announced in Daubert. E.g., United States v. Sherlin, 67 F.3d 1208 (6th Cir.1995); United States v. Toth, 91 F.3d 136 (4th Cir.). The Fifth Circuit, in United States v. Posado, 57 F.3d 428 (5th Cir.1995), has held that its per se rule excluding polygraph evidence can no longer be adhered to in view of Daubert, but has not yet expressed itself on the results of applying Daubert's principles.

The admission of polygraph evidence against a criminal defendant arguably presents questions under the Confrontation Clause and the hearsay rule. See pp. 362, 473. Likewise exclusion of polygraph evidence when offered by a criminal defendant presents questions under the Compulsory Process and Due Process Clauses. See Rock v. Arkansas, supra p. 256, invalidating state's per se rule excluding hypnotically induced memories. Recently in United States v. Scheffer, 44 M.J. 442 (1996), cert. granted, ___ S.Ct. ___, 1997 WL 28681 (1997), the United States Court of Appeals for the Armed Forces held that Mil. R. Evid. 707, when interpreted as a per se rule and applied to exclude polygraph evidence offered by an accused to rebut an attack on his credibility, violates the Sixth Amendment. The use of polygraph evidence against a criminal defendant might also implicate the privilege against self-incrimination. See infra pp. 1333–34.

In some jurisdictions, judicial use of polygraph evidence in certain non-trial contexts is permitted, for instance on motions for a new trial and in sentencing. See McCall, Misconceptions and Reevaluation—Polygraph Admissibility After Rock and Daubert, 1996 U. Ill. L. Rev. 363, 378–79. The polygraph is widely used in law enforcement, in intelligence work and in government and private employment, both for pre-employment screening and to detect employee misconduct. In 1988, the Employee Polygraph Protection Act, 29 U.S.C. § 2006 (1996), was adopted, which prohibits employer use of the polygraph. However, the act does not apply to government employment and to investigations into employee wrongdoing.

In addition to the articles mentioned above, useful references are: Barland, The Polygraph Test in the USA and Elsewhere, in The Polygraph Test 73 (A. Gale, ed., 1988); Raskin, The Polygraph in 1986: Scientific, Professional and Legal Issues Surrounding Application and Acceptance of Polygraph Evidence, 1986 Utah L.Rev. 29; Gudjonsson, Lie Detection: Techniques and Countermeasures, in Evaluating Witness Evidence 137 (S. Lloyd–Bostock and B. Clifford, eds., 1983); A. Yarmey, The Psychology of Eyewitness Testimony 171–74 (1979); E. Block, Lie Detectors—Their History and Use (1977); Annot. 43 A.L.R. Fed. 70 (1974).

A related development is the psychological stress evaluator (PSE), which is a device that attempts to detect stress in the voice. It is closely linked in theory to the polygraph, but uses certain voice tones as the relevant physical response instead of respiration, pulse, blood pressure, and galvanic skin reflex. Most of the courts that have considered the issue have rejected expert opinion based upon the results of the test. E.g., Barrel of Fun, Inc. v. State Farm Fire & Casualty Co., 739 F.2d 1028 (5th Cir.1984) (no showing of scientific acceptance or reliability); Underwood, Truth Verifiers: From the Hot Iron to the Lie Detector, 84 Ky. L. J. 597, 633 (1995–96). But see Simon Neustadt Family Center, Inc. v. Bludworth, 641 P.2d 531, 535–37 (N.M.Ct.App.1982) (exclusion of expert testimony based upon test upheld, but would be admissible in discretion of trial court). For discussions, see Horvath, Detecting Deception: The Promise and the Reality of Voice Stress Analysis, 27 J.Forensic Sci. 340 (1982); Kenety, The Psychological Stress Evaluator: The Theory, Validity and Legal Status of an Innovative "Lie Detector," 55 Ind.L.J. 349 (1980).[2]

2. TRUTH SERUM

Less prominent than the lie detector is narco-interrogation, the use of so-called "truth-serums." The various "truth-serums" are actually drugs that act as a depressant on the central nervous system and temporarily alter the psychological adjustment of the subject. Dession, Freedman, Donnelly and Redlich, Drug–Induced Revelation and Criminal Investigation, 62 Yale L.J. 315, 317 (1952); Kubis, Instrumental, Chemical and Psychological Aids in the Interrogation of Witnesses, 13 J.Soc.Issues (1957). See also Ahrens, Scientific Evidence and the Law, 13 N.Y.L.For. 612, 655 (1968); Note, Evolving Methods of Scientific Proof, 13 N.Y.L.For. 679, 697–700 (1968); Matthieson, The Truth

---

2. Mention should also be made of work that has been done on a technique that attempts to detect guilt by word association. See Guttmacher & Weihofen, Psychiatry and the Law 366 (1952); Spencer, Methods of Detecting Guilt: Word Association, Reaction–Time Method, 8 Or.L.Rev. 158 (1929).

Drug: Trial by Psychiatrist, 1967 Crim.L.Rev. 645; Polen, The Admissibility of Truth Serum Tests in the Courts, 35 Temp.L.Q. 401 (1962); Note, An Analysis of the Limited Value of Truth Serum, 11 Syracuse L.Rev. 64 (1959).

It is generally agreed that the results of narco-interrogation are not sufficiently reliable to be admissible on the issue of the truth of the matter stated. See, e.g., State v. Levitt, 176 A.2d 465, 470 (N.J.1961); Dugan v. Commonwealth, 333 S.W.2d 755 (Ky.1960); State v. Linn, 462 P.2d 729 (Idaho 1969); Meuhlberger, Interrogation Under Drug Influence, 42 J.Crim.L. Crim., & Police Sci. 513, 525 (1952); Underwood, Truth Verifiers: From the Hot Iron to the Lie Detector, 84 Ky. L. J. 597, 638–39 (1995–96). Cf. Brock v. United States, 223 F.2d 681 (5th Cir.1955) (responses to questions while asleep inadmissible).

Narco-interrogation can, however, be a valuable adjunct to psychiatric investigation. For this reason, Dession et al., supra at 322–26, argue that a psychiatrist who has examined a person by use of drugs should be allowed to use the results to support his opinion. Hearsay and self-incrimination issues may be involved. Cases finding objectionable the use of evidence founded upon narco-analysis often do not state clearly whether the objection lies in the unreliability of the technique or the particular use sought to be made of its results. In some cases objection seems to lie primarily against the subject matter of the expert opinion. Commonwealth v. Butler, 247 A.2d 794 (Pa.Super.1968) (motion for new trial; defendant offered opinion of doctors who examined him under sodium amytal that he was telling the truth when he said he did not commit the crime; not error to deny motion); Merritt v. Commonwealth, 386 S.W.2d 727, 729–30 (Ky.1965); Queen v. McKay, 1967 N.Z.L.R. 139; People v. Hiser, 72 Cal.Rptr. 906 (App.1968) (not error to exclude taped sodium pentothal interviews offered as basis for psychiatric opinion that defendant did not have capacity to form certain state of mind and do criminal act); People v. Myers, 220 N.E.2d 297 (Ill.1966), cert. denied, 385 U.S. 1019 (1967) (not error to refuse to allow psychiatrist who testified on defendant's sanity to disclose statements made by defendant under sodium pentothal); People v. Seipel, 247 N.E.2d 905, 907–08 (Ill.App.1969), cert. denied, 397 U.S. 1057 (1970); State v. Cypher, 438 P.2d 904, 916 (Idaho 1968); Annot., 41 A.L.R.3d 1369 (1972).

Lindsey v. United States, 237 F.2d 893 (9th Cir.1956): Prosecutrix in a rape case impeached by letters admitting that her accusation was false; solely to "rehabilitate" the witness, the government introduced a recording of her subsequent interview with a psychiatrist while she was under the influence of sodium-pentothal; after considering the authorities, the court reversed. United States v. Solomon, 753 F.2d 1522 (9th Cir.1985): Not abuse of discretion to exclude defendant's exculpatory statements made under the influence of sodium amytal when offered to rehabilitate; no showing drug reliably induces truthful statements. But not error to admit in-court testimony of prosecution witness who also had been questioned while under the influence of the drug.

For studies of the brain that may lead some day to a method of detecting deception and to determining whether seeming memories are true, see supra p. 245.

For issues relating to hypnosis, see supra pp. 267, 389.

CHAPTER 4

HEARSAY

INTRODUCTION

The hearsay rule is a consequence of our system's preference for testimonial proof—for trials in which witnesses who actually discerned the event in question inform the judge and jury about their sensory perceptions. Cf. Fed. R.Civ.Pro.43(a)("in every trial, the testimony of witnesses shall be taken in open court, unless a federal law, these rules, the Federal Rules of Evidence, or other rules adopted by the Supreme Court provide otherwise.").

Testimonial evidence has been termed "our surrogate stimulus—it is the event that we, through the jury, actually see." And "[t]he sin of hearsay is that it robs us of the believability of the surrogate stimulus. The witness who is before the jury did not actually see anything, but is merely relaying the account of someone who did see something." Nesson & Benkler, Constitutional Hearsay: Requiring Foundational Testing and Corroboration Under the Confrontation Clause, 81 Va. L. Rev. 149, 155 (1995). The authors suggest that trials based on second-hand stories may not command social conviction because we fear that inaccuracies in these second-hand reports will not be exposed.

On the other hand, we all make decisions in our everyday lives on the basis of other persons' accounts of what happened, and verdicts are usually sustained and affirmed even if they are based on hearsay erroneously admitted, or admitted because no objection was made. See Shepp v. Uehlinger, 775 F.2d 452, 454–455 (1st Cir.1985)(hearsay evidence alone can support a verdict). Although volumes have been written suggesting ways to revise the hearsay rule, no one advocates a rule that would bar all hearsay evidence. Indeed, the decided historical trend has been to exclude categories of highly probative statements from the definition of hearsay (sections 2 and 3, infra), and to develop more class exceptions to the hearsay rule (sections 4–11, infra). Furthermore, many states have added to their rules the residual, or catch-all, exceptions first pioneered by the Federal Rules which authorize the admission of hearsay that does not satisfy a class exception, provided it is adequately trustworthy and probative (section 12, infra).

Moreover, some commentators believe that the hearsay rule should be abolished altogether instead of being loosened. See, e.g., Note, The Theoretical Foundation of the Hearsay Rules, 93 Harv.L.Rev. 1786, 1804–1805, 1815 (1980)(footnotes omitted):

> The Federal Rules of Evidence provide that "[a]lthough relevant, evidence may be excluded if its probative value is substantially outweighed by the danger of unfair prejudice." Under this structure, exclusion is justified by fears of how the jury will be influenced by the evidence. However, it is not traditional to think of hearsay as merely a subdivision of this structure, and the Federal Rules do not conceive of hearsay in that manner. Prejudice refers to the jury's use of evidence for inferences other than those for which the evidence is legally relevant; by contrast, the rule against hearsay questions the jury's ability to evaluate the strength of a

legitimate inference to be drawn from the evidence. For example, were a judge to exclude testimony because a witness was particularly smooth or convincing, there would be no doubt as to the usurpation of the jury's function. Thus, unlike prejudices recognized by the evidence rules, such as those stemming from racial or religious biases or from the introduction of photographs of a victim's final state, the exclusion of hearsay on the basis of misperception strikes at the root of the jury's function by usurping its power to process quite ordinary evidence, the type of information routinely encountered by jurors in their everyday lives.

. . .

Since virtually all criteria seeking to distinguish between good and bad hearsay are either incoherent, inconsistent, or indeterminate, the only alternative to a general rule of admission would be an absolute rule of exclusion, which is surely inferior. More important, the assumptions necessary to justify a rule against hearsay . . . seem insupportable and, in any event, are inconsistent with accepted notions of the function of the jury. Therefore, the hearsay rules should be abolished.

Some support for this view can be found in the limited empirical research now available—which is, however, derived from simulations—that suggests that admitting hearsay has little effect on trial outcomes because jurors discount the value of hearsay evidence. See Rakos & Landsman, Researching the Hearsay Rule: Emerging Findings, General Issues, and Future Directions, 76 Minn. L.Rev. 655 (1992); Miene, Park, & Borgida, Jury Decision Making and the Evaluation of Hearsay Evidence, 76 Minn.L.Rev. 683 (1992); Kovera, Park, & Penrod, Jurors' Perceptions of Eyewitness and Hearsay Evidence, 76 Minn. L.Rev. 703 (1992); Landsman & Rakos, Research Essay: A Preliminary Empirical Enquiry Concerning the prohibition of Hearsay Evidence in American Courts, 15 Law & Psychol. Rev. 65 (1991).

Others, even if they concede that restrictions on hearsay have some utility, question whether the benefits outweigh the cost.

The cost of maintaining the rule is not just a function of its contribution to justice. It also includes the time spent on litigating the rule. And of course this is not just a cost voluntarily borne by the parties, for in our system virtually all the cost of the court—salaries, administrative costs, and capital costs—are borne by the public. As expensive as litigation is for the parties, it is supported by an enormous public subsidy. Each time a hearsay question is litigated, the public pays. The rule imposes other costs as well. Enormous time is spent teaching and writing about the hearsay rule, which are both costly enterprises. In some law schools, students spend over half their time in evidence classes learning the intricacies of the hearsay rule, and . . . enormous academic resources are expended on the rule.

Allen, Commentary on Professor Friedman's Article: The Evolution of the Hearsay Rule to a Rule of Admission, 76 Minn.L.Rev. 797, 800 (1992)(but would abolish rule only in civil cases). See also Friedman, Toward a Partial Economic, Game–Theoretic Analysis of Hearsay, 76 Minn. L. Rev. 723 (1992).

What benefits does the hearsay rule provide? Various justifications have been offered beyond the central concern with more reliable determinations: protecting the competitive advantage of lawyers with expertise in the hearsay doctrine; restraining the untrammeled discretion of judges; forcing the party with the burden of proof to come forward with better evidence. Do these factors have sufficiently different ramifications in civil and criminal cases to warrant a non-uniform approach to hearsay in criminal, quasi-criminal and civil cases?

What role, if any, should the Supreme Court's interpretation of the Confrontation Clause play in formulating a hearsay rule for criminal cases? Read literally, the Sixth Amendment provision that "the accused shall enjoy the right ... to be confronted with the witnesses against him" would require the exclusion of any statement made by a person not testifying at the trial. The Supreme Court has, however, "long rejected as unintended and too extreme" such an interpretation which would "abrogate virtually every hearsay exception." Ohio v. Roberts, 448 U.S. 56, 63 (1980). Of late, even though the Court insists that the "overlap is not complete" (United States v. Inadi, 475 U.S. 387, 393, n. 5 (1986)), it has conflated evidentiary and constitutional doctrine so that evidence that modern codifications exempt from the hearsay rule, or that fits within a traditional hearsay exception is found to simultaneously satisfy constitutional requirements. See Owens v. United States, infra p. 554; Bourjaily v. United States, infra p. 590; White v. United States, infra p. 796. Does this suggest that a tightening of the hearsay rule is needed in criminal cases in order adequately to protect defendants against unreliable evidence? Section 13 returns to a consideration of the constitutional issues.

SECTION 1.   DEFINITION AND RATIONALE

Leake v. Hagert

Supreme Court of North Dakota, 1970.
175 N.W.2d 675.

■ PAULSON, JUDGE. This is an appeal by the plaintiff, Allen Leake, from a judgment of dismissal of his cause of action entered in the District Court of Grand Forks County, North Dakota, and from an order of the trial court denying his motion for a new trial.

Allen Leake's complaint was predicated upon the alleged negligence of the defendant, Charlotte Hagert, in her operation of a motor vehicle on October 25, 1966, wherein she negligently and carelessly drove her automobile into the rear of the plow being towed by a tractor which Leake was operating, causing injuries to Leake and damages to his plow and tractor. Leake's complaint included allegations of damages for hospital and doctor bills; for permanent injuries to his chest and right arm; for pain and suffering; and for damages to his plow and tractor; and he prayed for a judgment against Charlotte Hagert in the sum of $27,600. Charlotte Hagert, in her answer, admitted that the collision occurred, but, as a defense, denied that the collision was proximately caused by her negligence in the operation of her motor vehicle, and she alleged that the sole and proximate cause of the collision was the negligence of the plaintiff in the maintenance and operation of his tractor and plow, upon a public highway after sunset, without proper lights, reflectors, or other warnings. Charlotte Hagert counterclaimed for damages caused by the alleged negligence of Allen Leake for permanent injuries, for pain and suffering, for hospitalization and medical expenses, and for damages to her 1966 Plymouth automobile; and she prayed for a judgment against him in the sum of $32,000.

All claims and defenses of both Allen Leake and Charlotte Hagert were submitted to a jury, which returned a verdict dismissing the complaint of Allen Leake as well as dismissing the counterclaim of Charlotte Hagert.

. . .

Allen Leake, after the judgment was entered, made a motion for a new trial which was denied by the trial court.

. . .

Leake's first contention on appeal is that certain errors at law occurred during the course of the trial, at the time that the trial court overruled objections to the admission of certain evidence. The evidence objected to was certain testimony adduced from Edward Gross, an adjuster who investigated the accident. Gross testified that Allen Leake's son told him, with reference to the small rear light on the tractor, that the red lens had been out for some time. Edward Gross's testimony concerning the statement of Allen Leake's son was hearsay.

The hearsay rule prohibits use of a person's assertion, as equivalent to testimony of the fact asserted, unless the assertor is brought to testify in court on the stand, where he may be probed and cross-examined as to the grounds of his assertion and his qualifications to make it. Grand Forks B. & D. Co. v. Iowa Hardware Mut. Ins. Co., 75 N.D. 618, 31 N.W.2d 495 (1948). See 5 Wigmore on Evidence (3d ed.) §§ 1361, 1364. Allen Leake contends that whether or not the red lens was out at the time of the accident is a material question of fact, determinative as to the contributory negligence by Allen Leake, and whether he complied with the standards set forth in § 39–21–15, N.D.C.C., which requires that every tractor, when operating upon a highway of this state at any time from one-half hour after sunset to a half-hour before sunrise, be equipped with at least one lamp displaying a red light visible, when lighted, from a distance of one thousand feet to the rear of such tractor. Leake's son did not testify in the present action; he was not a party to the action; his statement was not made under oath; his statement was not subject to cross-examination; and he was not available as a witness at the time of trial because he was in the Army and overseas. We find that it was error for the trial court to admit into evidence the testimony concerning what Leake's son said to Edward Gross; the son's statement was hearsay and should have been excluded.

Having found that the trial court erred in admitting the statement of Allen Leake's son into evidence, we must determine on this appeal whether such an erroneous admission was prejudicial and constitutes reversible error.... Reviewing the record concerning the testimony submitted with reference to the condition of the light and the lens at the time of the accident, we find that the hearsay statement of Allen Leake's son was erroneously admitted by the trial court, but that such error was not prejudicial.

. . .

For reasons stated in the opinion, the motion for a new trial and the judgment are affirmed.

NOTES

1. Is it significant that the declaration attributed to plaintiff's son was not made in plaintiff's presence? If plaintiff had been present and had cross-examined his son, would the evidence still be objectionable? See Morgan, Hearsay and Non–Hearsay, 48 Harv.L.Rev. 1138, 1140 (1935).

If the son's statement had been written, would the evidence still be objectionable? Dowdney v. Shadix, 176 S.E.2d 512, 513 (1970)("A hearsay statement not otherwise admissible is not made admissible merely because it is reduced to writing"). Is this so if the writing is in a diary? See Morgan, Hearsay

Dangers and the Application of the Hearsay Concept, 62 Harv.L.Rev. 177, 189–190 (1948).

2. What is the significance, if any, of the circumstance that the maker of the out-of-court statement is in the courtroom when evidence of the extrajudicial statement is offered? Does this remove the hearsay taboo? No, says the court in Sartin v. Stinecipher, 348 S.W.2d 492 (Tenn.1961), approving the trial court's opinion that the evidence was "rank hearsay" or "pure, pure hearsay". See also Pettus v. Casey, 358 S.W.2d 41 (Mo.1962) and Butler v. Butler, 461 P.2d 727 (Utah 1969). If the maker is on the witness stand, further problems arise. These are treated in Section 2, infra.

3. Suppose the maker of the out-of-court statement is a party who appears pro se but fails to take the stand. In Fine v. Kolodny, 284 A.2d 409, 411–412 (Md.1971), the court found that statements made by a plaintiff in the course of appearing pro se, in argument, in questioning witnesses, and in colloquy with the court, did not constitute testimony to be considered in passing on the sufficiency of the evidence. Why would plaintiff's statements not be equated with testimony?

4. State in Interest of D.C., 277 A.2d 402, 403 (N.J.Super.A.D.1971): Juvenile delinquency complaint against D.C., charging him with possession of a stolen automobile.

> The only evidence presented by the State as to the automobile being a stolen vehicle was the testimony of arresting officer Paz. While he was being cross-examined by D.C.'s counsel, the trial judge asked Paz whether he had checked out ownership of the car. When he answered that he had, the judge inquired, "What was it?" Counsel's immediate objection that this was not competent testimony was overruled, and Paz then said that he had called headquarters which, in turn, "called NCIC for a look-up on the vehicle and they found it was stolen out of Rutherford, your Honor."

> This double hearsay should not have been permitted.

5. People v. Eady, 294 N.W.2d 202, 203 (Mich.1980): D charged with criminal sexual assault. Defense: consent. Victim claimed she had struggled, screamed and honked car horn for one-half hour before police arrived. Police officer testified that police were responding to a radio report from a dispatcher who repeated a telephone report of someone screaming and honking a car horn. Reversible error: "There is no 'radio run' exception to the hearsay rule."

6. Schaffer v. State, 777 S.W.2d 111 (Tex.Crim.App.1989)(en banc): In a narcotics trial, defendant unexpectedly testified that he had been working as an informant for the past two years with a police officer named Jimmy Seals. On rebuttal, a narcotics investigator testified that he had contacted Officer Seals that morning. The prosecutor then asked:

> Q. Without telling us what he told you ... would you, at this time, ask the State to drop charges against Mr. Schaffer?

> A. No, sir.

Id. At 113. Held, reversible error to admit such "backdoor hearsay." The dissent objected that "a witness may testify that his or her opinion or action was based on hearsay information." Id. at 116. See further discussion of "background" hearsay, infra.

> See also Egede–Nissen v. Crystal Mountain, Inc., 584 P.2d 432 (Wash.App. 1978), modified on other grounds, 606 P.2d 1214 (1980)(en banc): On the issue of damages, P replied "No" when asked by her counsel: "After the physical examination were you allowed to return ... to your work with SAS." Held,

hearsay: "Here, it is clear that plaintiff must have been told by someone, either a doctor or an SAS official, that she could no longer work for the airline." Id. at 442. Professor Falknor designates such evidence as "Indirect Hearsay". See his article so entitled in 31 Tul.L.Rev. 3 (1956).

NOTES ON THE SCOPE OF THE HEARSAY RULE

1. Evidence codifications generally classify as hearsay assertions offered for the truth of the matter asserted. See, e.g., Fed.R.Evid., Rule 801(a), (c); Cal.Evid.Code § 1200. For a list of states which have adopted the federal definition see 4 J. Weinstein & M. Berger, Weinstein's Evidence ¶ 801(1)–(c)[02].

2. More than twenty-five years ago, Professor Morgan inquired whether "the rational basis for the hearsay classification is not the formula, 'assertions offered for the truth of the matter asserted,' but rather the presence of substantial risks of insincerity and faulty narration, memory, and perception?" Morgan, Hearsay Dangers and the Application of the Hearsay Concept, 62 Harv.L.Rev. 177, 218 (1948).

Professor Tribe in his article, Triangulating Hearsay, 87 Harv.L.Rev. 957, 958–60 (1974), developed a way to diagram out-of-court acts or utterances in order to ascertain whether evidentiary use of the act or utterance will require reliance on the credibility of the declarant:

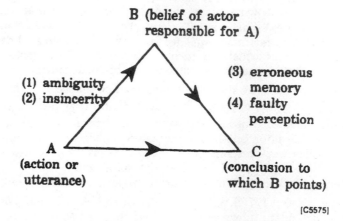

[C5575]

Professor Tribe explains:

The basic hearsay problem is that of forging a reliable chain of inferences, from an act or utterance of a person not subject to contemporaneous in-court cross-examination about that act or utterance, to an event that the act or utterance is supposed to reflect. Typically, the first link in the required chain of inferences is the link from the act or utterance to the belief it is thought to express or indicate. It is helpful to think of this link as involving a "trip" into the head of the person responsible for the act or utterance (the declarant) to see what he or she was really thinking when the act occurred. The second link is the one from the declarant's assumed belief to a conclusion about some external event that is supposed to have triggered the belief, or that is linked to the belief in some other way. This link involves a trip out of the head of the declarant, in order to match the declarant's assumed belief with the external reality sought to be demonstrated.

. . .

If we use the diagram to trace the inferential path the trier must follow, we begin at the lower left vertex of the triangle (A), which represents the declarant's (X's) act or assertion. The path first takes us to the upper vertex (B), representing X's belief in what his or her act or assertion suggests, and then takes us to the lower right vertex (C), representing the external reality suggested by X's belief. When "A" is used to prove "C" along the path through "B," a traditional hearsay problem exists and the use of the act or assertion as evidence is disallowed upon proper objection in the absence of some special reason to permit it.

It is of course a simple matter to locate the four testimonial infirmities on the triangle to show where and how they might impede the process of inference. To go from "A" to "B", the declarant's belief, one must remove the obstacles of (1) ambiguity and (2) insincerity. To go from "B" to "C", the external fact, one must further remove the obstacles of (3) erroneous memory and (4) faulty perception.

. . .

By contrast, when the trier's inference can proceed from "A" directly to "C," the infirmities of hearsay do not arise. For example, the out-of-court statement "I can speak" would be admissible as nonhearsay to prove that the declarant was capable of speech, for it is the fact of his speaking rather than the content of the statement which permits the inference, and that involves no problems of the statement's ambiguity, or of sincerity, memory, or perception.

3. Professor Tribe identifies one of the hearsay dangers as "ambiguity." What does ambiguity mean? Does it refer to the possibility of faulty, but innocent, errors in communication as when a declarant with diminished communicative abilities confuses two words, or does the danger exist because of inherent features of our language? The latter view is proposed by Professor Bergman in his article, Ambiguity: The Hidden Hearsay Danger Almost Nobody Talks About, 75 Ky.L.J. 841 (1987). Relying in part on recent work by linguistics researchers, he discusses a number of factors in the English language that may make it imperative to cross-examine the declarant in order to ensure that the listener is receiving the same message the speaker intended to send.

4. McCormick's Treatise on Evidence defines hearsay as follows:

Hearsay evidence is testimony in court, or written evidence, of a statement made out of court, the statement being offered as an assertion to show the truth of matters asserted therein, and thus resting for its value upon the credibility of the out-of-court asserter.

McCormick, Evidence § 246 (2d ed., Cleary, 1972). For a criticism of this view, see Park, McCormick on Evidence and the Concept of Hearsay: A Critical Analysis Followed by Suggestions to Law Teachers, 65 Minn.L.Rev. 423 (1981).

5. United States v. Barbati, 284 F.Supp. 409, 411 (E.D.N.Y.1968):

There is more force to defendant's contention that the testimony with respect to the identification by the barmaid at the scene of the crime constituted hearsay. Whether made orally, or by pointing him out, the barmaid was then, the argument goes, making an extra-judicial testimonial statement. This out-of-court statement was being relied upon at the trial to prove its truth, namely, that the man she pointed out was the one who passed a counterfeit bill to her. Since its use required reliance upon all elements of her credibility—observation power, memory, truthfulness and ability to communicate—the barmaid's testimony, defendant concludes, involved serious hearsay dangers.

This analysis is not conclusive. Much that might be classified as hearsay is held not to be hearsay. Much that is hearsay is, nonetheless, admissible.

Courts have not hesitated to characterize as non-hearsay evidence whose use involves hearsay dangers when it is highly probative and necessary.

Central of Georgia Railway Co. v. Reeves

Supreme Court of Alabama, 1972.
288 Ala. 121, 257 So.2d 839.

■ BLOODWORTH, JUSTICE. Appellee, W.R. Reeves (plaintiff below), filed suit under The Federal Employers Liability Act against his employer, appellant Central of Georgia Railway Company (defendant below), seeking damages for injuries arising out of the derailment of one of appellant's trains at Griffin, Georgia. There was a jury verdict and judgment for appellee for $50,000. Appeal is from this judgment and the overruling of motion for a new trial.

There are a number of assignments of error. But, the determinative issue before this court is whether the admission of appellee's testimony as to what an examining physician told him concerning the nature and extent of his injuries was a violation of the hearsay rule.

We are of the opinion that the admission of such testimony was violative of the hearsay rule and that the judgment must be reversed on account of its erroneous admission.

Appellant's assignment of error raising this issue is as follows:

"(45) The Trial Court erred in overruling the Defendant's (Appellant's) Motion for a New Trial, which contained the following ground:

" '45. For that the Court erred in allowing the following testimoney (sic) which was properly objected to by the defendant's counsel:

" 'Q. (BY MR. RIVES): Did you go see Dr. Bunderant?

" 'A. (BY MR. REEVES): Yes, sir, I went to see Dr. Bunderant, and he gave me a complete physical. Dr. Bunderant, he examined me. When he got through examining me, he told me I had—

" 'MR. SHARP: Judge, I object to what Dr. Bunderant said as being hearsay.

" 'MR. RIVES: Your Honor, he is the agent selected by the company.

. . .

" 'MR. SHARP: Yes, sir. If they wanted to get some testimony about what Dr. Bunderant said, I think the proper way to do it is to schedule his deposition over there and let Dr. Bunderant state what he said.

" '.'I think this is hearsay. It is not the best evidence to allow this man to come in and give hearsay testimoney (sic) to what Dr. Bunderant said. And I object to it on that basis.

" 'THE COURT: Overrule the objection.

. . .

" 'A. Dr. Bunderant examined me. When he got through examining me he told me that I had a weakness in my right arm, a dead place on the inside of my arm, and stiffness in the neck, and had nerve trouble in the roots of my back, said I wasn't physically able to do the work, and just too many people's lives were involved.' "

It is well established in Alabama that testimony by a witness in court as to statements made out-of-court by a physician is inadmissible as hearsay. . . .

However, appellee insists that the testimony should be admissible in this instance to show that appellee suffered mental anguish and to explain his mental condition which he says resulted from the statements having been made to him. Counsel for appellee articulates this position in brief as follows:

"There are two reasons this testimony was admissible in this case and both involve the fact that the validity of the opinion and the truth of the facts as stated by Dr. Bondurant were not in issue. First, there was a claim in the complaint for mental anguish undergone by the plaintiff as a result of the injuries which he received in the accident. Second, the plaintiff's injuries were inextricably involved with his mental condition by virtue of a conversion hysteria reaction brought upon by the accident itself and his inability to work thereafter. Certainly, any testimony which contributed to an understanding of his mental condition was relevant. The fact of the advice to him by Dr. Bundurant (whether his opinion was correct or not) that he had a weakness in his arm, a stiffness in his neck, nerve trouble and that he would be able to work no longer played a part in his mental condition, and thereby in his physical condition. His mind acted upon these statements. The question is whether the statements were made to him; not whether they were true. Dr. Bondurant may have been incorrect in his diagnosis and in his opinion that Mr. Reeves could not work, but it would make no difference. Mr. Reeves accepted it. Thus, there was no need to cross-examine Dr. Bondurant."

[The court finds the argument "unique", with little support in local precedents. It declines to follow out-of-state decisions supporting the argument and concludes that "the proposition that a patient may testify in court as to statements made to him out-of-court by his doctor in order to show that he, the patient, was caused mental anguish as a result of such statements" would " 'open wide the door to hearsay evidence,' without the opportunity afforded to cross-examine the declarant." Judgment reversed.]

NOTES

In deciding whether the Alabama view should be classed as a parochial error, consider the materials which follow.

1. 194th St. Hotel Corp. v. Hopf, 383 So.2d 739, 740–41 (Fla.App.1980):

    The plaintiff, Janet Hopf, a 17–year old guest of the appellant's hotel, was severely injured when she slipped on a wet spot on a wooden walkway at the rear of the lobby. . . .

    . . . [A]s a result of the fall, Ms. Hopf sustained a pneumothorax—a collapsed lung—which was repaired only by a painful operative procedure. When, soon afterwards, she returned home to New York, her lung collapsed again and further hospitalization was required. . . . Janet and her mother both stated that, because of her "constant fear" that her lung would again collapse, she no longer engaged in any of the myriad of activities in which she had participated before the accident. She testified that she felt "that it is just not fair that this should happen and that I always have to be afraid."

During the course of her testimony, Janet was permitted, over the defendant's hearsay objection, to testify as to what her doctor had told her about her future. Specifically, she stated that

> "He told me that I would have to live with myself and to be careful never to strain myself."

The trial court ruled, and specifically instructed the jury, that this testimony was to be received and considered only for the purpose of demonstrating "the state of mind of this witness as she received this information from [the doctor]." We conclude, contrary to the defendant's contention here, that the admission of this evidence for the limited purpose stated, was entirely correct. Since the statement was specifically not admitted to prove the truth of its contents, that is, the accuracy of the medical opinion that the plaintiff must avoid future strain, it should not technically be regarded as "hearsay" at all. See Lombardi v. Flaming Fountain, Inc., 327 So.2d 39 (Fla. 2d DCA 1976); § 90.801(1), Fla.Stat. (1979). In any case, whether treated as "nonhearsay," or, far less accurately, as an "exception" to the hearsay rule, it is well-settled that evidence of an out-of-court statement to show its effect upon the mental attitude of the person who hears it is properly admissible. 6 Wigmore on Evidence § 1789 (3rd ed. 1976); McCormick on Evidence § 249, text and cases at nn. 82–88 (2nd ed. 1972). In this case, it was obviously pertinent to the plaintiff's damage claims that her actions were restricted because of a reasonable belief that she must avoid future physical stress. Hence, it was perfectly proper for the jury to know one of the bases for that concern. [Footnote omitted.]

See also Brown v. Coca–Cola Bottling, Inc., 344 P.2d 207, 208–210 (Wash. 1959) (patient claimed damages for the pain and nervous shock he incurred in swallowing glass contained in Coca–Cola bottle; in arguing that plaintiff could testify that physician had told him that he might have to be operated on if his stomach didn't get better, counsel stated: "I am not offering this for the truth of the matter. I am not offering it to show that he would have had to be cut open, but I think I am entitled to show the state of mind created by this hearsay testimony."). And see Ferrara v. Galluchio, 152 N.E.2d 249 (N.Y.1958)(plaintiff's testimony that dermatologist told her she had cancer from allegedly improper X-ray treatments was admissible to show basis for her cancerphobia).

2. Wolfson v. Mutual Life Ins. Co. 455 F.Supp. 82 (M.D.Pa.), aff'd. mem., 588 F.2d 825 (3d Cir.1978): Action on life insurance policies. Insurer claimed fraud because insured failed to disclose that he had diabetes. Court admitted testimony of decedent's business partner that he overheard insurance agent assuring decedent that his diabetes would not have to be reported because no insulin treatment was involved. Would testimony by wife of decedent that her husband told her of insurance agent's assurances be admissible?

3. Kingdon v. Sybrant, 158 N.W.2d 863, 868 (N.D.1968): Lotus contests the will of her father, Fred, on the ground that he had the insane delusion that she was the off-spring of an illicit affair between her mother and one Sig. Proponents of the will offer evidence of scandalous neighborhood rumors respecting the mother and Sig. Held, admissible.

The primary question to be determined in this case is whether the decedent, Fred W. Kingdon, had any evidential basis that the contestant, Lotus Irene Korner, was not a child of his body. The existence of rumors as to an affair between Jessie Corkill Kingdon and Sig Boeman would be relevant insofar as the presence of such rumors could have affected the decedent's belief and given substance thereto. Since the basis of the contestant's case was the absence of such rumors, which established that the decedent had no basis for his belief, it is only just that the proponents could offer any evidence of the existence of such rumors in favor of their case. Thus, the trial court's reasoning in excluding testimony of this sort is not tenable, because the proponents were in no way attempting to prove that such an affair was an actual fact, or that Lotus Irene Korner was actually illegitimate. They were attempting to prove that such rumors existed and that, therefore, such rumors could form the basis for the belief of the testator that Lotus Irene Korner was not his child.

4. United States v. Ebens, 800 F.2d 1422, 1430 (6th Cir.1986): Defendant had pleaded guilty to manslaughter in state court after he killed a United States citizen of Chinese descent. After he was sentenced to probation and a small fine, public outrage, especially within the Chinese–American community, led to a federal indictment charging defendant under the Civil Rights Act with seeking to intimidate a person because of his race, color, religion, or national origin. At trial, three principal government witnesses testified to statements purportedly made by defendant on the evening of the killing from which racism could be inferred. Over defense objections, the court excluded as hearsay, tape recordings of interviews with the three witnesses conducted by Lisa Chan, the attorney who was instrumental in organizing the publicity that led to the federal prosecution. The defense offered the recordings to demonstrate that the witnesses' testimony concerning defendant's racist statements was false and that it resulted from improper coaching by Chan in preparation for trial. Held: reversible error to exclude the recordings. "Plainly, Chan's out of court utterances were admissible to show not the truth of what she said but the effect on [the witnesses] as bearing on whether the witnesses' subsequent sworn testimony was coached and hence inaccurate."

5. Other cases that employ a non-hearsay rationale to justify admitting evidence of one person's extra-judicial statements to show another's state of mind are noted below. In these cases what is the state of mind that is being proved?

United States v. Harris, 942 F.2d 1125 (7th Cir.1991)(in criminal prosecution of a young woman for "willfully" failing to report as income substantial sums received from a wealthy widower, now deceased, error to exclude love letters from decedent to taxpayer in which he told her that he would arrange for her financial security).

Pace v. Insurance Co. of N. Am., 838 F.2d 572 (1st Cir.1988)(in suit against insurer to recover for bad faith refusal to pay claim, letters containing results of interviews not hearsay when offered to prove that insurer had refused claim on counsel's advice).

United States v. Carter, 801 F.2d 78, 84 (2d Cir.), cert. denied, 479 U.S. 1012 (1986)(in prosecution for selling firearms without a license, defense sought to show that undercover agent had outrageously pressured defendant into selling him guns without any basis for believing that defendant was interested in doing so; not error to introduce recording of telephone conversation between employee of defendant and undercover agent in which employee told agent that defendant had been trying to reach agent).

United States v. Norwood, 798 F.2d 1094 (7th Cir.), cert. denied, 479 U.S. 1011 (1986)(defendant claimed that he was unaware that the credit card he used had been stolen; error, but harmless, to exclude testimony that card was handed to defendant by person who owed defendant money, who stated that card belonged to his "date" and that he was authorized to use it).

United States v. Rubin, 591 F.2d 278 (5th Cir.), cert. denied, 444 U.S. 864 (1979)(in prosecution of union official for taking unauthorized salary increases with criminal intent, error to exclude testimony of present and past presidents of the union who would have testified to telling him that the union constitutions were to be interpreted flexibly).

United States v. Sackett, 598 F.2d 739 (2d Cir.1979)(prosecution for fraudulently obtaining loan for mother secured by life insurance on her life; mother's hospital records properly admitted to show that defendant thought she was dying).

Morrison v. Lowe, 590 S.W.2d 299 (Ark.1979)(action to recover for personal injuries sustained in shoot-out with neighbors; testimony by plaintiff as to having been told of threats by defendants admissible to show that plaintiffs had reason to fear defendants and acted in self-defense).

People v. Duran, 545 P.2d 1322 (Cal.1976)(en banc)(error to exclude testimony by defendant as to warnings by correction officers that he could not afford to be involved in any further investigations to prove his reason for fleeing scene of crime).

Hickey v. Settlemier

Supreme Court of Oregon, 1993.
318 Or. 196, 864 P.2d 372 (en banc).

■ PETERSON, JUDGE.

. . .

Defendant, who is plaintiff's neighbor, was interviewed by the nationally televised program "²⁰⁄₂₀" in connection with a segment that "²⁰⁄₂₀" was producing that focused on "pet bandits." The record in this case contains a videotape of the program that shows defendant making certain statements and an ABC reporter saying:

"[M]ore than 300 people in central Oregon have complained that their pets were stolen and delivered to [plaintiff's] operation. Many want [plaintiff's] facility] closed down, including [plaintiff's] own godmother, [defendant], who lives next door. *She says there's no doubt in her mind that he's mistreating animals and dealing in stolen pets.*" (Emphasis added.) ...

Plaintiff then brought this defamation action. His complaint alleged that defendant made three false statements:

"1. That plaintiff is mistreating animals and dealing in stolen pets. [Hereinafter referred to as allegation 1.]

"2. That plaintiff subjects the animals to inhuman [sic] conditions, including crowding of animals in dirty cages, denying the animals food, water, and shade. [Hereinafter referred to as allegation 2.]

"3. That weekly, or more often, plaintiff shoots animals that are not suitable for research, leaving shell casings and pools of blood as evidence. [Hereinafter referred to as allegation 3.]"

Plaintiff's defamation action is based on [these] three statements allegedly made by defendant. Plaintiff offered the videotape as evidence that the statements were made. The videotape shows defendant herself making two statements, statements relevant to allegations 2 and 3 above. In addition, the videotape shows the reporter stating, "[Defendant] says there's no doubt in her mind that [plaintiff is] is mistreating animals and dealing in stolen pets." The reporter's statement is relevant to allegation 1 and, because the statement only appears in the record on the videotape, it presents a potential hearsay problem under OEC 801(3).

Some statements are themselves significant legal facts, that is, the substantive law attaches certain consequences to utterances so that the mere making of the statement becomes an issue in the case. Utley v. City of Independence, 240 Or 384, 393, 402 P.2d 91 (1965). Such statements made out-of-court are not offered for the truth of what they state and, therefore, are not hearsay. Instead, they are classified as verbal acts....

Defamation is one example of a verbal act. The making of the defamatory statement is itself of legal significance. Therefore, when an allegedly defamatory out-of-court statement is offered, it is not being offered to prove its truth, but that it was made. Indeed, it is legally significant because of its alleged untruth. Therefore, the allegedly defamatory statements made directly by defendant on the videotape are not hearsay.

Defendant denied making the statement attributed to her by the reporter concerning allegation 1. In the absence of the reporter's comment attributing those statements to defendant, there was no evidence of publication of allegation 1 by defendant. The question, then, is whether the reporter's statement is hearsay.

When statements made to a television reporter are sought to be proven by offering a videotape of the broadcast, as in the instant case, a problem of multiple hearsay is presented. OEC 805 states that multiple hearsay is admissible provided that each level of hearsay satisfies an exception to the hearsay rule ... The videotape is being offered to prove what the reporter heard defendant say. That is the first level of hearsay, because this brings into play the perception, recollection, narration, and sincerity of the reporter. If defendant's words are also being offered for their truth, a second level of hearsay exists, because this brings into play the perception, recollection, narration, and sincerity of defendant.

The statement made by the reporter on the tape is hearsay within the definition of OEC 801(3), because it is being offered to prove its truth (that defendant said that plaintiff was "mistreating animals and dealing in stolen pets"). Defendant's alleged statement within the reporter's statement is not hearsay, because it is a verbal act. The requirement of OEC 805 applies to nonhearsay statements within hearsay.... Therefore, in order for the reporter's account to be admissible, the reporter's statement must come within an exception to the hearsay rule under OEC 803 or 804.

Analytically, a television videotape is analogous to a newspaper article.... Cf. Tate v. North Pacific College, 70 Or. 160, 169, 140 P. 743 (1914) (newspaper article is "mere hearsay"). See also Horta v. Sullivan, 4 F.3d 2, 8 (1st Cir.1993)("The [newspaper] account is hearsay, inadmissible at trial to establish the truth of the reported facts."). The reporter's hearsay statement on the videotape is not within any hearsay exception and is, therefore, inadmissible to establish publication by defendant ...

1. Per Wisdom, J., in Safeway Stores, Inc. v. Combs, 273 F.2d 295 (5th Cir.1960), holding that a judgment for plaintiff should be reversed:

"This is a slip-and-fall case.

[Plaintiff] was shopping in a Safeway Store in El Paso, Texas, when she stepped into a puddle of ketchup that had spilled on the floor from a broken bottle.... [Defendant] relies upon [plaintiff's] alleged failure ... to heed an alleged warning ...

[Defendant's] manager's wife ... was in the store at the time of the accident. She testified that she ... told her husband that there was a broken bottle of ketchup in the frozen-food aisle [and that he] stopped what he was doing, hurried toward the ketchup bottle, picked up the glass, then started toward the back to get a mop. As he came out with a mop she heard him call out [to plaintiff]. When she was asked what he had said, plaintiff's counsel objected that the question called for hearsay. The trial judge sustained the objection and refused to permit the question to be answered. Had she been permitted to answer—it was stipulated—she would have testified that [he] said 'Lady, please don't step in that ketchup'.

"The hearsay rule is inapplicable to an utterance proved as an operative fact....

... Failure to permit [the manager's wife] to testify as to the fact of the warning deprived the defendant of the opportunity of showing whether the plaintiff exercised due care. The trial judge's ruling on this point is sufficient in itself to require the Court to reverse and remand.

See also Auseth v. Farmers Mut. Auto. Ins. Co., 99 N.W.2d 700 (Wis.1959)(plaintiff pedestrian, suing for injuries when struck by defendant's automobile, should be allowed to testify that another motorist motioned plaintiff and said to her that she could cross over. The testimony, material on the issue of comparative negligence, was not "offered to establish the truth of what the man said, but merely that he said it," and, "a jury could well conclude that [plaintiff] was less negligent ... than she would have been if she had not been given such assurance at all."); Ferriss v. Texaco, Inc., 599 P.2d 161 (Alaska 1979)(warning by co-worker). Cf. State Highway Dep't v. Buzzuto, 264 A.2d 347 (Del.1970)(doctor's instructions to driver of ambulance involved in collision with Highway Dept. truck); Kemnitz v. United States, 369 F.2d 389 (7th Cir.1966)(similar).

2. Query: in the case first cited in Note 1 supra, suppose defendant proposed that the manager's wife should testify that after plaintiff fell the manager said to his wife, "I begged the lady not to step in the ketchup." Admissible? Suppose defendant's proposal is that the manager should testify, "I begged the lady not to step in the ketchup." Admissible?

3. Per Wilson, C.J. in Hanson v. Johnson, 201 N.W. 322 (Minn.1924).

Action in conversion. Appeal from judgment by defendants.... It is claimed that the court erred in the reception of evidence.

Plaintiff owned and leased a farm to one Schrik under a written lease, the terms of which gave plaintiff ⅖ of the corn grown. The tenant gave a mortgage to defendant bank on his share of the crops. The tenant's mortgaged property was sold at auction by the bank with his permission. At this sale a crib of corn containing 393 bushels was sold by the bank to defendant Johnson. If plaintiff owned the corn it was converted by defendants.

. . .

In an effort to prove that the corn was owned by plaintiff, and that it was a part of his share, he testified, over the objection of hearsay and self-serving, that when the tenant was about through husking corn he was on the farm and the tenant pointed out the corn in question (and a double crib of corn) and said:

> "Mr. Hanson, here is your corn for this year, this double crib here and this single crib here is your share for this year's corn; this belongs to you, Mr. Hanson." . . .

There is no question but that plaintiff owned some corn. It was necessary to identify it. The division made his share definite. This division and identity was made by the acts of tenant in husking the corn and putting it in separate cribs and then his telling Hanson which was his share, and the latter's acquiescence therein. The language of the tenant was the very fact necessary to be proved. The verbal part of the transaction between plaintiff and the tenant was necessary to prove the fact. The words were the verbal acts. They aid in giving legal significance to the conduct of the parties. They accompanied the conduct. There could be no division without words or gestures identifying the respective shares. This was a fact to be shown in the chain of proof of title. It was competent evidence. It was not hearsay nor self-serving. 3 Wigmore on Ev. (2d Ed.) §§ 1770, 1772–1777. As between plaintiff and the tenant, this evidence would be admissible. It was original evidence. The issues here being between different persons does not change the rule.

4. Koury v. Follo, 158 S.E.2d 548, 556–557 (N.C.1968). Action for deafness of plaintiff's infant, allegedly caused by excessive dosage of Strep–Combiotic prescribed by defendant pediatrician. Evidence held admissible that the label on the bottle of the drug stated "Not for pediatric use".

> The Hearsay Rule does not apply where the purpose of offering the extra-judicial statement is not to prove the truth of the statement, but merely to prove the fact that it was made and that the circumstances under which it was made were such as should reasonably have made it known to the litigant. Wilson v. Hartford Accident and Indemnity Corp., 272 N.C. 183, 158 S.E.2d 1. The display of a red flag bearing the word "DANGER," a shouted warning or a printed warning by a person other than the witness testifying thereto, may be shown, not to prove the fact of danger, but to prove the giving of a warning which the person in question should have seen or heard and taken into account. For this purpose, the label on the bottle of Strep–Combiotic was properly admitted in evidence. It is not proof that the drug was unsafe for use upon a child. See Salgo v. Leland Stanford Jr. University Board of Trustees, 154 Cal.App.2d 560, 317 P.2d 170. It is evidence of a warning which the physician disregards at his peril, and his disregard of it is relevant upon the issue of his use of reasonable care, where other evidence shows the drug is, in fact, dangerous to a child.

5. Other instances in which the fact that particular words were spoken or written has legal consequences can be found in: Island Directory Co., v. Iva's Kinimaka Enterprises, Inc., 859 P.2d 935 (Haw.App.1993)(contract); Ries Biologicals, Inc. v. Bank of Santa Fe, 780 F.2d 888 (10th Cir.1986)(guaranty of payment); United States v. Jones, 663 F.2d 567, 571 (5th Cir.1981)(threats are "paradigmatic nonhearsay"); Freeman v. Metro. Life Ins. Co., 468 F.Supp. 1269 (W.D.Va.1979)(cancellation of insurance policy); Cohen v. Maine Sch. Admin. Dist. No. 71, 393 A.2d 547 (Me.1978)(approval required by statute).

6. State v. Gomez, 889 P.2d 729, 732–34 (Idaho.Ct.App.1994):

At trial Officer Creech testified about his investigation of the drug-dealing activity of Gail Philbrick. The officer said that he had delivered marked money to a confidential informant who was to use the money to purchase cocaine from Philbrick. The informant wore a transmitter during the meeting with Philbrick which allowed Creech to overhear their conversations. Philbrick did not deliver drugs at that meeting, but took the money and immediately travelled to the residence on Linden Street where Gomez was staying. As evidence that Gomez intended to deliver drugs to Philbrick, the prosecution asked officer Creech about the conversation he heard between the informant and Philbrick regarding the transfer of money for drugs:

Q: During the course of the conversation with Mr. Philbrick, did you overhear any conversation indicating a transfer of the funds?

MR. BUTLER: Your Honor, I'll object as basing an answer based on hearsay of what he overheard, Judge. It's inadmissible in evidence.

THE COURT: Overruled. I'll permit it.

. . .

THE WITNESS: Yes, I could clearly hear the conversation and when the transfer of funds occurred.

Gomez asserts that this testimony was hearsay and should have been excluded.

. . .

Not all out-of-court statements are hearsay, however. If the statement is not an assertion of fact or is not offered to prove the fact asserted, it is not hearsay. Thus, words which accompany acts and are considered "verbal parts of acts" fall outside of the hearsay definition. "Explanatory words which accompany and give character to [a] transaction are not hearsay when under the substantive law the pertinent inquiry is directed only to objective manifestations rather than to the actual intent or other state of mind of the actor." McCORMICK, § 249 at 102. Such verbal parts of acts may include words accompanying the handing of money from one person to another. Id.; REPORT OF THE IDAHO STATE BAR EVIDENCE COMMITTEE, Comment to Rule 801 at 403 (1983 & Supp.1985) citing 4 J. WEINSTEIN & M. BERGER, WEINSTEIN'S EVIDENCE ¶ 801(a)[02] at 62 (Supp.1983).

The prosecutor's question to Officer Creech in this case may have elicited hearsay. The question as phrased asked whether Officer Creech overheard a conversation indicating a particular fact—that funds were transferred. Hence, even an answer stating only, "yes," would relate some content or purport of what was said even though the question did not request and the witness did not relate the actual statements that were heard.

It is possible, however, that the statements upon which Officer Creech relied for his conclusion that the money was transferred were not hearsay but, rather, fell within the category of the "verbal part of the act," of transferring money [or were statements that contained no factual assertion, such as, "Go ahead and count the money."] This Court cannot determine whether Officer Creech's response related the "purport" of factual assertions made by the out-of-court declarants, which would constitute hearsay, or related a conclusion that Officer Creech drew from non-hearsay statements.

In this circumstance, where it appears that a question directed to the witness may call for hearsay, the appropriate response is for the trial court to sustain the objection unless the proponent of the testimony shows, by an offer of proof, that the out-of-court statement upon which the testimony is grounded is not hearsay. Accordingly, the district court here should have sustained the defense objection to the prosecutor's question unless and until it was shown through an offer of proof that the out-of-court statements on which Officer Creech would base his testimony were not hearsay.

[The court then found that any error in admitting the evidence was harmless "because other non-hearsay evidence amply proved that the informant gave the money to Philbrick."]

Can you construct a conversation between the informant and Philbrick that would be classified as a verbal act? a conversation that would be classified as hearsay?

7.   United States v. Jackson, 588 F.2d 1046, 1049–1050 n. 4 (5th Cir.), cert. denied, 442 U.S. 941 (1979).

Miss Johnson testified that she was unaware that the canvas bag she transported from Los Angeles to Birmingham contained heroin, and the prosecutor stated in court that the government considered her to be an innocent participant in the criminal scheme. She testified that she met Porter in Los Angeles in June 1977 and that he invited her to his family reunion in Birmingham. On July 6 a woman Miss Johnson did not know came by her apartment and gave her $130 as air fare to Birmingham. She also handed her a small canvas bag and requested that she pack it with the things she was carrying on her trip. The stranger told Miss Johnson that Porter would pick her up at the Birmingham airport. Appellants contend that the witness' testimony as to what the unidentified woman said when she brought the money and canvas bag to the witness at her Los Angeles apartment violated the hearsay rule and the Confrontation Clause of the Sixth Amendment. We disagree. The Federal Rules of Evidence exclude from the operation of the hearsay rule any oral statement not intended as an assertion. F.Rule Evid. 801(a). Furthermore, an out-of-court statement that is not offered as proof of the matter asserted therein is not hearsay. F.Rule Evid. 801(c). We think that the out-of-court statements fall within that class of " 'cases in which the utterance is contemporaneous with a nonverbal act, independently admissible, relating to that act and throwing some light upon it.' " United States v. Annunziato, 293 F.2d 373, 377 (2d Cir.1961)(quoting Morgan, A Suggested Classification of Utterances Admissible as Res Gestae, 31 Yale L.J. 229, 236 (1922)).

Under some circumstances, courts will admit a statement by a declarant from which the declarant's state of mind may be deduced. As you read the materials below, consider the hearsay and nonhearsay uses of such statements and other factors that bear on the statement's admissibility.

Banks v. State

Court of Appeals of Maryland, 1992.
92 Md.App. 422, 608 A.2d 1249.

■ MOTZ, JUDGE.

[Defendant was convicted and sentenced to twenty years imprisonment for fatally stabbing her boyfriend, McDonald] . . .

Appellant testified at trial that McDonald physically abused her when he drank, and that she was defending herself against an attack by him "with a sickle" when she stabbed him.... Five witnesses corroborated appellant's testimony about prior abuse of her by McDonald. On the other hand, McDonald's mother and sister, as well as two police officers, who had been to the house separately on various occasions to investigate complaints of domestic violence, testified that McDonald had told them that he was afraid of appellant because she physically abused him....

. . .

Appellant argues that the trial court erred in permitting the State to present evidence of statements made by McDonald to others at various points during his relationship with appellant, claiming that these statements are irrelevant and inadmissible hearsay. The State asserts that these statements were properly admitted to rebut defense counsel's opening statement that appellant would rely on the "battered spouse syndrome in defense of the murder charge."

The challenged statements can be briefly summarized as follows. McDonald's mother, Lucille McDonald (Lucille), testified that the day before the stabbing, she had a telephone conversation with her son during which he told her that appellant "was trying to hit him with a sickle that you cut the grass with." Ilene Muse, McDonald's sister (Muse), testified that McDonald asked her, on the day he was stabbed, to find other housing for him because "he was tired of the arguing [with Banks] and he was just ready to go." Officer Benjamin Braxton testified that during the summer months of 1990, he responded to the home of appellant and McDonald on three occasions to investigate "a domestic situation." Officer Braxton stated that on those three occasions, McDonald told him "that he had been assaulted" by appellant. Officer Richard Carter testified that he had responded to calls from "unknown complainants" at the home of appellant and McDonald on three or four occasions during the summer of 1988. He was unable to recall the exact dates of the complaints, but testified that each time he responded, McDonald stated that he and appellant "were having a[n] argument, and that he [McDonald] was trying to leave the house to keep from fighting." On one occasion, Carter testified, appellant was "highly intoxicated" while McDonald was sober and "on the defense."

. . .

It is not clear from the record the precise grounds on which the trial court admitted the above testimony, although it appears that the trial court believed that the statements were "verbal acts" and thus, not inadmissible hearsay.... The court went on to say that the testimony was not admissible "for the truth of whether she [appellant] was indeed going after him [McDonald] with the sickle at the time, but whether he was in fear of her acts as expressed excitedly over the telephone while [Lucille] was on the phone with him." Finally, the trial court instructed the jury, before admitting the testimony, that it was admissible, "not for the purpose of showing whether it [the alleged attack] actually was occurring, but just to show his [McDonald's] state of mind as expressed to his mother."

Verbal acts are those "out-of-court statements [that] are operative legal facts which constitute the basis of a claim, charge or defense ... and are nonhearsay." L. McLain, 6 Maryland Evidence § 801.7 at 278

(1987)(McLain).... Since the law accords the making of such statements a certain legal effect, the sincerity and reliability of the declarant is of no consequence; the simple fact that such statements are made is relevant....

... In the case at hand, the fact that McDonald made the statements, without more, is not relevant. The State argues that the making of the statements is evidence of McDonald's "fear" and "conflict avoidance." Neither fear nor conflict avoidance, however, has any legal significance in establishing the elements of murder or manslaughter. Nor is McDonald's fear relevant in rebutting evidence of battered spouse syndrome or self-defense or hot-blooded provocation. Rather, the relevance of the statements to the State's case depends entirely upon their truth, i.e., that appellant had previously been violent toward McDonald, and thus are hearsay.

The State further argues that, even if the statements were not verbal acts, they were nonhearsay for another reason—that is, because they were offered, not for their truth, but rather to show the state of mind of McDonald when he was stabbed....

"Statements offered, not to prove the truth of the matters asserted therein, but as circumstantial evidence that the declarant had ... a particular state of mind, when that ... state of mind is *relevant*, are nonhearsay." McLain, § 801.10 at 282–83 (citations omitted)(emphasis added). Here, even if the statements were not being offered for their truth, but rather as evidence of McDonald's state of mind, i.e., fear of appellant, this would not resolve the issue of their admissibility because evidence must also be both relevant and not unduly prejudicial. As Professor McCormick explains:

> A recurring problem arises in connection with the admissibility of accusatory statements made before the act by the victims of homicide. If the statement is merely an expression of fear, i.e. "I am afraid of D," no hearsay problem is involved since the statement falls within the hearsay exception for statements of mental or emotional condition. *This does not, however, resolve the question of admissibility. Since nothing indicates that the victim's emotional state is in issue in the case, the purpose of the offer of the statement must be to suggest the additional step of inferring some further fact from the existence of the emotional state.* The obvious inference from the existence of fear is that some conduct of D, probably mistreatment or threats, occurred to cause the fear. *The possibility of overpersuasion, the prejudicial character of the evidence, and the relative weakness and speculative nature of the inference, all argue against admissibility as a matter of relevance.* Even if one is willing to allow the evidence of fear standing alone, however, the fact is that such cases seem to occur but rarely. In life, the situation assumes the form either of a statement by the victim that D has threatened him, from which fear may be inferred, or perhaps more likely a statement of fear because D has threatened him. In either event, the cases have generally excluded the evidence. Not only does the evidence possess the weaknesses suggested above for expressions of fear standing alone, but in addition it seems unlikely that juries can resist using the evidence for forbidden purpose in the presence of specific disclosure of misconduct of D.

McCormick on Evidence § 296 at 853–54 (3d ed. 1984) (citations omitted)(emphasis added).

Here, McDonald's state of mind as a victim was irrelevant to the commission of the crime. (It was only appellant's state of mind that was relevant.) Further, any probative value of the statements as to the victim's state of mind would be outweighed by the extremely prejudicial nature of the evidence.

Accordingly, the trial court erred in admitting the disputed testimony. See Buckeye Powder Co. v. Dupont Powder Co., 248 U.S. 55, 65, 39 S.Ct. 38, 40, 63 L.Ed. 123 (1918)(where state of mind testimony is sought to be used in an attempt to demonstrate the truth of the underlying facts rather than solely to show state of mind, evidence must be excluded); United States v. Day, 591 F.2d 861, 881 (D.C.Cir.1978)(testimony of threats made by defendant to victim excluded on grounds of "hearsay problems and questions of relevancy and prejudice"); United States v. Brown, 490 F.2d 758, 763 n. 10 (D.C.Cir. 1973)(where state of mind testimony is sought to be used in an attempt to demonstrate the truth of the underlying facts rather than solely to show state of mind, evidence must be excluded); Commonwealth v. DelValle, 351 Mass. 489, 221 N.E.2d 922, 924 (1966)(testimony of threats made by defendant against victim inadmissible to rebut suicidal state of mind where introduced in State's case-in-chief and there was no evidence from the defense of victim's suicidal tendencies).

. . .

In sum, McDonald's statements to his mother, sister, and the two police officers about appellant's alleged violent behavior toward him were hearsay offered for their truth, and not admissible under any exception to the rule against hearsay. Thus, the trial court erred in admitting the testimony. Because of the highly prejudicial nature of the statements, we must reverse.

NOTES

1. In Evans–Smith v. Commonwealth, 361 S.E.2d 436, 442 (Va.App.1987), the court stated:

> A victim's state of mind would be relevant in cases where the defense contends that the death was the result of suicide, accident or self-defense. In those cases, hearsay statements made by the victim illustrating his or her state of mind would be relevant, material and admissible.

2. People v. Green, 609 P.2d 468, 480–82 (Cal.1980)(en banc): Defendant was charged with robbery, kidnapping and first-degree murder of his wife, Karen.

> The next contention relates to an incident occurring during the direct testimony of Pamela Robison. According to police reports, the witness was prepared to testify that Karen stated to her she had a telephone conversation with defendant on the morning of October 11 in which she told defendant she intended to get an annulment and he replied he would kill her if she left him. Prior to the giving of such testimony, and outside the presence of the jury, defendant moved to exclude the evidence of Karen's statement reporting his threat to her life. He conceded the statement was not subject to a hearsay objection because it was not offered for the truth of the matter asserted, i.e., to prove that he actually uttered the threat; rather, it was offered as circumstantial evidence of the fact that Karen was in fear of him on the morning of the crime.[1] Evidence of Karen's fear, in

---

1. When offered for such purpose the statement was simply not hearsay. (Evid. Code, § 1200; People v. Duran (1976) 16 Cal.3d 282, 295, 127 Cal.Rptr. 618, 545 P.2d 1322.) Both parties make the common mistake of treating this statement as an item of hearsay that is saved by an exception to the hearsay rule for statements of a declarant's then-existing "state of mind." (Evid.Code, § 1250.) Yet the writers have long pointed out the distinction between (1) using an out-of-court declarant's assertion of his state of mind (e.g., A testifies that he heard the declarant B say, "I am afraid of C") to prove that mental state directly, and (2) using his assertion of *other facts* (e.g., A testifies that

turn, was relevant to an issue in the case, i.e., to the question whether she accompanied defendant later that day against her will and without her consent, within the meaning of the law of kidnapping. On its face, therefore, Karen's statement was admissible.

Defendant's objection, however, was that because of the nature of the statement "any probative value is greatly outweighed by its prejudicial effect." He thereby specifically invoked the discretion vested in the court by Evidence Code section 352 to exclude relevant evidence "if its probative value is substantially outweighed by the probability that its admission will . . . create substantial danger of undue prejudice. . . . " After arguing the point at some length, defendant reiterated that "this statement is the essence of what the case is all about," and called on the court to "exercise its jurisdiction, its authority to guarantee the fairness of the proceeding and exclude it."

As defendant correctly points out, the record does not show that the court did in fact discharge its statutory duty in these circumstances by weighing the statement's potential for prejudice against its probative value and concluding that the latter was not "substantially outweighed" by the former. . . .

. . .

The Attorney General next contends that the foregoing requirement was satisfied by the trial court's admonition to the jury (and later instruction to the same general effect) limiting consideration of Karen's statement to its nonhearsay use as circumstantial evidence of her state of mind. Again the argument is untenable. When evidence is admissible for one purpose but not for another, the decision of the trial court to give such an instruction is merely a prerequisite to admitting the evidence at all. (Evid.Code, § 355.) The party opponent is still entitled to have it excluded on motion under section 352 if the nature of the evidence is such that despite a cautionary instruction its limited probative value is substantially outweighed by the danger of undue prejudice from the jury's misuse thereof for an inadmissible purpose. . . .

That rule is applicable here. Testimony that a defendant threatened his victim prior to committing the crime charged is a particularly sensitive form of evidence of the victim's state of mind. In the case at bar it created a substantial danger that despite the limiting instruction, the jury— consciously or otherwise—might consider Karen's statement as evidence not only of her mental state but also of that of defendant, i.e., of the fact that defendant actually threatened to kill her if she left him and inferentially harbored an intent to do so; and the relevance of that intent to the crime charged should have been obvious. Accordingly, under the foregoing authorities the court erred in admitting Robison's testimony of Karen's

he heard B say, "C threatened to kill me") to prove the same mental state indirectly. The first is hearsay because it is used *testimonially*, i.e., it is offered for the purpose of inducing the trier of fact to believe in the truth of the assertion itself, just as if the declarant had so testified on the witness stand. The second is not hearsay because it is used *circumstantially*, i.e., it is offered as evidence of conduct on the part of the declarant (B reported that C threatened to kill him) from which the trier of fact is asked to draw an inference as to the declarant's state of mind at the time (B fears C). (See, e.g., 6 Wigmore, Evidence (Chadbourn rev. ed. 1976) §§ 1715, 1790; Assem.Com. on Judiciary, com. foll. Evid.Code, § 1250, 2d par.; Jefferson Cal.Evidence Benchbook (1972) § 14.1, p. 168, caveat; Witkin, Cal.Evidence (1966) §§ 466–467, 556.) For present purposes, however, the failure to observe this distinction is immaterial. [Other footnotes to the court's opinion have been omitted and this footnote renumbered.]

statement without making an explicit determination that this risk of undue prejudice did not substantially outweigh the probative value of the evidence.

3.   After an award of custody to the father of a five year old girl, Tracey, who had been living in foster care, the mother claimed on appeal that the trial court had erred in admitting out-of-court statements made by Tracey to her foster mother. The child was placed in a foster home after her two-year old brother died while both children were living with their mother and her lover. The lover was charged with murder but the trial resulted in a hung jury, and the charges were dismissed. The foster mother testified that when she told Tracey that her mother had married her lover, Tracey started crying and said, "He killed my brother and he'll kill my mommie too." Betts v. Betts, 473 P.2d 403, 407 (Wash.Ct.App.1970). Should the court have admitted Tracey's statement? To prove what?

4.   Action for the wrongful death of a wife. The amount of damages to which the plaintiff-husband would be entitled depended on the pecuniary benefits he would have received from his wife had she lived. Defendants offered the will which was executed by the wife within four months of her death and which recited:

> "Whereas I have been a faithful, dutiful and loving wife to my husband . . . and whereas he reciprocated with acts of cruelty and indifference . . . I limit my bequest to him to one dollar."

Loetsch v. New York City Omnibus Corp., 52 N.E.2d 448 (N.Y.1943), noted in 30 Va.L.Rev. 343 and discussed in Morgan, Hearsay Dangers and The Application of The Hearsay Concept, 62 Harv.L.Rev. 177, 201–202 (1948).

5.   Prosecution for murder. Defendant interposed defense of insanity. The defendant offered in evidence letters written by him while a patient at a psychiatric hospital which were intercepted by the hospital and made a part of the hospital file. They were characterized by the identifying witness, a hospital official and expert witness for the defendant, as "classic paranoid letters." They were addressed to Pope Pius XII, the Commander–In–Chief, the F.B.I., the United State Counter Intelligence, the United States Secret Service, Walter Winchell and others. Sollars v. State, 316 P.2d 917 (Nev.1957). See also State v. Tryon, 142 A.2d 54, 56 (Conn.1958)(when asked to submit to the "balloon test" for intoxication, X told the policeman "She wouldn't blow up any balloon, but she would blow my head off").

6.   Action on life insurance policy. Insurance company defends on ground that insured committed suicide by jumping from an office building window. X's brother seeks to testify that about ten days before the fatal occurrence he asked X where he hid his drugs and X replied: "Don't worry about it. I keep them in the window sill outside my office. Nobody knows they are there." Simonton v. Continental Casualty Co., 507 P.2d 1132, 1135 (Colo.App.1973). Hearsay?

United States v. Reyes

United States Court of Appeals, Second Circuit, 1994.
18 F.3d 65.

■ LEVAL, CIRCUIT JUDGE:

Jeffrey Stein was convicted of conspiracy to import more than 5 kilograms of cocaine after a jury trial before Warren W. Eginton, Judge, in the District of Connecticut, and was sentenced to 135 months imprisonment, and other penalties. We reverse because of prejudicial improper evidence that the Government placed before the jury.

The prosecution arose out of an investigation conducted by the United States Customs Service after receiving a tip that the cargo ship Potomac, arriving in Bridgeport harbor, would have cocaine secured to the hull. Upon the ship's arrival, Customs supervised an underwater search by scuba divers who discovered a tube attached to the ship's keel. The tube was found to contain 66 kilograms of cocaine. Expecting drug traffickers to attempt to remove the cocaine during the ship's brief stop in port, Customs established a surveillance and investigation, which led the agents first to Francisco, Fernando and Berta Reyes, and from them to Rafael Reyes and the defendant Jeffrey Stein.

The indictment charged Stein together with the four members of the Reyes family. Before trial Fernando, Francisco and Rafael Reyes pleaded guilty, and the charges against Berta were dismissed. Stein accordingly stood trial alone.

The principal witness against Stein was Rafael Reyes, who had agreed to cooperate with the Government. Rafael thoroughly implicated Stein in the plot.

The Government offered corroborative evidence, partly through the testimony of Customs Agent Maryann Caggiano. Agent Caggiano's testimony was presented in the form of a narration of the exciting story of the investigation. Starting with Customs' receipt of the tip about narcotics affixed to the hull of the Potomac, she testified that Customs set up a scuba operation in Bridgeport harbor and discovered the tube affixed to the keel containing 66 kilos of cocaine; she established surveillance of the port, and received a tip from a tavern owner giving the license plates of a suspicious red van; she traced the license to a Stamford car rental agency and learned that the van had been rented to a Francisco Reyes; she watched the car rental agency awaiting the return of the van and confronted Fernando and Francisco Reyes following its return; she interviewed them, searched the trunk of their other car with their consent, finding scuba gear and tools appropriate for the removal of the cocaine canister from the hull of the ship; and arrested them. Caggiano went on to testify that the investigation led from those three members of the Reyes family to Rafael Reyes in Chicago and to the defendant Stein in Queens. From there, she described the early phases of the prosecution—the grand jury's return of an indictment, the issuance of a warrant to arrest Stein and proceedings on a motion to suppress evidence. (While much of Caggiano's testimony was relevant to the scope of the conspiracy and its membership, the narrative included many facts that were irrelevant to the question of Stein's guilt, including testimony concerning her own state of mind as the investigation progressed and the early events in the institution of the prosecution.)

During Caggiano's testimony (and the prosecutor's summation references to it), there occurred episodes which, in our view, require reversal of Stein's conviction.

A. Fernando and Francisco implicate Stein. During Caggiano's narration of her initial confrontations of Francisco and Fernando, following the return of the red van, the following testimony was given:

Q. Now, did you have further discussions with [Fernando and Francisco] at sometime after one o'clock on September 20 of 1990?

A. Yes.

Q. And did those further discussions with these individuals cause you to believe that there were other people involved with them in this particular criminal activity?

A. Yes, I did.

Q. And who were those other individuals?

. . .

A. Rafael Reyes and Jeffrey Stein.

Then after testifying about the discovery of the scuba gear and the tools in the Reyeses' car, Caggiano testified as follows:

Q. After you made those observations, did you have any further discussions with these two individuals?

A. Yes.

Q. And as a result of those discussions, did you learn whether Mr. Stein had been in Connecticut?

A. Yes, I did.

In both cases, this testimony was received over the defendant's hearsay objection and provoked a motion for a mistrial. In answer the Government successfully argued that the evidence should be received not for the truth of the matter asserted but as background, showing the agent's state of mind and the reasons for her actions.

B. Fernando describes the matchbook. After narrating her arrest of Fernando and Francisco, Caggiano was asked whether Fernando "directed [her] to a particular document that he thought was significant." The agent said "yes" and referred to a matchbook cover, later introduced as GX 23–A. The Assistant United States Attorney asked, "Ms. Caggiano, what was the significance of that matchbook?" to which the agent answered, "Mr. Reyes had stated that the numbers on the matchbook cover were beeper numbers for two people in Colombia that he was to get in contact with." Also written in the matchbook was Stein's address in Queens.

Upon summation, referring to the matchbook cover, the Assistant said:

Special Agent Caggiano told you that while they were in the—questioning Mr. Francisco and Fernando Reyes, there was a statement made about a matchbook cover *with numbers of individuals who were responsible for the cocaine*....

If you look at the matchbook cover that the Reyeses said contained *the information about the people responsible for this load of cocaine*, what appears on it? You have the name Herman. You have the name Bolero and Carlos, telephone numbers next to it, and *on the bottom of the matchbook cover you've got once again 1418 31st Drive, Astoria, Queens. Once again, Mr. Stein's address* and the very piece of paper they pulled out *being important to the owners of this cocaine, the people responsible for this cocaine.* (emphasis added).

Defense counsel objected to this use of Fernando's out-of-court statement for the truth of what he had said and further to the misrepresentation of Caggiano's testimony as to what he had said.

As to the objection to the use of hearsay, the Assistant responded, "There was no objection at the time [of the receipt of the evidence], so any objection is waived." As to the accuracy of his representation of the testimony, the Assistant said, "My recollection is that indeed was in the evidence, and I commented upon—over that which was in the evidence. That's my recollection." The objection was overruled and the motion for mistrial denied.

C.   The prejudicial question asked and withdrawn. A third episode narrowly averted an additional reason to reverse the conviction:

After her narration of the arrest of Fernando and Francisco Reyes, Caggiano was asked whether she had conducted another interview of Fernando Reyes, which she confirmed.

> Q.   Did the results of that interview confirm your earlier suspicions about the other co-conspirators in this conspiracy venture?

The defendant again objected on the grounds of hearsay. The Assistant responded:

> The Government's position is that it's perfectly appropriate. As both Mr. Ward and the court obviously knows, I haven't made any attempt to elicit the substance of those conversations. The reason the Government is eliciting it is it shows what effect that had on the mind of Ms. Caggiano.
>
> . . . . .
>
> However, that being said, the Government is going to withdraw the question, despite the fact I think it's perfectly appropriate under the rules . . . .

Had the witness answered the leading question, this would have compounded the prejudice by telling the jurors that Fernando had again confirmed Stein's complicity in the conspiracy.

Discussion

I.   Hearsay

. . .

The government contends that the passages quoted under A involved no hearsay because (i) the declarant's words were not repeated and (ii) in any event the jury was instructed that the Reyeses' statements were received not for their truth but only to explain Agent Caggiano's state of mind.

We reject the first contention: although the jury was not told exactly what words Francisco and Fernando had spoken, Caggiano's testimony clearly conveyed the substance of what they had said. The clear message conveyed to the jury (especially when connected to the hearsay about the numbers on the matchbook) was that Francisco and Fernando had admitted their role in a conspiracy to import the cocaine and had implicated Rafael and the defendant Jeffrey Stein. It also effectively communicated their assertion that Stein (who lived in Queens) had been in Connecticut with them.

As to the government's second argument, it is technically correct. Because the jury was instructed not to consider the out-of-court declarations as proof of the truth of what was said, technically no hearsay evidence was received. However, when the likelihood is sufficiently high that the jury will not follow the limiting instructions, but will treat the evidence as proof of the truth of the declaration, the evidence is functionally indistinguishable from hearsay. Whether such evidence may be received turns not merely on the delivery of a limiting instruction that the jury may be unable to follow, but on a more complex balancing of factors that is discussed below.

In the episode involving the matchbook cover (B above), Caggiano explicitly repeated Fernando's words, telling that Fernando had said the matchbook contained the "beeper numbers for two people in Colombia that he was to get in contact with." The defense attorney, whose hearsay objections had already been rejected repeatedly upon the Government's representation that the Reyeses' statements were offered not for their truth but for background and the agent's state of mind, did not renew the objection.

In addition, the account given to the jury in the summation differed significantly from what Fernando was reported by Caggiano to have said. Caggiano's testimony of Fernando's statement was that the matchbook showed the "beeper numbers for two people in Colombia that he was to get in contact with." That statement clearly could not have referred to Stein's address in Queens. However, when the Assistant referred to this testimony in his summation, he told the jury that "the Reyeses said [the matchbook cover] contained the information about the people responsible for this load of cocaine" and then pointed to Stein's address on the matchbook cover. Thus, whereas Fernando had in fact spoken only of the beeper numbers of the Colombians, the account reported to the jury in the summation sounded as if the Reyeses had explicitly identified Stein as one of the "people responsible for the cocaine."

We are assured by the Government and are fully convinced that the discrepancy between Caggiano's testimony and the summation was not intentional. Although the mistake had innocent origins, our concern is for its possible effect on the jury, especially in that it was coupled with the other hearsay testimony that communicated Fernando's implication of Stein.

II.   The Balance of Probative Value Against Prejudice

It is true, as the Government contends, that, in some instances, information possessed by investigating agents is received at trial not for the truth of the matter, but as "background" to explain the investigation, or to show an agent's state of mind so that the jury will understand the reasons for the agent's subsequent actions.... Such evidence can be helpful in clarifying noncontroversial matter without causing unfair prejudice on significant disputed matters. In other instances, it can constitute appropriate rebuttal to initiatives launched by the defendant.... However, neither circumstance obtained here. At trial and on this appeal, the Government has displayed so egregious a misunderstanding of the circumstances that will justify such evidence that the subject requires some explanation.

The proffer of such evidence generally raises two questions: first, whether the non-hearsay purpose by which the evidence is sought to be justified is relevant, i.e., whether it supports or diminishes the likelihood of any fact "that is of consequence to the determination of the action," see Fed.R.Evid. 401, and second, whether the probative value of this evidence for its non-hearsay purpose is outweighed by the danger of unfair prejudice resulting from the impermissible hearsay use of the declarant's statement. See Fed.R.Evid. 403.... Thus, contrary to the government's contention, the mere identification of a relevant non-hearsay use of such evidence is insufficient to justify its admission if the jury is likely to consider the statement for the truth of what was stated with significant resultant prejudice. The greater the likelihood of prejudice resulting from the jury's misuse of the statement, the greater the justification needed to introduce the "background" evidence for its non-hearsay uses.

Questions involved in the determination of the relevance and importance of such evidence include: (i) Does the background or state of mind evidence contribute to the proof of the defendant's guilt? (ii) If so, how important is it to the jury's understanding of the issues? (iii) Can the needed explanation of background or state of mind be adequately communicated by other less prejudicial evidence or by instructions? (iv) Has the defendant engaged in a tactic that justifiably opens the door to such evidence to avoid prejudice to the Government?

Questions involved in the assessment of potential prejudice include: (v) Does the declaration address an important disputed issue in the trial? Is the same information shown by other uncontested evidence? (vi) Was the statement made by a knowledgeable declarant so that it is likely to be credited by the jury? (vii) Will the declarant testify at trial, thus rendering him available for cross-examination? If so, will he testify to the same effect as the out-of-court statement? Is the out-of-court statement admissible in any event as a prior consistent, or inconsistent, statement? (viii) Can curative or limiting instructions effectively protect against misuse or prejudice?

In this case, virtually every variable argues against receipt of this evidence.

First, as to the relevance and importance of the asserted non-hearsay purpose: Agent Caggiano's state of mind as her investigation progressed was probably not relevant and was certainly not important to any issue properly in the trial. Her state of mind may be relevant to the history of the investigation, but the history of the investigation was not relevant to the guilt or innocence of the defendant. Prosecutors sometimes adopt a tactic of structuring the evidence in the form of the history of the investigation, because it makes the evidence more exciting and perhaps also because it suggests a guilty verdict as a logical, satisfying conclusion. It is not improper for prosecutors to use this tactic in presenting relevant evidence. But the fact that the prosecutor chooses this narrative device does not enlarge the scope of relevant evidence. The investigating agent's state of mind, although perhaps important to the story of the investigation, nonetheless remains irrelevant to the issue being tried: The question of the defendant's guilt.

Even if there had been sufficient reason to explain to the jury why the agent investigated Stein, that explanation was amply provided by the fact that his address had been used by the Reyeses in renting the red van and appeared again on Fernando's matchbook cover.

Nor had the defendant engaged in tactics that would justify rebuttal through the state of mind evidence, such as imputing bias, or likelihood of fabrication of evidence, to the Government agent. Where this happens, it can be important for the Government to show the jury that the agent had a valid reason to investigate the defendant. Such tactics by the defendant can result in opening the door to the receipt of even prejudicial declarations for the non-hearsay purpose of explaining the agent's actions. The Government makes no contention that any tactic of Stein called for such response at trial.

As to the capacity for prejudice: The co-conspirators' statements addressed the most important disputed issue in the trial; they directly implicated the defendant in the crime.[1] In addition, the declaration implicating the defendant in the crime came from a highly credible source. Caggiano's testimony conveyed that Fernando and Francisco admitted their complicity in the cocaine conspiracy, and immediately implicated their relative Rafael and the defendant Stein. Under the circumstances, the hearsay declaration communicated to the jury a powerful message that the defendant was guilty.

Fernando and Francisco did not testify at the trial. Accordingly, the defendant had no opportunity to discredit their declarations to Agent Caggiano by cross-examination.

---

1. In contrast, consider Agent Caggiano's testimony about the tip received by Customs that the Potomac would arrive in Bridgeport harbor with cocaine secured to the exterior hull. Because it was undisputedly proved at trial that the Potomac in fact had cocaine attached to the hull, and because the evidence of the tip did not implicate the defendant, the receipt of the hearsay (without objection) contributed to the jury's understanding of the background and the reasons for the agent's actions without prejudice to the defense. (Footnote of the court renumbered; other footnotes omitted).

Ordinarily we assume that juries will follow limiting and curative instructions. There are, however, occasions where the prejudice is so severe that such instructions are unlikely to be effective. Given the high potency of these declarations, their determinative significance for the only important issue in the trial, and their lack of significance for any other purpose, the limiting instructions given by the court were unlikely to prevent the jury from considering the declarations for their truth. The instructions given, furthermore, did not clearly explain the difficult mental task of considering information for one purpose but not for another. In our view, they did not effectively guard against the prejudicial impact of the declarations as highly persuasive evidence of the defendant's guilt. No limiting instruction was given, furthermore, with respect to the matchbook evidence.

In conclusion, the resulting prejudice from the receipt of such incriminating declarations was considerable and far exceeded the minimal or non-existent probative value of the non-hearsay uses of this evidence. We conclude that the receipt of this evidence was error.

. . .

We cannot conclude that it was " 'highly probable' that the[se] error[s] did not contribute to the verdict," Tussa, 816 F.2d at 67 (citations omitted), or that these errors had a "very slight effect" on the jury. United States v. Zackson, 12 F.3d 1178, 1184 (2d Cir.1993) cert. denied, 114 S. Ct. 2717. These errors do not pass the harmless error test. The judgment of conviction must be reversed. . . .

We add a note of caution to criminal prosecutors. Because in criminal cases there has been little prior discovery, and the defense lawyers often do not know in advance what will be the testimony of prosecution witnesses, trial judges have little ability to prevent error if prosecutors act without due caution. The need for retrial of this case could easily have been avoided if the Assistant U.S. Attorney, recognizing that he was about to elicit potentially incendiary evidence as to which there are arguable grounds for exclusion, had begun by a proffer, preferably in writing, explaining the issues in full, so that the defendant had the chance to object and the judge to rule before the harm was done.

. . .

NOTE

Compare United States v. Walker, 636 F.2d 194, 194–95 (8th Cir. 1980)(agent testified that he met defendant initially after he had received a call from a confidential informant; "It is appellant's contention that Agent Shurn's testimony, with respect to his actions following the phone conversation with the confidential informant, was not offered for any reason other than to establish the content of the phone conversation, which was clearly hearsay and inadmissible. We do not agree. . . . Agent Shurn did not testify as to any statement made by the confidential informant. He merely testified as to his own behavior based on information he received from the informant. This type of testimony is not hearsay and is properly admissible.").

Wright v. Doe D. Tatham

House of Lords, 1838.
5 Clark & Finnelly 670.

[On exceptions. The House of Lords put a question to the judges as to the admissibility of certain letters addressed to a testator, Marsden. One of these letters from Marsden's cousin, dated October 12, 1784, recounted the details of a sea voyage and described conditions at the destination, and wished Marsden good health; another from a vicar, dated May 20, 1786, requested Marsden to direct his attorney to propose some terms for a settlement of a dispute between Marsden and the parish or township; a third from a curate, dated October 3, 1799, expressed thanks for past favors received. The will and codicil were made in 1822 and 1825 respectively. The parties were at issue on the sanity of Marsden, and at the trial the letters were rejected.]

■ MR. JUSTICE COLERIDGE: In answer to the question stated by your Lordships, I beg humbly to express my opinion that neither of the letters was properly admissible in evidence. . . .

The first ground on which the admissibility of the letters is rested, lays all participation, all acts by Mr. Marsden in regard to them, out of the question: it becomes indifferent whether the letters ever reached him or not; the only things material are the writing and sending. The former shows the opinion of the writer, the latter vouches it. But, if the writer were alive, and producible in court, although the same reasoning would apply, it could hardly be contended that the letters could be read; the first principles of the law of evidence would prevent it, and I do not think it can be said that the death of the writer necessarily varies the rule. It is every day's experience that the death of a witness deprives the party of the testimony he would have given, although his statement of it, and his having acted upon the faith of it, may be capable of the clearest proof. Nor does the rule vary because the remoteness of the period, and the absence of any dispute on the matter at the time, put aside all suspicion of insincerity. The general rule still remaining the same, that evidence must be given upon oath; and it being certain that this case does not fall within any of the known exceptions hitherto stated in our books, is there any new principle on which it may be rested? As all the participation by Mr. Marsden is by the supposition excluded, the letters stand on exactly the same footing as if they had been addressed or their contents really stated to a third person; and the argument for the defendant below has met this view of the case, as it was bound to do. One learned Counsel . . . contends that the opinion expressed in or to be collected from the letter is evidence because it is a declaration accompanying the acts of writing and sending the letter. But the answer to this is irresistible; wherever a declaration, in itself inadmissible, is admitted as part of an act, because it explains, qualifies, or completes it, the act itself must be evidence in the cause without the declaration; but, in the present case, dismiss the declaration, and the act itself becomes wholly irrelevant, and therefore inadmissible. It is merely arguing in a circle, first to pray in aid the declaration to make the act relevant, and then to make the declaration admissible by showing it to be a part of the act. Another learned Counsel . . . has therefore more boldly asserted that in this case mere opinion as such is evidence, and that this is the expression of opinion legitimately proved as any other act. Suppose, says he, his fellow townsmen had elected Mr. Marsden to be their representative in Parliament, might I not prove that fact as evidence of their opinion of his competency? Assuming, as the argument does, that Mr. Marsden is connected with such election by no act on his part before, at the time, or after, I distinctly answer, no. The question seems to me based on the fallacy, that, whatever is morally convincing, and whatever reasonable beings would form their judgments and act upon, may be submitted to a jury. The mere word of a man of character, the mere opinion of a man of experience and prudence where by some act he vouches its sincerity, will naturally and properly influence our opinions; but the law of England requires the sanction of an oath to that which is to influence the verdict of a jury. I do not, indeed, concede though it is not perhaps necessary now to decide the point, that the mere opinion of a witness, even on oath, is, as such, admissible evidence upon a question of competency. Where you can bring the decision of that question, as you sometimes may, to depend upon deductions from scientific premises, you may hear those deductions expressed as opinions by scientific men. The necessity of the case justifies this departure from the general rule; but competency, in the main, is a question of fact, and the jury are to draw their conclusion from the evidence of the facts before them, not from the opinions which others may have formed from facts not before the jury. I admit that, in practice, where the witness to facts is present, it is by no means uncommon to ask directly for his opinion: such a question it would be idle to object to; for, the objection would only lead to a detailed inquiry into particular facts, which the witness is there ready to go into. Nothing, therefore, would be gained by it. I am not, however, aware that this question has ever, upon argument, been decided to be correct in form. But if it be, the argument is by no means relieved from another insuperable difficulty: if opinion, merely as such, be evidence, it cannot be proved by hearsay in the case supposed, of an election to Parliament offered to prove the opinion: such election can amount to no more than this, that each elector may be considered to say, I vote for Mr. Marsden, because I believe him to be competent: the number makes no difference. Now, proof of this declaration per se would not be legitimate evidence of the elector's opinion; and it is not made evidence by the fact that he votes in accordance: that fact, indeed, may make the declaration morally more convincing; but it is not in itself admissible, because irrelevant to the question of competency. One other case, put by the same learned Counsel in this part of the argument, it may be as well to notice here: Mr. Marsden had executed a bond to the late Mr. Bell, for a large sum of money lent. Proof of the execution of the bond, let in proof of all the circumstances attending the loan—that Mr. Bell had known him (with the remark that he must have thought him competent)—and that he was a very good judge of such matters. No doubt it did. The act of executing the bond was an act of Mr. Marsden's. To see what its quality was, and what inferences were to be drawn from it, it was necessary to look into all the surrounding circumstances; and those circumstances therefore becoming evidence, it became impossible to restrain either Counsel or jury from a consideration of Mr. Bell's opinion, which in itself would not have been evidence. But it is overlooking solid distinctions thence to infer, as was attempted in argument, that it might have been shown that Mr. Bell had made him his executor; because that would be only doing directly what in the admitted evidence in the cause had been done indirectly. Could that fact have been shown in Mr. Bell's lifetime without calling him? If not, how would his death have made it evidence?

Upon principle, then, I think it abundantly clear, that, upon the first ground suggested, these letters are not receivable.

■ MR. BARON ALDERSON: After fully considering the question which your Lordships have put to the Judges, I have also arrived at the conclusion that all the three letters ought to be rejected as evidence upon the trial in question. These letters were addressed to the testator by persons acquainted with him, and whose opinion as to his capacity, if properly proved, would be received as evidence in the cause.... If, therefore, the letters are to be used as proofs of the opinion of the writers respecting Mr. Marsden's capacity, the objection to their admissibility is, that this opinion is not upon oath, nor is it possible for the opposite party to test by cross-examination the foundation on which it rests.

The object of laying such testimony before the jury is, to place the whole life and conduct of the testator, if possible before them, so that they may judge of his capacity: for this purpose, you call persons who have known him for years, who have seen him frequently, who have conversed with him or corresponded with him. After having thus ascertained their means of knowledge, the question is put generally as to their opinion of his capacity. I conceive this question really means to involve an inquiry as to the effect of all the acts which the witnesses have seen the testator do for a long series of years, and the manner in which he was during that period treated by those with whom he was living in familiar intercourse. This is not properly opinion, like that of experts; but is rather a compendious mode of putting one instead of a multitude of questions to the witness under examination, as to the acts and conduct of the testator. Instances of such questions are not uncommon. A witness in a case of assault is frequently asked his opinion which of the two, the plaintiff or defendant, began the affray; no one considers the opinion of a witness in such a case as evidence; but when it is obvious that he has seen the whole, and can, if required, state all the circumstances in detail, such a compendious mode of putting the question is often allowed without objection. But there, the real meaning of the question is, what were the circumstances of the transaction: and unless the witness be then capable of deposing to them, the opinion could not be received at all.

A letter, therefore, as a mere opinion, is not evidence at all; for it cannot give these sanctions. If it were receivable, a letter to a third person, or an oral declaration to a third person, would be evidence equally. But no one has contended that these are receivable.

■ Mr. Baron Parke. ... These letters are sufficiently proved to have been written and sent to the house of the deceased by persons now dead, and they indicate the opinion of the writers that the alleged testator was a rational person, and capable of doing acts of ordinary business. But it is perfectly clear that in this case an opinion not given upon oath in a judicial inquiry between the parties, is no evidence; for the question is not what the capacity of the testator was reputed to be, but what it really was in point of fact; and though the opinion of a witness upon oath as to that fact might be asked, it would be only a compendious mode of ascertaining the result of the actual observation of the witness, from acts done, as to the habits and demeanor of the deceased. Nor is the evidence the more admissible because the persons writing the letters do not merely express an opinion in writing, but prove their belief of it by acting upon it to the extent of sending the letters and putting them in the course of reaching the person addressed. After all, it is but an expression of an opinion vouched by an act, and by an act not so strong by any means as others done to third persons which are allowed on all hands to be inadmissible; not even so strong nor so confirmatory of the truth of the communication as a simple letter written to another man. If the opinion of a person be of itself inadmissible, the act which only proves the belief of that person in its truth, and is irrelevant to the issue, except for that purpose, cannot render it admissible....

NOTES

1. In the Exchequer Chamber the learned Baron said:

> For example, if a wager to a large amount had been made as to the matter in issue by two third persons, the payment of that wager, however large the sum, would not be admissible to prove the truth of the matter in issue. You would not have had any right to present it to the jury as raising an inference of the truth of the fact, on the ground that otherwise the bet would not have been paid. It is, after all, nothing but the mere statement

of that fact, with strong evidence of the belief of it by the party making it. Could it make any difference that the wager was between the third person and one of the parties to the suit? Certainly not. The payment by other underwriters on the same policy to the plaintiff could not be given in evidence to prove that the subject insured had been lost. Yet there is an act done, a payment strongly attesting the truth of the statement, which it implies, that there had been a loss. To illustrate this point still further, let us suppose a third person had betted a wager with Mr. Marsden that he could not solve some mathematical problem, the solution of which required a high degree of capacity; would payment of that wager to Mr. Marsden's banker be admissible evidence that he possessed that capacity? The answer is certain; it would not. It would be evidence of the fact of competence given by a third party not upon oath. . . .

Many other instances of a similar nature, by way of illustration, were suggested by the learned counsel for the defendant in error, which on the most cursory consideration, any one would at once declare to be inadmissible in evidence. Others were supposed on the part of the plaintiff in error, which at first sight, have the appearance of being mere facts, and therefore admissible, though on further consideration they are open to precisely the same objection. Of the first description are the supposed cases of a letter by a third person to any one demanding a debt, which may be said to be a treatment of him as a debtor, being offered as proof that the debt was really due; a note, congratulating him on his high state of bodily vigour, being proposed as evidence of his being in good health; both of which are manifestly at first sight objectionable. To the latter class belong the supposed conduct of the family or relations of a testator, taking the same precautions in his absence as if he were a lunatic; his election, in his absence, to some high and responsible office; the conduct of a physician who permitted a will to be executed by a sick testator; the conduct of a deceased captain on a question of seaworthiness, who, after examining every part of the vessel, embarked in it with his family; all these when deliberately considered, are, with reference to the matter in issue in each case, mere instances of hearsay evidence, mere statements, not on oath, but implied in or vouched by the actual conduct of persons by whose acts the litigant parties are not to be bound. 7 A. & E. 313, 386–88 (1837).

All the judges agreed that the letters were inadmissible without evidence that they had been acted upon by Marsden. Barons Gurney and Bolland and Mr. Justice Park believed all three letters admissible, and Mr. Justice Vaughan, Mr. Justice Littledale and Lord Chief Justice Tindal believed one letter admissible, on the ground that the evidence showed such action by Marsden.

The judgment of The Exchequer Chamber was affirmed. Picturesque details of the setting of the case are extracted from the trial record and other sources and summarized in Maguire, The Hearsay System: Around and Through The Thicket, 14 Vand.L.Rev. 741, 749–760, 777 (1961).

2. It is, of course, possible to express thought, even profanity, in sign language. E.g., see the note entitled "Profanity in The Sign Language," 74 N.Y.L.Rev. 558 (1940). For cases where evidence of the nonverbal conduct of a third person, intended to assert the matter to be proved, was excluded, see Wells v. State, 67 S.W. 1020 (Tex.Cr.App.1902)(assault by husband upon D soon after alleged attack of wife by D); People v. Bush, 133 N.E. 201 (Ill.1921)(housing prosecutrix with nonvenereal inmates after Wasserman test); McCurdy v. Flibotte, 139 A. 367 (N.H.1927)(revocation of driving license of D). Cf. voluntary and involuntary reactions to tests given by physician to patient

(Greinke v. Chicago City Ry. Co., 85 N.E. 327 (Ill.1908)); and the testing of hearing of blindfolded patient by holding watch and vibrating tuning fork near his ears and noting his response (Edwards v. Druien, 32 S.W.2d 411 (Ky.1930)).

3. Evidence that boys used to make fun of the testatrix as she went about the streets was received by the trial judge as tending to show her abnormality. Error? See In re Hine, 37 A. 384 (Conn.1897). Evidence that members of the family of testatrix treated her as incompetent to manage her affairs was received at the trial. Hearsay? If accompanied by evidence of her reaction to such treatment, hearsay? See Estate of DeLaveaga, 133 P. 307 (Cal.1913). On the issue whether father or daughter died first in a common disaster, evidence that he was put on a stretcher and she was not, was offered as tending to show that he survived her. Hearsay? See Estate of Loucks, 117 P. 673 (Cal.1911). In a narcotics prosecution, court admitted evidence that taxi driver whom defendant had just met in Harvard Square fled when DEA agents appeared. Hearsay? See United States v. Abou–Saada, 785 F.2d 1, 7–8 (1st Cir.1986).

Headley v. Tilghman

United States Court of Appeals, Second Circuit, 1995.
53 F.3d 472.

[After the Connecticut appellate court affirmed defendant's conviction for possession of narcotics with intent to sell and conspiracy to sell narcotics, defendant sought a writ of habeas corpus in federal district court. The district court granted the petition, holding that the Connecticut trial court had improperly admitted (1) expert testimony of an arresting officer, and (2) statements made by an unidentified co-conspirator during a telephone call.]

■ McLAUGHLIN, CIRCUIT JUDGE:

. . .

BACKGROUND

In late 1987, Connecticut police officers searched Denise McCrary's apartment in Hartford, Connecticut pursuant to a valid search warrant. They seized close to $30,000 in cash, a handgun, and small amounts of cocaine and marijuana. In addition, they seized items consistent with drug dealing including a sifter, small plastic bags, a small hand-held scale, and a triple-beam scale. The officers arrested the defendant, Denise McCrary, and two others who were in the apartment at the time of the search. Detective Michael Manzi, a narcotics officer for the Hartford police department, searched Headley incident to the arrest and found $890 in cash and a beeper.

At the police station, while Manzi was processing the evidence, Headley's beeper was activated by an incoming call. Manzi called the number displayed on the beeper screen, and a man with a Jamaican accent answered, saying "Are you up? Can I come by? Are you ready?" When Manzi began to speak, the unidentified man hung up.

. . .

Manzi testified as both a fact witness regarding Headley's arrest and as an expert on narcotics investigations. In his capacity as an expert, Manzi stated his opinion concerning the drug-related use of the items seized in McCrary's apartment, the relationship between the amount of money and the amount of drugs found, and the "characteristics" of a "drug distribution house." He also recounted, over the defense's objection, the questions asked by the unidentified

Jamaican male who answered the call that Manzi made to the number that appeared on Headley's beeper screen. The trial court admitted these questions on the theory that they were those of a co-conspirator made in furtherance of the conspiracy. It also admitted, again over defense objection, Manzi's expert opinion that, based on his experience with Jamaican drug dealers during numerous narcotics investigations, the caller was seeking to purchase cocaine.

Next, Denise McCrary testified that, in exchange for money and drugs, she allowed Headley to use her apartment to distribute cocaine. She said that the week before their arrest, Headley arrived at her apartment with a large amount of cocaine, plastic bags, a triple-beam scale, a handgun and a pager. According to her, Headley had sold all the cocaine before the police raid on her apartment. She admitted, however, that the cocaine in her handbag, a hand-held scale, another bag of cocaine with a straw, and a sifter found in her apartment belonged to her. She testified that $28,000 in cash found in the cushions of her couch belonged to one of the other persons arrested at her apartment. She further stated that a phone message she took for Headley, which she wrote down on the back of an envelope, was from an individual she believed wanted to purchase cocaine.

In summation, the prosecutor recounted Manzi's testimony concerning Headley's arrest. Based on Manzi's expert testimony about "distribution houses," he argued that a conspiracy existed despite the absence of large amounts of drugs in McCrary's apartment. He also discussed Manzi's testimony about the unidentified caller's statements. He relied primarily on the extent and credibility of McCrary's testimony, but additionally argued that Manzi's testimony and the items seized provided further evidence that Headley was guilty of the crimes charged.

. . .

DISCUSSION

. . .

I. Expert Testimony

[The court held that the expert testimony did not impermissibly bolster McCrary's testimony, but "show[ed] that the physical evidence seized from the apartment was consistent with evidence that might be found at a distribution house."]

. . .

II. Statements of the Unidentified Caller

. . .

... Here the trial court admitted the statements as those of a co-conspirator made during and in furtherance of the conspiracy. We need not enter that troublesome thicket, however, because we find that the caller's statements were admissible as non-hearsay under United States v. Oguns, 921 F.2d 442, 448–49 (2d Cir.1990).

In Oguns, a police officer answered a telephone call while searching the defendant's house pursuant to a valid warrant. The unidentified caller asked, "Have the apples arrived there?" Id. at 448. The district court allowed the officer to recount this question, and admitted additional evidence demonstrating that narcotics traffickers often use code words when discussing drugs on the telephone. Id. at 445, 449. We affirmed, reasoning that:

the government legitimately used the phone call as circumstantial evidence of Oguns' knowledge and intent regarding the importation and distribution charges. The fact that an out-of-court statement is used to provide circumstantial evidence of a conspiracy does not require that the statement be analyzed under the co-conspirator exception to the hearsay rule.

Id. at 449 (citations omitted).

Here, as in Oguns, the questions asked by the unidentified Jamaican caller—"Are you up? Can I come by? Are you ready?"—were not admitted for their truth, but rather as circumstantial evidence that Headley used his beeper to receive requests for drugs. Evidence scholars are wont to characterize such statements as "mixed acts and assertions," see generally 4 Christopher B. Mueller & Laird C. Kirkpatrick, Federal Evidence 101–12 (2d ed. 1994), and admissibility is won by emphasizing the performance aspect of the statement. Thus, the question implies the speaker's belief that he is talking to a drug dealer; and that belief is regarded as circumstantial evidence of the nature of the business. By intellectual corner-cutting, the cases treat this as an assumption by the speaker that he has reached a drug den, rather than a direct assertion by him that "you are a drug dealer," an assertion that would surely trigger the hearsay rule, with its risks of insincerity, distorted perception, imperfect memory, and ambiguity of utterance. An assumption has a fair claim to be treated as non-hearsay since the attendant risks are not as intensively implicated as when the idea is directly enunciated in a statement. See United States v. Long, 905 F.2d 1572, 1579–80 (D.C.Cir.), cert. denied, 498 U.S. 948, 111 S.Ct. 365, 112 L.Ed.2d 328 (1990).

Accordingly, the questions are non-hearsay, the exclusion of which is not mandated by any other evidentiary rule. In addition, although, as in Oguns, the caller's questions were seemingly innocuous, Manzi's expert opinion that the caller was seeking to purchase cocaine provided an alternative interpretation based upon his experience eavesdropping on numerous drug deals between Jamaican individuals. The jury was free to reject the government's interpretation in favor of the defense's construction that the caller was merely asking Headley to go out for the night.

. . .

REVERSED and REMANDED with directions to deny the petition.

NOTES ON IMPLIED ASSERTIONS

1. In 1992, in Regina v. Kearly, 2 App.Cas.228 (1992), the House of Lords dealt with the admissibility of police testimony about phone calls and visits that the police received while present at defendant's premises in connection with a drug raid. The police found only a small quantity of amphetamines at the premises, which were occupied as well by defendant's wife and a lodger, but defendant was charged with intent to supply in addition to possession. At defendant's trial, police officers testified about ten telephone calls they intercepted during which the caller inquired for "Chippie" (the defendant's nickname), and asked for drugs. In addition, the police testified that seven persons came to the door seeking to purchase drugs, some of whom asked for their "usual amount." None of the telephone callers or in-person callers were called as witnesses; nor did the police explain their absence. The trial judge overruled defendant's hearsay objection.

The House of Lords overturned defendant's conviction for intent to supply, relying on the authority of Wright v. Doe d. Tatham to find that the requests were hearsay. The majority was unimpressed by the many callers; one Lord stated that "the probative force of hearsay evidence in particular circumstances has never afforded a ground for disregarding the hearsay rule." 2 All ER 345, 357 (1992). (English law does not contain a residual hearsay exception.) Dissenting opinions pointed to the corroborative effect of other identical calls, but agreed that evidence of a single intercepted call by the police would have to be excluded.

2. For a discussion of Kearley, see Symposium on Hearsay and Implied Assertions: How Would (or Should) the Supreme Court Decide the Kearley Case? 16 Miss.C.L.Rev. 1 (1995). Contributors debated how differing models of a hearsay rule would classify implied assertions. How would the statements in Wright, Headley and Kearley be analyzed pursuant to the following approaches?

• Classification as hearsay hinges on the nature of the declaration seeking admission. See United States v. Long, 905 F.2d 1572, 1579 (D.C.Cir.)(phone call received while police were searching defendant's premises asking if he "still had any stuff" admissible as non-hearsay; unintentional messages are outside the hearsay rule), cert. denied, 498 U.S. 948 (1990); United States v. Zenni, 492 F.Supp. 464 (E.D.Ky.1980)(an assertion is a "forceful or positive declaration;" to prove the premises were used for illegal conduct, court admitted phone calls seeking to place bets that police answered while raiding an alleged betting parlor); State v. Carter, 651 N.E.2d 965, 971 (Ohio 1995)(in murder prosecution, an inquiry by accomplice about where a gun and ammunition could be obtained was not hearsay; "We hold that because a true question or inquiry is by its nature incapable of being proved either true or false and cannot be offered 'to prove the truth of the matter asserted,' it does not constitute hearsay as defined by Evid.R. 801.").

• Classification as hearsay depends on the danger/s that a particular statement poses. The Advisory Committee in its Notes to Rule 801 views the possibility of fabrication as the central hearsay risk; the common law was concerned in addition about ambiguity, misperception and lack of memory. How much importance would the Supreme Court ascribe to the Advisory Committee Note? See Berger, How Would or Should the Supreme Court Interpret the Definitions in Rule 801? 16 Miss.C.L.Rev. 13 (1995). Are there risks other than insincerity with statements that are not explicit assertions? Consider Rex v. Wysochan, 54 C.C.C. 172 (Sask.App.1930), criticized in 1 Alberta Law Q. 58 (1934): In the presence of SK and W, AK, wife of SK, receives a bullet wound from which she later dies. About a half-hour after the shooting, she states to SK, "Stanley, help me out because there is a bullet in my body". Shortly thereafter, when placed upon a sleigh and covered, preparatory to being taken to the hospital, she says, "Stanley, help me, I am too hot". Upon the trial of W, charged with the murder of AK, SK's testimony charges W with the fatal shooting, whereas W's evidence lays the blame upon SK. One Tony is permitted to testify to AK's statements to SK. The judge charges the jury that asking her husband for help would be an "improbable thing" if he had been "author of her death." Conviction. Sentence of death. Affirmed, citing Wigmore, § 1790 and arguing that the utterances in question were not hearsay.

• Classification as hearsay rests on the context in which the words seeking admission were spoken. Hearsay dangers are minimized when communications are primarily actions rather than assertions. Professors Mueller and Kirkpatrick use the term "performative" for verbal behavior that is intertwined with conduct. See Mueller & Kirkpatrick, Evidence § 8.22 (1995). See also Mueller,

Incoming Drug Calls and Performative Words: They're Not Just Talking About It, Baron Parke! 16 Miss.C.L.Rev. 1, 117 (1995).

• Classification as hearsay follows whenever "communicative behavior [is] offered to show any proposition that the communicator could have expected the audience to understand from the communication." Cullen, Foreword to the First Virtual Forum: Wallace Stevens, Blackbirds and the Hearsay Rule, 16 Miss.C.L.Rev. 1, 11 (1995). In the Texas Rules of Evidence, the definition of "hearsay" is identical to that in the Federal Rules, but Texas Rule 801(c) adds: " 'Matter asserted' includes any matter explicitly asserted, and any matter implied by a statement, if the probative value of the statement as offered flows from declarant's belief as to the matter." Consider R v. Alice Ghaui (Tanganyika Territory), 62 Law Q.Rev. 226 (1946). The prisoner is charged with murder of her husband by poisoning him with arsenic. A witness is offered to testify that, three days before the murder, witness, seeing a boy with a basket loitering in the street, looked in the basket, saw a bottle of green fluid, and asked the boy what it was; that the boy replied it was poison he was taking to someone who wanted to kill a dog. Shortly thereafter witness saw the boy hand the basket to the prisoner. The trial judge refuses to permit the testimony as to what the boy said, rejecting the argument of the Crown that the evidence is not hearsay because it is not sought to prove the truth of the statement. The prisoner is acquitted.

3. In United States v. Reyes, supra, would the hearsay rule have been violated if Agent Caggiano had pointed out defendant's phone number on the match book? Consider in this connection.

United States v. Hensel, 699 F.2d 18, 31 (1st Cir.), cert. denied, 461 U.S. 958 (1983)(hearsay rule not violated by admission into evidence of a glass bearing the defendant's distinctive nickname that was found at a place where conspirators met):

>   The fact that the word "Dink" appears on the glass does not itself make the glass hearsay evidence, for no assertion intended by the act of putting the word on the glass was relevant to the chain of inferences the government wished the jury to draw. The jury was not asked to infer anything about the person who put the name on the glass, who for all we know or care works in a factory that turns out "name" glasses by the score. Rather, the jury was asked to infer that Dink Hensel was likely to have possessed a glass with the name "Dink" on it and that he, or someone he knew, placed it in the house at Turkey Cove. The first of these inferences is merely circumstantial. There is no obvious way it depends upon the statement or state of mind of any out-of-court declarant.

>   The second of these inferences could involve hearsay only if one accepts a highly complex line of argument: Hensel might claim that he would like to cross-examine the "unknown" person who brought the glass to Turkey Cove on the ground that this out-of-court person's state of mind is relevant to the validity of the second inference. In order to invoke the hearsay rule, Hensel would have to argue that this individual's "nonverbal conduct" in placing the glass in the house was "intended by him as an assertion," Fed.R.Evid. 801(a)(2), that "Hensel was here." Even were one to make the heroic assumption that this was Hensel's argument, it fails. It fails because Hensel did not preliminarily show the district judge that placing the glass in the house was intended as an "assertion" (e.g., that it was designed to "frame" Hensel). Yet, the Federal Rules of Evidence "place the burden [of proving such an assertive intent] upon the party

claiming that the intention existed." Fed.R.Evid. 801 Advisory Committee note (a).

See also United States v. McIntyre, 997 F.2d 687, 701 (10th Cir.1993)(surveys cases admitting documents to link various defendants together), cert. denied, 510 U.S. 1063 (1994).

4.   Does evidence of silence constitute hearsay? See Silver v. New York Cent. R. R. Co., 105 N.E.2d 923 (Mass.1952)(in suit by passenger claiming that she was injured because of extreme cold in railroad car, testimony by the porter that the other passengers did not complain should have been admitted if the circumstances of the plaintiff and the other passengers were substantially the same, and the porter was available to receive complaints). See Weinstein, Probative Force of Hearsay, 46 Iowa L.Rev. 331, 343 (1961) suggesting the unlikelihood that the non-complaining passengers were Eskimos or stockholders of the Railroad or masochists. Compare Smith v. Korn Indus. Inc., 262 S.E.2d 27 (S.C.1980)(testimony of friend that he had never heard plaintiff complain of physical condition prior to accident sued on is negative hearsay and inadmissible); Farm Bureau Mut. Ins. Co. v. Horne, 510 S.W.2d 70 (Ark. 1974)(in order to show that boat was not stolen until after effective date of insurance policy, plaintiff called owner of marina to testify that no report of missing boat was made to him on day in question; reversible error). How should these cases be analyzed under the Federal Rules of Evidence?

5.   Suppose a witness testifies about an observation made by a machine, such as a radar gun, a thermometer, a cat-scan or a polygraph? Does the hearsay rule apply? See City of Webster Groves v. Quick, 323 S.W.2d 386 (Mo.Ct.App. 1959). Suppose the observer is a dog? For a thorough analysis of bloodhound testimony see Taslitz, Does the Cold Nose Know? The Unscientific Myth of the Dog Scent Lineup, 42 Hastings L.J. 17, 110–112 (1990).

For a discussion of the admissibility of expert testimony based on hearsay, see pp. 1045–1063.

Kinder v. Commonwealth

Court of Appeals of Kentucky, 1957.
306 S.W.2d 265.

■ MONTGOMERY, JUDGE.

Don Kinder, the appellant, and Hayes Kinder, his father, were jointly indicted for grand larceny of certain personal property of the value of $425 belonging to the Bevander Coal Corporation. On a separate trial, appellant was convicted and sentenced to a year's confinement in the state reformatory. He alleges as grounds for reversal of the judgment that: (1) Incompetent evidence was admitted; (2) the evidence was insufficient to sustain the verdict; and (3) the court failed to instruct the jury properly.

John C. Nicewander, vice president of the coal company, testified to the loss of the missing property. He said that he recognized a part of the stolen property in a load of scrap on a truck parked at a service station. The truck was being operated by the Kinders. Hayes Kinder was asked where he obtained a radiator, purportedly a part of the stolen property. He answered that he bought it from a boy on Hackney's Creek, but was unable to recall his name or to describe his appearance.

The truck left the service station. The state police was furnished a description of the truck and its license number. It was later stopped by the police, but the stolen property was missing. The items of stolen property recognized by Nicewander were located later by the officers underneath a shack about 200 feet from the service station.

Appellant objected to the introduction of the following testimony by police officers as being inadmissible hearsay:

"We started home with this little boy and we was up at Millard, Junction 80 and 460, going east toward Grundy, and we got to talking to this boy and—

. . .

"Did you have information that the stuff could be found there?

"Yes, sir, I did.

. . .

"Sergeant Cornette, did anyone point out to you where this radiator could be found?

"Yes, sir, they did.

. . .

"Who did that?

"This small Kinder boy that I was taking home.

. . .

"Is that the same child that was with the defendants at the time you stopped the truck and took them in custody?

"Yes sir.

. . .

"Who pointed out where you could find the radiator at the building there, if anyone?

"This little Kinder boy."

The officers were not permitted to say what the little boy had said.

The boy referred to was identified as Danny Hackney, five years of age, the child of appellant's sister. He had been with the Kinders in the truck and had been taken home by the officers after the arrests. At the time of the trial, the child was purportedly in Ohio.

The objectionable testimony admitted is not hearsay. Hearsay has been defined as evidence which derives its value not solely from the credit to be given to the witness upon the stand but, in part, from the veracity and competency of some other person. The hearsay rule signifies a rule rejecting assertions offered testimonially which have not been in some way subjected to the test of cross-examination under oath. It is an extra-judicial testimonial assertion which may be either written or spoken. The theory of the rule is that the many possible deficiencies, suppressions, sources of error and untrustworthiness, which lie underneath the bare untested assertion of a witness, may be best brought to light and exposed by the fundamental test of cross-examination. 5 Wigmore, Evidence, Sections 1361–1362, pages 2 and 3; Sections 1395–1397, pages 122–127; 31 C.J.S. Evidence §§ 192, 193, page 919; 20 Am.Jur., Evidence, Section 451, page 400; Davis v. Bennett's Adm'r, 279 Ky. 799, 132 S.W.2d 334.

The statements objected to were made subject to cross-examination and were based upon personal knowledge. The officers were testifying to what they had seen and heard. Similar testimony has been held admissible. Johnson v. State, 254 Wis. 320, 36 N.W.2d 86. No merit is found in the objection to the testimony because of the age of the child since the child did not testify, and for the further reason that the child's age would not necessarily have rendered his testimony incompetent. The competency of an infant as a witness is determined by the witness' intelligence. Roberson's Criminal Law, Section 1843, at 1959.

. . .

Judgment affirmed.

United States v. Muscato

United States District Court, E. D. New York, 1982.
534 F.Supp. 969.

■ WEINSTEIN, CHIEF JUDGE.

. . .

I. Facts

The story begins with Walter Gollender, a self-styled part-time talent promotor. Though a fastidious and intelligent man, Gollender had been forced to leave the teaching profession by a psychiatric disability. In need of protection from Newark's dangers, real and imagined, he purchased a small, single shot firearm of simple design, in appearance resembling a large pen.

Gollender revealed his purchase to an acquaintance named Stanley Szostek, Jr., a former Newark police officer, who assisted his father in operating a neighborhood liquor and food store. In turn, Szostek showed the pen gun to his friend and business partner, Joseph Kirchner, a truck driver who delivered soft drinks to the store. Together, this enterprising pair had contrived to provide their community with a variety of services. They had invested in a rock concert, conducted a desultory loan-sharking business, and sold patent remedies as illicit drugs. Upon observing the simple construction of Gollender's weapon and learning that he had paid $40.00 for it, they decided to enter the arms trade.

Szostek took the prototype to a friend on the Newark police force, the defendant, John Muscato. Despairing of ever making the down payment for a new home on a modest policeman's salary, Muscato was moonlighting as a machinist in his father's basement. Muscato agreed to make copies of the pen gun in commercial quantities.

One problem with this plan was that it left Gollender defenseless. Accordingly, Muscato temporarily lent Gollender a twenty-five calibre pistol to replace his pen gun. Awed by the complexity and dangers of this new acquisition, Gollender carefully marked the pistol with a gummed label to indicate the safety position and the firing position. After the model pen gun had served its purpose, it was returned to him and he relinquished the pistol to Szostek.

As Muscato began producing pen guns, Szostek and Kirchner began casting about for markets for their product. They were particularly concerned to sell the guns outside of their home territory, perhaps so as not to embarrass the Newark police force with which they had such close connections. To this end they contacted a business acquaintance, Patrick Monteforte. Monteforte, who worked for one of the food wholesalers that supplied Szostek's store, provided

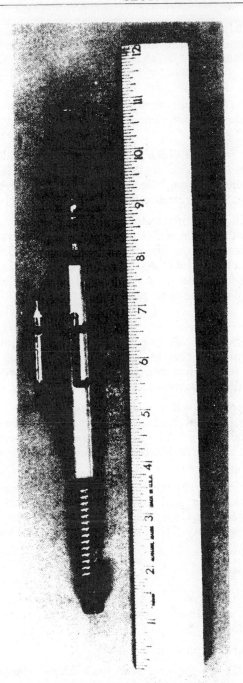

Szostek and Kirchner with stolen food in repayment of high interest loans. He began looking for potential buyers of pen guns on Staten Island.

As it turned out, the demand for pen guns in this part of the Eastern District of New York was substantial. It was Monteforte's fortune to land as a customer one of the world's major armaments purchasers, the United States Government. Though presenting himself as the representative of a large New York area crime syndicate, the buyer was in fact Special Agent Matthew Raffa of the United States Treasury Department, Bureau of Alcohol, Tobacco and

Firearms. As quickly as the basement factory could produce the pen guns, the Treasury Department bought them. Eventually, the government placed an order for 1,000 at $20,000.

. . .

Delivery of the final shipment was arranged to be in neutral territory, a diner in the shadow of the George Washington Bridge, in Fort Lee, New Jersey....

To the surprise of Kirchner, Szostek and McDonald [a recruit to the conspiracy], instead of enriching them by $20,000, Raffa and his colleagues arrested them. From McDonald the federal agents recovered a .25 calibre pistol, bearing the remnants of a gummed label at the safety catch.

Eventually, all of the conspirators were rounded up ... During his debriefing by government officials, Gollender chanced to describe the gun that he claimed he had received from Muscato and returned to Szostek, recalling that he had placed a gummed label at the safety catch. At this point, the government agents retrieved from a safe the pistol found on McDonald. Gollender promptly identified it as the same pistol he had described.

. . .

[Muscato's] defense consisted of a denial of criminal intent. The hypothesis suggested to the jury was that Muscato was a law-abiding policeman who had been making the various pen gun parts independently without knowing what they were or how they fit together....

The defense position was ... seriously undercut by the testimony of the other conspirators [who testified for the government]. Now, if these witnesses were not quite your run-of-the-mill mobsters, neither were they particularly solid citizens, and the defense attacked their credibility on cross-examination with considerable gusto.

Given Gollender's psychiatric history, he was by no means an ideal witness and the defense attorney had a field day with him on cross-examination. Particularly stressed was Gollender's difficulty in distinguishing reality from fancy and his suggestability. The following exchanges are typical:

Mr. Richman:

. . .

Q. And it is true that ... Dr. Howard Davidman, said that you have a great need to be noticed and appreciated which sometimes leads you to bizarre behavior? ...

A. It has happened on occasion, yes.

Q. And on those occasions you don't know whether you behavior is bizarre or not, isn't that correct?

A. I would hope it would not be, but maybe perhaps it has been.

Q. You can't distinguish sometimes from reality to perhaps not so reality?

A. I can distinguish from reality but I can't always predict what effect my behavior would have on other people.

Q. Sometimes you become panicky and overdo some things, isn't that correct? ...

A. Sometimes.

Given this attack on Gollender's credibility, one piece of real proof took on added weight. Linking Muscato to the conspiracy was the pistol he allegedly lent Gollender, which ultimately turned up in the hands of McDonald at the time of his arrest. Gollender identified the pistol in open court as follows:

Mr. (A.U.S.A.) Kirby: Did you have any conversation with Mr. Muscato at that time?

A. No, I did not. Except he gave me a .25 calibre gun while we were in the car. He came to an intersection in Irvington and he stopped and gave me the pistol....

Q. Mr. Gollender, I show you what has been marked as Government's Exhibit 12.

Would you take a look at that object and tell the Court and jury whether you recognize it?

A. Yes, it's the gun.

Q. I'm sorry?

A. Yes, I recognize it as the .25 caliber pistol.

Q. How do you recognize it as such?

A. It has the same marking on it, same scuff mark and mainly the remnants of the gum label I marked it with, safe or unsafe. It still has a piece of the paper indicating how it was safe or unsafe.

The fact that Gollender had provided an accurate description of the pistol prior to his being shown it or being told that it had been discovered on the person of Charles McDonald provided important confirmation of his testimony. The government petitioned the court for permission to elicit this fact from Special Agent Raffa. (It was clear that Muscato would deny from the witness stand Gollender's testimony about the source of the pistol.) The defense objected on the ground of hearsay. Ruling that it would permit Raffa to testify, the court on its own motion directed that Gollender be brought back to the courthouse and made available for cross examination concerning his out-of-court description and identification of the pistol.

For the tactical purpose of reducing the impression Raffa's proposed testimony would make on the jury, the defense brought it out on cross examination of the Special Agent. That cross examination proceeded as follows:

By Mr. Richman:

Q. Sir, Mr. Raffa, did there come a time in the conversation with Mr. Kirby where you-where Mr. Gollander said to you, "I have a 25 caliber gun which I received from John Muscato which has a sticky substance on it next to the safety"?

A. Yes, sir.

Q. Did you make any notations concerning that particular conversation?

A. No, I didn't.

Q. But, you remember it?

A. I most certainly do....

Q. Now, how many times did you speak to Mr. Gollander concerning the sticky substance?

A. I spoke to him the first day that he had mentioned it, and every time thereafter that he was interviewed by....

Q. How many times was that?

A. Eight to ten times, I believe.

Q. And you kept refreshing his recollection concerning this sticky substance?

Is that right?

A. No, on the contrary, he refreshed my recollection that he was the one that originally put a piece of paper on the firearm given to him by Mr. Muscato to show him where the safety position would be and the firing position. . . .

He told me first-I had never known that this, in fact, was the same gun.

He told me that the 25 caliber Titan gun that Mr. Muscato had given him, he put a small piece of paper on the frame of the gun to show when it was in the firing position or safe position.

I went into the evidence vault of the U.S. Attorney's Office upstairs and I took the 25 Titan that we had seized from Mr. McDonald.

I brought the gun in and I asked him to examine it and to tell me whether or not he recognized that.

He looked at the gun and he said, "This is the gun that Muscato gave me. And, I know that because I can see the remnants of the piece of paper that I had put on there, and it was a sticky substance that I put on the piece of paper to keep the paper on the gun."

So, when he looked at that, he said, "This is the remnants of it, and that is how I know it is the same gun."

Neither side wished to examine Gollender further. He was released on consent. We can assume that Gollender would have confirmed the agent's testimony about their conversations before the trial.

II.   Law

. . .

In theory the admissibility of this evidence turns on two apparently distinct questions: whether the testimony was hearsay, and, if so, whether it was admissible hearsay. In practice, however, the line between admissible hearsay and non-hearsay is often difficult to trace. The same fundamental concerns with reliability and need that shape the concept of hearsay are also expressed in the numerous exceptions to the hearsay rules, especially the catchall exception, Rule 803(24) of the Federal Rules of Evidence.

In this case, the extrajudicial declaration was both reliable and useful. Admission furthered "the end" of the Federal Rules of Evidence, "that the truth may be ascertained and proceedings justly determined." F.R.Evid. 102. It was highly "probative" and there was no "danger of unfair prejudice, confusion of the issues, or misleading the jury." F.R.Evid. 403. Moreover, both good sense and precedent supported admissibility. Nevertheless, the government's case, insofar as it rested on the out-of-court identification of the pistol found on Charles McDonald, contained both hearsay and non-hearsay components.

1) Was the extrajudicial declaration hearsay under the Federal Rules?

For purposes of analysis one way of treating the case with respect to the gun might be to consider only the following testimony: One member of the conspiracy testified that he had received a gun from the defendant, an alleged coconspirator, that this gun had a unique characteristic, observable upon examination, and that he had returned the gun to a third conspirator. The arresting officer testified that he had obtained a gun with the same unique characteristic from an alleged fourth conspirator. The jury could examine the gun, which had been admitted as an exhibit, to help it determine if the two witnesses were describing the same object. This part of the case presents no hearsay problem. Both witnesses testified with respect to characteristics and events they themselves observed.

The evidence was significant in two respects. First, the prosecution's ability to produce a gun matching Gollender's description lent circumstantial support to Gollender's story of having received such a gun from the defendant in furtherance of the conspiracy. Second, the fact that this gun was found on the person of another conspirator while engaged in acts furthering the conspiracy linked Muscato to the conspiracy.

What made the production of the gun useful as corroboration of Gollender's story is the improbability of his describing a gun with such a unique characteristic if he had not seen it. The physical evidence of the gun provided some assurance (unless the jury believed that this real evidence was fabricated by the prosecution) that the tale was not cut out of whole cloth. It did not by itself insure that Gollender saw the gun under the circumstances he related. If he first described the gun after having identified it while it was in the agent's possession, much of the effect of this line of proof would have been eroded. If, on the other hand, he described the gun before being shown it by a law enforcement official, production of the gun would have a substantial corroborative effect.

If we then add to the case the extrajudicial declaration of Gollender to the agent we have 1) testimony revealing the existence of a memory in the mind of a witness (a description of a gun with unique characteristics and its source), 2) a physical object matching that memory, and 3) an extrajudicial declaration made under circumstances indicating that the reported memory was acquired in a manner consistent with the witness' testimony.

It is the third leg which involved a hearsay danger since it depended on the truth of an extrajudicial declaration to the agent by Gollender. Gollender said outside of court, in essence, "the gun given to me by Muscato had a unique characteristic; this is that gun." On its face, thus parsed, his statement to the agent would appear to fall squarely within the definition of hearsay ...

. . .

The fact that the extrajudicial declarant, like his auditor, was a witness subject to cross examination does not eliminate the hearsay problem. While many writers proposed treating extrajudicial declarations by witnesses as non-hearsay or as falling within a broad hearsay exception ... the Federal Rules reject this approach except in special cases. See F.R.Evid. 801(d)(1); 803(5).

. . .

Despite the fact that it could be analyzed as hearsay under the Federal Rules of Evidence, this extrajudicial declaration posed minimal hearsay dangers; it was highly probative while being essentially corroborative in function. Admitting it may be justified under a number of different theories: that it was circumstantial rather than testimonial evidence and, therefore, was not hearsay; that it was offered on the issue of credibility rather than for its truth as evidence-in-chief; and that it was admissible under Rule 803(24).

2) The extrajudicial declaration as circumstantial evidence One way of characterizing the extrajudicial declaration in this case is as "circumstantial non-assertive use" of the utterance "to show state of mind." Statements used in this way, according to Professor McCormick, need not be denominated hearsay. This, he wrote, is especially true of "declarations evincing knowledge, notice, consciousness or awareness of some fact, which fact is established by other evidence in the case." McCormick, Evidence, § 249, p. 592 (2nd Cleary Ed.1972). According to this analysis, the extrajudicial declaration was offered not to prove the truth of the proposition asserted-the description of the gun-but to prove that the declarant had knowledge of the truth of that proposition. . . .

. . .

The evidence before us is much like the extrajudicial declaration at issue in Bridges v. State, 247 Wis. 350, 19 N.W.2d 529, 534 (1945), the case McCormick cited as the paradigm. A seven year old child described to a police officer several exterior and interior details of the house in which she was allegedly assaulted. Subsequently, it was discovered that this description closely fit defendant's home. The court, relying on 6 Wigmore §§ 1788, 1790, 1791 (3rd Ed.1940), reasoned that the statement to the police officer was circumstantial evidence of the child's state of mind which, in turn, was evidence of what caused that state of mind.

Additional support for such treatment of extrajudicial declarations (or behavior) evincing knowledge may be sought in Kinder v. Commonwealth, 306 S.W.2d 265 (Ky.App.1957), in which a defendant was convicted of larceny on the basis of his young son's knowledge of the location of the cache of stolen goods. Another such case is State v. Galvan, 297 N.W.2d 344 (Iowa 1980) . . .

The Bridges approach to cases of this sort cuts the gordian knot of hearsay. Not surprisingly, however, it leaves a few loose ends.

First, it involves an oversimplification of the function of the declaration involved. It is not quite accurate to characterize the extrajudicial declarations in any of these cases as mere descriptions of places of things or of "traces" on the mind. They are essentially accounts of events implicating criminal defendants and, ultimately, they will be used by the trier in support of the accounts they suggest, even if, as an intermediate step, they indicate only states of mind consistent with the truth and accuracy of these implied accounts. Thus, there is a sense in which they are offered to prove the proposition asserted.

Second, it does not sufficiently distinguish between the use of an extrajudicial declaration as evidence of past state of mind and its use as evidence of current state of mind. Yet there may be a difference in reliability between these two uses of an extrajudicial declaration. Where a prior statement is adduced to show the basis of a current memory trace, it can be checked and tested against the current statement. This is not necessarily the case for evidence such as that offered in Bridges or Galvan, concerning an ephemeral mental impression. In the present case, the extrajudicial declaration corroborates in-court testimony. In a case like Galvan, where the extrajudicial declarant is unavailable to testify, that is not the situation. This is cause for a sense of disquiet which cannot be adequately dispelled since there can be no in-court current explanation and testing of the declarant.

Third, and most important, a rule admitting all such material ignores important distinctions in reliability. There are dangers implicit in allowing into evidence material like that offered in Bridges, Kinder and Galvan-dangers which McCormick acknowledges but which the trier may fail to give proper weight. The ability of declarants to recall details observed in incriminating situations, before being exposed to those details by law enforcement officials or others, is bound to impress a trier. The probative force of such evidence, however, is dependent on the assumption that the extrajudicial declarant had no other way of learning the details described than by having witnessed the events described. If declarants in such cases were exposed to the objects they identified in some fashion other than one which squares with their implied account, or if the information was otherwise suggested to them, as by the form of questioning or what they inadvertently overheard, then their extrajudicial descriptions have little probative force. There is always a danger that even the least suggestive auditor will read into a conversation details put forward by one party and adopted by the other as his own thoughts....

Where the assumption that the extrajudicial declarant has not been previously exposed to the objects or events in question or their description remains unchecked by vigorous cross-examination or other evidence tested under adversarial fire, dangerous consequences can result. A well-documented Swedish case presented facts analogous to those in Bridges but with a twist. While a young boy claiming to be the victim of an assault could accurately identify the interior of the accused's apartment, it turned out that he had been previously exposed to an identical apartment. Then further investigation demonstrated inconsistencies in the boy's story that revealed that the accusation was fabricated in an attempt to deflect attention from the child's own disobedience. Trankell, "Was Lars Sexually Assaulted?", 56 Journal of Abnormal and Social Psychology, 385 ff. (1958); A. Trankell, Reliability of Evidence, 106 ff. (1972).

One way of coping with the incompleteness of the Bridges approach is to turn to criteria of admissibility other than the hearsay rule-i.e., those of Rule 403-for evaluating circumstantial non-assertive uses of extrajudicial declarations. See, e.g., Note, Theoretical Foundations of the Hearsay Rule, 93 Harv. L. Rev. 1786 (1980)....

Much would, of course, depend upon the court's evaluation of the witness. Moreover, in Bridges the circumstances were such as to make it highly unlikely that the details of the description could have been derived from anything but the child's experience of the event in question.

. . .

The out-of-court declaration [in the case before us] is accompanied by the declarant's in-court identification and availability for cross examination as well as the auditor's testimony respecting the declarant's limited opportunities for prior contact with the object identified.

3) The extrajudicial declaration as evidence of credibility

The government's contention that defendant Muscato had provided Gollender with the gun ultimately used by McDonald was dependent in the main upon the present recollection at the trial of Gollender and Special Agent Raffa; both testified. The principal role of the extrajudicial declaration was, in concert with Special Agent Raffa's testimony as to the conditions of the declaration, to bolster Gollender's credibility....

... As such it was a "prior statement by a witness ... and consistent with his testimony and ... offered to rebut an express or implied charge of recent fabrication or improper influence or motive" and so non-hearsay under Rule 801(d)(1)(B).

Even if it did not fall within the definition of non-hearsay in Rule 801(d)(1)(B), however, the extrajudicial declaration would be admissible on the issue of Gollender's credibility. . . .

. . .

4) Rule 803(24)

The twenty three specific classes of exceptions to the hearsay rule enumerated in Rule 803 identify situations in which there is a circumstantial guarantee of an extrajudicial declarant's credibility and special need for this class of hearsay. Rule 803(24), the catchall exception, is designed to permit the court to identify situations not enumerated in the other exceptions in which unique circumstances supply proof of reliability and need. . . .

Here, as provided by 803(24), there were "circumstantial guarantees of trustworthiness" "equivalent" to those in Rules 803(1) to 803(23). Corroborating circumstances included the physical features of the gun readily observable by the jury and the fact that it was under lock and key from the time of the initial arrest to the time of the extrajudicial declaration. In addition the fact that both parties to the out-of-court conversation were available for full cross examination on the details of the statement and the surrounding circumstances as well as on the events it described provided extraordinary guarantees that the jury could properly evaluate the extrajudicial declarant's credibility at the time he made the declaration. . . .

. . .

III.   Conclusion

Gollender's out-of-court statement was properly admitted. Whether or not this extrajudicial declaration is denominated hearsay turns on how one characterizes its function in the development of the government's case. It may be viewed as admissible hearsay, non-hearsay evidence-in-chief, or non-hearsay insofar as it is admissible on the issue of credibility. Admission of evidence of this sort does not derive its ultimate justification from any one theory, but from notions of reliability and the ability of the trier to properly evaluate probative force.

Absent a constitutional issue of confrontation-and there is none here-the central question is whether the jury could accurately evaluate the probative value of Gollender's out-of-court statement. Essentially this is an issue implicated in Rules 401 to 403, requiring the court's exercise of sound judgment and discretion. See, e.g., United States v. Barbati, 284 F.Supp. 409, 413 (E.D.N.Y. 1968) ("We cannot permit the mechanical and unreasoned application of the hearsay rule to deny evidence vital for our search for the truth."). In the circumstances of this case there can be no doubt that admitting this evidence enhanced the search for the truth without any possible unfairness or prejudice to the defendant. Motion for a new trial denied.

NOTES

1. In State v. Galvan, 297 N.W.2d 344 (Iowa 1980), cited in the principal case, the defendant was charged with aiding and abetting in the murder of a man whose hands and feet had been bound, and who had been repeatedly stabbed. The trial court admitted testimony by the defendant's wife that on the night of the murder he left the house with his youngest daughter, then age two, and that two days later "she observed her two-year old daughter, the one who had accompanied the defendant, behaving in a way that was, for the child, unique.

The child had taken a belt from her mother's robe and bound her own hands with it. Then she made several gestures as if beating her own chest."

The State argued:

> The testimony of Jenny Perez concerning her daughter's conduct was offered to prove that the child had knowledge of the fact that someone had been bound and stabbed, not to prove that the victim was bound and stabbed. As such, the Perez testimony is part of the State's circumstantial evidence, from which a reasonable juror could infer from the fact of the young child's conduct that she had seen the stabbing of someone who was tied up....

2. In Reed v. State, 438 So.2d 169 (Fla.Dist.Ct.App.1983), defendant, charged with murdering his wife Denise, argued that the court should have allowed testimony that a man called Frank had stated that Denise was dead and that she had been stabbed in the chest about twelve times, and that he had made this statement ten to fifteen minutes before the police announced that Denise had been found dead of multiple stab wounds. The trial judge had earlier excluded another statement, saying:

> Well, how do you—how do you get around—I know that expression, I have heard it a hundred times and I have never understood what it means. We don't offer this for the truth for what it was said, but for the state of mind of the declarant that it was said. If you don't—to me it's so obviously hearsay that the State or the other party cannot rebut it insofar as the state of mind or the truthfulness or anything else. I don't understand, I have never understood what that rule means, I am sorry, I am obtuse, I remember it in law school. It came across once a week, but I have never understood what it means.

> I have never understood how you can possibly say, okay, but this is hearsay, but we are going to let it in because we are not asserting the truth of what was said but rather the state of mind of the declarant. Seems to me that's the reason for hearsay. Id. at 170.

The appellate court affirmed. A concurring opinion concluded that Frank's statement was hearsay because "it depended for its value upon the observations and veracity of the declarant," but that even if it could be said "not to fall within the definition of hearsay, it would still be inadmissible under McCormick's theory because its trustworthiness could not be established.... Only the unavailable witnesses to the declaration could state with any certainty that Frank had not gotten his information from one or more of the officers at the scene, rather than from his personal observations of the decedent's body at a time when no one else was present." Id. at 173.

NOTE

Additional references. In addition to articles cited elsewhere in this section see Symposium, Hearsay Reform Conference, 76 Minn.L.Rev. 363–889 (1992); Symposium on Hearsay and Implied Assertions: How Would (or Should) the Supreme Court Decide the Kearley Case?, 16 Miss.C.L.Rev. 1 (1995); Callen, Hearsay and Informal Reasoning, 47 Vand. L.Rev. 43 (1994); Fenner, Law Professor Reveals Shocking Truth About Hearsay, 62 UMKC L.Rev. 1 (1993): Friedman, Improving the Procedure for Resolving Hearsay Issues, 13 Cardozo L.Rev. 883 (1991); Friedman, Route Analysis of Credibility and Hearsay, 96 Yale L.J. 667 (1987); Millich, Hearsay Antinomies: The Case for Abolishing the Rule and Starting Over, 71 Or. L. Rev. 723 (1992); Park, A Subject Matter

Approach to Hearsay Reform, 86 Mich. L. Rev. 51 (1987); Schum, Hearsay From a Layperson, 14 Cardozo L. Rev. 1 (1992); Siegel, Rationalizing Hearsay: A Proposal for a Best Evidence Hearsay Rule, 72 B.U.L.Rev. 893 (1992); Swift, A Foundation Fact Approach to Hearsay, 75 Cal.L.Rev. 1339 (1987); Swift, Abolishing the Hearsay Rule, 75 Cal.L.Rev. 495 (1987).

SECTION 2. PRIOR STATEMENTS OF WITNESSES

Rowe v. Farmers Insurance Company, Inc.

Supreme Court of Missouri, 1985.
699 S.W.2d 423 (en banc).

■ WELLIVER, JUDGE.

. . .

I

Respondent's car was found burning by Missouri Highway Patrol Officer Overbey, at about 1:00 A.M., on August 13, 1982. The 1981 Ford L.T.D. was aflame in a lonely rural field approximately 7 miles from respondent's home. Respondent filed a claim with appellant, his automobile insurance company. The claim was disallowed and respondent brought this action.

At trial, appellant contended that respondent either had his car torched to collect the insurance proceeds or later learned who burned his car and did not report this information to the police or to appellant. Appellant called Chester Carroll as a witness. Carroll is respondent's first cousin. On November 22, 1982, Carroll allegedly made several statements to Officer Overbey. Officer Overbey was prepared to testify that Carroll told him on November 22, 1982, that he overheard respondent tell another man that respondent was going to burn his Ford L.T.D. in order to acquire a four wheel drive pickup truck. This conversation, overheard by Carroll, occurred before the Ford was burned.

Carroll's deposition had been taken on June 23, 1983. Respondent visited Carroll about one week before the deposition. In this meeting, respondent and Carroll talked about respondent's suit against the appellant. At trial and in his deposition, Carroll denied overhearing any conversation between respondent and another man. The trial court did not allow the appellant to introduce evidence and expose Carroll's prior inconsistent statement made to Officer Overbey, relying on the rule that a party may not impeach his own witness.

. . .

The jury returned a verdict for respondent.

II

Missouri has consistently followed the ancient rule that a party cannot impeach his own witness. . . .

No valid reason for this anachronistic rule would seem to exist today. . . .

. . .

Based upon our own analysis and the experience of the vast majority of jurisdictions including the federal courts, we conclude that the time has come for us to recognize the right of any party to introduce a prior inconsistent statement to impeach any witness regardless of by whom the witness may have been subpoenaed or called. To the extent that prior civil cases have held to the contrary, they shall no longer be followed.

III

Having decided that a party may introduce prior inconsistent statements to impeach his own witness, we must now address the related question of whether prior inconsistent statements can be considered as substantive evidence in civil trials. Missouri generally has followed the orthodox standard that inconsistent statements made by a witness out of court are hearsay and inadmissible for the truth of the matter asserted.

The traditional rule requiring the exclusion of all prior inconsistent statements as substantive evidence is flawed. See generally, State v. Granberry, 491 S.W.2d 528, 534, (Mo. banc 1973)(Finch, J., concurring). The United States Court of Appeals for the Second Circuit has observed:

> The rule limiting the use of prior statements by a witness subject to cross-examination to their effect on his credibility has been described by eminent scholars and judges as "pious fraud," "artificial," "basically misguided," "mere verbal ritual," and an anachronism "that still impede(s) our pursuit of the truth."

United States v. DeSisto, 329 F.2d 929 (2d Cir.1964)(quoting Morgan, Hearsay Dangers and the Application of the Hearsay Concept, 62 Harv.L.Rev. 177, 193 (1948)). The chief flaw is that the inconsistent statements of witnesses often are relevant to more than just the credibility of the witness. State v. Copeland, 278 S.C. 572, 300 S.E.2d 63 (1982); Nugent v. Commonwealth, 639 S.W.2d 761 (Ky.1982). The inconsistent statement made by a witness may be more reliable and believable than a statement made at trial.

The possible relevance of inconsistent statements can be seen in the facts of the present case. The trial court did not allow the jury to learn of the statements made by Chester Carroll to Officer Overbey. Carroll had told Officer Overbey that he heard the respondent tell a man that he was going to burn his Ford L.T.D. to collect the insurance and buy a four wheel drive automobile. After a meeting between the respondent and Carroll, Carroll denied in his deposition and at trial that he ever overheard the respondent. A reasonable person could find this statement helpful in resolving the truth or falsity of the witness's testimony.

While the majority of jurisdictions have dealt with this question by statute or rule, some have done so by opinion. In Gibbons v. State, 248 Ga. 858, 286 S.E.2d 717 (1982), the Supreme Court of Georgia held that prior inconsistent statements may be admitted as substantive evidence when the witness is available for cross-examination. The Georgia court noted that allowing inconsistent statements to be used as substantive evidence has several salutary effects: (1) trial courts will become more adept at determining truth; (2) parties will be partially protected from the erratic witness who changes his story; (3) parties will be protected from the efforts of the other to influence witness testimony; and (4) witnesses will be partially protected from efforts to influence their testimony since the rewards of changing testimony are less. Gibbons v. State, 248 Ga. 858, 286 S.E.2d 717, 722 (1982).

Research regarding human memory indicates several advantages prior inconsistent statements have over trial testimony. Studies have disclosed that the ability to remember an incident declines as time passes. J. Marshall, Law and Psychology in Conflict 29–30 (2d ed. 1980). McCormick explains that "[t]he prior statement is always nearer and usually very much nearer to the event than is the testimony. The fresher the memory, the fuller and more accurate [any statement] is." McCormick, Handbook of the Law of Evidence § 251, at 745 (3d ed. 1984). See also 3A Wigmore, Evidence § 1018 (Chadbourn rev. 1970); Morgan, Hearsay Dangers and the Application of the Hearsay Concept, 62 Harv.L.Rev. 177, 192 (1948).

Investigations into human recall also have shown that witnesses are more prone to forget facts which support propositions with which they disagree. J. Marshall, Law and Psychology in Conflict 29 (Second Edition 1980). Once a legal dispute is created, the honest recollection of witnesses may change and favor the side they favor. Prior inconsistent statements are not as prone to this phenomenon as trial testimony. Inconsistent statements are often made before a legal dispute has been commenced and they are made sooner after the event when less time has elapsed allowing selective forgetting to operate. Prior inconsistent statements also may be made before a motive for perjury has arisen and perhaps are less likely to be untruthful.

The instruction to jurors to use a prior inconsistent statement only for assessing the credibility of the declarant, but not for the truth of the matter asserted in the inconsistent statement, is at best confusing. The repetitive effect of calling attention to the prior inconsistent statement by the instruction probably cannot do other than highlight the matter in the minds of the jurors thereby making them more inclined to rely on the statement than to disregard it. See generally Broeder, The University of Chicago Jury Project, 38 Neb. L.Rev. 744, 754 (1959).

It has been said that when the declarant is available for cross-examination enough of the dangers of hearsay are absent. State v. Copeland, 278 S.C. 572, 300 S.E.2d 63, 69 (1982), cert. denied, 460 U.S. 1103, 103 S.Ct. 1802, 76 L.Ed.2d 367 (1983); Advisory Committee's Note to Fed.R.Evid. 801(d)(1)(A); Comment, Prior Inconsistent Statements: Conflict Between State and Federal Rules of Evidence, 34 Mercer L.Rev. 1495, 1498 (1983). Wigmore supports the proposition that when the witness is present and subject to cross-examination on his prior inconsistent statements, "[t]he whole purpose of the hearsay rule has already been satisfied." 3A Wigmore, Evidence § 1018 (Chadbourn rev. 1970). Justice Learned Hand asserted: "If, from all that the jury see of the witness, they conclude that what he says now is not the truth, but what he said before [is the truth], they are nonetheless deciding from what they see and hear of that person in court." DiCarlo v. United States, 6 F.2d 364, 368 (2d Cir.1925).

The more "sensible and realistic view" and the weight of authority would appear to be to reject the orthodox rule and to view cross-examination of the declarant at trial as sufficient. 2 Jones on Evidence § 10.18 (6th ed. 1972). The Model Code of Evidence and the Uniform Rules of Evidence both allow the use of inconsistent statements as substantive evidence when the declarant is available for cross-examination. Model Code of Evidence Rule 503(b) (1942); Uniform Rule of Evidence 63(1) (1974).

The Federal Rule of Evidence 801(d)(1)(A), as submitted by the United States Supreme Court to Congress, would have allowed a prior inconsistent statement of any witness who was available for cross-examination to be admitted. Report of Senate Committee on the Judiciary to Fed.R.Evid. 801. Out of a political compromise, the present Federal Rule of Evidence arose, with the requirement that for a prior inconsistent statement to be admissible as substantive evidence the inconsistent statement must have been made under oath, in a proceeding, subject to the penalty of perjury. Report of Senate Committee on the Judiciary to Fed.R.Evid. 801. These limitations have been criticized for disregarding the benefits of allowing inconsistent statements to be considered as substantive evidence and the adequacy of cross-examination of the witness at trial. Ordover, *Surprise: That Damaging Turncoat Witness Is Still With Us: An Analysis of Federal Rules of Evidence*, 607, 801(d)(1)(A) and 403, 5 Hofstra L.Rev. 65 (1976–1977); Graham, *Employing Inconsistent Statements For Impeachment And As Substantive Evidence: A Critical Review and Proposed Amendments of Federal Rules of Evidence* 801(d)(1)(A), 613, and 607, 75 Mich.L.Rev. 1565 (1976–1977).

Nineteen American jurisdictions allow the prior inconsistent statements of a witness to be used substantively where the witness is available for cross-examination. A number of other jurisdictions also admit the prior inconsistent statements as substantive evidence subject to certain limitations. Only a handful of jurisdictions now refuse to permit prior inconsistent statements to be used as substantive evidence. It should be noted that the Missouri Legislature passed a law providing that the prior inconsistent statement of any witness in a criminal trial is substantive evidence. Mo.Rev.Stat. § 491.074 (1985). There has been no evidence from the experience of other jurisdictions that the admissibility of prior inconsistent statements has resulted in any abuse. J. Maguire, *Evidence Common Sense and Common Law* 63 (1947); McCormick, *Handbook of the Law of Evidence* § 251 (3d ed. 1984).

We believe that only when the declarant is available for cross-examination are enough of the dangers of hearsay and unreliability absent to justify the substantive use of prior inconsistent statements in civil cases. The cause is reversed and remanded for a new trial consistent with this opinion.

■ HIGGINS, C.J., and FINCH, SENIOR JUDGE, concur.

■ BLACKMAR and DONNELLY, JJ., concur in separate opinions filed.

■ BILLINGS, J., dissents in separate opinion filed.

■ RENDLEN, J., dissents and concurs in separate dissenting opinion of BILLINGS, J.

■ ROBERTSON, J., not participating because not a member of the Court when cause was submitted.

■ BLACKMAR, JUDGE, concurring.

. . .

. . . I opt in favor of giving the jury full information and letting it make the decision. The law of evidence deals in probabilities. Neither certainty nor absence of the possibility of abuse is required as a condition of admissibility.

I do not agree with the assertion that there may be no meaningful cross-examination about a claimed prior inconsistent statement which a witness disavows at trial. (Cf. concurring opinion of Judge Seiler in Granberry, 491 S.W.2d at 532, and Judge Billings' similar arguments). Cross-examination is not simply an effort to get a witness to disaffirm his testimony. There is ample room for exploration. Does the witness deny making the statement, or does he profess lack of memory? Did he initiate the conversation or was he questioned? Was he in a position to observe? If the witness admits making the earlier statement, he may explain the inconsistency. If he does not, then the person reporting the statement is subject to cross-examination. The surrounding circumstances may be fully explored so that the jury may be better enabled to determine where the truth lies.

One of my earlier concerns was as to whether an essential element of a case could be established simply by a prior statement of a witness which the witness repudiates at trial. The Washington Council of Lawyers expresses similar concern. Missouri, however, disclaims the *scintilla* rule and holds that every element of a case must be established by substantial evidence. So the courts do not have to countenance the submission of wholly unsubstantial cases to juries.

The enactment of Senate Committee Substitute for House Committee Substitute for House Bills 366, 248, 372 and 393, 83rd General Assembly, represents a recognition that prior inconsistent statements of a witness who is present at trial have value as evidence. I do not find, in that bill's limitation of the change to certain chapters of the criminal statutes, an affirmative policy of maintaining the orthodox view elsewhere. It is absolutely unnecessary, moreover, to deal with the problem of face to face confrontation in criminal cases as expounded by Judge Donnelly.

I concur in reversal and remand.

■ DONNELLY, JUDGE, concurring.

. . .

. . . I believe that it is now time . . . in civil cases [to] allow prior inconsistent statements to be used both for impeachment and for substantive evidence where the witness is at trial and subject to cross-examination by either party.

However, in my view, admission of prior inconsistent statements as substantive evidence in criminal cases would violate the Missouri Constitution, Article I, Section 18(a) which provides: "That in criminal prosecutions the accused shall have the right . . . to meet the witnesses against him face to face. . . . "

. . .

■ BILLINGS, JUDGE, dissenting.

. . .

Preliminarily, I wish to point out that the principal opinion's imperceptive and seemingly unquestioning support for a common law rule that gives a party the unrestricted right to impeach his own witness is intimately connected to the misguided theory that *any* prior inconsistent statement should be deemed substantive evidence if the declarant is presently available for cross-examination. This being so, I direct my remarks first to the general question of whether any prior inconsistent statement should be used as substantive evidence when the declarant is available for cross-examination at the time the prior statement is sought to be admitted into evidence.

When Congress conducted hearings on the Proposed Federal Rules of Evidence, they wisely solicited the views of dozens of leading lawyers, respected jurists, law professors and professional associations. Mr. Herbert Semmel, representing the Washington Council of Lawyers, directed part of his testimony to the Advisory Committee's version of Rule 801(d)(1)(A), which as then proposed, would have made any prior inconsistent statement non-hearsay and thus, admissible as substantive evidence. Mr. Semmel articulated with chilling eloquence the unreliability of and dangers inherent in coloring any prior inconsistent statement as substantive evidence.

There are substantial dangers in allowing any prior inconsistent statement to be introduced in evidence.

1. Inaccurate repetition of oral statements made months or years before the trial.

2.   Misleading statements subject to unintended interpretations made when the witness had no appreciation for the necessity for accurate reporting.

3.   Incomplete statements leading to unintended meaning, made when the witness had no appreciation for the necessity of complete reporting.

4.   Inaccurate or unintended statements made by a witness as a result of suggestion or coercion.

Trials occur months and often years after the events sought to be recreated at trial. Memory lapses are an obvious problem in the trial process. The problem becomes more acute when a witness tries to repeat what are often casual remarks by another person at a time when the listener may not have even been aware of the importance of the remarks or that he will later be called upon to repeat them. Moreover, people often hear what they want to hear and remember what they want to remember. A perfectly "honest" witness who favors one party to a lawsuit may have a distorted memory of what a witness for the other party said months or years before trial. And, of course, there are cases of out-right perjury by one witness testifying as to prior statements by an earlier witness. These dangers are not entirely alleviated because both the principal witness and the secondary witness, who testifies as to the former's alleged inconsistent statements, are both present at trial and available for corss-examination [sic]. The jury becomes diverted from the principal issues of the case to collateral questions of what one witness said on a prior occasion.

Many seemingly inconsistent statements are the result of casual comments made by persons who are unaware of the significance which may later be attached to these remarks. The comment may be incomplete; details are omitted which were unimportant to the declarant at the time but which may be crucial at a trial. Language may be employed in a loose, ambiguous manner which later aapears [sic] contradictory to testimony at trial. An observation may be conclusory. Or the declarant may have indulged in the very human tendency to subconsciously fill in the details where only a portion of an observed event remains in the memory.

The problems of inaccurate repetition, ambiguity and incompleteness of out-of-court statements may be found in both written and oral statements, although the problem is more acute in oral statements. But written statements are also subject to distortion. We are all familiar with the way a skilled investigator, be he a lawyer, police officer, insurance claim agent, or private detective, can listen to a potential witness and then prepare a statement for signature by the witness which reflects the interest of the investigator's client or agency. Adverse details are omitted; subtle changes of emphasis are made. It is regrettable but true that some lawyers will distort the truth to win a case and that some police officers will do the same to "solve" a crime, particularly one which has aroused the public interest or caused public controversy. Or the police officer may be seeking to put away a "dangerous criminal" who the officer "knows" is guilty but ngnist [sic] whom evidence is lacking. Examples of such conduct sometimes become public and undoubtedly represent the tip of the iceberg. The latest of such incident was reported in the New York Times of June 2, 1974, revealing testimony by a New York policeman who admitted perjury in courtroom testimony on a number of occasions to cover up illegal wiretaps.

The potential witness may very well sign a distorted statement. He may have little interest in whether it is accurate or he may not perceive the significance of an omission or a change. He may sign what is put before him out of a genuine desire to cooperate or out of fear of reprisals if he objects. Witnesses in criminal cases often are those who themselves have police records, are awaiting sentencing, or are on probation or parole. The Supreme Court in its current Term has again emphasized the danger that such witnesses may tailor their statements or testimony to appease the police or even to divert suspicion from themselves to others. Davis v. Alaska, 415 U.S. 308, 94 S.Ct. 1105, 39 L.Ed.2d 347 (1974).

It is one thing to admit such extra-judicial statements for impeachment purposes and quite another to allow a finding of guilt or a determination of liability or non-liability to rest on such statements. Use of prior inconsistent statements to impeach is an inherent part of the adversary system. Each party may make its own judgment as to whether the value of a witness's [sic] testimony at trial will be outweighed by adverse consequences when a prior inconsistent statement is introduced to impeach. On the other hand, under the Rules as proposed by the Advisory Committee and pronounced by the Supreme Court, any party to litigation could call a witness whose testimony at trial might be vague, incomplete or who might even be unable to recall the events in issue after the passage of considerable time. At that point, any prior statement, oral or written, inconsistent with testimony at trial could be introduced as substantive evidence. (Proposed Federal Rules of Evidence, promulgated November 20, 1972, Rule 801(d)(1)(A)). In theory, a criminal conviction or civil liability could rest solely on such evidence. (Emphasis ours.)

Statement of Herbert Semmel, Hearings on H.R. 5463, Before the Senate Committee on the Judiciary, 93d Congress, 2d Sess. at 302–03 (1974).

The principal opinion suggests that these dangers are rendered harmless if the declarant is available for cross-examination at the time the prior inconsistent statement is offered for admission into evidence. In State v. Granberry, 491 S.W.2d 528 (Mo. banc 1973), five members of this Court refused to adopt the position advanced today by the principal opinion. I submit that the position taken by the principal opinion elevates theory over the demanding realities of litigation and grossly underestimates the crucial role that timely cross-examination has in the search for truth.

The essential importance of the hearsay rule was noted by Professor Wigmore in his exhaustive treatise. Wigmore described the common law rule prohibiting the use of hearsay as "that most characteristic rule of the Anglo–American Law of Evidence—a rule which may be esteemed, next to jury trial, the greatest contribution of that eminently practical legal system to the world's method of procedure." 5 Wigmore, Evidence § 1364 (Chadbourn rev. 1974).

Hearsay is excluded from admission into evidence primarily because it has not been subjected to the penetrating heat of an effective cross-examination. A cross-examination which is postponed and stale simply cannot substitute for one which is fresh and immediate. The disparity between the former and the latter was delineated with unparalleled cogency and insight by the Michigan Supreme Court in Ruhala v. Roby, 379 Mich. 102, 150 N.W.2d 146 (1967).

Ruhala involved a witness to an automobile accident who at the scene of the accident stated that he saw a man driving the car. The estate of a woman killed in the accident, the plaintiff, filed an action and at trial the witness was going to testify that the woman was driving. The plaintiff sought to introduce the prior inconsistent statement and rely upon it as substantive evidence. The trial court excluded the statement for its substantive value and the Michigan Supreme Court affirmed. In so holding, the court made the following observations concerning the utility of postponed cross-examination:

Cross-examination presupposes a witness who affirms a thing being examined by a lawyer who would have him deny it, or a witness who denies a thing being examined by a lawyer who would have him affirm it. Cross-examination is in its essence an adversary proceeding

. . .

. . . If [a witness] refuses to adopt his prior statement as true, there can be no adversary cross-examination upon it. If he refuses to affirm, no question can be put to him which would shake his own confidence in his affirmation.

. . .

The would-be cross-examiner is not only denied the right to be the declarant's adversary, he is left with no choice but to become the witness' friend, protector and savior.

Id. at 156.

The court went on to state further that "no matter how deadly the thrust of the cross-examiner, the ghost of the prior statement stands." Id. at 157.

I wholly subscribe to Professor Wigmore's view that cross-examination is "beyond any doubt the greatest legal engine ever invented for the discovery of truth." 5 Wigmore, Evidence, § 1367 (Chadbourn rev. 1974). However, if this great legal engine for the discovery of truth is allowed to run out of time and with a better late than never attitude, I fail to see how it can any longer be depended upon to consistently satisfy the purpose of the hearsay rule. For all of these reasons, I cannot subscribe to the principal opinion's view that any prior inconsistent statement should be relied upon for its substantive value if the declarant is presently available for cross-examination.

. . .

NOTES

1. By 1996, only three American jurisdictions retained the orthodox rule that prior inconsistent statements are admissible solely for impeachment. See La. Code Evid. Ann. art. 607(D); State v. Miller, 408 S.E.2d 846 (N.C.1991); Tenn. R.Evid. 801 (admits only prior statements of identification for substantive use). The other states, by statute, rule, or common law fall into three groups: (1) those that have rules identical to Rule 801(d)(1)(A) of the Federal Rules of Evidence; (2) those that follow the more expansive rule initially proposed by the federal drafters, which authorizes the substantive use of all prior statements; and (3) those that concur with the Federal Rules in endorsing selective substantive use, but differ in their choice of prior inconsistent statements that qualify for such use. For example, see Rule 801(e)(1)(a) of the Texas Rules of Criminal Evidence which is identical to the federal rule except that it specifically excludes statements given at a grand jury proceeding. See also State v. Whelan, 513 A.2d 86 (Conn.) (admits for substantive use prior written inconsistent statement signed by the declarant), cert. denied, 479 U.S. 994 (1986); Ohio Rules of Evidence, Rule 801(D)(1)(a) (prior statement must have been subject to cross-examination when made). In New York, substantive use is permissible in civil cases (Letendre v. Hartford Accident & Indem. Co., 289 N.Y.S.2d 183, 236 N.E.2d 467 (N.Y.1968)) (in absence of statutory pre-emption or strong public policy, court free to fashion new exceptions to the hearsay rule), but prior inconsistent statements are limited to impeachment in criminal cases

(N.Y.Crim.Proc. § 60.35). What reasons can be offered in support of these different formulas?

2. Not infrequently the orthodox view forbidding substantive use of the prior statement precludes plaintiff or the prosecution from making out a prima facie case. See, e.g., Eisenberg v. United States, 273 F.2d 127 (5th Cir.1959); United States v. Rainwater, 283 F.2d 386 (8th Cir.1960) (contains extensive criticism of orthodox view). Moreover, in jury cases, the orthodox view requires extreme care in framing the charge. See, e.g., Slade v. United States, 267 F.2d 834 (5th Cir.1959) (reversal for inadequate charge).

3. To what extent may a prosecutor in a jurisdiction that has adopted the federal limitation impeach a turn-coat witness pursuant to Rule 607 with prior inconsistent statements that fail to satisfy Rule 801(d)(1)(A)? What is the efficacy of limiting instructions under these circumstances? See, p. 399, supra. Will there be instances where a prior inconsistent statement may be used as substantive evidence although it could not be used for impeachment? In this regard consider the Comment to § 1235 of the California Evidence Code:

> Because Section 1235 permits a witness' inconsistent statements to be considered as evidence of the matters stated and not merely as evidence casting discredit on the witness, it follows that a party may introduce evidence of inconsistent statements of his own witness whether or not the witness gave damaging testimony and whether or not the party was surprised by the testimony, for such evidence is no longer irrelevant (and, hence, inadmissible).

California v. Green

Supreme Court of the United States.
399 U.S. 149, 90 S.Ct. 1930, 26 L.Ed.2d 489 (1970).

■ MR. JUSTICE WHITE delivered the opinion of the Court.

Section 1235 of the California Evidence Code, effective as of January 1; 1967, provides that "[e]vidence of a statement made by a witness is not made inadmissible by the hearsay rule if the statement is inconsistent with his testimony at the hearing and is offered in compliance with Section 770."[1] In People v. Johnson, 68 Cal.2d 646, 68 Cal.Rptr. 599, 441 P.2d 111 (1968), cert. denied, 393 U.S. 1051, 89 S.Ct. 679, 21 L.Ed.2d 693 (1969), the California Supreme Court held that prior statements of a witness that were not subject to cross-examination when originally made, could not be introduced under this section to prove the charges against a defendant without violating the defendant's right of confrontation guaranteed by the Sixth Amendment and made applicable to the States by the Fourteenth Amendment. In the case now before us the California Supreme Court applied the same ban to a prior statement of a witness made at a preliminary hearing, under oath and subject to full cross-examination by an adequately counseled defendant. We cannot agree with the California court for two reasons, one of which involves rejection of the holding in People v. Johnson.

---

1. Cal.Evid.Code, § 1235 (1966). Section 770 merely requires that the witness be given an opportunity to explain or deny the prior statement at some point in the trial. (See Cal.Evid.Code, § 770 (1966); People v. Johnson, 68 Cal.2d 646, 650, n. 2, 68 Cal. Rptr. 599, 441 P.2d 111, 114 n. 2 (1968), cert. denied, 393 U.S. 1051, 89 S.Ct. 679, 21 L.Ed.2d 693 (1969). [The footnotes are the Court's and have been renumbered. Some have been omitted.]

I

In January 1967, one Melvin Porter, a 16–year–old minor, was arrested for selling marihuana to an undercover police officer. Four days after his arrest, while in the custody of juvenile authorities, Porter named respondent Green as his supplier. As recounted later by one Officer Wade, Porter claimed that Green had called him earlier that month, had asked him to sell some "stuff" or "grass," and had that same afternoon personally delivered a shopping bag containing 29 "baggies" of marihuana. It was from this supply that Porter had made his sale to the undercover officer. A week later, Porter testified at respondent's preliminary hearing. He again named respondent as his supplier, although he now claimed that instead of personally delivering the marihuana, Green had showed him where to pick up the shopping bag, hidden in the bushes at Green's parents' house. Porter's story at the preliminary hearing was subjected to extensive cross-examination by respondent's counsel—the same counsel who represented respondent at his subsequent trial. At the conclusion of the hearing, respondent was charged with furnishing marihuana to a minor in violation of California law.

Respondent's trial took place some two months later before a court sitting without a jury. The State's chief witness was again young Porter. But this time Porter, in the words of the California Supreme Court, proved to be "markedly evasive and uncooperative on the stand." People v. Green, 70 Cal.2d 654, 657, 75 Cal.Rptr. 782, 783, 451 P.2d 422, 423 (1969). He testified that respondent had called him in January 1967, and asked him to sell some unidentified "stuff." He admitted obtaining shortly thereafter 29 plastic "baggies" of marihuana, some of which he sold. But when pressed as to whether respondent had been his supplier, Porter claimed that he was uncertain how he obtained the marihuana, primarily because he was at the time on "acid" (LSD), which he had taken 20 minutes before respondent phoned. Porter claimed that he was unable to remember the events that followed the phone call, and that the drugs he had taken prevented his distinguishing fact from fantasy. See, e.g., App. 7–11, 24–25.

At various points during Porter's direct examination, the prosecutor read excerpts from Porter's preliminary hearing testimony. This evidence was admitted under § 1235 for the truth of the matter contained therein. With his memory "refreshed" by his preliminary hearing testimony, Porter "guessed" that he had indeed obtained the marihuana from the backyard of respondent's parents' home, and had given the money from its sale to respondent. On cross-examination, however, Porter indicated that it was his memory of the preliminary testimony which was "mostly" refreshed, rather than his memory of the events themselves, and he was still unsure of the actual episode. See App. 25. Later in the trial, Officer Wade testified, relating Porter's earlier statement that respondent had personally delivered the marihuana. This statement was also admitted as substantive evidence. Porter admitted making the statement, App. 59, and insisted that he had been telling the truth as he then believed it both to Officer Wade and at the preliminary hearing; but he insisted that he was also telling the truth now in claiming inability to remember the actual events.

Respondent was convicted. The District Court of Appeal reversed, holding that the use of Porter's prior statements for the truth of the matter asserted therein, denied respondent his right of confrontation under the California Supreme Court's recent decision in People v. Johnson, supra. The California Supreme Court affirmed, finding itself "impelled" by recent decisions of this Court to hold § 1235 unconstitutional insofar as it permitted the substantive use of prior inconsistent statements of a witness, even though the statements were subject to cross-examination at a prior hearing. We granted the State's petition for certiorari, 396 U.S. 1001, 90 S.Ct. 547, 24 L.Ed.2d 492 (1970).

II

The California Supreme Court construed the Confrontation Clause of the Sixth Amendment to require the exclusion of Porter's prior testimony offered in evidence to prove the State's case against Green because, in the court's view, neither the right to cross-examine Porter at the trial concerning his current and prior testimony, nor the opportunity to cross-examine Porter at the preliminary hearing satisfied the commands of the Confrontation Clause. We think the California court was wrong on both counts.

Positing that this case posed an instance of a witness who gave trial testimony inconsistent with his prior, out-of-court statements,[2] the California court, on the authority of its decision in People v. Johnson, supra, held that belated cross-examination before the trial court, "is not an adequate substitute for the right to cross-examination contemporaneous with the original testimony before a different tribunal." People v. Green, supra, 70 Cal.2d, at 659, 75 Cal.Rptr., at 785, 451 P.2d, at 425. We disagree.

Section 1235 of the California Evidence Code represents a considered choice by the California Legislature[3] between two opposing positions concerning the extent to which a witness' prior statements may be introduced at trial without violating hearsay rules of evidence. . . .

. . .

Our task in this case is not to decide which of these positions, purely as a matter of the law of evidence, is the sounder. The issue before us is the considerably narrower one of whether a defendant's constitutional right "to be confronted with the witnesses against him" is necessarily inconsistent with a State's decision to change its hearsay rules to reflect the minority view described above. While it may readily be conceded that hearsay rules and the Confrontation Clause are generally designed to protect similar values, it is quite a different thing to suggest that the overlap is complete and that the Confrontation Clause is nothing more or less than a codification of the rules of hearsay and their exceptions as they existed historically at common law. Our decisions have never established such a congruence; indeed, we have more than once found a violation of confrontation values even though the statements in issue were admitted under an arguably recognized hearsay exception. See Barber v. Page, 390 U.S. 719, 88 S.Ct. 1318, 20 L.Ed.2d 255 (1968); Pointer v. Texas, 380 U.S. 400, 85 S.Ct. 1065, 13 L.Ed.2d 923 (1965). The converse is equally true: merely because evidence is admitted in violation of a long-established hearsay rule does not lead to the automatic conclusion that confrontation rights have been denied.[4]

Given the similarity of the values protected, however, the modification of a State's hearsay rules to create new exceptions for the admission of evidence against a defendant, will often raise questions of compatibility with the defendant's constitutional right to confrontation. Such questions require attention to

---

2. See People v. Green, 70 Cal.2d 654, 657 n. 1, 75 Cal.Rptr. 782, 451 P.2d 422, 424 n. 1 (1969).

3. See the comments of the California Law Revision Commission. Cal.Evid.Code, § 1235 (1966).

4. See The Supreme Court, 1967 Term, 82 Harv.L.Rev. 63, 236 (1968); Note, Confrontation and the Hearsay Rule, 75 Yale L.J. 1434, 1436 (1966).

the reasons for, and the basic scope of, the protections offered by the Confrontation Clause.

The origin and development of the hearsay rules and of the Confrontation Clause have been traced by others and need not be recounted in detail here. It is sufficient to note that the particular vice that gave impetus to the confrontation claim was the practice of trying defendants on "evidence" which consisted solely of ex parte affidavits or depositions secured by the examining magistrates, thus denying the defendant the opportunity to challenge his accuser in a face-to-face encounter in front of the trier of fact. Prosecuting attorneys "would frequently allege matters which the prisoner denied and called upon them to prove. The proof was usually given by reading depositions, confessions of accomplices, letters, and the like; and this occasioned frequent demands by the prisoner to have his 'accusers,' i.e. the witnesses against him, brought before him face to face. . . . "[5]

But objections occasioned by this practice appear primarily to have been aimed at the failure to call the witness to confront personally the defendant at his trial. So far as appears, in claiming confrontation rights no objection was made against receiving a witness' out-of-court depositions or statements, so long as the witness was present at trial to repeat his story and to explain or repudiate any conflicting prior stories before the trier of fact.

Our own decisions seem to have recognized at an early date that it is this literal right to "confront" the witness at the time of trial that forms the core of the values furthered by the Confrontation Clause:

"The primary object of the constitutional provision in question was to prevent depositions or ex parte affidavits, such as were sometimes admitted in civil cases, being used against the prisoner in lieu of a personal examination and cross-examination of the witness, in which the accused has an opportunity, not only of testing the recollection and sifting the conscience of the witness, but of compelling him to stand face to face with the jury in order that they may look at him, and judge by his demeanor upon the stand and the manner in which he gives his testimony whether he is worthy of belief." Mattox v. United States, 156 U.S. 237, 242–243, 15 S.Ct. 337, 339, 39 L.Ed. 409 (1895).

Viewed historically, then, there is good reason to conclude that the Confrontation Clause is not violated by admitting a declarant's out-of-court statements, as long as the declarant is testifying as a witness and subject to full and effective cross-examination.

This conclusion is supported by comparing the purposes of confrontation with the alleged dangers in admitting an out-of-court statement. Confrontation: (1) insures that the witness will give his statements under oath—thus impressing him with the seriousness of the matter and guarding against the lie by the possibility of a penalty for perjury; (2) forces the witness to submit to cross-examination, the "greatest legal engine ever invented for the discovery of

---

5. 1 J. Stephen, A History of the Criminal Law of England 326 (1883). See also 9 Holdsworth, supra, n. 9, at 225–228.

A famous example is provided by the trial of Sir Walter Raleigh for treason in 1603. A crucial element of the evidence against him consisted of the statements of one Cobham, implicating Raleigh in a plot to seize the throne. Raleigh had since received a written retraction from Cobham, and believed that Cobham would now testify in his favor. After a lengthy dispute over Raleigh's right to have Cobham called as a witness, Cobham was not called, and Raleigh was convicted. See 1 Stephen, supra, at 333–336; 9 Holdsworth, supra, at 216–217, 226–228. At least one author traces the Confrontation Clause to the common-law reaction against these abuses of the Raleigh trial. See F. Heller, The Sixth Amendment 104 (1951).

truth";[6] (3) permits the jury that is to decide the defendant's fate to observe the demeanor of the witness in making his statement, thus aiding the jury in assessing his credibility.

It is, of course, true that the out-of-court statement may have been made under circumstances subject to none of these protections. But if the declarant is present and testifying at trial, the out-of-court statement for all practical purposes regains most of the lost protections. If the witness admits the prior statement is his, or if there is other evidence to show the statement is his, the danger of faulty reproduction is negligible and the jury can be confident that it has before it two conflicting statements by the same witness. Thus, as far as the oath is concerned, the witness must now affirm, deny, or qualify the truth of the prior statement under the penalty of perjury; indeed, the very fact that the prior statement was not given under a similar circumstance may become the witness' explanation for its inaccuracy—an explanation a jury may be expected to understand and take into account in deciding which, if either, of the statements represents the truth.

Second, the inability to cross-examine the witness at the time he made his prior statement cannot easily be shown to be of crucial significance as long as the defendant is assured of full and effective cross-examination at the time of trial. The most successful cross-examination at the time the prior statement was made could hardly hope to accomplish more than has already been accomplished by the fact that the witness is now telling a different, inconsistent story, and—in this case—one that is favorable to the defendant. We cannot share the California Supreme Court's view that belated cross-examination can never serve as a constitutionally adequate substitute for cross-examination contemporaneous with the original statement. The main danger in substituting subsequent for timely cross-examination seems to lie in the possibility that the witness' "[f]alse testimony is apt to harden and become unyielding to the blows of truth in proportion as the witness has opportunity for reconsideration and influence by the suggestions of others, whose interest may be, and often is, to maintain falsehood rather than truth." State v. Saporen, 205 Minn. 358, 362, 285 N.W. 898, 901 (1939). That danger, however, disappears when the witness has changed his testimony so that, far from "hardening," his prior statement has softened to the point where he now repudiates it.[7]

The defendant's task in cross-examination is, of course, no longer identical to the task that he would have faced if the witness had not changed his story and hence had to be examined as a "hostile" witness giving evidence for the prosecution. This difference, however, far from lessening, may actually enhance the defendant's ability to attack the prior statement. For the witness, favorable to the defendant, should be more than willing to give the usual suggested explanations for the inaccuracy of his prior statement, such as faulty perception or undue haste in recounting the event. Under such circumstances, the defendant is not likely to be hampered in effectively attacking the prior statement, solely because his attack comes later in time.

Similar reasons lead us to discount as a constitutional matter the fact that the jury at trial is foreclosed from viewing the declarant's demeanor when he first made his out-of-court statement. The witness who now relates a different story about the events in question must necessarily assume a position as to the truth value of his prior statement, thus giving the jury a chance to observe and

---

6. 5 Wigmore § 1367.

7. See Comment, Substantive Use of Extrajudicial Statements of Witnesses Under the Proposed Federal Rules of Evidence, 4 U.Rich.L.Rev. 110, 117–118 (1969); 82 Harv. L.Rev. 475 n. 16 (1968).

evaluate his demeanor as he either disavows or qualifies his earlier statement. The jury is alerted by the inconsistency in the stories, and its attention is sharply focused on determining either that one of the stories reflects the truth or that the witness who has apparently lied once, is simply too lacking in credibility to warrant its believing either story. The defendant's confrontation rights are not violated, even though some demeanor evidence that would have been relevant in resolving this credibility issue is forever lost.

It may be true that a jury would be in a better position to evaluate the truth of the prior statement if it could somehow be whisked magically back in time to witness a gruelling cross-examination of the declarant as he first gives his statement. But the question as we see it must be not whether one can somehow imagine the jury in "a better position," but whether subsequent cross-examination at the defendant's trial will still afford the trier of fact a satisfactory basis for evaluating the truth of the prior statement. On that issue, neither evidence[8] nor reason convinces us that contemporaneous cross-examination before the ultimate trier of fact is so much more effective than subsequent examination that it must be made the touchstone of the Confrontation Clause.

Finally, we note that none of our decisions interpreting the Confrontation Clause requires excluding the out-of-court statements of a witness who is available and testifying at trial. The concern of most of our cases has been focused on precisely the opposite situation—situations where statements have been admitted in the absence of the declarant and without any chance to cross-examine him at trial. These situations have arisen through application of a number of traditional "exceptions" to the hearsay rule, which permit the introduction of evidence despite the absence of the declarant usually on the theory that the evidence possesses other indicia of "reliability" and is incapable of being admitted, despite good-faith efforts of the State, in any way that will secure confrontation with the declarant.[9] Such exceptions, dispensing altogether with the literal right to "confrontation" and cross-examination, have been subjected on several occasions to careful scrutiny by this Court....

. . .

We find nothing, then, in either the history or the purposes of the Confrontation Clause, or in the prior decisions of this Court, that compels the conclusion reached by the California Supreme Court concerning the validity of California's § 1235. Contrary to the judgment of that court, the Confrontation Clause does not require excluding from evidence the prior statements of a witness who concedes making the statements, and who may be asked to defend or otherwise explain the inconsistency between his prior and his present version of the events in question, thus opening himself to full cross-examination at trial as to both stories.

. . .

8. The California Supreme Court in its earlier decision on this issue stated that "[t]his practical truth [the importance of immediate cross-examination] is daily verified by trial lawyers, not one of whom would willingly postpone to both a later date and a different forum his right to cross-examine a witness against his client." People v. Johnson, 68 Cal.2d 646, 655, 68 Cal.Rptr. 599, 606, 441 P.2d 111, 118 (1968), cert. denied 393 U.S. 1051, 89 S.Ct. 679, 21 L.Ed.2d 693 (1969). The citations that follow this sentence are to books on trial practice that shed little empirical light on the actual comparative effectiveness of subsequent, as opposed to timely, cross-examination. As the text suggests, where the witness has changed his story at trial to favor the defendant he should, if anything, be more rather than less vulnerable to defense counsel's explanations for the inaccuracy of his former statement.

9. See generally, e.g., 5 Wigmore §§ 1420–1422.

IV

There is a narrow question lurking in this case concerning the admissibility of Porter's statements to Officer Wade. In the typical case to which the California court addressed itself, the witness at trial gives a version of the ultimate events different from that given on a prior occasion. In such a case, as our holding in Part II makes clear, we find little reason to distinguish among prior inconsistent statements on the basis of the circumstances under which the prior statements were given. The subsequent opportunity for cross-examination at trial with respect to both present and past versions of the event, is adequate to make equally admissible, as far as the Confrontation Clause is concerned, both the casual, off-hand remark to a stranger, and the carefully recorded testimony at a prior hearing. Here, however, Porter claimed at trial that he could not remember the events that occurred after respondent telephoned him and hence failed to give any current version of the more important events described in his earlier statement.

Whether Porter's apparent lapse of memory so affected Green's right to cross-examine as to make a critical difference in the application of the Confrontation Clause in this case[10] is an issue which is not ripe for decision at this juncture. The state court did not focus on this precise question, which was irrelevant given its broader and erroneous premise that an out-of-court statement of a witness is inadmissible as substantive evidence, whatever the nature of the opportunity to cross-examine at the trial. Nor has either party addressed itself to the question. Its resolution depends much upon the unique facts in this record, and we are reluctant to proceed without the state court's views of what the record actually discloses relevant to this particular issue. What is more, since we hold that the admission of Porter's preliminary hearing testimony is not barred by the Sixth Amendment despite his apparent lapse of memory, the reception into evidence of the Porter statement to Officer Wade may pose a harmless-error question which is more appropriately resolved by the California courts in the first instance. Similarly, faced on remand with our decision that § 1235 is not invalid on its face, the California Supreme Court may choose to dispose of the case on other grounds raised by Green but not passed upon by that court; for example, because of its ruling on § 1235, the California court

---

10. Even among proponents of the view that prior statements should be admissible as substantive evidence, disagreement appears to exist as to whether to apply this rule to the case of a witness who disclaims all present knowledge of the ultimate event. Commentators have noted that in such a case the opportunities for testing the prior statement through cross-examination at trial may be significantly diminished. See Falknor, The Hearsay Rule and Its Exceptions, 2 U.C.L.A.L.Rev. 43, 53 (1954); 31 N.Y.U.L.Rev. 1101, 1105 (1956). While both the Model Code and the Uniform Rules would apparently admit prior inconsistent statements even where the witness claims to have no present knowledge or recollection of the event, see Model Code of Evidence Rule 503(b), Comment *b*, at 234 (1942); Uniform Rule of Evidence 63(1), Comment (1953), the preliminary draft of proposed rules of evidence for lower federal courts seems to limit admissibility to the case where the witness actually testifies concerning the substance of the event at issue, see Committee on Rules of Practice and Procedure of the Judicial Conference of the United States, Preliminary Draft of Proposed Rules of Evidence for the United States District Courts and Magistrates, rule 8–01(c)(2)(i), Advisory Comm. Notes at 165 (1969). See Comment, Substantive Use of Extrajudicial Statements of Witnesses Under the Proposed Federal Rules of Evidence, 4 U.Rich.L.Rev. 110, 119 and n. 40 (1969). The latter position accords with the common-law practice of not permitting prior inconsistent statements to be introduced even for impeachment purposes until and unless the witness has actually given "inconsistent" testimony concerning the substance of the event described in the prior statement. Id., at 119, 121; see e.g., Westinghouse Electric Corp. v. Wray Equipment Corp., 286 F.2d 491, 493 (C.A.1), cert. denied, 366 U.S. 929, 81 S.Ct. 1650, 6 L.Ed.2d 388 (1961); 3 Wigmore § 1043.

deliberately put aside the issue of the sufficiency of the evidence to sustain conviction.[11]

We therefore vacate the judgment of the California Supreme Court and remand the case to that court for further proceedings not inconsistent with this opinion. It is so ordered.

[Judgment of California Supreme Court vacated and case remanded.]

■ MR. JUSTICE MARSHALL took no part in the decision of this case.

■ MR. JUSTICE BLACKMUN took no part in the consideration or decision of this case.

■ MR. CHIEF JUSTICE BURGER, concurring.

[Opinion omitted.]

■ MR. JUSTICE HARLAN, concurring.

The precise holding of the Court today is that the Confrontation Clause of the Sixth Amendment does not preclude the introduction of an out-of-court declaration, taken under oath and subject to cross-examination, to prove the truth of the matters asserted therein, when the declarant is available as a witness at trial. With this I agree.

The California decision that we today reverse demonstrates, however, the need to approach this case more broadly than the Court has seen fit to do, and to confront squarely the Confrontation Clause because the holding of the California Supreme Court is the result of an understandable misconception, as I see things, of numerous decisions of this Court, old and recent, that have indiscriminately equated "confrontation" with "cross-examination." . . .

. . .

I reach two conclusions. First, the Confrontation Clause of the Sixth Amendment reaches no farther than to require the prosecution to *produce* any *available* witness whose declarations it seeks to use in a criminal trial. Second, even were this conclusion deemed untenable as a matter of Sixth Amendment law, it is surely agreeable to Fourteenth Amendment "due process," which, in my view, is the constitutional framework in which state cases of this kind should be judged. For it could scarcely be suggested that the Fourteenth Amendment takes under its umbrella all common-law hearsay rules and their exceptions.

. . .

The fact that the witness, though physically available, cannot recall either the underlying events that are the subject of an extra-judicial statement or previous testimony or recollect the circumstances under which the statement was given, does not have Sixth Amendment consequence. The prosecution has no less fulfilled its obligation simply because a witness has a lapse of memory. The witness is, in my view, available. To the extent that the witness is, in a

---

11. This issue is not insubstantial. Conviction here rests almost entirely on the evidence in Porter's two prior statements which were themselves inconsistent in some respects. See, e.g., Brief for Respondent 3 and n. 2, 49–50. The California Supreme Court also found it unnecessary to reach respondent's additional contentions of suppression of evidence and prejudicial misconduct. See People v. Green, 70 Cal.2d 654, 665, 451 P.2d 422, 429 (1969). Moreover, as noted earlier in this opinion, . . . the California court suggested that Porter's prior statements may not even have been admissible under § 1235 as "inconsistent" with his testimony at trial. . . .

practical sense, unavailable for cross-examination on the relevant facts, ... I think confrontation is nonetheless satisfied.

. . . .

■ Mr. Justice Brennan, dissenting.

. . . .

... [T]he facts of this case present two questions regarding the application of California Evidence Code § 1235: first, whether the Confrontation Clause permits a witness' extrajudicial statement to be admitted at trial as substantive evidence when the witness claims to be unable to remember the events with which his prior statement dealt, and, second, whether the clause permits a witness' preliminary hearing statement, made under oath and subject to cross-examination, to be introduced at trial as substantive evidence when the witness claims to be unable to remember the events with which the statement dealt. In my view, neither statement can be introduced without unconstitutionally restricting the right of the accused to challenge incriminating evidence in the presence of the factfinder who will determine his guilt or innocence.

[Extensive discussion omitted.]

In sum, I find that Porter's real or pretended lapse of memory about the pertinent events casts serious doubt upon the reliability of his preliminary hearing testimony. It is clear that so long as a witness, such as Porter, cannot or will not testify about these events at trial, the accused remains unable to challenge effectively that witness' prior assertions about them. The probable unreliability of the prior testimony, coupled with the impossibility of its examination during trial, denies the accused his right to probe and attempt to discredit incriminating evidence. Accordingly, I would hold California Evidence Code § 1235 in violation of the Confrontation Clause to the extent that it permits the substantive use at trial of prior statements, whether extrajudicial or testimonial, when the declarant is present at trial but unable or unwilling to be questioned about the events with which the prior statements dealt. I would therefore affirm the reversal of respondent's conviction.

NOTES

1. On remand, the California Supreme Court examined the trial transcript and concluded that Porter's evasions "must be deemed to constitute an implied denial that defendant did in fact furnish him with the marijuana as charged. His testimony was thus materially inconsistent with his preliminary hearing testimony and his extrajudicial declaration to Officer Wade...." It also found that under the circumstances, the prescribed purposes of the confrontation clause—"(1) to insure reliability by means of the oath, (2) to expose the witness to the probe of cross-examination, and (3) to permit the trier of fact to weigh his demeanor"—had been fulfilled since defendant had an opportunity, which he declined to exercise, to cross-examine Porter after Porter "grudgingly conceded" making the statements. People v. Green, 479 P.2d 998, 1002, 1003 (Cal.1971) (en banc). .

2. In a concurring opinion in Dutton v. Evans, 400 U.S. 74, 94 (1970), Justice Harlan repudiated the view which he expressed in the principal case "that the core purpose of the Confrontation Clause of the Sixth Amendment is to prevent overly broad exceptions to the hearsay rule." He instead urged that the Constitution requires only that the defendant have a right to cross-examine those witnesses who actually testify against him at trial.

3. *Past recollection recorded.* The distinction between past recollection recorded and refreshing recollection is explored in the Riccardi case, p. 340, supra. As the Riccardi court notes, a recorded recollection is a substitute for the witness' present memory that may be offered for its truth when certain conditions are met. In a footnote omitted in the materials above, the court states that the writing must have been made soon after the event, that the witness must state that the matter was recorded truthfully, and the original of the writing must be produced if possible. Compare Fed.R.Evid. 803(5).

The drafters of the Federal Rules of Evidence considered placing the recorded recollection doctrine in Rule 801(d)(1) before they decided to treat the prior writing as a hearsay exception in Rule 803(5). See Vermont v. Robar, 601 A.2d 1376, 1379 (1991) ("[W]e see little difference between prior statements admitted under Rule 801(d)(1)(A) and those admitted under Rule 803(5). Indeed, the operation of the rules is very similar."). What are the differences in how the two rules operate? Why did the Advisory Committee ultimately classify a recorded recollection as hearsay that is then made subject to a Rule 803 exception?

In United States v. Porter, 986 F.2d 1014 (6th Cir.), cert. denied, 510 U.S. 933 (1993), a written statement that defendant's 17 year-old girlfriend, Niswonger, had given to the FBI was read into evidence as past recollection recorded. Niswonger testified that "while she did recall giving the written statement and signing it, she now really did not remember much about what she had said in the statement because, she testified, she was confused and on drugs at the time the statement was made." She further testified that "although she tried to tell the truth in the statement, she was not sure she had done so." The court found the statement had properly been admitted:

> Rule 803(5) does not specify any particular method of establishing the knowledge of the declarant nor the accuracy of the statement. It is not a sine qua non of admissibility that the witness actually vouch for the accuracy of the written memorandum. Admissibility is, instead, to be determined on a case-by-case basis upon a consideration, as was done by the district court in this case, of factors indicating trustworthiness, or the lack thereof.
>
> While Rule 803(5) treats recorded recollection as an exception to the hearsay rule, the hearsay is not of a particularly unreliable genre. This is because the out-of-court declarant is actually on the witness stand and subject to evaluation by the finder of fact, in this case the jury. If the jury chose to believe what Niswonger said in the recorded statement rather than what she said while testifying, that decision was at least made based upon what it observed and heard from her in court.

Id. at 1017. The district court had found the statement reliable because Niswonger admitted making it; it was made soon after the events related; Niswonger had signed each page and had made 11 changes which she had initialed; the statement was made under penalty of perjury; the statement was detailed and internally consistent and corroborated by other evidence that had been admitted; the statement was made at a time that Niswonger feared reprisals from the defendant. The district court also determined that Niswonger was being "disingenuous" and "evasive" in attempting to distance herself from the prior statement and was acting in this manner either because she wished to marry the defendant or because she feared him.

In Boehmer v. LeBoeuf, 650 A.2d 1336 (Me.1994), the court declined to admit notes of an investigator, Kane, regarding statements made by an eyewitness, Bonnie, to an automobile accident. The proponents argued that the notes were admissible because Kane testified to their accuracy. They relied primarily on decisions in which courts have admitted memoranda as past recollection recorded when information, often a license plate number, is relayed by an eyewitness to a third party who records the information. See, e.g., United States v. Booz, 451 F.2d 719, 724–25 (3d Cir.1971); Commonwealth v. Galvin, 535 N.E.2d 623, 625 (Mass.App.1989). While the appellate court agreed that such memoranda have been admitted even though the eyewitness could not remember the license plate number and had never verified the memoranda, the court found the cases inapplicable:

> The cases relied on … are examples of circumstances surrounding the creation of the notes or memoranda wherein courts within their considerable discretion have concluded that such evidence is sufficiently trustworthy even in the absence of a personal adoption or verification. The circumstances in those cases typically have involved the persons with the information affirmatively seeking to convey it and initiating the contact with the people to whom the information was given.
>
> In this case, however, it was reasonable for the court to consider that at the time of the interview Bonnie was a thirteen-year-old child. She did not initiate the interview nor seek out Kane. Rather, she was approached by Kane, an adult private investigator in the employ of the Boehmers, and talked about the accident only at his behest. Kane made notes of their conversation. Those notes were not seen by Bonnie, much less acknowledged or adopted by her at the time when her memory of the accident was fresh. In view of such circumstances, it was neither error nor an abuse of the court's discretion for it to have concluded that the foundational requirements of Rule 803(5) had not been met.

620 A.2d at 1340.

See also United States v. Schoenborn, 4 F.3d 1424 (7th Cir.1993)(error to have admitted FBI agent's report of interview with prisoner which prisoner had refused to sign; agent testified that he had transcribed prisoner's statements accurately and that prisoner had reviewed report and told him that it was accurate).

Tome v. United States

Supreme Court of the United States, 1995.
513 U.S. 150, 115 S.Ct. 696, 130 L.Ed.2d 574.

■ JUSTICE KENNEDY delivered the opinion of the Court, except as to Part II–B.

Various federal Courts of Appeals are divided over the evidence question presented by this case. At issue is the interpretation of a provision in the Federal Rules of Evidence bearing upon the admissibility of statements, made by a declarant who testifies as a witness, that are consistent with the testimony and are offered to rebut a charge of a "recent fabrication or improper influence or motive." Fed.Rule Evid. 801(d)(1)(B). The question is whether out-of-court consistent statements made after the alleged fabrication, or after the alleged improper influence or motive arose, are admissible under the Rule.

I

Petitioner Tome was charged in a one-count indictment with the felony of sexual abuse of a child, his own daughter, aged four at the time of the alleged crime. The case having arisen on the Navajo Indian Reservation, Tome was tried by a jury in the United States District Court for the District of New

Mexico, where he was found guilty of violating 18 U.S.C. §§ 1153, 2241(c), and 2245(2)(A) and (B).

Tome and the child's mother had been divorced in 1988. A tribal court awarded joint custody of the daughter, A.T., to both parents, but Tome had primary physical custody. In 1989 the mother was unsuccessful in petitioning the tribal court for primary custody of A.T., but was awarded custody for the summer of 1990. Neither parent attended a further custody hearing in August 1990. On August 27, 1990, the mother contacted Colorado authorities with allegations that Tome had committed sexual abuse against A.T.

The prosecution's theory was that Tome committed sexual assaults upon the child while she was in his custody and that the crime was disclosed when the child was spending vacation time with her mother. The defense argued that the allegations were concocted so the child would not be returned to her father. At trial A.T., then six and one half years old, was the Government's first witness. For the most part, her direct testimony consisted of one-and two-word answers to a series of leading questions. Cross-examination took place over two trial days. The defense asked A.T. 348 questions. On the first day A.T. answered all the questions posed to her on general, background subjects.

The next day there was no testimony, and the prosecutor met with A.T. When cross-examination of A.T. resumed, she was questioned about those conversations but was reluctant to discuss them. Defense counsel then began questioning her about the allegations of abuse, and it appears she was reluctant at many points to answer. As the trial judge noted, however, some of the defense questions were imprecise or unclear. The judge expressed his concerns with the examination of A.T., observing there were lapses of as much as 40–55 seconds between some questions and the answers and that on the second day of examination the witness seemed to be losing concentration. The trial judge stated, "We have a very difficult situation here."

After A.T. testified, the Government produced six witnesses who testified about a total of seven statements made by A.T. describing the alleged sexual assaults: A.T.'s babysitter recited A.T.'s statement to her on August 22, 1990, that she did not want to return to her father because he "gets drunk and he thinks I'm his wife"; the babysitter related further details given by A.T. on August 27, 1990, while A.T.'s mother stood outside the room and listened after the mother had been unsuccessful in questioning A.T. herself; the mother recounted what she had heard A.T. tell the babysitter; a social worker recounted details A.T. told her on August 29, 1990 about the assaults; and three pediatricians, Drs. Kuper, Reich and Spiegel, related A.T.'s statements to them describing how and where she had been touched by Tome. All but A.T.'s statement to Dr. Spiegel implicated Tome. (The physicians also testified that their clinical examinations of the child indicated that she had been subjected to vaginal penetrations. That part of the testimony is not at issue here.)

A.T.'s out-of-court statements, recounted by the six witnesses, were offered by the Government under Rule 801(d)(1)(B). The trial court admitted all of the statements over defense counsel's objection, accepting the Government's argument that they rebutted the implicit charge that A.T.'s testimony was motivated by a desire to live with her mother. The court also admitted A.T.'s August 22d statement to her babysitter under Rule 803(24), and the statements to Dr. Kuper (and apparently also to Dr. Reich) under Rule 803(4)(statements for purposes of medical diagnosis). The Government offered the testimony of the social worker under both Rules 801(d)(1)(B) and 803(24), but the record does not indicate whether the court ruled on the latter ground. No objection was made to Dr. Spiegel's testimony. Following trial, Tome was convicted and sentenced to 12 years imprisonment.

On appeal, the Court of Appeals for the Tenth Circuit affirmed.... The court reasoned that "the pre-motive requirement is a function of the relevancy rules, not the hearsay rules" and that as a "function of relevance, the pre-motive rule is clearly too broad ... because it is simply not true that an individual with a motive to lie always will do so." 3 F.3d 342, 350 (C.A.10 1993). "Rather, the relevance of the prior consistent statement is more accurately determined by evaluating the strength of the motive to lie, the circumstances in which the statement is made, and the declarant's demonstrated propensity to lie." Ibid.... Applying this balancing test to A.T.'s first statement to her babysitter, the Court of Appeals determined that although A.T. might have had "some motive to lie, we do not believe that it is a particularly strong one." 3 F.3d at 351. The court held that the district judge had not abused his discretion in admitting A.T.'s out-of-court statements. It did not analyze the probative quality of A.T.'s six other out-of-court statements, nor did it reach the admissibility of the statements under any other rule of evidence.

. . .

II

The prevailing common-law rule for more than a century before adoption of the Federal Rules of Evidence was that a prior consistent statement introduced to rebut a charge of recent fabrication or improper influence or motive was admissible if the statement had been made before the alleged fabrication, influence, or motive came into being, but it was inadmissible if made afterwards. As Justice Story explained: "[W]here the testimony is assailed as a fabrication of a recent date ... in order to repel such imputation, proof of the *antecedent* declaration of the party may be admitted." Ellicott v. Pearl, 35 U.S. (10 Pet.) 412, 439, 9 L. Ed. 475 (1836)(emphasis supplied)....

McCormick and Wigmore stated the rule in a more categorical manner: "[T]he applicable principle is that the prior consistent statement has no relevancy to refute the charge unless the consistent statement was made before the source of the bias, interest, influence or incapacity originated." E. Cleary, McCormick on Evidence § 49, p. 105 (2d ed. 1972)(hereafter McCormick).... The question is whether Rule 801(d)(1)(B) embodies this temporal requirement. We hold that it does.

A

. . .

Rule 801 defines prior consistent statements as nonhearsay only if they are offered to rebut a charge of "recent fabrication or improper influence or motive." Fed.Rule Evid. 801(d)(1)(B). Noting the "troublesome" logic of treating a witness' prior consistent statements as hearsay at all (because the declarant is present in court and subject to cross-examination), the Advisory Committee decided to treat those consistent statements, once the preconditions of the Rule were satisfied, as nonhearsay and admissible as substantive evidence, not just to rebut an attack on the witness' credibility. See Advisory Committee Notes on Fed.Rule Evid. 801(d)(1), 28 U.S.C.App., p. 773. A consistent statement meeting the requirements of the Rule is thus placed in the same category as a declarant's inconsistent statement made under oath in another proceeding, or prior identification testimony, or admissions by a party opponent. See Fed.Rule Evid. 801.

The Rules do not accord this weighty, nonhearsay status to all prior consistent statements. To the contrary, admissibility under the Rules is confined to those statements offered to rebut a charge of "recent fabrication or improper influence or motive," the same phrase used by the Advisory Committee in its description of the "traditiona[l]" common law of evidence, which was the background against which the Rules were drafted. See Advisory Committee Notes, supra, at 773. Prior consistent statements may not be admitted to counter all forms of impeachment or to bolster the witness merely because she has been discredited. In the present context, the question is whether A.T.'s out-of-court statements rebutted the alleged link between her desire to be with her mother and her testimony, not whether they suggested that A.T.'s in-court testimony was true. The Rule speaks of a party rebutting an alleged motive, not bolstering the veracity of the story told.

This limitation is instructive, not only to establish the preconditions of admissibility but also to reinforce the significance of the requirement that the consistent statements must have been made before the alleged influence, or motive to fabricate arose. That is to say, the forms of impeachment within the Rule's coverage are the ones in which the temporal requirement makes the most sense. Impeachment by charging that the testimony is a recent fabrication or results from an improper influence or motive is, as a general matter, capable of direct and forceful refutation through introduction of out-of-court consistent statements that predate the alleged fabrication, influence or motive. A consistent statement that predates the motive is a square rebuttal of the charge that the testimony was contrived as a consequence of that motive. By contrast, prior consistent statements carry little rebuttal force when most other types of impeachment are involved. McCormick § 49, p. 105 ("When the attack takes the form of impeachment of character, by showing misconduct, convictions or bad reputation, it is generally agreed that there is no color for sustaining by consistent statements. The defense does not meet the assault." (footnote omitted)). . . .

There may arise instances when out-of-court statements that postdate the alleged fabrication have some probative force in rebutting a charge of fabrication or improper influence or motive, but those statements refute the charged fabrication in a less direct and forceful way. Evidence that a witness made consistent statements after the alleged motive to fabricate arose may suggest in some degree that the in-court testimony is truthful, and thus suggest in some degree that that testimony did not result from some improper influence; but if the drafters of Rule 801(d)(1)(B) intended to countenance rebuttal along that indirect inferential chain, the purpose of confining the types of impeachment that open the door to rebuttal by introducing consistent statements becomes unclear. If consistent statements are admissible without reference to the time frame we find imbedded in the Rule, there appears no sound reason not to admit consistent statements to rebut other forms of impeachment as well. Whatever objections can be leveled against limiting the Rule to this designated form of impeachment and confining the rebuttal to those statements made before the fabrication or improper influence or motive arose, it is clear to us that the drafters of Rule 801(d)(1)(B) were relying upon the common-law temporal requirement.

The underlying theory of the Government's position is that an out-of-court consistent statement, whenever it was made, tends to bolster the testimony of a witness and so tends also to rebut an express or implied charge that the testimony has been the product of an improper influence. Congress could have adopted that rule with ease, providing, for instance, that "a witness' prior consistent statements are admissible whenever relevant to assess the witness's truthfulness or accuracy." The theory would be that, in a broad sense, any prior statement by a witness concerning the disputed issues at trial would have some relevance in assessing the accuracy or truthfulness of the witness's in-court testimony on the same subject. The narrow Rule enacted by Congress, however, cannot be understood to incorporate the Government's theory.

Our analysis is strengthened by the observation that the somewhat peculiar language of the Rule bears close similarity to the language used in many of the common law cases that describe the premotive requirement. "Rule 801(d)(1)(B) employs the precise language—'rebut[ting] ... charge[s] ... of recent fabrication or improper influence or motive'—consistently used in the panoply of pre–1975 decisions." E.O. Ohlbaum, The Hobgoblin of the Federal Rules of Evidence: An Analysis of Rule 801(d)(1)(B), Prior Consistent Statements and a New Proposal, 1987 B.Y.U.L.Rev. 231, 245....

. . .

B

Our conclusion that Rule 801(d)(1)(B) embodies the common-law premotive requirement is confirmed by an examination of the Advisory Committee Notes to the Federal Rules of Evidence. We have relied on those well-considered Notes as a useful guide in ascertaining the meaning of the Rules. See, e. g., Huddleston v. United States, 485 U.S. 681, 688, 108 S.Ct. 1496, 1500, 99 L. Ed. 2d 771 (1988); United States v. Owens, 484 U.S. 554, 562, 108 S.Ct. 838, 844, 98 L. Ed.2d 951 (1988). Where, as with Rule 801(d)(1)(B),"Congress did not amend the Advisory Committee's draft in any way ... the Committee's commentary is particularly relevant in determining the meaning of the document Congress enacted." Beech Aircraft Corp. v. Rainey, 488 U.S. 153, at 165–166, n. 9, 109 S.Ct. 439, at 447–448, n. 9 (1988). The Notes are also a respected source of scholarly commentary. Professor Cleary was a distinguished commentator on the law of evidence, and he and members of the Committee consulted and considered the views, criticisms, and suggestions of the academic community in preparing the Notes.

The Notes disclose a purpose to adhere to the common law in the application of evidentiary principles, absent express provisions to the contrary. Where the Rules did depart from their common-law antecedents, in general the Committee said so.... The Notes give no indication, however, that Rule 801(d)(1)(B) abandoned the premotive requirement. The entire discussion of Rule 801(d)(1)(B) is limited to the following comment:

> "Prior consistent statements traditionally have been admissible to rebut charges of recent fabrication or improper influence or motive but not as substantive evidence. Under the rule they are substantive evidence. The prior statement is consistent with the testimony given on the stand, and, if the opposite party wishes to open the door for its admission in evidence, no sound reason is apparent why it should not be received generally." Notes on Rule 801(d)(1)(B); id., at 773.

Throughout their discussion of the Rules, the Advisory Committee Notes rely on Wigmore and McCormick as authority for the common-law approach. In light of the categorical manner in which those authors state the premotive requirement, see supra, ... it is difficult to imagine that the drafters, who noted the new substantive use of prior consistent statements, would have remained silent if they intended to modify the premotive requirement....

Observing that Edward Cleary was the Reporter of the Advisory Committee that drafted the Rules, the Court has relied upon his writings as persuasive authority on the meaning of the Rules.... Cleary also was responsible for the 1972 revision of McCormick's treatise, which included an examination of the changes introduced by the proposed federal rules to the common-law practice of impeachment and rehabilitation. The discussion, which occurs only three paragraphs after the treatise's categorical description of the common-law premotive rule, also lacks any indication that the proposed rules were abandoning that temporal limitation. See McCormick § 50, p. 107.

Our conclusion is bolstered by the Advisory Committee's stated "unwillingness to countenance the general use of prior prepared statements as substantive evidence." See Notes on Rule 801(d)(1), 28 U.S.C.App., p. 773. Rule 801(d), which "enumerates three situations in which the statement is excepted from the category of hearsay," ibid., was expressly contrasted by the Committee with Uniform Rule of Evidence 63(1) (1953), "which allows *any* out-of-court statement of a declarant who is present at the trial and available for cross-examination." Notes on Rule 801(d)(1), supra, at 773 (emphasis added). When a witness presents important testimony damaging to a party, the party will often counter with at least an implicit charge that the witness has been under some influence or motive to fabricate. If Rule 801 were read so that the charge opened the floodgates to any prior consistent statement that satisfied Rule 403, as the Tenth Circuit concluded, the distinction between rejected Uniform Rule 63(1) and Rule 801(d)(1)(B) would all but disappear.

That Rule 801(d)(1)(B) permits prior consistent statements to be used for substantive purposes after the statements are admitted to rebut the existence of an improper influence or motive makes it all the more important to observe the preconditions for admitting the evidence in the first place. The position taken by the Rules reflects a compromise between the views expressed by the "bulk of the case law ... against allowing prior statements of witnesses to be used generally as substantive evidence" and the views of the majority of "writers ... [who] ha[d] taken the opposite position." Ibid. That compromise was one that the Committee candidly admitted was a "judgment ... more of experience than of logic." Ibid.

"A party contending that legislative action changed settled law has the burden of showing that the legislature intended such a change." Green v. Bock Laundry Machine Co., 490 U.S. 504, 521, 109 S.Ct. 1981, 1990, 104 L. Ed. 2d 557 (1989) (applying that presumption in interpreting Federal Rule of Evidence 609). Nothing in the Advisory Committee's Notes suggests that it intended to alter the common-law premotive requirement.

C

The Government's final argument in favor of affirmance is that the common-law premotive rule advocated by petitioner is inconsistent with the Federal Rules' liberal approach to relevancy and with strong academic criticism, beginning in the 1940's, directed at the exclusion of out-of-court statements made by a declarant who is present in court and subject to cross-examination. This argument misconceives the design of the Rules' hearsay provisions.

Hearsay evidence is often relevant. "The only way in which the probative force of hearsay differs from the probative force of other testimony is in the absence of oath, demeanor, and cross-examination as aids in determining credibility." Advisory Committee's Introduction to Article VIII, 28 U.S.C.App., p. 771. That does not resolve the matter, however. Relevance is not the sole criterion of admissibility. Otherwise, it would be difficult to account for the Rules' general proscription of hearsay testimony (absent a specific exception), see Fed.Rule Evid. 802, let alone the traditional analysis of hearsay that the Rules, for the most part, reflect. Ibid. ("The approach to hearsay in these rules is that of the common law.... The traditional hearsay exceptions are drawn upon for the exceptions ..."). That certain out-of-court statements may be relevant does not dispose of the question whether they are admissible.

The Government's reliance on academic commentators critical of excluding out-of-court statements by a witness, see Brief for United States 40, is subject to like criticism. To be sure, certain commentators in the years preceding the adoption of the Rules had been critical of the common-law approach to hearsay, particularly its categorical exclusion of out-of-court statements offered for substantive purposes. See, e.g., Weinstein, The Probative Force of Hearsay, 46 Iowa L.Rev. 331, 344–345 (1961) (gathering sources).... As an alternative, they suggested moving away from the categorical exclusion of hearsay and toward a case-by-case balancing of the probative value of particular statements against their likely prejudicial effect. See Weinstein, supra, at 338.... The Advisory Committee, however, was explicit in rejecting this balancing approach to hearsay:

> "The Advisory Committee has rejected this approach to hearsay as involving too great a measure of judicial discretion, minimizing the predictability of rulings, [and] enhancing the difficulties of preparation for trial." Advisory Committee's Introduction, supra, at 771 (emphasis added).

. . .

The statement-by-statement balancing approach advocated by the Government and adopted by the Tenth Circuit creates the precise dangers the Advisory Committee noted and sought to avoid: It involves considerable judicial discretion; it reduces predictability; and it enhances the difficulties of trial preparation because parties will have difficulty knowing in advance whether or not particular out-of-court statements will be admitted. See Advisory Committee's Introduction, supra, at 771.

D

... If the Rule were to permit the introduction of prior statements as substantive evidence to rebut every implicit charge that a witness' in-court testimony results from recent fabrication or improper influence or motive, the whole emphasis of the trial could shift to the out-of-court statements, not the in-court ones. The present case illustrates the point. In response to a rather weak charge that A.T.'s testimony was a fabrication created so the child could remain with her mother, the Government was permitted to present a parade of sympathetic and credible witnesses who did no more than recount A.T.'s detailed out-of-court statements to them. Although those statements might have been probative on the question whether the alleged conduct had occurred, they shed but minimal light on whether A.T. had the charged motive to fabricate. At closing argument before the jury, the Government placed great reliance on the prior statements for substantive purposes but did not once seek to use them to rebut the impact of the alleged motive.

We are aware that in some cases it may be difficult to ascertain when a particular fabrication, influence, or motive arose. Yet, as the Government concedes, a majority of common-law courts were performing this task for well over a century, see Brief for United States 39, and the Government has presented us with no evidence that those courts, or the judicial circuits that adhere to the rule today, have been unable to make the determination. Even under the Government's hypothesis, moreover, the thing to be rebutted must be identified, so the date of its origin cannot be that much more difficult to ascertain. By contrast, as the Advisory Committee commented, see supra ..., the Government's approach, which would require the trial court to weigh all of the circumstances surrounding a statement that suggest its probativeness against the court's assessment of the strength of the alleged motive, would entail more of a burden, with no guidance to attorneys in preparing a case or to appellate courts in reviewing a judgment.

III

... When a party seeks to introduce out-of-court statements that contain strong circumstantial indicia of reliability, that are highly probative on the material questions at trial, and that are better than other evidence otherwise available, there is no need to distort the requirements of Rule 801(d)(1)(B). If its requirements are met, Rule 803(24) exists for that eventuality. We intimate no view, however, concerning the admissibility of any of A.T.'s out-of-court statements under that section, or any other evidentiary principle. These matters, and others, are for the Court of Appeals to decide in the first instance.

. . . .

The judgment of the Court of Appeals for the Tenth Circuit is reversed, and the case is remanded for further proceedings consistent with this opinion.

It is so ordered.

■ JUSTICE SCALIA, concurring in part and concurring in the judgment.

I concur in the judgment of the Court, and join its opinion except for Part II–B. That Part, which is devoted entirely to a discussion of the Advisory Committee's Notes pertinent to Rule 801(d)(1)(B), gives effect to those Notes not only because they are "a respected source of scholarly commentary," ante, at [544] but also because they display the "purpose," ante, at [544] or "inten[t]," ante, at [545], of the draftsmen.

... Having been prepared by a body of experts, the Notes are assuredly persuasive scholarly commentaries—ordinarily *the* most persuasive—concerning the meaning of the Rules. But they bear no special authoritativeness as the work of the draftsmen, any more than the views of Alexander Hamilton (a draftsman) bear more authority than the views of Thomas Jefferson (not a draftsman) with regard to the meaning of the Constitution. It is the words of the Rules that have been authoritatively adopted—by this Court, or by Congress if it makes a statutory change.... Like a judicial opinion and like a statute, the promulgated Rule says what it says, regardless of the intent of its drafters. The Notes are, to be sure, submitted to us and to the Members of Congress as the thoughts of the body initiating the recommendations ...; but there is no certainty that either we or they read those thoughts, nor is there any procedure by which we formally endorse or disclaim them. That being so, the Notes cannot, by some power inherent in the draftsmen, change the meaning that the Rules would otherwise bear.

... [T]he case can be adequately resolved without resort to the Advisory Committee at all. It is well established that " ' "the body of common law knowledge" ' " must be " ' "a source of guidance" ' " in our interpretation of the Rules. Daubert v. Merrell Dow Pharmaceuticals, Inc., 509 U.S. 579, 113 S.Ct. 2786, 2794, 125 L.Ed.2d 469 (1993)(quoting United States v. Abel, 469 U.S. 45, 52, 105 S. Ct. 465, 83 L.Ed.2d 450 (1984)(quoting Cleary, Preliminary Notes on Reading the Rules of Evidence, 57 Neb.L.Rev. 908, 915 (1978))). Rule 801(d)(1)(B) uses language that tracks common-law cases and prescribes a result that makes no sense except on the assumption that that language indeed adopts the common-law rule. . . .

■ JUSTICE BREYER, with whom THE CHIEF JUSTICE, JUSTICE O'CONNOR and JUSTICE THOMAS join, dissenting.

The basic issue in this case concerns, not hearsay, but relevance. As the majority points out, the common law permitted a lawyer to rehabilitate a witness (after a charge of improper motive) by pointing to the fact that the witness had said the same thing earlier—but only if the witness made the earlier statement *before* the motive to lie arose. The reason for the time limitation was that, otherwise, the prior consistent statement had no *relevance* to rebut the charge that the in-court testimony was the product of the motive to lie. . . .

The majority believes that a hearsay-related rule, Federal Rule of Evidence 801(d)(1)(B), codifies this absolute timing requirement. I do not. Rule 801(d)(1)(B) has nothing to do with relevance. Rather, that Rule carves out a subset of prior consistent statements that were formerly admissible only to rehabilitate a witness (a nonhearsay use that relies upon the fact that the statement was made). It then says that members of that subset are "not hearsay." This means that, *if* such a statement is admissible for a particular rehabilitative purpose (to rebut a charge of recent fabrication, improper influence or motive), its proponent now may use it substantively, for a hearsay purpose (i.e., as evidence of its truth), as well.

. . .

. . . I would read the Rule's plain words to mean exactly what they say: if a trial court properly admits a statement that is "consistent with the declarant's testimony" for the purpose of "rebut[ting] an express or implied charge . . . of recent fabrication or improper influence or motive," then that statement is "not hearsay," and the jury may also consider it for the truth of what it says.

. . .

. . . [O]ne can find examples where the timing rule's claim of "no relevancy" is simply untrue. A postmotive statement *is* relevant to rebut, for example, a charge of recent fabrication based on improper motive, say, when the speaker made the prior statement while affected by a far more powerful motive to tell the truth. A speaker might be moved to lie to help an acquaintance. But, suppose the circumstances *also* make clear to the speaker that only the truth will save his child's life. Or, suppose the postmotive statement was made spontaneously, or when the speaker's motive to lie was much weaker than it was at trial. In these and similar situations, special circumstances may indicate that the prior statement was made for some reason other than the alleged improper motivation; it may have been made not *because of*, but *despite*, the improper motivation. Hence, postmotive statements can, *in appropriate circumstances*, directly refute the charge of fabrication based on improper motive, not because they bolster in a general way the witness' trial testimony, see ante, at [543] but because the circumstances indicate that the statements are not causally connected to the alleged motive to lie.

. . .

. . . Trial judges may find it easier to administer an absolute rule. Yet, there is no indication in any of the cases that trial judges would, or do, find it particularly difficult to administer a more flexible rule in this context. And, there is something to be said for the greater authority that flexibility grants the trial judge to tie rulings on the admissibility of rehabilitative evidence more closely to the needs and circumstances of the particular case. 1 Weinstein's Evidence ¶ 401[01], pp. 401–8 to 401–9 ("A flexible approach . . . is more apt to yield a sensible result than the application of a mechanical rule."). Furthermore, the majority concedes that the premotive rule, while seemingly bright-line, poses its own administrative difficulties. Ante, at [546].

This Court has acknowledged that the Federal Rules of Evidence worked a change in common-law relevancy rules in the direction of flexibility. See Daubert v. Merrell Dow Pharmaceuticals, Inc., 509 U.S. 579, 113 S.Ct. 2786, 125 L.Ed.2d 469 (1993) . . .

. . . Daubert suggests that the liberalized relevancy provisions of the Federal Rules can supersede a pre-existing rule of relevance, at least where no compelling practical or logical support can be found for the pre-existing rule. It is difficult to find any strong practical or logical considerations for making the premotive rule an absolute condition of admissibility here. Perhaps there are other circumstances in which categorical common-law rules serve the purposes of Rules 401, 402, and 403, and should, accordingly, remain absolute in the law. But, for the reasons stated above, this case, like Daubert, does not present such a circumstance. Thus, considered purely as a matter of relevancy law (and as though Rule 801(d)(1)(B) had not been written), I would conclude that the premotive rule did not survive the adoption of the Rules.

. . .

. . . In most cases, this approach will not yield a different result from a strict adherence to the premotive rule for, in most cases, postmotive statements will not be significantly probative. And, even in cases where the statement is admitted as significantly probative (in respect to rehabilitation), the effect of admission on the trial will be minimal because the prior consistent statements will (by their nature) do no more than repeat in-court testimony.

In this case, the Court of Appeals, applying an approach consistent with what I have described above, decided that A.T.'s prior consistent statements were probative on the question of whether her story as a witness reflected a motive to lie. There is no reason to reevaluate this factbound conclusion. Accordingly, I would affirm the judgment of the Court of Appeals.

NOTES

1. Skepticism has been expressed as to whether "it will ever actually matter whether a prior consistent statement is admitted for substantive as well as nonhearsay purposes" because "a prior consistent statement will never be the only substantive evidence on a vital point." Blakey, An Introduction to the Oklahoma Evidence Code: Hearsay, 14 Tulsa L.J. 635, 677–78 (1979). But suppose the out-of-court statement contains details not contained in the trial testimony. Professor Friedman terms this the "overhang" problem and suggests that "[i]n some cases, the court should ensure—by outright exclusion, severance of the statement, limitation of the testimony, or instruction—that the jury does not use the prior statement to prove propositions to which the witness has not testified." Friedman, Prior Statements of a Witness: A Nettlesome Corner of the Hearsay Thicket, 1995 The Supreme Court Review 277, 309 (1996)(notes also that in Tome "[t]he Court gave no suggestion that it would be troubled by the use of A.T.'s prior statements to sweep in a great deal of substance to which she did not testify." Id. at 310). Cf. State v. Morales, 620 A.2d 1034 (N.H.1993)(court found no error in trial judge's having admitted victim's entire statement after the defendant had impeached the victim's credibility by pointing to some inconsistencies; appropriate for jury to consider these inconsistencies in the context of the entire statement; judge had instructed the jury not to consider the statement as substantive evidence).

2. Does Tome mean that in a federal jurisdiction a prior consistent statement that is used solely to rehabilitate an impeached witness must meet the requirements of Rule 801(d)(1)(B)? See Friedman, Prior Statements of a Witness: A Nettlesome Corner of the Hearsay Thicket, 1995 The Supreme Court Review 277, 319 (1996)("The Court's language (inadvertently, I think) seems to treat the Rule as one setting out the exclusive circumstances in which a prior consistent statement may be used to rehabilitate the testimony of a witness. Lower courts may infer from this that a statement that does not satisfy the Rule may not be used for rehabilitation."). Compare the approach of the California Evidence Code: section 791 governs the use of prior consistent statements for rehabilitation and section 1236 requires compliance with section 791 when the statement is used as substantive evidence.

3. Prior to Tome, federal courts disagreed on whether statements not used substantively had to satisfy the criteria of Rule 801(d)(1)(B).

United States v. Pierre, 781 F.2d 329 (2d Cir.1986): Prosecution for smuggling drugs. Drugs were found in defendant's suitcase when he came through immigration at Kennedy International Airport. He told the agent who questioned him after the discovery of the drugs that he did not know the drugs were in the suitcase and that the suitcase had been given him by a friend for delivery to a bar in Philadelphia. At the trial, the agent testified for the Government that during the airport interview, the defendant had declined a request that he cooperate in a controlled delivery of the suitcase to the bar in Philadelphia. On cross-examination, the agent acknowledged that his handwritten notes, taken during the interview, contained no reference to a request that defendant make a controlled delivery or to defendant's refusal to cooperate. On redirect, the agent was permitted to testify that his formal typewritten report, made several days after the airport interview, did contain a reference to defendant's refusal to cooperate in a controlled delivery.

In Quinto [United States v. Quinto, 582 F.2d 224 (2d Cir.1978)] an agent of the Internal Revenue Service testified to a damaging admission made to him by the defendant taxpayer. On cross-examination the agent's credibility was attacked, but not by use of a prior inconsistent statement. Responding on redirect examination to "a general attack on the agent's credibility," 582 F.2d at 229, the prosecution offered the agent's memorandum of an interview at which the defendant had made the admission. The memorandum was offered both to corroborate the agent's testimony and as substantive evidence that the admission had been made, id. This Court reversed. Judge Waterman ruled that the memorandum could not be used as substantive evidence because it failed to satisfy the criteria of Rule 801(d)(1)(B), notably the requirement that a prior consistent statement antedate a motive to fabricate trial testimony. Whatever motive the agent had to fabricate his trial testimony, presumably a desire to obtain a conviction, was "as operative at the time" the memorandum was prepared as at the time of the trial testimony. Id. at 234. Then, in the portion of the opinion subsequently disputed by Judge Friendly, Judge Waterman ruled that the memorandum could not be used for the rehabilitative purpose of bolstering the agent's credibility, id. at 235, because the same criteria required for use as substantive evidence applied to use for rehabilitation, id. at 232.

In Rubin [United States v. Rubin, 609 F.2d 51 (2d Cir.1979)], a Government agent, Cox, testified to admissions made by the defendant in a series of interviews conducted during a three-year period. On cross-examination Cox was impeached with memoranda of several of these interviews prepared by other agents. The memoranda contained versions of the defendant's interviews allegedly at variance with those recounted by Cox at trial. To rebut the force of these allegedly prior inconsistent statements (though the statements were those of other agents, not those of Cox), the Government was permitted to offer memoranda of four other interviews, conducted during a five-month period, in which the defendant was reported to have made statements consistent with those recounted by the agent's trial testimony. The use of these prior consistent statements (again, those of other agents, not those of Cox) was upheld in a decision that produced three opinions.

Writing for the Court, Judge Mansfield noted that if the allegedly consistent statements had been offered as substantive evidence (to prove the truth of Cox's account of the defendant's statements), the criteria of Rule 801(d)(1)(B) would have to be met, especially the requirement that the statements had been made before a motive to fabricate arose. He then observed that "[w]hether or not some lesser standard would be required if the prior statements had been offered merely to bolster Cox's credibility as a witness may be debated, as our esteemed brother, Judge Friendly, forcefully explains, notwithstanding our indication in Quinto that the standards for use of such statements for rehabilitative purposes should be the same as those under Fed.R.Evid. 801(d)(1)(B), 582 F.2d at 233." United States v. Rubin, supra, 609 F.2d at 61. Judge Mansfield then upheld use of the prior consistent statements because the defendant's objection had not been precise, because any error was harmless and, significantly, because the statements were "clearly admissible under the doctrine of completeness, Fed.R.Evid. 106." Id. at 63. Rule 106 provides that when part or all of a writing is introduced, the opponent may require introduction of any other part "or any other writing" if "in fairness" it ought to be considered contemporaneously with the first document.

The debate to which Judge Mansfield adverted was taken up by Judge Friendly in a concurring opinion and by Judge Meskill in dissent. Judge Friendly endeavored to demonstrate that Judge Waterman had been mistaken in Quinto in stating that the criteria for admitting a prior consistent statement as substantive evidence applied in determining whether the statement could be used solely to rehabilitate the credibility of a trial witness, a view he characterized as dictum, id. at 69 & n. 2.... Judge Friendly argued that a prior consistent statement could in some circumstances be used to rehabilitate credibility. Agreeing with one of Judge Mansfield's points, Judge Friendly concluded that the prior consistent statements in Rubin were properly used under the doctrine of completeness.

In dissent, Judge Meskill expressed the view that Quinto had correctly equated the criteria for admitting prior consistent statements as substantive evidence with those for using such statements only for rehabilitation. He also disagreed that this expression of equivalence could be dismissed as dictum since Quinto had rejected use of the prior consistent statement in that case both as substantive evidence and for rehabilitation. Judge Meskill did not consider whether the statements could be used under Rule 106 since the Government had not invoked the rule of completeness at trial.

... [W]e entirely agree with Judge Friendly that the broad statement in Quinto seeming to require *every* use of a prior consistent statement for rehabilitation to satisfy the criteria of Rule 801(d)(1)(B) for use as substantive evidence was dictum in the traditional sense: It was a statement broader than required for decision of the issue presented. The memorandum in Quinto had been offered to rebut only a generalized attack on credibility. It had no probative force beyond showing that the witness had at an earlier time been consistent with his trial testimony.... [A] prior consistent statement may be used for rehabilitation when the statement has a probative force bearing on credibility beyond merely showing repetition. When the prior statement tends to cast doubt on whether the prior inconsistent statement was made or on whether the impeaching statement is really inconsistent with the trial testimony, its use for rehabilitation purposes is within the sound discretion of the trial judge. Such use is also permissible when the consistent statement will amplify or clarify the allegedly inconsistent statement. It matters not whether such use is deemed a permissible type of rehabilitation or only an invocation of the principle of completeness, though not a precise use of Rule 106.

Applying what we take to be the governing principles from our prior cases, there can be no doubt that the District Judge in the instant case did not err in permitting the DEA agent to testify that his formal typewritten report mentioned Pierre's refusal to participate in a controlled delivery. Unlike the agent in Quinto, the agent here had not been subjected merely to a generalized attack on his credibility. Nor was this a case where a witness, confronted with a prior statement contradicting his trial testimony, was sought to be rehabilitated merely by the fact of his having given on a prior occasion a version consistent with his trial testimony. Here the defense sought to draw from the fact that the agent's notes omitted reference to the controlled delivery an inference that this proposal had not been mentioned in the post-arrest interview. It was obviously pertinent to the strength of that inference to show that the agent's formal report included the proposal for the controlled delivery. The issue for the jury was whether the omission from the notes meant that the topic had not been discussed or only that the agent had not included it among the fragmentary phrases he wrote down during the interview. The defense was entitled to argue the first possibility, but the prosecution was entitled to argue the second possibility and to support that argument with the fact that the controlled delivery proposal was mentioned in the agent's formal report.[1]

See also United States v. Castillo, 14 F.3d 802 (2d Cir.), cert. denied, 115 S.Ct. 101 (1994). Compare United States v. Miller, 874 F.2d 1255, 1272–73 (9th Cir.1989) (pre-Tome; statement is either admissible under Rule 801(d)(1)(B) or it is not admissible at all; court did not impose a temporal requirement for substantive use), cert. denied, 510 U.S. 894 (1993).

4. In Beech Aircraft Corp. v. Rainey, 488 U.S. 153, 170–173 (1988), the only seriously disputed issue was whether the fatal crash was due to pilot error or equipment malfunction. Plaintiff, the husband of the Navy pilot killed in the crash and himself a flight instructor, was called as an adverse witness by the defense and questioned about a letter he had sent to the officer investigating the accident. He admitted making two statements that suggested pilot error as the cause of the crash. On cross-examination, the trial court sustained a defense objection when plaintiff's counsel sought to ask him whether the letter did not also say that the most likely cause of the crash was a loss of power due

---

1. Footnotes omitted.

to equipment malfunction. The Supreme Court held that the trial court had erred in refusing to permit plaintiff "to present a more complete picture of what he had written:"

> We have no doubt that the jury was given a distorted and prejudicial impression of Rainey's letter. The theory of Rainey's case was that the accident was the result of a power failure, and, read in its entirety, his letter to Morgan was fully consistent with that theory. While Rainey did discuss problems his wife had encountered the morning of the accident which led her to attempt to cancel the flight, and also agreed that her airplane had violated pattern integrity in turning left prematurely, the thrust of his letter was to challenge Morgan's theory that the crash had been caused by a stall that took place when the pilots turned sharply right and pitched up in attempting to avoid the other plane. Thus Rainey argued that Morgan's hypothesis was inconsistent with the observations of eyewitnesses, the physical findings in the wreckage, and the likely actions of the two pilots. He explained at length his theory of power failure and attempted to demonstrate how the various pieces of evidence supported it. What the jury was told, however, through the defendants' direct examination of Rainey as an adverse witness, was that Rainey had written six months after the accident (1) that his wife had attempted to cancel the flight, partly because her student was tired and emotionally drained, and that "unnecessary pressure" was placed on them to proceed with it; and (2) that she or her student had abruptly initiated a hard right turn when the other aircraft unexpectedly came into view. It is plausible that a jury would have concluded from this information that Rainey did not believe in his theory of power failure and had developed it only later for purposes of litigation. Because the court sustained defense counsel's objection, Rainey's counsel was unable to counteract this prejudicial impression by presenting additional information about the letter on cross-examination.

> The common-law "rule of completeness," which underlies Federal Rule of Evidence 106, was designed to prevent exactly the type of prejudice of which Rainey complains. In its aspect relevant to this litigation, the rule of completeness was stated succinctly by Wigmore: "[T]he opponent, against whom a part of an utterance has been put in, may in his turn complement it by putting in the remainder, in order to secure for the tribunal a complete understanding of the total tenor and effect of the utterance." 7 J. Wigmore, Evidence in Trials at Common Law § 2113, p. 653 (J. Chadbourn rev. 1978).[2] The Federal Rules of Evidence have partially codified the doctrine of completeness in Rule 106:

> > "When a writing or recorded statement or part thereof is introduced by a party, an adverse party may require the introduction at that time of any other part or any other writing or recorded statement which ought in fairness to be considered contemporaneously with it."

> In proposing Rule 106, the Advisory Committee stressed that it "does not in any way circumscribe the right of the adversary to develop the matter on cross-examination or as part of his own case." Advisory Committee's Notes on Fed.Rule Evid. 106, 28 U.S.C.App., p. 682. We take this to be a reaffirmation of the obvious: that when one party has made use of a

---

2. In addition to this concern that the court not be misled because portions of a statement are taken out of context, the rule has also addressed the danger that an out-of-context statement may create such prejudice that it is impossible to repair by a *subsequent* presentation of additional material. The issue in this litigation, however, involves only the first concern. [Footnotes are the Court's renumbered].

portion of a document, such that misunderstanding or distortion can be averted only through presentation of another portion, the material required for completeness is ipso facto relevant and therefore admissible under Rules 401 and 402. See 1 J. Weinstein & M. Berger, Weinstein's Evidence ¶ 106[02], p. 106–20 (1986). The District Court's refusal to admit the proffered completion evidence was a clear abuse of discretion.

While much of the controversy in this suit has centered on whether Rule 106 applies, we find it unnecessary to address that issue. Clearly the concerns underlying Rule 106 are relevant here, but, as the general rules of relevancy permit a ready resolution to this litigation, we need go no further in exploring the scope and meaning of Rule 106.[3]

Is the rule of completeness stated in Rule 106 solely an offer of proof rule that does not make otherwise inadmissible evidence admissible, or does it create an additional basis for admissibility? In Beech, the Court stated in a footnote that "a hearsay objection [would not] have been availing."

> Although the question called for Rainey to testify to an out-of-court statement, that statement was not offered "to prove the truth of the matter asserted." Rule 801(c). Rather, it was offered simply to prove what Rainey had said about the accident six months after it happened, and to contribute to a fuller understanding of the material the defense had already placed in evidence.

488 U.S. at 173 n.18. See also U.S. Football League v. National Football League, 842 F.2d 1335, 1377 (2d Cir.1988)(excluding on the basis of hearsay and Rule 403 earlier letter to which letter admitted into evidence had replied), aff'd, 887 F.2d 408 (2d Cir.1989), cert. denied, 493 U.S. 1071 (1990); United States v. Sutton, 801 F.2d 1346, 1368–70 (C.A.D.C.1986)(error, but harmless, for court to have excluded statement offered by defendant on the ground of hearsay). See also Nance, A Theory of Verbal Completeness, 80 Iowa L. Rev. 825 (1995)(suggesting that the completeness doctrine trumps exclusionary rules, such as the rule against hearsay, that would otherwise prevent the opponent's response).

United States v. Owens

Supreme Court of the United States, 1988.
484 U.S. 554, 108 S.Ct. 838, 98 L.Ed.2d 951.

■ JUSTICE SCALIA delivered the opinion of the Court.

This case requires us to determine whether either the Confrontation Clause of the Sixth Amendment or Rule 802 of the Federal Rules of Evidence bars testimony concerning a prior, out-of-court identification when the identifying witness is unable, because of memory loss, to explain the basis for the identification.

I

On April 12, 1982, John Foster, a correctional counselor at the federal prison in Lompoc, California, was attacked and brutally beaten with a metal pipe. His skull was fractured, and he remained hospitalized for almost a month. As a result of his injuries, Foster's memory was severely impaired. When

---

3. Nor, in view of our disposition of the action, need we address the alternative ground cited by the Court of Appeals for its decision, namely that Rainey's proposed testimony would have constituted a "prior consistent statement" under Rule 801(d)(1)(B).

Thomas Mansfield, an FBI agent investigating the assault, first attempted to interview Foster, on April 19, he found Foster lethargic and unable to remember his attacker's name. On May 5, Mansfield again spoke to Foster, who was much improved and able to describe the attack. Foster named respondent as his attacker and identified respondent from an array of photographs.

Respondent was tried in Federal District Court for assault with intent to commit murder under 18 U.S.C. § 113(a). At trial, Foster recounted his activities just before the attack, and described feeling the blows to his head and seeing blood on the floor. He testified that he clearly remembered identifying respondent as his assailant during his May 5th interview with Mansfield. On cross-examination, he admitted that he could not remember seeing his assailant. He also admitted that, although there was evidence that he had received numerous visitors in the hospital, he was unable to remember any of them except Mansfield, and could not remember whether any of these visitors had suggested that respondent was the assailant. Defense counsel unsuccessfully sought to refresh his recollection with hospital records, including one indicating that Foster had attributed the assault to someone other than respondent. Respondent was convicted and sentenced to 20 years' imprisonment to be served consecutively to a previous sentence.

On appeal, the United States Court of Appeals for the Ninth Circuit considered challenges based on the Confrontation Clause and Rule 802 of the Federal Rules of Evidence. By divided vote it upheld both challenges (though finding the Rule 802 violation harmless error), and reversed the judgment of the District Court. 789 F.2d 750 (1986). We granted certiorari, 479 U.S. 1084 (1987), to resolve the conflict with other Circuits on the significance of a hearsay declarant's memory loss both with respect to the Confrontation Clause, see, e.g., United States ex rel. Thomas v. Cuyler, 548 F.2d 460, 462–463 (C.A.3 1977), and with respect to Rule 802, see, e.g., United States v. Lewis, 565 F.2d 1248, 1252 (C.A.2 1977), cert. denied, 435 U.S. 973 (1978).

II

The Confrontation Clause of the Sixth Amendment gives the accused the right "to be confronted with the witnesses against him." This has long been read as securing an adequate opportunity to cross-examine adverse witnesses. See, e.g., Mattox v. United States, 156 U.S. 237, 242–243 (1895); Douglas v. Alabama, 380 U.S. 415, 418 (1965). This Court has never held that a Confrontation Clause violation can be founded upon a witness' loss of memory, but in two cases has expressly left that possibility open.

In California v. Green, 399 U.S. 149, 157–164 (1970), we found no constitutional violation in the admission of testimony that had been given at a preliminary hearing, relying on (as one of two independent grounds) the proposition that the opportunity to cross-examine the witness at trial satisfied the Sixth Amendment's requirements. We declined, however, to decide the admissibility of the same witness' out-of-court statement to a police officer concerning events that at trial he was unable to recall. In remanding on this point, we noted that the state court had not considered, and the parties had not briefed, the possibility that the witness' memory loss so affected the petitioner's right to cross-examine as to violate the Confrontation Clause.[1] Id., at 168–169.

---

1. On remand, the California Supreme Court concluded that the Confrontation Clause was not violated by the out-of-court statement, because the declarant testified under oath, subject to cross-examination, and the jury was able to observe his demeanor. People v. Green, 3 Cal.3d 981, 479 P.2d 998, cert. dism'd, 404 U.S. 801 (1971). [Footnote of the Court renumbered; some footnotes omitted].

Justice Harlan, in a scholarly concurrence, stated that he would have reached the issue of the out-of-court statement, and would have held that a witness' inability to "recall either the underlying events that are the subject of an extra-judicial statement or previous testimony or recollect the circumstances under which the statement was given, does not have Sixth Amendment consequence." Id., at 188.

In Delaware v. Fensterer, 474 U.S. 15 (1985)(per curiam), we determined that there was no Confrontation Clause violation when an expert witness testified as to what opinion he had formed, but could not recollect the basis on which he had formed it. We said:

> "The Confrontation Clause includes no guarantee that every witness called by the prosecution will refrain from giving testimony that is marred by forgetfulness, confusion, or evasion. To the contrary, the Confrontation Clause is generally satisfied when the defense is given a full and fair opportunity to probe and expose these infirmities through cross-examination, thereby calling to the attention of the factfinder the reasons for giving scant weight to the witness' testimony." Id., at 21–22.

Our opinion noted that a defendant seeking to discredit a forgetful expert witness is not without ammunition, since the jury may be persuaded that "his opinion is as unreliable as his memory." Id., at 19. We distinguished, however, the unresolved issue in Green on the basis that that involved the introduction of an out-of-court statement. 474 U.S., at 18. JUSTICE STEVENS, concurring in the judgment, suggested that the question at hand was in fact quite close to the question left open in Green. 474 U.S., at 23–24.

Here that question is squarely presented, and we agree with the answer suggested 18 years ago by Justice Harlan. "[T]he Confrontation Clause guarantees only 'an *opportunity* for effective cross-examination, not cross-examination that is effective in whatever way, and to whatever extent, the defense might wish.'" Kentucky v. Stincer, 482 U.S. 730, 739 (1987), quoting from Fensterer, supra, at 20 (emphasis added); Delaware v. Van Arsdall, 475 U.S. 673, 679 (1986); Ohio v. Roberts, 448 U.S. 56, 73, n. 12 (1980). As Fensterer demonstrates, that opportunity is not denied when a witness testifies as to his current belief but is unable to recollect the reason for that belief. It is sufficient that the defendant has the opportunity to bring out such matters as the witness' bias, his lack of care and attentiveness, his poor eyesight, and even (what is often a prime objective of cross-examination, see 3A J. Wigmore, Evidence § 995, pp. 931–932 (J. Chadbourn rev. 1970)) the very fact that he has a bad memory. If the ability to inquire into these matters suffices to establish the constitutionally requisite opportunity for cross-examination when a witness testifies as to his current belief, the basis for which he cannot recall, we see no reason why it should not suffice when the witness' past belief is introduced and he is unable to recollect the reason for that past belief. In both cases the foundation for the belief (current or past) cannot effectively be elicited, but other means of impugning the belief are available. Indeed, if there is any difference in persuasive impact between the statement "I believe this to be the man who assaulted me, but can't remember why" and the statement "I don't know whether this is the man who assaulted me, but I told the police I believed so earlier," the former would seem, if anything, more damaging and hence give rise to a greater need for memory-testing, if that is to be considered essential to an opportunity for effective cross-examination. We conclude with respect to this latter example, as we did in Fensterer with respect to the former, that it is not. The weapons available to impugn the witness' statement when memory loss is asserted will of course not always achieve success, but successful cross-examination is not the constitutional guarantee. They are, however, realistic weapons, as is demonstrated by defense counsel's summation in this very case, which emphasized Foster's memory loss and argued that his identification of respondent was the result of the suggestions of people who visited him in the hospital.

Our constitutional analysis is not altered by the fact that the testimony here involved an out-of-court identification that would traditionally be categorized as hearsay. See Advisory Committee's Notes on Fed. Rule Evid. 801(d)(1)(C), 28 U.S.C.App., p. 717. This Court has recognized a partial (and somewhat indeterminate) overlap between the requirements of the traditional hearsay rule and the Confrontation Clause. See Green, 399 U.S., at 155–156; id., at 173 (Harlan, J., concurring). The dangers associated with hearsay inspired the Court of Appeals in the present case to believe that the Constitution required the testimony to be examined for "indicia of reliability," Dutton v. Evans, 400 U.S. 74, 89 (1970), or "particularized guarantees of trustworthiness," Roberts, supra, at 66. We do not think such an inquiry is called for when a hearsay declarant is present at trial and subject to unrestricted cross-examination. In that situation, as the Court recognized in Green, the traditional protections of the oath, cross-examination, and opportunity for the jury to observe the witness' demeanor satisfy the constitutional requirements. 399 U.S., at 158–161. We do not think that a constitutional line drawn by the Confrontation Clause falls between a forgetful witness' live testimony that he once believed this defendant to be the perpetrator of the crime, and the introduction of the witness' earlier statement to that effect.

Respondent has argued that this Court's jurisprudence concerning suggestive identification procedures shows the special dangers of identification testimony, and the special importance of cross-examination when such hearsay is proffered. See, e.g., Manson v. Brathwaite, 432 U.S. 98 (1977); Neil v. Biggers, 409 U.S. 188 (1972). Respondent has not, however, argued that the identification procedure used here was in any way suggestive. There does not appear in our opinions, and we decline to adopt today, the principle that, because of the mere possibility of suggestive procedures, out-of-court statements of identification are inherently less reliable than other out-of-court statements.

III

Respondent urges as an alternative basis for affirmance a violation of Federal Rule of Evidence 802, which generally excludes hearsay. Rule 801(d)(1)(C) defines as not hearsay a prior statement "of identification of a person made after perceiving the person," if the declarant "testifies at the trial or hearing and is subject to cross-examination concerning the statement." The Court of Appeals found that Foster's identification statement did not come within this exclusion because his memory loss prevented his being "subject to cross-examination concerning the statement." Although the Court of Appeals concluded that the violation of the Rules of Evidence was harmless (applying for purposes of that determination a "more-probable-than-not" standard, rather than the "beyond-a-reasonable-doubt" standard applicable to the Confrontation Clause violation, see Delaware v. Van Arsdall, 475 U.S., at 684), respondent argues to the contrary.

It seems to us that the more natural reading of "subject to cross-examination concerning the statement" includes what was available here. Ordinarily a witness is regarded as "subject to cross-examination" when he is placed on the stand, under oath, and responds willingly to questions. Just as with the constitutional prohibition, limitations on the scope of examination by the trial court or assertions of privilege by the witness may undermine the process to such a degree that meaningful cross-examination within the intent of the rule no longer exists. But that effect is not produced by the witness' assertion of memory loss—which, as discussed earlier, is often the very result sought to be produced by cross-examination, and can be effective in destroying the force of the prior statement. Rule 801(d)(1)(C), which specifies that the cross-examination need only "concer[n] the statement," does not on its face require more.

This reading seems even more compelling when the Rule is compared with Rule 804(a)(3), which defines "[u]navailability as a witness" to include situations in which a declarant "testifies to a lack of memory of the subject matter of the declarant's statement." Congress plainly was aware of the recurrent evidentiary problem at issue here—witness forgetfulness of an underlying event—but chose not to make it an exception to Rule 801(d)(1)(C).

The reasons for that choice are apparent from the Advisory Committee's Notes on Rule 801 and its legislative history. The premise for Rule 801(d)(1)(C) was that, given adequate safeguards against suggestiveness, out-of-court identifications were generally preferable to courtroom identifications. Advisory Committee's Notes on Rule 801, 28 U.S.C.App., p. 717. Thus, despite the traditional view that such statements were hearsay, the Advisory Committee believed that their use was to be fostered rather than discouraged. Similarly, the House Report on the Rule noted that since, "[a]s time goes by, a witness' memory will fade and his identification will become less reliable," minimizing the barriers to admission of more contemporaneous identification is fairer to defendants and prevents "cases falling through because the witness can no longer recall the identity of the person he saw commit the crime." H.R. Rep. No. 94–355, p. 3 (1975). See also S. Rep. No. 94–199, p. 2 (1975). To judge from the House and Senate Reports, Rule 801(d)(1)(C) was in part directed to the very problem here at issue: a memory loss that makes it impossible for the witness to provide an in-court identification or testify about details of the events underlying an earlier identification.

Respondent argues that this reading is impermissible because it creates an internal inconsistency in the Rules, since the forgetful witness who is deemed "subject to cross-examination" under 801(d)(1)(C) is simultaneously deemed "unavailable" under 804(a)(3). This is the position espoused by a prominent commentary on the Rules, see 4 J. Weinstein & M. Berger, Weinstein's Evidence 801–120 to 801–121, 801–178 (1987). It seems to us, however, that this is not a substantive inconsistency, but only a semantic oddity resulting from the fact that Rule 804(a) has for convenience of reference in Rule 804(b) chosen to describe the circumstances necessary in order to admit certain categories of hearsay testimony under the rubric "Unavailability as a witness." These circumstances include not only absence from the hearing, but also claims of privilege, refusals to obey a court's order to testify, and inability to testify based on physical or mental illness or memory loss. Had the rubric instead been "unavailability as a witness, memory loss, and other special circumstances" there would be no apparent inconsistency with Rule 801, which is a definition section excluding certain statements entirely from the category of "hearsay." The semantic inconsistency exists not only with respect to Rule 801(d)(1)(C), but also with respect to the other subparagraphs of Rule 801(d)(1). It would seem strange, for example, to assert that a witness can avoid introduction of testimony from a prior proceeding that is inconsistent with his trial testimony, see Rule 801(d)(1)(A), by simply asserting lack of memory of the facts to which the prior testimony related. See United States v. Murphy, 696 F.2d 282, 283–284 (C.A.4 1982), cert. denied, 461 U.S. 945 (1983). But that situation, like this one, presents the verbal curiosity that the witness is "subject to cross-examination" under Rule 801 while at the same time "unavailable" under Rule

804(a)(3). Quite obviously, the two characterizations are made for two entirely different purposes and there is no requirement or expectation that they should coincide.[2]

For the reasons stated, we hold that neither the Confrontation Clause nor Federal Rule of Evidence 802 is violated by admission of an identification statement of a witness who is unable, because of a memory loss, to testify concerning the basis for the identification. The decision of the Court of Appeals is reversed, and the case is remanded for proceedings consistent with this opinion.

So ordered.

■ JUSTICE KENNEDY took no part in the consideration or decision of this case.

■ JUSTICE BRENNAN, with whom JUSTICE MARSHALL joins, dissenting.

In an interview during his month-long hospitalization, in what was apparently a singular moment of lucid recollection, John Foster selected respondent James Owens' photograph from an array of possible suspects and informed FBI Agent Thomas Mansfield that it was respondent who had attacked him with a metal pipe on the morning of April 12, 1982. Had Foster subsequently died from his injuries, there is no doubt that both the Sixth Amendment and the Federal Rules of Evidence would have barred Mansfield from repeating Foster's out-of-court identification at trial. Fortunately, Foster survived the beating; his memory, however, did not, and by the time of respondent's trial he could no longer recall his assailant or explain why he had previously identified respondent as such. This profound memory loss, therefore, rendered Foster no less a conduit for stale and inscrutable evidence than Mansfield would have been, yet the Court nevertheless concludes that because defense counsel was afforded an unrestricted opportunity to cross-examine him, Foster's unadorned reiteration of his earlier statement did not deprive respondent of his constitutional right to confront the witness against him. In my view, the Court today reduces the right of confrontation to a purely procedural protection, and a markedly hollow one at that. Because I believe the Sixth Amendment guarantees criminal defendants the right to engage in cross-examination sufficient to "affor[d] the trier of fact a satisfactory basis for evaluating the truth of [a] prior statement," California v. Green, 399 U.S. 149, 161 (1970), and because respondent clearly was not afforded such an opportunity here, I dissent.

I

On April 12, 1982, Foster was brutally assaulted while on duty as a correctional counselor at the federal prison in Lompoc, California. His attacker beat him repeatedly about the head and upper body with a metal pipe, inflicting numerous and permanently disabling injuries, one of which was a profound loss of short-term memory. Foster spent nearly a month in the hospital recuperating from his injuries, much of that time in a state of semiconsciousness. Although numerous people visited him, including his wife who visited daily, Foster remembered none except Agent Mansfield. While he had no recollection of Mansfield's first visit on April 19, he testified that his memory of the interview Mansfield conducted on May 5 was "vivid." App. 28. In particular, he recalled telling Mansfield: "[A]fter I was hit I looked down and saw the blood

---

2. The dissent disagreed: "Because I believe such a construction of Rule 801(d)(1)(C) renders it unconstitutional under the Confrontation Clause, I would require, consistent with Rule 804(a), that the declarant be subject to cross-examination as to the subject matter of the prior statement. See 4 J. Weinstein & M. Berger, Weinstein's Evidence 801-120 to 801-121 (1987) (endorsing such a construction of Rule 801(d)(1)(C))." 484 U.S. 569, 571, n. 2 [Footnote by editors].

on the floor, and jammed my finger into Owens' chest, and said, 'That's enough of that,' and hit my alarm button." Id., at 31.

Foster testified that at the time he made these statements, he was certain that his memory was accurate. In addition, he recalled choosing respondent's photograph from those Mansfield showed him. There is no dispute, however, that by the time of trial Foster could no longer remember who had assaulted him or even whether he had seen his attacker. Nor could he recall whether any of the prison officials or other persons who visited him in the hospital had ever suggested that respondent had beaten him. A medical expert who testified on behalf of the prosecution explained that Foster's inability to remember most of the details of the assault was attributable to a gradual and selective memory loss caused by his head injuries.

II

The principal witness against respondent was not the John Foster who took the stand in December 1983—that witness could recall virtually nothing of the events of April 12, 1982, and candidly admitted that he had no idea whether respondent had assaulted him. Instead, respondent's sole accuser was the John Foster who, on May 5, 1982, identified respondent as his attacker. This John Foster, however, did not testify at respondent's trial: the profound memory loss he suffered during the approximately 18 months following his identification prevented him from affirming, explaining, or elaborating upon his out-of-court statement just as surely and completely as his assertion of a testimonial privilege, or his death, would have. Thus, while the Court asserts that defense counsel had "realistic weapons" with which to impugn Foster's prior statement, . . . it does not and cannot claim that cross-examination could have elicited any information that would have enabled a jury to evaluate the trustworthiness or reliability of the identification. Indeed, although the Court suggests that defense counsel was able to explore Foster's "lack of care and attentiveness," his "bad memory," and the possibility that hospital visitors suggested respondent's name to him, . . . Foster's memory loss precluded any such inquiries: he simply could not recall whether he had actually seen his assailant or even whether he had had an opportunity to see him, nor could he remember any of his visitors, let alone whether any of them had suggested that respondent had attacked him. Moreover, by the time of trial, Foster was unable to shed any light on the accuracy of his May 1982 recollection of the assault; the most he could state was that on the day of the interview he felt certain that his statements were true. As the court below found, "[c]learly two of the three dangers surrounding Foster's out-of-court identifications—misperception and failure of memory—could not be mitigated in any way by the only cross-examination of Foster that was available to [respondent]." 789 F.2d 750, 759 (C.A.9 1986).

In short, neither Foster nor the prosecution could demonstrate the basis for Foster's prior identification. Nevertheless, the Court concludes that the Sixth Amendment presents no obstacle to the introduction of such an unsubstantiated out-of-court statement, at least not where the declarant testifies under oath at trial and is subjected to unrestricted cross-examination. According to the Court, the Confrontation Clause is simply a procedural trial right that "guarantees only an *opportunity* for effective cross-examination, not cross-examination that is effective in whatever way, and to whatever extent, the defense might wish." . . .

Although the Court suggests that the result it reaches today follows naturally from our earlier cases, we have never before held that the Confrontation Clause protects nothing more than a defendant's right to question live witnesses, no matter how futile that questioning might be.... While we have rejected the notion that effectiveness should be measured in terms of a defendant's ultimate success, we have never until today, equated effectiveness with the mere opportunity to pose questions. Rather, consistent with the Confrontation Clause's mission of "advanc[ing] a practical concern for the accuracy of the truth-determining process in criminal trials," Dutton v. Evans, 400 U.S. 74, 89 (1970), we have suggested that the touchstone of effectiveness is whether the cross-examination affords " 'the trier of fact ... a satisfactory basis for evaluating the truth of the prior statement.' " Ibid. (quoting California v. Green, supra, at 161)....

NOTE

1.   In California v. Green, supra, the Court asked the state court to consider on remand whether Porter's alleged lapse of memory made a critical difference in the application of the Confrontation Clause, and added that resolving that question "depends much upon the unique facts in this record." After Owens, need the trial court concern itself with evaluating a declarant-witness' claim not to remember?

2.   Rule 801(d)(1)(C) applies regardless of whether the prior identification was made at the scene of the crime, at a later chance encounter, or at a police line-up. Infraction of the constitutional requirements for identification procedures, discussed above at pp. 246–47 may, of course, vitiate evidence that would otherwise have been admissible. The rule has been held to apply to photographic as well as in person identifications. See United States v. Fosher, 568 F.2d 207, 210 (1st Cir.1978). Does the rule allow the introduction at trial of composite sketches made by the police based on eye witness descriptions? See Lacy, Hearsay and Relevancy Obstacles to the Admission of Composite Sketches in Criminal Trials, 64 Boston U.L.Rev. 1101 (1984).

3.   Is testimony that a witness had previously identified a physical object within the rationale of the rule? See State v. Jenkins, 766 P.2d 499, 501–02 (Wash.Ct.App.1989)(car); Harley v. United States, 471 A.2d 1013, 1015–16 (D.C.1984)(handgun).

4.   Is the prior statement of identification admissible if the witness who made the pretrial identification 1) admits having made the identification but now recants, or 2) denies ever having made a pretrial identification? In reversing a conviction, the court stated in Commonwealth v. Daye, 469 N.E.2d 483, 488 (Mass.1984):

> Prior identifications are admissible as probative evidence notwithstanding their hearsay attributes because of the superior probative worth of an identification made closer in time to the events in question ... Where, however, the extrajudicial identification is established not by the identifying witness but by a person who observed the identification, we believe that probative worth is outweighed by "the hazard of error or falsity in the reporting." McCormick, The Turncoat Witness: Previous Statements as Substantive Evidence, 25 Tex.L.Rev. 573, 588 (1947). Where there is a dispute not only as to the accuracy of a pretrial identification, but also as to whether the identification was in fact made, "the evidential value of the prior identification is almost completely dissipated." Commonwealth v. Swenson, 368 Mass. 268, 273 n. 3, 331 N.E.2d 893 (1975). Thus, a police officer's attribution to a witness of a positive identification denied by

the witness at trial is not admissible to prove the identification. Its effect is limited to impeachment.

Compare United States v. Jarrad, 754 F.2d 1451, 1456 (9th Cir.), cert. denied, 474 U.S. 830 (1985)(FBI agent had properly been permitted to testify that witness who denied having selected defendant's picture from a photospread had in fact stated that defendant's picture was "similar to or reminded her of" the person in question: "Where, as here, both the agent and the witness testify and are available for cross-examination, the statement of identification is not hearsay.... [T]he rule was intended to solve the problem of a witness who identifies a defendant before trial, but then at trial refuses to acknowledge the identification because of fear of reprisal."); Commonwealth v. Floyd, 498 A.2d 816 (Pa.1985)(extensive survey of cases in which third person testifies to statement of identification); Nance v. State, 629 A.2d 633, 639 (Md.Ct.App.1993)("Ample authority supports the admission of extrajudicial identification even where the witness recants at trial.").

Sufficiency. Is a prior inconsistent statement or a statement of identification, standing alone, sufficient to support a conviction? Compare State v. Moore, 485 So.2d 1279, 1281 (Fla.1986)(prior inconsistent statement insufficient to support a conviction); United States v. Orrico, 599 F.2d 113, 119 (6th Cir.1979)(prior inconsistent statements "may be used to corroborate evidence which otherwise would be inconclusive, may fill in gaps in the Government's reconstruction of events, or may provide valuable detail which would otherwise have been lost through lapse of memory. But the Government having offered such statements as the sole evidence of a central element of the crime charged, we hold that the Government has failed to sustain its burden of proving guilt beyond a reasonable doubt") with Vermont v. Robar, 601 A.2d 1376 (Vt. 1991)("In general, we find the reasoning [of Orrick] persuasive, but ... the result may be overly rigid in circumstances where the prior statement is particularly reliable.")

In People v. Cuevas, 906 P.2d 1290 (Cal.1995), the court overruled a prior decision requiring corroboration in all cases regardless of the identification's probative value or the existence of other record evidence. The court noted

> the many varied circumstances that may attend an out-of-court identification and affect its probative value. These circumstances include, for example: (1) the identifying witness's prior familiarity with the defendant; (2) the witness's opportunity to observe the perpetrator during the commission of the crime; (3) whether the witness has a motive to falsely implicate the defendant; and (4) the level of detail given by the witness in the out-of-court identification and any accompanying description of the crime.

Id. at 1299.

The court also pointed out

> the many varied circumstances relating to the witness's failure to identify the defendant at trial. Among these circumstances are: (1) whether the identifying witness admits, denies, or fails to remember making the out-of-court identification; (2) whether the witness remembers the underlying events of the crime but no longer believes in the accuracy of the out-of-court identification; (3) whether, if the witness claims the identification was false or erroneous, the witness offers an explanation for making a false or erroneous identification; (4) whether, if the witness claims a failure of recollection, there are reasons supporting the loss of memory; (5) whether there is evidence that the witness's failure to confirm the identification in court resulted from the witness's appreciation that doing so would result in

the defendant's conviction; or (6) whether there is evidence that, as the Attorney General suggests occurred here, the witness's failure to confirm the identification arises from fear or intimidation.

Id. at 1299–1300.

NOTE ON CHILD SEX ABUSE CASES

Many states have recently adopted special "tender years" hearsay exceptions that make admissible prior statements by child victims in sexual abuse prosecutions. In 1982, only two states, Washington and Kansas, had such statutes; in 1996 more than thirty states have enacted some form of such a statute. These statutes supplement other hearsay exceptions under which much child hearsay is admitted, such as excited utterances, present sense impressions, statements for medical diagnosis and treatment and residual or catch-all exceptions. See Note, Should We Believe the People Who Believe the Children?: The Need for a New Sexual Abuse Tender Years Hearsay Exception Statute, 32 Harv.J.on Legis. 207, 235 (1995). These new statutes differ in detail, but some authorize admission of the prior statement only if the child was cross-examined when the statement was made, or if the child is subject to cross-examination when the statement is introduced. See, e.g., Alaska Stat. § 12.40.110 (1995); Ga. Code Ann. § 24–3–16 (1996); Mich.R.Evid. 803A. Other of the new statutes, however, eliminate the need for cross-examination if the child is unavailable or if corroborating evidence is available. See Montoya, Something Not So Funny Happened on the Way to Conviction: The Pretrial Interrogation of Child Witnesses, 35 Ariz.L.Rev. 927 (1993); Mosteller, Remaking Confrontation Clause and Hearsay Doctrine Under the Challenge of Child Sexual Abuse Prosecutions, 1993 U.Ill.L.Rev. 691 (1993). The constitutional ramifications of child hearsay are discussed infra at p. 778.

When a child testifies at trial outside the presence of the defendant by one-way closed circuit television, the Supreme Court has described such testimony as an in-court procedure rather than as hearsay. See Maryland v. Craig, 497 U.S. 836, 851 (1990) (closed-circuit television testimony "may be said to be technically given out of court though we do not so hold."). See discussion, supra at p. 367.

SECTION 3.   ADMISSIONS

Bill v. Farm Bureau Life Insurance Co.

Supreme Court of Iowa, 1963.
254 Iowa 1215, 119 N.W.2d 768.

■ THOMPSON, JUSTICE. The plaintiffs are beneficiaries in a policy of insurance issued by the defendant upon the life of their son, LeRoy Leo Bill, who died on January 12, 1961. Liability being denied by the insurer, this action was brought by the plaintiffs. The defendant alleged that the death of the insured was the result of suicide, which raises the only substantial question in the case. There is no denial of the issuance of the policy or that it was otherwise in effect on the date of LeRoy Bill's death; nor is there any contention that the policy was not voided under its terms if death was brought about by suicide. The trial court held that the question of suicide was for the determination of the jury and submitted it accordingly. The jury returned its verdict for the plaintiffs, judgment was rendered on the verdict, and we have this appeal. The defendant contends it was entitled to a peremptory verdict; it raised the question in various ways, and also challenges certain rulings on evidence and instructions given the jury.

The evidence disclosed that LeRoy, a 17 year old boy approximately five feet eleven inches tall, weighing about two hundred and eight pounds, had been employed as a farm hand by Howard Niedert, a farmer residing near Riceville, Iowa, since September 21, 1960. . . .

On the late afternoon of January 12, 1961, he was engaged in doing the chores and, when Mrs. Niedert arrived home about five o'clock, she talked with him. She observed nothing unusual about him and he went on about his tasks. She later saw him riding a saddle horse driving the cattle from the pasture, and that was the last anyone saw him alive. Apparently all the chores had been done except for the task of throwing down some hay or straw from the barn loft.

When Mr. Niedert arrived home about six o'clock that evening, LeRoy had not returned to the house for his evening meal. When the lad had not appeared by 6:30 o'clock, Niedert went to look for him and observed a light on in the barn. Upon entering the door he saw LeRoy's legs extending through a small opening 22″ × 20″ in the floor of the hay mow, used to lower bales of hay and straw for the stock. He thought LeRoy was sitting on the loft floor asleep, until he climbed the ladder in another chute to the floor above. Then "he could see the string to him and went over to him." The "string" was a piece of binder twine tied to an overhead two by eight inch beam some five feet and eleven inches above the floor, and attached to LeRoy's neck by a noose. Mr. Niedert felt the boy's neck, realized it was too late to give him aid and returned to the house. The authorities and LeRoy's parents were called and arrived a short time thereafter.

LeRoy's parents, the plaintiffs herein, arrived first but only Mr. Bill entered the barn. He went no closer than the top of the ladder to the second floor and then returned to the house. . . . [E]rror is assigned upon the refusal of the trial court to admit the testimony of the medical examiner, Dr. Willis K. Dankle, as to a conversation he had with the plaintiff Ernest Bill, in the presence of the other plaintiff, Norma Bill. Dr. Dankle testified that he had such a conversation at the Niedert farm on the evening after the death of LeRoy Bill. To the question "What was said at that time?" he answered "I asked him if there were any doubt in his mind that his son committed suicide." Then came a motion from plaintiffs' counsel to strike "as a conclusion and opinion on his part, in no way binding on this plaintiff, and certainly improper in a civil suit, what the man said at the time, what the doctor said." The court said: "Well, I think that originated with this witness and not with the plaintiffs. I think under the—". Taking this as an expression of intent to sustain the motion to strike, defendant's counsel said "Your Honor, we would like to make an offer of proof in chambers." This was agreed to by the court, and later, in chambers, Dr. Dankle was interrogated in this way: "Q. Doctor, did you have a conversation with Ernest Bill in the presence of Norma Bill at the Niedert farmhouse just before you left on the night of January 12th? A. Yes. Q. What did that conversation consist of in your part and on his? A. I said to Mr. Bill, 'Is there any doubt in your mind that your son committed suicide?' and if I might describe the situation, he and his wife were sitting at the table, mourning and tearful, and he just shook his head. Q. In what direction, Doctor, if you will say it so that the record can pick it up? A. A lateral motion of the head. Q. That is commonly interpreted as a negative sign? A. Which I interpreted as a negative sign."

No objections were lodged by the plaintiffs until all of the foregoing questions had been asked and answered. Then counsel for plaintiffs said: "We object to the proposed offer because there is no question that he died by his own hand. The issue in the case is whether his death was intention[al] or unintentional." After some discussion not material here, the court ruled: "Well, I will tell you, I am going to follow my judgment on this. I think that if the plaintiff had volunteered that there wasn't any doubt in his mind the boy committed suicide that would be perfectly admissible but here we have got an entirely negative approach; somebody puts this subject of suicide out there in the form of a question; he doesn't make any audible answer to it at all. I think there is too much ground for conjecture there on the part of the jury as to the implications they can draw from that. If this goes into the record it surely would be argued to the jury that he admitted that it was suicide and I don't believe that is a fair inference to draw from this sort of thing. Now, if he had said, 'No, there isn't any doubt in my mind but what the boy committed suicide, everything tends to show that,' then I think you would have a different situation but here he doesn't say anything. He shakes his head; maybe it was a negative shake, but he was under stress and strain here. The record shows that there was some mourning; there was some crying going on there at the table where the husband and wife sat. I just don't believe that is enough that I dare let that go to the jury.

"My ruling is going to be that it is not going to be admitted."

It will be noted that no objections were made until all of the questions put to Dr. Dankle had been asked and answered. There is no doubt that the matter inquired into was a proper one, and the doctor should have been permitted to answer all of the questions with the possible exception of the final one, which dealt with his interpretation of the negative sign, the head shake. That the plaintiff Ernest Bill had no doubt his son had committed suicide was an admission against interest; and the error of the court in excluding it was further compounded by the fact that both plaintiffs were permitted to testify, over objection, that they knew of no reason why their son should have intentionally taken his life. The excluded testimony would not only have shown an admission against interest, but would have tended to counter and contradict the testimony last above referred to.

Neither the plaintiffs' motion to strike nor their objection made after all the offered questions had been answered raised any real or substantial question as to the validity of the testimony. Neither raised the point decided by the court, which seems to have been that the lateral motion of the head made by Ernest Bill was too uncertain in its meaning and so was so speculative the jury should not have been permitted to pass upon it. With this we do not agree. A nod of the head is universally understood to be an affirmative or "yes" answer; a shake of the head is equally well understood to mean a negative or "no" reply. It is true the lateral motion might in some circumstances mean merely bewilderment or confusion, and "I don't know" answer. But this was an interpretation to be made by the jury.

. . .

The evidence was on an important point, and we cannot say it was not sufficiently prejudicial to require reversal. An admission by one of the plaintiffs, in the presence of the other who made no objection or comment, that he had no doubt his son committed suicide if so interpreted by the jury would certainly have been an important matter for its consideration. Error appears at this point.

. . .

Reversed and remanded.

[Dissenting opinions omitted.]

NOTES ON ADMISSION BY PARTY

1. The attempt to construct a satisfactory theory or doctrinal basis of admissions has produced much commentary. See, e.g., Morgan, Admissions as an Exception to the Hearsay Rule, 30 Yale L.J. 355 (1921); Morgan, Admissions, 12 Wash.L.Rev. 181 (1937); Strahorn, A Reconsideration of The Hearsay Rule and Admissions, 85 U.Pa.L.Rev. 484 (1937); Morgan, Some Suggestions for Defining and Classifying Hearsay, 86 U.Pa.L.Rev. 258 (1938); Harper, Admissions of Party–Opponent, 8 Mercer L.Rev. 252 (1957); Fisch, Extra Judicial Admissions, 4 Syracuse L.Rev. 90 (1953).

2. *Personal Knowledge.* Scherffius v. Orr, 442 S.W.2d 120, 124–125 (Mo.App. 1969): Motorist's action against farmer for accident allegedly caused by calf on highway.

> We ... find it necessary to disagree with defendant's insistence that there was no evidence the defendant owned the black calf and that defendant's alleged admissions against interest do not merit credence because defendant, not being a witness to the accident, could not have known it was his calf which plaintiff says was on the highway. "A party's admission against interest of a material fact relevant to an issue in the case [including admissions as to the ownership of personal property, Kidd v. Kidd, 216 S.W.2d 942, 946 (Mo.App.1949); 31A C.J.S. Evidence § 317 at p. 807] is competent against him as substantive evidence of the fact admitted. And for a statement by a party to be competent as an admission against interest, it is not necessary that it be a direct admission of the ultimate fact in issue, but it may be competent and of probative value if it bears on the issue incidentally or circumstantially." Gaddy v. State Board of Registration For Healing Arts, 397 S.W.2d 347, 354 (Mo.App.1965). Plaintiff's evidence of defendant's reported statements that "These are my cattle.... The black cows and calves are mine.... I believe I can take you where my calf got out ... I think I know where my calf got out," may have constituted an oblique method of proving a material fact in issue, but such admissions, nevertheless, were against the defendant's interest and "incidentally and circumstantially" provided competent evidence of probative value on the issue of ownership. Although there is nothing in the record which suggests defendant was possessed of any personal knowledge the calf in question was his and the jury admittedly was not advised how he came by the conclusion he was the owner of the animal, an extrajudicial admission of a litigant against his interest, although it be in the nature of a conclusion, is admissible whether the admission was based on personal knowledge or hearsay—where a party believes a fact upon evidence sufficient to convince him of its existence, even though it relates to a fact concerning which he could have no personal knowledge, his declaration of the existence of that fact, if against his interest, is competent evidence against him. Such evidence, though not conclusive and of a very unsatisfactory character, is for the jury to weigh and accord such value as they see fit.

P, three years old, accompanies her mother to D's beauty parlor. D suggests that P retire to D's backyard to play with D's children and dog Tippy. A few minutes later cries from the yard summon D, who then finds P bleeding from the nose and cheek. D then carries P inside and expresses regret to P's mother that Tippy has bitten P. In the trial of P's action against D, P's mother proposes to testify to D's statement that Tippy bit P. D objects that the statement is "predicated upon hearsay and therefore inadmissible". Overruled. Berkowitz v. Simone, 188 A.2d 665 (R.I.1963). See also Mahlandt v. Wild Canid Survival & Research Center, Inc., infra p. 582, Matthews v. Carpenter, 97 So.2d 522 (Miss.1957)(defendant's statement as to the cause of a fire in his shop, defendant having been out of town at the time of the fire); Pekelis v. Transcontinental & Western Air, 187 F.2d 122, 129 (2d Cir.1951). Suppose that in Berkowitz, D's statement to P's mother was, "My children said Tippy bit P". Would this be admissible against D? See Liebow v. Jones Store Co., 303 S.W.2d 660 (Mo.1957) and cf. Cox v. State, 148 N.E.2d 879 (N.Y.1958), noted in 34 N.Y.U.L.Rev. 966. Suppose in Berkowitz D offered to prove a statement by P that Tippy had not bitten P. Objection: P is too young to be a witness. See DeSouza v. Barber, 263 F.2d 470 (9th Cir.1959).

See also the discussion at p. 297, supra of the interrelationship between the personal knowledge requirement in Rule 602 and the hearsay rule.

3. *Application of opinion rule.* A motorist involved in an accident tells a police officer, "It was all my fault". Later, when proof of this statement is offered against him, he objects that the statement is inadmissible, because it is his conclusion or opinion. See Mason v. Shook, 127 So.2d 658 (Miss.1961); Eakins v. Nash, 194 N.E.2d 148 (Ohio.Ct.App.1963).

See also People v. Lazare, 542 P.2d 1290 (Colo.1975)(en banc)(defendant's statement, "There's been a murder."); Overnite Transportation Co. v. Hart, 191 S.E.2d 308 (Ga.Ct.App.1972) (plaintiff's statement that fall was not caused by prior accident); Kraxberger v. Rogers, 373 P.2d 647 (Or.1962) (defendant's statement that a car driven by his son was the "family automobile" was not "subject to objection that it was a conclusion or opinion"); Alires v. Southern Pacific Co., 378 P.2d 913 (Ariz.1963) (defendant fireman's statement that a certain railway crossing is "a particularly bad crossing").

4. *Self–serving nature of statement.* The modern cases make it clear that the self-serving characteristic of the admission when made is immaterial; indeed it is rarely mentioned even when it is most striking. The situation frequently arises when an owner's tax valuation of his property is used as an admission in litigation where he is claiming a higher value on the land. See East Kentucky Rural Electric Co–op. Corp. v. Phelps, 275 S.W.2d 592, 595 (Ky.1955); Commonwealth, Department of Highways v. Ward, 461 S.W.2d 380 (Ky.1970); 32 A.L.R.2d 209, 230 (1953). See also Krajewski v. Western & Southern Life Insurance Co., 217 N.W. 62 (Mich.1928), where a wife's allegation in a personally verified complaint for divorce that the husband was an habitual drunkard was received against her in an action to recover on a policy insuring his life, when offered by the insurer as evidence of the falsity of the insured's representation that he had never used stimulants to excess. For other instances see Kaiser v. United States, 60 F.2d 410 (8th Cir.1932); Manning v. Lowell, 53 N.E. 160 (Mass.1899); Wade v. Lane, 189 F.Supp. 661 (D.D.C.1960). Cf. 36 Texas L.Rev. 517 (1958).

5. *Conduct as an admission.* If while in custody upon a charge of robbing, D attempts to escape, may such attempt be proved against him at trial? Should the evidence be admitted if an additional charge had been pending against D at the time of his attempt? See People v. Yazum, 196 N.E.2d 263 (N.Y.1963), with which cf. State v. Thomas, 385 P.2d 532 (1963). See Annot., 3 A.L.R.4th 1085 (Wash.1981). Is such evidence properly classified as an admission pursuant to the Federal Rules of Evidence? See United States v. Lobo, 516 F.2d 883 (2d Cir.), cert. denied, 423 U.S. 837 (1975). As to evidence by accused in explanation of his flight, see People v. Davis, 193 N.E.2d 841 (Ill.1963). As to attempts by accused to commit suicide, see 7 N.C.L.Rev. 290 (1928), 1964 Wash.U.L.Q. 204, and Annot., 22 A.L.R.3d 840 (1968); People v. Butler, 90 Cal.Rptr. 497 (Cal.Ct.App.1970). Cf. Hutchins and Slesinger, Some Observations on The Law of Evidence—Consciousness of Guilt, 77 U.Pa.L.Rev. 725 (1929). See also Bush v. Jackson, 552 P.2d 509 (Colo.1976) (en banc)(consciousness of liability by disposing of property after accident); State v. Graves, 301 So.2d 864 (La. 1974)(wife's attempt to induce alibi witness to lie); People v. Haitz, 411 N.Y.S.2d 57 (4th Dept.1978)(failure to take breathalyzer test). See Hickman v. Pace, 198 A.2d 123 (N.J.Super.A.D.1964); Connolly v. Nicollet Hotel, 104 N.W.2d 721 (Minn.1960); Notes, 74 U.Pa.L.Rev. 746 (1926); 6 B.U.L.Rev. 50 (1926) regarding a party's failure to call a witness. See generally Maguire and Vincent, Admissions Implied from Spoliation or Related Conduct, 45 Yale L.J. 227 (1935).

6. *Constitutional constraints.* In Bruton v. United States, 391 U.S. 123 (1968), defendant and Evans, a co-defendant, were tried jointly. A prosecution witness testified that Evans, who never took the stand, had orally admitted his guilt, and had implicated the defendant. The trial judge instructed the jury to consider the confession only against Evans. The Supreme Court reversed defendant's conviction holding that admission of Evans' confession violated defendant's right of cross-examination secured by the confrontation clause. The Court stressed the unreliability of accomplice testimony, an "unreliability [which] is intolerably compounded when the alleged accomplice, as here, does not testify and cannot be tested by cross-examination." 391 U.S. at 136. The Court declined to treat the limiting instruction given by the trial judge as an adequate substitute for cross-examination. The Court noted, however, there was not before it any issue of Evans' statement being admissible against defendant as a recognized exception to the hearsay rule. "[W]e intimate no view whatever that such exceptions necessarily raise questions under the Confrontation Clause." 391 U.S. at 128 n. 3, See Bourjaily v. United States, infra.

Rule 14 of the Federal Rules of Criminal Procedure provides that in ruling on a motion by a defendant for a trial separate from other defendants "the court may order the attorney for the government to deliver to the court for inspection in camera any statements of confessions made at the trial." If the court orders a severance, no Bruton error can occur at trial. But suppose the court allows the joint trial to go forward. Can the confession of a non-testifying co-defendant which implicates the defendant ever be admitted without causing reversible error?

In Richardson v. Marsh, 481 U.S. 200 (1987), the Court held that a nontestifying codefendant's statement may be introduced at a joint trial if the statement does not incriminate the defendant on its face because all references to the defendant have been redacted. Under these circumstances the defendant has been adequately protected, even though the statement becomes incriminating when linked with evidence subsequently introduced, such as, in the instant case the testimony of the defendant. According to the majority, requiring separate trials in all cases of joint crimes where incriminating statements exist "would impair both the efficiency and the fairness of the criminal justice system." Id. at 210.

If, however, the statement of the nontestifying codefendant implicates the defendant on its face, Bruton mandates that it may not be admitted at a joint trial even though the statement is corroborated by the defendant's own statement which is admitted against the defendant, and the jury is instructed to consider the codefendant's statement only against the codefendant. Cruz v. New York, 481 U.S. 186, 193 (1987). The interlocking nature of the statements is, however, a factor to be considered on appeal in determining whether the Bruton violation was harmless. Id. at 194 and see Harrington v. California, 395 U.S. 250 (1969). See discussion of constitutional and harmless error at pp. 92–93.

In Cruz, supra, the Court suggested that the interlocking nature of the defendant's and codefendant's statements is a factor to be considered "in assessing whether [the] codefendant's statements are supported by sufficient 'indicia of reliability' to be directly admissible" against the defendant despite the lack of opportunity for cross-examination. 481 U.S. at 192.

NOTES ON ADOPTIVE ADMISSIONS

1. *Silence and other conduct.* If a party remains silent after he or she hears or receives a damaging statement, the statement may be admitted as an adoptive admission on the theory that the normal human reaction would have been to deny such a statement if it were untrue. What kind of foundational facts must the profferer present? In connection with the Bill case consider State v. Carlson, 808 P.2d 1002, 1005–1010 (Or.1991)(court held inadmissible as an adoptive admission defendant's nonverbal reaction—he "hung his head and shook his head back and forth"—when his wife accused him of having gotten tracks on his arms from "shooting up" and not from working on his car as defendant claimed; court noted that the record did not disclose "whether defendant's shaking his head back and forth was positive or negative in character;" under these circumstances, the court found the defendant's reaction "so ambiguous that it cannot reasonably be deemed sufficient to establish that any particular interpretation, consistent with the trial judge's ruling, is more probably correct." The court admitted the wife's statement, however, as an excited utterance.).

In cases of a continuing commercial relationship a response is normally expected. See Megarry Brothers, Inc. v. United States, 404 F.2d 479, 488 (8th Cir.1968)(failure to respond to two invoices admitted as evidence tending to show that invoices were not disputed). See also Graybar Elec. Co., Inc. v. Sawyer, 485 A.2d 1384 (Me.1985)(plaintiff sued defendant on oral personal guarantee defendant allegedly made at meeting with plaintiff's representatives; court held that since there was a presumption of receipt after proof of regular mailing, a letter referring to the guarantee which was written by plaintiff's financial manager and which defendant claimed never to have received was admissible as an adoptive admission).

The assenting-silence rationale has been illuminatingly critiqued by Goldman, S.J., in State v. Garcia, 199 A.2d 860 (N.J.Super.1964) and Musmanno, J., in Commonwealth v. Dravecz, 227 A.2d 904 (Pa.1967). See also Maguire, Adoptive Admissions in Massachusetts, 14 Mass.L.Q. # 6 p. 62 (1929); Brody, Admissions Implied From Silence, Evasion and Equivocation in Massachusetts in Criminal Cases, 42 B.U.L.Rev. 46 (1962); Gamble, The Tacit Admission Rule: Unreliable and Unconstitutional–A Doctrine Ripe for Abandonment, 14 Ga. L.Rev. 27 (1979); Gaynor, The Admission in Evidence of Statements "Made in The Presence of The Defendant", 48 J.Cr.L. & Crim. 193 (1957); Horan,

Admissibility of Declarations Made in The Presence of A Litigant, 27 Dicta 27 (1950); Heller, Admissions by Acquiescence, 15 U.Miami L.Rev. 161 (1960).

In order to constitute an admission by silence, must the statement to which the accused fails to reply be an accusation? State v. Peebles, 569 S.W.2d 1 (Mo.App.1978)(guards entered room to stop altercation and inquired as to what defendant was doing); United States v. Flecha, 539 F.2d 874 (2d Cir.1976)(statement by co-defendant to which defendant did not respond was: "If we are caught, we are caught."). Suppose the accused's response is not an express denial. See People v. Morgan, 358 N.E.2d 280 (Ill.App.1976)("How do you know I did it?"). Suppose the accused's response is a smile? See United States v. Disbrow, 768 F.2d 976 (8th Cir.1985). Suppose the defendant "just looked at . . . [the speaker], you know, like he had better hush"? State v. Hunt, 381 S.E.2d 453, 457 (N.C.1989).

Does possession of a written statement constitute an adoption of what its contents reveal? See United States v. Paulino, 13 F.3d 20, 24 (1st Cir.1994). Money order receipt that bore a misspelled version of defendant's name and notation that receipt was for May rent admitted to prove that defendant had paid the rent for the apartment in which the receipt was found for the period it was in use as a drug distribution center:

> "[P]ossession plus" can evidence adoption. Put another way, so long as the surrounding circumstances tie the possessor and the document together in some meaningful way, the possessor may be found to have adopted the writing and embraced its contents. Over and above possession, the tie is very strong here: appellant held the only known key to the apartment; he had frequented the premises; the saved document bore his name; and he was, at the very least, privy to the criminal enterprise. Consequently, the record is sufficient to permit a finding that appellant possessed and adopted, the receipt.

See also United States v. Carrillo, 16 F.3d 1046, 1048–1049 (9th Cir.1994)(defendant convicted of conspiracy to distribute more than five kilograms of cocaine; undercover agent testified that negotiations had been for 20 kilograms but that defendant had only produced 1 kilogram; court admitted unsigned, undated slip of paper found in defendant's shirt pocket that contained numbers consistent with some of the prices and quantities negotiated with the agent; defendant "manifested adoption of the statement . . . by possessing the slip of paper and negotiating sale prices and quantities for cocaine that were consistent with the figures on the slip of paper.").

2. *Statements of another.* Obviously, if a party expressly assents to the truth of a statement made by another, he is in the same position as if he had personally made the statement. The most frequent illustration of the adoption of a third person's statements which do not express what the party himself had perceived is found where the beneficiary of a life insurance policy in furnishing proofs of death attaches and incorporates, by reference or otherwise, certificates of physicians or written assertions of others. In the great majority of cases the attached documents are treated, so far as admissibility is concerned, as if they had been written by the beneficiary himself. This is particularly true of certificates of physicians. A few jurisdictions, however, refuse to receive them on the ground that the request or requirement by the insurance company that they be furnished prevents the conclusion that they were expressly adopted. See Bebbington v. California Western States Life Insurance Co., 180 P.2d 673, 1 A.L.R.2d 361 (Cal.1947), 61 Harv.L.Rev. 535 (1948). See also Wade v. Lane, 189 F.Supp. 661 (D.D.C.1960); Michael v. World Insurance Co., 254 F.2d 663 (6th Cir.1958).

See also Wagstaff v. Protective Apparel Corp. of America, 760 F.2d 1074, 1078 (10th Cir.1985)(plaintiff sued defendants for fraud in sale of distributorship to plaintiff's decedent; district court excluded as hearsay reprints of newspaper articles that plaintiff's decedent had received from defendants and which were offered to show that defendants inflated their financial situation: "This decision was incorrect ... By reprinting the newspaper articles and distributing them to persons with whom defendants were doing business, defendants unequivocally manifested their adoption of the inflated statements made in the newspaper articles."). White Industries, Inc. v. Cessna Aircraft Co., 611 F.Supp. 1049, 1062–65 (D.C.Mo.1985) contains a helpful discussion of when a business' internal use of information furnished by another constitutes an adoptive admission.

3. What is the role of the judge and jury in dealing with an adoptive admission? Is the question of adoption a preliminary question of fact for the trial judge or a question of conditional relevancy? See extensive discussion in State v. Carlson, 808 P.2d 1002, 1006–1009 (Or.1991) of courts' differing approaches. The court concludes that the jury may not hear the evidence unless the judge first finds that the proponent of the evidence established by a preponderance of the evidence that the opposing party intended "to adopt, agree with or approve of the statement." Compare United States v. Barletta, 652 F.2d 218, 219–20 (1st Cir.1981):

> [T]he "adoption" question comes within a special subclass of preliminary questions, those which present precisely the same question as an ultimate issue of fact in the case, which we think demands a different standard: to preserve the proper allocation of responsibilities between judges and juries, such questions ought to be decided by the latter. Thus the court's role in these instances is not to make a factual determination, but rather to rule as a matter of law whether a reasonable jury could properly find the ultimate fact in favor of the proponent of the evidence. Indeed, to hold otherwise—to deny the jury the possibility of making a particular factfinding simply because the court would determine the fact otherwise—might in criminal cases deprive a defendant of his Sixth Amendment right to have his case tried to a jury.

Is the court's conclusion in Barletta maintainable after the Supreme Court's decision in Bourjaily v. United States, infra?

4. Rule 806 specifically provides for the impeachment of the declarant of "a hearsay statement, or a statement defined in Rule 801(d)(2), (C), (D), or (E)." The rule does not refer to statements admitted against a party as individual or adoptive admissions under Rule 801(d)(2)(A) or (B). Suppose a prosecution witness testified that defendant admitted committing the crime or adopted someone else's statement implying his guilt. Is it fair to preclude the defendant from then impeaching himself as, for instance, by introducing prior inconsistent statements in which he denied his guilt? See Cordray, Evidence Rule 806 and the Problem of Impeaching the Nontestifying Declarant, 56 Ohio St. L.J. 495, 531–50 (1995).

5. *Constitutional constraints.* In a criminal case, the constitutional principles discussed supra at p. 463 may prohibit drawing an inference from the accused's silence. Clearly, silence which may not be used for impeachment because of constitutional restrictions may not be used as substantive evidence either. But suppose defendant's silence—such as his failure to offer an explanation for his actions—was not induced by assurances contained in Miranda warnings. Fletcher v. Weir, 455 U.S. 603 (1982) and Jenkins v. Anderson, 447 U.S. 231 (1980) hold that when no Miranda warnings were given, neither due process nor the privilege against self-incrimination prohibits use of the defendant's silence for impeachment purposes. Does this mean that the defendant's failure to tell the authorities that he had killed in self-defense can be used substantively on a consciousness of guilt theory? Justice Stevens and Stewart concurring in Jenkins would so have found. But see Friendly, J., in United States v. Caro, 637 F.2d 869, 876 (2d Cir.1981) ("[W]e are not confident that Jenkins permits ... evidence that a suspect remained silent before he was arrested or taken into custody to be used in the Government's case in chief."). On what basis can one distinguish between impeachment and substantive use? In this connection consider Judge Bazelon's opinion in Miller v. United States, 320 F.2d 767, 772 (D.C.Cir.1963) (extensive discussion of the ambiguity of flight as indicating feelings of guilt because "feelings of guilt may be present without actual guilt in so-called normal as well as neurotic people ...").

United States v. McKeon

United States Court of Appeals, Second Circuit, 1984.
738 F.2d 26.

■ WINTER, J.

. . .

BACKGROUND

On October 31, 1979, Irish police in Dublin found firearms in crates sent from New York supposedly containing electric paper drills. The alleged shipper of the crates, "Standard Tools," was a fictitious New York corporation which gave as its address a building in Queens, New York, owned by Bernard McKeon.

Officials of the United States Customs Service investigated the origin of the seized shipment and unearthed several shipping and warehousing documents relating to the shipment signed by one "John Moran." On at least one of these documents, which bore the Standard Tools letterhead, they discovered fingerprints of McKeon and his wife, Olive McKeon. After learning that McKeon owned the building given by Standard Tools as its mailing address, Customs Service agents interviewed him. McKeon told the agents that he had rented space to Standard Tools for use as a mail drop, explaining that this arrangement had been worked out after he had been approached on the street by John Moran or a party claiming to represent John Moran.

McKeon's first trial on federal firearms charges took place in December, 1982 and ended in a mistrial when the jury was unable to reach a verdict. Prior to McKeon's second trial, a government handwriting and photocopy expert concluded that warehousing and shipping documents supposedly prepared by representatives of Standard Tools, were photocopies produced on the xerox machine located in the bank in which Olive McKeon worked. The defense was apprised both of the expert's identity and his conclusions. In his opening statement at the second trial, Michael Kennedy, McKeon's lawyer[1] told the jury that the evidence would show that McKeon had innocently helped build packing crates for his tenant, John Moran, and that Moran alone was responsible for the Standard Tools' shipment of weapons. Kennedy then declared:

> With reference to the place where Olive McKeon works, expert testimony is going to be brought in to show that the Xerox machine ... where

1. Kennedy did not represent McKeon at the first trial.

Mrs. McKeon worked is not—I repeat—is not the same kind of Xerox machine that prepared any of the Standard Tools Xeroxed documents.

The evidence will also indicate that Mrs. McKeon had absolutely nothing to do with this case other than doing what many wives do, which is, picking up mail and opening it. That is the extent, the sum and substance of her involvement.

The second trial ended in a mistrial before the conclusion of the prosecution's case-in-chief when the defense moved for access to classified documents regarding alleged foreign wiretaps. As a consequence, the expert testimony promised by Kennedy in his opening statement was never offered.

Kennedy's opening statement at the third trial depicted Olive McKeon's role in the events differently than had his opening statement at the second trial. At the third trial, Kennedy told the jury that Bernard McKeon gave his wife the warehouse receipt and some Standard Tools stationery so that she might make two photocopies on the stationery using the bank's xerox machine. This was done, Kennedy said, as a favor to John Moran. He thus continued to picture Bernard McKeon as the innocent dupe of John Moran.

The next day, outside the presence of the jury, the prosecution moved to introduce as evidence the above-quoted portion of Kennedy's opening statement from the second trial. Arguing that the statement was the admission of a party-opponent under Fed.R.Evid. 801(d)(2), the prosecution suggested that it should be imputed to McKeon for any of the following reasons: (i) it was a statement in which McKeon had "manifested his adoption or belief in its truth," id. 801(d)(2)(B); (ii) it was "a statement by a person authorized by [McKeon] to make a statement concerning the subject," id. 801(d)(2)(C); and (iii) it was "a statement made by [McKeon's] agent ... concerning a matter within the scope of his agency," id. 801(d)(2)(D). The government argued that the inconsistencies in Kennedy's statements were relevant to prove McKeon's consciousness of guilt under Fed.R.Evid. 404(b). Judge Platt ruled that Kennedy's opening statement at the second trial was admissible as an admission under Rule 801(d)(2)....

As part of its case-in-chief, the government introduced the above-quoted portions of Kennedy's opening statement from the second trial. It also put on its expert witness in photocopying, James Kelly, who testified that between the second and third trials he met a former student, Jim Horan, and told him that he, Kelly, had been hired by the prosecution to testify at the third McKeon trial. Horan had been hired as the expert witness for the defense; until his meeting with Kelly, the defense had believed that the prosecution's expert witness would be one Peter Tytell, another former Kelly student. In summation, the prosecution argued that so long as the defense believed that Horan and Tytell would offer conflicting testimony about the xerox machine on which the copies were produced, it was prepared to contend that Olive McKeon did not xerox the warehouse receipt. Once it discovered that the teacher, Kelly, would dispute his pupil, Horan, at the third trial, the defense elected to present a different version of the facts—viz. that the receipt had been xeroxed by Olive McKeon at her workplace but for innocent reasons. The prosecution's summation dwelt at length on the change in stories as manifested by the opening statements, arguing that it established McKeon's consciousness of guilt.

This appeal followed McKeon's conviction on a single count of conspiracy.

DISCUSSION

1. *The Admissibility of the Opening Statement*

The parties agree that the evidentiary use against a criminal defendant of his counsel's argument to a jury in an earlier trial is without direct precedent. Although guidance is found in the rules and underlying policies of the law of evidence, the issue raises a number of difficulties since it touches upon numerous sensitive areas including: communications between criminal defendants and their attorneys, the privilege against self-incrimination, fear of impeachment by a prior conviction, the work product, legal theories and trial tactics of the attorney, the freedom of the attorney to engage in uninhibited and robust advocacy, the right to counsel of one's choice, and the usual issues of relevance, confusion and unfair prejudice as well.

We begin with the general proposition that "[s]tatements made by an attorney concerning a matter within his employment may be admissible against the party retaining the attorney," United States v. Margiotta, 662 F.2d 131, 142 (2d Cir.1981), cert. denied, 461 U.S. 913, 103 S.Ct. 1891, 77 L.Ed.2d 282 (1983), a proposition which extends to arguments to a jury. The binding effect on a party of a clear and unambiguous admission of fact made by his or her attorney in an opening statement was acknowledged by the Supreme Court in Oscanyan v. Arms Co., 103 U.S. 261, 263, 26 L.Ed. 539 (1880) and has been frequently recognized in subsequent lower court decisions involving civil cases. See, e.g., Rhoades, Inc. v. United Air Lines, 340 F.2d 481, 484 (3d Cir.1965); Collins v. Texas Company, 267 F.2d 257, 258 (5th Cir.1959). An admission by a defense attorney in his opening statement in a criminal trial has also been held to eliminate the need for further proof on a given element of an offense, Dick v. United States, 40 F.2d 609, 611 (8th Cir.1930)(attorney's opening statement that defendant previously had been convicted of an offense involving sale of liquor sufficient evidence as to that fact).

The general admissibility of an attorney's statements, as well as the binding effect of an opening statement within the four corners of a single trial, are thus well established. The specific issue before us, however, is somewhat different. It involves not the binding effect of an attorney's statements within a trial, but rather the evidentiary use against a criminal defendant of an attorney's seemingly inconsistent statement at an earlier trial to prove that fundamental portions of the defendant's present case are fabricated. Authority on this specific issue is scant, although in at least one civil action it has been suggested that while a previous opening statement is not binding on a litigant, the statement can, under certain circumstances be considered by the trier of fact.[2] Beyer Co. v. Fleischmann Co., 15 F.2d 465, 466 (6th Cir.1926).

We believe that prior opening statements are not *per se* inadmissible in criminal cases. To hold otherwise would not only invite abuse and sharp practice but would also weaken confidence in the justice system itself by denying the function of trials as truth-seeking proceedings. That function cannot be affirmed if parties are free, wholly without explanation, to make fundamental changes in the version of facts within their personal knowledge between trials and to conceal these changes from the final trier of fact.

Support for this conclusion may be found in the analogous issue of the admissibility of superseded pleadings in civil litigation. The law is quite clear that such pleadings constitute the admissions of a party-opponent and are

2. A distinction is generally recognized between an attorney's judicial admissions, which, like any stipulation, can bind a party within a given lawsuit, and an attorney's less formal evidentiary admissions, which are statements made as a party's agent and which the trier of fact may evaluate as it sees fit. Note, Judicial Admissions, 64 Colum.L.Rev. 1121, 1121 (1964). We are of course concerned only with evidentiary admissions since no one claims that the opening statement from the second trial estopped McKeon from claiming that his wife had photocopied the receipts at his request.

admissible in the case in which they were originally filed as well as in any subsequent litigation involving that party. Contractor Utility Sales Co. v. Certain–Teed Products Corp., 638 F.2d 1061, 1084 (7th Cir.1981); Raulie v. United States, 400 F.2d 487, 526 (10th Cir.1968); D. McCormick, Handbook of the Law of Evidence 633–36 (2d ed.1972). A party thus cannot advance one version of the facts in its pleadings, conclude that its interests would be better served by a different version, and amend its pleadings to incorporate that version, safe in the belief that the trier of fact will never learn of the change in stories. . . . Although we by no means equate the admissibility of inconsistent pleadings with the admissibility of inconsistent opening statements, we believe the analogy is correct insofar as consideration of whether a *per se* rule against the admission of the latter exists.[3]

We conclude, therefore, that there is no absolute rule preventing use of an earlier opening statement by counsel as an admission against a criminal defendant in a subsequent trial. We are not willing, however, to subject such statements to the more expansive practices sometimes permitted under the rule allowing use of admissions by a party-opponent. The rule itself has caused a substantial expenditure of ink by legal commentators seeking a coherent doctrinal theory explaining the use of admissions, D. McCormick, supra at 628–31, and has resulted in "a lengthy academic dispute in which most courts have evinced little interest." 4 J. Weinstein & M. Berger, Evidence 801–135 (rev. perm.ed. 1981).

Although we share that lack of interest, we note that the admissions rule is itself something of an anomaly since it is in some respects an exception to the general proposition that probative value and reliability are the touchstone of the law of evidence where non-privileged matters are concerned. Admissions may thus be used even though the statement was plainly self-serving when made, was not based upon the personal knowledge of the speaker and is in a form which would otherwise be inadmissible. D. McCormick, supra at 631–33; J. Weinstein & M. Berger, supra at 801–136. Why probative value and reliability carry so little weight in the case of the admissions rule is not clear, particularly since the use of admissions may be the trial equivalent of a deadly weapon. In all probability, these aspects of the rule are derived vestigially from an older, rough and ready view of the adversary process which leaves each party to bear the consequences of its own acts, no matter how unreliable these acts may be as proof. Whatever its derivation, however, we conclude that the evidentiary use of prior jury argument must be circumscribed in order to avoid trenching upon other important policies.

First, the free use of prior jury argument might consume substantial time to pursue marginal matters. Some witnesses may be available only at one trial, their testimony may change or other evidence may differ. Trial tactics may also change because of the earlier trial. If prior jury argument may be freely used for evidentiary purposes, later triers of fact will be forced to explore the evidence offered at earlier trials in order to determine the quality of the inconsistency between positions taken by a party. This will result in a substan-

---

3. This principle is not inconsistent with the long-established federal rule that a withdrawn guilty plea is not admissible in subsequent civil or criminal proceedings. Fed. R.Evid. 410; Kercheval v. United States, 274 U.S. 220, 47 S.Ct. 582, 71 L.Ed. 1009 (1927). The Kercheval rule is intended to permit a criminal defendant to exercise his right to a trial without imposing on that right conditions which make its exercise meaningless, id. at 224, 47 S.Ct. at 583. A criminal defendant's right to a trial does not carry with it a right to present in multiple trials contradictory versions of the facts that vary according to the nature of the prosecution's case.

tial loss of time on marginal issues, diversion from the real issues and exposure to evidence which may be otherwise inadmissible and prejudicial.

Second, inferences drawn from an inconsistency in arguments to a jury may be unfair. In criminal cases, the burden rests on the government to present a coherent version of the facts, and defense counsel may legitimately emphasize the weaker aspects of the government's case. Where successive trials occur, the evidentiary use of earlier arguments before the jury may lead to seemingly plausible but quite prejudicial inferences. A jury hearing that in the first trial defense counsel emphasized the weakness of the prosecution's case as to the defendant's criminal intent, may well, when lack of proof of identity is argued at the second, be misled as to the government's obligation to prove all the elements at both trials.

Third, the free use of prior jury argument may deter counsel from vigorous and legitimate advocacy. Argument to the jury is a crucial aspect of any trial, and the truth-seeking process itself demands that the professional adversaries be allowed to put before the trier of fact all relevant argument regarding the inferences or factual conclusions possible in a particular case. Counsel should not, except when the truth-seeking purpose clearly demands otherwise, be deterred from legitimate argument by apprehension about arguments made to a jury in an earlier trial.

Fourth, where an innocent factual explanation of a seeming inconsistency created by the prior opening statement exists, the offer of that explanation may seriously affect other rights of the defense. Where the explanation may be offered to the trier of fact only through the defendant as a witness, the defendant may have to choose between forgoing the explanation or facing the introduction of a prior criminal record for impeachment purposes and waiver of the attorney-client privilege. Even if defense counsel can offer the explanation in a hearing under Fed.R.Evid. 104(a) outside the presence of the jury, that offer may expose work product, trial tactics or legal theories to the prosecution. These Hobson's choices may thus seriously impair the defense.

Fifth, as is clear from our disposition of this case, the admissibility of a prior opening statement may lead to the disqualification of counsel chosen by the defendant, a most serious consequence.

For these reasons, we circumscribe the evidentiary use of prior jury argument. Before permitting such use, the district court must be satisfied that the prior argument involves an assertion of fact inconsistent with similar assertions in a subsequent trial. Speculations of counsel, advocacy as to the credibility of witnesses, arguments as to weaknesses in the prosecution's case or invitations to a jury to draw certain inferences should not be admitted. The inconsistency, moreover, should be clear and of a quality which obviates any need for the trier of fact to explore other events at the prior trial. The court must further determine that the statements of counsel were such as to be the equivalent of testimonial statements by the defendant. The formal relationship of the lawyer as agent and the client as principal by itself will rarely suffice to show this since, while clients authorize their attorneys to act on their behalf, considerable delegation is normally involved and such delegation tends to drain the evidentiary value from such statements. Some participatory role of the client must be evident, either directly or inferentially as when the argument is a direct assertion of fact which in all probability had to have been confirmed by the defendant.

Finally, the district court should, in a Fed.R.Evid. 104(a) hearing outside the presence of the jury, determine by a preponderance of the evidence that the inference the prosecution seeks to draw from the inconsistency is a fair one and that an innocent explanation for the inconsistency does not exist. Where the evidence is in equipoise or the preponderance favors an innocent explanation, the prior opening statement should be excluded. We impose this requirement so as to allow leeway for advocacy and to lessen the burden of choice between the defendant's not explaining the inconsistency to the jury or sacrificing other valuable rights. Moreover, where the attorney-client privilege, the privilege against self-incrimination, the fear of impeachment by a prior conviction, apprehension over having to change attorneys, the revelation of work product, trial tactics, or legal theories of defense counsel may be involved in explaining the changes in the defendant's version of events, the court should offer an opportunity to the defense to present those reasons in camera, outside the presence of the jury and of the prosecution. In camera hearings are permitted where the government seeks to use grand jury testimony to overcome the attorney-client privilege or work product immunity, In re John Doe Corp., 675 F.2d 482, 489–91 (2d Cir.1982), and similar considerations apply in the present circumstances.

Applying these principles to the present case, we conclude that the prior opening statement was properly admitted against McKeon under Fed.R.Evid. 801(d)(2)(B) and (C). The expert testimony about the xerox machine promised by Kennedy in the opening statement at the second trial was in support of a factual claim that Olive McKeon had not copied the documents. Kennedy's opening argument at the third trial, stating that Olive McKeon had indeed copied the documents at the request of her husband, was facially and irreconcilably at odds with the earlier assertion.

This inconsistency was not the result of differences in the evidence at the trials over which the defendant had no control or even of the behavior of a neutral witness.[4] An expert witness such as that promised by Kennedy differs from an ordinary witness in that the expert has no personal knowledge of the events underlying the lawsuit and is hired only after the relevant events occur. We have no reason to believe that McKeon's expert was not selected by McKeon's counsel with a view to the content of the testimony he would give, namely, testimony supporting the version in which Olive McKeon did not xerox the documents. The truth of this version of the facts was on a matter within McKeon's personal knowledge and which went to the heart of his defense. Absent some explanation to the trial judge, there was every reason to believe that McKeon participated in the development of trial strategy regarding this issue at both trials. He may reasonably be said, therefore, to have manifested a belief in the differing versions of the facts, Fed.R.Evid. 801(d)(2)(B), and to have authorized Kennedy to present them at trial. Fed.R.Evid. 801(d)(2)(C).

The offer of the expert testimony was a calculated act factually inconsistent with the version of events offered at the third trial. McKeon did not stand mute and put the government to its proof at the last trial. Rather, the defense offered the new version of the facts relating to the xeroxing of the documents at the very outset of trial. Having affirmatively opened the issue, McKeon had no more right to keep the later jury ignorant of the fact that he had earlier hired and promised another jury expert testimony supporting a different version of

---

4. A defendant is free to call witnesses who have personal knowledge of material facts even though the defendant believes the witness is mistaken, so long as the witness is believed to be testifying in good faith. A defendant is also free not to call in a subsequent trial a witness who previously testified without an unfavorable inference being drawn. Indeed, under Fed.R.Evid. 607, a party may impeach a witness he or she has called, in recognition of the fact that parties have to take their witnesses as they find them.

the facts than he would have had to preclude it from learning of inconsistent testimony he himself had given.

We thus conclude that the circumstances described above amply support an inference that the offer of expert testimony on the use of the bank's xerox machine may be regarded as the equivalent of a testimonial statement by McKeon that he did not ask his wife to copy the documents. They further support an inference that, knowing the expert's testimony was weak because it was untrue and would now be challenged by the expert's instructor, McKeon fabricated a new version of events. Absent an explanation for the radically different version of the facts offered at the third trial, we believe that Judge Platt had little choice but to admit the prior opening statement as evidence of fabrication demonstrating consciousness of guilt. No such explanation was proffered even though Judge Platt offered an *in camera* hearing on the reasons for the new version of events. If an innocent explanation for the inconsistency existed, but McKeon's counsel was unwilling to reveal it in open court for reasons explained above, this offer gave him ample opportunity to apprise the trial judge of that explanation without risk of a waiver of McKeon's rights or exposure of work product, trial tactics or legal theories.

NOTES ON AUTHORIZED ADMISSIONS

1. In United States v. GAF Corporation, 928 F.2d 1253, 1260 (2d Cir.1991), the court relied on McKeon to reverse a security fraud conviction because the trial court refused to admit evidence that the government's version of the facts had shifted. Before the first trial, the government filed a bill of particulars which detailed October and November trades that the government viewed as fraudulent transactions. The first trial ended in a deadlocked jury. At the second trial, defendants argued that since there was reasonable doubt about a particular defendant's responsibility for the November trades there was also reasonable doubt about who was responsible for the October purchases. The jury deadlocked again. Between the second and the third trial, the government amended its bill of particulars to include only the October transactions. At the third trial, the trial judge refused to allow defendants to introduce the original bill of particulars. In response to defendants' argument that the November trades were identical to the October trades and that defendants were not responsible for the November trades, the government replied that the November trades were a "smokescreen." In reversing the court explained:

> We think that the same considerations of fairness and maintaining the integrity of the truth-seeking function of trials that led this Court to find that opening statements of counsel and prior pleadings constitute admissions also require that a prior inconsistent bill of particulars be considered an admission by the government in an appropriate situation. Although the government is not bound by what it previously has claimed its proof will show any more than a party which amends its complaint is bound by its prior claims, the jury is at least entitled to know that the government at one time believed and stated, that its proof established something different from what it currently claims. Confidence in the justice system cannot be affirmed if any party is free, wholly without explanation, to make a fundamental change in its version of the facts between trials, and then conceal this change from the final trier of the facts ... A bill of particulars ... is prepared, reviewed, and presented by an agent of the United States ... [E]vidence that the government itself once possessed the view that the October and November trades were linked is certainly relevant to the defense.

For a detailed analysis of the McKeon and GAF decisions, see Mansfield, Evidential Use of the Litigation Activity of the Parties, 43 Syracuse L.Rev. 695, 707–22 (1992).

2. What effect does the attorney client privilege have on the admissibility of an attorney's statement as an authorized admission? See Transcript of Motion in United States v. Biaggi, No. CR 87 151 (E.D.N.Y. July 8, 1987), pp. 2–4, 6, 11–12:

THE COURT: Where is Mr. Slotnick?

MR. MC DONALD: He was in the courtroom a few moments ago.

THE COURT: You'd better get him. He's Hamlet on this motion.

I will hear the Government in connection with the Slotnick matter.

MR. MC DONALD: We believe that the statement that Mr. Slotnick made on January 6, 1987 is admissible on the basis of three provisions in the Federal Rules of Evidence. Sections 801 B, C and D.

Under B, a statement in which a party has manifested his adoption is an admissible statement, when made by another.

Under C, a statement made by a person authorized by the party to make that statement is admissible, and

Under D, a statement made by an agent making the statement about a matter within the scope of his employment at the time that he was an agent is admissible.

I think the facts of this case as demonstrated in the affidavit which we've submitted before, your Honor, and also on the basis of the facts stated by Mr. Slotnick in his affidavit and the affidavit of Mr. Biaggi, show that, one, the statement was authorized by Mario Biaggi, two, that Mr. Slotnick was an agent making a statement about a matter in the scope of his employment during that employment and, three, that Mr. Biaggi on the basis of all the circumstances considered in their entirety manifested his adoption of Mr. Slotnick's statement.

. . .

MR. SLOTNICK: Most respectfully, we'd suggest to the court based upon the documents submitted, there is no manifested adoption by the defendant with regard to the statement made of someone who appears as his attorney and someone who appears before a television camera at 9:30 at night and makes statements that are clearly, one, unauthorized and, two, not within the scope of his employment as an attorney.

THE COURT: . . . You claim that you are not acting as his attorney when you make these statements? What are you acting as, his public relations specialist?

MR. SLOTNICK: I think quite clearly those statements were in the vain of a public relations area, yes.

THE COURT: All right, if you take that position you understand that whatever you said to him or he said to you about these events will not come within the attorney-client privilege. Do you appreciate the road you are taking?

. . .

MR. SLOTNICK: My position is a simple one. I did—the reason that WNBC came to my office was not because of the fact that I was a friend of

Mario Biaggi or retained to be his public relations counsel, because I was his lawyer.

. . .

THE COURT: If you were an attorney, then there is a more serious question about a waiver. I myself think that it's highly probable that you'll be a witness at this trial, I'm willing under 403—Rule 403 to consider forcing the Government not to bring you into the case in the opening, referring only to the admissions of your client and not putting it in as part of its direct case, until it sees and we see how the case developes [sic], what you said publically [sic] and what your client said to you, and what you said to your client. If I rule that there has been a waiver of the attorney-client privilege, we're dealing with very serious problems here and there is simply no room for offhand, ill-considered, baseless statements by attorneys to the media. And your affidavits and brief suggest that this is the kind of statement that we're dealing with.

. . .

MR. SLOTNICK: It's our position respectfully and I respect the Court's statement. The statement that I made, Judge, based upon what you just said only shores up our position as an unauthorized statement—

THE COURT: That may be so. Then we're going to have a problem because your client may have to take the stand and you may have to take the stand and we're going to have inquiry whether it was authorized or unauthorized.

I believe the two affidavits arguably constitute a waiver of the attorney-client privilege.

3. *Admissions in judicial proceedings*

Superseded pleadings. As the principal case indicates, superseded pleadings qualify as admissions of a party-opponent. Must a court admit the prior pleadings, or does it have discretion to exclude? In Vincent v. Louis Marx & Co., 874 F.2d 36, 40 (1st Cir.1989), the plaintiff's complaint in a now-settled state court action alleged that the defendant driver did or should have had a clear view of plaintiff on her tricycle. The federal trial court stated it felt bound to admit this complaint in an action against the manufacturer of the tricycle which claimed that the tricycle was constructed too low to the ground to be seen by approaching motorists. After surveying the case law, the appellate court vacated a verdict for the defendant and remanded to the district court for reconsideration:

> Considering the disparate approaches to this issue, we are not disposed to lay down a flat rule admitting or excluding inconsistent allegations in a prior pleading. We think that the initial decision should be left to the discretion of the trial judge under Fed.R.Evid. 403. We have been unable to find any case holding that Fed.R.Evid. 403 cannot be invoked on this evidentiary issue. In light of the uncertain state of the law on the admissibility of prior inconsistent pleadings, this would appear to be the type of question that calls for the balancing approach under Fed.R.Evid. 403.

Compare Andrews v. Metro North Commuter RR. Co., 882 F.2d 705, 706–07 (2d Cir.1989)(grossly intoxicated plaintiff who was struck by train originally alleged that defendants failed to keep a proper lookout, to keep train under proper control, to give sufficient warnings; his amended complaint alleged that he had fallen from a railroad platform because of defective condition of platform and was struck by train because he could not get back on platform; court held that "district court's refusal to permit jurors to be informed of the amendment and to examine the original complaint was a substantial abuse of discretion.") To what extent should it matter that the pleading is offered in a different action rather than in the same action?

For a helpful discussion of when allegations are inconsistent and admissible, rather than hypothetical or alternative, as permitted by modern pleading rules, and inadmissible, see Dugan v. EMS Helicopters, Inc., 915 F.2d 1428, 1431–35 (10th Cir.1990)(plaintiffs asserted that the defendants were solely responsible; in state court action they had alleged that other defendants had contributed to the accident in question; reversible error not to admit prior pleadings about other defendants' negligence; court noted that evidence was relevant not only to the allocation of fault but also to the existence and amount of punitive damages).

Is the pleading admissible even if it is not verified, or if the inconsistency can be explained? See Contractor Utility Sales Co., Inc. v. Certain–Teed Products Corp., 638 F.2d 1061 (7th Cir.1981). See also Williams v. Union Carbide Corp., 790 F.2d 552, 556 (6th Cir.)("Absent unauthorized conduct on the part of the attorney, there is nothing unfair about having to explain one's past lawsuits."), cert. denied, 479 U.S. 992 (1986).

Briefs. Should briefs be analogized to pleadings or be treated with the sort of caution that McKeon suggests for opening statements? See Hardy v. Johns–Manville Sales Corp., 851 F.2d 742, 745 (5th Cir.1988)("Because appellate briefs must of necessity refer to what the record reflects as distinguished from what the real world facts actually are, and because these two sets of facts are not necessarily identical (indeed, they may well diverge at crucial junctures), using statements about record facts as substantive evidence, i.e., to establish the truth of the matter asserted in those statements, is bound to be uncertain in the best of circumstances and dangerously misleading in most others. Further, allowing in evidence, as party admissions, statements in appellate briefs has a special danger of creating jury confusion, because appellate briefs address the facts shown by the record below only as they are relevant to the specific legal questions presented by that particular appeal."), cert. denied, 504 U.S. 955 (1992); Dartez v. Owens–Illinois, Inc., 910 F.2d 1291 (5th Cir.1990)(extending Hardy to post-trial briefs); Kassel v. Gannett Co., Inc., 875 F.2d 935 (1st Cir.1989)(in libel action by VA psychologist against newspaper alleging that libelous article led to an involuntary job transfer, trial court erred in excluding a pro se brief filed in a labor grievance proceeding against the VA in which plaintiff stated that the article was a pretext as the VA had wanted to get rid of him long before it was written; court granted new trial on damages).

Guilty pleas. The rationale for excluding evidence that an initial plea of guilty has been superseded by a plea of not guilty is discussed at pp. 944–47 infra. See Federal Rule 410.

4. Federal Rule 801(d)(1)(C) provides that a statement that is offered against a party is not hearsay if it is "a statement by a person authorized by the party to make a statement concerning the subject." Compare this formulation which requires an agent to have "speaking authority" with the broader wording of Rule 801(d)(1)(D) which is considered below at pp. 582–89.

Problems of whether an agent is authorized to speak for his principal arise in many different contexts. See, for example, Carter v. Public Service Coordinated Transport, 136 A.2d 15 (N.J.Super.1957)(bus driver); Partin v. Great Atlantic & Pacific Tea Co., 149 A.2d 860 (N.H.1959)(store manager); Griffiths v. Big Bear Stores, Inc., 347 P.2d 532 (Wash.1959)(same); Mann v. Safeway

Stores, Inc., 518 P.2d 1194 (Idaho 1974)(grocery checker); McDonnell v. Montgomery Ward & Co., 154 A.2d 469 (Vt.1959) (manager of service department); Presidential Life Insurance Co. v. Calhoun, 325 S.W.2d 732 (Tex.Civ.App.1959)(corporate officer); Killen v. Brazosport Memorial Hospital, 364 S.W.2d 411 (Tex.Civ.App.1963)(doctor); McNerney v. New York Polyclinic Hospital, 238 N.Y.S.2d 729 (N.Y.App.Div.1963)(same); Southern Ry. Co. v. Birmingham, 122 So.2d 599 (Ala.1960)(city attorney); Collins v. Wayne Corp., 621 F.2d 777 (5th Cir.1980) (expert hired by party; reviews cases); People v. Tucker, 156 N.E.2d 873 (Ill.App.1959), cert. denied, 362 U.S. 950 (1960) (inmate of house of ill-fame); United States v. Draiman, 784 F.2d 248, 256–57 (7th Cir.1986)(accountant); United States v. DaSilva, 725 F.2d 828 (2d Cir. 1983)

May the agency of the alleged agent be established by his own declarations? May such declarations be used to establish that he was acting within the scope of his employment? See Kapelski v. Alton & Southern Railroad, 343 N.E.2d 207 (Ill.App.1976); Austin v. Gulf States Finance Co., 308 So.2d 90 (Miss.1975).

May statements made within the scope of authority but only to the principal himself be admitted? See, e.g., Big Mack Trucking Co., Inc. v. Dickerson, 497 S.W.2d 283, 287 (Tex.1973) (two employees of Big Mack, each driving a tractor-trailer, stopped and parked; L left his vehicle which rolled forward and crushed the other driver who had gotten out of his truck; in the ensuing wrongful death action, a Big Mack vice-president testified that L told him after the accident that he had been having air pressure problems (in which case he should not have parked without taking special precautions); court found reversible error: "If there be any special facts to show that Big Mack authorized [L] to speak to the world as well as to [the vice-president], those facts have not been introduced . . ."). Compare Kingsley v. Baker/Beech–Nut Corp., 546 F.2d 1136, 1141 (5th Cir.1977):

> [W]e must initially determine whether Baker/Beech–Nut had authorized Jackson to make statements about terminating Kingsley's employment. Trial evidence established that Jackson was Kingsley's superior within the Baker/Beech–Nut Sales Division, that Jackson was responsible for appraising Kingsley's work, and that Jackson reported these evaluations to his superiors who in turn acted upon them. It is clear, therefore, that Jackson had the authority from Baker/Beech–Nut to make the statements quoted from his telephone conversation. Since the proof did not conclusively establish to whom Jackson was speaking during his telephone conversation, the further question arises whether Rule 801(d)(2)(C) is phrased broadly. We construe it to encompass both type of statements.

Mahlandt v. Wild Canid Survival & Research Center, Inc.

United States Court of Appeals, Eighth Circuit, 1978.
588 F.2d 626.

■ VAN SICKLE, DISTRICT JUDGE.

This is a civil action for damages arising out of an alleged attack by a wolf on a child. The sole issues on appeal are as to the correctness of three rulings which excluded conclusionary statements against interest. Two of them were made by a defendant, who was also an employee of the corporate defendant; and the third was in the form of a statement appearing in the records of a board meeting of the corporate defendant.

On March 23, 1973, Daniel Mahlandt, then 3 years, 10 months, and 8 days old, was sent by his mother to a neighbor's home on an adjoining street to get his older brother, Donald. Daniel's mother watched him cross the street, and then turned into the house to get her car keys. Daniel's path took him along a walkway adjacent to the Poos' residence. Next to the walkway was a five foot chain link fence to which Sophie had been chained with a six foot chain. In other words, Sophie was free to move in a half circle having a six foot radius on the side of the fence opposite from Daniel.

Sophie was a bitch wolf, 11 months and 28 days old, who had been born at the St. Louis Zoo, and kept there until she reached 6 months of age, at which time she was given to the Wild Canid Survival and Research Center, Inc. It was the policy of the Zoo to remove wolves from the Children's Zoo after they reached the age of 5 or 6 months. Sophie was supposed to be kept at the Tyson Research Center, but Kenneth Poos, as Director of Education for the Wild Canid Survival and Research Center, Inc., had been keeping her at his home because he was taking Sophie to schools and institutions where he showed films and gave programs with respect to the nature of wolves. Sophie was known as a very gentle wolf who had proved herself to be good natured and stable during her contacts with thousands of children, while she was in the St. Louis Children's Zoo.

Sophie was chained because the evening before she had jumped the fence and attacked a beagle who was running along the fence and yapping at her.

A neighbor who was ill in bed in the second floor of his home heard a child's screams and went to his window, where he saw a boy lying on his back within the enclosure, with a wolf straddling him. The wolf's face was near Daniel's face, but the distance was so great that he could not see what the wolf was doing, and did not see any biting. Within about 15 seconds the neighbor saw Clarke Poos, about seventeen, run around the house, get the wolf off the boy, and disappear with the child in his arms to the back of the house. Clarke took the boy in and laid him on the kitchen floor.

Clarke had been returning from his friend's home immediately west when he heard a child's cries and ran around to the enclosure. He found Daniel lying within the enclosure, about three feet from the fence, and Sophie standing back from the boy the length of her chain, and wailing. An expert in the behavior of wolves stated that when a wolf licks a child's face that it is a sign of care, and not a sign of attack; that a wolf's wail is a sign of compassion, and an effort to get attention, not a sign of attack. No witness saw or knew how Daniel was injured. Clarke and his sister ran over to get Daniel's mother. She says that Clarke told her, "a wolf got Danny and he is dying." Clarke denies that statement. The defendant, Mr. Poos, arrived home while Daniel and his mother were in the kitchen. After Daniel was taken in an ambulance, Mr. Poos talked to everyone present, including a neighbor who came in. Within an hour after he arrived home, Mr. Poos went to Washington University to inform Owen Sexton, President of Wild Canid Survival and Research Center, Inc., of the incident. Mr. Sexton was not in his office so Mr. Poos left the following note on his door:

> Owen, would call me at home, 727–5080? Sophie bit a child that came in our back yard. All has been taken care of. I need to convey what happened to you. (Exhibit 11)

Denial of admission of this note is one of the issues on appeal.

Later that day, Mr. Poos found Mr. Sexton at the Tyson Research Center and told him what had happened. Denial of plaintiff's offer to prove that Mr.

Poos told Mr. Sexton that, "Sophie had bit a child that day," is the second issue on appeal.

A meeting of the Directors of the Wild Canid Survival and Research Center, Inc., was held on April 4, 1973. Mr. Poos was not present at that meeting. The minutes of that meeting reflect that there was a "great deal of discussion ... about the legal aspects of the incident of Sophie biting the child." Plaintiff offered an abstract of the minutes containing that reference. Denial of the offer of that abstract is the third issue on appeal.

Daniel had lacerations of the face, left thigh, left calf, and right thigh, and abrasions and bruises of the abdomen and chest. Mr. Mahlandt was permitted to state that Daniel had indicated that he had gone under the fence. Mr. Mahlandt and Mr. Poos, about a month after the incident, examined the fence to determine what caused Daniel's lacerations. Mr. Mahlandt felt that they did not look like animal bites. The parallel scars on Daniel's thigh appeared to match the configuration of the barbs or tines on the fence. The expert as to the behavior of wolves opined that the lacerations were not wolf bites or wounds caused by wolf claws. Wolves have powerful jaws and a wolf bite will result in massive crushing or severing of a limb. He stated that if Sophie had bitten Daniel there would have been clear opposition of teeth and massive crushing of Daniel's hands and arms which were not injured. Also, if Sophie had pulled Daniel under the fence, tooth marks on the foot or leg would have been present, although Sophie possessed enough strength to pull the boy under the fence.

The jury brought in a verdict for the defense.

The trial judge's rationale for excluding the note, the statement, and the corporate minutes, was the same in each case. He reasoned that Mr. Poos did not have any personal knowledge of the facts, and accordingly, the first two admissions were based on hearsay; and the third admission contained in the minutes of the board meeting was subject to the same objection of hearsay, and unreliability because of lack of personal knowledge.

. . .

... [T]he statement in the note pinned on the door is not hearsay, and is admissible against Mr. Poos. It was his own statement, and as such was clearly different from the reported statement of another. Example, "I was told that...." See Cedeck v. Hamiltonian Fed. Sav. & L. Ass'n., 551 F.2d 1136 (8th Cir.1977). It was also a statement of which he had manifested his adoption or belief in its truth. And the same observations may be made of the statement made later in the day to Mr. Sexton, that "Sophie had bit a child...."

Are these statements admissible against Wild Canid Survival and Research Center, Inc.? They were made by Mr. Poos when he was an agent or servant of the Wild Canid Survival and Research Center, Inc., and they concerned a matter within the scope of his agency, or employment, i.e., his custody of Sophie, and were made during the existence of that relationship.

Defendant argues that Rule 801(d)(2) does not provide for the admission of "in house" statements; that is, it allows only admissions made to third parties.

The notes of the Advisory Committee on the Proposed Rules (28 U.S.C.A., Volume on Federal Rules of Evidence, Rule 801, p. 527 at p. 530), discuss the problem of "in house" admissions with reference to Rule 801(d)(2)(C) situations. This is not a (C) situation because Mr. Poos was not authorized or directed to make a statement on the matter by anyone. But the rationale developed in that comment does apply to this (D) situation. Mr. Poos had actual physical custody of Sophie. His conclusions, his opinions, were obviously accepted as a basis for action by his principal. See minutes of corporate meeting. As the Advisory Committee points out in its note on (C) situations.

> ... communication to an outsider has not generally been thought to be an essential characteristic of an admission. Thus a party's books or records are usable against him, without regard to any intent to disclose to third persons. V Wigmore on Evidence § 1557.

[J. Weinstein and M. Berger, Weinstein's Evidence ¶ 801(d)(2)(D)[01]], states that:

> Rule 801(d)(2)(D) adopts the approach ... which, as a general proposition, makes statement made by agents within the scope of their employment admissible.... Once agency, and the making of the statement while the relationship continues, are established, the statement is exempt from the hearsay rule so long as it relates to a matter within the scope of the agency.

After reciting a lengthy quotation which justifies the rule as necessary, and suggests that such admissions are trustworthy and reliable, Weinstein states categorically that although an express requirement of personal knowledge on the part of the declarant of the facts underlying his statement is not written into the rule, it should be. He feels that is mandated by Rules 805 and 403.

Rule 805 recites, in effect, that a statement containing hearsay within hearsay is admissible if each part of the statement falls within an exception to the hearsay rule. Rule 805, however, deals only with hearsay exceptions. A statement based on the personal knowledge of the declarant of facts underlying his statement is not the repetition of the statement of another, thus not hearsay. It is merely opinion testimony. Rule 805 cannot mandate the implied condition desired by Judge Weinstein.

Rule 403 provides for the exclusion of relevant evidence if its probative value is substantially outweighed by the danger of unfair prejudice, confusion of the issues, or misleading the jury, or by consideration of undue delay, waste of time, or needless presentation of cumulative evidence. Nor does Rule 403 mandate the implied condition desired by Judge Weinstein.

Thus, while both Rule 805 and Rule 403 provide additional bases for excluding otherwise acceptable evidence, neither rule mandates the introduction into Rule 801(d)(2)(D) of an implied requirement that the declarant have personal knowledge of the facts underlying his statement. So we conclude that the two statements made by Mr. Poos were admissible against Wild Canid Survival and Research Center, Inc.

As to the entry in the records of a corporate meeting, the directors as primary officers of the corporation had the authority to include their conclusions in the record of the meeting. So the evidence would fall within 801(d)(2)(C) as to Wild Canid Survival and Research Center, Inc., and be admissible. The "in house" aspect of this admission has already been discussed, Rule 801(d)(2)(D), supra.

But there was no servant, or agency, relationship which justified admitting the evidence of the board minutes as against Mr. Poos.

None of the conditions of 801(d)(2) cover the claim that minutes of a corporate board meeting can be used against a non-attending, non-participating employee of that corporation. The evidence was not admissible as against Mr. Poos.

There is left only the question of whether the trial court's rulings which excluded all three items of evidence are justified under Rule 403. He clearly found that the evidence was not reliable, pointing out that none of the statements were based on the personal knowledge of the declarant.

Again, that problem was faced by the Advisory Committee on Proposed Rules. In its discussion of 801(d)(2) exceptions to the hearsay rule, the Committee said:

> The freedom which admissions have enjoyed from technical demands of searching for an assurance of trustworthiness in some against-interest circumstances, and from the restrictive influences of the opinion rule and the rule requiring first hand knowledge, when taken with the apparently prevalent satisfaction with the results, calls for generous treatment of this avenue to admissibility. 28 U.S.C.A., Volume of Federal Rules of Evidence, Rule 801, p. 527, at p. 530.

So here, remembering that relevant evidence is usually prejudicial to the cause of the side against which it is presented, and that the prejudice which concerns us is unreasonable prejudice; and applying the spirit of Rule 801(d)(2), we hold that Rule 403 does not warrant the exclusion of the evidence of Mr. Poos' statements as against himself or Wild Canid Survival and Research Center, Inc.

But the limited admissibility of the corporate minutes, coupled with the repetitive nature of the evidence and the low probative value of the minute record, all justify supporting the judgment of the trial court under Rule 403.

The judgment of the District Court is reversed and the matter remanded to the District Court for a new trial consistent with this opinion.

NOTES ON VICARIOUS ADMISSIONS

1. Under the common law, the admission of declarations by a joint obligor or obligee, or by a joint tenant offered against another joint tenant, or by a predecessor in title against a successor was often justified on the ground of privity. For instance, see Bailey v. Chicago Burlington & Quincy Railroad Co., 179 N.W.2d 560 (Iowa 1970) discussing when evidence of decedent's statements are admissible against plaintiff in an action for wrongful death. Compare Huff v. White Motor Corp., 609 F.2d 286 (7th Cir.1979). Federal Rules 801(d)(2)(D) rejects privity as a ground of admissibility by making no provision for it, thereby adopting the view of Morgan who had railed against "the ignis fatuus of privity." Morgan, Admissions, 12 Wash.L.Rev. 181, 203 (1937). See also Morgan, The Rationale of Vicarious Admissions, 42 Harv.L.Rev. 461 (1929). But see Falknor, Hearsay, 1969 Law & The Social Order 591, 604 ("I have a lingering doubt. It is true that there is no 'magic' in privity, so far as trustworthiness is concerned. But is there any more 'magic' in the mere fact of agency, so far as the trustworthiness of agents' declarations are concerned? . . . In other words, what gives to 'agency' any more significance than 'privity'? If privity as a ground of admissibility is an ignis fatuus, is not the fact of representation alone, as a ground of admissibility, similarly a misleading notion?").

2. In United States v. Valencia, 826 F.2d 169 (2d Cir.1987), the court held that a statement made by an attorney during informal conversations with a prosecutor in his efforts to secure bail for his client would not be admissible pursuant to Rule 801(d)(2)(C). After an extensive discussion of the McKeon case, supra p. 572, the court found that the district court had not exceeded its discretion in finding that the statement should not be admitted pursuant to Rule 801(d)(2)(D) either:

Unlike an opening statement, which is transcribed, or a written pleading, the statements of Maloney would have to be proved through the testimony of a person who heard them, thereby generating dispute as to precisely what was said. Moreover, a pleading or an opening statement to a jury is more likely to be worded with precision than informal remarks made during discussions with a prosecutor.

Second, unlike McKeon, the admission of Maloney's statements would pose some threat to chilling the prospects for plea negotiations . . .

Third, as we noted in McKeon, the opening statement was offered in that case to counter a position taken by the defense at the retrial that was directly inconsistent with the position set forth in the prior jury argument. By contrast, Maloney's statements are sought to be used as consciousness of guilt arising from an out-of-court denial of facts that the prosecutor is prepared to prove at trial are true. The statements are also sought to be used for impeachment in the event that the defendant testifies at trial. The justification for using the statements is far less substantial then those relied on to uphold the trial judge's decision in McKeon. Id. at 173.

Compare United States v. Harris, 914 F.2d 927, 932 (7th Cir.1990)(defense theory was that defendant's brother was the robber; court found that former attorney had acted as the agent of his client when he interviewed eyewitness, so that eyewitness' testimony that he had told attorney that he was confident that he had seen defendant and not his brother was admissible: "The fact that a lawyer's unsuccessful maneuver might be used against his client will not unduly chill legitimate advocacy.").

3. *Personal knowledge.* Brookover v. Mary Hitchcock Memorial Hospital, 893 F.2d 411, 417–18 (1st Cir.1990)(in action against hospital for injuries sustained by mentally retarded patient who fell when he got out of bed, father of patient testified that hospital nurses told him that bed restraints should have been used; court upheld admission of testimony over defendant's objection that the nurses lacked knowledge of the circumstances of the fall; the court stated that Rule 801(d)(2)(D) does not require personal knowledge, and added:

> No-one would be more knowledgeable about bed restraints than a hospital nurse, except possibly a doctor. So although the nurses did not have personal knowledge of all the circumstances surrounding the fall, the information they did have, albeit based on hearsay, was accurate and by virtue of their training and experience they were qualified to comment on whether or not a bed restraints [sic] should have been used. We are not here dealing with "gossip.").

Compare Litton Systems, Inc. v. American Tel. & Tel. Co., 700 F.2d 785, 816–17 (2d Cir.1983), cert. denied, 464 U.S. 1073 (1984) (court noted that hearsay which attorney summarized in notes of interviews with plaintiff's employees "may well have been inadmissible even if testified to by the employees interviewed;"); Oreck Corp. v. Whirlpool Corp., 639 F.2d 75, 80–81 n. 3 (2d Cir.1980), cert. denied, 454 U.S. 1083 (1981) (even if admissible court would regard statements by defendant's salesman "as having little probative value" in view of plaintiff's failure to establish whether statements "were based on rumor, innuendo, or his own conclusions"). See also Union Mut. Life Ins. Co. v. Chrysler Corp., 793 F.2d 1, 8, 9 (1st Cir.1986)(dispute about whether sublease had been modified; court admitted letter by accountant which amounted to an admission that Chrysler was not liable for payments under the sublease agreement; court found that even though accountant was a low level employee, nothing in the record required a finding that the matter should have appeared to him "as so important that he lacked the authority to write his routine response;" as to the objection that the accountant lacked personal knowledge, the court responded: "The authorities imposing such a requirement, however, seem concerned lest the admission serve as a vehicle for admitting other *hearsay,* where, for example, the out-of-court declarant's statement simply reflects the statements of other people which statements may themselves amount to inadmissible hearsay.... Here, however, the source of [the accountant's] knowledge apparently was the sublease itself, which he found while inspecting the file (at least, the district court may have thought so). Hence, [the] complaint is not so much about the *source* of Janowski's knowledge, but about the conclusion that he drew from that source. This complaint, as we have said, appropriately takes the form of an objection based on Fed.R.Evid. 403 or Fed.R.Evid. 701—and as we have also said, these latter objections here were not made, and, in any event, they would have proved unavailing.").

4. *Scope of employment.* In Wilkinson v. Carnival Cruise Lines, Inc., 920 F.2d 1560, 1566 (11th Cir.1991), the court observed that it is not the individual's position in the corporate hierarchy that is decisive of a Rule 801(d)(2)(D) issue, but rather whether the declarant was authorized "to act for his principal ... concerning the matter about which he allegedly spoke." In order to prove defendant had notice of problems with sliding glass doors on its cruise ship before the accident in question, plaintiff's cabin-mate testified at a deposition to a room steward's comments about such problems. The court found reversible error in the admission of this deposition. It noted that "plaintiff has offered not one whit of evidence at any phase of this proceeding to lay a predicate for the admissibility of the statement," or to contradict defendant's affidavit about a room steward's functions.

Consider also Precision Piping & Instruments, Inc. v. E.I. du Pont de Nemours & Co., 951 F.2d 613, 619–20 (4th Cir.1991), an anti-trust action in which plaintiff alleged that a number of corporations had illegally conspired to stop doing business with plaintiff. PPI sought to prove the conspiracy by calling employees of PPI to testify to statements made by employees of one of the defendants. The trial court excluded the statements and granted a directed verdict for the defendants. The appellate court affirmed:

> [W]e are in agreement with the district court that the relevant question is whether Marks and Zicherman had the authority to hire and fire PPI. If not, statements concerning PPI's contracts with Borg–Warner were made outside the scope of their employment.

> Our holding in Cline v. Roadway Express, Inc., 689 F.2d 481 (4th Cir.1982), is instructive. In Cline, an age discrimination case, this court considered a witness's testimony that persons at a managers meeting had referred to a company policy replacing older workers with younger, better educated ones. The district court admitted the evidence under Rule 801(d)(2)(D), and we affirmed. Unlike the circumstances here, however, the managers in Cline had the specific authority to hire and fire workers. There is no evidence that Marks possessed similar actual or apparent authority.

> In Portsmouth Paving, [694 F.2d 312, 321 (4th Cir.1982)], we affirmed the admission of testimony under Rule 801(d)(2)(D) concerning statements by a secretary as to what her boss said to her via car radio. Although the secretary admittedly did not have the specific responsibility or authority for the decision in issue, we found significant the fact that she did have the responsibility and authority to relay messages, in that case, to the testifying witness. In contrast, here Marks not only had no actual or apparent

authority to hire or fire contractors, but his authority did not extend to relaying messages to contractors regarding policies of Borg–Warner.

Turning to Hale's proffered testimony concerning Emerick's statements, the district court concluded that the proffered statements by Emerick were merely recitations of what Zicherman had said. Even if Emerick had the authority to relay Zicherman's statements, the statements would not get past the hearsay barrier because Zicherman's remarks were not made within the scope of his employment. More troublesome is the fact that Emerick had the ultimate responsibility for suspending PPI. Thus, if he, as the declarant, had related information about his actions suspending PPI, they clearly would have been within the scope of his employment. Instead, he was relating a statement about an apparent unauthorized action by Zicherman. An obvious inference is that Emerick approved and we, as was the district court, are presented with a nice technical evidentiary question. It is in such trial settings, however, where the discretion of trial courts in administering evidentiary rules is designed to reach optimum utility in their truth-finding roles. As stated in Boren v. Sable, 887 F.2d 1032, 1036 (10th Cir.1989):

> Certainly, the trial judge has discretion under Rule 403 to exclude a statement of multiple hearsay, even if each included portion meets the requirements of an exception, when he finds the statement so unreliable that its probative value is substantially outweighed by the danger of prejudice and confusion.

(quoting 4 J. Weinstein & M. Berger, Weinstein's Evidence, ¶ 805[01] (1990)).

. . . Under all the trial circumstances, the question of the propriety vel non of the district court's exercise of discretion is a close one. Had the district court ruled the statements admissible we would be hard put to fault that exercise of discretion. Rule 805 allows hearsay within hearsay, and we have previously extended the rule to include admissions within hearsay, see Portsmouth Paving, 694 F.2d at 321. We are, however, equally hard put to fault the court's exercise of discretion in excluding the testimony. Apart from the question of reliability, the proffered statements and the circumstances under which they purportedly were made are confusing and the inevitable arguing of possible inferences from them obviously could have resulted in untoward prejudice. The bottom line is that we likewise affirm the exclusion of the proffered statements as within the discretion of the district court.

5. When is a statement by an employee of a subsidiary corporation admissible against the parent corporation? Zenith Radio Corp. v. Matsushita Electric Industrial Co., Limited, 505 F.Supp. 1190, 1248 (E.D.Pa.1980), rev'd on related ground but aff'd on this point, 723 F.2d 238 (3d Cir.1983), rev'd on other grounds, 475 U.S. 574 (1986). In a criminal prosecution of a state governor, should the statements of his legislative aides and a state senator, one of his chief spokesmen on the Senate floor, be characterized as admissions? United States v. Mandel, 591 F.2d 1347 (4th Cir.1979), cert. denied, 445 U.S. 961 (1980).

6. Rad Services, Inc. v. Aetna Cas. and Sur. Co., 808 F.2d 271 (3d Cir. 1986)(fact that agents of plaintiff corporation claimed their privilege against self-incrimination at a deposition was properly introduced against plaintiff as a vicarious admission even though the declarants were no longer employees of plaintiff by time of trial; corporations could otherwise stymie the discovery process by firing workers responsible for improper conduct).

Bourjaily v. United States

Supreme Court of the United States, 1987.
483 U.S. 171, 107 S.Ct. 2775, 97 L.Ed.2d 144.

■ CHIEF JUSTICE REHNQUIST delivered the opinion of the Court.

Federal Rule of Evidence 801(d)(2)(E) provides, "A statement is not hearsay if ... [t]he statement is offered against a party and is ... a statement by a coconspirator of a party during the course and in furtherance of the conspiracy." We granted certiorari to answer three questions regarding the admission of statements under Rule 801(d)(2)(E): (1) whether the court must determine by independent evidence that the conspiracy existed and that the defendant and the declarant were members of this conspiracy; (2) the quantum of proof on which such determinations must be based; and (3) whether a court must in each case examine the circumstances of such a statement to determine its reliability. 479 U.S. 881, 107 S.Ct. 268, 93 L.Ed.2d 246 (1986).

In May 1984, Clarence Greathouse, an informant working for the Federal Bureau of Investigation, arranged to sell a kilogram of cocaine to Angelo Lonardo. Lonardo agreed that he would find individuals to distribute the drug. When the sale became imminent, Lonardo stated in a tape-recorded telephone conversation that he had a "gentleman friend" who had some questions to ask about the cocaine. In a subsequent telephone call, Greathouse spoke to the "friend" about the quality of the drug and the price. Greathouse then spoke again with Lonardo, and the two arranged the details of the purchase. They agreed that the sale would take place in a designated hotel parking lot, and Lonardo would transfer the drug from Greathouse's car to the "friend," who would be waiting in the parking lot in his own car. Greathouse proceeded with the transaction as planned, and FBI agents arrested Lonardo and petitioner immediately after Lonardo placed a kilogram of cocaine into petitioner's car in the hotel parking lot. In petitioner's car, the agents found over $20,000 in cash.

Petitioner was charged with conspiring to distribute cocaine, in violation of 21 U.S.C. § 846, and possession of cocaine with intent to distribute, a violation of 21 U.S.C. § 841(a)(1). The Government introduced, over petitioner's objection, Angelo Lonardo's telephone statements regarding the participation of the "friend" in the transaction. The District Court found that, considering the events in the parking lot and Lonardo's statements over the telephone, the Government had established by a preponderance of the evidence that a conspiracy involving Lonardo and petitioner existed, and that Lonardo's statements over the telephone had been made in the course of and in furtherance of the conspiracy. App. 66–75. Accordingly, the trial court held that Lonardo's out-of-court statements satisfied Rule 801(d)(2)(E) and were not hearsay. Petitioner was convicted on both counts and sentenced to 15 years. The United States Court of Appeals for the Sixth Circuit affirmed. 781 F.2d 539 (1986). The Court of Appeals agreed with the District Court's analysis and conclusion that Lonardo's out-of-court statements were admissible under the Federal Rules of Evidence. The court also rejected petitioner's contention that because he could not cross-examine Lonardo, the admission of these statements violated his constitutional right to confront the witnesses against him. We affirm.

Before admitting a co-conspirator's statement over an objection that it does not qualify under Rule 801(d)(2)(E), a court must be satisfied that the statement actually falls within the definition of the rule. There must be evidence that there was a conspiracy involving the declarant and the nonoffering party, and that the statement was made "in the course and in furtherance of the conspiracy." Federal Rule of Evidence 104(a) provides: "Preliminary questions concerning ... the admissibility of evidence shall be determined by the court." Petitioner and respondent agree that the existence of a conspiracy and petitioner's involvement in it are preliminary questions of fact that, under Rule 104, must be resolved by the court. The Federal Rules, however, nowhere define the standard of proof the court must observe in resolving these questions.

We are therefore guided by our prior decisions regarding admissibility determinations that hinge on preliminary factual questions....

Therefore, we hold that when the preliminary facts relevant to Rule 801(d)(2)(E) are disputed, the offering party must prove them by a preponderance of the evidence.

Even though petitioner agrees that the courts below applied the proper standard of proof with regard to the preliminary facts relevant to Rule 801(d)(2)(E), he nevertheless challenges the admission of Lonardo's statements. Petitioner argues that in determining whether a conspiracy exists and whether the defendant was a member of it, the court must look only to independent evidence—that is, evidence other than the statements sought to be admitted. Petitioner relies on Glasser v. United States, 315 U.S. 60, 62 S.Ct. 457, 86 L.Ed. 680 (1942), in which this Court first mentioned the so-called "bootstrapping rule." The relevant issue in Glasser was whether Glasser's counsel, who also represented another defendant, faced such a conflict of interest that Glasser received ineffective assistance. Glasser contended that conflicting loyalties led his lawyer not to object to statements made by one of Glasser's co-conspirators. The Government argued that any objection would have been fruitless because the statements were admissible. The Court rejected this proposition:

> "[S]uch declarations are admissible over the objection of an alleged co-conspirator, who was not present when they were made, only if there is proof aliunde that he is connected with the conspiracy.... Otherwise, hearsay would lift itself by its own bootstraps to the level of competent evidence." Id., at 74–75, 62 S.Ct., at 467.

The Court revisited the bootstrapping rule in United States v. Nixon, 418 U.S. 683, 94 S.Ct. 3090, 41 L.Ed.2d 1039 (1974), where again, in passing, the Court stated, "Declarations by one defendant may also be admissible against other defendants upon a sufficient showing, by independent evidence, of a conspiracy among one or more other defendants and the declarant and if the declarations at issue were in furtherance of that conspiracy." Id., at 701, and n. 14, 94 S.Ct., at 3104 (emphasis added) (footnote omitted). Read in the light most favorable to petitioner, Glasser could mean that a court should not consider hearsay statements at all in determining preliminary facts under Rule 801(d)(2)(E). Petitioner, of course, adopts this view of the bootstrapping rule. Glasser, however, could also mean that a court must have some proof aliunde, but may look at the hearsay statements themselves in light of this independent evidence to determine whether a conspiracy has been shown by a preponderance of the evidence. The Courts of Appeals have widely adopted the former view and held that in determining the preliminary facts relevant to co-conspirators' out-of-court statements, a court may not look at the hearsay statements themselves for their evidentiary value.

Both Glasser and Nixon, however, were decided before Congress enacted the Federal Rules of Evidence in 1975. These Rules now govern the treatment of evidentiary questions in federal courts. Rule 104(a) provides: "Preliminary questions concerning ... the admissibility of evidence shall be determined by the court.... In making its determination it is not bound by the rules of evidence except those with respect to privileges." Similarly, Rule 1101(d)(1) states that the Rules of Evidence (other than with respect to privileges) shall not apply to "[t]he determination of questions of fact preliminary to admissibility of evidence when the issue is to be determined by the court under rule 104." The question thus presented is whether any aspect of Glasser's bootstrapping rule remains viable after the enactment of the Federal Rules of Evidence.

Petitioner concedes that Rule 104, on its face, appears to allow the court to make the preliminary factual determinations relevant to Rule 801(d)(2)(E) by considering any evidence it wishes, unhindered by considerations of admissibility. Brief for Petitioner 27. That would seem to many to be the end of the matter. Congress has decided that courts may consider hearsay in making these factual determinations. Out-of-court statements made by anyone, including putative co-conspirators, are often hearsay. Even if they are, they may be considered, Glasser and the bootstrapping rule notwithstanding. But petitioner nevertheless argues that the bootstrapping rule, as most Courts of Appeals have construed it, survived this apparently unequivocal change in the law unscathed and that Rule 104, as applied to the admission of co-conspirator's statements, does not mean what it says. We disagree.

Petitioner claims that Congress evidenced no intent to disturb the bootstrapping rule, which was embedded in the previous approach, and we should not find that Congress altered the rule without affirmative evidence so indicating. It would be extraordinary to require legislative history to confirm the plain meaning of Rule 104. The Rule on its face allows the trial judge to consider any evidence whatsoever, bound only by the rules of privilege. We think that the Rule is sufficiently clear that to the extent that it is inconsistent with petitioner's interpretation of Glasser and Nixon, the Rule prevails.[1]

Nor do we agree with petitioner that this construction of Rule 104(a) will allow courts to admit hearsay statements without any credible proof of the conspiracy, thus fundamentally changing the nature of the co-conspirator exception. Petitioner starts with the proposition that co-conspirators' out-of-court statements are deemed unreliable and are inadmissible, at least until a conspiracy is shown. Since these statements are unreliable, petitioner contends that they should not form any part of the basis for establishing a conspiracy, the very antecedent that renders them admissible.

Petitioner's theory ignores two simple facts of evidentiary life. First, out-of-court statements are only *presumed* unreliable. The presumption may be rebutted by appropriate proof. See Fed.Rule Evid. 803(24) (otherwise inadmissible hearsay may be admitted if circumstantial guarantees of trustworthiness demonstrated). Second, individual pieces of evidence, insufficient in themselves

---

1. The Advisory Committee Notes show that the Rule was not adopted in a fit of absent-mindedness. The Note to Rule 104 specifically addresses the process by which a federal court should make the factual determinations requisite to a finding of admissibility:

"If the question is factual in nature, the judge will of necessity receive evidence pro and con on the issue. The rule provides that the rules of evidence in general do not apply to this process. McCormick § 53, p. 123, n. 8, points out that the authorities are 'scattered and inconclusive,' and observes:

"'Should the exclusionary law of evidence, "the child of the jury system" in Thayer's phrase, be applied to this hearing before the judge? Sound sense backs the view that it should not, and that the judge should be empowered to hear *any relevant evidence,* such as affidavits *or other reliable hearsay.*'" 28 U.S.C.App., p. 681 (emphasis added).

The Advisory Committee further noted, "An item, offered and objected to, *may itself be considered in ruling on admissibility,* although not yet admitted in evidence." Ibid. (emphasis added). We think this language makes plain the drafters' intent to abolish any kind of bootstrapping rule. Silence is at best ambiguous, and we decline the invitation to rely on speculation to import ambiguity into what is otherwise a clear rule.

[The footnotes are the Court's and have been renumbered. Some have been omitted.]

to prove a point, may in cumulation prove it. The sum of an evidentiary presentation may well be greater than its constituent parts. Taken together, these two propositions demonstrate that a piece of evidence, unreliable in isolation, may become quite probative when corroborated by other evidence. A *per se* rule barring consideration of these hearsay statements during preliminary factfinding is not therefore required. Even if out-of-court declarations by co-conspirators are presumptively unreliable, trial courts must be permitted to evaluate these statements for their evidentiary worth as revealed by the particular circumstances of the case. Courts often act as factfinders, and there is no reason to believe that courts are any less able to properly recognize the probative value of evidence in this particular area. The party opposing admission has an adequate incentive to point out the shortcomings in such evidence before the trial court finds the preliminary facts. If the opposing party is unsuccessful in keeping the evidence from the factfinder, he still has the opportunity to attack the probative value of the evidence as it relates to the substantive issue in the case. See, e.g., Fed.Rule Evid. 806 (allowing attack on credibility of out-of-court declarant).

We think that there is little doubt that a co-conspirator's statements could themselves be probative of the existence of a conspiracy and the participation of both the defendant and the declarant in the conspiracy. Petitioner's case presents a paradigm. The out-of-court statements of Lonardo indicated that Lonardo was involved in a conspiracy with a "friend." The statements indicated that the friend had agreed with Lonardo to buy a kilogram of cocaine and to distribute it. The statements also revealed that the friend would be at the hotel parking lot, in his car, and would accept the cocaine from Greathouse's car after Greathouse gave Lonardo the keys. Each one of Lonardo's statements may itself be unreliable, but taken as a whole, the entire conversation between Lonardo and Greathouse was corroborated by independent evidence. The friend, who turned out to be petitioner, showed up at the prearranged spot at the prearranged time. He picked up the cocaine, and a significant sum of money was found in his car. On these facts, the trial court concluded, in our view correctly, that the Government had established the existence of a conspiracy and petitioner's participation in it.

We need not decide in this case whether the courts below could have relied solely upon Lonardo's hearsay statements to determine that a conspiracy had been established by a preponderance of the evidence. To the extent that *Glasser* meant that courts could not look to the hearsay statements themselves for any purpose, it has clearly been superseded by Rule 104(a). It is sufficient for today to hold that a court, in making a preliminary factual determination under Rule 801(d)(2)(E), may examine the hearsay statements sought to be admitted. As we have held in other cases concerning admissibility determinations, "the judge should receive the evidence and give it such weight as his judgment and experience counsel." United States v. Matlock, 415 U.S. 164, 175, 94 S.Ct. 988, 995, 39 L.Ed.2d 242 (1974). The courts below properly considered the statements of Lonardo and the subsequent events in finding that the Government had established by a preponderance of the evidence that Lonardo was involved in a conspiracy with petitioner. We have no reason to believe that the District Court's factfinding of this point was clearly erroneous. We hold that Lonardo's out-of-court statements were properly admitted against petitioner.

We also reject any suggestion that admission of these statements against petitioner violated his rights under the Confrontation Clause of the Sixth Amendment. That Clause provides, "In all criminal prosecutions, the accused shall enjoy the right ... November 5, 1996. to be confronted with the witnesses against him." At petitioner's trial, Lonardo exercised his right not to testify.

Petitioner argued that Lonardo's unavailability rendered the admission of his out-of-court statements unconstitutional since petitioner had no opportunity to confront Lonardo as to these statements. The Court of Appeals held that the requirements for admission under Rule 801(d)(2)(E) are identical to the requirements of the Confrontation Clause, and since the statements were admissible under the Rule, there was no constitutional problem. We agree.

While a literal interpretation of the Confrontation Clause could bar the use of any out-of-court statements when the declarant is unavailable, this Court has rejected that view as "unintended and too extreme." Ohio v. Roberts, 448 U.S. 56, 63, 100 S.Ct. 2531, 2537, 65 L.Ed.2d 597 (1980). Rather, we have attempted to harmonize the goal of the Clause—placing limits on the kind of evidence that may be received against a defendant—with a societal interest in accurate factfinding, which may require consideration of out-of-court statements. To accommodate these competing interests, the Court has, as a general matter only, required the prosecution to demonstrate both the unavailability of the declarant and the "indicia of reliability" surrounding the out-of-court declaration. Id., at 65–66, 100 S.Ct., at 2538–2539. Last Term in *United States v. Inadi*, 475 U.S. 387, 106 S.Ct. 1121, 89 L.Ed.2d 390 (1986), we held that the first of these two generalized inquiries, unavailability, was not required when the hearsay statement is the out-of-court declaration of a co-conspirator. Today, we conclude that the second inquiry, independent indicia of reliability, is also not mandated by the Constitution.

The Court's decision in Ohio v. Roberts laid down only "a general approach to the problem" of reconciling hearsay exceptions with the Confrontation Clause. See 448 U.S., at 65, 100 S.Ct., at 2538. In fact, *Roberts* itself limits the requirement that a court make a separate inquiry into the reliability of an out-of-court statement. Because " 'hearsay rules and the Confrontation Clause are generally designed to protect similar values,' California v. Green, 399 U.S. [149, 155, 90 S.Ct. 1930, 1933, 26 L.Ed.2d 489 (1970),] and 'stem from the same roots,' Dutton v. Evans, 400 U.S. 74, 86, 91 S.Ct. 210, 218, 27 L.Ed.2d 213 (1970)," id., at 66, 100 S.Ct., at 2539, we concluded in Roberts that no independent inquiry into reliability is required when the evidence "falls within a firmly rooted hearsay exception." Ibid. We think that the co-conspirator exception to the hearsay rule is firmly enough rooted in our jurisprudence that, under this Court's holding in Roberts, a court need not independently inquire into the reliability of such statements. Cf. Dutton v. Evans, 400 U.S. 74, 91 S.Ct. 210, 27 L.Ed.2d 213 (1970)(reliability inquiry required where evidentiary rule deviates from common-law approach, admitting co-conspirators' hearsay statements made after termination of conspiracy). The admissibility of co-conspirators' statements was first established in this Court over a century and a half ago in United States v. Gooding, 12 Wheat. *460, 6 L.Ed. 693 (1827)(interpreting statements of co-conspirator as *res gestae* and thus admissible against defendant), and the Court has repeatedly reaffirmed the exception as accepted practice. In fact, two of the most prominent approvals of the rule came in cases that petitioner maintains are still vital today, Glasser v. United States, 315 U.S. 60, 62 S.Ct. 457, 86 L.Ed. 680 (1942), and United States v. Nixon, 418 U.S. 683, 94 S.Ct. 3090, 41 L.Ed.2d 1039 (1974). To the extent that these cases have not been superseded by the Federal Rules of Evidence, they demonstrate that the co-conspirator exception to the hearsay rule is steeped in our jurisprudence. In Delaney v. United States, 263 U.S. 586, 590, 44 S.Ct. 206, 207, 68 L.Ed. 462 (1924), the Court rejected the very challenge petitioner brings today, holding that there can be no separate Confrontation Clause challenge to the admission of a co-conspirator's out-of-court statement. In so ruling, the Court relied on established precedent holding such statements competent evidence.

We think that these cases demonstrate that co-conspirators' statements, when made in the course and in furtherance of the conspiracy, have a long tradition of being outside the compass of the general hearsay exclusion. Accordingly, we hold that the Confrontation Clause does not require a court to embark on an independent inquiry into the reliability of statements that satisfy the requirements of Rule 801(d)(2)(E).[2]

The judgment of the Court of Appeals is affirmed.

■ JUSTICE STEVENS, concurring.

... In my view, Glasser holds that a declarant's out-of-court statement is inadmissible against his alleged co-conspirators unless there is some corroborating evidence to support the triple conclusion that there was a conspiracy among those defendants, that the declarant was a member of the conspiracy, and that the statement furthered the objectives of the conspiracy. An otherwise inadmissible hearsay statement cannot provide the sole evidentiary support for its own admissibility—it cannot lift itself into admissibility entirely by tugging on its own bootstraps. It may, however, use its own bootstraps, together with other support, to overcome the objection. In the words of the Glasser opinion, there must be proof "aliunde," that is, evidence from another source, that together with the contents of the statement satisfies the preliminary conditions for admission of the statement. Id., at 74, 62 S.Ct., at 467.[1] This interpretation of Glasser as requiring some but not complete proof "aliunde" is fully consistent with the plain language of Rule 104(a). If, as I assume they did, the drafters of Rule 104(a) understood the Glasser rule as I do, they had no reason to indicate that it would be affected by the new Rule.

Thus, the absence of any legislative history indicating an intent to change the Glasser rule is entirely consistent with the reasoning of the Court's opinion, which I join.

■ JUSTICE BLACKMUN, with whom JUSTICE BRENNAN and JUSTICE MARSHALL join, dissenting.

I disagree with the Court in three respects: First, I do not believe that the Federal Rules of Evidence changed the long-and well-settled law to the effect that the preliminary questions of fact, relating to admissibility of a nontestifying co-conspirator's statement, must be established by evidence independent of that statement itself. Second, I disagree with the Court's conclusion that allowing the co-conspirator's statement to be considered in the resolution of these factual questions will remedy problems of the statement's unreliability. In my view, the abandonment of the independent-evidence requirement will lead, instead, to the opposite result. This is because the abandonment will

2. We reject any suggestion that by abolishing the bootstrapping rule, the Federal Rules of Evidence have changed the co-conspirator hearsay exception such that it is no longer "firmly rooted" in our legal tradition. The bootstrapping rule relates only to the method of proof that the exception has been satisfied. It does not change any ele-ment of the co-conspirator exception, which has remained substantively unchanged since its adoption in this country.

1. Glasser had argued that "independently of the statements complained of, there is *no proof* connecting him with the conspiracy." 315 U.S., at 75, 62 S.Ct., at 467 (emphasis added).

eliminate one of the few safeguards of reliability that this exemption from the hearsay definition possesses. Third, because the Court alters the traditional hearsay exemption—especially an aspect of it that contributes to the reliability of an admitted statement—I do not believe that the Court can rely on the "firmly rooted hearsay exception" rationale, see Ohio v. Roberts, 448 U.S. 56, 66, 100 S.Ct. 2531, 2539, 65 L.Ed.2d 597 (1980), to avoid a determination whether any "indicia of reliability" support the co-conspirator's statement, as the Confrontation Clause surely demands.

I

. . .

A

In order to understand why the Federal Rules of Evidence adopted without change the common-law co-conspirator exemption from hearsay, and why this adoption signified the Advisory Committee's intent to retain the exemption's independent-evidence requirement, it is useful to review briefly the contours of this exemption as it stood before enactment of the Rules. By all accounts, the exemption was based upon agency principles, the underlying concept being that a conspiracy is a common undertaking where the conspirators are all agents of each other and where the acts and statements of one can be attributed to all. See 4 J. Weinstein & M. Berger, Weinstein's Evidence ¶ 801(d)(2)(E)[01], pp. 801–232 and–233 (1985)(Weinstein & Berger); Davenport, The Confrontation Clause and the Co–Conspirator Exception in Criminal Prosecutions: A Functional Analysis, 85 Harv.L.Rev. 1378, 1384 (1972)(Davenport). As Judge Learned Hand explained this in a frequently quoted remark,

"When men enter into an agreement for an unlawful end, they become ad hoc agents for one another, and have made a 'partnership in crime.' What one does pursuant to their common purpose, all do, and, as declarations may be such acts, they are competent against all." Van Riper v. United States, 13 F.2d 961, 967 (CA2), cert. denied sub nom., Ackerson v. United States, 273 U.S. 702, 47 S.Ct. 102, 71 L.Ed. 848 (1926).

Each of the components of this common-law exemption, in turn, had an agency justification. To fall within the exemption, the co-conspirator's statement had to be made "in furtherance of" the conspiracy, a requirement that arose from the agency rationale that an agent's acts or words could be attributed to his principal only so long as the agent was acting within the scope of his employment. See Levie, Hearsay and Conspiracy: A Reexamination of the Co–Conspirators' Exception to the Hearsay Rule, 52 Mich.L.Rev. 1159, 1161 (1954)(Levie); 4 D. Louisell & C. Mueller, Federal Evidence § 427, p. 348 (1980)(Louisell & Mueller). The statement also had to be made "during the course of" the conspiracy. This feature necessarily accompanies the "in furtherance of" requirement, for there must be an employment or business relationship in effect between the agent and principal, in accordance with which the agent is acting, for the principal to be bound by his agent's deeds or words. See Levie, 52 Mich.L.Rev., at 1161; 4 Louisell & Mueller, at 337.

The final feature of the co-conspirator hearsay exemption, the independent-evidence requirement, directly corresponds to the agency concept that an agent's statement cannot be used alone to prove the existence of the agency relationship.

"Evidence of a statement by an agent concerning the existence or extent of his authority is not admissible against the principal to prove its existence or extent, unless it appears *by other evidence* that the making of such statement was within the authority of the agent or, as to persons dealing with the agent, within the apparent authority or other power of the agent" (emphasis added). Restatement (Second) of Agency § 285 (1957). See Levie, 52 Mich.L.Rev., at 1161. The reason behind this concept is that the agent's authority must be traced back to some act or statement by the alleged principal. See 1 F. Mechem, Law of Agency § 285, p. 205 (1914).

Thus, unlike many common-law hearsay exceptions, the co-conspirator exemption from hearsay with its agency rationale was not based primarily upon any particular guarantees of reliability or trustworthiness that were intended to ensure the truthfulness of the admitted statement and to compensate for the fact that a party would not have the opportunity to test its veracity by cross-examining the declarant. See Davenport, 85 Harv.L.Rev., at 1384. As such, this exemption was considered to be a "vicarious admission."[1] Although not an admission by a defendant himself, the vicarious admission was a statement imputed to the defendant from the co-conspirator on the basis of their agency relationship. As with all admissions, an "adversary system," rather than a reliability, rationale was used to account for the exemption to the ban on hearsay: it was thought that a party could not complain of the deprivation of the right to cross-examine himself (or another authorized to speak for him) or to advocate his own, or his agent's, untrustworthiness. See McCormick on Evidence § 262, p. 775 (E. Cleary ed. 1984). The co-conspirator "admission" exception was also justified on the ground that the need for this evidence, which was particularly valuable in prosecuting a conspiracy, permitted a somewhat reduced concern for the reliability of the statement. See Saltzburg, Standards of Proof and Preliminary Questions of Fact, 27 Stan.L.Rev. 271, 303 (1975); R. Lempert & S. Saltzburg, A Modern Approach to Evidence 395 (2d ed. 1982)(Lempert & Saltzburg).

Although, under common law, the reliability of the co-conspirator's statement was never the primary ground justifying its admissibility, there was some recognition that this exemption from the hearsay rule had certain guarantees of trustworthiness, albeit limited ones. This justification for the exemption has been explained:

> "Active conspirators are likely to know who the members of the conspiracy are and what they have done. When speaking to advance the conspiracy, they are unlikely to describe non-members as conspirators, and they usually will have no incentive to mis-describe the actions of their fellow members." Lempert & Saltzburg, at 395.

See also 4 J. Wigmore, Evidence § 1080a, p. 199 (Chadbourn rev. 1972)("the general idea of receiving vicarious admissions, is that where the third person was, at the time of speaking, in *circumstances that gave him substantially the same interest* to know something about the matter in hand as had the now opponent, and the *same motive* to make a statement about it, that person's statements have approximately the same testimonial value as if the now opponent had made them")(emphasis in original). And the components of the

---

1. As explained by Dean McCormick, the "vicarious" or "representative" admission concept was justified by an agency rationale. Such admissions were statements of an agent either expressly authorized by a principal or made within the scope of the agent's authority to speak for the principal. See McCormick on Evidence § 267, pp. 787–788 (E. Cleary ed. 1984). In speaking of these statements, I refer here to those by an agent or co-conspirator that are truly hearsay, i.e., used to prove the truth of the matter asserted—not statements that might be considered to be verbal *acts* of the agency or conspiracy that do not fall within the hearsay category and thus are otherwise admissible. As the above quotation from Judge Learned Hand suggests, this distinction is not always made. See McCormick, at 792.

exemption were understood to contribute to this reliability. When making a statement "during the course of" and "in furtherance of" a conspiracy, a conspirator could be viewed as speaking from the perspective of all the conspirators in order to achieve the common goals of the conspiracy, not from self-serving motives. See Davenport, 85 Harv.L.Rev., at 1387. In particular, the requirement that a conspiracy be established by independent evidence also is seen to contribute to the reliability issue. Yet that requirement goes not so much to the reliability of the statement itself, as to the reliability of the process of admitting it: a statement cannot be introduced *until* independent evidence shows the defendant to be a member of an existing conspiracy. See id., at 1390 ("Independent evidence of the conspiracy's existence and of the defendant's participation in it may supply inferences as to the reliability of the declaration"); Lempert & Saltzburg, at 395.

The Federal Rules of Evidence did not alter in any way this common-law exemption to hearsay. The Rules essentially codify the components of this exemption: Rule 801(d)(2)(E) provides that the co-conspirator's statement, to be admissible against a party, must be "by a coconspirator of a party during the course and in furtherance of the conspiracy." Moreover, the exemption was placed within the category of "not hearsay," as an admission, in contrast to the hearsay exceptions of Rules 803 and 804. The Advisory Committee explained that the exclusion of admissions from the hearsay category is justified by the traditional "adversary system" rationale, not by any specific "guarantee of trustworthiness" used to justify hearsay exceptions. See Advisory Committee's Notes on Fed.Rule Evid. 801, 28 U.S.C.App., p. 717, 56 F.R.D. 183, 297 (1972); see also Note, Federal Rule of Evidence 801(d)(2)(E) and the Confrontation Clause: Closing the Window of Admissibility for Coconspirator Hearsay, 53 Ford.L.Rev. 1291, 1295 and n. 25 (1985).

More importantly, by explicitly retaining the agency rationale for the exemption, the Advisory Committee expressed its intention that the exemption would remain identical to the common-law rule and that it would not be expanded in any way. The Advisory Committee recognized that this agency rationale had been subject to criticism. The drafters of the American Law Institute's Model Code of Evidence had gone so far as to abandon the agency justification and had eliminated the "in furtherance of" requirement, observing that "[t]hese statements are likely to be true, and are usually made with a realization that they are against the declarant's interest." Model Code of Evidence, Rule 508(b) commentary, p. 251 (1942). The Advisory Committee, however, declined to accept without reservation a reliability foundation for Rule 801(d)(2)(E).

The Advisory Committee thus decided to retain the agency justification, in general, and the "in furtherance of" language, in particular, as a compromise position. It thought that the traditional exemption appropriately balanced the prosecution's need for a co-conspirator's statements and the defendant's need for the protections against unreliable statements, protections provided by the components of the common-law exemption. See 4 Weinstein & Berger, ¶ 801(d)(2)(E)[01], p. 801–235. The Advisory Committee, however, expressed its doubts about the agency rationale and, on the basis of these doubts, plainly stated that the exemption should not be changed or extended: "the agency theory of conspiracy is at best a fiction and ought not to serve as a basis for admissibility beyond that already established." Advisory Committee's Notes on Fed.Rule Evid. 801, 28 U.S.C.App., p. 718, 56 F.R.D., at 299. In light of this intention not to alter the common-law exemption, the Advisory Committee's Notes thus make very clear that Rule 801(d)(2)(E) was to include *all* the components of this exemption, including the independent-evidence requirement.

B

Accordingly, when Rule 801(d)(2)(E) and Rule 104(a) are considered together—an examination that the Court neglects to undertake—there appears to be a conflict between the fact that no change in the co-conspirator hearsay exemption was intended by Rule 801(d)(2)(E) and the freedom that Rule 104(a) gives a trial court to rely on hearsay in resolving preliminary factual questions. Although one must be somewhat of an interpretative funambulist to walk between the conflicting demands of these Rules in order to arrive at a resolution that will satisfy their respective concerns, this effort is far to be preferred over accepting the easily available safety "net" of Rule 104(a)'s "plain meaning." The purposes of both Rules can be achieved by considering the relevant preliminary factual question for Rule 104(a) analysis to be the following: "whether a conspiracy that included the declarant and the defendant against whom a statement is offered has been demonstrated to exist on the basis of evidence *independent of the declarant's hearsay statements* "(emphasis added). Saltzburg & Redden, Federal Rules of Evidence Manual 735 (4th ed. 1986). This resolution sufficiently answers Rule 104(a)'s concern with allowing a trial court to consider hearsay in determining preliminary factual questions, because the only hearsay not available for its consideration is the statement at issue. The exclusion of the statement from the preliminary analysis maintains the common-law exemption unchanged.

As the Court recognizes, ante, at [592], in the more than 10 years since the enactment of the Federal Rules of Evidence, the Courts of Appeals, almost uniformly, have found no conflict between Rule 104(a) and the independent evidence requirement understood to adhere in Rule 801(d)(2)(E). Indeed, some courts have rejected the suggestion that Rule 104(a) has changed this component of the common-law exemption, because, like the Advisory Committee, they recognize the incremental protection against unreliable statements that this requirement gives to defendants. See, e.g., United States v. Bell, 573 F.2d 1040, 1044 (C.A.8 1978). Yet the Court cavalierly disregards these years of interpretative experience, as well as the rich history of this exemption, and arrives at its conclusion solely on the basis of its "plain meaning" approach.

II

. . .

As explained above, despite the recognized need by prosecutors for co-conspirator statements, these statements often have been considered to be somewhat unreliable. It has long been understood that such statements in some cases may constitute, at best, nothing more than the "idle chatter" of a declarant or, at worst, malicious gossip. See 4 Weinstein & Berger, ¶ 801(d)(2)(E)[01], p. 801–235. Moreover, when confronted with such a statement, an innocent defendant would have a difficult time defending himself against it, for, if he were not in the conspiracy, he would have no idea why the conspirator made the statement. See United States v. Stipe, 517 F.Supp. 867, 871 (W.D.Okla.), aff'd, 653 F.2d 446 (C.A.10 1981)("The dangers that an accused may be confronted with numerous statements made by someone else which he never authorized, intended, or even knew about . . . cannot be ignored"). Even an experienced trial judge might credit an incriminatory statement that a defendant could not explain, precisely because the defendant had no ready explanation for it. Because of this actual "real world" experience with the possible unreliability of these statements, the Advisory Committee retained the agency rationale for this exemption in Rule 801(d)(2)(E), as well as the safeguards, albeit limited, against unreliability that this rationale provided the defendant. The independent-evidence requirement was one such safeguard.

If this requirement is set aside, then one of the exemption's safeguards is lost. From a "real world" perspective, I do not believe that considering the statement together with the independent evidence will cure this loss. Contrary to the Court's suggestion, the situation in which a trial court now commonly will rely on the co-conspirator's statement to establish the existence of a conspiracy in which the defendant participated will not be limited to instances in which the statement constitutes just another "piece of evidence," to be considered as no more important than the independent evidence. Rather, such a statement will serve the greatest purpose, and thus will be introduced most frequently, in situations where all the other evidence that the prosecution can muster to show the existence of a conspiracy will not be adequate. In this situation, despite the use of hearsay admissible under other exceptions and the defendant's and other conspirators' actions, the co-conspirator's statement will be necessary to satisfy the trial court by a preponderance of the evidence that the defendant was a member of an existing conspiracy. Accordingly, the statement will likely control the interpretation of whatever other evidence exists and could well transform a series of innocuous actions by a defendant into evidence that he was participating in a criminal conspiracy. This is what "bootstrapping" is all about. Thus, the Court removes one reliability safeguard from an exemption, even though the situation in which a co-conspirator's statement will be used to resolve the preliminary factual questions is that in which the court will rely most on the statement.

. . .

III

. . .

The weakness of the Court's assertion—that the Confrontation Clause concern about reliability vanishes because Rule 801(d)(2)(E)'s exemption of a co-conspirator's statement from the hearsay definition is a "firmly rooted hearsay exception"—... becomes immediately apparent. First, as has been explained and as its inclusion under the admissions rubric would indicate, this exemption has never been justified primarily upon reliability or trustworthiness grounds and its reliability safeguards are not extensive. See also 53 Ford. L.Rev., at 1311–1312. Thus, it is surprising that, without any hesitation, the Court in this case turns to the "firmly rooted hearsay exception" rationale, which is based upon a confidence in adequate "indicia of reliability."

Second, and more astounding, is the Court's reliance upon the "firmly rooted hearsay exception" rationale as it simultaneously removes from the exemption one of the few safeguards against unreliability that it possesses.

. . .

I respectfully dissent.

NOTES ON COCONSPIRATORS' STATEMENTS

1. *The "in furtherance" requirement.* As the dissenters in the Bourjaily case note, the traditional coconspirators exception rests on an agency rationale: "When men enter into an agreement for an unlawful end, they become ad hoc agents for one another, and have made a 'partnership in crime.' What one does pursuant to their common purposes all do, and, as declarations may be such acts, they are competent against all." Van Riper v. United States, 13 F.2d 961, 967 (2d Cir.1926)(L. Hand, J.). Even though the drafters of the Federal Rules considered "the agency theory of conspiracy ... at best a fiction," they judged it a useful device for imposing some limits on the admission of coconspirators' statements. A concomitant of the agency rationale is that only those statements that tend to advance the objectives of the illegal design are authorized because the acts of an agent bind the principal only when the agent acts within the scope of his or her authority. Consequently, unlike the 1942 Model Code of Evidence and the 1953 Uniform Rules of Evidence which made admissible all statements relevant to the conspiracy and made during its pendency, the Federal Rules and the 1974 Uniform Rule require the statement to further the conspiracy.

How broadly should the "in furtherance" requirement be construed in view of this drafting history? Should admission hinge on showing that the statement actually furthered the conspiracy's objectives, or is admission authorized when the proponent or court is able to suggest a possible motive?

In United States v. Urbanik, 801 F.2d 692, 698–700 (4th Cir.1986), the majority found reversible error in the admission of statements that identified the defendant as the supplier of drugs where the witness testified that the statements were made while the witness and the declarant "were just 'hanging out' and 'shooting the breeze' about weight-lifting." The dissent would have admitted the statements:

> The challenged statement was made by Pelino while Haselhuhn, who was a drug distributor obtaining in part his supplies from Pelino, was at Pelino's gym, where apparently Pelino handled his drug operations, for the purpose of paying for and picking up cocaine. Both Haselhuhn and Pelino were weightlifters. After Haselhuhn had paid for the cocaine, he and Pelino had a conversation in Pelino's weightroom. They unquestionably talked about weightlifting at the time and about weightlifters. Pelino told Haselhuhn that there was an expert weightlifter in Florida, who supplied him "pot" at a "thousand pounds a clip." In this statement, Pelino identified Urbanik as a weightlifter but he also identified to his customer that this weightlifter was his source for controlled materials. This statement was made by Pelino to an individual who shared a common interest with him both in weightlifting and in the availability of drugs. The majority would treat this statement between the two as one relating only to weightlifting and would treat the fact that Pelino was simultaneously indicating to his customer that this weightlifter represented an ample source for him to supply the customer with controlled materials as mere innocent chatter without purpose or intention to influence Haselhuhn in continued purchases of controlled materials from him (Pelino). I do not think it is for us to assume that Pelino was not intending by this statement to impress on his customer that he had in Florida a supplier of drugs who could meet any requirement, even a "thousand pounds (of marijuana) at a clip" and that Haselhuhn could confidently rely on him (Pelino) to supply him (Haselhuhn) with his requirements of marijuana or other drugs; that is a question to be resolved by the jury.

> Haselhuhn was not at Pelino's gym to discuss weightlifting or to exercise; he was there to carry out a transaction in drugs. Any conversation about weightlifting was the idle chatter; the real interest of the parties was in drugs and marijuana and their availability. And it can be inferred that

Pelino was using the subject of weightlifting to provide him with an opportunity to emphasize his access to a substantial source and to assure Haselhuhn of his ability to supply material easily through his Florida source. If Pelino had intended his conversation to be strictly limited to weightlifting as the majority concludes, there would have been no reason for him to add the significant statement that this other individual was one of his suppliers and, more than that, a large one who could make delivery of substantial amounts "at a clip." If, however, the purpose of the added statement was to induce Haselhuhn to continue dealing with Pelino for drugs—and that could be a reasonable inference—then the statement would have been in clear furtherance of the conspiracy. Whether that was its purpose was—in my opinion—a question for the jury.

United States v. Guyton, 36 F.3d 655, 659 (7th Cir.1994) ("It is plausible that Morris and Calhoun, after seeing Phinnessee's well-established customer base, could have revealed their supplier to Phinnessee in an attempt to familiarize her with the other members of the Guyton conspiracy, with the expectation that she would eventually be induced to join it. This may not have been the exclusive, or even the primary, basis for making these statements. But such is not the standard; rather, the question is whether there exists some reasonable basis for making the statement.").

See United States v. Roberts, 14 F.3d 502, 516 (10th Cir.1993), cert. denied, 115 S.Ct. 1417 (1995) in which the following taped conversation— "devoted entirely to Lee Roberts' financial difficulties"—conducted by two indicted defendants, Lee Roberts and Carolynn Roberts, "became the corner- stone of the government's case" against Susan Byers in a narcotics prosecution:

On February 9, 1991, with bills overdue and front money slow to come in, Lee Roberts complained:

See and that's what I keep runnin' into up there, people don't pay me.

Carolynn Roberts: Well, Suzie does don't she and . . .

Lee Roberts: Suzie pays me, she's the best god damn hand I got.

The appellate court agreed with the district judge that Lee Roberts' comment, repeated six times in closing argument, "reflected Lee Roberts' intent to keep Carolynn Roberts, a member of the conspiracy 'abreast of what is going on, that is abreast of the status of another person within the alleged conspiracy and their performance under the conspiracy and their role.' "

United States v. Simmons, 923 F.2d 934, 945 (2d Cir.1991), cert. denied, 500 U.S. 919 (1991) and 502 U.S. 943 (1991). In prosecution of the "Montsan- to Crew" for their participation in a vast wholesale and retail heroin network, the prosecution offered as statements in furtherance of a conspiracy testimony by a former lieutenant in the Montsanto Crew about conversations with coconspirators about a murder they had committed:

The co-conspirators' discussions of Walker's brutal murder, and the rea- sons for it, may well have served to promote the criminal activities of the Monsanto Crew by enforcing discipline among its members. If nothing else, the story of Walker's murder warned members of the Crew that a similar fate awaited those who failed to follow Peter Monsanto's orders. Because these statements may have promoted cohesiveness among the Crew and helped induce Crew member assistance in the affairs of the criminal enterprise, the district court did not abuse its discretion in admitting the disputed testimony.

2. *"During the course."* The requirement in Rule 801(d)(2)(E) that the statement has to have been made "during the course" of the conspiracy states the usual rule in the United States. But see Dutton v. Evans, note 4, infra. Determining when the conspiracy began or ended or when a particular conspirator joined or terminated his membership can be difficult to ascertain. Suppose A joins the conspiracy after it has been in operation. Should statements made before he became a member be admissible against him? See Calif. Evidence Code § 1223. Suppose A is arrested, should statements subsequently made by the other conspirators be usable against him? See United States v. Taylor, 802 F.2d 1108, 1117 (9th Cir.1986), cert. denied, 479 U.S. 1094 (1987)("Although statements made by a co-conspirator after his arrest cannot be used against fellow conspirators ... the converse is not true; statements made by an *unarrested* co-conspirator who is still operating in furtherance of the on-going conspiracy may be introduced against the arrested conspirator"—declarant did not know of arrest). See also United States v. Pecora, 798 F.2d 614 (3d Cir.1986), cert. denied, 479 U.S. 1064 (1987).

3. *Independent corroborating evidence.* Although Bourjaily reserved decision on whether a court could rely solely on the hearsay statement seeking admission to determine by a preponderance of the evidence the existence of a conspiracy, all circuits addressing the issue have held that some independent corroborating evidence is required. See, e.g., United States v. Tellier, 83 F.3d 578 (2d Cir.1996)(court reversed RICO conviction because of insufficient evidence of two predicate acts as required; one of the predicate acts alleged was a conspiracy to distribute stolen marijuana but a hearsay statement was the only evidence of defendant's participation).

In 1996, the Committee on Rules of Practice and Procedure recommended to the Judicial Conference that it adopt an amendment to Rule 801(d)(2)(E) proposed by the Advisory Committee on the Federal Rules of Evidence that would add the following at the end of Rule 801:

> The contents of the statement shall be considered but are not alone sufficient to establish the declarant's authority under subdivision (C), the agency or employment relationship and scope thereof under subdivision (D), or the existence of the conspiracy and the participation therein of the declarant and the party against whom the statement is offered under subdivision (E).

The Proposed Committee Note explained:

> The court must consider in addition [to the contents of the statement] the circumstances surrounding the statement, such as the identity of the speaker, the context in which the statement was made, or evidence corroborating the contents of the statement in making its determination as to each preliminary question.

The proposed amendment also explicitly extended the reasoning of Bourjaily to statements proffered under Rules 801(d)(2)(C) or (D).

4. *Constitutional constraints.* In United States v. Inadi, 475 U.S. 387 (1986), the Supreme Court held that the confrontation clause does not require the government to show the unavailability of a co-conspirator-declarant in order to introduce his out-of-court statement. The Court explained:

> There are good reasons why the unavailability rule, developed in cases involving former testimony, is not applicable to co-conspirators' out-of-court statements. Unlike some other exceptions to the hearsay rules, or the exemption from the hearsay definition involved in this case, former testimony often is only a weaker substitute for live testimony. It seldom has

independent evidentiary significance of its own, but is intended to replace live testimony. If the declarant is available and the same information can be presented to the trier of fact in the form of live testimony, with full cross-examination and the opportunity to view the demeanor of the declarant, there is little justification for relying on the weaker version. When two versions of the same evidence are available, longstanding principles of the law of hearsay, applicable as well to Confrontation Clause analysis, favor the better evidence. See Graham, The Right of Confrontation and the Hearsay Rule: Sir Walter Raleigh Loses Another One, 8 Crim.L.Bull. 99, 143 (1972). But if the declarant is unavailable, no "better" version of the evidence exists, and the former testimony may be admitted as a substitute for live testimony on the same point.

Those same principles do not apply to co-conspirator statements. Because they are made while the conspiracy is in progress, such statements provide evidence of the conspiracy's context that cannot be replicated even if the declarant testifies to the same matters in court. When the Government—as here—offers the statement of one drug dealer to another in furtherance of an illegal conspiracy, the statement often will derive its significance from the circumstances in which it was made. Conspirators are likely to speak differently when talking to each other in furtherance of their illegal aims than when testifying on the witness stand. Even when the declarant takes the stand, his in court testimony seldom will reproduce a significant portion of the evidentiary value of his statements during the course of the conspiracy.

. . .

... [A]n unavailability rule is not likely to produce much testimony that adds anything to the "truth-determining process" over and above what would be produced without such a rule ... Some of the available declarants already will have been subpoenaed by the prosecution or the defense, regardless of any Confrontation Clause requirements. Presumably only those declarants that neither side believes will be particularly helpful will not have been subpoenaed as witnesses. There is much to indicate that Lazaro was in that position in this case. Neither the Government nor the defense originally subpoenaed Lazaro as a witness. When he subsequently failed to show, alleging car trouble, respondent did nothing to secure his testimony. If respondent independently wanted to secure Lazaro's testimony he had several options available, particularly under Federal Rule of Evidence 806, which provides that if the party against whom a co-conspirator statement has been admitted calls the declarant as a witness, "the party is entitled to examine him on the statement as if under cross-examination." Rule 806 would not require respondent to make the showing necessary to have Lazaro declared a hostile witness, although presumably that option also was available to him. The Compulsory Process Clause would have aided respondent in obtaining the testimony of any of these declarants. If the Government has no desire to call a co-conspirator declarant as a witness, and if the defense has not chosen to subpoena such a declarant, either as a witness favorable to the defense, or as a hostile witness, or for cross-examination under Federal Rule of Evidence 806, then it is difficult to see what, if anything, is gained by a rule that requires the prosecution to make that declarant "available." Id. at 393–399, 106 S.Ct. at 1126–1128.

Taken together, do the Court's holdings in Bourjaily and Inadi mean that a statement that satisfies Rule 801(d)(2)(E) of the Federal Rules always meets the constitutional test? Consider United States v. Salim, 664 F.Supp. 682, 684 (E.D.N.Y.1987)("While the Bourjaily ruling may govern reversible error (Federal Rule of Evidence 103), it does not exhaust the trial judge's responsibility to ensure a fair trial."), aff'd, 855 F.2d 944 (2d Cir.1988). Suppose, however, that the statement was admitted at a state trial in a state whose evidentiary requirements for co-conspirators' statements are less stringent than the federal model? In Dutton v. Evans, 400 U.S. 74 (1970), the statements in question satisfied Georgia law but could not have been admitted pursuant to the Rule 801(d)(2)(E) formula because they were made after the conspiracy had ended while all the conspirators were in custody. The Supreme Court affirmed the conviction. After first pointing out that the evidence in question was neither "crucial" nor "devastating", the Court then examined the statement and the circumstances under which it had been made. The majority concluded that there were sufficient indicia of reliability so that "the possibility that cross-examination of [the declarant] could conceivably have shown the jury that the statement, though made, might have been unreliable was wholly unreal." Id. at 89.

5. Most jurisdictions refuse to admit as vicarious admissions a statement made by a police officer, prosecutor or other government agent that the criminal defendant seeks to introduce against the government. See, e.g., United States v. Santos, 372 F.2d 177 (2d Cir.1967). This result has been criticized as inconsistent with the liberal receipt of co-conspirators statements against the accused, and violative of equal protection. Imwinkelried, Of Evidence and Equal Protection: The Unconstitutionality of Excluding Government Agents' Statements Offered As Vicarious Admissions Against the Prosecution, 71 Minn. L.Rev. 269 (1986).

6. Suppose a nontestifying defendant's statement is admitted as a coconspirator's statement? Does Rule 806 then authorize the impeachment of the defendant-declarant with prior convictions even though he has chosen not to take the stand? See Cordray, Evidence Rule 806 and the Problem of Impeaching the Nontestifying Declarant, 56 Ohio St. L.J. 495, 519 (1995)(suggests adding to Rule 807: "If the declarant is an accused, the credibility of the declarant may be attacked with prior convictions only if the declarant has affirmatively placed the declarant's credibility in issue.")

7. *Additional references.* See e.g., Davenport, the Confrontation Clause and the Co–Conspirator Exception in Criminal Prosecutions: A Functional Analysis, 85 Harv.L.Rev. 1387 (1972); Comment, Federal Rule of Evidence 801(d)(2)(E) and the Confrontation Clause: Closing the Window of Admissibility for Coconspirator Hearsay, 53 Fordham L.Rev. 1291 (1985); Comment, Restructuring the Independent Evidence Requirement of the Co–Conspirator Hearsay Exception, 127 U.Pa.L.Rev. 1439, 1443–1444 (1979).

SECTION 4. DECLARATIONS AGAINST INTEREST

Cole v. Cole

Court of Appeals of Georgia, 1992.
205 Ga.App. 332, 422 S.E.2d 230.

■ CARLEY, JUDGE. Mr. Harold Cole died intestate. He was survived by appellee Mrs. Audrey Cole, his second wife, and by appellants, the children of his first marriage. Relying upon the statutory presumption of a gift between spouses, the probate court found that the decedent had a one-half interest in the marital home. See OCGA § 53–12–92 (c). On appeal to the superior court, a jury found that the marital home belonged entirely to appellee pursuant to a purchase money resulting trust. See OCGA § 53–12–92 (a). Appellants appeal from the judgment entered on the jury's verdict.

. . .

Without objection, appellee testified that, after the marriage, she had sold her own home and, with no contribution from the decedent, used the proceeds to purchase a new home. Title was conveyed to appellee and the decedent jointly without any right of survivorship. Over a hearsay objection, appellee was further allowed to testify that the decedent had told her that he would be unable to contribute toward the purchase of the property until such time as he was no longer obligated to pay child support for appellants. On appeal, the trial court's failure to sustain the hearsay objection to this testimony is the sole enumeration of error.

"Declarations . . . made by a person since deceased against his interest and not made with a view to pending litigation shall be admissible in evidence in any case." OCGA § 24–3–8. . . . Appellants urge that appellee's testimony would not be admissible pursuant to OCGA § 24–3–8, but would be excludable as hearsay because the statement attributed to the decedent was wholly in favor of appellee's interest.

A decedent's declarations in disparagement of his title would be admissible pursuant to OCGA § 24–3–8, as they negate the existence of a gift and are, therefore, against the decedent's pecuniary interest. Wiley v. Luke, 259 Ga. 861, 862 (1b) (389 S.E.2d 223) (1990); Freeman v. Saxton, 240 Ga. 309, 311 (1) (240 S.E.2d 708) (1977). That such declarations are proffered by one who would benefit from their admission into evidence is not a valid ground for excluding them from the jury's consideration. Swain v. C & S Bank of Albany, 258 Ga. 547, 550 (1) (372 S.E.2d 423) (1988). Accordingly, appellee's testimony in the instant case was admissible under OCGA § 24–3–8, in rebuttal of the presumption arising under OCGA § 53–12–92 (c) that she had made a gift to him of a one-half interest in the real property and the improvements thereon.

Judgment affirmed.

NOTES

1. Barrera v. Gonzalez, 341 S.W.2d 703, 705–706 (Tex.Civ.App.1960). Defendant, a widow, sought to show that the deed which plaintiff claimed entitled him to the property on which defendant was living had in fact been intended by the parties as a mortgage. The deed from defendant and her husband to plaintiff recited that plaintiff had assumed the balance of an indebtedness owed by the husband to a lumber company. The husband had committed suicide. Defendant offered in evidence a suicide note, an entry made in a book found in Barrera's bed room, and some notations on the back of an envelope. The substance of these notations is the same in each document. Each document was offered as exceptions to the hearsay rule, and specifically as admissions against Barrera's interest. The declaration which defendants claim is against their interest is the recitation that the declarant was indebted to Gonzalez in the sum of $2,919.24. . . .

We regard the statements offered in this case as self-serving rather than disserving. The issue involved is not whether Barrera owed money. If that were the issue, the offered statements would be against interest. Instead, the statements are offered to prove that he did owe money and for that reason, he still owned the property. Unless the debt continued, title to the property was lost. The declarant served his own interest in making statements by which he would retain or recover the title to property he had deeded away. Statements which tend to prove the fact of debt serve his interest instead of defeating his interest. We do not reach the contention briefed by defendants, that any disserving statement will admit all, even the self-serving statements contained in the same document. In this case, even the statement that declarant owed $2,919.24 is self-serving to one who wishes to prove that he owes a debt secured by the property. The documents were properly excluded. [Footnotes omitted.]

2. Suppose a person testifies under a grant of immunity in a criminal antitrust case thereby avoiding criminal prosecution. Does his testimony become admissible in a subsequent civil antitrust action because of the possibility that the testimony might lead to the declarant's civil liability? See State ex rel. McGraw v. Meadow Gold Dairies, Inc., 875 F.Supp. 340, 344 (W.D.Va.1994).

3. A common instance of a statement self-serving in one aspect and disserving in another is a writing by a payee, whether by way of indorsement or separate memorandum, acknowledging part payment of a debt. If the statement was made a reasonable time before the statutory period of limitations had expired, it is held to be preponderatingly disserving although it starts the statutory period running anew; if made after the statutory period has expired, it is held to be preponderatingly self-serving, for it removes the bar which has already fallen. Whether the date appearing on the writing is presumed to be the date when the writing was made is the subject of conflicting decisions. See 59 A.L.R. 903 et seq. (1929). See also Handley v. Limbaugh, 162 S.E.2d 400, 404–405 (Ga.1968): Proceeding to establish the right to inherit as the child of decedents by virtue of their contract to adopt him. The natural father's declarations held admissible. "Code § 38–309 provides: 'The declarations and entries by a person, since deceased, against his interest, and not made with a view to pending litigation, shall be admissible in evidence in any case.' The testimony in regard to statements of the father of the appellee concerning the agreement of the Limbaughs to adopt the appellee was given by witnesses having no pecuniary interest in the case. The declarations of the deceased were made by one of the few persons having personal knowledge of the facts of the agreement in connection with the surrender of the appellee to the Limbaughs. The declarations were not self-serving, and they were made at a time when no litigation was in view. The surrender by the father of his child to another for adoption, while having the material advantage to the father of relieving him of the support of his child, had the immeasurable detriment of irrevocably depriving the father of the love and companionship of the child. Such a detriment to a parent has been held to be of sufficient value to constitute a consideration for the contract of adoption, which is enforceable in equity. McWilliams v. Pair, 151 Ga. 168(1), 106 S.E. 96; Savannah Bank & Trust Co. v. Wolff, 191 Ga. 111, 116, 11 S.E.2d 766, 770; Foster v. Cheek, 212 Ga. 821, 825, 96 S.E.2d 545, 548. These declarations of the appellee's father were therefore admissible under Code § 38–309, as declarations by a person, since deceased, against his interest, and not made with a view to pending litigation."

4. Duncan v. Smith, 393 S.W.2d 798 (Tex.1965) (bus driver's statement that he was passing a car on the right and his braking was inadequate held a statement against interest); Home Insurance Co. v. Allied Telephone Co., 442 S.W.2d 211 (Ark.1969) (bailee-driver's statement that he was in the right place at the wrong time, that the accident looks like "something that couldn't be helped", held a statement against interest).

Cf. Potter v. Finan, 150 N.W.2d 539, 542–543 (Mich.Ct.App.1967): Action against tavern operator for injuries received in a collision with automobile driven by a patron of the tavern. Latter's statement that he had ten beers preceding the accident, that he was intoxicated but not "too much", held not against his pecuniary interest.

5. Should there be a requirement of unavailability for this exception? See discussion in Orr v. State Farm Mutual Automobile Insurance Co., 494 S.W.2d 295 (Mo.1973) (en banc). Cf. Chambers v. Mississippi, 410 U.S. 284 (1973), supra p. 364.

Carpenter v. Davis

Supreme Court of Missouri, 1968.
435 S.W.2d 382.

■ DONNELLY, JUDGE. In this jury-tried action involving an intersectional vehicular collision in Osage County, Missouri, which occurred March 17, 1965, plaintiff seeks damages for the death of his wife, Opal Carpenter. The jury returned a verdict for defendants. Plaintiff appealed.

The collision occurred at the intersection of Highways 50 and 63. Highway 50 extends east and west. Highway 63 extends south from its intersection with Highway 50. A stop sign and red light at the intersection govern vehicles traveling north on Highway 63.

Opal Carpenter was a passenger in a car driven by her brother, Loren Babbitt, in a northerly direction on Highway 63. Defendant Thomas Grothoff was driving a Central Dairy Truck in an easterly direction on Highway 50. The truck struck the left side of the car near the center of the intersection.

The parties have narrowed the issues on this appeal. The question is whether, in this negligence action, an opinion as to fault is admissible as a declaration against interest. We hold that it is not.

Defendant Grothoff testified as follows:

"Q Now, what did you do immediately following the collision?

"A I run over and checked the car. This man was laying up against—this woman was kinda turned around and this man was laying up against her, and—

. . .

"Q (by Mr. Burruss) Did you have any conversation with the lady in the right front seat, Mrs. Carpenter, the lady who died?

"A Not at this time I didn't. I went and called the Highway Patrol and ordered an ambulance before I talked to anybody.

"Q All right. So you went to the car and looked in?

"A Yes, sir.

"Q But then you left this car, this Dodge Dart, is that right?

"A That's right.

"Q You went to call for assistance?

"A That's right.

"Q Where did you go to do that, Mr. Grothoff?

"A Willibrand's have a—has an outside pay telephone booth right next to its service station there, and I run over to it and I called the Highway Patrol.

"Q This is Willibrand's service station, right there at the intersection; is that right?

"A That's right.

"Q All right, sir. Then what did you do after you called the Highway Patrol?

"A Well, I had come back to the car and this time I went around to the other side of the car to where the lady was and she was trying to get out of the car, then.

"Q Did you have any conversation with her at that time?

"A Yes, sir, I did.

"Q And what did you say to her, Mr. Grothoff?

"MR. COIL: I object to this conversation. The witness is not—

"THE COURT: Step up, gentlemen.

(The following proceedings were had at the bench, outside the hearing of the jury:

"MR. COIL: The witness is not competent to testify to any statement—

"THE COURT: Suppose he makes his offer of proof and you make your objection?

"MR. BURRUSS: I want to show by this witness that he stated to the decedent, at this time, 'I'm sorry, lady, but you pulled right out in front of me.' And that she said to him, 'Yes. Yes, I know. It wasn't your fault.'

"I offer that as a declaration against interest.

"MR. COIL: I object to the offer on the ground this witness, being a party to the action, is not competent to testify to any statement made by the deceased person, and on the further ground that the proffered statement constitutes a legal conclusion and not part of the res gestae and is not a dying declaration.

"THE COURT: Are you sure he is going to testify to all that?

"MR. BURRUSS: All I can tell you, this is what the man said was said at the time and place.

"THE COURT: If he testifies to all that, I'll overrule the objection.

"Q (by Mr. Burruss) Now, Mr. Grothoff, my question to you was, what did you say to the woman who later died, Mrs. Carpenter, at that time?

"A I said, 'I'm sorry, lady, you pulled right out in front of me.'

"Q What did she reply to you when you said that?

"A *She said, 'Yes, I'm sorry, it's not your fault', something like that—'Yes, I know, it's not your fault,' I believe is what she said.*"

Plaintiff contends the trial court committed reversible error in admitting in evidence the statement, italicized above, attributed by the witness to Opal Carpenter. In determining the question of admissibility of the statement, we must first recognize the difference between admissions against interest and declarations against interest.

"There is a vital distinction between *admissions* against interest and *declarations* against interest. Admissions against interest are those made by a party to the litigation or by one in privity with or identified in legal interest with such party, and admissible whether or not the declarant is available as a witness. Declarations against interest are those made by persons not a party or in privity with a party to the suit, are secondary evidence and constitute an exception to the hearsay rule, admissible only when the declarant is unavailable as a witness." Neely v. Kansas City Public Service Co., 241 Mo.App. 1244, 1247, 252 S.W.2d 88, 91.

We reach the following preliminary conclusions:

(1) The statement in question is: " 'Yes, I know, it's not your fault,'...." The statement of fact, " 'Yes, I know,' " will be admissible upon retrial, if offered alone, as a declaration against interest. Graham v. Stroh, 342 Mo. 686, 696, 117 S.W.2d 258, 262; Straughan v. Asher, Mo.App., 372 S.W.2d 489, 494–495. However, the balance of the statement is an opinion as to fault.

(2) This opinion as to fault would have been admissible as an *admission* against interest had Opal Carpenter survived and this were her action for damages for personal injuries. Grodsky v. Consolidated Bag Co., 324 Mo. 1067, 26 S.W.2d 618; Annotation, 118 A.L.R. 1230.

(3) This opinion as to fault is not admissible in Missouri as an *admission* against interest because it was not made by a party to this action or by someone identified in legal interest with a party to this action. In McComb v. Vaughn, 358 Mo. 951, 956, 218 S.W.2d 548, 551, the Court stated: "... It seems to us deceased in his lifetime could not have had any identity as one in privity, in any legal sense, with plaintiff Lagatha in her new and distinct cause of action which arose and accrued to her only upon his death and only by virtue of statute."

In the Grodsky case, supra, this Court approved a ruling by the trial court admitting a statement by plaintiff that in her opinion someone other than defendant was entirely responsible for the accident. The Grodsky case involved an *admission* against interest. The declarant was a party. The question is whether the Grodsky holding should be extended to this case wherein declarant is not a party.

The Grodsky case, supra, and other cases involving *admissions* against interest, such as Costello v. M.C. Slater, Inc., Mo.App., 220 S.W.2d 947, cited by defendants, do not assist us in determining the question. They represent recognition, in an adversary proceeding, that a party should be held responsible for statements of fact or opinion, previously made, which conflict with the position taken by him in the judicial proceeding. Such statements may affect credibility and proof, and may aid the jury in arriving at the truth. In any event, the declarant is available in court to advance or defend his position.

An opinion as to fault in a negligence action is particularly susceptible to error. A witness at trial may, intentionally or otherwise, change a word and convey a meaning completely different from that intended by the declarant. An opinion as to fault may be ambiguous, and yet persuasive, where, as here, no opportunity exists for explanation or denial. In these circumstances, are the available safeguards sufficient to offset the risks of inaccuracy? We think not. See Wigmore on Evidence, 3rd Ed., Vol. V, § 1420; and McKelvey on Evidence, 5th Ed., § 258. We hold that an opinion as to fault is not admissible as a *declaration* against interest.

The case of Costello v. M.C. Slater, Inc., supra, insofar as it may infer that an opinion as to fault, coupled with a statement of fact, is admissible as a *declaration* against interest, should no longer be followed.

The trial court prejudicially erred in permitting the jury to consider, as an exception to the hearsay rule, an opinion as to fault, attributed to one not a party.

The judgment is reversed and the cause remanded.

■ FINCH, JUDGE (dissenting).

I concurred in division in an opinion substantially similar to the principal opinion herein. However, after reargument of the case before the court en banc I have concluded to dissent.

If Mrs. Carpenter had lived and had brought suit to recover for her injuries, the statement attributed to her by defendant Grothoff would have been admissible therein as an admission against interest. The principal opinion so recognizes. However, Mrs. Carpenter died and her husband seeks to recover for her death resulting from those same injuries. The principal opinion points out that Mrs. Carpenter, of course, is not a party to the present suit and that under the doctrine of McComb v. Vaughn, 358 Mo. 951, 218 S.W.2d 548, the cause of action by her husband is a new statutory cause of action and there is no privity between plaintiff Carpenter and his deceased wife. On that basis, the opinion concludes that the statement in question is not admissible as an admission against interest. It further holds that the statement is not admissible as a declaration against interest on the basis that the words spoken constitute an opinion as to fault rather than a statement of facts or deductions from other facts related by declarant in the same conversation.

We thus have, under the principal opinion, the anomalous situation wherein the husband, seeking a recovery for death caused by injuries to his wife, may prevent the introduction in evidence of the statement made by his wife at the time, although such statement would have been admissible against the wife in her own suit to recover for those same injuries. As a result, the husband has a greater chance to recover for the death of his wife than she would have had to recover for her own injuries.

The rule excluding such statement in a suit by the husband on the basis of absence of privity seems highly technical and neither just nor logical. I have concluded that we should not permit such a result. I would hold that where a deceased has made a statement which would have been admissible against him or her as an admission against interest in an action for personal injuries, such statement also is admissible against one maintaining an action for death resulting from those same injuries, even though the death action is one created by statute. It seems to me that in this limited type of situation we could reasonably waive the requirement of privity. The husband really stands in the shoes of the deceased (even though the death action is created by statute). An alternative basis, of course, would be to hold that privity exists in such a situation.[1]

Accordingly, I would hold that the statement by Mrs. Carpenter made to Grothoff was properly admitted in evidence, and I would affirm the judgment.

■ SEILER, JUDGE (dissenting).

I respectfully dissent, because it seems to me the declaration before us, "Yes, I know, it's not your fault" made in direct response to the statement of the driver to the injured person, "I'm sorry, lady, you pulled right out in front

---

1. Some states do find privity even though the death action is statutory. This was recognized in McComb v. Vaughn, 358 Mo. 951, 218 S.W.2d 548, 551. See, for exam-ple, Hovey v. See, Tex.Civ.App., 191 S.W. 606, and Georgia Railroad and Banking Co. v. Fitzgerald, 108 Ga. 507, 34 S.E. 316, 49 L.R.A. 175. [Judge's footnote.]

of me", does contain the necessary circumstantial probability of trustworthiness to qualify it for admission as an exception to the hearsay rule, and does not run afoul of the opinion rule. As Wigmore states, Wigmore on Evidence, 3rd Ed., Vol. V, § 1422, the "... practicable substitute for the ordinary test of cross-examination ..." as to declarations against interest is "Where the circumstances are such that a sincere and accurate statement would naturally be uttered, and no plan of falsification be formed." The entirety of what Mrs. Carpenter said meets this test.

As to the opinion rule, Wigmore points out that it should not apply to extra-judicial statements of deceased persons, anymore than it should to dying declarations, because the theory of the opinion rule "... is that, wherever the witness can state specifically the detailed facts observed by him, the inferences to be drawn from them can equally well be drawn by the jury, so that the witness' inferences become superfluous. Now, since the declarant is here deceased, it is no longer possible to obtain from him by questions any more detailed data than his statement may contain, and hence his inferences are not in this instance superfluous, but are indispensable", Wigmore, supra, Vol. V, §§ 1569 and 1447.

In addition, I doubt if Mrs. Carpenter's statement, under the circumstances, which I understood from oral argument were that the Carpenter car drove out in front of the dairy truck (a matter which Mrs. Carpenter as an occupant of the car would likely know about), is as much opinion as it is fact. As said in State v. Proctor (Mo.Sup.) 269 S.W.2d 624, 630, 48 A.L.R.2d 724, "... what constitutes a statement of opinion or a statement of fact depends not alone upon the statement itself but upon the surrounding circumstances as well...." I do not think it is a distortion to regard all of what she said as being drawn from facts immediately under her observation as to the operation of the car in which she was riding. No doubt under some circumstances an expression as to fault is not admissible as a declaration against interest. But it is too broad a rule in my opinion to say this is always the case, as the majority opinion indicates.

The fact that hindsight might indicate that Mrs. Carpenter may have been too harsh on herself in what she did say (if it should later prove by reason of some fact or facts unknown to her that it was Grothoff's responsibility despite her car pulling out in front of him) goes to the weight to be given to her declaration and would be a matter of argument to the jury, but should not affect its admissibility.

The majority opinion also seems to rest the exclusion of the fault part of Mrs. Carpenter's statement to some extent on the fear that the witness "at a trial may, intentionally or otherwise, change a word and convey a meaning completely different from that intended by the declarant". The possibility always exists, of course, that a witness may testify falsely or mistakenly. But usually we do not let this possibility keep out otherwise admissible evidence. If we did, very little oral testimony would ever be admitted. Rather than excluding evidence because of this possibility (as, for example, the testimony of interested parties was at one time excluded on the theory that they were likely to testify falsely) we should receive it, leaving its weight and value to be determined by other considerations. We can rely on cross-examination, the scrutiny to which the witness is subjected by the court and jury, and the efficacy of the investigation of the facts by counsel prior to trial, as our safeguards against falsity and mistake.

I would therefore hold that the trial court was correct in admitting the entire statement and would affirm the judgment.

■ STORCKMAN, JUDGE (dissenting).

I cannot agree that this court should undertake to divide the statement attributed to Mrs. Carpenter and indicate that the words "Yes, I know" be admitted on a retrial. The speaker is dead and cannot be heard to deny, verify or explain. The statement comes to us through repetition by the truck driver, a party defendant. The principal opinion points out that: "A witness at trial may, intentionally or otherwise, change a word and convey a meaning completely different from that intended by the declarant."

We go a step further in this case. The statement was transcribed and *punctuated* by the court reporter. Punctuation can vary the meaning and the court should not be bound by the punctuation supplied by the court reporter. As reported in the transcript, the statement is: "Yes, I know, it's not your fault." If the second comma is omitted, the statement is: "Yes, I know it's not your fault." Or all punctuation could be omitted with the same result that the whole statement would unquestionably relate to an opinion as to fault.

In any event, it is quite speculative to say that the statement, or any part of it, is a factual declaration. The matter of punctuation, however, makes it more so and demonstrates that the statement should be rejected as an entirety.

I am further convinced that the statement, in whole or in part, is not admissible as a declaration against interest as an exception to the hearsay rule. Fairly definite standards have been established which must be met to qualify a statement as such an exception.

The principal opinion cites and quotes from the case of Neely v. Kansas City Public Service Co., 241 Mo.App. 1244, 252 S.W.2d 88, with respect to the distinction between admissions against interest and declarations against interest which is helpful. The Neely opinion also sets out standards to which a statement must conform to qualify as a declaration against interest which are as follows: "To be admissible such a declaration (a) must spring from the peculiar means of knowledge of the matter stated, (b) must be against the interest of the declarant at the time made, and (c) such interest must be so apparent as to have been presumably in the declarant's mind when made." 252 S.W.2d at page 91. The letters in parentheses are added for emphasis and easy reference. This statement from the Neely case is based on McComb v. Vaughn, 358 Mo. 951, 218 S.W.2d 548, 551, and other Missouri cases and textbooks. More recently the standards are recited and discussed comprehensively in Straughan v. Asher, Mo.App., 372 S.W.2d 489, at pages 494, 495, n. 5, 6. By reason of her death Mrs. Carpenter is not available as a witness, but her alleged statement does not meet the other three standards imposed.

The declaration attributed to Mrs. Carpenter (a) "must spring from the peculiar means of knowledge of the matter stated". Mrs. Carpenter was not shown to have any "peculiar means" of knowing the position of the automobiles in the sense of being special or singular, such as the person who endorses a payment on a note or declares or disclaims his title to land. Mr. Grothoff or any bystander might have as good or better opportunity to observe the occurrence. Her means of knowledge would have to be inferred from her statement in conjunction with the self-serving statement of Mr. Grothoff. Furthermore, Mrs. Carpenter is not shown to have had knowledge sufficient to form an opinion as to whether the truck driver in the exercise of the highest degree of care could have slackened his speed or swerved in time to avoid the collision. In short, she is not shown to have any means of knowing whose fault it was.

Further, in order to be admissible, the declaration (b) "must be against the interest of the declarant at the time made". The interest of the declarant must be either proprietary, pecuniary or perhaps a penal interest. 31A C.J.S. Evidence § 219; Moore v. Metropolitan Life Insurance Co., Mo.App., 237 S.W.2d 210, 212[4]. The only possible pecuniary interest that Mrs. Carpenter could have had was a cause of action against the truck owner and its driver. It is well settled in this state that a husband's action for the wrongful death of his wife is purely statutory and not derivative or in privity with the wife. McComb v. Vaughn, 358 Mo. 951, 218 S.W.2d 548, 551[5]. In this case Mrs. Carpenter received serious injuries which caused her death. She had not asserted any claim and had no opportunity to do so.

The final requirement is that (c) "such interest must be so apparent as to have been presumably in the declarant's mind when made". There is no basis for any presumption that Mrs. Carpenter had in mind a lawsuit for her injuries at the time she was talking to Mr. Grothoff. The defendant driver's statement was self-serving and would ordinarily have been excluded. He had looked into the wrecked automobile and saw Mrs. Carpenter but apparently made no effort to extricate her before he left to call the highway patrol. When he returned she was trying to get out of the automobile in which she was trapped and fatally injured. That appeared to be her sole interest and concern. I would hold on these facts that the statement did not qualify as a declaration against interest. Her response was more in the nature of an amenity rather than giving attention to a pecuniary interest.

As previously stated, we are dealing with an exception to the hearsay rule. No Missouri decision has been found that justifies the admission of Mrs. Carpenter's statement as a declaration against interest or on any other basis. This is hardly a proper case in which to enlarge the scope of this exception to the hearsay rule. The rule as presently recognized has received the careful scrutiny of this court on previous occasions and has been approved. It has functioned well and no need for a change has been demonstrated.

I would rule the statement inadmissible on the grounds that it is an entire expression of opinion as to fault and that it does not qualify as a declaration against interest. I would reverse and remand on both grounds.

NOTES

1. Ferrebee v. Boggs, 263 N.E.2d 574 (Ohio.Ct.App.1970): Collision between Volkswagen and tractor-trailer. Infant passenger in Volkswagen killed. Tractor-trailer driver, who died later, said to Volkswagen driver while both were in an ambulance en route to hospital, "I did not mean to kill your baby, it was all my fault". In an action against Volkswagen driver (a) for pain and suffering and (b) for death of tractor driver, the statement is admitted on claim (a) as an admission and on claim (b) as a declaration against interest.

2. Action v. Bus Co., its driver and another automobilist. The automobilist offers evidence of the bus driver's statement, characterizing it as a "statement against interest" and pointing out that its "author is not in court". Objection sustained. Upon appeal, the automobilist argues that the statement should have been admitted "as an admission". Held, no error. The evidence was inadmissible as a declaration against interest, and the question whether it would have been admissible had it been claimed as an admission is not properly before the court. Johnson v. Rockaway Bus Corp., 140 A.2d 708 (Conn.1958). Cf. Smith v. Perdue, 129 S.E.2d 293 (N.C.1963) (two actions consolidated for trial: the same item of evidence was admitted as an admission in one action and as a declaration against interest in the other). See also Elms v. Kansas City

Public Service Co., 335 S.W.2d 26 (Mo.1960) (evidence admissible against one defendant as admission, but not against plaintiff as that defendant's declaration against interest); Pennsylvania R. Co. v. Rochinski, 158 F.2d 325 (D.C.Cir. 1946), noted in 15 Geo.Wash.L.Rev. 486 (evidence admissible either as declaration against interest or impeachment, depending upon identity of declarant); Straughan v. Asher, 372 S.W.2d 489 (Mo.Ct.App.1963) (evidence admissible to impeach but not as declaration against interest).

3. How apparent must it be to the declarant that the statement is against interest? See Gichner v. Antonio Troiano Tile & Marble Co., 410 F.2d 238, 242, 249 (D.C.Cir.1969): Ps alleged that their warehouse, a part of which was leased to D, was extensively damaged in a fire started by negligent smoking after four employees of D entered the warehouse at night after a drinking spree. One of the employees, Faulds, made a statement to the fire inspector the morning of the fire, in which he admitted that the group had been smoking. The majority found the statement to be against Fauld's interest:

> A statement is against pecuniary and proprietary interest when it threatens the loss of employment, or reduces the chances for future employment, or entails possible civil liability ... Here Faulds' statement is an important link in providing a basis for concluding that Faulds and the other nighttime visitors to the warehouse were responsible for starting the fire; the possibility of civil liability against him arising from the statement is thus evident. Indeed, an effort was made to make him a defendant in this case.... Further, even though [D] did not have a rule against smoking on the premises, Faulds' admission that he had been there after hours, for a purpose unrelated to his employment, and while there did something which may have caused the destruction of his employer's stock in trade, reflects on his responsibility and trustworthiness, and can reasonably be said to jeopardize his standing with his employer.

The court rejected D's argument that "Faulds only stated that they had been smoking, not that they had been carelessly smoking." "[I]t is not necessary for the statement to include every aspect of negligence; it is enough if the statement could reasonably provide an important link in a chain of evidence which is a basis for civil liability."

Dissent:

> ... Here we have a "bad case" with the traditional legal result. The majority, then, admit the statement of an off-duty laborer, made completely outside the scope of his employment and concerning conduct completely unrelated to the nature, scope, purpose or bounds of that employment, concerning an occurrence when he, after an all night drinking orgy, was a trespasser upon the employer's premises, outside the hours (and apparently the days) of his employment. The employee has disappeared. He is consequently unavailable for cross examination, and the factors that normally go into the determination of a witness' credibility are completely withheld from the trier of facts. I cannot subscribe to the majority action which puts a label of admissible evidence upon such a statement on the ludicrous conclusion that this laborer's employment constituted such a pecuniary or financial interest as to guarantee the accuracy of this statement.

Would Faulds' statement be admissible as a vicarious admission? Would Faulds' statement have been admissible if it had been against his employer's interest but not against his interest? See Gilmour v. Strescon Industries, Inc., 66 F.R.D. 146, 150 (E.D.Pa.), aff'd mem., 521 F.2d 1398 (3d Cir.1975).

See also Fisher v. Duckworth, 738 S.W.2d 810, 815 (Ky.1987): Ps brought personal injury action against owner of the car which hit them that was being driven by his employee (who was named as a co-defendant but who was never served and apparently unavailable at trial). The employer-owner introduced a tape recording of a telephone call in which the employee told the employer's insurance adjuster that he was on a personal errand at the time of the accident. In answer to a special interrogatory, the jury found that the employee was on a frolic of his own and the claim against the owner was dismissed. Reversed:

> We have no proof that Duckworth was a person sufficiently familiar with insurance law to know that the insurance coverage for Grisanti's vehicle might not extend to him if he had deviated from the scope of his employment to perform a personal errand. To the contrary, we note that ... Duckworth was employed by Grisanti, that he was an unskilled laborer, and that he was talking to his employer's insurance adjuster. The record does not show what conversation took place before the recorder was turned on.

4. Houck v. DeBonis, 379 A.2d 765 (Md.Ct.App.1977), cert. denied, 434 U.S. 967 (1977). P sustained personal injuries in an accident while driving a station wagon and attached trailer, both of which were owned by her husband, who was deceased by the time of trial. In P's suit against the dealer from whom the husband had purchased the trailer, D offers a statement by the husband in which he imputed negligence to P in her driving and towing. Admissible? On what theory?

Cf. State v. Lyman, 812 P.2d 23 (Or.App.1991) (in prosecution of D for driving while intoxicated, reversible error for trial court to admit statement of D's wife that D was driving while drunk; even though D's and wife's finances were interrelated, the risk of pecuniary loss to wife if D went to jail was "too attenuated" for a reasonable person in her position to conclude that the risk was so great "that she would not tell a lie.").

5. Uniform Rule of Evidence, Rule 804(b)(3) includes as being against interest, a statement that tended "to make [the declarant] an object of hatred, ridicule, or disgrace." This provision, which was also contained in the Federal Rule as promulgated by the Supreme Court, was deleted by Congress. See Sills v. State, 846 S.W.2d 392, 397 (Tex.Ct.App.1992) ("The State argues Chambers's statement subjected him to appellant's hatred and retaliation. Logically, it can be argued that any statement made by a declarant against another will subject the declarant to hatred and retaliation by the person or persons the statement implicates. The State does not refer us to any case law that supports this type of broad argument. To be admissible, a statement against interest that makes the declarant the object of hatred, ridicule, or disgrace must be in the context of the declarant's social interests, such as a confession by a small-town minister of homosexual conduct, Purtell v. State, 761 S.W.2d 360, 369 (Tex.Crim.App.1988), cert. denied, 490 U.S. 1059, 109 S.Ct. 1972, 104 L.Ed.2d 441 (1989), or a statement by a husband that he was responsible for an automobile accident whereby his wife became a paraplegic. Robinson v. Harkins & Co., 711 S.W.2d 619, 621 (Tex.1986). If the State's broad argument was accepted then virtually every statement a declarant made against another would be admissible.").

People v. Brown

Court of Appeals of New York, 1970.
26 N.Y.2d 88, 308 N.Y.S.2d 825, 257 N.E.2d 16.

■ BERGAN, JUDGE. The main issue in this case, where appellant has been convicted of murder in the second degree, is whether he acted in self-defense.

In turn this depends on the proof of appellant's contention that the deceased had a pistol drawn when appellant shot him.

One witness for appellant testified to this effect; but several prosecution witnesses testified decedent did not have a pistol in hand when defendant shot him and the police found no pistol on decedent's clothes or on the floor of the premises where the shooting occurred.

This brings into focus the importance of an admission made both to the police and to appellant's lawyer by one Shelton Seals, who at the time of trial was being held in jail on a charge of robbery, that he had "picked up the gun" apparently which he used in the robbery "immediately after the shooting" for which appellant has been convicted. This admission was made in a conversation at the jail with appellant's counsel; another and similar admission was made by Seals in a confession to the police.

If it had been true that Seals picked up a gun from the floor of the premises immediately after the shooting for which defendant has been convicted, this could have a significant bearing on defendant's contention that decedent was armed and that defendant acted in his own defense.

Seals was called as a defense witness. He refused to answer questions on constitutional grounds. Appellant then offered proof of his admissions. The court sustained objections to them. The ruling was clearly proper upon settled authority in this State. Thus the important question presented by this appeal is whether the existing rule should be continued or abandoned in favor of a more rational view of admissibility of declarations against interest.

In discussing the admissibility of such declarations against interest as an exception to the hearsay rule, Richardson makes the categorical statement that "The fact that the declaration alleged to have been made would subject the declarant to criminal liability is held not to be sufficient to bring it within the declaration against interest exception to the rule against hearsay evidence" (Richardson, Evidence [9th ed.], § 241, pp. 232, 233).

This, as it has been noted, has undoubtedly been the rule in New York (Kittredge v. Grannis, 244 N.Y. 168, 175, 176, 155 N.E. 88, 90; Ellwanger v. Whiteford, 15 A.D.2d 898, 225 N.Y.S.2d 734, affd. 12 N.Y.2d 1037, 239 N.Y.S.2d 680, 190 N.E.2d 24); in the Federal Courts (Donnelly v. United States, 228 U.S. 243, 33 S.Ct. 449, 57 L.Ed. 820); and in a majority of the States (31A C.J.S. Evidence § 219, pp. 608–609).

Yet the distinction which would authorize a court to receive proof that a man admitted he never had title to an Elgin watch, but not to receive proof that he had admitted striking Jones over the head with a club, assuming equal relevancy of both statements, does not readily withstand analysis.

Holmes attacked the distinction in his notable dissent in Donnelly (supra, 228 U.S. pp. 277–278, 33 S.Ct. p. 461) in which, among other things, he said: "The rules of evidence in the main are based on experience, logic, and common sense, less hampered by history than some parts of the substantive law. There is no decision by this court against the admissibility of such a confession; the English cases since the separation of the two countries do not bind us; the exception to the hearsay rule in the case of declarations against interest is well known; no other statement is so much against interest as a confession of murder; it is far more calculated to convince than dying declarations, which would be let in to hang a man (Mattox v. United States, 146 U.S. 140, 13 S.Ct. 50, 36 L.Ed. 917); and when we surround the accused with so many safeguards, some of which seem to me excessive; I think we ought to give him the benefit of a fact that, if proved, commonly would have such weight. The history of the law and the arguments against the English doctrine are so well and fully stated by Mr. Wigmore that there is no need to set them forth at greater length. 2 Wigmore, Ev. §§ 1476, 1477.''

Wigmore, as Holmes notes, developed the argument against the distinction, not only on the basis of sheer logic, but on the historical ground that the English cases which created the distinction, particularly the Sussex Peerage Case (11 Cl. & Fin. 85, 109) were a departure from the basic rule of long standing that admissions against interest generally were received, where relevant, and the declarant dead. The Peerage decision was regarded by Wigmore as "not strongly argued and not considered by the judges in the light of the precedents" (5 Wigmore Evidence, [3d ed.], § 1476, p. 283). Wigmore concludes his comprehensive analysis of the problem with the statement: "It is therefore not too late to retrace our steps, and to discard this barbarous doctrine." (op. cit., p. 290).

There seems to be developing in this country a gradual change of viewpoint which would abolish the distinction. In 1964 the Supreme Court of California decided People v. Spriggs, 60 Cal.2d 868, 36 Cal.Rptr. 841, 389 P.2d 377, opn. per Traynor, J. This held that proof defendant's companion admitted to the police that the heroin found on the ground was hers was admissible.

Justice Traynor, discussing the usual rule that admission against pecuniary interest was admissible, said: "A declaration against penal interest is no less trustworthy. As we pointed out in People v. One 1948 Chevrolet Conv. Coupe, 45 Cal.2d 613, 622, 290 P.2d 538, 55 A.L.R.2d 1272, a person's interest against being criminally implicated gives reasonable assurance of the veracity of his statement made against the interest. Moreover, since the conviction of a crime ordinarily entails economic loss, the traditional concept of a 'pecuniary interest' could logically include one's 'penal interest.' " (60 Cal.2d pp. 874–875, 36 Cal.Rptr. p. 845, 389 P.2d p. 381).

In the same direction in Missouri, see Moore v. Metropolitan Life Ins. Co., Mo.App., 237 S.W.2d 210 and Sutter v. Easterly (354 Mo. 282, 189 S.W.2d 284) where there is a good discussion of Wigmore's analysis; and in Arizona, Deike v. Great Atlantic & Pacific Tea Co., 3 Ariz.App. 430, 415 P.2d 145.

If, as it is argued, Seals picked up a gun on the floor after the shooting (a gun with which he subsequently committed a robbery) it would be a matter of importance in reaching the truth as to whether or not decedent was armed and it would tend to substantiate defendant's self-defense argument. This kind of admission might well be more important and reliable than the testimony of defendant's witness that decedent had a gun in hand.

There is another facet. The rule on admissions against interest was based on the absence of the witness; and usually this meant that he was dead. But whether the person is dead, or beyond the jurisdiction, or will not testify, and cannot be compelled to testify because of a constitutional privilege, all equally spell out unavailability of trial testimony. If the rule is to be changed to include penal admissions against interest, it ought to embrace unavailability because of the assertion of constitutional right which might be fairly common in the area of penal admissions.

This is the way the St. Louis Court of Appeals approached the question in Moore v. Metropolitan Life Ins. Co., Mo.App., 237 S.W.2d 210, 212, supra: "In other words, having regard for the principle of necessity which justifies resort to secondary evidence, a witness who stands upon his constitutional rights is, as a practical proposition, just as fully unavailable as though he were insane or dead or prevented from testifying because of some other acceptable reason. Sutter v. Easterly, 354 Mo. 282, 189 S.W.2d 284, 162 A.L.R. 437."

In People v. Spriggs, 60 Cal.2d 868, 36 Cal.Rptr. 841, 389 P.2d 377, supra, the California Supreme Court held the admission against penal interest admissible without reaching, on that record, the kind of lack of availability which would become a basis for taking the admission. The record of that trial did not show whether she was available.

But Judge Traynor's footnote 3 (p. 875, 36 Cal.Rptr. p. 845, 389 P.2d p. 381) was to the effect that "If Mrs. Roland had taken the witness stand, but refused to testify regarding possession of narcotics, invoking her constitutional right not to incriminate herself, she would not have been available as a witness."

The rule in New York should be modernized to hold that an admission against penal interest will be received where material and where the person making the admission is dead, beyond the jurisdiction and thus not available; or where he is in court and refuses to testify as to the fact of the admission on the ground of self incrimination.

Since there is to be a new trial two other points raised by appellant require discussion. The first is that the People were permitted excessive cross-examination of defendant when he took the stand as a witness in his own behalf. One line of questions related to his participation in a fight in which the victim was cut with a knife. Another concerned his paternity of a child, and his relationship with Pamela Sargent, one of the prosecution witnesses. This included inquiry concerning a paternity action in the Family Court.

The District Attorney contends that the questions relating to the assault and other matters were in good faith which is supported by files in his office. Some of this cross-examination was improper, especially the references to the paternity proceedings and perhaps also the incidents of relationships. But if the questions about the assault were asked in good faith they would be proper (see, e.g., People v. Alamo, 23 N.Y.2d 630, 298 N.Y.S.2d 681, 246 N.E.2d 496; People v. Van Gaasbeck, 189 N.Y. 408, 82 N.E. 718, 22 L.R.A., N.S., 650).

Appellant also argues he should have been allowed to examine a witness who testified for the defense concerning an attempt by that witness' wife to influence his testimony and to influence him not to testify. The witness' wife, who was a sister of decedent, had been an important prosecution witness. One of the questions excluded was her conversation with her husband (the defense witness) on "whether or not you should testify in this lawsuit".

The sister was, as it has been noted, an important prosecution witness, and her interest or bias would have been relevant. And it would not have been necessary to ask her about the conversation to lay a foundation for showing her bias or interest (People v. Brooks, 131 N.Y. 321, 30 N.E. 189; People v. Lustig, 206 N.Y. 162, 99 N.E. 183; People v. Michalow, 229 N.Y. 325, 128 N.E. 228). The inquiry should have been allowed.

The judgment should be reversed and a new trial ordered.

NOTES

1. In determining whether the statement is against interest, should the court look to the declarant's subjective understanding of whether the statement was disserving, or should it apply an objective standard, asking how an ordinary person would evaluate the nature of the statement? Does the "reasonable person" formulation in Federal Rule 804(b)(3) resolve this issue? Cf. N.Y.Proposed Code of Evidence § 804(b)(3): "A statement which at the time of its making the declarant knew ... tended to subject the declarant to ... criminal liability...."

Compare United States v. Bagley, 537 F.2d 162 (5th Cir.1976), cert. denied, 429 U.S. 1075 (1977) (reasonable man would not falsely admit serious crime to cellmate) with United States v. Satterfield, 572 F.2d 687, 693 (9th Cir.), cert. denied, 439 U.S. 840 (1978) (court approved exclusion of evidence of argument in which defendant asked declarant why he refused to admit that defendant was not his accomplice, and declarant replied that he did not wish to jeopardize his appeal: "The low likelihood of the success of Merriweather's appeal makes the declaration almost risk-free from his perspective.... Merriweather's stated optimism about the outcome of his appeal is simply not very credible."). See also State v. Standifur, 526 A.2d 955 (Md.1987) (layman would not have appreciated that by suspecting that he was dealing with stolen property he was subjecting himself to liability).

Compare State v. Gold, 431 A.2d 501 (Conn.)(declarant confessed to murder with which D was charged shortly before declarant committed suicide; admissible), cert. denied, 449 U.S. 920 (1980) with Commonwealth v. Pope, 491 N.E.2d 240, 243 (Mass.1986) ("A person who is about to commit suicide faces no penal consequences for any statement made just before death."); People v. Shortridge, 480 N.E.2d 1080, 1083 (N.Y.1985) (before committing suicide, father of defendant wrote letters in which he claimed responsibility for decedent's death; no independent corroborating evidence; "presence of strong motivation to fabricate or the absence of supporting evidence can, without more, be sufficient to render a declaration inadmissible as a matter of law."). See also United States v. Hoyos, 573 F.2d 1111, 1115 (9th Cir.1978) (statements by co-defendant to his wife which "could have been suppressed at a subsequent criminal prosecution under a claim of the confidential marital communications privilege;" inadmissible); United States v. Barrett, 539 F.2d 244 (1st Cir.1976) (statements to a friend while playing cards admissible); United States v. Atkins, 558 F.2d 133 (3d Cir.1977) (statement overheard by eavesdropper admissible), cert. denied, 434 U.S. 1071 (1978).

2.   People v. Edwards, 242 N.W.2d 739, 745–46 (Mich.1976):

The Committee on Rules of Practice and Procedure of the Judicial Conference of the United States, on the recommendation of the Advisory Committee on Rules of Evidence, proposed that an exception to the hearsay rule be recognized for declarations against penal as well as pecuniary or proprietary interest. The committee noted that "[q]uestions of possible fabrication are better trusted to the competence of juries than made the subject of attempted treatment by rule". Preliminary Draft of Proposed Rules of Evidence for the United States District Courts and Magistrates (March, 1969), p. 214.

The recommendation was not accepted. The rule which was enacted recognizes an exception to the hearsay rule for declarations against penal interest, but where such declarations are offered to exculpate the accused they are not admissible "unless corroborating circumstances clearly indicate the trustworthiness of the statement."

The nature of the "corroborating circumstances" which would "clearly indicate the trustworthiness" of a declaration against penal interest is neither defined in the rules nor discussed in the notes. It appears from the Editorial Comments to the Rules, however, that an important factor in the decision to require corroboration where defendants seek to introduce exculpatory declarations against penal interest was the fear of fabricated evidence, both perjured testimony by witnesses and false confessions of crime by declarants.

We are of the opinion that the circumstances surrounding the making or reporting of a third-party statement, whether "assuring reliability," "indicating trustworthiness," or "rendering totally incredible," go to the weight to be given the testimony, not its admissibility. For a judge to exclude evidence because he does not believe it has been described as "altogether atypical, extraordinary...."[1] "[O]ur adversary system reposes judgment of the credibility of all witnesses in the jury." Brooks v. Tennessee, 406 U.S. 605, 611, 92 S.Ct. 1891, 1894, 32 L.Ed.2d 358 (1972). Cross-examination of the witness, penalties for perjury, and the good sense of the trier of fact to whom all other questions of possible fabrication are entrusted are adequate safeguards against false testimony.

We reject the apparent double standard[2] of the congressional compromise that a preliminary showing of trustworthiness is required only where the defendant offers a declaration against penal interest to exculpate himself. Such a rule is based on an assumption that criminal defendants are more likely to use perjured testimony. We refuse to predicate a rule of law upon such an assumption.

When Michigan adopted Rules of Evidence in 1978, it included a corroboration requirement for exculpatory declarations against penal interest that is identical to the provision in Federal Rule 804(b)(3). See Chapter 3, section 1(D), supra for other contexts in which corroboration is required.

3.   What must be corroborated—the credibility of the witness, the credibility of the declarant, or the truth of the statement? Compare United States v. Bagley, supra note 1 with United States v. Atkins, 558 F.2d 133, 135 (3d Cir.1977), cert. denied, 434 U.S. 1071 (1978). See also United States v. Salvador, 820 F.2d 558, 561, 562 (2d Cir.1987) ("Exactly what needs to be corroborated, though, is not absolutely clear from the rule or from much of the case law. Corroboration of the trustworthiness of the statement could mean that the district judge is to require corroboration of the declarant's trustworthiness, focusing on declarant's reliability when the statement was made, or corroboration of the truth of the declarant's statement, focusing on whether the evidence in the record supported or contradicted the statement, or both ... Our court seems to require corroboration of both.").

A number of courts have used the trustworthiness factors which the Supreme Court relied upon in Chambers v. Mississippi, supra p. 399, as a guide in determining corroboration. See, e.g. State v. Russell, 617 P.2d 467 (Wash.Ct.

---

1.   Chadbourn, Bentham and the Hearsay Rule—A Benthamic View of Rule 63(4)(c) of the Uniform Rules of Evidence, 75 Harv. L.Rev. 932, 947 (1962), cited in Notes of Advisory Committee on Rules of Evidence to Committee on Rules of Practice and Procedure of the Judicial Conference of the United States, Preliminary Draft of Proposed Rules of Evidence for the District Courts and Magistrates (March, 1969), p. 155. [The footnotes are the court's renumbered. Others are omitted.]

2.   A police officer or an informer can testify to extrajudicial statements of the defendant without a foundation showing circumstances indicating reliability or trustworthiness.

Nor is there any requirement of a showing of trustworthiness where the people offer hearsay statements of alleged co-conspirators or co-defendants, usually reported by undercover agents or informants. The predicate of admissibility—proof by independent evidence that a crime was committed and that defendant was connected to it—does not require the people to show that the hearsay statement is itself trustworthy....

App.1980); United States v. Guillette, 547 F.2d 743 (2d Cir.1976), cert. denied, 434 U.S. 839 (1977). How persuasive is the Chambers analogy?

4. How high is the defendant's burden in proving corroboration? See, e.g., State v. Higginbotham, 212 N.W.2d 881 (Minn.1973) (D claimed his friend, O'Neal, who was with him at the time of the killing, fired the fatal shots; court excluded, for lack of corroboration, written confession O'Neal had made to the police five days after the shooting while wearing vest which eyewitnesses identified as having been worn by the killer; O'Neal, who pleaded not guilty, invoked Fifth Amendment when called as witness by D; court stressed that two eyewitnesses had identified D, that O'Neal stated he was on LSD the day of his confession, and that O'Neal was so close to D that he was often referred to as his brother); United States v. Metz, 608 F.2d 147, 157 (5th Cir.1979) (D offered affidavit by declarant, who had pleaded guilty to charged drug conspiracy, stating that he had never known or seen D during the course of conspiracy; D sought to show corroboration in three ways: 1) declarant's repeated affirmance of the exculpatory statement; 2) D's alibi witness placed him away from scene of narcotics transaction; 3) the only prosecution witness who claimed to have seen D at scene had earlier claimed never to have seen him; held, no corroboration), cert. denied, 449 U.S. 821 (1980). Compare United States v. Nagib, 56 F.3d 798 (7th Cir.1995) (in multi-defendant narcotics prosecution, transcript of co-defendant's change of plea should have been admitted as exculpatory declaration against interest; declarant admitted that he delivered a package containing LSD for air transportation and involved defendant in order to deceive airline employees; court pointed to following corroborating factors: that declarant did not exonerate other defendants with whom he had closer personal ties; that statement was voluntary, made while counsel was present and after declarant was advised of Miranda rights; statement was not made to curry favor as there was no plea agreement or downward departure in sentencing).

The corroboration requirement has been termed "constitutionally suspect." See Tague, Perils of the Rulemaking Process: The Development, Application, and Unconstitutionality of Rule 804(b)(3)'s Penal Interest Exception, 69 Geo.L.J. 851, 980 (1981) ("As formulated, the rule is constitutionally suspect in four respects. First, Congress relied on several unwarranted assumptions to justify the high corroboration burden imposed on the defendant. Second, the rule improperly discriminates between the defendant and the Government because the defendant alone must satisfy the corroboration requirement. Third, if the defendant does not satisfy the corroboration requirement, the rule forecloses jury assessment of the declarant's credibility. Finally, the rule clashes with the defendant's fifth and sixth amendment rights to introduce evidence.").

Williamson v. United States

Supreme Court of the United States, 1994.
512 U.S. 594, 114 S.Ct. 2431, 129 L.Ed.2d 476.

■ JUSTICE O'CONNOR delivered the opinion of the Court, except as to Part II–C.

In this case we clarify the scope of the hearsay exception for statements against penal interest. Fed.Rule Evid. 804(b)(3).

I

A deputy sheriff stopped the rental car driven by Reginald Harris for weaving on the highway. Harris consented to a search of the car, which revealed 19 kilograms of cocaine in two suitcases in the trunk. Harris was promptly arrested.

Shortly after Harris' arrest, Special Agent Donald Walton of the Drug Enforcement Administration (DEA) interviewed him by telephone. During that conversation, Harris said that he got the cocaine from an unidentified Cuban in Fort Lauderdale; that the cocaine belonged to petitioner Williamson; and that it was to be delivered that night to a particular dumpster. Williamson was also connected to Harris by physical evidence: The luggage bore the initials of Williamson's sister, Williamson was listed as an additional driver on the car rental agreement, and an envelope addressed to Williamson and a receipt with Williamson's girlfriend's address were found in the glove compartment.

Several hours later, Agent Walton spoke to Harris in person. During that interview, Harris said he had rented the car a few days earlier and had driven it to Fort Lauderdale to meet Williamson. According to Harris, he had gotten the cocaine from a Cuban who was Williamson's acquaintance, and the Cuban had put the cocaine in the car with a note telling Harris how to deliver the drugs. Harris repeated that he had been instructed to leave the drugs in a certain dumpster, to return to his car, and to leave without waiting for anyone to pick up the drugs.

Agent Walton then took steps to arrange a controlled delivery of the cocaine. But as Walton was preparing to leave the interview room, Harris "got out of [his] chair ... and ... took a half step toward [Walton] ... and ... said, ... 'I can't let you do that,' threw his hands up and said 'that's not true, I can't let you go up there for no reason.' " App. 40. Harris told Walton he had lied about the Cuban, the note, and the dumpster. The real story, Harris said, was that he was transporting the cocaine to Atlanta for Williamson, and that Williamson was traveling in front of him in another rental car. Harris added that after his car was stopped, Williamson turned around and drove past the location of the stop, where he could see Harris' car with its trunk open. Ibid. Because Williamson had apparently seen the police searching the car, Harris explained that it would be impossible to make a controlled delivery. Id., at 41.

Harris told Walton that he had lied about the source of the drugs because he was afraid of Williamson. Id., at 61, 68; see also id., at 30–31. Though Harris freely implicated himself, he did not want his story to be recorded, and he refused to sign a written version of the statement. Id., at 24–25. Walton testified that he had promised to report any cooperation by Harris to the Assistant United States Attorney. Walton said Harris was not promised any reward or other benefit for cooperating. Id., at 25–26.

Williamson was eventually convicted of possessing cocaine with intent to distribute, conspiring to possess cocaine with intent to distribute, and traveling interstate to promote the distribution of cocaine, 21 U.S.C. §§ 841(a)(1), 846; 18 U.S.C. § 1952. When called to testify at Williamson's trial, Harris refused, even though the prosecution gave him use immunity and the court ordered him to testify and eventually held him in contempt. The District Court then ruled that, under Rule 804(b)(3), Agent Walton could relate what Harris had said to him:

"The ruling of the Court is that the statements ... are admissible under [Rule 804(b)(3)], which deals with statements against interest.

"First, defendant Harris' statements clearly implicated himself, and therefore, are against his penal interest.

"Second, defendant Harris, the declarant, is unavailable.

"And third, as I found yesterday, there are sufficient corroborating circumstances in this case to ensure the trustworthiness of his testimony. Therefore, under [United States v. Harrell, 788 F.2d 1524 (C.A.11 1986)], these statements by defendant Harris implicating [Williamson] are admissible." App. 51–52.

Williamson appealed his conviction, claiming that the admission of Harris' statements violated Rule 804(b)(3) and the Confrontation Clause of the Sixth Amendment. The Court of Appeals for the Eleventh Circuit affirmed without opinion, judgt. order reported at 981 F.2d 1262 (1992), and we granted certiorari. 510 U.S. 1039, 114 S.Ct. 681, 126 L.Ed.2d 649 (1994).

II

A

The hearsay rule, Fed.Rule Evid. 802, is premised on the theory that out-of-court statements are subject to particular hazards. The declarant might be lying; he might have misperceived the events which he relates; he might have faulty memory; his words might be misunderstood or taken out of context by the listener. And the ways in which these dangers are minimized for in-court statements—the oath, the witness' awareness of the gravity of the proceedings, the jury's ability to observe the witness' demeanor, and, most importantly, the right of the opponent to cross-examine—are generally absent for things said out of court.

Nonetheless, the Federal Rules of Evidence also recognize that some kinds of out-of-court statements are less subject to these hearsay dangers, and therefore except them from the general rule that hearsay is inadmissible. One such category covers statements that are against the declarant's interest: "statement[s] which ... at the time of [their] making ... so far tended to subject the declarant to ... criminal liability ... that a reasonable person in the declarant's position would not have made the statement[s] unless believing [them] to be true." Fed.Rule Evid. 804(b)(3).

To decide whether Harris' confession is made admissible by Rule 804(b)(3), we must first determine what the Rule means by "statement," which Federal Rule of Evidence 801(a)(1) defines as "an oral or written assertion." One possible meaning, "a report or narrative," Webster's Third New International Dictionary 2229, defn. 2(a) (1961), connotes an extended declaration. Under this reading, Harris' entire confession—even if it contains both self-inculpatory and non-self-inculpatory parts—would be admissible so long as in the aggregate the confession sufficiently inculpates him. Another meaning of "statement," "a single declaration or remark," ibid., defn. 2(b), would make Rule 804(b)(3) cover only those declarations or remarks within the confession that are individually self-inculpatory. See also id., at 131 (defining "assertion" as a "declaration"); id., at 586 (defining "declaration" as a "statement").

Although the text of the Rule does not directly resolve the matter, the principle behind the Rule, so far as it is discernible from the text, points clearly to the narrower reading. Rule 804(b)(3) is founded on the commonsense notion that reasonable people, even reasonable people who are not especially honest, tend not to make self-inculpatory statements unless they believe them to be true. This notion simply does not extend to the broader definition of "statement." The fact that a person is making a broadly self-inculpatory confession does not make more credible the confession's non-self-inculpatory parts. One of the most effective ways to lie is to mix falsehood with truth, especially truth that seems particularly persuasive because of its self-inculpatory nature.

In this respect, it is telling that the non-self-inculpatory things Harris said in his first statement actually proved to be false, as Harris himself admitted during the second interrogation. And when part of the confession is actually self-exculpatory, the generalization on which Rule 804(b)(3) is founded becomes even less applicable. Self-exculpatory statements are exactly the ones which people are most likely to make even when they are false; and mere proximity to other, self-inculpatory, statements does not increase the plausibility of the self-exculpatory statements.

We therefore cannot agree with JUSTICE KENNEDY's suggestion that the Rule can be read as expressing a policy that collateral statements—even ones that are not in any way against the declarant's interest—are admissible, post, at [629]. Nothing in the text of Rule 804(b)(3) or the general theory of the hearsay Rules suggests that admissibility should turn on whether a statement is collateral to a self-inculpatory statement. The fact that a statement is self-inculpatory does make it more reliable; but the fact that a statement is collateral to a self-inculpatory statement says nothing at all about the collateral statement's reliability. We see no reason why collateral statements, even ones that are neutral as to interest, post, at [631], should be treated any differently from other hearsay statements that are generally excluded.

Congress certainly could, subject to the constraints of the Confrontation Clause, make statements admissible based on their proximity to self-inculpatory statements. But we will not lightly assume that the ambiguous language means anything so inconsistent with the Rule's underlying theory. See Cooter & Gell v. Hartmarx Corp., 496 U.S. 384, 394–395, 408–409, 110 S.Ct. 2447, 2455–2456, 2462–2463, 110 L.Ed.2d 359 (1990). In our view, the most faithful reading of Rule 804(b)(3) is that it does not allow admission of non-self-inculpatory statements, even if they are made within a broader narrative that is generally self-inculpatory. The district court may not just assume for purposes of Rule 804(b)(3) that a statement is self-inculpatory because it is part of a fuller confession, and this is especially true when the statement implicates someone else. "[T]he arrest statements of a codefendant have traditionally been viewed with special suspicion. Due to his strong motivation to implicate the defendant and to exonerate himself, a codefendant's statements about what the defendant said or did are less credible than ordinary hearsay evidence." Lee v. Illinois, 476 U.S. 530, 541, 106 S.Ct. 2056, 2062, 90 L.Ed.2d 514 (1986) (internal quotation marks omitted); see also Bruton v. United States, 391 U.S. 123, 136, 88 S.Ct. 1620, 1628, 20 L.Ed.2d 476 (1968); Dutton v. Evans, 400 U.S. 74, 98, 91 S.Ct. 210, 224 (1970) (HARLAN, J., concurring in result).

Justice KENNEDY suggests that the Advisory Committee Notes to Rule 804(b)(3) should be read as endorsing the position we reject—that an entire narrative, including non-self-inculpatory parts (but excluding the clearly self-serving parts, post, at [629]), may be admissible if it is in the aggregate self-inculpatory. See post, at [631].... Without deciding exactly how much weight to give the Notes in this particular situation, compare Schiavone v. Fortune, 477 U.S. 21, 31, 106 S.Ct. 2379, 2385, 91 L.Ed.2d 18 (1986) (Notes are to be given some weight), with Green v. Bock Laundry Machine Co., 490 U.S. 504, 528, 109 S.Ct. 1981, 1994–1995, 104 L.Ed.2d 557 (1989) (SCALIA, J., concurring in judgment) (Notes ought to be given no weight), we conclude that the policy expressed in the statutory text points clearly enough in one direction that it outweighs whatever force the Notes may have. And though Justice KENNEDY believes that the text can fairly be read as expressing a policy of admitting collateral statements, post, at [630], for the reasons given above we disagree.

B

We also do not share Justice KENNEDY's fears that our reading of the Rule "eviscerate[s] the against penal interest exception" . . . or makes it lack "meaningful effect," post, at [630]. There are many circumstances in which Rule 804(b)(3) does allow the admission of statements that inculpate a criminal defendant. Even the confessions of arrested accomplices may be admissible if they are truly self-inculpatory, rather than merely attempts to shift blame or curry favor.

For instance, a declarant's squarely self-inculpatory confession—"yes, I killed X"—will likely be admissible under Rule 804(b)(3) against accomplices of his who are being tried under a co-conspirator liability theory. See Pinkerton v. United States, 328 U.S. 640, 647, 66 S.Ct. 1180, 1184, 90 L.Ed. 1489 (1946). Likewise, by showing that the declarant knew something, a self-inculpatory statement can in some situations help the jury infer that his confederates knew it as well. And when seen with other evidence, an accomplice's self-inculpatory statement can inculpate the defendant directly: "I was robbing the bank on Friday morning," coupled with someone's testimony that the declarant and the defendant drove off together Friday morning, is evidence that the defendant also participated in the robbery.

Moreover, whether a statement is self-inculpatory or not can only be determined by viewing it in context. Even statements that are on their face neutral may actually be against the declarant's interest. "I hid the gun in Joe's apartment" may not be a confession of a crime; but if it is likely to help the police find the murder weapon, then it is certainly self-inculpatory. "Sam and I went to Joe's house" might be against the declarant's interest if a reasonable person in the declarant's shoes would realize that being linked to Joe and Sam would implicate the declarant in Joe and Sam's conspiracy. And other statements that give the police significant details about the crime may also, depending on the situation, be against the declarant's interest. The question under Rule 804(b)(3) is always whether the statement was sufficiently against the declarant's penal interest "that a reasonable person in the declarant's position would not have made the statement unless believing it to be true," and this question can only be answered in light of all the surrounding circumstances.[1]

C

In this case, however, we cannot conclude that all that Harris said was properly admitted. Some of Harris' confession would clearly have been admissible under Rule 804(b)(3); for instance, when he said he knew there was cocaine in the suitcase, he essentially forfeited his only possible defense to a charge of cocaine possession, lack of knowledge. But other parts of his confession, especially the parts that implicated Williamson, did little to subject Harris himself to criminal liability. A reasonable person in Harris' position might even think that implicating someone else would decrease his practical exposure to criminal liability, at least so far as sentencing goes. Small fish in a big conspiracy often get shorter sentences than people who are running the whole show, see, e.g., United States Sentencing Commission, Guidelines Manual

---

1. Of course, an accomplice's statements may also be admissible under other provisions of Rules 801–804. For instance, statements made in furtherance of the conspiracy may be admissible under Rule 801(d)(2)(E), and other statements that bear circumstantial guarantees of trustworthiness may be admissible under Rule 804(b)(5), the catch-all hearsay exception. [Footnote of the Court.]

§ 3B1.2 (Nov. 1993), especially if the small fish are willing to help the authorities catch the big ones, see, e.g., id., at § 5K1.1.

Nothing in the record shows that the District Court or the Court of Appeals inquired whether each of the statements in Harris' confession was truly self-inculpatory. As we explained above, this can be a fact-intensive inquiry, which would require careful examination of all the circumstances surrounding the criminal activity involved; we therefore remand to the Court of Appeals to conduct this inquiry in the first instance.

In light of this disposition, we need not address Williamson's claim that that the statements were also made inadmissible by the Confrontation Clause, see generally White v. Illinois, 502 U.S. 346, 112 S.Ct. 736, 116 L.Ed.2d 848 (1992), and in particular we need not decide whether the hearsay exception for declarations against interest is "firmly rooted" for Confrontation Clause purposes. Compare, e.g., United States v. Seeley, 892 F.2d 1, 2 (C.A.1 1989) (holding that the exception is firmly rooted), with United States v. Flores, 985 F.2d 770 (C.A.5 1993) (holding the contrary). We note, however, that the very fact that a statement is genuinely self-inculpatory—which our reading of Rule 804(b)(3) requires—is itself one of the "particularized guarantees of trustworthiness" that makes a statement admissible under the Confrontation Clause. See Lee v. Illinois, 476 U.S. 530, 543–545, 106 S.Ct. 2056, 2063–2064, 90 L.Ed.2d 514 (1986). We also need not decide whether, as some Courts of Appeals have held, the second sentence of Rule 804(b)(3)—"A statement tending to expose the declarant to criminal liability and offered to exculpate the accused is not admissible unless corroborating circumstances clearly indicate the trustworthiness of the statement" (emphasis added)—also requires that statements inculpating the accused be supported by corroborating circumstances. See, e.g., United States v. Alvarez, 584 F.2d 694, 701 (C.A.5 1978); United States v. Taggart, 944 F.2d 837, 840 (C.A.11 1991). The judgment of the Court of Appeals is vacated, and the case is remanded for further proceedings consistent with this opinion.

So ordered.

■ JUSTICE SCALIA, concurring.

I join the Court's opinion, which I do not understand to require the simplistic view of statements against penal interest that Justice KENNEDY attributes to it.

. . .

The relevant inquiry . . .—and one that is not furthered by clouding the waters with manufactured categories such as "collateral neutral" and "collateral self-serving," . . .—must always be whether the particular remark at issue (and *not* the extended narrative) meets the standard set forth in the Rule.

■ JUSTICE GINSBURG, with whom JUSTICE BLACKMUN, JUSTICE STEVENS, and JUSTICE SOUTER join, concurring in part and concurring in the judgment.

I join Parts I, II–A, and II–B of the Court's opinion. I agree with the Court that Federal Rule of Evidence 804(b)(3) excepts from the general rule that hearsay statements are inadmissible only "those declarations or remarks within [a narrative] that are individually self-inculpatory." Ante, at [624]. As the Court explains, the exception for statements against penal interest "does not allow admission of non-self-inculpatory statements, even if they are made within a broader narrative that is generally self-inculpatory," . . . the exception applies only to statements that are "sufficiently against the declarant's penal interest 'that a reasonable person in the declarant's position would not have made the statement unless believing it to be true.' "....

Further, the Court recognizes the untrustworthiness of statements implicating another person.... A person arrested in incriminating circumstances has a strong incentive to shift blame or downplay his own role in comparison with that of others, in hopes of receiving a shorter sentence and leniency in exchange for cooperation. For this reason, hearsay accounts of a suspect's statements implicating another person have been held inadmissible under the Confrontation Clause. See Lee v. Illinois, 476 U.S. 530, 541, 106 S.Ct. 2056, 2062, 90 L.Ed.2d 514 (1986) ("when one person accuses another of a crime under circumstances in which the declarant stands to gain by inculpating another, the accusation is presumptively suspect and must be subjected to the scrutiny of cross-examination"); ibid. (" '[T]he arrest statements of a co-defendant have traditionally been viewed with special suspicion. Due to his strong motivation to implicate the defendant and to exonerate himself, a co-defendant's statements about what the defendant said or did are less credible than ordinary hearsay evidence.' ")(quoting Bruton v. United States, 391 U.S. 123, 141, 88 S.Ct. 1620, 1630–1631, 20 L.Ed.2d 476 (1968) (White, J., dissenting)).

Unlike Justice O'CONNOR, however, I conclude that Reginald Harris' statements, as recounted by DEA Special Agent Donald E. Walton, do not fit, even in part, within the exception described in Rule 804(b)(3), for Harris' arguably inculpatory statements are too closely intertwined with his self-serving declarations to be ranked as trustworthy. Harris was caught red-handed with 19 kilos of cocaine—enough to subject even a first-time offender to a minimum of 12 ½ years' imprisonment. See United States Sentencing Commission, Guidelines Manual § 2D1.1(c) (1993); id., ch. 5, pt. A (sentencing table). He could have denied knowing the drugs were in the car's trunk, but that strategy would have brought little prospect of thwarting a criminal prosecution. He therefore admitted involvement, but did so in a way that minimized his own role and shifted blame to petitioner Fredel Williamson (and a Cuban man named Shawn).

Most of Harris' statements to DEA Agent Walton focused on Williamson's, rather than Harris' conduct.

.   .   .

I concur in the Court's decision to vacate the Court of Appeals' judgment, however, because I have not examined the entire trial court record; I therefore cannot say the Government should be denied an opportunity to argue that the erroneous admission of the hearsay statements, in light of the other evidence introduced at trial, constituted harmless error.

■ JUSTICE KENNEDY, with whom THE CHIEF JUSTICE and JUSTICE THOMAS join, concurring in the judgment.

I

.   .   .

There has been a long-running debate among commentators over the admissibility of collateral statements. Dean Wigmore took the strongest position in favor of admissibility, arguing that "the statement may be accepted, not merely as to the specific fact against interest, but also as to every fact contained in the same statement." 5 J. Wigmore, Evidence § 1465, p. 271 (3d ed. 1940) (emphasis deleted); see also 5 J. Wigmore, Evidence § 1465, p. 339 (J. Chadbourn rev. 1974); Higham v. Ridgway, 10 East. 109, 103 Eng.Rep. 717 (K.B. 1808). According to Wigmore, because "the statement is made under circumstances fairly indicating the declarant's sincerity and accuracy," the entire statement should be admitted. 5 J. Wigmore § 1465, p. 271 (3d ed. 1940). Dean McCormick's approach regarding collateral statements was more guarded. He argued for the admissibility of collateral statements of a neutral character; and for the exclusion of collateral statements of a self-serving character. For example, in the statement "John and I robbed the bank," the words "John and" are neutral (save for the possibility of conspiracy charges). On the other hand, the statement "John, not I, shot the bank teller" is to some extent self-serving and therefore might be inadmissible. See C. McCormick, Law of Evidence § 256, pp. 552–553 (1954)(hereinafter McCormick). Professor Jefferson took the narrowest approach, arguing that the reliability of a statement against interest stems only from the disserving fact stated and so should be confined "to the proof of the fact which is against interest." Jefferson, Declarations Against Interest: An Exception to the Hearsay Rule, 58 Harv.L.Rev. 1, 62–63 (1944). Under the Jefferson approach, neither collateral neutral nor collateral self-serving statements would be admissible.

. . .

[W]e should not assume that the text of Rule 804(b)(3), which is silent about collateral statements, in fact incorporates one of the competing positions. The Rule's silence no more incorporates Jefferson's position respecting collateral statements than it does McCormick's or Wigmore's.

II

... In my view, three sources demonstrate that Rule 804(b)(3) allows the admission of some collateral statements: the Advisory Committee Note, the common law of the hearsay exception for statements against interest, and the general presumption that Congress does not enact statutes that have almost no effect.

First, the Advisory Committee Note establishes that some collateral statements are admissible. In fact, it refers in specific terms to the issue we here confront: "[o]rdinarily the third-party confession is thought of in terms of exculpating the accused, but this is by no means always or necessarily the case: it may include statements implicating him, and under the general theory of declarations against interest they would be admissible as related statements." 28 U.S.C.App., p. 790. This language seems a forthright statement that collateral statements are admissible under Rule 804(b)(3), but the Court reasons that "the policy expressed in the statutory text points clearly enough in one direction that it outweighs whatever force the Notes may have." Ante, at [625]. Again, however, that reasoning begs the question: What is the policy expressed in the text on the admissibility of collateral statements? As stated above, the text of the Rule does not answer the question whether collateral statements are admissible. When as here the text of a Rule of Evidence does not answer a question that must be answered in order to apply the Rule, and when the Advisory Committee Note does answer the question, our practice indicates that we should pay attention to the Advisory Committee Note. We have referred often to those Notes in interpreting the Rules of Evidence, and I see no reason to jettison that well-established practice here. See Huddleston v. United States, 485 U.S. 681, 688, 108 S.Ct. 1496, 1500–1501, 99 L.Ed.2d 771 (1988); United States v. Owens, 484 U.S. 554, 562, 108 S.Ct. 838, 844, 98 L.Ed.2d 951 (1988); Bourjaily v. United States, 483 U.S. 171, 179, n. 2, 107 S.Ct. 2775, 2780, n. 2,

97 L.Ed.2d 144 (1987); United States v. Abel, 469 U.S. 45, 51, 105 S.Ct. 465, 468–469, 83 L.Ed.2d 450 (1984).

Second, even if the Advisory Committee Note were silent about collateral statements, I would not adopt a rule excluding all statements collateral or related to the specific words against penal interest.... Rule 804(b)(3) does not address the issue, but Congress legislated against the common law background allowing admission of some collateral statements, and I would not assume that Congress gave the common law rule a silent burial in Rule 804(b)(3).

There is yet a third reason weighing against the Court's interpretation, one specific to statements against penal interest that inculpate the accused.... [W]e should assume that Congress intended the penal interest exception for inculpatory statements to have some meaningful effect.... That counsels against adopting a rule excluding collateral statements. As commentators have recognized, "the exclusion of collateral statements would cause the exclusion of almost all inculpatory statements." Comment, 66 Calif.L.Rev., at 1207; see also Note, Inculpatory Statements Against Penal Interest and the Confrontation Clause, 83 Colum.L.Rev. 159, 163 (1983) ("most statements inculpating a defendant are only collateral to the portion of the declarant's statement that is against his own penal interest. The portion of the statement that specifically implicates the defendant is rarely directly counter to the declarant's penal interest") (footnote omitted) ...

. . .

To be sure, under the approach adopted by the Court, there are some situations where the Rule would still apply. For example, if the declarant said that he stole certain goods, the statement could be admitted in a prosecution of the accused for receipt of stolen goods in order to show that the goods were stolen. See 4 J. Weinstein & M. Berger, Weinstein's Evidence § 804(b)(3)[04], p. 804–164 (1993).... But as the commentators have recognized, it is likely to be the rare case where the precise self-inculpatory words of the declarant, without more, also inculpate the defendant. I would not presume that Congress intended the penal interest exception to the Rule to have so little effect with respect to statements that inculpate the accused.

I note finally that the Court's decision applies to statements against penal interest that exculpate the accused as well as to those that inculpate the accused. Thus, if the declarant said, "I robbed the store alone," only the portion of the statement in which the declarant said "I robbed the store" could be introduced by a criminal defendant on trial for the robbery. See Note, Declarations Against Penal Interest: Standards of Admissibility Under an Emerging Majority Rule, 56 B.U.L.Rev. 148, 165, n. 95 (1976). That seems extraordinary. The Court gives no justification for such a rule and no explanation that Congress intended the exception for exculpatory statements to have this limited effect. See id., at 166 ("A strict application of a rule excluding all collateral statements can lead to the arbitrary rejection of valuable evidence").

III

Though I would conclude that Rule 804(b)(3) allows admission of statements collateral to the precise words against interest, that conclusion of course does not answer the remaining question whether all collateral statements related to the statement against interest are admissible; and if not, what limiting principles should apply....

In the criminal context, a self-serving statement is one that tends to reduce the charges or mitigate the punishment for which the declarant might be liable.

See M. Graham, Federal Practice and Procedure § 6795, p. 810, n. 10 (1992). For example, if two masked gunmen robbed a bank and one of them shot and killed the bank teller, a statement by one robber that the other robber was the triggerman may be the kind of self-serving statement that should be inadmissible. See ibid. (collateral self-serving statement is "John used the gun"). (The Government concedes that such a statement may be inadmissible. See Brief for United States 12.) By contrast, when two or more people are capable of committing a crime and the declarant simply names the involved parties, that statement often is considered neutral, not self-serving. See Graham, supra, at 810, n. 10 ("the statement 'John and I robbed the bank' is collateral neutral"); Note, 56 B.U.L.Rev., at 166, n. 96 ("An examination of the decisions reveals that, with very few exceptions, collateral facts offered as part of a declaration against penal interest are neutral rather than self-serving"); see generally United States v. York, 933 F.2d 1343, 1362–1364 (C.A.7 1991); United States v. Casamento, 887 F.2d 1141, 1171 (C.A.2 1989).

Apart from that limit on the admission of collateral, self-serving statements, there is a separate limit applicable to cases in which the declarant made his statement to authorities; this limit applies not only to collateral statements but also to the precise words against penal interest. A declarant may believe that a statement of guilt to authorities is in his interest to some extent, for example as a way to obtain more lenient treatment, or simply to clear his conscience....

. . .

In sum, I would adhere to the following approach with respect to statements against penal interest that inculpate the accused. A court first should determine whether the declarant made a statement that contained a fact against penal interest. See ante ... (opinion of O'CONNOR, J.) ("Some of Harris' confession would clearly have been admissible under Rule 804(b)(3)"). If so, the court should admit all statements related to the precise statement against penal interest, subject to two limits. Consistent with the Advisory Committee Note, the court should exclude a collateral statement that is so self-serving as to render it unreliable (if, for example, it shifts blame to someone else for a crime the defendant could have committed). In addition, in cases where the statement was made under circumstances where it is likely that the declarant had a significant motivation to obtain favorable treatment, as when the government made an explicit offer of leniency in exchange for the declarant's admission of guilt, the entire statement should be inadmissible.

... District Judges, who are close to the facts and far better able to evaluate the various circumstances than an appellate court ... must be given wide discretion to examine a particular statement to determine whether all or part of it should be admitted. Like the Court, then, I would remand this case, but for application of the analysis set forth in this opinion.

NOTES

1. After Williamson, to what extent is a statement admissible that directly implicates another?

In Ciccarelli v. Gichner Systems Group, Inc., 862 F.Supp. 1293, 1298 (M.D.Pa.1994), plaintiffs sought to recover pension benefits that had been terminated on the ground of fraud. On a motion for summary judgment, defendants proffered an affidavit by a retired executive, now deceased, in which he admitted his fraudulent conduct and implicated plaintiffs. The court admitted only those portions of the affidavit that described potentially culpable conduct on the affiant's part:

> [O]nly those words that are actually self-inculpatory fit within the Rule 804(b)(3) exception. Thus, a sentence that is generally self-inculpatory might have portions that are collateral and inadmissible. For example, in the following sentence, only the parts referring to culpable conduct by the declarant would be admissible: "Matthew, Derek, and I robbed Kenneth." The references to Matthew and Derek would have to be redacted.

Is this per se rule of exclusion consistent with Justice O'Connor's opinion? Doesn't her opinion contain an example of a statement referring to Sam and Joe that "might be against the declarant's interest if a reasonable person in the declarant's shoes would realize that being linked to Joe and Sam would implicate the declarant in Joe and Sam's conspiracy"?

Compare United States v. Sasso, 59 F.3d 341, 349–50 (2d Cir.1995). The witness testified that one of the defendants, Armienti, told her that he could not leave his wife because she had incriminating information that she would report to the authorities if he left. Pressed by the witness (his girlfriend), he admitted that he was running guns for Sasso. The court upheld the admission of Armienti's statement against Sasso:

> A statement incriminating both the declarant and the defendant may possess adequate reliability if (a) the statement was made to a person whom the declarant believes is an ally, not a law enforcement official, and (b) the circumstances surrounding the portion of the statement that inculpates the defendant provide no reason to suspect that that portion is any less reliable than the part that directly incriminates the declarant....

> ... In Williamson, the Court interpreted the term "statement" within 804(b)(3) narrowly because it recognized that a declarant might attempt to shift blame to another by mixing within a narrative true self-inculpatory statements and false blame shifting ones....

> The circumstances of Armienti's statements to Kramer strongly suggest that his inculpation of Sasso was reliable. First, Armienti's statements inculpating Sasso equally inculpated Armienti himself in the gun-running conspiracy. There was no effort to shift blame from himself to Sasso. Second, ... [i]mplicating Sasso added nothing to the reason Armienti could not leave his wife. If his wife was holding it over his head that he was gun-running, she would be doing so whether his confederate was Sasso or someone else. Thus, even if Armienti were lying about the reason he would not leave his wife, there would have been no reason to falsely bring Sasso into the picture. Armienti also made later statements to Kramer implicating Sasso; those statements by Armienti apparently had no connection with any attempt to explain his marital status. Third, the statements were made to Kramer in private; there was no police or other official interrogation. There was no indication that, when Armienti made his statements to Kramer, the authorities had any knowledge of Armienti's crimes; hence there was no possibility that Sasso was implicated solely to curry favor with the authorities. Finally, it is unlikely that Armienti would have named Sasso as a participant in Armienti's gun-running activities in an attempt to curry favor with Kramer himself. Sasso points out in his brief on appeal that Armienti knew Kramer disliked Sasso. Since, in seeking to placate Kramer, Armienti would be quite unlikely to fabricate his association with someone of whom she disapproved, his statement to Kramer that his gun-running partner was Sasso must be viewed as having strong indicia of truthfulness.

Is Armienti's statement self-inculpatory when viewed in context? Is the language in Sasso consistent with Justice O'Connor's approach or with Justice Kennedy's reasoning? How does the Sasso court's analysis compare to the inquiry required when a statement is being offered pursuant to the catch-all hearsay exception? See infra and see footnote 1 in Williamson.

2. In Sasso, Armienti's statements were being challenged on confrontation clause grounds so that the court is not explicitly ruling on an evidentiary objection. But the hearsay and constitutional inquiry are intertwined. Although Justice O'Connor's opinion in Williamson declined to address whether defendant's right to confrontation was violated by the admission of Harris' statements, her opinion did note that "the very fact that a statement is genuinely self-inculpatory—which our reading of Rule 804(b)(3) requires—is itself one of the 'particularized guarantees of trustworthiness' that makes a statement admissible under the Confrontation Clause. See Lee v. Illinois, 476 U.S. 530, 543–545, 106 S.Ct. 2056, 2063–2064, 90 L.Ed.2d 514 (1986)." In Lee, the Court had found that an in-custody statement by an accomplice incriminating a defendant "was presumptively unreliable and that it did not bear sufficient independent 'indicia of reliability' to overcome that presumption." Does Justice O'Connor's language mean that any statement that satisfies Rule 804(b)(3) as interpreted in Williamson will automatically meet the requirements of the Confrontation Clause as well? As Justice O'Connor indicates, prior to Williamson there was some disagreement in the circuits as to whether a declaration against penal interest is "firmly rooted." Compare United States v. York, 933 F.2d 1343, 1363 (7th Cir.1991)(declaration that is not presumptively unreliable as in Lee is firmly rooted) with United States v. Flores, 985 F.2d 770, 772, 775 (5th Cir.1993)(Supreme Court's holding in Lee precludes a finding that the exception is firmly rooted).

3. Does the narrow construction of the term "statement" in Williamson apply to exculpatory as well as inculpatory statements? If "I robbed a bank with Joe" is not inculpatory when offered against Joe, is it exculpatory when offered by George?

See Justice Kennedy's concurrence in Williamson. See also United States v. Butler, 71 F.3d 243, 253 n. 7 (7th Cir.1995) and United States v. Thomas, 62 F.3d 1332 (11th Cir.1995)(applying Williamson to exculpatory statements), cert. denied, 116 S.Ct. 1058 (1996). But see Chambers v. Mississippi, 410 U.S. 284 (1973), supra p. 399 and Green v. Georgia, 442 U.S. 95, 97 (1979): D and M were indicted together, but tried separately, for rape and murder. After being convicted, D, at the penalty stage of the trial, sought to introduce testimony which W had given at M's trial. W had testified that M had confessed killing the victim after ordering D to run an errand. The proffered evidence was excluded as hearsay. Held:

> Regardless of whether the proffered testimony comes within Georgia's hearsay rule, under the facts of this case its exclusion constituted a violation of the Due Process Clause of the Fourteenth Amendment. The excluded testimony was highly relevant to a critical issue in the punishment phase of the trial, ... and substantial reasons existed to assume its reliability. Moore made his statement spontaneously to a close friend. The evidence corroborating the confession was ample, and indeed sufficient to procure a conviction of Moore and a capital sentence. The statement was against interest, and there was no reason to believe that Moore had any ulterior motive in making it. Perhaps most important, the State considered the testimony sufficiently reliable to use it against Moore, and to base a sentence of death upon it. In these unique circumstances, "the hearsay

rule may not be applied mechanistically to defeat the ends of justice." Chambers v. Mississippi, 410 U.S. 284, 302 (1973). Because the exclusion of Pasby's testimony denied petitioner a fair trial on the issue of punishment, the sentence is vacated and the case is remanded for further proceedings not inconsistent with this opinion.

Id. at 97.

For an interesting analysis of how the constitutional dictates of Chambers and Green affect the admissibility of an exculpatory declaration against interest see Carson v. Peters, 42 F.3d 384 (7th Cir.1994).

SECTION 5.   SPONTANEOUS, CONTEMPORANEOUS AND EXCITED UTTERANCES

Commonwealth v. Coleman

Supreme Court of Pennsylvania, 1974.
458 Pa. 112, 326 A.2d 387.

■ JONES, CHIEF JUSTICE.

On May 3, 1971, at approximately 6:00 a. m., Diane McCarthy was awakened by her boyfriend, James Coleman, who lived with her at her apartment in Allentown, Pennsylvania. At 6:15 a. m., Diane telephoned her mother in East Stroudsburg, saying that Coleman would not let her leave the apartment, that he would hang up the phone and that he was going to kill her. At approximately 6:25 a. m., the telephone connection was broken in Allentown, and the mother, Marilyn McCarthy, called the police as Diane had implored her to do. Five minutes later, Coleman, blood-spattered and cut about the face and hands, hailed a patrol car on a nearby street and said that he had hurt his girlfriend. The police found Diane in her apartment dead of multiple stab wounds at 6:35 a. m.

Appellant was tried before a jury in the Court of Common Pleas of Lehigh County and convicted of aggravated assault and battery, assault with intent to kill and second-degree murder on September 24, 1971. Timely motions for new trial and in arrest of judgment were denied, and appellant was sentenced to a term of ten to twenty years' imprisonment. This appeal followed.

Appellant contends that the trial judge erred in permitting the decedent's mother to testify for the Commonwealth as to the decedent's statements in the aforementioned telephone conversation prior to her death. He maintains that admission of this testimony under the res gestae exception to the hearsay rule was improper in that the decedent voiced only opinions without factual support at the time given. He argues that the effect of the judge's ruling was to preclude a successful plea of self-defense and to deter the jury from a verdict of voluntary manslaughter by evidencing the existence of malice. Appellant testified at trial that he had stabbed the decedent, but claimed that she had precipitated his action by an unprovoked attack upon him with a letter opener. He submits now, in essence, that the decedent's statements to her mother over the telephone are inadmissible as both hearsay and pure opinion. There is, however, no contention that the verdict was against the weight of the evidence.

The issue raised by this appeal is one of first impression in this Commonwealth. There is no doubt that the challenged testimony of decedent's mother comports with the classical definition of hearsay as an out-of-court utterance offered to prove the truth of the fact asserted, i.e. that appellant had made manifest an intent to kill Diane McCarthy. This Court must determine whether a declaration rendered in conclusory terms over a telephone conveying the substance of one's observation of another's apparently threatening behavior is properly admissible as evidence under any exception to the hearsay rule.

This Court has consistently recognized the validity and rationality of the res gestae exception to the bar against admissibility of hearsay evidence at trial. . . .

In an enlightened analysis of the historical application of the res gestae doctrine, Professor McCormick has indicated that the term res gestae is more generic than particular in nature. See McCormick, Evidence § 274 at 585 (1954). He concludes and we agree that within the scope of res gestae there exist four distinct exceptions to the hearsay rule, all possessing different indicia of reliability: (1) declarations of present bodily condition; (2) declarations of present mental state and emotion; (3) excited utterances; and (4) declarations of present sense impression. The practice in many courts, including those of this Commonwealth, has been to refer to the particular exception by the generic designation. Res gestae statements as defined by this Court . . . partake of the characteristics of excited utterances. The exception for excited utterances is not applicable to the present circumstances.

We note that the decedent's statements to her mother resemble more a verbalization of her perception of appellant's attitude and behavior than a declaration of emotion engendered by a prior physical occurrence. In a well-reasoned essay on the subject of res gestae, Professor Morgan asserted that there should be an exception to the hearsay rule for present sense impressions, i.e., declarations concerning conditions or non-exciting events which the declarant is observing at the time of his declaration. Morgan, Res Gestae, 12 Wash.L.Rev. 91, 96 (1937). The indicium of reliability for such a declaration is in his view its contemporaneousness with the observation of the occurrence or condition. Relative immediacy of the declaration insures that there will have been little opportunity for reflection or calculated misstatement. There is no necessity for the presence of a startling occurrence or accident to serve as a source of reliability, for:

> "The declaration is 'instictive, [sic] rather than deliberative—in short, the reflex product of immediate sensual impressions, unaided by restrospective [sic] mental action. These are the indicia of verity which the law accepts as a substitute for the usual requirements of an oath and opportunity for cross-examination.' "

Morgan, Res Gestae, 12 Wash.L.Rev. at 96, citing Illinois Central R.R. Co. v. Lowery, 184 Ala. 443, 448, 63 So. 952 (1913); see McCormick, Evidence § 298 at 710 [2d ed., Cleary (1972)].

Various courts throughout the United States have embraced the precepts underlying an exception to the hearsay rule for declarations of present sense impressions.[1] Of particular pertinence to our considerations in this case is the decision of the Supreme Court of Texas in Houston Oxygen Co. v. Davis, 139 Tex. 1, 161 S.W.2d 474 (1942). Therein, the defendant in an automobile collision case offered through a witness the declaration of one Mrs. Cooper that

---

1. We, of course, recognize that no declaration of present sense impression of a condition or another person's behavior will issue without a tinge of excitement. Excitement and spontaneity are well-accepted as the rationale underlying other exceptions to the hearsay rule, e.g., the admissibility of excited utterances. Their presence should cast no detrimental aspersions upon the reliability to be found in the decedent's statements to her mother in this case. [Footnote of the court, renumbered.]

when the plaintiff's car passed her at a point some four miles prior to that of the eventual accident, she had said: "[T]hey must have been drunk, that we would find them somewhere on the road wrecked if they keep that rate of speed up." Objection to the admissibility of this testimony was sustained at trial, but the Supreme Court reversed. It found that the evidential value of the remark was more than merely cumulative and that the comment possessed exceptional reliability in that it was contemporaneous in time with the observation, was safe from any defect in memory or opportunity for calculated misstatement, and had been made to the testifying witness who had an equal opportunity to observe and hence to check a misstatement. See also Hastings v. Ross, 211 Kan. 732, 508 P.2d 514 (1973) (statement of witness when she saw automobile pass her house that "that boy is going to kill somebody one of these days," uttered prior to the actual collision, held admissible); Claybrook v. Acreman, 373 S.W.2d 287 (Tex.Civ.App.1963) (statement of bystanders that "they won't last long at that rate of speed" held admissible); McCullom v. McClain, 227 S.W.2d 333 (Tex.Civ.App.1949) (declarations of bystanders relating to high speed of plaintiff's motorcycle just before collision held admissible); Marks v. I.M. Pearlstine & Sons, 203 S.C. 318, 26 S.E.2d 835 (1943) (statement by witness to racing by trucks that "the trucks are going to kill somebody yet" held admissible). Indeed, Rule 803(1) of the Federal Rules of Evidence provides for the admissibility of declarations of present sense impression made either during or immediately after perception of the event or condition.

Thorough consideration of the decedent's statements to her mother over the telephone in light of the present sense impression exception to the hearsay rule leads us to agree with the decision of the Court of Common Pleas that they are properly admissible as evidence. The decedent told her mother that appellant would not let her leave the apartment, that he would hang up the phone and that as soon as the phone had been hung up, he would kill her. The mother testified that appellant could be heard shouting in the background, and appellant himself testified that he and the decedent had engaged in a loud argument immediately prior to the telephone call. Contemporaneity of the declarations with the observation seems clear. There existed a sufficient confluence of time and events to vest special reliability in the statements. Moreover, we do not consider the inability of the mother to have observed the situation in the apartment to be sufficiently persuasive in effect to disallow application of the exception. Verification has never been deemed an absolute prerequisite to admissibility of testimony under this Court's previous treatment of res gestae exceptions to the hearsay rule. In view of the facts and corroborative testimony of the appellant, we can see no reason to alter that practice in this case.

In concluding that the mother's testimony is properly admissible under the present sense impression exceptions [sic] to the hearsay rule, we feel it necessary to re-examine this Court's holding in Shadowski v. Pittsburg Rys., 226 Pa. 537, 75 A. 730 (1910). In that case, a bystander, upon seeing a streetcar rapidly approach the point at which a child was running or playing on the track, exclaimed: "Look at that damn fool; he will run over that little girl up there." This Court held this statement inadmissible, finding that the exclamatory remark by a bystander neither emanated from the litigated act (the accident) nor had any causal connection therewith. Shadowski v. Pittsburgh Rys., 226 Pa. at 538, 75 A. at 731. The rationale underlying this Court's decision in Shadowski is not persuasive; indeed, it runs contrary to a reasoned consideration of reliability as the groundstone for admissibility of evidence. It is, therefore, expressly overruled. A declaration need not follow the litigated act to be admissible where other indices of reliability are present.

In coincidence with the allegation of hearsay, appellant contends that decedent's out-of-court statement—"He is going to kill me"—expresses a mere opinion without basis in fact. This contention is based upon the classic legal doctrine that witnesses shall testify in court only to facts and not to inferences, conclusions or opinions. Smith v. Clark, 411 Pa. 142, 190 A.2d 441 (1963); Delair v. McAdoo, 324 Pa. 392; 188 A. 181 (1936); Graham v. Pennsylvania Co., 139 Pa. 149, 21 A. 151 (1891). By definition, however, our holding that the decedent's statements are admissible under the exception for present sense impressions to the hearsay rule disposes of appellant's contention. An impression of contemporaneous events or conditions is not at all similar to an opinion rendered on evidence presented at trial. Moreover, we cannot say that admission of the decedent's declaration will subvert the historic function of the jury to pass on the credibility of witnesses, to determine facts and to decide the weight to be given evidence. The challenged testimony is competent and admissible.

Judgment affirmed.

■ Pomeroy, Justice (concurring).

While I concur with the majority's conclusion that the victim's statement to her mother was admissible into evidence under an exception to the hearsay rule and was not excludible as being an opinion, I disagree with the majority's holding that it is admissible only under the "present sense impression" exception. Assuming that this exception would be a useful addition to the law of Pennsylvania relative to hearsay evidence, it is not, in my view, applicable to the case at bar. On the other hand, I am satisfied that the challenged statement is admissible under the so-called "excited utterance" exception, another variant of the res gestae exception, and I am at a loss to explain the majority's conclusion to the contrary.

In the case of Allen v. Mack, 345 Pa. 407, 28 A.2d 783 (1942), this Court defined what is known as the res gestae exception to the hearsay rule: "A res gestae declaration may be defined as a spontaneous declaration by a person whose mind has been suddenly made subject to an overpowering emotion caused by some unexpected and shocking occurrence, which that person has just participated in or closely witnessed, and made in reference to some phase of that occurrence which he perceived, and this declaration must be made so near the occurrence both in time and place as to exclude the likelihood of its having emanated in whole or in part from his reflective faculties." 345 Pa. at 410, 28 A.2d at 784. The opinion of the Court concludes, and I agree, that as so defined, this exception is preferably described as the "excited utterance" exception. McCormick, Evidence § 297 at 704 (2d ed. [, Cleary,] 1972).

Professor McCormick has said that there are two basic requirements for the applicability of this exception: "First, there must be some occurrence or event sufficiently startling to render normal reflective thought processes of an observer inoperative. Second, the statement of the declarant must have been a spontaneous reaction to the occurrence or event and not the result of reflective thought." McCormick, op. cit., supra. See also A.L.I. Model Code of Evidence, Rule 512(b); proposed Rules of Evidence for the United States Courts and Magistrates, Rule 803(2) (1973).

From the evidence in the case at bar it is manifest that both elements of the "excited utterance" exception are present: a sufficiently shocking or (in McCormick's word) "startling" occurrence and a statement which is a "spontaneous reaction" to that occurrence. The victim's mother testified that her daughter, Diane McCarthy, telephoned her on the morning she died and told her mother that she had just been awakened by the defendant punching her seven times in the face. The mother further testified that throughout the call she could hear Coleman yelling loudly and angrily in the background. Certainly this episode in which Diane was caught up may be truly characterized as "sufficiently startling to render normal reflective thought processes . . . inoperative." McCormick, op. cit. supra. In Commonwealth v. Noble, 371 Pa. 138, 88 A.2d 760 (1952), this Court said "[s]pontaneous exclamations or declarations uttered during or immediately preceding or following the actual infliction of wounds or springing out of the actual commission of the crime, are admissible as within the res gestae rule." 371 Pa. at 145, 88 A.2d at 763. See also Commonwealth v. Edwards, 431 Pa. 44, 244 A.2d 683 (1968); Commonwealth v. Stokes, 409 Pa. 268, 186 A.2d 5 (1962). In the present case, Diane's declaration immediately followed defendant's first assault upon her and preceded only by moments the further threatened attack. Again, such an attack and such a threat surely qualify as "startling" (McCormick) or as "shocking" (Allen v. Mack, supra).

The element of "spontaneity" is likewise present here. The victim's mother testified that when she suggested to Diane that she would hang up and call the police, her daughter begged her not to do so " '[b]ecause as soon as the phone is hung up,' he was going to kill her." The conclusion is irresistible that this declaration was the victim's spontaneous reaction to the attack upon her only minutes before. There was no evidence that the statement was premeditated or in any way the product of design on the declarant's part. The fact that her fear was indeed justified was tragically borne out by the fact that only minutes after her frantic telephone call to her mother, Diane McCarthy was found dying of 102 stab wounds.

Since it is my belief that the challenged statement did come within the "excited utterance" exception to the hearsay rule, I think the Court is mistaken in using this case as a vehicle for the adoption of the "present sense impression" exception. In its effort to get away from the "res gestae" label for the hearsay exception applicable to a fact situation such as this case presents, the Court has, in my opinion, unnecessarily adopted a new and, on these facts, inapplicable exception.

For the above reason, I concur that, hearsay though it was, the statement was properly admitted into evidence.

■ ROBERTS and NIX, JJ., join in this concurring opinion.

NOTES

1. People v. Brown, 610 N.E.2d 369, 373–74 (N.Y.1993): Tape recordings of 911 calls reporting a burglary in progress were played for the jury:

> The remaining questions concern the nature and extent of the corroboration required to assure reliability. To be sure, some textual versions of the present sense impression rule require no corroboration at all (see, e.g., Fed.Rules Evid., rule 803[1], . . . State v. Flesher, 286 N.W.2d 215, 218 [Iowa 1979] [holding that corroboration, or the lack of it, will affect the weight given to the declaration but not its admissibility]). . . .
>
> Defendant argues that if we are to adopt the present sense impression exception in any form it must be with the strictest corroboration rule—i.e., requiring corroboration at trial by an "equally percipient witness", a witness at the scene who had an equal opportunity to perceive the event and who will be subject to cross-examination as to the accuracy of the declarant's statement. . . . If corroboration by an "equally percipient wit-

ness" were required in this case, defendant properly points out, the 911 tape should not have been admitted. The police who testified to the conditions and events at the scene were not present when the calls were made and could not have observed the events at the precise moment that they were being described by the 911 caller.

. . .

... Insisting that the declarant's descriptions of the events must be corroborated in court by a witness who was present with the declarant and who observed the very same events would deprive the exception of most, if not all, of its usefulness. If such an eyewitness is available to testify to the events, there is certainly no pressing need for the hearsay testimony. And *excluding* the statement of the declarant in all cases *when such eyewitness is not available* may bar the fact finder from hearing relevant testimony that is perfectly reliable. Nor do we agree with defendant that, at a minimum, there must be a corroborating witness who—although not necessarily percipient of all that declarant observed—did at least *simultaneously* see or hear some aspect of it (see, e.g., Commonwealth v. Coleman, 458 Pa. 112, 326 A.2d 387 [1974]). We see no reason why the contemporaneity of the declaration with the events as well as the accuracy of the declarant's description cannot be corroborated by other means.

We do, however, decline to adopt the People's argument that no corroboration should be required. The admission of a hearsay statement under any exception deprives the defendant of the right to test the accuracy and trustworthiness of the statement by cross-examination. The defendant's only protection against the admission of fabricated testimony or unfounded rumor is that there be sufficient safeguards to assure the statement's reliability [citations omitted]. With the excited utterance exception, this assurance is found in the fact that the statement is made under the stress of nervous excitement from the event and before there has been time to contrive and misrepresent [citations omitted]. We think that when statements are admitted under the present sense exception without the assurance of reliability that excitement affords, it is reasonable and prudent to require some additional indicia of reliability.

In this case, the testimony of the police officers who arrived at the restaurant shortly after the first call and who apprehended two suspects fitting the description of "one male black and one male white, wearing a blue t-shirt" given by the caller "Henry" was sufficient corroboration. The police observed what the 911 caller had described only moments before. The suspects were seen running out of the restaurant through the broken glass door and seeking refuge on the roof, lending credence to the report that there was a burglary in progress. That the circumstances and events at the scene were still very much as described by "Henry" corroborates what seems evident from the calls themselves—that "Henry's" reports were spontaneous and made contemporaneously with the events described.

In a subsequent New York case in which a tape recording had been admitted of a 911 call by a homeowner reporting a burglary in progress, a majority of the court refused to adopt an unavailability requirement over the objection that admission of the tape improperly "bolstered" the homeowner's testimony at trial. The concurring judges disagreed. They distinguished Brown "because those facts could not be proven by any other evidence" but found error, though harmless, in admitting a 911 tape as a present sense impression unless "there is some necessity for it." People v. Buie, 658 N.E.2d 192, 199–202 (N.Y.1995).

2. In State v. Flesher, cited in Brown, note 1 supra, the victim said during a telephone conversation with her husband shortly before her death, that there was someone at the door. When she came back on the line, the victim said, "It's Joan," and indicated that she had let Joan in. The court also admitted the witness' response: "Well, just be careful". See also Booth v. State, 508 A.2d 976 (Md.1986) (survey of cases).

3. Is the statement admissible as a present sense impression or an excited utterance if the declarant cannot be identified? In Brown, supra note 1, the opinion states: "It was stipulated that the name and telephone number given by the 911 caller in the transmissions were not correct." 594 N.Y.S.2d at 698.

See United States v. Medico, 557 F.2d 309 (2d Cir.), cert. denied, 434 U.S. 986 (1977): Bank robbery. Unidentified bystander who observed getaway car called out license plate number and description of car to other unidentified bystander who relayed information through bank door to witness, bank employee. Court found that testimony met all the requirements specified in Federal Rules of Evidence 803(1). See also State v. Smith, 285 So.2d 240 (La.1973): Victim of robbery was locked into back of truck. After he was let out, a woman whose identity was unknown handed him a piece of paper which contained a license number that led the police to defendant. Court found the slip of paper to be admissible either as an excited utterance or as a present sense impression. Compare Myre v. State, 545 S.W.2d 820, 826–27 (Tex.Crim.App.1977):

> Appellant also says that the court erred in admitting improper hearsay testimony before the jury. Sandra Tharp, the complaining witness in the robbery at the One Hour Martinizing laundry, testified that after appellant stole the money from her at gunpoint he made her lie down on the floor in the back of the laundry. When she heard the door close she ran to the front of the shop just as a customer came in who had seen the robber leave. She told the customer, who she later learned was Jerry Beacroft, "Could you follow that man? He has just robbed me and he has a gun; be careful." The customer ran out the door and she called the police. The court permitted her to testify, over appellant's objection that the customer told her the license plate number of the robber's car was HDG 145.

> Appellant contends this was hearsay. We agree. The out-of-court statement was offered to prove the truth of the matter asserted therein. The court ruled that the statement was res gestae of the offense. The statement may well have been an excited utterance, an exception to the hearsay rule; however, in the record before us a sufficient predicate was not laid for us to determine whether the statement was in fact an excited utterance. The State contends that the statement was a present sense impression. It was not admissible as a present sense impression because the witness did not have an equal opportunity to observe and check a possible misstatement of Beacroft. See Anderson v. State, 454 S.W.2d 740 (Tex.Cr.App.1970); McCormick, [Evidence § 298 (2d ed., Cleary, 1972)].

4. As to the requirement of personal knowledge, see McLaughlin v. Vinzant, 522 F.2d 448, 451 (1st Cir.), cert. denied, 423 U.S. 1037 (1975) (W testified that declarant came running into second floor apartment shouting that D had shot someone; shooting occurred in doorway to entrance of apartment house: "It is true that there is no evidence of precisely where Dellamano was and what events she witnessed leading her to announce that McLaughlin had shot Sheridan. But, it was permissible to draw an inference not only from the force of the statement itself but from the fact that she was accompanying McLaughlin and was somewhere in the immediate vicinity of the fatal event, that she possessed firsthand knowledge of the killing. See McCormick, Evidence § 297 at 705 (2d ed., [Cleary,] 1972).").

Compare State v. Bean, 337 So.2d 496, 498 (La.1976): Declarant who was holding victim, told W when he arrived on scene that D had stabbed victim: "In the present case, the record is insufficient to support a reasonable inference that the declarant actually witnessed the crime. Whether or not his identification of the assailant was based on personal observation is not disclosed in the context of the utterance or in the foundation for its admission."

See also, Miller v. Keating, 754 F.2d 507 (3d Cir.1985); People v. Poland, 174 N.E.2d 804 (Ill.1961); Watson v. State, 387 P.2d 289 (Alaska 1963); Johnson v. Newell, 278 A.2d 776 (Conn.1971); Ungefug v. D'Ambrosia, 58 Cal.Rptr. 223 (Cal.Ct.App.1967); Warfield v. Shell Oil Co., 472 P.2d 50 (Ariz. 1970).

For a discussion of the "personal knowledge" requirement in Fed.R.Evid. 602 see Chapter 3, section 1(F), supra.

5. Is excitement a guarantor of trustworthiness? See Moorehead, Compromising the Hearsay Rule: The Fallacy of Res Gestae Reliability, 29 Loy.L.A.L.Rev. 203, 237–38 (1995) (discusses empirical studies which suggest that stress may have a negative impact on cognition and perception). Cf. People v. Miklejohn, 585 N.Y.S.2d 454, 455 (N.Y.App.Div.1992) (homicide conviction reversed because trial court excluded victim's statement that he did not know his assailant; defendant and declarant had known each other for approximately fifteen years; victim made statement after he had been punched, hit in the head with a baseball bat, was bleeding profusely, and suffering from what proved to be a fatal bullet wound to the head and brain; court found that statement, made when victim appeared "dazed and confused," qualified as excited utterance).

6. Federal Rule 803(1) speaks of "[a] statement describing or explaining ... made while the declarant was perceiving ... or immediately thereafter." Federal Rule 803(2) is worded in terms of "[a] statement relating ... made while the declarant was under the stress of excitement...." Is the opinion rule equally applicable depending on which of the two exceptions is relied upon? See State v. Blackburn, 247 S.E.2d 334 (S.C.1978). See also Wright v. Swann, 493 P.2d 148 (Or.1972); Galveston Transit Co. v. Morgan, 408 S.W.2d 728 (Tex.Civ. App.1966); Elek v. Boyce, 308 F.Supp. 26 (D.S.C.1970); Bass v. Muenchow, 146 N.W.2d 923 (Iowa 1966). Should the opinion rule apply to hearsay statements? See discussion in Chapter 3, supra and chapter 6, infra.

7. How close in time must the statement be to the event to satisfy the "immediately thereafter" formulation in Rule 803(1), and the rationale for the exception? See United States v. Obayagbona, 627 F.Supp. 329, 340 (E.D.N.Y. 1985) (statement by undercover agent that defendant had delivered the heroin to him, which was made 15 minutes after the drug transaction, was "as spontaneous as possible: there had elapsed only two minutes and 25 seconds after the arrest ... By its nature the statement could not have been made in the presence of ... the defendant. It was repressed and then exploded almost as a reflex as soon as Agent Turner was free to speak."). Are there instances where because of the lapse of time the statement will be admissible pursuant to one exception but not the other? See Hilyer v. Howat Concrete Co., 578 F.2d 422 (D.C.Cir.1978) (statement made 15 to 45 minutes after event admissible as excited utterance but not as present sense impression).

8. Among the many cases discussing the time factor with regard to excited utterances, see State v. Henderson, 362 So.2d 1358, 1362 (La.1978):

[T]he trial court must determine whether the interval between the event and the statement was long enough to permit a subsidence of emotional upset and a restoration of a reflective thought process. Several additional factors which may indicate that the statement was the result of reflective thought, but which do not automatically justify exclusion, are as follows: Evidence that the statement was self-serving or made in response to an inquiry; Expansion of the excited utterance beyond a description of the exciting event into past facts or the future; Proof that the declarant performed tasks requiring reflective thought processes between the event and the statement.

Compare, Mason v. Mootz, 253 P.2d 240, 241–42 (Idaho 1953) (statement of deceased, "[W]atch where you are going and don't drive so fast" made immediately upon regaining consciousness—"and not made in response to interrogation"—in hospital where he was taken following an accident held admissible) with Cummings v. Illinois Cent. R.R. Co., 269 S.W.2d 111, 118 (Mo.1954)(statements of deceased made to fellow employee in response to questions one and one half hours after an explosion in which he was fatally burned held inadmissible as he was conscious and rational for the entire period and hence there was no evidence that he was unable to reflect or reason, but statements made seven minutes after the explosion while he was screaming in pain admissible) and People v. Seymour, 588 N.Y.S.2d 551, 554, 555 (N.Y.App.Div.1992) (statement of victim made one hour and 20 minutes after he was found unconscious in his apartment where he had been lying bound up for at least 24 hours, and possibly 48 hours, found admissible, because he had not yet had an opportunity for "studied reflection," but reversible error to admit statement made 20 minutes later after a break in the questioning at which time victim "was apparently conscious, reasonably comfortable, and capable of reflection.").

See also Newbury v. State, 695 P.2d 531 (Okla.Crim.App.1985) (homicide; father of children being cared for by babysitter—the victim—arrived home to find children sleeping and babysitter gone; defendant, a television installer who had been working at the house where the babysitter was employed on the evening in question, contended that the trial court erred in allowing testimony that when the four-year old child awoke the next morning she went into her mother's bedroom and answered her mother's inquiry about where the babysitter went by stating, " 'She went with the television man' "; after a hearing, court found the child incompetent to testify due to immaturity; court admitted statement as an excited utterance on the ground that being left alone with her 18 month old brother constituted an exciting event and that there had been no opportunity for fabrication or reflection since the child was asleep for virtually the entire time between the exciting event and the statement).

Also compare Allen v. McLain, 69 N.W.2d 390, 396 (S.D.1955) (doctor who attended plaintiff in hospital on the night of the accident was permitted to testify that while recovering consciousness she kept saying, "Slow down, please slow down." Held: "there should be no question of the competency of such a statement on account of an alleged unconscious state of the declarant unless the language is incoherent and the speaker delirious") with Wilson v. Toliver, 285 S.W.2d 575, 584 (Mo.1955) (not error to refuse to permit bystander who arrived fifteen minutes after the accident to testify that declarant said "Why did he keep swerving." Declarant's foot was nearly severed by the accident but she never lost consciousness and the trial court might therefore decide that she was not under such influence of shock or pain as to be unable to reflect or reason so as to make her statement a spontaneous utterance).

9. Is the fact that the statement is made in response to a question fatal to a finding of spontaneity? See People v. Edwards, 392 N.E.2d 1229, 1232 (N.Y. 1979):

> The natural reaction of any person arriving to aid one exposed to a startling event is to inquire "What happened?". To pivot the admissibility of a subsequent statement, however spontaneous, on the question of whether it was prompted by an equally spontaneous inquiry would serve no useful purpose. Instead, this is merely one of the factors to be weighed in determining whether the surrounding circumstances demonstrate that the utterance was instinctive. To be sure, if the question propounded or the identity of the questioner may suggest or influence the response or if it is asked an appreciable length of time after the startling event, the declarations might very well lack the inherent reliability basic to the rule. But where, as here, the responses are uttered under the stress of nervous excitement without opportunity for reasoned reflection, they should be submitted to the trier of fact.

Does this reasoning apply to present sense impressions as well?

10. May the spontaneous declaration of one who is incompetent as a witness be proved? See Newbury v. State, supra, note 8; Moster v. Bower, 286 N.E.2d 418 (Ind.Ct.App.1972) (dead man's statute). Does alcohol affect visual and auditory perceptions or dull pain sufficiently to allow reflection? See United States v. Glenn, 473 F.2d 191 (D.C.Cir.1972). See also Annot., Admissibility of testimony regarding spontaneous declarations made by one incompetent to testify at trial, 15 A.L.R.4th 1043 (1982).

11. What constitutes a startling event? See, David by Berkeley v. Pueblo Supermarket of St. Thomas, 740 F.2d 230 (3d Cir.1984) (seeing an eight month pregnant woman slip and fall on her stomach). Cf. United States v. Napier, 518 F.2d 316, 317 (9th Cir.), cert. denied, 423 U.S. 895 (1975) (approximately one week after a seven week hospitalization necessitated by assault, victim saw defendant's picture in newspaper and said, "He killed me, he killed me;" Held: admissible; display of the photograph constituted the startling event for purposes of calculating elapsed time).

12. May proof of the startling event be made by the statement itself? P's husband, for whose death she is claiming damages, said to her over the telephone about 8 P.M. August 15: "Mother, in washing the boiler when I lifted that manhead I was severely hurt, because I have got severe pains in the abdomen and I am suffering intensely." After 1 A.M. August 16, the husband said to his son, who went to the husband's place of work to bring him home: "I strained myself bad lifting that manhead; I had an awful strain; I went to put it up in place and felt an awful pain, . . . " August 17, the husband was taken to a hospital where an operation disclosed a ruptured appendix, which caused his death. P and the son were permitted, over objection, to testify to the above statements as tending to prove that the husband died as a result of an accident arising out of his employment. Held "admissible under an exception to the hearsay rule, and as part of the res gestae." Industrial Comm'n. of Colorado v. Diveley, 294 P. 532, 533 (Colo.1930).

The court relied upon two previous Colorado cases. The first of these relied expressly upon Travellers' Insurance Co. of Chicago v. Mosley, 75 U.S. (8 Wall.) 397, 399, 403 (1869). In Mosley, the action was upon an insurance policy covering loss of life by accident. The assured left his bedroom between 12 and 1 o'clock at night. His son testified that about 12 o'clock he saw assured downstairs "lying with his head on the counter." His wife testified that when he returned to the bedroom, "his voice trembled; he complained of his head, and appeared to be faint and in great pain." Both wife and son were permitted over objection to testify that assured said he had fallen downstairs. The issue was whether assured died from the result of falling downstairs or from natural causes. Verdict and judgment for P. Writ of error. Affirmed. Query, was the testimony concerning the assured's physical appearance and his declarations of presently existing pain sufficient to justify the trial judge in concluding that assured had experienced some shock producing nervous excitement? See also Silver Seal Prods. Co. v. Owens, 523 P.2d 1091 (Okla.1974)(statement by decedent that he had fallen on employer's ice-covered parking lot).

A case strikingly contra is Truck Ins. Exchange v. Michling, 364 S.W.2d 172 (Tex.1963)(able opinion by Culver, J.). See also Commonwealth v. Barnes, 456 A.2d 1037, 1042 (Pa.Super.1983)(court excluded extrajudicial statement of the alleged victim—"There's the son-of-a-bitch right there that took my money"—which was the only evidence that a crime had been committed; court held that there must be independent evidence that a startling event had occurred because it is the very existence of the startling event that guarantees reliability). See also discussion in Fagan v. Newark, 188 A.2d 427, 432–34 (N.J.Super.1963) and Maguire and Epstein, Rules of Evidence in Preliminary Controversies as to Admissibility, 36 Yale L.J. 1101, 1101, 1122–25 (1927).

13. *Child sex abuse cases.* The excited utterance exception has been the most frequently utilized of the traditional hearsay exceptions in child abuse prosecutions. See Note, A Comprehensive Approach to Child Hearsay in Sex Abuse Cases, 83 Colum.L.Rev. 1745, 1753 (1983). Admissibility is not a problem when a child who would be a competent witness spontaneously reports a sexual attack shortly after its occurrence while the child is in an obvious state of distress. But one or more of these factors is frequently absent when the child makes a statement. In the 1980's, many state legislatures reacted by creating a special hearsay exception for a child's complaint. In addition, some courts have responded by interpreting the traditional excited utterance exception broadly. See, e.g., State v. Smith, 337 S.E.2d 833 (N.C.1985) (statement by four-year-old to her grandmother made three days after sexual assault by mother's boyfriend; court noted that children had been threatened, and that close re¹ :ionship with defendant may have discouraged immediate complaint); St .te v. Logue, 372 N.W.2d 151, 159 (S.D.1985) (statement by four-year-old l᠈ y day after event to his younger brother complaining that his bottom hurt wh ᠈h was overheard by mother, who then elicited further statements: "The statements were made to the child's mother within the normal course of his daily activities. These circumstances, coupled with the inability we perceive of the child to fabricate an account of such a heinous sexual encounter, warrant a finding that the statements were excited utterances."); United States v. Nick, 604 F.2d 1199 (9th Cir.1979) (babysitter charged with sexual assault; child had been asleep when mother picked him up at babysitter's and told story after mother asked him if anything had happened); Lancaster v. People, 615 P.2d 720, 723 (Colo.1980) (en banc) (child taken for medical examination by police after D's landlady observed her on D's bed, half-undressed, but seemingly unharmed; examination revealed a pubic hair in child's vaginal area; court permitted mother to testify to remark made by child one-half hour after she was brought home by police).

But see State v. D.R., 518 A.2d 1122, 1127, 1130, 1132 (N.J.Super.1986) (court found that child was traumatized by experience but her description of the sexual assault "was not accompanied by evident 'stress of nervous excitement' as required by" New Jersey rule; consequently, the court, relying on precedent, refused to admit statement pursuant to a spontaneous statement exception, although it noted "that this reading of the rule is more restrictive than that employed by many courts;" after reviewing cases in other jurisdictions and legislative developments, court concluded that it had the power to create a new hearsay exception for children's statements in child sex abuse cases, rev'd, 537 A.2d 667 (N.J.1988) (court agreed on need for new exception but found that it had to be adopted by legislature).

See the extensive analysis in Myers, Hearsay Statements by the Child Abuse Victim, 38 Baylor L.Rev. 775, 859–875 (1986); Note, State v. Smith: Facilitating the Admissibility of Hearsay Statements in Child Sex Abuse Cases, 64 N.C.L.Rev. 1352 (1986). See also Swift, The Hearsay Rule at Work: Has It Been Abolished De Facto by Judicial Discretion? 76 Minn. L.Rev. 507 (1992)(survey concludes that federal courts are importing a "trustworthiness" factor into their analysis of victims' statements with the result that statements, particularly of children, are admitted when offered by the prosecution).

14. For an extensive treatment of spontaneous declarations, see Thayer, Bedingfield's Case—Declarations as a Part of the Res Gestae, 14 Am.U.L.Rev. 817 (1880); Morgan, A Suggested Classification of Utterances Admissible as Res Gestae, 31 Yale L.J. 229 (1922); and Hutchins and Slesinger, Some Observations on the Law of Evidence, 28 Colum.L.Rev. 432 (1928). See also, Waltz, The Present Sense Impression Exception to the Rule Against Hearsay: Origins and Attributes, 66 Iowa L.Rev. 869 (1981); Foster, Present Sense Impressions: An Analysis and a Proposal, 10 Loy.U.Chi.L.J. 299 (1979); Waltz, Present Sense Impressions and the Residual Exceptions: A New Day for "Great" Hearsay? 2 Litigation 22 (1975).

SECTION 6.   PHYSICAL OR MENTAL CONDITION OF DECLARANT

Fidelity Service Insurance Co. v. Jones

Supreme Court of Alabama, 1966.
280 Ala. 195, 191 So.2d 20.

■ COLEMAN, JUSTICE. Defendants appeal from a judgment for plaintiff in an action on a policy of accident insurance on the life of plaintiff's son, Kenny Jones.

By the policy, defendants agreed as follows:

"... the Company hereby insures the person named in said schedule against loss of life through accidental means and against loss of sight and limb from injury, subject to all the provisions and limitations hereinafter set out.

"... If the insured sustains drowning or bodily injury effected solely through violent, external and accidental means, and if such drowning or bodily injury is the direct, independent and proximate cause of the death of the insured within 90 days from the date of such injury, and if such death is not caused or contributed to by disease or infirmity, the Company will on surrender of the policy pay the principal sum specified herein;...."

The evidence tends to show the following facts. Insured spent the night at his father's home. The next morning, insured ate breakfast and walked about a mile to get help to start his truck which he used to haul coal. After work, around 6:00 p.m. that day, insured drove his truck to the home of his father-in-law and parked the truck which was loaded with five or six tons of coal. Insured had coal dust on his clothes. He came into the house. He did not complain of being sick and appeared to be normal. He drank a coca-cola with his father-in-law. Insured went outside and moved his own truck and the father-in-law's truck. Insured came back into the house and they talked "Maybe fifteen or twenty minutes." Insured went into the bathroom to clean up. The bathroom had a hard surface, linoleum floor. A small, cloth throw rug, 18 by 30 or 36 inches, was on the floor. Insured closed the bathroom door. The father-in-law heard a noise which sounded "like he knocked something off a shelf" and went to the bathroom door. He heard "him splashing water" and went back and sat down approximately "four minutes, maybe."

After the interval, the father-in-law jerked the bathroom door open. It, apparently, had been latched with a hook and eye latch. He found insured "slumped over in the tub, with his head under water." The water was eight or ten inches deep. Insured's mouth and nose were under the water. He had on his undershirt and shorts. The "little throw rug was sorter around his feet." The floor was wet and appeared to be slick. The father-in-law found a straight razor under the bath tub. He pulled insured out of the tub. Insured was dead.

The father-in-law saw no bruises or blood on insured's head. The water in the tub appeared to be dirty and it appeared to the father-in-law that insured had bathed. His body appeared to be clean. No autopsy was performed.

. . .

The evidence seems to us to compel the inference that insured fell and his head struck the tub, breaking his nose; that he was unconscious either before or after his head struck the tub; and that, because he was unconscious, his head remained under the water and he drowned.

The evidence supports at least two theories as to the cause of the fall. The evidence is that the bathroom floor was covered with hard surface linoleum and a small rug, was wet, and appeared to be slick. The common experience of mankind on wet, slick bathroom floors supports the inference that insured may have slipped and fallen, striking his head on the tub, thereby becoming unconscious and drowning. If such was the case, then his drowning was not caused or contributed to by any disease or infirmity and plaintiff was clearly entitled to recover. This explanation of the death is consistent with the absence of disease or infirmity as a contributing cause of the accident and brings the case within the terms of the policy.

The other theory is that insured suffered a blackout, became unconscious, and fell onto the tub with his head into the water. In such a case, he may have been unconscious before the fall, and it may fairly be said that the fall was caused or contributed to by the blackout. . . .

Defendants argue that the court erred in overruling defendants' objections to three questions propounded to plaintiff's witnesses as follows:

"Q. Did he complain of any sickness or anything like that?

" . . .

"Q. Had your son complained any during that time as to being sick or not feeling well?

" . . .

"Q. Did you know of him complaining about any blackout at any time?"

The inquiries were whether insured had made the complaints referred to. Defendants say the evidence called for by the questions was not admissible because it was hearsay.

The general rule is that, whenever the bodily or mental feelings of an individual are material to be proved, the usual expression of such feelings, made at the time in question, are original evidence. So, also, the representations by a sick person, of the nature, symptoms, and effect of the malady under which he is laboring at the time, are received as original evidence, whether made to a medical attendant or any other person, though not, in the latter case of so much weight. . . .

In the case at bar, defendants introduced evidence of statements made by insured to the effect that he had had a blackout. We are of opinion that, under the stated rule, plaintiff had a right to offer contradictory evidence and that the court did not err in overruling defendants' objections to the three questions.

Affirmed.

NOTES

1. If the alleged sufferer is a personal injury plaintiff who does not testify, may he have witnesses testify to his complaints of pain? See Inman v. Harper, 162 S.E.2d 629, 631 (N.C.Ct.App.1968)("We find no authority that the general rule is not applicable when the plaintiff does not testify. The reason for the rule would seem to require no distinction."). Cf. Kometani v. Heath, 431 P.2d 931 (Haw.1967)(proof of complaints of pain by plaintiff who claimed want of recollection of his condition); Capelouto v. Kaiser Foundation Hospitals, 500 P.2d 880 (Cal.1972)(en banc)(methods of proving pain and suffering of child too young to speak). Statements of a personal injury defendant may also be admissible. See Hansen v. Heath, 852 P.2d 977 (Utah 1993)(automobile accident; driver died before his deposition was taken; in action against driver's estate, court found admissible statement driver made to treating physician that he had suddenly lost consciousness before accident; statement was exculpatory because it absolved him of liability for accident under state law).

2. As to the admissibility of statements of present pain and symptoms when made to a physician to enable him to give expert testimony, see discussion at pp. 1053–56, infra.

United States v. Tome

United States Court of Appeals, Tenth Circuit, 1995.
61 F.3d 1446.

■ TACHA, CIRCUIT JUDGE.

[Defendant's jury conviction for sexually abusing his daughter A.T. was affirmed by the Tenth Circuit. The United States Supreme Court reversed because of the erroneous admission of prior consistent statements, see page 540, supra and remanded the case to the Tenth Circuit for further consideration.]

I. Background

. . .

. . . On remand, we must first determine whether the challenged evidence could have been admitted under another rule of evidence. See Fortier v. Dona Anna Plaza Partners, 747 F.2d 1324, 1331 (10th Cir.1984)("We may affirm the rulings on admission of evidence if that evidence is admissible under any of the Federal Rules of Evidence."). If we find that any of the statements were inadmissible, we must then assess whether the district court's error in admitting them was nevertheless harmless. See United States v. Flanagan, 34 F.3d 949, 955 (10th Cir.1994).

. . .

III. DISCUSSION

A. Testimony of Karen Kuper, Laura Reich, and Jean Spiegel

We first address the testimony of three pediatricians who examined A.T. In their testimony, the three doctors relayed statements made by A.T. either before or during the doctors' physical examinations of the child. At trial, the district court admitted the doctors' hearsay testimony under both Rules 801(d)(1)(B) and 803(4).

. . . Rule 803(4) . . . is premised on the theory that a patient's statements to her physician are likely to be particularly reliable because the patient has a self-interested motive to be truthful: She knows that the efficacy of her medical treatment depends upon the accuracy of the information she provides to the doctor. United States v. Joe, 8 F.3d 1488, 1493 (10th Cir.1993), cert. denied, 127 L. Ed. 2d 579, 114 S. Ct. 1236 (1994). Stated differently, "a statement made in the course of procuring medical services, where the declarant knows that a false statement may cause misdiagnosis or mistreatment, carries special guarantees of credibility." White v. Illinois, 502 U.S. 346, 356, 112 S.Ct. 736, 116 L. Ed. 2d 848 (1992).

A declarant's statement to a physician that identifies the person responsible for the declarant's injuries is ordinarily inadmissible under Rule 803(4) because the assailant's identity is usually unnecessary either for accurate diagnosis or effective treatment. Joe, 8 F.3d at 1494. This court held in Joe, however, that a hearsay statement revealing the identity of a sexual abuser who is a member of the victim's family or household "is admissible under Rule 803(4) where the abuser has such an intimate relationship with the victim that the abuser's identity becomes 'reasonably pertinent' to the victim's proper treatment." Id. at 1495. In so holding, we reasoned that

> [a]ll victims of domestic sexual abuse suffer emotional and psychological injuries, the exact nature and extent of which depend on the identity of the abuser. The physician generally must know who the abuser was in order to render proper treatment because the physician's treatment will necessarily differ when the abuser is a member of the victim's family or household. In the domestic sexual abuse case, for example, the treating physician may recommend special therapy or counseling and instruct the victim to remove herself from the dangerous environment by leaving the home and seeking shelter elsewhere.

Id. at 1494–95 (footnote omitted). Although the victim in Joe was an adult, we stated that "the identity of the abuser is reasonably pertinent in virtually every domestic sexual assault case," including those in which the victim is a child. Id. at 1494. Thus, when a victim of domestic sexual abuse identifies her assailant to her physician, the physician's recounting of the identification is admissible under Rule 803(4) when it is "reasonably pertinent" to the victim's treatment or diagnosis. Id. at 1495; see also John W. Strong et al., 2 McCormick on Evidence § 277, at 248 (4th ed. 1992)(hereinafter McCormick). After reviewing the testimony of each pediatrician, we conclude that A.T.'s statements to those doctors were reasonably pertinent to her diagnosis or treatment.

1. Testimony of Karen Kuper

Kae Ecklebarger of Child Protection Services referred A.T. to Dr. Karen Kuper, a board certified pediatrician, for a physical examination. Kuper testified that she examined A.T. on two occasions, in September and October 1990. Prior to the first examination, Kuper interviewed A.T. Kuper testified that the purpose of the interview was "to ascertain exactly what injuries had occurred." In response to Kuper's questions, A.T. told Kuper about the sexual abuse, at times pointing to the appropriate areas of dolls to answer Kuper's questions. A.T. also identified defendant as her abuser. After the interview, Kuper performed a complete physical examination of A.T.

We find it clear that A.T.'s statement to Kuper was reasonably pertinent to Kuper's proper diagnosis and treatment of A.T. The information contained in the statement was important to Kuper's determination of A.T.'s condition. This statement was therefore admissible under Rule 803(4).

2.   Testimony of Laura Reich

A.T. saw Dr. Laura Reich on September 21, 1990, for treatment of a skin rash in the vaginal area that was unrelated to any sexual abuse. At the time of Reich's examination of A.T., Reich was aware of the allegations of sexual abuse. Reich testified that, prior to conducting the physical examination, she asked A.T. several personal questions. One of these questions was whether "anybody had ever touched her in her private area." According to Reich's testimony, A.T. replied "that her father had put his thing in her." The remainder of Reich's testimony concerned her findings and conclusions from the physical examination.

Reich testified that the reason she had conducted a preexamination interview with A.T was "that the child needs to be comfortable with me before I examine her." Because the adequacy of Reich's examination in part depended on the child's comfort with her, we find that A.T.'s statement was reasonably pertinent to Reich's diagnosis or treatment. It consequently was admissible under Rule 803(4).

3.   Testimony of Jean Spiegel

Dr. Jean Spiegel, an assistant professor of pediatrics at the University of New Mexico, testified that she examined A.T. for the purpose of offering a second opinion as to whether the child had been sexually abused. Spiegel had extensive training in the area of child sexual abuse, and teaches other doctors how to examine children to detect molestation. Most of Spiegel's testimony focused on the technical aspects of her examination of A.T. and her conclusion that A.T. had experienced chronic vaginal penetration.

On redirect examination, Spiegel testified that A.T. told her where on her body she had been touched during the abuse. Spiegel did not ask, nor did A.T. volunteer, who had touched her. Clearly, A.T.'s statement regarding where she had been touched was pertinent to Spiegel's diagnosis of A.T. The district court therefore properly admitted the statement under Rule 803(4).

B.   Testimony of Kae Ecklebarger

Kae Ecklebarger, a caseworker for Colorado Springs Child Protection Services, interviewed A.T. on August 29, 1990. Ecklebarger testified that during the interview, A.T. gave Ecklebarger a detailed account of the alleged abuse, at times using anatomically correct dolls to demonstrate what had occurred. Ecklebarger also testified that A.T. claimed she had told her grandmother and aunt of the abuse. . . .

For a hearsay statement to be admissible under Rule 803(4), the declarant need not have necessarily made the statement to a physician. As the advisory committee's note to the rule explains, "statements to hospital attendants, ambulance drivers, or even members of the family might be included." Fed. R.

Evid. 803(4) advisory committee's note. Accordingly, the government argues that A.T.'s statement to Ecklebarger is admissible because the job of a Child Protection Services caseworker "was equivalent to that of a doctor under Fed. R. Evid. 803(4)," and because A.T. understood that Ecklebarger's role was to "help kids."

As stated previously, however, the test for admissibility under Rule 803(4) is "whether the subject matter of the statements is reasonably pertinent to diagnosis or treatment." McCormick § 277, at 248. Ecklebarger neither diagnosed nor treated A.T. She described her role as "the initial short-term investigator." Ecklebarger spoke to A.T. two times, after which "the case was sent on to an ongoing protection worker." Clearly, Ecklebarger did not treat A.T. in any way.

Nor did Ecklebarger diagnose A.T. Indeed, Ecklebarger referred the child to Dr. Kuper for a medical opinion regarding the allegations of abuse. Moreover, Ecklebarger testified that she interviewed A.T. only to the extent necessary to make a decision whether a protective order was appropriate. Because Ecklebarger did not diagnose or treat A.T., the child's statement to Ecklebarger could not have been for the "purpose[ ] of medical diagnosis or treatment," and thus was not properly admitted under Rule 803(4).

. . .

[The court concluded that A.T.'s statement to Ecklebarger did not satisfy the residual hearsay exception either. The court also found that other statements of A.T.'s—to her babysitter and her mother—had been erroneously admitted.]

E.   Harmless Error Analysis

. . .

Given the strength of the erroneously admitted statements, this court is left in grave doubt as to whether the testimony substantially influenced the outcome of defendant's trial. Because we cannot say that the district court's errors in admitting these statements were harmless, defendant's conviction cannot stand.

. . .

■ Holloway, Circuit Judge, concurring and dissenting:

. . .

... I disagree with the majority's conclusion that A.T.'s out-of-court statements to Drs. Kuper, Reich, and Spiegel were admissible under Fed. R.Evid.803(4)....

. . .

Here the majority opinion correctly notes that the exception of Rule 803(4) "is premised on the theory that a patient's statements to her physician are likely to be particularly reliable because the patient has a self-interested motive to be truthful: She knows that the efficacy of her medical treatment depends upon the accuracy of the information provided to the doctor." Majority Opinion at 4, citing Joe. The majority thus appropriately recognizes the selfish treatment interest rationale supporting the exception. However, without proof that A.T. had such knowledge, the guarantee of trustworthiness disappears, and the statement then stands on no more reliable grounds than any other hearsay statement.

Turning to the trial record, there is no showing which demonstrates that A.T., who was four years old at the time of the alleged abuse, five at the time she saw Drs. Kuper and Reich, and six when she saw Dr. Spiegel, had the necessary understanding that "the efficacy of her medical treatment depended upon the accuracy of the information she provided to the doctor." Majority Opinion at 4 . . . .

Thus, A.T.'s testimony is insufficient to establish that she knew the importance of telling the truth to Drs. Kuper, Reich, and Spiegel, and is therefore insufficient to satisfy the selfish interest rationale under Rule 803(4). Likewise, the testimony of the doctors themselves and of Beverly Padilla, A.T.'s mother, shows no such proof. See Appendix to this opinion. Because the record does not show that A.T. appreciated the importance of telling the truth to the doctors, I must conclude that A.T.'s out-of-court statements to the doctors are not admissible under Rule 803(4).

. . .

NOTES

1. Rule 803(4) of the Federal Rules of Evidence liberalized prior practice by including statements concerning past symptoms and those which relate to the cause of the injury if relevant to diagnosis or treatment, and by eliminating the distinction between treating physicians and doctors who are consulted solely for purposes of diagnosis even when they are consulted in order to testify at trial. See United States v. Iron Shell, 633 F.2d 77, 83 (8th Cir.1980), cert. denied, 450 U.S. 1001 (1981). A number of states have retained the treating restriction by limiting the rule to "statements made for purposes of medical treatment and medical diagnosis in connection with medical treatment." See La. Code Evid. art. 803(4) and Michigan R. Evid. 803(4) and see Rhode Island R. Evid. 803(4)("but not including statements made to a physician consulted solely for the purpose of preparing for litigation or obtaining testimony for trial.").

Are statements to a psychiatrist within the rationale for the exception? Cf. United States v. Lechoco, 542 F.2d 84 (D.C.Cir.1976).

2. *Statements of identification.* In United States v. Renville, 779 F.2d 430, 438 (8th Cir.1985), in approving the admission of the 11–year old victim's statement to a physician in which she identified the defendant as her abuser, the court explained that physicians have an obligation under state law to prevent an abused child from being returned to an abusive environment. The court also stated: "Before questioning the child, Dr. Likness explained to her that the examination and his prospective questions were necessary to obtain information to treat her and help her overcome any physical and emotional problems which may have been caused by the recurrent abuse . . . Nothing in the record indicates that the child's motive in making these statements was other than as a patient responding to a physician questioning for prospective treatment." Id. at 438–39.

In United States v. Joe, 8 F.3d 1488, 1494 n. 5 (10th Cir.1993), cert. denied, 510 U.S. 1184 (1994), discussed in Tome, supra, the court surveyed the admissibility of statements of identification in federal courts and rejected a "motive" test:

> The Fourth, Eighth and Ninth Circuits agree that the crucial question in determining admissibility under Rule 803(4) is whether the statement is "reasonably pertinent to diagnosis or treatment." [United States v.] George, 960 F.2d [97,] 99 [(9th Cir.1992)]; Morgan [v. Foretich], 846 F.2d

[941,] 949 [(4th Cir.1988)]; [United States v.] Renville, 779 F.2d at 436. The Fourth and Eighth Circuits, however, have employed the following two-part test to determine a statement's admissibility under Rule 803(4): "first, the declarant's motive in making the statement must be consistent with the purposes of promoting treatment; and second, the content of the statement must be such as is reasonably relied on by a physician in treatment or diagnosis." Renville, 779 F.2d at 436; Morgan, 846 F.2d at 949 (quoting Renville). This two-part test is not contemplated by the rule and is not necessary to ensure that that the rule's purpose is carried out.

The first prong of this two-part test inquires into the declarant's motive. Such inquiries, however, were not contemplated by the rule; the rule itself has built-in guarantees that assure the trustworthiness of a statement made for purposes of medical diagnosis or treatment. See White, 502 U.S. at 354 (noting that such statements "are made in contexts that provide substantial guarantees of their trustworthiness"). The second prong, which assures that the contents of the statement (in these cases the identity of the abuser) is reasonably relied on by the physician in treatment or diagnosis, merely rephrases the Rule 803(4) requirement that the statement be "reasonably pertinent to diagnosis or treatment." In short, the plain language of Rule 803(4) should guide us in determining the admissibility of statements made for purposes of medical diagnosis or treatment.

For a criticism that objects to the admission of statements "regardless of the circumstances surrounding the examination" see Marks, Should We Believe the People Who Believe the Children: The Need for a New Sexual Abuse Tender Years Hearsay Exception Statute, 32 Harv.J.Legis. 207, 231–232 (1995):

> First, there is no reason to believe that statements made by the child in order to prepare the doctor to testify are any more trustworthy than other out-of-court statements made by the child. Second, the child's relationship with the testifying doctor is not the typical doctor-patient relationship; it may often border on a police detective-witness interaction. Finally, the doctor does not see the child for treatment unless there has been a claim that the child has been abused. The doctor, therefore, is predisposed to confirm what she has already been told by other adults.

[Footnotes omitted.] See also Mosteller, Child Sexual Abuse and Statements for the Purpose of Medical Diagnosis or Treatment, 67 N.C.L.Rev. 257 (1989).

See also United States v. Yazzie, 59 F.3d 807, 813 (9th Cir.1995)(alleged victim's mother made statements to physician in which she identified the child's stepfather as the perpetrator; court found that although "[t]he plain language of the Rule does not limit its application to patient-declarants," a parent's statement of identification

> in a child molestation case must be treated as suspect ... [T]he perpetrators are usually parents or relatives who are supposed to act in the child's best interest.... In the drama that unfolds during the medical examination of a child molestation victim, a parent or guardian's motive for casting blame may or may not be in the child's best interest or for the purpose of medical diagnosis. For example, a parent might misidentify the assailant in an effort to protect the other spouse, to avoid reprisal from the other spouse, to avoid having suspicion cast upon him or her, or to incriminate falsely the other spouse for personal motives.

> Since child molestation cases challenge our assumptions about why certain statements might have been made, inquiry into the declarant's

purpose must be exacting. When a party seeks to introduce the statement of parent or guardian identifying a sex offender, the proponent must demonstrate from the context and content of the statements that they were made for the purpose of medical diagnosis or treatment.

. . .

Determining whether Sarah Yazzie's purpose was to obtain proper medical treatment for her son requires examination of the content of the notes and statements, and the context in which they were made. When they arrived at the clinic, Sarah Yazzie told Dr. Wolfe that they had come to see a doctor because of sexual abuse. In the first note, Sarah Yazzie demonstrated that she knew her son was denying abuse, and explained why he was denying abuse ("Step-dad brain-washed him."). She also pleaded with the Dr. Wolfe to help her and her son ("I ask help, please[.]"). These words express concern for her son and desire to obtain help for him from Dr. Wolfe. In addition, her later descriptions of the manner, duration, and frequency of Yazzie's abuse were necessary for treatment since the victim was denying abuse).

The victim in Joe, supra was the estranged adult wife of the defendant who was charged with first degree murder in her death. Defendant admitted the killing but denied having the requisite intent. A physician testified that while treating the victim for an alleged rape 8 days before her death she identified the defendant as her assailant and stated that defendant had threatened to kill her. The court found that "the domestic sexual abuser's identity is admissible under Rule 803(4)" when as here the assailant's identity "was important for [the physician's] recommendation regarding Ms. Joe's after-care, including appropriate counseling." 8 F.3d at 1495. Does the court's reasoning also authorize other statements of identification? See State v. Moen, 786 P.2d 111, 117–21 (Or.1990)(en banc)(defendant charged with murdering wife and mother-in-law; court approved admission of statement by mother-in-law to her physician that she was depressed by her son-in-law's physical abuse of her daughter, and that "she felt he might kill them both.").

3. The extent to which the physician may rely on other material which has not been introduced into evidence—such as reports by other physicians, laboratory reports, etc.—in formulating his opinion is discussed infra at pp. 1045–1063.

4. United States v. Narciso, 446 F.Supp. 252, 284–292 (E.D.Mich.1977): Two nurses at V.A. Hospital were charged with murder after an extensive investigation undertaken when 35 patients suffered a total of 51 cardiopulmonary arrests in a two-month period. After suffering such an arrest, one of the victims, McCrery (dead by the time of trial), was asked later in the day by his attending physician as to whether he had been given an injection and, if so, by whom. McCrery wrote: "PIA"; there was testimony indicating that one of the defendants was known as "PI." The court on a motion in limine by the defendants to exclude the note ruled that it did not qualify as a present sense impression or an excited utterance. As to the government's assertion that the note was admissible under Federal Rule of Evidence 803(4), the court wrote:

> The government argues that these questions were asked of Mr. McCrery for purposes of medical diagnosis and treatment and this argument is certainly supported by the testimony of Dr. Goodenday who indicated that her motivation for questioning McCrery subsequent to his recovery from the arrest was to discover (1) if any medication had been administered to him and (2) if so, who did it. Dr. Goodenday indicated that it would be necessary to find out who administered the medication to find

out what it was and thus what further medical treatment would be required.

Yet while the doctor's motive was further diagnosis, the underlying assumption of the rule requires the Court to inquire as to the *declarant's* motivation for giving the information. If his motive is to disclose the information to aid in his own diagnosis and treatment, this, it is assumed, guarantees the statement's trustworthiness. However, if the declarant makes the statement while under the impression that he is being asked to indicate "who was responsible" for what happened, his response may very well be accusatory in nature and any inherent reliability of such a statement is thereby destroyed. In this instance it is not clear that Dr. Goodenday communicated to McCrery that she wanted to know who had administered the injection to find out what the medication was. Once he indicated that he had indeed been given an injection, she merely asked him who gave it to him. Dr. Goodenday herself admitted that the possibility of someone deliberately injecting a muscle relaxant was being considered by the staff. Moreover, the McCrery arrest was one of the last of a series of arrests which began on July 18 and the record discloses that rumors of these arrests and the possibility that they were deliberately induced were prevalent among both the staff and patients.

Based on the entirety of this record this Court is not convinced that McCrery's response to Dr. Goodenday's questions was motivated solely by a desire to assist her in later diagnosis and treatment. Absent such assurance the government may not rely on the hearsay exception in FRE 803(4).

For other cases dealing with statements of causation, see Gosser v. Ohio Valley Water Co., 90 A. 540 (Pa.1914)(patient, who developed typhoid on February 8th, tells doctor he drank two glasses of water supplied by defendant on the night of January 15th—inadmissible in action against Water Company for death of patient); Redding v. State, 85 N.W.2d 647 (Neb.1957)(inmate of state hospital tells doctor he was beaten by attendant—inadmissible in prosecution of attendant for manslaughter); Schoenrock v. City of Sisseton, 103 N.W.2d 649 (S.D.1960)(patient's statement to doctor relating how automobile accident occurred—inadmissible). However, in Valentine v. Weaver, 228 S.W. 1036 (Ky.1921), a physician was permitted to testify that the patient said he had run a splinter into his finger at a particular time, but not at what place, and in Shell Oil Co. v. Industrial Commission, 119 N.E.2d 224, 231 (Ill.1954), the treating physician was permitted to testify to P's statement that he injured himself when he slipped while pulling on a pipe.

As to the similar problem in cases where patients' statements are recorded in hospital entries, see pp. 722–723 infra.

5. Good general discussions of statements of present and past bodily condition are Slough, Spontaneous Statements and State of Mind, 46 Iowa L.Rev. 224 (1961); Notes, 31 Ill.L.Rev. 1107 (1937); 51 Mich.L.Rev. 902 (1953); 8 Wis. L.Rev. 284 (1933); 24 Texas L.Rev. 387 (1946); 13 N.C.L.Rev. 228 (1934); 21 Ga.B.J. 97 (1958); 47 Geo.L.J. 747 (1959); 1964 Wash.U.L.Q. 192. See also Comment, 12 Duq.L.Rev. 375 (1973)(Workmen's Compensation Cases).

United States v. DiMaria

United States Court of Appeals, Second Circuit, 1984.
727 F.2d 265.

■ FRIENDLY, CIRCUIT JUDGE:

[A tractor-trailer truck carrying 950 cases of cigarettes, each containing 12,000 cigarettes, was hijacked on the New Jersey Turnpike. After a week of surveillance of various persons, the FBI moved in as the cigarettes were being off-loaded from a trailer to a van. The defendant had earlier arrived on the scene in a Cadillac and had directed the van as it backed up to the trailer. He was intercepted and arrested by the agents as he started to drive away from the scene. Defendant was convicted on three counts of an indictment charging, 1) possession of cigarettes stolen while moving in interstate commerce, 2) possession of contraband cigarettes, i.e. possession of an excess of 60,000 cigarettes which show no evidence of having been taxed by any state, and 3) conspiracy to commit both substantive offenses. He was sentenced to ten years imprisonment on the possession of stolen cigarettes count, and five years on the other two counts, the sentences to run concurrently.]

. . . The defense sought to elicit from FBI Special Agent MacDonald that as the agents approached him, DiMaria said:

> I thought you guys were just investigating white collar crime; what are you doing here? I only came here to get some cigarettes real cheap.

The defense contended that cheap or even "real cheap" cigarettes meant bootleg cigarettes, i.e., cigarettes brought from a low-tax state for sale in a high-tax state, rather than stolen cigarettes, and that the statement thus tended to disprove the state of mind required for conviction under 18 U.S.C. § 659 (Count III), and also under the conspiracy count which charged a conspiracy to violate both 18 U.S.C. § 659 and 18 U.S.C. § 2342, since the jury was charged that it could convict if it found DiMaria guilty of conspiring to commit either crime. The defense did not explain with particularity why the statement was not inculpatory rather than exculpatory with regard to Count IV which charged possession of contraband cigarettes in violation of 18 U.S.C. § 2342; the theory must be that the reference to getting "some cigarettes real cheap" could be considered by the jury as negating an intention to possess a quantity in excess of 60,000 which § 2341(2) requires for a conviction. Admissibility was predicated on Fed.R.Evid. 803(3) which excepts from the hearsay rule, even though the declarant is available as a witness:

> A statement of the declarant's then existing state of mind, emotion, sensation, or physical condition (such as intent, plan, motive, design, mental feeling, pain, and bodily health), but not including a statement of memory or belief to prove the fact remembered or believed unless it relates to the execution, revocation, identification or terms of declarant's will.[1]

After hearing argument, the judge excluded the statement.

Our decision in United States v. Marin, 669 F.2d 73, 84 (1982), which the Government cited to the judge as dispositive in its favor, is totally irrelevant. We there upheld the exclusion of a portion of a post-arrest statement by the defendant Romero that a co-defendant, Marin, had placed a bag of narcotics in Romero's car. This was not a statement of Romero's existing state of mind; it

---

1. DiMaria contends on appeal that the statement was also admissible because it was a "verbal act" and thus not within the definition of hearsay in Rule 801. Even if this contention were properly before us, which we doubt, see McCormick, Evidence § 51, at 112 n. 15 (Cleary 2d ed. 1972), and cases there cited; United States v. Lara–Hernandez, 588 F.2d 272, 274 (9th Cir.1978)(per curiam); Huff v. White Motor Corp., 609 F.2d 286, 290 (7th Cir.1979); United States v. Anderson, 618 F.2d 487, 491 (8th Cir.1980), we find no merit in the contention despite its endorsement in 6 Wigmore, Evidence § 1781, at 307 (Chadbourn rev. 1976). We prefer Judge Weinstein's view that the "verbal act" doctrine applies only when "the utterance is an operative fact which gives rise to legal consequences," e.g., notice, 4 Weinstein's Evidence ¶ 801(c)[01], at 801–65 (1981). [Footnote of the court renumbered; other footnotes omitted].

fell squarely within the exception to the Rule 803(3) exception banning "a statement of memory or belief to prove the fact remembered or believed."

The Government's claim that, apart from the authority of Marin, DiMaria's statement falls within the exception to the exception is baseless. . . .

. . . .

DiMaria's statement had none of these characteristics. It stated, or so the jury could find, that his existing state of mind was to possess bootleg cigarettes, not stolen cigarettes. It was not offered to prove that the cigarettes were not stolen cigarettes but only to show that DiMaria did not think they were. It would defy reality to predicate any contrary conclusion on the use of the words "I came" rather than "I am". DiMaria's remark was not a statement . . . of what he or someone else had done in the past. It was a statement of what he was thinking in the present. See, e.g., United States v. Zito, 467 F.2d 1401, 1404 & n. 4 (2d Cir.1972); United States v. Partyka, 561 F.2d 118, 125 (8th Cir.1977), cert. denied, 434 U.S. 1037, 98 S.Ct. 773, 54 L.Ed.2d 785 (1978). The trial judge initially recognized this, before being distracted by the Government's erroneous reliance on Marin, when he said "this statement goes directly to the 659 count, and his state of mind", App. at 302.

The Assistant United States Attorney also stated in objection that DiMaria's remark was "an absolutely classic false exculpatory statement", App. at 302. False it may well have been but if it fell within Rule 803(3), as it clearly did if the words of that Rule are read to mean what they say, its truth or falsity was for the jury to determine. Dean Wigmore strongly endorsed the admissibility of such a statement at common law, 6 Wigmore, Evidence § 1732, at 159–62 (Chadbourn rev. 1976). Dealing with the argument that declarations of a mental state by an accused could readily be trumped up, he protested "the singular fallacy . . . of taking the possible trickery of guilty persons as a ground for excluding evidence in favor of a person not yet proved guilty", id. at 160, and contended that to sustain the argument would be inconsistent with the presumption of innocence.

It is true that Dean Wigmore would permit the exclusion of a statement of existing state of mind if "the circumstances indicate plainly a motive to deceive", id. (footnote omitted). McCormick, Evidence § 294, at 695 n. 56 (Cleary 2d ed. 1972), cited two cases, Elmer v. Fessenden, 151 Mass. 359, 24 N.E. 208 (1889), and Hall v. American Friends Service Committee, Inc., 74 Wash.2d 467, 445 P.2d 616 (1968), overruled on other grounds, McGugart v. Brumback, 77 Wash.2d 441, 463 P.2d 140 (1969), which required that, in applying the state of mind exception, there be " 'no apparent motive for misstatement' " or " 'circumstantial probability' " of trustworthiness, and another, Smith v. Smith, 364 Pa. 1, 70 A.2d 630 (1950), which held that the self-serving nature of such a declaration went only to its weight. The Federal Rules of Evidence have opted for the latter view. The Advisers' Introductory Note: The Hearsay Problem, endorses Professor Chadbourn's criticism of § 63(4)(c) of the Commissioner's proposed Uniform Rules of Evidence, saying, "For a judge to exclude evidence because he does not believe it has been described as 'altogether atypical, extraordinary' ", citing Chadbourn, Bentham and the Hearsay Rule—A Benthamic View of Rule 63(4)(c) of the Uniform Rules of Evidence, 75 Harv.L.Rev. 932, 947 (1962).

It is doubtless true that all the hearsay exceptions in Rules 803 and 804 rest on a belief that declarations of the sort there described have "some particular assurance of credibility." See Introductory Note, supra. But the scheme of the Rules is to determine that issue by categories; if a declaration comes within a category defined as an exception, the declaration is admissible without any preliminary finding of probable credibility by the judge, save for the "catch-all" exceptions of Rules 803(24) and 804(b)(5) and the business records exception of Rule 803(6)("unless the source of information or the method or circumstance of preparation indicate lack of trustworthiness"). As Judge Weinstein has stated, "the scheme adopted for the hearsay article in the federal rules is that of a system of class exceptions coupled with an open-ended provision in Rules 803(24) and 804(b)(5), and with the exemption of certain prior statements from the definition of hearsay", 4 Weinstein's Evidence ¶ 800[02], at 800–13 (1981), even though this excludes certain hearsay statements with a high degree of trustworthiness and admits certain statements with a low one. This evil was doubtless thought preferable to requiring preliminary determinations of the judge with respect to trustworthiness, with attendant possibilities of delay, prejudgment and encroachment on the province of the jury. There is a peculiarly strong case for admitting statements like DiMaria's, however suspect, when the Government is relying on the presumption of guilty knowledge arising from a defendant's possession of the fruits of a crime recently after its commission.

The Government argues that if exclusion of the statement was erroneous, the error was harmless because of the strength of the evidence against DiMaria, the ambiguous nature of the statement, the doubt that the jury would credit it, and the fact that counsel was allowed to argue that DiMaria was only trying to buy some cigarettes cheap and did not know they were stolen. The evidence with respect to guilty knowledge, while entirely sufficient, was not overpowering. As indicated above, the interpretation and the credibility of DiMaria's statement were for the jury. Counsel's argument was no substitute for the argument that could have been made if DiMaria's statement had been admitted. As we have often remarked, we cannot but wonder why, if the statement was so insignificant as the Government now claims, the prosecutor was at such pains to have it excluded.

The judgment of conviction is reversed and the cause is remanded for a new trial consistent with this opinion.

■ Mansfield, Circuit Judge (dissenting):

I respectfully dissent. As the majority recognizes (Opin. p. 270), DiMaria's statement upon arrest that he "came ... to get some cigarettes real cheap" is ambiguous, since the term "real cheap" could refer either to "bootleg" (i.e., lower-taxed) or to stolen cigarettes. It would be of defensive use only if it meant the former, in which event to admit the self-serving statement without exposure to the crucible of cross-examination would in my view not only introduce an element of confusion but violate the spirit of the Hearsay Rule. However, although no guarantee of trustworthiness for the defendant's interpretation is offered, I am persuaded by Judge Friendly's customary careful and thorough analysis that the Federal Rules of Evidence required its admission.

Where I part company with my colleagues is in the appraisal of the seriousness of the error. In my view, when one examines the obviously weak nature of the statement in the light of the powerful case against DiMaria, the error was harmless.

NOTES

1. There are many other contexts in which the declarant's state of mind at the time the statement was made constitutes a material fact. See, e.g., Reserve Life Insurance Co. v. Goodloe, 316 S.W.2d 443 (Tex.Civ.App.1958)(state of mind

in re mutual mistake); Deane Buick Co. v. Kendall, 417 P.2d 11 (Colo.1966); Sloma v. Pfluger, 261 N.E.2d 323 (Ill.App.1970)(state of mind in re scope of employment); Seattle–First National Bank v. Randall, 532 F.2d 1291 (9th Cir.1976)(diaries of decedent admitted to show her incompetency at time she pledged stock); Estate of Lampkin, 21 Cal.Rptr. 513 (App.1962)(testamentary intent); Bedsole v. State, 150 So.2d 696 (Ala.1963)(state of mind in re self defense).

2.   When is the state of mind of the victim a material fact?

In United States v. Joe, 8 F.3d 1488 (10th Cir.1993), cert. denied, 510 U.S. 1184 (1994), the court found that the victim's statement to a physician that she was afraid of her husband because he had threatened her should not have been admitted under Rule 803(3), although the statement was admissible under Rule 803(4). See page 653, supra. The assertion of *why* she was afraid was a "statement of memory or belief" expressly excluded by Rule 803. Id. at 1493. The court stated, however, that "Ms. Joe's statement that she was afraid of her husband was admissible under Rule 803(3)." Id. What is the evidential hypothesis that makes such a statement relevant?

Compare United States v. Brown, 490 F.2d 758, 766 (D.C.Cir.1973)(error to allow murder victim's wife to testify that her husband was afraid he would be killed by defendant: "The principal danger is that the jury will consider the victim's statement of fear as somehow reflecting on defendant's state of mind rather then the victim's—i.e., as a true indication of defendant's intentions, actions, or culpability.") with State v. Alston, 461 S.E.2d 687, 704 (N.C. 1995)("we conclude that the conversations between the victim and the five witnesses related directly to the victim's fear of defendant and that the victim's statements were properly admitted pursuant to the state of mind exception to the hearsay rule to show the nature of the victim's relationship with the defendant and the impact of defendant's behavior on the victim's state of mind prior to her murder"), cert. denied, 116 S.Ct. 1021 (1996). Cf. Partin v. Commonwealth, 918 S.W.2d 219, 221–22 (Ky.1996)(testimony by witnesses that they observed victim's fear of defendant when they saw her in his presence was not hearsay and relevant). See also Banks v. State, p. 489, supra.

State v. Phillips, 461 S.E.2d 75, 90–92 (W.Va.1995)(husband charged with murdering his wife claimed that shooting was accidental; reversible error to have admitted statements by victim-wife that she knew of her husband's extramarital affairs and intended to get a divorce).

United States v. Veltmann, 6 F.3d 1483, 1493–94 (11th Cir.1993)(prosecution of husband and son of victim for maliciously destroying house by fire while victim was inside, and for mail and wire fraud stemming from related life and property insurance claims; defendants claimed that victim set fire in order to commit suicide; reversible error to have excluded videotaped deposition of witness who testified about victim's threats of suicide in months preceding her death and of his conversation with victim five hours before her death in which he told her that he was not giving her any more money; witness had provided large sums of money to victim, who was drug addict, over twenty-five year period; court held that "deposition was relevant, admissible state of mind evidence because it contained not merely references to suicide, but information pertinent to decedent's desperate mental condition regarding finances on the date of her death.").

United States v. Hartmann, 958 F.2d 774, 783 (7th Cir.1992)(wife of murder victim and her lover were charged with defrauding insurance companies as to policies on life of victim; government claimed that victim's signature designating wife as beneficiary was forged; statements of victim that he feared his wife and thought she and her lover would murder him were properly admitted as evidencing his present state of mind and making it unlikely that he would have made his wife a beneficiary). May the court consider prejudice under Rule 403 and exclude?

3. *Domestic Homicide Hearsay Exception.* In the wake of the O.J. Simpson trial, Professor Raeder has suggested the need for a new exception that would make admissible in a homicide prosecution statements by the victim about the victim's relationship with the defendant if

> (A) the circumstances surrounding its making indicate the trustworthiness of the statement; and (B) on at least three occasions prior to the declarant's death, the defendant was the primary aggressor in one or more of following behaviors directed at the declarant: sexual assault, physical assault, stalking, threats of physical or sexual assault or any other conduct characterized as domestic violence.

Raeder, The Admissibility of Prior Acts of Domestic Violence: Simpson and Beyond, 69 S.Cal.L.Rev. 1463, 1516 (1996). What is the rationale for such an exception? Are there advantages to treating victims' statements under a domestic violence exception rather than under Rule 803(3)? Should the rule be the same in the criminal murder prosecution, the civil case for damages by the relatives of a victim, and the child custody dispute between the father (accused of murdering his wife) and grandparents of the children of a victim? See the broader exception that California enacted as § 1370 of the California Evidence Code.

4. How contemporaneous must the statement be with the state of mind in issue? In United States v. Veltmann, supra note 2, the court discussed the "continuity of time" concept, relevant to a state of mind inquiry that allows a court to conclude in light of the "totality of the circumstances" that the "statement mirror[s] a state of mind which ... has some probability of being the same condition existing at the material time." 6 F.3d at 1494 (quoting from In re Fill, 68 B.R. 923, 928 (Bankr.S.D.N.Y.1987)). Court reviews cases in which statements were made considerably earlier than the relevant state of mind. Statements made after the time in question have also been admitted. See People v. One 1948 Chevrolet Conv. Coupe, 290 P.2d 538, 543 (Cal.1955).

5. Statements about the declarant's state of mind may also be admissible to prove what acts the declarant would have performed in the future. In wrongful death actions, for instance, statements indicating the degree of affection between the deceased and the plaintiff bear on the damages to be awarded because pecuniary loss is measured by how much support the plaintiff would have received from the deceased had he or she lived. See, e.g., Loetsch v. New York City Omnibus Corporation, 52 N.E.2d 448 (N.Y.1943); Benwell v. Dean, 57 Cal.Rptr. 394 (1967); Phoenix Mut. Life Ins. Co. v. Adams, 30 F.3d 554, 566 (4th Cir.1994)(intention to change beneficiary on life insurance policy). Cf. Blackburn v. Aetna Freight Lines, Inc., 368 F.2d 345 (3d Cir.1966)(wrongful death action in which decedent's statements of intent were admitted on the issue of his earning capacity).

6. Not all courts agree with Judge Friendly's conclusion in the principal case that an untrustworthy hearsay statement that falls within the parameters of an exception may never be excluded pursuant to Rule 403. See United States v. Mandel, p. 676, infra.

Mutual Life Insurance Co. v. Hillmon

Supreme Court of the United States, 1892.
145 U.S. 285, 12 S.Ct. 909, 36 L.Ed. 706.

[In error to the Circuit Court of the United States for the District of Kansas. Action to recover on a life insurance policy on the life of John W.

Hillmon. The letters referred to in the opinion were from Walters to his sister and to his sweetheart. Each of them contained irrelevant matter of the sort to be expected in such communications and expressed the intention of leaving Wichita with Hillmon on a journey to Colorado and elsewhere. Three actions, each of which was on a policy of life insurance, were consolidated for trial and in the Supreme Court on writ of error. The death occurred in March, 1879. The action was begun in 1880. At the first trial in 1882, the jury stood 7 to 5 for plaintiff; at the second trial in 1885, 6 to 6. The third jury in 1888 awarded plaintiff $37,500, and from the judgments entered thereon, the writ of error in the principal case was taken. At the fourth trial in 1895 and at the fifth in 1896, the juries disagreed. The New York Life Insurance Company settled with plaintiff in 1898. At the sixth trial in 1899, plaintiff recovered against Mutual Life and Connecticut Life. The Mutual Life paid the judgment rendered against it, but Connecticut Mutual secured a reversal on writ of error. Connecticut Mutual Life Ins. Co. v. Hillmon, 188 U.S. 208, 23 S.Ct. 294 (1903). Thereafter plaintiff dismissed the action probably as the result of a compromise. In 1896 the three insurance companies were barred from doing business in Kansas, and it was to secure the right to do business that the New York Life settled in 1898. After the Populist administration was defeated, the bar against the other two companies was removed.]

■ MR. JUSTICE GRAY, after stating the case as above, delivered the opinion of the court. . . .

[The learned justice pointed out a procedural error requiring reversal, and continued:]

There is, however, one question of evidence so important, so fully argued at the bar, and so likely to arise upon another trial, that it is proper to express an opinion upon it.

This question is of the admissibility of the letters written by Walters on the first days of March, 1879, which were offered in evidence by the defendants, and excluded by the court. In order to determine the competency of these letters, it is important to consider the state of the case when they were offered to be read.

The matter chiefly contested at the trial was the death of John W. Hillmon, the insured; and that depended upon the question whether the body found at Crooked Creek on the night of March 18, 1879, was his body, or the body of one Walters.

Much conflicting evidence had been introduced as to the identity of the body. The plaintiff had also introduced evidence that Hillmon and one Brown left Wichita in Kansas on or about March 5, 1879, and travelled together through Southern Kansas in search of a site for a cattle ranch, and that on the night of March 18, while they were in camp at Crooked Creek, Hillmon was accidentally killed, and that his body was taken thence and buried. The defendants had introduced evidence, without objection, that Walters left his home and his betrothed in Iowa in March, 1878, and was afterwards in Kansas until March, 1879; that during that time he corresponded regularly with his family and his betrothed; that the last letters received from him were one received by his betrothed on March 3 and postmarked at Wichita, March 2, and one received by his sister about March 4 or 5, and dated at Wichita a day or two before; and that he had not been heard from since.

The evidence that Walters was at Wichita on or before March 5, and had not been heard from since, together with the evidence to identify as his the body found at Crooked Creek on March 18, tended to show that he went from

Wichita to Crooked Creek between those dates. Evidence that just before March 5 he had the intention of leaving Wichita with Hillmon would tend to corroborate the evidence already admitted, and to show that he went from Wichita to Crooked Creek with Hillmon. Letters from him to his family and his betrothed were the natural, if not the only attainable, evidence of his intention.

The position, taken at the bar, that the letters were competent evidence, within the rule stated in Nicholls v. Webb, 8 Wheat. 326, 337, as memoranda made in the ordinary course of business, cannot be maintained, for they were clearly not such.

But upon another ground suggested they should have been admitted. A man's state of mind or feeling can only be manifested to others by countenance, attitude or gesture, or by sounds or words, spoken or written. The nature of the fact to be proved is the same, and evidence of its proper tokens is equally competent to prove it, whether expressed by aspect or conduct, by voice or pen. When the intention to be proved is important only as qualifying an act, its connection with that act must be shown, in order to warrant the admission of declarations of the intention. But whenever the intention is of itself a distinct and material fact in a chain of circumstances, it may be proved by contemporaneous oral or written declarations of the party.

The existence of a particular intention in a certain person at a certain time being a material fact to be proved, evidence that he expressed that intention at that time is as direct evidence of the fact, as his own testimony that he then had that intention would be. After his death, there can hardly be any other way of proving it; and while he is still alive, his own memory of his state of mind at a former time is no more likely to be clear and true than a bystander's recollection of what he then said, and is less trustworthy than letters written by him at the very time and under circumstances precluding a suspicion of misrepresentation.

The letters in question were competent, not as narratives of facts communicated to the writer by others, nor yet as proof that he actually went away from Wichita, but as evidence that, shortly before the time when other evidence tended to show that he went away, he had the intention of going, and of going with Hillmon, which made it more probable both that he did go and that he went with Hillmon, than if there had been no proof of such intention. In view of the mass of conflicting testimony introduced upon the question whether it was the body of Walters that was found in Hillmon's camp, this evidence might properly influence the jury in determining that question.

The rule applicable to this case has been thus stated by this court: "Wherever the bodily or mental feelings of an individual are material to be proved, the usual expressions of such feelings are original and competent evidence. Those expressions are the natural reflexes of what it might be impossible to show by other testimony. If there be such other testimony, this may be necessary to set the facts thus developed in their true light, and to give them their proper effect. As independent explanatory or corroborative evidence, it is often indispensable to the due administration of justice. Such declarations are regarded as verbal facts, and are as competent as any other testimony, when relevant to the issue. Their truth or falsity is an inquiry for the jury." Travellers' Insurance Co. of Chicago v. Mosley, 8 Wall. 397, 404, 405.

In accordance with this rule, a bankrupt's declarations, oral or by letter, at or before the time of leaving or staying away from home, as to his reason for going abroad, have always been held by the English courts to be competent, in an action by his assignees against a creditor, as evidence that his departure was with intent to defraud his creditors, and therefore an act of bankruptcy.

Bateman v. Bailey, 5 T.R. 512; Rawson v. Heigh, 9 J.B. Moore, 217; s.c. 2 Bing. 99; Smith v. Cramer, 1 Scott, 541; s.c. 1 Bing.N.C. 585. . . .

Even in the probate of wills, which are required by law to be in writing, executed and attested in prescribed forms, yet where the validity of a will is questioned for want of mental capacity or by reason of fraud and undue influence, or where the will is lost and it becomes necessary to prove its contents, written or oral evidence of declarations of the testator before the date of the will has been admitted, in Massachusetts and in England, to show his real intention as to the disposition of his property, although there has been a difference of opinion as to the admissibility, for such purposes, of his subsequent declarations. Shailer v. Bumstead, 99 Mass. 112; Sugden v. St. Leonards, 1 P.D. 154; Woodward v. Goulstone, 11 App.Cas. 469, 478, 484, 486. . . .

Upon an indictment of one Hunter for the murder of one Armstrong at Camden, the Court of Errors and Appeals of New Jersey unanimously held that Armstrong's oral declarations to his son at Philadelphia, on the afternoon before the night of the murder, as well as a letter written by him at the same time and place to his wife, each stating that he was going with Hunter to Camden on business, were rightly admitted in evidence. Chief Justice Beasley said: "In the ordinary course of things, it was the usual information that a man about leaving home would communicate, for the convenience of his family, the information of his friends, or the regulation of his business. At the time it was given, such declarations could, in the nature of things, mean harm to no one; he who uttered them was bent on no expedition of mischief or wrong, and the attitude of affairs at the time entirely explodes the idea that such utterances were intended to serve any purpose but that for which they were obviously designed. If it be said that such notice of an intention of leaving home could have been given without introducing in it the name of Mr. Hunter, the obvious answer to the suggestion, I think, is that a reference to the companion who is to accompany the person leaving is as natural a part of the transaction as is any other incident or quality of it. If it is legitimate to show by a man's own declarations that he left his home to be gone a week, or for a certain destination, which seems incontestible, why may it not be proved in the same way that a designated person was to bear him company? At the time the words were uttered or written, they imported no wrongdoing to any one, and the reference to the companion who was to go with him was nothing more, as matters then stood, than an indication of an additional circumstance of his going. If it was in the ordinary train of events for this man to leave word or to state where he was going, it seems to me it was equally so for him to say with whom he was going." Hunter v. State, 11 Vroom, 40 N.J.L. 495, 534, 536, 538.

Upon principle and authority, therefore, we are of opinion that the two letters were competent evidence of the intention of Walters at the time of writing them, which was a material fact bearing upon the question in controversy; and that for the exclusion of these letters, as well as for the undue restriction of the defendants' challenges, the verdicts must be set aside, and a new trial had. . . .

Judgment reversed, and case remanded to the Circuit Court with directions to set aside the verdict and to order a new trial.

United States v. Pheaster

United States Court of Appeals, Ninth Circuit, 1976.
544 F.2d 353, cert. denied, 429 U.S. 1099, 97 S.Ct. 1118, 51 L.Ed.2d 546 (1977).

[Defendants were charged with conspiracy to kidnap and the mailing of requests for ransom and extortionate threats.]

■ RENFREW, DISTRICT JUDGE:

. . .

This case arises from the disappearance of Larry Adell, the 16–year–old son of Palm Springs multi-millionaire Robert Adell. At approximately 9:30 P.M. on June 1, 1974, Larry Adell left a group of his high school friends in a Palm Springs restaurant known as Sambo's North. . . . Larry never returned to his friends in the restaurant that evening, and his family never saw him thereafter.

. . .

Appellant Inciso argues that the district court erred in admitting hearsay testimony by two teenaged friends of Larry Adell concerning statements made by Larry on June 1, 1974, the day that he disappeared. Timely objections were made to the questions which elicited the testimony on the ground that the questions called for hearsay. In response, the Government attorney stated that the testimony was offered for the limited purpose of showing the "state of mind of Larry". After instructing the jury that it could only consider the testimony for that limited purpose and not for "the truth or falsity of what [Larry] said", the district court allowed the witnesses to answer the questions. Francine Gomes, Larry's date on the evening that he disappeared, testified that when Larry picked her up that evening, he told her that he was going to meet Angelo at Sambo's North at 9:30 P.M. to "pick up a pound of marijuana which Angelo had promised him for free". R.T. Vol. 5, p. 286. She also testified that she had been with Larry on another occasion when he met a man named Angelo, and she identified the defendant as that man. Miss Gomes stated that it was approximately 9:15 P.M. when Larry went into the parking lot. Doug Sendejas, one of Larry's friends who was with him at Sambo's North just prior to his disappearance, testified that Larry had made similar statements to him in the afternoon and early evening of June 1st regarding a meeting that evening with Angelo. Mr. Sendejas also testified that when Larry left the table at Sambo's North to go into the parking lot, Larry stated that "he was going to meet Angelo and he'd be right back." R.T. Vol. 5, p. 338.

Inciso's contention that the district court erred in admitting the hearsay testimony of Larry's friends is premised on the view that the statements could not properly be used by the jury to conclude that Larry did in fact meet Inciso in the parking lot of Sambo's North at approximately 9:30 P.M. on June 1, 1974. The correctness of that assumption is, in our view, the key to the analysis of this contention of error. The Government argues that Larry's statements were relevant to two issues in the case. First the statements are said to be relevant to an issue created by the defense when Inciso's attorney attempted to show that Larry had not been kidnapped but had disappeared voluntarily as part of a simulated kidnapping designed to extort money from his wealthy father from whom he was allegedly estranged. In his brief on appeal, Inciso concedes the relevance and, presumably, the admissibility of the statements to "show that Larry did not voluntarily disappear". However, Inciso argues that for this limited purpose, there was no need to name the person with whom Larry intended to meet, and that the district court's limiting instruction was insufficient to overcome the prejudice to which he was exposed by the testimony.[1] Second, the Government argues that the statements are relevant and

1. Were this the only theory under which the testimony could come in, we would tend to agree with Inciso. In such a context, the potential prejudice would far outweigh the potential relevance of the testimony, and a limiting instruction would not sufficiently safeguard the defendant. . . . [Footnotes by the court unless otherwise indicated; some renumbered; others omitted.]

admissible to show that, as intended, Larry did meet Inciso in the parking lot at Sambo's North on the evening of June 1, 1974. If the Government's second theory of admissibility is successful, Inciso's arguments regarding the excision of his name from the statements admitted under the first theory is obviously mooted.

. . .

The Government's position that Larry Adell's statements can be used to prove that the meeting with Inciso did occur raises a difficult and important question concerning the scope of the so-called "Hillmon doctrine", a particular species of the "state of mind" exception to the general rule that hearsay evidence is inadmissible. The doctrine takes its name from the famous Supreme Court decision in Mutual Life Insurance Co. v. Hillmon, 145 U.S. 285, 12 S.Ct. 909, 36 L.Ed. 706 (1892). That the Hillmon doctrine should create controversy and confusion is not surprising, for it is an extraordinary doctrine. Under the state of mind exception, hearsay evidence is admissible if it bears on the state of mind of the declarant and if that state of mind is an issue in the case. For example, statements by a testator which demonstrate that he had the necessary testamentary intent are admissible to show that intent when it is in issue. The exception embodied in the Hillmon doctrine is fundamentally different, because it does not require that the state of mind of the declarant be an actual issue in the case. Instead, under the Hillmon doctrine the state of mind of the declarant is used inferentially to prove other matters which are in issue. Stated simply, the doctrine provides that when the performance of a particular act by an individual is an issue in a case, his intention (state of mind) to perform that act may be shown. From that intention, the trier of fact may draw the inference that the person carried out his intention and performed the act. Within this conceptual framework, hearsay evidence of statements by the person which tend to show his intention is deemed admissible under the state of mind exception. Inciso's objection to the doctrine concerns its application in situations in which the declarant has stated his intention to do something *with another person,* and the issue is whether he did so. There can be no doubt that the theory of the Hillmon doctrine is different when the declarant's statement of intention necessarily requires the action of one or more others if it is to be fulfilled.

When hearsay evidence concerns the declarant's statement of his intention to do something with another person, the Hillmon doctrine requires that the trier of fact infer from the state of mind of the declarant the probability of a particular act not only by the declarant but also by the other person. Several objections can be raised against a doctrine that would allow such an inference to be made. One such objection is based on the unreliability of the inference but is not, in our view, compelling.[2] A much more significant and troubling objection is based on the inconsistency of such an inference with the state of mind exception. This problem is more easily perceived when one divides what is really a compound statement into its component parts. In the instant case, the statement by Larry Adell, "I am going to meet Angelo in the parking lot to get

---

2. The inference from a statement of present intention that the act intended was in fact performed is nothing more than an inference. Even where no actions by other parties are necessary in order for the intended act to be performed, a myriad of contingencies could intervene to frustrate the fulfillment of the intention. The fact that the cooperation of another party is necessary if the intended act is to be performed adds another important contingency, but the difference is one of degree rather than kind. The possible unreliability of the inference to be drawn from the present intention is a matter going to the weight of the evidence which might be argued to the trier of fact, but it should not be a ground for completely excluding the admittedly relevant evidence.

a pound of grass", is really two statements. The first is the obvious statement of Larry's intention. The second is an implicit statement of Angelo's intention. Surely, if the meeting is to take place in a location which Angelo does not habitually frequent, one must assume that Angelo intended to meet Larry there if one is to make the inference that Angelo was in the parking lot and the meeting occurred. The important point is that the second, implicit statement has nothing to do with Larry's state of mind. For example, if Larry's friends had testified that Larry had said, "Angelo is going to be in the parking lot of Sambo's North tonight with a pound of grass", no state of mind exception or any other exception to the hearsay rule would be available. Yet, this is in effect at least half of what the testimony did attribute to Larry.

Despite the theoretical awkwardness associated with the application of the Hillmon doctrine to facts such as those now before us, the authority in favor of such an application is impressive, beginning with the seminal Hillmon decision itself....

    . . .

The Hillmon doctrine has been applied by the California Supreme Court in People v. Alcalde, 24 Cal.2d 177, 148 P.2d 627 (1944).... In Alcalde the defendant was tried and convicted of first degree murder for the brutal slaying of a woman whom he had been seeing socially. One of the issues before the California Supreme Court was the asserted error by the trial court in allowing the introduction of certain hearsay testimony concerning statements made by the victim on the day of her murder. As in the instant case, the testimony was highly incriminating, because the victim reportedly said that she was going out with Frank, the defendant, on the evening she was murdered. On appeal, a majority of the California Supreme Court affirmed the defendant's conviction, holding that Hillmon was "the leading case on the admissibility of declarations of intent to do an act as proof that the act thereafter was accomplished." 148 P.2d at 631. Without purporting to "define or summarize all the limitations or restrictions upon the admissibility of" such evidence, id. at 632, the court did mention several prudential considerations.... Thus, the declarant should be dead or otherwise unavailable, and the testimony concerning his statements should be relevant and possess a high degree of trustworthiness. Id. at 631. The court also noted that there was other evidence from which the defendant's guilt could be inferred. Applying these standards, the court found no error in the trial court's admission of the disputed hearsay testimony. "Unquestionably the deceased's statement of her intent and the logical inference to be drawn therefrom, namely, that she was with the defendant that night, were relevant to the issue of the guilt of the defendant." Id. at 632.[3]

In addition to the decisions in Hillmon and Alcalde, support for the Government's position can be found in the California Evidence Code and the new Federal Rules of Evidence, although in each instance resort must be made to the comments to the relevant provisions.

Section 1250 of the California Evidence Code carves out an exception to the general hearsay rule for statements of a declarant's "then existing mental or physical state". The Hillmon doctrine is codified in Section 1250(2) which allows the use of such hearsay evidence when it "is offered to prove or explain

---

3. Mr. Justice Traynor, dissenting, said (24 Cal.2d at p. 189, 146 P.2d at p. 633): "The declaration of the deceased in this case that she was going out with Frank is also a declaration that he was going out with her, and it could not be admitted for the limited purpose of showing that she went out with him at the time in question without necessarily showing that he went out with her." He quoted Mr. Justice Cardozo: "Discrimination so subtle is a feat beyond the compass of ordinary minds." [Footnote by eds.]

acts or conduct of the declarant." The comment to Section 1250(2) states that, "Thus, a statement of the declarant's intent to do certain acts is admissible to prove that he did those acts." Although neither the language of the statute nor that of the comment specifically addresses the particular issue now before us, the comment does cite the Alcalde decision and, therefore, indirectly rejects the limitation urged by Inciso.

Although the new Federal Rules of Evidence were not in force at the time of the trial below, we refer to them for any light that they might shed on the status of the common law at the time of the trial. The codification of the state of mind exception in Rule 803(3) does not provide a direct statement of the Hillmon doctrine.... Although Rule 803(3) is silent regarding the Hillmon doctrine, both the Advisory Committee on the Proposed Rules and the House Committee on the Judiciary specifically addressed the doctrine. After noting that Rule 803(3) would not allow the admission of statements of memory, the Advisory Committee stated broadly that

> "The rule of Mutual Life Ins. Co. v. Hillmon [citation omitted] allowing evidence of intention as tending to prove the doing of the act intended is, of course, left undisturbed." Note to Paragraph (3), 28 U.S.C.A. at 585.

Significantly, the Notes of the House Committee on the Judiciary regarding Rule 803(3) are far more specific and revealing:

> "However, the Committee intends that the Rule be construed to limit the doctrine of Mutual Life Insurance Co. v. Hillmon [citation omitted] so as to render statements of intent by a declarant admissible *only to prove his future conduct, not the future conduct of another person.*" House Report No. 93–650, Note to Paragraph (3), 28 U.S.C.A. at 579 (emphasis added).

Although the matter is certainly not free from doubt, we read the note of the Advisory Committee as presuming that the Hillmon doctrine would be incorporated in full force, including necessarily the application in Hillmon itself. The language suggests that the Advisory Committee presumed that such a broad interpretation was the prevailing common law position. The notes of the House Committee on the Judiciary are significantly different. The language used there suggests a legislative intention to cut back on what that body also perceived to be the prevailing common law view, namely, that the Hillmon doctrine could be applied to facts such as those now before us.[4]

Although we recognize the force of the objection to the application of the Hillmon doctrine in the instant case, we cannot conclude that the district court erred in allowing the testimony concerning Larry Adell's statements to be introduced.

. . .

NOTES

1. For other cases in which declarant's statement referred to future acts by another see:

4. In United States v. Mangan, 575 F.2d 32, 43 n. 12 (2d Cir.) cert. denied, 439 U.S. 931 (1978), the court refused to rely on Rule 803(3) to admit statement by declarant about his plans with another "[b]ecause of confusion generated by the Federal Rules of Evidence.... The Senate Committee was silent and the Conference Report consequently did not comment. Are the Senate and the President or, for that matter, the members of the House who were not on the Committee to be considered to have adopted the text of the Rule, as glossed by the Advisory Committee's Note that Rule 803(3) enacted Hillmon, or the House Committee's 'construction' which, in effect, seriously restricts Hillmon?" [Footnote by eds.]

State v. Vestal, 180 S.E.2d 755, 769–789 (N.C.1971), cert. denied, 414 U.S. 874 (1973). Prosecution of Vestal for the murder of Pennisi. Question as to admissibility of declaration of Pennisi to his wife that he was going on a trip with Vestal.

> The circumstances under which the statements were made supply the reasonable probability of trustworthiness. It is a matter of everyday experience that a man leaving his home, or his business establishment, for an out-of-town trip will, for domestic and business purposes, inform his family or business associates as to his destination, traveling companion, purpose and anticipated time of return. Such statements customarily have no purpose other than the orderly arrangement of his domestic and business affairs and their proper handling in his absence. It is this circumstance which supplies the required probability of truthfulness.

Concurring justices expressed disapproval:

> Whether a particular person is more inclined to tell the truth to his wife, his friend, or a stranger, when he is about to depart on a journey rather than on occasions unrelated to such departure, is subject to question. Certainly, the reasonable probability of the truthfulness of such declarations cannot be compared to the reasonable probability of the truthfulness of a dying declaration.

See also United States v. Delvecchio, 816 F.2d 859, 863 (2d Cir.1987)(informant's statement that he intended to meet with two defendants; admissible against the defendant as to whom there was corroborating eyewitness evidence that meeting took place, but error to have admitted against other defendant whom eyewitness was unable to identify as having attended the meeting; there must be "independent evidence which connects the declarant's statement with the non-declarant's activities."). Compare United States v. Houlihan, 871 F.Supp. 1495, 1501 & n. 4 (D.Mass.1994)(admitting statement of victim-declarant of intention to meet with defendant on evening of victim's murder as circumstantial evidence of meeting):

> As Rule 803(3) is unambiguous,[1] this Court is unpersuaded by appeals to legislative history.... Even if the Court were properly to engage in an examination of Rule 803(3)'s legislative history, the conflicting nature of that evidence ... would nevertheless lead us right back to the text.... Therefore, such an inquiry is unnecessary.
>
> Likewise, this Court is not persuaded by the decisions of the Fourth and Second Circuits requiring independent evidence before such testimony can be admitted. Indeed, this requirement is without foundation in either the text or the legislative history of Rule 803(3). Thus, while the approach adopted by the Second and Fourth Circuits may seem practical and fair, it is really little more than judicial policymaking.

2. State v. Weedon, 342 So.2d 642 (La.1977): Prosecution of husband for murder of wife. Witness testified that wife had called her the afternoon preceding the day of wife's presumed death to state that she intended to leave

---

1. One might argue that Rule 803(3) is ambiguous because on its face it provides no guidance as to whether it includes statements implicating the conduct of third parties. This, however, is a misunderstanding of the "plain meaning rule." Under this canon of construction, legislative history may only be consulted when the meaning of the words is in dispute; questions regarding the application of a statute to the facts of a particular case do not render a statute ambiguous ... [T]he text of the rule is in fact plain and the use of legislative history is therefore unwarranted. [Footnote is the court's, renumbered]

her husband the following morning, after he left on a trip, without telling him of her intention. Admissible?

In Commonwealth v. Santos, 119 A. 596 (Pa.1923), D's defense to a charge of manslaughter was that deceased shot D, and, then, either she committed suicide or D shot her, having been rendered irresponsible by the shot he received. It was held that D should be allowed to prove that, shortly before the day of the fatal encounter, deceased declared her intention of shooting D and then killing herself. As to proof of threats of violence in support of a plea of self defense, see Washington v. State, 307 So.2d 430 (Miss.1975).

3.   On appeal from a workmen's compensation award, defendant argued that the statements of decedent to his wife that he was going on a trip to complete some business (the only evidence of his intent), were inadmissible to prove that the accident in which decedent was killed arose out of and in the course of his employment. In overruling defendant's objections that the statements were hearsay and self-serving, the court said: "declarations made contemporaneously with, or immediately preparatory to, a particular litigated act, which tend to illustrate and give character to the act in question are admissible as a part of the res gestae.... However, we are convinced that if, under the evidence, it may reasonably be inferred that these statements were made by Lewis [the decedent] as spontaneous declarations of a then present intent on his part to make the trip for the purposes stated by him, then they are admissible, not as part of the res gestae, but as circumstances tending to prove the fact that the trip was made for these purposes." Lewis v. Lowe & Campbell Athletic Goods Co., 247 S.W.2d 800, 804 (Mo.1952). Accord: Firemen's Fund Ins. Co. v. Thien, 8 F.3d 1307, 1312 (8th Cir.1993)(district court properly admitted statements by decedent that he would be working next day; court should also have admitted contradictory statements that he was going on trip to log flight time or on vacation).

4.   Plaintiff sued estate on a contractual claim for compensation due for services rendered to the deceased in the 11 years she lived with him and worked for him in his business establishments. Executor contended that evidence of the decedent's statements should have been excluded as hearsay. Held: "The deceased's assertions that he would 'take care of her', clearly reflected his state of mind at the time he made the statements, namely, his understanding that Kirk was to be compensated for her services. That evidence tended to prove that he understood she was not working for him gratuitously." Kirk v. Marquis, 391 A.2d 335, 336 (Me.1978)(per curiam). See also Parkhill Trucking Co. v. Hopper, 256 P.2d 810 (Okl.1953)(wrongful death action; statement of deceased that he intended to care for mother).

5.   For discussion of the Hillmon doctrine and collections of authorities bearing upon the point, see Seligman, An Exception to the Hearsay Rule, 26 Harv.L.Rev. 146 (1912); Chafee, 35 id. 444–46 (1922); Maguire, The Hillmon Case—Thirty-three Years After, 38 id. 709 (1925); and Hutchins and Slesinger, Some Observations on The Law of Evidence—State of Mind to Prove an Act, 38 Yale L.J. 283 (1929). See also Weissenberger, Hearsay Puzzles: An Essay on Federal Evidence Rule 803(3), 64 Temp.L.Rev. 145 (1991); McFarland, Dead Men Tell Tales: Thirty Times Three Years of the Judicial Process After *Hillmon,* 30 Vill.L.Rev. 1 (1985); Rice, The State of Mind Exception to the Hearsay Rule: A Response to "'Secondary' Relevance," 14 Duq.L.Rev. 219 (1976); Seidelson, The State of Mind Exception to the Hearsay Rule, 13 Duq.L.Rev. 251 (1974); Rucker, The Twilight Zone of Hearsay, 9 Vand.L.Rev. 475 (1956); Payne, The Hillmon Case—An Old Problem Revisited, 41 Va.L.Rev. 1011 (1955); Slough, Res Gestae, 2 Kan.L.Rev. 121, 131 et seq. (1953).

Shepard v. United States

Supreme Court of the United States, 1933.
290 U.S. 96, 54 S.Ct. 22, 78 L.Ed. 196.

[Certiorari to the Circuit Court of Appeals for the Tenth Circuit. The defendant was convicted of the murder of his wife. On rebuttal, over the objection of the defendant, a nurse was permitted to testify that the wife asked the nurse to go to defendant's room and bring a bottle of whiskey. When the bottle was brought, the wife said that this was the liquor she had taken just before collapsing, asked whether there was enough left to make a test for the presence of poison, insisted that the smell and taste were strange, and then added the words "Dr. Shepard has poisoned me." After holding that the reception of this evidence could not be justified under the rule which makes dying declarations admissible, the court, speaking through Mr. Justice Cardozo, continued:]

We pass to the question whether the statements to the nurse, though incompetent as dying declarations, were admissible on other grounds.

The Circuit Court of Appeals determined that they were. Witnesses for the defendant had testified to declarations by Mrs. Shepard which suggested a mind bent upon suicide, or at any rate were thought by the defendant to carry that suggestion. More than once before her illness she had stated in the hearing of these witnesses that she had no wish to live, and had nothing to live for, and on one occasion she added that she expected some day to make an end to her life. This testimony opened the door, so it is argued, to declarations in rebuttal that she had been poisoned by her husband. They were admissible, in that view, not as evidence of the truth of what was said, but as betokening a state of mind inconsistent with the presence of suicidal intent.

(a) The testimony was neither offered nor received for the strained and narrow purpose now suggested as legitimate. It was offered and received as proof of a dying declaration. What was said by Mrs. Shepard lying ill upon her deathbed was to be weighed as if a like statement had been made upon the stand. The course of the trial makes this an inescapable conclusion. The government withdrew the testimony when it was unaccompanied by proof that the declarant expected to die. Only when proof of her expectation had been supplied was the offer renewed and the testimony received again. For the reasons already considered, the proof was inadequate to show a consciousness of impending death and the abandonment of hope; but inadequate though it was, there can be no doubt of the purpose that it was understood to serve. There is no disguise of that purpose by counsel for the government. They concede in all candor that Mrs. Shepard's accusation of her husband, when it was finally let in, was received upon the footing of a dying declaration, and not merely as indicative of the persistence of a will to live. Beyond question the jury considered it for the broader purpose, as the court intended that they should. A different situation would be here if we could fairly say in the light of the whole record that the purpose had been left at large, without identifying token. There would then be room for argument that demand should have been made for an explanatory ruling. Here the course of the trial put the defendant off his guard. The testimony was received by the trial judge and offered by the government with the plain understanding that it was to be used for an illegitimate purpose, gravely prejudicial. A trial becomes unfair if testimony thus accepted may be used in an appellate court as though admitted for a different purpose, unavowed and unsuspected. People v. Zackowitz, 254 N.Y. 192, 200, 172 N.E. 466. Such at all events is the result when the purpose in reserve is so obscure and artificial that it would be unlikely to occur to the minds of uninstructed jurors, and even if it did, would be swallowed up and lost in the one that was disclosed.

(b) Aside, however, from this objection, the accusatory declaration must have been rejected as evidence of a state of mind, though the purpose thus to limit it had been brought to light upon the trial. The defendant had tried to show by Mrs. Shepard's declarations to her friends that she had exhibited a weariness of life and a readiness to end it, the testimony giving plausibility to the hypothesis of suicide. Wigmore, sec. 1726; Commonwealth v. Trefethen, 157 Mass. 180, 31 N.E. 961. By the proof of these declarations evincing an unhappy state of mind, the defendant opened the door to the offer by the government of declarations evincing a different state of mind, declarations consistent with the persistence of a will to live. The defendant would have no grievance if the testimony in rebuttal had been narrowed to that point. What the government put in evidence, however, was something very different. It did not use the declarations by Mrs. Shepard to prove her present thoughts and feelings, or even her thoughts and feelings in times past. It used the declarations as proof of an act committed by some one else, as evidence that she was dying of poison given by her husband. This fact, if fact it was, the government was free to prove, but not by hearsay declarations. It will not do to say that the jury might accept the declarations for any light that they cast upon the existence of a vital urge, and reject them to the extent that they charged the death to some one else. Discrimination so subtle is a feat beyond the compass of ordinary minds. The reverberating clang of those accusatory words would drown all weaker sounds. It is for ordinary minds, and not for psychoanalysts, that our rules of evidence are framed. They have their source very often in considerations of administrative convenience of practical expediency, and not in rules of logic. When the risk of confusion is so great as to upset the balance of advantage, the evidence goes out. Thayer, Preliminary Treatise on the Law of Evidence, 266, 516; Wigmore, Evidence, secs., 1421, 1422, 1714.

These precepts of caution are a guide to judgment here. There are times when a state of mind, if relevant, may be proved by contemporaneous declarations of feeling or intent. Mutual Life Ins. Co. v. Hillmon, 145 U.S. 285, 295, 12 S.Ct. 909; Shailer v. Bumstead, 99 Mass. 112; Wigmore, secs. 1725, 1726, 1730. Thus, in proceedings for the probate of a will, where the issue is undue influence, the declarations of a testator are competent to prove his feelings for his relatives, but are incompetent as evidence of his conduct or of theirs. Throckmorton v. Holt, 180 U.S. 552, 571, 572, 573, 21 S.Ct. 474; Waterman v. Whitney, 11 N.Y. 157; Matter of Kennedy, 167 N.Y. 163, 172, 60 N.E. 442. In suits for the alienation of affections, letters passing between the spouses are admissible in aid of a like purpose, Wigmore, sec. 1730; Ash v. Prunier, 105 F. 722; Mutual Life Ins. Co. v. Hillmon, supra, page 297; Jameson v. Tully, 178 Cal. 380, 173 P. 577; Cottle v. Johnson, 179 N.C. 426, 102 S.E. 769; Curtis v. Miller, 269 Pa. 509, 512, 112 A. 747. In damage suits for personal injuries, declarations by the patient to bystanders or physicians are evidence of sufferings or symptoms (Wigmore, secs. 1718, 1719), but are not received to prove the acts, the external circumstances, through which the injuries came about. Wigmore, sec. 1722; Amys v. Barton, [1912] 1 K.B. 40; Chicago & A. R. Co. v. Industrial Board, 274 Ill. 336, 113 N.E. 629; Peoria Cordage Co. v. Industrial Board, 284 Ill. 90, 119 N.E. 996; Larrabee's Case, 120 Me. 242, 113 A. 268; Maine v. Maryland Casualty Co., 172 Wis. 350, 178 N.W. 749. Even statements of past sufferings or symptoms are generally excluded (Wigmore, sec. 1722[b]; Cashin v. N.Y., N.H. & H.R.R. Co., 185 Mass. 543, 70 N.E. 930), though an exception is at times allowed when they are made to a physician. Roosa v. Boston Loan Co., 132 Mass. 439, 440; Cleveland C., C. & I. R. Co. v. Newell, 104

Ind. 264, 271, 3 N.E. 836; contra, Davidson v. Cornell, 132 N.Y. 228, 237, 30 N.E. 573. So also in suits upon insurance policies, declarations by an insured that he intends to go upon a journey with another, may be evidence of a state of mind lending probability to the conclusion that the purpose was fulfilled. Mutual Life Ins. Co. v. Hillmon, supra. The ruling in that case marks the high-water line beyond which courts have been unwilling to go. It has developed a substantial body of criticism and commentary. Declarations of intention, casting light upon the future, have been sharply distinguished from declarations of memory, pointing backwards to the past. There would be an end, or nearly that, to the rule against hearsay if the distinction were ignored.

The testimony now questioned faced backward and not forward. This at least it did in its most obvious implications. What is even more important, it spoke to a past act, and more than that, to an act by some one not the speaker. Other tendency, if it had any, was a filament too fine to be disentangled by a jury.

The judgment should be reversed and the cause remanded to the District Court for further proceedings in accordance with this opinion.

[Footnote omitted]

United States v. Annunziato

United States Court of Appeals, Second Circuit, 1961.
293 F.2d 373, cert. denied, 368 U.S. 919, 82 S.Ct. 240.

■ FRIENDLY, CIRCUIT JUDGE. The trial of this seemingly simple criminal case, involving an alleged violation of 29 U.S.C.A. § 186(b), which at the time made it unlawful "for any representative of any employees who are employed in an industry affecting commerce to receive or accept, or to agree to receive or accept, from the employer of such employees any money or other thing of value," has raised a host of problems, to the proper solution of which the Government's seven page brief, filed, in violation of our Rule 15(a), 28 U.S.C.A. on the eve of the argument, has rendered almost no assistance.

In 1957 the Terry Contracting Company, Inc., a New York City concern, was engaged in constructing the Connecticut turnpike in Bridgeport, using materials from outside the state. Annunziato was business agent for the International Union of Operating Engineers, members of which were engaged in work on the site. The indictment alleged two violations of 29 U.S.C.A. § 186(b) by Annunziato—the receipt of $300 on or about July 3, 1957, and the receipt of $50 on or about December 24, 1957. Prior to trial the Government filed an information charging him with the same offense stated in the second count; without objection on his part, Count 2 of the indictment was nolled and Count 1 and the information were tried together. The jury brought in a verdict of guilty on the former, of not guilty on the latter. The court gave Annunziato the maximum prison sentence, one year, and imposed a fine of $2,500 plus costs of prosecution, 29 U.S.C.A. § 186(d).

The Government's proof on Count 1 was presented primarily through five employees of the Terry company, hereafter Terry, whose testimony can be summarized as follows:

(1) Walter Haas was timekeeper on the Bridgeport job, identified as Job No. 719, during June and July, 1957. He worked in a trailer, with a small office at one end, the other end open, and a door between. He first saw Annunziato on an occasion when the latter said "in a very loud voice" to Van Dommellen, the Terry superintendent, and to Frattini (later identified as the master

mechanic), that "The job was to be covered—the letter of the contract was to be covered by regarding the handling of all the operating machines whereby the operating local was under their jurisdiction," and that the contract would be enforced "Right to the 'T.' " A week or two later Annunziato appeared in the trailer and asked whether Mayhew, Terry's general superintendent who was located in New York, was on the job site. Haas said Mayhew was not but was expected. Mayhew arrived in the office with a Mr. Wolf, chief estimator, also from New York. When Haas saw Annunziato approaching, he left the office. He saw and heard Mayhew attempt to introduce Wolf; Annunziato declined the proffer, saying "This ain't no social call," whereupon Wolf also left the office. Haas then saw Annunziato pick up a small manila envelope from a table in the office.

(2) Arthur Van Dommellen, field superintendent of the Bridgeport job, recalled that late in June or early in July, 1957, Annunziato came into the trailer office and asked if someone from New York was there to see him. Van Dommellen answered "There's nobody here now, but I expect Mr. Mayhew later." Later Annunziato returned; Van Dommellen met him outside the trailer and told him Mayhew and Wolf were in the office if Annunziato wanted to see them. He did.

(3) William ("Bill") Mayhew was in general charge of all Terry construction projects. In June, 1957, the president of Terry was Harry Terker, deceased at the time of the trial. Mayhew was permitted to testify over objection that in the summer of 1957, on a day before he was scheduled to make a trip to New Haven, Harry Terker gave him a small manila envelope to deliver to the business agent for the operating engineers at Bridgeport. Mayhew asked the purpose; Harry Terker replied "It's for a commitment that I have made." When Mayhew demurred, Terker said, "Well, I have made the commitment, and I would like to keep up with it, and I would like you to do it, to take it with you, since you are going to New Haven." Arriving at Bridgeport, Mayhew and Wolf entered the trailer office. Annunziato came in and identified himself; Mayhew sought to introduce him to Wolf and proposed going out for a cup of coffee. Annunziato "said that he had not come for a social call; he was not interested in going for coffee." Mayhew handed the small envelope to Annunziato, who put it in his pocket. The envelope was about half an inch thick and flexible.

(4) Ralph Cohen was comptroller of Terry. He identified a Cash Voucher dated June 28, 1957, for $300, bearing the name "B. Mayhew" at the top and reading "Job # 719, Sundries." It also bore the legend "Receipt of above is hereby acknowledged," with Cohen's initials. If in fact Cohen had given the money to Mayhew, he would have made Mayhew sign the receipt; instead Cohen had put it in an envelope and given it to Harry Terker. Cohen was allowed to testify, over objection, that Harry Terker had told him to draw the petty cash "For Mr. Mayhew's use to pay somebody" on the job.

(5) Richard Terker, son of Harry Terker, had been secretary and treasurer of Terry; after his father's death he became president. He was allowed, over objection, to testify to a luncheon conversation with his father late in June or early in July, 1957. The father informed the son "that he had received a call from Mr. Annunziato" and "that he had been requested by Mr. Annunziato for some money on the particular project in question, the Bridgeport Harbor Bridge. I asked him what he intended to do, and he had agreed to send some up to Connecticut for him." Cross-examination developed that the sum of money mentioned was $250.

. . .

Our statement of the evidence has surely presaged another and more serious set of attacks—alleged violations of the hearsay rule. Appellant asserts this with respect to Mayhew's testimony that Harry Terker asked him to take the money to Bridgeport in order to keep a commitment that Terker had made to Annunziato, to Cohen's testimony that Harry Terker told him to draw $300 "For Mr. Mayhew's use to pay somebody" on the Bridgeport job, and most importantly, to Richard Terker's account of his luncheon talk with his father.

We need not tarry long over the first two statements. These fall so clearly within Professor Morgan's sixth class, "Cases in which the utterance is contemporaneous with a nonverbal act, independently admissible, relating to that act and throwing some light upon it," A Suggested Classification of Utterances Admissible as Res Gestae, 31 Yale L.J. 229, 236 (1922), see Beaver v. Taylor, 1863, 1 Wall. 637, 642, 17 L.Ed. 601; Lewis v. Burns, 1895, 106 Cal. 381, 39 P. 778; Shapiro v. United States, 2 Cir., 1948, 166 F.2d 240, 242, certiorari denied 1948, 334 U.S. 859, 68 S.Ct. 1533, 92 L.Ed. 1779; McCormick, Evidence (1954), pp. 586–587, that we do not need here to consider other possible grounds of admissibility.

Richard Terker's account seems to have been admitted on the basis that his father's luncheon statement was a declaration of a co-conspirator; the Government now seeks to sustain admissibility both on that ground and as a declaration of the father's intention. We think it was admissible on both grounds.

If the manila envelope had popped out of Harry Terker's wallet as he was settling the luncheon check and Harry had told Richard "This is money I'm sending up to Annunziato," admissibility would clearly follow from the combination, logically unassailable although practically debatable, of two principles, "that the existence of a *design* or *plan to do* a specific act is relevant to show that the act was probably done as planned" and that the plan or design may be evidenced, under an exception to the hearsay rule, "by the *person's own statements* as to its existence." 6 Wigmore, Evidence (3d ed.), pp. 79–80; Mutual Life Ins. Co. of New York v. Hillmon, 1892, 145 U.S. 285, 295, 12 S.Ct. 909, 36 L.Ed. 706. The question is whether a different result is demanded because here the declarant accompanied his statement of future plan with an altogether natural explanation of the reason, in the very recent past, that had prompted it.

We do not think such nicety is demanded either by good sense or by authority. State v. Farnam, 1916, 82 Or. 211, 161 P. 417; People v. Alcalde, 1944, 24 Cal.2d 177, 148 P.2d 627. As Professor Morgan has pointed out, Basic Problems of Evidence (1954), p. 293, the famous letter from Walters, oral evidence of which was held admissible in the Hillmon case, was actually a declaration of Walters' intention not simply to travel to Colorado but to travel with Hillmon, and the inference the jury would almost certainly draw was that this represented a previous arrangement between them.[1] Shepard v. United States, 1933, 290 U.S. 96, 103–106, 54 S.Ct. 22, 23, 78 L.Ed. 196, does not hold that a declaration of design is rendered inadmissible because it embodies a statement why the design was conceived. In that case there was no relevant declaration of design; the statement, "Dr. Shepard has poisoned me", was wholly of past fact and was offered and received as a dying declaration, erroneously as the Supreme Court held. In Mr. Justice Cardozo's words, the Government "did not use the declarations by Mrs. Shepard to prove her

---

1. Professor Morgan may overstate this slightly when he says "that to draw the inference that Walters went with Hamilton required an assumption that he had made an arrangement with Hillmon" before Walters wrote the letter. [Footnote is court's, renumbered. Others omitted.]

present thoughts and feelings, or even her thoughts and feelings in times past ... The testimony ... faced backward and not forward ... at least ... in its most obvious implications." Here the "most obvious implications" of Harry Terker's statement looked forward—he was going to send money to Bridgeport. To say that his portion of his statement is sufficiently trustworthy for the jury to consider without confrontation, but that his reference to the telephone call from Annunziato which produced the decision to send the money is not, would truly be swallowing the camel and straining at the gnat. The "vigorous leap" with respect to the hearsay exception for declarations of state of mind was taken when this was extended from cases where "it is material to prove the state of a person's mind, or what was passing in it, and what were his intentions," Sugden v. St. Leonards, L.R. 1 P.D. 154, 251 (1876), as to which the declaration may well be the most reliable evidence attainable, to cases where the state of mind is relevant only to prove other action, where it surely is not. See Maguire, The Hillmon case—Thirty–Three Years After, 38 Harv.L.Rev. 709, 714 (1925); Hutchins and Slesinger, State of Mind to Prove an Act, 38 Yale L.J. 283, 284–288 (1929). True, inclusion of a past event motivating the plan adds the hazards of defective perception and memory to that of prevarication; but this does not demand exclusion or even excision, at least when, as here, the event is recent, is within the personal knowledge of the declarant and is so integrally included in the declaration of design as to make it unlikely in the last degree that the latter would be true and the former false. True also, the statement of the past event would not be admitted if it stood alone, as the Shepard case holds; but this would not be the only hearsay exception where the pure metal may carry some alloy along with it. See 5 Wigmore Evidence (3d ed.), § 1465, and cases cited, and American Law Institute, Model Code of Evidence, Rule 509(2), for the application of such a principle under the hearsay exception for statements of fact against interest—an exception that would itself be applicable here but for the rather indefensible limitation that it does not relate to statements only against penal interest, see Wigmore, § 1476, American Law Institute, Model Code of Evidence, Rule 509(1).

. . .

Affirmed.

NOTES

1. Would Harry Terker's statement be admissible under Rule 804(b)(3)?

2. Other interesting cases in which the proffered statements referred to past, present, and future events include:

In United States v. DeCarlo, 458 F.2d 358, 362, 365 (3d Cir.), cert. denied, 409 U.S. 843 (1972), defendants were charged with violations of 18 U.S.C.A. §§ 892, 894, prohibiting extortionate credit transactions. Section 894(b) provides: "In any prosecution under this section ... evidence may be introduced tending to show that one or more extensions of credit by the creditor were, to the knowledge of the person against whom the implicit threat was alleged to have been made, collected or attempted to be collected by extortionate means.... " The following letter, written by a debtor of the defendants, DeCarlo and Cecere, and mailed to the FBI the day before the debtor's death from acute arsenic poisoning, was admitted by the court with instructions to consider the letter only for the purpose of determining the writer's state of mind:

Federal Bureau of Investigation, Newark, New Jersey.

Gentlemen: I am writing you, maybe others can be helped by my plight. On September 13, 1968, I was severely beaten at a place in the rear of Weiland's Restaurant, Route 22, DeCarlo's headquarters. I was then told and given 3 months until December 13, 1968 to pay the entire accumulated amount under threat of death. Cecere, DeCarlo and Polverino, also stated many times my wife and son would be maimed or killed. Please protect my family—I am sure they mean to carry out this threat.

Last night from my home I called DeCarlo and pleaded for time but to no avail. Over the phone DeCarlo stated unless further monies was paid the threats would be carried out.

Louis B. Saperstein

On appeal, defendants argued that the letter constituted inadmissible hearsay, and that it was irrelevant for the purpose of proving the crime for which the defendants had been indicted. The convictions were affirmed:

Had the letter been admitted for the truth of its assertions, it would have tended to show that Saperstein was beaten on September 13th and in fact owed DeCarlo and Cecere a sum of money. It would have fallen then within the definition of hearsay, and would not have been admissible unless it came within one of the recognized exceptions to the hearsay rule. However, it was not offered for the truth of the matter stated.

When the letter was proffered, the United States Attorney began his argument by stating, "These documents are offered for the limited purpose of showing the state of mind of the victim in this case, Louis B. Saperstein ... [I]t is our position that ... the explanations, whether they be written or oral, of the victim of an extortion are admissible for the limited purpose of proving his state of mind, what fears were operating his mind." ...

. . .

Undue prejudice to the defendants from the admission of the Saperstein letter could arise only if the jury considered the statements contained therein for the truth of their assertions rather than for their value as showing Saperstein's state of mind. Similarly, the probative value properly accrues when the jury considers the letters only with regard to the state of mind of the writer. The defendants contend that asking the jury to separate the concepts of state of mind and truth of the assertions is similar to requiring them to answer the classic query: "How many angels can dance on the head of a needle?" For this proposition they rely on Shepard v. United States, 290 U.S. 96 (1933), and in particular on the statement by Justice Cardozo, "When the risk of confusion is so great as to upset the balance of advantage, the evidence goes out." Id. at 104.

. . .

In the present case, the record is clear that the Government had no theory other than state of mind for the admissibility of the Saperstein letter, and the Court accepted the proffer on no other basis. In the charge, the jury was instructed, "You may consider [the letter] only for the purpose of deciding whether on the part of Mr. Saperstein there was a state of apprehension and fear of harm." The judge then requested each juror to sign a pledge that he would consider the letter only to determine Saperstein's state of mind because each side conceded that any consideration of the letter by the jury for the truth of its assertions would be improper. Thus we are not confronted with a *Shepard*-type, *post hoc* rationale for the admission of evidence. Rather, the letter was admitted for a narrow purpose, the trial court properly instructed the jury concerning their use of the contents of the letter, and the jury was capable of drawing the required distinction in order that the defendants would not be unduly prejudiced.

The defendants also argued "that the victim's state of mind is relevant only at the time the extortionate extension of credit is made, while the letter would show state of mind at the time the letter was written—more than two months after the extortion charged by the indictment."

The court held that Saperstein's state of mind at the time he wrote the letter was relevant:

> Section 894(b) makes clear the relevance of the victim's state of mind concerning attempts to collect the money owed. Even if the Saperstein letter could rationally show only his state of mind when the letter was written, this apprehension goes directly to the means by which the defendants attempted to collect the money he owed them, and the letter was therefore admissible for this purpose.

[Footnotes omitted.]

United States v. Mandel, 437 F.Supp. 262, 264, 266 (D.Md.1977) Ex-governor, who was charged with wrongdoing in connection with the acquisition of a race track, sought to introduce testimony of the wife of one of his co-defendants that on a number of occasions persons in her presence had said that the governor knew nothing about the race track acquisition and had instructed her not to tell anyone, including the governor, about the acquisition. The court excluded the testimony:

> Three separate inferences can be drawn from a statement which implies that Hess and Rodgers were keeping their ownership interests secret from Mandel:
>
> (1) They entered into an agreement *in the past* to keep their interests secret.
>
> (2) They were in the process of keeping the interests a secret *at the time* the statements were made.
>
> (3) They intended to keep their interests secret *in the future.*
>
> . . .
>
> In the Hillmon and Annunziato cases, as well as the other cases cited by the defendant in his brief, there was a pressing need for the hearsay testimony. The need in the present case is absent, as presumably defendants . . . can and will testify of the alleged secrecy agreed upon by them.
>
> The problem that gives the Court much concern is that if testimony of this character is received, it could open the door for widespread fabrication. This Court has tried many cases in which a defendant was charged with aiding and abetting the operation of a moonshine still. The usual defense in such a case is that the defendant was rabbit hunting when he happened to see the still and, through curiosity, planted himself nearby. Defendant will usually offer to bring forth witnesses who will say that he told them, either before he was found at the still or afterwards that he was rabbit hunting . . . Often these self-serving statements are concocted or fabricated.
>
> What is said is certainly *not* intended to imply that the proposed testimony of Mrs. Rogers is concocted, in any form or fashion. The

thing uppermost in this Court's mind is the precedential effect of admitting this type of evidence when the need is not overwhelming.

. . .

Accordingly, the Court holds that the testimony of Mrs. Rogers ... is not to be received into evidence at this time as the Court desires to hear more testimony in the case before a final decision is reached.

United States v. Day, 591 F.2d 861, 883 (D.C.Cir.1978): Government sought to introduce evidence that shortly before fatal shooting, Williams, the victim, gave witness, Mason, a piece of paper on which he had written names of defendants and telephone number, and had told Mason that if he (Williams) was not home by 3:00 P.M. the next day, witness should call the police, tell them what he had said, and give them the number.

We think that the inference to be drawn from Williams' statement to Mason which accompanied his handing over of the slip of paper, involving as it did somewhat of a prophecy of what might happen to him, has too great a potential for *unfair* prejudice, and we do not think that a limiting instruction can correct that deficiency.... Had Williams referred to prior harmful acts or threats by Day, such statements would be even more unfairly prejudicial, but even here "a palpable danger exists" that the jury will infer from the statement, "if anything happens to me, call the police and give them the names on this slip [i.e., Day and Sheffey]," that Day and Sheffey were capable of murder, or that they had done things in the past to justify Williams' apprehension. Such inferences insofar as they reflect on defendants' intentions or past conduct would be improperly drawn. See 160 U.S.App.D.C. at 210, 490 F.2d at 778. In fact, on the present record, Williams' state of mind, from which such inferences would be drawn, is immaterial. Of course, the situation will be different if the defendant seeks to adduce evidence tending to show self-defense or accident....

Even though we affirm the district court's ruling that the statement accompanying the delivery of the slip cannot be admitted, the slip of paper itself is admissible and Mason can testify that sometime in the hour before the shooting Williams gave him the slip of paper, that he telephoned the police after witnessing the shooting, and that he gave the police the information on the slip.

No hearsay problem is presented by the slip of paper and the writing on it ("Beanny, Eric, 635–3135"). Written assertions are not immune from the hearsay rule, Fed.R.Evid. 801(a)(1). However, the information on the slip was not hearsay. The words themselves do not assert anything except that Beanny and/or Eric might have a particular telephone number. The statement is not being offered as proof that Beanny and/or Eric had that telephone number, and hence, we conclude that the statement is not within the definition of hearsay evidence, Fed.R.Evid. 801(c).

See Notes on Implied Assertions, supra p. 507.

3. How should the court have ruled in the following cases? On what theory?

Smith v. Slifer, 81 Cal.Rptr. 871 (App.1969): In wrongful death action, plaintiffs sought to show that decedent, who rode to work daily with defendant, was a paying passenger in defendant's car. To prove payment, plaintiffs offered three statements made by decedent: 1) A statement made to her husband to the effect that defendant had run out of gas on the way home but that it had not been her fault since she had already paid defendant for the week; 2) another statement to her husband telling him that she had had to pay for parking that day but that she would deduct it from what she owed defendant for the coming week; 3) a statement to her sister that she needed to get the correct change to pay for her ride for the coming week. Are all or any of the statements admissible?

Trustees of University of Pennsylvania v. Lexington Insurance Co., 815 F.2d 890, 905 (3d Cir.1987): Corporate owner of hospital brought action against its excess insurance carrier because of its denial of coverage in medical malpractice suit which insured hospital had settled. One of the issues raised by the defendant was whether the settlement was reasonable. To prove reasonableness, plaintiff offered, pursuant to Rule 803(3), statements made by the state court judge who had approved the settlement as being fair and reasonable. Are these statements that reflect a then existing state of mind or are they statements of memory or belief, or are they not hearsay at all?

4.   In re Anderson's Estate, 198 P. 407 (Cal.1921). Will challenged on the ground that aunt of testatrix had exercised undue influence:

The declarations in the present case are of three sorts: First, there are the declarations indicative simply of the fact that at the time they were made, some three months after the execution of the will, the testatrix had changed her mind in regard to the disposition she wished to make of her property, and regretted the will she had made. If that change of mind and regret had been material, evidence of the declarations would have been competent. The point is that the fact that she had changed her mind and regretted what she had done was not material. It made no difference whether she had or not. The only evidentiary bearing of the fact on the issue before the jury, that of undue influence at the time of the execution of the will, lay in the possibility of reasoning from the fact that the testatrix had changed her mind and regretted what she had done that she had possibly acted only under undue pressure in the first instance. But this bearing is exceedingly slight and remote, or, in other words, the probative value of the fact that she had changed her mind as showing that she had not acted freely in the first instance, is almost, if not quite, nil. On the other hand, the fact that the testatrix had changed her mind was one which, if put before the jury, would almost certainly affect them greatly, and would in and of itself be given great weight by them, regardless of what its bearing on the real issue before them might or might not be. Under such circumstances, where the true evidentiary bearing of the evidence is at best slight and remote, and yet the evidence is of a nature such as to make it very prejudicial to the party against whom it is offered, the evidence should be excluded. See Adkins v. Brett, 193 P. 251 (Cal. 1920).

The second sort of declaration is the one contained in the letter by the testatrix to her aunt to the effect that the will had been made at the latter's request. This was not properly admissible for a reason just the converse of that applicable to declarations of the first sort. The fact declared, that the will was made at the request of the aunt, did have a very direct bearing on the issue in the case, and was quite material. But the declaration of this fact was not admissible because it was merely a declaration as to a past event, and was not indicative of the condition of mind of the testatrix at the time she made it. It was therefore not within the exception to the hearsay rule. Estate of Jones, 135 P. 288 (Cal.1913).

The third sort of declaration is the request by the testatrix of her husband that if they returned to Reno he [sic] protect her against her aunt and uncle, as they would be cruel toward her. This is the only declaration which meets both requirements necessary in order to bring a declaration within the exception. It (a) indicated her then state of mind toward her aunt, and (b) her then state of mind as so indicated was material, since the fact that she then feared her aunt had a reasonably direct bearing on what her mental attitude toward her aunt may have been at a previous and not far distant time, when she executed the will. Order reversed. Id. at 198 P. at 415–16.

How would the three kinds of declarations in the Anderson case be treated under the formulation in Rule 803(3) which treats as an exception to the hearsay rule "a statement of memory or belief to prove the fact remembered or believed [if] it relates to the execution, revocation, identification, or terms of declarant's will?" Cf. Okken v. Okken Estate, 348 N.W.2d 447, 449–50 (N.D. 1984)(in action by son claiming undue influence, wife of other son who had been named the sole beneficiary of mother's estate was permitted to testify about what her mother-in-law had told her over the years about disinherited son's behavior and the impact of this behavior on testatrix).

5.   Commonwealth v. Trainor, 374 N.E.2d 1216, 1220–1221 (Mass.1978):

A properly conducted public opinion survey, offered through an expert in conducting such surveys, is admissible in an obscenity case if it tends to show relevant standards in the Commonwealth. . . .

We are not inclined to pause long to resolve whether a survey of people's opinions is hearsay and, if it is, whether it is admissible under the state of mind exception to the hearsay rule. Numerous authorities have admitted particular surveys under that hearsay exception. See Zippo Mfg. Co. v. Rogers Imports, Inc., supra at 683; Holiday Inns, Inc. v. Holiday Out in America, supra at 447; Morelli v. Board of Educ., Pekin Community High School Dist. No. 303, 42 Ill.App.3d 722, 730–731, 1 Ill.Dec. 312, 356 N.E.2d 438 (1976); 2 Jones on Evidence, supra, § 10:8 at 278–279; Regina v. Prairie Schooner News Ltd., 1 C.C.C.2d 251, 266 (Man.Ct. of App.1970). The focus should be on the techniques employed rather than on whether hearsay is involved. See Fed.R.Evid. 703 and Note of the Advisory Committee, 56 F.R.D. 183, 283 (1972). A properly conducted public opinion survey itself adequately ensures a good measure of trustworthiness, and its admission may be necessary in the sense that no other evidence would be as good as the survey evidence or perhaps even obtainable as a practical matter. See Zippo Mfg. Co. v. Rogers Imports, Inc., supra at 683–684; American Luggage Works, Inc. v. United States Trunk Co., 158 F.Supp. 50, 53 (D.Mass.1957). Of course, the judge will have to determine in his discretion whether the methodology of the survey was adequate to justify its admission. In certain instances, any weaknesses in the manner in which a poll was conducted might affect only the weight to be accorded the survey results rather than the admissibility of the survey in evidence.

What factors enter into an analysis of the need for the survey at trial and its trustworthiness? In addition to the sources cited in the excerpt above see McElroy, Public Surveys—The Latest Exception to the Hearsay Rule, 28 Baylor L.Rev. 59 (1976).

SECTION 7.   BUSINESS ENTRIES AND PUBLIC RECORDS

HISTORICAL NOTE

Business Entries. The exception for business entries is probably utilized more than any of the other hearsay exceptions. Although it has some roots in common law doctrines, the modern exception came into existence in the 1920s when legislatures began enacting business records acts in response to an influential study produced under the leadership of Professor Edmund M. Morgan, one of the original authors of this casebook. With the advent of large corporations engaged in complex data production, these acts were needed because it had become too cumbersome to produce as witnesses all persons who had participated in the creation of a record through the gathering, transmitting and entering of information. The reliability of business records has been explained as resting "in general on a complex organization's need to keep accurate records, and on its internal discipline: employees who keep inaccurate records will be reprimanded or lose their jobs." United States of America, v. Hing Shair Chan, 680 F.Supp. 521 (E.D.N.Y.1988).

Public records. Like the business entries exception, the public records exception has common law antecedents, but no uniform rule had been codified before the enactment of the Federal Rules, and most existing statutes were very narrowly drawn. Because of this pattern, litigants often resorted to the business entries exception even when introducing public records. The drafters of the Federal Rules believed that public records were sufficiently reliable to warrant greater admissibility than under existing law. In drafting Federal Rule 803(8), the Advisory Committee sought to accomplish for the public records exception what the drafters of the model business records acts had achieved—a more generally applicable rule with a considerably wider scope. By far the most controversial aspect of Rule 803(8) is subdivision (C), the section dealing with investigatory reports, and issues remain about the inter-relationship between the business entries and public records exceptions.

See Steinmetz, Official Written Statements, 1945 Wis.L.Rev. 270; McCormick, Can The Courts Make Wider Use of Reports of Official Investigations? 42 Iowa L.Rev. 363 (1957); Knepper, "Official Records" as Evidence, 20 Ins.Counsel J. 88 (1953); Wallace, Official Written Statements, 46 Iowa L.Rev. 256 (1961).

United States v. Jacoby

United States Court of Appeals, Eleventh Circuit, 1992.
955 F.2d 1527, cert. denied, 507 U.S. 920, 113 S.Ct. 1282 (1993).

■ FRIEDMAN, SENIOR CIRCUIT JUDGE:

This criminal prosecution arose from the mid-eighties financial debacle of the Sunrise Savings and Loan Association (Sunrise) in South Florida. A jury convicted two former Sunrise officials of several financial crimes involving Sunrise. . . .

I

In 1987, a federal grand jury indicted three former Sunrise officers, including the appellants, and two of Sunrise's largest borrowers, William Frederick and Thomas Moye. (The third indicted officer, William Frame, suffered a heart attack during trial; his case was severed and will be retried.) Jacoby was Sunrise's president and chairman of its board of directors; Skubal was vice-president of Sunrise Mortgage Corporation, a wholly-owned subsidiary of Sunrise.

The indictment charged that from January 1983 to July 1985, Jacoby and Skubal engaged in a series of closely related acts calculated to conceal the dubious financial condition of Frederick and Moye from Sunrise's board of directors, from federal and state banking regulators, and from the public.

. . .

A.   Background. Sunrise commenced operations in 1980; the Federal Savings and Loan Insurance Corporation (FSLIC) insured its deposits. Jacoby was Sunrise's president from the beginning, and became chairman of its board of directors in 1983. Skubal joined Sunrise in November 1983, and became vice-president of Sunrise Mortgage Corporation shortly thereafter. In that position, Skubal was responsible for determining whether loans complied with federal regulations, and for construction disbursements.

Frederick and Moye were co-owners of Commercial Center Development Corporation, a real estate company involved in the development of strip shopping centers, and formed subsidiary "shell" corporations for planned centers. They entered into a banking relationship with Sunrise in 1982; by mid–1984 Sunrise had loaned Frederick, Moye, and their companies more than $150 million, and Sunrise was their exclusive lender.

The Boca Raton, Florida branch of the Philadelphia law firm of Blank, Rome, Comisky and McCauley (Blank, Rome), was involved substantially in Sunrise's formation, organization and day-to-day operations until Sunrise was declared insolvent in 1985 and the government took it over.

Under FSLIC regulations, Sunrise's total loans to any one borrower could not exceed approximately $50 million at any given time. Sunrise circumvented these regulations by treating Frederick and Moye as separate entities, and by advancing loans to nominee third parties, including employees and relatives of Frederick and Moye, for the benefit of Frederick and Moye.

In early 1984, when interest reserves on millions of dollars in loans Sunrise made in 1982 and 1983 became depleted, representatives of the FSLIC and the Florida Comptroller's Office met with Sunrise's board of directors regarding problems with Sunrise's loan practices, including loans made to Frederick and Moye. At the meeting, the Sunrise board executed a supervisory agreement designed to assure Sunrise's adherence to prudent and safe banking practices in making loans. One provision of the agreement required that, as a prerequisite to approval, all future loans greater than $500,000 include specific supporting documentation demonstrating compliance with underwriting and credit requirements.

. . .

II

Admission and Exclusion of Evidence

A.   The Scheer Memorandum. Jacoby's principle contention on appeal is that the district court committed reversible error when it received into evidence a memorandum to the file prepared by Blank, Rome attorney Dana Scheer, an associate in the Boca Raton office.

1.   Scheer was deeply involved in Sunrise's day-to-day operations. The memorandum, dated August 29, 1984, which Scheer initialed, related to the "Frederick Work Out." It stated:

> I was requested by Rob Jacoby in a telephone conversation on this date (Rob Jacoby was in New York) to close each of these loans. Mr. Jacoby indicated that he had presented these loans before Executive Committee in evening session August 28, 1984, and had received their approval. Mr. Jacoby indicated that upon his return to Palm Beach he would immediately

sign and forward a memo authorizing me to close these loans notwithstanding having no surveys, appraisals, title commitments, utility letters,
permits, opinions of counsel, and notwithstanding the fact that by making
several of these loans we might be violating doing business laws in the
State of Maryland and placing mortgages on parcels which were not legally
able to be subdivided in the event of foreclosure. Mr. Jacoby indicated that
no Board approval would be necessary for any of these loans and that it
was necessary to immediately close as soon as possible. A letter to file has
been dictated by me and is in Mr. Jacoby's office awaiting his return.

The loans to which this memorandum referred were the seven loans of
$500,000 or less to Powell, Valosin, and Wood for the purchase of real estate,
closed on August 30, 1984 and designed to remove Frederick's overdrafts from
Sunrise's books by August 31, 1984.

The memorandum was offered in conjunction with the testimony of Tabor,
Valosin, Wood, Berkovitz, and Frederick to demonstrate that the August 30,
1984 loans were fixed at $500,000 or less to circumvent the Sunrise board and
the underwriting and documentation requirements of the supervisory agreement, and that the loans were closed at Jacoby's direction and with his
awareness of the deficiencies in and problems with the loans.

The government contended that the memorandum was admissible under
two exceptions to the hearsay rule: (1) the business records exception, Fed.
R.Evid. 803(6); and (2) the residual hearsay exception for declarants who are
unavailable as a witness, Fed.R.Evid. 804(b)(5). Because Scheer declined to
testify on the basis of his fifth amendment privilege against self-incrimination,
he was unavailable as a witness.

Jacoby opposed admission under either theory, contending that the document did not meet the requirements of the business records exception, and that
it was inadmissible under the residual exception because it lacked adequate
guarantees of trustworthiness and raised sixth amendment confrontation
clause problems.

The district court questioned admissibility under the business records
exception, because "it is not a routine type of thing." The court, although
stating it was "not an easy question," admitted the memorandum under the
residual exception of Rule 804(b)(5), finding that "it does have the necessary
ingredients of authenticity and the words used, guarantees of trustworthiness,
circumstantial guarantees of trustworthiness are sufficient to justify its admission" and "I do think it is relevant."

2. In admitting the memorandum, the district court did not hold it
inadmissible under the business records exception. It merely questioned its
admissibility under that exception, but did not decide the question because it
admitted the memorandum under the residual exception of Rule 804(b)(5).

We conclude, however, that the memorandum was admissible under the
business records exception (which, the government stated in its brief in this
court, page 33, footnote 41, it continued to rely upon), and we therefore need
not determine its admissibility under Rule 804(b)(5).

. . . .

3.

... The government laid a foundation for the introduction of the Scheer
memorandum under the business records exception through the testimony of
Lucy Holton, a real estate paralegal in the Blank, Rome, office where Scheer
worked, and Lessie Younquist, Scheer's legal secretary, who worked exclusively

for him. Holton stated that Scheer would "from time to time dictate memos to the file explaining his actions in a particular closing" if "anything needed explaining in the closing;" that if "something needed explaining," it was his "habit" to "do a memo to the file"; that such memos would "be done at or about the time" of the transaction; and that it was the regular course of business of Blank, Rome and of Scheer to keep such a memorandum in the Blank, Rome files. She testified that Scheer did not prepare such memoranda for every transaction in which he was involved, but did so "more than occasionally," but not "day in and day out."

Younquist authenticated the memorandum as one that Scheer dictated and initialed and that she typed. She testified that Scheer would dictate memoranda to his files of notes and concerns regarding transactions as often as once a week or twice a month, or possibly only once a month, or perhaps occasionally, that Scheer dictated these memos in the regular course of business, and that is was his regular practice to do so. She recollected that this memorandum was dictated and typed on August 29, 1984. She testified that, normally, less than one hour would elapse between Scheer's dictation and her typing of it. She stated that other Blank, Rome attorneys also "engaged in that same practice from time to time."

This evidence established that: (1) Scheer dictated and Younquist typed the memorandum on August 29, 1984 (the memorandum was "made at or near the time by, or from information transmitted by, a person with knowledge"); (2) it was Scheer's regular practice to dictate memoranda to his files whenever something about a transaction needed to be explained or noted ("it was the regular practice of that business activity to make the memorandum"); and (3) it was Scheer's and Blank, Rome's practice to maintain these memoranda in the files as part of the regular course of business (it was "kept in the course of a regularly conducted business activity").

In admitting the Scheer memorandum under Rule 804(b)(5), the district court found that "it does have the necessary ingredients of authenticity and the words used, guarantees of trustworthiness, circumstantial guarantees of trustworthiness are sufficient to justify its admission." This finding is not clearly erroneous, and it satisfies the requirement in the business records exception that such a record is admissible if it meets the other requirements of Rule 803(6)—and we have held that the Scheer memorandum does so—"unless the source of information or the method or circumstances of preparation indicate lack of trustworthiness." Neither the "source of information" the document contained—a telephone conversation with Scheer's client, Jacoby—nor the "circumstances of preparation"—a frequent act by Scheer in the practice of his profession—"indicate lack of trustworthiness."

Moreover, Jacoby's own testimony on cross-examination supports the district court's finding of trustworthiness. He testified that he knew of no reason why the content of Scheer's memorandum would have been less than truthful, that the memorandum "was probably a standard sort of letter to the file," that the memorandum indicated they were "missing some documentation" for the loans, and that it was "urgent" that they close the loans by August 30.

Jacoby argues that Scheer had the motive to fabricate the memo to cover himself if he were accused of improprieties in connection with the closing of the Powell loans. On the other hand, an associate in a large firm whose client instructed him to close loans with serious flaws the following day—and, as we have shown, closing the Powell loans on August 30th was critical to the Sunrise management scheme to conceal the company's seriously-flawed financial position—would be most likely to write a memorandum to the files, of the type that

Scheer did, explaining that he had closed the loans only in response to his client's direction. Other Blank Rome attorneys also wrote such memoranda to record special circumstances. In the language of Rule 803(6), neither "the source of information" contained in the Scheer memorandum "nor the method or circumstances of preparation indicate lack of trustworthiness."

4.   The problem the district court discerned in considering the admissibility of the Scheer memorandum under the business records exception was that the memorandum was "not a routine type of thing." Jacoby challenged its admissibility as a business record essentially for the same reason, arguing that it did not record a routine transaction and indeed was "prepared because of a non-routine event."

The routineness or repetitiveness with which a record is prepared is not the touchstone of admissibility under the business records exception. ". . . Rule 803(6) should be interpreted so that the absence of routineness without more is not sufficiently significant to require exclusion of the record. Nonroutine records made in the course of a regularly conducted 'business' should be admissible if they meet the other requirements of Rule 803(6) unless 'the sources of information or other circumstances indicate lack of trustworthiness.' " 4 J. Weinstein and M. Berger, Weinstein's Evidence ¶ 803(6)03, at 803–182 (1991) [hereinafter Weinstein's Evidence]. It is significant, and essential to admissibility under this exception, that the record be the product of a "regular practice" of the business, see United States v. Freidin, 849 F.2d 716, 719–22 (2d Cir.1988), in the "usual course" of that business. See Hawkins, 905 F.2d at 1494 ("Admission of hearsay under this exception requires evidence 'sufficient to support the trustworthiness of the document, and to prove that it was prepared in the usual course of business.' ")(quoting United States v. Parker, 749 F.2d 628, 633 (11th Cir.1984)). These elements are present in the Scheer memorandum.

The evidence was that whenever Scheer believed it necessary to explain something or make a record of an unusual circumstance, he prepared a memorandum to the file. A significant part of his "regularly conducted business activity" was the closing of real estate loans and transfers and he frequently dictated memoranda to the files as part of that activity.

We are guided by the Advisory Committee Notes to Rule 803(6), which state:

> The element of unusual reliability of business records is . . . supplied by . . . actual experience of business in relying upon them, or by a duty to make an accurate record as part of a continuing job or occupation. . . . The model statutes and rules have sought to capture these factors and to extend their impact by employing the phrase "regular course of business," in conjunction with a definition of "business" far broader than its ordinary accepted meaning. The result is a tendency unduly to emphasize a requirement of routineness and repetitiveness and an insistence that other types of records be squeezed into the fact patterns which give rise to traditional business records. The rule therefore adopts the phrase "the course of a regularly conducted activity" as capturing the essential basis of the hearsay exception. . . .

(Citation omitted).

The record leaves no doubt that Scheer prepared his memorandum in "the course of a regularly conducted business activity" in which it was "the regular practice" to make such memoranda. The Scheer memorandum was properly admissible under the business records exception to the hearsay rule in Rule 803(6).

5. Our ruling that the Scheer memorandum was admissible under the business records exception makes it unnecessary to consider Jacoby's argument, made in support of his contention that the memorandum was improperly admitted under the residual exception because it was unreliable, that admission of the memorandum violated his Sixth Amendment right to confront the witnesses against him.

. . .

This court recently held that the prosecution is not required to demonstrate the unavailability of the declarant or independent indicia of reliability when evidence falls within the business records exception. "By analogy [to Bourjaily], we find the business records exception to the hearsay rule to be 'firmly enough rooted in our jurisprudence' to satisfy the requirements of the Confrontation Clause...." United States v. Norton, 867 F.2d 1354, 1363 (11th Cir.), cert. denied, 491 U.S. 907, 109 S. Ct. 3192, 105 L.Ed.2d 701 and 493 U.S. 871, 110 S. Ct. 200, 107 L. Ed.2d 154 (1989).

. . .

NOTES

1. Compare United States v. Strother, 49 F.3d 869, 875–76 (2d Cir.1995). D was convicted of defrauding a financial institution by inducing a bank employee, W, to authorize payment of a $82,500 check despite insufficient funds in his account by falsely representing that he would provide funds to cover the check. At trial, W testified to a phone conversation in which D had asked her to pay the check. The government conceded on appeal that no crime would have occurred if D had asked W to hold, rather than pay, the check. D argued that the trial court had erred in refusing to admit as business records two internal bank memoranda recounting the phone conversation: 1. a memorandum prepared by W at the direction of her branch manager 13 days after the telephone conversation with D; and 2. a memorandum placed in W's employment file that she read and signed two months after the conversation when she was put on probation in connection with the incident. Neither memorandum mentioned D's asking W to pay the check. See Fed.R.Evid. 803(7). W had testified as to both memoranda that it was the ordinary practice of the bank to make such memoranda.

The appellate court found that the district court had not abused its discretion in refusing to admit either memorandum as a business record:

> Arguably both memoranda were created as a regular practice of a regularly conducted business activity, even though situations such as the one at issue did not arise on a daily basis. On the other hand, we have not subscribed to the view that "the absence of routineness without more is not sufficiently significant to require exclusion of [a] record." [United States v.] Freidin, 849 F.2d [716], 720–21 [(2d Cir.1988)] (quoting 4 J. Weinstein & M. Berger, Weinstein's Evidence ¶ 803(6)[03], at 803–182). We are reluctant to adopt a rule that would permit the introduction into evidence of memoranda drafted in response to unusual or "isolated" events, see Freiden, 849 F.2d at 720, particularly where the entrant may have a motive to be less than accurate, see, e.g., Romano v. Howarth, 998 F.2d 101, 108 (2d Cir.1993); Fed.R.Evid.803(6) advisory committee's note ("Absence of routineness raises lack of motivation to be accurate.").

The majority concluded, however, that the trial court had erred in not admitting the memoranda as prior inconsistent statements of W, and reversed the conviction. The dissenting judge agreed that W's memorandum was not a business record and would have affirmed the conviction on harmless error grounds.

See also Palmer v. Hoffman, infra p. 692.

2. The Advisory Committee Note quoted in the Jacoby case accompanied a version of the rule that was subsequently amended by Congress. The excerpt below indicates in italics the words added by Congress and in brackets the words proposed by the Advisory Committee that were deleted by Congress:

> A memorandum, report, record, or data compilation [,] in any form, of acts, events, conditions, opinions, or diagnoses, made at or near the time by, or from information transmitted by, a person with knowledge, [all] *if kept* in the course of a regularly conducted *business* activity, *and if it was the regular practice of that business activity to make the memorandum, report, record, or data compilation, all* as shown by the testimony of the custodian or other qualified witness, unless the source[s] of information or *the method or* [other] circumstances *of preparation* indicate lack of trustworthiness. *The term "business" as used in this paragraph includes business, profession, occupation, and calling of every kind.*

How did the congressional changes affect the meaning of the rule?

The Jacoby court's focus is on Scheer's regular practices, not on Blank, Rome's practices, or on the practices of law firms in general. Does this comport with the rationale for the exception? Cf. Brodersen v. Sioux Valley Memorial Hospital, 902 F.Supp. 931, 954 (N.D.Iowa 1995)(reviews cases and concludes: "This court has found no case in which the court looked beyond the particular business in question to see if businesses of the same type, rather than that particular business, normally kept the records in question.").

3. *Foundation testimony.* Consider United States v. Pelullo, 964 F.2d 193, 198–202 (3d Cir.1992), a wire fraud prosecution in which the testimony of FBI agent, Wolverton, "was very significant" in establishing that the wire transfers were fraudulent:

> At trial, Wolverton, who is a certified public accountant, described how he traced funds diverted by Pelullo, by examining subpoenaed wire transfer documents, statements and checks. Wolverton testified that wire transfer documents are bank-generated documents that record the date, amount and source and destination account numbers of each wire transfer. The court admitted these documents over Pelullo's objections that the evidence was hearsay.

> The documents were hearsay. Each was an out-of-court statement offered to prove the truth of the facts described in the document, such as the identity of the sender and recipient, and the amount of the transaction....

> . . .

> [T]he government argues that, even if the documents were hearsay, they were admissible under the business records exception to the hearsay rule. Fed.R.Evid. 803(6). The business records exception permits admission of documents containing hearsay provided foundation testimony is made by "the custodian or other qualified witness," that: (1) the declarant in the records had personal knowledge to make accurate statements; (2) the declarant recorded the statements contemporaneously with the actions

that were the subject of the reports; (3) the declarant made the record in the regular course of the business activity; and (4) such records were regularly kept by the business.... With the exception of certain documents relating to counts 7, 11, 14, 549 and 54 ... however, no such foundation was ever laid for their admission.

The Government ... contends that the documents could have been admitted even without testimony of a custodian since surrounding circumstances provided the necessary foundation for trustworthiness. Here, the Government maintains that there are sufficient circumstantial guarantees of trustworthiness since: (1) the records were obtained in response to grand jury subpoenas directed to the corporations and their banks; (2) testimony of witnesses involved in the transactions corroborated the information in the bank records; and (3) Pelullo has not stated any reason why the records are not reliable. However, these reasons are not sufficient to overcome the express requirements of Rule 803(6).

It is, of course, true that Rule 803(6) does not require foundation testimony from the custodian of records for the rule states that such testimony may be provided by either the custodian or "other qualified witness." Furthermore, "[t]he phrase 'other qualified witness' should be given the broadest interpretation; he need not be an employee of the entity so long as he understands the system." 4 Jack B. Weinstein & Margaret A. Berger, Weinstein's Evidence ¶ 803(6)[02], at 803–178 (footnote omitted)(hereinafter "Weinstein & Berger"). Thus, courts have held that a government agent may provide a foundation where the agent is familiar with the record-keeping system. See, e.g., United States v. Franco, 874 F.2d 1136, 1139–40 (7th Cir.1989); see also Hathaway, 798 F.2d at 906 ("there is no reason why a proper foundation for application of Rule 803(6) cannot be laid, in part or in whole, by the testimony of a government agent"). In In re Japanese Elec. Prod. Antitrust Litig., 723 F.2d 238, 288 (3d Cir.1983), rev'd on other grounds sub. nom. Matsushita Elec. Indus. Co. v. Zenith Radio Corp., 475 U.S. 574, 106 S.Ct. 1348, 89 L.Ed.2d 538 (1986), we approved of the district court's holding that:

> 'the testimony of the custodian or other qualified witness is not a sine qua non of admissibility in the occasional case *where the requirements for qualification as a business record can be met* by documentary evidence, affidavits, or admissions of the parties, i.e., by circumstantial evidence, or by a combination of direct and circumstantial evidence.'

Id. (quoting Zenith Radio Corp. v. Matsushita Elec. Indus. Co., 505 F.Supp. 1190, 1236 (E.D.Pa.1980))(emphasis added).

However, none of these authorities holds that the court may admit into evidence under the business exception to the hearsay rule documents containing hearsay simply because there are some indicia of the trustworthiness of the statements. While a noncustodial witness such as a government agent, or even documentary evidence, may be used to lay the foundation required by Rule 803(6), that witness or those documents must still demonstrate that the records were made contemporaneously with the act the documents purport to record by someone with knowledge of the subject matter, that they were made in the regular course of business, and that such records were regularly kept by the business. Cf. Franco, 874 F.2d at 1140 (agent gave thorough description of the manner in which records were prepared and maintained based on agent's conversations with owner and employee of business as well as agent's own observations); Hathaway, 798 F.2d at 906 (FBI agent permitted to lay foundation where agent had familiarity with the record-keeping system). But see United States v. Hines, 564 F.2d 925, 928 (10th Cir.1977)(automobile manufacturers' invoices admissible without foundation since such documents possess a high degree of trustworthiness and necessity of admitting them outweighs inconvenience in having custodian testify), cert. denied, 434 U.S. 1022, 98 S.Ct. 748, 54 L.Ed.2d 770 (1978). Here, Agent Wolverton did not purport to have familiarity with the record-keeping system of the banks, nor did he attest to any of the other requirements of Rule 803(6). Therefore, as proponent of the evidence, the Government failed to lay a proper foundation as required by the business records exception.

See also United States v. Kail, 804 F.2d 441 (8th Cir.1986)(in prosecution of coin dealer for mail fraud for selling coins at inflated prices, court found that there was sufficient circumstantial evidence to admit ledger which had been kept by bookkeeper, who was the defendant's wife and not available to testify; entries were consistent with invoices in evidence and testimony of witnesses: receptionist testified that she had seen bookkeeper make entries in ledger, and bookkeeper had told postal inspectors who seized ledger that she needed photocopies in order to carry on business). Compare Saks International, Inc. v. M/V "Export Champion," 817 F.2d 1011 (2d Cir.1987)(in order to establish amount of coffee that had actually been loaded onto vessel, court relied on tallies prepared by unidentified employees of company that had provided stevedoring services; no employee of that company testified, but chief mate testified that it is the customary course of cargo business for ship to retain and rely on tallies prepared by shore-side stevedores to establish the actual loading count, doing only a spot-check for accuracy which mate had done) with National Labor Relations Board v. First Termite Control Co., Inc., 646 F.2d 424 (9th Cir.1981)(testimony of bookkeeper of corporation A that she had made payment on freight bill received from corporation B for a shipment of lumber was inadequate to admit freight bill, where bill was being offered to prove origin of shipment, since corporation A had no interest in ascertaining accuracy of the place of origin of shipment).

Is the usual insistence on a foundation witness who testifies at trial too cumbersome? In federal criminal trials, 18 U.S.C. § 3500 provides that foreign records "shall not be excluded by the hearsay rule" when accompanied by a certificate by the "custodian or a person with knowledge" that states the facts to which the certifier would have to testify if the records were being introduced under Rule 803(6). Courts to date have uniformly upheld 18 U.S.C. § 3500 as constitutional when attacked on Confrontation Clause grounds (see, e.g., United States v. Ross, 33 F.3d 1507, 1515–16 (11th Cir.1994), cert. denied, 115 S.Ct. 2558 (1995)), A number of states have extended the certification procedure to civil cases and domestic business records. See McClain, Self–Authentication of Certified Copies of Business Records, 24 Balt.L.Rev. 27 (1994).

As to foundation requirements for public records cf. Federal Rules of Evidence Rule 902. See also Calif.Evid.Code, Comment to § 1280. And see Federal Rules of Evidence Rule 803(12) and the Advisory Committee's Note.

4. A "data compilation" as well as records "in any form," are specifically mentioned in Rule 803(6). Do non-traditional technologies pose any special admissibility issues? How does the contemporaneity requirement apply to a printout? See United States v. Catabran, 836 F.2d 453, 456–457 (9th Cir.1988). Should the proponent of computer records have to account for the creation of the printout and the proper functioning of the software and/or the hardware? See, e.g., Monarch Federal Savings & Loan Ass'n v. Genser, 383 A.2d 475 (N.J.Super.1977)(requiring a complete and comprehensive description of the method and circumstances by which a computer printout was prepared); United States v. Briscoe, 896 F.2d 1476, 1494 (7th Cir.1990)(proponent not required to establish that computers were tested for programming errors), cert. denied, 498 U.S. 863 (1990); United States v. Young Bros., Inc., 728 F.2d 682 (5th Cir.), cert. denied, 469 U.S. 881 (1984)(only testimony of custodian of computer-generated records required; testimony of software programmer not needed to complete foundation); United States v. Vela, 673 F.2d 86 (5th Cir.1982)(court rejected need for unique foundation in admitting computerized telephone records). The view that computer data should be accorded a presumption of trustworthiness has been severely criticized by Peritz, Computer Data and Reliability: A Call for Authentication of Business Records Under the Federal Rules of Evidence, 80 Nw.U.L.Rev. 956 (1986). Professor Peritz believes that it is virtually impossible to detect either intentional fraud or unintentional error when looking at a perfect-looking printout. Consequently, he would give the proponent of the record the burden of proving the reliability of the computer equipment and the data processing techniques used, and would make the underlying data and programs available to the opposing party in advance of trial.

How about e-mails? Is their inherent nature such that they do not qualify as the record of a systematic business activity? See Monotype Corp. PLC v. International Typeface Corp., 43 F.3d 443, 450 (9th Cir.1994), criticized in Dreyer, When the Postman Beeps Twice: The Admissibility of Electronic Mail Under the Business Records Exception of the Federal Rules of Evidence, 64 Ford.L.Rev. 2285, 2316 (1996) for focusing exclusively on the medium of the message at the expense of the contents and the business context in which the message was sent. Will e-mails made by the federal government be admissible under Rule 803(8)? See 36 C.F.R. § 1234.26 (1996):

> Judicial use of electronic records. Electronic records may be admitted in evidence to Federal courts for use in court proceedings (Federal Rules of Evidence 803(8)) if trustworthiness is established by thoroughly documenting the recordkeeping system's operation and the controls imposed upon it.

Extensive guidelines for managing electronic records, including e-mails, are set forth at 36 C.F.R. § 1234.24(b)(1)(i)-(vi). What is the effect of such a regulation?

5. Under what circumstances, if any, may the following qualify as business records? Personal diaries? In re Japanese Electronic Products Antitrust Litigation, 723 F.2d 238, 289–293 (3d Cir.1983), rev'd on other grounds, 475 U.S. 574 (1986). Dun & Bradstreet reports? United States v. Beecroft, 608 F.2d 753 (9th Cir.1979); Del Monte Corp. v. Stark & Son Wholesale, Inc., 474 S.W.2d 854 (Mo.App.1971). Check stubs? Hanna Lumber Co. v. Neff, 579 S.W.2d 95 (Ark.1979); In re Levi's Will, 157 N.Y.S.2d 320 (Surr.Ct.1956); Sabatino v. Curtiss National Bank of Miami Springs, 415 F.2d 632 (5th Cir.1969), cert. denied, 396 U.S. 1057 (1970). Graphs? Evans v. Tanner, 244 So.2d 782 (Ala.1971). Newspapers? Samuel Sheitelman, Inc. v. Hoffman, 255 A.2d 807 (N.J.Super.1969). Hotel registration card filled out by guest? United States v. Lieberman, 637 F.2d 95 (2d Cir.1980). Letters? Higgins v. Martin Marietta Corp., 752 F.2d 492 (10th Cir.1985). Notes taken at meeting? Hoselton v. Metz Baking Co., 48 F.3d 1056, 1061 (8th Cir.1995). School attendance records? In re Welfare of L.Z., 396 N.W.2d 214 (Minn.1986). See Abelle, Evidentiary Problems Relevant to Checks and Computers, 5 Rutgers J. Computers & Law 323 (1976); Annot., Admissibility of records other than police reports, under Rule 803(6), Federal Rules of Evidence, providing for business records exception to hearsay rule, 61 A.L.R.Fed. 524 (1983).

6. Interrelationship between Rule 803(6) and Rule 1006. Ford Motor Co. v. Auto Supply Co., Inc., 661 F.2d 1171, 1174–76 (8th Cir.1981): Ford brought action against defendant for fraudulently representing that automotive parts were manufactured by Ford. In order to prove the amount of profits it lost, Ford introduced exhibit 30, a single sheet statement of sales and costs of the five specific parts involved in this litigation for the years 1972–1975:

Terrence Marrs, manager of the financial analysis department of the parts and service division of Ford Motor, prepared exhibit 30. Marrs testified in detail concerning the origin of the figures and summary. The major source for the material is what is called the Product Line Profitability Analysis (PLPA). The PLPA is prepared annually by Ford and compiles the performance of Ford parts by product line. . . .

Marrs testified that the PLPA were prepared in the ordinary course of business and were compiled each year to aid Ford in making decisions concerning pricing and purchasing. He stated that the PLPA were based on "actuals," the detailed accounting statements compiled on an on-going basis. Thus, the PLPAs are summaries of the "actuals" and were prepared at the close of each year. Marrs also testified that he did not prepare the PLPAs nor was he the custodian for these financial statements at the time they were prepared. The PLPAs and other "back up" material were not offered into evidence but were available in the court room.

The defendants-appellees argue that exhibit 30 was inadmissible because it is a summary of a summary, none of which contained original entries kept in the ordinary course of business and because it was based on records not prepared by the witness through whom it was offered.

There are two rules which govern this issue: Rules 803(6), 1006 Fed.R.Evid. Rule 1006 states that the contents of voluminous writings which cannot be conveniently examined in court may be presented in the form of a summary or calculation. The rule also states that the "originals" shall be made available for examination at a reasonable time and place, and that the court may order that they be produced during trial. . . .

. . .

Rule 1006 clearly permits the use of a summary such as exhibit 30. The issue here is whether the summary is based on admissible evidence, i.e., the PLPAs. A summary, if drawn from data that is inadmissible, likewise must be excluded. . . .

The question of whether the PLPAs are admissible and therefore a proper source for the exhibit 30 summary can be answered by rule 803(6). That rule allows admission of a record or data compilation, in any form, of events made at or near the time by a person with knowledge *if* kept in the course of a regularly conducted business activity and *if* it was the regular practice of that business to make the data compilation. This showing is required to be made by the custodian or other qualified witness.

By its terms rule 803(6) encompasses the PLPA. They are a record or data compilation made at the end of the business year. Marrs testified, and it is undisputed, that the PLPAs were kept in the course of regularly conducted business and that it was an annual practice to prepare these financial statements. Further, the rule expressly permits these elements to be shown by a "qualified witness" as opposed to the custodian. Marrs, as manager of the financial analysis department, was certainly a qualified witness. . . .

See also United States v. Kim, 595 F.2d 755, 764 n. 43 (D.C.Cir.1979):

Computer print-outs have been admitted despite the unavailability of the underlying documents, but only when the evidentiary foundation proved that the information was put into machine-readable form in the regular course of business. E.g. United States v. Russo, 480 F.2d 1228, 1241 (6th Cir.1973); United States v. De Georgia, 420 F.2d 889, 893 n. 11 (9th Cir.1969). In such a case, the Sixth Circuit was careful to explain that the print-out was being admitted as a business record and not as a summary. In fact, the court held that the computer print out was an "original" document, and not a summary. Russo, supra.

Similarly, Williams v. Humble Oil & Refining Co., 53 F.R.D. 694, 698 (E.D.La.1971) held that reports summarizing the history of the defendant's oil wells were admissible despite the unavailability of the underlying documents. The Court stated:

Nor does it matter that these reports are compilations. Many books of record are books of secondary entry. In order to evidence a sale, a journal may be admitted even though it reflects merely the entry originally made on an invoice. If this is the situation even when the original record is available, it should be so a fortiori when the original record appears to be no longer at hand.

But like the computer cases, Williams is distinguishable. The journals involved there were admitted under the business records exception, not as summaries of business records. They were "prepared within a reasonable time after the occurrence of the events reflected in them." And critically, the journals were prepared as a regular part of the company geologist's duties and were relied on by the company. Here the telex is not admissible as a business record, so the defendant must try to have it admitted as a summary. Under such circumstances, the underlying documents must be available for inspection.

Can a hearsay objection be raised to the admissibility of summaries that satisfy Federal Rules of Evidence Rule 1006? May the court choose to admit the underlying documents and to instruct the jury that the summaries are not in evidence? Compare United States v. Smyth, 556 F.2d 1179 (5th Cir.), cert. denied, 434 U.S. 862 (1977) with United States v. Nathan, 536 F.2d 988 (2d Cir.), cert. denied, 429 U.S. 930 (1976).

Rule 1006 does not govern the use of summaries or charts that are offered as pedagogical devices under Rule 611(a) to clarify testimony or otherwise assist the factfinder. See United States v. Porter, 821 F.2d 968, 975 (4th Cir.1987)("Summary charts may be admitted if they are based upon and fairly represent competent evidence already before the jury."), cert. denied, 485 U.S. 934 (1988). Consequently, a court may instruct the jury not to consider these summaries as evidence, see, e.g., United States v. Duncan, 919 F.2d 981, 988 (5th Cir.1990), cert. denied, 500 U.S. 926 (1991), and should generally not allow non-Rule 1006 summaries into the jury room. (United States v. Possick, 849 F.2d 332, 339 (8th Cir.1988)). See also the helpful discussion in United States v. Bertoli, 854 F.Supp. 975, 1049–56 (D.N.J.1994), aff'd and rev'd on other grounds, 40 F.3d 1384 (3d Cir.1994) of the differences between the two kinds of charts. Quesada, Summarizing Prior Witness Testimony: Admissible Evidence, Pedagogical Device, or Violation of the Federal Rules of Evidence, 24 Fla. S.U.L.Rev. 161 (1995)(author suggests that only objective evidence that does not rest on the credibility of witnesses ought to be allowed on pedagogic summaries as otherwise proponent gets another chance to prove its case).

Annots., 16 A.L.R.Fed. 542 (1973), 80 A.L.R.3d 405 (1977), 50 A.L.R.Fed. 319 (1980).

Palmer v. Hoffman

Supreme Court of the United States, 1943.
318 U.S. 109, 63 S.Ct. 477, 87 L.Ed. 645, 144 A.L.R. 719.

■ Mr. Justice Douglas delivered the opinion of the Court.

This case arose out of a grade crossing accident which occurred in Massachusetts. Diversity of citizenship brought it to the federal District Court in New York. There were several causes of action. The first two were on behalf of respondent individually, one being brought under a Massachusetts statute, Mass.Gen.L. (1932) c. 160, §§ 138, 232, the other at common law. The third and fourth were brought by respondent as administrator of the estate of his wife and alleged the same common law and statutory negligence as the first two counts. On the question of negligence the trial court submitted three issues to the jury—failure to ring a bell, to blow a whistle, to have a light burning in the front of the train. The jury returned a verdict in favor of respondent individually for some $25,000 and in favor of respondent as administrator for $9,000. The District Court entered judgment on the verdict. The Circuit Court of Appeals affirmed, one judge dissenting. 2 Cir., 129 F.2d 976. The case is here on a petition for a writ of certiorari which presents three points.

I. The accident occurred on the night of December 25, 1940. On December 27, 1940, the engineer of the train, who died before the trial, made a statement at a freight office of the petitioners where he was interviewed by an assistant superintendent of the road and by a representative of the Massachusetts Public Utilities Commission. See Mass.Gen.L. (1932), c. 159, § 29. This statement was offered in evidence by petitioners under the Act of June 20, 1936, 49 Stat. 1561, 28 U.S.C. § 695, 28 U.S.C.A. § 695.[1] They offered to prove (in the language of the Act) that the statement was signed in the regular course of business, it being the regular course of such business to make such a statement. Respondent's objection to its introduction was sustained.

We agree with the majority view below that it was properly excluded.

We may assume that if the statement was made "in the regular course" of business, it would satisfy the other provisions of the Act. But we do not think that it was made "in the regular course" of business within the meaning of the Act. The business of the petitioners is the railroad business. That business like other enterprises entails the keeping of numerous books and records essential to its conduct or useful in its efficient operation. Though such books and records were considered reliable and trustworthy for major decisions in the industrial and business world, their use in litigation was greatly circumscribed or hedged about by the hearsay rule—restrictions which greatly increased the

---

1. "In any court of the United States and in any court established by Act of Congress, any writing or record, whether in the form of an entry in a book or otherwise, made as a memorandum or record of any act, transaction, occurrence, or event, shall be admissible as evidence of said act, transaction, occurrence, or event, if it shall appear that it was made in the regular course of any business, and that it was the regular course of such business to make such memorandum or record at the time of such act, transaction, occurrence, or event or within a reasonable time thereafter. All other circumstances of the making of such writing or record, including lack of personal knowledge by the entrant or maker, may be shown to effect its weight, but they shall not affect its admissibility. The term 'business' shall include business, profession, occupation, and calling of every kind." [Footnotes are the Court's.]

time and cost of making the proof where those who made the records were numerous.[2] 5 Wigmore, Evidence (3d ed., 1940) § 1530. It was that problem which started the movement towards adoption of legislation embodying the principles of the present Act. See Morgan et al., The Law of Evidence, Some Proposals for its Reform (1927) c. V. And the legislative history of the Act indicates the same purpose.[3]

The engineer's statement which was held inadmissible in this case falls into quite a different category.[4] It is not a record made for the systematic conduct of the business as a business. An accident report may affect that business in the sense that it affords information on which the management may act. It is not, however, typical of entries made systematically or as a matter of routine to record events or occurrences, to reflect transactions with others, or to provide internal controls. The conduct of a business commonly entails the payment of tort claims incurred by the negligence of its employees. But the fact that a company makes a business out of recording its employees' versions of their accidents does not put those statements in the class of records made "in the regular course" of the business within the meaning of the Act. If it did, then any law office in the land could follow the same course, since business as defined in the Act includes the professions. We would then have a real perversion of a rule designed to facilitate admission of records which experience has shown to be quite trustworthy. Any business by installing a regular system for recording and preserving its version of accidents for which it was potentially liable could qualify those reports under the Act. The result would be that the Act would cover any system of recording events or occurrences provided it was "regular" and though it had little or nothing to do with the management or operation of the business as such. Preparation of cases for trial by virtue of being a "business" or incidental thereto would obtain the benefits of this liberalized version of the early shop book rule. The probability of trustworthiness of records because they were routine reflections of the day to day operations of a business would be forgotten as the basis of the rule. See Conner v. Seattle, R. & S. Ry. Co., 56 Wash. 310, 312, 313, 105 P. 634, 635, 636, 25 L.R.A., N.S., 930, 134 Am.St.Rep. 1110. Regularity of preparation would become the test rather than the character of the records and their earmarks of reliability (Chesapeake & Delaware Canal Co. v. United States, 250 U.S. 123,

2. The problem was well stated by Judge Learned Hand in Massachusetts Bonding & Ins. Co. v. Norwich Pharmacal Co., 2 Cir., 18 F.2d 934, 937: "The routine of modern affairs, mercantile, financial and industrial, is conducted with so extreme a division of labor that the transactions cannot be proved at first hand without the concurrence of persons, each of whom can contribute no more than a slight part, and that part not dependent on his memory of the event. Records, and records alone, are their adequate repository, and are in practice accepted as accurate upon the faith of the routine itself, and of the self-consistency of their contents. Unless they can be used in court without the task of calling those who at all stages had a part in the transactions recorded, nobody need ever pay a debt, if only his creditor does a large enough business."

3. Thus the report of the Senate Committee on the Judiciary incorporates the recommendation of the Attorney General who stated in support of the legislation, "The old common-law rule requires that every book entry be identified by the person making it. This is exceedingly difficult, if not impossible, in the case of an institution employing a large bookkeeping staff, particularly when the entries are made by machine. In a recent criminal case the Government was prevented from making out a prima-facie case by a ruling that entries in the books of a bank, made in the regular course of business, were not admissible in evidence unless the specific bookkeeper who made the entry could identify it. Since the bank employed 18 bookkeepers, and the entries were made by bookkeeping machines, this was impossible." S.Rep. No. 1965, 74th Cong., 2d Sess., pp. 1–2.

4. It is clear that it does not come within the exceptions as to declarations by a deceased witness. See Shepard v. United States, 290 U.S. 96, 54 S.Ct. 22, 78 L.Ed. 196; Wigmore, supra, chs. xli–xliv.

128, 129, 39 S.Ct. 407, 408, 409, 63 L.Ed. 889) acquired from their source and origin and the nature of their compilation. We cannot so completely empty the words of the Act of their historic meaning. If the Act is to be extended to apply not only to a "regular course" of a business but also to any "regular course" of conduct which may have some relationship to business, Congress not this Court must extend it. Such a major change which opens wide the door to avoidance of cross-examination should not be left to implication. Nor is it any answer to say the Congress has provided in the Act that the various circumstances of the making of the record should affect its weight not its admissibility. That provision comes into play only in case the other requirements of the Act are met.

In short, it is manifest that in this case those reports are not for the systematic conduct of the enterprise as a railroad business. Unlike payrolls, accounts receivable, accounts payable, bills of lading and the like these reports are calculated for use essentially in the court, not in the business. Their primary utility is in litigating, not in railroading.

It is, of course, not for us to take these reports out of the Act if Congress has put them in. But there is nothing in the background of the law on which this Act was built or in its legislative history which suggests for a moment that the business of preparing cases for trial should be included. In this connection it should be noted that the Act of May 6, 1910, 36 Stat. 350, 45 U.S.C. § 38, 45 U.S.C.A. § 38, requires officers of common carriers by rail to make under oath monthly reports of railroad accidents to the Interstate Commerce Commission, setting forth the nature and causes of the accidents and the circumstances connected therewith. And the same Act, 45 U.S.C. § 40, 45 U.S.C.A. § 40, gives the Commission authority to investigate and to make reports upon such accidents. It is provided, however, that "Neither the report required by section 38 of this title nor any report of the investigation provided for in section 40 of the title nor any part thereof shall be admitted as evidence or used for any purpose in any suit or action for damages growing out of any matter mentioned in said report or investigation." 45 U.S.C. § 41, 45 U.S.C.A. § 41. A similar provision, 36 Stat. 916, 54 Stat. 148, 45 U.S.C. § 33, 45 U.S.C.A. § 33, bars the use in litigation of reports concerning accidents resulting from the failure of a locomotive boiler or its appurtenances. 45 U.S.C. §§ 32, 33, 45 U.S.C.A. §§ 32, 33. That legislation reveals an explicit Congressional policy to rule out reports of accidents which certainly have as great a claim to objectivity, as the statement sought to be admitted in the present case. We can hardly suppose that Congress modified or qualified by implication these long standing statutes when it permitted records made "in the regular course" of business to be introduced. Nor can we assume that Congress having expressly prohibited the use of the company's reports on its accidents impliedly altered that policy when it came to reports by its employees to their superiors. The inference is wholly the other way.

The several hundred years of history behind the Act (Wigmore, supra, §§ 1517–1520) indicate the nature of the reforms which it was designed to effect. It should of course be liberally interpreted so as to do away with the anachronistic rules which gave rise to its need and at which it was aimed. But "regular course" of business must find its meaning in the inherent nature of the business in question and in the methods systematically employed for the conduct of the business as a business.

. . .

Affirmed.

NOTES

1. Compare Lewis v. Baker, 526 F.2d 470, 472–73 (2d Cir.1975): Plaintiff, a railroad employee claimed he was injured when he leaped off a box-car with defective brakes.

At the trial, defendants sought to rebut plaintiff's allegations of a faulty brake with evidence that the brake had functioned properly immediately prior to the accident when the plaintiff tested it, and immediately after the accident when it was checked in connection with the preparation of an accident report. It was the defendants' contention that plaintiff improperly set, or forgot to set, a necessary brake handle, panicked, and then leapt from the car.

In support of their interpretation of the events, defendants offered into evidence a "personal injury report" and an "inspection report." Frank Talbott, a trainmaster, testified that the personal injury report was signed by him and prepared under his supervision. The information had been provided to him by William F. Campbell, the night trainmaster. Talbott confirmed the authenticity of the record and testified that he was required to make out such reports of injuries as part of the regular course of business. At the trial David W. Halderman, an assistant general foreman for the defendants, identified the inspection report which had been prepared by Campbell and by Alfred Zuchero, a gang foreman. This report was based upon an inspection of the car Campbell and Zuchero had conducted less than four hours after the accident. Halderman testified that Zuchero was dead and that Campbell was employed by a railroad in Virginia. The latter was thus beyond the reach of subpoena. Halderman also confirmed that following every accident involving injury to an employee his office was required to complete inspection reports, and that such reports were regularly kept in the course of business. Over objection, the court admitted both reports into evidence.

. . .

... Appellant argues ... that ... the Supreme Court's decision in Palmer v. Hoffman, 318 U.S. 109, 63 S.Ct. 477, 87 L.Ed. 645 (1943), precludes their admission into evidence....

In Palmer v. Hoffman, the engineer preparing the report had been personally involved in the accident, and, as Circuit Judge Frank stated in his opinion for the Court of Appeals, the engineer knew "at the time of making it that he [was] very likely, in a probable law suit relating to that accident, to be charged with wrongdoing as a participant in the accident, so that he [was] almost certain, when making the memorandum or report, to be sharply affected by a desire to exculpate himself and to relieve himself or his employer of liability." 129 F.2d 976, 991 (2d Cir.1942)(italics omitted). Here there could have been no similar motivation on the part of Talbott, Campbell or Zuchero, for not one of them was involved in the accident, or could have possibly been the target of a lawsuit by Lewis. In United States v. New York Foreign Trade Zone Operators, 304 F.2d 792 (2d Cir.1962), we sustained the admissibility of a similar report by the co-employee of the injured party which had been prepared as part of the regular business of the defendant pier-owner and operator. As we explained there, the mere fact that a record might ultimately be of some value in the event of litigation does not per se mandate its exclusion. In Palmer v. Hoffman, "[o]bviously the Supreme Court was concerned about a likely untrustworthiness of materials prepared specifically by a prospective litigant for courtroom use." 304 F.2d at 797. The fact that a report embodies an employee's version of the accident, Taylor v. Baltimore & Ohio R.R. Co., 344 F.2d 281 (2d Cir.1965), or happens to work in favor of the entrant's employer, Naylor v. Isthmian S.S. Co., 187 F.2d 538 (2d Cir.1951) does not, without more, indicate untrustworthiness. See Pekelis v. Transcontinental & Western Air, Inc., 187 F.2d 122 (2d Cir.), cert. denied, 341 U.S. 951, 71 S.Ct. 1020, 95 L.Ed. 1374 (1951). In the absence of a motive to fabricate, a motive so clearly spelled out in Palmer v. Hoffman, the holding in that case is not controlling to emasculate the Business Records Act. Therefore the trial court must look to those earmarks of reliability which otherwise establish the trustworthiness of the record. See Gaussen v. United Fruit Co., 412 F.2d 72, 74 (2d Cir.1969).

Here the ICC requires the employer to prepare and file monthly reports of all accidents involving railroad employees. Assistant general foreman Halderman testified that following every injury he was required to inspect the equipment involved and to report the results of the inspection on a regular printed form. As we stated in Taylor v. Baltimore & Ohio R.R. Co., supra, "[i]t would ill become a court to say that the regular making of reports required by law is not in the regular course of business." 344 F.2d at 285. In addition to their use by the railroad in making reports to the ICC, the reports here were undoubtedly of utility to the employer in ascertaining whether the equipment involved was defective so that future accidents might be prevented. These factors, we think, are sufficient indicia of trustworthiness to establish the admissibility of the reports into evidence under the Federal Business Records Act.

2. Newark Electronics Corp. v. City of Chicago, 264 N.E.2d 868, 873 (Ill.App. 1970): action by electronics corporation for damages for flooding of basement; plaintiff's "compilation-computation" of water-damaged items held admissible.

The argument goes that a compilation-computation of water damaged items was not made in the regular course of business because it was not the business of Newark to make such compilation-computations. A literal reading of the rule would support this stance as correct. Obviously, Newark's business is not being flooded, even periodically—which might help under a literal interpretation. But if periodicity of flooding helps, the absurdity of a literal interpretation in our context is immediately apparent. Newark's business is selling merchandise via catalogs, and both suffered water damage. However, having suffered such damage, even for the first time, it seems reasonably businesslike to us to ascertain the damages by making a compilation-computation of such which flowed from the flooding (event) since such would be in the regular course of business, (ascertaining damages) and it would certainly be in the regular course of business to make such a record at the time of such flooding (event) or within a reasonable time thereafter. In our opinion, prior, regular floodings are not a precondition for the admission of a compilation-computation of a business' first experience with a disaster in order to make such admissible within the confines of Rule 236. Being in business—any kind—demands records for the routine day-by-day transactions, but regular, in our opinion, need not be day-by-day as to transactions or events that do not occur and have not occurred. A given event, transaction, or occurrence may occur only once and simply because it has never happened before it is not a contradiction to say that in making a record of such event, transaction or occurrence, singular though it may be, it was not made in the regular course of business. Because a company may eschew damages—who does like them—does not mean that suffering same, however, bizarre, is something unexpected or at least not to be expected in business.

But, the city argues that the compilation was made with litigating in mind, or at the very least, to be used if a dispute arose as to 'how much'. Thus, since they were made with an eye towards possible litigation, their sanctity and integrity is suspect. But if we look at it that way, all business records have their basis in the recordation of day-to-day occurrences and transactions and it is safe to say that such memorialization has as one of its uses the resolution of possible future disputes as to exactly what a particular occurrence, transaction or event partook of.

Cf. Smith v. Milwaukee & Suburban Transport Co., 147 N.W.2d 233 (Wis.1967)(record prepared post litem motam); Bradley v. Phelps, 260 N.E.2d 894 (Ind.App.1970); Pompa v. Hojancki, 281 A.2d 886 (Pa.1971)(same).

Johnson v. Lutz

Court of Appeals of New York, 1930.
253 N.Y. 124, 170 N.E. 517.

■ HUBBS, J. This action is to recover damages for the wrongful death of the plaintiff's intestate, who was killed when his motorcycle came into collision with the defendants' truck at a street intersection. There was a sharp conflict in the testimony in regard to the circumstances under which the collision took place. A policeman's report of the accident filed by him in the station house was offered in evidence by the defendants under section 374–a of the Civil Practice Act and was excluded. The sole ground for reversal urged by the appellants is that said report was erroneously excluded. That section reads: "Any writing or record, whether in the form of an entry in a book or otherwise, made as a memorandum or record of any act, transaction, occurrence or event, shall be admissible in evidence in proof of said act, transaction, occurrence or event, if the trial judge shall find that it was made in the regular course of any business, and that it was the regular course of such business to make such memorandum or record at the time of such act, transaction, occurrence or event, or within a reasonable time thereafter. All other circumstances of the making of such writing or record, including lack of personal knowledge by the entrant or maker, may be shown to affect its weight, but they shall not affect its admissibility. The term business shall include business, profession, occupation and calling of every kind."

Prior to the decision in the well-known case of Vosburgh v. Thayer (12 Johns. 461), decided in 1815, shopbooks could not be introduced in evidence to prove an account. The decision in that case established that they were admissible where preliminary proof could be made that there were regular dealings between the parties, that the plaintiff kept honest and fair books, that some of the articles charged had been delivered, and that the plaintiff kept no clerk. At that time it might not have been a hardship to require a shopkeeper who sued to recover an account to furnish the preliminary proof required by that decision. Business was transacted in a comparatively small way, with few if any clerks. Since the decision in that case, it has remained the substantial basis of all decisions upon the question in this jurisdiction prior to the enactment in 1928 of section 374–a, Civil Practice Act.

Under modern conditions the limitations upon the right to use books of account, memoranda or records made in the regular course of business, often resulted in a denial of justice, and usually in annoyance, expense and waste of time and energy. A rule of evidence that was practical a century ago had become obsolete. The situation was appreciated and attention was called to it by the courts and text writers. (Woods, Practice Evidence [2d ed.], 377; 3 Wigmore on Evidence [1923], sec. 1530.)

The report of the Legal Research Committee of the Commonwealth Fund, published in 1927, by the Yale University Press, under the title "The Law of Evidence—Some Proposals for its Reform," dealt with the question in chapter 5 under the heading "Proof of Business Transactions to Harmonize with Current Business Practice." That report, based upon extensive research, pointed out the confusion existing in decisions in different jurisdictions. It explained and illustrated the great need of a more practical, workable and uniform rule, adapted in modern business conditions and practices. The chapter is devoted to a discussion of the pressing need of a rule of evidence which would "give evidential credit to the books upon which the mercantile and industrial world relies in the conduct of business." At the close of the chapter the committee proposed a statute to be enacted in all jurisdictions. In compliance with such proposal the Legislature enacted section 374–a of the Civil Practice Act in the very words used by the committee.

It is apparent that the Legislature enacted section 374–a to carry out the purpose announced in the report of the committee. That purpose was to secure the enactment of a statute which would afford a more workable rule of evidence in the proof of business transactions under existing business conditions.

In view of the history of section 374–a and the purpose for which it was enacted, it is apparent that it was never intended to apply to a situation like that in the case at bar. The memorandum in question was not made in the regular course of any business, profession, occupation or calling. The policeman who made it was not present at the time of the accident. The memorandum was made from hearsay statements of third persons who happened to be present at the scene of the accident when he arrived. It does not appear whether they saw the accident and stated to him what they knew, or stated what some other persons had told them.

The purpose of the Legislature in enacting section 374–a was to permit a writing or record, made in the regular course of business, to be received in evidence without the necessity of calling as witnesses all of the persons who had any part in making it, provided the record was made as a part of the duty of the person making it, or on information imparted by persons who were under a duty to impart such information. The amendment permits the intro- duction of shopbooks without the necessity of calling all clerks who may have sold different items of account. It was not intended to permit the receipt in evidence of entries based upon voluntary hearsay statements made by third parties not engaged in the business or under any duty in relation thereto. It was said in Mayor, etc. v. Second Ave. R.R. Co. (102 N.Y. 572, at p. 581, 7 N.E. 905, 909): "It is a proper qualification of the rule admitting such evidence, that the account must have been made in the ordinary course of business, and that it should not be extended so as to admit a mere private memorandum, not made in pursuance of any duty owing by the person making it, or when made upon information derived from another who made the communication casually and voluntarily, and not under the sanction of duty or other obligation."

An important consideration leading to the amendment was the fact that in the business world credit is given to records made in the course of business by persons who are engaged in the business upon information given by others engaged in the same business as part of their duty.

"Such entries are dealt with in that way in the most important undertakings of mercantile and industrial life. They are the ultimate basis of calculation, investment, and general confidence in every business enterprise. Nor does the practical impossibility of obtaining constantly and permanently the verification of every employee affect the trust that is given to such books. It would seem that expedients which the entire commercial world recognizes as safe could be sanctioned, and not discredited, by Courts of justice. When it is a mere question of whether provisional confidence can be placed in a certain class of statements, there cannot profitably and sensibly be one rule for the business world and another for the court-room. The merchant and the manufacturer must not be turned away remediless because methods in which the entire community places a just confidence are a little difficult to reconcile with technical judicial scruples on the part of the same persons who as attorneys have already employed and relied upon the same methods. In short, Courts must here cease to be pedantic and endeavor to be practical." (3 Wigmore on Evidence [1923], sec. 1530, p. 278.)

The Legislature has sought by the amendment to make the courts practical. It would be unfortunate not to give the amendment a construction which will enable it to cure the evil complained of and accomplish the purpose for which it was enacted. In construing it we should not, however, permit it to be applied in a case for which it was never intended.

The judgment should be affirmed, with costs.

■ Cardozo, Ch. J., Pound, Crane, Lehman, Kellogg and O'Brien, JJ., concur.

Judgment affirmed.

NOTES

1. Matter of Leon RR, 397 N.E.2d 374, 377–78 (N.Y.1979). Proceeding to terminate parental rights on grounds of neglect instituted by county department of Social Services. Order terminating parental rights reversed:

> At the fact-finding hearing, petitioner offered its entire case file on the child and his parents into evidence. . . .

> Each report in the files and each of the statements contained in those reports were admissible only if they qualified as business records (CPLR 4518, subd. [a]). To constitute a business record exception to the hearsay rule, the proponent of the record must first demonstrate that it was within the scope of the entrant's business duty to record the act, transaction or occurrence sought to be admitted. But this satisfies only half the test. In addition, each participant in the chain producing the record, from the initial declarant to the final entrant, must be acting within the course of regular business conduct or the declaration must meet the test of some other hearsay exception (Johnson v. Lutz, 170 N.E. 517, 518; Toll v. State, 299 N.Y.S.2d 589, 592). Thus, not only must the entrant be under a business duty to record the event, but the informant must be under a contemporaneous business duty to report the occurrence to the entrant as well (Richardson, Evidence [10th ed. Prince], § 299). The reason underlying the business records exception fails and, hence, the statement is inadmissible hearsay if any of the participants in the chain is acting outside the scope of a business duty (Johnson v. Lutz, supra).

> In this case, petitioner was under a statutory duty to maintain a comprehensive case record for Leon containing reports of any transactions or occurrences relevant to his welfare (Social Services Law, § 372; 18

NYCRR 441.7[a]), thus satisfying this aspect of the business records test (see Kelly v. Wasserman, 5 N.Y.2d 425, 429, 185 N.Y.S.2d 538, 541, 158 N.E.2d 241, 243). Some of the entries in the case file were based on firsthand observations of Leon's caseworker which were recorded shortly after the occurrences, rendering them admissible. Many of the remaining entries, however, consisted of statements, reports and even rumors made by persons under no business duty to report to petitioner. Especially in the context of this case, it is essential to emphasize that the mere fact that the recording of third-party statements by the caseworker might be routine, imports no guarantee of the truth, or even reliability, of those statements. To construe these statements as admissible simply because the caseworker is under a business duty to record would be to open the floodgates for the introduction of random, irresponsible material beyond the reach of the usual tests for accuracy—cross-examination and impeachment of the declarant. Unless some other hearsay exception is available (Toll v. State, supra), admission may only be granted where it is demonstrated that the informant has personal knowledge of the act, event, or condition and he is under a business duty to report it to the entrant (Johnson v. Lutz, supra; cf. Model Code of Evidence, rule 514).

See also the analytical and exceptionally helpful opinion of Tenney, J. in Yates v. Bair Transport, Inc., 249 F.Supp. 681, 687–688 (S.D.N.Y.1965), concluding as follows, after a lengthy review of the authorities and literature:

> Based on the foregoing authorities, it appears that the Business Records Act overcomes the initial hurdle to the admissibility of evidence, but goes no further. Thus the hearsay statement (of a volunteer) contained in the police officer's report is no more admissible than the testimony of the police officer on the stand as to the hearsay statement made at the scene of the accident. If the making of the statement itself is relevant, it can be proved both by the report, which is a record kept in the ordinary course of business, as well as by the in-Court testimony of the officer. However, if the report is offered to prove the truth of the statement contained therein, the statement must either have been made in the regular course of business of the person making it, or must have an independent ground of admissibility such as an admission, etc., the same as the in-Court testimony of the officer as to the statements made, offered to prove the truth of what was said, must have an independent ground of admissibility, since all that can be shown under the Business Records Act is that in the regular course of business of the officer he wrote that X made the following statement to prove the truth of the fact that X made the statement, not the proof of the facts contained in the statement.

2.   State v. Lungsford, 400 A.2d 843, 849–50 (N.J.Super.A.D.1979). Prosecution for knowing possession of motor vehicle known to have been stolen and belonging to James Wilton. The only evidence in the case establishing that car had been stolen was police report containing a summary of information obtained from Wilton. One of the police officers who recorded the information knew Wilton and the car. Held: error to have admitted report:

> While police records may qualify as business records for certain purposes and in certain respects, they are nevertheless not vehicles by which substantive evidential status may be conferred upon the otherwise hearsay declarations of a victim of or witness to a crime, accident or other occurrence. If the declarant is not available to testify and if the statement is not admissible under some other exception to the hearsay rule, such as excited utterance or dying declaration, then admissibility cannot be predi-

cated exclusively upon the circumstance that the statement was made to a police officer who paraphrased its content in his report.

... [I]t is clear that one of the critical circumstances importing reliability is the fact that the informant whose declaration is so recorded is under a duty, in the context of the activity in which the record is made, to make an honest and truthful report. Thus, the business record exception is predicated not only on the circumstance that the record itself is kept in the usual course of the business but also on the circumstance that the recorded information is obtained by the recorder from a declarant having a "business" duty to communicate it truthfully....

... Here, the second of these criteria was not met. Obviously, the making of investigations and the receiving of information concerning crime is usual police business. Hence a police record is admissible to prove, for example, that a report of crime was made by a member of the public and when the report was made and received. It is not, however, admissible to prove the truth of the contents of that report since members of the public, whether targets of investigation, witnesses or victims, are not under a duty, in the nature of a business duty, to make an honest and truthful report. Thus, such "citizen" declarations are virtually universally held to constitute excluded hearsay in respect of otherwise admissible police reports....

The trial judge here evidently admitted the police report as proof of the truth of Wilton's declaration because of his personal belief that it was probably true. If, however, a hearsay declaration does not meet the threshold test of circumstantial reliability applicable to its category of hearsay exception—in this instance the declarant's business duty—the probable trustworthiness of a particular hearsay declaration is irrelevant.

Compare People v. Meyers, 340 N.Y.S.2d 505, 509 (N.Y.Crim.Ct.1973). Court found a "business duty" basis for accepting a police report to demonstrate ownership of a stolen motor vehicle: "The Court takes judicial notice of the fact that the Rating Bureau of the New York State Department of Insurance, with which all casualty insurance policies operative in this state are filed, reports that virtually all automobile theft policies carry a condition requiring the insured to notify the insurer in writing of the particulars of an accident, occurrence or loss, and, in the event of theft, also to notify the police."

Would an accident report filed by the plaintiff with the police department pursuant to statute be admissible as a business record? Kelly v. O'Neil, 296 N.E.2d 223 (Mass.App.Ct.1973). Cf. In re Ollag Construction Equipment Corp., 665 F.2d 43 (2d Cir.1981)(financial statements furnished to bank by debtor were found to be business records of bank; court noted that furnishing false financial statements to a bank constitutes a felony).

Beech Aircraft Corp. v. Rainey *

Supreme Court of the United States, 1988.
488 U.S. 153, 109 S.Ct. 439, 102 L.Ed.2d 445.

■ JUSTICE BRENNAN delivered the opinion of the Court.

In this case we address a longstanding conflict among the federal courts of appeal over whether Federal Rule of Evidence 803(8)(C), which provides an exception to the hearsay rule for public investigatory reports containing "factu-

---

* The "completeness" issue in Beech is discussed supra at p. 552.

al findings," extends to conclusions and opinions contained in such reports. We also consider whether, on the facts of this case, the trial court abused its discretion in refusing to admit, on cross-examination, testimony intended to provide a more complete picture of a document about which the witness had testified on direct.

I

This litigation stems from the crash of a Navy training aircraft at Middleton Field, Alabama, on July 13, 1982, which took the lives of both pilots on board, Lieutenant Commander Barbara Ann Rainey and Ensign Donald Bruce Knowlton. The accident took place while Rainey, a Navy flight instructor, and Knowlton, her student, were flying "touch-and-go" exercises in a T–34C Turbo–Mentor aircraft, number 3E955. Their aircraft and several others flew in an oval pattern, each plane making successive landing/takeoff maneuvers on the runway. Following its fourth pass at the runway, 3E955 appeared to make a left turn prematurely, cutting out the aircraft ahead of it in the pattern and threatening a collision. After radio warnings from two other pilots, the plane banked sharply to the right in order to avoid the other aircraft. At that point it lost altitude rapidly, crashed, and burned.

Because of the damage to the plane and the lack of any survivors, the cause of the accident could not be determined with certainty. The two pilots' surviving spouses brought a product liability suit against petitioners Beech Aircraft Corporation, the plane's manufacturer, and Beech Aerospace Services, which serviced the plane under contract with the Navy. The plaintiffs alleged that the crash had been caused by a loss of engine power, known as "rollback," due to some defect in the aircraft's fuel control system. The defendants, on the other hand, advanced the theory of pilot error, suggesting that the plane had stalled during the abrupt avoidance maneuver.

At trial, the only seriously disputed question was whether pilot error or equipment malfunction had caused the crash. Both sides relied primarily on expert testimony. One piece of evidence presented by the defense was an investigative report prepared by Lieutenant Commander William Morgan on order of the training squadron's commanding officer and pursuant to authority granted in the Manual of the Judge Advocate General. This "JAG Report," completed during the six weeks following the accident, was organized into sections labeled "finding of fact," "opinions," and "recommendations," and was supported by some 60 attachments. The "finding of fact" included statements like the following:

> "13. At approximately 1020, while turning crosswind without proper interval, 3E955 crashed, immediately caught fire and burned.

> "27. At the time of impact, the engine of 3E955 was operating but was operating at reduced power." App. 10–12.

Among his "opinions" Lieutenant Commander Morgan stated, in paragraph five, that due to the deaths of the two pilots and the destruction of the aircraft "it is almost impossible to determine exactly what happened to Navy 3E955 from the time it left the runway on its last touch and go until it impacted the ground." He nonetheless continued with a detailed reconstruction of a possible set of events, based on pilot error, that could have caused the accident. The next two paragraphs stated a caveat and a conclusion:

> "6. Although the above sequence of events is the most likely to have occurred, it does not change the possibility that a 'rollback' did occur.

"7. The most probable cause of the accident was the pilots [sic] failure to maintain proper interval." Id., at 15.

The trial judge initially determined, at a pretrial conference, that the JAG Report was sufficiently trustworthy to be admissible, but that it "would be admissible only on its factual findings and would not be admissible insofar as any opinions or conclusions are concerned." Id., at 35. The day before trial, however, the court reversed itself and ruled, over the plaintiffs' objection, that certain of the conclusions would be admitted. Id., at 40–41. Accordingly, the court admitted most of the report's "opinions," including the first sentence of paragraph five about the impossibility of determining exactly what happened, and paragraph seven, which opined about failure to maintain proper interval as "[t]he most probable cause of the accident." Id., at 97. On the other hand, the remainder of paragraph five was barred as "nothing but a possible scenario," id., at 40, and paragraph six, in which investigator Morgan refused to rule out rollback, was deleted as well.

This case also concerns an evidentiary ruling as to a second document. Five or six months after the accident, plaintiff John Rainey, husband of the deceased pilot and himself a Navy flight instructor, sent a detailed letter to Lieutenant Commander Morgan. Based on Rainey's own investigation, the letter took issue with some of the JAG Report's findings and outlined Rainey's theory that "[t]he most probable primary cause factor of this aircraft mishap is a loss of useful power (or rollback) caused by some form of pneumatic sensing/fuel flow malfunction, probably in the fuel control unit." Id., at 104, 111.

At trial Rainey did not testify during his side's case-in-chief, but he was called by the defense as an adverse witness. On direct examination he was asked about two statements contained in his letter. The first was to the effect that his wife had unsuccessfully attempted to cancel the ill-fated training flight because of a variety of adverse factors including her student's fatigue. The second question concerned a portion of Rainey's hypothesized scenario of the accident:

"Didn't you say, sir, that after Mrs. Rainey's airplane rolled wings level, that Lieutenant Colonel Habermacher's plane came into view unexpectedly at its closest point of approach, although sufficient separation still existed between the aircraft. However, the unexpected proximitely [sic] of Colonel Habermacher's plane caused one of the aircrew in Mrs. Rainey's plane to react instinctively and abruptly by initiating a hard right turn away from Colonel Habermacher's airplane?" Id., at 75.

Rainey admitted having made both statements. On cross-examination, Rainey's counsel asked the following question: "In the same letter to which Mr. Toothman made reference to in his questions, sir, did you also say that the most probably [sic] primary cause of this mishap was rollback?" Id., at 77. Before Rainey answered, the court sustained a defense objection on the ground that the question asked for Rainey's opinion. Further questioning along this line was cut off.

Following a two-week trial, the jury returned a verdict for the petitioners. A panel of the Eleventh Circuit reversed and remanded for a new trial. 784 F.2d 1523 (C.A.11 1986). Considering itself bound by the Fifth Circuit precedent of Smith v. Ithaca Corp., 612 F.2d 215 (C.A.5 1980), the panel agreed with Rainey's argument that Federal Rule of Evidence 803(8)(C), which excepts investigatory reports from the hearsay rule, did not encompass evaluative conclusions or opinions. Therefore, it held, the "conclusions" contained in the JAG Report should have been excluded. One member of the panel, concurring specially, urged however that the Circuit reconsider its interpretation of Rule

803(8)(C), suggesting that "Smith is an anomaly among the circuits." 784 F.2d, at 1530 (opinion of Johnson, J.). The panel also held, citing Federal Rule of Evidence 106, that it was reversible error for the trial court to have prohibited cross-examination about additional portions of Rainey's letter which would have put in context the admissions elicited from him on direct.[1]

On rehearing en banc, the Court of Appeals divided evenly on the question of Rule 803(8)(C). 827 F.2d 1498 (C.A.11 1987). It therefore held that Smith was controlling and consequently reinstated the panel judgment. On the Rule 106 question, the court unanimously reaffirmed the panel's decision that Rule 106 (or alternatively Rule 801(d)(1)(B)) required reversal. We granted certiorari to consider both issues. 485 U.S. 903, 108 S.Ct. 1073, 99 L.Ed.2d 233 (1988).

II

Federal Rule of Evidence 803 provides that certain types of hearsay statements are not made excludable by the hearsay rule, whether or not the declarant is available to testify. Rule 803(8) defines the "public records and reports" which are not excludable, as follows:

> "Records, reports, statements, or data compilations, in any form, of public offices or agencies, setting forth (A) the activities of the office or agency, or (B) matters observed pursuant to duty imposed by law as to which matters there was a duty to report, . . . or (C) in civil actions and proceedings and against the Government in criminal cases, factual findings resulting from an investigation made pursuant to authority granted by law, unless the sources of information or other circumstances indicate lack of trustworthiness."

Controversy over what "public records and reports" are made not excludable by Rule 803(8)(C) has divided the federal courts from the beginning. In the present case, the Court of Appeals followed the "narrow" interpretation of Smith v. Ithaca Corp., 612 F.2d 215, 220–223 (C.A.5 1980), which held that the term "factual findings" did not encompass "opinions" or "conclusions." Courts of appeal other than those of the Fifth and Eleventh Circuits, however, have generally adopted a broader interpretation. For example, the Court of Appeals for the Sixth Circuit, in Baker v. Elcona Homes Corp., 588 F.2d 551, 557–558 (1978), cert. denied, 441 U.S. 933, 99 S.Ct. 2054, 60 L.Ed.2d 661 (1979), held that "factual findings admissible under Rule 803(8)(C) may be those which are made by the preparer of the report from disputed evidence. . . ." The other courts of appeal that have squarely confronted the issue have also adopted the broader interpretation. We agree and hold that factually based conclusions or opinions are not on that account excluded from the scope of Rule 803(8)(C).

Because the Federal Rules of Evidence are a legislative enactment, we turn to the "traditional tools of statutory construction," INS v. Cardoza–Fonseca, 480 U.S. 421, 446, 107 S.Ct. 1207, 1221, 94 L.Ed.2d 434 (1987), in order to construe their provisions. We begin with the language of the Rule itself. Proponents of the narrow view have generally relied heavily on a perceived dichotomy between "fact" and "opinion" in arguing for the limited scope of the phrase "factual findings." Smith v. Ithaca Corp., supra, contrasted the term "factual findings" in Rule 803(8)(C) with the language of Rule 803(6)(records of regularly conducted activity), which expressly refers to "opinions" and "diag-

---

1. In the alternative the court held that Rainey's testimony should have been admitted as a prior consistent statement under Rule 801(d)(1)(B). [The footnotes are the Court's and have been renumbered. Some have been omitted.]

noses." "Factual findings," the court opined, must be something other than opinions. Smith, supra, at 221–222.[2]

For several reasons, we do not agree. In the first place, it is not apparent that the term "factual findings" should be read to mean simply "facts" (as opposed to "opinions" or "conclusions"). A common definition of "finding of fact" is, for example, "[a] conclusion by way of reasonable inference from the evidence." Black's Law Dictionary 569 (5th ed. 1979). To say the least, the language of the Rule does not compel us to reject the interpretation that "factual findings" includes conclusions or opinions that flow from a factual investigation. Second, we note that, contrary to what is often assumed, the language of the Rule does not state that "factual findings" are admissible, but that "reports ... setting forth ... factual findings" (emphasis added) are admissible. On this reading, the language of the Rule does not create a distinction between "fact" and "opinion" contained in such reports.

Turning next to the legislative history of Rule 803(8)(C), we find no clear answer to the question of how the Rule's language should be interpreted. Indeed, in this case the legislative history may well be at the origin of the dispute. Rather than the more usual situation where a court must attempt to glean meaning from ambiguous comments of legislators who did not focus directly on the problem at hand, here the Committees in both Houses of Congress clearly recognized and expressed their opinions on the precise question at issue. Unfortunately, however, they took diametrically opposite positions. Moreover, the two Houses made no effort to reconcile their views, either through changes in the Rule's language or through a statement in the Report of the Conference Committee.

Clearly this legislative history reveals a difference of view between the Senate and the House that affords no definitive guide to the congressional understanding. It seems clear however that the Senate understanding is more in accord with the wording of the Rule and with the comments of the Advisory Committee.[3]

The Advisory Committee's comments are notable, first, in that they contain no mention of any dichotomy between statements of "fact" and "opinions"

2. The court in Smith found it significant that different language was used in Rules 803(6) and 803(8)(C): "Since these terms are used in similar context within the same Rule, it is logical to assume that Congress intended that the terms have different and distinct meanings." 612 F.2d, at 222. The Advisory Committee notes to Rule 803(6) make clear, however, that the Committee was motivated by a particular concern in drafting the language of that Rule. While opinions were rarely found in traditional "business records," the expansion of that category to encompass documents such as medical diagnoses and test results brought with it some uncertainty in earlier versions of the Rule as to whether diagnoses and the like were admissible. "In order to make clear its adherence to the [position favoring admissibility]," the Committee stated, "the rule specifically includes both diagnoses and opinions, in addition to acts, events, and conditions, as proper subjects of admissible entries." Advisory Committee's Notes on Fed. Rule Evid. 803(6),

28 U.S.C.App., p. 723. Since that specific concern was not present in the context of Rule 803(8)(C), the absence of identical language should not be accorded much significance. See Rainey v. Beech Aircraft Corp., 827 F.2d 1498, 1511–1512 (C.A.11 1987)(en banc)(Tjoflat, J., concurring). What is more, the Committee's report on Rule 803(8)(C) strongly suggests that that Rule has the same scope of admissibility as does Rule 803(6): "Hence the rule, as in Exception [paragraph] (6), assumes admissibility in the first instance but with ample provision for escape if sufficient negative factors are present." Advisory Committee's Notes on Fed.Rule Evid. 803(8), 28 U.S.C.App., p. 725.

3. See Advisory Committee's Notes on Fed.Rule Evid. 803(8), 28 U.S.C.App., pp. 724–725. As Congress did not amend the Advisory Committee's draft in any way that touches on the question before us, the Committee's commentary is particularly relevant in determining the meaning of the document Congress enacted.

or "conclusions." What was on the Committee's mind was simply whether what it called "evaluative reports" should be admissible. Illustrating the previous division among the courts on this subject, the Committee cited numerous cases in which the admissibility of such reports had been both sustained and denied. It also took note of various federal statutes that made certain kinds of evaluative reports admissible in evidence. What is striking about all of these examples is that these were reports that stated conclusions. E.g., Moran v. Pittsburgh–Des Moines Steel Co., 183 F.2d 467, 472–473 (C.A.3 1950)(report of Bureau of Mines concerning the cause of a gas tank explosion admissible); Franklin v. Skelly Oil Co., 141 F.2d 568, 571–572 (C.A.10 1944)(report of state fire marshal on the cause of a gas explosion inadmissible); 42 U.S.C. § 269(b)(bill of health by appropriate official admissible as prima facie evidence of vessel's sanitary history and condition). The Committee's concern was clearly whether reports of this kind should be admissible. Nowhere in its comments is there the slightest indication that it even considered the solution of admitting only "factual" statements from such reports.[4] Rather, the Committee referred throughout to "reports," without any such differentiation regarding the statements they contained. What the Committee referred to in the Rule's language as "reports . . . setting forth . . . factual findings" is surely nothing more or less than what in its commentary it called "evaluative reports." Its solution as to their admissibility is clearly stated in the final paragraph of its report on this Rule. That solution consists of two principles: First, "the rule . . . assumes admissibility in the first instance. . . . " Second, it provides "ample provision for escape if sufficient negative factors are present."

That "provision for escape" is contained in the final clause of the Rule: evaluative reports are admissible "unless the sources of information or other circumstances indicate lack of trustworthiness." This trustworthiness inquiry— and not an arbitrary distinction between "fact" and "opinion"—was the Committee's primary safeguard against the admission of unreliable evidence, and it is important to note that it applies to all elements of the report. Thus, a trial judge has the discretion, and indeed the obligation, to exclude an entire report or portions thereof—whether narrow "factual" statements or broader "conclusions"—that she determines to be untrustworthy.[5] Moreover, safe-

---

4. Our conclusion that the Committee was concerned only about the question of the admissibility vel non of "evaluative reports," without any distinction between statements of "fact" and "conclusions," draws support from the fact that this was the focus of scholarly debate on the official reports question prior to adoption of the Federal Rules. Indeed, the problem was often phrased as one of whether official reports could be admitted in view of the fact that they contained the investigator's conclusions. Thus Professor McCormick, in an influential article relied upon by the Committee, stated his position as follows: "that evaluative reports of official investigators, though partly based upon statements of others, and though embracing conclusions, are admissible as evidence of the facts reported." McCormick, Can the Courts Make Wider Use of Reports of Official Investigations?, 42 Iowa L.Rev. 363, 365 (1957).

5. The Advisory Committee proposed a nonexclusive list of four factors it thought would be helpful in passing on this question:

(1) the timeliness of the investigation; (2) the investigator's skill or experience; (3) whether a hearing was held; and (4) possible bias when reports are prepared with a view to possible litigation (citing Palmer v. Hoffman, 318 U.S. 109, 63 S.Ct. 477, 87 L.Ed. 645 (1943)). Advisory Committee's Notes on Fed. Rule Evid. 803(8), 28 U.S.C. App., p. 725; see Note, The Trustworthiness of Government Evaluative Reports under Federal Rule of Evidence 803(8)(C), 96 Harv.L.Rev. 492 (1982).

In a case similar in many respects to this one, the trial court applied the trustworthiness requirement to hold inadmissible a JAG Report on the causes of a Navy airplane accident; it found the report untrustworthy because it "was prepared by an inexperienced investigator in a highly complex field of investigation." Fraley v. Rockwell Int'l Corp., 470 F.Supp. 1264, 1267 (S.D.Ohio 1979). In the present case, the District Court found the JAG Report to be trustworthy. App. 35. As no party has challenged that finding, we have no occasion to express an opinion on it.

guards built into other portions of the Federal Rules, such as those dealing with relevance and prejudice, provide the court with additional means of scrutinizing and, where appropriate, excluding evaluative reports or portions of them. And of course it goes without saying that the admission of a report containing "conclusions" is subject to the ultimate safeguard—the opponent's right to present evidence tending to contradict or diminish the weight of those conclusions.

Our conclusion that neither the language of the Rule nor the intent of its framers calls for a distinction between "fact" and "opinion" is strengthened by the analytical difficulty of drawing such a line. It has frequently been remarked that the distinction between statements of fact and opinion is, at best, one of degree:

> "All statements in language are statements of opinion, i.e., statements of mental processes or perceptions. So-called 'statements of fact' are only more specific statements of opinion. What the judge means to say, when he asks the witness to state the facts, is: 'The nature of this case requires that you be more specific, if you can, in your description of what you saw.' "W. King & D. Pillinger, Opinion Evidence in Illinois 4 (1942)(footnote omitted), quoted in 3 J. Weinstein & M. Berger, Weinstein's Evidence ¶ 701[01], p. 701–6 (1988).

See also E. Cleary, McCormick on Evidence 27 (3d ed. 1984)("There is no conceivable statement however specific, detailed and 'factual,' that is not in some measure the product of inference and reflection as well as observation and memory"); R. Lempert & S. Saltzburg, A Modern Approach to Evidence 449 (2d ed. 1982)("A factual finding, unless it is a simple report of something observed, is an opinion as to what more basic facts imply"). Thus, the traditional requirement that lay witnesses give statements of fact rather than opinion may be considered, "[l]ike the hearsay and original documents rules . . . a 'best evidence' rule." McCormick, Opinion Evidence in Iowa, 19 Drake L.Rev. 245, 246 (1970).

In the present case, the trial court had no difficulty in admitting as a factual finding the statement in the JAG Report that "[a]t the time of impact, the engine of 3E955 was operating but was operating at reduced power." Surely this "factual finding" could also be characterized as an opinion, which the investigator presumably arrived at on the basis of clues contained in the airplane wreckage. Rather than requiring that we draw some inevitably arbitrary line between the various shades of fact/opinion that invariably will be present in investigatory reports, we believe the Rule instructs us—as its plain language states—to admit "reports . . . setting forth . . . factual findings." The Rule's limitations and safeguards lie elsewhere: First, the requirement that reports contain factual findings bars the admission of statements not based on factual investigation. Second, the trustworthiness provision requires the court to make a determination as to whether the report, or any portion thereof, is sufficiently trustworthy to be admitted.

A broad approach to admissibility under Rule 803(8)(C), as we have outlined it, is also consistent with the Federal Rules' general approach of relaxing the traditional barriers to "opinion" testimony. Rules 702–705 permit experts to testify in the form of an opinion, and without any exclusion of opinions on "ultimate issues." And Rule 701 permits even a lay witness to testify in the form of opinions or inferences drawn from her observations when testimony in that form will be helpful to the trier of fact. We see no reason to strain to reach an interpretation of Rule 803(8)(C) that is contrary to the liberal thrust of the Federal Rules.[6]

We hold, therefore, that portions of investigatory reports otherwise admissible under Rule 803(8)(C) are not inadmissible merely because they state a conclusion or opinion. As long as the conclusion is based on a factual investigation and satisfies the Rule's trustworthiness requirement, it should be admissible along with other portions of the report.[7] As the trial judge in this case determined that certain of the JAG Report's conclusions were trustworthy, he rightly allowed them to be admitted into evidence. We therefore reverse the judgment of the Court of Appeals in respect of the Rule 803(8)(C) issue.

. . . .

NOTES

1. Suppose the investigator who prepared a report being offered under Rule 803(8)(C) relied in part on hearsay statements. Suppose, for instance, the investigator is a police expert in accident reconstruction. May the investigator consider eyewitnesses' statements? Should the court automatically exclude a report that considered hearsay statements because the declarant lacked personal knowledge or because the findings are untrustworthy? May the court admit the report under Rule 803(8) even though it would be inadmissible under Rule 803(6)? See Johnson v. Lutz, supra. Should the court admit the report but redact any references to the hearsay statements? Is it significant that the maker of the report could be qualified as an expert? Cf. Rule 703 (permitting experts to base their opinions on facts and data "reasonably relied upon by experts in the field.") and see discussion in chapter 6, infra.

Miller v. Field, 35 F.3d 1088, 1091–1092 (6th Cir.1994):

> This court has previously recognized "that factual findings, which are based on inadmissible hearsay, are not admissible under Rule 803(8)(C) because the underlying information is untrustworthy." Complaint of Paducah Towing Co., Inc. (United States v. Paducah Towing Co., Inc.), 692 F.2d 412, 420–21 (6th Cir.1982). See also Miller v. Caterpillar Tractor Co., 697 F.2d 141, 144 (6th Cir.1983)(court did not abuse discretion in refusing to admit as untrustworthy a document that relied upon hearsay statements of witnesses made to the investigator). . . .
>
> Such a result appears eminently reasonable in light of the stated justification for the Rule 803(8)(C) exception to the general prohibition on receipt of hearsay evidence. While a court may presume that a *preparer of a report*, under a duty to relate information, will perform the task required and formulate justified conclusions and reasonable opinions based on evidence *actually observed by the preparer*, no such presumption arises when the preparer relies on potentially untrustworthy hearsay evidence from another individual under no duty to provide unbiased information.

---

6. The cited Rules refer, of course, to situations—unlike that at issue—where the opinion testimony is subject to cross-examination. But the determination that cross-examination was not indispensable in regard to official investigatory reports has already been made, and our point is merely that imposing a rigid distinction between fact and opinion would run against the Rules' tendency to de-emphasize that dichotomy.

7. We emphasize that the issue in this case is whether Rule 803(8)(C) recognizes any difference between statements of "fact" and "opinion." There is no question in this case of any distinction between "fact" and "law." We thus express no opinion on whether legal conclusions contained in an official report are admissible as "findings of fact" under Rule 803(8)(C).

The bulk of the Michigan State Police reports introduced as evidence at trial contains neither factual findings made by the report's preparers nor conclusions and opinions based upon such factual findings. Instead, the reports are largely a recitation of statements of other individuals that fall under no other exception to the hearsay rule. Because those statements of the victim, the alleged assailants, other witnesses, and the local prosecutor are, therefore, hearsay within hearsay, that evidence should not have been placed before the jury in this case.

Clark v. Clabaugh, 20 F.3d 1290, 1295 (3d Cir.1994)(in a civil rights action charging violations in connection with a race riot, court found that the district court, in granting summary judgment, had properly relied on an evaluative report prepared by the Pennsylvania State Police):

Although [the investigating officers and authors] did interview persons who are parties to the litigation and incorporated their statements into the PSP Report, the bias of those interviewed does not render the PSP Report itself inherently untrustworthy, and such bias cannot be imputed to the investigating officers. Furthermore, the investigating officers interviewed representatives from all factions involved . . .").

United States v. Davis, 826 F.Supp. 617, 623–624 (D.R.I.1993)(CERCLA action to recover cleanup costs):

Finally, the United States does not dispute that the [remedial investigation] report contains some hearsay. Instead, they argue that a government record admissible under FRE 803(8)(C) should only be excluded if it is "pervaded" by hearsay such that it becomes untrustworthy. . . . [R]eports such as the report in the instant case do not merely repeat what was told to the investigators by the witnesses, but also draw inferences as to what in fact happened. The conclusions cannot be disentangled from the facts. Absent a specific showing of untrustworthiness, such multiple layers of hearsay clearly fall within the scope of FRE 803(8)(C).

[Footnotes omitted]

In re Air Disaster at Lockerbie, Scotland, 37 F.3d 804, 827 (2d Cir.1994)(admitting Scottish constable's report on luggage aboard plane that was based on information provided by friends and relatives of victims and physical evidence found at scene), cert. denied, 115 S.Ct. 934 (1995).

Cf. Baker v. Elcona Homes Corp., 588 F.2d 551 (6th Cir.1978)(admitting accident report by policeman qualified in accident reconstruction that contained statement of defendant about position of cars and concluded that plaintiff entered intersection against light; court found that defendant's statement made in hospital after accident was a prior consistent statement and therefore "we need not determine to what extent, where factual findings are admissible, the underlying data considered by the investigating officer are also admissible under Rule 803(8)."), cert. denied, 441 U.S. 933 (1979). See also Vanderpoel v. A–P–A Transport Corp., 1992 WL 158418 (E.D.Pa.1992)(court denied defendant's motion in limine to exclude entire state trooper's accident investigation report but excluded the portion of the report regarding the recorded statement of the driver of the defendant's tractor trailer).

2. What criteria should be applied in asserting the "trustworthiness" of an evaluative report? See Advisory Committee note to Rule 803(8). Compare Fraley v. Rockwell International Corp., 470 F.Supp. 1264 (S.D.Ohio 1979)(in action against airplane manufacturer arising out of crash of Navy plane, court held that report prepared by Naval Rework Facility would satisfy Rule 803(8)(C) but that report prepared by Judge Advocate General's office would not since the document was prepared by an inexperienced investigator in a highly complex field and therefore lacks reliability) with Sage v. Rockwell International Corp., 477 F.Supp. 1205 (D.N.H.1979)(companion case arising out of same crash as in Fraley; court admitted both reports holding that lack of experience of JAG investigator went only to weight, not admissibility). See also Baker v. Firestone Tire & Rubber Co., 793 F.2d 1196, 1199 (11th Cir. 1986)(court refused to admit report of House of Representatives Subcommittee which had investigated Firestone tires: "The subcommittee report did not contain the factual findings necessary to an objective investigation, but consisted of the rather heated conclusions of a politically motivated hearing.").

For a comprehensive analysis of evidentiary issues that arise with respect to reports offered under Rule 803(8)(C) see Gentile v. County of Suffolk, 129 F.R.D. 435 (E.D.N.Y.1990), aff'd, 926 F.2d 142 (2d Cir.1991). See also Schwartz, Admissibility of Investigatory Reports in § 1983 Civil Rights Actions—A User's Manual, 79 Marq.L.Rev. 453 (1996); Note, The Trustworthiness of Government Evaluative Reports Under Federal Rule of Evidence 803(8)(C), 96 Harv.L.Rev. 492 (1982).

3. Who has the burden of demonstrating "lack of trustworthiness?" In Ellis v. International Playtex Inc., 745 F.2d 292, 301 (4th Cir.1984), a wrongful death action brought against manufacturer of tampons by husband whose wife had allegedly died of toxic shock syndrome, the defendant contested causation; trial judge had excluded epidemiological studies prepared by the Federal Center for Disease Control and state agencies on the ground that they could not be admitted pursuant to Rule 803(8)(C) because plaintiff had failed to establish that the methodology used in the studies was sufficiently trustworthy; error:

> Placing the burden on the opposing party makes considerable practical sense. Most government sponsored investigations employ well accepted methodological means of gathering and analyzing data. It is unfair to put the party seeking admission to the test of "re-inventing the wheel" each time a report is offered. Rather than requiring the moving party to spend considerable time and money to ensure that the experts who conducted the study are available at trial, it is far more equitable to place that burden on the party seeking to demonstrate why a time tested and carefully considered presumption is not appropriate.

Cf. Bradford Trust Co. v. Merrill Lynch, Pierce, Fenner and Smith, Inc., 805 F.2d 49, 54–55 (2d Cir.1986)(FBI reports concluding that signature in question was genuine technically fell under Rule 803(8)(C) and therefore had to be admitted unless there was an affirmative showing of untrustworthiness; district court erred in refusing to give reports any weight on the ground that the preparer was unavailable for cross-examination; this "was simply another way of saying that the report was hearsay. Ignoring it on this ground is inconsistent with the notion of having exceptions to the hearsay rule").

4. The Federal Rules treat a statement of past recollection recorded as hearsay that is made subject to an exception in Rule 803(5). See p. 539, supra.

5. In criminal cases, what is the interrelationship between Rule 803(8) and Rules 803(5) and 803(6)? Subdivisions (B) and (C) of Rule 803(8) provide that reports of "matters observed by police officers and other law enforcement personnel" and investigatory reports offered against a criminal defendant are inadmissible. Are such reports admissible as business records or recorded recollection?

In United States v. Oates, 560 F.2d 45, 78 (2d Cir.1977), the trial court admitted a United States Customs Service chemist's worksheets and report which concluded that the white powdery substance he had analyzed was heroin. The appellate court found that admission of the chemist's documents constituted reversible error. The court characterized chemists of the United States Customs Service as "law enforcement personnel" and found that the chemist's reports could not be admitted under the Rule 803(6) business records exception:

> [I]n view of the articulated purpose behind the narrow drafting of FRE 803 in general and FRE 803(8) in particular, FRE 803(6) must be read in conjunction with FRE 803(8)(B) and (C). Specifically, the pervasive fear of the draftsmen and of Congress that interference with an accused's right to confrontation would occur was the reason why in criminal cases evaluative reports of government agencies and law enforcement reports were expressly denied the benefit to which they might otherwise be entitled under FRE 803(8). It follows that this explanation of the reason for the special treatment of evaluative and law enforcement reports under FRE 803(8) applies with equal force to the treatment of such reports under *any* of the other exceptions to the hearsay rule. . . .

Courts have retreated from the expansiveness of the Oates ruling in a variety of ways. See United States v. Rosa, 11 F.3d 315, 332 (2d Cir.1993), cert. denied, 114 S.Ct. 1565 (1994)(admitting autopsy results; "Congress did not mean the term 'police officers and other law enforcement personnel,' whose reported observations were not to be admissible by way of Rule 803(8) against defendants in criminal prosecutions, to include other types of public servants such as medical examiners.").

United States v. Orozco, 590 F.2d 789, 793–94 (9th Cir.), cert. denied, 442 U.S. 920 (1979):

> At trial, customs officials explained the procedure for recording the license plate numbers of vehicles passing through the border at San Ysidro. The procedure is a relatively simple one. As vehicles approach the border station, the primary customs inspector enters the license plate number into a computer. The computer then scans its system to determine whether that license number has appeared within the previous 72–hour period.

> While the district court admitted these computer cards under the "business records" exception, we feel that the proper inquiry is directed toward the "public records" exception of rule 803(8). While governmental functions could be included within the broad definition of "business" in rule 803(6), such a result is obviated by rule 803(8), which is the "business records" exception for public records such as those in issue here. . . .

> . . . In excluding "matters observed by . . . law enforcement personnel" from the coverage of the exception, Congress did not intend to exclude records of routine, nonadversarial matters such as those in question here. The legislative history indicates that

>> [o]stensibly, the reason for this exclusion is that observations by police officers at the scene of the crime or the apprehension of the defendant are not as reliable as observations by public officials in other cases because of the adversarial nature of the confrontation between the police and the defendant in criminal cases.

> S.Rep. No. 1277, 93d Cong., 2d Sess., reprinted in [1974] U.S.Code Cong. & Admin.News 7051, 7064. The customs inspector is one of the "law enforcement personnel" included in rule 803(8). However, the simple recordation of license numbers of all vehicles which pass his station is not

of the adversarial confrontation nature which might cloud his perception....

Therefore, the TECS cards were admissible "unless the sources of information or other circumstances indicate lack of trustworthiness." Fed. R.Evid. 803(8). There was testimony at trial that as the license numbers are entered, they appear on the computer's screen, allowing the inspector to see if a mistake has been made in his entry. The customs agents have no motive to fabricate entries into the computer and the possibility of an inaccurate entry is no greater here than it would be in any other recording system. The reliability of computers has been demonstrated in similar contexts.

Accord: United States v. Brown, 9 F.3d 907, 911–12 (11th Cir.1993)(per curiam)(regularly kept property receipts; "The police custodian in the instant case had no incentive to do anything other than mechanically record the relevant information on the property receipt."), cert. denied, 115 S.Ct. 152 (1994); United States v. Dancy, 861 F.2d 77 (5th Cir.1988)(fingerprint card); United States v. Gilbert, 774 F.2d 962, 965 (9th Cir.1985)(criminologist's notations on a fingerprint card); United States v. Quezada, 754 F.2d 1190, 1194 (5th Cir.1985)(Immigration and Naturalization form indicating that defendant had been arrested and deported); United States v. King, 590 F.2d 253 (8th Cir.1978)(certified documents from Missouri Department of Revenue showing ownership of automobile), cert. denied, 440 U.S. 973 (1979); United States v. Wilmer, 799 F.2d 495, 501 (9th Cir.1986)(calibration report of a breathalyzer maintenance operator), cert. denied, 481 U.S. 1004 (1987); United States v. Hernandez–Rojas, 617 F.2d 533, 534–35 (9th Cir.) (immigration officer's notation that defendant was previously deported to Mexico in a warrant deportation), cert. denied, 449 U.S. 864 (1980). See also Minner v. Kerby, 30 F.3d 1311, 1314 (10th Cir.1994)(court need not decide whether police chemist's notes satisfied Rule 803(6) or 803(8); notes had sufficient indicia of reliability because they concerned "mechanically objective tests performed on the powder and were taken contemporaneously with the performance of the tests.")

In United States v. Sokolow, 91 F.3d 396, 404–05 (3d Cir.1996), the court rejected an Oates challenge to the admissibility of an investigatory report:

Criticizing Oates as an unduly broad interpretation of Rule 803(8), many courts have declined to import the limitations of Rule 803(8)(B) and (C) into other hearsay exceptions. See, e.g., United States v. Picciandra, 788 F.2d 39, 44 (1st Cir.)(upholding admission of DEA report against criminal defendants under Rule 803(5)(past recollection recorded)), cert. denied, 479 U.S. 847, 107 S.Ct. 166, 93 L.Ed.2d 104 (1986); United States v. Metzger, 778 F.2d 1195, 1201 (6th Cir.1985)(declining to read Rule 803(8)(C) limitations into Rule 803(10)(absence of public record or entry)), cert. denied, 477 U.S. 906, 106 S.Ct. 3279, 91 L.Ed.2d 568 (1986). Although we have not specifically addressed this issue, the Seventh and Tenth Circuits have held that Rule 803(8)(C) does not compel the exclusion of documents properly admitted under Rule 803(6) where the author testifies. See United States v. Hayes, 861 F.2d 1225, 1230 (10th Cir.1988); United States v. King, 613 F.2d 670, 672–73 (7th Cir.1980). The Hayes court stated that the Oates rule does not apply in such circumstances "because such [investigator] testimony protects against the loss of an accused's confrontation rights, the underlying rationale for Rule 803(8) and the basis of the court's concern in Oates." 861 F.2d at 1230 (citation omitted). We reach the same conclusion here.

United States v. Sawyer, 607 F.2d 1190 (7th Cir.1979), cert. denied, 445 U.S. 943 (1980): Police and investigative report records that fall within scope of Rule 803(8) are admissible if they satisfy another hearsay exception and author of report testifies. Court used this analysis in admitting reports under Rule 803(5) notwithstanding their inadmissibility under Rule 803(8)(B). How helpful is the declarant's testimony when a record is being admitted as a past recollection recorded? Cf. United States v. Owens, supra, page 554.

Military Rules of Evidence, Rule 803(8)(1980) has added an exception to subdivision (B) which provides:

> Notwithstanding (B), the following are admissible under this paragraph as a record of a fact or event if made by a person within the scope of the person's official duties and those duties included a duty to know or to ascertain through appropriate and trustworthy channels of information the truth of the fact or event and to record such fact or event: enlistment papers, physical examination papers, outline-figure and fingerprint cards, forensic laboratory reports, chain of custody documents, morning reports and other personnel accountability documents, service records, officer and enlisted qualification records, records of court-martial convictions, logs, unit personnel diaries, individual equipment records, guard reports, daily strength records of prisoners, and rosters of prisoners.

United States v. Yakobov, 712 F.2d 20 (2d Cir.1983)(in a prosecution for dealing in firearms without a license, the government introduced two documents to the effect that a diligent search of Alcohol, Tobacco and Firearms (ATF) records had revealed no firearms license for defendant. Defendant contended on the basis of the Second Circuit's opinion in Oates, supra, that Rule 803(8) forecloses the receipt of such a certificate under Rule 803(10)):

> Several factors lead us to the conclusion that Oates should not be extended to Rule 803(10). First, there is a significant difference between the nature of a statement envisioned by Rule 803(8) and that of a statement envisioned by Rule 803(10). Rule 803(8) deals with statements setting forth "matters observed" and "findings of fact resulting from an investigation." The contents of these statements normally are direct affirmative assertions as to elements of the offense charged ... The assertion made by a statement envisaged by Rule 803(10) is normally a step removed from any element of the offense charged: it is not a statement that the defendant has failed to perform a given act or that he does not enjoy a certain status. Rather it is a statement that, among the records regularly kept by a public office or agency, a certain record, entry, report, etc., has not been found. This type of statement is an inferential step away from any element of the offense charged. It is not a finding of the material fact but is an assertion from which a finding of such a fact may be made.

> Further, though a statement envisioned by Rule 803(8) may have evaluative aspects—for example, a chemist's analysis of a substance as heroin, or a policeman's interpretation of a suspect's actions as checking for surveillance—a statement envisioned by Rule 803(10) has none. The latter statement merely states that a certain datum has not been located in records regularly made and preserved. Assuming there are sufficient indicia of the trustworthiness of such a statement to satisfy Rule 803(10)'s requirement of a diligent search, there is not the same need to cross-examine the maker of the statement as might exist with respect to a statement envisioned by Rule 803(8).

The court, nevertheless reversed Yakobov's conviction because the ATF certificate misspelled his name and the court concluded that the search that was conducted could not have been diligent.

6. What is the interrelationship between the confrontation clause and hearsay exceptions that make admissible statements in business records and public records, or evidence of the absence of statements in business and public records? If the record satisfies the evidentiary rule will it satisfy constitutional requirements as well, or must the prosecutor show reliability and/or unavailability of the declarant? In the Oates case, the court declined to decide the confrontation issue, but stated that "serious questions of constitutional dimension" reinforced its holding. 560 F.2d 45, 83 (2d Cir.1977). See United States v. White, infra p. 796.

Annots., Admissibility, over hearsay objection, of police observations and investigative findings offered by government in criminal prosecution, excluded from public records exception to hearsay rule under Rule 803(8)(B) or (C), 56 A.L.R.Fed. 524 (1982); Construction and application of provision of Rule 803(8)(B), Federal Rules of Evidence, excluding from exception to hearsay cases matters observed by law enforcement officers, 37 A.L.R.Fed. 831 (1978).

Commonwealth v. DiGiacomo

Supreme Court of Pennsylvania, 1975.
463 Pa. 449, 345 A.2d 605.

[Murder prosecution. Defendant admitted he fired the fatal shot but claimed justification because done to protect the life of his friend, Hruska, who was being beaten by the deceased. Pursuant to the business records exception, defendant sought to introduce the hospital records of Hruska who had been hospitalized after the fracas.]

■ NIX, J.

.   .   .

Appellant's second and final argument concerns the trial judge's refusal to permit the introduction of certain hospital records where the doctor who made the records was unavailable to testify. The records were permitted to prove the fact of hospitalization and the duration of the hospital stay, but not to show diagnosis or medical opinion. Appellant asserts that they were admissible to show Mr. Hruska's injuries as well.

The law is clear that hospital records are admissible to show the fact of hospitalization, treatment prescribed, and symptoms given. . . . Medical opinion contained in the records and proffered as expert testimony is not admissible however where the doctor is not available for cross-examination. See Jones Appeal, 449 Pa. 543, 297 A.2d 117 (1972). Here, appellant attempted to have the custodian of records testify as to the admitting diagnosis of the injuries sustained. Such testimony is in the nature of expert opinion testimony and accordingly was properly excluded. See, generally, McCormick, Handbook of the Law of Evidence, 732 (2d ed. 1972).

Judgment of sentence affirmed.

■ ROBERTS, JUSTICE (concurring).

Because I cannot agree with the majority's assertion that diagnoses contained in hospital records are never admissible under the business records exception to the hearsay rule, I cannot join in the opinion of the Court.

.   .   .

The trial court admitted the records only in so far as they proved the fact of the friend's hospitalization and the duration of his stay in the hospital. It refused to admit that part of the record that contained the diagnosis of the physician who treated the friend.

The majority today breezily affirms the trial court's ruling, concluding that hospital records are admissible only to show the fact of hospitalization, treatment prescribed and symptoms given. It asserts, moreover, because the physician's diagnosis is opinion evidence, it is not admissible where the physician is not available to testify.

In my view, the majority's resolution of this issue is inconsistent with the rationale underlying the business and professional records exception to the hearsay rule. McCormick gives the following reasons for the exception:

"The exception is justified on grounds analogous to those underlying other exceptions to the hearsay rule. Unusual reliability is regarded as furnished by the fact that in practice regular entries have a comparatively high degree of accuracy (as compared to other memoranda) because such books and records are customarily checked as to correctness by systematic balance-striking, because the very regularity and continuity of the records is calculated to train the recordkeeper in habits of precision, and because in actual experience the entire business of the nation and many other activities constantly function in reliance upon entries of this kind."

McCormick's Handbook of the Law of Evidence § 306, at 720 (2d ed. E. Cleary, 1972). Wigmore finds that the fact that hospital records are "made and relied upon in affairs of life and death" renders them especially reliable. VI Wigmore, Evidence § 1707, at 36 (3d ed. 1940).

The physician's diagnosis is probably the most important element in the hospital record in determining what treatment is necessary to preserve the patient's life and health. It would seem, therefore, that the reliability of the diagnosis is sufficiently safeguarded to allow its admission even where there is no opportunity for the non-offering party to cross-examine the recording physician. Cf. Commonwealth v. Harris, 351 Pa. 325, 41 A.2d 688 (1945).

Furthermore, I question the efficacy of cross-examination to uncover discrepancies in the physician's diagnosis. As Professor Wigmore has recognized,

"[A]midst the day-to-day details of sources of hospital cases, the physicians and nurses can ordinarily recall from actual memory few or none of the specific data entered; they themselves rely upon the record of their own action; hence to call them to the stand would ordinarily add little or nothing to the information furnished by the record alone. The occasional errors and omissions, occurring in the routine work of a large staff, are no more an obstacle to the general trustworthiness of such records than are the errors of witnesses on the stand."

Wigmore, supra. See generally, 4 Weinstein's Evidence, ¶ 803(6)[04] (1975); but see McCormick, supra, § 313.

Finally, although the use of the record deprives the non-offering party of the opportunity to explore the physician's qualifications, the fact that the diagnostician is a physician on the staff of a hospital assures at least minimal qualifications. The fact that no greater competence is indicated by the record can be adequately communicated to the jury.

However, even assuming that there may be some danger in admitting diagnoses without cross-examination of the recording physician, this does not dictate that all records containing diagnoses must be excluded from evidence. Judge Weinstein reports that "most federal courts reached an accommodation between the need for relevant information and the fear of uncross-examined opinion. They drew a distinction between diagnoses involving 'conjecture and opinion' and diagnoses upon which 'competent physicians would not differ.' " 4 Weinstein's Evidence, ¶ 803(b)[04] at 803–158 (1975). Records containing diagnoses tending toward the former were excluded, those tending toward the latter were not.[1] McCormick finds a similar development in several state courts. McCormick, supra, § 313. A sample of cases in which other jurisdictions have held that, at least in some situations, diagnoses are admissible include Thomas v. Hogan, 308 F.2d 355 (4th Cir.1962); Bailey v. Tennessee Coal, Iron & RR. Co., 261 Ala. 526, 75 So.2d 117 (1954); Tryon v. Casey, Mo.App., 416 S.W.2d 252 (1967); Brown v. St. Paul City Ry. Co., 241 Minn. 15, 62 N.W.2d 688 (1954)(dictum); Allen v. St. Louis, 365 Mo. 677, 285 S.W.2d 663 (1956); Weis v. Weis, 147 Ohio St. 416, 72 N.E.2d 245 (1947)(dictum); McReynolds v. Howland, 218 Or. 566, 346 P.2d 127 (1959); Travis Life Insurance Co. v. Rodriguez, 326 S.W.2d 256 (Tex.Civ.App.1959); Joseph v. W.H. Groves Latter Day Saints Hospital, 7 Utah 2d 39, 318 P.2d 330 (1957); Noland v. Mutual of Omaha Insurance Co., 57 Wis.2d 633, 205 N.W.2d 388 (1973).

On the basis of these authorities, I cannot agree that a prohibition on the admission of all hospital records containing diagnoses is necessary. However, I need not determine in what circumstances diagnoses should be admissible or whether in the present case the report in question was admissible. In my view, the exclusion of the report if it were error, was harmless.

As stated previously, appellant sought to have admitted the hospital record to show that his friend had been badly beaten by the deceased. Although the trial court refused to admit the part of the record containing the physician's diagnosis, it did permit the admission of the part of the record indicating that the friend had to be hospitalized as a result of the struggle and that he remained thereafter in the hospital for two months. From this evidence, the jury must have realized that the deceased had inflicted an awful beating on appellant's friend. The evidence describing the exact nature of the friend's injuries which was contained in the physician's diagnosis would have virtually no additional effect on the jury in light of other testimony about the beating. I am therefore convinced beyond a reasonable doubt that had the excluded evidence been admitted, it would have had no effect upon the judgment. Thus the error was harmless.

■ POMEROY, JUSTICE (concurring).

. . .

. . . I add this statement for the purpose of pointing out that, under the terms of the Business Records Act, a record is admissible "if, in the opinion of the court, the sources of information, method and time of preparation were such as to justify its admission." Thus, the trial judge has discretion in deciding whether business records are admitted into evidence, and his decision is reviewable only for an abuse of that discretion. The trial judge in this case, however, did not purport to exercise this discretion, but rather limited the admission of the hospital records because he believed them to be per se

---

1. Fed.R.Evid. 803(6) now permits the admission of diagnoses whether they are routine or speculative. The rule, however, permits the trial court to exclude a particular record where indications of trustworthiness are lacking. [Court's footnote, renumbered and partly omitted; other notes have been omitted.]

inadmissible for diagnostic purposes. In my view this was error, albeit harmless error.

NOTES

1. Commonwealth v. Campbell, 368 A.2d 1299, 1301–1303 (Pa.Super.1976): Rape. Issue: Is finding in a hospital record of spermatozoa in the prosecutrix' vagina admissible as a fact contained in a business record, or is this a medical conclusion barred by DiGiacomo, supra. Held,

> Turning to the situation at hand we feel that the court below correctly analyzed the finding of spermatozoa in the prosecutrix' vagina as one of fact. Tests to determine the presence of sperm are basic and routine and leave little room for error. Either there was spermatozoa present in her vagina or there was not. The medical records of the hospital indicated the presence of the substance. The defendant's counsel had been in contact with the doctor who had examined the prosecutrix and had not attempted to have him testify otherwise. . . .

> . . .

Dissent:

> . . .

> The hospital records offered in the present case included both entries of fact and of opinion. The entries that there was an abrasion to the left hand and no evidence of trauma to the neck, head, or extremities are entries of fact; they are indistinguishable, for example, from the entry in Platt v. John Hancock Mut. Life Ins. Co., supra, that the plaintiff's decedent had expectorated a cup of blood. The entry that there were spermatozoa in the vagina is an entry of opinion; it reports a conclusion that the untrained layman would not be competent to make; one may assume that the person who made the entry was a laboratory technician who made a vaginal smear, and after transferring the smear to a slide, examined it under a microscope. Accordingly, under the majority opinion in Commonwealth v. DiGiacomo, supra, this entry should not have been admitted, and a new trial should be granted.

> The majority reasons that admission was nevertheless proper because "defendant's counsel had been in contact with the doctor who had examined the prosecutrix and had not attempted to have him testify. . . . " These facts are in my view quite immaterial. Inadmissible hearsay does not become admissible because the party objecting to the hearsay could call the declarant. [Footnotes omitted.]

2. Taylor v. Anderson, 474 S.W.2d 541, 542–543, 545 (Tex.Civ.App.1971): Automobile collision; plaintiff claims a "whiplash" injury; record made by doctor at military hospital, "Unable to find anything on physical examination" held properly admitted. "Although our Business Records Act, Article 3737e, Tex.Rev.Civ.Stat.Ann., in unqualified terms makes a memorandum or record of a condition 'competent evidence of the . . . existence of the condition' if certain requirements relating to the making of the record are satisfied, our Supreme Court has given the statute a restricted interpretation insofar as hospital records reflecting a medical diagnosis are concerned. In Loper v. Andrews, 404 S.W.2d 300, 305 (Tex.1966), it was said that the statute permits the reception in evidence of diagnostic entries in hospital records only if 'the diagnosis records a condition resting in reasonable medical certainty.' A diagnosis rests in reasonable medical certainty if (1) it concerns a condition which is apparent and observable by all, such as a severed limb or an open wound, or (2) if it is based on facts and findings which, while requiring expert interpretation, nevertheless involve a medical condition which is well recognized and reasonably certain such as according to Loper, a diagnosis of leukemia. The net effect of Loper is to limit the admissibility of diagnostic entries to those which record diagnoses upon which competent physicians would normally agree. Eubanks v. Winn, 469 S.W.2d 292, 296 (Tex.Civ.App.—Houston, 14th Dist.1971, Ref.n.r.e.).

"In which category shall we place an entry which recites that the examining physician was 'unable to find anything.' Is this merely a routine entry consisting of a report of the 'patient's temperature, blood pressure . . ., external bruises, skin rash . . ., lacerations or injuries observable to persons generally, . . . noticeable external physical marks or defects, and similar facts not involving medical opinion . . .'? If so, then the entry is admissible as falling within the first example of a 'non-controversial' diagnosis described in Loper. . . . We find nothing in the record which would justify our setting aside the determination of the trial judge on the theory that the entry which he received in evidence shows a condition or diagnosis upon which competent doctors would likely disagree. Stated more simply, appellants have failed to establish that the trial court erred in allowing the hospital record to be read to the jury. Eubanks v. Winn, supra."

Cf. Bond v. Greenwood, 190 N.W.2d 731 (Mich.Ct.App.1971)(the entry "is in good physical condition" held admissible, as being "a general description of physical condition as distinguished from a diagnosis"). See also Johnson v. Mobile Crane Co., 463 P.2d 250 (Wash.App.1970)(diagnosis of alcoholism); Sarrio v. Reliable Contracting Co., 286 A.2d 183 (Md.1972)("drunk, had been drinking, had alcoholic breath"); Kraner v. Coastal Tank Lines, Inc., 257 N.E.2d 750 (Ohio.Ct.App.1970), rev'd, 269 N.E.2d 43 (Ohio 1971)(electroencephalogram test); Reed v. Aetna Casualty and Surety Co., 535 S.W.2d 377 (Tex.Civ.App.1976)(myositis, bursitis, arthritis; divided court); LeClaire v. Hovey, 237 N.W.2d 895 (S.D.1976)("I did not find anything very remarkable wrong with him;" divided court).

3. As to a record of a physician or hospital containing a diagnosis pertaining to the patient's mental condition, see New York Life Insurance Co. v. Taylor, 147 F.2d 297, 304 (D.C.App.1944)(leading case; "diagnosis of a psychoneurotic state involves conjecture and opinion . . . [and] must . . . be subjected to the safeguard of cross-examination of the physician who makes it."). See also Collins v. Collins, 464 S.W.2d 910 (Tex.Civ.App.1971)(opinion relating to mental incompetency cannot meet test of reasonable medical certainty). Contra: Pratt v. State, 387 A.2d 779 (Md.App.1978), aff'd, 398 A.2d 421 (Md.1979)(but reserving decision on whether report is admissible if prepared for a purpose other than treatment, especially if prepared in anticipation of litigation).

4. Must the proponent of a record containing "diagnoses" or "conclusions" establish affirmatively the qualifications of the person who expressed the opinion? Cf. Federal Rule 702. See United States v. Licavoli, 604 F.2d 613 (9th Cir.1979), cert. denied, 446 U.S. 935 (1980).

5. For an interesting case discussing problems relating to the admissibility of a physician's office records which contained abbreviations as to which the profferor did not lay a foundation see Wilson v. Bodian, 519 N.Y.S.2d 126 (2d Dept.1987).

Wadena v. Bush

Supreme Court of Minnesota, 1975.
305 Minn. 134, 232 N.W.2d 753.

■ KNUTSON, JUSTICE.

This is an appeal by defendant and third-party plaintiff, Lorraine A. Bush, from an order for judgment and order denying her motion for judgment n.o.v. or in the alternative, for a new trial in an automobile accident case.

John S. Wadena and David Deegan were passengers in a vehicle owned by John S. Wadena and driven by Byron Deegan which collided with a vehicle owned and driven by Mrs. Bush.

. . .

All of the persons involved in the accident admitted drinking intoxicating liquor on the evening prior to the collision. Mrs. Bush admitted drinking part of three drinks over the course of the evening. Diane Christopherson admitted having four or five drinks. The Deegans, John Wadena, and another friend consumed a six-pack of malt liquor that evening, but contended it was approximately five hours prior to the accident. Byron Deegan admitted having had two cans. John Wadena admitted having a can or two and two shots of whiskey. Another friend apparently had some of the malt liquor. Beer and beer cans were found in the Deegan vehicle after the crash, including an open can of malt liquor.

Respondents introduced into evidence Hennepin County General Hospital emergency room records. At the pretrial hearing the trial court granted the motions of respondents to delete from the records certain references to the alleged intoxication of respondents. Specifically, the trial court deleted an entry in a space on the hospital records for David Deegan—apparently provided for the use of "police"—which contained the word "drunk" and an entry in a space provided for "type of accident" which contained the words, "Disorderly conduct car vs. car." On the hospital record of Byron Deegan the words: "drunk," "unable to give history because of stupor," and "apparently intoxicated" were deleted, and on the record of John Wadena under the blank provided for "diagnosis" the word "Drunk" was deleted. . . .

. . .

Mrs. Bush argues that the trial court erred in deleting the portions of the records relating to the intoxicated condition of the parties in the Deegan automobile. She argues that it should have been admitted to show the negligence of the driver, Byron Deegan, and to show that the observations of passengers John Wadena and David Deegan might have been impaired on account of their intoxication. She also argues that the entries should have been admitted for impeachment purposes.

Minn.St. 600.02 of the Uniform Business Records as Evidence Act, under which the hospital records were admitted, constitutes an exception to the hearsay rule and permits the admission into evidence of certain records made in the ordinary course of business. It states:

> "A record of an act, condition, or event shall, *in so far as relevant,* be competent evidence *if the custodian or other qualified witness testified to its identity and the mode of its preparation,* and if it was made in the regular course of business, at or near the time of the act, condition, or event, and if, in the opinion of the court, the sources of information, method, and time of preparation were such as to justify its admission." (Italics supplied.)

Respondents contend that the trial court properly excluded the evidence. . . . First, the hospital entries were not medically relevant and thus were not within the scope of the Uniform Business Records as Evidence Act. Second, there was no proper foundation for the admission of the entries. . . .

This court has long taken the position that hospital entries are made within the regular course of business of the hospital under Minn.St. 600.02 only if they are germane to medical history, diagnosis, or treatment. For the purposes of this rule it does not matter whether the records are offered by plaintiff or defendant or whether they are introduced as substantive evidence or for impeachment....

Though this court has had numerous opportunities to deal with the general question of whether entries in hospital records are germane to medical history, treatment, or diagnosis, it has never considered this issue with respect to entries regarding intoxication....

. . .

... Here, the notations on the record are arguably germane to medical history, diagnosis, or treatment. In fact, counsel for Mrs. Bush made an offer of proof in an attempt to establish their contention that the emergency room personnel needed to know whether respondents were intoxicated in order to render proper treatment. Defendant Bush called Dr. Robert L. Meller for cross-examination under the rules. His connection with the parties does not appear from the record. The gist of Dr. Meller's testimony was that if a patient is brought into an emergency room in shock, it would be germane to treatment to know whether that patient was intoxicated. The combination of alcohol and shock, he said, could cause respiratory failure and death, and thus it could become necessary to administer a respiratory stimulant to such a patient. He also testified that if the patient merely needed to have facial lacerations stitched up, the amount of alcohol in his system would not be medically relevant. There was even some indication that his earlier comments applied only when the patient had been admitted in an unconscious condition. His final statements were:

"Q You are assuming that he is unconscious and you have to start from there?

"A Yes, that he'd come in—

"Q (Interrupting) Yes.

"A (Continuing)—in shock and in bad shape and you had to do something about it.

"Q If he is conscious and you are going to stitch up his face and forehead, whether he has got a high degree of alcohol or not, won't make any difference.

"A At that point."

The evidence as to the condition of the respondents when admitted to the hospital emergency room was inconclusive. A police officer testified that David Deegan was in shock after the accident. The hospital records, however, contained no such diagnosis. Instead, the diagnosis was "(1) Scalp laceration, (2) Possible fracture of nasal bridge, (3) Drunk"; the diagnosis of Byron Deegan's condition was "(1) Fracture alveolar ridge, (2) superficial laceration on chin." The diagnosis of John Wadena's condition was "Multiple lacerations—Fractured nose—Drunk." Officer Donald Hopson, who investigated the accident, stated that all of the parties were unconscious at the scene. His partner, Officer Raymond Morse, disagreed: David Deegan testified that he lost consciousness at the scene. Byron Deegan testified that he regained consciousness at General Hospital. John Wadena testified that he, too, had awakened at General Hospital. The hospital records, however, state, "no loss of consciousness" for both Byron and David Deegan. Thus, the evidence was not conclusive on the issue of whether plaintiffs' alleged intoxication was germane to the medical treatment they required.

. . .

Mrs. Bush relies upon Sarrio v. Reliable Contracting Co., Inc., 14 Md.App. 99, 286 A.2d 183 (1972), one of the few cases to consider the problem raised here in some detail. There, the trial court had admitted hospital records that showed that appellant was drunk and had alcoholic breath. The appellate court held that the notations were "pathologically germane," noting that appellant was seriously injured and suffered from a broken leg, a shoulder separation, and a cerebral concussion, and that his intoxication might well affect the course of his treatment.

Attempting to compare Sarrio to this case is difficult because of the different types of injuries suffered by the patients in question. The medical relevance of intoxication notations must turn upon the types of injuries suffered by the patient and the types of treatment contemplated by the hospital. Whether the notation is medically relevant under differing circumstances seems to be a technical question, difficult to make without expert medical testimony.

There are a few cases which appear to solve this problem by holding that the medical relevance of intoxication notations is a question of fact for the trial court and that its determination of the issue should be reversed on appeal only if clearly erroneous.

D'Amato v. Johnston, 140 Conn. 54, 97 A.2d 893 (1953), on which Mrs. Bush relies, expressly treats the question as one of fact for the trial court. There, plaintiff was admitted to the hospital emergency room with fractures and a history of unconsciousness following the accident. The hospital records contained several references to his apparent intoxication. In resolving the question of whether the entries were medically germane, the appellate court deferred to the finding of the trial court, stating:

> "In the present case, therefore, the question is whether the fact that D'Amato was intoxicated when he entered the hospital was relevant to a proper diagnosis of his injuries and a proper treatment of them. The statute provides that an entry shall be admissible '*if the trial judge shall find that it was made in the regular course of any business.*'[1] This means that the relevancy of the entries concerning D'Amato's intoxication to the hospital's business was a preliminary question of fact for the trial judge to decide. We may not interfere with the trial judge's decision unless it is one which he could not reasonably have reached. Obviously, his decision in this case was not unreasonable." (Italics supplied.) 140 Conn. 61, 97 A.2d 897.

. . .

On the facts of this case, it is very difficult to determine from the record whether the intoxication notations were medically relevant. The testimony of Dr. Robert L. Meller, the only witness called to establish their relevance, is susceptible of two determinations. Resolving the fact issue created by his testimony from the record is almost impossible. The trial court, who had the opportunity to actually hear the testimony and observe the demeanor of the doctor, would seem to be in a far better position to resolve the question of whether the notations were germane to medical history, diagnosis, or treat-

1. Our statute does not contain this provision. [Footnote is the court's, renumber- ed. Other footnotes have been omitted.]

ment. As the evidence created a fact issue, the trial court did not abuse its discretion in excluding the notations, and thus its decision should not be disturbed on appeal.

Respondents argue that the trial court could also have properly excluded the stricken portions of the hospital records on the grounds that no proper foundation had been laid for their admission. It appears that respondents are claiming that some of the comments made in the entries could have been hearsay statements of third persons . . .

. . .

. . . It seems clear that such notations are inadmissible in the absence of a showing of the identity of the person who made them and his source of information. See, Meeks v. Lunsford, 106 Ga.App. 154, 126 S.E.2d 531 (1962); Ward v. Thistleton, 32 A.D.2d 846, 302 N.Y.S.2d 339 (1969).

Because Mrs. Bush's counsel failed to make an offer of proof, the entries must be held inadmissible for want of foundation, even if they would otherwise be admissible.

NOTES

1. Ricciardi v. Children's Hospital Medical Center, 811 F.2d 18, 20–23 (1st Cir.1987)(medical malpractice suit; plaintiff claimed that his neurological difficulties stemmed from someone's negligence while he was undergoing surgery for the replacement of his aortic valve; plaintiff's only evidence of negligence consisted of a handwritten note on his medical chart, made by a neurology resident two days after the operation, which stated that an aortic cannula came out for forty to sixty seconds during the operation; the resident did not have personal knowledge of the incident and could not recall speaking with any members of the surgical team, although he assumed that he obtained the information from "professional people;" court found that note was not admissible under either the Massachusetts hospital or business records statutes or under Rule 803(6); "An unknown source is hardly trustworthy.").

2. Kelly v. Sheehan, 259 A.2d 605, 607 (Conn.1969): Plaintiff and defendant, two teen-agers alone in an automobile, are injured when the vehicle collides with a guide post. Each claims the other was the driver. Hospital record stating plaintiff was driver admitted in defendant's behalf. Held, error.

Since the enactment, in 1931 (see Cum.Sup.1935 § 1675c.), of the predecessor of § 52–180 of the General Statutes, which allows the admissibility of entries made in the regular course of business as an exception to the hearsay rule, hospital records detailing diagnosis, treatment and condition of a patient and facts helpful to understanding the medical and surgical aspects of the case have been admissible in evidence but not events or narration pertaining to the patient's resort to the hospital which have no reference to his treatment or medical or surgical history in the hospital. . . .

The mere fact that a record is generally admissible under § 52–180 "does not mean that anything and everything contained in the record is necessarily admissible in any given case." Maggi v. Mendillo, 165 A.2d 603, 605 (Conn.1960). "The real business of a hospital is the care and treatment of sick and injured persons. It is not to collect and preserve information for use in litigation. Accordingly, even though it might be the custom of a hospital to include in its records information relating to questions of

liability for injuries which had been sustained by its patients, such entries
... would not be made admissible by the statute unless they also contained
information having a bearing on diagnosis or treatment." D'Amato v.
Johnston, 97 A.2d 893, 897 (Conn.1953), 38 A.L.R.2d 772. The recital in
the hospital report that the minor plaintiff was driving the vehicle in which
he sustained his injury had no bearing on the diagnosis or treatment of his
injuries.

See also Williams v. Alexander, 129 N.E.2d 417 (N.Y.1955), in which a portion
of the hospital record containing the statement of plaintiff that "an automobile
ran into another automobile that was at a standstill causing his car ... to run
into him", was excluded by a 4 to 3 decision because it was "not germane to
diagnosis or treatment." Compare Skillern & Sons, Inc. v. Rosen, 359 S.W.2d
298 (Tex.1962)(hospital record of patient's statement that she fell while walking in the slushy snow in front of a local drug store); Pollack v. Metropolitan
Life Insurance Co., 138 F.2d 123 (3d Cir.1943), noted in 43 Mich.L.Rev. 411
(1944)(hospital record of patient's age); Mayor v. Dowsett, 400 P.2d 234
(Or.1965)(hospital record of wife's medical history obtained from husband).

3.   Cestero v. Ferrara, 273 A.2d 761 (N.J.1971): Collision at an intersection
governed by traffic lights. One driver sued the other, who counterclaimed. Each
contended that the light was green in his favor. Defendant in support of the
counterclaim, offered the hospital record stating "Pt. stopped for red light,
started up on green light and got hit". Held, admissible as an excited utterance
of patient.

Sullivan v. United States, 404 A.2d 153, 158–59 (D.C.App.1979), considers
the admissibility of an entry in a hospital record based upon complainant's
statements: "[n]o injury by accident, but after accident, in fight." Court held
that business record exception did not apply because declarant was under no
duty to relate, but statement was admissible as made for purposes of medical
diagnosis where there was "no evidence of a deliberate attempt to lay the
foundation for expert medical testimony in future litigation ... [and] no
assignment of blame." See also Felice v. Long Island Railroad Co., 426 F.2d
192, cert. denied, 400 U.S. 820 (1970). The exception for statements made for
purposes of medical diagnosis is discussed at pp. 647 to 654, above.

4.   See, Hale, Hospital Records as Evidence, 14 So.Calif.L.Rev. 99 (1941);
Braham, Case Records of Hospitals and Doctors as Evidence Under The
Business Records Act, 21 Temp.L.Q. 113 (1947); McCormick, The Use of
Hospital Records as Evidence, 26 Tul.L.Rev. 371 (1952); Pegg, Hospital Rec-
ords, 21 Ohio St.L.J. 190 (1960); Powell, Admissibility of Hospital Records Into
Evidence, 21 Md.L.Rev. 22 (1961); Arnold, Hospital and Medical Reports as
Evidence in a Personal Injury Case, 30 Ins. Counsel J. 240 (1963); Annots., 9
A.L.R.Fed. 457 (1971); 69 A.L.R.3d 22 (1976); 80 A.L.R.3d 456 (1977).

SECTION 8.   FORMER TESTIMONY

Gaines v. Thomas

Supreme Court of South Carolina, 1962.
241 S.C. 412, 128 S.E.2d 692.

■ BRAILSFORD, JUSTICE. In October of 1957, an automobile driven by William
Joseph Martin, Jr., defendant's intestate, and a truck of Peerless Mattress
Company, driven by Clyde Byars, collided on U.S. Highway # 1 in Aiken

County. Martin was killed and Melvin Gaines, the plaintiff in this action, who was working on the shoulder of the highway near the point of impact, was injured. Gaines brought this action in the Common Pleas Court for Aiken County against Martin's personal representative, and this appeal is from a judgment in his favor.

Previously, Byars, the truck driver, testified in an action in the U.S. District Court, brought by Martin's administrator against Peerless Mattress Company to recover damages for the alleged wrongful death of Martin. Byars died before the trial of this action, at which the plaintiff offered in evidence a transcript of his testimony at the previous trial. The court admitted it over the objection of the defendant. The correctness of this ruling is the first question involved here.

We must determine whether the testimony was properly admitted under the exception to the hearsay rule relating to the admission of the former testimony of a witness since deceased. The exception is generally stated to be that such testimony is admissible when the trial at which it is offered is between the same parties, or their privies, and involves the same issues. It has been applied in a long line of cases in this State (from Drayton ads. Wells, 1 Nott & McC. (10 S.C.L.) 409 in 1818 to Brown v. Bailey, 215 S.C. 175, 54 S.E.2d 769, in 1949); and identity of parties and issues has usually been referred to as necessary. Literally applied, this statement of the rule would exclude Byars' testimony, because Gaines was not a party to the former action. However, no case has been cited from this jurisdiction in which former testimony, otherwise admissible, has been rejected for lack of identity of parties when, as here, the party against whom the testimony is offered, as a party to the former action, had full opportunity to cross-examine the witness. The facts here are different from those involved in any of our prior decisions and require an examination of the rule and of the reasons for it.

These vehicles collided upon meeting each other on the open highway. At the former trial, the issue of liability depended upon the jury's conclusion as to which driver swerved across the center line and caused the collision. Byars' testimony was on this issue and he was cross-examined by counsel for the present defendant. At the trial of this action, Gaines rested his right to recover on the charge that the proximate cause of the collision, which resulted in injury to him, was the negligence of the defendant's intestate in swerving across the center line. It was on this issue that Byars' former testimony was offered and admitted. If he had been present to testify, there would have been no reason to conduct a different cross-examination from that to which he was subjected in the former trial. In short, the party against whom this testimony was received had a fair and adequate opportunity to cross-examine the witness at the former trial.

In Jones v. Charleston & W.C. Ry. Co., 144 S.C. 212, 142 S.E. 516, the following statement of the impelling reasons underlying the rule excluding hearsay testimony was quoted with approval:

"The reason for this rule of exclusion is that hearsay is not subject to the ordinary tests required by law for ascertaining its truth, the author of the statements not being subject to cross-examination in the presence of a court of justice, and not speaking under the penal sanction of an oath, there being no opportunity to investigate his character and motives, and his deportment not being subject to observation. And the misconstruction to which such evidence is exposed, from the ignorance or inattention of the hearers, or from criminal motives, is a powerful additional objection."

Where the parties and issues are the same, former testimony is free from all of these objections, except that the jury must weigh the credibility of the witness without having the opportunity to observe his demeanor on the stand. To preserve this opportunity, the witness must ordinarily appear in person. However, where he has died, the court yet has available relevant testimony, which has been delivered under oath, on the impressive occasion of a trial, at which the opposing party had the opportunity to cross-examine. The available evidence having been tested by the conventional means, the jury ought to have the benefit of it in its search for the truth. Hence, the exception letting in former testimony developed, on which all of the authorities are agreed when the parties and issues are the same.

The rule was formulated to insure fairness to the opposing party by limiting the admission of former testimony to situations in which he has had an adequate opportunity to cross-examine. The requirement that there be identity of parties and issues is but a means to that end. 31 C.J.S. Evidence § 390; Wigmore on Evidence, (3d Ed.), Section 1386. As stated in McCormick on Evidence, Sec. 232, "It is a convenient phrase to indicate a situation where the underlying requirement of adequacy of the present opponent's opportunity of cross-examination would usually be satisfied."

Our decisions have recognized that the assurance of an adequate opportunity for cross-examination by the opposing party is the end in view.

. . . .

The admission of Byars' testimony at this trial was equally as free of the objections to hearsay evidence as its use at a re-trial of the former action would have been. The facts with which we deal jibe with the rationale of the rule letting in former testimony. The "convenient phrase" must yield to the underlying principle that properly tested, relevant testimony of a deceased witness should be available to the jury, when no unfairness to the adverse party is involved. The testimony falls within this principle and was properly admitted.

. . . .

Affirmed.

NOTES

On the issue of former testimony generally, see: Martin, The Former-Testimony Exception in the Proposed Federal Rules of Evidence, 57 Iowa L.Rev. 547 (1972); Falknor, Former Testimony and the Uniform Rules: A Comment, 38 N.Y.U.L.Rev. 651 (1963); Glicksberg, Former Testimony Under The Uniform Rules of Evidence and in Florida, 10 U.Fla.L.Rev. 269 (1957); Isaksen, Use of Former Testimony, 1945 Wis.L.Rev. 445. See annotation: Admissibility or Use in Criminal Trial of Testimony Given at Preliminary Hearing by Witness Not Available at Trial, 38 A.L.R.4th 378 (1985).

Lloyd v. American Export Lines, Inc.

United States Court of Appeals, Third Circuit, 1978.
580 F.2d 1179, cert. denied, 439 U.S. 969, 99 S.Ct. 461, 58 L.Ed.2d 428 (1978).

■ ALDISERT, JUDGE.

. . . .

I.

This lawsuit emanates from a violent altercation between Alvarez and a fellow crew member, electrician Frank Lloyd, that occurred on September 7,

1974, when their ship, the SS EXPORT COMMERCE, was in the port of Yokohama, Japan. Lloyd filed an action against Export in the district court, alleging negligence under the Jones Act, 46 U.S.C. § 688, and unseaworthiness under general maritime law, seeking redress for the injuries sustained in the fight. Export joined Alvarez as a third-party defendant and Alvarez, in turn, counterclaimed against Export, alleging, as did Lloyd, negligence and unseaworthiness. Lloyd did not proceed in his case as plaintiff, failing to appear on seven occasions for a pretrial deposition, and failing to appear when the case was called for trial on November 18, 1976. Accordingly, his complaint was dismissed by the district court for failure to prosecute, and thereafter trial was had on Alvarez' counterclaim....

It was Alvarez' theory that Export negligently failed to use reasonable precautions to safeguard him from Lloyd after Export had knowledge of Lloyd's dangerous propensities. Alvarez testified ... to an incident occurring in July 1974 in the port of New York, when he ordered Lloyd to assist in loading electrical stores, and the latter refused....

Alvarez testified that on the day in question he had been ordered to perform electrical work in a resistor house aboard ship after an officer was unable to rouse Lloyd to do it. The court received into evidence a statement by Chief Officer Goslin that, prior to the fight, he went to Lloyd's quarters to inform him of a winch failure and discovered him lying fully clothed in his bunk, apparently intoxicated and unable to perform his duties. The only description of the fight that occurred when Lloyd subsequently entered the resistor house was offered by Alvarez, and is summarized in his brief as follows:

> Lloyd sneaked through the open door unnoticed by Alvarez and without any warning or provocation, Lloyd viciously attacked Alvarez, striking him in the head with an unidentified object while screaming he would "kill him." During this life-threatening struggle, Alvarez was able to pick up a turnbuckle[1] and end the fight by striking Lloyd once.

Appellee's Brief at 7.

The jury was not permitted to hear any version of the fight other than that of Alvarez; it was denied the opportunity of hearing the account rendered by Lloyd, who was the other participant in the affray and its only other eyewitness. It is the refusal of the district court to admit a public record of a prior proceeding and excerpts of Lloyd's testimony therein that constitutes the major thrust of Export's appeal. Export contends that this evidence was admissible in the form of transcripts and a final report from a Coast Guard hearing conducted intermittently from January 20, 1975 through January 6, 1976, the purpose of which was to determine whether Lloyd's merchant mariner's document should have been suspended or revoked on the basis of charges of misconduct brought against him for the fight with Alvarez. At that hearing, both Lloyd and Alvarez were represented by counsel and testified under oath.

II.

A.

[The court determines that excerpts from the transcript of the Decision and Order of the Coast Guard hearing examiner are admissible pursuant to Rule 803(8)(C) of the Federal Rules of Evidence.]

---

1. The turnbuckle wielded by Alvarez is a rod-like iron tool, approximately 2.5 feet in length, "with a screw thread at one end and a swivel at the other ... used for tightening a rod or stay." Webster's Third New International Dictionary (1961). [The footnotes are the court's and some have been omitted. Others have been renumbered.]

B.

Our examination of the transcript of Frank Lloyd's testimony at the Coast Guard hearing convinces us that it is highly relevant to the negligence issue raised by Alvarez. Because Lloyd testified not only to the incident of September 1974, but to the history of his relationship with Alvarez as well, his testimony would have been most helpful to the jury in determining the ultimate issue of whether the officers and crew of the SS EXPORT COMMERCE failed to take reasonable precautions to safeguard Alvarez against an attack by Lloyd. Indeed, Lloyd's testimony directly refuted the Alvarez theory....

. . .

C.

Alvarez objects to the admission of Lloyd's testimony on two grounds: first, there was insufficient proof that Lloyd was unavailable to testify at trial as contemplated in Rule 804(a)(5), and, second, the Coast Guard proceeding did not qualify under Rule 804(b)(1).

In order for the hearsay exceptions of Rule 804 to apply, it is required that the declarant be "unavailable"—in this case, that he be "absent from the hearing and the proponent of his statement [be] unable to procure his attendance ... by process or other reasonable means." Rule 804(a)(5). In preparation for trial, as has been noted, numerous attempts were made by Export to depose Lloyd, but he repeatedly failed to appear. Finally, on the day set for trial, Export learned that Lloyd would not appear to prosecute his case. Lloyd's counsel represented to the court that extensive efforts had been made to obtain his appearance, but they had failed, due at least in part to his seafaring occupation. Transcript at 27a–28a, Appendix Vol. I. We are satisfied that where Export and Lloyd's own counsel were unable to obtain his appearance in an action in which he had a formidable interest as a plaintiff, his unavailability status was sufficient to satisfy the requirement of Rule 804.

D.

We turn now to the more difficult question: did Alvarez or a "predecessor in interest" have the "opportunity and similar motive to develop the testimony by direct, cross or redirect examination" as required by Rule 804(b)(1)? In rejecting the proffered evidence, the district court took a strict view of the new rule, one that we do not share.

We note at the outset that inasmuch as Congress did not define "predecessor in interest", that interpretive task is left to the courts. We find no definitive guidance in the reports accompanying language changes made as the Rules were considered, in turn, by the Supreme Court and the houses of Congress. As originally submitted by the Supreme Court, Rule 804(b)(1) would have allowed prior testimony of an unavailable witness to be received in evidence if the party against whom it was offered, or a person with "motive and interest similar", had an opportunity to examine the witness. The House of Representatives adopted the present language, the Committee on the Judiciary offering this rationale:

> Rule 804(b)(1) as submitted by the Court allowed prior testimony of an unavailable witness to be admissible if the party against whom it is offered or a person "with motive and interest similar" to his had an opportunity to examine the witness. The Committee considered that it is generally unfair to impose upon the party against whom the hearsay evidence is being offered responsibility for the manner in which the witness was previously

handled by another party. The sole exception to this, in the Committee's view, is when a party's predecessor in interest in a civil action or proceeding had an opportunity and similar motive to examine the witness. The Committee amended the Rule to reflect these policy determinations.[2]

The Senate Committee on Judiciary viewed the import of this change as follows:

> Former testimony.—Rule 804(b)(1) as submitted by the Court allowed prior testimony of an unavailable witness to be admissible if the party against whom it is offered or a person "with motive and interest similar" to his had an opportunity to examine the witness.
>
> The House amended the rule to apply only to a party's predecessor in interest. Although the committee recognizes considerable merit to the rule submitted by the Supreme Court, a position which has been advocated by many scholars and judges, we have concluded that the difference between the two versions is not great and we accept the House amendment.[3]

We, too, fail to see a compelling difference between the two approaches.

In our analysis of this language change, we are aware of the basic thrust of subdivision (b) of Rule 804. It was originally designed by the Advisory Committee on Rules of Evidence of the Judicial Conference of the United States to strike a proper balance between the recognized risk of introducing testimony of one not physically present on a witness stand and the equally recognized risk of denying to the fact-finder important relevant evidence. Even in its slightly amended form as enacted by Congress, Rule 804 still serves the original intention of its drafters: "The rule expresses preferences: testimony given on the stand in person is preferred over hearsay, and hearsay, if of the specified quality, is preferred over complete loss of the evidence of the declarant."

Although Congress did not furnish us with a definition of "predecessor in interest," our analysis of the concept of interests satisfies us that there was a sufficient community of interest shared by the Coast Guard in its hearing and Alvarez in the subsequent civil trial to satisfy Rule 804(b)(1). Roscoe Pound has taught us that interests in law are "the claims or demands or desires which human beings, either individually or in groups or associations or relations, seek to satisfy...."[4] The interest implicated here was a claim or desire or demand which Alvarez as an individual, and the Coast Guard as a representative of a larger group, sought to satisfy, and which has been recognized as socially valid by authoritative decision-makers in our society.

Individual interests, like those of Alvarez, are involved immediately in the individual life, in the Pound formulation, and asserted in title of that life.[5] Public interests, like those of the Coast Guard, are involved in the life of a politically organized society, here the United States, and asserted in title of that entity.[6] Thus, Alvarez sought to vindicate his individual interest in recovering for his injuries; the Coast Guard sought to vindicate the public interest in safe

---

2. H.R.Rep. No. 650, 93rd Cong., 1st Sess. 15 (1973), Report of the House Committee on the Judiciary, reprinted in 4 J. Weinstein & M. Berger, Weinstein's Evidence, at 804–7 & 804–8.

We do not accept the view that this change in wording signalled a return to the common law approach to former testimony, requiring privity or a common property interest between the parties. See Weinstein, supra, Par. 804(b)(1)[04].

3. S.Rep. No. 1277, 93rd Cong., 2d Sess. 28 (1974), reprinted in Weinstein, supra, at 804–9.

4. Pound, A Survey of Social Interests, 57 Harv.L.Rev. 1 (1943).

5. Id. at 2.

6. Id.

and unimpeded merchant marine service. Irrespective of whether the interests be considered from the individual or public viewpoints, however, the nucleus of operative facts[7] was the same—the conduct of Frank Lloyd and Roland Alvarez aboard the SS EXPORT COMMERCE. And although the results sought in the two proceedings differed—the Coast Guard contemplated sanctions involving Lloyd's mariner's license, while Alvarez sought private substituted redress, i.e., monetary damages—the basic interest advanced by both was that of determining culpability and, if appropriate, exacting a penalty for the same condemned behavior thought to have occurred.[8] The Coast Guard investigating officer not only preferred charges against Lloyd but functioned as a prosecutor at the subsequent proceeding as well. Thus, he attempted to establish at the Coast Guard hearing what Alvarez attempted to establish at the later trial: Lloyd's intoxication, his role as the aggressor, and his prior hostility toward Alvarez. Dean Pound recognized that there can be such a community of individual and public interests as this: "It must be borne in mind that often we have here different ways of looking at the same claims or same type of claims as they are asserted in different titles."[9]

Moreover, although our precise task is to decide whether the Coast Guard investigating officer was Alvarez' predecessor in interest, it is equally important to respect always the fundamentals that underlie the hearsay rule, and the reasons for the exceptions thereto. Any fact-finding process is ultimately a search for truth and justice, and legal precepts that govern the reception of evidence must always be interpreted in light of this. Whether it be fashioned by rules of decision in cases or controversies, or promulgated by the Supreme Court with the approval of Congress, or designed and adopted by Congress, every rule of evidence is a means to an end, not an end in itself. We strive to avoid interpretations that are wooden or mechanical, like obsolete common law pleadings, and to favor those that facilitate the presentation of a complete picture to the fact-finder. With this approach in mind, we are satisfied that there existed, in the language of Rule 804(b)(1), sufficient "opportunity and similar motive [for the Coast Guard investigating officer] to develop [Lloyd's] testimony" at the former hearing to justify its admission against Alvarez at the later trial.

While we do not endorse an extravagant interpretation of who or what constitutes a "predecessor in interest," we prefer one that is realistically generous over one that is formalistically grudging. We believe that what has been described as "the practical and expedient view" expresses the congressional intention: "if it appears that in the former suit a party having a like motive to cross-examine about the same matters as the present party would have, was accorded an adequate opportunity for such examination, the testimony may be received against the present party."[10] Under these circumstances, the previous

---

7. Karl Llewellyn has defined an interest as "a social fact or factor of some kind, existing [in]dependent of the law", with "value independent of the law". Llewellyn, A Realistic Jurisprudence—The Next Step, 30 Colum.L.Rev. 430, 441 (1930).

8. In this regard, McCormick takes the position that "insistence upon precise identity of issues, which might have some appropriateness if the question were one of res judicata or estoppel by judgment, are out of place with respect to former testimony where the question is not of binding anyone, but merely of the salvaging, for what it may be worth, of

the testimony of a witness not now available in person.... It follows that neither the form of the proceeding, the theory of the case, nor the nature of the relief sought needs be the same." McCormick, Handbook of the Law of Evidence § 257 at 261 (2d ed. 1972).

9. Pound, supra, at 3.

10. McCormick, supra, § 256 at 619–20. The approach of the Federal Rules of Evidence is to examine proffered former testimony in light of the prior opportunity and motive to develop the testimony, whether in the form of direct, redirect or cross-examina-

party having like motive to develop the testimony about the same material facts is, in the final analysis, a predecessor in interest to the present party.

. . .

■ STERN, DISTRICT JUDGE, concurring.

... The majority here holds that because the Coast Guard investigating officer shared a community of interest with Alvarez he was Alvarez's predecessor in interest. I believe that this analysis is contrary to the Rule's clear language and is foreclosed by its legislative history.

I do, however, agree with the result which the majority reaches. The testimony Lloyd gave at the Coast Guard hearing should have been admitted into evidence. I would hold that it is admissible, not under 804(b)(1), but rather under the catch-all exception to the hearsay rule, 804(b)(5).

As the majority points out, the rule enacted as 804(b)(1) as originally submitted by the Supreme Court, would have permitted the introduction of former testimony if the party against whom it was offered, or a person "with motive and interest similar" to the party, had an opportunity to examine the witness. But Congress rejected this approach.

. . .

The Senate accepted the House change, although it may not have fully appreciated its significance. See S.Rep. No. 1277, 93d Cong., 2d Sess. 28 (1974), quoted in Majority op., supra, at 1185.

It is true that Congress nowhere defined "predecessor in interest," but it seems clear that this phrase, a term of art, was used in its narrow, substantive law sense. Although the commentators have expressed disapproval of this traditional and restrictive rule, they recognize that a "predecessor in interest" is defined in terms of a privity relationship.

> " 'The term "privity" denotes mutual or successive relationships to the same rights of property, and privies are distributed into several classes, according to the manner of this relationship. Thus, there are privies in estate, as donor and donee, lessor and lessee, and joint tenants; privies in blood, as heir and ancestor, and co-parceners; privies in representation, as executor and testator, administrator and intestate; privies in law, where the law, without privity of blood or estate casts the land upon another, as by escheat.' "

Metropolitan St. Ry. v. Gumby, 99 F. 192 (2d Cir.1900), quoted in 11 Moore's Federal Practice § 804.04[2], at VIII–265. See also 4 J. Weinstein & M. Berger, Weinstein's Evidence, at 804–65.

The majority rejects the view that the Rule's wording signals a return to the common law approach requiring privity or a common property interest between the parties, Majority op., supra, at 1185, n. 5, and finds it sufficient that the Coast Guard investigator shared a community of interest with Alvarez. But community of interest seems to mean only that the investigating officer sought to establish the same facts as Alvarez attempted to prove in the instant suit. Used in this sense, community of interest means nothing more than similarity of interest or similarity of motive. But similar motive is a separate prerequisite to admissibility under 804(b)(1) and thus the majority's analysis

tion. This less restrictive approach finds support among commentators. See McCormick, supra, § 255 at 617; Falknor, Former Testimony and the Uniform Rules: A Comment, 38 N.Y.U.L.Rev. 651 n. 1 (1963).

which reads "predecessor in interest" to mean nothing more than person with "similar motive" eliminates the predecessor in interest requirement entirely.

Moreover, while I appreciate the fact that the Coast Guard investigator sought to establish Lloyd's wrongdoing and that Alvarez sought to do the same, I do not believe that this establishes the kind of "common motive" sufficient to satisfy 804(b)(1).

A prosecutor or an investigating officer represents no ordinary party. He shoulders a peculiar kind of duty, even to his very adversary, a duty which is foreign to the adversarial process among ordinary litigants. The prosecutor, it is true, must seek to vindicate the rights of the alleged victim, but his interests go far beyond that. His interest in a prosecution is not that he shall win a case, but that justice shall be done. See Berger v. United States, 295 U.S. 78, 55 S.Ct. 629, 79 L.Ed. 1314 (1935).

The interests of an attorney representing the government surely overlap with those of the private litigant, but they do not coincide. The investigating officer was under no duty to advance every arguable issue against Lloyd in the vindication of Alvarez's interests, as Alvarez's own counsel would have been. He simply did not represent Alvarez.

. . . .

NOTES

1. *Predecessor in interest.* How broadly should the "predecessor in interest" requirement be construed? Given the facts in the Gaines case, supra, suppose a passenger in Martin's automobile were to bring an action against the Peerless Mattress Co. Would the defendant be able to offer in evidence a transcript of Byers' testimony at the previous trial? See Bartlett v. Kansas City Public Service Co., 160 S.W.2d 740 (Mo.1942), questioned in Falknor, The Hearsay Rule and Its Exceptions, 2 U.C.L.A.L.Rev. 43, 57–58 (1954). What would be the result pursuant to Federal Rule 804(b)(1) as submitted to the Supreme Court? Under Rule 804(b)(1) as construed by the majority in Lloyd? In this context consider the following explanation in Zenith Radio Corp. v. Matsushita Electric Industrial Co., 505 F.Supp. 1190, 1254 (E.D.Pa.1980), rev'd on related grounds, 723 F.2d 238 (3d Cir.), rev'd on other grounds, 475 U.S. 574 (1986): "In our view, it is highly significant that the 'previous party' in Lloyd was a government investigator, presumably impartial, who had no role in the subsequent legal action." See also In re Master Key Antitrust Litigation, 72 F.R.D. 108, 109 (D.Conn.), aff'd without published opinion, 551 F.2d 300 (2d Cir.1976)(court, after weighing "special considerations," concluded that the United States was a predecessor in interest of the present private plaintiffs: "The unique relationship between the Government's antitrust enforcement suits and the private actions which follow has Congressional recognition and ratification, which has in turn provided special benefits to the private plaintiffs. It has, for example, tolled the applicable statute of limitations, and thus allowed them to extend the period for which they may recover.... Furthermore, the judgment in the earlier decision will be admissible in evidence (although it too is hearsay) and serves to establish their prima facie case."). Compare the court's approach in Azalea Fleet, Inc. v. Dreyfus Supply & Machinery Co., 782 F.2d 1455, 1460–1461 (8th Cir.1986)(in a prior action arising out of property damage caused by a barge breakaway, the court had found equal liability on the part of the owner of the barges, Consolidated, and Archway, the owner of the boats towing the barges; in a second action, Consolidated was awarded indemnity from Azalea, and Azalea was granted indemnity against Dreyfus; court found no error in

Azalea's introduction of testimony that Lewis, the pilot of a harbor boat, gave at first trial; "we agree with Azalea that Consolidated was a 'predecessor in interest' of Dreyfus, with an 'opportunity and similar motive' to develop Lewis' testimony at the Eagle Marine trial. Both Consolidated in Eagle Marine and Dreyfus in this case had an interest in establishing that Archway's negligence was the sole cause of the breakaway.").

Cf. Federal Deposit Insurance Corp. v. Glickman, 450 F.2d 416 (9th Cir.1971)(in the prosecution of a federal criminal action the Government produces certain testimony; later the FDIC brings a civil action in which proof of the former testimony is offered against it. Held, the United States and FDIC are not the same person for the purposes of West's Ann.Cal.Evid.Code § 1291(a) which makes admissible against the party who formerly offered it the testimony of a witness now unavailable).

2. *Same or different proceeding.* Fleury v. Edwards, 200 N.E.2d 550, 553–54 (N.Y.1964). A collision occurs between a car driven by Fleury and another driven by defendant's wife. At a hearing held by the State Motor Vehicle Bureau to determine whether the driver's licenses or car registrations of the persons involved should be cancelled, Fleury and defendant's wife are examined and cross-examined under oath. Fleury and defendant are both represented by counsel. Fleury institutes a personal injury action against defendant. Fleury having died, his administratrix is substituted as plaintiff. Upon the trial of the action she offers to prove Fleury's testimony at the Bureau hearing. Objection under C.P.A. § 348 (later superseded by CPLR 4517). Held, though admissibility is not authorized by § 348, the evidence is nevertheless admissible under the common law which remains operative. The concurring opinion of Fuld, J. (in which all participating members of the court concur) follows:

> Death prevented a key witness from appearing at the trial of this negligence action. The testimony which he had previously given under oath upon a hearing before the Deputy Commissioner of Motor Vehicles was excluded below. We are asked, in support of that ruling, to say, in effect that, despite their responsibility to come as close as possible to the truth, the courts in civil cases are required to deny themselves the best available hearsay evidence, namely, testimony previously given under oath at an administrative hearing by the now deceased witness and tested by the cross-examination of the very party against whom it is sought to be used. Procedural rules are best calculated to serve justice if they permit admission of such testimony, provided only that the jury is adequately instructed by the court on the difficulties in evaluating hearsay and the opposing party is given an opportunity to investigate and produce evidence in derogation of the challenged hearsay. (See, e.g., Weinstein, Probative Force of Hearsay, 46 Iowa L.Rev. 331.)

> The precise issue posed, therefore, is whether the Legislature, by adopting section 348 of the Civil Practice Act (now CPLR 4517), limited the power of the courts to admit this evidence. I agree with the Chief Judge that history and the statutory scheme reveal no such limitation.

>   . . .

> Our statutory provisions cover only a few of the hearsay exceptions developed by the courts and recognized in New York. (Compare CPLR 4517–4518, 4520–4534 with Uniform Rules of Evidence, rules 62–66; Wigmore, Evidence [3d ed., 1940], vol. 5, §§ 1420–1684; vol. 6, §§ 1690–1810.) The fact, therefore, that the Legislature has adopted a rule sanctioning the admission of testimony previously given in a related "action" or "special

proceeding" does not imply a design to exclude the introduction of testimony given in an adversarial setting before an administrative officer or other administrative tribunal. (See 5 Weinstein–Korn–Miller, N.Y.Civ.Prac., par. 4517.27, at p. 45–266.)

Whether prior testimony before an administrative body would have been admissible in 1879, when the predecessor of CPLR 4517 was adopted, is not significant. The common law of evidence is constantly being refashioned by the courts of this and other jurisdictions to meet the demands of modern litigation. Exceptions to the hearsay rules are being broadened and created where necessary. (See, e.g., In re White's Will, 2 N.Y.2d 309, 160 N.Y.S.2d 841, 141 N.E.2d 416 (1957); Dallas County v. Commercial Union Assurance Co., 286 F.2d 388, 395 (5th Cir.1961)). Absent some strong public policy or a clear act of pre-emption by the Legislature, rules of evidence should be fashioned to further, not frustrate, the truth-finding function of the courts in civil cases.

Compare People v. Harding, 332 N.E.2d 354, 356–357 (N.Y.1975)(criminal statute which admits only former testimony given at a trial, a hearing on a felony complaint, or a conditional examination, is exclusive so that testimony given at a police disciplinary hearing should not have been admitted, distinguishing Fleury—although the error was harmless). Cf. People v. Okafor, 495 N.Y.S.2d 895 (1985)(in murder prosecution in which defendant admitted firing gun but claimed that he had not intended to hurt wife, court admitted former testimony of wife at Family Court hearing in which she testified to defendant's threats to kill her; court held that although Harding case does not authorize use of testimony, defendant by his own misconduct waived his right to object to evidence otherwise barred by criminal statute; court relied on Mastrangelo line of cases, infra at p. 760).

3. *Similar motive.* In State v. Ayers, 468 A.2d 606, 610, 611 (Me.1983), cert. denied, 466 U.S. 941 (1984), defendant and Donald Ayers, whom she subsequently married, were convicted of the murder of her husband. The defendants both testified and were found guilty. After the convictions were reversed, Barbara Ayers was separately retried. When Donald refused to testify, the court admitted his prior testimony describing the murder plot and the commission of the crime. On appeal, Barbara argued that she did not have a similar motive to develop the testimony at the first trial because she had then relied on a justification defense, but was now attempting to show that others had committed the murder:

> The "opportunity and similar motive" test of Rule 804(b)(1) has been usefully analyzed in terms of whether "an attorney making every effort within reason [at the prior trial] to bring out facts on behalf of his client might have developed the testimony fully." Martin, The Former–Testimony Exception in the Proposed Federal Rules of Evidence, 57 Iowa L.Rev. 547, 559 (1972)(emphasis in original). The author noted: It is unfair to hold a party to the former examination if no reasonable attorney would be expected to have elicited the now-relevant facts; but if the circumstances were such that those facts could have been brought out if they were available, the present opponent can fairly be held. Id. (emphasis added). The author further states that any inquiry into matters of tactical choice is precluded; that "it is ... indisputable that no authority considers them sufficient factors for excluding former testimony; the question is always phrased in terms of 'opportunity' and 'motive and interest,' rather than 'actual examination' and 'ability' to develop the testimony fully." Id. As so analyzed, the trial justice's preliminary determination on the admissibility

of prior testimony is a fact-finding, subject to review only for clear error. We can find no such error in the admission against Barbara Ayers of the prior testimony of Donald Ayers directly incriminating her in the murder for which she was standing trial in both cases.

Dissent: First, it is simplistic indeed to suggest, as the majority does, that guilt or innocence was "all-encompassing" and "the identical issue of both trials." They close their eyes to the fact that if a new trial is to be just that, client and counsel must have the opportunity to decide anew the trial strategy to be pursued.

Second, after the defense has settled upon their strategy for a jury trial, it is unrealistic to imply, as today's majority does, that instead of presenting their case in the manner and with a selectivity counsel deem most persuasive to the jury, they must digress by cross-examining witnesses at length on matters not relevant to the issues of the day, all at the peril that at some possible second trial the witnesses' former testimony would be admitted on the "all-encompassing" issue of "guilt or innocence." Jury persuasion becomes subordinated to making a record for an appellate court.

See also Hannah v. Overland, Mo., 795 F.2d 1385 (8th Cir.1986). P brought a § 1983 action alleging that he had been arrested without probable cause on a murder charge and that the police had used excessive force in arresting him. At trial, court excluded the depositions of two persons, taken in connection with the murder prosecution, in which they stated that they felt they were being pressured and threatened by the police to implicate P in the murder. A prosecutor represented the State at the depositions, but no representatives of the defendants were present. Affirmed: even assuming that the prosecutor was a "predecessor in interest" of the defendants, the prosecutor did not have a similar motive to develop the testimony at the deposition. At the time the State thought it had sufficient evidence to prove P guilty, and the deposition testimony posed little danger to the State's case.

In Lohrmann v. Pittsburgh Corning Corp., 782 F.2d 1156 (4th Cir.1986), the court excluded a deposition given in an action claiming that defendant had failed to protect its plant workers from the hazardous effects of raw asbestos in a manufacturing environment. In the second case, plaintiff was a pipefitter who worked in close proximity to processed asbestos products. Court noted that the state of the art differs considerably with regard to the health of plant workers exposed to raw asbestos and persons working in the vicinity of asbestos products and that this distinction was not relevant in the first case.

Commonwealth v. Canon, 368 N.E.2d 1181, 1185 (Mass.1977), cert. denied, 435 U.S. 933 (1978):

The defendant contends that evidence given at a prior civil trial is not admissible at a subsequent criminal trial, since the parties and issues are not the same. We disagree. There is no requirement of "privity," "reciprocity," or "mutuality"; it is only the party against whom the prior testimony is now offered whose presence in the prior suit is significant. See McCormick, Evidence § 256 (2d ed. 1972); 5 J. Wigmore, Evidence § 1388 (Chadbourn rev. 1974). The significant feature is whether that party had an adequate opportunity for cross-examination at the prior trial. . . .

. . . The defendant in the present case called Curley as a witness in the prior civil case, and was entitled to cross-examine him as an adverse party. G.L. c. 233, § 22. The substantial question is whether the defendant then had an adequate motive for the testing on cross-examination of the credibility of Curley's testimony. See 4 J. Weinstein & M. Berger, supra, par. 804(b)(1)[04]; McCormick, supra, § 257. The defendant was the plaintiff in the civil case, and Curley as one of the defendants in the civil case was defending on the ground that the agreement of the parties was illegal by reason of violation of G.L. c. 268A. That issue was substantially the same as the issue tried in the present case. It is not fatal that, as a tactical matter, the examination of Curley at the civil trial was primarily directed to the formation and terms of the agreement rather than to its illegality. Cf. Poe v. Turner, 490 F.2d 329, 331 (10th Cir.1974)(cross-examination waived "on a matter that was not a real issue"). The formation and terms of the agreement were very damaging to the defendant on the issue of illegality in both trials.

4. *Opportunity.* United States v. Feldman, 761 F.2d 380 (7th Cir.1985)(at the defendants' criminal trial for wire fraud in connection with the sale of precious metal futures, the government introduced a deposition of a former business associate taken without any cross-examination in an earlier civil "disgorgement" proceeding brought against the defendants by the Commodity Futures Trading Commission; defendants had not been indicted at the time of the deposition and neither defendant had attended the deposition nor was represented by counsel at the deposition although they were represented by counsel at the time; unknown to the defendants, the deponent had agreed to testify against them in return for a promise that he would not be a target of a grand jury investigation; lower court found that the defendants had an adequate opportunity to appear; reversed; there must be a perceived "real need or incentive to thoroughly cross-examine," quoting United States v. Franklin, 235 F.Supp. 338, 341 (D.D.C.1964)).

See also People v. Brock, 695 P.2d 209, 219 (Cal.1985)(court excluded preliminary hearing testimony given by patient in the hospital where the witness' physical and mental condition precluded meaningful cross-examination).

United States v. King, 552 F.2d 833, 844 (9th Cir.1976), cert. denied, 430 U.S. 966 (1977): Videotape deposition of two Ws in prison in Japan. After four days, defendants and their counsel left because of restrictive conditions imposed by the Japanese government.

> By absenting themselves from the proceedings, by failing to avail themselves of the opportunity to cross-examine the Government witnesses, even if under less than perfect conditions, the appellants intentionally and knowingly gave up both the right to be present and to object to future use of the testimony. It was a calculated act, undertaken with knowledge of the potential consequences. Appellants argue, however, that they gave up no *existing* rights since alleged constitutional defects emasculated the rights in any event. Since we have already found the exercise of those rights not to have been unconstitutionally infringed upon, the waiver was effective.

> Section 3503 itself supports this result. It provides that "failure, absent good cause shown, to appear after notice and tender of expenses shall constitute a waiver of [the] right [to be present] and of any objection to the taking and use of the deposition based upon that right." 18 U.S.C. § 3503(b). Since appellants can offer no reason for their absence other than the alleged harassments which we have found not to be constitutionally infirm, they have not shown "good cause" and have waived objections to the further taking and use of deponents' testimony.

5. *Depositions.* A jurisdiction's hearsay exception for prior testimony may not be the exclusive means by which a deposition becomes admissible at trial. See, e.g., Complaint of Bankers Trust Co., 752 F.2d 874, 888 n. 17 (3d Cir. 1984)("The exceptions to the requirement of oral testimony at trial appearing in Rule 32 and in the Federal Rules of Evidence are cumulative. Thus, even though a deposition does not fall within the exceptions to the hearsay rule set forth in Rule 804 of the Federal Rules of Evidence, it is admissible if it falls within the provisions of Rule 32(a)(3).").

See also Federal Rule of Civil Procedure 28(b) on taking depositions abroad ("evidence obtained in response to a letter of request need not be excluded merely because it is not a verbatim transcript, because the testimony was not taken under oath, or because of any similar departure from the requirements for depositions taken within the United States under these rules."). The interrelationship between Rule 28 and the Hague Convention on the Taking of Evidence Abroad in Civil or Commercial Matters is extensively explored in Societe Nationale Industrielle Aerospatiale v. United States District Court for the Southern District of Iowa, 482 U.S. 522 (1987)(majority holds that Convention does not provide the exclusive and mandatory procedure for obtaining information located within territory of foreign signatory, but is one method of seeking evidence that a court may elect to employ). Rule 28(b) was amended in 1993 to incorporate language from the Hague Convention and to provide that depositions may be taken in a foreign country "pursuant to any applicable treaty or convention." For an extensive discussion of the procedures that were prescribed to ensure fairness when a key prosecution witness who was incarcerated in France was deposed there pursuant to letters rogatory see United States v. Salim, 664 F.Supp. 682 (E.D.N.Y.1987), aff'd, 855 F.2d 944 (2d Cir.1988)(although defense counsel was not permitted to be present, the French court conducting the deposition asked questions which had been submitted in writing by the attorneys for both sides; defense counsel had an opportunity to confer with his client in person and by phone during the course of the deposition proceedings and proposed additional questions; because she was incarcerated, French law did not permit deponent to be sworn).

The admissibility of videotaped depositions in a criminal proceeding is considered in State v. Washington, 494 A.2d 335 (N.J.Super.Ct.App.Div.1985).

Note, Admissibility of Prior–Action Depositions and Former Testimony under Federal Rules of Civil Procedure 32(a)(4) and Federal Rules of Evidence 804(b)(1): Courts' Differing Interpretations, 41 Wash. & Lee L.Rev. 155 (1984); Annot., Admissibility of depositions under Federal Evidence Rule 804(b)(1), 84 A.L.R.Fed. 668 (1987).

6. *Objections.* If a deposition satisfies the exception for former testimony is the opponent precluded from raising other evidentiary objections? See Moss v. Ole South Real Estate, Inc., 933 F.2d 1300, 1311–12 (5th Cir.1991): In a civil rights action, the plaintiffs offered the deposition of Johnson, a HUD investigator, who was unavailable as a witness.

> [P]arts of Johnson's deposition should have been admitted. The relevant parts of Johnson's deposition, i.e. not the sections involving her investigatory technique or the results of her investigation, primarily addressed what individuals told her about the case. These quoted statements in Johnson's deposition are a classic example of hearsay within hearsay. Both levels of hearsay must conform to a hearsay exception to be admissible. See Fed. R. Evid. 805. The first level of hearsay consists of Johnson's statements as to what people told her. These statements are hearsay because the declarant, Johnson, who is not available as a witness, made the statements outside of the courtroom, and because the statements are offered to prove the truth of the matters asserted. Fed. R. Evid. 801. Johnson's statements, however,

are excluded from the application of the hearsay rule under Rule 804(b)(1)
. . .

The second level of hearsay consists of the statements made by other
persons to Johnson. These statements are generally inadmissible as hearsay, even though they were reported in the Johnson deposition, because
they are statements made outside the courtroom and are offered to prove
the truth of the matter asserted. See Fed. R. Evid. 801, 802. If parties to
the lawsuit or agents of the parties made the statements, however, the
statements are not within the definition of hearsay and are admissible
against the parties. Fed. R. Evid. 801(d)(2).

The defendants can still argue that such statements are inadmissible
under other evidence rules, i.e., the statements may be irrelevant, cumulative, or unduly prejudicial. We properly leave these determinations to the
trial court.[1]

Does the court's reasoning as to permissible objections to admitting a
deposition apply equally to admitting testimony from a previous trial? Consider
Paulk v. Housing Authority of City of Tupelo, 228 So.2d 871 (Miss.1969); Bauer
v. Pullman Co., 239 N.E.2d 226 (Ohio App.1968)(effect of supervening changes
between the two trials creating need for further cross-examination at second
trial); Monahan v. Monahan, 289 N.Y.S.2d 812 (1968)(inadequate opportunity
for cross-examination at prior trial because witness was emotionally upset). A
careful study of problems of waiver is Letwin, Waiver of Objections to Former
Testimony, 15 U.C.L.A.L.Rev. 118 (1967).

Ohio v. Roberts

Supreme Court of the United States, 1980.
448 U.S. 56, 100 S.Ct. 2531, 65 L.Ed.2d 597.

■ MR. JUSTICE BLACKMUN delivered the opinion of the Court.

This case presents issues concerning the constitutional propriety of the
introduction in evidence of the preliminary hearing testimony of a witness not
produced at the defendant's subsequent state criminal trial.

I

Roberts was charged with forgery of a check in the name of Bernard Isaacs,
and with possession of stolen credit cards belonging to Isaacs and his wife Amy.

A preliminary hearing was held in Municipal Court on January 10. The
prosecution called several witnesses, including Mr. Isaacs. Respondent's appointed counsel had seen the Isaacs' daughter, Anita, in the courthouse
hallway, and called her as the defense's only witness. Anita Isaacs testified that
she knew respondent, and that she had permitted him to use her apartment for
several days while she was away. Defense counsel questioned Anita at some
length and attempted to elicit from her an admission that she had given
respondent checks and the credit cards without informing him that she did not
have permission to use them. Anita, however, denied this. Respondent's attorney did not ask to have the witness declared hostile and did not request
permission to place her on cross-examination. The prosecutor did not question
Anita.

1. [Footnote of the court omitted.]

A county grand jury subsequently indicted respondent for forgery, for receiving stolen property (including the credit cards), and for possession of heroin. The attorney who represented respondent at the preliminary hearing withdrew upon becoming a Municipal Court Judge, and new counsel was appointed for Roberts.

Between November 1975 and March 1976, five subpoenas for four different trial dates were issued to Anita at her parents' Ohio residence. The last three carried a written instruction that Anita should "call before appearing." She was not at the residence when these were executed. She did not telephone and she did not appear at trial.

In March 1976, the case went to trial before a jury in the Court of Common Pleas. Respondent took the stand and testified that Anita Isaacs had given him her parents' checkbook and credit cards with the understanding that he could use them. Tr. 231–232. Relying on Ohio Rev.Code Ann. § 2945.49 (1975), which permits the use of preliminary examination testimony of a witness who "cannot for any reason be produced at the trial," the State, on rebuttal, offered the transcript of Anita's testimony. Tr. 273–274.

Asserting a violation of the Confrontation Clause and indeed, the unconstitutionality thereunder of § 2945.49, the defense objected to the use of the transcript. The trial court conducted a voir dire hearing as to its admissibility. Tr. 194–199. Amy Isaacs, the sole witness at voir dire, was questioned by both the prosecutor and defense counsel concerning her daughter's whereabouts. Anita, according to her mother, left home for Tucson, Ariz., soon after the preliminary hearing. About a year before the trial, a San Francisco social worker was in communication with the Isaacs about a welfare application Anita had filed there. Through the social worker, the Isaacs reached their daughter once by telephone. Since then, however, Anita had called her parents only one other time and had not been in touch with her two sisters. When Anita called, some seven or eight months before trial, she told her parents that she "was traveling" outside Ohio, but did not reveal the place from which she called. Mrs. Isaacs stated that she knew of no way to reach Anita in case of an emergency. App. 9. Nor did she "know of anybody who knows where she is." Id. at 11. The trial court admitted the transcript into evidence. Respondent was convicted on all counts. [The conviction was overturned on appeal].

II

A

The Court here is called upon to consider once again the relationship between the Confrontation Clause and the hearsay rule with its many exceptions. . . .

B

. . .

Reflecting its underlying purpose to augment accuracy in the factfinding process by ensuring the defendant an effective means to test adverse evidence, the Clause countenances only hearsay marked with such trustworthiness that "there is no material departure from the reason of the general rule." Snyder v. Massachusetts, 291 U.S., at 107, 54 S.Ct., at 333. The principle recently was formulated in Mancusi v. Stubbs:

> "The focus of the Court's concern has been to insure that there 'are indicia of reliability which have been widely viewed as determinative of whether a statement may be placed before the jury though there is no

confrontation of the declarant,' Dutton v. Evans, supra, at 89, 91 S.Ct., at 220 and to 'afford the trier of fact a satisfactory basis for evaluating the truth of the prior statement,' California v. Green, supra, 399 U.S., at 161, 90 S.Ct., at 1936. It is clear from these statements, and from numerous prior decisions of this Court, that even though the witness be unavailable his prior testimony must bear some of these 'indicia of reliability.'" 408 U.S., at 213, 92 S.Ct., at 2313.

. . .

III

A

. . .

This passage and others in the Green opinion suggest that the opportunity to cross-examine at the preliminary hearing—even absent actual cross-examination—satisfies the Confrontation Clause. Yet the record showed, and the Court recognized, that defense counsel in fact had cross-examined Porter at the earlier proceeding. Id., at 151, 90 S.Ct., at 1931. Thus, MR. JUSTICE BRENNAN, writing in dissent, could conclude only that "[p]erhaps" "the mere opportunity for face-to-face encounter [is] sufficient." Id., at 200, n. 8, 90 S.Ct., at 1957. See Note, 52 Texas L.Rev. 1167, 1170 (1974).

We need not decide whether the Supreme Court of Ohio correctly dismissed statements in Green suggesting that the mere opportunity to cross-examine rendered the prior testimony admissible. See Westen, The Future of Confrontation, 77 Mich.L.Rev. 1185, 1211 (1979)(issue is "truly difficult to resolve under conventional theories of confrontation"). Nor need we decide whether *de minimis* questioning is sufficient, for defense counsel in this case tested Anita's testimony with the equivalent of significant cross-examination.

B

Counsel's questioning clearly partook of cross-examination as a matter of form. His presentation was replete with leading questions,[2] the principal tool and hallmark of cross-examination. In addition, counsel's questioning comported with the principal purpose of cross-examination: to challenge "whether the declarant was sincerely telling what he believed to be the truth, whether the declarant accurately perceived and remembered the matter he related, and whether the declarant's intended meaning is adequately conveyed by the language he employed." Davenport, The Confrontation Clause and the Co-Conspirator Exception in Criminal Prosecutions: A Functional Analysis, 85 Harv.L.Rev. 1378 (1972). Anita's unwillingness to shift the blame away from respondent became discernible early in her testimony. Yet counsel continued to explore the underlying events in detail. He attempted, for example, to establish that Anita and respondent were sharing an apartment, an assertion that was critical to respondent's defense at trial and that might have suggested ulterior personal reasons for unfairly casting blame on respondent. At another point, he directly challenged Anita's veracity by seeking to have her admit that she had given the credit cards to respondent to obtain a television. When Anita denied

---

2. No less than 17 plainly leading questions were asked, as indicated by phrases in counsel's inquiries: "is[n't] it a fact . . . that"; "is it to your knowledge, then, that . . ."; "is[n't] that correct"; "you never gave them . . ."; "this wasn't then in the pack . . ."; "you have never [not] seen [discussed; talked] . . ."; "you never gave . . . ."

this, defense counsel elicited the fact that the only television she owned was a "Twenty Dollar ... old model." App.21. Cf. Davis v. Alaska, 415 U.S. 308, 316–317, 94 S.Ct. 1105, 1110–1111, 39 L.Ed.2d 347 (1974).

Respondent argues that, because defense counsel never asked the court to declare Anita hostile, his questioning necessarily occurred on direct examination. See State v. Minneker, 27 Ohio St.2d 155, 271 N.E.2d 821 (1971). But however state law might formally characterize the questioning of Anita, it afforded "substantial compliance with the purposes behind the confrontation requirement," Green, 399 U.S., at 166, 90 S.Ct., at 1939, no less so than classic cross-examination. Although Ohio law may have authorized objection by the prosecutor or intervention by the court, this did not happen. As in Green, respondent's counsel was not "significantly limited in any way in the scope or nature of his cross-examination." Ibid.

We are also unpersuaded that Green is distinguishable on the ground that Anita Isaacs—unlike the declarant Porter in Green—was not personally available for questioning at trial. This argument ignores the language and logic of Green:

> "Porter's statement would, we think, have been admissible at trial even in Porter's absence if Porter had been actually unavailable.... That being the case, we do not think a different result should follow where the witness is actually produced." Id., at 165, 90 S.Ct., at 1938–39.

Nor does it matter that, unlike Green, respondent had a different lawyer at trial from the one at the preliminary hearing. Although one might strain one's reading of Green to assign this factor some significance, respondent advances no reason of substance supporting the distinction. Indeed, if we were to accept this suggestion, Green would carry the seeds of its own demise; under a "same attorney" rule, a defendant could nullify the effect of Green by obtaining new counsel after the preliminary hearing was concluded.

Finally, we reject respondent's attempt to fall back on general principles of confrontation, and his argument that this case falls among those in which the Court must undertake a particularized search for "indicia of reliability." Under this theory, the factors previously cited—absence of face-to-face contact at trial, presence of a new attorney, and the lack of classic cross-examination—combine with considerations uniquely tied to Anita to mandate exclusion of her statements. Anita, respondent says, had every reason to lie to avoid prosecution or parental reprobation. Her unknown whereabouts is explicable as an effort to avoid punishment, perjury, or self-incrimination. Given these facts, her prior testimony falls on the unreliable side, and should have been excluded.

In making this argument, respondent in effect asks us to disassociate preliminary hearing testimony previously subjected to cross-examination from previously cross-examined prior-trial testimony, which the Court has deemed generally immune from subsequent confrontation attack. Precedent requires us to decline this invitation. In Green the Court found guarantees of trustworthiness in the accouterments of the preliminary hearing itself; there was no mention of the inherent reliability or unreliability of Porter and his story. See also Mancusi v. Stubbs, 408 U.S., at 216, 92 S.Ct., at 2314.

In sum, we perceive no reason to resolve the reliability issue differently here than the Court did in Green. "Since there was an adequate opportunity to cross-examine [the witness], and counsel ... availed himself of that opportunity, the transcript ... bore sufficient 'indicia of reliability' and afforded ' "the trier of fact a satisfactory basis for evaluating the truth of prior statement." ' " 408 U.S., at 216, 92 S.Ct., at 2314.[3]

IV

Our holding that the Supreme Court of Ohio erred in its "indicia of reliability" analysis does not fully dispose of the case, for respondent would defend the judgment on an alternative ground. The State, he contends, failed to lay a proper predicate for admission of the preliminary hearing transcript by its failure to demonstrate that Anita Issacs was not available to testify in person at the trial. All the justices of the Supreme Court of Ohio rejected this argument. 55 Ohio St.2d, at 195 and 199, 378 N.E.2d, at 495 and 497.

A

The basic litmus of Sixth Amendment unavailability is established: "[A] witness is not 'unavailable' for purposes of the ... exception to the confrontation requirement unless the prosecutorial authorities have made a good-faith effort to obtain his presence at trial." Barber v. Page, 390 U.S., at 724–725, 88 S.Ct., at 1322 (emphasis added). Accord, Mancusi v. Stubbs, supra; California v. Green, 399 U.S., at 161–162, 165, 167, n. 16, 90 S.Ct., at 1936–1937, 1938–1939, n. 16; Berger v. California, 393 U.S. 314, 89 S.Ct. 540, 21 L.Ed.2d 508 (1969).

Although it might be said that the Court's prior cases provide no further refinement of this statement of the rule, certain general propositions safely emerge. The law does not require the doing of a futile act. Thus, if no possibility of procuring the witness exists (as, for example, the witness' intervening death), "good faith" demands nothing of the prosecution. But if there is a possibility, albeit remote, that affirmative measures might produce the declarant, the obligation of good faith may demand their effectuation. "The lengths to which the prosecution must go to produce a witness ... is a question of reasonableness." California v. Green, 399 U.S., at 189, n. 22, 90 S.Ct., at 1951 (concurring opinion, citing Barber v. Page, supra). The ultimate question is whether the witness is unavailable despite good-faith efforts undertaken prior to trial to locate and present that witness. As with other evidentiary proponents, the prosecution bears the burden of establishing this predicate.

---

3. We need not consider whether defense counsel's questioning at the preliminary hearing surmounts some inevitably nebulous threshold of "effectiveness." In Mancusi, to be sure, the Court explored to some extent the adequacy of counsel's cross-examination at the earlier proceeding. See 408 U.S., at 214–215, 92 S.Ct., at 2313–2314. That discussion, however, must be read in light of the fact that the defendant's representation at the earlier proceeding, provided by counsel who had been appointed only four days prior thereto, already had been held to be ineffective. See id., at 209, 92 S.Ct. at 2311. Under those unusual circumstances, it was necessary to explore the character of the actual cross-examination to ensure that an adequate opportunity for full cross-examination had been afforded to the defendant. Cf.

Pointer v. Texas, 380 U.S., at 407, 85 S.Ct., at 1069. We hold that in all but such extraordinary cases, no inquiry into "effectiveness" is required. A holding that every case involving prior testimony requires such an inquiry would frustrate the principal objective of generally validating the prior-testimony exception in the first place—increasing certainty and consistency in the application of the Confrontation Clause.

The statement in Mancusi quoted in the text indicates the propriety of this approach. To the same effect is Mattox v. United States, 156 U.S., at 244, 15 S.Ct., at 340. ("The substance of the constitutional protection is preserved to the prisoner in the advantage he has once had of seeing the witness face to face, and of subjecting him to the ordeal of a cross-examination").

B

On the facts presented we hold that the trial court and the Supreme Court of Ohio correctly concluded that Anita's unavailability, in the constitutional sense, was established.

At the voir dire hearing, called for by the defense, it was shown that some four months prior to the trial the prosecutor was in touch with Amy Isaacs and discussed with her Anita's whereabouts. It may appropriately be inferred that Mrs. Isaacs told the prosecutor essentially the same facts to which she testified at voir dire: that the Isaacs had last heard from Anita during the preceding summer; that she was not then in San Francisco, but was traveling outside Ohio; and that the Isaacs and their other children knew of no way to reach Anita even in an emergency. This last fact takes on added significance when it is recalled that Anita's parents earlier had undertaken affirmative efforts to reach their daughter when the social worker's inquiry came in from San Francisco. This is not a case of parents abandoning all interest in an absent daughter.

The evidence of record demonstrates that the prosecutor issued a subpoena to Anita at her parents' home, not only once, but on five separate occasions over a period of several months. In addition, at the voir dire argument, the prosecutor stated to the court that respondent "witnessed that I have attempted to locate, I have subpoenaed, there has been a voir dire of the witness' parents, and they have not been able to locate her for over a year." App. 12.

Given these facts, the prosecution did not breach its duty of good-faith effort. To be sure, the prosecutor might have tried to locate by telephone the San Francisco social worker with whom Mrs. Isaacs had spoken many months before and might have undertaken other steps in an effort to find Anita. One, in hindsight, may always think of other things. Nevertheless, the great improbability that such efforts would have resulted in locating the witness, and would have led to her production at trial, neutralizes any intimation that a concept of reasonableness required their execution. We accept as a general rule, of course, the proposition that "the possibility of a refusal is not the equivalent of asking and receiving a rebuff." Barber v. Page, 390 U.S., at 724, 88 S.Ct., at 1322, quoting from the dissenting opinion in that case in the Court of Appeals (381 F.2d 479, 481 (C.A.10 1966)). But the service and ineffectiveness of the five subpoenas and the conversation with Anita's mother were far more than mere reluctance to face the possibility of a refusal. It was investigation at the last-known real address, and it was conversation with a parent who was concerned about her daughter's whereabouts.

Barber and Mancusi v. Stubbs, supra, are the cases in which this Court has explored the issue of constitutional unavailability. Although each is factually distinguishable from this case, Mancusi provides significant support for a conclusion of good-faith effort here,[4] and Barber has no contrary significance. Insofar as this record discloses no basis for concluding that Anita was abroad, the case is factually weaker than Mancusi; but it is stronger than Mancusi in

---

4. In Mancusi, the declarant "who had been born in Sweden but had become a naturalized American citizen, had returned to Sweden and taken up permanent residence there." 408 U.S., at 209, 92 S.Ct., at 2311. While in this country, he had testified against Stubbs at his Tennessee trial for murder and kidnaping. Stubbs was convicted, but obtained habeas corpus relief 10 years later, and was retried by Tennessee. Before the second trial, the prosecution sent a subpoena to be served in Texas, the declarant's last place of residence in this country. It could not be served. The Court rejected Stubbs' assertion that the prosecution had not undertaken good-faith efforts in failing to do more. "Tennessee ... was powerless to compel his attendance ... either through its own process or through established procedures." Id., at 212, 92 S.Ct., at 2313.

the sense that the Ohio prosecutor, unlike the prosecutor in Mancusi, had no clear indication, if any at all, of Anita's whereabouts. In Barber, the Court found an absence of good-faith effort where the prosecution made no attempt to secure the presence of a declarant incarcerated in a federal penitentiary in a neighboring State. There, the prosecution knew where the witness was, procedures existed whereby the witness could be brought to the trial, and the witness was not in a position to frustrate efforts to secure his production. Here, Anita's whereabouts were not known, and there was no assurance that she would be found in a place from which she could be forced to return to Ohio.

We conclude that the prosecution carried its burden of demonstrating that Anita was constitutionally unavailable for purposes of respondent's trial.

The judgment of the Supreme Court of Ohio is reversed, and the case is remanded for further proceedings not inconsistent with this opinion.

It is so ordered.

■ MR. JUSTICE BRENNAN, with whom MR. JUSTICE MARSHALL and MR. JUSTICE STEVENS join, dissenting.

In the present case, I am simply unable to conclude that the prosecution met its burden of establishing Anita Isaacs' unavailability. From all that appears in the record—and there has been no suggestion that the record is incomplete in this respect—the State's *total* effort to secure Anita's attendance at respondent's trial consisted of the delivery of five subpoenas in her name to her parents' residence, and three of those were issued after the authorities had learned that she was no longer living there. At least four months before the trial began, the prosecution was aware that Anita had moved away; yet during that entire interval it did nothing whatsoever to try to make contact with her. It is difficult to believe that the State would have been so derelict in attempting to secure the witness' presence at trial had it not had her favorable preliminary hearing testimony upon which to rely in the event of her "unavailability." The perfunctory steps which the State took in this case can hardly qualify as a "good-faith effort." In point of fact, it was no effort at all.

.   .   .

NOTES

1. *Defendant's "opportunity and similar motive" in preliminary hearings.* Rodriguez v. State, 711 P.2d 410, 413–14 (Wyo.1985):

The key question, then, is whether appellant's motive to cross-examine Mrs. McIntosh at the preliminary hearing was similar to the motive he would have had to cross-examine her at trial. The courts of other states have approached the question in three ways. They have held that defense attorneys never have similar motives to cross-examine at both preliminary hearings and trials; that defense attorneys always have similar motives to cross-examine at preliminary hearings and trials; and that defense attorneys' motives at preliminary hearings and trials must be compared on a case-by-case basis.

The Colorado Supreme Court has held that a defense attorney never has a motive to cross-examine a witness at a preliminary hearing which is similar to his motive to cross-examine that witness at trial. In People v. Smith, 597 P.2d 204, 207 (Colo.1979), the Colorado court stated that a preliminary hearing has the limited purpose of establishing probable cause. In most cases, even the most searching cross-examination will not prevent a finding of probable cause which is a considerably lesser burden of proof than the reasonable-doubt standard required at trial. Therefore, according to the Colorado court, defense attorneys will rarely, if ever, waste their time with effective cross-examination at the preliminary hearing. They will wait until trial where they will be highly motivated to attack the credibility of the witness in front of the jury.

The Colorado court's position is rejected by a majority of states. 4 Louisell and Mueller, Federal Evidence § 487, p. 1092 (1980). Most courts that have decided the issue have refused to adopt a per se rule against admission of preliminary hearing testimony at trial. In fact, several courts have held that preliminary hearing testimony is always admissible at trial if the declarant is unavailable. They reason that a defense attorney's "motive and interest are the same" in both the preliminary hearing and trial settings. Defense counsel "acts in both situations in the interest of and [is] motivated by establishing the innocence of the client." State v. Brooks, 638 P.2d 537, 541 (Utah 1981). See also, State v. Martinez, 691 P.2d 887, 889 (N.M.App.1984).

Unlike the Colorado, New Mexico, and Utah courts, the Supreme Court of Arkansas has refused to adopt a per se rule of either admission or exclusion of former testimony from a preliminary hearing. That court has held that the "similar motive" requirement of the former-testimony exception should be analyzed on a case-by-case basis. Scott v. State, 612 S.W.2d 110, 113 (Ark.1981). In Scott, the Arkansas court held that preliminary hearing testimony should not have been admitted at trial under the facts of that case, but, in the proper case, preliminary hearing testimony would be admissible.

We adopt the case-by-case approach taken by the Arkansas court. There will undoubtedly be cases in which preliminary hearing testimony should not be admitted at trial because the defense attorney did not have a similar motive to cross-examine the witness at the preliminary hearing but has a compelling motive to undertake that cross-examination at trial. There will also be cases, like the case at bar, in which the defense attorney has a motive at the preliminary hearing to cross-examine the witness which is similar to his motive to cross-examine at trial. The motive may exist whether or not cross-examination actually occurs. The per se rules adopted by Colorado on the one hand, and Utah and New Mexico on the other, do not account for the varying factual situations, strategies, and approaches to the case.

In this case, it is clear that appellant's motive to develop Mrs. McIntosh's testimony at the preliminary hearing was similar to his motive to develop her testimony at trial. One of his motives for cross-examination at the preliminary hearing was to show that there was no probable cause to believe that the appellant was the robber. If he could show that Mrs. McIntosh's identification testimony was so weak that there was no probable cause that "an offense has been committed *and that the defendant committed it,*" (emphasis added) Rule 7(b), W.R.Cr.P., the appellant would have been released.

Here, appellant's attorney undertook extensive cross-examination of Mrs. McIntosh at the preliminary hearing. That cross-examination is evidence that the attorney was motivated to attack Mrs. McIntosh's identification of his client as the robber. She was closely interrogated concerning her health, eyesight, nature and extent of her acquaintance with appellant, her observations of him, and the firmness of her identification.

Appellant's motive to cross-examine Mrs. McIntosh at trial, had she been available, would have been similar.

United States v. Zurosky, 614 F.2d 779, 791–793 (1st Cir.1979), cert. denied, 446 U.S. 967 (1980): D and others, including S, were indicted for possessing marijuana with intent to distribute. At a suppression hearing S took the stand and implicated himself and others including D. The district judge cautioned defense counsel that pursuant to Federal Rules of Evidence, Rule 804(b)(1), S's testimony might be admissible at a subsequent trial should S choose not to testify.

When asked if he would permit a full cross-examination, the judge responded that he would. . . .

. . . The court granted a recess so that counsel could ponder the matter. Counsel then decided to forego cross-examination. . . . The lengthy suppression hearing was then closed, with the court's astute observation that, based upon his reading of Rule 804, "it looks like you may be between the devil and a hard place, as they say on Cape Cod."

. . .

[D] contends that during the motion to suppress, he had no motive to show that [S's] incriminating statements were untrue. We disagree. Once it became evident that the guilt or innocence of [D] was in issue, especially given the district court's repeated warning about the potentially damaging nature of the testimony, the focus of the motion to suppress widened. [S's] testimony invited, if not compelled, cross-examination. . . .

Defense counsel made a tactical decision not to question [S]; this does not mean that they were denied an opportunity to do so. Again, we turn to the district court's forthright appraisal of the situation. "You have to make tactical decisions, but that is not the same as being blocked from cross-examination, and lots of times people as a tactical matter don't ask certain questions, but that doesn't say you don't have the opportunity within the meaning of 804(b)(1)." See United States v. Richman, 600 F.2d 286, 299 (1st Cir.1979)(counsel's decision to restrict cross-examination of a witness a trial tactic to which defendant was held).

2. *Unavailability.* State v. Shepherd, 442 S.E.2d 440, 442–43 (W.Va.1994):

In the case now before us, Mr. Tingler's preliminary hearing testimony was admitted at trial pursuant to W.Va.R.Evid. 804(b)(1). According to the trial testimony of Wood County Deputy Sheriff William Bruce Riffle, the State was aware that Mr. Tingler was in the Warren, Ohio area, where he stayed at the home of a distant relative several nights a month. Deputy Riffle further testified that he had the address and telephone number of the relative and had left several unanswered messages for Mr. Tingle there. However, there is no evidence that the State ever sought out the relative in an effort to gather information on Mr. Tingler's whereabouts. In fact, the record fails to describe what steps, if any, the State, took in its effort to procure Mr. Tingler for the final trial.

Furthermore, though the State unsuccessfully attempted to subpoena Mr. Tingler for the three previous trial dates, each of which was continued, it, by its own admission, did not even request that a summons be issued for Mr. Tingler to appear on the final trial date. According to the State's brief, it most recently attempted to procure Mr. Tingler for trial when a summons was issued for the December 2, 1991 trial. However, that summons was returned on November 29, 1991 indicating that Mr. Tingler had not been found. Mr. Shepard's malicious wounding trial was ultimately continued until March 24, 1992, a date approximately four months after the latest summons was issued and returned. Despite this lengthy time span, the State failed to even request the issuance of a subpoena for the final trial. We believe that the State should have, at the very least, sought a subpoena for Mr. Tingler for the trial on March 24, 1992.

On this record, it was not shown that a diligent search was made to find Mr. Tingler and to procure his attendance at the March 24, 1992 trial. Accordingly, the admission of Mr. Tingler's preliminary hearing testimony was reversible error.[1]

What should be the test for unavailability in civil cases?

Kirk v. Raymark Industries, Inc., 61 F.3d 147, 165–66 (3d Cir.1995):

[W]e note that it is an abuse of discretion for a district court to admit former testimony into evidence under Rule 804(b)(1) without a finding of unavailability. See O'Banion v. Owens–Corning Fiberglas Corp., 968 F.2d 1011, 1014 (10th Cir.1992)(district court abused its discretion in admitting former testimony of expert where there was no showing of unavailability). Because there was no finding on the record as to unavailability, if the district court based admitting this testimony on Rule 804(b)(1), we hold that the district court abused its discretion in allowing this former testimony into evidence.

Normally, our inquiry would end here after determining that former testimony cannot be admitted absent specific findings of unavailability. However, because of the likelihood that an offer may be made during the retrial of this matter to admit this testimony as former testimony, we believe further discussion is warranted.

We observe that it is the proponent of the statement offered under Rule 804 who bears the burden of proving the unavailability of the declarant. United States v. Eufracio–Torres, 890 F.2d 266, 269 (10th Cir.1989), cert. denied, 494 U.S. 1008, 110 S.Ct. 1306, 108 L.Ed.2d 482 (1990)(citing Ohio v. Roberts, 448 U.S. 56, 65, 100 S.Ct. 2531, 2538–39, 65 L.Ed.2d 597 (1980)); 2 John William Strong et al., McCormick on Evidence § 253, at 134 (4th ed. 1992)("The proponent of the hearsay statement must ... show that the witness cannot be found"). We can find nothing in the record that indicates any "reasonable means" employed by Kirk to procure the services of Dr. Burgher so that he might testify at trial. See McCormick § 253, at 134 (mere absence of the declarant, standing alone, does not establish unavailability); see also Moore v. Mississippi Valley State University, 871 F.2d 545, 552 (5th Cir.1989)(deposition inadmissible in civil trial where no evidence to establish unavailability offered).

Kirk claims that Dr. Burgher, who is a resident of Nebraska, was beyond her ability to subpoena and was thus unavailable. See Fed.R.Civ.P. 45(c)(3)(A)(ii). However, Kirk made no independent attempt to contact Dr. Burgher, offer him his usual expert witness fee, and request his attendance at trial.[2] Because Dr. Burgher was never even as much as contacted, Kirk has failed to prove that she used "reasonable means" to enlist his services.

---

1. [Footnotes of the court omitted.]

2. At oral argument, Kirk argued that it was the responsibility of Owens–Corning to locate and contact Dr. Burgher and establish his availability because the district court requested Owens–Corning to determine wheth-

What if proponent has voluntarily taken declarant's deposition knowing of his prior testimony, and failed to confront the declarant with the substance of his testimony at the taking of the deposition? Should the prior testimony be admissible if declarant is not now amenable to a subpoena? Cf. Zenith Radio Corp. v. Matsushita Electric Industrial Co., Limited, 505 F.Supp. 1190, 1249–1251 (E.D.Pa.1980), rev'd on related grounds, 723 F.2d 238 (3d Cir.), rev'd on other grounds, 475 U.S. 574 (1986). Suppose a party who has refused to produce a witness for a deposition offers the witness' testimony at a prior trial? May the court treat the witness as not unavailable? See discussion in Hoppe v. G.D. Searle, 779 F.Supp. 1413, 1415–16 (S.D.N.Y.1991).

If the witness is out of state but his return is imminent, should his former testimony be received? See Coakley v. Crow, 457 S.W.2d 431 (Tex.Civ.App. 1970), cert. denied, 402 U.S. 906 (1971). Cf. Williams v. Calloway, 201 So.2d 506 (1967).

How does proponent discharge the burden of proving unavailability? As to proving unavailability of the witness by affidavit, see State v. Howard, 168 N.W.2d 370 (Neb.1969).

United States v. DiNapoli

United States Court of Appeals, Second Circuit, 1993 (en banc).
8 F.3d 909.

■ NEWMAN, CHIEF JUDGE:

On this criminal appeal, which is before our Court on remand from the Supreme Court, we have given in banc consideration to a fairly narrow issue of evidence that has potentially broad implications for the administration of criminal justice. The issue concerns Rule 804(b)(1) of the Federal Rules of Evidence, which provides that testimony given by a currently unavailable witness at a prior hearing is not excluded by the hearsay rule if "the party against whom the testimony is now offered ... had an opportunity and similar motive to develop the testimony by direct, cross, or redirect examination." Fed.R.Evid. 804(b)(1)(emphasis added). Our precise issue is whether the prosecution had a "similar motive to develop" the testimony of two grand jury witnesses compared to its motive at a subsequent criminal trial at which the witnesses were unavailable. We hold that the "similar motive" requirement of Rule 804(b)(1) was not met and that the witnesses' grand jury testimony, offered by the defendants, was therefore properly excluded....

Background

[After a thirteen-month trial, defendants were convicted of participating in a racketeering scheme to rig bids for concrete work on high-rise buildings in Manhattan by obtaining control over the concrete industry through a "Club." Contrary to the prosecution's expectations, two witnesses, Bruno and DeMat-

er he would be available to testify. To the extent that the district court placed the burden on Owens–Corning to establish the unavailability of Dr. Burgher, the district court made an error of law in shifting the burden of proof. Kirk then articulated what we term a "convenience" argument, that is, she argued that Dr. Burgher was Owens Corning's expert and Owens–Corning was in a better position to locate Dr. Burgher because it had Dr. Burgher's telephone number. To the extent that Kirk is advocating that Owens–Corning should undertake the task of locating a witness for Kirk so that she may use that testimony against Owens–Corning, we reject any such notion.... [W]e do not believe that Owens–Corning had any duty to assist Kirk in preparing her case. [Footnote of the court; other footnotes omitted.]

teis, principals of a company that was an alleged member of the "Club," denied any knowledge that such a "Club" existed when they testified before a grand jury. The prosecutor responded by asking the witnesses a few questions and by confronting them with the substance of an inconsistent wiretapped conversation. At trial, Bruno and DeMatteis invoked the privilege against self-incrimination when subpoenaed by defendants. Thereupon, the defendants sought to admit the grand jury testimony under Rule 804(b)(1). The district court ruled that the "similar motive" requirement was not satisfied. On appeal, United States v. Salerno, 937 F.2d 797 (2d Cir.1991), the panel reversed the convictions for failure to admit the grand jury testimony, ruling that the "similar motive" requirement did not have to be met because the government could have compelled the witnesses to testify by granting them use immunity.]

Thereafter, the Supreme Court reversed the panel's reversal of the convictions. United States v. Salerno, 505 U.S. 317, 112 S.Ct. 2503, 120 L.Ed.2d 255 (1992). The Supreme Court ruled that all of the requirements of Rule 804(b)(1) must be met, including the "similar motive" requirement. The Court declined to decide whether the "similar motive" requirement was satisfied in this case, believing it "prudent to remand the case for further consideration" of that issue. Id. at ___, 112 S.Ct. at 2509.[1] In dissent, Justice Stevens reached the "similar motive" issue and concluded that a similar motive was present in this case. Id. at ___, 112 S.Ct. at 2509–12.

Upon remand, the panel ruled that the "similar motive" requirement was satisfied. United States v. Salerno,[2] 974 F.2d 231 (2d Cir.1992). The panel considered the questioning of the witnesses conducted by an Assistant United States Attorney and concluded that what occurred "was the equivalent of what would have been done if the opportunity to examine them had been presented at trial." Id. at 241.

Discussion

Our initial task is to determine how similarity of motive at two proceedings will be determined for purposes of Rule 804(b)(1). In resolving this matter, we do not accept the position, apparently urged by the appellants, that the test of similar motive is simply whether at the two proceedings the questioner takes the same side of the same issue. The test must turn not only on whether the questioner is on the same side of the same issue at both proceedings, but also on whether the questioner had a substantially similar interest in asserting that side of the issue. If a fact is critical to a cause of action at a second proceeding but the same fact was only peripherally related to a different cause of action at a first proceeding, no one would claim that the questioner had a similar motive at both proceedings to show that the fact had been established (or disproved). This is the same principle that holds collateral estoppel inapplicable when a small amount is at stake in a first proceeding and a large amount is at stake in a second proceeding, even though a party took the same side of the same issue

---

1. In a concurring opinion, Justice Blackmun stated:

> Because "similar motive" does not mean "identical motive," the similar-motive inquiry, in my view, is inherently a *factual* inquiry, depending in part on the similarity of the underlying issues and on the context of the grand jury questioning. It cannot be that the prosecution either *always* or *never* has a similar motive for questioning a particular witness with re-

spect to a particular issue before the grand jury at trial. 505 U.S. at 326, 112 S.Ct. at 2509.

[Footnote by editors; emphasis in original; footnotes of the court omitted.]

2. Salerno, the lead defendant, died during the pendency of the petition for rehearing en banc, causing the name of the case to change to DeNapoli. [Footnote by editors.]

at both proceedings.... This suggests that the questioner must not only be on the same side of the same issue at both proceedings but must also have a substantially similar degree of interest in prevailing on that issue.

Whether the degree of interest in prevailing on an issue is substantially similar at two proceedings will sometimes be affected by the nature of the proceedings. Where both proceedings are trials and the same matter is seriously disputed at both trials, it will normally be the case that the side opposing the version of a witness at the first trial had a motive to develop that witness's testimony similar to the motive at the second trial. The opponent, whether shouldering a burden of proof or only resisting the adversary's effort to sustain its burden of proof, usually cannot tell how much weight the witness's version will have with the fact-finder in the total mix of all the evidence. Lacking such knowledge, the opponent at the first trial normally has a motive to dispute the version so long as it can be said that disbelief of the witness's version is of some significance to the opponent's side of the case; the motive at the second trial is normally similar.

The situation is not necessarily the same where the two proceedings are different in significant respects, such as their purposes or the applicable burden of proof. The grand jury context, with which we are concerned in this case, well illustrates the point. If a prosecutor is using the grand jury to investigate possible crimes and identify possible criminals, it may be quite unrealistic to characterize the prosecutor as the "opponent" of a witness's version. At a preliminary stage of an investigation, the prosecutor is not trying to prove any side of any issue, but only to develop the facts to determine if an indictment is warranted. Even if the prosecutor displays some skepticism about particular testimony (not an uncommon response from any questioner interested in eliciting the truth), that does not mean the prosecutor has a motive to show the falsity of the testimony, similar to the motive that would exist at trial if an indictment is returned and the witness's testimony is presented by a defendant to rebut the prosecutor's evidence of guilt.

Even in cases like the pending one, where the grand jury proceeding has progressed far beyond the stage of a general inquiry, the motive to develop grand jury testimony that disputes a position already taken by the prosecutor is not necessarily the same as the motive the prosecutor would have if that same testimony was presented at trial. Once the prosecutor has decided to seek an indictment against identified suspects, that prosecutor may fairly be characterized as "opposed" to any testimony that tends to exonerate one of the suspects. But, because of the low burden of proof at the grand jury stage, even the prosecutor's status as an "opponent" of the testimony does not necessarily create a motive to challenge the testimony that is similar to the motive at trial. At the grand jury, the prosecutor need establish only probable cause to believe the suspect is guilty. By the time the exonerating testimony is given, such probable cause may already have been established to such an extent that there is no realistic likelihood that the grand jury will fail to indict. That circumstance alone will sometimes leave the prosecutor with slight if any motive to develop the exonerating testimony in order to persuade the grand jurors of its falsity.

. . .

[W]e do not accept the position, urged by the Government upon the Supreme Court, that a prosecutor "generally will not have the same motive to develop testimony in grand jury proceedings as he does at trial." See Salerno, 505 U.S. at 323–24, 112 S.Ct. at 2508–09. Though the Supreme Court declined to assess that contention and left its consideration to this Court in the first instance, we discern in its opinion a reluctance to engraft any general exception onto Rule 804(b)(1). "This Court cannot alter evidentiary rules merely because litigants might prefer different rules in a particular class of cases." Id. at 321, 112 S.Ct. at 2507. Our point is simply that the inquiry as to similar motive must be fact specific, and the grand jury context will sometimes, but not invariably, present circumstances that demonstrate the prosecutor's lack of a similar motive. We accept neither the Government's view that the prosecutor's motives at the grand jury and at trial are almost always dissimilar, nor the opposing view, apparently held by the District of Columbia Circuit, that the prosecutor's motives in both proceedings are always similar, see United States v. Miller, 904 F.2d 65, 68 (D.C.Cir.1990). . . .

Nor are we persuaded by the Government's contention that the absence of similar motive is conclusively demonstrated by the availability at the grand jury of some cross-examination opportunities that were forgone. In virtually all subsequent proceedings, examiners will be able to suggest lines of questioning that were not pursued at a prior proceeding. . . .

The proper approach, therefore, in assessing similarity of motive under Rule 804(b)(1) must consider whether the party resisting the offered testimony at a pending proceeding had at a prior proceeding an interest of substantially similar intensity to prove (or disprove) the same side of a substantially similar issue. The nature of the two proceedings—both what is at stake and the applicable burden of proof—and, to a lesser extent, the cross-examination at the prior proceeding—both what was undertaken and what was available but forgone—will be relevant though not conclusive on the ultimate issue of similarity of motive.

Having identified the proper approach to the determination of whether a similar motive existed, we might ordinarily remand to the District Court to apply the governing principles to the precise facts of this case. We decline to do so, however, both to avoid further delay in this already long-delayed matter and because this is the unusual case in which it can be shown beyond reasonable dispute that the prosecutor had no interest at the grand jury in proving the falsity of the witnesses' assertion that the "Club" did not exist. Two circumstances independently suffice. First, the defendants had already been indicted, and, as appellants' counsel conceded at argument, there existed no putative defendant as to whom probable cause was in issue. At most the Government had an interest in investigating further to see whether there might be additional defendants or additional projects within the criminal activity of the existing defendants. As to these matters, the prosecutor had no interest in showing that the denial of the Club's existence was false. The grand jury had already been persuaded, at least by the low standard of probable cause, to believe that the Club existed and that the defendants had participated in it to commit crimes. It is fanciful to think that the prosecutor would have had any substantial interest in showing the falsity of the witnesses' denial of the Club's existence just to persuade the grand jury to add one more project to the indictment.

Second, the grand jurors had indicated to the prosecutor that they did not believe the denial. The record is clear on this point. After a consultation with the grand jury, the prosecutor told Bruno, in the grand jurors' presence, that there was "strong concern on the part of the grand jury" that his testimony had "not been truthful." A prosecutor has no interest in showing the falsity of testimony that a grand jury already disbelieves.

. . . The District Court's exclusion of the witnesses' grand jury testimony was therefore entirely correct, and this ground for reversal of the convictions is rejected. . . .

■ PRATT, CIRCUIT JUDGE, (joined by MINER and ALTIMARI, CIRCUIT JUDGES), dissenting:

. . .

On remand from the Supreme Court ..., the panel determined that the government's motive was similar, primarily because (1) the government had examined both Bruno and DeMatteis extensively on whether a "Club" existed, (2) the government had vigorously examined both witnesses before the grand jury, and (3) the government was seeking at trial to prove the same issue as before the grand jury—the existence of a "Club" of concrete contractors. 974 F.2d at 240–41. . . .

The in banc majority, however, now concludes, as a matter of law, that the prosecutor's motive was not "similar". In doing so, it applies a gloss to the language of the rule that would find a similar motive only when the party against whom the testimony is offered had "an interest of substantially similar intensity to prove (or disprove) the same side of a substantially similar issue". Op. at 915. As a practical matter, the gloss effectively rewrites the rule from "similar motive" to "same motive".

Not only is the majority's test more stringent than the rule itself, it could also prove to be extremely difficult to administer, for on its face this test would require the district judge to compare the "intensity of interest" that the prosecutor possessed before the grand jury with his "intensity of interest" at the trial. . . . At the very least, this issue of fact should be decided in the first instance by a district judge, not an in banc appellate court.

One final, troubling aspect of the majority's decision is its acceptance of and reliance on the prosecutor's assertions that he already had an indictment against the defendants, that no new defendants were being contemplated at the time these witnesses were examined, and that, as a result, probable cause was not even an issue before the grand jury when Bruno and DeMatteis were testifying. If all these things were true, then why was the prosecutor using the grand jury at all? Could it have been simply a discovery device to develop more evidence to present at trial on the indictment he already had? If that were the case, however, the prosecutor's continuing use of the grand jury would have been improper. [citations omitted].

The effect of the in banc majority's decision will be to leave the determination of whether grand jury testimony may be presented at trial by a defendant entirely in the prosecutor's control, a result that seems at odds with the main objective of going to trial—permitting the jury, not the prosecutor, to determine what is the truth.

. . .

■ MINER, CIRCUIT JUDGE, (joined by GEORGE C. PRATT and ALTIMARI, CIRCUIT JUDGES), dissenting:

. . .

The majority examines the record and finds it "beyond reasonable dispute" that the prosecution had no motive in proving at the grand jury proceedings that the two witnesses falsely denied that a bid-rigging "Club" existed. I examine the record and come to the opposite conclusion. Whatever the reason behind the strategy, the prosecution strove to establish the falsity of the testimony of Bruno and DeMatteis through the use of a number of impeaching questions that are set forth in detail in the panel opinion.

. . .

NOTES

1. Is the majority's analysis in DiNapoli consistent with decisions that admit preliminary hearing testimony against an accused? See pp. 737–746, supra. See Note, United States v. DiNapoli: Admission of Exculpatory Grand Jury Testimony Against the Government Under Federal Rule of Evidence 804(b)(1), 61 Bklyn L.Rev. 543 (1995).

2. *Child sex abuse cases.* More than thirty states have enacted statutes authorizing the admissibility of videotaped testimony of a child sex crime victim taken before trial. See Montoya, Something Not So Funny Happened on the Way to Conviction: the Pretrial Interrogation of Child Witnesses, 35 Ariz. L. Rev. 927 (1993). These statutes differ in a number of respects. Some require preliminary findings by the trial court before the videotape may be made or used. See, e.g., § 1346 of the California Penal Code which provides that the preliminary examination testimony of a child, who is 15 years of age or under, may be videotaped, and that the tape may be introduced as former testimony, "if at the time of trial the court finds that further testimony would cause the victim emotional trauma so that the victim is medically unavailable or otherwise unavailable within the meaning of section 240 of the Evidence Code." Other statutes simply give the court discretion in ordering the videotape. Some of the statutes mandate procedural details such as who must be present at the videotaping, or that the defendant and witness must be placed so that the former can see and hear the child, but not vice versa. See, e.g., 18 U.S.C. § 3509 (b)(2)(B)(iv) which provides that the defendant may be present at the videotaped deposition unless the court has made a preliminary finding "that the child is unable to testify in the physical presence of the defendant" in which case the defendant shall be excluded from the deposition room and "the court shall order that 2–way closed circuit television equipment relay the defendant's image into the room in which the child is testifying, and the child's testimony into the room in which the defendant is viewing the proceeding, and that the defendant be provided with a means of private, contemporaneous communication with the defendant's attorney during the deposition" who will be in the deposition room. Some, but not all, of the statutes state that the defendant or his counsel have the right to cross-examine the child. See Bulkley, Evidentiary and Procedural Trends in State Legislation and Other Emerging Legal Issues in Child Sexual Abuse Cases, 84 Dick.L.Rev. 645, 657–658 (1985).

Do evidentiary or constitutional concerns require the unavailability of the child to be established before videotaped testimony is admissible? May a court assume without proof that all children or children under a certain age are unavailable because testimony at trial would be unduly traumatic? Or must the court make a determination in each case that the particular child is unavailable? If so, what standard of proof should the court use in ruling on unavailability, and what type of proof may the court rely upon? Must the child be found to be competent? See discussion p. 367 supra as to when child witnesses in child sex abuse prosecutions may testify outside the presence of the defendant.

Does replaying the testimony in the jury room unduly prejudice the defendant? In United States v. Binder, 769 F.2d 595 (9th Cir.1985), the majority of the court found that videotaped testimony is "the functional equivalent of a live witness" and is not analogous to audiotaped testimony which can be replayed. Id. at 601, n.i. The majority suggested that if the jury requests a review of videotaped testimony, a transcript should be prepared and the testimony may be read to the jurors.

SECTION 9. DYING DECLARATIONS

Wilson v. State

Supreme Court of Nevada, 1970.
86 Nev. 320, 468 P.2d 346.

■ BATJER, JUSTICE. At approximately 3:15 a.m., on December 8,1967, Henry Feltus was struck with a blast from a shotgun. He died at approximately 4:30 a.m., that same morning. The appellant was accused of killing Feltus; tried before a jury; convicted of murder in the first degree; and sentenced to life imprisonment without the possibility of parole. This appeal is taken from that conviction.

During the early morning of December 8, 1967, Feltus was at Ruben's Supper Club in Las Vegas, Nevada. The appellant entered the establishment, approached Feltus and indicated he wanted to converse with him outside the premises.

At the trial, witnesses testified that they had observed the appellant and Feltus leave by the back door of Ruben's, and that within a matter of seconds they heard what was thought to be a gunshot. Cleveland Ramsey stated that shortly after he heard the gunshot he observed Feltus come back into the club through the back door. At that time Feltus was holding his side with his hand, blood was gushing out between his fingers, and his clothes were covered with blood from his chest to his feet. As Feltus made his way to the bar, Dorothy Mae Willings rushed to help him, and he said to her, "Oh, Baby, I've been shot," and fell to the floor near the bar. Ramsey testified that Feltus had a large hole in his right chest area. Vera Maxine Bullock, the wife of one of the co-owners of the club, asked Feltus who had shot him. After he was given a drink of brandy Feltus answered that Stan had shot him. At approximately 3:30 a.m., Merlin John Dingle, an officer of the Las Vegas Police Department, arrived at the scene. The officer observed that Feltus, who was covered with blood from the top of his chest to his shoes, was moaning, gasping and thrashing around on the floor; that there were large quantities of blood pouring from a wound in his chest; and that it took three men to hold him down. Officer Dingle knelt down and stated, "Henry, this is Dingle. Who shot you?" Feltus responded, "Stan." This response was given two or three times. Officer Dingle then asked, "Do you mean Stanley Wilson?" The declarant nodded his head yes, and went "Um, hum."

Further attempts at conversation failed to evoke intelligible responses. Feltus died at 4:30 a.m., at the Southern Nevada Memorial Hospital. Dr. John C. Bovill testified that Feltus "[H]ad an obvious open massive wound of the right chest and you could see into the right chest, which is a little unusual." The doctor further testified that Feltus was conscious after he had arrived at the hospital and concluded that Feltus had the type of wound that frequently would cause death.

The trial court conducted a hearing, outside the presence of the jury, where the state's witnesses testified to facts surrounding the dying declaration of Feltus. After that hearing the trial court concluded that the declaration was made when Feltus was in extremis; that he was conscious of that condition, and that the state had laid a sufficient foundation for the presentation of the dying declarant's testimony. Ex parte Wheeler, 81 Nev. 495, 406 P.2d 713 (1965);

State v. Teeter, 65 Nev. 584, 200 P.2d 657 (1948); State v. Scott, 37 Nev. 412, 142 P. 1053 (1914). Over the appellant's objection the state's witnesses were then allowed to repeat the testimony before the jury.

The appellant contends that the trial court erred when it admitted such declarations into evidence. He further contends that the prosecutor committed reversible error when he asked one of the appellant's witnesses whether or not he had been convicted of a felony without having acceptable proof of that fact, and that an additional error was committed when the prosecutor, upon cross-examination of the appellant, asked a question which indicated that the appellant was a pimp.

The appellant conceded that the declarant was in extremis and realized that he was dying when he stated that the appellant had shot him. He further concedes that the trial court properly followed and applied the law of this state when it allowed testimony of the dying declaration before the jury, but he contends that the trial court erred when it did not require the prosecution to affirmatively prove, beyond a reasonable doubt, that the declarant believed in an Almighty Being and a life hereafter. The appellant insists that this requirement be added in this case because testimony was presented which tended to prove that the victim was a pimp.

The appellant is asking this court to establish an additional rule which would require the state to prove, through the introduction of affirmative evidence, that the presumption of truthfulness raised by the declarant's awareness of impending death is believable beyond a reasonable doubt. This we refuse to do. He misconceives the function of the court and jury. Once the trial judge reasonably finds, from the evidence, that there is a sufficient foundation to admit the dying declaration, then the statement is presented to the jury to be considered and weighed along with the credibility of the declarant.

As a general rule an accused, during the presentation of his defense is free to introduce whatever relevant evidence may be available to establish that the declarant was a person of dissolute and immoral character and in that manner discredit the dying declaration. Here the appellant did introduce testimony discrediting the victim, but because it was apparently discounted or disregarded by the jury, he asks us to impose upon the prosecution a burden of proof unheard of in the common law and unsupported by any authority, although he purports to rely on Barber v. Page, 390 U.S. 719, 88 S.Ct. 1318, 20 L.Ed.2d 255 (1968).

It has long been the established law in this state that dying declarations are competent evidence for or against the accused upon preliminary proof of certain existing conditions. In State v. Scott, 37 Nev. 412 at 429, 142 P. 1053 at 1059 (1914), this court said: "The question whether the alleged dying declarations were made under such circumstances as to render them admissible in evidence was in the first instance to be determined by the court upon the preliminary proof or predicate for their admission. All that was required to let the statements go to the jury was the making of a prima facie case that the utterances were made by the declarant when he was in extremis, and when he was fully conscious of that condition. However this may be, the ultimate facts and the weight, credence, and significance to be given to the statement when admitted is for the jury, and it is error to remove this question from their consideration. People v. Thomson, 145 Cal. 717, 79 P. 435; State v. Hendricks, 172 Mo. 654, 73 S.W. 194; 21 Cyc. 987."[1]

---

1. See also Commonwealth v. Edwards, 431 Pa. 44, 51–52, 244 A.2d 683, 686–687 (1968): "In the cases relied upon by appellant, the following passage appears: 'Wheth-

In State v. Teeter, supra, a case where the facts were very similar to the case at hand, although the declarant lived for several days after he received the fatal wound, this court said: "The authorities, very generally, hold that for a court properly to conclude that the declarant making the statement believed death was impending, it is not necessary for the declarant to state to anyone, expressly, that he knows or believes he is going to die, or that death is certain or near, or to indulge in any like expression; ... It is sufficient if the wounds are of such a nature that the usual or probable effect upon the average person so injured would be mortal; and that such probable mortal effect is not hidden, but, from experience in like cases, it may be reasonably concluded that such probable effect has revealed itself upon the human consciousness of the

er the attendant facts and circumstances of the case warrant the admission of a statement as a dying declaration is in the first instance for the court, but, when admitted, the declarant's state of mind and the credibility, interpretation and weight to be given his statement are for the jury *under proper instructions*.' (Emphasis added). Commonwealth v. Brown, supra, 388 Pa. at page 616, 131 A.2d at page 369; Commonwealth v. Knable, supra, 369 Pa. at page 175, 85 A.2d at 116; and cases cited therein. The question is what are proper instructions. In our opinion, a general charge on credibility of witnesses and weight of evidence is what this Court meant by 'proper instructions.' It would run counter to the basic tenet of the common law—that questions of law are for the court, and questions of fact for the jury—to hold otherwise. Appellant would have the court instruct the jury that in order for a statement to be acceptable as a dying declaration, the declarant must have knowledge of impending death. Although he does not spell it out so clearly, he obviously would apply the same principle to res gestae statements and require the jury to find that they were spontaneous utterances emanating from the event and so near in time as to exclude the possibility of premeditation or design. Clearly, if we were to follow appellant's suggestion, we would allow the jury to become usurpers of the judge's function to decide the law. That such a result was not intended by this Court is evident from the citation in Knable, supra, of Wigmore on Evidence, Third Edition, Vol. 5, § 1451(b). That subsection states:

'After a dying declaration, or any other evidence, has been admitted, the *weight* to be given to it is a matter exclusively for the jury. They may believe it or may not believe it; but, so far as they do or do not, their judgment is not controlled by rules of law. Therefore, though they themselves do not suppose the declarant to have been conscious of death, they may still believe the statement; conversely, though they do suppose him to have been thus conscious, they may still not believe the statement to be true. In other words, their canons of ultimate belief are not necessarily the same as the preliminary legal

conditions of Admissibility, whose purpose is an entirely different one (ante, § 29).

'It is therefore erroneous for the judge, after once admitting the declaration, to instruct the jury that they *must* reject the declaration, or exclude it from consideration, if the legal requirement as to consciousness of death does not in their opinion exist. No doubt they *may* reject it, on this ground or on any other; [footnote omitted] but they are not to be expected to follow a definition of law intended only for the judge....' (Emphasis in original). We thus hold that the trial judge did not err in failing to instruct the jury on conditions of admissibility of dying declarations and res gestae statements."

Patrick v. State, 436 S.W.2d 275, 278 (Ark.1969)("The court properly instructed the jury that the dying declaration was not to be considered unless the jury found it to have been made under a sense of impending death"); State v. Chaplin, 286 A.2d 325, 332 (Me.1972)("We are satisfied and now hold that the presiding Justice in a preliminary hearing, absent the jury, should examine the evidence to be tendered in support of the facts essential to admission of dying declarations. If he is satisfied that there is credible evidence which if believed would permit but not compel the jury to find the preliminary facts proven beyond a reasonable doubt, he should, unléss they violate other legal principles, admit the dying declarations into evidence. The jury may then determine the weight and credibility to be given to the declarations, assigning to them no weight whatsoever if in their judgment the preliminary facts are not so proven. In our view the practice outlined above better accords with the proper functions of judge and jury and will tend to eliminate some of the confusion readily apparent in the case law on this subject."); Commonwealth v. Key, 407 N.E.2d 327, 330 (Mass.1980)("Under traditional Massachusetts procedure, the judge and then the jury are to determine whether the requirements for a dying declaration have been established by a preponderance of evidence."). [This footnote is by the editors; the other footnote is the court's, renumbered.]

wounded person, so that he knows, or strongly believes, that death impends. Wharton's Criminal Evidence, Eleventh Edition, Sec. 530, pp. 852–854, and the many cases cited.''

Fundamentally we are precluded by the Nevada Constitution, Art. 1, Sec. 4,[2] from adopting any rule that would impinge upon the liberty of conscience and this applies equally to the dead as well as to the living.

In Barber v. Page, supra, cited by the appellant, the United States Supreme Court quotes with approval from Mattox v. United States, 156 U.S. 237, 242–243, 15 S.Ct. 337, 39 L.Ed. 409.

We quote with approval from a different part of that same case (Mattox v. United States, supra, 243–244, 15 S.Ct. 340): "The law, in its wisdom, declares that the rights of the public shall not be wholly sacrificed in order that an incidental benefit may be preserved to the accused.

"We are bound to interpret the constitution in the light of the law as it existed at the time it was adopted, not as reaching out for new guaranties of the rights of the citizen, but as securing to every individual such as he already possessed as a British subject,—such as his ancestors had inherited and defended since the days of Magna Charta. Many of its provisions in the nature of a bill of rights are subject to exceptions, recognized long before the adoption of the constitution, and not interfering at all with its spirit. Such exceptions were obviously intended to be respected. A technical adherence to the letter of a constitutional provision may occasionally be carried farther than is necessary to the just protection of the accused, and farther than the safety of the public will warrant. For instance, there could be nothing more directly contrary to the letter of the provision in question than the admission of dying declarations. They are rarely made in the presence of the accused; they are made without any opportunity for examination or cross-examination, nor is the witness brought face to face with the jury; yet from time immemorial they have been treated as competent testimony, and no one would have the hardihood at this day to question their admissibility. They are admitted, not in conformity with any general rule regarding the admission of testimony, but as an exception to such rules, simply from the necessities of the case, and to prevent a manifest failure of justice. As was said by the chief justice when this case was here upon the first writ of error, (Mattox v. United States, 146 U.S. 140, 152, 13 S.Ct. 50, 36 L.Ed. 917) the sense of impending death is presumed to remove all temptation to falsehood, and to enforce as strict an adherence to the truth as would the obligation of an oath.''

The High Court has clearly indicated that once the prosecution has clearly established that the declarant is in extremis and he is aware of that status, his statement is admissible, as an exception to the hearsay rule, to be considered by the jury. After the dying declaration has been presented to the jury, the accused then has wide latitude in impeaching the declarant and discrediting his dying statement, but the ultimate fact and the weight, credence and significance to be given to the statement is for the jury.

We now turn to the appellant's contention that the prosecutor committed reversible error, first when he asked one of the appellant's witnesses if he had ever been convicted of a felony, to which the witness replied in the negative;

---

2. Nevada Constitution, Art. 1, Sec. 4: "The free exercise and enjoyment of religious profession and worship without discrimination or preference shall forever be allowed in this State, and no person shall be rendered incompetent to be a witness on account of his opinions on matters of his religious belief, but the liberty of consciene [conscience] hereby secured, shall not be so construed, as to excuse acts of licentiousness or justify practices inconsistent with the peace, or safety of this State.''

secondly, when upon cross-examination one of his questions posed to the appellant inferred that the appellant was a pimp. When those questions were asked, during the trial, the appellant neither objected to them, nor moved to strike them from the record. The trial court was given no opportunity to rule on their propriety or admissibility. Neither question was so inherently unfair or damaging as to require the trial court to *sua sponte* preclude them.

When an appellant fails to specifically object to questions asked or testimony elicited during trial, but complains about them, in retrospect upon appeal, we do not consider his contention as a proper assignment of error. Wyatt v. State, Nev., 468 P.2d 338 (1970); Cross v. State, 85 Nev. 580, 460 P.2d 151 (1969); Cranford v. State, 76 Nev. 113, 349 P.2d 1051 (1960); State v. Ceja, 53 Nev. 272, 298 P. 658 (1931).

Appellant's counsel were appointed to prosecute this appeal. We direct the trial court to give each of them the certificate specified in NRS 7.260(3), to enable them to receive compensation for their services rendered on appeal.

The judgment of the trial court is affirmed.

NOTES

1. No one "who is immediately going into the presence of his Maker, will do so with a lie on his lips." Lush, L.J. in Regina v. Osman, 15 Cox C.C. 1, 3 (Eng.1881). But suppose the declarant is an atheist. Is it not true, as eloquently urged in the original majority opinion in Wright v. State, 135 So. 636 (Ala.Ct. App.1931), that the dying declaration of such an unbeliever carries no guaranty of its truthfulness?

Does this exception comport with modern religious attitudes? In Kidd v. State, 258 So.2d 423, 429–430 (Miss.1972), Smith J., concurring, called for a reexamination of the admissibility of dying declarations:

Perhaps, at the time that this exception was engrafted upon the exclusionary hearsay rule, it was not too violent an assumption to suppose that every dying man, who realized that he was dying, entertained a devout belief in divine judgment and punishment after death and that this justified the admission into evidence against an accused of his statements, without benefit of oath, notwithstanding that it deprived the accused absolutely of any opportunity to cross-examine him, and also of his constitutional right to be confronted by the witnesses against him. Moreover, the witness who plays the role of conduit in testifying to these supposedly sanctified statements will be, more often than not, a relative, friend or confidant of the deceased, whose testimony is subject to all of the human frailties of poor recollection, misunderstanding and downright dishonesty, as well as to the very human motivations of revenge or ill will against the alleged slayer.

Napoleon is reported to have said that Mohammed was a success because he invented a religion without any hell. Today, considering all of the many, many denominations of the Christian faith alone and their different concepts and teachings, and leaving out of consideration entirely the millions who, sadly enough, profess no religious faith whatever, as well as the multiplied millions who adhere to Buddhism, Confucianism and other non-Christian faiths, can it be said that a man who has been wounded and feels that he is dying, is by those circumstances alone automatically stripped of all human malice, anger and desire for revenge and is transformed *ipso facto* into a devout believer in a life after death and in divine punishment? I cannot think so. Certainly, an accused should not be deprived of his constitutional right to confrontation by the witnesses against him on a theory that meets neither the test of reason nor of the facts of common knowledge and human experience. This harmful effect of the admission of this type of hearsay is enhanced by a recital of dramatic circumstances under which the statement is alleged to have been made, and, the law having in effect declared this type of hearsay sacrosanct, there is no effective way to challenge its truth and it is more than just likely that the jury will attach undue importance to it and give it undue weight in arriving at a verdict.

It is my opinion that the admission of this type hearsay evidence should not be countenanced by the courts in any case, but certainly, in criminal cases, where a man may lose his liberty as the result of it, it should never be admitted.

See also, Note, 38 Ford.L.Rev. 509 (1970).

Compare People v. Calahan, 356 N.E.2d 942, 945 (Ill.App.1976):

While the original religious justification for the exception may have lost its conviction over the years, it can scarcely be doubted that powerful psychological pressures are present. At the moment wherein the deceased realizes his own death is imminent there can no longer be any temporal self-serving purpose to be furthered regardless of the speaker's personal religious beliefs. Indeed, given the physiological revulsion peculiar to the moment and common to all men, an express showing of the declarant's theological beliefs is immaterial. See 5 Wigmore on Evidence § 1443, at 241–42 (3d ed. 1940); McCormick on Evidence, § 281 et seq. (2d ed. 1972).

Most courts rule that evidence of lack of religious conviction or evidence indicating blatant irreverence is admissible only to affect the weight to be given to the declaration. But see Reeves v. State, 64 So. 836 (Miss.1914); Marley v. State, 69 So. 210 (Miss.1915); Tracy v. People, 97 Ill. 101, 106, 107 (1880); 167 A.L.R. 178–179 (1947). See also Rex v. Pike, 3 Car. & P. 598 (Eng.1829)(dying declaration of four year old child rejected because she did not and could not have any idea of a future state).

Relevant literature includes: Brazil, A Matter of Theology, 34 Aust.L.J. 195 (1960); Swancara, Religion in The Law of Dying Declarations, 66 U.S.L.Rev. 192 (1932); Notes, 38 W.Va.L.Q. 170 (1932); 5 U.Cinc.L.Rev. 490 (1931); 8 Tenn.L.Rev. 56 (1929); 24 Harv.L.Rev. 484 (1911); 36 Law Notes 43 (1932). See also Klicks, Impeachment of Dying Declarations, 19 Or.L.Rev. 265 (1940).

2. Numerous cases refuse to recognize the impropriety of insisting upon requiring the declaration to be in the form which might be demanded of a living witness. See Hardeman v. State, 61 So.2d 797, 802 (Miss.1953), excluding the statement, "He wouldn't have done it for anything intentionally"; State v. Hegel, 273 A.2d 383 (N.J.Super.1971)(victim's statement that she had been robbed); People v. Little, 371 N.Y.S.2d 726, 736 (N.Y.Co.Ct.1975)("He meant to kill me.") See, however, Powell v. State, 118 So.2d 304 (Miss.1960)(statement, "It was accidental" should be admitted); United States v. Etheridge, 424 F.2d 951 (6th Cir.1970), cert. denied, 400 U.S. 993, 91 S.Ct. 463 (1971)(victim's opinion as to cause of his murder admitted); Munoz v. State, 524 S.W.2d 710 (Tex.Cr.App.1975)(victim's opinion as to motive for shooting admitted); Shuman v. State, 578 P.2d 1183, 1185 (Nev.1978)(concluding that statute based on proposed federal rule "dispenses with the fact/opinion distinction"). In Broughton v. Commonwealth, 202 S.W.2d 1014, 1015 (Ky.1947), the statement "What did he shoot me for?" was excluded when introduced to rebut a claim of self-

defense. See also Comer v. State, 204 S.W.2d 875, 877 (Ark.1947)(dictum), excluding "They ought to turn [him] loose". See Wigmore's comment, "Are not some of these exclusion-rulings equal to any of the medieval witch formulas and conjurors' spells, as a means of getting at the truth?" 5 Wigmore, Evidence § 1447, n. 1 (3d ed. 1940). See also Notes, 53 W.Va.L.Rev. 170, 322 (1951); 10 U.Pitt.L.Rev. 209 (1948); 22 Md.L.Rev. 42 (1962).

3. The declarant must have "a settled hopeless expectation of immediate death". Immediate death means "death impending not on the instant, but within a very very short distance indeed." See Lord Alverstone in King v. Perry, [Eng.1909] 2 K.B. 697, 703. "There must be 'a settled hopeless expectation' ... that death is near at hand, and what is said must have been spoken in the hush of its impending presence.... The patient must have spoken with the consciousness of a swift and certain doom". Mr. Justice Cardozo in Shepard v. United States, 290 U.S. 96, 100 (1933).

This "hopeless expectation" is normally established by decedent's own statements. However, other means of proof are acceptable in order to infer decedent's expectation of death. Commonwealth v. Edwards, 110 A.2d 216, 219–220 (Pa.1955), found the requisite state of mind solely on the basis of the severity of the declarant's wounds. See People v. Nieves, 492 N.E.2d 109 (N.Y.1986)(requisite expectation of death could not be inferred where the severity of the wound would not have been apparent to the victim, although it was fatal; the victim took no actions normally associated with an expectation of imminent death; victim made the statements while her condition was stabilizing, and neither the doctor nor nurse told her that she was dying or even in a critical condition); Commonwealth v. Cooley, 348 A.2d 103 (Pa.1975); State v. Bowden, 228 S.E.2d 414 (N.C.1976); McFadden v. United States, 395 A.2d 14 (D.C.App.1978). See also Commonwealth v. Nolin, 364 N.E.2d 1224 (Mass.1977)(doctor told declarant "he had no chance to live."). In People v. Tilley, 94 N.E.2d 328, 332 (Ill.1950), the fact that last rites had been administered upon request of decedent was probative of the sense of impending death, but this was not sufficient in People v. Allen, 90 N.E.2d 48, 51 (N.Y.1949), where the statements were made "casually and not solemnly [and were] ... not shown to have any near relation, in time or thought, to those earlier expressions as to nearness of death." See Batten v. Commonwealth, 56 S.E.2d 231, 234–235 (Va.1949)(declarations made several days apart required independent proof of declarant's mental state). See also Notes, 12 Ohio St.L.J. 130 (1951); 4 Ford.L.Rev. 507 (1935); 16 Brooklyn L.Rev. 284 (1950); 34 Marq.L.Rev. 128 (1950); 6 So.Calif.L.Rev. 241 (1933); 14 Mo.L.Rev. 318 (1949); 47 Geo.L.J. 747, 755 (1959); 22 La.L.Rev. 651 (1962). Annot., 53 A.L.R.3d 1196 (1973).

4. The declaration must relate to the circumstances immediately surrounding or leading up to the conduct which caused the death. Pritchett v. State, 874 S.W.2d 168, 177 (Tex.App. 1994)(declarant explained that he and defendant had robbed store; declarant shot by proprietor). The decisions exhibit varying degrees of liberality. For a strict limitation see State v. Brooks, 186 N.W. 46 (Iowa 1922), and Jones v. State, 236 P.2d 102, 109–111 (Okla.Crim.App.1951). For a much more liberal view, see People v. Kreutzer, 188 N.E. 422 (Ill.1933). See also People v. Liccione, 407 N.Y.S.2d 753 (N.Y.App.Div.1978), aff'd mem., 407 N.E.2d 1333 (N.Y.1980)(victim stated that her assailant told her he had been hired by her husband). And see State v. Satterfield, 457 S.E.2d 440, 448–450 (W.Va.1995)(after witness testified for prosecution in homicide case, defense suggested on cross that he had taken part in murder; witness killed himself before court reconvened the next day and left a suicide note denying complicity which was admitted as a dying declaration).

Must the declarations relate to the death of the declarant? In Commonwealth v. Key, 407 N.E.2d 327 (Mass.1980), E and F were intentionally set on fire. Only F lived long enough to make a statement. Would F's statement be admissible in D's trial for murdering E? See also People v. Coniglio, 361 N.Y.S.2d 524 (Crim.Ct.1974).

5. What is the appropriate allocation of function as between judge and jury in resolving factual issues governing the admissibility of dying declarations? In addition to the principal case, and the cases cited in footnote 1, see also Commonwealth v. Key, 407 N.E.2d 327 (Mass.1980) and Commonwealth v. Polian, 193 N.E. 68 (Mass.1934)("humane practice" requires a judge and then the jury to pass on whether the requirements for a dying declaration have been satisfied); State v. Sprague, 394 A.2d 253, 255 (Me.1978)(reaffirming that judge must admit dying declaration if he is satisfied that there is credible evidence that would permit the jury to find the preliminary facts "proven beyond a reasonable doubt").

6. Until recently English and American cases had restricted this exception to statements by a victim of a homicide, or, in a few cases, to dying declarations of a victim of a criminal abortion. See People v. Murawski, 117 N.E.2d 88, 91 (Ill.1954). In Blair v. Rogers, 89 P.2d 928 (Okla.1939), and Cummings v. Illinois Central Railroad Co., 269 S.W.2d 111, 119–121 (Mo.1954), the courts excluded dying declarations in a civil case on the theory that any change should be legislative. Codifications are now in effect in many jurisdictions. Compare Federal Rule of Evidence Rule 804(b)(2) with Uniform Rule 804(b)(2)(1974) which eliminates the introductory language limiting the dying declaration exception to a prosecution for homicide or a civil action or proceeding. The restriction in the federal rule was added by Congress.

7. Should the statement be admitted if made in response to prompting and questioning by police, insurance agents, investigators or the like? Suppose that declarant, unable to speak, is shown a photograph of D and nods his head. See McFadden v. United States, 395 A.2d 14 (D.C.App.1978). See also Commonwealth v. Nolin, 364 N.E.2d 1224 (Mass.1977).

As to the admissibility of a taped dying declaration see State v. Larson, 281 N.W.2d 481 (Minn.), cert. denied, 444 U.S. 973 (1979). See also People v. Siler, 429 N.W.2d 865 (Mich.Ct.App.1988)(taped 911 call by victim stating that he had been stabbed in the heart by defendant).

SECTION 10. FORFEITURE

The Advisory Committee on the Federal Rules of Evidence has proposed adding a new subdivision to Rule 804:

(6) Forfeiture by wrongdoing. A statement offered against a party that has engaged or acquiesced in wrongdoing that was intended to, and did, procure the unavailability of the declarant as a witness.

PROPOSED COMMITTEE NOTE

Subdivision (b)(6). Rule 804(b)(6) has been added to provide that a party forfeits the right to object on hearsay grounds to the admission of a declarant's prior statement when the party's deliberate wrongdoing or acquiescence therein procured the unavailability of the declarant as a witness. This recognizes the need for a prophylactic rule to deal with abhorrent behavior "which strikes at the heart of the system of justice itself." United States v. Mastrangelo, 693 F.2d 269, 273 (2d Cir.1982), cert. denied, 467 U.S. 1204 (1984). The wrongdoing need not consist of a criminal act. The rule applies to all parties, including the government.

Every circuit that has resolved the question has recognized the principle of forfeiture by misconduct, although the tests for determining whether there is a forfeiture have varied. See, e.g., United States v. Aguiar, 975 F.2d 45, 47 (2d Cir.1992); United States v. Potamitis, 739 F.2d 784, 789 (2d Cir.), cert. denied, 469 U.S. 918 (1984); Steele v. Taylor, 684 F.2d 1193, 1199 (6th Cir.1982), cert. denied, 460 U.S. 1053 (1983); United States v. Balano, 618 F.2d 624, 629 (10th Cir.1979), cert. denied, 449 U.S. 840 (1980); United States v. Carlson, 547 F.2d 1346, 1358–59 (8th Cir.), cert. denied, 431 U.S. 914 (1977). The foregoing cases apply a preponderance of the evidence standard. Contra United States v. Thevis, 665 F.2d 616, 631 (5th Cir.)(clear and convincing standard), cert. denied, 459 U.S. 825 (1982). The usual Rule 104(a) preponderance of the evidence standard has been adopted in light of the behavior the new Rule 804(b)(6) seeks to discourage.

As the proposed note indicates, numerous cases have recognized that conduct by a party that results in a witness' unavailability may waive a party's right to exclude prior statements of the unavailable witness. The cases have concluded that the conduct waives the defendant's Sixth Amendment rights and a fortiori any hearsay objections. The proposed rule uses the word "forfeiture" rather than "waiver," the word which predominates in the case law, because "waiver" is ordinarily a term reserved for the "intentional relinquishment ... of a known right or privilege." Johnson v. Zerbst, 304 U.S. 458, 464 (1938).

Unavailability. See Steele v. Taylor, 684 F.2d 1193, 1199 (6th Cir.1982) (court found that defendant had procured the silence of a prostitute who had been working for him by control through marriage), cert. denied, 460 U.S. 1053 (1983). See also cases in which courts have found that defendant's threats caused a witness's refusal to testify. See, e.g., United States v. Aguiar, 975 F.2d 45, 47 (2d Cir.1992); United States v. Potamitis, 739 F.2d 784, 789 (2d Cir.), cert. denied, 469 U.S. 918 (1984); United States v. Balano, 618 F.2d 624, 629 (10th Cir.1979), cert. denied, 449 U.S. 840 (1980). In Aguiar, the statement itself was used in determining whether the defendant had caused the declarant's unavailability. See also United States v. Thevis, 665 F.2d 616 (5th Cir.), cert. denied, 459 U.S. 825 (1982).

"Acquiesced in wrongdoing." In United States v. Mastrangelo, the only witness who could link defendant to the drug conspiracy was shot dead in the street on his way to the courthouse. The murder victim's grand jury testimony was admitted under the residual hearsay exception and defendant was convicted. On appeal, the Second Circuit remanded the case for an evidentiary hearing on whether Mastrangelo had waived his confrontation rights:

> If the District Court finds that Mastrangelo was in fact involved in the death of Bennett through knowledge, complicity, planning or in any other way, it must hold his objections to the use of Bennett's testimony waived. Bare knowledge of a plot to kill Bennett and a failure to give warning to appropriate authorities is sufficient to constitute a waiver.

United States v. Mastrangelo, 693 F.2d 269, 273–74 (2d Cir.1982). On remand, the trial court found that circumstantial evidence allowed the inference that defendant had "general knowledge" of a plot to kill Bennett. The trial court further found that the Government had established this prior knowledge by a preponderance of the evidence, but not by "clear and convincing" evidence. 561

F.Supp. 1114 (E.D.N.Y.1983). The Second Circuit affirmed the conviction. 722 F.2d 13 (2d Cir.1983), cert. denied, 467 U.S. 1204 (1984).

Compare United States v. White, 838 F.Supp. 618, 623 (D.D.C.1993):

> Mere failure to prevent the murder, or mere participation in the alleged drug conspiracy at the heart of this case, must surely be insufficient to constitute a waiver of a defendant's constitutional confrontation rights. The Court believes a ruling to that effect would provide too little protection for so important a right.... [T]he government [must] show that the particular defendant participated in some manner in the planning or execution of the murder of Arvell Williams.

And see United States v. Houlihan, 887 F.Supp. 352, 364-65 (D.Mass.1995)(adopting rule of White, supra and holding that "being a part of a conspiracy to murder where one of the members of the conspiracy had the motive of silencing a witness" does not suffice; each member of conspiracy must know that "one of the motives for the killing was the silencing of a potential witness."), aff'd on point, 92 F.3d 1271 (1st Cir.1996).

"Procuring the unavailability of the declarant as a witness." When the government seeks to admit the grand jury testimony of a now unavailable declarant, the declarant has been identified as a potential witness. But suppose the statement was made before any legal proceedings were commenced. See, e.g., United States v. White, 838 F.Supp. 618 (D.D.C.1993)(finding that statements made by informant to police fit within waiver doctrine); United States v. Houlihan, 887 F.Supp. 352, 360-61 & note 17 (D.Mass.1995)(admitting statements made by alleged "foot-soldier" in a cocaine trafficking enterprise who cooperated with the police prior to his murder almost two and a half years before trial; defendant argued that waiver doctrine applies only to statements made on "eve of trial"; court found that there had been "showing that the victim was in fact cooperating with law enforcement authorities and was likely to have testified at trial and that these facts provided a motive for the murder"; court noted "that it is not necessary that the desire to silence a potential witness be the only motivation a defendant had for murdering that victim"), aff'd on point, 92 F.3d 1271, 1279 (1st Cir.1996)("no principled reason why the waiver-by-misconduct doctrine should not apply with equal force if a defendant intentionally silences a potential witness.").

Evidentiary consequences. United States v. White, 838 F.Supp. 618, 625 (D.D.C.1993)("purpose of finding a waiver is limited to allowing the adverse party to present statements made by the unavailable witness as if the witness were actually able to take the stand.... [Only] the initial layer of hearsay—the fact that the testifying officers are relating statements made to them by [the murdered declarant] will be ignored."); Steele v. Taylor, 684 F.2d 1193, 1207 (6th Cir.1982)(state habeas; dissenting judge objected that statement admitted pursuant to waiver doctrine consists of "the purest of doubly attenuated hearsay"), cert. denied, 460 U.S. 1053 (1983). Cf. United States v. Aguiar, 975 F.2d 45, 47 (2d Cir.1992)(admission of "facially unreliable hearsay would raise a due process issue, although it is hard to imagine circumstances in which such evidence would survive Fed.R.Evid. 403's test of weighing probative value against prejudicial effect, an objection that is not waived by procuring a witness's absence."). See also United States v. Houlihan, 92 F.3d 1271, 1283 (1st Cir.1996)(holding that trial court properly redacted some first-level hearsay).

References. Jonakait, Texts, or Ad Hoc Determinations: Interpretations of the Federal Rules of Evidence, 71 Ind.L.J. 551, 576-79 (1996); Markland, The

Admission of Hearsay Evidence Where Defendant Misconduct Causes the Unavailability of a Prosecution Witness, 43 Am.U.L.Rev. 995 (1994).

SECTION 11.   MISCELLANEOUS EXCEPTIONS

Numerous other exceptions to the hearsay rule exist that have not been discussed in the materials above. See, e.g., Federal Rules of Evidence Rule 803(9)–(23), Rule 804(b)(4); California Evidence Code §§ 1224–1227, 1281–1284, 1300–1302, 1310–1316, 1320–1324, 1330–1331, 1340–1341. See generally Binder, The Hearsay Handbook: The Hearsay Rule and Its 40 Exceptions (1975).

A few of the more significant of these miscellaneous exceptions are discussed in the materials below. The evolving concept of non-class exceptions, or catch-all exceptions, or residual hearsay, is the subject of Section 12, infra.

A.   ANCIENT DOCUMENTS

Bowers v. Fibreboard Corporation

Court of Appeals of Washington, Division Two, 1992.
66 Wash.App. 454, 832 P.2d 523.

■ SEINFELD, J.

. . .

Marlene Bowers is the personal representative of the estate of her stepfather, Richard Williams. Williams was a boilermaker in the United States Navy from 1946 until June 1962 and worked in the Puget Sound Naval Shipyard from 1977 to 1986. He served on the U.S.S. Manchester between 1946 and 1950 and on the U.S.S. Iowa in 1952 during the Korean war. Williams died in 1986 of mesothelioma. Here, also, it is undisputed that the cause of the mesothelioma was asbestos exposure.

The defendants manufactured asbestos products used as insulation on Navy ships. Navy boilermakers came into contact with such products when removing insulation from pipes and valves to prepare them for inspection and repairs. They also combined asbestos powder and water to create a compound for small repairs.

. . .

In Bowers' case, the defendants assign error to the trial court's decision to admit excerpts from the United States Navy publication, Dictionary of American Naval Fighting Ships, under the "ancient document" exception to the hearsay rule, ER 803(a)(16). . . .

Bowers sought to admit the excerpts to establish that the ships on which Williams served were in specific ports at a time when defendants' products were used on ships in those ports. One such excerpt, which the court admitted as an exhibit, stated that the Manchester was "laid down" in the Fore River Shipyard in Quincy, Massachusetts, in 1944 and launched in March 1946. Another excerpt, read into the record but not admitted as an exhibit, stated that the "Iowa departed from Yokosuka, Japan 19 October 1952 for overhaul at Norfolk." The deposition testimony of certain shipyard workers put defendants' products in the Fore River Shipyard at the time the Manchester was built,

1944, and at the Norfolk Naval Shipyard between 1942 and 1975. A worker at Norfolk stated that he worked on the Iowa during this time period.

Defendants contend that these excerpts do not fit under the hearsay rule's ancient document exception. They argue, rather, that the Dictionary of American Naval Fighting Ships (Dictionary) is more like a "learned treatise" that might be admissible under ER 803(a)(18) if called to the attention of a testifying expert, but that no such expert was presented in this case. We find, however, that the "ancient document" exception is broad enough to encompass these particular excerpts and that this ruling meets the purpose of the hearsay rule and the policies underlying the "ancient document" exception.

. . . .

Evidence is authentic if it is in fact what its proponent claims. ER 901(a), (b)(8). The defendants do not argue that the Dictionary is not authentic or that the portions admitted are less than 20 years old. In any event, the Dictionary in question is self-authenticating. ER 902. The rule does not require extrinsic evidence of authenticity as a condition precedent to admissibility for books, pamphlets, or other publications purporting to be issued by a public authority. ER 902(e). The title page of the Dictionary announces that its source is the Navy Department, Office of the Chief of Naval Operations.

The purpose of the rule prohibiting the use of hearsay testimony, except in limited circumstance, is to increase the probability that evidence shall be trustworthy and reliable. Chmela v. Department of Motor Vehicles, 88 Wn.2d 385, 392–93, 561 P.2d 1085 (1977). Certain categories of statements, including ancient document evidence, contain independent indicia of reliability and, thus, are excepted from the hearsay prohibition. E. Cleary, McCormick on Evidence § 253 (3d ed. 1984); ER 803(a)(1)-(23).

The requirement that an "ancient document" be at least 20 years old when offered enhances the probability that it will be trustworthy. First, the lengthy time period between preparation of the document and litigation provides assurance that the work was not fabricated in anticipation of litigation. In addition, in a case such as this, the 20 years between publication and the use of the Dictionary at trial provided readers an extended opportunity to point out any errors and suggest corrections to the information.

Necessity is the second policy reason for admitting certain hearsay evidence. 5 J. Wigmore, Evidence § 1420 (1974). As living witnesses to historical events are difficult to find, the trier of fact likely will lose the benefit of such evidence entirely if not admissible under an exception to the hearsay rule. 5 J. Wigmore § 1421. Furthermore, we recognize that the difficulty of assembling the pieces necessary to tell the entire story about an incident that occurred more than 20 years ago may be so great that the evidence is practically, though perhaps not technically, unavailable.

In support of their contention that ER 803(a)(18), the "learned treatise" exception, rather than the ER 803(a)(16) "ancient document" exception, should apply, defendants cite Most Worshipful Prince Hall Grand Lodge v. Most Worshipful Universal Grand Lodge, 62 Wn.2d 28, 381 P.2d 130, cert. denied, 375 U.S. 945 (1963). However, Prince Hall Lodge is distinguishable. The evidence at issue there involved several books introduced by both parties on the history of what was then called "colored Masonry". The trial court admitted all but one of the books into evidence, apparently under a then existing exception to the hearsay rule for treatises dealing with events of general history. Appellants challenged the trial court's exclusion of the one book: a supplement to a treatise written by a person other than the author of the treatise. The reviewing court noted that, in contrast to the works that the trial court admitted, in this one case the proponent did not qualify the book's author or provide any other basis for considering the work an authoritative history. Therefore, it was not an abuse of discretion to refuse to admit it. Prince Hall Lodge, 62 Wn.2d at 42.

Defendants argue that Bowers, likewise, offered no testimony in support of the Dictionary excerpts. However, a testimonial foundation, although required for admission of evidence from learned treatises, ER 803(a)(18), is not demanded by the rule excepting ancient documents. ER 803(a)(16). We need not decide the remaining question, whether the trial court must exclude a properly authenticated 20–year-old document absent additional evidence of its reliability, because here we do have such evidence. In deciding whether to admit the Dictionary, the trial court properly considered a letter offered by plaintiff from the head of the Ships' Histories Branch of the Department of the Navy. (The trial court must make the preliminary determination as to the admissibility of challenged evidence. ER 104(a). In doing so, the trial court is not bound by the Rules of Evidence. ER 104(a)). The letter stated that the Dictionary, an official publication, is contained in many reference libraries and that it has been "well-received" and "favorably reviewed" and that its primary sources are documents in the Naval Historical Center and National Archives.

In contrast to the treatise supplement by an unrecognized author in Prince Hall Lodge, the Dictionary is a government publication, compiled from data contained in government archives, maintained in numerous libraries, and reviewed by several journals. This combination of facts increases its probability of reliability and supports the admission of the Dictionary as an authoritative history.

Furthermore, there is no reason to exclude compilations of data such as those contained in the Dictionary from the term "ancient document". One commentator, referring to the "ancient document" exception to the hearsay rule, ER 803(a)(16), states:

> Nothing in the rule restricts its application to dispositive instruments such as deeds. The text of the rule is broad enough to include other documents, apparently including newspapers and treatises. Nothing in the rule requires that the author of the document be established as an expert.

(Footnotes omitted.) 5B K. Tegland, Wash. Prac., Evidence § 382 (3d ed. 1989).

Finally, defendants suggest that it is arbitrary to eliminate the additional foundational requirements for admission of a learned treatise merely because the document has reached the age of 20. We recognize that the selection of a specific time period for the general application of ER 803(a)(16) involved some subjective judgment. However, the fundamental reasons for the rule, necessity and high degree of reliability, encompass the inclusion of the Dictionary in this case. Further, the trier of fact can understand and utilize the Dictionary, a compilation of facts rather than a treatise of analysis, opinion, and theory, without expert interpretation. The testimony of an expert witness regarding his or her use of this text would add little.

The court acted within its discretion in admitting these Dictionary excerpts as "ancient documents".

. . .

NOTES

1. In another asbestos case, George v. Celotex Corp., 914 F.2d 26, 29–30 (2d Cir.1990), plaintiff sought to prove that defendant should reasonably have

known about asbestos dangers by introducing an unpublished 1947 report that questioned the industry threshold exposure limits then in effect. The court held that the report had been properly admitted as an ancient document under Rule 803(16). It rejected the defendant's argument "that the need to test the reliability of the report's conclusions makes it inadmissible." The court explained: "Defendant cites neither caselaw nor commentary in support of its argument, nor could we find any that limit the scope and application of the ancient documents exception to the hearsay rule in a manner suggested by the defendant."

2. In Skipper v. Yow, 105 S.E.2d 205 (N.C.1958), recitals in an ancient deed were admitted. Cf. the various ancient documents admitted in Seaway Co. v. Attorney General, 375 S.W.2d 923 (Tex.Civ.App.1964) and see Walker v. Town of Fruithurst, 130 So.2d 12 (Ala.1961)(map); Matter of Estate of Egbert, 306 N.W.2d 525 (Mich.Ct.App.1981)(photograph); Moore v. Horn, 359 S.W.2d 947 (Tex.Civ.App.1962)(pleading); Estate of Nidever, 5 Cal.Rptr. 343 (App.1960)(application for pension). Cf. King v. Schultz, 375 P.2d 108 (Mont.1962)(desert land entry documents). See also Wickes, Ancient Documents and Hearsay, 8 Tex.L.Rev. 451 (1930); Notes, 83 U.Pa.L.Rev. 247 (1934); 46 Iowa L.Rev. 448 (1961); 34 Tex.L.Rev. 323 (1955).

3. Bell v. Combined Registry Co., 397 F.Supp. 1241, 1247 (E.D.Ill.1975), aff'd, 536 F.2d 164 (7th Cir.), cert. denied, 429 U.S. 1001 (1976)(letters and newspaper articles from the 1930s and 1940s were admitted pursuant to Federal Rules of Evidence Rule 803(16) to show that owner of copyright had forfeited his copyright by publishing his work without a copyright notice). See also Calif.Evid.Code § 1331.

4. See also Federal Rules of Evidence Rule 803(20) which makes admissible reputation concerning boundaries or general history. See Gibson v. Pencader Presbyterian Church, 20 A.2d 134 (Del.Ch.1941) with which cf. International Free and Accepted Modern Masons v. Most Worshipful Prince Hall Grand Lodge, Free & Accepted Masons Etc., 318 S.W.2d 46 (Ky.1958) and Most Worshipful Prince Hall Grand Lodge v. Most Worshipful Universal Grand Lodge, 381 P.2d 130 (Wash.1963), cert. denied 375 U.S. 945 (1963). See also Guerrero v. Guerrero, 2 N.M.I. 61, 1991 WL 70062 (N. Mariana Islands 1991)(Rule 803(20) covers statements about ownership of land); Hudson, Historical Treatises as Evidence, 122 Just.P. 54 (1958), 123 id. 105 (1959).

B.   LEARNED TREATISES

Graham v. Wyeth Laboratories

United States Court of Appeals, Tenth Circuit.
906 F.2d 1399, cert. denied, 498 U.S. 981, 111 S.Ct. 511 (1990).

■ GARTH, CIRCUIT JUDGE:

. . .

This appeal originated from a $15,000,000 jury verdict in favor of Michelle Graham ("Graham") and against Wyeth for the defective manufacture of Wyeth's DTP vaccine. Wyeth manufactured a DTP vaccine which is used to immunize children against the diseases of diphtheria, tetanus (lockjaw) and pertussis (whooping cough) . . .

. . .

This lawsuit had its origins in the tragic history of the plaintiff, Michelle Graham, a child who has suffered, and is suffering from brain damage, and who requires continuous treatment and care. Michelle Graham (by her parents) alleged that she sustained severe and irreversible brain damage after being vaccinated against diphtheria, pertussis and tetanus with a defective vaccine produced by Wyeth.

. . .

Wyeth also argues that the district court abused its discretion when it admitted an American Medical Association Ad Hoc Panel Report, "Pertussis Vaccine Injury," 245 JAMA 21:3083 (December 6, 1985)(PX376) into evidence, when it redacted the Report, and when it, contrary to the provision of Fed.R.Evid. 803(18), not only permitted the report to be read to the jury in its redacted form but then permitted the jury to receive the document as an exhibit. Wyeth charges that this document was so fatal to Wyeth's case that Wyeth was obliged to move for a mistrial.[1]

The Report's first sentence stated its objective: ·

> In an effort to ensure an adequate and uninterrupted supply of vaccines for mandated pediatric immunization and to encourage the continued timely administration of these vaccines, the American Medical Association formed a commission to explore the need for a compensation system for vaccine-injured patients.

The remainder of that paragraph and a portion of the succeeding paragraph addressed itself to the issue of establishing a federal vaccine compensation program as an exclusive remedy for any individual injured by a mandated vaccine and noted that there was only one remaining supplier of DTP—a supplier who might be unable to obtain insurance renewal.

Other portions of the exhibit, while acknowledging that the Report did not have as its purpose stringent proof of causation of injury by the vaccine, did refer to injuries "reputed" to be vaccine-related and reported by television and radio news programs, newspapers or parents groups but whose relationship to DTP vaccine was not necessarily supported by medical evidence. It went on to state that it was the impression of the AMA panel that about 10% of patients exhibiting seizures may have residual brain damage after one year. Other probabilities of related injuries were discussed in the Report, although the panel noted that there was "no evidence that killed vaccine (such as [Wyeth's] pertussis vaccine) can cause any prolonged insidious or delayed deleterious effects (in contrast to live attenuated organism vaccine)." While the Report did not address the issue of whether DTP could cause retardation—but rather addressed itself to a proposed legislative solution to compensate vaccine victims—some of its content could be read as relating to the issues in this case. . . .

Wyeth objected to the admission of the Report in its entirety, claiming that the Report was neither a scientific nor a clinical study nor a learned treatise. It also objected to the court's sua sponte redaction of the introductory portion of the Report which, as noted, dealt with a proposed compensatory and insurance scheme. In addition, Wyeth contended that when the district court permitted the jury to have the redacted document in its possession during deliberations as a written exhibit, the district court had acted contrary to the express provision

---

1. The district court characterized the AMA Report as "the smoking gun we have been looking for . . ." (Tr. 1627) and denied Wyeth's motion. [Footnote of the court renumbered; some footnotes have been omitted.]

of Fed.R.Evid. 803(18) which provides that if a learned treatise is admitted "the statements may be read into evidence but may not be received as exhibits."

A.

Wyeth claimed among other things that the Report did not qualify as a learned treatise because Graham's expert had not established that it was a reliable authority within the meaning of Fed.R.Evid. 803(18). Wyeth also claimed that in order to be admitted into evidence, the Report would have to be demonstrated to be relevant to the facts of the case at issue.

Dr. Gilmartin, who testified on behalf of Graham, testified only that the panel was a prestigious panel, and that the Journal of the American Medical Association, in which the Report appeared, was an authoritative publication. Significantly, Dr. Gilmartin did not testify that the Report itself was a reliable authority or that it constituted a learned treatise. Moreover, because the Report did not deal with the causal relationship between DTP and stroke, Wyeth asserted that a specific issue in this case which focused on causation was not addressed and therefore the Report was irrelevant.

Our reading of the record does not disclose Wyeth's specific objection to the introduction of this Report on the ground that the foundation for its introduction was inadequate. Rather, Wyeth objected strenuously to the Report on the grounds that its purpose was not to establish causation, but was rather tangential in the sense that it advocated a legislative compensatory scheme. Indeed, Wyeth's strongest objection was to the sua sponte redaction of a portion of the Report which deprived the jury of knowledge that the Report did no more than propose a plan to compensate any DTP victims. In the absence of a specific objection to the manner in which Graham laid the foundation for the Report's introduction, we cannot say that the district court judge would have abused his discretion had he permitted the entire Report in evidence, leaving it to Wyeth to cross-examine Dr. Gilmartin on the purpose of the Report. By doing so, Wyeth could have clarified the relevance and import of the Report itself.

B.

Whether or not the full Report was admissible in evidence within the ambit of Fed. R. Evid. 803(18), the district court's subsequent action in sua sponte redacting a significant portion of the Report stands on a different footing. After Wyeth had objected to the relevancy of the Report because the panel had not established a causal relationship between DTP vaccine and encephalopathy, the district court on its own motion redacted the first paragraph and a substantial portion of the second paragraph of the Report. The sentences redacted, as we have noted earlier, contained a statement as to the purpose of the Report (compensation) and a reference to the possibility that insurance might be unavailable. The district court recognized that the issue of compensation as presented in the Report was irrelevant to the issues of this case, but by redacting all reference to compensation the court unwittingly distorted the thrust of the Report. Not only was the purpose and theme of the article withdrawn from the jury's consideration, but the district court explicitly ordered that Wyeth could not cross-examine any witness on the material which appeared in the redacted paragraphs.

. . .

Through its redaction, the district court admitted evidence into the case which could only mislead the jury. By prohibiting cross-examination about the true purpose of the Report the district court compounded its error. Moreover, although Dr. Gilmartin testified to some statements in the redacted Report having to do with the panel's recitation of probability of vaccine causation, (Tr. 1631) the entire redacted Report was given to the jury for their study during deliberations. What the last provision in Fed.R.Evid. 803(18) seeks to preclude by prohibiting the receipt of the written exhibit into evidence is described in Weinstein's Evidence as:

> To insure that the jurors will not be unduly impressed by the treatise, and that they will not use the text as a starting point for conclusions untested by expert testimony, the last paragraph of Rule 803(18) bars the admission of treatises as exhibits so that they cannot be taken into the juryroom.

J. Weinstein & M. Berger, 4 Weinstein's Evidence ¶ 803(18)[02].

. . .

We are satisfied that the district court abused its discretion in redacting the portions of the Report which explained the Report's purpose and background and in prohibiting Wyeth from addressing those issues on cross-examination or through its own witnesses. We are also satisfied that it was improper to submit the Report in its redacted version to the jury in contravention of Fed.R.Evid. 803(18). We need not decide if this abuse of discretion on the part of the district court, even though it may have been well intentioned, would by itself require a reversal of the judgment in favor of Graham.

[The court found other errors and reversed and remanded.]

NOTES

1. Which types of publication would constitute a learned treatise under Federal Rules of Evidence Rule 803(18)? Safety codes and standards? See Johnson v. William C. Ellis & Sons Iron Works, Inc., 609 F.2d 820 (5th Cir.1980). Reports prepared by United States Department of Transportation? See Dawson v. Chrysler, 630 F.2d 950 (3d Cir.1980), cert. denied, 450 U.S. 959 (1981). Text written by registered nurses offered in a malpractice action brought against physicians? Hemingway v. Ochsner Clinic, 608 F.2d 1040 (5th Cir.1979). See Note, 27 S.C.L.Rev. 766 (1976). See also Schneider v. Cessna Aircraft Co., 722 P.2d 321 (Ariz.Ct.App.1985)(in a wrongful death action that arose out of the crash of a Cessna aircraft, Cessna argued that the crash was caused by pilot inattention; in support of its theory, Cessna offered a FAA training film dealing with stall-spins caused by pilot inexperience or inattention; the court held that the video had properly been admitted pursuant to the learned treatises exception; plaintiff's expert had stated on cross-examination that FAA materials are an authoritative source and that their films are a good training source). See discussion in chapter 6, section 2 at p. 1063.

2. In a jurisdiction that has adopted the text of Federal Rule 803(18) are statements admissible if they are contained in a treatise which W1 on cross-examination declares to be inaccurate but W2 on direct testifies he relied upon extensively and has personally verified? Runkle v. Burlington Northern, 613 P.2d 982 (Mont.1980). See also Carroll v. Morgan, 17 F.3d 787, 790 (5th Cir.1994).

3. As to the difficulty a plaintiff may encounter in trying to establish the standard of medical practice in the community by a medical treatise rather than an expert, see Walker v. North Dakota Eye Clinic, Ltd., 415 F.Supp. 891 (D.N.D.1976). Cf. Schneider v. Revici, 817 F.2d 987, 991 (2d Cir.1987)(court held that even if defendant's text qualified as a learned treatise, admission would remain subject to Rule 403's balancing test, "a balancing that would favor exclusion because of the danger of prejudice inherent in recognizing a book authored by the defendant in a medical malpractice case as a learned treatise."). For the difficulties that arise in a jurisdiction that permits use of a learned treatise for impeachment but not as substantive evidence see Stinson v. England, 633 N.E.2d 532 (Ohio 1994).

5. Can one establish a medical standard by introducing a learned treatise to show that it does not require a particular practice? See, e.g., Haney v. DeSandre, 692 S.W.2d 214 (Ark.1985)(medical malpractice suit charged that defendant should have tested for pregnancy before performing hysterectomy; defense expert testified that nowhere in authoritative gynecological treatise does it state that pregnancy test should routinely be ordered; court held that a failure to state is not a statement).

6. See also Walsh & Rose, Increasing the Useful Information Provided by Experts in the Courtroom: A Comparison of Federal Rules of Evidence 703 and 803(18) with the Evidence Rules in Illinois, Ohio, and New York, 26 Seton Hall L.Rev. 183 (1995); Notes, 14 Val.U.L.Rev. 329 (1980), 9 Loyola U. of Chi.L.J. 193 (1977), 5 Val.U.L.Rev. 126 (1970), 66 Mich.L.Rev. 183 (1967).

7. Under what circumstances might a book for which no foundation was laid as a learned treatise be admissible under Rule 803(17), which allows admission of "tabulations, lists, directories, or other published compilations, generally used and relied upon by the public or by persons in particular occupations?" In United States v. Mount, 896 F.2d 612, 624–25 (1st Cir.1990), cert. denied, 510 U.S. 957 (1993), defendant was charged with transporting rare historical documents, including documents written or signed by Abraham Lincoln, knowing them to be stolen. The dealer to whom the defendant offered the letters testified that she alerted the FBI after consulting a multi-volume set that lists the owners of all known Lincoln documents. The court found that "the volumes comfortably fit within the hearsay exception in Rule 803(17)," after the dealer satisfied the foundational requirement by testifying that manuscript dealers like herself rely on this work. The volumes were therefore receivable as exhibits.

8. Compare Crane v. Crest Tankers, Inc., 47 F.3d 292, 295–96 (8th Cir. 1995)(in action under Jones Act to recover damages for personal injuries, reversible error to have given the jurors as an exhibit a slide rule device labeled a "Future Damage Calculator" marketed and distributed by "Lawyers and Judges Publishing Co.;" exhibit did not satisfy Rule 803(17) because proponent "made no showing and offered no foundation that the exhibit is generally used or relied upon by the public or persons in the legal or other professions;" court indicated that it was not concerned with the admission of the life expectancy table, which was part of the device, but with the present value table, which did not indicate how it was calculated, and with the suggestion that the judiciary had vouched for the device). See also United States v. Cassiere, 4 F.3d 1006, 1018–19 (1st Cir.1993)(admitting monthly published reports listing property sales and prices that testimony indicated real estate brokers and appraisers generally rely upon); In re Byington, 197 B.R. 130 (Bkrtcy.D.Kan.1996)(NADA "blue book" values of automobiles); Cosgrove v. Merrell Dow Pharmaceuticals, Inc., 788 P.2d 1293 (Idaho 1989)(sales charts listing drug sales were admissible where they were compiled by independent sources and regularly purchased by pharmaceutical companies); United States v. Grossman, 614 F.2d 295 (1st Cir.1980)(in prosecution for receiving stolen cigarette lighters, catalog issued by manufacturer of lighters was properly admitted to identify the stolen lighters where testimony by a purchasing agent of the manufacturer had established that the catalog "was a published compilation generally used and relied upon by retailers of Colibri lighters."). See also the extensive discussion in State v. Lungsford, 400 A.2d 843 (N.J.Super.App.Div.1979) of the foundational requirements that need to be satisfied before evidence is admitted under the exception codified in Rule 803(17).

9.   Non-published lists may at times also be admissible. See Madden v. State, 799 S.W.2d 683 (Tex.Crim.App.1990)(murder prosecution; court held that list found in victim's safe deposit box recording serial numbers of weapons owned by victim was admissible as a statement affecting an interest in property under Rule 803(15); numbers matched those of weapons that defendant had sold after murder thus establishing that defendant was in possession of victim's property).

D.   JUDGMENT OF PREVIOUS CONVICTION

NOTES

1.   There has been a growing tendency in civil actions to admit a judgment of conviction in a criminal action as proof of the facts on which the conviction was obtained. See McCormick, Evidence § 318 (2d ed., Cleary, 1972); Motomura, Using Judgments as Evidence, 70 Minn.L.Rev. 979 (1986); Cowen, The Admissibility of Criminal Convictions in Subsequent Civil Proceedings, 40 Calif.L.Rev. 225 (1952); Coutts, The Effect of a Criminal Judgment on a Civil Action, 18 Mod.L.Rev. 231 (1955). Annot., 18 A.L.R.2d 1287 (1951).

2.   Should admissibility be limited to judgments for felonies? Does the policy limiting the application of Federal Rules of Evidence Rule 803(22) to judgments "adjudging a person guilty of a crime punishable by death or imprisonment in excess of one year" mean that a guilty plea to a misdemeanor charge should also be excluded? In Hancock v. Dodson, 958 F.2d 1367, 1371 (6th Cir.1992), the majority rejected the appellant's argument that "individuals have little motivation to defend the charges, and so the resulting guilty plea is unreliable." The majority admitted a guilty plea to a misdemeanor as admissible non-hearsay under FRE 801(d)(2)(A), and stated that in the alternative the evidence was admissible under the residual exception. The dissenting judge found that the facts of the case presented a classic example of why pleas in non-felony cases should not be allowed under other hearsay exceptions:

> Faced with felony charges, Mr. Hancock was motivated to, and did in fact, defend against the charges. But then the state offered a deal. It offered to drop the felony charges in return for a guilty plea to misdemeanor charges and the payment of a $60 fine. Now Mr. Hancock had to weigh $60 against legal fees. He had to weigh $60 against the possibility of conviction, no matter how remote. In short, the state's offer of such an outstanding plea bargain effectively removed any motivation that Mr. Hancock may have had to defend against the charges. The majority rejects the straightforward application of Rule 803(22). First, it erroneously reasons that the record of conviction is itself an admission of Mr. Hancock, rather than merely hearsay containing an admission. This reasoning, however, leads to the anomalous result that misdemeanor convictions entered after a trial or a hearing would still be excluded, because they are not admissions. To admit misdemeanor convictions upon a guilty plea yet exclude misdemeanor convictions following a hearing is inconsistent with the first line of Rule 803(22), which treats "[e]vidence of a final judgment, entered after a trial

or upon a plea of guilty'' in equal terms. Furthermore, there is no reason to assume that one is any more probative of guilt than the other....

Id. at 1376–77. See also United States v. Loera, 923 F.2d 725, 730 (9th Cir.)(admitting prior misdemeanor conviction under Rule 803(8)), cert. denied, 502 U.S. 854 (1991); United States v. Gotti, 641 F.Supp. 283, 290 (E.D.N.Y.1986)(admitting misdemeanor plea as admission but stating that untrustworthy plea could be excluded under Rule 403).

Is the conviction admissible if it was obtained in a foreign country? Should there be a blanket rule of admission or exclusion? See Lloyd v. American Export Lines, Inc., 580 F.2d 1179, 1187–1190 (3d Cir.), cert. denied, 439 U.S. 969 (1978).

3. Rozier v. Ford Motor Co., 573 F.2d 1332, 1346–1348 (5th Cir.1978): Widow of passenger killed in automobile crash brought suit against car manufacturer claiming that Ford's negligent design of gas tank caused death of her husband.

Mrs. Rozier alleged that the district court erred in admitting into evidence over plaintiff's objection the plea of guilty by Benjamin Wilson, the driver of the impacting vehicle, to charges of involuntary manslaughter in the deaths of Mr. Rozier and Frank Mitchell, the driver of the Ford Galaxie....

Ford introduced a certified copy of Wilson's guilty plea for two stated purposes: (1) to corroborate the testimony of the investigating officer, Trooper Swindell, that Wilson's car was traveling at approximately 68 m.p.h. at the moment of impact, and (2) as evidence that Mr. Rozier's death was caused by Wilson's criminal act and not by Ford's negligence. While we agree with Ford that this evidence is not excluded by the hearsay rule by virtue of Rule 803(22), Fed.R.Evid., we hold that it is inadmissible under the test for legal relevancy set forth in Rule 403.

. . .

The jury in this case hardly needed Wilson's guilty plea to demonstrate what had caused the accident in which Mr. Rozier lost his life. The fact of the accident was conceded by the plaintiff, and numerous photographs put in evidence by both parties graphically depicted the devastating consequences of the impact. Certainly, the jury realized that the fuel tank would not have ruptured had it not been for the crushing blow inflicted by Wilson's car.

The real purpose for introducing the guilty plea would seem to be as evidence of legal cause. It is here that the danger of confusion arises. Because Wilson's admission of responsibility for Mr. Rozier's death was made in the context of a criminal action to deter reckless driving, its relevance in a civil action based on a legal doctrine presumably intended to deter the negligent manufacture of automobiles is attenuated at best. The liability which Wilson admitted in his guilty plea is based on a different social policy than that with which Mrs. Rozier charged Ford Motor Company. Furthermore, the second collision doctrine *assumes* that the primary collision is caused by a party other than the manufacturer. Here, Mrs. Rozier has alleged that the primary collision with Wilson caused the secondary collision with the fuel tank which, in turn, caused the death of her husband by creating the fire that incinerated him. The key question in the case is whether Ford owed a duty to Mr. Rozier to build a fuel tank that could withstand an impact such as that inflicted by Wilson's car. If Ford owed such a duty then, other considerations aside, Ford caused Mr. Rozier's death. We think that the interrelationship between cause and duty in the second collision context was difficult enough for the jury to grasp so that it should not have been further complicated by the unnecessary, confusing, and potentially misleading element of the Wilson guilty plea. We hold that the trial court abused its discretion in admitting this evidence. [Footnotes omitted.]

4. Seattle–First National Bank v. Cannon, 26 Wn.App. 922, 615 P.2d 1316, 1319–1321 (1980): Bank brought civil action against Ds who had been convicted of embezzling funds from bank. Trial court granted summary judgment against Ds based upon their conviction and awarded damages of $43,000:

> The trend, which we adopt here, has been to admit criminal convictions as evidence in a civil case as to those factual issues determined in the criminal case.

> . . . Those courts that have considered the matter, however, have divided on the question of whether it is only prima facie evidence or is conclusive evidence of the facts previously determined. The majority of courts have decided the evidence is conclusive as to those facts previously determined. Others hold the conviction is prima facie evidence of those facts.

> . . .

> . . . Although both these defendants deny any complicity in the acts of embezzlement, that matter has been conclusively decided against them. They were accorded all the procedural protections of a criminal trial which requires a higher burden of proof than pertains in a civil action. Thus, we find the doctrine of collateral estoppel is applicable to those issues determined in the criminal conviction. See Haslund v. Seattle, 86 Wn.2d 607, 622, 547 P.2d 1221 (1976).

> The ultimate facts decided in the criminal trial were that the Cannons were guilty of conspiracy and in aiding and abetting the embezzlement of bank funds. The federal government, however, was not required to prove an exact amount in excess of $100. . . .

> . . .

> While the federal district court required restitution by the Cannons for a specific sum and the Ninth Circuit in its opinion recited a figure of $43,000, those facts were evidentiary and collateral to the claim asserted by the government, i.e., conspiracy and aiding and abetting embezzlement. See Peterson v. Department of Ecology, 92 Wn.2d 306, 312–13, 596 P.2d 285 (1979). The amount of the damages is not within the doctrine of collateral estoppel. Nor may the evidence on that issue in the criminal trial be considered prima facie or conclusive evidence here. Damages must be proven anew. [Footnotes omitted.]

See also Jordan v. McKenna, 573 So.2d 1371 (Miss.1990)(civil action for assault and battery; defendant's rape conviction given conclusive effect where defendant had been adequately represented by counsel).

May judgments of conviction be given conclusive effect in federal court? Are there circumstances in which they must be given such an effect? See Warren v. Applebaum, 526 F.Supp. 586 (E.D.N.Y.1981): Plaintiff, who had been convicted in state court of armed robbery of defendant, subsequently brought a civil rights action alleging that defendant, a key witness at the criminal trial, had committed perjury and suppressed exculpatory evidence thereby violating plaintiff's constitutional rights. How should the court rule on defendant's motion to dismiss? Cf. United States Fidelity & Guaranty Co. v. Moore, 306 F.Supp. 1088, 1095 n. 17 (N.D.Miss.1969).

5. Should a court permit the admission of a prior judgment of acquittal in a later civil suit? See the dictum in Wolff v. Employers Fire Insurance Co., 140 S.W.2d 640, 645 (Ky.1940) and Bush, Criminal Convictions as Evidence in Civil Proceedings, 29 Miss.L.J. 276, 278 (1958). What of a civil judgment in a subsequent criminal action? See United States v. Konovsky, 202 F.2d 721, 726 (7th Cir.1953).

SECTION 12.   NON-CLASS EXCEPTIONS

Robinson v. Shapiro

United States Court of Appeals, Second Circuit, 1981.
646 F.2d 734.

■ MESKILL, CIRCUIT JUDGE:

In this diversity action, Village Towers Company (Village Towers), a partnership owning an apartment building in New York City, appeals from a judgment of the United States District Court for the Southern District of New York, 484 F.Supp. 91, Lasker, J., entered on a jury verdict awarding plaintiff Rita Robinson $1,180,000 for the wrongful death and conscious pain and suffering of her late husband, Joseph, both New Jersey residents....

. . .

The facts surrounding the accident in question are largely undisputed. In early 1977, Village Towers contracted with Wasoff Contractors, Inc. (Wasoff) for the installation of a new heating system and chimney for its 19–story apartment building at 15 Charles Street in Greenwich Village. Wasoff subcontracted the chimney work to Modern Sheet Metal, Inc. (Modern), which completed the job by March 1977. Nearly ten months after the job was finished, portions of the chimney blew down during a severe windstorm and fell on the roof of the apartment building's adjoining one-story garage. The next day, Village Towers called Wasoff, which had guaranteed the work for one year; Wasoff, in turn, contacted its subcontractor, Modern, and Modern dispatched a three-man crew, led by the decedent, to clean up the debris and appraise the damage.

A clear description of the premises is essential to understanding the events that followed. Around the edge of the garage roof was a brick "parapet wall" approximately fourteen inches thick and three to four feet high.... Along the front of the garage to the edge of the building, an iron fence extended above the parapet wall an additional three feet. A metal staircase led from the alleyway at ground level to a gap in the parapet wall. In this gap was a large iron "gate," fashioned in the same style as the iron fence and extending a foot above the fence, or about four feet higher than the parapet wall. This "gate" was not hinged; rather, it was wedged into the gap with wooden shims and tied to the surrounding fence with electrical wire. Thus, the "gate" could be "opened" only by taking it down.

The Modern crew arrived around 9:15 a.m. on January 9 and, after a brief discussion between Robinson and John Rendo, the building superintendent, they began work. To get onto the roof, the Modern workmen had to walk up the metal staircase to the "gate" and, using the "gate" for support, hoist themselves onto the parapet wall. Then they walked along the parapet wall to the building's side, where they stepped through an opening in the fence onto the garage roof. During the course of the day, officers of Modern visited the premises and reached the roof in the same manner. Around 3:00 p.m., the crew decided to stop for the day because of inclement weather. Robinson was the last to leave. As he was using the gate to step down onto the staircase, the gate gave way and Robinson fell to the bottom of the stairs with the gate on top of him. Robinson was taken to a nearby hospital, where he died three days later as a result of head injuries sustained in the fall.

. . .

At trial, much of the evidence concerned the parties' knowledge of and responsibility for the dangerous gate. Samuel Greenberg, an owner of Village Towers, testified that a Village Towers maintenance man had been responsible for reinstalling the fence and gate after the initial construction of the chimney in early 1977. James Castro, a member of Robinson's crew on the day of the accident, testified that the gate appeared to be locked and securely fastened to the parapet wall. Harold Shictman, an officer of Modern who also climbed onto the roof, testified that the gate seemed "sturdy enough." Craig Wasoff, an officer of Wasoff, also visited the site, but could not recall how he gained access to the garage roof. Finally, Castro testified that Robinson had told him prior to the accident that Superintendent Rendo had forbidden the crew to remove the gate, because Rendo used the roof area as a makeshift pen for his dog, and the resultant opening would allow the dog to escape. Castro testified further that Robinson also had said that Rendo refused to let the crew reach the garage roof through his apartment window because he did not want his rugs soiled.

. . .

Village Towers also argues that Robinson's co-worker, James Castro, should not have been allowed to testify as to what Robinson told him concerning the conversation with Superintendent Rendo. The plaintiff and the third-party defendants counter that the evidence was not objected to, Fed.R.Evid. 103, and in any event was properly admitted under the "residual hearsay exception" for unavailable declarants, Fed.R.Evid. 804(b)(5). The evidence was properly admitted.

Six weeks before trial, Modern had sought the addresses of all employees at 15 Charles Street, including Rendo, who Modern mistakenly believed was still superintendent. Village Towers did not respond to these interrogatories. Finally, Modern served notice to Village Towers of its intention to introduce testimony concerning specific statements that were made by Rendo to Robinson, pursuant to the residual hearsay exception of Fed.R.Evid. 803(24) and 804(b)(5). It was not until the first day of trial that Modern learned that Rendo had left Village Towers and could not be located. In a pretrial ruling, Judge Lasker decided to admit the testimony under Fed.R.Evid. 804(b)(5). See J.App. at 34–35.[1]

---

1. In denying Village Towers' motion for a new trial, the court also justified admission of the testimony under Fed.R.Evid. 803(1), which allows admission of "[a] statement describing or explaining an event or condition made while the declarant was perceiving the event or condition, or immediately thereafter." The court reasoned:

There is no "double hearsay" here because Rendo's statement was a "verbal act" it was an "event" that established the "condition" under which the men were to work. Robinson's statement to Castro, then, was "a statement describing or explaining an event or condition"

We recognize that the residual exception should be invoked sparingly, see Committee on the Judiciary, Note to Paragraph (24) S.Rep.No.93–1277 at 19–20; Huff v. White Motor Corp., 609 F.2d 286, 291 (7th Cir.1979), but conclude that the Castro testimony satisfied the conditions of Rule 804(b)(5). There is no dispute that the evidence was material, nor can there be any serious argument that the statement was not "more probative on the point for which it [was] offered" than other reasonably available evidence. Castro's testimony was the only evidence indicating that a Village Towers employee who was clearly aware of the condition of the gate prohibited the crew from removing the obstruction or using a safe passage. Such testimony was highly relevant to the negligence of Modern, Village Towers, and the decedent. Finally, the notice provided in this case is conceded to be adequate. Thus, the only issues are whether the testimony bore "equivalent circumstantial guarantees of trustworthiness" and whether "the general purposes of these rules and the interests of justice [were] best ... served" by admitting the testimony.[2]

In this case, Robinson immediately returned from Rendo's apartment to his crew and relayed to them the superintendent's instructions. He had little motive to dissemble, since following Rendo's directions made the job considerably more difficult. The wet and snowy weather conditions supported Robinson's account of why Rendo forbade the use of his apartment to gain access to the garage roof. Moreover, the condition of the garage roof clearly revealed that the area was frequently used by a dog, thus corroborating Robinson's explanation of why Rendo would not permit removal of the gate.[3] It strains credulity that Robinson would have fabricated such a story. Thus, the circumstances surrounding Robinson's statement in this case demonstrate a level of trustworthiness at least equivalent to that of evidence admitted under traditional

made immediately after the "event" and contemporaneously with the "condition."

484 F.Supp. at 95. Since we agree that the evidence was properly admitted under Rule 804(b)(5), we need not pass upon the correctness of the district court's alternate holding. [Footnotes are the court's, renumbered; some have been omitted.]

2. Village Towers argues that "the legislative history of the Evidence Rules demonstrates that Congress intended to bar the admission" of testimony such as Castro's. The owners point out that the originally proposed rules allowed hearsay evidence of an unavailable declarant's recent sense perceptions (proposed Rule 802(b)(2)) and contained a far broader catchall provision. These provisions, they contend, would have allowed the admission of Castro's testimony. But, they argue, the subsequent elimination of the "recent sense perception" exception and the substantial narrowing of the catchall provisions indicate that testimony such as Castro's is inadmissible.

This argument is unpersuasive. That Congress was unwilling to allow the admission of all recent sense perceptions is no indication that it intended to *exclude all* such perceptions. In the proper circumstances, Rule 804(b)(5) is an appropriate vehicle for admitting certain recent sense impressions. See United States v. Medico, 557 F.2d 309,

315 (2d Cir.), cert. denied, 434 U.S. 986, 98 S.Ct. 614, 54 L.Ed.2d 480 (1977). Moreover, the tightening of the requirements of Rule 804(b)(5) does not suggest that in an appropriate case the rule should not be applied, but merely indicates that Congress was concerned lest the exception swallow the rule. See Committee on the Judiciary, Note to Paragraph (24), S.Rep.No.93–1277 at 18–20.

3. There is disagreement among the circuits as to the scope of a court's inquiry in determining "circumstantial guarantees of trustworthiness." Compare Huff v. White Motor Corp., supra, 609 F.2d at 293 ("[T]he probability that the statement is true, as shown by corroborative evidence, is not, we think, a consideration relevant to its admissibility under the residual exception to the hearsay rule.") with United States v. Bailey, 581 F.2d 341, 349 (3d Cir.1978)("[T]he trustworthiness of a statement should be analyzed by evaluating not only the facts corroborating the veracity of the statement, but also the circumstances in which the declarant made the statement and the incentive he had to speak truthfully or falsely."). In United States v. Medico, supra, 557 F.2d at 315–16, this Court seemed to use the broader inquiry employed in Bailey. We need not decide this issue, however, since we are convinced that even under the narrower test of Huff, the testimony was properly admitted.

hearsay exceptions. See United States v. Iaconetti, 406 F.Supp. 554, 559 (E.D.N.Y.)(Weinstein, J.), aff'd, 540 F.2d 574 (2d Cir.1976), cert. denied, 429 U.S. 1041, 97 S.Ct. 739, 50 L.Ed.2d 752 (1977). Nor do we feel that admission of the evidence poorly served the interests of justice. We note that this requirement essentially a restatement of Fed.R.Evid. 102 is commended to the sound discretion of the trial judge.... Given Modern's good faith efforts to discover the whereabouts of Rendo, the importance and apparent truthfulness of the evidence, and the lack of diligence of Village Towers in responding to the interrogatories or otherwise attempting to locate Rendo,[4] we cannot say that Judge Lasker abused his discretion in determining that admission of the evidence would best serve the interests of justice. See Huff v. White Motor Corp., supra, 609 F.2d at 295.

NOTES

1. Other interesting civil cases in which evidence was admitted pursuant to the residual exceptions are: Furtado v. Bishop, 604 F.2d 80 (1st Cir.1979), cert. denied, 444 U.S. 1035 (1980)(civil rights action brought by prison inmates to recover for alleged beatings; affidavit by now-deceased attorney about his conversation with prison official); Muncie Aviation Corp. v. Party Doll Fleet, Inc., 519 F.2d 1178 (5th Cir.1975)(plane collision; Federal Aviation Administration advisory circulars on recommended landing procedures); Turbyfill v. International Harvester Co., 486 F.Supp. 232 (E.D.Mich.1980)(unsworn account of accident written on afternoon of accident by defendant's since-deceased mechanic); Grimes v. Employers Mut. Liab. Ins. Co., 73 F.R.D. 607 (D.Alaska 1977)(film of plaintiff in negligence action performing daily tasks and clinical tests); United States v. American Tel. & Tel. Co., 516 F.Supp. 1237 (D.C.D.C.1981)(antitrust suit; documents authored by employees or agents of companies in competition with defendant, such as memoranda of discussions, correspondence, diaries and calendars).

2. Should the proponent of the hearsay evidence have the obligation to obtain the testimony of witnesses other than the declarant who have knowledge of the subject matter of the hearsay evidence? See deMars v. Equitable Life Assurance Soc'y, 610 F.2d 55, 60–61 (1st Cir.1979)(admissibility of written opinion of non-treating physician who died prior to trial); In re Sterling Navigation Co., 444 F.Supp. 1043 (S.D.N.Y.1977)(other witnesses with knowledge were not deposed).

3. At least eight states impose a requirement that the trial court must make express findings that the requirements of the residual exception are met. See, e.g., State v. Horsley, 792 P.2d 945, 953 (Idaho 1990)("unless the trial court makes specific findings ... we will not be able to determine whether the trial court considered all of the requirements that must be met.") Compare Brookover v. Mary Hitchcock Memorial Hosp., 893 F.2d 411, 420 (1st Cir.1990)(although explicit findings would have been helpful to the appellate court, "[t]here is nothing in the Rule itself that requires explicit findings.").

4. If the proponent of the hearsay statement failed to give pre-trial notice, may the statement be admitted pursuant to the residual hearsay exception? Compare United States v. Oates, 560 F.2d 45, 73 n. 30 (2d Cir.1977)("There is absolutely no doubt that Congress intended that the requirement of advance

---

4. When Village Towers finally answered the interrogatory on the first day of trial, it informed Modern that Rendo could not be located. However, when Rendo's whereabouts later became an issue, the court was able to locate him in Florida within a matter of hours by calling his successor at Village Towers. See 484 F.Supp. at 95–96.

notice be rigidly enforced") with United States v. Bailey, 581 F.2d 341, 348 (3d Cir.1978)("advance notice requirement ... satisfied when, as here, the proponent of the evidence is without fault in failing to notify his adversary prior to trial and the trial judge has offered sufficient time, by means of granting a continuance, for the party against whom the evidence is to be offered to prepare to meet and contest its admission.") and People v. Fuller, 788 P.2d 741, 746 (Colo.1990)(notice requirement "should be interpreted flexibly and 'with a sense of trial realities'"). See also United States v. Baker, 985 F.2d 1248 (4th Cir.1993), cert. denied, 510 U.S. 1040 (1994); United States v. Benavente Gomez, 921 F.2d 378, 384–85 (1st Cir.1990); United States v. Furst, 886 F.2d 558 (3d Cir.1989), cert. denied, 493 U.S. 1062 (1990).

5.   In a jurisdiction that does not have a residual hearsay exception does a court have discretion to admit hearsay evidence that does not satisfy a specific class exception? In a federal case decided before the enactment of the Federal Rules of Evidence, the court admitted a 58–year old newspaper account of a fire not because it fell into any "readily identifiable and happily tagged species of hearsay exception", but because "[t]he usual dangers inherent in hearsay evidence such as lack of memory, faulty narration, intent to influence the court proceedings, and plain lack of truthfulness are not present here." Dallas County v. Commercial Union Assurance Co., 286 F.2d 388, 397–398 (5th Cir.1961). Is such a statement admissible in a jurisdiction that has codified its hearsay rule but has chosen not to adopt a residual exception?

6.   A study by Professor Raeder compared the Dallas County case's effect in the federal courts with the impact of the residual hearsay exceptions (or catchalls):

> From their enactment in 1975 to July 1991, more than 400 decisions have considered the admissibility of hearsay pursuant to the catchalls, or roughly eight times the entire number of cases that cited Dallas County in a comparable timeframe. In a complete turnaround, however, approximately sixty percent of the catchall cases are criminal, in contrast to the negligible references to expansive hearsay interpretation in criminal proceedings prior to 1975. In fact, more than forty percent of all hearsay sought to be introduced under the catchalls is proffered by prosecutors.

Raeder, The Effect of the Catchalls on Criminal Defendants: Little Red Riding Hood Meets the Hearsay Wolf and Is Devoured, 25 U.C.Loy.L.A.L.Rev. 925, 933–34 (1992). Professor Raeder also reported widely differing rates in admission of the hearsay depending on who was offering the evidence:

Civil plaintiffs	(offered in 113 cases)	43% success rate
Civil defendants	(offered in 49 cases)	49% success rate
Prosecutors	(offered in 171 cases)	81% success rate
Accused	(offered in 75 cases)	15% success rate

Raeder, The Hearsay Rule at Work: Has It Been Abolished De Facto by Judicial Discretion?, 76 Minn.L.Rev. 507, 508, note 2 (1992).

Idaho v. Wright

Supreme Court of the United States, 1990.
497 U.S. 805, 110 S.Ct. 3139, 111 L.Ed.2d 638.

■ JUSTICE O'CONNOR delivered the opinion of the Court.

This case requires us to decide whether the admission at trial of certain hearsay statements made by a child declarant to an examining pediatrician violates a defendant's rights under the Confrontation Clause of the Sixth Amendment.

I

Respondent Laura Lee Wright was jointly charged with Robert L. Giles of two counts of lewd conduct with a minor under 16, in violation of Idaho Code § 18–1508 (1987). The alleged victims were respondent's two daughters, one of whom was 5½ and the other 2½ years old at the time the crimes were charged.

Respondent and her ex-husband, Louis Wright, the father of the older daughter, had reached an informal agreement whereby each parent would have custody of the older daughter for six consecutive months. The allegations surfaced in November 1986 when the older daughter told Cynthia Goodman, Louis Wright's female companion, that Giles had had sexual intercourse with her while respondent held her down and covered her mouth, App. 47–55; 3 Tr. 456–460, and that she had seen respondent and Giles do the same thing to respondent's younger daughter, App. 48–49, 61; 3 Tr. 460. The younger daughter was living with her parents—respondent and Giles—at the time of the alleged offenses.

Goodman reported the older daughter's disclosures to the police the next day and took the older daughter to the hospital. A medical examination of the older daughter revealed evidence of sexual abuse. One of the examining physicians was Dr. John Jambura, a pediatrician with extensive experience in child abuse cases. App. 91–94. Police and welfare officials took the younger daughter into custody that day for protection and investigation. Dr. Jambura examined her the following day and found conditions "strongly suggestive of sexual abuse with vaginal contact," occurring approximately two to three days prior to the examination. Id., at 105, 106.

At the joint trial of respondent and Giles, the trial court conducted a voir dire examination of the younger daughter, who was three years old at the time of trial, to determine whether she was capable of testifying. Id., at 32–38. The court concluded, and the parties agreed, that the younger daughter was "not capable of communicating to the jury." Id., at 39.

At issue in this case is the admission at trial of certain statements made by the younger daughter to Dr. Jambura in response to questions he asked regarding the alleged abuse. Over objection by respondent and Giles, the trial court permitted Dr. Jambura to testify before the jury as follows:

"Q. [By the prosecutor] Now, calling your attention then to your examination of [Kathy Wright] on November 10th. What—would you describe any interview dialogue that you had with [Kathy] at that time? Excuse me, before you get into that, would you lay a setting of where this took place and who else might have been present?

"A. This took place in my office, in my examining room, and, as I recall, I believe previous testimony I said that I recall a female attendant being present, I don't recall her identity.

"I started out with basically, 'Hi, how are you,' you know, 'What did you have for breakfast this morning?' Essentially a few minutes of just sort of chitchat.

"Q. Was there response from Kathy to that first—those first questions?

"A. There was. She started to carry on a very relaxed animated conversation. I then proceeded to just gently start asking questions about,

'Well, how are things at home,' you know, those sorts. Gently moving into the domestic situation and then moved into four questions in particular, as I reflected in my records, 'Do you play with daddy? Does daddy play with you? Does daddy touch you with his pee-pee? Do you touch his pee-pee?' And again we then established what was meant by pee-pee, it was a generic term for genital area.

"Q. Before you get into that, what was, as best you recollect, what was her response to the question 'Do you play with daddy?'

"A. Yes, we play—I remember her making a comment about yes we play a lot and expanding on that and talking about spending time with daddy.

"Q. And 'Does daddy play with you?' Was there any response?

"A. She responded to that as well, that they played together in a variety of circumstances and, you know, seemed very unaffected by the question.

"Q. And then what did you say and her response?

"A. When I asked her 'Does daddy touch you with his pee-pee,' she did admit to that. When I asked, 'Do you touch his pee-pee,' she did not have any response.

"Q. Excuse me. Did you notice any change in her affect or attitude in that line of questioning?

"A. Yes.

"Q. What did you observe?

"A. She would not—oh, she did not talk any further about that. She would not elucidate what exactly—what kind of touching was taking place, or how it was happening. She did, however, say that daddy does do this with me, but he does it a lot more with my sister than with me.

"Q. And how did she offer that last statement? Was that in response to a question or was that just a volunteered statement?

"A. That was a volunteered statement as I sat and waited for her to respond, again after she sort of clammed-up, and that was the next statement that she made after just allowing some silence to occur." Id., at 121–123.

On cross-examination, Dr. Jambura acknowledged that a picture that he drew during his questioning of the younger daughter had been discarded. Id., at 124. Dr. Jambura also stated that although he had dictated notes to summarize the conversation, his notes were not detailed and did not record any changes in the child's affect or attitude. Id., at 123–124.

The trial court admitted these statements under Idaho's residual hearsay exception, which provides in relevant part:

"Rule 803. Hearsay exceptions; availability of declarant immaterial.— The following are not excluded by the hearsay rule, even though the declarant is available as a witness.

. . .

"(24) Other exceptions. A statement not specifically covered by any of the foregoing exceptions but having equivalent circumstantial guarantees of trustworthiness, if the court determines that (A) the statement is offered as evidence of a material fact; (B) the statement is more probative on the point for which it is offered than any other evidence which the proponent can procure through reasonable efforts; and (C) the general purposes of these rules and the interests of justice will best be served by admission of the statement into evidence." Idaho Rule Evid. 803(24).

Respondent and Giles were each convicted of two counts of lewd conduct with a minor under 16 and sentenced to 20 years' imprisonment. Each appealed only from the conviction involving the younger daughter. Giles contended that the trial court erred in admitting Dr. Jambura's testimony under Idaho's residual hearsay exception. The Idaho Supreme Court disagreed and affirmed his conviction. State v. Giles, 115 Idaho 984, 772 P.2d 191 (1989). Respondent asserted that the admission of Dr. Jambura's testimony under the residual hearsay exception nevertheless violated her rights under the Confrontation Clause. The Idaho Supreme Court agreed and reversed respondent's conviction. 116 Idaho 382, 775 P.2d 1224 (1989).

The Supreme Court of Idaho held that the admission of the inculpatory hearsay testimony violated respondent's federal constitutional right to confrontation because the testimony did not fall within a traditional hearsay exception and was based on an interview that lacked procedural safeguards. Id., at 385, 775 P.2d, at 1227. The court found Dr. Jambura's interview technique inadequate because "the questions and answers were not recorded on videotape for preservation and perusal by the defense at or before trial; and, blatantly leading questions were used in the interrogation." Ibid. The statements also lacked trustworthiness, according to the court, because "this interrogation was performed by someone with a preconceived idea of what the child should be disclosing." Ibid. Noting that expert testimony and child psychology texts indicated that children are susceptible to suggestion and are therefore likely to be misled by leading questions, the court found that "[t]he circumstances surrounding this interview demonstrate dangers of unreliability which, because the interview was not [audio or video] recorded, can never be fully assessed." Id., at 388, 775 P.2d, at 1230. The court concluded that the younger daughter's statements lacked the particularized guarantees of trustworthiness necessary to satisfy the requirements of the Confrontation Clause and that therefore the trial court erred in admitting them. Id., at 389, 775 P.2d, at 1231. Because the court was not convinced, beyond a reasonable doubt, that the jury would have reached the same result had the error not occurred, the court reversed respondent's conviction on the count involving the younger daughter and remanded for a new trial. Ibid.

We granted certiorari, 493 U.S. 1041 (1990), and now affirm.

II

. . .

Although we have recognized that hearsay rules and the Confrontation Clause are generally designed to protect similar values, we have also been careful not to equate the Confrontation Clause's prohibitions with the general rule prohibiting the admission of hearsay statements. See California v. Green, 399 U.S. 149, 155–156 (1970); Dutton v. Evans, 400 U.S. 74, 86 (1970)(plurality opinion); United States v. Inadi, 475 U.S. 387, 393, n. 5 (1986). The Confrontation Clause, in other words, bars the admission of some evidence that would otherwise be admissible under an exception to the hearsay rule. See, e.g., Green, supra, at 155–156; Bruton v. United States, 391 U.S. 123 (1968); Barber v. Page, 390 U.S. 719 (1968); Pointer, supra.

In Ohio v. Roberts, we set forth "a general approach" for determining when incriminating statements admissible under an exception to the hearsay rule also meet the requirements of the Confrontation Clause. 448 U.S., at 65. We noted that the Confrontation Clause "operates in two separate ways to restrict the range of admissible hearsay." Ibid. "First, in conformance with the Framers' preference for face-to-face accusation, the Sixth Amendment establishes a rule of necessity. In the usual case . . ., the prosecution must either produce, or demonstrate the unavailability of, the declarant whose statement it wishes to use against the defendant." Ibid. (citations omitted). Second, once a witness is shown to be unavailable, "his statement is admissible only if it bears adequate 'indicia of reliability.' Reliability can be inferred without more in a case where the evidence falls within a firmly rooted hearsay exception. In other cases, the evidence must be excluded, at least absent a showing of particularized guarantees of trustworthiness." Id., at 66 (footnote omitted); see also Mancusi v. Stubbs, 408 U.S. 204, 213 (1972).

. . .

We have applied the general approach articulated in Roberts to subsequent cases raising Confrontation Clause and hearsay issues. In United States v. Inadi, supra, we held that the general requirement of unavailability did not apply to incriminating out-of-court statements made by a non-testifying co-conspirator and that therefore the Confrontation Clause did not prohibit the admission of such statements, even though the Government had not shown that the declarant was unavailable to testify at trial. 475 U.S., at 394–400. In Bourjaily v. United States, supra, we held that such statements also carried with them sufficient "indicia of reliability" because the hearsay exception for co-conspirator statements was a firmly rooted one. 483 U.S., at 182–184.

Applying the Roberts approach to this case, we first note that this case does not raise the question whether, before a child's out-of-court statements are admitted, the Confrontation Clause requires the prosecution to show that a child witness is unavailable at trial—and, if so, what that showing requires. The trial court in this case found that respondent's younger daughter was incapable of communicating with the jury, and defense counsel agreed. App. 39. The court below neither questioned this finding nor discussed the general requirement of unavailability. For purposes of deciding this case, we assume without deciding that, to the extent the unavailability requirement applies in this case, the younger daughter was an unavailable witness within the meaning of the Confrontation Clause.

The crux of the question presented is therefore whether the State, as the proponent of evidence presumptively barred by the hearsay rule and the Confrontation Clause, has carried its burden of proving that the younger daughter's incriminating statements to Dr. Jambura bore sufficient indicia of reliability to withstand scrutiny under the Clause. The court below held that, although the trial court had properly admitted the statements under the State's residual hearsay exception, the statements were "fraught with the dangers of unreliability which the Confrontation Clause is designed to highlight and obviate." 116 Idaho, at 389, 775 P.2d, at 1231. The State asserts that the court below erected too stringent a standard for admitting the statements and that the statements were, under the totality of the circumstances, sufficiently reliable for Confrontation Clause purposes.

In Roberts, we suggested that the "indicia of reliability" requirement could be met in either of two circumstances: where the hearsay statement "falls within a firmly rooted hearsay exception," or where it is supported by "a showing of particularized guarantees of trustworthiness." 448 U.S., at 66. . . .

We note at the outset that Idaho's residual hearsay exception, Idaho Rule Evid. 803(24), under which the challenged statements were admitted, App. 113–115, is not a firmly rooted hearsay exception for Confrontation Clause purposes. Admission under a firmly rooted hearsay exception satisfies the constitutional requirement of reliability because of the weight accorded longstanding judicial and legislative experience in assessing the trustworthiness of certain types of out-of-court statements. See Mattox, 156 U.S., at 243; Roberts, 448 U.S., at 66; Bourjaily, 483 U.S., at 183; see also Lee, supra, at 552 (Blackmun, J., dissenting)("[S]tatements squarely within established hearsay exceptions possess 'the imprimatur of judicial and legislative experience' . . . and that fact must weigh heavily in our assessment of their reliability for constitutional purposes")(citation omitted). The residual hearsay exception, by contrast, accommodates ad hoc instances in which statements not otherwise falling within a recognized hearsay exception might nevertheless be sufficiently reliable to be admissible at trial. See e.g., Senate Judiciary Committee's Note on Fed. Rule Evid. 803(24), 28 U.S.C. App., pp. 786–787; E. Cleary, McCormick on Evidence § 324.1, pp. 907–909 (3d ed. 1984). Hearsay statements admitted under the residual exception, almost by definition, therefore do not share the same tradition of reliability that supports the admissibility of statements under a firmly rooted hearsay exception. Moreover, were we to agree that the admission of hearsay statements under the residual exception automatically passed Confrontation Clause scrutiny, virtually every codified hearsay exception would assume constitutional stature, a step this Court has repeatedly declined to take. See Green, 399 U.S., at 155–156; Evans, 400 U.S., at 86–87 (plurality opinion); Inadi, 475 U.S., at 393, n. 5; see also Evans, supra, at 94–95 (Harlan, J., concurring in result).

The State in any event does not press the matter strongly and recognizes that, because the younger daughter's hearsay statements do not fall within a firmly rooted hearsay exception, they are "presumptively unreliable and inadmissible for Confrontation Clause purposes," Lee, 476 U.S., at 543, and "must be excluded, at least absent a showing of particularized guarantees of trustworthiness," Roberts, 448 U.S., at 66. The court below concluded that the State had not made such a showing, in large measure because the statements resulted from an interview lacking certain procedural safeguards. The court below specifically noted that Dr. Jambura failed to record the interview on videotape, asked leading questions, and questioned the child with a preconceived idea of what she should be disclosing. See 116 Idaho, at 388, 775 P.2d, at 1230.

Although we agree with the court below that the Confrontation Clause bars the admission of the younger daughter's hearsay statements, we reject the apparently dispositive weight placed by that court on the lack of procedural safeguards at the interview. Out-of-court statements made by children regarding sexual abuse arise in a wide variety of circumstances, and we do not believe the Constitution imposes a fixed set of procedural prerequisites to the admission of such statements at trial. The procedural requirements identified by the court below, to the extent regarded as conditions precedent to the admission of child hearsay statements in child sexual abuse cases, may in many instances be inappropriate or unnecessary to a determination whether a given statement is sufficiently trustworthy for Confrontation Clause purposes. See, e.g., Nelson v. Farrey, 874 F.2d 1222, 1229 (C.A.7 1989)(videotape requirement not feasible, especially where defendant had not yet been criminally charged), cert. denied, 493 U.S. 1042 (1990); J. Myers, Child Witness Law and Practice § 4.6, pp. 129–134 (1987)(use of leading questions with children, when appropriate, does not necessarily render responses untrustworthy). Although the procedural guidelines propounded by the court below may well enhance the reliability of out-of-court statements of children regarding sexual abuse, we decline to read into the Confrontation Clause a preconceived and artificial litmus test for the procedural propriety of professional interviews in which children make hearsay statements against a defendant.

The State responds that a finding of "particularized guarantees of trustworthiness" should instead be based on a consideration of the totality of the circumstances, including not only the circumstances surrounding the making of the statement, but also other evidence at trial that corroborates the truth of the statement. We agree that "particularized guarantees of trustworthiness" must be shown from the totality of the circumstances, but we think the relevant circumstances include only those that surround the making of the statement and that render the declarant particularly worthy of belief. This conclusion derives from the rationale for permitting exceptions to the general rule against hearsay:

> "The theory of the hearsay rule . . . is that the many possible sources of inaccuracy and untrustworthiness which may lie underneath the bare untested assertion of a witness can best be brought to light and exposed, if they exist, by the test of cross-examination. But this test or security may in a given instance be superfluous; it may be sufficiently clear, in that instance, that the statement offered is free enough from the risk of inaccuracy and untrustworthiness, so that the test of cross-examination would be a work of supererogation." 5 J. Wigmore, Evidence § 1420, p. 251 (J. Chadbourn rev. 1974).

In other words, if the declarant's truthfulness is so clear from the surrounding circumstances that the test of cross-examination would be of marginal utility, then the hearsay rule does not bar admission of the statement at trial. The basis for the "excited utterance" exception, for example, is that such statements are given under circumstances that eliminate the possibility of fabrication, coaching, or confabulation, and that therefore the circumstances surrounding the making of the statement provide sufficient assurance that the statement is trustworthy and that cross-examination would be superfluous. See, e.g., 6 Wigmore, supra, §§ 1745–1764; 4 J. Weinstein & M. Berger, Weinstein's Evidence ¶ 803(2)[01] (1988); Advisory Committee's Note on Fed. Rule Evid. 803(2), 28 U.S.C.App., p. 778. Likewise, the "dying declaration" and "medical treatment" exceptions to the hearsay rule are based on the belief that persons making such statements are highly unlikely to lie. See, e.g., Mattox, 156 U.S., at 244 ("[T]he sense of impending death is presumed to remove all temptation to falsehood, and to enforce as strict an adherence to the truth as would the obligation of oath"); Queen v. Osman, 15 Cox Crim.Cas. 1, 3 (Eng.N.Wales Cir.1881)(Lush, L.J.)("[N]o person, who is immediately going into the presence of his Maker, will do so with a lie upon his lips"); Mosteller, Child Sexual Abuse and Statements for the Purpose of Medical Diagnosis or Treatment, 67 N.C.L.Rev. 257 (1989). "The circumstantial guarantees of trustworthiness on which the various specific exceptions to the hearsay rule are based are those that existed at the time the statement was made and do not include those that may be added by using hindsight." Huff v. White Motor Corp., 609 F.2d 286, 292 (C.A.7 1979).

We think the "particularized guarantees of trustworthiness" required for admission under the Confrontation Clause must likewise be drawn from the totality of circumstances that surround the making of the statement and that render the declarant particularly worthy of belief. Our precedents have recognized that statements admitted under a "firmly rooted" hearsay exception are so trustworthy that adversarial testing would add little to their reliability. See Green, 399 U.S., at 161 (examining "whether subsequent cross-examination at the defendant's trial will still afford the trier of fact a satisfactory basis for evaluating the truth of the prior statement"); see also Mattox, 156 U.S., at 244; Evans, 400 U.S., at 88–89 (plurality opinion); Roberts, 448 U.S., at 65, 73. Because evidence possessing "particularized guarantees of trustworthiness" must be at least as reliable as evidence admitted under a firmly rooted hearsay exception, see Roberts, supra, at 66, we think that evidence admitted under the former requirement must similarly be so trustworthy that adversarial testing would add little to its reliability. See Lee v. Illinois, 476 U.S., at 544 (determining indicia of reliability from the circumstances surrounding the making of the statement); see also State v. Ryan, 103 Wash.2d 165, 174, 691 P.2d 197, 204 (1984)("Adequate indicia of reliability [under Roberts] must be found in reference to circumstances surrounding the making of the out-of-court statement, and not from subsequent corroboration of the criminal act"). Thus, unless an affirmative reason, arising from the circumstances in which the statement was made, provides a basis for rebutting the presumption that a hearsay statement is not worthy of reliance at trial, the Confrontation Clause requires exclusion of the out-of-court statement.

The state and federal courts have identified a number of factors that we think properly relate to whether hearsay statements made by a child witness in child sexual abuse cases are reliable. See, e.g., State v. Robinson, 153 Ariz. 191, 201, 735 P.2d 801, 811 (1987)(spontaneity and consistent repetition); Morgan v. Foretich, 846 F.2d 941, 948 (C.A.4 1988)(mental state of the declarant); State v. Sorenson, 143 Wis.2d 226, 246, 421 N.W.2d 77, 85 (1988)(use of terminology unexpected of a child of similar age); State v. Kuone, 243 Kan. 218, 221–222, 757 P.2d 289, 292–293 (1988)(lack of motive to fabricate). Although these cases (which we cite for the factors they discuss and not necessarily to approve the results that they reach) involve the application of various hearsay exceptions to statements of child declarants, we think the factors identified also apply to whether such statements bear "particularized guarantees of trustworthiness" under the Confrontation Clause. These factors are, of course, not exclusive, and courts therefore have considerable leeway in their consideration of appropriate factors. We therefore decline to endorse a mechanical test for determining "particularized guarantees of trustworthiness" under the Clause. Rather, the unifying principle is that these factors relate to whether the child declarant was particularly likely to be telling the truth when the statement was made.

As our discussion above suggests, we are unpersuaded by the State's contention that evidence corroborating the truth of a hearsay statement may properly support a finding that the statement bears "particularized guarantees of trustworthiness." To be admissible under the Confrontation Clause, hearsay evidence used to convict a defendant must possess indicia of reliability by virtue of its inherent trustworthiness, not by reference to other evidence at trial. Cf. Delaware v. Van Arsdall, 475 U.S. 673, 680 (1986). "[T]he Clause countenances only hearsay marked with such trustworthiness that 'there is no material departure from the reason of the general rule.' " Roberts, 448 U.S., at 65 (quoting Snyder v. Massachusetts, 291 U.S. 97, 107 (1934)). A statement made under duress, for example, may happen to be a true statement, but the circumstances under which it is made may provide no basis for supposing that the declarant is particularly likely to be telling the truth—indeed, the circumstances may even be such that the declarant is particularly *un*likely to be telling the truth. In such a case, cross-examination at trial would be highly useful to probe the declarant's state-of-mind when he made the statements; the presence of evidence tending to corroborate the truth of the statement would be no substitute for cross-examination of the declarant at trial.

In short, the use of corroborating evidence to support a hearsay statement's "particularized guarantees of trustworthiness" would permit admission of a presumptively unreliable statement by bootstrapping on the trustworthiness of other evidence at trial, a result we think at odds with the requirement that hearsay evidence admitted under the Confrontation Clause be so trustworthy that cross-examination of the declarant would be of marginal utility. Indeed, although a plurality of the Court in Dutton v. Evans looked to corroborating evidence as one of four factors in determining whether a particular hearsay statement possessed sufficient indicia of reliability, see 400 U.S., at 88, we think the presence of corroborating evidence more appropriately indicates that any error in admitting the statement might be harmless, rather than that any basis exists for presuming the declarant to be trustworthy. See id., at 90 (Blackmun, J., joined by Burger, C.J., concurring)(finding admission of the statement at issue to be harmless error, if error at all); see also 4 D. Louisell & C. Mueller, Federal Evidence § 418, p. 143 (1980)(discussing Evans).

Moreover, although we considered in Lee v. Illinois the "interlocking" nature of a codefendant's and a defendant's confessions to determine whether the codefendant's confession was sufficiently trustworthy for confrontation purposes, we declined to rely on corroborative physical evidence and indeed rejected the "interlock" theory in that case. 476 U.S., at 545–546. We cautioned that "[t]he true danger inherent in this type of hearsay is, in fact, its selective reliability." Id., at 545. This concern applies in the child hearsay context as well: Corroboration of a child's allegations of sexual abuse by medical evidence of abuse, for example, sheds no light on the reliability of the child's allegations regarding the identity of the abuser. There is a very real danger that a jury will rely on partial corroboration to mistakenly infer the trustworthiness of the entire statement. Furthermore, we recognized the similarity between harmless-error analysis and the corroboration inquiry when we noted in Lee that the harm of "admission of the [hearsay] statement [was that it] poses too serious a threat to the accuracy of the verdict to be countenanced by the Sixth Amendment." Ibid. (emphasis added).

Finally, we reject respondent's contention that the younger daughter's out-of-court statements in this case are per se unreliable, or at least presumptively unreliable, on the ground that the trial court found the younger daughter incompetent to testify at trial. First, respondent's contention rests upon a questionable reading of the record in this case. The trial court found only that the younger daughter was "not capable of communicating to the jury." App. 39. Although Idaho law provides that a child witness may not testify if he "appear[s] incapable of receiving just impressions of the facts respecting which they are examined, or of relating them truly," Idaho Code § 9–202 (Supp.1989); Idaho Rule Evid. 601(a), the trial court in this case made no such findings. Indeed, the more reasonable inference is that, by ruling that the statements were admissible under Idaho's residual hearsay exception, the trial court implicitly found that the younger daughter, at the time she made the statements, was capable of receiving just impressions of the facts and of relating them truly. See App. 115. In addition, we have in any event held that the Confrontation Clause does not erect a per se rule barring the admission of prior statements of a declarant who is unable to communicate to the jury at the time of trial. See, e.g., Mattox, 156 U.S., at 243–244; see also 4 Louisell & Mueller, supra, § 486, pp. 1041–1045. Although such inability might be relevant to whether the earlier hearsay statement possessed particularized guarantees of trustworthiness, a per se rule of exclusion would not only frustrate the truth-seeking purpose of the Confrontation Clause, but would also hinder States in their own "enlightened development in the law of evidence," Evans, 400 U.S., at 95 (Harlan, J., concurring in result).

III

The trial court in this case, in ruling that the Confrontation Clause did not prohibit admission of the younger daughter's hearsay statements, relied on the following factors:

"In this case, of course, there is physical evidence to corroborate that sexual abuse occurred. It would also seem to be the case that there is no motive to make up a story of this nature in a child of these years. We're not talking about a pubescent youth who may fantasize. The nature of the statements themselves as to sexual abuse are such that they fall outside the general believability that a child could make them up or would make them up. This is simply not the type of statement, I believe, that one would expect a child to fabricate.

We come then to the identification itself. Are there any indicia of reliability as to identification? From the doctor's testimony it appears that the injuries testified to occurred at the time that the victim was in the custody of the Defendants. The [older daughter] has testified as to identification of [the] perpetrators. Those—the identification of the perpetrators in this case are persons well known to the [younger daughter]. This is not a case in which a child is called upon to identify a stranger or a person with whom they would have no knowledge of their identity or ability to recollect and recall. Those factors are sufficient indicia of reliability to permit the admission of the statements." App. 115.

Of the factors the trial court found relevant, only two relate to circumstances surrounding the making of the statements: whether the child had a motive to "make up a story of this nature," and whether, given the child's age, the statements are of the type "that one would expect a child to fabricate." Ibid. The other factors on which the trial court relied, however, such as the presence of physical evidence of abuse, the opportunity of respondent to commit the offense, and the older daughter's corroborating identification, relate instead to whether other evidence existed to corroborate the truth of the statement. These factors, as we have discussed, are irrelevant to a showing of the "particularized guarantees of trustworthiness" necessary for admission of hearsay statements under the Confrontation Clause.

We think the Supreme Court of Idaho properly focused on the presumptive unreliability of the out-of-court statements and on the suggestive manner in which Dr. Jambura conducted the interview. Viewing the totality of the circumstances surrounding the younger daughter's responses to Dr. Jambura's questions, we find no special reason for supposing that the incriminating statements were particularly trustworthy. The younger daughter's last statement regarding the abuse of the older daughter, however, presents a closer question. According to Dr. Jambura, the younger daughter "volunteered" that statement "after she sort of clammed-up." Id., at 123. Although the spontaneity of the statement and the change in demeanor suggest that the younger daughter was telling the truth when she made the statement, we note that it is possible that "[i]f there is evidence of prior interrogation, prompting, or manipulation by adults, spontaneity may be an inaccurate indicator of trustworthiness." Robinson, 153 Ariz., at 201, 735 P.2d, at 811. Moreover, the statement was not made under circumstances of reliability comparable to those required, for example, for the admission of excited utterances or statements made for purposes of medical diagnosis or treatment. Given the presumption of inadmissibility accorded accusatory hearsay statements not admitted pursuant to a firmly rooted hearsay exception, Lee, 476 U.S., at 543, we agree with the court below that the State has failed to show that the younger daughter's incriminating statements to the pediatrician possessed sufficient "particularized guarantees of trustworthiness" under the Confrontation Clause to overcome that presumption.

The State does not challenge the Idaho Supreme Court's conclusion that the Confrontation Clause error in this case was not harmless beyond a reasonable doubt, and we see no reason to revisit the issue. We therefore agree with that court that respondent's conviction involving the younger daughter must be reversed and the case remanded for further proceedings. Accordingly, the judgment of the Supreme Court of Idaho is affirmed.

It is so ordered.

■ JUSTICE KENNEDY, with whom THE CHIEF JUSTICE, JUSTICE WHITE, and JUSTICE BLACKMUN join, dissenting.

. . .

... The majority errs, in my view, by adopting a rule that corroboration of the statement by other evidence is an impermissible part of the trustworthiness inquiry. The Court's apparent ruling is that corroborating evidence may not be considered in whole or in part for this purpose.[1] This limitation, at least on a facial interpretation of the Court's analytic categories, is a new creation by the Court; it likely will prove unworkable and does not even square with the examples of reliability indicators the Court itself invokes; and it is contrary to our own precedents.

I see no constitutional justification for this decision to rescind corroborating evidence from consideration of the question whether a child's statements are reliable. It is a matter of common sense for most people that one of the best ways to determine whether what someone says is trustworthy is to see if it is corroborated by other evidence. In the context of child abuse, for example, if part of the child's hearsay statement is that the assailant tied her wrists or had a scar on his lower abdomen, and there is physical evidence or testimony to corroborate the child's statement, evidence which the child could not have fabricated, we are more likely to believe that what the child says is true. Conversely, one can imagine a situation in which a child makes a statement which is spontaneous or is otherwise made under circumstances indicating that it is reliable, but which also contains undisputed factual inaccuracies so great that the credibility of the child's statements is substantially undermined. Under the Court's analysis, the statement would satisfy the requirements of

---

1. The Court also states that the child's hearsay statements are "presumptively unreliable." Ante, at [783]. I take this to mean only that the government bears the burden of coming forward with indicia of reliability sufficient for the purposes of the Confrontation Clause, and that if it fails to do so the statements are inadmissible. A presumption of unreliability exists as a counterweight to the indicia of reliability offered by the government only where there is an affirmative rea-son to believe that a particular category of hearsay may be unreliable. See, e.g., Lee v. Illinois, 476 U.S. 530, 545 (1986)("[A] codefendant's confession is presumptively unreliable as to the passages detailing the defendant's conduct or culpability because those passages may well be the product of the codefendant's desire to shift or spread blame, curry favor, avenge himself, or divert attention to another").

the Confrontation Clause despite substantial doubt about its reliability. Nothing in the law of evidence or the law of the Confrontation Clause countenances such a result; on the contrary, most federal courts have looked to the existence of corroborating evidence or the lack thereof to determine the reliability of hearsay statements not coming within one of the traditional hearsay exceptions. . . .

. . .

The short of the matter is that both the circumstances existing at the time the child makes the statements and the existence of corroborating evidence indicate, to a greater or lesser degree, whether the statements are reliable. If the Court means to suggest that the circumstances surrounding the making of a statement are the best indicators of reliability, I doubt this is so in every instance. And, if it were true in a particular case, that does not warrant ignoring other indicators of reliability such as corroborating evidence, absent some other reason for excluding it. If anything, I should think that corroborating evidence in the form of testimony or physical evidence, apart from the narrow circumstances in which the statement was made, would be a preferred means of determining a statement's reliability for purposes of the Confrontation Clause, for the simple reason that, unlike other indicators of trustworthiness, corroborating evidence can be addressed by the defendant and assessed by the trial court in an objective and critical way.

In this case, the younger daughter's statements are corroborated in at least four respects: (1) physical evidence that she was the victim of sexual abuse; (2) evidence that she had been in the custody of the suspect at the time the injuries occurred; (3) testimony of the older daughter that their father abused the younger daughter, thus corroborating the younger daughter's statement; and (4) the testimony of the older daughter that she herself was abused by their father, thus corroborating the younger daughter's statement that her sister had also been abused. These facts, coupled with the circumstances surrounding the making of the statements acknowledged by the Court as suggesting that the statements are reliable, give rise to a legitimate argument that admission of the statements did not violate the Confrontation Clause. . . .

NOTES

1. In Wright, the majority rejected relying on corroborative evidence in determining whether evidence admitted under a residual exception satisfies the constitutional test of trustworthiness. Does corroboration count in deciding whether the evidentiary standard is satisfied? Compare Jonakait, Text, Texts, or Ad Hoc Determinations: Interpretation of the Federal Rules of Evidence, 71 Ind.L.J. 551, 590 (1996)(arguing that "since both confrontation and the evidence rules have as their prime purpose the advancement of the accuracy of the truth-determination process of our trials," the similarly worded confrontation and residual requirements should have the same meaning and should be interpreted consistently with Wright; consequently corroboration should not be considered in determining admissibility under a residual exception even in civil cases or when the accused offers the hearsay) with United States v. Valdez–Soto, 31 F.3d 1467, 1471 (9th Cir.1994), cert. denied, 115 S.Ct. 1969 (1995):

> In the absence of concerns about the accused's right to confrontation, the trial judge has a fair degree of latitude in deciding whether to admit statements under Fed.R.Evid. 803(24). The rule requires only that the hearsay have "equivalent circumstantial guarantees of trustworthiness" to any of the rule's enumerated exceptions. In addition to factors such as "the

declarant's perception, memory, narration, or sincerity concerning the matter asserted," United States v. Friedman, 593 F.2d 109, 119 (9th Cir.1979), we've recognized that corroborating evidence is a valid consideration in determining the trustworthiness of out-of-court statements for purposes of Rule 803(24). See, e.g., Larez v. City of Los Angeles, 946 F.2d 630, 643 n. 6 (9th Cir.1991)(declarants' out-of-court statements were "especially reliable" under Rule 803(24) because they corroborated one another). The district court thus did not err in considering corroborative evidence here.

See also United States v. Mokol, 939 F.2d 436, 439–40 (7th Cir.1991)(court held that district court had not abused its discretion in excluding murdered witness' statement after focusing on corroboration; no mention of Wright) and Huff v. White Motor Corp., 609 F.2d 286, 292 (7th Cir.1979)("guarantees to be considered in applying [Rule 803(24)] are those that existed when the statement was made").

For further consideration of corroboration requirements see chapter 3, section 1(D), supra.

2. In United States v. Canan, 48 F.3d 954 (6th Cir.1995), cert. denied, 116 S.Ct. 716 (1996), a drug prosecution, the district court admitted a videotaped statement made by a prosecution witness 15 days before his death of cancer. Although the defendant was present at the taping, his counsel was not. The appellate judges disagreed on whether the totality of the circumstances provided the necessary guarantees of trustworthiness.

The majority, which found the statement admissible, relied on the following factors: the witness expected defense counsel to be present so that he did not know that he would not be cross-examined when he agreed to testify; his testimony was consistent with testimony he had given in a different case; he knew he was being videotaped so that the jury would be able to observe his demeanor; videotaping is a circumstance that bears on the totality of the circumstances; the witness knew that he was dying so that he had no further incentive to curry favor with the government. Id. at 964.

The dissenting judge found that admission of the statement constituted reversible error:

> I do not agree with the district court's conclusion that Canan's presence alone "made fabrication difficult," and thus ensured the reliability of Kimbler's statement. Kimbler did not make the challenged statement at a formal proceeding; due to the absence of Canan's attorney and the lack of cross-examination, Kimbler's statement did not qualify as a deposition. Moreover, the questions were posed in such a fashion as to elicit damaging statements regarding Canan. In addition, as the district court observed, Kimbler "was in a grave condition at the time he gave this statement" and "must have realized that he would soon die." Rather than destroying any potential motive to craft his statement in order to curry favor with the government, as the district court found, however, Kimbler's condition may actually have diminished his truth-telling incentive—if Kimbler knew that he was approaching death, then he also knew that any threats of future prosecution were hollow.

Id. at 961–62.

3. In United States v. Valdez–Soto, 31 F.3d 1467 (9th Cir.1994), cert. denied, 115 S.Ct. 1969 (1995), Cortez, who was arrested selling drugs, agreed to cooperate with the government and made post-arrest statements implicating the defendants as his suppliers. At trial, however, Cortez testified very differently. The district court admitted the post-arrest statements under Rule 803(24). The appellate court affirmed:

Valdez–Soto and Gomez–Tello also claim the admission of these statements violated Rule 803(24)'s requirement that "the general purposes of these rules and the interests of justice will be best served by the admission of the statement." Relying on Rule 803(24)'s legislative history, defendants claim this hearsay exception must be interpreted narrowly. We decline the defendants' invitation to go skipping down the yellowbrick road of legislative history. Rule 803(24) exists to provide courts with flexibility in admitting statements traditionally regarded as hearsay but not falling within any of the conventional exceptions. And we review admission of evidence under this provision, like all other evidentiary rulings, for abuse of discretion.

Nor are we persuaded by defendants' related argument that prior inconsistent statements must be admitted, if at all, under those provisions of the hearsay rule dealing expressly with admission of such statements. Specifically, defendants assert that Rule 801(d)(1)(A) provides the *only* test for admission of unsworn prior inconsistent statements as substantive evidence: if that test is not met, they contend, the evidence can never be admitted. But the existence of a catch-all hearsay exception is a clear indication that Congress did *not* want courts to admit hearsay only if it fits within one of the enumerated exceptions. And the reference to guarantees of trustworthiness equivalent to those in the enumerated exceptions strongly suggests that almost fitting within one of these exceptions cuts in favor of admission, not against. Rule 803(24) easily encompasses a case like ours where the evidence has the requisite indicia of trustworthiness but is not otherwise admissible. . . .

Id. at 1471.

Dissent:

It is clear from the legislative history of Rules 801(d)(1) and 803(24) that Congress considered permitting the admission of the type of evidence at issue in this case. It is equally clear that Congress declined to do so. It is not the court's function to expand an exception which was explicitly considered and rejected by Congress.

Id. at 1477.

4. In Zenith Radio Corp. v. Matsushita Elec. Indus. Co., 505 F.Supp. 1190, 1262–1263 (E.D.Pa.1980), Judge Becker discussed the "near-miss" problem:

The defendants contend that the residual hearsay exceptions cannot be invoked as the basis for the admissibility of evidence which is generically of a type covered by another specific hearsay exception, but which fails to meet the precise requirements of that specific exception. For instance, they contend that if a document is a "business record" it must qualify for admission under Rule 803(6), and not under the residual exceptions. The plaintiffs counter that there is no such rule of law, and cite a number of cases in which courts have considered the admissibility of evidence under the residual exceptions after finding that the evidence failed to meet the terms of one or more of the specific exceptions. E.g., United States v. Hitsman, 604 F.2d 443 (5th Cir.1979).

We agree in principle with the defendants. The Advisory Committee explained its proposed residual exception, which was broader than the one enacted by Congress, as designated for "new and presently unanticipated situations." The Senate Judiciary Committee, which drafted the present rule, commented that "an overly broad residual hearsay exception could emasculate the hearsay rule and the recognized exceptions or vitiate the rationale behind codification of the rules." The Senate Committee also stated its intent "that the residual hearsay exceptions will be used very rarely, and only in exceptional circumstances." U.S.Code Cong. & Admin.News 1974, p. 7066. We find it clear from the history of the rules that neither the Advisory Committee nor the Senate Judiciary Committee intended that the residual exceptions be used to qualify for admission evidence which is of a type covered by a specific exception, but which narrowly fails to meet the standards of the specific rule. Instead, they intended that the residual exceptions be used in exceptional and unanticipated situations which are not specifically covered by the specific exceptions. [Footnotes omitted.]

The Third Circuit rejected Judge Becker's "near miss" theory in In re Japanese Elec. Prod. Antitrust Litig., 723 F.2d 238, 302 (3d Cir.1983), rev'd on other grounds, 475 U.S. 574 (1986)(further proceedings in the same case Judge Becker was considering). The Third Circuit found that the theory "conflicts with the general function of Rules 803(24) and 804(b)(5) [and] puts the federal evidence rules back into the straightjacket from which the residual exceptions were intended to free them."

See also United States v. Deeb, 13 F.3d 1532, 1536–37 (11th Cir.1994)(rejects "near miss" argument in admitting testimony that declarant had given at prior trial at which defendant was neither present nor represented by counsel), cert. denied, 115 S.Ct. 1093 (1995); United States v. Clarke, 2 F.3d 81, 83 (4th Cir.1993)("We believe that 'specifically covered' means exactly what it says: if a statement does not meet all of the requirements for admissibility under one of the prior exceptions, then it is not 'specifically covered.' " Court admitted testimony of defendant's brother implicating defendant given at brother's suppression hearing.), cert. denied, 510 U.S. 1166 (1994).

5. *Grand jury testimony.* Soon after the Federal Rules of Evidence were enacted some circuits began to admit grand jury testimony under the residual exception. In one early case, United States v. Garner, 574 F.2d 1141 (4th Cir.1978), Robinson, who had been indicted in connection with a heroin importation scheme, agreed to testify fully before the grand jury in consideration of a plea agreement. Robinson did testify extensively before the grand jury, but then at trial fluctuated between refusing to answer, recanting his grand jury testimony, and disclaiming knowledge about the defendants' activities. The trial court found Robinson unavailable for purposes of Rule 804(b) and admitted the grand jury testimony. The appellate court affirmed, finding that the grand jury testimony had been corroborated by other evidence. Justice Stewart, joined by Justice Marshall, dissented from the denial of certiorari:

Although they are not coextensive, the Confrontation Clause and the hearsay rule "stem from the same roots." Dutton v. Evans, 400 U.S. 74, 86 (1970). Considered under either the Sixth Amendment or the Federal Rules of Evidence, I have grave doubts about the admissibility of Robinson's grand jury testimony.

That the evidence was first given before a grand jury adds little to its reliability. In grand jury proceedings, the ordinary rules of evidence do not apply. Leading questions and multiple hearsay are permitted and common. Grand jury investigations are not adversary proceedings. No one is present to cross-examine the witnesses, to give the defendant's version of the story, or to expose weaknesses in the witnesses' testimony.

The only factor that generally makes grand jury testimony more trustworthy than other out-of-court statements is the fact that it is given under oath. The witnesses speak under the threat of prosecution for material false statements. But that usual indication of trustworthiness was missing here. Robinson recanted his grand jury testimony at the trial. By disclaiming under oath his earlier sworn statements, he put himself in a position where one of his two sworn statements had to be false. Without further proof, Robinson would appear to have violated federal law, and, after the petitioners' trial, the Government did, indeed, indict Robinson for violation of 18 U.S.C. § 1623. The charges were dismissed only after he pleaded guilty to a contempt citation.

The Courts of Appeals are struggling with the problem of the admissibility of hearsay evidence not falling within one of the traditional exceptions to inadmissibility. The Fourth Circuit has taken a relatively liberal view of the admissibility of grand jury testimony, both in this case and in United States v. West, 574 F.2d 1131 (4th Cir.1978). In a similar situation the Fifth Circuit concluded that grand jury testimony was inadmissible. United States v. Gonzalez, 559 F.2d 1271 (5th Cir.1977). Before the adoption of the Federal Rules of Evidence, the Second Circuit held that the use of grand jury testimony in a situation like this violated both the hearsay rule and the Sixth Amendment. United States v. Fiore, 443 F.2d 112 (2d Cir.1971). The Eighth Circuit, in a case in which the grand jury witness had not recanted his testimony, allowed the grand jury testimony to be admitted. United States v. Carlson, 547 F.2d 1346 (8th Cir.1976).

While those cases may be factually distinguishable, the conflict in interpretation among the Circuits remains.[1] In some Circuits Rule 804(b)(5) is being used to admit grand jury testimony when the witness is unavailable at trial; in others, it is not. Here, the witness recanted his grand jury testimony under oath at the trial, yet it was the crucial evidence in these petitioners' convictions.

I would grant certiorari to determine the limits placed upon the admissibility of this kind of evidence by either the Federal Rules of Evidence or the Constitution.

McKethan v. United States, 439 U.S. 936, 936–940 (1978).

As of this writing, the Supreme Court has not directly considered either the evidentiary or constitutional issues that arise when grand jury testimony is offered against a criminal defendant. It has, however, decided cases that bear on the issue. The notes below explore the applicability of Wright, p. 778 and Salerno, p. 748 supra.

In United States v. Gomez–Lemos, 939 F.2d 326, 332–33 (6th Cir.1991), the court held that the admission of grand jury testimony of alleged coconspirators who refused to testify at trial violated the confrontation clause:

> None of the other appellate decisions that have upheld the use of uncross-examined grand jury testimony under a residual exception to the hearsay rule provide persuasive authority for altering the outcome in this case. In Wright, the Court clearly stated that, unless a hearsay statement comes within one of the general exceptions to the hearsay rule, a trial judge must only look to the relevant circumstances "that surround the

---

1. It seems to me open to serious doubt whether Rule 804(b)(5) was intended to provide case-by-case hearsay exceptions, rather than only to permit expansion of the hearsay exceptions by categories. [Footnote is the Justice's, renumbered; other footnotes have been omitted.]

making of the [hearsay] statement and that render the declarant particularly worthy of belief" in determining whether the hearsay statement possesses "particularized guarantees of trustworthiness." 110 S.Ct. at 3148. Contrary to this rule, many courts have taken into consideration corroborative evidence in deciding whether the uncross-examined testimony of a witness meets the trustworthiness requirements.... The Wright case overrules these cases.

After the decision in Gomez–Lemos, a defendant whose conviction had previously been affirmed by the sixth circuit sought habeas corpus on the ground that the admission of grand jury testimony against him constituted reversible error under Wright. The sixth circuit affirmed the denial of the petition. It found that given the totality of the circumstances the grand jury testimony was properly admitted:

> Louzon, the witness, had testified consistently on two separate occasions before two grand juries; on one occasion the testimony was under a grant of immunity and on the other occasion it was a statement against penal interest (a separate and distinct exception to the hearsay rule); and Louzon felt that he was at risk when he was testifying.

Curro v. United States, 4 F.3d 436, 437 (6th Cir.1993). Compare United States v. Flores, 985 F.2d 770 (5th Cir.1993)(finding violation of confrontation clause rights in admission of grand jury testimony that was against declarant's penal interest; statements against penal interest are not firmly rooted hearsay exceptions and therefore Wright test must be applied).

In United States v. Dent, 984 F.2d 1453, 1465–67 (7th Cir.), cert. denied, 510 U.S. 858 (1993), a concurring opinion by Judge Easterbrook argued that the Supreme Court's opinion in United States v. Salerno, 505 U.S. 317, 112 S.Ct. 2503 (1992)(see discussion supra at pp. 747–751) "requires a fresh look at the introduction of grand jury testimony under Fed.R.Evid. 804(b)(5)":

> Defendants in criminal cases are not represented before the grand jury, and hence lack an "opportunity" to develop the witness' testimony by direct or cross examination. Grand jury testimony is accordingly inadmissible under Rule 804(b)(1) against a defendant in a criminal case.
>
> Bypassing Rule 804(b)(1), the district judge relied on Rule 804(b)(5), one of the residual exceptions to the hearsay rule ...
>
> Roger Elayyan testified before the grand jury but was out of the country during defendants' trial. The district judge permitted the prosecutor to use a transcript of Elayyan's testimony as substantive evidence. The court today holds that Elayyan's statement was inadmissible because not sufficiently trustworthy. That conclusion enables the court to avoid the question whether Rule 804(b)(5) applies to grand jury testimony in the first place.
>
> United States v. Boulahanis, 677 F.2d 586, 588–89 (7th Cir.1982), holds that it does.... But Boulahanis does not mention the introductory language limiting Rule 804(b)(5) to "[a] statement not specifically covered by any of the foregoing exceptions". Although Boulahanis assumed that Rule 804(b)(1) does not even *apply* to grand jury testimony, so clear is the inadmissibility of such testimony against the defendant under its standards, we know from Salerno that Rule 804(b)(1) indeed "applies." Prior testimony of every description is "specifically covered by" Rule 804(b)(1). Boulahanis treats Rule 804(b)(5) as if it began: "A statement not specifically *admissible under* any of the foregoing exceptions ...". Evidence that flunks an express condition of a rule can come in anyway. Rule 804(b)(5)

reads more naturally if we understand the introductory clause to mean that evidence of a kind specifically addressed ("covered") by one of the four other subsections must satisfy the conditions laid down for its admission, and that other kinds of evidence not covered (because the drafters could not be exhaustive) are admissible if the evidence is approximately as reliable as evidence that would be admissible under the specific subsections.

. . .

In Salerno the United States persuaded the Supreme Court that to introduce prior testimony by an unavailable declarant the proponent of the evidence must satisfy the conditions in Rule 804(b)(1). In our case the United States, concededly unable to satisfy the conditions in Rule 804(b)(1), contends that the judge may admit the evidence anyway after ascertaining that the testimony was trustworthy. I doubt that the Solicitor General took Salerno to the Supreme Court in order to change the citation of authority from Rule 804(b)(1) to Rule 804(b)(5) while leaving the result untouched, or that the Court thought that its opinion would do nothing beyond correcting a typographical error.

True, Salerno does not discuss Rule 804(b)(5); neither side suggested that the grand jury testimony would be admissible under that Rule. The district judge had held that the testimony in question did not satisfy the "trustworthiness" requirement, which appears in Rule 804(b)(5) but not in Rule 804(b)(1). Salerno therefore does not discuss whether resort to that subsection is appropriate when testimony appears to be more reliable. It would be ironic, though, if the upshot of Salerno were that *only* the prosecutor may employ grand jury testimony in criminal cases. Any asymmetry should run the other way: the confrontation clause of the sixth amendment protects defendants, not prosecutors, from out-of-court statements. Although historical exceptions to the hearsay rule do not violate the confrontation clause, new exceptions must overcome a presumption against them. White v. Illinois, 502 U.S. 346 (1992).

Trial by affidavit was the bugbear that led to the confrontation clause; trial by grand jury testimony is not far removed. Grand jury testimony, like an affidavit, is one-sided, an *ex parte* narration over which the prosecutor has ample control. To avoid the introduction of unilateral narrations, Rule 804(b)(1) provides that prior testimony is admissible only if the party against whom the evidence is offered had both opportunity to examine the declarant and motive to do so. That the testimony has indicia of trustworthiness cannot be controlling; many affidavits *appear* to be trustworthy. A defendant's entitlement to confront the witnesses against him is not limited to confronting apparently-untrustworthy witnesses. Confrontation is valuable in large measure because it may establish that what seems to be accurate is misleading or deceitful or rests on inadequate foundation. Conditions on the use of Rule 804(b)(1) ensure that the defendant retains the right of confrontation in circumstances that lie at the core of the constitutional guarantee. Temptation to get 'round this limitation by moving to Rule 804(b)(5) and slighting its introductory language should be resisted.

6. *Child sex abuse cases.* After Wright, courts continue to admit statements of a child victim under the residual exceptions. See, e.g., State v. Edwards, 485 N.W.2d 911 (Minn.1992)(statement made by child to police interviewer after defendant's arrest for criminal sexual conduct); In re A.S.W., 834 P.2d 801 (Alaska 1992). See also State v. Plant, 461 N.W.2d 253 (Neb.1990)(tape recorded statement four-year old child made to police officer about her father's physical abuse of her brother admitted; tape recorder had not been started until at least 20 minutes after interview began, and statements on tape were made in response to leading questions), partly vacated on other grounds, 532 N.W.2d 619 (Neb.1995).

Special hearsay exception. Many state legislatures have responded to the perceived epidemic of child sex abuse by enacting statutes that create a special "tender years" exception to the hearsay rule for a child's complaint of sexual abuse. See State v. Robinson, 735 P.2d 801, 806–808 (Ariz.1987)(en banc)(holding that statute conflicts with Arizona Rules of Evidence and is therefore an unconstitutional infringement of court's authority to make procedural rules); State v. Zimmerman, 829 P.2d 861 (Idaho 1992)(tender years statute is of no force and effect to the extent that it conflicts with Idaho Rules of Evidence); People v. Bowers, 801 P.2d 511 (Colo.1990)(tender years statute precludes resort to residual exceptions, but if child's statement satisfies a more specific exception such as Rules 803(2) or (4) then requirements of tender years statute "should never come into play"). See also Vann v. State, 831 S.W.2d 126 (Ark.1992)(provision in Arkansas statute requiring child's statement to possess a "reasonable likelihood" of trustworthiness is too permissive a standard in light of Wright and therefore unconstitutional).

The Washington statute, which has served as a model for other states, provides:

> A statement made by a child when under the age of ten describing any act of sexual contact performed with or on the child by another ... [and] not otherwise admissible by statute or court rule, is admissible in evidence in ... criminal proceedings, ... if:
>
> > (1) The court finds, in a hearing conducted outside the presence of the jury that the time, content, and circumstances of the statement provide sufficient indicia of reliability; and
> >
> > (2) The child either:
> >
> > > (a) Testifies at the proceedings; or
> > >
> > > (b) Is unavailable as a witness: PROVIDED, That when the child is unavailable as a witness, such statement may be admitted only if there is corroborative evidence of the act.

Wash.Rev.Code Ann. § 9A.44.120.

SECTION 13.   CONSTITUTIONAL RESTRAINTS

White v. Illinois

Supreme Court of the United States, 1992.
502 U.S. 346, 112 S.Ct. 736, 116 L.Ed.2d 848.

■ THE CHIEF JUSTICE delivered the opinion of the Court.

In this case we consider whether the Confrontation Clause of the Sixth Amendment requires that, before a trial court admits testimony under the "spontaneous declaration" and "medical examination" exceptions to the hearsay rule, the prosecution must either produce the declarant at trial or the trial court must find that the declarant is unavailable. The Illinois Appellate Court concluded that such procedures are not constitutionally required. We agree with that conclusion.

Petitioner was convicted by a jury of aggravated criminal sexual assault, residential burglary, and unlawful restraint. Ill.Rev.Stat., ch. 38, ¶¶ 12–14, 19–3, 10–3 (1989). The events giving rise to the charges related to the sexual assault of S.G., then four years old. Testimony at the trial established that in the early morning hours of April 16, 1988, S.G.'s babysitter, Tony DeVore, was awakened by S.G.'s scream. DeVore went to S.G.'s bedroom and witnessed petitioner leaving the room and petitioner then left the house. 6 Tr. 10–11. DeVore knew petitioner because petitioner was a friend of S.G.'s mother, Tammy Grigsby. Id., at 27. DeVore asked S.G. what had happened. According to DeVore's trial testimony, S.G. stated that petitioner had put his hand over her mouth, choked her, threatened to whip her if she screamed and had "touch[ed] her in the wrong places." Asked by DeVore to point to where she had been touched, S.G. identified the vaginal area. Id., at 12–17.

Tammy Grigsby, S.G.'s mother, returned home about 30 minutes later. Grigsby testified that her daughter appeared "scared" and a "little hyper." Id., at 77–78. Grigsby proceeded to question her daughter about what had happened. At trial, Grigsby testified that S.G. repeated her claims that petitioner choked and threatened her. Grigsby also testified that S.G. stated that petitioner "put his mouth on her front part." Id., at 79. Grigsby also noticed that S.G. had bruises and red marks on her neck that had not been there previously. Id., at 81. Grigsby called the police.

Officer Terry Lewis arrived a few minutes later, roughly 45 minutes after S.G.'s scream had first awakened DeVore. Lewis questioned S.G. alone in the kitchen. At trial, Lewis' summary of S.G.'s statement indicated that she had offered essentially the same story as she had first reported to DeVore and to Grigsby, including a statement that petitioner had "used his tongue on her in her private parts." Id., at 110–112.

After Lewis concluded his investigation, and approximately four hours after DeVore first heard S.G.'s scream, S.G. was taken to the hospital. She was examined first by Cheryl Reents, an emergency room nurse, and then by Dr. Michael Meinzen. Each testified at trial and their testimony indicated that, in response to questioning, S.G. again provided an account of events that was essentially identical to the one she had given to DeVore, Grigsby, and Lewis.

S.G. never testified at petitioner's trial. The State attempted on two occasions to call her as a witness but she apparently experienced emotional difficulty on being brought to the courtroom and in each instance left without testifying. App. at 14. The defense made no attempt to call S.G. as a witness and the trial court neither made, nor was it asked to make, a finding that S.G. was unavailable to testify. 6 Tr. 105–106.

Petitioner objected on hearsay grounds to DeVore, Grigsby, Lewis, Reents, and Meinzen being permitted to testify regarding S.G.'s statements describing the assault. The trial court overruled each objection. With respect to DeVore, Grigsby, and Lewis the trial court concluded that the testimony could be permitted pursuant to an Illinois hearsay exception for spontaneous declarations. Petitioner's objections to Reents' and Meinzen's testimony was similarly overruled, based on both the spontaneous declaration exception and an exception for statements made in the course of securing medical treatment. The trial court also denied petitioner's motion for a mistrial based on S.G.'s "presence [and] failure to testify." App. 14.

Petitioner was found guilty by a jury, and the Illinois Appellate Court affirmed his conviction. It held that the trial court operated within the discretion accorded it under state law in ruling that the statements offered by DeVore, Grigsby and Lewis qualified for the spontaneous declaration exception and in ruling that the statements offered by Reents and Meinzen qualified for the medical examination exception. 198 Ill.App.3d 641, 647, 657, 555 N.E.2d 1241, 1246–1251 (1990). The court then went on to reject petitioner's Confrontation Clause challenge, a challenge based principally on language contained in this Court's decision in Ohio v. Roberts, 448 U.S. 56 (1980). It concluded that our later decision in United States v. Inadi, 475 U.S. 387 (1986), foreclosed any rule requiring that, as a necessary antecedent to the introduction of hearsay testimony, the prosecution must either produce the declarant at trial or show that the declarant is unavailable. The Illinois Supreme Court denied discretionary review, and we granted certiorari, 500 U.S. 904 (1991), limited to the constitutional question whether permitting the challenged testimony violated petitioner's Sixth Amendment Confrontation Clause right.

We consider as a preliminary matter an argument not considered below but urged by the United States as amicus curiae in support of respondent. The United States contends that petitioner's Confrontation Clause claim should be rejected because the Confrontation Clause's limited purpose is to prevent a particular abuse common in 16th and 17th century England: prosecuting a defendant through the presentation of ex parte affidavits, without the affiants ever being produced at trial. Because S.G.'s out-of-court statements do not fit this description, the United States suggests that S.G. was not a "witness against" petitioner within the meaning of the Clause. The United States urges this position, apparently in order that we might further conclude that the Confrontation Clause generally does not apply to the introduction of out-of-court statements admitted under an accepted hearsay exception. The only situation in which the Confrontation Clause would apply to such an exception, it argues, would be those few cases where the statement sought to be admitted was in the character of an ex parte affidavit, i.e., where the circumstances surrounding the out-of-court statement's utterance suggest that the statement has been made for the principal purpose of accusing or incriminating the defendant.

Such a narrow reading of the Confrontation Clause, which would virtually eliminate its role in restricting the admission of hearsay testimony, is foreclosed by our prior cases. The discussions in these cases, going back at least as far as Mattox v. United States, 156 U.S. 237 (1895), have included historical examination of the origins of the Confrontation Clause, and of the state of the law of evidence existing at the time the Sixth Amendment was adopted and later. We have been careful "not to equate the Confrontation Clause's prohibitions with the general rule prohibiting the admission of hearsay statements," Idaho v. Wright, (1990) 497 U.S. 805, 814 (1990) (citations omitted). Nonetheless we have consistently sought to "stee[r] a middle course," Roberts, supra, at 68, n. 9, that recognizes that "hearsay rules and the Confrontation Clause are generally designed to protect similar values," California v. Green, 399 U.S. 149, 155 (1970), and "stem from the same roots." Dutton v. Evans, 400 U.S. 74, 86 (1970). In Mattox itself, upon which the Government relies, the Court allowed the recorded testimony of a witness at a prior trial to be admitted. But, in the Court's view, the result was justified not because the hearsay testimony was unlike an ex parte affidavit, but because it came within an established exception to the hearsay rule. We think that the argument presented by the Government comes too late in the day to warrant reexamination of this approach.

We therefore now turn to petitioner's principal contention that our prior decision in Roberts requires that his conviction be vacated. In Roberts we considered a Confrontation Clause challenge to the introduction at trial of a transcript containing testimony from a probable-cause hearing, where the transcript included testimony from a witness not produced at trial but who had been subject to examination by defendant's counsel at the probable-cause hearing. In the course of rejecting the Confrontation Clause claim in that case, we used language that might suggest that the Confrontation Clause generally requires that a declarant either be produced at trial or be found unavailable before his out-of-court statement may be admitted into evidence. However, we think such an expansive reading of the Clause is negated by our subsequent decision in Inadi, supra.

In Inadi we considered the admission of out-of-court statements made by a co-conspirator in the course of the conspiracy. As an initial matter, we rejected the proposition that Roberts established a rule that "no out-of-court statement would be admissible without a showing of unavailability." 475 U.S., at 392. To the contrary, rather than establishing "a wholesale revision of the law of evidence" under the guise of the Confrontation Clause, ibid., we concluded that "Roberts must be read consistently with the question it answered, the authority it cited, and its own facts." Id., at 394. So understood, Roberts stands for the proposition that unavailability analysis is a necessary part of the Confrontation Clause inquiry only when the challenged out-of-court statements were made in the course of a prior judicial proceeding. Ibid.

Having clarified the scope of Roberts, the Court in Inadi then went on to reject the Confrontation Clause challenge presented there. In particular, we refused to extend the unavailability requirement established in Roberts to all out-of-court statements. Our decision rested on two factors. First, unlike former in-court testimony, co-conspirator statements "provide evidence of the conspiracy's context that cannot be replicated, even if the declarant testifies to the same matters in court," Inadi, 475 U.S., at 395. Also, given a declarant's likely change in status by the time the trial occurs, simply calling the declarant in the hope of having him repeat his prior out-of-court statements is a poor substitute for the full evidentiary significance that flows from statements made when the conspiracy is operating in full force. Ibid.

Second, we observed that there is little benefit, if any, to be accomplished by imposing an "unavailability rule." Such a rule will not work to bar absolutely the introduction of the out-of-court statements; if the declarant either is unavailable, or is available and produced for trial, the statements can be introduced. Id., at 396. Nor is an unavailability rule likely to produce much testimony that adds meaningfully to the trial's truth-determining process. Ibid. Many declarants will be subpoenaed by the prosecution or defense, regardless of any Confrontation Clause requirement, while the Compulsory Process Clause and evidentiary rules permitting a defendant to treat witnesses as hostile will aid defendants in obtaining a declarant's live testimony. Id., at 396–398. And while an unavailability rule would therefore do little to improve the accuracy of factfinding, it is likely to impose substantial additional burdens on the factfinding process. The prosecution would be required to repeatedly locate and keep continuously available each declarant, even when neither the prosecution nor the defense has any interest in calling the witness to the stand. An additional inquiry would be injected into the question of admissibility of evidence, to be litigated both at trial and on appeal. Id., at 398–399.

These observations, although expressed in the context of evaluating co-conspirator statements, apply with full force to the case at hand. We note first that the evidentiary rationale for permitting hearsay testimony regarding spontaneous declarations and statements made in the course of receiving medical care is that such out-of-court declarations are made in contexts that provide substantial guarantees of their trustworthiness.[1] But those same factors that contribute to the statements' reliability cannot be recaptured even by later in-court testimony. A statement that has been offered in a moment of excitement—without the opportunity to reflect on the consequences of one's exclamation—may justifiably carry more weight with a trier of fact than a similar statement offered in the relative calm of the courtroom. Similarly, a statement made in the course of procuring medical services, where the declarant knows that a false statement may cause misdiagnosis or mistreatment, carries special guarantees of credibility that a trier of fact may not think replicated by courtroom testimony. They are thus materially different from the statements at issue in *Roberts,* where the out-of-court statements sought to be introduced were themselves made in the course of a judicial proceeding, and where there was consequently no threat of lost evidentiary value if the out-of-court statements were replaced with live testimony.

The preference for live testimony in the case of statements like those offered in Roberts is because of the importance of cross examination, "the greatest legal engine ever invented for the discovery of truth." Green, 399 U.S., at 158. Thus courts have adopted the general rule prohibiting the receipt of hearsay evidence. But where proffered hearsay has sufficient guarantees of reliability to come within a firmly rooted exception to the hearsay rule, the Confrontation Clause is satisfied.

We therefore think it clear that the out-of-court statements admitted in this case had substantial probative value, value that could not be duplicated simply by the declarant later testifying in court. To exclude such probative statements under the strictures of the Confrontation Clause would be the height of wrong-headedness, given that the Confrontation Clause has as a basic purpose the promotion of the "'integrity of the factfinding process.' " Coy v. Iowa, 487 U.S. 1012, 1020 (1988) (quoting Kentucky v. Stincer, 482 U.S. 730, 736 (1987)). And as we have also noted, a statement that qualifies for admission under a "firmly rooted" hearsay exception is so trustworthy that adversarial testing can be expected to add little to its reliability. Wright, 497 U.S., at pp. 820–821. Given the evidentiary value of such statements, their reliability, and that establishing a generally applicable unavailability rule would have few practical benefits while imposing pointless litigation costs, we see no reason to treat the out-of-court statements in this case differently from those we found admissible in Inadi. A contrary rule would result in exactly the kind of "wholesale revision" of the laws of evidence that we expressly disavowed in Inadi. We therefore see no basis in Roberts or Inadi for excluding from trial, under the aegis of the Confrontation Clause, evidence embraced within such exceptions to the hearsay rule as those for spontaneous declarations and statements made for medical treatment.

---

1. Indeed, it is this factor that has led us to conclude that "firmly rooted" exceptions carry sufficient indicia of reliability to satisfy the reliability requirement posed by the Confrontation Clause. See Idaho v. Wright, 497 U.S. 805–35 (1990); Bourjaily v. United States, 483 U.S. 171, 182–184 (1987). There can be no doubt that the two exceptions we consider in this case are "firmly rooted." The exception for spontaneous declarations is at least two centuries old, see 6 J. Wigmore, Evidence, § 1747, 195 (J. Chadbourn rev. 1976), and may date to the late 17th century. See Thompson v. Trevanion, 90 Eng.Rep. 179 (K.B. 1694). It is currently recognized under the Federal Rules of Evidence, Rule 803(2), and in nearly four-fifths of the States. See Brief of *Amici Curiae* for the State of California, et al., pp. 15–16, n. 4 (collecting state statutes and cases). The exception for statements made for purposes of medical diagnosis or treatment is similarly recognized in the Federal Rules of Evidence, Rule 803(4), and is equally widely accepted among the States. See Brief of *Amici Curiae* for the State of California, et al., at 31–32, n. 13 (same). [Footnote of the Court; renumbered]

As a second line of argument, petitioner presses upon us two recent decisions involving child-testimony in child-sexual assault cases, Coy v. Iowa, supra, and Maryland v. Craig, 497 U.S. 836 (1990). Both Coy and Craig required us to consider the constitutionality of courtroom procedures designed to prevent a child witness from having to face across an open courtroom a defendant charged with sexually assaulting the child. In Coy we vacated a conviction that resulted from a trial in which a child witness testified from behind a screen, and in which there had been no particularized showing that such a procedure was necessary to avert a risk of harm to the child. In Craig we upheld a conviction that resulted from a trial in which a child witness testified via closed circuit television after such a showing of necessity. Petitioner draws from these two cases a general rule that hearsay testimony offered by a child should be permitted only upon a showing of necessity—i.e., in cases where necessary to protect the child's physical and psychological well-being.

Petitioner's reliance is misplaced. Coy and Craig involved only the question of what *in-court* procedures are constitutionally required to guarantee a defendant's confrontation right once a witness is testifying. Such a question is quite separate from that of what requirements the Confrontation Clause imposes as a predicate for the introduction of out-of-court declarations. Coy and Craig did not speak to the latter question. As we recognized in Coy, the admissibility of hearsay statements raises concerns lying at the periphery of those that the Confrontation Clause is designed to address, 487 U.S., at 1016. There is thus no basis for importing the "necessity requirement" announced in those cases into the much different context of out-of-court declarations admitted under established exceptions to the hearsay rule.

For the foregoing reasons, the judgment of the Illinois Appellate Court is

Affirmed.

■ JUSTICE THOMAS, with whom JUSTICE SCALIA, joins, concurring in part and concurring in the judgment.

The Court reaches the correct result under our precedents. I write separately only to suggest that our Confrontation Clause jurisprudence has evolved in a manner that is perhaps inconsistent with the text and history of the Clause itself. The Court unnecessarily rejects, in dicta, the United States' suggestion that the Confrontation Clause in general may not regulate the admission of hearsay evidence. See ante, at 4–5. The truth may be that this Court's cases unnecessarily have complicated and confused the relationship between the constitutional right of confrontation and the hearsay rules of evidence.

The Confrontation Clause provides simply that "[i]n all criminal prosecutions, the accused shall enjoy the right ... to be confronted with the witnesses against him...." U.S. Const., Amdt. 6. It is plain that the critical phrase within the Clause for purposes of this case is "witnesses against him." Any attempt at unraveling and understanding the relationship between the Clause and the hearsay rules must begin with an analysis of the meaning of that phrase. Unfortunately, in recent cases in this area, the Court has *assumed* that *all* hearsay declarants are "witnesses against" a defendant within the meaning of the Clause, see, e.g., Ohio v. Roberts, 448 U.S. 56 (1980); Lee v. Illinois, 476 U.S. 530 (1986); Idaho v. Wright, 497 U.S. 805 (1990), an assumption that is neither warranted nor supported by the history or text of the Confrontation Clause.

There is virtually no evidence of what the drafters of the Confrontation Clause intended it to mean. See California v. Green, 399 U.S. 149, 176, n. 8 (1970) (Harlan, J., concurring); Dutton v. Evans, 400 U.S. 74, 95 (1970)

(Harlan, J., concurring in result); Baker, The Right to Confrontation, The Hearsay Rules, and Due Process—A Proposal for Determining When Hearsay May be Used in Criminal Trials, 6 Conn.Law Rev. 529, 532 (1974). The strictest reading would be to construe the phrase "witnesses against him" to confer on a defendant the right to confront and cross-examine only those witnesses who actually appear and testify at trial. This was Wigmore's view:

> "The net result, then, under the constitutional rule, is that, so far as testimony is required under the hearsay rule to be taken infrajudicially, *it shall be taken in a certain way,* namely, subject to cross-examination—not secretly or ex parte away from the accused. The Constitution does not prescribe what kinds of testimonial statements (dying declarations or the like) shall be given infrajudicially—this depends on the law of evidence for the time being—but only what mode of procedure shall be followed—i.e., a cross-examining procedure—in the case of such testimony as is required by the ordinary law of evidence to be given infrajudicially." 5 J. Wigmore, Evidence § 1397, p. 159 (J. Chadbourn rev. 1974) (footnote omitted) (emphasis modified).

The Wigmore view was endorsed by Justice Harlan in his opinion concurring in the result in Dutton v. Evans, supra, at 94. It also finds support in the plain language of the Clause.... The difficulty with the Wigmore–Harlan view in its purest form is its tension with much of the apparent history surrounding the evolution of the right of confrontation at common law and with a long line of this Court's precedent, discussed below. For those reasons, the pure Wigmore–Harlan reading may be an improper construction of the Confrontation Clause.

Relevant historical sources and our own earlier decisions, nonetheless, suggest that a narrower reading of the Clause than the one given to it since 1980 may well be correct. In 16th-century England, magistrates interrogated the prisoner, accomplices, and others prior to trial. These interrogations were "intended only for the information of the court. The prisoner had no right to be, and probably never was, present." 1 J. Stephen, A History of the Criminal Law of England 221 (1883). At the trial itself, "proof was usually given by reading depositions, confessions of accomplices, letters, and the like; and this occasioned frequent demands by the prisoner to have his 'accusers,' i.e., the witnesses against him, brought before him face to face.... " Id., at 326. See also 5 Wigmore, supra, § 1364, at 13 ("there was ... no appreciation at all of the necessity of calling a person to the stand as a witness"; rather, it was common practice to obtain "information by consulting informed persons not called into court"); 9 W. Holdsworth, History of English Law 227–229 (3d ed. 1944). The infamous trial of Sir Walter Raleigh on charges of treason in 1603 in which the Crown's primary evidence against him was the confession of an alleged co-conspirator (the confession was repudiated before trial and probably had been obtained by torture) is a well-known example of this feature of English criminal procedure. See Pollitt, The Right of Confrontation: Its History and Modern Dress, 8 J.Pub.L. 381, 388–389 (1959); 1 Stephen, supra, at 333–336; 9 Holdsworth, supra, at 216–217, 226–228.

Apparently in response to such abuses, a common-law right of confrontation began to develop in England during the late 16th and early 17th centuries. 5 Wigmore, supra, § 1364, at 23; Pollitt, supra, at 389–390. Justice Story believed that the Sixth Amendment codified some of this common law, 3 J. Story, Commentaries on the Constitution of the United States 662 (1833), and this Court previously has recognized the common-law origins of the right. See Salinger v. United States, 272 U.S. 542, 548 (1926) ("The right of confrontation did not originate with the provision in the Sixth Amendment, but was a common-law right having recognized exceptions"). The Court consistently has indicated that the primary purpose of the Clause was to prevent the abuses which had occurred in England. See Mattox v. United States, 156 U.S. 237, 242 (1895) ("The primary object of the [Confrontation Clause] was to prevent depositions or ex parte affidavits, such as were sometimes admitted in civil cases, being used against the prisoner in lieu of a personal examination and cross-examination of the witness . . ."); California v. Green, 399 U.S., at 156 ("It is sufficient to note that the particular vice that gave impetus to the confrontation claim was the practice of trying defendants on 'evidence' which consisted solely of ex parte affidavits or depositions secured by the examining magistrates, thus denying the defendant the opportunity to challenge his accuser in a face-to-face encounter in front of the trier of fact"); id., at 179 (Harlan, J., concurring) ("From the scant information available it may tentatively be concluded that the Confrontation Clause was meant to constitutionalize a barrier against flagrant abuses, trials by anonymous accusers, and absentee witnesses"); Dutton v. Evans, 400 U.S., at 94 (Harlan, J., concurring in result) (the "paradigmatic evil the Confrontation Clause was aimed at" was "trial by affidavit").

There appears to be little if any indication in the historical record that the exceptions to the hearsay rule were understood to be limited by the simultaneously evolving common-law right of confrontation. The Court has never explored the historical evidence on this point.[2] As a matter of plain language, however, it is difficult to see how or why the Clause should apply to hearsay evidence as a general proposition. As Justice Harlan observed:

> "If one were to translate the Confrontation Clause into language in more common use today, it would read: 'In all criminal prosecutions, the accused shall enjoy the right to be present and to cross-examine the witnesses against him.' Nothing in this language or in its 18th–century equivalent would connote a purpose to control the scope of the rules of evidence. The language is particularly ill-chosen if what was intended was a prohibition on the use of any hearsay. . . . " Id., at 95 (opinion concurring in result).

The standards that the Court has developed to implement its assumption that the Confrontation Clause limits admission of hearsay evidence have no basis in the text of the Sixth Amendment. Ever since Ohio v. Roberts, 448 U.S. 56 (1980), the Court has interpreted the Clause to mean that hearsay may be admitted only under a "firmly rooted" exception, id., at 66, or if it otherwise bears "particularized guarantees of trustworthiness," ibid. See, e.g., Idaho v. Wright, 497 U.S., at ___; Bourjaily v. United States, 483 U.S. 171, 183 (1987). This analysis implies that the Confrontation Clause bars only unreliable hearsay. Although the historical concern with trial by affidavit and anonymous accusers does reflect concern with the reliability of the evidence against a defendant, the Clause makes no distinction based on the reliability of the evidence presented. Nor does it seem likely that the drafters of the Sixth

---

2. The only recent decision to address this question explicitly was Ohio v. Roberts, 448 U.S. 56 (1980), in which the Court simply stated that "[t]he historical evidence leaves little doubt, however, that the Clause was intended to exclude some hearsay." Id., at 63 (citing California v. Green, 399 U.S. 149, 156–157 (1970)). The cited passage in *Green* simply reiterates the previously noted point that the right of confrontation evolved as a response to the problem of trial by affidavit. Thus, the statement in *Roberts* that "the Clause was intended to exclude *some* hearsay" is correct as far as it goes (affidavits and depositions are hearsay), but the opinion should not be read as having established that the drafters intended the Clause to encompass *all* hearsay, or even hearsay in general. [footnote of the Court; renumbered]

Amendment intended to permit a defendant to be tried on the basis of ex parte affidavits found to be reliable. Cf. U.S. Const., Art. III, § 3 ("No person shall be convicted of Treason unless on the Testimony of two Witnesses to the same overt Act, or on Confession in open Court"). Reliability is more properly a due process concern. There is no reason to strain the text of the Confrontation Clause to provide criminal defendants with a protection that due process already provides them.

The United States, as amicus curiae, has suggested that the Confrontation Clause should apply only to those persons who provide in-court testimony or the functional equivalent, such as affidavits, depositions, or confessions that are made in contemplation of legal proceedings. This interpretation is in some ways more consistent with the text and history of the Clause than our current jurisprudence, and it is largely consistent with our cases. If not carefully formulated, however, this approach might be difficult to apply, and might develop in a manner not entirely consistent with the crucial "witnesses against him" phrase.

In this case, for example, the victim's statements to the investigating police officer might be considered the functional equivalent of in-court testimony because the statements arguably were made in contemplation of legal proceedings. Attempts to draw a line between statements made in contemplation of legal proceedings and those not so made would entangle the courts in a multitude of difficulties. Few types of statements could be categorically characterized as within or without the reach of a defendant's confrontation rights. Not even statements made to the police or government officials could be deemed automatically subject to the right of confrontation (imagine a victim who blurts out an accusation to a passing police officer, or the unsuspecting social-services worker who is told of possible child abuse). It is also not clear under the United States' approach whether the declarant or the listener (or both) must be contemplating legal proceedings. The United States devotes little attention to the application of its proposed standard in this case.

Thus, we are faced with a situation in which the text of the Sixth Amendment supports the Wigmore–Harlan view but history and our earlier cases point away from that strictest reading of the text. Despite this tension, I believe it is possible to interpret the Confrontation Clause along the lines suggested by the United States in a manner that is faithful to both the provision's text and history. One possible formulation is as follows: The federal constitutional right of confrontation extends to any witness who actually testifies at trial, but the Confrontation Clause is implicated by extrajudicial statements only insofar as they are contained in formalized testimonial materials, such as affidavits, depositions, prior testimony, or confessions. It was this discrete category of testimonial materials that was historically abused by prosecutors as a means of depriving criminal defendants of the benefit of the adversary process, see, e.g., Mattox v. United States, 156 U.S. 237, 242–243 (1895), and under this approach, the Confrontation Clause would not be construed to extend beyond the historical evil to which it was directed.

Such an approach would be consistent with the vast majority of our cases, since virtually all of them decided before Ohio v. Roberts involved prior testimony or confessions exactly the type of formalized testimonial evidence that lies at the core of the Confrontation Clause's concern. This narrower reading of the Confrontation Clause would greatly simplify the inquiry in the hearsay context. Furthermore, this interpretation would avoid the problem posed by the Court's current focus on hearsay exceptions that are "firmly rooted" in the common law. See ante, at 8, n. 8. The Court has never explained the Confrontation Clause implications of a State's decision to adopt an exception not recognized at common law or one not recognized by a majority of the States. Our current jurisprudence suggests that, in order to satisfy the Sixth Amendment, the State would have to establish in each individual case that hearsay admitted pursuant to the newly created exception bears "particularized guarantees of trustworthiness," and would have to continue doing so until the exception became "firmly rooted" in the common law, if that is even possible under the Court's standard. This result is difficult to square with the Clause itself. Neither the language of the Clause nor the historical evidence appears to support the notion that the Confrontation Clause was intended to constitutionalize the hearsay rule and its exceptions. Although the Court repeatedly has disavowed any intent to cause that result, see, e.g., ante, at 5; Idaho v. Wright, 497 U.S., at ___; United States v. Inadi, 475 U.S. 387, 393, n. 5 (1986); Dutton v. Evans, 400 U.S., at 86; California v. Green, 399 U.S., at 155, I fear that our decisions have edged ever further in that direction.

For the foregoing reasons, I respectfully suggest that, in an appropriate case, we reconsider how the phrase "witness against" in the Confrontation Clause pertains to the admission of hearsay. I join the Court's opinion except for its discussion of the narrow reading of this phrase proposed by the United States.

NOTES

1. Before turning to the constitutional issue, consider first how and whether each of the five out-of-court statements proffered in White satisfied a traditional hearsay exception. Are there objections you would have made if these statements were being offered under the Federal Rules? In reviewing a state court judgment as in White, the Supreme Court does not, of course, deal with purely evidentiary issues, but does not the practice of courts in applying hearsay doctrine bear on the trustworthiness of the evidence that is admitted? Is an interpretation of the Confrontation Clause that ignores the way in which exceptions are applied desirable?

2. The White opinion indicates that the Confrontation Clause is satisfied when "trustworthy", "reliable" hearsay evidence is admitted. It also endorses the "integrity of the fact-finding process" as the principal goal of the Confrontation Clause. Cf. Fed.R.Evid. 102. If the Court means that accuracy in ascertaining the truth is paramount, how do its holdings with regard to the admissibility of various kinds of out-of-court statements promote this objective? In light of Owens, p. 554, supra, Bourjaily, p. 590, supra, and Roberts, p. 737, supra does the prosecution have any constitutional obligation to demonstrate trustworthiness and reliability with regard to evidence proffered pursuant to Rules 801(d)(1),(d)(2), 803(1)-(23), or 804(b)(1)-(4)? Do you agree with the Court that evidence admitted under firmly rooted hearsay exceptions "is so trustworthy that adversarial testing can be expected to add little to its reliability"? Do the cases you have read confirm that cross-examination of the declarant is unlikely to furnish any useful information to the trier of fact regardless of the nature of the statement, or the declarant, or the circumstances in which the statement is made? Is the majority's assumption in White that the admission of firmly-rooted hearsay will result in more accurate verdicts verifiable?

3. When does an exception become firmly rooted? Is the White Court using a historical test in treating as firmly rooted the statements of causation admitted under the exception for medical diagnosis and treatment? See pp. 647–654, supra. Does the Court's analysis mean that new class exceptions that evolve under federal or state law should be analyzed under White, or under Wright, supra p. 778?

4. After White, under what circumstances is there a burden on the prosecution to produce a hearsay declarant at trial? Is there a constitutional unavailability requirement? Cf. Ohio v. Roberts, p. 737, supra. Do you agree with the Court that an unavailability requirement is not needed to promote accuracy in factfinding because the defendant can produce the declarant himself? See Swift, Smoke and Mirrors: The Failure of the Supreme Court's Accuracy Rationale in White v. Illinois Requires a New Look at Confrontation, 22 Cap.U.L.Rev. 145, 165–69 (1993) (after White, prosecutors have the tactical advantage of choosing between using the same person, who may be a poor performer or susceptible to particular impeachment techniques, as a hearsay declarant or live witness; the burden and cost on the defendant are increased, and defendant must wait until defense case while prosecutor's hearsay remains unchallenged). In Wright, the Court assumed that the declarant was unavailable. Is there an unavailability prong that must be satisfied when evidence is admitted under a nonfirmly rooted hearsay exception?

5. Are there values other than the evidentiary value of accuracy in factfinding that would be served by an interpretation of the Confrontation Clause requiring the prosecution to produce available hearsay declarants? A number of recent articles suggest that the government's enormous power to prosecute and to shape evidence through its investigative practices requires the production of available declarants so that the defendant has a fair opportunity to test the probative value of the evidence and to expose the government's role in its creation. See, e.g., Berger, The Deconstitutionalization of the Confrontation Clause: A Proposal for a Prosecutorial Restraint Model, 76 Minn.L.Rev. 557, 561 (1992) ("Hearsay statements procured by agents of the prosecution or police should ... stand on a different footing than hearsay created without governmental intrusion" because central missions of the Confrontation Clause and the Sixth Amendment are to keep the prosecutorial powers of the government in check and to make visible crucial workings of the government); Kirst, The Procedural Dimensions of Confrontation Doctrine, 66 Neb.L.Rev. 485, 487 (1987) (suggesting that the Confrontation Clause is "a limit on the procedure the government [can] use" to prosecute); Jonakait, The Origins of the Confrontation Clause: An Alternative History, 27 Rutgers L.J. 77, 82 (1995) ("confrontation should operate with other Sixth Amendment rights that affirmatively grant an accused the opportunity for meaningful defense advocacy.").

See also Scallen, Constitutional Dimensions of Hearsay Reform: Toward a Three–Dimensional Confrontation Clause, 76 Minn.L.Rev. 623 (1992) (confrontation increases legitimacy of trial process by having a "societal" dimension that focuses on relationships between the accused, accusers and the state); Taslitz, Catharsis, The Confrontation Clause, and Expert Testimony, 22 Cap. U.L.Rev. 103, 130 (1993)("Confrontation is part of the defense's right to present its case, its story.").

And see Graham, The Right of Confrontation and the Hearsay Rule: Sir Walter Raleigh Loses Another One, 8 Crim.L.Bull. 99 (1972); Haddad, The Future of Confrontation Clause Developments: What Will Emerge When the Supreme Court Synthesizes the Diverse Lines of Confrontation Decisions? 81 J.Crim.L. & Criminology 77 (1990); Imwinkelried, The Constitutionalization of Hearsay: The Extent to Which the Fifth and Sixth Amendments Permit or Require the Liberalization of the Hearsay Rules, 76 Minn.L.Rev. 521 (1992); Jonakait, Restoring Confrontation to the Sixth Amendment, 35 UCLA L.Rev. 557 (1988); Mosteller, Remaking Confrontation Clause and Hearsay Doctrine

Under the Challenge of Child Sexual Abuse Prosecutions, 1993 U.Ill.L.Rev. 691; Swift, supra note 4 at 170–75 (reviews recent writings discussing values other than accuracy in factfinding).

6. Has the Supreme Court's insistence on the essential congruence between the hearsay rules and the Confrontation Clause led to a dead-end in which the clause has become insignificant in protecting a criminal defendant on constitutional grounds? Is a consequence that the Court will interpret the federal hearsay rules more strictly? Cf. Williamson, supra p. 622, Tome p. 540.

7. *Due process.* Justice Harlan in his concurring opinion in California v. Green, p. 530, supra proposed the due process clause as "the constitutional framework" for judging the admissibility of hearsay in state cases. Professor Swift has suggested that the factors the Court looks to in White resemble the criteria developed by the Court in Mathews v. Eldridge, 424 U.S. 319 (1976) to test whether administrative proceedings conform to procedural due process. Swift, Smoke and Mirrors: The Failure of the Supreme Court's Accuracy Rationale in White v. Illinois Requires a New Look at Confrontation, 22 Cap.U.L.Rev. 145, 176 (1993). She concludes, however, that "the Supreme Court's own due process calculus, were it applied to the procedural protection of confrontation sought by the defendant in White, would weigh in favor of the confrontation claim." Id. at 183. She explains:

> [T]he Matthews test requires a classic judgment of justification: whether the social benefits of confrontation, enforced through an unavailability requirement, are outweighed by the social costs of such a requirement. The social value of the private interest at stake in criminal prosecutions is high; the benefits of confrontation are significant; the possible social costs [of producing the declarant, litigating "unavailability" when the declarant is not produced, and the risk of acquitting a guilty defendant if the hearsay cannot be used because the government cannot prove unavailability] do not outweigh these benefits.

Id. at 182.

CHAPTER 5

CIRCUMSTANTIAL PROOF: FURTHER PROBLEMS

SECTION 1. EVIDENCE OF OTHER CRIMES

People v. Zackowitz

Court of Appeals of New York, 1930.
254 N.Y. 192, 172 N.E. 466.

[Appeal from a judgment of the Kings County Court, rendered March 25, 1930, upon a verdict convicting the defendant of the crime of murder in the first degree.]

■ CARDOZO, CH.J. On November 10, 1929, shortly after midnight, the defendant in Kings county shot Frank Coppola and killed him without justification or excuse. A crime is admitted. What is doubtful is the degree only.

Four young men, of whom Coppola was one, were at work repairing an automobile in a Brooklyn street. A woman, the defendant's wife, walked by on the opposite side. One of the men spoke to her insultingly, or so at least she understood him. The defendant, who had dropped behind to buy a newspaper, came up to find his wife in tears. He was told she had been insulted, though she did not then repeat the words. Enraged, he stepped across the street and upbraided the offenders with words of coarse profanity. He informed them, so the survivors testify, that "if they did not get out of there in five minutes, he would come back and bump them all off." Rejoining his wife, he walked with her to their apartment house located close at hand. He was heated with liquor which he had been drinking at a dance. Within the apartment he induced her to tell him what the insulting words had been. A youth had asked her to lie with him, and had offered her two dollars. With rage aroused again, the defendant went back to the scene of the insult and found the four young men still working at the car. In a statement to the police, he said that he had armed himself at the apartment with a twenty-five calibre automatic pistol. In his testimony at the trial he said that this pistol had been in his pocket all the evening. Words and blows followed, and then a shot. The defendant kicked Coppola in the stomach. There is evidence that Coppola went for him with a wrench. The pistol came from the pocket, and from the pistol a single shot, which did its deadly work. The defendant walked away and at the corner met his wife who had followed him from the home. The two took a taxicab to Manhattan where they spent the rest of the night at the dwelling of a friend. On the way the defendant threw his pistol into the river. He was arrested on January 7, 1930, about two months following the crime.

At the trial the vital question was the defendant's state of mind at the moment of the homicide. Did he shoot with a deliberate and premeditated design to kill? Was he so inflamed by drink or by anger or by both combined that, though he knew the nature of his act, he was the prey to sudden impulse, the fury of the fleeting moment? (People v. Caruso, 246 N.Y. 437, 446, 159 N.E.

390). If he went forth from his apartment with a preconceived design to kill, how is it that he failed to shoot at once? How reconcile such a design with the drawing of the pistol later in the heat and rage of an affray? These and like questions the jurors were to ask themselves and answer before measuring the defendant's guilt.... Delicate enough and subtle is the inquiry, even in the most favorable conditions, with every warping influence excluded. There must be no blurring of the issues by evidence illegally admitted and carrying with it in its admission an appeal to prejudice and passion.

Evidence charged with that appeal was, we think, admitted here. Not only was it admitted, and this under objection and exception, but the changes were rung upon it by prosecutor and judge. Almost at the opening of the trial the People began the endeavor to load the defendant down with the burden of an evil character. He was to be put before the jury as a man of murderous disposition. To that end they were allowed to prove that at the time of the encounter and at that of his arrest he had in his apartment, kept there in a radio box, three pistols and a tear-gas gun. There was no claim that he had brought these weapons out at the time of the affray, no claim that with any of them he had discharged the fatal shot. He could not have done so, for they were all of different calibre. The end to be served by laying the weapons before the jury was something very different. The end was to bring persuasion that here was a man of vicious and dangerous propensities, who because of those propensities was more likely to kill with deliberate and premeditated design than a man of irreproachable life and amiable manners. Indeed, this is the very ground on which the introduction of the evidence is now explained and defended. The District Attorney tells us in his brief that the possession of the weapons characterized the defendant as "a desperate type of criminal," a "person criminally inclined." The dissenting opinion, if it puts the argument less bluntly, leaves the substance of the thought unchanged. "Defendant was presented to the jury as a man having dangerous weapons in his possession, making a selection therefrom and going forth to put into execution his threats to kill." The weapons were not brought by the defendant to the scene of the encounter. They were left in his apartment where they were incapable of harm. In such circumstances, ownership of the weapons, if it has any relevance at all, has relevance only as indicating a general disposition to make use of them thereafter, and a general disposition to make use of them thereafter is without relevance except as indicating a "desperate type of criminal," a criminal affected with a murderous propensity....

If a murderous propensity may be proved against a defendant as one of the tokens of his guilt, a rule of criminal evidence, long believed to be of fundamental importance for the protection of the innocent, must be first declared away. Fundamental hitherto has been the rule that character is never an issue in a criminal prosecution unless the defendant chooses to make it one (Wigmore, Evidence, vol. 1, §§ 55, 192). In a very real sense a defendant starts his life afresh when he stands before a jury, a prisoner at the bar. There has been a homicide in a public place. The killer admits the killing but urges self-defense and sudden impulse. Inflexibly the law has set its face against the endeavor to fasten guilt upon him by proof of character or experience predisposing to an act of crime (Wigmore, Evidence, vol. 1, §§ 57, 192; People v. Molineux, 168 N.Y. 264, 61 N.E. 286). The endeavor has been often made, but always it has failed. At times, when the issue has been self-defense, testimony has been admitted as to the murderous propensity of the deceased, the victim of the homicide (People v. Druse, 103 N.Y. 655, 8 N.E. 733; People v. Rodawald, 177 N.Y. 408, 70 N.E. 1; Wigmore, Evidence, vol. 1, §§ 63, 246), but never of such a propensity on the part of the killer. The principle back of the exclusion is one, not of logic, but of policy (Wigmore, vol. 1, §§ 57, 194; People v. Richardson, 222 N.Y. 103, 109, 110, 118 N.E. 514). There may be cogency in the argument that a quarrelsome defendant is more likely to start a quarrel than one of milder type, a man of dangerous mode of life more likely than a shy recluse. The law is not blind to this, but equally it is not blind to the peril to the innocent if character is accepted as probative of crime. "The natural and inevitable tendency of the tribunal—whether judge or jury—is to give excessive weight to the vicious record of crime thus exhibited, and either to allow it to bear too strongly on the present charge, or to take the proof of it as justifying a condemnation irrespective of guilt of the present charge" (Wigmore, Evidence, vol. 1, § 194, and cases cited).

A different question would be here if the pistols had been bought in expectation of this particular encounter. They would then have been admissible as evidence of preparation and design (Wigmore, Evidence, vol. 1, § 238; People v. Scott, 153 N.Y. 40, 46 N.E. 1028). A different question would be here if they were so connected with the crime as to identify the perpetrator, if he had dropped them, for example, at the scene of the affray (People v. Hill, 198 N.Y. 64, 91 N.E. 272). They would then have been admissible as tending to implicate the possessor (if identity was disputed), no matter what the opprobrium attached to his possession. Different, also, would be the question if the defendant had been shown to have gone forth from the apartment with all the weapons on his person. To be armed from head to foot at the very moment of an encounter may be a circumstance worthy to be considered, like acts of preparation generally, as a proof of preconceived design. There can be no such implication from the ownership of weapons which one leaves behind at home.

The endeavor was to generate an atmosphere of professional criminality. It was an endeavor the more unfair in that, apart from the suspicion attaching to the possession of these weapons, there is nothing to mark the defendant as a man of evil life. He was not in crime as a business. He did not shoot as a bandit shoots in the hope of wrongful gain. He was engaged in a decent calling, an optician regularly employed, without criminal record, or criminal associates. If his own testimony be true, he had gathered these weapons together as curios, a collection that interested and amused him. Perhaps his explanation of their ownership is false. There is nothing stronger than mere suspicion to guide us to an answer. Whether the explanation be false or true, he should not have been driven by the People to the necessity of offering it. Brought to answer a specific charge, and to defend himself against it, he was placed in a position where he had to defend himself against another, more general and sweeping. He was made to answer to the charge, pervasive and poisonous even if insidious and covert, that he was a man of murderous heart, of criminal disposition....

The judgment of conviction should be reversed, and a new trial ordered.

■ POUND, J. (dissenting) ... The possession of these dangerous weapons was a separate crime. (Penal Law, § 1897.) The broad question is whether it had any connection with the crime charged. The substantial rights of the defendant must be protected. Where the penalty is death, we may grant a new trial if justice requires it, even though no exception was taken in the court below. (Code Crim.Pro. § 528.)

The People may not prove against a defendant crimes not alleged in the indictment committed on other occasions than the crime charged as aiding the proofs that he is guilty of the crime charged unless such proof tends to establish (1) motive; (2) intent; (3) absence of mistake or accident; (4) a common scheme or plan embracing the commission of two or more crimes so related to each other that proof of the one tends to establish the other; (5) the identity of the person charged with the commission of the crime on trial. These exceptions are stated generally and not with categorical precision and may not be all-inclusive. (People v. Molineux, 168 N.Y. 264, 61 N.E. 286; People v. Pettanza, 207 N.Y. 560, 101 N.E. 428; People v. Moran, 246 N.Y. 100, 106, 158 N.E. 35.) None of them apply here nor were the weapons offered under an exception to the general rule. They were offered as a part of the transaction itself. The accused was tried only for the crime charged. The real question is whether the matter relied on has such a connection with the crime charged as to be admissible on any ground. If so, the fact that it constitutes another distinct crime does not render it inadmissible. (Commonwealth v. Snell, 189 Mass. 12, 21, 75 N.E. 75.) The rule laid down in the Molineux case has never been applied to prevent the People from proving all the elements of the offense charged, although separate crimes are included in such proof. Thus in this case no question is made as to the separate crime of illegal possession of the weapon with which the killing was done. It was "a part of the history of the case" having a distinct relation to and bearing upon the facts connected with the killing. (People v. Governale, 193 N.Y. 581, 86 N.E. 554; People v. Rogers, 192 N.Y. 331, 85 N.E. 135; People v. Hill, 198 N.Y. 64, 91 N.E. 272; People v. Rodawald, 177 N.Y. 408, 70 N.E. 1.)

As the District Attorney argues in his brief, if defendant had been arrested at the time of the killing and these weapons had been found on his person, the People would not have been barred from proving the fact, and the further fact that they were nearby in his apartment should not preclude the proof as bearing on the entire deed of which the act charged forms a part. Defendant was presented to the jury as a man having dangerous weapons in his possession, making a selection therefrom and going forth to put into execution his threats to kill; not as a man of a dangerous disposition in general, but as one who, having an opportunity to select a weapon to carry out his threats, proceeded to do so. . . .

The judgment of conviction should be affirmed.

■ LEHMAN, KELLOGG, and O'BRIEN, JJ., concur with CARDOZO, CH. J.; POUND, J., dissents in opinion in which CRANE and HUBBS, JJ., concur.

Judgment reversed; etc.

NOTES

1. United States v. Himelwright, 42 F.3d 777, 786 & n. 8 (3d Cir.1994): In prosecution of postal worker for making threatening telephone calls, held error to allow the introduction of evidence of the defendant's purchase and possession of guns.

Himelwright's two-day trial took place on November 15 and 16, 1993, following a series of well publicized shooting sprees by postal workers. See, e.g., Workers Kill Workers; Yet Again, Violence in the Post Office, New York Times, May 9, 1993, Sec. 4, at 2; Inside Post Offices, the Mail is Only Part of the Pressure, New York Times, May 15, 1993, at A1; Postal Study Aims to Spot Violence–Prone Workers, New York Times, July 1, 1993, at A9. As reported in the New York Times on August 3, 1993, "There have been at least 11 shooting incidents involving aggrieved emotionally disturbed postal workers in the United States in the last decade with 35 people killed and 18 wounded." Police Arrest Postal Worker in Pistol Threat to His Wife, New York Times, Aug. 3, 1993, at B5. We believe the government's portrait of Himelwright as the stereotypical violence-prone postal worker had serious potential for prejudice to him in two different ways. First, it had the potential for frightening the jury into ignoring evidence that otherwise might have raised a reasonable doubt about whether he intended a serious threat. Second, if the jury was persuaded that Himelwright was violence-prone by character, it might have inferred that he intended violence in this particular instance. That inference is precisely what [Fed.] Rule [Evid.] 404(b) prohibits. Moreover, the manner in which this evidence was used at trial exacerbated the error of its admission: the prosecutor was permitted to introduce into evidence, and display before the jury, the firearms themselves. Such a method of introduction is not proscribed. But because of the remote connection between the possession (or purchase) of the firearms and telephone calls, the display of weaponry was far more prejudicial than probative under the circumstances of this case. We believe that this enabled, if not invited, the jury to draw impermissible inferences which might well have deprived Himelwright of a fair trial.[1]

State v. Spraggin, 252 N.W.2d 94 (Wis.1977). Defendant was convicted of intentionally aiding and abetting the delivery of heroin. A state narcotics agent bought the heroin not from the defendant but from a third person in the street near defendant's home. Shortly after the purchase, police converged on defendant's house, arrested her and conducted searches that turned up firearms, a possibly stolen television set and other materials. These materials, along with accompanying testimony about their discovery, were introduced into evidence.

At the trial, the State laid the foundation for introducing into evidence weapons and stolen goods found in the defendant's house. The State had Officer Wells, a narcotics officer with the Wisconsin Department of Justice, Division of Criminal Investigation, testify that he had been involved in about 100 transactions involving the sale of heroin and that in almost every deal in which he was involved "there has been a weapon involved" and that "most of the dealers are totally involved with getting payments from heroin addicts via stolen goods." The court asked whether the State was trying to show that it is customary for heroin dealers to be in possession of stolen property. The witness responded: "I have seen it frequently on the street. Whether it could be considered customary more than 50 percent of the time, I don't know." The judge permitted the jury to hear Officer Wells' testimony that on the basis of his experience he believed that heroin dealers usually have weapons and stolen goods on the premises. The guns and allegedly stolen goods were introduced into evidence.

The defendant objected to this testimony and these exhibits. Again the defendant contended that such evidence indicated bad character, had little probative value, caused unfair prejudice, and did not have "anything to do with the merits of this charge." Before the close of the case the defense counsel again requested—with no success—that the jury be instructed to disregard the material taken from the defendant's home.

· · ·

This evidence indicates that the defendant's home was a den of iniquity and that she had a propensity and disposition toward criminal activity. The evidence was designed to convince the jury that the defendant's possession of weapons and stolen goods was indicative of her guilt of the act charged in this case—intentionally aiding and abetting in the delivery of heroin. No specific connection was shown between this evidence

---

1. Footnote omitted.

and the defendant's alleged criminal acts. Weapons and stolen goods may constitute the protection and currency necessary in the realm of heroin trafficking, but the State did not demonstrate in any manner that this particular evidence was so employed. The inference of such use must be supported by more than the mere introduction of these exhibits into evidence and the broad assertion that guns and stolen goods are commonly used by those in the heroin trade. The very purpose of the other-conduct rule is to exclude evidence which is relevant only for showing a disposition to commit a crime. The very purpose of the rule was violated here. Id. at 98–99.

The court held that the introduction of the evidence violated section 904.04(2) of the Wisconsin Rules of Evidence and reversed defendant's conviction for that reason. Section 904.04(2) provides: "Evidence of other crimes, wrongs, or acts is not admissible to prove the character of a person in order to show that he acted in conformity therewith. This subsection does not exclude the evidence when offered for other purposes, such as proof of motive, opportunity, intent, preparation, plan, knowledge, identity, or absence of mistake or accident."

United States v. Shelton, 628 F.2d 54 (D.C.Cir.1980): Prosecution for assaulting a federal officer. The sharply disputed issue was whether defendant had simply run from the scene or pointed a gun at the officer. The court reversed defendant's conviction because during cross-examination of defendant and a witness who was with defendant at the time of the incident, the prosecutor had elicited the information that they were unemployed and yet at the time of the incident in possession of $2600, and also that the witness had been in the neighborhood where the incident took place—a well-known center of narcotics activity—on several earlier occasions.

> The evidence produced by the prosecutor's line of cross-examination is not rendered more acceptable by the fact that it is less focused and more subtly adduced than traditional "other crimes" evidence. Quite the contrary. Where the "other crime" alleged is not specified, it is more difficult for the defendant to refute the charge or to demonstrate its insignificance. Where the evidence is presented by innuendo, it is less likely that the jury will guard against manipulation. Therefore, the likelihood that a jury will draw an improper inference is even greater in a case like the one before us than it is in the traditional "other crimes" case. Id. at 57.

2. If in the Zackowitz case it was certain the jury would not find defendant guilty simply because he had a collection of guns or because of an interest or disposition revealed by the collection, would there be any reason to exclude the evidence of the guns?

3. Does it make any difference whether the possession of the guns shown in the Zackowitz case was or was not a crime under New York law? In White v. United States, 279 F.2d 740, 748–49 (4th Cir.), cert. denied, 364 U.S. 850 (1960), a prosecution for robbing a bank, evidence of a plan by defendant to rob another bank was conditionally admitted and then excluded. The appellate court stated that it would not have been error to allow the jury to consider the evidence since the mere formation of a plan to rob is not illegal. But in Huff v. United States, 273 F.2d 56, 60 (5th Cir.1959), a prosecution for smuggling jewels into the United States, the court's discussion of evidence that defendant intended to use the jewels in a fraudulent scheme does not suggest that any less caution need be exercised in determining the admissibility of such evidence simply because it does not indicate independent criminality. See also Commonwealth v. Peay, 85 A.2d 425 (Pa.1951) (evidence that defendants were members of the Communist Party and organizers for an allegedly communist dominated union in a prosecution for assault and for obstructing an officer arising out of a picket line affray).

4. Do the same considerations apply in deciding whether to admit other crime evidence in trial to a judge as in trial to a jury? United States v. Hamrick, 293 F.2d 468 (4th Cir.1961), a nonjury case, suggests not. There the trial court was reversed for, among other things, asking for and receiving from the prosecutor evidence of defendant's criminal record before he had determined the question of defendant's guilt. But this was an extreme case, since not only did the judge initiate the inquiry, but remarked as he did so: "You can tell more what kind of a snake you are dealing with if you can see his color." In United States v. Martinez, 333 F.2d 80 (2d Cir.), cert. denied, 379 U.S. 907 (1964), another nonjury case, defense counsel refused to answer the court's question whether defendant had a prior criminal record. On appeal the court held that the question should not have been asked, but rejected defendant's argument that from his counsel's answer and his own failure to take the stand, the court must have concluded that he had a criminal record. If other crime evidence is offered in a nonjury case and "excluded," would the mere offer in some circumstances provide ground for a mistrial or reversal? In the Martinez case the court observed: "Even if the Government had offered the record of a prior conviction which was then excluded, it could scarcely be argued that a conviction must nevertheless be reversed; yet the judge would have had more knowledge of the earlier offense than here. . . ." Id. at 82.

5. No part of the law of evidence is more litigated than that having to do with the admissibility of evidence of other crimes. A treatise on this subject, which appears to catalogue all the cases and which keeps abreast of developments with annual supplements, states: "[A]lleged errors in the admission of uncharged misconduct are the most frequent ground for appeal in criminal cases; in many states such errors are the most common ground for reversal; and the Federal Rule in point, Rule 404(b), has generated more reported cases than any other subsection of the rules." E. Imwinkelried, Uncharged Misconduct Evidence viii (1984).

6. The principles governing the admission of evidence of other crimes or noncriminal misconduct to establish an element of the offense should be compared with the principles governing the admission of such evidence for purpose of impeachment. See supra pp. 416–38.

7. Useful references are: Lacy, Admissibility of Evidence of Crimes Not Charged in the Indictment, 31 Or.L.Rev. 267 (1952); Stone, The Rule of Exclusion of Similar Fact Evidence: America, 51 Harv.L.Rev. 988 (1938). See also Reed, Trial by Propensity: Admission of Other Criminal Acts Evidenced in Federal Criminal Trials, 50 U.Cin.L.Rev. 713 (1981), and Reed, The Development of the Propensity Rule in Federal Criminal Causes 1840–1975, 51 U.Cin.L.Rev. 299 (1982) (extensive historical inquiry); Thomas, Looking Logically at Evidence of Other Crimes in Oklahoma, 15 Okla.L.Rev. 431 (1962); Slough, Other Vices, Other Crimes: An Evidentiary Dilemma, 20 U.Kan.L.Rev. 411 (1972); Comments, Developments in Evidence of Other Crimes, 7 U.Mich. J.L.Ref. 535 (1974); Admissibility of Prior Criminal Acts as Substantive Evidence in Criminal Prosecutions, 36 Tenn.L.Rev. 515 (1969); A Proposed Analytical Method for the Determination of the Admissibility of Evidence of Other Offenses in California, 7 UCLA L. Rev. 463 (1960); Annot., Propriety, on Voir Dire in Criminal Case, of Inquiries as to Juror's Possible Prejudice If Informed of Defendant's Prior Convictions, 43 A.L.R.3d 1081 (1972).

United States v. Accardo

United States Court of Appeals, Seventh Circuit, 1962.
298 F.2d 133.

■ KILEY, CIRCUIT JUDGE. This is an appeal by defendant from a judgment, upon a verdict, convicting him, after a trial of nearly nine weeks, on three counts charging violations of § 7206(1)[1] of the Internal Revenue Code of 1954. He was sentenced to a total of six years in prison and fined $15,000.00.

Defendant, before 1956, reported income from gambling and undisclosed sources. In February, 1954, the District Director of Internal Revenue wrote him ordering him to maintain detailed records "from that time forward." On October 5, 1955, the Director wrote asking him to submit records to support income and deductions reported in his 1954 return. His attorney told the Director there were no records.

In 1956 defendant reported income of $42,862.25 from Premium Beer Sales, Inc. In an "addenda" he scheduled "expenses incurred in promoting beer sales and automobile expenses" to support a deduction of $515.51. In 1957 he reported income from Premium of $67,540.85 and claimed deductions of $1,726.76 for automobile expense as "agent" for Premium. In 1958 he reported income from Premium of $68,871.70 and claimed automobile expense deduction of $1,753.66 as "agent" for Premium. April 25, 1960, the January Special Grand Jury indicted him.

The indictment is in three counts, each charging substantially the same violations in 1956, 1957, and 1958. In essence, it is charged that defendant stated in his income tax returns that he was employed by Premium and falsely stated that 80% of his automobile expenses were incurred by him in promoting beer sales in 1956, and 90% of that expense as "agent" for Premium in 1957 and 1958....

Defendant contends the court erred in denying various motions, for mistrial and to poll the jury, based upon prejudicial newspaper publicity.

The selection of the jury began September 12, 1960. The court directed and ordered the jurors, at the end of the first day of voir dire, not to read the daily press or listen to television or radio accounts in connection with the case. That afternoon and evening, and the next morning, newspapers reported that defendant had been arrested fourteen times with "no major conviction"; that he had been found guilty of disorderly conduct; that in 1930 he was indicted for carrying concealed weapons; that in 1948 he was charged with conspiracy to defraud the Government as a result of a trip under an assumed name to visit "syndicate hoodlums" at Leavenworth. "He beat both charges...."

The morning of September 14 there was a newspaper headline: "THERE'S A CAPONE ECHO AT ACCARDO TRIAL." The article compared defendant's trial with that of "Al Capone" twenty-nine years before, and said "In the villain's part this time was Chicago's jet-age Capone—stonyfaced ... Accardo, the master of muscling legitimate business." The article said the evidence that convicted Capone was "practically negligible."

---

1. "§ 7206. Fraud and false statements. Any person who—(1) ... Willfully makes and subscribes any return, statement, or other document, which contains or is verified by a written declaration that it is made under the penalties of perjury, and which he does not believe to be true and correct as to every material matter; ... shall be guilty of a felony and, upon conviction thereof, shall be fined not more than $5,000, or imprisoned not more than 3 years, or both, together with the costs of prosecution." [Footnotes are those of the court. Some of the court's footnotes have been omitted.]

On September 27 Joseph Bronge, Jr., a Government witness, testified that Accardo worked for his father as a distributor of Fox Head beer, that he knew Accardo, had visited his home; that his father was now dead; and that he had heard defendant was engaged in the sale of beer.

The next morning there were front page headlines: "MURDER VICTIM'S SON TAKES STAND AGAINST ACCARDO" and "GANGSTER UPSET BY TESTIMONY OF BRONGE." On page 14 appeared the headline: "ACCARDO JURY HEARS SON OF GANG VICTIM." The stories related that the father of the witness appeared before the grand jury which indicted Accardo, had been indicted for perjury, and was murdered "in a West Side beer war last year"; that "the shooting was blamed on fear by hoodlums that he would tell how they forced him and other beer distributors to put them on the payroll."

The jury separated each night and was exposed to the prejudicial publicity. In view of that fact and of defendant's publicity value, it was essential that the judge frequently, prior to separation, call the attention of the jurors *specifically* to the possibility of newspaper accounts carrying statements of facts about the case. Coppedge v. United States, D.C.Cir., 272 F.2d 504, 507 (1959).

The judge's general admonitions at the beginning of the jury selection, his assumption of their effectiveness, and his instructions, were inadequate protection. His general inquiry during the voir dire examination did not supply the deficiency. There is no certainty that all jurors would volunteer information about violating the admonitions or admit that they were influenced by the publicity. Coppedge v. United States, D.C.Cir., 272 F.2d 504, 508 (1959). He should have, by the careful examination of each juror, out of the presence of the others, determined the effect of the articles on those who had read them and whether they had discussed the articles with others. Coppedge v. United States, D.C.Cir., 272 F.2d 504, 508 (1959). These individual interviews would have tended to overcome reluctance to speak out.

The published material would have been inadmissible in evidence because it would prejudice defendant. Its effect would be at least as great if it reached the jury through news accounts. Marshall v. United States, 360 U.S. 310, 312–313, 79 S.Ct. 1171, 3 L.Ed.2d 1250 (1959)....

There was prejudicial error also in the trial court's admission, over objection, of evidence of defendant's income tax returns for the years 1940 through 1955. The court admitted the evidence to show "motive, intent or willful conduct."

No case has been cited, or found, which would support the instant ruling. Government relies upon United States v. Iacullo, 7 Cir., 226 F.2d 788 (1955), cert. denied, 350 U.S. 966, 76 S.Ct. 435, 100 L.Ed. 839 (1956). That case is not applicable because there evidence of a prior similar violation was held admissible under an exception to the general rule,[2] the earlier transaction was "in remarkable conformity" to the pattern of the offenses charged, and there was not a jury. Here there was a jury; and most of the disputed evidence, indicating violations of Illinois anti-gambling laws, showed no "remarkable conformity" to the offenses charged in the instant indictment, since it has never been claimed that the prior returns violated the law.

The Supreme Court has said that it would "expect willfulness" in felonies of this class "to include some element of evil motive and want of justification...." Spies v. United States, 317 U.S. 492, 498, 63 S.Ct. 364, 368, 87 L.Ed. 418 (1943). The Court there equated "bad faith" and "evil motive." Morissette

---

2. "As a general rule, upon the trial of an accused person, evidence of another of- fense, wholly independent of the one charged, is inadmissible." 226 F.2d 788, 793.

v. United States, 342 U.S. 246, 265, 72 S.Ct. 240, 96 L.Ed. 288 (1952). And in United States v. Murdock, 290 U.S. 389, 394, 54 S.Ct. 223, 225, 78 L.Ed. 381 (1933), the Court said that in a criminal statute willful generally means "an act done with a bad purpose ...; without justifiable excuse ...; stubbornly, obstinately, perversely .... also ... to characterize a thing done without ground for believing it is lawful ... or conduct marked by careless disregard whether or not one has the right so to act,...." It is because of this element that a defendant is entitled to produce evidence, and to an instruction, with respect to his good faith and actual belief. United States v. Murdock, 290 U.S. 389, 396, 54 S.Ct. 223, 78 L.Ed. 381 (1933).

The income tax returns were introduced, and several witnesses testified to the preparation of the returns and to conversations with defendant about the sources of his income for those years. A Government witness testified to a summary of the returns and the written summary was introduced into evidence. The effect of all this testimony was to show that defendant had an income from gambling in 1940 through 1955 of about "one million two hundred thousand dollars."

The element of willfulness or motive, in the sense of "bad faith," involved in the offense charged is in the implied charge of an affirmative deliberate claim of a business expense deduction made when defendant knew he was not lawfully entitled to the deduction. The willful, or "bad faith," element is the deliberate making of the false statement, not the making of an honest mistake of judgment. Spies v. United States, 317 U.S. 492, 63 S.Ct. 364, 87 L.Ed. 418 (1943); United States v. Murdock, 290 U.S. 389, 54 S.Ct. 223, 78 L.Ed. 381 (1933). The motive for the willfulness is not an element. Testimony that defendant was not employed furnishes a basis upon which the jury may draw inferences that defendant knew or ought to have known that he was not a "promoter of beer sales," and "agent," for Premium and therefore could not lawfully claim the deduction, and consequently was willful in making the false statement. So far as the offense charged is concerned, proof of an ulterior motive or intent of defendant in making the "switch" in reporting income in 1956 or in creating a "facade"[3] is not a relevant circumstance to support an inference that defendant was willful, in the sense of harboring "bad faith," in making the false statement. The disputed evidence is not admissible on authority of the illustrations given in Spies v. United States, 317 U.S. 492, 499, 63 S.Ct. 364, 87 L.Ed. 418 (1943). The Court there was discussing the willful element in a tax evasion case, and not the willful element in a charge under § 7206(1).

The impact of this testimony on the trial judge indicates the probable prejudicial impact the testimony had on the jury. In denying the defendant's motion for a new trial, the trial court said:

"I don't know how a defendant could have been engaged in that kind of enterprise, it would seem to me, without relying on the connivance of certain public officials. That is not in evidence, but I think that a reasonable inference from the record in this case.... I think the only conclusion one can draw from the huge amounts of income reported by the defendant and as revealed from the evidence is that this is a malignancy, this professional gambling, which has penetrated all levels of our society, and that it is a national calamity."

3. The Government presented the evidence to show that defendant made the alleged false statement as part of a facade behind which (in 1956) he made a switch to falsely reporting employment income from Premium instead of reporting gambling income from undisclosed sources.

We conclude that the highly prejudicial evidence was not relevant and was inadmissible, that the court had no discretion to admit it, and that the careful instruction with respect to the evidence could not cure the error because the evidence should not have been admitted.

. . .

For prejudicial error at the trial, the judgment is reversed and the cause remanded for new trial, consistent with the rules announced in this opinion.

■ DUFFY, CIRCUIT JUDGE (concurred) [opinion omitted].

■ SCHNACKENBERG, CIRCUIT JUDGE (dissenting).

. . .

The government's theory was that defendant's purported employment by Premium was in name only and hence that the deductions claimed for automobile business expenses for 1956, 1957 and 1958 were false; and that defendant thus sought to convey to the Internal Revenue Service the false impression that he was devoting his time and effort to the sale and promotion of beer products, and by this means to interfere with the Service's investigation and determination of his true tax liability. According to the government's theory, the motive for defendant's falsification was to establish records to support income and deductions appearing on his 1954 income tax return, as requested by the Service on October 5, 1955.

The evidence offered by the government and admitted, as above referred to, was clearly relevant and no error occurred in that respect. Nothing was said in Spies v. United States, 317 U.S. 492, 63 S.Ct. 364, 87 L.Ed. 418, which is inconsistent with the admission of this evidence. In fact, its language clearly supports an affirmance herein. For instance, the court said, at 499, 63 S.Ct. at 368:

> "... we would think affirmative willful attempt may be inferred from conduct such as ... covering up sources of income, ... and any conduct, the likely effect of which would be to mislead or to conceal. If the tax-evasion motive plays any part in such conduct the offense may be made out even though the conduct may also serve other purposes such as concealment of other crime."

Judge Kiley recognizes the distinction between the willfulness or bad faith element involved in the deliberate making of a false statement and the making of an honest mistake of judgment. The law entrusted to the jury the function of deciding which factor motivated defendant. This was a question of fact. The answer is evident in the verdict, which was approved by the district court.

. . .

For these reasons I would affirm the judgment of the district court.

NOTES

1. Marshall v. United States, 360 U.S. 310 (1959), cited in the Accardo case, was a prosecution for dispensing drugs without a prescription from a physician. The trial court refused to allow the government to prove that defendant had previously practiced medicine without a license on the ground that "[It] would be just like offering evidence that he picked pockets or was a petty thief or something of that sort which would have no bearing on the issue and would tend to raise a collateral issue and I think would be prejudicial to the defendant." Id. at 311. Nevertheless, during the trial, a substantial number of jurors obtained newspapers containing the information that defendant not only had previously practiced medicine without a license, including writing out prescriptions for drugs, but also that he had been convicted of forgery. The jurors who had seen the newspapers were examined by the trial judge, and stated that they would not be influenced by what they had read, could decide the case on the basis of the evidence alone, and felt no prejudice against defendant. The trial judge denied defendant's motion for a mistrial. The Supreme Court reversed, stating: "We have here the exposure of jurors to information of a character which the trial judge ruled was so prejudicial it could not be directly offered as evidence. The prejudice to the defendant is almost certain to be as great when that evidence reaches the jury through news accounts as when it is a part of the prosecution's evidence. Cf. Michelson v. United States, 335 U.S. 469, 475 (1948). It may indeed be greater for it is then not tempered by protective procedures. In the exercise of our supervisory power to formulate and apply proper standards for enforcement of the criminal law in the federal courts ... we think a new trial should be granted." Id. at 312–13. Murphy v. Florida, 421 U.S. 794 (1975), applies a more lenient standard to state convictions being tested under the Due Process Clause of the Fourteenth Amendment when jurors have learned of defendant's other crimes from the media. Reversal is required only if community sentiment has been poisoned against the defendant or the jurors have displayed animus towards him.

2. In the Accardo case, could the fact that witness Bronge's father was murdered because hoodlums feared he would tell how they forced him and other beer distributors to put them on the payroll be put in evidence? United States v. Howard, 228 F.Supp. 939 (D.Neb.1964) (overruling motion for judgment notwithstanding verdict or for new trial), concerns this question. A complaint was filed against defendant on December 23, 1959, charging him with a narcotics violation. He was arrested, but released on bond for a hearing on December 28, 1959. The hearing was not held because of the death of Ellis, who was to have been the government's principal witness. Defendant was indicted for the narcotics violation in February, 1960, but not brought to trial until March, 1964. At the trial, the court admitted evidence that defendant had been convicted in a state court of murdering Ellis on December 27, 1959, and also that on December 24, 1959, defendant had learned that Ellis was an informer against him. In admitting this evidence, the court instructed the jury: "This evidence has been received for a limited purpose only and is to be considered by you only insofar as an inference may arise therefrom of an admission of guilt or an act inconsistent with the innocence of the defendant to the charge on which he is on trial herein." Id. at 941. See also People v. Baptist, 389 N.E.2d 1200, 1204–05 (Ill. 1979) (not error to admit evidence of murder and attempted murder of eye-witnesses, these crimes having been sufficiently connected to defendant). But see People v. West, 278 N.E.2d 233, 242 (Ill.Ct.App.1971) (conviction for sale of narcotics reversed because, inter alia, informer allowed to testify that sometime after sale he was beaten up by someone who called him a stool pigeon, although he did not know who it was).

In Kostal v. People, 357 P.2d 70 (Colo.1960), cert. denied, 365 U.S. 804 (1961), defendants Kostal and Watson were indicted for the murder of a policeman in the course of a robbery of a store in Jefferson County, Colorado. The killing occurred on December 9, 1956. At defendants' trial, evidence of the following occurrences was admitted over their objection. (1) Defendants escaped from Folsum Prison, California, on November 21, 1956. (2) Following their escape, defendants stole an automobile in Sacramento and drove to Los Angeles. (3) In Los Angeles they burglarized a pawnshop and took two guns found in their possession at a later time when they were arrested. (4) Defendants stole an automobile in Los Angeles and drove to Colorado. (5) After the slaying of the policeman, and on the same day, December 9, 1956, defendants stole two automobiles from an automobile agency in Lakewood, Colorado. (6) On December 14 and 15, 1956, defendants robbed a tavern and a grocery store in Kansas City. [Kostal was then arrested in Kansas City and was found in possession of the gun that fired the shot that killed the policeman, which was also one of the guns taken from the pawnshop. Watson was arrested in Detroit and was then in possession of another gun taken from the pawnshop.] (7) In November, 1957, a few days before they were to stand trial for the murder, defendants escaped from the Jefferson County jail. Their escape was accompanied by violence, robbery, theft of an automobile, a running gunfight and injury to a policeman. (8) Kostal was apprehended in the course of a gunfight in Times Square, New York, on January 10, 1958. An officer attempting to make the arrest suffered a gunshot wound from a gun in Kostal's hands. This occurred during a scuffle for possession of the gun drawn by Kostal in an effort to avoid arrest. Which of these incidents was it permissible to prove? The Supreme Court of Colorado said (5), (7) and (8), but not the others, and reversed for a new trial.

Other cases finding no error in admission of evidence of criminal conduct giving rise to an inference of consciousness of guilt are United States v. Posey, 611 F.2d 1389 (5th Cir.1980) (defendant offered bribe to sheriff to allow him to escape); Wilson v. State, 344 So.2d 739 (Miss.1977) (when pursued by officer because his vehicle met description of vehicle used in robbery, defendant failed to stop and when overtaken fired on officer); Mackiewicz v. State, 114 So.2d 684 (Fla.1959), cert. denied, 362 U.S. 965 (1960) (theft of automobile shortly after killing and subsequent escape from prison); State v. Nelson, 338 P.2d 301, 304, 307 (N.M.), cert. denied, 361 U.S. 877 (1959) (defendant arrested for reckless driving some days after killing, attempted to bribe officer, then broke arrest and fled). May a defendant introduce evidence that although he had an opportunity to escape from jail he did not take it? See People v. Bandhauer, 463 P.2d 408 (Cal. 1970). If evidence is introduced that the defendant escaped from jail while awaiting trial, he may have a difficult decision whether to introduce evidence that he was being held on other charges as well as that for which he is being tried. See Annot., 3 A.L.R.4th 1085 (1981).

3.   That evidence of another crime tends to establish a motive for the crime with which defendant is charged is a frequently invoked exception to the general rule against other crime evidence. A dramatic example of this is Fuller v. State, 113 So.2d 153, 172–76 (Ala.1959), cert. denied, 361 U.S. 936 (1960). There Fuller, Chief Deputy Sheriff of Russell County, Alabama, was prosecuted for the murder of Albert L. Patterson, Democratic nominee for the office of Attorney General of the state. The identity of Patterson's killer was a central issue in the case. On appeal from a conviction, the court held that there had been no error in admitting evidence, first, that during his campaign for Attorney General, Patterson had made many public statements pledging to eradicate gambling and other vices in the state and particularly in Russell County, and second, that after the killing defendant had stated that he had received money from slot machine operations in Russell County and had accepted bribes in connection with operation of houses of prostitution.

In Gill v. United States, 285 F.2d 711 (5th Cir.1961), cert. denied, 373 U.S. 944 (1963), a prosecution for robbery, evidence was held to have been properly admitted that ten days before the robbery the defendant gave a worthless check to a grocery store.

The question whether evidence of narcotics use or addiction is admissible to show a motive to commit crime has received conflicting answers. United States v. Saniti, 604 F.2d 603 (9th Cir.), cert. denied, 444 U.S. 969 (1979) (in robbery prosecution not error to admit evidence of defendant's $250–a-day heroin and morphine habit); State v. Sutfield, 354 So.2d 1334 (La.1978) (in robbery prosecution, error to admit evidence of defendant's narcotics addiction).

Consider also the following cases where evidence of other crimes was offered to show motive. People v. Edwards, 323 P.2d 484, 488–89 (Cal.Ct.App. 1958) (in prosecution for theft of trailer, not error to permit prosecutor to ask defendant whether shortly after trailer was taken he was apprehended attempting to burglarize a safe and whether he had not taken the trailer to carry off the safe); United States v. Peltier, 585 F.2d 314, 321–22 (8th Cir.1978), cert. denied, 440 U.S. 945 (1979) (in prosecution for murder of FBI agents, not error to admit evidence that at the time of the slayings there was a warrant out for defendant's arrest on a charge of attempted murder); State v. Martineau, 368 A.2d 592, 594 (N.H.1976) (in prosecution for murder not error to admit evidence that defendant had been incarcerated on complaint of the murder victim that defendant had raped her). State v. Robinette, 383 S.E.2d 32 (W.Va.1989) (in prosecution for murder of wife, not error to admit evidence that defendant had forged his wife's signature on an application for life insurance). As far as probative value is concerned, what is the difference between evidence of motive and evidence indicating consciousness of guilt? Between evidence of motive and evidence of conduct of defendant indicating a disposition to commit crime?

United States v. Montalvo

United States Court of Appeals, Second Circuit, 1959.
271 F.2d 922, cert. denied, 361 U.S. 961, 80 S.Ct. 589, 4 L.Ed.2d 543 (1960).

[Defendants were convicted under an indictment charging them with receiving, possessing, concealing and facilitating the transportation and concealment of narcotics illegally imported, in violation of 21 U.S.C. §§ 173 and 174, and with conspiracy to violate the same sections.

Testimony of agents and employees of the Bureau of Narcotics tended to establish the following facts. Defendants Montalvo, William Rovira, and Rose Rovira drove from Manhattan to a housing project in the Bronx. There they obtained a brown paper bag of a certain description. Shortly after leaving the housing project, Montalvo, carrying a brown paper bag of the same description, left the Rovira automobile and took a taxi to his apartment on West 73rd Street in Manhattan. Almost immediately after Montalvo's arrival at his apartment, agents of the Bureau of Narcotics searched the apartment and the basement of the apartment building and discovered a brown paper bag, containing heroin, similar to the bag that had been earlier observed in defendants' possession. Agents arrested Montalvo. William Rovira was observed twice slowly driving by Montalvo's apartment house. Rovira was then arrested in a nearby drugstore. A search of his person disclosed a penknife, the blade of which was caked with a small quantity of heroin.]

■ FRIENDLY, CIRCUIT JUDGE. ... Appellants question the sufficiency of the evidence and allege various errors by the trial judge. We think the evidence was ample to warrant submission to the jury, and we find no errors in Judge Dimock's conduct of the trial.

. . .

Defendants misconceive the theory of the admissibility of the penknife. The evidence was not admitted to show that since William Rovira had committed another narcotics offense at some unspecified date, he might be supposed capable of committing another one now. The government was seeking to show that Rovira, who had been with Montalvo earlier, was about to rejoin him to carry forward the illegal enterprise. Rovira's possession of a tool whose suitability to that end was made plain by its previous use in a similar one, was relevant to that issue. The fact that evidence which is relevant and not otherwise inadmissible may also tend to show a previous crime does not bar its admissibility, 1 Wigmore on Evidence §§ 215–16 (3d ed. 1940). The trial judge must have wide discretion to determine whether the probative value of the evidence is outweighed by its prejudicial character. McCormick, Evidence, § 157 at 332 (1954). The discretion here was not abused. For if the evidence did not have a great tendency to lead, it had equally little to mislead.

. . .

Judgments affirmed.

NOTE

In connection with the Montalvo case consider the following: Prosecution for burglary of pay telephone A on November 28. W1 testified he saw defendant and two others outside telephone booth A, that one of the others went into the booth and defendant handed him something that he applied to the bottom of the telephone, that at that point the witness was observed and the person in the booth handed defendant something that defendant threw away. W1 identified Exhibit 1 as an object he found on the ground at the place he saw defendant throw something. W2 testified that on November 29 he inspected pay telephone B, located about 7 miles from telephone A, and found it broken open. He identified Exhibit 2 as telephone B. W3, an expert, testified that he had examined Exhibits 1 and 2 and that Exhibit 1 had been used to open the coin box of Exhibit 2. Should the testimony of W2 and W3 and Exhibit 2 be admitted? See State v. Latta, 425 P.2d 186 (Or.1967), where the issues and evidence differ in some respects from the case stated.

People v. Steele

Supreme Court of Illinois, 1961.
22 Ill.2d 142, 174 N.E.2d 848.

■ SCHAEFFER, CHIEF JUSTICE. The defendant, Stephen Steele, pleaded not guilty to an indictment which charged that he "did offer to unlawfully sell a narcotic drug and then did unlawfully ... sell to John Stribling, Junior ... a quantity ... of a certain purported narcotic drug...." (See Ill.Rev.Stat.1959, chap. 38, par. 192.28–38.) He waived a jury trial, was found guilty after a trial before a judge, and was sentenced to the penitentiary for a term of not less than two nor more than six years. Upon this writ of error he contends that the allegations of the indictment were not proved beyond a reasonable doubt, and that prejudicial testimony was admitted over his objection.

An informer, Robert Jackson, a Federal narcotics agent, Joseph Dino, Jr., and a State narcotics agent, John Stribling, Jr., testified for the People. Jackson testified that about two weeks before December 11, 1958, the defendant had told him that he could buy narcotics from the defendant and had given him his phone number. Several narcotics agents were present about 6:30 P.M. on December 11, when Jackson telephoned the defendant. The defendant was not in, but he returned the call later. Jackson told him that he wanted to buy an ounce of raw heroin. The defendant said it would cost $400, and they arranged to meet. Agent Dino listened to the conversation on an extension telephone, and corroborated Jackson's testimony with respect to it.

Stribling accompanied Jackson to the meeting place. There the defendant questioned Stribling's presence, saying to Jackson, "Aw, what's this here?" Jackson replied "He's all right. He's with me." Jackson testified that he then "stepped out of the picture and Officer Stribling and him transacted the business." Stribling gave the defendant a roll of bills, the serial numbers of which had been recorded, and the defendant gave him a small package wrapped in paper. Stribling then returned to Jackson's apartment and performed a field test which showed that the substance in the package was not narcotics. Chemical analysis later disclosed it to be quinine hydrochloride.

Agent Dino testified that he observed the meeting while sitting in a parked automobile and that he placed the defendant under arrest after the transaction was completed. Stribling testified that after the defendant was arrested, he denied dealing in narcotics but said that he needed the money and "When you find a sucker, bump his head." Dino's testimony corroborated this conversation.

The defendant denied that he had offered to sell narcotics....

The statute under which the defendant was prosecuted provides: "Whoever agrees, consents or in any manner offers to unlawfully sell ... any narcotic drugs to any person, ... and then sells ... to any person any nonnarcotic ... substance or material shall be imprisoned...." (Ill.Rev.Stat.1959, chap. 38, par. 192.28–38.) The defendant contends, and the People agree, that to establish guilt the proof must show beyond a reasonable doubt that the defendant offered to sell narcotics to Stribling, and sold a nonnarcotic substance to him....

The defendant also contends that the court erred in admitting prejudicial evidence over his objection. Jackson was the first witness for the prosecution. On direct examination, after he had given his name and address and had stated that he used narcotics, he was asked, "What kind of business dealings did you have with the defendant prior to December 11, 1958." Over objection he was permitted to answer, "Buying narcotics." The defendant's motion for a mistrial was denied.

The People suggest that this evidence of other offenses may be justified by our decision in People v. Aldridge, 19 Ill.2d 176, 180, 166 N.E.2d 563, 565. The circumstances here, however, differ from those in the Aldridge case. There the reference to prior offenses was not elicited at the outset of the prosecution's case, but came in the course of the defendants' assertion of their innocence upon direct examination by their own attorney. It was in that context that we pointed out that the "testimony tended to negative the possibility of innocent or inadvertent conduct on the part of the defendants, and to establish their guilty knowledge, and so would apparently have been admissible even if offered by the prosecution."

The unique nature of the crime with which the defendant was here charged must be taken into account in determining the admissibility of the evidence. This case does not involve a prosecution for the sale of narcotics, but rather a prosecution for offering to sell narcotics and then selling a different substance. The element of deceit is thus a principal ingredient in the offense, and the overtones are those of confidence game, or of obtaining money under false pretenses. Evidence of earlier transactions in narcotics supports an inference that those earlier sales were part of a course of conduct designed to induce the belief that what was now offered for sale was also a narcotic drug. That evidence also makes it more likely that on the present occasion the defendant offered to sell narcotics rather than some other substance, and it tends to show that the defendant knew that what he was selling was not a narcotic drug. (See Wigmore on Evidence, 3rd ed. secs. 321, 304.) The evidence of other transactions was thus independently relevant apart from its tendency to show the bad character of the accused, and so its admission was not improper. People v. Lehman, 5 Ill.2d 337, 342–343, 125 N.E.2d 506; McCormick on Evidence, sec. 157.

The judgment of the criminal court of Cook County is affirmed.

Judgment affirmed.

NOTES

The foregoing cases give some idea of the virtually endless variety of situations in which it can be claimed that under the circumstances of the particular case the other crime evidence has some special bearing on a disputed issue that justifies admission. Here are some further examples.

Gaddis v. State, 360 P.2d 522 (Okl.Crim.App.1960). Defendant was prosecuted for a burglary committed at Carol's apartment on November 14, 1958. Carol testified that defendant appeared at her door and asked for June May. When Carol said that June May had moved, defendant left, but then returned and asked to use the telephone. When Carol refused, defendant came in, knocked her down and took her purse. June May then testified that she had previously lived in the apartment. On October 13, 1958, a person who looked like defendant came to the door and asked to use the telephone. When she refused, he knocked her down and took her purse. The purse contained a glasses case with June May's name on it. June May's testimony was held to have been properly admitted.

People v. Cole, 194 N.E.2d 269, 271 (Ill.1963). Defendant was prosecuted for selling narcotics to an agent on October 10. Evidence of earlier sales to the same agent, on July 20 and September 26, was held to have been properly admitted. "Prior transactions between agent Cook and defendant strengthened the identification of defendant as the person with whom Cook dealt on October 10, and tended to remove any doubt that the defendant's conduct on October 10, if the jury believed Cook's version, was inadvertent or innocent. We think that it also showed the relationship between the parties and therefore explained Cook's account of the transaction of October 10. Considering the stealth with which narcotics transactions are conducted, it is not likely that agent Cook could have merely walked up to defendant, asked for a spoon of heroin, given him $120, gone to the Woods Lounge and had defendant give him the heroin.... This account becomes plausible, however ... [in the light of the prior transactions]." See also United States v. Magnano, 543 F.2d 431 (2d Cir.1976), cert. denied, 429 U.S. 1091 (1977). Prosecution for violation of narcotics laws. Not error to admit testimony of government witness that he had had earlier drug dealings with several of the defendants. The testimony explained how the witness was able to become a member of the conspiracy on his release from jail. People v. Ellis, 186 N.E.2d 269 (Ill.1962). Prosecution for robbing a milkman on October 31. Not error to admit testimony of the milkman that defendant had also robbed him on October 27; it was relevant to the witness's ability to identify defendant.

People v. Montanez, 359 N.E.2d 371 (N.Y. 1976): Prosecution for second degree manslaughter—recklessly causing the death of another. The disputed question was whether the gun that killed the victim had gone off while the defendant was brandishing it, possibly in a threatening manner, or when the victim handed it to defendant to show it to him. Held: It was not error to admit testimony of witnesses who had passed through the room where the defendant and the victim were talking shortly before the firearm discharged that they were talking about narcotics and a shortage of money in connection with a narcotics transaction. It was error, however, to admit testimony that the victim had previously smuggled large quantities of drugs into the country, testimony that in view of the other evidence carried a suggestion that defendant was in the midst of a large scale drug traffic. "The defendant was on trial for recklessly causing the death of his friend. There was no intent to kill or even injure alleged or proven and the crime charged involved a low degree of criminal culpability. But the evidence of the uncharged drug activities involved the fullest measure of evil intent and culpability.... Obviously this testimony could radically alter the jury's conception of the case and the defendant's culpability. In short this is a classic example of a case where the prejudice to the defendant out-weighed the probative value of the evidence...." Id. at 375.

Snead v. State, 8 So.2d 269 (Ala.1942). Defendant's assertion of physical incapacity to commit assault countered by evidence that he had committed another assault.

People v. Gutierrez, 622 P.2d 547, 552 (Colo.1981). Prosecution for felony menacing and burglary. Evidence of assault by defendant on same evening properly admitted to rebut alibi. See also McLendon v. United States, 13 F.2d 777, 778 (6th Cir.1926). Unsuccessful attempt to justify use of evidence that defendant had been imprisoned by arguing that this tended to establish his ignorance of certain material events.

Massey v. State, 371 N.E.2d 703, 707 (Ind.1978): In prosecution for armed robbery, not error to admit testimony that defendant had kidnapped the witness and locked him in the trunk of the witness's car and that while in the trunk the witness heard the defendant plan the robbery. State v. Morgan, 246 N.W.2d 165, 167–68 (Minn.1976), cert. denied, 430 U.S. 936 (1977): In a prosecution for murders, not error to allow testimony that defendant admitted the murders to the witness while he held the witness hostage.

State v. Abercrombie, 375 So.2d 1170, 1174–77 (La.1979), cert. denied, 446 U.S. 935 (1980): Prosecution for murder of a Catholic priest. The priest was shot when he answered his front doorbell. One issue was the identity of the killer. Held: Not error to admit evidence that defendant had earlier assaulted another priest and employees of a Catholic agency. "The defendant's behavior illustrated a particular feeling against a small particular group, Catholic employees." See also Dillard v. State, 477 S.W.2d 547 (Tex.Crim.App.1971): In prosecution for murder of negro prostitute, not error to admit evidence that on two subsequent occasions defendant had shot at negroes.

Government of Virgin Islands v. Harris, 938 F.2d 401, 420 (3d Cir.1991): When issue was whether defendant's wife was dead and if so, whether defendant had murdered her, not error to admit evidence of defendant's past acts of violence towards his wife.

A number of decisions have reversed convictions when the use of "mug shots" for purposes of identification has been made known to the jury in such a way as to indicate defendant's prior involvement with the law. See United States v. Harrington, 490 F.2d 487 (2d Cir.1973); Commonwealth v. Allen, 292 A.2d 373 (Pa.1972).

People v. Santarelli

Court of Appeals of New York, 1980.
425 N.Y.S.2d 77, 401 N.E.2d 199.

■ GABRIELLI, JUDGE, for the Court.

On the morning of August 24, 1975, the defendant shot and killed his brother-in-law, Joseph Foti, by firing five shotgun blasts at him, two of which proved to be fatal. There was no apparent motive for the killing; in fact, the evidence indicated that the victim and defendant had enjoyed a very close and warm relationship over the years. Following a protracted trial, defendant was convicted of having committed murder in the second degree (Penal Law, § 125.25, subd. 1) by shooting his brother-in-law with a sawed-off shotgun. At his jury trial, defendant acknowledged having committed the acts charged in the indictment, but contended that his conduct should be excused because he was legally insane at the time of the alleged crime and, consequently, could not be held criminally responsible for his actions (see Penal Law, § 30.05). The People, in an effort to rebut this claim, sought to establish that the shooting was merely a product of defendant's "explosive personality", a character trait not rising to the level of legal insanity. To this end, the District Attorney offered proof through the testimony of witnesses that defendant had committed a number of unprovoked, violent acts, unconnected with his brother-in-law, prior to the shooting. It is the trial court's ruling permitting the use of all of this testimony that forms the basis of the present controversy.

The People's direct case at trial consisted solely of testimony by several police officers, each of whom described the circumstances surrounding the shooting. Lieutenant Fusco, a criminologist, explained that the dwelling in which the shooting occurred was divided into two apartments which were separated by a staircase and a doorway. Defendant and his wife occupied the upper apartment, while the defendant's in-laws occupied the floor below. On the basis of information derived from the autopsy and from the position of the bullet holes in the woodwork, Lieutenant Fusco was able to conclude that the victim, Joseph Foti, had been standing on the lower landing of the staircase leading to defendant's apartment when he was struck by gun discharges fired from above. After the first shot was fired, according to Lieutenant Fusco, the victim had enough strength to exit the building through the lower apartment in a vain attempt to effect an escape via the driveway. It was at this point, Lieutenant Fusco stated, that Foti was struck by the fatal shots, which were fired from a second-floor patio connected to defendant's apartment. Defendant was apprehended shortly after the shooting and promptly acknowledged his responsibility for his brother-in-law's death.

Following the close of the People's direct case, defendant called a number of lay and expert witnesses in an effort to demonstrate that the shooting was the product of a "paranoid delusion" which caused him to believe that his brother-in-law was trying to kill him and that immediate defensive action was necessary to ward off an imminent attack. Several acquaintances of defendant were called to attest to the fact that defendant appeared distracted and unusually tense in the days immediately preceding the shooting. Defendant's sister and several other relatives confirmed these observations and further noted that defendant's attack on his brother-in-law was particularly uncharacteristic, since the two men had always enjoyed a very close and warm relationship. Nola Santarelli, defendant's wife, testified that in the weeks preceding the killing, her husband had become increasingly disturbed as a result of efforts by members of the FBI to convince him to become a witness in a criminal action on the government's behalf. Defendant had been especially unnerved, according to Mrs. Santarelli, when his close friend, Vincent Christina, also tried to persuade him to become a witness for the government.

Testimony concerning the events of the day of the shooting was supplied by Mrs. Santarelli, defendant's father and the victim's widow. All three testified that on the morning of the day in question, defendant had had a violent argument with his wife in which he accused her of working with the FBI. Mrs. Santarelli fled from the couple's apartment as a result of the quarrel, and defendant's brother-in-law, Joseph Foti, was called in to act as a peacemaker. Defendant immediately indicated his desire not to speak with Foti, but Foti persisted in pursuing the conversation. Finally, when Foti attempted to follow defendant into the latter's apartment, defendant opened his apartment door and fired upon his brother-in-law.

To support his contention that his acts had been the product of a "paranoid delusion", defendant also called to the stand two expert witnesses who were familiar with his background. On direct examination, both psychiatrists stated their professional beliefs that defendant had been in a psychotic state aggravated by amphetamine abuse when he shot his brother-in-law and that, at the time of the crime, he lacked substantial capacity to apprehend the nature and consequences of his acts or that his conduct was wrong (see Penal Law, § 30.05). Upon cross-examination of defendant's expert witnesses, however, the District Attorney attempted to establish that defendant's conduct also could be explained as a symptom of a "personality disorder" commonly termed an "explosive personality". He elicited through questioning that an individual suffering from such a disorder would probably have a history of violent, antisocial conduct and would have a tendency to react with disproportionate violence in the face of relatively mild provocation. Moreover, the psychiatrists stated, although an individual with a "personality disorder" will often exhibit poor impulse control, especially when placed under stress, such an individual is generally considered to be in touch with reality and cannot be classified as legally insane within the meaning of section 30.05 of the Penal Law.

Having thus established the medical and legal significance of the term "explosive personality", the prosecutor then attempted to demonstrate that defendant was suffering from that condition rather than from the more serious condition of "delusional psychosis" and that, consequently, his conduct in shooting his brother-in-law could not be legally excused. By using the technique of hypothetical questioning, the District Attorney initially elicited from the expert witnesses that the shooting could be considered symptomatic of an "explosive personality" if it were assumed that the actor had committed certain specific acts of violence in the past and it were further assumed that he was laboring under considerable emotional stress at the time of the crime. The prosecutor then offered to prove through witnesses that defendant had, in fact, committed a number of irrational, violent acts in his past and that his tendency to react with violence had been exacerbated by the pressure that was being placed upon him in the weeks preceding the shooting as a result of his involvement with organized crime.

Defense counsel promptly objected to the admission of such proof on the ground that it would be highly prejudicial and would be probative only of defendant's propensity to commit violent crimes. Arguing that the evidence was not relevant to any material element of the People's case, defendant took the position that it should be excluded under the standards articulated in People v. Goldstein, 295 N.Y. 61, 65 N.E.2d 169 and People v. Molineux, 168 N.Y. 264, 61 N.E. 286. The trial court, however, rejected defense counsel's argument and permitted the prosecutor to proceed with his rebuttal witnesses, while granting defendant a "continuing objection". Santarelli ultimately was convicted of murder in the second degree, and his conviction was affirmed by the Appellate Division. Noting that the challenged evidence "carried little potential for prejudice in this case", the Appellate Division upheld the trial court's ruling on the basis of what it perceived to be a "general rule" that once a defendant asserts the insanity defense, "any and all prior conduct of the accused having a bearing on the subject is admissible, even though it might also tend to show him guilty of other crimes" (64 A.D.2d 803, 804, 407 N.Y.S.2d 744, 746).

We note at the outset that we agree in principle with the Appellate Division's conclusion that the People are entitled to introduce evidence of prior criminal conduct which is probative of the defendant's sanity once the question of the defendant's sanity is made an issue in the case. We nonetheless hold that the present conviction must be reversed, since we find that much of the evidence admitted by the Trial Judge failed to meet the test of "relevancy" long established in our earlier decisions.

. . .

There is no pre-established formula for determining when a particular uncharged criminal or immoral act may be admitted in evidence against a defendant (see McCormick, Evidence [2d ed.], § 190). Although we have suggested certain "categories" for use as a guide in evaluating the relevance of such evidence (see People v. Molineux, 168 N.Y. 264, 61 N.E. 286, supra), we have consistently stated that these categories are not exhaustive, but rather represent "illustrations" of the type of analysis to be applied in cases involving potentially prejudicial information. . . . Similarly, when a defendant interposes the "insanity defense", he necessarily puts in issue some aspects of his character and personal history. By coming forward with sufficient evidence to rebut the presumption of sanity, the defendant in effect injects a new factual issue into the case, and the People are consequently required to bear the additional burden of proving the defendant sane beyond a reasonable doubt (see, e.g., People v. Silver, 33 N.Y.2d 475, 354 N.Y.S.2d 915, 310 N.E.2d 520). It would strain the rules of evidence beyond anything ever intended by our prior decisions to hold, as defendant urges, that the People are precluded from introducing evidence to counter a defendant's claim of insanity solely because the evidence involves the defendant's previous immoral or unlawful conduct.

We hold instead that evidence of uncharged criminal or immoral conduct may be admitted as part of the People's case on rebuttal if it has a tendency to disprove the defendant's claim that he was legally insane at the time of the crime. Background information which sheds light upon a defendant's personal history is often of crucial significance in cases involving the insanity defense, and we decline to adopt a blanket rule which would exclude such information solely because it is indicative of the defendant's prior antisocial conduct. Having placed his mental state before the trier of fact, the defendant cannot complain when the People seek to bring forth additional evidence bearing upon that issue.

This is not to suggest, however, that a defendant automatically places his entire character in issue when he interposes the defense of legal insanity. To the contrary, a defendant who asserts an insanity defense "opens the door" to the People's "character evidence" only to the extent that such evidence has a natural tendency to disprove his specific claim. In the present case, for example, defendant's claim was that he suffered from a form of "temporary insanity" that prevented him from apprehending the nature and consequences of his acts and from knowing that his conduct was wrong. He attempted to establish this claim through lay testimony concerning his "unusual" behavior in the weeks preceding the shooting and through expert testimony indicating that his symptoms were consistent with an ultimate "break with reality" in the form of a "paranoid delusion". The presumption of sanity having thus been rebutted, the People were faced with the burden of having to prove defendant sane beyond a reasonable doubt. Given the nature of defendant's insanity claim, it was reasonable for the prosecutor to counter defendant's evidence with evidence that defendant's conduct also was consistent with a "personality disorder" not rising to the level of legal insanity. To the extent that evidence of defendant's prior violent acts and his relationship with organized crime had a direct bearing upon the validity of the People's "explosive personality" theory, we think it was clearly admissible.

The problem arises in this case, however, because the Trial Judge failed to evaluate with sufficient particularity whether each piece of evidence offered by the People was actually relevant and material to their "explosive personality" theory (cf. People v. Allweiss, 48 N.Y.2d 40, 49, 421 N.Y.S.2d 341, 346, 396 N.E.2d 735, 739, supra).[1] It is on this point, in fact, that we depart from the views expressed by the Appellate Division. In deciding whether to admit evidence of prior criminal or immoral conduct in rebuttal to an insanity claim, the trial court must take special care to ensure not only that the evidence bears some articulable relation to the issue, but also that its probative value in fact warrants its admission despite the potential for prejudice. As we noted in People v. Allweiss, 48 N.Y.2d 40, 47, 421 N.Y.S.2d 341, 344, 396 N.E.2d 735, 738, supra: "If the evidence is actually of slight value when compared to the possible prejudice to the accused, it should not be admitted, even though it might technically relate to some fact to be proven" (accord McCormick, Evidence, § 190). This observation is particularly apt in cases involving the insanity defense, where virtually every fact in the accused's life may in some sense be said to have a bearing upon the issue of his mental state.[2] Indeed, in

---

1. This is not to suggest, of course, that the prosecution was limited to building a single, integrated theory of "sanity" as a means of rebutting defendant's insanity claim. To the contrary, the prosecutor was free to present his rebuttal case in any manner he deemed most effective. Here, the prosecutor chose to concentrate on establishing an alternate theory of defendant's mental state to demonstrate that the shooting was the act of a legally sane man. Since the prosecutor himself elected to chart his own course in this manner and, indeed, relied exclusively upon his "explosive personality" hypothesis as a justification for introducing evidence of defendant's prior immoral and illegal acts, his offer of proof can only be

evaluated with reference to that hypothesis. [Footnotes are the court's; one footnote has been omitted.]

2. It is true that in People v. Carlin, 194 N.Y. 448, 452, 87 N.E. 805, 807, we stated that "[t]he whole previous career of a man, in its general aspects at least, may throw some light on his mental condition at the time when he is alleged to have committed a criminal offense, and when insanity is relied on as a defense". This statement, however, was intended only as an indication of the considerable latitude which should be afforded to a *defendant* who is seeking to prove his own insanity as a defense to a criminal charge. The statement certainly was not in-

insanity cases such as this, the danger is particularly great that the jury will become confused by the mass of evidence presented and will decide to convict the defendant not because they find he was legally sane at the time of the act, but rather because they are convinced that he is a person of general criminal bent.

With these considerations in mind, we turn our attention to an analysis of the individual pieces of evidence that were admitted below over objection by defense counsel. The first witness to testify for the People on rebuttal was one Robert Grover, who stated that he had observed defendant participate in a barroom scuffle. Grover, however, had no information regarding how the fight started and was unable to state whether defendant had reacted without adequate provocation. Thus, while Grover's testimony may have served to demonstrate that defendant actually did engage in violence on at least one occasion, it could not logically be used to support the People's theory that defendant had a chronically "explosive" temperament or a "hair trigger" temper. Since there was at least some potential for prejudice in Grover's testimony, and since the testimony was not directly relevant to the question of defendant's sanity, we think that it should have been excluded.

Similarly objectionable was the admission of testimony by a police officer, Charles Monroney, who stated that he observed defendant standing behind a bar throwing bottles and glasses around the room. Like the testimony offered by Robert Grover, Officer Monroney's testimony shed no light on the questions of how the incident began and whether there might be some rational explanation for defendant's conduct. In light of the ambiguity of this testimony, it cannot be said that its probative value with respect to defendant's mental condition outweighed its potentially prejudicial effect, and accordingly, we find that the testimony should not have been placed before the jury.

The most serious trial error occurred, however, when the Trial Judge permitted the jury to hear the testimony of Vincent Christina, defendant's close friend, and one Eugene Heath, a teamster shop steward. Heath stated under oath that he had been attacked and badly beaten by two men, but he was unable to identify his assailants. Christina supplied the missing information, testifying that he and his friend, Joseph Santarelli, had traveled to Heath's place of business and had beaten the shop steward in accordance with a preestablished plan. The admission of this testimony plainly posed a danger that the jury would be influenced by the implication that defendant was a vicious individual who was given to cold-blooded acts of violence. Yet, there was nothing in the testimony that was indicative of an "explosive personality" or a penchant for *impulsive* violence; if anything, the contrary was suggested. Since there could have been no logical purpose for the evidence concerning the Heath incident other than to demonstrate defendant's general propensity toward criminality, there was no justification for the admission of this highly prejudicial information.

Finally, we hold that it was also error to permit testimony by defendant's probation officer, John Caram, that defendant had previously been convicted of possession of a sawed-off shotgun. We can see no logical relationship between

tended to suggest that the *People* may bring in "the whole previous career of a man" whenever the insanity defense is interposed. Indeed, such a rule would impose an unwarranted burden upon a defendant who has a potential defense on grounds of insanity, since it would force him to choose between foregoing the defense on the one hand and, raising it on the other hand and taking the risk that the People will use the occasion to place all of his past immoral or illegal conduct before the jury, regardless of its relevance.

the ownership of a weapon, legal or not, and the symptoms of an "explosive personality", and we therefore conclude that whatever probative value the evidence may have had was greatly outweighed by its potential for prejudicing the jury.

It should be noted that not all of the evidence offered by the People to support their "explosive personality" hypothesis suffered from the same infirmity. Probation Officer Caram, for example, also testified concerning several incidents in which defendant had resorted to violence in the face of relatively mild provocation. Since Officer Caram was able to give some information about the precipitating events preceding these incidents, this testimony was directly relevant to the question of defendant's reaction patterns. Thus, it was properly admitted despite the danger of prejudice.

Similarly, the testimony elicited by the prosecutor regarding defendant's relationship to organized crime had a tendency to support the People's trial theory and was therefore properly admitted in evidence. An important aspect of the People's case on rebuttal was its contention that defendant was not suffering from "paranoid delusions", but rather was under considerable emotional stress at the time of the shooting as a result of circumstances that were firmly rooted in reality. It was shown that defendant had been made aware that an attempt had been made on the life of his friend, Vincent Christina, and that this knowledge had caused him to be fearful enough for his own safety to make inquiries concerning the possibility of receiving FBI protection. Although the connections were not drawn definitively, there was a clear implication that defendant's fears were based upon his familiarity with local organized crime activities. The prosecutor's purpose in bringing out these facts was to demonstrate that defendant was under very real stress at the time of the shooting. As indicated by the testimony of the expert witnesses, such a stressful situation would likely accentuate the characteristics of an individual with an "explosive" personality and cause him to react with disproportionate force when faced with frustration or mild provocation. Hence, if the facts concerning defendant's problems with respect to organized crime were proven, the jury could infer that the shooting had simply been precipitated by the considerable emotional pressure under which defendant had been laboring, rather than by any "temporary psychosis" sufficient to satisfy the definition of legal insanity. For this reason, we conclude that the testimony offered by the People to demonstrate that defendant was familiar with organized crime activities and had become fearful for his life was relevant to the central issue in this case, the defendant's sanity. Accordingly, the testimony was properly admitted in evidence.

We note in passing that we are not insensitive to the problems encountered by the Trial Judge in cases such as this. It is often difficult, if not impossible, for the Trial Judge to determine in advance whether the testimony of a particular witness will be relevant to a specific issue in the case. Here, the Trial Judge made a commendable effort in this direction by conducting an inquiry out of the jury's hearing to ascertain the nature and relevance of the People's rebuttal proof. It is apparent from our holding, however, that his inquiry was not sufficiently detailed to permit him to make an informed determination as to the relevance of each piece of evidence offered by the District Attorney. Indeed, in view of the unpredictability of live testimony, we note that it is sometimes almost impossible for a Trial Judge to ascertain in advance whether the evidence offered through a witness regarding a defendant's past crimes would be sufficiently relevant to justify its admission at trial.

It is for this reason that we disapprove of defense counsel's decision in this case to rely upon a "continuing objection" to the District Attorney's entire line of proof. While defense counsel's anticipatory "continuing objection" may have served the technical function of preserving a "question of law" for appellate review (see CPL 470.05, subd. 2), it did not provide the Trial Judge with an opportunity to consider the specific relevance of each fact as it was being presented through testimony. Had individual objection been taken each time prejudicial information was elicited, the Trial Judge might have been moved to require the prosecutor to articulate his theory of relevancy with more specificity, and the defects in the instant proceeding might have been avoided (cf. People v. Michael, 48 N.Y.2d 1, 6, 420 N.Y.S.2d 371, 373, 394 N.E.2d 1134, 1136). In light of the difficulties encountered in this case, we find that the trial court's acceptance of defendant's "continuing objection" was ill-advised and that the interests of all parties would have been better served had individual objection been required.

Finally, we note that the Trial Judge acted properly in instructing the jury that it could consider defendant's prior criminal history only in relation to the question of his sanity and not as an indication of his general propensity to commit the crime for which he was on trial. While such limiting instructions could not serve to cure the errors in admitting the objectionable testimony, they did serve the salutary purpose of minimizing any prejudicial effect that the otherwise properly admitted evidence might have had on the minds of the jurors.

For the foregoing reasons, the order of the Appellate Division should be reversed and the case remitted for further proceedings on the indictment.

■ JASEN, JUDGE (dissenting).

I would affirm the order of the Appellate Division. In my opinion, the rule adopted by the majority today unfairly restricts the People's use of evidence of prior crimes and antisocial conduct offered solely for the purpose of proving defendant's mental condition. The majority, in adopting a new restrictive rule, overemphasizes the possibility of prejudice to the defendant and, in so doing, has withheld from the jury logically probative and clearly relevant proof of defendant's sanity which the trial court, in its discretion, may accept into evidence.

. . .

In the case before us, defendant admitted killing his brother-in-law. His plea of not guilty by reason of insanity made the issue of defendant's sanity the sole question to be decided by the jury. Thus, the traditional concern as to whether evidence of prior crimes and antisocial conduct will lead the jury to improperly infer criminal predisposition, if not altogether absent from the case, is at least greatly attenuated. As a result, the rule articulated in People v. Molineux, 168 N.Y. 264, 61 N.E. 286, and its progeny—where the issue was whether the defendant actually committed the acts complained of—has little application to the instant case, except insofar as it reaffirms the general proposition that evidence bearing upon the character and prior history of the defendant may be excluded when its probative force is outweighed by its potential for prejudice.

. . .

The majority suggests that in order to be relevant, evidence of prior crimes and antisocial conduct must be consonant with the prosecutor's theory of sanity—in this case, a "personality disorder", also termed an "explosive personality". However, the majority cites no authority for this proposition other than the general rule that the probative value of such evidence must outweigh its potential for prejudicing the defendant. In fact, where the defendant's sanity is in issue, the weight of authority is to the contrary.

It has long been recognized that the scope of evidence which is admissible on the issue of insanity is very broad indeed. In People v. Carlin, 194 N.Y. 448, 452, 87 N.E. 805, 807, for example, this court noted "[t]he whole previous career of a man, in its general aspects at least, may throw some light on his mental condition at the time when he is alleged to have committed a criminal offense, and when insanity is relied upon as a defense in his behalf." A similar view has also been articulated by Professor Wigmore in his treatise on evidence. He states: "The first and fundamental rule, then, will be that *any and all conduct* of the person is admissible in evidence. There is no restriction as to the kind of conduct. There can be none; for if a specific act does not indicate insanity it may indicate sanity. It will certainly throw light one way or the other upon the issue." (2 Wigmore, Evidence [3d ed.], § 228, p. 9; emphasis in original.) Other leading treatises are in agreement....

The majority asserts that this concept of admissibility was not intended to apply to proof of sanity offered by the People, but only to proof of insanity offered by the defense. However, the majority fails to explain why the same proof offered on the same issue is relevant when offered by the defendant and irrelevant when offered by the People. It would seem that if a criminal defendant may offer any proof of his previous career to the jury in support of his claimed infirmity, the People should be equally free to do so with respect to their claim that the defendant is sane. This is especially true in view of the People's burden of establishing defendant's sanity beyond a reasonable doubt.

Although the majority suggests that it has not done so, it has effectively restricted the People to only one theory of sanity. In my opinion, such a restriction is inappropriate. The defendant in this case has grounded his defense on a type of insanity in the nature of a "paranoid delusion", and contends that he was only temporarily incapacitated at the time he killed his brother-in-law. In order to rebut the defense of temporary insanity, the People attempted to show that the defendant suffered from a "personality disorder" and that, although quite sane, he tended to react violently at the slightest provocation. The majority has chosen to exclude from evidence the testimony of several witnesses which indicated antisocial and violent behavior in the defendant's past and evidence of prior criminal activity. The proffered reason for this exclusion is that the evidence was either unclear as to the amount of provocation involved or concerned intentional unprovoked violence. This analysis, however, defies reason.

Although the prosecutor relied to a great extent upon the theory that defendant suffered from a "personality disorder", in so doing he did not bind himself to do so to the exclusion of every other possible theory of sanity. It must be remembered that the prosecutor's burden in this case was to prove defendant's sanity beyond a reasonable doubt, not to set forth a single unitary theory of sanity. He was free to offer a number of theories of sanity so long as each was material and relevant to a reasonable alternative explanation which could rebut defendant's claim of temporary insanity. In my opinion, the excluded evidence was relevant on this issue. The sheer number of violent acts committed by the defendant, both premeditated and as a reaction to whatever amount of provocation and his prior criminal possession of a weapon might well lead the jury to infer that the defendant's claim of temporary insanity was not worthy of belief in light of his past history of sane but antisocial behavior. This evidence does not become irrelevant merely because the prosecutor failed to label his theory properly.

I would also point out that this inference of "predisposition toward violence" is altogether different from the inference of "criminal predisposition" which the authorities cited by the majority seek to prevent. In fact, a sane yet antisocial predisposition toward violence is an entirely acceptable and relevant theory with which a prosecutor may rebut a claim of temporary insanity. This is equally true whether such predisposition toward antisocial conduct arises from a "personality disorder" or from any other sort of sane yet antisocial behavior. In short, it seems quite clear that most, if not all, of the prosecutor's proof was material and relevant on the issue of sanity and was, therefore, admissible.

. . .

Accordingly, the order of the Appellate Division should be affirmed.

NOTES

1. United States v. Emery, 682 F.2d 493, 498 (5th Cir.), cert. denied, 459 U.S. 1044 (1982): Prosecution for bank robbery. Defense that at the time of the robbery defendant was experiencing paranoia that produced such compulsion that he was unable to conform his conduct to the requirements of law and so was legally insane. Psychiatric testimony was introduced and testimony was offered describing defendant's robbery of another bank a month before the crime with which he was charged. The trial court admitted the evidence of the other robbery, finding it "relevant on the basis of a psychiatrist's opinion that it was a factor leading to his diagnosis and, after listening to lay witnesses describe appellant's behavior during the [uncharged] Atlanta robbery...." Held: No error under Fed. R. Evid. 404(b) and 403.

2. Crawley v. State, 513 S.W.2d 62 (Tex.Crim.App.1974): Prosecution for wilful injury to the personal property of another. An automobile driven by defendant collided with another automobile. Held: Not error to admit evidence that defendant had been involved in six similar collisions at the same place within the preceding four months. In Adkinson v. State, 611 P.2d 528 (Alaska), cert. denied, 449 U.S. 876 (1980), a prosecution of a landowner for manslaughter of person who had come upon his land, the disputed issue was whether the defendant had intentionally pointed his gun at the victim. Held: Not error to admit evidence that on two other occasions defendant had pointed his gun at persons who came upon his land. State v. Wyman, 270 A.2d 460 (Me.1970), was a prosecution for assault with an automobile. Defendant denied that he had intentionally run into the victim. Held: Not error to admit evidence that shortly after the alleged assault and in the same vicinity, defendant had narrowly missed two other persons with his automobile and called out to them, "Do you want to be No. 2?" State v. Stevens, 558 A.2d 833, 843 (N.J.1989): In prosecution of policeman for unauthorized exercise of official function, knowing it was unauthorized, and for misconduct in order to obtain a benefit for himself, not error to admit evidence of earlier instances of arresting women and making them disrobe.

> On those issues—defendant's purpose for conducting the searches and his knowledge that such conduct was an unauthorized exercise of his official position—evidence of the circumstances in which defendant had previously used his office to intimidate women into disrobing or providing sexual favors was highly probative. Although "intent" and "state of mind"—the phrases used by the courts below to sustain admissibility of the other-crimes evidence—fairly suggest the evidence's relevance to these statutory elements of the crime of official misconduct, we would encourage an

enhanced degree of precision in explicating the specific grounds for admitting such evidence.

Child abuse cases frequently present the question whether evidence of other misconduct should be admitted to negative accident. See, e.g., People v. Taggart, 621 P.2d 1375 (Colo.1981), holding it not error to admit evidence of five other instances of abuse by defendant of the same child to negative claims of accident and justification. Some courts stress the difficulty in these cases of obtaining evidence of the defendant's conduct and state of mind. E.g., United States v. Woods, 484 F.2d 127, 133 (4th Cir.1973), cert. denied, 415 U.S. 979 (1974). On the other hand, in Harvey v. State, 604 P.2d 586 (Alaska 1979), where the issue was whether defendant had caused the injury that resulted in the child's death, it was held error to admit evidence that earlier defendant had beaten another woman's child. A similar caution is shown in State v. Morris, 362 So.2d 1379 (La.1978), involving earlier beatings of two children of the defendant.

In Roe v. United States, 316 F.2d 617, 622–25 (5th Cir.1963), defendant was prosecuted for using the mails to sell investment contracts without having filed a registration statement with the SEC. Defendant had sold mineral leases that the government contended were, under the circumstances, "investment contracts." The trial court instructed that it was necessary for conviction to find that the sales were made with knowledge that the conduct was unlawful. The court of appeals held that there was no error in admitting evidence that another person, with whom defendant had close business associations, had been convicted for violating the same statute under which defendant was indicted.

In Andresen v. Maryland, 427 U.S. 463 (1976), a prosecution for fraudulent misrepresentation in connection with the sale of a lot in a subdivision, defendant's records in regard to this lot and other lots in the subdivision were seized under a warrant and subsequently admitted into evidence. Held: Suppression of the evidence regarding the other lots was not constitutionally required. The relevance of the documents pertaining to the other lots and their admissibility to show intent or lack of mistake in regard to the litigated lot would have been apparent to the investigators.

Imwinkelried, The Use of Evidence of an Accused's Uncharged Misconduct to Prove Mens Rea: The Doctrines Which Threaten to Engulf the Character Evidence Prohibition, 51 Ohio St. L.J. 575, 580 (1990): "Intent is an element of every true crime. Accepting the premise that the character evidence prohibition is inapplicable to evidence offered to establish mens rea, the courts could rationalize admitting evidence of any similar uncharged crimes as a matter of course."[1]

See, generally, McKusick, Techniques in Proof of Other Crimes to Show Guilty Knowledge and Intent, 24 Iowa L.Rev. 471 (1939).

United States v. Figueroa

United States Court of Appeals, Second Circuit, 1980.
618 F.2d 934.

■ NEWMAN, CIRCUIT JUDGE:

This criminal appeal concerns primarily the admissibility of prior crime evidence in a multi-defendant trial. Jose Figueroa, Angel Lebron, and Ralph Acosta were convicted after a two-day trial in the United States District Court

---

1. Footnote omitted.

for the Eastern District of New York (Thomas C. Platt, Jr., Judge) upon jury verdicts finding them guilty of conspiracy to possess and distribute heroin in violation of 21 U.S.C. § 846 (1976) and the substantive offense of possession of heroin with intent to distribute in violation of 21 U.S.C. § 841(a)(1) (1976).

The Government's evidence disclosed the following. On October 5, 1978, an informant of the Drug Enforcement Administration (DEA) placed two telephone calls from a DEA office to Figueroa. In these calls the informant arranged for the purchase of eight ounces of heroin. The conversations, conducted in Spanish, were tape recorded by a DEA agent with the informant's consent, and translated transcripts were introduced into evidence only against Figueroa.

Later that day, DEA agent Victor Aponte accompanied the informant to a meeting with Figueroa. Figueroa discussed the proposed transaction with Aponte, counted the $8,500 that Aponte displayed, and agreed to take Aponte to the place where the heroin was kept. After the group was joined by Lebron and Acosta, Aponte was told that they were going to "La Teresa," a social club managed by Lebron. Aponte drove to the club while the others proceeded on foot. Upon entering the club, which was located on the second floor of a building, Acosta looked out the window and told Lebron that everything was clear. Lebron then went into the club's bar area and emerged with a brown paper bag, which Lebron, accompanied by Aponte and the informant, took into an office. There, Lebron emptied eight cellophane packets from the paper bag onto a desk. Aponte opened one of the packets and noted a brown powdery substance with a vinegar-like odor, which he concluded was brown rock heroin.

Aponte told Lebron he wished to conclude the deal outside the club. He left to get the $8,500 from his car, instructing Lebron to have Acosta meet him with the heroin outside the building entrance. Returning from his car, Aponte saw Acosta outside the building, next to the informant. The informant had taken off his coat, a pre-arranged signal that the person next to him was carrying heroin. Aponte testified he could see a portion of the brown paper bag sticking out of Acosta's jeans pocket and could see the outline of some of the cellophane packets inside the bag, which was inside the pocket. Aponte asked Acosta if they were going ahead with the deal and was told no. When Acosta began to walk away, Aponte went to his car to pursue him. Finding Acosta on a nearby street, Aponte got out of his car and identified himself as a police officer. According to Aponte, Acosta then reached into the pocket that contained the brown paper bag. As Aponte grabbed Acosta and wrestled him to the ground, Acosta pulled the bag out of his pocket and threw it into a crowd of passers-by who had gathered to watch the arrest. The bag and its contents were never found.

For virtually all the critical events—the conversations concerning heroin, Lebron's display of the heroin, and Acosta's throwing the paper bag on the street, the only witness was Aponte. Only the fact of the two telephone calls and the identification of the voices of the informant and Figueroa on the tape recordings were testified to by another DEA agent. The informant was identified by name, and his last known address disclosed, but he was not located by either side and did not testify. The defendants called no witnesses.

The principal claim of all three appellants concerns the introduction into evidence of a 1968 conviction of Acosta for selling heroin. Since that claim presents different issues with respect to Acosta and his co-defendants, separate consideration is required.

Acosta

In a series of recent cases, this Court has endeavored to clarify the standards that apply and the procedure to be followed when the Government offers evidence of a defendant's similar crimes or acts. To be admissible the evidence must be relevant to some disputed issue in the trial, Fed.R.Evid. 404(b), and its probative value must not be substantially outweighed by the risk of unfair prejudice. Fed.R.Evid. 403; United States v. Mohel, 604 F.2d 748 (2d Cir.1979); United States v. Lyles, 593 F.2d 182 (2d Cir.1979); United States v. Manafzadeh, 592 F.2d 81 (2d Cir.1979); United States v. O'Connor, 580 F.2d 38 (2d Cir.1978); United States v. DeVaugn, 579 F.2d 225 (2d Cir.1978); United States v. Benedetto, 571 F.2d 1246 (2d Cir.1978). The procedure for determining admissibility depends on the grounds on which the Government offers the evidence. If the evidence is offered to prove that the defendant committed the act charged in the indictment, for example, by proving identity or common scheme, the evidence may be offered during the prosecution's case-in-chief, unless the defendant's commission of the act is not a disputed issue. On the other hand, if the evidence is offered to prove the defendant's knowledge or intent, the offer of similar acts evidence should await the conclusion of the defendant's case and should be aimed at a specifically identified issue. This enables the trial judge to determine whether the issue sought to be proved by the evidence is really in dispute and, if so, to assess the probative worth of the evidence on this issue against its prejudicial effect. United States v. Danzey, 594 F.2d 905 (2d Cir.), cert. denied, 441 U.S. 951, 99 S.Ct. 2179, 60 L.Ed.2d 1056 (1979); United States v. Halper, 590 F.2d 422 (2d Cir.1978); United States v. Benedetto, supra; United States v. Leonard, 524 F.2d 1076, 1092 (2d Cir.1975), cert. denied, 425 U.S. 958, 96 S.Ct. 1737, 48 L.Ed.2d 202 (1976).

Despite the frequency with which these principles have been expressed and the reversals that have occurred when they have not been followed ... , the Government persists in jeopardizing convictions by offering evidence of similar crimes or acts either in disregard of the standards or without assisting the trial judge to make sure that they are correctly applied.

In this case, the Government offered evidence of defendant Acosta's 1968 conviction for sale of narcotics. The offer was made at the conclusion of the prosecution's case-in-chief, but before it had been ascertained that the defendants would rest without presenting evidence.[1] More significantly, the prosecutor neglected to inform the trial judge of the issue to which the evidence was claimed to be relevant.[2] When Acosta's counsel then endeavored to oppose the

---

1. Since the defendants rested without presenting evidence, the slightly premature timing of the offer of the similar act evidence was of no consequence here. See United States v. Williams, 577 F.2d 188 (2d Cir.), cert. denied, 439 U.S. 868, 99 S.Ct. 196, 58 L.Ed.2d 179 (1978). Defendants frequently do not disclose whether there will be a defense case until the prosecution has rested its case. Consequently, the safer course in offering similar act evidence that should normally await the prosecution's rebuttal case, see United States v. Danzey, supra, is for the prosecution to rest, reserving, out of the presence of the jury, the right to reopen to present such evidence in the event the defendants rest without introducing evidence. If that occurs and the evidence is subsequently admitted, the trial judge can inform the jury that

court procedure obliged the prosecution to defer its similar act evidence, thereby avoiding any unwarranted inference that the prosecution was desperately using a last-minute tactic. [Footnotes are the court's. Some have been omitted. Footnote 3 is the editors'.]

2. This Circuit's use of the inclusionary approach to similar act evidence does not obviate the need to identify the fact or issue to which the evidence is relevant. All evidence objected to on relevancy grounds must be claimed to prove some fact or issue "of consequence to the determination of the action." Fed.R.Evid. 401. The exclusionary approach to similar act evidence obliges the trial court to determine whether the issue sought to be proved is among the traditional exceptions to the rule barring prior act evi-

offer because of both its timing and inadmissibility, the trial judge undertook to suggest a basis for admissibility. Referring to an issue raised during the cross-examination of Agent Aponte as to whether the evidence that Lebron had displayed to Aponte was really heroin, Judge Platt observed: "[W]hen there is a question here of the substance and you all challenged the substance I would think the evidence was highly probative that this man has been convicted of the prior sale of the very substance." (Tr. 230).

Contrary to Judge Platt's suggestion, the issue as to whether the substance was heroin had been raised in the cross-examination of Aponte only by counsel for Lebron and Figueroa, and not by counsel for Acosta. . . .

Confronted with Judge Platt's suggestion that the prior crime evidence was admissible because of a defense suggestion that the substance may not have been heroin, Acosta's counsel responded, "That is not my position. . . . I have never taken the position that these were coffee grinds. . . . I have never taken a position, nor will I take the position that my man was involved in any plan, in any ripoff. . . ." (Tr. 231). Acosta's counsel made clear that his defense was denial that the alleged conduct of his client had occurred at all. He did not claim that Acosta threw away something other than heroin nor did he claim that Acosta threw away heroin, unaware of what it was. He claimed that Aponte was fabricating the episode alleged to have occurred on the street. When Judge Platt insisted that the issue was "whether there was an intent to deal in narcotics here or whether there was an intent to deal in coffee grinds or some other brown substance," (Tr. 234), Acosta's counsel unequivocally stated, "There is no issue of intent." (Tr. 235).

It was error to admit Acosta's prior conviction. His counsel's cross-examination had raised no issue concerning his intent, and his counsel had sufficiently removed that issue from the case. The Government has things backwards when it depicts Acosta as "on the one hand enjoying the benefit of a defense of lack of intent because it was raised by a co-defendant, but on the other hand seeking to exclude relevant evidence of a past conviction simply by stating that he, after all, was not the one raising the defense." (Appellee's Br. 17). It is the Government that is trying to enjoy the benefit of having put Acosta on trial with two co-defendants and then offering evidence against him on grounds available, if at all, only as to his co-defendants. The advantages to the prosecution of a joint trial do not include that maneuver. Cf. United States v. DeCicco, 435 F.2d 478, 483 (2d Cir.1970) (condemning prosecution's evidence of a defendant's prior similar act as a basis for inferring the intent of a co-defendant).

Moreover, Acosta's prior conviction would not have been admissible even if he had been claiming that the Government's evidence proved at most a "rip-off," i.e., a sale of a substance the defendants knew was not heroin. Evidence of similar acts or crimes is relevant to the issue of intent, not to the issue of the nature of the substance that was in the cellophane bag. No one in the case claimed that the trio was unwittingly selling Aponte heroin, thinking it was some other substance. Their point was that the prosecution had failed to prove what was in the bag, not what was in their minds. While the prosecution is entitled to prove that a substance is heroin without producing either the substance or a chemical analysis, United States v. Bermudez, 526 F.2d 89 (2d Cir.1975), cert. denied, 425 U.S. 970, 96 S.Ct. 2166, 48 L.Ed.2d 793 (1976),

dence; the inclusionary approach permits the evidence to be used to prove any issue other than propensity, but the trial court is still obliged to ask, "Is the evidence in any way relevant to a fact in issue otherwise than by merely showing propensity?" Stone, The Rule of Exclusion of Similar Fact Evidence: America, 51 Harv.L.Rev. 988, 1004 (1938).

defendants are entitled to question the persuasiveness of whatever evidence is presented. But such probing puts in issue only the true nature of the substance, not what the defendants intended or knew it to be.

Having failed to specify at the time the prior crime evidence was offered the issue it tended to prove, the Government on appeal advances a theory of admissibility other than the one relied upon by the District Court. The Government now suggests that cross-examination by Acosta's counsel created an issue as to whether Acosta intended to join the conspiracy alleged to have existed between Figueroa and Lebron. While Acosta's principal line of defense was that Aponte's entire account of the events of October 5 was not to be believed, his counsel did elicit on cross-examination Aponte's acknowledgment that when, according to Aponte's version, Lebron displayed the cellophane packets inside the office of the social club, Acosta was not in the office, and that Aponte never discussed price or quantity with Acosta.

There is an ambiguity as to whether this brief cross-examination was designed to show only that Acosta had taken no action to join the conspiracy or also to show that regardless of Acosta's acts, he was unaware of the nature of the conspiracy and did not intend to join it. Judge Platt at one point suggested that the latter point was being pressed. As he suggested to Acosta's counsel, "On the basis of your whole case the presentation so far has been it's a mistake or accident or other innocent reason that your man happened to be around." (Tr. 232). Acosta's counsel responded, "It is not a mistake or accident.... I am saying and I have taken the position throughout that this didn't happen." (Tr. 232–34). This renewal of Acosta's basic denial of the whole episode appears to have satisfied Judge Platt, who then discussed with counsel and ultimately relied upon the theory that Acosta was challenging the nature of the substance in the bag.

In United States v. Williams, 577 F.2d 188, 192 (2d Cir.), cert. denied, 439 U.S. 868 ... (1978), this Court ruled that a prior conviction was properly admitted on the issue of intent where counsel had argued that the defendant had not attended a crucial meeting and that, even if he had been present, his attendance did not constitute intentional participation in the conspiracy. No such alternative argument was advanced by counsel for Acosta. On the contrary, he represented to Judge Platt that there was no claim of accident or mistake and that intent was not an issue in the case.

Finally, the Government contends that Acosta's counsel had not indicated with sufficient definiteness that intent was not a disputed issue in Acosta's case. The decisions in this Circuit have used various expressions to describe when a dispute concerning an issue has been sufficiently removed to bar use of similar act evidence. Thus, the question has been stated to be whether an issue like intent is "really in dispute," United States v. Williams, supra, 577 F.2d at 191; United States v. Benedetto, supra, 571 F.2d at 1249, or "truly in dispute," United States v. O'Connor, supra, 580 F.2d at 43, or whether the defendant has "affirmatively take[n] the issue of intent out of the case," United States v. Williams, supra, 577 F.2d at 191, or "offered to stipulate" to the requisite intent, United States v. Manafzadeh, supra, 592 F.2d at 85, or made "an unequivocal concession of the element," United States v. Mohel, supra, 604 F.2d at 754.

Whether an issue remains sufficiently in dispute for similar acts evidence to be material and hence admissible, unless the prejudicial effect of the evidence substantially outweighs its probative value, depends not on the form of words used by counsel but on the consequences that the trial court may properly attach to those words. When the Government offers prior act evidence to prove an issue, counsel must express a decision not to dispute that issue with sufficient clarity that the trial court will be justified (a) in sustaining objection to any subsequent cross-examination or jury argument that seeks to raise the issue and (b) in charging the jury that if they find all the other elements established beyond a reasonable doubt, they can resolve the issue against the defendant because it is not disputed. See United States v. Mohel, supra, 604 F.2d at 754. While those consequences can be attached to a formal stipulation that the issue has been conceded, a formal stipulation is not required or necessarily appropriate. With respect to intent, defense counsel will understandably be reluctant to tell the jury that while he contends his client was not present, he concedes that if he had been present, he had the requisite intent. The conditional nature of such a stipulation may easily be misunderstood. That risk is substantially lessened if the matter is handled by the trial judge in the jury instructions.

Despite the prosecution's failure in this case to identify the issue to which Acosta's prior conviction was material, Acosta's counsel clearly stated that he was not disputing the issues suggested by the trial court as providing the basis for admissibility, primarily intent. Counsel's disclaimers were repeated and emphatic, and, had they been relied upon to exclude Acosta's conviction would have justified preclusion of cross-examination and argument on intent and supported an instruction taking the issue out of Acosta's case. In these circumstances, it was error to admit Acosta's prior conviction.

The trial court also erred in failing to determine whether the probative value of the evidence was "substantially outweighed by the danger of unfair prejudice." Fed.R.Evid. 403. Initially, it appears that after the judge identified intent as the issue to which he believed Acosta's conviction was material, there was inadequate consideration of the probative value of the evidence. The judge noted that under Rule 609 a prior conviction offered to impeach a witness's credibility may be more readily admitted if the witness's incarceration ended no more than ten years prior to the trial. The judge ascertained that Acosta's incarceration for his conviction had ended at a point just within the ten-year period prior to the trial. Apparently purporting to analogize from Rule 609, the judge considered the prior conviction to have sufficient probative value simply because it satisfied the ten-year provision of Rule 609. But both Rule 609 and Rule 403, which is pertinent here, oblige the trial court to assess the probative value of every prior conviction offered in evidence and the remoteness of a conviction, whatever its age, is always pertinent to this assessment. Satisfying the ten-year provision of Rule 609 does not justify the automatic admission of a prior conviction under that rule nor assure that it has the requisite probative value under Rule 403.

More significantly, the trial judge failed to consider the risk of unfair prejudice and to balance this risk against probative value. Judge Platt expressed the not uncommon misconception that "Everything that is introduced against a defendant in a criminal case is prejudicial," and then said of Acosta's prior conviction, "The sole question is its probative value." (Tr. 239).

All evidence introduced against a defendant, if material to an issue in the case, tends to prove guilt, but is not necessarily prejudicial in any sense that matters to the rules of evidence. See United States v. Briggs, 457 F.2d 908, 911 (2d Cir.), cert. denied, 409 U.S. 986 . . . (1972). Evidence is prejudicial only when it tends to have some adverse effect upon a defendant beyond tending to prove the fact or issue that justified its admission into evidence. See Advisory Committee Note to Rule 403; S. Saltzburg and K. Redden, Federal Rules of Evidence Manual 43 (2d ed. 1978 Supp.). The prejudicial effect may be created by the tendency of the evidence to prove some adverse fact not properly in issue or unfairly to excite emotions against the defendant. A prior conviction is material to a defendant's intent (when intent is in issue), but it is also prejudicial to the extent that it tends to prove a defendant's propensity to commit crimes. When material evidence has an additional prejudicial effect, Rule 403 requires the trial court to make a conscientious assessment of whether the probative value of the evidence on a disputed issue in the case is substantially outweighed by the prejudicial tendency of the evidence to have some other adverse effect upon the defendant.

In assessing the risk of prejudice against the defendant, the trial court should carefully consider the likely effectiveness of a cautionary instruction that tries to limit the jury's consideration of the evidence to the purpose for which it is admissible. Whatever the criticism of such instructions, they remain an accepted part of our present trial system. However, while their utility is not to be invariably rejected, neither should it be invariably accepted. When a prior conviction, not involving falsity, is offered to impeach the credibility of a defendant who testifies, the Federal Rules of Evidence require the trial judge to assess whether "the probative value of admitting this evidence outweighs its prejudicial effect to the defendant." Fed.R.Evid. 609(a). If an instruction limiting consideration of the conviction to the issue of credibility always sufficed to insure requisite fairness, there would be no need to make the balance mandated by Rule 609(a). Similarly, the balancing required by Rule 403 for all evidence would not be needed if a limiting instruction always insured that the jury would consider the evidence only for the purpose for which it was admitted. Giving the instruction may lessen but does not invariably eliminate the risk of prejudice notwithstanding the instruction. Rule 403 balancing must therefore take into account the likelihood that the limiting instruction will be observed. This involves no burden upon the conduct of the trial. No jury inquiry is required or appropriate. The trial judge, sensitive to the realities of the courtroom context as in all other trial rulings, must simply include a sound estimate of the likely force of limiting instructions in the overall Rule 403 determination.

Some cases have gone far toward assuming that the trial court tacitly made the balance required by Rule 403. See, e.g., United States v. Hayes, 553 F.2d 824, 828 (2d Cir.), cert. denied, 434 U.S. 867 ... (1977). No such assumption can be made here where the trial court explicitly identified as the "sole question" the "probative value" of the evidence.

Erroneous admission of a defendant's prior conviction normally warrants a new trial, United States v. Rinaldi, 301 F.2d 576 (2d Cir.1962), and there is no basis for escaping that conclusion here. The case against Acosta rested entirely on the testimony of Aponte, whose credibility was a seriously contested issue in the trial. The impact upon Acosta of the introduction of his prior narcotics conviction may well have been decisive to the outcome of the jury's deliberation. It is inconceivable that knowledge of Acosta's prior conviction did not play some significant part in the decision of at least some of the jurors to find Aponte's accusations of Acosta credible.

. . .

[Convictions reversed and remanded for new trial.][3]

[Dissenting opinion omitted.]

3. For an explanation of the reversal of the convictions of Lebron and Figueroa, see infra p. 873.

NOTES

1. Both Fed. R. Evid. 403 and Fed. R. Evid. 404(b) are applied in Figueroa. Rule 404(b) provides:

> Evidence of other crimes, wrongs, or acts is not admissible to prove the character of a person in order to show action in conformity therewith. It may, however, be admissible for other purposes, such as proof of motive, opportunity, intent, preparation, plan, knowledge, identity, or absence of mistake or accident, provided that upon request by the accused, the prosecution in a criminal case shall provide reasonable notice in advance of trial, or during trial if the court excuses pretrial notice on good cause shown, of the general nature of any such evidence it intends to introduce at trial.

Note that if the evidence is not offered as a basis for an inference to "character," it does not come with the first sentence of 404(b). Note also that if the evidence is not offered as a basis for an inference from "character" to "action in conformity therewith," it does not come with the first sentence of 404(b). Finally, the list in the second sentence of 404(b) is preceded by the words "such as," making it clear that the list is not exhaustive.

2. The prosecution's "need" for evidence as a factor bearing on the admissibility of evidence of other crimes receives considerable attention in the cases. In Figueroa, the government had no need of the evidence because the defendant did not contest the issue to which it related. See also United States v. Crowder, 87 F.3d 1405 (D.C.Cir.1996): An unequivocal offer to stipulate elements of the crime—in the litigated case intent and knowledge—and agreement to an instruction that the government need not prove these elements, renders evidence of crimes offered solely to prove these elements inadmissible. See supra p. 25 on stipulations generally. Old Chief v. United States, 117 S.Ct. 644 (1997): Defendant was prosecuted for assault with a dangerous weapon and for using a firearm in relation to a crime of violence. In addition, he was charged under a statute making it unlawful for anyone who has been convicted of a crime punishable by imprisonment for more than one year (except certain business offenses and state law misdemeanors punishable by imprisonment for two years or less) to possess a firearm. Held: Abuse of discretion under FRE 403 to allow the prosecution, in order to establish that defendant had been previously convicted, to introduce a record of defendant's conviction that showed the conviction was for an assault resulting in serious bodily injury, in view of the fact that defendant was ready to admit or stipulate that he had been convicted of a crime of the sort described in the statute.

In United States v. Beechum, 582 F.2d 898, 914 (5th Cir.1978), cert. denied, 440 U.S. 920 (1979), cited supra p. 373, the court stated: Probative value under Fed. R. Evid. 404(b) "must be determined with regard to the extent to which the defendant's unlawful intent is established by other evidence, stipulation, or inference. It is the incremental probity of the evidence that is to be balanced against its potential for undue prejudice."[1] In United States v. McMahon, 592 F.2d 871 (5th Cir.), cert. denied, 442 U.S. 921 (1979), admission of other crime evidence was justified on an appraisal of the government's case in the absence of such evidence. The court found that the government had "substantial need" of evidence bearing on the issue of intent. The court in United States v. Dolliole, 597 F.2d 102 (7th Cir.), cert. denied, 442 U.S. 946 (1979), speaks of the other crime evidence being "reasonably necessary."

---

1. Footnote omitted.

On the other hand, consider United States v. Carter, 516 F.2d 431, 434 (5th Cir.1975): Prosecution for possession of sugar with intent to make moonshine. Defendants went from supermarket to supermarket buying sugar until they had over 1000 pounds. They acted openly and when their automobile was stopped by revenue agents made no effort to flee. At the trial, evidence was introduced of five liquor law convictions of one of the defendants over a twenty-three year period, the most recent being ten years before the litigated offense. In reversing the convictions the court observed:

> [W]e view the factor of the prosecution's need for the evidence with particular caution in this case because the appellants were accused of an offense consisting of an essentially innocent act, the possession of sugar, which is converted into a criminal misdemeanor solely by their subjective intent in possessing the substance; furthermore, there was virtually no evidence of their intent, other than Carter's criminal record. The lack of independent evidence of the appellant's intent would seem to make the factor of the government's need for the evidence weigh heavily on the balancing scales. However, under these circumstances, the risk is particularly great that the jury was unfairly prejudiced and that the appellants were found guilty primarily, if not exclusively, because of wrongdoings long past.

In deciding the admissibility of other crime evidence, should there be consideration of the availability of other evidence to the prosecution? State v. Castro, 756 P.2d 1033, 1042 (Hawai'i 1988): In prosecution for attempting to murder defendant's estranged girlfriend, abuse of discretion to admit evidence of earlier acts of violence by the defendant against the girlfriend. "Arguably, the evidence . . . helped to prove the defendant's conduct was intentional. Yet, the introduction of such evidence can hardly be justified on the basis of need or the inefficacy of alternative proof. For there was much more from which an inference of intentional conduct could be drawn in the evidence of the offense for which the defendant was being tried." See State v. Lyle, 118 S.E. 803, 812 (S.C.1923) (forgery case in which authorship of allegedly forged writing was in issue; despite availability of neutral standards of defendant's handwriting, prosecution chose to rely on standards indicating his guilt of other forgeries); State v. Wofford, 114 N.W.2d 267 (Minn.1962) (possible to show defendant's possession of gun subsequently used in commission of litigated crime without revealing fact that earlier possession was in connection with a burglary). See the last sentence in the Advisory Committee's Note to Fed. R. Evid. 403.

State v. Bock

Supreme Court of Minnesota, 1949.
229 Minn. 449, 39 N.W.2d 887.

■ KNUTSON, JUSTICE. Defendant was convicted of forgery in the second degree. He appeals from an order denying his motion for a new trial and from the judgment.

During the night of November 11, 1947, the General Roofing Company, located at 1837 East Lake street, Minneapolis, was broken into and 27 blank checks and a check-writing machine were stolen. About 1 p.m. on November 12, a man appeared at the National Tea Company store, located at 1510 Nicollet avenue, purchased groceries amounting to $3.21, and in payment thereof presented a check drawn on the check blank of General Roofing Company payable to Harold A. Camden in the amount of $62.20. The clerk, Myrtle P. Long, who received the check, referred the customer to the cashier, Miriam J.

Nigon, whose duty it was to approve checks before they could be cashed. The person presenting the check offered some identifications which he had, but they were not examined. Mrs. Nigon was suspicious of the check and stated that she would call the bank on which it was drawn, whereupon the person presenting the check excused himself, stating that he would be back in a minute. He failed to return. The check was not endorsed at the time it was presented.

Both Mrs. Nigon and Miss Long identified defendant as the person who presented this check, which is identified in the record as state's exhibit A. In describing the person who presented the check, Mrs. Nigon testified that he wore a light tan jacket and pants and a tan hat. Miss Long testified that he wore khaki-colored jacket and trousers and a tan or light hat. The amount and name of the General Roofing Company on exhibit A were made with the check-writing machine of the company. The check bore the forged signature of Roy A. Drew, the owner of the company, and Carol Saunders, a nonexistent person so far as is disclosed by the record. Genuine checks drawn on the General Roofing Company were signed by Roy A. Drew, the owner, and Carole M. Basken, the office manager. The office manager, who testified at the trial, did not know any person by the name of Harold A. Camden. Neither Mrs. Nigon nor Miss Long had ever seen defendant prior to the time he presented exhibit A.

The conviction of defendant is based on the attempt to pass exhibit A.

Over the objection of defendant, evidence was admitted showing that on December 13, 1947, a man called at the Town Market Furniture Company, located at 116–120 Washington avenue south, and purchased two lamps costing $39.80. He offered to make a down payment of $15 and to pay the balance when he called for the lamps, which he stated he would do later. He identified himself as James Wagner, living at 2321 Second street northeast. He presented a check for $46.30, payable to James Wagner, purported to have been drawn on the account of and signed by Arthur Martin. Over the signature of Arthur Martin appeared the name Arthur Martin Contractors, 521 South Ninth street, which was typewritten on the check. After deducting the down payment of $15, the individual presenting this check was given cash amounting to $31.30. Both the salesman, Alfred Gudmundson, and the acting cashier, Agnes L. James, identified defendant as the person who presented the check. Mr. Gudmundson testified that the individual who presented the check wore dark trousers, a light grey hat, and a red-and-black checkered jacket. Agnes L. James testified to substantially the same effect. This check is identified as state's exhibit B in the record.

On the same day, a man made a similar purchase of two lamps from the Community Furniture Company of Minneapolis and in a similar manner offered to make a down payment of $15. He presented a check identical with exhibit B, except as to a slight difference in the amount, receiving $31.70 in cash. Elmer W. Axelson, who handled the transaction, identified defendant as the person who presented this check. He did not remember what clothes the man wore, but testified that the man presenting the check gave his name as James Wagner and his address as 2331 Second street northeast. This check is identified in the record as state's exhibit F. On December 16, a man called at the Walden Furniture Company and in a like manner purchased two lamps, for which he offered a down payment of $15, presenting a check identical with exhibits B and F and again receiving cash in the sum of $31.70. David C. Walden, the owner of the store, identified the individual who presented this check as defendant. He described the person presenting the check as having worn light tan or brown pants, a tan jacket, and a tan hat. This check is identified in the record as state's exhibit D.

Exhibits B, D, and F were all drawn on the Northwestern National Bank. There was no account in this bank in the name of Arthur Martin or Arthur Martin Contractors. All three checks had been endorsed at the time they were presented.

Later in December, after defendant had been questioned concerning these checks and exhibit A, his apartment was searched by a detective of the Minneapolis police force, but no clothing resembling any of that covered by a description of the person who passed or attempted to pass exhibit A or exhibits B, D, and F was found in his apartment aside from a light-colored hat. Both defendant and his wife testified that he had never owned clothing similar to that described by any of these witnesses. There is some testimony by the manager of the Richmond Apartments, located at 521 South Ninth street, that a man by the name of Arthur J. Martin had lived in the Richmond Apartments until October 21, 1947, but no attempt was made to connect this with defendant or any acquaintance of defendant. Defendant lived at 629 East Eighteenth street.

Defendant's defense consists largely of an alibi. The identification of defendant by the state's witnesses is positive, but equally positive are the witnesses for defendant that he was at home on the occasion when the above-mentioned checks were presented. The evidence is conclusive that he was at home during the early part of the evening of November 11, during which evening the blank checks of the General Roofing Company were stolen.

Defendant, as part of his defense, offered to prove that on November 12, 1947, a check drawn on the General Roofing Company, payable to Harold A. Camden in the amount of $62.20, identical with exhibit A, was presented to the Rydell Clothing Company at Washington avenue south and Hennepin avenue in payment for merchandise purchased, amounting to $4.50. This check, like exhibit A, bore the forged signature of Roy Drew and the additional signature of Carol Saunders. He offered to show by the clerk who received the check that the person who presented it was not defendant and further offered to show by the testimony of Detective Hillner of the Minneapolis police force that the check had been turned over to Hillner for investigation. This check is identified in the record as defendant's exhibit 1. He also offered to show that a check identical in form and amount was presented to an employe of the Washington Shirt Company on November 12 in payment for merchandise amounting to $12, and that when the man, who represented himself to be Harold A. Camden, was told that the employe of the store wished to call the bank to verify the check he stated that he would go outside to change the parking of his car and that he did not return. He further offered to show by the clerk who accepted the check that the man who presented it was not defendant. This check is identified as defendant's exhibit 2. The offer of proof respecting defendant's exhibits 1 and 2 was rejected by the court upon the objection of the state.

After the trial and conviction of defendant, one Roland William Miller, on April 1, 1948, was charged by information with having committed the crime of forgery. He entered a plea of guilty and was placed on probation. In support of his motion for a new trial, defendant submitted an affidavit of Miller, wherein Miller positively stated that it was he who presented and cashed exhibits B, D, and F and that he, in company with police officers, had identified himself to all three concerns wherein these checks had been cashed; that he had presented to the county attorney a statement of all facts pertaining to these transactions; and that he does not know defendant or any member of his family.

The record shows that defendant had twice before been convicted of a felony, once for forgery and once for theft from a military reservation.

This appeal presents three questions for our determination.

(1) Was it error to admit in evidence exhibits B, D, and F and the testimony of witnesses identifying defendant as the person who cashed these checks?

(2) Was it error to refuse to admit evidence of other checks cashed by someone other than defendant on the same day and identical with exhibit A?

(3) Was it an abuse of discretion to deny a new trial after the admissions of Roland Miller that it was he who had cashed exhibits B, D, and F, as set forth in his affidavit?

1–2.   It is a general rule that evidence of separate and independent crimes is inadmissible to prove the guilt of a person charged with having committed a crime. But to this rule there are several well-established exceptions. State v. Stuart, 203 Minn. 301, 281 N.W. 299. Thus, where it is necessary to prove the identity of a person, evidence of other similar crimes of the accused closely connected in time, place, and manner is admissible. State v. Lucken, 129 Minn. 402, 152 N.W. 769; State v. Barrett, 40 Minn. 65, 41 N.W. 459; Annotations, 3 A.L.R. 1540; 22 A.L.R. 1016; 27 A.L.R. 357; 63 A.L.R. 602. Such evidence is also admissible to show a common system, scheme, or plan embracing the crime charged. State v. Sweeney, 180 Minn. 450, 231 N.W. 225, 73 A.L.R. 380. Exhibits B, D, and F were within these exceptions to the general rule and therefore admissible.

Objection to the admission of exhibits B, D, and F, in addition to the general grounds that they were incompetent, immaterial, and irrelevant, was based on the remoteness in point of time and generally on the lack of sufficient foundation. Whether separate offenses are so closely connected with that with which defendant is charged as to show a general scheme or plan or permit an inference of guilt to be drawn is a matter resting largely within the discretion of the trial court. State v. Robbins, 185 Minn. 202, 240 N.W. 456. We will not reverse unless there is a clear abuse of discretion. State v. Voss, 192 Minn. 127, 255 N.W. 843. We find no abuse of judicial discretion in admitting exhibits B, D, and F.

3.   Objection to the admission of defendant's exhibits 1 and 2 was not based upon an insufficient foundation, but for the reason "that there isn't any showing in the offer of evidence by the defendant's attorney that this defendant did not offer the check for payment to the National Tea Company, on November 12, 1947, nor the other checks in evidence relative to the Community Furniture Company, the Walden Furniture Company, and the Town Market Furniture Company; there isn't any showing by this evidence that this defendant was not the person who offered and passed these checks."

Of course, defendant denied having passed any of the above checks. His defense was an alibi. Proof of similar acts constituting separate and distinct crimes is admissible under an exception to the general rule, not for the purpose of showing specifically that defendant committed the crime with which he has been charged, but for the purpose of permitting the trier of facts to draw an inference from the evidence showing a general plan or scheme, consisting of a series of acts similar to that with which defendant is charged, that he did commit the crime with which he is charged. 2 Wigmore, Evidence, 3d Ed., § 304. In determining defendant's guilt, the identity of the person who presented exhibit A is the decisive factor. Inasmuch as an inference that defendant uttered exhibit A is permissible from evidence showing that he passed exhibits B, D and F, there appears to us no good reason why an opposite inference that defendant was not the person who offered exhibit A is not permissible from a showing that checks identical with exhibit A were offered or passed on the same day and in a like manner by someone other than defendant. In discussing this question, Wigmore, in his work on Evidence, 3d Ed., § 304, has this to say: "It should be noted that this kind of evidence may be also available to negative the accused's guilt. E.g. if A is charged with forgery, and denies it, and if B can be shown to have done a series of similar forgeries connected by a plan, this plan of B is some evidence that B and not A committed the forgery charged. This mode of reasoning may become the most important when A alleges that he is a victim of mistaken identification." Again, in Id. § 341, p. 245, we find the following: "Notice that here, as throughout this series of offenses, the principle of similar acts (ante, § 304) can be used to exonerate an innocent accused, where the acts evidencing the plan are those of a third person not the defendant."

. . .

4.   Where the state has introduced evidence of other crimes to establish identity, the defendant is entitled to rebut the inference that might be drawn therefrom by showing that the crimes have been committed by someone else. 22 C.J.S., Criminal Law, § 622, p. 953. He should also have the right to show that crimes of a similar nature have been committed by some other person when the acts of such other person are so closely connected in point of time and method of operation as to cast doubt upon the identification of defendant as the person who committed the crime charged against him. State v. Harris, 153 Iowa 592, 133 N.W. 1078.

Here, the crimes relied upon by the state were much more remote in point of time than those defendant sought to show. State's exhibits B, D, and F were passed or offered about a month later than the check upon which defendant's prosecution rests. They were not the same either as to payee or payer. On the other hand, the checks which defendant offered to prove had been passed by some other individual were identical with that upon which defendant's prosecution is based, both as to date, payee, and payer, and were offered or passed on the identical day that the check charged against defendant was offered. The method of operation was also identical with that which the state claims defendant used. Defendant was entitled to have the jury pass upon the credibility and weight of this evidence, together with that of the state, in determining the identity of the person who committed the crime charged against defendant. It was error to exclude the evidence offered by defendant.

5.   There remains for consideration the third and final contention of defendant. This relates to the affidavit of Miller. The affidavit is not controverted by the state, and, for the purpose of this decision, we accept it as true.

There can be little doubt that the positive identification of defendant as the person who presented and cashed exhibits B, D and F by those to whom the checks were presented, in view of defendant's former convictions, would have a serious impact upon the minds of the members of the jury in determining whether defendant was the person who cashed exhibit A. The trial court was of the opinion, and the state now contends, that at best the affidavit was only of an impeaching nature and cumulative of the other denials of defendant that he cashed any of these checks. The identification of defendant, while positive, was based upon a slight opportunity to observe defendant. None of the witnesses had any previous acquaintance with him. That they could easily have been mistaken has now been demonstrated by the affidavit of Miller, assuming that to be true, as we must.

While it is true that the matter of granting a new trial on the ground of newly discovered evidence rests largely in the discretion of the trial court and that a new trial will not ordinarily be granted where the newly discovered evidence is only of a cumulative or corroborative nature, it is also true that cumulative evidence of an untrue or erroneous nature is as apt to lead to an unjust result as cumulative evidence that is true may lead to a correct one. It can hardly be supposed that the erroneous multiplication of the identification of defendant by all these witnesses would fail to impress the jury when considered with the evidence of defendant's former convictions. Balanced against the testimony of the witnesses, who identified defendant was the evidence pertaining to his alibi. Whether the jury would have been willing to believe his witnesses concerning his alibi had they had the benefit of the admissions of Miller, and possibly the elimination of exhibits B, D, and F entirely, is something we cannot tell. However, in view of the prejudicial nature of the testimony concerning the passing of exhibits B, D, and F and the identification of defendant as the person who passed them by several witnesses, we feel that in the interest of justice defendant should be granted a new trial.

Reversed.

NOTES

1. In Lyles v. State, 109 S.E.2d 785 (Ga.1959), defendant was convicted of murdering her daughter by arsenic poisoning in order to obtain money under an insurance policy. The court found no error in the admission of evidence that defendant had previously murdered three other persons—two husbands and a mother-in-law. The court listed these similarities: (1) each of the victims occupied a close relationship to defendant, (2) each died from arsenic poisoning, (3) each died from multiple doses built up to a lethal level, (4) defendant showed little or no grief for any of the victims, (5) defendant collected a substantial amount of money as a result of the death of each victim, (6) defendant gave each victim a lavish burial, (7) all victims were taken to the same hospital and attended there by defendant, (8) defendant expressed intense dislike for each victim either before or after death, and (9) defendant predicted the deaths of three of the victims. State v. Moore, 440 S.E.2d 797, 812–14 (N.C.), cert. denied, 115 S.Ct. 253 (1994): In prosecution of wife for murdering husband with arsenic, evidence of arsenic poisonings of two other husbands admissible. People v. Peete, 169 P.2d 924 (Cal.), cert. denied, 329 U.S. 790 (1946): Defendant was convicted of a murder committed in 1944. The court found no error in the admission of evidence that over twenty years before, defendant had been convicted of a murder committed under strikingly similar and peculiar circumstances. In both instances defendant explained the victim's disappearance by saying that the victim had been wounded by a third person and had gone away because ashamed of the wound; in both cases defendant had exercised dominion over the victim's property after the victim's disappearance; in both cases the victim had been shot in the neck. The dissent pointed out the unlikelihood that defendant would have committed a second crime in exactly the way that had led to her conviction of the first. State v. Speer, 501 N.W.2d 429 (Wis.1993): In prosecution for daytime burglary of house with for sale sign outside, not error to admit evidence of daytime burglary in California two years before of another house with a for sale sign outside.

United States v. Woods, 484 F.2d 127, 133 (4th Cir.1973), cert. denied, 415 U.S. 979 (1974): Prosecution for murder of defendant's infant foster child. Expert testimony was given that the child died of suffocation, although the expert agreed that there was some probability that he died of a disease unknown to medical science. Held: Not error to admit evidence that defendant had custody of or access to nine other children who suffered episodes of cyanosis, of whom five had died. "Thus, with regard to no single child was there any legally sufficient proof that defendant had done any act which the law forbids. Only when all of the evidence concerning the nine other children and Paul is considered collectively is the conclusion impelled that the probability that some or all of the other deaths, cyanotic seizures, and respiratory deficiencies were accidental or attributable to natural causes was so remote, the truth must be that Paul and some or all of the other children died at the hands of the defendant."

The most famous case of this sort is Rex v. Smith, 11 Cr.App.R. 229, 84 L.J.K.B. 2153 (1915), the "Brides in the Bath Case." Defendant was indicted for the murder of a woman with whom he had gone through a form of marriage, who had then mysteriously died in her bath, and who had made defendant the sole beneficiary under her will. Evidence was admitted that subsequently defendant had "married" two other women who had also died in their baths and who had also left their property to defendant. For an interesting account of this case see Marjoribanks, For the Defence—The Life of Sir Edward Marshall Hall 312–44 (1929).

State v. Johnson, 832 P.2d 443, 449 (Or.1992):

Tragically, many murders involve single women who are sexually assaulted and physically battered. Ligature strangulation homicide is not per se distinctive or unique. Evidence submitted in the pretrial hearing in this case indicates that there were 19 ligature strangulations in Multnomah County, where both the Wilder and Bobbie Jean murders took place, between 1982 and February 1989. Dr. Larry Lewman, the Oregon State Medical Examiner, who performed the autopsy on Wilder, testified as a witness for the state that ligature strangulations are very common in sex crimes.

The fact that the ligature device used in both crimes was a portion of a telephone cord between the wall jack and the base of the telephone is not sufficient to earmark the homicides as the handiwork of one criminal. Telephone cords are common. Using them to strangle someone is terrible; it is not, however, unique or distinctive by itself.[1] Further characteristics could make telephone cord strangulation unique, such as tying a certain kind of knot or painting the cord a certain color, but it would be those characteristics which make use of the telephone cord distinctive, not the use of the cord itself.

In this case, the characteristics of the modus of the prior and charged crimes point to a lack of distinctiveness—one cord was ripped from the wall, the other was removed; one was wrapped around the victim's neck nine times, the other five times; bedding was caught up in the telephone cord in the Wilder murder, but not in Bobbie Jean's murder; the person who killed Wilder used only a telephone cord, while Bobbie Jean's murderer used hands as well as the cord to strangle her. Rather, the characteristics of the modus of each crime suggest nothing more than that a person committing a murder grabbed what was available. That is not distinctive. Murderers who strangle their victims without premeditation use what is at

1. Rarity, by itself, is not to be equated with distinctiveness. If there were an abnormal year with only two murders by gunshot in the City of Portland, could we conclude that a gunshot is a signature for that year and therefore conclude that the same person did both? Of course not. Many people have guns; even more have telephone cords. [Footnote of the court.]

hand. Wilder and Bobbie Jean were killed in apartments, where telephone cords were available. The telephone cord ligature strangulations of Wilder and Bobbie Jean do not have a signature quality.

We conclude that the record does not support a finding that there is either a very high degree of similarity between the prior and charged misconduct or a methodology that is so distinctive so as to earmark the crimes as the handiwork of one criminal. . . .

Commonwealth v. Brusgulis, 548 N.E.2d 1234, 1238 (Mass.1990):

The fact is that the circumstances of each incident were characteristic of numerous assaults on women walking or jogging in unpopulated portions of public parks or in similar areas. If we were to uphold the admission of the evidence of prior bad acts in this case, we would be endorsing a rule that evidence of prior assaults by a person is admissible in the trial of every future assault charge against that person, provided that there is a general, although less than unique or distinct, similarity between the incidents. . . .

With State v. Speer, supra, compare State v. Rutchik, 341 N.W.2d 639 (Wis. 1984): In prosecution for burglary in which there was evidence that defendant knew by reading obituary notices that the house would be empty at a certain time, not error to introduce evidence of defendant's conviction of earlier burglary in which same method was employed, at least to prove intent. A dissent observed that the modus operandi was frequently used by burglars and that publications by law enforcement agencies advise the public to take special precautions to protect against burglars during funerals.

In Robinson v. State, 108 So.2d 188 (Ala.Ct.App.1959), defendant was prosecuted under a statute making it an offense for one already convicted of committing or attempting to commit a crime of violence to own or have in his possession or control a pistol. At the trial, police testified that they had found a pistol in the gas station run by defendant. Defendant testified that this pistol did not belong to him but to his bookkeeper, and by her testimony she confirmed this. On cross-examination of defendant, the following exchange took place.

Q. Do you remember the time, Ural, when you were tried and acquitted up here for possession of a pistol sometime ago? A. Yes, sir.

Q. Who claimed to own that pistol?

Mr. Crosland: We object to that, if the Court please. He was acquitted by a jury and—

Mr. Stewart: He is very good at getting other folks to claim pistols—

The Court: I overrule the objection.

Mr. Crosland: We except, if the Court please.

Q. Ural, who claimed to own this pistol when you were tried for possession of this pistol? A. If that's the gun, that gun belonged to a first cousin of mine.

Q. It belonged to a first cousin of yours? A. Yes, sir. If that's the one.

Q. And your wife? A. Yes, sir.

Mr. Crosland: Your Honor, I have no objections to trying that case over and we can go and get the record and read it word for word, and read where a Not Guilty verdict was returned by the jury.

Mr. Stewart: We admit that he was tried and acquitted. I just want to show—. Id. at 191.

People v. Ewoldt, 867 P.2d 757, 770 (Cal. 1994), distinguishes the degree of similarity required for admissibility of other crime evidence according to the nature of the issue in dispute. According to the court, the greatest similarity is required when the issue is identity, less when the question is whether the act occurred at all, and still less when the question is state of mind. The Ewoldt case itself involved a conviction for molesting and committing lewd acts on the defendant's stepdaughter; the disputed evidence concerned other instances of such conduct with the stepdaughter and with another daughter when she was the stepdaughter's age. The Ewoldt decision also addressed the meaning of "plan" in the oft-repeated statement—e.g., Fed. R. Evid. 404 (b)—that evidence of another crime is admissible if introduced to show a plan on the part of the defendant and not simply to show a propensity to commit crimes. The court overruled earlier decisions that in order for there to be a plan such as would make other crime evidence admissible, the other crime and the charged offense had to flow from the same conception or plot, and held that it was enough that both crimes expressed the same trait or inclination. (That there was a plan did not guarantee admissibility, however, because in addition a certain degree of similarity was required.)

With Ewoldt compare People v. Fiore, 312 N.E.2d 174, 178 (N.Y. 1974): Prosecution of president of school board for soliciting bribe from contractor in connection with school construction. Held: Error to admit evidence that defendant had obtained a bribe from the architect on the same project. "[M]erely showing two or more similar crimes does not necessarily establish a *common scheme*. To some extent every criminal repeater has a modus operandi. But a modus operandi alone is not a common scheme; it is only a repetitive pattern." See also Imwinkelried, Using a Contextual Construction to Resolve the Dispute Over the Meaning of the Term "Plan" in Federal Rule of Evidence 404(b), 43 Kan. L. Rev. 1005 (1995), distinguishing an "unlinked plan" (similarity of charged and uncharged crimes); a "linked methodology" (each time the crime is committed it is committed in the same way, but nothing unique about the method); and a grand design encompassing the charged and uncharged crimes. The author argues only the last should be considered to involve a plan within the meaning of Fed. R. Evid. 404(b). See also Bryden and Park, "Other Crimes" Evidence in Sex Offense Cases, 78 Minn. L. Rev. 529, 546–51 (1994).

2. The Bok case presents the question of possible use of evidence of misconduct by persons other than the defendant.

State v. Garfole, 388 A.2d 587 (N.J.1978): Defendant was convicted of a sexual assault. At the trial he was not allowed to introduce evidence of four or five other sexual assaults similar in certain respects to the litigated assault, most of which had taken place in the same neighborhood as the litigated assault and close in time to it. The defendant had alibis for four of these other assaults, but no alibi for the litigated assault. Defendant had been indicted for the other assaults as well as for the litigated assault, but the charges relating to the other assaults had been dismissed on motion of the prosecution at the outset of the trial. The Supreme Court of New Jersey remanded the case:

> The crucial legal issue in this case is the extent to which Evid.R. 55 and the decisions expounding it in the context of use of similar other crimes evidence by the State against an accused are applicable when a defendant seeks to use such evidence for purposes of exculpation.

. . .

[T]he basis of the Appellate Division's affirmance was the supposed insufficiency of similarity of the series of offenses relied upon by defendant. In this regard the court imposed upon the defendant the same standards of degree of similarity of the several incidents as would apply if the offer of evidence was by the State. It required that "'the device used [in the prior crimes] . . . be so unusual and distinctive as to be like a signature',," citing authority applicable to efforts by the prosecutor to establish by other offenses by the defendant that all, including the charge being tried, were committed by the accused. 148 N.J. Super. 127 at 130, 372 A.2d 340 at 342.

We are of the view, however, that a lower standard of degree of similarity of offenses may justly be required of a defendant using other-crimes evidence defensively than is exacted from the State when such evidence is used incriminatorily. As indicated above, other-crimes evidence submitted by the prosecution has the distinct capacity of prejudicing the accused. Even instructions by the trial judge may not satisfactorily insulate the defendant from the hazard of the jury using such evidence improperly to find him guilty of the offense charged merely because they believe he has committed a similar offense before. Therefore a fairly rigid standard of similarity may be required of the State if its effort is to establish the existence of a common offender by the mere similarity of the offenses. State v. Sempsey, . . . 141 N.J.Super. at 323, 358 A.2d 212. But when the defendant is offering that kind of proof exculpatorily, prejudice to the defendant is no longer a factor, and simple relevance to guilt or innocence should suffice as the standard of admissibility, since ordinarily, and subject to rules of competency, an accused is entitled to advance in his defense any evidence which may rationally tend to refute his guilt or buttress his innocence of the charge made. See Evid.R. 1(2). The application of a modified requirement of relevancy to the proffer by a defendant is additionally justified by the consideration that the defendant need only engender reasonable doubt of his guilt whereas the State must prove guilt beyond a reasonable doubt.

. . .

If no other considerations came into play it might thus well be concluded that defendant's proffer of proof, as expanded at the Appellate Division level, was of sufficient probative value to warrant its admission into evidence for appraisal by the jury. But important coordinate factors, highly material to the sound administration of the trial process, require appraisal along with the factor of the degree of relevance of defendant's proffered proofs. These are those mentioned in Evid.R. 4 which, to the extent here material, reads:

> The judge may in his discretion exclude evidence if he finds that its probative value is substantially outweighed by the risk that its admission will either (a) necessitate undue consumption of time or (b) create substantial danger of . . . confusing the issues or of misleading the jury.

Defendant's proffer, as argued by the State, does create the possibility of undue consumption of time and of danger that the jury might be confused or misled. A trial of defendant's guilt of the misfeasances of June 14, 1971 would become expanded into one of determination as to his guilt vel non of each of the four prior occurrences and possibly of the sixth.

Defendant's proofs of the other occurrences and his tendered alibis for four of them would generate four mini-trials as to the truth of those claims.

. . .

Accordingly, what is called for in the present case is a highly discretionary determination as to the admissibility of the defendant's proffered evidence which weighs and takes into account the degree of relevance of the disputed evidence as against the Rule 4 considerations which militate for rejection of it. Id. at 450–57, 388 A.2d at 589, 590–93.[2]

See also United States v. Stevens, 935 F.2d 1380 (3d Cir.1991) (accord).

United States v. Aboumoussallem, 726 F.2d 906, 911–12 (2d Cir.1984): In a prosecution for smuggling heroin into the United States, the defendant, Yagih, claimed he had been duped by his cousins Nazih and Pierre and that he did not know the attaché case he carried from Beirut to Kennedy Airport contained heroin. Yagih claimed the case had been handed to him by Pierre just as Yagih was boarding his flight to New York, and that Pierre had asked him to take it to Nazih, who was in the United States. Yagih offered the testimony of Wendy Golding that five and a half months before the smuggling incident with which Yagih was charged, she had been duped by Pierre and Nazih into transporting hashish oil from Lebanon to the United States. The trial court excluded the evidence. Held: Defendant's evidence was not inadmissible under Fed.R.Evid. 404(b):

> [W]e believe the standard of admissibility when a criminal defendant offers similar acts evidence as a shield need not be as restrictive as when a prosecutor uses such evidence as a sword.... [R]isks of prejudice are normally absent when the defendant offers similar acts evidence of a third party to prove some fact pertinent to the defense.... In such cases the only issue arising under Rule 404(b) is whether the evidence is relevant to the existence or nonexistence of some fact pertinent to the defense.[3]

The court held, however, that the trial court had not abused its discretion in excluding the evidence under Rule 403. Although the dangers of jury confusion and trial delay were slight, the court said, the probative value of evidence that five and a half months earlier Pierre and Nazih had duped a stranger was not great.

But see State v. Savino, 567 So.2d 892 (Fla.1990): When defendant seeks to introduce evidence of a crime committed by a third person to prove the third person committed the litigated crime, the other crime must have been of such a nature that it would be admissible against the third person if he were on trial for the litigated crime.

In Macklin v. United States, 410 F.2d 1046 (D.C.Cir.1969), it was the prosecution that sought advantage from showing the crimes of others. Conviction for carrying dangerous weapon reversed because of error in admitting evidence that at the time defendant was arrested his companions were in possession of weapons.

See generally Comment, Of Propensity, Prejudice and Plain Meaning: The Accused's Use of Exculpatory Specific Acts Evidence and the Need to Amend Rule 404(b), 87 Nw. Univ. L. Rev. 651 (1993).

---

2. Footnotes omitted.   3. Footnote omitted.

Fed. R. Evid. 413 and 414

[See Rules, Statute and Case Supplement.]

NOTE

Congress enacted Rules 413 and 414[1] pursuant to Pub. L. 103–322, Title XXXII, § 320935, September 13, 1994, 108 Stat. 2135, with a contingent effective date. The legislation required the Judicial Conference to make recommendations regarding the legislation within 150 days after enactment. The Judicial Conference disapproved of the policies expressed in the rules and recommended that Congress should reconsider its decision, or that it should adopt an amendment to Rule 404 that embodies the policies of Rules 413 and 414. As provided in the 1994 legislation, the rules took effect on July 10, 1995— 150 days after the Judicial Conference's recommendation—because Congress failed to act.

Among the questions that arise under Rules 413 and 414 are these: May evidence admissible under these rules be excluded by virtue of Rule 403? May evidence admissible under these rules be excluded by virtue of other exclusionary rules, such as the hearsay rule? What is the relation between Rules 413 and 414 and Fed. R. Evid. 405, which governs the manner of proving character when character is permitted to be proved? (See infra p. 875 for discussion of proof of character through reputation and opinion.) Rules 413 and 414 permit introduction of evidence of offenses committed by the defendant. What of evidence that the defendant has not committed certain offenses or has engaged in good acts? What of evidence that a third person committed a sexual offense, offered by the defendant to show that the third person, rather than the defendant, committed the litigated offense?

Lannan v. State

Supreme Court of Indiana, 1992.
600 N.E.2d 1334.

ON CRIMINAL PETITION TO TRANSFER

■ SHEPARD, CHIEF JUSTICE.

A jury convicted appellant Donald Lannan of molesting young V.E., after hearing testimony from another girl who said Lannan had molested her in the past and testimony from the victim regarding several other instances of molestation which were not charged. Lannan's petition for transfer asks this Court to abandon the so-called "depraved sexual instinct" exception under which evidence about these uncharged acts was admitted. We grant transfer to reexamine the exception, its rationales, and whether they remain compelling enough to justify its continued application.... We have concluded that Rule 404(b) of the Federal Rules of Evidence provides a better basis for testing the admissibility of this sort of evidence than our existing caselaw provides.

I. History of the Exception

It has long been settled that in prosecutions for incest, sodomy, criminal deviate conduct or child molesting, evidence of certain kinds of prior sexual conduct is admissible under Indiana's depraved sexual instinct exception to the general rule of inadmissibility of prior bad acts. See Stewart v. State (1990), Ind., 555 N.E.2d 121; State v. Robbins (1943), 221 Ind. 125, 46 N.E.2d 691;

---

1. Rule 415 was enacted at the same time. It is cited infra p. 916.

State v. Markins (1884), 95 Ind. 464. This exception has been carved out of the general rule for two reasons. First, the exception has been based on a recidivist rationale: " 'Acts showing a perverted sexual instinct are circumstances which with other circumstances may have a tendency to connect an accused with a crime of that character.' " Kerlin v. State (1970), 255 Ind. 420, 424, 265 N.E.2d 22, 25 (quoting Lovely v. United States, 169 F.2d 386, 390 (4th Cir.1948)). Second, the exception has been based on the need to bolster the testimony of victims: to lend credence to a victim's accusations or testimony which describe acts which would otherwise "seem improbable standing alone." Stwalley v. State (1989), Ind., 534 N.E.2d 229, 231.

The desire to level the playing field by bolstering the testimony of a solitary child victim-witness (recounting unspeakable acts, often in embarrassing detail in the intimidating forum of a courtroom while subject to aggressive cross-examination) was central to the holding in Robbins, the forerunner in a long line of modern era cases developing the depraved sexual instinct exception.[1] In Robbins, the defendant was the superior court judge in Vincennes during the late 1930s. He was indicted on two counts of sodomy with a twelve-year-old girl. The case might fairly have been characterized as a credibility contest between a child and a pillar of the community. To even up this contest, the State sought to introduce testimony from other children regarding other instances of sexual misconduct committed by the defendant against children. The trial court excluded the evidence; this Court held that the testimony of the other children should have been allowed.[2]

Indiana has not stood alone in fashioning exceptions to the rules of evidence in cases where children are victims of sexual abuse. Approximately twenty other states have or have had such exceptions.[3] Some, such as Missouri and Kansas, explicitly recognize a depraved sexual instinct exception, State v. Lachterman, 812 S.W.2d 759 (Mo.Ct.App.1991), cert. denied, 503 U.S. 983, 112 S.Ct. 1666, 118 L.Ed.2d 387 (1992), or allow evidence of prior bad acts to prove defendant's "lustful disposition or nature." State v. Whiting, 173 Kan. 711, 252 P.2d 884 (1953). Others, such as Illinois, South Dakota and Wisconsin, follow rules similar to Federal Rule of Evidence 404(b), but stretch the definition of the common scheme and plan doctrine to allow prior occurrences of sexual misconduct into evidence, in effect to prove proclivity. See People v. Partin, 156 Ill.App.3d 365, 509 N.E.2d 662 (1987); State v. Means, 363 N.W.2d 565 (S.D.1985); State v. Friedrich, 135 Wis.2d 1, 398 N.W.2d 763 (1987). One court has likened this contortion of the traditional 404(b) exceptions to "forcing a square peg into a round hole." Lachterman, 812 S.W.2d at 768.

The Supreme Court of Wisconsin has been particularly forthright in explaining the justification for what has come to be known in that state as the

---

1. See, e.g., Lamar v. State (1964), 245 Ind. 104, 195 N.E.2d 98; Miller v. State (1971), 256 Ind. 296, 268 N.E.2d 299; Lawrence v. State (1984), Ind., 464 N.E.2d 923; Kuchel v. State (1991), Ind., 570 N.E.2d 910. [Footnotes are the court's; some footnotes omitted, others renumbered.]

2. The State appealed on reserved questions of law following the defendant's acquittal after the trial judge instructed the jury to find him not guilty. This Court found error in the directed verdict, as well, and in so doing shed light on its motivation.

> We can well understand the trial judge's reluctance to believe that *a man occupying appellee's position in the com-*

munity could be guilty of such infamous misconduct but . . . the jury had the first right to pass upon its credibility.

> Perhaps the girl's testimony would not have seemed so improbable if the court had admitted other evidence . . . erroneously excluded.

Robbins, 221 Ind. at 134–35, 46 N.E.2d 691 (emphasis added).

3. See Chris Hutton, Commentary: Prior Bad Acts Evidence in Cases of Sexual Contact with a Child, 34 S.D.L.Rev. 604, 614 n. 47 (1989); Edward J. Imwinkelried, Uncharged Misconduct Evidence §§ 4.11–4.18 at 34–52 (1984 & 1992 Supp.).

"greater latitude" doctrine. Friedrich, 398 N.W.2d at 775. The justification is, quite simply, protection of children, the most sexually vulnerable in society. Like our Court in Robbins, Wisconsin has sought to level the playing field in service to the desirable social end of convicting child molesters. . . .

II.   The Recidivism Rationale

Implicit in the application of our exception and those applied across the country under different names is the assumption that sexual offenders repeat their crimes more often than other criminals. "To a person of normal, social and moral sensibility, the idea of the sexual exploitation of the young is so repulsive that it's almost impossible to believe that none but the most depraved and degenerate would commit such an act." Friedrich, 398 N.W.2d at 763. The Indiana Association of Criminal Defense Lawyers, amicus curiae, calls such a belief "ignorant" and "founded on myth," (amicus brief at 35), yet we are inclined to accept the conclusion that recidivisim among sexual deviates is quite high.[4] This alone, however, cannot justify continued adherence to the depraved sexual instinct exception. We have no doubt that recidivism among those who violate drug laws, for instance, is extraordinarily high.[5] We do not allow the State to introduce previous drug convictions in its case-in-chief in a prosecution for selling illegal drugs, however, even though it can hardly be disputed that such evidence would be highly probative. This exclusionary rule renders inadmissible character evidence offered solely to show the accused's propensity to commit the crime with which he is charged. The rationale behind this general rule, sometimes termed "the propensity rule," is that the prejudicial effect of such evidence outweighs any probative value. See Warner v. State (1991), Ind., 579 N.E.2d 1307. If a high rate of recidivism cannot justify a departure from the propensity rule for drug defendants, logic dictates it does not provide justification for departure in sex offense cases.

III.   The Bolstering Rationale

We turn then to the second rationale frequently offered for the depraved sexual instinct exception—that allowing such evidence lends credence to a

---

4. An Emory University psychiatrist who has accumulated data on more than 500 sexual offenders reports that the average number of sex crimes committed by the adult offender is usually in the hundreds. See Discovering and Dealing with Deviant Sex, Psychology Today, April 1985, at 8, 10. Conversely, defendant and amicus argue that those convicted of sex crimes have a lower rate of recidivism than those convicted of most other crimes. See amicus brief at 17 (citing Blinder, Psychiatry in the Everyday Practice of Law 213 (2d ed. 1982 & 1991 supp.)). We believe studies which show a low recidivism rate among sex offenders are of questionable value, since often they utilize arrest and conviction rates, which are inadequate measures of recidivism due to the low number of cases which actually make it that far into the system. See A. Nicholas Groth, Robert E. Longo & J. Bradley McFadin, Undetected Recidivism among Rapists and Child Molesters, 28 Crime & Delinquency 450 (1982).

It is generally true that most criminals get away with more crimes than

they are convicted of, but it would appear that this is especially true of offenders who commit sexual assaults. The low recidivism rate generally attributed to such offenders can be understood due to the low visibility of such offenses. Although the sexual offender's behavior is repetitive, most of his recidivism goes undetected. This may be attributable in part to how recidivism is defined.

Then, too, there is a wide variety of factors that serve to deter many victims of sexual assault from reporting their victimization. Even if the offense is reported, in the majority of cases, no suspect is apprehended; few of the cases in which a suspect is apprehended reach trial level, and still fewer result in conviction.

Id. at 457–58.

5. See M.C. Slough, Other Vices, Other Crimes: An Evidentiary Dilemma, 20 Kan. L.Rev. 411, 424 (1972).

victim's testimony describing acts which would otherwise seem improbable standing alone.

This rationale has its origins in an era less jaded than today. When the accusations were brought in Robbins, in the late 1930s, the idea that an adult male who occupied a position of responsibility in the community would force himself sexually upon a child bordered on the preposterous. Sadly, it is our belief that fifty years later we live in a world where accusations of child molest no longer appear improbable as a rule. This decaying state of affairs in society ironically undercuts the justification for the depraved sexual instinct exception at a time when the need to prosecute is greater.

Indeed, there remains what might be labeled the "rationale behind the rationale," the desire to make easier the prosecution of child molesters, who prey on tragically vulnerable victims in secluded settings, leaving behind little, if any, evidence of their crimes. Nearly four decades ago, the Minnesota Law Review, noting the trend toward admissibility of depraved sexual instinct-type evidence, attributed it to a feeling "that handicapping the state in the prosecution of criminals is undesirable. It is also likely that a realization of the difficulty of obtaining proof of sexual offenses has been partially responsible for the trend." Note, Evidence of Similar Transactions in Sex Crime Prosecutions; A New Trend Toward Liberal Admissibility, 40 Minn.L.Rev. 694, 704 (1956). The emotional appeal of such an argument is powerful, given the special empathy that child victims of sexual abuse evoke. But even this cannot support continued application of an exception which allows the prosecution to accomplish what the general propensity rule is intended to prevent.

In the interest of aiding the prosecution, we could of course *expand* the exception and abrogate the general rule. After all, our empathy for victims of all crimes is considerable. But the general rule prohibiting the state from offering character evidence merely to show the defendant is a "bad guy" and therefore probably committed the crime with which he is charged remains as fundamental today as ever. "We indeed live in a vulgar age," Lee v. Weisman, 505 U.S. 577, 637, 112 S.Ct. 2649, 2681, 120 L.Ed.2d 467 (1992) (Scalia, J., dissenting), when recidivists flout the law and routinely violate the behavioral norms of civilized society. We have not yet reached the point, though, where we are prepared to abandon a basic tenet of criminal evidence law older than the republic itself,[6] however desirable the social end may be. As we said in Penley v. State (1987), Ind., 506 N.E.2d 806, 808:

> The notion that the State may not punish a person for his character is one of the foundations of our system of jurisprudence. Evidence of misconduct other than that with which one is charged ("uncharged misconduct") will naturally give rise to the inference that the defendant is of bad character. This, in turn, poses the danger that the jury will convict the defendant solely on this inference.

IV. Disadvantages of Present Rule

We do not wish to imply that the rationales put forth on behalf of the depraved sexual instinct exception are entirely without merit. They are not.

---

6. See Commonwealth v. Boulden, 179 Pa.Super. 328, 116 A.2d 867, 871 (1955) (quoting 1 Wigmore on Evidence 646 (3d ed. 1940)):

"[F]or nearly three centuries, ever since the liberal reaction which began with the Restoration of the Stuarts, this policy of exclusion, in one or another of its reasonings, has received judicial sanction, more emphatic with time and experience. It represents a revolution in the theory of criminal trials, and is one of the peculiar features, of vast moment, which distinguishes the Anglo–American from the Continental system of Evidence."

Each retains some measure of validity. Yet it seems to us that any justification for maintaining the exception in its current form is outweighed by the mischief created by the open-ended application of the rule.

For instance, the current rule does not oblige the State to give notice of its intention to present evidence of a defendant's depraved sexual instinct (although local discovery rules requiring both sides to exchange witness lists would seem to provide adequate protection if defense counsel is industrious enough to discern through investigation the nature and substance of the witness' testimony). Nor does the rule as it now stands require particular similarity between the prior bad act and the crime charged. See Jarrett v. State (1984), Ind., 465 N.E.2d 1097 (uncharged crime need not be identical, sufficient if same sexual instinct is involved).

Then, too, this Court has allowed evidence of extremely remote instances of sodomy, molest or sexual assault, under the theory that remoteness goes to weight and not admissibility. See Lawrence v. State (1984), Ind., 464 N.E.2d 923 (evidence of sexual crime committed twenty-two years earlier admitted to show depraved sexual instinct); Kerlin v. State (1970), 255 Ind. 420, 265 N.E.2d 22 (in prosecution for sodomy with fifteen-year-old boy, evidence admitted showing defendant committed sodomy with two adult males seven and eight years before). The Kerlin decision drew a strong dissent from Justice DeBruler, who wrote:

> There was no connection between the [prior acts] and the offense being tried. This testimony was not offered as bearing on an issue such as motive, intent, identity; nor could it evince any common scheme or plan, etc. This evidence was offered for the purpose of showing the appellant's character was bad and that he had a tendency to commit acts of sodomy. As such it was inadmissible. *Evidence of other offenses cannot be admitted merely in an attempt to show some predisposition of the accused to commit criminal acts or to establish some likelihood that he might do so.*

255 Ind. at 427, 265 N.E.2d at 26 (emphasis added). Twenty-two years later, Justice DeBruler has carried the day. His reasoning tracks the language of Federal Rule of Evidence 404(b), which we hereby adopt in its entirety, effective from this day forward.

V.   Use of Rule 404(b)

We hasten to add that abandoning the depraved sexual instinct exception does not mean evidence of prior sexual misconduct will never be admitted in sex crimes prosecutions. It means only that such evidence will no longer be admitted to show action in conformity with a particular character trait. It will continue to be admitted, however, for other purposes such as proof of motive, opportunity, intent, preparation, plan, knowledge, identity, or absence of mistake. "That is, such evidence may be admissible *despite its tendency to show bad character or criminal propensity*, if it makes the existence of an element of the crime charged more probable than it would be without such evidence." Bedgood v. State (1985), Ind., 477 N.E.2d 869, 872–73 (emphasis added).

. . .

VI.   Lannan's Claim

Finally, we turn to the facts of appellant's trial to determine whether the adoption of Rule 404(b) requires reversal in this case.

Donald Lannan, age twenty-three at the time of his arrest, was charged with one count of child molesting, a class C felony. Ind.Code Ann. § 35–42–4–

3(c) (West 1986). The charging information alleged that on June 17, 1989, he engaged in sexual intercourse with V.E., age fourteen.

At trial, V.E. testified that she was spending the evening at her grandmother's house. She shared a room with T.W., her cousin of similar age. V.E. said Lannan came into the room and asked T.W. to "mess around with him," but T.W. refused. V.E. said Lannan then had intercourse with her.

T.W. testified that she was in the bedroom when Lannan came in late at night, and that Lannan had fondled her before moving on to V.E. She testified that Lannan was naked, and that he had removed V.E.'s shorts. T.W. also said she heard V.E. telling Lannan to stop because it hurt.

Both girls also testified about an incident in Lannan's truck during the summer of 1988 in which he allegedly fondled both of them. And V.E. told the jury of submitting to sex with Lannan on at least three other occasions after the crime alleged. This testimony was neither detailed nor lengthy. V.E. said it happened once at defendant's grandmother's house, at "Aunt Belinda's", and at her house after defendant and his wife Debbie had moved in with V.E.'s family. "If he didn't do it with Debbie, he would came over and did it and had intercourse with me," she said. Record at 193. Testimony as to all of these uncharged acts was admitted pursuant to the depraved sexual instinct exception. Under the new rule announced today, this was an insufficient basis for admitting evidence of uncharged misconduct.

As we noted above, however, it does not necessarily follow that all testimony revealing uncharged misconduct was inadmissible. T.W.'s eyewitness account of the crime—including her allegation that Lannan fondled her before having intercourse with V.E.—helped complete the story of the crime in a way that incidentally revealed uncharged misconduct. Hence, her allegations as to Lannan's misconduct in the house were admissible under the theory of res gestae. See Wilson v. State, (1986), Ind., 491 N.E.2d 537.

The testimony regarding the incident in Lannan's truck is more troublesome. Had the State filed an additional count (or counts) charging Lannan with fondling V.E. (or both girls), their testimony would have been admissible as direct evidence of a fact in issue. However, these crimes and V.E.'s allegations of additional instances of intercourse were uncharged. As such, given our abandonment of the depraved sexual instinct exception, our inquiry is whether these prior acts were admissible under any 404(b) exception. We can find none without forcing a square peg in a round hole.

In determining whether the introduction of this evidence warrants reversal, we must assess the probable impact of the evidence upon the jury.... Ordinarily, evidence of uncharged crimes of the character introduced in this case could be said to have a major impact on the jury. Today we are persuaded otherwise, however, in large measure because of the testimony of Alfred Sage, an uncle of V.E. and T.W. Sage testified that in May 1990, Lannan drove to the home where the molest occurred and shouted, "I'm going to f . . . them again." Record at 274. This declaration, coupled with the victim's testimony and T.W.'s corroboration, leads us to conclude that the impact of this other evidence on the jury was not of sufficient weight to require reversal.

We therefore affirm the judgment of the trial court.

■ DeBruler, Dickson, and Krahulik, JJ., concur.

■ Givan, Justice, concurring in result.

I concur in the result of the majority opinion. I strongly disagree with the majority's abolition of the depraved sexual instinct rule. The majority opinion very accurately has set forth the reasons for the adoption of this rule and the long history of its usage in this State. I find no need to repeat the statements made in the majority opinion. Suffice it to say that based upon those reasons given, I believe the necessity to protect children from the devastating harm of molestation justifies the invocation of the rule.

I fully recognize, as stated by the majority, that in most cases the evidence of prior conduct probably will come in under accepted rules which the majority leaves intact. However, I do not believe this fact justifies the abrogation of the rule. I believe a jury is entitled to know that a defendant in a child molesting case has a history of sexual deviate conduct because of the heinous nature of the crime and the possible unbelievability of a small child. To me, the abrogation of this rule is an erosion, albeit small, of the protection of children. I would not diminish that protection one iota.

I concur with the majority in their affirmance of the conviction of appellant.

NOTES

1. Agreeing with the Lannan decision in rejecting an exception to the other crimes rule for sex offenses are Getz v. State, 538 A.2d 726 (Del.1988), and State v. Rickman, 876 S.W.2d 824 (Tenn.1994). The latter decision rests rejection on the state's adoption of Rule 404.

2. People v. Oliphant, 250 N.W.2d 443, 457–58 (Mich.1976): Prosecution for rape in which evidence that defendant had raped other women was admitted. Held: No error. The other rapes involved similar circumstances: the defendant picked up college-age women and after a period of friendly discussion, drove them to an unfamiliar place and achieved intercourse by threats of force; the circumstances manifested a plan to act in such a way as to make it difficult for the women to prove non-consent.

The dissenting opinion observed:

[A] man's propensity to use force when he encounters resistance does not tend to show whether a woman resisted, submitted under duress or consented freely. Such a propensity does not tend to show that the woman did not consent but rather what may have occurred if she did not. The evidence of other rapes tends to show that Oliphant is a rapist and may be guilty of the offense charged, that if he thought it necessary he would have used force or a show of force to have intercourse with the complainant. Although the evidence is probative of propensity to use force (propensity to rape) it is not admissible for that purpose. Such evidence does not negate complainant's consent or tend to show nonconsent, the issue it is said to be probative of and admissible to prove.

State v. Lamoureux, 623 A.2d 9, 14 (R.I.1993): In prosecution for sexual assault, not error to admit evidence of another sexual assault on a different victim under nearly identical circumstances to prove lack of consent. The court repudiated its statement in an earlier case that "[t]he fact that one woman was raped ... has no tendency to prove that another woman did not consent."

Compare cases in which claims of self-defense may let in evidence of other crimes. State v. Monroe, 364 So.2d 570 (La.1978): Prosecution for murder. The victim, an elderly white male, was found strangled to death at a place reputed to be a haunt of derelicts and winos. On the night following the litigated homicide, another elderly white male was found strangled to death in the same area. The bodies had similar bruises and marks on the necks. Defendant admitted to police that he killed both victims, but claimed self-defense. Held: Not error to admit evidence of the second incident. Halliburton v. State, 528 S.W.2d 216 (Tex.Crim.App.1975), held that in a prosecution of a wife for the murder of her husband, once the defendant had taken the stand and testified that she acted in self-defense, it was not error to admit evidence that several weeks after the litigated homicide, she had shot another man, an acquaintance, when he told her that he could not pay a debt.

For discussion of other crime evidence relating to sexual offenses, some of it directed to Fed. R. Evid. 413 and 414, see Bryden and Park, "Other Crimes" Evidence in Sex Offense Cases, 78 Minn. L. Rev. 529 (1994); Imwinkelried, A Small Contribution to the Debate Over the Proposed Legislation Abolishing the Character Evidence Prohibition in Sex Offense Prosecutions, 44 Syracuse L. Rev. 1125 (1993); Symposium on the Admission of Prior Offense Evidence in Sexual Assault Cases, 70 Chicago–Kent L. Rev. 3 (1994); Gregg, Other Acts of Sexual Misbehavior and Perversion as Evidence in Prosecution for Sexual Offenses, 6 Ariz. L. Rev. 212 (1965); Annot., Admissibility, in Rape Case, of Evidence That Accused Raped or Attempted to Rape Person Other Than Prosecutrix, 2 A.L.R.4th 330, 1980 WL 130990 (1980).

Huddleston v. United States

Supreme Court of the United States, 1988.
485 U.S. 681, 108 S.Ct. 1496.

■ CHIEF JUSTICE REHNQUIST delivered the opinion of the Court.

Federal Rule of Evidence 404(b) provides:

> "Other crimes, wrongs, or acts.—Evidence of other crimes, wrongs, or acts is not admissible to prove the character of a person in order to show action in conformity therewith. It may, however, be admissible for other purposes, such as proof of motive, opportunity, intent, preparation, plan, knowledge, identity, or absence of mistake or accident."

This case presents the question whether the district court must itself make a preliminary finding that the Government has proved the "other act" by a preponderance of the evidence before it submits the evidence to the jury. We hold that it need not do so.

Petitioner, Guy Rufus Huddleston, was charged with one count of selling stolen goods in interstate commerce, 18 U.S.C. § 2315, and one count of possessing stolen property in interstate commerce, 18 U.S.C. § 659. The two counts related to two portions of a shipment of stolen Memorex videocassette tapes that petitioner was alleged to have possessed and sold, knowing that they were stolen.

The evidence at trial showed that a trailer containing over 32,000 blank Memorex videocassette tapes with a manufacturing cost of $4.53 per tape was stolen from the Overnight Express yard in South Holland, Illinois, sometime between April 11 and 15, 1985. On April 17, 1985, petitioner contacted Karen Curry, the manager of the Magic Rent-to-Own in Ypsilanti, Michigan, seeking her assistance in selling a large number of blank Memorex videocassette tapes. After assuring Curry that the tapes were not stolen, he told her he wished to sell them in lots of at least 500 at $2.75 to $3 per tape. Curry subsequently arranged for the sale of a total of 5,000 tapes, which petitioner delivered to the various purchasers—who apparently believed the sales were legitimate.

There was no dispute that the tapes which petitioner sold were stolen; the only material issue at trial was whether petitioner knew they were stolen. The District Court allowed the Government to introduce evidence of "similar acts" under Rule 404(b), concluding that such evidence had "clear relevance as to [petitioner's knowledge]." App. 11. The first piece of similar act evidence offered by the Government was the testimony of Paul Toney, a record store owner. He testified that in February 1985, petitioner offered to sell new 12" black and white televisions for $28 apiece. According to Toney, petitioner indicated that he could obtain several thousand of these televisions. Petitioner and Toney eventually traveled to the Magic Rent-to-Own, where Toney purchased 20 of the televisions. Several days later, Toney purchased 18 more televisions.

The second piece of similar act evidence was the testimony of Robert Nelson, an undercover FBI agent posing as a buyer for an appliance store. Nelson testified that in May 1985, petitioner offered to sell him a large quantity of Amana appliances—28 refrigerators, 2 ranges, and 40 icemakers. Nelson agreed to pay $8,000 for the appliances. Petitioner was arrested shortly after he arrived at the parking lot where he and Nelson had agreed to transfer the appliances. A truck containing the appliances was stopped a short distance from the parking lot, and Leroy Wesby, who was driving the truck, was also arrested. It was determined that the appliances had a value of approximately $20,000 and were part of a shipment that had been stolen.

Petitioner testified that the Memorex tapes, the televisions, and the appliances had all been provided by Leroy Wesby, who had represented that all of the merchandise was obtained legitimately. Petitioner stated that he had sold 6,500 Memorex tapes for Wesby on a commission basis. Petitioner maintained that all of the sales for Wesby had been on a commission basis and that he had no knowledge that any of the goods were stolen.

In closing, the prosecution explained that petitioner was not on trial for his dealings with the appliances or the televisions. The District Court instructed the jury that the similar acts evidence was to be used only to establish petitioner's knowledge, and not to prove his character. The jury convicted petitioner on the possession count only.

A divided panel of the United States Court of Appeals for the Sixth Circuit initially reversed the conviction, concluding that because the Government had failed to prove by clear and convincing evidence that the televisions were stolen, the District Court erred in admitting the testimony concerning the televisions. 802 F.2d 874 (1986).[1] The panel subsequently granted rehearing to address the decision in United States v. Ebens, 800 F.2d 1422 (C.A.6 1986), in which a different panel had held: "Courts may admit evidence of prior bad acts if the proof shows by a preponderance of the evidence that the defendant did in fact commit the act." Id., at 1432. On rehearing, the court affirmed the conviction. "Applying the preponderance of the evidence standard adopted in Ebens, we cannot say that the district court abused its discretion in admitting evidence of the similar acts in question here." 811 F.2d 974, 975 (1987) (per curiam). The court noted that the evidence concerning the televisions was admitted for a proper purpose and that the probative value of this evidence was not outweighed by its potential prejudicial effect.

_____

1. "[T]he government's only support for the assertion that the televisions were stolen was [petitioner's] failure to produce a bill of sale at trial and the fact that the televisions were sold at a low price." 802 F.2d, at 876, n. 5. [Footnotes are the Court's; some footnotes omitted, others renumbered.]

We granted certiorari, 484 U.S. 894, 108 S.Ct. 226, 98 L.Ed.2d 185 (1987), to resolve a conflict among the Courts of Appeals as to whether the trial court must make a preliminary finding before "similar act" and other Rule 404(b) evidence is submitted to the jury. We conclude that such evidence should be admitted if there is sufficient evidence to support a finding by the jury that the defendant committed the similar act.

Federal Rule of Evidence 404(b)—which applies in both civil and criminal cases—generally prohibits the introduction of evidence of extrinsic acts that might adversely reflect on the actor's character, unless that evidence bears upon a relevant issue in the case such as motive, opportunity, or knowledge. Extrinsic acts evidence may be critical to the establishment of the truth as to a disputed issue, especially when that issue involves the actor's state of mind and the only means of ascertaining that mental state is by drawing inferences from conduct. The actor in the instant case was a criminal defendant, and the act in question was "similar" to the one with which he was charged. Our use of these terms is not meant to suggest that our analysis is limited to such circumstances.

Before this Court, petitioner argues that the District Court erred in admitting Toney's testimony as to petitioner's sale of the televisions.[2] The threshold inquiry a court must make before admitting similar acts evidence under Rule 404(b) is whether that evidence is probative of a material issue other than character. The Government's theory of relevance was that the televisions were stolen, and proof that petitioner had engaged in a series of sales of stolen merchandise from the same suspicious source would be strong evidence that he was aware that each of these items, including the Memorex tapes, was stolen. As such, the sale of the televisions was a "similar act" only if the televisions were stolen. Petitioner acknowledges that this evidence was admitted for the proper purpose of showing his knowledge that the Memorex tapes were stolen. He asserts, however, that the evidence should not have been admitted because the Government failed to prove to the District Court that the televisions were in fact stolen.

Petitioner argues from the premise that evidence of similar acts has a grave potential for causing improper prejudice. For instance, the jury may choose to punish the defendant for the similar rather than the charged act, or the jury may infer that the defendant is an evil person inclined to violate the law. Because of this danger, petitioner maintains, the jury ought not to be exposed to similar act evidence until the trial court has heard the evidence and made a determination under Federal Rule of Evidence 104(a) that the defendant committed the similar act. Rule 104(a) provides that "[p]reliminary questions concerning the qualification of a person to be a witness, the existence of a privilege, or the admissibility of evidence shall be determined by the court, subject to the provisions of subdivision (b)." According to petitioner, the trial court must make this preliminary finding by at least a preponderance of the evidence.

We reject petitioner's position, for it is inconsistent with the structure of the Rules of Evidence and with the plain language of Rule 404(b). Article IV of the Rules of Evidence deals with the relevancy of evidence. Rules 401 and 402 establish the broad principle that relevant evidence—evidence that makes the existence of any fact at issue more or less probable—is admissible unless the Rules provide otherwise. Rule 403 allows the trial judge to exclude relevant evidence if, among other things, "its probative value is substantially out-

---

2. Petitioner does not dispute that Nelson's testimony concerning the Amana appliances was properly admitted under Rule 404(b).

weighed by the danger of unfair prejudice." Rules 404 through 412 address specific types of evidence that have generated problems. Generally, these latter Rules do not flatly prohibit the introduction of such evidence but instead limit the purpose for which it may be introduced. Rule 404(b), for example, protects against the introduction of extrinsic act evidence when that evidence is offered solely to prove character. The text contains no intimation, however, that any preliminary showing is necessary before such evidence may be introduced for a proper purpose. If offered for such a proper purpose, the evidence is subject only to general strictures limiting admissibility such as Rules 402 and 403.

Petitioner's reading of Rule 404(b) as mandating a preliminary finding by the trial court that the act in question occurred not only superimposes a level of judicial oversight that is nowhere apparent from the language of that provision, but it is simply inconsistent with the legislative history behind Rule 404(b). The Advisory Committee specifically declined to offer any "mechanical solution" to the admission of evidence under 404(b). Advisory Committee's Notes on Fed. Rule Evid. 404(b), 28 U.S.C.App., p. 691. Rather, the Committee indicated that the trial court should assess such evidence under the usual rules for admissibility: "The determination must be made whether the danger of undue prejudice outweighs the probative value of the evidence in view of the availability of other means of proof and other factors appropriate for making decisions of this kind under Rule 403." Ibid. see also S.Rep. No. 93–1277, p. 25 (1974) ("[I]t is anticipated that with respect to permissible uses for such evidence, the trial judge may exclude it only on the basis of those considerations set forth in Rule 403, i.e. prejudice, confusion or waste of time").

Petitioner's suggestion that a preliminary finding is necessary to protect the defendant from the potential for unfair prejudice is also belied by the Reports of the House of Representatives and the Senate. The House made clear that the version of Rule 404(b) which became law was intended to "plac[e] greater emphasis on admissibility than did the final Court version." H.R.Rep. No. 93–650, p. 7 (1973). The Senate echoed this theme: "[T]he use of the discretionary word 'may' with respect to the admissibility of evidence of crimes, wrongs, or other acts is not intended to confer any arbitrary discretion on the trial judge." S.Rep. No. 93–1277, supra, at 24. Thus, Congress was not nearly so concerned with the potential prejudicial effect of Rule 404(b) evidence as it was with ensuring that restrictions would not be placed on the admission of such evidence.

We conclude that a preliminary finding by the court that the Government has proved the act by a preponderance of the evidence is not called for under Rule 104(a).[3] This is not to say, however, that the Government may parade past the jury a litany of potentially prejudicial similar acts that have been established or connected to the defendant only by unsubstantiated innuendo. Evidence is admissible under Rule 404(b) only if it is relevant. "Relevancy is not an inherent characteristic of any item of evidence but exists only as a relation between an item of evidence and a matter properly provable in the case." Advisory Committee's Notes on Fed.Rule Evid. 401, 28 U.S.C. App., p. 688. In

---

3. Petitioner also suggests that in performing the balancing prescribed by Federal Rule of Evidence 403, the trial court must find that the prejudicial potential of similar acts evidence substantially outweighs its probative value unless the court concludes by a preponderance of the evidence that the defendant committed the similar act. We reject this suggestion because Rule 403 admits of no such gloss and because such a holding would be erroneous for the same reasons that a preliminary finding under Rule 104(a) is inappropriate. We do, however, agree with the Government's concession at oral argument that the strength of the evidence establishing the similar act is one of the factors the court may consider when conducting the Rule 403 balancing. Tr. of Oral Arg. 26.

the Rule 404(b) context, similar act evidence is relevant only if the jury can reasonably conclude that the act occurred and that the defendant was the actor. See United States v. Beechum, 582 F.2d 898, 912–913 (C.A.5 1978) (en banc). In the instant case, the evidence that petitioner was selling the televisions was relevant under the Government's theory only if the jury could reasonably find that the televisions were stolen.

Such questions of relevance conditioned on a fact are dealt with under Federal Rule of Evidence 104(b). Beechum, supra, at 912–913; see also E. Imwinkelried, Uncharged Misconduct Evidence § 2.06 (1984). Rule 104(b) provides:

> "When the relevancy of evidence depends upon the fulfillment of a condition of fact, the court shall admit it upon, or subject to, the introduction of evidence sufficient to support a finding of the fulfillment of the condition."

In determining whether the Government has introduced sufficient evidence to meet Rule 104(b), the trial court neither weighs credibility nor makes a finding that the Government has proved the conditional fact by a preponderance of the evidence. The court simply examines all the evidence in the case and decides whether the jury could reasonably find the conditional fact—here, that the televisions were stolen—by a preponderance of the evidence. See 21 C. Wright & K. Graham, Federal Practice and Procedure § 5054, p. 269 (1977). The trial court has traditionally exercised the broadest sort of discretion in controlling the order of proof at trial, and we see nothing in the Rules of Evidence that would change this practice. Often the trial court may decide to allow the proponent to introduce evidence concerning a similar act, and at a later point in the trial assess whether sufficient evidence has been offered to permit the jury to make the requisite finding.[4] If the proponent has failed to meet this minimal standard of proof, the trial court must instruct the jury to disregard the evidence.

We emphasize that in assessing the sufficiency of the evidence under Rule 104(b), the trial court must consider all evidence presented to the jury. "[I]ndividual pieces of evidence, insufficient in themselves to prove a point, may in cumulation prove it. The sum of an evidentiary presentation may well be greater than its constituent parts." Bourjaily v. United States, 483 U.S. 171, 179–180, 107 S.Ct. 2775, 2781, 97 L.Ed.2d 144 (1987). In assessing whether the evidence was sufficient to support a finding that the televisions were stolen, the court here was required to consider not only the direct evidence on that point— the low price of the televisions, the large quantity offered for sale, and petitioner's inability to produce a bill of sale—but also the evidence concerning petitioner's involvement in the sales of other stolen merchandise obtained from Wesby, such as the Memorex tapes and the Amana appliances. Given this evidence, the jury reasonably could have concluded that the televisions were stolen, and the trial court therefore properly allowed the evidence to go to the jury.

---

4. "When an item of evidence is conditionally relevant, it is often not possible for the offeror to prove the fact upon which relevance is conditioned at the time the evidence is offered. In such cases it is customary to permit him to introduce the evidence and 'connect it up' later. Rule 104(b) continues this practice, specifically authorizing the judge to admit the evidence 'subject to' proof of the preliminary fact. It is, of course, not the responsibility of the judge sua sponte to insure that the foundation evidence is offered; the objector must move to strike the evidence if at the close of the trial the offeror has failed to satisfy the condition." 21 C. Wright & K. Graham, Federal Practice and Procedure § 5054, pp. 269–270 (1977) (footnotes omitted).

We share petitioner's concern that unduly prejudicial evidence might be introduced under Rule 404(b). See Michelson v. United States, 335 U.S. 469, 475–476, 69 S.Ct. 213, 218–219, 93 L.Ed. 168 (1948). We think, however, that the protection against such unfair prejudice emanates not from a requirement of a preliminary finding by the trial court, but rather from four other sources: first, from the requirement of Rule 404(b) that the evidence be offered for a proper purpose; second, from the relevancy requirement of Rule 402—as enforced through Rule 104(b); third, from the assessment the trial court must make under Rule 403 to determine whether the probative value of the similar acts evidence is substantially outweighed by its potential for unfair prejudice,[5] see Advisory Committee's Notes on Fed.Rule Evid. 404(b), 28 U.S.C. App., p. 691; S.Rep. No. 93–1277, at 25; and fourth, from Federal Rule of Evidence 105, which provides that the trial court shall, upon request, instruct the jury that the similar acts evidence is to be considered only for the proper purpose for which it was admitted. See United States v. Ingraham, 832 F.2d 229, 235 (C.A.1 1987).

Affirmed.

NOTES

1. How is the evidence of the sale of the TV's relevant to defendant's knowledge that the tapes were stolen? What is the source of the Court's requirement that in order for other crime evidence to be admissible, there must be sufficient evidence to support a finding that the defendant committed the other crime? Rule 404(b)? Rule 403? Rule 402? Rule 104?

2. One of the fullest discussions of burden of proof in regard to other crime evidence is People v. Albertson, 145 P.2d 7, 20–22, 30–32 (Cal.1944), demanding "substantial evidence" but not proof beyond a reasonable doubt. At the penalty phase of a trial, on the other hand, the California court does demand that other crimes be established beyond a reasonable doubt, People v. Polk, 406 P.2d 641 (Cal. 1965), cert. denied, 384 U.S. 1010 (1966), but not non-criminal misconduct. People v. Coleman, 459 P.2d 248, 254 (Cal. 1969).

The states take different positions on the question: People v. Garner, 806 P.2d 366 (Colo.1991): Trial court must determine that more probably than not the other crime was committed and the defendant committed it; Huddleston rejected; adoption of Rule 404 had the effect of displacing the earlier clear and convincing test. State v. Trainor, 540 A.2d 1236 (N.H.1988): There must be clear and convincing evidence. Benson v. State, 395 A.2d 361 (Del.1978): Evidence must be "substantial," "plain, clear and conclusive." Cross v. State, 386 A.2d 757, 764 (Md.1978): Evidence must be clear and convincing to the trial judge. People v. Duncan, 260 N.W.2d 58, 60–61 (Mich.1977): "Sufficient to convince the jury of the probability of the defendant's actions."

3. Should an instruction be given to the jury? In Ernster v. State, 308 S.W.2d 33 (Tex.Crim.App. 1957), defendant was prosecuted for "misrepresenting a written instrument affecting property." The charge was that defendant had secured a veteran's signature on an application and contract of sale covering a certain parcel of land by misrepresenting the contents of these documents. Testimony of other veterans was admitted that defendant had, through similar misrepresentations, also obtained their signatures on applications and contracts

---

5. As petitioner's counsel conceded at oral argument, petitioner did not seek review of the Rule 403 balancing performed by the courts below. Tr. of Oral Arg. 14. We therefore do not address that issue.

of sale for parcels of land included in the same subdivision as the litigated parcel. This testimony was limited to showing defendant's "intent and motive" in respect to the misrepresentation with which he was charged. Defendant requested, but was refused, an instruction that before the jury could consider the other transactions, it must find beyond a reasonable doubt that the other misrepresentations had been made, that they had been made with intent to defraud, and that the persons to whom the misrepresentations were made had relied upon them. The appellate court reversed because of the failure to instruct that the jury could not consider the other offenses unless they believed beyond a reasonable doubt that defendant was guilty of them. One judge, dissenting, maintained that no such burden rested on the state, and that "[i]t was the fact that appellant made the same or similar misrepresentations as to the contents of the instruments to others of the group, and not the fact that other veterans relied upon such misrepresentations that was material and was relied upon by the state to show an intent to defraud the veteran named in the indictment."

United States v. Sampson, 980 F.2d 883 (3d Cir.1992): When other crime evidence is admitted for a noncharacter use, court must guide jury as to that use. See Imwinkelried, A Small Contribution to the Debate over the Proposed Legislation Abolishing the Character Evidence Prohibition in Sex Offense Prosecutions, 44 Syracuse L. Rev. 1125, 1140–44 (1993), discussing the effectiveness of limiting instructions with particular reference to other crime evidence.

Acquittal of the Other Crime

In Dowling v. United States, 493 U.S. 342 (1990), the Supreme Court held that the collateral estoppel component of the Double Jeopardy Clause of the Fifth Amendment does not bar use of evidence of another crime—in the litigated case as tending to show identity—even though the defendant has been acquitted of the other crime. According to the Court, the meaning of an acquittal is only that the guilt of the defendant has not been established beyond a reasonable doubt and that such a burden need not be satisfied to justify use of evidence of the other crime in another case. The Court added that even if collateral estoppel applied, it was not relevant to the litigated case because the defendant had not carried his burden of showing that his not being one of the intruders in the earlier case was necessarily established in that case: he may have been acquitted for some other reason. See also United States v. Watts, 117 S.Ct. 633 (1997): Federal sentencing judge may take into account defendant's commission of another offense, even though there has been an acquittal, if the other offense is proved by a preponderance of the evidence.

With Dowling compare State v. Little, 350 P.2d 756, 762, 764 (Ariz.1960):

We do not agree, however, that the effect of the prior acquittal should be determined by a strict application of the rules of res judicata or collateral estoppel. Although a verdict of acquittal may not necessarily mean that the jury found that the prior sale did not in fact take place, such a finding is a possible and indeed reasonable inference to be drawn from the verdict. Further, the relevance of the alleged prior sale as part of a plan or scheme may be doubted in the absence of proof of criminality of that prior sale. Thus, if the acquittal is based on an implied finding that the product sold was not sufficiently proved to be a narcotic or that defendant did not know that it was such, the sale could not reasonably be part of a plan knowingly to sell narcotics unless the jury in the instant action is permitted to find, contrary to the finding of the jury in the first action, that the defendant illegally and knowingly sold what was in fact a narcotic.

. . .

The fact of an acquittal, we feel, when added to the tendency of such evidence to prove the defendant's bad character and criminal propensities, lowers the scale to the side of inadmissibility of such evidence. The factors which lead us to this balancing may, perhaps, not be subject to precise articulation, but we note two points. As discussed in connection with the third assignment of error above, the relevance of the evidence of the prior offense depends upon the court's or jury's drawing two separate inferences, thus lessening the probative weight of such evidence; where the significance of such evidence must, if the doctrine of res judicata or collateral estoppel is to be given any effect, be determined in the light of the record and verdict of the former trial, the evidence of such former offense tends to become remote, speculative or confusing.

Further, to the extent that evidence of the prior offense tends to prove the instant offense, the defendant is required, in order to avoid conviction and punishment for the instant offense, to refute, for the second time, his commission of the prior offense. A verdict of acquittal should relieve the defendant from having to answer again, at the price of conviction for that crime or another, evidence which amounts to a charge of a crime of which he has been acquitted.

We hold that the evidence herein of the prior offense of which defendant was acquitted is inadmissible. . . .

United States v. Felix, 503 U.S. 378, 112 S.Ct. 1377 (1992): Introduction of evidence of crime X in prosecution for crime Y, perhaps under Fed. R. Evid. 404(b), does not bar subsequent prosecution for crime X. People v. Griffin, 426 P.2d 507 (Cal. 1967): Not error to admit evidence of a crime of which defendant had been acquitted, but error not to allow evidence of the acquittal to be introduced. The hearsay problem is discussed. In People v. Peete, 169 P.2d 924 (Cal.), cert. denied, 329 U.S. 790 (1946), supra p. 848, the prosecution suggested on the appeal that the fact that defendant had been convicted of the earlier murder made the question res judicata. But the court did not find it necessary to deal with this contention, since at the trial defendant had been allowed, without objection, to testify that she did not commit the earlier crime. In some contexts collateral estoppel has been successfully employed against a criminal defendant. See United States v. Bejar–Matrecios, 618 F.2d 81 (9th Cir.1980).

People v. Castillo

Court of Appeals of New York, 1979.
417 N.Y.S.2d 915, 391 N.E.2d 997.

Opinion of the Court

■ FUCHSBERG, JUDGE.

After a jury trial, defendant Leonel Castillo was convicted on charges that grew out of two separate criminal incidents two days apart. The counts relating to the earlier criminal episode—first degree robbery, first degree burglary and first degree sexual abuse—were dismissed by the Appellate Division on the facts and in the interest of justice. The case was then remanded for sentencing on the surviving count, one for attempted burglary that resulted from his participation in the later incident. Castillo now contends that there was no proof of his intention to commit attempted burglary and that that charge must now be dismissed or, alternatively, that in any event the jury's consideration of his guilt or innocence on that count was so infected (1) by the evidence and charge relating to the now dismissed counts, and (2) by evidence that he was walking around in the vicinity of the crimes on a day subsequent to his arrest that a new trial is required. For the reasons that follow, we agree that retrial and not dismissal is warranted.

The first incident occurred at approximately 4:00 A.M. on August 27, 1975 at the third floor apartment of a Bronx family when their adult daughter was awakened by a male intruder. The man threatened her, took a sum of money, kissed her face, fondled parts of her body and then fled when she screamed. Because the room was unlit, she could describe her assailant to the police only as a Black teenage male and provided no further identifying characteristics. In particular, though the intruder spoke during the incident, she noticed nothing distinctive about his speech.

On August 29, again in the early morning hours, the victim's father and brother awoke to discover a man walking along a window ledge outside the apartment. According to the father, the man was trying to pull open the bathroom window. The police were summoned but the intruder was gone when they arrived. However, they found defendant, who answered the general description of the perpetrator furnished to them, walking on the street a short distance from the building. He was then taken to the premises, where he was identified by the father and son as the man they had seen on the ledge. The daughter, viewing Castillo through a peephole in the door, at that time also identified him as the man who had assaulted her two nights previously.

Defendant, a Guatemalan native who speaks halting and heavily accented English, was at the time of these crimes 28 years of age. At his trial, after producing several character witnesses, he took the stand in his own defense and denied any involvement in either crime. His version of the events of August 29 was simply that he had been walking on his way to the butcher shop where he was employed when the police came upon him. According to Castillo, his job commenced at 5:00 A.M. and the street on which the apartment house, where the crimes occurred, is located was roughly half way between his home and his place of employment. As to the August 27 incident, Castillo asserted that he had taken a bus to work that morning and did not leave his home until 4:15 A.M.

In reversing the counts pertaining to the August 27 episode, the Appellate Division found that "under all the circumstances, there exists a substantial possibility of misidentification leading inevitably to the creation of a reasonable doubt" (62 A.D.2d 938, 939, 403 N.Y.S.2d 746, 747). In remanding for resentencing on the remaining count, the court did so to afford the Trial Judge the opportunity to cure the taint that the dismissed counts might have worked on his exercise of sentencing discretion; it otherwise allowed the conviction on that count to stand. We hold that this limited remedy was insufficient. As it turned out, the joinder of the August 29 count with the counts that must now be viewed as based entirely upon a misidentification worked ineradicable prejudice on Castillo's right to a fair trial on the charge of attempted burglary.

That prejudice was preordained by the very tenor of defendant's trial, the product of an assiduous effort by the prosecutor to orchestrate the evidence relevant to both incidents into a single theme: that Castillo was engaged in a pattern of criminal activity. Doubtless the Assistant District Attorney's strenuous opposition to the defendant's prompt motion for severance was motivated in part by a desire to use to full advantage the undeniable similarities as to time and place in the two criminal episodes, a motivation at least conceptually proper before the weakness of the identification testimony revealed itself (see People v. Molineux, 168 N.Y. 264, 305–306, 61 N.E. 286, 299–300). Thus, the trial strategy blurred the separate features of each incident to a point where it cannot be said that the proofs relating to one episode did not supplement deficiencies in the proof on key elements of the other.

Specifically, the earlier incident tended not merely to bolster the witnesses' identification of Castillo as the man on the ledge and to undermine Castillo's defense, but, further, provided the prosecution with a compelling argument as to the defendant's intent on August 29. In fact, the Trial Judge instructed the jury that "On the question of the intent to commit a crime in the dwelling . . . you may infer such intent from the manner of attempted entry and considering the time of night *or if you find that this defendant was, in fact, the perpetrator of the acts alleged to have occurred on August 27th . . . then you may infer from such prior acts on these premises an intent to commit the same or similar crimes on August 29th.*" (Italics supplied.) Defendant's counsel took exception and the court twice reformulated the latter half of its instruction, but it only served to emphasize to the jury that the inference could be drawn from defendant's participation in the earlier incident: "if as I say you find he was the person on both occasions . . . you may infer from the acts on August 27th an intent on August 29th to repeat the same or similar criminal action or conduct." Despite the phrasing of the intent charge in the alternative, the *option* to determine that intent from the subsequently dismissed counts could easily have overborne the jury's consideration of the circumstances of the attempted entry.

In comparison to the bare circumstance of Castillo's having been seen on the window ledge tugging at the window, the impact of the August 27 proof was utterly damning. Most obvious was its almost irresistible tendency to connect the defendant with a prior course of criminality, curious in its similarity. This evidence, since found to be admissible against Castillo on the dismissed counts only, was calculated to play upon the jury's natural inclination to view a defendant who has been accused of committing such crimes in the past as either the kind of person likely to have committed the crime charged or as deserving of punishment in any event (see People v. Jackson, 39 N.Y.2d 64, 67–68, 382 N.Y.S.2d 736, 737–738, 346 N.E.2d 537, 538–539; People v. Molineux, 168 N.Y. 264, 293, 61 N.E. 286, 294, supra; cf. People v. Davis, 44 N.Y.2d 269, 274, 405 N.Y.S.2d 428, 430, 376 N.E.2d 901, 903). Aggravating the prejudice was the inflammatory nature of that prior crime. Further, and most devastating when combined with the Judge's charge on intent, was the fact that the prior crime placed Castillo *inside* the apartment.

All this tended to deny the defendant his right to have the jury fairly evaluate only the evidence admissible against him on the attempted burglary count. Left to infer the defendant's intent to commit a crime within the apartment from the proof relating to that uncompleted event alone, the jury could have found he had engaged only in trespassing or voyeurism or, since only one witness testified that he "pulled on the window" and it is conceded that he never gained access to the apartment, even the lesser included offense of attempted trespass (see People v. Henderson, 41 N.Y.2d 233, 236–237, 391 N.Y.S.2d 563, 566–567, 359 N.E.2d 1357, 1359–1360). These outcomes were precluded by the Appellate Division's restriction of its remand to the matter of the sentence.

. . .

For all these reasons, the order of the Appellate Division, insofar as appealed from, should be reversed and a new trial ordered on the fourth count of the indictment.

■ CHIEF JUDGE COOKE, and JUDGES JASEN, GABRIELLI, JONES and WACHTLER concur with JUDGE FUCHSBERG.

Order, insofar as appealed from, reversed, etc.

NOTES

1. Leaving aside the complication arising from the weakness of the identification testimony relating to the incident of August 27th and the dismissal of the counts relating to that incident, was it proper in People v. Castillo to join the charges relating to the August 27th and August 29th incidents? Was evidence relating to one incident admissible to prove the other?

In Drew v. United States, 331 F.2d 85 (D.C.Cir.1964), defendant was indicted for a robbery committed on July 27, 1962, and for an attempted robbery on August 13, 1962. His motions for separate trials of the two offenses were denied and he was convicted on both counts. In reversing the convictions for failure to grant separate trials, the court made the following observations:

> The justification for a liberal rule on joinder of offenses appears to be the economy of a single trial. The argument against joinder is that the defendant may be prejudiced for one or more of the following reasons: (1) he may become embarrassed or confounded in presenting separate defenses; (2) the jury may use the evidence of one of the crimes charged to infer a criminal disposition on the part of the defendant from which is found his guilt of the other crime or crimes charged; or (3) the jury may cumulate the evidence of the various crimes charged and find guilt when, if considered separately, it would not so find.

> . . .

> If, then, under the rules relating to [the admissibility of evidence of] other crimes, the evidence of each of the crimes on trial would be admissible in a separate trial for the other, the possibility of "criminal propensity" prejudice would be in no way enlarged by the fact of joinder. . . .

> The federal courts, including our own, have, however, found no prejudicial effect from joinder when the evidence of each crime is simple and distinct, even though such evidence might not have been admissible in separate trials under the rules just discussed. This rests upon the assumption that, with a proper charge, the jury can easily keep such evidence separate in their deliberations and, therefore, the danger of the jury's cumulating the evidence is substantially reduced. [The court here cited Judge Learned Hand's opinion in United States v. Lotsch, 102 F.2d 35 (2d Cir.1939).]

> . . .

> Judge Hand recognizes the possibility, of course, that the jury may misuse the evidence, no matter how simple and separable; his position is merely that the possibility is somewhat reduced. However, the possibility of the jury's becoming hostile or inferring guilt from belief as to criminal disposition is just as substantial. For this reason great care must be exercised to protect the defendant from this possibility when joinder is tolerated under this theory.

In summary, then, even where the evidence would not have been admissible in separate trials, if, from the nature of the crimes charged, it appears that the prosecutor might be able to present the evidence in such a manner that the accused is not confounded in his defense and the jury will be able to treat the evidence relevant to each charge separately and distinctly, the trial judge need not order a severance or election at the commencement of the trial. If, however, it appears at any later stage in the trial that the defendant will be embarrassed in making his defense or that there is a possibility that the jury will become or has become confused, then, upon proper motion, the trial judge should order severance.

The court went on to examine the facts of the particular case and to conclude that in a separate trial for either offense the evidence of the other offense would not have been admissible. The circumstances of the crimes were not of sufficient similarity, nor were they part of a single transaction or continuing state of affairs, so as to justify admission under any exception to the general rule excluding evidence of other crimes. The court concluded, moreover, that the jury could well have been confused by the presentation of the evidence, for the record indicated uncertainty at times in the questions of counsel and the answers of witnesses as to which crime was being referred to.

These lapses do not appear to have been purposeful, but lack of improper motivation does not lessen their impact on the jury. If separate crimes are to be tried together—and we are not to be understood as intimating any conclusion that this can never, as a practical matter, be successfully undertaken—both court and counsel must recognize that they are assuming a difficult task the performance of which calls for a vigilant precision in speech and action far beyond that required in the ordinary trial. The confusion here was probably the result of the superficial similarity of the two crimes and the way in which they were committed.[1] On this record, we cannot say that the jury probably did not misuse the evidence, as Judge Hand was able to hold in Lotsch.

For these reasons we find that there was prejudice in the joinder and the court below should have granted separate trials. Id. at 88, 90–94.

United States v. Halper, 590 F.2d 422 (2d Cir.1978): Defendant, owner of a diagnostic laboratory, was convicted of filing fraudulent medicaid claims and failure to report taxable income. The charges were tried together. The appellate court held that the joinder was prejudicial and in violation of Fed.R.Crim.Proc. 8(a) (governing joinder of counts) and Fed.R.Crim.Proc. 13 (governing the trial together of two or more indictments), and remanded for separate trials. The court held that evidence of the two crimes with which defendant was charged was not mutually admissible in separate trials. The court endorsed the rule laid down in Drew v. United States, supra. It added, furthermore: "[E]ven where evidence of the joined offenses might be mutually admissible in separate trials, we advise prosecutors and trial courts to exercise caution with regard to the joinder of 'same or similar character' offenses. . . . '[T]he evidence put forth to prove an offense for which a defendant is tried will generally be more extensive, and thus more damaging, than that which would be adduced to establish a prior crime as proof of such matters as motive or intent.' " Id. at 431.

---

1. The Government strenuously argues that the two crimes were sufficiently similar to come within the "identity" exception to the "other crimes" rule. However, once that argument has been rejected, the "similarity" point cuts the other way. Every suggestion at the trial that the two crimes were closely parallel increases the likelihood that the jury may become confused or misuse the evidence. The more similar the crime, the more careful the trial court and Government counsel must be to keep the evidence separate. [Footnote of the court. Other footnotes of the court have been omitted.]

United States v. Daniels, 770 F.2d 1111 (D.C.Cir.1985): Prosecution for armed robbery (count 1), unlicensed possession of a pistol (count 2), and possession of a firearm after being convicted of a felony (count 3). In order to establish count 3, a stipulation was read to the jury that defendant had been convicted of an unspecified felony. It was conceded that this fact would not have been admissible in a separate trial of counts 1 and 2. Held: The joinder of count 3 with counts 1 and 2 did not in the circumstances of the case cause undue prejudice. The court observed, however: "Unfortunately, a side consequence of the law [making it illegal for an ex-felon to possess firearms] has been to provide federal prosecutors with a powerful tool for circumventing the traditional rule against introduction of other crimes evidence. Whenever an ex-felon is charged with committing a crime involving the use of a gun, prosecutors may inform the jury of the defendant's prior convictions merely by taking the time to include a charge of firearms possession." Id. at 1118.

United States v. Figueroa, 618 F.2d 934 (2d Cir.1980), supra p. 835, involved a joint trial of three defendants for heroin trafficking. After finding that evidence of a prior crime of one of the defendants had been erroneously admitted against him and required a new trial for him, the court went on to hold that a new trial was also required for the other defendants. Notwithstanding a limiting instruction, they had been unfairly prejudiced. The court's opinion includes a careful discussion of all aspects of the problem of other crimes evidence in joint trials and compares it with the problem in such trials of hearsay statements made by defendants. See also People v. Chambers, 41 Cal.Rptr. 551 (App.1964); Dawson, Joint Trials of Defendants in Criminal Cases: An Analysis of Efficiencies and Prejudices, 77 Mich.L.Rev. 1379, 1444–47 (1979).

2. See Lynch, RICO: The Crime of Being a Criminal, 87 Colum.L.Rev. 661, 920 (1987), on the wide admissibility of evidence of criminal activity under 18 U.S.C. § 1962(c) (1982), a section of the Racketeer Influenced and Corrupt Organization Act (RICO) that makes it a crime "for any person employed by or associated with any enterprise" in or affecting commerce "to conduct or participate, directly or indirectly, in the conduct of such enterprise's affairs through a pattern of racketeering activity or collection of unlawful debt."

Such a commitment is not, in any conventional sense, an "act." The jury's task is to assess in a global way the nature of the defendant's involvement in a network of criminal activities and associations, to determine whether the total picture of the defendant's criminal career permits the judgment that he has become part of an underworld "enterprise." If character can be defined as the residue of a series of moral decisions, the jury in a very real sense is being asked to make a judgment on the defendant's character.

In making such a judgment, the jury is entitled to rely not only on evidence of the defendant's own crimes, but also on evidence of the crimes of those with whom he is alleged to have thrown in his lot. Such evidence is excluded from the transaction-model trial, precisely because it may distract the jury from its responsibility of deciding what the evidence shows about a particular act. In an illicit-enterprise RICO trial, it is admitted, precisely because the jury is asked to make a judgment not only about what discrete acts the defendant committed at particular moments in time, and what his intention was with respect to each act at those moments, but also about how those acts fit into his entire moral life: Were they parts of a pattern? Were they committed as part of his association with a subculture of crime?

Id. at 944.[2]

3. Courts have dealt extensively with the use of other crimes evidence in the context of the defense of entrapment. When the defendant claims entrapment, the prosecution may meet this claim by showing that the defendant was predisposed to commit the crime. See Sherman v. United States, 356 U.S. 369 (1958). In order to show predisposition, the prosecution may introduce evidence of the defendant's criminal record. However, if the probative value of the evidence is weak and the danger of use to show guilt of the crime with which the defendant is charged is great, the evidence may be excluded. See Hansford v. United States, 303 F.2d 219 (D.C.Cir.1962); State v. Gibbons, 519 A.2d 350 (N.J.1987); United States v. Blankenship, 775 F.2d 735, 739–40 (6th Cir.1985). But see United States v. Mack, 643 F.2d 1119 (5th Cir.1981); United States v. Segovia, 576 F.2d 251 (9th Cir.1978). How is the admission of evidence of other crimes to show predisposition justified under Fed.R.Evid. 404? See United States v. Murzyn, 631 F.2d 525 (7th Cir.1980), cert. denied, 450 U.S. 923 (1981).

4. The admission of other crimes evidence on the question of penalty has presented difficult questions. Under the United States Sentencing Guidelines, § 1B1.3, the penalty may be increased if it is established that the defendant has committed an offense "relevant" to the offense for which he is convicted. In the federal courts before the Guidelines, and in many state courts, a sentencing judge could take into account the defendant's past crimes and a wide range of information relating to his life and character. See Williams v. New York, 337 U.S. 241 (1949). A range of information nearly as broad is often presented to the jury when it is to determine the penalty, at least when it determines the penalty in a separate proceeding after guilt has been determined. See, e.g., People v. Terry, 390 P.2d 381 (Cal.), cert. denied, 379 U.S. 866 (1964). What use may be made of other crime evidence, however, when the jury is to determine guilt and punishment in a single proceeding? See Spencer v. Texas, 385 U.S. 554 (1967), and McGautha v. California, 402 U.S. 183 (1971), for partial answers to this question under the Due Process Clause.

5. Is there a constitutional barrier to the use of other crime evidence to show guilt? If there is, what is its relation to the nonconstitutional other crimes rule explored in this section of the casebook? McKinney v. Rees, 993 F.2d 1378 (9th Cir.), cert. denied, 510 U.S. 1020 (1993): The defendant was convicted in a state court of murdering his mother. Her throat had been cut with a knife. The issue in dispute was the identity of the killer. Held: Due Process was violated and the trial rendered fundamentally unfair by the admission of evidence that some months before the mother's death, defendant had possessed two knives, one of which had been taken from him before the crime and the other he also probably did not possess at the time of the crime, and that he was interested in knives, proud of his knife collection and sometimes wore camouflage pants with a knife strapped to his leg. Compare People v. Zackowitz, supra p. 808. See Spencer v. Texas, 385 U.S. 554, 562–64 (1967); id. at 572–75 (Warren, C.J., dissenting); Estelle v. McGuire, 502 U.S. 62, 75 n. 5 (1991) (not reaching question whether Due Process violated by propensity use of other crime evidence); Advisory Committee Note to Fed. R. Evid. 404(a); Liebman, Proposed Evidence Rules 413 to 415—Some Problems and Recommendations, 20 U. Dayton L. Rev. 753, 757–58 (1995) (cases raising question of constitutional status of other crime rule); Patterson, Evidence of Prior Bad Acts: Admissibility Under the Federal Rules, 38 Baylor L. Rev. 331, 336 n. 20, 359–61 (1986). In Estelle v. Williams, 425 U.S. 501 (1976), the Court held that the Fourteenth Amendment would be

---

2. Footnote omitted.

violated if the accused were compelled to stand before the jury in identifiable prison clothes.

SECTION 2.   EVIDENCE OF A CRIMINAL DEFENDANT'S REPUTATION AND OPINION EVIDENCE OF HIS CHARACTER; EVIDENCE OF VICTIM'S CHARACTER

Michelson v. United States

Supreme Court of the United States, 1948.
335 U.S. 469, 69 S.Ct. 213, 93 L.Ed. 168.

■ MR. JUSTICE JACKSON delivered the opinion of the Court.

In 1947 petitioner Michelson was convicted of bribing a federal revenue agent. The Government proved large payment by accused to the agent for the purpose of influencing his official action. The defendant, as a witness on his own behalf, admitted passing the money but claimed it was done in response to the agent's demands, threats, solicitations, and inducements that amounted to entrapment. It is enough for our purposes to say that determination of the issue turned on whether the jury should believe the agent or the accused.

On direct examination of defendant, his own counsel brought out that, in 1927, he had been convicted of a misdemeanor having to do with trading in counterfeit watch dials. On cross-examination it appeared that in 1930, in executing an application for a license to deal in second-hand jewelry, he answered "No" to the question whether he had theretofore been arrested or summoned for any offense.

Defendant called five witnesses to prove that he enjoyed a good reputation. Two of them testified that their acquaintance with him extended over a period of about thirty years and the others said they had known him at least half that long. A typical examination in chief was as follows:

"Q. Do you know the defendant Michelson? A. Yes.

"Q. How long did you know Mr. Michelson? A. About 30 years.

"Q. Do you know other people who know him? A. Yes.

"Q. Have you had occasion to discuss his reputation for honesty and truthfulness and for being a law-abiding citizen? A. It is very good.

"Q. You have talked to others? A. Yes.

"Q. And what is his reputation? A. Very good."

These are representative of answers by three witnesses; two others replied, in substance, that they never had heard anything against Michelson.

On cross-examination, four of the witnesses were asked, in substance, this question: "Did you ever hear that Mr. Michelson on March 4, 1927, was convicted of a violation of the trademark law in New York City in regard to watches?" This referred to the twenty-year-old conviction about which defendant himself had testified on direct examination. Two of them had heard of it and two had not.

To four of these witnesses the prosecution also addressed the question the allowance of which, over defendant's objection, is claimed to be reversible error:

"Did you ever hear that on October 11th, 1920, the defendant, Solomon Michelson, was arrested for receiving stolen goods?"

None of the witnesses appears to have heard of this.

The trial court asked counsel for the prosecution, out of presence of the jury, "Is it a fact according to the best information in your possession that Michelson was arrested for receiving stolen goods?" Counsel replied that it was, and to support his good faith exhibited a paper record which defendant's counsel did not challenge.

The judge also on three occasions warned the jury, in terms that are not criticized, of the limited purpose for which this evidence was received.[1]

Defendant-petitioner challenges the right of the prosecution so to cross-examine his character witnesses. The Court of Appeals held that it was permissible. The opinion, however, points out that the practice has been severely criticized and invites us, in one respect, to change the rule.[2] Serious

1. In ruling on the objection when the question was first asked, the Court said: "... I instruct the jury that what is happening now is this: the defendant has called character witnesses, and the basis for the evidence given by those character witnesses is the reputation of the defendant in the community, and since the defendant tenders the issue of his reputation the prosecution may ask the witness if she has heard of various incidents in his career. I say to you that regardless of her answer you are not to assume that the incidents asked about actually took place. All that is happening is that this witness' standard of opinion of the reputation of the defendant is being tested. Is that clear?"

In overruling the second objection to the question the Court said: "Again I say to the jury there is no proof that Mr. Michelson was arrested for receiving stolen goods in 1920, there isn't any such proof. All this witness has been asked is whether he had heard of that. There is nothing before you on that issue. Now would you base your decision on the case fairly in spite of the fact that that question has been asked? You would? All right."

The charge included the following: "In connection with the character evidence in the case I permitted a question whether or not the witness knew that in 1920 this defendant had been arrested for receiving stolen goods. I tried to give you the instruction then that the question was permitted only to test the standards of character evidence that these character witnesses seemed to have. There isn't any proof in the case that could be produced before you legally within the rules of evidence that this defendant was arrested in 1920 for receiving stolen goods, and that fact you are not to hold against him; nor are you to assume what the consequences of that arrest were. You just drive it from your mind so far as he is concerned, and take it into consideration only in weighing the evidence of the character witnesses."

[Footnotes 1–23 inclusive are parts of the original report, any editorial addition being bracketed. Some of the Court's footnotes have been omitted.]

2. Footnote 8 to that court's opinion reads as follows [165 F.2d at 735]:

"Wigmore, Evidence (3d ed. 1940) § 988, after noting that 'such inquiries are almost universally admitted,' not as 'impeachment by extrinsic testimony of particular acts of misconduct,' but as means of testing the character 'witness' grounds of knowledge,' continues with these comments: 'But the serious objection to them is that practically the above distinction—between rumors of such conduct, as affecting reputation, and the fact of it as violating the rule against particular facts—cannot be maintained in the mind of the jury. The rumor of the misconduct, when admitted, goes far, in spite of all theory and of the judge's charge, towards fixing the misconduct as a fact upon the other person, and thus does three improper things,—(1) it violates the fundamental rule of fairness that prohibits the use of such facts, (2) it gets at them by hearsay only, and not by trustworthy testimony, and (3) it leaves the other person no means of defending himself by denial or explanation, such as he would otherwise have had if the rule had allowed that conduct to be made the subject of an issue. Moreover, these are not occurrences of possibility, but of daily practice. This method of inquiry or cross-examination is frequently resorted to by counsel for the very purpose of injuring by indirection a character which they are forbidden directly to attack in that way; they rely upon the mere putting of the question (not caring that it is answered negatively) to convey their covert insinuation. The value of the inquiry for testing purposes is often so small and the opportunities of its abuse by underhand ways are so great that the practice may amount to little more than a mere subterfuge, and should be strictly supervised by forbidding it to counsel who do not use it in good faith.'

"Because, as Wigmore says, the jury almost surely cannot comprehend the judge's

and responsible criticism has been aimed, however, not alone at the detail now questioned by the Court of Appeals but at common-law doctrine on the whole subject of proof of reputation or character.[3] It would not be possible to appraise the usefulness and propriety of this cross-examination without consideration of the unique practice concerning character testimony, of which such cross-examination is a minor part.[4]

Courts that follow the common-law tradition almost unanimously have come to disallow resort by the prosecution to any kind of evidence of a defendant's evil character to establish a probability of his guilt.[5] Not that the law invests the defendant with a presumption of good character, Greer v. United States, 245 U.S. 559, 38 S.Ct. 209, 62 L.Ed. 469, but it simply closes the whole matter of character, disposition and reputation on the prosecution's case-in-chief. The State may not show defendant's prior trouble with the law, specific criminal acts, or ill name among his neighbors, even though such facts might logically be persuasive that he is by propensity a probable perpetrator of the crime.[6] The inquiry is not rejected because character is irrelevant,[7] on the contrary, it is said to weigh too much with the jury and to so overpersuade them as to prejudge one with a bad general record and deny him a fair opportunity to defend against a particular charge. The overriding policy of excluding such evidence, despite its admitted probative value, is the practical experience that its disallowance tends to prevent confusion of issues, unfair surprise and undue prejudice.[8]

But this line of inquiry firmly denied to the State is opened to the

limiting instruction, the writer of this opinion wishes that the United States Supreme Court would tell us to follow what appears to be the Illinois rule, i.e., that such questions are improper unless they relate to offenses similar to those for which the defendant is on trial. See Aiken v. People, 183 Ill. 215, 55 N.E. 695; cf. People v. Hannon, 381 Ill. 206, 44 N.E.2d 923."

3. A judge of long trial and appellate experience has uttered a warning which, in the opinion of the writer, we might well have heeded in determining whether to grant certiorari here: "... evidence of good character is to be used like any other, once it gets before the jury, and the less they are told about the grounds for its admission, or what they shall do with it, the more likely they are to use it sensibly. The subject seems to gather mist which discussion serves only to thicken, and which we can scarcely hope to dissipate by anything further we can add." L. Hand in Nash v. United States, 2 Cir., 54 F.2d 1006, 1007.

In opening its cyclopedic review of authorities from many jurisdictions, Corpus Juris Secundum summarizes that the rules regulating proof of character "have been criticized as illogical, unscientific, and anomolous, explainable only as archaic survivals of compurgation or of states of legal development when the jury personally knew the facts on which their verdict was based." 32 C.J.S., Evidence, § 433.

4. See Maguire, Evidence: Common Sense and Common Law (1947). Compare pp. 203–209 and pp. 74–76.

5. Greer v. United States, 245 U.S. 559, 38 S.Ct. 209, 62 L.Ed. 469; 1 Wigmore, Evidence (3d ed., 1940) § 57; 1 Wharton, Criminal Evidence (11th ed., 1935) § 330. This was not the earlier rule in English common law and is not now the rule in some civil law countries. 1 Wigmore, Evidence (3d ed., 1940) § 193.

6. This would be subject to some qualification, as when a prior crime is an element of the later offense; for example, at a trial for being an habitual criminal. There are also well-established exceptions where evidence as to other transactions or a course of fraudulent conduct is admitted to establish fraudulent intent as an element of the crime charged....

7. As long ago as 1865, Chief Justice Cockburn said, "The truth is, this part of our law is an anomaly. Although logically speaking, it is quite clear that an antecedent bad character would form quite as reasonable a ground for the presumption and probability of guilt as previous good character lays the foundation of innocence, yet you cannot, on the part of the prosecution, go into evidence as to character." Regina v. Rowton, 10 Cox's Criminal Cases 25, 29–30. And see 1 Wigmore, Evidence (3d ed., 1940) § 55.

8. 1 Wigmore, Evidence (3d ed., 1940) § 57.

defendant because character is relevant in resolving probabilities of guilt.[9] He may introduce affirmative testimony that the general estimate of his character is so favorable that the jury may infer that he would not be likely to commit the offense charged. This privilege is sometimes valuable to a defendant for this Court has held that such testimony alone, in some circumstances, may be enough to raise a reasonable doubt of guilt and that in the federal courts a jury in a proper case should be so instructed. Edgington v. United States, 164 U.S. 361, 17 S.Ct. 72, 41 L.Ed. 467.

When the defendant elects to initiate a character inquiry, another anomalous rule comes into play. Not only is he permitted to call witnesses to testify from hearsay, but indeed such a witness is not allowed to base his testimony on anything but hearsay.[10] What commonly is called "character evidence" is only such when "character" is employed as a synonym for "reputation." The witness may not testify about defendant's specific acts or courses of conduct or his possession of a particular disposition, or of benign mental and moral traits; nor can he testify that his own acquaintance, observation, and knowledge of defendant leads to his own independent opinion that defendant possesses a good general or specific character, inconsistent with commission of acts charged. The witness is, however, allowed to summarize what he has heard in the community, although much of it may have been said by persons less qualified to judge than himself. The evidence which the law permits is not as to the personality of defendant but only as to the shadow his daily life has cast in his neighborhood. This has been well described in a different connection as "the slow growth of months and years, the resultant picture of forgotten incidents, passing events, habitual and daily conduct, presumably honest because disinterested, and safer to be trusted because prone to suspect.... It is for that reason that such general repute is permitted to be proven. It sums up a multitude of trivial details. It compacts into the brief phrase of a verdict the teaching of many incidents and the conduct of years. It is the average intelligence drawing its conclusion." Finch, J., in Badger v. Badger, 88 N.Y. 546, 552, 42 Am.Rep. 263.

While courts have recognized logical grounds for criticism of this type of opinion-based-on-hearsay testimony, it is said to be justified by "overwhelming considerations of practical convenience" in avoiding innumerable collateral issues which, if it were attempted to prove character by direct testimony, would complicate and confuse the trial, distract the minds of jurymen and befog the chief issues in the litigation. People v. Van Gaasbeck, 189 N.Y. 408, 418, 82 N.E. 718, 22 L.R.A., N.S., 650, 12 Ann.Cas. 745.

Another paradox in this branch of the law of evidence is that the delicate and responsible task of compacting reputation hearsay into the "brief phrase of a verdict" is one of the few instances in which conclusions are accepted from a witness on a subject in which he is not an expert. However, the witness must qualify to give an opinion by showing such acquaintance with the defendant, the community in which he has lived and the circles in which he has moved, as to speak with authority of the terms in which generally he is regarded. To require affirmative knowledge of the reputation may seem inconsistent with the latitude given to the witness to testify when all he can say of the reputation is that he has "heard nothing against defendant." This is permitted upon

---

9. 1 Wigmore, Evidence (3d ed., 1940) § 56; Underhill, Criminal Evidence (4th ed., 1935) § 165; 1 Wharton, Criminal Evidence (11th ed., 1935) §§ 330, 336.

10. 5 Wigmore, Evidence (3d ed., 1940) § 1609; Underhill, Criminal Evidence (4th ed., 1935) § 170; 1 Wharton, Criminal Evidence (11th ed., 1935) § 333.

assumption that, if no ill is reported of one, his reputation must be good.[11] But this answer is accepted only from a witness whose knowledge of defendant's habitat and surroundings is intimate enough so that his failure to hear of any relevant ill repute is an assurance that no ugly rumors were about.[12]

Thus the law extends helpful but illogical options to a defendant. Experience taught a necessity that they be counterweighted with equally illogical conditions to keep the advantage from becoming an unfair and unreasonable one. The price a defendant must pay for attempting to prove his good name is to throw open the entire subject which the law has kept closed for his benefit and to make himself vulnerable where the law otherwise shields him. The prosecution may pursue the inquiry with contradictory witnesses[13] to show that damaging rumors, whether or not well-grounded, were afloat—for it is not the man that he is, but the name that he has which is put in issue. Another hazard is that his own witness is subject to cross-examination as to the contents and extent of the hearsay on which he bases his conclusions, and he may be required to disclose rumors and reports that are current even if they do not affect his own conclusion.[14] It may test the sufficiency of his knowledge by asking what stories were circulating concerning events, such as one's arrest, about which people normally comment and speculate. Thus, while the law gives defendant the option to show as a fact that his reputation reflects a life and habit incompatible with commission of the offense charged, it subjects his proof to tests of credibility designed to prevent him from profiting by a mere parade of partisans.

To thus digress from evidence as to the offense to hear a contest as to the standing of the accused, at its best opens a tricky line of inquiry as to a shapeless and elusive subject matter. At its worst it opens a veritable Pandora's box of irresponsible gossip, innuendo and smear. In the frontier phase of our law's development, calling friends to vouch for defendant's good character, and its counterpart—calling the rivals and enemies of a witness to impeach him by testifying that his reputation for veracity was so bad that he was unworthy of belief on his oath—were favorite and frequent ways of converting an individual litigation into a community contest and a trial into a spectacle. Growth of urban conditions, where one may never know or hear the name of his next-door neighbor, have tended to limit the use of these techniques and to deprive them of weight with juries. The popularity of both procedures has subsided, but courts of last resort have sought to overcome danger that the true issues will be obscured and confused by investing the trial court with discretion to limit the number of such witnesses and to control cross-examination. Both propriety and

---

11. People v. Van Gaasbeck, 189 N.Y. 408, 420, 82 N.E. 718, 22 L.R.A., N.S., 650, 12 Ann.Cas. 745. The law apparently ignores the existence of such human ciphers as Kipling's Tomlinson, of whom no ill is reported but no good can be recalled. They win seats with the righteous for character evidence purposes, however hard their lot in literature.

12. Id.; 5 Wigmore, Evidence (3d ed., 1940) § 1614; Underhill, Criminal Evidence (4th ed., 1935) § 171; 1 Wharton, Criminal Evidence (11th ed., 1935) § 334.

13. 1 Wigmore, Evidence (3d ed., 1940) § 58; Underhill, Criminal Evidence (4th ed., 1935) § 167; 1 Wharton, Criminal Evidence (11th ed., 1935) § 330.

14. A classic example in the books is a character witness in a trial for murder. She testified she grew up with defendant, knew his reputation for peace and quiet, and that it was good. On cross-examination she was asked if she had heard that the defendant had shot anybody and, if so, how many. She answered, "Three or four," and gave the names of two but could not recall the names of the others. She still insisted, however, that he was of "good character." The jury seems to have valued her information more highly than her judgment, and on appeal from conviction the cross-examination was held proper. People v. Laudiero, 192 N.Y. 304, 309, 85 N.E. 132. See also People v. Elliott, 163 N.Y. 11, 57 N.E. 103.

abuse of hearsay reputation testimony, on both sides, depend on numerous and subtle considerations, difficult to detect or appraise from a cold record, and therefore rarely and only on clear showing of prejudicial abuse of discretion will Courts of Appeals disturb rulings of trial courts on this subject.[15]

Wide discretion is accompanied by heavy responsibility on trial courts to protect the practice from any misuse. The trial judge was scrupulous to so guard it in the case before us. He took pains to ascertain, out of presence of the jury, that the target of the question was an actual event, which would probably result in some comment among acquaintances if not injury to defendant's reputation. He satisfied himself that counsel was not merely taking a random shot at a reputation imprudently exposed or asking a groundless question to waft an unwarranted innuendo into the jury box.[16]

The question permitted by the trial court, however, involves several features that may be worthy of comment. Its form invited hearsay; it asked about an arrest, not a conviction, and for an offense not closely similar to the one on trial; and it concerned an occurrence many years past.

Since the whole inquiry, as we have pointed out, is calculated to ascertain the general talk of people about defendant, rather than the witness' own knowledge of him, the form of inquiry, "Have you heard?" has general approval, and "Do you know?" is not allowed.[17]

A character witness may be cross-examined as to an arrest whether or not it culminated in a conviction, according to the overwhelming weight of authority.[18] This rule is sometimes confused with that which prohibits cross-examination to credibility by asking a witness whether he himself has been arrested.

Arrest without more does not, in law any more than in reason, impeach the integrity or impair the credibility of a witness. It happens to the innocent as

---

15. See, e.g., Mannix v. United States, 4 Cir., 140 F.2d 250. It has been held that the question may not be hypothetical nor assume unproven facts and ask if they would affect the conclusion, Little v. United States, 8 Cir., 93 F.2d 401; Pittman v. United States, 8 Cir., 42 F.2d 793; Filippelli v. United States, 9 Cir., 6 F.2d 121; and that it may not be so asked as to detail evidence or circumstances of a crime of which defendant was accused. People v. Marendi, 213 N.Y. 600, 107 N.E. 1058. It has been held error to use the question to get before the jury a particular derogatory newspaper article. Sloan v. United States, 8 Cir., 31 F.2d 902. The proof has been confined to general reputation and that among a limited group such as fellow employees in a particular building held inadmissible. Williams v. United States, 168 U.S. 382, 18 S.Ct. 92, 42 L.Ed. 509.

16. This procedure was recommended by Wigmore. But analysis of his innovation emphasizes the way in which law on this subject has evolved from pragmatic considerations rather than from theoretical consistency. The relevant information that it is permissible to lay before the jury is talk or conversation about the defendant's being arrested. That is admissible whether or not an actual arrest had taken place; it might even be more significant of repute if his neighbors

were ready to arrest him in rumor when the authorities were not in fact. But before this relevant and proper inquiry can be made, counsel must demonstrate privately to the court an irrelevant and possibly unprovable fact—the reality of arrest. From this permissible inquiry about reports of arrest, the jury is pretty certain to infer that defendant had in fact been arrested and to draw its own conclusions as to character from that fact. The Wigmore suggestion thus limits legally relevant inquiries to those based on legally irrelevant facts in order that the legally irrelevant conclusion which the jury probably will draw from the relevant questions will not be based on unsupported or untrue innuendo. It illustrates Judge Hand's suggestion that the system may work best when explained least. Yet, despite its theoretical paradoxes and deficiencies, we approve the procedure as calculated in practice to hold the inquiry within decent bounds.

17. See Stewart v. United States, 70 App.D.C. 101, 104 F.2d 234; Little v. United States, 8 Cir., 93 F.2d 401; Filippelli v. United States, 9 Cir., 6 F.2d 121.

18. See Mannix v. United States, 4 Cir., 140 F.2d 250; Josey v. United States, 77 U.S.App.D.C. 321, 135 F.2d 809; Spalitto v. United States, 8 Cir., 39 F.2d 782, and authorities there cited.

well as the guilty. Only a conviction, therefore, may be inquired about to undermine the trustworthiness of a witness.

Arrest without more may nevertheless impair or cloud one's reputation. False arrest may do that. Even to be acquitted may damage one's good name if the community receives the verdict with a wink and chooses to remember defendant as one who ought to have been convicted. A conviction, on the other hand, may be accepted as a misfortune or an injustice, and even enhance the standing of one who mends his ways and lives it down. Reputation is the net balance of so many debits and credits that the law does not attach the finality to a conviction, when the issue is reputation, that is given to it when the issue is the credibility of the convict.

The inquiry as to an arrest is permissible also because the prosecution has a right to test the qualifications of the witness to bespeak the community opinion. If one never heard the speculations and rumors in which even one's friends indulge upon his arrest, the jury may doubt whether he is capable of giving any very reliable conclusions as to his reputation.

In this case the crime inquired about was receiving stolen goods; the trial was for bribery. The Court of Appeals thought this dissimilarity of offenses too great to sustain the inquiry in logic, though conceding that it is authorized by preponderance of authority. It asks us to substitute the Illinois rule which allows inquiry about arrest, but only for very closely similar if not identical charges, in place of the rule more generally adhered to in this country and in England.[19] We think the facts of this case show the proposal to be inexpedient.

The good character which the defendant had sought to establish was broader than the crime charged and included the traits of "honesty and truthfulness" and "being a law-abiding citizen." Possession of these character-istics would seem as incompatible with offering a bribe to a revenue agent as with receiving stolen goods. The crimes may be unlike, but both alike proceed from the same defects of character which the witnesses said this defendant was reputed not to exhibit. It is not only by comparison with the crime on trial but by comparison with the reputation asserted that a court may judge whether the prior arrest should be made subject of inquiry. By this test the inquiry was permissible. It was proper cross-examination because reports of his arrest for receiving stolen goods, if admitted, would tend to weaken the assertion that he was known as an honest and law-abiding citizen. The cross-examination may take in as much ground as the testimony it is designed to verify. To hold otherwise would give defendant the benefit of testimony that he was honest and law-abiding in reputation when such might not be the fact; the refutation was founded on convictions equally persuasive though not for crimes exactly repeated in the present charge.

The inquiry here concerned an arrest twenty-seven years before the trial. Events a generation old are likely to be lived down and dropped from the present thought and talk of the community and to be absent from the knowledge of younger or more recent acquaintances. The court in its discretion may well exclude inquiry about rumors of an event so remote, unless recent misconduct revived them. But two of these witnesses dated their acquaintance with defendant as commencing thirty years before the trial. Defendant, on direct examination, voluntarily called attention to his conviction twenty years

19. The Supreme Court of Illinois, in considering its own rule which we are urged to adopt, recognized that "the rule adhered to in this State is not consistent with the great weight of authority in this country and in England." People v. Hannon, 381 Ill. 206, 209, 44 N.E.2d 923, 924. Authorities in all states are collected in State v. Shull, 131 Or. 224, 282 P. 237, 71 A.L.R. 1504.

before. While the jury might conclude that a matter so old and indecisive as a 1920 arrest would shed little light on the present reputation and hence propensities of the defendant, we cannot say that, in the context of this evidence and in the absence of objection on this specific ground, its admission was an abuse of discretion.

We do not overlook or minimize the consideration that "the jury almost surely cannot comprehend the Judge's limiting instructions," which disturbed the Court of Appeals. The refinements of the evidentiary rules on this subject are such that even lawyers and judges, after study and reflection, often are confused, and surely jurors in the hurried and unfamiliar movement of a trial must find them almost unintelligible. However, limiting instructions on this subject are no more difficult to comprehend or apply than those upon various other subjects; for example, instructions that admissions of a codefendant are to be limited to the question of his guilt and are not to be considered as evidence against other defendants, and instructions as to other problems in the trial of conspiracy charges. A defendant in such a case is powerless to prevent his cause from being irretrievably obscured and confused; but, in cases such as the one before us, the law foreclosed this whole confounding line of inquiry, unless defendant thought the net advantage from opening it up would be with him. Given this option, we think defendants in general and this defendant in particular have no valid complaint at the latitude which existing law allows to the prosecution to meet by cross-examination an issue voluntarily tendered by the defense. See Greer v. United States, 245 U.S. 559, 38 S.Ct. 209, 62 L.Ed. 469.

We end as we began, with the observation that the law regulating the offering and testing of character testimony may merit many criticisms. England, and some states have overhauled the practice by statute.[20] But the task of modernizing the longstanding rules on the subject is one of magnitude and difficulty which even those dedicated to law reform do not lightly undertake.[21]

The law of evidence relating to proof of reputation in criminal cases has developed almost entirely at the hands of state courts of last resort, which have such questions frequently before them. This Court, on the other hand, has contributed little to this or to any phase of the law of evidence, for the reason, among others, that it has had extremely rare occasion to decide such issues, as the paucity of citations in this opinion to our own writings attests. It is obvious that a court which can make only infrequent sallies into the field cannot recast the body of case law on this subject in many, many years, even if it were clear what the rules should be.

We concur in the general opinion of courts, textwriters and the profession that much of this law is archaic, paradoxical and full of compromises and compensations by which an irrational advantage to one side is offset by a poorly

---

20. Criminal Evidence Act, 61 & 62, Vict. c. 36. See also 51 L.Q.Rev. 443, for discussion of right to cross-examine about prior arrests. For review of English and state legislation, see 1 Wigmore, Evidence (3d ed., 1940) § 194, et seq. The Pennsylvania statute, Act of March 15, 1911, P.L. 20, § 1, discussed by Wigmore has been amended, Act of July 3, 1947, P.L. 1239, § 1, 19 P.S. § 711. The current statute and Pennsylvania practice were considered recently by the Superior Court of that state. Commonwealth v. Hurt, 163 Pa.Super. 232, 60 A.2d 828.

21. The American Law Institute, in promulgating its "Model Code of Evidence," includes the comment, "Character, whenever used in these Rules, means disposition not reputation. It denotes what a person is, not what he is reputed to be. No rules are laid down as to proof of reputation, when reputation is a fact to be proved. When reputation is a material matter, it is proved in the same manner as is any other disputed fact." Rule 304. The latter sentence may seem an over-simplification in view of the decisions.

reasoned counter-privilege to the other. But somehow it has proved a workable even if clumsy system when moderated by discretionary controls in the hands of a wise and strong trial court. To pull one misshapen stone out of the grotesque structure is more likely simply to upset its present balance between adverse interests than to establish a rational edifice.

The present suggestion is that we adopt for all federal courts a new rule as to cross-examination about prior arrest, adhered to by the courts of only one state and rejected elsewhere.[22] The confusion and error it would engender would seem too heavy a price to pay for an almost imperceptible logical improvement, if any, in a system which is justified, if at all, by accumulated judicial experience rather than abstract logic.[23]

The judgment is

Affirmed.[24]

NOTES

1. If a character witness is asked on cross-examination whether he has heard that some bad act was committed by the defendant and he answers that he has not, he is not impeached is he? If the bad act could be shown by extrinsic evidence, perhaps the witness would be impeached, but the Michelson opinion states that extrinsic evidence may not be introduced for this purpose. Why may it not be? If the witness is a reputation witness and he admits having heard of the bad act, what is the reasoning that leads to the conclusion that he has been impeached? Fed. R. Evid. 405(a) states: "On cross-examination, inquiry is allowable into relevant specific instances of conduct." But see People v. Nyberg, 656 N.E.2d 65, 75 (Ill.App.1995): Cross-examination of reputation witness must be confined to his knowledge of disparaging rumors and conversations and may not extend to the witness's knowledge of the defendant's acts.

Contrary to the situation that existed at the time of the Michelson decision, Fed. R. Evid. 405 now permits opinion of character testimony as well as testimony about reputation. How does this change affect permissible cross-examination? United States v. Curtis, 644 F.2d 263, 268–70 (3d Cir.1981):

> If, as here, their [the character witnesses'] direct testimony is addressed to community reputation, inquiry may be about conduct, and even about charges, which may have come to the attention of the relevant community.... If, on the other hand, opinion evidence is offered in proof of character, relevant cross examination is only that which bears on the fact or factual basis for formation of the opinion.

. . .

Evidence Rule 405(a) has not effected a merger between reputation and opinion evidence. The reference in the rule's second sentence to cross examination on "relevant specific instances of conduct" is to instances of conduct relevant to the type of testimony offered on direct examination. Thus an opinion witness can be cross examined only on matters bearing on his own opinion, while a reputation witness can only be examined on

---

22.   See note 19.

23.   It must not be overlooked that abuse of cross-examination to test credibility carries its own corrective. Authorities on practice caution the bar of the imprudence as well as the unprofessional nature of attacks on witnesses or defendants which are likely to be resented by the jury. Wellman, Art of Cross Examination (1927) p. 167 et seq.

24.   The concurrence of Justice Frankfurter and the dissent of Justice Rutledge, in which Justice Murphy joined, are omitted.

matters reasonably proximate to the time of the alleged offense and likely to have been known to the relevant community at that time.

But see People v. Hurd, 85 Cal.Rptr. 718, 726–28 (App. 1970): Defendant's witness testified to his opinion of defendant's moral character based upon his own contact with defendant and conversations with others. On cross-examination the prosecutor asked the witness whether he had heard of arrests and convictions of defendant for various offenses. The trial court's allowance of such cross-examination was upheld by the appellate court. Cf. State v. Martin, 365 A.2d 104, 107 (Conn.1976).

United States v. Oshatz, 912 F.2d 534, 539 (2d Cir.1990), cert. denied, 500 U.S. 910 (1991): Error, though not prejudicial, for prosecutor to ask defendant's character witness whether he would have the same opinion of the defendant's character if he assumed the defendant's guilt of the offense with which he was charged.

> We do not doubt that to some extent a guilt-assuming hypothetical question might be probative of the credibility of testimony given by a non-expert character witness. Steadfast adherence to a favorable opinion by a witness asked to assume the defendant's guilt might provide some basis for concluding that the witness is simply supporting the defendant, rather than providing credible testimony about his character. But we share the view ... that such cross-examination is nevertheless to be prohibited because it creates too great a risk of impairing the presumption of innocence. Moreover, after a jury has repeatedly heard a prosecutor assure a trial judge that he has a good-faith basis for asking permitted hypothetical questions, the jury might infer from the judge's permission to ask a guilt-based hypothetical question that the prosecutor has evidence of guilt beyond the evidence in the record.

Compare United States v. White, 887 F.2d 267, 274 (D.C.Cir.1989): Hypothetical assuming guilt of offense with which defendant charged permissible if witness testified to his opinion of the defendant's character, although perhaps not if witness testified to reputation.

2.   People v. Kramer, 66 Cal.Rptr. 638, 648 (App. 1968): Abortion prosecution. Defendant introduced testimony of witnesses (doctors, the president of a medical school, a lawyer, a dentist, a pharmacist and a minister) to his reputation as an ethical medical practitioner. On cross-examination the prosecutor asked some of these witnesses whether they had heard reports among students at the University of California at Riverside, frequenters of bars in Riverside, nurses in Riverside and the Mexican–American community in Riverside that defendant was the one to see for an abortion. In affirming the order of the trial court from which defendant appealed, the appellate court stated:

> [G]ood faith requires, in addition to factual support for the matters inferred in the question, that the question be asked in anticipation of an affirmative response and not simply for the purpose of getting an innuendo before the jury.... While questions pertaining to defendant's reputation in a particular segment of the community may be proper on cross-examination of character witnesses where, as here, the trait involved is the professional reputation of a doctor as an ethical general medical practitioner, good faith requires a preliminary showing that the witness has acquaintances among or contacts with the particular segment either through foundational questions to the witness or by other good faith showing outside the presence of the jury which would satisfy the judge that there is a reasonable basis for anticipating an affirmative response from the witness that he has heard such reports.... In the instances when objections

were interposed, the record shows that the witnesses, a dentist and an attorney, testified that they did have professional contacts with persons in the group mentioned in the question.

See also People v. Pratt, 759 P.2d 676, 683–85 (Colo.1988): Necessity of good faith; determination of basis should be in absence of jury. In Awkard v. United States, 352 F.2d 641 (D.C.Cir.1965), a conviction was reversed because the prosecutor had been allowed to ask about arrests and convictions that had taken place in communities and at times that it was clear from the reputation witnesses' testimony were not within their knowledge.

People v. Dorrikas, 92 N.W.2d 305 (Mich.1958), reversed a conviction because the trial court had failed to make a determination, out of the presence of the jury, as to whether the arrests and convictions that the prosecutor asked defendant's reputation witnesses about had actually occurred. The error was serious enough to warrant reversal even though defendant had made no objection at trial. What standard of proof should govern the determination by the trial court? In People v. Alamo, 246 N.E.2d 496 (N.Y.), cert. denied, 396 U.S. 879 (1969), the court found there was an adequate basis for believing the defendant had committed the offenses inquired about, but there was a strong dissent. The case also involved the related question of the "good faith" requirement in asking a witness, for purposes of impeachment, about his misconduct. See supra p. 435.

3. The Court's opinion in Michelson justifies cross-examining reputation witnesses about whether they heard that defendant had been arrested for receiving stolen goods on the ground that "the crimes may be unlike, but both alike proceed from the same defects of character which the witnesses said this defendant was reputed not to exhibit." In United States v. Wooden, 420 F.2d 251 (D.C.Cir.1969), a prosecution for burglary, it was held error to allow cross-examination of witnesses who had testified to defendant's reputation for honesty, integrity, peaceableness and good order concerning a conviction for drunkenness. On the other hand, see Travis v. United States, 247 F.2d 130, 132–33, 136 (10th Cir.1957), a prosecution of a union official for filing a false non-Communist affidavit. Although defendant's witnesses only testified to his good reputation for truth and veracity, the prosecutor was allowed to ask them if they had heard that defendant had been convicted of contempt for disobeying a court order. On appeal, this was found not to be error. In State v. Moorman, 321 P.2d 236 (Mont.1958), a statutory rape case, defendant's witnesses testified to his reputation for "morality." It was held to be permissible to ask them on cross-examination whether they had heard that defendant did not support his child and had shot at his wife.

4. There is authority contrary to the statement made in footnote 15 of the Michelson opinion that only "general" reputation may be testified to. In People v. Bouton, 405 N.E.2d 699, 704 (N.Y. 1980), the court stated: Admissible reputation "may grow wherever an individual's associations are of such quantity and quality as to permit him to be personally observed by a sufficient number of individuals to give reasonable assurance of reliability." Under this test, reputation in business circles may be admissible. See also State v. McEachern, 194 S.E.2d 787, 790–94 (N.C.1973) ("any community or society in which the person has a well-known or established reputation"); United States v. Parker, 447 F.2d 826, 830–31 (7th Cir.1971) (reputation among co-workers in the Internal Revenue Service). See supra p. 444 for the same issue regarding reputation for truth and veracity bearing on credibility.

5. United States v. Lewis, 482 F.2d 632 (D.C.Cir.1973), holds inadmissible testimony as to good reputation subsequent to the conduct with which defendant is charged and State v. Hobbs, 172 N.W.2d 268, 274–75 (Iowa 1969), testimony as to good reputation based upon comments made about defendant after prosecution was commenced. United States v. Null, 415 F.2d 1178, 1180 (4th Cir.1969), accepts the general principle stated in Lewis and Hobbs:

> The reason why evidence of reputation of a defendant as of a time subsequent to the time of the act in issue is usually objectionable is, not because it is not relevant, but because of the likelihood that a false reputation has been created as a result of public discussion and partisan feeling about the very act charged or as a result of interested utterances of persons concerned with the prosecution. In short, the objectionable feature is the lack of safeguards of trustworthiness.

However, because in that case the character witnesses in fact had testified to the defendant's reputation at the time of trial, and also because defendant had testified, the prosecutor was allowed to ask the reputation witnesses how defendant's reputation had been affected by the bringing of charges. Even if on direct examination the reputation testified to must be confined to that which existed before the conduct with which the defendant is charged or before the prosecution was begun, might there be theoretical justification for asking on cross-examination whether the witness has heard about later events? State v. Howard, 385 N.E.2d 308 (Ohio.Ct.App.1978), says no, and United States v. Lewis, supra at 643, says perhaps.

6.   In the discussion of character evidence introduced to attack the credibility of a witness, supra p. 445, a question was posed why more than relevance should be required of such evidence. The same question recurs with respect to character evidence, whether of reputation or opinion, offered for substantive use. Justice Jackson addresses himself in Michelson to the qualifications of reputation witnesses and in particular to the necessity for adequate exposure to talk, or lack of talk, about the defendant. Some cases appear to be more demanding than Michelson. An example is State v. Hobbs, supra. There it was held proper to reject the testimony of a reputation witness because the type, number, place, duration and representative nature of the comments he heard from others about the defendant had not been established. In State v. Cross, 343 S.W.2d 20, 24 (Mo.1961), defendant's offer of testimony of a reputation witness was rejected. The witness had been specially employed by defense counsel during the week of the trial to investigate the reputation of defendant in the community in which he lived. Within "more than one day's period of time" he had talked with eighteen or twenty persons living in the immediate area of defendant's residence. On appeal, the rejection of this testimony was sustained on the ground that the witness was not qualified. The court observed, however, that

> Our review convinces us that we should not and we need not hold that a stranger-investigator may never, under any circumstances, acquire the necessary testimonial qualifications on the fact issue of one's general reputation. On the contrary, we are of the view that an investigation and inquiry made for the specific purpose of discovering one's general reputation, may extend over a sufficient time, be broad enough in scope, and be otherwise conducted in such a manner as to enable the investigator reasonably to arrive at a probatively valuable conclusion as to the manner in which a community regards one. We observe, however, that usually it would be safer practice to adhere to the usual and generally approved procedures in adducing general reputation testimony.

7.   The witnesses in Michelson testified to the defendant's good reputation for honesty and truthfulness and for being a peaceable and law-abiding citizen.

Such traits were arguably relevant to the conduct with which he was charged—bribing a revenue agent. Fed. R. Evid. 404(a)(1) permits an accused to introduce evidence of "a pertinent trait of character." In United States v. Angelini, 678 F.2d 380 (1st Cir.1982), the court held that evidence that the defendant was law-abiding was evidence of a pertinent trait of character within the meaning of 404(a)(1): "Pertinent" requires only relevance and being law-abiding constitutes a "trait," although the "defendant's character generally" would not. In United States v. Hewitt, 634 F.2d 277 (5th Cir.1981), a prosecution for unlawful possession or receipt of firearms, it was held not error under 404(a)(1) to exclude evidence of defendant's good character for truth and veracity, this not being a trait pertinent to the crime charged, but it was error to exclude evidence of defendant's character for lawfulness. State v. Vogel, 526 N.W.2d 80 (Neb.1995): Error in prosecution for bribery to exclude evidence of character for honesty. People v. Miller, 890 P.2d 84 (Colo.1995): Not error in prosecution for drug offense to exclude evidence of character for truthfulness. United States v. Diaz, 961 F.2d 1417, 1419 (9th Cir.1992): In prosecution for large scale drug dealing, not error to exclude defendant's character trait of not being prone to large scale drug dealing. "Such an inquiry would be misleading if addressed to a defendant with a record of criminal offenses other than drug dealing.... [T]he impression may be given that the defendant is a law-abiding person although he has a record of other crimes." Is this reasoning persuasive? Did the court believe the evidence did not show a trait of "character"? See Government of Virgin Islands v. Petersen, 553 F.2d 324 (3d Cir.1977): Inquiry into whether defendant had religious beliefs that reject violence did not qualify as evidence of character.

See supra p. 444 on the character admissible to attack the credibility of a witness.

8. As indicated above, Fed. R. Evid. 405(a) permits testimony as to opinion of character as well as about reputation. In the following case, the opening provided by Rule 405(a) was taken advantage of with a vengeance, but to what effect?

> The lawyer for a union leader charged with 12 others in a bribery case faced the problem of countering secretly recorded tapes portraying the defendants as thugs. The answer was nearly 500 character witnesses, many testifying in groups.

> For a week, a parade of union members, widows, priests, nuns and other friends of the union leader, Stephen Traitz Jr., went before the Federal jury to praise him.

> . . .

> In the first day of the defense phase of the trial last week, Mr. Kidd presented about 140 union members, 20 at a time standing shoulder to shoulder, to testify on Mr. Traitz's behalf.

> "Did any of you feel that when Mr. Traitz was handing out those gifts to your kids at Christmas he was bribing them?" Mr. Kidd asked.

> "No," each of the seven groups of roofers answered in unison. Most wore union jackets and one had a tee shirt emblazoned with the message, "Steve-'O, We Love You,"

New York Times, Nov. 8, 1987, p. 32, col. 1.

9. In an earlier discussion of the admissibility of expert testimony relevant to witness credibility, a question was raised whether such testimony concerned character within the meaning of Fed. R. Evid. 405(a). See supra p. 448 and Fed.

R. Evid. 608(a). The same question is presented when expert opinion is offered for substantive use, for instance to show that the defendant did or did not act in a certain way or that he had a certain state of mind at the time he acted. As in the case of expert evidence on credibility, full consideration of this subject must await discussion of the general topic of expert testimony, infra p. 954.

Many cases support the admissibility of expert testimony to show that a person did or did not perform a particular act or form a certain state of mind. People v. Stoll, 783 P.2d 698 (Cal. 1989): In prosecution for sexual abuse of children, error to exclude testimony of psychologist, based on standardized personality tests and an interview, that defendant showed a normal personality function and no indication of deviancy and was not likely to have committed the acts charged. The court adhered to the principles it had laid down in People v. Jones, 266 P.2d 38 (Cal.1954). United States v. Rahm, 993 F.2d 1405, 1411–15 (9th Cir.1993): In prosecution for possessing and attempting to pass counterfeit currency, in which an element of the offense was whether the defendant knew the currency was counterfeit, error to exclude testimony of psychologist that standardized tests showed defendant had a tendency to overlook important visual details and that her personality style might be marked by lack of insight. United States v. Roberts, 887 F.2d 534 (5th Cir.1989): In prosecution for possession of cocaine with intent to distribute, error to exclude expert testimony that defendant had a naive and autocratic personality that made it unlikely his intention was to violate the law, but likely that he would engage in an unauthorized, one-man undercover operation. United States v. Hill, 655 F.2d 512 (3d Cir.1981), cert. denied, 464 U.S. 1039 (1984): In a narcotics prosecution in which the defense was entrapment, error to exclude testimony of a psychologist that defendant had a unique susceptibility to inducement. State v. Christensen, 628 P.2d 580 (Ariz.1981): In a prosecution for murder, error to exclude testimony of a psychologist that defendant had difficulty dealing with stress and that in a stressful situation his reactions would be more reflexive than reflective, as bearing on premeditation.

However, there is substantial resistance. United States v. Webb, 625 F.2d 709 (5th Cir.1980): Prosecution for shooting at a helicopter. Not error to exclude testimony of witnesses called by defendant that, based on psychological tests, he was nonviolent and not likely to shoot at a helicopter. Painter v. Commonwealth, 171 S.E.2d 166, 171–72 (Va.1969): In prosecution for murder, not error to exclude testimony of doctors as to defendant's mental make-up bearing on his state of mind at the time of the homicide. State v. Hulbert, 481 N.W.2d 329 (Iowa 1992): In prosecution for sexual abuse of child, not abuse of discretion to exclude testimony of psychologist, based on tests, that defendant did not fit the profile of child molester. United States v. Williams, 957 F.2d 1238 (5th Cir.1992): Error to admit prosecution evidence of drug courier profile.

Lowery v. The Queen, [1974] A.C. 85, [1973] 3 All E.R. 662 (P.C.) (Australia). In a prosecution for the brutal and sadistic murder of a young girl, the contention of the Crown was that both defendants acted in concert as principals or that one was a principal and the other an aider and abetter. Each of the defendants attempted to place primary responsibility on the other. Defendant L introduced evidence to the effect that he had no motive to kill the girl and that he was a person who would not have been interested in the sort of behavior manifested by the killer. Held, in these circumstances, it was error to allow defendant K to introduce the testimony of a psychologist who had examined both defendants and administered intelligence and personality tests to both, that defendant L had a sadistic streak in his personality, whereas defendant K did not, and that K was a person likely to be dominated by others.

And yet, "If in imaginary circumstances similar to those of this case it was apparent that one of the accused was a man of great physical strength whereas the other was a weakling it could hardly be doubted that in forming an opinion as to the probabilities it would be relevant to have the disparity between the two in mind." Id. at 671.

Compare Regina v. McMillan, 23 C.C.C.2d 160 (Ont.Ct.App.1975), aff'd, 33 C.C.C.2d 360 (S.Ct.1977): Prosecution of a father for murder of his infant child. A defense theory was that defendant's wife, not defendant, had caused the injuries that led to the child's death. The defendant introduced psychiatric evidence that his wife was a psychopath. The admission of this evidence was held not to be error. However, this evidence and the fact that "the entire nature of the defence involved an assertion that the respondent was a person of normal make-up," opened the way for prosecution evidence of the defendant's mental make-up. Id. at 177.

State v. Loebach, 310 N.W.2d 58 (Minn.1981): Defendant was charged with the murder of a 3–year-old child. The child had been born when the defendant was married to its mother, but it was biologically the child of another man. The child died of injuries to the head. To establish that defendant had inflicted these injuries, the prosecution introduced the testimony of a caseworker, who had known defendant when he was a juvenile, that defendant's mother had abused him and that defendant was not good at controlling his anger; the testimony of an employee of a school for disturbed adolescents, which defendant had attended for three years, that defendant often withdrew from others and had a low frustration level; and the testimony of a doctor that adults who abuse their children often have been abused themselves, and that "battering parents" frequently exhibit low empathy, short temper and lack of self-esteem. Held: Error, although harmless, to admit evidence of the "battering parent" syndrome or to establish the character of the defendant as a "battering parent." "We feel this finding is required until further evidence of the scientific accuracy and reliability of syndrome or profile diagnoses can be established." Id. at 64.

See Curran, Expert Psychiatric Evidence of Personality Traits, 103 U.Pa. L.Rev. 999 (1955), 42 Calif.L.Rev. 880 (1954); Falknor & Steffen, Evidence of Character: From the "Crucible of the Community" to the "Couch of the Psychiatrist," 102 U.Pa.L.Rev. 980 (1954). See also Ahrens, Scientific Evidence and the Law: Identification, Verification of Verbal Testimony and Psychological Proof, 13 N.Y.L.For. 612, 632–34 (1967); Allen, Admission of Psychiatric Evidence, 8 Ariz.L.Rev. 205, 225 (1967).

10. A defendant ordinarily may not prove good character by particular instances of his conduct. See Fed. R. Evid. 405(a). In United States v. White, 225 F.Supp. 514, 519, 521–22 (D.D.C.1963), a murder prosecution, the court held it had not committed error in refusing to admit evidence of defendant's conduct as a boy, employee and husband tending to establish his peaceful disposition. State v. Reeder, 904 P.2d 644 (Or.Ct.App.1995): In prosecution for sexual abuse of child, not error to exclude evidence focused on defendant's activities with other children and his not engaging in misconduct with them. State v. Galliano, 639 So.2d 440 (La.Ct.App.1994): In rape prosecution in which consent was the issue, testimony of another woman with whom defendant had had an intimate relationship, that defendant had never forced sex on her inadmissible. United States v. Burke, 781 F.2d 1234 (7th Cir.1985): Prosecution of private investigator for extorting money from his clients by falsely representing to them that there was a criminal investigation of their business underway and that it was necessary to pay FBI agents to stop the investigation. Defendant contended his purpose was to lead the clients on to find out why they would pay so much money to escape indictment and then turn them over to the FBI, thereby obtaining publicity for his business. Held: Not abuse of discretion to exclude evidence, offered by defendant, that in earlier years he had provided information to the FBI. Did the evidence in this case fall under the ban of Fed. R. Evid. 404? Would its admission risk prejudice to the government?

If the prosecution has been allowed to introduce evidence of prior crimes under an exception to the general exclusionary rule, defendant may be allowed to introduce evidence of particular instances of his conduct to rebut the inference arising from the prosecution's evidence. Thus in United States v. Shavin, 287 F.2d 647, 652–54 (7th Cir.1961), defendant was prosecuted for mail fraud in presenting to insurance companies copies of medical bills alleged to be larger than the doctors' actual bills. The government was allowed to introduce evidence of other occasions on which defendant had presented overstated bills to insurance companies to bear on his intent on the litigated occasions. Under these circumstances, the court held, it was error not to allow defendant to present evidence of further instances in which he had presented correct bills.

11.   Moves by a defendant designed to put his character in a good light may expose him to retaliation that would not otherwise be allowed. In Bond v. State, 403 N.E.2d 812 (Ind.1980), a prosecution for murder and kidnapping, the court held that because the defendant had introduced the testimony of a psychologist that he had no homicidal tendencies, it was not error to admit prosecution evidence of prior acts of violence. Other cases hold that if a defendant makes a sweeping assertion of virtue and good character, the way is open for the prosecution to introduce evidence of his criminal record. See People v. Westek, 190 P.2d 9, 13–18 (Cal.1948); State v. Wilson, 320 S.W.2d 525 (Mo.1959); State v. Costakos, 169 A.2d 383 (R.I.1961). Jackson v. State, 48 S.E.2d 864, 870 (Ga.1948), was an automobile homicide case. Defendant did not testify but made an unsworn statement, which included assertions that he had never been in trouble before with anybody and had only been in jail twice. It was held that the prosecution was properly allowed to give evidence that three or four weeks before the death in issue, defendant had driven while under the influence of liquor and had had a collision. In State v. Gregory, 488 P.2d 757, 763 (Wash.1971), the defendant opened himself to questions about being AWOL from the Army by wearing his uniform during the trial and testifying about his distinguished military career. But see State v. Martin, 365 A.2d 104 (Conn. 1976): Defendant introduced opinion testimony concerning his non-aggressiveness; error to allow the prosecution to rebut this testimony with evidence of specific instances of aggressive conduct.

12.   Fed. R. Evid. 405(b) allows proof by evidence of specific instances of conduct, as well as by evidence of reputation and opinion, when "character or a trait of character of a person is an essential element of a charge, claim, or defense." Should reputation evidence be admissible against a defendant in a prosecution for being a "common prostitute"? See State v. McCorvey, 114 N.W.2d 703 (Minn.1962). In State v. Roda, 103 S.E.2d 305 (W.Va.1958), a prosecution for maintaining a common nuisance—illegally serving liquor— evidence of the reputation of the place was held inadmissible. But the court said that such evidence would be admissible in a prosecution for maintaining a house of ill-repute.

13.   Consider the problems involved in proof of reputation under the Consumer Credit Protection Act of 1968, 18 U.S.C. §§ 891–94. See United States v. DeCarlo supra p. 674. In United States v. Dennis, 625 F.2d 782, 799–802 (8th Cir.1980), a prosecution under this statute, it was held not error to admit testimony of defendant's reputation for violence known to the witnesses, debtors of the defendant, and acts of violence by defendant in the collection of debts from others, seen by these witnesses, as bearing upon the witnesses' belief that such means would be used against them. Furthermore, evidence of defendant's reputation for violence, the court held, would also be admissible to prove his intent to use illegal means to collect the debts. " 'If a man makes vaguely menacing statements, aware that he is commonly known as a violent man, then it is a reasonable inference that he intends to instill fear. If this were not his intention, we may infer that he would take special care to counteract the communication of an implied threat. It is unlikely that the defendant is unaware of his own reputation for violence; reputation, by definition, reflects general knowledge in the community, and, if anyone is a member of the relevant community, it is the defendant himself.' " Id. at 800, quoting Goldstock and Coenen, Controlling the Contemporary Loan Shark: The Law of Illicit Lending and the Problem of Witness Fear, 65 Cornell L.Rev. 127, 200–01 (1980). An understanding between debtor and creditor that violence or illegal means will be used to collect the debt is an element of the offense under the statute.

Burgeon v. State

Supreme Court of Nevada, 1986.
102 Nev. 43, 714 P.2d 576.

■ PER CURIAM:

This is an appeal from a judgment of conviction upon jury verdict of one count of second degree murder with the use of a deadly weapon. For the reasons expressed below, we affirm.

At appellant Burgeon's jury trial, the state presented testimony by Jesus Salas, the state's only eyewitness to the events which led to the death of the victim, Luis Badillo. Salas testified that he and the victim had driven to a local convenience store on the evening in question. The victim went into the store and Salas remained in the car in the parking lot. Appellant approached the vehicle and asked Salas if he wanted to buy a revolver. Salas told appellant that he did not have the money to purchase the revolver. At this point, the victim returned to the car and entered the passenger's side of the vehicle.

Appellant was standing outside the car when another individual, Eddie Bustamante, approached the car, spoke to the victim, and hit the victim in the face. Salas testified that appellant attempted to stop the altercation between the victim and Bustamante and that Salas simultaneously put the car in reverse and began to back away. As Salas was backing up the car, Eddie Bustamante threw a beer can at the car, hitting the windshield. Finally, Salas testified that appellant then drew a gun and fired approximately three shots, one of which hit the victim in the head and killed him.

Appellant testified on his own behalf at trial. His testimony was consistent with Salas' with one major exception. Appellant stated that as the car was backing away, the victim had pointed a gun at appellant and Eddie Bustamante. Appellant, believing that his life was in danger, then drew his gun and fired.

Eddie Bustamante also testified at trial, and his testimony corroborated appellant's version of the events. In particular, Bustamante also stated that he and the victim disliked each other and had previously fought.

Appellant also presented the testimony of Luis Talavera, who had been standing in the parking lot of the convenience store during the altercation. Talavera testified that he saw the victim point a gun at appellant before appellant drew a gun.

Appellant's theory at trial was that he acted in self-defense. Before closing his case-in-chief, appellant's counsel moved to introduce evidence of specific acts of violence previously committed by the deceased victim for the purpose of showing that the victim was the likely aggressor. A detailed offer of proof was presented in support of the motion. Appellant's counsel also sought to call the victim's father to testify regarding his son's character and reputation for violent behavior. The state opposed both motions. The district court denied appellant's motions and refused to allow the testimony of the father relating to his son's reputation or the testimony of other witnesses concerning specific acts of violence attributable to the victim, for the purpose of proving the issue of self-defense. The court's ruling was apparently based on the fact that appellant did not have any knowledge of the victim's reputation or specific acts of violence. Appellant contends that this ruling was in error.

When it is necessary to show the state of mind of the accused at the time of the commission of the offense for the purpose of establishing self-defense, specific acts which tend to show that the deceased was a violent and dangerous person may be admitted, provided that the specific acts of violence of the deceased were known to the accused or had been communicated to him. See State v. Sella, 41 Nev. 113, 138, 168 P. 278, 286 (1917). In the present case, appellant concedes that the specific acts of violence of the victim were not previously known to him. Since appellant did not have knowledge of the acts, evidence of the victim's specific acts of violence were therefore not admissible to establish the reasonableness of appellant's fear or his state of mind.

Appellant also admits that he did not have any knowledge of the deceased's general character. NRS 48.045(1)(b), however, permits the admission of evidence of the character of the victim of the crime when it is offered by the accused, whether or not the accused had knowledge of the victim's character.[1] Appellant's lack of knowledge of the victim's character was irrelevant to the issue of the admissibility of evidence of general reputation tending to prove that the victim was the likely aggressor. See State v. Jacoby, 260 N.W.2d 828 (Iowa 1977). Under NRS 48.055(1), proof of character may be established by testimony as to reputation or in the form of an opinion.[2] The character of the victim cannot be established by proof of specific acts. See also Government of Virgin Islands v. Carino, 631 F.2d 226 (3d Cir.1980) (interpreting similar federal statutes). Thus, although the district court correctly excluded evidence of the deceased's prior acts of violence, we conclude that evidence of the victim's general reputation would have been admissible. See State v. Helm, 66 Nev. 286,

---

1. NRS 48.045 provides in pertinent part:

   1. Evidence of a person's character or a trait of his character is not admissible for the purpose of proving that he acted in conformity therewith on a particular occasion, except:

       . . .

   (b) Evidence of the character or a trait of character of the victim of the crime

offered by an accused.... [Footnotes are the court's.]

2. NRS 48.055(1) provides:

   In all cases in which evidence of character or a trait of character of a person is admissible, proof may be made by testimony as to reputation or in the form of an opinion. On cross-examination, inquiry may be made into specific instances of conduct.

300–01, 209 P.2d 187, 193–94 (1949); State v. Sella, 41 Nev. at 136–37, 168 P. at 285–86.

. . .

[The court concluded, however, that there had been an insufficient offer of proof regarding the testimony of the father of the victim and, therefore, that the trial court had not erred in refusing to allow the father to testify. Also, since the jury had heard substantial testimony concerning the victim's gang-related activities of a violent nature, exclusion of the father's testimony was not prejudicial. Judgment of conviction affirmed.]

NOTE

Fed. R. Evid. 404(a)(2) and Fed. R. Evid. 405 are the same as the Nevada rules applied in the Burgeon case. Under these rules, reputation and opinion evidence may be introduced to show the victim was the aggressor, but not evidence of particular acts by the victim. On the other hand, evidence of particular acts might have such probative value as not to fall within the category of character evidence at all, and so not be excluded by Rule 404. Likewise, if evidence is introduced of the victim's acts or reputation not as the basis for an inference to the victim's actions, but as the basis for an inference to the defendant's apprehension for his safety, Rule 404 would seem inapplicable. See Adams, Admissibility of Proof of an Assault Victim's Specific Instances of Conduct As an Essential Element of a Self–Defense Claim Under Iowa Rule of Evidence 405, 39 Drake L. Rev. 401, 419–20 (1989–90).

Williams v. Lord, 996 F.2d 1481, 1483 (2d Cir.1993), cert. denied, 510 U.S. 1120 (1994): In a prosecution for murder, the defendant, a prostitute, testified that the victim, after smoking crack for a while, went crazy, tried to strangle her and cut her with a knife, and that she seized the knife and stabbed him in self-defense. In support of her version of what had happened, the defendant sought to introduce the testimony of another woman that the victim had raped her at knife's point. Concededly, the defendant did not know of this earlier incident. Defendant's proffered evidence was excluded by the New York courts because the defendant did not know of the prior incident and because it did not have particular probative value. Held: No violation of defendant's constitutional right to present a defense.

> We believe that the limitation on Williams' ability to introduce evidence of Bennett's prior rape satisfies the balancing test set forth in Rock [Rock v. Arkansas, supra p. 256]. The rule at issue serves two legitimate state interests. First, New York has an interest in seeing that every person, regardless of his worth to the community is not unlawfully assaulted.... Moreover, "there is a very real danger that the trier of fact will overestimate [the evidence's] significance." ... Second, by avoiding the need to establish the truth of Doe's [the other woman's] accusation about the rape, the rule narrows the issues for the jury, preventing "undue diversion to collateral matters." ...

> Moreover, this evidence has little probative value....

Some jurisdictions allow evidence of specific acts even if not known to the defendant. Chandler v. State, 405 S.E.2d 669, 673 (Ga.1991); Pitchess v. Superior Court, 522 P.2d 305 (Cal. 1974): Prosecution for battery against police officers. Defendant claimed he acted in self-defense and that the police had used excessive force. The court upheld the trial court's order for the production of records of investigations into other instances of the use of excessive force by the police the defendant was alleged to have assaulted, on the ground, among others, that such evidence would be relevant and admissible. Evans v. United States, 277 F.2d 354, 355–56 (D.C.Cir.1960), was an appeal from a conviction of second degree murder. Defendant contended she had inflicted the fatal knife wounds in repelling a sexual assault by the decedent. Prior to the incident defendant and decedent were complete strangers to each other. There was evidence that the decedent was drunk at the time of the incident. The court reversed the conviction, holding that the trial court committed error in excluding the following testimony of the decedent's widow, offered by defendant. "[He] was ill mentally, not insane . . . a lost soul who wanted to be with people, get along with the rest, and did not know how to do it; that at times, that he would like to drink and at times on drinking and otherwise he would even go to the extent of being psychotic, perhaps, and with her at least she would know— acted belligerent and in a really bellicose type of manner." The court took the position that the admission of this testimony was but a logical extension of the rule, already accepted in the District of Columbia, admitting in evidence the uncommunicated threats of the deceased against defendant, and observed: "We think that, in the circumstances of this case, almost any evidence showing what kind of a man the decedent was would be highly relevant in helping the jury to determine whether appellant's story of a sexual assault was truthful, and would therefore serve the interests of justice."

Defendant crossed a picket line to apply for a job. On recrossing the picket line in order to leave the area, defendant killed a picket, he claimed in self-defense. Should defendant be allowed to introduce newspaper articles read by him recounting acts of violence at other times and places by members of a different union from that conducting the picket line that defendant crossed? See Commonwealth v. Irwin, 381 A.2d 444 (Pa.1977). When a white pleads self-defense in a prosecution for the murder of a black, should he be allowed to testify that he believed that blacks are especially prone to violence and that he believed this because of a widespread attitude among whites in the community to this effect? Cf. State v. Smith, 470 P.2d 214 (Wash.Ct.App.1970).

Someone killed a tavern owner at his tavern with a shotgun, transported his body to a river and dumped it in. A large sum of money that the tavern owner usually kept with him was missing. There was no other evidence that cast light on the killing or the events immediately surrounding it. Defendant pleaded not guilty. The evidence against him consisted mostly of testimony about behavior on his part after the homicide that could have been for the purpose of destroying evidence. For example, he had his pickup truck washed, possibly to get rid of mud from the scene of the killing. Should the defendant be allowed to introduce evidence of the victim's reputation for violence and specific acts of shooting and killing others and fighting with patrons of his tavern? See Broz v. State, 472 S.W.2d 907 (Tenn.Crim.App.1971), cert. denied, 406 U.S. 949 (1972).

Mode v. State, 350 S.W.2d 675, 680 (Ark.1961), cert. denied, 370 U.S. 909 (1962): Murder prosecution in which self-defense was claimed. The court held that in view of the fact that the defendant had introduced evidence of numerous instances of threats, carrying of weapons and acts of violence by the victim directed at the defendant and known to him, it was not error to admit evidence of the victim's good reputation for being peaceable and law-abiding. "[W]hen, under the claim of self-defense, there is offered—as here—such an abundance of testimony of specific acts of bad conduct as to present a picture of the deceased being a violent and turbulent man, then the defense has, in effect, attacked the good reputation of the deceased and has opened the door for the

State to show on rebuttal the general reputation of the deceased as a peaceable and law-abiding citizen."

Arthur v. State, 339 S.W.2d 538 (Tex.Crim.App.1960): The fact that defendant put in evidence of the defendant's reputation for being peaceable did not open the way for the prosecution to put in evidence of the victim's reputation for being peaceable.

Stearns v. State, 96 So.2d 306 (Ala.1957): Defendant testified to decedent's reputation for violence and that it was known to him. The prosecution was then allowed to introduce evidence of defendant's reputation for violence. This was held to be error.

White v. State

Court of Appeals of Maryland, 1991.
598 A.2d 187.

■ Argued before MURPHY, C.J., and ELDRIDGE, RODOWSKY, McAULIFFE, CHASANOW and KARWACKI, J.J.

■ CHASANOW, JUDGE.

Richard Junior White and his cousin, Adrian Raymond White (the Whites), were charged with kidnapping a woman in Anne Arundel County, raping her in a van, and robbing her of four dollars she had in her purse. At the trial, the Whites wanted to put on the witness stand a man who they said would testify that the victim had previously offered or exchanged sex for drugs. The trial court refused, saying that such testimony would violate Maryland's rape shield statute, Maryland Code (1957, 1987 Repl.Vol.), Article 27, § 461A. The statute reads:

"(a) Evidence relating to victim's chastity.—Evidence relating to a victim's reputation for chastity and opinion evidence relating to a victim's chastity are not admissible in any prosecution for commission of a rape or sexual offense in the first or second degree. Evidence of specific instances of the victim's prior sexual conduct may be admitted only if the judge finds the evidence is relevant and is material to a fact in issue in the case and that its inflammatory or prejudicial nature does not outweigh its probative value, and if the evidence is:

(1) Evidence of the victim's past sexual conduct with the defendant; or

(2) Evidence of specific instances of sexual activity showing the source or origin of semen, pregnancy, disease, or trauma; or

(3) Evidence which supports a claim that the victim has an ulterior motive in accusing the defendant of the crime; or

(4) Evidence offered for the purpose of impeachment when the prosecutor puts the victim's prior sexual conduct in issue.

(b) In camera hearing.—Any evidence described in subsection (a) of this section, may not be referred to in any statements to a jury nor introduced at trial without the court holding a prior in camera hearing to determine the admissibility of the evidence. If new information is discovered during the course of the trial that may make the evidence described in subsection (a) admissible, the court may order an in camera hearing to determine the admissibility of the proposed evidence under subsection (a)."

In an unreported opinion, the Court of Special Appeals affirmed the Whites' convictions. We granted the Whites' petition for certiorari to consider whether the trial court correctly applied the rape shield law in excluding the proffered testimony. We believe that the trial court properly exercised its discretion and, therefore, affirm the judgments below.

At trial, the victim, whom we shall identify only as "Nicole," testified that on the evening of December 19, 1988 she was at the home she shared with her fiancé and their son. At about midnight, when the rest of the household was asleep, she went to a local phone booth at the side of the street to make some calls. While she was at the phone, a white van drove by, and one of its occupants asked her if she knew where any crack cocaine could be found. Nicole told them she did not "do" drugs, and the van drove off.

A short distance away, the van made a U-turn and came back. This time, according to Nicole, the men jumped out and pulled her into the vehicle so harshly that she dropped the beer she was drinking, lost one of her shoes, and urinated in her pants. The pair told her they would not kill her if she kept quiet. After the van stopped, the men, for one to two hours, repeatedly raped her on the vehicle's back seat. The men also took four dollars they found in her purse and released her near the spot where they had grabbed her. Nicole returned home and banged on the door. She told her fiancé that she had been raped by two men. Police later found Nicole's shoe in the street near the phone.

The Whites admit that they were in a van with Nicole that night, but their version of what happened differs dramatically from hers. Richard White testified that he picked up his cousin, Adrian, and drove to the Pioneer City area in Anne Arundel County to buy a video game from a friend of Adrian's. He dropped Adrian off at the friend's house and drove away, planning to return to his home in Baltimore City.

According to Richard, Nicole, whom he did not know, approached the van and asked for a ride to Freetown, another county neighborhood a few miles to the east. After he told her he couldn't take her there, Nicole asked to be driven to Meade Village, a community next to Pioneer City; Richard agreed. As they approached Meade Village, Nicole asked Richard for some cocaine. She then ducked down in the back of the van, telling Richard that her boyfriend's brother lived in the area. Nicole then made "suggestive moves" and offered her body to Richard if he would buy her some cocaine. He declined the offer, saying he had a fiancee, two children, and a fear of AIDS.

Eventually, Richard said, he bought about $35 worth of cocaine from two men, using some of his money and some that Nicole had put toward the purchase. He made the drug buy, he claimed, because he felt sorry for Nicole. She consumed the cocaine, and he asked her if she still wanted to go to Freetown. Now she wanted to go back to Pioneer City. Nicole said she wanted more cocaine, and she resumed making "suggestive moves" and grabbed Richard's penis. This time, Richard got excited but told her he wasn't going to engage in any sex because he didn't "bring any protection."

Again, Richard said, they came across the two men who had sold him the drugs earlier. This time Adrian was there arguing with the men. Adrian got in, and the van pulled away. They drove for about five or ten minutes and stopped in a wooded area. They never found any more cocaine, and eventually Nicole asked to be let out at a school near Pioneer Village. There was no sexual activity other than Nicole's "suggestive moves" and the grab at his penis, according to Richard. He said Nicole was mad about not getting any additional drugs and told them that her boyfriend would be angry if he knew that she was using cocaine. Eventually Nicole got out near a school close to the spot where she had been picked up.

Adrian White testified that, after he swapped the video game he had just acquired for what he thought was cocaine but turned out to be ground macadamia nuts, he began arguing with the fraudulent vendors. During the argument, the white van driven by Richard returned. He got in, he said, and saw Nicole. Adrian described her as "more hyper than upset"; she said she wanted cocaine, but they could not give her any. They dropped her off at a school.

Defense counsel wanted to put a final witness on the stand, a man named Luther Moore. According to the proffer, "He is a witness who is familiar with [Nicole and the area], and he's going to testify that he has previous occasions when he has known that [Nicole] has asked people to provide cocaine in return for sex." When the State objected, citing the rape shield law, defense counsel told the court that the evidence was being offered under the exception covering evidence supporting a claim that the victim has an ulterior motive in accusing the defendant of a crime.

Defense counsel observed that the testimony's relation to sexual activity was "only peripheral in that she was going to provide her body in return for drugs." When the trial judge then asked whether Nicole had offered sex to Luther Moore, defense counsel expanded his proffer: "He's going to testify that he has had instances when she participated in sex with him for drugs." The judge sustained the prosecutor's objection.

The case was submitted to the jury, which found the Whites guilty of first and second degree rape, assault with intent to rape, assault, kidnapping, and theft. The trial court sentenced each of the Whites to life imprisonment for rape, one year consecutive for theft, and ten years consecutive for kidnapping. Convictions for the remaining charges were merged into the first degree rape convictions at sentencing. A three-judge panel later amended the sentences to make the ten years for kidnapping to run concurrently with the life sentences. The sole issue before us is the propriety of the trial court's refusal to admit the proffered defense testimony of Luther Moore.

Rape shield statutes have been enacted in a number of states throughout the country. One purpose of the statute is to protect rape victims from unscrupulous defense attorneys who try to shift the focus away from their clients and onto the victims. See Stephens v. Morris, 756 F.Supp. 1137, 1142 (N.D.Ind.1991) ("The principal reason for the rape shield statutes is to shield victims of sex crimes from general inquiry into their past sexual conduct and to keep these victims from feeling that they are on trial."); Lucado v. State, 40 Md.App. 25, 35–39, 389 A.2d 398, 404–06 (1978); Galvin, Shielding Rape Victims in the State and Federal Courts: A Proposal for the Second Decade, 70 Minn.L.Rev. 763, 791–98 (1986); McCormick on Evidence, § 193 at 573–74 (E. Cleary 3d ed. 1984); 5 L. McClain, Maryland Evidence, § 412.1 at 449–50 (1987).

Another reason to protect rape victims from harassment on the witness stand has been to encourage more victims to report the crimes and help bring rapists to justice. In analyzing its rape shield law, Mississippi's Supreme Court recently observed that the rule's purpose is

"to prevent defense counsel from putting the victim 'on trial,' from unfairly invading the victim's privacy and from deflecting the jury's attention from the true issue. The rule reflects recognition that the trial process at best is traumatic to the victim of sexual abuse. If she has reason to believe the most intimate details of her life are going to be bandied about the courtroom, many victims will decide the game is not worth the candle and decline to file a complaint."

Goodson v. State, 566 So.2d 1142, 1149–50 (Miss.1990). See also State v. Patnaude, 140 Vt. 361, 438 A.2d 402, 407 (1981) ("The restrictions on the admissibility of certain evidence imposed by the rape victim shield law will encourage reluctant rape victims to come forward and report the crime, encourage these same victims to testify in court against their assailant, and produce more prosecutions and convictions, and thus be a greater deterrent."); People v. Khan, 80 Mich.App. 605, 264 N.W.2d 360, 364 (1978) (Before the enactment of Michigan's rape shield statute, "countless victims, already scarred by the emotional (and often physical) trauma of rape, refused to report the crime or testify for fear that the trial proceedings would veer from an impartial examination of the accused's conduct on the date in question and instead take on aspects of an inquisition in which complainant would be required to acknowledge and justify her sexual past."); ... V. Berger, Man's Trial, Woman's Tribulation: Rape Cases in the Courtroom, 77 Col.L.Rev. 1, 54 (1977) (In addition to protecting the victim's privacy and sparing her undue harassment, rape shield laws "encourage the victim to report the assault and assist in bringing the offender to justice by testifying against him in court. Insofar as the laws in fact increase the number of prosecutions, they support the government's aim of deterring would-be rapists as well as its interest in going after actual suspects." (Footnote omitted)).

In 1978 Congress enacted Fed.R.Evid. 412, which was intended to accomplish the same purposes as its state counterparts, particularly "to protect rape victims from the degrading and embarrassing disclosure of intimate details about their private lives." Statement of Representative Mann, quoted in 2 J. Weinstein and M. Berger, Weinstein's Evidence, at 412–5 (1989). Speaking for the proposed federal rule, Representative Holtzman said:

> "Too often in this country victims of rape are humiliated and harassed when they report and prosecute the rape. Bullied and cross-examined about their prior sexual experiences, many find the trial almost as degrading as the rape itself. Since rape trials become inquisitions into the victim's morality, not trials of the defendant's innocence or guilt, it is not surprising that it is the least reported crime. It is estimated that as few as one in ten rapes is ever reported."

Quoted in 2 Weinstein's Evidence, at 412–6. See United States v. Cardinal, 782 F.2d 34, 36 (6th Cir.1986), cert. denied, 476 U.S. 1161, 106 S.Ct. 2282, 90 L.Ed.2d 724 (1986).

The General Assembly originally enacted Maryland's statute in 1976 as part of a major revision of the state's sex offense laws. In its report on the rape shield bill, the Senate Judicial Proceedings Committee said that it

> "took cognizance of the broad based support of the concept of limiting evidence relating to prior sexual conduct of a rape victim and that such a limitation would probably result in an increase in the percentage of rapes reported; that a statutory response to the inherent sensitivities of a traumatized victim could accommodate the constitutionally mandated rights and protections properly afforded a defendant in our criminal justice system; and that the weighing of inflammatory nature versus the probative value of evidence of specific instances of prior sexual conduct precludes possible admission of highly prejudicial evidence of limited probative value. Presently, it is the practice of some courts to admit evidence of any probative value irrespective of its inflammatory nature."

Report of Senate Judicial Proceedings Committee on Senate Bill No. 399 at 4.

The statute, however, is not inflexible. The exceptions written into the law provide ways for a defendant to bring up a victim's conduct when necessary to the defense. The Whites argue that Luther Moore's testimony about Nicole's prior sexual conduct fits the third exception to the rape shield statute, which permits evidence of prior sexual conduct if it "supports a claim that the victim has an ulterior motive in accusing the defendant of the crime." In order for them to succeed in getting that evidence to the jury, however, they must convince the trial judge first that it "is relevant and is material to a fact in issue," and second "that its inflammatory or prejudicial nature does not outweigh its probative value." Art. 27, § 461A(a)....

The Whites proffered that Luther Moore's testimony would establish Nicole's motives to make a false complaint of rape. Their first contention is that Nicole may have falsely accused them of rape because she was angry that they had not obtained more cocaine for her. Her anger was the result of their failure to procure drugs, not their failure to trade drugs for sex. Even adopting the Whites' contention, it was not their declining Nicole's offer of sex that motivated the false charge; it was their declining her request for drugs. Any prior sexual acts or prior sexual solicitations by Nicole could have little, if any, relevance to her alleged anger at the Whites. In addition, the fact that Nicole may have successfully offered or traded sex for drugs in the past does not tend to show that she would become enraged with the Whites for failing to supply her with drugs and declining her alleged sexual solicitation. Luther Moore's testimony would have dubious relevance to establishing that Nicole had an ulterior motive to lie, whereas its prejudice to Nicole and the State would be extreme.

The Whites also allege that Nicole might have fabricated a rape story so that her fiancé would not get mad because she had been out smoking cocaine with two men. Luther Moore's proffered testimony provides no support for this contention. Whether Nicole may have smoked cocaine in the past is irrelevant to any alleged fear of her fiancé's reaction if he ever found out that she had been smoking cocaine. In fact, Luther Moore's proposed testimony seems to run counter to this part of the Whites' argument, since the proffer contains the claim that Nicole had consumed cocaine in the past without reference to any fear she had of her fiancé's reaction. Proffered evidence of past sexual conduct must contain a direct link to the facts at issue in a particular case before it can be admitted. Other courts have given some guidance for the instant case. See, e.g., Hall v. State, 500 So.2d 1282, 1285–86 (Ala.Crim.App.1986) (Defense wanted to offer evidence that victim and her boyfriend had a sexual relationship in order to show that victim had a motive to fabricate the rape and justify her late return to her boyfriend; court held that such evidence is barred by rape shield statute); Commonwealth v. Folino, 293 Pa.Super. 347, 439 A.2d 145, 149–50 (1981) (Statement of teenage, runaway victim to police officer a week after assault that she was "living with" truck driver did not show plan to engage in sex as means of support and was not admissible; also proffered evidence that victim approached another man prior to defendant and offered to engage in sex with him barred by rape shield statute despite defense claim that it would show a continuing course of conduct).

What Luther Moore's testimony would do is paint a picture of the victim as an immoral person who sells herself for illegal drugs. In that manner, the Whites might refocus the trial on Nicole's character, one of the results that the rape shield statute is meant to guard against. Even if we were to assume that the proffered testimony may have had some relevancy, albeit minimal, the trial judge may exclude it under § 461A if its inflammatory or prejudicial nature outweighs its probative value, having due regard for the defendant's right of confrontation, right to present an effective defense and right to due process. Thomas v. State, 301 Md. at 318–19, 483 A.2d at 18–19; Annotation 1 A.L.R.4th 283 (1980). The testimony in question would have invited the jurors to stray into collateral matters that would have obscured the issues before them. Its probative value, if any, was far outweighed by its prejudicial effect. . . .

The Whites contend that the trial judge failed to balance the inflammatory nature of the proffered evidence against its probative value. They are wrong. The transcript of the bench conference reveals that, as the prosecutor and defense lawyer started sparring over the proffer, the judge read the rape shield statute twice. The second time, he specifically read out loud the section calling for him to balance the probative value of the evidence against its potential for prejudice. After that, the two lawyers continued to debate before the trial court ruled. It is apparent to us that the judge acted according to his responsibilities as outlined in the statute.

An additional reason for rejecting the proffer of Luther Moore's testimony exists independent of the rape shield statute. A trial judge has discretion in determining whether evidence is relevant to bias or motive. As we have already indicated, Nicole's alleged bias against the Whites was because they failed to supply her with drugs, not because they failed to have sexual relations with her. Even if she had exchanged sexual favors for drugs in the past, it would not necessarily indicate that she would become enraged and vindictive if someone were unable or unwilling to trade drugs for sex. In fact, nothing in the proffer is at odds with Nicole's version of what happened. Wide latitude must be given to a criminal defendant to establish bias or motive of a witness. Smallwood v. State, 320 Md. at 307–08, 577 A.2d at 359. The trial judge, however, still has discretion in determining whether particular evidence is relevant to the issue of bias or motive.

. . .

[W]e find no violation of the Whites' constitutional rights. The United States Supreme Court recently upheld a notice requirement in Michigan's rape shield law. In doing so, the Court reiterated the principle that " 'trial judges retain wide latitude' to limit reasonably a criminal defendant's right to cross-examine a witness 'based on concerns about, among other things, harassment, prejudice, confusion of the issues, the witness' safety, or interrogation that is repetitive or only marginally relevant.' " Michigan v. Lucas, 500 U.S. 145, 149, 111 S.Ct. 1743, 1746, 114 L.Ed.2d 205, 212 (1991), quoting Delaware v. Van Arsdall, 475 U.S. 673, 679, 106 S.Ct. 1431, 1435, 89 L.Ed.2d 674 (1986). The Court noted that the Michigan law "represents a valid legislative determination that rape victims deserve heightened protection against surprise, harassment, and unnecessary invasions of privacy." 500 U.S. at 150, 111 S.Ct. at 1746, 114 L.Ed.2d at 212.

Of course, the state's interest in excluding evidence must at times yield to a defendant's due process right to present a defense and 6th Amendment right to confront witnesses, especially where the proffered testimony has a direct link to the defendant or establishes a possible motive for the witness to implicate the defendant in a crime. But with this in mind, the trial court in the proper exercise of discretion may exclude evidence under Art. 27, § 461A without offending a defendant's constitutional rights of confrontation and due process. Thomas v. State, 301 Md. at 318–19, 483 A.2d at 18–19.

We hold that the trial judge did not abuse his discretion in excluding the proffered evidence. We therefore affirm the judgment of the Court of Special Appeals.

Judgment of the court of special appeals affirmed.[1]

FED. R. EVID. 412

[See Rules, Statute and Case Supplement.]

NOTES

1.   The term relevance is used in the heading to Rule 412 but not in the text. The provision in the rule relating to civil cases uses the term probative value. The Advisory Committee's Note recites as one of the reasons for the rule "to safeguard the victim [of sexual misconduct] against ... sexual stereotyping...." Does Rule 412 exclude a class of evidence that in any case is irrelevant under Rule 401, or does it substitute a standard of relevance different from the one in 401? If it substitutes a different standard, why has this been done for the particular class of evidence in the particular kind of case covered by Rule 412? Note that Rule 412 overrides both Rule 404 and Rule 608: it extends to both evidence introduced for substantive purposes and evidence introduced for its bearing on credibility. Does Rule 412 alter the substantive law of consent?

2.   Under Rule 412, evidence of the victim's sexual behavior or predisposition is excluded regardless of the nature of the inference to be drawn from the evidence. Compare Rule 404, which excludes evidence of a person's character introduced for the purpose of showing action in conformity therewith. A consequence would appear to be that evidence of a victim's behavior and reputation known to the defendant, which does not fall within Rule 404 when offered in self-defense cases, see supra p. 893, does fall within the prohibition of Rule 412. See People v. Wilhelm, 476 N.W.2d 753 (Mich..App.1991), cert. denied, 508 U.S. 917 (1993): In rape prosecution in which the disputed issue was consent, testimony by the defendant that shortly before the alleged rape he was in a bar and saw the victim lift her dress and expose her breasts to two men sitting at her table, barred by the state rape shield statute. But see State v. Colbath, 540 A.2d 1212, 1216–17 (N.H.1988):

> On the one hand, describing a complainant's open, sexually suggestive conduct in the presence of patrons of a public bar obviously has far less potential for damaging the sensibilities than revealing what the same person may have done in the company of another behind a closed door. On the other hand, evidence of public displays of general interest in sexual activity can be taken to indicate a contemporaneous receptiveness to sexual advances that cannot be inferred from evidence of private behavior with chosen sex partners.
>
> In this case, for example, the jury could have taken evidence of the complainant's openly sexually provocative behavior toward a group of men as evidence of her probable attitude toward an individual within that group. Evidence that the publicly inviting acts occurred closely in time to the alleged sexual assault by one such man could have been viewed as indicating the complainant's likely attitude at the time of the sexual activity in question.

3.   One of the defendant's characterizations of the evidence excluded in the White case, evidently intended to suggest special probative value, was that it showed the victim was interested in exchanging sex for drugs. See State v. Crims, 540 N.W.2d 860, 868 (Minn..App.1995): In rape prosecution in which defendant claimed the victim had consented to sex in return for money to buy

---

1.   Footnotes omitted.

drugs, evidence that the victim had on other occasions exchanged sex for drugs with third persons did not establish such a pattern of clearly similar behavior as to make exclusion erroneous. See the Advisory Committee's Note to Rule 412 stating that the rule extends to "pattern witnesses." At the same time, the Committee states: "Evidence offered to prove allegedly false prior claims by the victim is not barred by Rule 412." See State v. Boggs, 588 N.E.2d 813, 817 (Ohio 1992): Evidence of a prior false accusation of rape is not evidence of the victim's prior sexual activity and so not excluded by the rape shield statute. The trial court should determine whether the accusation was false, and only if it was "totally unfounded" is the evidence admissible. United States v. Stamper, 766 F.Supp. 1396 (W.D.N.C.1991): If it is assumed that Rule 412 bars evidence of a prior false accusation of rape in circumstances similar to the litigated case, exclusion would be unconstitutional. Commonwealth v. Wall, 606 A.2d 449, 463 (Pa.Super.1992): "Here, the evidence of the victim's prior participation in the *successful prosecution* of an adult male which led to her removal from the home in which she had been molested was offered to show that the victim was aware of both the content and the *consequence* of making a sexual abuse claim against an adult male." State v. Guthrie, 621 N.E.2d 551 (Ohio.App.1993): In child sexual abuse prosecution, not abuse of discretion to exclude evidence that the child had been abused by someone else on another occasion, offered to show an alternative source of the child's sexual knowledge.

4. State v. Sexton, 444 S.E.2d 879, 898–901 (N.C.1994): In prosecution for rape and murder in which defendant contended the victim had initiated the sexual encounter and consented to intercourse, not error to allow prosecution to introduce in rebuttal testimony by persons who worked with the victim that she was not flirtatious, was a strong family person, did not have a reputation for being flirtatious and had a reputation for being a family person.

> [T]he sexual assault victim herein, Kimberly Crews, was dead and could neither rebut the defense of consent nor risk subjecting herself to possible cross-examination about her previous sexual behavior. Therefore, the policies designed to protect rape victims personally and which support a conclusion that previous sexual behavior must in every instance be deemed irrelevant to prosecution of sexual assaults are of less importance.... [P]ermitting this rebuttal evidence does not conflict with the underlying statutory policy of eliminating prejudice to the State's case caused by introducing evidence of the victim's unfavorable personal characteristics or the policy that the issue of the victim's character is a collateral one.... [T]he statute was intended as a shield for the victims of sexual assault and not as a sword for defendants. Therefore, we hold that in the limited circumstance where the rape victim is deceased and the defendant's own testimony brings into question the victim's sexual behavior, the prosecution may present rebuttal evidence relating to the victim's prior sexual conduct to challenge the credibility of defendant's testimony....

> Defendant also contends the trial court erred in permitting the rebuttal testimony about the victim's general good moral character, devotion to family, and reputation for marital fidelity. Defendant argues that the general rule is that evidence of a victim's character cannot be introduced to prove that she acted in accord therewith, but acknowledges that an exception exists for character evidence introduced to rebut defense evidence which puts it at issue. Defendant contends, however, that he did not introduce any evidence which permitted rebuttal evidence of the victim's good character; therefore, the evidence was erroneously admitted to defendant's prejudice. We do not find defendant's arguments persuasive.

Rule 404 prohibits the admission of evidence of a person's character offered for the purpose of proving conduct in conformity therewith. N.C.G.S. § 8C–1, Rule 404(a) (1992). An exception exists for evidence of a pertinent trait of character of the victim if offered by the accused "or by the prosecution to rebut the same." N.C.G.S. § 8C–1, Rule 404(a)(2). . . .

In the instant case, defendant's testimony was that the victim was the instigator of the consensual sexual acts. His defense to the rape and sexual assault charges went beyond consent, however, when he testified that the victim stated positively that she wanted to cheat on her husband. Ordinarily, the exception created by Rule 404(a)(2) "applies to all kinds of prosecutions, except those for 'rape' or 'assault with intent to commit' rape, where the question of admitting evidence of the character of the complaining witness is governed by Rule 412." 2 Louisell, Federal Evidence § 139. Notwithstanding, by attacking the victim's character for marital fidelity, defendant went beyond what was necessary for his defense and opened the door to the rebuttal evidence.

In Commonwealth v. McKay, 294 N.E.2d 213, 218 (Mass.1973), the court held it was not error to allow the complaining witness to testify that she had been a virgin, even though the defendant would have been prohibited from initiating this line of inquiry by introducing evidence that the complaining witness had sexual relations with other men. "The victim's lack of virginity . . . has little probative value on the issue of consent because the victim's consent to intercourse with one man does not imply her consent in the case of another. . . . On the other hand, the status of the victim as a virgin at the time of the alleged crime has far more probative value on the issue of consent." But see State v. Gavigan, 330 N.W.2d 571 (Wis.1983): In rape prosecution in which consent was the only issue, it was error under the rape shield statute to admit testimony that before the intercourse at issue in the case the complainant had been a virgin. But it would not have been error, if there was a limiting instruction, to admit evidence that just before the intercourse complainant had said to defendant that she didn't do that sort of thing and that she wasn't that type of girl. People v. Sandoval, 552 N.E.2d 726, 731 (Ill.), cert. denied, 498 U.S. 938 (1990): In rape prosecution in which defendant was charged with engaging in anal sex with complainant against her will, rape shield statute prevented the prosecution from bringing out on direct examination of the complainant that she had never engaged in anal sex with others.

5. The 1994 amendment of Rule 412, as submitted by the Advisory Committee to the Supreme Court, included the provision extending the rule to civil cases. The Supreme Court promulgated the rule except for this provision. However, Congress restored the provision. An important consequence of the extension to civil cases is to make the rule applicable in suits for sexual harassment under Title VII of the Civil Rights Act. Note the difference between 412(b)(1), dealing with criminal cases, and 412(b)(2), dealing with civil cases, especially the provision in 412(b)(2) requiring that probative value substantially outweigh harm and prejudice before evidence may be admitted. Compare Fed. R. Evid. 403 and Fed. R. Evid. 609(a)(1) and (b).

6. As noted in the White decision, the Supreme Court of the United States has upheld the constitutionality of a pretrial notice requirement included in a state rape shield statute. Michigan v. Lucas, 500 U.S. 145 (1991). On the other hand, see Olden v. Kentucky, 488 U.S. 227 (1988), supra p. 363, holding that the defendant in a rape case has a constitutional right to inquire into the alleged victim's cohabitation with another man in order to show bias. Stephens v. Miller, 13 F.3d 998 (7th Cir.) (en banc), cert. denied, 115 S.Ct. 57 (1994): In a prosecution for rape in which the defendant claimed consent, the defendant was prohibited from testifying to certain statements he made to the complainant during the encounter.

BAUER, J. for the court:

> The [state trial court] ... did nothing arbitrary or disproportionate to the purposes the Indiana Rape Shield Statute was designed to serve when it excluded the "doggy fashion" and "partner switching" statements. The Indiana Rape Shield Statute was enacted to prevent just this kind of generalized inquiry into the reputation or past sexual conduct of the victim in order to avoid embarrassing her and subjecting her to possible public denigration.... Its application to exclude references here to "doggy fashion" sexual intercourse and partner switching effectuate its purpose. The Indiana trial court properly balanced Stephens' right to testify with Indiana's interests because it allowed him to testify about what happened and that he said something that upset Wilburn. The Constitution requires no more than this. The interests served by the Indiana Rape Shield Statute justify this very minor imposition on Stephens' right to testify.

Id. at 1002.

FLAUM, J. concurring:

> [O]nce it is acknowledged that a defendant's right to tell his story is not boundless, one is compelled to seek the broad and elemental contours of this right that *are* inviolate. As an initial matter, it is apparent that a defendant cannot be denied the opportunity to elicit the core of operative facts that comprise his theory of defense. In a rape case, where the defendant asserts the defense of consent, this essential center certainly would include both the facts that arguably manifest consent and those that diminish the credibility of inculpatory evidence accumulated against the defendant. More germane to this case, but related in principle, is the notion that a defendant's opportunity to develop not only the rudiments but also the details of his story cannot be so cramped as to leave his defense drained of its effectiveness. Ascertaining which details are essential in a particular case admittedly may be an exacting and imprecise examination. However, until we are benefitted by further teachings of the Supreme Court, I conclude that this is the inquiry that should be conducted.
>
> In this case, I cannot adopt the majority's characterization that the application of the rape shield statute constitutes a "very minor imposition on Stephens' right to testify." ... Nevertheless, I accept that Stephens' testimony was appropriately excludable because the testimony was not sufficiently central to his defense to outweigh the interests served by the statute.

Id. at 1006.

CUMMINGS, J., joined by CUDAHY and MANION, JJ., dissenting:

> The plausibility of Stephens' defense turned in substantial part on whether the jury could be persuaded that something Stephens had said to the complainant could have so enraged her that she would have responded in the manner he alleged. Central to Stephens' case then are the words he claims to have said that night, words the jury never heard. Stephens proposed to testify that while he and the complainant were engaged in intercourse "doggy fashion," he said to her "Don't you like it like this? ... Tom Hall said you did." ... Stephens instead was permitted only to testify without elaboration that he had said something that angered the complainant. The judge required Stephens to convince the jury of the truth of his

story without allowing him to reveal the fragments on which its plausibility turned. He was asked to counter the detailed and vivid depiction offered by the prosecution with a version whose essential elements had been expunged.

Id. at 1010.

CUDAHY J. dissenting:

The testimony that Stephens sought to offer, however, neither sought to prove the victim's character nor was intended to address the question of consent. Rather than attempting to prove the truth of any matter about Wilburn's character, Stephens ostensibly wanted to offer his story to show its effect on the listener. This, of course, is a common distinction in the law of evidence. See generally 6 John Henry Wigmore Evidence § 1789 (Chadbourn Rev.1976). Nor was Stephens' testimony intended as evidence of consent, but rather it is evidence of a motive to fabricate. Stephens' theory was that what he said so enraged Wilburn that it led her to concoct a rape charge.[1]

. . . .

The Supreme Court [in Davis v. Alaska, 415 U.S. 308, 94 S.Ct. 1105 (1974), supra p. 363], however, struck the balance otherwise. It held that the defendant's interest in using this evidence—to suggest that the witness had a motive to lie—outweighed the state's interest in protecting the witness's reputation. Since Davis, the Court has consistently reaffirmed a defendant's right to introduce evidence suggesting that a witness had a motive to fabricate. . . .

The analogy between Davis and the instant case is compelling. As in Davis, Stephens sought to show that the prosecution witness had a reason to lie. In addressing a constitutional challenge to rape shield legislation, "Davis is clearly apropos when the rape victim's prior sexual conduct has some relevance to establish a *motive for false accusation*." 23 Charles Alan Wright & Kenneth W. Graham, Jr., Federal Practice and Procedure: Evidence § 5387, at 568 (1980) (emphasis added). . . .

. . . .

Applying this principle to the case at bar presents a difficult question. On the one hand, to suggest that a woman who is shown to have been sexually active would become so angry that she would invent a rape charge may be more than a bit old-fashioned. But on the other, it is the former pervasiveness of this traditionalist view that ultimately led the Congress and forty-eight state legislatures to enact rape shield legislation, protecting rape victims from having to endure trials in which they are cross-examined about their entire sexual past. It is paradoxically *because* being confronted with one's sexual activity—or at least with its more lurid aspects—is thought to be the source of extreme embarrassment that Stephens has a right to present this evidence. Thus, I ultimately conclude that Stephens' claim—that what he told Wilburn so enraged her that it led her to accuse him of rape—is some evidence of a motive to fabricate. As such, the Constitution requires that he be permitted to introduce this evidence at trial. . . .

---

1. There is some force to the suggestion that this evidence was not introduced solely to show a motive to fabricate but also to explain why Wilburn withdrew her consent and threw Stephens out of the trailer. . . . [Footnote to the opinion.]

Id. at 1012–15.[2]

Ripple, J. dissenting:

Today's decision will no doubt be hailed as a very "contemporary" one. However, the correctness of a ruling by Judges of the Third Article is not measured by whether it is "contemporary" but by whether it protects the basic constitutional values that undergird our political and legal order. When viewed from this perspective, the court's decision represents a radical departure from the standards established by the Supreme Court of the United States for the protection of the right of an accused to give evidence in his or her own defense. It also condones an injustice that raises the distinct possibility that an innocent person has been convicted of a most heinous crime. . . .

. . .

Whether the complainant consented to have sexual intercourse with the defendant and whether the statement that was allegedly made to her would have caused her to withdraw that consent and become so infuriated as to recharacterize the encounter when it suited her convenience is an issue upon which the cold record reveals little. Ascertaining THE TRUTH required a careful assessment of personalities, demeanor, and temperament of the two individuals. To limit the defendant to testifying that he said "something" that angered her is to deprive the jury of the essence of his testimony. It was the rawness of what he allegedly said that would have given substance to his testimony. Only after being apprised of that statement and ascertaining whether such an utterance, made when it was made, would produce the reaction it did in this particular complainant could the jury have determined whether the statement was made and, if made, whether it produced the alleged reaction.

. . .

The trial court's decision not only deprived the defendant of the ability to give, from his own mouth, his own version of the event, but the bland substitution also portrayed him to the jury as someone less than frank. A juror, realizing the importance of the testimony to the defendant's case, certainly would expect that he be quite a bit more specific than "I said something to make her angry." . . .

. . .

This case thus leaves us with the haunting fear that, had the jury been allowed to hear both sides of the story and evaluate the demeanor of both witnesses as they told what happened, the result may well have been different. The responsibility for this result must rest on other shoulders.[3]

Id. at 1019, 1023–24.

7. Consider the relation between Fed. R. Evid. 412 and Fed. R. Evid. 413 and 414. Suppose evidence of prior sexual behavior of the defendant is admitted under 413 or 414, but evidence of the victim's behavior is excluded under 412. Does this present a constitutional problem?

8. In addition to the articles cited in the White decision, there is much other commentary on rape shield statutes. E.g., Fishman, Consent, Credibility, and the Constitution: Evidence Relating to a Sex Offense Complainant's Past

---

2. A footnote is omitted.   **3.** Footnotes omitted.

Sexual Behavior, 44 Cath. U. L. Rev. 709 (1995); Tanford and Bocchino, Rape Victim Shield Laws and the Sixth Amendment, 128 U. Pa. L. Rev. 544 (1980); Letwin, "Unchaste Character," Ideology, and the California Rape Evidence Laws, 54 S. Cal. L. Rev. 35 (1980); Ordover, Admissibility of Patterns of Similar Sexual Conduct: The Unlamented Death of Character for Chastity, 63 Cornell L. Rev. 90 (1977); Rudenstein, Rape Shield Laws: Some Constitutional Problems, 18 Wm. & Mary L. Rev. 1 (1976); Note, Proving Welcomeness: The Admissibility of Evidence of Sexual History in Sexual Harassment Claims Under the 1994 Amendments to Federal Rule of Evidence 412, 48 Vand. L. Rev. 1155 (1995).

SECTION 3.   EVIDENCE OF REPUTATION AND OPINION OF CHARACTER IN CIVIL CASES

Crumpton v. Confederation Life Ins. Co.

United States Court of Appeals, Fifth Circuit, 1982.
672 F.2d 1248.

■ JOHN R. BROWN, CIRCUIT JUDGE:

Vicki Crumpton, the beneficiary of an accidental death policy, sued Confederation Life Insurance Co. (Confederation) for the benefits under the policy. From a jury verdict and judgment in favor of the beneficiary, Confederation appeals. The asserted errors are twofold: (1) improper admission of prejudicial evidence of the character of the insured; and (2) incorrect denial of motions for j.n.o.v. or new trial since as a matter of law the death of the insured was not accidental. Finding no error by the District Court, we affirm.

I.   Facts

The facts in this suit on an insurance policy are unusual for that genre of cases. The insured, Titus Crumpton (Crumpton), was shot by Joanne Petton, a neighbor who lived just a little more than a block away. While Confederation's defense to the policy was that Crumpton's death was not accidental, the focus of the trial was on the alleged rape of Ms. Petton by the deceased insured. Thus we find it necessary briefly to summarize the circumstances claimed to have led to Crumpton's death.

On the afternoon of November 8, 1978, Ms. Petton, a housewife with three children, was allegedly raped and beaten in her home by Crumpton. The assailant apparently threatened to kill Petton's children if she informed the police or anyone about the rape. Ms. Petton did report the incident to the police five days later, on the morning of November 13, 1978, stating that the attack had occurred on the morning of November 8 and that she could not identify her assailant. Between the time of the alleged rape and her report to the police, Ms. Petton did inform her parents and her husband, but she never revealed to her husband that the assailant had made threats against her. On November 13, Ms. Petton was also examined by her physician who found multiple bruises on Petton's body "more consistent with a sex assault than just would be a general beating of some sort".

At approximately 9 p.m. on November 13, 1978, Ms. Petton asked her husband to pick up some medication at the drug store. After he left, Ms. Petton then delivered to her next door neighbor a sealed envelope containing a handwritten note stating "Mr. Crumpton attacked and raped me in afternoon not morning". Subsequently, Ms. Petton, with a pistol in her possession, went out to the garage at which time she observed Crumpton standing out on the street. Apparently, he proceeded toward her so she pulled out the gun and, without any verbal warning, shot Crumpton at close range.

II.   Suit on the Policy

Titus Crumpton was insured by Confederation as part of a group policy obtained by his employer to cover accidental death and dismemberment. The policy, in the amount of $150,000, designated Vicki Crumpton as the beneficiary. The policy provided benefits for accidental death, defined as "death resulting from ... accidental bodily injury visible on the surface of the body or disclosed by an autopsy."

Vicki Crumpton brought this suit seeking recovery of the proceeds of this policy, claiming that her father, Titus Crumpton, died of gunshot wounds inflicted by another person. Confederation, while admitting that Crumpton was insured under the policy, denied coverage, asserting that Crumpton's death did not result from an accidental bodily injury within the meaning of the policy. Specifically, Confederation, while not disputing the death, contended that Crumpton had raped his neighbor who fatally shot him in the belief that he had returned to inflict further harm on her or her children. For this reason, Confederation asserted that Crumpton should have anticipated that his actions would result in bodily injury, and thus his death was not accidental under the meaning of the policy.

The beneficiary denied that the rape occurred or alternatively asserted that Crumpton could not reasonably have anticipated his death five days after the rape. The case was tried to a jury to whom one special interrogatory was submitted: "Did plaintiff Vicki Crumpton prove by a preponderance of the evidence that the bodily injuries of T.B. Crumpton which resulted in his death were accidental?" The jury responded that "Plaintiff did prove." The District Court entered judgment awarding the beneficiary the benefits under the policy as well as statutory penalties and attorney's fees. Confederation's subsequent motion for j.n.o.v. or for new trial was denied. From this denial, Confederation appeals.

III.   Character Evidence

Confederation's primary assertion of error concerns the admission by the District Court of evidence regarding Crumpton's character. Prior to trial, Confederation by motion in limine sought an order prohibiting the admission into evidence of "any fact regarding or relating to T.B. Crumpton's character or reputation in the community." This motion was denied by the District Court judge who found that under the peculiar fact circumstances, Crumpton's character was at issue. Also, the District Court determined that the evidence would be admissible in a criminal case under F.R.Evid. 404(a), which rule, although appearing to apply only to criminal cases, should properly apply to the type of case at hand.[1]

---

1. The following exchange occurred between the District Court judge and counsel for Confederation on the motion to prohibit character evidence.

THE COURT: ... [T]hat will be overruled and the basic reasons are that I think that in the peculiar fact circumstances of this case that Crumpton's character is in issue and character evidence would not be offered for collateral purposes and secondly, that I think under the circumstances, although the precise language of Rule 404(a) would appear to apply only to criminal cases, that the proper construction should be that it should apply to this type of case also. And that the

At the trial Vicki Crumpton called as witnesses several persons who testified to Crumpton's "character". The witnesses included the pastor of a church, who testified that Crumpton did not have a violent temper, did not use profanity, and did not make passes at women; the church secretary who testified similarly; a "good friend" who testified that Crumpton did not use profanities or make obscene gestures or indecent proposals to women, was not violent, and did not drink; Crumpton's sister-in-law who testified similarly; and the beneficiary who testified that her father was not violent and did not use threats.

Confederation contends that the admission of this testimony not only violated F.R.Evid. 404 but was also prejudicial, constituting "virtually the only direct evidence adduced to satisfy the Beneficiary's burden. . . ." The propriety of the admission of evidence of character depends in part on the purpose for which that evidence is offered. Generally this type of evidence is offered for one of two purposes: (1) when a person's possession of a particular character trait is an operative fact in determining the legal rights and liabilities of the party and thus is one of the ultimate issues in the case; or (2) to prove circumstantially that a person acted in conformity with his character on a particular occasion.[2]

The use of character evidence for the first purpose above is generally referred to as "character at issue". When used for such a purpose, it is not within the scope of F.R.Evid. 404 which applies instead to the second use, that of showing that the person acted in conformity with his character. Reyes v. Missouri Pacific Railroad, 589 F.2d 791, 793 n. 4 (5th Cir.1979). F.R.Evid. 404(a) governs the admission of character evidence when used for the circumstantial purpose and generally excludes such evidence unless within one of the three exceptions. These exceptions are formulated in terms of whose character is being offered as evidence. They allow the admission of character evidence to prove action in conformity with character of the accused, of a victim in certain circumstances, and of a witness. With these exceptions, character evidence is generally excluded because it is viewed as having slight probative value and yet may be very prejudicial. Reyes, supra, at 793–94 n. 6. Where character is part of the ultimate issue of a case, F.R.Evid. 404(a) is not relevant.

The District Court, in denying the motion to exclude evidence of Crumpton's character, based the decision first on a finding that character was at issue.

evidence would certainly be admissible if we were trying a criminal case. . . .

THE COURT: I want you to have a continuing objection to all of the evidence that comes in that does not pertain to the actual event so that you don't need to repeat that during trial. So, if you want to just state your objection right now for record purposes, I will overrule it, even though I will listen very carefully to it.

MR. LESH: Let me do that. We do want a continuing objection to all evidence pertaining to the character or reputation of Titus Crumpton on the ground that it is not relevant to the issue before the Court. It is expressly excluded by Rule 404. We would like that to be a continuing objection.

We would also make the statement that in view of the Court's ruling we will be compelled ourselves to put in evidence pertaining to the character of Mr. Crumpton and his conduct preceding the events in question which we would not have to do but for the Court's ruling. So, we do not want the introduction of that evidence to constitute a waiver of our objection to the admissibility of all of this evidence.

THE COURT: Okay. The objection is overruled for the reasons I outlined briefly which I will probably incorporate in an opinion, if necessary, after the case is over.

MR. LESH: Now, we do have—

THE COURT: As to the second point, your putting on evidence obviously does not waive your objection to character.

[Footnotes are the court's.]

2. McCormick on Evidence §§ 186–188, at 442–45 (2d ed. 1972); 1 Wigmore on Evidence §§ 55–81 (3d ed. 1940).

We agree with this conclusion. While the evidence of Crumpton's character might create an inference that he acted in accordance with that character on the night of the shooting, his character is also a fact upon which the liabilities of the parties turn. Crumpton's character was at issue given the defense raised by Confederation that Crumpton should have anticipated bodily injury because he committed a violent criminal act. Since his character was at issue and therefore not within Rule 404(a), the admission of the evidence was within the discretion of the trial court.[3] ... Given the unusual nature of this case, the decision whether to admit the evidence of character, although perhaps a close call, was reached after carefully weighing all factors. We thus find no abuse of discretion by the District Court in admitting such evidence.

Even if the evidentiary ruling were erroneous, reversal would not be necessary since the evidence of Crumpton's character was not prejudicial to the rights of Confederation. As discussed later in this opinion, there was sufficient evidence—aside from this testimony concerning Crumpton's character—from which the jury could find that Crumpton's death was accidental under the terms of the policy. Even if the jury believed Ms. Petton's claim that Crumpton had raped her previously, the jury did not necessarily have to find that Crumpton would reasonably anticipate Ms. Petton's delayed response. Absent a showing that substantial rights of the party were adversely affected, reversal for an erroneous ruling on evidence is not warranted.... The burden of demonstrating that such substantial rights were affected is on the party who asserts an error, here, Confederation.

The District Court also found that even if F.R.Evid. 404(a) were applicable, the evidence of character would be admissible under the exceptions. While Rule 404(a) generally applies to criminal cases, the unusual circumstances here place the case very close to one of a criminal nature.[4] The focus of the civil suit on the insurance policy was the issue of rape, and the resulting trial was in most respects similar to a criminal case for rape. Had there been a criminal case against Crumpton, evidence of his character that was pertinent would have been admissible. We do not view the notes of the Advisory Committee as contravening this interpretation.[5]

3. The evidence is also clearly relevant within the meaning of F.R.Evid. 401. Confederation's challenge to the admission of the evidence focuses on F.R.Evid. 404(a) and does not specifically assert error under F.R.Evid. 401 or 403, both of which Rules allow broad discretion to the District Court.

4. The application of Rule 404 within the context of a civil suit for injuries was not questioned in Hackbart v. Cincinnati Bengals, Inc., 601 F.2d 516 (10th Cir.), cert. denied, 444 U.S. 931 (1979). In that case, a football player sued for injuries received in a game and the District Court allowed evidence of prior acts of the plaintiff designed to show that the plaintiff was a "dirty player". The Tenth Circuit, after quoting F.R.Evid. 404, focused not on the Rule but on relevancy and whether the plaintiff's character was at issue. We interpret the Court's failure to discuss whether F.R.Evid. 404 is applicable to civil suits as impliedly approving its use, although not necessarily in the case at hand, to civil suits.

5. The Advisory Committee stated:

The argument is made that circumstantial use of character ought to be allowed in civil cases to the same extent as in criminal cases, i.e., evidence of good (nonprejudicial) character would be admissible in the first instance, subject to rebuttal by evidence of bad character.... Uniform Rule 47 goes further, in that it assumes that character evidence in general satisfies the conditions of relevancy, except as provided in Uniform Rule 48. The difficulty with expanding the use of character evidence in civil cases is set forth by the California Law Revision Commission in its ultimate rejection of Uniform Rule 47 ...:

"Character evidence is of slight probative value and may be very prejudicial. It tends to distract the trier of fact from the main question of what actually happened on the particular occasion. It subtly permits the trier of fact to reward the good man to punish the bad man because of their respective characters despite what

IV.   J.N.O.V. or New Trial

Confederation's second asserted error is that the District Court should have granted its motion for j.n.o.v. or for new trial. Confederation claims that the evidence established conclusively that Crumpton's death did not result from accidental bodily injury. To find such error, we would have to find that the evidence left no doubt that (1) Crumpton raped Ms. Petton and (2) rape and assault would likely lead to the death of the rapist.

Our standard of review on motions for j.n.o.v. is well-established in this Circuit. Boeing Co. v. Shipman, 411 F.2d 365, 374–75 (5th Cir.1969) (en banc). Viewing the evidence as a whole and in the light most favorable to the party opposing the motion, if reasonable men could not reach a contrary result, granting the motion is proper. . . .

In Texas, in insurance cases a presumption of accidental death from evidence of death by violent and external means has been recognized. Republic National Life Insurance Co. v. Heyward, 536 S.W.2d 549, 558 (Tex.1976).

> [T]he test of whether the killing is accidental within the terms of an insurance policy is not to be determined from the viewpoint of the one who does the killing, but rather from the viewpoint of the insured.

Heyward, 536 S.W.2d at 552, quoting Hutcherson v. Sovereign Camp, W.O.W., 112 Tex. 551, 251 S.W. 491 (1923). If from the viewpoint of the insured his conduct was such that he should have anticipated that in all reasonable probability he would be killed, his death is not accidental. McGowen v. Travelers Insurance Co., 448 F.2d 1315 (5th Cir.1971). "Unless some evidence to the contrary is produced, we think it is reasonable to presume that insured did not act in such a way that he should have reasonably known his actions would probably result in his death. The law assumes that one's natural instinct is to avoid injury and preserve his own life." Heyward, 536 S.W.2d at 559.

There was sufficient evidence under the Boeing standard for the jury to determine that Crumpton could not or should not have anticipated that his actions at that time would result in his death. Under the evidence presented, there were three probable theories of what had occurred. The first theory was that no rape was ever committed. Ms. Petton did not report the rape immediately, nor did she go to a doctor for tests to confirm the rape until five days later, when it was too late for a conclusive determination. The beneficiary also introduced forensic evidence that no traces of seminal fluid were found on Ms. Petton's dress, nor on the portion of the prophylactic allegedly worn by

---

the evidence in the case shows actually happened."

Much of the force of the position of those favoring greater use of character evidence in civil cases is dissipated by their support of Uniform Rule 48 which excludes the evidence in negligence cases, where it could be expected to achieve its maximum usefulness. Moreover, expanding concepts of "character" which seem of necessity to extend into such areas as psychiatric evaluation and psychological testing, coupled with expanded admissibility, would open up such vistas of mental examinations as caused the court concern in Schlagenhauf v. Holder [370 U.S. 104, 85 S.Ct. 234, 13 L.Ed.2d 152]. . . . It is believed that those espousing change have not met the burden of persuasion.

While the Committee's notes reject the expanded use of character evidence in civil cases, we do not view this as determinative of the circumstances of this case, which while actually civil, in character is akin to a criminal case. In Reyes, supra, we said that the "general rule of exclusion" was applicable to both civil and criminal proceedings. Reyes, 589 F.2d at 793 and n. 5. Thus by implication, when evidence would be admissible under Rule 404(a) in a criminal case, we think that it should also be admissible in a civil suit where the focus is on essentially criminal aspects, and the evidence is relevant, probative, and not unduly prejudicial.

Crumpton during the rape. Also, the fact that Ms. Petton's accounts of the rape were inconsistent, varying as to the time and place in the version told to the police prior to the shooting and that told after the shooting, presented a credibility issue for the jury. The second theory is that the rape was committed but not by Crumpton. The beneficiary introduced some testimony that Crumpton had been seen ironing just minutes prior to his death and that he had told his sister-in-law less than an hour before his death that he was going to try to find and feed his cat. Thus he could have been looking for his cat when he was mistakenly identified as the rapist by Ms. Petton who panicked and shot him. The third theory is that Crumpton committed the rape.

Even if Crumpton did commit the rape, the jury was not required to find that this action would naturally result in his subsequent murder. Crumpton, at the time of the shooting, was dressed in house shoes and had left his TV set on. Evidence presented by the beneficiary indicated that the powder markings showed that Crumpton had the back of his hands facing the murder weapon, rather than reaching for the weapon. Ms. Petton testified that she had had no contact with Crumpton between the time of the rape and the shooting five days later. Also, Petton testified that she gave no warning before she fired at Crumpton. Thus the jury, even if it believed that Crumpton had raped Ms. Petton five days earlier, could find that he would not reasonably have anticipated that she would shoot him. In a somewhat analogous situation, where an insured was slain while in the act of intercourse with the assailant's wife, a Texas court stated that the killing of the adulterer was not a natural and probable consequence of the act of adultery. In that case, the court found that an adulterer was not bound to anticipate that his death was the inevitable result of his act. Great American Reserve Insurance Co. v. Sumner, 464 S.W.2d 212 (Tex.Civ.App.—Tyler 1971, writ ref'd n.r.e.). See Wallace v. Connecticut General Life Insurance Co., 477 F.2d 680, 682 (5th Cir.1973). While rape and assault are violent actions, one does not necessarily anticipate that the victim will sometime later take the law into her own hands. Had Crumpton been shot at the time of the rape, the question might be a closer one.

We find that there was sufficient evidence from which reasonable men could find that either Crumpton did not rape Ms. Petton and thus had no reason to anticipate that his actions would cause his death or that even if he did rape Ms. Petton, he would not reasonably anticipate her subsequent actions.

Affirmed.

NOTES

1. In Hess v. Marinari, 94 S.E. 968, 970–71 (W.Va.1919), an action for battery with a meat cleaver, the court observed:

It must be borne in mind that in this case the plaintiff was seeking to recover and did a verdict for very heavy punitive damages. In order for him to recover such damages it was necessary for the jury to believe that the defendant had acted with malice toward the plaintiff; in other words, the jury would have to believe the very same things that would have to be shown in order to find him guilty of a criminal offense. What good reason is there for admitting evidence of character in a criminal case to overcome the evidence of criminal intent and rejecting it in a civil case in which the very same intent has to be established in order to recover? ... [W]here in a civil case it is necessary that the jury find that the defendant acted with criminal intent there is no good reason why he should not be allowed to prove his good character in the respect which it is necessarily questioned by charging him with the offense.... [W]e conclude that where it is necessary to the recovery which the plaintiff seeks that he prove against the defendant facts which constitute a crime, and that in order to [be liable to?] such recovery the defendant must have had criminal intent when he did the acts complained of, it is proper for the defendant to introduce character evidence such as was offered in this case for the purpose of overcoming the proof offered to show criminal intent.

There is another very good reason why this sort of evidence is admissible in a case like this where punitive damages are sought and recovered. Anything allowed to the plaintiff as damages in addition to what is necessary to compensate him for his injury is purely punishment to the defendant. It is true the damages which are allowed him as compensation are also punishment as far as the defendant is concerned, but whatever is allowed in addition to this is giving the plaintiff something to which he is in no wise entitled, except upon the theory that the defendant ought to be punished, and that the amount allowed as compensation is not sufficient for the purpose. How may the jury arrive at these punitive damages? What would be punishment for one man might be inadequate punishment for another. Surely the jury would not conclude that a man of good character for peace and quietude in the community should be punished by a fine as large as one who is a notorious bully. In fixing the punishment for crime, one of the very important elements to be considered is the subject of the punishment, and no reason is perceived why the jury should not be advised as to the character of a man who committed the acts complained of, not only for the purpose of weighing this evidence upon the question of criminal intent, or the malice charged against him, but upon the question of ascertaining the amount they think necessary to fine him in order to inflict adequate punishment....

2.   Bolton v. Tesoro Petroleum Corp., 871 F.2d 1266, 1277–78 (5th Cir.1989): In securities fraud case, not plain error to allow introduction of testimony of former President Ford as to his high esteem for the CEO of the defendant corporation, the CEO also being a defendant, when during the course of the trial the CEO had been accused of fraud, obstructing justice, perjury and bribery.

3.   The exclusionary rule in Fed. R. Evid. 404(a) is not limited to criminal cases, but the exception in 404(a)(1) speaks of "evidence of a pertinent trait of character offered by an accused." In Ginter v. Northwestern Mut. Life Ins. Co., 576 F.Supp. 627 (E.D.Ky.1984), the court expressly disagreed with the Crumpton decision. Ginter was also a suit to recover under a life insurance policy. The insurance company defended on the ground that there had been material omissions in the application for insurance. The beneficiary sought to introduce evidence that the insured was a man of good character who would be unlikely to submit a fraudulent or erroneous application. The court held that the language of Rule 404(a), taken with the Advisory Committee's Note, deprived the court of authority to admit character evidence in civil cases, "even though the case may be considered as analogous to a criminal prosecution," "except where character itself is an element of the claim or defense, as in cases involving defamation." Id. at 628, 630. See also Nakasian v. Incontrade, Inc., 78 F.R.D. 229 (S.D.N.Y.1978): Action for breach of stock sale agreement. The defense was that the agreement had been secured by duress, undue influence and conduct inconsistent with professional standards applicable to plaintiff as a lawyer. Held: Plaintiff would not be permitted under Rule 404 to call as witnesses members of the law firm for which he had worked to testify to his good character.

4. In Carrick v. McFadden, 533 P.2d 1249 (Kan.1975), an action for battery in which each party claimed that the other was the aggressor, the court, interpreting a statute, held it error to have excluded reputation and opinion testimony concerning plaintiff's character and propensity for violence even though not known to defendant. In Strickland v. Jackson, 209 S.E.2d 859 (N.C.Ct.App. 1974), a similar case, it was held not error to admit evidence of the reputation for peaceableness or violence of both parties. But in Sims v. Sowle, 395 P.2d 133 (Or.1964), another case involving a claim of self-defense, the court held it error to allow plaintiff to show his good reputation for peace and quiet.

5. Note that Fed. R. Evid. 412, supra p. 901, is applicable in civil proceedings. See especially 412(b)(2).

6. Nance v. Veazey, 312 S.W.2d 350 (Ky.1958), was a will contest in which the mental capacity of the testator was disputed. Exclusion of evidence of the reputation of the lawyer who drew the will was sustained. Presumably it was his reputation as an able lawyer that was sought to be proved.

7. As mentioned in the Crumpton case, character or reputation may be "directly in issue." In International Security Life Ins. Co. v. Melancon, 463 S.W.2d 762 (Tex.Civ.App.1971), an action for damages for negligently certifying to a licensing board that a person had a good reputation for honesty and truthfulness, evidence was introduced that the person had a bad reputation. Note, Vague Defamatory Statements and the Libel Plaintiff's Burden of Proving Falsity, 87 Colum.L.Rev. 623, 634–35 (1987), advocates allowing plaintiff to introduce good character evidence in a defamation action for "vague defamatory statements," on the ground that the plaintiff's character is in issue. See Fed.R.Evid. 405(b).

SECTION 4.   SIMILAR OCCURRENCES

Dallas Railway & Terminal Co. v. Farnsworth

Supreme Court of Texas, 1950.
148 Tex. 584, 227 S.W.2d 1017.

■ SMEDLEY, JUSTICE. The Court of Civil Appeals affirmed a judgment against petitioner, Dallas Railway & Terminal Company, in the sum of $12,518.00, for damages on account of injuries suffered by respondent, Mrs. Letta M. Farnsworth, when struck by petitioner's street car immediately after she had alighted from it. Tex.Civ.App., 221 S.W.2d 981.

. . .

It should be sufficient, without discussing at length the evidence above set out, to express our opinion that it makes issues of fact as to primary negligence on the part of the operator of the street car and contributory negligence on the part of respondent. In other words, there is some evidence to support the jury's finding that the operator was negligent in failing to give respondent an opportunity to get beyond the overhang of the car and some evidence to support the finding that respondent was not negligent in failing to step from the path of the car's overhang. The evidence, or part of it, as to negligence on the part of the operator is respondent's testimony that she was struck by the street car before she had time to take a step, almost instantaneously, after she alighted, the testimony of another witness that the movement of the car was abrupt and of another that the car "was moving rapidly for that intersection". . . .

. . .

Respondent was permitted to testify, over objections, that when she entered the street car at the Sears–Roebuck store on Lamar Street the operator started the car before she could get to a seat and was in a great hurry, that he stopped at Lamar and Young Streets and passengers "scarcely got off before he started", and that the same was true at Lamar and Main Streets. This testimony when first considered may appear to be forbidden by the general rule announced in Missouri, K. & T. Ry. Co. v. Johnson, 92 Tex. 380, 382, 48 S.W. 568, 569, that "when the question is whether or not a person has been negligent in doing, or in failing to do, a particular act, evidence is not admissible to show that he has been guilty of a similar act of negligence, or even habitually negligent upon a similar occasion." The reason for the rule is the fundamental principle that evidence must be relevant to the facts in issue in the case on trial and tend to prove or disprove those facts, evidence as to collateral facts not being admissible. 20 Am.Jur., p. 278, Sec. 302. There are some modifications of the general rule as applied to particular cases. It has been said that evidence of similar transactions or *conduct on other occasions* is not competent to prove the commission of a particular act charged *"unless the acts are connected in some special way, indicating a relevancy beyond mere similarity in certain particulars."* (Emphasis added.) 20 Am.Jur. pp. 278–279, Sec. 302.

Cunningham v. Austin & N.W. Ry. Co., 88 Tex. 534, 31 S.W. 629, 631, recognized in Missouri, K. & T. Ry. Co. v. Johnson, 92 Tex. 380, 48 S.W. 568, as a modification of the general rule is very closely in point here. In that case the negligence charged against a railway company was failure of its inspector to inspect a car wheel, and there was an issue as to the inspector's competency. The court held admissible testimony offered for the purpose of proving that the inspector had failed to inspect the wheels of the company's trains on several days a short time subsequent to the date of the accident. In so holding, the court said that evidence of the failure of the employee to perform this duty at different times tended to prove his mental condition or quality, that is, that he was inattentive and thoughtless and that "such mental quality was a relevant fact upon the issue as to whether he probably inspected the cars on the particular morning of the accident."

In the case before us testimony that the operator of the street car hurried his starting of the car, after making three stops a short time before the accident in which respondent was injured, tended to prove the state of his mind or the condition of his nerves, that is, that he was in a hurry, and so was relevant and of some probative value on the issue as to whether he failed to give respondent an opportunity to get beyond the overhang of the car before starting it. See also Harshbarger v. Murphy, 22 Idaho 261, 125 P. 180, 44 L.R.A.N.S. 1173, Am.Ann.Cas. 1914A,958. The three stops about which respondent testified over objection were made on the same run as that on which she was injured, and occurred within a distance of one mile, or three or four miles, from the place where she was injured, and within seven to ten minutes of the time of her injury. They were not so far removed either in place or in time as to be considered "conduct on other occasions," but were so closely related to the occurrence on which this suit is based that they may be considered, as in effect, part of the conduct of the operator that caused respondent's injury. We believe that the testimony was relevant and admissible.

. . .

The judgment of the Court of Civil Appeals is reversed and the cause is remanded to that Court for further consideration of the assignments of error as to excessiveness of the verdict.

NOTES

1. Wilson v. City of Chicago, 6 F.3d 1233, 1238 (7th Cir.1993), cert. denied, 114 S.Ct. 1844 (1994): In suit against city and policemen for the actions of the policemen in torturing the plaintiff to extract a confession, the torture allegedly including electroshock, held, error to have excluded evidence that ten days before the alleged torture, one of the policemen had subjected another person to electroshock and that shortly before the plaintiff's arrest, another of the policemen had taken a person to the police station and beaten him. But see Brett v. Berkowitz, 1995 WL 270146 at 7 (Del.Super.): Suit against lawyer by female divorce client for intentional infliction of mental distress in that the lawyer had engaged in sexually related behavior toward the client. The plaintiff sought discovery of similar behavior by the lawyer towards other female divorce clients. Held: Discovery denied because the evidence would not be admissible under Rule 404(b). The exception in Rule 404(b) would apply only if the prior acts were "so unusual and distinctive that their relationship to the charged offense may establish identity" or "form part of the background of the alleged act, to which it is inextricably related and without which a full understanding of the charged offense is not gained."

2. Does Fed. R. Evid. 404 exclude evidence of other acts of a person to prove character to show action in conformity therewith if there is nothing reprehensible or offensive about the other acts or the character they reveal that might lead the trier of fact to rest decision upon an improper ground? This question has already been asked supra p. 420. See the general language of Rule 404(a) and the reference in 404(b) to "other crimes, wrongs, or *acts....*" (emphasis added.) If in the case of evidence of similar acts more than relevance is required even though there is no risk of prejudice, why should this be so? Why should evidence of similar acts to prove character to prove action in conformity therewith be treated differently than any other circumstantial evidence? Does Rule 404 exclude evidence of similar acts when an animal, a machine or a process of nature is involved, rather than a human being?

See the possible application of Fed. R. Evid. 412 or Federal R. Evid. 415 to similar act evidence in civil cases.

3. Is evidence of other accidents admissible to prove that defendant's instrumentality caused the injury? In Poston v. Clarkson Construction Co., 401 S.W.2d 522, 527 (Mo.Ct.App.1966), where the issue was whether cracks in plaintiff's house were caused by defendant's blasting, it was held error to have excluded plaintiff's evidence of damage to other houses that "pretty well surrounded" plaintiff's house when there was nothing in the record to show dissimilarities in regard to factors such as construction. Arkansas Power & Light Co. v. Johnson, 538 S.W.2d 541 (Ark.1976), was a wrongful death action in which an issue was whether decedent died because his ladder came into contact with defendant's power line. The court held it not error to admit evidence that another person had suffered electrical injury at the same place under identical conditions six weeks after the litigated incident. In Carter v. Yardley & Co., 64 N.E.2d 693 (Mass.1946), plaintiff received a second degree burn when she applied defendant's perfume to her skin. Plaintiff was permitted to introduce the testimony of three witnesses that each had applied perfume from the same bottle to his or her skin and that it had irritated and injured the skin. Note the possibility in a case of this sort that evidence may be admissible to prove that the plaintiff was not extraordinarily susceptible. Koch v. Sports Health Home Care Corp., 54 F.3d 773 (4th Cir.1995): In negligence suit against manufacturer, not abuse of discretion to admit evidence of plaintiff's psychiatric history, including instances of inflicting injury on herself, as tending to show that the litigated injury was self-inflicted rather than caused by defendant's product, at least when one of the plaintiff's witnesses first mentioned the possibility of self-infliction. In Board v. Thomas Hedley & Co., [1951] 2 T.L.R. 779 (England), a food poisoning case, plaintiff was granted discovery of all complaints submitted to the defendant by other purchasers, since the testimony of these purchasers would be relevant on the issue of whether the food was bad. In Union Paint & Varnish Co. v. Dean, 137 A. 469 (R.I.1927), defendant had sought to return unopened to plaintiff a drum of paint warranted to waterproof a roof for ten years. Exclusion of defendant's evidence that paint of the same brand, bought from the same salesman five months earlier, when applied to a roof had ruined the shingles and caused leakage was held error. This case is discussed in James, Relevancy, Probability and the Law, 29 Calif.L.Rev. 689, 692 (1941). If defendant were not defending an action for the price of the paint but was suing for damages to his roof, would evidence that the earlier purchased paint had damaged his roof be admissible to prove that the paint was the harmful factor?

Strauss v. Douglas Aircraft Co., 404 F.2d 1152, 1154, 1158 and n. 10 (2d Cir.1968): Suit by passenger against airplane manufacturer. As a result of air turbulence and an alleged defect in his "seat belt cable disconnect assembly," the passenger was hurled from his seat and struck his head against the ceiling of the aircraft. The trial judge permitted a

> design engineer employed by Douglas, to testify that improper and ineffective repairs were made by Delta [the owner of the aircraft] to the cable assemblies of another DC–8 which Delta had also purchased from Douglas. Photographs of these repairs were received in evidence. The testimony was admitted, over objection, to show that Delta had abused the cable assemblies.... This evidence was presumably accorded considerable weight by the jury, because it asked to see the photographs of the repairs on the other plane shortly before it emerged from the jury room with a verdict for Douglas.... Here there was evidence of but a single instance of repairs to another plane, with no showing of any correlation between the two planes. Thus, there was not a sufficient basis from which a jury could reasonably infer that the seat belts in Strauss' plane were also improperly repaired by Delta. And, any probative value of such evidence was greatly outweighed by its possibly prejudicial effect.... Douglas argues that if we find the evidence of the repairs to be improper, we should also direct the exclusion of evidence of frayed cables in other Delta aircraft, which were admitted over Douglas' objection. But that evidence involved 191 instances of frayed cables on five of Delta's six DC–8s, including eight frayed cables on the plane involved in this accident. We believe this is a sufficiently large number of instances on which the jury might base an inference of systematic conduct.

Bonilla v. Yamaha Motors Corp., 955 F.2d 150 (1st Cir.1992): In motorcycle accident case in which issue was whether the accident was caused by defectively designed brakes or excessive speed, error, under Fed. R. Evid. 404(b), to admit evidence of speeding violations by plaintiff, one four years before the accident, the other two years afterwards. Amatucci v. Delaware & Hudson Ry. Co., 745 F.2d 180 (2d Cir.1984): In FELA case in which plaintiff sought to recover for heart condition allegedly caused by the stressful job of being an extra-board engineer, error to admit evidence that seven or eight other engineers had suffered heart attacks while driving locomotives for defendant.

4. When an attempt is made to introduce evidence of other occurrences in actions based upon theories of negligence, breach of warranty or strict liability, careful consideration must be given to the elements of liability under each theory and the possible relevance of the evidence to these elements. In addition to causation, there may be questions of foreseeability and whether a product was "defective" or "unreasonably dangerous" in use.

Ault v. International Harvester Co., 528 P.2d 1148 (Cal.1974): Plaintiff was injured when a vehicle in which he was riding, which had been manufactured by defendant, suddenly went off the road and plunged into a canyon. In a suit to recover for his injuries, plaintiff alleged that the accident occurred because the gearbox in the vehicle broke as a result of metal fatigue. Plaintiff claimed that the metal used in the gearbox constituted a "design defect." The court held that it was not error to admit plaintiff's evidence that gearboxes in two other vehicles manufactured by defendant which had physical properties similar to those of the gearbox in plaintiff's vehicle had broken as a result of metal fatigue. Farner v. Paccar, Inc., 562 F.2d 518, 528 (8th Cir.1977): Action against a truck manufacturer on theories of negligence and strict liability. The plaintiff's decedent died when his truck veered off the highway, allegedly because of the failure of the suspension system. The court held it was not error to allow owners of similar trucks manufactured by the defendant to testify that the suspension systems in their trucks had failed. Eagleburger v. Emerson Elec. Co., 794 S.W.2d 210, 215–20, 244–46 (Mo.Ct.App.1990): When issue was whether 40–foot aluminum ladder was unreasonably dangerous because of risk of electrocution from power lines, not error to admit Consumer Products Safety Commission Report of 426 accidents involving aluminum ladders and power lines during a ten-year period. Dissent: Insufficient similarity of conditions.

Exum v. General Elec. Co., 819 F.2d 1158 (D.C.Cir.1987): Defendant's Model 811 "french fryer" required the operator, in order to filter grease, to lift a six-pound pan containing 15 pounds of grease at a temperature of 350 degrees and pour the grease through a paper cone filter into a second pan placed on the floor. Wendy's, the fast food company, used the Model 811 in its eating establishments. Plaintiff, an employee of Wendy's, was injured while carrying out the grease filtering operation: a pressurized asthma inhaler in his shirt pocket fell into the pan of grease on the floor, causing an explosion. Plaintiff sued defendant on a theory of negligent design. Plaintiff was allowed to introduce evidence that defendant manufactured a manual siphon costing less than $100, which could have been incorporated into the Model 811 to eliminate the need for pouring grease from one pan into another. However, plaintiff was not allowed to introduce evidence of other accidents in which Wendy's employees had been injured while pouring hot grease. Some of these accidents occurred before plaintiff's accident and involved spillage during the pouring operation. One accident occurred after plaintiff's accident and involved an object being dropped into the pan of grease on the floor. Held: Error to exclude the evidence of other accidents: the prior accidents were relevant to dangerousness and notice and the subsequent accident was relevant to dangerousness.

5. In regard to using evidence of other accidents to establish that defendant knew or should have known of the dangerous conditions, see Texas & New Orleans R.R. Co. v. Davis, 210 S.W.2d 195 (Tex.Civ.App.1948), where a sheriff testified that there were one or two accidents a year at the railroad crossing involved. See also Rader v. Gibbons & Reed Co., 494 P.2d 412 (Or.1972) (motorist killed by rock crashing through windshield; evidence of rocks on highway and a rock hitting the windshield of another motorist before the litigated incident); Kinney v. Mason Elevator, 194 N.W.2d 408 (Mich.Ct.App. 1971) (recognizing admissibility of prior accidents to show knowledge, but finding the accidents sought to be proved stemmed from unique and different causes). Clark v. Stewart, 185 N.E. 71 (Ohio 1933), was an action for injuries resulting from an automobile accident in which the son had been driving defendant father's car. Recovery was sought both on the basis of respondeat superior and the personal negligence of the father in allowing the son to drive. No error was found in the allowance of questions to the father about prior accidents of the son, known to him. But see Richmond v. Norwich, 115 A. 11, 16–19 (Conn.1921): Plaintiff shot by guard employed by city and claimed to be irresponsible and unfit; error to admit evidence of another incident, after the incident in which plaintiff was injured, in which the guard acted irresponsibly in the use of firearms. Cf. Kurn v. Radencic, 141 P.2d 580 (Okl.1943), where plaintiff-trespasser was beaten up by a railroad policeman after having been removed from a freight train and sought punitive as well as compensatory damages from the railroad. Plaintiff was permitted to introduce evidence that the particular policeman had previously committed violent assaults on other trespassers. The court said that this evidence went to the amount of punitive damages, since there is a difference in the degree of wrong committed by a principal having an employee who, without prior misconduct, commits an aggravated tort of this nature, and a principal having an employee with a previously demonstrated inclination wilfully to injure others.

6. Suppose defendant wishes to prove that an instrumentality was safe or that he had no reason to know of the danger. May he introduce evidence that no other accidents have occurred or no other complaints been received? In Greiten v. LaDow, 235 N.W.2d 677, 682 (Wis.1975), an action for negligence against the designer and installer of equipment, the court held it was not error to admit evidence of no prior accidents with the equipment since it was installed, six years before the litigated accident. In Pittman v. Littlefield, 438 F.2d 659 (1st Cir.1971), where plaintiff was injured when a pallet tipped over and heavy bags fell on him, the court held that an inadequate foundation as to similarity of conditions had been laid for testimony by a witness that he had never seen supplies of this sort tip over from a pallet. The hearsay problem in no-complaint evidence is perceived and neatly handled in Menard v. Cashman, 55 A.2d 156, 160 (N.H.1947). See also Silver v. New York Cent. R. Co., supra p. 510.

7. Consider the admissibility of other acts evidence in suits under civil rights statutes, especially for the purpose of demonstrating racial motivation. In Miller v. Poretsky, 595 F.2d 780 (D.C.Cir.1978), a suit by a tenant against a landlord for racial discrimination, the court held it was error, although harmless, to exclude plaintiff's evidence that the defendant had discriminated against someone else in the same apartment complex. At least it was error, the court held, when the defendant had been allowed to put in testimony of others that defendant did not discriminate against them and the trial judge indicated at the pretrial conference that the plaintiff would be allowed to introduce his evidence. Federal Rules of Evidence 403 and 404, the court held, did not justify the exclusion of the evidence. A concurring opinion stated:

> An important public policy is subserved by admission of evidence of other acts of discrimination or nondiscrimination on the part of a defendant whose motivation vis-a-vis the plaintiff has been drawn into question. As the populace has become more and more aware of the illegality of disparate treatment attributable to racial or some other invidious classification, discriminatory practices have become increasingly subtle. Absent something amounting well nigh to an open admission of discriminatory

purpose, victims may find it virtually impossible to prove that fact unless permitted to introduce evidence that the defendant has engaged in one or more acts of discrimination against others. At the same time, a defendant falsely accused of discriminating against the plaintiff should not be made to forego an opportunity to demonstrate lack of bias—more palatably than by his unsupported disavowal alone—by evidence reflecting nondiscriminatory activity on other occasions.

Id. at 796. The same opinion carefully reviews the use of other acts evidence in civil rights cases and concludes that the plaintiff's evidence should have been admitted even in the absence of the special circumstances pointed to by the majority. Garvey v. Dickinson College, 763 F.Supp. 799 (M.D.Pa.1991): In suit under Title VII for sexual harassment, evidence that defendant professor had harassed other female students and staff would be admissible to show intent to discriminate: those involved in the other incidents were in the same department. But see Hogan v. AT&T, 812 F.2d 409, 410 (8th Cir.1987): In suit by employee for discrimination on grounds of race and sex, assuming error in the exclusion of evidence that a supervisor previously had made an unsubstantiated claim that a black woman employee's performance was poor, offered on the issue of intent, the error did not affect the substantial rights of the plaintiff.

8. Proof of similar occurrences can be significant in property valuation cases, especially condemnation proceedings. This subject will be discussed further in connection with expert testimony, infra pp. 1065–67. Here emphasis is on the independent use of evidence of similar occurrences, rather than on evidence of such occurrences in the basis of expert opinion.

Village of Lawrence v. Greenwood, 90 N.E.2d 53 (N.Y.1949), was a condemnation proceeding in which the village was allowed to prove market value by evidence of the purchase price paid on two recent sales of comparable property in the neighborhood. For a comprehensive review of the factors to be considered in determining whether properties are comparable, see Sengstock and McAuliffe, What is the Price of Eminent Domain? 44 J.Urb.L. 185, 195–97 (1967). 85 A.L.R.2d 110 (1962), deals with the admissibility of sales prices of comparable realty to prove value. 155 A.L.R. 262 (1945), deals with evidence of sales price or contract sales price of the very property. There is authority for the proposition that the test of comparability is stricter when other sales are introduced independently than when they are the basis of expert opinion. E.g., Kamrowski v. State, 155 N.W.2d 125 (Wis.1967).

Should sales of comparable property be admitted when either the acquiring party or the landowner or both have been subject to abnormal pressures, as where a sale was made under threat of eminent domain or where the proprietor of a small parcel of land could hold out and block a large development? See Epstein v. Boston Housing Authority, 58 N.E.2d 135 (Mass.1944).

Should offers to purchase property be admitted to prove its value? Hardaway v. City of Des Moines, 166 N.W.2d 578, 581 (Iowa 1969), was a condemnation proceeding in which it was held not error to exclude evidence of an offer. "We believe as a general rule an unaccepted offer for the purchase of real estate should not be received as evidence of the value of such real estate. However, that is not to say there might not be exceptional cases in which the evidence establishes a foundation for a bona fide offer so firmly and completely that the trial court would not abuse its discretion in receiving evidence of such offer.... To these limitations we would add the requirement that the proof come from the offeror. We do not intend to deprive the person against whom such offer is made of the right to cross-examination." For further discussion of the hearsay problem in respect to both offers and sales, see infra p. 1066.

What about options? United States v. Smith, 355 F.2d 807, 812 (5th Cir.1966): Error to allow testimony as to options on other comparable property and to admit expert testimony based on such options, even though consideration was given. "The payment ... merely binds the landowner and indicates the bona fides of his asking price. It does not in any way bind the holder to buy at that price or indicate that he regards that price as a fair one from a purchaser's standpoint." The court distinguishes options that have been exercised and become binding contracts of sale.

Should condemnation awards for comparable property be admissible? See Comment, Valuation Evidence in California Condemnation Cases, 12 Stan. L.Rev. 766, 781 n. 93 (1960).

SECTION 5.   HABIT AND CUSTOM

Halloran v. Virginia Chemicals, Inc.

Court of Appeals of New York, 1977.
41 N.Y.2d 386, 393 N.Y.S.2d 341, 361 N.E.2d 991.

■ BREITEL, CHIEF JUDGE.

Defendant Virginia Chemicals appeals in a personal injury products liability action. Plaintiff Frank Halloran, an automobile mechanic, obtained a verdict in his favor, after a jury trial on the issue of liability only, for injuries he sustained while using a can of refrigerant packaged and sold by the chemical company. A divided Appellate Division affirmed, and certified a question of law for review in this court.

. . .

There is one other issue meriting extended discussion: whether evidence that the injured mechanic had previously used an immersion heating coil to heat the can of the refrigerant should be admissible to show that on the particular occasion he was negligent and ignored the labeled warnings on the can. Evidently relying on the rubric excluding prior instances of carelessness to create an inference of carelessness on a particular occasion, both the Trial Judge and the Appellate Division, save for two dissenting Justices, agreed that such evidence was not admissible.

There should be a reversal and a new trial. If plaintiff, when necessary to stimulate the flow of the refrigerant, a highly compressed liquefied gas, habitually or regularly used an immersion coil to heat the water in which the container was placed, evidence of that habit or regular usage should be admissible to prove he followed such a procedure on the day of the explosion. Evidence of habit or regular usage, if properly defined and therefore circumscribed, involves more than unpatterned occasional conduct, that is, conduct however frequent yet likely to vary from time to time depending upon the surrounding circumstances; it involves a repetitive pattern of conduct and therefore predictable and predictive conduct. On this view, the excluded evidence was offered to show a particular method of executing a task followed by the mechanic, who, on his own testimony, had serviced "hundreds" of air-conditioning units and used "thousands" of cans of the refrigerant. If on remittal the evidence tends to show that the mechanic used an immersion coil a sufficient number of times to warrant a finding of habit, or regular usage, it would be admissible to aid the jury on its inquiry whether he did so on the occasion in question.

On June 1, 1970, the day of the accident, Frank Halloran, a mechanic for 15 years, had been employed by the Hillcrest Service station for over three years. Among his duties was the servicing and charging of automobile air-conditioning units, a job for which he had been specially trained, and for which he used "all [his] own tools." The particular task involved that day was the changing of the air-conditioning compressor on a 1967 Chrysler automobile. Plaintiff testified that he had emptied the system, removed the old compressor, and installed a new one. He then began to charge the unit.

The first two cans of the refrigerant, Freon, flowed into the system without difficulty. By the time he was emptying the third can, however, plaintiff found it necessary to accelerate the flow of the refrigerant. The mechanic described how he filled an empty two-pound coffee tin with warm tap water, used a thermometer to determine that the water temperature was about 90 to 100 degrees, and inserted into the coffee tin the third can of Freon. Having a similar problem with the flow of the fourth can, Halloran again dropped the Freon into the warm water. Noticing that his low pressure gauge showed a rapid increase in the pressure, and aware that "something was wrong", Halloran reached down to remove the can from the water, but was too late. The can exploded before he could touch it.

Neither the thermometer Halloran claimed to have used nor the bottom of the exploded can of Freon was produced at trial. Halloran knew that excessive heating of the can would cause damage, and that the warnings on the can specified 130 degrees as the maximum permissible safe temperature. As discussed earlier, he proved no particular defect in the can, its contents, or in so much of the exploded can which was produced at the trial. Having worked alone that day, Halloran was the only eyewitness to the explosion.

Defendant Virginia Chemicals, on cross-examination of Halloran and on its defense, sought to establish that it was Halloran's "usage and practice" to use an immersion coil to heat the water in which the Freon was placed. Halloran denied ever making such use of an immersion coil. But defendant offered a witness prepared to testify not only that he had seen Halloran on previous occasions using an immersion coil to heat Freon, but that he had warned plaintiff of the danger as well. Plaintiff, relying on the rule that extrinsic evidence cannot be introduced to impeach a witness on collateral matters, objected to the admissibility of such testimony. The Trial Judge sustained the objection.

Of course, had an immersion heating coil been used at the time of the accident the unexplained and thus far unexplainable explosion would have been fully explained.

Were the evidence defendant sought to produce collateral, defendant generally would be bound by plaintiff's denial. For it is now well settled that extrinsic evidence introduced solely to impeach credibility on a collateral issue is, with special exceptions, inadmissible (People v. Schwartzman, 24 N.Y.2d 241, 245, 299 N.Y.S.2d 817, 820, 247 N.E.2d 642, 644; Potter v. Browne, 197 N.Y. 288, 293, 90 N.E. 812, 814; Richardson, Evidence [10th ed.], § 491).

To be sure, Halloran's practice prior to June 1, 1970 is not conclusive proof of the method he employed in working on the 1967 Chrysler. "Collateral", however, it is not. Logically probative it is and ought to be. While courts of this State have in negligence cases traditionally excluded evidence of carefulness or carelessness as not probative of how one acted on a particular occasion, in other cases evidence of a consistent practice or method followed by a person has routinely been allowed (compare, e.g., Zucker v. Whitridge, 205 N.Y. 50, 58–66, 98 N.E. 209, 210–213 [carefulness], and Hartley v. Szadkowski, 32 A.D.2d 550,

300 N.Y.S.2d 82 [carelessness], with People v. Bombard, 5 A.D.2d 923, 172 N.Y.S.2d 1, cert. den., 358 U.S. 849, 79 S.Ct. 75, 3 L.Ed.2d 83, [prosecutor's practice of insisting defendant be advised of right to counsel]). That a kind of habit, practice, or method was proffered in this case to establish negligence should not, without more, affect its admissibility.

Because one who has demonstrated a consistent response under given circumstances is more likely to repeat that response when the circumstances arise again, evidence of habit has, since the days of the common-law reports, generally been admissible to prove conformity on specified occasions (e.g., Miller v. Hackley, 5 Johns. 375, 384; 1 Wigmore, Evidence [3d ed.], § 92; Richardson, Evidence [10th ed.], § 185; Fed.Rules Evidence, rule 406 [in U.S.Code, tit. 28, Appendix]; see, generally, Lewan, Rationale of Habit Evidence, 16 Syracuse L.Rev. 39). Hence, a lawyer, to prove due execution of a will, may testify that he always has wills executed according to statutory requirements (Matter of Kellum, 52 N.Y. 517, 519–520). So too, to prove that notice is mailed on a specified day of the month, one is allowed to testify that he is in the habit of being home on that day of the month to transact such business (Beakes v. Da Cunha, 126 N.Y. 293, 298, 27 N.E. 251, 252).

When negligence is at issue, however, New York courts have long resisted allowing evidence of specific acts of carelessness or carefulness to create an inference that such conduct was repeated when like circumstances were again presented (e.g., Warner v. New York Cent. R.R. Co., 44 N.Y. 465, 472; Grenadier v. Surface Transp. Corp. of N.Y., 271 App.Div. 460, 461, 66 N.Y.S.2d 130, 131; Lefcourt v. Jenkinson, 258 App.Div. 1080, 18 N.Y.S.2d 160; Richardson, Evidence, § 186; Fisch, New York Evidence, § 202; cf. Cabezudo v. New York's Eldorado, 50 A.D.2d 794, 795, 378 N.Y.S.2d 75, 77). Hence, evidence of a plaintiff's habit of jumping on streetcars may not be offered to prove he was negligent on the day of the accident (Eppendorf v. Brooklyn City & Newtown R.R. Co., 69 N.Y. 195, 197). Nor could testimony that the deceased had usually looked both ways before crossing railroad tracks be introduced to establish his care on the particular occasion (Zucker v. Whitridge, 205 N.Y. 50, 58–66, 98 N.E. 209, 210–213, supra). Whether a carryover from the prohibition against using so-called "character" evidence in civil cases, or grounded on the assumption that even repeated instances of negligence or care do not sufficiently increase the probability of like conduct on a particular occasion, the statement that evidence of habit or regular usage is never admissible to establish negligence is too broad (see 1 Wigmore, Evidence [3d ed.], § 97, esp. p. 532).

At least, as in this kind of case, where the issue involves proof of a deliberate and repetitive practice, a party should be able, by introducing evidence of such habit or regular usage, to allow the inference of its persistence, and hence negligence on a particular occasion (see McCormick, Evidence [2d ed.], § 195, advocating an even more expansive approach; see, also, 1 Wigmore, Evidence [3d ed.], § 97). Far less likely to vary with the attendant circumstances, such repetitive conduct is more predictive than the frequency (or rarity) of jumping on streetcars or exercising stop-look-and-listen caution in crossing railroad tracks. On no view, under traditional analysis, can conduct involving not only oneself but particularly other persons or independently controlled instrumentalities produce a regular usage because of the likely variation of the circumstances in which such conduct will be indulged. Proof of a deliberate repetitive practice by one in complete control of the circumstances is quite another matter and it should therefore be admissible because it is so highly probative.

As previously noted, Halloran, in the course of his work as a mechanic, had serviced "hundreds" of automobile air conditioners and had used "thousands" of cans of Freon. From his testimony at trial it seems clear that in servicing these units he followed, as of course he would, a routine. If, indeed, the use of an immersion coil tended to be part of this routine whenever it was necessary to accelerate the flow of the refrigerant, as he indicated was often the case, the jury should not be precluded from considering such evidence as an aid to its determination.

Of course, to justify introduction of habit or regular usage, a party must be able to show on voir dire, to the satisfaction of the Trial Judge, that he expects to prove a sufficient number of instances of the conduct in question (see Fed.Rules Evidence, rule 406; Model Code of Evidence, rule 307, subd. [3], par. [b], including Comment, Illustrations 2, 3 [1942]; Uniform Rules of Evidence, rule 406, subd. [b]; see, also, 2 Wigmore, Evidence [3d ed.], § 376). If defendant's witness was prepared to testify to seeing Halloran using an immersion coil on only one occasion, exclusion was proper. If, on the other hand, plaintiff was seen a sufficient number of times, and it is preferable that defendant be able to fix, at least generally, the times and places of such occurrences, a finding of habit or regular usage would be warranted and the evidence admissible for the jury's consideration.

. . .

■ Jasen, Gabrielli, Jones, Wachtler, Fuchsberg and Cooke, JJ., concur.

Order modified, and the case remitted to Supreme Court, Queens County, for a new trial in accordance with the opinion herein. . . .

NOTES

1. Fed.R.Evid. 406 provides: "Evidence of the habit of a person or of the routine practice of an organization, whether corroborated or not and regardless of the presence of eyewitnesses, is relevant to prove that the conduct of the person or organization on a particular occasion was in conformity with the habit or routine practice." In the discussion of Rule 412, supra p. 901, a question was asked whether that rule establishes a different standard of relevance than the standard included in Rule 401. Rule 406 states that a certain kind of evidence—evidence of habit—is relevant. Does this rule state a different standard of relevance than the standard included in Rule 401? If not, why do we need to be told in Rule 406 that habit evidence is relevant?

2. What is the difference between "habit" and "character"? Frase v. Henry, 444 F.2d 1228, 1231–32 (10th Cir.1971): Wrongful death actions arising out of highway collision.

We pass on to the other question on appeal, whether it was prejudicial error to allow two witnesses for appellee to testify that appellee's deceased was a good driver. Witness Mrs. Bodge testified that she had ridden with appellee's deceased and she thought he was a good driver who did not drive over the speed limit but usually drove five miles per hour under the limit. Witness Frase also testified that appellee's deceased was a good driver, cautious, obeyed the rules of the road, and in the recollection of the witness never drove over 60 miles per hour. The issue posed by the parties is whether the testimony was inadmissible under K[ansas] S.A. § 60–448 which excludes evidence of a trait of a person's character with respect to care or skill, or whether the testimony was admissible under K.S.A. § 60–449, which allows testimony of habit or custom.

"Character" is a generalized description of one's disposition in respect to a general trait such as honesty, temperance, or carefulness, while "habit" is more specific. The latter designates a regular practice of meeting a particular kind of situation with a certain type of conduct, or a reflex behavior in a specific set of circumstances. Evidence of habit or custom is relevant to an issue of behavior on a specific occasion because it tends to prove that the behavior on such occasion conformed to the habit or custom.

While the distinction between trait of character and habit or custom is easy in statement, it is more difficult in application.... Certain things are abundantly clear though. Obviously had the testimony been merely that the deceased was a careful, cautious man, it would not have been admissible because such testimony is not specific enough to tend to prove that the deceased was careful in a specific instance in specific circumstances. However, testimony regarding the deceased's care in driving, his practice of driving under the speed limit, and his regard to the rules of the road is testimony which devolved into specific aspects of the deceased's conduct. Such testimony showed more than a general disposition to be careful and showed a regular practice of meeting a particular kind of situation with a specific type of conduct. The testimony is all the more cogent because of the lack of an eyewitness account of what transpired that morning on U.S. 36.

In view of the trial judge's wide discretion in receiving evidence, and since in the absence of state rulings a trial judge's view is highly persuasive as to what the law of the State of Kansas is or would be, we are not convinced that the reception of the evidence was erroneous under § 60–448.[1]

Simplex, Inc. v. Diversified Energy Systems, Inc., 847 F.2d 1290, 1293–94 (7th Cir.1988): In contract suit in which defendant claimed the items delivered by the plaintiff were defective and not delivered on time, not error to exclude evidence of plaintiff's inadequate performance under other contracts:

We are cautious in permitting the admission of habit or pattern-of-conduct evidence under Rule 406 because it necessarily engenders the very real possibility that such evidence will be used to establish a party's propensity to act in conformity with its general character, thereby thwarting Rule 404's prohibition against the use of character evidence except for narrowly prescribed purposes....

We are extremely dubious of Diversified's contention that late and inadequate performance of other contracts approaches the level of specificity necessary to be considered semi-automatic conduct.... [T]he production of defective products could take an endless variety of forms. Beyond the conclusory assertion that "numerous examples of other instances of lateness and defective performance on similar contracts" exist, Diversified fails to allege any specific, repetitive conduct that might approach evidence of habit. Mere similarity of contracts does not present the kind of "sufficiently similar circumstances to outweigh the danger ... of prejudice and of confusion." See McCormick on Evidence § 162 (1964).[2]

3. Evidence of a habit may be admissible for the sake of an inference from its nonobservance. State v. Clemons, 1988 WL 37129 (Ohio.Ct.App.): When the issue was whether a woman was killed during an early period or at a later time and evidence showed that she had not come home to her baby during the early

---

1. Footnotes omitted.

2. Footnote omitted.

period, permissible under Rule 406 to admit testimony that the woman habitually was attentive to the baby and did not leave it for an extended period.

4. It is difficult to draw from the cases a clear statement as to how specific a habit must be in order to be admissible. Consider the following: Glatt v. Feist, 156 N.W.2d 819 (N.D.1968): Action for injuries to pedestrian from collision with vehicle. Plaintiff was hit at or near an intersection on Main Street as she was returning home from church. The disputed issue was whether plaintiff was in the cross-walk or just to the east of it when she was hit. Held: Error to exclude defendant's evidence of plaintiff's habit, on returning from church, of angling across Main Street at the place where the accident occurred in such a way as to go outside the cross-walk. See also Charmley v. Lewis, 729 P.2d 567 (Or.1986): Not error to admit similar evidence; Haider v. Finken, 239 N.W.2d 508, 520 (N.D.1976): Not error to exclude testimony as to plaintiff's habit of dimming his lights when approaching an oncoming vehicle. State v. Lewis, 225 P.2d 428 (Wash.1950): Manslaughter case arising out of hunting accident; defendant not permitted to prove by the testimony of hunting companions that he was a careful hunter.

5. How many recurrences must be shown to add up to a habit? Over how long a period must the recurrences extend? Must the person whose habit is sought to be proved invariably act in accordance with the habit, or will some deviations be permitted? Will evidence of a habit be admitted even though it consists only of a sampling of the person's behavior when confronted by a particular kind of situation? Crawford v. Fayez, 435 S.E.2d 545 (N.C.Ct.App.1993), cert. denied, 441 S.E.2d 113 (1994): In medical malpractice suit in which plaintiffs contended the doctor had not told them of the risk of a certain side effect of the drug he prescribed, not error to admit testimony of five of the 26 patients for whom the doctor had prescribed the drug that he had warned them about the side effect. State v. Wadsworth, 210 So.2d 4 (Fla.1968): Prosecution for "manslaughter by an intoxicated motorist"; not error to admit as corroborative evidence testimony of a liquor store clerk that two or three times a week over a two year period, defendant had purchased miniature bottles of vodka and said that he "had a problem." State v. Radziwil, 563 A.2d 856 (N.J.Super.1989), aff'd, 582 A.2d 1003 (N.J.1990): In a prosecution for manslaughter and death by automobile in which as a practical matter the only disputed issue was whether the defendant was drunk when his vehicle collided with the decedent's, not abuse of discretion to admit evidence that during the period preceding the accident, almost every weekend the defendant went to a bar about six miles from the scene of the accident and became drunk. The accident occurred shortly after midnight on a weekend night. But see Reyes v. Missouri Pacific Railroad Co., 589 F.2d 791 (5th Cir.1979): Action for negligence with defense of contributory negligence. Plaintiff was run over by defendant's train while lying on the track. Held, error to admit evidence of plaintiff's four convictions for public drunkenness. These incidents, spanning three and a half years, "are of insufficient regularity to rise to the level of 'habit' evidence." Petricevich v. Salmon River Canal Co., 452 P.2d 362 (Idaho 1969): Not error to exclude evidence defendant started fires to prove started fire on particular occasion; insufficient number of prior instances and similarity with litigated instance not shown. Stanton v. Morrison Mills, Inc., 47 A.2d 112 (N.H.1946) (very frequent routine action but for less than three days).

Wilson v. Volkswagen of America, Inc., 561 F.2d 494, 511–12 (4th Cir. 1977), cert. denied, 434 U.S. 1020 (1978): In overturning a default judgment entered against defendants on the ground that they had deliberately withheld discoverable materials and lied to the trial court about their existence, the appellate court disapproved of the trial court's reliance on information concerning three other cases in which default judgments had been entered against defendants. The information concerning these other cases was fragmentary and did not establish their similarity with the litigated case. Furthermore, "[I]t is obvious that no finding is supportable under Rule 406, Federal Rules of Evidence, which fails to examine critically the 'ratio of reactions to situations.' "The court observed that compared with the large number of cases filed against the defendants in which no claim of misconduct was apparently made, the mere fact that in three cases default judgments had been entered, especially in view of the paucity of exact information about them and that default seemed to have been vacated in two of them, "can hardly be thought sufficient to establish 'regularity of response' so automatic as to represent habit or pattern." Thompson v. Boggs, 33 F.3d 847, 855 (7th Cir.1994), cert. denied, 115 S.Ct. 1692 (1995): In suit against police officer for use of excessive force, not error to exclude evidence of the officer's use of excessive force on five other occasions. "[W]ithout any evidence of the total number of contacts Officer Boggs had with citizens or the number of arrests he performed, [the evidence] fail[ed] to satisfy the plaintiff's burden of demonstrating that Boggs' 'regular response to a repeated specific situation' was the 'systematic' use of excessive force."

Levin v. United States, 338 F.2d 265, 269–74 (D.C.Cir.1964), cert. denied, 379 U.S. 999 (1965), involved admissibility of evidence of defendant's observance of the Sabbath to establish that late on a certain Friday afternoon he was not in the Statler Hotel in Washington, D.C., receiving money from the prosecution witness, but at home in Queens. "It seems apparent to us that an individual's religious practices would not be the type of activities which would lend themselves to the characterization of 'invariable regularity.' Certainly the very volitional basis of the activity raises serious questions as to its invariable nature, and hence its probative value.... Needless to say, the observance of the Sabbath in a particular manner involves a volitional assent, however guided or instructively urged."

6.   Convenience and compactness of proof are important factors. When a single witness can testify that he saw the asserted actor behave identically on 50 occasions, the testimony will be more acceptable then if it is proposed to call 50 witnesses, each with only one occasion to tell about. In Crawford v. Fayez, supra, where the issue was whether the doctor had told the plaintiffs of the risk of a side effect, the evidence introduced was not only the testimony of other patients that the doctor had told them of the side effect, but also the testimony of the doctor that it was his habit and routine practice to tell patients of the side effect. See generally Lewan, The Rationale of Habit Evidence, 16 Syracuse L. Rev. 39 (1964), cited in the Halloran opinion. As adopted by the Supreme Court, Federal Rule of Evidence 406 included a subdivision (b), which provided: "Habit or routine practice may be proved by testimony in the form of an opinion or by specific instances of conduct sufficient in number to warrant a finding that the habit existed or that the practice was routine." Congress eliminated this subdivision, the House Judiciary Committee Report explaining: "The Committee deleted this subdivision believing that the method of proof of habit and routine practice should be left to the courts to deal with on a case-by-case basis. At the same time, the Committee does not intend that its action be construed as sanctioning a general authorization of opinion evidence in this area." When a witness testifies to his opinion about habit, is this simply a way of communicating the numerous particular instances he has observed or more than this?

7.   Habit or custom evidence as to the routine practice of a business is generally admissible to prove what was done on a particular occasion. Baldridge v. Matthews, 106 A.2d 809 (Pa.1954): In an action for criminal conversation, it was held not error to admit testimony of a hotel clerk that it was the hotel's invariable practice to require payment in advance when a person was without luggage, in order to establish that defendant and plaintiff's wife had luggage with them when they took a room and thus intended an overnight stay. Spartan Grain & Mill Co. v. Ayers, 517 F.2d 214 (5th Cir.1975): Error to exclude evidence of plaintiff's pick-up practices in handling defendant's eggs offered to prove plaintiff's rough handling of defendant's eggs on particular occasions. Commonwealth v. Torrealba, 54 N.E.2d 939, 942 (Mass.1944) (to prove that store made no sale on particular occasion, testimony was introduced that it was customary to give a sales slip with each purchase—defendant produced no such slip); United States v. Lopez, 328 F.Supp. 1077, 1086 (E.D.N.Y.1971) (on legality of frisk of air passenger after use of magnetometer, permissible to accept testimony of practice of adjusting machine, the person who actually adjusted the machine not being available).

United States v. Angelilli, 660 F.2d 23, 37–42 (2d Cir.1981), cert. denied, 455 U.S. 910 (1982): Four marshals of the Civil Court of the City of New York were prosecuted under the Racketeer Influenced and Corrupt Organizations Act, 18 U.S.C. § 1962(c) (1976) (RICO), and various other federal statutes for conducting fraudulent auctions of judgment debtors' assets and for conspiracy. The defendants were alleged to have auctioned or arranged for the auction of the assets at less than their true value, in return for which they received "top money" from the buyers at the sham auctions. Testimony was introduced by the government that it was the regular custom and practice of New York City marshals to demand and accept "top money". In regard to the admissibility of this testimony, the Court of Appeals stated: "Such testimony could properly be considered in determining whether or not the government had proven the existence of a broad conspiracy among marshals to demand top money, as alleged in the indictment, but it could not be considered in reaching a finding as to whether or not any of the defendants themselves demanded or received top money." "[T]he ... instruction permitted the jury to infer conduct of an individual on the basis of the custom of an organization. It may be that the ambiguous structure of Rule 406—which does not link the conduct of a person expressly with proof as to the habit of that person, nor the conduct of an organization expressly with proof as to the routine practice of that organization ...—was intended to make admissible the evidence of the practice of the organization to prove the conduct of any of its members. As a matter of policy, however, we cannot countenance that application of the Rule here ... since it would defy the principle of the individuality of guilt to hold that a defendant's mere membership in an organization practicing a particular type of crime could be used to show that the defendant himself committed such a crime."

United States v. Rangel–Arreola, 991 F.2d 1519, 1523 (10th Cir.1993): Prosecution for possession of marijuana found in a hidden compartment in the fuel tank of a truck. Not error to exclude defense testimony of two truck drivers and an investigator that it was the common practice of truck drivers to accept trucking jobs without checking the fuel tanks or knowing the purpose of the journey.

> [I]n order to utilize Rule 406, Mr. Rangel must demonstrate the two truck drivers were part of an organization or group to which he belonged and that their testimony would have related the routine practice of the group. The record does not support a finding that free-lance truck drivers in the El Paso region form a cohesive organization. The underlying rationale for applying Rule 406 to organizations is that as a practical matter, organizations must make many of their practices routine and this routine lends a degree of reliability to habit evidence.... The district court did not abuse

its discretion in finding Rule 406 inapplicable to a loose-knit group with no apparent structure or routine.

When studying the topic of expert testimony and Fed. R. Evid. 702, infra p. 954, consider whether the evidence in Rangel–Arreola could gain admission under that rule.

Fed. R. Evid. 404 excludes evidence of the character of a person to prove action in conformity therewith. Does a "person" include an organization? Possibly, since an organization is made up of persons. If the prohibition of Rule 404 does not extend to organizations, is there anything in the Federal Rules of Evidence to prevent introduction of evidence of the practice of an organization to prove how an individual acted even though the practice does not amount to a "routine practice" within the meaning of Rule 406? If the practice of an organization introduced to prove how an individual acted does fall within the prohibition of Rule 404, does it if the evidence is introduced not to prove how an individual acted, but to prove his state of mind? Cf. Imwinkelried & Margolin, The Case for the Admissibility of Defense Testimony About Customary Political Practices in Official Corruption Prosecutions, 29 Am. Cr. L. Rev. 1 (1991) (evidence of practice of members of legislative body to channel bona fide contributions through legislative aides introduced to rebut inference individual legislator had mens rea required for crime).

8. As is the case with respect to evidence of similar occurrences, evidence of habit may be admissible as conveying knowledge or putting on notice. E.g., Brogan v. City of Philadelphia, 29 A.2d 671, 673 (Pa.1943) (habit of bad boys to throw missiles into street from defendant's premises as imposing a duty on him to stop the practice); Condel v. Savo, 39 A.2d 51 (Pa.1944) (responsibility of parents who knew their child habitually hit other children with sticks).

SECTION 6. REPAIRS, LIABILITY INSURANCE

Phar–Mor, Inc. v. Goff

Supreme Court of Alabama, 1992.
594 So.2d 1213.

■ INGRAM, Justice.

Phar–Mor, Inc., the defendant in this negligence action, appeals, contending that the trial court erred in admitting photographs taken at the time of the trial that Phar–Mor says showed subsequent remedial measures.

This action arose out of an accident that occurred at a Mobile Phar–Mor store. Mrs. Edna Goff allegedly fell when her foot was caught under a display basket in the store. She alleges that Phar–Mor negligently or wantonly maintained the aisles of the store in an unreasonably dangerous condition, negligently or wantonly failed to maintain the aisles in a reasonably safe condition, negligently or wantonly placed displays and/or other objects in the aisles of the store that she and other business invitees of the defendant would reasonably be expected to traverse, and negligently or wantonly failed to warn her of dangerous conditions existing in the aisles of the store. She alleges that the negligence or wantonness of Phar–Mor, Inc., was the proximate cause of her injuries. Her husband, Dan Goff, joined the action, claiming loss of Mrs. Goff's services and consortium.

The Goffs allege that Mrs. Goff fell because of an unsafe condition in the store, namely, a display basket set up to show certain merchandise. The Goffs allege that the basket was set up so that protruding wire prongs located on the bottom (in the toe space) could "snag" a person's foot. Phar–Mor contends that the basket was set up according to the manufacturer's instructions and that it was not aware that the basket presented a dangerous condition. Phar–Mor presented evidence that showed that the proper manner to set up the basket was with the metal legs, which the Goffs call "protruding wire prongs," supporting the basket, which was how the basket was set up at the time Mrs. Goff fell.

The Goffs called as their first witness Michael Broughton, the store manager. Broughton was called as an adverse witness. He testified that the basket Mrs. Goff allegedly caught her foot under had been erected in accordance with the manufacturer's instruction. He testified that, when erected, the basket rested upon metal legs, which created a toe space underneath the basket. He also testified that the basket could be set up to eliminate the toe space.

During the trial, the Goffs' counsel moved to be allowed to take pictures of the Phar–Mor store where the accident occurred, to show that the baskets were at that time being used upside down and on pallets. The trial court allowed this, over the objection of Phar–Mor. The next day the Goffs introduced the time-of-trial photographs into evidence, again over the objection of Phar–Mor, for the express purpose of proving feasibility and proving product misuse. The jury verdict was for the Goffs.

The Goffs alleged that Phar–Mor negligently or wantonly failed to maintain its premises in a reasonably safe condition. In order to prevail, the Goffs had to show that the premises were not in a reasonably safe condition and that Phar–Mor knew or should have known of the unsafe condition.

. . .

The issue on appeal is whether the trial court erred in admitting the time-of-trial photographs over Phar–Mor's objection that the photographs were inadmissible as evidence of subsequent remedial measures offered to prove prior culpable conduct.

[It is axiomatic that rulings as to the admissibility of evidence rest largely within the discretion of the trial court]. . . . In this case, the trial court's discretion is circumscribed by the well established rule that subsequent remedial measures are not admissible to prove antecedent negligence or culpable conduct.

The general rule excluding evidence of subsequent remedial measures is that "evidence of repairs or alterations made, or precautions taken, by the defendant after the injury to the plaintiff in an accident [are] not admissible as tending to show the defendant's antecedent negligence [or culpable conduct]." Charles W. Gamble, McElroy's Alabama Evidence § 189.02(1) (4th ed. 1991). . . . Under the rule, subsequent remedial measures have been excluded on two grounds: (1) that evidence of a subsequent repair or change was irrelevant to show antecedent negligence . . . and (2) that public policy favored promoting safety by removing the disincentive to repair. . . . Even though the rule was established to exclude evidence of subsequent remedial repairs or alterations, evidence of such repairs or alterations can be introduced for certain purposes other than proving antecedent negligence or culpable conduct:

" '[E]vidence of subsequent remedial repairs . . . may be admissible to show identity of ownership, to show control of the locus, to contradict or impeach a witness, or to lessen the weight of an expert opinion. Norwood Clinic v. Spann, 240 Ala. 427, 199 So. 840 (1941). Another permissible use may occur where such evidence is offered to establish a condition existing at the time of the accident. Leeth v. Roberts, 295 Ala. 27, 322 So.2d 679 (1975).' "

Holland v. First National Bank of Brewton, 519 So.2d 460, 462 (Ala.1987) (quoting Banner Welders, Inc. v. Knighton, 425 So.2d 441, 444–45 (Ala.1982)).

. . .

The record here reflects that Phar–Mor objected to the Goffs' request to the trial court that they be permitted to "photograph the display basket as [it was] at the time of trial." Later, Phar–Mor moved for a mistrial, and the following discussion was had on the record:

"THE COURT: All right. Mr. Carr, what do you have?

"MR. CARR: A motion for mistrial in violation of subsequent remedial measures.

"THE COURT: Violating what?

"MR. CARR: Subsequent remedial measures. [The Goffs' attorney] did an excellent job trying to set it up so that he could argue it with [sic] something else, but it is clear and if it was anything other than that I challenge him to tell me.

"MR. CUNNINGHAM: I can tell you exactly what it is. If you assume it's a subsequent remedial measure, once the witness denies that it is feasible, you are then permitted to talk about it all day long. Once he says it can't be done that way, if you've got evidence that in fact they did it that way, it comes into evidence, number one. Number two, it's not a subsequent remedial measure, it's misuse of a product, they misused the product. They had it upside down and that's the point of my—

"THE COURT: You know, that's what I thought he was talking about.

"MR. CARR: [Broughton] did not say it wasn't feasible, first. Second, it is no evidence that it's misuse of products—They could have sued the manufacturer if they thought there was some problem or something with that, but—

"MR. CUNNINGHAM: Not if you're putting it upside down.

"THE COURT: All right. Motion denied."

The trial court allowed the photographs taken at the time of trial to come into evidence. The Goffs' attorney argued the following in closing argument:

"Let me put it this way. If we had tried this case and the only evidence you had seen, and the only evidence you had heard about were these photographs [meaning the photographs taken by Mr. Goff shortly after the incident], you would have never known and probably like me would have never figured out that you can pull the bottom out of the basket, turn it over, stick it back in and use it for the same purpose without any hazard there. You would have never known that. And would it be the same case without knowing that? Would you be deciding this case on complete evidence without you knowing that? And I suggest to you that if we hadn't brought that fact to your attention that the baskets out there now are precisely the opposite of what they were at the time of this accident, you would have never known it because Phar–Mor wasn't about to tell you that. And if you believe that Mr. Broughton didn't know when he testified yesterday how they use those baskets now, where the hazard is eliminated, that he is just totally unaware of that, I have trouble believing that. He had to have been aware of it. They had to have been aware of it. And as long as everybody just kept riding down that same railroad track without ever knowing that they used them the other way this case would have been decided without some very significant important evidence; *which shows an appreciation on their part and knowledge on their part that it needed to be in a condition and set up in a way where nobody could get caught up in it.* And now the store doesn't have that hazard in it. And now nobody is going to trip in it. But that's not the way it was at the time this lady suffered her fall, the way it should have been but not the way it was and that's not her fault. It's not her fault."

(Emphasis supplied.)

On appeal Phar–Mor argues that the evidence was not properly admitted to show feasibility or product misuse. The Goffs contend on appeal that the photographs are not evidence of subsequent remedial measures or, in the alternative, that they were offered to impeach the testimony of Broughton.

The Goffs argue that the photographs do not show a subsequent remedial measure because Broughton testified that Phar–Mor used the baskets upside down in order to put heavier objects in the baskets. However, in closing argument the Goffs' attorney stated that the photographs showed "an appreciation on their part and knowledge on their part that it needed to be in a condition and set up in a way where nobody could get caught up in it." Obviously the Goffs cannot argue both ways. Either changing the way the baskets were set up made them safer or it did not. If the subsequent change made the condition safer, that subsequent change cannot be used to prove that the condition was unsafe before. This is the basic exclusionary rule, which prohibits the admission into evidence of subsequent remedial measures except for a qualified purpose. It is undisputed that using the baskets up on pallets and upside down with the legs on top made the baskets safer, because when they were in that position a person's foot could not get caught under them; therefore, we hold that this use of the baskets cannot be used against Phar–Mor to prove its alleged antecedent negligence.

As stated before, evidence of subsequent remedial measures cannot be used to prove prior culpable conduct. However, it can be used for other purposes. The Goffs raise three other purposes: (1) product misuse, (2) feasibility, and (3) impeachment.

. . .

The Goffs, at trial, raised the issue of product misuse by Phar–Mor. Phar–Mor introduced evidence, which was not disputed, that the basket the Goffs alleged had caused Mrs. Goff's fall was set up according to the manufacturer's instruction at the time of Mrs. Goff's fall. Therefore, the fact that Phar–Mor at the time of trial had some baskets set up in a manner contrary to the manufacturer's intended use is not material to the case at hand.

. . .

At trial the Goffs also asserted that the time-of-trial photographs were being introduced to show feasibility. However, contrary to the argument of the Goffs, feasibility was never controverted. Phar–Mor never claimed that the baskets could not be set up in a manner different from the manner in which they were set up the day of Mrs. Goff's fall. Moreover, Broughton, Phar–Mor's representative, testified that the baskets could be used upside down from the way they were intended to be used, but that he was not aware of any baskets set up in that manner. This obviously does not put into controversy whether it was feasible to use the baskets upside down. Therefore, the photographs were not admissible to show feasibility, because feasibility was not controverted.

On appeal the Goffs argue that the photographs were admissible to impeach the credibility of Broughton's testimony. Broughton was called as an adverse witness by the Goffs. During his testimony he stated that the basket involved was not upside down and that he was not aware of any baskets that were being used upside down at the time of trial. The Goffs argue that photographs of the baskets turned upside down at the time of trial are sufficient to impeach the credibility of Broughton's testimony.

The trial court gave the Goffs the opportunity to show that the basket could be used upside down. Broughton admitted that it was possible to eliminate the toe space underneath by placing the basket up on a pallet and erecting it upside down. He merely stated that he was unaware of any baskets being used upside down.

This Court recently stated in Blythe v. Sears, Roebuck & Co., 586 So.2d 861 (Ala.1991), that the trial court must apply the impeachment exception with care so that the exception does not swallow the rule. In so holding, we established that in order to impeach the credibility of a witness through the introduction of a subsequent remedial measure, the testimony providing grounds for impeachment must have been initiated by the witness. Id.

The impeachment exception to the exclusionary rule was created to prevent a defendant from gaining an unfair advantage from self-serving, false, or misleading statements that would go unchallenged under the exclusionary rule. Id. Because the exception arose in order to protect a plaintiff from an aggressive defendant attempting to manipulate the exclusionary nature of the rule for his own advantage, it follows that a plaintiff who is on the offensive should not be allowed to manipulate the impeachment exception in order to introduce evidence for purposes otherwise inadmissible. In such a situation, the defendant is in greater need of protection than the plaintiff who is seeking to prove the defendant's negligence under the guise of impeachment.

In this case the Goffs repeatedly asked Broughton questions seemingly pointed toward setting up the introduction of the subsequent remedial measure. . . .

. . .

The statements the Goffs claim they sought to impeach were statements elicited by the Goffs from Phar–Mor's representative, Broughton. However, the rule is an exclusionary one. If the evidence is offered to prove prior culpable conduct, it is inadmissible. In his closing argument, the Goffs' counsel described the time-of-trial photographs as "very significant important evidence; *which shows an appreciation on their part and knowledge on their part that it needed to be in a condition and set up in a way where nobody could get caught up in it.*" (Emphasis supplied.) Clearly, the Goffs used the photographs to argue that the mere existence of the baskets, at the time of trial, being used upside down and on pallets, was sufficient to show that Phar–Mor appreciated the danger posed by using the baskets as the manufacturer intended. This appreciation of the danger is the keystone of premises liability. Therefore, the introduction of subsequent remedial measures to prove this point was improper.

Furthermore, we cannot hold that the evidence was properly admitted for any other purpose. Although we recognize that the decision whether to admit evidence rests largely with the trial court and that its ruling will not be disturbed on appeal in the absence of a gross abuse of discretion, we hold that the trial court committed reversible error in allowing the Goffs to introduce photographs of the baskets as they were being used at the time of trial. At trial, the Goffs offered the evidence to prove feasibility and product misuse; these issues were not material in this case, because they were not controverted. On appeal the Goffs argue that the evidence was offered to impeach Broughton. This impeachment evidence was inadmissible, because the statement sought to be impeached was not initiated by the witness.

. . .

Reversed and Remanded.

NOTES

1. Fed. R. Evid. 407 is the federal equivalent of the common law exclusionary rule applied in the Phar–Mor case. The Advisory Committee's Note to Rule 407 suggests that lack of relevance alone cannot explain the exclusionary rule. Why can it not, at least in negligence cases? Suppose in the Phar–Mor case another customer, after seeing Mrs. Goff fall and hurt herself, turned the offending basket upside down. Would this fact be relevant? No doubt the other customer would have supposed he was reducing the risk, but would this warrant altering judgment concerning the risk a reasonable store owner would have appreciated before Mrs. Goff's fall or concerning how a prudent store owner would have acted in view of that risk? Why should it make a difference, so far as relevance is concerned, that it was one of the store's employees who turned the basket over? If evidence of subsequent remedial measures is irrelevant, there is no need for Rule 407: the evidence is excluded by Rule 402. If such evidence is irrelevant in a negligence case, would it be irrelevant in a case based upon strict liability? The answer to this question may depend upon the theory of strict liability that obtains. Suppose the theory of strict liability in the case of injury by a manufactured product requires that the product have been defective and unreasonably dangerous at the time of distribution by the manufacturer. Although this standard of liability does not require fault, it does call for assessment of risk as it would have appeared at a certain time and a balancing of utility and cost against that risk. How could this judgment be affected by the fact that the manufacturer made the product safer after the plaintiff's injury?

2. The opinion in the Phar–Mor case lists as a reason for excluding evidence of subsequent remedial measures the removal of a disincentive to increase safety. The Advisory Committee in its Note to Rule 407 characterizes this reason as the "more impressive" ground for exclusion. In Polansky v. Ryobi America Corp., 760 F.Supp. 85, 86 (D.Md.1991), the court held that this policy does not apply if the defendant continues to market the product that injured the plaintiff, along with a new model with additional safety features. Is this correct?

3. A third reason for excluding evidence of subsequent remedial measures is suggested in Columbia & P.S. Ry. v. Hawthorne, 144 U.S. 202, 207 (1892): "[T]he evidence is incompetent, because the taking of such precautions against the future is not to be construed as an admission of responsibility for the past, has no legitimate tendency to prove that the defendant had been negligent before the accident happened, and is calculated to distract the minds of the jury from the real issue, and to create a prejudice against the defendant." In other words, even if the evidence is relevant, it invites decision on an improper basis.

4. A majority of the federal Courts of Appeal have held that Rule 407 applies in strict liability cases as well as in negligence cases, but a minority have disagreed. The meaning of the term "culpable conduct" in the rule has been a subject of dispute. The legislative history of Rule 407 is not helpful. A majority of state courts appear to have taken a position contrary to the majority of the federal courts. On these matters, see Note, Design Defects in the Rules Enabling Act: The Misapplication of Federal Rule of Evidence 407 to Strict Liability, 65 N.Y.U. L. Rev. 736, 737 (1990). The arguments brought up in this debate are exemplified in the following cases.

Werner v. Upjohn Co., Inc., 628 F.2d 848, 857 (4th Cir.1980), cert. denied, 449 U.S. 1080 (1981):

> Plaintiff argues that a fundamental distinction exists between negligence and strict liability since in a negligence action it is the reasonableness of the defendant's conduct which is in issue while in a strict liability case the issue is whether the product is unreasonably dangerous. Thus, the argument goes, in a negligence action the focus is on the defendant while in strict liability the focus is on the product. We concede the obvious distinction between negligence and strict liability, but we do not believe that this distinction should produce a different result. The rationale behind Rule 407 is that people in general would be less likely to take subsequent remedial measures if their repairs or improvements would be used against them in a lawsuit arising out of a prior accident. By excluding this evidence defendants are encouraged to make such improvements. It is difficult to understand why this policy should apply any differently where the complaint is based on strict liability as well as negligence. From a defendant's point of view it is the fact that the evidence may be used against him which will inhibit subsequent repairs or improvement. It makes no difference to the defendant on what theory the evidence is admitted; his inclination to make subsequent improvements will be similarly repressed. The reasoning behind this asserted distinction we believe to be hypertechnical, for the suit is against the manufacturer, not against the product.

Ault v. International Harvester Co., 528 P.2d 1148 (Cal.1974):

> While the provisions of section 1151 [a section of the California Evidence Code similar to Federal Rule of Evidence 407] may fulfill this antideterrent function [in avoiding giving the defendant reason for not taking steps to improve safety] in the typical negligence action, the provision plays no comparable role in the products liability field. Historically, the common law rule codified in section 1151 was developed with reference to the usual negligence action, in which a pedestrian fell into a hole in a sidewalk ... or a plaintiff was injured on unstable stairs ...; in such circumstances, it may be realistic to assume that a landowner or potential defendant might be deterred from making repairs if such repairs could be used against him in determining liability for the initial accident.
>
> When the context is transformed from a typical negligence setting to the modern products liability field, however, the "public policy" assumptions justifying this evidentiary rule are no longer valid. The contemporary corporate mass producer of goods, the normal products liability defendant, manufactures tens of thousands of units of goods; it is manifestly unrealistic to suggest that such a producer will forego making improvements in its product, and risk innumerable additional lawsuits and the attendant adverse effect upon its public image, simply because evidence of adoption of such improvement may be admitted in an action founded on strict liability for recovery on an injury that preceded the improvement. In the products liability area, the exclusionary rule of section 1151 does not affect the primary conduct of the mass producer of goods, but serves merely as a

shield against potential liability. In short, the purpose of section 1151 is not applicable to a strict liability case and hence its exclusionary rule should not be gratuitously extended to that field. 528 P.2d at 1151–52.

The dissent in Ault observes:

Lack of probative value is the basis for the exclusionary rule according to Professor Wigmore, although he recognizes that some courts have also relied on public policy to avoid discouraging persons from making repairs following an accident. (2 Wigmore on Evidence (3d ed. 1940) pp. 151–159.)

There is even less probative value when evidence of subsequent change is offered to prove an admission in product liability cases. Change in a product is frequently made for reasons unrelated to the remedial nature of the change. Among the motivations for change are the desires to decrease production cost or to increase efficiency or salability. The most striking illustration of lack of probative value is supplied by the automobile industry. Each year hundreds of changes are made in a new model. It is absurd to suggest that each change reflects an admission the modification was made to remedy a defect.

Notwithstanding the lack of probative value, juries, in the heat of negligence or product liability trials—learning only of a single change—may conclude the change reflects an admission of negligence or defect and may give great and decisive weight to the perceived admission. The danger of such misuse of evidence is at least as great in product liability cases as in negligence cases.

The lack of probative value and the danger of misuse of evidence of subsequent change are not cured when the issue before the jury is defect rather than negligence, and no reason exists for refusing to give the word "culpable" its common meaning. Accordingly, I conclude that section 1151 should be applicable in product liability cases. 528 P.2d at 1155.

A footnote accompanying the dissent states:

The policy of encouraging modification following an accident may not be viewed as the basis of the section 1151 exclusionary rule when the rule is considered in light of present California law. Section 1151 by its terms only excludes evidence when offered to prove negligence or culpability; the section does not necessarily exclude evidence when it is probative to other relevant issues. A party contemplating change in his real property, chattel, or product prior to trial cannot know with certainty that evidence of his change will not be received as relevant on issues other than negligence and culpability, frustrating the policy of encouraging safety modification. Because lack of admissibility is not predictable under the California rules but may only be determined on the basis of issues developed at trial, the goal of encouraging modifications is not substantially furthered by section 1151.

The majority argue it is unlikely that potential admission of evidence of change will deter manufacturers from making changes toward increased safety. But, because encouraging change is not the purpose of section 1151, the reasoning does not furnish a basis to reject application of the section to product liability cases.

In 1996, the Judicial Conference of the United States approved for submission to the Supreme Court an amended Rule 407:

Rule 407. Subsequent Remedial Measures

When, after an injury or harm allegedly caused by an event, measures are taken that, if taken previously, would have made the event less likely to occur, evidence of the subsequent measures is not admissible to prove negligence, culpable conduct, a defect in a product, a defect in a product's design, or a need for a warning or instruction. Evidence of subsequent measures may be offered for another purpose, such as impeachment or—if controverted—proof of ownership, control, or feasibility of precautionary measures.

It will be seen that the amended rule adopts the position taken by the majority of the Courts of Appeal that 407 should apply to strict liability cases.

5. If a defendant has made a modification in its product after distribution of the particular item that injured the plaintiff but before the plaintiff's injury occurred, is evidence of the modification excluded by Rule 407? Courts have gone both ways on this question. Kelly v. Crown Equipment Co., 970 F.2d 1273, 1277 (3d Cir.1992) (Rule 407 applies); Raymond v. Raymond Corp., 938 F.2d 1518, 1522–24 (1st Cir.1991) (Rule 407 inapplicable but not abuse of discretion to exclude under Rule 403 because liability under state law depended on whether product unreasonably dangerous at time of sale and evidence of modification might mislead the jury). See Note, Subsequent Remedial Measures and Strict Products Liability, 81 Va. L. Rev. 1144 (1995). Note that the proposed amended Rule 407 does not apply when the remedial measure was taken before the injury.

6. A repair or modification made after the accident by someone other than the party against whom the evidence is sought to be introduced has been held not to fall within the antideterrent policy of 407. At the same time, the evidence may be excluded because irrelevant or because it is of slight probative value and may confuse the jury. See Raymond v. Raymond Corp., 938 F.2d 1518, 1524–25 (1st Cir.1991) (not abuse of discretion to exclude). But see Espeaignnette v. Gene Tierney Co., 43 F.3d 1 (1st Cir.1994) (error to exclude because relevant to feasibility). See also Dixon v. International Harvester Co., 754 F.2d 573, 583 (5th Cir.1985); Comment, Federal Rule of Evidence 407 and Its State Variations, 49 UMKC L. Rev. 338, 347–49 (1981).

7. Rule 407 states that the rule does not require the exclusion of evidence of subsequent measures when offered for purpose of impeachment. Pitasi v. Stratton Corp., 968 F.2d 1558, 1561 (2d Cir.1992), was a suit by an injured skier against a ski resort for negligently failing to place ropes across entrances to a dangerous ski trail. The ski resort contended that no rope was necessary because the dangerousness of the trail was obvious and that the skier was contributorily negligent. Held: Error to exclude plaintiff's evidence that immediately after the accident, the defendant put up ropes. "Pitasi did not seek to introduce Stratton's subsequent remedial measures in order to prove that Stratton was negligent. Rather Pitasi sought to impeach Stratton's witnesses and to rebut its defense that Pitasi was contributorily negligent because the dangerous conditions on East Meadow were so obvious and apparent that warning signs or ropes at the trail's side entrances were unnecessary. Rule 407 clearly allows a plaintiff to introduce evidence of remedial measures to rebut such assertions." But see Wusinich v. Aeroquip Corp., 843 F.Supp. 959, 961–62 (E.D.Pa.1994), rejecting argument that evidence of safety features added to type of machine after sale of particular machine that injured plaintiff should be admissible to rebut defense evidence that the accident was the result of plaintiff's contributory negligence, not defective design. "To permit Plaintiffs to proffer evidence of subsequent remedial measures in order to prove an element of the tort because such element was controverted by Defendants would in essence, permit the exception to swallow the rule," citing Kelly v. Crown Equipment Co., 970 F.2d 1273, 1278 (3d Cir.1992) (just because defense expert testified he believed machine properly designed, plaintiff may not put in evidence expert knew of subsequent modification). See also D. L. by Friederichs v. Huebner, 329 N.W.2d 890, 897–902 (Wis.1983). But see Muzyka v. Remington Arms Co., Inc., 774 F.2d 1309 (5th Cir.1985): Where the issue was the adequacy of a safety mechanism on a rifle and defendant's experts had testified the rifle was the safest on the market, error to exclude evidence that following the accident, defendant had changed the safety mechanism on this type of rifle; Cyr v. J. I. Case Co., 652 A.2d 685, 694 (N.H.1994): If a defense witness testified that a certain device would reduce safety or not improve it, perhaps permissible to introduce evidence that defendant had installed the device after the accident. See generally Note, The Impeachment Exception to Rule 407: Limitations on the Introduction of Evidence of Subsequent Measures, 42 U. Miami L. Rev. 901 (1988).

8. For discussions of whether federal or state law applies to the admissibility of subsequent remedial measures in diversity suits in federal courts, see Kelly v. Crown Equipment Co., 970 F.2d 1273, 1278 (3d Cir.1992) (federal law applies); Note, Design Defects in the Rules Enabling Act: The Misapplication of Federal Rule of Evidence 407 to Strict Liability, 65 N.Y.U. L. Rev. 736, 760–81 (1990) (state law should apply).

9. The fact that defendant was covered by liability insurance is treated in the same manner as evidence of subsequent repairs. Such evidence is inadmissible as tending to prove negligence or other wrong-doing, but can come in when relevant to another issue. Fed.R.Evid. 411; 2 Wigmore, Evidence § 282a (Chadbourn rev. 1979). Approaches to the topic raise questions of relevance and prejudice. The problem can come up in reverse if defendant attempts to prove lack of coverage. Wilbur v. Tourangeau, 71 A.2d 565 (Vt.1950), held such evidence improperly admitted.

SECTION 7. COMPROMISES

Hiram Ricker & Sons v. Students Intern'l Meditation Soc'y

United States Court of Appeals, First Circuit, 1974.
501 F.2d 550.

■ Before COFFIN, CHIEF JUDGE, MCENTEE and CAMPBELL, CIRCUIT JUDGES.

■ MCENTEE, CIRCUIT JUDGE.

This is a diversity action based on a contract. Plaintiff-appellee Ricker owns a 2500–acre resort complex in Poland Springs, Maine, which includes lodgings, a golf course and a beach. At the beginning of 1970, only the golf course and a single adjacent building, the Poland Springs Lodge, were actually in use and open to the public. In February 1970, representatives of the defendant-appellant Society contacted Ricker about taking over some of the unused facilities from June 28 to July 26 for a course to train new instructors of transcendental meditation. After some negotiation, Ricker agreed to furnish rooms, facilities and three vegetarian meals and a snack per day for the course participants.[1] In exchange, the Society was to pay Ricker based on a specified

---

1. There was no formal contract. Instead, the basic agreement was embodied in certain correspondence admitted into evidence. Some modifications were made subsequently and several others were disputed at

schedule of room rates and the number of persons who would attend. The Society would be responsible for the headcount necessary to determine its final bill. The training course was held at the Poland Springs complex on the dates scheduled. The Society paid Ricker a total of $185,000 in a series of payments, some in advance and some during the course.

Ricker brought this action seeking $77,508.36 as the balance allegedly due on the contract. Alternatively, Ricker sought the same amount on the theory of quantum meruit. In response, the Society counterclaimed for return of the $185,000 in payments already made. At trial, Ricker presented evidence tending to show that more persons attended the training course than were accounted for in the Society's payments. Ricker also presented evidence that the Society improperly reduced some of the agreed-upon room rates as it made its calculations. The Society presented evidence to rebut these assertions. With respect to its counterclaim, it also presented evidence tending to show that the rooms and dining facilities which Ricker provided were dirty and inadequate....

. . .

The district court submitted all issues to the jury....

The jury returned a verdict for Ricker in the amount of $65,780.00 and rejected the Society's counterclaim. The court entered judgment on the verdict, adding $9,494.16 in interest.

. . .

The Society contends that the district court improperly admitted evidence of an offer to settle Ricker's claim. However, we hold that the evidence to which the Society objects was not an offer to settle within the meaning of the rule calling for exclusion.

The precise testimony was this. Saul Feldman, the president of Ricker, became increasingly dissatisfied with the size of the periodic payments the Society made to him during the one-month training course. Feldman felt that more persons had attended the course than the Society would concede. On July 26, the last day of the course, he called on Jerry Jarvis, a Society executive. At this time, pursuant to their contract, Feldman anticipated receipt of the final payment. He testified:

"[Jarvis] passed me a yellow sheet of paper saying, 'This is what we owe you. If you agree and sign a release absolving us from any and all damage and all future bills we will pay you.' It was $44,000."

Counsel for the Society moved to strike this testimony on the ground that it was an inadmissible offer of settlement. The court refused. Whereupon the yellow sheet itself was received in evidence and read to the jury by Ricker's counsel, again over objection. Nothing on the sheet referred to an offer of settlement. It was entirely a series of calculations, which concluded that the Society owed Ricker a final bill of $44,163.25.

It is, of course, true that evidence of settlement negotiations is generally inadmissible. On the other hand, there is a "well-recognized exception regarding admissions of fact as distinguished from hypothetical or provisional concessions conditioned upon the settlement's completion." NLRB v. Gotham Indus., Inc., 406 F.2d 1306, 1313 (1st Cir.1969). See generally 4 Wigmore, Evidence § 1061 (Chadbourn rev. 1972). In the instant case, the yellow sheet handed to Feldman on the final day of the course represented the Society's "unconditional assertion" of what it thought it actually owed Ricker based on the contract. See

trial. [Footnote by the court, renumbered; other footnotes omitted.]

4 Wigmore, supra, at 34. It was not a hypothetical or conditional sum intended only to forestall the additional costs of litigation. Indeed, although Ricker was unhappy about the size of the early payments, until it received the Society's final payment offer of $44,000, it could not determine whether it had an actual controversy with the Society. The rule excluding offers of settlement is designed to encourage settlement negotiations after a controversy has actually arisen. It also prevents admission of evidence that does not represent either party's true belief as to the facts. Neither policy would have been served by excluding Feldman's testimony about the Society's final payment offer, or the yellow sheet on which that offer was calculated.

. . .

[Reversed and remanded for other reasons.]

NOTES

1. Fed. R. Evid. 408, adopted by Congress the year after the Hiram Ricker decision provides:

> Evidence of (1) furnishing or offering or promising to furnish, or (2) accepting or offering or promising to accept, a valuable consideration in compromising or attempting to compromise a claim which was disputed as to either validity or amount, is not admissible to prove liability for or invalidity of the claim or its amount. Evidence of conduct or statements made in compromise negotiations is likewise not admissible. This rule does not require the exclusion of any evidence otherwise discoverable merely because it is presented in the course of compromise negotiations. This rule does not require exclusion when the evidence is offered for another purpose, such as proving bias or prejudice of a witness, negativing a contention of undue delay, or proving an effort to obstruct a criminal investigation or prosecution.

2. The Advisory Committee's Note to Rule 408 refers to irrelevance as a possible explanation for the rule, although it characterizes as "a more consistently impressive ground" "promotion of the public policy favoring the compromise and settlement of disputes." How does the argument for irrelevance in the case of settlements compare with the same argument in the case of subsequent remedial measures?

3. The opinion in Hiram Ricker refers to the necessity of a dispute. Why does the policy favoring settlements require that there have been a dispute? If there must have been a dispute, from whose or from what point of view must there have been a dispute? Was there a dispute in Hiram Ricker? At the time Saul Feldman called on Jerry Jarvis, Feldman believed that more persons had attended the course than the Society would concede. How probable must a dispute have been? Must there have been a likelihood of litigation? See Brazil, Protecting the Confidentiality of Settlement Negotiations, 39 Hast. L. J. 955, 961–63, 973 (1988) ("Courts should not construe rule 408 ... to discourage parties from being the first to put an offer or demand on the table...."). Is the requirement in Rule 408 that the action or statement have been made "in compromising or attempting to compromise" distinct from the requirement that there have been a dispute?

4. The opinion in Hiram Ricker refers to a "well-recognized exception regarding admissions of fact as distinguished from hypothetical or provisional concessions conditioned upon the settlement's completion." Has this exception been abolished by the sentence in 408 "Evidence of conduct or statements made in compromise negotiations is likewise not admissible"? How is the policy of Rule 408 advanced by this sentence?

5. May agreement of the parties make admissible what is stated in Rule 408 to be inadmissible, or make inadmissible what is not excluded by 408? See Brazil, supra, at 1026–27 and United States v. Mezzanatto, 513 U.S. 196 (1995), infra p. 944.

6. Fed. R. Evid. 409 provides:

> "Evidence of furnishing or offering or promising to pay medical, hospital, or similar expenses occasioned by an injury is not admissible to prove liability for an injury."

Brown v. Wood, 160 S.E. 281, 282–83 (N.C.1931): "It has never been suggested that the fact that the Good Samaritan placed an injured and unfortunate man upon his own beast, pouring wine and oil into his wounds, paying his maintenance charges at the inn, and promising even to give more, if necessary, upon his return, was an implied admission that the agents of the Good Samaritan, in the course of their employment, actually inflicted the injury upon the wounded man found on the Jericho Highway"; but from the decision, it seems that if the Good Samaritan had said he would see "that everything was all right," there would have been a jury question as to whether he had admitted liability.

Why does Rule 409, unlike Rule 408, omit a requirement of a dispute? Why are medical and hospital expenses singled out for special treatment? What is included within the term "similar expenses"? Compensation for lost earnings? For pain and suffering? The Good Samaritan paid more than medical expenses.

John McShain, Inc. v. Cessna Aircraft Co.

United States Court of Appeals, Third Circuit, 1977.
563 F.2d 632.

■ Before VAN DUSEN, ADAMS and HUNTER, CIRCUIT JUDGES.

Per Curiam:

The appeal in this diversity case turns primarily on challenges to the evidentiary rulings of a trial court.

In May 1969, John McShain, Inc. purchased an aircraft manufactured by Cessna Aircraft Co. from Wings, Inc. for $282,136. In December 1969, several hundred landings and 147 hours of flight later, the main landing gear of the plane collapsed as the plane alighted on the runway in Baltimore. After notifying Cessna, McShain had the aircraft repaired by Butler Aviation–Friendship, Inc. at a cost of $11,734. During the course of the overhaul, Cessna representatives visited the Butler repair facilities. The plane was then returned to McShain.

After 5 hours of further flight, the plane's landing gear once more gave way upon touchdown. The cost of repairs this time totaled $24,681. McShain refused to fly the craft again.

Negotiations between McShain and Cessna regarding a new plane terminated when McShain filed an action in Pennsylvania Common Pleas Court seeking rescission of the original sales contract and the return of the purchase price.

McShain then instituted the present action against Cessna in district court, alleging defective design in the landing gear and Cessna's failure to correct that design despite knowledge of the defects. McShain requested judgment for (a) the cost of the repairs, (b) consequential damages, and (c) $5,000,000 in punitive damages. Cessna joined Butler as a third party defendant on the theory that the second crash was the result of inept repairs.

Before the conclusion of the eighteen-day trial, Cessna accepted liability for the first collapse on the ground that the existence of an understrength bolt had been discovered in the landing gear, and that that bolt was the cause of the original breakdown.

The jury returned a verdict of $11,734 for the plaintiff as to the first accident, and a special verdict finding that there was no design defect in the landing gear. McShain moved for a new trial on the ground of six allegedly improper evidentiary rulings. The trial court denied the motion, and McShain has appealed from that denial.

McShain's two most substantial objections to the rulings below challenge Judge McGlynn's admission of McShain's pre-trial release of Butler from liability, and the trial court's refusal to admit copies of National Transportation Safety Board accident files. We conclude, however, that neither of these rulings, nor indeed any of the other rulings referred to on this appeal, warrants a new trial.

A. THE BUTLER–McSHAIN AGREEMENT

Before the action was filed in the district court, the plaintiff signed an agreement releasing Butler from any liability for the accident in exchange for $10 and the right to engage as a consultant Ralph Harmon, who was at the time an employee of Butler's sister corporation, Mooney Aircraft Corp. Mr. Harmon was thereupon retained by McShain, and ultimately testified as an expert witness in support of the design-defect contention. Judge McGlynn allowed the release to be entered into evidence and read to the jury for the purpose of impeaching Mr. Harmon's testimony.

McShain urges that, under Federal Rule of Evidence 408, agreements in compromise of a claim are generally inadmissible on the issue of liability on such claim. Cessna's reference to the Butler–McShain agreement, McShain insists, is such a proscribed use of evidence, since Cessna's counsel implicitly attempted to shift blame for the second failure from Cessna to Butler.

In response, Cessna maintains that the evidence was in fact admitted for the purpose of establishing the bias of Mr. Harmon, thus falling squarely within the exception to Rule 408. The rule by its terms "does not require the exclusion [of] evidence" when offered for the purpose of "proving bias or prejudice of a witness."

We believe that Judge McGlynn did not commit reversible error in admitting the agreement and in allowing comments upon it. The fact that a sister corporation of Harmon's employer had been released from liability in exchange for Harmon's testimony cast doubt upon Harmon's impartiality. Thus, as counsel for McShain appeared to contend at oral argument, McShain's claim is in reality that the potential prejudice from the admission of the agreement outweighed the agreement's probative value. See Fed. Rule Evid. 403.

In evaluating such an argument, we acknowledge that the trial judge's familiarity with the tone and scope of the evidence presented to the jury puts him in an advantageous position to gauge the relative importance of potential prejudice and probative value. Nonetheless, the balance required is not a pro forma one. A sensitive analysis of the need for the evidence as proof on a contested factual issue, of the prejudice which may eventuate from admission, and of the public policies involved is in order before passing on such an objection. The substantiality of the consideration given to competing interests can be best guaranteed by an explicit articulation of the trial court's reasoning.

Here, the trial judge clearly took notice of the arguments presented by both sides regarding the admissibility of the release. And while his ruling does not fully set forth his underlying rationale, we conclude that admission of the release was not an abuse of discretion so "inconsistent with substantial justice" as to require a new trial.

. . .

The judgment of the district court will be affirmed.[1]

NOTES

1. With the McShain case compare Fenberg v. Rosenthal, 109 N.E.2d 402 (Ill.App.1952): A defense witness had been paid money by defendant for injuries received in the same accident out of which the action arose. Plaintiff sought to get this fact to the jury to show bias of the witness in favor of defendant. The court held that the rule excluding evidence of settlements must prevail over the rule permitting a party to show that a witness has received money. Evidence of the payment to the witness can, however, come in, the court said, if the trial judge finds that fraud or other questionable practice was used to influence the testimony of the witness.

A somewhat different situation was involved in Esser v. Brophey, 3 N.W.2d 3 (Minn.1942). Defendant claimed that the negligence of X was the cause of the collision between the automobiles of plaintiff and defendant. Plaintiff called X as a witness and on cross-examination defendant proved that he had sued X for damages to his car and that X had paid him $50 in settlement of this action. Defendant argued that this evidence was admissible to show that X was biased against the defendant. The court held the evidence irrelevant to show bias. See also Granville v. Parsons, 66 Cal.Rptr. 149 (Cal.App.1968).

2. Rule 408 expressly excludes from its coverage "evidence offered for another purpose, such as proving bias or prejudice of a witness...." Compare the language of Rule 407 regarding evidence offered for impeachment. Why this difference in scope? The possibility of completely undermining the policy of Rule 407 by admitting evidence of subsequent repairs for impeachment has been pointed out supra p. 937. Under Rule 408, would introduction of evidence of a settlement or a statement made in settlement negotiations to impeach a party-witness through self contradiction have a similar potential? See Brazil, Protecting the Confidentiality of Settlement Negotiations, 39 Hast. L. J. 955, 969–78 (1988).

3. Many purposes for the introduction of evidence of settlements other than "to prove liability for or invalidity of the claim or its amount" are possible. Charlotte Motor Speedway, Inc. v. International Ins. Co., 125 F.R.D. 127 (M.D.N.C.1989): In suit under indemnity policy for amounts paid to settle minority shareholder suit, discovery of attorney work-product relevant to whether the settlement was entered into in good faith permissible; Fed. R. Evid. 408 not cited. Dierks Lumber & Coal Co. v. Tollett, 10 S.W.2d 5, 6 (Ark.1928): Evidence of settlement negotiations to explain delay in bringing action. Lake v. Wright, 53 S.W.2d 233 (Ark.1932): Evidence to establish concealment of cause of action. Fletcher v. Western National Life Ins. Co., 89

---

1. Footnotes omitted.

Cal.Rptr. 78 (App.1970): In action for infliction of emotional distress, defendant's offer to settle an insurance claim was itself part of the conduct alleged to have caused the distress.

4. Manko v. United States, 87 F.3d 50, 54 (2d Cir.1996): Fed. R. Evid. 408 interpreted not to exclude evidence of government settlement of civil tax claim offered by defendant in criminal prosecution for same behavior that constituted the basis of the civil claim. "The policy favoring the encouragement of civil settlements, sufficient to bar their admission in civil actions, is insufficient, in our view, to outweigh the need for accurate determinations in criminal cases where the stakes are higher."

5. If a settlement receives judicial approval, there is a possibility a party will be precluded by the doctrine of "judicial estoppel" from taking the opposite position in a proceeding against a third party. See Reynolds v. Commissioner of Internal Revenue, 861 F.2d 469, 474 (6th Cir.1988): Where the Commissioner in a bankruptcy proceeding involving the estate of the wife secured "final judicial acceptance" of the position that the capital gain was to be taxed to the wife, he was judicially estopped from asserting in a proceeding against the husband that the gain was to be taxed to the husband.

Offers to Plead Guilty and Withdrawn Pleas of Guilty

Under Fed. R. Evid. 410, a plea of guilty that is later withdrawn is generally inadmissible in any criminal or civil proceeding against the defendant who made the plea. This is in accord with the generally accepted common law rule. See, e.g., Kercheval v. United States, 274 U.S. 220 (1927); People v. Quinn, 393 P.2d 705 (Cal.1964); State v. Boone, 327 A.2d 661 (N.J.1974); People v. Smith, 404 N.Y.S.2d 947 (Sup.1978). But see Morrissey v. Powell, 23 N.E.2d 411 (Mass.1939) (withdrawn guilty plea admissible against defendant in related civil action).

United States v. Mezzanatto, 513 U.S. 196 (1995): As a condition to entering into discussions with the defendant for the purpose of determining whether there was a possibility of the defendant's cooperating with the government and obtaining favorable treatment, the prosecutor required the defendant to agree that any statements the defendant made during the discussions could be used to impeach contradictory testimony the defendant might give at a trial, if the case proceeded that far. Defendant agreed to this condition. During the course of the discussion, the prosecutor decided that the defendant was not being truthful, terminated the discussion and proceeded with a prosecution of the defendant. At the trial, the court allowed the introduction of statements made by the defendant during the discussion to impeach his testimony. The defendant contended this violated Fed. R. Evid. 410.

THOMAS, J. for the Court:

> We agree with respondent's basic premise: There may be some evidentiary provisions that are so fundamental to the reliability of the factfinding process that they may never be waived without irreparably "discredit[ing] the federal courts." See 21 Wright & Graham § 5039 ... at 207–208 [Federal Practice and Procedure (1977)].... But enforcement of agreements like respondent's plainly will not have that effect. The admission of plea statements for impeachment purposes *enhances* the truth-seeking function of trials and will result in more accurate verdicts....
>
>   . . .
>
> Respondent also contends that waiver is fundamentally inconsistent with the Rules' goal of encouraging voluntary settlement. See Advisory

Committee Notes on Fed. Rule Evid. 410.... Because the prospect of waiver may make defendants "think twice" before entering into any plea negotiation, respondent suggests that enforcement of waiver agreements acts "as a brake, not as a facilitator, to the plea-bargain process." Brief for Respondent 23, n. 17. The Ninth Circuit expressed similar concerns, noting that Rules 410 and 11(e)(6) [Fed. R. Crim. Proc.] "aid in obtaining th[e] cooperation" that is often necessary to identify and prosecute the leaders of a criminal conspiracy and that waiver of the protections of the Rules "could easily have a chilling effect on the entire plea bargaining process." 998 F.2d, at 1455. According to the Ninth Circuit, the plea-statement Rules "permit the plea bargainer to maximize what he has 'to sell' " by preserving "the ability to withdraw from the bargain proposed by the prosecutor without being harmed by any of his statements made in the course of an aborted plea bargaining session." Ibid.

We need not decide whether and under what circumstances substantial "public policy" interests may permit the inference that Congress intended to override the presumption of waivability, for in this case there is no basis for concluding that waiver will interfere with the Rules' goal of encouraging plea bargaining. The court below focused entirely on the *defendant's* incentives and completely ignored the other essential party to the transaction: the prosecutor. Thus, although the availability of waiver may discourage some defendants from negotiating, it is also true that prosecutors may be unwilling to proceed without it. ... Because prosecutors have limited resources and must be able to answer "sensitive questions about the credibility of the testimony" they receive before entering into any sort of cooperation agreement [Hughes, Agreements for Cooperation in Criminal Cases, 45 Vand. L. Rev. 1, 10 (1992)] ... prosecutors may condition cooperation discussions on an agreement that the testimony provided may be used for impeachment purposes....

Indeed, as a logical matter, it simply makes no sense to conclude that mutual settlement will be encouraged by precluding negotiation over an issue that may be particularly important to one of the parties to the transaction. A sounder way to encourage settlement is to permit the interested parties to enter into knowing and voluntary negotiations without any arbitrary limits on their bargaining chips....

. . .

Finally, respondent contends that waiver agreements should be forbidden because they invite prosecutorial overreaching and abuse. Respondent asserts that there is a "gross disparity" in the relative bargaining power of the parties to a plea agreement and suggests that a waiver agreement is "inherently unfair and coercive." Brief for Respondent 26. Because the prosecutor retains the discretion to "reward defendants for their substantial assistance" under the Sentencing Guidelines, respondent argues that defendants face an " 'incredible dilemma' " when they are asked to accept waiver as the price of entering plea discussions....

The dilemma flagged by respondent is indistinguishable from any of a number of difficult choices that criminal defendants face every day. The plea bargaining process necessarily exerts pressure on defendants to plead guilty and to abandon a series of fundamental rights, but we have repeatedly held that the government "may encourage a guilty plea by offering substantial benefits in return for the plea." Corbitt v. New Jersey, 439 U.S. 212, 219, 99 S.Ct. 492, 497–498, 58 L.Ed.2d 466 (1978)....

[T]he appropriate response to respondent's predictions of abuse is to permit case-by-case inquiries into whether waiver agreements are the product of fraud or coercion. We hold that absent some affirmative indication that the agreement was entered into unknowingly or involuntarily, an agreement to waive the exclusionary provisions of the plea-statement Rules is valid and enforceable.

SOUTER, J., with whom STEVENS, J. joins, dissenting:

Since the zone of unrestrained candor is diminished whenever a defendant has to stop to think about the amount of trouble his openness may cause him if the plea negotiations fall through, Congress must have understood that the judicial system's interest in candid plea discussions would be threatened by recognizing waivers under Rules 410 and 11(e)(6).... There is, indeed, no indication that Congress intended merely a regime of such limited openness as might happen to survive market forces sufficient to supplant a default rule of inadmissibility. Nor may Congress be presumed to have intended to permit waivers that would undermine the stated policy of its own Rules....

The unlikelihood that Congress intended the modest default rule that the majority sees in Rules 11(e)(6) and 410 looms all the larger when the consequences of the majority position are pursued. The first consequence is that the Rules will probably not even function as default rules, for there is little chance that they will be applied at all. Already, standard forms indicate that many federal prosecutors routinely require waiver of Rules 410 and 11(e)(6) rights before a prosecutor is willing to enter into plea discussions....

[A]lthough the erosion of the Rules has begun with this trickle, the majority's reasoning will provide no principled limit to it. The Rules draw no distinction between use of a statement for impeachment and use in the Government's case in chief. If objection can be waived for impeachment use, it can be waived for use as affirmative evidence, and if the government can effectively demand waiver in the former instance, there is no reason to believe it will not do so just as successfully in the latter. When it does, there is nothing this Court will legitimately be able to do about it. The Court is construing a congressional Rule on the theory that Congress meant to permit its waiver. Once that point is passed, as it is today, there is no legitimate limit on admissibility of a defendant's plea negotiation statements beyond what the Constitution may independently impose or the traffic may bear. Just what the traffic may bear is an open question, but what cannot be denied is that the majority opinion sanctions a demand for waiver of such scope that a defendant who gives it will be unable even to acknowledge his desire to negotiate a guilty plea without furnishing admissible evidence against himself then and there. In such cases, the possibility of trial if no agreement is reached will be reduced to fantasy. The only defendant who will not damage himself by even the most restrained candor will be the one so desperate that he might as well walk into court and enter a naked guilty plea. It defies reason to think that Congress intended to invite such a result, when it adopted a Rule said to promote candid discussion in the interest of encouraging compromise.

Id. at 204–10, 214–18.

The 1980 amendment to Fed.R.Evid. 410 made inadmissible "any statement made in the course of any proceedings under Rule 11 of the Federal Rules of Criminal Procedure [which deals comprehensively with pleas and plea agreements] or comparable state procedure" regarding guilty pleas, and "any statement made in the course of plea discussions with an attorney for the prosecuting attorney...." The amendment was intended to narrow the broader language of former Rule 410, which made statements inadmissible if "made in connection with, and relevant to" an "offer to plead guilty," without regard to whom the statements were made. As the Advisory Committee observes in its Note to the 1980 amendment, under the former rule voluntary admissions were rendered inadmissible simply because they were made to law enforcement officers in the hope of obtaining leniency. See United States v. Herman, 544 F.2d 791 (5th Cir.1977); United States v. Brooks, 536 F.2d 1137 (6th Cir.1976). For a criticism of the 1980 amendment, see H.R.Rep. No. 96–1302, 96th Cong., 2d Sess. 4–7 (1980): "In fact to so limit the rule is inconsistent with Congress's expressed intention to promote candor in plea discussions." Nevertheless, the Advisory Committee notes: "This change, it must be emphasized, does not compel the conclusion that statements made to law enforcement agents, especially when the agents purport to have authority to bargain, are inevitably admissible. Rather, the point is that such cases are not covered by the per se rule of 11(e)(6) and thus must be resolved by that body of law dealing with police interrogations."

Prior to the 1980 amendment, the issue of whether discussions between the accused and government agents other than attorneys could be characterized as plea negotiations and were, therefore, inadmissible, was the subject of much litigation. E.g., United States v. Robertson, 582 F.2d 1356 (5th Cir.1978) (en banc); United States v. Doe, 655 F.2d 920, 924–25 (9th Cir.1980); United States v. Castillo, 615 F.2d 878 (9th Cir.1980) (conversations with prison counselor). State v. O'Blasney, 297 N.W.2d 797 (S.D.1980); People v. Friedman, 403 N.E.2d 229 (Ill.1980). The question of whether a statement was "made in the course of plea discussions" may still require judicial resolution even though a government attorney was involved. United States v. Robertson, supra, laid down this test: "[W]hether the accused exhibited an actual subjective expectation to negotiate a plea at the time of the discussion, and, second, whether the accused's expectation was reasonable given the totality of the objective circumstances." 582 F.2d at 1366. "There is plea bargaining only when 'the accused *contemplates entering a plea* to obtain a concession from the government [and] the government contemplates making some concession *to obtain the accused's plea.*' " United States v. Cross, 638 F.2d 1375, 1379 (5th Cir.1981) (quoting from United States v. Robertson; emphasis in original). See United States v. Castillo and United States v. Doe, supra (both adopting the Robertson test); People v. Friedman, supra (adopting Robertson); State v. Traficante, 636 A.2d 692 (R.I.1994); Peters v. State, 586 P.2d 749 (Okl.Cr.App.1978); Armes v. State, 540 S.W.2d 279 (Tenn.Cr.App.1976). See generally Note, Guilty Plea Bargaining: Compromises by Prosecutors to Secure Guilty Pleas, 112 U.Pa.L.Rev. 865 (1964); Annot., Admissibility of Defense Communications Made in Connection With Plea Bargaining, 59 A.L.R.3d 441 (1974).

As to the admissibility of statements made subsequent to pleas later withdrawn, see Hutto v. Ross, 429 U.S. 28 (1976) (confession made subsequent to plea bargain not per se inadmissible in criminal trial); United States v. Perry, 643 F.2d 38, 52 (2d Cir.), cert. denied, 454 U.S. 835 (1981).

Section 8. Forensic Argument

Harvey v. Aubrey

Supreme Court of Arizona, 1939.
53 Ariz. 210, 87 P.2d 482.

■ Lockwood, Judge. This is an action in forcible detainer by John L. Aubrey, hereinafter called plaintiff, against Robert E. Harvey and Nell Harvey, his wife, hereinafter called defendants, to recover possession of certain real property. Judgment went for plaintiff, and defendants have appealed....

... It is the general rule that counsel are allowed considerable latitude in arguing a case to a jury, and that they may argue not only as to the existence of the facts which some evidence shows directly, but also as to the reasonable inferences of fact to be drawn from the evidence. They have not, however, the right to argue any matter which is not in issue, except as it may bear on a matter which is in issue.... [T]he record does not show precisely the line of argument which the court forbade, but apparently counsel for the defendants desired to argue that it was reasonable to infer from the fact that a clause in the original lease permitted a new lease under certain conditions, that the new lease had actually been made. The position of the court apparently was that though it was admitted by both parties that under the provisions of the old lease the parties might, if they desired, agree upon a new one, this provision in the old lease could not reasonably raise an inference that by reason thereof a new lease had been made, and it was, therefore, improper for counsel to argue the clause in the old lease as a basis for such an inference.

The question is not without doubt, but we are inclined to think that the court was correct in its ruling. The clause in the old lease that the parties might, if they so desired, make a new lease is no evidence that they did make one, and we think it would have been improper to argue from that clause that the jury might infer that a new lease was made. Suppose for example, that the defendants had offered the original written lease in support of their plea that a new lease had been made, and had then rested. It is obvious that a verdict in favor of defendants could not have been sustained by such evidence. Nor could such lease be taken as corroborative evidence of their direct testimony that a new lease had been made. This being the case, we think the court did not err in refusing to permit counsel for defendants to make such an argument.

The judgment of the trial court is affirmed.

NOTE

In argument counsel have wide latitude in drawing inferences from the evidence and in attempting to persuade the jury as to the probability of these inferences; the court need not enlighten the jury as to contrary inferences from the same facts. Kercher v. City of Conneaut, 65 N.E.2d 272 (Ohio.App.1945); Keal Driveway Co. v. Car and General Ins. Co., 145 F.2d 345 (5th Cir. 1944). However, the court should insist at least that a reasonable person might make the inference urged. Thus, courts have refused to disapprove inferences so long as they were not "wholly unreasonable." Hayes v. Coleman, 61 N.W.2d 634 (Mich.1953). Compare this test with that in Traders and General Ins. Co. v. Stone, 258 S.W.2d 409 (Tex.Civ.App.1953) (any inference made in good faith is valid as long as it is not unreasonable), and Tilbury v. Welberg, 55 N.W.2d 685 (Minn.1952) (if the inference made by counsel is "clearly unjustifiable" then the trial judge should so inform the jury). Other courts have declared that the question of whether an argument is logical or not is always one for the jury's unaided determination. Anderson v. Erberich, 112 S.W.2d 634 (Ark.1938); Southeastern Greyhound Lines v. Durham, 8 S.E.2d 99 (Ga.App.1940) ("the fact that such deductions ... are not logical, is a matter of reply by adverse counsel and not rebuke by the courts"); Lawyer v. Stansell, 250 N.W. 887 (Iowa 1933). Sometimes, on the other hand, the court's standards of probative force required of an inference seem unreasonably high. See Arnett v. Dalton, 257 S.W.2d 585 (Ky.1953) (improper to infer that driver was drunk after testimony that he had been observed having one drink and there were five empty beer cans in the back of the car). See the analysis in Levin and Levy, Persuading the Jury With Facts not in Evidence: The Fiction–Science Spectrum, 105 U.Pa. L.Rev. 139 (1956); Mansfield, Jury Notice, 74 Geo.L.J. 395, 422–24 (1985).

Robinson v. Pennsylvania Railroad Co.

United States Court of Appeals, Third Circuit, 1954.
214 F.2d 798.

■ STALEY, CIRCUIT JUDGE. This Federal Employers' Liability Act case resulted in a verdict and judgment for plaintiff, and defendant appeals.

. . .

Of the many remaining matters urged upon us by both sides, the only one that stands out with any degree of clarity on this record is that, because of the bickering and brawling of both counsel, the jury could not possibly have decided the real issues on their merits but was sidetracked into passing judgment on the character of the attorneys.

We will set out some of the more flagrant statements contained in the arguments to the jury. The closing summation of plaintiff's counsel began like this:

> "As usual, my good friend in these cases always attacks every lawyer, no matter who he is. The case is always a fake and it is always a phony, and everybody is a liar, and everybody is pulling something to try to get something from the client he represents, everybody is a thief."

Then, taking a wholly unjustified view of defense counsel's comment upon plaintiff's complaint of pain in his back, plaintiff's counsel said, "Now, look who he has made a thief out of. He made a thief out of Dr. Goldsmith.... So Dr. Goldsmith is now a liar and he is putting something on to try to put something over on the railroad." At this point there was a defense objection, followed by some bickering, with no admonition from the court except to say " ... the jury will be the judge of what was said.... let us go ahead." Plaintiff's counsel then returned to the same vein of argument, saying: "Now he comes around and makes a thief out of Dr. John Farrell ... now Dr. Farrell is also a thief, and he is trying to put something over on the railroad." Referring to the defense comments on plaintiff's testimony, plaintiff's counsel said, "He [plaintiff] is seventy years old and he did not come in here to be made a thief of, and a liar, and a perjurer." These inflammatory accusations had no factual foundation and had absolutely nothing to do with the real issues which the jury was to decide. Defense counsel had pointed to certain physical characteristics of the power saw, used to cut the planks on the bridge, as supporting his view of the way the work was being done when plaintiff was injured. Plaintiff's counsel replied: "Now let us get down to this little tricky stunt that he pulled here with this saw.... Don't you see what the whole stunt here is?" In his summation defense counsel said that the railroad was defending the case because it felt that the accident was plaintiff's own doing. Counsel for the plaintiff replied that the defense theory of the accident was " ... to distort facts ... in an effort to do what? ... To fit this story of why the railroad defends this case. Why didn't he tell you why they are defending the thousands of others? Everybody is a thief, the railroad never lies. Is that nice?" One final statement by plaintiff's counsel deserves mention. He said near the end of his closing summation:

"But the very idea to the whole argument, this whole plan, this whole idea, is to take this man and make a nonentity out of him, to destroy the existence of an Alfred Robinson of any kind upon their books or upon their records, to make it appear as if he were no one, as if he meant nothing to this company, as if the forty years of honest service had been nothing. How far up the echelons of this company do you have to go before they kick you out like a sawdust bag?"

Here a defense motion to withdraw a juror was denied.

Enough has been set out to make it evident that the closing speech of counsel for the plaintiff dealt with many matters which were prejudicial because totally irrelevant and confusing to the jury. But, says plaintiff's counsel, defense counsel started the improper arguments and the former merely replied. To an extent that appears to be true, but if so, "... then the trial had degenerated even more than we have indicated." United States v. American Die & Instrument Works, Inc., 3 Cir., 1954, 213 F.2d 731. If it is at all relevant to determine who started the improper arguments, it is worth noting that in the opening summation of plaintiff's counsel, in making light of the testimony and argument that the floor of the bridge was being sawed a whole section at one time, he said, "And that whole switch has been made for the purpose of trying to show contributory negligence on this man ... there is not an iota of contributory negligence in this case, and any attempt to reduce this verdict that is being made on sheer imagination, somebody has been doing a little mixing here, twisting the dog around a little to try to keep this man from what the law says he should get under these circumstances.... They are trapped in this concoction of their own making." At any rate, recrimination has no place in counsel's jury speeches. New York Central R.R. v. Johnson, 1929, 279 U.S. 310, 49 S.Ct. 300, 73 L.Ed. 706; Chicago & N.W. Ry. v. Kelly, 8 Cir., 1936, 84 F.2d 569; Mittleman v. Bartikowsky, 1925, 283 Pa. 485, 129 A. 566.[1] Especially is this so when dealing with conduct that shows not a mere isolated lapse from propriety in the heat of argument but repeated accusations against opposing counsel and client and repeated references to matters entirely foreign to the real issues before the jury. On the other hand, defense counsel's conduct was far from being a model of propriety. A few examples are in order. He began by saying that "... it is part of the act to come in and say: Well, of course, there is no question about the negligence here...." Later, in telling the jury not to confuse the evidence from the stand with what the lawyers said, especially what the plaintiff's lawyer said, defense counsel stated, "... because what he has told you about the way this cut was made was just as phony and just as inaccurate and just as unreliable [as another contention]. That contention ... was just a false statement, just as phony as the pretense...." He accused plaintiff's counsel of manufacturing his case, in the following language, "You are not expected to throw your commonsense and wits out of the window when you come into a courtroom and just accept some cock-and-bull story invented by the lawyer ... that is a complete fabrication and invention on the

---

1. His own improper remarks may estop counsel from objecting to arguments of his opponent that would be unjustified were they not required to overcome the prejudicial effect of the original impropriety. Smith v. Schwartz, 96 P.2d 816 (Cal.Ct.App.1940); Logan v. Jacobs, 119 P.2d 53 (Okla.1941). Nevertheless, "while improper argument by one counsel may elicit a response by his opponent which is also improper, without requiring a reversal, it does not open up the entire field to improper argument." Chicago and North Western Railway v. Kelly, 84 F.2d 569, 574 (8th Cir.1936). Such unseemly exchanges can be avoided, and should be, as the main case points out, by firm exercise of the trial court's broad discretion and initiative in restricting argument. Cf. Taylor v. F.W. Woolworth Co., 98 P.2d 114 (Kan.1940). [The footnotes are the editors'; the court's footnotes have been omitted.]

part of the lawyer to try to get you bamboozled, to bring you around to some conclusion about this case that just is not so." Again referring to the alleged direction of sawing the planks, he said, "... but for the purposes of this case Mr. Richter is willing to turn him around in the hope that that will turn you around too...." Finally, commenting on plaintiff's theory that his fellow workers were negligent in failing to warn him not to step on the sawed planks, which warning defendant contended was unnecessary because the danger was obvious, he said, "And yet that is the only way that the lawyer has been able to think up a story that might lead you to believe that Mr. Robinson ought to get any money in this." To none of these improper statements did plaintiff object. Indeed, plaintiff's attorney seemed more than happy to meet defendant's attorney on these grounds, and he showed that readiness to engage in personal abuse in his closing summation. The jury was empaneled, however, to pass upon entirely different issues, to be fought out on entirely different grounds. It is at least probable that the jury was utterly confused by these diversionary tactics, so that in the end their verdict might well represent their judgment of which lawyer was in the right as to the false issues, leaving the real issues undecided. See Kroger Grocery & Baking Co. v. Stewart, 8 Cir., 1947, 164 F.2d 841, 844. This conclusion is strengthened by the fact that none of the improper remarks evoked a reprimand from the trial judge or even a direction that they should be disregarded by the jury. Worse yet, in his charge the judge told the jury that "The lawyers in this case have argued the facts thoroughly and well...." This apparent approval of the accusatory statements of counsel might well have led the jury to believe that it could and should consider them in its deliberations. In short, we are firmly convinced that the conduct of both counsel was of such nature as to vitiate the entire trial. Both of these men are experienced and able lawyers, and there is no excuse for such conduct.

Plaintiff points out that only a few of the statements about which defendant complains were objected to at the time and that a motion to withdraw a juror was made to only one such statement. For lack of objection and specific motion, it is argued that an appellate court may not interfere. As to the ordinary case, we agree, but we have never understood it to be the law that flagrantly abusive statements, unsupported by the evidence and introducing matters clearly irrelevant to the jury's deliberation of the issues on the law and evidence, in the absence of an admonition to the jury, are immune from appellate redress simply because there was not an objection to each such statement. This field of improper trial arguments is not one where the citation of cases is of much help, but, to the extent that precedents are at all relevant, there is authority for the proposition that lack of an objection is not always a bar to correction and that, in the obvious case such as this, plain error may, indeed must, be noticed and rectified. New York Central R.R. v. Johnson, 1929, 279 U.S. 310, 318, 49 S.Ct. 300; Aetna Life Ins. Co. of Hartford, Conn. v. Kelley, 8 Cir., 1934, 70 F.2d 589, 594, 93 A.L.R. 471; Rouse v. Burnham, 10 Cir., 1931, 51 F.2d 709, 713. See also United States v. Socony–Vacuum Oil Co., 1940, 310 U.S. 150, 239, 60 S.Ct. 811, 84 L.Ed. 1129.

As we are convinced that the jury did not have an opportunity fairly to pass upon the real issues because of the conduct of the attorneys, no purpose can be served in discussing the other matters raised on this appeal. Minneapolis, St. P. & S. Ste. M. Ry. v. Moquin, 1931, 283 U.S. 520, 51 S.Ct. 501, 75 L.Ed. 1243.

The judgment of the district court will be reversed and the cause remanded for a new trial, each party to bear its own costs on this appeal.[2]

2. Louisiana & Arkansas Railway v. Johnson, 214 F.2d 290, 293–94 (5th Cir.), cert. denied, 348 U.S. 875 (1954): "Appellant's investigation in preparing its defense

NOTES

1. It is highly improper for counsel to make themselves unsworn witnesses to facts that have not been introduced in evidence. Strong v. Abner, 105 S.W.2d 599 (Ky.1937). However, they may urge the jury to accept as true a proposition that was not established by evidence if it is part of the general and common knowledge of laymen, for example, that an automobile will not start unless the ignition is turned on. Levlon v. Dallas Railway & Terminal Co., 117 S.W.2d 876 (Tex.Civ.App.1938).

Compare Model Rules of Professional Conduct, Rule 3.4 (1983): "Fairness to Opposing Party and Counsel. A Lawyer shall not: . . . (e) in trial, allude to any matter that the lawyer does not reasonably believe is relevant or that will not be supported by admissible evidence, assert personal knowledge of facts in issue except when testifying as a witness, or state a personal opinion as to the justness of a cause, the credibility of a witness, the culpability of a civil litigant or the guilt or innocence of an accused. . . ." In Henderson v. United States, 218 F.2d 14, 19 (6th Cir.), cert. denied, 349 U.S. 920 (1955), the court said: "It is not misconduct on his [the prosecutor's] part to express his individual belief in the guilt of the accused if such belief is based solely on the evidence introduced and the jury is not led to believe that there is other evidence, known to the prosecutor but not introduced, justifying that belief."

2. Does mere withdrawal of offensive remarks remove the basis for a mistrial? Can the judge eliminate prejudice by striking the offensive words and instructing the jury to disregard them? See Yellow Cab Co. v. Adams, 31 S.E.2d 195 (Ga.Ct.App.1944); Meyer v. Capital Transit Co., 32 A.2d 392 (D.C.Mun.App. 1943).

3. The right to address the jury in order to persuade it with respect to the probabilities of disputed propositions is of great value and the opportunity to address the jury first and last is much sought after. Errors with respect to these matters may result in reversal. See 38 A.L.R.2d 1396 (1954). One of the procedural consequences of affirmative defenses may be the transfer of this opportunity. See Michael, The Elements of Legal Controversy 708–22 (1948). In 1975 the Federal Rules of Criminal Procedure were amended to provide: "Closing Argument. After the closing of evidence the prosecution shall open the argument. The defense shall be permitted to reply in rebuttal." Rule 29.1. The Advisory Committee Note states: "The rule is drafted in the view that fair and effective administration of justice is best served if the defendant knows the arguments actually made by the prosecution in behalf of conviction before the

included placing the appellee under the surveillance of a detective, who admitted on cross-examination that he tried to induce the appellee to drink alcoholic liquors when the appellee had expressed a preference for soft drinks. There was also evidence that appellant's chief surgeon, at the direction of its vice-president, had reprimanded its division surgeon for giving the appellee a statement to the Railroad Retirement Board that he needed retirement on account of shock and injury to his ankle. Appellee's counsel, in arguing the case to the jury, stated in part: 'Now in this case you will note that the plaintiff was dealing with a very very resourceful defendant; a defendant which in many respects would stop at nothing; a very resourceful defendant.' The district court overruled appellant's objection to this argument. In the part of the argument immediately preceding, counsel for the appellee had commented on the employment and conduct of the private detective and immediately following he commented on the reprimand to the doctor. We cannot say, under the circumstances of this case, that the district court abused its discretion in overruling the objection to this argument. That was the only objection made to the argument which is set out in full in the transcript, and which as a whole, was a fair though vigorous presentation of the issues."

defendant is faced with the decision whether to reply and what to reply."
Should the defendant be entirely happy with this explanation?

4. McCullough v. Langer, 73 P.2d 649 (Cal.Ct.App.1937):

It is the custom and the prevailing rule of procedure that the party
upon whom the burden of proof rests has the right to open and close the
arguments subject to a reasonable discretion on the part of the court to
regulate the time and manner of presenting the arguments. Section 607,
subd. 4, Code Civ.Proc. It is ordinarily true that when the party who is
entitled to open the argument waives that privilege he may not be
permitted to close the argument when his adversary also waives argument.
It is usually true that when counsel for the respondent declines to reply to
a fair opening argument, the one upon whom the burden rests may not
then be permitted to further continue his argument. . . .

In the interest of justice, there is and should be an exception to this
last-mentioned rule. When it is previously understood from a specific order
of court that each side is allotted a fixed period of time for arguments to be
divided between two or more attorneys for respective sides, and one of the
attorneys upon whom the burden of the affirmative rests makes a full and
a fair presentation of the issues upon which he relies for judgment, it is
within the sound discretion of the trial judge to require the opposing
counsel to then make his reply, or, upon his refusal to do so, he may be
precluded from following the closing argument of his adversary. This is
based on the established custom of granting to the affirmative side of a
controversy the opening and closing of the arguments. It sometimes occurs
that after the time for arguments has been fixed by the court, the attorney
having the affirmative seeks to reserve his theory of the case for his final
argument by waiving his right to the opening. He then runs the risk of
losing his opportunity of making the closing argument if his opponent sees
fit to submit the cause without argument. Since there is then no argument
to answer, it has been held the court will not abuse its discretion by
refusing to permit the plaintiff to make a closing argument, for such
strategy would have the effect of depriving the defendant of the opportunity to answer his opponent's argument and might result in possible injustice. . . .

When the court has previously allowed a specified period of time for
arguments to be divided between adverse counsel and an attorney representing the affirmative of the controversy has made a reasonably fair
opening argument, it is not an abuse of discretion to allow him or an
associate to complete the argument within the allotted time, even though
adverse counsel may waive his argument at the close of the opening
presentation. . . .

CHAPTER 6

EXPERT EVIDENCE

SECTION 1. THE NATURE AND FUNCTION OF EXPERT EVIDENCE

In Chapter 3 on Testimonial Evidence, the Opinion Rule was examined. A version of this rule is found in Fed. R. Evid. 701. As noted earlier—supra p. 359—the purpose of the Opinion Rule is to enforce a distinction between information that is permitted to enter into consideration through the formal process of proof—sworn and cross-examined witnesses, authenticated documents and so forth—and information that is permitted to enter into consideration through the informal process—the trier of facts' ways of acquiring information before the trial begins. Inquiry into the topic of relevance has provided an opportunity for consideration of what this principle of allocation between formal and informal processes may be and the reasons for it, because an item of evidence offered through the formal process will be relevant only if certain background information, available to the trier of facts through the informal process, is permitted to be taken into account. The Opinion Rule enforces the principle of allocation by forbidding a witness to testify in a way that unnecessarily exposes the trier of fact to information that is permitted to come into consideration only through the informal process. Thus a witness will not be allowed to testify that someone was in the garden when all he saw was a footprint in the flowerbed. On the other hand, if a witness can communicate information that is permitted to be brought in through the formal process only if he testifies to an opinion or draws an inference that reflects information that is not permitted to be brought in through that process—e.g., if he is not allowed to say that a person was drunk, he will not have communicated fully what he perceived of that person's demeanor—he may do so, but the trier of fact will be required, so far as possible, to rely only on its own ideas and not the witness's about the significance of demeanor on the issue of drunkenness.

The law relating to the admissibility of expert testimony—in the Federal Rules, in the first instance, Rule 702—repeats the principle allocating information between the formal and informal processes. In addition, Rule 702 calls attention to the fact that much important information admissible through the formal process will concern cases other than the litigated case and general principles. A witness may expressly recite this sort of information or he may communicate it by means of an opinion on an issue in the litigated case.

If the distinction between information that may come in through the formal process and information that may come through the informal process is clear, less clear is the distinction between lay and expert testimony, a distinction that seems to receive recognition in Fed. R. Evid. 701 and 702. Are these subclasses of the whole class of information that may come through the formal process? If so, what distinguishes the two subclasses? It cannot be that the expert is someone who knows something that the trier of fact does not know, whereas the lay witness does not have such knowledge: the "lay" witness who testifies that the light was red when the car entered the intersection knows something that the trier of fact does not know just as much as the witness who tells the trier of fact about the principles of DNA. Perhaps in a rough and ready way it can be said that the lay witness testifies about the facts of the litigated case, whereas the expert testifies about the facts of other cases and general principles. But at the borderline, the distinction is hard to apply: Is a witness who testifies that it was not the defendant but the defendant's brother who held up the bank, testifying about the facts of the litigated case, whereas a witness who testifies that many members of the defendant's ethnic group look like the defendant, so that there is a certain probability that the defendant was not the holdup man, testifying to the facts of other cases or to a general principle?

Assuming there is an intelligible category "expert" testimony, what are the requirements for the admissibility of evidence that falls within this category? Is it enough that such evidence be relevant? Is the category to be subdivided into subcategories, for instance into scientific evidence and nonscientific evidence? Are these subcategories subject to different requirements for admissibility? What would be the reason for a difference in treatment? These questions are explored in the materials that follow.

United States v. Robinson

United States Court of Appeals, Second Circuit, 1976.
544 F.2d 110, cert. denied, 434 U.S. 1050 (1978).

■ Before SMITH, OAKES and MESKILL, CIRCUIT JUDGES.

■ MESKILL, CIRCUIT JUDGE:

On February 18, 1975, three armed men robbed the Trap Falls office of the Connecticut National Bank in Shelton, Connecticut, and fled with $2,034. Tellers, Retta Mondulick and Robert Welch, were present in the bank at the time of the robbery, and the entire 84-second incident was captured on film by a bank surveillance camera that was activated by Mrs. Mondulick when she saw the first man enter the bank.

Appellant Robinson came under suspicion as a result of an informant's tip. He surrendered voluntarily after learning that the FBI had, with the consent of his wife, searched his apartment and taken his coat, which resembled a coat worn by one of the bank robbers.

At Robinson's first trial, the jury was unable to reach a verdict, and Judge Newman declared a mistrial. At a second jury trial before Judge Zampano, Robinson was found guilty of bank robbery in violation of 18 U.S.C. §§ 2113(a) and (b). Because certain erroneous evidentiary rulings prejudiced Robinson's alibi defense, we reverse his conviction.

I.   The Third Man

There is no dispute over the identity of two of the three bank robbers. One was Luther Fleming, who is apparently still at large. The other was David Tate, who pled guilty and was given a ten year sentence. Tate did not testify at Robinson's first trial.

On the day after the bank robbery, the FBI took a bank surveillance photograph to the Bridgeport jail and enlisted the aid of Correctional Officer George Maher and his staff in identifying the third man involved in the robbery. Maher was prepared to testify that, based on an examination of their files, he and his staff concluded that the individual in the picture resembled one Eli Turner. If Judge Zampano had admitted the evidence of the resemblance to

Turner, the government would have stipulated that Bridgeport Police Captain Anthony Fabrizi, if called, would testify that Eli Turner was suspected of committing two local armed robberies in early February, 1975, and was still at large. Judge Zampano excluded Maher's testimony because he was concerned that its admission would open the door to testimony by numerous witnesses that the bank surveillance photographs either did or did not resemble Robinson. On appeal, Robinson claims that the exclusion of the Maher/Fabrizi testimony was error. We agree.

The central issue in this case was one of identification. The government maintained that the third man in the bank was Robinson, and Robinson claimed that it was not. Robinson's claim was more plausible than it might at first appear. The photographic identification procedures employed by the FBI had been mildly suggestive, and the defense argued that the in-court identifications made by the two tellers were the products of pretrial misidentification. The bank surveillance photographs were of such quality that the defense was able to argue to the jury that an examination of the film would prove that the third bank robber was not Robinson. The testimony of Tate, who agreed to testify on the eve of the second trial, was subject to attack on the ground that it was the product of a "deal" with the government.

It was entirely proper for Robinson to disprove the government's contention by proving that the third man was someone else. 1 J. Wigmore, Evidence § 34 (3d ed. 1940) [hereinafter cited as Wigmore]; 2 Wigmore § 413. If it was, then obviously Robinson was innocent. Evidence to the effect that the third man in the bank resembled an individual suspected of two armed robberies that occurred in the Bridgeport area within six days prior to the bank robbery was clearly probative of the issue Robinson sought to prove, namely, that the third man was someone else.

The reasons given by Judge Zampano for the exclusion of this evidence were based upon his desire to avoid repetitive opinion testimony by witnesses for both the prosecution and the defense concerning whether or not Robinson resembled the individual in the bank surveillance photographs. This concern was, of course, legitimate.[1] The jury could look at the pictures and look at Robinson and decide that issue for itself. The Advisory Committee Notes to Fed. R. Evid. 701 indicate that if "attempts are made to introduce meaningless assertions which amount to little more than choosing up sides, exclusion for lack of helpfulness is called for by the rule." However, the Maher/Fabrizi testimony had a different purpose. Maher was going to testify about the resemblance of the individual in the picture to Turner, not Robinson. Turner was not before the court, and he could not have been brought to court because he was still at large. The comparison that Maher was going to make was one which the jury could not have made for itself, so his testimony did not suffer from a "lack of helpfulness." The reasons given by Judge Zampano for the exclusion of the Maher/Fabrizi testimony simply do not justify his evidentiary ruling.

---

1. We note that the first time anyone offered evidence of that kind was at the first trial when, over the objection of defense counsel, the government introduced the testimony of a Bridgeport police officer who said that he recognized the individual in one of the bank surveillance photographs as Robinson. The government's argument at the first trial, of course, was somewhat different from the one they advance on this appeal. Nevertheless, we are inclined to agree with the government that, despite the broad language of Fed. R. Evid. 701, it is not improper to exclude the testimony of lay witnesses asked to render an opinion whether the individual in a bank photograph is the defendant. Our agreement with that abstract proposition does not help the government, however, for it is inapplicable to the facts of this case. [Footnote by the court. Other footnotes to the court's opinion have been omitted and this footnote renumbered.]

The government argues that opinion testimony based on only general features is inadmissible, particularly when the opinion comes from a lay witness. Even assuming the correctness of that proposition, ... we cannot agree that it is dispositive on the facts of this case. As indicated above, Maher was not going to testify about the defendant, he was going to testify about another individual. His opinion was "rationally based on [his] perception" because he had seen Turner, and it was "helpful to ... the determination of a fact in issue" because Turner was unavailable. Therefore, his opinion was admissible under Rule 701, and it would not have been "objectionable because it embrace[d] an ultimate issue to be decided by the trier of fact." Fed. R. Evid. 704. We cannot agree with the government that Maher's testimony amounted to "meaningless assertions which amount to little more than choosing up sides." Advisory Committee Notes to Rule 701. On the contrary, it was testimony from a disinterested government official that bore directly on the principal issue in the case, namely, the identity of the third man in the bank.

. . .

Reversed and remanded.

NOTES

1. Is the court in Robinson justified in seeing the case as involving Fed. R. Evid. 701 or should it be looking to Rule 702?

2. In United States v. Saniti, 604 F.2d 603 (9th Cir.), cert. denied, 444 U.S. 969 (1979), the court held it not error in a bank robbery prosecution to allow witnesses to identify the robber in surveillance photographs to be the defendant. "The two witnesses who identified Saniti as the person in the surveillance photographs were his roommates. Their perceptions of his appearance and clothing were rationally based upon their association with him. The two witnesses were able to identify the clothing on the person in the photograph as belonging to Saniti. That clothing was not available to the jury for comparison." See also United States v. Butcher, 557 F.2d 666 (9th Cir.1977): Not error to allow police officers and a parole officer acquainted with defendant to testify that defendant was the person in the surveillance photographs; State v. Benton, 567 So.2d 1067, 1068 (Fla.Dist.Ct.App.1990): Error to exclude testimony of witness who had known defendant for a number of years that person in bank camera surveillance photograph of holdup man was defendant: such evidence is admissible "if there is some basis for concluding that the witness is more likely to correctly identify the defendant from the photograph than is the jury." On the other hand, in United States v. Calhoun, 544 F.2d 291 (6th Cir.1976), it was held error to admit testimony of the defendant's probation officer that defendant was the person in the surveillance photographs. There was evidence that the robber had a mustache, goatee and sideburns. Evidently at the trial defendant was clean shaven. The probation officer could not remember whether at the time of his contacts with defendant he had a mustache, goatee or sideburns, but only that he had facial hair. The court stated that the evidence "teases the outer limits of Rule 701." Important to the holding was the danger that in cross-examining the identification witness the fact of the defendant's criminal record would come out. There was no showing that persons acquainted with the defendant other than the probation officer could not have been called.

With United States v. Robinson and the cases just cited, compare cases involving "photographic identification experts" in which the question presented was whether the witness should be allowed to compare photographs of the defendant with photographs of the bank robber taken by bank surveillance cameras. In United States v. Trejo, 501 F.2d 138, 142–43 (9th Cir.1974), it was held error to allow such testimony when all that the witness could point to was the shape of the face, nose, mouth and hair. The court distinguished United States v. Cairns, 434 F.2d 643 (9th Cir.1970), where the witness talked about specific details such as the folds in the ear and a facial crease. In United States v. Brown, 501 F.2d 146, 148–50 (9th Cir.1974), it was error to allow an opinion based on one surveillance photograph because the image was so clear and on another because it was so vague, but admission of an opinion based on a third was in the discretion of the trial court. What is the asserted subject of expertise in these cases?

Een v. Consolidated Freightways

United States District Court, District of North Dakota, 1954.
120 F.Supp. 289, aff'd, 220 F.2d 82 (8th Cir.1955).

■ VOGEL, DISTRICT JUDGE. This is an action for damages for personal injuries arising out of a collision between a car driven by the plaintiff Clarence O. Een, now an incompetent, and a truck driven by the defendant Dulski and owned by the defendant Consolidated Freightways. The jury returned a verdict for the defendants. The Court is now presented with plaintiffs' motion for a new trial. Such motion is based principally upon the grounds that the Court erred in allowing a defendants' witness, one John Holcomb, to testify, over objection, that from his observations he believed the collision had occurred on the west (defendants') side of the highway.

Holcomb was a deputy sheriff and former city policeman with over 17 years' experience investigating accidents as a law enforcement officer. He arrived at the scene of the accident approximately an hour and twenty minutes after its occurrence but before the damaged vehicles had been moved from the positions in which they had come to rest after the impact, and before the highway had been open to other traffic. He was accompanied by a patrolman who also testified in the case, first at the instance of the plaintiffs, later being called by the defendants, but who was not asked by either party concerning his opinion as to where the collision took place. These two were the first police officials to arrive at the scene of the accident. Immediately after arriving, Holcomb took charge of unblocking the road and then in directing traffic past the stalled truck which he had had pulled to one side of the road. Holcomb also visited the scene of the accident on the morning after its occurrence.

After establishing Holcomb's qualifications and having him describe what he found and what he did, defendants' counsel asked him if, from his observations, he had formed an opinion as to where the impact occurred. Upon receiving an affirmative answer, he was asked to state the opinion. Plaintiffs' counsel objected on the grounds that it was incompetent, irrelevant and immaterial, calling for speculation, guess and conjecture, invading the province of the jury and called for a conclusion. The objections were overruled and the witness was allowed to state that in his opinion the impact occurred in the west lane of traffic. There was no objection to the qualifications of the witness and plaintiffs make no point of this in the motion for a new trial. In any event, whether an expert is sufficiently qualified to give an opinion is clearly within the discretion of the trial court. Chicago, Great Western Ry. Co. v. Beecher, 8 Cir.1945, 150 F.2d 394, 400; 2 Wig., Ev'd., 3d Ed., sec. 561. The issue, then, seems to be whether the matter was a proper subject for opinion testimony. The objection, while not specifically so stating, nevertheless raises that issue.

.   .   .

The United States Court of Appeals for this Circuit has indicated that it is largely within the discretion of the trial court to accept or reject opinion testimony by expert witnesses.

In Redding v. Long–Bell Lumber Co., 8 Cir., 1953, 207 F.2d 371, 376, the Court said:

> "We think too the general subject of inquiry was a matter of common knowledge rather than a subject for expert testimony, at least it was within the discretion of the court to hear or decline to hear expert testimony."

See also 32 C.J.S., Evidence, § 449. Indeed, Wigmore advocates that the matter be left entirely within the discretion of the trial court. 7 Wig., Ev'd., 3d Ed., sec. 1929.

It should be noted that the objection that the testimony invades the province of the jury or that it is upon the very issue that the jury must decide has no validity. 7 Wig., Ev'd., secs. 1920, 1921. In Builders Steel Co. v. Commissioner of Internal Revenue, 8 Cir., 1950, 179 F.2d 377, at page 380 the Court stated:

> "Where the matter under inquiry is properly the subject of expert testimony, it is no objection that the opinion sought to be elicited is upon the issue to be decided. Svenson v. Mutual Life Ins. Co. of New York, 8 Cir., 87 F.2d 441, 445 and cases cited."

The issue herein, then, is whether the point of collision upon the highway is properly the subject of expert testimony by a witness who personally observed the scene of the collision soon after its occurrence and who had had many years' experience in the investigation of automobile accidents.

. . .

In the case at hand, contrary inferences as to which side of the road the accident occurred on were earnestly argued by opposing counsel from the physical facts existing immediately after the accident. It would seem, therefore, that this is not a case where the conclusion as to where the collision occurred is so obvious that any reasonable person, trained or not, could easily draw the inference. Rather, it would seem to be a case where trained experts in the field would be of considerable assistance to the jurors in arriving at their conclusions.

Modern legal thinking indicates quite clearly that the rule excluding opinion evidence is to be applied sparingly, if at all, so that the jury may have all evidence that may aid them in their determination of the facts. Thus, Wigmore states that, rightfully understood, the true test of the rule is whether opinion testimony upon this subject matter from this particular witness may appreciably assist the jury. 7 Wig., Ev'd., 3d Ed., sec. 1923. He even suggests that the rule should be that all opinion testimony is admissible subject only to the trial court's discretion to exclude it upon considerations of trial convenience. 7 Wig., Ev'd., 3d Ed., sec. 1929.

. . .

This Court is of the opinion that under the circumstances as they existed and in considering the evidence introduced at the trial, the opinion of the witness Holcomb was properly admitted. It was the view of this Court at the time the ruling was made during the trial that the subject was a proper one for the admission of an opinion of a concededly qualified expert. The physical facts and circumstances found immediately after the accident prompted contrary inferences to be argued with equal earnestness by able and experienced counsel.

The witness had personally observed the physical facts and circumstances soon after the accident occurred, before the damaged vehicles had been moved, and before the highway had been opened to other traffic, and the witness was qualified through long years of experience in the investigation of automobile accidents. Where the inference or conclusion to be drawn is not so obvious that it can be said that the jurors were as equally competent to reach it as one skilled through long experience, then the opinion of one who is so skilled is not only admissible but may be of aid to the jurors. The witness was subject to cross-examination concerning the basis for his opinion but plaintiffs' counsel did not see fit to inquire into it and refused to permit the witness to state his reasons when he offered to do so. In the instructions of the Court to the jurors, they were told specifically that they were not bound by the opinions of expert witnesses, that the testimony of expert witnesses was purely advisory and that they should give such weight and value to such opinions as they thought right and proper under the circumstances. If this Court had been sitting as the trier of the facts, then under the peculiar circumstances here existing it would have felt that the opinion of the witness Holcomb would have been of assistance in determining the ultimate facts.

The motion for a new trial must be denied.

It will be so ordered.

NOTES

1. See Parker, Automobile Accident Analysis By Expert Witnesses, 44 Va. L. Rev. 789 (1958); Miller v. Pillsbury, 211 N.E.2d 733 (Ill.1965) (not error to admit testimony of accidentologist as to which vehicle over center line); Zellers v. Chase, 197 A.2d 206 (N.H.1964) (whether vehicle accelerating from dirt thrown back in wheel marks); Housman v. Fiddyment, 421 S.W.2d 284, 291–92 (Mo.1967) (error to allow witness to give opinion as to point of maximum engagement of vehicles; with data available, question could be determined by jurors possessed of ordinary knowledge). Krizak v. W.C. Brooks and Sons, Inc., 320 F.2d 37 (4th Cir.1963), declines to hold that the trial judge erred in excluding testimony of accidentologist, emphasizing discretion of trial judge. In Hagan Storm Fence Co. v. Edwards, 148 So.2d 693 (Miss.1963), the admission of testimony of an accidentologist was held to be reversible error, but there is a potent dissent.

The Law Reform Committee in England made the interesting observation that with the institution of pretrial discovery of accidentologists' reports, use of the testimony of these experts went out of fashion in England. Evidence of Opinion and Expert Evidence, Law Reform Committee, 17th Report, Cmnd. 4489, pp. 23, 42 (1970).

2. Bennett v. International Shoe Co., 80 Cal.Rptr. 318 (Cal.App.1969): Appellant purchased a pair of shoes manufactured by appellee. The shoes had waxed soles. Shortly after purchasing the shoes and while he was wearing them, appellant slipped going down stairs and injured himself. He sued the manufacturer on a theory of strict liability: the product was defective and appellee had placed it on the market knowing it would be used without inspection for defects. The court of appeals held that the trial court did not err in refusing to allow a mechanical engineer to testify for appellant as to the results of certain tests made by him on the sole of one of the shoes and as to his general observations and opinion on the slipperiness and safety of shoes treated in the way the shoes purchased by appellant had been treated.

De Long v. Erie County, 457 N.E.2d 717, 723 (N.Y.1983): In wrongful death action, not error to admit testimony of economist on market value of services performed by average housewife in decedent's circumstances. "Undoubtedly most jurors have at least a general awareness of the various services performed by a housewife. It is doubtful, however, that they are equally knowledgeable with respect to the monetary equivalent of those services. Although it was once thought that this was not a subject which would lend itself to scientific inquiry and analysis ... that can no longer be said today. It is now apparent, as a majority of courts have held ..., that qualified experts are available and may aid the jury in evaluating the housewife's services not only because jurors may not know the value of those services, but also to dispel the notion that what is provided without financial reward may be considered of little or no financial value in the marketplace." See also Har–Pen Truck Lines, Inc. v. Mills, 378 F.2d 705, 710–12 (5th Cir.1967) (sufficient evidence to support verdict in wrongful death action in view of testimony of economist as to value of deceased mother's household services to her children).

United States v. DiDomenico, 985 F.2d 1159, 1166, 1169 (2d Cir.1993): Held not error to exclude psychiatric testimony that defendant had a dependent personality disorder claimed to be relevant to whether she knew property was stolen. Dissent: "[R]ather than supporting the district court's assertion that defendant's alleged mental state was 'relatively commonplace,' the expert witness would have testified to precisely the opposite point, namely that DiDomenico's Dependent Personality Disorder was a mental disease or defect that fell beyond 'one of the host of attitudes and syndromes that are a part of daily living'.... To hear DiDomenico's self-description of her emotional state at the time of her crime, without more, is not to understand 'to the best possible degree' how this emotional state might affect her ability to have guilty knowledge. A psychiatrist can provide this 'specialized understanding.' "

United States v. Brown, 776 F.2d 397, 399–402 (2d Cir.1985), cert. denied, 475 U.S. 1141 (1986): Not error to permit police officer with experience in the drug traffic to testify to his observations of defendant's behavior and to state his opinion that defendant was acting as a "steerer," one whose task was to make sure a buyer was an addict or user of drugs and not an undercover policeman. See also People v. Hardy, 76 Cal.Rptr. 557 (Cal.App.1969), approving expert testimony by police as to the professional modus operandi of criminal "till tapping," and People v. Crooks, 59 Cal.Rptr. 39 (Cal.App.1967), approving vice squad members' testimony as to modus operandi known as "the creeper," used by prostitutes. But see Central Mut. Ins. Co. v. D. & B., Inc., 340 S.W.2d 525 (Tex.Civ.App.1960), excluding testimony of an "experienced expert burglar" as to how a professional would conduct a safe robbery.

United States v. Nersesian, 824 F.2d 1294, 1307–08 (2d Cir.), cert. denied, 484 U.S. 957 (1987):

On direct-examination, Agent Nolan, who had read most of the voluminous English transcripts of tape recordings that had been played for the jury but had not actually listened to the Arabic tapes themselves, drew upon his specialized knowledge and experience to explain patterns of speech and language that, in his experience, narcotics dealers commonly use in their conversations. For instance, he pointed out that caution, pauses, excessive use of pronouns, and the participants' apparent knowledge of what they were talking about were indicia that could be relied upon in assessing whether a conversation was drug-related. He also identified certain key words or phrases used in certain intercepted conversations as narcotics-related. For instance, he testified that, depending on the context, words such as cheese, land, room, house, car, horse, and stick-shift, could carry a hidden meaning related to narcotics. . . . [W]e perceive no error in the district court's decision to allow the government to elicit expert testimony from a properly qualified expert witness regarding the parlance of the narcotics trade and the meaning thereof. The district court's decision to allow Agent Nolan to testify was within the wide latitude provided by Fed. R. Evid. 702.

See also United States v. Skowronski, 968 F.2d 242, 246 (2d Cir.1992): Not error to allow government "to introduce evidence as to the meanings of terms such as 'stand-up' (i.e., unlikely to inform), likely to 'flip' (i.e., likely to inform), and 'made guy' (i.e., a documented and sworn member of an organized crime family)."

Daubert v. Merrell Dow Pharmaceuticals, Inc.

Supreme Court of the United States, 1993.
509 U.S. 579, 113 S.Ct. 2786, 125 L.Ed.2d 469.

■ JUSTICE BLACKMUN delivered the opinion of the Court.

In this case we are called upon to determine the standard for admitting expert scientific testimony in a federal trial.

I

Petitioners Jason Daubert and Eric Schuller are minor children born with serious birth defects. They and their parents sued respondent in California state court, alleging that the birth defects had been caused by the mothers' ingestion of Bendectin, a prescription anti-nausea drug marketed by respondent. Respondent removed the suits to federal court on diversity grounds.

After extensive discovery, respondent moved for summary judgment, contending that Bendectin does not cause birth defects in humans and that petitioners would be unable to come forward with any admissible evidence that it does. In support of its motion, respondent submitted an affidavit of Steven H. Lamm, physician and epidemiologist, who is a well-credentialed expert on the risks from exposure to various chemical substances.[1] Doctor Lamm stated that he had reviewed all the literature on Bendectin and human birth defects—more than 30 published studies involving over 130,000 patients. No study had found Bendectin to be a human teratogen (i.e., a substance capable of causing malformations in fetuses). On the basis of this review, Doctor Lamm concluded that maternal use of Bendectin during the first trimester of pregnancy has not been shown to be a risk factor for human birth defects.

Petitioners did not (and do not) contest this characterization of the published record regarding Bendectin. Instead, they responded to respondent's motion with the testimony of eight experts of their own, each of whom also possessed impressive credentials.[2] These experts had concluded that Bendectin

---

1. Doctor Lamm received his master's and doctor of medicine degrees from the University of Southern California. He has served as a consultant in birth-defect epidemiology for the National Center for Health Statistics and has published numerous articles on the magnitude of risk from exposure to various chemical and biological substances. App. 34–44. [Footnotes by the Court. Some footnotes omitted, some renumbered.]

2. For example, Shanna Helen Swan, who received a master's degree in biostatics from Columbia University and a doctorate in statistics from the University of California at Berkeley, is chief of the section of the California Department of Health and Services that determines causes of birth defects, and has served as a consultant to the World Health Organization, the Food and Drug Adminis-

can cause birth defects. Their conclusions were based upon "in vitro" (test tube) and "in vivo" (live) animal studies that found a link between Bendectin and malformations; pharmacological studies of the chemical structure of Bendectin that purported to show similarities between the structure of the drug and that of other substances known to cause birth defects; and the "reanalysis" of previously published epidemiological (human statistical) studies.

The District Court granted respondent's motion for summary judgment. The court stated that scientific evidence is admissible only if the principle upon which it is based is " 'sufficiently established to have general acceptance in the field to which it belongs.' " 727 F. Supp. 570, 572 (S.D.Cal.1989), quoting United States v. Kilgus, 571 F.2d 508, 510 (C.A.9 1978). The court concluded that petitioners' evidence did not meet this standard. Given the vast body of epidemiological data concerning Bendectin, the court held, expert opinion which is not based on epidemiological evidence is not admissible to establish causation. 727 F. Supp., at 575. Thus, the animal-cell studies, live-animal studies, and chemical-structure analyses on which petitioners had relied could not raise by themselves a reasonably disputable jury issue regarding causation. Ibid. Petitioners' epidemiological analyses, based as they were on recalculations of data in previously published studies that had found no causal link between the drug and birth defects, were ruled to be inadmissible because they had not been published or subjected to peer review. Ibid.

The United States Court of Appeals for the Ninth Circuit affirmed. 951 F.2d 1128 (1991). Citing Frye v. United States, 54 App. D.C. 46, 47, 293 F. 1013, 1014 (1923), the court stated that expert opinion based on a scientific technique is inadmissible unless the technique is "generally accepted" as reliable in the relevant scientific community. 951 F.2d, at 1129–1130. The court declared that expert opinion based on a methodology that diverges "significantly from the procedures accepted by recognized authorities in the field ... cannot be shown to be 'generally accepted as a reliable technique.' " id., at 1130, quoting United States v. Solomon, 753 F.2d 1522, 1526 (C.A.9 1985).

The court emphasized that other Courts of Appeals considering the risks of Bendectin had refused to admit reanalyses of epidemiological studies that had been neither published nor subjected to peer review. 951 F.2d, at 1130–1131. Those courts had found unpublished reanalyses "particularly problematic in light of the massive weight of the original published studies supporting [respondent's] position, all of which had undergone full scrutiny from the scientific community." Id., at 1130. Contending that reanalysis is generally accepted by the scientific community only when it is subjected to verification and scrutiny by others in the field, the Court of Appeals rejected petitioners' reanalyses as "unpublished, not subjected to the normal peer review process and generated solely for use in litigation." Id., at 1131. The court concluded that petitioners' evidence provided an insufficient foundation to allow admission of expert testimony that Bendectin caused their injuries and, accordingly, that petitioners could not satisfy their burden of proving causation at trial.

We granted certiorari, 506 U.S. 914, 113 S. Ct. 320, 121 L. Ed. 2d 240 (1992), in light of sharp divisions among the courts regarding the proper standard for the admission of expert testimony....

tration, and the National Institutes of Health. App. 113–114, 131–132. Stewart A. Newman, who received his master's and a doctorate in chemistry from Columbia University and the University of Chicago, respectively, is a professor at New York Medical College and has spent over a decade studying the effect of chemicals on limb development. App. 54–56. The credentials of the others are similarly impressive. See App. 61–66, 73–80, 148–153, 187–192, and Attachment to Petitioners' Opposition to Summary Judgment, Tabs 12, 20, 21, 26, 31, 32.

II

A

In the 70 years since its formulation in the Frye case, the "general acceptance" test has been the dominant standard for determining the admissibility of novel scientific evidence at trial. See E. Green & C. Nesson, Problems, Cases, and Materials on Evidence 649 (1983). Although under increasing attack of late, the rule continues to be followed by a majority of courts, including the Ninth Circuit.

The Frye test has its origin in a short and citation-free 1923 decision concerning the admissibility of evidence derived from a systolic blood pressure deception test, a crude precursor to the polygraph machine. In what has become a famous (perhaps infamous) passage, the then Court of Appeals for the District of Columbia described the device and its operation and declared:

> "Just when a scientific principle or discovery crosses the line between the experimental and demonstrable stages is difficult to define. Somewhere in this twilight zone the evidential force of the principle must be recognized, and while courts will go a long way in admitting expert testimony deduced from a well-recognized scientific principle or discovery, *the thing from which the deduction is made must be sufficiently established to have gained general acceptance in the particular field in which it belongs.*" 54 App. D.C., at 47, 293 F., at 1014 (emphasis added).

Because the deception test had "not yet gained such standing and scientific recognition among physiological and psychological authorities as would justify the courts in admitting expert testimony deduced from the discovery, development, and experiments thus far made," evidence of its results was ruled inadmissible. Ibid.

The merits of the Frye test have been much debated, and scholarship on its proper scope and application is legion.[3] Petitioners' primary attack, however, is not on the content but on the continuing authority of the rule. They contend that the Frye test was superseded by the adoption of the Federal Rules of Evidence. We agree.

We interpret the legislatively-enacted Federal Rules of Evidence as we would any statute. Beech Aircraft Corp. v. Rainey, 488 U.S. 153, 163, 102 L. Ed. 2d 445, 109 S. Ct. 439 (1988). Rule 402 provides the baseline:

> "All relevant evidence is admissible, except as otherwise provided by the Constitution of the United States, by Act of Congress, by these rules, or by

---

3. See, e.g., Green, Expert Witnesses and Sufficiency of Evidence in Toxic Substances Litigation: The Legacy of Agent Orange and Bendectin Litigation, 86 Nw. U. L. Rev. 643 (1992) (hereinafter Green); Becker & Orenstein, The Federal Rules of Evidence After Sixteen Years—The Effect of "Plain Meaning" Jurisprudence, the Need for an Advisory Committee on the Rules of Evidence, and Suggestions for Selective Revision of the Rules, 60 Geo. Wash.L.Rev. 857, 876–885 (1992); Hanson, "James Alphonso Frye is Sixty–Five Years Old; Should He Retire?," 16 W. St. U. L. Rev. 357 (1989); Black, A Unified Theory of Scientific Evidence, 56 Ford. L. Rev. 595 (1988); Imwinkelried, The "Bases" of Expert Testimony: The Syllogistic Structure of Scientific Testimony, 67 N.C. L. Rev.

1 (1988); Proposals for a Model Rule on the Admissibility of Scientific Evidence, 26 Jurimetrics J. 235 (1986); Gianelli, The Admissibility of Novel Scientific Evidence: Frye v. United States, A Half–Century Later, 80 Colum. L. Rev. 1197 (1980); The Supreme Court, 1986 Term, 101 Harv. L. Rev. 7, 119, 125–127 (1987).

Indeed, the debates over Frye are such a well-established part of the academic landscape that a distinct term—"Frye-ologist"—has been advanced to describe those who take part. See Behringer, Introduction, Proposals for a Model Rule on the Admissibility of Scientific Evidence, 26 Jurimetrics J., at 239, quoting Lacey, Scientific Evidence, 24 Jurimetrics J. 254, 264 (1984).

other rules prescribed by the Supreme Court pursuant to statutory authority. Evidence which is not relevant is not admissible."

"Relevant evidence" is defined as that which has "any tendency to make the existence of any fact that is of consequence to the determination of the action more probable or less probable than it would be without the evidence." Rule 401. The Rule's basic standard of relevance thus is a liberal one.

Frye, of course, predated the Rules by half a century. In United States v. Abel, 469 U.S. 45, 83 L. Ed. 2d 450, 105 S. Ct. 465 (1984), we considered the pertinence of background common law in interpreting the Rules of Evidence. We noted that the Rules occupy the field, id., at 49, but, quoting Professor Cleary, the Reporter, explained that the common law nevertheless could serve as an aid to their application:

> "In principle, under the Federal Rules no common law of evidence remains. 'All relevant evidence is admissible, except as otherwise provided....' In reality, of course, the body of common law knowledge continues to exist, though in the somewhat altered form of a source of guidance in the exercise of delegated powers." Id., at 51–52.

We found the common-law precept at issue in the Abel case entirely consistent with Rule 402's general requirement of admissibility, and considered it unlikely that the drafters had intended to change the rule. id., at 50–51. In Bourjaily v. United States, 483 U.S. 171, 97 L. Ed. 2d 144, 107 S. Ct. 2775 (1987), on the other hand, the Court was unable to find a particular common-law doctrine in the Rules, and so held it superseded.

Here there is a specific Rule that speaks to the contested issue. Rule 702, governing expert testimony, provides:

> "If scientific, technical, or other specialized knowledge will assist the trier of fact to understand the evidence or to determine a fact in issue, a witness qualified as an expert by knowledge, skill, experience, training, or education, may testify thereto in the form of an opinion or otherwise."

Nothing in the text of this Rule establishes "general acceptance" as an absolute prerequisite to admissibility. Nor does respondent present any clear indication that Rule 702 or the Rules as a whole were intended to incorporate a "general acceptance" standard. The drafting history makes no mention of Frye, and a rigid "general acceptance" requirement would be at odds with the "liberal thrust" of the Federal Rules and their "general approach of relaxing the traditional barriers to 'opinion' testimony." Beech Aircraft Corp. v. Rainey, 488 U.S., at 169 (citing Rules 701 to 705). See also Weinstein, Rule 702 of the Federal Rules of Evidence is Sound; It Should Not Be Amended, 138 F.R.D. 631, 631 (1991) ("The Rules were designed to depend primarily upon lawyer-adversaries and sensible triers of fact to evaluate conflicts"). Given the Rules' permissive backdrop and their inclusion of a specific rule on expert testimony that does not mention "general acceptance," the assertion that the Rules somehow assimilated Frye is unconvincing. Frye made "general acceptance" the exclusive test for admitting expert scientific testimony. That austere standard, absent from and incompatible with the Federal Rules of Evidence, should not be applied in federal trials.

B

That the Frye test was displaced by the Rules of Evidence does not mean, however, that the Rules themselves place no limits on the admissibility of purportedly scientific evidence.[4] Nor is the trial judge disabled from screening such evidence. To the contrary, under the Rules the trial judge must ensure that any and all scientific testimony or evidence admitted is not only relevant, but reliable.

The primary locus of this obligation is Rule 702, which clearly contemplates some degree of regulation of the subjects and theories about which an expert may testify. "If *scientific*, technical, or other specialized *knowledge will assist the trier of fact* to understand the evidence or to determine a fact in issue" an expert "may testify *thereto*." The subject of an expert's testimony must be "scientific ... knowledge."[5] The adjective "scientific" implies a grounding in the methods and procedures of science. Similarly, the word "knowledge" connotes more than subjective belief or unsupported speculation. The term "applies to any body of known facts or to any body of ideas inferred from such facts or accepted as truths on good grounds." Webster's Third New International Dictionary 1252 (1986). Of course, it would be unreasonable to conclude that the subject of scientific testimony must be "known" to a certainty; arguably, there are no certainties in science. See, e.g., Brief for Nicolaas Bloembergen et al. as Amici Curiae 9 ("Indeed, scientists do not assert that they know what is immutably 'true'—they are committed to searching for new, temporary theories to explain, as best they can, phenomena"); Brief for American Association for the Advancement of Science and the National Academy of Sciences as Amici Curiae 7–8 ("Science is not an encyclopedic body of knowledge about the universe. Instead, it represents a *process* for proposing and refining theoretical explanations about the world that are subject to further testing and refinement") (emphasis in original). But, in order to qualify as "scientific knowledge," an inference or assertion must be derived by the scientific method. Proposed testimony must be supported by appropriate validation—i.e., "good grounds," based on what is known. In short, the requirement that an expert's testimony pertain to "scientific knowledge" establishes a standard of evidentiary reliability.[6]

Rule 702 further requires that the evidence or testimony "assist the trier of fact to understand the evidence or to determine a fact in issue." This condition goes primarily to relevance. "Expert testimony which does not relate to any issue in the case is not relevant and, ergo, non-helpful." 3 Weinstein & Berger ¶ 702, p. 702–18. See also United States v. Downing, 753 F.2d 1224,

---

4. The Chief Justice "does not doubt that Rule 702 confides to the judge some gatekeeping responsibility," post, at 971, but would neither say how it does so, nor explain what that role entails. We believe the better course is to note the nature and source of the duty.

5. Rule 702 also applies to "technical, or other specialized knowledge." Our discussion is limited to the scientific context because that is the nature of the expertise offered here.

6. We note that scientists typically distinguish between "validity" (does the principle support what it purports to show?) and "reliability" (does application of the principle produce consistent results?). See Black, A Unified Theory of Scientific Evidence, 56 Ford. L. Rev. 595, 599 (1988). Although "the difference between accuracy, validity, and reliability may be such that each is distinct

from the other by no more than a hen's kick," Starrs, Frye v. United States Restructured and Revitalized: A Proposal to Amend Federal Evidence Rule 702, 26 Jurimetrics J. 249, 256 (1986), our reference here is to evidentiary reliability—that is, trustworthiness. Cf., e. g., Advisory Committee's Notes on Fed. Rule Evid. 602 (" 'The rule requiring that a witness who testifies to a fact which can be perceived by the senses must have had an opportunity to observe, and must have actually observed the fact' is a 'most pervasive manifestation' of the common law insistence upon 'the most reliable sources of information.' " (citation omitted)); Advisory Committee's Notes on Art. VIII of the Rules of Evidence (hearsay exceptions will be recognized only "under circumstances supposed to furnish guarantees of trustworthiness"). In a case involving scientific evidence, evidentiary reliability will be based upon scientific validity.

1242 (C.A.3 1985) ("An additional consideration under Rule 702—and another aspect of relevancy—is whether expert testimony proffered in the case is sufficiently tied to the facts of the case that it will aid the jury in resolving a factual dispute"). The consideration has been aptly described by Judge Becker as one of "fit." Ibid. "Fit" is not always obvious, and scientific validity for one purpose is not necessarily scientific validity for other, unrelated purposes. See Starrs, Frye v. United States Restructured and Revitalized: A Proposal to Amend Federal Evidence Rule 702, and 26 Jurimetrics J. 249, 258 (1986). The study of the phases of the moon, for example, may provide valid scientific "knowledge" about whether a certain night was dark, and if darkness is a fact in issue, the knowledge will assist the trier of fact. However (absent creditable grounds supporting such a link), evidence that the moon was full on a certain night will not assist the trier of fact in determining whether an individual was unusually likely to have behaved irrationally on that night. Rule 702's "helpfulness" standard requires a valid scientific connection to the pertinent inquiry as a precondition to admissibility.

That these requirements are embodied in Rule 702 is not surprising. Unlike an ordinary witness, see Rule 701, an expert is permitted wide latitude to offer opinions, including those that are not based on first-hand knowledge or observation. See Rules 702 and 703. Presumably, this relaxation of the usual requirement of first-hand knowledge—a rule which represents "a 'most pervasive manifestation' of the common law insistence upon 'the most reliable sources of information,'" Advisory Committee's Notes on Fed. Rule Evid. 602 (citation omitted)—is premised on an assumption that the expert's opinion will have a reliable basis in the knowledge and experience of his discipline.

C

Faced with a proffer of expert scientific testimony, then, the trial judge must determine at the outset, pursuant to Rule 104(a), whether the expert is proposing to testify to (1) scientific knowledge that (2) will assist the trier of fact to understand or determine a fact in issue.[7] This entails a preliminary assessment of whether the reasoning or methodology underlying the testimony is scientifically valid and of whether that reasoning or methodology properly can be applied to the facts in issue. We are confident that federal judges possess the capacity to undertake this review. Many factors will bear on the inquiry, and we do not presume to set out a definitive checklist or test. But some general observations are appropriate.

Ordinarily, a key question to be answered in determining whether a theory or technique is scientific knowledge that will assist the trier of fact will be whether it can be (and has been) tested. "Scientific methodology today is based on generating hypotheses and testing them to see if they can be falsified; indeed, this methodology is what distinguishes science from other fields of human inquiry." Green, at 645. See also C. Hempel, Philosophy of Natural Science 49 (1966) ("The statements constituting a scientific explanation must be capable of empirical test"); K. Popper, Conjectures and Refutations: The Growth of Scientific Knowledge 37 (5th ed. 1989) ("The criterion of the scientific status of a theory is its falsifiability, or refutability, or testability").

---

7. Although the Frye decision itself focused exclusively on "novel" scientific techniques, we do not read the requirements of Rule 702 to apply specially or exclusively to unconventional evidence. Of course, well-established propositions are less likely to be challenged than those that are novel, and they are more handily defended. Indeed, theories that are so firmly established as to have attained the status of scientific law, such as the laws of thermodynamics, properly are subject to judicial notice under Fed. Rule Evid. 201.

Another pertinent consideration is whether the theory or technique has been subjected to peer review and publication. Publication (which is but one element of peer review) is not a sine qua non of admissibility; it does not necessarily correlate with reliability, see S. Jasanoff, The Fifth Branch: Science Advisors as Policymakers 61–76 (1990), and in some instances well-grounded but innovative theories will not have been published, see Horrobin, The Philosophical Basis of Peer Review and the Suppression of Innovation, 263 J. Am. Med. Assn. 1438 (1990). Some propositions, moreover, are too particular, too new, or of too limited interest to be published. But submission to the scrutiny of the scientific community is a component of "good science," in part because it increases the likelihood that substantive flaws in methodology will be detected. See J. Ziman, Reliable Knowledge: An Exploration of the Grounds for Belief in Science 130–133 (1978); Relman and Angell, How Good Is Peer Review?, 321 New Eng. J. Med. 827 (1989). The fact of publication (or lack thereof) in a peer-reviewed journal thus will be a relevant, though not dispositive, consideration in assessing the scientific validity of a particular technique or methodology on which an opinion is premised.

Additionally, in the case of a particular scientific technique, the court ordinarily should consider the known or potential rate of error, see, e. g., United States v. Smith, 869 F.2d 348, 353–354 (C.A.7 1989) (surveying studies of the error rate of spectrographic voice identification technique), and the existence and maintenance of standards controlling the technique's operation. See United States v. Williams, 583 F.2d 1194, 1198 (C.A.2 1978) (noting professional organization's standard governing spectrographic analysis), cert. denied, 439 U.S. 1117, 59 L. Ed. 2d 77, 99 S. Ct. 1025 (1979).

Finally, "general acceptance" can yet have a bearing on the inquiry. A "reliability assessment does not require, although it does permit, explicit identification of a relevant scientific community and an express determination of a particular degree of acceptance within that community." United States v. Downing, 753 F.2d, at 1238. See also 3 Weinstein & Berger ¶ 702[03], pp. 702–41 to 702–42. Widespread acceptance can be an important factor in ruling particular evidence admissible, and "a known technique that has been able to attract only minimal support within the community," Downing, supra, at 1238, may properly be viewed with skepticism.

The inquiry envisioned by Rule 702 is, we emphasize, a flexible one.[8] Its overarching subject is the scientific validity—and thus the evidentiary relevance and reliability—of the principles that underlie a proposed submission. The focus, of course, must be solely on principles and methodology, not on the conclusions that they generate.

Throughout, a judge assessing a proffer of expert scientific testimony under Rule 702 should also be mindful of other applicable rules. Rule 703 provides that expert opinions based on otherwise inadmissible hearsay are to be admitted only if the facts or data are "of a type reasonably relied upon by experts in the particular field in forming opinions or inferences upon the subject." Rule

---

8. A number of authorities have presented variations on the reliability approach, each with its own slightly different set of factors. See, e. g., Downing, 753 F.2d at 1238–1239 (on which our discussion draws in part); 3 Weinstein & Berger ¶ 702[03], pp. 702–41 to 702–42 (on which the Downing court in turn partially relied); McCormick, Scientific Evidence: Defining a New Approach to Admissibility, 67 Iowa L. Rev. 879, 911–912 (1982); and Symposium on Science and the Rules of Evidence, 99 F.R.D. 187, 231 (1983) (statement by Margaret Berger). To the extent that they focus on the reliability of evidence as ensured by the scientific validity of its underlying principles, all these versions may well have merit, although we express no opinion regarding any of their particular details.

706 allows the court at its discretion to procure the assistance of an expert of its own choosing. Finally, Rule 403 permits the exclusion of relevant evidence "if its probative value is substantially outweighed by the danger of unfair prejudice, confusion of the issues, or misleading the jury...." Judge Weinstein has explained: "Expert evidence can be both powerful and quite misleading because of the difficulty in evaluating it. Because of this risk, the judge in weighing possible prejudice against probative force under Rule 403 of the present rules exercises more control over experts than over lay witnesses." Weinstein, 138 F.R.D., at 632.

III

We conclude by briefly addressing what appear to be two underlying concerns of the parties and amici in this case. Respondent expresses apprehension that abandonment of "general acceptance" as the exclusive requirement for admission will result in a "free-for-all" in which befuddled juries are confounded by absurd and irrational pseudoscientific assertions. In this regard respondent seems to us to be overly pessimistic about the capabilities of the jury, and of the adversary system generally. Vigorous cross-examination, presentation of contrary evidence, and careful instruction on the burden of proof are the traditional and appropriate means of attacking shaky but admissible evidence. See Rock v. Arkansas, 483 U.S. 44, 61, 97 L. Ed. 2d 37, 107 S. Ct. 2704 (1987). Additionally, in the event the trial court concludes that the scintilla of evidence presented supporting a position is insufficient to allow a reasonable juror to conclude that the position more likely than not is true, the court remains free to direct a judgment, Fed. Rule Civ. Proc. 50 (a), and likewise to grant summary judgment, Fed. Rule Civ. Proc. 56. Cf., e.g., Turpin v. Merrell Dow Pharmaceuticals, Inc., 959 F.2d 1349 (CA6) (holding that scientific evidence that provided foundation for expert testimony, viewed in the light most favorable to plaintiffs, was not sufficient to allow a jury to find it more probable than not that defendant caused plaintiff's injury), cert. denied, 506 U.S. 826 (1992); Brock v. Merrell Dow Pharmaceuticals, Inc., 874 F.2d 307 (C.A.5 1989) (reversing judgment entered on jury verdict for plaintiffs because evidence regarding causation was insufficient), modified, 884 F.2d 166 (C.A.5 1989), cert. denied, 494 U.S. 1046 (1990); Green 680–681. These conventional devices, rather than wholesale exclusion under an uncompromising "general acceptance" test, are the appropriate safeguards where the basis of scientific testimony meets the standards of Rule 702.

Petitioners and, to a greater extent, their amici exhibit a different concern. They suggest that recognition of a screening role for the judge that allows for the exclusion of "invalid" evidence will sanction a stifling and repressive scientific orthodoxy and will be inimical to the search for truth. See, e.g., Brief for Ronald Bayer et al. as Amici Curiae. It is true that open debate is an essential part of both legal and scientific analyses. Yet there are important differences between the quest for truth in the courtroom and the quest for truth in the laboratory. Scientific conclusions are subject to perpetual revision. Law, on the other hand, must resolve disputes finally and quickly. The scientific project is advanced by broad and wide-ranging consideration of a multitude of hypotheses, for those that are incorrect will eventually be shown to be so, and that in itself is an advance. Conjectures that are probably wrong are of little use, however, in the project of reaching a quick, final, and binding legal judgment—often of great consequence—about a particular set of events in the past. We recognize that in practice, a gatekeeping role for the judge, no matter how flexible, inevitably on occasion will prevent the jury from learning of authentic insights and innovations. That, nevertheless, is the balance that is struck by Rules of Evidence designed not for the exhaustive search for cosmic understanding but for the particularized resolution of legal disputes.[9]

IV

To summarize: "general acceptance" is not a necessary precondition to the admissibility of scientific evidence under the Federal Rules of Evidence, but the Rules of Evidence—especially Rule 702—do assign to the trial judge the task of ensuring that an expert's testimony both rests on a reliable foundation and is relevant to the task at hand. Pertinent evidence based on scientifically valid principles will satisfy those demands.

The inquiries of the District Court and the Court of Appeals focused almost exclusively on "general acceptance," as gauged by publication and the decisions of other courts. Accordingly, the judgment of the Court of Appeals is vacated and the case is remanded for further proceedings consistent with this opinion.

It is so ordered.

■ CHIEF JUSTICE REHNQUIST, with whom JUSTICE STEVENS joins, concurring in part and dissenting in part.

The petition for certiorari in this case presents two questions: first, whether the rule of Frye v. United States, 54 App. D.C. 46, 293 F. 1013 (1923), remains good law after the enactment of the Federal Rules of Evidence; and second, if Frye remains valid, whether it requires expert scientific testimony to have been subjected to a peer-review process in order to be admissible. The Court concludes, correctly in my view, that the Frye rule did not survive the enactment of the Federal Rules of Evidence, and I therefore join Parts I and II–A of its opinion. The second question presented in the petition for certiorari necessarily is mooted by this holding, but the Court nonetheless proceeds to construe Rules 702 and 703 very much in the abstract, and then offers some "general observations." . . .

"General observations" by this Court customarily carry great weight with lower federal courts, but the ones offered here suffer from the flaw common to most such observations—they are not applied to deciding whether or not particular testimony was or was not admissible, and therefore they tend to be not only general, but vague and abstract. This is particularly unfortunate in a case such as this, where the ultimate legal question depends on an appreciation of one or more bodies of knowledge not judicially noticeable, and subject to different interpretations in the briefs of the parties and their amici. Twenty-two amicus briefs have been filed in the case, and indeed the Court's opinion contains no less than 37 citations to amicus briefs and other secondary sources.

The various briefs filed in this case are markedly different from typical briefs, in that large parts of them do not deal with decided cases or statutory language—the sort of material we customarily interpret. Instead, they deal with definitions of scientific knowledge, scientific method, scientific validity, and peer review—in short, matters far afield from the expertise of judges. This is not to say that such materials are not useful or even necessary in deciding how Rule 703 should be applied; but it is to say that the unusual subject matter

---

9. This is not to say that judicial interpretation, as opposed to adjudicative factfinding, does not share basic characteristics of the scientific endeavor: "The work of a judge is in one sense enduring and in another ephemeral. . . . In the endless process of testing and retesting, there is a constant rejection of the dross and a constant retention of whatever is pure and sound and fine." B. Cardozo, The Nature of the Judicial Process 178, 179 (1921).

should cause us to proceed with great caution in deciding more than we have to, because our reach can so easily exceed our grasp.

But even if it were desirable to make "general observations" not necessary to decide the questions presented, I cannot subscribe to some of the observations made by the Court. In Part II–B, the Court concludes that reliability and relevancy are the touchstones of the admissibility of expert testimony.... Federal Rule of Evidence 402 provides, as the Court points out, that "evidence which is not relevant is not admissible." But there is no similar reference in the Rule to "reliability." The Court constructs its argument by parsing the language "if scientific, technical, or other specialized knowledge will assist the trier of fact to understand the evidence or to determine a fact in issue ... an expert ... may testify thereto...." Fed. Rule Evid. 702. It stresses that the subject of the expert's testimony must be "scientific ... knowledge," and points out that "scientific" "implies a grounding in the methods and procedures of science," and that the word "knowledge" "connotes more than subjective belief or unsupported speculation." ... From this it concludes that "scientific knowledge" must be "derived by the scientific method." ... Proposed testimony, we are told, must be supported by "appropriate validation." ... Indeed, in footnote 6, the Court decides that "in a case involving scientific evidence, *evidentiary reliability* will be based upon *scientific validity*." ...

Questions arise simply from reading this part of the Court's opinion, and countless more questions will surely arise when hundreds of district judges try to apply its teaching to particular offers of expert testimony. Does all of this dicta apply to an expert seeking to testify on the basis of "technical or other specialized knowledge"—the other types of expert knowledge to which Rule 702 applies—or are the "general observations" limited only to "scientific knowledge"? What is the difference between scientific knowledge and technical knowledge; does Rule 702 actually contemplate that the phrase "scientific, technical, or other specialized knowledge" be broken down into numerous subspecies of expertise, or did its authors simply pick general descriptive language covering the sort of expert testimony which courts have customarily received? The Court speaks of its confidence that federal judges can make a "preliminary assessment of whether the reasoning or methodology underlying the testimony is scientifically valid and of whether that reasoning or methodology properly can be applied to the facts in issue." ... The Court then states that a "key question" to be answered in deciding whether something is "scientific knowledge" "will be whether it can be (and has been) tested." ... Following this sentence are three quotations from treatises, which speak not only of empirical testing, but one of which states that "the criterion of the scientific status of a theory is its falsifiability, or refutability, or testability"....

I defer to no one in my confidence in federal judges; but I am at a loss to know what is meant when it is said that the scientific status of a theory depends on its "falsifiability," and I suspect some of them will be, too.

I do not doubt that Rule 702 confides to the judge some gatekeeping responsibility in deciding questions of the admissibility of proffered expert testimony. But I do not think it imposes on them either the obligation or the authority to become amateur scientists in order to perform that role. I think the Court would be far better advised in this case to decide only the questions presented, and to leave the further development of this important area of the law to future cases.

NOTES

1. The Frye test, found by the Court in Daubert not to be adopted by Fed. R. Evid. 702, presents numerous difficulties in application. Who is it that must have accepted the principle or discovery in question or, to put it another way, what is the field to which the principle or discovery belongs? What is meant by "general acceptance"? What degree of dissent will render the evidence inadmissible? As to those who accept the principle or discovery, in what sense must they accept it? Must they hold it to be a basis for reaching conclusions that are certainly correct? To what subjects is the Frye test applicable? To all scientific matters or only to "novel" scientific matters? To "scientific" matters but not to nonscientific matters? These difficulties and others are pointed out in Giannelli, The Admissibility of Novel Scientific Evidence: Frye v. United States a Half-Century Later, 80 Colum.L.Rev. 1197 (1980). See also Giannelli, Frye v. United States, 99 F.R.D. 202, 204–07 (1984); Moenssens, Admissibility of Scientific Evidence—An Alternative to the Frye Rule, 25 Wm. & M. L.Rev. 545, 548 (1984). To the extent that the Daubert decision retains the Frye test as one factor to be considered, all these questions remain. Notwithstanding the difficulties of the Frye test, some jurisdictions retain it even in the face of Daubert. E.g., People v. Leahy, 882 P.2d 321 (Cal.1994).

Even when Frye was the predominant test, some jurisdictions rejected it. In Coppolino v. State, 223 So.2d 68 (Fla.Dist.Ct.App.1968), cert. denied, 399 U.S. 927 (1970), a murder case, a toxicologist testified that as a result of certain tests made upon tissue from the body of the deceased, he had determined the presence of unusual amounts of the component parts of succinylcholine chloride and was of the opinion that the deceased had received a toxic dose of the substance. Prior to the performance of these tests by the witness, it was believed by medical scientists to be impossible to demonstrate the presence of this substance. There was no scientific literature about these tests. The court held that the trial judge in finding the expert opinion based upon the new tests sufficiently reliable for admission had not abused his discretion. A concurring opinion observed: "The tests ... were novel and devised specifically for this case. This does not render the evidence inadmissible. Society need not tolerate homicide until there develops a body of medical literature about some particular lethal agent." 223 So.2d at 75. See also State v. Buller, 517 N.W.2d 711 (Iowa 1994): Not error to admit testimony of behavior of dog trained to detect fire accelerants even though dog's handler had developed the specialty himself.

As indicated in Daubert, the Frye test was announced in a case involving polygraph evidence and applied to exclude such evidence. United States v. Galbreth, 908 F.Supp. 877 (D.N.M.1995), holds that the Daubert requirement applies to polygraph evidence and that the evidence satisfies the requirement. See supra p. 467 for discussion of polygraph evidence.

2. Giannelli, Daubert: Interpreting the Federal Rules of Evidence, 15 Cardozo L. Rev. 1999, 2016–17 (1994):

> Citing Rule 702, the Daubert Court commented that "there is a specific Rule that speaks to the contested issue." I disagree. Rule 702 concerns (1) the subject matter of expert testimony and (2) the qualifications of expert witnesses. However, the subject matter of expert testimony raises two distinct issues. In an insightful passage in his 1947 book, Professor Maguire commented on the subject matter of expert testimony:
>
>> The field of expertness is bounded on one side by the great area of the *commonplace*, supposedly within the ken of every person of moderate intelligence, and on the other by the even greater area of the specula-

tive and uncertain. Of course both these boundaries constantly shift, as the former area enlarges and the latter diminishes.[1]

A simple chart illustrates these two aspects of the subject matter requirement:

A	B
/_____	/_____

speculative-uncertain   expert testimony   commonplace
(experimental)   (demonstrable)

Boundaries A and B raise distinct issues, and thus the evidentiary standards for these two boundaries are different. Frye deals with boundary A. The Frye Court simply used different terms; it spoke of the "line between the experimental and demonstrable stages."

In contrast, Rule 702 was directed at boundary B, distinguishing expert testimony from the commonplace. Rule 702 changed the common law formulation ("beyond the ken of laymen") to one of assistance to the trier of fact. The Advisory Committee's Note addresses only the difference between expert and lay knowledge (boundary B).[2] The Note cites an article by Professor Ladd,[3] which also addresses only the latter issue.[4] This is not surprising because prior codification efforts, the Model Code of Evidence[5] and the Uniform Rules of Evidence[6] also did not address the Frye issue.

3. Schwartz, There is No Archbishop of Science, 69 B.U. L. Rev. 517, 520–21 (1989):

Because judges (like others in the mainstream of our society) believe that scientific evidence is objective, neutral, and particularly powerful, they have been unwilling to allow juries to review "wrong" scientific evidence. They fear that the presentation of such evidence would be too powerful a potion for lay jurors. The screening solutions . . . aim to ensure that jurors receive only "correct" science or, at least, are informed through court-appointed truth squads about which science is "correct" and which is quackery.

The problem is that there is no adequate way to screen good science from bad science. We do not have to look to Galileo or Lysenko to see the danger in recognizing orthodoxy in science; we do not even have to look to the eugenics theories that were generally accepted when Frye was decided in 1923. We can look to modern neonatology (and its now discredited practices of giving oxygen or sulfa drugs to newborns) or psychiatry (and its history of using insulin shock and lobotomy) or oncology to see misguided orthodoxy overthrown almost weekly. Whether science is good or bad is no different from other contested factual issues that are routinely submit-

---

1. John M. Maguire, Evidence: Common Sense and Common Law 30 (1947) (emphasis added). . . . [Footnotes of the author, some omitted, others renumbered.]

2. Fed. R. Evid. 702 advisory committee's note ("Whether the situation is a proper one for the use of expert testimony is to be determined on the basis of assisting the trier.").

3. Mason Ladd, Expert Testimony, 5 Vand. L. Rev. 414 (1952).

4. Ladd notes the use of handwriting, fingerprints, and ballistics but does not dis-

cuss a threshold standard to determine admissibility. The only comment that may have been intended to cover the issue is: "Furthermore, the issue must be such that the expert may answer by giving an opinion that is a reasonable probability rather than conjecture or speculation." Id. at 419. He never elaborates on this sentence.

5. Model Code of Evidence Rule 402 (1942).

6. Unif. R. Evid. 56(2) (1953).

ted to juries. Indeed, our unstated assumptions about the objectivity, neutrality, and truth of anything purporting to be scientific drive us to limit jury access to scientific testimony just when that access is most important: when there is a genuine dispute between litigants that depends upon the truth of a scientific assertion. Judicial screening for scientific acceptability, whatever form that screening may take, is usurpation of the jury's fact-finding role by the judge or by the judge's delegate (usually some scientist who is respected by the judge).

Even if there were "right science" and "wrong science," and even if there were an American Archbishop of Science to tell them apart and declare scientific truth, "bad" science, from the scientist's viewpoint, might still be helpful to a court faced with a particular issue. The goals of the scientific and judicial processes are different; their procedures and techniques are different. Not surprisingly, the certainty they require in order to do their work is different.

Scientists, working to reach generalizable and universal knowledge without any externally imposed time deadline, are not willing to tolerate half-completed research or poorly tested hypotheses. To scientists, such research is nothing more than bad science. The judicial system, however, driven to quickly resolve matters of concern to defined parties, with res judicata effects on those parties alone and not on society as a whole, will be better served by incomplete scientific work than by none at all.

Courts must answer each question "yes" or "no"; it is as harmful for the court (at least in civil cases) to err in answering any question "yes" as to err in answering "no." Scientists can answer analogous questions "yes," "no," or "we don't know yet." A great many of the "we don't know yet" answers given by scientists are really "probably yes" or "probably no" answers. While in such cases science is best advanced if scientists continue to say "we don't know yet," litigation would be substantially improved if scientists were willing to admit that the underlying question could be considered "probably yes" or "probably no." Stated another way, the confidence level necessary to make scientific research useful in the courtroom may be much lower than the level necessary to make it generally acceptable for scientific purposes. This is not to say that scientific truth is better than legal truth. Rather, it is different, because scientists and courts have different functions. A scientist may properly decry as bad science some research that will result in good law.

4. In what circumstances does the requirement laid down in Daubert apply? Only if the evidence is "scientific"? What is "scientific" evidence? Does the Daubert requirement apply to all expert evidence? If it does not, what is required of expert nonscientific evidence?

United States v. Starzecpyzel, 880 F.Supp. 1027 (S.D.N.Y.1995): Prosecution for forgery. Memorandum and order on pretrial motion to exclude the testimony of forensic document examiners offered by the prosecution:

While the Court originally considered Daubert to be controlling as to the admissibility of the forensic testimony at issue—relating to the comparison of a large body of genuine writings to claimed forgeries—the Court now concludes that Daubert, which focuses on the "junk science" problem, is largely irrelevant to the challenged testimony. The Daubert hearing established that forensic document examination, which clothes itself with the trappings of science, does not rest on carefully articulated postulates, does not employ rigorous methodology, and has not convincingly documented the accuracy of its determinations. The Court might well have concluded that forensic document examination constitutes precisely the sort of junk science that Daubert addressed.

Yet, as distinguished from such discredited ventures as hedonic damage expertise, clinical ecology, trauma-cancer expertise or the Bendectin plaintiffs' statistical machinations, forensic document examination does involve true expertise, which may prove helpful to a fact-finder. FDE expertise is not properly characterized as scientific, but as practical in character. In a nutshell, over a period of years, FDEs gradually acquire the skill of identifying similarities and differences between groups of handwriting exemplars. Such expertise is similar to that developed by a harbor pilot who has repeatedly navigated a particular waterway. The Court therefore treats forensic document expertise under the "technical, or other specialized knowledge" branch of Rule 702, which is apparently not governed by Daubert.

Such experts, who acquire their skills through practical training, apprenticeships, and long years of practice, are generally not expected to be able to articulate and justify the theoretical bases underlying their practice, to expose their techniques to a larger community of practitioners through peer-reviewed publication, or to subject those techniques to extensive testing. Although Daubert standards do not apply to such "skilled" witnesses, trial courts need not certify every individual accomplished at a particular task as an expert. The Federal Rules of Evidence have long imposed a "gatekeeping" function on trial judges to ensure relevance and helpfulness to the fact-finder before admitting expert witness testimony. Finding this standard satisfied for the proffered testimony, Defendants' motion to exclude the testimony is denied.

FDE testimony, while acceptable under Rule 702, does suffer from a substantial problem of prejudice, which is the subject of Fed.R.Evid. 403. The problem arises from the likely perception by jurors that FDEs are scientists, which would suggest far greater precision and reliability than was established by the Daubert hearing. This perception might arise from several sources, such as the appearance of the words "scientific" and "laboratory" in much of the relevant literature, and the overly precise manner in which FDEs describe their level of confidence in their opinions as to whether questioned writings are genuine. The Court has determined that the problem of prejudice can be sufficiently diminished with the use of procedural safeguards, including a pre-testimony jury instruction, that FDE testimony need not be excluded pursuant to Rule 403.

. . .

FDEs certainly find "general acceptance" within their own community, but this community is devoid of financially disinterested parties, such as academics. Were the community expanded to include other forensic sciences, such as medical examination and forensic psychiatry, there is no indication that these additional practitioners would concern themselves with the reliability of forensic document examination.

A logical choice for a relevant scientific community would seem to be a collection of such mainstream sciences as pattern recognition (within the field of computer science) and motor control (within the field of medicine). It appears to the Court that such scientists are either unfamiliar with forensic document examination, or are critical of the field. Professor Stelmach, whom the Court views as a mainstream scientist, expressed his strong conviction that FDEs are not scientists, and have not demonstrated an ability to do what they claim to do. The government, on the other hand, produced no evidence of mainstream scientific support for forensic document examination. The Court also found relevant the apparent stagnation of research within the FDE community. Even the most recent texts and training materials in the field cite to Osborn's Questioned Documents, published in 1910 and 1929, with disturbing frequency. Michael J. Saks & Jonathan J. Koehler, What DNA "Fingerprinting" Can Teach the Law About the Rest of Forensic Science, 13 Cardozo L.Rev. 363 (1991) ("[A] handful of seminal works ... some of them generations old ... remain the principal works to which contemporary analysts turn"). More than half a century later, one would have expected scientists to have either rigorously confirmed the methods described in these texts, to have rejected them as unreliable, or to have replaced them with substantially improved methods. By way of explanation, Defendants note that "[u]nlike DNA profiling technology or epidemiology, this discipline has no counterpart in industry or academia with an economic incentive to study and refine its scientific basis." ...

In sum, the testimony at the Daubert hearing firmly established that forensic document examination, despite the existence of a certification program, professional journals and other trappings of science, cannot, after Daubert, be regarded as "scientific ... knowledge." ...

. . .

The fact that Daubert does not apply to nonscientific expertise does not suggest that judges are without an obligation to evaluate proffered expert testimony for reliability.

. . .

Within Rule 702 itself, there are several requirements imposed on "technical, or other specialized knowledge" witnesses. First, of course, the witness must possess such a relevant form of "knowledge." Second, the knowledge must "assist the trier of fact." Finally, the witness must be "qualified as an expert." Each of these clauses presents a possible barrier to expert testimony. The latter clause, for example, could bar the testimony of weekend sailors professing expertise as harbor pilots, since they would be unable to point to relevant training or experience.

. . .

Balancing the probative value of FDE testimony against the danger of unfair prejudice, the Court, with due respect for the abilities of jurors, concludes that the prejudice problem does not require the exclusion of the proffered testimony. Certain protections are called for, however. First, the jury will be instructed, in advance of any forensic document testimony, that FDEs offer practical, rather than scientific expertise. A similar expert witness instruction will appear in the jury charge....

Second, the Court will consider restricting the testimony of FDEs as regards their degree of certainty in determining the genuineness of a signature....[7]

Thomas v. Newton Intern'l Enterprises, 42 F.3d 1266, 1270 n. 3 (9th Cir.1994): Error to exclude testimony of longshoreman with 29 years experience that an unguarded deck opening within two feet of the bottom of an access

7. Footnotes omitted.

ladder was an extremely unusual and hazardous condition. Daubert's standard inapplicable because this was not scientific evidence. "While a scientific conclusion must be linked in some fashion to the scientific method ... [the witness's] non-scientific testimony need only be linked to some body of specialized knowledge or skills."

State v. Cressey, 628 A.2d 696 (N.H.1993): In prosecution for child sexual abuse, error to admit testimony of psychologist that behavior of child consistent with sexual abuse: under New Hampshire Evidence Rule 702 (same as Fed. R. Evid. 702), expert testimony must be reliable to be admissible, citing Daubert.

What standard controls the admissibility of the testimony of a historian? Denson v. Stack, 997 F.2d 1356 (11th Cir.1993) (whether watercourse was navigable in 1845), an anthropologist? Dang Vang v. Vang Xiong X. Toyed, 944 F.2d 476, 480–82 (9th Cir.1991) (attitude of Hmong women toward men and persons holding government positions).

5. In re Paoli R.R. Yard PCB Litigation, 35 F.3d 717, 744–47 (3d Cir.1994), cert. denied, 115 S.Ct. 1253 (1995): Suit for physical ailments allegedly caused by PCB's manufactured or used by defendant. Summary judgment for defendants reversed:

> As we explained in Paoli I, "the reliability requirement must not be used as a tool by which the court excludes all questionably reliable evidence." Paoli I, 916 F.2d at 857. The "ultimate touchstone is helpfulness to the trier of fact, and with regard to reliability, helpfulness turns on whether the expert's 'technique or principle [is] sufficiently reliable so that it will aid the jury in reaching accurate results.' " DeLuca, 911 F.2d at 956 (quoting 3 J. Weinstein & M. Berger, Weinstein's Evidence 702[03], at 702–35 (1988)). A judge frequently should find an expert's methodology helpful even when the judge thinks that the expert's technique has flaws sufficient to render the conclusions inaccurate. He or she will often still believe that hearing the expert's testimony and assessing its flaws was an important part of assessing what conclusion was correct and may certainly still believe that a jury attempting to reach an accurate result should consider the evidence. See Paoli I, 916 F.2d at 857 (helpfulness requires more than bare logical relevance, but there is a strong preference for admission) (citing Downing, 753 F.2d at 1235).

> The same standard of reliability extends to the step in the expert's analysis that "fits" his or her conclusions to the case at hand. Once again, we emphasize that the standard is not that high. For example, in Paoli I, we held that testimony that PCBs cause liver cancer "fit" the case even in the absence of plaintiffs who had liver cancer, because an expert's affidavit suggested that increased risk of liver cancer was probative of increased risk of other forms of cancer. See Paoli I, 916 F.2d at 858. Nonetheless, the standard is higher than bare relevance.[8]

> In addition to arguing that the district court usurped the role of the jury by requiring more than a prima facie showing of reliability, plaintiffs submit that the district court mistakenly applied the reliability inquiry to expert testimony that should not have been subject to that inquiry. Both

---

8. Daubert's statement that fit "goes primarily to relevance" is not to the contrary.... This statement elucidates what the fit requirement is about—that the scientific knowledge must be connected to the question at issue—rather than the standard for evaluating that connection. The passages in Dau- bert quoted in the text supra, which indicate that the connection between the scientific knowledge and the case must itself constitute scientific knowledge, demonstrate that the standard for fit is higher than bare relevance. [Footnotes of the court. Some footnotes omitted, others renumbered.]

Daubert and Downing require that expert testimony be based on the methods and procedures, the processes and techniques of science. In Paoli I we suggested that so long as any deviation the expert made from a reliable method merely constituted a change in the *application* of that method, the expert's testimony remained based on a reliable scientific method. We thought that ferreting out misapplication fell within the province of the jury, and that only if the expert so altered a reliable methodology as to skew it would the reliability inquiry of Downing be applicable to the altered methodology. See Paoli I, 916 F.2d at 858. Plaintiffs assert that the district court applied the Downing inquiry to methodologies that merely constituted slight alterations of reliable methodologies.

However, after Daubert, we no longer think that the distinction between a methodology and its application is viable. To begin with, it is extremely elusive to attempt to ascertain which of an expert's steps constitute parts of a "basic" methodology and which constitute changes from that methodology. If a laboratory consistently fails to use certain quality controls so that its results are rendered unreliable, attempting to ascertain whether the lack of quality controls constitutes a failure of methodology or a failure of application of methodology may be an exercise in metaphysics. Moreover, any misapplication of a methodology that is significant enough to render it unreliable is likely to also be significant enough to skew the methodology.

As suggested, Daubert inters any need for us to make such a distinction, for Daubert's requirement that the expert testify to scientific knowledge—conclusions supported by good grounds for each step in the analysis—means that any step that renders the analysis unreliable under the *Daubert factors renders the expert's testimony inadmissible. This is true whether the step completely changes a reliable methodology or merely misapplies that methodology.*[9]

Finally, plaintiffs contend that the district court usurped the role of the jury by making admissibility decisions based on its disagreement with the *conclusions* of plaintiffs' experts. Plaintiffs are correct, of course, that Daubert requires the judge's admissibility decision to focus not on the expert's conclusions but on his or her principles and methodology. But we think that this distinction has only limited practical import. When a judge disagrees with the conclusions of an expert, it will generally be because he or she thinks that there is a mistake at some step in the investigative or reasoning process of that expert. If the judge thinks that the conclusions of some other expert are correct, it will likely be because the judge thinks that the methodology and reasoning process of the other expert are superior to those of the first expert. This is especially true given that the expert's view that a particular conclusion "fits" a particular case must itself constitute scientific knowledge—a challenge to "fit" is very close to a challenge to the expert's ultimate conclusion about the particular case, and yet it is part of the judge's admissibility calculus under Daubert.[10]

. . .

---

9. Of course, if a court finds that an expert has employed a methodology only slightly different from a methodology that the court thinks is clearly reliable, the court should be more likely to accept the altered methodology than if it was evaluating that methodology as an original matter.

10. The methodology/conclusion distinction remains of some import, however, to the extent that there will be cases in which a party argues that an expert's testimony is unreliable because the conclusions of an expert's study are different from those of other experts. In such cases, there is no basis for

In Downing we explained that under Rule 702, admissibility of scientific testimony turns not only on reliability but also on the possibility that admitting the evidence would overwhelm, confuse, or mislead the jury. We held that in conducting this balancing inquiry, there is a presumption of helpfulness.... The extent to which an adverse party has had notice and the opportunity to present his or her own experts is also relevant. Moreover, a district court cannot exclude a scientific technique as too confusing and overwhelming simply based on its conclusion that scientific techniques by their very nature confuse and overwhelm the jury. There must be something about the particular scientific technique such as its posture of mythic infallibility that makes it especially overwhelming....

We explained in Downing that Rule 702 analysis partly incorporates Rule 403 analysis but leaves some room for Rule 403 to operate independently. For example, we noted that a judge might use Rule 403 to exclude an expert's critique of eyewitness testimony even though the critique met the requirements of Rule 702 if there was evidence of defendant's guilt other than eyewitness testimony which would make efforts to criticize eyewitness testimony a waste of time.

In Daubert, the Supreme Court seems to have inverted our view that much of Rule 403 analysis conflates into Rule 702; rather the Court seems to have conflated the confusion/overwhelming impact prong of our Rule 702 analysis into its Rule 403 analysis. The Daubert Court did not mention the confusion/overwhelming prong when discussing Rule 702 but did provide support for application of essentially similar analysis under the rubric of Rule 403. The Court noted that Rule 403's balancing test of the probative against the prejudicial value of evidence has a special role in cases involving expert witnesses. It stated that because expert evidence is often more misleading than other evidence, Rule 403 gives a judge more power over experts than over lay witnesses.... This, however, does not change our opinion that in order for a district court to exclude scientific evidence, there must be something particularly confusing about the scientific evidence at issue—something other than the general complexity of scientific evidence.[11]

See Faigman, Porter and Saks, Check Your Crystal Ball at the Courthouse Door, Please: Exploring the Past, Understanding the Present, and Worrying About the Future of Scientific Evidence, 15 Cardozo L. Rev. 1799, 1831–33 (1994) (questioning the possibility of distinguishing between method and conclusion).

6. In Daubert, the Court cites Judge Weinstein's observation that "expert evidence can be both powerful and quite misleading because of the difficulty in evaluating it." There may be an implication in this citation that in certain

---

holding the expert's testimony inadmissible. See Hines v. Consolidated Rail Corporation, 926 F.2d 262, 274 (3d Cir.1991) ("though [the expert's] opinion could be considered to be 'novel,' it appears that ... his methods were not"); Kenneth J. Chesebro, Taking Daubert's "Focus" Seriously: The Methodology/Conclusion Distinction, 15 Cardozo L.Rev. 1747, 1748 (1994) ("it is completely inappropriate for either the proponent of scientific testimony or her opponent to advance Rule 702 admissibility arguments that depend on the ultimate conclusion reached by an expert.").

11. The fact that Daubert held that Rule 702 is the primary locus of a court's gatekeeping role indicates that exclusion under Rule 403 should be rare despite the Court's later statement that Rule 403 gives judges greater power over experts than over ordinary witnesses. Daubert's view of the judge's substantive power under Rule 403 is thus similar to our view of the judge's substantive power under the overwhelming/confusion prong of Rule 702—both give the judge slightly more power than is ordinarily the case under Rule 403 to find that evidence is more prejudicial than probative.

circumstances juries are not competent to evaluate scientific or expert evidence. In what sense might juries not be competent? There is a substantial body of literature on the way juries think about expert evidence. E.g., Jacobs, Testing the Assumptions Underlying the Debate about Scientific Evidence: A Closer Look at Juror "Incompetence" and Scientific "Objectivity," 25 Conn. L. Rev. 1083 (1993); Gross, Expert Evidence, 1991 Wis. L. Rev. 1113, 1164, 1179–86; Cecil, Hans and Wiggins, Citizen Comprehension of Difficult Issues, 40 Am. U. L. Rev. 727 (1991). The idea that juries are incompetent to evaluate certain kinds of evidence was one of the notions that in the 1970s and 1980s led to an effort to exclude juries entirely from "complex" cases. For an account see Campbell, Current Understanding of the Seventh Amendment: Jury Trials in Complex Litigation, 66 Wash. U. L. Q. 63 (1988).

7. Should the Court's opinion in Daubert have discussed and distinguished Barefoot v. Estelle, 463 U.S. 880, 899 (1983)? In Barefoot, the Court held it did not violate Due Process to put before the jury in the penalty phase of a murder trial testimony of psychiatrists, based upon hypothetical questions, regarding defendant's future dangerousness. "We are not persuaded that such testimony is almost entirely unreliable and that the factfinder and the adversary system will not be competent to uncover, recognize and take due account of its shortcomings." The Court cited with approval the lower court's statement that the purpose of the jury was to sort out the true from the false. In Barefoot, the question was whether it violated the Constitution to admit against a criminal defendant relevant but unreliable evidence. Compare the question presented in Rock v. Arkansas, supra p. 256, whether it violates the Constitution to exclude relevant but unreliable evidence when offered by a criminal defendant. What constitutional questions are presented by Daubert?

8. For a discussion of some of the issues raised by Daubert, see Walker, The Siren Songs of Science: Toward a Taxonomy of Scientific Uncertainty for Decisionmakers, 23 Conn. L. Rev. 567, 581–98 (1991). See also Carnegie Comm'n on Science, Technology and Government, Science and Technology in Judicial Decisionmaking: Creating Opportunities and Meeting Challenges (1993); Reference Manual on Scientific Evidence (Fed. Judicial Center, 1994); Berger, Procedural Paradigms for Applying the Daubert Test, 78 Minn.L.Rev. 1345 (1994); Mansfield, Scientific Evidence Under Daubert, 28 St. Mary's L.J. 1 (1996).

9. Further light may be shed on the meaning of Daubert when the Supreme Court decides Joiner v. General Elec. Co., 78 F.3d 524 (11th Cir.1996), cert. granted, 117 S.Ct. 1243 (1997). In Joiner, the Court of Appeals reversed the District Court for excluding expert opinion on whether PCBs caused plaintiff's lung cancer and entering summary judgment for defendant. There was disagreement between the majority and dissenter in the Court of Appeals as to the proper standard for appellate review of trial court applications of Daubert.

United States v. Chischilly

United States Court of Appeals, Ninth Circuit, 1994.
30 F.3d 1144, cert. denied, 115 S.Ct. 946 (1995).

[Appeal from conviction for aggravated sexual assault and murder. One of the grounds of appeal was the erroneous admission of DNA evidence.]

■ CHOY, CIRCUIT JUDGE:

. . .

Following completion of the competency hearing, Chischilly learned from the Government that FBI tests had established a match between his blood sample and semen found on the victim's clothing. Chischilly filed a motion in limine and requested a hearing pursuant to Frye v. United States, 293 F. 1013 (D.C.Cir.1923), to examine the admissibility of this identification evidence, never before presented in the District of Arizona, derived from DNA profiling analysis.[1] After an extensive hearing involving the testimony of eight scientists and the admission of 152 exhibits, the district court denied Chischilly's motion in limine.

At trial the jury heard further testimony from expert witnesses retained by each side on the FBI's findings, methodology and procedures and was presented findings from the recent report of the Committee on DNA Technology in Forensic Science of the National Research Council of the National Academy of Sciences (the "NRC Report"). According to the testimony of Government witnesses, DNA analysis conducted by the FBI later indicated a match between a sample of Chischilly's blood and sperm found on the victim. A Government expert witness, Dr. Chakraborty, further testified that one in 2563 would be a "conservative estimate" of the probability of a similar match between the DNA of a randomly selected American Indian and either the evidentiary sample or the defendant's DNA.

. . .

In view of the "raging controversy" in the scientific community over DNA testing, Chischilly contends that the district court committed reversible error by admitting evidence of a match between his blood samples and semen found on the victim's clothing, as well as testimony regarding the random probability of such a match. We review evidentiary rulings for abuse of discretion substantially prejudicing the defendant's rights.

. . .

Compounding the obstacle this standard of review poses for Chischilly's fourth contention of error is the Supreme Court's ruling in Daubert v. Merrell Dow Pharmaceuticals, Inc. . . . handed down after the submission of the parties' initial briefs on appeals. . . .

. . .

Chischilly first challenged the reliability of the Government's DNA extraction and matching procedures on the following grounds: (1) the Government's experts were either drawn from the overly narrow field of forensic scientists, a group predisposed to accept new forensic techniques, or had a career interest in testifying on behalf of the FBI; (2) contaminants could have affected some of the samples relied on by the FBI in its DNA analysis and led to unreliable results; (3) inconsistencies in the gel used by the FBI in the electrophoresis process may affect the mobility of the alleles[2] in the DNA fragments; (4)

1. For a reasonably clear, current and concise description of DNA identification profiling as conducted by FBI laboratories, see United States v. Jakobetz, 955 F.2d 786 (2d Cir.), cert. denied, 506 U.S. 834 . . . (1992) (taking judicial notice of the DNA identification analysis theories and procedures adopted by the FBI). [Footnotes of the court. Some footnotes omitted, others renumbered.]

2. An allele is "any alternative form of a gene that can occupy a particular chromo-somal locus. In humans and other diploid organisms there are two alleles, one on each chromosome of a homologous pair." Dorland's Illustrated Medical Dictionary 48 (27th ed. 1988). Forensic DNA tests compare allele combinations at loci where the alleles tend to be highly variable across individuals and ethnic groups. If there is no match between the alleles from the evidence DNA and the potential suspect's DNA, the suspect is generally ruled out as the source of the evidence, un-

ethidium bromide, used by the FBI but not most research laboratories in gel electrophoresis, may retard the migration of DNA fragments through the electrophoretic gel; (5) the presence of additional bands on the autorads[3] interpreted in the RFLP[4] test may have indicated that the DNA samples were degraded; (6) the FBI's match criteria are subjective, imprecise, insufficiently stringent and not uniformly applied; and (7) the FBI's quality assurance program is inadequate and is subject to insufficient peer-reviewed publication.

Chischilly then questioned the FBI's statistical methods for determining the random probability of a match between his DNA sample and the relevant population and raised the following additional objections: (8) the product rule is a novel statistical procedure whose reliability is not generally accepted by the scientific community; (9) substructuring[5] within the Native American and Navajo populations invalidates use of the product rule to determine the probability of a coincidental match within the FBI's I–3 database for Native American populations; and (10) the FBI's I–3 database is too small and contains too few Navajos.

Chischilly marshals an impressive body of academic commentary in support of several of his contentions and points out areas where the FBI's DNA testing and statistical procedures may warrant review and revision. Nonetheless, we conclude that under Daubert the district court did not abuse its discretion in admitting evidence of a DNA match and testimony regarding the probability of a coincidental match.

Challenging the motivations and impartiality of Government-retained expert witnesses, Chischilly's first objection is clearly conjectural and raises a

less the failure is attributable to inadequate test conditions or contaminated samples. If there is a match, analysts use the frequency of the alleles' appearance in the relevant population to calculate the probability that another person could have the same pattern of allele pairs. See Georgia Sargeant, DNA Evidence Finding Stricter Scrutiny, New Uses, Trial, Apr. 1993, at 15.

3. An autorad (a.k.a. autoradiograph) is "a radiograph of an object or tissue made by recording the radiation emitted by radioactive material within it, especially after the purposeful introduction of radioactive material." Dorland's Illustrated Medical Dictionary 172. In DNA profiling, forensic scientists employ autorads in an extraction process known as "Southern Transfer", in which DNA fragments are placed atop a gel subjected to an electric current. DNA fragments comprised of alleles are then soaked up by capillary action into a nylon membrane. The membrane is then immersed in a solution containing a radioactive probe. These probes bind to portions of the DNA fragments containing complementary sequences of allelic base pairs (e.g., a radioactive probe with the sequence CCGGACAT would target a sample strand containing the nucleotide sequence GGCCTGTA). The membrane is then placed against a sheet of X-ray film known as an autorad. The radioactive molecules in the probe expose the autorad and leave traces known as "bands" indicating the location and distance travelled by the migrating al-

leles through the gel. A computer then scans the autorad and measures this distance, a variable corresponding to the size of a particular allele type (larger types of alleles tend to migrate more slowly through the gel). Differences in band length at a given loci are analyzed to match or distinguish the alleles in the evidentiary DNA and the potential suspect's sample. For a fuller description of gel electrophoresis as applied to DNA forensic testing, see Lempert, Some Caveats Concerning DNA as Criminal Identification Evidence: With Thanks to the Reverend Bayes, 13 Cardozo L.Rev. 303, 304 n. 4 (1991)....

4. RFLP (i.e., restriction fragment length polymorphism) analysis refers to the process of cutting the evidence DNA and the potential suspect's DNA into fragments at particular loci with "restriction enzymes". The resulting restriction fragments, comprised of "alleles" (i.e., one of two forms of a gene which may occur at any given gene locus ...), are subjected to gel electrophoresis, as described supra.

5. "Substructuring" refers to the tendency toward decreasing genetic heterogeneity and allelic independence ... exhibited by ethnically homogeneous, non-randomly mating populations; that is, a substructured population may be defined as one in which the probability of a random match between two of its members is greater than the likelihood of such a match between two members of the population at large.

credibility issue which the trial court was in a superior position to ours to weigh. In light of Daubert, Chischilly's second, third and fourth objections, regarding potential faults in the DNA sample extraction processes conducted in FBI laboratories, go to the weight to be accorded the evidence, not to its admissibility in the first instance. . . .

The fifth objection, regarding the possible degrading of the DNA samples, is more troubling, insofar as it was based on data specific to Chischilly's DNA test and was not rebutted with especial force by experts retained by the Government. Nevertheless, Chischilly failed to demonstrate that the degradation is the result of a faulty methodology or theory as opposed to imperfect execution of laboratory techniques whose theoretical foundation is sufficiently accepted in the scientific community to pass muster under Daubert. See United States v. Martinez, 3 F.3d 1191, 1198 (8th Cir.1993) (finding under Daubert's flexible standard that "[a]n alleged error in the application of a reliable methodology should provide the basis for exclusion of the opinion only if that error negates the basis for the reliability of the principle itself"). The impact of imperfectly conducted laboratory procedures might therefore be approached more properly as an issue going not to the admissibility, but to the weight of the DNA profiling evidence.

We reach the same conclusion with respect to Chischilly's sixth objection. Chischilly presented expert testimony that other laboratories, even one in which FBI protocols are used to prepare autorads, would have declared a nonmatch when comparing Chischilly's DNA sample with the evidentiary sample. With regard to admissibility, the mere existence of scientific institutions that would interpret data more conservatively scarcely indicates a "lack of general acceptance" under Daubert's fourth factor. Similarly, the testimony indicates disagreement over, not an absence of, controlling standards for purposes of the second part of Daubert's third factor, focussing on whether such standards exist and are maintained. . . . Suggesting similar treatment of Chischilly's sixth objection, Daubert cautions lower courts not to confuse the role of judge and jury by forgetting that "vigorous cross-examination, presentation of contrary evidence, and careful instruction on the burden of proof", rather than exclusion, "are the traditional and appropriate means of attacking shaky but admissible evidence."

In regard to the first part of Daubert's third factor, the known or potential rate of error, some commentators have objected that "the potential rate of error in the forensic DNA typing technique is unknown." See, e.g., Hoeffel, The Dark Side of DNA Profiling: Unreliable Scientific Evidence Meets the Criminal Defendant, 42 Stan.L.Rev. 465, 509 (1990). However, we note that scientific institutions have undertaken on numerous occasions in recent years to estimate error rates attending DNA profiling. See Koehler, DNA Matches and Statistics: Important Questions, Surprising Answers, 76 Judicature 222, 229 (1993) . . . In addition, some commentators have cautioned against accepting overly permissive error rates, at least for false positives, in view of the high stakes involved in a criminal trial. See id. ("before deciding an error rate of, say, 1 percent is acceptable or even 'good,' consider the error rate that would be tolerated in a commercial airliner"). Nevertheless, we conclude that there was a sufficient showing of low error rates so that the third factor does not weigh against the admissibility of DNA profiling evidence.

Chischilly's seventh objection, that FBI procedures are insufficiently exposed to the light of peer review, deserves but does not withstand close attention under Daubert's second factor, relating to degree of publication. We note that in a learned opinion rejecting a claim that the FBI has failed to share its DNA testing data and methodology, the California Court of Appeals has commented upon the existence of "numerous published articles on DNA analysis as performed by the FBI." Barney, 8 Cal.App.4th at 813, 10 Cal. Rptr.2d 731. In addition, the NRC Report, frequently cited by Chischilly for its recommended improvements of the FBI's DNA analysis, is at least the functional equivalent of a publication subject to peer-review under Daubert's liberally framed second factor.

Chischilly's eighth, ninth and tenth objections, aimed at the FBI's statistical techniques for determining the probability of a coincidental match, are perhaps his weightiest against admission of DNA profiling evidence in this case. However, under Daubert, they fail to demonstrate that the district court abused its discretion by admitting into evidence testimony regarding the results of the FBI's DNA analysis. Chischilly asserts rather persuasively and with considerable scientific backing that where an individual's DNA sample is tested against samples from a population in which persons of that individual's ethnic group are underrepresented, calculations based on the product rule[6] may tend to understate the probability that a random match would occur between the evidentiary sample and that individual's ethnic group. Chischilly called numerous experts who testified that the more homogeneous a population remains through intermarriage, the less random the relationship becomes between the coincidence of certain sequences of alleles at different test sites across the two samples (i.e., matches of nucleotide base pairs at given segments of the defendant's sample and the crime scene DNA). In analyzing the DNA evidence in this case, the FBI used its I-3 database, composed of DNA samples from Native Americans.[7] Nevertheless, Chischilly's objection remains because his distinct tribe (Navajo) may have been underrepresented in the I-3 database.

Chischilly asserts that, "[t]he scientific community is torn by controversy about the appropriateness of the FBI's databases, the effects of substructuring within their databases, and their statistical methodologies. This controversy has divided the scientific community into opposing camps." Chischilly goes on to cite studies offered by proponents of the FBI techniques and to note that "[b]oth sides of this continuing controversy find support in the journals and research, and both sides have prominent spokespeople." While perhaps support for exclusion of Chischilly's DNA test results under the superseded Frye test, with its requirement of general acceptance of a theory in the scientific community, these same statements take on the hue of adverse admissions under Daubert's more liberal admissibility test: evidence of opposing academic camps arrayed in virtual scholarly equipoise amidst the scientific journals is scarcely an indication of the "minimal support within a community" that would give a trial court cause to view a known technique with skepticism under Daubert's fourth factor.

Accordingly, we conclude that under Daubert, the three chief components of DNA profiling as performed in this case, sample processing, match determi-

---

6. Whereas no two individuals (apart from identical twins) share the same overall DNA profile, "no individual has a unique profile at a given locus." DNA Profiling at 488. Under the product rule the probabilities of finding a match at each given locus on the samples satisfying statistical criteria for a match are multiplied together to calculate the random probability that the trace DNA found at the crime scene could have come from another member of the population represented by the defendant.

7. It is only helpful to use an ethnic-specific database when it is reasonable to assume that the perpetrator of the crime is a member of that group. Crimes occurring in areas that are populated by a particular ethnic group are typical instances in which an ethnic-specific database will be used. Use of ethnic-specific databases generally strengthens the probative value of statistical data.

nation and statistical analysis, pass muster under Rule 702. Nevertheless, we take seriously the Court's admonition in Daubert that scientific evidence must withstand close scrutiny under Rule 403.... We therefore consider whether the probative value of the evidence is outweighed by its prejudicial potential. We will not reverse unless the district court abused its discretion in admitting the evidence. We conclude that it did not.

Notwithstanding Daubert's express preference for exposing novel scientific theories and methodologies to the glare of the adversarial process, Daubert enjoins watchful assessment of the risk that a jury would assign undue weight to DNA profiling statistics even after hearing appellant's opposing evidence, the testimony of Government witnesses under vigorous cross-examination and the careful instructions of the district court on burdens of proof. Of particular concern is where the Government seeks to present probability testimony derived from statistical analysis, the third main phase of DNA profiling. Numerous hazards attend the courtroom presentation of statistical evidence of any sort. Accordingly, Rule 403 requires judicial vigilance against the risk that such evidence will inordinately distract the jury from or skew its perception of other, potentially exculpatory evidence lacking not so much probative force as scientific gloss.

With regard to DNA evidence, there are two general tendencies that should be guarded against: (1) that the jury will accept the DNA evidence as a statement of source probability (i.e., the likelihood that the defendant is the source of the evidentiary sample); and (2) that once the jury settles on a source probability, even if correctly, it will equate source with guilt, ignoring the possibility of non-criminal reasons for the evidentiary link between the defendant and the victim. As to the second concern, there is little chance in this case that the jury could have mistakenly equated source probability with guilt because it is clear that the evidentiary sample was criminally linked with the victim. The presence of sperm in the circumstances of this case undermined Chischilly's claim of innocence, as well as any hapless bystander or good samaritan defense, by clearly establishing a causal, and not merely a casual, link between the crime and the evidentiary sample.

The first concern is somewhat more complex. The FBI matching statistic does not represent source probability. Rather, the test results reflect the statistical probability that a match would occur between a randomly selected member of the database group and either the evidentiary sample or the defendant. To illustrate, suppose the FBI's evidence establishes that there is a one in 10,000 chance of a random match. The jury might equate this likelihood with source probability by believing that there is a one in 10,000 chance that the evidentiary sample did not come from the defendant. This equation of random match probability with source probability is known as the prosecutor's fallacy.

There is also a corresponding defense fallacy. Suppose there were 10,000,000 members of the group represented in the database used. The defense may claim that there is then only a one in 1,000 ($10,000/10,000,000$) chance that the evidentiary sample came from the defendant because 1,000 matches would occur if the entire population were tested. This claim resembles the prosecutor's fallacy in making an illogical leap, but differs in understating the tendency of a reported match to strengthen source probability and narrow the group of potential suspects. Lying somewhere between the two, the real source probability will reflect the relative strength of circumstantial evidence connecting the defendant and other persons with matching DNA to the scene of the crime.

Often acute even for Caucasian suspects, these pitfalls become more perilous where the defendant is a member of a substructured population, such as Navajo Indians. Underrepresentation of persons of like ethnicity in the profile data bases and questionable assumptions of allelic independence[8] may inflate the odds against a random match with the defendant's sample. In such a situation the jury may be ill-suited to discount properly the probative value of DNA profiling statistics.

Geographic factors may further increase the potential of prejudice from the FBI's database selection. Although "the fact that certain alleles occur more frequently in the Navajos than they do in European and West African populations is of little consequence for a crime committed in Boston, where few Navajos reside," this fact is of considerable consequence for a crime committed on a reservation in Arizona, where many Navajos make their home. In such instances, the troubling possibility arises with singular force that the product rule, founded on the questionable premise of allelic independence at different test sites, will understate the random probability that some other nearby resident with a similar genetic profile could have been the source of the sample found on the victim.

On the other side of the Rule 403 ledger, statistical evidence derived from sample processing and match analysis, properly documented and performed in compliance with established, peer-reviewed laboratory protocols, is certainly probative of the defendant's guilt or innocence. Where the district court provides careful oversight, the potential prejudice of the DNA evidence can be reduced to the point where this probative value outweighs it.

In this case, the district court provided such oversight, the prosecution was careful to frame the evidence properly and the defense was adequately equipped to contest its validity. Confronted with an unusually informed, capable and zealous challenge from the defense, the Government was careful to frame the DNA profiling statistics presented at trial as the probability of a random match, not the probability of the defendant's innocence that is the crux of the prosecutor's fallacy. While not calculated pursuant to the NRC Report's controversial recommendation to adopt the ceiling principle[9], the one in 2563 probability that was introduced at trial was nonetheless arguably calculated on the basis of somewhat conservative statistical assumptions[10], was premised on the favorable assumption that the source of the sperm was a Native American[11]

---

8. "Allelic independence" refers to the absence of correlation between the inheritance of an allele controlling one genetic characteristic, such as eye color, with the inheritance of other alleles governing other traits and occurring at other loci.

9. Under the ceiling principle, as advocated by the NRC Report, in the statistical calculation phase each allele will be assigned a value equal to the greater of five percent or the highest frequency resulting from tests of the relevant population. This procedure places what some scientists and statisticians regard as a rather conservative, arbitrary limit on the odds against a member of a given population having the same array of alleles at each locus tested. See Statistical Evaluation of DNA Fingerprinting at 749 (criticizing the National Research Council's suggestion that the ceiling principle be adopted for substructured populations).

10. Dr. Chakraborty testified that in calculating the one in 2563 probability, the FBI "follows something like ceiling principle (sic)" in that "they looked at the allele frequencies in several American Indian segment tribal populations and picked up the one containing largest frequency (sic)."

11. As noted by Dr. Chakraborty in his testimony for the Government, calculations based on the data base for the American public at large could have reduced the probability of a random match by more than two orders of magnitude. Conversely, further "closing the window" through adoption of a strictly Navajo database, not yet established by the FBI, might have further increased the likelihood of a random match. However, undermining somewhat the significance of substructuring, the "raging controversy" over DNA profiling evidence also encompasses a dispute over the extent to which individual

and was emphasized at the expense of a much smaller probability of a random match that Government witnesses testified would be statistically defensible.[12]

In sum, we conclude that the district court did not abuse its discretion in admitting the DNA evidence in this case. The evidence is admissible under Daubert and Rule 702. Moreover, the potential prejudicial effect in this case did not outweigh the probative value of the evidence under Rule 403.

. . .

For the foregoing reasons, we affirm Chischilly's conviction of murder and aggravated sexual abuse. . . .

[Dissenting opinion omitted.]

Karjala, Evidentiary Uses of Neutron Activation Analysis

59 Cal.L.Rev. 997, 1020–24, 1028–29, 1031–32 (1971).[1]

Some cases involve questions that are capable of reasonably precise definition and to which the expert can give firm, objective answers, including most particularly the limitations on his conclusions. In other types of cases, the expert may have to rely mainly on the depth of his general background in the subject, and he may not be able to articulate the precise foundations for his conclusions or the limitations thereon.[2] Evidence derived from [neutron] activation analysis provides a good example of the former type of expert opinion, and it is useful to compare this type of evidence with that produced by experts in such areas as fingerprints, handwriting, and firearms identification, all of which are examples of the latter.

Identification by trace element characterization rests on the hypothesis that materials of similar type but which derive from different sources[3] (for example, two hairs, two pieces of glass, two blood samples) will usually be sufficiently different in their minute concentrations of trace elements that they can be distinguished, at least to some extent. Thus, a "match" by NAA may tend to show that they come from a common source. Similar considerations are involved in the other types of identification procedures. For example, the fingerprint expert compares types of characteristics, such as ridge endings and bifurcations, and their locations, and depending on the number of points of agreement he draws conclusions as to whether identification has been estab-

---

and ethnic differences, as opposed to differences among substructured groups, are primarily responsible for genetic diversity. See Statistical Evaluation of DNA Fingerprinting at 748.

12. Besides, even if the denominator in the one in 2563 probability should have been further reduced to guard against the risks inherent in a substructured population, "[i]t may well be that a match is so improbable that an exaggerated picture of its improbability caused by an inappropriate data base does not prejudice a defendant because the true probability would have been more than enough to persuade a jury that the defendant was the source of the evidence sample." Caveats Concerning DNA at 321, n. 44.

2. See the comparison of the testimony of an orthopedic surgeon in a personal injury suit and that of a psychiatrist in a murder trial in Diamond & Louisell, The Psychiatrist as an Expert Witness, 63 Mich.L.Rev. 1335 (1965).

3. In using NAA it is always crucial to be very clear as to what is meant by the "same source."

lished.[4] Similarly, the handwriting expert compares peculiarities of letter formation and the firearms expert compares such things as the rifling marks on the bullets fired by a given gun. Yet these latter procedures differ in a fundamental way from a comparison of the results of an NAA measurement: the characteristics which are compared are not amenable to what has been called a *total-ordering*.[5]

Basically, totally-orderable data is simply that which can be catalogued in a systematic manner. If the results of measurements on a true random sample are thus catalogued, it is easy to calculate the probability that a particular measurement will "match" from a random choice by finding the number of measurements on the random sample which gave the same results and taking the ratio to the total number of measurements in the sample.[6] Comparison techniques which are not amenable to total-ordering are necessarily somewhat subjective, at least in the sense that adequate criteria do not exist which would permit the expert to articulate the precise foundations for his conclusion that a "match" exists or that there is a certain probability of identity. Thus, one expert may feel that a positive result is established while another feels equally strongly that the same evidence does not warrant such a conclusion. These identifications thus depend on the "intuitive ability" and "common sense" of the expert. Numerous authors have called for more recognition and investigation of the logical processes which lie behind these methods, but it is not the purpose of this Comment to weigh the conflicting factors involved in the evidentiary use of such subjective procedures. The different considerations involved in the use of NAA evidence, however, are crucial. In the first place, the quantitative values of element concentrations and their respective experimental errors determined by activation analysis do lend themselves well to total-ordering.[7] Therefore, it is always possible, at least in principle, to build up the background data required to evaluate definitively the significance of the analysis. Equally important, if practical problems make the necessary data collection difficult, or if sufficient background data are simply not yet available in a particular case, the expert can nevertheless state clearly and precisely what inferences his measurements warrant and how these conclusions must be limited. Thus, a subjective approach to the interpretation and presentation of NAA results is unnecessary.

4. Osterburg, The Evaluation of Physical Evidence in Criminalistics, in Law Enforcement Science and Technology 419, 420–21.

5. Kingston, Statistical Concepts in Evidence Evaluation, Law Enforcement Science and Technology, 437, 438–39.

6. Fingerprints provide an example of nontotally-orderable data. Although claims have been made to the effect that millions of fingerprints have been compared with no two found to be identical [M. Houts, From Evidence to Proof 133 (1956)], other commentators have questioned whether the number of direct fingerprint comparisons is as large as most people think. Kingston, supra note 5, at 440. It is very time consuming to make such comparisons because there is no truly systematic way to go about it. Id. This is probably a major reason for the disagreement as to the number of points that must "match" before identity is positively established. See M.K. Mehta, The Identification of Thumb Impressions and the Cross Examination of Finger Print Experts 28 (1963), quoted in Osterburg, supra note 4, at 421. Similar problems arise in handwriting and bullet comparisons. The quotations in Osterburg [Id. at 421–22] illustrate the nonobjective character of these and other types of identification procedures.

7. This is because the results of NAA are themselves expressed in numerical amounts. The graphs shown in the discussion of hair comparisons ... [omitted] are essentially total-orderings of the results of measurements for that element (called element A), and the elements themselves are easy to order because they are unambiguously defined and there are only about 100 of them. Contrast this with the essentially infinite number of ways one can deviate from the "normal" way of writing a given letter, for example.

Second, the subjective approach can claim much less validity in the interpretation of NAA results than it can in, say, fingerprint analysis. There is no group of activation analysis experts, comparable to fingerprint analysts, who can claim to possess valuable funds of experience comparing objects in general and finding that they can identify two objects with a common origin. On the contrary, the NAA expert's ability to trace an object's origin stems not from his background experience and intuition, but solely from the statistical analysis of the trace element compositions of similar objects. Ideally, the background information required for the statistical analysis should be performed by analysts other than the expert testifying at trial, but, in any event, the testifying expert's knowledge does not extend beyond its statistical foundation. Any claim that he has a subjective or intuitive ability to identify objects with a common origin is unfounded and misleading.

Third, the risks involved in employing a subjective approach to neutron activation analysis are extremely great. The jury may give undue weight to the expert's opinion simply because of his scientific reputation or because his field is so esoteric. Furthermore, the meanings of terms such as "common origin" or "same batch," which must be precisely defined in an objective analysis, become hazy and confused under the subjective approach, rendering it even more difficult for the trier of fact to understand how the evidence should be interpreted. Finally, subjective testimony is much more easily colored by the natural self-interest that government laboratory scientists have in obtaining convictions than is objective testimony based on scientifically-accepted background information and well-established statistical interpretation procedures.

These considerations distinguish NAA evidence from fingerprint data and other more or less subjective identification techniques. They make it extremely important that experts present their NAA conclusions as carefully and precisely as possible. A general feeling that two pieces of material came from a common source—based, for example, on an examination of their gamma-ray spectra—contains little or no probative value and can be seriously misleading.

. . .

[T]he expert should present his results in the form of a quantitative statement regarding the elemental composition of the samples he analyzes. He should simply state that the samples contain elements A, B, C ... in amounts X, Y, Z ... within corresponding experimental errors. This information should be presented as simply as possible, without the introduction of new terms, so that the focus of attention is on the more important problem: understanding the probability evidence and properly taking it into consideration in reaching a verdict.

. . .

The qualifications of the expert as an analytical chemist do not necessarily establish his competence to interpret the legal relevance of his measurements. The legal relevance depends on the existence of statistical background information regarding the distribution of trace element concentrations over a valid sample of similar materials.[8] Therefore, the validity of the sampling proce-

---

8. Similar materials in this context means materials similar to those which present the issue in the immediate case. Thus, if the hair of a defendant is being compared to hairs found on a murder victim, the background information would be the distribution of trace element concentrations in hair among persons in the sample group.

The "valid sample" referred to may be random, but it will be partially nonrandom if it is necessary that the defendant be compared only to members randomly chosen

dure—the number of samples and the method of collection—must be established, and the analytical chemist may not have the necessary background. Furthermore, the expert must be sufficiently skilled that he can avoid the many pitfalls of probability theory.[9] Fortunately, the same expert need not be responsible for both the elemental analysis and its statistical interpretation. It is true that measurements constituting the background information in a particular case will usually themselves have been NAA measurements. However, if testimony establishes the elemental compositions of the samples within a given experimental error, there is no reason a nonchemist expert in statistics cannot interpret it, which means that the NAA expert need only present the NAA results themselves. In fact, a stipulation as to the NAA measurement may often be possible, and the only qualifications at issue then will be those necessary to interpret the relevance of the measurement. In such an event the statistical expert may replace the analytical chemist entirely.

NOTES

1. For a detailed description of DNA, the methods used to ascertain the characteristics of a sample as well as the problems involved in determining frequencies in populations and expressing them statistically, see Springfield v. State, 860 P.2d 435 (Wyo.1993). In that case the court held that evidence of a "match" without accompanying statistical evidence of frequencies would be meaningless. It also rejected the contention of the defendant, a Crow Indian, that it was error to use a Native American data base that included no Crow. See also the discussion of statistical evidence in Chapter 1, supra, pp. 51–79, including the need for reliable statistical bases of relative frequency of characteristics in subject populations, p. 66; Kaye, DNA Evidence: Probability, Population Genetics and the Courts, 7 Harv. J. L. & Tech. 101 (1993); Lempert, The Suspect Population and DNA Identification, 34 Jurimetrics J. 1 (1993); Committee on DNA Forensic Science, The Evaluation of Forensic DNA Evidence (1996) (updating and revising in certain respects the 1992 report of the National Research Council referred to in United States v. Chischilly).

2. Three related topics of claimed expertise merit special mention because of the number of recent cases that involve them and because they present Frye/Daubert issues in an interesting way. These topics are commonly designated: "battered woman syndrome," "rape trauma syndrome" and "sexually abused child syndrome." In each case the claim is that a body of special knowledge has been developed which permits an inference from the behavior or condition of a person to the cause of that behavior or condition. In each case courts and commentators are divided on admissibility of the evidence.

Battered woman syndrome. State v. Allery, 682 P.2d 312, 316 (Wash.1984): In a prosecution for murder in which self-defense was pleaded, it was error to exclude testimony regarding battered woman syndrome. "We find that expert testimony explaining why a person suffering from the battered woman syn-

from a specific group. Choosing the sample group against which the defendant should be compared is often a difficult problem, especially in the case of hair comparisons.

9. For example, in the case of hair, it is not sufficient merely to state the probability of finding a "match" between a hair chosen at random from the general population and the hair found on the victim's body. This probability may be very low, but if the trace element concentrations among the hairs on defendant's own head are highly variable, then it may also be highly improbable that a hair chosen at random from *his* head would "match." Since the hair found on the victim is essentially one which was chosen at random from the assailant, it is only the comparison of these two probabilities that is relevant to the probative value of the evidence against this particular defendant.

drome would not leave her mate, would not inform police or friends, and would fear increased aggression against herself would be helpful to a jury in understanding a phenomenon not within the competence of an ordinary person." See also Smith v. State, 277 S.E.2d 678 (Ga.1981) (error to exclude). But see State v. Thomas, 423 N.E.2d 137 (Ohio 1981) (not error to exclude).

Blackman and Brickman, The Impact of Expert Testimony on Trials of Battered Women Who Kill Their Husbands, 2 Behav.Sci. & L. 413 (1984); Comment, Legal and Psychiatric Concepts and the Use of Psychiatric Evidence in Criminal Trials, 73 Cal.L.Rev. 411, 420–24 (1985); Note, A Trend Emerges: A State Survey on the Admissibility of Testimony Concerning the Battered Women's Syndrome, 25 J. Fam. L. 373 (1986–87).

Rape trauma syndrome. People v. Taylor, 552 N.E.2d 131 (N.Y.1990): Testimony admissible that victims of rape often are calm when they report the rape and delay in identifying the rapist. State v. Allewalt, 517 A.2d 741, 746–51 (Md.1986): In a rape prosecution in which the defense was consent, held, not error under the circumstances to admit the testimony of a psychiatrist called by the state concerning rape trauma syndrome:

> Dr. Spodak's opinion that the PTSD [post-trauma stress disorder] which he diagnosed in Mrs. Lemon was caused by the rape which she described is as evidentiarily reliable as an opinion by an orthopedist who has been engaged only to testify ascribing a plaintiff's subjective complaints of low back pain to soft tissue injury resulting from an automobile accident described in the history given by the plaintiff. Maryland evidence law recognizes such medical opinions to be competent on, and relevant to, the issue of causation in addition to the fact of bodily harm.

> . . .

> Read literally, the opinion by the Court of Special Appeals [which had held it error to admit the psychiatrist's testimony] would require Dr. Spodak's opinion to "establish" that a rape had occurred and indeed, to establish that fact "conclusively." A slavish application of so rigid a requirement would eliminate most of the evidence at trials of all kinds....

> . . .

> We find nothing in the record now before us which justifies the Court of Special Appeals' apparent concern that Dr. Spodak was presenting a kind of mystical infallibility. He did not purport to have invented a scientific test for determining consent to sexual intercourse had months earlier. He did claim that he could use his special knowledge and the interviewing techniques of his profession to diagnose whether Mrs. Lemon, at the time of his examination of her, suffered from a medically recognized anxiety disorder. He did not claim that psychiatry could demonstrate conclusively that the cause of the PTSD was rape. He did claim the special knowledge and experience to be able to identify the cause of the PTSD by utilizing the history furnished by the patient....

> . . .

> Lurking in the background is the nice question of whether the absence of PTSD is provable by the accused in defense of a rape charge, as tending to prove that there was consent....[1]

1.   Footnotes omitted.

See also State v. McQuillen, 689 P.2d 822, 827–29 (Kan.1984): Trial court erred in ruling that prosecution's expert testimony regarding RTS would be excluded.

People v. Bledsoe, 681 P.2d 291, 300–01 (Cal.1984): Error, although not prejudicial, to admit testimony of rape counselor, who had treated alleged victim of rape, that the alleged victim was suffering from rape trauma syndrome:

> Thus, as a rule, rape counselors do not probe inconsistencies in their clients' descriptions of the facts of the incident, nor do they conduct independent investigations to determine whether other evidence corroborates or contradicts their clients' renditions. Because their function is to help their clients deal with the trauma they are experiencing, the historical accuracy of the clients' descriptions of the details of the traumatizing events is not vital in their task. To our knowledge, all of the studies that have been conducted in this field to date have analyzed data that have been gathered through this counseling process and, as far as we are aware, none of the studies has attempted independently to verify the "truth" of the clients' recollections or to determine the legal implication of the clients' factual accounts.

> [Rape trauma syndrome] does not consist of a relatively narrow set of criteria or symptoms whose presence demonstrates that the client or patient has been raped; rather, as the counselor in this case testified, it is an "umbrella" concept, reflecting the broad range of emotional trauma experienced by clients of rape counselors. Although there are patterns that have been observed, the ongoing studies reveal that a host of variables contribute to the effect of rape on its victims....

> Given the history, purpose, and nature of the rape trauma syndrome concept, we conclude that expert testimony that a complaining witness suffers from rape trauma syndrome is not admissible to prove that the witness was raped. We emphasize that our conclusion in this regard is not intended to suggest that rape trauma syndrome is not generally recognized or used in the general scientific community from which it arose, but only that it is not relied on in that community for the purpose for which the prosecution sought to use it in this case, namely, to prove that a rape in fact occurred. Because the literature does not even purport to claim that the syndrome is a scientifically reliable means of proving that a rape occurred, we conclude that it may not properly be used for that purpose in a criminal trial.

> We hasten to add that nothing in this opinion is intended to imply that evidence of the emotional and psychological trauma that a complaining witness suffers after an alleged rape is inadmissible in a rape prosecution. As discussed in the statement of facts, in this case numerous witnesses—in addition to the rape counselor—described the severe emotional distress that Melanie exhibited both in the house immediately following the attack and in subsequent weeks, and, as defendant implicitly concedes, there is no question but that such evidence was properly received. Lay jurors are, however, fully competent to consider such evidence in determining whether a rape occurred, and "[p]ermitting a person in the role of an expert to suggest that because the complainant exhibits some of the symptoms of rape trauma syndrome, the victim was therefore raped, unfairly prejudices the appellant by creating an aura of special reliability and trustworthiness." (State v. Saldana ... 324 N.W.2d at p. 230 [Minn.1982] ...).[2]

---

2.   Footnotes omitted.

See also Massaro, Experts, Psychology, Credibility and Rape: The Rape Trauma Syndrome Issue and Its Implications for Expert Psychological Testimony, 69 Minn.L.Rev. 395 (1985); McCord, The Admissibility of Expert Testimony Regarding Rape Trauma Syndrome in Rape Prosecutions, 26 B.C.L.Rev. 1143 (1985).

Sexually abused children. State v. Myers, 359 N.W.2d 604, 609 (Minn. 1984): In a prosecution for criminal sexual conduct with a child, not error to permit psychologist to describe traits typically found in sexually abused children and those she had observed in complainant. In re Cheryl H., 200 Cal.Rptr. 789, 799–801 (Cal.App.1984): In proceeding to have child declared dependent of court, not error to admit testimony of psychiatrist based on child's behavior while playing with anatomically correct dolls, that child had been sexually abused.

State v. Foret, 628 So.2d 1116 (La.1993): Prosecution for sexual abuse of juvenile. Error to admit testimony of psychologist who relied on Child Sexual Abuse Accommodation Syndrome that juvenile had been abused and that he believed juvenile was telling the truth. The court held that state law embodied the Daubert standard and that the evidence failed that standard. Evidence of the syndrome would be admissible, however, if it described the syndrome in general terms and was introduced to rebut evidence that the juvenile had made an inconsistent statement or delayed in reporting. State v. Cressey, 628 A.2d 696 (N.H.1993): Error to admit testimony that behavior of child consistent with sexual abuse. People v. Taylor, 552 N.E.2d 131 (N.Y.1990): Error to admit testimony that child's having nightmares, waking in a cold sweat, being frightened and running away from home consistent with having been raped. See Roe, Expert Testimony in Child Sexual Abuse Cases, 40 U.Miami L.Rev. 97 (1985); Note, The Unreliability of Expert Testimony on the Typical Characteristics of Sexual Abuse Victims, 74 Geo. L.J. 429 (1985). For discussion of expert testimony on the credibility of children, see supra p. 449.

An article discussing all three topics of expert testimony set forth in this Note is McCord, Syndromes, Profiles and Other Mental Exotica: A New Approach to the Admissibility of Nontraditional Psychological Evidence in Criminal Cases, 66 Or.L.Rev. 19 (1987). See also Murphy, Assisting the Jury in Understanding Victimization: Expert Psychological Testimony on Battered Woman Syndrome and Rape Trauma Syndrome, 25 Colum. J.L. & Soc. Prob. 277 (1992).

Meier v. Ross General Hospital

Supreme Court of California, 1968.
69 Cal.2d 420, 71 Cal.Rptr. 903, 445 P.2d 519.

■ TOBRINER, JUSTICE. Plaintiffs, the widow and minor children of decedent Kurt Meier, brought this action against defendants Ross General Hospital and James M. Stubblebine, to recover damages for the alleged wrongful death of the decedent. While a patient in the psychiatric wing of the hospital and under the care and supervision of Dr. Stubblebine, decedent committed suicide by jumping headfirst through an open window of his second floor room. Following a trial before a jury, the verdict favored both defendants. Plaintiffs appeal from the judgment.

.   .   .

[W]e hold that the conditional res ipsa instruction, properly qualified, should be given in this case. If those charged with the care and treatment of a mentally disturbed patient know of facts from which they could reasonably conclude that the patient would be likely to harm himself in the absence of preclusive measures, then they must use reasonable care under the circumstances to prevent such harm. (Wood v. Samaritan Institution (1945) 26 Cal.2d 847, 853, 161 P.2d 556.) Given this duty and the fact that defendants placed decedent, following an attempted suicide, in a second floor room with a fully openable window, the jury could find from the fact of decedent's suicidal plunge through this window that defendants more probably than not breached the duty of care owed to decedent. Even in the absence of expert testimony which describes the probability that the death or injury resulted from negligence, the jury may competently decide that defendant more probably than not breached his duty of care when the evidence supports a conclusion that the cause of the accident (here, the openable window) was not inextricably connected with a course of treatment involving the exercise of medical judgment beyond the common knowledge of laymen.

Finally, we conclude that we must reverse the judgment and remand for a new trial because the jury's verdict may have been based on the erroneous instruction; prejudice appears from the probability of a determinative application of an erroneous instruction, and this court should not speculate upon the actual basis of the verdict. . . .

On July 5, 1962, decedent Kurt Meier attempted to commit suicide by slashing his wrists. After treatment for his physical injury, the decedent's family brought him to the Ross General Hospital. Defendant Stubblebine, director of the hospital's psychiatric wing, attended decedent upon his admission and during his hospitalization became his personal physician.

The hospital had adopted the "open door" policy for its psychiatric patients. This method of treatment de-emphasizes physical restraint by providing a "homelike" atmosphere in the hospital. The patients are free to move about and even to leave the hospital if they are so inclined. No mechanical security devices are regularly used; the doors are not locked; the windows are not barred.

The policy rests upon the premise that freedom of movement and personal responsibility of patients, even potential suicides, improve the process of their rehabilitation and reduce possible emotional stress. The proponents of the "open door" policy concede, however, that the lessening of physical security exposes a potentially suicidal patient to greater risk. They assert that no amount of security or physical restraint short of rendering the patient unconscious can effectively prevent suicide. Nevertheless, recognizing the risk of suicide in certain patients, the proponents of "open door" therapy normally employ larger staffs to facilitate surveillance and administer chemotherapy to those patients whose symptomatic restlessness and agitation indicate severe depression which may lead to suicide.

The window through which the decedent jumped was not barred in any way; it had no security screen; it was fully openable by means of a crank. The crank could have been removed, and the window secured at a fixed width, by removing a screw. Evidence introduced by plaintiffs at trial indicated that other hospitals employ security windows of a type which would have prevented the accident in this case. Plaintiffs also offered evidence which tended to show that secured windows would not have been incompatible with the "open door" policy. Defendant physician and other defense experts testified that the operation of the psychiatric facilities at Ross Hospital, including the openable windows, comported with accepted hospital and medical standards. Plaintiffs produced no expert witness.

To alleviate decedent's depression, defendant Stubblebine had prescribed a program of chemotherapy. The record indicates, however, that decedent refused to take the medication as prescribed. Although various members of the hospital staff saw and observed decedent on several occasions, the record does not reveal whether the hospital supplied any formal observation or guard. On July 13, 1962, while decedent was alone in his room, he plunged through the window to his death.

At trial, plaintiffs characterized the openable window in decedent's room as an invitation to commit suicide, a patent violation of defendant's duty of care to the decedent, and a fact of negligence wholly unrelated to the "open door" policy. Plaintiffs also attacked the adequacy of the chemotherapy prescribed and administered to the decedent. In answer, defendants described the treatment and supervision given decedent while in the hospital as exceeding the standard of due care and comporting with good medical practice. Defendants' expert witnesses testified that the "open door" policy as administered at Ross Hospital complied with accepted professional standards. Defendants suggested that the openable window constituted as much a part of "open door" therapy as the unlocked doors. Finally, defendants offered evidence of the difficulty, bordering on impossibility, of preventing an attempted suicide by any sort of physical restraint.

The trial judge gave three distinct negligence instructions: ordinary negligence, medical malpractice, and the questionable res ipsa loquitur instruction. The jury's verdict (10 to 2) favored both defendants.

The trial judge instructed the jury on the doctrine of res ipsa loquitur: "With respect to the doctrine of res ipsa loquitur mentioned by counsel we have this question for you to decide in this case. The question is stated in this way: Whether the accident involved occurred under the following three conditions. First, that it is the kind of accident which ordinarily does not occur in the absence of someone's negligence; second, that it was caused by an agency or instrumentality in the exclusive control of the defendants; and third, that the accident was not due to any voluntary action or contribution on the part of the decedent. And only in the event that you should find all these conditions to exist, you are instructed that an inference arises that a proximate cause of the occurrence was some negligent conduct on the part of the defendants."

Although this instruction meets the requirements set forth by this court in Ybarra v. Spangard . . . 25 Cal.2d 486, 489, 154 P.2d 687, . . . we held in Vistica v. Presbyterian Hospital, . . . 67 Cal.2d 465, 468–469, 62 Cal.Rptr. 577, 432 P.2d 193, that an instruction must be measured by the circumstances of the case in which it was given. . . . In the present case, the plaintiffs offered an instruction which would have explained to the jury that "A plaintiff may properly rely on res ipsa loquitur although he [the decedent] participated in events leading to the accident if the evidence excludes his conduct as the responsible cause." The trial judge refused to give this qualification. We held in Vistica v. Presbyterian Hospital, . . . 67 Cal.2d at pages 470–471, 62 Cal.Rptr. 577, 432 P.2d 193, that just such a qualification must be given whenever the facts of a case support a theory of liability based on a duty to protect plaintiff (decedent) from his own actions, voluntary or involuntary.

. . .

Defendants argue that any error in the form in which the trial judge instructed the jury on res ipsa loquitur must be adjudged harmless. They contend that, when the question of negligence involves a determination of what constitutes proper medical treatment the jury cannot competently assess the "probabilities of negligence" without the assistance of expert witnesses and that, therefore, the trial judge should not have given any res ipsa instruction in the first instance. They point out that the res ipsa loquitur instruction may properly be given in medical malpractice cases only when laymen (the jury) can infer as a matter of common knowledge that the accident would not have occurred unless the defendant were negligent, or when expert testimony supports the same inference, namely that the accident was more probably than not caused by defendant's negligence. (Siverson v. Weber (1962) 57 Cal.2d 834, 836, 22 Cal.Rptr. 337, 372 P.2d 97; cf. Prosser, Res Ipsa Loquitur in California (1949) 37 Cal.L.Rev. 183, 193, 210–212.) Since plaintiffs here could offer no expert testimony on the "probabilities of negligence," defendants contend that the trial court should not have given the res ipsa instruction because the propriety of treatment for mentally ill patients raises questions of professional judgment and accepted medical practice which fall outside the realm of lay or common knowledge.

Defendants' contention raises the issue whether, as a matter of law, the jury could find, without the aid of expert testimony, the conditions precedent to an application of the doctrine of res ipsa loquitur. Stated differently, could the jury find from the mere occurrence of the accident under the circumstances that it probably was the result of negligence by someone and that defendant is probably the person who is responsible? (Clark v. Gibbons (1967) 66 Cal.2d 399, 408, 58 Cal.Rptr. 125, 426 P.2d 525.) The former probability must concern us here: defendants assert that the jury requires the aid of experts because the questions raised lie exclusively within the province of medical science.

The facts of this case preclude our acceptance of defendants' contention. Ordinarily, if a plaintiff seeks to hold a hospital or a physician liable for a breach of a duty as to the medical care and treatment of a patient, the courts refuse to give a res ipsa loquitur instruction unless the plaintiff has produced some expert testimony[1] which supports an inference of negligence from the fact of the accident itself. (Siverson v. Weber, supra, 57 Cal.2d 834, 22 Cal.Rptr. 337, 372 P.2d 97; cf. Quintal v. Laurel Grove Hosp. (1964) 62 Cal.2d 154, 41 Cal.Rptr. 577, 397 P.2d 161; Clark v. Gibbons, supra, 66 Cal.2d 399, 58 Cal.Rptr. 125, 426 P.2d 525.)[2] The reason for this requirement appears from the following statement: "The law demands only that a physician or surgeon have the degree of learning and skill ordinarily possessed by practitioners of the medical profession in the same locality and that he exercise ordinary care in applying such learning and skill to the treatment of his patient.... Ordinarily, a doctor's failure to possess or exercise the requisite learning or skill can be established only by the testimony of experts." (Lawless v. Calaway, supra, 24 Cal.2d 81, 86, 147 P.2d 604, 606.)

---

1. Under our law, the plaintiff may call the defendant physician and make him the plaintiff's "expert witness" for the purposes of this requirement. (Code Civ.Proc., § 2055; Lawless v. Calaway (1944) 24 Cal.2d 81, 89–91, 147 P.2d 604.) [Footnotes of the court. Some footnotes omitted, others renumbered.]

2. Quintal and Clark permit the application of res ipsa loquitur to cases in which the only basis for the jury's competence to determine the "probabilities of negligence" are the rarity of the accident and some expert testimony supporting a negligent cause. That this development constitutes a more liberal interpretation of the scope of res ipsa loqui-

tur has been noted (see Clark v. Gibbons, supra, 66 Cal.2d 399, 421–424, 58 Cal.Rptr. 125, 426 P.2d 525, Traynor, C.J., concurring; cf. Prosser, Res Ipsa Loquitur in California, supra, 37 Cal.L.Rev. 183, 189–196.) We mention these recent precedents in this context only to point out that the present case is not governed by them. For the reasons presented infra, we hold that the question of res ipsa must go to the jury even without any expert testimony when the facts support a finding of probable negligence without regard to the propriety of any distinctly "medical" course of treatment.

The courts, however, have established an exception to this requirement for the testimony of experts if the subject matter of the litigation is such that laymen could infer *as a matter of common knowledge* that the injury would not have occurred unless the defendant were negligent. (Note, The Application of Res Ipsa Loquitur in Medical Malpractice Cases (1966) 60 Nw.L.Rev. 852, 857–864.) The requirement for expert testimony disappears if "during the performance of surgical or other skilled operations an ulterior act or omission occurs, the judgment of which does not require scientific opinion to throw light upon the subject." (Ales v. Ryan (1936) 8 Cal.2d 82, 98, 64 P.2d 409, 417; see, e.g., Leonard v. Watsonville Community Hosp. (1956) 47 Cal.2d 509, 305 P.2d 36, leaving a clamp in the incision following abdominal surgery; Davis v. Memorial Hosp. (1962) 58 Cal.2d 815, 26 Cal.Rptr. 633, 376 P.2d 561, rectal abscess following routine pre-surgical enema; Friedman v. Dresel (1956) 139 Cal.App.2d 333, 293 P.2d 488, failure to examine or X–ray hip despite complaints of pain in that area.)

In order to sustain the application of res ipsa loquitur in the particular circumstances of this case, however, we need not rely upon the above "common knowledge" exception to the requirement of expert testimony in medical malpractice cases. An obvious instance in which we do not call for expert testimony arises when the facts of a case support a finding of negligence of the ordinary type unrelated to questions involving materia medica.[3] (Cf. Ales v. Ryan, supra, 8 Cal.2d 82, 100, 64 P.2d 409.)

In this case Dr. Stubblebine, testifying as plaintiffs' witness under Code of Civil Procedure section 2055, acknowledged that a secured type of window was compatible with the "open door" policy.

"Q: Did you consider the fact that he [decedent] might go out the window?

"A: Not very much, because there were so many other means available, closer at hand, more certain.

"Q: You didn't know what means he might take?

"A: No.

"Q: The window was one of them?

"A: Yes.

"Q: You gave the window no concern at all? . . . [Objection.] . . .

"Q: Your answer was 'not very much.' Did you consider it—to what extent did you consider it?

"A: I don't know how much weight I gave it. I was more concerned about the many other ways.

"Q: You told me that the cranks of the windows—they would crank open?

"A: Yes.

3. When the evidence is conflicting, or subject to different inferences, as to whether the alleged negligence is to be measured by reference to the ordinary standard of due care or by reference to the standard of good medical practice set by physicians of good standing in the community, a question of fact arises which must be left to the jury under proper instructions. (Cf. Davis v. Memorial Hospital, supra, 58 Cal.2d 815, 817, 26 Cal. Rptr. 633, 376 P.2d 561.) Such a question emerges in a case like the one before us in which the facts show a possibly negligent act or omission (i.e., leaving decedent alone in a room with an openable window) which defendant seeks to justify as part of a course of "medical" treatment involving the exercise of professional judgment ("open door" therapy). The jury must determine whether the defendants instituted a course of conduct, or act or omission, for a good faith "medical" reason. The appropriate standard of care to be applied depends on the results of such a determination. (See fn. 4, infra.)

"Q: And the crank may be removed?

"A: Yes.

"Q: You could open it a certain distance and remove the crank, and the only way you could close or open it further would be with the crank?

"A: Yes.

"Q: Did you give any thought to providing proper ventilation, to remove the crank and—.

"A: No.

" . . .

"Q: You could have a secured type of window and still leave the doors open, and it would still be the open door policy?

"A: Yes.

" . . .

"Q: The kind of window a facility might have doesn't change the fact it might otherwise be an open type hospital?

"A: That is correct."

No testimony introduced by defendants, either specifically or substantially or as a matter of law, rebutted the inference from Dr. Stubblebine's statement that the openable window did not constitute an essential, or even relevant, element of the "open door" policy.

The jury could therefore find negligence in the present case without regard to the propriety or impropriety of an asserted medical justification. We hold that the trial court must submit a conditional res ipsa instruction, even absent expert testimony on the "probabilities of negligence," when the evidence supports a conclusion that the cause of the accident (the openable window) was not inextricably bound up in a course of treatment involving the exercise of medical judgment beyond the common knowledge of laymen.[4] In brief, the "open door" policy does not necessarily call for an openable window; the objectives of the policy can be achieved without leaving an openable window available to the patient.

. . .

The judgment is reversed and the case remanded to the trial court for a new trial in accordance with this opinion.

NOTES

1. Runnells v. Rogers, 596 S.W.2d 87 (Tenn.1980):

In this medical malpractice action the sole question is the necessity for expert medical testimony.

---

4. The judge should instruct the jury, however, that if it finds that defendants allowed the decedent to remain in the room with an openable window for a good faith medical reason that is inextricably bound up in a course of treatment involving the exercise of medical judgment beyond the knowledge of common laymen, they must assess this medical reason in the light of the standard of medical learning and skill prevalent in the community. The need for expert testimony in such a case will depend upon whether the subject matter in issue falls within the "common knowledge" exception discussed supra. . . .

On the trial, the jury awarded plaintiff the sum of $1,224.48. The Court of Appeals reversed and dismissed, holding that such testimony was required.

I.

. . .

The basic facts are not in dispute. On April 14, 1976, petitioner, while operating this power lawnmower, ran over a piece of wire throwing it into his foot, resulting in a puncture wound, with the wire being imbedded in the foot. He went immediately to the Baptist Hospital where he was seen by the respondent, Dr. Rogers. Dr. Rogers examined the foot, took X-rays, and made an unsuccessful effort to remove the imbedded bit of wire. He gave petitioner some capsules for infection and told him to go home, stay off his feet and come back the following Friday, two days later. No effort was made after this initial consultation to remove the wire.

Petitioner returned on Friday. Dr. Rogers again examined the foot, redressed the wound, told him to continue on antibiotics and told him to return the following Monday. On Monday, April 19, 1976, petitioner reported for work but his foot was in such pain that he was unable to perform his duties. By that time his foot had swollen and was turning red. He was unable to get his shoe on. That same day he went back to the hospital, where he saw another doctor in the absence of Dr. Rogers. He gave him some antibiotics and told him to return to see Dr. Rogers on Wednesday.

On April 21, 1976, he returned to Dr. Rogers, who examined his foot and removed the stitches. By this time his foot was turning a dark color. The doctor prescribed more antibiotics, told him to stay off that week and to return to work on Monday.

On April 26, 1976, after working two days on light duty, petitioner went back to Dr. Rogers. By this time he was walking with difficulty, his foot had turned blue, and it was "running" or oozing some sort of liquid substance. Dr. Rogers examined him, told him to soak his foot, stay off it and return the following Monday. He continued on antibiotics.

On Monday, April 29, 1976, petitioner again tried to return to work and was able to work some that week; however, his foot was black and swollen, still running and he continued to be unable to get a shoe on it. On May 5, 1976, he again saw Dr. Rogers who examined him, told him to take antibiotics, soak his foot and go back to work the following week. He tried to return to work but by this time his foot "was so sore I couldn't hardly walk." It was still black and running and he could not wear a shoe. Following each visit and at all times petitioner relied upon Dr. Rogers and followed his advice and instructions. Finally, on May 10, 1976, he consulted Dr. John C. Brothers, who X-rayed and dressed the foot, gave him a "larger" prescription for antibiotics and made an appointment for the following Monday.

On May 16, 1976, Dr. Brothers put him in West Side Hospital, reduced the infection and surgically removed the wire. After a four-day hospital stay he was released and gradually recovered.

The plaintiff did not call an expert medical witness.

This suit was filed on September 23, 1976, against Dr. Rogers and the Baptist Hospital. At the conclusion of all the proof, the Trial Judge sustained a motion for a directed verdict as to the hospital.

The requirement for expert testimony and the "common knowledge" exception thereto are firmly entrenched in our law. The difficulty arises when an effort is made to apply the rules to a given set of facts in a case wherein the application of the exception is fairly debatable. This is such a case.

In the totality of the circumstances, however, we perceive this to be a proper case for the application of the common knowledge exception. It is evident from reading and studying this record that this wire imbedded in plaintiff's foot should have been removed. We held in Baldwin [Baldwin v. Knight, 569 S.W.2d 450 (Tenn.1978)] ... that the negligent failure of a physician to discover a piece of wire lodged in the plaintiff's foot by a lawnmower was within the knowledge of a layman. We see no difference in principle between a failure to discover on the one hand and a failure to treat properly after discovery on the other.

It is within the common knowledge of laymen that where a patient is injured by a piece of wire imbedded in his foot, the foot has swollen to the point that the shoe may not be worn, the patient has difficulty in walking, there is soreness resulting from probing in an unsuccessful effort to remove it, and the foot is oozing and running, then the wire must be removed. These facts must be considered in the light of the action of Dr. Brothers in reducing the infection and removing the wire.

Even a barefoot boy knows that when his foot is infested by a sticker, splinter, thorn, pin or other foreign object, it must be removed. Most assuredly this lies within the ken of a layman.

Dr. Rogers apparently thought so. He tried to remove it and upon failure merely treated Runnells with antibiotics, resting and soaking, during all of which time the patient grew steadily worse.

The fact that Dr. Brothers removed the wire and the patient promptly healed would lead an average layman to conclude that this was the proper practice and failure to do so was a deviation. Medical testimony could hardly have made the case stronger....

Reversed.

Dissent:

I am unable to concur in the majority's "barefoot boy" philosophy concerning foreign objects. It is a known fact that thousands of veterans of World War I and World War II have lived for years with fragments of shrapnel and other foreign objects in arms, legs, and other portions of the anatomy because of medical judgment that removal would be ill-advised or detrimental. Andrew Jackson was shot in a duel in 1806. The ball was embedded in the rib cage near the heart, and it remained there until Jackson's death in 1845 some thirty-nine years later. Although the wound was troubling to Jackson on frequent occasions, it was the medical judgment of surgeons of that day that removal could not be safely accomplished.

While that case is hardly analogous to the facts presented here, nevertheless it is my opinion that whether and when removal should have been attempted in the present case were clearly questions for expert evaluation and judgment and were not decisions for determination by lay persons. I do not consider Baldwin v Knight ... to be controlling here, and it seems to me, contrary to the statement in the majority opinion, that there is a vast difference between the failure of a physician to discover a foreign body for lack of a proper history on the one hand and his professional judgment as to whether or when to remove it on the other.

Even a casual glance at medical literature will demonstrate the foregoing. For example, in a discussion of injuries to the hand found in a treatise on traumatic medicine, the following statement is made:

> "Complications following removal of a foreign body may well be precipitated by ill-advised attempts at removal in the first place. Small inert foreign bodies such as BB shot are frequently better left alone since the exploration for their removal may entail considerable dissection amongst vital anatomical structures. . . .

> "The secondary removal of foreign bodies has all the problems inherent in the removal at the time of injury. It is also often made more difficult because the track of injury can no longer be located and because considerable scar tissue surrounds the foreign body. An ever-present and severe risk is that the surgery may 'light up' a tetanus infection from bacteria introduced at the time of the original injury. Appropriate precautions must always be taken before such surgery is undertaken." 2 Traumatic Medicine and Surgery for the Attorney, 182–83 (P.D. Cantor ed. 1960).

While the foregoing discussion pertains to a hand injury, an examination of any medical or surgical textbook will reveal that the anatomy and structure of the foot are also extremely complex. See e. g., Legal Anatomy and Surgery, 309–19 (2d ed. B.S. Maloy 1955). Without detailed medical testimony as to the location of a foreign body, its size and relation to surrounding tissues, muscles and bones, in my opinion, it would be sheer guesswork on the part of lay persons to know whether surgical removal of a foreign object should be attempted and at what point in the course of treatment such attempt should be made. Apparently in the present case Dr. Rogers at first attempted removal but later felt that another and different course of treatment was advisable. Statutes governing medical malpractice actions now require that expert testimony be used to establish the appropriate standard of care in the first place and its violation in the second place. The instances in which these requirements need not be met are few indeed. In my opinion the present case is not such an exception.

. . .

2. Cramer v. Theda Clark Memorial Hosp., 172 N.W.2d 427 (Wis.1969): The trial court erred in taking the issue of negligence from the jury on the ground of the plaintiff's failure to introduce evidence of the standard of care observed by hospitals in the area. While plaintiff was recovering from an operation, he slid off the end of his bed, attempted to stand, fell and was hurt. He had been in restraints in the bed, but a nurse released one of his arms so that he could eat. After the nurse left the room, plaintiff used his free arm to get out of the other restraints. "In such cases the standard of care is not what the practice is in hospitals in the area, but the ordinary care which the condition of the patient then requires. One does not need to be an expert to be able to determine whether a person should be in or out of restraints." There was evidence that plaintiff had been irrational and had tried to get out of bed before.

A case similar to Meier v. Ross Gen. Hospital, with an interesting opinion by Bazelon, J., is Lucy Webb Hayes National Training School v. Perotti, 419 F.2d 704 (D.C.Cir.1969). See also Duling v. Bluefield Sanitarium, Inc., 142 S.E.2d 754 (W.Va.1965) (hospital nurses failed to look at child although mother had told them of symptoms; no expert testimony on nurses' practice in area needed); Washington Hosp. Center v. Butler, 384 F.2d 331 (D.C.Cir.1967) (patient fell during x-rays; nurse failed to tell radiologist of patient's history of dizziness; no need for expert testimony); Pederson v. Dumouchel, 431 P.2d 973 (Wash.1967) (patient unconscious for month following operation to reduce fractured jaw; error not to give res ipsa instruction even though no expert testimony introduced). But see Rosenberg by Rosenberg v. Cahill, 492 A.2d 371, 375 (N.J.1985): Expert testimony required as to whether it was negligent for chiropractor not to recognize soft tissue abnormalities from x-rays and to appreciate need for medical attention. Hansel v. Ford Motor Co., 473 P.2d 219, 226–27 (Wash.Ct.App.1970): Auto accident due to allegedly faulty repair of brakes. Plaintiff's expert testified that brakes did not work because "piston rod was not installed in its proper position on the web of a shoe." Held, no need for expert testimony that defendant mechanic failed to exercise skill possessed by other mechanics in the area. This is more nearly analogous to the surgical removal of the wrong leg than to the course of treatment where there are several alternatives."

3. Mason v. Ellsworth, 474 P.2d 909, 915–919 (Wash.Ct.App.1970), was a suit for injuries resulting from the perforation of plaintiff's esophagus during the performance of a diagnostic esophagoscopy. One theory of recovery was premised upon failure to inform plaintiff of the danger of perforation.[1]

The crux of the informed-consent problem as it has been developed in the various courts lies in the necessity for, and use of, expert medical testimony. The majority of jurisdictions treat informed consent in the same manner as medical malpractice. As a result, plaintiff is required to establish: (1) by expert medical testimony what a reasonable practitioner, under the same or similar circumstances, would have disclosed to his patient concerning risks incident to a proposed procedure, and (2) that the physician has deviated from this standard to the injury of the plaintiff. This categorization, in effect, tends to emasculate the patient's right to know— it measures that right entirely in terms of the standard of practice of those who are obligated to inform him. The particular standard of practice by physicians in this area may be unreasonable or even negligent under the law. The majority of cases concentrate on defining the physician's duty while merely alluding to the patient's right to know.

We are aware that a given case may require the use of medical expertise to determine what is medically sound in a physician's explanation of a *procedure* to his patient. The medical explanation in the instant case concerning the procedure is not in issue. But it is imperative that it be understood that the basis of the theory of informed consent is *both* the *patient's right* to be reasonably informed of all *material* elements, including risks, which may affect his consent to the procedure *and* the *physician's duty* to inform his patient in a medically sound fashion. The former's right inheres in the long recognized inviolability of the human body; while the latter's duty is grounded upon the strong fiduciary bond which is the basis of the patient-physician relationship.

---

1. Footnotes omitted.

In contrast to the majority approach described above are two apparent positions that have developed in reaction to the grouping of informed consent with malpractice. The first is best expressed by the following excerpt from Myers, Informed Consent in Medical Malpractice, 55 Calif.L.Rev. 1396 (1967):

> A physician is under an obligation (1) to make a full disclosure of all known material risks in a proposed operation or course of treatment except for those risks of which the patient is likely to know or (2) to prove the reasonableness of any lesser disclosure or the immateriality of the undisclosed risk.

(Footnotes omitted.) At a glance such a rule appears to remedy the fault of following strictly the malpractice approach. The plaintiff's onerous burden of establishing a standard of medical practice is eliminated and the so-called "conspiracy of silence" is pierced. However, the correlative of such a rule, if carried to its conclusion, could serve as the basis for a different claim against a physician in malpractice, i.e., one for having told too much to the patient, contrary to good, sound medical practice, so that the procedure is refused or complications arise out of fear or other emotional distress, to his injury, even though the risk revealed is minimal.

The second may be characterized by the case of Berkey v. Anderson, 1 Cal.App.3d 790, 805, 82 Cal.Rptr. 67, 78 (1969) (2d Dist., Div. 5):

> We cannot agree that the matter of informed consent must be determined on the basis of medical testimony any more than that expert testimony of the standard practice is determinative in any other case involving a fiduciary relationship. We agree with appellant that a physician's duty to disclose is not governed by the standard practice of the physicians' community, but is a duty imposed by law which governs his conduct in the same manner as others in a similar fiduciary relationship. To hold otherwise would permit the medical profession to determine its own responsibilities....

> We believe a valid distinction exists between the traditional theory of malpractice and the instant cause of action. The milieu which may surround a particular patient's reaction to a proposed procedure, coupled with a physician's personal rapport with that patient and his response to that patient's reaction is a highly personal relationship. That is why it has been designated as a fiduciary relationship. Such a personal relationship cannot be categorized within the same standard, for example, as the objective procedure to be used to remove a gallstone or an appendix. In the latter case there exists objective standards of medical procedure which can be readily ascertained and placed into evidence, while in the former an attempt to establish an objective standard of disclosure is nothing more than a Procrustean machination employed for the sake of utility.

> The law applicable to informed consent must balance the conflicting right of the patient and duty of the doctor in an equitable fashion. The inviolability of the patient's body, which is firmly grounded in Anglo–American law, must be a starting point. Thus, the physician, absent an emergency, must not only explain the nature and consequences of a procedure, but also describe material risks peculiar to the procedure which may reasonably be foreseeable. In this framework, expert medical testimony to establish a standard of disclosure by the plaintiff becomes unnecessary. However, this does not prevent the physician from introducing evidence of such a standard, if in fact one exists; nor does it eliminate the

necessity for some medical testimony to establish what is a reasonably foreseeable risk.

See also Pauscher v. Iowa Methodist Medical Center, 408 N.W.2d 355 (Iowa 1987): Patient with life-threatening illness was subjected to diagnostic procedure without being informed of a 1 in 100,000 chance that she might die of the procedure. She did in fact die of the procedure. The court held it was error to have directed a verdict for defendant doctors because of plaintiff's failure to introduce expert testimony that defendants had violated a professional standard in failing to inform the patient of this risk—"the authoritarian rationale that undergirds the professional role is apparent in the record before us"—but that a directed verdict for the defendant doctors was warranted, because no reasonable jury could have found defendants negligent: the small risk that defendants failed to disclose would not have been deemed material by a reasonable patient.

4. See Dorf v. Relles, 355 F.2d 488 (7th Cir.1966), a malpractice suit against a lawyer in which negligence was charged in failure to conduct proper negotiations for settlement and to keep in communication with the client regarding such negotiations. Judgment for the plaintiff reversed because of the absence of expert testimony concerning the care usually exercised by lawyers when confronted with situations of this sort. The absence of expert testimony regarding the care exercised by lawyers was also fatal to the plaintiff in Baker v. Beal, 225 N.W.2d 106, 112–13 (Iowa 1975), and Wright v. Williams, 121 Cal.Rptr. 194 (Cal.App.1975) (maritime law specialist). See also Ambrosio and McLaughlin, The Use of Expert Witnesses in Establishing Liability in Legal Malpractice Cases, 61 Temple L. Rev. 1351 (1988); Klaus and Mallen, The Misguiding Hand of Counsel—Reflections on "Criminal Malpractice," 21 UCLA L.Rev. 1191 (1974); Leibson, Legal Malpractice Cases: Special Problems of Identifying Issues of Law and Fact in the Use of Expert Testimony, 75 Ky.L.J. 1 (1986–87).

5. Stiver v. Parker, 975 F.2d 261, 272–73 (6th Cir.1992): Action for negligence brought by surrogate mother and her husband against lawyer who organized surrogacy program and doctors who participated in it, for damages resulting from transmission through insemination to the mother and child of a disease that infected the donor of the semen. The claim was that the program was not organized to protect against the kind of danger that in fact occurred.

The District Court gave summary judgment for all parties and against the Stivers on all claims, holding that the Stivers had not established a genuine issue as to a material fact concerning an essential element of the case for which they had the burden of proof. . . .

The District Court framed the cause of action as sounding in medical and legal malpractice against Keane and all the professionals. It held that claims against them failed because the Stivers failed to present expert witnesses as to the appropriate standard of care, a requirement under Michigan law for a medical or legal malpractice case to go to the jury. . . . Michigan law requires similar expert evidence in a legal malpractice case. Beattie v. Firnschild, 152 Mich.App. 785, 394 N.W.2d 107 (1986) (holding that in legal malpractice case, plaintiff must establish malpractice or violations of Professional Code or Rules by expert testimony).

Insofar as the cases against the defendants are framed narrowly as malpractice causes of action, the District Court is correct. We do not read the complaint or the papers on summary judgment or on appeal, however, as so narrowly framed. The plaintiffs' theory is based rather on general principles of tort law establishing affirmative duties to act. The malpractice requirement of expert witness testimony does not apply in circumstances involving negligence liability of those who undertake to operate a surrogacy program.

In the instant case the purpose of Michigan's expert witness rule in professional malpractice cases is not served. The rule is based on an assumption that there is an existing custom and practice in the profession which defines the standard of liability applicable to the particular professional conduct in question. An expert witness is needed so that the fact finder will understand the professional norm. The instant case is one of first impression involving an entirely new area of practice for doctors, lawyers and surrogacy brokers. The legal standards and policy and professional norms are just in the process of being established. General principles of tort law outside the standard malpractice area are at stake. Therefore, we conclude that the District Court erred in dismissing the plaintiffs' case because they did not produce expert malpractice witnesses.

What characteristics of an activity produce the consequence that a nongovernmentally established standard of behavior, rather than the general standard of reasonable care, is applicable? This question is presented whether observance of the nongovernmental standard conclusively establishes reasonable care or is only evidence of it. In United Blood Services v. Quintana, 827 P.2d 509 (Colo.1992) (blood provided by defendant tainted with AIDS virus infected plaintiff), the court, influenced by the language of a statute regulating blood banks, held that supplying blood was a medical service, not the sale of a product, and so a professional standard of care was applicable rather than the standard of ordinary care. The court stated, however, that the way was open for the plaintiff to show that the national professional standard was unreasonably deficient in not adopting available practices that were substantially more protective against harm. Consequently, the court said, the trial court erred in excluding expert testimony, offered by the plaintiff, that the professional standard was indeed unreasonably deficient. Why allow experts to testify to opinions regarding the adequacy of the national professional standard?

Samples v. City of Atlanta, 916 F.2d 1548, 1551 (11th Cir.1990): In action against policemen for excessive use of force, not error to allow "use of force expert" to testify that policemen's conduct did not violate prevailing standards in field of law enforcement. Rutter v. Northeastern Beaver County School Dist., 437 A.2d 1198, 1201–02 (Pa.1981): In action for injuries sustained in football practice in which "jungle football" was played without protective gear and the coaches participated, with result that they could not supervise, held, error to exclude testimony of former coach regarding safety standards maintained at Pennsylvania high schools and the rules of an interscholastic athletic league. Matulevich v. Matulevich, 498 A.2d 939, 940, 942 (Pa.Super.1985): Action for injuries suffered in hunting accident. In a north-south line of hunters, defendant was the first in the line, counting from the south, plaintiff the third. As the line moved toward the east, a deer crossed the line between the second man and the plaintiff. A shot fired from defendant's gun struck plaintiff in the chest. Held: Not error to exclude expert testimony. "[O]nce the configuration of the hunting drive, which all parties agree was an acceptable method of hunting, was explained to the jury, they were perfectly able to evaluate the reasonableness of the parties' conduct without the aid of an expert."

Washington v. United States

United States Court of Appeals, District of Columbia Circuit, 1967.
390 F.2d 444.

[Defendant sought reversal of a conviction for rape on the ground that the trial court should have entered judgment of acquittal because of insanity. The

Court of Appeals held that the trial court had not erred in refusing to enter judgment of acquittal and affirmed defendant's conviction. The court, per Bazelon, J., made the following observations concerning the role of expert psychiatric testimony in relation to the insanity defense.][1]

In Durham v. United States,[2] we announced a new test for insanity: "An accused is not criminally responsible if his unlawful act was the product of a mental disease or defect."[3] We intended to widen the range of expert testimony in order to enable the jury "to consider all information advanced by relevant scientific disciplines."

This purpose was not fully achieved, largely because many people thought Durham was only an attempt to identify a clearly defined category of persons—those classified as mentally ill by the medical profession—and excuse them from criminal responsibility. In fact, the medical profession has no such clearly defined category, and the classifications it has developed for purposes of treatment, commitment, etc., may be inappropriate for assessing responsibility in criminal cases. Since these classifications were familiar, however, many psychiatrists understandably used them in court despite their unsuitability. And some psychiatrists, perhaps unwittingly, permitted their own notions about blame to determine whether the term mental illness should be limited to psychoses, should include serious behavior disorders, or should include virtually all mental abnormalities. To ensure that the views of the experts would not bind the fact-finder, we decided to give mental illness a legal definition independent of its medical meaning. We announced in McDonald v. United States that mental illness "includes any abnormal condition of the mind which substantially affects mental or emotional processes and which substantially impairs behavior control."[4]

. . .

[We have] described the steps taken in Durham and McDonald to enable the jury to consider all the relevant information about the defendant. Durham and McDonald were also attempts to clarify the respective roles of the expert[5] and the jury by reducing the emphasis on conclusory labels. We thought the new test announced in Durham would allow the expert to testify in *medical* terms familiar to him and to his profession. The jury would no longer be forced to focus on the conclusory labels used by the expert.

Soon after Durham we found that, although the jury was being given more information, still too much emphasis was being placed upon the labels used by the psychiatrist, upon whether he concluded that the defendant did or did not have a "mental illness." In Carter v. United States[6] we pointed out again that Durham was designed to eliminate this kind of labeling.

1. Except for footnote 3, footnotes are those of the court. The footnotes have been renumbered. Some footnotes have been omitted and material in others has been omitted.

2. 94 U.S.App.D.C. 228, 214 F.2d 862 (1954).

3. The Insanity Defense Reform Act of 1984, 18 U.S.C. § 17 (1986 Supp.), provides: "Affirmative defense.—It is an affirmative defense to a prosecution under any Federal statute that, at the time of the commission of the acts constituting the offense, the defendant, as a result of a severe mental disease or defect, was unable to appreciate the nature and quality or the wrongfulness of his acts. Mental disease or defect does not otherwise constitute a defense." Eds.

4. 114 U.S.App.D.C. 120, 124, 312 F.2d 847, 851 (1962) (en banc).

5. The term "expert" is not necessarily limited to psychiatrists. See, e.g., Jenkins v. United States, 113 U.S.App.D.C. 300, 307 F.2d 637 (1962).

6. 102 U.S.App.D.C. 227, 252 F.2d 608 (1957).

Unexplained medical labels—schizophrenia, paranoia, psychosis, neurosis, psychopathy—are not enough. Description and explanation of the origin, development and manifestations of the alleged disease are the chief functions of the expert witness. The chief value of an expert's testimony in this field, as in all other fields, rests upon the material from which his opinion is fashioned and the reasoning by which he progresses from his material to his conclusion; in the explanation of the disease and its dynamics, that is, how it occurred, developed and affected the mental and emotional processes of the defendant; it does not lie in his mere expression of conclusion.... Durham was intended to restrict to their proper medical function the part played by the medical experts.[7]

This warning was not effective enough, so in McDonald v. United States we gave the terms "disease" and "defect" a *legal* definition independent of their medical meanings.

Our eight-year experience under Durham suggests a *judicial* definition, however broad and general, of what is included in the terms "disease" and "defect." In Durham, rather than define either term we simply sought to distinguish disease from defect. Our purpose now is to make it very clear that neither the court nor the jury is bound by ad hoc definitions or conclusions as to what experts state is a disease or defect. What psychiatrists may consider a "mental disease or defect" for clinical purposes, where their concern is treatment, may or may not be the same as mental disease or defect for the jury's purpose in determining criminal responsibility. Consequently, for that purpose the jury should be told that a mental disease or defect includes any abnormal condition of the mind which substantially affects mental or emotional processes and substantially impairs behavior controls. Thus the jury would consider testimony concerning the development, adaptation and functioning of these processes and controls.

We emphasize that, since the question of whether the defendant has a disease or defect is ultimately for the triers of fact, obviously its resolution cannot be controlled by expert opinion. The jury must determine for itself, from all the testimony, lay and expert, whether the nature and degree of the disability are sufficient to establish a mental disease or defect as we have now defined those terms. What we have said, however, should in no way be construed to limit the latitude of expert testimony.[8]

---

7. Id. at 236, 252 F.2d at 617.

8. 114 U.S.App.D.C. at 124, 312 F.2d at 850–851. An alternative to Durham–McDonald would be to make the ultimate test whether or not it is just to blame the defendant for his act. If the question were simply whether it is "just" to "blame" the defendant, then mental illness, productivity, ability to control oneself, etc., might be factors which the jury could consider in reaching its conclusion on the justness of punishment. Since the words "just" and "blame" do not lend themselves to refined definition, the charge to the jury under this test probably would not be detailed. But the words that have been used in other charges, such as "defect of reason," "disease of the mind," "nature and quality of the act," "behavior controls," "mental disease or defect," "capacity ... to appreciate the criminality of his conduct," and "capacity to conform his conduct to the requirements of law," are also vague—the chief difference being that these words give a false impression of scientific exactness, an impression which may lead the jury to ignore its own moral judgment and defer to the moral judgment of scientific "experts." However, we are unaware of any test for criminal responsibility which does not focus on the term "mental illness," or some closely similar term. This focus may be unfortunate, but we are not deciding that question now, and are not proposing to abandon the term. Contrast Dershowitz, Psychiatry in the Legal Process: A Knife That Cuts Both Ways, 51 Judicature 370 (1968), recommending that "no legal rule should ever be phrased in medical terms...."

We clearly separated the legal and moral question of culpability from the medical-clinical concept of illness. We hoped thereby to separate the roles of the psychiatrist and the jury, with the former stating medical-clinical facts and opinions and the latter making the judgments required by the legal and moral standard. Also, we hoped that the expert's conclusion would not be so heavily weighted in the jury's minds if we made plain that the expert and the jury had different judgments to make.

Even after McDonald, though, we allowed the experts to state whether they thought the defendant had a mental disease or defect. We assumed that the expert could separate the medical judgments which he was supposed to make from the legal and moral judgments which he was not supposed to make. It has become abundantly apparent that this theory has not worked out. Too often conclusory labels—both medical and legal—have substituted, albeit unwittingly, for the facts and analysis which underlie them. The transcript in this case illustrates that they may have served more to confuse the jury than to guide it. Also, testimony in terms of "mental disease or defect" seems to leave the psychiatrist too free to testify according to his judgment about the defendant's criminal responsibility.

This kind of testimony does not give the jury a satisfactory basis for determining criminal responsibility. A proper adjudication requires that the jury be fully informed about the defendant's mental and emotional processes and, insofar as it affects these processes, his social situation. Of course, we cannot hope to obtain *all* the relevant information about a defendant. We cannot explore in full the effects of his genetic structure, his family relationships, his upbringing in slum or suburb. But within the limits imposed by the courtroom context and the level of scientific knowledge we should provide the jury with as much of this information as is reasonably available. We are not excused from doing what we can do simply because there are things we cannot do.

With the relevant information about defendant, and guided by the legal principles enunciated by the court, the jury must decide, in effect, whether or not the defendant is blameworthy. Undoubtedly, the decision is often painfully difficult, and perhaps its very difficulty accounts for the readiness with which we have encouraged the expert to decide the question. But our society has chosen not to give this decision to psychiatrists or to any other professional elite but rather to twelve lay representatives of the community. The choice was not made on a naive assumption that all jurors would be fully capable of dealing with these difficult questions or with the underlying information. Nonetheless, this decision, along with many equally difficult ones in other areas, ranging from negligence to antitrust, was given to a jury.[9] As long as this is our system, we should try to make it work.

The trial judge should limit the psychiatrists' use of medical labels—schizophrenia, neurosis, etc. It would be undesirable, as well as difficult, to eliminate completely all medical labels, since they sometimes provide a convenient and meaningful method of communication. But the trial judge should ensure that their meaning is explained to the jury and, as much as possible,

---

9. The phrase "mental disease or defect" has been criticized for not giving enough guidance to the jury. In this regard the phrase is similar to other conclusory labels in the law. For example, "negligence" is a vague label given content primarily by the conclusions for which it stands. A person is "negligent" if he is at "fault" (blameworthy?), or if he has not exercised "due care," or if he has not met some standard of reasonable conduct. We are comfortable with a concept like negligence because we understand that it is a conclusion based on other considerations. Similarly, we can accept the term "mental disease or defect" if we understand what it represents.

that they are explained in a way which relates their meaning to the defendant.[10]

The problem with labels, such as, "product" and "mental disease or defect," is even more difficult. Because these labels are employed in the legal test for responsibility, there is a danger that the psychiatric witness will view them as a legal-moral rather than a medical matter. There are two possible solutions. We could simply prohibit testimony in terms of "product" and "mental disease or defect." Or we could clearly instruct the expert to stick to medical judgments and leave legal-moral judgments to the jury.

A strong minority of this court has consistently advocated that psychiatrists be prohibited from testifying whether the alleged offense was the "product" of mental illness, since this is part of the ultimate issue to be decided by the jury.[11] We now adopt that view.

. . .

10. "A diagnosis of the defendant's condition, while involving conclusions of a kind, is admissible even though a jury is not bound by a diagnosis or a particular diagnostic label on a mental disorder. The jury wants and needs help from the expert, but it does not help a jury of laymen to be told of a diagnosis limited to the esoteric and swiftly changing vocabulary of psychiatry. Every technical description ought to be 'translated' in terms of 'what I mean by this,' followed by a down-to-earth concrete explanation in terms which convey meaning to laymen. A psychiatrist who gives a jury a diagnosis, for example, of 'psychoneurotic reaction, obsessive compulsive type' and fails to explain fully what this means, would contribute more to society if he were permitted to stay at his hospital post taking care of patients.

. . .

"It is at this point where trial counsel's responsibility comes into play. It is for him to elicit, either by direct or cross-examination, 'the material from which [the psychiatric] opinion is fashioned' and the steps by which the raw material of the tests, observations and other data led to the diagnosis and opinion. The value of an expert opinion can rise no higher than the facts and premises on which it is based. But it is only a rare medical witness who is so skilled in the forensic art that he can present testimony adequately even where there is inept interrogation by counsel. If trial counsel fail in their role the trial judge would be well advised to urge them, out of the presence of the jury, to explore and develop the subject so that the witness can translate all of his medical observations to the jury. This is the area in which the deterioration if not breakdown of the trials of these 'insanity' cases is to a large extent the fault of the trial counsel. If lawyers want the views of the experts to be accepted by lay jurors their first duty is to draw out expert testimony in terms which are intelligible and meaningful." Campbell v.

United States, 113 U.S.App.D.C. 260 at 277–278, 307 F.2d 597 at 614–615 (1962) (Burger, J., dissenting).

11. "In a number of cases in this court appellants have protested the 'trial by label' especially the practice of allowing a psychiatrist to tell the jury that the defendant's act, for which he is on trial, is *not* the 'product' of mental disease. The reason is obvious: when a qualified expert psychiatrist with the mantle of professional standing, and medical degrees in a high calling, tells a jury that the act charged is *not* the 'product' of any 'mental disease' he is stating a conclusion *that the defendant ought to be found guilty.* As I view it, no witness, expert or otherwise, should ever be allowed to state that conclusion to a jury. . . .

"I suggest also that if contending counsel and the psychiatrists are forbidden to take the 'easy way' by testifying on the causal connection in terms of 'product' this very fact will *compel* compliance with our unanimous opinion in Carter. . . .

"The pernicious practice of allowing the conclusion opinions on 'product' by experts, apart from its other vices, has operated to *narrow* and constrict the scope of psychiatric testimony when what we want is to *broaden* that scope. . . . The function of the psychiatrist is not to try to tell the jurors what verdict they should render but rather to portray, as fully and completely as possible, the mental and emotional makeup of the defendant, how his emotional and intellectual processes work and how they affected his capacity to control his conduct, both generally and in the specific situation surrounding the crime charged. They should try to portray the 'inner man' as best they can without fanciful speculation. The opinions must be based on 'reasonable medical certainty' which has always been the legal standard for expert medical opinions. The experts cannot be expected to know all these answers as to every defen-

The term "product" has no clinical significance for psychiatrists. Thus there is no justification for permitting psychiatrists to testify on the ultimate issue. Psychiatrists should explain how defendant's disease or defect relates to his alleged offense, that is, how the development, adaptation and functioning of defendant's behavioral processes may have influenced his conduct. But psychiatrists should not speak directly in terms of "product," or even "result" or "cause."

It can be argued that psychiatrists should also be prohibited from testifying whether the defendant suffered from a "mental disease or defect," since this too is part of the ultimate issue. But unlike the term "product," the term "mental disease or defect" may have some clinical significance to the psychiatrist. Moreover, prohibition of testimony about "mental disease or defect" would not be a panacea. Other words and other concepts may similarly be transformed into labels. For example, in McDonald we spoke about "abnormal" conditions of the mind, about impairment of mental and emotional processes, and about control mechanisms. The transcript of this trial illustrates how easily these concepts can become slogans, hiding facts and representing nothing more than the witness's own conclusion about the defendant's criminal responsibility.

At least for now, rather than prohibit testimony on "mental disease or defect," we shall try to help the psychiatrists understand their role in court, and thus eliminate a fundamental cause of unsatisfactory expert testimony. A copy of the explanatory instruction to psychiatrists which we have set out in the Appendix should accompany all orders requiring mental examinations so that the psychiatrists will be advised of the kind of information they are expected to provide. To ensure that counsel and the jury are also so advised, the trial judge should give the explanatory instruction in open court to the first psychiatric witness immediately after he is qualified as an expert. It need not be repeated to later witnesses. Some of it will be repeated in the court's instruction to the jury at the end of the trial, but we think the jury should hear

dant but these are the areas in which they should be examined and cross-examined extensively. Only by doing this can we avoid the sterile, atrophying process of letting these trials continue to be contests of labels in which the prosecution strains to get at least one expert to say 'no disease' or 'no product' and defense strains for the opposing labels. The natural tendency of advocates is to stop as soon as they have made a record which will assure that they will get to the jury—or get a directed verdict. The ultimate responsibility—and power—to prevent witnesses from violating rules of evidence lies with judges." Campbell v. United States, 113 U.S.App.D.C. at 276–77, 307 F.2d at 613–614 (Burger, J., dissenting).

. . .

There are many cases in this jurisdiction holding that an expert cannot testify on the ultimate issue before the jury.... There are cases to the contrary, but they seem to be based on the theory that the conclusion was simply a summary of the underlying facts.... A conclusion about "product" is not merely a summary of the underlying medical psychological and social facts. It is an opinion on whether or not the defendant should be found guilty. "... [T]here is a kind of statement by the witness which amounts to little more than an expression of his belief as to how the case should be decided.... Such extreme expressions as these all courts, it is believed, would exclude. [Citing cases.] There is no necessity for such evidence, and to receive it would tend to suggest that the judge and jury may shift responsibility for decision to the witnesses." McCormick, Evidence 25 (1954). According to McCormick, even Dean Wigmore, the leading proponent of opinion testimony, would exclude this kind of conclusion, Id. at 26.

If testimony about "product" were prohibited, then, the reason would not simply be that it is part of the ultimate conclusion but that it is a legal and moral conclusion about which psychiatrists and other experts have no more expertise than jurors. See Suarez, A Critique of the Psychiatrist's Role as Expert Witness, 12 Jo.For.Sci. 172, 178 (1967).

it in full and *before* the testimony....[12]

. . .

[Appendix and concurring opinion of Judge Fahy omitted.]

Korn, Law, Fact and Science in the Courts

66 Colum.L.Rev. 1080, 1095–97 (1966).[1]

. . .

A rule of law may require reference to science either because it expressly uses a scientific concept as part of the definition of the situations it means to embrace, or because it makes material a subject that has been the object of special study by science even though the rule is not itself framed in scientific terms. Illustrative of the first type of rule are prohibitions against the sale of "hallucinogenic drugs" and the familiar body of antitrust doctrine framed in terms of "monopoly" and "competition." The second type includes, for example, the nature and extent of plaintiff's injuries as the measure of damages in personal injury suits and the many rules that turn upon physical or mental abnormality, such as whether a person is "permanently disabled," "competent" to make a will, or responsible for criminal behavior. Thus, whether the test of criminal responsibility is framed in terms of "mental disease or defect" or in terms of capacity to know "right from wrong," adjudication would proceed foolishly if it failed to seek guidance from the discipline that makes abnormal mental condition its special province of study.

Use of a generalized scientific concept as part of a legal rule or standard presumptively fosters correct and consistent adjudication. The function of the rule of law is, after all, to define in general terms the various real world phenomena that the rule means to embrace. Much of the work of scientists consists in carefully observing, classifying, and naming these same phenomena. A rule incorporating the scientist's conceptual scheme takes advantage of this endeavor and should therefore facilitate more accurate identification of the particular phenomena sought to be covered than ordinary legal standards, such as "due care," "consideration," or "holder in due course."

But the extent of this advantage depends mainly on two factors: first, the degree to which the legal rule adopts the scientific knowledge simpliciter or skews it with value and policy considerations; and, second, the sophistication of the science itself in classifying the phenomena within its scope and verifying the existence of particular instances of a class. For example, adjudication under a law prohibiting the sale of "hallucinogenic" drugs or foods that are "adulterated" or "decomposed" could be expected to be effective. With regard to the first factor, the rule would probably be construed to accept the scientist's definitions unqualifiedly, since in these instances the purposes of law and

---

12. The writer of this opinion would make the following observations for himself. It may be that this instruction will not significantly improve the adjudication of criminal responsibility. Then we may be forced to consider an absolute prohibition on the use of conclusory legal labels. Or it may be that psychiatry and the other social and behavioral sciences cannot provide sufficient data relevant to a determination of criminal responsibility no matter what our rules of evidence are. If so, we may be forced to eliminate the insanity defense altogether, or refashion it in a way which is not tied so tightly to the medical model.... But at least we will be able to make that decision on the basis of an informed experience. For now the writer is content to join the court in this first step.

1. Footnotes omitted. Copyright © 1966 by The Directors of the Columbia Law Review Assoc., Inc. All Rights Reserved. Reprinted by permission.

science are in accord. In terms of the second factor, the scientist either has already identified the particulars that the standard embraces or has available techniques for doing so with a high degree of precision.

At the other extreme, on both counts, is a standard such as "substantially lessening competition." First, it is clear that the legal concept is intended to incorporate social values and purposes quite independently of whatever definition economists may choose to give the term. Second, even if this were not the case, the degree of consensus among economists themselves as to what the standard embraces would be fairly low: analogous scientific concepts are themselves highly intellectualized and abstract; differences in economic theory aggravate the difficulty of verifying their existence empirically by reference to external phenomena; and the economist's techniques for such empirical verification are in any event less precise than, say, the chemist's in dealing with "adulterated" or "decomposed" food. Similar difficulties are shared by the sciences that study human behavior, and most acutely by those concerned with mental and emotional conditions.

. . .

NOTE ON EXPERT TESTIMONY IN OBSCENITY CASES

Obscenity cases make ideally challenging occasions for analyzing the nature and function of expert testimony. This is because of the difficult and indefinite nature of the substantive law standards involved. In Roth v. United States, 354 U.S. 476, 489 (1957), the Supreme Court propounded as the constitutional test for obscenity "whether to the average person, applying contemporary standards, the dominant theme of the material taken as a whole appeals to the prurient interest." Obscenity thus defined was held not to be speech protected by the First Amendment. The constitutional test was further elaborated in Miller v. California, 413 U.S. 15, 24 (1973): "The basic guidelines for the trier of fact must be: (a) whether 'the average person, applying contemporary community standards' would find that the work, taken as a whole, appeals to the prurient interest ... (b) whether the work depicts or describes, in a patently offensive way, sexual conduct specifically defined by the applicable state law, and (c) whether the work, taken as a whole, lacks serious literary, artistic, political, or scientific value." Regarding the community standards referred to in the first "guideline," the Court held in Miller and other decisions that a state need not look to a national standard, but may define an obscenity offense in terms of "contemporary community standards" without further specification, or it may define it in more precise geographical terms, e.g., state-wide. The Court has not yet decided whether a state may adopt a national standard if it wishes. Miller v. California, 413 U.S. 15, 31 (1973); Jenkins v. Georgia, 418 U.S. 153, 157 (1974); Smith v. United States, 431 U.S. 291, 304 n. 11 (1977). In Pope v. Illinois, 481 U.S. 497, 500–01 (1987), the Court held regarding the third "guideline"—that relating to value—that "[t]he proper inquiry is not whether an ordinary member of any given community would find serious literary, artistic, political, or scientific value in allegedly obscene material, but whether a reasonable person would find such value in the material, taken as a whole."

In his concurring opinion in Smith v. California, 361 U.S. 147, 160–61, 164–67 (1959), Justice Frankfurter discussed the use of expert testimony in obscenity cases.

The second constitutional infirmity urged by appellant is the exclusion of appropriately offered testimony through duly qualified witnesses regarding the prevailing literary standards and the literary and moral criteria by which books relevantly comparable to the book in controversy are deemed not obscene. This exclusion deprived the appellant, such is the claim, of important relevant testimony bearing on the issue of obscenity and therefore restricted him in making his defense. The appellant's ultimate contention is that the questioned book is not obscene and that a bookseller's possession of it could not be forbidden.

. . .

The uncertainties pertaining to the scope of scienter requisite for an obscenity prosecution and the speculative proof that the issue is likely to entail, are considerations that reinforce the right of one charged with obscenity—a right implicit in the very nature of the legal concept of obscenity—to enlighten the judgment of the tribunal, be it the jury or as in this case the judge, regarding the prevailing literary and moral community standards and to do so through qualified experts. It is immaterial whether the basis of the exclusion of such testimony is irrelevance, or the incompetence of experts to testify to such matters. The two reasons coalesce, for community standards or the psychological or physiological consequences of questioned literature can as a matter of fact hardly be established except through experts. Therefore, to exclude such expert testimony is in effect to exclude as irrelevant evidence that goes to the very essence of the defense and therefore to the constitutional safeguards of due process. The determination of obscenity no doubt rests with judge or jury. Of course the testimony of experts would not displace judge or jury in determining the ultimate question whether the particular book is obscene, any more than the testimony of experts relating to the state of the art in patent suits determines the patentability of a controverted device.

There is no external measuring rod for obscenity. Neither, on the other hand, is its ascertainment a merely subjective reflection of the taste or moral outlook of individual jurors or individual judges. Since the law through its functionaries is "applying contemporary community standards" in determining what constitutes obscenity, Roth v. United States, 354 U.S. 476, 489, 77 S.Ct. 1304, . . . it surely must be deemed rational, and therefore relevant to the issue of obscenity, to allow light to be shed on what those "contemporary community standards" are. Their interpretation ought not to depend solely on the necessarily limited, hit-or-miss, subjective view of what they are believed to be by the individual juror or judge. It bears repetition that the determination of obscenity is for juror or judge not on the basis of his personal upbringing or restricted reflection or particular experience of life, but on the basis of "contemporary community standards." . . . Unless we disbelieve that the literary, psychological or moral standards of a community can be made fruitful and illuminating subjects of inquiry by those who give their life to such inquiries, it was violative of "due process" to exclude the constitutionally relevant evidence proffered in this case. . . . For the reasons I have indicated, I would make the right to introduce such evidence a requirement of due process in obscenity prosecutions.

Justice Harlan addressed the same subject in his concurring and dissenting opinion, id. at 171–72.[1]

I am also not persuaded that the ordinance in question was unconstitutionally applied in this instance merely because of the state court's

_____

1. Footnotes omitted.

refusal to admit expert testimony. I agree with my brother Frankfurter that the trier of an obscenity case must take into account "contemporary community standards," Roth v. United States, 354 U.S. 476, 489, 77 S.Ct. 1304, 1311.... This means that, regardless of the elements of the offense under state law, the Fourteenth Amendment does not permit a conviction such as was obtained here unless the work complained of is found substantially to exceed the limits of candor set by contemporary community standards. The community cannot, where liberty of speech and press are at issue, condemn that which it generally tolerates. This being so, it follows that due process ... requires a State to allow a litigant in some manner to introduce proof on this score. While a State is not debarred from regarding the trier of fact as the embodiment of community standards, competent to judge a challenged work against those standards, it is not privileged to rebuff *all* efforts to enlighten or persuade the trier.

However, I would not hold that any particular kind of evidence must be admitted, specifically, that the Constitution requires that oral opinion testimony by experts be heard. There are other ways in which proof can be made, as this very case demonstrates. Appellant attempted to compare the contents of the work with that of other allegedly similar publications which were openly published, sold and purchased, and which received wide general acceptance. Where there is a variety of means, even though it may be considered that expert testimony is the most convenient and practicable method of proof, I think it is going too far to say that such a method is constitutionally compelled, and that a State may not conclude, for reasons responsive to its traditional doctrines of evidence law, that the issue of community standards may not be the subject of expert testimony. I know of no case where this Court, on constitutional grounds, has required a State to sanction a particular mode of proof.

In my opinion this conviction is fatally defective in that the trial judge, as I read the record, turned aside *every* attempt by appellant to introduce evidence bearing on community standards. The exclusionary rulings were not limited to offered expert testimony. This had the effect of depriving appellant of the opportunity to offer any proof on a constitutionally relevant issue....

In Paris Adult Theatre I v. Slaton, 413 U.S. 49, 56 & n. 6 (1973), the Court held that generally in obscenity cases expert testimony is not required.

Nor was it error to fail to require "expert" affirmative evidence that the materials were obscene when the materials themselves were actually placed in evidence.

This is not a subject that lends itself to the traditional use of expert testimony. Such testimony is usually admitted for the purpose of explaining to lay jurors what they otherwise could not understand.... No such assistance is needed by jurors in obscenity cases; indeed the "expert witness" practices employed in these cases have often made a mockery out of the otherwise sound concept of expert testimony.... We reserve judgment, however, on the extreme case, not presented here, where contested materials are directed at such a bizarre deviant group that the experience of the trier-of-fact would be plainly inadequate to judge whether the material appeals to the prurient interest....

But see Luke Records, Inc. v. Navarro, 960 F.2d 134, 139 (11th Cir.), cert. denied, 506 U.S. 1022 (1992): Declaratory judgment that rap recording had no artistic value reversed because of absence of expert testimony.

Should public opinion surveys be admissible in obscenity cases? "To date, there has been no attempt to accumulate empirical data concerning national standards; nor is it clear that this could ever satisfactorily be done.... This statement is based on a limited survey of selected sociologists and professors of law who have had considerable acquaintance with the problem." Note, The Use of Expert Testimony in Obscenity Litigation, 1965 Wis.L.Rev. 113, 120. In Hamling v. United States, 418 U.S. 87, 108–09 (1974), the Court said it was possibly error, but not harmful, to exclude a defense witness who had made a survey of local community standards. See St. John v. North Carolina Parole Comm'n, 764 F.Supp. 403, 408–12 (W.D.N.C.1991), aff'd, 953 F.2d 639 (4th Cir.1992), cert. denied, 506 U.S. 825 (1992), on the difficulty of designing an admissible survey of whether material appeals to prurient interest or is patently offensive to the average person in the community.

See, generally, Kalven, The Metaphysics of the Law of Obscenity, 1960 Sup.Ct.Rev. 1, 38–40; Lockhart and McClure, Censorship of Obscenity: The Developing Constitutional Standards, 45 Minn.L.Rev. 5, 95–99 (1960); Frank, Obscenity: Some Problems in Values and the Use of Experts, 41 Wash.L.Rev. 631 (1966); Stern, Toward a Rationale for the Use of Expert Testimony in Obscenity Litigation, 20 Case–W.Res.L.Rev. 527 (1969). See infra pp. 1272–73 on the judicial notice aspect of these problems.

United States v. Scop

United States Court of Appeals, Second Circuit, 1988.
846 F.2d 135.

■ WINTER, CIRCUIT JUDGE:

In 1980 and 1981, appellants Alan Scop, Raphael Bloom, Herbert Stone and Jack Ringer were variously involved in the initial offering and subsequent trading of the stock of an automobile dealership. Each was indicted for mail fraud in violation of 18 U.S.C. § 1341 (1982), securities fraud in violation of Section 10(b) of the Securities Exchange Act of 1934, 15 U.S.C. § 78j(b) (1982), and conspiracy to commit those offenses in violation of 18 U.S.C. § 371 (1982).[1] Appellants Bloom and Stone were also charged with making false declarations before a grand jury in violation of 18 U.S.C. § 1623 (1982). After a jury trial before Judge Pollack, appellants were convicted on all counts.

Several investors in the dealership's stock testified at trial, but the government's case was based primarily upon the testimony of a co-conspirator who testified pursuant to a plea agreement and upon that of a government investigator who testified as an expert witness. On appeal, appellants argue inter alia that their mail fraud, securities fraud and conspiracy convictions are time-barred and that the government's expert witness was wrongly allowed to give

---

1. The mail fraud statute, 18 U.S.C. § 1341, prohibits the use of the mails for the purpose of executing "any scheme or artifice to defraud." Section 10(b), 15 U.S.C. § 78j(b), outlaws the use of "any manipulative or deceptive device or contrivance in contravention" of rules promulgated by the Securities and Exchange Commission in connection with the purchase and sale of securities. The relevant SEC rule is Rule 10b–5, 17 C.F.R. § 240.10b–5 (1987), which makes unlawful the use of "manipulative and deceptive devices" in connection with the purchase and sale of any securities. "Manipulative and deceptive devices" are defined to include employing "any device, scheme, or artifice to defraud," making "any untrue statement of a material fact or ... omit[ting] to state a material fact necessary in order to make the statements made, in the light of the circumstances under which they are made, not misleading," or engaging "in any act, practice or course of business which operates or would operate as a fraud or deceit upon any person." [Footnote of the court.]

opinions that embodied legal conclusions and were based upon his assessment of the credibility of the testimony of other witnesses. Because we believe that the expert witness's opinions were inadmissible, we reverse all but the false-declaration convictions.

A. The Scheme

We of course view the evidence in the light most favorable to the government. In 1979, Gary Brustein, a manager of a teenage discotheque, was approached by Ringer about financing the teenage discotheque through a public offering of stock. Brustein, however, was more interested in the automobile business than in the discotheque. He suggested to Ringer that they confer with Keith Sheldon, an old friend in the car business, about forming a new company, European Auto Classics ("EAC"), to sell foreign antique and classic cars to members of the affluent community of Great Neck, Long Island.

Money for the venture was to come from a public offering of stock in the new company. Because Brustein and Sheldon knew little about stock offerings or running a business, the decisions concerning the public offering and the start-up of the company were made by Ringer. Ringer brought in Martin Klein as vice-president to provide business experience while Ringer served as general manager, a job for which he was paid a weekly salary of about $275 and given the use of an automobile. Ringer selected the lawyer to handle the preparation and filing of the offering circular and other documents needed to take the company public. Because Ringer had "problems in the past with the SEC," however, these documents made no mention of his involvement. Finally, Ringer secured the services of Amfco Securities and Norbay Securities as co-underwriters for the public offering. Ringer was associated with Amfco, whose president and sole broker was Scop. Stone was a broker at Norbay.

Meanwhile, EAC leased a showroom and began renovating it, largely with borrowed money. In February 1980, Amfco and Norbay opened the public offering of fifty million shares of EAC stock at one cent per share. When the offering closed on April 3, 1980, all fifty million shares had been sold, and EAC had achieved its goal of a total initial financing of $500,000.

As participants in the EAC public offering, Ringer, Scop and Stone were prohibited from purchasing any of the company's stock during the public offering period by SEC Rule 10b–6, 17 C.F.R. § 240.10b–6 (1987). Nevertheless, Ringer and Scop attempted to circumvent this prohibition by the use of accounts in other names. For example, Ringer had his accounts in the name of his wife, brother-in-law and some friends, while Scop used the names of friends.

After the close of the public offering, EAC's stock was traded on the over-the-counter market through several brokerage firms acting as "market makers" willing to buy or sell EAC stock on a continuing basis. These included Amfco, Norbay and Jay W. Kaufmann & Co., a securities firm through which Bloom traded in the stock.

By May 1980, the price of the stock reached four cents per share although EAC had operated in the red from its inception. Ringer met that month with Sam Sarcinelli, later a key government witness, at a hotel in New York. At the time he testified, Sarcinelli had three previous felony convictions for tax, narcotics and firearms violations. He also had plead guilty to two counts of the indictment in the present case and had agreed to testify against the other defendants in return for the government's recommendation that his sentence be concurrent with those he was already serving. It came out at trial that in the early 1970's Sarcinelli had been barred by the SEC from dealing in securities and that he had lied under oath to the SEC in 1980

At the time of the meeting with Ringer, Sarcinelli was involved in buying and selling stocks and cocaine. By all appearances he was a wealthy man, and Ringer originally approached him to obtain a loan, offering stock in EAC and other companies as collateral. According to Sarcinelli's testimony, the idea of a loan was soon superseded by a plan in which Sarcinelli would aid Ringer, Scop and Stone in "working" the EAC stock, artificially moving its price to a target of fifteen cents per share by means of a series of controlled purchases and sales at successively higher prices.

Sarcinelli also testified about another meeting with Ringer, Brustein and some of Sarcinelli's associates in a Los Angeles hotel in July 1980, at which the artificial inflation of the share price and a proposed misleading letter to EAC's stockholders concerning the company's prospects were discussed. According to Sarcinelli, he brought Bloom into the scheme a few weeks later.

Sarcinelli and his associates soon began bringing in customers for the stock and setting up "matched orders" or "matched trades" to be executed by Scop, Stone and Bloom. These "matched orders" involved Sarcinelli covering "both sides" of a transaction by providing the buyer, seller and price. Nevertheless, the stock price did not move as he had expected, reaching a price of no more than six cents per share. By late August or early September, Sarcinelli began to suspect that one of his partners was "back dooring" him by selling the stock on the open market, thereby undermining the scheme to control the stock's price. Sarcinelli severed all involvement in the scheme in November 1980.

After Sarcinelli withdrew, attempts to inflate the price of the stock appear to have ceased, and the stock generally declined, eventually becoming worthless. Nevertheless, after July 22, 1981, the critical date for purposes of the statute of limitations, defendants' nominees sold shares of EAC stock at prices that were still higher than what they had paid, defendants mailed stock certificates for purchases made in the previous year, and Bloom and Stone told nervous customers to hold on to their shares. Promised financial information on the company was never sent to shareholders despite requests.

B. Whitten's Expert Testimony

The government called Stanley Whitten, the chief investigator for the SEC regional office in Chicago, as its final witness. Whitten had been a stockbroker for eight years prior to joining the SEC as an investigator in its Enforcement Division in 1974. He had spent over one thousand hours during four years of working on the present case and had interviewed approximately seventy witnesses. He had also assisted in the preparation of the indictment.

Whitten did not testify at trial as a witness with personal knowledge of relevant events. Claiming to be an expert in securities trading practices, he purported to base his testimony not on information obtained from his four-year investigation, but solely on the testimony and documentary evidence introduced at trial.

Whitten was allowed to answer over defense objections a question concerning his opinion as to whether there was a scheme to defraud investors in EAC stock from 1979 to 1982. He answered, "It is my opinion that the stock of European Auto Classics was manipulated and that certain individuals were active participants and material participants in the manipulation of that stock. And that these individuals engaged in a manipulative and fraudulent scheme in furtherance of that manipulation." Whitten consciously used the same formulation throughout his testimony. For example, when asked to name the "participants" in the scheme and the roles that they played, he corrected himself in mid-sentence to include the same elements in his answer: "I believe that the role at the inception, in terms of the participants and the manipulation—excuse me, the fraudulent manipulative practices that were engaged in...." He also repeatedly described the defendants as "active participants" and "material participants" in the manipulation of EAC stock. On cross-examination Whitten acknowledged that his positive assessment of the testimony of the government's witnesses, including Sarcinelli, was a basis for his opinions.

. . .

We agree with defendants that Whitten's repeated statements embodying legal conclusions exceeded the permissible scope of opinion testimony under the Federal Rules of Evidence. It is true that Fed.R.Evid. 704 states that "testimony in the form of an opinion or inference otherwise admissible is not objectionable because it embraces an ultimate issue to be decided by the trier of fact." However, Rule 704 was not intended to allow experts to offer opinions embodying legal conclusions....

. . .

Had Whitten merely testified that controlled buying and selling of the kind alleged here can create artificial price levels to lure outside investors, no sustainable objection could have been made. Instead, however, Whitten made no attempt to couch the opinion testimony at issue in even conclusory factual statements but drew directly upon the language of the statute and accompanying regulations concerning "manipulation" and "fraud". See supra note 1. In essence, his opinions were legal conclusions that were highly prejudicial and went well beyond his province as an expert in securities trading. Moreover, because his opinions were calculated to "invade the province of the court to determine the applicable law and to instruct the jury as to that law," FAA v. Landy, 705 F.2d 624, 632 (2d Cir.), cert. denied, 464 U.S. 895 ... (1983) they could not have been helpful to the jury in carrying out its legitimate functions. "The admission of such testimony would give the appearance that the court was shifting to witnesses the responsibility to decide the case." Marx & Co. v. Diners' Club, Inc., 550 F.2d 505, 510 (2d Cir.) (citation omitted), cert. denied, 434 U.S. 861 ... (1977). "It is not for witnesses to instruct the jury as to applicable principles of law, but for the judge." Id. at 509–10; see also Torres v. County of Oakland, 758 F.2d 147, 150 (6th Cir.1985) ("The problem with testimony containing a legal conclusion is in conveying the witness' unexpressed, and perhaps erroneous, legal standards to the jury."); McCormick on Evidence § 12 (3d ed. 1984); 3 J. Weinstein & M. Berger, Weinstein's Evidence § 704[02] (1987); ABA Section of Litigation, Emerging Problems under the Federal Rules of Evidence, 217–29 (1983).

"Manipulation," "scheme to defraud," and "fraud" are not self-defining terms but rather have been the subject of diverse judicial interpretations....

The government argues, however, that Whitten's testimony was proper under three of our recent decisions upholding opinion testimony by government investigators. In United States v. Carson, 702 F.2d 351, 369–70 (2d Cir.), cert. denied, 462 U.S. 1108 ... (1983), two Drug Enforcement Agency agents were allowed to testify concerning their opinion that conduct they observed involved a narcotics transaction. Because "the clandestine manner in which drugs are bought and sold[ ]is unlikely to be within the knowledge of the average layman," id., the conclusions of the agents based on their years of experience were held admissible under Rule 702. In United States v. Young, 745 F.2d 733, 760–61 (2d Cir.1984), cert. denied, 470 U.S. 1084 ... (1985), a police detective was allowed to testify, based on his observations, that he believed a narcotics transaction had taken place. In the same case, a DEA agent testifying as an expert witness was permitted to describe a typical chain of heroin distribution, including the characteristics and operating methods of a heroin "mill." The district judge instructed the jury that this general description was unrelated to the facts or circumstances of the particular case. The agent was then allowed to testify that what he found in defendant's apartment was precisely what he would have expected to find in a heroin "mill." Id. at 761. In United States v. Brown, 776 F.2d 397, 400 (2d Cir.1985), cert. denied, 475 U.S. 1141 . . . (1986), a police officer testifying as an expert was permitted to describe a typical drug buy in Harlem, including the role of the "steerer." He was then permitted to testify over objection that the defendant acted as a "steerer" in a transaction the officer had observed.

In each of these cases, we upheld the convictions. We noted in Brown, however, that "there is something rather offensive in allowing an investigating officer to testify not simply that a certain pattern of conduct is often found in narcotics cases, leaving it for the jury to determine whether the defendant's conduct fits the pattern, but also that such conduct fitted the pattern." Id. at 401. Nevertheless, the Advisory Committee's Note to Rule 704 cautions against limiting experts to "might or could" formulations when they are prepared to say "did," and Carson, Young and Brown appear to be consistent with that admonition. Whether these results are desirable is not for us to say in light of the Rules' generally liberated approach to expert testimony.

None of our prior cases, however, has allowed testimony similar to Whitten's repeated use of statutory and regulatory language indicating guilt. For example, telling the jury that a defendant acted as a "steerer" or participated in a narcotics transaction differs from opining that the defendant "possessed narcotics, to wit, heroin, with the intent to sell," or "aided and abetted the possession of heroin with intent to sell," the functional equivalent of Whitten's testimony in a drug case. It is precisely this distinction, between ultimate factual conclusions that are dispositive of particular issues if believed, e.g., medical causation, and "inadequately explored legal criteria," that is drawn by the Advisory Committee's Note.

. . .

All convictions on counts one through thirteen are therefore reversed. . . .

[Concurring opinions omitted.]

NOTES

1.   Korn, Law, Fact and Science in the Courts, 66 Colum.L.Rev. 1080, 1100–01 (1966):

> When, on the other hand, the question involves application of a mixed "legal-scientific" concept, application of the "ultimate issue" doctrine may be justified; then it is not simply a denial to the trier of fact of an informed opinion but may reflect a considered judgment that the expert's view regarding the inferential jump between the scientific and the legal conception is not wanted. The expert's view may be unwanted, for example, because the court feels that it would unduly influence the jury's exercise of policy or value judgment, or because some determinants of the legal standard that are not at all referable to science cannot be separated from decision of the ultimate issue, or because decision of that issue involves elaboration of the standard—a form of lawmaking which the court may choose to perform unaided. . . . The "ultimate issue" doctrine should probably have no place at all in cases in which the requisite inferences call

for purely scientific knowledge. When issues involve the application of mixed "legal-scientific" concepts, the mechanical operation of the doctrine should give way to direct inquiry about when it is desirable to have the expert in his testimony bridge the gap between scientific and legal conception; when to have the jury do so unassisted by either expert or court; and when to have the court narrow the gap by elaborating to some extent the application of the rule of law to the particulars of the case.

2. United States v. Hearst, 563 F.2d 1331, 1351–52 (9th Cir.1977), cert. denied, 435 U.S. 1000 (1978): Prosecution for bank robbery in which defendant claimed she had acted under duress:

> As her final argument, appellant contends that the district court erred in permitting the government's experts to express their opinions on the "ultimate issues" of duress and voluntariness. In response to a question from the prosecutor, one expert, Dr. Fort, gave as his opinion that appellant "did not perform the bank robbery because she was in fear of her life. She did it as a voluntary member of the SLA." The other expert, Dr. Kozol, stated: "I think she entered that bank voluntarily in order to participate in the robbing of that bank. This was an act of her own free will."

> Fed.R.Evid. 704 states the law regarding expert opinion testimony on ultimate issues. It provides:

>> Testimony in the form of an opinion or inference otherwise admissible is *not objectionable* because it embraces an ultimate issue to be decided by the trier of fact.

(Emphasis added.) Appellant makes two arguments in an effort to establish that Rule 704 does not render Fort's and Kozol's opinions admissible. First, she contends that those opinions were not "otherwise admissible" within the meaning of Rule 704 because Fort and Kozol were qualified to testify only within the realm of their expertise, psychology and psychiatry. She argues that because the ultimate issues of duress and voluntariness are "commonsense" concepts that combine "moral and empirical considerations with a legal conclusion," the doctors' testimony on those issues went beyond their expertise and became merely statements of "personal morality."

> We find this argument without merit. The doctors' discipline is concerned with both the motives of human conduct and the variety of behavioral responses to physical, emotional and mental stimuli. Such matters were critical to the defense raised by appellant. She conceded as much by calling three expert witnesses and building her defense on their testimony regarding the effects of the captors' coercion on her behavior and mental state. Once it is conceded that experts in psychology and psychiatry can be of help to a jury faced with a defense such as appellant raised, we see no basis in this case for limiting their opinions to subsidiary issues and prohibiting them from opining whether appellant entered and robbed the bank voluntarily or under duress.

> Appellant constructs her second argument regarding the applicability of Rule 704 on a portion of the Advisory Committee's note on that rule:

>> The abolition of the ultimate issue rule does not lower the bars so as to admit all opinions.... [Rules 403, 701, and 702] also stand ready to exclude opinions phrased in terms of inadequately explored legal criteria. Thus the question, "Did T have capacity to make a will?" would be excluded, while the question, "Did T have sufficient mental

capacity to know the nature and extent of his property and the natural objects of his bounty and to formulate a rational scheme of distribution?" would be allowed.

Appellant contends that the question, "Did appellant voluntarily rob the bank?" is legally and conceptually identical to the question, "Did T have capacity to make a will?" thus requiring exclusion of the question and the opinion it elicited.

We disagree. The Advisory Committee's phrase "inadequately explored legal criteria" refers to terminology, the meaning of which is not reasonably clear to laymen. The term "capacity to make a will" is an example of that type of terminology because the average layman would not know that it encompasses the ability, first, to know the nature and extent of one's property, second, to identify the natural objects of one's bounty, and third, to formulate a rational plan of distribution. The terms "voluntarily rob a bank" or "act under fear of death or grave bodily harm" do not suffer from that same disability. The average layman would understand those terms and ascribe to them essentially the same meaning intended by the expert witness. Rejecting all of appellant's arguments on this issue, we conclude that the opinions of Kozol and Fort were properly admitted under Fed. R.Evid. 704.

We are reinforced in this conclusion by our review of the testimony of appellant's expert witnesses. They repeatedly made statements on and references to the "ultimate issues" of coercion, duress and voluntariness. In their testimony on direct examination, for example, they stated that she "was coerced into doing" the bank robbery and that "she complied with everything they [her captors] told her to do." Significantly, this testimony came after the government objected to it on the ground that such opinion testimony regarding coercion would usurp the jury's function. Appellant succeeded in having those objections overruled. The Kozol and Fort opinions elicited by the government were no more than responsive to the testimony of appellant's experts. Cf. McCormick on Evidence § 57, at p. 132–33 (2d ed. Cleary 1972); Teague v. United States, 268 F.2d 925, 927 (9th Cir.1959); Meyers v. United States, 147 F.2d 663, 667 (9th Cir.1945).[1]

3. 3–M Corp. McGhan Medical Reports Div. v. Brown, 475 So.2d 994, 997 (Fla.App.1985): Error to allow expert to testify product was defective; Riess v. A.O. Smith Corp. 556 A.2d 68 (Vt.1988): Error to allow expert to testify as to negligence and proximate cause. See also Steinbock et als., Expert Testimony on Proximate Cause, 41 Vand. L. Rev. 261 (1988).

Specht v. Jensen

United States Court of Appeals, Tenth Circuit, 1988.
853 F.2d 805, cert. denied, 488 U.S. 1008 (1989).

On rehearing en banc

■ JOHN P. MOORE, CIRCUIT JUDGE.

This case is before the court for rehearing en banc of one issue.... The question considered is whether Fed.R.Evid. 702 will permit an attorney, called as an expert witness, to state his views of the law which governs the verdict

---

1. Footnote omitted.

and opine whether defendants' conduct violated that law. We conclude the testimony was beyond the scope of the rule and thus inadmissible.

. . .

This case is an action for damages pursuant to 42 U.S.C. § 1983 grounded upon allegedly invalid searches of the plaintiffs' home and office. The underlying facts are set forth in the panel opinion and need not be restated here. What is germane for present consideration is whether defendants' conduct involved a "search" within the meaning of the Fourth Amendment and whether plaintiffs consented to the search were issues to be determined by the jury. [sic]

After testimony had been presented by the plaintiffs to establish the underlying facts, plaintiffs' counsel informed the court he wished to call an attorney who, after being given "a hypothetical of the facts that are in evidence in this case," would be asked if he believed that a search took place in the plaintiffs' home and business. Counsel stated that the witness would then be asked "based on the same facts in evidence whether he believed a consent search of either the business or the residence had been taken or undertaken." Finally, counsel proposed to ask the witness:

> [B]ased on his knowledge in these areas what would constitute a proper search, or the proper documents constituting or allowing a search and would expect that he would say as follows: That if there is no search warrant, if there is no consent, if there are no exigent circumstances, that the search is illegal per se. And that would be the extent of his testimony.[1]

Defense counsel objected to the propriety of the testimony, suggesting that the subject was beyond the scope of Rule 702. He argued, "here we have an issue involving whether or not this [testimony] intrudes on the province of this court in terms of the law." Counsel continued:

> [W]hat constitutes [a] reasonable or unreasonable search is a matter of law. How the jury applies that law to these facts is the province of the jury. But the law must be defined by the Court, not by an expert witness. . . . [I]n order for [the expert] to testify, he must first presume what the Court is going to instruct as to the law; and if he doesn't presume what he thinks the Court is going to instruct as to the law, he must . . . define his own definitions of the law; and that's where the intrusion of the Court is germane.

. . .

> Now, is [the expert] going to tell the jury what the law is upon which he is going to apply a hypothetical set of facts, or is this court going to tell the jury what the standard is?

Following those remarks, the court ruled:

> The Court: Although the Court doesn't have the precise instruction that it intends to give, the instruction would be along the line that the Constitu-

---

1. When questioned by the court whether the witness would be testifying on "an area of fact," plaintiffs' counsel did not directly answer but explained the witness would render opinions on whether there had been a search, whether there had been consent to the search, whether the consent was voluntary, and whether there were exigent circumstances to permit a warrantless search. Because the testimony was to be based upon hypothetical questions which assumed the existence of the essential facts, we believe there could be no "area of fact" involved. Thus, contrary to the plaintiffs' present assertions, counsel's representation clearly indicated the expert's testimony would cover only questions of law. [Footnotes of the court. Some footnotes omitted, others renumbered.]

tion protects citizens against unreasonable searches; that this means that a search warrant must be obtained from a judicial officer before a search can be made of a home or an office; that there are exceptions to this requirement, one being a search by consent. Where there is consent, the law enforcement officers may reasonably conduct a search to the extent of the consent.

With this ruling, the expert was allowed to testify, and he did so at length. On the basis of hypothetical questions tailored to reflect plaintiffs' view of the evidence, the expert concluded there had been no consent given, and illegal searches had occurred.

. . .

Our judgment must . . . be guided by consideration of whether the testimony of the attorney expert aided the jury in its determination of critical issues in this case. We must also consider, however, whether the expert encroached upon the trial court's authority to instruct the jury on the applicable law, for it is axiomatic that the judge is the sole arbiter of the law and its applicability. As one scholar noted:

> A witness cannot be allowed to give an opinion on a question of law. . . . In order to justify having courts resolve disputes between litigants, it must be posited as an a priori assumption that there is one, but only one, legal answer for every cognizable dispute. There being only one applicable legal rule for each dispute or issue, it requires only one spokesman of the law, who of course is the judge. . . . To allow anyone other than the judge to state the law would violate the basic concept. Reducing the proposition to a more practical level, it would be a waste of time if witnesses or counsel should duplicate the judge's statement of the law, and it would intolerably confound the jury to have it stated differently.

Stoebuck, Opinions on Ultimate Facts: Status, Trends, and a Note of Caution, 41 Den.L.Cent.J. 226, 237 (1964) (footnote omitted).

The concern that an expert should not be allowed to instruct the jury is also emphasized in Fed.R.Evid. 704, which allows witnesses to give their opinions on ultimate issues. In the advisory notes to this rule, the committee stated:

> The abolition of the ultimate issue rule does not lower the bars so as to admit all opinions. Under Rules 701 and 702, opinions must be helpful to the trier of fact, and Rule 403 provides for exclusion of evidence which wastes time. These provisions afford ample assurances against the admission of opinions which would merely tell the jury what result to reach, somewhat in the manner of the oath-helpers of an earlier day. They also stand ready to exclude opinions phrased in terms of inadequately explored legal criteria. Thus the question, "Did T have capacity to make a will?" would be excluded, while the question, "Did T have sufficient mental capacity to know the nature and extent of his property and the natural object of his bounty and to formulate a rational scheme of distribution?" would be allowed.

The committee's illustration establishes the starting point for analysis of admissibility by distinguishing between testimony on issues of law and testimony on ultimate facts. While testimony on ultimate facts is authorized under Rule 704, the committee's comments emphasize that testimony on ultimate questions of law is not favored. The basis for this distinction is that testimony on the ultimate factual questions aids the jury in reaching a verdict; testimony which articulates and applies the relevant law, however, circumvents the jury's decision-making function by telling it how to decide the case.

Following the advisory committee's comments, a number of federal circuits have held that an expert witness may not give an opinion on ultimate issues of law. In Marx & Co. v. Diners' Club, Inc., 550 F.2d 505 (2d Cir.), cert. denied, 434 U.S. 861 ... (1977), for example, the Second Circuit held it was error for the trial court to allow a lawyer to render his opinions on the legal obligations arising from a contract and on the legal significance of various facts in evidence. The court stated, "legal opinions as to the meaning of the contract terms at issue ... was testimony concerning matters outside [the witness's] area of expertise.... It is not for witnesses to instruct the jury as to the applicable principles of law, but for the judge." 550 F.2d at 509–10. Similarly, the Fourth Circuit decided the testimony of an attorney on the meaning and applicability of "domestic" (as opposed to foreign) law would be inadmissible as an invasion of the province of the judge.... Finally, in United States v. Zipkin, 729 F.2d 384 (6th Cir.1984), the Sixth Circuit reversed the trial court's decision to allow a bankruptcy judge to testify regarding his interpretation of the Bankruptcy Act and his own orders. "It is the function of the trial judge to determine the law of the case," the court stated. "It is impermissible to delegate that function to a jury through the submission of testimony on controlling legal principles." 729 F.2d at 387.

The courts in these decisions draw a clear line between permissible testimony on issues of fact and testimony that articulates the ultimate principles of law governing the deliberations of the jury. These courts have decried the latter kind of testimony as directing a verdict, rather than assisting the jury's understanding and weighing of the evidence. In keeping with these decisions, we conclude the expert in this case was improperly allowed to instruct the jury on how it should decide the case. The expert's testimony painstakingly developed over an entire day the conclusion that defendants violated plaintiffs' constitutional rights. He told the jury that warrantless searches are unlawful, that defendants committed a warrantless search on plaintiffs' property, and that the only applicable exception to the warrant requirement, search by consent, should not vindicate the defendants because no authorized person voluntarily consented to allow a search of the premises. He also stated that the acts of the private individual could be imputed to the accompanying police officer to constitute sufficient "state action" for a § 1983 claim. By permitting the jury to hear this array of legal conclusions touching upon nearly every element of the plaintiffs' burden of proof under § 1983, the trial court allowed the expert to supplant both the court's duty to set forth the law and the jury's ability to apply this law to the evidence.

Given the pervasive nature of this testimony, we cannot conclude its admission was harmless. There is a significant difference between an attorney who states his belief of what law should govern the case and any other expert witness. While other experts may aid a jury by rendering opinions on ultimate issues, our system reserves to the trial judge the role of adjudicating the law for the benefit of the jury. When an attorney is allowed to usurp that function, harm is manifest in at least two ways.

First, as articulated in Marx & Co. v. Diners' Club, Inc., the jury may believe the attorney-witness, who is presented to them imbued with all the mystique inherent in the title "expert," is more knowledgeable than the judge in a given area of the law.... Indeed, in this case, the expert's knowledge and experience was made known to the jury by both the court and counsel in a manner which gave his testimony an aura of trustworthiness and reliability.

Thus, there is a substantial danger the jury simply adopted the expert's conclusions rather than making its own decision. Notwithstanding any subsequent disclaimers by the witness that the court's instructions would govern, a practical and experienced view of the trial world strongly suggests the jury's deliberation was unduly prejudiced by the expert's testimony.[2]

Second, testimony on ultimate issues of law by the legal expert is inadmissible because it is detrimental to the trial process. If one side is allowed the right to call an attorney to define and apply the law, one can reasonably expect the other side to do the same. Given the proclivity of our brothers and sisters at the bar, it can be expected that both legal experts will differ over the principles applicable to the case. The potential is great that jurors will be confused by these differing opinions, and that confusion may be compounded by different instructions given by the court. . . . We therefore conclude the expert's testimony on the ultimate issues of law was not harmless as contended by the dissent.

. . .

The line we draw here is narrow. We do not exclude all testimony regarding legal issues. We recognize that a witness may refer to the law in expressing an opinion without that reference rendering the testimony inadmissible. Indeed, a witness may properly be called upon to aid the jury in understanding the facts in evidence even though reference to those facts is couched in legal terms. For example, we have previously held that a court may permit an expert to testify that a certain weapon had to be registered with the Bureau of Alcohol, Tobacco, and Firearms. United States v. Buchanan, 787 F.2d 477, 483 (10th Cir.1986). In that case, however, the witness did not invade the court's authority by discoursing broadly over the entire range of the applicable law. Rather, the expert's opinion focused on a specific question of fact.[3] See also Huddleston v. Herman & MacLean, 640 F.2d 534, 552 (5th Cir.1981), modified on other grounds, 459 U.S. 375 . . . (1983) (attorney expert in securities law allowed to testify that a statement in a prospectus was standard language for the issuance of a new security because this information helped the jury weigh the evidence of defendants' scienter); United States v. Garber, 607 F.2d 92 (5th Cir.1979) (trial court erred in refusing to let experts on income tax law testify regarding whether failure to report funds received for sale of blood plasma constituted income tax evasion).

These cases demonstrate that an expert's testimony is proper under Rule 702 if the expert does not attempt to define the legal parameters within which the jury must exercise its fact-finding function. However, when the purpose of testimony is to direct the jury's understanding of the legal standards upon which their verdict must be based, the testimony cannot be allowed. In no instance can a witness be permitted to define the law of the case.

Plaintiffs seek to avoid this conclusion by arguing the expert testimony here was no different from a medical expert testifying that specific conduct constitutes medical malpractice. We do not believe, however, there is an analog between the testimony of the medical expert and that of the legal expert because the former does not usurp the function of the court. The testimony of

2. Indeed, one is constrained to ask why it is helpful to the jury to present expert testimony on the law if the witness himself states, as he did here, that anything he says is subject to correction by the judge. Is this not more confusing than helpful? The question is rhetorical and stands as further exam- ple why a lawyer's testimony on ultimate issues of law is improper.

3. By contrast, the expert in the instant case did not testify on issues of fact because he based his opinions on hypothetical facts. The expert added nothing to resolve the salient factual issues of the case.

the medical expert in plaintiffs' hypothesis is more like that of the legal expert who explains a discrete point of law which is helpful to the jury's understanding of the facts.

. . .

■ SEYMOUR, CIRCUIT JUDGE, with whom McKAY, CIRCUIT JUDGE, joins, dissenting.

In testifying here, the expert, Daniel Sears, followed a format which is expressly contemplated by the Federal Rules of Evidence and is typical of expert testimony in general: Sears gave "a dissertation or exposition of . . . principles relevant to the case," and he took "the further step of suggesting the inference which should be drawn from applying the specialized knowledge to the facts." Fed.R.Evid. 702 advisory committee's note. Although the majority opinion concludes that the admission of this testimony is reversible error, the opinion does not clearly articulate the ground upon which it holds the testimony inadmissible. The rationale upon which the majority then holds the error prejudicial is correspondingly murky, is without persuasive support, and is contrary to the weight of authority. In my view, when the expert testimony is considered in light of the record below and in the context of the rules governing the admissibility of such testimony, the error in its admission, if any, must be considered harmless. . . . .

In this case, the only reason offered by defendants at trial for excluding Sears' testimony was that, in giving his opinion on the issues of search and consent, Sears would articulate the law applicable to those issues and would thereby usurp the province of the court. I agree with the majority opinion to the extent that it holds excludable expert testimony which merely sets out for the jury the applicable principles of law. Although the Federal Rules of Evidence generally permit an expert to state principles of "specialized knowledge" within his area of expertise, see Fed.R.Evid. 702 advisory committee's note, when a lawyer/expert does so he sets out legal principles. Because it is the law as articulated by the court that governs the jury's deliberations, the expert's evidence on the law may be excludable under Fed.R.Evid. 702 because it is not helpful to the jury.[1]

. . .

A review of the record here establishes that defendants cannot sustain their burden of demonstrating a prejudicial effect on their substantial rights arising from Sears' testimony on his view of the law. . . . Defendants pointed out on cross-examination that Sears' opinions were based on his own view of the law, and that Sears did not know what the court's instructions on the law would be. Although Sears agreed that his view of the law in the area of search and seizure could very well differ from that of the trial judge, his definition of

---

1. An interesting contrary view on presenting expert legal testimony to the trier of fact is found in Note, Expert Legal Testimony, 97 Harv.L.Rev. 797, 811–12 (1984) (footnotes omitted).

"Expert testimony in harmony with the judge's view of the law may be completely appropriate. Allowing legal testimony before the jury only when the testimony is consistent with the judge's view of the law will eliminate the concern that such testimony may usurp the role of the judge or jury. As long as an expert does not present a legal conclusion that merely tells the jury what result to reach, expert legal testimony does not impinge upon the jury's function of applying the law to the facts of the case. Moreover, although there is a danger that such testimony will partially usurp the judge's role of instructing the jury on the law, such testimony may enhance rather than interfere with the judge's charge to the jury if the expert testifies consistently with the judge's view of the law."

[Footnotes are the judge's.]

an illegal search was essentially the same as the one the judge gave to the jury.[2] ... Significantly, Sears himself further stated that the trial court's "understanding of the law is controlling in this case." ... The court instructed the jury that it must apply the law as stated in the court's instructions, and also informed the jury that it should determine what weight, if any, to give to the expert testimony.

. . .

The majority's statement that Sears' testimony was excludable because it supplanted the jury's ability to apply the law to the evidence may be meant as a holding that this testimony created the danger that the jury would rely on the expert rather than make an independent determination of the ultimate issues. However, the jury in this case was instructed that it should determine what weight, if any, to give the expert testimony, as with the testimony of any other witness. The jury was further instructed that it was the judge of the facts, that it was to follow the law as stated in the court's instructions, and that it was to apply this law to the facts as the jury found them. Courts and commentators have overwhelmingly concluded that such instructions preclude a finding of prejudice because they eliminate any possibility that expert testimony on the ultimate fact could overbear the jury's independence....

NOTE

United States v. Ingredient Technology Corp., 698 F.2d 88, 96–97 (2d Cir.), cert. denied, 462 U.S. 1131 (1983):

> The more sophisticated argument is made that the district court's exclusion of the testimony offered by two of defendant's experts, coupled with the decision of the trial court not to instruct the jury in terms of Treasury Regulation § 1.471–1, thwarted the defense that the defendants could not have formed a willful intent. Rapaport argues that the clarity of whatever legal duty was owed has become, in this case, an issue of fact and not of law. The defendants point to United States v. Garber, 607 F.2d 92 (5th Cir.1979) (en banc), a case involving a prosecution for tax evasion for having failed to report income from the sale of the taxpayer's blood containing a rare and valuable antibody, where the Fifth Circuit held exclusion of the testimony of a tax expert that in his opinion the income was not taxable was erroneous and reversed the conviction. Indeed, it is pointed out, the Fifth Circuit went further to say that the relevance of a dispute in the law "does not depend on whether the defendant actually knew of the conflict." Id. at 98, citing United States v. Critzer, 498 F.2d 1160 (4th Cir.1974). See also United States v. Clardy, 612 F.2d 1139, 1153 (9th Cir.1980) (government expert's testimony relative to issue of willfulness admissible where defense theory is that there is good faith dispute as to tax law interpretation). We decline to apply the Garber reasoning for two reasons. First, the holding of that case was that in view of the defense that Ms. Garber "subjectively thought that proceeds from the sale of part of her body were not taxable" exclusion of an accountant's expert testimony that money obtained from the sale of blood plasma was not taxable income was reversible error. Here, however, there was no evidence that

---

2. In their brief filed after rehearing was granted, defendants for the first time asserted that Sears misstated the law in two material respects. A careful examination of the record reveals that any discrepancy between Sears' articulation of the law and the court's instructions is so de minimis as to be irrelevant, which perhaps explains why defendants did not raise this argument in a timely manner.

Rapaport or anyone else at SuCrest genuinely thought that what they were doing was lawful and proper; on the contrary, their conduct indicated a subjective belief in the *un*lawfulness of the conduct. Second, as pointed out in Note, Criminal Liability for Willful Evasion of an Uncertain Tax, 81 Colum.L.Rev. 1348, 1360 (1981), the Garber majority's approach permits juries to find that uncertainty in the law negates willfulness whether or not the defendants are actually confused about the extent of their tax liability. In contrast, prior cases on willfulness consistently require factual evidence of the defendants' state of mind to negate willfulness under any theory. See id. at 1357. We agree with the Garber dissent, 607 F.2d at 105, that it would be very confusing to a jury to have opposing opinions of law admitted into evidence as involving a factual question for them to decide. Indeed, as that dissent points out, the inevitable logic of the majority's decision in Garber is that if the tax law is uncertain, the indictment should be dismissed. Questions of law are for the court. United States v. Bronston, 658 F.2d 920, 930 (2d Cir.1981), cert. denied, 456 U.S. 915 ... (1982); Marx & Co. v. Diners' Club, Inc., 550 F.2d 505, 509–10 (2d Cir.), cert. denied, 434 U.S. 861 ... (1977). See also 7 Wigmore, Evidence § 1952 at 81. To the extent that Garber is inconsistent with our Bronston and Marx cases, we decline to follow it. We note that the Fifth Circuit has itself limited Garber in United States v. Herzog, 632 F.2d 469, 473 (5th Cir. 1980) (expert's view of tax laws irrelevant to willfulness issues since complexity of laws sheds no light on defendant's intent).

United States v. West

United States Court of Appeals, Seventh Circuit, 1992.
962 F.2d 1243.

■ WILL, SENIOR DISTRICT JUDGE.

Peter Elliot West was charged with holding up the First National Bank in Champaign and at trial his sole defense was going to be that he was legally insane at the time of the holdup. The video tape from the bank's surveillance camera made the possibility of any other defense difficult. In addition, the fact that he was arrested on his way home from the bank still holding his mask, his gun and the money made any other defense virtually impossible but left insanity as a plausible possibility.

To assist West in preparing his defense, the district judge appointed a board-certified psychiatrist, Dr. Lawrence L. Jeckel, to examine him and Jeckel concluded, in a written report, that West was suffering at the time of the alleged crime from a severe mental disease, "schizoaffective disorder." American Psychiatric Association Diagnostic and Statistical Manual of Mental Disorders (3d ed. 1980) § 295.70. He also concluded, however, that notwithstanding his condition West "understood the wrongfulness of his actions at the time of the alleged crime," a conclusion which was inconsistent with West's planned defense—that his schizoaffective disorder made him legally insane.

West says he leaves dollar bills on his dresser as a way of reaching George Washington, whom he has talked to and first contacted at Valley Forge. He also has conversations with dead bunnies. When the police arrested him after the holdup he was wearing eight T-shirts and two sweatshirts. (It was January. But West told Dr. Jeckel that he was wearing layers because everybody is always taking things from him). A government psychiatrist at the United States Medical Center for Federal Prisoners in Springfield, Missouri diagnosed West as a probable manic depressive and a possible schizophrenic and alcohol abuser with a mix of character disorders.

In federal court, a defendant's mental disorder is not an affirmative defense unless (1) it is "severe" and (2) as a result of it the defendant was unable at the time of the crime "to appreciate the nature and quality or the wrongfulness of his acts." 18 U.S.C. § 17. Jeckel's conclusion that West's mental condition, though severe, did not keep him from knowing what he was doing or that doing it was wrong meant that, in Jeckel's opinion, West was not legally insane at the time of the holdup. Not surprisingly, the government moved at the close of its case to bar Jeckel from testifying for West.

The motion was resolved by voir dire. Jeckel was called to the stand and on direct, on cross and in response to questions from the court he repeated exactly what he had stated in his written report: (1) that West suffers from a severe mental disease or defect, specifically a schizoaffective disorder, and (2) that West was suffering from that disorder on the day he robbed the bank but that, notwithstanding his condition, West knew he was robbing a bank and understood that robbing banks is wrong.

Having heard that offer of proof, but no other evidence as to West's mental condition, the district judge (over strong objection) granted the government's motion to exclude Jeckel's testimony, and also announced that he would not charge the jury on the question of insanity, thereby eliminating West's only possible defense on the sole basis of Jeckel's opinion that West knew what he was doing and that it was wrong; an opinion which was inadmissible under Rule 704(b) of the Federal Rules of Evidence as discussed later herein. The judge's position was straightforward. As he put it:

> Under Section 17, the defense of insanity is bottomed on the lack of cognitive ability to know it's wrong to rob the bank or not know you are robbing the bank. [But] [h]ere is the psychiatrist, qualified [and] board certified, who forthrightly says that from his examination this person's mental condition didn't prevent him from knowing he was robbing the bank and didn't prevent him from knowing that it was wrong to rob the bank ... [And] it is outrageous to say that a psychiatrist whose opinion is that the defendant knew what he did was wrong and knew what he was doing should testify in support of an insanity defense when the physician says that under the definition of the statute ... there is no insanity.... There is no causative relationship, and the doctor says so right out....
>
> Added to that, added to the Section 17 reason, Rule 403 would also require the exclusion on the basis of Dr. Jeckel's statements to me, and I accept them. I respect his opinion....
>
> [Also,] I am not going to charge jury on the question of insanity where there is no sufficient clear and convincing evidence to support it.... To permit a lawyer ... to get up and make an argument that the defendant was insane at the time of the occurrence when the defendant's own psychiatrist says the defendant doesn't meet the criteria for Section 17 to me is nonsense....

Thus prevented from presenting an insanity defense (though having announced to the jury, in his opening statement, that insanity would be virtually his only defense), West's counsel put on just two witnesses, each to testify as to West's peaceful nature, and then rested. The jury, uninstructed on insanity, returned a verdict of guilty.

We reverse with some observations as to the appropriate procedure under the Federal Rules of Evidence.

Rule 704(b) of the Federal Rules of Evidence forbids experts in criminal cases from testifying with respect to the "ultimate issues" of a defendant's "mental state or condition."[1] In a case where the defendant makes insanity his or her defense, those "ultimate issues" are whether at the time of the crime the defendant "appreciated the nature and quality or the wrongfulness of his acts," 18 U.S.C. § 17, or, in other words, whether the defendant knew what he or she was doing and that it was wrong. On those issues, because of Rule 704(b), no expert may testify. These are questions, under 704(b), *"for the trier of fact alone,"* which means that it was error to exclude Dr. Jeckel's testimony as to West's mental condition, thereby foreclosing jury consideration of West's defense.

Dr. Jeckel said, in his written report and during voir dire, that it was his opinion that West knew what he was doing and knew it was wrong. That was an opinion on a subject that was clearly relevant to the merits of West's defense. To the extent it was a believable opinion, it was an opinion highly probative on the issue of insanity, and it was an opinion, moreover, which court-ordered psychiatric reports routinely do include.... It was testimony, from West's own court-appointed witness, that his defense was invalid. But it was also an opinion on the ultimate issue with respect to West's defense, whether at the time of the alleged crime West appreciated what he was doing and that doing it was wrong, 18 U.S.C. § 17, and under Rule 704(b) it was, therefore, inadmissible testimony.

More importantly, under Rule 704(b) Dr. Jeckel's opinion as to what West understood or didn't understand during the holdup was not only inadmissible but was also legally insignificant, an argument that West's lawyer made repeatedly during the voir dire but without convincing the district judge. Jeckel's views on the "ultimate issues" of whether West understood that he was robbing a bank and appreciated that robbing banks was wrong were from a legal standpoint beside the point. Because of Rule 704(b), they had nothing at all to do with whether Jeckel should have been allowed to testify or whether West should have been allowed to present his insanity defense to the jury. In logic of course, Dr. Jeckel's opinion is the ultimate point; it refutes the contention that West was legally insane. But in law (as Holmes said, the life of the law has not been logic), his opinion wins no points at all. Under Rule 704(b) an expert's opinion about what the defendant did or didn't appreciate at the time of the crime is not evidence that a jury may consider in returning its verdict on the sanity of the defendant, nor is it a valid basis for the district judge to exclude the testimony of the psychiatrist—to do so would deny the jury its statutorily mandated role.

A judge is entitled to *hear* the opinion of the psychiatrist—under Rule 104(a) a judge is not bound by the rules of evidence. That does not mean, however, that a judge can exclude all of the psychiatrist's testimony on the basis of the psychiatrist's inadmissible opinion on the ultimate issue. The at least theoretical effect of Rule 704(b) is to make it possible for juries to find a defendant not guilty by reason of insanity even if no expert would draw that same conclusion. Conversely, the rule also permits juries to find a defendant sane and guilty even if every expert would opine that the defendant was insane. The purpose of Rule 704(b) is to have jurors decide whether the defendant was

---

1. "No expert witness testifying with respect to the mental state or condition of a defendant in a criminal case may state an opinion or inference as to whether the defendant did or did not have the mental state or condition constituting an element of the crime charged or of a defense thereto. Such ultimate issues are matters for the trier of fact alone."…. [Footnotes of the court. Some footnotes omitted, others renumbered.]

sane or not without being told what conclusion an expert might draw.[2] A judge may take this decision from the jury, like any other, if the *admissible* evidence, not including psychiatrists' opinions, would not permit a reasonable jury to return a verdict of insanity. To allow the judge to exclude expert and other testimony as to a defendant's severe mental illness in cases in which the psychiatrist believes, notwithstanding that defendant suffers from a severe mental illness, that the defendant is legally sane, would provide for an uneven application of the rule, interpreting it one way when the psychiatrist agrees with the government, and a different way when the psychiatrist agrees with the defendant.

For these reasons, it was improper in this case for the district judge to foreclose West from presenting evidence and arguing his insanity defense merely because Dr. Jeckel's inadmissible ultimate issue testimony undermined that defense. What Jeckel thought about the ultimate issue, whether West understood that he was robbing a bank and understood that it was wrong, was inadmissible. And that his inadmissible opinion contradicted West's insanity defense was not a proper ground for precluding other admissible evidence as to that defense—just as it would not be proper, in any other criminal case, to bar a particular defense simply because the success of the defense might depend on denying facts that earlier had been conceded in inadmissible statements (facts, for example, that the defendant might have acknowledged during an involuntary confession or during failed plea discussions).

The exclusion of Dr. Jeckel's testimony was also not permissible under Rule 403. The district court said that Dr. Jeckel's testimony would mislead the jury with confusing psychiatric terminology. Almost every psychiatrist's testimony in almost every case involves unfamiliar psychiatric terminology—there was nothing more technical or confusing about Dr. Jeckel's testimony here than the psychiatric testimony in most cases. In fact, if Dr. Jeckel had concluded that West was legally insane, no court could have properly excluded his underlying testimony as being too confusing, although under Rule 704(b) he still would not have been permitted to state an ultimate conclusion that West was or was not insane.

---

2.   Congress gave two reasons for wanting to take the decision from the experts and give it to the jury. The first is described in the Senate Report, which says that "[t]he purpose [of 704(b)]is to eliminate the confusing spectacle of competing expert witnesses testifying to contradictory conclusions as to the ultimate legal issue to be found by the trier of fact." S.Rep. No. 225, 98th Cong., 1st Sess. 231 (1983) reprinted in 1984 U.S.Code Cong. & Admin.News 3182, 3412. The second rationale Congress gave for 704(b), contained in both the Senate and House Reports, evinces a skepticism not about the spectacle of competing mental health experts and their conflicting testimony but about their competence to testify about moral questions of criminal responsibility. The House Judiciary Committee's report emphasizes that:

> While the medical and psychological knowledge of expert witnesses may well provide data that will assist the jury in determining the existence of the defense, no person can be said to have expertise

regarding the legal and moral decision involved. Thus, with regard to the ultimate issue, the psychiatrist, psychologist or other similar expert is no more qualified than a lay person.

H.R.Rep. No. 577, 98th Cong. 1st Sess. 2, 16 (1983). And similarly, the Senate Report, quoting from a statement by the American Psychiatric Association, stresses that:

> [P]sychiatrists are experts in medicine, not the law.... When ... "ultimate issue" questions are formulated by the law and put to the expert witness who must then say "yea" or "nay," then the expert witness is required to make a leap in logic. He no longer addresses himself to medical concepts but instead must infer or intuit what is in fact unspeakable, namely, the probable relationship between medical concepts and legal or moral constructs such as free will.

S.Rep., supra, in 1984 U.S.Code Cong. & Admin.News at 3413.

The suggestion that the testimony would be misleading assumes what the trial was to decide—whether or not West was insane. The district court seemed to be primarily concerned with the possibility of the jury coming back with the "wrong" verdict. What the right and wrong verdicts are, was, of course, determined by the district court solely on the inadmissible ultimate opinion of the expert, Dr. Jeckel. However, this would allow a district court to do under Rule 403 precisely what it may not do: exclude all testimony on insanity because of the inadmissible opinion of a psychiatrist on the ultimate issue, and thus subvert clear congressional policy that the question is for the jury to decide. The exclusion of testimony by Dr. Jeckel about West's mental condition and bizarre conduct is no more justifiable under Rule 403 than it would be under § 17.

Dr. Jeckel's testimony as to West's mental condition was relevant and it was probative. Dr. Jeckel's underlying testimony clearly supported his medical diagnosis that West suffered from a severe mental disease, which is what West needed in part to prove if his defense was to prevail. It is true that much of Dr. Jeckel's testimony, while showing a severe mental disease, did not show an inability to determine right from wrong. However, insufficiency of evidence is not a reason to exclude it. Bourjaily v. United States, 483 U.S. 171, 175, 107 S.Ct. 2775, 2778 ... (1987) ("The inquiry ... is not whether the proponent of the evidence wins or loses his case on the merits, but whether the evidentiary Rules have been satisfied.") Sufficiency was for the jury to decide. Furthermore, the testimony about West's conversations with dead bunnies or with George Washington, and other evidence of his mental disorder might well have helped the jury determine whether West knew that what he was doing was wrong. In any event, under Rule 704(b) that was clearly for the jury, not Dr. Jeckel or the court, to decide.

. . .

It is true that, after the John Hinckley case in which psychiatrists testified that Hinckley was insane when he fired at President Reagan, one overall goal of Congress in passing the Insanity Defense Reform Act was to lessen the availability of and narrow the scope of the insanity defense, as § 17's standards do. There was also, in addition, an intention to take the decision on sanity away from the psychiatrist and give it to the jury. Under the system Congress established, the jury can find a defendant sane when the psychiatrists would not, as well as finding a defendant, such as West, insane when the psychiatrists would not. Congress may have believed that this system would decrease the number of defendants found to be insane. At any rate, it is certainly the system that Congress set up, and it is not the courts' prerogative to change it and make it more draconian than Congress provided.

The wisdom of such a system may be doubted. The evidence that would probably be most helpful to a jury on the question of sanity is an expert's opinion on whether the defendant knew what he or she was doing and whether or not it was wrong. We, however, are obligated to follow the rules Congress has made, and not rewrite nor avoid them, unwise though they may be. Congress wrote them and Congress, not the courts, should change them.

. . .

In sum, because of Rule 704(b) it was legally incorrect both (a) to preclude Dr. Jeckel from testifying as to West's mental condition merely because of his ultimate opinion that West was legally sane and (b) by foreclosing all evidence on the subject, to prevent West from presenting an insanity defense. Beyond what he had to say on the ultimate issue, Jeckel also stated during voir dire and in his report that in his opinion West suffers from a severe mental disease or defect and was suffering from it on the day he robbed the bank. *That* was relevant and admissible evidence, which the district judge did not reject as incredible.... Considering all the admissible evidence, including West's own statements as to his knowledge and conduct, there may have been a sufficient quantum of it to get West's insanity defense to the jury.... If not, the trial judge, after having heard all the admissible evidence, could have refused to instruct on insanity.

The district judge's rulings completely deprived West of the only defense he had, see Chambers v. Mississippi, 410 U.S. 284, 93 S.Ct. 1038 ... (1973); Washington v. Texas, 388 U.S. 14, 87 S.Ct. 1920 ... (1967), and led to a jury verdict which, within the area of reasonable doubt, Chapman v. California, 386 U.S. 18, 24, 87 S.Ct. 824, 828 ... (1967), might not have been the same if the insanity defense had gone to the jury. West's conviction must therefore be reversed.

In this case, if there is a retrial, Rule 704(b) would allow Dr. Jeckel to testify that West suffers from a severe schizoaffective disorder but forbid him from telling the jury that, in his opinion, the disorder did not impair his understanding that what he was doing was robbing a bank and did not cloud his judgment so as to make him think that robbing a bank wasn't wrong. It will allow West to testify and present other evidence as to his conduct, practices and mental condition, e.g. the government psychiatrist from Springfield, Missouri. It will allow the government to introduce expert testimony that West does not suffer from severe mental disease and other evidence, except expert opinions, as to West's knowledge of what he was doing and that it was wrong. Finally, ... if the trial judge believes the admissible evidence, excluding any expert opinions as to whether West knew he was robbing a bank and that it was wrong, is insufficient for a jury to find that West was insane, the judge may refuse to instruct the jury on insanity or to submit a verdict form on insanity. This procedure is consistent with both the language of Rule 704(b) and its legislative history.

The judgment of the district court is reversed.

[Concurring opinion of Cudahy, T. omitted.]

■ MANION, CIRCUIT JUDGE, concurring.

This case presents a most difficult puzzle involving the relationship among 18 U.S.C. § 17, Fed.R.Evid. 704(b) and Fed.R.Evid. 403. I agree with the district court that to permit counsel "to get up and make an argument that the defendant was insane at the time of the occurrence when the defendant's own psychiatrist says the defendant doesn't meet the criteria for Section 17 ... is nonsense." Nonetheless, I must join my colleagues in reversing West's conviction because, under Rule 704(b), Dr. Jeckel's opinion that West was not legally insane alone cannot be grounds to foreclose West from presenting any evidence on his insanity defense.

I do not agree, however, that Dr. Jeckel's testimony could never be properly excluded under Rule 403. Although Congress only forbade psychiatrists from expressing their ultimate conclusions and did not bar them from testifying, this congressional scheme should not be used to nullify Rule 403.

In addition, I think it is important to remember that neither the government nor the district court will be powerless on retrial to point out the weaknesses of Dr. Jeckel's testimony to the jury. Rule 704(b) does not prohibit psychiatrists from " 'presenting and explaining their diagnoses, such as whether the defendant had a severe mental disease or defect and what *the character-*

istics of such disease or defect, if any, may have been.' " United States v. Davis, 835 F.2d 274, 276 (11th Cir.), cert. denied, 487 U.S. 1219 . . . (1988) (quoting S.Rep. No. 225, 98th Cong., 1st Sess. 230) (emphasis in original). Thus, a skilled attorney can avoid some of the pernicious effects of Rule 704(b) by asking a psychiatrist whether the ability to discern right from wrong is a characteristic of the defendant's illness. Id. . . . On retrial, for example, the government could ask Dr. Jeckel: "Does a finding that a person suffers from schizoaffective disorder, in and of itself, indicate that a person is unable to understand the wrongfulness of his acts?" The government could even go on to explore what particular characteristics of schizoaffective disorder render a person able or unable to appreciate the wrongfulness of his acts. Such questions are merely questions about the characteristics of the mental disease, as opposed to subjective questions leading to conclusions about the defendant's personal knowledge, intent or ability.

. . .

NOTE

United States v. Kristiansen, 901 F.2d 1463 (8th Cir.1990): Under Rule 704 (b), error not to allow defendant's psychiatrist to state whether defendant's mental condition would affect his ability to appreciate the nature and quality of his actions. United States v. Freeman, 804 F.2d 1574, 1576 (11th Cir.1986): Rule 704 (b) does not violate Due Process.

Supplementary Note on Expert Medical Testimony

A general practitioner is not usually considered disqualified from testifying against a specialist in a malpractice case, nor are doctors trained in other specialities necessarily disqualified. Steinberg v. Indem. Ins. Co., 364 F.2d 266, 272–73 (5th Cir.1966): Not error to allow general practitioner to testify that plastic surgeons fell below accepted standard in failing to remove splint when certain symptoms appeared. Frost v. Mayo Clinic, 304 F.Supp. 285 (D.Minn. 1969): Doctors who were not orthopedic or neurosurgeons qualified to testify concerning negligence of defendants, orthopedic and neurosurgeons, in failing to appraise properly and act upon pain and neurological deficits following disc operation. Rosenberg v. Cahill, 492 A.2d 371, 375–80 (N.J.1985): In malpractice action against chiropractor, medical doctor should have been allowed to testify that chiropractor should have recognized soft-tissue abnormalities from x-rays and referred patients for medical treatment. "[T]here is an overlap between the medical and chiropractic professions with respect to both the use of x-rays and the diagnoses of conditions that may require medical attention." Baerman v. Reisinger, 363 F.2d 309 (D.C.Cir.1966): General practitioner with experience in treating hyperthyroidism might be qualified to testify to standard applicable to cardiologist in diagnosing hyperthyroidism. Kosberg v. Washington Hosp. Center, Inc., 394 F.2d 947 (D.C.Cir.1968): Internist qualified to testify against psychiatrist concerning electro-shock therapy. But see Lundgren v. Eustermann, 370 N.W.2d 877 (Minn.1985): Psychologist not qualified to testify to standard of care applicable to internist who prescribed thorazine, because although knowledgeable about psychology and pharmacology, psychologist did not have knowledge of how physicians customarily use thorazine in treatment. Swanson v. Chatterton, 160 N.W.2d 662 (Minn.1968): Internist disqualified in malpractice action against orthopedic surgeon not because unlicensed in defendant's specialty, but because he did not have necessary experience. Simpsen v. Madison Gen. Hosp. Ass'n., 180 N.W.2d 586 (Wis.1970): Not error to exclude testimony of podiatrist as to whether trauma to foot shortly after operation on foot caused infection.

People v. Davis, 402 P.2d 142 (Cal. 1965): Murder conviction reversed because of exclusion of testimony of psychologist offered by defendant on issue of sanity. The psychologist, although he did not attend medical school, was "the fastest man to go through the University of Chicago," having passed from freshman to Ph.D. in four and one-half years. Per Traynor, J.: "It does not follow that all psychologists are competent to give an expert opinion on sanity. Many practicing psychologists are not concerned with problems of abnormal psychology and are not familiar with the clinical branch of their field. A certain level of training and experience is also necessary; one with only an undergraduate interest in psychology who has since pursued other fields would certainly not be qualified to give an expert opinion.... Moreover, not all questions relating to legal sanity can be answered by a psychologist.... The interpretation of an electroencephalogram or the physiological effect of drugs, for example, may be beyond the ken of a psychologist without medical training. Whether a psychologist qualifies as an expert on sanity in a particular case depends on the facts of that case, the questions propounded to the witness, and his peculiar qualifications." Id. at 148.

There is a problem about the qualification of a practitioner of one school to testify against a practitioner of another school. People v. Chatfield, 77 Cal.Rptr. 118 (Cal.App.1969), cert. denied, 402 U.S. 951 (1971): Defendant, a chiropractor, was convicted of theft in obtaining money from persons by representing that a certain machine called the Drown Machine was capable of diagnosing and curing diseases. The use of the machine was known as "Drown Therapy." The prosecution offered the testimony of Dr. Greenfield, a professor in the Department of Radiology of the UCLA Medical School. Dr. Greenfield had a Ph.D. in Physics and specialized in medical physics. He testified that the Drown machine was not capable of diagnosing or curing any pathology. The appellate court affirmed defendant's conviction, finding no error in the admission of Dr. Greenfield's testimony over the objection that "he was neither a medical doctor nor a chiropractor nor a student of 'Drown Therapy.' " "It was not unreasonable for the trial court to conclude that the testimony of this witness could be helpful in evaluating the Drown machine as a diagnostic or therapeutic instrument. By this standard his testimony was admissible." Id.

Increasing liberality is shown by courts in regard to whether an expert witness in a medical malpractice case must know the standard of care prevailing in the particular community in which the defendant practices. The required qualifications for an expert witness and the standard of care to which the defendant is held are, of course, two sides of the same coin. Pederson v. Dumouchel, 431 P.2d 973, 978 (Wash.1967): Error to instruct that doctors are held to the standard of care prevailing in local community or similar community; they are held to the standard the average practitioner observes acting in the same or similar circumstances, local practice being only one factor to consider; opinion gives reasons for abandonment of former rule. Wickliffe v. Sunrise Hosp., Inc., 706 P.2d 1383 (Nev.1985): Locality rule overthrown: witness familiar with standard of care of reasonably competent hospital in similar circumstances wherever located may testify in negligence action against hospital or its employees. Duling v. Bluefield Sanitarium, Inc., 142 S.E.2d 754, 765 (W.Va.1965): Expert need not be familiar with standard of care for hospital nurses in same locality. Annot., Modern Status of "Locality Rule" in Malpractice Action Against Physician Who is Not a Specialist, 99 A.L.R.3d 1133 (1980). But see Murphy v. Dyer, 409 F.2d 747 (10th Cir.1969): Not error in action against Colorado Springs obstetrician-gynecologist for injury to patient from spinal anesthetic to exclude testimony of renowned anesthesiologist from Seattle whose books were standard because not shown to be familiar with standard of practice in Colorado Springs or a similar community or with standard observed by obstetricians administering anesthetic.

<u>Supplementary References on Expert Evidence</u>

Rosenthal, The Development of the Use of Expert Testimony, 2 L. & Contemp. Probs. 403 (1935) (illuminating historical account); L. Hand, Historical and Practical Considerations Regarding Expert Testimony, 15 Harv. L. Rev.40 (1901); Moenssens, Admissibility of Fingerprint Evidence and Constitutional Objections to Fingerprinting Raised in Criminal and Civil Cases, 40 Chi.-Kent L. Rev. 85 (1963); Orth, The Use of Expert Witnesses in Musical Infringement Cases, 16 U. Pitt. L. Rev. 232 (1955); Bullen, The Role of Literary Experts in Plagarism Trials, 7 Am. U. L. Rev. 55 (1958); Rose, The Social Scientist as an Expert Witness, 40 Minn. L. Rev. 205 (1956); Louisell, The Psychologist in Today's Legal World, 39 Minn. L. Rev. 235 (1955); Salzman, Psychiatric Interviews as Evidence: The Role of the Psychiatrist in Court— Some Suggestions and Case Histories, 30 Geo. Wash. L. Rev. 853 (1962); Lassen, The Psychologist as an Expert in Assessing Mental Disease or Defect, 50 A.B.A.J. 239 (1964); Wells, The 1984 ABA Criminal Justice Mental Health Standards and the Expert Witness: New Therapy for a Troubled Relationship? 13 West. St. U. L. Rev. 79 (1985); Comment, Legal and Psychiatric Concepts and the Use of Psychiatric Evidence in Criminal Trials, 73 Cal.L.Rev. 411 (1985); Ahrens, Scientific Evidence and the Law: Identification, Verification of Verbal Testimony and Physiological Proof, 13 N.Y.L.For. 612 (1968); Van Duizend and Sacks, Report on the Use of Scientific and Technological Evidence in Litigation (1983) (case studies and extensive bibliography); McCormick, Some Observations Upon the Opinion Rule and Expert Testimony, 13 Tex. L.Rev. 109 (1945); Morris, The Role of Expert Testimony in the Trial of Negligence Issues, 26 Tex.L.Rev. (1947).

SECTION 2.   THE BASIS OF EXPERT TESTIMONY

Even though expert opinion testimony may be admissible under the principles explored in the preceding section, may it nevertheless be inadmissible because of a defect in the basis upon which it rests? If under Fed. R. Evid. 702 a certain degree of reliability is required for the admission of the evidence—at least in the case of scientific evidence—is the same or a similar demand to be found in Fed. R. Evid. 703, which concerns the basis of expert opinion? In other words, what is the significance of the Daubert decision for the correct interpretation of Rule 703? It is clear that under certain circumstances, expert opinion is admissible even though there is to be found in the basis of the opinion material that because of one of the exclusionary rules would not be independently admissible. But what are the circumstances that permit this exception and the justifications for recognizing it? In the case of the hearsay rule, how do the justifications for allowing hearsay in the basis of expert opinion compare with the justifications for exceptions to the hearsay rule? If inadmissible material is permitted in the basis of expert opinion, may it be disclosed to the jury on direct examination as an aid in evaluating the opinion? May it be disclosed on cross-examination?

Rabata v. Dohner

Supreme Court of Wisconsin, 1969.
45 Wis.2d 111, 172 N.W.2d 409.

[Action for damages for personal injuries resulting from an automobile accident. The trial court entered judgment for plaintiff. Defendant appealed.]

■ HEFFERNAN, JUSTICE.

. . .

Rabata's attorney called Harold Vik, who testified that he had been retained by Rabata's counsel a few weeks after the accident, that he had then viewed the scene, had examined the vehicles, and had photographed them prior to the time that any parts had been scavenged. He stated that he had also studied the police photographs that had been placed in evidence showing the road conditions at the time of the accident and the position of the cars. Counsel for Rabata then asked Vik the following question:

"Q Now, Mr. Vik, based on your education and on your training and experience of reconstruction of automobile accidents, and based upon the police pictures, and your examination of the vehicles, and the other pictures which are in evidence here in this case, do you have an opinion as to how this accident occurred?

"A I do.

"Q Will you state that opinion as to the position of the vehicles at impact, and what if any opinions you have as to speed of the vehicles?"

Opposing counsel objected on the grounds that the question was not in hypothetical form and that no sufficient foundation had been laid. The following exchange then took place:

"The Court: All right. It seems to me, Mr. Bannen, that you should establish through this witness that he has some background knowledge of the alleged facts in this case before you proceed to have him give his opinions.

"Mr. Bannen: Your Honor, I don't want to ask him a hypothetical question.

"The Court: I wasn't requiring you to. I think you ought to at least attempt to establish that he has some knowledge of the general testimony that has been involved here.

"Mr. Conway: He wasn't present at the time of the occurrence.

"The Court: No, I know.

"Mr. Conway: He proposes to put something on this scale drawing for which there is no foundation.

"Mr. Bannen: I'm asking him from the physical facts, your Honor.

"Mr. Metzner: Then the objection goes to the ground that the physical facts produced up to this time by this witness are inadequate—grossly inadequate—on which to lay a foundation.

"Mr. Bannen: I think that should be brought out on cross examination.

"The Court: I think, Mr. Bannen, you should show, briefly—and I'm not going to spend too much time on this—but I think you should show briefly that this witness at least has some factual knowledge of the testimony that has been brought out here relative to directions and so forth.

"Mr. Bannen: Q Well, you were present when Mr. Rabata testified, were you not?

"The Witness: A I was.

"Q And you heard his testimony as to the directions of the automobiles?

"A Yes.

"Mr. Bannen: I would like to ask my questions now, your Honor.

"Mr. Conway: We would renew our objection that there isn't a foundation for this witness.—

"The Court: Well, go ahead, Mr. Bannen."

Mr. Vik proceeded to give his opinion that Dohner had invaded Rabata's lane of traffic at the time of the accident. He was exhaustively cross-examined as to the basis of his conclusion and what facts he had considered in arriving at the conclusion and how those facts had been determined. Under cross-examination, Vik conceded that the location of debris had not been considered in determining the point of impact; and when asked whether this was an important factor in determining a point of impact, he stated, "We like to know about debris, if there is anything to know about it."

The defendant on this appeal contends that the court erred in allowing Harold Vik to testify on an ultimate issue of fact without a hypothetical question. We do not agree. It is well-established law in Wisconsin that an expert may give an opinion in answer to a direct, as contrasted to, a hypothetical question, where the facts upon which he relies are either undisputed or are the result of firsthand knowledge. This is the case here.

. . .

In the instant case, the attorney for the plaintiff Rabata refused to use a hypothetical question in examining the reconstruction expert, Harold Vik. He was invited to do so and stated that he did not wish to ask a hypothetical question. He stated that defense counsel could, if he wished, explore the background premises by cross-examination. On the other hand, counsel for the defendant, in eliciting the opinion of Professor Archie Easton in regard to where the collision took place, propounded a lengthy hypothetical question which covered almost four pages of the transcript and took several minutes to state. The question propounded by defense counsel is an example of an impeccably tailored hypothetical question. The points at issue, which at that time had not been proved, were stated as assumptions, and all the facts assumed that were material to answering the hypothetical question were clearly spelled out. Factual points involving the location of the accident, the type of vehicles, the direction in which the vehicles were traveling, the nature of the surface of the highway, the weather conditions, the type and condition of the tires on the vehicles, the speed of the vehicles, the grade of the road, the nature of the surface of the intersecting road, the number of passengers in each vehicle, the assumed conduct of the drivers in respect to brake application and maneuvers to avoid the accident, the position in which the automobiles came to rest, the nature and exact location of the debris on the highway, the damage to the vehicles, the effect of the position at which the vehicles came to rest upon the ability of traffic to proceed on the road, etc., were all set forth meticulously in the question.

In response to the question propounded to the defendant's reconstruction expert, Professor Easton unequivocally stated that he had an opinion. He pointed out that, in his opinion based on these assumed facts, the accident took place in Dohner's lane of traffic. The jury, however, apparently gave more weight to Rabata's expert, who expressed his opinion in response to a direct question, than they did to Dohner's witness, who answered only after being propounded a lengthy hypothesis.

This court is of the opinion that the use of a hypothetical question frequently has a stultifying, somniferous, effect upon a jury and presents to them at one time so great a quantity of assumed facts that it is not reasonable to expect them to have any clear idea of the basis on which the opinion is formed.

Moreover, the members of this court, based on their experience gleaned as practicing lawyers and trial judges, are satisfied that a mechanistic hypothetical question has the effect of boring and confusing a jury. Rather than inducing a clear expression of expert opinion and the basis for it, it inhibits the expert and forecloses him from explaining his reasoning in a manner that is intelligible to a jury.

The question is therefore posed in this case whether this court should require as a matter of general rule that the opinions of an expert should be elicited by hypothetical questions in those cases where they have heretofore been required. It was apparent herein that the very skilled trial counsel for Dohner believed, and he had good reason to believe, that the safe and proper procedure to use was to question Professor Easton by the use of a hypothetical question.

Almost all courts which have approached the subject have concluded that the hypothetical question, although logically a useful method of separating the premises from the conclusions, is potentially, and in actuality, a dangerous device which can lead to slanted questions, jury fatigue, and obfuscation of the facts. They have usually attempted to eradicate these inherent vices by setting up, on a case-by-case basis, elaborate rules detailing what facts should be included in a hypothetical question and setting forth exceptions to the rule requiring their use.

It is apparent that such tinkering with the hypothetical-question rule has not solved the problems.

McCormick has pointed out that courts throughout the country have attempted to limit the complexities of hypothetical questions by requiring, as Wisconsin has done, that only material facts be embraced in the hypothesis. He points out, however:

"... this seems undesirable as likely to multiply disputes as to the sufficiency of the hypothesis, and as tending to cause counsel, out of abundance of caution, to propound questions so lengthy as to be wearisome and almost meaningless to the jury." McCormick, Evidence (hornbook series), sec. 14, pp. 31, 32.

Despite the valiant attempts of courts to overcome the inherent vice of the hypothetical question, they have been far from successful, and legal writers who have addressed themselves to the problem have been almost unanimous in advocating their elimination.

. . .

In recent years the requirement that a hypothetical question be used to secure an expert opinion has been abandoned in California, Kansas, New Jersey, and New York.... The proposed Federal Rules of Evidence (46 F.R.D. 161) dispense with the requirements of hypothetical questions and state the new rule thus:

"Rule 7–03 Opinion Testimony by Experts

"The facts or data in the particular case upon which an expert bases an opinion or inference may be those perceived by or made known to him at or before the hearing. If of a type reasonably relied upon by experts in forming opinions or inferences upon the subject, the facts or data need not be admissible in evidence." P. 315.

The philosophy expressed by Wigmore and McCormick has also been codified in Rule 409 of the Model Code of Evidence, and we accept that rule as one properly to be applied in trial matters, both civil and criminal, in the courts of Wisconsin and in the discretion of the trial judge. That rule provides:

"An expert witness may state his relevant inferences from matters perceived by him or from evidence introduced at the trial and seen or heard by him or from his special knowledge, skill, experience or training, whether or not any such inference embraces an ultimate issue to be decided by the trier of fact, and he may state his reasons for such inferences and need not, unless the judge so orders, first specify, as an hypothesis or otherwise, the data from which he draws them; but he may thereafter during his examination or cross-examination be required to specify those data." P. 210–211.

We believe that this rule makes sense and would avoid the dilemma in which counsel for the defendant obviously found himself when he thought it necessary to propound a lengthy hypothetical question. It also preserves the right of counsel to use a hypothetical question if he considers it the best method of securing an expert opinion and it gives to the trial judge the authority to require a hypothetical question if direct questioning is not likely to be helpful to the jury. The rule, of course, assumes that the witness is an expert and is competent to qualify as such. It does not contemplate any change in our existing Wisconsin practice for the proper qualification of a witness who, in the sound discretion of the trial judge, may or may not be accepted as an expert. It does contemplate that the complete foundation for the opinion need not be put to the witness by hypothesis or otherwise prior to eliciting the opinion. This was the position taken by Judge Gollmar in the instant case when he allowed the opinion of Harold Vik without a hypothetical question and also permitted the defense attorney an unlimited opportunity in cross-examination to test the foundation upon which the opinion was based.[1] This cross-examination was skillfully conducted by defense counsel and pointed out lacunae in the foundation upon which Harold Vik's opinion was based. For example, cross-examination forced an admission that Vik had not taken into consideration the location of the debris on the highway and that the location of such debris was a matter that should be considered when it is available. There is no obligation on counsel on cross-examination of an expert to elicit premises for the opinion that would damage the cross-examiner's position. He need not prove that his adversary's witness had a sound basis for his opinion.

Of course, it is within the discretion of counsel eliciting the opinion to use a hypothetical question if he so desires; but under the rule which we herein adopt, he will no longer be forced to do so if the use of such question, in his opinion, is likely to dull the effect of the point at issue. The trial judge, however, when he feels that the propounding of the question without a clear statement of the assumptions upon which it is based would confuse rather than aid the jury, may in his discretion insist that a hypothesis be used. He may also, of course, insist that some foundation be put in the record if he believes that the elicitation of an opinion without a foundation is likely to mislead or confuse the jury. In general, however, if the premises upon which the conclusion is reached are to be attacked as being inadequate to support the opinion, even in light of the expert qualifications, it becomes the duty and obligation of opposing counsel to draw out the data on which the expert has arrived at his opinion.

1. The trial lawyer's ability to prepare to cross-examine his adversary's expert witness is, of course, dependent to a large degree upon his diligence in pursuing the pre-trial discovery procedures that are available in Wisconsin.... [Footnote by the court]

This is what was done in the instant case, and it became apparent after cross-examination that a substantial foundation existed for Harold Vik's opinion.

Under the circumstances of this case, we conclude that, even under the rules existing heretofore, the plaintiff was not required to propound a hypothetical question to its expert witness; and under the rule which we adopt herein, no hypothetical questions will be routinely required and attacks upon the premises upon which expert opinions are based must ordinarily be reached by cross-examination.

Judgment affirmed.

NOTES

1. Diamond and Louisell, The Psychiatrist As An Expert Witness, 63 Mich. L. Rev. 1335, 1346–47 (1965):[1]

It is recognized that a few situations exist in law (as for example, an issue of testamentary capacity) where no approach other than the hypothetical question is normally possible. But if one accepts the principle that the validity of the psychiatrist's observations and inferences is dependent upon the totality of his approach, upon his taking everything, including his own personal and subjective interaction with his patient into account, then the hypothetical question generally becomes a dubious technique.

No hypothetical question can ever be formulated which would contain sufficient facts to justify a really valid psychiatric inference. This is because the modern psychodynamically oriented psychiatrist simply does not assemble diagnostic facts, A, B, and C about his patient and thus arrive at conclusion D. The psychiatrist may be very much interested in observed phenomena, such as mannerisms, delusional and hallucinated behavior, and the like, but he can not derive a valid conclusion from such phenomena until he puts them together with his own subjective relationship to the examinee within the context of the latter's total background. There are few, if any, pathognomonic signs of mental disease.

The problem of the hypothetical question usually arises in a criminal trial under two circumstances. First, it arises when the psychiatrist has not actually examined the defendant. Such hypothetical testimony is of doubtful worth and often of dubious ethical quality. Secondly, it arises when it is used as a device to restrict the information admitted to the jury. A defendant many demand that all sorts of information about the crime and the criminal be withheld from the jury's knowledge, including evidence of previous offenses. The hypothetical question can be used for this purpose, restricting the psychiatrist to only certain facts and aspects of the case. This is the defendant's constitutional right. But it is not necessarily the psychiatrist's ethical duty to cooperate with such strategy. He should not and, if he is conscientious, he will not, wholly shrug off the responsibility for the consequences of his testimony.

2. What may be included in a hypothetical question? Dickinson v. Mailliard, 175 N.W.2d 588, 593–94 (Iowa 1970): "Plaintiff also complains of the hypothetical question which defendant was permitted to pose to Dr. Graham in the deposition cross-examination. Plaintiff had told a nurse he was experiencing pain and numbness in his hand and arm. This information was given the doctor, who asked him about these symptoms. The doctor says plaintiff just

1. Michigan Law Review, 1966. Reprinted with permission.

'brushed it off' and replied that 'perhaps he had laid on it wrong.' Dr. Graham was asked a hypothetical question which assumed plaintiff had denied complaining of pain or numbness in his hand or arm. It is claimed this was error because the record contains no evidence of such denial. There was no error here."

Carnival Cruise Lines v. Rodriguez, 505 So.2d 550, 552 (Fla.Ct.App.1987): Plaintiff contracted toxoplasmosis choreoretinitis and lost vision in one eye. In a suit against the steamship company that employed plaintiff, the issue was whether he had contracted the disease from undercooked meat served aboard defendant's ship or otherwise. Verdict for plaintiff. "The second error mandating reversal arises from the omission of a material fact in a hypothetical question posed to one of Rodriguez's expert witnesses. The question omits the critical fact that Rodriguez had vacationed in Costa Rica for approximately six weeks during his employment and thus had not consumed all his meals on board ship. This omission is especially prejudicial because another of Rodriguez's experts testified that Rodriguez may have acquired the disease while he was on vacation. The trial court erred in overruling counsel's objection to the question." Grand Island Grain Co. v. Roush Mobile Home Sales, Inc., 391 F.2d 35, 41 (8th Cir.1968): "[T]he questions omitted pertinent established facts essential to the formation of a rational opinion and embraced assumptions far too frail and speculative in the light of the evidence adduced ...," and so the disallowance of the hypothetical was proper. Are these cases correct?

3. For a lucid description of the emergence in the eighteenth and nineteenth centuries of the requirement of a detailed hypothetical question and the reasons thought to justify it, see Rosenthal, The Development of the Use of Expert Testimony, 2 L. & Contemp. Probs. 403, 414–18 (1935). Other useful references on hypotheticals are Ladd, Expert and Other Opinion Testimony, 40 Minn. L. Rev. 437, 447–49 (1956); Tyree, The Opinion Rule, 10 Rutgers L. Rev. 601, 614–16 (1956); McCormick, Some Highlights of the Uniform Evidence Rules, 33 Tex. L. Rev. 559, 566–67 (1955); McCoid, Opinion Evidence and Expert Witnesses, 2 UCLA L. Rev. 356, 364–66 (1955); Miller, Beyond the Law of Evidence, 40 S. Cal. L. Rev. 1, 30–33 (1967) (criticizing the failure of the California Evidence Code expressly to abolish the hypothetical question requirement); Goldstein, Trial Technique 452–86 (1935); Busch, Law and Tactics in Jury Trials § 426 (1949).

4. Abolition of the hypothetical question requirement is, of course, closely related to Fed. R. Evid. 705: "The expert may testify in terms of opinion or inference and give reasons therefor without first testifying to the underlying facts or data, unless the court requires otherwise. The expert may in any event be required to disclose the underlying facts or data on cross-examination." A Committee Comment to Minnesota Evidence Rule 705, which is identical to the Federal Rule, suggests that the court's discretion to require that facts and data be disclosed might be exercised, on request of the adverse party, "in the case where the adverse party has not been provided with the necessary information to conduct an effective cross-examination...." 50 Minn. Stat. Ann. 471 (West 1980).

Arkansas State Highway Comm'n v. Roberts, 441 S.W.2d 808, 813–17 (1969) (concurring opinion) (failure to give reasons for expert opinion may so affect probative value as to undermine admissibility or sufficiency to support verdict); Walters v. State Road Dept., 239 So.2d 878 (Fla.Ct.App.1970) (inability of land value expert in condemnation case to explain how he reached his opinion rendered verdict based on opinion violative of constitutional guarantee of full compensation).

United States v. Scop

United States Court of Appeals, Second Circuit, 1988.
846 F.2d 135.

[For other parts of the court's opinion, see supra pp. 1015–19.]

. . .

We turn now to a second fatal objection to Whitten's opinion testimony. On cross-examination, defense counsel brought out that Whitten's opinions were based on his positive assessment of the trustworthiness and accuracy of the testimony of the government's witnesses, in particular that of Sarcinelli. We believe that expert witnesses may not offer opinions on relevant events based on their personal assessment of the credibility of another witness's testimony. The credibility of witnesses is exclusively for the determination by the jury, United States v. Richter, 826 F.2d 206, 208 (2d Cir.1987), and witnesses may not opine as to the credibility of the testimony of other witnesses at the trial. Even apart from the gross invasion of the province of the jury that Whitten's testimony represented, his only claim to expertise was limited to securities trading and did not encompass the evaluation of testimony. Moreover, even expert witnesses possessed of medical knowledge and skills that relate directly to credibility may not state an opinion as to whether another witness is credible, United States v. Azure, 801 F.2d 336, 340–41 (8th Cir.1986), although such witnesses may be permitted to testify to relevant physical or mental conditions. See generally Annotation, Necessity and Admissibility of Expert Testimony as to Credibility of Witnesses, 20 A.L.R.3d 684 (1968).

It is true that Rule 705 allows an expert to state an opinion without disclosing the basis for it, and that a cross-examiner thus may elect not to probe into whether an expert witness's personal assessment of other witnesses' credibility is a basis of the opinion. In a sense, therefore, defendants caused Whitten's credibility opinions to be exposed to the jury. Our objection to testimony on credibility is not limited, however, to the prejudicial effect such testimony may have on the jury. Rather, we believe that such testimony not only should be excluded as overly prejudicial but also renders inadmissible any secondary opinion based upon it. Our holding, therefore, is that witness A may not offer an opinion as to relevant facts based on A's assessment of the trustworthiness or accuracy of witness B where B's credibility is an issue to be determined by the trier of fact. Were we to rule otherwise, triers of fact would be called upon either to evaluate opinion testimony in ignorance of an important foundation for that opinion or to hear testimony that is otherwise inadmissible and highly prejudicial. The present case exemplifies this dilemma. On the one hand, the jury could not accurately evaluate Whitten's testimony in ignorance of the fact that it was based in large part on his opinion that Sarcinelli was telling the truth. That judgment went well beyond the witness's purported expertise and vitiated whatever value his testimony had. On the other hand, testimony by one witness concerning the credibility of other testimony is objectionable in light of the presumption that the trier of fact is the best evaluator of credibility. Such testimony is thus not helpful to the trier of fact and is likely to be prejudicial.

Indeed, Whitten's offering of such an opinion was particularly objectionable. He had spent years investigating this case and had reached a conclusion well before trial as to the credibility of the various witnesses and parties. We believe it to be virtually impossible for an investigator so deeply involved in a case to put aside previous judgments regarding the credibility of witnesses and to render de novo judgments on their credibility after listening to the trial.

Even if Whitten had such a sharply compartmentalized mind as to allow segregation of his various credibility analyses, such testimony by an investigator and opinions based thereon are clearly prejudicial when offered to a jury. In Young, 745 F.2d at 766 (Newman, J., concurring), Judge Newman noted that a jury may infer from an investigating agent's opinion that the agent has knowledge about the defendant beyond the evidence offered at trial, an observation we commended to district judges in Brown, 776 F.2d at 401 & n. 6. Certainly, the risk of a jury believing that an opinion offered as to credibility by an agent such as Whitten was based on his investigation as a whole rather than solely on evidence adduced at trial is particularly great.

We find nothing in Rule 703 inconsistent with our ruling. That Rule permits inadmissible evidence to be the basis of an expert's opinion where it is of "a type reasonably relied upon by experts in the particular field." As the Advisory Committee's Note makes plain in its illustration of decisions by physicians, the purpose of the rule is to align the law with the extrajudicial "practice of experts" who may base their opinions on technically inadmissible evidence, such as unauthenticated x-rays and oral reports by nurses. The Rule in no way purports to allow witnesses to assess the trustworthiness or accuracy of testimony given in the same case or to offer opinions based on such an assessment.

Our ruling thus does not preclude use of an expert such as Whitten to testify to methods by which share prices may be artificially inflated. Simple hypotheticals based on assumptions about testimony in the record can also be posed to the witness in a way that allows his or her opinions to be given but leaves the credibility issues to the jury.... Our ruling thus also does not conflict with Rule 703's provision that the "facts or data in the particular case upon which an expert bases an opinion or inference may be thus ... made known to the expert at ... the hearing." Fed.R.Evid. 703; see also Fed.R.Evid. 703 advisory committee's note ("expert [may] attend trial and hear the testimony establishing the facts"). Where such facts or data are based on the trial testimony of a witness whose credibility is not in dispute, the expert need not make a judgment about credibility. Where the credibility of the witness is an issue, the expert may assume the truth of his or her trial testimony and thereafter offer an opinion based on the substance of the testimony. There is thus no need for an expert to make, much less state to the jury, an assessment of credibility when offering an opinion based on trial testimony.

. . .

All convictions on counts one through thirteen are therefore reversed....

■ PIERCE, CIRCUIT JUDGE, concurring:

I concur in all of Judge Winter's thorough opinion except for the portion discussing the "second fatal objection" to Whitten's expert testimony. A question remains in my mind as to whether Judge Winter's conclusion that "expert witnesses may not offer opinions on relevant events based on their personal assessment of the credibility of another witness's testimony" is consistent with Rules 703 and 705 of the Federal Rules of Evidence and the Advisory Committee Notes. As I understand it, the expert's reliance on the testimony of a witness whose credibility is in question may be brought out on cross-examination and may not affect the foundation for admission of the opinion itself. See, e.g., Polk v. Ford Motor Co., 529 F.2d 259, 271 (8th Cir.), cert. denied, 426 U.S. 907, 96 S.Ct. 2229 ... (1976); Twin City Plaza, Inc. v. Central Surety and Ins. Corp., 409 F.2d 1195, 1200 (8th Cir.1969); 3 J. Weinstein & M. Berger,

Weinstein's Evidence ¶705[01], at 705–6 to–10 (1987); McCormick on Evidence § 14, at 35 (E. Cleary 3d ed. 1984).

.   .   .

NOTE

For criticism of the Scop decision, see Berger, United States v. Scop: The Common–Law Approach to an Expert's Opinion About a Witness's Credibility Still Does Not Work, 55 Brook. L. Rev. 559 (1989).

Pelster v. Ray

United States Court of Appeals, Eighth Circuit, 1993.
987 F.2d 514.

[Action by the Pelsters against the Mortons for fraud in passing through the Mortons' used car auction sale (South Central Auction) an Oldsmobile Cutlass Ciera owned by U.S. Wholesales, the odometer of which the Mortons knew had been rolled back. At the trial, the Pelsters were allowed to introduce the testimony of Ley, an investigator into automobile theft and odometer fraud.]

■ WOLLMAN, CIRCUIT JUDGE.

.   .   .

Ley described the general investigative techniques that he customarily uses in his work. He testified that he attempts to trace a vehicle's title history back through its various owners to the manufacturer. He stated that in the course of an investigation he speaks with dealers and obtains from them whatever documentation they can provide, usually titles, odometer statements, repair records, and bills of sale. He further stated that he also talks to auto auctions; he seeks similar documents from them, often including the auction's check-in sheets (also known as "block sheets"), which contain a description of the car and its current odometer reading. He testified that he contacts former owners of the vehicle, seeking oral and written information about the vehicle's mileage. Finally, he stated that he obtains copies of titles, odometer statements, and other documents from government agencies in the various states in which the vehicle had been titled. He testified that he had followed this procedure in investigating the roll-back of the Ciera.

Ley described generally how the roll-back game operates. He explained how people alter or roll back a car's odometer. Ley also explained how people physically alter the vehicle's documentation (titles and odometer statements) to match the new numbers on the odometer. . . .

Counsel for the Pelsters then directed Ley's testimony to the history of the Ciera. Counsel walked Ley through the various documents that accompanied the Ciera through its transfers, including copies of titles, odometer statements, and auction check-in sheets. Having explained the contents of these various documents, Ley opined that the Ciera had been rolled back during the time that it was in the possession of U.S. Wholesales and before it passed through South Central.

.   .   .

The Mortons challenge the admission of Ley's testimony on several grounds. They assert that his testimony violated the rule against hearsay because he based his testimony on out-of-court statements made in oral conversations and written documents; concerned matters on which Ley lacked personal knowledge; and, to the extent it was based on the contents of documents, violated the best evidence rule.

Ley admitted in his testimony that he had obtained his information (oral and written) from numerous out-of-court sources, including previous owners, dealers, auctions, state agencies, a "confidential informant," and various individuals connected with U.S. Wholesales. During most of his testimony, it was unclear upon which of those sources of information Ley was basing his testimony. Presumably, Ley's ultimate conclusions that 300 of 350 cars auctioned at South Central had been rolled back and that U.S. Wholesales had been responsible for 204 of those 300 rolled-back cars were based on all of the sources he identified.

We find that Ley's testimony constituted inadmissible hearsay. The out-of-court documents and declarants "stated" that a particular vehicle's odometer registered a specific number of miles on a given date. Another document or declarant told Ley that the same vehicle's odometer registered a smaller number of miles on a later date. From those two out-of-court statements, Ley testified that the odometer had been rolled back in the intervening period of time. Neither the Mortons nor the jury, however, had an opportunity to examine those out-of-court statements. Moreover, Ley did not testify individually regarding all of the cars that he had investigated; he merely stated his general conclusion that people or documents had told him the mileage figures 350 times and that 300 times they had led him to conclude that a vehicle's odometer had been rolled back before the car passed through South Central.

The Pelsters claim that they did not offer Ley's testimony to prove that 300 rolled-back cars passed through South Central, 204 of which came from U.S. Wholesales. They assert that they offered Ley's testimony to show the Mortons' knowledge, intent, and common plan. They fail to acknowledge, however, that in order to prove that the Mortons knew that U.S. Wholesales was selling rolled-back cars through South Central or that they intended to defraud subsequent purchasers through a common plan, the Pelsters must first show that U.S. Wholesales was, in fact, selling rolled-back cars through South Central. To make that intermediate showing, they must initially prove that, at some point before the cars passed through South Central, the mileage readings on the cars' odometers had decreased by comparing the readings on two dates. If the Pelsters did not offer the out-of-court statements upon which Ley relied to prove the truth of those mileage figures, then the Pelsters cannot prove the first proposition in their evidentiary chain (that an initial mileage reading was higher than a subsequent reading). Consequently, they could never support an inference to prove the final proposition, that the Mortons knew of the fraud.

Of greater moment is the Pelsters' second justification for the admission of the hearsay in Ley's testimony. The Pelsters claim that Ley was an expert witness, who may base his opinions upon facts or data "of a type reasonably relied upon by experts in the particular field in forming inferences or opinions." Fed.R.Evid. 703. They repeatedly assert that Ley conducted a two-year investigation according to his standard investigative procedures, which "establishes Ley's reasonabl[e] reliance on the results of that procedure."

A district court's ruling on the admissibility of expert testimony is reviewed under an abuse of discretion standard.... In this case, however, the Pelsters never qualified Ley as an expert, and the magistrate judge never ruled that he was. They never identified a field of expertise or demonstrated that experts in that field reasonably rely on the sources of information actually used by Ley. We have no ruling by the magistrate judge to review, so we cannot know whether the magistrate judge considered the testimony admissible under the theory that Ley was an expert or on some other grounds, such as the non-hearsay theory discussed above. The magistrate judge merely overruled defense counsel's hearsay objections without comment.

Nevertheless, we find that Ley's conclusions were inadmissible, even if he had been properly qualified as an expert. The Federal Rules of Evidence provide for the admission of expert testimony where it will "assist the trier of fact to understand the evidence or to determine a fact in issue." Fed.R.Evid. 702. Conversely, "[w]here the subject matter is within the knowledge or experience of lay people, expert testimony is superfluous." Ellis v. Miller Oil Purchasing Co., 738 F.2d 269, 270 (8th Cir.1984).... The test for determining the appropriateness of expert testimony is "the common sense inquiry whether the untrained layman would be qualified to determine intelligently and to the best possible degree the particular issue without enlightenment from those having a specialized understanding of the subject involved in the dispute." Fed.R.Evid. 702 advisory committee's note.

In this case, any lay person has the ability to compare the odometer readings on two titles, odometer statements, or check-in sheets and decide whether and when the vehicle's odometer had been rolled back. Cf. Zimmer v. Miller Trucking Co., 743 F.2d 601, 604 (8th Cir.1984) (proper to exclude "expert" testimony of police officer regarding whether a roadside "emergency" existed because jurors are as capable as officers of answering that question). Thus, Ley's testimony that the odometers on 204 U.S. Wholesales cars and 96 other vehicles had been rolled back before those cars passed through South Central was not necessary to aid the jury. Instead, Ley's testimony provided the Pelsters with a shortcut to a proposition further up their evidentiary chain. Moreover, it was a shortcut that was based on evidence in Ley's investigative file that may or may not have been admissible on its own and that the Mortons had no opportunity to examine or rebut.

Ley's testimony presents an especially dangerous use of expert testimony. Ordinarily, an expert sets forth the general principles or procedures relied on by experts in the field or in a school of thought within the field. The expert then draws inferences and reaches conclusions that the jury would find difficult to do on its own. The expert does so, however, on the facts of the case as they have been proven by other witnesses or by the expert's own personal investigation, which may include the taking of third party statements if of a type reasonably relied upon by experts in the field. Here, Ley relied solely on hearsay statements to prove the truth of the statements themselves, not as a basis for a conclusion that the jury was not competent to draw.

The added factor of Ley's position as a "criminal investigator" for the state further increased the danger inherent in his testimony. His testimony is analogous to a police detective testifying that several witnesses had said that a drug dealer was wearing a blue jacket at the time he sold drugs to prove that the dealer had been so attired and that the defendant, who was arrested with a blue jacket, was guilty of distributing illegal drugs.

Having determined that Ley's conclusions were based on hearsay and were not proper subjects of expert testimony, we find that Ley's testimony regarding the results of his investigation prejudiced the defendants. It was only on the basis of Ley's inadmissible testimony that the Pelsters were able to assert in their closing argument that the chances were 86% that any car sold at South Central had been rolled back and 100% that a U.S. Wholesales car sold at South

Central had been rolled back. Consequently, we must remand the case for a new trial.

On retrial, it seems likely that the Pelsters will once again call Ley to the stand. We do not hold that the entirety of Ley's testimony is inadmissible, nor do we conclude that Ley may not testify as an expert witness on some topics, if the Pelsters properly qualify him. The trial judge may well find that the jury needs the assistance of expert testimony on various issues, including what information is contained on titles, odometer statements, and check-in sheets; how titles are altered; how wholesale auto auctions operate; or any number of other subjects. What the Pelsters may not do is bring inadmissible hearsay and documents before the jury in the guise of expert testimony to prove subsidiary facts in their evidentiary chain that the jury is entitled to decide for itself by examining evidence that meets the requirements for admissibility.

We acknowledge that the Pelsters are now faced with a formidable and tedious task on retrial. In addition to presenting evidence to show the presence of a representation, their reliance, and causation, they must produce admissible documents or testimony on enough rolled-back vehicles to persuade the jury that the Mortons knew of the falsity of the Ciera's odometer reading. How many vehicles they will need to trace for the jury and how to present such evidence are questions of their trial strategy.

. . .

Because the Mortons' challenge to Ley's testimony merits a new trial, we need not reach their other claims of error. The judgment is reversed, and the case is remanded to the district court for a new trial.

[Concurring opinion omitted.]

Christophersen v. Allied–Signal Corp.

United States Court of Appeals, Fifth Circuit, 1991.
939 F.2d 1106, cert. denied, 503 U.S. 912 (1992).[1]

■ Before CLARK, CHIEF JUDGE, REAVLEY, KING, JOHNSON, GARWOOD, JOLLY, HIGGINBOTHAM, DAVIS, JONES, SMITH, DUHE, WIENER and BARKSDALE, CIRCUIT JUDGES.

PER CURIAM:

The issue presented by this appeal is how a court should determine the admissibility of expert opinion testimony. At the summary judgment stage of this case, plaintiff attempted to establish medical causation of a toxic tort through the testimony of a single expert witness. The district court held that the basis of the expert's opinion was insufficiently reliable and, in the alternative, that the expert's testimony would have been more prejudicial than probative. With the expert's testimony ruled inadmissible, plaintiff was left without proof of causation. The district court entered summary judgment for the defendants. We affirm.

. . .

Christophersen died in March of 1986 as a result of a rare, small-cell form of cancer that originated in his colon and metastasized to his liver. During the fourteen years preceding his death, Christophersen worked for Marathon at its plant in Waco, Texas. At that plant, Marathon produces nickel/cadmium batteries. Christophersen never was directly involved in the production of these

---

1. Footnotes to the opinions omitted.

batteries. The record, however, indicates that over a number of years Christophersen's job duties required him to visit the area of the plant in which the batteries were manufactured. During these visits, Christophersen was allegedly exposed to fumes resulting from the manufacturing process. Plaintiffs, Christophersen's surviving spouse and child, contend that these fumes contained particles of nickel and cadmium and that Christophersen's exposure to these heavy metals caused the cancer that resulted in his death.

. . .

The district court ... granted Marathon's motion for summary judgment on the marketing defect claim because the plaintiffs did not present sufficient evidence of causation. In reaching this conclusion, the court focused on the affidavit of the plaintiffs' expert witness, Dr. Miller, who concluded that Christophersen's exposure to nickel and cadmium at Marathon caused the cancer that resulted in his death. The district court undertook an in-depth review of the basis for Dr. Miller's conclusion and determined that his opinion should be excluded....

. . .

[I]f the expert is qualified, are the facts and data that serve as a basis for the expert's opinion the same type of facts as other experts in the same field reasonably rely upon in forming their opinions? Fed.R.Evid. 703. While testimony based on the personal observations of the expert is preferable, neither the rules nor our cases have insisted on personal examinations. The reports and statements of others such as doctors, nurses, or medical personnel, while not as valuable as testimony based on the expert's own observations, can provide a reliable basis for the expert's opinion, at least when reliance on such sources is the custom of the discipline. At the same time, a common-sense skepticism may be warranted when an expert's factual basis is derived, not from treatment or observation, but from subjective information obtained from counsel or client in preparation for trial. But such skepticism should not necessarily lead us to exclude the expert's opinion. So long as the facts upon which the expert bases his opinion are those "perceived or made known to the expert at or before the hearing" and are "of a type reasonably relied upon by experts in the particular field," we should proceed to evaluate the expert's methodology. Fed.R.Evid. 703.

. . .

Dr. Miller premised his opinion that Marathon caused Christophersen's cancer on his belief that Christophersen had approximately a twenty-year history of "extensive exposure to nickel and cadmium fumes in the work place." The district court, pursuant to Rule 703, analyzed the underlying "facts and data" of Dr. Miller's opinion to determine whether it was based on the types of facts reasonably relied upon by experts in the field. Dr. Miller testified at his deposition that the level and duration of the patient's exposure are important considerations when evaluating the effect of exposure to a toxic substance.

The district court found that virtually all of the factual data concerning Christophersen's exposure to nickel and cadmium came from the affidavit of a Marathon employee named Edgar Manoliu (Manoliu), who described the fumes and Christophersen's exposure to them. The district court criticized this affidavit, however, as being inaccurate and incomplete. The Manoliu affidavit appears to have over-estimated the number of times per week Christophersen visited the manufacturing area, as well as the average length of time he would remain there on each visit. The affidavit was also devoid of any information about the type of fumes to which Christophersen was exposed or the type of fumes generated by the battery manufacturing process.

We find particularly telling Manoliu's admission in his deposition that he did not know the chemical composition of the fumes nor the mix of chemicals in the impregnation and soak tanks.

Nor was Dr. Miller informed as to the physical facilities at the Marathon plant, including the size of the plant or the impregnation and soak area, or the ventilation available in these areas or in Christophersen's office. In addition, Dr. Miller did not always rely upon the accurate data that were contained in the affidavit. For example, the affidavit correctly indicated that Christophersen worked for fourteen years at the Waco plant before his death. Dr. Miller, however, based his opinion upon the assumption that Christophersen worked in the plant for twenty years. Thus Dr. Miller over-estimated the duration of Christophersen's exposure by approximately fifty percent. Accordingly, accurate dosage and exposure information was not used by Dr. Miller.

> . . .

Plaintiffs do not contest the district court's findings as to the deficiencies in the Manoliu affidavit. Rather, they argue that Dr. Miller stated in his opinion that dosage was less important when determining individual causation. Plaintiffs accordingly argue that any deficiencies in the underlying facts and data go to the weight of Dr. Miller's opinion rather than its admissibility. We disagree. If the dosage of the harmful substance and the duration of exposure to it are the types of information upon which experts reasonably rely when forming opinions on the subject, then the district court was justified in excluding Dr. Miller's opinion that is based upon critically incomplete or grossly inaccurate dosage or duration data. . . .

As we have noted, Rule 703 seeks to ensure that the "facts and data" not otherwise admissible in evidence that form the basis of an expert's opinion are "of a type reasonably relied upon by experts in the particular field in forming opinions or inferences upon the subject." Although this rule is primarily directed toward permitting an expert to base his opinion on hearsay or otherwise inadmissible sources, Barrel of Fun, Inc. v. State Farm Fire & Casualty Co., 739 F.2d 1028, 1033 (5th Cir.1984), the inquiry into the "types" of "facts and data" underlying an expert's testimony is not limited to the admissibility of that data. District judges may reject opinions founded on critical facts that are plainly untrustworthy, principally because such an opinion cannot be helpful to the jury.

The argument that Rule 703 addresses only generic facts and data and is unconcerned with the sufficiency and accuracy of underlying facts as they relate to the case at hand, will lead to the irrational result that Rule 703 requires the court to admit an expert's opinion even if those facts and data upon which the opinion are based are crucially different from the undisputed record. Such an interpretation often will render Rule 703 impotent as a tool for testing the trustworthiness of the facts and data underlying the expert's opinion in a given trial. Certainly nothing in Rule 703 requires a court to admit an opinion based on facts that are indisputably wrong. Even if Rule 703 will not require the exclusion of such an unfounded opinion, general principles of relevance will. In other words, an opinion based totally on incorrect facts will not speak to the case at hand and hence will be irrelevant. In any event such an opinion will not advance the express goal of "assisting the trier of fact" under Rule 702.

We do not of course say that Rule 703 requires that all facts and data underlying the opinion must relate perfectly to the record facts. As we have pointed out, only when the facts and data are critically inaccurate or incomplete, as determined by what other experts would or would not be willing to base opinions upon, would the facts and data lack the necessary requisites of Rule 703. The district court in this case did not abuse its discretion.

. . .

Affirmed.

■ CLARK, CHIEF JUDGE, concurring in the result:

. . .

The second sentence of Rule 703 adopted a new approach to trustworthiness. It allows the expert to rely on inadmissible facts or data if they are of a type reasonably relied upon within the expert's community. See United States v. Williams, 447 F.2d 1285, 1290–91 (5th Cir.1971) (en banc), cert. denied, 405 U.S. 954 . . . (1972). Trustworthiness of facts or data not tested for admissibility is gained through the assurance that the expert's scientific community reasonably relies on them for the same purpose. See id. at 1290. For example, Rule 703 would permit a doctor to give a diagnostic opinion based upon facts contained in examination or test reports made by hospital technicians even if such reports were inadmissible hearsay, if it is shown that other doctors reasonably rely on such reports when forming similar opinions. Rule 703 says nothing more than that the facts or data need not be admissible in evidence if the reliability inquiry is otherwise satisfied.

If the facts or data are admissible, Rule 703 does not authorize exclusion of the expert opinion. If they are admissible, the inquiry ends, and nothing in Rule 703 authorizes exclusion of the expert's testimony. If they are not admissible, the district court must determine whether the reliability inquiry is satisfied. If it is satisfied, Rule 703 does not authorize exclusion. If it is not, the district court should exclude the testimony. No other reading is consistent with the plain language, history, and purpose of Rule 703.

Both sentences of Rule 703 apply just to the "facts or data" upon which an expert bases an opinion. Rule 703 does not address "methodology"—how the expert uses the facts or data to form an opinion. Rule 703 does not authorize a court to approve or disapprove the expert's conclusion. The words of Rule 703 allow use of facts or data "of a *type* reasonably relied upon by experts in the particular field in forming opinions or inferences upon the *subject*...." The court's inquiry is not whether experts in the relevant field would reasonably rely on the *particular* facts or data used by the expert witness. Nor does Rule 703 require a court to determine whether experts in the field would reasonably rely on the same type of facts or data to reach the expert witness's *actual* opinion. The rule is met if similar experts use facts or data of the same kind to form opinions on the subject in issue. . . .

. . .

In Viterbo v. Dow Chem. Co., 826 F.2d 420 (5th Cir.1987), this circuit began disregarding the plain language of Rule 703. Viterbo held that expert opinion testimony may be excluded under Rule 703 if, without regard to the admissibility of the underlying facts or data, other experts in the field would reasonably rely on the facts and data assumed by the expert witness. See id. at 422–24. This interpretation is erroneous for two reasons. First, it disregards the fact that the reliability of the facts and data underlying the expert's opinion only comes into question if the facts and data are not admissible. Second, it disregards the fact that Rule 703's reliability inquiry addresses only the "type" of facts and data used by the expert witness and whether experts in the field would reasonably rely on facts or data of that type in forming opinions "upon the subject." This reliability inquiry provides the only necessary and proper guarantee of trustworthiness.

. . .

The majority says that giving the rule its plain meaning "often will render Rule 703 impotent as a tool for testing the trustworthiness of the facts and data underlying the expert's opinion in a given trial." This criticism grafts onto the rule a function that is incompatible with its language and purpose. The trustworthiness aspect of the reliability inquiry has nothing to do with whether the expert's facts or data provide sufficient support for the expert's opinion. Rule 703 does not say that the facts or data upon which an expert witness bases an opinion must supply reasonably reliable support for that opinion. Rather, the rule treats the reliability inquiry as a sufficient guarantee that an expert's inadmissible facts or data are sufficiently trustworthy to overcome the reasons why they are inadmissible. The rules deal with fundamentally unsupported but relevant expert opinions only in terms of probity versus prejudice under Rule 403. . . .

. . .

In today's case, the facts and data upon which Dr. Miller based his opinion were the Manoliu affidavit, Christophersen's medical records, and medical literature. . . . In rendering summary judgment, the district court did not expressly determine that these facts and data could not have been admitted in evidence. For summary judgment purposes, the facts contained in Manoliu's affidavit should have been considered admissible at trial in the form of Manoliu's direct testimony. The facts contained in the medical records should have been considered admissible in the form of direct testimony by those who made the records or as records of regularly conducted activity. See Fed. R. Evid. 803(6). Medical records also might be the type of sources of information upon which cancer experts reasonably rely when forming their opinions as to the causes of a person's cancer. No competent summary judgment proof suggests that they were not. The data contained in the medical literature would have been admissible over a hearsay objection under the learned treatise exception to the hearsay rule. See Fed. R. Evid. 803(18). The majority and the district court did not consider whether the facts and data relied on by Dr. Miller were admissible.

The district court also attempted to determine whether experts in the field of cancer research would have reasonably relied on the particular facts and data used by Dr. Miller (the Manoliu affidavit, medical literature, and medical records) to form his actual opinion (that nickel and cadmium caused Christophersen's colon cancer). This analysis was also improper. Rule 703 only asks the court to determine whether experts in the field of cancer research would have reasonably relied on facts or data of this "type" in forming opinions or inferences "upon the subject" of cancer causation.

Insistence on a punctilious observance of the intended operation of Rules 702 and 703 does not put form over substance. Rather it enforces the spirit of the Federal Rules of Evidence which provide the trier of fact with all but a narrow band of relevant evidence. Evidence authorized by the literal terms of Rules 702 and 703 may not be excluded unless the court balances probity against substantially greater prejudice as required by Rule 403. . . . The majority opinion destroys the value of that weighing because it allows district courts to exclude expert opinions under Rules 702 and 703 for reasons those rules do not permit.

Because the district court's analysis of Dr. Miller's testimony was premised on an incorrect legal interpretation of Rule 703 that would deprive a jury of evidence it should be able to consider, I agree with Judge Reavley that exclusion on the basis of Rule 703 was manifestly erroneous and that the majority erred in basing affirmance on this rule.

. . .

While I reject Viterbo's departure from the plain meaning of Rule 703, I agree with its reasoning that if an opinion is fundamentally unsupported, then it offers no expects assistance to the jury; and that lack of reliable support can render an opinion substantially more prejudicial than probative, making it inadmissible under Rule 403. . . .

. . .

I do not disagree with the dissent's view that Dr. Miller's testimony passed Rules 702 and 703. I very much disagree with its view that the court was required to admit his opinion testimony because the provisions of these two rules were met. The trial court was requested to review the evidence under Rule 403. He did so and concluded that Dr. Miller's testimony should be excluded.

. . .

■ REAVLEY, CIRCUIT JUDGE, with whom KING, JOHNSON and WIENER, CIRCUIT JUDGES, join, dissenting:

. . .

An expert may base an opinion on "facts or data" otherwise inadmissible, if "of a type reasonably relied upon by experts in the particular field in forming opinions or inferences on the subject." Courts properly defer "to the expert's view that experts in his field reasonably rely on such sources of information." Greenwood Utilities Comm'n v. Mississippi Power Co., 751 F.2d 1484, 1495 (5th Cir.1985); see also In re Japanese Electronic Products, 723 F.2d at 277 (district court misinterpreted Rule 703 by "substituting its own opinion as to what constitutes reasonable reliance"). . . .

If Judge Clark would override that fact issue with Rule 403, he fashions a rule with the following new and drastic effect. Judges may weigh contradictory evidence and exclude any proffered evidence considered unreliable. The judge's opinion about the contested evidence determines unreliability. The force of the proffered evidence on the very point at issue becomes the prejudice.

. . .

■ [Opinion of KING, CIRCUIT JUDGE, with which JUDGES REAVLEY, JOHNSON and WIENER, joined, dissenting, omitted.]

People v. Anderson

Supreme Court of Illinois, 1986.
113 Ill.2d 1, 99 Ill.Dec. 104, 495 N.E.2d 485, cert. denied, 479 U.S. 1012.

■ JUSTICE SIMON delivered the opinion of the court:

On September 5, 1978, the defendant, Clifford Anderson, shot and killed the manager and the engineer of the apartment building where he lived and was employed as a janitor. He was indicted on two counts of murder and two counts of armed violence. At trial he defended on the ground of insanity. . . .

The defendant concedes that the only material issue at trial was his sanity, and thus an extended discussion of the facts is unnecessary. To establish his defense, the defendant called a psychiatrist, his roommate, and his sister. The psychiatrist had interviewed Anderson and reviewed various psychiatric and criminal records, as well as letters written by or at the direction of Anderson. In response to a hypothetical question, the expert testified that the defendant could not conform his conduct to the requirements of the law at the time of the shootings. On cross-examination he stated that the defendant probably was unable to appreciate the criminality of his acts.

. . .

A . . . question which arose at both of the defendant's previous trials, and which is likely to recur at a new trial, is to what extent the defendant's expert witness could disclose to the jury the basis for his diagnosis. Specifically, the defendant challenges the judge's ruling that his psychiatric expert could not reveal facts or opinions contained in reports upon which he relied in making his diagnosis. The defendant also argues that the court was incorrect in preventing the psychiatrist from recounting specific statements made by the defendant to him. Because these questions are of importance to the proper consideration of the insanity defense, we proceed to address them in turn.

The trial judge refused to allow any disclosure of the contents of the reports upon which the defendant's expert witness, Dr. Jerome Katz, relied in forming his opinion. These reports included evaluations by psychiatrists, doctors, and counselors made while Anderson was in the army and while he was incarcerated in California, reports by the State's psychiatric experts, and information relating to a previous criminal offense. Dr. Katz was allowed only to state that he utilized these reports.

After this court's decisions in People v. Ward (1975), 61 Ill.2d 559, 338 N.E.2d 171, and Wilson v. Clark (1981), 84 Ill.2d 186, 49 Ill.Dec. 308, 417 N.E.2d 1322, it is undisputed that even though reports made by others may be substantively inadmissible, an expert may utilize them in forming his opinion as long as experts in the field reasonably rely on such materials. Nor is there any question that the psychiatric profession reasonably and customarily relies on records of the kind at issue here; both Dr. Katz and the State's expert, Dr. Gerson Kaplan, testified that a patient's psychiatric history is one of the most important criteria in making a diagnosis. . . . The only question is whether the rationale of Ward and Wilson also allows the psychiatric expert to explain the basis of his opinion by referring to relevant matters in the reports.

At issue in Ward was a diagnosis by the prosecution's psychiatric expert which was grounded in a personal interview with the accused as well as a review of other reports, including evaluations by another psychiatrist and a psychologist. In addition to stating his opinion that the defendant was sane, the doctor disclosed the findings of some of the secondhand sources. This court, relying on Rule 703 of the Federal Rules of Evidence . . . , held that expert medical opinion on the question of sanity based in part on records compiled by others which had not been admitted into evidence was permissible if the reports "are of a type customarily utilized by the medical profession." People v. Ward (1975), 61 Ill.2d 559, 568, 338 N.E.2d 171.

The State correctly notes that Ward did not explicitly hold that it was proper for the psychiatrist to reveal the contents of the reports he relied upon in arriving at his diagnosis. The majority of appellate cases following Ward, however, have interpreted it as implicitly deciding that the underlying facts and opinions could be disclosed. . . .

The defendant points to Ward and the appellate court decisions for support, and adds that this court's opinion in Wilson v. Clark (1981), 84 Ill.2d 186, 49 Ill.Dec. 308, 417 N.E.2d 1322, clarifies that expert witnesses may disclose the contents of otherwise inadmissible materials upon which they reasonably rely. In Wilson, the court prospectively adopted Rules 703 and 705 of the Federal Rules of Evidence to govern all cases involving expert testimony. . . .

. . .

Rule 705, which was enacted to eliminate the necessity for the hypothetical question and to place the burden for eliciting the facts upon which an expert opinion is based on the cross-examiner . . ., does not clearly answer whether such facts may be brought out on direct examination. Nor does Rule 703 by its terms resolve this issue. However, in our judgment the logic underlying Rule 703 and this court's decisions in Ward and Wilson compels the conclusion that an expert should be allowed to reveal the contents of materials upon which he reasonably relies in order to explain the basis of his opinion.

Rule 703 was designed to " 'broaden the basis for expert opinions . . . and to bring the judicial practice into line with the practice of the experts themselves when not in court.' " (People v. Ward (1975), 61 Ill.2d 559, 567, 338 N.E.2d 171, quoting Advisory Committee Note to Rule 703.) The rule thus expands the range of information available, at least indirectly, to the trier of fact. Inasmuch as the opinion based on these materials—which are deemed trustworthy by the profession—is allowed, it would be both illogical and anomalous to deprive the jury of the reasons supporting that opinion.

This conclusion accords with the overwhelming weight of authority from other jurisdictions as well as a great deal of persuasive scholarly commentary. . . .

To prevent the expert from referring to the contents of materials upon which he relied in arriving at his conclusion "places an unreal stricture on him and compels him to be not only less than frank with the jury but also . . . to appear to base his diagnosis upon reasons which are flimsy and inconclusive when in fact they may not be." (State v. Myers (1976), 159 W.Va. 353, 358, 222 S.E.2d 300, 304.) Absent a full explanation of the expert's reasons, including underlying facts and opinions, the jury has no way of evaluating the expert testimony . . . and is therefore faced with a "meaningless conclusion" by the witness (State v. Griffin (1965), 99 Ariz. 43, 49, 406 P.2d 397, 401).

We reject the State's suggestion that the jury was adequately apprised of the basis of Dr. Katz' opinion because he identified the sources of the reports. The mere fact that the doctor utilized specified background material did not tell the jury "which opinions he credited, which he rejected, and why." (See United States v. Harper (5th Cir.1971), 450 F.2d 1032, 1037.) As the court in Harper aptly stated:

"In a case such as this, in which expert witnesses express different conclusions as to the defendant's mental condition at the time of the alleged offense, it is important that the jury know upon what facts the expert witness based his conclusion. As we have said on several occasions, 'expert opinion as to insanity rises no higher than the reasons upon which it is based.' " 450 F.2d 1032, 1037.

The trial court ruled, and the State maintains here, that the information in the records utilized by Dr. Katz constitutes inadmissible hearsay and that Rule 703 was not intended to create an exception to the hearsay rule. Of course, by even allowing an expert to consider such materials in forming an opinion they are indirectly brought before the jury. More fundamentally, however, the State's argument misapprehends the hearsay rule. Hearsay is an extrajudicial statement offered in court "to show the truth of the matters asserted." . . . Although the contents of the reports relied upon by Dr. Katz would clearly be inadmissible if offered for their truth, the defense seeks to allow the expert to disclose the underlying facts and conclusions not for their truth but for the limited purpose of explaining the basis for the expert witness' opinion. For this limited purpose the statements do not constitute hearsay, and can therefore be allowed. See, e.g., Paddack v. Dave Christensen, Inc. (9th Cir.1984), 745 F.2d 1254, 1262; United States v. Ramos (11th Cir.1984), 725 F.2d 1322.

It is true that an uninformed jury could misuse this type of information as substantive proof of insanity. We do not believe that this possibility is a sufficient reason to deny the jury an adequate basis for assessing the weight and credibility of expert opinion. A limiting instruction, advising the jury to consider the underlying statements only to evaluate the basis of the expert's opinion, should forestall any such misuse. (United States v. Madrid (10th Cir.1982), 673 F.2d 1114; United States v. Harper (5th Cir.1971), 450 F.2d 1032, 1037; Brown Mechanical Contractors, Inc. v. Centennial Insurance Co. (Ala.1983), 431 So.2d 932, 944; Saltzburg and Redden, Federal Rules of Evidence Manual 671 (4th ed. 1986).) A trial judge, of course, need not allow the expert to recite secondhand information when its probative value in explaining the expert's opinion pales beside its likely prejudicial impact or its tendency to create confusion.

The final question to be addressed, which was expressly left open in People v. Gacy (1984), 103 Ill.2d 1, 71, 82 Ill.Dec. 391, 468 N.E.2d 1171, is whether a psychiatric expert may be precluded from relating statements made to him by the defendant which figure in his diagnosis. Because, as Dr. Katz testified, psychiatrists customarily rely on statements made by a patient in forming a diagnosis (Diamond and Louisell, The Psychiatrist as an Expert Witness: Some Ruminations and Speculations, 63 Mich.L.Rev. 1335, 1350 (1965); Dieden and Gasparich, Psychiatric Evidence and Full Disclosure in the Criminal Trial, 52 Calif.L.Rev. 543, 550 (1964)), an expert must be allowed to repeat those statements if relevant to explaining the opinion to the jury. . . .

. . .

The convictions are reversed and the cause remanded for a new trial.

NOTES

1. *Hearsay in the Basis of Expert Opinion.* Why should expert opinion be allowed to rest upon otherwise inadmissible hearsay? Finnegan v. Fall River Gas Works Co., 34 N.E. 523 (Mass.1893): The issue was whether the victim of fatal inhalation of gas had undergone conscious suffering. A physician was allowed to testify that there had been conscious suffering, although deceased died alone without medical attendance and the witness had no experience personally or through patients with this kind of asphyxiation. Holmes J. wrote an opinion approving attribution of weight to the testimony: "Although it might not be admissible merely to repeat what a witness had read in a book not itself admissible, still, when one who is competent on the general subject accepts from his reading as probably true a matter of detail which he has not verified, the fact gains an authority which it would not have had from the printed page alone, and, subject perhaps to the exercise of some discretion, may be admitted." See also United States v. Sims, 514 F.2d 147, 149 (9th Cir.), cert. denied, 423 U.S. 845 (1975): "Years of experience teach the expert to separate the wheat from the chaff and to use only those sources and kinds of information which are of a type reasonably relied upon by similar experts in arriving at sound opinions on the subject." Brown v. United States, 375 F.2d 310, 318 (D.C.Cir.1966), cert. denied, 388 U.S. 915 (1967): "The information is winnowed through the mental process of the expert, and is by him either accepted or rejected." State v. Weber, 496 N.W.2d 762, 767 (Wis.App.1993): "The expert is assumed ... to have the skill to properly evaluate the hearsay as a basis for a judgment upon which he or she would act in the practice of his or her profession, and to give it the probative force appropriate to the circumstances."

Do these explanations justify allowing expert opinion to rest upon hearsay in the following cases? United States v. Lundy, 809 F.2d 392, 395–96 (7th Cir.1987): Not ground for exclusion of expert's opinion that fire was of incendiary origin that he relied not only on his long experience in investigating fires and observation of burned premises, but also on statements made to him by many people "involved in the fire." The witness "presented uncontroverted evidence that interviews with many witnesses to a fire are a standard investigatory technique in cause and origin inquiries." United States v. Elkins, 885 F.2d 775, 786 (11th Cir.1989), cert. denied, 494 U.S. 1005 (1990): Expert in Libyan history allowed to testify as to who was head of the Libyan military, relying in part on the Libyan press. United States v. McCollum, 732 F.2d 1419, 1422–23 (9th Cir.), cert. denied, 469 U.S. 920 (1984): Prosecution for attempted bank robbery. The defense was that defendant had been under hypnosis at the time of the attempted robbery. A forensic hypnotist called by defendant gave his opinion that defendant had been under hypnosis at the time of the attempted robbery. In reaching this conclusion, the hypnotist relied on statements made to him by the defendant recounting how defendant had been hypnotized prior to the attempted robbery. In the opinion of the hypnotist, when the defendant made these statements, he was under hypnosis induced by the hypnotist. United States v. Rollins, 862 F.2d 1282, 1293 (7th Cir.1988), cert. denied, 490 U.S. 1074 (1989): Not error to admit opinion of narcotics agent regarding the meaning of certain code words, based in part on the statement of an informant regarding what certain words meant. "[A]gent Wright testified that although he had heard many of the code words that Wells and Slaughter used in other narcotics cases that he had worked on, he had never heard the specific term 't-shirts' used as a code word before. According to Agent Wright's testimony, however, the term 't-shirts' is the type of word that would normally be used by narcotics dealers to disguise the true nature of their conversations. Thus, although Agent Wright testified that Wells told him that 't-shirts' meant cocaine, he also based his opinion regarding the meaning of this term on the context of Wells' and Slaughter's conversations, and his vast prior experience with narcotics trafficking and the use of code words."[1]

McLellan v. Morrison, 434 A.2d 28, 30 (Me.1981): Not error to admit testimony of a physician that an injury to plaintiff's ulnar nerve was not caused by an automobile accident even though the opinion was based in part on a telephone conversation with another physician. "In conferring with another

---

1.   Footnote omitted.

medical expert, Dr. Griffin was merely following a procedure similar to consulting a medical textbook to obtain a confirmation of his own tentative conclusion." Drexler v. Seaboard System R.R., 530 So.2d 754 (Ala.1988): Error to admit opinion of economist on present value of future wages when he had obtained interest and inflation rates his calculation took into account by a telephone call to the public library.

Does it make a difference to the acceptability of hearsay in the basis of expert opinion that the hearsay relates to the facts of the litigated case, to the facts of other cases or general propositions more or less directly employed in reaching a conclusion about the litigated case, or to the range of information and background propositions that constitute the witness an expert in his field generally? As seen at the beginning of the discussion of the nature and function of expert testimony, supra p. 955, it is not easy to draw a line between "the facts of the litigated case" and other matters. At the same time it is clear, as a practical matter, that unless hearsay is allowed in the basis of expert opinion at least in regard to the general educational background of the witness, no expert opinion testimony would be possible. Furthermore, the educational process that has made the witness an expert in his field ordinarily has built-in mechanisms for countering unreliable information.

2. *Fed. R. Evid. 703.* Christopherson v. Allied Signal Corp. presents the question whether Fed. R. Evid. 703, as well as Rule 702, imposes a requirement of reliability for the admission of expert testimony, even though there may be nothing in the basis of the expert opinion that brings into play any exclusionary rule. The citation to Rule 703 in the Court's opinion in Daubert may suggest that it does. There is the further question regarding the conditions that must be satisfied in order for expert opinion based upon inadmissible hearsay to be allowed into evidence. Considerable controversy surrounds the second sentence in Rule 703—"If of a type reasonably relied upon by experts in the particular field in forming opinions or inferences upon the subject, the facts or data need not be admissible in evidence." The idea that experts rely upon hearsay in forming an opinion could mean, not that they attach some specific probative value to the hearsay, but that they attach a probative value different from that which would be attached by nonexperts. Under Rule 703, is it enough that the particular expert has relied on the hearsay statement in this sense, or is it also required that some group of experts also would rely, and, furthermore, that the group would attach to the hearsay statement the same probative value as the witness? If reference to a group is required, then the difficulties encountered in application of the Frye test are present: What group? How is it to be determined what the group thinks? Finally, is it enough that the witness gives the hearsay statement a different probative value than would nonexperts and that the probative value he gives is the same as would be given by some group of experts or, additionally, must it be determined that the reliance is "reasonable"?

In re Paoli R. R. Yard PCB Litigation, 35 F.3d 717, 747–48 (3d Cir.1994), cert. denied, 115 S.Ct. 1253 (1995):

> Under our case law on Rule 703, "the proper inquiry is not what the court deems reliable, but what experts in the relevant discipline deem it to be." In re Japanese Elect. Prod., 723 F.2d at 277. See also DeLuca, 911 F.2d at 952; Paoli I, 916 F.2d at 853. We have held that the district judge must make a factual finding as to what data *experts* find reliable ..., and that if an expert avers that his testimony is based on a type of data on which experts reasonably rely, that is generally enough to survive the Rule 703 inquiry.... [W]e think that our former view is no longer tenable in

light of Daubert.... By requiring the judge to look to the views of other experts rather than allowing the judge to exercise independent judgment, current Third Circuit case law eviscerates the judge's gatekeeping role with respect to an expert's data and instead gives that role to other experts....

We now make clear that it is the judge who makes the determination of reasonable reliance, and that for the judge to make the factual determination under Rule 104(a) that an expert is basing his or her opinion on a type of data *reasonably* relied upon by experts, the judge must conduct an independent evaluation into reasonableness. The judge can of course take into account the particular expert's opinion that experts reasonably rely on that type of data, as well as the opinions of other experts as to its reliability, but the judge can also take into account other factors he or she deems relevant.

State v. Henze, 356 N.W.2d 538 (Iowa 1984): Prosecution for driving under the influence of alcohol. Dr. Berstler, a witness called by defendant, had examined defendant at a clinic shortly after his arrest and later consulted medical records prepared by other doctors in the clinic before the date of the arrest. The records stated that defendant had an anxiety neurosis, was depressed and took Valium. If restricted to his own observations of defendant on the night of the arrest, Dr. Berstler could testify only that he was unable to form an opinion whether defendant was or was not intoxicated on the night of the arrest; if allowed to take into account the medical records, Dr. Berstler could testify that defendant's appearance and behavior on the night of the arrest did not require the conclusion that he was intoxicated, but could be explained by anxiety, depression and the use of Valium. Held: Error, under Iowa Rule of Evidence 703 (identical with Fed. R. Evid. 703), not to allow Dr. Berstler to include the medical records in the basis for his opinion. The court took judicial notice that doctors customarily rely on medical records prepared by others in forming their opinions. Dissent:

> More importantly, Dr. Berstler did not say, and no other evidence suggests, that the specific medical records on which he was basing his opinion were of the type usually relied upon by medical experts in forming the specific type of opinion defendant wished Dr. Berstler to present to the jury.
>
> I do not doubt that medical doctors often rely upon medical records prepared by other persons in forming their own opinions or drawing some kinds of inferences. I am unwilling to stretch that general observation into a judicially noticed fact that would satisfy rule 703 whenever a medical doctor wishes to give opinion testimony based in part on another doctor's medical records, regardless of the type of record, type of medical specialty, and type of opinion or inference to be drawn. The admissibility of opinion testimony based on hearsay should depend on the circumstances of each specific case, not on judicial notice of what doctors routinely rely upon in general.

Id. at 541.

In re "Agent Orange" Product Liability Litigation, 611 F.Supp. 1223, 1246 (E.D.N.Y.1985), aff'd, 818 F.2d 187 (2d Cir.1987), cert. denied, 487 U.S. 1243 (1988): The court held that the testimony of an expert that the cause of diseases suffered by Vietnam veterans was the herbicide "Agent Orange" was inadmissible because the expert relied upon affidavits and checklists that had been prepared by the veterans detailing the veterans' diseases and their exposure to Agent Orange in Vietnam. The affidavits and checklists "are not material that experts in this field would reasonably rely upon and so must be excluded under Rule 703. Although the court would usually hold a full Rule

104(a) hearing prior to making such a determination, the unreasonableness of Dr. Singer's ... [opinion] is so blatant that a hearing would be useless. The court takes judicial notice—based on hundreds of trials—that no reputable physician relies on hearsay checklists by litigants to reach a conclusion with respect to the cause of their afflictions." See also In re "Agent Orange" Product Liability Litigation, 611 F.Supp. 1267, 1280–81 (1985), aff'd, 818 F.2d 187 (2d Cir.1987), cert. denied, 487 U.S. 1234 (1988). The opinions in the Agent Orange case are not entirely clear whether an expert's opinion should be excluded only if experts in the field would not rely upon the sort of hearsay he relied upon, or also if the court finds that the hearsay is unreliable.

3. *Confrontation Clause.* Extrajudicial declarations in the basis of expert opinion can raise questions not only under the hearsay rule, but also under the Confrontation Clause as well. United States v. Smith, 869 F.2d 348, 355 (7th Cir.1989): Not a violation of Rule 703 or the Confrontation Clause to admit voice identification testimony of Dr. Nakasone based upon examination of spectrograms made by Lieutenant Smrkovski, who was originally to have been a prosecution witness but became unavailable.

4. *Summaries.* In certain cases a witness is allowed to summarize the reports of others. It may be asked in what sense such testimony should be viewed as expert opinion testimony. United States v. Aluminum Co. of America, 35 F.Supp. 820, 823 (S.D.N.Y.1940): An issue was the quality and quantity of remote and scattered ore deposits. Expert testimony based on drill hole reports made by others was approved. "Opinion testimony by an acceptable expert resting wholly or partly on information, oral or documentary, recited by him as gathered from others, which is trustworthy and which is practically unobtainable by other means, is competent even though the firsthand sources from which the information came be not produced in court.... In other words, when hearsay evidence is offered it is admissible if resort to it be essential in order to discover the truth and if the surroundings persuade the court that the information adduced by the expert as a basis of his opinion is reliable." See the valuable discussion of the question in Dession, The Trial of Economic and Technological Issues of Fact: I, 58 Yale L.J. 1242 (1949). See also Keen v. O'Rourke, 290 P.2d 976 (Wash.1955): In action for amounts due on contract, not error to allow plaintiff to introduce written summaries of credits and debits of defendant's accounts. These summaries were prepared from office records by plaintiff's bookkeeper. The court stated that the summaries were admitted for the purpose of illustrating the bookkeeper's testimony. The records from which the summaries were made were also admitted into evidence. For discussions of Fed. R. Evid. 1006, dealing with summaries of voluminous writings, see supra pp. 234–35 and 690–91. For expert testimony and public opinion polls, see supra p. 679 and infra pp. 1274–75.

5. *Revealing Hearsay on Direct Examination of the Expert.* This issue, which is addressed in People v. Anderson, is much disputed. People v. Nicolaus, 817 P.2d 893, 909–10 (Cal.1991), cert. denied, 505 U.S. 1224 (1992): Not abuse of discretion to refuse to admit into evidence journal articles relied upon by expert. State v. Barrett, 445 N.W.2d 749 (Iowa 1989): Error to allow expert to state on redirect that none of his colleagues had given him persuasive reason to disregard his opinion that a death was murder and not suicide. Schuchman v. Stackable, 555 N.E.2d 1012, 1024–28 (Ill.App.), cert. denied, 561 N.E.2d 708 (Ill.1990): Not error to prohibit expert who relied upon medical treatises and articles to read from or summarize them. Dissent:

> To suggest that the use of authorities in cross-examination is different because they are used for impeachment only and not offered as substantive

evidence ignores the fact that when they are submitted as bases of the expert's opinion (as they were in this case) they are not being offered as substantive evidence either. In both situations they are being offered for non-substantive reasons, in both situations there is the danger that the jury will fail to recognize this distinction, but in both cases that danger can hopefully be overcome by an appropriate limiting instruction.

Henriksen v. Cameron, 622 A.2d 1135, 1144 (Me.1993):

> Pursuant to Rule 703, Dr. Collins could testify that he relied on Dr. Voss's report in order to establish the factual foundation necessary for the admissibility of his opinion. Testimony regarding the substance of Dr. Voss's report, however, is not necessary to establish factual foundation under Rule 703 and remains hearsay not within any exception.... Rule 703 does not make the substance of Dr. Voss's report admissible and, therefore, admitting Dr. Collins' testimony about the substance of the report was error.

> The trial court's error in admitting this evidence, however, was harmless.... From Dr. Collins' testimony that he relied on Dr. Voss's report which was properly admitted, a jury could infer that Dr. Voss's report essentially supported Dr. Collins' opinion. Therefore, the admission of evidence confirming that Dr. Voss agreed with Dr. Collins was cumulative and thus its admission constitutes harmless error not requiring reversal.[2]

United States v. Affleck, 776 F.2d 1451, 1456–58 (10th Cir.1985): In prosecution for securities fraud, accountant who testified for the government regarding whether financial information was altered or misrepresented to investors, relied not only on an examination of the records of defendant's companies, but also on interviews with defendant's employees, former accountants and the trustee in bankruptcy. During the course of the accountant's direct testimony, he related what he had been told by these persons. Held: No error because these were statements reasonably relied upon by accountants and because the evidence was used only to explain how the witness had formed his conclusion and was not offered to prove the truth of the out of court assertions.

Carlson, Experts as Hearsay Conduits: Confrontation Abuses in Opinion Testimony, 76 Minn. L. Rev. 859 (1992) (would not allow recital of inadmissible hearsay on direct when it concerns case-specific facts); Carlson, In Defense of a Constitutional Theory of Experts, 87 Nw. U. L. Rev. 1182 (1993).

In 1989, Minnesota's Rule 703, identical to Fed. R. Evid. 703, was amended to add subsection (b):

> Underlying expert data must be independently admissible in order to be received upon direct examination; provided that when good cause is shown in civil cases and the underlying data is particularly trustworthy, the court may admit the data under this rule for the limited purpose of showing the basis for the expert's opinion. Nothing in this rule restricts admissibility of underlying expert data when inquired into on cross-examination.

50 Minn. Stat. Annot. 87 (West 1996).

6. *Cross-Examination of the Expert.* United States v. A & S Council Oil Co., 947 F.2d 1128, 1135 (4th Cir.1991): Jackson, a government witness, incriminated defendant. Some of Jackson's direct testimony cast doubt on Jackson's sanity. After Jackson had testified, the government called a psychiatrist who testified that although Jackson suffered from a schizophrenic affective disorder,

---

2. Footnote omitted.

he could distinguish reality from imagination. On cross-examination, the defendant sought to question the psychiatrist regarding the results of a polygraph examination that Jackson had taken and the opinion of the examiner that Jackson was not telling the truth when he incriminated the defendant, which circumstances the psychiatrist had considered when forming his opinion about Jackson's mental state. Held: "Full examination of the underpinnings of an expert's opinion is permitted because the expert, like all witnesses, puts his credibility in issue by taking the stand. Jackson's polygraph result is relevant to ... [the psychiatrist's] credibility because ... [the psychiatrist] must have necessarily discounted it to reach the opinion he stated in court.... We emphasize that the polygraph result is admissible as an attack on ... [the psychiatrist's] opinion, not directly on Jackson's credibility...." Is allowing defendant to cross-examine the psychiatrist in this fashion consistent with the position, possibly dictated by Daubert, that the psychiatrist's opinion would not be admissible if based upon the polygraph result?

Lewandowski v. Preferred Risk Mut. Ins. Co., 146 N.W.2d 505, 509 (Wis.1966): Plaintiff's expert relied upon letters from another doctor not called as a witness; error not to permit defendant to introduce the letters "for impeachment purposes or to test the validity of the opinion." But see Shinn v. Francis, 404 P.2d 1017, 1022 (Okla.1965): Error to permit defendant on cross-examination of plaintiff's expert witness to ask him, for purpose of "test[ing] his opinion in the light of the facts and tests reported to him," about the findings of other doctors, contradictory to the opinion of plaintiff's expert, contained in reports that had been submitted to him. "On direct examination of the doctor, plaintiff's counsel very carefully confined his questions to opinions of the doctor based upon the doctor's own examinations and the case history furnished by plaintiff and not upon the reports of the other doctors." Vinicky v. Midland Mut. Cas. Ins. Co., 151 N.W.2d 77, 82–83 (Wis.1967): Not error to permit plaintiff to introduce report defendant's expert referred to on direct and relied upon in forming his opinion, but error to permit plaintiff to introduce report which, although expert admitted on cross-examination he had seen and read, had not formed a basis of his opinion.

In Ruth v. Fenchel, 121 A.2d 373, 377 (N.J.1956), the court made the following statement regarding references to treatises in the examination and cross-examination of expert witnesses:

> Thus the law settled ... was this: Experts may state what books they relied on in forming their opinions but may not give the contents unless these are asked for in cross-examination (in which case "the treatise may be read to show that it does not contain ... corroboration, on the principle of discrediting a witness by showing misstatements on a material point." 6 Wigmore, Evidence (3d ed.) sec. 1700, p. 19), and the witness may also be cross-examined as to whether he admits other books to be recognized and standard authorities, and upon such admission may be confronted with statements in those books. The statements from such books and documents may be thus admitted on the cross-examination of the witness either when the authorities have been cited by him or are admitted by him to be recognized and standard authorities on the subject. Even then the work itself is not to be admitted in evidence, but the statements only may be read by the cross-examiner so far as they are material and have first been brought to the attention of the witness....

Ellison v. Simmons, 447 S.W.2d 66, 70–71 (Mo.1969):

> The other point we will consider relates to the cross-examination of plaintiff's witness Carter. He testified concerning a test he performed at

plaintiff's request to determine the stopping distance of a car being operated at 65 m.p.h. on the road in question. He had with him while on the witness stand a book entitled 'Traffic Accident Investigation Manual.' In cross-examining the witness defendant had him read from a chart in the book which showed a stopping distance at 65 m.p.h. which was much farther than the result of the test performed by the witness. Plaintiff contends that the court erred in overruling his objection to that evidence because the chart in the manual constituted hearsay.... We think ... that the manner in which defendant used the manual in this instance was improper in that it resulted in the admission of the stopping distance shown in the manual as independent evidence of that fact.... Under certain circumstances it has been held not to be an abuse of the trial court's discretion to permit the use of such a manual in testing the knowledge of an expert on cross-examination.... However, we do not think such would have been proper in this instance because the witness did not testify generally concerning his knowledge of the stopping distances but simply related the result of this specific test.

In Darling v. Charleston Community Memorial Hosp., 211 N.E.2d 253, 259 (Ill.1965), cert. denied, 383 U.S. 946 (1966), the court abandoned the rule that an expert may be cross-examined only about treatises upon which he expressly based his opinion and allowed cross-examination as to recognized authorities: "The author's competence is established if the judge takes judicial notice of it, or if it is established by a witness expert in the subject." See also Hemminghaus v. Ferguson, 215 S.W.2d 481, 488 (Mo.1948) (approving reading passages from recognized authorities to witness on cross and redirect examination and asking about his agreement).

Federal Rule of Evidence 803 (18) provides:

"The following are not excluded by the hearsay rule ... To the extent called to the attention of an expert witness upon cross-examination or relied upon by the expert witness in direct examination, statements contained in published treatises, periodicals or pamphlets on a subject of history, medicine, or other science or art, established as a reliable authority by the testimony or admission of the witness or by other expert testimony or by judicial notice. If admitted, the statements may be read into evidence but may not be received as exhibits."

See also California Evidence Code §§ 721, 1341. For further discussion and citations, see supra p. 766.

See Holz, Learned Treatises As Evidence in Wisconsin, 51 Marq. L. Rev. 271 (1967) (touching upon such questions as pretrial notice of treatise passages to be used and certification of authoritative treatises by professional societies); Note, Medical Treatises to Be Admitted as Direct Evidence in Wisconsin, 66 Mich. L. Rev. 183 (1967) (suggesting advantage of nonpartisan, nonlitigation-oriented treatise over expert witnesses called by parties); Seidelson, Medical Malpractice Cases and the Reluctant Expert, 16 Cath. U. L. Rev. 158, 169–71 (1966) (excellent discussion of the failure of statutes and judicially adopted rules embodying the "learned treatise" exception to the hearsay rule to solve plaintiffs' problems in medical malpractice cases).

7. *Material in the Basis of Expert Opinion Violating Exclusionary Rules Other than the Hearsay Rule.* International Adhesive Coating v. Bolton Emerson International, Inc., 851 F.2d 540, 543–45 (1st Cir.1988): Action for damages for breach of warranty covering the electrical elements in a boiler manufactured by defendant. Because of a breakdown in the boiler function, the plaintiff suffered business losses.

The damage amounts had been calculated by Stephen Vesey, an accounting expert, who reviewed International's financial records and prepared a report outlining the documentable costs assignable to each of International's claimed losses....

With these principles in mind, we have no trouble concluding that Vesey's testimony was properly admitted under Rule 703. Vesey testified that he derived his damage estimates by reviewing International's business and financial records and through interviews with company personnel. We think it obvious that these are sources of information normally and reasonably relied upon by accountants, and Vesey testified to this effect as well. The jury was entitled to believe Vesey's testimony. The verdict demonstrates that it did.

To be sure, Vesey's description of the underlying documentation was sometimes abbreviated and conclusory, but that went to the weight of his testimony, not its admissibility. Both in the district court and on appeal, Emerson has failed to come to terms with Rules 703 and 705, maintaining that Vesey was obligated, as a condition of admissibility, to present "invoices, statements, documents, breakdown or ... supporting data to support the areas damages that he testified about." As we have already pointed out, this is contrary to the words of the Rules and the case law. We find it especially significant that, throughout the pretrial period, Emerson had access to all of the International business and financial documents upon which Vesey relied. Emerson also received a copy of Vesey's report two years before trial. Emerson thus had ample opportunity to investigate, expose and rebut any of Vesey's allegedly insupportable opinions.

See also United States v. Williams, 447 F.2d 1285 (5th Cir.1971) (en banc), cert. denied, 405 U.S. 954 (1972). In Fuller v. Lemmons, 434 P.2d 145 (Okla.1967), it was held that expert opinion based upon x-rays is inadmissible unless the x-rays are introduced into evidence and that it is not enough that they are produced and made available to the opponent.

Are the reasons that justify admitting expert opinion based upon hearsay equally applicable to expert opinion based upon writings covered by the Best Evidence Rule? The authentication requirement?

Nachtsheim v. Beech Aircraft Corp., 847 F.2d 1261, 1270–71 (7th Cir. 1988): When in testifying to the cause of an aircraft crash expert relied upon information about another crash of the same model plane, which information was not independently admissible—see supra pp. 914–21—not an abuse of discretion under Fed. R. Evid. 403 to prohibit disclosure of this information on direct examination.

8. *Impeachment of Expert Witnesses.* There are of course other ways of impeaching expert witnesses than the methods referred to supra p. 1061. There may be technical attacks on their training and special competency. See Gresham, Cross–Examination of the Medical Witness, 29 Ins. C.J. 252 (1962); Kripke, Cross–Examination of the Defendant's Medical Expert, 36 Dicta 312 (1959); Brock, Cross–Examination of the Orthopedic Surgeon, 22 Ala. Law. 323 (1961); Vogel, Cross–Examination of Medical Experts, 7 DePaul L. Rev. 149 (1958); Trial Tactics in Handling the Medical Expert Witness, 29 Tenn. L. Rev. 208 (1962); Hilton, Cross–Examination of a Handwriting Expert by Test Problem, 13 Rutgers L. Rev. 306 (1958); Moore, Cross-Examining the Incompetent Document Examiner, 1 Washburn L.J. 533 (1962). Also, there may be inquiry into their interest or bias, as in the case of lay witnesses, but here often specialized on the ground of receipt of compensation over and above normal witness fees. E.g., State v. Creech, 51 S.E.2d 348, 355 (N.C.1949) (witness asked about having come to court "in the capacity of a paid employee and a paid witness"). Barrios v. Davis, 415 S.W.2d 714 (Tex.Civ.App.1967) (questions on cross-examination allowed as to number of cases expert had testified in, fees in those cases, amount earned per year from lawyers' referrals). Madsen v. Obermann, 22 N.W.2d 350, 354 (Iowa 1946), allows impeachment of expert by using his prior inconsistent testimony with respect to a similar state of facts in another case. Sanchez v. Black Brothers Co., 423 N.E.2d 1309, 1314–15, 1320–21 (Ill.App.1981): Error not to allow plaintiff to cross-examine defendant's expert concerning a speech he had given to a group of engineers about how he handles cross-examination.

> The way I counteracted the thing, I used another technique. I used the technique as science as a foreign language. I made a statement to the attorney that absolutely nobody could understand. Now, what it amounts to, it's going to terminate it in a hurry.

> I want the jury to understand what I say when I feel there are certain conditions. Under direct examination, the jury understands everything that I say. Under cross examination, there are some things I will allow the jury to understand and there are some things which I will not allow the jury to understand.

> If you don't want the jury to understand something, then what you do is you answer the question precisely, you see. If somebody is working with a form of inertia, why I use a form of inertia. I say, "Do you mean the second bolt above the first bolt," you know. Just get into something which is a very precise way of saying something.

> The interval of minus infinity to plus infinity of X times X, X^2, and you know the—no one is going to be able to do much with that kind of thing.

> And he says, "Can you simplify it?" You say, "See, there's too much simplification already. This is the only way that I can state it to you so there will be no misunderstanding."

See also Goldstein, Trial Technique 437–38 (1935); Busch, Law and Practice in Jury Trials 736–40, 764–66, 857–59, 865–70 (1935).

9. *Expert Testimony in Property Valuation Cases.* Expert testimony concerning property values provides an opportunity to review many of the problems considered in this section and to perceive their interrelation.

Consider, for instance, Arkansas State Highway Comm'n v. Russell, 398 S.W.2d 201 (Ark.1966). This was a condemnation suit in which the owner was allowed to give his opinion as to the value of his land. On cross-examination he admitted that his opinion was influenced by an offer he had received. The trial court rejected the contention that the owner's testimony should be stricken. The appellate court held this not to be error.

In these property valuation cases the meaning of "value" is critical. It affects all the other questions. "Value" is sometimes stated to be the price that a willing buyer and a willing seller would agree upon, neither required to enter into the transaction, both taking account of all relevant factors. In the development of the meaning of "value", it is possible that the profession of real estate appraisers plays a significant role. See Comment, Valuation of Real Property— Role of the Expert Witness, 44 Wash. L. Rev. 687, 699 (1969). For a helpful discussion of the meaning of value in condemnation proceedings, see Sengstock and McAuliffe, What is the Price of Eminent Domain? 44 J. Urb. L. 185 (1967).

The meaning of "value" determines whether what is involved is one of those subjects that lay triers of fact are so familiar with that expert testimony is not allowed, one of those subjects so unfamiliar that expert testimony is required, or a subject that permits but does not require expert testimony. The meaning of "value" also determines who is qualified to give an opinion. Most courts allow the owner of the litigated property to give his opinion of its value. E.g., McInnis and Co. v. Western Tractor & Equipment Co., 410 P.2d 908 (Wash.1966).

The meaning of "value" determines the kind of information that may or must be considered by an expert for his opinion to be admissible. Sale prices of comparable property are one factor upon which an expert may base his opinion.

There are hearsay problems that arise in the use of comparable property to determine value. First there is the question of whether the sale is itself hearsay. Then there is the question of whether statements of persons who are not witnesses may be used to establish the fact of the sale. In many jurisdictions experts are permitted to base opinions upon such statements. E.g., State Highway Comm'n v. Conrad, 139 S.E.2d 553 (N.C.1965). They are also allowed to base opinions upon statements by persons not witnesses concerning other relevant factors. Some jurisdictions allow experts to testify to these statements for the purpose of setting forth the basis of their opinion. E.g., State v. Wineberg, 444 P.2d 787, 792–95 (Wash.1968). Others do not. See Annot., Admissibility of Hearsay Evidence as to Comparable Sales of Other Land as Basis for Expert's Opinion as to Land Value, 12 A.L.R.3d 1064 (1967).

Sales of comparable property may be introduced to establish value independently and not simply as part of the basis of expert opinion. E.g., State Highway Comm'n v. Fisch–Or, Inc., 406 P.2d 539 (Or.1965). In this situation the sales may not be proved by hearsay. See Sengstock and McAuliffe, supra at 195–97. There is authority for the proposition that the test of comparability is stricter when the sales are used independently than when they are used as part of the basis of expert opinion. In the latter situation, "whether or not the property is sufficiently similar, and the sale sufficiently close in point of time, is evidence from which the jury many determine the credibility of the expert and, even though of doubtful probative value, is admissible for this purpose.... Where value is sought to be proved directly by comparable sales the foundation must first be laid by showing the similarity of the properties, and whether such foundation has been properly laid is for the determination of the trial judge.... Suppose, for example, that a witness who has by preliminary questioning been qualified as an expert should state as his conclusion the value of improved city property, and, on cross examination it should appear that he arrived at this figure by comparison with sales of unimproved rural property on the basis that both properties were owned by nonresidents. Should such testimony by stricken insofar as it involves the dissimilar property? The effect of the evidence would be, not to prove the value of the land, but to disprove the capacity of the appraiser. For this reason much latitude must be allowed in the admission of this sort of testimony, its effect, if necessary, to be limited by proper instructions from the trial judge." Hollywood Baptist Church v. State Highway Dept., 150 S.E.2d 271, 274–75 (Ga.Ct.App.1966). See also Jordan v. Department of Transp., 342 S.E.2d 482, 483–84 (Ga.Ct.App.1986) (error to prevent expert from stating that his opinion of value was based in part on sales of comparable property, so that jury could consider weight of opinion, even though other sales might not be admissible as direct proof because too remote in time.)

The admissibility of offers to buy raises questions as to whether such evidence is relevant, whether it is hearsay, whether in view of its arguable hearsay nature and probative value it may be used in the basis of expert opinion or independently. See State Highway Comm'n v. Fisch–Or, Inc., 406 P.2d 539 (Or.1965).

See generally Comment, Valuation Evidence in California Condomnation Cases, 12 Stan. L. Rev. 766 (1960). The California Evidence Code makes special provision for evidence of value in condemnation cases in §§ 810–22. Note particularly that §§ 815–16 do not permit evidence of other sales to be admitted except as part of the basis of expert opinion and that § 822(b) does not permit offers to be admitted even for this purpose. For further discussion of other sales to prove value, see supra pp. 920–21.

10. *Further References on the Basis of Expert Testimony.* Imwinkelried, A Comparativist Critique of the Interface between Hearsay and Expert Opinion in American Evidence Law, 33 B.C. L. Rev. 1 (1991); Maguire and Hahesy, Requisite Proof of Basis for Expert Opinion, 5 Vand. L. Rev. 433 (1952), Selected Writings on Evidence and Trial 503 (1957); Rheingold, The Basis of Medical Testimony, 15 Vand. L. Rev. 473 (1962); Deiden and Gasparitch, Psychiatric Evidence and Full Disclosure in the Criminal Trial, 52 Cal. L. Rev. 543 (1964); Overlooked Hearsay Medical Opinions: Erroneous Medical Testimony Based on Information Obtained by the Doctor's Assistants, 2 Current Med. for Att'ys 14 (May, 1955); Comment, The Admissibility of Expert Medical Testimony Based in Part Upon Information Received from Third Persons, 35 S.Cal.L.Rev. 193 (1962); Seidel and Gingrich, Hearsay Objections to Expert Psychiatric Opinion Testimony and the Proposed Federal Rules of Evidence, 39 UMKC L.Rev. 141 (1970–71).

On the Federal Rules of Evidence and the basis of expert testimony, including the hearsay question, see Carlson, Policing the Bases of Modern Expert Testimony, 39 Vand. L. Rev. 577 (1986); Carlson, Collision Course in Expert Testimony: Limitations on Affirmative Introduction of Underlying Data, 36 U. Fla. L. Rev. 234 (1984); McElhaney, Expert Witnesses and the Federal Rules of Evidence, 28 Mercer L. Rev. 463 (1977).

SECTION 3.   COURT-APPOINTED EXPERTS, DISCOVERING EXPERT OPINION, COMPELLING EXPERT TESTIMONY

The numerous challenges and difficulties in the use of expert evidence seen in the materials in the two preceding sections have led in some instances to experts being appointed by the court rather than chosen by the parties. Such court-appointed experts, it is suggested, will bring about increased understanding by the trier of facts and increased accuracy of findings. The need for the judge to take the initiative, it is argued, is greater in the case of expert testimony than with other evidence. It is not suggested that court-appointed experts should replace entirely experts chosen by the parties, but only that they can be a useful supplement. Nevertheless, it has proved difficult to establish a standard for when an expert should be appointed and to fit the use of court-appointed experts into a system that primarily relies upon the parties to introduce evidence. These uncertainties may explain why experts are rarely appointed by courts.

Dissatisfaction with the present system of expert evidence finds expression in other ways as well: the appointment of expert special masters to assist the court in various tasks; the use of experts as informal technical advisors to the court; and the creation of specialized tribunals to deal with cases involving technical knowledge. Sometimes these procedures are employed without much attention to the conflict they may create with rights to a judicial determination of facts and to an opportunity to question the reliability of materials upon which decision is to rest.

Dissatisfaction with the traditional approach to expert evidence is reflected also in increased emphasis on pretrial discovery of expert opinion and its basis. A pretrial conference may be held to reduce the area of conflict between experts and to enhance the intelligibility of expert testimony for the trier of facts. Limitations on pretrial discovery are encountered, however, in the parties' power to "capture" experts by consulting or retaining them and then deciding not to call them, and in the social interest in not overburdening experts and scientific research by excessive demands from the legal system.

Scott v. Spanjer Bros., Inc.

United States Court of Appeals, Second Circuit, 1962.
298 F.2d 928.

[Action for personal injuries by infants and their parents. Judgment for plaintiffs affirmed. Held: Not error for court to appoint physician to examine plaintiff Wayne Scott and no substantial prejudice to defendants in lack of earlier notice of court's action.]

■ HINCKS, CIRCUIT JUDGE (dissenting in part).

I dissent from so much of the opinion as holds that the trial judge acted without error in appointing at the very outset of the trial a physician of his own choice to examine the plaintiff Wayne Scott out of court and to testify to his findings, conclusions and prognosis at the trial without any prior report thereof to the parties.

My brothers say that "the appointment of an impartial medical expert by the court ... is an equitable and forward-looking technique for promoting the fair trial of a lawsuit." I agree that this is so when the appointment is safeguarded to insure the impartiality of the expert and to protect the parties from surprise. But that was not done here.

The desirability of the selection of unbiased experts by the judge is discussed by Wigmore in § 563 of his treatise. The preferred procedure is outlined in ¶ (3)(C) of that section (3rd ed., Vol. II, p. 648). There Wigmore accepts as "the final solution" of the underlying problem the model uniform Act proposed in 1937 by the National Conference of Commissioners on Uniform State Laws after years of debate and study. Perusal of the Act which is set forth in § 563 (Vol. II, p. 651 et seq.) will show numerous vital safeguards provided by the Act not taken by the court below.

Thus §§ 2 and 4 of the model Act require that before making an appointment the judge shall give reasonable notice to the parties of the names of the experts proposed for appointment and shall appoint the experts agreed on by the parties. Here the notice on the very eve of trial was far less than reasonable: it was so short that an expert on whom the parties apparently could have agreed could not be obtained in time—an obstacle which could have been avoided by but a few days' notice. The unreasonableness of notice on the eve of trial is further pointed up by the fact that at pretrial three months earlier the trial judge had indicated no intention of himself appointing an expert or any need therefor. Yet the only reason given for an appointment at the eve of trial was that because the plaintiff Wayne was an infant the "Court has the very important duty to protect an infant's rights" and "wanted to appoint a doctor to examine that infant as of today for the purpose of ascertaining the extent of his injuries, etc." One may question whether a court is under a duty to appoint expert witnesses for infant plaintiffs represented by counsel. But even so, the duty could have been as well discharged under a more seasonable notice which would have given time for the parties to agree on an expert.

Section 6 of the model Act makes provision for written reports by the court's experts to be filed and open to inspection by any party and later to be read by the witness in court. Here, appellants' counsel was not advised of what the expert would say until he actually testified. This was after counsel had completed his cross-examination of Wayne's mother on whose version of Wayne's "history" the expert's testimony was solely based. And of course at that stage it was too late to consult and perhaps call other psychiatrists.

Section 10 of the model Act provides that the compensation of the court's expert, as approved by the court, may eventually be taxed as costs against the losing party. In the absence of enabling legislation or of provision for compensation by agreement between the parties, there is no authority for compelling a party to compensate the court's expert. The party who calls an expert is generally the only available source of his compensation, except of course for the insignificant per diem of $4 allowed under 28 U.S.C.A. § 1821 and taxable under 28 U.S.C.A. § 1920. I think it would be a clear abuse of discretion for a judge to order a professional man, medical or engineering, to go to the labor of examining a patient or other subject-matter out of court and then testify as to his expert opinion without provision for compensation more nearly adequate than the meagre fee provided by 28 U.S.C.A. § 1821. Indeed, it would be unfair to expect physicians and scientists to serve as experts on that basis in cases in which the lawyers presumably have retainers carrying adequate compensation. Without adequate authorized compensation for court-appointed experts there is danger of some sub rosa arrangement for compensation by a party—a situation under which the court's expert in fact would be no more unbiased than one called by a party.

It is true that the model Act above discussed has not been widely adopted—only in South Dakota and Vermont so far as my researches show. But the failure of an Act such as this with all its restrictive safeguards to achieve enactment, is scant reason for judges, at least in run-of-the-mill cases such as this, to arrogate to themselves unrestricted powers which under traditional trial procedure are reserved to counsel.

Any consideration of the desirability of court-appointed experts should not overlook the fact that in the medical field, as well as in other sciences, there are many areas in which the experts are divided into opposing schools of thought. Under the conventional trial technique, the opposing parties will each generally proffer experts favorable to his position thus leaving it to the trier to decide, with such aid as cross and redirect examination may afford, which view rests upon the more reliable base—a difficult task especially for a jury. On the other hand, a judge making an a priori appointment often unaware of the existence of opposing schools in the area may inadvertently appoint an expert who, by his professional and personal attitudes, is precommitted to a particular school and his views, with the accolade flowing from a judicial appointment, may well be decisive. Thus the outcome of unilateral judicial appointment may be not so much an improvement of justice as the fortuitous product of arbitrary—albeit well-intended—judicial action.

The procedure adopted here did not comply with that prescribed for criminal cases by Fed.Rules Crim.Proc. rule 28. It was in violation of the spirit of Fed.Rules Civ.Proc. rule 38(b). Surely a party needs protection from surprise caused by a judge as much as that caused by his adversary. And I cannot understand my brothers' reliance on Ex parte Peterson, 253 U.S. 300, 40 S.Ct.

543, 64 L.Ed. 919, which involved the power of a judge to appoint an auditor whose task it was to organize and report on independent evidence—not to contribute new evidence as does a witness.

. . .

Students of California School for the Blind v. Honig

United States Court of Appeals, Ninth Circuit, 1984.
736 F.2d 538.

[Appeal from order granting preliminary injunction against opening a school until additional tests were made to determine seismic safety.]

■ Before CHOY, PREGERSON and REINHARDT, CIRCUIT JUDGES.

■ PREGERSON, CIRCUIT JUDGE.

. . .

The District Court's Use of a Court–Appointed Expert

After a lengthy trial and much conflicting expert testimony, the judge could not decide the merits of the students' seismic safety claims on the basis of evidence presented at trial, so he reopened the case and appointed a neutral expert to evaluate the adequacy of seismic testing at the Fremont site. The state defendants have several objections to this procedure on this appeal, all of which we find unpersuasive.

A.   Reopening the Case

The state defendants object to the district court's sua sponte reopening the case to obtain evidence from a neutral expert. Sua sponte reopening is an unusual procedure, but it is within the discretion of the trial court. See Calage v. University of Tennessee, 544 F.2d 297, 302 (6th Cir.1976) (district court did not abuse its discretion in sua sponte reopening sex discrimination case for additional evidence to explain wage differentials); Arthur Murray, Inc. v. Oliver, 364 F.2d 28, 34 (8th Cir.1966) (district court abused discretion in sua sponte reopening antitrust case for additional evidence on lost profits where there was sufficient evidence in the record and no exceptional circumstances).

The court's discretion was not abused here. Both Calage and Arthur Murray emphasize that "such evidence as a judge may properly seek to have added to a record on his own motion should appear both to be important as a matter of preventing injustice and to be reasonably available." Calage, 544 F.2d at 302 (citing Arthur Murray, 364 F.2d at 34). The district court specifically found reopening was necessary to prevent injustice and that the evidence was reasonably available. Only one additional expert testified, and his testimony was based primarily on the existing trial record. Although the procedure is somewhat unusual, the circumstances of the case appear to justify it.

B.   Rule 706

The district court expressly relied on Rule 706, Fed.R.Evid. as a source of power to appoint a neutral expert. Rule 706 allows the court to appoint a neutral expert on its own motion, whether or not the expert is agreed upon by the parties. Rule 706 also allows the court to assess the cost of the expert's compensation as it deems appropriate. Appointments under Rule 706 are reviewable only for abuse of discretion. See Fugitt v. Jones, 549 F.2d 1001, 1006 (5th Cir.1977). As required by Rule 706, the judge allowed both parties to thoroughly cross-examine its appointed expert. Thus, under Rule 706, the district court's appointment of a neutral expert was proper.

The state defendants argue that the district court treated the neutral expert, Dr. Jahns, not as a neutral expert, but as a special master. Appointments of special masters are subject to stricter standards of review than appointments of neutral experts under Rule 706. Rule 53, Fed.R.Civ.P. governs the appointment of special masters. Rule 53(b) provides, "A reference to a master shall be the exception and not the rule." The court in Arthur Murray, supra, used the lack of an "exceptional condition" as grounds for reversing the appointment of a special master in an antitrust case.

Here, the district court first appointed Dr. Jahns expressly as a court-appointed neutral expert under Rule 706. He was not appointed a special master until later. After his testimony convinced the court to order additional testing, Dr. Jahns was appointed special master to oversee the court-ordered tests. The state defendants argue, however, that his role was akin to that of a special master throughout the proceeding, because the district court relied upon him so heavily. The argument is not persuasive. Even if Jahns is characterized as a special master from the time of his original appointment, the case is complex enough to fit the exceptional circumstances requirement of Rule 53(b).

C. Dr. Jahns's Qualifications

The state defendants contend that Dr. Jahns was unqualified. They argue that Jahns was not experienced in investigating school sites, that he was not familiar with California law regulating the construction of schools in seismically dangerous areas, and that he was not an expert on the effects of liquefaction, a potential seismic problem at the Fremont site. The students argue that Dr. Jahns was well-qualified, pointing out that Jahns was formerly dean of Stanford's Earth Sciences Department, and had extensive experience doing seismic safety evaluations for such critical facilities as nuclear power plants and hydroelectric dams. They also point out that Jahns was somewhat familiar with school sites, having reviewed at least ten school site investigations within the past five years, and that he generally understood seismic safety standards applicable to school sites under California law.

We find the attack on Jahns' qualifications without merit. Under Rule 706, the court is free to appoint an expert of its own choosing without the consent of either party. Moreover, the question of whether an expert is qualified rests within the sound discretion of the trial judge. J. Weinstein & M. Berger, 3 Weinstein's Evidence ¶ 702[04] at 702–22 (1982). Nothing indicates that the trial court abused its discretion in selecting the qualified expert here.

. . .

Affirmed.[1]

NOTES

1. On the influence of court-appointed experts with juries, compare Rubin and Ringenbach, The Use of Court Experts in Asbestos Litigation, 137 F.R.D. 35, 41

---

1. The Supreme Court granted certiorari and vacated the judgment of the Court of Appeals with instructions to remand to the District Court on the ground that by the time the case reached the Supreme Court, the requirements of the District Court's preliminary injunction—that additional tests be conducted—had been complied with, so that the issue presented by the petition for certiorari—whether the District Court had abused its discretion in issuing the preliminary injunction—was moot. 471 U.S. 148, 105 S.Ct. 1820 (1985). Eds.

(1991) (suggesting influence on juries, but study of limited number of cases), with Diamond, What Jurors Think: Expectations and Reactions of Citizens Who Serve as Jurors, in Verdict 282, 293–94 (Litan, ed. 1993) (no evidence suggests juries give greater weight to non-adversarial expert). Among the questions that arise in connection with the use of court-appointed experts are: What are the circumstances that call for the appointment of an expert? How should the expert be told what he is to do? How should the expert be informed about the facts of the litigated case? Should the judge have contact with the expert outside the presence of the parties? Should the expert have contact with the parties?

It is often asked why courts use their power to call experts so rarely. Gross, Expert Evidence, 1991 Wis.L.Rev. 1113, 1205: "In short, court-appointed experts are not used in American trials because they are beyond the control of lawyers. As a result, they threaten the prerogatives of the trial attorneys, and they are likely to be inadequately prepared for testimony and uncomfortably unpredictable."

It should be noted that if the court has power to appoint experts under Fed.R.Evid. 706, it also has power under Fed.R.Evid. 614 to call other witnesses and to interrogate witnesses called by the parties. When should it use these powers?

2. Langbein, The German Advantage in Civil Procedure, 52 U.Chi.L.Rev. 823, 836–40 (1985).[1]

The Continental tradition. European legal systems are, by contrast, expert-prone. Expertise is frequently sought. The literature emphasizes the value attached to having expert assistance available to the courts in an age in which litigation involves facts of ever-greater technical difficulty. The essential insight of Continental civil procedure is that credible expertise must be neutral expertise. Thus, the responsibility for selecting and informing experts is placed upon the courts, although with important protections for party interests.

Selecting the expert. German courts obtain expert help in lawsuits the way Americans obtain expert help in business or personal affairs. If you need an architect, a dermatologist, or a plumber, you do not commission a pair of them to take preordained and opposing positions on your problem, although you do sometimes take a second opinion. Rather, you take care to find an expert who is qualified to advise you in an objective manner; you probe his advice as best you can; and if you find his advice persuasive, you follow it.

When in the course of winnowing the issues in a lawsuit a German court determines that expertise might help resolve the case, the court selects and instructs the expert. The court may decide to seek expertise on its own motion, or at the request of one of the parties. The code of civil procedure allows the court to request nominations from the parties— indeed, the code requires the court to use any expert upon whom the parties agree—but neither practice is typical. In general, the court takes the initiative in nominating and selecting the expert.

The only respect in which the code of civil procedure purports to narrow the court's discretion to choose the expert is a provision whose significance is less than obvious: "If experts are officially designated for certain fields of expertise, other persons should be chosen only when

---

1. Footnotes omitted.

special circumstances require." One looks outside the code of civil procedure, to the federal statutes regulating various professions and trades, for the particulars on official designation. For the professions, the statutes typically authorize the official licensing bodies to assemble lists of professionals deemed especially suited to serve as experts. In other fields, the state governments designate quasi-public bodies to compile such lists. For example, under section 36 of the federal code on trade regulation, the state governments empower the regional chambers of commerce and industry (Industrie-und Handelskammern) to identify experts in a wide variety of commercial and technical fields. That statute directs the empowered chamber to choose as experts persons who have exceptional knowledge of the particular specialty and to have these persons sworn to render professional and impartial expertise. The chamber circulates its lists of experts, organized by specialty and subspecialty, to the courts. German judges receive sheaves of these lists as the various issuing bodies update and recirculate them.

Current practice. In 1984 I spent a little time interviewing judges in Frankfurt about their practice in selecting experts. My sample of a handful of judges is not large enough to impress statisticians, but I think the picture that emerges from serious discussion with people who operate the system is worth reporting. Among the judges with whom I spoke, I found unanimity on the proposition that the most important factor predisposing a judge to select an expert is favorable experience with that expert in an earlier case. Experts thus build reputations with the bench. Someone who renders a careful, succinct, and well-substantiated report and who responds effectively to the subsequent questions of the court and the parties will be remembered when another case arises in his specialty. Again we notice that German civil procedure tracks the patterns of decision-making in ordinary business and personal affairs: If you get a plumber to fix your toilet and he does it well, you incline to hire him again.

When judges lack personal experience with appropriate experts, I am told, they turn to the authoritative lists described above. If expertise is needed in a field for which official lists are unavailing, the court is thrown upon its own devices. The German judge then gets on the phone, working from party suggestions and from the court's own research, much in the fashion of an American litigator hunting for expertise. In these cases there is a tendency to turn, first, to the bodies that prepare expert lists in cognate areas; or, if none, to the universities and technical institutes.

If enough potential experts are identified to allow for choice, the court will ordinarily consult party preferences. In such circumstances a litigant may ask the court to exclude an expert whose views proved contrary to his interests in previous litigation or whom he otherwise disdains. The court will try to oblige the parties' tastes when another qualified expert can be substituted. Nevertheless, a litigant can formally challenge an expert's appointment only on the narrow grounds for which a litigant could seek to recuse a judge.

Preparing the expert. The court that selects the expert instructs him, in the sense of propounding the facts that he is to assume or to investigate, and in framing the questions that the court wishes the expert to address. In formulating the expert's task, as in other important steps in the conduct of the case, the court welcomes adversary suggestions. If the expert should take a view of premises (for example, in an accident case or a building-construction dispute), counsel for both sides will accompany him.

Safeguards. The expert is ordinarily instructed to prepare a written opinion. When the court receives the report, it is circulated to the litigants. The litigants commonly file written comments, to which the expert is asked to reply. The court on its own motion may also request the expert to amplify his views. If the expert's report remains in contention, the court will schedule a hearing at which counsel for a dissatisfied litigant can confront and interrogate the expert.

The code of civil procedure reserves to the court the power to order a further report by another expert if the court should deem the first report unsatisfactory. A litigant dissatisfied with the expert may encourage the court to invoke its power to name a second expert. The code of criminal procedure has a more explicit standard for such cases, which is worth noticing because the literature suggests that courts have similar instincts in civil procedure. The court may refuse a litigant's motion to engage a further expert in a criminal case, the code says,

> if the contrary of the fact concerned has already been proved through the former expert opinion; this [authority to refuse to appoint a further expert] does not apply if the expertise of the former expert is doubted, if his report is based upon inaccurate factual presuppositions, if the report contains contradictions, or if the new expert has available means of research that appear superior to those of a former expert.

When, therefore, a litigant can persuade the court that an expert's report has been sloppy or partial, that it rests upon a view of the field that is not generally shared, or that the question referred to the expert is exceptionally difficult, the court will commission further expertise.

A litigant may also engage his own expert, much as is done in the Anglo–American procedural world, in order to rebut the court-appointed expert. The court will discount the views of a party-selected expert on account of his want of neutrality, but cases occur in which he nevertheless proves to be effective. Ordinarily, I am told, the court will not in such circumstances base its judgment directly upon the views of the party-selected expert; rather, the court will treat the rebuttal as ground for engaging a further court-appointed expert (called an *Oberexperte*, literally an "upper" or "superior" expert), whose opinion will take account of the rebuttal.

To conclude: In the use of expertise German civil procedure strikes an adroit balance between nonadversarial and adversarial values. Expertise is kept impartial, but litigants are protected against error or caprice through a variety of opportunities for consultation, confrontation, and rebuttal.

See also Basten, The Court Expert in Civil Trials—A Comparative Appraisal, 40 Mod.L.Rev. 174 (1977); Travis, Impartial Expert Testimony Under the Federal Rules of Evidence: A French Perspective, 8 Int'l Law. 492 (1974).

3.   A wealth of literature has developed on court-appointed experts: Cecil & Willging, Accepting Daubert's Invitation: Defining a Role for Court–Appointed Experts in Assessing Scientific Validity, 43 Emory L.J. 995 (1994) (survey of judges on use of court-appointed experts and discussion of difficulties encountered in use); T. Willging, Court–Appointed Experts (Federal Judicial Center 1986) (comprehensive list of federal cases and discussion of procedural issues in use of court-appointed experts in federal courts); Sink, The Unused Power of a Federal Judge to Call His Own Expert Witnesses, 29 S.Cal.L.Rev. 195 (1950); Goldstein & Fine, The Indigent Accused, The Psychiatrist, and The Insanity Defense, 110 U.Pa.L.Rev. 1061 (1962); Klein, Judicial Administration—A Bibli-

ography 393–97 (1963); Myers, "The Battle of the Experts": A New Approach to an Old Problem in Medical Testimony, 44 Neb.L.Rev. 539 (1965).

4. Students of the California School for the Blind v. Honig involved both the use of a court-appointed expert and the use of a special master. The use of court-appointed experts may be compared with other available procedures.

Special Masters. Special masters are appointed by federal courts either under Fed.R.Civ.Proc. 53 or in an exercise of the court's inherent power. A special master may take evidence and he files a report. In trial to a judge, this report must be accepted unless it is clearly erroneous. This procedure could be argued to violate the parties' right to a judicial determination. In trial to a jury, the master's report is read to the jury as evidence. In neither trial to a judge nor trial to a jury does the master testify or become subject to cross-examination. See Johnson Controls v. Phoenix Control Systems, 886 F.2d 1173, 1176 (9th Cir.1989); Farrell, Coping with Scientific Evidence: The Use of Special Masters, 43 Emory L.J. 927 (1994). Thus a question arises whether the policy against hearsay is violated. Sometimes special masters are appointed because of their possession of expertise in a particular field. In this situation, although the parties may learn from the master's report what expert information the master believed himself to possess and what use he made of it, they will not have the same opportunity to explore the reliability of this information that they would have if the master were a witness. See generally Degraw, Rule 53, Inherent Powers, and Institutional Reform: The Lack of Limits on Special Masters, 66 N.Y.U.L.Rev. 800 (1991). See also Hart v. Community School Bd., 383 F.Supp. 699 (E.D.N.Y.1974) (review of authorities on when court justified in appointing expert special master).

Technical Advisors. Reilly v. United States, 863 F.2d 149, 152–61 (1st Cir.1988): In suit by infant negligently injured by doctor at birth, not error to appoint economist to advise court how to calculate lost earning power and the cost of future care. Since the advisor was not appointed as a witness under Rule 706, the procedural requirements of that rule did not apply. Although in some cases it may be desirable to notify the parties of an advisor's identity, to prepare formal instructions for the advisor and to have him file a report, these actions are not always required and may interfere with the informal nature of the advisor's role. An opportunity to cross-examine the advisor is not required because he is not intended to be an evidentiary source. See also Renaud v. Martin Marietta Corp., 972 F.2d 304, 308 n. 8 (10th Cir.1992) (not abuse of discretion to deny right to take deposition of expert who functioned more in role of advisor than witness); Danville Tobacco Ass'n v. Bryant–Buckner Associates, Inc., 333 F.2d 202 (4th Cir.1964) (not error to appoint expert on tobacco marketing to recommend to court formula for allotment of selling time for tobacco warehouses). See Note, Improving Judicial Gatekeeping: Technical Advisors and Scientific Evidence, 110 Harv.L.Rev. 941, 952–58 (1997).

In a recent silicone breast implant case, the District Court employed technical advisors to aid the Court in determining the admissibility, under Daubert v. Merrell Dow, of plaintiffs' expert testimony regarding causation. Hall v. Baxter Healthcare Corp., 947 F.Supp. 1387 (D.Or.1996). The advisors, along with the Court, heard testimony offered by the parties, considered questions submitted by the court and filed reports, which were appended to the court's opinion. The court held the plaintiffs' expert evidence inadmissible. In appointing the advisors, the Court expressly disclaimed reliance on Fed. R. Evid. 706, invoking instead Fed. R. Evid. 104 and the court's inherent authority. In multidistrict litigation also involving silicone breast implants, on the other hand, expert witnesses have been appointed under Rule 706. See N.Y.L.J., pp. 3, 6, Jan. 13, 1997.

Specialized Tribunals. See Note, Fighting Fire with Firefighters: A Proposal for Expert Judges at the Trial Level, 93 Colum.L.Rev. 473, 490–93 (1993) (judges in Court of Appeals for the Federal Circuit, which has jurisdiction over patent and other cases with technical aspects, have expertise when appointed or acquire it in the course of sitting on cases); Ayer, Allocating the Costs of Determining "Just Compensation," 21 Stan.L.Rev. 693, 724–25 (1969) (proposal for "independent appraisers" in condemnation suits); Korn, Law, Fact and Science in the Courts, 66 Colum. L.Rev. 1080, 1083 (1966) (discussing use of specialized tribunals for cases involving technical issues); Luneburg and Nordenberg, Specially Qualified Juries and Expert Nonjury Tribunals: Alternatives for Coping with the Complexities of Modern Civil Litigation, 67 Va.L.Rev. 887 (1981); Wessel, Alternative Dispute Resolution for the Socioscientific Dispute, 1 J.L. & Tech. 1 (1986); Yellin, High Technology and the Courts: Nuclear Power and the Need for Institutional Reform, 94 Harv.L.Rev. 489, 555–60 (1981) (suggesting committee of scientists, engineers and lawyers to act as "standing masters" for complex environmental cases); Note, Scientific Evidence and the Question of Judicial Capacity, 25 Wm. & Mary L.Rev. 675, 686–702 (1984) (discussing proposal for a "science court," advisory panels, special masters, court-appointed experts).

For discussion and citations relevant to different forms of assistance to courts in dealing with technical and scientific subjects, see J. Weinstein, Individual Justice in Mass Tort Litigation, chap. 7 (1995).

5. In certain jurisdictions screening panels of doctors and lawyers have been established by medical societies and bar associations to deal with medical malpractice cases. If a complainant makes a showing satisfactory to the panel, he will be provided with expert testimony for litigation. Seidelson, Medical Malpractice Cases, 16 Cath.U.L.Rev. 158, 162–68 (1966), points out the difficulty the complainant may have in making his case before the panel without the assistance of an expert and asks why an injured party should have to satisfy such a panel before he has a chance to succeed in litigation. In Mattos v. Thompson, 421 A.2d 190 (Pa.1980), the court held unconstitutional a statute requiring arbitration of medical malpractice cases before resort to jury trial, because the application of the statutory procedures in practice resulted in such delays as unduly to burden the right to jury trial. See also Bernier v. Burris, 497 N.E.2d 763, 766–71 (Ill.1986) (statute unconstitutional). See also Goldschmidt, Where Have All the Panels Gone? A History of the Arizona Medical Liability Review Panel, 23 Ariz.St.L.J. 1013 (1991) (recent trend against panels because of tendency to increase costs and time required for disposing of claims).

Professional societies sometimes have committees charged with reviewing court testimony given by their members and taking disciplinary action in appropriate cases. See Medical–Legal Screening Panels As An Alternative Approach to Medical Malpractice Claims, 13 Wm. & Mary L.Rev. 695 (1972), studying the effect of such procedures, the volume of court cases, number of settlements and cost of medical malpractice insurance.

Rancourt v. Waterville Urban Renewal Authority

Supreme Court of Maine, 1966.
223 A.2d 303.

■ WILLIAMSON, CHIEF JUSTICE. This is an appeal by the Waterville Urban Renewal Authority, the defendant, from the assessment of damages by a jury for the taking of plaintiff's property by eminent domain.... In the words of the defendant's counsel "The sole issue in this case is whether or not the expert witness engaged by the condemning authority to appraise the premises in question should have been allowed to testify as an expert in behalf of the opposing party to this action, namely the landowner."

The facts are not in dispute. Mr. St. Pierre, called by the plaintiff in rebuttal, testified that he had made an appraisal of the plaintiff's property in January 1963 for the defendant, and that in his opinion the fair market value of the property was then $27,500. The witness was offered for the purpose of impeaching the testimony of an expert offered by the defendant.

Objection was made by the defendant to the use of the witness by the plaintiff on three grounds: (1) That the witness had made the appraisal for and at the expense of the defendant, (2) that by contract with the defendant the witness was prohibited from divulging any information which he gathered as a result of his appraisal, and (3) that the opinion of the witness was a privileged communication.

The defendant contends that the evidence was privileged (1) under a privilege analogous to that of an attorney and client, and (2) by virtue of Rule 26(b) M.R.C.P. relating to Discovery and Depositions.

In the first place the relationship between the defendant Authority and the witness was not that of an attorney and client. A privilege existing on the facts before us prohibiting the witness from testifying without the consent of the defendant would extend the rule of privileged communication far beyond its present bounds.

We have no physician-patient privilege under our common law. The priest-penitent privilege comes by statute. 16 M.R.S.A. §§ 57, 58, enacted 1965, c. 117.

Here we do not find that need of confidential relationship existing between attorney and client. The reasons for the privilege in the attorney-client relationship are not present in the expert witness area under consideration. There is nothing about an opinion on the fair value of real estate that requires secrecy. Surely with no physician-patient privilege and the priest-penitent privilege only by statute, we cannot expect to find, and we do not find, an employer-expert privilege excluding the opinion on the value of real estate by the expert.

The defendant urges that Rule 26(b) M.R.C.P. in denying the right to compel the production of the conclusions of an expert under the facts of this case, effectively creates a privilege against the use of the expert as a witness at trial by the opposing party.

Rule 26(b) reads in part as follows:

"... nor shall the deponent be required to produce or submit for inspection any part of a writing which reflects an attorney's mental impressions, conclusions, opinions, or legal theories, or, except as provided in Rule 35(b)[1] the conclusions of an expert."

In Field & McKusick, Maine Civil Practice, we find in Reporter's Notes, p. 249:

"The sweep of disclosure is, however, limited by the last sentence of Rule 26(b), which is taken from the New Jersey rule. It forbids discovery of a written statement taken by or for an attorney in anticipation of litigation or in preparation for trial unless the court otherwise orders to prevent injustice or undue hardship. This reflects the holding of the Supreme Court

---

1. Relating to mental and physical ex-   aminations under certain conditions. Eds.

of the United States in Hickman v. Taylor, 329 U.S. 495, 67 S.Ct. 385 [91 L.Ed. 451] (1947), but is broader than that holding."

And from the text:

"§ 26.17 *Scope of Examination—Discovery From Experts.* Rule 26(b) makes any writing which reflects the conclusions of an expert completely immune from discovery. The reason for this is plainly to prevent a party from obtaining without cost the benefit of an expert's opinion for which his adversary has paid in preparation for trial. It stems from the same principle that protects the attorney's working files from discovery. The policy behind the rule applies equally to the taking of an expert's deposition."

Rule 26(b) is neither limited by nor does it limit, the admissibility of evidence at trial. No new privilege operative to keep otherwise admissible evidence from the Court and jury was thereby created. The Rule was designed to regulate the discovery and deposition process before the trial and as a part thereof to protect a party against the necessity of disclosing the "work product", so-called. The opinion of the expert, although it might be admissible at trial, was for purposes of Rule 26(b) placed in the category of the "work product".

The expert under Rule 26(b) is not thereby taken from the witness stand. He remains a live person, available to give testimony and in particular to give his informed opinion. The fact that the opinion was obtained at the expense of the defendant and for its information and use only, does not force the conclusion that the expert may not testify from the stand at the request of the opposing party without the consent of his employer.

The opinion of the expert is a fact which the fact finders may be entitled to know. The cry of "privilege" does not stop the Court and jury from hearing the opinion of the expert in the search for the truth.

Whether an expert called to the stand by the opposing party should be compelled to testify presents issues not strictly before us. The principle that there is no privilege on the part of the employer of the witness, as here the Authority, arising from a confidential relationship is, however, implicit in decisions relating to compelling an expert to testify.

Mr. St. Pierre, the witness, did not object to testifying, either for lack of fee or for any other reason. The question of whether the evidence of the witness was "necessary for the purposes of justice" was not raised by the witness or the plaintiff. It is too late for objection to be made that the presiding Justice failed properly to exercise his judicial discretion in permitting the witness to take the stand.

. . .

We find no error in the admission of Mr. St. Pierre's testimony.

Appeal denied.

Buchanan, Plaintiff American Motors Corp., Defendant–Appellant In re Snyder, Non–Party Appellee

United States Court of Appeals, Sixth Circuit, 1983.
697 F.2d 151.

■ Before ENGEL and MERRITT, CIRCUIT JUDGES, and MORTON, CHIEF DISTRICT JUDGE.

■ MERRITT, CIRCUIT JUDGE.

Appellant, a defendant in a federal, diversity, products liability, wrongful death action in North Carolina for injury arising from a claimed design defect in a Jeep manufactured by appellant, seeks to subpoena appellee, an expert residing in Michigan who has published a lengthy adverse research study about the safety of appellant's product. The subpoena reads in pertinent part as follows:

> To Richard G. Snyder, Highway Safety Research Institute of the University of Michigan, Ann Arbor, Michigan.
>
> You are commanded to appear at 290 City Center Building at the offices of Huron Reporting Service in the city of Ann Arbor on the 23rd day of July, 1981, at 10:00 A.M. to testify ... at the taking of a deposition in the above-entitled action pending in the United States District Court for the Western District of North Carolina and bring with you any and all research data, memoranda, correspondence, lab notes, reports, calculations, moving pictures, photographs, slides, statements and the like pertaining to the on-road crash experience of utility vehicles study by the Highway Safety Research Institute of the University of Michigan for the Insurance Institute for Highway Safety in which you participated.

(Appendix, p. 3.) Appellee is a stranger to the North Carolina litigation and is not an expert witness or adviser to any party to that litigation under Rule 26(b)(4) of the Federal Rules of Civil Procedure or to the Court under Rule 706(a) of the Federal Rules of Evidence. Appellant states that its reason for seeking discovery from the expert is that it expects its adversary in the North Carolina litigation to use the research study as one basis for expressing an adverse expert opinion about the safety of appellant's product.

Assuming without deciding that the expert here, whose testimony and data have been subpoenaed, has neither an absolute nor qualified privilege to refuse discovery and is subject to the same general evidentiary rules requiring discovery as any other witness, it is nevertheless clear that the question of the scope of discovery addresses itself to the sound discretion of the District Court in the first instance. See Judge Friendly's opinion for the Second Circuit in Kaufman v. Edelstein, 539 F.2d 811, 822 (2d Cir.1976) (trial court's decision respecting quashing subpoena addressed to expert who is a stranger to litigation "represent[s] an exercise of discretion"). Our review of the record indicates that the District Court did not abuse its discretion in quashing the subpoena duces tecum in the instant case on grounds that it is unreasonably burdensome. Compliance with the subpoena would require the expert who has no direct connection with the litigation to spend many days testifying and disclosing all of the raw data, including thousands of documents, accumulated over the course of a long and detailed research study. Like the District Court, we note that the expert is not being called because of observations or knowledge concerning the facts of the accident and injury in litigation or because no other expert witnesses are available. Appellant wants to attempt to prove that the expert's written opinions stated in the research study are not well founded.

The District Court did not err in finding improper the practice of calling an eminent expert witness (who is a stranger to the litigation) under a burdensome subpoena duces tecum that would require him to spend a large amount of time itemizing and explaining the raw data that led him to a research opinion adverse to the interest of a party which is the author of the subpoena.

Accordingly, the judgment of the District Court quashing the subpoena in question is affirmed.

NOTES

1. Healy v. Counts, 100 F.R.D. 493 (D.Colo.1984): Defendant may not list as experts he intends to call as witnesses persons plaintiff has consulted but does not intend to call. Compare Atlantic Coast Line R. Co. v. Dixon, 207 F.2d 899 (5th Cir.1953): Plaintiff's attorney asked defendant's medical expert on cross-examination what he thought of the qualifications of plaintiff's medical expert. The appellate court held this permissible.

For discussion of objections founded on the lawyer-client privilege and the Sixth Amendment right to counsel to the prosecution's calling a psychiatrist consulted by a criminal defendant on the instructions of his lawyer, see infra pp. 1458–61, 1493–94.

On making the other party one's own expert, see Oleksiw v. Weidener, 207 N.E.2d 375 (Ohio 1965), reversing judgment in medical malpractice case because of trial court's refusal to allow plaintiff to elicit expert opinion from defendant doctors.

2. Kaufman v. Edelstein, 539 F.2d 811, 821 (2d Cir.1976), cited in the Buchanan case, dealt with the question of compelling testimony from an expert who was a stranger to the litigation. Judge Friendly's opinion contains the following observation:

> We can find no justification for a federal rule that would wholly exempt experts from placing before a tribunal factual knowledge relating to the case in hand, opinions already formulated, or, even, in the rare case when the party may seek this and the witness feels able to answer, a freshly formed opinion, simply because they have become expert in a particular calling. We likewise see no basis for recognizing a narrower principle that an expert is privileged against being called against his will in the absence of a preliminary showing of the unavailability of a voluntary expert equally qualified.

Deitchman v. E.R. Squibb and Sons, Inc., 740 F.2d 556 (7th Cir.1984): In action for injuries allegedly caused by DES, District Court abused discretion in quashing subpoena directed against doctor who was custodian of research records regarding possible connection between DES and clear cell andenocarcinoma of the genital tract. The plaintiffs did not intend to call the doctor as a witness, but his published articles would be relied upon by plaintiffs' experts. The District Court should design an order that provides defendant with discovery that enables it to cross-examine plaintiffs' experts, but at the same time recognizes interests in confidentiality and not chilling scientific research. In re American Tobacco Co., 880 F.2d 1520 (2d Cir.1989): Order compelling production of research records upheld under similar facts: even if under state law the scientists have a privilege not to testify, it does not extend to data underlying published studies. See Marcus, Discovery Along the Litigation/Science Interface, 57 Brook.L.Rev. 381 (1991).

In 1991 Fed.R.Civ. Proc. 45 was amended to provide:

> If a subpoena . . . requires disclosure of an unretained expert's opinion or information not describing specific events or occurrences in dispute and resulting from the expert's study made not at the request of any party . . . the court may, to protect a person subject to or affected by the subpoena, quash or modify the subpoena or, if the party in whose behalf the subpoena is issued shows a substantial need for the testimony or material that cannot be otherwise met without undue hardship and assures that the person to whom the subpoena is addressed will be reasonably compensated,

the court may order appearance or production only upon specified conditions.

Fed.R.Civ.Proc. 45(c)(3)(B)(ii) and (iii).

3. "Impartial" medical testimony plans have been motivated largely by the desire to induce settlements and to obtain disinterested expert testimony that will enable the trier of fact to reach a decision in regard to the disputed issue more satisfactory than if guided exclusively by the testimony of experts called by the parties. A different motivation, that of securing expert testimony for plaintiffs in medical malpractice cases, has produced a similar but in some respects different proposal. It will be noted that in the "impartial" medical testimony plans, the doctors who participate do so on a voluntary basis. In Seidelson, Medical Malpractice Cases, 16 Cath.U.L.Rev. 158, 171–85 (1966), it is proposed that when a plaintiff cannot otherwise obtain expert testimony, experts be compelled to testify on his behalf. The author considers and rejects arguments against statutes authorizing courts to compel such testimony and arguments against the existence of judicial power to compel such testimony in the absence of statute. In answer to the question will this process produce testimony of the sort desired, the author suggests that doctors who are appointed and study the case for the purpose of testifying for the plaintiff, may cease to identify closely with the defendant, react critically to evidence of serious incompetence and sympathize with the injured plaintiff. Of course, if this psychological transformation does not take place, the resulting testimony may not be significantly different from that obtained under the "impartial" plans. Indeed, if the doctor appointed to testify for the plaintiff allows resentment at being drafted to support a cause in which he does not believe to get the better of him, the result may be worse for the plaintiff than under the "impartial" plans. A plaintiff may be so uncertain about the testimony that he will consider it prudent to ask the court to call the expert as its own witness. The truth of the matter may be that there is no sure-fire way of obtaining for the plaintiff expert testimony that will put his case in the best possible light.

4.   Pretrial Discovery Relating to Experts. Fed.R.Civ.Proc. 26 provides:

(a) Required Disclosures . . .

. . .

(2) Disclosure of Expert Testimony

(A) In addition to the disclosures required by paragraph (1), a party shall disclose to other parties the identity of any person who may be used at trial to present evidence under Rules 702, 703, or 705 of the Federal Rules of Evidence.

(B) Except as otherwise stipulated or directed by the court, this disclosure shall, with respect to a witness who is retained or specially employed to provide expert testimony in the case or whose duties as an employee of the party regularly involve giving expert testimony, be accompanied by a written report prepared and signed by the witness. The report shall contain a complete statement of all opinions to be expressed and the basis and reasons therefor; the data or other information considered by the witness in forming the opinions; any exhibits to be used as a summary of or support for the opinions; the qualifications of the witness, including a list of all publications authored by the witness within the preceding ten years; the compensation to be paid for the study and testimony; and a listing of any other cases in which the witness has testified as an expert at trial or by deposition within the preceding four years.[1]

(b) Discovery Scope and Limits....

. . .

(4) Trial Preparation: Experts

(A) A party may depose any person who has been identified as an expert whose opinions may be presented at trial. If a report from the expert is required under subdivision (a)(2)(B), the deposition shall not be conducted until after the report is provided.

(B) A party may, through interrogatories or by deposition, discover facts known or opinions held by an expert who has been retained or specially employed by another party in anticipation of litigation or preparation for trial and who is not expected to be called as a witness at trial, only as provided in Rule 35(b)[2] or upon a showing of exceptional circumstances under which it is impracticable for the party seeking discovery to obtain facts or opinions on the same subject by other means.

(C) Unless manifest injustice would result, (i) the court shall require that the party seeking discovery pay the expert a reasonable fee for time spent in responding to discovery under this subdivision; and (ii) with respect to discovery obtained under subdivision (b)(4)(B) of this rule the court shall require the party seeking discovery to pay the other party a fair portion of the fees and expenses incurred by the latter party in obtaining facts and opinions from the expert.

. . .

Eliasen v. Hamilton, 111 F.R.D. 396 (N.D.Ill.1986): Defendants were not entitled to depose plaintiffs' nontestifying expert about the preparation of a report for plaintiffs:

"Gruy is an expert who has been 'retained or specially employed' by plaintiffs in preparation for trial. Plaintiffs hired Gruy to prepare a report; plaintiffs furnished information to Gruy for the report; and plaintiffs paid Gruy for his services. This is all the rule [Fed.R.Civ.Proc. 26(b)(4)] requires for Gruy to become a 'captured' expert. This is undoubtedly a harsh rule. It may be a bad rule. We could join in the voices already criticizing it as a bad rule. See, e.g., United States v. Meyer, 398 F.2d 66, 76 (9th Cir.1968); Note, Discovery of Expert Information, 47 N.C.L.Rev. 401, 406 (1969). [Footnote by the court: "The court in Meyer criticized the rule by stating: '[W]e do not believe that "fear that one side will benefit unduly from the other side's better preparation" ... is a sufficient justification for the application ... of a rule which would deny a litigant the testimony of a witness rejected by his opponent simply because his opponent reached the witness first and paid for his services.' "]But this would not help defendants, because good or bad, it is the rule, and we must apply it as written."

---

1. Fed.R.Crim.Proc. requires the government to provide, at the defendant's request, a similar report for any expert who will testify for the government, such a request from the defendant in turn entitling the government to receive a report from any expert who will testify for the defendant. Fed.R.Crim.Proc. 16(a)(E) and (b)(1)(C). Eds.

2. Rule 35(b) provides for the right of a party to receive a physician's report following a court-ordered mental or physical examination. Eds.

Id. at 401–02. The court said, however, that defendants could have discovery from the expert of facts known and opinions held by him prior to the time he began to work for the plaintiffs on the litigation.

See also In re "Agent Orange" Product Liability Litigation, 105 F.R.D. 577, 581 (E.D.N.Y.1985), interpreting and applying the requirement for discovery under Fed.R.Civ.Proc. 26(b)(4)(B) of a "showing of exceptional circumstances under which it is impracticable for the party seeking discovery to obtain facts or opinions on the same subject by other means," and Pearl Brewing Co. v. Joseph Schlitz Brewing Co., 415 F.Supp. 1122 (S.D.Tex.1976), also applying 26(b)(4).

For the extensive commentary on 26(b)(4), see, e.g., Pielemeier, Discovery of Non-Testifying "In–House" Experts Under Federal Rule of Civil Procedure 26, 58 Ind.L.J. 597 (1983); Day, The Ordinary Witness Doctrine: Discovery of the Pre–Retention Knowledge of a Nonwitness Expert Under Federal Rule 26(b)(4)(B), 38 Ark.L.Rev. 763 (1985); Graham, Expert Witness Testimony and the Federal Rules of Evidence: Insuring Adequate Assurance of Trustworthiness, 1986 U.Ill.L.Rev. 43, 80–88 (discussing "Saturday night experts," experts selected to testify just before trial, and other devices employed by some lawyers to avoid pretrial discovery and to frustrate the purpose of 26(b)(4)(A)); Graham, Discovery of Experts Under Rule 26(b)(4) of the Federal Rules of Civil Procedure, 1976 Ill.L.For. 895, 1977 Ill.L.For. 169. See also Note, Federal Discovery Practices Concerning Expert Witnesses, 14 Okla. City U.L.Rev. 391 (1989), suggesting category of expert not "retained or specially employed" by a party but only informally consulted, whose opinions should be more easily discoverable than experts who fall under 26(b)(4)(B).

For commentary on the general topic of compelling expert testimony, see Maurer, Compelling the Expert Witness, 19 Ga.L.Rev. 71 (1984); Meyer, The Expert Witness: Some Proposals for Change, 45 St. John's L.Rev. 105 (1970); Eberhardt, Right to Compel Testimony of Expert Witness Employed by Adverse Party, 73 Dick.L.Rev. 675 (1969); Schuck, Techniques for Proof of Complicated Scientific and Economic Facts, 40 F.R.D. 33 (1966) (noting that discovery may lead to use of stipulated written expert testimony supplemented when necessary by oral testimony); Von Kalinowski, Use of Discovery Against the Expert Witness, 40 F.R.D. 43 (1966); Friedenthal, Discovery and Use of an Adverse Party's Expert Information, 14 Stan.L.Rev. 455 (1962); Note, Compelling Experts to Testify: A Proposal, 44 U.Chi.L.Rev. 851 (1977); Annot., Right of Independent Expert to Refuse to Testify as to Expert Opinion, 50 A.L.R. 4th 680 (1986).

5.   Various pretrial procedures have been used by some courts to deal with the challenge of expert testimony. A pretrial meeting may be held with the judge, the lawyers and the experts in an effort to clarify what is in dispute. One result of such a meeting may be to enable stipulated reports of the experts to be read into the record. The experts may be brought to agree on a glossary of technical terms. The meeting may also make it possible to require that some objections to expert testimony be made before trial and disposed of by rulings in limine. For discussion of these developments, see Moenssens, Admissibility of Scientific Evidence—An Alternative to the Frye Rule, 25 Wm. & Mary L.Rev. 545, 569–71 (1984); Weinstein, Improving Expert Testimony, 20 U.Rich.L.Rev. 473, 481–84 (1986); Weinstein, Role of Expert Testimony and Novel Scientific Evidence in Proof of Causation, Proceeding ABA, Managing Mass Torts, Aug. 9, 1987, at 18–21.

6.   If compelled to testify, how much compensation should an expert receive? Not more than ordinary witness fees if he testifies only to facts? See City and

County of San Francisco v. Superior Court, 231 P.2d 26, 29 (Cal.1951). Crawford Fitting Co. v. J.T. Gibbons, Inc., 482 U.S. 437 (1987): The statutory amount of $30 per day per witness is the most a federal court may tax as costs to the losing party for the prevailing party's expert witnesses; court-appointed witnesses are not subject to this limitation.

7. Obtaining adequate expert assistance for indigent criminal defendants poses a particular problem. In Ake v. Oklahoma, 470 U.S. 68 (1985), the Court held that in a criminal trial, when sanity at the time of the offense is to be a significant factor, due process requires the court to assure an indigent defendant access to a competent psychiatrist who will conduct an appropriate examination and assist in evaluation, preparation and presentation of the defense. Psychiatric assistance is also constitutionally required, the Court said, in the context of a capital sentence proceeding, when the state presents psychiatric evidence of the defendant's future dangerousness. See also Little v. Armontrout, 835 F.2d 1240 (8th Cir.1987) (en banc): In prosecution for rape in which hypnosis-enhanced testimony identifying defendant as the rapist was admitted, the Due Process Clause required that defendant be provided with a state-appointed expert on hypnosis; Note, The Right to a Partisan Psychiatric Expert: Might Indigency Preclude Insanity? 61 N.Y.U.L.Rev. 703 (1986) (arguing that Ake can be read to entitle defendant to partisan psychiatrist). Cf. Little v. Streater, 452 U.S. 1, 16 (1981): "Without aid in obtaining blood test evidence in a paternity case, an indigent defendant, who faces the State as an adversary when the child is a recipient of public assistance and who must overcome the evidentiary burden Connecticut imposes, lacks 'a meaningful opportunity to be heard.' "[3] Apart from constitutional rights, federal law and the law of many states make psychiatric assistance available to indigent criminal defendants. See Ake v. Oklahoma, 470 U.S. at 77, 105 S.Ct. at 1094. 18 U.S.C. § 3006A provides that indigent defendants shall receive the assistance of all experts "necessary for an adequate defense." But see Decker, Access to Expertise, 101 F.R.D. 599, 636–38 (1984) (inadequacy of state assistance and importance of assistance because of mistakes made by laboratories). See also Decker, Expert Services in the Defense of Criminal Cases, 51 U.Cin.L.Rev. 574 (1984).

---

3. Laboratories surveyed in a 1977 study sponsored by the Department of Health, Education and Welfare (now the Department of Health and Human Services) charged an average of approximately $245 for a battery of test systems that led to a minimum exclusion rate of 80%. HEW Office of Child Support Enforcement, Blood Testing to Establish Paternity 35–37 (1977). According to appellant, blood grouping tests were available at the Hartford Hospital for $250 at the time this paternity action was pending trial, but the cost has since been increased to $460. . . . [Footnote by the Court, moved and renumbered.]

CHAPTER 7

PROCEDURAL CONSIDERATIONS

Justice is pictured as passive, blindfolded and holding evenly balanced scales. In fact modern courts take an active role in litigation, oversee the litigants and lean towards one side or the other in a variety of acceptable and unacceptable ways. They are in the business of deciding disputes and that often requires active intervention and decisions without a full sense of how the facts have been, or can be, fully developed so that the truth is known. Burdens of proof and presumptions are designed to favor one side of the dispute or the other. When this is justified as a matter of general policy and practice and how it is accomplished is the subject of Sections 1 and 2 of this chapter. Note, for example, the different burdens placed on the state in proving guilt and in proving that evidence was not illegally obtained or in sentencing. While a relic of an earlier view of evidence, Section 3, Fixed Evaluation of Evidence, infra, also reflects policies affording one class of litigants advantages over another.

The prejudices or predilections of the particular trier towards one side have been implicit in much of the material already studied. The judge's charge marshalling the evidence and the opportunity of litigants to argue their side fully in closings as well as to challenge prospective jurors and judges are intended to prevent this idiosyncratic, non-law authorized, favoring of one side or another.

The dangers of a judge interjecting his views in the case to favor one side in the charge is serious, no matter how even-handed he may try to be. This explains, in part, limits in fact and in theory on summing up and comment by the judge which are prohibited in some states. A rule promulgated by the Supreme Court as part of the Federal Rules of Evidence specifically acknowledging this power in federal judges was omitted by Congress in adopting the Rules. Judges tend to use this power very sparingly. See generally, J. Weinstein & M. Berger, 1 Weinstein's Evidence 107–1 ff.

Use of the power of the court to call and question witnesses and to control such aspects of the trial as order of proof may also have an effect on which side is more likely to prevail. See, e.g., Fed.R.Evid. 611(a). Certainly the power of the judge to pass on preliminary questions of fact, will have a great and often determinative effect on the outcome of the litigation, particularly in view of the wide discretion incorporated in the Federal Rules of Evidence and much modern practice. See, e.g., Fed.R.Evid. 102, 104, 403.

Possible abuse of discretion and the danger of the trier favoring one side or the other are enhanced when the rules of evidence can be ignored almost entirely by the trier. See, e.g., Fed.R.Evid. 104 (preliminary questions).

Whatever limits are placed on the trier by rules of evidence in order to ensure fairness, accuracy and impartiality depend largely upon the attorney's taking the proper steps to see that the trial is conducted fairly and that his client's right to correct errors on appeal is protected. See Ch. 1, E., Preserving Issues For Appeal, supra.

Most judges are scrupulously fair in their intent to allow the adversarial system to proceed without unnecessary judicial intervention both because they believe it will in most cases achieve the most accurate and fair result and because their own lack of knowledge of the details of the litigation make intervention too hazardous. Moreover, they recognize that at least some jurors will rely on them for guidance as a symbol of impartiality and skilled professionalism. This means that any hint that the judge believes one side's position is more meritorious than another may critically affect a juror's decision. Most judges are sincere when they tell the jury that they have no view as to guilt or innocence and are indifferent as to the result. Litigants should leave the court with the sense that cool impartiality has ruled from the bench. Occasionally, however, because of frustration by what it conceives to be incompetent counsel, the pressure of other cases or its own lack of judicial temperament, the court may intervene improperly leaving the litigants without the feeling of impartiality.

In Johnson v. Metz, 609 F.2d 1052, 1057–1058 (2d Cir.1979), a writ of habeas corpus was sought on the basis of partiality of the state trial judge. Concurring in the decision to dismiss for failure to exhaust state remedies, Judge Newman wrote:

The petitioners' claim on the merits is not limited to an assertion that the trial judge rendered their convictions constitutionally unfair by his excessive intervention. Were the claim so limited, it would indeed be a novel basis for alleging that a conviction has been obtained in violation of the Due Process Clause. Intervention per se would normally be a matter of concern to a court with supervisory authority. In that capacity, the New York Court of Appeals only recently reversed a conviction where the trial judge intervened to ask more than one-third of all the questions asked during the trial. People v. Mees, 47 N.Y.2d 997, 420 N.Y.S.2d 214, 394 N.E.2d 283 (1979). No doubt that Court will not lightly forgo the opportunity to reexamine this record, in which the trial judge asked more questions than either the prosecutor or the defense attorneys.

But the degree of intervention provides only the context in which petitioners' claim arises. The essence of the claim is that the nature of all of the trial judge's conduct—his questions, his comments to defense counsel, his comments to the defendants, and his comments to the jury—combined to deny petitioners the "fair trial in a fair tribunal" that is "a basic requirement of due process." In re Murchison, 349 U.S. 133, 136 (1955). This claim goes far beyond what occurred in Davis v. Craven, 485 F.2d 1138 (9th Cir.1973) (en banc), cert. denied, 417 U.S. 933 (1974), where the trial judge had expressed a circumspect opinion as to the petitioner's guilt. The claim here is that the trial judge so far departed from his role as a "symbol of even-handed justice," United States ex rel. Elksnis v. Gilligan, 256 F.Supp. 244, 254 (S.D.N.Y.1966) (Weinfeld, J.), as to join forces with the prosecution and help secure the convictions.

A claim of this nature is well within the mainstream of due process adjudication. A federal court, exercising habeas jurisdiction, has overturned a state conviction where even isolated comments of a trial judge to a jury created prejudice sufficient to establish a denial of due process. United States ex rel. Harding v. Marks, 403 F.Supp. 946 (E.D.Pa.1975). A trial judge's one-sided intrusion into the process of criminal adjudication has also precipitated federal court reversal of a state conviction when the trial judge exerted improper influence over the decision of a defendant's witness to testify, Webb v. Texas, 409 U.S. 95 (1972), and when a trial judge exerted improper influence over a defendant's decision to plead guilty, United States ex rel. Elksnis v. Gilligan, supra.

Due process violations sufficient to avoid state criminal convictions have been found when the role of the trial judge created only the risk or the appearance of partiality. Ward v. Village of Monroeville, 409 U.S. 57 (1972) (fine payable to judge or his administration); Tumey v. Ohio, 273 U.S. 510 (1927) (same); Mayberry v. Pennsylvania, 400 U.S. 455 (1971) (trial for contemptuous behavior that had been directed toward the judge); In re Murchison, 349 U.S. 133 (1955) (prior role of trial judge as one man grand jury); In re Oliver, 333 U.S. 257 (1948) (same). Surely actual conduct by a trial judge conveying to a jury not merely his opinion of a defendant's guilt but his determination to secure a conviction is at least as serious a denial of due process as cases where state court convictions have been vacated because the jury was subjected to the risk of improper influence from other sources. Sheppard v. Maxwell, 384 U.S. 333 (1966) (excessive publicity); Turner v. Louisiana, 379 U.S. 466 (1965) (prosecution witnesses attending the jury); Moore v. Dempsey, 261 U.S. 86 (1923) (threat of mob violence).

Petitioners' claim, now returned for what will surely be sensitive examination by the state courts, is that the trial judge failed to observe the enduring admonition of Judge Learned Hand: "[The trial judge] must not take on the role of a partisan; he must not enter the lists; he must not by his ardor induce the jury to join in a hue and cry against the accused. Prosecution and judgment are two quite separate functions in the administration of justice; they must not merge." United States v. Marzano, 149 F.2d 923, 926 (2d Cir.1945).

SECTION 1.   BURDENS OF PROOF

A.   HISTORY

Under the Anglo–American common law system of administering justice the court theoretically knows the law applicable to every controversy which is brought before it. It has at its command a major premise from which the correct conclusion, to be expressed in an order or a judgment, will inevitably follow as soon as the minor premise is ascertained. The proposition of the major premise will assert that if a specified state of facts exists, the controversy must be resolved in favor of one or the other of the parties. This state of facts will include all which create or change legal relations between the parties with reference to the matter in controversy. Put in the conditional form the rule of law (major premise) might read: if A (negligence) and if B (causing damage) and if C (non-negligence of person damaged) then liability of negligent party to party damaged for amount of damages. The material propositions in the case (minor premise) might be: a (defendant drove through a red light on December 31, 1981, hitting plaintiff's car in an intersection of A Avenue and 1st Street), b (plaintiff's fender was crumpled by the collision requiring $1,000 for repairs) and c (plaintiff was proceeding through a green light, keeping a sharp lookout and otherwise acting prudently). The conclusion would be plaintiff is liable to defendant for $1,000.

But the court has no knowledge of the existence of the controversy or of the pertinent facts until the parties have been properly brought before it and the matter in dispute has been placed before it for adjudication. The party desiring the status quo changed must take the proper action to bring his adversary before the court. The next step requires the parties to disclose to the court the exact point or points in dispute—as exactly as modern pleading and pretrial practice will permit.

Assume that plaintiff at common law is claiming damages for breach of contract by defendant. The court's major premise will assert defendant's responsibility if a specified state of fact exists as to the act of promising, the capacity of promisor and of promisee, fraud, duress, mistake, consideration, novation, breach, accord and satisfaction, former recovery, and every other pertinent matter. As to the facts concerning each of these the court knows nothing. As to how many of them will it require the plaintiff to make an assertion in his first pleading? Conceivably, as to every matter which might affect legal relations between him and defendant, and thus to make plain his contention as to each fact in the conditional clause of the major premise. The defendant might then be called upon to admit or deny each of plaintiff's assertions and in this way make specific the matters in dispute.

Of course, no such requirements are imposed. The court distributes the burden of pleading between the parties according to what it believes to be good policy in the light of its previous experience and its concept of the proper function of pleadings. See Cleary, Presuming and Pleading: An Essay on Juristic Immaturity, 12 Stan.L.Rev. 5 (1959); James, Jr., Burdens of Proof, 47 Virginia L.Rev. 51, 58–63 (1961). In so doing it cannot avoid making, for this limited purpose, an assumption, tacit or express, as to each undisclosed operative fact. Thus suppose that a court rules that a complaint which contains no allegation of consideration for the promise for breach of which plaintiff is suing states no cause of action. Its major premise prescribes as a condition of defendant's liability that his promise must have been supported by consideration. Before the pleadings began, the court knew nothing about consideration or lack of it in this case. Neither litigant has made any assertion about it. The decision is for defendant. Consequently, the court must, for this purpose, be assuming that there was no consideration. In like manner when the court fixes upon defendant the burden of pleading accord and satisfaction, thus denominating it an affirmative defense, it assumes in the absence of any allegation about the matter, that no accord and satisfaction occurred.

Should the opponent not contest the allegations of a complaint or answer they are deemed admitted. If all of plaintiff's allegations or any allegation of an affirmative defense is not denied there is no factual dispute and no need for a trial.

Where, as is the usual case, a material proposition of fact is contested then a trial will be necessary to decide whether the material proposition is true— e.g., there was or was not consideration or defendant was or was not going through a red light when his car struck plaintiff's.

As to each issue of fact to be resolved at the trial a modern Anglo–American court has no knowledge. In the evolution of our trial by jury the procedure for fact-finding has gone through five stages.

In the first the jury answers the question in issue of its own knowledge. Neither party has any burden of making the facts known, though each has a limited privilege of presenting pertinent data. Each party carries the risk that the jury may find against him because the data known to the jurors may be inadequate or may be given too little or too great persuasive effect. The jury's answer is final as between the parties.

In the second stage the situation is the same, except that after the original jury has answered the question, the defeated litigant may in certain cases have the same question submitted to an attaint jury. The answer of the attaint jury, whether it coincide with that of the original jury or not, is final.

About the middle of the seventeenth century the third stage is reached. The court now assumes the power to set aside the verdict of the jury on the ground that it is against the facts. Though the jury may still act upon its own private knowledge, its main reliance has come to be upon the evidence presented in open court. A litigant may now lose the benefit of a verdict if the evidence at the trial makes it plain that nothing which the jury could have known could reasonably have led it to find such a verdict. The litigant still has no burden of producing any evidence as a condition of having the issue submitted to the jury, nor has he any burden of persuading the jury, for they may find in his favor without a word of evidence. But if he is to keep any verdict he may secure from the jury, he must see to it that there is produced at the trial, whether by himself, by his adversary or by the judge, whatever evidence, if any, may be necessary to convince the court that the jury may reasonably find in his favor.

In the fourth stage, which begins near the end of the 1600's, the trial judge is empowered to direct the jury to return a specified verdict if the evidence at the trial demonstrates that the jury's private knowledge would not warrant any other verdict. Henceforth one of the litigants has the burden of seeing to it that there is presented at the trial sufficient evidence to convince the trial judge that the jury may, taking into account its private knowledge, reasonably return a verdict in his favor, and this, as a condition of having the issue submitted to the jury. Still neither can be said to have any burden of persuading the jury for the jury may still act upon its own knowledge, though obviously one of them must carry the risk of the jury's nonpersuasion.

By the middle of the eighteenth century it has become established that the jury must base its verdict solely upon evidence presented in court. This is the final stage. One or the other of the litigants now has the burden of seeing to it that sufficient evidence is produced at the trial to convince the judge that the jury may reasonably find in his favor and sufficient evidence to persuade the jury actually to find in his favor. Cf. Note, The Changing Role of the Jury in the Nineteenth Century, 74 Yale L.J. 170 (1964). With some degree of self-pride, the United States Supreme Court remarked, "One of the rightful boasts of Western Civilization is that the [prosecution] has the burden of establishing guilt solely on the basis of evidence produced in court and under circumstances assuring an accused all the safeguards of a fair procedure." Deutch v. United States, 367 U.S. 456, 471 (1961).

Even though the trier may remain in doubt about the facts in the case, the court may not equivocate. It must find for the plaintiff or the defendant. Cf. Vanosdol v. Henderson, 22 N.E.2d 812 (Ind.1939) ("We don't know" evasive); Morris v. Vining, 49 So.2d 458 (La.App.1950) (improper to divide four cows among parties where evidence on right to possession equally balanced). As Professors Hart and McNaughton put the matter in Evidence and Inference, 48, 53 (Lerner ed., 1959):

> The law does not require absolute assurance of the perfect correctness of particular decisions. While it is of course important that the court be right in its determinations of fact, it is also important that the court decide the case when the parties ask for the decision and on the basis of the evidence presented by the parties. A decision must be made now, one way or the other. To require certainty or even near-certainty in such a context would be impracticable and undesirable.

The rules governing burdens of proof provide the chief procedural device for resolving the dilemma of the necessity for precision and certainty in fact finding by the courts, and the lack of capacity to meet these standards. Even in arbitrations where the arbitrator is free to ignore the concept of burdens of proof, "most arbitrators recognize the usefulness of the burden of proof/burden of proceeding concept as it has developed in Anglo–American jurisprudence." Gorske, Burden of Proof in Grievance Arbitration, 43 Marq.L.Rev. 135, 179 (1959).

B.   Points at Trial at Which Question Is Raised

Because the jury must base its finding upon the evidence presented in court and because the judge has the power, by ordering a nonsuit or dismissal or by directing a verdict, to prevent the jury from passing upon a question where the evidence is such that reasonable people could give but one answer, the burdens which a party may have to bear in a jury trial merit detailed description. Assume an action for breach of an express promise by defendant to do act X in which defendant denies having made the promise. Assume too that the burden of pleading and the burden of proof rests on the same party—a result which is not logically or practically necessary. See Fed.R.Civ.P. 8(c) (affirmative defenses); 2A Moore's Federal Practice ¶ 8.27(c).

1.   At the trial, plaintiff will begin with two burdens if he desires to get a verdict in his favor from the jury and an additional burden if he desires a direction in his favor by the judge. The defendant will begin without a burden.

(a) Plaintiff's initial burden will be to introduce evidence which would support a finding that defendant made the promise. Whether he has discharged this burden is a question to be decided by the judge after plaintiff has rested. This question may be raised by the judge of his own motion, but it will usually be raised by motion of the defendant. In some jurisdictions the proper motion is for a dismissal of the action; in others, for a compulsory nonsuit; in still others a motion for a directed verdict will be entertained. E.g., Fed.R.Civ.P. 50(a). Whatever the form, it is assumed in this discussion that the defendant, in case the motion is denied, may go forward with evidence on his own behalf. Cf. 9 Wigmore, Evidence § 2496(2) (Chadbourn rev. 1981). If the judge decides that plaintiff has not discharged this first burden, he will terminate the action by granting the motion. If he denies the motion, the plaintiff no longer has to discharge any burden to avoid a nonsuit, dismissal or directed verdict, and the defendant has acquired the burden of introducing evidence if he is to secure such mandatory action by the judge. The judge's denial of defendant's motion determines only that plaintiff is entitled, on the evidence thus far introduced, to have the jury decide whether or not the defendant made the promise.

(b) At this stage of the trial it is impossible for either the litigants or the judge to ascertain whether the plaintiff still has the second of his original burdens, namely, to persuade the jury to find that the defendant made the promise. It may be that if the case were submitted to the jury without further evidence and without argument, it would find for the plaintiff. If so, the plaintiff has discharged his burden of persuasion, at least temporarily, and the defendant has acquired a correlative burden of dissuading the jury from finding that he made the promise. On the other hand, it may be that the jury would find for defendant because not yet persuaded to find for plaintiff. Its non-persuasion may be either because the evidence, no matter how persuasively presented and explained, lacks the requisite convincing power, or because without argument its real value is not appreciated by the jury. If the former, the plaintiff has the burden of introducing additional evidence, if the latter, he has the burden of making the requisite argument or explanation. If, as previously suggested, the jury is already persuaded to find for plaintiff, it may be that, despite any explanation or argument that might be made to the contrary, the evidence is in the minds of the jury decisive, or it may be that without argument or explanation the jury is attributing to the evidence a value which explanation or argument would totally destroy or at least so weaken as to deprive it of the required convincing force. If the former, defendant has the burden of introducing evidence which will dissuade the jury from finding that he made the promise; if the latter, the burden of making the dissuading argument or explanation.

Whether the plaintiff has yet discharged his burden of persuasion and the defendant has acquired the correlative burden of dissuasion, only the jury could know. The court has probably told the jury to keep an open mind until the case is submitted to it and the jury does not usually know what the precise issue before it is at this stage. No motion by either party, no order by the judge, can call for a disclosure of the jury's state of persuasion or non-persuasion at the close of plaintiff's evidence. And the same is true at every later stage of the trial short of final verdict. In a word, there is no procedural device by the use of which the parties can ascertain whether the plaintiff has discharged his burden of persuading the jury until the judge submits the issue to the jury after the close of all the evidence.

(c) What of plaintiff's third possible burden, that the introducing evidence in order to secure a directed verdict in his own favor? Has he yet discharged it and thereby imposed upon defendant a correlative burden to escape a directed verdict? That will depend upon the quality and quantity of the evidence already in the case. If that evidence is such that it could not fail to convince any reasonable person that defendant made the promise, defendant must, in most cases, come forward with evidence to the contrary or suffer a directed verdict. In some states a verdict may never be directed for the party having the burden of persuasion upon oral testimony, for such a direction would permit the judge to be the judge of the credibility of the witnesses. See, e.g., MacDonald v. Pennsylvania Railway Co., 36 A.2d 492 (Pa.1944). For one aspect of the problem in criminal cases see Note, Submission of Lesser Crimes, 56 Colum.L.Rev. 888 (1956).

But neither of his own motion nor on motion of plaintiff can the judge direct a verdict for plaintiff without affording defendant an opportunity to present his evidence. Such a motion may not properly be made without violating our notions of due process until defendant rests.

Ordinarily then at the close of plaintiff's evidence in chief, the parties by proper motion can ascertain whether plaintiff has satisfied his first burden of coming forward. It is possible that he has temporarily satisfied the burden of persuading the jury to find in his favor and also the burden of introducing sufficient evidence to secure a directed verdict, but there is no procedural device by which he can at this stage of the trial determine whether he has done so.

2.   Now assume that after defendant's motion to terminate the case at the close of plaintiff's evidence in chief has been denied, the defendant rests without offering any evidence. At this point the plaintiff, by moving for a directed verdict, can discover whether defendant had the burden of introducing evidence sufficient to justify a jury in failing to find that defendant made the promise. If the judge grants the motion, it will mean that on the evidence introduced by plaintiff no jury could reasonably refuse to find that defendant had made the promise. If the judge denies the motion, he will be ruling that there is no burden upon defendant to produce evidence to entitle him to have the jury pass upon the question. Since he has already denied defendant's motion for a directed verdict, the situation is now this (and it is the usual one in practice): of the burdens with which the plaintiff began, he has discharged

the first; he has not discharged the third; whether he has discharged the second is to be determined by the jury. Though the defendant began with no burden, there has been placed upon him the burden of introducing evidence if he is to secure a directed verdict. The opportunity to discharge this burden he has waived by resting without offering any evidence. Whether he has also a burden of so expounding the evidence as to convince the jury that they should not find that he made the promise, he has no means of ascertaining. In this situation the parties will present their respective arguments to the jury, each attempting to persuade the jury that on the evidence it should return a verdict in his favor. If the jury is not persuaded to find for plaintiff, it must find for defendant.

If the defendant's motion for nonsuit, dismissal, or directed verdict, made at the close of the plaintiff's case, is denied, the defendant will not usually rest without offering evidence. By introducing evidence, the defendant risks waiving the right to appellate review of the adequacy of plaintiff's case standing alone because in a criminal case his own evidence may sufficiently buttress the government's case to uphold a guilty verdict. McGautha v. California, 402 U.S. 183 (1971); United States v. Evans, 572 F.2d 455, 479 n. 27 (5th Cir.), cert. denied, 439 U.S. 870 (1978); United States v. Trotter, 529 F.2d 806, 809 n. 3 (3d Cir.1976) ("By introducing evidence, [defendant] waived his motion for acquittal. Since he renewed his motion at the end of all the evidence, we must examine the record as a whole for sufficient evidence to sustain a conviction."); United States v. Martinez, 514 F.2d 334, 337 (9th Cir.1975); United States v. Brown, 456 F.2d 293, 294 (2d Cir.), cert. denied, 407 U.S. 910 (1972) (court applied waiver rule even though trial judge had erroneously reserved judgment on motion to acquit; see Fed.R.Crim.P. 29(a)); United States v. Maffei, 450 F.2d 928, 930 (6th Cir.1971), cert. denied, 406 U.S. 938 (1972) (but note the dissent on certiorari by Douglas, J., pointing out the conflict among the circuits and calling for a resolution of the conflict); United States v. Rosengarten, 357 F.2d 263, 266 (2d Cir.1966). Contra, United States v. Rizzo, 416 F.2d 734, 736 n. 3 (7th Cir.1969) ("[I]n reviewing the denial of the motion for acquittal, this Court must consider the record as it existed when the motion was made, at the end of the Government's case in chief."); State v. Stuart, 51 Hawai'i 656, 664, 466 P.2d 444, 450 (1970) (per J. Levinson, concurring). But cf. United States v. House, 551 F.2d 756, 759 (8th Cir.), cert. denied, 434 U.S. 850 (1977) (court refused to apply the waiver rule when a motion to acquit was erroneously reserved at close of plaintiff's case, and defendant made a clear demand for a ruling). See also, Note, the Motion for Acquittal: A Neglected Safeguard, 70 Yale L.J. 1151 (1961). Note that in Regina v. Onufrejczyk, infra, the jury was told to consider the people's case without respect to defendant's evidence.

After he has introduced his evidence and rested, the plaintiff may move for a directed verdict in the same way as if the defendant had rested without tendering any evidence. If plaintiff's motion is denied, he may introduce evidence in rebuttal; usually this will terminate the testimony, but each party ordinarily has the opportunity to meet new matter introduced by his opponent. Whenever one party rests, the other party may move for a directed verdict, and when the evidence is closed, each party may move for a directed verdict in his favor. Each motion raises the same problems for the judge as the motion at the close of plaintiff's case, except in those few jurisdictions which hold that if both parties move for a directed verdict, both waive trial by jury.

Now let it be assumed that the plaintiff's claim is met not by a denial but by a plea of the affirmative defense of accord and satisfaction, which in turn is denied by the plaintiff. If it is assumed that upon this issue the burdens are upon the defendant, the situation will be the same as that heretofore described, except that the parties will be reversed. If the defendant interposes both a denial and a plea of accord and satisfaction which is traversed by the plaintiff, then the burdens on the first issue will be upon the plaintiff, and on the second issue will be upon the defendant. A verdict for the plaintiff may be directed only if the jury could not reasonably fail to find that defendant made the promise and could not reasonably find the alleged accord and satisfaction; a verdict for the defendant may be directed if the jury could not reasonably find that the defendant made the promise or could not reasonably fail to find the alleged accord and satisfaction.

The foregoing paragraphs use the terms, burden of producing evidence and burden of persuasion. In the hypothetical case, it is literally true that plaintiff will begin the trial with the burden of introducing evidence that the defendant made the promise, for no evidence at all has yet been introduced. It is also literally true that at the commencement of the trial defendant has the burden of producing evidence on the issue of accord and satisfaction, and for the same reason. The defendant may win the lawsuit without introducing any evidence upon that issue if plaintiff fails to discharge the burden of production or persuasion as to the issue of promise; but if the result of the litigation depends upon the issue of accord and satisfaction, defendant must lose in the absence of meeting the burden of production and persuasion on accord and satisfaction. After the close of plaintiff's evidence, however, defendant may or may not have a burden with reference to the alleged accord and satisfaction. Whatever evidence has been introduced during the presentation of plaintiff's case inures to the benefit of defendant as well as to that of plaintiff, not only upon the issue of promise but also upon the issue of accord and satisfaction. It is entirely without significance whether this evidence was given when plaintiff was examining his witnesses or when defendant was examining them. Hence if the evidence thus introduced, had it been offered by the defendant, would have discharged any burden of defendant, that burden is effectively discharged. In like manner any evidence introduced by defendant may discharge, or assist in discharging, any burden of plaintiff. In short, the question is not whether the plaintiff or the defendant has introduced the evidence which discharges the burden but whether such evidence has been introduced. Consequently, it would be more accurate to say that the plaintiff begins the trial with the risk of nonproduction of evidence that defendant made the promise and the defendant begins both the trial and the presentation of his case carrying the risk of nonproduction of evidence of accord and satisfaction. Similarly the burden of persuasion is more accurately described as the risk of nonpersuasion. Since the courts have almost always talked in terms of burden, however, it may be well to continue to do so.

The term burden of proof is often used interchangeably with burden of persuasion and burden of producing evidence. Compare the definitions of the Model Code of Evidence (Rule 1(2), (3)): "Burden of producing evidence of a fact means the burden which is discharged when sufficient evidence is introduced to support a finding that the fact exists.

"Burden of persuasion of a fact means the burden which is discharged when the tribunal which is to determine the existence or nonexistence of the fact is persuaded by sufficient evidence to find that the fact exists." In the notes that follow the terminology of the Model Code will be used.

C.   ALLOCATING BURDENS

Allocating burdens of persuasion involves distinct substantive policies favoring one class of litigant over another. Thus, in diversity cases, while federal procedural law controls pleading, state law determines burdens of proof.

Palmer v. Hoffman, 318 U.S. 109 (1943); C. Wright, Law of Federal Courts 316–17 (3rd Ed.1976). Even burdens of coming forward, while often not as devastating to a case, may be crucial in shifting the possibility of victory towards one side or the other, thus implicating policies about which side ought to be favored where evidence is sparse or nonexistent.

Generally courts have deferred to the legislature when the later body has spoken, however delphian. Steadman v. Securities and Exchange Commission, 450 U.S. 91, 95 & n. 10 (1981) (note 5 has been incorporated in the text): "[W]here Congress has spoken, we have deferred to 'the traditional powers of Congress to prescribe rules of evidence and standards of proof in the federal courts', absent countervailing constitutional restraints. Vance v. Terrazas, 444 U.S. 252, 265, 100 S.Ct. 540, 548, 62 L.Ed.2d 461 (1980).... ([T]he task of determining the appropriate standard of proof ... may be one of discerning Congressional intent ...)." Cf. Wilson v. Scripps–Howard Broadcasting Co., 642 F.2d 371 (6th Cir.1981) (the First amendment requires the plaintiff to establish falsity in libel action).

These materials are designed to distinguish the issues of who has what burdens, how high they are, and how the jury should be instructed about them. But, as is apparent, these three concepts are often intertwined in the statutes and cases as are the closely related problems of shifting burdens of proof through presumptions and otherwise. Cf. E.I. du Pont de Nemours v. Berkley & Co., Inc., 620 F.2d 1247, 1266–1267 (8th Cir.1980) (under 35 U.S.C. § 282 a patent is presumed valid and the burden of going forward as well as the burden of persuasion rests upon the party asserting invalidity). The power of the court to comment on evidence and on possible inferences which may be drawn from it are also closely related in practical effect to burdens.

AMERICAN LAW INSTITUTE MODEL PENAL CODE
TENTATIVE DRAFT NO. 4, 1955, PP. 7, 108–111.

Section 1.13. Proof Beyond a Reasonable Doubt; Affirmative Defenses; Burden of Proving Fact When Not an Element of an Offense; Presumptions.

(1) No person may be convicted of an offense unless each element of such offense is proved beyond a reasonable doubt. In the absence of such proof, the innocence of the defendant is assumed.

(2) Paragraph (1) of this section does not:

(a) require the disproof of an affirmative defense unless and until there is evidence supporting such defense; or

(b) apply to any defense which the Code or another statute plainly requires the defendant to prove by a preponderance of evidence.

(3) A ground of defense is affirmative, within the intendment of paragraph (2)(a) of this section, when:

(a) it arises under a section of the Code which so provides; or....

(d) it involves a matter of excuse or justification peculiarly within the knowledge of the defendant on which he can fairly be required to adduce supporting evidence.

COMMENTS

The problems dealt with are, of course, procedural in nature. But they involve such fundamental policy that, though there is some fragmentary treatment in state codes of criminal procedure, they are omitted from the most important modern formulations in that field.... Moreover, students of procedure often have admonished that the underlying legislative considerations relevant to the solution of these problems have as large a substantive as adjective dimension.

. . .

1.   Paragraph (1) sets forth the general requirement. It calls for proof beyond a reasonable doubt of "every element of the offense." The term "element of an offense" is broadly defined in section 1.14(9) to mean "such conduct or such attendant circumstances or such a result of conduct as (a) is included in the definition of the offense or (b) establishes the required culpability or (c) negatives an excuse or justification for such conduct or (d) negatives a defense under the statute of limitations or (e) establishes jurisdiction or venue."

In treating venue as an element of the offense for this purpose, the draft imposes a more rigorous demand than many states, which as to venue, and sometimes even jurisdiction, call for proof only by preponderance of evidence.... Much as there is to say for a distinction between facts which establish the criminality of the defendant's conduct and those which merely satisfy procedural requirements, with a lighter burden for the latter than the former, there is larger difficulty in presenting to a jury different standards for appraising different features of the prosecution's case. So long as venue and jurisdiction present questions for the jury on the general issue, the prosecutors among the Advisory Committee were agreed that no slight relaxation of the burden possibly can compensate for the confusion likely to be caused by utilizing any double standard of this kind.

. . .

3.   Paragraph (2) is addressed to the first qualification of the reasonable doubt provision, namely, the case of an affirmative defense.

Sub-paragraph (a) deals with the most frequent case where the denomination of a defense as affirmative relieves the prosecution of the burden of adducing evidence in the first instance on the issue; the evidential burden is imposed on the defendant. Unless there is evidence supporting the defense, there is no issue on the point to be submitted to the jury. When, however, there is evidence supporting the defense (whether presented by the prosecution or defendant), the prosecution has the normal burden; the defense must be negatived by proof beyond a reasonable doubt.

The draft does not attempt to state how strong the evidence must be to satisfy the test that "there is evidence" supporting the defense. The Council of the Institute thought it the wiser course to leave this question to the courts. It may be noted, however, that Rule 1(2) of the A.L.I. MODEL CODE OF EVIDENCE defines the "burden of producing evidence of a fact" to call for "sufficient evidence ... to support a finding that the fact exists." We have no doubt that such a standard is too onerous to be accepted for the present purpose. It should suffice to put the prosecution to its proof beyond a reasonable doubt that the defendant shows enough to justify such doubt upon the issue. We think that most courts would construe the section in this way.

Affirmative defenses, in this sense, are very common in existing penal law—even as to matters which in any ordinary meaning of the term involve the proof or disproof of elements of the crime charged. Typical illustrations are: Self-defense and similar claims of justification for conduct that would otherwise be criminal; excuses such as necessity, duress and claim of right; some exculpating mistakes, such as those based upon intoxication; license; many claims of exemption from a statutory prohibition based on a proviso or exception. See, e.g. McCormick, Evidence (1953) pp. 683–85; Williams, Criminal Law: The General Part §§ 224–232; Wigmore, Evidence (3d ed.) vol. 9, §§ 2486, 2501, 2512. In many states, indeed, with respect to some of these claims the defendant has more than an evidential burden; he also has a burden of persuasion. See e.g. as to self-defense: West's Ann.Cal.Penal Code § 1105; Commonwealth v. Troup, 153 A. 337 (Pa.1931); Quillen v. State, 23 L.W. 2323 (Del.1955); as to insanity: Leland v. Oregon, 343 U.S. 790 (1952) (proof beyond reasonable doubt).

No single principle can be conscripted to explain when these shifts of burden to defendants are defensible, even if the burden goes no further than to call for the production of some evidence. Neither the logical point that the prosecution would be called upon to prove a negative, nor the grammatical point that the defense rests on an exception or proviso divorced from the definition of the crime is potently persuasive, although both points have been invoked. See e.g. Rossi v. United States, 289 U.S. 89 (1933); United States v. Fleischman, 339 U.S. 349, 360–363 (1950); State v. McLean, 196 N.W. 278 (Minn.1923). What is involved seems rather a more subtle balance which acknowledges that a defendant ought not to be required to defend until some solid substance is presented to support the accusation but, beyond this, perceives a point where need for narrowing the issues, coupled with the relative accessibility of evidence to the defendant, warrants calling upon him to present his defensive claim. No doubt this point is reached more quickly if, given the facts the prosecution must establish, the normal probabilities are against the defense but this is hardly an essential factor. Given the mere fact of an intentional homicide, no one can estimate the probability that it was or was not committed in self-defense. The point is rather that purposeful homicide is an event of such gravity to society, and the basis for a claim of self-defense is so specially within the cognizance of the defendant, that it is fair to call on him to offer evidence if the defense is claimed. This is in essence the classic analysis by Justice Cardozo in Morrison v. California, 291 U.S. 82, 88–90 (1934), although the statute there involved seemingly also shifted burden of persuasion. See also Williams v. United States, 78 U.S.App.D.C. 147, 138 F.2d 81 (1943) (justification for abortion). So long as this criterion is satisfied, it is submitted that no constitutional objection is presented, though language in Tot v. United States, 319 U.S. 463 (1943), but not the decision, must be distinguished. See Morgan, Comment, 56 Harv.L.Rev. 1324, 1328–1330.

Patterson v. New York

Supreme Court of the United States, 1977.
432 U.S. 197, 97 S.Ct. 2319, 53 L.Ed.2d 281.

■ MR. JUSTICE WHITE delivered the opinion of the Court.

The question here is the constitutionality under the Fourteenth Amendment's Due Process Clause of burdening the defendant in a New York State murder trial with proving the affirmative defense of extreme emotional disturbance as defined by New York law.

I

After a brief and unstable marriage, the appellant, Gordon Patterson, Jr., became estranged from his wife, Roberta. Roberta resumed an association with

John Northrup, a neighbor to whom she had been engaged prior to her marriage to appellant. On December 27, 1970, Patterson borrowed a rifle from an acquaintance and went to the residence of his father-in-law. There, he observed his wife through a window in a state of semiundress in the presence of John Northrup. He entered the house and killed Northrup by shooting him twice in the head.

Patterson was charged with second-degree murder. In New York there are two elements of this crime: (1) "intent to cause the death of another person"; and (2) "caus[ing] the death of such person or of a third person." N.Y.Penal Law § 125.25 (McKinney 1975). Malice aforethought is not an element of the crime. In addition, the State permits a person accused of murder to raise an affirmative defense that he "acted under the influence of extreme emotional disturbance for which there was a reasonable explanation or excuse."[1]

New York also recognizes the crime of manslaughter. A person is guilty of manslaughter if he intentionally kills another person "under circumstances which do not constitute murder because he acts under the influence of extreme emotional disturbance." Appellant confessed before trial to killing Northrup, but at trial he raised the defense of extreme emotional disturbance.[2]

The jury was instructed as to the elements of the crime of murder. Focusing on the element of intent, the trial court charged:

> "Before you, considering all of the evidence, can convict this defendant or anyone of murder, you must believe and decide that the People have established beyond a reasonable doubt that he intended, in firing the gun, to kill either the victim himself or some other human being. . . .

.   .   .

> "Always remember that you must not expect or require the defendant to prove to your satisfaction that his acts were done without the intent to kill. Whatever proof he may have attempted, however far he may have gone in an effort to convince you of his innocence or guiltlessness, he is not obliged, he is not obligated to prove anything. It is always the People's burden to prove his guilt, and to prove that he intended to kill in this instance beyond a reasonable doubt." App. A70–A71.

The jury was further instructed, consistently with New York law, that the defendant had the burden of proving his affirmative defense by a preponderance of the evidence. The jury was told that if it found beyond a reasonable doubt that appellant had intentionally killed Northrup but that appellant had demonstrated by a preponderance of the evidence that he had acted under the

---

1. Section 125.25 provides in relevant part:

"A person is guilty of murder in the second degree when:

> "1. With intent to cause the death of another person, he causes the death of such person or of a third person; except that in any prosecution under this subdivision, it is an affirmative defense that:

> "(a) The defendant acted under the influence of extreme emotional disturbance for which there was a reasonable explanation or excuse, the reasonableness of which is to be determined from the viewpoint of a person in the defen-

dant's situation under the circumstances as the defendant believed them to be. Nothing contained in this paragraph shall constitute a defense to a prosecution for, or preclude a conviction of, manslaughter in the first degree or any other crime." [Some footnotes are omitted; others are renumbered; footnotes by the Court.]

2. Appellant also contended at trial that the shooting was accidental and that therefore he had no intent to kill Northrup. It is here undisputed, however, that the prosecution proved beyond a reasonable doubt that the killing was intentional.

influence of extreme emotional disturbance, it had to find appellant guilty of manslaughter instead of murder.

The jury found appellant guilty of murder. Judgment was entered on the verdict, and the Appellate Division affirmed. While appeal to the New York Court of Appeals was pending, this Court decided Mullaney v. Wilbur, 421 U.S. 684, 95 S.Ct. 1881, 44 L.Ed.2d 508 (1975), in which the Court declared Maine's murder statute unconstitutional. Under the Maine statute, a person accused of murder could rebut the statutory presumption that he committed the offense with "malice aforethought" by proving that he acted in the heat of passion on sudden provocation. The Court held that this scheme improperly shifted the burden of persuasion from the prosecutor to the defendant and was therefore a violation of due process. In the Court of Appeals appellant urged that New York's murder statute is functionally equivalent to the one struck down in Mullaney and that therefore his conviction should be reversed.

The Court of Appeals rejected appellant's argument, holding that the New York murder statute is consistent with due process. 39 N.Y.2d 288, 383 N.Y.S.2d 573, 347 N.E.2d 898 (1976). The Court distinguished Mullaney on the ground that the New York statute involved no shifting of the burden to the defendant to disprove any fact essential to the offense charged since the New York affirmative defense of extreme emotional disturbance bears no direct relationship to any element of murder. This appeal ensued, and we noted probable jurisdiction. 429 U.S. 813, 97 S.Ct. 52, 50 L.Ed.2d 72 (1976). We affirm.

II

It goes without saying that preventing and dealing with crime is much more the business of the States than it is of the Federal Government, Irvine v. California 347 U.S. 128, 134, 74 S.Ct. 381, 384, 98 L.Ed. 561 (1954) (plurality opinion), and that we should not lightly construe the Constitution so as to intrude upon the administration of justice by the individual States. Among other things, it is normally "within the power of the State to regulate procedures under which its laws are carried out, including the burden of producing evidence and the burden of persuasion," and its decision in this regard is not subject to proscription under the Due Process Clause unless "it offends some principle of justice so rooted in the traditions and conscience of our people as to be ranked as fundamental." Speiser v. Randall, 357 U.S. 513, 523, 78 S.Ct. 1332, 1341, 2 L.Ed.2d 1460 (1958)....

In determining whether New York's allocation to the defendant of proving the mitigating circumstances of severe emotional disturbance is consistent with due process, it is therefore relevant to note that this defense is a considerably expanded version of the common-law defense of heat of passion on sudden provocation and that at common law the burden of proving the latter, as well as other affirmative defenses—indeed, "all ... circumstances of justification, excuse or alleviation"—rested on the defendant. 4 W. Blackstone, Commentaries * 201; M. Foster, Crown Law 255 (1762); Mullaney v. Wilbur, supra, 421 U.S., at 693–694, 95 S.Ct., at 1886–1887. This was the rule when the Fifth Amendment was adopted, and it was the American rule when the Fourteenth Amendment was ratified. Commonwealth v. York, 50 Mass. 93 (1845).

In 1895 the common-law view was abandoned with respect to the insanity defense in federal prosecutions. Davis v. United States, 160 U.S. 469, 16 S.Ct. 353, 40 L.Ed. 499 (1895). This ruling had wide impact on the practice in the federal courts with respect to the burden of proving various affirmative defenses, and the prosecution in a majority of jurisdictions in this country sooner or later came to shoulder the burden of proving the sanity of the accused and of disproving the facts constituting other affirmative defenses, including provocation. Davis was not a constitutional ruling, however, as Leland v. Oregon, supra, made clear.[3]

At issue in Leland v. Oregon was the constitutionality under the Due Process Clause of the Oregon rule that the defense of insanity must be proved by the defendant beyond a reasonable doubt. Noting that Davis "obviously establish[ed] no constitutional doctrine," 343 U.S., at 797, 72 S.Ct. at 1007, the Court refused to strike down the Oregon scheme, saying that the burden of proving all elements of the crime beyond reasonable doubt, including the elements of premeditation and deliberation, was placed on the State under Oregon procedures and remained there throughout the trial. To convict, the jury was required to find each element of the crime beyond a reasonable doubt, based on all the evidence, including the evidence going to the issue of insanity. Only then was the jury "to consider separately the issue of legal sanity per se...." Id., at 795, 72 S.Ct. at 1006. This practice did not offend the Due Process Clause even though among the 20 States then placing the burden of proving his insanity on the defendant, Oregon was alone in requiring him to convince the jury beyond a reasonable doubt.

3. Meanwhile, the Court had explained that although the State could go too far in shifting the burden of proof to a defendant in a criminal case, the Due Process Clause did not invalidate every instance of burdening the defendant with proving an exculpatory fact. In Morrison v. California, 291 U.S. 82, 54 S.Ct. 281, 78 L.Ed. 664 (1934), a state law made it illegal for an alien ineligible for citizenship to own or possess land. Initially, in a summary dismissal for want of a substantial federal question, Morrison v. California, 288 U.S. 591, 53 S.Ct. 401, 77 L.Ed. 970 (1933), the Court held that it did not violate the Due Process Clause for the State to place on the defendant "the burden of proving citizenship as a defense," 291 U.S., at 88, 54 S.Ct. at 284, once the State's evidence had shown that the defendant possessed the land and was a member of a race barred from citizenship. In the later Morrison case the Court reiterated and approved its previous summary holding, even though it struck down more drastic burden shifting permitted under another section of the statute. The Court said that its earlier per curiam ruling "was not novel":

"The decisions are manifold that within limits of reason and fairness the burden of proof may be lifted from the state in criminal prosecutions and cast on a defendant. The limits are in substance these, that the state shall have proved enough to make it just for the defendant to be required to repel what has been proved with excuse or explanation, or at least that upon a balancing of convenience or of the opportunities for knowledge the shifting of the burden will be found to be an aid to the accuser without subjecting the accused to hardship or oppression. Cf. Wigmore, Evidence, Vol.

5, §§ 2486, 2512 and cases cited. Special reasons are at hand to make the change permissible when citizenship *vel non* is the issue to be determined. Citizenship is a privilege not due of common right. One who lays claim to it as his, and does this in justification or excuse of an act otherwise illegal, may fairly be called upon to prove his title good." Id., at 88–89, 54 S.Ct., at 284.

In ruling that in the other section of the statute then at issue the State had gone too far, the Court said:

"For a transfer of the burden, experience must teach that the evidence held to be inculpatory has at least a sinister significance (Yee Hem v. United States, [268 U.S. 178, 45 S.Ct. 470, 69 L.Ed. 904 (1925)]; Casey v. United States, [276 U.S. 413, 48 S.Ct. 373, 72 L.Ed. 632 (1928)]), or if this at times be lacking, there must be in any event a manifest disparity in convenience of proof and opportunity for knowledge, as, for instance, where a general prohibition is applicable to every one who is unable to bring himself within the range of an exception. Greenleaf, Evidence, Vol. 1, § 79." Id., at 90–91, 54 S.Ct., at 285.

The Court added that, of course, the possible situations were too variable and that too much depended on distinctions of degree to crowd them all into a simple formula. A sharper definition was to await specific cases. Of course, if the Morrison cases are understood as approving shifting to the defendant the burden of disproving a fact necessary to constitute the crime, the result in the first Morrison case could not coexist with In re Winship, 397 U.S. 358, 90 S.Ct. 1068, 25 L.Ed.2d 368 (1970), and Mullaney.

In 1970, the Court declared that the Due Process Clause "protects the accused against conviction except upon proof beyond a reasonable doubt of every fact necessary to constitute the crime with which he is charged." In re Winship, 397 U.S. 358, 364, 90 S.Ct. 1068, 1073, 25 L.Ed.2d 368 (1970). Five years later, in Mullaney v. Wilbur, 421 U.S. 684, 95 S.Ct. 1881, 44 L.Ed.2d 508 (1975), the Court further announced that under the Maine law of homicide, the burden could not constitutionally be placed on the defendant of proving by a preponderance of the evidence that the killing had occurred in the heat of passion on sudden provocation. The Chief Justice and Mr. Justice Rehnquist, concurring, expressed their understanding that the Mullaney decision did not call into question the ruling in Leland v. Oregon, supra, with respect to the proof of insanity.

Subsequently, the Court confirmed that it remained constitutional to burden the defendant with proving his insanity defense when it dismissed, as not raising a substantial federal question, a case in which the appellant specifically challenged the continuing validity of Leland v. Oregon. This occurred in Rivera v. Delaware, 429 U.S. 877, 97 S.Ct. 226, 50 L.Ed.2d 160 (1976), an appeal from a Delaware conviction which, in reliance on Leland, had been affirmed by the Delaware Supreme Court over the claim that the Delaware statute was unconstitutional because it burdened the defendant with proving his affirmative defense of insanity by a preponderance of the evidence. The claim in this Court was that Leland had been overruled by Winship and Mullaney. We dismissed the appeal as not presenting a substantial federal question. . . .

III

We cannot conclude that Patterson's conviction under the New York law deprived him of due process of law. The crime of murder is defined by the statute, which represents a recent revision of the state criminal code, as causing the death of another person with intent to do so. The death, the intent to kill, and causation are the facts that the State is required to prove beyond a reasonable doubt if a person is to be convicted of murder. No further facts are either presumed or inferred in order to constitute the crime. The statute does provide an affirmative defense—that the defendant acted under the influence of extreme emotional disturbance for which there was a reasonable explanation—which, if proved by a preponderance of the evidence, would reduce the crime to manslaughter, an offense defined in a separate section of the statute. It is plain enough that if the intentional killing is shown, the State intends to deal with the defendant as a murderer unless he demonstrates the mitigating circumstances.

Here, the jury was instructed in accordance with the statute, and the guilty verdict confirms that the State successfully carried its burden of proving the facts of the crime beyond a reasonable doubt. Nothing in the evidence, including any evidence that might have been offered with respect to Patterson's mental state at the time of the crime, raised a reasonable doubt about his guilt as a murderer; and clearly the evidence failed to convince the jury that Patterson's affirmative defense had been made out. It seems to us that the State satisfied the mandate of Winship that it prove beyond a reasonable doubt "every fact necessary to constitute the crime with which [Patterson was] charged." 397 U.S., at 364, 90 S.Ct., at 1073.

In convicting Patterson under its murder statute, New York did no more than Leland and Rivera permitted it to do without violating the Due Process Clause. Under those cases, once the facts constituting a crime are established beyond a reasonable doubt, based on all the evidence including the evidence of the defendant's mental state, the State may refuse to sustain the affirmative defense of insanity unless demonstrated by a preponderance of the evidence.

The New York law on extreme emotional disturbance follows this pattern. This affirmative defense, which the Court of Appeals described as permitting "the defendant to show that his actions were caused by a mental infirmity not arising to the level of insanity, and that he is less culpable for having committed them," 39 N.Y.2d, at 302, 383 N.Y.S.2d, at 582, 347 N.E.2d, at 907, does not serve to negative any facts of the crime which the State is to prove in order to convict of murder. It constitutes a separate issue on which the defendant is required to carry the burden of persuasion; and unless we are to overturn Leland and Rivera, New York has not violated the Due Process Clause, and Patterson's conviction must be sustained.

We are unwilling to reconsider Leland and Rivera. But even if we were to hold that a State must prove sanity to convict once that fact is put in issue, it would not necessarily follow that a State must prove beyond a reasonable doubt every fact, the existence or nonexistence of which it is willing to recognize as an exculpatory or mitigating circumstance affecting the degree of culpability or the severity of the punishment. Here, in revising its criminal code, New York provided the affirmative defense of extreme emotional disturbance, a substantially expanded version of the older heat-of-passion concept; but it was willing to do so only if the facts making out the defense were established by the defendant with sufficient certainty. The State was itself unwilling to undertake to establish the absence of those facts beyond a reasonable doubt, perhaps fearing that proof would be too difficult and that too many persons deserving treatment as murderers would escape that punishment if the evidence need merely raise a reasonable doubt about the defendant's emotional state. It has been said that the new criminal code of New York contains some 25 affirmative defenses which exculpate or mitigate but which must be established by the defendant to be operative.[4] The Due Process Clause, as we see it, does not put New York to the choice of abandoning those defenses or undertaking to disprove their existence in order to convict of a crime which otherwise is within its constitutional powers to sanction by substantial punishment.

The requirement of proof beyond a reasonable doubt in a criminal case is "bottomed on a fundamental value determination of our society that it is far worse to convict an innocent man than to let a guilty man go free." Winship, 397 U.S., at 372, 90 S.Ct., at 1077 (Harlan, J., concurring). The social cost of

4. The State of New York is not alone in this result:

"Since the Model Penal Code was completed in 1962, some 22 states have codified and reformed their criminal laws. At least 12 of these jurisdictions have used the concept of an 'affirmative defense' and have defined that phrase to require that the defendant prove the existence of an 'affirmative defense' by a preponderance of the evidence. Additionally, at least six proposed state codes and each of the four successive versions of a revised federal code use the same procedural device. Finally, many jurisdictions that do not generally employ this concept of 'affirmative defense' nevertheless shift the burden of proof to the defendant on particular issues." Low & Jeffries, DICTA: Constitutionalizing the Criminal Law?, 29 Va.Law Weekly, No. 18, p. 1 (1977) (footnotes omitted).

Even so, the trend over the years appears to have been to require the prosecution to disprove affirmative defenses beyond a reasonable doubt. See W. LaFave & A. Scott, Criminal Law § 8, p. 50 (1972); C. McCormick, Evidence § 341, pp. 800–802 (2d ed. 1972). The split among the various jurisdictions varies for any given defense. Thus, 22 jurisdictions place the burden of proving the affirmative defense of insanity on the defendant, while 28 jurisdictions place the burden of disproving insanity on the prosecution. Note, Constitutional Limitations on Allocating the Burden of Proof of Insanity to the Defendant in Murder Cases, 56 B.U.L.Rev. 499, 503–505 (1976).

placing the burden on the prosecution to prove guilt beyond a reasonable doubt is thus an increased risk that the guilty will go free. While it is clear that our society has willingly chosen to bear a substantial burden in order to protect the innocent, it is equally clear that the risk it must bear is not without limits; and Mr. Justice Harlan's aphorism provides little guidance for determining what those limits are. Due process does not require that every conceivable step be taken, at whatever cost, to eliminate the possibility of convicting an innocent person. Punishment of those found guilty by a jury, for example, is not forbidden merely because there is a remote possibility in some instances that an innocent person might go to jail.

It is said that the common-law rule permits a State to punish one as a murderer when it is as likely as not that he acted in the heat of passion or under severe emotional distress and when, if he did, he is guilty only of manslaughter. But this has always been the case in those jurisdictions adhering to the traditional rule. It is also very likely true that fewer convictions of murder would occur if New York were required to negative the affirmative defense at issue here. But in each instance of a murder conviction under the present law New York will have proved beyond a reasonable doubt that the defendant has intentionally killed another person, an act which it is not disputed the State may constitutionally criminalize and punish. If the State nevertheless chooses to recognize a factor that mitigates the degree of criminality or punishment, we think the State may assure itself that the fact has been established with reasonable certainty. To recognize at all a mitigating circumstance does not require the State to prove its nonexistence in each case in which the fact is put in issue, if in its judgment this would be too cumbersome, too expensive, and too inaccurate.

We thus decline to adopt as a constitutional imperative, operative country-wide, that a State must disprove beyond a reasonable doubt every fact constituting any and all affirmative defenses related to the culpability of an accused. Traditionally, due process has required that only the most basic procedural safeguards be observed; more subtle balancing of society's interests against those of the accused have been left to the legislative branch. We therefore will not disturb the balance struck in previous cases holding that the Due Process Clause requires the prosecution to prove beyond a reasonable doubt all of the elements included in the definition of the offense of which the defendant is charged. Proof of the nonexistence of all affirmative defenses has never been constitutionally required; and we perceive no reason to fashion such a rule in this case and apply it to the statutory defense at issue here.

This view may seem to permit state legislatures to reallocate burdens of proof by labeling as affirmative defenses at least some elements of the crimes now defined in their statutes. But there are obviously constitutional limits beyond which the States may not go in this regard. "[I]t is not within the province of a legislature to declare an individual guilty or presumptively guilty of a crime." McFarland v. American Sugar Rfg. Co., 241 U.S. 79, 86, 36 S.Ct. 498, 500, 60 L.Ed. 899 (1916). The legislature cannot "validly command that the finding of an indictment, or mere proof of the identity of the accused, should create a presumption of the existence of all the facts essential to guilt." Tot v. United States, 319 U.S. 463, 469, 63 S.Ct. 1241, 1246, 87 L.Ed. 1519 (1943). See also Speiser v. Randall, 357 U.S., at 523–525, 78 S.Ct., at 1340–1341. Morrison v. California, 291 U.S. 82, 54 S.Ct. 281, 78 L.Ed. 664 (1934), also makes the point with sufficient clarity.

Long before Winship, the universal rule in this country was that the prosecution must prove guilt beyond a reasonable doubt. At the same time, the long-accepted rule was that it was constitutionally permissible to provide that various affirmative defenses were to be proved by the defendant. This did not lead to such abuses or to such widespread redefinition of crime and reduction of the prosecution's burden that a new constitutional rule was required. This was not the problem to which Winship was addressed. Nor does the fact that a majority of the States have now assumed the burden of disproving affirmative defenses—for whatever reasons—mean that those States that strike a different balance are in violation of the Constitution.

. . .

■ MR. JUSTICE REHNQUIST took no part in the consideration or decision of this case.

■ MR. JUSTICE POWELL, with whom MR. JUSTICE BRENNAN and MR. JUSTICE MARSHALL join, dissenting.

. . .

II

It is unnecessary for the Court to retreat to a formalistic test for applying Winship. Careful attention to the Mullaney decision reveals the principles that should control in this and like cases. Winship held that the prosecution must bear the burden of proving beyond a reasonable doubt " 'the existence of every fact necessary to constitute the crime charged.' " 397 U.S., at 363, 90 S.Ct. at 1073 quoting Davis v. United States, 160 U.S. 469, 493, 16 S.Ct. 353, 360, 40 L.Ed. 499 (1895). In Mullaney we concluded that heat of passion was one of the "facts" described in Winship—that is, a factor as to which the prosecution must bear the burden of persuasion beyond a reasonable doubt. 421 U.S., at 704, 95 S.Ct. at 1892. We reached that result only after making two careful inquiries. First, we noted that the presence or absence of heat of passion made a substantial difference in punishment of the offender and in the stigma associated with the conviction. Id., at 697–701, 95 S.Ct. at 1888. Second, we reviewed the history, in England and this country, of the factor at issue. Id., at 692–696, 95 S.Ct. at 1886–1888. Central to the holding in Mullaney was our conclusion that heat of passion "has been, almost from the inception of the common law of homicide, the single most important factor in determining the degree of culpability attaching to an unlawful homicide." Id., at 696, 95 S.Ct. at 1888.

Implicit in these two inquiries are the principles that should govern this case. The Due Process Clause requires that the prosecutor bear the burden of persuasion beyond a reasonable doubt only if the factor at issue makes a substantial difference in punishment and stigma. The requirement of course applies a fortiori if the factor makes the difference between guilt and innocence. But a substantial difference in punishment alone is not enough. It also must be shown that in the Anglo–American legal tradition the factor in question historically has held that level of importance. If either branch of the test is not met, then the legislature retains its traditional authority over matters of proof. But to permit a shift in the burden of persuasion when both branches of this test are satisfied would invite the undermining of the presumption of innocence, "that bedrock 'axiomatic and elementary' principle whose 'enforcement lies at the foundation of the administration of our criminal law.' "

. . .

I hardly need add that New York's provisions allocating the burden of persuasion as to "extreme emotional disturbance" are unconstitutional when judged by these standards. "Extreme emotional disturbance" is, as the Court of Appeals recognized, the direct descendant of the "heat of passion" factor considered at length in Mullaney. I recognize, of course, that the differences between Maine and New York law are not unimportant to the defendant; there is a somewhat broader opportunity for mitigation. But none of those distinctions is relevant here. The presence or absence of extreme emotional disturbance makes a critical difference in punishment and stigma, and throughout our history the resolution of this issue of fact, although expressed in somewhat different terms, has distinguished manslaughter from murder. See 4 W. Blackstone, Commentaries *190–193, 198–201.

. . .

Martin v. Ohio

Supreme Court of the United States, 1987.
480 U.S. 228, 107 S.Ct. 1098, 94 L.Ed.2d 267.

■ Justice White delivered the opinion of the Court.

The Ohio Code provides that "[e]very person accused of an offense is presumed innocent until proven guilty beyond a reasonable doubt, and the burden of proof for all elements of the offense is upon the prosecution. The burden of going forward with the evidence of an affirmative defense, and the burden of proof by a preponderance of the evidence, for an affirmative defense, is upon the accused." Ohio Rev.Code Ann. § 2901.05(A) (1982). An affirmative defense is one involving "an excuse or justification peculiarly within the knowledge of the accused, on which he can fairly be required to adduce supporting evidence." Ohio Rev.Code Ann. § 2901.05(C)(2) (1982). The Ohio courts have "long determined that self-defense is an affirmative defense," 21 Ohio St.3d 91, 93, 488 N.E.2d 166, 168 (1986), and that the defendant has the burden of proving it as required by § 2901.05(A).

As defined by the trial court in its instructions in this case, the elements of self-defense that the defendant must prove are (1) that the defendant was not at fault in creating the situation giving rise to the argument; (2) the defendant had an honest belief that she was in imminent danger of death or great bodily harm and that her only means of escape from such danger was in the use of such force; and (3) the defendant must not have violated any duty to retreat or avoid danger. App. 19. The question before us is whether the Due Process Clause of the Fourteenth Amendment forbids placing the burden of proving self-defense on the defendant when she is charged by the State of Ohio with committing the crime of aggravated murder, which, as relevant to this case, is defined by the Revised Code of Ohio as "purposely, and with prior calculation and design, caus[ing] the death of another." Ohio Rev.Code Ann. § 2903.01 (1982).

The facts of the case, taken from the opinions of the courts below, may be succinctly stated. On July 21, 1983, petitioner Earline Martin and her husband, Walter Martin, argued over grocery money. Petitioner claimed that her husband struck her in the head during the argument. Petitioner's version of what then transpired was that she went upstairs, put on a robe, and later came back down with her husband's gun which she intended to dispose of. Her husband saw something in her hand and questioned her about it. He came at her, she lost her head and fired the gun at him. Five or six shots were fired, three of them striking and killing Mr. Martin. She was charged with and tried for aggravated murder. She pleaded self-defense and testified in her own defense.

The judge charged the jury with respect to the elements of the crime and of self-defense and rejected petitioner's Due Process Clause challenge to the charge placing on her the burden of proving self-defense. The jury found her guilty.

Both the Ohio Court of Appeals and the Supreme Court of Ohio affirmed the conviction. Both rejected the constitutional challenge to the instruction requiring petitioner to prove self-defense. The latter court, relying upon our opinion in Patterson v. New York, 432 U.S. 197, 97 S.Ct. 2319, 53 L.Ed.2d 281 (1977), concluded that, the State was required to prove the three elements of aggravated murder but that Patterson did not require it to disprove self-defense, which is a separate issue that did not require Mrs. Martin to disprove any element of the offense with which she was charged. The court said, "the state proved beyond a reasonable doubt that appellant purposely, and with prior calculation and design, caused the death of her husband. Appellant did not dispute the existence of these elements, but rather sought to justify her actions on grounds she acted in self defense." 21 Ohio St.3d, at 94, 488 N.E.2d, at 168. There was thus no infirmity in her conviction. We granted certiorari, 475 U.S. 1119, 106 S.Ct. 1634, 90 L.Ed.2d 180 (1986), and affirm the decision of the Supreme Court of Ohio.

In re Winship, 397 U.S. 358, 364, 90 S.Ct. 1068, 1072, 25 L.Ed.2d 368 (1970), declared that the Due Process Clause "protects the accused against conviction except upon proof beyond a reasonable doubt of every fact necessary to constitute the crime with which he is charged." A few years later, we held that Winship's mandate was fully satisfied where the State of New York had proved beyond reasonable doubt, each of the elements of murder, but placed on the defendant the burden of proving the affirmative defense of extreme emotional disturbance, which, if proved, would have reduced the crime from murder to manslaughter. Patterson v. New York, supra. We there emphasized the preeminent role of the States in preventing and dealing with crime and the reluctance of the Court to disturb a State's decision with respect to the definition of criminal conduct and the procedures by which the criminal laws are to be enforced in the courts, including the burden of producing evidence and allocating the burden of persuasion. 432 U.S., at 201–202, 97 S.Ct., at 2322. New York had the authority to define murder as the intentional killing of another person. It had chosen, however, to reduce the crime to manslaughter if the defendant proved by a preponderance of the evidence that he had acted under the influence of extreme emotional distress. To convict of murder, the jury was required to find beyond a reasonable doubt, based on all the evidence, including that related to the defendant's mental state at the time of the crime, each of the elements of murder and also to conclude that the defendant had not proved his affirmative defense. The jury convicted Patterson, and we held there was no violation of the Fourteenth Amendment as construed in Winship. Referring to Leland v. Oregon, 343 U.S. 790, 72 S.Ct. 1002, 96 L.Ed. 1302 (1952) and Rivera v. Delaware, 429 U.S. 877, 97 S.Ct. 226, 50 L.Ed.2d 160 (1976), we added that New York "did no more than Leland and Rivera permitted it to do without violating the Due Process Clause" and declined to reconsider those cases. 432 U.S., at 206, 207, 97 S.Ct., at 2324, 2325. It was also observed that "the fact that a majority of the States have now assumed the burden of disproving affirmative defenses—for whatever reasons—[does not] mean that those States that strike a different balance are in violation of the Constitution." Id., at 211, 97 S.Ct., at 2327.

As in Patterson, the jury was here instructed that to convict it must find, in light of all the evidence, that each of elements of the crime of aggravated murder must be proved by the State beyond reasonable doubt and that the burden of proof with respect to these elements did not shift. To find guilt, the jury had to be convinced that none of the evidence, whether offered by the State or by Martin in connection with her plea of self-defense, raised a reasonable doubt that Martin had killed her husband, that she had the specific purpose and intent to cause his death, or that she had done so with prior calculation and design. It was also told, however, that it could acquit if it found by a preponderance of the evidence that Martin had not precipitated the confrontation, that she had an honest belief that she was in imminent danger of death or great bodily harm, and that she had satisfied any duty to retreat or avoid danger. The jury convicted Martin.

We agree with the State and its Supreme Court that this conviction did not violate the Due Process Clause. The State did not exceed its authority in defining the crime of murder as purposely causing the death of another with prior calculation or design. It did not seek to shift to Martin the burden of proving any of those elements, and the jury's verdict reflects that none of her self-defense evidence raised a reasonable doubt about the state's proof that she purposefully killed with prior calculation and design. She nevertheless had the opportunity under state law and the instructions given to justify the killing and show herself to be blameless by proving that she acted in self-defense. The jury thought she had failed to do so, and Ohio is as entitled to punish Martin as one guilty of murder as New York was to punish Patterson.

It would be quite different if the jury had been instructed that self-defense evidence could not be considered in determining whether there was a reasonable doubt about the state's case, i.e., that self-defense evidence must be put aside for all purposes unless it satisfied the preponderance standard. Such instruction would relieve the state of its burden and plainly run afoul of Winship's mandate. 397 U.S., at 364, 90 S.Ct., at 1072. The instructions in this case could be clearer in this respect, but when read as a whole, we think they are adequate to convey to the jury that all of the evidence, including the evidence going to self-defense, must be considered in deciding whether there was a reasonable doubt about the sufficiency of the state's proof of the elements of the crime.

We are thus not moved by assertions that the elements of aggravated murder and self-defense overlap in the sense that evidence to prove the latter will often tend to negate the former. It may be that most encounters in which self-defense is claimed arise suddenly and involve no prior plan or specific purpose to take life. In those cases, evidence offered to support the defense may negate a purposeful killing by prior calculation and design, but Ohio does not shift to the defendant the burden of disproving any element of the state's case. When the prosecution has made out a prima facie case and survives a motion to acquit, the jury may nevertheless not convict if the evidence offered by the defendant raises any reasonable doubt about the existence of any fact necessary for the finding of guilt. Evidence creating a reasonable doubt could easily fall far short of proving self-defense by a preponderance of the evidence. Of course, if such doubt is not raised in the jury's mind and each juror is convinced that the defendant purposely and with prior calculation and design took life, the killing will still be excused if the elements of the defense are satisfactorily established. We note here, but need not rely on it, the observation of the Supreme Court of Ohio that "Appellant did not dispute the existence of [the elements of aggravated murder], but rather sought to justify her actions on grounds she acted in self-defense." 21 Ohio St.3d, at 94, 488 N.E.2d, at 168.**

** The dissent believes that the self-defense instruction might have led the jury to believe that the defendant had the burden of proving prior calculation and design. Indeed,

Petitioner submits that there can be no conviction under Ohio law unless the defendant's conduct is unlawful and that because self-defense renders lawful what would otherwise be a crime, unlawfulness is an element of the offense that the state must prove by disproving self-defense. This argument founders on state law, for it has been rejected by the Ohio Supreme Court and by the Court of Appeals for the Sixth Circuit. White v. Arn, 788 F.2d 338, 346–347 (C.A.6 1986); State v. Morris, 8 Ohio App.3d 12, 18–19, 455 N.E.2d 1352, 1359–1360 (1982). It is true that unlawfulness is essential for conviction, but the Ohio courts hold that the unlawfulness in cases like this is the conduct satisfying the elements of aggravated murder—an interpretation of state law that we are not in a position to dispute. The same is true of the claim that it is necessary to prove a "criminal" intent to convict for serious crimes, which cannot occur if self-defense is shown: the necessary mental state for aggravated murder under Ohio law is the specific purpose to take life pursuant to prior calculation and design. See White v. Arn, supra, at 346.

As we noted in Patterson, the common law rule was that affirmative defenses, including self-defense, were matters for the defendant to prove. "This was the rule when the Fifth Amendment was adopted, and it was the American rule when the Fourteenth Amendment was ratified." 432 U.S., at 202, 97 S.Ct., at 2322. Indeed, well into this century, a number of States followed the common law rule and required a defendant to shoulder the burden of proving that he acted in self-defense. Fletcher, Two Kinds of Legal Rules: A Comparative Study of Burden-of-Persuasion Practices in Criminal Cases, 77 Yale L.J. 880, 882, and n. 10 (1968). We are aware that all but two of the States, Ohio and South Carolina, have abandoned the common law rule and require the prosecution to prove the absence of self-defense when it is properly raised by the defendant. But the question remains whether those States are in violation of the Constitution; and, as we observed in Patterson, that question is not answered by cataloging the practices of other States. We are no more convinced that the Ohio practice of requiring self-defense to be proved by the defendant is unconstitutional than we are that the Constitution requires the prosecution to prove the sanity of a defendant who pleads not guilty by reason of insanity. We have had the opportunity to depart from Leland v. Oregon but have refused to do so. Rivera v. Delaware, 429 U.S. 877, 97 S.Ct. 226, 50 L.Ed.2d 160 (1976). These cases were important to the Patterson decision and they, along with Patterson, are authority for our decision today.

The judgment of the Ohio Supreme Court is accordingly

Affirmed.

■ JUSTICE POWELL, with whom JUSTICE BRENNAN and JUSTICE MARSHALL join, and with whom JUSTICE BLACKMUN joins with respect to Parts I and III, dissenting.

Today the Court holds that a defendant can be convicted of aggravated murder even though the jury may have a reasonable doubt whether the accused acted in self-defense, and thus, whether he is guilty of a crime. Because I think this decision is inconsistent with both precedent and fundamental fairness, I dissent.

its position is that no instruction could be clear enough not to mislead the jury. As is evident from the test, we disagree. We do not harbor the dissent's mistrust of the jury; and the instructions were sufficiently clear to convey to the jury that the state's burden of proving prior calculation did not shift and that self-defense evidence had to be considered in determining whether the state's burden had been discharged. We do not depart from Patterson v. New York, 432 U.S. 197, 97 S.Ct. 2319, 53 L.Ed.2d 281 (1977), in this respect, or in any other.

I

Petitioner Earline Martin was tried in state court for the aggravated murder of her husband. Under Ohio law, the elements of the crime are that the defendant ... purposely killed another with "prior calculation and design." Ohio Rev.Code Ann. § 2903.01 (1982). Martin admitted that she shot her husband, but claimed that she acted in self-defense. Because self defense is classified as an "affirmative" defense in Ohio, the jury was instructed that Martin had the burden of proving her claim by a preponderance of the evidence. Martin apparently failed to carry this burden, and the jury found her guilty.

The Ohio Supreme Court upheld the conviction, relying in part on this Court's opinion in Patterson v. New York, 432 U.S. 197, 97 S.Ct. 2319, 53 L.Ed.2d 281 (1977). The Court today also relies on the Patterson reasoning in affirming the Ohio decision. If one accepts Patterson as the proper method of analysis for this case, I believe that the Court's opinion ignores its central meaning.

In Patterson, the Court upheld a state statute that shifted the burden of proof for an affirmative defense to the accused. New York law required the prosecutor to prove all of the statutorily defined elements of murder beyond a reasonable doubt, but permitted a defendant to reduce the charge to manslaughter by showing that he acted while suffering an "extreme emotional disturbance." See N.Y. Penal Law §§ 125.25, 125.20 (McKinney 1975 and Supp.1987). The Court found that this burden-shifting did not violate due process, largely because the affirmative defense did "not serve to negative any facts of the crime which the State is to prove in order to convict of murder." 432 U.S., at 207, 97 S.Ct., at 2325. The clear implication of this ruling is that when an affirmative defense does negate an element of the crime, the state may not shift the burden. See White v. Arn, 788 F.2d 338, 344–345 (C.A.6 1986). In such a case, In re Winship, 397 U.S. 358, 90 S.Ct. 1068, 25 L.Ed.2d 368 (1970), requires the state to prove the nonexistence of the defense beyond a reasonable doubt.

The reason for treating a defense that negates an element of the crime differently from other affirmative defenses is plain. If the jury is told that the prosecution has the burden of proving all the elements of a crime, but then also is instructed that the defendant has the burden of disproving one of those same elements, there is a danger that the jurors will resolve the inconsistency in a way that lessens the presumption of innocence. For example, the jury might reasonably believe that by raising the defense, the accused has assumed the ultimate burden of proving that particular element. Or, it might reconcile the instructions simply by balancing the evidence that supports the prosecutor's case against the evidence supporting the affirmative defense, and conclude that the state has satisfied its burden if the prosecution's version is more persuasive. In either case, the jury is given the unmistakable but erroneous impression that the defendant shares the risk of nonpersuasion as to a fact necessary for conviction.[1]

---

1. Indeed, this type of instruction has an inherently illogical aspect. It makes no sense to say that the prosecution has the burden of proving an element beyond a reasonable doubt and that the defense has the burden of proving the contrary by a preponderance of the evidence. If the jury finds that the prosecutor has not met his burden, it of course will have no occasion to consider the affirmative defense. And if the jury finds that each element of the crime has been proved beyond a reasonable doubt, it necessarily has decided that the defendant has not disproved an element of the crime. In either situation the instructions on the affirmative defense are surplusage. Because a reasonable jury

Given these principles, the Court's reliance on Patterson is puzzling. Under Ohio law, the element of "prior calculation and design" is satisfied only when the accused has engaged in a "definite process of reasoning in advance of the killing," i.e., when he has given the plan at least some "studied consideration." App. 14 (jury instructions, emphasis added). In contrast, when a defendant such as Martin raises a claim of self-defense, the jury also is instructed that the accused must prove that she "had an honest belief that she was in imminent danger of death or great bodily harm."[2] Id., at 19 (emphasis added). In many cases, a defendant who finds himself in immediate danger and reacts with deadly force will not have formed a prior intent to kill. The Court recognizes this when it states:

> "It may be that most encounters in which self-defense is claimed arise suddenly and involve no prior plan or specific purpose to take life. In those cases, evidence offered to support the defense may negate a purposeful killing by prior calculation and design...." Ante, at 1102.

Under Patterson, this conclusion should suggest that Ohio is precluded from shifting the burden as to self-defense. The Court nevertheless concludes that Martin was properly required to prove self-defense, simply because "Ohio does not shift to the defendant the burden of disproving any element of the state's case." Ibid.

The Court gives no explanation for this apparent rejection of Patterson. The only justification advanced for the Court's decision is that the jury could have used the evidence of self-defense to find that the state failed to carry its burden of proof. Because the jurors were free to consider both Martin's and the state's evidence, the argument goes, the verdict of guilt necessarily means that they were convinced that the defendant acted with prior calculation and design, and were unpersuaded that she acted in self-defense. Ante, at 1101. The Court thus seems to conclude that as long as the jury is told that the state has the burden of proving all elements of the crime, the overlap between the offense and defense is immaterial.

This reasoning is flawed in two respects. First, it simply ignores the problem that arises from inconsistent jury instructions in a criminal case. The Court's holding implicitly assumes that the jury in fact understands that the ultimate burden remains with the prosecutor at all times, despite a conflicting instruction that places the burden on the accused to disprove the same element. But as pointed out above, the Patterson distinction between defenses that negate an element of the crime and those that do not is based on the legitimate concern that the jury will mistakenly lower the state's burden. In short, the Court's rationale fails to explain why the overlap in this case does not create the risk that Patterson suggested was unacceptable.[3]

will attempt to ascribe some significance to the court's instructions, the likelihood that it will impermissibly shift the burden is increased.

Of course, whether the jury will in fact improperly shift the burden away from the state is uncertain. But it is "settled law ... that when there exists a reasonable possibility that the jury relied on an unconstitutional understanding of the law in reaching a guilty verdict, that verdict must be set aside." Francis v. Franklin, 471 U.S. 307, 323 n. 8, 105 S.Ct. 1965, 1976 n. 8, 85 L.Ed.2d 344 (1985).

2. The accused also must have avoided the danger if possible, and must not have been at fault in creating the threatening situation. See State v. Robbins, 58 Ohio St.2d 74, 79–80, 388 N.E.2d 755, 758 (1979).

3. This risk could have been reduced— although in my view, not eliminated—if the instructions had made it clear that evidence of self-defense can create a reasonable doubt as to guilt, even if that same evidence did not rise to the level necessary to prove an affirmative defense. But the instructions gave little guidance in this respect. The trial court simply told the jury that the prosecution

Second, the Court significantly, and without explanation, extends the deference granted to state legislatures in this area. Today's decision could be read to say that virtually all state attempts to shift the burden of proof for affirmative defenses will be upheld, regardless of the relationship between the elements of the defense and the elements of the crime. As I understand it, Patterson allowed burden-shifting because evidence of an extreme emotional disturbance did not negate the mens rea of the underlying offense. After today's decision, however, even if proof of the defense does negate an element of the offense, burden-shifting still may be permitted because the jury can consider the defendant's evidence when reaching its verdict.

I agree, of course, that States must have substantial leeway in defining their criminal laws and administering their criminal justice systems. But none of our precedents suggests that courts must give complete deference to a State's judgment about whether a shift in the burden of proof is consistent with the presumption of innocence. In the past we have emphasized that in some circumstances it may be necessary to look beyond the text of the State's burden-shifting laws to satisfy ourselves that the requirements of Winship have been satisfied. In Mullaney v. Wilbur, 421 U.S. 684, 698–699, 95 S.Ct. 1881, 1889, 44 L.Ed.2d 508 (1975) we explicitly noted the danger of granting the State unchecked discretion to shift the burden as to any element of proof in a criminal case.[4] The Court today fails to discuss or even cite Mullaney, despite our unanimous agreement in that case that this danger would justify judicial intervention in some cases. Even Patterson, from which I dissented, recognized that "there are obviously constitutional limits beyond which the States may not go [in labeling elements of a crime as an affirmative defense]."[5] 432 U.S., at 210, 97 S.Ct., at 2327. Today, however, the Court simply asserts that Ohio law properly allocates the burdens, without giving any indication of where those limits lie.

Because our precedent establishes that the burden of proof may not be shifted when the elements of the defense and the elements of the offense conflict, and because it seems clear that they do so in this case, I would reverse the decision of the Ohio Supreme Court.

II

Although I believe that this case is wrongly decided even under the principles set forth in Patterson, my differences with the Court's approach are more fundamental. I continue to believe that the better method for deciding when a state may shift the burden of proof is outlined in the Court's opinion in Mullaney and in my dissenting opinion in Patterson. In Mullaney, we emphasized that the state's obligation to prove certain facts beyond a reasonable

must prove the elements of the crime, and the defendant must prove the existence of the defense. The instructions gave no indication how the jury should evaluate evidence that affected an element of both the crime and the defense. Cf. Francis v. Franklin, supra, 471 U.S., at 322, 105 S.Ct., at 1975 ("Nothing in these specific sentences or in the [jury] charge as a whole makes clear ... that one of these contradictory instructions carries more weight than the other").

4. We noted, for example:

"[I]f Winship were limited to those facts that constitute a crime as defined by state law, a State could undermine many of the interests that decision sought to protect without effecting any substantive change in its law. It would only be necessary to redefine the elements that constitute different crimes, characterizing them as factors that bear solely on the extent of punishment." 421 U.S., at 698, 95 S.Ct., at 1889.

5. See also McMillan v. Pennsylvania, 106 S.Ct. 2411, 2417, 91 L.Ed.2d 67 (1986) ("[I]n certain limited circumstances Winship's reasonable-doubt requirement applies to facts not formally identified as elements of the offense charged").

doubt was not necessarily restricted to legislative distinctions between offenses and affirmative defenses. The boundaries of the state's authority in this respect were elaborated in the Patterson dissent, where I proposed a two-part inquiry:

> "The Due Process Clause requires that the prosecutor bear the burden of persuasion beyond a reasonable doubt only if the factor at issue makes a substantial difference in punishment and stigma. The requirement of course applies a fortiori if the factor makes the difference between guilt and innocence.... It also must be shown that in the Anglo–American legal tradition the factor in question historically has held that level of importance. If either branch of the test is not met, then the legislature retains its traditional authority over matters of proof." 432 U.S., at 226–227, 97 S.Ct., at 2335 (footnotes omitted).

Cf. McMillan v. Pennsylvania, 477 U.S. 79, 106 S.Ct. 2411, 2421, 91 L.Ed.2d 67 (1986) (STEVENS, J., dissenting) ("if a State provides that a specific component of a prohibited transaction shall give rise both to a special stigma and to a special punishment, that component must be treated as a 'fact necessary to constitute the crime' within the meaning of our holding in In re Winship").

There are at least two benefits to this approach. First, it ensures that the critical facts necessary to sustain a conviction will be proved by the state. Because the Court would be willing to look beyond the text of a state statute, legislatures would have no incentive to redefine essential elements of an offense to make them part of an affirmative defense, thereby shifting the burden of proof in a manner inconsistent with Winship and Mullaney. Second, it would leave the states free in all other respects to recognize new factors that may mitigate the degree of criminality or punishment, without requiring that they also bear the burden of disproving these defenses. See Patterson v. New York, 432 U.S., at 229–230, 97 S.Ct., at 2336–2337 (POWELL, J., dissenting) ("New ameliorative affirmative defenses ... generally remain undisturbed by the holdings in Winship and Mullaney" (footnote omitted)).

Under this analysis, it plainly is impermissible to require the accused to prove self-defense. If petitioner could have carried her burden, the result would have been decisively different as to both guilt and punishment. There also is no dispute that self-defense historically is one of the primary justifications for otherwise unlawful conduct. See e.g., Beard v. United States, 158 U.S. 550, 562, 15 S.Ct. 962, 966, 39 L.Ed. 1086 (1895). Thus, while I acknowledge that the two-part test may be difficult to apply at times, it is hard to imagine a more clear-cut application than the one presented here.

III

In its willingness to defer to the State's legislative definitions of crimes and defenses, the Court apparently has failed to recognize the practical effect of its decision. Martin alleged that she was innocent because she acted in self-defense, a complete justification under Ohio law. See State v. Nolton, 19 Ohio St.2d 133, 249 N.E.2d 797 (1969). Because she had the burden of proof on this issue, the jury could have believed that it was just as likely as not that Martin's conduct was justified, and yet still have voted to convict. In other words, even though the jury may have had a substantial doubt whether Martin committed a crime, she was found guilty under Ohio law. I do not agree that the Court's authority to review state legislative choices is so limited that it justifies increasing the risk of convicting a person who may not be blameworthy. See Patterson v. New York, supra, 432 U.S., at 201–202, 97 S.Ct., at 2322 (state definition of criminal law must yield when it " 'offends some principle of justice so rooted in the traditions and conscience of our people as to be ranked as fundamental' " (quoting Speiser v. Randall, 357 U.S. 513, 523, 78 S.Ct. 1332, 1340, 2 L.Ed.2d 1460 (1958)). The complexity of the inquiry as to when a state may shift the burden of proof should not lead the Court to fashion simple rules of deference that could lead to such unjust results.

NOTE

1. For a comprehensive discussion of burdens of proof in criminal cases see Robinson, Criminal Law Defenses, 82 Colum.L.Rev. 199 (1982).

The 1975 decision in Mullaney v. Wilbur described in the 1977 decision in Patterson v. New York created considerable confusion. See, e.g., Farrell v. Czarnetzky, 566 F.2d 381, 384 (2d Cir.1977), cert. denied, 434 U.S. 1077 (1978) (concurring: "Mullaney, while not expressly overruled, has been drained of much of its vitality . . . and for present purposes all."); Warren v. State, 350 A.2d 173, 176 (Md.Ct.Spec.App.1976) ("In the Chinese tradition, the legal aftermath of the Supreme Court's ruling in Mullaney v. Wilbur . . . would have entitled this year of our Lord to the epithet 'The Year of the Mullaney.' . . ."). Does the distinction between an affirmative defense and an essential element of the principal offense justify a different constitutional standard for the weight of the burden of persuasion?

Commenting on Mullaney v. Wilbur: Allen, The Restoration of In re Winship: A Comment on Burdens of Persuasion in Criminal Cases After Patterson v. New York, 76 Mich.L.Rev. 30 (1977); Note, The Constitutionality of Affirmative Defenses After Patterson v. New York, 78 Colum.L.Rev. 655 (1978); Comment, Constitutionality of Affirmative Defenses in the Texas Penal Code, 28 Baylor L.Rev. 120 (1976) (applying Mullaney v. Wilbur to Texas law); Comment, Constitutionality of the Common Law Presumption of Malice in Maine, 54 B.U.L.Rev. 973 (1974); Tushnet, Constitutional Limitation of Substantive Criminal Law: An Examination of the Meaning of Mullaney v. Wilbur, 55 B.U.L.Rev. 775 (1975); Note, Affirmative Defenses in Ohio After Mullaney v. Wilbur, 36 Ohio St.L.J. 828 (1975); Comment, Constitutional Limitations Upon the Use of Statutory Criminal Presumptions and the Felony–Murder Rule, 46 Miss.L.J. 1021 (1975); Note, Constitutionality of Presumptions on Receiving Stolen Property: Turning the Thumbscrew in Michigan and Other States, 21 Wayne L.Rev. 1437 (1975).

Two criminal cases dealing with presumptions, County Court of Ulster County v. Allen, 442 U.S. 140 (1979), and Sandstrom v. Montana, 442 U.S. 510 (1979), are discussed under Presumptions, Section 2, infra. Does the use of presumptions give the legislature greater freedom than it would have in creating affirmative burdens of proof?

Will the Court give greater weight to the creation of an affirmative burden when it is explicitly created by the legislature after a considered inquiry than if it is created by the courts? Should an affirmative burden have more favorable treatment if the burden is by a preponderance rather than beyond a reasonable doubt?

2. Professor Allen argues that the due process analysis in Patterson is more consistent than is Mullaney with the analysis in In re Winship:

> II. The Federal Interest in the Reasonable Doubt
> Standard: The "Restoration" of Winship
>
> In his dissent in Patterson, Justice Powell accused the Court of "drain[ing] In re Winship . . . of much of its vitality." [432 U.S. at 216, 97

S.Ct. at 2330, 53 L.Ed.2d at 296] Justice Powell was wrong. Patterson did not "drain Winship of its vitality"; rather, it rejected Mullaney's extension of Winship beyond the latter's legitimate boundaries, and thus it restored Winship to its original purpose. Careful examination of these three cases shows not only that Patterson rightly rejected the due process analysis employed in Mullaney, but also indicates the proper scope of the federal interest in the reasonable doubt standard. ... Justice White's opinion alludes to several different arguments that conceivably could be used to articulate the federal interest in the reasonable doubt standard, but the opinion fails to elaborate upon any of them. Only one of the Court's allusions makes sense, however. It is contained in the following passage of the opinion:

The Due Process Clause, as we see it, does not put New York to the choice of abandoning [affirmative] defenses or undertaking to disprove their existence in order to convict of a crime which otherwise is within its constitutional powers to sanction by substantial punishment. [432 U.S. at 207–08, 97 S.Ct. at 2325–26, 53 L.Ed.2d at 290–91]

The key to this passage is the word "otherwise." What the Court is saying, I think, is that if a state may "otherwise" impose a particular sentence on the basis of what the state has proven beyond a reasonable doubt, then permitting a defendant to reduce the sentence he receives below the permissible level through proof of an affirmative defense is constitutional.

If the Court now subscribes to this theory—sometimes referred to as the theory that "the greater includes the lesser"—the analysis of the constitutionality of an affirmative defense must proceed to another level. One must ask whether the greater punishment—the punishment authorized in the event the defendant fails to establish the affirmative defense—is constitutional. To answer that question, one must turn to the eighth amendment.

Through most of the nineteenth century, the eighth amendment was thought to forbid only rather hideous punishments, but within the last century the cruel and unusual punishment clause has been interpreted to require a rough proportionality between the culpability of an offense and the punishment that is imposed. This requirement of proportionality provides the method of testing the accuracy of the assumption found in my hypothetical, and it also provides the means of delineating the extent of the federal interest in the reasonable doubt standard. If the courts conclude that a given punishment is not disproportional to what the state has proved beyond reasonable doubt notwithstanding the presence or absence of any mitigating factors, then a defendant's liberty interest would obviously be satisfied by a statute that required proof of only those elements and that imposed that particular punishment. Accordingly, the mere addition to that statute of an affirmative defense, which after all could constitutionally be ignored, should be equally satisfactory. The import of the proportionality principle is, then, that the state should be required to prove enough to justify the imposition of the maximum sentence permissible under the statute. Once that is accomplished, the accused has been fully protected against an unwarranted deprivation of liberty, and the state should be permitted to elaborate on the basic statute as it sees fit.

Allen, The Restoration of In re Winship: A Comment on Burdens of Persuasion in Criminal Cases after Patterson in New York, 76 Mich.L.Rev. 30, 36–46 (1977) (footnotes omitted). See also Jeffries and Stephan III, Defenses, Presumptions, and Burden of Proof in the Criminal Law, 88 Yale L.J. 1325, 1365–

79 (1979) ("[T]he only sensible construction of Winship is one that demands, as an essential of due process, proof beyond a reasonable doubt of facts sufficient to justify penalties of the sort contemplated;" the constitutional minima for criminal punishment should include the requirements of an act (actus reus), culpability (mens rea), and severity of the punishment should be relative to the gravity of the underlying offense (proportionality principle)). But see Fletcher, Two Kinds of Legal Rules: A Comparative Study of Burden–of–Persuasion Practices in Criminal Cases, 77 Yale L.J. 880 (1968) (criticizing rules tending to place burden on defendants respecting "affirmative defenses" as contrary to the trend of western rationales of criminal law); Underwood, The Thumbs on the Scales of Justice: Burdens of Persuasion in Criminal Cases, 86 Yale L.J. 1299 (1977) (The rules of proof may affect the public's perception of the risk of punishment for a given crime. Altering these rules of proof may be deceptive to the public because of the widely shared expectation that defendants are treated as innocent until proven guilty, and that the prosecution must prove its case beyond a reasonable doubt. That widely shared expectation poses a serious problem of fair notice for any attempt to adjust the rules of proof that govern the trial of a criminal case; The "greater-includes-the-lesser" argument is difficult to confine within reasonable bounds).

3. Courts continue to be troubled by the insanity defense. Cf. Rivera v. Delaware, 429 U.S. 877 (1976); Buzynski v. Oliver, 538 F.2d 6 (1st Cir.), cert. denied, 424 U.S. 984 (1976) (court questions the vitality of Leland v. Oregon). See generally Commonwealth v. Kostka, 50 N.E.2d 444 (Mass.1976) (footnotes omitted):

> Twenty-eight jurisdictions, including the Federal government and Massachusetts, provide that, after evidence of insanity has been introduced into the case, the burden devolves on the prosecution to prove the defendant's sanity beyond a reasonable doubt. Twenty-three jurisdictions, including the District of Columbia, consider insanity to be an affirmative defense, and require that the defendant prove insanity by a preponderance of the evidence. One jurisdiction, Wisconsin, employs both of these rules, depending on which definition of insanity the defendant relies on.

The degree of evidence required to raise the issue of insanity varies from jurisdiction to jurisdiction, see e.g., United States v. Hartfield, 513 F.2d 254 (9th Cir.1975); United States v. Milne, 487 F.2d 1232 (5th Cir.1973) ("slight evidence"); United States v. Schultz, 431 F.2d 907 (8th Cir.1970) ("some evidence"); United States v. Currier, 405 F.2d 1039, 1042 (2d Cir.), cert. denied, 395 U.S. 914 (1969) ("It takes more than a mere claim of irresponsibility to raise the issue."); State v. Ortiz, 560 P.2d 803 (Ariz.1977) ("evidence which generates substantial and reasonable doubt"); People v. Ware, 528 P.2d 224 (Colo.1974) ("any evidence"). Even where a defendant has the burden of proving insanity by a preponderance of the evidence, some courts will shift the burden to the State if the defendant introduces an unvacated judgment of insanity, see Nilsson v. State, 477 S.W.2d 592, 599 (Tex.Cr.App.1972).

4. An Iowa rule shifting to the defendant the burden of proving his alibi by a preponderance of the evidence was held to violate the Fourteenth Amendment: only a shift in the burden of going forward is constitutional. Stump v. Bennett, 398 F.2d 111 (8th Cir.), cert. denied, 393 U.S. 1001 (1968). See also Adkins v. Bordenkircher, 517 F.Supp. 390 (S.D.W.Va.1981) (instruction shifting burden of persuasion on alibi to defendant unconstitutional). Is alibi a material proposition or is it evidence negativing a material proposition—e.g., the defendant was not present, therefore he could not have fired the shot? The issue of burden of proof must be distinguished from that of discovery and notice to permit the prosecution to prepare and investigate. Notice is required in many jurisdictions. E.g., Pressler, New Jersey Court Rules, R.3:11–1 (1981) (rule requires defendant to furnish a bill of particulars, upon demand of prosecuting attorney, stating specific places defendant claims to have been at time of the offense and names and addresses of the witnesses upon whom he intends to rely to establish such alibi). See also Fed.R.Crim.P. 12.1(a) (notice of alibi by defendant). Cf. Williams, Advance Notice of the Defense, 1959 Criminal L.Rev. 548 (Eng.).

5. James, Burdens of Proof, 47 Va.L.Rev. 51, 58–61 (1961) (footnotes omitted):

There is no satisfactory test for allocating the burden of proof in either sense on any given issue. The allocation is made on the basis of one or more of several variable factors. Before considering these, however, we should note three formal tests which have some currency but are not very helpful.

1. It is often said that the party who must establish the affirmative proposition has the burden of proof on the issue. But language can be manipulated so as to state most propositions either negatively or affirmatively. . . .

2. It is sometimes said that the burden of proof is upon the party to whose case the fact in question is essential, and so it is, but this test simply poses another question: to which party's case is the fact essential? And the second question is no easier to answer than the first; indeed it is but a restatement of the same question.

3. It is often said that the party who has the burden of pleading a fact must prove it. This is in large part true and where there is clear authority on the pleading rule this is a fairly good, though not infallible, indication that the rule of burden of proof will parallel it. Three things should, however, be noted. The burden of proof does not follow the burden of pleading in all cases. Many jurisdictions for example require a plaintiff to plead non-payment of an obligation sued upon but do not require him to prove it. In federal courts defendant must plead contributory negligence as an affirmative defense to an action for injuries negligently caused, but federal courts in diversity of citizenship cases will follow a local rule which puts on plaintiff the burden of proving his freedom from contributory negligence. The second difficulty with the suggested test is that there is often no clear authority upon the pleading rule. The burden of pleading is itself allocated on the basis of pragmatic considerations of fairness, convenience, and policy, rather than on any general principle of pleading. Since the burden of proof is allocated on very much the same basis, a similar inquiry must be made to determine the pleading rule (where there is no clear authority) as would suffice to answer the burden of proof rule in the first instance. This fact, incidentally, suggests why burden of pleading and burden of proof are usually parallel; they are both manifestations of the same or similar considerations. A third difficulty with the proposed rule is that under modern systems, pleadings are cut off with the answer so that issues often have to be tried that do not appear in the pleadings at all.

. . .

Substantive considerations may also be influential. For real or supposed reasons of policy the law sometimes disfavors claims and defenses which it nevertheless allows. Where that is the case procedural devices like burden of proof are often used as handicaps, to use Judge Clark's felicitous phrase, against the disfavored contention. Thus whoever charges his adversary with fraud, be he plaintiff or defendant, must prove it. And although falsity is often included in the definitions of defamatory statements, yet the defendant in libel or slander must plead and prove the truth of the objectionable words if he would use that as a defense. In many of the older states, plaintiff, in a negligence action, had to prove his own due care, but as the defense of contributory negligence became increasingly unpopular with courts and legislatures, the tendency has been increasingly to make defendants plead and prove it.

See also Bolding, Scandinavian Studies in Law, Aspects of the Burdens of Proof, 12, 25–27 (1960):

> It might . . . be suggested that burden-of-proof rules are sometimes required because we want to influence the mode of behaviour within a special group of people; it may happen, for instance, that contractors, knowing themselves to be obliged to carry the burden of proof, e.g. on the question whether a price has been agreed upon or not, are induced to be more careful when making their contracts, from which it may follow—among other consequences—that questions concerning what a contractor may charge will not so often be left in doubt as would be the case if a principle of preponderance were to be applied.

6. As noted above, there is a tendency to place the burden on the party who "has peculiar knowledge or control of the evidence as to such matter." Nader v. Allegheny Airlines, 512 F.2d 527, 538 (D.C.Cir.1975), rev'd on other grounds, 426 U.S. 290 (1976) (action against airline for overbooking); Trans–American Van Service, Inc. v. United States, 421 F.Supp. 308, 330 (N.D.Tex.1976) (action involving application for a common carrier certificate; once the applicant has proven a prima facie case of "public convenience and necessity," the existing carrier opposing the application has the burden of proving such application should be denied; for "[t]he capabilities of protesting carriers are matters peculiarly within their knowledge."); Nemeth v. Pankost, 224 Cal.App.2d 351, 36 Cal.Rptr. 600, 604 (1964) (in suit by real estate salesman against broker for commission, if broker disputed assertion that it received a commission, it should have produced its records to show receipt or lack of receipt of commission). But cf. Tortora v. General Motors Corp., 130 N.W.2d 21, 24 (Mich.1964) (employer's knowledge of prior record of driving violations; but "in view of the availability . . . of modern discovery" devices which enable evidence to be ferreted out before trial, this consideration is less important than it once was); Browzin v. Catholic University of America, 527 F.2d 843 (App.D.C.1975) (litigant who does not have the burden of establishing a fact because it is peculiarly within the knowledge of the opposing party fails to raise that issue at trial, waives right to insist upon it on appeal).

7. Does the consideration of peculiar knowledge apply in criminal cases? Cf. Orfield, Burden of Proof and Presumptions in Federal Criminal Cases, 31 Univ. of Kansas City L.Rev. 30, 49 (1963): "The federal courts are in accord with the modern trend to treat affirmative defenses as situations where the defendant has merely the burden of going forward with the evidence, but the burden of persuasion rests on the government." See also Underwood, The Thumb on the Scales of Justice: Burdens of Persuasion in Criminal Cases, 86 Yale L.J. 1325, 1334–35 & n. 97 (1977), where the author recognizes that the device of assigning the burden of persuasion to the defendant may help produce relevant evidence, while avoiding "constitutional objection to more direct devices for eliciting evidence from a criminal defendant, an objection rooted in the Fifth Amendment's ban on compulsory self-incrimination." She points out, however, that "the Fifth Amendment limits the government only with respect to evidence that is both testimonial in character, ... and within the personal control of the defendant, ... leaving considerable room for the exercise of legal compulsion to obtain evidence from other sources, of nontestimonial evidence from the defendant." Professor Underwood concludes that use of a less drastic device, namely, assigning the defendant only the burden of producing evidence, is sufficient to elicit the relevant evidence.

8. Under one approach to entrapment, a defendant had the "relatively slight" burden of proving inducement by the government agent to commit the offense before the government had to prove propensity beyond a reasonable doubt. E.g., United States v. Greenberg, 444 F.2d 369 (2d Cir.), cert. denied, 404 U.S. 853 (1971); United States v. Sherman, 200 F.2d 880 (2d Cir.1952). Then in United States v. Braver, 450 F.2d 799, 805 (2d Cir.1971), the Second Circuit suggested a new jury charge: "if [the jury] finds some evidence of government initiation of the illegal conduct, the government has to prove beyond a reasonable doubt that the defendant was ready and willing to commit the crime." In accord, United States v. Hammond, 598 F.2d 1008 (5th Cir.1979), Kadis v. United States, 373 F.2d 370 (1st Cir.1967). But see People v. Laietta, 30 N.Y.2d 68, 330 N.Y.S.2d 351, 281 N.E.2d 157 (1972) (under the New York Penal Law the defendant carries both the burden of going forward and the burden of persuasion on the defense of entrapment); in accord, requiring defendant to prove entrapment by a preponderance of evidence: State v. Kelsey, 566 P.2d 1370 (Haw.1977); State v. Braun, 228 S.E.2d 466 (App.), appeal dismissed, 230 S.E.2d 766 (N.C.1976) ("to the satisfaction of the jury"). For a discussion of the objective and subjective approaches to entrapment see People v. Turner, 210 N.W.2d 336 (Mich.1973).

9. Is it possible to place all burdens of proof on a defendant? Cf. Upper Lakes Shipping, Ltd. v. Seafarers' International Union of Canada, 125 N.W.2d 324, 330 (Wis.1963) (civil contempt proceeding): "The party seeking the aid of the judicial process to reinforce his legal and economic position must present the information necessary for judgment to the court." See Thompson v. City of Louisville, 362 U.S. 199 (1960); Annot., Conviction of Criminal Offense Without Evidence as Denial of Due Process of Law, 80 A.L.R.2d 1362 (1961). Thompson was later extended so that a conviction must be supported by evidence, which, when construed in a light most favorable to the prosecution, a rational fact finder could find establishes guilt beyond a reasonable doubt. Jackson v. Virginia, 443 U.S. 307 (1979). But cf. R. Broughton, [1953] V.L.R. 572, requiring a person accused of bigamy to prove by the balance of probabilities that he thought he was not married to his first wife, criticized in MacDougall, The Burden of Proof in Bigamy, 21 Modern L.Rev. 510 (1958).

D. WEIGHT OF BURDEN OF PRODUCING EVIDENCE

United States v. Taylor[1]

United States Court of Appeals, Second Circuit, 1972.
464 F.2d 240.

■ FRIENDLY, CHIEF JUDGE:

The sole question meriting discussion in this opinion is the sufficiency of the evidence to warrant submission to the jury of the question whether Taylor "with intent to defraud" kept in possession and concealed a quantity of

---

1. Footnotes are omitted—Ed.

counterfeit Federal Reserve notes found in a car which Taylor, accompanied by one MacDonald, was driving from Canada into the United States.

I.

. . .

It is, of course, a fundamental of the jury trial guaranteed by the Constitution that the jury acts, not at large, but under the supervision of a judge. See Capital Traction Company v. Hof, 174 U.S. 1, 13–14, 19 S.Ct. 580, 43 L.Ed. 873 (1899). Before submitting the case to the jury, the judge must determine whether the proponent has adduced evidence sufficient to warrant a verdict in his favor. Dean Wigmore considered, 9 Evidence § 2494 at 299 (3d ed. 1940), the best statement of the test to be that of Mr. Justice Brett in Bridges v. Railway Co. [1874] L.R. 7 H.L. 213, 233:

> [A]re there facts in evidence which if unanswered would justify men of ordinary reason and fairness in affirming the question which the Plaintiff is bound to maintain?

It would seem at first blush—and we think also at second—that more "facts in evidence" are needed for the judge to allow men, and now women, "of ordinary reason and fairness" to affirm the question the proponent "is bound to maintain" when the proponent is required to establish this not merely by a preponderance of the evidence but, as all agree to be true in a criminal case, beyond a reasonable doubt. Indeed, the latter standard has recently been held to be constitutionally required in criminal cases. In re Winship, 397 U.S. 358, 361–364, 90 S.Ct. 1068, 25 L.Ed.2d 368 (1970). . . .

After acknowledging "that in their actual judgments the added gravity of the consequences [in criminal cases] makes them [the judges] more exacting," 140 F.2d at 594, Judge Hand based the refusal to require a higher standard of sufficiency in criminal cases on authority and a belief that "[w]hile at times it may be practicable" to "distinguish between the evidence which should satisfy reasonable men, and the evidence which should satisfy reasonable men beyond a reasonable doubt[,] . . . in the long run the line between them is too thin for day to day use." Id.

However the argument from authority may have stood in 1944, that battle has now been irretrievably lost. See 2 C. Wright, Federal Practice and Procedure § 467, at 255–257 (1969), and cases there cited. Almost all the circuits have adopted something like Judge Prettyman's formulation in Curley v. United States, 81 U.S.App.D.C. 389, 160 F.2d 229, 232–233, cert. denied, 331 U.S. 837, 67 S.Ct. 1511, 91 L.Ed. 1850 (1947). This, along with its rationale, reads as follows:

> The functions of the jury include the determination of the credibility of witnesses, the weighing of the evidence, and the drawing of justifiable inferences of fact from proven facts. It is the function of the judge to deny the jury any opportunity to operate beyond its province. The jury may not be permitted to conjecture merely, or to conclude upon pure speculation or from passion, prejudice or sympathy. The critical point in this boundary is the existence or non-existence of reasonable doubt as to guilt. If the evidence is such that reasonable jurymen must necessarily have such a doubt, the judge must require acquittal, because no other result is permissible within the fixed bounds of jury consideration. But if a reasonable mind might fairly have a reasonable doubt or might fairly not have one, the case is for the jury, and the decision is for the jurors to make. The law recognizes that the scope of a reasonable mind is broad. Its conclusion is

not always a point certain, but, upon given evidence, may be one of a number of conclusions. Both innocence and guilt beyond a reasonable doubt may lie fairly within the limits of reasonable conclusion from given facts. The judge's function is exhausted when he determines that the evidence does or does not permit the conclusion of guilt beyond a reasonable doubt within the fair operation of a reasonable mind.

The true rule, therefore, is that a trial judge, in passing upon a motion for directed verdict of acquittal, must determine whether upon the evidence, giving full play to the right of the jury to determine credibility, weigh the evidence, and draw justifiable inferences of fact, a reasonable mind might fairly conclude guilt beyond a reasonable doubt. If he concludes that upon the evidence there must be such a doubt in a reasonable mind, he must grant the motion; or, to state it another way, if there is no evidence upon which a reasonable mind might fairly conclude guilt beyond a reasonable doubt, the motion must be granted. If he concludes that either of the two results, a reasonable doubt or no reasonable doubt, is fairly possible, he must let the jury decide the matter. (footnotes omitted)

... The Supreme Court has recognized the feasibility of a standard intermediate between preponderance and proof beyond a reasonable doubt, to wit, clear and convincing evidence. ... Implicit in the Court's recognition of varying burdens of proof is a concomitant duty on the judge to consider the applicable burden when deciding whether to send a case to the jury.

. . .

II.

As happens not infrequently, appellant's victory on the legal point dealt with above is, for him, an empty one. Study of the transcript shows that the Government's case was far stronger than indicated in the briefs.

Taylor and MacDonald were stopped by a customs agent, while entering from Canada by car, at the border-crossing at Port Massena, N.Y., for routine questioning. Because Taylor had no proof of ownership of the vehicle, he and MacDonald were asked into the customs office for a more thorough investigation. When the two investigating customs agents began an inspection of the vehicle, thirty-four counterfeit $20 Federal Reserve notes fell from a magazine which was on the back seat. Forty-four $20 notes were subsequently found in four road maps of Ontario, Michigan, and two groups of other states, which had been lying on the dashboard. Taylor and MacDonald were placed under arrest. Four days later, Taylor admitted to one of the arresting agents, after proper warnings, that the magazine in which thirty-four of the bills were found belonged to him.

Warren Rudderow testified that he had given the car to Taylor in Orlando, Florida; that at the time of the transfer the car contained the magazine and maps other than those in which the bills were found; and that the car had not then contained any counterfeit bills. A Secret Service Agent testified that the bills were clearly counterfeit and not of "deceptive" quality. He based his conclusions on several factors, including the fact that the seventy-eight bills had only four different serial numbers, the printing of the Treasury seal was "poor" and "just a smudge," and the paper was heavy and lacked the distinctive red and blue fibers. The bills were offered in evidence.

It would be most unusual for a person having $1560 in what he believed to be lawful money to carry it scattered in the interior of an automobile rather than on his person or in a locked compartment. It would be still more unusual to select a magazine and four road maps as the places for custody. The evidence clearly warranted—indeed almost compelled—the inference that the defendants had placed the counterfeit bills in the car sometime after they received it from Rudderow and had secreted them in the durable magazine and in road maps acquired during their northbound journey. The curious method adopted for transporting the bills together with the testimony of the Secret Service Agent afforded ample basis for a reasonable man to be convinced beyond reasonable doubt that the appellant possessed both the knowledge that the bills were counterfeit and the required specific intent to defraud. . . .

Affirmed.

NOTES

1. McNaughton, in an interesting comment containing helpful diagrams, says that the judge should allow an issue to go to the jury in the usual civil case only if, after resolving all questions of credibility in favor of the proponent, he finds that a reasonable jury could be persuaded that it is more probable than not that a proposition of fact is true. McNaughton, Burden of Production of Evidence: A Function of a Burden of Persuasion, 68 Harv.L.Rev. 1382 (1955). In most jurisdictions, this analysis is sound, although the test is stated in various ways that reflect differing degrees of obeisance toward the right of the jury to be somewhat unreasonable. Compare the difference in the approach of Mr. Justice Rutledge writing for the majority—"the essential requirement is that mere speculation be not allowed to do duty for probative facts, after making due allowance for all reasonably possible inferences"—with Mr. Justice Black's dissenting statement "that a verdict should be directed, if at all, only when, without weighing the credibility of the witnesses, there is in the evidence no room whatever for honest difference of opinion over the factual issue in controversy." Galloway v. United States, 319 U.S. 372, 395 (1943). Cf. Jaffe, Judicial Review: Questions of Fact, 69 Harv.L.Rev. 1020, 1041 ff. (comparing review of jury and administrative agency). Where the scintilla test or one of its variations is used, the burden of producing bears little, if any, relation to the burden of persuasion. See, e.g., Barber v. Stephenson, 69 So.2d 251, 255–56 (Ala.1953) ("there need be only a scintilla of evidence to require reference of the issue raised thereby to the jury for decision. If there is a mere 'gleam,' 'glimmer,' 'spark,' 'the least particle,' the 'smallest trace'—'a scintilla' afforded from the evidence to sustain the issue, the court in duty bound must submit the question to the jury."). But see Palisi v. Louisville & Nashville Railroad Co., 226 F.Supp. 651 (S.D.Miss.1964), aff'd, 342 F.2d 799 (5th Cir.1965), cert. denied, 382 U.S. 834 (1965) (scintilla of evidence rule is not in effect in federal courts, or in Mississippi).

2. To the extent that McNaughton's analysis is followed by the courts, there should be a difference between the burden in civil and criminal cases. See, e.g., Parham v. Dell Rapids Township in Minnehaha County, 122 N.W.2d 548, 552 (S.D.1963) (preponderance of probability unlike criminal case). Since the burden of persuasion may differ as to different issues in civil cases, the burdens of coming forward should reflect this difference. In F.E.L.A. cases, for example, the burden of coming forward is "significantly different from the ordinary common-law negligence action ..." Rogers v. Missouri Pacific Railroad, 352 U.S. 500, 509–510 (1957); Fitzgerald v. A.L. Burbank & Co., 451 F.2d 670, 681 (2d Cir.1971) (plaintiff must show a "reasonable probability" that the employer's negligence was the proximate cause of death or the issue will be taken from the jury to avoid speculation); Fritts v. Toledo Terminal Railroad, 293 F.2d 361, 362 (6th Cir.1961) ("complete lack of probative facts"); Note F.E.L.A., Negligence and Jury—Trials—Speculation Upon a Scintilla, 11 W.Res.L.Rev. 123, 136 (1959) (this interpretation supported by the "spirit of the statute"). Cf. Paul v. Ribicoff, 206 F.Supp. 606, 610 (D.Colo.1962) ("The extent of a claimant's burden of proof is primarily a matter of policy based upon experience. ... In this connection the Social Security Act, being remedial in nature, is generally construed liberally in favor of the claimant if any substantial basis exists for relief ...").

In forfeiture proceedings, the government's burden of showing probable cause to seize is met by "less than prima facie legal proof and no more than reasonable ground for belief in guilt ... something more than mere suspicion and ... as reasonable under all the circumstances." Bush v. United States, 389 F.2d 485 (5th Cir.1968) (illegal exporting); United States v. One 1975 Lincoln Continental, 72 F.R.D. 535, 540 (S.D.N.Y.1976):

> [T]he question arises: has the Government demonstrated that it had "probable cause" to believe that the Lincoln Continental was used to transport heroin before its sale by James to Balmer and X? "Probable cause" is the litmus paper by which initiation of the forfeiture proceeding is measured. 21 U.S.C. § 881(b)(4). The Government is not required to prove the truth of its belief. 19 U.S.C. § 1615 provides that in forfeiture proceedings, where the vehicle is claimed by any person, "the burden of proof shall lie upon such claimant ..." Accordingly, the Government bears the initial burden of showing probable cause for the institution of the suit for forfeiture. Upon such a showing, the burden of absolving the vehicle from culpability rests upon the claimant.

In some civil cases a plaintiff may be able to meet his burden of coming forward with very little evidence. In Calvert v. Katy Taxi, Inc., 413 F.2d 841 (2d Cir.1969), an injured pedestrian sued for damages sustained when the defendant taxi collided with a car and immediately thereafter struck the plaintiff. The Second Circuit, while acknowledging the traditional principles that the mere fact of an accident does not constitute a prima facie case of negligence and that "unless the trial judge thinks reasonable men could infer from the evidence a greater likelihood of negligence on the part of the defendant, the plaintiff has no right to go to the jury", ruled that a nonparticipatory plaintiff is permitted to get to the jury on the naked proof of a collision, without having to show the defendant's negligence:

> Generally, where two moving vehicles (A's and B's) are involved in a collision, there are four possible explanations for an injury to a noncontributorily negligent bystander or passenger.
>
> (1) Both A and B were negligent.
>
> (2) Neither A nor B were negligent.
>
> (3) A alone was negligent.
>
> (4) B alone was negligent.
>
> In a case such as the one now before us, where plaintiff's suit is against B alone, and plaintiff himself is in no way contributorily negligent, most courts have consistently held that plaintiff does not have a sufficient case to get to the jury if he is unable to produce evidence explaining why the collision occurred. ... A rule to the contrary has been thought to be unfair due to the total lack of proof of any circumstance from which it might reasonably be inferred that the collision of two vehicles was solely caused by the want of care on the part of the one defendant B, for it also might reasonably be inferred that the unexplained collision was caused otherwise.

But, as noted by Professor James, while possibilities (1) and (4) above represent one half of the possible explanations for the accident, "it does not follow that they represent only fifty per cent of the probabilities." For it is entirely conceivable that the lack of care by both operators (possibility (1)) occurs with greater frequency than the other three possible explanations. And, "if it does, the balance of probabilities" should lie "with plaintiff in such a case," and a prima facie case of negligence thereby be established.

Id. at 846–847. See also Pfaffenbach v. White Plains Express Corp., 17 N.Y.2d 132, 269 N.Y.S.2d 115, 216 N.E.2d 324 (1966) (when defendant's truck skidded on a slippery road and collided with the car in which plaintiff was a passenger, a prima facie case of negligence was established without plaintiff having to eliminate an unknown defect in his host's car or the negligence of his host as possible reasons for the collision).

New York Pattern Jury Instructions, 1 N.Y.P.J.I.—Civil 2:84 (2d ed.) provides:

The fact that defendant's motor vehicle skidded, if you find that to be the fact, is a circumstance to be taken into consideration in determining whether defendant exercised reasonable care in its operation, but does not, standing alone, require that you find defendant negligent....

See generally, James, Functions of Judge and Jury in Negligence Cases, 58 Yale L.J. 667 (1949). Are courts creating or affecting substantive rules in cases such as Calvert or Pfaffenbach? Cf. Novis v. Sheinkin, 60 A.D.2d 623, 624, 400 N.Y.S.2d 161, 162 (1977) ("The rule of Pfaffenbach is, after all, merely a specific application of the doctrine of res ipsa loquitur to a particular class of automobile negligence cases. ....").

Compare the problem of the plaintiff suing as a group, only one of which is responsible for the injury. These issues are becoming more important as broad claims of disease generated by Agent Orange, asbestos and other carcinogens reach the courts. See, e.g., In re Agent Orange Product Liability Litigation, 597 F.Supp. 740, 816–843 (E.D.N.Y.1984), aff'd on other grounds, 818 F.2d 145 (2d Cir.1987) (indeterminate plaintiffs and defendants); Hall v. E.I. DuPont De Nemours & Co., 345 F.Supp. 353 (E.D.N.Y.1972) (blasting caps; industry wide liability); Sindell v. Abbott Laboratories, 26 Cal.3d 588, 163 Cal.Rptr. 132, 607 P.2d 924, cert. denied, 449 U.S. 912 (1980) (DES; percentage of market); Hardy v. Johns–Manville Sales Corp., 509 F.Supp. 1353, 1357 (E.D.Tex.1981) (asbestos; "Each defendant will be held liable for the proportion of the judgment represented by its share of that market unless it demonstrates that it could not have made the product which caused plaintiff's injuries."). Is this last requirement a fair burden to place on an individual defendant? See Comment, DES and a Proposed Theory of Enterprise Liability, 46 Fordham L.Rev. 963 (1978); Kaye, The Limits of Preponderance of Evidence Standard: Justifiability Naked Statistical Evidence and Multiple Causation, 1982 ABA Foundation Research J. 487.

3. Will the court, even in criminal cases, apply a varying standard of proof sufficient to go to the jury depending upon the nature of the crime? See Hellman v. United States, 298 F.2d 810, 812 (9th Cir.1961) (On the question of the sufficiency of the evidence to support a conviction the evidence is to be considered in the light most favorable to the Government); Noto v. United States, 367 U.S. 290, 296 (1961). It is to be borne in mind, however, that Smith Act offenses require strict standards of proof. Scales v. United States, 367 U.S. 203, at 232 (1961). ... With specific reference to the factor of intent, it is said in Scales, at page 229 ..., that there must be 'clear proof.' And in Noto at pages 299–300, ..., this view is further amplified as follows:

> ... this element of the membership crime, like its others must be judged *strictissimi juris,* for otherwise there is a danger that one in sympathy with the legitimate aims of such an organization, but not specifically intending to accomplish them by resort to violence, might be punished for his adherence to lawful and constitutionally protected purposes ... which he does not necessarily share.

A mistaken finding would impair legitimate political expression or association.

E. WEIGHT OF BURDEN OF PERSUASION

In re Winship

United States Supreme Court, 1970.
397 U.S. 358, 90 S.Ct. 1068, 25 L.Ed.2d 368.

■ MR. JUSTICE BRENNAN delivered the opinion of the Court.

... This case presents the single, narrow question whether proof beyond a reasonable doubt is among the "essentials of due process and fair treatment" required during the adjudicatory stage when a juvenile is charged with an act which would constitute a crime if committed by an adult.

Section 712 of the New York Family Court Act defines a juvenile delinquent as "a person over seven and less than sixteen years of age who does any act which, if done by an adult, would constitute a crime." During a 1967 adjudicatory hearing, conducted pursuant to § 742 of the Act, a judge in New York Family Court found that appellant, then a 12–year–old boy, had entered a locker and stolen $112 from a woman's pocketbook. The petition which charged appellant with delinquency alleged that his act, "if done by an adult, would constitute the crime or crimes of Larceny." The judge acknowledged that the proof might not establish guilt beyond a reasonable doubt, but rejected appellant's contention that such proof was required by the Fourteenth Amendment. The judge relied instead on § 744(b) of the New York Family Court Act which provides that "[a]ny determination at the conclusion of [an adjudicatory] hearing that a [juvenile] did an act or acts must be based on a preponderance of the evidence." ...

I

The requirement that guilt of a criminal charge be established by proof beyond a reasonable doubt dates at least from our early years as a Nation. The "demand for a higher degree of persuasion in criminal cases was recurrently expressed from ancient times, [though] its crystallization into the formula 'beyond a reasonable doubt' seems to have occurred as late as 1798. It is now accepted in common law jurisdictions as the measure of persuasion by which the prosecution must convince the trier of all the essential elements of guilt." C. McCormick, Evidence § 321, pp. 681–682 (1954); see also 9 J. Wigmore, Evidence § 2497 (3d ed. 1940). Although virtually unanimous adherence to the reasonable-doubt standard in common-law jurisdictions may not conclusively establish it as a requirement of due process, such adherence does "reflect a profound judgment about the way in which law should be enforced and justice administered." Duncan v. Louisiana, 391 U.S. 145, 155, 88 S.Ct. 1444, 1451 (1968).

Expressions in many opinions of this Court indicate that it has long been assumed that proof of a criminal charge beyond a reasonable doubt is constitutionally required. . . .

The reasonable-doubt standard plays a vital role in the American scheme of criminal procedure. It is a prime instrument for reducing the risk of convictions resting on factual error. The standard provides concrete substance for the presumption of innocence—that bedrock "axiomatic and elementary" principle whose "enforcement lies at the foundation of the administration of our criminal law." Coffin v. United States, supra, at 453. As the dissenters in the New York Court of Appeals observed, and we agree, "a person accused of a crime . . . would be at a severe disadvantage, a disadvantage amounting to a lack of fundamental fairness, if he could be adjudged guilty and imprisoned for years on the strength of the same evidence as would suffice in a civil case." 24 N.Y.2d, at 205, 247 N.E.2d, at 259.

. . .

Lest there remain any doubt about the constitutional stature of the reasonable-doubt standard, we explicitly hold that the Due Process Clause protects the accused against conviction except upon proof beyond a reasonable doubt of every fact necessary to constitute the crime with which he is charged.

. . .

Reversed.

■ MR. JUSTICE HARLAN, concurring. . . . First, in a judicial proceeding in which there is a dispute about the facts of some earlier event, the factfinder cannot acquire unassailably accurate knowledge of what happened.[1] Instead, all the factfinder can acquire is a belief of what *probably* happened. The intensity of this belief—the degree to which a factfinder is convinced that a given act actually occurred—can, of course, vary. In this regard, a standard of proof represents an attempt to instruct the factfinder concerning the degree of confidence our society thinks he should have in the correctness of factual conclusions for a particular type of adjudication. Although the phrases "preponderance of the evidence" and "proof beyond a reasonable doubt" are quantitatively imprecise, they do communicate to the finder of fact different notions concerning the degree of confidence he is expected to have in the correctness of his factual conclusions.

A second proposition, which is really nothing more than a corollary of the first, is that the trier of fact will sometimes, despite his best efforts, be wrong in his factual conclusions. In a lawsuit between two parties, a factual error can make a difference in one of two ways. First, it can result in a judgment in favor of the plaintiff when the true facts warrant a judgment for the defendant. The analogue in a criminal case would be the conviction of an innocent man. On the other hand, an erroneous factual determination can result in a judgment for the defendant when the true facts justify a judgment in plaintiff's favor. The criminal analogue would be the acquittal of a guilty man.

The standard of proof influences the relative frequency of these two types of erroneous outcomes. If, for example, the standard of proof for a criminal trial were a preponderance of the evidence rather than proof beyond a reasonable doubt, there would be a smaller risk of factual errors that result in freeing guilty persons, but a far greater risk of factual errors that result in convicting

---

1. For an interesting analysis of standards of proof see Kaplan, Decision Theory and the Factfinding Process, 20 Stan.L.Rev. 1065, 1071–1077 (1968). [Some footnotes omitted; this footnote renumbered and moved; Footnotes by the Court.]

the innocent. Because the standard of proof affects the comparative frequency of these two types of erroneous outcomes, the choice of the standard to be applied in a particular kind of litigation should, in a rational world, reflect an assessment of the comparative social disutility of each.

When one makes such an assessment, the reason for different standards of proof in civil as opposed to criminal litigation becomes apparent. In a civil suit between two private parties for money damages, for example, we view it as no more serious in general for there to be an erroneous verdict in the defendant's favor than for there to be an erroneous verdict in the plaintiff's favor. A preponderance of the evidence standard therefore seems peculiarly appropriate for, as explained most sensibly[2] it simply requires the trier of fact "to believe that the existence of a fact is more probable than its nonexistence before [he] may find in favor of the party who has the burden to persuade the [judge] of the fact's existence."[3]

In a criminal case, on the other hand, we do not view the social disutility of convicting an innocent man as equivalent to the disutility of acquitting someone who is guilty. As Mr. Justice Brennan wrote for the Court in Speiser v. Randall, 357 U.S. 513, 525–526, 78 S.Ct. 1332, 1341–1342 (1958):

"There is always in litigation a margin of error, representing error in factfinding, which both parties must take into account. Where one party has at stake an interest of transcending value—as a criminal defendant his liberty— this margin of error is reduced as to him by the process of placing on the other party the burden ... of persuading the factfinder at the conclusion of the trial of his guilt beyond a reasonable doubt."

In this context, I view the requirement of proof beyond a reasonable doubt in a criminal case as bottomed on a fundamental value determination of our society that it is far worse to convict an innocent man than to let a guilty man go free. It is only because of the nearly complete and long-standing acceptance of the reasonable-doubt standard by the States in criminal trials that the Court has not before today had to hold explicitly that due process, as an expression of fundamental procedural fairness, requires a more stringent standard for criminal trials than for ordinary civil litigation.

■ [Dissents of Mr. Chief Justice Burger and Justices Stewart and Black omitted.]

Lego v. Twomey

Supreme Court of the United States, 1972.
404 U.S. 477, 92 S.Ct. 619, 30 L.Ed.2d 618.

■ Mr. Justice White delivered the opinion of the Court.

In 1964, this Court held that a criminal defendant who challenges the voluntariness of a confession made to officials and sought to be used against him at his trial has a due process right to a reliable determination that the confession was in fact voluntarily given and not the outcome of coercion which the Constitution forbids. Jackson v. Denno, 378 U.S. 368, 84 S.Ct. 1774 (1964).

---

2. The preponderance test has been criticized, justifiably in my view, when it is read as asking the trier of fact to weigh in some objective sense the quantity of evidence submitted by each side rather than asking him to decide what he believes most probably happened. See J. Maguire, Evidence, Common Sense and Common Law 180 (1947).

3. F. James, Civil Procedure 250–51 (1965); see E. Morgan, Some Problems of Proof Under the Anglo–American System of Litigation 84–85 (1956).

While our decision made plain that only voluntary confessions may be admitted at the trial of guilt or innocence, we did not then announce, or even suggest, that the factfinder at a coercion hearing need judge voluntariness with reference to an especially severe standard of proof. Nevertheless, since Jackson, state and federal courts have addressed themselves to the issue with a considerable variety of opinions.[1] We granted certiorari in this case to resolve the question. 401 U.S. 992, 91 S.Ct. 1238 (1971).

Petitioner Lego was convicted of armed robbery in 1961 after a jury trial in Superior Court, Cook County, Illinois. The court sentenced him to prison for 25 to 50 years. The evidence introduced against Lego at trial included a confession he had made to police after arrest and while in custody at the station house. Prior to trial Lego sought to have the confession suppressed. He did not deny making it but did challenge that he had done so voluntarily. The trial judge conducted a hearing, out of the presence of the jury, at which Lego testified that police had beaten him about the head and neck with a gun butt. His explanation of this treatment was that the local police chief, a neighbor and former classmate of the robbery victim, had sought revenge upon him. Lego introduced into evidence a photograph which had been taken of him at the county jail on the day after his arrest. The photograph showed that petitioner's face had been swollen and had traces of blood on it. Lego admitted that his face had been scratched in a scuffle with the robbery victim but maintained that the encounter did not explain the condition shown in the photograph. The police chief and four officers also testified. They denied either beating or threatening petitioner and disclaimed knowledge that any other officer had done so. The trial judge resolved this credibility problem in favor of the police and ruled the confession admissible. At trial, Lego testified in his own behalf. Although he did not dispute the truth of the confession directly, he did tell his version of the events which had transpired at the police station. The trial judge instructed the jury as to the prosecution's burden of proving guilt. He did not instruct that the jury was required to find the confession voluntary before it could be used in judging guilt or innocence. On direct appeal the Illinois Supreme Court affirmed the conviction. People v. Lego, 32 Ill.2d 76, 203 N.E.2d 875 (1965).

Four years later petitioner challenged his conviction by seeking a writ of habeas corpus in the United States District Court for the Northern District of Illinois. He maintained that the trial judge should have found the confession voluntary beyond a reasonable doubt before admitting it into evidence. Although the judge had made no mention of the standard he used, Illinois law provided that a confession challenged as involuntary could be admitted into evidence if, at a hearing outside the presence of the jury, the judge found it voluntary by a preponderance of the evidence. In the alternative petitioner argued that the voluntariness question should also have been submitted to the jury for its separate consideration. After first denying the writ for failure to exhaust state remedies, the District Court granted a rehearing motion, concluded that Lego had no state remedy then available to him and denied relief on the

---

1. State courts which have considered the question since Jackson have adopted a variety of standards, most of them founded upon state law. Many have sanctioned a standard of proof less strict than beyond a reasonable doubt, including proof of voluntariness by a preponderance of the evidence or to the satisfaction of the court or proof of voluntariness in fact. 429 Pa. 141, 239 A.2d 426 (1968); Monts v. State, 218 Tenn. 31, 400 S.W.2d 722 (1966); State v. Davis, 73 Wash.2d 271, 438 P.2d 185 (1968).

Other States, using state law or not specifying a basis, require proof beyond a reasonable doubt. ... Two federal courts have held as an exercise of supervisory power that voluntariness must be proved beyond a reasonable doubt.

[Some footnotes are omitted; others are renumbered; footnotes by the Court.]

merits. United States ex rel. Lego v. Pate, 308 F.Supp. 38 (N.D.Ill.1970). The Court of Appeals for the Seventh Circuit affirmed.

I

Petitioner challenges the judgment of the Court of Appeals on three grounds. The first is that he was not proved guilty beyond a reasonable doubt as required by In re Winship, 397 U.S. 358, 90 S.Ct. 1068 (1970), because the confession used against him at his trial had been proved voluntary only by a preponderance of the evidence. Implicit in the claim is an assumption that a voluntariness hearing is designed to enhance the reliability of jury verdicts. To judge whether that is so we must return to Jackson v. Denno, 378 U.S. 368, 84 S.Ct. 1774 (1964).

In New York prior to Jackson, juries most often determined the voluntariness of confessions and hence whether confessions could be used in deciding guilt or innocence. Trial judges were required to make an initial determination and could exclude a confession, but only it could not under any circumstances be deemed voluntary. When voluntariness was fairly debatable, either because a dispute of fact existed or because reasonable men could have drawn differing inferences from undisputed facts, the question whether the confession violated due process was for the jury. This meant the confession was introduced at the trial itself. If evidence challenging its voluntariness were adduced, the jury was instructed first to pass upon voluntariness, and, if it found the confession involuntary, ignore it in determining guilt. If, on the other hand, the confession were found to be voluntary, the jury was then free to consider its truth or falsity and give the confession an appropriate weight in judging guilt or innocence.

We concluded that the New York procedure was constitutionally defective because at no point along the way did a criminal defendant receive a clear-cut determination that the confession used against him was in fact voluntary. The trial judge was not entitled to exclude a confession merely because he himself would have found it involuntary, and, while we recognized that the jury was empowered to perform that function, we doubted it could do so reliably. Precisely because confessions of guilt, whether coerced or freely given, may be truthful and potent evidence, we did not believe a jury could be called upon to ignore the probative value of a truthful but coerced confession; it was also likely, we thought, that in judging voluntariness itself the jury would be influenced by the reliability of a confession it considered an accurate account of the facts. "It is now axiomatic," we said,

> "that a defendant in a criminal case is deprived of due process of law if his conviction is founded, in whole or in part, upon an involuntary confession, without regard for the truth or falsity of the confession, Rogers v. Richmond, 365 U.S. 534, 81 S.Ct. 735, and even though there is ample evidence aside from the confession to support the conviction. Malinski v. New York, 324 U.S. 401, 65 S.Ct. 781; Stroble v. California, 343 U.S. 181, 72 S.Ct. 599; Payne v. Arkansas, 356 U.S. 560, 78 S.Ct. 844. Equally clear is the defendant's constitutional right at some stage in the proceedings to object to the use of the confession and to have a fair hearing and a reliable determination on the issue of voluntariness, a determination uninfluenced by the truth or falsity of the confession." Rogers v. Richmond, supra.

We did not think it necessary, or even appropriate, in Jackson to announce that prosecutors would be required to meet a particular burden of proof in a Jackson hearing held before the trial judge.[2] Indeed, the then-established duty to determine voluntariness had not been framed in terms of a burden of proof, nor has it been since Jackson was decided. We could fairly assume then, as we can now, that a judge would admit into evidence only those confessions which he reliably found, at least by a preponderance of the evidence, had been made voluntarily.

We noted in Jackson that there may be a relationship between the involuntariness of a confession and its unreliability.[3] But our decision was not based in the slightest on the fear that juries might misjudge the accuracy of confessions and arrive at erroneous determinations of guilt or innocence. That case was not aimed at reducing the possibility of convicting innocent men.

Quite the contrary, we feared that the reliability and truthfulness of even coerced confessions could impermissibly influence a jury's judgment as to voluntariness. The use of coerced confessions, whether true or false, is forbidden because the method used to extract them offends constitutional principles. Rogers v. Richmond, 365 U.S. 534, 540–541, 81 S.Ct. 735, 739 (1961). The procedure we established in Jackson was designed to safeguard the right of an individual, entirely apart from his guilt or innocence, not to be compelled to condemn himself by his own utterances. Nothing in Jackson questioned the province or capacity of juries to assess the truthfulness of confessions. Nothing in that opinion took from the jury any evidence relating to the accuracy or weight of confessions admitted into evidence. A defendant has been as free since Jackson as he was before to familiarize a jury with circumstances which attend the taking of his confession, including facts bearing upon its weight and voluntariness.[4] In like measure, of course, juries have been at liberty to disregard confessions which are insufficiently corroborated or otherwise deemed unworthy of belief.

Since the purpose that a voluntariness hearing is designed to serve has nothing whatever to do with improving the reliability of jury verdicts, we

---

2. "Judge" is used here and throughout the opinion to mean a factfinder, whether trial judge or jury, at a voluntariness hearing. The proscription against permitting the jury which passes upon guilt or innocence to judge voluntariness in the same proceeding does not preclude the States from impaneling a separate jury to determine voluntariness. Jackson v. Denno, 378 U.S., at 391 n. 19, 84 S.Ct., at 1788.

3. We noted that coerced confessions are forbidden in part because of their "probable unreliability." Jackson v. Denno, 378 U.S., at 385–386. However, it had been settled when this Court decided Jackson that the exclusion of unreliable confessions is not the purpose which a voluntariness hearing is designed to serve. Rogers v. Richmond, 365 U.S. 534, 81 S.Ct. 735 (1961). The sole issue in such a hearing is whether a confession was coerced. Whether it be true or false is irrelevant; indeed, such an inquiry is forbidden. The judge may not take into consideration evidence which would indicate that the confession, though compelled, is reliable, even highly so. Id. at 545, 81 S.Ct., at 741. As difficult as such tasks may be to accomplish, the judge is also duty-bound to ignore impli-

cations of reliability in facts relevant to coercion and to shut from his mind any internal evidence of authenticity which a confession itself may bear.

4. This is the course which petitioner pursued. Cf. Jackson v. Denno, 378 U.S., at 386 n. 13, 84 S.Ct., at 1785. Although 18 U.S.C.A. § 3501(a) is inapplicable here, it is relevant to note the provisions of that section:

> "(a) In any criminal prosecution brought by the United States or by the District of Columbia, a confession, as defined in subsection (e) hereof, shall be admissible in evidence if it is voluntarily given. Before such confession is received in evidence, the trial judge shall, out of the presence of the jury, determine any issue as to voluntariness. If the trial judge determines that the confession was voluntarily made it shall be admitted in evidence and the trial judge shall permit the jury to hear relevant evidence on the issue of voluntariness, and shall instruct the jury to give such weight to the confession as the jury feels it deserves under all the circumstances."

cannot accept the charge that judging the admissibility of a confession by a preponderance of the evidence undermines the mandate of In re Winship, 397 U.S. 358, 90 S.Ct. 1068 (1970). Our decision in Winship was not concerned with standards for determining the admissibility of evidence or with the prosecution's burden of proof at a suppression hearing when evidence is challenged on constitutional grounds. Winship went no further than to confirm the fundamental right that protects "the accused against conviction except upon proof beyond a reasonable doubt of every fact necessary to constitute the crime with which he is charged." Id., at 364, 90 S.Ct., at 1072. A high standard of proof is necessary, we said, to ensure against unjust convictions by giving substance to the presumption of innocence. Id., at 363, 90 S.Ct., at 1072. A guilty verdict is not rendered less reliable or less consonant with Winship simply because the admissibility of a confession is determined by a less stringent standard. Petitioner does not maintain that either his confession or its voluntariness is an element of the crime with which he was charged. He does not challenge the constitutionality of the standard by which the jury was instructed to decide his guilt or innocence; nor does he question the sufficiency of the evidence which reached the jury to satisfy the proper standard of proof. Petitioner's rights under Winship have not been violated.[5]

II

Even conceding that Winship is inapplicable because the purpose of a voluntariness hearing is not to implement the presumption of innocence, petitioner presses for reversal on the alternative ground that evidence offered against a defendant at a criminal trial and challenged on constitutional grounds must be determined admissible beyond a reasonable doubt in order to give adequate protection to those values which exclusionary rules are designed to serve. Jackson v. Denno, 378 U.S. 368, 84 S.Ct. 1774 (1964), an offspring of Brown v. Mississippi, 297 U.S. 278, 56 S.Ct. 461 (1936), requires judicial rulings on voluntariness prior to admitting confessions. Miranda v. Arizona, 384 U.S. 436, 86 S.Ct. 1602 (1966), excludes confessions flowing from custodial interrogations unless adequate warnings were administered and a waiver was obtained. Weeks v. United States, 232 U.S. 383, 34 S.Ct. 341 (1914), and Mapp v. Ohio, 367 U.S. 643, 81 S.Ct. 1684 (1961), make impermissible the introduction of evidence obtained in violation of a defendant's Fourth Amendment rights. In each instance, and without regard to its probative value, evidence is kept from the trier of guilt or innocence for reasons wholly apart from enhancing the reliability of verdicts. These independent values, it is urged, themselves require a stricter standard of proof in judging admissibility.

The argument is straightforward and has appeal. But we are unconvinced that merely emphasizing the importance of the values served by exclusionary rules is itself sufficient demonstration that the Constitution also requires admissibility to be proved beyond reasonable doubt. Evidence obtained in violation of the Fourth Amendment has been excluded from federal criminal trials for many years. Weeks v. United States, supra. The same is true of coerced confessions offered in either federal or state trials. Bram v. United

---

5. Nothing is to be gained from restating the constitutional rule as requiring proof of guilt beyond a reasonable doubt on the basis of constitutionally obtained evidence and then arguing that rights under Winship are diluted unless admissibility is governed by a high standard. Transparently, this assumes the question at issue, which is whether a confession is admissible if found voluntary by a preponderance of the evidence. United States v. Schipani, 289 F.Supp. 43 (E.D.N.Y.1968), aff'd 414 F.2d 1262 (2d Cir. 1969), followed this unsatisfactory course in a Fourth Amendment case but stopped short of basing the decision on the Constitution.

States, 168 U.S. 532, 18 S.Ct. 183 (1897); Brown v. Mississippi, supra. But, from our experience over this period of time no substantial evidence has accumulated that federal rights have suffered from determining admissibility by a preponderance of the evidence. Petitioner offers nothing to suggest that admissibility rulings have been unreliable or otherwise wanting in quality because not based on some higher standard. . . .

To reiterate what we said in Jackson: when a confession challenged as involuntary is sought to be used against a criminal defendant at his trial, he is entitled to a reliable and clear-cut determination that the confession was in fact voluntarily rendered. Thus, the prosecution must prove at least by a preponderance of the evidence that the confession was voluntary. Of course, the States are free, pursuant to their own law, to adopt a higher standard. They may indeed differ as to the appropriate resolution of the values they find at stake.

. . .

The decision of the Court of Appeals is affirmed.

■ Mr. Justice Powell and Mr. Justice Rehnquist took no part in the consideration or decision of this case.

■ Mr. Justice Brennan, with whom Mr. Justice Douglas and Mr. Justice Marshall join, dissenting.

. . .

If we permit the prosecution to prove by a preponderance of the evidence that a confession was voluntary, then, to paraphrase Mr. Justice Harlan, we must be prepared to justify the view that it is no more serious in general to admit involuntary confessions than it is to exclude voluntary confessions. I am not prepared to justify that view. Compelled self-incrimination is so alien to the American sense of justice that I see no way that such a view could ever be justified. If we are to provide "concrete substance" for the command of the Fifth Amendment that no person shall be compelled to condemn himself, we must insist, as we do at the trial of guilt or innocence, that the prosecution prove that the defendant's confession was voluntary beyond a reasonable doubt. In my judgment, to paraphrase Mr. Justice Harlan again, the command of the Fifth Amendment reflects the determination of our society that it is worse to permit involuntary self-condemnation than it is to deprive a jury of probative evidence. Just as we do not convict when there is a reasonable doubt of guilt, we should not permit the prosecution to introduce into evidence a defendant's confession when there is a reasonable doubt that it was the product of his free and rational choice.

I add only that the absolute bar against the admission of a defendant's compelled utterance at his criminal trial is fundamentally an expression of the American commitment to the moral worth of the individual. What we said in Winship bears repeating here. "[U]se of the reasonable-doubt standard is indispensable to command the respect and confidence of the community in applications of the criminal law. It is critical that the moral force of the criminal law not be diluted by a standard of proof that leaves people in doubt whether innocent men are being condemned." Id., 397 U.S., at 364, 90 S.Ct., at 1072. I believe that it is just as critical to our system of criminal justice that when a person's words are used against him, no reasonable doubt remains that he spoke of his own free will.

NOTES

1. The clear tendency of the Federal courts is to require a preponderance test as to all preliminary matters, including all predicates for admissibility. See, e.g., Bourjaily v. United States, 483 U.S. 171 (1987) (preponderance standard as to elements of conspirator hearsay rule, Rule 801(d)(1)(E)). Nevertheless, there are some areas where congressional or Constitutional policy may warrant a higher standard. Under the Bail Reform Act of 1984, for example, a defendant may be detained prior to trial where no release conditions "will reasonably assure ... the safety of any other person and the community." 18 U.S.C. § 1342(1e). United States v. Salerno, 481 U.S. 739 (1987):

> The government must first of all demonstrate probable cause to believe that the charged crime has been committed by the arrestee, but that is not enough. In a full-blown adversary hearing, the government must convince a neutral decisionmaker by clear and convincing evidence that no conditions of release can reasonably assure the safety of the community or of any person. 18 U.S.C. § 3142(f). While the government's general interest in preventing crime is compelling, even this interest is heightened when the government musters convincing proof that the arrestee, already indicted or held to answer for a serious crime, presents a demonstrable danger to the community. Under these narrow circumstances, society's interest in crime prevention is at its greatest.

In Crane v. Kentucky, 476 U.S. 683 (1986) the court apparently approved a finding of voluntariness of a confession based upon a preponderance ground. Defendant was, however, entitled to put the issue of its probative force to the jury, introducing evidence on the point. See also, e.g., United States v. DelVecchio, 800 F.2d 21 (2d Cir.1986) (preponderance to show separate conspiracy on motion to dismiss on double jeopardy grounds); United States v. Lee, 818 F.2d 1052 (2d Cir.1987) (disputed allegations in presentence reports by preponderance of the evidence). The Lee problem will become particularly acute in applying the guidelines of the United States Sentencing Commission pursuant to 28 U.S.C. § 994(a), requiring precise factual findings. See, e.g., U.S. Sentencing Comm., Sentencing Guidelines and Policy Statements, April 13, 1987; Supplementary Report, June 18, 1987; Draft Worksheets, May 29, 1987.

Congress sometimes sets out the applicable standard by statute. See, e.g., Comprehensive Crime Control Act of 1984, P.L. 98–473: claimant to forfeited goods, 18 U.S.C. § 1963 (preponderance); discharge of person found incapable of standing trial by reason of mental disease or defect, 18 U.S.C. § 4241 (preponderance); after finding of not guilty by reason of mental disease or defect, 18 U.S.C. § 4243 (clear and convincing or preponderance, depending upon offense); see also 18 U.S.C. § 4244.

2. United States v. Schipani, 193 F.Supp. 156 (E.D.N.Y.1968), aff'd, 414 F.2d 1262 (2d Cir.1969), cert. denied, 397 U.S. 922 (1970):

> In the case before us, the precise weight of the government's burden may affect the decision on the motion to suppress. We are, therefore, compelled to address the question with some attention. The matter presents inherent practical and theoretical difficulties.
>
> The problem will, perhaps, be more clearly exposed by considering a number of simple hypothetical situations. (The terminology used generally follows Michael and Adler, The Trial of an Issue of Fact, 34 Colum.L.Rev. 1224, 1252 (1934) and Michael and Adler, The Nature of Judicial Proof (1931). See also, e.g., Ball, The Moment of Truth: Probability Theory and

Standards of Proof, 14 Vand.L.Rev. 807 (1961); James, Relevancy, Probability and the Law, 29 Calif.L.Rev. 689 (1941)).

In a civil case involving a breach of contract where defendant claims that he did not execute the agreement, the court will admit the alleged written contract if a reasonable man might find that it was signed by or on behalf of the defendant. Admissibility depends purely on the document's meeting minimum standards of probative force. There may be mixed questions of law and fact relating to "execution" turning on whether, for example, the document was forged or whether the defendant was tricked into signing it. In determining whether the material proposition—the defendant "entered" into the contract—has been established, the jury will consider all of the admitted evidence, including the document before it. If there is some doubt about whether the defendant's signature was forged, or whether he had authorized an agent to execute it, the jury will consider this doubt in evaluating all the lines of proof bearing on the material proposition.

The level of burden of proof (persuasion) with respect to the material proposition will be, since this is an ordinary civil case, a preponderance— that is to say the trier must be convinced, on the basis of his evaluation of the evidence, that the proposition is more probably true than false (50 + % probable for purposes of this analysis). Thus, if the trier would have been just convinced that the material proposition was probably true absent this doubt about the authenticity of the document, doubt about this line of proof might sufficiently reduce his evaluation of the probability of the material proposition so that he might find that it was not proven (50% or less probable).

The jury's evaluation of the evidence relevant to a material proposition requires a gestalt or synthesis which seldom needs to be analyzed precisely. Any item of evidence must be interpreted in the context of all the evidence introduced (and often of that reasonably expected which was not produced). In giving appropriate, if sometimes unreflective, weight to a specific piece of evidence the trier will fit it into a shifting mosaic. If the trier concludes that one item of evidence is reliable, this may affect his evaluation of the credibility of a witness who gives testimony inconsistent with this evidence. His evaluation of the credibility of this witness may, in turn, affect his conclusion as to the probative force of the witness' testimony with respect to another line of proof. But confirming evidence of that other line of proof may require a reevaluation of the witness' credibility and a complex readjustment of the assessment of all the interlocking evidence.

Since so much of the evaluation of evidence depends upon varying hypotheses applied by triers with different backgrounds and views of life, fact finding differences among jurors and between judge and jury are to be expected. The court's function is, in the usual simple case, only to decide whether a reasonable man might have his assessment of the probabilities of a material proposition changed by the piece of evidence sought to be admitted. If it may affect that evaluation it is relevant and, subject to certain other rules, admissible. See Trautman, Logical or Legal Relevancy—A Conflict of Theory, 5 Vand.L.Rev. 385, 390 (1951). Even, therefore, if a juror decides that the probability is only 40% that the document referred to above is authentic, it may help him determine whether the material proposition is more probably true than not. This difference between the probabilities required of a material proposition and of relevant evidence and individual lines of proof partly explains why, in criminal cases, some courts have said that while the burden of proof of an element of the crime is beyond a reasonable doubt, individual items of evidence need not be proved by so high a standard....

It is apparent, then, that the judge's function in determining admissibility in a case such as is hypothesized above is relatively simple.... He need not be concerned unduly about mistakenly admitting evidence because, if the document lacks probative force, the jury can (absent factors such as prejudice) be counted on to ignore it. Only time has been lost by admitting evidence with probative force so low that it cannot affect the outcome.

Where admissibility of evidence depends upon extrinsic policies rather than upon probative force, the problem is more complex and the pressure on the trial judge is greater. Let us suppose, solely for the sake of analysis, that the burden on the government is to prove by a preponderance that a proffered document with high probative force was not obtained in violation of the law. Assume that exclusion depends upon an extrinsic policy designed to protect constitutional rights and to discourage obtaining evidence illegally. Suppose that the only material proposition in the case is whether defendant had certain knowledge (as that the powder he possessed was a narcotic). Let us suppose that the only evidence on the point is a letter from the defendant and that it would permit a jury to find beyond a reasonable doubt (95 + % probable, for the purposes of this analysis) that he did have knowledge.

Now, if we suppose that the judge has decided that there is a question about whether the document was illegally obtained but that there is a bare preponderance (50 + % probable) in favor of the government's contention that it was legally obtained, the judge will, on the assumptions made, admit it. The question of whether the document was or was not illegally obtained is not considered by the jury and normally it will not have before it evidence bearing on this question. Thus, the jury will give the document its full probative weight and it will find the defendant guilty beyond a reasonable doubt.

Whether such a result in a criminal case is proper depends upon how the rule of law is stated. If it is: "the material proposition of knowledge must be proven beyond a reasonable doubt *by evidence properly admitted in the trial*" the verdict should stand. The trier might have concluded that the probability of knowledge was 95 + % if he assessed the document solely on the basis of its probative force. However, if it is: "the material proposition of knowledge must be proven beyond a reasonable doubt *by legally obtained evidence,*" there is doubt about the validity of the conviction. If the probative force is discounted by the probabilities relating to the illegality, then the total probative force of all the relevant evidence might well have fallen below 95 + %. The documentary line of proof would not then have a force of 95 + % probability but of (95 + × 50 +) %, or somewhere in the order of 50 + %. See Ball, The Trial Court: Probability Theory and Jury Issues, in Communication Sciences and Law: Reflections from the Jurimetrics Conference, 189–90 (Allen and Caldwell, eds., 1965).

This attenuation of probabilities results from the fact that, where variables are independent and the probability of a combination of variables is to be determined, the probability of each variable is multiplied by the probability of each other variable. See, e.g., Hoel, Elementary Statistics, 56–63 (1966); Keynes, A Treatise on Probability, 121, 135–136 (1952). Probative force and illegality are sufficiently independent to justify multiplying them for the purposes of this analysis. Where the probability of one or two variables approaches 100% the product will, of course, approximate the probability of the less probable variable.

3. Does Lego sufficiently direct attention to the relative importance of the various policies favoring admission or exclusion? What are those policies? What is the implied view of the importance of protecting the integrity of the guilt-finding function of the courts and of the function in preventing violations of the Constitution by the police? Note the analogous distinction made in the treatment of the informer's privilege, infra. See United States v. Raddatz, 447 U.S. 667, 678 (1980) (allowing Magistrate to pass on suppression motion in first instance so long as Article III court makes ultimate decision since "the interests underlying a voluntariness hearing do not coincide with the criminal law objectives of determining guilt or innocence.").

4. Griffith v. State, 157 S.E.2d 894 (Ga.App.1967): In objecting on appeal to the admissibility of a confession, defendant claimed that he was indigent and that the State had failed to inform him of his right to have a lawyer appointed. Finding that the State had administered all the other warnings required by Miranda v. Arizona, 384 U.S. 436 (1966), the court declared a prima facie case for voluntariness had been made—thus relieving the State of the burden of showing that at the time of interrogation the defendant had been given his full warnings or that the police officers knew he was indigent. Cf. People v. Huntley, 15 N.Y.2d 72, 78, 255 N.Y.S.2d 838, 843, 204 N.E.2d 179, 183 (1965) (judge must find voluntariness beyond a reasonable doubt before the confession can be submitted to the jury); New York v. Valerius, 31 N.Y.2d 51, 334 N.Y.S.2d 871, 286 N.E.2d 254 (1972). Is voluntariness used in a technical sense? Was Miranda designed to avoid much of this kind of preliminary inquiry by requiring a detailed warning—including that of the right to have counsel appointed in case of need before further questions were put—in all cases as a predicate for admissibility?

5. Preferable practice in Federal courts, supported as convenient though not inexorably compelled and therefore less likely to be imposed upon State tribunals, calls for pretrial adjudication of objection when a litigant asserts unreasonable search and seizure as the ground for exclusion. Weeks v. United States, 232 U.S. 383, 387–388, 393, 396, 398 (1914). See F.R.Crim.Proc., Rule 41(e), 18 U.S.C.A. The pretrial hearing is before a judge sitting without jury. The expedient avoids retardation of the main trial by holding within it an independent subtrial; but the subtrial practice is allowed and usually followed with respect to reception of assertedly coerced confessions. See People v. Gerber, 43 Misc.2d 724, 252 N.Y.S.2d 167 (Cty. Ct.1964). Stimulated by the discussion of In re Fried, 161 F.2d 453, 457 et seq., 1 A.L.R.2d 996, 1001 et seq. (2d Cir.), cert. dismissed, 332 U.S. 807 (1947), a fair number of federal decisions reported from the lower courts use pretrial determinations in confession cases. A pretrial determination adverse to the government permits it to appeal before trial—an option denied if the verdict is for defendant under the double jeopardy clause. 18 U.S.C. § 3731.

6. New York places the burden of proof on the defendant who challenges, on grounds of illegal seizure, the admissibility of physical evidence. People v. Berrios, 28 N.Y.2d 361, 321 N.Y.S.2d 884, 270 N.E.2d 709 (1971). The defendants in Berrios protested the admissibility of envelopes containing heroin, claiming they had been obtained by an unlawful search. In disputing police statements that the envelopes had been dropped by defendants when police approached them, the defendants and the New York County District Attorney urged a change in the New York rule to avoid encouraging police fabrication.

The New York Court of Appeals rejected this plea with respect to what it referred to as "these 'dropsey' cases," 28 N.Y. at 365, 321 N.Y.S.2d at 886, placing upon the person who contends he is aggrieved the burden of proving the wrong:

The People must, of course, always show that police conduct was reasonable. Thus, though a defendant who challenges the legality of a search and seizure has the burden of proving illegality, the People are nevertheless put to "the burden of *going forward* to show the legality of the police conduct in the first instance (People v. Malinsky, 15 N.Y.2d 86, 91, n. 2, 262 N.Y.S.2d 65, 209 N.E.2d 694)" [emphasis in original]. These considerations require that the People show that the search was made pursuant to a valid warrant, consent, incident to a lawful arrest or, in cases such as those here, that no search at all occurred because the evidence was dropped by the defendant in the presence of the police officer.

28 N.Y. at 367, 321 N.Y.S.2d at 888–889. (Emphasis in original.)

Judge Fuld vigorously dissented: "Underlying the Fourth and Fourteenth Amendments is the basic proposition that 'no man is to be convicted on unconstitutional evidence.' (Mapp v. Ohio, 367 U.S. 643, 657, 81 S.Ct. 1684, 1692) In light of the situation as it today exists, the present rule—which imposes upon the accused the burden of proving the illegality of a seizure on a motion to suppress—subverts this principle by making it possible for some defendants to be convicted on evidence obtained in violation of constitutional guarantees. This follows from the fact that a trial judge who is unsure whether the prosecution's account of the seizure is credible must, nevertheless, resolve his doubt in favor of the People and admit the evidence. To thus increase the likelihood of a conviction on proof of dubious constitutionality must be stamped as highly unreasonable and unfair. A change in the rule [shifting the burden to the State] will help assure that a defendant's constitutional rights will not be violated since, by placing the burden on the People, the judge will be permitted to suppress evidence in cases where, for instance, he finds the testimony of each side evenly balanced on the scales of credibility and is unable to make up his mind as to who is telling the truth." 28 N.Y. at 370–71, 321 N.Y.S.2d at 891.

When a search and seizure is based upon consent, the New York courts have held that the burden of proof "rests heavily upon the People to establish the voluntariness of that waiver of a constitutional right." People v. Whitehurst, 25 N.Y.2d 389, 391, 306 N.Y.S.2d 673, 674, 254 N.E.2d 905, 906 (1969). Both the federal and some state courts have held that the prosecution must bear the burden of justifying a warrantless seizure of evidence. See, e.g., Bumper v. North Carolina, 391 U.S. 543, 548–549 (1968); United States v. Nolan, 420 F.2d 552 (5th Cir.1969), cert. denied, 400 U.S. 819 (1970); Abt v. Superior Ct., 1 Cal.3d 418, 82 Cal.Rptr. 481, 462 P.2d 10 (1969).

7. See American Law Institute, Proposed Official Draft No. 1 of the Model Code of Pre–Arraignment Procedure (1972):

Section SS 290.3. Challenge to Evidence of Reasonable Cause

(1) Contesting Evidence for Issuance of Warrant.

(a) Subject to the provisions of paragraph (b), in any proceeding on a motion to suppress evidence seized by authority of a search warrant, or incidental to an arrest made by authority of an arrest warrant, the moving party shall be entitled to contest, by cross-examination or offering evidence, the good faith of any testimony presented to the issuing authority and relied on to establish reasonable cause for issuance of the warrant.

(b) The moving party shall be allowed to make the contest authorized in paragraph (a) only upon preliminary motion, supported by affidavit, setting forth substantial basis for questioning the good faith of the testimony, and such party shall have the burden of proving the lack of good faith.

(2) Contesting Evidence for Officer's Determination of Reasonable Cause. In any proceeding on a motion to suppress evidence wherein authority for the seizure is based on an officer's determination that he had reasonable cause to arrest, search, or seize as the case may be, the moving party shall be entitled to contest, by cross-examination or offering evidence, the reasonableness of the officer's reliance upon the information.

How persuasive is the argument that the magistrate's ex parte investigation will be of such a high caliber that the burden should be placed on the defendant? See Id. at pp. 222 ff; United States v. Halsey, 257 F.Supp. 1002 (S.D.N.Y.1966). Will the requirement in (1)(b) of a "motion" supported by an affidavit setting forth "substantial basis for questioning" make it difficult for the defendant to challenge before trial the truth of evidence supporting reasonable cause, bearing in mind that an officer will normally be the affiant and will probably not talk to the defense counsel; that the informer's name will usually not be available; that grand jury testimony will not be shown to defense counsel; that a transcript of discussions between the issuing magistrate and the officer will not exist; and that, since the officer will not yet have testified, material under Section 3500 of Title 18 of the United States Code or its equivalent will not be shown to defense counsel? Supporting information may become available during the course of the trial because the affiant will probably be a witness and the informer's name may well become available in connection with a substantive issue. At this point the motion will be made. See Weinstein, Some Aspects of Search and Seizure Doctrine, 44 N.Y.S.Bar J. 298 (1972).

The critical information needed for this kind of proof will almost always come from the government. To what extent does this limited accessibility make unfair any burden of proof on the defendant? Cf. Kastigar v. United States, 406 U.S. 441, 92 S.Ct. 1653, 32 L.Ed.2d 212 (1972). The majority held that an "affirmative duty" on the prosecution to demonstrate that it had obtained its evidence from an independent source would suffice to protect the Fifth Amendment rights of a witness compelled to give grand jury testimony and later brought to trial. Justice Marshall, dissenting, argued that even this relatively heavy burden is not enough in light of the lack of countervailing evidence facing defendant when the burden of going forward shifts to him. Can the prosecution sustain its initial burden with a "mere assertion"?

United States v. Fatico

United States District Court, Eastern District of New York, 1978.
458 F.Supp. 388, aff'd, 603 F.2d 1053 (2d Cir.1979), cert. denied, 444 U.S. 1073, 100 S.Ct. 1018, 62 L.Ed.2d 755 (1980).

■ WEINSTEIN, DISTRICT JUDGE.

In view of prior proceedings, see United States v. Fatico, 441 F.Supp. 1285, 1287 (E.D.N.Y.1977), reversed, 579 F.2d 707 (2d Cir.1978), the key question of law now presented is what burden of proof must the government meet in establishing a critical fact not proved at a criminal trial that may substantially enhance the sentence to be imposed upon a defendant. There are no precedents directly on point.

The critical factual issue is whether the defendant was a "made" member of an organized crime family.

. . .

C. Burden of Proof

1. The Continuum

a. Burdens in General

We begin with the caution of Justice Brennan in Speiser v. Randall, 357 U.S. 513, 520–21, 78 S.Ct. 1332, 1339, 2 L.Ed.2d 1460 (1958), about the crucial nature of fact finding procedures:

> To experienced lawyers it is commonplace that the outcome of a lawsuit— and hence the vindication of legal rights—depends more often on how the factfinder appraises the facts than on a disputed construction of a statute or interpretation of a line of precedents. Thus the procedures by which the facts of the case are determined assume an importance fully as great as the validity of the substantive rule of law to be applied. And *the more important the rights at stake, the more important must be the procedural safeguards surrounding those rights.* (Emphasis supplied.)

> The "question of what degree of proof is required . . . is the kind of question which has traditionally been left to the judiciary to resolve. . . ." Woodby v. Immigration & Naturalization Serv., 385 U.S. 276, 284, 87 S.Ct. 483, 487, 17 L.Ed.2d 362 (1966).

> Broadly stated, the standard of proof reflects the risk of winning or losing a given adversary proceeding or, stated differently, the certainty with which the party bearing the burden of proof must convince the factfinder.

In re Ballay, 157 U.S.App.D.C. 59, 73, 482 F.2d 648, 662 (1973).

As Justice Harlan explained in his concurrence in In re Winship, 397 U.S. 358, 370, 90 S.Ct. 1068, 1075–76, 25 L.Ed.2d 368 (1970), the choice of an appropriate burden of proof depends in large measure on society's assessment of the stakes involved in a judicial proceeding.

> [I]n a judicial proceeding in which there is a dispute about the facts of some earlier event, the factfinder cannot acquire unassailably accurate knowledge of what happened. Instead, all the factfinder can acquire is a belief of what probably happened. The intensity of this belief—the degree to which a factfinder is convinced that a given act actually occurred—can, of course, vary. In this regard, a standard of proof represents an attempt to instruct the factfinder concerning the degree of confidence our society thinks he should have in the correctness of factual conclusions for a particular type of adjudication. Although the phrases "preponderance of the evidence" and "proof beyond a reasonable doubt" are quantitatively imprecise, they do communicate to the finder of fact different notions concerning the degree of confidence he is expected to have in the correctness of his factual conclusions. (Emphasis in original.)

Thus, the burden of proof in any particular class of cases lies along a continuum from low probability to very high probability.

. . .

b. Preponderance of the Evidence

As a general rule, a "preponderance of the evidence"—more probable than not—standard is relied upon in civil suits where the law is indifferent as between plaintiffs and defendants, but seeks to minimize the probability of error.

> In a civil suit between two private parties for money damages, for example, we view it as no more serious in general for there to be an erroneous verdict in the defendant's favor than for there to be an erroneous verdict in the plaintiff's favor. A preponderance of the evidence standard therefore seems peculiarly appropriate for, as explained most sensibly, it simply requires the trier of fact "to believe that the existence of a fact is more probable than its nonexistence before [he] may find in favor of the party who has the burden to persuade the [judge] of the fact's existence."

In re Winship, 397 U.S. 358, 371–72, 90 S.Ct. 1068, 1076, 25 L.Ed.2d 368 (1970) (Harlan concurring) (footnotes omitted). Quantified, the preponderance standard would be 50 + % probable. United States v. Schipani, 289 F.Supp. 43, 56 (E.D.N.Y.1968), aff'd, 414 F.2d 1262 (2d Cir.1969)... But cf. M. Finkelstein, Quantitative Methods in Law, 59–78 (1978) (equalization of errors between parties may require higher probability than minimization of errors—i.e., more than 50 + %).

The preponderance of the evidence test has also been used to determine the admissibility of evidence under the constitutional exclusionary rules.

. . .

See generally, Saltzburg, Standard of Proof and Preliminary Questions of Fact, 27 Stan.L.Rev. 271, 305 (1975) (suggesting that the Court's Lego rule be altered to provide that the beyond a reasonable doubt standard be substituted for the preponderance standard "whenever the defendant can demonstrate a need for protection that overrides any countervailing concerns of the criminal justice system.").

After sentencing, the defendant does not retain the opportunity to relitigate some questions that he has after an adverse pre-trial determination. In addition, in the case before us, the facts critical to sentencing are hardly collateral; they cut to the heart of the defendant's liberty. ... Since the factual determination of the sentencing judge is final, the defendant deserves substantial protection, including a burden of proof higher than that used in negligence cases.

c.   Clear and Convincing Evidence

In some civil proceedings where moral turpitude is implied the courts utilize the standard of "clear and convincing evidence"—a test somewhat stricter than preponderance of the evidence.

. . .

Where proof of another crime is being used as relevant evidence pursuant to rules 401 to 404 of the Federal Rules of Evidence, the most common test articulated is some form of the "clear and convincing" standard. ... A panel of the Ninth Circuit has even suggested a beyond a reasonable doubt test. United States v. Testa, 548 F.2d 847, 851 n. 1 (9th Cir.1977). The Second Circuit applies a preponderance of the evidence test. See United States v. Leonard, 524 F.2d 1076, 1090–91 (2d Cir.1975); United States v. Kahan, 572 F.2d 923, 932 (2d Cir.1978). These standards are designed to give defendants added protection not fully afforded by Rules 403 and 404. Since the crimes are merely evidence of intermediate propositions, not material elements of a crime being tried or of a sentence, there is theoretically no reason why any burden must be met as long as Rule 401's test of relevancy is satisfied—that is, the evidence has any tendency to make the material proposition "more probable or less probable than it would be without the evidence." See United States v. Schipani, 289 F.Supp. 43, 56 (E.D.N.Y.1968), aff'd, 414 F.2d 1262 (2d Cir.1969). The organized crime charge before us is more akin to a material proposition than to an intermediate evidentiary proposition. The line of cases dealing with other crime evidence is, therefore, not useful in determining an appropriate burden of proof on sentencing.

Quantified, the probabilities might be in the order of above 70% under a clear and convincing evidence burden.

d.   Clear, Unequivocal and Convincing Evidence

"[I]n situations where the various interests of society are pitted against restrictions on the liberty of the individual, a more demanding standard is frequently imposed, such as proof by clear, unequivocal and convincing evidence." In re Ballay, 157 U.S.App.D.C. 59, 73, 482 F.2d 648, 662 (1973). The Supreme Court has applied this stricter standard to deportation proceedings, see Woodby v. Immigration & Naturalization Serv., 385 U.S. 276, 285–86, 87 S.Ct. 483, 487–88, 17 L.Ed.2d 362 (1966), denaturalization cases, see Baumgartner v. United States, 322 U.S. 665, 64 S.Ct. 1240, 88 L.Ed. 1525 (1944); Chaunt v. United States, 364 U.S. 350, 81 S.Ct. 147, 5 L.Ed.2d 120 (1960), and expatriation cases, see Gonzales v. Landon, 350 U.S. 920, 76 S.Ct. 210, 100 L.Ed. 806 (1955); Nishikawa v. Dulles, 356 U.S. 129, 78 S.Ct. 612, 2 L.Ed.2d 659 (1958). In Woodby, the Court explained:

> To be sure, a deportation proceeding is not a criminal prosecution. But it does not syllogistically follow that a person may be banished from this country upon no higher degree of proof than applies in a negligence case. This Court has not closed its eyes to the drastic deprivations that may follow when a resident of this country is compelled by our Government to forsake all the bonds formed here and go to a foreign land where he often has no contemporary identification.

Supra, 385 U.S. at 285, 87 S.Ct. at 487–88 (citations omitted). See Friendly, Some Kind of Hearing, 123 U.Pa.L.Rev. 1267, 1296–97 (1975). In terms of percentages, the probabilities for clear, unequivocal and convincing evidence might be in the order of above 80% under this standard. See section II(C)(3) infra.

e.   Proof Beyond a Reasonable Doubt

The standard of "proof beyond a reasonable doubt" is constitutionally mandated for elements of a criminal offense. Mullaney v. Wilbur, 421 U.S. 684, 95 S.Ct. 1881, 44 L.Ed.2d 508 (1975); In re Winship, 397 U.S. 358, 364, 90 S.Ct. 1068, 25 L.Ed.2d 368 (1970). Cf. Gagnon v. Scarpelli, 411 U.S. 778, 789 n. 12, 93 S.Ct. 1756, 1763 n. 12, 36 L.Ed.2d 656 (1973) (because a probationer or parolee is "already-convicted," proof beyond a reasonable doubt standard not needed in revocation hearing). Writing for the majority in Winship, Justice Brennan enumerated the "cogent reasons" why the " 'reasonable-doubt' standard plays a vital role in the American scheme of criminal procedure" and "is a prime instrument for reducing the risk of convictions resting on factual error." Id. at 363, 90 S.Ct. at 1072.

> The accused during a criminal prosecution has at stake interest of immense importance, both because of the possibility that he may lose his liberty upon conviction and because of the certainty that he would be stigmatized by the conviction. Accordingly, a society that values the good name and freedom of every individual should not condemn a man for commission of a crime when there is reasonable doubt about his guilt. As

we said in Speiser v. Randall, supra, 357 U.S., at 525–526, 78 S.Ct., at 1342: "There is always in litigation a margin of error, representing error in fact finding, which both parties must take into account. Where one party has at stake an interest of transcending value—as a criminal defendant his liberty—this margin of error is reduced as to him by the process of placing on the other party the burden of . . . persuading the factfinder at the conclusion of the trial of his guilt beyond a reasonable doubt. Due process commands that no man shall lose his liberty unless the Government has borne the burden of . . . convincing the factfinder of his guilt."

. . .

Moreover, use of the reasonable-doubt standard is indispensable to command the respect and confidence of the community in applications of the criminal law. It is critical that the moral force of the criminal law not be diluted by a standard of proof that leaves people in doubt whether innocent men are being condemned.

Id. at 363–64, 90 S.Ct. at 1072–73. See generally, Underwood, The Thumb on the Scales of Justice: Burdens of Persuasion in Criminal Cases, 86 Yale L.J. 1299 (1977).

In capital cases, the beyond a reasonable doubt standard has been utilized for findings of fact necessary to impose the death penalty after a finding of guilt. See Gregg v. Georgia, 428 U.S. 153, 164, 96 S.Ct. 2909, 2921, 49 L.Ed.2d 859 (1976); Jurek v. Texas, 428 U.S. 262, 269, 96 S.Ct. 2950, 2955, 49 L.Ed.2d 929 (1976).

Many state courts, in interpreting state recidivism statutes, have held that proof of past crimes must be established beyond a reasonable doubt. See, e.g., ... Note, The Constitutionality of Statutes Permitting Increased Sentences for Habitual or Dangerous Criminals, 89 Harv.L.Rev. 356, 383 n. 140 (1975) (citing these and other cases).

In civil commitment cases, where the stakes most resemble those at risk in a criminal trial, some courts have held that the beyond a reasonable doubt standard is required.

. . .

If quantified, the beyond a reasonable doubt standard might be in the range of 95 + % probable. . . .

2.   Preponderance Standard of the "Dangerous Special Offenders" Act.

Only "a preponderance of the information" produced at a hearing after a plea or finding of guilt is needed to prove that a defendant is a "dangerous special offender" as a basis for an enhanced sentence. 18 U.S.C. § 3575(b). Sentences up to twenty-five years may follow such a finding. 18 U.S.C. § 3575(b). See generally, United States v. Bowdach, 561 F.2d 1160, 1171 (5th Cir.1977).

The statute provides three categories of factual predicates.

1.   Two previous felony convictions, imprisonment for one of these felonies, and less than five years elapsed between the commission of the present felony and the defendant's release from imprisonment or his commission of the last previous felony.

2.   Triggering offense part of a criminal pattern of conduct which provided a substantial source of income to the defendant, and in which he manifested special skill or expertise.

3. Triggering offense a conspiracy, or in furtherance of a conspiracy, involving three or more other persons in a pattern of criminal conduct initiated, organized, planned, financed, directed, managed, or supervised by defendant or bribe or force used.

18 U.S.C. § 3575(e). The facts required to be proved are technically defined. A substantial source of income is, for example, the minimum wage for a forty-hour, fifty-week year.

One reason this statute probably was not relied upon by the Government is that it is doubtful that it could demonstrate that the defendant fits within any of the three precise categories the statute prescribes. A more important reason is that notice must be given "a reasonable time" before trial or plea. 18 U.S.C. § 3575(a). This requirement is designed to advise defendant of the risk he runs should he plead guilty. See Federal Rules of Criminal Procedure, Rule 11(c)(1). Given the evidence against him and the prior hung jury, had he been faced with a twenty-five year sentence it is doubtful that this defendant would have pled guilty. This conclusion is suggested by eleventh-hour motions defendant, Daniel Fatico, and his brother, Carmine, have made to withdraw their pleas of guilt on the ground that,

> Had the Government made ... an announcement ... that they intended to establish that I was a high-ranking member of Organized Crime, I would not have pled guilty, but would have instead defended myself at a trial, where formal rules of evidence and procedure prevailed.

These motions were denied. More than a year, an appeal, and a full evidentiary hearing followed the original pleas. Under these circumstances, disappointment over the extent of a sentence that is within statutory limits is not a proper ground for setting aside a plea of guilt. ...

By not proceeding under the statute, the Government has also deprived the defendant of the considerable procedural protections it affords. See United States v. Stewart, 531 F.2d 326, 332 (6th Cir.), cert. denied, 426 U.S. 922, 96 S.Ct. 2629, 49 L.Ed.2d 376 (1976). "[T]he Act provides far more due process protection for a convicted offender at a hearing on an enhanced sentence than is required in normal criminal prosecutions in either state or federal jurisdictions.... " United States v. Ilacqua, 562 F.2d 399, 403 n. 7 (6th Cir.1977). We need not, therefore, consider the constitutional validity of the portion of the statute that might apply to defendant. ...

3. Higher Sentence Based on Proof of a Fact Not Established in Criminal Trial.

In 1967 the Supreme Court decided Specht v. Patterson, 386 U.S. 605, 87 S.Ct. 1209, 18 L.Ed.2d 326. Specht had been convicted for taking indecent liberties, under a Colorado statute that carried a maximum sentence of 10 years. A separate statute, the Sex Offenders Act, provided that if the trial court was "of the opinion that [a] ... person (convicted of specified sex offenses), if at large, constitutes a threat of bodily harm to members of the public, or is an habitual offender and mentally ill," he might receive an indeterminate sentence of from one day to life. Characterizing the invocation of the Colorado Sex Offenders Act as "the making of a new charge leading to criminal punishment," the Court held that the defendant must be afforded substantial due process. Id. at 610, 87 S.Ct. at 1212.

> Due process, in other words, requires that he be present with counsel, have an opportunity to be heard, be confronted with witnesses against him, have the right to cross-examine, and to offer evidence of his own. And there must be findings adequate to make meaningful any appeal that is allowed.

Id.

More recently, the Second Circuit in an opinion by Judge Friendly, decided a case similar to Specht involving a New York sex offender statute. Hollis v. Smith, 571 F.2d 685, 688 (2d Cir.1978). Unlike the Colorado statute, New York's did not, on its face, require proof of a new fact before imposition of the indeterminate sentence. Rather, it "simply enlarged the court's sentencing discretion without any standards whatever ..." from a maximum of five years to a maximum of life. Id. at 688. The state courts, however, had interpreted the statute to require a psychiatric study and finding that the defendant is a danger to society or is capable of benefiting from confinement.

In Hollis v. Smith, the Second Circuit determined that due process requires proof of the critical fact at issue by "clear, unequivocal and convincing evidence." 571 F.2d 685, 695–96 (2d Cir.1978). It found the evidence relied upon for the longer sentence did not measure up to that standard and granted a writ of habeas corpus.

In the instant case, proof by the Government that the defendant is a member of organized crime was not established in the criminal trial. As in Hollis, proof of this critical fact will result in a substantially longer period of incarceration. But, unlike Hollis, proof of the fact is not a previously defined prerequisite to a longer sentence. This difference, however, is of little consequence and Judge Friendly did not base his holding on it.

[T]he potential unfairness to defendant may be equally as great when an increase in sentence is based on facts not specified by the legislature as when the legislature has specifically delineated standards.

. . .

Note, The Constitutionality of Statutes Permitting Increased Sentences for Habitual or Dangerous Criminals, 89 Harv.L.Rev. 356, 375 (1975).

Following what we believe to be the letter and spirit of Hollis, and the need to protect critical rights of liberty, we hold that when the fact of membership in organized crime will result in a much longer and harsher sentence, it must be established by "clear, unequivocal and convincing evidence." Cf. Note, Burdens of Proof at Sentencing, 66 Geo.L.J. 1515 (1978) (clear and convincing). Since this is a federal conviction, not a habeas corpus proceeding, we need not determine whether this holding rests on due process, as Judge Friendly suggests, or upon the judicial responsibility to properly administer litigation. Woodby v. Immigration & Naturalization Serv., 385 U.S. 276, 284, 87 S.Ct. 483, 487, 17 L.Ed.2d 362 (1966).

It is important to note that we do not hold that this standard of proof is fixed for all possible disputed facts at sentencing. Where the sentencing judge will give a matter only slight weight, a preponderance standard might be suitable. In some instances, for example, a dispute may arise about how much support a defendant gave an estranged wife and, since the matter might require an extensive and bitter hearing, some rough approximation based on 50 + % probabilities will normally satisfy everyone. Cf. United States v. Sneath, 557 F.2d 149, 150 (8th Cir.1977) (collateral issue on sentence does not require "trial-type inquiry"). If the defendant challenges what the judge regards as a peripheral issue, the normal practice is for the court to state that it will assume defendant's version for the purposes of sentencing. At the other end of the spectrum, where there is a dispute about a recent serious felony conviction, ease of proof suggests that the court should require proof beyond a reasonable doubt if its existence will enhance the sentence. Cf. United States v. Tucker, 404 U.S. 443, 92 S.Ct. 589, 30 L.Ed.2d 592 (1972).

Flexibility is even reflected in the standard charge on reasonable doubt "a doubt sufficient to cause a prudent person to hesitate to act in the most important affairs of his life." Holt v. United States, 218 U.S. 245, 254, 31 S.Ct. 2, 6–7, 54 L.Ed. 1021 (1910); 1 E.J. Devitt and C.B. Blackmar, Federal Jury Practice and Instructions § 11.14, p. 310 (4th ed. 1977). The charge gives the trier considerable freedom to require greater probability for more important issues. As Professor Friedman sensibly observed, confirming what judges see happening in the courtroom:

> [J]udges and jurors alike must be "satisfied" of the truth of allegations or denials of fact. What amounts to satisfaction will vary with the issues involved. The more trivial the question, the more easily and swiftly will satisfaction materialize. The more momentous and serious its consequences, the greater the caution and deliberation demanded, that is, the greater the amount of cogent evidence before there can be any "satisfaction" about where the truth lies.

Friedman, Standards of Proof, 33 Can.Bar Rev. 665, 670 (1955).

The issue of membership in an organized crime family may be even more important than a prior conviction—and problems of proof are much more difficult. Considering the need to avoid extended sentencing hearings, the standard suggested by the Second Circuit in Hollis is appropriate. As indicated below, most judges in this district would place the probabilities of a "beyond a reasonable doubt" standard lower than would this court and would not find the Hollis test particularly high. For this and other reasons, this court believes a "beyond a reasonable doubt" burden more consonant with the tradition of American due process. Based on cases in this Circuit, however, Hollis probably articulates the highest burden acceptable to the Court of Appeals. Any lower standard under the circumstances would be imprudent. Kadish, Legal Norm and Discretion in the Police and Sentencing Process, 75 Harv.L.Rev. 904, 923 (1962). "The moral force of the criminal law [should] not be diluted by a standard of proof that leaves men in doubt whether innocent men are being condemned." In re Winship, 397 U.S. 358, 364, 90 S.Ct. 1068, 1072, 25 L.Ed.2d 368 (1970). As Chief Judge Cardozo so aptly put the matter: "[T]he genius of our criminal law is violated when punishment is enhanced in the face of a reasonable doubt as to the facts leading to enhancement." People v. Reese, 258 N.Y. 89, 179 N.E. 305, 308 (1932).

Professor Underwood, in a recent article cites a number of studies suggesting that judges, as well as laymen, will not always make the fine distinctions between preponderance, clear and convincing, clear unequivocal and convincing, and beyond a reasonable doubt described in this and other opinions. The Thumb on the Scales of Justice: Burdens of Persuasion in Criminal Cases, 86 Yale L.J. 1299, 1311 (1977). Those interviewed placed the probability standard higher than would be expected on theoretical grounds for a preponderance and somewhat lower than might be expected for beyond a reasonable doubt, indicating a narrower range in which to insert the two intermediate burdens.

> [A]lmost a third of the responding judges put "beyond a reasonable doubt" at 100%, another third put it at 90% or 95%, and most of the rest put it at 80% or 85%. For the preponderance standard, by contrast, over half put it between 60% and 75%. Questionnaires sent to jurors and students produced slightly lower results for the reasonable doubt instruction, and rather higher results for the preponderance standard; still, for most people the distinction was clear.

(Footnotes omitted). But cf. H. Kalven, Jr. and H. Zeisel, The American Jury, 187 (1966) ("the jury takes more generously than the judge the law's admonition not to convict unless guilt is proved beyond a reasonable doubt"); W.B. Fairley and F. Mosteller, Statistics and Public Policy, 182 (1977) (Harvard Business School students; "very high probability" and "practically certain" have median quantitative meaning of 90%, but distributions show "practically certain" "is generally a higher number.").

A survey of district judges in the Eastern District of New York indicates the following assessment of probabilities:

Probabilities Associated with Standards of Proof
Judges Eastern District of New York

Judge	Preponderance	Clear and Convincing	Clear, Unequivocal and Convincing	Beyond a Reasonable Doubt
1	50 + %	60–70%	65–75%	80%
2	50 + %	67%	70%	76%
3	50 + %	60%	70%	85%
4	51%	65%	67%	90%
5	50 + %	Standard is Elusive and Unhelpful		90%
6	50 + %	70 + %	70 + %	85%
7	50 + %	70 + %	80 + %	95%
8	50.1%	75%	75%	85%
9	50 + %	60%	90%	85%
10	51%	Cannot Estimate Numerically		

This wide variation confirms the wisdom of Maimonides, who justified the high probability requirement in criminal cases partly on the ground that some triers would tend to shave the barriers to a finding of guilt. He wrote:

> The 290th commandment is the prohibition to carry out punishment on a high probability, even close to certainty.... Do not think this law unjust. For among contingent things some are very likely, other possibilities are very remote, and yet others are intermediate. The "possible" is very wide. Had the torah permitted punishment to be carried out when the possibility is very likely—such that it is almost a necessity ... *some might inflict punishment when the chances are somewhat more distant than that, and then when they are even further still, until they would punish and execute people unjustly on slight probability according to the judge's imagination.* Therefore, the Almighty shut this door and commanded that no punishment be carried out except where there are witnesses who testify that the matter is established in certainty beyond any doubt, and, moreover, it cannot be explained otherwise in any manner. If we do not punish on very strong probabilities, nothing can happen other than that a sinner be freed; but if punishment be done on probability and opinion it is possible that one day we might kill an innocent man—and it is better and more desirable to free a thousand sinners, than ever to kill one innocent.

Maimonides, Safer HaMitzvot, Negative Commandment 290, quoted in N.L. Rabinovich, Probability and Statistical Inference in Ancient and Medieval Jewish Literature, 111 (1973) (emphasis supplied). The view, abhorring punishment on the basis of suspicion, is common among societies which respect the rule of law. According to Professor Sandy Zabell, Professor of Statistics at the University of Chicago, the earliest reference he has found in non-religious legal literature is in the Digest:

> The Divine Trajan stated in a Rescript to Assiduus [sic] Severus: "It is better to permit the crime of a guilty person to go unpunished than to condemn one who is innocent."

Justinian, Digest, 48.19.5 (collected in 9 S.P. Scott, The Civil Law 110 (1932)) (Trajan ruled A.D. 98–117)).

If, as suggested earlier in discussing the standard of "clear, unequivocal and convincing evidence," the probability is about 80%, it means we would rather have four cases decided in error against the Government than more than one against the defendant. If, in the case of proof "beyond a reasonable doubt," the figure of 95% or 99% is used, it means that we would rather have, respectively, twenty or one hundred guilty persons go free than more than one innocent person be convicted. Blackstone would have put the probability standard for proof "beyond a reasonable doubt" at somewhat more than 90%, for he declared: "It is better that ten guilty persons escape than one innocent suffer." W. Blackstone, The Law of England, Book the Fourth, Chapter 27, p. 358 (T. Wait and Co., Portland 1807). Undoubtedly both Blackstone and Maimonides had capital offenses in mind—where a mistake was generally not correctable.

The high probability required in criminal cases, however, does not mean that most guilty people who are tried are acquitted. In almost all cases the guilt is so clear or the doubt so great that precise quantification is of no moment. In some few instances—which this court would roughly estimate on the basis of experience as no more than one in ten cases—it may make a difference whether the trier's perception of the standard is 80, 90, 95, or 99%.

The standard can never be set at certainty or 100% probability, because

> Time is irreversible, events unique, and any reconstruction of the past at best an approximation. As a result of this lack of certainty about what happened, it is inescapable that the trier's conclusions be based on probabilities.

Maguire, et al., Cases and Materials on Evidence 1 (6th ed. 1973). Setting the standard at 100% in order to avoid any chance of convicting the innocent would thus result in a zero conviction rate and acquittal of all the guilty. As Professor Posner points out:

> If the standard of proof is set at so high a level that the probability of an innocent person's being convicted is zero, the conviction rate for guilty people will also be zero, since only with a zero conviction rate can all possibility of an innocent person's being convicted be eliminated.

Posner, An Economic Approach to Legal Procedure and Judicial Administration, 2 J. of Legal Studies 399, 411 (1973).

Quantification of these standards has not been well developed for reasons not now relevant. ... Cf. 9 J.H. Wigmore, Evidence (3rd Ed.1940), § 2497, p. 325 ("no one has yet invented or discovered a mode of measurement for the intensity of human belief"). But cf. 1 J. Bentham, Rationale of Judicial Evidence, ch. VI, 71 ff (1827) (importance of quantitative numerical scale in expressing degrees of persuasion); T. Starkie, Law of Evidence, 753–54 (9th Am.Ed. by G. Sharswood 1869) (notion that "moral probabilities could ever be represented by numbers ... and thus subjected to arithmetical analysis, cannot but be regarded as visionary and chimerical;" but analysis developed at p. 756; adopts "maxim of law ... that it is better that ninety-nine (i.e. an indefinite number of) offenders should escape, than that one innocent person should be condemned"); 1 W.M. Best, Law of Evidence, 97 (1st Am.Ed. by J.A. Morgan, 1878) (Bentham's suggestion "fantastic," quoting criticism by Dumont, French translator of Bentham). Nevertheless, there is little doubt that utilizing one rather than the other of the four burdens discussed in this opinion will make a difference in the results in some cases.[1]

III. FACTS APPLIED TO LAW

The testimony originally proffered by the Government would not have proved by a preponderance, and certainly not by "clear, unequivocal and convincing evidence," that defendant is a "made" member of the Gambino family. Montello and Llauget are hardly model witnesses. They have extensive criminal records, long histories of association with organized crime, and for some years they have been supported by the Government in its witness protection program. All of this leaves their credibility in doubt. Moreover, even if believed, much of their testimony is equivocal. The bulk of their specific testimony centered on the Fatico–Llauget–Dellacroce "sit-down." Montello was not a party to this meeting. Even if the "sit-down" occurred just as Llauget indicated, it is hardly conclusive of membership in the Gambino family. Attendance at the Gambino wake is also of little probative value. Nor is the 1966 arrest of Carmine Fatico for consorting with known criminals highly probative of his brother's alleged membership in the Gambino family. Finally, Daniel Fatico's arrest record for such activities as burglary, bookmaking, policy, illicit manufacture of alcohol and running a disorderly house is ambiguous on the issue of organized crime; it is often the hallmark of an incompetent individual hoodlum.

When viewed with the other evidence introduced at the sentencing hearing, however, a much more compelling case is made out. The fact that seven different government agents, four of them from the FBI, relying on a total of seventeen independent informants, testified that Daniel Fatico was a member of the Gambino family, is, in the court's view, highly probative. Even if one or several of these experienced agents miscalculated the reliability of an informant, the large number of agents and informants, greatly reduces the margin for error. There are also the independent police observations of the defendant and his associates consorting with criminals. The sheer magnitude of this proof offsets to some extent the enormous handicap placed upon the defendant by the Government's nonproduction of any of the informants and its withholding of material crucial to effective cross-examination. While we must remain dubious of any conclusions based upon hearsay, the Government's proof here meets the rigorous burden of "clear, unequivocal and convincing evidence." The probability is at least 80% that defendant is an active member of an organized crime family.

Conclusion

. . . .

Were it not for the organized crime issue, defendant would have been sentenced in the hijacking case to no more than a three year term, concurrent with the gambling sentence. This is in conformity with standard practice favoring concurrency. See A.B.A. Proj. on Standards for Criminal Justice, Sentencing Alternatives and Procedures § 3.4(iv) at pp. 171–72 (1968). A three year concurrent sentence would take into account defendant's age, health problems, close and stable family relationships, and the fact that because his prior convictions in the state courts have almost without exception been punished by relatively small fines and probations, this is his first major taste of

---

1. Commonwealth v. Sullivan, 20 Mass. App.Ct. 802, 482 N.E.2d 1198 (1985), reversed a conviction on the ground that trial judge's attempt at qualification of reasonable doubt was improper. [Footnote by eds.]

incarceration. In addition, the maximum penalty is five years and defendant is entitled to some consideration for his plea of guilty.

Based on the evidence presented at the sentencing hearing, the court concludes that defendant is a member of the Gambino crime family. It sentences him to a prison term of four years to be served consecutively with the three year sentence for gambling. This new sentence is necessary for purposes of incapacitation to protect the public from further criminal conduct by the defendant, a recidivist and member of a dangerous group of well-organized criminals.

Under normal Parole Board practice, without a finding of organized crime, the Probation Department estimated that defendant would have been subject to Parole Guidelines of twelve to sixteen months for the gambling conviction. See guideline Application Manual, United States Parole Commission Research Unit Report Sixteen (November 1977) (Adopted by the Commission as Appendix 4 United States Parole Commission Manual—May 1, 1978). He probably would have been kept in a medium or low security prison in Danbury, Connecticut or Allenwood, Pennsylvania, where he could be conveniently visited by his family. In about a year he probably would have been released to a half-way house in New York City where he would have been able to work during the day, see his family each evening, and spend weekends at home.

Given the finding of organized crime and the consecutive sentences, the chances of early parole are reduced to the vanishing point. Defendant will probably spend some six years in a penitentiary even with time off for good behavior. He will probably be sent to a secure facility such as Atlanta. Within the prison he will be treated as a person with dangerous potential, probably finding it more difficult to obtain furloughs and other privileges. In short, the result of the finding of organized crime membership will probably be five extra years of hard service in a high security prison far from his family.

NOTES

1. Is Fatico consistent with Lego v. Twomey? Fatico was decided by the same judge who wrote the opinion in Schipani, criticized in Lego v. Twomey, supra. Does Fatico suffer from the same defect, if it is one, referred to in the Court's footnote? The problem becomes much more important under Federal Sentencing Guideline procedures. Why?

2. Illustrative of how a variety of considerations may cause burdens to vary even with respect to a relatively narrow area of the law is the situation in the post-conviction remedy field. See, e.g., United States v. Keogh, 440 F.2d 737 (2d Cir.1971) (when the habeas corpus claim is nondeliberate prosecutorial non-disclosure at trial and the defense had made no request for disclosure but hindsight revealed that the defense could have put the evidence to significant use, the petitioner must show a substantially higher probability that disclosure of evidence would have altered the result than where non-disclosure was deliberate). If a petition for habeas corpus is based upon claimed denial of the effective assistance of counsel, some federal courts have held that the petitioner need only show a prima facie case to shift the burden to the state to prove lack of prejudice. See, e.g., Fields v. Peyton, 375 F.2d 624 (4th Cir.1967) (plea half hour after appointment of counsel); Commonwealth v. Clark, 279 A.2d 41 (Pa.1971) (on a claim of denial of right of speedy trial, the claimant's uncontradicted testimony of a seven year interval between indictment and trial raised a prima facie showing of resultant harm, thus shifting to the state the burden of affirmatively proving absence of prejudice). Cf. Pitts v. State of North Carolina,

395 F.2d 182 (4th Cir.1968) (delay of almost 16 years between initiation of prosecution and trial was a delay of such magnitude that it was not the defendant who was required to bear the burden of showing prejudice resulting from delay but the State which had to carry the burden of proving that accused suffered no serious prejudice beyond that which ensues from ordinary and inevitable delay). But cf. Jones v. Wainwright, 490 F.2d 1222, 1226 (5th Cir.1974) (the presumption of prejudice should not be applied where delay was purely "that an important witness was absent at the delayed trial, the absence is unexplained, the content of the witness's testimony is unknown, and there exists a possibility, but only a possibility, that the testimony might have been favorable to the accused"); Powell v. United States, 352 F.2d 705 (D.C.Cir. 1965) (defendant bears the burden of establishing prejudice as a result of delay). See in general Note, Constitutional Right to a Speedy Trial: The Element of Prejudice and the Burden of Proof, 44 Temp.L.Q. 310 (1971); Note, The Right to a Speedy Trial, 20 Stan.L.Rev. 476 (1968).

Judge Godbold in Speedy Trial–Major Surgery for a National Ill, 24 Ala.L.Rev. 265, 283–84 (1972) writes (footnotes omitted):

> The most substantial problem generated by the prejudice requirement involves the allocation of the burden of proof. As might be expected from the generally cautious and restrictive approach which the courts have taken towards speedy trial claims, this obligation has been imposed upon the accused, and the courts have required concrete evidence to meet it ... [I]n cases where the accused contends that his ability to defend himself was impaired, the burden of proof may be crucial. Although the disappearance of witnesses may be subject to proof, demonstrating their materiality may be difficult and "measur[ing] the cost of delay in terms of dimmed memories of the parties and available witnesses" may be almost impossible. In some instances, however, the rigors of this requirement have been mitigated. Moved by such factors as intentionally dilatory prosecution tactics or extremely protracted delays, the courts have either required the prosecution to prove the absence of prejudice or, in what amounts to the same thing, have presumed the existence of prejudice.

In Barker v. Wingo, 407 U.S. 514 (1972), the court held that a defendant's constitutional right to a speedy trial can be determined only by an ad hoc balancing test weighing the conduct of prosecutor and defendant, and considering factors such as length and reason for delay, the defendant's assertion of his right in lower courts, and prejudice to the defendant. There is some loose language used by the Court as to the effect of a delay: "The length of the delay is to some extent a triggering mechanism. Until there is some delay which is presumptively prejudicial there is no necessity for inquiry into the factors that go into the balance." 407 U.S. at 530. One commentator has concluded that a shift in the "vital burden" was unintended by the Court:

> Rather it is likely that the choice of the term "presumptively prejudicial" in the duration of the discussion was simply inadvertent. Probably the court meant to say simply that a claim of denial of speedy trial may be heard after the passage of a period of time which is prima facie, unreasonable in the circumstances.

Uviller, Barker v. Wingo: Speedy Trial Gets a Fast Shuffle, 72 Colum.L.Rev. 1376, 1384–85 (1972). See also, Amsterdam, Speedy Criminal Trial, Rights and Remedies, 27 Stan.L.Rev. 525 (1975), Rudstein, The Right to a Speedy Trial: Barker v. Wingo in the Lower Federal Courts, [1975] U.Ill.L.F. 11.

NOTES ON BURDEN IN CIVIL CASES

1. Theoretically, where the burden of proof is defined as "more probable than not," and where an issue is contested by the introduction of conflicting evidence, it is only when, in the trier's estimation, the case rests on the knife edge of doubt between more and less probable than not that the location of the burden can affect the outcome. In fact, the burden almost always has much more impact. Lawyers, whatever the articulation of the test, devote much time and ingenuity to seeing that the burden is placed on their opponent. See, e.g., Forman, The Burden of Proof [in Tax Cases], 39 Taxes 737 (1961); Comment, Burden of Proof in Priority Problems, 10 Baylor L.Rev. 42 (1958). James in his article, Burdens of Proof, 47 Va.L.Rev. 51–52, 54 (1961) sums up the view of the most thoughtful of the analysts such as Wigmore, Morgan and Michael when he says of the persuasion burden:

> Wherever in human affairs a question of the existence or non-existence of a fact is to be decided by somebody, there is the possibility that the decider, or trier of the fact, may at the end of his deliberations be in doubt on the question submitted to him. On all the material before him, he may, for example, regard the existence or non-existence of the fact as equally likely—a matter in equipoise. If, now, the trier is operating under a system which requires him to decide the question one way or the other, then to avoid caprice that system must furnish him with a rule for deciding the question when he finds his mind in this kind of doubt or equipoise. Where the parties to a civil action are in dispute over a material issue of fact, then that party who will lose if the trier's mind is in equipoise may be said to bear the risk that the trier will not be affirmatively persuaded or the risk of nonpersuasion upon that issue. . . . [A] more meaningful and accurate statement would require the jury to believe that the existence of a fact is more probable than its nonexistence before they may find in favor of the party who has the burden to persuade the trier of the fact's existence.

2. Civil cases involving allegations of moral turpitude frequently require a higher degree of proof than the ordinary case. In Weise v. Red Owl Stores, Inc., 175 N.W.2d 184 (Minn.1970), a fraud allegation required "clear and convincing evidence." A conspiracy to commit fraud allegation called for "clear and convincing" proof in O'Brien v. Larson, 521 P.2d 228 (Wash.App.1974). In Basic Chemicals, Inc. v. Benson, 251 N.W.2d 220 (Iowa, 1977) "substantial evidence" was required to prove that there was a conspiracy to misappropriate trade secrets and to engage in unfair competition. In Crocker v. United States, 130 Ct.Cl. 567, 127 F.Supp. 568, 572 (1955), "well nigh irrefragable proof" was needed (and supplied) to prove bad faith on the part of a government official who discharged a subordinate. An attorney disciplinary proceeding required "convincing proof to a reasonable certainty" in Medoff v. State Bar, 71 Cal.2d 535, 550, 78 Cal.Rptr. 696, 706, 455 P.2d 800, 810 (1969); a similar test was applied in an action to remove a judge, McComb v. Commission on Judicial Performance, 19 Cal.3d Spec. Trib. Supp. 1, 138 Cal.Rptr. 459, 564 P.2d 1 (1977) (the court rejected the application of In re Winship to the proceeding since the grounds for the removal of the judge did not require proof of criminal misconduct). But see Matter of Robson, 575 P.2d 771 (Alaska1978) which held that a preponderance of the evidence was sufficient to suspend an attorney; In re Lieberman, 125 N.E.2d 328 (Ohio1955) (same).

Similarly, a heavier burden may be required where the consequences of a victory are harsh. In a deportation hearing the government must show "clear, unequivocal, and convincing evidence," for it is impermissible for a person to be "banished from this country upon no higher degree of proof that applies in a negligence case." Woodby v. Immigration and Naturalization Service, 385 U.S. 276, 285 (1966). In Woodby, the Court pointed out the practical flexibility of a theoretically rigid standard by noting: "This standard of proof applies to all deportation cases, regardless of the length of time the alien has resided in this country. It is perhaps worth pointing out, however, that, as a practical matter, the more recent the alleged events supporting deportability, the more readily the Government will generally be able to prove its allegations by clear, unequivocal and convincing evidence." Id. at 266, n. 19. See also Addington v. Texas, 441 U.S. 418 (1979) (civil proceeding under state law to involuntarily commit an individual to a state hospital for an indefinite period must meet "clear and convincing" standard for this particularly important individual interest); In re Eichner, 73 A.D.2d 431, 426 N.Y.S.2d 517 (2d Dept.1980) ("clear and convincing evidence" that an unconscious patient is terminally ill and is in permanent vegetative coma "with extremely remote probability of regaining cognitive brain function" is necessary prerequisite to denying medical treatment).

3.   There seems to be sharp disagreement among some of the commonwealth authorities about whether allegations in a civil case which constitute elements of a criminal offense should be proved beyond a reasonable doubt. See Cohen, Allegation of Crime in a Civil Action: Burden of Proof, 20 U. of Toronto Faculty Law Review 20, 34 (1962). The overwhelming majority of decisions in this country require no greater measure of persuasion for such an allegation in a civil action than for other allegations. See Groom, Proof of Crime in a Civil Proceeding, 13 Minn.L.Rev. 556 (1929). Allen v. Illinois, 478 U.S. 364 (1986), a proceeding to have a person declared dangerous was not criminal for self incrimination purposes, but did require proof beyond a reasonable doubt. See also Sedima, S.P.R.L. v. Imrex Co., Inc., 473 U.S. 479 (1985).

Constitutional substantive policy may require a heavier burden as in a libel action to which the actual malice standard applies, where the burden is one of "clear and convincing" evidence. Anderson v. Liberty Lobby, Inc., 477 U.S. 242 (1986).

What should be the standard in determining whether an alien is entitled to political asylum? Compare INS v. Stevic, 467 U.S. 407, 429 (1984) (prosecution more likely than not under 8 U.S.C. § 243(h)) with Carcamo–Flores v. INS, 805 F.2d 60, 64 (2d Cir.1986) ("well founded fear" under 8 U.S.C. § 208(a)). See I.N.S. v. Cardoza Fonseca, 480 U.S. 421 (1987) ("well founded fear" does not require proof by preponderance of prosecution in home country).

4.   In will contest cases, where a stranger in a fiduciary capacity is a principal beneficiary and natural objects of bounty are excluded, the beneficiary has "the obligation of disproving, by a clear preponderance of evidence, the exertion of undue influence by him." Berkowitz v. Berkowitz, 162 A.2d 709, 710 (Conn. 1960). Cf. In re Estate of Button, 328 A.2d 480, 484 n. 7 (Pa.1974) (to avoid a will on grounds of undue influence "requires proof greater than a mere preponderance, . . . but less than beyond a reasonable doubt. . . .").

" 'He who attempts to establish title to property through a gift inter vivos as against the estate of a decedent takes upon himself a heavy burden which he must support by evidence of great probative force . . . ,' " the court noted in Matter of Estate of Kaminsky, 17 A.D.2d 690, 230 N.Y.S.2d 954 (3d Dept.1962). Is such a ruling based upon policy or an assumption that people are unlikely to make gifts? In this case the court indicated its skepticism about the alleged gift when it wrote: "It is difficult to conceive that a frugal widow already aged, beset with disease and injury, possessed of relatively small income and confronted with an obviously long period of expensive hospitalization would have been so improvident as to make the gifts contended for." Has the burden of proof problem been confused here with the problem of assessing probabilities?

5. The difficulties of obtaining proof to substantiate a claim or defense are often reflected in the instructions on burden of persuasion. The lapse of time between the events and the trial, led one court to require plaintiff to produce "clear and concise" proof in Detroit & Toledo Shore Line Railroad Co. v. United States, 105 F.Supp. 182 (N.D.Ohio 1952). In re Garrett's Estate, 94 A.2d 357, 359 (Pa.1953), saw claims on the estate made twenty-two years after the intestate's death. The court placed a "heavy" burden on the claimants for "... unlike Tennyson's brook the Garrett estate cannot go on forever ..."

See Noseworthy v. City of New York, 298 N.Y. 76, 80, 80 N.E.2d 744, 746 (1948) (finding that plaintiff, the estate of a dead victim of an accident, may prevail on a lesser degree of proof because the dead victim is unavailable to testify). In Schechter v. Klanfer, 28 N.Y.2d 228, 321 N.Y.S.2d 99, 269 N.E.2d 812 (1971), the New York Court of Appeals extended the Noseworthy rule by holding that an amnesiac plaintiff suing for negligence bears a lesser burden of persuasion in showing freedom from contributory negligence. To avoid the danger that amnesia would be feigned, the court held:

> Plaintiff has the burden of proof on the issue of amnesia as on other issues. A jury should be instructed that before the lesser burden of persuasion is applied, because of the danger of shamming, they must be satisfied that the evidence of amnesia is clear and convincing, supported by the objective nature and extent of any other physical injuries sustained, and that the amnesia was clearly a result of the accident.

See also Sawyer v. Dreis & Krump Mfg. Co., 67 N.Y.2d 328, 502 N.Y.S.2d 696, 493 N.E.2d 920 (1986); 1 N.Y. Pattern Jury Instructions 1:62 (1974); Stevens Linen Associates Inc. v. Mastercraft Corp., 656 F.2d 11, 14 (2d Cir.1981) ("We believe the district court erred in failing to award Stevens compensatory damages. In establishing lost sales due to sales of an infringing product, courts must necessarily engage in some degree of speculation.").

6. John Santosky II v. Kramer, 455 U.S. 745, 755–770 (1982) (footnotes omitted; emphasis in original):

> Standards of proof, like other "procedural due process rules[,] are shaped by the risk of error inherent in the truth-finding process as applied to the *generality of cases,* not the rare exceptions." Mathews v. Eldridge, 424 U.S., at 344 (emphasis added). Since the litigants and the factfinder must know at the outset of a given proceeding how the risk of error will be allocated, the standard of proof necessarily must be calibrated in advance. Retrospective case-by-case review cannot preserve fundamental fairness when a class of proceedings is governed by a constitutionally defective evidentiary standard.
>
> . . .
>
> In parental rights termination proceedings, the private interest affected is commanding; the risk of error from using a preponderance standard is substantial; and the countervailing governmental interest favoring that standard is comparatively slight. Evaluation of the three Eldridge factors compels the conclusion that use of a "fair preponderance of the evidence" standard in such proceedings is inconsistent with due process.

. . .

[T]he first Eldridge factor—the private interest affected—weighs heavily against use of the preponderance standard at a State-initiated permanent neglect proceeding.

. . .

Under Mathews v. Eldridge, we next must consider both the risk of erroneous deprivation of private interests resulting from use of a "fair preponderance" standard and the likelihood that a higher evidentiary standard would reduce that risk. See 424 U.S., at 335.

. . .

At such a proceeding, numerous factors combine to magnify the risk of erroneous factfinding. . . . Because parents subject to termination proceedings are often poor, uneducated, or members of minority groups, . . . such proceedings are often vulnerable to judgment based on cultural or class bias.

The State's ability to assemble its case almost inevitably dwarfs the parents' ability to mount a defense.

. . .

[Third, u]nlike a constitutional requirement of hearings, see, e.g., Mathews v. Eldridge, 424 U.S., at 347, or court-appointed counsel, a stricter standard of proof would reduce factual error without imposing substantial fiscal burdens upon the State. As we have observed, 33 States already have adopted a higher standard by statute or court decision without apparent effect on the speed, form, or cost of their factfinding proceedings.

. . .

A majority of the States have concluded that a "clear and convincing evidence" standard of proof strikes a fair balance between the rights of the natural parents and the State's legitimate concerns. . . . We hold that such a standard adequately conveys to the factfinder the level of subjective certainty about his factual conclusions necessary to satisfy due process.

7. One writer lists the following standards used in civil cases: "clear;" "clear and satisfactory;" "convincing;" "clear and convincing;" "clear, satisfactory and convincing;" "clear, cogent and convincing;" "clear, unequivocal and convincing;" "strong;" "strong and convincing;" "very clear;" "very clear and satisfactory;" "very clear and decisive;" and suggests as a research project that all the cases be examined on a "national" scale so that "the word or phrase used the greatest number of times to describe the degree of proof required in one particular type of case would be selected as the true standard for that particular type of case." Morse, Evidentiary Lexicology, 59 Dick.L.Rev. 86 (1954).

Compare with the foregoing the potent suggestions of Friedman, Standards of Proof, 33 Can.Bar Rev. 665, 670 (1955): ". . . [J]udges and jurors alike must be 'satisfied' of the truth of allegations or denials of fact. What amounts to satisfaction will vary with the issues involved. The more trivial the question, the more easily and swiftly will satisfaction materialize. The more momentous and serious its consequences, the greater the caution and deliberation demanded, that is, the greater amount of cogent evidence before there can be any 'satisfaction' about where the truth lies."

For an interesting discussion by Judge Jones of the derivation and meaning of the terms "clear and convincing" and of the "mishmash" of precedents, as well as of the counter-intuitive result that proof of deceit requires clear and convincing evidence, while punitive damages requires a preponderance, see Riley Hill Gen. Contr. v. Tandy Corp., 737 P.2d 595 (Or.1987).

8. The proponent may bear different burdens of proof on different issues in his case. For example, in Ramsey v. United Mine Workers, 401 U.S. 302 (1971), where coal mine operators accused the defendant union of violating the Sherman Antitrust Act by conspiring to drive them out of business, the Supreme Court held that under the Norris–LaGuardia Act the plaintiffs bore a statutory burden of "clear proof" only in proving union authorization or ratification of individual member acts. Once this was shown, only a preponderance of evidence was necessary to prove the union's violation of the Sherman Act. In Basic Chemicals Inc. v. Benson, 251 N.W.2d 220, 230, 232 (Iowa 1977), a preponderance of the evidence was sufficient to prove that the plant's chemical company's former president had misappropriated trade secrets and engaged in unfair competition, while "substantial evidence" was required to prove a conspiracy existed among the former president and competing chemical companies.

Is it possible for neither party to have the burden of persuasion? See Alaska v. 45,621 Square Feet of Land, 475 P.2d 553 (Alaska 1970) (in condemnation proceedings neither the landowner nor the state bore the burden of proving the fair market value of the condemned property; since the state constitution guaranteed just compensation, the jury's sole concern was to determine that amount).

9. See Gold: Causation in Toxic Torts: Burdens of Proof, Standards of Persuasion, and Statistical Evidence, 96 Yale L.J. 376, 378–79 (1986):

> [T]he use of statistical proof of causation has created confusion between the substantive burden of proof and the standard of persuasion which must be met to satisfy the burden. Formerly the "fact" of causation (burden) had to be supported by a "preponderance of the evidence" (standard). "Preponderance" was defined probabilistically: the jury had to be persuaded that the fact was "more likely than not" true. But in toxic torts, the statistical causation evidence is also expressed probabilistically—as a factual estimate of the defendant's contribution to the plaintiff's risk. The failure to distinguish between the two kinds of probability has led to the collapse of the factual burden and preponderance standard into a single test: does the factual probability of causation exceed 50%? The result ... is that the standard of persuasion loses its meaning. Furthermore, this "collapsing" works hidden doctrinal changes and encourages the application of simple-minded quantitative rules and narrow limits on evidence. [It is desirable to adopt] an approach which minimizes these consequences and, compared to either the status quo or other reform proposals, better meets diverse and sometimes conflicting tort law goals. It suggests adapting to the problems of toxic tort causation by (1) considering a broad range of evidence; (2) distinguishing clearly between burdens of proof (statistical probability as the fact being proven) and standards of persuasion (probabilities of belief); (3) replacing the]50% rule with a substantial factor test; and (4) allowing discounted recoveries to reflect uncertainty.

The author characterizes his third proposal as "Gestalt award discounting."

10. American Hospital Supply Corporation v. Hospital Products Limited, 780 F.2d 589, 593 (7th Cir.1986) (Posner, J.):

> [G]rant the preliminary injunction if but only if $P \times H_p > (1 - P) \times H_d$, or, in words, only if the harm to the plaintiff if the injunction is denied,

multiplied by the probability that the denial would be an error (that the plaintiff, in other words, will win at trial), exceeds the harm to the defendant if the injunction is granted, multiplied by the probability that granting the injunction would be an error. That probability is simply one minus the probability that the plaintiff will win at trial; for if the plaintiff has, say, a 40 percent chance of winning, the defendant must have a 60 percent chance of winning, $(1.00 - .40 = .60)$. The left-handed side of the formula is simply the probability of an erroneous denial weighted by the cost of denial to the plaintiff, and the right-handed side simply the probability of an erroneous grant weighted by the cost of grant to the defendant.

COMMITTEE OF SUPREME COURT JUSTICES, JUDICIAL CONFERENCE, NEW YORK PATTERN JURY INSTRUCTIONS (1965)

PJI 1:23 Burden of Proof

The burden of proof rests on the plaintiff. That means that it must be established by a fair preponderance of the credible evidence that the claim plaintiff makes is true. The credible evidence means the testimony or exhibits that you find to be worthy to be believed. A preponderance means the greater part of such evidence. That does not mean the greater number of witnesses or the greater length of time taken by either side. The phrase refers to the quality of the evidence, that is, its convincing quality, the weight and the effect that it has on your minds. The law requires that, in order for the plaintiff to prevail, the evidence that supports his claim must appeal to you as more nearly representing what took place than that opposed to his claim. If it does not, or if it weighs so evenly that you are unable to say that there is a preponderance on either side, then you must resolve the question in favor of the defendant. It is only if the evidence favoring the plaintiff's claim outweighs the evidence opposed to it that you can find in favor of plaintiff. (Footnote omitted.)

Anderson v. Chicago Brass Co.

Supreme Court of Wisconsin, 1906.
127 Wis. 273, 106 N.W. 1077.

[Action for personal injuries. From a judgment for defendant, plaintiff appeals.]

■ WINSLOW, J. . . . The serious questions in the case arise upon the charge of the court and the special verdict. The court charged the jury on the subject of burden of proof and preponderance of the evidence as follows:

"I shall use the term 'burden of proof' in connection with these instructions, and by burden of proof I mean that it is incumbent on the party affirmatively asserting an allegation to establish it by a fair preponderance of the credible evidence, facts, and circumstances proven on the trial. And by 'preponderance of evidence,' as I have used the term, is meant the greater convincing power of evidence. That is, in the trial of a lawsuit that side has furnished the preponderance of evidence which has produced evidence of greater convincing power in the minds of the jury than that produced by the other side. And when the law imposes upon a party the burden of proof it means that such party is bound to produce evidence in support of the proposition involved of greater convincing power than that produced by the other side. Such convincing power of evidence is not necessarily determined by the number of witnesses, for it may be that the testimony given by one witness has greater convincing power than that given by several witnesses contradicting or tending to contradict that given by the one."

The definition thus given of the term "preponderance of the evidence" was substantially correct, but not so with the definition of "burden of proof." It is well settled by a long series of decisions in this court that the party upon whom rests the burden of proof does not lift that burden by merely producing a preponderance of evidence. He may produce a preponderance, that is, he may produce evidence of a slightly greater convincing power to the mind than that produced by his opponent, but still his evidence may be weak and leave the mind in doubt. In order to entitle himself to a finding in his favor his evidence must not only be of greater convincing power, but it must be such as to satisfy or convince the minds of the jury of the truth of his contention. This idea, in some definite and certain form, must be given to the jury or the instruction will be incomplete and erroneous.... This idea was nowhere given to the jury in the charge before us, and the omission was fatal....

By the Court: Judgment reversed, and action remanded for a new trial.

NOTES

1. In Logeman Brothers Co. v. R.J. Preuss Co., 1111 N.W. 64 (Wis.1907), counsel attacked a charge drawn in accord with the decision in the principal case as "self-contradictory, illogical, misleading, and therefore erroneous." But the court was not swayed by this argument. See Mr. Wigmore's biting comment, "a wondrous cobweb of pedantry is here woven to occupy the jury's simple mind and the trial judge's tongue." 9 Wigmore, Evidence, § 2498, note 1 (3d ed. 1940).

2. Considerable conflict and confusion are to be found in the appellate search for an acceptable definition of the term.

One group of cases rejects the idea that a jury need only find the facts to be more probable than not. In Frazier v. Frazier, 89 S.E.2d 225, 235 (S.C.1955), the court declared: "A 'preponderance of the evidence' ... is that evidence which convinces us as to its truth." In Lampe v. Franklin American Trust Co., 96 S.W.2d 710, 723 (Mo.1936), the court in approving a trial judge's refusal to charge that the jury should find a fact if they believed it to be more probable than not, said: "They [the jury] must not attempt to base a verdict upon what facts may be 'more probable', if they cannot decide what facts are true". See Comment, Instructions to the Jury on Damages in Civil Cases in Missouri, 5 St. Louis U.L.J. 411, 420–25 (1959); Note, Variable Verbalistics—The Measure of Persuasion in Tennessee, 11 Vanderbilt L.Rev. 1413 (1958). These statements in a charge obviously can not be taken literally by the jury. Will it mean to them that the court is requiring a very high degree of proof?

Another line of cases places its emphasis on probabilities. In Burnett v. Reyes, 118 Cal.App.2d Supp. 878, 880, 256 P.2d 91, 93 (1953), the court stated: "[T]he burden was upon the plaintiff to prove his case by preponderance of the evidence and [that] means that the greater probability lies in favor of the decision."; Big Butte Ranch Inc. v. Grasmick, 415 P.2d 48, 51 n. 2 (Idaho1966) (preponderance of evidence means "such evidence as, when weighed with that opposed to it, has more convincing force and from which it results that the greater probability of truth lies therein"); Cruz v. Drezek, 397 A.2d 1335, 1339 (Conn.1978) (requiring a "reasonable belief that is more probable than otherwise that the fact or issue is true"); Scherling v. Kilgore, 599 P.2d 1352, 1359 (Wyo.1979) (preponderance of the evidence means "proof which leads trier to find that existence of contested fact is more probable than its non-existence.").

See also the discussion of Smith v. Rapid Transit, Inc., 58 N.E.2d 754 (Mass. 1945), supra.

3. One error that must not be committed is to give the jury the impression that there is some proprietary right to evidence. "The court in its charge specifically quoted that evidence three separate times treating it solely as proof to support a finding of guilt through premeditation and deliberation. That evidence, however, also had a real bearing upon the question of defendant's mental state, but the court did not specifically charge its relevance on the subject of insanity. From the court's instructions, the jurors might well have been led to conclude that that evidence offered by the People could properly be considered only as proof, on behalf of the prosecution, to point to defendant's guilt and support a conviction. They were not adequately apprised of the fact that the evidence adduced by the People may, by its very nature, have within it proof that defendant was not responsible for his actions." People v. Kelly, 302 N.Y. 512, 518, 99 N.E.2d 552, 554 (1951). See also Waynick v. Reardon, 72 S.E.2d 4, 7 (N.C.1952).

4. For interesting comments on the difficulty of conveying to the jury the correct idea of its task where a preponderance of the evidence is the guide, see Report of Proceedings on Trial by Jury, 11 U.Cin.L.Rev. 119, 195 (1937), which states that the result of an inquiry of jurors showed that preponderance of the evidence was one of the most difficult of all phrases used in instructions to understand; and see Judge Frank's discussion of the difficulties in Larson v. Jo Ann Cab Corp., 209 F.2d 929 (2d Cir.1954). See, also, Morgan, Instructing the Jury upon Presumptions and Burden of Proof, 47 Harv.L.Rev. 59 (1933); Morgan, Some Problems of Proof under the Anglo–American System of Litigation 82–85 (1956). McBaine in Burden of Proof: Presumptions, 2 U.C.L.A.L.Rev. 13, 19 (1954), suggests that the then Uniform Rules be amended to require extended charges on burdens.

For a study that focused on the different understanding between judges and jurors of the phrase "by a preponderance of the evidence," see Simon, Quantifying Burdens of Proof, 5 Law & Society Rev. 319, 325 (1971). Professor Simon found that when asking the two groups to express their beliefs in terms of numerical probabilities the jurors thought "preponderance of the evidence calls for a greater showing of probability than did the judges." See the discussion of this point in Fatico, supra.

NOTES ON INSTRUCTING JURIES IN CRIMINAL CASES

1. Judge May's statement, that the phrase, "beyond reasonable doubt" is not found in criminal prosecutions prior to the closing years of the eighteenth century, may be literally true. May, Some Rules of Evidence, 10 Am.L.Rev. 642, 656, 657 (1876). But Thayer has demonstrated that the idea has been consistently applied for centuries, citing Corpus Juris (4th century) and Coke's Third Institute among other authorities. Thayer, Preliminary Treatise on Evidence 558–559 (1898). See Slovenko, Establishing the Guilt of the Accused, 31 Tul.L.Rev. 173 (1956).

2. Whether intermediate evidentiary propositions must be proved beyond a reasonable doubt is the subject of conflicting decisions. People v. Klinkenberg, 90 Cal.App.2d 608, 632, 204 P.2d 47, 62 (1949) ("every fact in a chain of circumstances need not be proved beyond a reasonable doubt"); State v. Palumbo, 306 A.2d 793 (N.H.1973) (the decisive question is whether on all the evidence guilt has been established beyond a reasonable doubt); Commonwealth v. Petrisko, 275 A.2d 46, 49 (Pa.1971) ("[I]t is not necessary that each piece of evidence be linked to the defendant beyond a reasonable doubt. It is only necessary that each piece of evidence include [the defendant] in group who could be linked while excluding others, and that combination of evidence link [the defendant] to the crime beyond a reasonable doubt."); 9 Wigmore, Evidence § 2497 n. 7 (Chadbourn Rev.1981). As to the necessity of applying a like standard to every element of the offense charged, see Mullaney v. Wilbur, infra; State v. King, 256 N.W.2d 1 (Iowa 1977); People v. Newman, 46 N.Y.2d 126, 412 N.Y.S.2d 860, 385 N.E.2d 598 (1978); The American Law Institute, Model Penal Code, Tentative Draft No. 4, 7–8, 109 (1955). But cf. Patterson v. New York, infra.

3.   Some courts have declared that it is futile to attempt to explain "simple terms like 'reasonable doubt' so as to make them plainer.... Every attempt to explain them renders an explanation of the explanation necessary." Sherwood, J., in State v. Robinson, 23 S.W. 1066, 1069 (Mo.1893). In Rex v. Summers, C.Cr.A., [1952] 1 All.E.R. 1059, 1060, Lord Goddard advocates the abolition of the term stating: "I have never yet heard any court give a real definition of what is a 'reasonable doubt' and it would be much better if that expression was not used." The phrase is now apparently being abandoned in England. See R. v. Attfield, C.Cr.A., [1961] 3 All.E.R. 243, 247 ("the jury should be directed ... that the standard of proof required before a verdict of guilty can be returned is that the jury should be satisfied, that they should feel sure"); see also Cowen and Carter, Essays on the Law of Evidence, 245–249, 269–270 (1956); Cannon, Beyond Reasonable Doubt, 1961 Criminal L.Rev. (England) 235. Other courts have said that the trial judge may in his discretion refuse to explain the expression, United States v. Lawson, 507 F.2d 433 (7th Cir.1974), cert. denied, 420 U.S. 1004 (1975), but many have held that a failure to give "a clear and full instruction as to what is meant by the term" is reversible error. See, e.g., Friedman v. United States, 381 F.2d 155 (8th Cir.1967). Compare United States v. Gatzonis, 805 F.2d 72 (2d Cir.1986) (urging courts not to tell the jury that "the requirements of proof beyond a reasonable doubt operates on the whole case and not on the separate bits of evidence.").

There have been empirical studies of the effect on the jury of varying the instruction on the weight of the burden in a criminal case. One is the Jury Project at the London School of Economics reported in L.S.E. Jury Project, Juries and the Rules of Evidence, 1973 Crim.L.Rev. 208 (1973). It is briefly discussed in Underwood, The Thumb on the Scales of Justice: Burdens of Persuasion in Criminal Cases, 86 Yale L.J. 1299, 1309–1310 (1977); she notes that "[t]he result of [the study is] inconclusive, but [it suggests that] the instruction can affect the outcome of a case." Note the variation among judges described in the Fatico case, supra.

In California, the trial judge may find safety in sections 1096 and 1096a of the Penal Code. The former defines reasonable doubt thus: "It is not a mere possible doubt; because everything relating to human affairs, and depending on moral evidence, is open to some possible or imaginary doubt. It is that state of the case, which, after the entire comparison and consideration of all the evidence, leaves the minds of jurors in that condition that they cannot say they feel an abiding conviction, to a moral certainty, of the truth of the charge." Section 1096a provides that the court may read this to the jury and no further instruction defining reasonable doubt need be given. This statutory definition is taken from the charge of Chief Justice Shaw in Commonwealth v. Webster, 5 Cush. 295 (Mass.1850). Any variation on the instruction is likely to cause reversal. See, e.g., People v. Garcia, 54 Cal.App.3d 61, 126 Cal.Rptr. 275 (1975), cert. denied, 426 U.S. 911 (1976). In rejecting the California formulation, the Comments to the Model Penal Code declare: "No effort is made to define 'reasonable doubt,' in the view that definition can add nothing helpful to the phrase." American Law Institute: Model Penal Code, Tent.Draft No. 4, 109 (1955). For an acute criticism of the California definition see 9 Wigmore, Evidence 322 (3d ed. 1940).

SECTION 2.   PRESUMPTIONS AND RELATED SUBJECTS

The vast literature on presumptions treats many more details than is appropriate for a general course in evidence. Those wishing further exposure to the intricacies of the subject will find, in addition to discussions in the standard treatises, among the more comprehensive and illuminating articles, Morgan, Some Observations Concerning Presumptions, 44 Harv.L.Rev. 906 (1930); Morgan, Further Observations on Presumptions, 16 So.Calif.L.Rev. 245 (1943); McCormick, Charges on Presumptions and Burden of Proof, 5 N.C.L.Rev. 291 (1927); Cleary, Presuming and Pleading: An Essay on Juristic Immaturity, 12 Stan.L.Rev. 5 (1959); Ladd, Presumptions in Civil Actions, 1977 Ariz.St.L.J. 275 (1977); Mueller, Instructing the Jury Upon Presumptions in Civil Cases: Comparing Federal Rule 301 with Uniform Rule 301, 12 Land and Water L.Rev. 219 (1977); Finan, Presumptions and Modal Logic: A Hohfeldian Approach, 13 Akron L.Rev. 19 (1979); Louisell, Construing Rule 301: Instructing the Jury on Presumptions in Civil Actions and Proceedings, 63 Va.L.R. 281 (1977); Gordon and Tenebaum, Conclusive Presumption Analysis: The Principle of Individual Opportunity, 71 Nw.U.L.Rev. 579 (1977); Ladd, Presumptions in Civil Actions, 1977 Ariz.St.L.J. 275 (1977); Allen, Presumptions in Civil Actions Reconsidered, 66 Iowa L.Rev. 844 (1981); Allen, Structuring Decision-making in Criminal Cases: A Unified Constitutional Approach to Evidentiary Devices, 94 Harv.L.Rev. 321 (1981); Nesson, Rationality, Presumptions, and Judicial Comment: A Response to Professor Allen, 94 Harv.L.Rev. 1574 (1981); Allen, More on Constitutional Process-of-Proof Problems in Criminal Cases, 94 Harv.L.Rev. 1795 (1981).

Part of the difficulty with this subject is that the term presumption is used with different meanings.

1. Most text writers and many courts would define a presumption as a procedural rule requiring the court, once it concludes that the "basic" fact is established, to assume the existence of the "presumed fact" until the presumption is rebutted and becomes inoperative. Some of the theories on when and how a presumption is rebutted are mentioned below. It is generally agreed that a presumption always shifts the burden of producing evidence as to the presumed fact from the proponent to his opponent. For example, the unexplained absence of a person from his home for seven years gives rise to a presumption of death. If a widow suing on an insurance policy establishes the basic fact of unexplained absence the insurance company must come forward with evidence that the insured is not dead, or the presumed fact of the insured's death is treated as having been established. See, e.g., Tobin v. United States Railroad Retirement Board, 286 F.2d 480 (6th Cir.1961); Magers v. Western & Southern Life Insurance Co., 335 S.W.2d 355 (Mo.App.1960); 9 Wigmore Evidence (Chadbourn Rev.1981) § 2531a. As noted below some courts hold that a presumption shifts the burden of persuasion on the presumed fact as well as the burden of coming forward.

2. Courts and legislatures frequently use the term "irrebuttable presumption of law" or "conclusive presumption of law," as a euphemism in stating a rule of substantive law. They mean that once the basic fact is established the presumed fact must be assumed and evidence disproving it will not be considered. For example, in Wareham v. Wareham, 195 Cal.App.2d 64, 15 Cal.Rptr. 465 (1961), the ex-husband of the defendant was ordered to support a child of

the defendant's born eight and one half months after he moved out of the family domicile and filed for divorce, even though blood tests established that he could not have been the father. The court stated that a conclusive presumption of legitimacy applied whenever a wife was cohabiting with her husband at the time of possible conception. See People v. Thompson, 89 Cal.App.3d 193, 152 Cal.Rptr. 478 (1979) (upholding the application of the conclusive presumption stated in Cal.Evid.Code § 621; "[T]he issue of a wife cohabiting with her husband, who is not impotent or sterile, is conclusively presumed to be a child of the marriage," in a criminal prosecution for willful failure to support a son). Cf. In re Lisa R., 13 Cal.3d 636, 119 Cal.Rptr. 475, 532 P.2d 123, cert. denied, 421 U.S. 1014 (1975) (due process afforded alleged father, who never married the mother, standing to offer evidence that he was the natural father of a minor child, despite a statutory presumption that a child of a married woman is presumed to be legitimate). See generally 90 A.L.R.3d 1032 (1979) (standing of various persons to dispute the presumption of legitimacy of a child conceived or born during wedlock). Implicit in In re Lisa R. is the general proposition that like rules of substantive law conclusive presumptions are subject to the constitutional tests of due process and equal protection. See, e.g., Vlandis v. Kline, 412 U.S. 441 (1973) (held a conclusive statutory presumption of residency for university tuition purposes invalid as violative of due process). See generally, Gordon and Tenebaum, Conclusive Presumption Analysis: The Principle of Individual Opportunity, 71 N.W.U.L.Rev. (1977).

3. The term "permissive presumption" is sometimes used interchangeably with the term "inference." Thus, if the basic fact is established the trier of fact *may* infer the existence of the "presumed" fact. The difference between a presumption and inference was described as follows in State v. Corby, 145 A.2d 289, 293 (N.J.1958), overruled on other grounds, State v. Taylor, 217 A.2d 1, cert. denied, 385 U.S. 855 (1966):

> A presumption is an assumption of fact resulting from a rule of law which requires such fact to be assumed from another fact or set of facts. An inference is a deduction which may or may not be made from certain proven facts. The term "presumption" connotes that a force is accorded by law to a given evidential fact whereby the duty of producing further testimony is affected. An inference, however persuasive, does not affect the duty of producing testimony. A presumption is compulsory and *prima facie* establishes the fact to be true; it remains compulsory if it is not disproved. A presumption cannot be disregarded by the jury while an inference may or may not be, depending on the deductions made by the jury from all of the evidence. A presumption has a technical force or weight attached to it and the jury, in the absence of proof overcoming it, must find in accordance with it. An inference carries no such force as a matter of law. The jury is at liberty to find the ultimate fact one way or the other as they may be convinced by the testimony. In the one case, the law draws a conclusion from the evidence; in the other, the jury may draw the conclusion, depending upon how they view the impact of the proof. In short, a presumption is a mandatory deduction, born as a matter of law, while an inference is a permissive deduction which the reason of the jury may or may not reach without express direction of law.

Is this how the Supreme Court is dealing with the term in County Court of Ulster County v. Allen, 442 U.S. 140 (1979), infra, when it speaks of "permissive" rather than "mandatory" presumptions?

4. The term "prima facie" is sometimes used in the area of presumptions, particularly in statutes. Sometimes it is used in place of the term presumption as defined in paragraph 1, above. See, e.g., Cal.Evid.Code § 602, 630; cf. Me.R.Evid. 301(b) (prima facie evidence is said to create a presumption, and

such presumption shifts the burden of persuasion to the defendant). The draftsmen of the New York Civil Practice Law and Rules noted:

> The term "prima facie" has been substituted for "presumptive" throughout this title for reasons of consistency without intending any change in meaning. As used, the term means a presumption which shifts the burden of coming forward and not the burden of persuasion. It is rebutted when evidence contrary to the presumed fact sufficient to support a finding of its negative has been introduced.

N.Y.Adv.Comm. on Practice & Procedure, Second Prel.Rep., N.Y.Leg.Doc. No. 13, p. 267 (1958).

Often, however, "prima facie" is used in the sense of paragraph 3, above, to mean that the basic fact will, as a matter of law, permit an inference that the presumed fact exists—i.e., it permits the matter to go to the jury when it might find in the proponent's favor as to the basic fact.

In Rehm v. United States, 183 F.Supp. 157, 159–160 (E.D.N.Y.1960) the plaintiffs, seeking to recover on the basis of res ipsa loquitur, thought they were entitled to summary judgment because defendant offered no explanation of the occurrence. The court stated that plaintiff failed "to appreciate the procedural effects of the doctrine of res ipsa loquitur when held to apply in New York", which is merely to establish a prima-facie case of negligence by the defendant. It noted that

> the proper meaning of "prima-facie case" is that quantum of evidence tending to prove each material fact that a plaintiff must introduce to sustain his burden of going forward with the evidence, i.e. render himself immune from a nonsuit. With the evidence in this posture, the trier of the facts *may* reasonably find for the plaintiff by drawing the permissible inferences favorable to him. This does not mean that the plaintiff is entitled to a directed verdict or that the burden is shifted to the defendant. It merely means that the plaintiff has sustained his burden of going forward with the evidence.... A true presumption arises when the plaintiff establishes to the satisfaction of the fact-trier the basic facts which *require* a finding of the presumed fact. When a true presumption arises, the defendant must come forward and rebut the presumption or suffer a directed verdict....

5.   The applicability in an action of the rule of law which determines the connection between a basic fact and a presumed fact depends upon the establishment of the basic fact in that action. The basic fact is established if its existence is conceded by the parties in their pleadings or by stipulation or is judicially noticed by the judge. It may also be established by evidence. If the evidence is such that no reasonable trier of fact could fail to find the existence of the basic fact, the judge will either make the requisite finding or direct the jury to do so. If the evidence is not thus conclusive, the basic fact is not established until its existence is found by the trier of fact. Even if the presumption is rebutted, the basic fact continues to have its normal inferential value in permitting a finding as to the presumed fact.

UNIFORM RULES OF EVIDENCE

ARTICLE III. PRESUMPTIONS

Rule 301.

**PRESUMPTIONS IN GENERAL IN CIVIL
ACTIONS AND PROCEEDINGS**

(a) **Effect.** In all actions and proceedings not otherwise provided for by statute or by these rules, a presumption imposes on the party against whom it is directed the burden of proving that the nonexistence of the presumed fact is more probable than its existence.

(b) Inconsistent Presumptions. If presumptions are inconsistent, the presumption applies that is founded upon weightier considerations of policy. If considerations of policy are of equal weight neither presumption applies.

Rule 302.

APPLICABILITY OF FEDERAL LAW IN CIVIL CASES

In civil actions and proceedings, the effect of a presumption respecting a fact which is an element of a claim or defense as to which federal law supplies the rule of decision is determined in accordance with federal law.

Rule 303.

PRESUMPTIONS IN CRIMINAL CASES

(a) Scope. Except as otherwise provided by statute, in criminal cases, presumptions against an accused, recognized at common law or created by statute, including statutory provisions that certain facts are prima facie evidence of other facts or of guilt, are governed by this rule.

(b) Submission to Jury. The court is not authorized to direct the jury to find a presumed fact against the accused. If a presumed fact establishes guilt or is an element of the offense or negatives a defense, the court may submit the question of guilt or of the existence of the presumed fact to the jury, but only if a reasonable juror on the evidence as a whole, including the evidence of the basic facts, could find guilt or the presumed fact beyond a reasonable doubt. If the presumed fact has a lesser effect, the question of its existence may be submitted to the jury provided the basic facts are supported by substantial evidence or are otherwise established, unless the court determines that a reasonable juror on the evidence as a whole could not find the existence of the presumed fact.

(c) Instructing the Jury. Whenever the existence of a presumed fact against the accused is submitted to the jury, the court shall instruct the jury that it may regard the basic facts as sufficient evidence of the presumed fact but is not required to do so. In addition, if the presumed fact establishes guilt or is an element of the offense or negatives a defense, the court shall instruct the jury that its existence, on all the evidence, must be proved beyond a reasonable doubt.

NOTES

1. A number of states have refused to follow Federal Rule of Evidence 301. Some have adopted, instead, the Uniform Rule; others use a different approach for different presumptions; still others leave the matter to court interpretation as in Amodeo, supra. The provisions are collected in J.B. Weinstein & M. Berger, Weinstein's Evidence ¶ 301[04]. Is the California comprehensive approach treating different presumptions differently useful? See California Evidence Code, Division 5, Burden of Proof; Burden of Producing Evidence; Presumptions and Inferences. The California enumeration, lengthy as it is, is not exhaustive. See Cal.Evid.Code § 630, 660; Russell v. Pacific Grove, 54 Cal.App.3d 53, 60, 126 Cal.Rptr. 371, 375 (1975).

2. "In civil actions and proceedings, the effect of a presumption respecting a fact which is an element of a claim or defense as to which state law supplies the rule of decision is determined in accordance with state law." Fed.R.Evid. 302. Where a presumption is designed merely as a rule of convenience in proving an intermediate proposition, as in the case of establishing the receipt of a mailed letter, state law need not be applied. See also Berger, Privileges, Presumptions and Competency of Witnesses in the Federal Courts: A Federal Choice of Laws Rule, 42 Bklyn.L.Rev. 417 (1976); Mueller, Instructing the Jury Upon Presumptions in Civil Cases: Comparing Federal Rule 301 with Uniform Rule 301, 12 Land and Water L.Rev. 219, 272–77 (1977); Wellborn, The Federal Rule of Evidence and the Application of State Law in Federal Courts, 55 Tex.L.Rev. 371 (1977).

Hinds v. John Hancock Mutual Life Insurance Co.

Supreme Judicial Court of Maine, 1959.
155 Me. 349, 155 A.2d 721, 85 A.L.R.2d 703.

■ WEBBER, JUSTICE. Plaintiff is beneficiary of an insurance policy covering the life of his late father, Donald Hinds. The policy provides for payment of a death benefit of $9,000 and, in addition thereto, of a like sum in the event the death of the assured should be due to bodily injuries sustained solely through "violent, external and accidental means." Suit was brought in behalf of plaintiff, a minor, by Emily Hinds, his mother and legal guardian. It is not disputed that the death of the assured being shown, the plaintiff is entitled to recover the ordinary death benefit of $9,000. The jury, however, awarded double indemnity as reflected by a verdict of $18,000. Issues are raised both by general motion and exceptions.

At the outset it was stipulated that an analysis of the blood of the decedent, Donald Hinds, made shortly after his death, disclosed an alcoholic content of .267% by weight. During the presentation of the plaintiff's case, it was shown by competent medical and other testimony that the assured was found slumped unconscious in a chair at his kitchen table late in the evening; that he was removed to a hospital and died there without regaining consciousness; that the cause of death was a gunshot wound inflicted by a revolver fired while in contact with the skin in the region of the right temple; that the bullet pursued approximately a horizontal course through the head from right to left; that decedent was a "big man" over six feet tall and weighing about 200 pounds; that he was fifty years old and apparently in good health; that on a table at his right side were a revolver and an opened package of bullets; that there were present no cloths or other gun cleaning paraphernalia; that there were no outward or visible signs of any violent scuffle, quarrel or other disturbance on the premises; and that there were empty whiskey bottles near the decedent's body. The family physician, first to arrive at the scene, found Emily Hinds holding her husband's head. He described her as appearing confused and in a state of shock. Social and business friends gave testimony tending to negative any apparent motive for suicide. A medical expert stated that one in the decedent's state of intoxication would be confused, with his reactions markedly slow and his pain sensation diminished; that he would be unable to think clearly but would not be unconscious and would be able to "navigate" although not very steadily. Not one of the witnesses had ever before seen the decedent in this stage of intoxication. Emily Hinds, although inferentially an eyewitness to the tragedy, was not called by the plaintiff.

On this posture of the evidence, as will be shown, the plaintiff at the close of his main case had by no means offered sufficient proof of death by "accidental means." However, no request was made to the court to direct a verdict and we are satisfied that the election by counsel for the defendant to go forward with evidence stemmed largely from the uncertainty heretofore existing in this jurisdiction as to the evidentiary status of presumptions. We will have occasion to discuss this problem later in the opinion. Attention should first be given, however, to the evidence offered by the defendant.

The witness first called in defense was Emily Hinds. At the very beginning of her examination, she was asked if she was the widow of Donald Joseph Hinds. She then replied, "I refuse to *testify*, on the advice of counsel, on my constitutional right that it might tend to incriminate me." (Emphasis supplied.) She was then asked, "Do you consider that you would be incriminated by being the wife of Donald Joseph Hinds?" At this point the jury was ordered to retire and colloquy then ensued which resulted in a ruling by the presiding justice that the pending question and all further questions of this witness were *excluded* because of her claim of privilege. Defendant's counsel took no exception nor did he pursue the matter further with this witness. He next called a police officer who had investigated the death on the evening of its occurrence. This witness identified the gun which he had observed on the kitchen table as being a .22 caliber automatic pistol, designed to fire long rifle bullets. He testified that the broken box of ammunition scattered about the table contained short rifle bullets. The full box originally contained 50 cartridges, all of which were accounted for. The officer counted 47 cartridges on the table and found three in the gun, one of which had been fired. He further noted what appeared to be a few business papers scattered on the table. He noted the presence on the floor beside the table of two empty bottles, each designed to contain a fifth of a gallon of whiskey. He was permitted to testify that on the evening in question he had a conversation with Emily Hinds as to the events leading up to the shooting of her husband but, upon objection by the plaintiff, was not allowed to state the substance of that conversation. Thereupon, in the absence of the jury, the defendant made an offer to prove by the witness that Emily Hinds freely and voluntarily described to him the events of the evening which culminated when the decedent held the gun against his right temple and pulled the trigger. This proffered evidence was rejected by the court as hearsay. At this point the evidence on both sides was closed and the case submitted to the jury, with what result we have already noted.

In the case of Cox v. Metropolitan Life Ins. Co., 139 Me. 167, 28 A.2d 143, involving suit on a policy covering accidental death, our court recognized that the burden of proving accident rested upon the claimant throughout the trial and never shifted. The distinction is clearly made in Watkins v. Prudential Ins. Co., 1934, 315 Pa. 497, 173 A. 644, 649, 95 A.L.R. 869, 875, as "between suits on insurance policies like the one here sued on, which insure against death as a result 'of bodily injuries effected solely through external, violent and accidental means' and suits on those policies which insure against death but which contain a proviso avoiding the policy if the insured dies by his own act." As the court there pointed out, in the former situation the plaintiff has the unremitting burden of proof as to accident, whereas in the latter situation the plaintiff need only prove death while the defendant has from the inception the burden of proof as to suicide which is there raised as an affirmative defense. So in the case before us, the death of the insured person by violent and external means was conceded. The defendant by its pleadings having raised the issue, it remained for the plaintiff to prove by a fair preponderance of the whole evidence that those means were also accidental. . . .

The plaintiff in the first instance was aided by the so-called presumption against suicide. This presumption stems from and is raised by our common knowledge and experience that most sane men possess a natural love of life and an instinct for self-protection which effectively deter them from suicide or the self-infliction of serious bodily injury. It is commonly recognized that there is an affirmative presumption of death by accidental means which arises under appropriate circumstances from the negative presumption against suicide. Whether and to what extent the presumption persists in the face of contrary evidence is a matter of great and even decisive importance in the instant case.

Although a small minority of states adhere to an opposite view, it is now almost universally held that disputable presumptions are not themselves evidence nor are they entitled to be weighed in the scales as evidence. Rather are they recognized as "rules about evidence." They may be distinguished from inferences in that an inference is *permissible,* where as a presumption is *mandatory.* They compel a finding of the presumed fact in the absence of contrary evidence. They perform the office of locating the burden of going forward with evidence, but having performed that office they *disappear* in the face of countervailing evidence. . . .

The minority view that the presumption is itself evidence or has evidentiary weight has its adherents among the courts, some of which have felt constrained to that result by judicial interpretation of applicable statutes . . . No statute exists in Maine declaring that disputable presumptions are themselves evidence.

Although our own court has never found it necessary to contribute any extended academic discussion to the plethora of words which have been written on this controversial subject, we find no satisfactory indication from the language used, confusing though it may be, that our court has accepted the principle that presumptions are themselves evidence. . . . In determining whether evidence preponderates, the factfinder must of course scrutinize it in the light of common sense and common experience including the relative unlikelihood of criminal conduct. . . . Gratuitous expressions seeming to accord presumptions evidentiary weight in the scales were at best superfluous and at worst incorrect. We now hold unequivocally that presumptions serve their allotted procedural purpose but are not themselves evidence.

A far more difficult and troublesome question arises, however, in determining what quantum or quality of evidence is required to cause a rebuttable presumption to disappear. Conversely, to what extent will such a presumption persist in the fact of contrary evidence? And who is to evaluate that evidence, the trial judge or the jury? It is at this point that courts have gone their several ways and too often semantics have been substituted for logic. On the one hand is the risk that the jury may be confused by instructions relating to presumptions and may misapply them, especially by according to presumptions artificial evidentiary weight in the scales which they do not possess. On the other hand is the concern expressed by many writers of opinion and texts that if the presumption be regarded purely as a procedural tool *in the hands of the trial judge,* he will have in effect usurped the province of the jury as factfinder in determining the weight and credibility of such evidence as tends to negative the presumed fact. Efforts to reconcile these two desirable objectives have produced both compromise and confusion.

Many courts have adopted what is usually referred to as the Thayer theory of rebuttal which provides that disputable presumptions (other than the presumption of legitimacy) fall as a matter of law when evidence has been introduced which would support a finding of the nonexistence of the presumed fact. This rule has the virtue of uniformity and won approval in the American Law Institute, Model Code of Evidence, Rules 703 and 704. In the foreword of the Model Code, Professor Edmund M. Morgan, the reporter and a recognized authority in the field of evidence and procedure, makes this excellent analysis of the several views (page 55):

"As to the other consequences of the establishment of the basic fact, save only the basic fact of the presumption of legitimacy, the opinions reveal at least eight variant views, of which the following are the most important:

"1. The existence of the presumed fact must be assumed unless and until evidence has been introduced *which would justify a jury in finding the non-existence of the presumed fact.* When once such evidence has been introduced, the existence or non-existence of the presumed fact is to be determined exactly as if no presumption had ever been operative in the action; indeed, as if no such concept as a presumption had even been known to the courts. *Whether the judge or the jury believes or disbelieves the opposing evidence thus introduced is entirely immaterial.* In other words, the sole effect of the presumption is to cause the establishment of the basic fact to put upon the party asserting the non-existence of the presumed fact the risk of the non-introduction of evidence which would support a finding of its non-existence. This may be called the *pure Thayerian rule,* for if he did not invent it, he first clearly expounded it.

"2. The existence of the presumed fact must be assumed unless and until evidence has been introduced which would justify a jury in finding the non-existence of the presumed fact. When such evidence has been introduced, the existence or non-existence of the presumed fact is a question for the jury unless and until *'substantial evidence' of the non-existence of the presumed fact has been introduced. When such substantial evidence has been introduced, the existence or non-existence of the presumed fact is to be decided as if no presumption had ever been operative in the action.* Thus if the basic fact, by itself or in connection with other evidence, would rationally support a finding of the presumed fact, the existence or non-existence of the presumed fact is a question for the jury; if the basic fact is the only evidence of the presumed fact and would not rationally justify a finding of the presumed fact, the judge directs the jury to find the non-existence of the presumed fact. *Unfortunately the cases which support this rule do not define substantial evidence: it is certainly more than enough to justify a finding; sometimes it seems to be such evidence as would ordinarily require a directed verdict. . . .*

"3. The existence of the presumed fact must be assumed *unless and until the evidence of its non-existence convinces the jury that its non-existence is at least as probable as its existence.* This is sometimes expressed as requiring evidence which balances the presumption.

"4. The existence of the presumed fact must be assumed unless and until the jury finds *that the non-existence of the presumed fact is more probable than its existence.* In other words the presumption puts upon the party alleging the non-existence of the presumed fact both the burden of producing evidence and *the burden of persuasion of its non-existence.* This is sometimes called the Pennsylvania rule." (Emphasis supplied.)

Professor Morgan and his distinguished colleague, Professor John M. Maguire, have never concealed their preference for some form of the foregoing variants which would involve the shifting of the burden of *persuasion* at least as to certain classifications of presumptions, if not as to all. . . .

If we have, as we believe, because of the conflicting expressions and the lack of any definitive announcement in our own opinions, some freedom in determining what procedural effect we will assign to disputable presumptions, some examination of the cases which have employed the several variants may be helpful.

In the leading case of New York Life Ins. Co. v. Gamer, supra [303 U.S. 161, 58 S.Ct. 500], the court, without reviewing the evidence, pronounced that portion of it which was adverse to the presumption (of death by accidental means) to be "sufficient to sustain a finding that the death was not due to accident" in accordance with the Thayerian concept. It held that upon the introduction of this quantum of evidence, the presumption disappeared as a matter of law and should not have reached the jury. Mr. Justice Black, dissenting, first criticised the majority for its application of Montana law which in his view required that the presumption persist until the contrary evidence " '*all* points to suicide ... with such certainty as to preclude any other reasonable hypothesis.' " He then expressed his concern over the method of determination by saying: "The *jury*—not the *judge*—should decide when there has been 'substantial' evidence which overcomes the previous adequate proof."

It has frequently been stated that a disputable presumption disappears in the face of "substantial countervailing evidence" and the case is thereafter in the hands of the jury free of any presumption. As previously noted, what is meant by "substantial", however, is not always clear. In Alpine Forwarding Co. v. Pennsylvania R. Co., 2 Cir., 1932, 60 F.2d 734, another case which has been often cited, L. Hand, J., held that the determination as to whether the evidence contrary to the presumed fact is "substantial" is always and solely for the trial judge, and that in a properly conducted trial the presumption will never be mentioned to the jury at all....

The New York court in Chaika v. Vandenberg, 1929, 252 N.Y. 101, 169 N.E. 103, concluded that the presumption did not disappear in the face of the uncorroborated but uncontradicted denial of an interested party, but rather the credibility of such witness became an issue for the factfinder. Thus is presented a negative element in the definition of what constitutes "substantial" evidence.

The often cited case of McIver v. Schwartz, 1929, 50 R.I. 68, 145 A. 101, 102, involved the uncorroborated denial of the defendant which was not believed by either the trial judge or the jury. Affirming the principle that a presumption disappears as a matter of law in the face of "any credible evidence to the contrary," the court upset a jury verdict for the plaintiff. It would appear that "any credible evidence" here meant "any believable evidence even though not in fact believed by anyone."

Reaching an opposite conclusion, however, at least with respect to certain classes of presumptions, are such cases as O'Dea v. Amodeo, 1934, 118 Conn. 58, 170 A. 486; Koops v. Gregg, 1943, 130 Conn. 185, 32 A.2d 653; and United States v. Tot, 3 Cir., 1942, 131 F.2d 261, 267, which seem to require that the requisite contrary evidence must be in fact believed and any question of veracity raises an issue for the factfinder. The latter opinion voices the criticism which has often been made of the pure Thayerian rule that a presumption should not fall merely because words are uttered which nobody believes. "A gentle tapping on a window pane will not break it; so a mere attempt to refute a presumption should not cause it to vanish, if it is of any value at all." Hildebrand v. Chicago, B. & Q. R. R., 1933, 45 Wyo. 175, 17 P.2d 651, 657....

O'Dea v. Amodeo, supra, established an elaborate classification of disputable presumptions with a prescribed rebuttal requirement for each classification. It does not appear that this method of approach has won any substantial following perhaps because of the practical difficulties which might arise in applying the rule on a case by case basis in the trial courts.

Amid so much confusion there is the natural temptation toward oversimplification. Nevertheless, if the presumption is to be a useful procedural tool in the hands of the trial court, relative simplicity is a desirable goal. In the article in 47 Harvard Law Review 59 already cited, Professor Morgan has made a thorough and helpful analysis of this troublesome problem. As he points out, rebuttable presumptions have been created "(a) to furnish an escape from an otherwise inescapable dilemma or to work a purely procedural convenience, (b) to require the litigant to whom information as to the facts is the more easily accessible to make them known, (c) to make more likely a finding in accord with the balance of probability, or (d) to encourage a finding consonant with the judicial judgment as to sound social policy." Although the purposes for which presumptions are raised might properly and logically affect the method of their rebuttal, the writer, while suggesting that they should be permitted to shift the burden of persuasion, sees no serious or insurmountable objection to the establishment of a single procedural rule that a disputable presumption persists until the contrary evidence persuades the factfinder that the balance of probabilities is in equilibrium, or, stated otherwise, until the evidence satisfies the jury or factfinder that it is as probable that the presumed fact does not exist as that it does exist. We view the adoption of such a rule as a practical solution of a confusing procedural problem. In establishing the vanishing point for presumptions, it provides more certainty than do the varying definitions of "substantial countervailing evidence". It has also the virtue of reserving to the factfinder decisions as to veracity, memory and weight of testimony whenever they are in issue. In essence, the proposed rule recognizes that when an inference has hardened into a presumption compelling a finding in the absence of contrary evidence, it has achieved a status which should not vanish at the first "tapping on the window pane." It recognizes that "surely the courts do not raise such a presumption merely for the purpose of making the opponent of the presumption cause words to be uttered." We agree with Mr. Morgan that our objective should be to devise a "simple, sensible and workable" plan for the procedural use of disputable presumptions and are satisfied that the suggested rule achieves that end.

Such a rule gives to the presumption itself maximum coercive force short of *shifting the burden of persuasion*. Although we are keenly aware that there is severe criticism by respected authority of the widely accepted rule that the burden of persuasion on an issue never shifts, that rule has been thoroughly imbedded in the law of this state. An unbroken line of judicial pronouncements to this effect are to be found in our opinions. We would be most reluctant to make a radical change in the accepted rule unless forced to do so by some compelling logic. We feel no such compulsion here. Logic compels the conclusion that a mere procedural device is not itself evidence. But beyond that there seems to be a certain amount of judicial latitude which permits the court to determine how a disputable presumption, necessarily artificial in its nature, can best perform a useful function in forwarding the course of a trial. As already noted, it seems pointless to create a presumption and endow it with coercive force, only to allow it to vanish in the face of evidence of dubious weight or credibility. Neither does it seem to us necessary, in order to bring some order out of chaos, to overrule all precedent and permit the presumption to shift the burden of persuasion from him who first proposes the issue and seeks to change the status quo. These considerations prompt us to adopt the foregoing rule which seems to us a satisfactory middle course.

In our review of many opinions on this subject, we have discovered no more careful or accurate an analysis than is contained in a dissenting opinion by Mr. Justice Traynor appearing in Speck v. Sarver, supra, 128 P.2d at pages 19, 22.

Endorsing the view which we take of the effect of rebuttable presumptions as the "sounder one", he states: "Once such evidence (contrary to the presumed fact) is produced and believed, the jury should weigh it against any evidence introduced in support of the facts presumed and decide in favor of the party against whom the presumption operates if it believes that the non-existence of the facts is as probable as their existence. Nothing need be said about weighing the presumption as evidence."

With respect to the presumption against suicide in particular, Mr. Justice Taft concurring in Carson v. Metropolitan Life Ins. Co., supra [165 Ohio St. 238, 135 N.E.2d 259], said: "There may be instances where the only evidence produced or introduced to rebut the presumption against suicide is evidence which the jury may quite properly disbelieve in exercising its function as trier of the facts and judge of the credibility of witnesses. In such an instance, if the rule is as broadly stated as is suggested ... then incredible evidence or evidence having no weight whatever could be effective in making the presumption against suicide disappear. Obviously, that would be unreasonable.

"There may therefore be instances where it will be necessary for the trial court to mention the presumption against suicide in charging a jury, even though it is erroneous to advise the jury ... that that presumption may be weighed as evidence."

The rule for which we have expressed preference does not, as we interpret it, mean that the persistence or disappearance of a disputable presumption may never be resolved as a matter of law. Whenever no countervailing evidence is offered or that which is offered is but a scintilla, or amounts to no more than speculation and surmise, the presumed fact will stand as though proven and the jury will be so instructed. On the other hand, when the contrary evidence comes from such sources and is of such a nature that rational and unprejudiced minds could not reasonably or properly differ as to the non-existence of the presumed fact, the presumption will disappear as a matter of law. Where proof of the presumed fact is an essential element of the plaintiff's case, he would suffer the consequence of a directed verdict. Such would ordinarily be the result, for example, when evidence effectively rebutting the presumption is drawn from admissions by the plaintiff, evidence from witnesses presented and vouched for by the plaintiff, or from uncontroverted physical or documentary evidence.

Regardless of the view taken of the procedural effect of the presumption of death by accidental means, courts have not failed to be impressed by undisputed evidence of physical facts negativing accident. In Mitchell v. New England Mut. Life Ins. Co., 4 Cir., 1941, 123 F.2d 246, 248, the court, noting a contact wound and the horizontal course of the shot, concluded that "the nature of the wound itself bars any reasonable hypothesis of accident." ...

Bearing in mind the sage admonition of Chief Justice Clark, dissenting in McDowell v. Norfolk Southern R. Co., 1923, 186 N.C. 571, 120 S.E. 205, 42 A.L.R. 857, that too much technical and procedural "hair splitting" may impede the orderly course of litigation, let us turn to the facts before us. Applying the above stated rules of law to the facts of the instant case, it becomes at once apparent that the verdict of the jury was erroneous. As has been noted, the plaintiff undertook to satisfy his burden of proof, that is, the risk of nonpersuasion, that the death was caused by violent, external and accidental means. In the initial stages of the presentation of the plaintiff's case, there was undisputed and conclusive evidence that the means of death were both violent and external. Momentarily, as to the required proof of accidental means, the plaintiff was aided by the presumption, and the burden of going forward with evidence (as distinguished from the burden of proof) on this element of the case at once shifted to the defendant. This burden, however, could be as well satisfied by evidence adduced from plaintiff's witnesses as from those produced by the defendant. As the presentation of the plaintiff's main case proceeded, evidence of physical facts, emanating from the plaintiff's own witnesses and never disputed, clearly depicted an intentional, self-inflicted injury resulting in death. This evidence must be assessed in the light of inherent probabilities. Most significant is the fact that this was a *contact* wound at the right temple. Moreover, the course of the bullet on a horizontal plane through the head conclusively completes the picture of a fatal shot fired from a revolver held at and against the right temple and in a horizontal position. It is apparent that this evidence tends effectively to rule out any reasonable likelihood that there was an accidental discharge of the firearm while being cleaned or handled by either the decedent or his wife. The only reasonable inference is that the decedent placed a loaded revolver against his right temple and pulled the trigger. It matters not whether in so doing he intended to take his own life or was performing a grossly negligent and dangerous act reasonably calculated to produce grievous bodily harm or death. Where a shooting is the natural and probable consequence of the acts of the decedent, the result which should have been anticipated can hardly be termed an accident. ... We think the definition employed in Lickleider v. Iowa State Traveling Men's Ass'n, 1918, 184 Iowa 423, 166 N.W. 363, 366, 168 N.W. 884, 3 A.L.R. 1295 is entirely accurate. "It may be, and it is true, that if the insured does a voluntary act, the natural, usual, and to be expected result of which is to bring injury upon himself, then a death so occurring is not an accident in any sense of the word, legal or colloquial.... To illustrate, A. may be foolhardy enough to believe that he can leap from a fourth story window with safety, and, trying it, is killed. ... In no proper sense of the word is A.'s death accidental or caused by accidental means...." ... Whatever the thought processes of the decedent may have been when he placed a loaded revolver at right angles against his temple and pulled the trigger, the tragic results of that act can hardly be said to have been unusual, unexpected or unforeseen.

We note the negative evidence suggesting the absence of any apparent motive for self-destruction. The explanation of the decedent's conduct may well lie in his state of voluntary intoxication. Whatever may have been the reason for his act, we are satisfied that apparent absence of motive *alone* will not suffice under circumstances such as these to support a plaintiff's verdict or even to take the case to the jury. This is so because men without apparent motive do commit suicide and what prompts a man suddenly to succumb or appear to succumb to an excess of depression or despair is usually a secret locked in the recesses of his mind. Evidence tending either to demonstrate or negative any motive for self-destruction is always properly received in a case of this sort, but as already noted cannot *alone* suffice against undisputed physical evidence all pointing toward a voluntary act, the natural consequence of which was self-destruction. ...

The evidence offered by the defendant did no more than to bolster the evidence of physical facts which, uncontradicted and unexplained, conclusively destroyed any presumption against the intentional self-infliction of the fatal wound. The plaintiff failed to offer any further evidence tending to show that the decedent met his death other than by his own hand, even though the burden of going forward with evidence on this element of the case had shifted back again to him. Having lost the benefit of the presumption, he was left with nothing to support his theory of accident but the merest surmise and conjecture conjuring up the most unlikely possibilities. Such speculation will not suffice for evidence. With the evidence complete, there was then but one possible verdict which the jury could properly return, and that for the defendant as to the claim for double indemnity.

Why then did the jury reach a verdict so obviously contrary to the evidence?

. . .

. . . The jury had heard the only apparent eyewitness to the tragedy refuse to "testify", claiming the protection of Art. I, Sec. 6 of the Constitution of Maine. They had seen that action apparently sustained by the court and acceded to by the defendant. They had no knowledge of the contents of the offer of proof made by the defendant in connection with the proffered testimony of the officer. It is not unreasonable to suppose that the jury may have mistaken these developments for evidence and may have somehow drawn the erroneous inference that Mrs. Hinds had shot her husband. Although no such inference could properly be drawn from her refusal to answer, the impression that such an inference might be raised could easily have been created in the minds of the jury by one of the instructions given by the court. After reminding the jury that a witness had claimed privilege, the court said: "Now such an invocation of the constitutional provision against self-incrimination is not to be taken lightly and a person who invokes that privilege must be assumed to do so in good faith." No further explanatory instructions were given in this connection. Without more, the jury might have understood that they were free to draw such inferences as they chose from the act of the witness in claiming privilege. Obviously it would not have been proper for the jury to have speculated or conjectured that the witness had committed any particular crime, or especially that the witness had shot her husband.

. . .

One further factor plays a part in this case and may not be disregarded. As already noted, it is highly improbable that a contact wound on a horizontal plane at the temple was inflicted as a result of clumsy or accidental handling of the gun by Mrs. Hinds. If the act were hers, it would in the absence of explanation appear to fall into the category of wrongful and criminal conduct. Such conduct is never assumed but must be proven by evidence, in a civil case, which is full, clear and convincing. The total absence of such evidence in this case left no room for inference and could not be compensated for by conjecture.

In conclusion, then, the plaintiff had the burden of persuasion throughout to prove death by violent, external and accidental means. At the close of all the evidence there was an uncontradicted showing by strong evidence of physical facts drawn from disinterested witnesses presented by the plaintiff that death was self-inflicted and non-accidental. The plaintiff, not the defendant, needed the aid of supporting testimony from Mrs. Hinds if he were to satisfy his burden of proof. The plaintiff was left with no proof of accident whatever. Only one verdict was possible and that for the plaintiff in the sum of $9,000.

The entry will be

Exceptions overruled. Motion for new trial overruled if plaintiff within 30 days from filing of this mandate remit all of the verdict in excess of $9,000; otherwise motion sustained and new trial granted.

MAINE RULES OF EVIDENCE

ARTICLE III. PRESUMPTIONS

Rule 301.

PRESUMPTIONS IN GENERAL IN CIVIL ACTIONS AND PROCEEDINGS

(a) Effect. In all civil actions and proceedings, except as otherwise provided by statute or by these rules, a presumption imposes on the party against whom it is directed the burden of proving that the nonexistence of the presumed fact is more probable than its existence.

(b) Prima facie evidence. A statute providing that a fact or group of facts is prima facie evidence of another fact establishes a presumption within the meaning of this rule.

(c) Inconsistent presumptions. If two presumptions arise which are conflicting with each other, the court shall apply the presumption which is founded on the weightier considerations of policy and logic. If there is no such preponderance, both presumptions shall be disregarded.

Advisers' Note

The problems in dealing with presumptions are complex and difficult. First of all, the term has been used in very different senses by courts and legislatures. The generally prevailing view among the commentators is that the word presumption should be reserved for the convention that when a designated fact called the basic fact exists, another fact called the presumed fact *must* be taken to exist in the absence of adequate rebuttal. It has that meaning in this rule. Laymen, and courts as well, frequently use it as a synonym for "inference" ("Dr. Livingston, I presume"), a matter of logic and experience, not of law. The trier of fact is free to adopt or reject the inference. The phrase "conclusive presumption" is not a presumption in any useful sense, but a rule of law that if one fact, the basic fact, is proved, no one will be heard to say that another fact, the presumed fact, does not exist. Nor is the "presumption of innocence" in criminal cases really a presumption at all, but rather a forceful way of saying that the prosecution must prove guilt beyond a reasonable doubt and that there is to be no inference against the defendant because of his arrest, indictment, or presence in the dock.

Giving presumption the meaning stated, if the only evidence relates to B, the basic fact, it is universally conceded that when B is established, P, the presumed fact, has to be taken as true. The trouble begins when evidence that P is not true is introduced. One view, still followed in the majority of states, is that the presumption places on the party against whom it is directed the burden of going forward with evidence but that when there is testimony to support a finding of the nonexistence of the presumed fact, the presumption disappears like a bursting bubble and the case proceeds as though there never had been a presumption. Another view is that the presumption continues despite contradictory evidence, and the burden of persuasion is shifted so that the party against whom the presumption is directed must show that the nonexistence of the presumed fact is more probable than its existence.

This rule adopts for civil actions the second of these views and shifts the burden of persuasion to the party against whom the presumption operates. This is a change in Maine law as enunciated in the landmark opinion by Justice Webber in Hinds v. John Hancock Mutual Life Insurance Co., 155 Me. 349, 155 A.2d 721 (1959) where the Law Court took the position that a presumption persists "until the contrary evidence persuades the factfinder that the balance of probabilities is in equilibrium, or, stated otherwise, until the evidence satisfies the jury or factfinder that it is as probable that the presumed fact does not exist as that it does exist." The Hinds rule appears to have worked with reasonable satisfaction, but there have been difficulties in explaining to the jury the concept of probabilities being in equilibrium. Moreover, it involves the logical impossibility of treating a presumption as evidence to be balanced against other evidence when it is not evidence at all but a rule about evidence. The difficulties with the Hinds rule are enhanced because it does not take into account the different types of presumptions. Most presumptions are grounded upon an inference; that is, a deduction of fact that may logically and reasonably be drawn from another fact or group of facts. Evidence of these underlying facts can be balanced against evidence of contrary facts. It is not helpful, however, to say that the presumption persists to the point of equilibrium. On the other hand, some presumptions are not based upon rational inference but are created to reflect a desirable policy. An example is the presumption that goods received by the terminal carrier were in the same condition as when delivered to the initial carrier. See Ross v. Maine Central Railroad, 114 Me. 287, 96 A. 223 (1915). Here there is nothing to balance against evidence that the goods came to the last carrier in damaged condition, and the Hinds rule is particularly ill adapted to this situation.

The Federal Rule limits the effect of a presumption to fixing the burden of going forward, so that the presumption disappears when evidence is introduced which would support a contrary finding. Thus the offering of testimony which no one in the courtroom believes serves to drop the presumption out of the case. This gives too little weight to presumptions, especially those not based on rational inference.

In shifting the burden of persuasion this rule has the merit of making it unnecessary for the court ever to mention the presumption and making it possible to charge the jury in terms which it can readily understand. It may be thought to give too great an effect to some presumptions, but this seems preferable to the alternative of giving too little weight. In making its choice the Court has adopted the rule originally promulgated by the Supreme Court and incorporated in the newly approved Uniform State Law. It was also looked upon with favor in Justice Webber's opinion which finally settled upon the Hinds rule.

It should be noted that the rule preserves any statute giving a presumption a different effect. One such statute is the Uniform Commercial Code, 11 M.R.S.A. § 1–201(31), which defines a presumption in terms affecting only the burden of going forward.

There are numerous statutes which state that one fact is prima facie evidence of another fact. The purpose of subdivision (b) is to make it clear that such a statute creates a presumption within the meaning of this rule in a civil case. Rule 303(a) is to the same effect in a criminal case.

Subdivision (c) is designed to resolve the impasse when the court is confronted by inconsistent presumptions. It directs the application of the one founded upon weightier considerations of policy. If policy considerations are of equal weight, both presumptions are to be disregarded. The wording is taken from the Uniform Rules of Evidence approved in 1953 by the Commissioners on Uniform State Laws. The principal class of cases in which the problem has arisen is where rights are asserted under a second marriage but no direct evidence is available of a death or divorce terminating the first marriage before the second. Most courts say the presumption of innocence or of the validity of a marriage is stronger than the presumption of continuance of life or continuance of marriage.

NOTES

1. See generally, R.H. Field and P.B.L. Murray, Maine Evidence, pp. 35ff. (1976). What difference would there have been in the result reached in the principal case if the court had ignored the subject of presumptions?

2. Compare with the principal case, Life and Casualty Insurance Co. v. Daniel, 163 S.E.2d 577, 584 (Va.1968), also involving a suit to recover a sum of money under an accident policy that excluded recovery for self-destruction, in which the court took the view that a presumption against suicide has evidentiary value and does not disappear when rebutting evidence is introduced. The court said, "When positive evidence appears to indicate suicide it stands on one side, and the trier of fact must weigh them both in determining the question." Are presumptions useful in suicide—accident cases?

3. Should the jury be instructed about presumptions? Judge Learned Hand said that "if the trial is properly conducted, the presumption will not be mentioned at all." Alpine Forwarding Co. v. Pennsylvania Railroad, 60 F.2d 734, 736 (2d Cir.1932). Is this a consequence of his espousal of the Thayer rule? On the other hand, McCormick feels that silence "abandons one of the judge's useful opportunities for wise guidance of the trial, and runs counter to the traditions of the trial courts in most states." McCormick, Evidence § 314 (1954). See Hecht and Pinzler, Rebutting Presumptions: Order Out of Chaos, 58 B.U.L.Rev. 527, 552 (1978). Despite the Thayerian rule barring the giving of jury instructions on presumptions where rebuttal evidence has been introduced, many courts do in fact inform the jury. See, e.g., Life and Casualty Insurance Co. v. Daniel, 163 S.E.2d 577 (Va.1968). Closely allied is some commentators' feeling that courts at times resort to presumption terminology, even when there is no true presumption in the case, because it enables them to comment on the evidence in jurisdictions where there is no such right. Levin, Pennsylvania and the Uniform Rules of Evidence: Presumption and Dead Man Statutes, 103 U. of Pa.L.Rev. 1, 27–28 (1954); Note, Evidence—Presumptions—Statutory Presumption of Due Care in Wrongful Death Action, 60 Mich.L.Rev. 510 (1962). But there appears to be no correlation between those states in which comment on the evidence is permitted and those in which presumptions are not mentioned.

The Report of the New Jersey Supreme Court Committee on Evidence 51 (1963) suggests: ". . . that the judge need not use the term 'presumption,' and need not define it or spell out its function. In cases where the jury must treat the basic facts of the presumption as established, the judge 'need say nothing about the presumption for he need not tell the jury why one party rather than the other must carry a risk or burden.' 1 Morgan, Basic Problems of Evidence 40 (3d ed. 1961). He should limit himself to stating the appropriate burden of proof required. Where the existence of the basic facts is to be determined by the jury, 'the judge must instruct that if the jury find the basic fact, they must also find the presumed fact unless persuaded by the evidence that its non-existence is more probable than its existence.' Morgan, supra at 42. In the case of presumptions requiring clear and convincing evidence or proof beyond a reasonable doubt, the greater degree of proof should be instructed accordingly. Thus the instructions would be phrased entirely in terms of assuming facts and burden of proof. . . ." What view has New Jersey adopted as to the rebuttal of presumptions?

4. Federal Rule of Evidence 301 adopts a Thayerian rule imposing the "burden of going forward with evidence to rebut or meet the presumption" on the party against whom the presumption is directed.

What degree of proof is needed to rebut the presumption? A criticism of the pure Thayerian rule, or "bubble-bursting theory" as it is commonly called, is that any evidence no matter how incredible could rebut the presumption. As Lamm, J. put it in Mackowik v. Kansas City, St. Joseph & Council Bluffs Railroad Co., 94 S.W. 256, 262 (Mo.1906): " 'Presumptions' . . . may be looked on as the bats of the law, flitting in the twilight but disappearing in the sunshine of actual facts." Congress did not expressly state a standard which a judge could utilize in determining when sufficient evidence has been introduced to rebut the presumption. From this ambiguity, there may be room for courts to require a higher degree of rebuttal evidence. Two commentators suggest a modified Thayerian rule whereby "the presumption remains in the case until the judge finds credible rebutting evidence has been introduced." Hecht and Pinzler, Rebuttable Presumptions: Order Out of Chaos, 58 B.U.L.Rev. 527, 550 (1978). In fact, for many years the state courts adopting the Thayer rule have utilized various standards in determining the sufficiency of rebuttal evidence. See, e.g., Stephens v. Dichtenmueller, 207 So.2d 718, 725 (Fla.App.), rev'd on other grounds, 216 So.2d 448 (Fla.1968) (concurring opinion) ("A legal presumption will not disappear if no countervailing evidence is introduced or evidence is only scintilla, or amounts to no more than speculation, surmise, or conjecture"); J.D. v. M.D., 453 S.W.2d 661, 663 (Mo.App.1970) (presumption that child conceived in marriage may be rebutted by substantial evidence; evidence must, "in order to qualify as 'substantial,' amount to clear, convincing, and satisfactory proof that no copulation occurred or was possible between husband and wife during conception or must equate to proof so strong and persuasive as to leave no room for reasonable doubt"); Waters v. New Amsterdam Casualty Co., 144 A.2d 354 (Pa.1958) (presumption that use of vehicle is with permission of owner may be overcome with credible evidence); see also 5 A.L.R.3d 19, 55–63 (1966); cf. Breeden v. Weinberger, 493 F.2d 1002 (4th Cir.1974) (in action brought under Social Security Act to collect disability benefits, where there is an absence of wage entries it is presumed that no wages were paid; held, such presumption can be rebutted by substantial evidence and a presumption does not enhance the burden of persuasion requiring plaintiff to present clear and convincing evidence). Dean Ladd concludes that the Thayer–Wigmore rule cannot and has not been uniformly applied. Ladd, Presumptions in Civil Actions, 1977 Ariz.St.L.J. 275, 284–85 (1977). See also, Mueller, Instructing the Jury Upon Presumptions in Civil Cases: Comparing Federal Rule 301 with Uniform Rule 301, 12 Land and Water L.Rev. 219, 242–60 (1977) (in an analysis of the Thayerian rule as applied in practice he discovers five different approaches taken by the courts).

United States v. Jessup

United States Court of Appeals, First Circuit, 1985.
757 F.2d 378.

■ BREYER, CIRCUIT JUDGE.

This appeal challenges the constitutionality of a provision of the Bail Reform Act of 1984, 18 U.S.C. § 3141 et seq., that requires judicial officers making bail decisions to apply a rebuttable presumption that one charged with a serious drug offense will likely flee before trial. 18 U.S.C. § 3142(e). We find that Congress has acted within the Constitution's prescribed limits in creating this rebuttable presumption and that the magistrate and district court have acted within their lawful authority in applying it, and related statutory provisions, to the appellant Mark Jessup. We affirm the district court's decision to deny him bail and to hold him in custody pending his trial.

I

The Bail Reform Act of 1984 ("the Act") makes it, in one respect, harder and, in another respect, easier for judicial officers to order pretrial detention of those accused of crimes. It makes it harder by specifying explicitly what was implicit in prior law, namely that magistrates and judges cannot impose any "financial condition" that will result in detention. § 3142(c). ...High money bail cannot be used as a device to keep a defendant in custody before trial. The Act makes detention easier by broadening the category of persons whom the officer can order detained. ...

This case concerns one of the "rebuttable presumptions" that the Act creates. It states

Subject to rebuttal by the person, it shall be presumed that no condition or combination of conditions will reasonably assure the appearance of the person as required and the safety of the community if the judicial officer finds that there is probable cause to believe that the person committed an offense for which a maximum term of imprisonment of ten years or more is prescribed in the Controlled Substances Act (21 U.S.C. 801 et seq.). ...

§ 3142(e).

The magistrate here used the presumption in deciding to detain appellant Jessup. The magistrate found that Jessup posed a threat to the safety of the community in that, if released, he might continue to commit crimes. The magistrate also found that, if released, there was a substantial risk that Jessup would flee. ...

II

Before turning to the constitutional question, we must first decide what the rebuttable presumption means. What kind of burden is it designed to impose upon a defendant? Or, to cast the question in terms traditionally used in the law of evidence, does it impose a "burden of persuasion" or only a "burden of production"? See generally C. McCormick, Evidence § 342 et seq. (2d ed. 1972). If the former, the alleged drug offender would have to *prove* he would not flee—i.e., he would have to *persuade* the judicial officer on the point. If the latter, he would only have to introduce a certain amount of evidence contrary to the presumed fact; no change in the burden of persuasion is effected. Where the burden of persuasion lies may make a practical difference to a magistrate or judge genuinely uncertain on the basis of what the parties have presented.

The United States Attorney here suggests that Congress meant the presumption to shift the burden of persuasion to the defendant. ...

Our reasons for believing that the burden of persuasion does not shift include the following. First, we are chary of interpreting ambiguous language to mandate pretrial confinement where evidence before a magistrate is indeterminate. Although pretrial confinement to prevent flight is not punishment, but rather one of various restrictions on the freedom of an accused person aimed at facilitating trial, see Bell v. Wolfish, 441 U.S. 520, 535–39, 99 S.Ct. 1861, 1871–74, 60 L.Ed.2d 447 (1979), it is still a most severe restriction requiring clear cause.

Second, the Senate Judiciary Committee Report explaining the new presumption, while arguably ambiguous, does not suggest that Congress meant to impose a burden of persuasion on the defendant. To understand the relevance of the Report's description, one must realize that § 3142(e) creates not only the drug offender presumptions already mentioned (concerning "flight" and "danger") but it also creates a rebuttable presumption that one previously convicted of having committed a crime while free on bail is sufficiently "dangerous" to warrant detention. The Report describes both of these presumptions in the same place. It says that the object of this last presumption is to shift the burden

> to the defendant *to establish a basis for concluding* that there are conditions of release sufficient to assure that he will not again engage in dangerous criminal activity pending his trial.

S.Rep. No. 225, 98th Cong., 1st Sess. 19 (1983), reprinted in 1984 U.S.Code Cong. & Admin.News, pp. 1, 22 (emphasis added). The position of this sentence in the Report, its language, and the nature of the language of the statutory presumption all suggest that the words "establish a basis for concluding" aptly describe the intended effect of *both* § 3142(e) presumptions. And, these words do not say that the burden of persuasion shifts to the defendant, nor do they imply that it is up to the defendant to persuade the judicial officer.

Third, a later section in the Act, § 3148(b), establishes another similar presumption, this time in respect to a person who is released on bail (or the equivalent) and *then* commits a crime. The Act requires that such a person be brought back before the magistrate, who will consider whether to revoke his bail and detain him. The Act tells the magistrate that, if he finds probable cause to believe the person committed another crime while on release, he is to presume (subject to rebuttal) that detention is necessary to protect the community from still further crimes. That is to say, the Act applies a rebuttable presumption of "dangerousness." In describing the presumption, the Committee Report states that

> the establishment of probable cause to believe that the defendant has committed a serious crime while on release constitutes compelling evidence that the defendant poses a danger to the community, and, once such probable cause is established, it is appropriate that the burden rest on the defendant *to come forward with evidence* indicating that this conclusion is not warranted in his case.

S.Rep., supra, at 36 (emphasis added), 1984 U.S.Code Cong. & Admin.News, p. 39. This language ("come forward with evidence") is traditionally used to suggest a shift in the burden of production, not of persuasion. (Compare, for example, the language used by the congressional Conference Committee which, in preparing the Federal Rules of Evidence, noted that a

> presumption shifts to the party against whom it is directed the burden of *going forward with evidence* to meet or rebut the presumption, but it does not shift to that party the burden of persuasion on the existence of the presumed fact.

Fed.R.Evid. 301, Notes of Conference Committee (emphasis added).) The Act then does not impose a burden of persuasion even upon a defendant found likely to have just committed a crime while on bail. It would be anomalous to interpret the Act as imposing such a burden on those who committed such crimes in the past or on those charged with drug offenses, since they, if anything, present less risky cases.

Fourth, an examination of a related section of the Act, § 3143, shows that Congress knew how to create a "burden of persuasion" when it wanted to do so. Section 3143 creates a presumption that a defendant who has been convicted of a crime may not be released pending his appeal or sentencing unless he shows "by clear and convincing evidence that [he] is not likely to flee or pose a danger to the safety of any other person or the community." § 3143(a), (b). (This provision differs from the Bail Reform Act of 1966, in which even convicted defendants were presumptively entitled to the same opportunity for release on bail as defendants who had not already been convicted. See 18 U.S.C. former § 3148.) The Judiciary Committee Report notes that

> The Committee intends that in overcoming the presumption in favor of detention [in § 3143] *the burden of proof* rests with the defendant.

S.Rep., *supra,* at 27 (emphasis added), 1984 U.S.Code Cong. & Admin.News, p. 30. Congress could have used language similar to that of § 3143, or Report language similar to that just quoted, if it had intended § 3142(e) to impose a similar burden of persuasion. The absence of such language, and the proximity of §§ 3142 and 3143, reinforces our conclusion that § 3142 was meant to impose only a burden of production.

The government's strongest argument to the contrary rests upon two propositions:

> (a) Congress did not intend to create a set of presumptions with little or no practical effect; and

> (b) a 'burden of production' presumption would have little practical effect.

We agree with the first part of the argument: Congress did not intend the presumption to have a practical effect. This can be seen in the Report's discussion of the § 3142(e) presumptions, which says that in the circumstances that trigger the presumption (a serious drug offense charge; past commission of a crime on bail), a "strong probability arises that no form of conditional release will be adequate." S.Rep., supra, at 19 (emphasis added), 1984 U.S.Code & Admin.News, p. 22. In respect to the § 3148(b) presumption, the Report adds that

> the establishment of probable cause to believe that the defendant has committed a serious crime while on release constitutes compelling evidence that the defendant poses a danger to the community.

Id. at 36 (emphasis added), 1984 U.S.Code Cong. & Admin.News, p. 39.

We do not agree, however, with the second part of the argument. It is true that, under the prevailing judicial view, a "burden of production" presumption is a "bursting bubble." See C. McCormick, Evidence § 345 at 821 (2d ed. 1972) ("bursting bubble" theory is "the most widely followed theory of presumptions in American law"); Legille v. Dann, 544 F.2d 1, 6 (D.C.Cir.1976) (same). Under this theory, the presumption requires the "presumed against" party to introduce evidence, but, once he does so, the presumption "bursts" and totally disappears, allowing the judge (or jury) to decide the question without reference to the presumption. Since a defendant can always provide the magistrate with some reason to believe him a good risk, a "bursting bubble" approach might render the presumption virtually meaningless, contrary to Congress's clear intent.

Nonetheless, Congress does not have to make a "bursting bubble" of each "burden of production" presumption. We believe that here it has not done so; rather, it has created a "burden of production" presumption that does have significant practical impact. That is to say, the Report's language, together with the legislative history of the Act (with its emphasis on the importance of the presumption), indicates to us that Congress meant to impose a "burden of production" presumption, but it did not intend to make that presumption a "bursting bubble."

We are led to this conclusion in part by the strain of legal thought which has marked out a "middle ground" for some presumptions—holding that they neither shift the burden of persuasion nor "burst" once contrary evidence is presented. See Morgan, Instructing the Jury upon Presumptions and Burdens of Proof, 47 Harv.L.Rev. 59, 82–83 (1933); 21 C. Wright & K. Graham, Federal Practice and Procedure (Evidence) § 5122 at 566 (noting that while courts pay "lip service" to "bursting bubble" approach, "most of them [have] felt compelled to deviate from the 'bursting bubble' theory at one time or another in order to give greater effect to presumptions"); see generally Hecht & Pinzler, Rebutting Presumptions: Order Out of Chaos, 58 B.U.L.Rev. 527 (1978). Under this view, to remove the presumption entirely from a case once conflicting evidence has been presented could undercut the legislative purpose in creating the presumption (say, an intent to have courts follow the legislature's assessment of probabilities or the furtherance of some other specific public policy). The House Judiciary Committee adopted exactly this sort of "intermediate position" in its Report on Fed.R.Evid. 301. The Committee Report said that the "bursting bubble" approach gave presumptions "too slight an effect," and proposed a version of Fed.R.Evid. 301 under which presumptions would "not vanish upon the introduction of contradicting evidence" but would remain available "to be considered by the jury." See Fed.R.Evid. 301 and accompanying committee reports; Hearings on Proposed Rules of Evidence Before the Subcommittee on Criminal Justice of the House Comm. on the Judiciary (Supp.), 93d Cong., 1st Sess., ser. 2, at 364 (Comm.Print 1973). A number of courts have also adopted this "middle ground" view of presumptions. See, e.g., Montgomery County Fire Board v. Fisher, 53 Md.App. 435, 454 A.2d 394, 400 (1983) (statutory presumption that firefighter's heart disease is job related "does not disappear like the bursting bubble upon generation of a jury issue; rather it remains in the case as one of the elements to be considered"); Wright v. State Accident Insurance Fund, 289 Or. 323, 613 P.2d 755, 759–60 (1980) (same presumption) ("If there is opposing evidence, the trier of fact must weigh the evidence, giving the presumption the value of evidence, and determine upon which side the evidence preponderates."); Starr v. Campos, 134 Ariz. 254, 655 P.2d 794, 796 (1982) (jury weighs blood alcohol intoxication presumption along with other evidence); Walker v. Butterworth, 599 F.2d 1074, 1078 (1st Cir. 1979) (sanity presumption carries evidentiary value).

The case for a "middle ground" position is particularly strong in this setting of a detention hearing, where the procedures are informal and there is no jury. In such a setting, there is no occasion for the presumption to play its traditional practical role in the judge's decision about whether to direct a verdict (if no contrary evidence is produced) or whether, instead, to send an issue to the jury. In a detention hearing there is no jury. Thus a "bursting bubble" approach would call on the judge (or magistrate) to consider the presumption and then, if it is met with contrary evidence, to erase the presumption from his mind—not a task that is psychologically easy to accomplish.

Moreover, here the Act's history suggests a relatively obvious way to apply this presumption along the lines of the House Judiciary Committee's "intermediate position"—giving it some weight, without shifting the burden of persuasion. Congress investigated a general problem, the problem of drug offenders and flight. After hearing evidence, Congress concluded that "flight to avoid prosecution is particularly high among persons charged with major drug offenses." S.Rep., supra, at 20, 1984 U.S.Code Cong. & Admin.News, p. 23. It found that "drug traffickers often have established ties outside the United States ... [and] have both the resources and foreign contacts to escape to other countries...." Id. Congress then wrote its drug offender/flight presumption. These facts suggest that Congress intended magistrates and judges, who typically focus only upon the particular cases before them, to take account of the more general facts that Congress found. In order to "rebut" the presumption, the defendant must produce some evidence; and the magistrate or judge should then still keep in mind the fact that Congress has found that offenders, as a general rule, pose *special* risks of flight. The magistrate or judge should incorporate that fact and finding among the other special factors that Congress has told him to weigh when making his bail decision. See § 3142(g) (judicial officer shall weigh, among other things, "nature of circumstances of offense," "weight of evidence," "history and characteristics of the person including ... character, physical and mental condition, family history ..., past conduct ...," and so forth). Congress did not precisely describe just how a magistrate will weigh the presumption, along with (or against) other § 3142(g) factors. But the same can be said of each of the several § 3142(g) factors. It is not unusual for Congress to instruct a magistrate or judge conscientiously to weigh several different factors without specifying precise weights for each. See, e.g., Criminal Fine Enforcement Act of 1984, 18 U.S.C. § 3622.

Finally, the most common criticism of the "intermediate position" is that it is confusing; a jury, for example might not understand how to weigh a presumption against direct evidence. See Senate Judiciary Committee Notes on Fed.R.Evid. 301; C. McCormick, Handbook of the Law of Evidence § 345 at 825 & n. 60 (1972). This criticism has less weight in the context of a detention hearing, where no jury is involved, and the magistrate or judge is accustomed to the process of weighing several competing factors.

Since the presumption is but one factor among many, its continued consideration by the magistrate does not impose a burden of persuasion upon the defendant. And, since Congress seeks only consideration of the general drug offender/flight problem, the magistrate or judge may still conclude that what is true in general is not true in the particular case before him. He is free to do so, and to release the defendant, as long as the defendant has presented some evidence and the magistrate or judge has evaluated all of the evidence with Congress's view of the general problem in mind. It is worth noting that the Act requires that all detention orders "include written findings of fact and *a written statement of the reasons for the detention.*" § 3142(i)(1) (emphasis added). Thus, the defendant is protected from a weighing of factors that is arbitrary, or not in keeping with the Act.

In sum, the congressional report language about the presumption's nature and effect, the unsuitability of a "bursting bubble" presumption in an informal, nonjury hearing, and the availability of a "middle way," lead us to reject the government's "burden of persuasion" argument. Insofar as a magistrate or judge previously shared Congress's views about the general nature of the drug offender/flight problem, use of the new presumption might not make much difference. But, insofar as the magistrate or judge did not previously share those views, the presumption will have a significant practical effect. And this, we think, is what Congress intended.

III

We turn now to Jessup's claim that use of the drug offender/flight presumption is unconstitutional because it deprives him of his "liberty ... without due process of law." U.S. Constitution, Amendment V. In deciding whether this presumption makes Jessup's bail procedures constitutionally unfair, we shall ask 1) whether the presumption represents a reasonable congressional response to a problem of legitimate legislative concern, and 2) whether the presumption increases the risk of an erroneous deprivation of liberty—i.e., will it likely increase the risk that magistrates will release or detain the wrong people? See Schall v. Martin, 104 S.Ct. 2403, 2409, 81 L.Ed.2d 207 (1984); Mathews v. Eldridge, 424 U.S. 319, 335, 96 S.Ct. 893, 903, 47 L.Ed.2d 18 (1976) (determining procedural fairness by examining private interests, governmental interests, and risk of error).

... The drug offender/flight presumption seems a reasonable response to this general problem, requiring that a charged drug offender produce some evidence that he does not present a special risk and then requiring the magistrate to review the matter with Congress's general findings in mind.

Jessup, and a defendant in a related case, United States v. Lepere, 760 F.2d 251 (1st Cir.1985), attack the presumption in part by challenging the underlying congressional conclusions—by arguing that the evidence does not show a serious, special drug offender/flight problem. The Supreme Court, however, has cautioned us to give "significant weight" to the "capacity of Congress to amass the stuff of actual experience and cull conclusions from it." Usery v. Turner Elkhorn Mining, 428 U.S. 1, 28, 96 S.Ct. 2882, 2898, 49 L.Ed.2d 752 (1976). We cannot here reevaluate the statistical studies or other evidence presented at congressional hearings. To do so would invite potentially endless, unresolvable scholarly argument. (Statistical assumptions, for example, are almost always open to plausible attack.) And, doing so would overlook the fact that factual judgments in Congress (as elsewhere) often rest, less upon the gathering of numbers, than upon instinctive evaluation of the views of those with practical experience in the field—views that may reach the legislative ear both informally and formally. Given Congress's constitutional authority and practical factgathering power—a power far greater than that of courts—we are not persuaded that Congress's conclusions concerning the drug offender/flight problem are without substantial basis in fact, or that Congress's solution is unreasonable. And, we conclude that the government's interest in the presumption is a strong and legitimate one.

We also find that the presumption does not significantly increase the risk of an "erroneous deprivation" of liberty. Mathews v. Eldridge, 424 U.S. at 324–25, 96 S.Ct. at 897–98. The presumption shifts the burden of production, not the burden of persuasion. It applies only where there is probable cause to believe a person is guilty of a serious crime. The defendant can provide argument and evidence suggesting that he is not involved in the "highly lucrative" drug operations at the center of congressional concern. The Act further specifically provides a defendant with a hearing at which he

> has the right to be represented by counsel, and, if he is financially unable to obtain adequate representation, to have counsel appointed for him. The person shall be afforded an opportunity to testify, to present witnesses on his own behalf, to cross-examine witnesses who appear at the hearing, and to present information by proffer and otherwise.

§ 3142(f)(2)(B). Although the magistrate will keep the presumption in mind in making a decision, he will do so only as a reminder of Congress's findings. Given the Act's procedural protections, the fact that the presumption does not shift the burden of persuasion, and the presumption's relation to Congress's factfinding powers, we cannot say that it promotes less, rather than more, accurate decisionmaking Given the legitimate governmental interest in securing a defendant's appearance at trial, the presumption's restrictions on the defendant's liberty are constitutionally permissible.

Jessup's strongest argument to the contrary rests upon Leary v. United States, 395 U.S. 6, 89 S.Ct. 1532, 23 L.Ed.2d 57 (1969), which he cites for the proposition that a presumption in a criminal case is invalid unless there is "substantial assurance that the presumed fact is more likely than not to flow from the proved fact on which it is made to depend." Id. at 36, 89 S.Ct. at 1548. No one claims, he adds, that despite money bail and other release conditions, drug offenders are more likely than not to run away. We note, however, that the Leary Court applied this standard to a presumption in the context of a full blown criminal trial, where the presumption was used to establish an important element of the crime that was charged. Here, on the other hand, we deal with a presumption that is applied to a preliminary hearing, where decisions must be made quickly and where the purpose is not to punish but to increase the likelihood that the trial will go forward. It is well established that the constitutional guarantees at such hearings are less protective of defendants than at trial. Cf. Gerstein v. Pugh, 420 U.S. 103, 111–14, 95 S.Ct. 854, 861–63, 43 L.Ed.2d 54 (1975); United States v. Edwards, 430 A.2d 1321, 1333–37 (D.C.App. 1981), cert. denied, 455 U.S. 1022, 102 S.Ct. 1721, 72 L.Ed.2d 141 (1982). And, what is more to the point, the evidentiary burdens imposed upon the government are also less severe. Cf. Gerstein v. Pugh, 420 U.S. at 121, 95 S.Ct. at 866 (approving "informal modes of proof" in probable cause hearings). The Constitution does not require as great a degree of certainty for charging or for securing the presence at trial of one charged as for convicting that person at a criminal trial. In this context then, the substantial basis of information underlying "drug offender/flight" conclusions is sufficient to meet the Constitution's requirement of adequate support for a presumption. We reject Jessup's claim that more support is necessary.

We do not consider the government's claim that a still lesser test ("some rational connection," see Usery v. Turner Elkhorn Mining, 428 U.S. at 28, 96 S.Ct. at 2898) is all that the presumptions need satisfy. This lesser standard, applied by the Supreme Court typically in cases involving economic regulation, see id., may be insufficient here, where personal liberty is at stake.

Finally, Jessup contends that the real purpose of the presumption is not to detain those likely to flee but rather to impose extra punishment upon alleged drug offenders. In deciding whether this is, in fact, its purpose, we must ask whether there is "an alternative purpose" with which the presumption is "rationally ... connected ... [and to which it is] assignable," and whether the presumption is "excessive in relation to the alternative purpose assigned." Bell v. Wolfish, 441 U.S. 520, 538, 99 S.Ct. 1861, 1873, 60 L.Ed.2d 447 (1979) (quoting Kennedy v. Mendoza–Martinez, 372 U.S. 144, 168–69, 83 S.Ct. 554, 567–68, 9 L.Ed.2d 644 (1963)). Here, the "alternative purpose" is obvious, namely Congress's stated object: preventing pretrial flight. For reasons previously given, the presumption does not impose an excessive burden in respect to this purpose. We find no legal basis for viewing the presumption as imposing "punishment." For these reasons, we believe the presumption, as we have interpreted it, is constitutional.

IV

... The Act allows him to present all the special features of his case directly to the magistrate. The less those features resemble the congressional paradigm, the less weight the magistrate will likely give to Congress's concern for flight. The individual characteristics of a case and the precise weight to be given the presumption are matters for a magistrate to take into account within the framework of factors set out in § 3142(g). In other words, Jessup's argument goes not to the applicability of the presumption but rather to the weight that should properly be accorded it.

. . .

Finally, we have asked ourselves whether it is fair to Jessup to affirm the detention order on the basis of an interpretation of the presumption that the magistrate might not have followed. We now hold that the presumption shifts the burden of production not persuasion and that once the defendant produces evidence, the magistrate will keep in mind Congress's general factual view about special drug offender risks, using it where appropriate along with the factors set out in § 3142(g) to judge the risk of flight in the particular case. Did the magistrate here use the presumption more strongly to Jessup's disadvantage? Having reviewed the magistrate's findings, we think not. (See pp. 387–88, supra). The magistrate wrote that Jessup "has not rebutted" the presumption; but he also goes on to consider "all the circumstances" and then states his belief that Jessup would not be deterred from fleeing. Nothing in the record suggests the magistrate believed Jessup had to shoulder a "burden of persuasion" or that his decision turned upon that point. Of course, Jessup remains free to ask the magistrate for reconsideration of his detention order, United States v. Angiulo, 755 F.2d 969 (1st Cir.1985), a fact that allows Jessup a remedy if we have misread the magistrate's decision.

For these reasons, the judgment below is

Affirmed.

. . .

APPENDIX B

1. "Bail Reform," Hearings Before the Subcommittee on the Constitution of the Senate Judiciary Committee, 97th Cong., 1st Sess., Sept. 17 and Oct. 21, 1981 (Comm.Print 1982)

. . .

d. Statement of Mr. Kenneth Feinberg (p. 95)

If recent bail studies agree on any single conclusion it is that the bail system is most likely to break down in the area of narcotics enforcement and drug addiction. The ineffectiveness of existing bail procedures in dealing with the pervasive narcotics problem is proved by examining the type of person most likely to be arrested while on bail. Those rearrested usually have some relationship to narcotics trafficking or addiction. Although a convincing argument can be made that the rearrest rate of persons bailed is not serious enough to warrant a wholesale change in existing bail procedures, I think it is becoming increasingly obvious that, when it comes to narcotics, bail reform takes on an additional urgency.

I also believe that it is in the area of narcotics enforcement that one sees the most common abuses of the existing money bail system. The record is filled with examples of the influential narcotics dealer who posts the one million dollar bail set by the judge as a condition of release and then proceeds to flee the jurisdiction or continues to ply his trade. One can hardly point with pride to bail procedures which allow such highly publicized examples of the misuse of money bail.

e. Statement of Mr. Joel Hirschhorn, on behalf of National Association of Criminal Defense Lawyers (p. 106)

(Mr. Hirschhorn offered the following chart, based on data given him by Mr. Joseph Bogart, Clerk of the United States District Court for the Southern District of Florida.)

U.S. DISTRICT COURT—SOUTHERN DISTRICT OF FLORIDA

Year	Total number of cases filed	Total number of narcotics cases filed	Total number of bond-jumping indictments	Percentage of bond-jumping indictments	
				All cases	Narcotics cases
1978	920	439	16	2	4
1979	576	209	9	2	4
1980	739	289	12	2	4
Jan. 1, 1981, to June 30, 1981	352	168	16	5	10
Total	2,587	1,105	53	2	5

. . .

O'Dea v. Amodeo

Supreme Court of Errors of Connecticut, 1934.
118 Conn. 58, 170 A. 486.

■ MALTBIE, C.J. The plaintiff's injuries arose out of a collision between an automobile in which he was riding and one driven by the defendant Joseph Amodeo. It was alleged in the complaint that the car was maintained by the defendant Charles Amodeo for the use and enjoyment of his family and particularly his son Joseph, who was operating it with his father's consent and within the scope of his authority to do so. The jury returned a verdict against both defendants and the trial court set it aside as regards Charles Amodeo. The claim made by him was that there was no evidence that the automobile was a family car, which was sufficient to sustain the verdict against him; while the plaintiff claimed that, though the evidence offered was insufficient by itself to sustain the verdict, there was no evidence offered such that the jury as reasonable men could not reasonably conclude that the car was maintained as a family car, and he appealed to the statute, General Statutes, Cum.Supp.1931, sec. 600a, now Cum.Supp.1933, sec. 1152b. This provides as follows: "Proof that the operator of a motor vehicle was the husband, wife, father, mother, son or daughter of the owner, shall raise a presumption that such motor vehicle was being operated as a family car within the scope of a general authority from the owner, and shall impose upon the defendant the burden of rebutting such presumption."

The contention of the defendant Charles Amodeo, whom we shall hereafter refer to as the defendant, is that the effect of this statute is merely to carry the case to the jury and justifies a conclusion that an automobile is a family car when no substantial evidence is offered by the defendant that it was not, but that, as soon as substantial evidence to that effect is offered, the statute ceases to have any effect and the plaintiff then has the burden of proving that the car was a family car just as though no statute existed. In the case of Vincent v. Mutual Reserve Fund Life Ass'n, 77 Conn. 281, 58 A. 963, we discussed the nature and function of rebuttable presumptions and pointed out that whether they rest upon general experience or probability or merely on policy or convenience they have as such no probative force. No general rule can, however, be laid down as to the effect of a particular presumption in the actual trial of a case, for this depends upon the purpose it is designed to serve. Without attempting an exhaustive survey, we refer to the following examples as illustrating the varying effects produced: The presumption of innocence in a criminal case, a presumption which is of avail only to a defendant, merely emphasizes the burden which rests upon the State to prove the accused guilty. "It cannot add an additional burden to this. Its function is exhausted in putting such burden of proof on the state." State v. Smith, 65 Conn. 283, 285, 31 A. 206, 207. . . . Whether the defendant produces any evidence or not, it operates to its full extent. The same situation exists as regards the rule that fraud is not to be presumed. . . .

Presumptions which have their basis merely in convenience and serve to bring out the real issues in dispute, thus avoiding the necessity of producing evidence as to matters not really in issue, as the presumption which frees an insured in the first instance from offering evidence that he has performed all the conditions of the policy upon which he bases his action, operate only until the defendant has produced some substantial countervailing evidence, some evidence sufficient to raise an issue, and when that has been done they drop out of the case. . . . The same situation exists with reference to the presumption of sanity in a criminal case. It is a convenient device for avoiding the production of evidence as to a matter which in most cases will not present any issue. Thus, in State v. Gargano, 99 Conn. 103, 108, 121 A. 657, we said that the state might rest upon it as upon making out a prima facie case until evidence to the contrary is introduced.

It is also true that when the presumption rests upon common experience and inherent probability, it exhausts itself when the defendant produces substantial countervailing evidence. . . . Such presumptions differ, however, from those of which we have been speaking, in that as they are based upon the fact that common experience and reason justify the drawing of a certain inference from the circumstances of a given situation, it follows that, although the presumption as such disappears from the case when substantial countervailing evidence is produced, the facts and circumstances which give rise to it remain and afford the basis for a like inference by the trier, whether court or jury. "The facts which furnish the foundation of the presumption in question are entitled to count as evidence, and all fair inferences therefrom may be drawn, but the rule of law which gives to them an additional artificial effect may not be regarded as either contributing evidence or possessing probative quality." Vincent v. Mutual Reserve Fund Life Ass'n, supra, 77 Conn. page 290, 58 A. 963, 966. A somewhat similar situation arises in regard to the application of the doctrine *res ipsa loquitur,* with this distinction, that we do not regard that doctrine as giving rise to a presumption in the true sense of the term but consider that, where the necessary facts are proven, they afford the basis of a justifiable inference of negligence. . . .

It is true that our statements of the effect of a presumption arising out of common experience have not always been entirely precise. Thus in Weidlich v. New York, N.H. & H.R. Co., 93 Conn. 438, 440, 106 A. 323, 324, in speaking of a presumption of the continuance of life, we said: "This presumption of fact will then supply the place of evidence in setting up something which must be overcome by proof." . . . In Knapp v. Tidewater Coal Co., 85 Conn. 147, 155, 81 A. 1063, 1066, we said of certain presumptions: "It was incumbent upon the appellant to overcome these presumptions" and to establish its defense. In Barlow Brothers Co. v. Gager, 113 Conn. 429, 448, 155 A. 628, 636, we said of the presumption applied by some courts that a trustee sued for breach of trust has acted properly until the contrary is shown, that it went no farther than "to place the burden of proof upon the person alleging the breach." In these cases, however, we had no occasion carefully to define the effect of the presumptions we were considering. Presumptions of the classes we have been discussing lose their effect as soon as substantial countervailing evidence is introduced, and they may be said to have been rebutted when that evidence is offered.

But where the circumstances involved in an issue are peculiarly within the knowledge of one party and his power to bring them before the court, in certain instances the law deems it fit that he should have the burden not merely of offering some substantial countervailing evidence, but of proving such circumstances. An illustration of such a presumption is that which aids a bailor in an action against a bailee based upon his negligence. In such a case, we have said that the presumption of negligence makes out a prima facie case, "which may be overcome by the bailee by any explanation which shall satisfy the trier that the loss was not due to his failure to exercise reasonable care in the custody of the goods." Murray v. Paramount Petroleum & Products Co., Inc., 101 Conn. 238, 242, 125 A. 617, 619. In such a situation the policy of the law requires that, unless the defendant proves the actual circumstances involved in the loss of goods, the plaintiff should prevail; if the defendant does prove those circumstances, then the burden of showing that upon the whole case he was negligent rests upon the plaintiff. See Morgan, 47 Harvard Law Review, 59, 79.

Upon a somewhat different basis, policy dictates the rule that where, in a contest over a will, it is shown that the natural objects of a testator's bounty have been displaced by some person standing in a peculiar relationship of trust to him, as the lawyer who drew his will, or the guardian of his person or estate, the use of undue influence is presumed, and in such a situation the proponents of the will have the burden of disproving the actual exercise of such influence by a clear preponderance of the evidence.... In these instances the presumption is not rebutted when substantial countervailing evidence is produced, but the person in whose favor it operates continues to have its benefit until the adverse party has produced evidence which, believed by the trier, affords a basis for finding the circumstances relevant to the issue of the defendant's liability.

A presumption established by statute may fall into one or the other of these categories, or the language used may clearly indicate the effect which it is intended to have. Thus, General Statutes, Cum.Supp.1933, sec. 1149b, creates a presumption that one killed by the negligent operation of a motor vehicle was in the exercise of reasonable care, and then proceeds definitely to place the burden to plead and prove contributory negligence upon the defendant.

The statute involved in this case in terms goes no farther, after stating the presumption, than to put the burden of rebutting it upon the defendant, and our question is: What did the Legislature intend by this provision? If in this instance the intent of the Legislature was to do no more than to establish a presumption which would be rebutted by the production of substantial countervailing evidence, the last provision in the statute would serve no purpose, and we must assume that by its inclusion the Legislature intended some further effect. Nor, particularly in view of the fact to which we have referred, that the effect of presumptions has not always been precisely stated in our opinions, can we attribute too much of technical nicety to the language used by the Legislature. To conclude that it distinguished between the situations where a presumption is rebutted by the production of substantial countervailing evidence and those where it is only rebutted when the party against whom it has been invoked has proven certain countervailing facts, is to "impute to the lawmakers a subtlety of discrimination which they would probably disclaim." Cortes v. Baltimore Insular Line, Inc., 287 U.S. 367, 375, 53 S.Ct. 173, 176, 77 L.Ed. 368, quoted in Jewett City Savings Bank v. Board of Equalization, 116 Conn. 172, 183, 164 A. 643.

To construe the statute as meaning that the presumption would be rebutted as soon as substantial countervailing evidence was offered would necessarily mean that, when the defendant had offered such evidence, the presumption would not only cease to operate; but the burden of proof would be upon the plaintiff unaided by inferences from the facts which gave rise to the presumption, and in the absence of sufficient evidence to sustain that burden the defendant must prevail, even though the trier entirely disbelieved the testimony offered by the defendant. ... It may have been that the Legislature had in mind the language used by us, which we have quoted, in Weidlich v. New York, N.H. & H.R. Co., supra; Knapp v. Tidewater Coal Co., supra; and Barlow Brothers Co. v. Gager, supra, and may have taken it to mean that the burden rests upon the defendant to overcome the presumption by the weight of the evidence offered. However that may be, the situation presented is similar to those to which we have referred where the presumption rests upon the fact that the circumstances involved in the issue are peculiarly within the knowledge of the defendant, and as to which we have said that unless the defendant proves the actual circumstances of the case, the presumption is not rebutted.

We conclude that the intent of the statute is that the presumption shall avail the plaintiff until such time as the trier finds proven the circumstances of the situation with reference to the use made of the car and the authority of the person operating it to drive it, leaving the burden then upon the plaintiff to establish, in view of the facts so found, that the car was being operated at the time as a family car. From this it would follow that if the plaintiff offered no evidence upon the issue and the trier disbelieved the testimony offered by the defendant for the purpose of showing the circumstances of operation to have been such that it was not a family car, the plaintiff would be entitled to recover. In the instant case the plaintiff offered no evidence, other than that the car was operated by the son of the owner, to support his contention that the automobile which caused the accident was maintained by the defendant as a family car and that the son was operating it within the scope of a general authority to do so. The defendant testified that the car was not maintained for the general use of the members of his family, and both he and his son testified that the latter had no general permission to operate it, that on the occasion in question he had no permission to use it, and that the father did not know that he had taken it until after the accident occurred. It is evident from the trial court's memorandum of decision that it did not construe the statute as we have done, because it stated that even if the testimony of these two witnesses was disbelieved the plaintiff would not be entitled to recover.

It also appears from that memorandum that the trial court considered that the evidence of these witnesses was such that the jury could not disregard it and were obliged as matter of law to find in accordance with it. It is only in a rare case that it can be said as matter of law that the jury must accept as true evidence offered before them, for the credibility of witnesses is peculiarly within the field of the exercise of their function; and the trial court may not ordinarily substitute its conclusion for theirs. Porcello v. Finnan, 113 Conn. 730, 733, 156 A. 863. It appears in evidence that the car was maintained by the defendant for the pleasure of his family; and that the son, as he knew, had a license to operate motor vehicles. The son gave no testimony to indicate any attempt on his part, when he took the car from the garage at his home on the evening in question, to do so surreptitiously, although he knew his mother was at home at the time. When the father was told of the accident, he evinced no surprise, nor has he ever upbraided the son for taking the car. In certain respects the testimony of both father and son was contradicted and they were, of course, much interested witnesses. Except to prove certain formal matters they were called as witnesses in their own behalf and not by the plaintiff. The mother was not called as a witness to testify as to a lack of knowledge of the taking of the car by the son. The evidence discloses nothing in the case to arouse the jury's passion or prejudice. In this situation we cannot say that the jury was compelled to accept as true the testimony of the father and son.... The trial court was in error in setting the verdict aside.

There is error, and the case is remanded, with direction to enter judgment upon the verdict.

NOTES

1. How could the Connecticut statute have been rewritten to achieve the result reached in the main case without using the term presumption? Why do you think it was written as it was? Cleary, Presuming and Pleading: An Essay on Juristic Immaturity, 12 Stanford L.Rev. 1, 21, 22, 25–26 (1959):

> Can it be that much of the difficulty and controversy which have surrounded the subject of presumptions is due to using presumptions to achieve a result which, in many instances, may be reached more easily, more directly, and more clearly by the normal processes of pleading? ...

> ... take a case involving a controversy over the responsibility of defendant for negligence of the driver of a motor vehicle. Under the conventional pattern, plaintiff alleges in his complaint that the driver acting as defendant's agent in the scope of his employment drove negligently and injured plaintiff. Agency is denied in the answer. At the trial, plaintiff offers evidence that defendant owned the motor vehicle and then rests, invoking the presumption of agency arising from proof of ownership. If defendant relies on disputing the basic fact of ownership, the case will be resolved upon an issue never mentioned in the pleadings. If he relies on proof that no agency existed, the case will be decided on a pleaded issue but with the burden of persuasion exactly opposite the pattern worked out in the pleadings.

> Compare the straightforward approach, with the pleadings giving an accurate picture and notice of the course which the trial will actually follow.... In the driver case, the complaint alleges that D owned a motor vehicle and that X drove it negligently. D files an answer denying ownership, or alleging nonagency as an affirmative defense, or both. In each instance the pleadings reflect accurately the issues in the case and the incidence of the burdens of producing evidence and of persuasion as to them.

> Now the views advanced herein are not the product of a great affinity for pleading, though if we are to have pleadings it seems wise to make them accurate at least to the extent of not being downright misleading. Rather, these views result from the conviction that a large part of the confusion and controversy surrounding presumptions arises from the fact that we are expecting too much of them. Presumptions are a one-ton truck carrying a ten-ton load. They simply are not a suitable method of allocating

the elements in a case, and when we use them for that purpose, they groan and struggle and frequently break down.

. . .

Up to this point, presumptions have been considered only insofar as they operate to transfer one or both burdens of an element in the case. They may and do, of course, operate with regard to a lesser fragment of the case within the larger framework. Thus they may furnish convenient and desirable ready-made patterns of thought, or bridge minor but embarrassing gaps in proof or reasoning.

To illustrate: In an action upon an account, plaintiff, desiring to prove defendant's failure to deny as an admission of liability, may prove the mailing of a statement of account to defendant and rely upon the presumption that it was received by him in due course of the mails. The presumed fact of delivery is much smaller than an element in the case. The presumption of agency of a driver, on the other hand, clearly involves an element of the case.

. . .

The distinction is essential and fundamental. As we have seen, the use of presumptions as a means of allocating elements in a case should be abandoned entirely in favor of procedures more appropriate for the purpose. This would leave the field of presumptions to be occupied exclusively and sensibly by the tactical use.

2. For a more recent Connecticut case applying the principles set forth in the principal case concerning the "family car doctrine" see Sutphen v. Hagelin, 344 A.2d 270 (Conn.Super.1975); cf. Little v. Streater, 452 U.S. 1 (1981) (defendant in paternity action "faces an unusual evidentiary obstacle," since upon complaint of mother the reputed father must show lack of paternity by evidence other than his own testimony). Compare with the principal case, Waters v. New Amsterdam Casualty Co., 144 A.2d 354, 357 (Pa.1958) holding that "the burden of persuasion on the issue of the permission of the driver of the automobile remains with the plaintiff."

3. Swain v. Neeld, 145 A.2d 320, 323, 324 (N.J.1958) involved the construction of a statutory presumption that transfers without consideration were made in contemplation of death:

The effect to be afforded a presumption must ultimately lie in the reasons for its creation.... Suffice it to say that in this instance the language utilized, the introducer's statement, and the fact that the presumption is grounded not only in probability but in fairness and policy as well, cumulatively compel the result that the legislature intended to shift the burden of ultimate persuasion from the state to the taxpayer where the transfer was made within the specified period.

4. Gausewitz, Presumptions in a One Rule World, 5 Vand.L.Rev. 324, 331 (1952):

The one policy is to do actual, concrete, substantial justice in each individual case; the other policy is to do formal, procedural justice by having a uniform rule that is easily administered regardless of its effect in the particular case.... The first of these conflicting policies can be called the "particular justice policy" because it aims at actual justice in the particular, individual, case. The other can be called the "procedural justice policy" because it aims at an easily understood and administered uniform rule that will probably result in justice in the average case and also avoid injustices due to difficulties of administration. Almost everyone seems to agree, and always to have agreed, that the procedural justice policy should be followed in dealing with presumptions; that there should be one rule for all, or all but one or two or a very few presumptions.

5. The presumption of death from an unexplained absence is used 1) to allow the spouse of a missing person to marry; 2) to extinguish title and interest in property owned by the absentee; 3) to determine the enforceability of a life insurance policy; and 4) to determine whether the absentee predeceased a testator for the purpose of ascertaining the proper distribution of the testator's property. Should the rules with respect to burdens be the same in each of these situations? See 99 A.L.R.2d 296, 307 (1965), as to requisite search. See generally, Jalet, Mysterious Disappearance: The Presumption of Death and the Administration of Estates of Missing Persons or Absentees, 54 Iowa L.Rev. 177 (1968). Note, A Review of the Presumption of Death in New York, 26 Albany L.Rev. 231, 245 (1962), suggests that this presumption is an anachronism; it developed as a rule of necessity to fix property rights 300 years ago when there were poor facilities of communication and detection. Closely connected is the presumption fixing the time of death. The note suggests that a consideration of all the "unique ... facts which surround the disappearance and indicate the personal characteristics of the absentee ... would result in a more accurate determination of the absentee's time of death." This is the approach of the Uniform Absence as Evidence of Death and Absentees' Property Act, 8 U.L.A. 5 (1972), which has been adopted in Tennessee and Wisconsin; Section 1(1) provides:

> In any proceeding under this Act where the death of a person and the date thereof, or either, is in issue, the fact that he has been absent from his place of residence, unheard of for seven years, or for any other period, creates no presumption requiring the Court or the jury to find that he is now deceased. The issue shall go the Court or jury as one of fact to be determined upon the evidence.

New York has modified the traditional rule with regard to unexplained absences by a statute, E.P.T.L. 2–1.7 (1981), providing that it must be established that the person was absent for a continuous period of five years, there had been a diligent but fruitless search, and the person's absence cannot be satisfactorily explained.

Texas Department of Community Affairs v. Burdine

Supreme Court of the United States, 1981.
450 U.S. 248, 101 S.Ct. 1089, 67 L.Ed.2d 207.

■ JUSTICE POWELL delivered the opinion of the Court.

This case requires us to address again the nature of the evidentiary burden placed upon the defendant in an employment discrimination suit brought under Title VII of the Civil Rights Act of 1964, 42 U.S.C. § 2000e et seq. The narrow question presented is whether, after the plaintiff has proved a prima facie case of discriminatory treatment, the burden shifts to the defendant to persuade the court by a preponderance of the evidence that legitimate, nondiscriminatory reasons for the challenged employment action existed.

I

Petitioner, the Texas Department of Community Affairs (TDCA), hired respondent, a female, in January 1972, for the position of accounting clerk in the Public Service Careers Division (PSC). PSC provided training and employment opportunities in the public sector for unskilled workers. When hired, respondent possessed several years' experience in employment training. She was promoted to Field Services Coordinator in July 1972. Her supervisor resigned in November of that year, and respondent was assigned additional duties. Although she applied for the supervisor's position of Project Director, the position remained vacant for six months.

PSC was funded completely by the United States Department of Labor. The Department was seriously concerned about inefficiencies at PSC. In February, 1973, the Department notified the Executive Director of TDCA, B.R. Fuller, that it would terminate PSC the following month. TDCA officials, assisted by respondent, persuaded the Department to continue funding the program, conditioned upon PSC reforming its operations. Among the agreed conditions were the appointment of a permanent Project Director and a complete reorganization of the PSC staff.

After consulting with personnel within TDCA, Fuller hired a male from another division of the agency as Project Director. In reducing the PSC staff, he fired respondent along with two other employees, and retained another male, Walz, as the only professional employee in the division. It is undisputed that respondent had maintained her application for the position of Project Director and had requested to remain with TDCA. Respondent soon was rehired by TDCA and assigned to another division of the agency. She received the exact salary paid to the Project Director at PSC, and the subsequent promotions she has received have kept her salary and responsibility commensurate with what she would have received had she been appointed Project Director.

Respondent filed this suit in the United States District Court for the Western District of Texas. She alleged that the failure to promote and the subsequent decision to terminate her had been predicated on gender discrimination in violation of Title VII. After a bench trial, the District Court held that neither decision was based on gender discrimination. The court relied on the testimony of Fuller that the employment decisions necessitated by the commands of the Department of Labor were based on consultation among trusted advisors and a nondiscriminatory evaluation of the relative qualifications of the individuals involved. He testified that the three individuals terminated did not work well together, and that TDCA thought that eliminating this problem would improve PSC's efficiency. The court accepted this explanation as rational and, in effect, found no evidence that the decisions not to promote and to terminate respondent were prompted by gender discrimination.

The Court of Appeals for the Fifth Circuit reversed in part. 608 F.2d 563 (1979). The court held that the District Court's "implicit evidentiary finding" that the male hired as Project Director was better qualified for that position than respondent was not clearly erroneous. Accordingly, the court affirmed the District Court's finding that respondent was not discriminated against when she was not promoted. The Court of Appeals, however, reversed the District Court's finding that Fuller's testimony sufficiently had rebutted respondent's prima facie case of gender discrimination in the decision to terminate her employment at PSC. The court reaffirmed its previously announced views that the defendant in a Title VII case bears the burden of proving by a preponderance of the evidence the existence of legitimate nondiscriminatory reasons for the employment action and that the defendant also must prove by objective evidence that those hired or promoted were better qualified than the plaintiff. The court found that Fuller's testimony did not carry either of these evidentiary burdens. It, therefore, reversed the judgment of the District Court and remanded the case for computation of backpay. Because the decision of the Court of Appeals as to the burden of proof borne by the defendant conflicts with interpretations of our precedents adopted by other courts of appeals, we granted certiorari 447 U.S. 920, 100 S.Ct. 3009, 65 L.Ed.2d 1112 (1980). We now vacate the Fifth Circuit's decision and remand for application of the correct standard.

II

In McDonnell Douglas Corp. v. Green, 411 U.S. 792, 93 S.Ct. 1817, 36 L.Ed.2d 668 (1973), we set forth the basic allocation of burdens and order of presentation of proof in a Title VII case alleging discriminatory treatment. First, the plaintiff has the burden of proving by the preponderance of the evidence a prima facie case of discrimination. Second, if the plaintiff succeeds in proving the prima facie case, the burden shifts to the defendant "to articulate some legitimate, nondiscriminatory reason for the employee's rejection." Id., at 802, 93 S.Ct., at 1824. Third, should the defendant carry this burden, the plaintiff must then have an opportunity to prove by a preponderance of the evidence that the legitimate reasons offered by the defendant were not its true reasons, but were a pretext for discrimination. Id., at 804, 93 S.Ct., at 1825.

The nature of the burden that shifts to the defendant should be understood in light of the plaintiff's ultimate and intermediate burdens. The ultimate burden of persuading the trier of fact that the defendant intentionally discriminated against the plaintiff remains at all times with the plaintiff. See Board of Trustees of Keene State College v. Sweeney, 439 U.S. 24, 25, n. 2, 99 S.Ct. 295, 296, n. 2, 58 L.Ed.2d 216 (1979); id., at 29, 99 S.Ct., at 297 (STEVENS, J., dissenting). See generally 9 Wigmore, Evidence § 2489 (3d ed. 1940) (the burden of persuasion "never shifts"). The McDonnell Douglas division of intermediate evidentiary burdens serves to bring the litigants and the court expeditiously and fairly to this ultimate question.

The burden of establishing a prima facie case of disparate treatment is not onerous. The plaintiff must prove by a preponderance of the evidence that she applied for an available position, for which she was qualified, but was rejected under circumstances which give rise to an inference of unlawful discrimination.[1] The prima facie case serves an important function in the litigation: it eliminates the most common nondiscriminatory reasons for the plaintiff's rejection. See Teamsters v. United States, 431 U.S. 324, 358 & n. 44, 97 S.Ct. 1843, 1866, n. 44, 52 L.Ed.2d 396 (1977). As the Court explained in Furnco Construction Co. v. Waters, 438 U.S. 567, 577, 98 S.Ct. 2943, 2949, 57 L.Ed.2d 957 (1978), the prima facie case "raises an inference of discrimination only

---

1. In McDonnell Douglas, supra, we described an appropriate model for a prima facie case of racial discrimination. The plaintiff must show:

"(i) that he belongs to a racial minority; (ii) that he applied and was qualified for a job for which the employer was seeking applicants; (iii) that, despite his qualification, he was rejected; and (iv) that, after his rejection, the position remained open and the employer continued to seek applicants from persons of complainant's qualifications." 411 U.S., at 802, 93 S.Ct., at 1824.

We added, however, that this standard is not inflexible, as "[t]he facts necessarily will vary in Title VII cases, and the specification above of the prima facie proof required from respondent is not necessarily applicable in every respect in differing factual situations." Id., at 802, n. 13, 93 S.Ct., at 1824 n. 13.

In the instant case, it is not seriously contested that respondent has proved a prima facie case. She showed that she was a qualified woman who sought an available position, but the position was left open for several months before she finally was rejected in favor of a male who had been under her supervision. [Some footnotes are omitted; others are renumbered; footnotes by the Court.]

because we presume these acts, if otherwise unexplained, are more likely than not based on the consideration of impermissible factors.'' Establishment of the prima facie case in effect creates a presumption that the employer unlawfully discriminated against the employee. If the trier of fact believes the plaintiff's evidence, and if the employer is silent in the face of the presumption, the court must enter judgment for the plaintiff because no issue of fact remains in the case.[2]

The burden that shifts to the defendant, therefore, is to rebut the presumption of discrimination by producing evidence that the plaintiff was rejected, or someone else was preferred, for a legitimate, nondiscriminatory reason. The defendant need not persuade the court that it was actually motivated by the proffered reasons. See Sweeney, supra, at 25, 99 S.Ct., at 296. It is sufficient if the defendant's evidence raises a genuine issue of fact as to whether it discriminated against the plaintiff.[3] To accomplish this, the defendant must clearly set forth, through the introduction to admissible evidence, the reasons for the plaintiff's rejection.[4] The explanation provided must be legally sufficient to justify a judgment for the defendant. If the defendant carries this burden of production, the presumption raised by the prima facie case is rebutted,[5] and the factual inquiry proceeds to a new level of specificity. Placing this burden of production on the defendant thus serves simultaneously to meet the plaintiff's prima facie case by presenting a legitimate reason for the action and to frame the factual issue with sufficient clarity so that the plaintiff will have a full and fair opportunity to demonstrate pretext. The sufficiency of the defendant's evidence should be evaluated by the extent to which it fulfills these functions.

The plaintiff retains the burden of persuasion. She now must have the opportunity to demonstrate that the proffered reason was not the true reason for the employment decision. This burden now merges with the ultimate burden of persuading the court that she has been the victim of intentional discrimination. She may succeed in this either directly by persuading the court

---

2. The phrase "prima facie case" may denote not only the establishment of a legally mandatory, rebuttable presumption, but also may be used by courts to describe the plaintiff's burden of producing enough evidence to permit the trier of fact to infer the fact at issue. 9 Wigmore, Evidence § 2494 (3d ed. 1940). McDonnell Douglas should have made it apparent that in the Title VII context we use "prima facie case" in the former sense.

3. This evidentiary relationship between the presumption created by a prima facie case and the consequential burden of production placed on the defendant is a traditional feature of the common law. "The word 'presumption' properly used refers only to a device for allocating the production burden." F. James & G. Hazard, Civil Procedure § 7.9, at 255 (2d ed. 1977) (footnote omitted). See Fed.Rule Evid. 301. See generally 9 Wigmore, Evidence § 2491 (3d ed. 1940). Cf. J. Maguire, Evidence, Common Sense and Common Law, 185–186 (1947). Usually, assessing the burden of production helps the judge determine whether the litigants have created an issue of fact to be decided by the jury. In a Title VII case, the allocation of burdens and the creation of a presumption by the estab-

lishment of a prima facie case is intended progressively to sharpen the inquiry into the elusive factual question of intentional discrimination.

4. An articulation not admitted into evidence will not suffice. Thus, the defendant cannot meet its burden merely through an answer to the complaint or by argument of counsel.

5. See generally J. Thayer, Preliminary Treatise on Evidence 346 (1898). In saying that the presumption drops from the case, we do not imply that the trier of fact no longer may consider evidence previously introduced by the plaintiff to establish a prima facie case. A satisfactory explanation by the defendant destroys the legally mandatory inference of discrimination arising from the plaintiff's initial evidence. Nonetheless, this evidence and inferences properly drawn therefrom may be considered by the trier of fact on the issue of whether the defendant's explanation is pretextual. Indeed, there may be some cases where the plaintiff's initial evidence, combined with effective cross-examination of the defendant, will suffice to discredit the defendant's explanation.

that a discriminatory reason more likely motivated the employer or indirectly by showing that the employer's proffered explanation is unworthy of credence. See McDonnell Douglas, supra, at 804 805, 93 S.Ct., at 1825–1826

III

In reversing the judgment of the District Court that the discharge of respondent from PSC was unrelated to her sex, the Court of Appeals adhered to two rules it had developed to elaborate the defendant's burden of proof. First, the defendant must prove by a preponderance of the evidence that legitimate, nondiscriminatory reasons for the discharge existed. 608 F.2d, at 567. See Turner v. Texas Instruments, Inc., 555 F.2d 1251, 1255 (CA5 1977). Second, to satisfy this burden, the defendant "must prove that those he hired ... were somehow better qualified than was plaintiff; in other words, comparative evidence is needed." 608 F.2d, at 567 (emphasis in original). See East v. Romine, Inc., 518 F.2d 332, 339–340 (CA5 1975).

A

The Court of Appeals has misconstrued the nature of the burden that McDonnell Douglas and its progeny place on the defendant. See Part II, supra. We stated in Sweeney that "the employer's burden is satisfied if he simply 'explains what he has done' or 'produc[es] evidence of legitimate nondiscriminatory reasons.' "439 U.S., at 25, n. 2, 99 S.Ct., at 296 n. 2, quoting id., at 28, 29, 99 S.Ct., at 297–298 (Stevens, J., dissenting). It is plain that the Court of Appeals required much more: it placed on the defendant the burden of persuading the court that it had convincing, objective reasons for preferring the chosen applicant above the plaintiff.[6]

The Court of Appeals distinguished Sweeney on the ground that the case held only that the defendant did not have the burden of proving the absence of discriminatory intent. But this distinction slights the rationale of Sweeney and of our other cases. We have stated consistently that the employee's prima facie case of discrimination will be rebutted if the employer articulates lawful reasons for the action; that is, to satisfy this intermediate burden, the employer need only produce admissible evidence which would allow the trier of fact rationally to conclude that the employment decision had not been motivated by discriminatory animus. The Court of Appeals would require the defendant to introduce evidence which, in the absence of any evidence of pretext, would persuade the trier of fact that the employment action was lawful. This exceeds what properly can be demanded to satisfy a burden of production.

The court placed the burden of persuasion on the defendant apparently because it feared that "[i]f an employer need only *articulate*—not prove—a legitimate, nondiscriminatory reason for his action, he may compose fictitious, but legitimate, reasons for his actions." Turner v. Texas Instruments, Inc.,

---

6. The court reviewed the defendant's evidence and explained its deficiency:

"Defendant failed to introduce comparative factual data concerning Burdine and Walz. Fuller merely testified that he discharged and retained personnel in the spring shakeup at TDCA primarily on the recommendations of subordinates and that he considered Walz qualified for the position he was retained to do. Fuller failed to specify any objective criteria on which he based the decision to discharge Burdine and retain Walz.

He stated only that the action was in the best interest of the program and that there had been some friction within the department that might be alleviated by Burdine's discharge. Nothing in the record indicates whether he examined Walz' ability to work well with others. This court in *East* found such unsubstantiated assertions of 'qualification' and 'prior work record' insufficient absent data that will allow a true comparison of the individuals hired and rejected." 608 F.2d, at 568.

supra, at 1255 (emphasis in original). We do not believe, however, that limiting the defendant's evidentiary obligation to a burden of production will unduly hinder the plaintiff. First, as noted above, the defendant's explanation of its legitimate reasons must be clear and reasonably specific. Supra, at 5–6. See Loeb v. Textron, Inc., 600 F.2d 1003, 1011–1012, n. 5 (CA1 1979). This obligation arises both from the necessity of rebutting the inference of discrimination arising from the prima facie case and from the requirement that the plaintiff be afforded "a full and fair opportunity" to demonstrate pretext. Second, although the defendant does not bear a formal burden of persuasion, the defendant nevertheless retains an incentive to persuade the trier of fact that the employment decision was lawful. Thus, the defendant normally will attempt to prove the factual basis for its explanation. Third, the liberal discovery rules applicable to any civil suit in federal court are supplemented in a Title VII suit by the plaintiff's access to the Equal Employment Opportunity Commission's investigatory files concerning her complaint. See EEOC v. Associated Dry Goods Corp., 449 U.S. 596, 101 S.Ct. 817, 66 L.Ed.2d 762 (1981). Given these factors, we are unpersuaded that the plaintiff will find it particularly difficult to prove that a proffered explanation lacking a factual basis is a pretext. We remain confident that the McDonnell Douglas framework permits the plaintiff meriting relief to demonstrate intentional discrimination.

B

The Court of Appeals also erred in requiring the defendant to prove by objective evidence that the person hired or promoted was more qualified than the plaintiff. McDonnell Douglas teaches that it is the plaintiff's task to demonstrate that similarly situated employees were not treated equally. 411 U.S., at 804, 93 S.Ct., at 1825. The Court of Appeals' rule would require the employer to show that the plaintiff's objective qualifications were inferior to those of the person selected. If it cannot, a court would, in effect, conclude that it has discriminated.

The court's procedural rule harbors a substantive error. Title VII prohibits all discrimination in employment based upon race, sex and national origin. "The broad, overriding interest, shared by employer, employee, and consumer, is efficient and trustworthy workmanship assured through fair and ... neutral employment and personnel decisions." McDonnell Douglas, supra, at 801, 93 S.Ct., at 1823. Title VII, however, does not demand that an employer give preferential treatment to minorities or women. 42 U.S.C. § 2000e–2(j). See Steelworkers v. Weber, 443 U.S. 193, 205–206, 99 S.Ct. 2721, 2728–2729, 61 L.Ed.2d 480 (1979). The statute was not intended to "diminish traditional management prerogatives." Id., at 207, 99 S.Ct., at 2729. It does not require the employer to restructure his employment practices to maximize the number of minorities and women hired. Furnco Construction Co. v. Waters, 438 U.S., at 577–578, 98 S.Ct., at 2949–2950.

The views of the Court of Appeals can be read, we think, as requiring the employer to hire the minority or female applicant whenever that person's objective qualifications were equal to those of a white male applicant. But Title VII does not obligate an employer to accord this preference. Rather, the employer has discretion to choose among equally qualified candidates, provided the decision is not based upon unlawful criteria. The fact that a court may think that the employer misjudged the qualifications of the applicants does not in itself expose him to Title VII liability, although this may be probative of whether the employer's reasons are pretexts for discrimination. Loeb v. Textron, Inc., supra, at 1012, n. 6; see Lieberman v. Gant, 630 F.2d 60, 65 (CA2 1980).

IV

In summary, the Court of Appeals erred by requiring the defendant to prove by a preponderance of the evidence the existence of nondiscriminatory reasons for terminating the respondent and that the person retained in her stead had superior objective qualifications for the position. When the plaintiff has proved a prima facie case of discrimination, the defendant bears only the burden of explaining clearly the nondiscriminatory reasons for its actions. The judgment of the Court of Appeals is vacated and the case is remanded for further proceedings consistent with this opinion.

It is so ordered.

NOTES

1. In the sex and race discrimination cases courts refer constantly to shifting burdens, usually without resorting to the term presumptions. See, e.g., McDonnell Douglas Corp. v. Green, 411 U.S. 792 (1973); Furnco Construction Corp. v. Waters, 438 U.S. 567 (1978); NAACP v. Medical Center, Inc., 657 F.2d 1322 (3d Cir. en banc 1981); D.C. Baldus & J.W.L. Cole, Statistical Proof of Discrimination (1979). The basic statutes referred to in these cases do not use the term presumption.

2. See Batson v. Kentucky, 476 U.S. 79 (1986), using the burden shifting device to determine whether a state has unconstitutionally challenged jurors on the ground of race. Once the defendant has shown he is member of a cognizable racial group and that there is enough evidence to raise an inference of discriminatory challenges, the burden shifts to the state to come forward with a neutral explanation. See United States v. Biaggi, 673 F.Supp. 96 (E.D.N.Y. 1987) (Italo Americans a cognizable group).

3. Assuming that the case will be tried without a jury, what does the concept of presumption add in the main case; could the use of the term have been avoided? See, e.g., United States Postal Service Bd. of Governors v. Aikens, 460 U.S. 711 (1983) (in bench trial, once all evidence is in, court should decide question of discriminatory intent without reference to prima facie case analysis). If the case were tried by a jury, how would the jury be instructed?

4. Beltran v. Myers, 451 U.S. 625 (1981), is one of the many cases dealing with statutory presumptions. Some of the several hundred statutes are collected in J.B. Weinstein and M. Berger, Weinstein's Evidence 301–31. Typical is the statute described in Beltran:

> After our grant of certiorari on November 3, 1980, Congress passed § 5 of Pub.L. 96–611, 94 Stat. 3567 (Dec. 28, 1980) (the "Boren–Long Amendment"), which made material changes in the law in this area. This section creates a presumption that assets disposed of for less than full consideration within the preceding 24 months should be included in the resources of an applicant for SSI benefits. The applicant can overcome this presumption with "convincing evidence to establish that the transaction was exclusively for some ... purpose" other than establishing eligibility. Id., § 5(a) (amending § 1613 of the Social Security Act, 42 U.S.C. § 1382b). This section goes on to allow state Medicaid plans to apply similar rules to Medicaid recipients—including both the categorically needy and the medically needy. Pub.L. 96–611, § 5(b), 94 Stat. 3568 (1980) (amending § 1902 of the Social Security Act, 42 U.S.C. § 1396a). It states that if the state plan includes a transfer-of-assets rule, it shall specify a procedure for implementing the denial of benefits "which, except as provided in para-

graph (2), is not more restrictive than the procedure specified" for SSI. Paragraph (2) provides that where the uncompensated value of the disposed of resources exceeds $12,000, the States may impose a period of ineligibility exceeding 24 months, as long as this period bears "a reasonable relationship to such uncompensated value."

In sum, it would appear that in the future the States will be permitted to impose transfer-of-assets restrictions generally similar to that of California.[1]

5. Presumptions governing collateral attacks on judgments of conviction would have been added by the Supreme Court using its rule making power. Under the Supreme Court's draft, Rule 9(a) of the Rules Governing Section 2254 [Title 28 U.S.C.] Cases in the United States District Courts provided:

> If the petition [for a writ of habeas corpus] is filed more than five years after the judgment of conviction, there shall be a presumption, rebuttable by the petitioner, that there is prejudice to the state.

If there were such prejudice the petition could have been dismissed on the theory that the state's "ability to respond" to the petition was substantially reduced. The petitioner could have avoided dismissal by showing that the petition

> is based on grounds of which he could not have had knowledge by the exercise of reasonable diligence before the circumstances prejudicial to the state occurred.

Id. 28 U.S.C. § 2254 covers petitions from those in the custody of a state.

These presumptions were struck by Congress. Pub.L. 94–426 § 2(7) on the ground that they were "unsound policy." 3 U.S. Code Congressional and Administrative News, 94th Cong., Second Sess. 248 (1976). Could the Supreme Court have achieved the same result by interpreting section 2254? Would Congress have been likely to then pass a statute overruling this interpretation?

6. While the government retains the overall burden of proof in deportation hearings, the burden of coming forward may shift. Thus in Small v. Immigration and Naturalization Service, 438 F.2d 1125 (2d Cir.1971), once the government established alienage, marriage less than two years prior to entry, and annulment or termination of marriage within two years subsequent to entry, a statutory presumption of contracting marriage to evade immigration laws was deemed to arise and the burden of refuting the presumption shifted to the alien.

County Court of Ulster County v. Allen

Supreme Court of the United States, 1979.
442 U.S. 140, 99 S.Ct. 2213, 60 L.Ed.2d 777.

■ MR. JUSTICE STEVENS delivered the opinion of the Court.

1. The California rule is set out in Cal. Wel. & Inst. Code § 14015. This statute provides in part:

"[A]ny transfer of the holdings by gift or, knowingly, without adequate and reasonable consideration, shall be presumed to constitute a gift of property with intent to qualify for assistance and such act shall disqualify the owner for further aid for a period determined under standards established by the director, and in no event for less than half of the period that the capital value of the transferred property would have supplied the person's maintenance needs based on his circumstances at the time of his transfer plus the cost of any needed medical care." [Footnote by Court renumbered and moved.]

A New York statute provides that, with certain exceptions, the presence of a firearm in an automobile is presumptive evidence of its illegal possession by all persons then occupying the vehicle [1] The United States Court of Appeals for the Second Circuit held that respondents may challenge the constitutionality of this statute in a federal habeas corpus proceeding and that the statute is "unconstitutional on its face." 568 F.2d 998, 1009. We granted certiorari to review these holdings and also to consider whether the statute is constitutional in its application to respondents. 439 U.S. 815, 99 S.Ct. 75, 58 L.Ed.2d 106.

Four persons, three adult males (respondents) and a 16–year-old girl (Jane Doe, who is not a respondent here), were jointly tried on charges that they possessed two loaded handguns, a loaded machinegun, and over a pound of heroin found in a Chevrolet in which they were riding when it was stopped for speeding on the New York Thruway shortly after noon on March 28, 1973. The two large-caliber handguns, which together with their ammunition weighed approximately six pounds, were seen through the window of the car by the investigating police officer. They were positioned crosswise in an open handbag on either the front floor or the front seat of the car on the passenger side where Jane Doe was sitting. Jane Doe admitted that the handbag was hers.[2] The machinegun and the heroin were discovered in the trunk after the police pried it open. The car had been borrowed from the driver's brother earlier that day; the key to the trunk could not be found in the car or on the person of any of its occupants, although there was testimony that two of the occupants had placed something in the trunk before embarking in the borrowed car. The jury convicted all four of possession of the handguns and acquitted them of possession of the contents of the trunk.

1. New York Penal Law § 265.15(3):

"The presence in an automobile, other than a stolen one or a public omnibus, of any firearm, defaced firearm, firearm silencer, bomb, bombshell, gravity knife, switchblade knife, dagger, dirk, stiletto, billy, blackjack, metal knuckles, sandbag, sandclub or slungshot is presumptive evidence of its possession by all persons occupying such automobile at the time such weapon, instrument or appliance is found, except under the following circumstances:

"(a) if such weapon, instrument or appliance is found upon the person of one of the occupants therein;

"(b) if such weapon, instrument or appliance is found in an automobile which is being operated for hire by a duly licensed driver in the due, lawful and proper pursuit of his trade, then such presumption shall not apply to the driver; or

"(c) if the weapon so found is a pistol or revolver and one of the occupants, not present under duress, has in his possession a valid license to have and carry concealed the same." In addition to the three exceptions delineated in §§ 265.15(3)(a)-(c) above as well as the stolen-vehicle and public-omnibus exception in § 265.15(3) itself, § 265.20 contains various exceptions that apply when weapons are present in an automobile pursuant to certain military, law enforcement, recreational, and commercial endeavors. [Some footnotes omitted; some renumbered; footnotes by the Court.]

2. The arrest was made by two state troopers. One officer approached the driver, advised him that he was going to issue a ticket for speeding, requested identification and returned to the patrol car. After a radio check indicated that the driver was wanted in Michigan on a weapons charge, the second officer returned to the vehicle and placed the driver under arrest. Thereafter, he went around to the right side of the car and, in "open view," saw a portion of a .45 automatic pistol protruding from the open purse on the floor or the seat. 40 N.Y.2d 505, 508–509, 387 N.Y.S.2d 97, 99–100, 354 N.E.2d 836, 838–839 (1976). He opened the car door, removed that gun and saw a .38 caliber revolver in the same handbag. He testified that the crosswise position of one or both of the guns kept the handbag from closing. After the weapons were secured, the two remaining male passengers, who had been sitting in the rear seat, and Jane Doe were arrested and frisked. A subsequent search at the police station disclosed a pocket-knife and marihuana concealed on Jane Doe's person. Tr., at 187–192, 208–214, 277–278, 291–297, 408.

Counsel for all four defendants objected to the introduction into evidence of the two handguns, the machinegun, and the drugs, arguing that the State had not adequately demonstrated a connection between their clients and the contraband. The trial court overruled the objection, relying on the presumption of possession created by the New York statute. Tr., at 474–483. Because that presumption does not apply if a weapon is found "upon the person" of one of the occupants of the car, see n. 1, supra, the three male defendants also moved to dismiss the charges relating to the handguns on the ground that the guns were found on the person of Jane Doe. Respondents made this motion both at the close of the prosecution's case and at the close of all evidence. The trial judge twice denied it, concluding that the applicability of the "on the person" exception was a question of fact for the jury. Tr., at 544–557, 589–590.

At the close of the trial, the judge instructed the jurors that they were entitled to infer possession from the defendants' presence in the car. He did not make any reference to the "upon the person" exception in his explanation of the statutory presumption, nor did any of the defendants object to this omission or request alternative or additional instructions on the subject.

. . .

Respondents filed a petition for a writ of habeas corpus in the United States District Court for the Southern District of New York contending that they were denied due process of law by the application of the statutory presumption of possession. The District Court issued the writ. . . .

The Court of Appeals for the Second Circuit . . . concluded that the statute is unconstitutional on its face because the "presumption obviously sweeps within its compass (1) many occupants who may not know they are riding with a gun (which may be out of their sight), and (2) many who may be aware of the presence of the gun but not permitted access to it."[3] [4]

Inferences and presumptions are a staple of our adversarial system of factfinding. It is often necessary for the trier of fact to determine the existence of an element of the crime—that is, an "ultimate" or "elemental" fact—from the existence of one or more "evidentiary" or "basic" facts. E.g., Barnes v. United States, 412 U.S. 837, 843–844, 93 S.Ct. 2357, 2361–2362, 37 L.Ed.2d 380; Tot v. United States, 319 U.S. 463, 467, 63 S.Ct. 1241, 1244, 87 L.Ed.2d 1519; Mobile, J. & K.C. R. Co. v. Turnipseed, 219 U.S. 35, 42, 31 S.Ct. 136, 137, 55 L.Ed. 78. The value of these evidentiary devices, and their validity under the Due Process Clause, vary from case to case, however, depending on the strength of the connection between the particular basic and elemental facts involved and on the degree to which the device curtails the factfinder's freedom to assess the evidence independently. Nonetheless, in criminal cases, the ultimate test of any device's constitutional validity in a given case remains constant: the device must not undermine the factfinder's responsibility at trial,

---

3. The majority continued:

"Nothing about a gun, which may be only a few inches in length (e.g., a Baretta or Derringer) and concealed under a seat in a glove compartment or beyond the reach of all but one of the car's occupants, assures that its presence is known to occupants who may be hitchhikers or other casual passengers, much less that they have any dominion or control over it." 568 F.2d, at 1007.

4. [T]he assumption that it would be unconstitutional to apply the statutory presumption to a hitchhiker in a car containing a concealed weapon does not necessarily advance the constitutional claim of the driver of a car in which a gun was found on the front seat, or of other defendants in entirely different situations.

based on evidence adduced by the State, to find the ultimate facts beyond a reasonable doubt. See In re Winship, 397 U.S. 358, 364, 90 S.Ct. 1068, 1072, 25 L.Ed.2d 368; Mullaney v. Wilbur, 421 U.S. 684, 702–703 n. 31, 95 S.Ct. 1881, 1891–1892 n. 31, 44 L.Ed.2d 508.

The most common evidentiary device is the entirely permissive inference or presumption, which allows—but does not require—the trier of fact to infer the elemental fact from proof by the prosecutor of the basic one and that places no burden of any kind on the defendant. See, e.g., Barnes v. United States, 412 U.S., at 840 n. 3, 93 S.Ct., at 2360 n. 3. In that situation the basic fact may constitute prima facie evidence of the elemental fact. See, e.g., Turner v. United States, 396 U.S. 398, 402 n. 2, 90 S.Ct. 642, 645, n. 2, 24 L.Ed.2d 610. When reviewing this type of device, the Court has required the party challenging it to demonstrate its invalidity as applied to him. E.g., Barnes v. United States, supra, 412 U.S., at 845, 93 S.Ct., at 2362; Turner v. United States, supra, 396 U.S., at 419–424, 90 S.Ct., at 653–656. See also United States v. Gainey, 380 U.S. 63, 67–68, 69–70, 85 S.Ct. 754, 757–758, 758–759, 13 L.Ed.2d 658. Because this permissive presumption leaves the trier of fact free to credit or reject the inference and does not shift the burden of proof, it affects the application of the "beyond a reasonable doubt" standard only if, under the facts of the case, there is no rational way the trier could make the connection permitted by the inference. For only in that situation is there any risk that an explanation of the permissible inference to a jury, or its use by a jury, has caused the presumptively rational factfinder to make an erroneous factual determination.

A mandatory presumption is a far more troublesome evidentiary device. For it may affect not only the strength of the "no reasonable doubt" burden but also the placement of that burden; it tells the trier that he or they must find the elemental fact upon proof of the basic fact, at least unless the defendant has come forward with some evidence to rebut the presumed connection between the two facts. E.g., Turner v. United States, supra, 396 U.S., at 401–402, and n. 1, 90 S.Ct., at 644–645, and n. 1; Leary v. United States, 395 U.S. 6, 30, 89 S.Ct. 1532, 1545, 23 L.Ed.2d 57; United States v. Romano, 382 U.S. 136, 137, and n. 4, 138, 143, 86 S.Ct. 279, 280, and n. 4, 281, 283, 15 L.Ed.2d 210; Tot v. United States, supra, 319 U.S., at 469, 63 S.Ct., at 1245.[5] In this situation, the Court has generally examined the presumption on

---

5.   This class of more or less mandatory presumptions can be subdivided into two parts: presumptions that merely shift the burden of production to the defendant, following the satisfaction of which the ultimate burden of persuasion returns to the prosecution; and presumptions that entirely shift the burden of proof to the defendant. The mandatory presumptions examined by our cases have almost uniformly fit into the former subclass, in that they never totally removed the ultimate burden of proof beyond a reasonable doubt from the prosecution. E.g., Tot v. United States, 319 U.S. at 469, 63 S.Ct., at 1245. See Roviaro v. United States, 353 U.S. 53, 63, 77 S.Ct. 623, 629, 1 L.Ed.2d 639, describing the operation of the presumption involved in Turner, Leary, and Romano.

To the extent that a presumption imposes an extremely low burden of production— e.g., being satisfied by "any" evidence—it may well be that its impact is no greater than that of a permissive inference and it may be proper to analyze it as such. See generally Mullaney v. Wilbur, supra, 421 U.S. 684, 703 n. 31, 95 S.Ct., 1881, 1892 n. 31, 44 L.Ed.2d 508.

In deciding what type of inference or presumption is involved in a case, the jury instructions will generally be controlling, although their interpretation may require recourse to the statute involved and the cases decided under it. Turner v. United States, supra, provides a useful illustration of the different types of presumptions. It analyzes the constitutionality of two different presumption statutes (one mandatory and one permissive) as they apply to the basic fact of possession of both heroin and cocaine, and the presumed facts of importation and distribution of narcotic drugs. The jury was charged essentially in the terms of the two statutes.

The importance of focusing attention on the precise presentation of the presumption

its face to determine the extent to which the basic and elemental facts coincide. E.g., Turner v. United States, supra, 396 U.S., at 408–418, 90 S.Ct., at 648–653; Leary v. United States, supra, 395 U.S., at 45–52, 89 S.Ct., at 1552–1553; United States v. Romano, supra, 382 U.S., at 140 141, 86 S.Ct., at 281 282; Tot v. United States, supra, 319 U.S. at 468, 63 S.Ct., at 1245. To the extent that the trier of fact is forced to abide by the presumption, and may not reject it based on an independent evaluation of the particular facts presented by the State, the analysis of the presumption's constitutional validity is logically divorced from those facts and based on the presumption's accuracy in the run of cases.[6] It is for this reason that the Court has held it irrelevant in analyzing

to the jury and the scope of that presumption is illustrated by a comparison of United States v. Gainey, 380 U.S. 63, 85 S.Ct. 754, 13 L.Ed.2d 658, with United States v. Romano. Both cases involved statutory presumptions based on proof that the defendant was present at the site of an illegal still. In Gainey the Court sustained a conviction "for carrying on" the business of the distillery in violation of 26 U.S.C. § 5601(a)(4), whereas in Romano, the Court set aside a conviction for being in "possession, custody, and . . . control" of such a distillery in violation of § 5601(a)(1). The difference in outcome was attributable to two important differences between the cases. Because the statute involved in Gainey was a sweeping prohibition of almost any activity associated with the still, whereas the Romano statute involved only one narrow aspect of the total undertaking, there was a much higher probability that mere presence could support an inference of guilt in the former case than in the latter.

Of perhaps greater importance, however, was the difference between the trial judge's instructions to the jury in the two cases. In Gainey the judge had explained that the presumption was permissive; it did not require the jury to convict the defendant even if it was convinced that he was present at the site. On the contrary, the instructions made it clear that presence was only "a circumstance to be considered along with all the other circumstances in the case." As we emphasized, the "jury was thus specifically told that the statutory [presumption] was not conclusive." 380 U.S. at 69–70, 85 S.Ct., at 758–759. In Romano the trial judge told the jury that the defendant's presence at the still "shall be deemed sufficient evidence to authorize conviction." 382 U.S. at 182, 86 S.Ct., at 281. Although there was other evidence of guilt, that instruction authorized conviction even if the jury disbelieved all of the testimony except the proof of presence at the site. This Court's holding that the statutory presumption could not support the Romano conviction was thus dependent, in part, on the specific instructions given by the trial judge. Under those instructions it was necessary to decide whether, regardless of the specific circumstances of the particular case, the statu-

tory presumption adequately supported the guilty verdict.

6. In addition to the discussion of Romano in n. [5], supra, this point is illustrated by Leary v. United States, supra. In that case, Dr. Timothy Leary, a professor at Harvard University was stopped by customs inspectors in Laredo, Texas as he was returning from the Mexican side of the international border. Marihuana seeds and a silver snuff box filled with semirefined marihuana and three partially smoked marihuana cigarettes were discovered in his car. He was convicted of having knowingly transported marihuana which he knew had been illegally imported into this country in violation of 21 U.S.C. § 176a. That statute includes a mandatory presumption: "possession shall be deemed sufficient evidence to authorize conviction [for importation] unless the defendant explains his possession to the satisfaction of the jury." Leary admitted possession of the marihuana and claimed that he had carried it from New York to Mexico and then back.

Justice Harlan for the Court noted that under one theory of the case, the jury could have found direct proof of all of the necessary elements of the offense without recourse to the presumption. But he deemed that insufficient reason to affirm the conviction because under another theory the jury might have found knowledge of importation on the basis of either direct evidence or the presumption, and there was accordingly no certainty that the jury had not relied on the presumption. 395 U.S., at 31–32, 89 S.Ct., at 1545–1546. The Court therefore found it necessary to test the presumption against the Due Process Clause. Its analysis was facial. Despite the fact that the defendant was well educated and had recently traveled to a country that is a major exporter of marihuana to this country, the Court found the presumption of knowledge of importation from possession irrational. It did so not because Dr. Leary was unlikely to know the source of the marihuana but instead because "a majority of possessors" were unlikely to have such knowledge. Id., at 53, 89 S.Ct., at 1557. Because the jury had been instructed to rely on the presumption even if it did not believe the Government's direct evidence of knowledge of impora mandatory presumption, but not in analyzing a purely permissive one, that there is ample evidence in the record other than the presumption to support a conviction. E.g., Turner v. United States, supra, 396 U.S., at 407, 90 S.Ct., at 647; Leary v. United States, supra, 395 U.S., at 31–32, 89 S.Ct., at 1545–1546; United States v. Romano, supra, 382 U.S., at 138–139, 86 S.Ct., at 280–281.

Without determining whether the presumption in this case was mandatory, the Court of Appeals analyzed it on its face as if it were. In fact, it was not, as the New York Court of Appeals had earlier pointed out. 40 N.Y.2d, at 510–511, 387 N.Y.S.2d, at 100, 354 N.E.2d, at 840.

The trial judge's instructions make it clear that the presumption was merely a part of the prosecution's case,[7] that it gave rise to a permissive inference available only in certain circumstances, rather than a mandatory conclusion of possession, and that it could be ignored by the jury even if there was no affirmative proof offered by defendants in rebuttal.[8] The judge explained that possession could be actual or constructive, but that constructive possession could not exist without the intent and ability to exercise control or dominion over the weapons.[9] He also carefully instructed the jury that there is a mandatory presumption of innocence in favor of the defendants that controls unless it, as the exclusive trier of fact, is satisfied beyond a reasonable doubt that the defendants possessed the handguns in the manner described by the judge.[10] In short, the instructions plainly directed the jury to consider all the

tation (unless, of course, the defendant met his burden of "satisfying" the jury to the contrary), the Court reversed the conviction.

7. "It is your duty to consider all the testimony in this case, to weigh it carefully and assess the credit to be given to a witness by his apparent intention to speak the truth and by the accuracy of his memory to reconcile, if possible, conflicting statements as to material facts and in such ways to try and get at the truth and to reach a verdict upon the evidence." Tr., at 739–740.

"To establish the unlawful possession of the weapons, again the People relied upon the presumption and, in addition thereto, the testimony of Anderson and Lemmons who testified in their case in chief." Id., at 744.

"Accordingly, you would be warranted in returning a verdict of guilt against the defendants or defendant if you find the defendants or defendant was in possession of a machine gun and the other weapons and that the fact of possession was proven to you by the People beyond a reasonable doubt, and an element of such proof is the reasonable presumption of illegal possession of a machine gun or the presumption of illegal possession of firearms, as I have just before explained to you." Id., at 746.

8. "Our Penal Law also provides that the presence in an automobile of any machine gun or of any handgun or firearm which is loaded is presumptive evidence of their unlawful possession.

"In other words, these presumptions or this latter presumption upon proof of the

presence of the machine gun and the hand weapons, you may infer and draw conclusions that such prohibitive weapon was possessed by each of the defendants who occupied the automobile at the time when such instruments were found. The presumption or presumptions is effective only so long as there is no substantial evidence contradicting the conclusion flowing from the presumption, and the presumption is said to disappear when such contradictory evidence is adduced." Id., at 743.

"The presumption or presumptions which I discussed with the jury relative to the drugs or weapons in this case need not be rebutted by affirmative proof or affirmative evidence but may be rebutted by an evidence or lack of evidence in the case." Id., at 760.

9. "As so defined, possession means actual physical possession, just as having the drugs or weapons in one's hand, in one's home, or other place under one's exclusive control, or constructive possession which may exist without personal dominion over the drugs or weapons but with the intent and ability to retain such control or dominion." Id., at 742.

10. "[Y]ou are the exclusive judge of all the questions of fact in this case. That means that you are the sole judges as to the weight to be given to the evidence and to the weight and probative value to be given to the testimony of each particular witness and to the credibility of any witness." Id., at 730.

"Under our law, every defendant in a criminal trial starts the trial with the pre-

circumstances tending to support or contradict the inference that all four occupants of the car had possession of the two loaded handguns and to decide the matter for itself without regard to how much evidence the defendants introduced.[11]

Our cases considering the validity of permissive statutory presumptions such as the one involved here have rested on an evaluation of the presumption as applied to the record before the Court. None suggests that a court should pass on the constitutionality of this kind of statute "on its face." It was error for the Court of Appeals to make such a determination in this case.

III

As applied to the facts of this case, the presumption of possession is entirely rational. Notwithstanding the Court of Appeals' analysis, respondents were not "hitch-hikers or other casual passengers," and the guns were neither "a few inches in length" nor "out of [respondents'] sight." See n. 4, supra, and text accompanying. The argument against possession by any of the respondents was predicated solely on the fact that the guns were in Jane Doe's pocketbook. But several circumstances—which, not surprisingly, her counsel repeatedly emphasized in his questions and his argument, e.g., Tr., at 282–283, 294–297, 306—made it highly improbable that she was the sole custodian of those weapons.

Even if it was reasonable to conclude that she had placed the guns in her purse before the car was stopped by police, the facts strongly suggest that Jane Doe was not the only person able to exercise dominion over them. The two guns were too large to be concealed in her handbag. The bag was consequently open, and part of one of the guns was in plain view, within easy access of the driver of the car and even, perhaps, of the other two respondents who were riding in the rear seat.

Moreover, it is highly improbable that the loaded guns belonged to Jane Doe or that she was solely responsible for their being in her purse. As a 16–year-old girl in the company of three adult men she was the least likely of the four to be carrying one, let alone two, heavy handguns. It is far more probable that she relied on the pocket-knife found in her brassiere for any necessary self-protection. Under these circumstances, it was not unreasonable for her counsel to argue and for the jury to infer that when the car was halted for speeding, the other passengers in the car anticipated the risk of a search and attempted to conceal their weapons in a pocketbook in the front seat. The inference is surely more likely than the notion that these weapons were the sole property of the 16–year-old girl.

---

sumption in his favor that he is innocent, and this presumption follows him throughout the entire trial and remains with him until such time as you, by your verdict find him or her guilty beyond a reasonable doubt or innocent of the charge. If you find him or her not guilty, then, of course, this presumption ripens into an established fact. On the other hand, if you find him or her guilty then this presumption has been overcome and is destroyed." Id., at 734.

"Now, in order to find any of the defendants guilty of the unlawful possession of the weapons, the machine gun, the .45 and the .38, you must be satisfied beyond a reasonable doubt that the defendants possessed the machine gun and the .45 and the .38, possessed it as I defined it to you before." Id., at 745.

11. The verdict announced by the jury, clearly indicates that it understood its duty to evaluate the presumption independently and to reject it if it was not supported in the record. Despite receiving almost identical instructions on the applicability of the presumption of possession to the contraband found in the front seat and in the trunk, the jury convicted all four defendants of possession of the former but acquitted all of them of possession of the latter....

Under these circumstances, the jury would have been entirely reasonable in rejecting the suggestion—which, incidentally, defense counsel did not even advance in their closing arguments to the jury[12]—that the handguns were in the sole possession of Jane Doe. Assuming that the jury did reject it, the case is tantamount to one in which the guns were lying on the floor or the seat of the car in the plain view of the three other occupants of the automobile. In such a case it is surely rational to infer that each of the respondents was fully aware of the presence of the guns and had both the ability and the intent to exercise dominion and control over the weapons. The application of the statutory presumption in this case therefor comports with the standard laid down in Tot v. United States, 319 U.S., at 467, 63 S.Ct. at 1244, and restated in Leary v. United States, supra, 395 U.S., at 36, 89 S.Ct., at 1548. For there is a "rational connection" between the basic facts that the prosecution proved and the ultimate fact presumed, and the latter is "more likely than not to flow from" the former.[13]

12. Indeed, counsel for two of the respondents virtually invited the jury to find to the contrary:

"One more thing. You know, different people live in different cultures and different societies. You may think that the way [respondent] Hardrick has his hair done up is unusual; it may seem strange to you. People live differently.... For example, if you were living under their times and conditions and you traveled from a big city, Detroit, to a bigger city, New York City, *it is not unusual for people to carry guns, small arms to protect themselves, is it?* There are places in New York City policemen fear to go. But you have got to understand; you are sitting here as jurors. These are people, live flesh and blood, the same as you, different motives, different objectives." Tr., at 653–654 (emphasis added). See also Id. at 634.

It is also important in this regard that respondents passed up the opportunity to have the jury instructed not to apply the presumption if it determined that the handguns were "upon the person" of Jane Doe.

13. The New York Court of Appeals first upheld the constitutionality of the presumption involved in this case in People v. Russo, 303 N.Y. 673, 102 N.E.2d 834 (1951). That decision relied upon the earlier case of People v. Terra, 303 N.Y. 332, 102 N.E.2d 576 (1951), which upheld the constitutionality of another New York statute that allowed a jury to presume that the occupants of a room in which a firearm was located possessed the weapon. The analysis in Terra, which this Court dismissed for want of a substantial federal question, 342 U.S. 938, 72 S.Ct. 561, 96 L.Ed. 698, is persuasive:

"There can be no doubt about the 'sinister significance' of proof of a machine gun in a room occupied by an accused or about the reasonableness of the connection between its illegal possession and occupancy of the room where it is kept. Persons who occupy a room, who either reside in it or use it in the conduct and operation of a business or other venture—and that is what in its present context the statutory term 'occupying' signifies ...—normally know what is in it; and, certainly, when the object is as large and uncommon as a machine gun, it is neither unreasonable nor unfair to presume that the room's occupants are aware of its presence. That being so, the legislature may not be considered arbitrary if it acts upon the presumption and erects it into evidence of a possession that is 'conscious' and 'knowing'." 303 N.Y., at 335–336, 102 N.E.2d, at 578–579.

See also Controlled Substances, Dangerous Unless Used as Directed, N.Y.Leg.Doc. No. 10, at 69 (1972), in which the drafters of the analogous automobile/narcotics presumption in N.Y.Pen.L. § 220.25 (McKinney Supp. 1978), explained the basis for that presumption:

"We believe, and find, that it is rational and logical to presume that all occupants of a vehicle are aware of, and culpably involved in, possession of dangerous drugs found abandoned or secreted in a vehicle when the quantity of the drug is such that it would be extremely unlikely for an occupant to be unaware of its presence....

"We do not believe that persons transporting dealership quantities of contraband are likely to go driving around with innocent friends or that they are likely to pick up strangers. We do not doubt that this can and does in fact occasionally happen, but because we find it more reasonable to believe that the bare presence in the vehicle is culpable, we think it reasonable to presume culpability in the direction which the proven facts already point. Since the presumption is an evidentiary one, it may be offset by any evidence including the testimony of the defendant, which would negate the defendant's culpable involvement." Legislative judgments such as

Respondents argue, however, that the validity of the New York presumption must be judged by a "reasonable doubt" test rather than the "more likely than not" standard employed in Leary.[14] Under the more stringent test, it is argued that a statutory presumption must be rejected unless the evidence necessary to invoke the inference is sufficient for a rational jury to find the inferred fact beyond a reasonable doubt. See Barnes v. United States, 412 U.S. at 842–843, 93 S.Ct., at 2361–2362. Respondents' argument again overlooks the distinction between a permissive presumption on which the prosecution is entitled to rely as one not-necessarily-sufficient part of its proof and a mandatory presumption which the jury must accept even if it is the sole evidence of an element of the offense.

In the latter situation, since the prosecution bears the burden of establishing guilt, it may not rest its case entirely on a presumption unless the fact proved is sufficient to support the inference of guilt beyond a reasonable doubt. But in the former situation, the prosecution may rely on all the evidence in the record to meet the reasonable doubt standard. There is no more reason to require a permissive statutory presumption to meet a reasonable doubt standard before it may be permitted to play any part in a trial than there is to require that degree of probative force for other relevant evidence before it may be admitted. As long as it is clear that the presumption is not the sole and sufficient basis for a finding of guilt, it need only satisfy the test described in Leary.

The permissive presumption, as used in this case, satisfied the Leary test. And, as already noted, the New York Court of Appeals has concluded that the record as a whole was sufficient to establish guilt beyond a reasonable doubt.

The judgment is reversed.

■ MR. CHIEF JUSTICE BURGER, concurring [omitted].

■ MR. JUSTICE POWELL, with whom MR. JUSTICE BRENNAN, MR. JUSTICE STEWART, and MR. JUSTICE MARSHALL join dissenting.

I

. . . I do not agree with the Court's conclusion that the only constitutional difficulty with presumptions lies in the danger of lessening the burden of proof the prosecution must bear. As the Court notes, the presumptions thus far reviewed by the Court have not shifted the burden of persuasion, see ante, at 2224 n. 16; instead they either have required only that the defendant produce some evidence to rebut the inference suggested by the prosecution's evidence, see Tot v. United States, 319 U.S. 463, 63 S.Ct. 1241, 87 L.Ed.2d 1519 (1943), or merely have been suggestions to the jury that it would be sensible to draw certain conclusions on the basis of the evidence presented.[1] See Barnes v.

this one deserve respect in assessing the constitutionality of evidentiary presumptions. E.g., Leary v. United States, 395 U.S., at 39, 89 S.Ct., at 1549; United States v. Gainey, 380 U.S., at 67, 85 S.Ct., at 757.

14. "The upshot of Tot, Gainey, and Romano is, we think, that a criminal statutory presumption must be regarded as 'irrational' or 'arbitrary,' and hence unconstitutional, unless it can at least be said with substantial assurance that the presumed fact is more likely than not to flow from the proved fact on which it is made to depend."

1. The Court suggests as the touchstone for its analysis a distinction between "mandatory" and "permissive" presumptions. See ante, at 2224–2225. For general discussions of the various forms of presumptions, see Jeffries & Stephan, Defenses, Presumptions, and Burden of Proof in the Criminal Law, 88 Yale L.J. 1325 (1979); F. James, Civil Procedure § 7.9 (1965). I have found no recognition in the Court's prior decisions that this distinction is important in analyzing presumptions used in criminal cases. Cf. F. James, Civil Procedure, ibid. (distinguishing true "presumptions" from "permissible in-

United States, supra, 412 U.S. at 840 n. 3, 93 S.Ct., at 2360 n. 3. Evolving from our decisions, therefore, is a second standard for judging the constitutionality of criminal presumptions which is based—not on the constitutional requirement that the State be put to its proof—but rather on the due process rule that when the jury is encouraged to make factual inferences, those inferences must reflect some valid general observation about the natural connection between events as they occur in our society.

This due process rule was first articulated by the Court in Tot v. United States, supra, in which the Court reviewed the constitutionality of § 2(f) of the Federal Firearms Act. That statute provided in part that "possession of a firearm or ammunition by any ... person [who has been convicted of a crime of violence] shall be presumptive evidence that such firearm or ammunition was shipped or transported [in interstate or foreign commerce]." As the Court interpreted the presumption, it placed upon a defendant only the obligation of presenting some exculpatory evidence concerning the origins of a firearm or ammunition, once the Government proved that the defendant had possessed the weapon and had been convicted of a crime of violence. Noting that juries must be permitted to infer from one fact the existence of another essential to guilt, "if reason and experience support the inference," 319 U.S., at 467, 63 S.Ct., at 1244, the Court concluded that under some circumstances juries may be guided in making these inferences by legislative or common-law presumptions, even though they may be based "upon a view of relation broader than that a jury might take in a specific case," at 468, 63 S.Ct., at 1245. To provide due process, however, there must be at least "a rational connection between the facts proved and the fact presumed"—a connection grounded in "common experience." Id., at 467, 63 S.Ct., at 1245. In Tot, the Court found that connection to be lacking.

Subsequently, in Leary v. United States, 395 U.S. 6, 89 S.Ct. 1532, 23 L.Ed.2d 57 (1969), the Court reaffirmed and refined the due process requirement of Tot that inferences specifically commended to the attention of jurors must reflect generally accepted connections between related events. At issue in Leary was the constitutionality of a federal statute making it a crime to receive, conceal, buy, or sell marihuana illegally brought into the United States, knowing it to have been illegally imported. The statute provided that mere possession of marihuana "shall be deemed sufficient evidence to authorize conviction unless the defendant explains his possession to the satisfaction of the jury." After reviewing the Court's decisions in Tot v. United States, supra, and other criminal presumption cases, Mr. Justice Harlan, writing for the Court, concluded "that a criminal statutory presumption must be regarded as 'irrational' or 'arbitrary,' and hence unconstitutional, unless it can be said with substantial assurance that the presumed fact is more likely than not to flow from the proved fact on which it is made to depend." 395 U.S., at 36, 89 S.Ct., at 1548 (footnote omitted). The Court invalidated the statute, finding there to be insufficient basis in fact for the conclusion that those who possess marihuana are more likely than not to know that it is imported illegally.

Most recently, in Barnes v. United States, supra, we considered the constitutionality of a quite different sort of presumption—one that suggested to the jury the "[p]ossession of recently stolen property, if not satisfactorily explained, is ordinarily a circumstance from which you may reasonably draw the inference ... that the person in possession knew the property had been stolen." 412 U.S. at 840 n. 3, 93 S.Ct., at 2360 n. 3. After reviewing the various formulations used by the Court to articulate the constitutionally required basis

ferences"). [Some footnotes omitted; some re-numbered.]

for a criminal presumption, we once again found it unnecessary to choose among them. As for the presumption suggested to the jury in Barnes, we found that it was well founded in history, common sense, and experience, and therefore upheld it as being "clearly sufficient to enable the jury to find beyond a reasonable doubt" that those in the unexplained possession of recently stolen property know it to have been stolen. Id., at 845, 93 S.Ct., at 2363.

In sum, our decisions uniformly have recognized that due process requires more than merely that the prosecution be put to its proof. In addition, the Constitution restricts the court in its charge to the jury by requiring that, when particular factual inferences are recommended to the jury, those factual inferences be accurate reflections of what history, common sense, and experience tell us about the relations between events in our society. Generally this due process rule has been articulated as requiring that the truth of the inferred fact be more likely than not whenever the premise for the inference is true. Thus, to be constitutional a presumption must be at least more likely than not true.

II

In the present case, the jury was told that,

"Our Penal Law also provides that the presence in an automobile of any machine gun or of any handgun or firearm which is loaded is presumptive evidence of their unlawful possession. In other words, [under] these presumptions or this latter presumption upon proof of the presence of the machine gun and the hand weapons, you may infer and draw a conclusion that such prohibited weapon was possessed by each of the defendants who occupied the automobile at the time when such instruments were found. The presumption or presumptions is effective only so long as there is no substantial evidence contradicting the conclusion flowing from the presumption, and the presumption is said to disappear when such contradictory evidence is adduced."

Undeniably, the presumption charged in this case encouraged the jury to draw a particular factual inference regardless of any other evidence presented: to infer that respondents possessed the weapons found in the automobile "upon proof of the presence of the machine gun and the hand weapon" and proof that respondents "occupied the automobile at the time such instruments were found." I believe that the presumption thus charged was unconstitutional because it did not fairly reflect what common sense and experience tell us about passengers in automobiles and the possession of handguns. People present in automobiles where there are weapons simply are not "more likely than not" the possessors of those weapons.

Under New York law, "to possess" is "to have physical possession or otherwise to exercise dominion or control over tangible property." N.Y. Penal Law § 10.00(8). Plainly the mere presence of an individual in an automobile—without more—does not indicate that he exercises "dominion or control over" everything within it. As the Court of Appeals noted, there are countless situations in which individuals are invited as guests into vehicles the contents of which they know nothing about, much less have control over. Similarly, those who invite others into their automobile do not generally search them to determine what they may have on their person; nor do they insist that any handguns be identified and placed within reach of the occupants of the automobile. Indeed, handguns are particularly susceptible to concealment and therefore are less likely than are other objects to be observed by those in an automobile.

In another context, this Court has been particularly hesitant to infer possession from mere presence in a location, noting that "[p]resence is relevant and admissible evidence in a trial on a possession charge; but absent some showing of the defendant's function at [the illegal] still, its connection with possession is too tenuous to permit a reasonable inference of guilt—'the inference of the one from proof of the other is arbitrary....' Tot v. United States, 319 U.S. 463, 467, 63 S.Ct. 1241, 1245, 87 L.Ed.2d 1519." United States v. Romano, 382 U.S., at 141, 86 S.Ct., at 282. We should be even more hesitant to uphold the inference of possession of a handgun from mere presence in an automobile, in light of common experience concerning automobiles and handguns. Because the specific factual inference recommended to the jury in this case is not one that is supported by the general experience of our society, I cannot say that the presumption charged is "more likely than not" to be true. Accordingly, respondents' due process rights were violated by the presumption's use.

As I understand it, the Court today does not contend that in general those who are present in automobiles are more likely than not to possess any gun contained within their vehicles. It argues, however, that the nature of the presumption here involved requires that we look, not only to the immediate facts upon which the jury was encouraged to base its inference, but to the other facts "proved" by the prosecution as well. The Court suggests that this is the proper approach when reviewing what it calls "permissive" presumptions because the jury was urged "to consider all the circumstances tending to support or contradict the inference." Ante, at 2227.

It seems to me that the Court mischaracterizes the function of the presumption charged in this case. As it acknowledges was the case in Romano, supra, the "instruction authorized conviction even if the jury disbelieved all of the testimony except the proof of presence" in the automobile.[2] Ante, at 2225 n. 15. The Court nevertheless relies on all of the evidence introduced by the prosecution and argues that the "permissive" presumption could not have prejudiced defendants. The possibility that the jury disbelieved all of this evidence, and relied on the presumption, is simply ignored.

I agree that the circumstances relied upon by the Court in determining the plausibility of the presumption charged in this case would have made it reasonable for the jury to "infer that each of the respondents was fully aware of the presence of the guns and had both the ability and the intent to exercise dominion and control over the weapons." But the jury was told that it could conclude that respondents possessed the weapons found therein from proof of the mere fact of respondents' presence in the automobile. For all we know, the jury rejected all of the prosecution's evidence concerning the location and origin of the guns, and based its conclusion that respondents possessed the weapons solely upon its belief that respondents had been present in the automobile.[3] For

---

2. In commending the presumption to the jury, the court gave no instruction that would have required a finding of possession to be based on anything more than mere presence in the automobile. Thus, the jury was not instructed that it should infer that respondents possessed the handguns only if it found that the guns were too large to be concealed in Jane Doe's handbag, ante, at 2227–2228; that the guns accordingly were in the plain view of respondents, ante, at 2228; that the weapons were within "easy access of the driver of the car and even, perhaps, of the

other two respondents, who were riding in the rear seat," ibid.; that it was unlikely that Jane Doe was solely responsible for the placement of the weapons in her purse, id.; or that the case was "tantamount to one in which the guns were lying on the floor or the seat of the car in the plain view of the three other occupants of the automobile." Ante, at 2228.

3. The Court is therefore mistaken in its conclusion that, because "respondents were not 'hitch-hikers or other casual passengers,' and the guns were neither 'a few

purposes of reviewing the constitutionality of the presumption at issue here, we must assume that this was the case. See Bollenbach v. United States, 326 U.S. 607, 613, 66 S.Ct. 402, 405, 90 L.Ed. 350 (1946); cf. Leary v. United States, 395 U.S., at 31, 89 S.Ct., at 1545.

The Court's novel approach in this case appears to contradict prior decisions of this Court reviewing such presumptions. Under the Court's analysis, whenever it is determined that an inference is "permissive," the only question is whether, in light of all of the evidence adduced at trial, the inference recommended to the jury is a reasonable one. The Court has never suggested that the inquiry into the rational basis of a permissible inference may be circumvented in this manner. Quite the contrary, the Court has required that the "evidence *necessary to invoke the inference* [be] sufficient for a rational juror to find the inferred fact...." Barnes v. United States, 412 U.S., at 843, 93 S.Ct., at 2362 (emphasis supplied). See Turner v. United States, 396 U.S. 398, 407, 90 S.Ct. 642, 647, 24 L.Ed.2d 610 (1970). Under the presumption charged in this case, the only evidence necessary to invoke the inference was the presence of the weapons in the automobile with respondents—an inference that is plainly irrational.

In sum, it seems to me that the Court today ignores the teaching of our prior decisions. By speculating about what the jury may have done with the factual inference thrust upon it, the Court in effect assumes away the inference altogether, constructing a rule that permits the use of any inference—no matter how irrational in itself—provided that otherwise there is sufficient evidence in the record to support a finding of guilt. Applying this novel analysis to the present case, the Court upholds the use of a presumption that it makes no effort to defend in isolation. In substance, the Court—applying an unarticulated harmless error standard—simply finds that the respondents were guilty as charged. They may well have been but rather than acknowledging this rationale, the Court seems to have made new law with respect to presumptions that could seriously jeopardize a defendant's right to a fair trial. Accordingly, I dissent.

NOTES

1. In upholding the "rationality" of the permissive presumption the Court in Allen quoted from the "analogous automobile/narcotics presumption in N.Y.Pen.L. 220.25." But cf. Lopez for and in Behalf of Garcia v. Curry, 583 F.2d 1188 (2d Cir.1978), which stated that a New York statute allowing possession of narcotics to be inferred from defendant's presence in an automobile with narcotics could only be upheld where dealership quantity is present. The court stressed that there had been a comprehensive commission report and public hearings providing a factual basis for upholding such presumption, unlike in Allen where the same court "[n]oting the absence of legislative findings to support the presumptions, ... found no rational basis for the

inches in length' nor 'out of [respondents'] sight,' " reference to these possibilities is inappropriate in considering the constitutionality of the presumption as charged in this case. Ante, at 2227. To be sure, respondents' challenge is to the presumption as charged to the jury in this case. But in assessing its application here, we are not free, as the Court apparently believes, to disregard the possibility that the jury may have disbelieved all other evidence supporting an inference of possession. The jury may have concluded that respondents—like hitchhikers—had only an incidental relationship to the auto in which they were traveling, or that, contrary to some of the testimony at trial, the weapons were indeed out of respondents' sight.

inference of possession from presence." 583 F.2d at 1192 n. 8. But the Lopez court granted a writ of habeas corpus on the judge's charge

> that "the Penal Law says in effect that from this evidence [that both the cocaine and the defendants were present in the automobile] each of the defendants possessed the cocaine, knowingly possessed the cocaine." If the foundation was laid, he added, the state was "entitled to the presumption . . . charging them with possession."
>
> These instructions ran afoul of the guarantee of In re Winship, 397 U.S. 358, 364, 90 S.Ct. 1068, 1073, 25 L.Ed.2d 368 (1970).

Id. at 1192.

In State v. Christianson, 404 A.2d 999 (Me.1979), a defendant convicted of trafficking in a schedule drug challenged a Maine statute providing that

> [a] laboratory which receives a drug or substance from a law enforcement officer or agency for analysis . . . shall, if it is capable of so doing, analyze . . ., and shall issue a certificate stating the results of such analysis [which] . . . shall be prima facie evidence that the composition and quality of the drug or substance is as stated therein, unless with 10 days written notice to the prosecution, the defendant requests that a qualified witness testify as to such composition and quality.

17—A.M.R.S.A. § 1112(1). That is, the existence of one fact—chemist's certification of the drug's composition—is "prima facie" evidence of the existence of another fact necessary for conviction—the actual composition of the drug. Under Me.R.Evid. 303(a) a statutory-provision which provides "that certain facts are prima facie evidence of other facts" is to be treated as a presumption and governed by Me.R.Evid. 303(b)(c). Under Me.R.Evid. 303(b) the existence of a presumed fact must be capable of being inferred beyond a reasonable doubt from proof of the existence of the basic fact. The court concluded that there was nothing irrational in the legislature believing that a "sworn representation by a laboratory chemist (certified to perform certain tests) that a properly performed test showed a substance to be a particular schedule drug is reliable enough to support a fact-finding inference beyond a reasonable doubt that the substance in question is in fact that particular drug." 404 A.2d at 1003.

2. Highly critical of the mandatory-permissive distinction is Collier, The Improper Use of Presumptions in Recent Criminal Law Adjudications, 38 Stanf.L.Rev. 423, 460 (1986) ("All presumptions should be treated as 'mandatory' and their empirical premises subject to reasonable-doubt scrutiny."). In Lushing, Faces Without Features: The Surface Validity of Criminal Inferences, 72 Nw.U.Journal of Criminal L. and Crim. 82, 90 (1980), Professor Lushing creates the term "instructed inference" to describe the Allen instruction, since "The Allen problem revolves around a variation lying between the poles of a naturally drawn inference and a presumption: the judge tells the jury. 'If you find the letter was mailed you may, if you wish, conclude that the letter was received.' This is an instruction of an inference. . . ."

> The notorious complexity of the subject of deduction devices is no excuse for the Allen Court's insensitivity to the effect instructions have upon jurors. Interpretation of a judge's instructions in a lawyerlike manner—a methodology apparently abandoned by the Court two weeks later in Sandstrom—avoids the crucial dimension of impact on the layman. Ironically enough, the famous earlier decision in Allen v. United States, [164 U.S. 492, 17 S.Ct. 154, 41 L.Ed. 528 (1896)]which upheld the "dynamite charge," also proceeded from a one-dimensional analysis of instructions. In the earlier Allen case, a charge that juror hold-outs should question their

position and take into account that a majority disagreed with them was approved, the Court stating that "[i]t certainly cannot be the law that each juror should not listen with deference to the arguments and with a distrust of his own judgment, if he finds a large majority of the jury taking a different view of the case...." [164 U.S. at 501]. That certainly cannot be the law, but the issue the giving of an instruction raises is not simply what is the law, but also how will the jurors interpret the instruction. County Court v. Allen was a triumph of pedantry over realism. (Footnotes omitted.)

In Allen, Structuring Jury Decisionmaking in Criminal Cases: A Unified Constitutional Approach to Evidentiary Devices, 94 Harv.L.Rev. 321, 367 (1980), Professor Allen argues that presumptions, burdens of proof, instructions on inferences and comments on evidence by the court are all functionally similar methods for shifting burdens of persuasion, that may intrude on the jury's freedom to find facts and undermine the reasonable doubt standard. He concludes:

Because these various evidentiary devices are merely differing ways of allocating burdens of persuasion, an adequate method of analysis is available. Thus, the Court is in a position to begin addressing the real issues: What facts must constitutionally be established at trials, and to what extent will trial courts be permitted to give rational guidance to juries on such factual issues that must be established at trial? Despite the flaws in its reasoning, Ulster may have moved the analysis in that direction by, in essence, analyzing the instruction as though it were a comment on the evidence. And the primary point of Sandstrom may very well be a reiteration of the necessity for giving carefully composed jury instructions when they affect constitutionally significant factual issues.

Responding in a variety of ways, Professor Nesson suggests as a possible "model instruction" in Ulster the following:

It is often possible to infer from the presence of loaded firearms in an automobile that the occupants of the automobile possessed the weapons. You must decide whether, in the context of this case, such a conclusion is justified as to each defendant. You should consider all the facts. For example, consider where the guns were found, whether they were in plain sight, how easy they were to reach. Based on your consideration of all the evidence, you must decide whether the prosecution has proved beyond reasonable doubt that each defendant is guilty as charged.

Nesson, Rationality, Presumptions, and Judicial Comment: A Response to Professor Allen, 94 Harv.L.Rev. 1574, 1589 (1981). See also Allen, More on Constitutional Process-of-Proof Problems in Criminal Cases, 94 Harv.L.Rev. 1795 (1981). Is the Nesson suggestion one you would wish the court to adopt were you counsel for the prosecutor? For the defendant? Might the Nesson charge have an impact on the jury even greater than the presumption charge actually used since the jury would understand better what the judge is saying and might it interpret his comment as an indication that the judge thought that this was strong evidence of guilt?

What does "possession" really mean in these cases? How can this legal term be defined in a helpful way to the jury in a state case? In federal cases the court can utilize the conspiracy and aider and abetter charges. See generally the discussion in United States v. Weaver, 594 F.2d 1272 (9th Cir.1979). Possession then would mean physical possession as by having your hands on it or having it in your control intending to be able to use it when needed, or being associated with people in that category when you are engaged on a joint criminal enterprise. Whether or not a defendant actually knew it was there might under special circumstances be of little probative force. Contrariwise, even if the defendant saw a gun in open view, if he was not associated in the criminal enterprise he would not be guilty; mere passive knowledge would not suffice. Theoretically you might go along with a group of friends who were bent on a bank robbery knowing that they were going to rob a bank and had weapons; if you had no intention of joining the enterprise you would not be in the possession of the weapons. Once the court comes to grips with the problem of what constitutes "possession" can the sample charge be omitted with no loss and possibly some gain? Given the general competency of our attorneys, should the court rely upon both prosecution and the defense counsel to analyze the evidence sufficiently in the light of the charge? Do they or the jury need the court's analysis of the evidence? Even in federal courts, where the power to comment on evidence is acknowledged, courts show a tendency to define the law in light of the particular fact pattern presented and not to define or comment on inferences. See, J.B. Weinstein and M. Berger, 1 Weinstein's Evidence, 107–1 ff.

What is the value of the classic approach of Thayer and Morgan in treating presumption rules as directions for judges that operate only when determining whether a case may go to the jury and who should be assigned what burdens? Is it preferred to the kinds of instructions used and suggested?

3. "The power to create presumptions is not a means of escape from constitutional restrictions." Bailey v. State, 219 U.S. 219, 239 (1911) (holding that it would be a violation of the constitutional prohibition against involuntary servitude to require specific performance of personal service contracts by creating a presumption that breach was committed with intent to defraud). Cf. Lavine v. Milne, 424 U.S. 577 (1976), where the Court upheld as constitutional a statute providing for Home Relief benefits that contained a rebuttable presumption that a person who applied for benefits within 75 days after voluntarily terminating his employment is deemed to have terminated his employment for purposes of qualifying for benefits, which causes a denial of such benefits. The Court said, "Outside the criminal law area, where special concerns attend, the locus of the burden of persuasion is normally not an issue of federal constitutional moment," 424 U.S. at 585. See also Note, Constitutionality of Rebuttable Statutory Presumptions, 55 Colum.L.Rev. 527 (1955).

4. In Jeffries & Stephan, Defenses, Presumptions, and Burden of Proof in the Criminal Law, 88 Yale L.J. 1325, 1393–97 (1979), the authors criticize the Tot–Leary approach discussed in the main case dealing with the constitutionality of presumptions. They argue that the lack of a "rational connection" between the proved and presumed fact should not be dispositive of the presumption's validity. Rather, the critical issue is whether the Constitution permits a felony conviction to be based on the proven fact alone, where the presumed fact, which is an ultimate fact, has not been proven. "The search for a 'rational connection' implies that the important issue is formal conformity between proved and presumed facts rather than substantive adequacy of an established basis for punishment." Id. at 1396–97.

Francis v. Franklin

Supreme Court of the United States, 1985.
471 U.S. 307, 105 S.Ct. 1965, 85 L.Ed.2d 344.

■ JUSTICE BRENNAN delivered the opinion of the Court.

This case requires that we decide whether certain jury instructions in a criminal prosecution in which intent is an element of the crime charged and the only contested issue at trial satisfy the principles of Sandstrom v. Montana, 442 U.S. 510, 99 S.Ct. 2450, 61 L.Ed.2d 39 (1979). Specifically, we must evaluate jury instructions stating that: (1) "[t]he acts of a person of sound mind and discretion are presumed to be the product of a person's will, but the presumption may be rebutted" and (2) "[a] person of sound mind and discretion is presumed to intend the natural and probable consequences of his acts, but the presumption may be rebutted." App. 8a–9a. The question is whether these instructions, when read in the context of the jury charge as a whole, violate the Fourteenth Amendment's requirement that the State prove every element of a criminal offense beyond a reasonable doubt. See Sandstrom, supra; In re Winship, 397 U.S. 358, 364, 90 S.Ct. 1068, 1072, 25 L.Ed.2d 368 (1970).

I

Respondent Raymond Lee Franklin, then 21 years old and imprisoned for offenses unrelated to this case, sought to escape custody on January 17, 1979, while he and three other prisoners were receiving dental care at a local dentist's office. The four prisoners were secured by handcuffs to the same 8-foot length of chain as they sat in the dentist's waiting room. At some point Franklin was released from the chain, taken into the dentist's office and given preliminary treatment, and then escorted back to the waiting room. As another prisoner was being released, Franklin, who had not been reshackled, seized a pistol from one of the two officers and managed to escape. He forced the dentist's assistant to accompany him as a hostage.

In the parking lot Franklin found the dentist's automobile, the keys to which he had taken before escaping, but was unable to unlock the door. He then fled with the dental assistant after refusing her request to be set free. The two set out across an open clearing and came upon a local resident. Franklin demanded this resident's car. When the resident responded that he did not own one, Franklin made no effort to harm him but continued with the dental assistant until they came to the home of the victim, one Collie. Franklin pounded on the heavy wooden front door of the home and Collie, a retired 72-year-old carpenter, answered. Franklin was pointing the stolen pistol at the door when Collie arrived. As Franklin demanded his car keys, Collie slammed the door. At this moment Franklin's gun went off. The bullet traveled through the wooden door and into Collie's chest killing him. Seconds later the gun fired again. The second bullet traveled upward through the door and into the ceiling of the residence.

Hearing the shots, the victim's wife entered the front room. In the confusion accompanying the shooting, the dental assistant fled and Franklin did not attempt to stop her. Franklin entered the house, demanded the car keys from the victim's wife, and added the threat "I might as well kill you." When she did not provide the keys, however, he made no effort to thwart her escape. Franklin then stepped outside and encountered the victim's adult daughter. He repeated his demand for car keys but made no effort to stop the daughter when she refused the demand and fled. Failing to obtain a car, Franklin left and remained at large until nightfall.

Shortly after being captured, Franklin made a formal statement to the authorities in which he admitted that he had shot the victim but emphatically denied that he did so voluntarily or intentionally. He claimed that the shots were fired in accidental response to the slamming of the door. He was tried in the Superior Court of Bibb County, Georgia, on charges of malice murder[1]—a

---

1. The malice murder statute at the time in question provided:

"A person commits murder when he unlawfully and with malice aforethought, either

capital offense in Georgia and kidnaping. His sole defense to the malice murder charge was a lack of the requisite intent to kill. To support his version of the events Franklin offered substantial circumstantial evidence tending to show a lack of intent. He claimed that the circumstances surrounding the firing of the gun, particularly the slamming of the door and the trajectory of the second bullet, supported the hypothesis of accident, and that his immediate confession to that effect buttressed the assertion. He also argued that his treatment of every other person encountered during the escape indicated a lack of disposition to use force.

On the dispositive issue of intent, the trial judge instructed the jury as follows:

"A crime is a violation of a statute of this State in which there shall be a union of joint operation of act or omission to act, and intention or criminal negligence. A person shall not be found guilty of any crime committed by misfortune or accident where it satisfactorily appears there was no criminal scheme or undertaking or intention or criminal negligence. The acts of a person of sound mind and discretion are presumed to be the product of the person's will, but the presumption may be rebutted. A person of sound mind and discretion is presumed to intend the natural and probable consequences of his acts, but the presumption may be rebutted. A person will not be presumed to act with criminal intention but the trier of facts, that is, the Jury, may find criminal intention upon a consideration of the words, conduct, demeanor, motive and all other circumstances connected with the act for which the accused is prosecuted." App. 8a–9a.

Approximately one hour after the jury had received the charge and retired for deliberation, it returned to the courtroom and requested reinstruction on the element of intent and the definition of accident. Id., at 13a–14a. Upon receiving the requested reinstruction, the jury deliberated 10 more minutes and returned a verdict of guilty. The next day Franklin was sentenced to death for the murder conviction.

. . . .

II

The Due Process Clause of the Fourteenth Amendment "protects the accused against conviction except upon proof beyond a reasonable doubt of every fact necessary to constitute the crime with which he is charged." In re Winship, 397 U.S. 358, 364, 90 S.Ct. 1068, 1073, 25 L.Ed.2d 368 (1970). This "bedrock, 'axiomatic and elementary'" [constitutional] principle, id., at 363, 90 S.Ct., at 1072, prohibits the State from using evidentiary presumptions in a jury charge that have the effect of relieving the State of its burden of persuasion beyond a reasonable doubt of every essential element of a crime. Sandstrom v. Montana, supra, at 520–524, 99 S.Ct., at 2457–2459; Patterson v. New York, 432 U.S. 197, 210, 215, 97 S.Ct. 2319, 53 L.Ed.2d 281 (1977); Mullaney v. Wilbur, 421 U.S. 684, 698–701, 95 S.Ct. 1881, 1889–1890, 44 L.Ed.2d 508 (1975); see also Morissette v. United States, 342 U.S. 246, 274–275, 72 S.Ct. 240, 255, 96 L.Ed. 288 (1952). The prohibition protects the "fundamental value determination of our society," given voice in Justice Harlan's concurrence in Winship, "that it is far worse to convict an innocent man than to let a guilty man go free." 397 U.S., at 372, 90 S.Ct., at 1077. See Speiser v.

express or implied, causes the death of another human being.... Malice shall be implied where no considerable provocation appears and where all the circumstances of the killing show an abandoned and malignant heart." Ga.Code Ann. § 26–1101(a) (1978).

Randall, 357 U.S. 513, 525–526, 78 S.Ct. 1332, 1341–1342, 2 L.Ed.2d 1460 (1958). The question before the Court in this case is almost identical to that before the Court in Sandstrom: "whether the challenged jury instruction had the effect of relieving the State of the burden of proof enunciated in Winship on the critical question of . . . state of mind," 442 U.S., at 521, 99 S.Ct., at 2458, by creating a mandatory presumption of intent upon proof by the State of other elements of the offense.

The analysis is straightforward. "The threshold inquiry in ascertaining the constitutional analysis applicable to this kind of jury instruction is to determine the nature of the presumption it describes." Id., at 514, 99 S.Ct., at 2454. The court must determine whether the challenged portion of the instruction creates a mandatory presumption, see id., at 520–524, 99 S.Ct., at 2457–2459, or merely a permissive inference, see Ulster County Court v. Allen, 442 U.S. 140, 157–163, 99 S.Ct. 2213, 2224–2227, 60 L.Ed.2d 777 (1979). A mandatory presumption instructs the jury that it must infer the presumed fact if the State proves certain predicate facts.[2] A permissive inference suggests to the jury a possible conclusion to be drawn if the State proves predicate facts, but does not require the jury to draw that conclusion.

Mandatory presumptions must be measured against the standards of Winship as elucidated in Sandstrom. Such presumptions violate the Due Process Clause if they relieve the State of the burden of persuasion on an element of an offense. Patterson v. New York, supra, 432 U.S., at 215, 97 S.Ct., at 2329 ("a State must prove every ingredient of an offense beyond a reasonable doubt and . . . may not shift the burden of proof to the defendant by presuming that ingredient upon proof of the other elements of the offense"). See also Sandstrom, supra, 442 U.S., at 520–524, 99 S.Ct., at 2457–2459; Mullaney v. Wilbur, supra, 421 U.S., at 698–701, 95 S.Ct., at 1889–1890.[3] A permissive inference does not relieve the State of its burden of persuasion because it still requires the State to convince the jury that the suggested conclusion should be inferred based on the predicate facts proven. Such inferences do not necessarily implicate the concerns of Sandstrom. A permissive inference violates the Due Process Clause only if the suggested conclusion is not one that reason and common sense justify in light of the proven facts before the jury. Ulster County Court, supra, 442 U.S., at 157–163, 99 S.Ct., at 2224–2227.

Analysis must focus initially on the specific language challenged, but the inquiry does not end there. If a specific portion of the jury charge, considered in isolation, could reasonably have been understood as creating a presumption that relieves the State of its burden of persuasion on an element of an offense, the potentially offending words must be considered in the context of the charge as a whole. Other instructions might explain the particular infirm language to the extent that a reasonable juror could not have considered the charge to have created an unconstitutional presumption. Cupp v. Naughton, 414 U.S. 141, 147, 94 S.Ct. 396, 400, 38 L.Ed.2d 368 (1973). This analysis "requires careful

---

2. A mandatory presumption may be either conclusive or rebuttable. A conclusive presumption removes the presumed element from the case once the State has proven the predicate facts giving rise to the presumption. A rebuttable presumption does not remove the presumed element from the case but nevertheless requires the jury to find the presumed element unless the defendant persuades the jury that such a finding is unwarranted. See Sandstrom v. Montana, 442 U.S. 510, 517–518, 99 S.Ct. 2450, 2455–2456, 61 L.Ed.2d 39 (1979).

3. We are not required to decide in this case whether a mandatory presumption that shifts only a burden of production to the defendant is consistent with the Due Process Clause, and we express no opinion on that question.

attention to the words actually spoken to the jury . . ., for whether a defendant has been accorded his constitutional rights depends upon the way in which a reasonable juror could have interpreted the instruction." Sandstrom, supra, 442 U.S., at 514, 99 S.Ct., at 2454.

A

Franklin levels his constitutional attack at the following two sentences in the jury charge: "The acts of a person of sound mind and discretion are presumed to be the product of a person's will, but the presumption may be rebutted. A person of sound mind and discretion is presumed to intend the natural and probable consequences of his acts, but the presumption may be rebutted." App. 8a–9a.[4] The Georgia Supreme Court has interpreted this language as creating no more than a permissive inference that comports with the constitutional standards of Ulster County Court v. Allen, supra. See Skrine v. State, 244 Ga. 520, 521, 260 S.E.2d 900 (1979). The question, however, is not what the State Supreme Court declares the meaning of the charge to be, but rather what a reasonable juror could have understood the charge as meaning. Sandstrom, 442 U.S., at 516–517, 99 S.Ct., at 2455 (state court "is not the final authority on the interpretation which a jury could have given the instruction"). The federal constitutional question is whether a reasonable juror could have understood the two sentences as a mandatory presumption that shifted to the defendant the burden of persuasion on the element of intent once the State had proved the predicate acts.

The challenged sentences are cast in the language of command. They instruct the jury that "acts of a person of sound mind and discretion are presumed to be the product of the person's will," and that a person "is presumed to intend the natural and probable consequences of his acts," App. 8a–9a (emphasis added). These words carry precisely the message of the language condemned in Sandstrom, supra, at 515, 99 S.Ct., at 2454 (" '[t]he law presumes that a person intends the ordinary consequences of his voluntary acts' "). The jurors "were not told that they had a choice, or that they might infer that conclusion, they were told only that the law presumed it. It is clear that a reasonable juror could easily have viewed such an instruction as mandatory." 442 U.S., at 515, 99 S.Ct., at 2454 (emphasis added). The portion of the jury charge challenged in this case directs the jury to presume an essential element of the offense—intent to kill—upon proof of other elements of the offense—the act of slaying another. In this way the instructions "undermine the factfinder's responsibility at trial, based on evidence adduced by the State, to find the ultimate facts beyond a reasonable doubt." Ulster County Court v. Allen, supra, 442 U.S., at 156, 99 S.Ct., at 2224 (emphasis added).

The language challenged here differs from Sandstrom, of course, in that the jury in this case was explicitly informed that the presumptions "may be rebutted." App. 8a–9a. The State makes much of this additional aspect of the instruction in seeking to differentiate the present case from Sandstrom. This distinction does not suffice, however, to cure the infirmity in the charge. Though the Court in Sandstrom acknowledged that the instructions there challenged could have been reasonably understood as creating an irrebuttable presumption, 442 U.S., at 517, 99 S.Ct., at 2455, it was not on this basis alone that the instructions were invalidated. Had the jury reasonably understood the instructions as creating a mandatory rebuttable presumption the instructions would have been no less constitutionally infirm. Id., at 520–524, 99 S.Ct., at 2457–2459.

---

4. Intent to kill is an element of the offense of malice murder in Georgia. See Pat-terson v. State, 239 Ga. 409, 416–417, 238 S.E.2d 2, 8 (1977).

An irrebuttable or conclusive presumption relieves the State of its burden of persuasion by removing the presumed element from the case entirely if the State proves the predicate facts. A mandatory rebuttable presumption does not remove the presumed element from the case if the State proves the predicate facts, but it nonetheless relieves the State of the affirmative burden of persuasion on the presumed element by instructing the jury that it must find the presumed element unless the defendant persuades the jury not to make such a finding. A mandatory rebuttable presumption is perhaps less onerous from the defendant's perspective, but it is no less unconstitutional. Our cases make clear that "[s]uch shifting of the burden of persuasion with respect to a fact which the State deems so important that it must be either proved or presumed is impermissible under the Due Process Clause." Patterson v. New York, 432 U.S., at 215, 97 S.Ct., at 2329. In Mullaney v. Wilbur we explicitly held unconstitutional a mandatory rebuttable presumption that shifted to the defendant a burden of persuasion on the question of intent. 421 U.S., at 698–701, 95 S.Ct., at 1889–1890. And in Sandstrom we similarly held that instructions that might reasonably have been understood by the jury as creating a mandatory rebuttable presumption were unconstitutional. 442 U.S., at 524, 99 S.Ct., at 2459.[5]

When combined with the immediately preceding mandatory language, the instruction that the presumptions "may be rebutted" could reasonably be read as telling the jury that it was required to infer intent to kill as the natural and probable consequence of the act of firing the gun unless the defendant persuaded the jury that such an inference was unwarranted. The very statement that the presumption "may be rebutted" could have indicated to a reasonable juror that the defendant bore an affirmative burden of persuasion once the State proved the underlying act giving rise to the presumption. Standing alone, the challenged language undeniably created an unconstitutional burden-shifting presumption with respect to the element of intent.

B

The jury, of course, did not hear only the two challenged sentences. The jury charge taken as a whole might have explained the proper allocation of

---

5. The dissent's suggestion that our holding with respect to the constitutionality of mandatory rebuttable presumptions "extends" prior law, post, at 1978 (REHNQUIST, J., dissenting), is simply inaccurate. In Sandstrom v. Montana our holding rested on equally valid alternative rationales: "the question before this Court is whether the challenged jury instruction had the effect of relieving the State of the burden of proof enunciated in Winship on the critical question of petitioner's state of mind. We conclude that under either of the two possible interpretations of the instruction set out above, precisely that effect would result, and that the instruction therefore represents constitutional error." 442 U.S., at 521, 99 S.Ct., at 2458 (emphasis added). In any event, the principle that mandatory rebuttable presumptions violate due process had been definitively established prior to Sandstrom. In Mullaney v. Wilbur, it was a mandatory rebuttable presumption that we held unconsti-

tutional. 421 U.S., at 698–701, 95 S.Ct., at 1889–1890. As we explained in Patterson v. New York:

"Mullaney surely held that a State . . . may not shift the burden of proof to the defendant by presuming that ingredient upon proof of the other elements of the offense. . . . Such shifting of the burden of persuasion with respect to a fact which the State deems so important that it must be either proved or presumed is impermissible under the Due Process Clause." 432 U.S., at 215, 97 S.Ct., at 2329.

An irrebuttable presumption, of course, does not shift any burden to the defendant; it eliminates an element from the case if the State proves the requisite predicate facts. Thus the Court in Patterson could only have been referring to a mandatory rebuttable presumption when it stated that "such shifting of the burden of persuasion . . . is impermissible." Ibid. (emphasis added).

burdens with sufficient clarity that any ambiguity in the particular language challenged could not have been understood by a reasonable juror as shifting the burden of persuasion. See Cupp v. Naughton, 414 U.S. 141, 94 S.Ct. 396, 38 L.Ed.2d 368 (1973). The State argues that sufficient clarifying language exists in this case. In particular, the State relies on an earlier portion of the charge instructing the jurors that the defendant was presumed innocent and that the State was required to prove every element of the offense beyond a reasonable doubt.[6] The State also points to the sentence immediately following the challenged portion of the charge, which reads: "[a] person will not be presumed to act with criminal intention...." App. 9a.

As we explained in Sandstrom, general instructions on the State's burden of persuasion and the defendant's presumption of innocence are not "rhetorically inconsistent with a conclusive or burden-shifting presumption," because "[t]he jury could have interpreted the two sets of instructions as indicating that the presumption was a means by which proof beyond a reasonable doubt as to intent could be satisfied." 442 U.S., at 518–519, n. 7, 99 S.Ct., at 2456, n. 7. In light of the instructions on intent given in this case, a reasonable juror could thus have thought that, although intent must be proved beyond a reasonable doubt, proof of the firing of the gun and its ordinary consequences constituted proof of intent beyond a reasonable doubt unless the defendant persuaded the jury otherwise. Cf. Mullaney v. Wilbur, 421 U.S., at 703, n. 31, 95 S.Ct., at 1891, n. 31. These general instructions as to the prosecution's burden and the defendant's presumption of innocence do not dissipate the error in the challenged portion of the instructions.

Nor does the more specific instruction following the challenged sentences— "A person will not be presumed to act with criminal intention but the trier of facts, that is, the Jury, may find criminal intention upon a consideration of the words, conduct, demeanor, motive and all other circumstances connected with the act for which the accused is prosecuted," App. 9a—provide a sufficient corrective. It may well be that this "criminal intention" instruction was not directed to the element of intent at all, but to another element of the Georgia crime of malice murder. The statutory definition of capital murder in Georgia requires malice aforethought. Ga.Code Ann. § 16–5–1 (1984) (formerly Ga.Code Ann. § 26–1101(a) (1978)). Under state law malice aforethought comprises two elements: intent to kill and the absence of provocation or justification. See Patterson v. State, 239 Ga. 409, 416–417, 238 S.E.2d 2, 8 (1977); Lamb v. Jernigan, 683 F.2d 1332, 1337 (CA11 1982) (interpreting Ga.Code Ann. § 16–5–1), cert. denied, 460 U.S. 1024, 103 S.Ct. 1276, 75 L.Ed.2d 496 (1983). At another point in the charge in this case, the trial court, consistently with this understanding of Georgia law, instructed the jury that malice is "the unlawful, deliberate intention to kill a human being without justification or mitigation or excuse." App. 10a.

The statement "criminal intention may not be presumed" may well have been intended to instruct the jurors that they were not permitted to presume the absence of provocation or justification but that they could infer this conclusion from circumstantial evidence. Whatever the court's motivation in

---

6. These portions of the instructions read:

"... I charge you that before the State is entitled to a verdict of conviction of this defendant at your hands ... the burden is upon the State of proving the defendant's guilt as charged ... beyond a reasonable doubt." App. 4a.

"Now ... the defendant enters upon his trial with the presumption of innocence in his favor and this presumption ... remains with him throughout the trial, unless it is overcome by evidence sufficiently strong to satisfy you of his guilt ... beyond a reasonable doubt." Id., at 5a.

giving the instruction, the jury could certainly have understood it this way. A reasonable juror trying to make sense of the juxtaposition of an instruction that "a person of sound mind and discretion is presumed to intend the natural and probable consequences of his acts," App. 8a–9a and an instruction that "[a] person will not be presumed to act with criminal intention," App. 9a, may well have thought that the instructions related to different elements of the crime and were therefore not contradictory—that he could presume intent to kill but not the absence of justification or provocation.[7]

Even if a reasonable juror could have understood the prohibition of presuming "criminal intention" as applying to the element of intent, that instruction did no more than contradict the instruction in the immediately preceding sentence. A reasonable juror could easily have resolved the contradiction in the instruction by choosing to abide by the mandatory presumption and ignore the prohibition of presumption. Nothing in these specific sentences or in the charge as a whole makes clear to the jury that one of these contradictory instructions carries more weight than the other. Language that merely contradicts and does not explain a constitutionally infirm instruction will not suffice to absolve the infirmity. A reviewing court has no way of knowing which of the two irreconcilable instructions the jurors applied in reaching their verdict.[8] Had the instruction "[a] person ... is presumed to

---

7. Because the jurors heard the divergent intent instructions before they heard the instructions about absence of justification, the dissent argues that no reasonable juror could have understood the criminal intent instruction as referring to the absence of justification. The dissent reproves the Court for reading the instructions "as a 'looking-glass charge' which, when held to a mirror, reads more clearly in the opposite direction." Post, at 1984 (REHNQUIST, J., dissenting). A reasonable juror, however, would have sought to make sense of the conflicting intent instructions not only at the initial moment of hearing them but also later in the jury room after having heard the entire charge. One would expect most of the juror's reflection about the meaning of the instructions to occur during this subsequent deliberative stage of the process. Under these circumstances, it is certainly reasonable to expect a juror to attempt to make sense of a confusing earlier portion of the instruction by reference to a later portion of the instruction. The dissent obviously accepts this proposition because much of the language the dissent marshals to argue that the jury would not have misunderstood the intent instruction appears several paragraphs after the conflicting sentences about intent. Indeed much of this purportedly clarifying language appears after the portion of the charge concerning the element of absence of justification. See post, at 1982 (REHNQUIST, J., dissenting), quoting App. 10a.

It is puzzling that the dissent thinks it "defies belief" to suggest that a reasonable juror would have related the contradictory intent instructions to the later instructions about the element of malice. Post, at 1984. As the portion of the charge quoted in the dissent makes clear, the later malice instruc-

tions specifically spoke of intent: "Malice ... is the unlawful, deliberate intention to kill a human being without justification or mitigation or excuse, which intention must exist at the time of the killing." App. 10a. See post, at 1982 (REHNQUIST, J., dissenting). A reasonable juror might well have sought to understand this language by reference to the earlier instruction referring to criminal intent.

Finally, the dissent's representation of the language in this part of the charge as a clarifying "express statement[ ] ... that there was no burden on the defendant to disprove malice," post, at 1984, is misleading. The relevant portion of the charge reads: "it is not required of the accused to prove an absence of malice, if the evidence for the State shows facts which may excuse or justify the homicide." App. 10a. This language is most naturally read as implying that if the State's evidence does not show mitigating facts the defendant does have the burden to prove absence of malice. Thus, if anything, this portion of the charge exacerbates the potential for an unconstitutional shifting of the burden to the defendant.

8. The dissent would hold a jury instruction invalid only when "it is at least likely" that a reasonable juror would have understood the charge unconstitutionally to shift a burden of persuasion. Post, at 1985 (REHNQUIST, J., dissenting). Apparently this "at least likely" test would not be met even when there exists a reasonable possibility that a juror would have understood the instructions unconstitutionally, so long as the instructions admitted of a "more 'reasonable' " constitutional interpretation. Post, at 1985. Apart from suggesting that application

intend the natural and probable consequences of his acts," App. 8a–9a, been followed by the instruction "this means that a person will not be presumed to act with criminal intention but the jury may find criminal intention upon consideration of all circumstances connected with the act for which the accused is prosecuted," a somewhat stronger argument might be made that a reasonable juror could not have understood the challenged language as shifting the burden of persuasion to the defendant. Cf. Sandstrom, 442 U.S., at 517, 99 S.Ct., at 2455 ("given the lack of qualifying instructions as to the legal effect of the presumption, we cannot discount the possibility that the jury may have interpreted the instruction" in an unconstitutional manner). See also Corn v. Zant, 708 F.2d 549, 559 (CA11 1983), cert. denied, 467 U.S. 1220, 104 S.Ct. 2670, 81 L.Ed.2d 375 (1984). Whether or not such explanatory language might have been sufficient, however, no such language is present in this jury charge. If a juror thought the "criminal intention" instruction pertained to the element of intent, the juror was left in a quandary as to whether to follow that instruction or the immediately preceding one it contradicted.[9]

of the "at least likely" standard would lead to the opposite result in the present case, the dissent leaves its proposed alternative distressingly undefined. Even when faced with clearly contradictory instructions respecting allocation of the burden of persuasion on a crucial element of an offense, a reviewing court apparently would be required to intuit, based on its sense of the "tone" of the jury instructions as a whole, see Ibid., whether a reasonable juror was more likely to have reached a constitutional understanding of the instructions than an unconstitutional understanding of the instructions.

This proposed alternative standard provides no sound basis for appellate review of jury instructions. Its malleability will certainly generate inconsistent appellate results and thereby compound the confusion that has plagued this area of the law. Perhaps more importantly, the suggested approach provides no incentive for trial courts to weed out potentially infirm language from jury instructions; in every case, the "presumption of innocence" boilerplate in the instructions will supply a basis from which to argue that the "tone" of the charge as a whole is not unconstitutional. For these reasons, the proposed standard promises reviewing courts, including this Court, an unending stream of cases in which ad hoc decisions will have to be made about the "tone" of jury instructions as a whole.

Most importantly, the dissent's proposed standard is irreconcilable with bedrock due process principles. The Court today holds that contradictory instructions as to intent—one of which imparts to the jury an unconstitutional understanding of the allocation of burdens of persuasion—create a reasonable likelihood that a juror understood the instructions in an unconstitutional manner, unless other language in the charge explains the infirm language sufficiently to eliminate this possibility. If such a reasonable possibility of an unconstitutional understanding exists, "we have no way of knowing that [the defendant] was not convicted on the basis of the unconstitutional instruction." Sandstrom, 442 U.S., at 526, 99 S.Ct., at 2460. For this reason, it has been settled law since Stromberg v. California, 283 U.S. 359, 51 S.Ct. 532, 75 L.Ed. 1117 (1931), that when there exists a reasonable possibility that the jury relied on an unconstitutional understanding of the law in reaching a guilty verdict, that verdict must be set aside. See Leary v. United States, 395 U.S. 6, 31–32, 89 S.Ct. 1532, 1545–1546, 23 L.Ed.2d 57 (1969); Bachellar v. Maryland, 397 U.S. 564, 571, 90 S.Ct. 1312, 1316, 25 L.Ed.2d 570 (1970). The dissent's proposed alternative cannot be squared with this principle; notwithstanding a substantial doubt as to whether the jury decided the State proved intent beyond a reasonable doubt, the dissent would uphold this conviction based on an impressionistic and intuitive judgment that it was more likely that the jury understood the charge in a constitutional manner than in an unconstitutional manner.

9.   Rejecting this conclusion, the dissent "simply do[es] not believe" that a reasonable juror would have paid sufficiently close attention to the particular language of the jury instructions to have been perplexed by the contradictory intent instructions. See post, at 1984 (REHNQUIST, J., dissenting). See also Sandstrom v. Montana, 442 U.S., at 528, 99 S.Ct., at 2461 (REHNQUIST, J., concurring) ("I continue to have doubts as to whether this particular jury was so attentively attuned to the instructions of the trial court that it divined the difference recognized by lawyers between 'infer' and 'presume' "). Apparently the dissent would have the degree of attention a juror is presumed to pay to particular jury instructions vary with whether a pre-

Because a reasonable juror could have understood the challenged portions of the jury instruction in this case as creating a mandatory presumption that shifted to the defendant the burden of persuasion on the crucial element of intent, and because the charge read as a whole does not explain or cure the error, we hold that the jury charge does not comport with the requirements of the Due Process Clause.

III

Petitioner argues that even if the jury charge fails under Sandstrom this Court should overturn the Court of Appeals because the constitutional infirmity in the charge was harmless error on this record. This Court has not resolved whether an erroneous charge that shifts a burden of persuasion to the defendant on an essential element of an offense can ever be harmless. See Connecticut v. Johnson, 460 U.S. 73, 103 S.Ct. 969, 74 L.Ed.2d 823 (1983). We need not resolve the question in this case. The Court of Appeals conducted a careful harmless-error inquiry and concluded that the Sandstrom error at trial could not be deemed harmless. 720 F.2d, at 1212. The Court noted:

> "[Franklin's] only defense was that he did not have the requisite intent to kill. The facts did not overwhelmingly preclude that defense. The coincidence of the first shot with the slamming of the door, the second shot's failure to hit anyone, or take a path on which it would have hit anyone, and the lack of injury to anyone else all supported the lack of intent defense. A presumption that Franklin intended to kill completely eliminated his defense of 'no intent.' Because intent was plainly at issue in this case, and was not overwhelmingly proved by the evidence ... we cannot find the error to be harmless." Ibid.

Even under the harmless-error standard proposed by the dissenting Justices in Connecticut v. Johnson, supra, 460 U.S., at 97, n. 5, 103 S.Ct., at 973, n. 5 (evidence "so dispositive of intent that a reviewing court can say beyond a reasonable doubt that the jury would have found it unnecessary to rely on the presumption") (POWELL, J., dissenting), this analysis by the Court of Appeals is

---

sumption of attentiveness would help or harm the criminal defendant. See, e.g., Parker v. Randolph, 442 U.S. 62, 73, 99 S.Ct. 2132, 2139, 60 L.Ed.2d 713 (1979) (opinion of REHNQUIST, J.) ("A crucial assumption underlying that system [of trial by jury] is that juries will follow the instructions given them by the trial judge. Were this not so, it would be pointless for a trial court to instruct a jury, and even more pointless for an appellate court to reverse a criminal conviction because the jury was improperly instructed.... [A]n instruction directing the jury to consider a codefendant's extrajudicial statement only against its source has been found sufficient to avoid offending the confrontation right of the implicated defendant"); see also id., at 75, n. 7, 99 S.Ct., at 2140, n. 7 ("The 'rule'—indeed, the premise upon which the system of jury trials functions under the American judicial system—is that juries can be trusted to follow the trial court's instructions"). Cf. Wainwright v. Witt, 469 U.S. 412, 105 S.Ct. 844, 83 L.Ed.2d 841 (1985).

The Court presumes that jurors, conscious of the gravity of their task, attend closely the particular language of the trial court's instructions in a criminal case and strive to understand, make sense of, and follow the instructions given them. Cases may arise in which the risk of prejudice inhering in material put before the jury may be so great that even a limiting instruction will not adequately protect a criminal defendant's constitutional rights. E.g., Bruton v. United States, 391 U.S. 123, 88 S.Ct. 1620, 20 L.Ed.2d 476 (1968); Jackson v. Denno, 378 U.S. 368, 84 S.Ct. 1774, 12 L.Ed.2d 908 (1964). Absent such extraordinary situations, however, we adhere to the crucial assumption underlying our constitutional system of trial by jury that jurors carefully follow instructions. As Chief Justice Traynor has said, "we must assume that juries for the most part understand and faithfully follow instructions. The concept of a fair trial encompasses a decision by a tribunal that has understood and applied the law to all material issues in the case." Quoted in Connecticut v. Johnson, 460 U.S. 73, 85, n. 14, 103 S.Ct. 969, 977, n. 14, 74 L.Ed.2d 823 (1983) (opinion of BLACKMUN, J.).

surely correct.[10] The jury's request for reinstruction on the elements of malice and accident, App. 13a–14a, lends further substance to the court's conclusion that the evidence of intent was far from overwhelming in this case. We therefore affirm the Court of Appeals on the harmless-error question as well.

IV

Sandstrom v. Montana made clear that the Due Process Clause of the Fourteenth Amendment prohibits the State from making use of jury instructions that have the effect of relieving the State of the burden of proof enunciated in Winship on the critical question of intent in a criminal prosecution. 442 U.S., at 521, 99 S.Ct., at 2457. Today we reaffirm the rule of Sandstrom and the wellspring due process principle from which it was drawn. The Court of Appeals faithfully and correctly applied this rule and the court's judgment is therefore

Affirmed.

■ JUSTICE POWELL, dissenting.

In Sandstrom v. Montana, 442 U.S. 510, 99 S.Ct. 2450, 61 L.Ed.2d 39 (1979), we held that instructing the jury that "the law presumes that a person intends the ordinary consequences of his voluntary acts" violates due process. We invalidated this instruction because a reasonable juror could interpret it either as "an irrebuttable direction by the court to find intent once convinced of the facts triggering the presumption" or "as a direction to find intent upon proof of the defendant's voluntary actions ... unless the defendant proved the contrary by some quantum of proof which may well have been considerably greater than 'some' evidence—thus effectively shifting the burden of persuasion on the element of intent." Id., at 517, 99 S.Ct., at 2456 (original emphasis). Either interpretation, we held, would have relieved the State of its burden of proving every element of the crime beyond a reasonable doubt. See id., at 521, 99 S.Ct., at 2457; Mullaney v. Wilbur, 421 U.S. 684, 698–701, 95 S.Ct. 1881, 1889–1890, 44 L.Ed.2d 508 (1975).

Unlike the charge in Sandstrom, the charge in the present case is not susceptible of either interpretation. It creates no "irrebuttable direction" and a reasonable juror could not conclude that it relieves the State of its burden of persuasion. The Court, however, believes that two sentences make the charge infirm:

> "The acts of a person of sound mind and discretion are presumed to be the product of the person's will, but the presumption may be rebutted. A person of sound mind and discretion is presumed to intend the natural and probable consequences of his acts but the presumption may be rebutted."
> App. 8a–9a.

I agree with the Court that "[s]tanding alone," the challenged language could be viewed as "an unconstitutional burden-shifting presumption with respect to the element of intent." Ante, at 1973 (emphasis added). The fact is, however, that this language did not stand alone. It is but a small part of a lengthy charge, other parts of which clarify its meaning. Although the Court states that it considered the effect the rest of the charge would have had on a reasonable juror, its analysis overlooks or misinterprets several critical instructions. These

---

10. The primary task of this Court upon review of a harmless-error determination by the Court of Appeals is to ensure that the court undertook a thorough inquiry and made clear the basis of its decision. See Con-necticut v. Johnson, supra, at 102, 103 S.Ct., at 985 (POWELL, J., dissenting) (harmless error "is a question more appropriately left to the courts below").

instructions, I believe, would have prevented a reasonable juror from imposing on the defendant the burden of persuasion on intent. When viewed as a whole, see Cupp v. Naughten, 414 U.S. 141, 146–147, 94 S.Ct. 396, 400, 38 L.Ed.2d 368 (1973), the jury charge satisfies the requirements of due process.

The trial court repeatedly impressed upon the jury both that the defendant should be presumed innocent until proven guilty and that the State bore the burden of proving guilt beyond a reasonable doubt. It stated:

"[T]he burden is upon the State of proving the defendant's guilt as charged in such count beyond a reasonable doubt. . . .

". . . If, upon a consideration of all the facts and circumstances of this case, your mind is wavering, unsettled, not satisfied, then that is the reasonable doubt under the law and if such a doubt rests upon your mind, it is your duty to give the defendant the benefit of that doubt and acquit him.

"Now, the defendant enters upon his trial with the presumption of innocence in his favor and this presumption . . . remains with him throughout the trial, unless and until it is overcome by evidence sufficiently strong to satisfy you of his guilt to a reasonable and moral certainty and beyond a reasonable doubt.

. . .

"Now, Ladies and Gentlemen, the burden is upon the State to prove to a reasonable and moral certainty and beyond a reasonable doubt every material allegation in each count of this indictment and I charge you further, that there is no burden on the defendant to prove anything. The burden is on the State.

. . .

"Members of the Jury, if, from a consideration of the evidence or from a lack of evidence, you are not satisfied beyond a reasonable doubt and to a reasonable and moral certainty that the State has established the guilt of the defendant . . . then it would be your duty to acquit him. . . ." App. 4a–12a.

We noted in Sandstrom, supra, 442 U.S., at 518, n. 7, 99 S.Ct., at 2456, n. 7, that general instructions may be insufficient by themselves to make clear that the burden of persuasion remains with the State. In this case, however, the trial court went well beyond the typical generality of such instructions. It repeatedly reiterated the presumption of innocence and the heavy burden imposed upon the State. In addition, the jury was told that the "presumption of innocence . . . remains with [the defendant] throughout the trial," App. 5a, and that "there is no burden on the defendant to prove anything. The burden is on the State," id., at 8a.

More important is the immediate context of the two suspect sentences. They appeared in a paragraph that stated:

"A crime is a violation of a statute of this State in which there shall be a union of joint operation of act or omission to act, and intention or criminal negligence. A person shall not be found guilty of any crime committed by misfortune or accident where it satisfactorily appears there was no criminal scheme or undertaking or intention or criminal negligence. The acts of a person of sound mind and discretion are presumed to be the product of the person's will, but the presumption may be rebutted. A person of sound mind and discretion is presumed to intend the natural and probable consequences of his acts but the presumption may be rebutted. A person will not be presumed to act with criminal intention but the trier of fact, that is, the Jury, may find criminal intention upon a consideration of the words, conduct, demeanor, motive and all other circumstances connected with the act for which the accused is prosecuted." App. 8a–9a (emphasis added).

The final sentence clearly tells the jury that it cannot place on the defendant the burden of persuasion on intent. The Court, however, holds that in context it could not have had this effect. It believes that the term "criminal intention" refers not to intent at all, but to "absence of provocation or justification," ante, at 1974, a separate element of malice murder. Despite the fact that provocation and justification are largely unrelated to intent, the Court believes that "the jury could certainly have understood [the term] this way." Ibid. Such a strained interpretation is neither logical nor justified.*

The instructions on circumstantial evidence further ensured that no reasonable juror would have switched the burden of proof on intent. Three times the trial court told the jury that it could not base a finding of any element of the offense on circumstantial evidence unless the evidence "exclude[d] every other reasonable hypothesis, save that of the [accused's] guilt...." App. 6a. Under these instructions, a reasonable juror could not have found intent unless the State's evidence excluded any reasonable hypothesis that the defendant had acted unintentionally. This requirement placed a burden of excluding the possibility of lack of intent on the State and would have made it impossible to impose on the defendant the burden of persuasion on intent itself.

Together, I believe that the instructions on reasonable doubt and the presumption of innocence, the instruction that "criminal intention" cannot be presumed, and the instructions governing the interpretation of circumstantial evidence removed any danger that a reasonable juror could have believed that the two suspect sentences placed on the defendant the burden of persuasion on intent. When viewed as a whole, the jury instructions did not violate due process. I accordingly dissent.

JUSTICE REHNQUIST, with whom THE CHIEF JUSTICE and JUSTICE O'CONNOR join, dissenting.

In In re Winship, 397 U.S. 358, 90 S.Ct. 1068, 25 L.Ed.2d 368 (1970), the trial judge in a bench trial held that although the State's proof was sufficient to warrant a finding of guilt by a preponderance of the evidence, it was not sufficient to warrant such a finding beyond a reasonable doubt. The outcome of the case turned on which burden of proof was to be imposed on the prosecution. This Court held that the Constitution requires proof beyond a reasonable doubt in a criminal case, and Winship's adjudication was set aside.

Today the Court sets aside Franklin's murder conviction, but not because either the trial judge or the trial jury found that his guilt had not been proven beyond a reasonable doubt. The conviction is set aside because this Court

---

* The term's context also precludes such an interpretation. The term "criminal intention" appears in a paragraph describing the general requirements of all crimes without discussing the specific requirements of any particular one. The Court offers no reason why a reasonable juror might have believed that this paragraph referred to only one of the crimes charged—malice murder—especially when a different crime—kidnapping— was described in the immediately following paragraphs. It is much more reasonable to interpret the term "criminal intention" as shorthand for "intention or criminal negligence," the traditional *mens rea* requirement. In this view, the final sentence informs the jury that whatever else a rebuttable presumption might establish it cannot by itself establish *mens rea*.

concludes that one or two sentences out of several pages of instructions given by the judge to the jury could be read as allowing the jury to return a guilty verdict in the absence of proof establishing every statutory element of the crime beyond a reasonable doubt. The Court reaches this result even though the judge admonished the jury at least four separate times that they could convict only if they found guilt beyond a reasonable doubt. The Court, instead of examining the charge to the jury as a whole, seems bent on piling syllogism on syllogism to prove that someone might understand a few sentences in the charge to allow conviction on less than proof beyond a reasonable doubt. Such fine parsing of the jury instructions given in a state court trial is not required by anything in the United States Constitution.

Today's decision needlessly extends our holding in Sandstrom v. Montana, 442 U.S. 510, 99 S.Ct. 2450, 61 L.Ed.2d 39 (1979), to cases where the jury was not required to presume conclusively an element of a crime under state law. But even assuming the one or two sentences singled out by the Court might conceivably mislead, I do not believe that a reasonable person reading that language "in the context of the overall charge," see Cupp v. Naughten, 414 U.S. 141, 94 S.Ct. 396, 38 L.Ed.2d 368 (1973), could possibly arrive at the Court's conclusion that constitutional error occurred here. I disagree with the Court's legal standard, which finds constitutional error where a reasonable juror could have understood the charge in a particular manner. But even on the facts, the Court's approach to the charge is more like that of a zealous lawyer bent on attaining a particular result than that of the "reasonable juror" referred to in Sandstrom.

In Sandstrom the jury was charged that "[t]he law presumes that a person intends the ordinary consequences of his voluntary acts." 442 U.S., at 515, 99 S.Ct., at 2454 (emphasis supplied). As in this case, intent was an element of the crime charged in Sandstrom, and the Court was of the opinion that given the mandatory nature of the above charge it was quite possible that the jury "once having found [Sandstrom's] act voluntary, would interpret the instruction as automatically directing a finding of intent." Id., at 515–516, 99 S.Ct., at 2455. Such a presumption would have relieved the State entirely of the burden it had undertaken to prove that Sandstrom had killed intentionally—i.e., "purposefully or knowingly"—and would have mandated a finding of that intent regardless of whether other evidence in the case indicated to the contrary. Id., at 521, 99 S.Ct., at 2457.

The Sandstrom Court went on, however, to discuss the constitutionality of a presumption "that did not conclusively establish intent but rather could be rebutted." Id., at 515, 99 S.Ct., at 2455. The Court opined that such a presumption would be unconstitutional because it could be understood as shifting the burden to the defendant to prove that he lacked the intent to kill. Id., at 524, 99 S.Ct., at 2459 (citing Mullaney v. Wilbur, 421 U.S. 684, 95 S.Ct. 1881, 44 L.Ed.2d 508 (1975)). In addition, the Court in a footnote stated that such a burden-shifting "mandatory rebuttable presumption" could not be cured by other language in the charge indicating that the State bore the burden of proving guilt beyond a reasonable doubt, because "the jury could have interpreted the ... instructions as indicating that the presumption was a means by which proof beyond a reasonable doubt as to intent could be satisfied." Id., 442 U.S., at 519, n. 7, 99 S.Ct., at 2456, n. 7.

It should be clear that the instructions at issue here—which provide that the challenged presumptions "may be rebutted"—are very different from the conclusive language at issue in Sandstrom. The conclusive presumption eliminates an element of the crime altogether; the rebuttable presumption here indicates that the particular element is still relevant, and may be shown not to exist. Nevertheless, the Court relies on the latter portion of the Sandstrom opinion, outlined above, as the precedent dictating its result. Ante, at 1972, 1973. The language relied upon is, of course, manifestly dicta, inasmuch as the Sandstrom Court had already held (1) that a mandatory conclusive presumption on intent is unconstitutional and (2) that a reasonable juror could have understood the instruction at issue as creating such a conclusive presumption.

Even if one accepts the Sandstrom dicta at face value, however, I do not agree with the Court that a "reasonable juror" listening to the charge "as a whole" could have understood the instructions as shifting the burden of disproving intent to the defendant. Before examining the convoluted reasoning that leads to the Court's conclusion, it will be useful to set out the relevant portions of the charge as the jury heard them, and not in scattered pieces as they are found in the Court's opinion. The trial court began by explaining the general presumption of innocence:

"I charge you that before the State is entitled to a verdict of conviction . . . the burden is upon the State of proving the defendant's guilt as charged in such count beyond a reasonable doubt. . . .

"Now, reasonable doubt is just what that term implies. It's a doubt based on reason. . . . [A] reasonable doubt is the doubt of a fair-minded, impartial juror actively seeking for the truth and it may arise from a consideration of the evidence, from a conflict in the evidence or from a lack of evidence. If, upon a consideration of all the facts and circumstances of this case, your mind is wavering, unsettled, not satisfied, then that is the reasonable doubt under the law and if such a doubt rests upon your mind, it is your duty to give the defendant the benefit of the doubt and acquit him. If, on the other hand, no such doubt rests upon your mind, it would be equally your duty to return a verdict of guilty.

"Now, the defendant enters upon his trial with the presumption of innocence in his favor and this presumption, while not evidence, is yet in the nature of evidence and it remains with him throughout the trial, unless and until it is overcome by evidence sufficiently strong to satisfy you of his guilt to a reasonable and moral certainty and beyond a reasonable doubt."

The court stated the burden of proof once more in its general instructions concerning evaluation of witness credibility, and then stated it again before it turned to more specific instructions:

"Now, Ladies and Gentlemen, the burden is upon the State to prove to a reasonable and moral certainty and beyond a reasonable doubt every material allegation in each count of this indictment and I charge you further, *that there is no burden on the defendant to prove anything. The burden is on the State*.

"Now I give you in charge, certain definitions as found in the Criminal Code of the State of Georgia.

"A crime is a violation of a statute of this State in which there shall be a union of joint operation of act or omission to act, and intention or criminal negligence. A person shall not be found guilty of any crime committed by misfortune or accident where it satisfactorily appears there was no criminal scheme or undertaking or intention or criminal negligence. *The acts of a person of sound mind and discretion are presumed to be the product of the person's will, but the presumption may be rebutted. A person of sound mind and discretion is presumed to intend the natural and probable consequences of his acts but the presumption may be rebutted. A person will not be presumed to act with criminal intention but the trier of facts, that is, the Jury, may find criminal intention upon a consideration of the words, conduct, demeanor, motive and all other circumstances connected with the act for which the accused is prosecuted.*" (Emphasis supplied.)

After instructing the jury on the specific elements of Count I, charging respondent with the kidnapping of the nurse, the Court went on to instruct on the elements of murder:

"I charge you that the law of Georgia defines murder as follows: A person commits murder when he unlawfully and with malice aforethought, either express or implied, causes the death of another human being. Express malice is that deliberate intention unlawfully to take away the life of a fellow creature which is manifested by external circumstances capable of proof. Malice shall be implied where no considerable provocation appears and where all the circumstances of the killing show an abandoned and malignant heart.

"Now, you will see that malice is an essential ingredient in murder as charged in this indictment in Count II, and it must exist before the alleged homicide can be murder. *Malice in its legal sense is not necessarily ill will or hatred; it is the unlawful, deliberate intention to kill a human being without justification or mitigation or excuse, which intention must exist at the time of the killing....*

"Members of the Jury, *I charge you that it is not encumbent upon the accused to prove an absence of malice, if the evidence for the prosecution shows facts which may excuse or justify the homicide. The accused is not required to produce evidence of mitigation, justification or excuse on his part to the crime of murder. Whether mitigation, justification or excuse is shown by the evidence on the part of the State, it is not required of the accused to prove an absence of malice, if the evidence for the State shows facts which may excuse or justify the homicide.* But it is for you, the members of the Jury to say after a consideration of all the facts and circumstances in the case, whether or not malice, express or implied, exists in the case." (Emphasis supplied.)

In Cupp v. Naughten, 414 U.S. 141, 94 S.Ct. 396, 38 L.Ed.2d 368 (1973), we dealt with a constitutional challenge to an instruction that "every witness is presumed to speak the truth," in the context of a criminal trial where the defense presented no witnesses. We there reaffirmed "the well-established proposition that a single instruction to a jury may not be judged in artificial isolation, but must be viewed in the context of the overall charge." Id., at 146–147, 94 S.Ct., at 400 (citing Boyd v. United States, 271 U.S. 104, 107, 46 S.Ct. 442, 443, 70 L.Ed. 857 (1926)). We noted that if a particular instruction was erroneous a reviewing court still must ask "whether the ailing instruction by itself so infected the entire trial that the resulting conviction violates due process." Id. In reaching our conclusion that the instruction at issue in Cupp did not violate due process, we noted that the jury had been fully informed of the State's burden to prove guilt beyond a reasonable doubt. We also pointed out that the instruction concerning the presumption of truthfulness had been accompanied by an instruction that in assessing a witness's credibility the jury should be attentive to the witness's own manner and words. We concluded that these instructions sufficiently allowed the jury to exercise its own judgment on the question of a witness's truthfulness; we also found no undue pressure on the defendant to take the stand and rebut the State's testimony, since the instruction indicated that such rebuttal could be founded on the State's own evidence. Id., 414 U.S., at 149, 94 S.Ct., at 401.

I see no meaningful distinction between Cupp and the case at bar. Here the jury was instructed no less than four times that the State bore the burden of proof beyond a reasonable doubt. This language was accompanied early in the charge by a detailed discussion indicating that the jurors were the judges of their own reasonable doubt, that this doubt could arise after taking into account all the circumstances surrounding the incident at issue, and that where such doubt existed it was the jurors' duty to acquit. Four sentences prior to the offending language identified by the Court the jury was explicitly charged that "there is no burden on the defendant to prove anything." Immediately following that language the jury was charged that a person "will not be presumed to act with criminal intention," but that the jury could find such intention based upon the circumstances surrounding the act. The jury was then charged on Georgia's definition of malice, an essential element of murder which includes (1) deliberate intent to kill (2) without justification or mitigation or excuse. Again, the jury was explicitly charged that "it is not incumbent upon the accused to prove an absence of malice, if the evidence for the prosecution shows facts which may excuse or justify the homicide."

The Court nevertheless concludes, upon reading the charge in its entirety, that a "reasonable juror" could have understood the instruction to mean (1) that the State had satisfied its burden of proving intent to kill by introducing evidence of the defendant's acts—drawing, aiming and firing the gun—the "natural and probable consequences" of which were the death in question; (2) that upon proof of these acts the burden shifted to the defendant to disprove that he had acted with intent to kill; and (3) that if the defendant introduced no evidence or the jury was unconvinced by his evidence, the jury was *required* to find that the State had proved intent to kill even if the State's proof did not convince them of the defendant's intent.

The reasoning which leads to this conclusion would appeal only to a lawyer, and it is indeed difficult to believe that "reasonable jurors" would have arrived at it on their own. It runs like this. First, the Court states that a "reasonable juror" could understand the particular offending sentences, considered in isolation, to shift the burden to the defendant of disproving his intent to kill. Ante, at 1973. The Court then proceeds to examine other portions of the charge, to determine whether they militate against this understanding. It casually dismisses the "general instructions on the State's burden of persuasion," relying on the *Sandstrom* footnote which stated that the burden-shifting instruction could be read consistently with the State's general burden because "[t]he jury could have interpreted the two sets of instructions as indicating that the presumption was a means by which proof beyond a reasonable doubt was satisfied."

Pausing here for a moment, I note that I am not at all sure that this expository fast footwork is as applicable where, unlike in *Sandstrom*, the presumption created by the charge is not conclusive, but rebuttable. Since in this case the presumption was "rebuttable," the obvious question is: "rebuttable by what?" The Court's analysis must assume that a "reasonable juror" understood the presumption to be a means for satisfying the State's burden unless rebutted *by the defendant*. The italicized words, of course, are not included in the charge in this case, but if the jurors reasonably believed that the presumption could be rebutted by other means—for example, by the circumstances surrounding the incident—then the Court's analysis fails. But I find the Court's assumption unrealistic in any event, because if the jurors understood the charge as the Court posits then that conclusion was reached in the face of the contradictory preceding statement that *the defendant had no burden to prove anything.*

Undaunted, the Court does not even mention the italicized portion of the charge. Instead, it proceeds to dispose of the sentence immediately following the challenged sentences, which states that a person will *not* be presumed to act with *"criminal intent."* With respect to this language, the Court first speculates that it might have been directed, not to the "intent" element of malice, but rather to the element of malice which requires that the defendant act without justification or excuse. Thus, the Court explains that its "reasonable juror" could have reconciled the two apparently conflicting sentences by deciding "that the instructions related to different elements of the crime and were therefore not contradictory—that he could presume intent to kill but not the absence of justification or provocation." Ante, at 1974.

This statement defies belief. Passing the obvious problem that both sentences speak to the defendant's "intent," and not to "justification or provocation," the Court has presumed that the jurors hearing this charge reconciled two apparently contradictory sentences by neatly attributing them to separate elements of Georgia's definition of "malice"—no small feat for laymen—and did so *even though they had not yet been charged on the element of malice.* Either the Court is attributing qualities to the average juror that are found in very few lawyers, or it perversely reads the instructions as a "looking-glass charge" which, when held to a mirror, reads more clearly in the opposite direction.[1]

Alternatively, the Court suggests that the sentences dealing with the presumptions on intent are flatly contradictory, and that the charge therefore is defective since there is no way to determine which instruction a reasonable juror would have followed. The Court reasoned in this regard:

"Nothing in these specific sentences or in the charge as a whole makes clear to the jury that one of these contradictory instructions carries more weight than the other. Language that merely contradicts and does not explain a constitutionally infirm instruction will not suffice to absolve the infirmity."

It may well be that the Court's technical analysis of the charge holds together from a legal standpoint, but its tortured reasoning is alone sufficient to convince me that no "reasonable juror" followed that path. It is not that I think jurors are not conscientious, or that I believe jurors disregard troublesome trial court instructions; I agree with the Court that we generally must assume that jurors strive to follow the law as charged. See ante, at 1976, n. 9. Rather, I simply do not believe that a "reasonable juror," upon listening to the above charge, could have interpreted it as shifting the burden to the defendant to disprove intent, and as requiring the juror to follow the presumption *even if he was not satisfied with the State's proof on that element.*

To reach this conclusion the juror would have had to disregard three express statements—that the defendant had no burden to prove anything, that "criminal intent" was not to be presumed, and that there was no burden on the defendant to disprove malice. In addition, he would have had to do so under circumstances where a far more "reasonable" interpretation was available. The challenged language stated that the presumption could be rebutted. Throughout the charge the jury was told that they were to listen to all the evidence and draw their own conclusions, based upon a witness's demeanor and words and their own common sense. They were told that the burden of proof rested on the

---

1. "[Alice] puzzled over this for some time, but at last a bright thought struck her. 'Why, it's a Looking-glass book, of course! And, it I hold it up to a glass, the words will also go the right way again.' " L. Carroll, Through the Looking Glass, at 22–23.

State, and they were told that circumstances surrounding the acts in question would provide a basis for drawing various conclusions with respect to intent and malice. The reasonable interpretation of the challenged charge is that, just as in Cupp, the presumption could be rebutted by the circumstances surrounding the acts, whether presented by the State or the defendant. Such an interpretation would not require a juror to disregard any possibly conflicting instructions; it also would have been consistent with the entire tone of the charge from start to finish. See McInerney v. Berman, 621 F.2d 20, 24 (CA1 1980) ("[I]t will be presumed that [a juror] will not isolate a particular portion of the charge and ascribe to it more importance than the rest.").

Perhaps more importantly, however, the Court's reasoning set out above indicates quite clearly that where a particular isolated instruction can be read as burden-shifting the Court is not disposed to find that instruction constitutionally harmless in the absence of specific language elsewhere in the charge which addresses and cures that instruction. See also ante, at 1975, n. 8. This reasoning cannot be squared with Cupp, in which this Court emphasized that "the question is not whether the trial court failed to isolate and cure a particular ailing instruction, but rather whether the ailing instruction by itself so infected the entire trial that the resulting conviction violates due process." Cupp, 414 U.S., at 147, 94 S.Ct., at 400. It is true that the problems raised here probably could be alleviated if the words "is presumed" were merely changed to "may be presumed," thereby making the presumption permissive, see ante, at 1972; Lamb v. Jernigan, 683 F.2d 1332, 1339–1340 (CA11 1982); McInerney, supra, 621 F.2d, at 24, and admittedly the Court's analysis of the charge establishes a rule that is easier in application in the appellate courts. But that is not the question. Cupp indicates that due process is not violated in every case where an isolated sentence implicates constitutional problems, and the Court's hypertechnical arguments only highlight how far it has strayed from the norm of "fundamental fairness" in order to invalidate this conviction.

Thus, even accepting the Court's reasonable juror test, I cannot agree that the charge read as a whole was constitutionally infirm. But quite apart from that, I would take a different approach than the Court does with respect to the applicable legal standard. It appears that under the Court's approach it will reverse a conviction if a "reasonable juror" hypothetically might have understood the charge unconstitutionally to shift a burden of proof, even if it was unlikely that a single juror had such an understanding. I believe that it must at least be *likely* that a juror so understood the charge before constitutional error can be found. Where as here a Sandstrom error is alleged involving not a conclusive presumption, but a rebuttable presumption, language in the charge indicating the State's general burden of proof and the jury's duty to examine all surrounding facts and circumstances generally should be sufficient to dissipate any constitutional infirmity. Otherwise we risk finding constitutional error in a record such as this one, after finely parsing through the elements of state crimes that are really far removed from the problems presented by the burden of proof charge in Winship. I do not believe that the Court must inject itself this far into the state criminal process to protect the fundamental rights of criminal defendants. I dissent and would reverse the judgment of the Court of Appeals.

NOTES

1. Does Francis prohibit all presumptions in criminal cases which have the consequence of shifting the burden of persuasion to defendant as to any issue, or do they hinge on the fact that the instruction may have relieved the prosecution of the burden on the only contested issue in the case. Note, too, the question of whether burden-shifting presumptions are covered, left open in footnote 3 of the majority opinion in Francis. Does the result turn on the fact that this is a capital case? Does Francis show the wisdom of not using the term presumption when instructing the jury? How would you have reframed the instruction?

2. In Hammontree v. Phelps, 605 F.2d 1371 (5th Cir.1979), the defendant had been convicted in State court under a negligent homicide statute which provided that, "[t]he violation of a statute or ordinance shall be considered only as presumptive evidence of such negligence." The federal district court granted a writ of habeas corpus finding that the provision violated due process because it created an unconstitutional presumption that violation of a statute constitutes criminal negligence. Hammontree v. Phelps, 462 F.Supp. 366 (W.D.La.1978). The Court of Appeals pointed out that the construction of the statute by the Louisiana Supreme Court in State v. Hammontree, 363 So.2d 1364, 1372 (La.1978), did not shift any burden from the prosecution to the defendant. However, the Court of Appeals disagreed with the Louisiana Supreme Court as to the appropriateness of the following jury charge:

> The particular statute that defines "the crime of negligent homicide also provides that" "'the violation of a statute or ordinance shall be considered only as presumptive evidence of such negligence.' "This has reference to criminal negligence, which is an essential element of the crime charged. The use of the word "only" in this part of the law means that such presumption is merely a rebuttable one and not conclusive. The presumption does not deprive the accused of the right of showing evidence that he was free from criminal negligence even though he has violated a statute or ordinance. This presumption of law does not change the rule heretofore mentioned as to the presumption of innocence that attends the accused throughout the trial, for upon its conclusion and after all of the evidence has been presented, in order to convict, the State must have proved to your satisfaction and beyond a reasonable doubt that the defendant was criminally negligent, under the definition of criminal negligence given to you in this charge, and that such negligence was the cause of the killing.

As Judge Wisdom wrote for the Court of Appeals,

> On these instructions, a reasonable juror could conclude, as in *Sandstrom*, that the criminal negligence statute created a mandatory presumption requiring the defendant to produce a "quantum of proof which may well have been considerably greater than 'some evidence'—thus effectively shifting the burden of persuasion".... The trial judge did not state that the presumption placed no "affirmative burden" on the accused.

605 F.2d at 1379–1380. See also, Nesson, Reasonable Doubt and Permissive Inferences: The Value of Complexity, 92 Harv.L.Rev. 1187, 1208–215 (1979). The author discusses the inappropriateness of the "unless satisfactorily explained" instruction which is likely to be understood by jurors as an invitation to draw an inference from the defendant's silence which might itself be sufficient to invalidate it on fifth amendment grounds; however, one situation considered appropriate for a jury to draw an inference from a lack of satisfactory explanation is where "the prosecution not only proves the suggestive predicate fact but also proves affirmatively, that there is no satisfactory explanation for it."

3. How should "the presumption of innocence" be treated? Carr v. State, 4 So.2d 887, 888 (Miss.1941):

[T]he so-called presumption of innocence is not, strictly speaking, a presumption in the sense of an inference deduced from a given premise. It is more accurately an assumption which has for its purpose the placing of the burden of proof upon anyone who asserts any deviation from the socially desirable ideal of good moral conduct. ... As a procedural aid it compels the state to assume and maintain the burden of proving guilt. ... There seems to be no reason why this assumption, although it may be conceded that it "enters the trial with the defendant," should "go throughout" the trial despite its early or complete liquidation by overwhelming proof. And we should not indulge the fiction that it necessarily "goes into the jury room" with the jury. On the contrary, each juror under his oath should carry into the jury room a conviction of guilt if, under the instructions and testimony, this assumption has been met and overcome.

People v. Roman, 35 N.Y.2d 978, 979, 365 N.Y.S.2d 527, 528, 324 N.E.2d 885, 886 (1975) holding that "[t]o forbid a defendant to wear his own clothing and to require him to appear in convict's attire—a continuing visual communication to the jury—is to deny" the defendant his right to a presumption of innocence.

In Kentucky v. Whorton, 441 U.S. 786, 789 (1979), it was held that "the failure to give a requested instruction on the presumption of innocence does not in and of itself violate the Constitution ...; [s]uch a failure must be evaluated in light of the totality of circumstances, including all instructions to the jury, arguments of counsel, whether the weight of the evidence was overwhelming, and other relevant factors—to determine whether the defendant received a constitutionally fair trial."

4. What, if any, effect will the rebuttable presumption that those accused of certain crimes present special threats to the community warranting pretrial detention have? See, e.g., United States v. Jessup, 757 F.2d 378, 380 (1st Cir.1985).

Rose v. Clark

Supreme Court of the United States, 1986.
478 U.S. 570, 106 S.Ct. 3101, 92 L.Ed.2d 460.

■ JUSTICE POWELL delivered the opinion of the Court.

This case presents the question whether the harmless error standard of Chapman v. California, 386 U.S. 18, 87 S.Ct. 824, 17 L.Ed.2d 705, 24 A.L.R.3d 1065 (1967), applies to jury instructions that violate the principles of Sandstrom v. Montana, 442 U.S. 510, 99 S.Ct. 2450, 61 L.Ed.2d 39 (1979), and Francis v. Franklin, 471 U.S. 307, 105 S.Ct. 1965, 85 L.Ed.2d 344 (1985).

I

On December 30, 1978, Charles Browning and Joy Faulk were shot to death while they sat in Browning's pickup truck in a remote area of Rutherford County, Tennessee. Respondent Stanley Clark, Faulk's former boyfriend, was charged with the murders.

The evidence introduced at trial showed that Browning, Faulk, and Faulk's two young children (ages 6 and 3) had been driving in Rutherford County on the night of the murders. According to the older child, another vehicle followed Browning's truck for about an hour. Browning pulled his truck into a private driveway, apparently to let the other vehicle pass. The driver of the second vehicle then pulled in behind Browning, thereby blocking any exit. The driver left his vehicle, walked up to the cab of Browning's truck, and fired four shots at pointblank range. One shot struck Browning in the head, two others struck Faulk in the head, and the fourth struck Faulk in the left shoulder. The killer left the scene in his vehicle. Both Browning and Faulk died.

Faulk's children, who had not been shot, went for help, telling a local resident that "Clicker" (the nickname by which the children knew respondent) had shot Browning and their mother. Earlier that night, police had seen respondent following Browning's truck. Police soon located respondent, but apprehended him only after a high-speed chase. Police found the murder weapon, a .25–caliber pistol that respondent had borrowed from a friend, near respondent's home. At trial, the State relied on the foregoing evidence, and on evidence showing that respondent and Joy Faulk had a stormy love affair that Faulk ended in the fall of 1978. Several times after their break-up, respondent threatened to kill Faulk if he ever found her with another man.

Respondent offered two lines of defense. First, he contended that Sam Faulk, Joy's ex-husband, killed the victims because of a dispute concerning custody of the two Faulk children. The State rebutted this contention by introducing evidence that no such dispute existed, and that Sam Faulk was elsewhere when the murders were committed. Second, respondent argued that he was either insane or incapable of forming the requisite criminal intent. To support this argument, respondent introduced evidence that he was suffering from amnesia and could not remember the events of the night of the murders. In addition, some testimony suggested that respondent had been drinking heavily the entire day before the murders. Finally, two defense psychiatrists testified that respondent was legally insane at the time the murders were committed because his depression concerning his recent break-up with Joy Faulk made it impossible for him to conform his conduct to the law.

At the close of trial, the court instructed the jury on the elements of both first-and second-degree murder. Under Tennessee law, first-degree murder requires proof of premeditation and deliberation, while second-degree murder requires proof of malice. The court's instructions defined malice as "an intent to do any injury to another, a design formed in the mind of doing mischief to another." App. 186. Malice did not require proof of planning or premeditation; a killing "upon a sudden impulse of passion" sufficed if committed with intent to harm another. Id., at 187. The court then charged the jury:

"All homicides are presumed to be malicious in the absence of evidence which would rebut the implied presumption. Thus, if the State has proven beyond a reasonable ... doubt that a killing has occurred, then it is presumed that the killing was done maliciously. But this presumption may be rebutted by either direct or circumstantial evidence, or by both, regardless of whether the same be offered by the Defendant, or exists in the evidence of the State." Ibid.

The jury found respondent guilty of first-degree murder for killing Faulk and of second-degree murder for killing Browning.

The Tennessee Court of Criminal Appeals affirmed the convictions, reject-ing respondent's argument that the jury instructions had impermissibly shifted the burden of proof as to malice.[1] Respondent then sought habeas corpus relief

---

1. The Court of Criminal Appeals noted that, almost immediately following the "presumption" instruction, the judge charged:

"The question of whether the alleged killing was done with malice is for you to determine from the entire case, and you should look to all of the facts and circum- stances developed by the evidence to determine whether the State has ... proven beyond a reasonable doubt the existence of malice. If you have a reasonable doubt as to whether the alleged killing was done with malice, then the Defendant cannot be guilty

in the Middle District of Tennessee. The District Court held that the malice instruction had violated respondent's right to have his guilt proved beyond a reasonable doubt, as that right was defined in Sandstrom v. Montana. The court went on to find that the error could not be deemed harmless because respondent had "relied upon a mens rea defense" in contesting his guilt. 611 F.Supp. 294, 302 (1983).

The Court of Appeals for the Sixth Circuit affirmed. The court agreed that the malice instruction was unconstitutional under Sandstrom. Turning to the question whether the error was harmless, the court reasoned that because respondent contested malice at his trial, an erroneous burden-shifting instruction could not be harmless under governing precedent. App. to Pet. for Cert. A–5 (citing Engle v. Koehler, 707 F.2d 241, 246 (CA6 1983), aff'd by an equally divided Court, 466 U.S. 1, 104 S.Ct. 1673, 80 L.Ed.2d 1 (1984)). The court reached this conclusion "despite the substantial evidence of petitioner's guilt," and added:

> "Were we writing on a clean slate, we would direct our inquiry to that suggested by Justice Powell (dissenting) in Connecticut v. Johnson, 460 U.S. at 97 n. 5 [103 S.Ct. 969, 74 L.Ed.2d 823]: the inquiry is whether the evidence is so dispositive of intent that a reviewing court can say beyond a reasonable doubt that the jury would have found it unnecessary to rely on the presumption. If that were the question in this case ... we might be able to respond in the affirmative." App. to Pet. for Cert. A–6.

The court nevertheless affirmed the order granting habeas corpus relief. We granted certiorari limited to the question whether the Court of Appeals' harmless-error analysis was correct. 106 S.Ct. 59, 88 L.Ed.2d 48 (1985).

II

A

In Chapman v. California, 386 U.S. 18, 87 S.Ct. 824, 17 L.Ed.2d 705, 24 A.L.R.3d 1065 (1967), this Court rejected the argument that errors of constitutional dimension necessarily require reversal of criminal convictions. And since Chapman, "we have repeatedly reaffirmed the principle that an otherwise valid conviction should not be set aside if the reviewing court may confidently say, on the whole record, that the constitutional error was harmless beyond a reasonable doubt." Delaware v. Van Arsdall, 475 U.S. 673, ___, 106 S.Ct. 1431, 89 L.Ed.2d 674 (1986). That principle has been applied to a wide variety of constitutional errors. E.g., id., at 106 S.Ct. 1431, 89 L.Ed.2d 674 (failure to permit cross-examination concerning witness bias); Rushen v. Spain, 464 U.S. 114, 118, 104 S.Ct. 453, 78 L.Ed.2d 267 (1983) (per curiam) (denial of right to be present at trial); United States v. Hasting, 461 U.S. 499, 508–509, 103 S.Ct. 1974, 76 L.Ed.2d 96 (1983) (improper comment on defendant's failure to testify); Moore v. Illinois, 434 U.S. 220, 232, 98 S.Ct. 458, 54 L.Ed.2d 424 (1977) (admission of witness identification obtained in violation of right to counsel); Milton v. Wainwright, 407 U.S. 371, 92 S.Ct. 2174, 33 L.Ed.2d 1 (1972) (admission of confession obtained in violation of right to counsel); Chambers v. Maroney, 399 U.S. 42, 52–53, 90 S.Ct. 1975, 26 L.Ed.2d 419 (1970) (admission of evidence obtained in violation of the Fourth Amendment)....

---

of murder in the second degree and you must acquit him of that offense." App. 188.

The Court of Criminal Appeals reasoned that this instruction adequately informed the jurors that the burden of proof on malice remained on the State at all times. App. to Pet. for Cert. A–37 to A–39. [Footnote of Court renumbered; other footnotes are omitted]

Despite the strong interests that support the harmless-error doctrine, the Court in Chapman recognized that some constitutional errors require reversal without regard to the evidence in the particular case. 386 U.S. at 23, n. 8, 87 S.Ct. 824, 17 L.Ed.2d 705, 24 A.L.R.3d 1065, citing Payne v. Arkansas, 356 U.S. 560, 78 S.Ct. 844, 2 L.Ed.2d 975 (1958) (introduction of coerced confession); Gideon v. Wainwright, 372 U.S. 335, 83 S.Ct. 792, 9 L.Ed.2d 799, 23 Ohio Ops.2d 258, 93 A.L.R.2d 733 (1963) (complete denial of right to counsel); Tumey v. Ohio, 273 U.S. 510, 47 S.Ct. 437, 71 L.Ed.2d 749, 5 Ohio L.Abs. 159, 5 Ohio L.Abs. 185, 50 A.L.R. 1243 (1927) (adjudication by biased judge). This limitation recognizes that some errors necessarily render a trial fundamentally unfair. The State of course must provide a trial before an impartial judge, Tumey v. Ohio, supra, with counsel to help the accused defend against the State's charge, Gideon v. Wainwright, supra. Compare Holloway v. Arkansas, 435 U.S. 475, 488–490, 98 S.Ct. 1173, 55 L.Ed.2d 426 (1978) with Cuyler v. Sullivan, 446 U.S. 335, 348–350, 100 S.Ct. 1708, 64 L.Ed.2d 333 (1980). Without these basic protections, a criminal trial cannot reliably serve its function as a vehicle for determination of guilt or innocence, see Powell v. Alabama, 287 U.S. 45, 53 S.Ct. 55, 77 L.Ed.2d 158, 84 A.L.R. 527 (1932), and no criminal punishment may be regarded as fundamentally fair. Harmless-error analysis thus presupposes a trial, at which the defendant, represented by counsel, may present evidence and argument before an impartial judge and jury.[2] See Delaware v. Van Arsdall, supra, at 106 S.Ct. 1431, 89 L.Ed.2d 674 (constitutional errors may be harmless "in terms of their effect on *the factfinding process at trial*") (emphasis added); Chapman, supra, at 24, 87 S.Ct. 824, 17 L.Ed.2d 705, 24 A.L.R.3d 1065 (error is harmless if, beyond a reasonable doubt, it "did not *contribute to the verdict* obtained") (emphasis added).

. . .

B

Applying these principles to this case is not difficult. Respondent received a full opportunity to put on evidence and make argument to support his claim of innocence. He was tried by a fairly selected, impartial jury, supervised by an impartial judge. Apart from the challenged malice instruction, the jury in this case was clearly instructed that it had to find respondent guilty beyond a reasonable doubt as to every element of both first-and second-degree murder. See also n. [1], supra. Placed in context, the erroneous malice instruction does not compare with the kinds of errors that automatically require reversal of an otherwise valid conviction. We therefore find that the error at issue here—an instruction that impermissibly shifted the burden of proof on malice—is not "so basic to a fair trial" that it can never be harmless. Cf. Chapman, 386 U.S., at 23, 87 S.Ct. 824, 17 L.Ed.2d 705, 24 A.L.R.2d 1065.

The purpose behind the rule of Sandstrom v. Montana supports this conclusion. Sandstrom was a logical extension of the Court's holding in In re Winship, 397 U.S. 358, 90 S.Ct. 1068, 25 L.Ed.2d 368, 51 Ohio Ops.2d 323 (1970), that the prosecution must prove "every fact necessary to constitute the crime with which [the defendant] is charged" beyond a reasonable doubt. Id., at 364, 90 S.Ct. 1068, 25 L.Ed.2d 368, 51 Ohio Ops.2d 323; see Sandstrom, 442 U.S., at 520, 523, 99 S.Ct. 2450, 61 L.Ed.2d 39; Francis v. Franklin, 471 U.S., at

---

2. Each of the examples Chapman cited of errors that could never be harmless either aborted the basic trial process, Payne v. Arkansas, 356 U.S. 560, 78 S.Ct. 844, 2 L.Ed.2d 975 (1958) (use of coerced confession), or denied it altogether, Gideon v. Wainwright, 372 U.S. 335, 83 S.Ct. 792, 9 L.Ed.2d 799, 23 Ohio Ops.2d 258, 93 A.L.R.2d 733 (1963) (denial of counsel); Tumey v. Ohio, 273 U.S. 510, 47 S.Ct. 437, 71 L.Ed. 749, 5 Ohio L.Abs. 159, 5 Ohio L.Abs. 185, 50 A.L.R. 1243 (1927) (biased adjudicator).

___, 105 S.Ct. 1965, 85 L.Ed.2d 344. The purpose of that rule is to ensure that only the guilty are criminally punished. As the Court stated last term in Francis v. Franklin, the rule "protects the 'fundamental value determination of our society,' given voice in Justice Harlan's concurrence in Winship, that 'it is far worse to convict an innocent man than to let a guilty man go free.' " Ibid., quoting Winship, supra, at 372, 90 S.Ct. 1068, 25 L.Ed.2d 368, 51 Ohio Ops.2d 323 (Harlan, J., concurring). When the verdict of guilty reached in a case in which Sandstrom error was committed is correct beyond a reasonable doubt, reversal of the conviction does nothing to promote the interest that the rule serves.

Nor is Sandstrom error equivalent to a directed verdict for the State.[3] When a jury is instructed to presume malice from predicate facts, it still must find the existence of those facts beyond a reasonable doubt. Connecticut v. Johnson, 460 U.S. 73, 96–97, 103 S.Ct. 969, 74 L.Ed.2d 823 (1983) (Powell, J., dissenting). In many cases, the predicate facts conclusively establish intent, so that no rational jury could find that the defendant committed the relevant criminal act but did not intend to cause injury. See, e.g., Lamb v. Jernigan, 683 F.2d 1332, 1342–1343 (CA11 1982), cert. denied, 460 U.S. 1024, 103 S.Ct. 1276, 75 L.Ed.2d 496 (1983). In that event the erroneous instruction is simply superfluous: the jury has found, in Winship's words, "every fact necessary" to establish every element of the offense beyond a reasonable doubt. See Connecticut v. Johnson, supra, at 97, 103 S.Ct. 969, 74 L.Ed.2d 823 (Powell, J., dissenting); Jeffries & Stephan, Defenses, Presumptions, and Burden of Proof in the Criminal Law, 88 Yale LJ 1325, 1388, n. 192 (1979).

No one doubts that the trial court properly could have instructed the jury that it could infer malice from respondent's conduct. See Francis v Franklin, 105 S.Ct. 1965, 85 L.Ed.2d 344; Ulster County Court v. Allen, 442 U.S. 140, 157–163, 99 S.Ct. 2213, 60 L.Ed.2d 777 (1979). Indeed, in the many cases where there is no direct evidence of intent, that is exactly how intent is established. For purposes of deciding this case, it is enough to recognize that in some cases that inference is overpowering. See Hopper v. Evans, 456 U.S., at 613, 102 S.Ct. 2049, 72 L.Ed.2d 367. It would further neither justice nor the purposes of the Sandstrom rule to reverse a conviction in such a case.[4] We accordingly hold

---

3. "Because a presumption does not remove the issue of intent from the jury's consideration, it is distinguishable from other instructional errors that prevent a jury from considering an issue." Connecticut v. Johnson, 460 U.S. at 95, n. 3, 103 S.Ct. 969, 74 L.Ed.2d 823 (Powell, J., dissenting). Cf. Jackson v. Virginia, 443 U.S. 307, 320, n. 14, 99 S.Ct. 2781, 61 L.Ed.2d 560 (1979) (suggesting that failure to instruct a jury as to the reasonable-doubt standard cannot be harmless).

4. We think the dissent, and not the Court, "asks and answers the wrong question" in this case. Post, at 92 L.Ed.2d 482 (Blackmun, J., dissenting). We agree that the determination of guilt or innocence, according to the standard of proof required by Winship and its progeny, is for the jury rather than the court. See id., at 92 L.Ed.2d 480–481. Harmless-error analysis addresses a different question: what is to be done about a trial error that, in theory, may have altered the basis on which the jury decided the case, but in practice clearly had no effect

on the outcome? This question applies not merely to Sandstrom violations, but to other errors that may have affected either the instructions the jury heard or the record it considered—including errors such as mistaken admission of evidence, or unconstitutional comment on a defendant's silence, or erroneous limitation of a defendant's cross-examination of a prosecution witness. All of these errors alter the terms under which the jury considered the defendant's guilt or innocence, and therefore all theoretically impair the defendant's interest in having a jury decide his case. The dissent's argument—that the Sixth Amendment forbids a reviewing court to decide the impact of a trial error on the outcome, post, 92 L.Ed.2d 480 logically implies that all such errors are immune from harmless-error analysis. Yet this Court repeatedly has held to the contrary. E.g., Delaware v. Van Arsdall, 106 S.Ct. 1431, 89 L.Ed.2d 674 (1986) (limitation on defendant's cross-examination); United States v. Hasting, 461 U.S. 499, 103 S.Ct.

that Chapman's harmless error standard applies in cases such as this one.[5]

III

Although the Court of Appeals acknowledged that Sandstrom error might in some cases be harmless, its analysis of the issue cannot square with Chapman. The court concluded that a Sandstrom error could never be harmless where a defendant contests intent. App. to Pet. for Cert. A–5. But our harmless error cases do not turn on whether the defendant conceded the factual issue on which the error bore. Rather, we have held that "Chapman mandates consideration of the entire record prior to reversing a conviction for constitutional errors that may be harmless." United States v. Hasting, 461 U.S., at 509, n. 7, 103 S.Ct. 1974, 76 L.Ed.2d 96. The question is whether, "on the whole record ... the error ... [is] harmless beyond a reasonable doubt." Id., at 510, 103 S.Ct. 1974, 76 L.Ed.2d 96. See also Chapman, 386 U.S., at 24, 87 S.Ct. 824, 17 L.Ed.2d 705, 24 A.L.R.3d 1065 ("before a federal constitutional error can be held harmless, the court must be able to declare a belief that it was harmless beyond a reasonable doubt"); Connecticut v. Johnson, 460 U.S., at 97, n. 5, 103 S.Ct. 969, 74 L.Ed.2d 823 (Powell, J., dissenting) (in cases of Sandstrom error, "the inquiry is whether the evidence was so dispositive of intent that a reviewing court can say beyond a reasonable doubt that the jury would have found it unnecessary to rely on the presumption"). Thus, the fact that respondent denied that he had "an intent to do any injury to another," App. 186, does not dispose of the harmless-error question.

Although we "plainly have the authority" to decide whether, on the facts of a particular case, a constitutional error was harmless under the Chapman standard, we "do so sparingly." United States v. Hasting, supra, at 510, 103 S.Ct. 1974, 76 L.Ed.2d 96. The Court of Appeals has not yet applied Chapman to the facts of this case. We therefore remand to that court for determination of whether the error committed in this case was harmless beyond a reasonable doubt.

1974, 76 L.Ed.2d 96 (1983) (improper comment on defendant's failure to testify); Moore v. Illinois, 434 U.S. 220, 98 S.Ct. 458, 54 L.Ed.2d 424 (1977) (admission of improperly obtained witness identification). Indeed, Chapman v. California, 386 U.S. 18, 87 S.Ct. 824, 17 L.Ed.2d 705, 24 A.L.R.3d 1065 (1967), the beginning of this line of cases, applied harmless-error analysis to an error that placed an improper argument before the jury. Id., at 24–25, 87 S.Ct. 824, 17 L.Ed.2d 705, 24 A.L.R.3d 1065 (finding comment on defendant's silence harmful). See also Hopper v. Evans, 456 U.S., at 613–614, 102 S.Ct. 2049, 72 L.Ed.2d 367 (citing Chapman, and finding error in jury instructions harmless). These decisions, ignored by the dissent, strongly support application of harmless-error analysis in the context of Sandstrom error.

5. The dissent contends that the jury's decision to convict respondent of only one count of premeditated murder "aptly illustrate[s] why harmless-error analysis is inappropriate" in cases where intent is at issue.

Post, at 92 L.Ed.2d 481 (Blackmun, J., dissenting). This argument is without merit. The jury determined that respondent was guilty beyond a reasonable doubt of "intend[ing] to take the life" of Joy Faulk "with cool purpose." App. 185 (trial court's charge defining premeditation). The jury then determined that respondent was guilty of the malicious, but not premeditated, murder of Charles Browning. The only alleged error in these instructions was the trial court's instruction that the jury could presume *malice* from a killing. Respondent's (and the dissent's) theory is that a proper instruction on the burden of proof on malice might have led the jury to find *neither* malice *nor* premeditation as to Faulk's killing. This argument is implausible on its face.

We leave the question whether the error in this case was harmless beyond a reasonable doubt to the Court of Appeals on remand. We do suggest that the different verdicts for the two killings in no way support respondent's contention that the Sandstrom error in this case was prejudicial.

IV

The judgment of the Court of Appeals is vacated, and the case is remanded for further proceedings consistent with this opinion ...

■ CHIEF JUSTICE BURGER, concurring.

I join the Court's opinion, although I see no need for remanding for application of harmless error analysis.

.   .   .

■ JUSTICE STEVENS, concurring in the judgment.

The Court correctly concludes that the harmless error standard of Chapman v. California, 386 U.S. 18, 87 S.Ct. 824, 17 L.Ed.2d 705, 24 A.L.R.3d 1065 (1967) applies to the erroneous jury instructions in this case. I do not agree, however, with the Court's dictum regarding the nature of harmless error analysis.

.   .   .

■ JUSTICE BLACKMUN, with whom JUSTICE BRENNAN and JUSTICE MARSHALL join, dissenting.

Stanley Clark was deprived of two rights: the right guaranteed by the Due Process Clause of the Fourteenth Amendment to compel the State of Tennessee to prove beyond a reasonable doubt every element of the crimes with which he was charged, and the right guaranteed by the Sixth Amendment to have a jury of his peers determine whether the State had met that burden. Today, the Court focuses entirely on the former right and disregards totally the latter. A reviewing court's conclusion that the record would support a conviction by a properly instructed jury has no bearing on the question whether a defendant was denied the right to have the jury that actually tried him make that determination. "To conform to due process of law, [defendants are] entitled to have the validity of their convictions appraised on consideration of the case ... as the issues were determined in the trial court." Cole v. Arkansas, 333 U.S. 196, 202, 68 S.Ct. 514, 92 L.Ed.2d 644 (1948). A trial that was fundamentally unfair at the time it took place, because the jury was not compelled to perform its constitutionally required role, cannot be rendered fundamentally fair in retrospect by what amounts to nothing more than an appellate review of the sufficiency of the evidence. I therefore dissent from the Court's holding that harmless-error analysis should be applied.

.   .   .

CHAPTER 8

JUDICIAL NOTICE

SECTION 1. GENERAL CONSIDERATIONS

THAYER, A PRELIMINARY TREATISE ON EVIDENCE AT THE COMMON LAW 278–80 (1898)

Whereabout in the law does the doctrine of judicial notice belong? Wherever the process of reasoning has a place, and that is everywhere. . . . The subject of judicial notice . . . belongs to the general topic of legal or judicial reasoning. It is, indeed, woven into the very texture of the judicial function. In conducting a process of judicial reasoning, as of other reasoning, not a step can be taken without assuming something which has not been proved; and the capacity to do this, with competent judgment and efficiency, is imputed to judges and juries as part of their necessary mental outfit.

ISAACS, THE LAW AND THE FACTS, 22 COLUM.L.REV. 1, 6–7 (1922)

Theoretically, the need of the court for information as to general facts is taken care of by the doctrine of judicial notice. What the court is presumed to know a lawyer may tell it, and very little formality need be resorted to in this process of theoretically reminding the court of what it already knows. But this very fiction of judicial notice is based on a medieval conception of learning. The learned man of the middle ages was supposed to be skilled, and probably was skilled, in all of the Seven Sciences. The entire amount of the world's information could have been compressed in a very few volumes, and as a matter of fact, there were many men who, with apparent success, made all knowledge their particular province. This conception of the learned man is, of course, entirely abandoned today. Consequently, the doctrine of judicial notice does not quite fit the needs of modern life. In the first place, some of the general facts needed in the decision of technical questions are so highly complicated that it is hopeless to expect to instruct even the most intelligent judge in the course of a single case to the extent necessary to enable him to come to an accurate conclusion. At least, if the court is not made up of specialists, it ought to have the aid of special investigators capable of subjecting the evidence on general facts so loosely presented in the lawyer's argument to the same degree of scrutiny that the far less important and less difficult special facts are subjected to when they are presented to a jury. The difficulty is that there is no method provided in our law, officially, for the instruction of a court in the facts and principles of economics, social science, politics, history, or any of the other fields whose facts are the subject of judicial notice.

DAVIS, JUDICIAL NOTICE, 1969 LAW AND THE SOCIAL ORDER 511, 515

The basic objective of a good system of judicial notice should be to achieve the maximum possible convenience that is consistent with procedural fairness. Proving facts with evidence takes time and effort. Noticing facts is simpler, easier, more convenient. Both the court and the parties benefit from the increased efficiency when a court notices facts and thereby makes proof of them unnecessary. Yet procedural fairness must always be protected. This means that any party adversely affected must always have a chance to challenge facts which are to be noticed or facts which have been noticed.

The ultimate principle is that extra-record facts should be assumed whenever it is convenient to assume them, except that convenience should always yield to the requirement of procedural fairness that parties should have opportunity to meet in the appropriate fashion all facts that influence the disposition of the case. (Emphasis in original.)

WEINSTEIN, KORN AND MILLER, 5 NEW YORK CIVIL PRACTICE[1], ¶ 4511.01

The term "judicial notice" incorporates a considerable number of related but distinct concepts. Like its analogue, "official notice," in the field of Administrative Law, it may, in its broadest sense, be considered to include all methods other than the formal introduction of evidence for informing the court during the course of litigation. Judicial notice may take place in any court at any stage of the litigation, from motion practice to appeals. Matters judicially noticed by an appellate court need not be limited to matters sustaining the judgment below; they may support a reversal. For purposes of analysis it is necessary to divide the field into at least four main categories, some of which, in turn, must be subdivided. The main headings are: legislative facts, adjudicative facts, political facts, and law. . . .

1. *Legislative Facts.* The term "legislative facts," as distinguished from "adjudicative facts," is helpful in analysis and is used by writers who have done most to clarify thinking in this field. The scope of inquiry in this area is quite broad and cannot be limited by anything but the court's own sense of proprieties without incapacitating the court from exercising its full creative function in lawmaking generally and in exercising limits on legislative activities based upon constitutional requirements. As indicated below, the limiting criteria of rule 201 of the Federal Rules of Evidence are useful only in considering some kinds of adjudicative facts; they are not helpful in determining when the court should take notice of legislative facts. Our adversarial system requires that, where practicable, the parties be informed of the lines of inquiry the court is embarked upon so that they can assist in furnishing information and in preventing misconceptions; this requirement is applicable to legislative facts as well as other kinds of facts determined through judicial notice.

"Legislative facts" may be subdivided into the following three forms:

(a) *Information about the impact of prior and proposed law.* This data is required so that lawmaking through judicial decisions or alternative interpretations of prior decisions or statutes may be based, so far as possible, on a realistic view of society. Appellate courts are not well equipped for this kind of inquiry and this inadequacy is a built-in limitation on the court's capacity to change the law. Reliance is usually placed upon briefs of the parties, briefs *amicus* and some research of the courts. While suggestions have been made that referees and special fact finding agencies be used for this purpose, they will probably not be acted upon because they require the courts to admit that they are making law in the same way as the legislature—an admission incompatible with our conception of limited and divided powers. Some courts are using rearguments usefully to inform themselves before assuming facts necessary to change the substantive law.

---

1. Footnotes omitted—Ed.

(b) *Information on legislative history to interpret a statute*. This kind of information about what leads to enactment of a statute is necessary for intelligent and creative statutory interpretation.

(c) *Information on bases for legislative exercise of constitutional power*. Information on societal needs sufficient to determine whether such constitutional substantive due process tests as rationality of purpose and classification were met by the legislature in enacting a statute is essential if the court is to meet its constitutional responsibility. This information is obtained, in part, by using such legislative history as committee hearings and reports and, in part, by judicial notice.

2. *Adjudicative Facts*. "Adjudicative facts" may be subdivided into two forms:

(a) *Hypotheses and generalized knowledge*. Obtaining information about the world generally sufficient to supply evidential hypotheses required to draw inferences from evidence presented at a trial is essential to the fact-finding function. This category includes information all jurors as well as judges are expected to bring to the trial, such as that commuters in a hurry to catch a train are more likely to have been speeding than commuters who are not in a hurry. It may include information of which laymen are only dimly aware, such as the incompatibility of certain blood types, and such hypotheses may need to be supplied by experts, statutes, or instruction from the judge after he has informed himself.

(b) *Specific facts*. Information about the nature of specific events or things such as the time of sunrise on a particular day or the commercial character of Times Square may be obtained by the court to save unnecessary proof about propositions of fact which are not really disputable. Properly includable under this heading are matters of record in courts of the state and knowledge by the court of the structure of government.

Information of specific adjudicative facts is properly described by [Rule 201(a) of the Federal Rules of Evidence].... This definition is probably adequate insofar as it describes information communicated to a jury by a trial judge but it does not fully describe the wide variety of background knowledge, prejudice and misinformation about people and things necessarily relied upon by jurors and judges in evaluating evidence through use of hypotheses and generalized knowledge. Most cases in fact turn upon the conflicting inferences from the evidence; the hypotheses of the jury *are* "the subject of dispute" and *are not*, "capable of immediate and accurate determination."

3. *Political Facts*. Obtaining information from another branch of the government which has power to bind the court is often treated as a matter of judicial notice. The clearest example of this is the suggestion from the State Department that a certain government is or is not recognized and should, therefore be accorded or denied certain rights in our courts. These are matters decided by the political branch of the government; the court is not really concerned with judicial notice of any fact but rather in getting a clear ruling from some authentic official communication of the proper authority.

4. *Law*. Deciding what is the substantive law which should be applied in the case being tried is a question for the court and not the jury.... Much of the difficulty the bench and the bar has had with this area might have been eliminated had the term judicial notice never been used to cover the substantive-law-determination-function of the judge. The judge's role is essentially the same whether he is determining the law of contributory negligence under New York law when an accident occurred in New York or under the law of a foreign

state or country when the accident took place in another jurisdiction and the New York law of conflict of laws makes the foreign law material. [Most American jurisdictions now reject] the contention that foreign law is a matter of fact and that, under the constitutional guarantee of trial by jury, such a question of fact could not be decided by the court. In the case of foreign countries, as well as local governmental agencies, the difficulties in ascertaining the law warrant certain procedural aids to judge and litigant to minimize the chance of a mistake about the content of the controlling law....

NOTES

1. In studying the materials in this chapter consider whether it is helpful to use the term judicial notice to refer to such a variety of concepts. Does incorporating a whole spectrum of ideas under one legal heading inhibit analysis? Does it affect litigation? Are the Federal Rules of Evidence adequate? Should they be amended? How? See, e.g., Turner, A Rule Ready for a Change, 45 U. of Pitt.L.Rev. 181 (1983).

2. See Bulova Watch Co., Inc. v. K. Hattori & Co., Ltd., 508 F.Supp. 1322 (E.D.N.Y.1981). Judicial notice was taken on a motion to dismiss for failure of jurisdiction. In determining whether a Japanese corporation exercised control over a New York corporation for "long arm" purposes, the court took "judicial notice of the nature of executive management relationships in Japan. The court noted (Id. at 1328):

USE OF JUDICIAL NOTICE

A common sense appraisal of economic relationships is often more useful than prior cases based on situations different in detail.... We tend to come closer to the mark when we examine a business relationship from the practical viewpoint of businessmen rather than through the distorting lens of a legal conceptual framework established in an earlier era. In the multidimensional complexity of real life a two dimensional straight line provides a misleading boundary. A court cannot simply "isolate each contact of the defendant with New York and say that each such contact does not constitute the doing of business." Potter's Photographic Applications Co. v. Ealing Corporation, 292 F.Supp. 92, 100 (E.D.N.Y.1968). Rather, it must look to the "cumulative significance" of all activities of a foreign corporation within the state in order to determine whether the corporation is doing business within the state for jurisdictional purposes. Id. In doing so it must make use of so much of judicial notice as is required to understand general commercial settings and the particular relationships of the parties and their dispute.

Judicial notice may be resorted to on a motion to dismiss for lack of jurisdiction. Fed.R.Evid. 201(f) ("judicial notice may be taken at any stage of the proceeding"); Singleton v. City of New York, 632 F.2d 185, 204 (2d Cir.1980) (dissent) (motion to dismiss for lack of timeliness); St. Louis Baptist Temple, Inc. v. Federal Deposit Insurance Corp., 605 F.2d 1169, 1172 (10th Cir.1979) (summary judgment); United States ex rel. McClaughlin v. People of the State of New York, 356 F.Supp. 988, 990 (E.D.N.Y. 1973) (motion to dismiss on merits); Fox v. Kane–Miller Corp., 398 F.Supp. 609, 651 (D.Md.1975), aff'd, 542 F.2d 915 (4th Cir.1976) (motion for judgment notwithstanding verdict); Webb v. Nolan, 361 F.Supp. 418, 420 (M.D.N.C.1972) (motion to dismiss for lack of jurisdiction).

The information that may be noticed where jurisdiction is sought over a multinational is much broader than the narrow form of "adjudicative" fact either "generally known within the territorial jurisdiction" or capable of "determination by resort to sources whose accuracy cannot reasonably be questioned." Fed.R.Evid. 201(a), (b)—e.g., the day of a week of a certain date. The judgments involved in determining questions of jurisdiction such as the one before us involve mixed questions of law and fact. Inextricably, intertwined in the decision is a normative judgment of what is fair and reasonable—a question primarily of law rather than an adjudicative fact. Thus the factual issues are closer on a spectrum to legislative facts necessary in interpreting the meaning of law and filling in its interstitial detail. The data noticed also provide the general knowledge needed to understand and draw inferences from the particular evidence in the controversy before the court to those material propositions of fact necessary in determining jurisdiction.

There is always danger in the superficial sociological musings of lawyers and judges who must perforce be relatively ignorant of the realities underlying the diverse situations with which they must deal and which they must try to understand. Yet, whether we explore the economic, political or social settings to which the law must be applied explicitly or suppress our assumptions by failing to take note of them, we cannot apply the law in a way that has any hope of making sense unless we attempt to visualize the actual world with which it interacts—and this effort requires judicial notice to educate the court.

A court's power to resort to less well known and accepted sources of data to fill in the gaps of its knowledge for legislative and general evidential hypothesis purposes must be accepted because it is essential to the judicial process. See, generally, Davis, Facts in Lawmaking, 80 Colum.L.Rev. 931 (1980). Here flexible judicial notice is required first, in interpreting N.Y.CPLR 301 and 302, and, second, in understanding the relationship of the Japanese parent to its American subsidiaries.

In view of the extensive judicial notice taken, based partly upon the court's own research, the court issued a preliminary memorandum and invited the parties to be heard on the "propriety of taking judicial notice and the tenor of the matter noticed" upon motion made within ten days. This procedure complies with the spirit of Rule 201(e) of the Federal Rules of Evidence reading as follows:

(e) Opportunity to Be Heard. A party is entitled upon timely request to an opportunity to be heard as to the propriety of taking judicial notice and the tenor of the matter noticed. In the absence of prior notification, the request may be made after judicial notice has been taken.

Inviting parties to participate in such ongoing colloquy has the advantage of reducing the possibility of egregious errors by the court and increases the probability that the parties may believe they were fairly treated, even if some of them are dissatisfied with the result.

Accepting this invitation, the defendant Hattori submitted affidavits and separate materials and reargued the motion. These submissions were most helpful and resulted in the court modifying a number of conclusions, but not the final result.

Was the court justified in taking judicial notice as it did?

Zenith Radio Corp. v. Matsushita Electric Industrial Co., Ltd., 505 F.Supp. 1125, 1190 (E.D.Pa.1980), rev'd, 723 F.2d 238 (3d Cir.1983), rev'd on other grounds, 475 U.S. 574 (1986), supra, discussed the relationship of Japanese subsidiaries to parents to determine whether the admission of one company could be used against another under Rule 801(d)(2) of the Federal Rules of Evidence. The court had to make certain assumptions about Japanese relationships. Was it proper to do so? Could the trial court have avoided the problem?

Both the Zenith Radio and the Bulova Watch litigation compelled the trial courts to attempt to arrive at some sense of foreign entities working in a foreign milieu. Both cases involved preliminary motions where the issues of fact, law and policy were intertwined. Note the way a court may lean towards one side or another by the extent of its judicial notice and its liberality in admitting evidence. Rule 201 provides only for judicial notice of "adjudicative facts." By taking judicial notice of "mixed questions of law and fact," did either of the courts in the principal cases violate rule 201?

Might the Zenith court have reached a different result had it made use of judicial notice and resorted to less well known and accepted sources of data to fill the gaps in its knowledge as the court did in the Bulova case? Was it proper for the court in Bulova to engage in such extensive judicial notice? Note that these courts have apparently opposing views of the burdens to be imposed on the proponent of evidence and the type of evidence that a court may consider. See United States v. American Telephone and Telegraph Co., 516 F.Supp. 1237, 1981–1 Trade Cas. p. 63,983 (D.D.C.1981) (criticizing the test applied in Zenith as excessively restrictive, the court noticed the existence of a close functional relationship among the component entities of the Bell System and found that an out-of-court statement by an employee of a subsidiary could be admitted against the parent corporation pursuant to Fed.R.Evid. 801(d)(2)).

3. May a court take judicial notice more freely when it is deciding a motion? If it can, is this because in a bench trial there is more flexibility in enforcing the rules of evidence? In Zenith, the court was ruling on admissibility; are there any limits on judicial notice under rule 201 in view of Fed.R.Evid. 104(a)? The matter is discussed in the trial court's Zenith opinion, supra. See also, e.g., Bishop v. Byrne, 265 F.Supp. 460, 464–465 (S.D.W.Va.1967) (tort action against physician; complaint failed to allege pain or suffering but court took judicial notice that this could be inferred from the necessity of a Caesarean section); Golaris v. Jewel Tea Co., 22 F.R.D. 16, 19 (N.D.Ill.1958) (information as to trichinosis; "it has long been recognized that the motion [to dismiss] and its forerunner the demurrer do not accept as true facts alleged in a complaint which are contrary to facts of which the court will take judicial notice."); see Comment, Not Looking the Complaint in the Face: Judicial Notice On Demurrer, 4 U.San Francisco L.Rev. 433 (1970).

SECTION 2.   FACTS

A.   ADJUDICATIVE

In re Marriage of Tresnak

Supreme Court of Iowa, 1980.
297 N.W.2d 109.

■ McCORMICK, JUSTICE.

This appeal involves a parental dispute over custody of two sons, Rick, age eleven, and Ryan, age nine. The parents are Emil James Tresnak (Jim) and Linda Lou Tresnak (Linda) who were married in 1965. In the August 1979 decree dissolving the marriage, the trial court awarded custody of the children to Jim. Linda appeals. We reverse and remand.

Jim was twenty-four at the time of the marriage and had three years of college. Linda was nineteen, had one year of college and had worked for one year. They resided in Dodge, Nebraska, where Jim worked with his father in the insurance business. In 1969 he sold his interest in the insurance agency and the parties sold their home. Jim returned to college and obtained his degree. In 1970 the family moved to Omaha where Jim taught in a private girls' college. In 1971 they moved to Chariton where Jim taught high school business courses, a position which he still held at the time of trial.

Linda worked in a nursing home in 1967 but otherwise was not employed outside the home during the marriage.

Jim obtained a master's degree in 1978 after three years of summer school study at Northeast Missouri State University in Kirksville.

In the fall of 1975 Linda entered junior college at Centerville. She attended summer sessions at the university in Kirksville in 1976 through 1978, while Jim was there. In addition, she attended the university fulltime from January 1978 until the spring of 1979. At that time she graduated with a B.A. degree in psychology. She planned to enter law school at the University of Iowa in the fall of that year.

The children stayed in Chariton with Jim from January through May 1978 while Linda was in school in Kirksville. The whole family was in Kirksville that summer while both parents were in school. In the fall, the children remained with Linda and enrolled in school in Kirksville for the 1978–79 school year while Jim returned to Chariton. The children have been in the continuous custody of Linda since then.

In awarding custody of the children to Jim, the trial court said:

The Petitioner at this time in life now desires to continue her education by attending law school at the University of Iowa. Although this is commendable insofar as her ambition for a career is concerned, in the opinion of the Court, it is not necessarily for the best interest and welfare of her minor children, who are now ten and eight years of age. Anyone who has attained a legal education can well appreciate the time that studies consume. Although the Petitioner, during her undergraduate work, was able to care for the children while attending the Northeast Missouri University at Kirksville by studying after the children were placed in bed, the study of law is somewhat different in that it usually requires library study, where reference material is required. Also, other than time in class during the day, there will be study periods during the day in the library necessary, as well as in the evening, and which would necessarily require the children being in the hands of a babysitter for many hours a day when not attending school. The weekends are usually occupied by study periods, and although the Petitioner has a high academic ability, she will find that by reason thereof there will be additional activities bestowed upon her, such as becoming a member of a law review, which is time-consuming. Although the Petitioner may believe that she would not have to engage in such, she by [not] doing so would be interfering with her own achievements for her own benefit and welfare in future years.

The Respondent father has a stable position in the Chariton school system, president of the teachers' association, and, so far as known now, can remain in the Chariton schools for many years in the future. The Respondent's salary, though not exceptionally high, is adequate to maintain the children properly, and give them all the necessities of life. The Respondent father will be able to engage in various activities with the boys, such as athletic events, fishing, hunting, mechanical training, and other activities that boys are interested in. It would also be a benefit to the children if they were allowed to remain in the Chariton school system where they have attended school and have many friends and acquaintances. Placing custody with the Petitioner would require the children to be placed in the Iowa City school system for only a temporary time of three years, and again undoubtedly removed and placed in another system where the Petitioner would locate to practice her profession.

Linda, supported by the amicus briefs, challenges the trial court's statements concerning the demands of law school and the appropriateness of awarding custody of male children to their fathers. She asks that the custody decision be reversed.

I. The trial court's analysis. In challenging the trial court's reasoning, Linda contends no evidentiary support existed for the court's assumptions about law school and the children's activities. She also contends the assumed facts are not a proper subject of judicial notice.

A. The demands of law school. The only evidence about the demands of law school appeared in Linda's testimony. She acknowledged on cross-examination that law school would require many hours of study. However, she also said she did not expect to leave the children with babysitters often, she would take them to the library with her if necessary, and she did not believe her studies would interfere with her care of the children. Thus, while the record supports the trial court's inference that law school studies would occupy much of Linda's time, it does not lend much support to the court's statements about the necessity of library work away from the children, the likelihood of her involvement in extra-curricular activities, or the effect of such factors on her care of the children.

Nor are these matters subject to judicial notice. "To be capable of being judicially noticed a matter must be of common knowledge or capable of certain verification." Motor Club of Iowa v. Department of Transportation, 251 N.W.2d 510, 517 (Iowa 1977). Courts are permitted to dispense with formal proof of matters which everyone knows. See City of Cedar Rapids v. Cox, 252 Iowa 948, 958, 108 N.W.2d 253, 259 (1961), appeal dismissed, 368 U.S. 3, 82 S.Ct. 16, 7 L.Ed.2d 17. In this case, in overruling Linda's motion for new trial, the trial court defended its findings by asserting a "personal acquaintanceship with the studies of law school." However, judicial notice " 'is limited to what a judge may properly know in his judicial capacity, and he is not authorized to make his personal knowledge of a fact not generally or professionally known the basis of his action.' " Bervid v. Iowa State Tax Commission, 247 Iowa 1333, 1339, 78 N.W.2d 812, 816 (1956). See J. Wigmore, 9 Evidence § 2569 at 540 (3d ed. 1961). It is common knowledge in the legal profession that law school studies are demanding and time-consuming, but the requirements of a specific law school curriculum are not generally or professionally known.

The trial court's statements about the necessity of extensive library study and likelihood of Linda's work on the law review of the University of Iowa law school are not matters of common knowledge or capable of certain verification within the meaning of the judicial notice principle. Because the statements have only tenuous support in the evidence, they are entitled to little weight in evaluating the merits of the custody dispute. In saying this, however, we do not suggest the court could not consider the demands of law school which were shown in the evidence.

B. The children's preferred activities. Linda testified that the boys enjoy fishing, reading, baking cookies, bicycling, swimming, soccer, and basketball. They do not play baseball or football. She fishes, reads, bakes cookies, bicycles and swims with them. Jim testified he swam and played soccer with the children, although he said his age and smoking limited his participation in soccer to about fifteen minutes. Linda said he refused to take the boys fishing.

This record does not support the court's statement that Jim "will be able to engage in various activities with the boys, such as athletic events, fishing, hunting, mechanical training and other activities that boys are interested in." No evidence was received that these boys were interested in hunting or mechanical training, that the enumerated pursuits are more appropriate to males, that "other activities" exist in which males have a necessary interest, or that these children will necessarily have the same interests as other males. Nor does the record contain any evidence that Jim was capable of participating in any activities with the children that Linda could not participate in with them equally well.

Apart from the lack of evidentiary support, the statement has at least two other flaws. It contains matters which are not subject to judicial notice, and it represents a stereotypical view of sexual roles which has no place in child custody adjudication.

We have emphasized that child custody cases are to be decided "upon what the evidence actually reveals in each case, not upon what someone predicts it will show in many cases." In re Marriage of Bowen, 219 N.W.2d 683, 688 (Iowa 1974). Each case must be decided on its own facts. In re Marriage of Dawson, 214 N.W.2d 131, 132 (Iowa 1974). As we said in Bowen, neither parent has an edge on the other based merely on sex: "The real issue is not the sex of the parent but which parent will do better in raising the children." 219 N.W.2d at 688. It logically follows that neither parent has an edge on the other based on the sex of the children either. We reject the idea that any a priori notion of parental fitness should be based on the sex of parent or child.

The trial court was not justified in basing the award in this case in part on assumptions related to the sex of the parents and children which are not supported by the record.

II. The merits of the custody award. Our review of the record is de novo. Although we give weight to the court's findings, we are not bound by them.

Because either parent would be a good custodian of the children, the decision on the merits is difficult. Linda and Jim are stable and responsible persons who love their children and are capable of giving them adequate care.

Prior to returning to school, Linda fulfilled a traditional role as housewife and mother while Jim was the breadwinner. Until Linda moved to Kirksville in January 1978, she continued to have primary responsibility for the day-to-day parenting of the children. This was true even when she was attending junior college full-time. Although Jim had primary responsibility for the children from January through May 1978, Linda came home each weekend to clean house, help with the laundry, cook meals, and prepare foods to be served during the following week. During that period Rick required assistance at home with his spelling. After first agreeing to help, Jim later asserted he was too busy to do so. Linda provided the assistance during her weekends at home. She has had primary care of the children since the fall of 1978.

Linda is a fastidious housekeeper and obviously a highly-motivated and organized person. She has been active in school affairs. She plays with the children and has counseled with them concerning their development as adolescents.

Jim likes his work and keeps busy with it. He is not as concerned about household cleanliness as Linda. Nor did he display her concern about the children's meals and clothing during the period he had their primary care. He has not been active in their school affairs, and he was not aware of several of their allergies. Although this is explained in part by the necessity of devoting his time and energy to making a living, the record shows that even when he had primary responsibility for the care of the children, he was not as attentive as Linda to the details of their lives. Moreover, she maintained her attentiveness even during the times when her studies were demanding as much time as Jim's work.

A psychologist who interviewed the children testified in Linda's behalf. He said the children were exceptionally well-adjusted and would not suffer from moving with their mother to Iowa City. He reasoned that the stability of their relationship with their mother was more important than continuity in their place of residence. The children are normal, although Rick has had problems with spelling and underachievement at school. Linda has worked with him on these problems. The children are close, well-mannered and disciplined.

The trial court believed Linda's pursuit of a legal education would be detrimental to the children's interests. We do not think the record bears out this concern. She very capably cared for the children during her undergraduate studies. During that time Jim did not complain of her ability to do so. Moreover, the children did not suffer when, by agreement of the parties, they lived with Linda and attended the Kirksville schools in the 1978–79 school year. No question existed about their moving again. The only issue was whether they would return to Chariton or accompany Linda to Iowa City.

Furthermore, no basis exists for characterizing Linda's law school years as unstable. She has demonstrated she can control the time she spends on her studies as well as Jim can control the time he spends on his work. Although she may move again when she finishes law school, this prospect differs little from Jim's readiness to move to a junior college teaching position if an opportunity arises.

It is common knowledge that in many homes today both parents have demanding out-of-home activities, whether in employment, school or community affairs. Neither should necessarily be penalized in child custody cases for engaging in such activities. In this case, Linda seeks a legal education for self-fulfillment and as a means of achieving financial independence. These goals are not inimical to the children's best interests. Because the record shows she is capable of continuing to provide the children with the same high quality of care she has given them in the past, her attendance at law school should not disqualify her from having their custody. We perceive no reason for believing she will not give the children excellent care during her law school years and thereafter.

Applying the criteria of In re Marriage of Winter, 223 N.W.2d 165, 166–67 (Iowa 1974), we believe the long-range best interests of the children will be better served if Linda has their custody. Therefore we reverse the trial court and remand to permit the court to enter appropriate orders relating to child support and visitation.

Reversed and remanded.

■ All Justices concur except REYNOLDSON, C.J., and LeGRAND, J., who concur in the result.

NOTES

1. See, generally, Wexler, Rethinking the Modification of Child Custody Decrees, 94 Yale L.J. 757 (1985); Symposium, Children, Divorce and the Legal System: The Direction for Reform, 19 Colum.J. of Law and Social Problems, 393 (1985). For other areas in which changing views of woman's roles and background have affected both substantive and procedural views, see, e.g., Berger, Man's Trial, Woman's Tribulations: Rape Cases in the Courtroom, 77 Col.L.Rev. 1 (1977); Krieger & Fox, Evidentiary Issues in Sexual Harassment, Berkeley Women's L.J. 115 (1987); Odgers, Evidence of Sexual History in Sexual Offense Trials, 11 Sydney L.Rev. 74 (1986).

2. Contrast with Tresnak, Sotiriades v. Mathews, 546 F.2d 1018, 1021 (D.C.Cir.1976). "It is a matter of common knowledge, confirmed by experience, that a woman's undocumented statement of her age is subject to discount, particularly when it makes her younger than she is." The court's judicial notice of this "fact" led to a reversal of the Secretary's reduction of Social Security benefits. The reduction was predicated on "fraud or similar act." See also Local Union No. 35 of Intern. Brotherhood of Electrical Workers v. Hartford, 625 F.2d 416 (2d Cir.1980), which held that discrimination in the construction trades on racial grounds has been found so often by courts, that it is a proper subject for judicial notice.

Doe v. Doe, 222 Va. 736, 284 S.E.2d 799 (1981): The Supreme Court of Virginia would not take judicial notice of effect of natural mother's openly lesbian lifestyle on her son's welfare. The natural mother's lifestyle was the sole reason foster parents sought custody.

3. To what extent did the Supreme Court in Gaines rely on judicial notice of the way law schools operate in Missouri ex rel. Gaines v. Canada, 305 U.S. 337 (1938) (violation to send Black law students out of state). Did the court consider that one of the benefits of law school is association with peers who would practice in state and the exposure to the state law? What is the difference between Gaines and Tresnak? Compare Monahan and Walker, Social Authority: Obtaining, Evaluating, and Establishing Social Science in Law, 134 U. of Pa.L.Rev. 477, 516 (1986) (whether social science is "used to create a legal rule is better analogized to fact or law should be pragmatic."). See also Davis, Judicial, Legislative, and Administrative Lawmaking: A Proposed research Service for the Supreme Court, 71 Minn.L.Rev. 1, 18 (1986) (informal consultation of law clerk of Justice reflected in opinion). See also Davis, "There is a book out ...": An analysis of Judicial Absorption of Legislative Facts, 100 Harv.L.Rev. 1539 (1987), quoting in title from Ross v. Hoffman, 364 A.2d 596 (Md.App.1976), aff'd as modified, 372 A.2d 582 (Md.1977). The author notes that the case "illustrates, in unselfconscious terms, the process of judicial absorption of legislative facts: on a child custody case." 100 Harv.L.Rev. 1539, n. 1. On the dangers of judicially noticing matters of social factors see Perry, Precedential Value of Judicial Notice of Social Facts: Parkham As An Example, 22 J. of Family Law, 633 (1984).

4. Many of the judicial notice provisions in the state codifications were taken from either the Uniform Rules of Evidence as promulgated in 1953, or the more recent 1974 Uniform Rules which were patterned after the Federal Rules of Evidence. See generally, 35 A.L.R.Fed. 440 (1977) (meaning of "adjudicative facts").

5. The 1969 draft of Rule 201 of the Federal Rules of Evidence received constructive criticism from Professor Kenneth Culp Davis. See Davis, 1969 Law and Social Order 513. Professor Davis sees three variables that bear on procedural fairness and control judicial notice of facts—(1) the degree to which the facts are debatable or indisputable, (2) the degree to which they are peripheral or central to the case, and (3) the degree to which they are adjudicative or legislative. Does Rule 201 deal with these variables? Are judges bound by the Rule precluded from doing so?

Among commentators there has been controversy over the degree of probability a proposition of fact must possess before notice can be taken. One school, led by Professor Morgan, has insisted that judicial notice be limited to indisputables. This means not only probability must be at, or close to, 100% but that reasonable men would not dispute it. Fairness to the parties is the prime concern here. The other view, supported by Wigmore and Thayer and now by Professor Davis, argues that it is convenient to assume all facts that are unlikely to be challenged, as well as those considered to be absolutely indisputable. Convenience is the principle goal and gives way only to objections on grounds of fairness. Rule 201 speaks with Morgan's voice. Does it, however, preclude Davis' view? Cf. Antitrust Commission Report, 80 F.R.D. 509, 564–65 (1979) (in its discussion of judicial notice as one method of simplifying complex antitrust litigation, the report recognizes that Rule 201 leans toward the more conservative school of Morgan, but it notes that "creative use of judicial notice nonetheless need not be precluded").

Judicial notice is not infrequently taken even when there can arise reasonable doubt as to whether the matter is disputable. See, e.g., Securities and Exchange Commission v. Capital Gains Research Bureau, 375 U.S. 180, 201 (1963) (involving non-disclosure by an investment advisor to his clients, where the lower court found insufficient proof, the Supreme Court apparently assumed that the market would be influenced by the activity from his recommendations); Alvary v. United States, 302 F.2d 790 (2d Cir.1962) (trial court erred in taking judicial notice of textbooks to reach conclusion that Hungarian realty had no value because of Communist takeover); Reinert v. Superior Court, 2 Cal.App.3d 36, 82 Cal.Rptr. 263 (1969) (the objective symptoms of marijuana are not so universally known as to be indisputable; defendant arrested in bed observed to have "thick speech and dilated eyes").

In formal jury trials is Rule 201 more appropriate, while in such matters as preliminary injunctions where short cuts for speed's sake are desirable is the Davis view sound? If a disputable fact is peripheral to the case, do such factors as reducing the speed of the trial and lessening jury confusion militate against strict enforcement of Rule 201? Is the good sense of counsel and trial judges together with power to stipulate a sufficient corrective? In practice will the freedom to judicially notice vary according to the function the court is performing—e.g., jury trial or ruling on a demurrer? See Note, The Presently Expanding Concept of Judicial Notice, 13 Vill.L.Rev. 528 (1968). Cf. Trans World Airlines, Inc. v. Hughes, 308 F.Supp. 679, 683–684. (S.D.N.Y.1969), modified on other grounds, 449 F.2d 51 (2d Cir.1971), rev'd on other grounds, 409 U.S. 363 (1973) (in ruling that judicially noticed facts could contradict allegations of the complaint in a default judgment, the court pointed out that only the most indisputable facts could be noticed and that the "more critical an issue is to the case, the more reluctant courts should be to determine it by taking judicial notice.").

6.   In Russo v. Russo, 21 Cal.App.3d 72, 98 Cal.Rptr. 501 (1971), an appeal from an order changing child custody as it was established pursuant to an interlocutory decree of divorce by granting custody to the father, the mother contended that the order was "totally unsupported by the evidence presented to the trial court" and must therefore be reversed. The father pointed to the fact that the young child was left at a bus stop in the morning by her mother and on the client's return had to walk three blocks to her baby-sitter's home. Significant was the nature of the neighborhood where this occurred. At a hearing, the father answered affirmatively to the leading question, "You know it is in a rather bad neighborhood?" A further attempt by the father to develop the character of the neighborhood by asking "Have you taken a look at that particular area ... during the daytime?" was preempted by the judge's remark, "Give me credit for some sense." In reversing the order, the court noted that "[w]hatever may be said for other characteristics of the ... district, it is not a matter of common information and experience, or one about which there can be no dispute, that it is unsafe for infants to walk in at 11:30 in the morning." Cf. Varcoe v. Lee, 180 Cal. 338, 181 P. 223 (1919) (court upheld an instruction predicated on judicial notice that a specific two blocks in San Francisco was a "business district" within the meaning of that term as used in a provision of the motor vehicle laws limiting speed in such districts). To what extent is the court in Russo or in Tresnack subconsciously relying on traditional notions of the female as primary nurturer of the child either in analyzing the facts or in interpreting the substantive law?

7. Suppose the appellate court and the trial court sit in different localities. How can the appellate court determine if a matter of fact is common knowledge at the place of trial, that is, if judicial notice could have been properly taken by the trial court? See Morgan, Judicial Notice, 57 Harv.L.Rev. 269, 291 (1944) ("an appellate court in dealing with a record made in a lower court may be in no position to take judicial knowledge of matter which the lower court judicially knew"). Compare Uniform Rule 12 (1953). In Pereza v. Mark, 423 F.2d 149, 151 (2d Cir.1970), the appellate court took judicial notice that the judge and jury were "better able to decide what constitutes careless handling of firearms in Saxton's River, Vermont" than the circuit court sitting in New York City.

8. Judicial notice may be used on an appeal to provide the appellate court with relevant information (adjudicative facts) not in the record and not considered below. See, e.g., Communist Party v. Subversive Activities Control Board, 351 U.S. 115 (1956) (in deciding whether to reverse and remand, the Court took into consideration newspaper reports and affidavits coming into existence subsequent to the trial). Cf. People v. Burt, 279 N.W.2d 299 (Mich.App.1979) (improperly allowed jury to look at T.V. Guide to determine that defendant's alibi that he was watching a certain football game on T.V. could not be true; but error harmless because appellate court took judicial notice of fact that no football game was broadcast that day).

In Boynton v. Virginia, 364 U.S. 454 (1960), the petitioner had been convicted for attempting to eat in a segregated bus line terminal lunch room. The Supreme Court—seeking to determine whether the interstate bus carrier exercised control over the operator of the lunch room—wrote to counsel for Respondent inquiring as to "the intercorporate relationship between the Trailways Bus Company and the Trailways Bus Terminal, Inc., set forth in any documents of which the Virginia courts can take judicial notice." Petitioner's Brief at 20. But cf. Melong v. Micronesian Claims Commission, 643 F.2d 10, 12 n. 5 (D.C.Cir.1980) (court refused to take judicial notice of 172 pages of unauthenticated documentary material: "Judicial notice was never intended to permit such a widespread introduction of substantive evidence at the appellate level, particularly when there has been absolutely no showing of special prejudice or need;" court further noted that material submitted did not satisfy Rule 201(b)(2)).

What dangers need to be avoided by an appellate court in supplementing the record by judicial notice? What techniques are available to an appellate court to obtain information it feels is necessary for a decision when the methods of judicial notice are not applicable?

9. Meredith v. Fair, 298 F.2d 696, 701 (5th Cir.1962): In affirming a decision denying plaintiff a preliminary injunction the court took judicial notice that the state of Mississippi had maintained a policy of segregation in its schools and colleges. The appellate court relied upon the state's statutes, allocation of funds and the requirement of alumni certificates for admission. The court rejected the contention that plaintiff "should have examined the genealogical records of all the students and alumni of the University and should have offered these records in evidence in order to prove the University's alleged policy...." Id. The court noted that the state's segregation policy was a "plain fact known to everyone...." Id. After a trial on the merits, the district court found "as a fact, that the University is not a racially segregated institution." Meredith v. Fair, 202 F.Supp. 224, 227 (S.D.Miss.), rev'd, 305 F.2d 343 (5th Cir.), cert. denied, 371 U.S. 828 (1962). The appellate court rejected the trial court's finding as beyond belief in view of its knowledge of segregation practices in the state's schools and colleges. 305 F.2d 343. Was it proper for the court to use its own knowledge in analyzing the evidence before the trial court?

Holland v. Board of Public Instruction, 258 F.2d 730, 731–32 (5th Cir. 1958):

> The school district in which the plaintiff resides was created originally for tax purposes in 1912. It is designated by city ordinance as a Negro residential area, and the constitutionality of that ordinance is not directly attacked.... [T]he record as a whole clearly reveals the basic fact that, by whatever means accomplished, a completely segregated school system was and is being maintained and enforced. No doubt that fact is well known to all of the citizens of the County, and the courts simply cannot blot it out of their sight. In the light of compulsory residential segregation of the races by city ordinance, it is wholly unrealistic to assume that the complete segregation existing in the public schools is either voluntary or the incidental result of valid rules not based on race.

Rowe v. General Motors Corp., 457 F.2d 348, 357–59 (5th Cir.1972) (Title VII discriminatory employment practices):

> Out of total of 114 employees promoted from hourly jobs to salaried jobs between 1963 and 1967, only 7 were blacks.... All we do today is recognize that promotional/transfer procedures which depend almost entirely upon the subjective evaluation and favorable recommendation of the immediate foreman are a ready mechanism for discrimination against Blacks much of which can be covertly concealed and, for that matter, not really known to management. We and others have expressed a skepticism that Black persons dependent directly on decisive recommendations from Whites can expect non-discriminatory action.

10. For what purpose is the court noticing facts in the Meredith cases cited in note 9, supra, and in the Boynton case in note 8, supra? Could a litigant establish through judicial notice that a segregationist policy exists when there are no state or local statutes requiring racial segregation and the school board denies maintaining such a policy? What kind of information would the attorney for the petitioner want to bring to the trial court's attention in such a case? Note that "the fact that the trial judge knew what the actual fact was, and that it was indisputable, would not of itself justify him in recognizing it." Varcoe v. Lee, 180 Cal. 338, 344, 181 P. 223, 225 (1919). Cf. Sims v. Baggett, 247 F.Supp.

96, 108–09 (M.D.Ala.1965) (in finding racial gerrymandering in the reapportionment plan for the Alabama legislature, a three judge court took judicial notice of the long history of the struggle to obtain the right to vote in Alabama and the number of counties under injunction under the Voting Rights Act of 1965).

Would the attorney for the school board or other governmental agency be likely to have recourse to judicial notice? Does it matter whether the litigation is north or south of the Mason–Dixon line? See Fed.R.Evid. 201(b); Kaplan, Segregation Litigation and the Schools [in the North], 58 Nw.U.L.Rev. 1, 157 (1963), 59 id. 121 (1964).

11.   For an interesting proposal for instructing the jury on evidential hypothesis for judicial notice purposes see Mansfield, Jury Notice, 74 Georgetown Law Journal 395 (1985).

Soley v. Star & Herald Co.

United States Court of Appeals, Fifth Circuit, 1968.
390 F.2d 364.

■ GOLDBERG, CIRCUIT JUDGE. *A Case of Libel.* On October 24, 1960, a Canal Zone bus stopped suddenly as one of its passengers, Benjamin Polycarpo Soley, was preparing to exit. Soley was thrown from the bus and landed on the ground in a sitting position. He sued the bus company for negligence, claiming damages due to back pains and impotence, but in 1964 the district court sitting without a jury ruled for the bus company. Four days after the judgment a newspaper owned by The Star & Herald Co. published an account of the trial, stating in part:

> "The case was postponed on several occasions, principally for the gathering of medical testimony. It was on this testimony, which proved inconclusive and *showed that the plaintiff had been treated prior to the accident for a condition that he claimed was caused by the fall from the bus,* that the case was dismissed." (Emphasis added.)

One year later Soley filed the suit at bar against The Star & Herald Co. (appellees) in the same district court for libel. His suit was dismissed for failure to state a claim, and he appealed.

Although this is not the first time that Soley has been cast in the role of a defamed,[1] his performance in this action has hardly been flawless. Nevertheless, as we extricate fact from fancy out of the uncoordinated allegations in his trial and appellate pleadings, we find some undue haste in dismissing a potential claim.

Soley filed his first libel complaint on April 7, 1965, without the benefit of legal counsel. His complaint alleged that the above account in the appellees' newspaper was "false and malicious" and that the account was "responsible for many attendant failures, which took a heavy toll both financially and physically from one of my next of kin." In an amended complaint, filed almost a year later and with assistance of counsel, he added:

> "[T]he facts stated in said publication were wholly false and untrue, scandalous and defamatory and were known to the defendant so to be ... exposing him [Soley] to disgrace in his occupation and mistrust on his

---

1. Soley v. Ampudia, 5 Cir.1950, 183   have been omitted; others are renumbered.]
F.2d 277, 19 A.L.R.2d 689. [Some footnotes

entire family...." He also referred to "the aforesaid false, scandalous, malicious and defamatory libel of and concerning plaintiff."

On March 21, 1966, the appellees filed a motion "to strike the complaint, as amended ... on the ground that the said complaint does not state a claim against defendant, upon which relief can be granted." The court granted two requests for continuances, one on Soley's motion. On August 3, 1966, the court heard arguments by Soley and two lawyers for the appellees and sustained the appellees' motion without giving any conclusory reason. No affidavits had been filed, but the trial judge did refer in the following manner to the record in the negligence suit against the bus company, which suit he had tried:

"... and the Court having heard the arguments of respective counsel and having referred to the record of the case of Benjamin Polycarpo Soley, Plaintiff, v. Canal Zone Bus Service, Defendant, Civil No. 5173, Balboa Division of the United States District Court for the Canal Zone, and finds that the motion to strike should be sustained and the plaintiff's complaint dismissed with prejudice.

"

We start from the proposition that Soley in his complaints did state a claim upon which relief could be granted. The "plaintiff's checklist" of allegations in a libel action—population, untruth, damages, and even malice—was presented to the court in some manner. Because the appellees' motion to strike the complaint failed to rebut any specific contention or to offer an affirmative defense, the trial judge evidently came upon some evidence outside the pleadings which he felt justified the dismissal. Perhaps Soley admitted during an oral hearing that his claim was groundless. (Unfortunately, the hearings were not transcribed.) More likely is the assumption that the trial judge found the newspaper article to be true. Although we have no such statement in the record before us, the trial judge's reference to the negligence action indicates that evidence of Soley's prior treatment for back pains and impotence had been adduced at the negligence trial.[2]

We are advised by Fed.R.Civ.P. 12(b) that a trial court may, in its consideration of a motion to dismiss, treat it as a motion for summary judgment and consider evidence outside the pleadings.... However, before summary judgment can be granted, the trial judge must be convinced "that there is no genuine issue as to any material fact and that the moving party is entitled to a judgment as a matter of law." Fed.R.Civ.P. 56(c).... He must not grant summary judgment merely because the complaint and papers in support thereof are drawn unskillfully.... Nor may he overlook a factual issue even if the parties stipulated that none existed. United States v. Mullins, 4 Cir.1965, 344 F.2d 128.

We are not chary of summary judgments, but the mechanics leading to such a judicial denouement should lend themselves to clarification rather than obfuscation.

In the case at bar the appellees submitted no affidavits to support the summary judgment, and yet such remedy was granted. The court sua sponte furnished the evidence. Moreover, although the judge evidently referred to

2. The appellees' brief, containing the following one-sentence analysis of the deciding issue in this case, reaffirms our assumption:

"Appellant has failed to include in the record on appeal a copy of the decision in case No. 5173 [the negligence action], hence he has failed to bring before this Court the touchstone upon which must be decided whether or not the Star & Herald's article of April 8, 1964, reports the substance of the said decision falsely."

something in the record of the negligence action, he did not advise the adverse litigants and counsel in their adversary pits. . . .

We are cognizant of the general rule which permits judicial notice of a court's prior cases to support a motion for summary judgment. . . . But the trial court in this case did not inform the parties as to what he noticed. In his order he said he "referred to" the record in the negligence action. Does this mean that he physically and contemporaneously had it before him? Was the record in the courtroom available to counsel and litigants and the court reporter? "To refer" means to allude to or consider. Perhaps the trial judge merely indulged in remembrances of things past.

The appellees would have us soothe our doubts by procedural sedative. They argue that, because Soley has failed to include in the record on appeal the complete transcript of the negligence action, we have no grounds upon which we can reverse the trial court. However, Soley did file a notice of appeal in which he listed assignments of error and points on appeal. Granted, his points, which were signed by Soley "in Defensa Propria," are sparse on relevancy and lack any sense of cohesion. But we find them sufficient to alert the appellees as to why the summary judgment was being challenged. Moreover, the appellees' own brief acknowledges their complete understanding of the nature of the challenge.

The appellees do not claim lack of notice, nor do they attempt to fill the substantive gap, with evidence supporting the summary judgment. Instead, they rest their case on the niceties of federal appellate practice. They rely on our Court's lack of patience with appellants who claim specific trial errors but neglect to use the available means of including such errors in the record. . . . However, appellees are not devoid of responsibility to inform us. . . . That responsibility increases when such appellees seek our stamp of approval on an unarticulated summary judgment for which no justification can be found in the record. . . .

Our shifting part of the burden to the appellees should not be taken as a comment on the merits. If the record of the negligence action in whole or in part can be identified and will support a summary judgment, our opinion will not prejudice the appellees' rights to avoid troublesome litigation. . . . But justifiable impatience does not in itself justify summary judgment.

On the other hand, if no such record exists or if the record does not clearly justify the challenged newspaper words, a trial may be required. We will not affirm a summary judgment based on the solitary cerebration of the trial court. Memories deceive, and litigants should have the opportunity to challenge even a judge's recollections.

Truth seeking in adversary litigation must entail a full panoply of informatory devices, and while many of the formalities of yore have succumbed, litigants and counsel must not be required to be clairvoyant. They cannot read over the judge's shoulder or penetrate his memory. Nor can we. From Shakespeare's Hamlet to Albee's Tiny Alice soliloquies and asides have been shared with the audience.

Reversed and Remanded for proceedings consistent with this opinion.

NOTES

1. Matters of record in other courts are, it is sometimes said, usually denied notice requiring proof. See McCormick, Evidence § 330 (2d ed., Cleary, 1972). There is, however more than a suspicion that in many unreported cases, the

trial judge does look at related court files. It takes a fairly brazen advocate to try to deny him this source of information. In analyzing the cases it is helpful sometimes to differentiate between records of the same and of different courts; it is also necessary in some instances to differentiate between evidence and a finding of fact in other and related litigations.

2. See South Shore Land Co. v. Petersen, 226 Cal.App.2d 725, 38 Cal.Rptr. 392, 402–403 (1964), where the California court took "judicial notice" of the court proceedings and records of a case in the federal courts using the record on appeal to determine what the federal court had decided. Both cases involved the same parcel of land. Does the propriety of the court's action depend upon the proper scope of judicial notice or of res judicata and collateral estoppel or both? Cf. Emich Motors Corp. v. General Motors Corp., 340 U.S. 558, 566, 569–571 (1951); Comment, Developments—Res Judicata, 65 Harv.L.Rev. 818, 880 (1952). See also Holmes v. United States, 231 F.Supp. 971 (N.D.Ga.1964), aff'd, 353 F.2d 785 (5th Cir.1965) (court, apparently sua sponte, took judicial notice of prior proceedings and applied res judicata on defendants' motion for summary judgment; "To prevent additional repetitive litigation with what seems to be continuing harassment of the defendants and to accomplish finality of litigation, this Court hereby takes judicial notice of these prior proceedings and applies the rule of res judicata to the complaint herein." Id. at 972.). Accord, Southern Pacific Railroad Co. v. United States, 168 U.S. 1, 55–61 (1897) (former judgment held conclusive even though estoppel not specially pleaded). See also Inmates, D.C. Jail v. Jackson, 416 F.Supp. 119 (D.D.C.1976) (court took judicial notice of prior action and invoked the doctrine of collateral estoppel in granting motion for summary judgment where different plaintiffs challenged the same conditions and requested the same relief).

3. Wigmore says that whether a court will notice a fact contained in the record of another case depends "more or less on the practical notoriety and certainty of the fact under the circumstances of each case," 9 Wigmore, Evidence § 2579 (Chadbourn rev. 1981), while McCormick considers the requirement of formal proof rather than informal presentation to be "needless." McCormick, Evidence § 330 (2d ed., E. Cleary, 1972).

Courts are more likely to notice the records of a prior case if the cases are "related." The term "related" has no fixed content. Cf. United States v. Montemayor, 666 F.2d 235 (5th Cir.1982) (at bail hearing district court relied upon case on civil docket in determining defendant's financial resources). Among some of the criteria used are the following: (1) whether the second case involved the same factual pattern. Shuttlesworth v. Birmingham, 394 U.S. 147, 157 (1969) (criminal prosecution of a black minister who had helped lead a civil rights march in violation of a city ordinance; the court looked to an earlier case, Walker v. Birmingham, 388 U.S. 307 (1967), to obtain the "surrounding relevant circumstances" of the march in order to find that the application of the ordinance had been contrary to the manner in which the Alabama Supreme Court had construed as unconstitutional); United States v. Moreno, 579 F.2d 371 (5th Cir.1978), cert. denied, 440 U.S. 908 (1979) (in a prosecution for importation of marijuana, the district court held that it was entitled under Fed.R.Evid. 201 to take judicial notice of its prior decisions concerning the characteristics of the border checkpoint at which defendant had crossed from Mexico; The prior decisions had held that the checkpoint was the "functional equivalent of the border."); Schweitzer v. Scott, 469 F.Supp. 1017 (C.D.Cal. 1979) (in determining if an applicant for leave in forma pauperis is bringing an appeal in good faith within the meaning of 28 U.S.C. § 1915, the court may take judicial notice of its own record for the purpose of ascertaining whether petitioner had exhibited any tendency toward initiating and carrying on harassing litigation in the district); United States v. Fatico, 441 F.Supp. 1285 (E.D.N.Y.1977), rev'd on other grounds, 579 F.2d 707 (2d Cir.1978), cert. denied, 444 U.S. 1073 (1980) (judicial notice of court's own records of the fact that there had been major hijacking gangs preying on interstate and international commerce at New York's Kennedy International Airport); Lowe v. McDonald, 221 F.2d 228 (9th Cir.1955) (judicial notice taken of prior case where title was established); Oeth v. Mason, 247 Cal.App.2d 805, 56 Cal.Rptr. 69 (1967) (prior action between same parties dismissed without prejudice; proper to take judicial notice on motion to dismiss because statute of limitations had run); Miller v. Smith, 282 P.2d 715, 718 (N.M.1955) ("but the cause of which judicial notice is taken must be so closely interwoven or so closely interdependent with the case on trial before the court as to require judicial notice when that notice is requested"); (2) Whether the evidence or finding of facts as to one of the parties in the first case, who is also a party to the second, is relevant to prove an issue in the second case: In re Phillips, 593 F.2d 356 (8th Cir.1979) (bankruptcy judge taking judicial notice of claimant's state court petition, which had resulted in the entry against the bankrupt, for the purpose of determining the nature of the debt created by the default judgment); Kinnett Dairies, Inc. v. Farrow, 580 F.2d 1260, 1277–78 n. 33 (5th Cir.1978) (proper for the district court to take judicial notice of materials in the court's own files—depositions and expert testimony—from an earlier proceeding brought in the court by the same plaintiff where such notice was requested by plaintiff and was not objected to by the defendant or by an intervening defendant, and where court was faced with issues similar, and in some respects identical to those considered in the prior proceeding); Yokozeki v. State Bar, 11 Cal.3d 436, 444, 113 Cal.Rptr. 602, 607, 521 P.2d 858, 863, cert. denied, 419 U.S. 900 (1974) ("[A]lthough findings in a civil action are not binding on us in this proceeding ..., we can take judicial notice of matters in a civil action which arise out of a course of conduct underlying the charges against an attorney in disbarment proceedings...."); People v. Simari, 25 A.D.2d 485, 266 N.Y.S.2d 584 (1966) (court took judicial notice of the records of the Surrogate Court in order to determine the proper parties to the suit in which a prisoner was attempting to recover money that was his own and not part of the avails of his burglary; unreasonable to require a prisoner to prove death of a person). See also Ly Shew v. Acheson, 110 F.Supp. 50, 55–56 (N.D.Cal.1953) (reviewing statistics in hundreds of cases involving Chinese claiming to have been sired by American citizens, in order to evaluate credibility of witnesses), rev'd on other but related grounds, 219 F.2d 413 (9th Cir.1954); In re Department of Buildings of City of New York, 14 N.Y.2d 291, 297, 251 N.Y.S.2d 441, 446, 200 N.E.2d 432, 436 (1964) (on the basis of the cases which had been before it over the years the court took judicial notice of the existence of a housing emergency); Bell v. Maryland, 378 U.S. 226, 242 (1964) (concurring opinion of Douglas, J.,) (reviewing the testimony and other evidence presented in prior cases heard by the Court involving "sit-in" demonstrations).

It is sometimes said that a lesser standard is used when the facts to be judicially noticed are peripheral facts rather than central or ultimate facts or general rather than specific facts. See McCormick, Evidence § 328 at 760 (2d ed., Cleary, 1972). But cf. C.H.O.B. Associates, Inc. v. Board of Assessors of Nassau County, 45 Misc.2d 184, 257 N.Y.S.2d 31, aff'd, 22 A.D.2d 1015, 256 N.Y.S.2d 550 (2d Dept.1964), aff'd, 16 N.Y.2d 779, 262 N.Y.S.2d 501, 209 N.E.2d 820 (1965), where the plaintiff sought to show, by selecting illustrative samples, that the Board of Assessors had illegally treated vacant land in a way different from improved land. The defendant County submitted the record of a prior case in the County in which a statistical expert had testified against the

County using scientifically selected samples; it asked the Court to utilize judicial notice, inter alia, to determine the proper way to make valid comparisons between types of property. Costs may be substantially reduced by obtaining expert opinion from the record of another case; but is this practice desirable? Cf. also M/V American Queen v. San Diego Marine Construction Corp., 708 F.2d 1483, 1491 (9th Cir.1983) ("court can properly notice a doctrine ... of law [but not fact] from such prior case and apply that principle under the theory of stare decisis.").

Taking judicial notice may impinge on the right to a jury trial, to cross-examine or to object to hearsay. See, e.g., In re Martin, 3 Wash.App. 405, 476 P.2d 134 (1970) (in custody hearing testimony in a former juvenile court hearing was not to be noticed because the parents would be deprived of their right to cross-examine and to object to incompetent evidence); People v. Billon, 266 Cal.App.2d 537, 72 Cal.Rptr. 198 (1968) (appellate court refused to judicially notice another court record to show a prior conviction which was an element of the offense of possessing a firearm because to notice a record never offered in evidence at the trial court for the purpose of proving an essential element of the criminal offense would be to deny the defendant his right to a trial by jury). Cf. Bragg v. Auburn, 253 Cal.App.2d 50, 61 Cal.Rptr. 284 (1967) (court refused to notice a document—the "declaration" of a legislator, apparently made for purposes of the litigation, as to his opinion regarding a piece of legislation—in the record which was inadmissible and had been filed outside the trial with the clerk and "bootstrapped into cognizability" by designation as part of the clerk's transcript on appeal).

4. See also Government of the Virgin Islands v. Testamark, 528 F.2d 742 (3d Cir.1976) (finding that court did not err in taking judicial notice of defendant's prior conviction for impeachment purposes, although better practice is for the prosecution to present official copies of the conviction records); United States v. Gordon, 634 F.2d 639 (1st Cir.1980) (where defendant claimed double jeopardy, trial court could take judicial notice of North Carolina indictment which was allegedly an "exact duplicate" of Massachusetts indictment).

5. Courts utilize their own records in the present litigation to notice facts about the structure of the legal system of which the court is a part. There are facts relating to his court which every judge knows or has the duty to find out. Thus judges notice the organization of their own court and lower courts under their supervision, e.g., State v. Superior Court, 422 P.2d 393 (Ariz.App.1967) (assignment of judges and grand jury matters); the identity and authority to act of fellow judges and other officers, e.g., Boston v. Freeman, 171 S.E.2d 206 (N.C.App.1969); and terms of court. See, e.g., Morgan v. Western Auto Supply Co., 117 S.E.2d 253 (Ga.App.1960) (named superior courts were not in vacation at time order was signed); A & M College of Texas v. Guinn, 280 S.W.2d 373, 376–77 (Tex.Civ.App.1955) ("[E]very judge judicially knows the terms of his own court[,] ... the Probate Court[,] ... [and] appellate courts should have judicial knowledge of facts judicially known by the court from which the appeal is taken.").

6. As Soley v. Star & Herald Co., supra, indicates, a trial court in taking judicial notice should make an adequate record in order that the appellate court can review the basis of the decision. Compare Kelley v. Kelley, 75 So.2d 191, 193 (Fla.1954), where the trial judge considered evidence he had heard in a prior criminal trial:

> All of the facts and circumstances were in the mind and memory of the Circuit Judge but not in the record of the cause he was then considering. It is a part of the fundamental law of this State that the final judgments and

final decrees of the Circuit Court are subject to review by this Court on proper proceedings. It is elemental that in reviewing the actions of Circuit Courts, we are confined to the record produced here. It is from that record that we must determine whether the judgment of the lower court is lawful.

State v. Finkle

Superior Court of New Jersey, 1974.
128 N.J.Super. 199, 319 A.2d 733, aff'd, 66 N.J. 139, 329 A.2d 65, cert. denied, 423 U.S. 836, 96 S.Ct. 61, 46 L.Ed.2d 54.

■ CONFORD, P.J.A.D.

Defendant challenges his conviction of driving 75.3 miles an hour in a 55 m.p.h. zone on U.S. Rt. 322 on May 5, 1973, primarily on the ground that the evidence of his guilt rests solely on a reading of his speed by a VASCAR [visual average speed computer and recorder] device operated by a state trooper. The contention is that expert testimony as to the reliability of the device, which was not here presented before the trial tribunals, is an essential prerequisite for the admissibility of such evidence. The State takes the position that the scientific reliability of the device is a proper subject of judicial notice and that both the accuracy of the instrument used and the qualifications of the trooper who employed it were fully established by evidence adduced at the trial before the Municipal Court of Folsom Borough. The conviction in that court was affirmed in a trial *de novo* on the municipal court transcript before the Atlantic County Court.

. . .

The substantial question before us on this appeal is whether sufficient indication of the general reliability of VASCAR is not now available to warrant the court's taking judicial notice thereof so as to dispense with the necessity in each of the scores (if not hundreds) of prosecutions annually based on use of the instrument of submitting expert proof to establish such reliability.

An understanding of the evidence in the present case and of our conclusions as to judicial notice require a description of the VASCAR device and of how it functions. . . .

The principles underlying VASCAR are simple. The apparatus is mounted in and powered by the battery of a motor vehicle. As the operator opens and closes a distance switch it measures the distance traversed by the vehicle during the interim and simultaneously feeds that information into a computer module. The distance is measured by an odometer module which is linked with the speedometer cable of the control car, but the measurement is not affected by the accuracy of the speedometer. The VASCAR unit also measures the period of time elapsing between the opening and closing by the operator of a time switch, and simultaneously feeds that information into the computer module. The switches can be opened and closed, as between distance and time, in any order. When both pieces of information (distance and time) have been stored in the computer there is within a second a computation by the computer module of the speed of a target vehicle, in terms of miles per hour to the nearest one-tenth of a mile, represented by the ratio of the inputs of distance to time as fed into the computer. This figure is flashed to a screen on the apparatus visible to the operator.

The method of use of VASCAR by a police officer in detecting the speed of a target vehicle depends upon whether the clocking car is following the target car, is being followed by it, the cars are approaching each other from opposite directions, or the clocking car is parked alongside the highway while the target car passes by. VASCAR can be used in any of these situations.

When the clocking car is stationary, as in the instant case, it is necessary that the reference points be predetermined and that the clocking vehicle travel the course in advance, thus locking the distance traversed into the computer module before the time measurement is made. That measurement is made as the target vehicle passes from one of the reference points to the other within the observation of the operator. . . .

The State's witness in the present case was Trooper Leach. His observation of the defendant's car was from a parked position in a diner driveway adjoining the eastbound lanes of U.S. Rt. 322. The observation took place at 8:30 p.m. on May 5, 1973. At 10:05 a.m. that day the trooper had calibrated the VASCAR unit in the following manner. Using a stop-watch, it self checked for accuracy by radio time, he fed 30 seconds of time into the unit and also a premeasured half-mile of distance, deriving a reading of 59.8 m.p.h. as against an accurate 60. On feeding 20 seconds of time into the unit (with the same distance input), he derived a reading of 89.8 m.p.h. as against an accurate 90. He adjusted the mechanism by turning a screw, thereby yielding perfect readings of 60 and 90 m.p.h. At 11:20 p.m. the same day another calibration check of the unit in the same manner again produced perfect readings without the need for adjustment. . . .

The Franklin Institute of Philadelphia prepared the first engineering evaluation of the initial model of this device. "Evaluation of a Device for Checking and Recording the Speed of a Moving Automotive Vehicle;" (1960), by Walter E. Onderko. Comparison of the performance of the machine, in checking the speed of vehicles traveling distances of one-half, one-quarter and one-eighth mile, with calculated speeds obtained from stop watch time and measured distances showed deviations within one mile an hour. An error of 25 feet in judging the position of a vehicle with respect to a marker would produce an error of 2½ m.p.h. based on a vehicle speed of 60 m.p.h. and a distance of one-eighth mile. With the distance increased to one-quarter mile the error is decreased to 1½ miles an hour.

A pamphlet compiled by the New Jersey Institute for Continuing Legal Education and copyrighted by Rutgers University, entitled "Understanding the Breathalyzer, Vascar and Speed Radar" (1974), includes reprints of purported evaluations of VASCAR by the University of North Carolina Highway Safety Research Center (1968), the Iowa Highway Patrol (1968), the IIT Research Institute of Chicago, Illinois (1970) and the Michigan State Police (1967). The IIT study was made for the advice of the Florida State Department of Highway Safety. We have secured independent verification of the authenticity of the North Carolina report. We accept the reprints of the others as authentic in view of the academic credentials of the publisher and compiler. We have also examined an evaluation of VASCAR made for the Indiana State Police.

The consensus of these studies is that VASCAR is soundly engineered and that when properly used by an adequately trained operator over minimum distances of one-eighth to one-tenth of a mile VASCAR has a high degree of reliability in detecting the rate of speed of suspect motorists. From a parked position a minimum distance of 300 feet can be used. Average error is rarely found to exceed two miles an hour, and usually is within a range of 1½ miles an hour or less.

Evid.R. 9(2)(d) provides that judicial notice may be taken of "such facts as are so generally known or of such common notoriety within the area pertinent to the event that they cannot reasonably be the subject of dispute"; also, under Evid.R. 9(2)(e), judicial notice may be taken of "specific facts and propositions of generalized knowledge which are capable of immediate determination by resort to sources of reasonably indisputable accuracy." And see State v. Dantonio, supra (taking judicial notice of the reliability of radar as a speed detection device); State v. Johnson, 42 N.J. 146, 170, 199 A.2d 809 (1964) (taking judicial notice of the reliability of the Harger Drunkometer); State v. Arnwine, 67 N.J.Super. 483, 171 A.2d 124 (App.Div.1961) (refusing judicial notice of reliability of polygraph); cf. State v. McDavitt, 62 N.J. 36, 44, 297 A.2d 849 (1972).

We are satisfied from the evidence herein and the materials which have been introduced before us that VASCAR now uses the criteria of the rule for judicial notice. The absence of extensive scientific writings on the subject, such as preceded judicial notice of radar, for example, is not an inhibiting factor. This device does not embody any presently novel scientific principle. Instruments for the automatic measurement of time and distance have long been familiar to our technology. More recent, but not less firmly established, are the numerous practical applications of computer and calculator science using electronic equipment. VASCAR simply integrates all these now well-established techniques into a composite instrument. There is no reason whatever to doubt its practical efficacy for the designed purpose in the hands of a properly trained operator; and the manifold instances, as here and in the tests reported in the studies cited above, in which calibration has demonstrated beyond dispute the accuracy of particular VASCAR instruments, confirm that the device is reliable beyond any reasonable doubt.

The foregoing conclusions gain added support from the widespread satisfactory experience of police departments here and across the country with VASCAR. Cf. State v. Dantonio, supra (18 N.J. at 579, 115 A.2d 35); State v. Andretta, 61 N.J. 544, 549, 551, 296 A.2d 644 (1972) (police work with voiceprints).

In deciding to accord judicial notice to the reliability of the Harger Drunkometer the Supreme Court stated, in State v. Johnson, supra:

This conclusion cannot be affected by the fact that there are some, like defendant's witness in this case, who dispute the precise accuracy of the device and that there is a possibility of error. Practically every new scientific discovery has its detractors and unbelievers, but neither unanimity of opinion nor universal infallibility is required for judicial acceptance of generally recognized matters. [42 N.J. at 171, 199 A.2d at 823]

Note also the caveat in McCormick, Evidence (1954), in discussing judicial notice, that the most frequent shortcoming of the courts in dealing with the doctrine is their failure "to employ the doctrine of judicial notice in this field [scientific and technological facts] to the full measure of its usefulness" (at 694).

Defendant challenges the use by this court of the data mentioned above on hearsay and due process grounds. In the latter regard he asserts he has been deprived of his rightful opportunity to confront and cross-examine the authors of the several reports mentioned. However, the very process of determination of whether grounds exist for the taking of judicial notice implies discretionary resort by the court to relevant authoritative literature in the particular field without any need for putting it through the adversarial trial process. See, e.g., the extensive consultation of relevant literature in State v. Dantonio, supra (18 N.J. at 573, 575, 576, 578–579, 115 A.2d 35), where the court decided to take judicial notice of radar as a speed measurement device. Evid.R. 10(2) provides that

> In determining the propriety of taking judicial notice of a matter or the tenor thereof, (a) any source of relevant information may be consulted or used, whether or not furnished by a party, and (b) no rule of evidence except Rule 4 [discretionary exclusion of evidence whose probative value is outweighed by risk of undue consumption of time or undue prejudice] or a valid claim of privilege shall apply.

Copies of all the material considered by the court have been furnished to defendant, and he has employed the opportunity to attack its probative force as well as its admissibility. See Evid.R. 10(1). It has been implicit that the court would have received from defendant any authoritative data disparaging the reliability of VASCAR. None has been received nor does the court know of any. The contentions in respect of the hearsay rule and due process rights are without merit.

We find that the conviction of defendant in the County Court of exceeding the speed limit is sustainable on the evidence adduced. In doing so, however, we point out that the factor of potential margin for error in VASCAR readings inherent in the intervention of the mental and physical processes of the operator of the device may well justify a court in declining to find guilt beyond a reasonable doubt where the reading is relatively close to the legal speed limit. But here there is no such problem in view of the wide disparity between the 55 m.p.h. limit and the 75.3 m.p.h. VASCAR reading. We also emphasize that in every future case there must be satisfactory proof of the good working order of the particular VASCAR instrument used and of the qualifications of the operator.

Affirmed; no costs on this appeal.

NOTES

1. The courts are generally in accord in holding that expert testimony is no longer needed to establish the scientific validity of radar. People v. Flaxman, 74 Cal.App.3d Supp. 16, 23, 141 Cal.Rptr. 799, 803 (1977) ("For a substantial period of time courts have taken judicial notice of the use, validity and accuracy of radar devices as a scientific method of measuring speed.... However, this is to be distinguished from a determination of the accuracy of a radar reading in a given case."). Latin, Tannehill & White, Remote Sensing Evidence and Environmental Law, 64 Cal.L.Rev. 1300, 1413–14 (1976); 47 A.L.R.3d 822 (1973).

Judicial notice extends only to the scientific accuracy of the Doppler-shift principle—the scientific principle upon which police radar commonly operates—as a means of measuring speed, but does not extend to the accuracy or efficiency of any given instrument designed to employ the principle. Some courts take the view that evidence tending to show the accuracy of the particular radar instrument involved in a given case is a necessary prerequisite to the admissibility of speed obtained by the use of the speedometer. See, e.g., State v. Tomanelli, 216 A.2d 625 (Conn.1966); People v. Flaxman, 74 Cal. App.3d Supp. 16, 141 Cal.Rptr. 799 (1977). Other courts take the view that evidence of accuracy affects only the sufficiency of the radar evidence. See, e.g., People v. Blattman, 50 Misc.2d 606, 270 N.Y.S.2d 903 (1966).

The device used in the principal case—"visual average speed computer and recorder" (VASCAR)—is a type of computerized stopwatch mechanism. As the principal case shows, although it is relatively new, the courts have begun to take notice of the reliability of the scientific principles upon which VASCAR operates. Contra, People v. Leatherbarrow, 69 Misc.2d 563, 330 N.Y.S.2d 676 (Cty. Ct.1972). See also People v. Donohoo, 54 Ill.App.3d 375, 377, 12 Ill.Dec. 49, 51, 369 N.E.2d 546, 548 (1977) ("speed gun" based on Doppler principle approved). Contra, State v. Boyington, 379 A.2d 486 (N.J.Super.1977) (similarity of speed gun to radar was not established by party).

In a radar case, is the court using judicial notice to admit the radar results or to hold the results conclusive on the issue of speeding? See People v. Flaxman, 74 Cal.App.3d Supp. 16, 141 Cal.Rptr. 799 (1977). Could the court on the same facts have reversed if there had been a jury verdict of not guilty? See Baer, Radar Goes to Court, 33 N.C.L. 355, 380–81 (1955).

2. Scientific speed measuring devices can be effectively used with presumptions. Camera, electrical contact and radar devices will enable police to sit by the side of the road copying license numbers and pressing buttons instead of risking their lives in wild chases if they can rely on a presumption that the owner was driving. See People v. Hildebrandt, 308 N.Y. 397, 126 N.E.2d 377 (1955), refusing to construct a judicial presumption although in an earlier case, People v. Rubin, 284 N.Y. 392, 31 N.E.2d 501 (1940), the court had approved a presumption that a car parked overtime had been driven to the curb by the owner. An inference alone would not support the conviction said the court. See 308 N.Y. at 401, 126 N.E.2d at 379. State v. Scoggin, 72 S.E.2d 54 (N.C.1952), refused to follow the Rubin case on the ground that the matter should be left to the legislature. Compare Dooley v. Commonwealth, 92 S.E.2d 348, 349 (Va. 1956), approving a statute making the results of radar checks "prima facie evidence of speed . . . in any court or legal proceeding where such speed is at issue."

3. Courts, when called upon to determine whether to admit scientific evidence, have often relied upon a test first expressed in Frye v. United States, 293 Fed. 1013 (D.C.Cir.1923). See generally the discussion in Chapter 4, section 3, Expert Witnesses.

4. See McCormick, Evidence 712, 688 (1954): "The emphasis is shifting from the ancient and now comparatively less important basis of 'common knowledge' to the more pregnant basis of verifiable certainty." Furthermore, "this principle of verifiability with certainty should prove to be the growth-principle in the evolution of judicial notice," and is of particular significance to judicial notice of scientific knowledge. Which of these approaches is used by the court in the Finkle case? See Fed.R.Evid. 201.

5. See United States v. Lopez, 328 F.Supp. 1077 (E.D.N.Y.1971), involving the use of a type of metal detector at airports to deter airplane hijacking:

The electronic weapons detector—appropriately named "Friskem"— utilized in this case depends upon magnetic field detectors called "flux-gate magnetometers". . . .

Its operation is based upon the physical fact that the earth is surrounded by a relatively constant magnetic field composed of lines of flux. Steel and other ferromagnetic metals are much better conductors than the air. As a result, when any such metal moves through an area, nearby magnetic lines of flux are distorted to some degree as they tend to converge and pass through the metal while seeking the path of least resistance. Such distortions occurring near a "flux-gate magnetometer" create a signal which can be amplified and calibrated to detect magnetic disturbances. See, e.g., Chapman, The Earth's Magnetism, 10–12, 17–19, 27, 28 (2d ed. 1951); J. Jaquet, No–Touch Frisk Electronic Weapons Detection paper presented at Conference on Electronic Crime Countermeasures, U. of Ky., April 22, 1971; Marshall, An Analytic Model for the Fluxgate Magnetometer, IEEE Transactions on Magnetics, Vol. MAG–3, No. 3 (Sept. 1967); Geyger, Flux–Gate Magnetometer Uses Toroidal Core, Electronics (June 1, 1962); Geyger, The Ring–Core Magnetometer—A New Type of Second–Harmonic Flux–Gate Magnetometer, Communication and Electronics (Mar. 1962).

Though these scientific principals are not matters of common knowledge they may be readily and accurately determined, are verifiable to almost a certainty and are not disputed. The literature was placed in the Court file, notice was given to the parties that the Court intended to rely upon it, and there was no objection by either party.

Under these circumstances the Court takes judicial notice of the scientific principles utilized in the design of the Friskem unit. It finds that such a machine, if properly constructed and operated, can perform in the manner described to the Court by testimony and manuals. [Extensive citation omitted.] Since no opinion was brought to the Court's attention taking judicial notice of magnetometer capabilities, the Court also relied upon expert testimony adduced at the hearing. Such reliance is often the first step in a process that passes through judicial notice to acceptance on a theory of stare decisis. . . . This has been the experience in connection with such scientific techniques as use of fingerprints, ballistic comparison and radar.

In a subsequent decision by another judge of the same court, extensive judicial notice of the testimony and conclusions in Lopez was taken, the court noting,

In taking judicial notice, despite the government's offer to make the same proof available at this hearing, the court concluded that the scientific reliability of the profile (and the magnetometer . . .) has been sufficiently proven in Lopez to permit conservation of judicial time and energy through the device of judicial notice. This type of stare decisis development is an application of black-letter law.

United States v. Bell, 335 F.Supp. 797, 800 n. 2 (E.D.N.Y.1971), aff'd 464 F.2d 667 (2d Cir.), cert. denied, 409 U.S. 991 (1972).

6. In Hardy v. Johns–Manville Sales Corp., 681 F.2d 334 (5th Cir.1982), the court refused to take notice that asbestos causes cancer. Contrast Bey v. Bolger, 540 F.Supp. 910 (E.D.Pa.1982) where the court noticed that a person suffering from hypertension is susceptible to stroke, heart attack, or other physical ailments.

7. For a discussion of blood grouping on paternity and identification issues see Chapter 1, supra. See Callison v. Callison, 687 P.2d 106, 112 (Okl.1984). In a paternity action the court admitted a human leukocyte test (HLA). It declared, the "test is so widely acknowledged and recognized that its accuracy can readily be determined by sources whose accuracy cannot reasonably be questioned." Was the court referring to the theory or the results?

8. Some courts have refused to admit the results of drunkometer tests. See, e.g., City of Sioux Falls v. Kohler, 118 N.W.2d 14, 15 (S.D.1962):

Like "drunkometer" the trade name "Intoximeter" itself carries with it a self-serving implication. This was pointed out by the New York Court in People v. Davidson, 5 Misc.2d 699, 152 N.Y.S.2d 762, 765 (1956), as follows: "the very name of the device—'drunkometer'—might very well be misinterpreted to mean that only those who were 'drunk' or intoxicated were to be tested by it; that the very name somehow lent weight to the result which it produced...." There is no supporting proof that ... the Intoximeter test is a reliable or scientifically accurate gauge of blood alcohol. It was clearly hearsay as to defendant and self-serving as to the City.

See also People v. Morse, 38 N.W.2d 322 (Mich.1949). The trend, however, is towards admitting the results of such tests. See Note of Commissioners, Uniform Chemical Test for Intoxication Act (1957). In State v. Miller, 165 A.2d 829, 833 (N.J.Super.1960), the court stated: "[T]here is a possibility of error, but, as of the present time, the Drunkometer is so well established that these considerations do not affect the admissibility of the Drunkometer evidence but simply affect its weight." Slough & Wilson, Alcohol and the Motorist: Practical and Legal Problems of Chemical Testing, 44 Minn.L.Rev. 673, 684 (1960); Watts, Some Observations on Police Administered Tests for Intoxication, 45 N.C.L. 34, 56 (1966) (discussion of underlying principles).

Some states have enacted statutes providing for the admissibility of breath tests—"drunkometer" or "breathalyzer"—and blood tests that measure alcoholic content in the bloodstream. See, e.g., N.Y.Veh. & Traf.Laws § 1193-94 (McKinney, Supp.1979); Ala.Code § 32-5A-194 (Supp.1980); Alaska Stat. § 28.35.033 (1971); Md.Courts & Judicial Proceedings Code Ann. §§ 10-302 to 10-309 (1974 & Supp.1980). Note that when the legislature provides for the admissibility of this type of evidence, it is not necessary for the courts to judicially notice the underlying scientific principles. Legislative provisions may thus obviate the judicial role in determining the admissibility of scientific test results and the weight to be given them. See, e.g., Alaska Stat. § 28.35.033:

Chemical analysis of blood. (a) Upon the trial of a civil or criminal action or proceeding arising out of acts alleged to have been committed by a person while operating a motor vehicle under the influence of intoxicating liquor, the amount of alcohol in the person's blood at the time alleged, as shown by chemical analysis of the person's breath, shall give rise to the following presumptions:

(1) If there was 0.05 per cent or less by weight of alcohol in the person's blood, it shall be presumed that the person was not under the influence of intoxicating liquor.

(2) If there was in excess of 0.05 per cent but less than 0.10 per cent by weight of alcohol in the person's blood, that fact does not give rise to any presumption that the person was or was not under the influence of intoxicating liquor, but that fact may be considered with other competent evidence in determining whether the person was under the influence of intoxicating liquor.

(3) If there was 0.10 per cent or more by weight of alcohol in the person's blood, it shall be presumed that the person was under the influence of intoxicating liquor.

(b) For purposes of this section, per cent by weight of alcohol in the blood shall be based upon milligrams of alcohol per 100 cubic centimeters of blood.

(c) The provisions of (a) of this section may not be construed to limit the introduction of any other competent evidence bearing upon the question of whether the person was or was not under the influence of intoxicating liquor.

(d) To be considered valid under the provisions of this section the chemical analysis of the person's breath shall have been performed according to methods approved by the Department of Health and Social Services.

The Department of Health and Social Services is authorized to approve satisfactory techniques, methods, and standards of training necessary to ascertain the qualifications of individuals to conduct the analysis. If it is established at trial that a chemical analysis of breath was performed according to approved methods by a person trained according to techniques, methods and standards of training approved by the Department of Health and Social Services, there is a presumption that the test results are valid and further foundation for introduction of the evidence is unnecessary.

[(e) and (f) omitted]

Note that the above provision assigns the determination of whether a scientific method is reliable to the Department of Health and Social Services. Compare such legislative provisions with the analysis undertaken by courts faced with the question of whether to admit scientific test results. Do legislative provisions provide greater certainty in planning for trial? Are these questions better decided on the judicial level? Applying the various meanings given to the term presumption, what aid will this statute give to the prosecutor? See State v. Childress, 274 P.2d 333 (Ariz.1954). What problems does it pose for the defendant? What charge or charges ought the trial judge be prepared to deliver? See also Uniform Act Regulating Traffic on Highways § 54(b) (determines weight to be given to results of blood tests in criminal prosecution for driving while under the influence of intoxicating liquor or drugs).

B.   LEGISLATIVE

United States v. Gould

United States Court of Appeals, Eighth Circuit, 1976.
536 F.2d 216.

■ GIBSON, CHIEF JUDGE.

Defendants, Charles Gould and Joseph Carey, were convicted of conspiring to import (Count I) and actually importing (Count II) cocaine from Colombia, South America, into the United States in violation of the Controlled Substances Import and Export Act. 21 U.S.C. § 951 et seq. (1970). Both defendants received five-year sentences on each count to run concurrently, as well as a special parole term of three years.

The evidence persuasively showed that defendants and David Miller enlisted the cooperation of Miller's sister, Barbara Kenworthy, who agreed to travel to Colombia with defendants and smuggle the cocaine into the United States by placing it inside two pairs of hollowed-out platform shoes. In May of 1975, defendants and Ms. Kenworthy travelled to Colombia where the cocaine was purchased and packed in Ms. Kenworthy's shoes. The success of the importation scheme was foiled when, upon Ms. Kenworthy's arrival to the Miami airport from Colombia, a customs agent insisted upon x-raying the cocaine-laden shoes. Approximately two pounds of cocaine were discovered and seized by customs officials. Ms. Kenworthy was thereafter interrogated by two agents of the Drug Enforcement Administration (DEA) and she informed them that she had been directed to deliver the cocaine to Miller in Des Moines, Iowa. She finally agreed to cooperate with the agents and make a controlled delivery of a cocaine substitute to Miller. DEA agents in Des Moines then secured a search warrant, the delivery was consummated and Miller was arrested.

Defendants do not challenge the sufficiency of the evidence but contend that the District Court erred in (1) improperly taking judicial notice and instructing the jury that cocaine hydrochloride is a schedule II controlled substance, . . .

As to the first issue, defendants contend that evidence should have been presented on the subject of what controlled substances fit within schedule II for the purpose of establishing a foundation that cocaine hydrochloride was actually within that schedule. Schedule II controlled substances, for the purpose of the Controlled Substances Import and Export Act, include the following:

(a) Unless specifically excepted or unless listed in another schedule, any of the following substances whether produced directly or indirectly by extraction from substances of vegetable origin, or independently by means of chemical synthesis, or by a combination of extraction and chemical synthesis:

. . .

(4) Coca leaves and any salt, compound, derivative, or preparation of coca leaves, and any salt, compound, derivative, or preparation thereof which is chemically equivalent or identical with any of these substances, except that the substances shall not include decocainized coca leaves or extraction of coca leaves, which extractions do not contain cocaine or ecgonine.

21 U.S.C. § 812 (1970); see 21 C.F.R. § 1308.12 (1975).

At trial, two expert witnesses for the Government testified as to the composition of the powdered substance removed from Ms. Kenworthy's platform shoes at the Miami airport. One expert testified that the substance was comprised of approximately 60 percent cocaine hydrochloride. The other witness stated that the white powder consisted of 53 percent cocaine. There was no direct evidence to indicate that cocaine hydrochloride is a derivative of coca leaves. In its instructions to the jury, the District Court stated:

If you find the substance was cocaine hydrochloride, you are instructed that cocaine hydrochloride is a schedule II controlled substance under the laws of the United States.

Our inquiry on this first assignment of error is twofold. We must first determine whether it was error for the District Court to take judicial notice of the fact that cocaine hydrochloride is a schedule II controlled substance. Secondly, if we conclude that it was permissible to judicially notice this fact, we must then determine whether the District Court erred in instructing the jury that it must accept this fact as conclusive.

The first aspect of this inquiry merits little discussion. In Hughes v. United States, 253 F. 543, 545 (8th Cir.1918), cert. denied, 249 U.S. 610, 39 S.Ct. 291, 63 L.Ed. 801 (1919), this court stated:

It is also urged that there was no evidence that morphine, heroin, and cocaine are derivatives of opium and coca leaves. We think that is a matter of which notice may be taken. In a sense the question is one of the definition or meaning of words long in common use, about which there is no obscurity, controversy, or dispute, and of which the imperfectly informed can gain complete knowledge by resort to dictionaries within reach of everybody. . . . Common knowledge, or the common means of knowledge, of the settled, undisputed, things of life, need not always be laid aside on entering a courtroom.

It is apparent that courts may take judicial notice of any fact which is "capable of such instant and unquestionable demonstration, if desired, that no party would think of imposing a falsity on the tribunal in the face of an intelligent adversary." IX J. Wigmore, Evidence § 2571, at 548 (1940). The fact that cocaine hydrochloride is derived from coca leaves is, if not common knowledge, at least a matter which is capable of certain, easily accessible and indisputably accurate verification. See Webster's Third New International Dictionary 434 (1961). Therefore, it was proper for the District Court to judicially notice this fact. Our conclusion on this matter is amply supported by the weight of judicial authority....

Our second inquiry involves the propriety of the District Court's instruction to the jurors that this judicially noticed fact must be accepted as conclusive by them. Defendants, relying upon Fed.R.Ev. 201(g), urge that the jury should have been instructed that it could discretionarily accept or reject this fact. Rule 201(g) provides:

> In a civil action or proceeding, the court shall instruct the jury to accept as conclusive any fact judicially noticed. In a criminal case, the court shall instruct the jury that it may, but is not required to, accept as conclusive any fact judicially noticed.[1]

It is clear that the reach of rule 201 extends only to adjudicative, not legislative, facts. Fed.R.Ev. 201(a). Consequently, the viability of defendants' argument is dependent upon our characterization of the fact judicially noticed by the District Court as adjudicative, thus invoking the provisions of rule 201(g). In undertaking this analysis, we note at the outset that rule 201 is not all-encompassing. "Rule 201 ... was deliberately drafted to cover only a small fraction of material usually subsumed under the concept of 'judicial notice.' "1 J. Weinstein, Evidence ¶ 201[01] (1975).

The precise line of demarcation between adjudicative facts and legislative facts is not always easily identified. Adjudicative facts have been described as follows:

> When a court ... finds facts concerning the immediate parties—who did what, where, when, how, and with what motive or intent—the court ... is performing an adjudicative function, and the facts are conveniently called adjudicative facts....
>
> Stated in other terms, the adjudicative facts are those to which the law is applied in the process of adjudication. They are the facts that normally go to the jury in a jury case. They relate to the parties, their activities, their properties, their businesses.

2 K. Davis, Administrative Law Treatise § 15.03, at 353 (1958). Legislative facts, on the other hand, do not relate specifically to the activities or characteristics of the litigants. A court generally relies upon legislative facts when it

---

1. In the proposed federal Rules of Evidence, forwarded by the Supreme Court of the United States to Congress on February 5, 1973, rule 201(g) did not draw this distinction between civil and criminal cases. The proposed rule 201(g) provided that "[t]he judge shall instruct the jury to accept as established any facts judicially noticed." Congress disagreed with this unqualified rule requiring mandatory instructions in all cases. It was feared that requiring the jury to accept a judicially noticed adjudicative fact in a criminal case might infringe upon the defendants' Sixth Amendment right to a trial by jury. H.Rep. No. 93–650, 93d Cong., 1st Sess. 6–7 (1973), reprinted in 4 U.S.Code Cong. & Admin.News pp. 7075, 7080 (1974). Consequently, Congress adopted the present text of rule 201(g) which requires a mandatory instruction in civil cases but a discretionary instruction in criminal cases. [Some footnotes omitted; others renumbered; footnotes by the Court.]

purports to develop a particular law or policy and thus considers material wholly unrelated to the activities of the parties.

> Legislative facts are ordinarily general and do not concern the immediate parties. In the great mass of cases decided by courts ..., the legislative element is either absent or unimportant or interstitial, because in most cases the applicable law and policy have been previously established. But whenever a tribunal engages in the creation of law or of policy, it may need to resort to legislative facts, whether or not those facts have been developed on the record.

2 K. Davis, Administrative Law Treatise, supra at § 15.03. Legislative facts are established truths, facts or pronouncements that do not change from case to case but apply universally, while adjudicative facts are those developed in a particular case.

Applying these general definitions, we think it is clear that the District Court in the present case was judicially noticing a legislative fact rather than an adjudicative fact. Whether cocaine hydrochloride is or is not a derivative of the coca leaf is a question of scientific fact applicable to the administration of the Comprehensive Drug Abuse Prevention and Control Act of 1970. 21 U.S.C. § 801 et seq. (1970). The District Court reviewed the schedule II classifications contained in 21 U.S.C. § 812, construed the language in a manner which comports with common knowledge and understanding, and instructed the jury as to the proper law so interpreted. It is undisputed that the trial judge is required to fully and accurately instruct the jury as to the law to be applied in a case. Bird v. United States, 180 U.S. 356, 361, 21 S.Ct. 403, 405, 45 L.Ed. 570, 573 (1901). When a court attempts to ascertain the governing law in a case for the purpose of instructing the jury, it must necessarily rely upon facts which are unrelated to the activities of the immediate parties. These extraneous, yet necessary, facts fit within the definition of legislative facts and are an indispensable tool used by judges when discerning the applicable law through interpretation.[2] The District Court, therefore, was judicially noticing such a legislative fact when it recognized that cocaine hydrochloride is derived from coca leaves and is a schedule II controlled substance within the meaning of § 812.

Through similar reasoning, this judicially noticed fact simply cannot be appropriately categorized as an adjudicative fact. It does not relate to "who did what, where, when, how, and with what motive or intent," nor is it a fact which would traditionally go to the jury. See 2 K. Davis, Administrative Law Treatise, supra at § 15.03. The fact that cocaine hydrochloride is a derivative of coca leaves is a universal fact that is unrelated to the activities of the parties to this litigation. There was no preemption of the jury function to determine what substance was actually seized from Ms. Kenworthy at the Miami airport. The jury was instructed that, if it found that the confiscated substance was cocaine hydrochloride, the applicable law classified the substance as a schedule II controlled substance.

---

2. The Notes of the Advisory Committee to rule 201 offer support for the proposition that courts utilize legislative facts when they interpret a statute.

> While judges use judicial notice of "propositions of generalized knowledge" in a variety of situations: *determining the validity and meaning of statutes,* formulating common law rules, deciding whether evidence should be admitted, assessing the sufficiency and effect of evidence, *all are essentially nonadjudicative in nature.* (Emphasis added.)

See State v. Freeman, 440 P.2d 744, 757 (Okl.1968); C. McCormick, Law of Evidence § 328, at 759 (2d ed. 1972); 1 J. Weinstein, Evidence ¶ 201[01] (1975).

It is clear to us that the District Court took judicial notice of a legislative, rather than an adjudicative, fact in the present case and rule 201(g) is inapplicable. The District Court was not obligated to inform the jury that it could disregard the judicially noticed fact. In fact, to do so would be preposterous, thus permitting juries to make conflicting findings on what constitutes controlled substances under federal law....[3]

The judgment of conviction is affirmed.

NOTES

1. Was the characterization in the main case calculated to avoid rule 201(g)? Is it inconsistent with the policy of that rule? See Advisory Committee's Note:

> Subdivision (g). Much of the controversy about judicial notice has centered upon the question whether evidence should be admitted in disproof of facts of which judicial notice is taken....
>
> The proponents of admitting evidence in disproof have concentrated largely upon legislative facts. Since the present rule deals only with judicial notice of adjudicative facts, arguments directed to legislative facts lose their relevancy.

See also H.R.Rep. No. 93–650, 93rd Cong., 1st Sess. 6–7 (1973):

> [B]eing of the view that mandatory instruction to a jury in a criminal case to accept as conclusive any fact judicially noticed is inappropriate because contrary to the spirit of the Sixth Amendment right to a jury trial, the Committee adopted the 1969 Advisory Committee draft of this subsection, allowing a mandatory instruction in civil actions and proceedings and a discretionary instruction in criminal cases.

Maine declined to follow the federal version of subdivision (g). Me.R.Evid. 201(g). The Maine Advisers' Note explains:

> The Federal Rule adds a sentence in subdivision (g) that in a criminal case the court shall instruct the jury that it may, but is not required to, accept as conclusive any fact judicially noted. Since judicial notice is limited to facts not subject to reasonable dispute, there is no reason for not making it mandatory in criminal as well as in civil cases. It would be as absurd in a criminal case as in a civil action to allow jurors to question the accuracy of the court's instruction as to what day of the week December 4, 1972, actually was.
>
> It is essential to bear in mind that resort to judicial notice in any case, civil or criminal, is permissible only if the judicially noticed fact is not subject to reasonable dispute. The court must not accept as sufficient the absence of actual dispute over, for example, a scientific conclusion found in a text or treatise. Such a misuse of judicial notice would deprive a criminal defendant of his constitutional right to jury trial.

---

3. Common sense dictates that the construction urged upon us by defendants is not well-taken. The fact that cocaine hydrochloride is derived from coca leaves is scientifically and pharmacologically unimpeachable, it would be incongruous to instruct the jurors on this irrefutable fact and then inform them that they may disregard it at their whim. It would be similarly illogical if we were to conclude that trial judges could rely upon generally accepted, undisputed facts in interpreting the applicable statutory law, yet obligate them to instruct the jury that it could disregard the factual underpinnings of the interpretation in its discretion.

Cf. Mont.R.Evid. 201 (identical to Federal Rule 201 except for the substitution of "all facts" for "adjudicative facts" in subdivision (a)). The Commission comment explains the change in language:

> The Commission believes that use of the terms "adjudicative" and "legislative" facts as is done with Federal Rule 201 is confusing and that they cannot be readily or easily be applied to all factual situations. The Commission rejects the approach under the Federal Rule 201 of limiting judicial notice to adjudicative facts because this is a basis which is totally new, not clearly defined, and contrary to existing Montana practice. The confusion and litigation bound to result are clearly contrary to a rule which is meant to save time and expense.

See United States v. Coffman, 638 F.2d 192, 194 (10th Cir.1980), where at issue was whether a court, in taking judicial notice that LSD is a controlled substance under federal law, is required to give the cautionary instruction contained in Fed.R.Evid. 201(g). The court found that it is not required to inform the jury that it could disregard the judicially noticed fact. In the court's view, to impose such a requirement "would be preposterous, thus permitting juries to make conflicting findings on what constitutes controlled substances under federal law;" See also United States v. Berrojo, 628 F.2d 368 (5th Cir.1980).

2. Is the proper balance drawn in Gould between the power of the court and the jury? Suppose the issue had been whether marijuana or cocaine is a narcotic? See United States v. Vila, 599 F.2d 21 (2d Cir.), cert. denied, 444 U.S. 837 (1979) (court determined that classification of cocaine as a narcotic was constitutional); National Organization for Reform of Marijuana Laws v. Bell, 488 F.Supp. 123 (D.D.C.1980) (court determined that marijuana falls within the statutory classification of the Controlled Substances Act). Is this a legal or a factual problem? Would expert testimony on the point be relevant? What exploration of the literature should be undertaken by the court if an attack on the constitutionality of the legislative categorization of one of these substances as a narcotic is being made? See Turner v. United States, infra note 3. How might new information on the effects of marijuana be used? See National Commission on Marijuana and Drug Abuse, Marihuana, A Signal of Understanding, 37–126 (N.Am.Lib.Ed.1972). See also United States v. Creswell, 515 F.Supp. 1268 (E.D.N.Y.1981), where the defendant, charged with importing substantial quantities of "hashish oil (marijuana)," moved for dismissal on the ground that the Administrator of the Drug Enforcement Agency had failed to follow the statutory procedures regarding the classification of controlled substances. Deferring to the judgment of the Administrator in meeting his obligation to reclassify drugs by taking into account current facts including the "current pattern of abuse" and "current scientific knowledge," the court noted:

> The evidentiary hearing and review sought here would ... require an investigation as to the state of the then-current scientific knowledge and abuse in the ... time period covered by the allegations of the indictment against this defendant. Since the Administrator's attention has not been focused on any particular time period, there can be no assurance that a coherent record has been made.

Did the Creswell court determine whether the classification was proper or whether the Administrator had satisfied the procedural requirements of classification? Did the court judicially notice a legislative or an adjudicative fact? For a discussion of judicial notice of facts authoritatively determined by non-judicial agencies see infra. Compare United States v. Malloy, 691 F.2d 498 (4th

Cir.1982) (unpublished),[1] where the trial court properly took judicial notice that cocaine hydrochloride was a Schedule II controlled substance, notwithstanding that the jury was not given an opportunity to reject this fact. See also with respect to cocaine and cocoa leaves, United States v. Whitley, 734 F.2d 1129 (6th Cir.1984).

3. Judicial notice of legislative fact is normally used to show that a particular condition existed at the time of statutory enactment. See Wyman v. Wallace, 615 P.2d 452 (Wash.1980) (court abolished cause of action for alienation of spouse's affection after it took judicial notice of legislative facts about the marital relationship and the subject of alienation of affections). In Roe v. Wade, 410 U.S. 113 (1973), the Supreme Court held unconstitutional a statute which prohibited abortions for any purpose except to save the mother's life. In finding that the right to privacy was a fundamental right that had been denied by the prohibition on abortion and that the state interests did not justify such denial, the court took notice of several factors including ancient attitudes, the common law, the dangers associated with abortion that had prompted the early legislation, modern medical advances that have minimized these dangers, and the current attitude that has been adopted by various organizations.

Is there substantive justification for bringing these facts up-to-date at the time of the trial or the appeal? See Turner v. United States, 396 U.S. 398 (1970). At issue was the validity of a statutory presumption of knowledge that heroin and cocaine had been illegally imported from the fact of possession. The Court found that since heroin is not produced in this country, the presumption was valid with respect to the heroin. With respect to the cocaine, however, since it is produced in this country and since the amount possessed by the defendant was small—less than one gram—the Court found that the presumption should not be applied. In Turner, the Court relied extensively on post legislation studies. Does that mean that a statute that passes constitutional muster when enacted might not when the Court has information available to it which the legislature could not have considered? See also Leary v. United States, 395 U.S. 6 (1969).

Compare with Turner, the opinion in United States v. Jiminez, 444 F.2d 67, 68 (2d Cir.1971):

> There can be little question that the 1.5 kilograms of cocaine involved in this case is far above the much smaller levels covered by the direct holding of Turner (Turner concerned less than one gram). The question of what to do with these larger amounts has been before the court in a number of recent cases, and is now settled for this circuit by United States v. Gonzales, Miranda and Ovalle, 442 F.2d 698 (2d Cir.1970), holding that, on the basis of judicial notice of statistics supplied by the Bureau of Narcotics and other sources, the presumption of importation for cocaine of large quantities such as one kilogram should stand.

See United States v. Gonzalez, 442 F.2d 698, 711 (2d Cir.1970), cert. denied, 404 U.S. 845 (1971) (Feinberg and Smith dissenting) (criticized the majority for not giving the defendants an opportunity to "contest at trial level the 'judicially noticed' facts" and statistical information supporting the presumption as to the importation of large amounts of cocaine); United States v. Bramble, 641 F.2d 681, 683 (9th Cir.1981) (court refused to judicially notice that 21 marijuana

---

1. Federal Courts of Appeals issue opinions which may not be cited. This is one of them. The student doing research should be aware that the vast bulk of opinions on evidence are either oral or unpublished. [Eds.]

plants in a hot house in defendant's yard must have been grown for purposes of sale).

4. In Durham v. United States, 94 U.S.App.D.C. 228, 214 F.2d 862 (1954), the court relied upon extensive writings to reject as obsolete the traditional M'Naughten Rules for insanity. This decision provoked a wealth of comment. See, e.g., 54 Colum.L.Rev. 1153 (1954); 68 Harv.L.Rev. 364 (1954); 30 Ind.L.J. 194 (1954). See also 45 A.L.R.2d 1430 (1956). Psychiatrists, while finding difficulty with the court's formulation, have generally approved the abandonment of the M'Naughten Rules and the court's use of psychiatric opinion. See Roche, Criminality and Mental Illness—Two Faces of the Same Coin, 22 U.Chi.L.Rev. 320 (1955); Guttmacher, The Psychiatrist as an Expert Witness, id. at 325; Zilboorg, A Step Toward Enlightened Justice, id. at 331. Durham was overruled by United States v. Brawner, 471 F.2d 969 (D.C.Cir.1972), which adopted the formulation of the American Law Institute. See Model Penal Code § 4.01(1) (1962); Wechsler, The Criteria of Criminal Responsibility, 22 U.Chi. L.Rev. 367 (1955); Symposium on Insanity as a Defense in Criminal Law, 45 Marq.L.Rev. 477 (1962); Wade v. United States, 426 F.2d 64, 69 (9th Cir.1970) (while finding no substantial difference between the two rules, the court adopted the A.L.I. provision).

Are advance notice to parties, briefs and oral presentations, briefs by amicus curiae, and independent research by the court enough to protect the public from inept presentation of important issues? See the excellent Note, Social and Economic Facts—Appraisal of Suggested Techniques for Presenting Them to the Courts, 61 Harv.L.Rev. 692 (1948). Compare Uniform Rule 10. Is a court well-equipped to carry out this kind of inquiry? Cf. Levy, Realist Jurisprudence and Prospective Overruling, 109 U. of Pa.L.Rev. 1 (1960).

Should the change in the law in Durham have been left to the legislature? Cf. McDonald v. United States, 114 U.S.App.D.C. 120, 312 F.2d 847, 850–851 (1962) (limiting the Durham Rule by defining "disease" and "defect").

5. Is there any difference between the use of published and unpublished works? In United States v. Roth, 237 F.2d 796, 814 (2d Cir.1956), involving allegedly obscene publications, Judge Frank in his concurring opinion relies not only on the published works of sociologists but also on a letter from a sociologist written to him in response to his own inquiry. While the final appeal in the Roth case was under consideration (Roth v. United States, 354 U.S. 476 (1957)), the Solicitor General sent the Supreme Court a carton of what he designated "hard-core pornography," Lockhart & McClure, Censorship of Obscenity: The Developing Constitutional Standards, 45 Minn.L.Rev. 5, 26 (1960). Was it proper for the court to resort to this material in formulating its definition of obscenity—"whether to the average person, applying contemporary community standards, the dominant theme of the material taken as a whole appeals to prurient interest." Is there any difference between utilizing information outside the record at the trial level or the appellate level? See Currie, Appellate Court's Use of Facts Outside of the Record by Resort to Judicial Notice and Investigation, 1960 Wis.L.Rev. 39. For refinements of the Roth Test see Miller v. California, 413 U.S. 15 (1973).

In People v. Finkelstein, 11 N.Y.2d 300, 305, 229 N.Y.S.2d 367, 371, 183 N.E.2d 661, cert. denied, 371 U.S. 863 (1962), the court excluded a book and magazines as irrelevant since "the fact that certain other and different publications were *seen* in bookstores and on magazine stands in New York City is no indication that they were *sold*, or *read*, or that to the average person applying contemporary community standards ... they were not obscene." In a concurring opinion, Judge Voorhis stated:

In my view the other publications offered in evidence might well have been admitted for whatever aid they might have supplied to the court in discerning what are contemporary community standards, but this is also a subject of judicial notice. As stated in Wigmore, Evidence (3d ed., vol. 9 § 2567, p. 535): "That a matter is judicially noticed means merely that it is taken as true without the offering of evidence by the party who would ordinarily have done so. This is because the Court *assumes* that the matter is so notorious that it will not be disputed. *But the opponent is not prevented from disputing* the matter by evidence, if he believes it disputable. It is true that occasionally a Court is found declaring a thing judicially noticed and at the same time refusing to listen to evidence to the contrary; but usually this is in truth laying down a new rule of substantive law by declaring certain facts immaterial.

. . .

Is the court dealing with legislative or adjudicative facts or both by taking judicial notice of general examples of pornography or by utilizing public opinion polls on community standards?

Does the consideration of other publications depend on whether the court is viewing the Roth test as a question of fact to be determined by a jury or of substantive law to be decided by a court? In either case, can a work be judged as "obscene" without some standard for comparison. See United States v. Manarite, 448 F.2d 583, 593 (2d Cir.), cert. denied, 404 U.S. 947 (1971) ("Evidence of mere availability of similar materials is not by itself sufficiently probative of community standards to be admissible in the absence of proof that the material enjoys a reasonable degree of acceptance"); See also Jacobellis v. State, 378 U.S. 184 (1964).

A random survey of San Diego residents asking whether they thought "adults should be able to buy and view this book and materials" was excluded by the trial judge in a case concerning the mailing of obscene material in violations of 18 U.S.C. § 1461. The exclusion was affirmed by the Supreme Court. Hamling v. United States, 418 U.S. 87 (1974). Was this sound? Suppose the survey had been utilized as a basis for an expert's opinion? See Rules 702–704, Federal Rules of Evidence. See discussion of the use of experts in obscenity cases under Expert Testimony, infra.

6. Do trademark and obscenity cases raise similar issues of methods of proof? Some of the problems are discussed under Hearsay, Physical or Mental Condition of Declarant. See Ives Laboratories, Inc. v. Darby Drug Co., 638 F.2d 538 (2d Cir.1981), rev'd sub nom. Inwood Laboratories v. Ives Laboratories, 456 U.S. 844 (1982), a trademark infringement suit against drug manufacturers in which plaintiff claimed that defendants suggested that retailers fill prescriptions with defendants' generic drugs rather than plaintiff's product, appellate court found no support for district court's conclusion that mislabeling occurs because of confusion rather than defendants' inducement; the appellate court stated:

we are now in possession of additional undisputed evidence, which we may judicially notice, suggesting that illegal substitution and mislabeling in New York are neither *de minimis* nor inadvertent. During the month of May, 1980, six indictments were handed down in the New York City area alleging illegal substitution [for plaintiff's product]. These indictments, which reflect the grand jurors' views that reasonable grounds exist for charging the druggists with engagement in such illegal activities are inconsistent with appellees contention that mislabeling is rare or unintentional.

The court conceded that "while ... somewhat unusual to take judicial notice of proceedings not directly involving the parties to an action," here "the appeal being heard is not from a criminal conviction.". In reversing Ives, the Supreme Court noted: "An appellate court cannot substitute its interpretation of the evidence for that of the trial court simply because the reviewing court 'might give the facts another construction, resolve the ambiguities differently, and find a more sinister cast to actions which the District Court apparently deemed innocent.' " "In reaching" its "conclusion the Court of Appeals took judicial notice of the fact that in May 1980, six indictments were handed down in New York City charging pharmacists with substituting cyclandelate for CYCLOS-PASMAOL. We note that the evidence of which the Court of Appeals took judicial notice not only involved no convictions but also involved knowledge that was not available when the District Court rendered its decision." Id. 857 + n. 19.

United States v. Various Articles of Obscene Merchandise, Schedule No. 2102, 709 F.2d 132 (2d Cir.1983) (in pornography confiscation case court noticed widespread community availability and patronage of such material as circumstantial evidence of contemporary community standards); Eden Toys, Inc. v. Marshall Field & Co., 675 F.2d 498 (2d Cir.1982) (in copyright case concerning toy snowman, court held features of snowmen are known generally). See Wells Fargo & Co. v. Wells Fargo Express Co., 358 F.Supp. 1065 (D.Nev. 1973), vacated on jurisdictional grounds, 556 F.2d 406 (9th Cir.1977) (court took judicial notice of the national knowledge of the historic name "Wells Fargo").

Do opinion polls furnish a satisfactory way of resolving the trademark questions? Does the answer to this question depend upon whether the courts are deciding issues of law or fact? Does it make any difference in classes of cases where there are no juries? Cf. Potts v. Coe, 145 F.2d 27, 140 F.2d 470 (D.C.Cir.1944), determining what a patentable article was in the light of well-known corporate research practices.

7. Courts generally admit the results of opinion polls and surveys in trademark confusion cases. See, e.g., United States v. 88 Cases, 187 F.2d 967, 974 (3d Cir.), cert. denied, 342 U.S. 861 (1951); Union Carbide Corp. v. Ever–Ready Inc., 531 F.2d 366, 386–388 (7th Cir.), cert. denied, 429 U.S. 830 (1976).

Courts also admit the results of opinion polls and surveys in false advertising cases. See, e.g., American Brands, Inc. v. R.J. Reynolds Tobacco Co., 413 F.Supp. 1352, 1356–57 (S.D.N.Y.1976) (issue was whether the cigarette advertisement "NOW. 2 mg. 'tar' is the lowest" had a tendency to mislead and deceive because it implied that no other cigarette had only 2 mg. tar when in fact, another brand had equally low tar content):

> Deceptive advertising or merchandising statements may be judged in various ways.... [W]here the defendant's trademark or trade name does not actually duplicate the plaintiff's, if there is such a substantial similarity between the plaintiff's mark or name and the defendant's that the likelihood of confusion must necessarily follow, a court can grant relief on its own findings without recourse to a survey of consumer reaction.

> The subject matter here is different.... [W]e are asked to determine whether a statement acknowledged to be literally true and grammatically correct nevertheless has a tendency to mislead, confuse or deceive. As to

such a proposition the public's reaction to [the] advertisement will be the starting point in any discussion of the likelihood of deception. . . .

See also American Home Products Corp. v. Johnson & Johnson, 436 F.Supp. 785, 792 (S.D.N.Y.1977), aff'd, 577 F.2d 160 (2d Cir.1978) (expert opinion excluded because court had "actual tests of consumer reaction" which were the "best evidence of what meaning consumers take from advertising").

Courts have been reluctant to admit surveys and polls in other types of cases. E.g. Irvin v. State, 66 So.2d 288 (Fla.1953), cert. denied, 346 U.S. 927 (1954) (Roper poll held inadmissible as a method of determining the likelihood of a defendant's being unable to receive a fair trial in a given community on request for change of venue).

8. In Williams v. Florida, 399 U.S. 78 (1970), the Supreme Court was presented with the issue of whether the constitutional guarantee of a trial by jury entitles a defendant in a criminal action to a 12–person jury. Florida law had provided for a six-person jury in all but capital cases. The defendant, charged in Florida court with robbery, had filed a pretrial motion to impanel a 12–person jury instead of the six-person jury provided by Florida law. The motion was denied and defendant was subsequently convicted and sentenced to life imprisonment. In holding that the 12–person jury is not a necessary ingredient of "trial by jury," the Supreme Court took notice of "[w]hat few experiments [had] occurred—usually in the civil area—indicat[ing] that there is no discernible difference between the results reached by the two different-sized juries." Williams has been highly criticized. See, generally, Note, Statistical Analysis and Jury Size: Ballew v. State of Georgia, 56 Den.L.J. 659 (1979) ("[T]he Court did not critically analyze the 'experiments' it relied upon. . . . [T]he studies relied upon did not really prove what the Court indicated they did." Id. at 664.); Lempert, Uncovering "Nondiscernible" Differences: Empirical Research and the Jury–Size Cases, 73 Mich.L.Rev. 645, 649 n. 9 (1975) (court found evidence to support its intuitive assumption that jury size had no relation to jury verdicts); Zeisel, . . . And Then There Were None: The Diminution of the Federal Jury, 38 U.Chi.L.Rev. 710, 714 (1971) (studies indicate that six-person jury is a less effective factfinder than a 12–person jury); O'Brien, Of Judicial Myths, Motivations and Justifications: A Postscript on Social Science and the Law, 64 Judicature 285 (1981); Zeisel & Diamond, "Convincing Empirical Evidence" on the Six Member Jury, 41 U.Chi.L.Rev. 281, 281 (1974):

> The Court generally cites "empirical" studies as lawyers cite cases, treating their summary conclusions as if they were holdings in prior cases. Applied to empirical research, this treatment encourages the notion that empirical findings, like case law, are infinitely mutable. The courts are thus diverted from using empirical studies for their intended purpose: to shed light on hitherto unknown facts.

> A more critical use of empirical data would better inform the courts and force them to face openly those instances in which their decisions are based on theory and merely ornamented by the "facts." Assurance of critical examination in the courts would also force researchers more carefully to connect their summary conclusions with the results of their studies.

Also critical are Kaye, Comment, Mathematical Models and Legal Realities: Reflection on the Poisson Model of Jury Behavior, 13 Conn.L.Rev. 1 (1980). Cf. Luneburg and Nordenberg, Specially Qualified Juries and Expert Nonjury Tribunals: Alternatives for Coping with the Complexities of Modern Civil Litigation, 67 Va.L.Rev. 887 (1981); M. Saks, Small–Group Decision Making and Complex Information Tasks (Fed.Jud.Center 1981).

In Ballew v. Georgia, 435 U.S. 223 (1978), the Supreme Court relied upon empirical data in finding that a five-person jury in a criminal case is unconstitutional. In so finding, did the Court withdraw from its position in Williams that there is no discernible difference between the results reached by six and 12–person juries? Did the Court in Ballew necessarily have superior empirical data to that used in Williams?

The reliability of empirical data in assessing human behavior has been scrutinized in other legal areas. E.g., Committee on Law Enforcement and the Administration of Justice, Forecasting the Impact of Legislation on Courts 3 (1980):

> We conclude that the basic theoretical and empirical knowledge necessary to develop good estimates of the impact of legislation on courts for broad classes of legislation is not yet available. The task of estimating impact is fundamentally one of predicting behaviors: the number and nature of transactions in the society that may eventually lead to litigation, the choices made by potential litigants to go to court or not, the behaviors of lawyers and others who broker entry to the legal system. Estimating the impacts of new legislation on courts involves predicting the effects of the legislation on all those behaviors and probably more, and they are all extremely difficult to predict.

9. Should the courts make use of empirical data to assess the effects of segregation and discrimination in public schools? See Weinstein, Equality, Liberty, and the Public Schools: The Role of the State Courts, 1 Cardozo L.Rev. 343, 353–55 n. 44 (1979):

> The literature is not conclusive, but it suggests that with sensitive and competent direction by school authorities there is no educational loss to white pupils and at least a possible benefit to black pupils. See J. Coleman, E. Campbell, C. Hobson, J. McPartland, A. Mood, F. Weinfeld & R. York, Equality of Educational Opportunity 307–08 (1966); C. Jencks, M. Smith, H. Acland, M.J. Bane, D. Cohen, H. Gintus, B. Heyne & S. Michelson, Inequality, A Reassessment of the Effect of Family and Schooling in America (1972); U.S. Comm'n on Civil Rights, Racial Isolation in the Public Schools 113–14 (1967); M. Weinberg, Minority Students (1977); Bussed Blacks and Whites Gain in Tests, Study Says, N.Y. Times, Dec. 24, 1978, at 22, col. 1; Who Gains From School Integration? N.Y. Times, Dec. 30, 1978, at 18, col. 1 (Berkeley, California test scores rise for both blacks and whites in fully integrated system).

> > Professor Weinberg's latest analysis of available research concludes that: Judging from actual cases of desegregated schooling, one may conclude under desegregation that:

> > 1. Academic achievement rises as the minority child learns more while the advantaged majority child continues to learn at his accustomed rate. Thus, the gap narrows. There is no evidence that the presence of middle-class children is required in desegregated schools before such an achievement effect begins to operate.

> > 2. Minority children gain a more realistic conception of their vocational and educational future. This process may involve a scaling up or a scaling down of older aspirations. Self-acceptance and self-concepts of minority children are higher than under segregation.

> > 3. Positive racial attitudes by black and white students develop as they attend school together. Attendance in one desegregated school facilitates attendance at other desegregated schools.

M. Weinberg, supra, at 327–28. Weinberg stresses, however, the need for a positive plan in order to make integration work and particularly the need for high expectations on the part of teachers and staff: "poor children will learn if the schools choose to educate them." Id. at 330. See Report of the United States Comm'n on Civil Rights, Fulfilling the Letter and Spirit of the Law, Desegregation of the Nation's Public Schools 112 (Aug.1976). See also Edwards, Components of Academic Success: A Profile of Achieving Black Adolescents, 45 J. Negro Educ. 408 (1976) (study of a 99% black high school in a large midwestern city); Hunt, The Schooling of Immigrants and Black Americans: Some Similarities and Differences, 45 J. Negro Educ. 423 (1976); Kiesling, The Value to Society of Integrated Education and Compensatory Education, 61 Geo.L.J. 857, 861 (1973) (response to policymakers' demand for empirical research regarding the efficacy of racial mixing has been "disappointing"); Nichols & McKinney, Black or White Socio–Economically Disadvantaged Pupils—They Aren't Necessarily Inferior, 46 J. Negro Educ. 443, 449 (1977) ("[A]pparent poor performance in the schools serving [poor] pupils reflects inferior social situations in society at large and/or inferior schools rather than inferior children."); Sizemore, Educational Research and Desegregation: Significance for the Black Community, 47 J. Negro Educ. 58 (1978) (Much scholarship subtly supports metropolitan desegregation and the reversal of white flight, rather than elevation of black achievement, and therefore a new approach to educational research is needed.).

The greater obstacles (including the dismal effects of slavery) encountered in the education of black children than in the education of white immigrant children are described in Hunt, The Schooling of Immigrants and Black Americans: Some Similarities and Differences, 45 J. Negro Educ. 423 (1976). Cf. Greeley, Debunking the Role of Social Scientists in Court, 7 Human Rights 34, 35 (1978) ("There may be moral, esthetic, legal and religious grounds for promoting more school integration; but do not expect that by doing so you will make much contribution to improving the income of minority groups—to say nothing of improving their education."). Compare Grayzel, Using Social Science Concepts in the Legal Fight Against Discrimination: Servant or Sorcerer's Apprentice? 64 A.B.A.J. 1239 (1978) (urging skeptical resistance to the incorporation of unsubstantiated and manipulable social science concepts into legal decisionmaking) with W. Taylor, The Supreme Court and Recent School Desegregation Cases 4–5 (March 16, 1978) (on file at Center for Nat'l Policy Rev., Catholic U. of Am.), in which the author states:

> While social science has not played a major role in determining the existence of constitutional violations, it has been a more important factor at the remedy stages, where the equitable powers of courts ordinarily afford them a good deal of flexibility in shaping relief. Recent decisions of the Supreme Court, notably Dayton, appear to limit the flexibility to use social science and educational expertise in framing a remedy by applying mechanistic legal formulations even at that stage. (footnote omitted).

See generally, DeVries, Edwards & Slavin, Biracial Learning Teams and Race Relations in the Classroom, 70 J.Educ.Psych. 356 (1978) (substantial increase in cross-friendships among blacks and whites produced by certain teaching techniques); Travis & Anthony, Some Psychological Consequences of Integration, 47 J. Negro Educ. 151, 157–58 (1978) (Although "integration is initially stressful for black students.... [u]ltimate adjustment and emotional health were not jeopardized for black or white students."); Roberts, Mixed Results of Integration Typified in Louisville School, N.Y.

Times, March 16, 1978, at B16, cols. 3–6 (citing in part studies showing higher gains for blacks when integration comes at earlier grades).

10.   Arguments Before the Court, Capital Punishment, The United States Law Week, volume 40, no. 28, January 25, 1972:

Mr. Justice Douglas: "Is there anything in this record to show the people on whom the death penalty is usually imposed—by income or anything such as that?"

Mr. Amsterdam: "There are published materials, such as the racial studies, that I think are judicially noticeable."

Mr. Justice Douglas: "Is there anything in the Georgia record that indicates what kind of people Georgia executes?"

The answer is plain from the statistics, counsel [for defendant] replied: "It is that Georgia executes black people." He explained that anti-capital punishment lawyers had been asking for evidentiary hearings on the statistical question for a long time, and that no court has ever consented. Of course, he added, we are very unsatisfied with the factual record in all these cases.

Mr. Justice Rehnquist wanted to know why Mr. Amsterdam thought his figures were judicially noticeable and the state figures not.

Counsel explained that the state's figures are all from confidential state corrections department statistics.

Studies that are judicially noticeable are those that have been in the public domain long enough to be commented upon, criticized, and evaluated.

In McCleskey v. Kemp, 481 U.S. 279 (1987), the Supreme Court rejected powerful statistical proof of the impact of capital punishment on Black defendants as a basis for outlawing capital punishment. No purposeful discrimination was shown, the court held. What policy—whether or not based upon judicial notice—distinguishes this case of statistical data from that in jury, job, and school desegregation cases?

11.   At the trial level, avoidance of some of the pitfalls of extensive judicial notice of scientific data by the courts has been suggested through: 1) greater reliance on experts, especially court appointed, see discussion of expert testimony infra, and references to special masters; 2) use of special science magistrates; 3) court advisors; 4) use of expert jurys; 5) specialized courts; 6) reference to science courts; 7) use of a scientific expert as an aide to the judge; and 8) use of the issue resolver. See e.g., J.D. Nyhart, J.A. Meldman, D.J. Gilbert, The Use of Scientific and Technical Evidence in Formal Judicial Proceedings, 41 (1977) (multilith). Assuming that the fact finding and normative issues can be separated, what are the advantages and disadvantages of such procedures? Need the procedures be the same at the appellate, trial, pretrial, office settlement, administrative and house counsel decision making levels?

Compare Horowitz, Overcoming Barriers to the Use of Applied Social Research in the Courts, in The Use/Nonuse/Misuse of Applied Social Research in the Courts 149 (1980):

This leaves the question of the adversary process and the use of experts. It is in that realm that most proposals for innovation have come— for social science masters; for social science staffs; for the use of dispassionate third-party experts, either ad hoc or on a continuing basis.

I am wary of these proposals. The beauty of the judicial process is that the judge himself actually decides. Where else does that happen in government these days? I am afraid that, by creating bodies of social science experts, we will tend to take the decision out of the hands of the judges, not formally, not officially, but tacitly and incrementally. I think the judges will have a strong tendency to defer to those social scientists whom they appoint to positions, if judges do the appointing, or to their organizational colleagues, if backup institutions are created.

In short, I think the problem with the adversary method of handling social science issues is the fact that it is both partisan and inconclusive, and the judge is left without a reliable answer; he is left with a choice between two polar positions. But the defects of proposals to find objective expertise may well be the opposite of this. Their perhaps too conclusive character, because of the deference factor that I mentioned, and their propensity for undercutting the participation of the parties in the decision-making process are two of their major problems. The availability of objective expertise, if that is what it is to be called, raises the possibility that the judge may refer to the objective expertise without the participation of the parties. That would be a fundamental alteration in our adversary system. If we are going to make it, we should first consider carefully the pros and cons of the adversary process, not merely in cases where social science is relevant but across the board.

If we do want to create a repository of specialized social science wisdom, I think perhaps the best approach is to integrate it into the adversary process, make sure that the parties have access to social science resources (a resource center, for example), and permit the parties to develop the material rather than encourage the judge to do so. If, on top of that, the rules of evidence are suitably altered to reduce judicial reliance on the expert witness and increase reliance on the studies themselves, the judge may be in a much better position to check the accuracy and the good sense of what the experts and the parties that hired them have said. This may well be the best that can be expected in a rather messy situation.

I am also wary of creating bodies of outside experts for the courts to call upon rather than merely for the parties to use, because those experts create the possibility of institutional rather than individually accountable decisions. Moreover, their very availability may increase the attention given to recurrent patterns and broad policies at the expense of what I take to be the generally commendable attention currently given to individual claims and grievances. The rules of evidence and the institutions for getting evidence before the judge have, in the end, substantive consequences.

Nevertheless, courts frequently resort to data of the United States Census Bureau. See opinion of Douglas, J. in Bell v. Maryland, 378 U.S. 226, 242 (1964). Is there any difference between census reports and other types of surveys? Do any other policies in the field of evidence come into play in determining what is admissible? See Zeisel, The Uniqueness of Survey Evidence, 45 Cornell L.Q. 322 (1960); 1 Moore's Federal Practice, Manual on Complex Litigation, ¶ 2.712 (2d ed. 1979):

Second Recommendation: Scientifically designed samples and polls meeting the tests of necessity and trustworthiness, are useful adjuncts to conventional methods of proof and may contribute materially to shortening the trial of the complex case.

Briggs v. Elliott

Supreme Court of the United States, October Term, 1952.
Transcript of Argument December 9, 10, 1952.[1]

Marshall for appellants

We are saying that there is a denial of equal protection of the laws [by state laws requiring segregation in the public schools]. [W]e produced expert witnesses. Appellees in their brief comment that they do not think too much of them. I do not think that the District Court thought too much of them. But they stand in the record as unchallenged as experts in their field. Dr. Redfield's testimony was to this effect, that there were no recognizable differences from a racial standpoint between children. [T]hat given a similar learning situation, a Negro child and a white child would tend to do about the same thing. [T]he state has made no effort up to this date to show any basis for that classification other than that it would be unwise to do otherwise.

Witnesses testified that segregation deterred the development of the personalities of these children. Two witnesses testified that it deprives them of equal status in the school community, that it destroys their self-respect. Two other witnesses testified that it denies them full opportunity for democratic social development. Another witness said that it stamps him with a badge of inferiority. [O]ne witness, Dr. Kenneth Clark, examined the appellants in this very case and found that they were injured as a result of this segregation.

Davis for respondents

I want to say something about the evidence offered by the plaintiffs upon which counsel so confidently relied.

I see that the evidence offered by the plaintiffs, be its merit what it may, deals entirely with legislative policy, and does not tread on constitutional right. Whether it does or not, it would be difficult for me to conceal my opinion that that evidence in and of itself is of slight weight and in conflict with the opinion of other and better informed sources.

I am tempted to digress, because I am discussing the weight and pith of this testimony, which is the reliance of the plaintiffs here to turn back this enormous weight of legislative and judicial precedent on this subject. I may have been unfortunate, or I may have been careless, but it seems to me that much of that which is handed around under the name of social science is an effort on the part of the scientist to rationalize his own preconceptions. They find usually, in my limited observation, what they go out to find.

Now, these learned witnesses do not have the whole field to themselves. They do not speak without contradiction from other sources. We quote in our brief—I suppose it is not testimony, but it is quotable material, and we are content to adopt it—Dr. Odum, of North Carolina, who is perhaps the foremost investigator of educational questions in the entire South; Dr. Frank Graham, former president of the University of North Carolina; ex-Governor Darden, president of the University of Virginia; Hodding Carter, whose recent works on Southern conditions have become classic; Gunnar Myrdal, Swedish scientist employed to investigate the race question for the Rockefeller Foundation; W.E.B. DuBois; Ambrose Caliver; and the witness Crow, who testified in this case, all of them opposing the item that there should be an immediate abolition of segregated schools.

---

1. Reported with Brown v. Board of Education, 347 U.S. 483, 74 S.Ct. 686 (1954). The transcript of the argument has necessarily been cut heavily to emphasize the judicial notice problem. Because of their number, these excisions have not been indicated.

If this question is a judicial question, if it is to be decided on the varying opinions of scholars, students, writers, authorities, and what you will, certainly it cannot be said that the testimony will be all one way. Certainly it cannot be said that a legislature conducting its public schools in accordance with the wishes of its people—it cannot be said that they are acting merely by caprice or by racial prejudice.

Marshall for appellants

[I]f it is true that there is a large body of scientific evidence on the other side, the place to have produced that was in the District Court, and I do not believe that the State of South Carolina is unable to produce such witnesses for financial or other reasons.

Justice Frankfurter: Can we not take judicial notice of writings by people who competently deal with these problems? Can I not take judicial notice of Myrdal's book without having him called as a witness?

Mr. Marshall: Yes, sir. But I think when you take judicial notice of Gunnar Myrdal's book, we have to read the matter, and not take portions out of context. Gunnar Myrdal's whole book is against the argument.

Justice Frankfurter: That is a different point. I am merely going to the point that in these matters this Court takes judicial notice of accredited writings, and it does not have to call the writers as witnesses. How to inform the judicial mind, as you know, is one of the most complicated problems. It is better to have witnesses, but I did not know that we could not read the works of competent writers.

Mr. Marshall: Mr. Justice Frankfurter, I did not say that it was bad. I said that it would have been better if they had produced the witnesses so that we would have had an opportunity to cross-examine and test their conclusions.

For example, the authority of Hodding Carter, the particular article quoted, was a magazine article of a newspaperman answering another newspaperman, and I know of nothing further removed from scientific work than one newspaperman answering another.

I am not trying—

Justice Frankfurter: I am not going to take issue with you on that.

Mr. Marshall: No sir. But it seems to me that in a case like this that the only way that South Carolina, under the test set forth in this case, can sustain that statute is to show that Negroes as Negroes—all Negroes—are different from everybody else.

Justice Frankfurter: Do you think it would make any difference to our problem if this record also contained the testimony of six professors from other institutions who gave contrary or qualifying testimony? Do you think we would be in a different situation?

Mr. Marshall: You would, sir, but I do not believe that there are any experts in the country who would so testify. I know of no scientist that has made any study, whether he be anthropologist or sociologist, who does not admit that segregation harms the child.

Justice Frankfurter: Yes. But what the consequences of the proposed remedy are, is relevant to the problem.

Mr. Marshall: I think, sir, that the consequences of the removal of the remedy are a legislative and not a judicial argument, sir. I rely on Buchanan v. Warley, where this Court said that the solution was not to deprive people of their constitutional rights.

Justice Frankfurter: Then the testimony is irrelevant to the question.

Mr. Marshall: I think the testimony is relevant as to whether or not it is a valid classification. That is on the classification point.

Justice Frankfurter: But the consequences of how you remedy a conceded wrong bear on the question of whether it is a fair classification.

I want to know from you whether I am entitled to take into account, in finally striking this judgment, whether I am entitled to take into account the reservation that Dr. Graham and two others, I believe, made in their report to the President. May I take that into account?

Mr. Marshall: Yes, sir.

Justice Frankfurter: May I weigh that?

Mr. Marshall: Yes, sir.

Justice Frankfurter: Then you have competent consideration without any testimony.

NOTES

1. The appellants in Brown v. Board of Education, submitted an appendix with their briefs entitled: "The Effects of Segregation and the Consequences of Desegregation: A Social Science Statement" (reprinted in 37 Minn.L.Rev. 427 (1953)). Did the Justices of the Supreme Court inform themselves by relying on this statement or on the testimony in the lower courts or on their own general knowledge? See Brown v. Board of Education, 347 U.S. 483, 493–96, especially footnotes 10 and 11 (1954); Kohn, Social Psychological Data, Legislative Fact, and Constitutional Law, 29 Geo.Wash.L.Rev. 136 (1960); Cahn, Jurisprudence, in Annual Survey of American Law, 809, 816–27 (1954).

Were the famous footnotes 10 and 11 designed to dress up the opinion by showing that the court had done some research? See Kaplan, Segregation, Litigation and the Schools, 58 Nw.U.L.Rev. 157, 172–73 (1963); Black, The Lawfulness of the Segregation Decisions, 69 Yale L.J. 421, 430, n. 25 (1960).

Extensive historical briefs on the legislative history of the 14th Amendment and a brief by sociologists were also submitted in the Brown case. Cf. Bell v. Maryland, 378 U.S. 226, 286 (1964) (Goldberg concurring) (resort to legislative history in construing the purpose of amendment to the Constitution); Fullilove v. Klutznick, 448 U.S. 448, 503, 504 (1980) (action to have "minority business enterprise" provision of Public Works Employment Act of 1977 declared in violation of the Equal Protection Clause because it requires that at least 10% of federal funds granted for local public works projects be used to procure services or supplies from businesses owned by minorities) (Powell, J., Concurring):

Congress is not an adjudicatory body called upon to resolve specific disputes between competing adversaries. Its constitutional role is to be representative rather than impartial, to make policy rather than to apply settled principles of law. The petitioners' contention that this Court should treat the debates on § 103(f)(2) as the complete "record" of congressional decisionmaking underlying that statute is essentially a plea that we treat Congress as if it were a lower federal court. But Congress is not expected to act as though it were duty bound to find facts and make conclusions of law. The creation of national rules for the governance of our society simply does not entail the same concept of recordmaking that is appropriate to a judicial or administrative proceeding. Congress has no responsibility to confine its vision to the facts and evidence adduced by particular parties. Instead, its special attribute as a legislative body lies in its broader mission to investigate and consider all facts and opinions that may be relevant to the resolution of an issue. One appropriate source is the information and expertise that Congress acquires in the consideration and enactment of earlier legislation. After Congress has legislated repeatedly in an area of national concern, its members gain experience that may reduce the need for fresh hearings or prolonged debate when Congress again considers action in that area.

Acceptance of petitioners' argument would force Congress to make specific factual findings with respect to each legislative action. Such a requirement would mark an unprecedented imposition of adjudicatory procedures upon a coordinate branch of Government. Neither the Constitution nor our democratic tradition warrants such a constraint on the legislative process. I therefore conclude that we are not confined in this case to an examination of the legislative history of § 103(f)(2) alone. Rather, we properly may examine the total contemporary record of congressional action dealing with the problems of racial discrimination against minority business enterprises.

B

In my view, the legislative history of § 103(f)(2) demonstrates that Congress reasonably concluded that private and governmental discrimination had contributed to the negligible percentage of public contracts awarded minority contractors.

2. Were the parties in Briggs v. Elliott asking the court to take judicial notice of facts for the purpose of proving or disproving a proposition of fact which was in issue—i.e., negro and white schools did not give equally valuable educations—or for the purpose of changing the rule of law—i.e., segregated schools were unconstitutional? Does it make any difference? How did the court use judicial notice?

Compare United States v. Dallas County Commission, 739 F.2d 1529 (11th Cir.1984), holding it error for the district court to have taken notice of Black voting apathy as an explanation of failure of Blacks to be elected. On a retrial, how would this problem be solved by the litigants?

Michael M. v. Superior Court of Sonoma County

Supreme Court of the United States, 1981.
450 U.S. 464, 101 S.Ct. 1200, 67 L.Ed.2d 437.

■ JUSTICE REHNQUIST announced the judgment of the Court and delivered an opinion in which THE CHIEF JUSTICE, JUSTICE STEWART, and JUSTICE POWELL joined.

The question presented in this case is whether California's "statutory rape" law, § 261.5 of the California Penal Code, violates the Equal Protection clause of the Fourteenth Amendment. Section 261.5 defines unlawful sexual intercourse as "an act of sexual intercourse accomplished with a female not the wife of the perpetrator, where the female is under the age of 18 years." The statute thus makes men alone criminally liable for the act of sexual intercourse.

In July 1978, a complaint was filed in the Municipal Court of Sonoma County, Cal., alleging that petitioner, then a 17½ year old male, had had unlawful sexual intercourse with a female under the age of 18, in violation of § 261.5. The evidence adduced at a preliminary hearing showed that at approximately midnight on June 3, 1978, petitioner and two friends approached Sharon, a 16½ year old female, and her sister as they waited at a bus stop. Petitioner and Sharon who had already been drinking, moved away from the others and began to kiss. After being struck in the face for rebuffing petitioner's initial advances, Sharon submitted to sexual intercourse with petitioner. Prior to trial petitioner sought to set aside the information on both state and federal constitutional grounds, asserting that § 261.5 unlawfully discriminated on the basis of gender. The trial court and the California Court of Appeal denied petitioner's request for relief and petitioner sought review in the Supreme Court of California.

The Supreme Court held that "Section 261.5 discriminates on the basis of sex because only females may be victims, and only males may violate the section." The court then subjected the classification to "strict scrutiny," stating that it must be justified by a compelling state interest. It found that the classification was "supported not by mere social convention but by the immutable physiological fact that it is the female exclusively who can become pregnant." Canvassing "the tragic human cost of illegitimate teenage pregnancies," including the large number of teenage abortions, the increased medical risk associated with teenage pregnancies, and the social consequences of teenage child bearing, the court concluded that the state has a compelling interest in preventing such pregnancies. Because males alone can "physiologically cause the result which the law properly seeks to avoid" the court further held that the gender classification was readily justified as a means of identifying offender and victim. For the reasons stated below, we affirm the judgment of the California Supreme Court.

As is evident from our opinions, the Court has had some difficulty in agreeing upon the proper approach and analysis in cases involving challenges to gender-based classifications. The issues posed by such challenges range from issues of standing, see Orr v. Orr, 440 U.S. 268, 99 S.Ct. 1102, 59 L.Ed.2d 306 (1979) to the appropriate standard of judicial review for the substantive classification. . . .

[T]he principle is that a legislature may not "make overbroad generalizations based on sex which are entirely unrelated to any differences between men and women or which demean the ability or social status of the affected class." Parham v. Hughes, 441 U.S. 347, 354, 99 S.Ct. 1742, 60 L.Ed.2d 269 (1979) (Stewart, J. plurality). But because the Equal Protection Clause does not "demand that a statute necessarily apply equally to all persons" or require "things which are different in fact . . . to be treated in law as though they were the same," Rinaldi v. Yeager, 384 U.S. 305, 309, 86 S.Ct. 1497, 1499, 16 L.Ed.2d 577 (1966) quoting Tigner v. Texas, 310 U.S. 141, 147, 60 S.Ct. 879, 882, 84 L.Ed. 1124 (1940) this Court has consistently upheld statutes where the gender classification is not invidious, but rather realistically reflects the fact that the sexes are not similarly situated in certain circumstances. . . . As the Court has stated, a legislature may "provide for the special problems of women." Weinberger v. Wiesenfeld, 420 U.S. 636, 653, 95 S.Ct. 1225, 1236, 43 L.Ed.2d 514 (1975).

Applying those principles to this case, the fact that the California Legislature criminalized the act of illicit sexual intercourse with a minor female is a sure indication of its intent or purpose to discourage that conduct. Precisely why the legislature desired that result is of course somewhat less clear. This Court has long recognized that "inquiries into congressional motives or purposes are a hazardous matter." United States v. O'Brien, 391 U.S. 367, 383–384, 88 S.Ct. 1673, 1682–1683, 20 L.Ed.2d 672 (1968); Palmer v. Thompson,

403 U.S. 217, 224, 91 S.Ct. 1940, 1944, 29 L.Ed.2d 438 (1971), and the search for the "actual" or "primary" purpose of a statute is likely to be elusive. . . . Here, for example, the individual legislators may have voted for the statute for a variety of reasons. Some legislators may have been concerned about preventing teenage pregnancies, others about protecting young females from physical injury or from the loss of "chastity," and still others about promoting various religious and moral attitudes towards premarital sex.

The justification for the statute offered by the State and accepted by the Supreme Court of California, is that the legislature sought to prevent illegitimate teenage pregnancies. That finding, of course, is entitled to great deference. Reitman v. Mulkey, 387 U.S. 369, 373–374, 87 S.Ct. 1627, 1629–1630, 18 L.Ed.2d 830 (1967). And although our cases establish that the State's asserted reason for the enactment of a statute may be rejected, "if it could not have been a goal of the legislation," Weinberger v. Wiesenfeld, supra, at 648, n. 16, 95 S.Ct. at 1233, this is not such a case.

We are satisfied not only that the prevention of illegitimate pregnancy is at least one of the "purposes" of the statute, but that the State has a strong interest in preventing such pregnancy. At the risk of stating the obvious, teenage pregnancies, which have increased dramatically over the last two decades,[1] have significant social, medical and economic consequences for both the mother and her child, and the State.[2] Of particular concern to the State is that approximately half of all teenage pregnancies end in abortion.[3] And of those children who are born, their illegitimacy makes them likely candidates to become wards of the State.[4]

We need not be medical doctors to discern that young men and young women are not similarly situated with respect to the problems and the risks of

---

1. In 1976 approximately one million 15–19 year olds became pregnant, one-tenth of all women in that age group. Two-thirds of the pregnancies were illegitimate. Illegitimacy rates for teenagers (births per 1,000 unmarried females ages) increased 75% for 14–17 year olds between 1961 and 1974 and 33% for 18–19 year olds. Alan Guttmacher Institute, 11 Million Teenagers 10, 13 (1976); C. Chilman, Adolescent Sexuality In A Changing American Society, 195 (NIH Pub. No. 80-1426, 1980). [Some footnotes omitted; others renumbered; footnotes by the Court.]

2. The risk of maternal death is 60% higher for a teenager under the age of 15 than for a woman in her early twenties. The risk is 13% higher for 15–19 year olds. The statistics further show that most teenage mothers drop out of school and face a bleak economic future. See, e.g., 11 Million Teenagers, supra, at 23, 25; Bennett & Bardon, The Effects of a School Program On Teenager Mother And Their Children, 47 Am.J. of Orthopsychiatry 671 (1977); Phipps–Yonas, Teenage Pregnancy and Motherhood, 50 Am.J. of Orthopsychiatry 403, 414 (1980).

3. This is because teenagers are disproportionately likely to seek abortions. Center for Disease Control, Abortion Surveillance 1976, 22–24 (1978). In 1978, for example, teenagers in California had approximately 54,000 abortions and 53,800 live births. California Center for Health Statistics, Reproductive Health Status of California Teenage Women 1, 23 (1980).

4. The policy and intent of the California Legislature evinced in other legislation buttresses our view that the prevention of teenage pregnancy is a purpose of the statute. The preamble to the "Maternity Care for Minors Act," for example, states "The legislature recognizes that pregnancy among unmarried persons under 21 years of age constitutes an increasing social problem in California." Cal. Welfare & Inst.Code § 16145 (West Supp.1979).

Subsequent to the decision below, the California Legislature considered and rejected proposals to render § 261.5 gender neutral, thereby ratifying the judgment of the California Supreme Court. That is enough to answer petitioner's contention that the statute was the "accidental by product of a traditional way of thinking about women." Califano v. Webster, 430 U.S. 313, 320, 97 S.Ct. 1192, 1196, 51 L.Ed.2d 360 (1977) (quoting Califano v. Goldfarb, 430 U.S. 199, 223, 97 S.Ct. 1021, 1035, 51 L.Ed.2d 270 (1977) (Stevens, J., concurring)). Certainly this decision of the California Legislature is as good a source as is this Court in deciding what is "current" and what is "outmoded" in the perception of women.

sexual intercourse. Only women may become pregnant and they suffer disproportionately the profound physical, emotional, and psychological consequences of sexual activity. The statute at issue here protects women from sexual intercourse at an age when those consequences are particularly severe.[5]

The question thus boils down to whether a State may attack the problem of sexual intercourse and teenage pregnancy directly by prohibiting a male from having sexual intercourse with a minor female.[6] We hold that such a statute is sufficiently related to the State's objectives to pass constitutional muster.

Because virtually all of the significant harmful and inescapably identifiable consequences of teenage pregnancy fall on the young female, a legislature acts well within its authority when it elects to punish only the participant who, by nature, suffers few of the consequences of his conduct. It is hardly unreasonable for a legislature acting to protect minor females to exclude them from punishment. Moreover, the risk of pregnancy itself constitutes a substantial deterrence to young females. No similar natural sanctions deter males. A criminal sanction imposed solely on males thus serves to roughly "equalize" the deterrents on the sexes.

We are unable to accept petitioner's contention that the statute is impermissibly underinclusive and must, in order to pass judicial scrutiny, be broadened so as to hold the female as criminally liable as the male. It is argued that this statute is not necessary to deter teenage pregnancy because a gender-neutral statute, where both male and female would be subject to prosecution, would serve that goal equally well. The relevant inquiry, however, is not

---

5. Although petitioner concedes that the State has a "compelling" interest in preventing teenage pregnancy, he contends that the "true" purpose of § 261.5 is to protect the virtue and chastity of young women. As such, the statute is unjustifiable because it rests on archaic stereotypes. What we have said above is enough to dispose of that contention. The question for us—and the only question under the Federal Constitution—is whether the legislation violates the Equal Protection Clause of the Fourteenth Amendment, not whether its supporters may have endorsed it for reasons no longer generally accepted. Even if the preservation of female chastity were one of the motives of the statute, and even if that motive be impermissible, petitioner's argument must fail because "it is a familiar practice of constitutional law that this court will not strike down an otherwise constitutional statute on the basis of an alleged illicit legislative motive." United States v. O'Brien, 391 U.S. 367, 383, 88 S.Ct. 1673, 1682, 20 L.Ed.2d 672 (1968). In Orr v. Orr, 440 U.S. 268, 99 S.Ct. 1102, 59 L.Ed.2d 306 (1979), for example, the Court rejected one asserted purpose as impermissible, but then considered other purposes to determine if they could justify the statute. Similarly, in Washington v. Davis, 426 U.S. 229, 243, 96 S.Ct. 2040, 2049, 48 L.Ed.2d 597 (1976) the Court distinguished Palmer v. Thompson, 403 U.S. 217, 91 S.Ct. 1940, 29 L.Ed.2d 438 (1971), on the grounds that the purposes of the ordinance there were not open to impeachment by evidence that the legislature

was actually motivated by an impermissible purpose. See also Arlington Heights v. Metropolitan Housing Corp., 429 U.S. 252, 270, n. 21, 97 S.Ct. 555, 566, 50 L.Ed.2d 450 (1977); Mobile v. Bolden, 446 U.S. 55, 91, 100 S.Ct. 1490, 1508, 64 L.Ed.2d 47 (1980) (Stevens, J., concurring).

6. We do not understand petitioner to question a state's authority to make sexual intercourse among teenagers a criminal act, at least on a gender-neutral basis. In Carey v. Population Services International, 431 U.S. 678, 694, n. 17, 97 S.Ct. 2010, 2021, 52 L.Ed.2d 675 (1977) (Brennan, J., plurality), four Members of the Court assumed for the purposes of that case that a State may regulate the sexual behavior of minors, while four other Members of the Court more emphatically stated that such regulation would be permissible. Id., at 702, 703, 97 S.Ct., at 2025, 2026 (White, J., concurring); Id., at 705–707, 709, 97 S.Ct., at 2026–2028, 2029 (Powell, J., concurring); Id., at 713, 97 S.Ct., at 2030–2031 (Stevens, J., concurring); Id., at 718, 97 S.Ct., at 2033 (Rehnquist, J., dissenting). The Court has long recognized that a State has even broader authority to protect the physical, mental, and moral well-being of its youth, than of its adults. See e.g., Planned Parenthood of Missouri v. Danforth, 428 U.S. 52, 72–74, 96 S.Ct. 2831, 2842–2843, 49 L.Ed.2d 788 (1976); Ginsberg v. New York, 390 U.S. 629, 639–640, 88 S.Ct. 1274, 1280–1281, 20 L.Ed.2d 195 (1968); Prince v. Massachusetts, 321 U.S. 158, 170, 64 S.Ct. 438, 444, 88 L.Ed. 645 (1944).

whether the statute is drawn as precisely as it might have been, but whether the line chosen by the California Legislature is within constitutional limitations. Kahn v. Shevin, 416 U.S., at 356, n. 10, 94 S.Ct., at 1737–1738.

In any event, we cannot say that a gender-neutral statute would be as effective as the statute California has chosen to enact. The State persuasively contends that a gender-neutral statute would frustrate its interest in effective enforcement. Its view is that a female is surely less likely to report violations of the statute if she herself would be subject to criminal prosecution. In an area already fraught with prosecutorial difficulties, we decline to hold that the Equal Protection Clause requires a legislature to enact a statute so broad that it may well be incapable of enforcement.

We similarly reject petitioner's argument that § 261.5 is impermissibly overbroad because it makes unlawful sexual intercourse with prepubescent females, who are, by definition, incapable of becoming pregnant. Quite apart from the fact that the statute could well be justified on the grounds that very young females are particularly susceptible to physical injury from sexual intercourse, see Rundlett v. Oliver, 607 F.2d 495 (C.A.1 1979), it is ludicrous to suggest that the Constitution requires the California Legislature to limit the scope of its rape statute to older teenagers and exclude young girls.

There remains only petitioner's contention that the statute is unconstitutional as it is applied to him because he, like Sharon, was under 18 at the time of sexual intercourse. Petitioner argues that the statute is flawed because it presumes that as between two persons under 18, the male is the culpable aggressor. We find petitioner's contentions unpersuasive. Contrary to his assertions, the statute does not rest on the assumption that males are generally the aggressors. It is instead an attempt by a legislature to prevent illegitimate teenage pregnancy by providing an additional deterrent for men. The age of the man is irrelevant since young men are as capable as older men of inflicting the harm sought to be prevented.

In upholding the California statute we also recognize that this is not a case where a statute is being challenged on the grounds that it "invidiously discriminates" against females. To the contrary, the statute places a burden on males which is not shared by females. But we find nothing to suggest that men, because of past discrimination or peculiar disadvantages, are in need of the special solicitude of the courts. Nor is this a case where the gender classification is made "solely ... for administrative convenience," as in Frontiero v. Richardson, 411 U.S. 677, 690, 93 S.Ct. 1764, 1772, 36 L.Ed.2d 583 (1973) or rests on "the baggage of sexual stereotypes" as in Orr v. Orr, 440 U.S. 268, 283, 99 S.Ct. 1102, 1114, 59 L.Ed.2d 306 (1979). As we have held, the statute instead reasonably reflects the fact that the consequences of sexual intercourse and pregnancy fall more heavily on the female than on the male.

Accordingly, the judgment of the California Supreme Court is affirmed.

Affirmed.

[concurring opinions omitted]

.   .   .

■ JUSTICE BRENNAN, with whom JUSTICES WHITE and MARSHALL join, dissenting.

.   .   .

[T]here are at least two serious flaws in the State's assertion that law enforcement problems created by a gender-neutral statutory rape law would make such a statute less effective than a gender-based statute in deterring sexual activity.

First, the experience of other jurisdictions, and California itself, belies the plurality's conclusion that a gender-neutral statutory rape law "may well be incapable of enforcement." There are now at least 37 States that have enacted gender-neutral statutory rape laws. Although most of these laws protect young persons (of either sex) from the sexual exploitation of older individuals, the laws of Arizona, Florida, and Illinois permit prosecution of both minor females and minor males for engaging in mutual sexual conduct. California has introduced no evidence that those states have been handicapped by the enforcement problems the plurality finds so persuasive. Surely, if those States could provide such evidence, we might expect that California would have introduced it.

In addition, the California Legislature in recent years has revised other sections of the Penal Code to make them gender-neutral. For example, Cal.Penal Code §§ 286(b)(1) and 288a(b)(1), prohibiting sodomy and oral copulation with a "person who is under 18 years of age," could cause two minor homosexuals to be subjected to criminal sanctions for engaging in mutually consensual conduct. Again, the State has introduced no evidence to explain why a gender-neutral statutory rape law would be any more difficult to enforce than those statutes.

The second flaw in the State's assertion is that even assuming that a gender-neutral statute would be more difficult to enforce, the State has still not shown that those enforcement problems would make such a statute less effective than a gender-based statute in deterring minor females from engaging in sexual intercourse. Common sense, however, suggests that a gender-neutral statutory rape law is potentially a greater deterrent of sexual activity than a gender-based law, for the simple reason that a gender-neutral law subjects both men and women to criminal sanctions and thus arguably has a deterrent effect on twice as many potential violators. Even if fewer persons were prosecuted under the gender-neutral law, as the State suggests, it would still be true that twice as many persons would be subject to arrest. The State's failure to prove that a gender-neutral law would be a less effective deterrent than a gender-based law, like the State's failure to prove that a gender-neutral law would be difficult to enforce, should have led this Court to invalidate § 261.5.

■ JUSTICE STEVENS, dissenting.

Local custom and belief—rather than statutory laws of venerable but doubtful ancestry—will determine the volume of sexual activity among unmarried teenagers. The empirical evidence cited by the plurality demonstrates the futility of the notion that a statutory prohibition will significantly affect the volume of that activity or provide a meaningful solution to the problems created by it. Nevertheless, as a matter of constitutional power, ... I would have no doubt about the validity of a state law prohibiting all unmarried teenagers from engaging in sexual intercourse. The societal interests in reducing the incidence of venereal disease and teenage pregnancy are sufficient, in my judgment, to justify a prohibition of conduct that increases the risk of those harms. ...I respectfully dissent.

NOTES

1. In how many ways did the judges take judicial notice in the main case? Was it possible for the court to have decided the case without extensive judicial notice? How was the court informed? See also the extensive notice of statutory and historical data in Roe v. Wade, 410 U.S. 113 (1973) (abortion); Bowers v.

Hardwick, 478 U.S. 186 (1986) (homosexual sodomy). Note the court's taking judicial notice of what Congress might have found in United States v. Jessup, 757 F.2d 378 (1st Cir.1985), supra.

In sex discrimination cases courts often look to pertinent legislative facts to determine whether a particular classification meets the appropriate constitutional standard. See also Stanton v. Stanton, 421 U.S. 7, 15 (1975) (issue was whether it was constitutional to permit a parent to support a son longer than a daughter on the basis of a statute establishing a greater age of majority for males. One factor considered by the court was that "[t]he presence of women in business, in the professions, in government and, indeed, in all walks of life where education is a desirable, if not always a necessary antecedent, is apparent and a proper subject of judicial notice"); Carey v. Population Services International, 431 U.S. 678 (1977) (in the context of a constitutional challenge of a law prohibiting the distribution of contraceptives to minors under 16, the court, although not relying on the scientific studies, took judicial notice of studies that indicated that limiting access to contraceptives will not discourage early sexual behavior).

2. It was once thought that the only facts usable as a basis for determining the validity of a statute attacked as violating the Fourteenth Amendment were those judicially noticeable, but as the principal case shows that notion has now gone by the boards, and the courts will consider any evidence upon which the legislature could have relied. See also Denman, Comment on Trials of Fact in Constitutional Cases, 21 A.B.A.J. 805 (1935); Notes, 49 Harv.L.Rev. 631 (1936); 61 id. 692 (1948). The same may be true as to an administrative tribunal acting in a legislative capacity. See N.L.R.B. v. Seven–Up Bottling Co., 344 U.S. 344 (1953); Republic Aviation Corp. v. N.L.R.B., 324 U.S. 793 (1945); Roberts, Preliminary Notes Toward a Study of Judicial Notice, 52 Cornell L.Q. 210, 233 (1967):

> Courts seen as super legislatures must be allowed to roam far and wide and must at all costs, not be inhibited by any requirement that the facts with which they deal must be either found in the record or attributable to common knowledge or sources of indisputable accuracy. The law, in short, must be seen as a creative process and the rules of judicial notice recast to expedite this creativity.

See also, Chayes, The Role of the Judge in Public Law Litigation, 89 Harv. L.Rev. 1281, 1316 (1976) ("Perhaps the most important consequence of the inevitably exposed position of the judiciary in our contemporary regulatory state is that it will force us to confront more explicitly the qualities of wisdom, viability, responsiveness to human needs—the justice—of judicial decisions."); Weinstein, Equality, Liberty, and the Public Schools, 48 U.Cin.L.Rev. 203, 205–06 (1979) (footnotes omitted):

> If we are to improve the probability of making decisions that will do more good than harm and that will be consistent with societal goals, our discretion must be informed not only by the details of the case but also by the historic currents of our society. Trial judges, no less than appellate judges, legislators, executives or bureaucrats, must analyze the policies they enforce. . . .

> Obviously, since the judge does not begin each case by forgetting all he has ever known, he will bring misconceptions, biases and gaps of knowledge to each dispute.

Metromedia, Inc., v. San Diego, 453 U.S. 490 (1981) (In deciding whether an ordinance which imposed substantial prohibitions on the erection of billboards was justified as a comprehensive commitment to making the physical environment in commercial and industrial areas more attractive the Supreme Court noted: "Of course, it is not for a court to impose its own notion of beauty on San Diego. But before deferring to a city's judgment, a court must be convinced that the city is seriously and comprehensively addressing aesthetic concerns with respect to its environment.").

3. How much does the scope and nature of judicial proof depend upon what the court conceives its role to be in settling disputes and laying down guidelines for the future? Cf. State Commission for Human Rights v. Farrell, 43 Misc.2d 958, 960, 252 N.Y.S.2d 649, 652 (1964) in which the court had before it the question of how to enforce an administrative determination that a union had discriminated against minorities in operating its apprenticeship program. It informed itself of the problems in extensive informal hearings with the parties, declaring:

> The court approaches this matter not simply as litigation between private parties, but rather views the instant proceedings as raising vital matters filled with greatest public concern. The issue herein, involving the development of nondiscriminatory shop training programs cannot be approached strictly within the conventional confines of an adversary proceeding. The people of this State, as well as groups throughout the country, are searching for guidelines in the handling of this volatile problem. To the end, the court enlisted the cooperation of the parties....

Chayes, The Role of the Judge in Public Law Litigation, 89 Harv.L.Rev. 1281, 1297 (1976) ("In public law litigation, ... factfinding is principally concerned with 'legislative' rather than 'adjudicative' fact. And 'fact evaluation' is perhaps a more accurate term than 'fact-finding.' The whole process begins to look like the traditional description of legislation...." (footnotes omitted).

4. Should courts take notice of current political trends? See Weinstein, The Effect of Austerity on Institutional Litigation, 6 Law and Human Behaviour 145, 150 (1982):

> In a society of finite resources, one can seldom feed Peter better without taking from Paul. And, of course, as resources become scarcer, the decision to transfer resources becomes increasingly difficult. System-reform litigation has always been criticized for involving judges in a process of resource allocation that is essentially legislative. As a theoretical matter, there are some arguments to refute this criticism, but as the pressures of the troubled economy continue to build, and the country swings towards the right, practical concerns will force the courts to consider even more critically the potential effects of sweeping decrees.

See also N.Y. Times, July 29, 1981, at 1, col. 1 ("The general trend all over the state is to put people in jail.... It's the get-tough policy that judges are picking up from their local populations.").

When a court decision implements current political trends or, in construing existing legislation, brings legislative facts up-to-date, is the court making law? E.g., United States v. Jacobs, 547 F.2d 772 (2d Cir.1976), cert. dismissed, 436 U.S. 31 (1978) (appellate court canvassed each United States Attorney in the circuit regarding practice of warning a potential defendant appearing before a grand jury that he was a target). Is judicial lawmaking an intrusion on the legislative role? See Tribe, Seven Pluralist Fallacies: In Defense of the Adversary Process—A Reply to Justice Rehnquist, 33 U.Miami L.Rev. 43, 56–57 (1978) ("The courts must stand ready to intervene when no other forum is available for the vindication of fundamental rights—this is the high mission of the American judiciary."). Judicial lawmaking may also serve to fill legislative gaps. But see, Weinstein, The Effect of Austerity on Institutional Litigation, 6 Law and Human Behaviour 145, 151 (1982):

> The message is clear. Those interested in the poor and disadvantaged will be doing a grave disservice to their clients if they rely so heavily on the courts to improve institutions that they fail to utilize other branches of the government in their search for relief. The primary resources are in the hands of the legislatures, the executive and the powerful private groups that exert both political and economic power on the decision-making process.... The courts, at best, are a sensitive conscience, educating us about the constitutional and equitable aspirations of our society, and exerting moderate pressure to move us back when we stray....

The decision on the extent of judicial notice at the appellate level will depend to some extent on the court's view of its role in reviewing trial or administrative determinations. Should judges, upon review of administrative decisions, confine themselves to the monitoring of the procedures of the decision-making process or delve into the technology issues?

Chief Judge David Bazelon of the Court of Appeals for the District of Columbia took a narrow view when he wrote:

> It follows that, in reviewing administrative decisions on scientific issues, it makes no sense to rely upon the courts to evaluate the agency's scientific and technological determinations; and there is perhaps even less reason for the courts to substitute their own value preferences for those of the agency, to which the legislature has presumably delegated the decisional power and responsibility ... what the courts and judges *can* do—and do well when conscious of their role and limitations—is scrutinize and monitor the decision-making process to make sure that it is thorough, complete and rational; that all relevant information has been considered; and that insofar as possible, those who will be affected by a decision have had an opportunity to participate in it.

D.L. Bazelon, Address Before Conference on U.S. Energy Policy, Atomic Industrial Forum, Washington, D.C., January 10, 1977 at 7–8.

A different view was stated by Judge Harold Leventhal in Ethyl Corp. of America v. EPA, 541 F.2d 1, 68–69 (D.C.Cir.1976):

> Our present system of review assumes judges will acquire whatever technical knowledge is necessary as background for decision of the legal questions. It may be that some judges are not initially equipped for this role, just as they may not be technically equipped initially to decide issues of obviousness and infringement in patent cases. If technical difficulties loom large, Congress may push to establish specialized courts. Thus far, it has proceeded on the assumptions that we can both have the important values secured by generalist judges and rely on them to acquire whatever technical background is necessary.... Better no review at all than a charade that gives the imprimatur without the substance of judicial confirmation that the agency is not acting unreasonably.

The differences were expounded further in International Harvester Co. v. Ruckelshaus, 478 F.2d 615, 632 (D.C.Cir.1973). In remanding an EPA decision not to grant a one year suspension on auto emission standards, Judge Leventhal delivered a lengthy economic-environmental risk analysis. His opinion involved examination of the available technology, EPA predictions, assumptions and statistical reliability. Chief Judge Bazelon, in a concurring opinion, avoided the technology questions. He stated:

The court's proper role is to see to it that the agency provides a "framework for principled decision-making." Such a framework, necessarily includes the right of interested parties to confront the agency's decisions and the requirement that the agency set forth with clarity the grounds for its reflection of opposing views.

Judge Edward Tamm recognized these two conflicting viewpoints in Essex Chemical Corp. v. Ruckelshaus, 486 F.2d 427, 434 (D.C.Cir.1973). Before conducting an investigation of the evidence supporting a stationary pollution source regulation, the judge added this statement of reserve:

The judgment of the Administrator is to be weighted against his statutory function and limitations, the record searched to determine if indeed his decisions and reasons therefore are themselves reasoned, and at that point our function terminates. Our expertise is not in setting standards for emission control but in determining if the standards as set are the result of reasoned decision-making. Yet, even this limited function required that we foray into the technical world to the extent necessary to ascertain if the Administrator's decision is reasoned. While we must bow to the acknowledged expertise of the Administrator in matters technical we should not automatically succumb thereto, overwhelmed as it were by the utter "scientificity" of the expedition.

See, generally, J.D. Nyhart, J.A. Meldman, D.J. Gilbert, The Use of Scientific and Technical Evidence in Formal Judicial Proceedings, 6 ff (Sept.1977) (multilith).

What of foreign political issues? See Orantes–Hernandez v. Smith, 541 F.Supp. 351 (C.D.Cal.1982) (court noticed that El Salvador is currently in the midst of a widespread civil war in an immigration case); McDonnell Douglas Corp. v. Islamic Republic of Iran, 758 F.2d 341 (8th Cir.1985) (plaintiff brought a declaratory judgment to relieve it of liability to Iran. Court judicially noticed that forum clause putatively requiring litigation in Iran would in effect deny plaintiff a fair trial); United States v. Salim, 664 F.Supp. 682 (E.D.N.Y.1987) (fairness of French criminal and civil procedure).

5. What legislative facts did the Court in the principal case judicially notice? Compare United States v. Fisher, 2 Cranch 358, 6 U.S. 358, 385 (1805) (Marshall, C.J.) ("Where the mind labours to discover the design of the legislature, it seizes everything from which aid can be derived....") with 3 Davis, Administrative Law Treatise, § 15.9 at 166 (2d ed. 1980):

The judicial notice problem is not whether facts should be noticed. The two problems are (1) whether the noticed facts, in all the circumstances, were inadequate to support the lawmaking, and (2) whether the parties should have had a pre-decision chance to challenge the facts the Court assumed. For a satisfactory system of judicial notice, both questions must be answered. The first question, the more neglected one, may be the more vital.

Worse than assuming facts that have not been proved, worse than using inadequate facts, and worse than using facts that parties have had no pre-decision chance to challenge, is making a decision without needed facts.

Were the facts judicially noticed in the principal case adequate? Is the entire notion of a collective legislative intent artificial? See Radin, Statutory Interpretation, 43 Harv.L.Rev. 863, 872 (1930) (Legislative intent is "a Queerly amorphous piece of slag"). See also Professor Llewellyn's discussion of how a court's sense of situation should affect statutory construction, Llewellyn, Remarks on the Theory of Appellate Decision and the Rules or Canons About How Statutes Are to Be Construed, 3 Vand.L.Rev. 395, 400 (1950):

If a statute is to make sense, it must be read in the light of some assumed purpose. A statute merely declaring a rule, with no purpose or objective, is nonsense.

If a statute is to be merged into a going system of law, moreover, the court must do the merging, and must in so doing take account of the policy of the statute—or else substitute its own version of such policy. Creative reshaping of the net result is thus inevitable.

6. Legislation that is challenged on grounds of violating due process guarantees under the 14th Amendment or similar state constitutional provisions often involves reliance on legislative facts. See, e.g., Johnson v. Opelousas, 488 F.Supp. 433 (W.D.La.1980) (in finding that a curfew ordinance was not repugnant to the 14th Amendment, the court took judicial notice of a rapidly increasing nocturnal crime rate); Flakes v. Percy, 511 F.Supp. 1325 (W.D.Wis. 1981) (court took judicial notice that it is unusual, within institutions in which persons are involuntarily confined, to lock persons into cells in which there are no toilets or sinks and that the right to gain access to such facilities without awaiting permission of the government is close to the core of the liberty guaranteed by the Due Process Clause of the Fourteenth Amendment).

7. Mason, Harlan Fiske Stone: Pillar of the Law, 785 (1956):

Judges might bear their awesome responsibility more easily, Stone believed, if they would recognize the role of the legislature as a coordinate branch of government, empowered, as is the Court, to define social policy, but with broader limits. As his approach was pragmatic, he did not, as he once remarked critically of John Marshall, always see things in "blacks and whites." "Reasonableness," the "weighing of evidence," "accommodation"—the reshaping of our fundamental law in harmony with "that sober second thought of the community"—these are the keys to Stone's theory. In this process it is not enough to lay the statute beside the Constitution or assemble matched judicial precedents. Unlike Sutherland, Stone did not dismiss economic data as "interesting but only mildly persuasive," or as throwing "no legitimate light" on matters which judges need consider. Stone, in fact, criticized lawyers who, like Sutherland, "seem to think it is sufficient to cite our decisions, without placing before us the economic data which would reveal the situation to which constitutional limitations are to be applied." On occasion he and Justice Brandeis accumulated such material—"as the Irishman played the fiddle, by main strength." In 1937 Stone expressed the "need for securing an economic service—a small group of men, who have had some training as economists and statisticians, who would be qualified to assemble material for use of the Court." "I have felt hitherto," he wrote, "that the time was not ripe to advocate the establishment of such a service, but it seems to me the time is now not far away." It would, he said, be of "great assistance in relieving us and our very limited staff from the drudgery. . . ."

C. AUTHORITATIVE DETERMINATION BY NON-JUDICIAL AGENCY

Ren–Guey v. Lake Placid 1980 Olympic Games, Inc.

New York Supreme Court, Appellate Division, 1980.
72 A.D.2d 439, 424 N.Y.S.2d 535, aff'd, 49 N.Y.2d 771, 426 N.Y.S.2d 473, 403 N.E.2d 178.

■ PER CURIAM.

The International Olympic Committee (IOC) governs the Olympic Games and owns the rights to them. The Olympic Charter provides that every person or organization that participates in the Games shall accept the supreme authority of the IOC. The charter gives the IOC complete control over the development and conduct of the Games and makes the IOC the final authority on all questions concerning the Games. The various National Olympic Committees (NOC) are the IOC representatives in their respective countries. The NOC from a given country is not free to define itself. The charter provides that the name of an NOC must reflect the territorial extent and tradition of its country subject to IOC approval. Competing athletes, such as plaintiff, must be affiliated with the NOC of their nation.

The problem of having two Chinas competing in the Olympics has confronted the IOC since 1960, when the IOC required athletes from the Republic of China (Taiwan) to compete under the name "Formosa".[1] At an IOC session in April of 1979, the IOC resolved to allow both Chinas to compete in the 1980 Games. However, the resolution left to the Executive Board of the IOC determinations regarding names, flags, anthems and constitutions. After receiving notification that the United States had withdrawn diplomatic recognition of Taiwan, the Executive Board, at a meeting held October 23 to 25, 1979, adopted a resolution allowing the NOC from the People's Republic of China to use the nation's official flag, anthem and emblem, while changing the name of the Taiwanese NOC and requiring submission of alternatives for the flag, anthem and emblem to be used by the Taiwanese at the Games.

The defendant is a not-for-profit corporation established under New York law to comply with the requirement of the Olympic Charter that the NOC of the host country establish an appropriate entity to serve as a surrogate of the IOC to operate the Games. Plaintiff is an athlete selected by the Taiwanese NOC to participate in the Winter Olympic Games at Lake Placid. In this action he seeks a permanent injunction staying the Games unless defendant allows plaintiff to use the flag, emblem, name and anthem of the Republic of China.

Initially, we grant the motion of the United States Attorney General to file a Statement of Interest of the United States with respect to this matter (28 U.S.Code, Tit. 28, § 517).

Both the plaintiff and Special Term focus on the narrow issue of plaintiff's rights as an individual. In our view, however, the issue is much broader since plaintiff seeks not only to express his own individual political beliefs, but also to carry a flag and wear an emblem symbolic of the country which he represents as a participant in the Games.

The President has the sole power to recognize foreign governments.... Whether a foreign government should be recognized is a political question that neither the United States Supreme Court nor any other American court may review....

The flag is the emblem of national sovereignty.... and since it is inextricably intertwined with the national identity, use of a flag, in an event such as the Olympic Games, creates an issue of sovereign representation. In effect, plaintiff asks this court to compel the defendant, as surrogate of the IOC, to recognize a symbol of national sovereignty. However, by its resolution, the IOC gave only conditional recognition to Taiwan and expressly rejected Taiwan's traditional anthem and flag. Since the Department of State, acting on behalf of the President, has elected to defer to the IOC in matters concerning national

---

1. The Taiwanese did so under protest. In 1976, the Taiwanese were not permitted to use their official name, flag and anthem at the Montreal Summer Olympics.

representation at the Olympics, the issue involved in this appeal is a political question, bound up as it is with difficult questions of foreign policy, and is, therefore, beyond the powers of this court to review.

The motion of the United States Attorney General should be granted, without costs.

The order should be reversed, on the law, without costs, the motion should be denied and the complaint dismissed.

Motion of the United States Attorney General granted, without costs.

Order reversed, on the law, without costs, motion denied and complaint dismissed.

NOTES

1. In a private contract case, should the court be bound by a state department finding? Is the main case one between private parties?

2. When a court obtains information from another branch of the government, the court is often not interested in judicially noticing a fact but rather in getting an authoritative, authentic communication that will dispose of the matter.

Someone alleging that he is acting for the Republic of China sues on an insurance policy. The defendant alleges that the plaintiff does not represent the Chinese government. Can the court judicially notice which of two contenders is the government of the territory known as China? Is this decision one for the executive branch of the government, which, once made known to the court, is not open to question? See Republic of China v. Merchants' Fire Assur. Corp., 30 F.2d 278 (9th Cir.1929), 42 Harv.L.Rev. 959 (1929). See also Republic of Vietnam v. Pfizer, Inc., 556 F.2d 892 (8th Cir.1977) (subsequent to the filing of suit by the Republic of Vietnam, that government surrendered unconditionally to the military forces of North Vietnam and thus became defunct. The new government was not recognized by the United States. The court dismissed the action "on the ground that the plaintiff ... no longer exists in any form recognizable by this Court and has not been succeeded by any government, entity or person that has capacity to sue in this Court." Id. at 894. The court, in refusing to give the new government the necessary recognition, noted, "[t]he recognition of foreign governments is a function of the executive branch and is wholly outside the competence of the judiciary." Id.); and Republic of China v. Pang–Tsu Mow, 101 F.Supp. 646, 648 (D.D.C.1951), aff'd, 201 F.2d 195 (D.C.Cir.1952), cert. denied, 345 U.S. 925 (1953) ("The recognition by the political department of the United States government of a foreign government is conclusive of its legal status as far as the United States Courts are concerned.").

3. Does the same rule apply when the issue is whether a certain government actually controls a given territory? See 9 Wigmore, Evidence § 2575 (Chadbourn rev.1981) and cases cited therein commenting; "although it is difficult to make generalizations, [c]ourts are apt to be extremely liberal in drawing the line so as to favor judicial notice.").

4. To what extent are these decisions explicable by what the courts conceive to be the proper distribution of functions between the judicial and political branches of the Government? See Guerra v. Guajardo, 466 F.Supp. 1046, 1056 (S.D.Tex.1978), aff'd, 597 F.2d 769 (5th Cir.1979) (footnotes omitted):

. . .

A case before a federal court involving a political question presents a nonjusticiable issue. The origin of the political question is found in the constitutional separation of powers among the three branches of government ... There are instances where the resolution of an issue revolves about standards that are incapable of judicial application or where the exercise of discretion is patently entrusted to the Executive or Legislative Branches. Such discretion is beyond the competence of the courts to decide....

When a court is forced to delve into foreign policy considerations which have already been considered by the Executive Branch with information both unobtainable to the courts and confidential, it must defer to the President's judgment. See, e.g., Chicago & Southern Air Lines, Inc. v. Waterman Steamship Corp., 333 U.S. 103, 114 (1948) (Presidential approval of overseas air transportation certificate of convenience); Occidential of Umm al Qaywayn, Inc., supra, (tortious conversion of oil suit involving a resolution of territorial disputes between sovereigns); Dole v. Carter, 569 F.2d 1109, 1110 (10th Cir.1977), (executive decision to return the Crown of St. Steven to the People of Hungary).

See also Timberg, Sovereign Immunity and Act of State Defenses: Transnational Boycotts and Economic Coercion, 55 Tex.L.Rev. 1, 31–36 (1976).

In Dames & Moore v. Regan, Iranian Assets case, 453 U.S. 654 (1981), the Supreme Court upheld an agreement between the United States and Iranian governments which lead to the release of the Americans held hostage by Iran. Pursuant to this agreement, the United States was obligated to terminate all legal proceedings in United States courts involving claims of United States nationals against Iran, to nullify all attachments and judgments obtained therein, and to bring about the termination of such claims through binding arbitration in an Iran–United States Claims Tribunal. Also upheld were Executive Orders issued by the President to implement the agreement. In finding that such action was within the grant of power by the constitution to the executive branch the court (Rehnquist, J.) noted:

Perhaps it is because it is so difficult to reconcile the ... definition of Article III judicial power with the broad range of vitally important day-to-day questions regularly decided by Congress or the Executive, without either challenge or interference by the judiciary, that the decisions of the Court in this area have been rare, episodic, afford little precedential value for subsequent cases.... It is to ... history that we now turn.... the United States has repeatedly exercised its sovereign authority to settle claims of its nationals against foreign countries.... [B]eing overly sanguine about the chances of United States claimants before the Claims Tribunal would require a degree of naivete which should not be demanded even of judges....

The Court was obviously noticing a great deal of American and world history. To what extent was it taking account of recent current events and, if so, what was its source of information? See Arguments Before the Court in the Iranian Assets case: "Justice Rehnquist, referring to preservation of U.S. citizen's rights through the [International] Tribunal, said, 'the more you read the newspapers the more doubts you have.' " 49 U.S.L.W. 3961, June 30, 1981. Should judges base their decision on what they read in the newspapers? See H.D. Thoreau, Essays, at 254 (1862) ("Blessed are they who never read a newspaper, for they shall see Nature, and, through her, God."); 2 Correspondence of Mr. Justice Holmes and Harold Laski, 1916–1935 at 1196 (M.D.Howe ed. 1953) (Holmes) ("I have given up all subscriptions to periodicals and take *no* newspaper—except by prescription."); United States v. Baker, 641 F.2d 1311 (9th Cir.1981) (court refused to take judicial notice of the news media as an unquestionably accurate source of publicity).

D.   PERSONAL KNOWLEDGE

1.   JUDGE

NOTES

1. The earliest case distinguishing the personal knowledge of the judge from his judicial knowledge seems to be that in Y.B. 7, Henry IV, 41:5 (1406). It is referred to and declared applicable by Mr. Newport in 3 Howell's State Trials 538, 662 (1696). Nevertheless, judges continue to be outraged by attempts to rely on the record to support propositions known by them to be false.

In Beychok v. St. Paul Mercury Indemnity Co., 119 F.Supp. 52 (W.D.La. 1954), the judge noticed that a certain stool in a luncheonette had been in the same state for about fifteen years prior to plaintiff's accident and that no one had been injured thereby. The court said, however, that this fact was common knowledge.

Gibson v. Von Glahn Hotel Co., 185 N.Y.S. 154 (Sup.Ct.1920). The issue was whether defendant's establishment was a hotel, so that defendant would be subject to the absolute liability of innkeepers at common law. The trial judge said: "I know the Von Glahn Hotel as well as the witness does himself; I will give you a ruling now it is a hotel." The judgment for plaintiff was reversed, the court stating: "The determination of the question by the court upon its own knowledge, without reference to the evidence, was improper. The determination of a fact can only be founded upon evidence of witnesses. The court has no right, irrespective of the testimony of witnesses, to determine a fact based upon its own knowledge." See also Riley v. Wallace, 222 S.W. 1085 (Ky.1920); State v. Armitage, 1118 So. 696 (La.1928); Shapleigh v. Mier, 299 U.S. 468, 113 A.L.R. 253, 258 (1938). See In re Bommer, 159 Misc. 511, 288 N.Y.S. 419 (Surr.Ct.1936), where in interpreting a statute the judge reluctantly decided to ignore what he knew as one of its draftsmen.

2. In Illinois Drovers National Bank v. Great Southwest Fire Ins. Co., 55 Ill.App.3d 953, 13 Ill.Dec. 763, 371 N.E.2d 855 (1977), at issue was whether a church had been occupied within the sixty day period preceding its destruction by fire. Had the church been vacant or unoccupied during that entire period, fire insurance coverage would have been precluded. In response to evidence put forward by the defendant insurance company that utilities had been cut off over sixty days before the fire thus leading to the inference that the premises had been vacant, the trial judge stated:

> I know of my own knowledge that it is possible for people to have currents of electricity of their premises under circumstances which is unbeknown to the Edison Company....

> I can tell you the one experience I had back two years ago, and I'm not saying it's applicable here; but I was asked by a clergyman one day to visit some very poor people of his particular parish....

> I recall it was in the summer months, and I did visit the premises. The father was half asleep on the couch with the TV blaring with the ballgame. While I was talking to him, I saw a long cord going from somewhere behind the TV out the window of the premises.

> While I was speaking with him, I walked out and followed the cord and looked out the window. This home happened to be next to a railroad embankment. What he or somebody had done was unscrewed a bulb or taken a bulb out of a railroad light standing and put a plug—I guess you call it—in there, and he was getting his electricity from one of our railroads in the City.
>
> So, I'm taking that into account reaching a decision here of the possibilities.

Id. at 955, 13 Ill.Dec. at 765, 371 N.E.2d at 857. The appellate court reversed because: "It is a well established principle of law that in a trial of a case, the trial judge may consider only that knowledge he has acquired by the introduction of evidence or of which he may take judicial notice." Id. at 951, 13 Ill.Dec. at 766, 371 N.E.2d at 858.

Compare Belcher v. Buesking, 371 N.E.2d 417, 420 (Ind.App.1978) ("[w]ithin the framework of judicial notice, or knowledge of certain physical laws going to an evaluation and understanding of evidence, and not to consideration of evidence other than that presented by the parties is not considered error.... [W]here ... the trial is to the court alone, it is presumed that the judge upon considering the facts of an automobile accident will draw on his own experience as a driver, as an observer of traffic and even as one who may understand elementary physics."), with, Castello v. Cassidy, 210 N.Y.S.2d 46, 47 (Sup.Ct.1960) ("It was error for the Trial Justice, in the guise of judicial notice, to substitute his own personal knowledge for evidence as to the grade of the streets where the accident occurred.").

In Government of Virgin Islands v. Gereau, 523 F.2d 140 (3d Cir.1975), cert. denied, 424 U.S. 917 (1976), the trial judge, in passing on a motion for a new trial (arising out of alleged jury tampering), erred in determining credibility as between juror and jury matron on the basis of his own knowledge about the matron's need for extra income. See also United States v. Sorrells, 714 F.2d 1522 (11th Cir.1983) (personal knowledge of reliability of informant not a proper basis for validating a search warrant).

In William H. Grossman, Inc. v. Quinn, 118 N.Y.S.2d 376 (Sup.Ct.), rev'd, 281 App.Div. 1028, 122 N.Y.S.2d 614 (1st Dept.1953), petitioner sought to remove his package liquor store from its present licensed premises to a new location. The State Liquor Authority disapproved the application on the ground that "public convenience and advantage" would not be served by the removal, since the proposed location is only 203 feet from another licensed liquor store. The determination of the Liquor Authority was annulled, the Justice stating:

> What I know as a man, I need not affect not to know as a judicial officer. Based on an intimate familiarity with the proposed locale—having lived in its general vicinity for almost fifty years and having represented the district in the Legislature for many years—it is compellingly clear to me that there is public advantage rather than disadvantage in petitioner moving the site of its business.

In Jacobellis v. State, 378 U.S. 184, 197 (1964) which reviewed a criminal prosecution for possessing and exhibiting an allegedly obscene film, Justice Stewart stated in a concurring opinion:

> I have reached the conclusion ... that ... criminal laws in this area are constitutionally limited to hard-core pornography. I shall not today attempt further to define the kinds of material I understand to be embraced within that short-hand description; and perhaps I could never succeed in intelligi-

bly doing so. But I know it when I see it, and the motion picture involved in this case is not that.

In view of the judicial function involved, should the rules governing the use of the judges' personal knowledge be the same in each of the above cases?

2. JURY

NOTES

1. Rostad v. Portland Railway, Light & Power Co., 201 P. 184 (Or.1921):

> Of course, jurors must act with legal discretion and in subordination to the rules of evidence.... The personal knowledge of any juror concerning any probative fact involved in the case under consideration is not to be used in deciding the case. Such a juror should communicate his information to the court, and if he is not excused from service and it is deemed proper to use his cognizance of such a fact in the trial, he must be sworn as a witness and examined, subject to cross-examination by the adverse party, the same as any other witness. But any juror must consider the testimony in the light of that knowledge and experience which is common to all men. For instance, it is a matter of common knowledge that a bullet piercing the brain of a human being will in all likelihood prove fatal. It is common knowledge, also, that a forest tree cut nearly in two at the butt will fall, if a high wind blows against it. If a witness should testify to the contrary to these ordinary phenomena, the common knowledge of the juror derived from his experience in such matters would naturally compel him to discredit that witness. Many illustrations might be given where men are normally and legitimately influenced in considering testimony by their general knowledge and experience. Probably as clear a statement of the true doctrine as can be found is that contained in the language of Mr. Justice Hackney in Jenney Electric Co. v. Branham, 145 Ind. 314, 41 N.E. 448, 33 L.R.A. 395. The court there had instructed the jury that—
>
> > "You may also, in considering whom you will or will not believe, take into account your experience and relations among men."

2. In Thomas v. Kansas Power and Light Co., 340 P.2d 379 (Kan.1959), the intestate, while assisting in the installation of a television antenna was killed as a result "of coming into contact with electricity." The plaintiff sought to recover pursuant to the wrongful death statute. The issue was whether the trial court decision in favor of plaintiff could stand where there was the following alleged jury misconduct:

> After the jury was discharged on the afternoon of November 13 juror Noll borrowed a book on electricity from a friend, took it home with him, and thereafter read from it extensively until the early hours of the next morning, paying particular attention to the arcing and jumping characteristics of electricity while being transmitted through electric transmission lines. The next morning, after the jury returned to the jury room to resume its deliberations, he proceeded, in the presence of all the jurors, to discuss with most, if not all, of them matters and things he had learned from the book about the subject in question.

This was held to be reversible error. Would the result in Thomas have differed had juror Noll not discussed his readings with the other members of the jury? Cf. State v. McNichols, 363 P.2d 467 (Kan.1961) (juror's looking up the word "culpable" to assist in interpreting the charge on "culpable negligence," was misconduct).

Assuming that the plaintiff had requested the court to take judicial notice of the contents of the same book which Juror Noll read:

a.   What factors would determine whether or not the court should take notice? What other policies and aspects of the law of evidence might enter into this determination?

b.   Before reaching a decision, should the court offer the defendant an opportunity to disprove the theory of the book? Should such a rebuttal argument be heard in the presence of the jury? Should plaintiff's request be heard in the presence of the jury?

c.   If the court decides to take judicial notice, what should be its instruction to the jury? Compare Palestroni v. Jacobs, 77 A.2d 183 (N.J.Super.1950) (trial court was reversed for allowing the jury to use a dictionary because the defendant was denied the opportunity to challenge the definition).

Do you think the result would have been different if (1) Juror Noll referred to the book but had read it several years before the trial or (2) had talked about Benjamin Franklin and his kite?

Should the attorneys for the parties not have assumed that the jury would be curious about this matter? Was it a part of plaintiff's case? Were the attorneys at fault?

3.   In Tennessee Gas Transmission Co. v. Hall, 277 S.W.2d 733 (Tex.Civ.App. 1955) the Jury, in determining the amount of compensation to which defendant was entitled for granting an easement to plaintiff for the construction and maintenance of a gas pipeline on defendant's land, considered the possibility of a decrease in the value of defendant's land if in the future defendant's use of a subsoiler broke the pipe and resulted in an explosion. There had been no evidence about subsoiling operations. The court held that the jury could "take into consideration matters of common knowledge though such facts have not been proved during the trial. . . . [I]n the jurisdiction of the trial court subsoiling or chiseling operations, as discussed by the jury, were matters of common knowledge."; See also Tudor v. Tudor, 311 S.W.2d 733, 737 (Tex.Civ.App.1958) (in action to recover profits from the operation of a gin, it was not improper for a juror to consider the fact that gin work in the "busy season required long hard hours," since that was common knowledge).

4.   Should juries be permitted to decide cases on the basis of factors not litigated by the parties? How can they be prevented from doing so? Does it make any difference whether the information used by the jurors is common knowledge in the locality or the specialized knowledge of one or more jurors? See Levin & Levy, Persuading the Jury with Facts not in Evidence: The Fiction–Science Spectrum, 105 U.Pa.L.Rev. 139 (1969); Manchester, Judicial Notice and Personal Knowledge, 42 Modern L.Rev. (1979) (England) (judge and jury).

Data from the University of Chicago Jury Project suggest that juror knowledge of local conditions, of witnesses, of lawyers, of the parties and of other jurors plays an important role in the outcome of many cases. In the survey, the decisions in ten of fourteen civil cases and three of seven criminal cases were found to have been influenced by this personal juror knowledge. Broeder, The Impact of the Vicinage Requirement: An Empirical Look, 45 Neb.L.Rev. 99 (1966). See Levin & Levy, Persuading the Jury with Facts not in Evidence: The Fiction–Science Spectrum, 105 U.Pa.L.Rev. 139 (1969).

5.   It is clear that a juror having personal knowledge of the particular facts in issue should be sworn and subject to cross-examination rather than use this knowledge in the jury room. But cf. Fed.R.Evid. 606 (declaring jurors incompetent as witnesses in the trial in which he sits). It is equally clear that jurors must use their personal general knowledge about men and affairs in order to weigh and analyze the evidence. See United States v. Ricciardi, 357 F.2d 91, 95–96 (2d Cir.), cert. denied, 384 U.S. 942 (1966). In determining whether a strike by building superintendents would "affect commerce" for purposes of the Labor Management Relations Act, the court noted:

> To be sure, there was no testimony which said in so many words that a strike by the superintendents of the buildings with 30 or less units, who were represented by Council 7 of Local 32 E, would tend to curtail interstate commerce; but the Government should not be penalized for its failure to belabor the obvious. As Mr. Justice Metcalf wrote in Commonwealth v. Peckham, 68 Mass. (2 Gray) 514, 515 (1854): "Jurors are not to be presumed ignorant of what everybody else knows. And they are allowed to act upon matters within their general knowledge, without any testimony on those matters." See also Rostad v. Portland R'y, Light & Power Co., 101 Or. 569, 581, 201 P. 184, 188 (1921) ("[t]riers of fact cannot, in the nature of things, be divested of general knowledge of practical affairs"); McCormick, Evidence § 324 at p. 691 (1954); 9 Wigmore, Evidence § 2569 (3d ed. 1940); Morgan, Judicial Notice, 57 Harv.L.Rev. 269, 272 (1944). If a jury does not need to be told that gin is intoxicating, Commonwealth v. Peckham, supra, or that good rugs are valuable, Shikany v. Salt Creek Transp. Co., 48 Wyo. 190, 45 P.2d 645 (1935), or that spare parts were difficult to obtain in this country during 1943 and 1944, Holt v. Pariser, 161 Pa.Super. 315, 54 A.2d 89 (1947), the jury here did not need to be told that a strike or a slow-down by employees who run machines would affect the amount of material used in the machines. Cf. Apex Hosiery Co. v. Leader, 310 U.S. 469, 60 S.Ct. 982, 84 L.Ed. 1311 (1940). To paraphrase Rule 9 of the Uniform Rules of Evidence, the proposition is one of generalized knowledge so universally known that it cannot reasonably be the subject of dispute. The jury could apply this proposition to the testimony before it as to the responsibilities of the building superintendents and as to the amount of fuel used in the buildings, and conclude that a labor dispute in the industry would interfere with the sale or distribution of out-of-state fuel on other than a *de minimis* basis.

But see Edelstein v. Roskin, 356 So.2d 38, 39 (Fla.App.1978) (automobile accident case; the jury's question as to whether a juror, who was personally familiar with the intersection at which the accident took place, could be allowed to "become a witness in the jury room" by telling other jurors his views with respect to the visibility and structures at the intersection should have been answered in the negative); Harden v. Illinois Central Railroad Co., 112 N.W.2d 324 (Iowa1961) (action arising from collision of an automobile with a train where automobile speed was an important factor; taking to the jury room by juror of a handbook, which was not admitted into evidence, showing stopping distances of cars being driven at various speeds, which distances were substantially different from testimony of patrolman, was reversible error).

6. Sometimes jury misconduct can be cured by special instructions from the judge. See United States v. Sisco, 392 F.Supp. 1347–50 (W.D.Mo.1974). The defendant in a prosecution for sale of narcotics was held not entitled to a new trial on grounds that a juror was discovered during trial to be reading and consulting a Bible "to determine whether or not God felt the defendant was guilty," where the juror's misconduct was brought to the attention of the trial judge during the jury's deliberation; jury was recalled; and cautionary instruction given.

Can formal judicial notice be applied to everyday inferences from personal experiences? In an automobile accident case, does not the juror have to apply his own knowledge to the fact that driving and putting on lipstick at the same time substantially increases the risk of collision? Is it improper for the jury to use its knowledge and experience when, in determining credibility, it considers the reasons a witness might have had to lie; when in considering whether defendant killed, that a movement of the finger against a trigger may cause a bullet to be expelled which, if it enters a living body, can cause serious damage?

Suppose you are trying an environmental pollution case. A prestigious academician tells you that both jurors and judges will have the following "misconceptions": 1) cancer rates are soaring, 2) manmade chemicals are present in significant amounts, 3) pollution causes cancer and birth defects, 4) only a small number of chemicals are carcinogens and reproductive toxins and the manufacturers can eliminate them and 5) technology is doing us in. See Ames, Six Common Errors relating to Environmental Pollution, 27 Water (National Assoc. of Water Companies) 20 (1986). Should you use this information as defendant's lawyer, plaintiff's lawyer, the trial court or the appellate court?

Can a judge in sentencing take account of his knowledge of special crime problems in his or her district?

E.   PROCEDURAL PROBLEMS

1.   EFFECT OF JUDICIAL NOTICE

United States v. Jones

United States Court of Appeals, Sixth Circuit, 1978.
580 F.2d 219.

■ Before CELEBREZZE, LIVELY and ENGEL, CIRCUIT JUDGES.

■ ENGEL, CIRCUIT JUDGE.

Appellee William Allen Jones, Jr. was convicted by a district court jury of illegally intercepting telephone conversations of his estranged wife and of using the contents of the intercepted communications, in violation of 18 U.S.C. §§ 2511(1)(a) and (d) (1976). The proofs at trial showed only that the telephone which Jones had tapped was furnished by South Central Bell Telephone Company. Other than this fact, the government offered no evidence to show that South Central Bell was at the time a "person engaged as a common carrier in providing or operating ... facilities for the transmission of interstate or foreign communications." 18 U.S.C. § 2510(1). See also 18 U.S.C. § 2510(10) and 47 U.S.C. § 153(h), defining common carrier.

Following the jury verdict of guilty on three of the five counts of the indictment, Jones' counsel moved the court for a new trial on the ground that the government had altogether failed to prove that the wire communication which the defendant tapped came within the definition of Section 2510. Upon a careful review of the evidence, United States District Judge Frank Wilson agreed and entered a judgment of acquittal. The government has appealed.

It is not seriously disputed that an essential element of the crimes charged, and one which the government was obligated to prove beyond a reasonable doubt, was that the conversation which was tapped was a "wire communication" as defined in the Act. Instead, the issue is whether the abbreviated proof offered by the government was minimally sufficient for the prima facie case which the government was obligated to place before the jury. In other words, was the proof that the tapped telephone was installed and furnished by "South Central Bell Telephone Company," without more, sufficient to enable the jury to find as a matter of fact that South Central Bell was a common carrier which provided facilities for the transmission of interstate or foreign communications? The government contends that, construing that evidence in the light most favorable to it, these facts could be permissibly inferred by the jury without any other proof.

The government's argument is essentially twofold. First, it urges that South Central Bell's status may reasonably be characterized as a fact within the common knowledge of the jury and that no further record evidence was necessary. Failing that, the government urges that such a fact is the proper subject of judicial notice which may be taken at any stage of the proceeding, including appeal, under Federal Rule of Evidence 201(f).

The government's first argument finds some support in Wigmore. 9 Wigmore on Evidence § 2570 at 542–43 (3d ed. 1940). Similarly, the legislative history of the Federal Rules of Evidence indicates that, even in criminal cases, "matters falling within the common fund of information supposed to be possessed by jurors need not be proved." Advisory Committee Note to Federal Rule of Evidence 201(g) (1969 draft), quoted, 1 Weinstein's Evidence 201–2 (1977). As that Note further indicates, however, such matters "are not, properly speaking, adjudicative facts but an aspect of legal reasoning." Id. Thus, while the jury may properly rely upon its own knowledge and experience in evaluating evidence and drawing inferences from that evidence, there must be sufficient record evidence to permit the jury to consult its general knowledge in deciding the existence of the fact.

While Wigmore notes that "[t]he range of [a jury's] general knowledge is not precisely definable," Wigmore, supra, § 2570 at 546, "the scope of this doctrine is narrow; it is strictly limited to a few matters of elemental experience in human nature, commercial affairs, and everyday life." Id. at 544. This category of fact is not so much a matter of noticing facts outside the record as it is a matter of the communication value of the words used, which can only be understood in the light of the common experience of those who employ them. See generally K. Davis, Administrative Law Text § 15.06 at 305 (3d ed. 1972).

While the issue is not without difficulty, we are satisfied that South Central Bell's status as a "common carrier . . . providing . . . facilities for the transmission of interstate . . . communications" is a fact which, if to be established without direct or circumstantial proof, must be governed by the judicial notice provisions of the Federal Rules of Evidence.

The government did not at any time during the jury trial specifically request the district court to take judicial notice of the status of South Central Bell. Nevertheless, it relies upon the provisions of Rule 201(f) which state that "[j]udicial notice may be taken at any stage of the proceeding." It is true that the Advisory Committee Note to 201(f) indicates that judicial notice is appropriate "in the trial court or on appeal." See 1 Weinstein's Evidence ¶ 201[06] (1976). It is also true that the language of 201(f) does not distinguish between judicial notice in civil or criminal cases.[1] There is, however, a critical difference

---

1. See also United States v. Blunt, 558 F.2d 1245 (6th Cir.1977), in which we held that proof that Blunt had committed an assault within the confines of the Federal Correctional Institution at Lexington, Kentucky, was a sufficient showing that the crime occurred within the territorial jurisdiction of the United States as defined in 18 U.S.C. § 7(3) (1976). We ruled that the record sufficiently demonstrated " 'practical usage and

in the manner in which the judicially noticed fact is to be submitted to the jury in civil and criminal proceedings:

> Instructing jury. In a civil action or proceeding, the court shall instruct the jury to accept as conclusive any fact judicially noticed. In a criminal case, the court shall instruct the jury that it may, but is not required to, accept as conclusive any fact judicially noticed.

Fed.R.Evid. 201(g). Thus under subsection (g) judicial notice of a fact in a civil case is conclusive while in a criminal trial the jury is not bound to accept the judicially noticed fact and may disregard it if it so chooses.

It is apparent from the legislative history that the congressional choice of language in Rule 201 was deliberate. In adopting the present language, Congress rejected a draft of subsection (g) proposed by the Supreme Court, which read:

> The judge shall instruct the jury to accept as established any facts judicially noticed.

The House Report explained its reason for the change:

> Rule 201(g) as received from the Supreme Court provided that when judicial notice of a fact is taken, the court shall instruct the jury to accept that fact as established. Being of the view that mandatory instruction to a jury in a criminal case to accept as conclusive any fact judicially noticed is inappropriate because contrary to the spirit of the Sixth Amendment right to a jury trial, the Committee adopted the 1969 Advisory Committee draft of this subsection, allowing a mandatory instruction in civil actions and proceedings and a discretionary instruction in criminal cases.

H.Rep. No. 93–650, 93d Cong., 1st Sess. 6–7 (1973), U.S.Code Cong. & Admin.News 7075, 7080 (1974). Congress intended to preserve the jury's traditional prerogative to ignore even uncontroverted facts in reaching a verdict. The legislature was concerned that the Supreme Court's rule violated the spirit, if not the letter, of the constitutional right to a jury trial by effectively permitting a partial directed verdict as to facts in a criminal case.[2]

As enacted by Congress, Rule 201(g) plainly contemplates that the jury in a criminal case shall pass upon facts which are judicially noticed. This it could not do if this notice were taken for the first time after it had been discharged and the case was on appeal. We, therefore, hold that Rule 201(f), authorizing judicial notice at the appellate level, must yield in the face of the express congressional intent manifested in 201(g) for criminal jury trials. To the extent

dominion exercised over the ... federal establishment by the United States government.' " Id. at 1247, quoting with approval United States v. Erdos, 474 F.2d 157, 159 (4th Cir.), cert. denied, 414 U.S. 876, 94 S.Ct. 42, 38 L.Ed.2d 122 (1973).

Blunt went on to note that "[t]he district court would have been correct in taking judicial notice under Rule 201, Federal Rules of Evidence, of the fact that the Institution was within the territorial jurisdiction of the United States." 558 F.2d at 1247. While concluding that territorial jurisdiction under 18 U.S.C. § 7(3) would have been an appropriate subject for judicial notice in the district court, our court did not take judicial notice and did not, as the government asserts, intimate that

it would be proper to do so at the appellate level in a criminal case. [Some footnotes omitted; others renumbered.]

2. The Supreme Court of Utah expressed a similar concern in State v. Lawrence, 120 Utah 323, 234 P.2d 600 (1951):

> If a court can take one important element of an offense from the jury and determine the facts for them because such fact seems plain enough to him, then which element cannot be similarly taken away, and where would the process stop?

234 P.2d at 603.

that the earlier practice may have been otherwise, we conceive that it has been altered by the enactment of Rule 201.

Accordingly, the judgment of the district court is affirmed.

NOTES

1. Did the Court in Jones reach the just result? Is it not likely that every member of the jury knew that Central Bell was a common carrier? See United States v. Deckard, 816 F.2d 426 (8th Cir.1987), where the court took judicial notice that the Southwestern Bell Telephone System, which served defendant, carried interstate communications. Approved was the instruction:

> [Y]ou may accept the court's declaration as evidence, and regard as proved the fact or event which has been judicially noticed, but you are not required to do so since you are the sole judge of the facts.

Compare with Jones, Government of Canal Zone v. Burjan, 596 F.2d 690 (5th Cir.1979) which involved a criminal prosecution for grand larceny in which the defendant had waived his right to a jury trial. For the purpose of resolving jurisdictional issues raised by the defendant, the Court of Appeals took judicial notice of the boundaries of the Canal Zone despite the fact that the trial court had not taken notice. The court, without "intimating [its] views as to the correctness of Jones," id. at 694, held that rule 201(g) did not preclude judicial notice since the rule was inapplicable in a nonjury case. See also Commonwealth v. Kingsbury, 393 N.E.2d 391 (Mass.1979) (dictum approving Jones); United States v. Dior, 671 F.2d 351 (9th Cir.1982) (lack of proof of Canadian–United States exchange rates, relying on Jones case to achieve absurd result). Compare cases ignoring Rule 201(g) to uphold sensible verdicts: United States v. Lavender, 602 F.2d 639 (4th Cir.1979); United States v. Piggie, 622 F.2d 486 (10th Cir.), cert. denied, 449 U.S. 863 (1980).

2. In State v. Lawrence, 234 P.2d 600 (Utah1951), the Supreme Court of Utah reversed a conviction for grand larceny of an automobile. The court found that the use of judicial notice by the trial judge had invaded the defendant's right to a jury trial by removing an element of the offense from the jury. Where the prosecution had neglected to prove the value of the automobile, the trial judge instructed the jury that the value of the car was over fifty dollars—the threshold level for grand larceny. Note that the statute involved in State v. Lawrence provided that facts judicially noticed are conclusive in both criminal and civil cases. What would the result have been under Fed.R.Evid. 201(g)?

3. Is there any merit to the notion that the right to a jury trial has been fundamentally infringed if the judge takes one element of the offense from the jury, no matter how indisputable? Does the court do this when it refuses to charge a lesser degree of the crime? See N.Y.CPL § 300.50 codifying the rule established in People v. Mussenden, 308 N.Y. 558, 127 N.E.2d 551 (1955); N.Y.CPL § 300.50 provides in part:

> In submitting a count of an indictment to the jury, the court in its discretion may, in addition to submitting the greatest offense which it is required to submit, submit in the alternative any lesser included offense if there is a reasonable view of the evidence which would support a finding that the defendant committed such lesser offense but did not commit the greater.

See People v. Henderson, 41 N.Y.2d 233, 236, 391 N.Y.S.2d 563, 565–566, 359 N.E.2d 1357, 1360 (1976) (construing N.Y.CPL § 300.50(1)). The test of whether a lesser included offense is to be submitted is whether there is a rational basis to submit the lesser charge "[t]o warrant a refusal to submit it 'every possible hypothesis' but guilt of the higher crime must be excluded ..." Mensah v. The King, [1946] A.C. 83, 91–94.

4. This problem was once important where membership in the Communist Party was involved. The applicable statute may be cast in terms of membership in an organization teaching or advocating the violent overthrow of the government. E.g., 18 U.S.C. § 2385 (1970) (Smith Act); 8 U.S.C. § 1251 (1970) (deportation of aliens affiliated with Communist Party or who advocate or teach opposition to all organized government; the predecessors of the section did not mention Communist Party by name); 50 U.S.C. § 2255 (1951 & Supp.1981) (civil defense loyalty oath). The issue is then whether the court will judicially notice that the Communist Party is such an organization. Courts have divided on the point. See Note, 55 Colum.L.Rev. 631, 711 (1955). Is the only issue whether the fact is commonly known or easily ascertainable? Or does every defendant—at least in a criminal case—have the statutory or constitutional right to relitigate the nature of the Communist Party; or, to have a decision in its favor even without the introduction of evidence? Does it matter that this question of fact has been decided by an agency specifically assigned to do this job? See id. at 714, n. 636.

5. Is it significant that prior cases have judicially noticed the point or have held that it had been established? See Spector v. United States, 193 F.2d 1002, 1006 (9th Cir.1952) (under no theory of res judicata or stare decisis are these defendants bound by the facts about the Communist Party which the Supreme Court said had been established in Dennis v. United States, 339 U.S. 162, reh. denied 339 U.S. 950 (1950)).

6. See Isaacs, The Law and the Facts, 22 Colum.L.Rev. 1, 3 (1922): "Whatever definition of law we adopt, there is a large and growing group of facts that tend to be dealt with as matters of law after courts have had a large experience with them in the course of which a uniform line of decisions on the facts has developed." See also Salmond, Jurisprudence 16 (6th ed. 1920) (what is today fact may become law by stare decisis).

7. Should evidence rebutting a judicially noticed fact be admitted? The controversy over admitting rebutting evidence is a corollary of the argument, supra, whether noticed fact must be indisputable.

Against Admissibility: Morgan, McCormick and the Codifications which espouse indisputability hold that permitting further evidence would be a waste of time since the judge has been convinced that the fact is indisputable. See McCormick, Judicial Notice, 5 Vand.L.Rev. 296, 321–22 (1952); Evidence 710–11 (1954); Morgan, Judicial Notice, 57 Harv.L.Rev. 269, 279 (1944); McNaughton, Judicial Notice—Excerpts Relating to the Morgan–Wigmore Controversy, 14 Vand.L.Rev. 779 (1961); Fed.R.Evid. 201(g) (facts judicially noticed conclusive in civil but not criminal cases). A few states with rules patterned after Fed.R.Evid. 201 have modified subsection (g) making all facts judicially noticed conclusive whether in a civil or a criminal action. They include: Arizona, Arkansas, Maine, North Dakota, and South Dakota. For other codifications following the Morgan approach see, e.g., Uniform Rule of Evidence 201(g) (1974 version); Cal.Evid.Code § 457; and N.J.R.Evid. 11. Cf. Beardsley v. Irving, 71 A. 580 (Conn.1909).

For Admissibility: The Thayer, Wigmore, Davis position that evidence rebutting the judicially noticed fact can be introduced has been endorsed by L. Hand, J., in United States v. Aluminum Co. of America, 148 F.2d 416, 446 (2d Cir.1945), by Cardozo, J., in Ohio Bell Telephone Co. v. P.U.C., 301 U.S. 292, 301 (1937), and by two circuit courts, Barr Rubber Products Co. v. Sun Rubber

Co., 425 F.2d 1114, 1126 n. 19 (2d Cir.), cert. denied, 400 U.S. 878 (1970) and United States v. Grady, 225 F.2d 410, 416–17 (7th Cir.), cert. denied, 350 U.S. 896 (1955). See Macht v. Hecht Co., 59 A.2d 754, 756 (Md.1948); Wells v. Pittsburgh Bd. of Public Education, 374 A.2d 1009 (Pa.Cmwlth.1977); see also 9 Wigmore § 2567 (Chadbourn rev. 1981); Davis, A System of Judicial Notice Based on Fairness and Convenience, in Perspectives of Law, 69, 76–77 (1964). Does this view make judicial notice anything more than a branch of the already complicated law of presumptions?

8. In a non-jury trial, the point at which the contrary information is considered is not important. But in a jury trial there is a practical difference between the two approaches. See Reception of Evidence to Contradict or Rebut Matters Judicially Noticed, 45 A.L.R.2d 1169 (1954). If the judge declared a fact indisputable and noticed after a hearing, permitting the jury to hear further evidence to the contrary would defeat the principal reasons for taking judicial notice. If the court can take judicial notice on the basis of records and texts which are hearsay and therefore non-admissible, while the jury is restricted to a consideration of admissible evidence, does Wigmore present a workable rule? Davis agrees with Wigmore, 3 Davis, Administrative Law Treatise, ¶ 15.13 (1980); Davis, Judicial Notice, 55 Colum.L.Rev. 945, 981–82 (1955). Is this because he is primarily concerned with the administrative-non-jury situation?

2. NOTIFYING THE PARTIES

NOTES

1. A court is not required to take judicial notice unless requested to do so by a party and supplied with the necessary information, Fed.R.Evid. 201(d), 201(e); see Clark v. South Central Bell Telephone Co., 419 F.Supp. 697, 703–04 (W.D.La.1976) (court would not take judicial notice of certain population and demographic data in a suit alleging racial discrimination by the utility in its hiring and promotion practices because, inter alia: "For a court to notice facts judicially, if they are not matters of general knowledge, the sources of those facts must be placed before the Court.... No facts or reliable sources were placed before the Court in this instance."). See Cal.Evid.Code § 454 (court may resort to "[a]ny source of pertinent information").

Rule 201(e) of the Federal Rules of Evidence grants each party "upon timely request to an opportunity to be heard as to the propriety of taking judicial notice and the tenor of the matter noticed." The Rules do not develop the procedures to carry out this "opportunity to be heard." No hearing before judicial notice is taken is required, but it would seem to be a good practice.

Implicit in 201(e) is a right of the parties to be notified when the other party requests judicial notice be taken or a judge takes judicial notice on his own. While no formal scheme is provided for in the Rules, the Rules do say such notice should be timely. This is important so that a judge may have time to carefully consider whether the matter should be judicially noticed and for opposing counsel to have time to present his rebuttal to the court. See Cal.Evid.Code § 453. If a trial court takes judicial notice on its own when must notice be given? See Kinnett Dairies Inc. v. Farrow, 580 F.2d 1260, 1277–78 n. 33 (5th Cir.1978) (it was held sufficient for the court acting upon a request for a preliminary injunction to reveal in its written opinion that it has taken judicial notice of certain records where one of the parties had requested such notice and others had not objected at the time).

May a judge take judicial notice on his own and not inform the parties? Does Fed.R.Evid. 201(e) allow the parties opportunity to be heard after such judicial notice is taken? See North American Van Lines Inc. v. United States, 412 F.Supp. 782, 806 (N.D.Ind.1976) (dictum; "A party may object to the taking of such [judicial] notice, and may thereafter challenge the propriety of such notice taking"). But see, United States v. Doss, 563 F.2d 265, 269 n. 2, 285 n. 5 (6th Cir.1977) (held, over dissent, that it could take judicial notice of its own records without giving notice to the parties and without giving them an opportunity to be heard).

If a party is not given this opportunity, are constitutional guarantees violated? See Ohio Bell Telephone Co. v. Public Utilities Commission, 301 U.S. 292, 302–303 (1937) (review of an administrative agency's decision, where the Court indicated that judicial notice without permitting the parties an opportunity to challenge the deductions was violative of due process). See also Chubbs v. City of New York, 324 F.Supp. 1183, 1187–1188 (E.D.N.Y.1971), a pro se prisoner civil rights case where an attempt to grant petitioner full constitutional protections without unnecessarily burdening the parties was made.

> On its own motion the Court ... obtained from various depositories in the state the records of the criminal trial and appeal. Such judicial notice at the pleading stage is authorized....

> Judicial notice on the Court's own motion can be exceedingly dangerous because, given an opportunity, the party adversely affected may be able to show why judicial notice should not be taken or why facts properly noticed do not have the significance attributed to them by the court.

2. If the judge in taking judicial notice relied on authoritative sources, should these sources be set out in the record? See United States v. Lopez, 328 F.Supp. 1077 (E.D.N.Y.1971) (the court listed the texts relied on in noticing certain scientific knowledge). If the court did not set out the sources consulted, would the parties have sufficient information to rebut effectively? Cf. Caterpillar Tractor Co. v. Illinois Pollution Control Board, 48 Ill.App.3d 655, 6 Ill.Dec. 737, 363 N.E.2d 419 (1977) (the court granted a lower court motion to expunge from the record scientific data and reports published after the hearings which the Board took judicial notice of and relied upon to support its findings, since "[b]asic notions of fair play require that the parties have an opportunity to cross-examine, explain, or refute facts which are the basis for an adjudication," citing Fed.R.Evid. 201(e)). Would the appellate court have a sufficient record for reviewing the propriety of judicial notice?

3. Rule 201(f) of the Federal Rules of Evidence allows judicial notice at any stage of the proceedings. Sometimes the result may be unfair. Colonial Leasing Company of New England, Inc. v. Logistics Control Group International, 762 F.2d 454 (5th Cir.1985), was a creditors' action for fraudulent conveyance. The appeals court held that post trial judicial notice of an Oregon judgment in favor of a purported creditor was improper. Defendant debtor correctly believed plaintiff had not made out a prima facie case at trial. Accordingly, defendant rested on its motion for a directed verdict, without producing any evidence (i.e., evidence that the Oregon judgment may have been procured through fraud or collusion). Judicial notice deprived the defendant of the opportunity to produce relevant evidence.

SECTION 3. LAW

One of the judge's primary functions is to decide what substantive law should be applied to the facts of the case before him. The methods a judge utilizes in finding and selecting the applicable law are determined in large measure by historical factors in the development of the common law.

In the case of law of the forum, the judge finds the law through judicial notice. Opposing counsel are usually relied upon to call the court's attention— by argument and brief—to the controlling legal material. On occasion a judge will conduct an independent investigation. In any event, no formal evidentiary requirements apply; flexibility and informality prevail. The only limitations are those inherent in the adversary system of keeping the other side informed. If the judge selects law which neither side has presented he may, but need not, request additional briefs prior to his final decision. The parties are protected in their right to appeal or ask for reargument in the event no further right of appeal exists.

Although the judge's function is essentially the same when selecting law foreign to the forum or administrative regulations or municipal ordinances, Anglo–American courts have historically characterized all questions of law, other than domestic statewide law, as questions of fact to be found by the jury. As questions of fact, they were also subject to the requirements of formal pleading and proof.

In the case of foreign law, two factors appear to have dictated the American practice of requiring formal pleading and proof: (1) the general unavailability of adequate law books and (2) the judge's need for expert assistance in translating and interpreting. Neither of these factors supports the practice in the case of sister-state law, or domestic private acts, ordinances and regulations, which nevertheless have been approached as matters of fact requiring pleading and proof.

A third factor of much greater historical than current significance is succinctly suggested by the following quotation from Professor Julius Goebel, Jr.'s first volume in the History of the Supreme Court of the United States, Antecedents and Beginnings to 1801, xv. (1971):

> In Thomas Jefferson's first catalogue of his library (1783) the laws of the American states other than his own were classified as "Foreign Laws." This insular outlook was shared by lawyers in other jurisdictions; it derived from the fact that as colonies each had had an identity impressed upon it by the circumstances of its founding that was to develop into a jealous particularism.

For an extended history of the treatment of foreign law as fact, see Miller, Federal Rule 44.1 and the "Fact" Approach to Determining Foreign Law: Death Knell for a Die–Hard Doctrine, 65 Mich.L.Rev. 613 (1967). While foreign causes of action were never viewed with hostility in the United States, Professor Miller offers several explanations for the American adherence to the English fact-theory of foreign law: the great size of the United States, the 19th century absorption of large territories with radically different cultural and legal frameworks, reinforcing the state court's tendency to characterize sister-state law as foreign, the relatively long isolation from other legal systems, and the philosophy of state sovereignty.

At common law the party relying on foreign law had to plead and prove it as if it were a material proposition of fact. Failure to plead in the requisite detail often led to a dismissal—usually with leave to replead. E.g., Harrison v. United Fruit Co., 143 F.Supp. 598 (S.D.N.Y.1956) (law of Honduras). Absence of proof of the foreign law was ground for dismissal on the merits. See, e.g., Cuba Railroad Co. v. Crosby, 222 U.S. 473 (1912) (dismissal of action for loss of hand in a machine on ground that Cuban law had not been proved). Since injustice resulted from strict adherence, the courts became restive with the harsh doctrine of dismissal. As noted by the New Jersey court in Leary v. Gledhill, 84 A.2d 725 (N.J.1951), a variety of techniques for filling the gap in proof with local law developed:

> [T]he courts frequently indulged in one or another of several presumptions: that the common law prevails in the foreign jurisdiction; that the law of the foreign jurisdiction is the same as the law of the forum, be it common law or statute; or that certain fundamental principles of the law exist in all civilized countries. As a fourth alternative, instead of indulging in any presumption as to the law of the foreign jurisdiction, the courts would merely apply the law of the forum as the only law before the court, on the assumption that by failing to prove the foreign law the parties acquiesce in having their controversy determined by reference to the law of the forum, be it statutory or common law. By the application of these various presumptions the courts have in effect treated the common law rule that foreign law could not be noticed but must be pleaded and proved as if it were a matter of fact merely as a permissive rule whereby either party could, if it were to his advantage, plead and prove the foreign law. Thus the failure to plead and prove the foreign law has not generally been considered as fatal.

In recent years, the courts developed a flexible approach in deciding whether to apply a domestic forum's law upon a failure to prove and plead foreign law. See, e.g., Watts v. Swiss Bank Corp., 27 N.Y.2d 270, 276, 317 N.Y.S.2d 315, 319–320, 265 N.E.2d 739, 743 (1970) (Breitel, J.) ("in the absence of manifest injustice, the court will allow the parties by default in pleading or proof to agree or acquiesce that forum law be applied.... "); Schlesinger, A Recurrent Problem in Transnational Litigation: The Effect of Failure to Invoke or Prove the Applicable Foreign Law, 59 Cornell L.Rev. 1, 12–15 (1973)....

Even when judicial notice will be taken, or where, as under Rule 44.1 of the Federal Rules of Civil Procedure, the term judicial notice is not used, lawyers must be prepared to aid the judge in determining foreign law. Instead of, or in addition to oral testimony, written depositions, citations and affidavits of an expert can be submitted. E.g., Albert v. Brownell, 219 F.2d 602 (9th Cir.1954); Murphy v. Bankers Commercial Corp., 111 F.Supp. 608 (S.D.N.Y.) aff'd 203 F.2d 645 (2d Cir.1953); Miele v. Miele, 95 A.2d 768 (N.J.Super.1953). See Nussbaum, Proving the Law of Foreign Countries, 3 Am.J.Comp.L. 60 (1954). If affidavits are used do they constitute hearsay? Can this method be used in the absence of a statute permitting judicial notice?

If the court insists that expert testimony be used to prove foreign law, can treatises be used to contradict the witnesses? In analyzing the foreign law may a judge call his own expert? See Fed.R.Evid. 706. There is no reason why a pretrial hearing should not be used to obtain an agreement by the parties to have experts' reports submitted. See Fed.R.Civ.P. Rule 16. Cf. Fed.R.Civ.P. Rule 26(b)(4), 28 U.S.C.A. (trial preparation of experts).

Federal courts faced with Erie and similar problems may refer the matter to the state for an advisory opinion on state law. Clay v. Sun Insurance Office Limited, 377 U.S. 179 (1964); American Law Institute, Study of the Division of Jurisdiction Between State & Federal Courts, p. 292 ff. (1969). In some instances a federal court may abstain to permit the state to interpret its own law. See, e.g., Railroad Commission of Texas v. Pullman Co., 312 U.S. 496 (1941); Hart & Wechsler, The Federal Courts and the Federal System, p. 988 ff. (2d Ed. 1973 by Bator, Miskin, Shapiro & Wechsler). Some doubt about the abstention doctrine to avoid deciding difficult questions of state law exists. See, e.g., Meredith v. City of Winter Haven, 320 U.S. 228 (1943); C.A. Wright, Law of Federal Courts, p. 202 ff. (2d Ed.1970).

Sometimes a question of fact determines what law applies. For example, if there is a question of whether the controlling event occurred in state A or in state B and the rules of law in these states are different, is this a judge or jury question? Opting for a jury decision is, e.g., Marra v. Bushee, 447 F.2d 1282 (2d Cir.1971), while taking a contrary position is, e.g., Chance v. E.I. Du Pont De Nemours & Co., Inc., 57 F.R.D. 165 (E.D.N.Y.1972). See Reese, Smit & Reese, The Role of the Jury in Choice of Law, 25 Case W.R.L.Rev. 82 (1974), following Chance.

In the state courts, the obvious undesirability of proving sister-state law by analogy to foreign law led to early demands for statutory reform. The majority of states have abolished the requirement of formal proof by adopting the Uniform Judicial Notice of Foreign Law Act or similar statutes. The Uniform Act provides that foreign law shall be determined by the judge. It authorizes judicial notice of the law of sister states. It does not, however, put sister-state law on the same informal basis as forum law, since section 4 requires that "reasonable notice shall be given to the adverse parties either in pleadings or otherwise." See, e.g., Gaipo v. Gaipo, 227 A.2d 581 (R.I.1967) (it is incumbent on the litigant to "either plead or otherwise give the defendant reasonable notice of her intention to invoke a foreign law"); Cliff v. Pinto, 60 A.2d 704 (R.I.1948) (act's objective is to provide a simple means of letting the forum ascertain the law).

A large number of states have adopted the Uniform Proof of Statutes Act, assuming the accuracy of published statutory compilations. Compare Federal Rules of Evidence, Rule 902(5) (authentication). See also Uniform Interstate and International Procedure Act, § 5.03.

International Law should be treated like the law of a sister or foreign state; to the extent that it is embodied in a treaty it becomes local law by virtue of the supremacy clause. See American Law Institute, Foreign Relations Law, Tent. Draft No. 1, § 133 (1980). Various printed versions of the treaties of the United States are "legal evidence" of them. 1 U.S.C. § 112a. As the reporter to the American Law Institute's draft, Professor Louis Henkin suggests the "analogy to proof of foreign law" is strong. Id. Because many judges are unfamiliar with foreign law, "there has grown a practice of looking to evidence, including expert testimony, on questions of international law," but this is a discretionary matter for the court. Id.

NOTES ON PRIVATE ACTS, ADMINISTRATIVE REGULATIONS AND MUNICIPAL ORDINANCES

The difficulty posed by private acts, regulations and ordinances is that a judge may be unaware of their existence and they may not always be readily available. As far as federal courts are concerned, these difficulties are resolved in large measure by the Public Printing and Document Act which provides that "[t]he contents of the Federal Register shall be judicially noticed...." (44 U.S.C.A. § 1507) It provides for the publication of:

"(1) Presidential proclamations and Executive orders, except those not having general applicability and legal effect or effective only against Federal agencies or persons in their capacity as officers, agents, or employees thereof; (2) documents or classes of documents that the President may determine from time to time have general applicability and legal effect; and (3) documents or classes of documents that may be required so to be published by Act of Congress." 44 U.S.C.A. § 1505(a).

The contents of the Code of Federal Regulations (which is also published as a special or supplemental edition of the Federal Register) are thus also required to be judicially noticed. 44 U.S.C.A. §§ 1507, 1510.

Under Rule 43(a) of the Federal Rules of Civil Procedure, federal courts might take notice of a state's private statutes, regulations, and ordinances if these matters were judicially noticeable under the law of the state in which the federal court was sitting, since under Rule 43(a) the statute or rule which favored the reception of the evidence governed. See, e.g., Marnell v. United Parcel Service of America, Inc., 260 F.Supp. 391, 398 (N.D.Cal.1966) (California Public Utilities Code and agency orders and decisions); Case v. Kelly, 133 U.S. 21, 27 (1890) (". . . we do not doubt the authority of the legislature of a State to enact that after the passage and publication of one of its [private] statutes the courts of the State shall be bound to take judicial notice of it without its being pleaded or proven before them. This rule, thus prescribed for the government of the courts of the States, must be binding in proceedings in federal courts in the same State."). Present practice is at least as broad as the states'.

The problem is not one of empowering a court to act but rather of working out a method of informing the court and of making the materials readily available. The Advisory Committee on Evidence suggested that the matter be dealt with by a further expansion of the first sentence of Rule 44.1 and Rule 26.1 to include "or a resolution, private act, regulation, ordinance, or similar official act of a branch, officer, agency, or public entity of the United States or of a State."

It would then be useful for the states to take action to codify and collect and publish administrative regulations, ordinances and private acts in a form readily accessible to the researcher. Even, however, in such states as New York where an official compilation of codes, rules and regulations by the Secretary of State is mandated (N.Y. Executive Law §§ 102–107), and where local laws must be centrally filed (N.Y. Municipal Home Rule Law § 27), many local regulations and ordinances are unavailable except from one of the hundreds of scattered municipalities. Given the present state of disorganization in availability of regulations and local ordinances and laws in most states, educating the court requires supplying it with copies of the applicable documents. The kind of notice required under Rule 26.1 of the Federal Rules of Criminal Procedure and Rule 44.1 of the Federal Rules of Civil Procedure when foreign law is relied upon is desirable for state regulations and local enactments.

While the Federal Register Act may not bind state courts, state courts will generally judicially notice federal administrative regulations. See, e.g., West's Ann.Cal.Evid.Code § 451. See also 5 Weinstein, Korn & Miller, New York Civil Practice § 4511.03 n. 23 (1971); But see Mastrullo v. Ryan, 105 N.E.2d 469, 470 (Mass.1952).

A federal court will generally judicially notice a state administrative regulation. E.g., Carter v. McGinnis, 320 F.Supp. 1092 (W.D.N.Y.1970) (court took judicial notice of state prison regulations); Marnell v. United Parcel Service of America, Inc., 260 F.Supp. 391, 398 (N.D.Cal.1966). But see Campbell v. Mincey, 413 F.Supp. 16, 19 (N.D.Miss.1975), aff'd, 542 F.2d 573 (5th Cir.1976) ("state regulations are beyond the scope of judicial notice provided for in the new Federal Rules of Evidence (rule 201) and also the common law doctrine of judicial notice."). See also 5 J. Moore, Federal Practice ¶ 43.09 (2d ed. 1971).

Several states by statute provide for judicial notice and private acts of the executive departments of their own state. See, e.g., West's Ann.Cal.Evidence Code § 451. The statutes of other states provide for judicial notice of published compilations of administrative regulations. For example, N.Y. CPLR 4511, in part, provides:

> (a) When judicial notice shall be taken without request. Every court shall take judicial notice without request ... of the official compilation of codes, rules and regulations of the state except those that relate solely to the organization or internal management of an agency of the state ...

> (b) When judicial notice may be taken without request. Every court may take judicial notice without request of the ... regulation of officers, agencies or governmental subdivisions of the state or of the United States.

The general common law rule is that judicial notice is not taken of municipal ordinances, but that they must be pleaded and proved. However, judicial notice is provided by statute in some states. E.g., Ill.S.N.A. ch. 51, § 48a, N.Y. CPLR 4511. It is common for courts—whether state or federal—of the jurisdiction encompassing the municipality to judicially notice local ordinances and regulations. Care must be taken to ensure that the provisions relied upon are up-to-date, since the local practice is often sloppy. It may, under such circumstances be desirable to obtain a certificate of the local clerk that the provision furnished is current and accurate. Does such a certificate present an authentication or hearsay issue?

CHAPTER 9

PRIVILEGES

SECTION 1. INTRODUCTION

The purpose of most evidentiary rules is to improve factfinding. The rules governing privileges are different. An evidentiary privilege is a rule that provides a basis for excluding otherwise relevant evidence in a formal proceeding because of extrinsic policy concerns that are deemed more important than the need to resolve the factual issues in the particular case. The privilege rules do not contribute to improved factfinding; to the contrary, by excluding probative evidence, they interfere with the factfinding process and thus add to the burdens and, in some measure, the costs of litigation, civil or criminal.

The subject of privileges has a broad sweep: in this Chapter, we have grouped the various evidentiary privileges according to categories, common attributes, and similar rationales. There is a basic privilege that belongs to the individual—the Privilege Against Self-incrimination. It takes two forms: the privilege of the witness not to answer questions and the privilege of a criminal defendant to not take the stand as a witness. There are a number of other privileges that share a common characteristic—they involve confidential communications between persons who are involved in some sort of professional relationship—such as attorney-client, physician-patient or psychotherapist-privilege, priest-penitent, and journalist-source (as well as other professional relationships to which an evidentiary privilege may be attached).

Another form of "relationship" privilege also involves confidential communications—between two parties to an officially favored relationship, such as husband and wife. A separate husband-wife privilege relates to the situation where one spouse is called to testify against the other.

Still a third general category consists of rules the purpose of which is to protect the effective functioning of institutions, public or private. Examples include executive privilege, official information privilege, and the peer review and critical self-analysis privileges.

The law governing privileges varies from jurisdiction to jurisdiction in the United States. In most states, evidentiary privileges are created by statute. Even where the basic source of privilege law is statutory, a question may be posed whether the courts can create new privileges or whether the statute provides an exhaustive list of the privileges. The original draft of the Federal Rules of Evidence contained thirteen provisions specifying nine different privileges. Before the Federal Rules were promulgated, however, Congress deleted all of the privilege provisions, and in Rule 501, the following language was substituted:

Except as otherwise required by the Constitution ... or provided by Act of Congress or in rules prescribed by the Supreme Court pursuant to statutory authority, the privilege of a witness ... shall be governed by the principles of the common law as they may be interpreted by the courts of the United States in the light of reason and experience. However, in civil actions ..., with respect to an element of a claim or defense as to which

State law supplies the rule of decision, the privilege of a witness, ... shall be determined in accordance with State law.

Congress has also enacted a provision, 28 U.S.C. section 2076, which requires the approval of Congress before any amendment creating, abolishing, or modifying a federal evidentiary privilege can go into effect.

The effect of Rule 501 was to leave the recognition of, and the interpretation of the scope of evidentiary privileges to the federal judiciary without legislative provisions creating specific privileges. In dealing with privilege issues in court cases, however, federal judges still have occasion to refer to the original proposed privilege provisions of the Federal Rules.

The evidentiary privileges are applicable to statements made in formal proceedings where witnesses are under oath and testimony is taken—judicial, administrative, and grand jury proceedings, coroner inquests, and legislative hearings. The privilege against self-incrimination has been extended to apply to statements made outside of any formal proceeding but in the context of "custodial interrogation." Insofar as oral statements are involved, we limit ourselves to testimony taken in formal proceedings; Miranda v. Arizona and its progeny which are typically treated in criminal procedure courses are not examined here.

The privileges also may apply to documentary and other kinds of physical evidence. Indeed, many of the most difficult privilege questions that have arisen in recent years involve matters where the government or a litigant is trying to obtain physical evidence through the use of a subpoena.

Those privileges which are tied to professional relationships should be distinguished from other sources of rules prohibiting a professional from disclosing information obtained in the context of a professional relationship— namely, rules of professional responsibility and professional ethics. The privileges generally only restrict disclosure of confidential communications in formal proceedings while the latter operate to prohibit any disclosure in any setting. The scope and application of the privileges may differ considerably from the professional ethics rules of confidentiality.

The privilege rules typically are enforced by exclusion of the evidence (or, occasionally, by contempt proceedings against a person who, claiming a privilege, refuses to disclose evidence which the court determines is not covered by a privilege). Breach of rules of professional ethics or professional responsibility governing confidentiality are subject to sanction by the appropriate professional association and in serious cases can even lead to loss of a professional license, for example, in the case of an attorney, to disbarment.

Of all the evidentiary privileges, only the privilege against self-incrimination has been created by a constitutional provision. Some of the other privileges derive some support from constitutional provisions and may have a constitutional dimension. A constitutional claim can be made, for example, in connection with the attorney-client privilege under the Sixth Amendment's right to counsel provision. A constitutional claim can also be made with respect to the physician-patient and spousal privileges—namely that the Constitution mandates protecting individual privacy by means of a privilege. Materials relating to constitutional issues of this type are presented at appropriate points in the sections that follow.

In connection with each of the privileges, a starting point for analysis and evaluation is to examine the extrinsic policy rationale(s) for the privilege. In some instances, for example, the confidential communication privileges growing out of a professional relationship, while there may be alternative theories, there is also an obvious, commonly offered rationale—to encourage free communication between attorney and client, doctor and patient, etc.

A key issue in connection with such a rationale is whether, in fact, enforcement of the privilege is necessary to accomplish the purpose of the privilege. This, of course, is an empirical question. The courts generally assume the answer to such questions without in fact trying to ascertain whether the policy has a sound empirical foundation. If you were going to test the rationale underlying the attorney client privilege, for example, how would you approach the question of obtaining empirical evidence on the issue?

In connection with each of the privileges, it is also appropriate to ask:

(1) Are the values being implemented by the rule of privilege important enough to justify the resulting interference with the fact-finding function in the litigation process?

(2) Are the values served by the rule of privilege A as important as those served by privilege B? The answer to this question may affect how broadly or narrowly A and B ought to be construed.

(3) Are the values served by existing rules of privilege more important than the values that would be served were rules of privilege adopted in some areas where they do not now generally exist?

(4) Is each of the intricate rules that have been developed relating to each of the privileges necessary to effectuate the policies underlying the privilege?

Not all privileges are treated in this chapter. Certain areas related to the subject of privileges are covered in other law school courses—e.g., the subject of search and seizure and the informer's privilege—and have therefore been omitted.

SECTION 2. PRIVILEGE BELONGING TO THE INDIVIDUAL: THE PRIVILEGE AGAINST SELF-INCRIMINATION

A. INTRODUCTION

CONSTITUTION OF THE UNITED STATES

AMENDMENT V

No person ... shall be compelled in any criminal case to be a witness against himself....

AMENDMENT XIV

Section 1 ... nor shall any State deprive any person of life, liberty, or property, without due process of law....

Invocation of the privilege against self-incrimination occurs in two kinds of contexts, the privilege of the witness not to answer specific questions and the privilege of the accused not to take the stand to testify. The privilege of the witness can arise in the course of any formal proceeding but probably occurs most frequently today in grand jury proceedings and court trials. In an earlier era, when legislative committees were quite active in an investigatory or inquisitorial mode, issues relating to the application of the witness's privilege in legislative hearings arose in a number of landmark cases.

Basic issues treated in this Section include an examination of the issues raised in connection with determining whether a statement is self-incriminatory. The privilege is deemed only to apply to compelled self-incrimination: what is the applicable doctrine on the compulsion issue, and how does it relate to the doctrine of waiver? Does a person who voluntarily discloses self-incriminatory information in one proceeding waive the privilege with respect to a later different proceeding?

Another basic feature of the privilege as interpreted by the courts is that it only applies to testimonial communications. In a series of recent decisions, including cases in the Supreme Court, the federal courts have wrestled with the application of that aspect of the privilege to efforts by the government to obtain documents that may be evidence of criminal conduct. In this connection, there is often an interplay with other topics, for example, the nonapplicability of the self-incrimination privilege to corporations and other entities and the simultaneous applicability of the attorney-client privilege.

Two major limitations on the scope and application of the self-incrimination privilege are the required records doctrine and the granting of immunity from prosecution in order to overcome a claim of the privilege. Under the required records doctrine, the government can require the maintenance of records and require the production of such records despite a claim of self-incrimination. The immunity issues arise out of the fact that under prevailing Fifth Amendment doctrine, if the government, as authorized by statute, grants immunity to a witness that is coextensive with the privilege against self-incrimination, the witness is required to answer, or be held in contempt. The courts are also beginning to develop some forms of judicially imposed immunity or restrictions on the use of evidence that has been obtained from a witness despite its self-incriminatory aspect.

The Section concludes with two topics that emphasize the privilege issues that relate particularly to the criminal defendant—the kinds of inferences that can be drawn from the fact that the privilege has been invoked and the limitations arising from the privilege that restrict the prosecutor's ability to obtain discovery against the criminal defendant.

B.   HISTORY AND RATIONALE

Legal historians actively continue to debate the origins of the privilege against self-incrimination, and the history is relevant in how the privilege is interpreted today. Thus Professor Meltzer has stated:

> The privilege, which is incorporated in the federal Bill of Rights and in all but two state constitutions, has, somewhat extravagantly, been considered a distinctive feature of the Anglo–American system. This difference easily became a mark of the "peculiar excellence" of our own system. The privilege reflected our preference for an accusatorial-adversary system as opposed to the inquisitorial system of the continental countries—and "inquisitorial procedure" carries a cluster of connotations which are repugnant to those bred in common-law traditions, particularly if they disregard administrative, legislative, and grand jury investigations, as well as police interrogations. Because it symbolizes the right of the individual not to be hounded by the state, the privilege has seemed more important, and limitations on its scope have seemed more alarming, whenever liberty has been threatened.

Meltzer, Required Records, the McCarran Act and the Privilege Against Self-Incrimination, 18 U.Chi.L.Rev. 687 (1951).

Today, however, there is active debate on the question of whether the privilege was indeed a peculiar Anglo–American development. Thus Professor Helmholz has concluded that this type of privilege had been recognized in an early period by the ius commune (the blend of Roman and canon law applied on the European Continent) and that the privilege first entered the body of English law through the ecclesiastical courts. See Helmholz, Origins of the Privilege Against Self–Incrimination: The Role of the European Ius Commune. 65 N.Y.U.L.Rev. 962 (1990).

Professor Langbein, on the other hand, while rejecting the views of scholars such as Wigmore and Levy who "located the origins of the common law privilege in the second half of the seventeenth century, as part of the aftermath of the constitutional struggles that resulted in the abolition of the courts of Star Chamber and High Commission," has concluded that the privilege entered the common law at the end of the eighteenth century as part of the rise of adversary criminal procedure and was "the work of defense counsel." See Langbein, The Historical Origins of the Privilege Against Self–Incrimination at Common Law, 92 Mich.L.Rev. 1047 (1994). For commentary on the on-going historical discussions, see Alschuler, A Peculiar Privilege in Historical Perspective: The Right To Remain Silent, 94 Mich.L.Rev. 2625 (1996). Alschuler notes:

> Linguistic confusion also may have affected historians of the privilege, and some of the apparent disagreement among them may have arisen from the ambiguity of phrases like "privilege against self-incrimination." When scholars like John H. Wigmore have concluded that the privilege was in place in common law courts by the end of the seventeenth century, they have meant, mostly, that sworn witnesses in these courts could decline to answer questions on the ground that their answers would incriminate them. When, however, scholars like John Langbein have maintained that the privilege did not come into effective existence until more than a century later, they have meant, mostly, that until the nineteenth century unsworn criminal defendants were expected to answer questions both before trial and at trial.

Also see Moglen, Taking the Fifth: Reconsidering the Constitutional Origins of the Privilege Against Self–Incrimination, 92 Mich.L.Rev. 1086 (1994). For a collection of articles on the history, see The Privilege Against Self–Incrimination: Its Origins and Development (R.H. Helmholz ed., forthcoming 1997).

The continuing historical debate, as active as it is, is exceeded in intensity by the continuing search for a rationale for the privilege which has intrigued scholars in this country and in England for more than a century. And the debate continues.

At an early date, Bentham and Wigmore took contrasting positions on the privilege, with Bentham arguing that the privilege served no defensible function. Professor Meltzer characterized the Bentham and Wigmore positions as follows:

> Bentham's classic attack on the privilege has dominated later criticism. He argued that only the guilty claimed the privilege or were protected by it, that it deprived the trier of the most serviceable evidence, that it fostered the use of illegal means in the gathering of evidence, and that its recognition was based on sentimentality and a confusion of interrogation with torture.

Bentham's argument did not persuade Wigmore, whose appraisal in turn deserves re-examination both because it has been so influential and because its underlying assumptions are not without their difficulties.

In justifying the defendant's immunity from compulsory incrimination at the trial stage, Wigmore implied that it was designed to protect the innocent. His principal emphasis, however, was on the stimulus which the privilege gives to effective and civilized detection practices by the police. He found that—

> The real objection is that any system of administration which permits the prosecution to trust habitually to compulsory self-disclosure as a source of proof must itself suffer morally thereby. The inclination develops to rely mainly upon such evidence, and to be satisfied with an incomplete investigation of the other sources. The exercise of the power to extract answers begets a forgetfulness of the just limitations of that power. The simple and peaceful process of questioning breeds a readiness to resort to bullying and to physical force and torture. If there is a right to an answer, there soon seems to be a right to the expected answer,—that is, to a confession of guilt. Thus the legitimate use grows into the unjust abuse; ultimately, the innocent are jeopardized by the encroachments of a bad system. Such seems to have been the course of experience in those legal systems where the privilege was not recognized.

See Meltzer, supra at 687–690.

Other rationales have been advanced. Thus a familiar argument is that in the absence of the privilege the defendant is put to a cruel trilemma—testify truthfully and incriminate oneself, or commit perjury and incur the risk of conviction for that crime, or remain silent and suffer the sanction of contempt. See Meltzer, supra at 693. It has been suggested that the cruel trilemma argument is conceptually linked to a theory of excuse, the criminal doctrine that individuals should not be held liable for conduct that law abiding citizens would have engaged in. See Stuntz, Self–Incrimination and Excuse, 88 Columb.L.Rev. 1227 (1988).

Another important claim is that compelled self-incrimination violates individual privacy and autonomy and that there is a moral right to silence against the state. See Gerstein, Privacy and Self–Incrimination, 80 Ethics 87 (1970); Gerstein, Punishment and Self–Incrimination, 16, Am.J.Juris. 84 (1971); Gerstein, The Demise of Boyd: Self–Incrimination and Private Papers in the Burger Court, 27 U.C.L.A.L.Rev. 343 (1979); Greenawalt, Silence as a Moral and Constitutional Right, 23 Wm. & Mary L.Rev. 15 (1981).

The Supreme Court has addressed the privacy rationale in the following terms:

> It is true that the Court has often stated that one of the several purposes served by the constitutional privilege against compelled testimonial self-incrimination is that of protecting personal privacy.... But the Court has never suggested that every invasion of privacy violates the privilege. Within the limits imposed by the language of the Fifth Amendment, which we necessarily observe, the privilege truly serves privacy interests; but the Court has never on any ground, personal privacy included, applied the Fifth Amendment to prevent the otherwise proper acquisition or use of evidence which, in the Court's view, did not involve compelled testimonial self-incrimination of some sort.

If the Fifth Amendment protected generally against the obtaining of private information from a man's mouth or pen or house, its protections would presumably not be lifted by probable cause and a warrant or by immunity. The privacy invasion is not mitigated by immunity; and the Fifth Amendment's strictures, unlike the Fourth's, are not removed by showing reasonableness. The Framers addressed the subject of personal privacy directly in the Fourth Amendment. They struck a balance so that when the State's reason to believe incriminating evidence will be found becomes sufficiently great, the invasion of privacy becomes justified and a warrant to search and seize will issue. They did not seek in still another Amendment—the Fifth—to achieve a general protection of privacy but to deal with the more specific issue of compelled self-incrimination.

We cannot cut the Fifth Amendment completely loose from the moorings of its language, and make it serve as a general protector of privacy—a word not mentioned in its text and a concept directly addressed in the Fourth Amendment.

Fisher v. United States, 425 U.S. 391 (1976).

Professor Schulhofer has justified the privilege on the ground that it protects innocent defendants who might be poor witnesses in their own behalf, Schulhofer, Some Kind Words for the Privilege Against Self–Incrimination, 26 Val.U.L.Rev. 311 (1991), while Professor Akhil Amar and Renee Lettow have advanced the related notion that the privilege should be interpreted as aimed at unreliable evidence, Amar and Lettow, Fifth Amendment First Principles: The Self–Incrimination Clause, 93 Mich.L.Rev. 857 (1995). Accordingly, compelled testimony should not be admitted but the fruits of such testimony should be admissible.

McCormick has also supported the claim that the privilege enhances the judicial process's access to reliable information, 1 McCormick on Evidence 432 (4th ed., Strong, 1992) and that it helps make the criminal trial more nearly a contest between equals, ibid.

For a good summary of the various theories and a critical analysis of the various rationales offered in support of the privilege, see Dolinko, Is There a Rationale for the Privilege Against Self–Incrimination, 33 UCLA L.Rev. 1063 (1986). Dolinko systematically reviews and criticizes each of the rationales for the privilege and concludes:

> Some claim that the privilege promotes the goals of the criminal justice system; others that it is a corollary of one or another fundamental right. I have argued that neither of these justificatory strategies succeeds. If I am correct, the role of the privilege in American Law can be explained by specific historical developments, but cannot be justified either functionally or conceptually. Id. at 1147.

Query: Does the scope and operation of the privilege depend on which, if any, of the foregoing reasons are adopted as the basis for the privilege? In examining the cases in this section, keep in mind the various possible justifications for the privilege.

The literature on the origins of, and rationale for, the privilege is quite extensive. In addition to the authorities cited above, see, e.g. 8 Wigmore, Evidence § 2250 (McNaughton rev. 1961); McNaughton, The Privilege Against Self–Incrimination: Its Constitutional Affectation, Raison d'Etre and Miscellaneous Implications, 51 J.Crim.L., Criminol. & Police Sci. 138 (1960); Levy, Origins of the Fifth Amendment (1968); Pittman, The Colonial and Constitutional History of the Privilege Against Self–Incrimination in America, 21

Va.L.Rev. 163 (1935); Wigmore, Nemo Tenetur Seipsum Prodere, 5 Harv.L.Rev. 71 (1891); Griswold, The Fifth Amendment Today (1955); Griswold, The Right to Be Let Alone, 55 Nw.U.L.Rev. 216 (1960); Fortas, The Fifth Amendment: Nemo Tenetur Prodere Seipsum, 25 Cleve.B.A.J. 98 (1954); Friendly, The Fifth Amendment Tomorrow: The Case for Constitutional Change, 37 U. of Cinn. L.Rev. 671 (1968); Schiller, On the Jurisprudence of the Fifth Amendment Right to Silence, 16 Am.Crim.L.Rev. 197 (1979); Greenawalt, Perspectives on the Right to Silence, in Crime, Criminology and Public Policy 259 (R. Hood ed. 1974); For useful comparative material, see Kirschenbaum, Self–Incrimination in Jewish Law (New York 1970); Enker, Self–Incrimination in Jewish Law—A Review Essay, Dine Israel IV p. cvii (1973); I. M. Rosenberg & Y. L. Rosenberg, The Talmudic Rule Against Self–Incrimination, 63 N.Y.U.L.Rev. 955 (1988); Mendelson, Self–Incrimination in American and French Law, 19 Crim.L.Bull. 34 (1983).

C. BASIC ELEMENTS

1. THE TEST FOR SELF–INCRIMINATION

Whether a court will accept a witness's fifth amendment claim not to be required to answer a specific question depends on whether the answer to the question would tend to incriminate under the applicable test for self-incrimination. That issue has several different dimensions-a) whether the answer has a sufficient evidentiary connection to possible criminal liability; b) whether prosecution would, as a practical matter, be sufficiently likely; and c) the jurisdictional feature—whether a risk of prosecution in another jurisdiction is sufficient to qualify under the privilege. Each of these dimensions is treated below.

a. *The Evidentiary Dimension*

In Hoffman v. United States, 341 U.S. 479 (1951), the Supreme Court described the evidentiary test to be applied:

> The privilege afforded not only extends to answers that would in them selves support a conviction under a federal criminal statute but likewise embraces those which would furnish a link in the chain of evidence needed to prosecute the claimant for a federal crime. But this protection must be confined to instances where the witness has reasonable cause to apprehend danger from a direct answer. The witness is not exonerated from answering merely because he declares that in so doing he would incriminate himself—his say-so does not of itself establish the hazard of incrimination. It is for the court to say whether his silence is justified, and to require him to answer if "it clearly appears to the court that he is mistaken." Temple v. Commonwealth, 75 Va. 892, 899 (1881). To sustain the privilege, it need only be evident from the implications of the question, in the setting in which it is asked, that a responsive answer to the question or an explanation of why it cannot be answered might be dangerous because injurious disclosure could result. The trial judge in appraising the claim "must be governed as much by his personal perception of the peculiarities of the case as by the facts actually in evidence." See Taft, J., in Ex parte Irvine, C.C.S.D.Ohio, 1896, 74 F. 954, 960.

In Hoffman, petitioner had been convicted of criminal contempt for refusing to obey a federal court order requiring him to answer certain questions asked in a grand jury investigation. In response to subpoena, petitioner had appeared to testify before a special federal grand jury that was investigating fraud and violations of the customs, narcotics and internal revenue liquor laws of the United States, the Mann Act, perjury, bribery, and other federal criminal laws. The pertinent interrogation, in which he refused to answer, proceeded as follows:

"Q. What do you do now, Mr. Hoffman?

"A. I refuse to answer.

"Q. Have you been in the same undertaking since the first of the year?

"A. I don't understand the question.

"Q. Have you been doing the same thing you are doing now since the first of the year?

"A. I refuse to answer.

"Q. Do you know Mr. William Weisberg?

"A. I do.

"Q. How long have you known him?

"A. Practically twenty years, I guess.

"Q. When did you last see him?

"A. I refuse to answer.

"Q. Have you seen him this week?

"A. I refuse to answer.

"Q. Do you know that a subpoena has been issued for Mr. Weisberg?

"A. I heard about it in Court.

"Q. Have you talked with him on the telephone this week?

"A. I refuse to answer.

"Q. Do you know where Mr. William Weisberg is now?

"A. I refuse to answer.

It was stipulated that petitioner declined to answer on the ground that his answers might tend to incriminate him of a federal offense.

In ruling upon petitioner's claim of privilege, the court set forth the following facts as "the background as indicated by the record":

The judge who ruled on the privilege had himself impaneled the special grand jury to investigate "rackets" in the district. He had explained to the jury that "the Attorney General's office has come into this district to conduct an investigation ... [that] will run the gamut of all crimes covered by Federal statute." "If rackets infest or encrust our system of government," he instructed, "just as any blight attacks any other growth, it withers and dies.... " Subpoenas had issued for some twenty witnesses, but only eleven had been served; as the prosecutor put it, he was "having trouble finding some big shots." Several of those who did appear and were called into the grand-jury room before petitioner had refused to answer questions until ordered to do so by the court. The prosecutor had requested bench warrants for eight of the nine who had not appeared the first day of the session, one of whom was William Weisberg. Petitioner had admitted having known Weisberg for about twenty years. In addition, counsel for petitioner had advised the court that "It has been broadly published that [petitioner] has a police record."

The court went on to state:

> [The court below] ... should have considered, in connection with the business questions, that the chief occupation of some persons involves evasion of federal criminal laws, and that truthful answers by petitioner to these questions might have disclosed that he was engaged in such proscribed activity.
>
> Also, the court should have recognized, in considering the Weisberg questions, that one person with a police record summoned to testify before a grand jury investigating the rackets might be hiding or helping to hide another person of questionable repute sought as a witness. To be sure, the Government may inquire of witnesses before the grand jury as to the whereabouts of unlocated witnesses; ordinarily the answers to such questions are harmless if not fruitless. But of the seven questions relating to Weisberg (of which three were answered), three were designed to draw information as to petitioner's contacts and connection with the fugitive witness; and the final question, perhaps an afterthought of the prosecutor, inquired of Weisberg's whereabouts at the time. All of them could easily have required answers that would forge links in a chain of facts imperiling petitioner with conviction of a federal crime. The three questions, if answered affirmatively, would establish contacts between petitioner and Weisberg during the crucial period when the latter was eluding the grand jury; and in the context of these inquiries the last question might well have called for disclosure that Weisberg was hiding away on petitioner's premises or with his assistance. Petitioner could reasonably have sensed the peril of prosecution for federal offenses ranging from obstruction to conspiracy.
>
> In this setting it was not "perfectly clear, from a careful consideration of all the circumstances in the case, that the witness is mistaken, and that the answer[s] cannot possibly have such tendency" to incriminate.
>
> This conclusion is buttressed by the supplemental record. It showed that petitioner had a twenty-year police record and had been publicly labeled an "underworld character and racketeer"; that the Senate Crime Investigating Committee had placed his name on a list of "known gangsters" from the Philadelphia area who had made Miami Beach their headquarters; that Philadelphia police officials had described him as "the king of the shore rackets who lives by the gun"; that he had served a sentence on a narcotics charge; and that his previous conviction was dramatized by a picture appearing in the local press while he was waiting to testify, in which petitioner was photographed with the head of the Philadelphia office of the United States Bureau of Narcotics in an accusing pose.

NOTES

1. The Hoffman case was decided in an era when many investigations were being undertaken by grand juries and legislative committees into the possibility of subversive activity. See, e.g., Rogers v. United States, 340 U.S. 367 (1951); Blau v. United States, 340 U.S. 159 (1950); Quinn v. United States, 349 U.S. 155 (1955); Emspak v. United States, 349 U.S. 190 (1955).

2. The principal case sets forth several different considerations relevant to establishing a legitimate claim to the privilege:

a) The basic requirement for asserting a claim to the privilege: Would the witness's answer "furnish a link in the chain of evidence" needed to prosecute the claimant for a crime?

b) The formula governing the witness's apprehension of the likelihood of incrimination: "reasonable cause to apprehend danger from a direct answer".

c) The standard of proof to be applied by the judge in ruling on the claim: whether or not it is "perfectly clear ... that the witness is mistaken, and that the answer[s] cannot possibly have" a tendency to incriminate.

d) The attitude with which the issue is to be approached: In making this determination the judge is to liberally construe the privilege "in favor of the right it was intended to secure."

e) The sources and kinds of facts to be considered in ruling on the claim: all the circumstances in the case including the trial judge's "personal perception of the peculiarities of the case," its setting and background and all other evidence in the record including supplemental facts offered by the witness in support of his claim of privilege. To what extent does Cal.Evid.Code § 404 capture the same factors covered by Hoffman?

b. The Likelihood of Prosecution

How realistic must the fear of prosecution be? To what extent should the court take into account that in point of fact a prosecution would not be likely to be undertaken?

NOTES

1. In United States v. Zappola, 646 F.2d 48 (2d Cir.1981), one of the victims of an attempted extortion claimed his privilege against self-incrimination with respect to conversations and meetings that occurred while he was acting in an undercover capacity for the government. The court of appeals rejected the claim on the ground that he could not reasonably fear prosecution with respect to his activities as a government agent. See also United States v. Damiano, 579 F.2d 1001 (6th Cir.1978) and United States v. Melchor Moreno, 536 F.2d 1042 (5th Cir.1976).

2. In Commonwealth v. Carrera, 227 A.2d 627 (Pa.1967) an unmarried woman who had undergone an abortion was called before a grand jury to give testimony about the perpetrators. The court assumed arguendo that the woman could not be prosecuted for her part in the abortion but sustained the claim of privilege on the ground that she could fear a fornication prosecution based upon the intercourse that led to conception.

3. The issue of the practical likelihood of prosecution also arises in connection with the witness's fear of the risk of prosecution in a foreign jurisdiction-see below.

c. The Jurisdictional Dimension

To what extent is the fear of prosecution in another jurisdiction a legitimate basis for invoking the privilege?

NOTES

1. Murphy v. Waterfront Commission, 378 U.S. 52 (1964) made it clear that the possibility of prosecution in another jurisdiction—state or federal—within our federal structure is a sufficient basis for applying the privilege.

2. What about the risk of prosecution in a foreign country? Is it a sufficient basis for legitimately invoking the privilege? Such issues often arise in connection with immunity grants, see infra p. 1373. In many of the cases, the courts have avoided having to reach the constitutional issue by concluding that, for one reason or another, there was no practical likelihood of prosecution in the foreign jurisdiction:

a) See, e.g., Zicarelli v. New Jersey State Commission of Investigation, 406 U.S. 472 (1972) where the court ruled that the witness was never in real danger of being compelled to disclose information that might incriminate him under foreign law.

b) If a witness's grand jury testimony would incriminate him under foreign law but the grand jury minutes are secret, does the possibility of a leak pose a sufficient reason to invoke the privilege? See In re Federal Grand Jury Witness, 597 F.2d 1166 (9th Cir.1979); In re Campbell, 628 F.2d 1260 (9th Cir.1980).

c) Also see In re Grand Jury Subpoena of Flanagan, 691 F.2d 116 (2d Cir.1982): The immunized grand jury witness's fear of prosecution in a foreign jurisdiction (Ireland or the UK) for IRA–related activities was "remote and speculative rather than real, reasonable, or substantial." There was no pending or prospective prosecution there, nor any effort to extradite him, nor any indication that his conduct was covered by extradition treaties. The unanswered questions all related to activities in the United States. There was no indication that Ireland or the UK claimed extraterritorial jurisdiction. Further, the grand jury testimony was secret, and the government gave assurances that it would not disclose his immunized testimony to anyone. See generally, Note, 14 Am.Crim.L.Rev. 275 (1976); Note, 10 Brooklyn J.Internat.Law 219 (1984).

d) Even where an arrest warrant had already been issued in the foreign jurisdiction, the witness' fear of foreign prosecution was deemed not to be substantial, since the likelihood that he would be extradited was considered to be low; moreover, it was assumed that the district court could keep the testimony secret. In re Application of the President's Commission on Organized Crime, 763 F.2d 1191 (11th Cir.1985). Also see In re Grand Jury Proceedings: Witness–Perdue, 819 F.2d 984 (11th Cir.1987); In re Sealed Case, 825 F.2d 494 (D.C.Cir.), cert. denied, 484 U.S. 963 (1987).

e) Because the cases described in the preceding paragraphs in this note all concluded that the immunized witness did not confront a "real and substantial" risk of foreign prosecution, they did not reach the constitutional question, whether, if fully immunized under domestic law, the witness could invoke a fifth amendment privilege based upon a fear of foreign prosecution. Finally, however, in United States v. (Under Seal) (Araneta), 794 F.2d 920 (4th Cir.), cert. denied, 479 U.S. 924 (1986), the court concluded that there was a risk of actual prosecution of the witnesses in the foreign jurisdiction (the witnesses were the daughter and son-in-law of Ferdinand E. Marcos, and the foreign jurisdiction was the Philippines). Accordingly, the court addressed the constitutional issue:

> To determine whether the Fifth Amendment protects from compelled self-incrimination a witness immunized under domestic law but exposed to a substantial risk of foreign prosecution, we reason by analogy to the extension of the Fifth Amendment to prosecutions under state law. When the Fifth Amendment was applied only to the federal government, the Supreme Court held that the protection it afforded did not forbid the United States from compelling testimony from a witness that would incriminate him under state law. Only when the Fifth Amendment was held applicable to the states, was the privilege held to protect a witness in

state or federal court from incriminating himself under either federal or state law.

From this history, we conclude that the Fifth Amendment privilege applies only where the sovereign compelling the testimony and the sovereign using the testimony are both restrained by the Fifth Amendment from compelling self-incrimination. Since the Fifth Amendment would not prohibit the use of compelled incriminating testimony in a Philippine court, it affords an immunized witness no privilege not to testify before a federal grand jury on the ground that his testimony will incriminate him under Philippine law.

Insofar as the privilege exists to promote the criminal justice system established by our Constitution, it can have no application to a prosecution by a foreign sovereign not similarly constrained. Comity among nations dictates that the United States not intrude into the law enforcement activities of other countries conducted abroad. With regard to insulating the individual from the moral hazards of self-incrimination, perjury or contempt, the United States has done everything in its power to relieve the pressure by granting the Aranetas use and derivative use immunity. Just as comity among nations requires the United States to respect the law enforcement processes of other nations, our own national sovereignty would be compromised if our system of criminal justice were made to depend on the actions of foreign governments beyond our control. It would be intolerable to require the United States to forego evidence legitimately within its reach solely because a foreign power could deploy this evidence in a fashion not permitted within this country. Our conclusion in this respect is reinforced by the authorities that hold, as a matter of domestic law, that the Fifth Amendment privilege does not protect the witness against all adverse uses of his compelled testimony but only those adverse uses specifically proscribed by the Fifth Amendment. Id. at 926–927.

Accord: In re Grand Jury Proceedings, Doe # 700; United States v. (Under Seal), 817 F.2d 1108 (4th Cir.1987). See generally, Note: The Reach of the Fifth Amendment Privilege When Domestically Compelled Testimony May Be Used in a Foreign Country's Court, 69 Va.L.Rev. 875 (1983).

2. COMPELLED DISCLOSURE AND WAIVER

NOTES

1. Suppose a witness in the course of testifying, without objecting thereto, discloses information which is self-incriminating? In Garner v. United States, 424 U.S. 648 (1976), the court addressed this issue as follows:

The Court has held that an individual under compulsion to make disclosures as a witness who revealed information instead of claiming the privilege lost the benefit of the privilege.... [I]n the ordinary case, if a witness under compulsion to testify makes disclosures instead of claiming the privilege, the Government has not "compelled" him to incriminate himself.

The Amendment speaks of compulsion. It does not preclude a witness from testifying voluntarily in matters which may incriminate him. If, therefore, he desires the protection of the privilege, he must claim it or he will not be considered to have been "compelled" within the meaning of the Amendment. United States v. Monia, supra, 317 U.S. at 427, 63 S.Ct. at 410, 87 L.Ed. at 380 ... Unless a witness objects, a government ordinarily may assume that its compulsory processes are not eliciting testimony that he deems to be incriminating. Only the witness knows whether the apparently innocent disclosure sought may incriminate him, and the burden appropriately lies with him to make a timely assertion of the privilege. If, instead, he discloses the information sought, any incriminations properly are viewed as not compelled....

In a footnote to the above quoted material, the court stated:

Some cases have indicated that a nonclaiming witness has "waived" the privilege ... others have indicated that such a witness testifies "voluntarily,".... Neither usage seems analytically sound. ... [I]t seems desirable to reserve the term "waiver" in these cases for process by which one affirmatively renounces the protection of the privilege.

The court thus, inter alia, rejected the use of the language of waiver in situations where a witness, without objecting, made incriminating disclosures in the course of testifying. Earlier cases had typically used the language of waiver in such situations.

Garner was characterized in CFTC v. Collins, 997 F.2d 1230 (7th Cir.1993) as follows: "Garner ... holds that the taxpayer who includes incriminating information on his return is like the witness who blurts out incriminating testimony rather than invoking the Fifth Amendment and keeping mum: He has not been compelled to testify against himself, he has no Fifth...."

2. In Rogers v. United States, 340 U.S. 367, 370–374 (1951), Chief Justice Vinson stated:

If petitioner desired the protection of the privilege against self-incrimination, she was required to claim it. The privilege "is deemed waived unless invoked." United States v. Murdock, 1931, 284 U.S. 141, 148, 52 S.Ct. 63, 76 L.Ed. 210....

Although the claim was made at the time of her second refusal to answer in the presence of the court, it came only after she had voluntarily testified to her status as an officer of the Communist Party of Denver. To uphold a claim of privilege in this case would open the way to distortion of facts by permitting a witness to select any stopping place in the testimony....

Since the privilege against self-incrimination presupposes a real danger of legal detriment arising from the disclosure, petitioner cannot invoke the privilege where response to the specific question in issue here would not further incriminate her. Disclosure of a fact waives the privilege as to details. As this Court stated in Brown v. Walker, 1896, 161 U.S. 591, 597, 16 S.Ct. 644, 647, 40 L.Ed. 819:

Thus, if the witness himself elects to waive his privilege, as he may doubtless do, since the privilege is for his protection and not for that of other parties, and discloses his criminal connections, he is not permitted to stop, but must go on and make a full disclosure.

Following this rule, federal courts have uniformly held that, where criminating facts have been voluntarily revealed, the privilege cannot be invoked to avoid disclosure of the details....

Requiring full disclosure of details after a witness freely testifies as to a criminating fact does not rest upon a further "waiver" of the privilege against self-incrimination. Admittedly, petitioner had already "waived" her privilege of silence when she freely answered criminating questions relating to her connection with the Communist Party. But when petitioner was asked to furnish the name of the person to whom she turned over Party records, the court was required to determine, as it must whenever the privilege is claimed, whether the question presented a reasonable danger of further crimination in light of all the circumstances, including any previous disclosures. . . .

3. The Court in Rogers favorably quoted (at n. 16) from VIII Wigmore Evidence (1940) § 2276 as follows: "The case of the ordinary witness can hardly present any doubt. He may waive his privilege, this is conceded. He waives it by exercising his option of answering: this is conceded. Thus the only inquiry can be whether, by answering as to fact X he waived it for fact Y. If the two are related facts, parts of a whole fact forming a single relevant topic, then his waiver as to a part is a waiver as to the remaining parts; because the privilege exists for the sake of the criminating fact as a whole."

Query: Is there often likely to be room for argument as to whether fact X and fact Y are sufficiently related to form "a single relevant topic" of crimination? See Justice Black dissenting in Rogers v. United States, 340 U.S. 367, 379 (1951). Compare the similar problem of characterization under the scope of cross-examination rules, supra, p. 371. Regarding the issue of waiver by the accused who testifies, see infra, p. 1385.

4. It has been suggested that the combination of the rule of Hoffman with that of Rogers poses a dilemma for witnesses:

> On the one hand they risk imprisonment for contempt by asserting the privilege prematurely. On the other, they might lose the privilege if they answer a single question. The court's view makes the protection depend on timing so refined that lawyers, let alone laymen, will have difficulty in knowing when to claim it.

Justice Black dissenting in Rogers v. United States, 340 U.S. 367, 378 (1951).

Might it have been argued in Hoffman that the witness had waived the privilege by the answers he had given to some of the questions? Consider, for example, the situation in In re Grand Jury Subpoena Dated April 9, 1996 (Smith) F.3d (11th Cir. 1996) No. 96–4676, 6/21/96: The sole officer and director of a corporation was served with a subpoena directed to her as the custodian of the corporate records. When called to testify before the grand jury, she testified that she did not have the records and refused to answer when asked where the records were located. The government, inter alia, argued that by stating to the grand jury that she did not have the records, she waived the privilege against self-incrimination. The court rejected the government's contention:

> If Smith possessed the records, she would have been required to turn them over. If she remained silent at the enforcement hearing, the inference would have been that she was refusing to comply with the order to produce the records. To treat her statement as a waiver would create an intolerable result; she would have had to choose between testifying and being held in contempt, and her Fifth Amendment right would have slipped between the cracks.

The suggestion that judicial decisions might create a no man's land through which testifying witnesses who wish to claim the privilege must tread has not generally been borne out by the cases, as the (Smith) case, supra, indicates, perhaps also because witnesses are usually able to invoke the privilege early enough under the doctrine of Hoffman to avoid the risk posed under Rogers. For consideration of whether Smith had a fifth amendment privilege, see infra p. 1353.

5. The Garner case, supra note 1, involved a nontax criminal prosecution in which the Government introduced at trial the defendant's income tax returns, which he had earlier filed without invoking the privilege. The question was whether the introduction of this evidence at trial, over petitioner's fifth amendment objection, violated the privilege against compulsory self-incrimination when petitioner had earlier made the incriminating disclosures on his returns instead of then claiming the privilege. As indicated in note 1, supra, the court in Garner concluded that it was not "analytically sound" to use the language of waiver or voluntariness in characterizing the action of an ordinary witness in freely giving incriminating testimony.

Despite Garner the lower courts have not generally switched from using the language of waiver to the language of non-compulsion. See, e.g., United States v. Miller, 904 F.2d 65 (D.C.Cir.1990). Were they to do so, would this change in language be likely to affect the result reached in individual cases? Should the result in a particular case depend on whether the issue is whether the witness is deemed to have waived the privilege, or whether self-incriminating testimony given by a witness is deemed not to have been compelled?

Would the privilege question be any different if a taxpayer made disclosures on her tax return without objection and then subsequently was called at a trial to testify as to the same matters? In that circumstance, applying the Garner analytical language, it can be argued that the fact that the taxpayer made uncompelled incriminatory disclosures on her return should not prevent her from invoking the privilege when a subsequent effort is made to compel her testimony regarding the same matter? Is it any easier to reach such a conclusion using the language of compulsion than it would be if the language of waiver were used?

6. The issue posed at the end of the preceding note has usually been addressed in waiver terms—that is, does testimony in one proceeding as to incriminating matter waive a witness's claim to the privilege against giving testimony regarding the same subject matter in a later proceeding? Wigmore and McCormick indicate that generally the prevailing answer is "no". See 8 Wigmore § 2276 (McNaughton rev. 1961). McCormick on Evidence § 140 at 347–348 (3d ed., Cleary, 1984). Query, why should a different rule apply to the witness's testimony in one proceeding than it does in two separate proceedings? Thus, if a witness testifies as to part of a transaction, he can be required to testify as to the whole, see note 3 supra; he will be deemed to have waived as to the rest. But if he testifies in one proceeding as to the whole, he can under the majority rule still invoke the privilege in a second proceeding as to the same subject matter.

The District of Columbia Circuit rejected the majority view in Ellis v. United States, 416 F.2d 791 (D.C.Cir.1969), where the court ruled that the prevailing doctrine was unsound, at least as applied to a witness who first testified in a grand jury proceeding voluntarily and with knowledge of his privilege and then refused to testify at a trial based on an indictment returned by the same grand jury that heard his testimony. Judge Leventhal wrote:

> Once a witness has voluntarily spoken out, we do not see how his protected interest is jeopardized by testifying in a subsequent proceeding, provided he is not required to disclose matters of substance which are unknown to the Government....

> It would impede sound law enforcement if an implicated but cooperating witness can decide, after he has made disclosure to the grand jury, that he will refuse to testify at trial.... [T]he witness is entitled to counsel [at the trial], either his own or court appointed, and may object to any question

that would require disclosure of new matter of substance. Ellis v. United States, 416 F.2d 791, 801, 805 (D.C.Cir.1969).

Judge Leventhal also indicated in a footnote: "Since the concept of waiver is a circumscribed one, it would be well for the prosecutor routinely to advise all grand jury witnesses waiving the privilege that they may be called to testify at trial, to avoid any possible subsequent contention that they did not knowingly waive what they thought was a right to be silent at trial."

Although the Ellis decision has not generally been followed in other circuits, see e.g. United States v. Johnson, 488 F.2d 1206, 1210 (1st Cir.1973); Ottomano v. United States, 468 F.2d 269, 273 (1st Cir.1972); United States v. Housand, 550 F.2d 818, 821, n. 3 (2d Cir.1977); United States v. Licavoli, 604 F.2d 613, 623 (9th Cir.1979), the doctrine has been reaffirmed in the District of Columbia. See United States v. Miller, 904 F.2d 65 (D.C.Cir.1990).

7. Compare with the waiver issues discussed in the previous notes the waiver doctrine applied with respect to the attorney-client and other confidential communication privileges, infra, pp. 1482 et seq. Is the privilege against self-incrimination different? In what respects?

Of course, in many circumstances, if hearsay concerns can be overcome (as they often will be), the earlier testimony may anyway be admissible (in the same way as the tax returns in Garner were admitted in the later prosecution). But the question remains: why should not the earlier disclosure bar the witness from subsequently invoking the privilege? Arguably, the answer to that question should not turn on terminology, that is, whether the language of compulsion or waiver is used, but rather on whether the conclusion reached is consonant with the underlying rationale of the privilege. Suppose, for example, that a protection of privacy rationale for the privilege were accepted by the courts. What conclusion should follow regarding the two proceedings-waiver issue? Suppose the cruel trilemma rationale were adopted.

8. Is the import of the Garner and Rogers cases that incriminating testimony obtained from an "ordinary witness" does not violate the privilege even though the witness has not made a "knowing and intelligent" waiver of the privilege? That there is no requirement that the ordinary witness be given warnings relating to the privilege before testifying? On the other hand, incriminating statements obtained from a criminal suspect in custody or a criminal accused are not admissible unless there has been a "knowing, intelligent waiver," Miranda v. Arizona, 384 U.S. 436, 444 (1966). Warnings must be given before interrogating such a person. Ibid. The fact, however, that the suspect is not made aware of all the crimes about which he may be questioned is not relevant in determining the validity of his decision to waive the privilege. Colorado v. Spring, 479 U.S. 564 (1987).

What might justify drawing distinctions between the ordinary witness and the criminal suspect? Is the ordinary witness at trial, in a grand jury or other formal proceeding, or in filling out a tax return, in a better position to protect himself against self-incrimination and thus less needy than a criminal suspect of the protection of warnings and a knowing, intelligent waiver requirement?

9. Other warnings decisions—

a) In United States v. Washington, 431 U.S. 181 (1977), the court ruled that the warnings given to a grand jury witness, inter alia, that he had a right to remain silent before the grand jury and that anything he said could be used against him in court were adequate to negate "any possible compulsion to self-incrimination which might otherwise exist." The Court expressly declined to decide "whether any Fifth Amendment warnings are constitutionally required for grand jury witnesses," indicating that in this case the witness was "clearly ... on notice that he was a suspect."

b) In United States v. Mandujano, 425 U.S. 564 (1976), a person suspected of criminal activity was called to testify before the grand jury. Before testifying, he was told generally of his right not to answer incriminating questions, about the possibility of liability for perjury for false answers and about his right to consult with counsel outside of the grand jury room. He was subsequently charged with perjury based upon his grand jury testimony. Eight justices (Justice Stevens did not participate) rejected his claim that his allegedly perjured grand jury testimony should be suppressed because prior to testifying he had not been given full Miranda warnings (including, e.g., warnings as to his right to remain silent, his right to have counsel with him and his right to have counsel appointed for him if he could not afford an attorney).

Four justices (Burger joined by White, Powell and Rehnquist) generally rejected his claim that Miranda warnings were required for a grand jury witness who was a putative defendant. Two justices (Brennan joined by Marshall) would require an effective warning and an intentional and intelligent waiver of the right to be free from compulsory self-incrimination before a putative defendant could be questioned by the grand jury; further, that the putative defendant should be told at least that he has a right to have counsel appointed for him if he cannot afford one and the right to consult with counsel before answering any question posed. Justice Stewart joined by Justice Blackmun wrote a brief opinion in which he did not reach the issues explored in the other two opinions because the "Fifth Amendment privilege ... provides no protection for the commission of perjury." Id. 425 U.S. 564, 609. See generally, McCormick on Evidence 337–340 (3rd ed., Cleary, 1984).

10. How does one establish the legitimacy of a claim of privilege without disclosing incriminating matter? In Hoffman, supra p. 1321, the court stated:

> However, if the witness, upon interposing his claim, were required to prove the hazard in the sense in which a claim is usually required to be established in court, he would be compelled to surrender the very protection which the privilege is designed to guarantee.

What implications flow from the quoted statement? That a court should not require the witness to prove very much in order to claim the privilege? Are there alternative approaches? Compare Cal.Evid.Code § 915. See United States v. Melchor Moreno, 536 F.2d 1042, 1046–1048 (5th Cir.1976).

11. In Rogers the witness had the opportunity to raise her privilege claim and obtain an immediate judicial ruling on the validity of the claim at the time she gave her testimony. In the Garner context, if the taxpayer claims the privilege on his return, there is no opportunity for a judicial ruling on the validity of the claim until a prosecution is instituted for failing to provide required information. In Garner, the Court held that a preliminary judicial ruling on the validity of the claim of privilege is not required by the Fifth Amendment guarantee. Accord: United States v. Murdock, 284 U.S. 141 (1931).

12. Maness v. Meyers, 419 U.S. 449 (1975) reversed a lower court ruling holding in contempt two lawyers who, in a civil proceeding that could lead to issuance of an injunction against distribution of obscene materials, by their advice had caused their client to decline on fifth amendment grounds to produce subpoenaed material. The court stated:

> We begin with the basic proposition that all orders ... of courts must be complied with promptly.... [C]ounsel should neither engage the court in

extended discussion once a ruling is made, nor advise a client not to comply. . . .

When a court during trial orders a witness to reveal information, however, a different situation may be presented. Compliance could cause irreparable injury because appellate courts cannot always "unring the bell" once the information has been released. . . . In those situations . . . the person to whom such an order is directed has an alternative . . . "resistance to that order with the concomitant possibility of an adjudication of contempt if his claims are rejected on appeal". . . .

This method of achieving precompliance review is particularly appropriate where the Fifth Amendment privilege against self-incrimination is involved.

In the present case the City Attorney argued that if petitioner's client produced the magazines he was amply protected because in any ensuing criminal action, he could always move to suppress, or object on Fifth Amendment grounds to the introduction of the magazines into evidence. Laying to one side possible waiver problems that might arise if the witness followed that course, cf. Rogers v. United States . . . , we nevertheless cannot conclude that it would afford adequate protection. Without something more "he would be compelled to surrender the very protection which the privilege is designed to guarantee." Hoffman v. United States. . . .

Although it is clear that non-compliance risked . . . a final criminal contempt judgment against the witness if, on appeal, petitioner's advice proved to be wrong, the issue here is whether petitioner, as counsel, can be penalized for good faith advice to claim the privilege. . . .

The witness, once advised of the right, can choose for himself whether to risk contempt in order to test the privilege before evidence is produced. . . . But, if his lawyer may be punished for advice so given there is a genuine risk that a witness exposed to possible self-incrimination will not be advised of his right. . . .

We conclude that an advocate is not subject to the penalty of contempt for advising his client, in good faith, to assert the Fifth Amendment privilege against self-incrimination in any proceeding embracing the power to compel testimony. . . . Id. 419 U.S. 449, 458–468, 42 L.Ed.2d 574, 583–589, 95 S.Ct. 584, 591–596.

Justice White concurred separately in Maness. He argued that if a witness's claim of privilege is overruled by the trial judge and his subsequent answer is self-incriminatory and later is offered in a criminal prosecution against the witness, his objection to the admissibility of the evidence should be sustained since he was coerced by court order to reveal it. [Compare Cal.Evid. Code § 919 (ed.).] Since such a result would adequately protect the interests of the witness, his refusal to answer originally should subject him to contempt. Under these circumstances his counsel "would have no business advising his client to disobey the court's order to answer." However, since in this case, the possibility of such an ultimate protection of the witness' interests "was hardly brought home to this petitioner or his client . . . therefore . . . it was error to hold the attorney in contempt for advising his client not to answer." Id. 419 U.S. 449, 472–476.

Justice Stewart joined by Justice Blackmun also separately concurred, on the ground that under the circumstances as explained in the Court's opinion and Justice White's opinion "[t]o punish [counsel] for performing his professional duty in good faith would be an arbitrary interference with his client's right to the presence and advice of retained counsel—and thus a denial of due process of law." Id. 419 U.S. 449, 470–472.

3. THE TESTIMONIAL COMMUNICATION REQUIREMENT

a. *In General*

The privilege has been held to protect a person only from being compelled to testify against himself or otherwise provide the state with evidence of "a testimonial or communicative nature." Schmerber v. California, 384 U.S. 757, 761 (1966). Thus Schmerber held that taking blood from a suspect over his objection was not barred by the privilege. Applying the Schmerber test, the Supreme Court also held that compelling an accused to provide handwriting exemplars does not violate the privilege, Gilbert v. California, 388 U.S. 263, 266 (1967), nor does compelling him to speak for identification purposes at a lineup. United States v. Wade, 388 U.S. 218, 221 (1967). The Court has also ruled that a person's refusal to take a breathalyzer test could be admitted into evidence; that the privilege was not violated since no impermissible coercion was involved when the suspect refused to take the test. South Dakota v. Neville, 459 U.S. 553 (1983). See generally, 8 Wigmore, Evidence § 2263 (McNaughton rev. 1961); Arenella, Schmerber and the Privilege Against Self–Incrimination: A Reappraisal, 20 Am.Crim.L.Rev. 31 (1982).

Why should the application of the privilege be limited to testimonial communications? Why should there be a difference, if there is, in the legal consequences of the following: compelling a witness to testify orally as to self-incriminating facts? compelling him to write a self-incriminating statement? compelling her to produce an self-incriminating letter she had written earlier? compelling her to produce a letter written by her brother that incriminates her? compelling her to produce a bloody handkerchief that incriminates her?

Is the requirement of a testimonial communication to be found in the language of the Amendment itself? or in its history? or in some other source?

In considering the materials in this section, particularly those that deal with documents and the possibility of implied statements that may be deemed testimonial, consider whether it would make sense to abandon or modify the testimonial communication requirement?

NOTES

1. Problem: Defendant is asked to give a handwriting exemplar. The government agent proposes to dictate what the defendant should write. The defendant refuses, insisting that he see what he is being asked to write. Can he be required by the court to provide the exemplar and adverse comment made thereon if he refuses? Consider United States v. Campbell, 732 F.2d 1017, 1021 (1st Cir.1984):

> The only difference we see between dictation and being shown the words to write would be to discover defendant's choice of spelling. . . .

> We agree that spelling may be an identifying characteristic no less than handwriting idiosyncrasies. That is, from the standpoint of the Fifth Amendment, that it may be something more. When he writes a dictated work, the writer is saying, "This is how I spell it,"—a testimonial message in addition to a physical display.

2. Consider in connection with the problem in note 1., supra, the Supreme Court's decision in Pennsylvania v. Muniz, 496 U.S. 582 (1990): The Court ruled that a videotape of the slurred nature of an arrested drunk driving suspect's answers to routine booking questions (name, address, height, weight, eye color, date of birth and correct age) was admissible, even in the absence of Miranda warnings because "[r]equiring a suspect to reveal the physical manner in which he articulates words ... does not, without more, compel him to provide a 'testimonial' response for purposes of the privilege."

However, a bare majority of the court also held, that requiring the suspect to give the date of his sixth birthday (to test his mental alertness) required a testimonial response because—

> [He] ... was left with the choice of incriminating himself by admitting that he did not then know the date of his sixth birthday, or answering untruthfully by reporting a date that he did not then believe to be accurate (an incorrect guess would be incriminating as well as untruthful) ... Hence, the incriminating inference of impaired mental faculties stemmed ... from a testimonial aspect of ... [his] response.

Four justices dissented from this ruling (per Rehnquist, C.J.):

> If the police may require Muniz to use his body in order to demonstrate the level of his physical coordination, there is no reason why they should not be able to require him to speak or write in order to determine his mental coordination. That was all that was sought here.

Do you agree with the majority or the dissent's conclusion regarding the sixth birthday question? Which aspect of Muniz is closer to the facts of the problem in note 1, the routine booking questions or sixth birthday question?

3. In Doe v. United States, 487 U.S. 201 (1988), often referred to as Doe II (see p. 1346 infra for a discussion of the issues in Doe I), the government had filed a motion requesting the lower court to order Doe to sign 12 forms consenting to disclosure of any bank records relating to 12 foreign bank accounts over which the government knew or suspected that Doe had control. The Supreme Court described the issue in the case as follows:

> The execution of the consent directive at issue in this case obviously would be compelled, and we may assume that its execution would have an incriminating effect. The question on which this case turns is whether the act of executing the form is a "testimonial communication." The parties disagree about both the meaning of the "testimonial" and whether the consent directive fits the proposed definitions.

In rendering a decision in favor of the government, the Supreme Court rejected the petitioner's contention that a compelled statement is testimonial if the government could use the content of the speech or writing, as opposed to its physical characteristics, to further a criminal investigation of the witness. Rather, the court indicated that—

> An examination of the Court's application of ... [fifth amendment] principles in other cases indicates the Court's recognition that, in order to be testimonial, an accused's communication must itself, explicitly or implicitly, relate a factual assertion or disclose information. Only then is a person compelled to be a "witness" against himself.

The court went on to conclude that the consent directive that the petitioner had been compelled to sign was not itself "testimonial":

> [The form] ... is carefully drafted not to make reference to a specific account, but only to speak in the hypothetical. Thus, the form does not acknowledge that an account in a foreign financial institution is in existence or that it is controlled by petitioner. Nor does the form indicate

whether documents or any other information relating to petitioner are present at the foreign bank, assuming that such an account does exist. The form does not even identify the relevant bank.... [T]he Government is not relying upon the "truthtelling" of Doe's directive to show the existence of, or his control over, foreign bank account records.

... By signing the form, Doe makes no statement, explicit or implicit, regarding the existence of a foreign bank account or his control over any such account. Nor would his execution of the form admit the authenticity of any records produced by the bank.

Finally, we cannot agree with petitioner's contention that his execution of the directive admits or asserts Doe's consent. The form does not state that Doe "consents" to the release of bank records. Instead, it states that the directive "shall be construed as consent" with respect to Cayman Islands and Bermuda bank-secrecy laws. Because the directive explicitly indicates that it was signed pursuant to a court order, Doe's compelled execution of the form sheds no light on his actual intent or state of mind.... In its testimonial significance, the execution of such a directive is analogous to the production of a handwriting sample or voice exemplar: it is a nontestimonial act.

We read the directive as equivalent to a statement by Doe that, although he expresses no opinion about the existence of, or his control over, any such account, he is authorizing the bank to disclose information relating to accounts over which, in the bank's opinion, Doe can exercise the right of withdrawal.

4.   JUSTICE STEVENS dissented from the majority view in Doe, supra note 3. In a footnote, he stated:

The forced production of physical evidence, which we have condoned ... involves no intrusion upon the contents of the mind of the accused. See Schmerber.... The forced execution of a document that purports to convey the signer's authority, however, does invade the dignity of the human mind; it purports to communicate a deliberate command. The intrusion on the dignity of the individual is not diminished by the fact that the document does not reflect the true state of the signer's mind.

JUSTICE STEVENS also stated:

[C]an he be compelled to use his mind to assist the prosecution in convicting him of a crime? I think not. He may in some cases be forced to surrender a key to a strong box containing incriminating documents, but I do not believe he can be compelled to reveal the combination to his wall safe—by word or deed.

Is it an implication of the majority's decision in Doe that the government could compel a person to reveal the combination to his wall safe? To what extent does the majority's decision turn on the peculiar hypothetical form and general language in which the consent directive was cast? Does the court's ruling open the door for the government to control the application of the fifth amendment privilege in certain kinds of circumstances? Is there an argument that, despite the form in which the consent directive was cast, it still communicates certain facts regarding the petitioner's state of mind?

5.   The Doe decision, supra notes 3–4, was handed down after the decision in Fisher v. United States, considered in the next section, p. 1336, and the court at several points in Doe related different aspects of Fisher. Consider the implications of the decision in Fisher for the issue in Doe.

b. *Subpoenaed Documents*

The testimonial communication-privilege issue frequently arises in connection with a subpoena to produce documents. Fisher v. United States, reproduced below, is the leading Supreme Court case on the subject.

Fisher v. United States

Supreme Court of the United States, 1976.
425 U.S. 391, 96 S.Ct. 1569, 48 L.Ed.2d 39.

■ MR. JUSTICE WHITE delivered the opinion of the Court.

In these two cases we are called upon to decide whether a summons directing an attorney to produce documents delivered to him by his client in connection with the attorney-client relationship is enforceable over claims that the documents were constitutionally immune from summons in the hands of the client and retained that immunity in the hands of the attorney.

. . .

II

All of the parties in these cases and the Court of Appeals for the Fifth Circuit have concurred in the proposition that if the Fifth Amendment would have excused a taxpayer from turning over the accountant's papers had he possessed them, the attorney to whom they are delivered for the purpose of obtaining legal advice should also be immune from subpoena. Although we agree with this proposition for the reasons set forth in Part III, infra, we are convinced that, under our decision in Couch v. United States, 409 U.S. 322, 93 S.Ct. 611, 34 L.Ed.2d 548 (1973), it is not the taxpayer's Fifth Amendment privilege that would excuse the attorney from production.

The taxpayer's privilege under this Amendment is not violated by enforcement of the summonses involved in these cases because enforcement against a taxpayer's lawyer would not "compel" the taxpayer to do anything—and certainly would not compel him to be a "witness" against himself. The Court has held repeatedly that the Fifth Amendment is limited to prohibiting the use of "physical or moral compulsion" exerted on the person asserting the privilege. . . .

In Couch v. United States, supra, we recently ruled that the Fifth Amendment rights of a taxpayer were not violated by the enforcement of a documentary summons directed to her accountant and requiring production of the taxpayer's own records in the possession of the accountant. We did so on the ground that in such a case "the ingredient of personal compulsion against an accused is lacking." 409 U.S., at 329, 93 S.Ct., at 616, 34 L.Ed.2d, at 554.

Here, the taxpayers are compelled to do no more than was the taxpayer in Couch. The taxpayers' Fifth Amendment privilege is therefore not violated by enforcement of the summonses directed toward their attorneys. This is true whether or not the Amendment would have barred a subpoena directing the taxpayer to produce the documents while they were in his hands.

The fact that the attorneys are agents of the taxpayers does not change this result. Couch held as much, since the accountant there was also the taxpayer's agent, and in this respect reflected a longstanding view. . . .

Nor is this one of those situations, which Couch suggested might exist, where constructive possession is so clear or relinquishment of possession so temporary and insignificant as to leave the personal compulsion upon the taxpayer substantially intact. 409 U.S., at 333, 93 S.Ct., at 618, 34 L.Ed.2d, at 556. In this respect we see no difference between the delivery to the attorneys in these cases and delivery to the accountant in the Couch case. As was true in Couch, the documents sought were obtainable without personal compulsion on the accused.

. . .

The Amendment protects a person from being compelled to be a witness against himself. Here, the taxpayers retained any privilege they ever had not to be compelled to testify against themselves and not to be compelled themselves to produce private papers in their possession. This personal privilege was in no way decreased by the transfer. It is simply that by reason of the transfer of the documents to the attorneys, those papers may be subpoenaed without compulsion on the taxpayer. The protection of the Fifth Amendment is therefore not available. "A party is privileged from producing evidence but not from its production."

. . . We adhere to the view that the Fifth Amendment protects against "compelled self-incrimination, not [the disclosure of] private information." United States v. Nobles, 422 U.S. 225, 233 n. 7, 95 S.Ct. 2160, 2167, 45 L.Ed.2d 141 (1975).

III

Our above holding is that compelled production of documents from an attorney does not implicate whatever Fifth Amendment privilege the taxpayer might have enjoyed from being compelled to produce them himself. The taxpayers in these cases, however, have from the outset consistently urged that they should not be forced to expose otherwise protected documents to summons simply because they have sought legal advice and turned the papers over to their attorneys. The Government appears to agree unqualifiedly. The difficulty is that the taxpayers have erroneously relied on the Fifth Amendment without urging the attorney-client privilege in so many words. They have nevertheless invoked the relevant body of law and policies that govern the attorney-client privilege.

. . .

[The Court at this point in its Opinion proceeded to address the question whether the attorney-client privilege protects documents in the hands of an attorney which would have been privileged in the hands of the client by reason of the Fifth Amendment. This portion of the Opinion is reproduced infra p. 1438. The Court answered this question in the affirmative and then continued. . . .]

. . .

We accordingly proceed to the question whether the documents could have been obtained by summons addressed to the taxpayer while the documents were in his possession. The only bar to enforcement of such summons asserted by the parties or the courts below is the Fifth Amendment's privilege against self-incrimination.

It is . . . clear that the Fifth Amendment does not independently proscribe the compelled production of every sort of incriminating evidence but applies only when the accused is compelled to make a testimonial communication that is incriminating....

. . .

[We] turn to the question of what, if any, incriminating testimony within the Fifth Amendment's protection, is compelled by a documentary summons.

A subpoena served on a taxpayer requiring him to produce an accountant's workpapers in his possession without doubt involves substantial compulsion. But it does not compel oral testimony; nor would it ordinarily compel the taxpayer to restate, repeat, or affirm the truth of the contents of the documents sought. Therefore, the Fifth Amendment would not be violated by the fact alone that the papers on their face might incriminate the taxpayer, for the privilege protects a person only against being incriminated by his own compelled testimonial communications....

The accountant's workpapers are not the taxpayer's. They were not prepared by the taxpayer, and they contain no testimonial declarations by him. Furthermore, as far as this record demonstrates, the preparation of all of the papers sought in these cases was wholly voluntary, and they cannot be said to contain compelled testimonial evidence, either of the taxpayers or of anyone else. The taxpayer cannot avoid compliance with the subpoena merely by asserting that the item of evidence which he is required to produce contains incriminating writing, whether his own or that of someone else.

The act of producing evidence in response to a subpoena nevertheless has communicative aspects of its own, wholly aside from the contents of the papers produced. Compliance with the subpoena tacitly concedes the existence of the papers demanded and their possession or control by the taxpayer. It also would indicate the taxpayer's belief that the papers are those described in the subpoena. Curcio v. United States, 354 U.S. 118, 125, 77 S.Ct. 1145, 1150, 1 L.Ed.2d 1225, 1231 (1957). The elements of compulsion are clearly present, but the more difficult issues are whether the tacit averments of the taxpayer are both "testimonial" and "incriminating" for purposes of applying the Fifth Amendment. These questions perhaps do not lend themselves to categorical answers; their resolution may instead depend on the facts and circumstances of particular cases or classes thereof. In light of the records now before us, we are confident that however incriminating the contents of the accountant's workpapers might be, the act of producing them—the only thing which the taxpayer is compelled to do—would not itself involve testimonial self-incrimination.

It is doubtful that implicitly admitting the existence and possession of the papers rises to the level of testimony within the protection of the Fifth Amendment. The papers belong to the accountant, were prepared by him, and are the kind usually prepared by an accountant working on the tax returns of his client. Surely the Government is in no way relying on the "truthtelling" of the taxpayer to prove the existence of or his access to the documents. 8 Wigmore § 2264, p. 380. The existence and location of the papers are a foregone conclusion and the taxpayer adds little or nothing to the sum total of the Government's information by conceding that he in fact has the papers.

When an accused is required to submit a handwriting exemplar he admits his ability to write and impliedly asserts that the exemplar is his writing. But in common experience, the first would be a near truism and the latter self-evident. In any event, although the exemplar may be incriminating to the accused and although he is compelled to furnish it, his Fifth Amendment privilege is not violated because nothing he has said or done is deemed to be sufficiently testimonial for purposes of the privilege....

Moreover, assuming that these aspects of producing the accountant's papers have some minimal testimonial significance, surely it is not illegal to seek accounting help in connection with one's tax returns or for the accountant to prepare workpapers and deliver them to the taxpayer. At this juncture, we are quite unprepared to hold that either the fact of existence of the papers or of their possession by the taxpayer poses any realistic threat of incrimination to the taxpayer.

As for the possibility that responding to the subpoena would authenticate[1] the workpapers, production would express nothing more than the taxpayer's belief that the papers are those described in the subpoena. The taxpayer would be no more competent to authenticate the accountant's workpapers or reports by producing them than he would be to authenticate them if testifying orally. The taxpayer did not prepare the papers and could not vouch for their accuracy. The documents would not be admissible in evidence against the taxpayer without authenticating testimony. Without more, responding to the subpoena in the circumstances before us would not appear to represent a substantial threat of self-incrimination.

Whether the Fifth Amendment would shield the taxpayer from producing his own tax records in his possession is a question not involved here; for the papers demanded here are not his "private papers," see Boyd v. United States, 116 U.S., at 634–635, 6 S.Ct., at 534, 29 L.Ed., at 752. We do hold that compliance with a summons directing the taxpayer to produce the accountant's documents involved in these cases would involve no incriminating testimony within the protection of the Fifth Amendment.

. . .

■ MR. JUSTICE BRENNAN, concurring in the judgment.

I concur in the judgment. Given the prior access by accountants retained by the taxpayers to the papers involved in these cases and the wholly business rather than personal nature of the papers, I agree that the privilege against compelled self-incrimination did not in either of these cases protect the papers from production in response to the summonses. . . .

. . .

1. The "implicit authentication" rationale appears to be the prevailing justification for the Fifth Amendment's application to documentary subpoenas. Schmerber v. California, 384 U.S., at 763–764, 86 S.Ct., at 1832, 16 L.Ed.2d, at 915–916 ("the privilege reaches . . . the compulsion of responses which are also communications, for example, compliance with a subpoena to produce one's papers. Boyd v. United States, 116 U.S. 616, 6 S.Ct. 524, 29 L.Ed. 746"); Couch v. United States, 409 U.S., at 344, 346, 93 S.Ct., at 611, 625, 34 L.Ed.2d, at 548, 564 (Marshall, J., dissenting) (the person complying with the subpoena "implicitly testifies that the evidence he brings forth is in fact the evidence demanded"); United States v. Beattie, 522 F.2d 267, 270 (C.A.2 1975) (Friendly, J.) ("[a] subpoena demanding that an accused produce his own records is . . . the equivalent of requiring him to take the stand and admit their genuineness"), cert. pending, Nos. 75–407, 75–700; 8 Wigmore § 2264, p. 380 (the testimonial component involved in compliance with an order for production of documents or chattels "is the witness' assurance, compelled as an incident of the process, that the articles produced are the ones demanded"); McCormick § 126, p. 268 ("[t]his rule [applying the Fifth Amendment privilege to documentary subpoenas] is defended on the theory that one who produces documents (or other matter) described in the subpoena duces tecum represents, by his production, that the documents produced are in fact the documents described in the subpoena"); People v. Defore, 242 N.Y. 13, 27, 150 N.E. 585, 590 (1926) (Cardozo, J.) ("A defendant is 'protected from producing his documents in response to a subpoena duces tecum, for his production of them in court would be his voucher of their genuineness.' There would then be 'testimonial compulsion' "). [Footnotes are those of the court. Some footnotes have been omitted, and others renumbered.]

. . . An individual's books and papers are generally little more than an extension of his person. They reveal no less than he could reveal upon being questioned directly. Many of the matters within an individual's knowledge may easily be retained within his head as set down on a scrap of paper. I perceive no principle which does not permit compelling one to disclose the contents of one's mind but does permit compelling the disclosure of the contents of that scrap of paper by compelling its production. Under a contrary view, the constitutional protection would turn on fortuity, and persons would, at their peril, record their thoughts and the events of their lives. The ability to think private thoughts, facilitated as it is by pen and paper, and the ability to preserve intimate memories would be curtailed through fear that those thoughts or the events of those memories would become the subjects of criminal sanctions however invalidly imposed. Indeed, it was the very reality of those fears that helped provide the historical impetus for the privilege. E. Griswold, The Fifth Amendment Today 8–9 (1955); 8 J. Wigmore, Evidence § 2250, pp. 277–281 (McNaughton rev.1961); id., § 2251, pp. 313–314; McKay, Self–Incrimination and the New Privacy, 1967 Supreme Court Review 193, 212.

The Court's treatment of the privilege falls far short of giving it the scope required by history and our precedents. It is, of course, true "that the Fifth Amendment protects against 'compelled self-incrimination, not [the disclosure of] private information,' "but it is also true that governmental compulsion to produce private information that might incriminate violates the protection of the privilege. Similarly, although it is necessary that the papers "contain no testimonial declarations by [the taxpayer]" in order for the privilege not to operate as a bar to production, it does not follow that papers are not "testimonial" and thus producible because they contain no declarations. And while it may be that the unavailability of the privilege depends on a showing that "the preparation of all of the papers sought in these cases was wholly voluntary," ibid., again it does not follow that the protection is necessarily unavailable if the papers were prepared voluntarily, for it is the compelled production of testimonial evidence, not just the compelled creation of such evidence, against which the privilege protects.

Though recognizing that a subpoena served on a taxpayer involves substantial compulsion, the Court concludes that since the subpoena does not compel oral testimony or require the taxpayer to restate, repeat, or affirm the truth of the contents of the documents sought, compelled production of the documents by the taxpayer would not violate the privilege, even though the documents might incriminate the taxpayer. This analysis is patently incomplete: the threshold inquiry is whether the taxpayer is compelled to produce incriminating papers. That inquiry is not answered in favor of production merely because the subpoena requires neither oral testimony from nor affirmation of the papers' contents by the taxpayer. To be sure, the Court correctly observes that "[t]he taxpayer cannot avoid compliance with the subpoena merely by asserting that the item of evidence which he is required to produce contains incriminating writing, whether his own or that of someone else." For it is not enough that the production of a writing, or books and papers, is compelled. Unless those materials are such as to come within the zone of privacy recognized by the Amendment, the privilege against compulsory self-incrimination does not protect against their production.

. . .

A precise cataloguing of private papers within the ambit of the privacy protected by the privilege is probably impossible. Some papers, however, do lend themselves to classification. See generally Comment, The Search and

Seizure of Private Papers: Fourth and Fifth Amendment Considerations, 6 Loyola (LA) L.Rev. 274, 300–303 (1973). Production of documentary materials created or authenticated by a State or the Federal Government, such as automobile registrations or property deeds, would seem ordinarily to fall outside the protection of the privilege. They hardly reflect an extension of the person.

Economic and business records may present difficulty in particular cases. The records of business entities generally fall without the scope of the privilege. But, as noted, the Court has recognized that the privilege extends to the business records of the sole proprietor or practitioner. Such records are at least an extension of an aspect of a person's activities, though concededly not the more intimate aspects of one's life. Where the privilege would have protected one's mental notes of his business affairs in a less complicated day and age, it would seem that that protection should not fall away because the complexities of another time compel one to keep business records. Nonbusiness economic records in the possession of an individual, such as canceled checks or tax records, would also seem to be protected. They may provide clear insights into a person's total lifestyle. They are, however, like business records and the papers involved in these cases, frequently, though not always, disclosed to other parties; and disclosure, in proper cases, may foreclose reliance upon the privilege. Personal letters constitute an integral aspect of a person's private enclave. And while letters, being necessarily interpersonal, are not wholly private, their peculiarly private nature and the generally narrow extent of their disclosure would seem to render them within the scope of the privilege. Papers in the nature of a personal diary are a fortiori protected under the privilege.

The Court's treatment in the instant cases of the question whether the evidence involved here is within the protection of the privilege is, with all respect, most inadequate. The gaping hole is in the omission of any reference to the taxpayer's privacy interests and to whether the subpoenas impermissibly invade those interests. The observations that the "accountant's workpapers are not the taxpayer's" and "were not prepared by the taxpayer," touch on matters relevant to the taxpayer's expectation of privacy, but do not of themselves determine the availability of the privilege. . . .

I also question the Court's treatment of the question whether the act of producing evidence is "testimonial." I agree that the act of production implicitly admits the existence of the evidence requested and possession or control of that evidence by the party producing it. It also implicitly authenticates the evidence as that identified in the order to compel. I disagree, however, that implicit admission of the existence and possession or control of the papers in this case is not "testimonial" merely because the Government could readily have otherwise proved existence and possession or control in these cases. I know of no Fifth Amendment principle which makes the testimonial nature of evidence and, therefore, one's protection against incriminating himself, turn on the strength of the Government's case against him.

Nor do I consider the taxpayers' implicit authentication an insubstantial threat of self-incrimination. Actually, authentication of the papers as those described in the subpoenas establishes the papers as the taxpayers', thereby supplying an incriminatory link in the chain of evidence against them. It is not the less so because the taxpayers' accountants may also provide the link, since the protection against self-incrimination cannot, I repeat, turn on the strength of the Government's case.

NOTES

1. Application of the privilege to documents and private papers has spawned a complex body of case law. The seminal case on the constitutional protection afforded to documents and private papers had long been Boyd v. United States, 116 U.S. 616 (1886). Boyd involved a forfeiture proceeding based upon a failure to pay duty on a shipment of imported glass. During the trial, the quantity and value of a previous shipment of glass came into issue, and the defendant was ordered, over his objection on constitutional grounds, to produce the relevant invoice. The Court per Justice Bradley, held the order to produce the invoice violated the defendant's constitutional rights, stating:

> [W]e are ... of opinion that a compulsory production of the private books and papers of the owner of goods sought to be forfeited ... is compelling him to be a witness against himself, within the meaning of the Fifth Amendment ... and is the equivalent of ... an unreasonable search and seizure ... within the meaning of the Fourth Amendment. Id. 116 U.S. 616, 634–635, 6 S.Ct. 524, 534–35, 29 L.Ed. 746, 752.

2. In a portion of the Fisher Opinion, omitted supra, the Court generally laid to rest the Boyd notion that a subpoena duces tecum or summons to produce private papers as a matter of course calls into question Fourth Amendment interests.

3. Subsequently, relying on the Fisher view that "the Fifth Amendment is limited to prohibiting the use of 'physical or moral compulsion' exerted on the person asserting the privilege," the Court held that the Fifth Amendment does not apply where personal business papers (containing statements that the claimant of the privilege had voluntarily committed to writing) are seized under a search warrant by law enforcement personnel and "the individual against whom the search is directed is not required to aid in the discovery, production or authentication of incriminating evidence." Andresen v. Maryland, 427 U.S. 463, 474 (1976).

4. In Couch v. United States, 409 U.S. 322 (1973), discussed in the Fisher opinion, the taxpayer had turned over possession of her business and tax records to her accountant, but she retained ownership of the material. A summons to produce these documents was directed to the accountant. In rejecting the taxpayer's claim of privilege, the Court stated:

> Petitioner would, in effect, have us read Boyd to mark ownership, not possession, as the bounds of the privilege, despite the fact that possession bears the closest relationship to the personal compulsion forbidden by the Fifth Amendment. To tie the privilege against self-incrimination to a concept of ownership would be to draw a meaningless line. It would hold here that the business records which petitioner actually owned would be protected in the hands of her accountant, while business information communicated to her accountant by letter and conversations in which the accountant took notes, in addition to the accountant's own workpapers and photocopies of petitioner's records, would not be subject to a claim of privilege since title rested in the accountant. Such a holding would thus place unnecessary emphasis on the form of communication to an accountant and the accountant's own working methods, while diverting the inquiry from the basic purposes of the Fifth Amendment's protections....
>
> Petitioner argues, nevertheless, that grave prejudice will result from a denial of her claim to equate ownership and the scope of the privilege. She alleges that "[i]f the IRS is able to reach her records the instant those records leave her hands and are deposited in the hands of her retainer

whom she has hired for a special purpose then the meaning of the privilege is lost." That is not, however, the import of today's decision. We do indeed believe that actual possession of documents bears the most significant relationship to Fifth Amendment protections against governmental compulsions upon the individual accused of crime. Yet situations may well arise where constructive possession is so clear or the relinquishment of possession is so temporary and insignificant as to leave the personal compulsions upon the accused substantially intact. But this is not the case before us. Here there was no mere fleeting divestment of possession: the records had been given to her accountant regularly since 1955 and remained in his continuous possession until the summer of 1969 when the summons was issued. Moreover, the accountant himself worked neither in petitioner's office nor as her employee. The length of his possession of petitioner's records and his independent status confirm the belief that petitioner's divestment of possession was of such a character as to disqualify her entirely as an object of any impermissible Fifth Amendment compulsion. . . .

Id. 409 U.S. 322, 331–35.

5. Would the result in Fisher have been different if the tax records in question had been prepared by the taxpayer rather than his accountant? Compare Justice Brennan's concurrence. The majority in Fisher, of course, expressly declined to decide whether the privilege protects a taxpayer from producing his own records. Consider also footnote 1 in Mr. Brennan's concurring opinion in Fisher in which he stated:

> [T]he Court's notation that [s]pecial problems of privacy which might be presented by subpoena of a diary . . . are not involved here . . . is only made in the context of discussion of the Fourth Amendment and thus may readily imply that even a subpoena of a personal diary containing forthright confessions of crime may not be resisted on grounds of privilege.

How much protection would be afforded under the majority's approach to various kinds of personal papers, e.g. a pocket calendar? a desk calendar? a diary? a personal letter? See generally Note, 90 Harv.L.Rev. 945 (1977). Has the court since Fisher provided a definitive answer as to whether the fifth amendment protects the private papers of an individual. See, Justice O'Connor concurring in United States v. Doe (Doe I), 465 U.S. 605 (1984):

> I write separately . . . just to make explicit what is implicit in the analysis of the opinion: that the Fifth Amendment provides no protection for the contents of private papers of any kind.

Justice Marshall joined by Justice Brennan concurring in part and dissenting in part responded to Justice O'Connor:

> Contrary to what Justice O'Connor contends, I do not view the Court's opinion in this case as having reconsidered whether the Fifth Amendment provides protection for the contents of "private papers of any kind." This case presented nothing remotely close to the question that Justice O'Connor eagerly poses and answers.

6. An accountant files an affidavit in support of his motion to quash a grand jury subpoena for his personal business records. In the affidavit he states that he prepared the records and they are in his possession. Does furnishing this much information about the records waive his privilege against providing further information that would authenticate the records? H: The individual does not thereby waive his privilege. "To hold that a custodian who attempts to establish the facts necessary to support a valid claim of self-incrimination thereby waives that privilege would make a mockery of the substantive constitutional right." United States v. Doe, 628 F.2d 694, 696 (1st Cir.1980). Compare the advice that counsel should refrain from acknowledging, in conversations with prosecutors and investigating agents, that the client possesses specific records because of a concern that, as a result, a court might "later determine that the compelled production of the very same records would add very little to the sum of the government's knowledge." Rosenblatt and Shevitz, Fifth Amendment and Production of Corporate Records, N.Y.Law Journal, July 31, 1985, p. 1, 3.

7. In light of Fisher, can the prosecutor, through a subpoena, obtain incriminating physical evidence from an individual, a gun, brass knuckles or the like? See Commonwealth v. Hughes, 404 N.E.2d 1239 (Mass.1980), reproduced infra, p. 1439.

D.   NON-APPLICATION OF THE PRIVILEGE

1.   COLLECTIVE ENTITIES

The Supreme Court has repeatedly affirmed that an individual cannot rely upon the privilege to refuse to produce the records of a collective entity which are in his possession in a representative capacity, even if these records might incriminate him personally. The collective entity itself has no privilege against self-incrimination; only individual persons may claim the benefit of the privilege.

The issues involved in this area are closely tied to those which were considered in the previous section. Because subpoenaed documents are involved, there is a question whether the custodian of the records of a collective entity may raise a claim of privilege regarding any implied statement that arises out of the act of production. The instant subject also has a close relationship to the Required Records doctrine which is treated in the next section.

The court has ruled in the case of a number of different kinds of collective entity forms that the privilege does not apply. In Bellis v. United States, 417 U.S. 85 (1974), the court summarized the relevant case law up to that time as follows:

> On the other hand, an equally long line of cases has established that an individual cannot rely upon the privilege to avoid producing the records of a collective entity which are in his possession in a representative capacity, even if these records might incriminate him personally. This doctrine was first announced in a series of cases dealing with corporate records. In Wilson v. United States, 221 U.S. 361, the Court held that an officer of a corporation could not claim his privilege against compulsory self-incrimination to justify a refusal to produce the corporate books and records in response to a grand jury subpoena duces tecum directed to the corporation. A companion case, Dreier v. United States, 221 U.S. 394, 31 S.Ct. 550, 55 L.Ed. 784 (1911), held that the same result followed when the subpoena requiring production of the corporate books was directed to the individual corporate officer. In Wheeler v. United States, 226 U.S. 478, 33 S.Ct. 158, 57 L.Ed. 309 (1913), the Court held that no Fifth Amendment privilege could be claimed with respect to corporate records even though the corporation had previously been dissolved. And Grant v. United States, 227 U.S. 74, 33 S.Ct. 190, 57 L.Ed. 423 (1913), applied this principle to the records of a dissolved corporation where the records were in the possession of the individual who had been the corporation's sole shareholder.

To some extent, these decisions were based upon the particular incidents of the corporate form, the Court observing that a corporation has limited powers granted to it by the State in its charter, and is subject to the retained "visitorial power" of the State to investigate its activities. But any thought that the principle formulated in these decisions was limited to corporate records was put to rest in United States v. White, 322 U.S. 694, 64 S.Ct. 1248 (1944). In White, we held that an officer of an unincorporated association, a labor union, could not claim his privilege against compulsory self-incrimination to justify his refusal to produce the union's records pursuant to a grand jury subpoena. White announced the general rule that the privilege could not be employed by an individual to avoid production of the records of an organization, which he holds in a representative capacity as custodian on behalf of the group. Relying on White, we have since upheld compelled production of the records of a variety of organizations over individuals' claims of Fifth Amendment privilege....

These decisions reflect the Court's consistent view that the privilege against compulsory self-incrimination should be "limited to its historic function of protecting only the natural individual from compulsory incrimination through his own testimony or personal records." United States v. White, supra, 322 U.S. at 701, 64 S.Ct. at 1252....

Since no artificial organization may utilize the personal privilege against compulsory self-incrimination, the Court found that it follows that an individual acting in his official capacity on behalf of the organization may likewise not take advantage of his personal privilege. In view of the inescapable fact that an artificial entity can only act to produce its records through its individual officers or agents, recognition of the individual's claim of privilege with respect to the financial records of the organization would substantially undermine the unchallenged rule that the organization itself is not entitled to claim any Fifth Amendment privilege, and largely frustrate legitimate governmental regulation of such organizations....

The analysis of the Court in White, of course, only makes sense in the context of what the Court described as "organized, institutional activity." ... This analysis presupposes the existence of an organization which is recognized as an independent entity apart from its individual members. The group must be relatively well organized and structured, and not merely a loose, informal association of individuals. It must maintain a distinct set of organizational records, and recognize rights in its members of control and access to them. And the records subpoenaed must in fact be organizational records held in a representative capacity. In other words, it must be fair to say that the records demanded are the records of the organization rather than those of the individual under White....

In Bellis, the issue before the Supreme Court was whether a partner in a small law firm could invoke the privilege to justify his refusal to comply with a subpoena requiring production of the partnership financial records. The court applied the collective entity doctrine to deny the use of the privilege in this circumstance, stating:

> We think it is similarly clear that partnerships may and frequently do represent organized institutional activity so as to preclude any claim of Fifth Amendment privilege with respect to the partnership's financial records.... Although none of the reported cases has involved a partnership of quite this magnitude, it is hardly surprising that all of the courts of appeals which have addressed the question have concluded that White's analysis requires rejection of any claim of privilege in the financial records

of a large business enterprise conducted in the partnership form. . . . Even those lower courts which have held the privilege applicable in the context of a smaller partnership have frequently acknowledged that no absolute exclusion of the partnership form from the White rule generally applicable to unincorporated associations is warranted. . . .

In this case, however, we are required to explore the outer limits of the analysis of the Court in White. Petitioner argues that in view of the modest size of the partnership involved here, it is unrealistic to consider the firm as an entity independent of its three partners; rather, he claims, the law firm embodies little more than the personal legal practice of the individual partners. Moreover, petitioner argues that he has a substantial and direct ownership interest in the partnership records, and does not hold them in a representative capacity.

Despite the force of these arguments, we conclude that the lower courts properly applied the White rule in the circumstances of this case. While small, the partnership here did have an established institutional identity independent of its individual partners. This was not an informal association or a temporary arrangement for the undertaking of a few projects of shortlived duration. Rather, the partnership represented a formal institutional arrangement organized for the continuing conduct of the firm's legal practice. The partnership was in existence for nearly 15 years prior to its voluntary dissolution. Although it may not have had a formal constitution or bylaws to govern its internal affairs, state partnership law imposed on the firm a certain organizational structure in the absence of any contrary agreement by the partners; for example, it guaranteed to each of the partners the equal right to participate in the management and control of the firm, . . . and prescribed that majority rule governed the conduct of the firm's business. The firm maintained a bank account in the partnership name, had stationery using the firm name on its letterhead, and, in general, held itself out to third parties as an entity with an independent institutional identity. It employed six persons in addition to its partners, including two other attorneys who practiced law on behalf of the firm, rather than as individuals on their own behalf. It filed separate partnership returns for federal tax purposes, ... State law permitted the firm to be sued, . . . and to hold title to property, . . . in the partnership name, and generally regarded the partnership as a distinct entity for numerous other purposes.

. . .

This might be a different case if it involved a small family partnership, . . . or, as the Solicitor General suggests, . . . if there were some other preexisting relationship of confidentiality among the partners. But in the circumstances of this case, petitioner's possession of the partnership's financial records in what can be fairly said to be a representative capacity compels our holding that his personal privilege against compulsory self-incrimination is inapplicable.

Subsequently, in United States v. Doe, 465 U.S. 605 (1984), frequently referred to as Doe I, the Supreme Court did not apply the collective entity doctrine to the business records of a sole proprietorship, apparently relying on the fact that the owner of a sole proprietorship acts in a personal, not a representative capacity. The court went on to rule that, applying Fisher, the contents of the business records, even if incriminating are not privileged because the preparation of the records had been voluntary, not compelled, and the subpoena did not compel the individual to restate, repeat or affirm the truth of the contents of the records. However, since the lower courts had made a finding that the act of producing the documents would involve testimonial self-incrimination—that is, by producing the records, the individual would be admitting that the records exist, that they are in his possession and that they are authentic—the court concluded that the production of the records could not be compelled without a statutory grant of immunity.

NOTES

1. Recall that United States v. Doe, supra (Doe I), involved a sole proprietorship. After Fisher, Bellis, and Doe I, where is the line to be drawn between collective entities to which the privilege does not apply and other kinds of business relationships? Consider the following:

a.   A husband-wife business partnership. See Matter of September, 1975 Special Grand Jury, 435 F.Supp. 538 (N.D.Ind.1977). A two man law partnership. See United States v. Kuta, 518 F.2d 947 (7th Cir.1975). A mother-son small family partnership operating a nursing home. See Sreter v. Hynes, 419 F.Supp. 546 (E.D.N.Y.1976). Suppose a law firm is organized as a partnership, but the senior partner runs it as a sole proprietorship under an arrangement whereby his word with respect to every decision is final and where every physical item of the partnership is in fact his personal property. See Matter of Grand Jury Impaneled on January 21, 1975, 529 F.2d 543 (3d Cir.1976).

b.   Sole shareholder of a one person corporation. See Braswell v. United States, 487 U.S. 99 (1988), reproduced infra p. 1348.

2. How long does a partnership continue in existence for purposes of the privilege? Consider United States v. Hankins, 565 F.2d 1344 (5th Cir.1978), where at the time a summons was issued to produce certain business records, one of the partners had died, his widow had sold her interest to the surviving partner who was the custodian of the records in question and the estate of the deceased partner had executed a bill of sale to sell its interest to the surviving partner. Nevertheless, because there was provision for the children of the deceased partner to buy shares in the successor corporation that was to be established, the court held that the partnership was "continuing in existence until the business was incorporated," and the records "were not the personal papers" of the surviving partner, Id. 565 F.2d 1344.

3. After United States v. Doe (Doe I), can a former officer of a corporation who still has corporate documents in his possession claim the privilege—that producing the documents will incriminate him? See In re Grand Jury Subpoenas Duces Tecum Dated June 13, 1983 and June 22, 1983, 722 F.2d 981 (2d Cir.1983): Former officer of corporation who retained certain corporate records after leaving corporate employment should be given opportunity to support his claim that compelled production of the records could reasonably be viewed as tending to incriminate him. The court also stated:

> It is true that if the witness were still a ... [corporate] officer or employer he would normally be obligated as a representative of the company to produce its documents, regardless of whether they contained information incriminating him.... But that is because there would rarely be any dispute over possession when the person subpoenaed is required to respond in his representative capacity. In producing records as an officer of the company he would not be attesting to his personal possession of them but to their existence and possession by the corporation, which is not entitled to claim a Fifth Amendment privilege with respect to them. Id. at 986.

For a former corporate officer case reaching a contrary result, see In re Grand Jury Subpoena, 784 F.2d 857 (8th Cir.1986).

4. When are records personal rather than corporate records? Suppose that a corporate executive keeps a diary and desk-type calendar at his office and uses it to record business meetings and transactions and also for personal notations of a non-business nature? See United States v. MacKey, 647 F.2d 898 (9th Cir.1981). Suppose that a doctor keeps personal records of the treatment of patients while he works for a clinic organized as a professional corporation? See United States v. Radetsky, 535 F.2d 556 (10th Cir.1976).

5. After the decisions in Fisher and United States v. Doe, (Doe I) supra, it was suggested by some commentators that the effect of those cases was to undermine the personal/organizational (held-in-a-representative capacity) approach to the privilege, that "[a] subpoena of organizational documents, no less than a subpoena of personal documents, compels an individual to hand over evidence: in each case, an act of production is compelled." Note, Organizational Papers and the Privilege Against Self–Incrimination, 99 Harv.L.Rev. 640, 647 (1986). The question was whether a person could invoke the act of production-implied authentication doctrine to resist production and authentication of corporate documents which she held only in a representative capacity. In the wake of Fisher and Doe I, a split developed concerning this issue in the U.S. courts of appeal. Thus, for example, the Second Circuit took the following approach to the problem in In re Two Grand Jury Subpoenae Duces Tecum, 769 F.2d 52 (2d Cir.1985):

> In certain limited circumstances, ... an individual may have a fifth amendment privilege against being personally compelled to produce corporate documents.... [T]he act of producing documents may constitute personal testimony concerning the document's existence, their possession or control, or the fact that the one producing them believes them to be the documents described in the subpoena. When this testimony would be self-incriminating, one has a personal fifth amendment privilege to refuse to comply with a subpoena requesting production.

> [E]ven if the situation is unusual and a corporation's custodian of records would incriminate himself if he were to act to produce the company's records, this still does not relieve the corporation of its continuing obligation to produce the subpoenaed documents. United States v. Barth, 745 F.2d 184, 189 (2d Cir.1984).... In such a situation the corporation must appoint some other employee to produce the records, and if no existing employee could produce the records without incriminating himself by such an act, then the corporation may be required to produce the records by supplying an entirely new agent.... There simply is no situation in which the fifth amendment would prevent a corporation from producing corporate records, for the corporation itself has no fifth amendment privilege. Id. at 56–57.

The split in the circuits on this issue was finally resolved in Braswell v. United States, reproduced below.

Braswell v. United States

Supreme Court of the United States, 1988.
487 U.S. 99, 108 S.Ct. 2284, 101 L.Ed.2d 98.

[Petitioner operated his business—selling and purchasing equipment, land, timber and oil and gas interests—initially as a sole proprietorship, but subsequently, he formed two corporations to carry on the business. A federal grand jury issued a subpoena requiring the petitioner to produce the books and records of the two corporations. The subpoena provided that petitioner could deliver the records to the agent serving the subpoena and did not require the petitioner to testify. Petitioner's motion to quash the subpoena was denied by the District Court, and the United States Court of Appeals for the Fifth Circuit affirmed.]

■ CHIEF JUSTICE REHNQUIST delivered the opinion of the Court.

This case presents the question whether the custodian of corporate records may resist a subpoena for such records on the ground that the act of production would incriminate him in violation of the Fifth Amendment. We conclude that he may not.

. . . Petitioner . . . relies solely upon the argument that his act of producing the documents has independent testimonial significance, which would incriminate him individually, and that the Fifth Amendment prohibits government compulsion of that act. The bases for this argument are extrapolated from the decisions of this Court in Fisher and Doe.

Had petitioner conducted his business as a sole proprietorship, Doe would require that he be provided the opportunity to show that his act of production would entail testimonial self-incrimination. But petitioner has operated his business through the corporate form, and we have long recognized that, for purposes of the Fifth Amendment, corporations and other collective entities are treated differently from individuals. This doctrine—known as the collective entity rule—has a lengthy and distinguished pedigree.

. . . .

[The court here reviewed the collective entity cases, summarized supra p. 1344, including Wilson v. United States, Dreier v. United States, United States v. White, and Bellis v. United States.]

The plain mandate of these decisions is that without regard to whether the subpoena is addressed to the corporation, or as here, to the individual in his capacity as a custodian, a corporate custodian such as petitioner may not resist a subpoena for corporate records on Fifth Amendment grounds. Petitioner argues, however, that this rule falls in the wake of Fisher v. United States, and United States v. Doe. In essence, petitioner's argument is as follows: In response to Boyd v. United States, 116 U.S. 616, 6 S.Ct. 524, 29 L.Ed. 746 (1886), with its privacy rationale shielding personal books and records, the Court developed the collective entity rule, which declares simply that corporate records are not private and therefore are not protected by the Fifth Amendment. The collective entity decisions were concerned with the contents of the documents subpoenaed, however, and not with the act of production. In Fisher and Doe, the Court moved away from the privacy-based collective entity rule, replacing it with a compelled-testimony standard under which the contents of business documents are never privileged but the act of producing the documents may be. Under this new regime, the act of production privilege is available without regard to the entity whose records are being sought. See In re Grand Jury Matter (Brown), 768 F.2d 525, 528 (CA3 1985) (en banc) ("[Fisher and Doe]make the significant factor, for the privilege against self-incrimination, neither the nature of entity which owns the documents, nor the contents of documents, but rather the communicative or noncommunicative nature of the arguably incriminating disclosures sought to be compelled").

To be sure, the holding in Fisher—later reaffirmed in Doe—embarked upon a new course of Fifth Amendment analysis. We cannot agree, however, that it rendered the collective entity rule obsolete. The agency rationale undergirding the collective entity decisions, in which custodians asserted that production of entity records would incriminate them personally, survives. From Wilson forward, the Court has consistently recognized that the custodian of corporate or entity records holds those documents in a representative rather than a personal capacity. Artificial entities such as corporations may act only through their agents, and a custodian's assumption of his representative capacity leads to certain obligations, including the duty to produce corporate records on proper demand by the Government. Under those circumstances, the custodian's act of production is not deemed a personal act, but rather an act of the corporation. Any claim of Fifth Amendment privilege asserted by the agent would be tantamount to a claim of privilege by the corporation—which of course possesses no such privilege.

Indeed, the opinion in Fisher—upon which petitioner places primary reliance—indicates that the custodian of corporate records may not interpose a Fifth Amendment objection to the compelled production of corporate records, even though the act of production may prove personally incriminating. The Fisher Court cited the collective entity decisions with approval and offered those decisions to support the conclusion that the production of the accountant's workpapers would "not ... involve testimonial self-incrimination." 425 U.S., at 411, 96 S.Ct., at 1581. The Court thus reaffirmed the obligation of a corporate custodian to comply with a subpoena addressed to him.

Petitioner also attempts to extract support for his contention from Curcio v. United States, 354 U.S. 118, 77 S.Ct. 1145, 1 L.Ed.2d 1225 (1957). But rather than bolstering petitioner's argument, we think Curcio substantiates the Government's position. Curcio had been served with two subpoenas addressed to him in his capacity as secretary-treasurer of a local union, which was under investigation. One subpoena required that he produce union books, the other that he testify. Curcio appeared before the grand jury, stated that the books were not in his possession, and refused to answer any questions as to their whereabouts. Curcio was held in contempt for refusing to answer the questions propounded. We reversed the contempt citation, rejecting the Government's argument "that the representative duty which required the production of union records in the White case requires the giving of oral testimony by the custodian." Id., at 123, 77 S.Ct., at 1149.

Petitioner asserts that our Curcio decision stands for the proposition that although the contents of a collective entity's records are unprivileged, a representative of a collective entity cannot be required to provide testimony about those records. It follows, according to petitioner, that because Fisher recognizes that the act of production is potentially testimonial, such an act may not be compelled if it would tend to incriminate the representative personally. We find this reading of Curcio flawed.

The Curcio Court made clear that with respect to a custodian of a collective entity's records, the line drawn was between oral testimony and other forms of incrimination. "A custodian, by assuming the duties of his office, undertakes the obligation to produce the books of which he is custodian in response to a rightful exercise of the State's visitorial powers. But he cannot lawfully be compelled, in the absence of a grant of adequate immunity from prosecution, to condemn himself by his own oral testimony." 354 U.S., at 123–24, 77 S.Ct., at 1149 (emphasis added).

We note further that recognizing a Fifth Amendment privilege on behalf of the records custodians of collective entities would have a detrimental impact on the Government's efforts to prosecute "white-collar crime," one of the most serious problems confronting law enforcement authorities. "The greater portion of evidence of wrongdoing by an organization or its representatives is usually found in the official records and documents of that organization. Were the cloak of the privilege to be thrown around these impersonal records and documents, effective enforcement of many federal and state laws would be impossible." White, 322 U.S., at 700, 64 S.Ct., at 1252.

Petitioner suggests, however, that these concerns can be minimized by the simple expedient of either granting the custodian statutory immunity as to the act of production, 18 U.S.C. §§ 6002, 6003, or addressing the subpoena to the corporation and allowing it to choose an agent to produce the records who can do so without incriminating himself. We think neither proposal satisfactorily addresses these concerns. Taking the last first, it is no doubt true that if a subpoena is addressed to a corporation, the corporation "must find some means by which to comply because no Fifth Amendment defense is available to it." In re Sealed Case, 266 U.S.App.D.C. 30, 44, n. 9, 832 F.2d 1268, 1282, n. 9 (1987). The means most commonly used to comply is the appointment of an alternate custodian. See, e.g., In re Two Grand Jury Subpoenae Duces Tecum, 769 F.2d 52, 57 (C.A.2 1985); United States v. Lang, 792 F.2d 1235, 1240–1241 (CA4), cert. denied, 479 U.S. 985, 107 S.Ct. 574, 93 L.Ed.2d 578 (1986); In re Grand Jury No. 86–3 (Will Roberts Corp.), 816 F.2d 569, 573 (CA11 1987). But petitioner insists he cannot be required to aid the appointed custodian in his search for the demanded records, for any statement to the surrogate would itself be testimonial and incriminating. If this is correct, then petitioner's "solution" is a chimera. In situations such as this—where the corporate custodian is likely the only person with knowledge about the demanded documents—the appointment of a surrogate will simply not ensure that the documents sought will ever reach the grand jury room; the appointed custodian will essentially be sent on an unguided search.

This problem is eliminated if the Government grants the subpoenaed custodian statutory immunity for the testimonial aspects of his act of production. But that "solution" also entails a significant drawback. All of the evidence obtained under a grant of immunity to the custodian may of course be used freely against the corporation, but if the Government has any thought of prosecuting the custodian, a grant of act of production immunity can have serious consequences. Testimony obtained pursuant to a grant of statutory use immunity may be used neither directly nor derivatively. 18 U.S.C. § 6002; Kastigar v. United States, 406 U.S. 441, 92 S.Ct. 1653, 32 L.Ed.2d 212 (1972). And "[o]ne raising a claim under [the federal immunity] statute need only show that he testified under a grant of immunity in order to shift to the government the heavy burden of proving that all of the evidence it proposes to use was derived from legitimate independent sources." Id., at 461–462, 92 S.Ct., at 1665. Even in cases where the Government does not employ the immunized testimony for any purpose—direct or derivative—against the witness, the Government's inability to meet the "heavy burden" it bears may result in the preclusion of crucial evidence that was obtained legitimately.

Although a corporate custodian is not entitled to resist a subpoena on the ground that his act of production will be personally incriminating, we do think certain consequences flow from the fact that the custodian's act of production is one in his representative rather than personal capacity. Because the custodian acts as a representative, the act is deemed one of the corporation and not the individual. Therefore, the Government concedes, as it must, that it may make no evidentiary use of the "individual act" against the individual. For example, in a criminal prosecution against the custodian, the Government may not introduce into evidence before the jury the fact that the subpoena was served upon and the corporation's documents were delivered by one particular individual, the custodian. The Government has the right, however, to use the corporation's act of production against the custodian. The Government may offer testimony—for example, from the process server who delivered the subpoena and from the individual who received the records—establishing that the corporation produced the records subpoenaed. The jury may draw from the corporation's act of production the conclusion that the records in question are authentic corporate records, which the corporation possessed, and which it produced in response to the subpoena. And if the defendant held a prominent position within the corporation that produced the records, the jury may, just as it would had someone else produced the documents, reasonably infer that he had possession of the documents or knowledge of their contents. Because the jury is not told that the defendant produced the records, any nexus between the defendant and the documents results solely from the corporation's act of production and other evidence in the case.

Consistent with our precedent, the United States Court of Appeals for the Fifth Circuit ruled that petitioner could not resist the subpoena for corporate documents on the ground that the act of production might tend to incriminate him. The judgment is therefore

Affirmed.

■ JUSTICE KENNEDY, with whom JUSTICE BRENNAN, JUSTICE MARSHALL, and JUSTICE SCALIA join, dissenting.

. . .

The heart of the matter, as everyone knows, is that the Government does not see Braswell as a mere agent at all; and the majority's theory is difficult to square with what will often be the Government's actual practice. The subpoena in this case was not directed to Worldwide Machinery Sales, Inc., or Worldwide Purchasing, Inc. It was directed to "Randy Braswell, President[,] Worldwide Machinery Sales, Inc.[,] Worldwide Purchasing, Inc." and informed him that "[y]ou are hereby commanded" to provide the specified documents. App. 6. The Government explained at oral argument that it often chooses to designate an individual recipient, rather than the corporation generally, when it serves a subpoena because "[we] want the right to make that individual comply with the subpoena." Tr. of Oral Arg. 43. This is not the language of agency. By issuing a subpoena which the Government insists is "directed to petitioner personally," Brief for United States 6 (filed Aug. 14, 1987), it has forfeited any claim that it is simply making a demand on a corporation that, in turn, will have to find a physical agent to perform its duty. What the Government seeks instead is the right to choose any corporate agent as a target of its subpoena and compel that individual to disclose certain information by his own actions.

The majority gives the corporate agent fiction a weight it simply cannot bear. In a peculiar attempt to mitigate the force of its own holding, it impinges upon its own analysis by concluding that, while the Government may compel a named individual to produce records, in any later proceeding against the person it cannot divulge that he performed the act. But if that is so, it is because the Fifth Amendment protects the person without regard to his status as a corporate employee; and once this be admitted, the necessary support for the majority's case has collapsed.

Perhaps the Court makes this concession out of some vague sense of fairness, but the source of its authority to do so remains unexplained. It cannot rest on the Fifth Amendment, for the privilege against self-incrimination does not permit balancing the convenience of the Government against the rights of a witness, and the majority has in any case determined that the Fifth Amendment is inapplicable. If Braswell by his actions reveals information about his state of mind that is relevant to a jury in a criminal proceeding, there are no grounds of which I am aware for declaring the information inadmissible, unless it be the Fifth Amendment.

The majority's abiding concern is that if a corporate officer who is the target of a subpoena is allowed to assert the privilege, it will impede the Government's power to investigate corporations, unions, and partnerships, to uncover and prosecute white-collar crimes, and otherwise to enforce its visitatorial powers. There are at least two answers to this. The first, and most fundamental, is that the text of the Fifth Amendment does not authorize exceptions premised on such rationales. Second, even if it were proper to invent such exceptions, the dangers prophesied by the majority are overstated.

In one sense the case before us may not be a particularly sympathetic one. Braswell was the sole stockholder of the corporation and ran it himself. Perhaps that is why the Court suggests he waived his Fifth Amendment self-incrimination rights by using the corporate form. One does not always, however, have the choice of his or her employer, much less the choice of the business enterprise through which the employer conducts its business. Though the Court here hints at a waiver, nothing in Fifth Amendment jurisprudence indicates that the acceptance of employment should be deemed a waiver of a specific protection that is as basic a part of our constitutional heritage as is the privilege against self-incrimination.

The law is not captive to its own fictions. Yet, in the matter before us the Court employs the fiction that personal incrimination of the employee is neither sought by the Government nor cognizable by the law. That is a regrettable holding, for the conclusion is factually unsound, unnecessary for legitimate regulation, and a violation of the Self–Incrimination Clause of the Fifth Amendment of the Constitution. For these reasons, I dissent.

NOTES

1. The court in Braswell endorsed the line drawn by the Curcio court between acts of production and oral testimony by a custodian of documents. In Curcio, the court also stated regarding this issue:

> [I]n the instant case, the Government is seeking to compel the custodian to do more than identify documents already produced. It seeks to compel him to disclose, by his oral testimony, the whereabouts of books and records which he has failed to produce. It even seeks to make the custodian name the persons in whose possession the missing books may be found. Answers to such questions are more than "auxiliary to the production" of unprivileged corporate or association records. . . .

> [F]orcing the custodian to testify orally as to the whereabouts of nonproduced records requires him to disclose the contents of his own mind. He might be compelled to convict himself out of his own mouth.

Are you persuaded that this is an appropriate line to draw? Consider further on this issue the decision in In re Grand Jury Subpoena Dated April 9, 1996 (Smith), F.3d (11th Cir. 1996) No. 96–4676, 6/21/9: The sole officer and director of a corporation had been served with a subpoena as the custodian of the corporate records. She moved to quash the subpoena, testifying before the grand jury that she did not have the records and refusing to answer when asked where the records were located. Relying on Curcio, the court of appeals held that a custodian of corporate records may not be compelled to testify regarding their location:

> In drawing a line between acts of production and oral testimony, the court [in Braswell] appears to have relied on one fact that distinguishes these two types of testimony: The corporation owns the documents. In contrast, to the extent that one's thoughts and statements can be said to "belong" to anyone, they belong to the witness herself. A custodian has no personal right to retain corporate books. . . . For Fifth Amendment analysis, oral statements are different. The government has no right to compel a person to speak the contents of her mind when doing so would incriminate that person.

> . . . [T]he government argues, and the district court held that Curcio does not apply on the ground that the witness in that case was called before the grand jury pursuant to a personal subpoena and not in his capacity as the records custodian.

> Had the court intended to rely on the distinction between types of subpoenas, it would have been unnecessary to analyze Curcio's rights under the Fifth Amendment . . . We see no basis for distinguishing Curcio on the ground that Curcio involved a personal subpoena.

> The line drawn between the act of production and oral testimony may be a purely formal one, but it is the line the Supreme Court has drawn. The refusal to provide testimony pertaining to the location of documents not in one's possession falls squarely on the side of the line that the Supreme Court has held is subject to Fifth Amendment protection.

2. Does the line drawn between "the act of production and oral testimony" open the door to manipulation by custodians of documents, making it difficult for the government to obtain corporate documents? Suppose the custodian turns over all of the corporate documents to someone else? Does the government have any recourse?

3. May the custodian of corporate documents be required orally to identify or authenticate them? The Curcio court stated: "Requiring the custodian to identify or authenticate the documents for admission into evidence merely makes explicit what is implicit in the production itself." Is requiring authentication testimony different from the facts involved in Curcio? See also United States v. Blackman, 72 F.3d 1418 (9th Cir.1995).

4. Note that the court in Braswell rejected the alternative of granting the custodian statutory immunity as to the act of production but nevertheless ruled that the government could not make any evidentiary use of the "individual act" of production against the custodian. In what other kinds of cases may the court require a custodian to produce documents but nevertheless bar the government from making any evidentiary use of the the "individual act" of production? This question can also be raised in connection with the required records doctrine. See infra, 1355. Also see the more general treatment of the subject of immunity and related issues, infra, p. 1367.

5. See generally Mosteller, Simplifying Subpoena Law: Taking the Fifth Amendment Seriously, 73 Va.L.Rev. 1 (1987); Alito, Documents and the Privilege Against Self–Incrimination, 48 U.Pitt.L.Rev. 27 (1986); Note, Fifth Amendment Privilege for Producing Corporate Documents, 84 Mich.L.Rev. 1544 (1986).

2. REQUIRED RECORDS

The Supreme Court in a series of cases has held that a statutory requirement that a report or registration must be supplied to the government may not run afoul of the Fifth Amendment, depending on the circumstances, even though the information required to be provided in the reports or inference from the registration may be self-incriminatory. The court has also applied the "required records" exception to the privilege in other contexts where it can be said that a person has been required to keep certain records or is subject to a regulatory scheme or regime.

The opinions in the required records cases articulate the factors that the court considers relevant in deciding whether the reporting requirement violates the privilege. The required records doctrine constitutes a major inroad on the applicability of the privilege against self-incrimination. It is not unrelated to the collective entity doctrine, and an important question is whether, and if so, to what extent, do features of the collective entity doctrine as developed by the Supreme Court apply in the required records context.

The leading early Supreme Court required records cases are reviewed in the following excerpt from the Sixth Circuit case of United States v. Alkhafaji, 754 F.2d 641 (6th Cir.1985):

In Albertson [v. Subversive Activities Control Board, 382 U.S. 70, 86 S.Ct. 194, 15 L.Ed.2d 165 (1965)] the Supreme Court set aside an order issued by the Subversive Activities Control Board requiring the petitioners to register under the Subversive Activities Control Act of 1950. The registration form required an admission that the registrant was a member of the Communist Party of the United States and this admission could be used to prosecute the registrant under various laws which made membership in that party illegal. The Supreme Court found that the registration requirement was "inconsistent" with the guarantee against compulsory self-incrimination. In doing so, the Court emphasized several factors. First, the requirement was directed at "a highly selective group inherently suspect of criminal activities," rather than the public at large. Second, the claim of constitutional protection was "not asserted in an essentially non-criminal and regulatory area of inquiry"; rather, the inquiry took place in an area "permeated with criminal statutes, where response to any of the form's questions in context might involve the petitioners in the admission of a crucial element of the crime." Id. at 79, 86 S.Ct. at 199. Finally, compliance with the requirement would create a substantial likelihood of prosecution.

The Albertson, criteria were applied by the Supreme Court in Haynes v. United States, 390 U.S. 85, 88 S.Ct. 722, 19 L.Ed.2d 923 (1968), a prosecution for failing to register a sawed-off shotgun for taxation. The Court found that the statute apparently was intended to require taxation only of "gangster type" weapons. Further, the registration requirement was part of a law which made possession and transportation of certain firearms illegal under many circumstances. It existed as part of an "area permeated with criminal statutes" rather than an area concerned primarily with government regulation in a non-criminal setting.

The Supreme Court decided two other cases on the same day as the Haynes decision. In Marchetti v. United States, 390 U.S. 39, 88 S.Ct. 697, 19 L.Ed.2d 889 (1968), the Court struck down a statute making it a crime to willfully fail to pay an occupational tax on wagering and to register as one conducting wagering. There were numerous laws making wagering a crime, and the Court found that the information obtained from the registration and issuance of a wager license would be readily available to prosecutors enforcing such laws. This information, divulged on pain of prosecution, "would surely prove a significant 'link in a chain' of evidence tending to establish his guilt." Id. at 48, 88 S.Ct. at 703. The Court also applied the Albertson criteria to reverse a conviction in Grosso v. United States, 390 U.S. 62, 88 S.Ct. 709, 19 L.Ed.2d 906 (1968). This to, was a case involving the tax on wagering. The opinion highlighted the additional duty of one engaged in the wagering business to file monthly returns with the Internal Revenue Service on a form which revealed the details of the wagering business actually being carried on. As in Marchetti, the Court found that the combination of state and federal anti-gambling laws placed Grosso "entirely within 'an area permeated with criminal statutes,' where he is 'inherently suspect of criminal activities.' " Id. at 64, 88 S.Ct. at 712.

In Leary v. United States, 395 U.S. 6 (1969), the Supreme Court reversed a conviction under the Marihuana Tax Act. Central to its determination of a Fifth Amendment violation was the finding that the purpose of the Act was to bring to light violations of the marihuana laws. Since possession of marihuana is illegal in every state, compliance with requirements of the Act would create a "real and appreciable" risk of incrimination. Id. at 18. By complying, a person identified himself as a member of a "selective" and "suspect" group, since persons legally in possession of marihuana were "virtually certain" either to be registered or to be exempt from obtaining an order form required by regulations. Id.

In United States v. Sullivan, 274 U.S. 259, 47 S.Ct. 607, 71 L.Ed. 1037 (1927), the Supreme Court upheld the conviction of one engaged in illegal liquor traffic for willfully refusing to file an income tax return. Writing for the Court, Justice Holmes found that "the protection of the Fifth Amendment was pressed too far" in the decision of the court of appeals reversing the conviction. Id. at 263, 47 S.Ct. at 607. The defendant could have objected to answering specific questions on grounds of Fifth Amendment privilege, but could not refuse to file the return. "It would be an extreme if not an extravagant application of the Fifth Amendment to say that it authorized a man to refuse to state the amount of his income because it had been made in crime." Id. at 263–264, 47 S.Ct. at 607–608. In Albertson and the other cases previously discussed the Court distinguished Sullivan on the ground that all persons with taxable income are required to file returns, and thus, the filing requirement is not directed at a "highly selective group inherently suspect of criminal activities" and the claim of privilege in Sullivan was not "against an inquiry in an area permeated with criminal statutes." Albertson, 382 U.S. at 79, 86 S.Ct. at 199.

In California v. Byers, 402 U.S. 424 (1971), the Court found Sullivan rather than Albertson controlling. At issue was the question whether a state "hit and run" statute which required a driver involved in a motor vehicle accident to stop at the scene and give his name and address infringed the constitutional privilege against compulsory self-incrimination. In a plurality opinion, Chief Burger wrote:

> Tension between the State's demand for disclosures and the protection of the right against self-incrimination is likely to give rise to serious questions. Inevitably these must be resolved in terms of balancing the public need on the one hand, and the individual claim to constitutional protections on the other; neither interest can be treated lightly. 402 U.S. at 427, 91 S.Ct. at 1537.

In conducting its close scrutiny of the California statute, the Court found the Albertson elements missing. All drivers of motor vehicles have the same responsibility under the law; the requirement of identifying one's self after an accident was not directed to a "selective" or "suspect" group. Moreover, involvement in an automobile accident does not ordinarily implicate any criminal activity. In addition, the purposes of the statute are non-criminal—to facilitate proper allocation of civil liabilities and to regulate the use of motor vehicles. The fact that the essentially neutral act of making the required disclosure might possibly have the collateral consequence of ultimately leading to prosecution is not sufficient:

> In order to involve the privilege it is necessary to show that the compelled disclosures will themselves confront the claimant with "substantial hazards of self-incrimination."402 U.S. at 429, 91 S.Ct. at 1538.

Justice Harlan, the author of Albertson, Haynes, Marchetti, Grosso and Leary, concurred in the judgment in Byers. He concluded that when a statute "operate[s] in the context of the ... collection of data for purposes essentially unrelated to criminal prosecution," id. at 436, 91 S.Ct. at 1542, "the presence of a 'real' and not 'imaginary' risk of self-incrimination is not a sufficient predicate for extending the privilege against self-incrimination" to such a regulatory scheme. Id. at 439, 91 S.Ct. at 1543.

The Second Circuit has found Byers controlling in upholding convictions under two quite different statutes which require potentially incriminating disclosures. In United States v. Stirling, 571 F.2d 708 (2d Cir.), cert. denied, 439 U.S. 824, 99 S.Ct. 93, 58 L.Ed.2d 116 (1978), the court affirmed a conviction for securities fraud. The defendants maintained that if they had disclosed the true facts surrounding certain transactions to the SEC and the public they would have been admitting sufficient facts to form a basis for criminal prosecution under federal labor laws. The court rejected this argument and conducted the "close scrutiny" dictated by Byers, using the balancing approach described in that decision. The court concluded that this balancing requires a finding that an "essentially regulatory statute" does not violate the Fifth Amendment privilege against self-incrimination where four conditions are found to exist: (1) self-reporting is essential to fulfillment of the regulatory objective, (2) the burden of disclosure is placed on the general public rather than a selective, suspect group, (3) the general activity is lawful and (4) the possibility of incrimination is not substantial. The court also pointed out that Byers held that the possibility that disclosed information might be "a link in the chain" of evidence leading to prosecution and conviction is not a sufficient basis for finding an infringement. 571 F.2d at 728.

The offense in United States v. Dichne, 612 F.2d 632 (2d Cir.1979), cert. denied, 445 U.S. 928 (1980), was failure to report to United States Customs the transportation out of the United States of "monetary instruments" having a value in excess of $5,000 as required by the Bank Secrecy Act. The court analyzed the reporting requirement under both the Albertson line of cases and under Byers and concluded that it was not inconsistent with the guarantee against compulsory self-incrimination. Important considerations were the fact that the transportation of money out of the United States is not itself illegal and that the majority of persons required to make the report would have no involvement in criminal activity. Thus the reporting requirement is not aimed at an "inherently suspect group" and it does not involve an area "permeated with criminal statutes." The court distinguished Haynes because the statute involved there required reports only with respect to weapons principally used in unlawful activities. The court found the legitimate regulatory, noncriminal interest of the government to be substantial and that the reporting requirements do not involve a "direct link to any related criminal activity." Id. at 640.

The most recent foray of the Supreme Court into the Required Records thicket occurred in the case of Baltimore City Department of Social Services v. Bouknight, reproduced below. Bouknight did not, however, involve a required report or registration; rather, the issue was whether a mother could rely upon the Fifth Amendment as a basis for her refusal to comply with a court order requiring her to produce her child.

Baltimore City Department of Social Services v. Bouknight

Supreme Court of the United States, 1990.
493 U.S. 549, 110 S.Ct. 900, 107 L.Ed.2d 992.

■ JUSTICE O'CONNOR delivered the opinion of the Court.

In this action, we must decide whether a mother, the custodian of a child pursuant to a court order, may invoke the Fifth Amendment privilege against self-incrimination to resist an order of the juvenile court to produce the child. We hold that she may not.

I

Petitioner Maurice M. is an abused child. When he was three months old, he was hospitalized with a fractured left femur, and examination revealed several partially healed bone fractures and other indications of severe physical abuse. In the hospital, respondent Bouknight, Maurice's mother, was observed shaking Maurice, dropping him in his crib despite his spica cast, and otherwise handling him in a manner inconsistent with his recovery and continued health. Hospital personnel notified the Baltimore City Department of Social Services (BCDSS) of suspected child abuse. In February 1987, BCDSS secured a court order removing Maurice from Bouknight's control and placing him in shelter care. Several months later, the shelter care order was inexplicably modified to return Maurice to Bouknight's custody temporarily. Following a hearing held shortly thereafter, the juvenile court declared Maurice to be a "child in need of assistance," thus asserting jurisdiction over Maurice and placing him under BCDSS' continuing oversight. BCDSS agreed that Bouknight could continue as custodian of the child, but only pursuant to extensive conditions set forth in a court-approved protective supervision order. The order required Bouknight to "cooperate with BCDSS," "continue in therapy," participate in parental aid and training programs, and "refrain from physically punishing [Maurice]." The order's terms were "all subject to the further Order of the Court." Bouknight's attorney signed the order, and Bouknight in a separate form set forth her agreement to each term.

Eight months later, fearing for Maurice's safety, BCDSS returned to juvenile court. BCDSS caseworkers related that Bouknight would not cooperate with them and had in nearly every respect violated the terms of the protective order. BCDSS stated that Maurice's father had recently died in a shooting incident and that Bouknight, in light of the results of a psychological examination and her history of drug use, could not provide adequate care for the child. On April 20, 1988, the court granted BCDSS' petition to remove Maurice from

Bouknight's control for placement in foster care. BCDSS officials also petitioned for judicial relief from Bouknight's failure to produce Maurice or reveal where he could be found. The petition recounted that on two recent visits by BCDSS officials to Bouknight's home, she had refused to reveal the location of the child or had indicated that the child was with an aunt whom she would not identify. The petition further asserted that inquiries of Bouknight's known relatives had revealed that none of them had recently seen Maurice and that BCDSS had prompted the police to issue a missing persons report and referred the case for investigation by the police homicide division. Also on April 20, the juvenile court, upon a hearing on the petition, cited Bouknight for violating the protective custody order and for failing to appear at the hearing. Bouknight had indicated to her attorney that she would appear with the child, but also expressed fear that if she appeared the State would " 'snatch the child.' " The court issued an order to show cause why Bouknight should not be held in civil contempt for failure to produce the child. Expressing concern that Maurice was endangered or perhaps dead, the court issued a bench warrant for Bouknight's appearance.

Maurice was not produced at subsequent hearings. At a hearing one week later, Bouknight claimed that Maurice was with a relative in Dallas. Investigation revealed that the relative had not seen Maurice. The next day, following another hearing at which Bouknight again declined to produce Maurice, the juvenile court found Bouknight in contempt for failure to produce the child as ordered. There was and has been no indication that she was unable to comply with the order. The court directed that Bouknight be imprisoned until she "purge[d] herself of contempt by either producing [Maurice] before the court or revealing to the court his exact whereabouts."

The juvenile court rejected Bouknight's subsequent claim that the contempt order violated the Fifth Amendment's guarantee against self-incrimination. The court stated that the production of Maurice would purge the contempt and that "[t]he contempt is issued not because she refuse[d] to testify in any proceeding ... [but] because she has failed to abide by the Order of this Court, mainly [for] the production of Maurice M." While that decision was being appealed, Bouknight was convicted of theft and sentenced to 18 months' imprisonment in separate proceedings. The Court of Appeals of Maryland ... found that the contempt order unconstitutionally compelled Bouknight to admit through the act of production "a measure of continuing control and dominion over Maurice's person" in circumstances in which "Bouknight has a reasonable apprehension that she will be prosecuted." We granted certiorari, 490 U.S. 1003, 109 S.Ct. 1636, 104 L.Ed.2d 152 (1989), and we now reverse.

II

The juvenile court concluded that Bouknight could comply with the order through the unadorned act of producing the child, and we thus address that aspect of the order. When the government demands that an item be produced, "the only thing compelled is the act of producing the [item]." The Fifth Amendment's protection may nonetheless be implicated because the act of complying with the government's demand testifies to the existence, possession, or authenticity of the things produced. But a person may not claim the Amendment's protections based upon the incrimination that may result from the contents or nature of the thing demanded. Bouknight therefore cannot claim the privilege based upon anything that examination of Maurice might reveal, nor can she assert the privilege upon the theory that compliance would assert that the child produced is in fact Maurice (a fact the State could readily establish, rendering any testimony regarding existence or authenticity insufficiently incriminating). Rather, Bouknight claims the benefit of the privilege because the act of production would amount to testimony regarding her control over, and possession of, Maurice. Although the State could readily introduce evidence of Bouknight's continuing control over the child—e.g., the custody order, testimony of relatives, and Bouknight's own statements to Maryland officials before invoking the privilege—her implicit communication of control over Maurice at the moment of production might aid the State in prosecuting Bouknight.

The possibility that a production order will compel testimonial assertions that may prove incriminating does not, in all contexts, justify invoking the privilege to resist production. Even assuming that this limited testimonial assertion is sufficiently incriminating and "sufficiently testimonial for purposes of the privilege," Bouknight may not invoke the privilege to resist the production order because she has assumed custodial duties related to production and because production is required as part of a noncriminal regulatory regime.

The Court has on several occasions recognized that the Fifth Amendment privilege may not be invoked to resist compliance with a regulatory regime constructed to effect the State's public purposes unrelated to the enforcement of its criminal laws. In Shapiro v. United States, 335 U.S. 1, 68 S.Ct. 1375, 92 L.Ed. 1787 (1948), the Court considered an application of the Emergency Price Control Act of 1942 and a regulation issued thereunder which required licensed businesses to maintain records and make them available for inspection by administrators. The Court indicated that no Fifth Amendment protection attached to production of the "required records," which the " 'defendant was required to keep, not for his private uses, but for the benefit of the public, and for public inspection.' " The Court's discussion of the constitutional implications of the scheme focused upon the relation between the Government's regulatory objectives and the Government's interest in gaining access to the records in Shapiro's possession:

> It may be assumed at the outset that there are limits which the Government cannot constitutionally exceed in requiring the keeping of records which may be inspected by an administrative agency and may be used in prosecuting statutory violations committed by the recordkeeper himself. But no serious misgiving that those bounds have been overstepped would appear to be evoked when there is a sufficient relation between the activity sought to be regulated and the public concern so that the Government can constitutionally regulate or forbid the basic activity concerned, and can constitutionally require the keeping of particular records, subject to inspection by the Administrator.

The Court has since refined those limits to the government's authority to gain access to items or information vested with this public character. The Court has noted that "the requirements at issue in Shapiro were imposed in 'an essentially non-criminal and regulatory area of inquiry,' " and that Shapiro's reach is limited where requirements "are directed to a 'selective group inherently suspect of criminal activities.' " [The court here cited Marchetti, Albertson, Grosso, and Haynes.]

California v. Byers confirms that the ability to invoke the privilege may be greatly diminished when invocation would interfere with the effective operation of a generally applicable, civil regulatory requirement. In Byers, the Court upheld enforcement of California's statutory requirement that drivers of cars involved in accidents stop and provide their names and addresses. A plurality found the risk of incrimination too insubstantial to implicate the Fifth Amendment, and noted that the statute "was not intended to facilitate criminal convictions but to promote the satisfaction of civil liabilities," " 'directed at the public at large,' " quoting Albertson, and required disclosure of no inherently illegal activity. See also United States v. Sullivan (rejecting Fifth Amendment objection to requirement to file income tax return). Justice Harlan, the author of Marchetti, Grosso, and Haynes, concurred in the judgment. He distinguished those three cases as considering statutory schemes that "focused almost exclusively on conduct which was criminal." While acknowledging that in particular cases the California statute would compel incriminating testimony, he concluded that the noncriminal purpose and the general applicability of the reporting requirement demanded compliance even in such cases.

When a person assumes control over items that are the legitimate object of the government's noncriminal regulatory powers, the ability to invoke the privilege is reduced. In Wilson v. United States, the Court surveyed a range of cases involving the custody of public documents and records required by law to be kept because they related to "the appropriate subjects of governmental regulation and the enforcement of restrictions validly established." The principle the Court drew from these cases is: "[W]here, by virtue of their character and the rules of law applicable to them, the books and papers are held subject to examination by the demanding authority, the custodian has no privilege to refuse production although their contents tend to criminate him. In assuming their custody he has accepted the incident obligation to permit inspection." [The court here cited Braswell and Curcio.] ("A custodian, by assuming the duties of his office, undertakes the obligation to produce the books of which he is custodian in response to a rightful exercise of the State's visitorial powers"). In Shapiro, the Court interpreted this principle as extending well beyond the corporate context, and emphasized that Shapiro had assumed and retained control over documents in which the Government had a direct and particular regulatory interest. Indeed, it was in part Shapiro's custody over items having this public nature that allowed the Court in Marchetti, Grosso, and Haynes, to distinguish the measures considered in those cases from the regulatory requirement at issue in Shapiro.

These principles readily apply to this case. Once Maurice was adjudicated a child in need of assistance, his care and safety became the particular object of the State's regulatory interests. ("This court has jurisdiction to require at all times to know the whereabouts of the minor child. We asserted jurisdiction over that child in the spring of 1987 ...”). Maryland first placed Maurice in shelter care, authorized placement in foster care, and then entrusted responsibility for Maurice's care to Bouknight. By accepting care of Maurice subject to the custodial order's conditions (including requirements that she cooperate with BCDSS, follow a prescribed training regime, and be subject to further court orders), Bouknight submitted to the routine operation of the regulatory system and agreed to hold Maurice in a manner consonant with the State's regulatory interests and subject to inspection by BCDSS. In assuming the obligations attending custody, Bouknight "has accepted the incident obligation to permit inspection." [citing] Wilson. The State imposes and enforces that obligation as part of a broadly directed, noncriminal regulatory regime governing children cared for pursuant to custodial orders. See Md.Cts. & Jud.Proc. Code Ann. § 3–802(a) (1984) (setting forth child protective purposes of subtitle, including "provid[ing] for the care, protection, and wholesome mental and physical development of children coming within the provisions of this subtitle").

Persons who care for children pursuant to a custody order, and who may be subject to a request for access to the child, are hardly a " 'selective group inherently suspect of criminal activities.' " Marchetti, quoting Albertson. The juvenile court may place a child within its jurisdiction with social service officials or "under supervision in his own home or in the custody or under the guardianship of a relative or other fit person, upon terms the court deems appropriate." Children may be placed, for example, in foster care, in homes of relatives, or in the care of state officials. Even when the court allows a parent to retain control of a child within the court's jurisdiction, that parent is not one singled out for criminal conduct, but rather has been deemed to be, without the State's assistance, simply "unable or unwilling to give proper care and attention to the child and his problems." The provision that authorized the juvenile court's efforts to gain production of Maurice reflects this broad applicability. See Md.Cts. & Jud.Proc.Code Ann. § 3–814(c) (1984) ("If a parent, guardian, or custodian fails to bring the child before the court when requested, the court may issue a writ of attachment directing that the child be taken into custody and brought before the court. The court may proceed against the parent, guardian, or custodian for contempt"). This provision "fairly may be said to be directed at ... parents, guardians, and custodians who accept placement of juveniles in custody." (McAuliffe, J., dissenting).

Similarly, BCDSS' efforts to gain access to children, as well as judicial efforts to the same effect, do not "focu[s] almost exclusively on conduct which was criminal." Many orders will arise in circumstances entirely devoid of criminal conduct. Even when criminal conduct may exist, the court may properly request production and return of the child, and enforce that request through exercise of the contempt power, for reasons related entirely to the child's well-being and through measures unrelated to criminal law enforcement or investigation. This case provides an illustration: concern for the child's safety underlay the efforts to gain access to and then compel production of Maurice. Finally, production in the vast majority of cases will embody no incriminating testimony, even if in particular cases the act of production may incriminate the custodian through an assertion of possession or the existence, or the identity, of the child. These orders to produce children cannot be characterized as efforts to gain some testimonial component of the act of production. The government demands production of the very public charge entrusted to a custodian, and makes the demand for compelling reasons unrelated to criminal law enforcement and as part of a broadly applied regulatory regime. In these circumstances, Bouknight cannot invoke the privilege to resist the order to produce Maurice.

We are not called upon to define the precise limitations that may exist upon the State's ability to use the testimonial aspects of Bouknight's act of production in subsequent criminal proceedings. But we note that imposition of such limitations is not foreclosed. The same custodial role that limited the ability to resist the production order may give rise to corresponding limitations upon the direct and indirect use of that testimony. See Braswell. The State's regulatory requirement in the usual case may neither compel incriminating testimony nor aid a criminal prosecution, but the Fifth Amendment protections are not thereby necessarily unavailable to the person who complies with the regulatory requirement after invoking the privilege and subsequently faces prosecution. In a broad range of contexts, the Fifth Amendment limits prosecutors' ability to use testimony that has been compelled. See Simmons v. United States, 390 U.S. 377, 391–394, 88 S.Ct. 967, 974–976, 19 L.Ed.2d 1247 (1968) (no subsequent admission of testimony provided in suppression hearing); Murphy v. Waterfront Comm'n of New York Harbor, 378 U.S. 52, 75–76, 79, 84 S.Ct. 1594, 1607–1608, 1609, 12 L.Ed.2d 678 (1964) (Fifth Amendment bars use, in criminal processes, in other jurisdictions of testimony compelled pursuant to a grant of use immunity in one jurisdiction); Maness v. Meyers, 419 U.S.

449, 474–475, 95 S.Ct. 584, 599, 42 L.Ed.2d 574 (1975) (WHITE, J., concurring in result); Adams v. Maryland, 347 U.S. 179, 181, 74 S.Ct. 442, 445, 98 L.Ed. 608 (1954) ("[A] witness does not need any statute to protect him from the use of self-incriminating testimony he is compelled to give over his objection....

III

The judgment of the Court of Appeals of Maryland is reversed, and the cases are remanded to that court for further proceedings not inconsistent with this opinion.

[Justice Marshall, with whom Justice Brennan joined, dissented in a separate opinion.]

NOTES

1. In United States v. Alkhafaji, quoted from supra p. 1355, the issue was whether the disclosure requirement of the Gun Control Act of 1968, 18 U.S.C. § 921 et seq. (1982), violates the Fifth Amendment privilege against compulsory self-incrimination. The defendant had been convicted of a violation of 18 U.S.C. § 922(e) for delivering firearms to an airline for transportation without written notice to the carrier. A few hours before boarding an airline to travel abroad, the defendant, a resident alien, had checked an unusually large number of pieces of luggage with the airline. Acting on a tip from the Federal Bureau of Investigation, a customs inspector searched the luggage and found three shotguns and eight handguns. The luggage also contained car parts and other miscellaneous items.

The statute under which Alkhafaji was convicted, 18 U.S.C. § 922(e), provides in pertinent part:

It shall be unlawful for any person knowingly to deliver ... to any common ... carrier for transportation ... in interstate or foreign commerce, ... any package or other container in which there is any firearm or ammunition without written notice to the carrier that such firearm or ammunition is being transported ...; except that any passenger who owns or legally possesses a firearm or ammunition being transported aboard any common ... carrier for movement with the passenger in interstate or foreign commerce may deliver said firearm or ammunition into the custody of the pilot, ... of such common ... carrier for the duration of the trip without violating any of the provisions of this chapter.

Addressing the Fifth Amendment issue, the Alkhafaji court stated:

It seems clear to us that § 922(e) falls somewhere between the statutes considered in the Albertson line and the one at issue in Byers. Though it is primarily a regulatory statute, it does reflect congressional concern with weapons and ammunition, an area permeated with criminal statutes. However, all persons who ship firearms or ammunition to someone other than a licensed importer, dealer, manufacturer or collector are required to give written notice to the carrier, with passengers being permitted to deliver legally possessed weapons and ammunition to a representative of the carrier in lieu of the written notice. Many people who would fall into this group would not be acting unlawfully. It cannot be said that this requirement is directed at a "highly selective and inherently suspect" group of people. This general requirement cannot be held to violate an individual passenger or shipper's constitutional right solely because compliance might supply evidence of other criminal activity.

We think it is significant that all of the statutes considered in Albertson and like cases required a report to a government agency. In contrast, § 922(e) requires a report only to the carrier. Though carriers may pass such reports along to governmental agencies concerned with enforcement of other laws relating to firearms, they are not required to do so. The carriers fulfill their responsibility by refusing to accept the firearms or ammunition for transportation if inquiry reveals that such transportation would be unlawful. Under these circumstances, the likelihood that required disclosures will be incriminating is much less substantial.

2. The required records and collective entity doctrines arguably have a common heritage. One of the earliest Supreme Court corporate records-collective entity cases, Wilson v. United States, discussed supra 1344, was also a foundational case for the required records doctrine. In Bouknight, Justice O'Connor called attention to these origins, first, by quoting a pertinent passage from Wilson:

> "[W]here, by virtue of their character and the rules of law applicable to them, the books and papers are held subject to examination by the demanding authority, the custodian has no privilege to refuse production although their contents tend to criminate him. In assuming their custody he has accepted the incident obligation to permit inspection."

and second, by stating: "In Shapiro [a foundational required records case], the court interpreted this principle [the Wilson principle as reflected in the previous quotation] as extending well beyond the corporate context."

Although there is some common origin and some overlap in rationale, the two doctrines clearly have some different elements, and there are various ways in which they can be compared or differentiated. For example, a required records situation may, but does not necessarily, involve a collective entity such as a corporation. One court has compared the two doctrines in the following terms:

> We have recognized that corporate records include but are not limited to required records. Thus required records are a subset of corporate records.

United States v. Dean, 989 F.2d 1205 (D.C.Cir.1993).

3. Bouknight suggests that the required records doctrine can be applied in a variety of contexts wherever it can be said that a "noncriminal regulatory regime" is applicable. Application of the doctrine to a juvenile court's exercise of supervision over a child, of course, involved a type of situation different from any previously considered by the Supreme Court.

For another kind of judicial supervision context in which the required records doctrine has been invoked, see In re Grand Jury Proceedings, 119 B.R. 945 (E.D.Mich.1990): A trustee in bankruptcy in a Chapter 11 proceeding who was suspected of embezzlement was ordered to turn over all banking and financial records relating to the estate of the debtor garage. The trustee was described as a officer of the court and a public official who had no right to refuse to turn over public documents.

Another arguably creative application of the doctrine is In re Dr. John Doe, 711 F.2d 1187 (2d Cir.1983): A physician's patient files were deemed required records on the ground that the state statutory scheme labels as unprofessional conduct a failure to maintain adequate records for each patient.

The required records doctrine also applies to records the maintenance of which is required by administrative regulation. In re Grand Jury Proceedings, 601 F.2d 162 (5th Cir.1979).

4. Are government records required records or collective entity records or both? If they are both, which doctrine applies to them—the collective entity doctrine or the required records doctrine? Does it make any difference? As to a particular kind of government record, see United States v. Dean, 989 F.2d 1205 (D.C.Cir.1993): The executive assistant of the Secretary of Housing and Urban Development was required to turn over office records, including an office diary and appointment books. The government argued that these records were not like corporate documents but rather were like required records. The court disagreed, ruling that these documents were not public documents which the official involved was required to keep: "There is no reason to treat government records as different from corporate records to the extent that the former similarly includes required records."

5. In the Dean case, supra note 4, in arguing that this was a required records rather than a collective entity case, the government was trying to avoid the application of the act of production doctrine as it was applied in Braswell. Although the district court had required Dean to produce the documents, the court had also granted a motion to suppress evidence of her act of producing the documents. The government was trying to overturn the ruling granting the motion, but the Court of Appeals, relying on Braswell, affirmed.

If the government had persuaded the D.C. Circuit that this was a required records case, should it necessarily have succeeded in overturning the ruling on the motion to suppress? Consider the following:

a) Prior to Bouknight, there was substantial authority supporting the proposition that the Fisher–Doe act-of-production doctrine does not apply to required records. The U.S. courts of appeal uniformly rejected the claim that an individual is protected by the Fifth Amendment from having to produce such records because the production would involve testimonial self-incrimination by the recordkeeper. In re Grand Jury Subpoena Duces Tecum Served Upon Randall Underhill, 781 F.2d 64 (6th Cir.), cert. denied, 479 U.S. 813 (1986); In re Grand Jury Subpoenas Duces Tecum Dated June 13, 1983 and June 22, 1983, 722 F.2d 981 (2d Cir.1983); In re Dr. John Doe, 711 F.2d 1187 (2d Cir.1983); In re Grand Jury Proceedings (McCoy), 601 F.2d 162 (5th Cir.1979).

b) Several rationales were offered in support of this result:

1) "[I]f an individual chooses to begin or continue to do business in an area in which the government requires record keeping, he may be deemed to have waived any Fifth Amendment protection which would otherwise be present in the absence of the record keeping regulation." In re Grand Jury Subpoena Duces Tecum Served Upon Randall Underhill, supra at 70.

2) "[S]ince ... [the records] are required to be kept, production of them can hardly provide the basis for an inference of criminality in possessing them." In re Grand Jury Subpoenas Duces Tecum Dated June 13 and June 22, 1983, supra at 987, n. 5.

3) "[T]he required records doctrine is an exception to the Fifth Amendment ... As such, the doctrine presupposes that compliance with the government's inquiry may be incriminating." In re Grand Jury Subpoena Duces Tecum Served Upon Randall Underhill, supra at 70.

c) Bouknight itself rejected the application of the act-of-production doctrine to the situation before it. Recall that the court stated:

Even assuming that this limited testimonial assertion is sufficiently incriminating and "sufficiently testimonial for purposes of the privilege," Bouknight may not invoke the privilege to resist the production order because she has assumed custodial duties related to production and because production is required as part of a noncriminal regulatory regime.

d) However, having approved the order requiring Bouknight to produce her child, Justice O'Connor proceeded to suggest that there might be some limits on the government's use of the fact of production in any subsequent prosecution of Bouknight, without defining the "precise" limitations ["we note that the imposition of such limitations is not foreclosed."] The fact that the court left some uncertainty about this aspect of the case, unlike Braswell where the court was quite clear on the subject, suggests that the court may be still feeling its way in this new doctrinal path—namely, requiring production despite the Fifth Amendment, while being prepared to impose some kind of limits on the government's evidentiary use of the act of production. Note, too, that the court cited a string of its previous decisions, all involving cases where the Fifth Amendment was interpreted to limit "prosecutors' ability to use testimony that has been compelled."

Is there a reason why the court could not simply apply the Braswell approach to the Bouknight situation? Is there a difference that makes the matter more difficult in cases like Bouknight and other non-collective agency required records situations? Consider in this connection the district court's action in Doe I, as described by Justice Powell in the Supreme Court's opinion:

> While not ruling out the possibility that the Government could devise a way to ensure that the act of turning over the documents would not incriminate respondent, the [district] court held that the Government had not made such a showing.

6. For a post-Bouknight required records case where the issues discussed in the previous note might have been expected to arise, see In re Grand Jury Subpoena: United States v. Spano, 21 F.3d 226 (8th Cir.1994): Spano (who had been ordered to produce tax and workmen's compensation records, automobile licensing and sales records and federally required odometer statements) argued that "because he is a sole proprietor, the requested records were his own personal business records, and the existence, authenticity, and possession of the requested records were not foregone conclusions; therefore, he is entitled to invoke the Fifth Amendment against a potentially self-incriminatory act of production." The court while, inter alia, noting that the Supreme Court in Bouknight had not "directly" relied upon the required records exception, nevertheless followed the reasoning in Bouknight and held that Spano was required to produce the records which were part of a noncriminal regulatory regime.

Should the court also have suggested that there were some limits on the evidentiary use to which the act of producing the records might be put? The court did not mention this possibility. How practical is this avenue in a sole proprietor situation?

7. Tax protestors have frequently invoked the Fifth Amendment in support of efforts to avoid the payment of taxes. A significant obstacle to their claims is United States v. Sullivan, discussed in the introduction to this section.

In United States v. Neff, 615 F.2d 1235 (9th Cir.1980), the court rejected a tax protestor's fifth amendment response to specific questions on his income tax form on the ground that he had not demonstrated a real and appreciable danger of incrimination. The court noted that the questions posed on the form did not themselves suggest that the response would be incriminating nor did the setting in which the questions were asked alter their non-incriminating nature. "At no point ... was the district judge presented with any indicia of potential incrimination." Id. at 1240–1241.

The facts in United States v. Carlson, 617 F.2d 518 (9th Cir.1980) should be compared with Neff. The defendant first filed false W–4 withholding statements and then asserted a privilege against self-incrimination objection to the filing of his income tax form, claiming that responding to the questions on the form would involve a real and appreciable hazard of incrimination with respect to the previous false filing of the W–4 forms. Acknowledging that the required responses would involve a substantial threat of incrimination, the court nevertheless affirmed the conviction, concluding that if his assertion of the privilege were upheld, it would license a form of conduct that would undermine the whole system of tax collection. The court stated its holding as follows:

> We therefore hold that an individual who seeks to frustrate the tax laws by claiming too many withholding exemptions, with an eye to covering that crime and evading the tax return requirement by assertion of the Fifth Amendment, is not entitled to the amendment's protection. Id. at 523.

8. There is a significant literature on the required records problem. See e.g., Meltzer, Required Records, the McCarran Act and the Privilege Against Self–Incrimination, 18 U.Chi.L.Rev. 687 (1951); Mansfield, The Albertson Case: Conflict Between the Privilege Against Self–Incrimination and the Government's Need for Information, 1966 S.Ct.Rev. 103; McKay, Self–Incrimination and the New Privacy, 1967 S.Ct.Rev. 193; Saltzburg, The Required Records Doctrine: Its Lessons for the Privilege Against Self–Incrimination (In Honor of Bernard D. Meltzer), 53 U.Chi.L.Rev. 6 (1986).

E.   IMMUNITY

Kastigar v. United States

Supreme Court of the United States, 1972.
406 U.S. 441, 92 S.Ct. 1653, 32 L.Ed.2d 212.

■ MR. JUSTICE POWELL delivered the opinion of the Court.

This case presents the question whether the United States Government may compel testimony from an unwilling witness, who invokes the Fifth Amendment privilege against compulsory self-incrimination, by conferring on the witness immunity from use of the compelled testimony in subsequent criminal proceedings, as well as immunity from use of evidence derived from the testimony.

Petitioners were subpoenaed to appear before a United States grand jury in the Central District of California on February 4, 1971. The Government believed that petitioners were likely to assert their Fifth Amendment privilege. Prior to the scheduled appearances, the Government applied to the District Court for an order directing petitioners to answer questions and produce evidence before the grand jury under a grant of immunity conferred pursuant to 18 U.S.C. §§ 6002, 6003. Petitioners opposed issuance of the order, contending primarily that the scope of the immunity provided by the statute was not coextensive with the scope of the privilege against self-incrimination, and therefore was not sufficient to supplant the privilege and compel their testimony. The District Court rejected this contention, and ordered petitioners to appear before the grand jury and answer its questions under the grant of immunity.

Petitioners appeared but refused to answer questions, asserting their privilege against compulsory self-incrimination. They were brought before the District Court, and each persisted in his refusal to answer the grand jury's questions, notwithstanding the grant of immunity. The court found both in contempt, and committed them to the custody of the Attorney General until either they answered the grand jury's questions or the term of the grand jury expired. The Court of Appeals for the Ninth Circuit affirmed. Stewart v. United States, 440 F.2d 954 (C.A.9 1971). This Court granted certiorari to resolve the important question whether testimony may be compelled by granting immunity from the use of compelled testimony and evidence derived therefrom ("use and derivative use" immunity), or whether it is necessary to grant immunity from prosecution for offenses to which compelled testimony relates ("transactional" immunity). 402 U.S. 971, 91 S.Ct. 1668, 29 L.Ed.2d 135 (1971).

I

The power of government to compel persons to testify in court or before grand juries and other governmental agencies is firmly established in Anglo–American jurisprudence. The power with respect to courts was established by statute in England as early as 1562, and Lord Bacon observed in 1612 that all subjects owed the King their "knowledge and discovery." While it is not clear when grand juries first resorted to compulsory process to secure the attendance and testimony of witnesses, the general common-law principle that "the public has a right to every man's evidence" was considered an "indubitable certainty" that "cannot be denied" by 1742....

But the power to compel testimony is not absolute. There are a number of exemptions from the testimonial duty, the most important of which is the Fifth Amendment privilege against compulsory self-incrimination. The privilege reflects a complex of our fundamental values and aspirations, and marks an important advance in the development of our liberty. It can be asserted in any proceeding, civil or criminal, administrative or judicial, investigatory or adjudicatory; and it protects against any disclosures that the witness reasonably believes could be used in a criminal prosecution or could lead to other evidence that might be so used. This Court has been zealous to safeguard the values that underlie the privilege.

Immunity statutes, which have historical roots deep in Anglo–American jurisprudence,[1] are not incompatible with these values. Rather, they seek a rational accommodation between the imperatives of the privilege and the legitimate demands of government to compel citizens to testify. The existence of these statutes reflects the importance of testimony, and the fact that many offenses are of such a character that the only persons capable of giving useful testimony are those implicated in the crime. Indeed, their origins were in the

---

1. Soon after the privilege against compulsory self-incrimination became firmly established in law, it was recognized that the privilege did not apply when immunity, or "indemnity," in the English usage, had been granted. See L. Levy, Origins of the Fifth Amendment 328, 495 (1968). Parliament enacted an immunity statute in 1710 directed against illegal gambling, 9 Anne, c. 14, §§ 3–4, which became the model for an identical immunity statute enacted in 1774 by the Colonial Legislature of New York. Law of Mar. 9, 1774, c. 1651, 5 Colonial Laws of New York 621, 623 (1894). These statutes provided that the loser could sue the winner, who was compelled to answer the loser's charges. After the winner responded and returned his ill-gotten gains, he was "acquitted, indemnified [immunized] and discharged from any further or other Punishment, Forfeiture or Penalty, which he ... may have incurred by the playing for, and winning such Money...." 9 Anne, c. 14, § 4 (1710); Law of Mar. 9, 1774, c. 1651, 5 Colonial Laws of New York, at 623.... [Footnotes are those of the court. Some footnotes have been omitted and others are renumbered.]

context of such offenses, and their primary use has been to investigate such offenses. Congress included immunity statutes in many of the regulatory measures adopted in the first half of this century. Indeed, prior to the enactment of the statute under consideration in this case, there were in force over 50 federal immunity statutes. In addition, every State in the Union, as well as the District of Columbia and Puerto Rico, has one or more such statutes. The commentators, and this Court on several occasions, have characterized immunity statutes as essential to the effective enforcement of various criminal statutes. As Mr. Justice Frankfurter observed, speaking for the Court in Ullmann v. United States, 350 U.S. 422, 76 S.Ct. 497, 100 L.Ed. 511 (1956), such statutes have "become part of our constitutional fabric." Id., at 438.

II

Petitioners contend, first, that the Fifth Amendment's privilege against compulsory self-incrimination, which is that "[n]o person ... shall be compelled in any criminal case to be a witness against himself," deprives Congress of power to enact laws that compel self-incrimination, even if complete immunity from prosecution is granted prior to the compulsion of the incriminatory testimony. In other words, petitioners assert that no immunity statute, however drawn, can afford a lawful basis for compelling incriminatory testimony. They ask us to reconsider and overrule Brown v. Walker, 161 U.S. 591, 16 S.Ct. 644, 40 L.Ed. 819 (1896), and Ullmann v. United States, supra, decisions that uphold the constitutionality of immunity statutes. We find no merit to this contention and reaffirm the decisions in Brown and Ullmann.

III

Petitioners' second contention is that the scope of immunity provided by the federal witness immunity statute, 18 U.S.C. § 6002, is not coextensive with the scope of the Fifth Amendment privilege against compulsory self-incrimination, and therefore is not sufficient to supplant the privilege and compel testimony over a claim of the privilege. The statute provides that when a witness is compelled by district court order to testify over a claim of the privilege:

"the witness may not refuse to comply with the order on the basis of his privilege against self-incrimination; but no testimony or other information compelled under the order (or any information directly or indirectly derived from such testimony or other information) may be used against the witness in any criminal case, except a prosecution for perjury, giving a false statement, or otherwise failing to comply with the order." 18 U.S.C. § 6002.

The constitutional inquiry, rooted in logic and history, as well as in the decisions of this Court, is whether the immunity granted under this statute is coextensive with the scope of the privilege. If so, petitioners' refusals to answer based on the privilege were unjustified, and the judgments of contempt were proper, for the grant of immunity has removed the dangers against which the privilege protects. Brown v. Walker, supra. If, on the other hand, the immunity granted is not as comprehensive as the protection afforded by the privilege, petitioners were justified in refusing to answer, and the judgments of contempt must be vacated. McCarthy v. Arndstein, 266 U.S. 34, 42, 45 S.Ct. 16, 17, 69 L.Ed. 158 (1924).

Petitioners draw a distinction between statutes that provide transactional immunity and those that provide, as does the statute before us, immunity from use and derivative use. They contend that a statute must at a minimum grant full transactional immunity in order to be coextensive with the scope of the privilege. In support of this contention, they rely on Counselman v. Hitchcock, 142 U.S. 547, 12 S.Ct. 195, 35 L.Ed. 1110 (1892), the first case in which this Court considered a constitutional challenge to an immunity statute. The statute, a re-enactment of the Immunity Act of 1868, provided that no "evidence obtained from a party or witness by means of a judicial proceeding ... shall be given in evidence, or in any manner used against him ... in any court of the United States...." Notwithstanding a grant of immunity and order to testify under the revised 1868 Act, the witness, asserting his privilege against compulsory self-incrimination, refused to testify before a federal grand jury. He was consequently adjudged in contempt of court. On appeal, this Court construed the statute as affording a witness protection only against the use of the specific testimony compelled from him under the grant of immunity. This construction meant that the statute "could not, and would not, prevent the use of his testimony to search out other testimony to be used in evidence against him." Since the revised 1868 Act, as construed by the Court, would permit the use against the immunized witness of evidence derived from his compelled testimony, it did not protect the witness to the same extent that a claim of the privilege would protect him. Accordingly, under the principle that a grant of immunity cannot supplant the privilege, and is not sufficient to compel testimony over a claim of the privilege, unless the scope of the grant of immunity is coextensive with the scope of the privilege, the witness' refusal to testify was held proper. In the course of its opinion, the Court made the following statement, on which petitioners heavily rely:

"We are clearly of opinion that no statute which leaves the party or witness subject to prosecution after he answers the criminating question put to him, can have the effect of supplanting the privilege conferred by the Constitution of the United States. [The immunity statute under consideration] does not supply a complete protection from all the perils against which the constitutional prohibition was designed to guard, and is not a full substitute for that prohibition. In view of the constitutional provision, a statutory enactment, to be valid, must afford absolute immunity against future prosecution for the offence to which the question relates." 142 U.S., at 585–586, 12 S.Ct., at 206.

Sixteen days after the Counselman decision, a new immunity bill was introduced by Senator Cullom, who urged that enforcement of the interstate Commerce Act would be impossible in the absence of an effective immunity statute. The bill, which became the Compulsory Testimony Act of 1893, was drafted specifically to meet the broad language in Counselman set forth above. The new Act removed the privilege against self-incrimination in hearings before the Interstate Commerce Commission and provided that:

"no person shall be prosecuted or subjected to any penalty or forfeiture for or on account of any transaction, matter or thing, concerning which he may testify, or produce evidence, documentary or otherwise...." Act of Feb. 11, 1893, 27 Stat. 444.

This transactional immunity statute became the basic form for the numerous federal immunity statutes until 1970, when, after re-examining applicable constitutional principles and the adequacy of existing law, Congress enacted the statute here under consideration. The new statute, which does not "afford [the] absolute immunity against future prosecution" referred to in Counselman, was drafted to meet what Congress judged to be the conceptual basis of Counselman, as elaborated in subsequent decisions of the Court, namely, that immunity from the use of compelled testimony and evidence derived therefrom is coextensive with the scope of the privilege.

The statute's explicit proscription of the use in any criminal case of "testimony or other information compelled under the order (or any information directly or indirectly derived from such testimony or other information)" is consonant with Fifth Amendment standards. We hold that such immunity from use and derivative use is coextensive with the scope of the privilege against self-incrimination, and therefore is sufficient to compel testimony over a claim of the privilege. While a grant of immunity must afford protection commensurate with that afforded by the privilege, it need not be broader. Transactional immunity, which accords full immunity from prosecution for the offense to which the compelled testimony relates, affords the witness considerably broader protection than does the Fifth Amendment privilege. The privilege has never been construed to mean that one who invokes it cannot subsequently be prosecuted. Its sole concern is to afford protection against being "forced to give testimony leading to the infliction of 'penalties affixed to ... criminal acts.' " Immunity from the use of compelled testimony, as well as evidence derived directly and indirectly therefrom, affords this protection. It prohibits the prosecutorial authorities from using the compelled testimony in any respect, and it therefore insures that the testimony cannot lead to the infliction of criminal penalties on the witness.

Our holding is consistent with the conceptual basis of Counselman. The Counselman statute, as construed by the Court, was plainly deficient in its failure to prohibit the use against the immunized witness of evidence derived from his compelled testimony....

In Murphy v. Waterfront Comm'n, 378 U.S. 52, 84 S.Ct. 1594, 12 L.Ed.2d 678 (1964), the Court carefully considered immunity from use of compelled testimony and evidence derived therefrom. The Murphy petitioners were subpoenaed to testify at a hearing conducted by the Waterfront Commission of New York Harbor. After refusing to answer certain questions on the ground that the answers might tend to incriminate them, petitioners were granted immunity from prosecution under the laws of New Jersey and New York. They continued to refuse to testify, however, on the ground that their answers might tend to incriminate them under federal law, to which the immunity did not purport to extend. They were adjudged in civil contempt, and that judgment was affirmed by the New Jersey Supreme Court.

The issue before the Court in Murphy was whether New Jersey and New York could compel the witnesses, whom these States had immunized from prosecution under their laws, to give testimony that might then be used to convict them of a federal crime. Since New Jersey and New York had not purported to confer immunity from federal prosecution, the Court was faced with the question what limitations the Fifth Amendment privilege imposed on the prosecutorial powers of the Federal Government, a nonimmunizing sovereign. After undertaking an examination of the policies and purposes of the privilege, the Court overturned the rule that one jurisdiction within our federal structure may compel a witness to give testimony which could be used to convict him of a crime in another jurisdiction.[2] The Court held that the privilege protects state witnesses against incrimination under federal as well as state law, and federal witnesses against incrimination under state as well as

---

2. Reconsideration of the rule that the Fifth Amendment privilege does not protect a witness in one jurisdiction against being compelled to give testimony that could be used to convict him in another jurisdiction was made necessary by the decision in Malloy v. Hogan, 378 U.S. 1, 84 S.Ct. 1489, 12 L.Ed.2d 653 (1964), in which the Court held the Fifth Amendment privilege applicable to the States through the Fourteenth Amendment. Murphy v. Waterfront Comm'n, 378 U.S., at 57, 84 S.Ct., at 1597.

federal law. Applying this principle to the state immunity legislation before it, the Court held the constitutional rule to be that:

> "[A] state witness may not be compelled to give testimony which may be incriminating under federal law unless the compelled testimony and its fruits cannot be used in any manner by federal officials in connection with a criminal prosecution against him. We conclude, moreover, that in order to implement this constitutional rule and accommodate the interests of the State and Federal Governments in investigating and prosecuting crime, the Federal Government must be prohibited from making any such use of compelled testimony and its fruits." 378 U.S., at 79, 84 S.Ct., at 1609.

The Court emphasized that this rule left the state witness and the Federal Government, against which the witness had immunity only from the use of the compelled testimony and evidence derived therefrom, "in substantially the same position as if the witness had claimed his privilege in the absence of a state grant of immunity." Ibid. . . .

Since the privilege is fully applicable and its scope is the same whether invoked in a state or in a federal jurisdiction, the Murphy conclusion that a prohibition on use and derivative use secures a witness' Fifth Amendment privilege against infringement by the Federal Government demonstrates that immunity from use and derivative use is coextensive with the scope of the privilege. As the Murphy Court noted, immunity from use and derivative use "leaves the witness and the Federal Government in substantially the same position as if the witness had claimed his privilege" in the absence of a grant of immunity. The Murphy Court was concerned solely with the danger of incrimination under federal law, and held that immunity from use and derivative use was sufficient to displace the danger. This protection coextensive with the privilege is the degree of protection that the Constitution requires, and is all that the Constitution requires even against the jurisdiction compelling testimony by granting immunity.

. . .

Petitioners argue that use and derivative-use immunity will not adequately protect a witness from various possible incriminating uses of the compelled testimony: for example, the prosecutor or other law enforcement officials may obtain leads, names of witnesses, or other information not otherwise available that might result in a prosecution. It will be difficult and perhaps impossible, the argument goes, to identify, by testimony or cross-examination, the subtle ways in which the compelled testimony may disadvantage a witness, especially in the jurisdiction granting the immunity.

This argument presupposes that the statute's prohibition will prove impossible to enforce. The statute provides a sweeping proscription of any use, direct or indirect, of the compelled testimony and any information derived therefrom:

> "[N]o testimony or other information compelled under the order (or any information directly or indirectly derived from such testimony or other information) may be used against the witness in any criminal case. . . ." 18 U.S.C. § 6002.

This total prohibition on use provides a comprehensive safeguard, barring the use of compelled testimony as an "investigatory lead," and also barring the use of any evidence obtained by focusing investigation on a witness as a result of his compelled disclosures.

A person accorded this immunity under 18 U.S.C. § 6002, and subsequently prosecuted, is not dependent for the preservation of his rights upon the integrity and good faith of the prosecuting authorities. As stated in Murphy:

> "Once a defendant demonstrates that he has testified, under a state grant of immunity, to matters related to the federal prosecution, the federal authorities have the burden of showing that their evidence is not tainted by establishing that they had an independent, legitimate source for the disputed evidence." 378 U.S., at 79 n. 18, 84 S.Ct., at 1609.

This burden of proof, which we reaffirm as appropriate, is not limited to a negation of taint; rather, it imposes on the prosecution the affirmative duty to prove that the evidence it proposes to use is derived from a legitimate source wholly independent of the compelled testimony.

. . . .

We conclude that the immunity provided by 18 U.S.C. § 6002 leaves the witness and the prosecutorial authorities in substantially the same position as if the witness had claimed the Fifth Amendment privilege. The immunity therefore is coextensive with the privilege and suffices to supplant it. The judgment of the Court of Appeals for the Ninth Circuit accordingly is

Affirmed.

MR. JUSTICE BRENNAN and MR. JUSTICE REHNQUIST took no part in the consideration or decision of this case.

[JUSTICES DOUGLAS and MARSHALL wrote dissenting opinions.]

NOTES

1. Congress repealed all of the federal statutes providing for transactional immunity in connection with the enactment of the Witness Immunity Act, 18 U.S.C. §§ 6001–6005 (1970), under the terms of which Kastigar was immunized. In addressing the immunity issue in a state proceeding, it is important to determine whether the state uses transactional or use immunity.

2. Is it significant that the immunity granted cannot, by its nature, be effective in foreign countries? See note supra, p. 1325.

3. The grant of immunity does not preclude all uses of immunized testimony. "[T]he privilege does not extend to consequences of a noncriminal nature, such as threats of liability in civil suits, disgrace in the community, or the loss of employment." United States v. Apfelbaum, 445 U.S. 115 (1980). See, e.g., Segretti v. State Bar, 15 Cal.3d 878, 126 Cal.Rptr. 793, 544 P.2d 929 (1976) (use of immunized testimony in state bar disciplinary proceedings); Patrick v. United States, 524 F.2d 1109 (7th Cir.1975) (use of immunized testimony in connection with tax liability).

4. Must the witness specifically claim the privilege in order to trigger the immunity grant? Generally yes, but see United States v. Monia, 317 U.S. 424 (1943) (Sherman Act). The decision to grant immunity is made by the prosecutor after weighing the possible value of the witness' testimony against the loss of the opportunity to prosecute the witness (although where only use immunity is given that opportunity may still exist). As to "automatic" immunity statutes, see generally McCormick on Evidence § 143 at pp. 542–544 (4th ed., Strong, 1992). For a description of the procedures applied in connection with federal grants of immunity, see Thornburgh, Reconciling Effective Federal Prosecution and the Fifth Amendment, 67 J.Crim.L. and Criminol. 155 (1976). U.S. Attorneys must obtain approval from the U.S. Department of Justice in order to make an immunity grant. Ibid. And see generally Symposium, The Granting of Witness Immunity, 67 J.Crim.L. and Criminol. 129–180 (1976).

5. The government may anyway prosecute the immunized witness. See, e.g., United States v. Montoya, 45 F.3d 1286 (9th Cir.1995). In Montoya, the defendant moved to dismiss the indictment on the ground that it was tainted by his earlier immunized testimony. The government responded with affidavits from nine prosecutors and agents who had been involved in the two relevant overlapping investigations. A number of procedural issues arose in connection with the determination of whether the government had met its burden of proving an independent source.

a) It is not necessary in every case to hold an evidentiary hearing to determine whether there was taint. In Montoya, the government was deemed to have met its burden of proof as to the existence of independent prior sources for the indictment through affidavits of prosecutors and federal agents.

b) In Montoya, the court ruled that the government must prove the independent source by a preponderance of the evidence.

c) The appellate court in Montoya indicated that it reviewed the district court finding on the taint issue under a clearly erroneous standard.

6. A trial court may hold a Kastigar hearing pre-trial, post-trial, mid-trial (as evidence is offered) or it may employ some combination of these methods. A pre-trial hearing is the most common choice. United States v. North, 910 F.2d 843, modified, 920 F.2d 940 (D.C.Cir.1990).

7. In Montoya, supra note 5, the court, quoting from earlier cases, addressed the issue raised by the fact that prosecutors and agents may have been exposed to immunized testimony:

> There is no per se rule requiring the withdrawal of a prosecutor or other government official who may have been exposed to immunized testimony. [citing United States v. Mapelli, 971 F.2d 284 (9th Cir.1992)] If the prosecution team has been exposed to the immunized testimony, the government may still use the evidence if it meets its burden of proof that the evidence is derived from independent sources. [citing United States v. Crowson, 828 F.2d 1427 (9th Cir.1987)] The question is not whether the prosecutor was aware of the contents of the immunized testimony, but whether he used the testimony in any way to build a case against the defendant. The government may protect against a claim of indirect use by assigning the case to others not exposed and barring communication between them and the prosecutors who obtained the compelled testimony.

In United States v. Crowson, supra, the court also noted that there was some disagreement among the circuits as to whether exposure to immunized testimony places a heavier burden on the government to show that it made no non-evidentiary use of the testimony (such as using it to help focus the investigation, in deciding to prosecute, refusing to plea bargain, or in planning trial strategy). Compare United States v. Byrd, 765 F.2d 1524 (11th Cir.1985) with United States v. McDaniel, 482 F.2d 305 (8th Cir.1973) and see note 9 infra.

8. A straightforward illustration of an independent source-exposure to im-munized testimony situation is United States v. Lipkis, 770 F.2d 1447 (9th Cir.1985): The defendant first made voluntary statements to the same FBI agent on three different occasions; later he made identical statements to the same agent under an immunity grant. The defendant argued at his trial that the FBI agent's testimony should have been excluded because it was tainted by the agent's exposure to the compelled statements. Held: The government had met its burden of proving that the evidence introduced at trial was derived from a legitimate source wholly independent of the immunized statements.

9. a) In United States v. Koon, 34 F.3d 1416 (9th Cir.1994), an appeal arising out of the Rodney King beating case, the court rejected a stringent, two part test for determining taint under Kastigar. This two part test had been adopted by the District of Columbia Circuit in United States v. North, 910 F.2d 843, modified, 920 F.2d 940 (D.C.Cir.1990), cert. denied 500 U.S. 941 (1991) and in United States v. Poindexter, 951 F.2d 369 (D.C.Cir.1991), cert. denied 506 U.S. 1021 (1992).

b) The North–Poindexter test requires the prosecutor, first, to prove an independent source for all matters concerning which the witness testifies, and, second, to prove that any witness exposed to compelled statements has not shaped or altered her testimony in any way, either directly or indirectly, as a result of that exposure. How would the D.C. Circuit's test have worked in United States v. Lipkis, supra note 8. Could the government have met its burden in that case under the D.C. test?

c) In the original North decision, supra a) above, the court indicated that the burden under its two part test could be met if the prosecutor "canned" the witness's testimony before the exposure to the immunized statements occurred. Subsequently, in the second North decision, supra a) above, the court made clear that canning the witness's testimony before exposure to the immunized statements was only an example of a way in which the prosecutor's Kastigar burden might be met.

10. The Civil Rights Division of the U.S. Department of Justice has described its handling of immunized statements as follows:

> When immunized statements are received in a case handled by the Criminal Section of the Civil Rights Division, personnel from the Criminal Section sanitize the reports by redacting statements and fruits of statements by the target of the investigation which could violate the standards of use immunity if used against the individual who made the statement.

Appellee's Brief, In re Grand Jury Subpoenas Dated December 7 and 8, Issued to Bob Stover, Chief of Albuquerque Police Department, 40 F.3d 1096 (10th Cir.1994). See also United States Attorneys' Manual 9–23.400.

11. The application of Kastigar sometimes occurs in a context where a statutory immunity grant is not involved. Thus, for example, United States v. Koon, supra note 9a., involved a Kastigar issue but did not involve an immunity grant. Rather it was related to a series of Supreme Court cases which established the proposition that public employees such as police officers can be required to give testimony in the course of an administrative investigation or face dismissal. However, where a police officer invokes his Fifth Amendment rights and then gives testimony under threat of removal from office, the statement is deemed compelled, and the government is precluded from using either the testimony or its fruits as evidence in a prosecution. The doctrine is sometime referred to as the Garrity doctrine. See Lefkowitz v. Cunningham, 431 U.S. 801 (1977); Lefkowitz v. Turley, 414 U.S. 70 (1973); Gardner v. Broderick, 392 U.S. 273 (1968); Uniformed Sanitation Men Association, Inc. v. Commissioner of Sanitation of the City of New York, 392 U.S. 280 (1968); Spevack v. Klein, 385 U.S. 511 (1967) Garrity v. New Jersey, 385 U.S. 493 (1967). See Warnken, The Law Enforcement Officer's Privilege Against Self-Incrimination, 16 U. Balt. L. Rev. 452 (1987).

United States v. Koon involved such a Fifth Amendment issue. Once a public employee has demonstrated that his testimony was compelled under the Garrity doctrine, the government has the burden of proving in a "Kastigar hearing" that the evidence to be introduced at trial was not tainted by the compelled statements. Thus, the same type of hearing is held in such cases as in the statutory use immunity cases discussed supra.

In Koon, the court compared the Garrity issue and the statutory use immunity context:

> [F]ederal immunity statutes provide a framework for a prosecuting attorney . . . to make a reasoned decision as to whether the benefits of obtaining compelled testimony justify the obstacles that may be created in any future prosecutions. The process of formal grants of immunity also provides time for the prosecutor to protect the testimony of potential witnesses by obtaining canned statements and by shielding these witnesses from exposure to the immunized testimony.

> In contrast . . . [i]n . . . [the Garrity] context, the individuals who question the employee are concerned about potential misconduct, and their goal is generally to learn the facts of a situation as quickly as possible. . . . [I]ndeed, they may not even have the prospect of prosecution and the requirements of the Fifth Amendment in mind.

12. Although only use immunity is available under the federal immunity statute, issues involving earlier grants of state transactional immunity may be litigated in the federal courts. Often the question is whether the federal prosecutor has established an independent source for the case where there has been a previous grant of state transactional immunity. See, e.g., United States v. Hampton, 775 F.2d 1479 (11th Cir.1985): A state attorney general's office turned over to federal agents its files relating to a marijuana smuggling investigation, without revealing to the federal officers that portions of the materials transferred included immunized testimony or were derived from such testimony. It was not until three years later that the federal government learned that these state investigative materials contained immunized testimony. (The witness in the state proceedings had been immunized under a Florida statute that automatically grants transactional immunity to a witness who gives testimony pursuant to a subpoena.) When the federal prosecutor subsequently filed an indictment against that witness, the reviewing court concluded that the government had not carried its burden of showing that its evidence was derived from a legitimate source wholly independent of the state immunized testimony.

The facts in Hampton illustrate the complexity of determining whether subsequent evidence has been tainted by the original immunized testimony. H, who had been immunized in the state proceedings, had given evidence against the then target of the state investigation, M. Later, as a result of the federal investigation M was indicted. M, however, entered into a plea agreement in which he agreed to testify against H, who in turn was then indicted. The court stated:

> Thus, in the instant case, if . . . [H's] immunized testimony or its fruits contributed directly or indirectly to the government's case against . . . [M], and thereby to . . . [M's] decision to plead guilty and testify against . . . [H], then . . . [M's] testimony would not be derived independently of . . . [H's] immunized statement.

> Although . . . [M] testified at the . . . hearing on behalf of the government, he was not asked about what factors motivated him to accept the plea

bargain.... The record is silent as to what, if anything, ... [M] knew or was told about the evidence ... [H] was expected to provide against him. Id. at 1485.

13.   One who is granted immunity is not immune from prosecution for perjury based upon false testimony given under the immunity grant. United States v. Wong, 431 U.S. 174 (1977); United States v. Mandujano, 425 U.S. 564 (1976); Glickstein v. United States, 222 U.S. 139 (1911).

14.   The truthful, immunized testimony that a witness has given may be introduced in his prosecution for perjury so as to put the allegedly perjurious statements in context and to show that the defendant knew the statements were false. United States v. Apfelbaum, 445 U.S. 115 (1980). In Apfelbaum, Justice Rehnquist speaking for the Court stated:

> [E]ven if both truthful and untruthful testimony from the immunized proceeding are admissible in a subsequent perjury prosecution, the exception surely would ... be properly regarded as "narrow" once it is recognized that the testimony remains inadmissible in all prosecutions for offenses committed prior to the grant of immunity that would have permitted the witness to invoke his Fifth Amendment privilege absent the grant.

> [W]e conclude that the Fifth Amendment does not prevent the use of respondent's immunized testimony at his trial for false swearing because, at the time he was granted immunity, the privilege would not have protected him against false testimony that he later might decide to give. ... We believe that it could not be fairly said that respondent, at the time he asserted his privilege and was consequently granted immunity, was confronted with more than a "trifling or imaginary" hazard of compelled self-incrimination as a result of the possibility that he might commit perjury during the course of his immunized testimony....

> We hold here that in our jurisprudence there ... is no doctrine of "anticipatory perjury." ... Similarly, a future intention to commit perjury or to make false statements if granted immunity because of a claim of compulsory self-incrimination is not by itself sufficient to create a "substantial and 'real' " hazard that permits invocation of the Fifth Amendment. Therefore, neither the immunity statute nor the Fifth Amendment preclude the use of respondent's immunized testimony at a subsequent prosecution for making false statements.... Id. 445 U.S. 115, 128–131, 100 S.Ct. 948, 956–957, 63 L.Ed.2d 250, 261–264.

15.   Compare with United States v. Apfelbaum, supra note 14, the following excerpt from United States v. Doe, 819 F.2d 11 (1st Cir.1987):

> Appellant's immunized testimony in a future appearance before the grand jury cannot be used as evidence to prove a charge of perjury in giving false testimony in his prior appearance, ... [citing United States v. Cintolo, 818 F.2d 980, 988 n. 5 (1st Cir.1987)]. The fact that appellant's testimony on both occasions would have been compelled by the same immunity order is of no consequence; a grant of immunity precludes the use of immunized testimony in a prosecution for past perjury, ... regardless of the context in which that past perjury occurred.

16.   In New Jersey v. Portash, 440 U.S. 450 (1979) the Court ruled that grand jury testimony given under a grant of immunity could not be used to impeach the defendant witness if he takes the stand at his subsequent trial on charges based upon the conduct to which his immunized testimony relates. Compare Harris v. New York, 401 U.S. 222 (1971), See generally Note, Standards for

Exclusion in Immunity Cases After Kastigar and Zicarelli, 82 Yale L.J. 171 (1972); Strachan, Self–Incrimination, Immunity, and Watergate, 56 Tex.L.Rev. 791 (1978).

17.   In United States v. Doe, 465 U.S. 605 (1984), (Doe I) the court stated:

> The Government did state several times before the District Court that it would not use respondent's act of production against him in any way. But counsel for the Government never made a statutory request to the District Court to grant respondent use immunity. We are urged to adopt a doctrine of constructive use immunity. Under this doctrine, the courts would impose a requirement on the Government not to use the incriminatory aspects of the act of production against the person claiming the privilege even though the statutory procedures have not been followed.

> We decline to extend the jurisdiction of courts to include prospective grants of use immunity in the absence of the formal request that the statute requires.... The decision to seek use immunity necessarily involves a balancing of the Government's interest in obtaining information against the risk that immunity will frustrate the Government's attempts to prosecute the subject of the investigation.... Congress expressly left this decision exclusively to the Justice Department.

United States v. Doe, 465 U.S. at 616–617.

18.   Compare the court's rejection of a constructive immunity in Doe I with what the court did in Braswell v. United States, supra p. 1348, and with the court's statements in Bouknight, supra p. 1358. Also consider the following statements:

a) "One approach to harmonizing these discordant interests would permit government subpoena of personal business records, together with an exclusionary rule to prevent government use in any way of the fact that the individual complied with the subpoena." In re Grand Jury Proceedings United States, 626 F.2d 1051, 1057 (1st Cir.1980).

b) "It is well settled in this circuit that if the government later attempts to implicate the custodian on the basis of the act of production, evidence of that fact is subject to a motion to suppress." In re Grand Jury Proceedings, (Morganstern) 771 F.2d 143, 148 (6th Cir.1985).

c) "We note, however, that should production itself be potentially incriminatory, the government could either by stipulation or by obtaining a grant of immunity pursuant to 18 U.S.C. §§ 6002–6003, immunize the act of production...." In re Grand Jury Subpoenas Duces Tecum Dated June 13, 1983 and June 22, 1983, 722 F.2d 981, 988 (2d Cir.1983).

Also consider the Garrity doctrine supra note 11 and how the court has dealt with evidence related to testimony compelled from a police officer on threat of dismissal. Is there a difference between statutory immunity, constructive immunity and the application of "an exclusionary rule to prevent government use in any way of the fact that the individual complied with the subpoena."

19.   Does a defendant have a right to obtain immunity for a defense witness who claims the privilege (sometimes called reverse immunity)? In this context, it has been suggested that a trial court does not have independent authority to grant a witness use immunity, that that authority resides exclusively in the Executive Branch. See e.g., United States v. Herbst, 641 F.2d 1161 (5th Cir.1981). Compare Virgin Islands v. Smith, 615 F.2d 964 (3d Cir.1980). Defendants may also try to persuade a court to order the prosecutor to immunize a defense witness through a statutory immunity grant, but the circuits are generally reluctant to issue such an order. For example:

> Very few situations will impose a duty on the government to grant a defense witness immunity.... To warrant an immunity request, it must be shown that the government has engaged in discriminatory use of immunity to gain a tactical advantage or, through its own overreaching, has forced the witness to invoke the Fifth Amendment; and ... the witness' testimony will be material, exculpatory and not cumulative and is not obtainable from any other source. United States v. Burns, 684 F.2d 1066, 1077 (2d Cir.1982).... Where, as here, the witness herself is a prosecution target, there can be no claim of discrimination or overreaching. United States v. Shandell, 800 F.2d 322 (2d Cir.1986).

20.   United States v. Turkish, 623 F.2d 769, 772–773 (2d Cir.1980) reviewed the arguments for and against granting defendants' claims for defense witness immunity. The court concluded:

> Without precluding the possibility of some circumstances not now anticipated, we simply do not find in the Due Process Clause a general requirement that defense witness immunity must be ordered whenever it seems fair to grant it. The essential fairness required by the Fifth Amendment guards the defendant against overreaching by the prosecutor,.... It does not create general obligations for prosecutors or courts to obtain evidence protected by lawful privilege.

> [W]e do not wish to see criminal trials regularly interrupted by wide-ranging inquiries concerning the specific pros and cons of defense witness immunity in a particular case. In fact, we think trial judges should summarily reject claims for defense witness immunity whenever the witness for whom immunity is sought is an actual or potential target of prosecution. Id. 623 F.2d 769, 777–778.

21.   Assuming that circumstances can arise where a trial court is justified in ordering the government to grant statutory immunity to a defense witness, are there sanctions short of a judgment of acquittal that the court can use to encourage the government to grant the immunity? See, for example, United States v. Horwitz, 622 F.2d 1101 (2d Cir.1980), cert. denied, 449 U.S. 1076 (1981) where the trial judge, in granting defendant Horwitz's motion for a new trial, had indicated that if the defendant's witnesses were not immunized by the government, he would at the retrial order suppression of the testimony of the government's immunized witnesses. The court of appeals remanded the case for reconsideration under Turkish. It has been held that a prosecutor's promise to a witness of non-statutory use immunity, if binding at all, is not co-extensive with the witness's privilege against self-incrimination. United States v. D'Apice, 664 F.2d 75 (5th Cir.1981).

22.   Problem: The prosecutor in a criminal case seeks to introduce the hearsay statement of a declarant who is physically present but unavailable because he has invoked his privilege against self-incrimination. He can be made available by granting him use immunity in connection with his testimony. Should the prosecutor be obligated to grant the immunity or forego the use of his hearsay statement? See United States v. Valente, 17 M.J. 1087, 1088–1099 (1984).

23.   Most of the literature concerning a defendant's right to have defense witnesses immunized is favorable to the idea. See Note, Right of the Criminal Defendant to the Compelled Testimony of Witnesses, 67 Colum.L.Rev. 953 (1967); Note, A Re-examination of Defense Witness Immunity: A New Use for Kastigar, 10 Harv.J.Legis. 74 (1974); Westen, The Compulsory Process Clause,

73 Mich.L.Rev. 71 (1974); Note, Separation of Powers and Defense Witness Immunity, 66 Geo.L.J. 51 (1977); Note, The Public Has a Claim to Every Man's Evidence: The Defendant's Constitutional Right to Witness Immunity, 30 Stan.L.Rev. 1211 (1978); Note, The Sixth Amendment Right to Have Use Immunity Granted to Defense Witnesses, 91 Harv.L.Rev. 1266 (1978).

F.   EXERCISE OF THE PRIVILEGE: COMMENT AND INFERENCE

Carter v. Kentucky

Supreme Court of the United States, 1981.
450 U.S. 288, 101 S.Ct. 1112, 67 L.Ed.2d 241.

■ JUSTICE STEWART delivered the opinion of the Court.

In this case a Kentucky criminal trial judge refused a defendant's request to give the following jury instruction: "The defendant is not compelled to testify and the fact that he does not cannot be used as an inference of guilt and should not prejudice him in any way." The Supreme Court of Kentucky found no error. We granted certiorari to consider the petitioner's contention that a defendant, upon request, has a right to such an instruction under the Fifth and Fourteenth Amendments of the Constitution. 449 U.S. 819, 101 S.Ct. 71, 66 L.Ed.2d 21.

I

A

In the early morning of December 22, 1978, Officer Deborah Ellison of the Hopkinsville, Kentucky Police Department, on routine patrol in downtown Hopkinsville, noticed something in the alley between Young's Hardware Store and Edna's Furniture Store. She backed her car up, flashed her spotlight down the alley, and saw two men stopped alongside one of the buildings. The men ran off. Officer Ellison drove her squad car down the alley and found a hole in the side of Young's Hardware Store. She radioed Officer Leroy Davis, whom she knew to be in the area, informing him that two men had fled from the alley.

Soon after receiving Ellison's call, Officer Davis saw two men run across a street near where he had been patrolling. The two ran in opposite directions, and Davis proceeded after one of them. Following a chase, during which he twice lost sight of the man he was pursuing, Davis was finally able to stop him. The man was later identified as the petitioner, Lonnie Joe Carter. During the course of the chase, Davis saw the petitioner drop two objects: a gym bag and a radio tuned to a police band. When apprehended, the petitioner was wearing gloves but no jacket. While Davis was pursuing the petitioner, Officer Ellison inspected the alley near the hole in the building wall. She found two jackets, along with some merchandise that had apparently been removed from the hardware store.

After arresting the petitioner, Davis brought him to Officer Ellison to see if she could identify him as one of the men she had seen in the alley. Ellison noted that he was of similar height and weight to one of the men in the alley, and that he wore similar clothing, but because it had been too dark to get a good view of the men's faces, she could not make a more positive identification. The petitioner was then taken to police headquarters.

B

The petitioner was subsequently indicted for third-degree burglary of Young's Hardware Store. The indictment also charged him with being a persistent felony offender, in violation of Ky.Rev.Stat. 532.080, on the basis of previous felony convictions. At the trial, the voir dire examination of prospective jurors was conducted solely by the judge. The prosecutor's opening statement recounted the evidence expected to be introduced against the petitioner. The opening statement of defense counsel began as follows:

"Let me tell you a little bit about how this system works. If you listened to Mr. Ruff [the prosecutor] you are probably ready to put Lonnie Joe in the penitentiary. He read you a bill, a true bill that was issued by the Grand Jury. Now, the Grand Jury is a group of people that meet back here in a room and the defendant is not able or not allowed to present any of his testimony before this group of people. The only thing that the Grand Jury hears is the prosecution's proof and I would say approximately what Mr. Ruff has said to you. I suppose that most of you would issue a true bill if Mr. Ruff told you what he has just told you and you didn't have a chance to hear what the defendant had to say for himself. Now, that is just completely contrary to our system of law. A man, as the Judge has already told you, ... is innocent until ... proved guilty ..."

The prosecution rested after calling Officers Ellison, Davis, another officer, and the owner of Young's Hardware Store. The trial judge then held a conference, outside of the hearing of the jury, to determine whether the petitioner would testify, and whether the prosecutor would be permitted to impeach the petitioner with his prior felony convictions. Defense counsel stated:

"Judge, I think possibly the only reservation Mr. Carter might have about testifying would be his impeachment by the use of these previous offenses that he is aware of and has told me about. I would like to explain to him in front of you what this all means."

Counsel then explained to the petitioner that if he testified the Commonwealth could "use the fact that you have several offenses on your record ... [to] impeach your ... propensity to tell the truth ..." Counsel added that in his experience this was "a heavy thing, it is very serious, and I think juries take it very seriously ..." The judge indicated that under Kentucky law he had "discretionary control" over the use of prior felony convictions for impeachment, and cautioned the prosecutor that he might be inviting a reversal if he introduced more than three prior felony convictions, strongly suggesting that the prosecutor rely on the most recent convictions only. The judge then addressed the petitioner:

"THE COURT: ... You can sit there and say nothing and it cannot be mentioned if you don't testify but if you do these other convictions can be shown to indicate to the jury that maybe you are not telling the truth.

.   .   .

"THE COURT: ... [Y]ou talk to Mr. Rogers [defense counsel] and then tell us what you want to do.

.   .   .

"THE COURT: Now, Lonnie, you have come back after a private conference with your lawyer, Mr. Rogers, and you have told me you have decided not to take the stand?

"LONNIE JOE CARTER: Yes, Sir."

Upon returning to open court, the petitioner's counsel advised the court that there would be no testimony introduced on behalf of the defense. He then requested that the following instruction be given to the jury:

"The defendant is not compelled to testify and the fact that he does not cannot be used as an inference of guilt and should not prejudice him in any way."

The trial court refused the request.

The prosecutor began his summation by stating that he intended to review the evidence "that we were privileged to hear," and cautioned the jury to "[c]onsider only what you have heard up here as evidence in this case and not something that you might speculate happened or could have happened...." After mentioning admissions that the petitioner had allegedly made at police headquarters, the prosecutor argued:

"Now that is not controverted whatsoever. It is not controverted that Lonnie Joe is the man that Miss Ellison saw here. It is not controverted that Lonnie Joe is the man that Davis caught up here (again pointing to blackboard sketch). It is not controverted that Lonnie Joe had that bag (pointing to bag on reporter's desk) and that radio (pointing to radio) with him. It is not controverted that both of those jackets belonged to Lonnie Joe. At least, that is what he told the police department. But, at any rate, that is all we have to go on ..."

The prosecutor continued that if there was a reasonable explanation why the petitioner ran when he saw the police, it was "not in the record."[2]

The jury found the petitioner guilty, recommending a sentence of two years. The recidivist phase of the trial followed. The prosecutor presented evidence of the previous felony convictions that had been listed in the indictment. The defense presented no evidence, and the jury found the petitioner guilty as a persistent offender, sentencing him to the maximum term of 20 years in prison.

. . .

II

The constitutional question presented by this case is one the Court has specifically anticipated and reserved, first in Griffin v. California, 380 U.S. 609, 615, n. 6, 85 S.Ct. 1229, 1233, n. 6, 14 L.Ed.2d 106, and more recently in Lakeside v. Oregon, 435 U.S. 333, 337, 98 S.Ct. 1091, 1093, 55 L.Ed.2d 319 (1978). But, as a question of federal statutory law, it was resolved by a unanimous Court over 40 years ago in Bruno v. United States, 308 U.S. 287, 60 S.Ct. 198, 84 L.Ed. 257. The petitioner in Bruno was a defendant in a federal criminal trial who had requested a jury instruction similar to the one requested by the petitioner in this case. The Court, addressing the question whether Bruno "had the indefeasible right" that his proffered instruction be given to the jury, decided that a federal statute, which prohibits the creation of any presumption from a defendant's failure to testify, required that the "substance

---

2. Defense counsel began his closing argument as follows:

"Ladies and Gentlemen of the jury, I am sure you all right now are wondering well what has happened? Why didn't Mr. Carter take the stand and testify? Let me tell you.

The judge just read to you that the man is presumed innocent and that it is up to the prosecution to prove him guilty beyond a reasonable doubt. He doesn't have to take the stand in his own behalf. He doesn't have to do anything."

of the denied request should have been granted ..." 308 U.S., at 294, 60 S.Ct., at 200.

The Griffin case came here shortly after the Court had held that the Fifth Amendment command that no person "shall be compelled in any criminal case to be a witness against himself" is applicable against the States through the Fourteenth Amendment. Malloy v. Hogan, 378 U.S. 1, 84 S.Ct. 1489, 12 L.Ed.2d 653. In Griffin, the Court considered the question whether it is a violation of the Fifth and Fourteenth Amendments to invite a jury in a state criminal trial to draw an unfavorable inference from a defendant's failure to testify. Griffin v. California, 380 U.S. 609, 85 S.Ct. 1229, 14 L.Ed.2d 106. The trial judge had there instructed the jury "that a defendant has a constitutional right not to testify," and that the defendant's exercise of that right "does not create a presumption of guilt or by itself warrant an inference of guilt" nor "relieve the prosecution of any of its burden of proof." But the instruction additionally permitted the jury to "take that failure into consideration as tending to indicate the truth of [the State's] evidence and as indicating that among the inferences that may be reasonably drawn therefrom those unfavorable to the defendant are the more probable." Id., at 610, 85 S.Ct., at 1230.

This Court set aside Griffin's conviction because "the Fifth Amendment ... forbids either comment by the prosecution on the accused's silence or instructions by the Court that such silence is evidence of guilt." Id., at 615, 85 S.Ct., at 1233. It condemned adverse comment on a defendant's failure to testify as reminiscent of the "inquisitorial system of criminal justice," id., at 614, 85 S.Ct., at 1232, quoting Murphy v. Waterfront Comm'n, 378 U.S. 52, 55, 84 S.Ct. 1594, 1596, 12 L.Ed.2d 678, and concluded that such comment effected a court-imposed penalty upon the defendant that was unacceptable because "[i]t cuts down on the privilege by making its assertion costly." 380 U.S., at 614, 85 S.Ct., at 1232.

The Court returned to a consideration of the Fifth Amendment and jury instructions in Lakeside v. Oregon, 435 U.S. 333, 98 S.Ct. 1091, 55 L.Ed.2d 319, where the question was whether the giving of a "no-inference" instruction over defense objection violates the Constitution. Despite trial counsel's complaint that his strategy was to avoid any mention of his client's failure to testify, a no inference instruction was given by the trial judge. The petitioner contended that when a trial judge in any way draws the jury's attention to a defendant's failure to testify, unless the defendant acquiesces, the court invades the defendant's privilege against compulsory self-incrimination. This argument was rejected.

The Lakeside Court reasoned that the Fifth and Fourteenth Amendments bar only adverse comment on a defendant's failure to testify, and that "a judge's instruction that the jury must draw *no* adverse inferences of any kind from the defendant's exercise of his privilege not to testify is 'comment' of an entirely different order." 435 U.S., at 339, 98 S.Ct., at 1094. The purpose of such an instruction, the Court stated, "is to remove from the jury's deliberations any influence of unspoken adverse inferences," and "cannot provide the pressure on a defendant found impermissible in Griffin." Ibid.

The Court observed in Lakeside that the petitioner's argument there rested on "two very doubtful assumptions:"

> First, that the jurors have not noticed that the defendant did not testify and will not, therefore, draw adverse inferences on their own. Second, that the jurors will totally disregard the instruction, and affirmatively give weight to what they have been told not to consider at all. Federal

constitutional law cannot rest on speculative assumptions so dubious as these. 435 U.S., at 340, 98 S.Ct., at 1095 (footnote omitted).

Finally, the Court stressed that "the very purpose" of a jury instruction is to direct the jurors' attention to important legal concepts "that must not be misunderstood, such as reasonable doubt and burden of proof," and emphasized that instruction "in the meaning of the privilege against compulsory self-incrimination is no different." Ibid.

. . .

The Griffin case stands for the proposition that a defendant must pay no court-imposed price for the exercise of his constitutional privilege not to testify. The penalty was exacted in Griffin by adverse comment on the defendant's silence; the penalty may be just as severe when there is not adverse comment, but when the jury is left to roam at large with only its untutored instincts to guide it, to draw from the defendant's silence broad inferences of guilt. Even without adverse comment, the members of a jury, unless instructed otherwise, may well draw adverse inferences from a defendant's silence.

The significance of a cautionary instruction was forcefully acknowledged in Lakeside, where the Court found no constitutional error even when a no-inference instruction was given over a defendant's objection. The salutary purpose of the instruction, "to remove from the jury's deliberations any influence of unspoken adverse inferences," was deemed so important that it there outweighed the defendant's own preferred tactics.

We have repeatedly recognized that "instructing a jury in the basic constitutional principles that govern the administration of criminal justice," Lakeside, 435 U.S., at 342, 98 S.Ct., at 1096, is often necessary. Jurors are not experts in legal principles; to function effectively, and justly, they must be accurately instructed in the law. Such instructions are perhaps nowhere more important than in the context of the Fifth Amendment privilege against compulsory self-incrimination, since "[t]oo many, even those who should be better advised, view this privilege as a shelter for wrongdoers. They too readily assume that those who invoke it are . . . guilty of crime . . ." Ullmann v. United States, 350 U.S. 422, 426, 76 S.Ct. 497, 500, 100 L.Ed. 511. And, as the Court has stated, "we have not yet attained that certitude about the human mind which would justify us in . . . a dogmatic assumption that jurors if properly admonished, neither could nor would heed the instructions of the trial court . . ." Bruno, 308 U.S., at 294, 60 S.Ct., at 200.

A trial judge has a powerful tool at his disposal to protect the constitutional privilege—the jury instruction—and he has an affirmative constitutional obligation to use that tool when a defendant seeks its employment. No judge can prevent jurors from speculating about why a defendant stands mute in the face of a criminal accusation, but a judge can, and must, if requested to do so, use the unique power of the jury instruction to reduce that speculation to a minimum.

. . .

[JUSTICE POWELL and JUSTICE STEVENS (joined by JUSTICE BRENNAN) concurred in separate opinions. JUSTICE REHNQUIST wrote a dissenting opinion.]

NOTES

The principal case arises out of the fact that the accused in a criminal case has a privilege not to take the stand to testify. Issues that relate to the accused's privilege usually involve problems relating to the drawing of an inference against him by the trier of fact and what happens when the accused does take the stand.

1. Another in the series of Supreme Court cases on the comment and inference issue is James v. Kentucky, 466 U.S. 341 (1984): The trial judge had rejected defendant's request that "an admonition be given to the jury that no emphasis be given to the defendant's failure to testify." On appeal, the state high court affirmed on the ground that under Kentucky practice there was a difference between the instruction required by Carter and an admonition as requested by the defendant. The Supreme Court reversed, concluding that the defendant had adequately invoked the substance of his federal constitutional right.

2. For cases where repeated "indirect" references by the prosecutor to the defendant's failure to testify were held to be reversible error, see United States ex rel. Burke v. Greer, 756 F.2d 1295 (7th Cir.1985); Williams v. Lane, 826 F.2d 654 (7th Cir.1987).

3. It would, of course, be improper for the prosecutor to call the accused to the stand and thereby force him to invoke the privilege in the presence of the jury. Suppose, however, that the accused takes the stand and then declines to answer certain questions, claiming the privilege. Consider United States v. Hearst, 563 F.2d 1331 (9th Cir.1977), cert. denied, 435 U.S. 1000 (1978), the facts of which are set forth supra at p. 378. The accused had claimed that the trial judge erred in allowing the prosecution to continue to ask questions which it knew would elicit repeated assertions of the privilege against self-incrimination. The appellate court rejected this contention, stating:

> [W]hen a defendant has voluntarily waived his ... privilege by testifying ..., the rationale for prohibiting privilege-invoking queries on cross-examination does not apply. The defendant has chosen to make an issue of his credibility.... [T]he government may ... successfully impeach him by asking questions which he refuses to answer. If the refusals could not be put before the jury, the defendant would have the unusual and grossly unfair ability to insulate himself from challenges merely by declining to answer embarrassing questions. Id. 563 F.2d 1331, 1341–1342.

Query: Does it follow from Hearst that the trial judge could have commented on the accused's silence in the face of questions about other possibly criminating activities? See Caminetti v. United States, 242 U.S. 470 (1917). Compare Griffin v. California, 380 U.S. 609 (1965).

4. The extent of waiver by an accused who takes the stand is treated more fully supra, pp. 377–378, in connection with materials on the scope of cross-examination. It has been held that an accused who takes the stand for the sole purpose of testifying upon the issue of the voluntariness of his out-of-court confession does not generally waive his privilege against self-incrimination. Calloway v. Wainwright, 409 F.2d 59 (5th Cir.), cert. denied, 395 U.S. 909 (1969). See Rules 104(d) and 608(b), Federal Rules of Evidence.

5. Problem: X is a defendant with nine others charged with RICO violations. After the indictment is filed, the government identifies X as an informant, a fact which he denies. His co-defendants file pre-trial motions to exclude X's hearsay statements that the government intends to offer under the co-conspirator's exception; they argue that since X was an informant, his statements could not have been in furtherance of the conspiracy. The government in response argues that X possessed the requisite criminal intent despite his status as an informant. To establish X's state of mind at the earlier time, the government calls X as its first witness at a pre-trial hearing. X invokes his privilege against self-incrimination, and the government applies to the court for a grant of use immunity under which X's testimony could not be used against him in any criminal proceeding including the instant one. The judge grants the use immunity and orders X to testify. X refuses, is held in contempt and appeals the ruling. What result? See United States v. Johnson, 801 F.2d 597 (2d Cir.1986) where the court did not reach the merits, concluding that the issue had become moot.

6.   When a defendant takes the stand in his own defense, he may be cross-examined about his failure to testify on his previous trial for the same offense, Raffel v. United States, 271 U.S. 494 (1926). Compare Grunewald v. United States, 353 U.S. 391 (1957) and also see Jenkins v. Anderson, 447 U.S. 231 (1980).

7.   The privilege operates differently with respect to the ordinary witness and the accused. The former can be called to testify and be asked but not compelled to answer incriminating questions. The line between the accused and the ordinary witness may not always be clear. See United States v. Washington, 431 U.S. 181 (1977) discussed supra, p. 1330, and consider the relevance of Miranda v. Arizona, 384 U.S. 436 (1966) extending the privilege to the criminal suspect in custody or its equivalent.

8.   As the facts in the principal case suggest, there are many reasons why an accused may decline to take the stand, which in themselves have nothing to do with the announced reason for invoking the privilege. Nevertheless there is no doubt that the inference of criminality may be drawn by the public. Is the same true for the ordinary witness? See Griswold, The Fifth Amendment Today (1955). Cf. Griswold, The Right to be Let Alone, 55 NW U.L.Rev. 216, 223 (1960). The inference-drawing issue with respect to the ordinary witness comes into sharp focus in the employee-dismissal cases, the so-called Garrity line of cases, discussed supra note 11, p. 1375.

9.   a) Suppose that a non-defendant witness is called by the prosecution and claims the privilege. Is it appropriate for the jury to draw an inference as to the nature of the testimony that would have been produced had the privilege not been claimed? See Billeci v. United States, 184 F.2d 394 (D.C.Cir.1950), 24 A.L.R.2d 881; State v. Sutterfield, 607 P.2d 789 (Or.App.1980). For a case in which the defendant tried to force a witness to invoke his privilege in front of the jury to support an inference that a contraband weapon was the witness's and not the defendant's, see United States v. Hart, 729 F.2d 662, 670 (10th Cir.1984).

b) In State v. Weber, 199 S.W. 147 (Mo.1917), evidence offered by D that X at D's preliminary hearing had claimed the privilege was excluded. See also State v. Howard, 619 P.2d 943 (Or.App.1980) where former testimony offered by the defendant was excluded in part because the witness in the previous proceeding while testifying had also claimed his privilege, and the only reason for defendant to offer that part of his testimony was to allow the jury to draw the inference that the witness had committed the crimes.

c) State v. Mitchell, 487 P.2d 1156 (Or.App.1971) refused to permit the defendant to call his co-defendant when he knew that the privilege would be claimed with respect to all relevant testimony. Compare State v. Addington, 147 P.2d 367 (Kan.1944), where the court allowed comment on D's failure to call his co-defendant as a witness.

In United States v. Lewis, 816 F.2d 683 (6th Cir.1987) cert. denied, sub nom. Lindsey v. United States, 484 U.S. 934 (1987) the government called as a witness an unindicted co-conspirator after having been informed that the witness would invoke the privilege if called to testify. Held (in an unpublished opinion): Not reversible error when the trial court gave a cautionary instruction not to consider the witness's actions as bearing on the guilt or innocence of any of the defendants. On the issue of the curative effect of the cautionary instruction, compare United States v. King, 461 F.2d 53, 57, n. 4 (8th Cir.1972); United States v. Ritz, 548 F.2d 510 (5th Cir.1977).

d) Trial of Bernhard H. Goetz: Defendant charged with attempted murder in a subway shooting of four persons. Defendant claimed that the shooting victims were attempting to rob him. One of the shooting victims invoked his privilege against self-incrimination and refused to testify for the prosecution. The defense urged that the jurors be told that he had invoked his privilege. The judge was reported to have rejected the defense request while indicating that he would tell the jurors that if the witness would have testified, his testimony would not have been helpful to the prosecution's case. New York Times, Sec. I, p. 51, col. 6, June 10, 1987.

e) United States v. Nunez, 668 F.2d 1116 (10th Cir.1981): An instruction to the jury that in assessing the credibility of a witness it should consider his invocation of the Fifth Amendment is improper.

f) A witness for the prosecution has been charged in a criminal complaint with crimes that may be relevant to his credibility. The prosecutor offers to stipulate that should the witness be questioned about the allegations in the complaint, he would say that they were true. The defense refuses to stipulate. It is anticipated that when asked about each of the crimes, the witness will invoke his privilege against self-incrimination. "[T]o simplify the case and move it forward," the judge instructs the jury that in assessing the credibility of the witness, whenever the witness pleads the Fifth, it can be assumed that he was guilty of that crime. United States v. Gallo, No. CR 86–452 (S–4) tr., unrptd. [E.D.N.Y., Oct. 19, 1987].

10. a) In Baxter v. Palmigiano, 425 U.S. 308 (1976), in declining to extend Griffin, the Court held that permitting an adverse inference to be drawn from an inmate's silence at a prison disciplinary hearing does not violate the Constitution. The Court also stated:

> [T]he Fifth Amendment does not forbid adverse inferences against parties to civil actions when they refuse to testify in response to probative evidence offered against them. 425 U.S. at 318, 96 S.Ct. at 1557.

b) In Rad Services Inc. v. Aetna Casualty and Surety Company, 808 F.2d 271 (3d Cir.1986), the court in a civil case ruled that the judge below did not err in permitting the jury to draw adverse inferences from the refusals to testify of non-party agents of the plaintiff who had claimed their privilege against self-incrimination in response to questioning regarding their employment and the crucial facts at issue. Further, the court indicated that the inference could be drawn even if the witness no longer worked for the party. "[A] witness truly bent on incriminating his former employer would likely offer damaging testimony directly, instead of hoping for an adverse inference from a Fifth Amendment invocation" and "a rule precluding evidence of a former employee's invocation would allow a corporate party ... to stymie the discovery process with expedience by discharging those potentially responsible for the alleged wrongdoing." The court also stated: "The aims supporting the privilege simply apply less forcefully in civil than in criminal cases. A non-party's silence in a civil proceeding implicates Fifth Amendment concerns to an even lesser degree."

Also see Brink's, Inc. v. City of New York, 717 F.2d 700 (2d Cir.1983).

c) In Brink's, Inc. v. City of New York, supra, Judge Winter dissented as follows:

My misgivings concern the ruling permitting the systematic interrogation of witnesses on direct examination by counsel who knows they will assert the privilege against self-incrimination. This holding allows juries to draw prejudicial inferences from leading questions put to witnesses, denies parties the right to cross-examine, and is an invitation to sharp practice.

The assertion of the privilege by the five witnesses in the instant case was hardly unexpected, and the direct examination did not cease once it became clear that they would not testify in the conventional sense. Indeed, the City was altogether uninterested in posing questions that elicited testimonial answers....

[T]he prejudicial impact of allowing juries to draw inferences against parties from assertions of the privilege by witnesses clearly outweighs any probative value. Fed.R.Evid. 403.

First, the supposed probative value is derived entirely from the questions put by counsel. Consider the following examination of Mr. Gargiulo, a discharged employee of Brink's:

Q: Did you carry a brown satchel while you were working on the parking meter contract?

A: I respectfully must decline to answer that question pursuant to my rights under the Fifth Amendment of the Constitution of the United States.

Q: And it's a fact, is it not, that you used that satchel to place monies from the coin cannisters into the satchel to take for your own personal use during the period of the parking meter contract?

A: I respectfully must decline to answer that question pursuant to my rights under the Fifth Amendment of the Constitution of the United States.

Q: On March 5, 1980, do you recall throwing a handful of slugs into a trash can in a Blimpie's near 42 Franklin Street?

A: I respectfully must decline to answer that question pursuant to my rights under the Fifth Amendment of the Constitution of the United States.

. . .

Obviously, the posing of fact-specific questions is designed to suggest to the jury that but for the privilege the answer in each case would have been "yes" ... This practice inevitably invites jurors to give evidentiary weight to questions rather than answers. Moreover, it leaves the examiner free, once having determined that the privilege will be invoked, to pose those questions which are most damaging to the adversary, safe from any contradiction by the witness no matter what the actual facts.

Second, the adversary is effectively denied the right of cross-examination since the witness cannot even be made to explain why the privilege has been invoked, much less to contradict the intended inference. Id. at 715–716.

Compare the issues raised by the examination of the witness in Brink's with the examination of the accused in United States v. Hearst, supra note 3.

d) See generally Heidt, The Conjurer's Circle, The Fifth Amendment Privilege in Civil Cases, 91 Yale L.J. 1062 (1982); Note, Adverse Inferences Based on

Non–Party Invocations: The Real Magic Trick in Fifth Amendment Civil Cases, 60 Notre Dame L.Rev. 370 (1985).

G.   PROSECUTORIAL DISCOVERY

How much information can the prosecutor obtain from the defendant by way of discovery in advance of trial? The answer may be influenced by the rules regarding the criminal defendant's right of discovery against the prosecution, on the ground that there ought to be some reciprocity in discovery. But the prosecutor's discovery rights are limited by any privileges applicable to the information being sought, including the privilege against self-incrimination.

In California, the issues raised by prosecutorial efforts to discover information from defendants has a long history which is recounted in In re Misener, 38 Cal.3d 543, 213 Cal.Rptr. 569, 698 P.2d 637(1985). In the Misener case, the Supreme Court of California ruled that discovery that compelled disclosures from the defendant that would aid the prosecution was unconstitutional under the state constitutional provision prohibiting compelled self-incrimination. In the wake of that decision, the electorate approved an initiative reinstating prosecutorial discovery. The constitutionality of the initiative's provisions was approved in the case of Izazaga v. Superior Court, reprinted below. Only the portions of the case dealing with the constitutional issue under the federal Constitution have been reproduced.

Izazaga v. Superior Court

Supreme Court of California, 1991.
54 Cal.3d 356; 285 Cal.Rptr. 231, 815 P.2d 304.

■ LUCAS C.J.

In this case we resolve several issues presented by the adoption on June 5, 1990, of an initiative measure designated on the ballot as Proposition 115 and entitled the "Crime Victims Justice Reform Act." Petitioner raises various challenges under the federal and state Constitutions to the provisions of the measure authorizing reciprocal discovery in criminal cases.

We conclude that, properly construed and applied, the discovery provisions of Proposition 115 are valid under the state and federal Constitutions, and that Proposition 115 effectively reopened the two-way street of reciprocal discovery in criminal cases in California.

I.   Facts

Petitioner was charged with two counts of forcible rape (Pen. Code, former § 261, subd. (2)), one count of kidnapping (Pen. Code, § 207), and numerous enhancement allegations. The acts were alleged to have occurred on June 18, 1990. The People served on petitioner an informal request for discovery pursuant to newly adopted Penal Code section 1054.5, subdivision (b) (section 1054.5(b)). After petitioner refused the informal discovery request, the People filed a formal motion for discovery in superior court, to which petitioner filed an opposition. Following a hearing, the court granted the motion and issued an order requiring discovery.

The Court of Appeal summarily denied petitioner's application for a writ of mandate or prohibition. We stayed the discovery order and issued an alternative writ of mandate to consider the important constitutional and interpretive questions presented. Petitioner raises several arguments regarding the constitutionality of the discovery provisions added by Proposition 115.

Before we consider these contentions, we first review these new discovery provisions.

II.   Constitutional and Statutory Provisions

Proposition 115 added both constitutional and statutory language authorizing reciprocal discovery in criminal cases. Section 30, subdivision (c), added to article I of the California Constitution (article I, section 30(c)) by Proposition 115, declares discovery to be "reciprocal" in criminal cases. ("In order to provide for fair and speedy trials, discovery in criminal cases shall be reciprocal in nature, as prescribed by the Legislature or by the People through the initiative process.")

Proposition 115 also added a new Penal Code chapter on discovery. (Pen. Code, § 1054 et seq. [hereafter, the new discovery chapter].) The new Penal Code sections relevant to the issues that arise in this case are section 1054 (providing for interpretation of the chapter to give effect to certain specified purposes), section 1054.1 (providing for defense discovery), section 1054.3 (providing for prosecutorial discovery), section 1054.5 (providing mechanism for compelled discovery), section 1054.6 (providing that discovery shall not be required of work product or otherwise privileged information and material), and section 1054.7 (requiring disclosure at least 30 days prior to trial, placing a continuing duty to disclose on both prosecution and defense, and providing for denial of disclosure on a showing of "good cause"). [1]

Proposition 115 also repealed several discovery provisions, including Penal Code former section 1102.5 (previously declared unconstitutional in In re Misener (1985) 38 Cal.3d 543 [213 Cal.Rptr. 569, 698 P.2d 637] and Penal Code former section 1430 (requiring prosecutor to furnish defendant with police and arrest reports).

III.   Discussion

A.   Privilege Against Self-Incrimination

Petitioner asserts application of the discovery provisions enacted by Proposition 115 would violate his state and federal constitutional privileges against compelled self-incrimination. We disagree.

1.   **Federal Constitutional Challenge.** The Fifth Amendment of the United States Constitution recites in pertinent part: "No person . . . shall be compelled in any criminal case to be a witness against himself. . . ." Petitioner asserts that the new discovery chapter enacted by Proposition 115 compels a criminal defendant to be a witness against oneself in violation of the foregoing self-incrimination clause.

First, petitioner argues that the requirement under section 1054.3 that the defense must disclose to the prosecution the names and addresses of all witnesses it intends to call at trial, rather than merely its alibi witnesses, violates the self-incrimination clause. Decisions of the Supreme Court compel a contrary conclusion.

In Williams v. Florida (1970) 399 U.S. 78 [26 L.Ed.2d 446, 90 S.Ct. 1893] (Williams), the high court upheld against a self-incrimination clause challenge Florida's "notice-of-alibi" rule, which required a criminal defendant intending to rely on an alibi defense to notify the prosecution of the place where the defendant claimed to be at the time in question, and of the names and

---

1. The new discovery chapter of the Penal Code also includes section 1054.2 (prohibiting disclosure to defendant, but not to defense counsel, of address and telephone number of victims and prosecution witnesses) and section 1054.4 (providing that the chapter does not limit law enforcement from lawfully gathering nontestimonial evidence).

addresses of the witnesses the defendant intended to call in support of the alibi. Petitioner, noting that section 1054.3 is not limited to situations involving an alibi defense, attempts to distinguish Williams and argues that the self-incrimination clause prohibits the compelled discovery of defense witnesses in the absence of an alibi defense and the special problems it presents. As support for this argument petitioner cites the language in Williams that, "Given the ease with which an alibi can be fabricated, the State's interest in protecting itself against an eleventh-hour defense is both obvious and legitimate." (Id. at p. 81 [26 L.Ed.2d at p. 450].)

Petitioner's argument is misguided. The language in Williams on which he relies relates to the due process and fair trial issues addressed in that case, and is not relevant to the Fifth Amendment analysis. Moreover, petitioner's argument misinterprets the scope of the self-incrimination clause, which "protects a person only against being incriminated by his own compelled testimonial communications." (Fisher v. United States (1976) 425 U.S. 391, 409 [48 L.Ed.2d 39, 55, 96 S.Ct. 1569], italics added.) Under cases of the Supreme Court, there are four requirements that together trigger this privilege: the information sought must be (i) "incriminating"; (ii) "personal to the defendant"; (iii) obtained by "compulsion"; and (iv) "testimonial or communicative in nature." (See United States v. Nobles (1975) 422 U.S. 225 [45 L.Ed.2d 141, 95 S.Ct. 2160] [Nobles]; Schmerber v. California (1966) 384 U.S. 757, 761 [16 L.Ed.2d 908, 914, 86 S.Ct. 1826]; Doe v. United States (1988) 487 U.S. 201, 207 [101 L.Ed.2d 184, 194–195, 108 S.Ct. 2341].)

Statutorily mandated discovery of evidence that meets these four requirements is prohibited. Conversely, discovery of evidence that does not meet each of these requirements is not barred by the self-incrimination clause. This is so even in the absence of special state interests such as protection against easily fabricated "eleventh hour" defenses. The absence of particular state interests in disclosure affects none of these four requirements, and thus cannot itself trigger the self-incrimination clause. (See New Jersey v. Portash (1979) 440 U.S. 450, 459 [59 L.Ed.2d 501, 510, 99 S.Ct. 1292].)

In Williams, supra, 399 U.S. 78, the high court held that discovery of the names and addresses of a defendant's alibi witnesses is not "compelled" self-incrimination, and therefore does not violate the Fifth Amendment. The court reasoned, "At most, the rule only compelled [defendant] to accelerate the timing of his disclosure, by forcing him to divulge at an earlier date information that the [defendant] from the beginning planned to divulge at trial." Thus, discovery of the names and addresses of the witnesses that the defense intends to call at trial, whether or not in support of an alibi defense, merely forces the defendant "to divulge at an earlier date information that the [defendant] from the beginning planned to divulge at trial." Under the rationale of Williams, such discovery does not constitute compelled self-incrimination, and therefore does not implicate the privilege.

We thus address petitioner's second contention, that insofar as section 1054.3 requires the defense to disclose before trial any statements of the witnesses it intends to call at trial, that section violates the self-incrimination clause. Once again, decisions of the Supreme Court compel a contrary conclusion.

Compelled disclosure of the statements of defense witnesses does not meet all of the requirements necessary to implicate the self-incrimination clause. We agree with petitioner that the acceleration doctrine of Williams discussed above is not dispositive here, for it is not a matter of merely forcing the defendant "to divulge at an earlier date information that the [defendant] from the beginning planned to divulge at trial." 26 L.Ed.2d 446, 452. Some statements of witnesses the defense intends to call might never be offered at trial by the defense. Thus, to the extent that the statements are incriminating, such incrimination is indeed compelled. And clearly such statements are "testimonial or communicative in nature." Such statements are not, however, "personal to the defendant."

As the high court stated in Nobles, supra, 422 U.S. 225, the privilege against self-incrimination " 'is a personal privilege: it adheres basically to the person, not to information that may incriminate him.' " In Nobles, the court rejected a self-incrimination challenge to a trial court order requiring the defense to disclose its investigator's report of statements made by prosecutorial witnesses once the defense called its investigator as a trial witness.

In Nobles the high court reasoned: "The fact that these statements of third parties were elicited by a defense investigator on [defendant's] behalf does not convert them into [defendant's] personal communications. Requiring their production from the investigator therefore would not in any sense compel [defendant] to be a witness against himself or extort communications from him." (Nobles, supra, 422 U.S. 225, 234 [45 L.Ed.2d 141, 151].) The court concluded, "the Fifth Amendment privilege against compulsory self-incrimination, being personal to the defendant, does not extend to the testimony or statements of third parties called as witnesses at trial." (Ibid. [45 L.Ed.2d 141, 151].)

The high court's reasoning in Nobles is controlling here. Section 1054.3 requires disclosure by the defense of statements, and reports of statements, of "persons, other than defendant," that the defense intends to call as witnesses at trial. Thus, the compelled statements are those of "third parties" within the meaning of Nobles and are therefore outside of the scope of the self-incrimination clause.

Petitioner attempts to distinguish Nobles, noting that the Supreme Court has never upheld disclosure of statements of defense witnesses before trial. He further observes that the Federal Rules of Criminal Procedure provide for disclosure of statements of defense witnesses only after they testify at trial, citing rule 26 of the Federal Rules of Criminal Procedure (18 U.S.C.).

Here again petitioner's argument misinterprets the scope of the self-incrimination clause. The timing of the disclosure, whether before or during trial, does not affect any of the four requirements that together trigger the privilege against self-incrimination, and therefore cannot implicate the privilege. The acceleration doctrine of Williams, supra, 399 U.S. 78, compels this conclusion. We conclude that statements of the witnesses that the defense intends to call at trial are not personal to the defendant, and therefore compelled discovery of such statements does not implicate the self-incrimination clause.

NOTES

1. In United States v. Nobles, discussed in the principal case, a defense investigator had interviewed the two key prosecutorial witnesses prior to trial and prepared a report of the interview. The defense proposed to have the investigator testify to facts derived from the interviews that would impeach the two prosecution witnesses. Specifically, the Supreme Court in Nobles ruled that refusing to permit the investigator to testify unless the defense turned over the relevant portions of the investigator's report for use in cross-examining him did not violate the defendant's self-incrimination privilege. Is there any way in which the turning over of the investigator's report might involve an implied communication by the defendant? In this connection, it should be noted that, in addition to the excerpts from the court's opinion in Nobles quoted in Izazaga, the court also stated: "Respondent did not prepare the report, and there is no suggestion that the portions subject to the disclosure order reflected any information that he conveyed to the investigator." For additional discussion of Nobles, see supra Ch. 3, p. 269.

2. Problem: Defendant is charged with murder by strangulation. His sisters, while going through his room, find some papers written in the defendant's handwriting. These contain threats to kill the deceased as well as what appears to be a murder checklist. The sisters give the papers to an attorney who gives them to a public defender investigator who gives them to the deputy public defender representing the defendant. The deputy public defender places the papers in a sealed envelope and, without informing the prosecutor, delivers them to the clerk of the court. [Query: Was this the proper thing for defense counsel to do? See infra p. 1436.]

The prosecutor learns of the writings from the husband of one of the defendant's sisters and files a motion with the trial court to produce and unseal the described documents. Defendant opposes the motion. How should the court rule? See People v. Sanchez, 24 Cal.App.4th 1012 , 30 Cal.Rptr.2d 111 (1994).

3. On the application of the provisions of Proposition 115 (granting a right of prosecutorial discovery) to other kinds of proceedings, see Hines v. Superior Court, 20 Cal.App.4th 1099, 12 Cal.Rptr.2d 216 (1992): Held: Prosecutorial discovery does not apply to the penalty phase of a capital case before there is a guilty verdict along with a finding of special circumstances (that make it a capital case); Robert S. v. Superior Court, 9 Cal.App.4th 1417, 12 Cal.Rptr.2d 489 (1992): Held: The discovery provisions of Proposition 115 do not as such apply to delinquency proceedings, but California courts have determined that discovery in delinquency proceedings should parallel that in criminal cases. Accordingly, the juvenile court's order granting prosecutorial discovery was not an abuse of discretion.

4. See generally, Mosteller, Discovery Against the Defense: Tilting the Adversarial Balance, 74 Cal.L.Rev. 1567 (1986); Blumenson, Constitutional Limitations on Prosecutorial Discovery, 18 Harv.Civ.Rts–Civ.Lib.L.Rev. 123 (1983); Allis, Limitations on Prosecutorial Discovery of the Defense Case in Federal Courts: The Shield of Confidentiality, 50 S.Cal.L.Rev. 461 (1977); Van Kessel, Prosecutorial Discovery and the Privilege Against Self–Incrimination: Accommodation or Capitulation, 4 Hastings Const.L.Q. 855 (1977).

SECTION 3. THE ATTORNEY-CLIENT PRIVILEGE

A. INTRODUCTION AND RATIONALE

In 1942, Professor Edmund M. Morgan in the Forward to the American Law Institute's Model Code of Evidence, pp. 24–28 (1942),* characterized the attorney-client privilege as follows:

The lawyer-client privilege has its roots in history. There was in early England no compulsory process for witnesses. Indeed persons ready and willing to furnish information in open court had to be careful to avoid the appearance of fomenting litigation. The Anglo–Norman jurors were really witnesses in a sense, since they were chosen because they probably had personal knowledge of the pertinent facts, and jury service was compulsory. But witnesses, as we know them, were first required to appear and testify in the reign of Elizabeth. It was not until the middle of the nineteenth century that a party to an action was competent to give evidence for himself and could be compelled to be a witness for his opponent. In these circumstances it was to be expected that the attorney, an officer of the court, who represented the client in legal proceedings, should not fall within the compulsory process. Furthermore there was in the early 1800s a great reluctance on the part of judges to compel anyone to violate a confidence, and naturally that reluctance operated in multiple measure where a member of the legal profession was asked to commit a breach of the code of a gentleman. So we find the English courts first treating the question from the standpoint of the attorney. The privilege was his, not his client's. The client by a bill of discovery might be required to disclose what he had told his attorney, while the attorney was privileged not to testify.

This notion could not well endure when other persons in whom trust had been reposed were not permitted to keep their vows of silence. Very early there was talk of the desirability of the privilege from the client's point of view and that of the public interest in the administration of justice. At present there is no question that the privilege is that of the client. If he does not object to disclosure, the attorney must disclose. The orthodox justification for the present privilege stresses first the function of the lawyer in the administration of justice. In a complex society such as ours, ... there can be no question of the need for trained technicians to advise men how to order their conduct. And under rules of procedure developed by courts and legislatures, the impossibility of a layman's preparing and conducting a lawsuit needs no demonstration. The next step posits the necessity of full disclosure by the client. Unless he makes known to the lawyer all the facts, the advice which follows will be useless, if not misleading; the lawsuit will be conducted along improper lines, the trial will be full of surprises, much useless litigation may result. Thirdly, unless the client knows that his lawyer cannot be compelled to reveal what is told him, the client will suppress what he thinks to be the unfavorable facts. When he consults a lawyer, he knows that a lawsuit or, in these days, an administrative or legislative investigation is possible or even likely. In such a proceeding all pertinent material will be sought. Hence, he has in contemplation the possible official inquiry, and he will not make revelations that may be used to his detriment. This is somewhat doubtful. And finally, it is said, that the harm done in the suppression of the truth in litigation or other official investigation is less than the good done in the public interest in the administration of justice by the existence of the privilege.

This last assertion merits examination. If the client suppresses pertinent facts, what will happen? First, suppose that no lawsuit results. The client by reason of withholding material matter gets bad advice, and acts upon it. He sustains a loss, gets into trouble. Whom has he to blame but himself? Why should he be saved from his own deceit? Suppose a lawsuit or official investigation results (and this is the case where the privilege counts): whether the client be a plaintiff or a defendant or a mere witness, he is subject to compulsory process and may be required to disclose at the trial or hearing every pertinent fact within his knowledge, under the sanction of an oath or its equivalent that obliges him to tell the whole truth. If he told his lawyer the truth, he must now tell the same thing from the witness box. If he told his lawyer a lie and sticks to it, he will tell the same story at the trial or hearing. If he told his lawyer the truth and now tells a lie, why should he be protected from exposure? Is the privilege retained in order to protect perjurors? How can that either directly or indirectly further the administration of justice? ...

There are no data to furnish a reasoned support for the privilege in general. The reason for its creation is exploded: the system into which it fitted as a rational part is gone. In situations where the privilege against self-incrimination is involved, the retention of the privilege is justified. There the justification rests not on the attorney-client privilege but upon a combination of the privilege against self-incrimination and the right of every person accused of crime to competent counsel. The practical policy against the combination of advocate and witness in the same lawsuit may justify an additional limitation.

On the other hand, a proposal to abolish so ancient a privilege—a privilege so closely connected with the administration of justice, ... arouses such strenuous opposition from the bar that it would be futile to attempt its enactment....

See also Winter J. in In re Shargel, 742 F.2d 61 (2d Cir.1984):

While the attorney-client privilege historically arose at the same time as the privilege against self-incrimination, it was early established that the privileges had distinct policies and that the "point of honor",the attorney's reluctance to incriminate his client,was not a valid reason to invoke the attorney-client privilege. 9 W. Holdsworth, A History of English Law, at 201-02 (1926).

The goal of enabling attorneys to offer informed professional advice and advocacy cannot be accomplished if courts may compel disclosure of communications between the client and attorney necessary to the provision of such services. Absent the privilege, an attorney could not even appraise the risk to the client of such a communication until it occurs. The attorney must thus decide early in the course of consultation whether to warn the client against communications which, however necessary to the rendering of competent legal advice, might be disclosed to an adversary in litigation. Lawyers would routinely have to choose between forgoing information indispensable to the provision of informed and competent legal representation or hearing the information and exposing the client to risk of subsequent disclosure to an adversary. Inadequate legal counsel would fall upon the innocent as well as upon the guilty and would in the long run impair the ability of courts to administer justice fairly. The privilege thus spares attorneys the necessity of making such Hobson's choices and protects the system of justice generally by allowing the client to shield confidential communications made in the course of seeking legal advice.

Where no such dilemma is created for the lawyer, information is not protected by the privilege even though the client may strongly fear the effects of disclosure, including incrimination.... Id. at 63.

Hazard, an Historical Perspective on the Attorney–Client Privilege*

66 Calif.L.Rev. 1061, 1065, 1066 (1978).

The law of attorney client privilege is the product of judicial decisions, augmented by statutes that usually incorporate the decisional law. This will be called the "privilege rule." The rules of professional ethics, on the other hand, emanate from the legislative process of the legal profession itself. For over a half century, the central legislative source in the legal profession has been the American Bar Association, acting through its House of Delegates. The A.B.A. has undertaken to state rules of professional ethics that it hopes will be adopted by the states through their own bar associations or courts. By this process of adoption, and perhaps simply through recognition of the rules within the profession at large, the bar seeks to establish prevailing norms governing the responsibilities of the attorney in the attorney-client relationship, including the responsibility to maintain confidentiality. The rules promulgated by the bar association therefore have considerable significance in defining the terms and conditions under which a client's communications to his attorney are to be kept confidential. The bar's rule as to the proper scope of confidentiality, which will be called the "confidence rule," is, perhaps not surprisingly, more expansive that the rule of attorney-client privilege developed by the courts.

[The ABA in 1983 approved Model Rules of Professional Conduct which comprise its recent statement of the rules of professional ethics.]

Thornburgh, Sanctifying Secrecy: the Mythology of the Corporate Attorney–client Privilege**

There are three traditional kinds of myths about the purpose of the attorney-client privilege: (1) the privilege is necessary to encourage clients to fully and honestly confide in their lawyers; (2) the privilege is necessary to encourage lawyers to thoroughly advise and interview their clients; and (3) the privilege is necessary to protect the relationship between the lawyer and the client. There is also a traditional myth about the effect of the privilege: the privilege is virtually cost free because it does not deprive the trier of fact of any relevant information.

Recently, the traditional mythology has been challenged by an aspiring replacement myth suggested by law and economics scholars. Having both purpose and effect components, this myth claims that the additional cost to opponents caused by the privilege motivates clients to communicate fully with their lawyers. Moreover, the privilege actually benefits the judicial system by discouraging perjury, because well-informed lawyers steer their clients away from baseless claims and defenses.

. . .

[The] assumption-that clients need the privilege to encourage them to communicate-purports to be an empirical one. The modest amount of empirical data available, however, is equivocal at best and casts doubt on the truth of this assertion. Taken together, these studies question the following assumptions: (1)

that clients know about the privilege and can, therefore, be influenced by it; (2) that clients are influenced by the privilege in making disclosures; and (3) that clients, even with the privilege, are honest with their lawyers.

NOTES

1. In addition to the historical treatment in the Morgan and Hazard sources quoted above, the history of the attorney-client privilege is addressed in Radin, The Privilege of Confidential Communication Between Lawyer and Client, 16 Cal. L.Rev. 487 (1928); Holdsworth, A History of English Law 201 (7th ed. 1956); 8 Wigmore, Evidence at 531 (McNaughton rev. ed. 1961).

2. As the excerpts quoted above indicate, the attorney-client privilege has been under some critical scrutiny and attack in recent years. Of course, many of these criticisms are not new: Professor Morgan's comments were published more than a half century ago. What is new, however, are some efforts to examine the empirical foundations for some of the assumptions underlying the privilege. Also the application to the privilege of the tools of economic analysis is a recent development. There is also increased attention to the moral and ethical issues related to confidentiality and the attorney-client relationship.

a) There is general agreement that the existing empirical evidence is inadequate to support a convincing case for or against the privilege. See, e.g. Developments in the Law–Privileged Communications, 98 Harv. L.Rev. 1450 (1985); 23 Wright & Graham, Federal Practice and Procedure: Evidence, section 5422.1 at 214 (Supp. 1993).

Empirical studies are reported in Note, Functional Overlap Between the Lawyer and Other Professionals: Its Implications for Privileged Communications Doctrine, 71 Yale L.J. 1226 (1962); Zacharias, Rethinking Confidentiality, 74 Ia. L.Rev. 351, 379 (1989); Empirical Research Project, Corporate Legal Ethics-An Empirical Study: The Model Rules, the Code of Professional Responsibility and Counsel's Continuing Struggle Between Theory and Practice, 8 J. Corp. L. 601 (1983); Alexander, The Corporate Attorney Client Privilege: A Study of the Participants, 63 St. John's L. Rev. 191 (1989).

b) For economic analysis arguments applied to the attorney-client privilege, see, e.g., Easterbrook, Insider Trading, Secret Agents, Evidentiary Privileges, and the Production of Information, 1981 Sup. Ct. Rev. 309; Allen, Grady, Polsby & Yashko, A Positive Theory of the Attorney–Client Privilege and the Work Product Doctrine, 19 J. Legal Stud. 359 (1990). The application of this economic analysis to the attorney-client privilege in the corporate setting is criticized in Thornburg, supra, 69 Notre Dame L.Rev. 157 (1993). Economic analysis argumentation applied to the attorney's work product doctrine, see infra p. 1454, is criticized in Thornburg, Rethinking Work Product, 77 Va. L.Rev. 1515 (1991). Her criticisms are responded to by Professor Allen, Work Product Revisited: A Comment on Rethinking Work Product, 78 Va. L.Rev. 949 (1992); and Professor Thornburg replies, Work Product Rejected: A Reply to Professor Allen, 78 Va.L.Rev. 957 (1992).

c) As to the moral and ethical aspects, see, e.g. Hazard, Ethics in the Practice of Law (1978); Luban, Lawyers and Justice, An Ethical Study (1988); Simon, Ethical Discretion in Lawyering, 101 Harv. L.Rev. 1083 (1988); Rhode, Ethical Perspectives on Legal Practice, 37 Stan. L.Rev. 589 (1985)

d) For comparative material on the lawyer-client relationship, see, e.g. Taruffo, The Lawyer's Role and the Model of Civil Process, 16 Israel L.Rev. 5 (1981); D. Rueschemeyer, Lawyers and Their Society (1973).

Also see generally Gardner, A Re-evaluation of the Attorney–Client Privilege, 8 Vill.L.Rev. 279 (1963); Comment, The Attorney–Client Privilege: Fixed Rules Balancing and Constitutional Entitlement, 91 Harv.L.Rev. 464 (1971); Developments in the Law, Privileged Communications, 98 Harv.L.Rev. 1451, 1501–1509 (1985).

B.   BASIC ELEMENTS

In re: Sealed Case

United States Court of Appeals, District of Columbia Circuit, 1984.
737 F.2d 94.

■ Before ROBINSON, GINSBURG and PALMIERI, CIRCUIT JUDGES.

■ GINSBURG, CIRCUIT JUDGE.

This is an expedited appeal from a district court order instructing an attorney to testify before a grand jury on matters the attorney's former client regards as privileged. Appellant is a corporation (hereafter, "the Company") targeted for investigation by the grand jury. The witness whose testimony is at stake formerly served as the Company's vice president-general counsel, and sole in-house attorney. The Company instructed its former counsel to raise the attorney-client privilege regarding several grand jury inquiries. Former counsel did so and the government moved to compel his testimony.

The district court granted the motion as to four conversations between the witness and the Company's president, and two "hunches" the witness entertained; it denied the motion as to one conversation between the witness and a Company senior executive.

I.   FACTS

The former vice president-general counsel whose grand jury testimony is at issue (hereafter, "C") was the Company's sole in-house attorney from 1976 until 1981. C was responsible for all Company legal affairs; he reported directly to the Company's president (hereafter, "P"). P and other Company personnel informed C about virtually all Company business activities, and C used the information thus received to render legal advice on a daily basis to a wide variety of Company employees.

In the course of the investigation, C appeared before the grand jury and testified at length about his activities and observations during his tenure with the Company. At certain "critical points," however, on instruction from the Company's current counsel, C asserted attorney-client privilege and refused to answer questions.

C's refusal to answer related to five matters:

(1) A 1980 disclosure by C to P concerning a conversation C overheard at the O'Hare Hilton;

(2) The bases for certain "hunches" C had regarding Company involvement in bid rigging;

(3) A 1978 or 1979 conversation between C and a Company senior executive at a St. Paul restaurant;

(4) Two 1979 or 1980 conversations between C and P in P's office in the course of periodic status reviews of the Company's legal affairs;

(5) A 1978 conversation between C and P aboard an airplane.

In response to the government's motion to compel C's testimony, the district court held two evidentiary hearings, received briefs, and entertained oral argument. The court then ruled that, as to all four conversations with P and two of C's "hunches," the Company had not established entitlement to privileged communication protection. The court upheld the attorney-client privilege plea on one matter: C's St. Paul restaurant conversation with a Company senior executive.

The Company maintains in this appeal that the attorney-client privilege shields all matters addressed in the government's motion to compel; the government seeks reversal of the district court's order as to the one matter on which it did not prevail.

II.   DISCUSSION

We set out initially, as did the district court and the parties, the concise summary of the attorney-client privilege composed by Judge Wyzanski in United States v. United Shoe Machinery Corp., 89 F.Supp. 357, 358–59 (D.Mass.1950):

> The privilege applies only if (1) the asserted holder of the privilege is or sought to become a client; (2) the person to whom the communication was made (a) is a member of the bar of a court or his subordinate and (b) in connection with this communication is acting as a lawyer; (3) the communication relates to a fact of which the attorney was informed (a) by his client (b) without the presence of strangers (c) for the purpose of securing primarily either (i) an opinion on law or (ii) legal services or (iii) assistance in some legal proceeding, and not (d) for the purpose of committing a crime or tort; and (4) the privilege has been (a) claimed and (b) not waived by the client.

To this we append two additional black letter statements. Communications from attorney to client are shielded if they rest on confidential information obtained from the client. Mead Data Central, Inc. v. United States Department of Air Force, 184 U.S. App. D.C. 350, 566 F.2d 242, 254 (D.C.Cir.1977). Correlatively, "when an attorney conveys to his client facts acquired from other persons or sources, those facts are not privileged." Brinton v. Department of State, 204 U.S. App. D.C. 328, 636 F.2d 600, 604 (D.C.Cir.1980), cert. denied, 452 U.S. 905, 101 S.Ct. 3030, 69 L.Ed.2d 405 (1981).

In practice, however, advice does not spring from lawyers' heads as Athena did from the brow of Zeus. Inevitably, attorneys' opinions reflect an accumulation of education and experience in the law and the large society law serves. In a given case, advice prompted by the client's disclosures may be further and inseparably informed by other knowledge and encounters. We have therefore stated that the privilege cloaks a communication from attorney to client " 'based, in part at least, upon a confidential communication [to the lawyer] from [the client].' " Brinton, 636 F.2d at 604.

It remains the claimant's burden, however, to present to the court sufficient facts to establish the privilege; the claimant must demonstrate with reasonable certainty, that the lawyer's communication rested in significant and inseparable part on the client's confidential disclosure.

We note one further general consideration. The lawyer whose testimony the government seeks in this case served as in-house attorney. That status alone does not dilute the privilege. United Shoe Machinery Corp., 89 F. Supp. at 360; See Upjohn Co. v. United States, 449 U.S. 383, 394–95, 101 S.Ct. 677, 66 L.Ed.2d 584 (1981). We are mindful, however, that C was a Company vice president, and had certain responsibilities outside the lawyer's sphere. The

Company can shelter C's advice only upon a clear showing that C gave it in a professional legal capacity.

We next explain our rulings on each of the alleged confidential communications.

1.   The conversation between C and P in which C reported what he overheard at the O'Hare Hilton.

The district court ordered C to testify regarding a discussion in which C disclosed to P the contents of a conversation C had overheard at the O'Hare Hilton between executives of two of the Company's competitors. The Company claims no privilege for the contents of the overheard conversation. Indeed, C has already told the grand jury what he overheard. The Company contends, however, that related portions of the discussion between C and P rested, in part at least, on confidential Company information.

The record does not support the Company's position. At the hearing on the motion to compel, C stated that in giving advice to P on this matter (1) he did not rely on information from any source other than the O'Hare Hilton meeting, and (2) P did not disclose any confidential information to him. These statements settle the question. The Company points to other statements indicating that C and P believed their exchange was confidential. Their expectation as to confidentiality, however, hardly demonstrates that confidential information gained from the client underpinned the conversation. The Company, in short, has not sustained its burden. We affirm the district court's ruling.[1]

2.   C's "hunches" concerning certain Company activities

The district court directed C to answer questions about:

1.   His "hunch" or opinion of the identity of the person with whom [P] met in the United Air Lines Red Carpet Room at O'Hare International Airport in Chicago on or about April 3, 1978;

2.   His "hunch" or opinion concerning whether there was an agreement among the bidders for the contracts to supply . . . construction services and equipment to the owners of the [X facility] and the [Y facility], both bid on or about [month and day], 1980. Seizing on broader language appearing in the district court's Memorandum, the Company argues that the "hunch" testimony would divulge confidential Company information and, to the extent not supported by facts or personal knowledge, would amount to speculation in which the Company's former lawyer ought not be heard to indulge.

We rule precisely and only on the directions expressed in the district court's order. C no doubt has hunches that would implicate confidential Company disclosures, and could speculate on many matters involving the Company. But the district court's order is riveted to hunches gleaned from C's direct observations at public places.

As to the first "hunch," C has already testified that he observed the president of one of the Company's competitors walking down the United Air Lines concourse some distance behind P as P returned from a meeting P earlier

---

1.   The district court thought the privilege inapplicable in part because C initiated the conversation and was not schooled in antitrust matters. We do not agree that these are privilege-stripping factors. A sheltered communication on one occasion may originate with the lawyer based on confidential disclosures the client made on an earlier occasion. A client does not lose protection for disclosures in special subject areas made to lawyers who are generalists. [Footnotes are those of the court. Some footnotes have been omitted, and others renumbered.]

told C he had with "someone" in the Red Carpet Room. As to the second, C similarly testified that he observed P making hurried calls from a public phone booth at Hobby Airport in Houston on the morning of the day projects X and Y were bid.

A grand jury can act on information from a wide variety of sources, including tips and rumors, even speculation. With this precedent in view, we affirm the "hunch" directions in the district court's order. C may be asked, and must respond to inquiries, about opinions formed from direct observations C made at O'Hare and Hobby Airports, coupled with other non-confidential information C may possess, concerning the identity of the person trailing P at O'Hare and bid rigging on the two named projects.

3. The conversation between C and a Company senior executive at a St. Paul restaurant.

Based on the evidence submitted, the district court properly concluded that the senior executive C met at a St. Paul restaurant sought C's legal advice, and that all of C's dealings with this executive involved Company legal matters, not non-law related Company operations. The record also supports the district court's determinations that the matters discussed concerned confidential Company information and were treated accordingly (no one else was at the restaurant table and the executive was not speaking loudly enough to be overheard). We find no tenable basis to upset the district court's ruling that this conversation was privileged.

4. Two conversations between C and P in the course of meetings to review the Company's legal affairs.

The district court held the privilege inapplicable to portions of two legal affairs conversations in P's office. In support of its ruling, the court found that: (1) the conversations took place after two regular legal status review meetings between C and P; (2) they were initiated by C; (3) P was not seeking legal advice; (4) C was acting as a corporate executive, not as a lawyer; and (5) the advice was not based on confidential information.

Mindful that FED. R. CIV. P. 52(a) secures the district court's findings of fact against reversal on appeal unless they are "clearly erroneous," we nevertheless conclude "on the entire evidence" that the district court erred. The record shows that C, in his capacity as general counsel, met with P on these occasions to give P status reports on the Company's legal affairs. In the course of these meetings, C raised concerns about the Company's antitrust compliance; there is no evidence in the record to substantiate the finding that the antitrust discussion took place after or apart from the regular meetings. Although the advice was unsolicited and P did not disclose confidential information to C at those meetings, C rendered legal advice, based, at least in part, on Company confidential information previously disclosed to him by management personnel generally, and by the St. Paul senior executive specifically. Under these circumstances, the conversations qualify for the privilege.

Although the record supports the district court's finding that C initiated the conversations, that factor alone does not strip a communication of its privileged status. Cf. Upjohn, 449 U.S. at 390 (privilege protects both lawyer's professional advice to client and client's disclosure of confidential information to lawyer to enable lawyer to give advice).

5. The conversation between C and P aboard an airplane.

We also reverse the district court's rejection of the attorney-client privilege to shield the conversation between C and P during their flight from Chicago to Omaha on or about April 3, 1978. The district court's ruling rests on findings that P did not expressly request C to keep the conversation confidential and that the "circumstances" were inconsistent with an intention to preserve confidentiality. The district court also stated that it seemed "rather incongruous" that confidential information would be discussed in the course of a commercial flight.

As the district court itself later recognized, D.D.C. Memorandum, an express request for confidentiality is not required. 8 Wigmore on Evidence § 2311, at 600 (McNaughton rev. ed. 1961).

Our review of the "circumstances," moreover, reveals no comprehensible basis for the district court's position. C and P were seated next to each other in the first-class section of the aircraft. There were no other parties to their conversation. Although C could not recall whether other people were seated nearby, C did testify that he and P were talking in "tones" not likely to be overheard.[2] He also testified that it was implicit from their relationship as president and general counsel that C should keep P's disclosures confidential at all times.

In view of all relevant portions of the record, we conclude that the Company has sustained its burden to show that the privilege applies to this conversation. We reverse as without foundation in the record or the governing law the segment of the district court's order requiring C to answer questions about the legal claims discussion held in the first-class compartment.

III. CONCLUSION

For the foregoing reasons, the district court's order is affirmed with regard to C's "hunches," his conversation with a Company senior executive in St. Paul, and his conversation with P about what he overheard at the O'Hare Hilton. It is reversed as to C's conversations with P regarding the Company's antitrust compliance and his conversation with P on the airplane.

It is so ordered.

NOTES

1. The excerpt from Judge Wyzanski's opinion quoted in the principal case toward the beginning of Judge (now Justice) Ginsburg's discussion is generally accepted as a sound basic statement of the attorney-client privilege. Compare sections 950–952, California Evidence Code.

2. As the principal case indicates, the communication in question must have a legal advice purpose. Where, as in the principal case, the attorney is corporate counsel and also has a management position, separating the legal advice role from the management role may be difficult. For further treatment of the role of in-house counsel in a corporate arrangement, see infra, p. 1451.

3. On the general issue of whether a communication between lawyer and client involves a legal advice purpose, see the following two excerpts from Wigmore:

2. C and P did not whisper. Nor did P make other overt attempts to safeguard the conversation. But there is no evidence that the discussion was overheard by anyone either passing or seated nearby.

The conversation itself dealt almost entirely with an analysis of legal claims that might arise in connection with an upcoming construction project. From the context of the conversation, it was apparent that P sought C's professional advice. C had worked as an attorney on this matter before the conversation and again after the flight. In this work, C relied on company confidential information furnished to him prior to the conversation, and he additionally used factual information P provided during the conversation.

The courts have not always used consistent language in answering the question whether the privilege is limited in some way to communications necessary or material or relevant to some purpose of the consultation.

It should be clear, on the one hand, that the actual necessity of making a particular statement, or the materiality to the cause of a particular fact, cannot determine the answer, for the client cannot know what is necessary or material, and the object of the privilege is that he should be unhampered in his quest for advice. On the other hand, when he knowingly departs from that purpose and interjects other matters not relevant to it, he is in that respect not seeking legal advice, and the privilege does not design to protect him. The test is, therefore, not whether the fact or the statement is actually necessary or material or relevant to the subject of the consultation, but whether the statement is made as a part of the purpose of the client to obtain advice on that subject. Some such rule would seem to have been in the minds of all the judges in spite of the occasional apparent inconsistency of their utterances. 8 Wigmore, Evidence § 2310 (McNaughton rev. 1961).

A lawyer is sometimes employed without reference to his knowledge and discretion in the law, as where he is charged with finding a profitable investment for trust funds.... It is not easy to frame a definite test for distinguishing legal from nonlegal advice. Where the general purpose concerns legal rights and obligations, a particular incidental transaction would receive protection, though in itself it were merely commercial in nature, as where the financial condition of a shareholder is discussed in the course of a proceeding to enforce a claim against a corporation. But apart from such cases, the most that can be said by way of generalization is that a matter committed to a professional legal adviser is prima facie so committed for the sake of the legal advice which may be more or less desirable for some aspect of the matter, and is therefore within the privilege unless it clearly appears to be lacking in aspects requiring legal advice.

Obviously, much depends upon the circumstances of the individual transactions. 8 Wigmore, Evidence § 2296 (McNaughton rev. 1961).

4. As the principal case indicates, the fact that both a client and his counsel had an expectation that their exchange would be confidential, by itself, is not enough to insure application of the privilege. Contrariwise, if communications occur between attorney and client that would otherwise be privileged but under circumstances that suggest an absence of a purpose to maintain confidentiality, the privilege is inapplicable. For example, see Bolyea v. First Presbyterian Church of Wilton, 196 N.W.2d 149, 55 A.L.R.3d 1304 (N.D.1972) (consultation in presence of others not related to the business in hand, preparation of deeds); People v. Poulin, 27 Cal.App.3d 54, 103 Cal.Rptr. 623 (1972) (communication in court in presence and within hearing of bailiff); Dobbins v. State, 483 P.2d 255, 260 (Wyo.1971) (trial upon a charge of sale of marijuana to a minor; defendant's statement to his counsel while a witness was testifying overheard by another witness sitting 12 feet away. Held: not privileged—the witness who heard defendant's statement may testify regarding it). The fact, however, that the conversation took place in a public place, e.g. a restaurant, (or, as in the principal case, in the first class section of an airplane), does not, by itself, suggest an absence of an expectation of confidentiality, if the parties were talking in tones not likely to be overheard.

Although listening in to cellular telephone calls is a criminal violation, it is apparently also quite easy to accomplish. Should the privilege be applicable to conversations between the attorney and the client over a cellular phone?

5. It seems obvious that a client instructing his lawyer to reveal the content of a specified communication either forestalls any privilege or else destroys it. Franzen v. Shenk, 192 Cal. 572, 584, 607, 221 P. 932, 937, 946 (1924) (threats to be told to parent of proposed victims); Dickerson v. Dickerson, 322 Ill. 492, 153 N.E. 740 (1926) (secrecy to end with client's life); United States v. McDonald, 313 F.2d 832, 835 (2d Cir.1963) (no privilege as to real estate transaction closing statements intended to be revealed to other parties); State v. Dombrowski, 171 N.W.2d 349 (Wis.1969) (location of dead body); People v. Werhollick, 45 Ill.2d 459, 259 N.E.2d 265 (1970) (offer to become prosecution witness); Esposito v. United States, 436 F.2d 603 (9th Cir.1970) (matter to be repeated in court on the day following the communication).

6. How does the rule of confidentiality established in professional ethics compare with that given effect under the attorney-client privilege? See the Comment to Rule 1.6, ABA, Model Rules of Professional Conduct (1983): "The confidentiality rule applies not merely to matters communicated in confidence by the client but also to all information relating to the representation, whatever its source." See also Doe v. A Corporation, 709 F.2d 1043, 1046 (5th Cir.1983).

7. As the principal case indicates, a communication from the attorney to the client, as well as from the client to the attorney, may be covered by the privilege. The principal case sets forth the basic doctrine. Consider the following cases involving related issues:

a) In re Grand Jury Testimony of Attorney X, 621 F.Supp. 590 (E.D.N.Y. 1985): A federal grand jury obtained evidence that attorney's client was involved in a fraud. Subsequently, the government, suspecting that the client had criminally obstructed the fraud investigation, sought to compel the attorney to testify before the grand jury: a) whether he had been told by a third party that his client's name had been mentioned in the fraud investigation; and b) whether he had informed his client of this fact. Rejecting the claim that the information sought was protected by the attorney-client privilege, the court stated:

> [A] communication from an attorney to his client is privileged if it would reveal confidential information communicated by the client to the lawyer, ... or if it consists of legal advice given to the client....
>
> The information about the grand jury investigation that the attorney obtained from a third person and relayed to his client is clearly not confidential. Where an attorney is a mere conduit the client may not invoke the privilege....
>
> The ... [client] argues that although the information sought may not be confidential its disclosure would permit inferences as to confidential matters such as the concerns of his client and the reasons for his seeking representation. However, the court is satisfied by the facts stated in the government's in camera affidavit that these concerns are no longer, if they ever were, confidential. Id. at 592.

b) United States v. Woodruff, 383 F.Supp. 696 (E.D.Pa.1974): The defendant free on bail did not appear for trial. In pursuit of a bail jumping charge, the government sought the testimony of the defendant's counsel, a public defender, as to whether he had advised his client of the time and place of trial and whether his client had acknowledged that he understood. The court held the attorney-client privilege inapplicable since the communications were not made with the purpose of securing legal advice nor were they incidental to or intertwined with the legal problem of the defendant. The court went on to say,

> Such communications are non-legal in nature. Counsel is simply performing a notice function.... For this reason, and the fact that any communication from the attorney to the client in this regard was based on facts obtained by the attorney from a source other than his client, we hold that the transmission to defendant from the attorney of the fact of the time of trial is not privileged. Id. at 698.

c) United States v. Ramirez, 608 F.2d 1261 (9th Cir.1979): Defendant asked a prosecution witness's counsel whether he had advised the witness (who was also under indictment) of the possibility of a misdemeanor disposition or dismissal in exchange for his cooperation with the government. In the text of its opinion, the applicability of the attorney-client privilege was assumed, but the court indicated in a footnote that there was a substantial question whether the privilege applied in this situation. There is a special interest in disclosing leniency agreements and negotiations between the government and its witnesses. See Giglio v. United States, 405 U.S. 150 (1972); Napue v. Illinois, 360 U.S. 264 (1959). How does this fact bear on the applicability of the privilege? Does the attorney-client privilege apply to the advice given by a lawyer to his client concerning his right not to testify? See United States v. Arthur, 602 F.2d 660 (4th Cir.1979).

d) Compare with the foregoing and with the principal case, In re Navarro, 93 Cal.App.3d 325, 155 Cal.Rptr. 522 (1979): Attorney was subpoenaed as a witness and asked whether she had shown a police report to her defendant-client. Whether the defendant-client had seen the arrest report was an important element in the prosecution's case since if the defendant was aware of the contents of the arrest report, it provided a motive for the murder with which the defendant was charged. Held: The showing of the arrest report to the client was a communication to the client and was privileged. The court cited in support of its decision the opinion of the California Supreme Court in In re Jordan, 12 Cal.3d 575, 116 Cal.Rptr. 371 (1974) which held privileged the sending of draft pleadings and a photocopy of an unreported decision to a prison inmate-client.

Was it significant to the decision in In re Navarro, supra that section 952 of the California Evidence Code provides:

> As used in this article, "confidential communication between client and lawyer" means information transmitted between a client and his lawyer in the course of that relationship ... and includes a legal opinion formed and the advice given by the lawyer....

8. The date set for a person's trial is a matter of public record. Is this fact relevant to the issue in Woodruff, supra note 7b. Can the communication of public record information be deemed a confidential communication from the attorney to the client? Compare United States v. Cochran, 546 F.2d 27 (5th Cir.1977) where the client's former attorney testified that defendant had in an earlier case freely and voluntarily pleaded guilty to a burglary charge and had been advised by the judge at the time as to the possible maximum sentence for the crime to which he was pleading guilty. The court rejected the application of the attorney-client privilege, stating: "[T]he attorney only testified to matters of public record or to matters which took place in open court." The court went on to state (at n. 5): "The mere appearance of an attorney testifying against a former client, even as to matters of public record, is distasteful and should only be used in rare instances." Id. at 546 F.2d 27, 29.

9. In Carl v. Children's Hospital, 657 A.2d 286 (D.C.App.1995) (reh. en banc granted, 665 A.2d 650 (1995)), in a wrongful discharge case, the plaintiff attempted to compel answers to questions regarding whether counsel had communicated to the employer at a meeting the fact that plaintiff had given expert testimony against the employer in a previous matter—which she alleged as the real reason for her discharge. The court held the communications privileged, stating:

> Here ... Murrays's uncontradicted affidavit established that the purpose of the meeting was to obtain legal advice concerning ... [plaintiff's] employment and that everyone present at the meeting participated in the discussion. During these communications, ... [the employer's] management relayed confidential information to the in-house counsel, and the attorneys, in giving legal advice, relied upon information they had received from their client and other sources including their previous experiences, backgrounds, and prior professional relationship with the client. Whatever the attorneys conveyed to ... [the employer] was intimately related to the information received from the client and was therefore privileged.

What is the impact of the fact that at the same time the attorney may have reported to the client about the key fact (that is, the fact that plaintiff had testified against the employer in a previous matter), the employer-client also communicated confidentially regarding other matters? Is it sufficient that the attorney demonstrates that the key communication derived from third party information is "inextricably intertwined with confidential communications from the client?" Is this conclusion consistent with the position taken by Judge Ginsburg in the principal case?

10. May an attorney testify as to his observations of the client's mental condition at the time of their consultation? as to whether client was responsive? whether he was logical in conversation or reasoning? Suppose that the attorney testified that his client admitted to him that he had lied to the examining psychiatrist in the hope that the latter would form an opinion that the client had been insane at the time he committed the homicide. Darrow v. Gunn, 594 F.2d 767 (9th Cir.), cert. denied, 444 U.S. 849 (1979) holds that to the extent that the client's former attorney's testimony was based on his observations of the client, his appearance, demeanor and so on, the client cannot claim the protection of the privilege.

11. A letter from the client to her attorney may be admitted into evidence for the limited purpose of comparing the type style on the letter with the type style of a letter the defendant is charged with having forged.

> [T]he attorney-client privilege protects only the substance of the communication and not its form.... No testimony was offered relating to the content of the letter itself. While it is true that the jury may have been able to observe the content of the letter by reading it when comparing the similarity in type style, we have reviewed the content of this letter and note that the 1978 letter does not relate to any of the crimes defendant is presently charged with....

United States v. Weger, 709 F.2d 1151 (7th Cir.1983).

12. The privilege assumes the existence or at least potential existence of the attorney-client relationship. Protection may arise, however, at the threshold even if that threshold, approached in good faith, is not crossed. Keir v. State, 11 So.2d 886 (Fla.1943) (inquiries by letter from potential client to attorney who was not retained).

13. The privilege attaches to the confidential communications between client and attorney but not to the facts or events that are the subject of such communications. Consider whether the privilege applies in the following cases, in each of which the client has communicated in confidence to his attorney regarding event X:

a) Client on the stand is asked questions regarding event X.

b) Client on the stand is asked questions about what he said to his attorney about event X; about what his attorney said to him in response.

c) Client on the stand volunteers information about his conversations with his attorney regarding event X. Has he waived his privilege?

d) Client on the stand volunteers information about event X. Has he waived his privilege? Compare the waiver by partial disclosure in connection with the privilege against self-incrimination, supra p. 1327.

e) Client is granted immunity in connection with his testimony regarding event X. Does the grant of immunity affect his attorney-client privilege? See People v. Lynch, 23 N.Y.2d 262, 296 N.Y.S.2d 327, 244 N.E.2d 29 (1968).

14. Is the mere fact that the statement was overheard sufficient to defeat confidentiality? See, e.g. Dobbins v. State, supra note 4: "It is academic that a confidential communication between an attorney and his client overheard by a third person is not privileged." Also see Clark v. State, infra p. 1473. The older rule is reflected in Wigmore's view that an eavesdropper could testify to otherwise privileged conversations. 8 Wigmore on Evidence 2326 (McNaughton rev. 1961). Under the modern codes, however, see proposed Federal Rule 503(b) and California Evidence Code 954, the attorney-client privilege can be invoked to bar the eavesdropper from testifying as to an overheard communication that otherwise falls under the privilege. Should the test be whether the attorney and the client took reasonable steps to maintain confidentiality and whether the overhearing was or was not reasonably foreseeable?

In this connection, suppose that copies of confidential letters from the client to the lawyer are retrieved by an opposing party from a trash bin outside of the client's office where they have been deposited by a member of the client's staff. May they be introduced into evidence? See Suburban Sew 'N Sweep, Inc. v. Swiss–Bernina, Inc., 91 F.R.D. 254 (N.D.Ill.1981). Is it reasonable to expect attorneys to shred all documents that are confidential before throwing them away? How will you handle this issue in your own practice?

Consider also the increasing use of e-mail to communicate in business and legal affairs. Security codes are in use, but determined hackers may be able to break into any system without ever coming near to the attorney's office. Further, consider the fact that even when you delete e-mail messages, they may still be retrievable. The technology may be moving in the direction of paperless office communication systems. What would be the implications of that kind of development?

15. Should the fact-finder be permitted to draw a negative inference from the invocation of the attorney-client privilege? See Bartel, Drawing Negative Inferences Upon a Claim of the Attorney–Client Privilege, 60 Brooklyn L.Rev. 1355 (1995).

16. The principal case also involved the question of whether the lower court's decision was immediately appealable. Regarding that issue, Judge Ginsburg stated:

It is the main rule that an order in an ongoing proceeding compelling testimony or documentary production is not immediately appealable; to obtain instant appellate review, the party to whom the command is addressed must refuse to respond and submit to a contempt citation. In Perlman v. United States, 247 U.S. 7, 38 S.Ct. 417, 62 L.Ed. 950 (1918), the Supreme Court indicated an exception to the main rule; the Company in this case dominantly relies on the Perlman exception.

In Perlman, a United States Attorney obtained a court order for the production before a grand jury of exhibits deposited with a district court clerk in prior litigation. Perlman alleged that the deposited materials belonged to him and moved to block their presentation to the grand jury. He asserted that government use of the exhibits would violate his rights under the Fourth and Fifth Amendments. The court clerk had no interest in resisting production and could not be expected to stand in contempt to aid Perlman. The district court denied Perlman's motion. The Supreme Court declared that ruling immediately appealable. Absent instant review, the Court said, Perlman would be "powerless to avert the mischief of the order." 247 U.S. at 13. n5.

Following High Court instruction, see United States v. Ryan, 402 U.S. 530, 533, 91 S.Ct. 1580, 29 L.Ed.2d 85 (1971), we have confined the Perlman exception to situations in which the contempt route to instant appellate review is unavailable. In re Sealed Case, 211 U.S. App.D.C. 68, 655 F.2d 1298 (D.C.Cir.1981). [The court here noted in a footnote that the circuit's views on this issue are not uniform, some circuits, for example, being willing to permit an immediate appeal without inquiry as to whether the attorney will stand in contempt.] C stated under oath that if the district court ordered his testimony he would not stand in contempt to permit an immediate appeal from the district court's ruling. The government acknowledges that this is the atypical case in which "the circumstances make it unlikely that a former attorney will stand in contempt." C is no longer in the Company's employ; he has no work product to protect; he is not likely to view the Company as an object of his continuing devotion.

[The court in a footnote here noted: The government urges that the Company "may obtain full and appropriate appellate review in the event that it is convicted with the use of this testimony or its fruits." Brief for the Government at 17. The purpose of the attorney-client privilege, however, is to protect the client's confidences. As the Company observes, "once the cat is out of the bag, it cannot be put back in."]

Because it is at least "unlikely that [C] would risk a contempt citation in order to allow immediate review of [the Company's] claim of privilege," we hold this case within the limited class to which Perlman applies, and therefore turn to the attorney-client privilege issues tendered for review.

17. The privilege being personal, its holder may waive the protection and testify adversely, or permit testimony adverse, to the interests of a non-holder. Suppose the holder, called to testify against a non-holder, claims privilege and the trial judge incorrectly overrules the claim with the holder yielding and giving the harmful testimony. Has the non-holder any legal recourse?

Alternatively, suppose the non-holder calls to testify for him a witness who claims privilege, and the trial judge incorrectly sustains the claim. What then? The decisions are few and in conflict probably because either the client or the attorney is usually the witness, and where the foundation for the privilege is established, it is generally honored and because the bar agrees with the statement of the court in Chicago Great Western Railway Co. v. McCaffrey, 160 N.W. 818 (Iowa1917), that when the attorney is called as a witness it is his duty to claim the privilege unless the client has waived it.

For cases holding that a party cannot take advantage of the privilege of a witness, see State v. Madden, 201 N.W. 297 (Minn.1924); State v. Dunkley, 39 P.2d 1097 (Utah1935). The Texas court, taking the position that the privilege is that of the client and that the client if a party has a complete and adequate remedy by appeal from an erroneous ruling, has held that an attorney who refuses to obey the trial judge's order to divulge the communication is punishable for contempt. Ex parte Lipscomb, 239 S.W. 1101 (Tex.1922). Cf. Dike v. Dike, 448 P.2d 490 (Wash.1968) (abuse of discretion to hold the attorney in contempt, except perhaps in extreme case). Also see §§ 953–955, 914, 918–919, California Evidence Code and Rule 512 of the proposed Fed.R.Evid.

C.   THE IDENTITY OF THE CLIENT, FEE INFORMATION AND RELATED MATTERS

1.   IN GENERAL

Over the past two decades, the federal government has directed numerous subpoenas to lawyers to testify or produce documents before a grand jury in order to obtain information regarding a client's identity or fees paid to the attorney. The government may obtain such subpoenas in order to obtain disclosure of the identity of an undisclosed client or client fee information that can be used as a lead to obtain further evidence of conspiratorial involvement to be used against a targeted suspect or as a lead to other persons involved in the group criminality under investigation. Such information may also be useful to identify a taxpayer who has made an anonymous tax payment through his attorney, or in a prosecution of the attorney to whom the subpoena is directed under federal money laundering provisions, or in connection with an effort to forfeit the attorney's fee to the government. See infra, p. 1426.

The cases in this area can be divided among the benefactor cases,i.e. where the government seeks the identity of a person who has paid a co-conspirator's legal fees; the "tax" cases,i.e. where the government seeks the client's fee arrangements as evidence of unexplained wealth or seeks to learn the client's identity in order to link the client to an already documented tax offense; and the "good samaritan" cases,i.e. where the government seeks the identity of a client who, anonymously, via the attorney, has volunteered information regarding another person's crimes, and the government wishes to contact the client for more information or to arrange to have him or her testify in court. See Note, Benefactor Defense Before the Grand Jury: The Legal Advice and Incrimination Theories of the Attorney Client Privilege, 6 Cardozo Law Rev. 537, 539 (1985).

The extensive use of such subpoenas has precipitated a continuing struggle, involving the U.S Department of Justice, the organized bar and the courts, as reflected in the case law and the scholarly and bar literature, regarding the permissibility and appropriateness of such practices.

Some government spokespersons have denied that attorneys were being targeted or even that there was an increase in the number of subpoenas directed to attorneys. See e.g. Nat.Law Journal. Dec. 9, 1985, p. 3; BNA, 38 Crim.L.Rep. 2199 (1985). Other government lawyers have contended that subpoenas to attorneys were being used mainly to investigate large criminal organizations and that they were needed to investigate certain types of cases. Ibid.

Early in this period, major bar organizations undertook studies and made recommendations regarding the practice, including the American Bar Association and the Association of the Bar of the City of New York. See e.g. Report, Committee on Criminal Advocacy, Association of the Bar of the City of New York, The Issuance of Subpoenas Upon Lawyers in Criminal Cases by State and Federal Prosecutors: A Call for Immediate Remedial Action (1985). Also see BNA, 38 Crim.L.Rep. 2386 (1986); BNA, 38 Crim.L.Rep. 2199 (1985).

In 1985, guidelines for the issuance of grand jury subpoenas used to obtain information from attorneys regarding clients were incorporated into the U.S. Attorneys' Manual (sec. 9–2.161(a)). Under the guidelines, before such a subpoena can be issued, a determination must be made by the Assistant Attorney General in charge of the Criminal Division that the information sought is not protected by a valid claim of privilege; is unavailable from other sources; is reasonably needed for the successful completion of the investigation or prosecution; is narrowly drawn; and that the need for the information outweighs the potential adverse effects on the attorney-client relationship, including the risk that the attorney will be disqualified. The Guidelines also contain the usual provision that they are solely for the purpose of internal Department of Justice guidance and may not be relied upon to create any rights enforceable at law in any matter civil or criminal. Also see BNA, 38 Crim. L.Rep. 3001 (1985).

Adoption of the guidelines apparently did little to reduce the number of subpoenas being sought. One United States Court of Appeals noted that in the District of Massachusetts alone, from 50 to 100 attorney subpoenas per year were served from 1983 through 1986. Those figures were compared with the criminal case load in the district during the same period (ranging from 306 to 463 cases filed per year) and it was concluded that the subpoena-of-attorney issue "could very well be present" in a "not ... insignificant proportion" of the cases. United States v. Klubock, 832 F.2d 664 (1st Cir.1987). Department of Justice statistics indicated that from October 1988 through September, 1989, the Department received 410 requests from federal prosecutors to subpoena 649 attorneys; during a similar period in 1987–88, the Department received 363 requests to subpoena 523 attorneys. (cited in Mckenna, A Prosecutor's Reconsideration of Rule 3.10, 53 U. Pitt. L. Rev. 489, 491 (1992).

The organized bar's principal response to these developments has been to develop ethical rules addressing the issue. After some states had adopted rules on the subject, in 1991, the American Bar Association incorporated into its Model Rules of Professional Conduct Rule 3.8(f), which provided, inter alia, that "the prosecutor in a criminal case shall ... not subpoena a lawyer in a grand jury or other criminal proceeding to present evidence about a past or present client unless ... the prosecutor obtains prior judicial approval after an opportunity for an adversarial proceeding," (reprinted in 6 Laws. Man. on Prof. Conduct (ABA/BNA25, 26 (Feb. 28, 1990)).

In response, the government mounted a series of judicial challenges directed against the state and United States district court rules that incorporated provisions similar to Rule 3.8(f). The results have been mixed. In the earliest decision on the issue, United States v. Klubock, 832 F.2d 664 (1st Cir.1987), the First Circuit sitting en banc affirmed, by an equally divided court, a decision sustaining the power of the United States District Court for Massachusetts to adopt a local rule similar to 3.8(f).

Subsequently, in Whitehouse v. United States District Court for the District of Rhode Island, 53 F.3d 1349 (1st Cir.1995), the First Circuit held that a rule similar to 3.8(f) that was initially promulgated by the Rhode Island Supreme Court and then incorporated by the United States District Court for Rhode Island into its local rules was within the power of the court to adopt and was not inconsistent with or preempted by Rule 17 and Rule 57 of the Federal Rules of Criminal Procedure. (Rule 17 contains general provisions for the issuance of subpoenas and Rule 57 deals with the rulemaking authority of the District Courts).

The court in Whitehouse expressly rejected the position of the Third Circuit in Baylson v. Disciplinary Bd. of the Supreme Court of Pennsylvania, 975 F.2d 102 (3d Cir.1992), cert. denied 507 U.S. 984 (1993), holding that a rule similar to 3.8(f) adopted by the Supreme Court of Pennsylvania was invalid as in conflict with Rules 17 and 57.

Faced with a similar provision the Tenth Circuit, in United States v. Colorado Supreme Court, 87 F.3d 1161 (10th Cir.1996), ruled that the United States has standing to challenge the application to federal prosecutors of Colorado ethics rules similar to 3.8(f).

In the wake of the foregoing litigation, the ABA repealed subsection (f) of Rule 3.8 which provided for prior judicial approval for attorney subpoenas. Meanwhile, in addition to the states already mentioned, rules similar to 3.8(f) have been adopted in Tennessee (Tenn. Ct. C.P.R. & DR 7–103(C)) and Virginia (Va. Sup. Ct. R. 3A:12(a)), while New York, Illinois and the District of Columbia are reported to have considered and rejected such a rule. See 6 Laws. Man.on Prof. Conduct (ABA/BNA) 28, 29, 53, 55, 172, 175.

See generally, Stern & Hoffman, Privileged Informers,: The Attorney Subpoena Problem and a Proposal for Reform, 136 U.Pa. L. Rev. 1783 (1988); Zacharias, A Critical Look at Rules Governing Grand Jury Subpoenas of Attorneys, 76 Minn.L.Rev. 917 (1992); Cramton & Udell, State Ethics Rules and Federal Prosecutors: The Controversies over the Anti–Contact and Subpoena Rules, 53 U.Pitt. L.Rev. 357 (1992); Bowman, A Bludgeon by Any Other Name: The Misuse of "Ethical Rules" against Prosecutors to Control the Law of the State, 9 Geo. J. Legal Ethics 665 (1996).

While this controversy has continued, decisions testing the application of the attorney-client privilege to the client information being sought have continued to be handed down. Consider whether you can observe any influence of the controversy on the trend of decisions applying the attorney-client privilege in such matters.

Ralls v. United States

United States Court of Appeals, Ninth Circuit, 1995.
52 F.3d 223.

■ Before ALDISERT, CHOY, SCHROEDER, CIRCUIT JUDGES.

■ CHOY, CIRCUIT JUDGE.

Stephen Ralls, Esq. ("Ralls"), a criminal defense attorney, appeals the district court's order denying in part his motion to quash a grand jury subpoena which required him to provide information regarding a client/fee-payer. Ralls also appeals from the district court's order holding him in contempt for failure to provide information pursuant to court orders.

Upon examination of Ralls' sealed affidavit, we find that the client/fee-payer's identity and the fee arrangements are inextricably linked to privileged communications and are therefore privileged. Having jurisdiction, we reverse the district court's partial denial of Ralls' motion to quash the grand jury subpoena, and we order that the subpoena be quashed in its entirety on the basis of attorney-client privilege. Furthermore, we reverse the district court's order holding Ralls in contempt for failing to comply with the subpoena.

Ralls was paid by a client/fee-payer to represent Philip Bonnette ("Bonnette") at his initial court appearance and at his detention hearing. Bonnette was arrested with another individual named Victor Tarrazon–Orduno ("Tarrazon") in connection with their attempt to transport approximately 300 pounds of cocaine from Arizona to California. The Government later issued a grand jury subpoena to Ralls, seeking to discover the name of the person who hired Ralls, the amount of money paid, method of payment, the existence of any retainer agreement, and conversations with the fee-payer. Ralls moved to quash the subpoena on November 22, 1993. The district court ordered Ralls to testify regarding the fee-payer's identity and the fee arrangements, but concluded that all conversations between Ralls and the fee-payer were privileged.

II

[W]e review the district court's decision not to quash a grand jury subpoena for abuse of discretion. The party asserting the attorney-client privilege has the burden of establishing the relationship and the privileged nature of the communication. Whether the party met these requirements is a mixed question of law and fact which is reviewed de novo. The district court's factual findings are reviewed for clear error.

III

Generally, the attorney-client privilege does not safeguard against the disclosure of either the identity of the fee-payer or the fee arrangement. This is so because the attorney-client privilege applies only to confidential professional communications, and the payment of fees is usually incidental to the attorney-client relationship. Matter of Grand Jury Proceeding (Cherney), 898 F.2d 565, 567 (7th Cir. 1990). However, a narrow exception to the general rule of disclosure exists.

An attorney may invoke the privilege to protect the identity of a client or information regarding a client's fee arrangements if disclosure would "convey information which ordinarily would be conceded to be part of the usual privileged communication between attorney and client." United States v. Horn, 976 F.2d 1314, 1317 (9th Cir.1992) (quoting Baird v. Koerner, 279 F.2d 623, 632 (9th Cir.1960)).

The application of the privilege is not triggered by the fact that the disclosure of the fee-payer's identity and the fee arrangements may incriminate the fee-payer. Id. Rather, the privilege is invoked where disclosure of the fee-payer/client identity and the fee information would infringe upon a privileged communication. In re Osterhoudt, 722 F.2d 591, 593–94 (9th Cir.1983).

The Fifth Circuit has held that "if the disclosure of the client's identity will also reveal the confidential purpose for which he consulted an attorney, we protect both the confidential communication and the client's identity as privileged." In re Grand Jury Subpoena (Deguerin), 926 F.2d 1423, 1431 (5th Cir.), cert. denied, 499 U.S. 959 (1991). Likewise, the Seventh Circuit has stated, "[It is a] well-supported proposition that where disclosure of the unknown client would, in effect, reveal the client's motive for seeking legal advice, the privilege precludes disclosure." Cherney, 898 F.2d at 569. Both the DeGuerin and Cherney courts found significant the fact that the fee-payers had already admitted, to the subpoenaed attorneys, their involvement in the crime for which the defendants had been charged.

In contrast, the attorney-client relationship does not exist where the attorney acts as a mere conduit for the transfer of money. In Vingelli v. United States Drug Enforcement Agency, 992 F.2d 449 (2d Cir. 1993), the client had hired an attorney to transmit funds to another attorney to represent a person facing drug charges. Despite the fact that the client sought legal advice regarding the ramifications of having contacts with and lending money to the criminal defendant, the Second Circuit held that disclosure of the fee-payer's identity does not necessarily reveal a confidential communication. In refusing to apply the attorney-client privilege, the Second Circuit stated:

> The rule governing the unprivileged nature of client identification implicitly accepts the fact that a client might retain or consult an attorney for numerous reasons. Thus, the fact that disclosure of [the client/fee-payer's identity] might suggest the possibility of wrongdoing on his or her part does not affect analysis of whether disclosure would reveal a confidential communication.

Vingelli, 992 F.2d at 453.

The facts of this case are more similar to Cherney and DeGuerin than Vingelli because Ralls has revealed through the sealed affidavit that the fee-payer specifically discussed his or her own criminal liability in connection with the same crime for which Bonnette was charged. See Cherney, 898 F.2d at 568; see also DeGuerin, 926 F.2d at 1432.

The district court failed to apply the correct test which is whether the fee-payer's identity and the fee arrangements are so intertwined with confidential communications that revealing either the identity or the arrangements would be tantamount to revealing a privileged communication.

An examination of Ralls' sealed affidavit, specifically paragraphs 5, 6, 10, 11, and 12, leaves no doubt that the fee arrangements and the fee-payer's identity are inextricably intertwined with confidential communications and fall within the attorney-client privilege. The fee-payer sought Ralls' advice regarding his involvement in the crime for which Bonnette was arrested. Further, the fee-payer paid for Bonnette's legal fees in the very same matter which gave rise to the attorney-client relationship. "In effect, therefore, disclosure of the [fee-payer's] identity would expose the substance of a confidential communication between the attorney and the [fee-payer]." Cherney, 898 F.2d at 568.

Where the district court "has failed to make a finding because of an erroneous view of the law, the usual rule is that there should be a remand for further proceedings.... unless the record permits only one resolution of the factual issue." Pullman–Standard v. Swint, 456 U.S. 273, 291–92, 102 S.Ct. 1781, 1791–92, 72 L.Ed.2d 66 (1982). Here, the facts are not in dispute, and the question to be resolved is one of mixed law and fact which is reviewed de novo. Hirsch, 803 F.2d at 496. We find that the fee-payer's identity and the fee arrangements are so intertwined with attorney-client communications that they are therefore privileged. In the interest of judicial economy, we rule that the subpoena be quashed in its entirety rather than remanding the matter to the district court.

The Government argues that there was a clear conflict of interest in Ralls' representation of both Bonnette and the fee-payer and argues that this conflict prevented the formation of an attorney-client relationship between the fee-payer and Ralls. The Government's argument is not persuasive. First, there is no evidence to indicate the existence of an actual conflict of interest. We take notice of the fact that Ralls' representation of Bonnette was limited to Bonnette's initial appearance and his detention hearing. Even if an actual conflict of interest exists, however, the proper course of action for the district court is to bar Ralls from representation.

Because we find in favor of Ralls, we do not address Ralls' two alternative arguments based upon the "last link"[1] and the "least intrusive means"[2] doctrines.

IV

We affirm the district court's decision to quash the subpoena pertaining to conversations between Ralls and the fee-payer and reverse the district court's decision not to quash the remainder of the subpoena. Ralls' sealed affidavit clearly establishes that he had an attorney-client relationship with the fee-payer and that the identity of the fee-payer and the fee arrangements are inextricably intertwined with privileged communications. Therefore, the fee information is privileged, and Ralls cannot be forced to testify regarding such information. We order that the grand jury subpoena be quashed in its entirety and reverse the district court's order holding Ralls in contempt.

NOTES

1. A foundational case on the issue of whether the client's identity falls within the attorney client privilege is Baird v. Koerner, 279 F.2d 623 (9th Cir.1960). Baird is summarized in the court's opinion in In the Matter of Witnesses Before the Special March 1980 Grand Jury: Appeal of United States, 729 F.2d 489 (7th Cir.1984) as follows:

> In Baird, an attorney had sent a check to the IRS on behalf of unnamed clients, and the IRS sought to compel him to reveal his clients' identities. The Ninth Circuit held that their identities were privileged. The court noted that disclosure of a client's identity "may well be the link that could form the chain of testimony necessary to convict an individual of a federal crime." 279 F.2d at 633. However, the court's opinion also suggests that the decision was based upon the fact that so much information had already

1. The "last link" doctrine prevents an attorney from disclosing a client's identity if disclosure would be the final step in the chain of evidence to indict or prosecute that client. United States v. Gray, 876 F.2d 1411, 1415–16 (9th Cir.1989), cert. denied, 495 U.S. 930, 110 S.Ct. 2168, 109 L.Ed.2d 497 (1990). This court has recognized the "last link" doctrine as it relates to fee information. See Horn, 976 F.2d at 1317; Alexiou v. United States, 39 F.3d 973, 976 (9th Cir.1994); Lahodny v. United States, 695 F.2d 363, 365 (9th Cir.1982). However, the application of the "last link" doctrine has been limited to situations where disclosure of the fee-payer's identity would be tantamount to disclosure of a privileged communication. See Gray, 876 F.2d at 1416; Alexiou, 39 F.3d at 976–77 (the court analyzed whether the communication was privileged in order to determine that the last link exception did not apply). Therefore, the decision of whether the last link doctrine applies turns on the court's ruling on whether the attorney-client privilege prevents the disclosure of the fee-payer's identity and fee arrangements.

2. The "least intrusive means" doctrine requires the Government to first exhaust all of its investigatory powers before "[it is] permitted to compel witness-attorneys to testify before a grand jury regarding matters which could be considered to be protected by the attorney-client privilege." In re Witness–Attorney Before Grand Jury No. 83–1, 613 F.Supp. 394, 398 (S.D.Fla.1984). The "least intrusive means" doctrine does not have application in the Ninth Circuit. In United States v. Perry, 857 F.2d 1346, 1348 (9th Cir.1988), this court firmly refused to require the Government to make a pre-indictment, preliminary showing of need before issuing a grand jury subpoena to an attorney-witness. Likewise, in In re Grand Jury Proceeding (Schofield), 721 F.2d 1221, 1222 (9th Cir. 1983), this court ruled that the Government need not make a preliminary showing of legitimate need and relevance before issuing a subpoena to an attorney who is representing the target of a grand jury investigation.

been disclosed that revelation of the clients' identities would have disclosed confidential communications such as their concern about their tax returns. In its discussion of the attorney-client privilege, the court emphasized that the privilege protects "confidential communications," including the client's motive for consulting the attorney. See 279 F.2d at 629–32. The court's statement of the law embodies the confidential communication rationale for the privilege:

If the identification of the client conveys information which ordinarily would be conceded to be part of the usual privileged communication between attorney and client, then the privilege should extend to such identification in the absence of other factors.

279 F.2d at 632. Thus in Baird, disclosure of the clients' identities would have revealed, under the circumstances, confidential communications between clients and their attorney, including the clients' motivations for seeking legal advice.

2. The circuits have generally been moving away from an incrimination test for determining whether the identity of the client is covered by the privilege. Thus, for example, see In the Matter of Witnesses, etc. supra note 1:

In addition, subsequent decisions of the Fifth and Ninth Circuits cast substantial doubt on whether those courts adhere to the incrimination rationale for these exceptions to the privilege. . . .

In the recent case of In re Osterhoudt, 722 F.2d 591 (9th Cir.1983), the Ninth Circuit clearly rejected the incrimination rationale and held that fee information about a known client was not privileged. The court's per curiam opinion does not disagree with the results in prior cases, but it criticizes other cases for having "mistakenly formulated the exception not in terms of the principle itself, but rather in terms of this example of circumstances in which the principle is likely to apply." 722 F.2d at 593. We agree. While the exception is often discussed in terms of whether the information would incriminate the client, the exception is better understood in terms of confidential communications. The client's identity or fee arrangements may be privileged where so much is already known that the identity or fees would reveal the client's confidential communication that he or she may, for example, have been involved in specific criminal conduct. The fact that the information is incriminating may provide all parties with their motives to seek its disclosure or protection; however, the application of the privilege turns not upon incrimination per se but upon whether disclosure would in effect reveal information which has been confidentially communicated.

Decisions in other circuits support our view of the privilege. . . .

3. In the principal case, the court treats as significant the fact that "[t]he feepayer sought Rall's advice regarding his involvement in the crime for which Bonnette was arrested" and that "the fee-payer paid for Bonnette's legal fees in the very same matter which gave rise to the attorney-client relationship." Do these facts "leave no doubt that the fee arrangements and the fee-payer's identity are inextricably intertwined with confidential communications"? Is there any other basis for the conclusion of "intertwinedness"?

In Baird, supra note 1, it was clear from the circumstances why the anonymous client had consulted the attorney—for advice about tax matters. In the principal case, was the reason why the unidentified client consulted the attorney clear from the circumstances, or did it only become clear from the attorney's sealed affidavit? Is this a significant distinction if the question is whether "disclosure of the [feepayer's] identity would expose the substance of a confidential communication between the attorney and the [feepayer]"? In the principal case, would "disclosure of the unknown client . . ., in effect, reveal the client's motive for seeking legal advice"?

4. Compare with the principal case:

a) The government concedes on oral argument that an attorney-client relationship existed between the fee-payer and the attorney prior to the attorney's representation of the second client (whose fees were paid by the fee-payer) and that the purpose for which the fee-payer sought advice was his involvement in the underlying drug conspiracy. See In the matter of Grand Jury Proceeding (Cherney), 898 F.2d 565 (7th Cir. 1990).

b) The government asserts that it already knows the fee-payer's incriminating motive for seeking legal advice so that disclosure of his identity will reveal nothing further. See In re Grand Jury Proceedings, 946 F.2d 746 (11th Cir.1991).

c) In arguing for application of the privilege to protect the fee-payer's identity, the attorney states that the fee-payer sought his advice concerning the same matter for which the second client had sought advice. See In re Grand Jury Subpoena for Attorney Representing Criminal Defendant Reyes–Requena II, 926 F.2d 1423 (5th Cir.1991).

In Reyes–Requena II, supra, the court stated:

> . . . [The attorney] rightly concluded that he could claim the privilege only by demonstrating a connection between Reyes–Requena's attorney's fees and the confidential purpose for which . . . [the fee-payer] consulted him concerning the very matter for which Reyes–Requena had been charged. We do not accept the Government's catch–22 argument that by revealing the information necessary to assert privilege, . . . [the attorney] destroyed the privilege.

Is this a sound application of the proposition that sometimes it is necessary to reveal privileged facts in order to demonstrate that the privilege is applicable?

5. A failure on the part of the attorney to assert that the fee-payer is a client of the attorney who sought legal advice defeats the claim that the identity of that person is protected by the attorney client privilege. In re Grand Jury Subpoenas, 906 F.2d 1485 (10th Cir.1990); In re Grand Jury Subpoena for Attorney Representing Criminal Defendant Reyes–Requena I, 913 F.2d 1118 (5th Cir.1990).

Compare Vingelli v. United States Drug Enforcement Agency, 992 F.2d 449 (2d Cir.1993), discussed in the principal case. In Vingelli, attorney No. 1 was given money by a client which he sent to attorney No. 2 to pay him for representing a person facing drug charges. Attorney No. 1 was called before the grand jury to identify the fee-payer client. He asserted that the fee-payer had consulted him in order to seek advice concerning the ramifications of lending $5,000 to a criminal defendant and having contacts with the defendant. Holding that the attorney client privilege did not protect the fee-payer client's identity nor information about the fee payment, the court stated:

> Revelation of the client's name—even in conjunction with the fee payment information—would not reveal the client's privilege communication. To the contrary, the disclosure of the client's name in this case would not compel a particular conclusion concerning that purpose. . . .

The unknown client may not have consulted appellant regarding any legal questions, He or she may have sought only to shield his or her identity from discovery while assisting a friend, relative, or associate with the payment of legal fees, or the client may have been enmeshed in a complex of legal problems, one aspect of which concerned the ... [second] client. The fact is that identifying the admittedly long-term client does not clarify the reason client sought counsel. As evidence by our present inability to divine the client's motive for seeking counsel, the purpose of the client's communication with the attorney would not become apparent merely upon disclosure of his or her identity.

With regard to the fee payment information.... [t]he information appellant is called upon to provide was narrowly defined, referring only to the source and transmission of the legal fees paid to attorney ... No. 2. Not only should such disclosure not inhibit open, full and frank discussion between appellant and his client concerning legal representation, but monetary transfers to attorney ... No. 2 via ... attorney No. 1 were obviously not made in order for the unknown client to obtain legal advice from attorney No. 1.

6. In In the Matter of Witnesses, etc. supra note 1, the court also stated: "As a general matter, information about a known client's fees appears far less likely to reveal confidential communications than would the revelation of an unknown client's identity." Should the issue of the client's identity and the fee arrangements have been treated separately in the principal case?

In In the Matter of Witnesses, etc. supra note 1, the court also noted:

[I]t does not necessarily follow that the grand jury may obtain "any and all records relating to moneys received" as demanded in the subpoenas. It is possible that records falling within the language of the subpoenas contain information which would reveal confidential communications between attorney and client. For example, billing sheets or time tickets which indicate the nature of documents prepared, issues researched or matters discussed could reveal the substance of confidential discussions between attorney and client.

7. Should the identity of the client and fee arrangements generally not be privileged because these matters do not involve a confidential communication, as suggested in the principal case, or because they are "preliminary, by their nature, establishing only the existence of the relation between client and counsel?" In re Grand Jury Subpoenas, United States v. Hirsch, 803 F.2d 493, 496 (9th Cir.1986).

8. In United States v. Pape, 144 F.2d 778 (2d Cir.1944), a majority of the court (Clark and Swann) sustained a ruling requiring an attorney to testify that the accused in a White Slave prosecution had earlier, in another city, retained him to represent both the woman and himself. Judge Learned Hand dissenting said:

Pape retained Buckley as his own lawyer at the same time that he retained him for the woman. I agree that his retainer of an attorney for himself involved no privileged communication; I have nothing to add to, or subtract from, what my brothers say on that. Moreover, it goes without saying that Pape's retainer of Buckley for the woman would not have been privileged, had he not retained him as his own attorney. On the other hand I attach no importance to the fact that he retained him in both capacities at the same time; the case stands as it would, if he had retained him for himself first. Yet if he had done that, when he told him to appear for her, I think it was a communication between attorney and client, a step in his own defence; it may have been also a step in hers but that, I submit, is irrelevant. That direction to his own attorney in his own interest was as much a privileged communication as any direction would have been, made in the course of preparing for a trial; as much, for example, as to tell one's attorney to interview a witness. That it was an important step in connecting him with the woman's prostitution, admits of no debate. Id. at 144 F.2d 778, 783–84.

9. In United States v. Strahl, 590 F.2d 10 (1st Cir.1978), cert. denied, 440 U.S. 918 (1979) the defendant had used a stolen Treasury note to pay his attorney for legal fees owed. The appellate court affirmed a ruling allowing the attorney to identify the defendant as the person who made the payment. Baird was distinguished on the ground that the payment related to past accumulated legal fees or to satisfy an unrelated debt. The court went on to say:

> We can find no furtherance of the policies behind the attorney-client privilege ... that would result from shielding the payment of an attorney with stolen goods, a fraudulent act as well as a convenient means of unloading highly incriminating evidence, possession of which was itself a crime.

10. Are there special reasons why the attorney-client privilege should not apply to information regarding the client's identity, legal fees and the like? Consider the following excerpt from In re Michaelson, 511 F.2d 882, 888–889 (9th Cir.), cert. denied, 421 U.S. 978 (1975):

> There are strong policy reasons why the existence of an attorney-client relationship, including the fee arrangement, should not be privileged.... The courts have inherent power to regulate the bar. The courts have the right to inquire into fee arrangements both to protect the client from excessive fees and to assist an attorney in collection of his fee, but more importantly, the court may inquire into fee arrangements to protect against suspected conflicts of interest. When an attorney is paid by some-one other than his client to represent that client there is a real and present danger that the attorney may in actuality be representing not the interests of his client, but those of his compensator. Not only does the client have a right to know who is paying his attorney, but the court retains the right to satisfy itself that no conflict exists and that the attorney is fulfilling his duty of loyalty to his client.

11. Is the identity of the lawyer consulted by the client protected by the privilege? Held: No. Howell v. Jones, 516 F.2d 53, 56 (5th Cir.1975); Goddard v. United States, 131 F.2d 220, 221 (5th Cir.1942).

12. Is an attorney sometimes able to invoke his own privilege against self-incrimination in refusing to answer questions seeking the identity of his client? See Matter of Grand Jury Empanelled, Feb. 14, 1978, 603 F.2d 469 (3d Cir.1979). In Reyes–Requena II, supra note 4c., the Justice Department authorized an application for use immunity for the attorney "thereby preventing ... [him] from asserting the privilege against self-incrimination as a reason for refusing to reveal the identity of the fee-payer and the amount paid." To be distinguished are cases where the attorney attempts to invoke the Fifth Amendment privilege of the client and instances where the attorney-client privilege is relied upon but where the applicability of that privilege turns on the presence of the client's privilege against self-incrimination. See supra, p. 1336 and infra, p. 1438.

13. Problems:

a) An attorney who specialized in tax law evaluated real estate partnerships for clients who wanted to invest for tax purposes. He charged a fee only to clients who invested and told each of them that the fee was deductible as a legal expense. The IRS contends that the fees are brokerage charges, and seeks through a summons to obtain the names of all of the clients who paid fees in connection with the acquisition of real estate partnership interests during a specified three year period. Should the summons be enforced over an objection based on the attorney-client privilege?

b) The government seeks to obtain information from a criminal attorney concerning any moneys transferred to him on behalf of eight individuals who have been indicted for violating the RICO statute. The information is sought as evidence of unexplained wealth, tax law violations, and payments of fees by benefactors. The attorney argues against enforcement of the subpoena on the ground that he is a prominent criminal law specialist and that the disclosure of the identity of a person consulting him would in effect divulge the communication, "I have a criminal problem." What result?

14. In re Grand Jury Matters, Appeal of United States, 751 F.2d 13 (1st Cir.1984): "Although grand jury subpoenas are issued in the name of the district court, they are issued pro forma and in blank to anyone requesting them without prior court approval or control. Fed.R.Crim.P. 17(a).... These subpoenas are in fact almost universally instrumentalities of the United States Attorney's office or of some other department of the executive branch.... Because this subpoena power may be abused, Fed.R.Crim.P. 17(c) gives the district court, on motion, the power to quash or modify a subpoena duces tecum if compliance would be unreasonable or oppressive." Id. at 16.

In In re Grand Jury Matters, Appeal of United States, supra, federal subpoenas seeking fee information were directed to attorneys who in state criminal prosecutions were serving as defense counsel for the same persons a federal grand jury was investigating. The attorneys argued that enforcement of the subpoenas would have a negative effect on their ability to defend their clients in the pending state criminal action and that forced disclosure would jeopardize the attorney-client relationship at a crucial point in defense preparations. The court of appeals ruled that the district court could reasonably have concluded that the timing of the subpoenas, i.e. while the attorneys were preparing for a major felony trial involving the same clients, made the subpoenas "unreasonable and oppressive." The court also stated:

> To call defense attorneys before the grand jury, in connection with an investigation of the same activities for which their clients were standing trial in state court, while the attorneys were preparing for this major felony trial, could be taken as a veiled threat, with such potential for harm to the state defendants and the defense bar as to require the government to show with some particularity why the grand jury's investigation required the execution of the subpoenas at this particularly sensitive moment....

> Appellees suggest a number of ways in which enforcement of these subpoenas during "the critical time between accusation and trial," could jeopardize not only their attorney-client relationships but also their clients' sixth amendment rights. First, they argue that the subpoenas create a conflict of interest between attorney and client. The lawyers' interest lies in avoiding potential contempt sanctions by complying with the subpoenas, or at least by expending the fewest possible resources in resisting them. By contrast, the clients' interest in lessening the likelihood of indictment on additional charges would require the lawyer to do his utmost, including incurring

contempt citations, to resist the subpoena. Second, appellees contend that requiring each attorney to become a witness against his client inevitably drives a wedge between attorney and client, may disqualify the attorneys from representing the clients in possible federal proceedings, and potentially may require the attorneys to withdraw from the state criminal cases. Appellees further contend that if the United States Attorney is allowed to enforce this subpoena, he will have a dangerous means by which to control the disqualification of defense attorneys. Finally, appellees point to the chilling message sent to defense attorneys by government prosecutors if, soon after embarking upon the defense of a case, the attorneys are themselves subpoenaed. Id. at 18–19.

15. Is it significant in deciding whether or not to quash a subpoena directed to an attorney to reveal the client's identity that the government might be able to find out the identity of the person they are seeking through other means, e.g. tracing persons who presented and cashed certain suspect checks? See footnote 2 in the principal case discussing the "least intrusive means" doctrine and see In re Grand Jury Investigation No. 83–2–35, 723 F.2d 447 (6th Cir.1983).

16. Are the whereabouts of the client protected by the privilege? See In re Stolar, 397 F.Supp. 520, 523–525 (S.D.N.Y.1975):

> In this case an attorney has been subpoenaed in order that he might be questioned regarding the whereabouts of his client so that, in turn, the client could then be interrogated as to the whereabouts of a person suspected of having violated federal law. The government apparently was not satisfied with the proposal made by the attorney that he would make his client available for questioning by the FBI. Instead, the government chose to compel the attorney's appearance before the grand jury to obtain the information it sought.
>
> . . .
>
> Sheperd was aware that he was being sought for questioning by the FBI, although apparently not in connection with any claimed crime on his part. He was not disposed to reveal his whereabouts to that agency. When Sheperd telephoned Stolar he made known his misgivings and sought counsel with respect to his legal rights. Stolar agreed to provide such legal advice. During the course of that conversation Sheperd gave the attorney his telephone number. As part of the attorney-client discussions which thereafter took place Sheperd also disclosed his home address and the name of the place where he was employed. The Court is of the opinion that the information sought was communicated to the attorney confidentially and solely for the purpose of receiving legal advice. Under the circumstances Sheperd had a legitimate basis to expect that such information disclosed to his attorney was made in confidence and would not be revealed. Legal advice that an individual may decline to be interviewed by the FBI will hardly be meaningful if the attorney at the behest of the FBI may then be compelled to disclose the very information which the client has legally sought to conceal.

17. Problem: As a result of a bank failure, the client is involved in numerous civil lawsuits (but no criminal investigation at the time). He requests counsel to review the laws of a number of named jurisdictions in connection with his desire to change his residence. In the course of communications on that subject, the client reveals to the attorney his new residence and requests that the location be kept confidential. Can the attorney be required to reveal the client's new location?

18. The issue of the location of a client-parent arises in child custody matters. Brennan v. Brennan, 422 A.2d 510 (Pa.Super.1980) holds that the privilege applies where the client has indicated that he wants his location kept confidential, and no crime or fraud is involved. Compare Dike v. Dike, 448 P.2d 490 (Wash.1968); In the Matter of Jacqueline F., 47 N.Y.2d 215, 417 N.Y.S.2d 884, 391 N.E.2d 967 (1979).

19. Another method the government might use to obtain fee and client identity information is to subpoena bank records relating to an attorney's trust account. For a decision holding that bank records do not fall under the attorney-client privilege merely because they derive from transactions involving an attorney's trust account maintained at the bank, see Gannet v. First National State Bank of New Jersey, 546 F.2d 1072 (3d Cir.1976).

2. SPECIAL INSTANCES

a. Required Reports Under 26 U.S.C. Section 6050I and the Bank Secrecy Act

In addition to seeking client identification and fee information by subpoena in the course of a trial or grand jury investigation, the government may also obtain such information from reports required filed under 26 U.S.C. § 6050I by individuals engaged in a trade or business reporting the receipt of more than $10,000 in cash; or by banks under the Bank Secrecy Act (15 U.S.C. § 5312 et seq.) regarding bank transactions involving more than $10,000.

Application of such reporting requirements to situations involving attorneys and their clients raises many of the same kinds of issues relating to the attorney-client privilege and Sixth Amendment right to counsel that were considered in the previous section. To what extent does the difference in the context, including the fact that the reports are supposed to be routinely made in connection with transactions and the fact that they are required by statute, affect the attorney-client privilege and Sixth Amendment issues?

United States of America v. Goldberger & Dubin

United States Court of Appeals, Second Circuit, 1991.
935 F.2d 501.

■ Before Van Graafeiland and Walker, Circuit Judges and Dearie, District Judge.

■ Van Graafeiland, Circuit Judge:

Attorneys Ronald P. Fischetti, Mark F. Pomerantz, Paul A. Goldberger, Lawrence A. Dubin, the law firms of Fischetti, Pomerantz & Russo and Goldberger & Dubin, P.C., and intervenors John Doe No. 1 and John Doe No. 2 appeal from orders of the United States District Court for the Southern District of New York (Broderick, J.) requiring the attorneys and their firms to provide the Internal Revenue Service, pursuant to 26 U.S.C. sec. 6050I, with the names of clients who paid them cash fees in excess of $10,000. We affirm.

Internal Revenue Code section 6050I requires "any person ... engaged in a trade or business, and who, in the course of such trade or business, receives more than $10,000 in cash in 1 transaction (or 2 or more related transactions) ..." to file a return specified as Form 8300. When completed, a Form 8300 contains the cash payor's name and other identifying information. During 1986 and 1987, Fischetti, Pomerantz & Russo received cash fees in excess of $10,000 from two individuals identified in this proceeding as John Doe No. 1 and John

Doe No. 2. Both payors retained the Fischetti firm to represent them in connection with criminal indictments; both were advised of section 6050I's reporting requirements, and both requested their attorneys not to disclose their identities as payors. Goldberger and Dubin, P.C. similarly received cash fees in excess of $10,000 from, or on behalf of, each of three individuals, one of these three has intervened. Respondents filed a Form 8300 disclosing the cash fee payment in each case but did not identify the payor. Following an unproductive exchange of correspondence with respondents, the IRS issued summonses directing them to appear and produce information identifying the payors. Upon respondents' refusal to comply, the government petitioned the district court for enforcement of the summonses. John Doe No. 1 and John Doe No. 2 were granted leave to intervene in the summons enforcement proceedings. In a bench ruling after oral argument, the district court held that respondents must comply with the IRS summonses and provide the payor information.

Financial-reporting legislation plays an important role in the economic life of our country. Prominent among statutes of this nature are those that require reports of substantial currency transactions. See, e.g., the Bank Secrecy or Currency and Foreign Transactions Reporting Act of 1970 (the Bank Secrecy Act), Pub. L. No. 91–508, 84 Stat. 1114 (codified as amended and revised at 31 U.S.C. §§ 5311–5326) ... [which has] survived constitutional challenges. See California Bankers, supra, 416 U.S. at 77.

The record-keeping and reporting provisions of the Bank Secrecy Act were based upon congressional findings that they "have a high degree of usefulness in criminal, tax, and regulatory investigations or proceedings."

Congress incorporated section 6050I(a) in the Tax Reform Act of 1984, Pub. L. No. 98–369, 98 Stat. 494, in an additional effort to unearth the "underground economy." Congress expanded the reporting requirements for cash transactions in excess of $10,000 to apply to "any person who is engaged in a trade or business." Extensive lobbying efforts to exempt attorneys from the reach of this amendment were unsuccessful. Appellants now seek to secure from the judiciary what their lobbyists were unable to get from Congress.

Appellants' allegations of unconstitutionality merit only brief discussion. Their contentions relative to the Fourth and Fifth Amendments have been rejected consistently in cases under the Bank Secrecy Act by both the Supreme Court and this court. See United States v. Miller, 425 U.S. 435, 444, 96 S.Ct. 1619, 48 L.Ed.2d 71 (1976); California Bankers, supra, 416 U.S. at 44–75.... The reporting requirements of the 1984 Tax Reform Act, like those of the Bank Secrecy Act, target transactions without regard to the purposes underlying them and do not require reporting of information that necessarily would be criminal.

Respondents' principal constitutional argument, that section 6050I deprives them of their Sixth Amendment right to counsel, is equally without merit.

Section 6050I stops far short of the forfeiture statutes that were at issue in Caplin & Drysdale, Chartered v. United States, 491 U.S. 617, 109 S. Ct. 2646, 109 S. Ct. 2667, 105 L.Ed.2d 528 (1989) and United States v. Monsanto, 491 U.S. 600, 109 S.Ct. 2657, 105 L.Ed.2d 512 (1989), in which the preclusion of the defendants from using seized assets to pay their attorneys was held not to violate the Sixth Amendment. Section 6050I does not preclude would-be clients from using their own funds to hire whomever they choose. To avoid disclosure under section 6050I, they need only pay counsel in some other manner than with cash. The choice is theirs. None of the appellants has advanced a legitimate reason why payment other than in cash cannot be made. Statements such as "some clients may not have non-cash assets" are somewhat less than persuasive. Equally unpersuasive is the argument that a would-be client might elect to take his business to an unscrupulous lawyer who would ignore the reporting requirements of section 6050I. Although the unscrupulous lawyer might not be the client's first choice, the Sixth Amendment does not guarantee the client the right to his first choice. In Morris v. Slappy, 461 U.S. 1, 13–14, 103 S.Ct. 1610, 75 L.Ed.2d 610 (1983), the Court rejected the claim that the Sixth Amendment guarantees a "meaningful relationship between an accused and his counsel."

In sum, we hold that section 6050I passes constitutional muster. Appellants' contention that section 6050I conflicts with the traditional doctrine of attorney-client privilege also is without merit. Certain general principles, hereafter discussed, are applicable to that doctrine. . . .

[The court here reviewed the doctrine of how the identity of the client is treated under the attorney-client privilege. See the materials in the previous section, 3C.1., of this Chapter.]

Application of the foregoing principles in the instant case makes it clear that, absent special circumstances, concerning which there is no evidence whatever herein, the identification in Form 8300 of respondents' clients who make substantial cash fee payments is not a disclosure of privileged information. This case readily is distinguishable from cases such as Marchetti v. United States, 390 U.S. 39, 48–49, 88 S.Ct. 697, 19 L.Ed.2d 889 (1968) (the gambler's registration case), in which the "direct and unmistakable consequence" of the disclosure requirements was the incrimination of the person making the disclosure. No such "direct linkage" is apparent in section 6050I.

When members of the Fischetti firm returned the incomplete 8300 Forms to the IRS, they included notes indicating that disclosure of the client information "would violate NYCPLR § 4503" which codifies the attorney-client privilege law of New York. They erred twice in so doing. In the first place, in actions such as the instant one, which involve violations of federal law, it is the federal common law of privilege that applies. United States v. Sykes, 697 F.2d 87, 89 n. 1 (2d Cir.1983); Gannet v. First Nat'l State Bank of New Jersey, 546 F.2d 1072, 1076 (3d Cir.1976), cert. denied, 431 U.S. 954, 97 S.Ct. 2674, 53 L.Ed.2d 270 (1977). Secondly, even if New York State law were to be applied, a communication to an attorney would not be considered confidential unless it was made in the process of obtaining legal advice; and fee arrangements between attorney and client do not satisfy this requirement in the usual case. Matter of Priest v. Hennessy, 51 N.Y.2d 62, 69, 431 N.Y.S.2d 511, 409 N.E.2d 983 (1980). Moreover, said the Priest court, "even where the technical requirements of the privilege are satisfied, it may, nonetheless, yield in a proper case, where strong public policy requires disclosure." Priest, supra, 51 N.Y.2d at 69. That surely should be the case where, as here, the attorney-client privilege doctrine collides head on with a federal statute that implicitly precludes its application. See Caplin & Drysdale, supra, 491 U.S. at 633 n.10.

The importance of client identification as a means of uncovering tax evasion is apparent from the briefs of appellants' amici, which state that "the wholesale enforcement of attorney 8300 Forms would require thousands of attorneys each year to provide client-information to the government" (Association of the Bar of the City of New York Committee on Criminal Advocacy a 7) and "threatens profoundly to affect the adversarial system of justice in the United States" (American Bar Association at 6). In its "General Explanation of the Revenue Provisions of the Deficit Reduction Act of 1984", the Staff of the Joint Committee on Taxation, 98th Cong., 2d Sess. stated:

Congress believed that reporting on the spending of large amounts of cash would enable the Internal Revenue Service to identify taxpayers with large cash incomes. Id. at 491.

The practice of law is treated as a "trade or business" under both the income tax laws, 6 Mertens, Law of Federal Income Taxation § 25.123, and the Sherman Act, Goldfarb v. Virginia State Bar, 421 U.S. 773, 786–88, 95 S.Ct. 2004, 44 L.Ed.2d 572 (1975). There is no indication that Congress intended those words to be interpreted any differently in section 6050I. Indeed, Congress's rejection of the lobbying efforts to secure a specific exclusion of the legal profession from this customary definition is strong evidence that Congress did not wish to do so. The clear and unmistakable intent of Congress in enacting the currency reporting statutes was to enable the IRS to identify taxpayers with large cash incomes. To the extent that the congressional intent, as expressed in section 6050I, conflicts with the attorney-client privilege, the latter must give way to the former.

Because attorneys are not excepted by the Constitution from complying with section 6050I, they are subject to the civil and criminal penalties designed to induce such compliance. Although sections 6721–6724 of the Internal Revenue Code, 26 U.S.C. §§ 6721–6724, provide specific penalties for failure to comply with information-reporting requirements of the code, such penalties are not necessarily exclusive. In short, "in the absence of allegations as to special circumstances—we see no reason why an attorney should be any less subject to questioning about fees received from a taxpayer than should any other person who has dealt with the taxpayer." In the instant case, as in most cases, the moving force behind nondisclosure is the client, not the lawyer. Indeed, it is the lawyer's duty to counsel against such wrongful nondisclosure, not to encourage it. A client, for whose benefit the attorney-client privilege exists, should not be permitted to claim the privilege, either directly or through his attorney, for the purpose of concealing his own ongoing or contemplated fraud. The IRS summons authority conferred by 26 U.S.C. § 7602 is not for the purpose of accusing but of inquiring.

Affirmed.

NOTES

1. In agreement with the Second Circuit decision in the principal case, court decisions in the Eighth, Ninth and Eleventh Circuits have also concluded that requiring client identity information in Form 8300 reports under section 6050I does not, absent special circumstances, violate the attorney-client privilege. United States v. Sindel, 53 F.3d 874 (8th Cir.1995); United States v. Leventhal, 961 F.2d 936 (11th Cir.1992); United States v. Blackman, 72 F.3d 1418 (9th Cir.1995). Also see United States v. Gertner, 873 F.Supp. 729 (D.Mass.1995). The Sindel case also sustained the reporting procedure against a Sixth Amendment right to counsel challenge. The court in Blackman stated:

> Only in the extremely rare case will the receipt of cash for fees be so intertwined with the subject of the representation as to obviate compliance with section 6050I. We are hardpressed to imagine such a case, and decline to provide an illustration.

Compare the decision in Sindel which concluded that in connection with the filing of Form 8300, the attorney "could not release information about the payments on behalf of Jane Doe without revealing the substance of a confidential communication" but did "not find any similar constraints upon the disclosure of information about the payments on behalf of John Doe." The court based its differing conclusions about the two clients on the attorney's in camera testimony about his clients' special circumstances, but did not in its opinion disclose the circumstances that it had taken into account.

2.   The reports required to be filed on Form 8300 must identify the nature of the transaction, the individual or organization for whom the transaction was completed, and "the person on whose behalf the transaction was conducted (if the recipient knows or has reason to know that the person from whom the cash was received conducted the transaction as an agent for another person)."

3.   a) As mentioned in the principal case, when section 6050I was enacted, there were immediate calls for exempting attorneys from the Act's reporting requirement. No exceptions for attorneys were made, however, when implementing regulations were promulgated. See 51 Fed.Reg. 31613, September 4, 1986.

b) Does a lawyer's filing of a Form 8300 report as required by section 6050I violate the rules of professional responsibility with respect to client confidentiality? For an opinion giving a negative answer, see Arizona State Bar Committee on Rules of Professional Conduct, Op. 87–3, reported in 3 ABA/BNA Lawyers' Manual on Professional Conduct 65 (1987).

4.   In January, 1990, a new version of Form 8300 was promulgated which asked the reporting party to check a box if the payment is a "suspicious transaction." The accompanying instructions defined a suspicious transaction as "[a] transaction in which it appears that a person is attempting to cause this report not to be filed or a false or incomplete report to be filed; or where there is an indication of possible illegal activity."

5.   A privilege against self incrimination issue under the required records doctrine may also be raised in connection with the Form 8300 reports. See supra, 1355. And see "Hollow Ritual[s]": The Fifth Amendment and Self–Reporting Schemes, 34 UCLA L.Rev. 467, 489–506 (1986).

6.   The Bank Secrecy Act requires the filing of a report to the IRS of every bank transaction involving currency of more than $10,000. The reports called Currency Transaction Reports (CTR's) are filed on Form 4789 which requires that specified information be provided including: the identity of the person conducting the transaction with the bank; the business, occupation or profession of that person; the individual or organization for whom the transaction was completed; and if a check was involved in the transaction, the names of the payee and drawer of the check.

7.   Attempts are sometimes made in connection with the filing of CTR'S to cloak the identity of the client by using intermediaries and corporate shells. See, for example, Gannet v. First National State Bank of New Jersey, 410 F.Supp. 585 (D.NJ.1976) where two attorneys were used in an attempt to conceal the client's identity. Such efforts are not necessarily successful. See Gannet v. First National State Bank of New Jersey, 546 F.2d 1072 (3d Cir.1976).

8.   Since 1996, under regulations issued under the Bank Secrecy Act, banks are required to file a new SAR (suspicious activity report) form. See Hall, Note, An Emerging Duty to Report Criminal Conduct: Banks, Money Laundering, and the Suspicious Activity Report, 84 Ky. L.J. 643 (1995–96).

9.   Rather than attempting to invoke the attorney-client or Fifth Amendment privileges, or shield the client's identity through the use of intermediaries, an attorney might be tempted to try to avoid the reporting requirements altogether by "structuring," that is, by breaking the sum of money into a series of transactions. See Ratzlaf v. United States, 510 U.S. 135 (1994) which held that under the Bank Secrecy Act in order to convict under the relevant statutory provision, the government had to prove that the defendant acted with the knowledge that the structuring acts engaged in were unlawful. Subsequently, Congress amended the relevant statute with the purpose of overruling Ratzlaf. See 31 U.S.C. sec. 5324(c).

10. The issues created by the breaking of the sum of money into a series of transactions also arise under 26 U.S.C. § 6050I which expressly requires the reporting of cash received in excess of $10,000 in "2 or more related transactions." Regulations issued in 1986, define "related transactions" to mean "any transaction conducted between a payer (or its agent) and a recipient of cash in a 24–hour period. Additionally, transactions conducted between a payer (or its agent) and a cash recipient during a period of more than 24 hours are related if the recipient knows or has reason to know that each transaction is one of a series of connected transactions." There is also an express prohibition against dividing a transaction into multiple transactions in order to avoid the reporting requirement. See 51 Fed.Reg. 31611, Sept. 4, 1986.

Significantly, the following example of a related transaction is used in the Regulations:

> An attorney agrees to represent a client in a criminal case with the attorney's fee to be determined on an hourly basis. In the first month, in which the attorney represents the client, the bill for the attorney's services comes to $8000 which the client pays in cash. In the second month in which the attorney represents the client, the bill for the attorney's services comes to $4,000, which the client again pays in cash. The aggregate amount of cash ..., the sale of legal services relating to the criminal case, and the receipt of cash must be reported under this section. Ibid.

b. Forfeiture of Attorneys' Fees

NOTES

1. Since the 1980's, the federal government has, in a significant number of cases, as part of its use of forfeiture against the money and property of persons convicted of RICO or drug violations, attempted to forfeit the fees paid to defense attorneys by convicted clients. The forfeiture provisions of the RICO statute are set forth at 18 U.S.C. § 1963 and the relevant drug provisions are found at 21 U.S.C. § 853.

2. In October, 1985, the Department of Justice issued guidelines on the forfeiture of attorneys' fees that were incorporated into the U.S. Attorneys' Manual. See 38 Crim.L.Rep. 3001 (1985). Relevant excerpts are set forth below:

9–111.230 Policy Limitations On Application Of Forfeiture Provisions To Attorney Fees.

While there are no constitutional or statutory prohibitions to application of the third party forfeiture provisions to attorneys fees, the Department recognizes that attorneys, who among all third parties uniquely may be aware of the possibility of forfeiture, may not be able to meet the requirements for equitable relief without hampering their ability to represent their clients. In particular, requiring an attorney to bear the burden of proving he was reasonably without cause to believe that an asset was subject to forfeiture may prevent the free and open exchange of information between an attorney and a client. The Department recognizes that the proper exercise of prosecutorial discretion dictates that this be taken into consideration in applying the third party forfeiture provision to attorney fees. Accordingly, it is the policy of the Department that application of the forfeiture provisions to attorney fees be carefully reviewed and that they be uniformly and fairly applied.

9-111.300 Division Approval.

No forfeiture proceedings under 18 U.S.C. 1963 or 21 U.S.C. 853 may be instituted to forfeit an asset transferred to an attorney as fees for legal services without the prior approval of the Assistant Attorney General, Criminal Division, pursuant to the guidelines herein.

9-111.410 Forfeiture of Assets Transferred To An Attorney In A Fraudulent Or Sham Transaction.

Forfeiture of an asset transferred to an attorney as fees for legal services may be pursued where there are reasonable grounds to believe that the transfer is a fraudulent or sham transaction designed to shield from forfeiture assets which otherwise are forfeitable.

9-111.430 Forfeiture of Assets Transferred To An Attorney For Representation In A Criminal Matter.

Forfeiture of an asset transferred to an attorney as payment for legal fees for representation in a criminal matter may be pursued, notwithstanding the fact that the asset may have been transferred for legitimate services actually rendered, where there are reasonable grounds to believe that the attorney had actual knowledge that the asset was subject to forfeiture at the time of the transfer. However, such reasonable grounds must be based on facts and information other than compelled disclosures of confidential communications made during the course of the representation.

3.   In Caplin & Drysdale Chartered v. United States, 491 U.S. 617 (1989), in a five to four opinion, the Supreme Court held that no exemption exists in the federal forfeiture statute for assets that a defendant wishes to use to pay defense counsel, and the statute does not violate the Fifth Amendment or the Sixth Amendment right to the assistance of counsel. Also in United States v. Monsanto, 491 U.S. 600 (1989), a companion case to Caplin & Drysdale, the court held that under the forfeiture statute, the judge could, consistent with the Constitution, enter a pretrial order freezing assets in the defendant's possession that he wishes to use to pay counsel fees.

4.   In 1986, Congress enacted two money laundering crimes. The first, 18 U.S.C. § 1956, makes it a crime to engage in a financial transaction, i.e. a bank or similar transaction, knowing that the money is derived from unlawful activity and with the specific intent to promote specified unlawful activity or having knowledge that the transaction is designed to conceal the source of specified unlawful activity. The second, 18 U.S.C. § 1957, creates the offense of knowingly engaging in a bank or similar transaction with criminally derived property of a value greater than $10,000 where the property is derived from specified unlawful activity. Compare California Penal Code § 186.10, a provision similar to 18 U.S.C. § 1957, but which provides in the case of attorneys' fees that the prosecution must prove "that the ... [money] was accepted ... with the intent to disguise ... the source of the funds or the nature of the criminal activity."

5.   In United States v. Saccoccia, 898 F.Supp. 53 (D.R.I.1995), defendants had been convicted of money laundering offenses, appealed and their convictions were affirmed. The government applied for an order to depose defense counsel in the case and to require the production of documents for the purpose of locating assets of the defendants to satisfy the forfeiture judgment that had been entered in connection with the conviction. The court held that the defendants failed to establish that information regarding the amount, form or source of the legal fees paid should be treated as confidential attorney-client communications necessary to obtain legal advice with respect to their money laundering activities. The court then proceeded to discuss the Sixth and Fifth Amendments issues in the case as follows:

> The Sixth Amendment protects against unwarranted interference with defense counsel's trial preparation and prevents unjustifiably placing defense counsel in a position that might result in disqualification. The prospect of disqualification looms especially large when an attorney is subpoenaed to testify regarding dealings with a client who is being investigated or prosecuted for a criminal offense. See In re Grand Jury Matters, 751 F.2d 13 (1st Cir.1984) (expressing concern that subpoenaing an attorney while the client is awaiting trial may drive a wedge between the attorney and client and may create a conflict of interest that could ultimately require disqualification of the attorney). However, that does not mean that counsel never may be subpoenaed when criminal charges are pending against the client.

> In any event, the concerns underlying the Sixth Amendment no longer are implicated in this case. The defendants' trials are over. Consequently, the depositions sought by the Government will neither interfere with counsel's trial preparation nor create any risk that counsel will be disqualified from continuing to represent their clients with respect to criminal charges for which they were prosecuted. Indeed, the defendants' Sixth Amendment rights are no longer applicable because their appeals have been exhausted. The mere possibility that counsel might represent the defendants in some future prosecution does not alter matters. To begin with, there is no indication that any future prosecution is contemplated. More importantly, the defendants' Sixth Amendment rights with respect to any possible future prosecution have not yet attached.

> The defendants and some of their attorneys argue that granting the Government's application would violate their Fifth Amendment privileges against self-incrimination with respect to the money laundering activities at issue in this case. The defendants' claims are unfounded for two reasons. First, once a defendant's conviction becomes final, he no longer is in danger of incriminating himself with respect to the crime charged and, therefore, the privilege against self-incrimination ceases to apply. Furthermore, the Fifth Amendment protects a defendant from being compelled to bear witness against himself. Defendant's Fifth Amendment rights are not violated by a subpoena directed to his attorney because such a subpoena does not compel the defendant, himself, to do anything.

> Counsel's rather surprising assertion of their privilege against self-incrimination presents different questions that are not as easily answered. A party claiming the privilege against self-incrimination must establish that the testimony being compelled creates a "substantial and real" as opposed to a "trifling and imaginary" risk of criminal prosecution. In this case, counsel assert that their testimony would subject them to possible prosecution for money laundering based on charges that they knowingly took tainted funds as payment for their services. The Court finds that argument unpersuasive for several reasons.

> First, among other things, conviction under the money laundering statutes requires proof that a defendant engaged in a monetary transaction involv-

ing the proceeds of unlawful activity and that the defendant knew that the money came from illegal sources. See 18 U.S.C. §§ 1956(a)(1), 1956(a)(2)(B), and 1957. Here, counsel do not even allege that they are under suspicion or investigation for money laundering. They argue that a possibility of prosecution exists because the Government apparently believes that the defendants used tainted funds to pay their legal fees. However, even assuming that the Government's belief is well-founded, counsel have provided no reason for inferring either that counsel knew that the money paid to them came from illegal sources or that their testimony would assist the Government in establishing such knowledge.

On the contrary, such an inference would be inconsistent with counsels' argument that the information sought is protected by the attorney-client privilege. Any use of tainted funds to pay the defendants' legal fees would have constituted a continuation of their money laundering efforts. ... [T]he crime/fraud exception renders the privilege inapplicable to communications regarding continuing or future criminal activity. Therefore, by arguing that the fee information at issue falls within the attorney-client privilege, counsel have implicitly represented that there was no reason for them to believe that any amounts paid to them were derived from illegal activities.

6. How persuasive are the reasons that the court offered in Saccoccia, supra note 5, for rejecting the attorneys' fifth amendment claim? Were the attorneys taking inconsistent positions? Is that a reason to reject their fifth amendment claim?

7. In re Moffitt, Zwerling & Kemler, P.C., 846 F.Supp. 463 (E.D.Va.1994): Defendant, facing indictment for drug trafficking offenses, paid a law firm $103,800 to retain services of defense counsel. Defendant was indicted, pled guilty to several drug trafficking offenses and, pursuant to the plea agreement, the court entered an order forfeiting various properties and cash including the cash paid to the law firm.

The law firm filed a petition under 21 U.S.C. sec. 853(n)(2) claiming that it was, in effect, a bona fide purchaser for value of the fee and that at the time the fee was received, the law firm was "reasonably without cause to believe that the property (i.e. the case fee) was subject to forfeiture." The court proceeded to conduct a two day evidentiary hearing on this issue. The defendant and several of his co-conspirators testified on behalf of the government. In support of the conclusion that the cash fee was subject to forfeiture, government agents also had examined IRS Form 8300's filed by the law firm. These forms revealed that deposits totaling $103,000 were made into the firm's account on the dates that a witness testified that proceeds of the criminal activities were paid by the defendant to the law firm. The law firm had not identified the source of the cash on the forms. The court found that the cash involved constituted proceeds from the defendant's drug trafficking and that there was no credible evidence to the contrary. The court stated:

> Quite apart from what the law firm knew, there is that which it chose not to know. Thus, the law firm partners did not ask ... [the defendant] directly and pointedly to identify the source of the funds. Nor did they inquire what, if any, legitimate sources of funds ... [defendant] had. None of the reasons adduced to explain these omissions are persuasive to convert the law firm's view as to the money's source from a forlorn hope to a reasonable belief. In these circumstances, especially where large sums of cash are involved, failure to make a direct inquiry may be tantamount to wilful blindness, which would invite the inference that an adverse answer

would have been given had the question been asked. Thus, when confronted with circumstances essentially similar to those at bar attorneys should inform prospective clients that they cannot pay fees with drug proceeds and that such proceeds are subject to forfeiture, even in the attorney's hands. If the prospective client answers that the money comes from legitimate sources, attorney should take whatever further steps or ask whatever further questions may be suggested by the circumstances to satisfy themselves that it is objectively reasonable to believe the answer.

The district court's decision on this issue was affirmed. United States v. Moffitt, Zwerling & Kemler, P.C., 83 F.3d 660 (4th Cir.1996).

7. Between 1985 and 1989, it has been reported that the Justice Department initiated 40 fee forfeiture actions against attorneys. Barnet & Fox, Trampling on the Sixth Amendment: The Continued Threat of Attorney Fee Forfeiture, 22 Ohio N.U.L. Rev. 1 at note 134 (1995).

8. Issues raised by the government's efforts to forfeit attorneys' fees have been extensively addressed in the legal literature: See Note, Attorney Fee Forfeiture, 86 Columb.L.Rev. 1021 (1986); Brickey, Forfeiture of Attorneys' Fees: The Impact of RICO and CCE Forfeitures on the Right to Counsel, 71 Va.L.Rev. 493 (1986); Note, Forfeiture of Attorneys' Fees: A Trap for the Unwary, 88 W.Va.L.Rev. 825 (1986); Note, Forfeiture of Attorneys' Fees: Should Defendants be allowed to Retain the "Rolls Royce of Attorneys" with the "Fruits of the Crime?" 39 Stan.L.Rev. 663 (1987); Winick, Forfeiture of Attorneys' Fees Under RICO and CCE and the Right to Counsel of Choice: The Constitutional Dilemma and How to Avoid It, 43 U. Miami. L.Rev. 765 (1989); Horwatt, Note, An Attorney Is Not a Rolls–Royce: The Comprehensive Forfeiture Act of 1984 and the Sixth Amendment Right to Effective Assistance of Counsel after United States v. Monsanto, 1 Wm. & Mary Bill Rts. J. 145 (1992); Barnet & Fox, Trampling on the Sixth Amendment: The Continued Threat of Attorney Fee Forfeiture, 22 Ohio N.U.L. Rev. 1 (1995).

D.   PHYSICAL EVIDENCE

People v. Meredith

Supreme Court of California, 1981.
29 Cal.3d 682, 175 Cal.Rptr. 612, 631 P.2d 46.

■ TOBRINER, JUSTICE.

Defendants Frank Earl Scott and Michael Meredith appeal from convictions for the first degree murder and first degree robbery of David Wade. Meredith's conviction rests on eyewitness testimony that he shot and killed Wade. Scott's conviction, however, depends on the theory that Scott conspired with Meredith and a third defendant, Jacqueline Otis, to bring about the killing and robbery. To support the theory of conspiracy the prosecution sought to show the place where the victim's wallet was found, and, in the course of the case this piece of evidence became crucial. The admissibility of that evidence comprises the principal issue on this appeal.

We first summarize the evidence other than that relating to the discovery and location of the victim's wallet. Our summary is based upon the testimony of Jacqueline Otis and Laurie Ann Sam, the key prosecution witnesses, upon the statement given the police by defendant Scott, and upon Scott's trial testimony.

On the night of April 3, 1976, Wade (the victim) and Jacqueline Otis, a friend of the defendants, entered a club known as Rich Jimmy's. Defendant Scott remained outside by a shoeshine stand. A few minutes later codefendant Meredith arrived outside the club. He told Scott he planned to rob Wade, and asked Scott to go into the club, find Jacqueline Otis, and ask her to get Wade to go out to Wade's car parked outside the club.

In the meantime, Wade and Otis had left the club and walked to a liquor store to get some beer. Returning from the store, they left the beer in a bag by Wade's car and reentered the club. Scott then entered the club also and, according to the testimony of Laurie Ann Sam (a friend of Scott's who was already in the club), Scott asked Otis to get Wade to go back out to his car so Meredith could "knock him in the head."

When Wade and Otis did go out to the car, Meredith attacked Wade from behind. After a brief struggle, two shots were fired; Wade fell, and Meredith, witnessed by Scott and Sam, ran from the scene.

Scott went over to the body and, assuming Wade was dead, picked up the bag containing the beer and hid it behind a fence. Scott later returned, retrieved the bag, and took it home where Otis and Meredith joined him.

We now recount the evidence relating to Wade's wallet, basing our account primarily on the testimony of James Schenk, Scott's first appointed attorney. Schenk visited Scott in jail more than a month after the crime occurred and solicited information about the murder, stressing that he had to be fully acquainted with the facts to avoid being "sandbagged" by the prosecution during the trial. In response, Scott gave Schenk the same information that he had related earlier to the police. In addition, however, Scott told Schenk something Scott had not revealed to the police: that he had seen a wallet, as well as the paper bag, on the ground near Wade. Scott said that he picked up the wallet, put it in the paper bag, and placed both behind a parking lot fence. He also said that he later retrieved the bag, took it home, found $100 in the wallet and divided it with Meredith, and then tried to burn the wallet in his kitchen sink. He took the partially burned wallet, Scott told Schenk, placed it in a plastic bag, and threw it in a burn barrel behind his house.

Schenk, without further consulting Scott, retained Investigator Stephen Frick and sent Frick to find the wallet. Frick found it in the location described by Scott and brought it to Schenk. After examining the wallet and determining that it contained credit cards with Wade's name, Schenk turned the wallet and its contents over to Detective Payne, investigating officer in the case. Schenk told Payne only that, to the best of his knowledge, the wallet had belonged to Wade.

Prior to trial, a third attorney, Hamilton Hintz, was appointed for Scott. Hintz unsuccessfully sought an in limine ruling that the wallet of the murder victim was inadmissible and that the attorney-client privilege precluded the admission of testimony concerning the wallet by Schenk or Frick.

At trial Frick, called by the prosecution, identified the wallet and testified that he found it in a garbage can behind Scott's residence. On cross-examination by Hintz, Scott's counsel, Frick further testified that he was an investigator hired by Scott's first attorney, Schenk, and that he had searched the garbage can at Schenk's request. Hintz later called Schenk as a witness: Schenk testified that he told Frick to search for the wallet immediately after Schenk finished talking to Scott. Schenk also stated that Frick brought him the wallet on the following day; after examining its contents Schenk delivered the wallet to the police. Scott then took the stand and testified to the information about the wallet that he had disclosed to Schenk.

The jury found both Scott and Meredith guilty of first degree murder and first degree robbery. It further found that Meredith, but not Scott, was armed with a deadly weapon. Both defendants appeal from their convictions.

Defendant Scott concedes, and we agree, that the wallet itself was admissible in evidence. Scott maintains, however, that Evidence Code section 954 bars the testimony of the investigator concerning the location of the wallet. We consider, first, whether the California attorney-client privilege codified in that section extends to observations which are the product of privileged communications. We then discuss whether that privileged status is lost when defense conduct may have frustrated prosecution discovery.

Section 954 provides, "[T]he client . . . has a privilege to refuse to disclose, and to prevent another from disclosing, a confidential communication between client and lawyer. . . ." Under that section one who seeks to assert the privilege must establish that a confidential communication occurred during the course of the attorney-client relationship. (8 Wigmore, Evidence (McNaughton rev. ed. 1961) § 2292; Witkin, Cal. Evidence (2d ed. 1966) § 794.)

Scott's statements to Schenk regarding the location of the wallet clearly fulfilled the statutory requirements. Moreover, the privilege did not dissolve when Schenk disclosed the substance of that communication to his investigator, Frick. Under Evidence Code section 912, subdivision (d), a disclosure which is "reasonably necessary" to accomplish the purpose for which the attorney has been consulted does not constitute a waiver of the privilege. If Frick was to perform the investigative services for which Schenk had retained him, it was "reasonably necessary," that Schenk transmit to Frick the information regarding the wallet. Thus, Schenk's disclosure to Frick did not waive the statutory privilege.

The statutes codifying the attorney-client privilege do not, however, indicate whether that privilege protects facts viewed and observed as a direct result of confidential communication. To resolve that issue, we turn first to the policies which underlie the attorney-client privilege, and then to the cases which apply those policies to observations arising from a protected communication.

The fundamental purpose of the attorney-client privilege is, of course, to encourage full and open communication between client and attorney. "Adequate legal representation in the ascertainment and enforcement of rights or the prosecution or defense of litigation compels a full disclosure of the facts by the client to his attorney. . . . Given the privilege, a client may make such a disclosure without fear that his attorney may be forced to reveal the information confided to him."

In the criminal context, as we have recently observed, these policies assume particular significance: " 'As a practical matter, if the client knows that damaging information could more readily be obtained from the attorney following disclosure than from himself in the absence of disclosure, the client would be reluctant to confide in his lawyer and it would be difficult to obtain fully informed legal advice.' . . . Thus, if an accused is to derive the full benefits of his right to counsel, he must have the assurance of confidentiality and privacy of communication with his attorney."

Judicial decisions have recognized that the implementation of these important policies may require that the privilege extend not only to the initial communication between client and attorney but also to any information which the attorney or his investigator may subsequently acquire as a direct result of that communication. In a venerable decision involving facts analogous to those in the instant case, the Supreme Court of West Virginia held that the trial court erred in admitting an attorney's testimony as to the location of a pistol which he had discovered as the result of a privileged communication from his client. That the attorney had observed the pistol, the court pointed out, did not nullify the privilege: "All that the said attorney knew about this pistol, or where it was to be found, he knew only from the communications which had been made to him by his client confidentially and professionally, as counsel in this case. And it ought therefore, to have been entirely excluded from the jury...." (State of West Virginia v. Douglass (1882) 20 W.Va. 770, 783.)

More recent decisions reach similar conclusions. In State v. Olwell (1964) 64 Wash.2d 828, 394 P.2d 681, the court reviewed contempt charges against an attorney who refused to produce a knife he obtained from his client. The court first observed that "[t]o be protected as a privileged communication ... the securing of the knife ... must have been the direct result of information given to Mr. Olwell by his client." (P. 683) The court concluded that defense counsel, after examining the physical evidence, should deliver it to the prosecution, but should not reveal the source of the evidence; "[b]y thus allowing the prosecution to recover such evidence, the public interest is served, and by refusing the prosecution an opportunity to disclose the source of the evidence, the client's privilege is preserved and a balance reached between these conflicting interests." (P. 685.)

Finally, we note the decisions of the New York courts in People v. Belge (Sup.Ct.1975) 83 Misc.2d 186, 372 N.Y.S.2d 798, affirmed in People v. Belge (App.Div.1975) 50 A.D.2d 1088, 376 N.Y.S.2d 771. Defendant, charged with one murder, revealed to counsel that he had committed three others. Counsel, following defendant's directions, located one of the bodies. Counsel did not reveal the location of the body until trial, 10 months later, when he exposed the other murders to support an insanity defense.

Counsel was then indicted for violating two sections of the New York Public Health Law for failing to report the existence of the body to proper authorities in order that they could give it a decent burial. The trial court dismissed the indictment, the appellate division affirmed, holding that the attorney-client privilege shielded counsel from prosecution for actions which would otherwise violate the Public Health Law.[1]

The foregoing decisions demonstrate that the attorney-client privilege is not strictly limited to communications, but extends to protect observations made as a consequence of protected communications. We turn therefore to the question whether that privilege encompasses a case in which the defense, by removing or altering evidence, interferes with the prosecution's opportunity to discover that evidence.[2]

---

1. In each of the cases discussed in text, a crucial element in the court's analysis is that the attorney's observations were the direct product of information communicated to him by his client. Two decisions, People v. Lee (1970) 3 Cal.App.3d 514, 83 Cal.Rptr. 715 and Morrell v. State (Alaska 1978) 575 P.2d 1200, held that an attorney must not only turn over evidence given him by third parties, but also testify as to the source of that evidence. Both decisions emphasized that the attorney-client privilege was inapplicable be-cause the third party was not acting as an agent of the attorney or the client. [Footnotes are those of the court. Some footnotes have been omitted and others renumbered.]

2. We agree with the parties' suggestion that an attorney in Schenk's position often may best fulfill conflicting obligations to preserve the confidentiality of client confidences, investigate his case, and act as an officer of the court if he does not remove evidence located as the result of a privileged communication. We must recognize, however,

In some of the cases extending the privilege to observations arising from protected communications the defense counsel had obtained the evidence from his client or in some other fashion removed it from its original location.... None of the decisions, however, confronts directly the question whether such removal or alteration should affect the defendant's right to assert the attorney-client privilege as a bar to testimony concerning the original location or condition of the evidence.

When defense counsel alters or removes physical evidence, he necessarily deprives the prosecution of the opportunity to observe that evidence in its original condition or location. As the Attorney General points out, to bar admission of testimony concerning the original condition and location of the evidence in such a case permits the defense in effect to "destroy" critical information; it is as if, he explains, the wallet in this case bore a tag bearing the words "located in the trash can by Scott's residence," and the defense, by taking the wallet, destroyed this tag. To extend the attorney-client privilege to a case in which the defense removed evidence might encourage defense counsel to race the police to seize critical evidence. (See In re Ryder (E.D.Va.1967) 263 F.Supp. 360, 369); ...

We therefore conclude that courts must craft an exception to the protection extended by the attorney-client privilege in cases in which counsel has removed or altered evidence. Indeed, at oral argument defense counsel acknowledged that such an exception might be necessary in a case in which the police would have inevitably discovered the evidence in its original location if counsel had not removed it. Counsel argued, however, that the attorney-client privilege should protect observations of evidence, despite subsequent defense removal, unless the prosecution could prove that the police probably would have eventually discovered the evidence in the original site.

We have seriously considered counsel's proposal, but have concluded that a test based upon the probability of eventual discovery is unworkably speculative. Evidence turns up not only because the police deliberately search for it, but also because it comes to the attention of policemen or bystanders engaged in other business. In the present case, for example, the wallet might have been found by the trash collector. Moreover, once physical evidence (the wallet) is turned over to the police, they will obviously stop looking for it; to ask where, how long, and how carefully they would have looked is obviously to compel speculation as to theoretical future conduct of the police.

We therefore conclude that whenever defense counsel removes or alters evidence, the statutory privilege does not bar revelation of the original location or condition of the evidence in question.[3] We thus view the defense decision to

---

that in some cases an examination of evidence may reveal information critical to the defense of a client accused of crime. If the usefulness of the evidence cannot be gauged without taking possession of it, as, for example, when a ballistics or fingerprint test is required, the attorney may properly take it for a reasonable time before turning it over to the prosecution. (Olwell, supra, 394 P.2d, pp. 684–685.) Similarly, in the present case the defense counsel could not be certain the burnt wallet belonged in fact to the victim: in taking the wallet to examine it for identification, he violated no ethical duty to his client or to the prosecution.

3. In offering the evidence, the prosecution should present the information in a manner which avoids revealing the content of attorney-client communications or the original source of the information. In the present case, for example, the prosecutor simply asked Frick where he found the wallet; he did not identify Frick as a defense investigator or trace the discovery of the wallet to an attorney-client communication.

In other circumstances, when it is not possible to elicit such testimony without identifying the witness as the defendant's attorney or investigator, the defendant may be willing to enter a stipulation which will simply inform the jury as to the relevant location

remove evidence as a tactical choice. If defense counsel leaves the evidence where he discovers it, his observations derived from privileged communications are insulated from revelation. If, however, counsel chooses to remove evidence to examine or test it, the original location and condition of that evidence loses the protection of the privilege. Applying this analysis to the present case, we hold that the trial court did not err in admitting the investigator's testimony concerning the location of the wallet.

[The court proceeded to affirm the judgment of conviction, although modifying it on other grounds.]

NOTES

1.   In the principal case, the attorney voluntarily turned over the wallet to the police. When an attorney receives information about physical evidence that incriminates the client, does the attorney have an obligation to turn over the evidence which comes into his or her possession or to inform the police of its location? Can the government obtain evidence in the attorney's possession through the issuance of a subpoena duces tecum? If the attorney has information about physical evidence, can he be required to testify about it? The prosecutor may also attempt to obtain physical evidence from the attorney through the issuance of a warrant to search his office. See e.g. People v. Nash, 341 N.W.2d 439 (Mich.1983). See infra p. 1437.

2.   There is limited authority on the question of the attorney's obligation voluntarily to turn over to the prosecutor physical evidence in his possession. In State v. Olwell, discussed in the principal case, the court in dictum stated:

> The attorney should not be a depository for criminal evidence (such as a knife, other weapons, stolen property, etc.), which in itself has little, if any, material value for the purposes of aiding counsel in the preparation of the defense of his client's case. Such evidence given the attorney during legal consultation for information purposes and used by the attorney in preparing the defense of his client's case, whether or not the case ever goes to trial, could clearly be withheld for a reasonable period of time. It follows that the attorney, after a reasonable period, should as an officer of the court, on his own motion turn the same over to the prosecution. 64 Wash.2d 828, 833–834, 394 P.2d 681, 684–685 (1964).

There is similar language in Morrell v. State, discussed in footnote 1 in the principal case. See also In re Ryder cited in the principal case. An attorney took possession of stolen money and a sawed-off shotgun and placed it in a safety deposit box with the purpose of retaining it until the client's trial was completed. The court held that the attorney's conduct was not encompassed by the attorney-client privilege and that he had violated the Canons of Professional Ethics. He was suspended from practice in that court for eighteen months.

In People v. Superior Court of San Mateo County (Fairbank), 192 Cal. App.3d 32, 237 Cal. Rptr.158 (1987), defense counsel argued that although they had an obligation to turn over to the prosecutor evidence that had come into their possession, they did not have to do so prior to trial. The court rejected the claim:

> or condition of the evidence in question. When such a stipulation is proffered, the prosecution should not be permitted to reject the stipulation in the hope that by requiring defense counsel personally to testify to such facts, the jury might infer that counsel learned those facts from defendant.

If counsel or an agent of counsel choose to remove, possess, or alter physical evidence pertaining to the crime, counsel must immediately inform the court of the action. The court, exercising care to shield privileged communications and defense strategies from prosecution view, must then take appropriate action to ensure that the prosecution has timely access to physical evidence possessed by the defense and timely information about alteration of any evidence.

We reject amicus's suggestion that prosecution access to the physical evidence should depend upon the prosecution's showing of "need" for the evidence. The obligation to provide the prosecution with access to physical evidence and information about its alteration is absolute. Defense counsel may not use seizure or alteration of evidence as an excuse to pretry the prosecution's case or test the court's sympathies.

3. The ABA's Model Rules of Professional Conduct do not contain any provisions expressly dealing with the obligations of criminal defense attorneys in regard to physical evidence. However, in 1983 the Criminal Justice Section of the ABA approved standards on this subject that had been prepared by the Section's Committee on Ethical Considerations in Criminal Cases. See 29 Crim.L.Rep. 2465 (Aug. 26, 1981). These standards provided as follows:

(a) A lawyer who receives a physical item under circumstances implicating a client in criminal conduct shall disclose the location of or shall deliver that item to law enforcement authorities only: (1) if such is required by law or court order, or (2) as provided in paragraph (d).

(b) Unless required to disclose, the lawyer shall return the item to the source from whom the lawyer receives it, except as provided in paragraphs (c) and (d). In returning the item to the source, the lawyer shall advise the source of the legal consequences pertaining to possession or destruction of the item.

(c) A lawyer may receive the item for a period of time during which the lawyer: (1) intends to return it to the owner; (2) reasonably fears that return of the item to the source will result in destruction of the item; (3) reasonably fears that return of the item to the source will result in physical harm to anyone; (4) intends to test, examine, inspect, or use the item in any way as part of the lawyer's representation of the client; or (5) cannot return it to the source. If the lawyer retains the item, the lawyer shall do so in a manner that does not impede the lawful ability of law enforcement to obtain the item.

(d) If the item received is contraband or if in the lawyer's judgment the lawyer cannot retain the item in a way that does not pose an unreasonable risk of physical harm to anyone, the lawyer shall disclose the location of or shall deliver the item to law enforcement authorities.

(e) If the lawyer discloses the location of or delivers the item to law enforcement authorities under paragraphs (a) or (d), or to a third party under paragraph (c)(1), the lawyer shall do so in the way best designed to protect the client's interests.

4. Do the standards set forth in the previous note strike the right balance between the duties of the defense attorney and the interests of society? Are they consistent with the principal case and its California progeny, namely the (Fairbank) case, supra note 2.

Consider in this connection, Hitch v. Superior Court, 708 P.2d 72 (Ariz. 1985): The girlfriend of the defendant in a murder case told the police that the murder victim had a wristwatch in his possession shortly before his death. Subsequently she told an investigator employed by defense counsel that she had found a wristwatch in defendant's suit jacket. The defense attorney took possession of the watch because, as he later asserted, he wanted to examine it to determine whether it was the same one the girlfriend had described to the police and because he was concerned that she might destroy or conceal it.

What was the attorney's obligation under the Criminal Justice Section standards? Note that the court in Hitch, purporting to apply those standards, ruled that the attorney must turn the watch over to the prosecution because he had reasonable grounds to believe that the evidence might be destroyed. Was this a correct application of the standards? If not, what should the attorney have done with the watch?

5. According to the standards set forth in note 3, under what circumstances should the attorney retain evidence in his possession? What problems can arise when the attorney returns the evidence to its source? Under what circumstances should defense counsel actively try to obtain evidence?

6. Under circumstances where an attorney turns over physical evidence in his possession to the prosecutor, there is authority for the proposition that he should not be identified in court as the source of the evidence. See footnote 3 in the principal case and the court's discussion of Olwell. Compare Justice Brickley's opinion in People v. Nash, 341 N.W.2d 439, 449 (Mich.1983), concluding that the fact that the incriminating gun was obtained from the attorney's office is admissible. Otherwise, it would "create a gap in the sequence of events that would link the gun to the accused, leaving the jury to speculate as to how the police had obtained the revolver." Justice Brickley cited the principal case in support of his conclusion. How might that proposition be derived from the principal case? Is not the import of the principal case that defendant Scott's attorney could not testify as to the source of the information he received regarding the location of the wallet? See footnotes 1 and 3. Did the attorney's testimony in the case directly reveal the source of the information? Indirectly? Does it matter whether the relevant testimony on that issue resulted from questions from the prosecution or from defense counsel?

Also compare State v. Green, 493 So.2d 1178 (La.1986): The defendant had delivered a gun to his attorney for safekeeping.

The court stated:

> Our holding today mandates the state prove the connection between the physical evidence and the defendant without in any way relying on the testimony of the client's attorney who initially received the evidence. The attorney may not be called to the stand and examined as to any of the circumstances which preceded his possession and subsequent delivery to police of a piece of physical evidence—here the gun. By thus allowing the prosecution to recover such evidence, the public interest is served, and by refusing the prosecution an opportunity to elicit the source of the evidence from the attorney, the client's privilege is preserved and a balance is reached between these conflicting interests.

7. One way an attorney can guard the identity of the client and himself as the source of an item of physical evidence voluntarily delivered to the prosecutor is to arrange to have the evidence delivered anonymously. For an argument that such anonymous deliveries should be prohibited, see Lefstein, Incriminating Physical Evidence, The Defense Attorney's Dilemma, and the Need for Rules, 64 N.C.L.Rev. 897, 935–938 (1986).

8. Of course, even if the identity of the attorney as the source of the evidence is not disclosed in the trial, the item of evidence itself may provide the link to the client-defendant,for example, his fingerprints may be on the item. Compare Lefstein, supra note 7, at 915.

9. Footnote 1 in the principal case is also relevant if the evidence was turned over to to the attorney by a third person, not the client. What result if the third person was acting as the agent of the client? As the agent of the attorney? See Clutchette v. Rushen, 770 F.2d 1469 (9th Cir.1985); United States v. Palmer, 536 F.2d 1278, 1281 (9th Cir.1976). See also Matter of Victor, 422 F.Supp. 475 (S.D.N.Y.1976); Bieber v. State, 261 A.2d 202 (Md.App.1970).

10. Additional questions arise if the prosecutor tries to subpoena physical evidence from the defendant. Consider in this connection Fisher v. United States, 425 U.S. 391 (1976), reprinted supra p. 1336.

In Fisher, the issue was whether the government, using a summons, could obtain from an attorney documents delivered to him by his client. The Supreme Court addressed the attorney-client issue in the case as follows:

> ... As a practical matter, if the client knows that damaging information could more readily be obtained from the attorney following disclosure than from himself in the absence of disclosure, the client would be reluctant to confide in his lawyer and it would be difficult to obtain fully informed legal advice. However, since the privilege has the effect of withholding relevant information from the factfinder, it applies only where necessary to achieve its purpose. Accordingly it protects only those disclosures,necessary to obtain informed legal advice,which might not have been made absent the privilege....

> This Court and the lower courts have thus uniformly held that pre-existing documents which could have been obtained by court process from the client when he was in possession may also be obtained from the attorney by similar process following transfer by the client in order to obtain more informed legal advice....

> The purpose of the privilege requires no broader rule. Pre-existing documents obtainable from the client are not appreciably easier to obtain from the attorney after transfer to him. Thus, even absent the attorney-client privilege, clients will not be discouraged from disclosing the documents to the attorney, and their ability to obtain informed legal advice will remain unfettered. It is otherwise if the documents are not obtainable by subpoena duces tecum or summons while in the exclusive possession of the client, for the client will then be reluctant to transfer possession to the lawyer unless the documents are also privileged in the latter's hands. Where the transfer is made for the purpose of obtaining legal advice, the purposes of the attorney-client privilege would be defeated unless the privilege is applicable. "It follows, then, that when the client himself would be privileged from production of the document, either as a party at common law ... or as exempt from self-incrimination, the attorney having possession of the document is not bound to produce." 8 Wigmore § 2307, p. 592.

Fisher v. United States, supra at 1344, 425 U.S. at 403–404.

Query: Can the prosecution in a criminal case charging assault with a deadly weapon by court order compel the defendant to produce the weapon?

Commonwealth v. Hughes

Supreme Judicial Court of Massachusetts, 1980.
380 Mass. 583, 404 N.E.2d 1239, cert. denied, 449 U.S. 900 (1980).

■ KAPLAN, JUSTICE.

A Berkshire County grand jury on October 4, 1978, indicted the defendant Edward H. Hughes on two counts of assault by means of a dangerous weapon, to wit, a pistol.

On March 28, 1979, the Commonwealth filed a "Motion to Order Defendant to Produce Weapon" for ballistics examination. The weapon was described in the motion as a "Smith and Wesson .38 Caliber Revolver Serial Number J354354." An accompanying affidavit stated that the defendant had registered the revolver with the firearms identification division of the Department of Public Safety The motion was allowed after hearing: the defendant was ordered to produce the described revolver within ten days; the Commonwealth was ordered to give the defendant a copy of any ballistics test results within ten days of receiving them; and "[a]ny question concerning the admissibility of evidence emanating from the allowance of this motion is deferred to the trial justice, if appropriately raised."

[T]he Commonwealth on August 21, 1979, instituted proceedings for contempt which were brought to hearing on August 30. A representative of the firearms identification division testified that on March 23, 1976 (twenty-seven months before the alleged assault) the defendant had registered the gun described, and had not since then filed any report of transfer of the gun. The defendant was held in contempt but given until 3 P.M. that day to produce the weapon or show present inability to do so, otherwise he would be incarcerated until purgation or further order of the court. Sentence being stayed by the judge, the parties applied jointly for direct appellate review, which we allowed. We reverse.

[T]he defendant must justify what would otherwise be contumacy by reference to his privilege not to be "compelled ... to be a witness against himself."

"[T]he Fifth Amendment does not independently proscribe the compelled production of every sort of incriminating evidence but applies only when the accused is compelled to make a testimonial communication that is incriminating." Fisher v. United States,

The upshot is that we have to say here whether the defendant's producing the revolver would have sufficient testimonial aspects to initiate Fifth Amendment consideration and whether in those aspects there can be found a tendency to incriminate him. "These questions perhaps do not lend themselves to categorical answers; their resolution may instead depend on the facts and circumstances of particular cases or classes thereof." Fisher v. United States,

[In Fisher] [t]he I.R.S., after interviewing certain taxpayers regarding possible civil or criminal infractions of the tax laws, learned that these persons had retrieved some of their accountants' work papers (which laid out analyses of the taxpayers' income and disbursements related to the years under investigation), and had passed the papers to their attorneys. Summons was then served on the attorneys to produce the work sheets. The issue reduced to whether the taxpayers themselves had a Fifth Amendment privilege to refuse production of the papers. On the particular facts, the Court held against the taxpayers.

The Court recognized that two kinds of testimonial assertions were implied in the production. First, "producing the documents tacitly admits their existence and their location in the hands of their possessor." Second, the production implicitly authenticated the papers as being those requested in the summons. Why, then, was the claim of privilege denied? The elements of existence, location, and control of the papers were "not in issue"; "[t]he existence and location of the papers are a foregone conclusion and the taxpayer adds little or nothing to the sum total of the Government's information by conceding that he in fact has the papers." The information added was trivial.

Coming to the element of authentication, the Court said that, while testimonial, it did not incriminate the taxpayer: the implicit assertion that the papers produced conformed to the summons would not serve to authenticate them at trial; it was the testimony of the accountants that would do that. Nor was the government using the taxpayer's "authentication" to prove that the figures were accurate.

The converse inference from Fisher, as indicated by the Court, is that assertions implied from production of things (whether or not documents) are within the Fifth Amendment, and thus justify the refusal to produce, when they are nontrivial and incriminating.

If the defendant should produce the revolver, he would be making implicitly a statement about its existence, location and control to which the Commonwealth says it would allude at trial to show he had possession and control at some point after the alleged crime. The implied statement would also function as an authentication. Nor would the statement amount to a "foregone conclusion" conveying merely trivial new knowledge. On the contrary, it would deal with just those matters about which the Commonwealth desires but does not have solid information. Apparently the Commonwealth does not know whether the gun exists or, if it does, where it is being kept; it has only some evidence to base a suspicion that the defendant may be able to produce it, if he will. In the language of the cases, the Commonwealth is seeking to be relieved of its ignorance or uncertainty by trying to get itself "informed of knowledge the defendant possesses."

The avowals sought from the defendant are not only significant but must be taken to be incriminating. The revolver is the supposed instrumentality of the crime, and control or possession after the event, taken together with the earlier ownership attested by the registration, would tend to establish possession at the critical time. It is partially on this declared theory that the Commonwealth has pursued the defendant with its motion to produce. The Commonwealth states that once it has the revolver in hand, it will run ballistics tests, and these may lead to expert testimony, of whatever strength, tying the revolver to the actual assault. This is a step beyond the production sought, but the constitutional privilege "does not merely encompass evidence which may lead to criminal conviction, but includes information which would furnish a link in the chain of evidence that could lead to prosecution." Maness v. Meyers, 419 U.S. 449, 461, 95 S.Ct. 584, 592, 42 L.Ed.2d 574 (1975). Hoffman v. United States, 341 U.S. 479, 488, 71 S.Ct. 814, 819, 95 L.Ed. 1118 (1951). In reviewing the contempt adjudication, it is right to assume, as the defendant does arguendo in his brief, that he has present possession of the registered gun, which makes very real the factor of self-incrimination that is involved.

The Commonwealth has not attempted to eliminate, as far as it could, the testimonial aspects of the defendant's producing the gun, by the expedient of undertaking that at trial it would authenticate the gun simply by the serial number (if that number appears), and would make no tender in the court room of the fact that it was the defendant who produced the gun. We go no further than to express doubt whether the case would have been materially altered by an offer of such an undertaking in the court below. Implicit statements as to existence, location, and control would nevertheless have been compelled and the information would have been delivered over to the Commonwealth. The Commonwealth could use such information, mediately, to secure other incriminating evidence to put before the jury, and it can be assumed that the testimonial statement as to the location of the gun would be used, mediately, to lead to ballistics tests and ballistics evidence and an opinion thereon. More generally, we express doubt whether a defendant may be compelled to deliver the corpus delicti, which may then be introduced by the government at trial, if only it is understood that the facts as to the source of the thing are withheld from the jury.

NOTES

1. Accord: Goldsmith v. Superior Court, 152 Cal.App.3d 76, 199 Cal.Rptr. 366 (1984). In Goldsmith, the trial court had ordered "the defendant and/or his attorney to produce the weapon" or to show cause why they had not complied with the order. At an in camera hearing on the matter, defense counsel represented to the court that he neither possessed the gun nor had control over it. He declined on grounds of attorney-client privilege to reveal whether he knew where the gun was. When the weapon was not produced, the court proceeded to impose sanctions on the defendant by restricting his introduction of certain kinds of evidence relating to the weapon. On appeal, relying heavily on the principal case, the court reversed the trial court's order.

Compare United States v. Authement, 607 F.2d 1129 (5th Cir.1979): Brass knuckles subpoenaed from defendant's attorney. Held: Production did not violate the defendant's privilege against self-incrimination even though it showed the knuckles existed, were carried at the time of the assault and were in his possession when subpoenaed. The fact that defendant's attorney produced the knuckles was not used against defendant at trial; he did not testify; that his attorney had produced the knuckles in response to the subpoena was not disclosed to the jury; and the knuckles were identified and authenticated by a third party.

2. The Fisher tacit admission-implied authentication doctrine was applied by the Supreme Court in United States v. Doe, 465 U.S. 605 (1984). See p. 1346, supra.

3. Problem: A savings and loan association is robbed. FBI agents obtain information identifying two suspects and that one of the suspects had previously been in the employ of an attorney named Genson. The agents also learn that that suspect had transferred $200.00 in cash to Genson within three hours after the robbery. A week later Genson is served with a subpoena duces tecum requesting the production of "any and all monies paid or delivered to you or into your care, custody, and control by ... [the named suspects] or their agents, subsequent to 9:00 A.M. on Tuesday, December 30, 1986."

Advise Genson how he should respond to the subpoena. Compare In re January 1976 Grand Jury, 534 F.2d 719 (7th Cir.1976).

4. A considerable literature has developed on the issues discussed in this section. In addition to Lefstein, supra, note 7, p. 1485, see Incriminating Criminal Evidence: Practical Solutions, 15 Pac.L.J. 807 (1984); Abramovsky, Confidentiality: The Future Crime—Contraband Dilemmas, 85 W.Va.L.Rev. 929 (1983); Bender, Incriminating Evidence: What to do with a Hot Potato, 11 Colo.Law. 880 (1982); Note, The Attorney–Client Privilege: Hear No Evil, See No Evil, Speak No Evil? 20 Hous.L.Rev. 921 (1983); Comment, Extending the Attorney Client Privilege: A Constitutional Criminal Defendant's Constitutional Rights, 70 Cal.L.Rev. 1048 (1982); Note, Ethics, Law, and Loyalty: The Attorney's Duty to Turn Over Incriminating Physical Evidence, 32 Stan.L.Rev. 977, 994 (1980); Comment, The Problem of an Attorney in Possession of

Evidence Incriminating His Client: The Need for a Predictable Standard, 47
U.Cin.L.Rev. 431, 441–43 (1978); Comment, The Right of a Criminal Defense
Attorney to Withhold Physical Evidence Received from his Client, 38 U.Chi.
L.Rev. 211 (1970).

E.   THE CORPORATION AS THE CLIENT, WORK PRODUCT AND RELATED MATTERS

Upjohn v. United States

Supreme Court of the United States, 1981.
449 U.S. 383, 101 S.Ct. 677, 66 L.Ed.2d 584.

■ JUSTICE REHNQUIST delivered the opinion of the Court.

We granted certiorari in this case to address important questions concerning the scope of the attorney-client privilege in the corporate context and the
applicability of the work-product doctrine in proceedings to enforce tax summonses. With respect to the privilege question the parties and various amici
have described our task as one of choosing between two "tests" which have
gained adherents in the courts of appeals. We are acutely aware, however, that
we sit to decide concrete cases and not abstract propositions of law. We decline
to lay down a broad rule or series of rules to govern all conceivable future
questions in this area, even were we able to do so. We can and do, however,
conclude that the attorney-client privilege protects the communications involved in this case from compelled disclosure and that the work-product
doctrine does apply in tax summons enforcement proceedings.

I

Petitioner Upjohn manufactures and sells pharmaceuticals here and
abroad. In January 1976 independent accountants conducting an audit of one of
petitioner's foreign subsidiaries discovered that the subsidiary made payments
to or for the benefit of foreign government officials in order to secure government business. The accountants so informed Mr. Gerard Thomas, petitioner's
Vice–President, Secretary, and General Counsel. Thomas is a member of the
Michigan and New York bars, and has been petitioner's General Counsel for 20
years. He consulted with outside counsel and R.T. Parfet, Jr., petitioner's
Chairman of the Board. It was decided that the company would conduct an
internal investigation of what were termed "questionable payments." As part
of this investigation the attorneys prepared a letter containing a questionaire
which was sent to "all foreign general and area managers" over the Chairman's
signature. The letter began by noting recent disclosures that several American
companies made "possibly illegal" payments to foreign government officials
and emphasized that the management needed full information concerning any
such payments made by Upjohn. The letter indicated that the Chairman had
asked Thomas, identified as "the company's General Counsel," "to conduct an
investigation for the purpose of determining the nature and magnitude of any
payments made by the Upjohn Company or any of its subsidiaries to any
employee or official of a foreign government." The questionnaire sought detailed information concerning such payments. Managers were instructed to
treat the investigation as "highly confidential" and not to discuss it with
anyone other than Upjohn employees who might be helpful in providing the
requested information. Responses were to be sent directly to Thomas. Thomas
and outside counsel also interviewed the recipients of the questionnaire and
some 33 other Upjohn officers or employees as part of the investigation.

On March 26, 1976, the company voluntarily submitted a preliminary report to the Securities and Exchange Commission on Form 8–K disclosing certain questionable payments. A copy of the report was simultaneously submitted to the Internal Revenue Service, which immediately began an investigation to determine the tax consequences of the payments. Special agents conducting the investigation were given lists by Upjohn of all those interviewed and all who had responded to the questionnaire. On November 23, 1976, the Service issued a summons pursuant to 26 U.S.C. § 7602 demanding production of:

> "All files relative to the investigation conducted under the supervision of Gerard Thomas to identify payments to employees of foreign governments and any political contributions made by the Upjohn Company or any of its affiliates since January 1, 1971 and to determine whether any funds of the Upjohn Company had been improperly accounted for on the corporate books during the same period.

> "The records should include but not be limited to written questionnaires sent to managers of the Upjohn Company's foreign affiliates, and memoranda or notes of the interviews conducted in the United States and abroad with officers and employees of the Upjohn Company and its subsidiaries." App. 17a–18a.

The company declined to produce the documents specified in the second paragraph on the grounds that they were protected from disclosure by the attorney-client privilege and constituted the work product of attorneys prepared in anticipation of litigation. On August 31, 1977, the United States filed a petition seeking enforcement of the summons under 26 U.S.C. §§ 7402(b) and 7604(a) in the United States District Court for the Western District of Michigan. . . .

II

Federal Rule of Evidence 501 provides that "the privilege of a witness . . . shall be governed by the principles of the common law as they may be interpreted by the courts of the United States in light of reason and experience." The attorney-client privilege is the oldest of the privileges for confidential communications known to the common law. . . . Admittedly complications in the application of the privilege arise when the client is a corporation, which in theory is an artificial creature of the law, and not an individual; but this Court has assumed that the privilege applies when the client is a corporation. United States v. Louisville & Nashville R. Co., 236 U.S. 318, 336, 35 S.Ct. 363, 369, 59 L.Ed. 598 (1915), and the Government does not contest the general proposition.

The Court of Appeals, however, considered the application of the privilege in the corporate context to present a "different problem," since the client was an inanimate entity and "only the senior management, guiding and integrating the several operations, . . . can be said to possess an identity analogous to the corporation as a whole." 600 F.2d at 1226. The first case to articulate the so-called "control group test" adopted by the court below, City of Philadelphia v. Westinghouse Electric Corp., 210 F.Supp. 483, 485 (E.D.Pa.), petition for mandamus and prohibition denied, General Electric Company v. Kirkpatrick, 312 F.2d 742 (C.A.3 1962), cert. denied, 372 U.S. 943, 83 S.Ct. 937, 9 L.Ed.2d 969 (1963), reflected a similar conceptual approach:

> "Keeping in mind that the question is, Is it the corporation which is seeking the lawyer's advice when the asserted privileged communication is made?, the most satisfactory solution, I think, is that if the employee

making the communication, of whatever rank he may be, is in a position to control or even to take a substantial part in a decision about any action which the corporation may take upon the advice of the attorney, ... then, in effect, he is (or personifies) the corporation when he makes his disclosure to the lawyer and the privilege would apply."

Such a view, we think, overlooks the fact that the privilege exists to protect not only the giving of professional advice to those who can act on it but also the giving of information to the lawyer to enable him to give sound and informed advice.... See ABA Code of Professional Responsibility, Ethical Consideration 4–1:

> "A lawyer should be fully informed of all the facts of the matter he is handling in order for his client to obtain the full advantage of our legal system. It is for the lawyer in the exercise of his independent professional judgment to separate the relevant and important from the irrelevant and unimportant. The observance of the ethical obligation of a lawyer to hold inviolate the confidences and secrets of his client not only facilitates the full development of facts essential to proper representation of the client but also encourages laymen to seek early legal assistance."

See also Hickman v. Taylor, 329 U.S. 495, 511, 67 S.Ct. 385, 393–394, 91 L.Ed. 451 (1947).

In the case of the individual client the provider of information and the person who acts on the lawyer's advice are one and the same. In the corporate context, however, it will frequently be employees beyond the control group as defined by the court below, "officers and agents ... responsible for directing [the company's] actions in response to legal advice"—who will possess the information needed by the corporation's lawyers. Middle-level—and indeed lower-level—employees can, by actions within the scope of their employment, embroil the corporation in serious legal difficulties, and it is only natural that these employees would have the relevant information needed by corporate counsel if he is adequately to advise the client with respect to such actual or potential difficulties. This fact was noted in Diversified Industries, Inc. v. Meredith, 572 F.2d 596 (C.A.8 1977) (en banc):

> "In a corporation, it may be necessary to glean information relevant to a legal problem from middle management or non-management personnel as well as from top executives. The attorney dealing with a complex legal problem 'is thus faced with a "Hobson's choice." If he interviews employees not having "the very highest authority" their communications to him will not be privileged. If, on the other hand, he interviews only those employees with the "very highest authority," he may find it extremely difficult, if not impossible, to determine what happened.' " Id. at 608–609 (quoting Weinschel, Corporate Employee Interviews and the Attorney-Client Privilege, 12 B.C. Ind. & Comm.L.Rev. 873, 876 (1970)).

The control group test adopted by the court below thus frustrates the very purpose of the privilege by discouraging the communication of relevant information by employees of the client to attorneys seeking to render legal advice to the client corporation. The attorney's advice will also frequently be more significant to noncontrol group members than to those who officially sanction the advice, and the control group test makes it more difficult to convey full and frank legal advice to the employees who will put into effect the client corporation's policy. See, e.g., Duplan Corp. v. Deering Milliken, Inc., 397 F.Supp. 1146, 1164 (D.S.C.1974) ("After the lawyer forms his or her opinion, it is of no immediate benefit to the Chairman of the Board or the President. It must be given to the corporate personnel who will apply it.").

The narrow scope given the attorney-client privilege by the court below not only makes it difficult for corporate attorneys to formulate sound advice when their client is faced with a specific legal problem but also threatens to limit the valuable efforts of corporate counsel to ensure their client's compliance with the law. In light of the vast and complicated array of regulatory legislation confronting the modern corporation, corporations, unlike most individuals, "constantly go to lawyers to find out how to obey the law," Burnham, The Attorney-Client Privilege in the Corporate Arena, 24 Bus.Law. 901, 913 (1969), particularly since compliance with the law in this area is hardly an instinctive matter, see, e.g., United States v. United States Gypsum Co., 438 U.S. 422, 440–441, 98 S.Ct. 2864, 2875–2876, 57 L.Ed.2d 854 (1978) ("the behavior proscribed by the [Sherman] Act is often difficult to distinguish from the gray zone of socially acceptable and economically justifiable business conduct"). The test adopted by the court below is difficult to apply in practice, though no abstractly formulated and unvarying "test" will necessarily enable courts to decide questions such as this with mathematical precision. But if the purpose of the attorney-client privilege is to be served, the attorney and client must be able to predict with some degree of certainty whether particular discussions will be protected. An uncertain privilege, or one which purports to be certain but results in widely varying applications by the courts, is little better than no privilege at all. The very terms of the test adopted by the court below suggest the unpredictability of its application. The test restricts the availability of the privilege to those officers who play a "substantial role" in deciding and directing a corporation's legal response. Disparate decisions in cases applying this test illustrate its unpredictability. . . .

The communications at issue were made by Upjohn employees to counsel for Upjohn acting as such, at the direction of corporate superiors in order to secure legal advice from counsel. As the magistrate found, "Mr. Thomas consulted with the Chairman of the Board and outside counsel and thereafter conducted a factual investigation to determine the nature and extent of the questionable payments and to be in a position to give legal advice to the company with respect to the payments." Pet.App. 13a. Information, not available from upper-echelon management, was needed to supply a basis for legal advice concerning compliance with securities and tax laws, foreign laws, currency regulations, duties to shareholders, and potential litigation in each of these areas. The communications concerned matters within the scope of the employees' corporate duties, and the employees themselves were sufficiently aware that they were being questioned in order that the corporation could obtain legal advice. The questionnaire identified Thomas as "the company's General Counsel" and referred in its opening sentence to the possible illegality of payments such as the ones on which information was sought. App. 48a. A statement of policy accompanying the questionnaire clearly indicated the legal implications of the investigation. The policy statement was issued "in order that there be no uncertainty in the future as to the policy with respect to the practices which are the subject of this investigation." It began "Upjohn will comply with all laws and regulations," and stated that commissions or payments "will not be used as a subterfuge for bribes or illegal payments" and that all payments must be "proper and legal." Any future agreements with foreign distributors or agents were to be approved "by a company attorney" and any questions concerning the policy were to be referred "to the company's General Counsel." App. 165a–166a. This statement was issued to Upjohn employees worldwide, so that even those interviewees not receiving a questionnaire were aware of the legal implications of the interviews. Pursuant to explicit instructions from the Chairman of the Board, the communications were considered "highly confidential" when made, App. 39a, 43a, and have been kept confidential by the company. Consistent with the underlying purposes of the attorney-client privilege, these communications must be protected against compelled disclosure.

The Court of Appeals declined to extend the attorney-client privilege beyond the limits of the control group test for fear that doing so would entail severe burdens on discovery and create a broad "zone of silence" over corporate affairs. Application of the attorney-client privilege to communications such as those involved here, however, puts the adversary in no worse position than if the communications had never taken place. The privilege only protects disclosure of communications; it does not protect disclosure of the underlying facts by those who communicated with the attorney:

> "The protection of the privilege extends only to communications and not to facts. A fact is one thing and a communication concerning that fact is an entirely different thing. The client cannot be compelled to answer the question, 'What did you say or write to the attorney?' but may not refuse to disclose any relevant fact within his knowledge merely because he incorporated a statement of such fact into his communication to his attorney." City of Philadelphia v. Westinghouse Electric Corp., 205 F.Supp. 830, 831 (E.D.Pa.1962).

... Here the Government was free to question the employees who communicated with Thomas and outside counsel. Upjohn has provided the IRS with a list of such employees, and the IRS has already interviewed some 25 of them. While it would probably be more convenient for the Government to secure the results of petitioner's internal investigation by simply subpoenaing the questionnaires and notes taken by petitioner's attorneys, such considerations of convenience do not overcome the policies served by the attorney-client privilege. As Justice Jackson noted in his concurring opinion in Hickman v. Taylor, 329 U.S., at 516, 67 S.Ct., at 396: "Discovery was hardly intended to enable a learned profession to perform its functions ... on wits borrowed from the adversary."

Needless to say, we decide only the case before us, and do not undertake to draft a set of rules which should govern challenges to investigatory subpoenas. Any such approach would violate the spirit of F.R.E. 501. See S.Rep. No. 93–1277, 93d Cong., 2d Sess., 13 ("the recognition of a privilege based on a confidential relationship ... should be determined on a case-by-case basis"); Trammel, 445 U.S., at 47, 100 S.Ct., at 910–911; United States v. Gillock, 445 U.S. 360, 367, 100 S.Ct. 1185, 1190, 63 L.Ed.2d 454 (1980). While such a "case-by-case" basis may to some slight extent undermine desirable certainty in the boundaries of the attorney-client privilege, it obeys the spirit of the Rules. At the same time we conclude that the narrow "control group test" sanctioned by the Court of Appeals, in this case cannot, consistent with "the principles of the common law as ... interpreted ... in light of reason and experience," F.R.E. 501, govern the development of the law in this area.

III

Our decision that the communications by Upjohn employees to counsel are covered by the attorney-client privilege disposes of the case so far as the responses to the questionnaires and any notes reflecting responses to interview questions are concerned. The summons reaches further, however, and Thomas has testified that his notes and memoranda of interviews go beyond recording responses to his questions. App. 27a–28a, 91a–93a. To the extent that the material subject to the summons is not protected by the attorney-client privilege as disclosing communications between an employee and counsel, we must reach the ruling by the Court of Appeals that the work-product doctrine does not apply to summonses issued under 26 U.S.C. § 7602.

The Government concedes, wisely, that the Court of Appeals erred and that the work-product doctrine does apply to IRS summonses. Gov.Br., at 16, 48. This doctrine was announced by the Court over 30 years ago in Hickman v. Taylor, 329 U.S. 495, 67 S.Ct. 385, 91 L.Ed. 451 (1947). In that case the Court rejected "an attempt, without purported necessity or justification, to secure written statements, private memoranda, and personal recollections prepared or formed by an adverse party's counsel in the course of his legal duties." Id., at 510, 67 S.Ct., at 393. The Court noted that "it is essential that a lawyer work with a certain degree of privacy" and reasoned that if discovery of the material sought were permitted

> "much of what is now put down in writing would remain unwritten. An attorney's thoughts, heretofore inviolate, would not be his own. Inefficiency, unfairness and sharp practices would inevitably develop in the giving of legal advice and in the preparation of cases for trial. The effect on the legal profession would be demoralizing. And the interests of the clients and the cause of justice would be poorly served." Id., at 511, 67 S.Ct., at 393–394.

The "strong public policy" underlying the work-product doctrine was reaffirmed recently in United States v. Nobles, 422 U.S. 225, 236–240, 95 S.Ct. 2160, 2169–2171, 45 L.Ed.2d 141 (1975), and has been substantially incorporated in Federal Rule of Civil Procedure 26(b)(3).

As we stated last Term, the obligation imposed by a tax summons remains "subject to the traditional privileges and limitations." United States v. Euge, 444 U.S. 707, 714, 100 S.Ct. 874, 879–880, 63 L.Ed.2d 141 (1980). Nothing in the language of the IRS summons provisions or their legislative history suggests an intent on the part of Congress to preclude application of the work-product doctrine. Rule 26(b)(3) codifies the work-product doctrine, and the Federal Rules of Civil Procedure are made applicable to summons enforcement proceedings by Rule 81(a)(3). See Donaldson v. United States, 400 U.S. 517, 528, 91 S.Ct. 534, 541, 27 L.Ed.2d 580 (1971). While conceding the applicability of the work-product doctrine, the Government asserts that it has made a sufficient showing of necessity to overcome its protections. The magistrate apparently so found, Pet.App. 30a. The Government relies on the following language in Hickman:

> "We do not mean to say that all written materials obtained or prepared by an adversary's counsel with an eye toward litigation are necessarily free from discovery in all cases. Where relevant and nonprivileged facts remain hidden in an attorney's file and where production of those facts is essential to the preparation of one's case discovery may properly be had.... And production might be justified where the witnesses are no longer available or may be reached only with difficulty." 329 U.S. at 511, 67 S.Ct., at 394.

The Government stresses that interviewees are scattered across the globe and that Upjohn has forbidden its employees to answer questions it considers irrelevant. The above-quoted language from Hickman, however, did not apply to "oral statements made by witnesses ... whether presently in the form of [the attorney's] mental impressions or memoranda." Id., at 512, 67 S.Ct., at 394. As to such material the Court did "not believe that any showing of necessity can be made under the circumstances of this case so as to justify production.... If there should be a rare situation justifying production of these matters petitioner's case is not of that type." Id., at 512–513, 67 S.Ct., at 394–395. See also Nobles, supra, 422 U.S., at 252–253, 95 S.Ct., at 2177 (White, J., concurring). Forcing an attorney to disclose notes and memoranda of witnesses' oral statements is particularly disfavored because it tends to reveal the attorney's mental processes, 329 U.S., at 513, 67 S.Ct., at 394–395 ("what he saw fit to write down regarding witnesses' remarks"); id., at 516–517, 67 S.Ct., at 396 ("the statement would be his [the attorney's] language, permeated with his inferences") (Jackson, J., concurring).

Rule 26 accords special protection to work product revealing the attorney's mental processes. The Rule permits disclosure of documents and tangible things constituting attorney work product upon a showing of substantial need and inability to obtain the equivalent without undue hardship. This was the standard applied by the magistrate, Pet.App. 26a–27a. Rule 26 goes on, however, to state that "[i]n ordering discovery of such materials when the required showing has been made, the court shall protect against disclosure of the mental impressions, conclusions, opinions or legal theories of an attorney or other representative of a party concerning the litigation." Although this language does not specifically refer to memoranda based on oral statements of witnesses, the Hickman court stressed the danger that compelled disclosure of such memoranda would reveal the attorney's mental processes. It is clear that this is the sort of material the draftsmen of the Rule had in mind as deserving special protection. See Notes of Advisory Committee on 1970 Amendment to Rules, reprinted in 48 F.R.D. 487, 502 ("The subdivision . . . goes on to protect against disclosure the mental impressions, conclusions, opinions, or legal theories . . . of an attorney or other representative of a party. The Hickman opinion drew special attention to the need for protecting an attorney against discovery of memoranda prepared from recollection of oral interviews. The courts have steadfastly safeguarded against disclosure of lawyers' mental impressions and legal theories . . .").

Based on the foregoing, some courts have concluded that no showing of necessity can overcome protection of work product which is based on oral statements from witnesses. See, e.g., In re Grand Jury Proceedings, 473 F.2d 840, 848 (C.A.8 1973) (personal recollections, notes and memoranda pertaining to conversation with witnesses); In re Grand Jury Investigation, 412 F.Supp. 943, 949 (E.D.Pa.1976) (notes of conversation with witness "are so much a product of the lawyer's thinking and so little probative of the witness's actual words that they are absolutely protected from disclosure"). Those courts declining to adopt an absolute rule have nonetheless recognized that such material is entitled to special protection. See, e.g., In re Grand Jury Investigation, 599 F.2d, at 1231 ("special considerations . . . must shape any ruling on the discoverability of interview memoranda . . . such documents will be discoverable only in a 'rare situation' "); Cf. In re Grand Jury Subpoena, 599 F.2d, at 511–512.

We do not decide the issue at this time. It is clear that the magistrate applied the wrong standard when he concluded that the Government had made a sufficient showing of necessity to overcome the protections of the work-product doctrine. The magistrate applied the "substantial need" and "without undue hardship" standard articulated in the first part of Rule 26(b)(3). The notes and memoranda sought by the Government here, however, are work product based on oral statements. If they reveal communications, they are, in this case, protected by the attorney-client privilege. To the extent they do not reveal communications, they reveal the attorneys' mental processes in evaluating the communications. As Rule 26 and Hickman make clear, such work product cannot be disclosed simply on a showing of substantial need and inability to obtain the equivalent without undue hardship.

While we are not prepared at this juncture to say that such material is always protected by the work-product rule, we think a far stronger showing of necessity and unavailability by other means than was made by the Government or applied by the magistrate in this case would be necessary to compel disclosure. Since the Court of Appeals thought that the work-product protection was never applicable in an enforcement proceeding such as this, and since the magistrate whose recommendations the District Court adopted applied too lenient a standard of protection, we think the best procedure with respect to this aspect of the case would be to reverse the judgment of the Court of Appeals for the Sixth Circuit and remand the case to it for such further proceedings in connection with the work-product claim as are consistent with this opinion.

Accordingly, the judgment of the Court of Appeals is reversed, and the case remanded for further proceedings.

■ CHIEF JUSTICE BURGER, concurring in part and concurring in the judgment.

I join in Parts I and III of the opinion of the Court and in the judgment. As to Part II, I agree fully with the Court's rejection of the so-called "control group" test, its reasons for doing so, and its ultimate holding that the communications at issue are privileged. As the Court states, however, "if the purpose of the attorney-client privilege is to be served, the attorney and the client must be able to predict with some degree of certainty whether particular discussions will be protected." Ante, at 684. For this very reason, I believe that we should articulate a standard that will govern similar cases and afford guidance to corporations, counsel advising them, and federal courts.

The Court properly relies on a variety of factors in concluding that the communications now before us are privileged. See ante, at 685. Because of the great importance of the issue, in my view the Court should make clear now that, as a general rule, a communication is privileged at least when, as here, an employee or former employee speaks at the direction of the management with an attorney regarding conduct or proposed conduct within the scope of employment. The attorney must be one authorized by the management to inquire into the subject and must be seeking information to assist counsel in performing any of the following functions: (a) evaluating whether the employee's conduct has bound or would bind the corporation; (b) assessing the legal consequences, if any, of that conduct; or (c) formulating appropriate legal responses to actions that have been or may be taken by others with regard to that conduct....

Other communications between employees and corporate counsel may indeed be privileged,as the petitioners and several amici have suggested in their proposed formulations,but the need for certainty does not compel us now to prescribe all the details of the privilege in this case.

NOTES

1. The principal case addresses a few of the many issues that arise out of the relationship between the lawyer and a corporation. The modern context in which these issues arise has been described as follows:

> As the operation of the modern corporation and the regulation under which it transacts business have grown increasingly complex, the involvement of corporate attorneys in their clients' affairs has comparably expanded. Corporate attorneys are increasingly acquiring responsibility for examining, through special investigations and routine oversight, the actions of the corporation and its employees for compliance with the law. Consequently, the corporate attorney has developed into a focal point for damaging

information about the corporation, and hence an invaluable potential source of information. Access to the attorney's knowledge and files provides an enormous boon to any legal adversary of the client, whether a governmental agency or private party.

For the most part, clients and even many lawyers are relatively insensitive to this problem, presuming that any disclosures to an attorney are magically rendered immune from later discovery; yet the only special limitations on obtaining information from a lawyer are the attorney-client privilege and the work product doctrine, both of which leave large holes in the cloak of protection. Even more unsettling, the uneven, confusing and contradictory administration of the general standards for these protections in the corporate setting have created a situation in which freedom from discovery can only be guaranteed for only a narrow class of information; often documents protected in one court will be discoverable in another.

Borow and Guth, The Attorney–Client Relationship in the Context of an SEC Investigation and Related Criminal Proceedings, SEC Enforcement and White Collar Crimes 253–254 (N.Y.L.J. Press 1981).

2. As the principal case indicates, the attorney-client privilege is generally held to be applicable to corporations. Compare the privilege against self-incrimination which is held not to apply to group entities such as corporations.

For a judicial argument that the attorney-client privilege should not be extended to corporations, see Chief Judge Campbell's opinion in Radiant Burners, Inc. v. American Gas Ass'n, 207 F.Supp. 771 (N.D.Ill.1962), reversed by the court of appeals, 320 F.2d 314 (7th Cir.1963), in an opinion that stated: "With deference to the ingenuity and judicial courage displayed by the district court ... we find ourselves in disagreement with the broad holding that a corporation is not entitled to make claim to the attorney-client privilege."

In Thornburg, Sanctifying Secrecy: The Mythology of the Corporate Attorney–Client Privilege, 69 Notre Dame L.Rev. 157 (1993), a vigorous attack is made on the application of the attorney-client privilege in the corporate setting. In reviewing the material in this section, consider the following excerpts from the Thornburg article:

The corporate attorney client privilege tends to give corporate and repeat litigants an advantage over individual litigants, and to give defendants an advantage over plaintiffs. This impacts the disadvantaged parties, and also the judicial system as a whole because of its tendency to affect case outcomes more consistently. A corporation that can plan for the occurrence of claims against it has the advantage of being able to structure its information flow so as to maximize the chance that internal communication will be held to be privileged and thus shielded from discovery. In many settings, then, a privilege claim is not a mere procedural rule. It is also, "in effect, an argument for a substantive advantage for generally identifiable interests." For example, the literature for corporate lawyers is replete with articles recommending strategies for protecting communications with a privilege and for performing "legal audits" to eliminate incriminating documents. A corporation that is a repeat litigant can choose to litigate a privilege issue, whatever its expense, because it is able to spread that expense over multiple lawsuits. It can also choose to litigate those cases that are most likely to produce proprivilege case law. As a class of litigants that are most likely to do early, extensive internal investigation, repeat corporate litigants are the primary beneficiaries of a privilege that protects the communications generated in those investigations from discovery....

Without an available privilege, the corporation and its employees would have to communicate the information required to secure reliable legal advice and to protect the corporation's interests during litigation. The party bearing the bad facts would bear the risk of communicating or not communicating that information to its attorney. But there would be no point in creating labyrinthine processes to maximize some privilege, because no privilege would exist.

Thornburg, supra, at 202–203, 221.

3. There is an extensive literature on the corporate attorney-client privilege and on the principal case. See, e.g., Leubsdorf, Pluralizing the Client Lawyer Relationship, 77 Cornell L.Rev. 825 (1992); Alexander, The Corporate Attorney–Client Privilege: A Study of the Participants, 63 St.John's L.Rev. 191 (1989); Waldman, Beyond Upjohn: The Attorney–Client Privilege in the Corporate Context, 28 Wm. & Mary L.Rev. 473 (1987); Saltzburg, The Federal Rules of Evidence: Corporate and Related Attorney–Client Privilege Claims: A Suggested Approach, 12 Hofstra L.Rev. 279 (1984); Note, The Attorney–Client Privilege and the Corporate Client: Where Do We Go After Upjohn? 81 Mich.L.Rev. 665 (1983); Sexton, A PostUpjohn Consideration of the Corporate Attorney–Client Privilege, 57 N.Y.U.L.Rev. 443 (1982); Gergacz, Attorney Corporate Client Privilege, 37 Bus. Law. 461 (1982); Rosenfeld, The Transformation of the Attorney Client Privilege: In Search of an Ideological Reconciliation of Individualism, the Adversary System, and the Corporate Client's S.E.C. Disclosure Obligations, 33 Hastings L.J. 495 (1982).

4. Note that in the principal case, the attorney involved in the claim based on the attorney-client privilege was in-house counsel. Should it matter whether in-house counsel or outside counsel is involved? Note that the attorney-client privilege is generally held to apply equally to in-house counsel and outside counsel. See the opinion of Judge Wyzanski, United States v. United Shoe Machinery Corp., 89 F.Supp. 357, 360 (D.Mass.1950) and see Forrow, The Corporate Law Department Lawyer, Counsel to the Entity, 34 Bus.Law 1797 (1979). Also see generally Spangler, Lawyers for Hire, Salaried Professionals at Work (1986).

Compare the approach in many European countries where in-house counsel are not permitted to be members of the bar because they are not deemed to be independent. Accordingly, the European Court of Justice of the European Community ruled that in-house counsel in the EC would not have the benefit of the attorney-client privilege that covers communications with independent attorneys. Case 1^{55}/₇₉, AM & S Europe Ltd. v. Commission, 1982 E.C.R. 1575. See Hill, Note: A Problem of Privilege: In–House Counsel and the Attorney–Client Privilege in the United States and the European Community, 27 Case W. Res. J. Int'l L. 145 (1995); Burkard, Attorney–Client Privilege in the EEC: The Perspective of the Multinational Corporate Counsel, 20 Int'l Law 677 (1986).

In 1990, it was reported that in excess of 55,000 attorneys in the United States, representing approximately 10% of the bar, were employed as in-house counsel. Metzloff, Ethical Considerations for the Corporate Legal Counsel, Westlaw, C566 Ali–Aba 109 (1990). For a study which identifies some differences in the perceptions of in-house and outside corporate counsel relating to the operation of the attorney-client privilege, see Alexander, The Corporate Attorney–Client Privilege: A Study of the Participants, 63 St.John's L.Rev. 191 (1989).

5. What kinds of considerations become important under the Court's approach in Upjohn? Is it significant, for example, that information is obtained by counsel from corporate employees to enable the lawyer to give legal advice regarding impending litigation? regarding possible litigation? regarding safety measures that might be taken to avoid future liability? How does one distinguish between "business advice" and "legal advice" if the source of the advice is a lawyer?

6. Which of the following factors is sufficiently crucial under Upjohn that its absence should defeat the application of the attorney-client privilege?

(a) The investigation was being conducted to enable counsel "to be in a position to give legal advice" to the company.

(b) The information "was needed to supply a basis for legal advice concerning compliance with ... [certain] laws, ... duties to stockholders and potential litigation...."

(c) The communications concerned matters within the scope of the employees' corporate duties.

(d) The employees were aware that they were being questioned so that the corporation could obtain legal advice.

(e) Various written statements accompanying the investigative questionnaire emphasized the legal implications of the information being sought and that corporate attorneys were involved.

(f) The fact that the communications were considered "highly confidential" was emphasized in the written statements.

(g) The communications were kept confidential by the company.

7. The control group test applied by many courts prior to Upjohn and the approach taken in Upjohn focus on whether the person(s) from whom communications are made to the corporate attorney are to be viewed as the client(s) in connection with a claim by the corporation that the privilege attached to their communications. Does Upjohn have implications for other issues in the corporate attorney-client setting?

8. To what kind of intra-corporate documents does the privilege apply? Suppose an interview of a corporate employee is conducted by a corporate attorney in the course of an investigation into possible criminal activities of employees, and the interview statement is also transmitted to other corporate departments. See Sierra Vista Hospital v. Superior Court, 248 Cal.App.2d 359, 368–369, 56 Cal.Rptr. 387, 392–393 (1967): A report of an incident in the hospital was prepared by the Director of Nursing Services and the Hospital Administrator. The report was sent to the carrier of the hospital's liability insurance company which in turn forwarded the report to the attorney representing the hospital in the event of litigation. The report was prepared on a form labeled "Confidential Report of Incident (Not a Part of Medical Record)." Held: Privileged. The hospital intended the report to be made as a confidential communication from it to its attorney through the agency of its insurance company. The court quoted from a leading California decision, D.I. Chadbourne Inc. v. Superior Court, 60 Cal.2d 723, 737, 36 Cal.Rptr. 468, 478, 388 P.2d 700 (1964): "[T]he number of hands through which the communication may travel without losing confidentiality must always depend on reason and the particular facts of the case...." Compare Bernardi v. Community Hospital Association, 166 Colo. 280, 443 P.2d 708, 715–716 (1968) where the court reached a contrary result in a case where the incident report prepared by a nurse was placed in the patient's hospital chart, another copy went to the hospital administrator and still another copy went to the director of nurses at the hospital. Counsel for the hospital did not see all incident reports that were prepared and did not see the report in question. He was only made aware of its contents after the action in this case was filed.

In Chadbourne supra, the court stated:

When the corporate employer has more than one purpose in directing ... [the] employee to make ... [the] report or statement, the dominant purpose will control, unless the secondary use is such that confidentiality has been waived.

9. In connection with the issues raised in the preceding note, and in light of Upjohn, consider the following excerpt from Thornburg, supra, note 2:

Let's return to XYZ corporation, the manufacturer of consumer widgets, and its employee Smith. A consumer who was injured by the widget has sued and alleges that the widget is defective.

If the plaintiff ... deposes Jones, the president, and asks him what Smith said, the president should be required testify about what Smith told him because the communication went straight from employee to employee for business purposes. Unfortunately, the claims and the case law are not so clear. Many corporations would still claim a privilege based on the attorney's need to gather information. The argument goes like this: no single corporate employee is likely to have all the information the lawyer needs to advise the corporation, and so corporate employees need to be able to gather this information for the lawyer. If there is no privilege for what Smith told Jones, Jones will be reluctant to seek out this information for fear that it will be used against the corporation, and the attorney will not get all the information needed to represent the corporation. After all, if the attorney interviewed Smith directly, their conversations would be privileged. Therefore, inserting Jones as investigator/lawyer's helper should not change the character of the conversation. Smith is still providing information for the lawyer, and Jones is serving as a mere conduit. ...

How, then, can the plaintiff learn anything if such privilege claims are sustained? He will need to somehow identify those employees who have personal knowledge of the relevant facts and depose each one. He must also identify and seek production of those documents that never went near the lawyer's office.

Thornburg, supra note 2 at 193–195.

10.   Problem: A large manufacturer is subject to numerous products liability suits. When the company receives notice of the filing of a claim, an in-house attorney sets a case reserve for the matter embodying the attorney's estimate of anticipated legal expenses, settlement value, length of time to resolve the litigation, geographic considerations and other factors. The documents containing the individual case reserves set by the legal department are then sent to and used by another department in the company, the risk management department, for a variety of business planning purposes involving budget, profit and insurance. Does the attorney-client privilege attach to these documents? See Simon v. G.D. Searle & Co., 816 F.2d 397 (8th Cir.1987).

The risk management department also uses the individual case reserve documents to generate risk management documents that aggregate the case reserve information in an attempt to keep track of the costs of the company's products liability litigation. Does the attorney client privilege attach to these documents? See Simon v. G.D. Searle & Co., supra.

11.   a) Problem: X corporation is in financial difficulty. On March 26, 1985, A, the President of the corporation, begins meeting with attorneys from the Y law firm regarding the matters that led to the corporation's financial difficulty, explaining that he is seeking both personal and corporate legal advice and indicating to the attorneys that "possibly you will represent me; possibly you will represent the firm." On March 31st, the Y law firm is retained to represent the X corporation, and the firm continues to consider whether it will represent A and other principals of the corporation. A's meetings with the attorneys of the firm continue until April 4th when the law firm informs A and other principals in the corporation that they should obtain separate counsel. On April 7th, the corporation files a petition for bankruptcy and a trustee is appointed. In connection with subsequent litigation, the trustee attempts to depose A regarding his conversations with the attorneys between March 26 and April 4, 1985. A invokes his personal attorney-client privilege. What result? See In the Matter of Bevill, Bresler & Schulman Asset Management Corporation, 805 F.2d 120 (3d Cir.1986).

b) Suppose the claim of privilege is made by the employee (but not by the corporation) with respect to an interview of the employee conducted by the corporate attorney in the course of an investigation into possible criminal activities of corporate employees. See United States v. Demauro, 581 F.2d 50, 55 (2d Cir.1978).

c) Does Upjohn apply where the interview that is sought by discovery was with an employee that the corporation intended to terminate? Held: interview statement to corporate counsel by employee scheduled to be terminated covered by attorney-client privilege. Admiral Insurance Company v. United States District Court, 881 F.2d 1486 (9th Cir.1989). The privilege has also been applied to information provided by former corporate employees. In re Coordinated Pretrial Proceedings, 658 F.2d 1355 (9th Cir.1981).

d) Suppose the employee when deposed claims the privilege against self-incrimination so that the third party has no way to get at the underlying facts. Should this affect the availability of the attorney-client privilege under Upjohn? Held: No, an unavailability exception would be inconsistent with the purpose of the privilege. Admiral Insurance Company v. United States District Court, supra c.

12. Upjohn also involved application of the work-product doctrine enunciated in Hickman v. Taylor, 329 U.S. 495 (1947). That doctrine was subsequently incorporated in Rule 26(b)(3) of the Federal Rules of Civil Procedure which in pertinent part provides:

[A] party may obtain discovery of documents and tangible things otherwise discoverable under subdivision (b)(1) of this rule and prepared in anticipation of litigation or for trial by or for another party or by or for that other party's representative (including his attorney, consultant, surety, indemnitor, insurer, or agent) only upon a showing that the party seeking discovery has substantial need of the materials in the preparation of his case and that he is unable without undue hardship to obtain the substantial equivalent of the materials by other means. In ordering discovery of such materials when the required showing has been made, the court shall protect against disclosure of the mental impressions, conclusions, opinions, or legal theories of an attorney or other representative of a party concerning the litigation.

13. Rule 26(b)(3) extends work-product protection where the material, discovery of which is sought, was "prepared in anticipation of litigation." See e.g. In re Grand Jury Proceedings in the Matter of Browning Arms Co., 528 F.2d 1301, 1303–1304 (8th Cir.1976). How should this limitation be interpreted? For example, should work-product protection extend to an attorney's investigation into possibly illegal actions taken by employees of the corporate client? Compare Diversified Industries v. Meredith, 572 F.2d 596 (8th Cir.1977) with In re Grand Jury Subpoena, 599 F.2d 504 (2d Cir.1979). Should it matter whether litigation has actually been initiated? Whether the material was also prepared for other than litigation purposes? See the advisory committee's notes to Rule 26(b)(3): "Materials assembled in the ordinary course of business . . . or for other nonlitigation purposes are not under the qualified immunity provided by this subdivision." See Simon v. G.D. Searle & Co., 816 F.2d 397, 401 (8th Cir.1987).

14. If the materials were prepared in anticipation of litigation, should it matter that discovery is sought in connection with the trial of a case other than that which was "anticipated"? See e.g. In re Subpoena Addressed to Samuel W. Murphy, 560 F.2d 326, 334–335 (8th Cir.1977).

15. As noted by the Court in Upjohn, the Hickman Opinion indicated that work-product materials might be discoverable when a sufficient showing was made that the materials could not otherwise be obtained or could be obtained "only with difficulty." This approach was codified into the Rule 26(b)(3) provision that the party seeking discovery must show "substantial need" and that he is "unable without undue hardship to obtain the substantial equivalent of the materials. . . ." But Rule 26, again following the Hickman doctrine recognized that no showing of necessity could force disclosure of "mental impressions, conclusions, opinions, or legal theories of an attorney. . . ." As noted by the Supreme Court in Upjohn supra, there is some disagreement within the courts of appeal as to how much protection, under this heading, should be afforded to notes and memoranda of witnesses' oral statements. Consider in this connection how much work-product protection should be afforded to the following:

a.   A verbatim transcription prepared by a stenographer of a series of the attorney's questions and the witness' answers.

b.   A verbatim transcription of a witness' narrative statement given in response to a single question by the attorney, "Tell me in your own words what happened."

c.   A verbatim transcription of an interview with the witness conducted by a private detective employed by the attorney.

d.   The notes of an interview with a witness conducted by a private detective employed by the attorney.

In connection with the last two examples, consider the following statement from the opinion of the Court in United States v. Nobles, 422 U.S. 225, 238–239 (1975), the facts of which are set forth, supra, p. 269:

> At its core, the work-product doctrine shelters the mental processes of the attorney, providing a privileged area within which he can analyze and prepare his client's case. But the doctrine is an intensely practical one, grounded in the realities of litigation in our adversary system. One of those realities is that attorneys often must rely on the assistance of investigators and other agents in the compilation of materials in preparation for trial. It is therefore necessary that the doctrine protect material prepared by agents for the attorney as well as those prepared by the attorney himself.

The Court went on to reject the work-product claim on the ground that the defendant waived the protection of the doctrine by calling the investigator to testify as to the statements described in his investigative report. Justice White, joined by Justice Rehnquist in a separate concurrence, argued that the Hickman Court intentionally treated work-product protection as a limitation on pretrial discovery and not as a qualified privilege in order to avoid imposing restrictions on the trial judge's ordering evidentiary matter at trial. Even as to evidentiary matter at trial, however, Justice White seemed to imply that work-product might be applicable where the matter consisted of an oral statement written down by the lawyer since requiring production of such statements would "create a substantial risk that the lawyer would have to testify," Id. at 252, a practice to be frowned upon. Where the statement sought as evidence at trial was written down by an investigator, Justice White concluded the policy against the lawyers testifying was not applicable, and no work-product protection should be afforded. He went on to conclude, however, that the notes of the lawyer and the investigator should be treated similarly in the context of pre-trial discovery:

> Where the purpose of the rule protecting the work product is to remove the incentive a party might otherwise have to rely solely on his opponent's preparation, it is sensible to treat preparation by an attorney and investigator alike.

United States v. Nobles, 422 U.S. 225, 254, at n. 16.

Also consider in this connection People v. Collie, 30 Cal.3d 43, 59–60, 177 Cal.Rptr. 458, 467, 634 P.2d 534, 543–544 (1981):

> The discovered documents in this case were reports to defense counsel from the defense investigator, in which the investigator paraphrased the [witness's] statements . . ., prefacing each with the expression, 'subject reports.' . . . If the only 'work' for which protection is claimed consists of prefacing the witness's statements with a phrase such as 'subject reports,' it is difficult to conceive how the policies served by the work-product doctrine would be offended by its disclosure, at least if it is the attorney's agent rather than the attorney who records the statements. On the other hand, courts should not hastily conclude that summarized or edited remarks, or statements in response to questions formulated by the attorney or his aides, are without potential for invading the protected provinces of thought and strategy.

Collie involved a discovery motion made during cross-examination of the defense witness.

16.   United States v. Nobles, supra, holds inter alia, that work-product protection applies to criminal as well as civil litigation. Does it apply to protect the files of the prosecution as well as the accused? See United States v. Nobles, supra at 238, n. 12.

17.   What kinds of comparisons can be made between the attorney-client privilege and the work-product doctrine? Under what kinds of circumstances might communications emanating from corporate employees be entitled to one kind of protection and not the other? It has often been emphasized that the work-product doctrine provides only qualified protection. Is the attorney-client privilege any less qualified?

Has the Court, by broadening the applicability of the attorney-client privilege in the corporate setting, thereby decreased the number of instances where the only bar to discovery is the work-product doctrine? At the same time, has the Court by its treatment of notes of witness statements under the work-product doctrine come close to creating for such materials absolute protection against discovery? Does the Court seem to be moving in the direction of creating a unitary doctrine under which the old distinctions between the attorney-client privilege and work-product doctrine may no longer be significant? Or do very important differences exist between these two sister doctrines that establish limitations on one party's ability to obtain materials from the other? Consider in this connection the following proposal:

> We believe that, except in one circumstance, only a qualified privilege is desirable in the corporate setting. The privilege should give way upon a substantial showing of need in much the same way as "work product" protection. The exceptional circumstance, where we would apply the privilege in full, is where the corporation can demonstrate that the confidential communications were elicited under circumstances, including potential liability, virtually identical to those facing natural persons. The Supreme Court has taken a different view in Upjohn.

Lempert and Saltzburg, A Modern Approach to Evidence 708 (2d ed. 1982). See also Note: Attorney–Client and Work Product Protection in a Utilitarian World: An Argument for Recomparison, 108 Harv. L.Rev. 1697 (1995).

F.   THE ATTORNEY'S AGENTS AND JOINT DEFENSE MATTERS

People v. Lines

Supreme Court of California, 1975.
13 Cal.3d 500, 119 Cal.Rptr. 225, 531 P.2d 793.

■ SULLIVAN, JUSTICE.

Defendant Richard Lee Lines was charged by information with the murder of his aunt, Rose Ethyl Hunt. He entered pleas of not guilty and not guilty by reason of insanity. After a bifurcated trial, a jury found defendant guilty of murder in the second degree and sane at the time the offense was committed. Defendant was sentenced to imprisonment for the term prescribed by law. He appeals from the judgment of conviction.

. . .

Several psychiatrists were appointed by the court at various stages in the proceeding to examine defendant's mental condition. As will appear, defendant objected to the admission of the testimony of ... Doctor Markman ...

The information was filed on December 17, 1971. On December 27, 1971, defendant entered a plea of not guilty. On January 25, 1972, on defendant's motion the court appointed pursuant to sections 730[1] and 1017[2] of the Evidence Code, Doctors Tweed and Markman to examine defendant. On April 17, 1972, defendant entered a plea of not guilty by reason of insanity and the court thereupon pursuant to section 1026 et seq. of the Penal Code and section 730 of

---

1. Section 730 provides: "When it appears to the court, at any time before or during the trial of an action, that expert evidence is or may be required by the court or by any party to the action, the court on its own motion or on motion of any party may appoint one or more experts to investigate, to render a report as may be ordered by the court, and to testify as an expert at the trial of the action relative to the fact or matter as to which such expert evidence is or may be required. The court may fix the compensation for such services, if any, rendered by any person appointed under this section, in addition to any service as a witness, at such amount as seems reasonable to the court." [Footnotes are those of the court. Some footnotes have been omitted and others renumbered.]

2. Section 1017 provides: "There is no privilege under this article if the psychotherapist is appointed by order of a court to examine the patient, but this exception does not apply where the psychotherapist is appointed by order of the court upon the request of the lawyer for the defendant in a criminal proceeding in order to provide the lawyer with information needed so that he may advise the defendant whether to enter or withdraw a plea based on insanity or to present a defense based on his mental or emotional condition."

the Evidence Code appointed Doctor Bielinski "to examine deft." and "reappointed" Doctors Markman and Tweed "previously appointed ... to examine deft. and report to the court...."[3]

[W]hen Doctor Markman was called defendant objected to the admission of his testimony insofar as it was based on the first two examinations of defendant on the ground the information gained from these examinations constituted confidential communications protected by the attorney-client privilege.

The attorney-client privilege enables a client to prevent disclosure of confidential communications between himself and his attorney, i.e., information transmitted in confidence between a client and his attorney in the course of the attorney-client relationship. (§§ 952, 954.) Confidentiality is not destroyed by disclosure of these communications to third persons "to whom disclosure is reasonably necessary for ... the accomplishment of the purpose for which the lawyer is consulted." (§ 952.) The Law Revision Commission comment to section 952 states that section 952 includes confidential communications made by the client to a physician for the purpose of transmitting such information to the attorney and indicates that this rule codifies the existing law as stated in City & County of San Francisco v. Superior Court (1951) 37 Cal.2d 227, 231 P.2d 26.

. . .

In the case at bench, Doctor ... Markman [was] ... appointed by the court for the purpose of examining defendant for his own benefit and of fully informing his counsel as to the nature and extent of defendant's mental condition to the end of assisting counsel in the preparation and presentation of a defense. What this arrangement amounted to in effect was that defendant, through the doctor as an intermediate agent, communicated to his attorney information as to his mental condition. To put it another way, all information obtained by the doctors from their examination of defendant and the reports thereof furnished to his attorney constituted confidential communications protected from disclosure by the attorney-client privilege. The fact that the psychiatrists were appointed by the court rather than privately employed by counsel in no way affects the confidentiality of these communications since they were appointed to prepare a confidential report for defendant.

The People apparently concede that these communications from Dr. Markman were originally protected by the attorney-client privilege but argue that they ceased to be so once defendant tendered the issue of his mental condition by pleading not guilty by reason of insanity. Under the patient-litigant exception to the physician-patient privilege "[t]here is no privilege ... as to a communication relevant to an issue concerning the condition of the patient if such issue has been tendered by ... [t]he patient...." (§ 996.) Similarly under the patient-litigant exception to the psychotherapist-patient privilege, "[t]here is no privilege ... as to a communication relevant to an issue concerning the mental or emotional condition of the patient if such issue has been tendered by ... [t]he patient...." (§ 1016.) But there is no statutory client-litigant exception to the attorney-client privilege (see §§ 950–962). Indeed this court has expressly so held, declaring that when communications by a client to his attorney regarding his physical or mental condition require the assistance of a

---

3. Penal Code section 1027 provides: "When a defendant pleads not guilty by reason of insanity the court must select and appoint two, and may select and appoint three, psychiatrists to examine the defendant and investigate his sanity. It is the duty of the psychiatrists so selected and appointed to examine the defendant and investigate his insanity, and to testify, whenever summoned, in any proceeding in which the sanity of the defendant is in question."

physician to interpret the client's condition to the attorney, the information obtained by the physician as a result remains protected from disclosure even if the client places his physical or mental condition in issue. (City & County of San Francisco v. Superior Court, supra, 37 Cal.2d 227, 237–238, 231 P.2d 26.)

. . .

The record in the instant case reveals that Doctor Markman was initially appointed by the court to examine defendant by order made on January 25, 1972, pursuant to sections 730 and 1017 on motion of defendant. The results and any report of such examination and all information and communications relating thereto were permanently protected by the attorney-client privilege unless such privilege was waived. However, on April 17, 1972, upon defendant's entering a plea of not guilty by reason of insanity, Doctor Markman (again along with Doctor Tweed) was reappointed to examine defendant and report to the court by a given date. As noted previously, this reappointment was made at the same time that Doctor Bielinski was appointed to examine defendant. . . .

It thus appears that . . ., the court appointed three psychiatrists pursuant to Penal Code section 1027, two of whom, Doctors Markman and Tweed, had been appointed on January 25, not pursuant to Penal Code section 1027 but pursuant to Evidence Code section 1017. When a defendant pleads not guilty by reason of insanity, the court is required to appoint two psychiatrists to examine defendant and investigate his sanity; these psychiatrists may be called to testify by either party or the court. The information gained from these examinations and communicated to the court, either by written medical report or in court testimony of the psychiatrist called as a witness by either party or by the court itself is clearly not protected by the attorney-client privilege. The psychiatrists so appointed are not appointed as agents of the attorney, but of the court; the communications are not made in confidence and are not made to the attorney. Therefore, the trial court did not err in allowing Doctor Markman to testify as to the results of his examination of defendant pursuant to his reappointment under section 1027 of the Penal Code. However, the results of the initial examination pursuant to section 1017 and communications thereof to defendant's attorney are, as stated earlier, protected by the attorney-client privilege. . . .

Nevertheless we do not believe that the admission of the testimony of Doctor . . . Markman, although error, was prejudicial to defendant. [His] testimony was essentially the same as that of Doctor . . . Tweed who testified, without objection by the defense, as to defendant's sanity. Defendant has failed to point out to us anything different or particularly prejudicial to him in the testimony of Doctor . . . Markman. After an examination of the entire cause, including the evidence, it does not appear to us to be reasonably probable that a result more favorable to defendant would have been reached in the absence of the above error. We cannot say that there has been a miscarriage of justice . . . .

NOTES

1. For other decisions holding that the attorney-client privilege applies to a criminal defendant's communications to a physician or psychiatrist engaged by his counsel and consulted in preparation for trial and that an insanity plea does not waive the privilege, see State v. Pratt, 398 A.2d 421, 422–425 (Md.1979) and cases cited therein. Compare People v. Edney, 39 N.Y.2d 620, 385 N.Y.S.2d 23, 350 N.E.2d 400 (1976). See also United States v. Alvarez, 519 F.2d 1036, 1046 (3d Cir.1975) where a psychiatrist was appointed with the approval of the court to examine the defendant in aid of preparation of an insanity defense.

The court concluded that: a) the attorney-client privilege covers conversations to the psychiatrist appointed for this purpose; b) the privilege is not waived by the assertion of an insanity defense; c) the privilege would be waived if the expert is later used as a witness on behalf of the defendant. Why should calling the psychiatrist to the stand waive the privilege while simply asserting the insanity defense does not?

2. In the principal case, the same psychiatrist was twice appointed by the court under two different statutory provisions, and it was held that the attorney-client privilege applied to the first appointment but not to the second. Suppose that the psychiatrist could not testify as to matters learned in the second examination without revealing matters learned in the first? It is noteworthy in this connection that the court in Lines in an omitted portion of the opinion indicated its disapproval of such reappointments. Suppose that the unprivileged appointment occurred first and at the second examination to which the attorney-client privilege did attach, the defendant repeated the same statements he had made at the first examination. Does the attorney-client privilege apply to the psychiatrist's testimony as to those statements?

3. Consider in connection with the principal case the following excerpt from United States ex rel. Edney v. Smith, 425 F.Supp. 1038 (E.D.N.Y.1976):

> The extent to which the privilege includes communications to a non-lawyer by the lawyer's client is determined by balancing two competing factors: 1) The need of the attorney for the assistance of the non-lawyer in effectively representing the client, and 2) The increased potential for inaccuracy in the truth-finding process as the trier of fact is deprived of valuable witnesses.

> Given the complexities of modern existence few, if any, lawyers could as a practical matter represent the interests of their clients without the assistance of a variety of trained legal associates not yet admitted to the bar, clerks, typists, messengers, and similar aides.

> The assistance of these agents being indispensable to his work and the communications of the client being often necessarily committed to them by the attorney or by the client himself, the privilege must include all the persons who act as the attorney's agents.

> 8 Wigmore, Evidence § 2301 at 583 (McNaughton rev. 1961).

> There has been a tendency to expand this class of privileged "agents" to include various specialists that an attorney must consult in effectively representing his client. As a consequence, in a number of states when a client, acting on his attorney's advice, consults a physician for the purpose of obtaining testimony, data or recommendations for litigation purposes, the resultant communications are protected by the attorney-client privilege. This is so even though the communication will not be afforded the physician-patient privilege because, either a) the consultation was for the purposes of preparation for litigation, rather than treatment, and no physician-patient relationship arose, or b) putting the patient's condition in issue in the case constituted a waiver of this privilege.

> One line of cases, originating in California, has justified this extension of the privilege on the ground that in these circumstances the physician is merely acting as a conduit, relating the client's communications to the attorney. Alternatively, the psychiatrist is likened to an interpreter, without whom neither attorney nor client could understand the significance of the client's information. . . .

The conceptual ground offered for the extension is not beyond criticism, for the doctor's observations and conclusions are based upon far more than the client's communications. As Professor Friedenthal has noted:

> The court[s fail] to discuss the fact that the doctor's observations and conclusions, apart from the client's communications to him, constituted knowledge on the part of the doctor which would be highly material to the case. Thus, in transmitting the "client's communication" the doctor became far more than a mere interpreter, for he added an important increment of knowledge of his own. It seems that this knowledge should be treated just like the knowledge of any other witness and should be discoverable from the doctor himself.

Friedenthal, Discovery and Use of an Adverse Party's Expert Information, 14 Stan.L.Rev. 455, 463–464 (1962).

Nonetheless, from a pragmatic perspective the extension is desirable. Only a foolhardy lawyer would determine tactical and evidentiary strategy in a case with psychiatric issues without the guidance and interpretation of psychiatrists and others skilled in this field....

As Chief Judge Haynsworth reminded us:

> The assistance of a psychiatrist is crucial in a number of respects to an effective insanity defense. In the first place, the presence or absence of psychiatric testimony is critical to presentation of the defense at trial. "In practical terms, a successful defense without expert testimony will be made only in cases so extreme, or so compelling in sympathy for the defendant, that the prosecutor is unlikely to bring them at all."
>
> Moreover the use of an expert for other, non-testimonial, functions can be equally important. Consultation with counsel attunes the lay attorney to unfamiliar but central medical concepts and enables him, as an initial matter, to assess the soundness and advisability of offering the defense. The aid of a psychiatrist informs and guides the presentation of the defense, and perhaps most importantly, it permits a lawyer inexpert in the science of psychiatry to probe intelligently the foundations of adverse testimony. "If an accused is to raise an effective insanity defense, it is clear that he will need the psychiatrist as a witness. He will need his aid in determining the kinds of testimony to be elicited, the specialists to be consulted, and the areas to be explored on cross-examination of opposing psychiatrists."

United States v. Taylor, 437 F.2d 371, 377 n. 9 (4th Cir.1971).

Prior to the adoption of the Federal Rules of Evidence parallel considerations led the Court of Appeals for this Circuit to extend the attorney-client privilege to communications made by a client to an accountant who was acting as a fact-gatherer and interpreter for the lawyer. See United States v. Kovel, 296 F.2d 918 (2d Cir.1961).

If it is necessary to protect accountant-client communications in this way, it is essential to similarly protect psychotherapist-patient communications....

4. Suppose it can be shown that it was necessary or at least useful for a third person to have been present at an attorney-client meeting but that that person was not an agent of either the client or the attorney. Suppose, for example, the third person is a prospective witness for the defense in a criminal case about which the attorney is advising the client? See United States v. Landof, 591 F.2d

36, 39 (9th Cir.1978). Should it make any difference that the third person is also an attorney?

United States v. McPartlin

United States Court of Appeals, Seventh Circuit, 1979.
595 F.2d 1321, cert. denied, 444 U.S. 833.

■ Before PELL, SPRECHER and TONE, CIRCUIT JUDGES.

■ TONE, CIRCUIT JUDGE.

The appellants were convicted, in a nine-week jury trial, of conspiring to violate the wire and travel fraud statutes and of substantive violations of those statutes.

The indictment charged that defendant Frederick B. Ingram, chairman of the board of the Louisiana-based Ingram Corporation, had paid defendant Robert F. McPartlin, an Illinois legislator, defendant Valentine Janicki, a trustee for the Metropolitan Sanitary District, and others more than $900,000 to secure for the Ingram Corporation a multi-million dollar sludge-hauling contract with the District. Defendants Franklin H. Weber, a businessman, and Edwin T. Bull, president of a towing company, were alleged to be intermediaries through whom many of the payments were made. William J. Benton, vice president of Ingram Corporation, was an unindicted co-conspirator who played a major role in the conspiracy and testified as a witness for the prosecution. . . .

Throughout the period covered by the indictment, Benton kept diaries, or appointment calendars, in which he made notes concerning meetings and telephone conversations, naming the persons involved and often recording the substance of the conversations. The Benton diaries figured prominently in the government's case, for they corroborated much of his testimony.

Destroying Benton's credibility was important to Ingram, as it was to the other defendants, even though Ingram's defense was based, in part, on the argument that he had made the payments in response to the threats Benton had reported to him, because Ingram's account of events in issue differed materially from Benton's, and because the government's case hinged largely on Benton's testimony. Since Benton's diaries corroborated so much of his testimony, it was imperative from the standpoint of all defendants that an effort be made to discredit them.

Such an effort was made, and Frederick Ingram and McPartlin cooperated in that effort. . . .

An investigator acting for Frederick Ingram's counsel twice interviewed McPartlin with the consent of the latter's counsel for the purpose of determining whether there was a basis for challenging the truth of some of the diary entries. In the second of these interviews McPartlin made certain statements, which Ingram argues tend to support his defense. At trial, when Ingram offered evidence of these statements, McPartlin's counsel objected on the ground, inter alia, of the attorney-client privilege, and the court, after an in camera hearing, sustained the objection on this and another ground. . . .

McPartlin was entitled to the protection of the attorney-client privilege, because his statements were made in confidence to an attorney for a co-defendant for a common purpose related to both defenses. They were made in connection with the project of attempting to discredit Benton, a project in which Ingram and McPartlin and their attorneys were jointly engaged for the benefit of both defendants. Ingram acknowledges that communications by a client to his own lawyer remain privileged when the lawyer subsequently shares them with co-defendants for purposes of a common defense. The common-defense rule, which is not as narrow as Ingram contends, has been recognized in cases spanning more than a century. Chahoon v. Commonwealth, 62 Va. (21 Gratt.) 822 (1871); Schmitt v. Emery, 211 Minn. 547, 2 N.W.2d 413 (1942); Continental Oil Co. v. United States, 330 F.2d 347 (9th Cir.1964); Hunydee v. United States, 355 F.2d 183 (9th Cir.1965); Matter of Grand Jury Subpoena, 406 F.Supp. 381, 387–389 (S.D.N.Y.1975); see State v. Emmanuel, 42 Wash.2d 799, 259 P.2d 845, 854–855 (1953); Note, "Waiver of Attorney–Client Privilege on Inter–Attorney Exchange of Information," 63 Yale L.J. 1030 (1954); Note, "The Attorney–Client Privilege in Multiple Party Situations," 8 Colum.J.L. & Soc.Prob. 179 (1972). Uninhibited communication among joint parties and their counsel about matters of common concern is often important to the protection of their interests. Note, supra, 8 Colum.J.L. & Soc.Prob. at 179–180. In criminal cases it can be necessary to a fair opportunity to defend. Therefore, waiver is not to be inferred from the disclosure in confidence to a co-party's attorney for a common purpose.

In the case at bar, the judge found, as a preliminary question of fact, from the evidence adduced at the hearing held pursuant to Rule 104(a), Fed.R.Evid., that McPartlin had made the statements to the investigator in confidence. That finding is not clearly erroneous.

Ingram argues that the co-defendants' defenses must be in all respects compatible if the joint-defense privilege is to be applicable. The cases do not establish such a limitation, and there is no reason to impose it. Rule 503(b)(3) of the proposed Federal Rules of Evidence, as approved by the Supreme Court, stated that the privilege applies to communications by a client "to a lawyer representing another in a matter of common interest." See 2 J. Weinstein, Evidence 503–552 (1977). The Advisory Committee's Note to proposed Rule 503(b) makes it clear that the joint-interest privilege is not limited to situations in which the positions of the parties are compatible in all respects.

. . . The privilege protects pooling of information for any defense purpose common to the participating defendants. Cooperation between defendants in such circumstances is often not only in their own best interests but serves to expedite the trial or, as in the case at bar, the trial preparation.

Ingram also seems to argue that the communication was not privileged because it was made to an investigator rather than an attorney. The investigator was an agent for Ingram's attorney, however, so it is as if the communication was to the attorney himself. "It has never been questioned that the privilege protects communications to the attorney's . . . agents . . . for rendering his services." 8 Wigmore, Evidence § 2301 at 583 (McNaughton rev. 1961)
. . .

Nor was it, as Ingram contends, fatal to the privilege that McPartlin made the statement, in effect, to Ingram's attorney rather than his own. When the Ingram and McPartlin camps decided to join in an attempt to discredit Benton, the attorney for each represented both for purposes of that joint effort. The relationship was no different than it would have been if during the trial the Ingram and McPartlin attorneys had decided that Ingram's attorney would cross-examine Benton on behalf of both, and during cross-examination McPartlin passed Ingram's attorney a note containing information for use in the cross-examination. The attorney who thus undertakes to serve his client's co-defendant for a limited purpose becomes the co-defendant's attorney for that purpose. . . .

NOTES

1. For another case upholding the application of the privilege in a joint defense context, see Eisenberg v. Gagnon, 766 F.2d 770, 787 (3d Cir.1985). For cases disallowing a joint defense privilege claim, see In Matter of Bevill, Bresler & Schulman Asset Management Corporation, 805 F.2d 120 (3d Cir.1986); United States v. Lopez, 777 F.2d 543 (10th Cir.1985), Government of Virgin Islands v. Joseph, 685 F.2d 857 (3d Cir.1982).

2. Suppose there are actual or potential adverse interests among co-defendants. May they be represented by the same attorney? See Wheat v. United States, 486 U.S. 153 (1988): Five days before trial, defendant moved to replace attorney A with attorney B, immediately after one of his co-defendants pleaded guilty. The trial court denied the motion despite the fact that the defendant and his co-defendants had agreed to waive any actual or potential conflict of interest problems arising out of the fact that attorney B also represented defendant's co-defendants. (Whether the interests of the defendant and his co-defendants were, in fact, adverse was disputed by the parties.) Admittedly, attorney B had received privileged information from the co-defendants, but he indicated that he did not intend to use in cross-examination any of the privileged information. The Supreme Court affirmed the court of appeals, approving the trial court's exercise of discretion to take such measures, particularly at the pretrial stage, in order to protect criminal defendants against nascent conflicts of interest.

3. The privilege does not apply to attorney-client communications arising out of a joint client situation when offered in an action between the clients. See proposed Federal Rule 503(d)(5) and California Evidence Code § 962. Should the logic underlying this exception be extended to the situation in the principal case? Compare the rule that the privilege does not apply where the issue is whether the attorney breached his duty to the client. See § 957, California Evidence Code and proposed Federal Rules of Evidence, Rule 503(d)(3). Thus, Armstrong v. United States, 440 F.2d 658 (5th Cir.1971) held that the privilege did not apply to attorney-client communications where the client's claim was that counsel had provided an inadequate defense.

4. Stockholders bring a derivative suit against the corporation. Management claims the privilege with respect to its communications with corporate counsel prior to the litigation. Does the privilege apply? Held: Privilege not applicable if the stockholders can "show cause why it should not be invoked in the particular instance." Garner v. Wolfinbarger, 430 F.2d 1093, 1103–1104 (5th Cir.1970). Garner described "good cause" as follows:

> There are many indicia that may contribute to a decision of presence or absence of good cause, among them the number of shareholders and the percentage of stock they represent; the bona fides of the shareholders; the nature of the shareholders' claim and whether it is obviously colorable; the apparent necessity or desirability of the shareholders having the information and the availability of it from other sources; whether, if the shareholders' claim is of wrongful action by the corporation, it is of action criminal, or illegal but not criminal, or of doubtful legality; whether the communication related to past or to prospective actions; whether the communication is of advice concerning the litigation itself; the extent to which the communication is identified versus the extent to which the shareholders are blindly fishing; the risk of revelation of trade secrets or other information in whose confidentiality the corporation has an interest for independent reasons. Id. at 1103–1104.

Garner has been applied where suit was brought against a majority shareholder in his individual capacity based upon his having "squeezed out" out the minority shareholder plaintiffs, allegedly by a fraudulent scheme. According to the plaintiffs' theory, which the court accepted, the defendant majority shareholder became the alter ego of the corporation. Fausek v. White, 965 F.2d 126 (1992). See Johnson, Evidence: Fausek v. White: The Sixth Circuit Garners Support for a Good Cause Exception the the Attorney Client Privilege, 18 Dayton L.Rev. 313 (1993); Comment, The Attorney–Client Privilege in Shareholders' Suits, 69 Colum.L.Rev. 309 (1969).

5. The privilege has been held not to apply in probate litigation between persons all of whom are claiming through the testator. Stevens v. Thurston, 289 A.2d 398 (N.H.1972). See proposed Federal Rule 503(d)(2).

6. May a client in a joint defense situation reveal his own statements made at the joint conference? See proposed Federal Rule 503(b) and the Advisory Committee's Note thereto.

G.   THE CRIME–FRAUD EXCEPTION

Even though an attorney-client relationship exists, and the client is consulting the attorney for the purpose of obtaining legal advice, application of the privilege may be defeated if a showing is made that the communications were in furtherance of an intended or present (as distinguished from, past) illegality involving a crime or fraud. This is the so-called crime-fraud exception to the attorney-client privilege. The crime-fraud doctrine has become one of the most frequently invoked ways to set aside the protections otherwise afforded to attorney-client communications.

United States v. Zolin

Supreme Court of the United States, 1989.
491 U.S. 554, 109 S.Ct. 2619, 105 L.Ed.2d 469.

■ JUSTICE BLACKMUN delivered the opinion of the Court.

This case arises out of the efforts of the Criminal Investigation Division of the Internal Revenue Service (IRS) to investigate the tax returns of L. Ron Hubbard, founder of the Church of Scientology (the Church), for the calendar years 1979 through 1983. We granted certiorari, 488 U.S. 907 (1988), to consider two issues. . . .

The second issue concerns the testimonial privilege for attorney-client communications and, more particularly, the generally recognized exception to that privilege for communications in furtherance of future illegal conduct—the so-called "crime-fraud" exception. The specific question presented is whether the applicability of the crime-fraud exception must be established by "independent evidence" (i. e., without reference to the content of the contested communications themselves), or, alternatively, whether the applicability of that exception can be resolved by an in camera inspection of the allegedly privileged material. We reject the "independent evidence" approach and hold that the district court, under circumstances we explore below, and at the behest of the party opposing the claim of privilege, may conduct an in camera review of the materials in question. Because the Court of Appeals considered only "independent evidence," we vacate its judgment on this issue and remand the case for further proceedings.

I

In the course of its investigation, the IRS sought access to 51 documents that had been filed with the Clerk of the Los Angeles County Superior Court in connection with a case entitled Church of Scientology of California v. Armstrong, No. C420 153. The Armstrong litigation involved, among other things, a charge by the Church that one of its former members, Gerald Armstrong, had obtained by unlawful means documentary materials relating to Church activities, including two tapes. Some of the documents sought by the IRS had been filed under seal.

Respondents asserted the privilege as a bar to disclosure of the tapes. The IRS argued, among other things, however, that the tapes fell within the crime-fraud exception to the attorney-client privilege, and urged the District Court to listen to the tapes in the course of making its privilege determination. In addition, the IRS submitted to the court two declarations by Agent Petersell. In the first, Petersell stated his grounds for believing that the tapes were relevant to the investigation. See Declaration para. 3 (March 8, 1985). In the second, Petersell offered a description of the tapes' contents, based on information he received during several interviews. Appended to this declaration—over respondents' objection—were partial transcripts of the tapes, which the IRS lawfully had obtained from a confidential source. See March 15, 1985, declaration (filed under seal). In subsequent briefing, the IRS reiterated its request that the District Court listen to the tapes in camera before making its privilege ruling.

. . .

III

Questions of privilege that arise in the course of the adjudication of federal rights are "governed by the principles of the common law as they may be interpreted by the courts of the United States in the light of reason and experience." Fed. Rule Evid. 501. We have recognized the attorney-client privilege under federal law, as "the oldest of the privileges for confidential communications known to the common law." Upjohn Co. v. United States, 449 U.S. 383, 389 (1981). Although the underlying rationale for the privilege has changed over time, see 8 J. Wigmore, Evidence § 2290 (McNaughton rev. 1961), courts long have viewed its central concern as one "to encourage full and frank communication between attorneys and their clients and thereby promote broader public interests in the observance of law and administration of justice." Upjohn, 449 U.S., at 389. That purpose, of course, requires that clients be free to "make full disclosure to their attorneys" of past wrongdoings, Fisher v. United States, 425 U.S. 391, 403 (1976), in order that the client may obtain "the aid of persons having knowledge of the law and skilled in its practice," Hunt v. Blackburn, 128 U.S. 464, 470 (1888).

The attorney-client privilege is not without its costs. Cf. Trammel v. United States, 445 U.S. 40, 50 (1980). "[S]ince the privilege has the effect of withholding relevant information from the factfinder, it applies only where necessary to achieve its purpose." Fisher, 425 U.S., at 403. The attorney-client privilege must necessarily protect the confidences of wrongdoers, but the reason for that protection—the centrality of open client and attorney communication to the proper functioning of our adversary system of justice—"ceas[es] to operate at a certain point, namely, where the desired advice refers not to prior wrongdoing, but to future wrongdoing." 8 Wigmore, § 2298, p. 573; see also Clark v. United States, 289 U.S. 1, 15 (1933). It is the purpose of the crime-fraud exception to the attorney-client privilege to assure that the "seal of secrecy," ibid., between lawyer and client does not extend to communications "made for the purpose of getting advice for the commission of a fraud" or crime. O'Rourke v. Darbishire , [1920] A. C. 581, 604

A variety of questions may arise when a party raises the crime-fraud exception. The parties to this case have not been in complete agreement as to which of these questions are presented here. In an effort to clarify the matter, we observe, first, that we need not decide the quantum of proof necessary ultimately to establish the applicability of the crime-fraud exception. Rather, we are concerned here with the type of evidence that may be used to make that ultimate showing. Within that general area of inquiry, the initial question in this case is whether a district court, at the request of the party opposing the privilege, may review the allegedly privileged communications in camera to determine whether the crime-fraud exception applies. If such in camera review is permitted, the second question we must consider is whether some threshold evidentiary showing is needed before the district court may undertake the requested review. Finally, if a threshold showing is required, we must consider the type of evidence the opposing party may use to meet it: i. e., in this case, whether the partial transcripts the IRS possessed may be used for that purpose.

A

We consider first the question whether a district court may ever honor the request of the party opposing the privilege to conduct an in camera review of allegedly privileged communications to determine whether those communications fall within the crime-fraud exception. We conclude that no express provision of the Federal Rules of Evidence bars such use of in camera review, and that it would be unwise to prohibit it in all instances as a matter of federal common law.

(1)

At first blush, two provisions of the Federal Rules of Evidence would appear to be relevant. Rule 104(a) provides: "Preliminary questions concerning the qualification of a person to be a witness, the existence of a privilege, or the admissibility of evidence shall be determined by the court.... In making its determination it is not bound by the rules of evidence except those with respect to privileges." (Emphasis added.) Rule 1101(c) provides: "The rule with respect to privileges applies at all stages of all actions, cases, and proceedings." Taken together, these Rules might be read to establish that in a summons-enforcement proceeding, attorney-client communications cannot be considered by the district court in making its crime-fraud ruling: to do otherwise, under this view, would be to make the crime-fraud determination without due regard to the existence of the privilege.

Even those scholars who support this reading of Rule 104(a) acknowledge that it leads to an absurd result.

"Because the judge must honor claims of privilege made during his preliminary fact determinations, many exceptions to the rules of privilege will become 'dead letters,' since the preliminary facts that give rise to these exceptions can never be proved. For example, an exception to the attorney-client privilege provides that there is no privilege if the communication was made to enable anyone to commit a crime or fraud. There is virtually no way in which the exception can ever be proved, save by compelling disclosure of the contents of the communication; Rule 104(a) provides that this cannot be done." 21 C. Wright & K. Graham, Federal Practice & Procedure: Evidence § 5055, p. 276 (1977).

We find this Draconian interpretation of Rule 104(a) inconsistent with the Rule's plain language. The Rule does not provide by its terms that all materials as to which a "clai[m] of privilege" is made must be excluded from consideration. In that critical respect, the language of Rule 104(a) is markedly different from the comparable California evidence rule, which provides that "the presiding officer may not require disclosure of information claimed to be privileged under this division in order to rule on the claim of privilege." Cal. Evid. Code Ann. § 915(a) (West Supp. 1989).[1] There is no reason to read Rule 104(a) as if its text were identical to that of the California rule.

Nor does it make sense to us to assume, as respondents have throughout this litigation, that once the attorney-client nature of the contested communications is established, those communications must be treated as presumptively privileged for evidentiary purposes until the privilege is "defeated" or "stripped away" by proof that the communications took place in the course of planning future crime or fraud. Although some language in Clark might be read as supporting this view, see 289 U.S., at 15, respondents acknowledged at oral argument that no prior holding of this Court requires the imposition of a strict progression of proof in crime-fraud cases.

We see no basis for holding that the tapes in this case must be deemed privileged under Rule 104(a) while the question of crime or fraud remains open. Indeed, respondents concede that "if the proponent of the privilege is able to sustain its burden only by submitting the communications to the court" for in camera review, the court is not required to avert its eyes (or close its ears) once it concludes that the communication would be privileged, if the court found the crime-fraud exception inapplicable. Rather, respondents acknowledge that the court may "then consider the same communications to determine if the opponent of the privilege has established that the crime-fraud exception applies." Id., at 15. Were the tapes truly deemed privileged under Rule 104(a) at the moment the trial court concludes they contain potentially privileged attorney-client communications, district courts would be required to draw precisely the counterintuitive distinction that respondents wisely reject. We thus shall not adopt a reading of Rule 104(a) that would treat the contested communications as "privileged" for purposes of the Rule, and we shall not interpret Rule 104(a) as categorically prohibiting the party opposing the privilege on crime-fraud grounds from relying on the results of an in camera review of the communications.

(2)

Having determined that Rule 104(a) does not prohibit the in camera review sought by the IRS, we must address the question as a matter of the federal

---

1. A good example of the effect of the California rule is provided by the record in this case. While the disputed matters were being briefed in Federal District Court, the State Superior Court held a hearing on a motion by Government attorneys seeking access to materials in the Armstrong case for ongoing litigation in Washington, D. C. The transcript of the hearing was made part of the record before the District Court in this case. Regarding the tapes, the Government argued to the Superior Court that the attorney-client conversations on the tapes reflect the planning or commission of a crime or fraud. Tr. of Hearing of February 11, 1985, in No. C420 153 (Super. Ct. Cal.), p. 52. That claim was supported by several declarations and other extrinsic evidence. The Government noted, however, that "the tape recordings themselves would ... be the best evidence of exactly what was going on." Id., at 53. The intervenors stressed that, as a matter of California law, "you can't show the tapes are not privileged by the contents." Id., at 58; see also id., at 68. The Superior Court acknowledged the premise that "you can't look at the conversation itself to make [the crime-fraud] determination," id., at 74, and concluded that the extrinsic evidence was not sufficient to make out a prima facie case that the crime-fraud exception applies, id., at 75–76. [Footnotes are those of the court. Some footnotes have been omitted, and others renumbered.]

common law of privileges. See Rule 501. We conclude that a complete prohibition against opponents' use of in camera review to establish the applicability of the crime-fraud exception is inconsistent with the policies underlying the privilege.

We begin our analysis by recognizing that disclosure of allegedly privileged materials to the district court for purposes of determining the merits of a claim of privilege does not have the legal effect of terminating the privilege. Indeed, this Court has approved the practice of requiring parties who seek to avoid disclosure of documents to make the documents available for in camera inspection, and the practice is well established in the federal courts. Respondents do not dispute this point: they acknowledge that they would have been free to request in camera review to establish the fact that the tapes involved attorney-client communications, had they been unable to muster independent evidence to serve that purpose.

Once it is clear that in camera review does not destroy the privileged nature of the contested communications, the question of the propriety of that review turns on whether the policies underlying the privilege and its exceptions are better fostered by permitting such review or by prohibiting it. In our view, the costs of imposing an absolute bar to consideration of the communications in camera for purpose of establishing the crime-fraud exception are intolerably high.

"No matter how light the burden of proof which confronts the party claiming the exception, there are many blatant abuses of privilege which cannot be substantiated by extrinsic evidence. This is particularly true ... of ... situations in which an alleged illegal proposal is made in the context of a relationship which has an apparent legitimate end." Note, The Future Crime or Tort Exception to Communications Privileges, 77 Harv. L. Rev. 730, 737 (1964). A per se rule that the communications in question may never be considered creates, we feel, too great an impediment to the proper functioning of the adversary process. See generally 2 D. Louisell & C. Mueller, Federal Evidence § 213, pp. 828–829 (1985); 2 J. Weinstein & M. Berger, Weinstein's Evidence [*570] para. 503(d)(1)[01], p. 503–71. This view is consistent with current trends in the law. Compare National Conference of Commissioners on Uniform State Laws, Uniform Rules of Evidence, Rule 26(2)(a) (1953 ed.) ("Such privileges shall not extend ... to a communication if the judge finds that sufficient evidence, aside from the communication, has been introduced to warrant a finding that the legal service was sought or obtained in order to enable or aid the client to commit or plan to commit a crime or a tort", reprinted in 1 J. Bailey & O. Trelles, The Federal Rules of Evidence: Legislative Histories and Related Documents (1980), with Uniform Rule of Evidence 502 (adopted 1974), 13A U. L. A. 256 (1986) (omitting explicit independent evidence requirement).

B

We turn to the question whether in camera review at the behest of the party asserting the crime-fraud exception is always permissible, or, in contrast, whether the party seeking in camera review must make some threshold showing that such review is appropriate. In addressing this question, we attend to the detrimental effect, if any, of in camera review on the policies underlying the privilege and on the orderly administration of justice in our courts. We conclude that some such showing must be made.

Our endorsement of the practice of testing proponents' privilege claims through in camera review of the allegedly privileged documents has not been without reservation. This Court noted in United States v. Reynolds, 345 U.S. 1 (1953), a case which presented a delicate question concerning the disclosure of military secrets, that "examination of the evidence, even by the judge alone, in chambers" might in some cases "jeopardize the security which the privilege is meant to protect." Id., at 10. Analogizing to claims of Fifth Amendment privilege, it observed more generally: "Too much judicial inquiry into the claim of privilege would force disclosure of the thing the privilege was meant to protect, while a complete abandonment of judicial control would lead to intolerable abuses." Id., at 8.

The Court in Reynolds recognized that some compromise must be reached. See also United States v. Weisman, 111 F.2d 260, 261–262 (C.A.2 1940). In Reynolds, it declined to "go so far as to say that the court may automatically require a complete disclosure to the judge before the claim of privilege will be accepted in any case." 345 U.S., at 10 (emphasis added). We think that much the same result is in order here.

A blanket rule allowing in camera review as a tool for determining the applicability of the crime-fraud exception, as Reynolds suggests, would place the policy of protecting open and legitimate disclosure between attorneys and clients at undue risk. There is also reason to be concerned about the possible due process implications of routine use of in camera proceedings. Finally, we cannot ignore the burdens in camera review places upon the district courts, which may well be required to evaluate large evidentiary records without open adversarial guidance by the parties.

There is no reason to permit opponents of the privilege to engage in groundless fishing expeditions, with the district courts as their unwitting (and perhaps unwilling) agents. Courts of Appeals have suggested that in camera review is available to evaluate claims of crime or fraud only "when justified," In re John Doe Corp., 675 F. 2d, at 490, or "[i]n appropriate cases," In re Sealed Case, 219 U. S. App. D. C. 195, 217, 676 F.2d 793, 815 (1982) (opinion of Wright, J.). Indeed, the Government conceded at oral argument (albeit reluctantly) that a district court would be mistaken if it reviewed documents in camera solely because "the government beg[ged it]" to do so, "with no reason to suspect crime or fraud."

In fashioning a standard for determining when in camera review is appropriate, we begin with the observation that "in camera inspection . . . is a smaller intrusion upon the confidentiality of the attorney-client relationship than is public disclosure." Fried, Too High a Price for Truth: The Exception to the Attorney–Client Privilege for Contemplated Crimes and Frauds, 64 N. C. L. Rev. 443, 467 (1986). We therefore conclude that a lesser evidentiary showing is needed to trigger in camera review than is required ultimately to overcome the privilege. Ibid. The threshold we set, in other words, need not be a stringent one.

We think that the following standard strikes the correct balance. Before engaging in in camera review to determine the applicability of the crime-fraud exception, "the judge should require a showing of a factual basis adequate to support a good faith belief by a reasonable person" that in camera review of the materials may reveal evidence to establish the claim that the crime-fraud exception applies.

Once that showing is made, the decision whether to engage in in camera review rests in the sound discretion of the district court. The court should make that decision in light of the facts and circumstances of the particular case, including, among other things, the volume of materials the district court has been asked to review, the relative importance to the case of the alleged privileged information, and the likelihood that the evidence produced through in camera review, together with other available evidence then before the court, will establish that the crime-fraud exception does apply. The district court is also free to defer its in camera review if it concludes that additional evidence in support of the crime-fraud exception may be available that is not allegedly privileged, and that production of the additional evidence will not unduly disrupt or delay the proceedings.

C

The question remains as to what kind of evidence a district court may consider in determining whether it has the discretion to undertake an in camera review of an allegedly privileged communication at the behest of the party opposing the privilege. Here, the issue is whether the partial transcripts may be used by the IRS in support of its request for in camera review of the tapes.

The answer to that question, in the first instance, must be found in Rule 104(a), which establishes that materials that have been determined to be privileged may not be considered in making the preliminary determination of the existence of a privilege. Neither the District Court nor the Court of Appeals made factual findings as to the privileged nature of the partial transcripts, so we cannot determine on this record whether Rule 104(a) would bar their consideration.

Assuming for the moment, however, that no rule of privilege bars the IRS' use of the partial transcripts, we fail to see what purpose would be served by excluding the transcripts from the District Court's consideration. There can be little doubt that partial transcripts, or other evidence directly but incompletely reflecting the content of the contested communications, generally will be strong evidence of the subject matter of the communications themselves. Permitting district courts to consider this type of evidence would aid them substantially in rapidly and reliably determining whether in camera review is appropriate.

Respondents suggest only one serious countervailing consideration. In their view, a rule that would allow an opponent of the privilege to rely on such material would encourage litigants to elicit confidential information from disaffected employees or others who have access to the information. We think that deterring the aggressive pursuit of relevant information from third-party sources is not sufficiently central to the policies of the attorney-client privilege to require us to adopt the exclusionary rule urged by respondents. We conclude that the party opposing the privilege may use any nonprivileged evidence in support of its request for in camera review, even if its evidence is not "independent" of the contested communications as the Court of Appeals uses that term. [2]

D

In sum, we conclude that a rigid independent evidence requirement does not comport with "reason and experience," Fed. Rule Evid. 501, and we decline to adopt it as part of the developing federal common law of evidentiary

---

2. In addition, we conclude that evidence that is not "independent" of the contents of allegedly privileged communications—like the partial transcripts in this case—may be used not only in the pursuit of in camera review, but also may provide the evidentiary basis for the ultimate showing that the crime-fraud exception applies. We see little to distinguish these two uses: in both circumstances, if the evidence has not itself been determined to be privileged, its exclusion does not serve the policies which underlie the attorney-client privilege. See generally Note, The Future Crime or Tort Exception to Communications Privileges, 77 Harv. L. Rev. 730, 737 (1964).

privileges. We hold that in camera review may be used to determine whether allegedly privileged attorney-client communications fall within the crime-fraud exception. We further hold, however, that before a district court may engage in in camera review at the request of the party opposing the privilege, that party must present evidence sufficient to support a reasonable belief that in camera review may yield evidence that establishes the exception's applicability. Finally, we hold that the threshold showing to obtain in camera review may be met by using any relevant evidence, lawfully obtained, that has not been adjudicated to be privileged.

■ JUSTICE BRENNAN took no part in the consideration or decision of this case.

1. THE SUBSTANTIVE STANDARD

NOTES

1. There are various formulations of the crime-fraud exception to the attorney-client privilege. As in the principal case, the courts refer to the exception to the privilege "for communications in furtherance of future illegal conduct," or "communications made for the purpose of getting advice for the commission of a fraud or crime." Similarly a sharp line is drawn between past conduct, on the one hand, and present or future conduct, on the other hand. Thus, "It is a truism that while the attorney-client privilege stands firm for client's revelations of past conduct, it cannot be used to shield ongoing or intended future criminal conduct." United States v. Tei Fu Chen, 99 F.3d 1495 (9th Cir.1996). Also see, e.g. In re Richard Roe, Inc. and John Doe, Inc. 68 F.3d 38 (2d Cir.1995)("not protected if they relate to client communications in furtherance of contemplated or ongoing criminal or fraudulent conduct.") A somewhat more elaborate formulation of the same notion is that set forth in In re Grand Jury (G.J. No. 87–03–A), 845 F.2d 896 (11th Cir. 1988):

> ... [T]here must be a ... showing that the client was engaged in criminal or fraudulent conduct when he sought the advice of counsel, that he was planning such conduct when he sought the advice of counsel, or that he committed a crime or fraud subsequent to receiving the benefit of counsel's advice.

2. With regard to the matter of on-going illegality, consider the following case:

President of a corporation is under investigation for tax evasion and immigration offenses based on allegations that she willfully employed a person in the United States, knowing that she lacked the necessary visas or work permits. The government served subpoenas on the corporation's attorneys to require them to identify documents they prepared in connection with obtaining work authorization for the employee and to testify regarding communications between the attorneys and the corporate president regarding the attempts to obtain the work permits for the employee. When counsel was consulted, the corporation continued to employ the person illegally, and when the corporation corresponded with the Immigration and Naturalization Service about its petition to legalize the status of the employee, it did not disclose that the individual had been working in the corporation's office illegally for more than a year. In re Grand Jury Proceedings. Appeal of the Corporation, 87 F.3d 377 (9th Cir.1996).

Consider in connection with the foregoing:

> ... [The] principle [relating to the crime-fraud exception] is easily applied when a lawyer is retained to defend a client in a criminal prosecution or civil litigation relating to an entirely completed course of conduct. But it is difficult to apply when the lawyer's role is more in the nature of business

planning or counseling or bringing the client into compliance for past wrongs, as opposed to simply defending the client against a charge relating to past wrongs. The act of bringing a client into compliance with the law ordinarily and properly engages the lawyer in an effort to assure the client is sanctioned no more harshly than the law requires. Because of the delicacy and importance of the attorney-client privilege in the counseling relationship, both the district court's task and ours are especially difficult when the United States Attorney insists upon using a person's own lawyer against him. United States v. Tei Fu Chen, 99 F.3d 1495 (9th Cir.1996).

3. In re Richard Roe, Inc. and John Doe, Inc., 68 F.3d 38 (2d Cir.1995): The government argued, after making an ex parte submission of documents relating to attorney-client communications, that the correct legal standard for applying the crime-fraud exception was whether the "documents, read collectively, have the real potential of being relevant evidence of activity in furtherance of a crime." The court rejected the government's contention on the grounds that: a) the client communication or attorney work product must itself be in further-ance of the crime or fraud; and b) the particular communication must have been intended in some way to facilitate or conceal the criminal activity. "Because a simple finding of relevance doe not demonstrate a criminal or fraudulent purpose, it does not trigger the exception."

4. The exception is applicable when the client consults the attorney to further the commission of a crime or fraud. It is the client's state of mind and actions and not the attorney's which are determinative. In re Grand Jury Proceedings. Appeal of the Corporation, supra note 2. The fact that "the lawyers ... were innocent of any wrongful intent, and had no knowledge that their services were being used to trick the ... [government agencies] ... does not preserve the attorney-client privilege against the crime-fraud exception." United States v. Tei Fu Chen, supra note 2. But see infra note 11, regarding the application of the crime fraud exception to the work product doctrine.

5. Suppose there is no indication in the client's portion of an attorney-client conversation that the client consulted the attorney for an illegal purpose, but in the course of the conversation the attorney counsels illegal activity. Consider the following excerpt from an attorney-client telephone conversation overheard by an eavesdropper in Clark v. State, 261 S.W.2d 339 (Tex.Crim.App.), cert. denied, 346 U.S. 855, rehearing denied, 346 U.S. 905 (1953):

The appellant: "Hello, Jimmy, I went to the extremes."

The voice in Dallas [the attorney]: "What did you do?"

The appellant: "I just went to the extremes."

The voice in Dallas: "You got to tell me what you did before I can help."

The appellant: "Well, I killed her."

The voice in Dallas: "Who did you kill; the driver?"

The appellant: "No, I killed her."

The voice in Dallas: "Did you get rid of the weapon?"

The appellant: "No, I still got the weapon."

The voice in Dallas: "Get rid of the weapon and sit tight and don't talk to anyone, and I will fly down in the morning."

The court in the Clark case went on to state:

The murder weapon was not found. The evidence indicates that appellant disposed of it as advised in the telephone conversation. Such advice or counsel was not such as merits protection because given by an attorney. It was not in the legitimate course of professional employment in making or preparing a defense at law.

Nothing is found in the record to indicate that appellant sought any advice from Mr. Martin other than that given in the conversation testified to by the telephone operator. We are not therefore dealing with a situation where the accused sought legitimate advice from his attorney in preparing his legal defense.

Do you agree with the court's conclusion?

6. Held: Crime-fraud exception applicable even when the alleged illegality being investigated is solely that of the law firm. In re Impounded Case (Law Firm), 879 F.2d 1211 (3d Cir. 1989). The court in this case went on to state:

> [T]he district concluded that all the seized documents fell within the crime-fraud exception, except those implicating the clients in the very criminal activity for which legal advice was sought.

> ... We think the district court's expansive reading of the crime-fraud exception here takes too narrow a view of a client's privilege. We believe that if the client is not implicated in criminal conduct the privilege obtains unless a document is pertinent to the accusation of criminal activity by the attorney alone.

7. Suppose the government claims that only one of two joint corporate holders of the attorney-client privilege was involved in a crime or fraud concerning which there were communications in furtherance. Should the crime-fraud exception apply where one of the two privilege-holders is innocent? The question was posed but not answered in In re Richard Roe, Inc. and John Doe, Inc., 68 F.3d 38 (2d Cir.1995).

8. Is it correct to describe a case in which the crime-fraud exception is applicable as one in which the client has "waived" the attorney-client privilege? See United States v. Davis, 1 F.3d 606 (7th Cir.1993) where this locution is used. Does the concept of waiver carry with it any substantive implications?

9. The crime-fraud exception has been invoked with respect to investigative reports prepared for the corporation-client. See generally, supra, p. 1442 et seq. See, e.g., Pritchard–Keang Nam Corporation v. Jaworski, 751 F.2d 277 (8th Cir.1984) where the court, in applying the exception, used the test, "was the report communicated with the purpose of perpetrating the fraud?"

10. Once it is determined that the privilege is lost because of ongoing or imminent crime or fraud, there is a further issue to be resolved: the scope of the loss. Compare the scope of waiver of the privilege issue, infra p. 1484. The privilege is lost with respect to misconduct that occurred during the period of representation. Any communications regarding past crimes remain privileged. What result with respect to past crimes that were the subject of a coverup during the period of representation? Under that circumstance, may communications regarding the past crimes be inquired into? See In re Sealed Case, 754 F.2d 395 (D.C.Cir.1985).

Compare United States v. Davis, supra note 8. Defendant had been indicted on a charge of obstruction of justice for allegedly having concealed a document that the government claimed fell within the scope of a subpoena duces tecum that had been issued. The government subpoenaed the attorney who had represented him at the time when the subpoena for documents had been issued. The court ruled that the privilege had been waived because the client had used the attorney-client relationship to engage in criminal activity—namely the withholding of the document from the grand jury. The court approved the district court's action in restricting the government's inquiry to "asking ... [the attorney] whether, during the course of his representation of ... [the client], [the client] admitted lying to him about the existence of the pertinent document and his compliance with the grand jury's subpoena."

11.   The crime fraud exception also applies to the work product doctrine. In re Impounded Case (Law Firm), 879 F.2d 1211 (3d Cir. 1989). Recall the fact that work product can be discovered upon a showing of substantial need and inability to secure the substantial equivalent of the materials by alternate means without undue hardship, supra p. 1454, while opinion work product representing the actual thoughts and impressions of the attorney is even more scrupulously protected, and the protection can be claimed by the client or the attorney. See In re Grand Jury Proceedings, Thursday Special Grand Jury September Term, 1991, 33 F.3d 342 (4th Cir.1994) and see p. 1455 supra.

Held: a prima facie showing of fraud is necessary to establish the application of the exception to the work product; documents containing the attorney's opinion work product must bear a close relationship to client's existing or future scheme to commit a crime or fraud. In re Sealed Case, 676 F.2d 793 (D.C.Cir.1982); In re Murphy, 560 F.2d 326 (8th Cir.1977).

In In re Grand Jury Proceedings, Thursday Special Grand Jury September Term, 1991, supra, the court ruled that if the government failed to establish that the attorney was aware or a knowing participant in the criminal conduct, and may therefore not be said to have waived his right to assert the work product privilege, the lower court should redact any portions of the subpoenaed materials containing the attorney's opinion work product.

12.   Judge Wright considered the application of the crime-fraud exception to the work product privilege in In re Sealed Case, 676 F.2d 793 (D.C.Cir.1982) at 812:

> [A]n attorney's opinion work product cannot be privileged if the work was performed in furtherance of a crime, fraud, or other type of misconduct fundamentally inconsistent with the basic premises of the adversary system. In some circumstances the attorney may be innocently involved in the client's crime or fraud. But a guilty client may not use the innocence or ignorance of its attorney to claim the court's protection against a grand jury subpoena. Unless the blameless attorney is before the court with an independent claim of privilege, the client's use of an attorney's efforts in furtherance of crime or fraud negates the privilege.

> In a footnote to these comments, id. at 812, n. 75, he added: "[S]ince the work product privilege belongs to the lawyer as well as the client, ... in some situations an attorney may be able to claim the privilege even though he or she was consulted in furtherance of the client's crime or fraud.... But there is no need to accord a guilty client standing to assert the claims of its innocent attorney."

13.   See generally Cohn, The Work–Product Doctrine: Protection, Not Privilege, 71 Georgetown L.Rev. 917 (1983); The Work Product Doctrine, 68 Cornell L.Rev. 760 (1983).

2.   PROCEDURAL CONSIDERATIONS

NOTES

1.   In the principal case, United States v. Zolin, the Supreme Court declined to decide the quantum of proof necessary ultimately to establish the applicability of the crime-fraud exception. Consider, however the following excerpts:

United States v. Tei Fu Chen, 99 F.3d 1495 (9th Cir.1996):

Mere allegations or suspicion by the government are insufficient. But proof beyond a reasonable doubt is not necessary to justify application of the crime-fraud exception. The test for invoking the crime-fraud exception to the attorney-client privilege is whether there is "reasonable cause to believe that the attorney's services were utilized in furtherance of the ongoing unlawful scheme." Reasonable cause is more than suspicion but less than a preponderance of evidence. The government must submit "evidence that if believed by the jury would establish the elements of an ongoing violation."

In re John Doe, Inc., 13 F.3d 633 (2d Cir.1994):

Appellants ... argue that under Zolin the court should have articulated a standard higher than "probable cause," such as "clear and convincing evidence."

In this case, we do not need to reach the issue of whether Zolin requires a higher standard of proof. Currently, we require that a party seeking to overcome the attorney-client privilege with the crime-fraud exception must show that there is "probable cause to believe that a crime or fraud ha[s] been committed and that the communications were in furtherance thereof." This standard has been rephrased as requiring "that a prudent person have a reasonable basis to suspect the perpetration or attempted perpetration of a crime or fraud, and that the communications were in furtherance thereof."

Haines v. Liggett Group, Inc., 975 F.2d 81 (3d Cir.1992):

In matters referring to fraud or crime generally we have required that the party seeking discovery must make a prima facie showing of fraud or crime. However, we have not defined the contours for a prima facie showing. . . .

Based on its analysis of the various standards applied by the courts of appeals, the district court concluded that "all of these proposed standards amount to the same basic proposition—has the party seeking discovery presented evidence which, if believed by the fact-finder, supports plaintiff's theory of fraud?" We interpret this statement to mean that the party seeking discovery must present evidence which, if believed by the the fact-finder, would be sufficient to support a finding that the elements of the crime-fraud exception were met. The court's opinion reflect that it carefully analyzed the various views on prima facie evidence announced by other courts of appeals and adopted a workable standard.

2. In Haines, supra note 1 (which is one of the cases litigating the effects of tobacco in a wrongful death action), the court also took cognizance of the fact that while Zolin requires a lower standard to trigger an in camera review of the attorney client materials than to ultimately establish the application of the crime fraud exception, there is "some similarity between the two standards." The court proceeded to distinguish them:

But at a very minimum, we must recognize that the objectives of the two proceedings are completely different. One merely seeks in camera examination of documents by the court; this is a comparatively non-dispositive procedural way station. The other seeks to break the seal of a highly protected privilege. For in camera inspection, it would sufficient for the district court, in its discretion, to consider only the presentation made by the party challenging the privilege.

Deciding whether the crime-fraud exception applies is another matter. If the party seeking to apply the exception has made its initial showing, than a more formal procedure is required than that entitling plaintiff to in camera review. The importance of the privilege as well as fundamental concepts of due process require that the party defending the privilege be given the opportunity to be heard, by evidence and argument, at the hearing seeking an exception to the privilege.

3. Compare with the last paragraph quoted from the Haines case in note 2 supra, the fact that cases in other circuits have held that denying to the claimants of the privilege the opportunity to inspect and rebut the government's submissions and excluding them from the in camera proceeding in order to preserve grand jury secrecy does not violate due process. In re John Doe, Inc., 13 F.3d 633 (2d Cir.1994); In re Grand Jury Proceedings, Thursday Special Grand Jury September Term, 1991, 33 F.3d 342 (4th Cir.1994).

4. It has been held that the Zolin standard to determine whether an in camera inspection of the communications is warranted can be met by an ex parte sealed affidavit from an FBI agent. In re John Doe, 13 F.3d 633 (2d Cir.1994).

5. Is the government entitled to in camera review of the relevant documents to ensure that the documents are truly privileged, that is, that the attorney-client privilege applies in the first place? If so, what standard of proof should be applied in determining whether an in camera review is justified? Held: The government may be entitled to in camera review and the standard to be applied when a party seeks in camera review to contest assertion of the privilege is that used in Zolin for crime-fraud in camera review. "The same two-stage process established in Zolin should be employed in this context." In re Grand Jury Investigation, 974 F.2d 1068 (9th Cir.1992). See generally, Fried, Too High a Price for Truth: The Exception to the Attorney–Client Privilege for Contemplated Crimes and Frauds, 64 N.C.L. Rev. 443 (1986); Galanek, Note: The Impact of the Zolin Decision on the Crime–Fraud Exception to the Attorney–Client Privilege, 24 Ga. L.Rev. 1115 (1990).

3.   AN ATTORNEY'S AFFIRMATIVE OBLIGATIONS WITH RESPECT TO CLIENT'S PRESENT OR FUTURE CRIMINAL OR FRAUDULENT CONDUCT

NOTES

1. Suppose that your client informs you that he is going to commit perjury. The Supreme Court has stated: "An attorney's duty of confidentiality, which totally covers the client's admission of guilt, does not extend to a client's announced plans to engage in future criminal conduct." Nix v. Whiteside, 475 U.S. 157, 173 (1986). See Silver, Truth, Justice and the American Way: The Case Against the Client Perjury Rules, 47 Vand. L.Rev. 339 (1994); Beckman, Sixth Amendment-Effective Assistance of Counsel: A Defense Attorney's Right to Refuse Cooperation in Defendant's Perjured Testimony, 77 J.Crim. L. & Criminology 692 (1986); Freedman, Client Confidences and Client Perjury: Some Unanswered Questions, 136 U.Pa. L.Rev. 1939 (1988). For additional discussion of issues relating to client perjury, see Ch. 3, supra, pp. 329–331.

2. See Rules 1.2(d) and 1.6, in the ABA's Model Rules of Professional Conduct (1983) for provisions dealing with an attorney's obligations with respect to the client's present or future criminal or fraudulent conduct. See Bainor & Batterman, Report On The Debate Over Whether There Should Be An Exception To Confidentiality For Rectifying A Crime Or Fraud: Committee on Professional

Responsibility, Association of the Bar of the City of New York, 20 Fordham Urb. L.J. 857 (1993):

> In the latest round of what has proven to be a lengthy debate, the American Bar Association's House of Delegates rejected a proposal ... by the Standing Committee on Ethics and Professional Responsibility ... to permit lawyers to disclose confidences of clients who use their legal services in committing fraudulent or criminal acts. In its Report and Recommendation to the House of Delegates, the Ethics Committee had proposed amendments to Model Rule 1.6(b) of the Model Rule of Professional Conduct that would have added an additional justification permitting lawyers to reveal, without the client's consent and to the extent reasonably necessary, information that relates to the representation of a client. The proposed amendments would have authorized disclosure "to rectify the consequences of a client's criminal or fraudulent act in the commission of which the lawyer's services had been used."

> Pursuant to Model Rule 1.6(b), lawyers already are authorized, but not mandated, to reveal such information in two situations. First, information can be revealed in order to prevent the client from committing a criminal act that the lawyer believes would likely result in imminent death or substantial bodily harm. Second, under certain enumerated circumstances, a lawyer can disclose information in order to establish a claim or defense on behalf of the lawyer.

> The Committee on Professional Responsibility of the Association of the Bar of the City of New York concluded that—

>> [T]he present state of the ethical rules governing lawyers' conduct provides little guidance to the practitioner; the rules are confusing and contradictory, and therefore, at the very least, these rules should be clarified to provide more meaningful guidance. Id.

3.   The problem of professional ethics, attorney-client confidentiality and the corporation has spawned a considerable literature: E.g., Symposium, Ethical Responsibilities of Corporate Lawyers, 31 Bus.Law 1173 (1978); Block and Barton, Internal Investigations: Maintaining the Confidentiality of a Corporate Client's Communication with Investigative Counsel, 35 Bus.Law 5 (1979); Weisenberger, Toward Precision in the Application of the Attorney–Client Privilege for Corporations, 65 Ia.L.Rev. 899 (1980); Tankersly, The Corporation Attorney–Client Privilege, Culpable Employees, Attorney Ethics, and the Joint Defense Doctrine, 58 Tex.L.Rev. 809 (1980); Note, Discovery of Internal Corporate Investigations, 32 Stan.L.Rev. 1163 (1980); Kutak, Coming: The New Model Rules of Professional Conduct, 66 A.B.A.J. 45 (1980); Hazard, Ethics in the Practice of Law 43–57 (1978); J.B. Weinstein & M.A. Berger, 2 Weinstein's Evidence ¶¶ 503[01]–503[03].

4.   What are the obligations of the attorney for a corporation who discovers that persons associated with the corporation are acting or intend to act in violation of a legal obligation to the corporation or in violation of law? See Rule 1.13, ABA, Model Rules of Professional Conduct (1983). See also Rule 1.6. Compare also Model Rule 3.3. Consider the application of these Rules to the following Problem:

PROBLEM

November 15, 1994

To the Members of the Ethics Committee:

I need to know what my responsibilities are under the following facts.

After I graduated from Law School last May, I took a job in the counsel's office of a large corporation which I will call Admiral Drug Co. It manufactures various routine pharmaceutical items, among other things. It is my job to handle many different routine problems, small litigations, contract drafting, some negotiations and labor problems, and to assist my direct superior, George Miller, who is associate general counsel.

After I was here several months, getting acquainted with the office files and procedures, I happened to review the papers in a 4 million share stock offering Admiral did about two years ago. In reading over the prospectus, I saw an error in the description of the terms under which Admiral had taken a large loan from a commercial bank. Under the securities laws, this could subject Admiral to substantial damages if buyers of the stock issue discover the error and bring a class action for their losses. They won't have losses unless the stock goes down below the price they paid. Right now it is about three points under that price. When I called this error to the attention of Mr. Miller, he expressed surprise and instructed me not to reveal it.

My first question is whether I have any obligation on the facts I just described.

My second question arises because Admiral is now about to make another stock offering. I am not directly responsible for it, but I have been tangentially involved and I have been watching how it is done. For both stock offerings, we have outside counsel to help us, the New York firm of Swift, Long & Lasser. I have looked over the page proofs of the prospectus for this second offering and discovered that the same misstatement about the terms of the debt is repeated. When I mentioned this to Mr. Miller, he said that the company didn't believe it had a choice because if it were to correct the error now, it would increase the chances of "some smart class action lawyer" catching the original error and filing a lawsuit. Mr. Miller said that Frank McDonald (I am making all these names up for obvious reasons), the general counsel of the company and a member of its Board of Directors, was fully aware of these facts.

So my second question is: Do these additional facts give me any obligation to do something?

My third question troubles me even more. Admiral markets a tampon called Relax. Recently, it supposedly "improved" the tampon by the addition of certain chemicals that increase its absorbability. Two weeks ago, a young biochemist in the research department, whom I know from college, was having lunch with me at her request and she told me that tests she performed revealed that the added chemicals could be dangerous to a user's health to an extent she could not determine. I didn't completely understand the science end of it, but I asked her if she had talked to her superiors. She said she had and that they thought her research was faulty for various reasons. They also said that the tests they did showed no health danger.

My friend told me she had inspected her superiors' research and thought it was sloppy. She also said she had been shown a memorandum from the marketing people to the research department urging the research department to approve the chemical additives as soon as possible for a major marketing campaign that was being planned. Finally, she told me that she had talked to five of the younger people in the research department and four agreed with her that the product needed further testing to be confident of its safety.

I mentioned all this to Mr. Miller, who said that half a dozen senior scientists had approved the product, that there would always be division of opinion in the research department and that it wasn't my job to decide whose conclusions were correct. The following day my biochemist friend showed me a paper in a scientific journal she had just received and which expressed preliminary concern about the harmful effects of the particular chemicals on humans based on tests on laboratory animals.

For each of these problems, I would like to know: (1) what am I required to do or not do; (2) what am I permitted to do even if not required?

Thank you.*

Without respect to the outcome of the above inquiry, assume shareholders sued and users brought a product liability case as foreseen by the young lawyer. He has in his file copies of the memoranda and reports of conversations he adverted to. Almost all of this information was sent by him to the head of the corporate legal department who has some additional memoranda respecting his own contemporaneous conversations with the heads and middle level people in various relevant operating departments.

Interrogatories sufficiently detailed to ferret out these documents have been served on outside counsel for Admiral Drug in both cases. Does the attorney-client or work product rule protect them from discovery? Explain.

5. Compare with the foregoing Problem the facts in Meyerhofer v. Empire Fire and Marine Insurance Co., 497 F.2d 1190 (2d Cir.1974): As a result of a dispute within his law firm as to a failure to adequately disclose certain possibly excessive fees in connection with a registration statement filed under the Securities Act, G resigned from the firm. He subsequently submitted an affidavit to the SEC concerning the non-disclosed fees, and when he was later charged as a defendant in a shareholder suit, to verify his non-participation in the allegedly fraudulent conduct that was the basis for the action, he turned over to plaintiff's counsel the affidavit he had prepared for the SEC. Did G violate the attorney-client privilege or professional ethics by making these disclosures?

6. For another similar case involving voluntary disclosures by corporate counsel that raises questions of both the lawyer's duty of confidentiality and the privilege, see SEC v. Gulf & Western Industries, 518 F.Supp. 675 (D.D.C. 1981): Outside general counsel to the corporation who also served as a corporate director and member of its pension fund advisory committee was charged with embezzlement from his law firm and the corporation. As part of a plea bargain, he agreed to disclose to the SEC improprieties of the corporation and its officers. The latter were as a result charged in a SEC civil action. They raised as an affirmative defense the claim that the SEC induced the breach of the attorney-client privilege by the outside general counsel "thus obtaining an insider's view of ... [the corporation] that only its principal lawyer could provide." Held: The defendants failed to sustain the burden of showing that: a) the information communicated to the SEC originated in connection with legal advice or was confidential; and b) the Commission or its staff solicited confidential information.

---

* The Editors wish to thank Professor Stephen Gillers of the N.Y.U. Law School for the material contained in this Problem.

The court in conclusion stated:

> The defendants express a concern that if ... [the general counsel's] cooperation with the SEC is sanctioned, attorneys would be tempted to reveal their client's confidences whenever they encountered trouble. This ruling should not be read to endorse such a practice.... Permitting this matter to proceed should not erode the policies underlying the privilege or place a chilling effect on future attorney-client relationships.

> In this case, the Commission, as protector of the public interest, could possibly show good cause to justify disclosure of any privileged information.... The Court does not reach this issue, however, since the defendants have failed to show a breach of the attorney-client relationship. Id. at 686.

7.   Are lawyers who resign representation of a client because they believe the client is committing, and may continue to commit fraud, permitted to communicate with another lawyer working for the same client regarding the client's wrongful activity? See Krach, Note, The Client–Fraud Dilemma: A Need for Consensus, 48 Md. L.Rev. 436 (1987); Inter-lawyer Communication and the Prevention of Client Fraud: A Look Back at O.P.M., 34 UCLA L.Rev. 925 (1987). The OPM case discussed in these two articles is widely cited as an illustration of the inadequacy of the existing rules. In OPM, while representing a leasing company, the law firm learned that its client had obtained millions of dollars of loans based on fraudulent leases and that the firm had unwittingly aided the client by issuing opinion letters that were based on falsified documents. Having been advised by outside counsel that it could not disclose the fraud and that it could continue to represent the client provided that it was assured that the fraudulent conduct had ended, the law firm continued the representation for a time, but the fraudulent conduct continued and the law firm finally withdrew from representing the client. It publicly stated its rationale for withdrawing as a mutual parting of the ways. As a result, OPM obtained new counsel and was able to obtain 15 million dollars of additional loans based on fraudulent leases.

A more recent case involved a suit filed by the Office of Thrift Supervision (OTS) against the law firm of Kaye, Scholer, Fierman, Hays & Handler in connection with firm's representation of Charles Keating and the Lincoln Savings & Loan Association. OTS charged that law firm had misled regulators and had done nothing while Lincoln Savings was providing false information and was purging its files of incriminating documents just before OTS was to examine its records. The Kaye Scholer law firm settled with OTS for 41 million dollars. See Koniak, When Courts Refuse to Frame the law and Others Frame It To Their Will, 66 S.Cal. L.Rev. 1075 (1993).

Professor Geoffrey Hazard of the Yale Law School, in anticipation of testifying, provided an expert opinion regarding the propriety of the law firm's conduct in which he reportedly opined that Kaye, Scholer had no duty to disclose weaknesses in Lincoln's position and that its conduct had not violated existing standards of ethical conduct and professional responsibility ... that Kaye Scholer would have violated the Code of Professional Responsibility if it had made the disclosures to the bank regulators. Id. 20 Fordham Urb. L.J. at 862, notes 19 and 20.

8.   See H. Weinstein, Client Confidences and the Rules of Professional Responsibility: Too Little Consensus and Too Much Confusion, 35 S.Tex. L.Rev. 727 (1994); Cahn, Critical Theories and Legal Ethics, Inconsistent Stories, 81 Geo.L.J. 2475 (1993); Hazard, the Future of Legal Ethics, 100 Yale L.J. 1239 (1991); Subin, The Lawyer as Superego: Disclosure of Client Confidences to

Prevent Harm, 70 Ia. L.Rev. 1091 (1985); Miller, Note, The Attorney's Duty to Reveal a Client's Intended Future Criminal Conduct, 1984 Duke L.J. 582.

H.   Waiver of the Attorney–Client Privilege and/or Work Product

NOTES

1.   The attorney-client privilege may be waived by action of the client or someone authorized to act on his or her behalf. Waiver may be by disclosure or other conduct indicating that there is no longer an expectation of confidentiality. An agent of the holder-client who has express or implied authority to act on the client's behalf may waive.

2.   A recurring problem area involves disclosures by the attorney. If the attorney is acting within the scope of his or her authority in making a disclosure, subsequently a court may conclude that there has been a waiver. There are cases where attorneys have waived inadvertently. Obviously, it behooves counsel to be careful. See Note, Inadvertent Disclosure of Documents Subject to the Attorney–Client Privilege, 82 Mich.L.Rev. 598 (1983). In Gray v. Bicknell, 86 F.3d 1472 (8th Cir.1996), the court reviewed three different approaches that have been followed with respect to attorney-client privilege waiver based on inadvertent disclosures:

> Under the lenient approach, the attorney-client privilege must be knowingly waived. Here the determination of inadvertence is the end of the analysis. The attorney-client privilege exists for the benefit of the client and cannot be waived except by an intentional and knowing relinquishment. Georgetown Manor, Inc. v. Ethan Allen, Inc., 753 F.Supp. 936 (S.D.Fla.1991).

> The lenient test creates little incentive for lawyers to maintain tight control over privileged material.

> The second approach is known as the strict test. Gray urges the Court to adopt such a test and refers to In re Sealed Case, 877 F.2d 976 (D.C.Cir. 1989), a case describing the D.C. Circuit's strict test. . . . Under the strict test, any document produced, either intentionally or otherwise, loses its privileged status with the possible exception of situations where all precautions were taken. Once waiver has occurred, it extends " 'to all other communications relating to the same subject matter.' " Id. at 981 (quoting In re Sealed Case, 676 F.2d 793, 809 (D.C.Cir.1982)).

> The strict test sacrifices the value of protecting client confidences for the sake of certainty of results. . . . If, when a document stamped "attorney-client privileged" is inadvertently released, it and all related documents lose their privileged status, then clients will have much greater hesitancy to fully inform their attorney.

> Finally, there is the middle test, sometimes called the Hydraflow test. . . . Hydraflow, Inc. v. Enidine, Inc., 145 F.R.D. 626 (W.D.N.Y.1993). Under the Hydraflow test, the court undertakes a five-step analysis of the unintentionally disclosed document to determine the proper range of privilege to extend. These considerations are (1) the reasonableness of the precautions taken to prevent inadvertent disclosure in view of the extent of document production, (2) the number of inadvertent disclosures, (3) the extent of the disclosures, (4) the promptness of measures taken to rectify the disclosure, (5) whether the overriding interest of justice would be served by relieving

the party of its error. [S]ee also Alldread v. City of Grenada, 988 F.2d 1425 (5th Cir.1993).... At the court's discretion, the privilege may also be determined to have been waived for related, but-as-yet undisclosed, documents.

We believe that ... the middle test ... strikes the appropriate balance between protecting attorney-client privilege and allowing, in certain situations, the unintended release of privileged documents to waive that privilege. The middle test is best suited to achieving a fair result. It accounts for the errors that inevitably occur in modern, document-intensive litigation, but treats carelessness with privileged material as an indication of waiver. The middle test provides the most thoughtful approach, leaving the trial court broad discretion as to whether waiver occurred and, if so, the scope of that waiver. It requires a detailed court inquiry into the document practices of the party who inadvertently released the document.

3. In United States v. Valencia, 826 F.2d 169 (2d Cir.1987), the prosecutor sought a pretrial ruling that an attorney's statements to the prosecutor, made in the course of discussions about bail and reporting his client's allegedly false exculpatory statements, were admissible at trial as vicarious admissions of the client. The trial court denied the motion on the ground that the attorney's statements could not be directly attributed to the defendant and that their use would contravene the attorney-client privilege; that to admit the statements "would set a dangerous precedent for the admission of all informal, out-of-court statements by attorneys against their clients."

On appeal, a majority of the court of appeals affirmed, on the ground that the trial judge has discretion in applying the admissions provisions of the Federal Rules to statements of a criminal defendant's attorney; that in this case the government's claim to this evidence was outweighed by the defendant's interest in retaining the services of his counsel, assuring uninhibited discussions between his counsel and the prosecutor and avoiding the risk of impairing the defendant's privilege against self incrimination. The majority declined to reach the attorney-client privilege issue. The dissent, inter alia, concluded that the defendant's attorney-client privilege had been waived, stating:

> Having implicitly granted his attorney this authority [to enter into bail negotiations] ... Valencia may not now be heard to complain about how that authority was exercised.

See also United States v. McKeon, 738 F.2d 26 (2d Cir.1984).

4. At trial, the issue of whether the attorney was authorized to speak may arise under two headings,whether the attorney-client privilege is waived when confidential communications are revealed by the attorney, and whether the statements are admissible against the client under the hearsay exception for vicarious admissions. Should the same standard be applied to each of these authority issues?

Generally, an attorney is viewed as having a very broad implied authority to speak for the client in the judicial context, in connection with negotiations on behalf of the client or in other legal settings where the lawyer is representing the client's interests. There are other contexts where, generally, the attorney does not have implied authority to speak. For example, absent special facts, one can assume that an attorney's disclosure of confidential facts to a group at a cocktail party is not within his implied authority. Suppose that in a case that commands media attention, a criminal defense attorney goes on TV to comment on various aspects of his client's case and, in the course of those comments, reveals confidential matters; suppose it is concluded that the attorney did not have authority to speak. What result when the prosecutor offers the attorney's TV statements into evidence? Are any ethical issues raised by the lawyer's conduct?

5. If the attorney's disclosures waive the protection of the privilege, there is a question as to the scope of the waiver. Where an attorney, acting within his authority, makes a statement revealing confidential matters, there is a waiver with respect to the matters revealed in the statement. Does the waiver extend beyond the matters already revealed?

   a. Where part of a confidential conversation has been disclosed, the waiver extends to the rest of the conversation. United States v. Tellier, 255 F.2d 441, 447 (2d Cir.1958).

   b. Should the waiver extend beyond the specific communication or other confidential matters revealed, to the subject matter of those disclosures, for example, all conversations on the same topic? See von Bulow by Auersperg v. von Bulow, 114 F.R.D. 71 (S.D.N.Y.1987): Plaintiffs sought discovery of discussions between the defendant and his attorneys, claiming a waiver of the attorney-client privilege based on the fact that one of the attorneys, who had represented the defendant in a prior case involving an appeal from a criminal conviction for attempted murder, had, with his client's encouragement, published a book about the criminal case; and that the book contained an account of the attorney's previously confidential conversations with his client. On appeal, the Second Circuit vacated the trial court's order granting discovery, concluding that where disclosures of privileged information are made extrajudicially and do not prejudice the opposing party, "there exists no reason in logic or equity to broaden the waiver beyond those matters actually revealed"; "that the extrajudicial disclosure of an attorney-client communication, one not subsequently used by the client in a judicial proceeding to his adversary's prejudice, does not waive the privilege as to the undisclosed portions of the communication." 828 F.2d 94, 102 (2d Cir.1987).

Accord: Chevron Corp. v. Pennzoil Co., 974 F.2d 1156 (9th Cir.1992) (alternative ground).

6. Consider the following statement in Wigmore:

   The client's offer of his own or the attorney's testimony as to a specific communication to the attorney is a waiver as to all other communications to the attorney on the same matter. This is so because the privilege of secret consultation is intended only as an incidental means of defense, and not as an independent means of attack, and to use it in the latter character is to abandon it to the former. 8 Wigmore on Evidence, 2327 (McNaughton rev. 1961). See generally, R. L. Marcus, The Perils of Privilege: Waiver and the Litigator, 84 Mich.L.Rev. 1605 (1986).

The doctrine to which Wigmore refers is the notion that the attorney-client privilege may not be used both as a sword and a shield. United States v. Bilzerian, 926 F.2d 1285 (2d Cir.1991). See e.g. Chevron Corp. v. Pennzoil Co., 974 F.2d 1156 (9th Cir.1992): Pennzoil claimed that it was reasonable for it to acquire Chevron stock for investment purposes and that it did so in reliance upon the advice of tax counsel. Chevron sought to compel disclosure of the documents that otherwise fell within the attorney-client privilege, arguing that Pennzoil waived the privilege by using advice of counsel both as a sword to defeat Chevron's tax arguments, and as a shield to protect against the basis for its claim that it was reasonably relying on the advice of counsel. Held: The attorney-client privilege was "implicitly waived":

> [T]o the extent that Pennzoil claims that its tax position is reasonable because it was based on advice of counsel, Pennzoil puts at issue the tax advice it received.... Pennzoil cannot invoke the attorney-client privilege to deny Chevron access to the very information that Chevron must refute in order to demonstrate the Pennzoil's Schedule 13D is materially misleading.

7. Does one attorney's disclosures that trigger a waiver determination operate to waive with respect to communications as to the same subject matter between the client and other attorneys representing him or her? See Nye v. Sage Products, Inc., 98 F.R.D. 452 (N.D.Ill.1982).

8. Of course, if a waiver as to the subject matter is deemed to have occurred, there may be a question as to how that subject matter is to be characterized.

9. Suppose the government using a lawfully issued search warrant searches the home of a target of investigation and finds and seizes a copy of a letter written by the target to his attorney for the purpose of seeking legal advice. Does the attorney-privilege apply to the letter? Held: Attorney-client privilege applicable. United States v. De La Jara, 973 F.2d 746 (9th Cir.1992). Suppose the target then fails to pursue the timely return of the letter. Held: Where the target did nothing to recover the letter or protect its confidentiality during the six month period between its seizure and introduction into evidence, he "allowed the mantle of confidentiality which once protected the document to be irretrievably breached, thereby waiving his privilege." Id.

10. Is the privilege waived when a writing consisting of a confidential attorney-client communication is examined by a witness-client prior to trial and in preparation for testifying? See the material on refreshing recollection, supra, p. 340 et seq.

11. In Upjohn v. United States, 449 U.S. 383 (1981), supra p. 1442, recall that the company voluntarily disclosed certain information to the SEC. This was done pursuant to the SEC's "voluntary disclosure" program begun in 1975 under which the SEC encouraged corporate self-investigations of political "slush fund" and under-the-table foreign and domestic payments. See In re Sealed Case, 676 F.2d 793, 800–801 (D.C.Cir.1982). Subsequent decisions have addressed the extent to which such voluntary disclosures waive the attorney-client privilege.

a) In re Sealed Case, supra: "When Company submitted its investigative counsel's report and notes to the SEC ... it bound itself to provide the SEC access to any documentation necessary to evaluate the report." Id. at 824.

b) Does a voluntary disclosure to the SEC waive as to other parties? Diversified Industries, Inc. v. Meredith, 572 F.2d 596 (8th Cir.1977) ruled that a disclosure to a federal investigatory agency of the results of an internal corporate investigation does not waive the attorney-client privilege when the documents are being sought by a rival corporation. Subsequent decisions in other circuits have, however, approved a broad waiver rule. Thus, waiver has been upheld where the other party seeking the documents was another federal agency. Permian Corp. v. United States, 665 F.2d 1214 (D.C.Cir.1981). Subsequently, the same circuit ruled that Permian was not limited to circumstances in which material disclosed to one federal agency was sought by another federal agency; the material was not protected by privilege in a later grand jury proceeding. In re Subpoenas Duces Tecum (Fulbright & Jaworski), 738 F.2d 1367, 1370 (C.A.D.C.1984). See also Westinghouse Corporation v. Republic of the Philippines, 951 F.2d 1414 (3d Cir.1991): Against a claim of limited waiver, the court held that by disclosing documents generated in an internal investigation to the SEC and the Department of Justice, Westinghouse had effected a complete waiver and therefore the Republic of the Philippines which had filed a lawsuit against Westinghouse could obtain the documents. Also see In re Martin Marietta Corporation, 856 F.2d 619 (4th Cir.1988), cert. denied 490 U.S. 1011 (1989) and see Willcox, Martin Marietta and the Erosion of the Attorney–Client Privilege and Work–Product Protection, 49 Md. L. Rev. 917 (1990).

See generally, Developments in the Law,Privileged Communications, 98 Harv.L.Rev. 1450, 1650–1659 (1985); Block and Barton, Securities Litigation,Waiver of the Attorney–Client Privilege by Disclosure to the SEC, 10 Sec.Reg.L.J. 170 (1982); Note, Corporate Disclosure and Limited Waiver of the Attorney–Client Privilege, 50 Geo.Wash.L.Rev. 812 (1982).

12. Who has authority to waive the privilege on behalf of the corporation? Suppose the person purporting to waive the privilege is house counsel and also an officer of the corporation and also a potential target of the grand jury investigation. Should it make any difference whether outside counsel has been engaged to represent the corporation in the matter? See generally Velsicol Chemical Corp. v. Parsons, 561 F.2d 671, 675 (7th Cir.1977).

13. In Commodity Futures Trading Commission v. Weintraub, 471 U.S. 343 (1985), the Supreme Court ruled that a bankruptcy trustee has the power to waive a corporate debtor's attorney-client privilege with respect to communications that occurred before the filing of the bankruptcy petition. The Court stated:

> The parties in this case agree that, for solvent corporations, the power to waive the corporate attorney-client privilege rests with the corporation's management and is normally exercised by its officers and directors. . . .

> The parties also agree that when control of a corporation passes to new management, the authority to assert and waive the corporation's attorney-client privilege passes as well. New managers installed as a result of a takeover, merger, loss of confidence by shareholders, or simply normal succession, may waive the attorney-client privilege with respect to communications made by former officers and directors. Displaced managers may not assert the privilege over the wishes of current managers even as to statements that the former might have made to counsel concerning matters within the scope of their corporate duties. . . .

> In light of the [Bankruptcy] Code's allocation of responsibilities, it is clear that the trustee plays the role most closely analogous to that of a solvent corporation's management. . . .

471 U.S. at 348–355.

14. Suppose that an individual goes into bankruptcy. Does the decision in Commodity Futures Trading Commission v. Weintraub, supra note 9, mean that a bankruptcy trustee in such a case would have the power to waive that individual's attorney-client privilege? See id. at 355–357.

15. The work product privilege may also be waived. Judge Wright specifically addressed the waiver issue with respect to work product protection in In re Sealed Case, 676 F.2d 793, 818 (D.C.Cir.1982):

> The purposes of the work product privilege are . . . not inconsistent with selective disclosure,even in some circumstances to an adversary. Yet at some point acceptable tactic may degenerate into,sharp practices,inimical to a healthy adversary system. When that occurs . . . then the balance of

interests ... shifts, and the courts need not impede a grand jury's legitimate efforts in the name of protecting the adversary system.

The circumstances of this case convince us that respecting Company's claim to work product privilege is not required to maintain a healthy adversary system. We evaluate in turn three general factors that justify an implied waiver as to some of the documents in this case: the basic conditions of the SEC's voluntary disclosure program, the express assurances Company offered regarding the completeness of the final report given to the SEC and the grand jury, and the importance of specific documents for a fair evaluation of Company's voluntary disclosure.

See also In re Subpoenas Duces Tecum (Fulbright & Jaworski), 738 F.2d 1367 (C.A.D.C.1984).

I. THE SIXTH AMENDMENT RIGHT TO COUNSEL AND THE ATTORNEY-CLIENT PRIVILEGE

The Sixth Amendment Right to Counsel protection and the attorney-client privilege intersect in two very different categories of cases. The first involves instances where a claim is made that governmental agents have gained access to confidential attorney-client communications. The second involves instances where a court has rejected a claim of attorney-client privilege, and the contention is made that this action has the effect of denying the defendant the effective assistance of counsel.

1. Government Intrusion Into Attorney-Client Confidences

The Sixth Amendment's right to counsel provision adds a constitutional dimension to a breaking of the confidentiality of attorney-client communications in the context of a criminal case. Like comparable issues that have arisen in connection with the confrontation clause and hearsay, questions may be posed regarding the relationship between traditional attorney-client privilege doctrine and the relevant constitutional principles.

Governmental intrusions into attorney-client communications have taken several different forms. The most frequent type of claimed intrusion involves a government informer or agent in the defense camp, either as a co-defendant or as an associate of the defendant, participating in conversations that involve the defendant's attorney. A second type involves surreptitious overhearing of attorney-client conversations. A third category involves governmental searches of attorney files.

a. The informer-in-the-defense-camp cases are part of a larger set, all of which involve a government agent who participates in a conversation with a person who does not realize that the agent is recording or transmitting the conversation or will report back to governmental authorities its contents. See United States v. White, 401 U.S. 745 (1971). The Supreme Court has consistently sustained the constitutionality of such law enforcement activity under the Fourth Amendment. The question discussed here is whether such activity becomes unconstitutional under the Sixth Amendment because the conversation at which the government agent is present takes place after a formal charging of the criminal defendant and involves not only the defendant but his attorney and perhaps others in the defense camp. If so, what is it specifically that triggers a constitutional violation?

The leading cases are Weatherford v. Bursey, 429 U.S. 545 (1977) and Hoffa v. United States, 385 U.S. 293 (1966). In Weatherford, W, a state undercover agent, had been charged as a co-defendant with B. W and B each retained his own attorney. At the insistence of B and his attorney, W met twice with them to discuss the approaching trial. W did not, however, "discuss with or pass on to his superiors or the prosecuting attorney or any of [his] ... staff 'any details or information regarding the plaintiff's trial plans, strategy, or anything having to do with the [pending] criminal action.... ' " Id. 429 U.S. 545, 548. B later brought an action against W and others under 42 U.S.C. § 1983, alleging, inter alia, that he had been deprived of the effective assistance of counsel as a result of W's meetings with him and his attorney. The Court of Appeals ruled in favor of B, applying a per se rule to the effect that "whenever the prosecutor knowingly arranges or permits intrusion into the attorney-client relationship" the right to counsel is violated. The Supreme Court reversed, relying principally on the fact that W had communicated nothing to his superiors or to the prosecution about B's trial plans. The Court expressly rejected the Court of Appeals' conclusion that treated W as a member of the prosecution team whose knowledge of B's trial plans violated B's right to counsel: "[T]his reasoning is not a realistic assessment of the relationship of ... [W] ... to the prosecuting staff or of the potential for detriment to ... [B] ... or benefit to the State that ... [W's] ... uncommunicated knowledge might pose." Id. 429 U.S. 545, 556. The Court, too, took into account the fact that W participated in the defense discussions not because the State wanted information about them but rather because he was asked and to refuse would have raised suspicions in the minds of B and his attorney.

The Court stated:

Had ... [W] testified at ... [B's] trial as to the conversation between [B] and ... [his attorney]; had any of the State's evidence originated in these conversations; had those overheard conversations been used in any other way to the substantial detriment of ... [B]; or even had the prosecution learned from ... [W] ... the details of the ... conversation about trial preparations, B would have a much stronger case. Id. 429 U.S. 545, 554.

In Hoffa, P, a government informer and an associate of defendant H, was present during his first trial in and around the hotel suite in which trial strategy was discussed by H and his lawyers. P was also present during discussions H had regarding endeavors to bribe jurors in the case then being tried. There was some question about the extent to which P actually heard and reported back to a government agent information concerning defense counsel activities, but the Court proceeded on the assumption that some intrusion on the lawyer-client relationship had occurred. However, the first trial ended in a hung jury; and the issue of a violation of H's right to counsel was posed in the context of a second trial on charges arising out of the jury tampering efforts in the first trial. The Court concluded that any assumed violation of H's right to counsel at the first trial [which might have made invalid a conviction, if there had been one in that case] in no way tainted the testimony of P in the second trial on a different charge. Also: "the clinching basic fact ... [was] that none of ... [H's] incriminating statements which ... P heard were made in the presence of counsel ... or in connection in any way with the legitimate defense of the ... [first] prosecution." Hoffa, supra, 385 U.S. 293 (1966).

Weatherford and Hoffa leave many questions unanswered. For example, the Court did not make clear whether communication of defense information to government officials would necessarily trigger a constitutional violation. All that the Court said in Weatherford was that had such communication occurred or had other specified acts been present, the claimant "would have a much stronger case." It is perhaps significant that the Court in Weatherford emphasized that in Hoffa the Court had only assumed for purposes of discussion that a Sixth Amendment violation had occurred at the first trial.

Lower court decisions since Weatherford (and also before) have wrestled with these questions. Two post-Weatherford court of appeals cases illustrate different approaches. In United States v. Levy, 577 F.2d 200, 208 (3d Cir.1978), the court concluded that communication by a co-defendant government informant to Drug Enforcement Administration agents of information regarding defense strategy obtained from conversations involving the two defendants and their joint attorney violated the Sixth Amendment and was ground for dismissal of the charges. In effect, the court said that a per se constitutional violation occurs once defense strategy information is communicated to government enforcement agents. It rejected the district court's view that actual prejudice must be shown, and it did not require proof that the prosecutors in the case received the information.

See also United States v. Ginsberg, 758 F.2d 823 (2d Cir.1985) which treated as presumed confidential defense camp discussions overheard by a co-defendant cooperating with the government.

The Court of Appeals in United States v. Melvin, 650 F.2d 641 (5th Cir.1981) reached a different conclusion: The defendants' attorneys and the defendants met several times with the secret government informant, trying to persuade him to let the attorneys represent him. The informant communicated to customs agents the information obtained at these meetings, and this information was conveyed to the prosecutor in the case. The court expressed doubts whether confidentiality attached to these meetings. On the assumption that it did, however, it concluded that there must be a showing of prejudice before any remedy is required, and then a determination must be made whether some remedy short of dismissal might suffice.

In reaching this conclusion, the Melvin court relied heavily on the decision in United States v. Morrison, 449 U.S. 361 (1981). In Morrison, government agents tried to persuade the defendant to cooperate in a related case after she had been indicted and retained counsel. The Supreme Court stated:

> The premise of our prior cases is that the constitutional infringement identified has had or threatens some adverse effect upon the effectiveness of counsel's representation or has produced some other prejudice to the defense. Absent such impact on the criminal proceeding ... there is no basis for imposing a remedy.... More particularly, absent demonstrable prejudice, or substantial threat thereof, dismissal of the indictment is plainly inappropriate even though the violation may have been deliberate.

It should, of course, be noted that although the constitutional doctrine invoked in Morrison was right to counsel, in that case there was no intrusion on defense strategy or attorney-client conversations.

In connection with the prosecution "team" concept see United States v. Natale, 494 F.Supp. 1114, 1124 (E.D.Pa.1979) where the court concluded that no information was communicated "to the prosecution team, although other information obtained from the defendants was disclosed to investigatory governmental officials who were carefully isolated from and did not divulge such information to any of the governmental officials who were prosecuting the charges against the defendants." For a situation where there appears to have been an intrusion by a federal agent into a state criminal defendant's meetings with his attorney but no communication of anything to the state prosecutor, see In re Pratt, 112 Cal.App.3d 795, 170 Cal.Rptr. 80, 114–119 (1980).

Compare United States v. Fortna, 796 F.2d 724 (5th Cir.1986), a case in which defendant's attorney who had also been involved in drug dealing began to cooperate with the FBI and to provide the government with incriminating information about the defendant.

For the view that to establish prejudice from the government's intrusion into attorney-client confidential communications, the defendant must show that the information was "used for the benefit of the government or the detriment of the defendant," see Bishop v. Rose, 701 F.2d 1150 (6th Cir.1983).

See generally, Lurie, Sixth Amendment Implications of Informant Participation in Defense Meetings, 58 Fordham L.Rev. 795 (1990); Note, Government Intrusions into the Defense Camp: Undermining the Right to Counsel, 97 Harv. L.Rev. 1143 (1984). Halpern, Government Intrusions into the Attorney–Client Relationship: An Interest Analysis of Rights and Remedies, 32 Buffalo L.Rev. 127 (1983);

b.   The Sixth Amendment issue is also posed where government agents surreptitiously eavesdrop on attorney-client conversations. Such eavesdropping may, of course, also violate the Fourth Amendment. Initially it might be thought that the same approach taken in the informer-in-the-defense-camp cases would be applicable to this group of cases. Not necessarily so. Under the Fourth Amendment, the Court has drawn a constitutional line between surreptitious eavesdropping and informer participation in private conversations. The Court has at least suggested that these two types of situations, occurring in a Sixth Amendment context, also involve different kinds of concerns:

> ... One threat to the effective assistance of counsel posed by government interception of attorney-client communications lies in the inhibition of free exchanges between defendant and counsel because of the fear of being overheard. However, a fear that some third party may turn out to be a government agent will inhibit attorney-client communication to a lesser degree than the fear that the government is monitoring those communications through electronic eavesdropping, because the former intrusion may be avoided by excluding third parties from defense meetings or refraining from divulging defense strategy when third parties are present at those meetings. Of course, in some circumstances the ability to exclude third parties from defense meetings may not eliminate the chilling effect on attorney-client exchanges, but neither Hoffa nor any other decision of this Court supports respondent's theory that the chill is the same whether induced by electronic surveillance or by undercover agents.... Weatherford v. Bursey, 429 U.S. 545, 554–555, 97 S.Ct. 837, 51 L.Ed.2d 30, 39 (1977).

The Supreme Court has not yet rendered a full opinion in a case involving surreptitious eavesdropping on attorney-client conversations. Two cases have been decided by the Court, Black v. United States, 385 U.S. 26, (1966) and O'Brien v. United States, 386 U.S. 345 (1967). In Black, the eavesdropping issue was raised after trial and conviction, and the Court wrote a per curiam opinion granting a new trial and opportunity for a hearing on the issues raised by the electronic surveillance. O'Brien involved similar facts, and the Court made the same disposition, citing Black.

The leading eavesdropping case involving a clear-cut decision on the merits of the Sixth Amendment claim is still the court of appeals decision in Coplon v. United States, 191 F.2d 749, 757–759 (D.C.Cir.1951) where the court held that surreptitious overhearing by government agents of attorney-client conversations before and during trial, if they occurred, deprived the defendant of her right to counsel and would entitle her to a new trial. The court there rejected the notion that "vindication of the right depend[ed] upon whether its denial resulted in demonstrable prejudice." [In Hoffa, the Supreme Court "assume[d]" that Coplon was correctly decided. In Weatherford, it was again emphasized that in Hoffa the Court had "assumed, without deciding," that Coplon was correctly decided.]

See also United States v. Orman, 417 F.Supp. 1126, 1136 (D.Colo.1976) where DEA agents surreptitiously eavesdropped on the defendant's conversations with the public defender who was representing her. The court dismissed the prosecution despite the fact that the information overheard was not communicated to the prosecutors because

[W]hat was learned by the agents would be of help to them in structuring a defense to the affirmative [entrapment] defense they anticipated and knowledge on the part of the agents of defense plans and strategy is all [that is] ... necessary to require dismissal.

United States v. Peters, 468 F.Supp. 364 (S.D.Fla.1979), also involved a type of eavesdropping on attorney-client conversations. One defendant had taped three-way telephone conversations relating to defense strategy involving himself, his co-defendant and their attorney. The tape was seized by government agents upon arresting the first defendant. The arresting drug enforcement agent listened at length to the tape and subsequently gave the tape to the prosecutor who listened, too. The district court, relying on United States v. Levy, supra, dismissed the indictment. Query: Does Peters involve an informer-in-the-defense-camp situation or surreptitious overhearing of attorney-client conversations?

See generally, Goldsmith & Balmforth, The Electronic Surveillance of Privileged Communications: A Conflict in Doctrines, 64 S.Cal.L.Rev. 903 (1991) which considers the issues that arise whenever privileged conversations, attorney-client, husband-wife, physician-patient, etc., are electronically overheard.

c.   Another factual setting in which governmental agents may gain access to attorney-client confidences arises out of governmental searches, pursuant to a warrant, of law offices and attorney files. In Zurcher v. Stanford Daily, 436 U.S. 547 (1978), the Supreme Court ruled that under the Fourth Amendment a search warrant could be issued against a third person nonsuspect and that the government was not required in such cases to proceed through the use of a subpoena duces tecum. But law office searches also raise a Sixth Amendment right to counsel issue as well as potentially involving a breach of the attorney-client privilege. Consider the statement of the court in People v. Nash, 341 N.W.2d 439, 447 (Mich.1983):

... [W]e express our dismay over what is reported to be an increasing trend toward law office searches, with concern that such a practice may take root in this state.... The specter of law-enforcement officers rummaging through the files and papers of a nonsuspect lawyer's office has grave implications involving not only the attorney-client privilege of the suspect and all other clients of the attorney, but also the constitutional rights against self-incrimination and of counsel.

For a case involving a search of an attorney's files without a warrant, see United States v. Sander, 615 F.2d 215 (5th Cir.1980): Local police rummaged through a murdered attorney's files and read a federal defendant's case file, but did not communicate anything to federal officials. For other law office search cases, see Law Offices of Bernard D. Morley, P.C. v. MacFarlane, 647 P.2d 1215 (Colo.1982); Deukmejian v. Los Angeles Superior Court, 103 Cal.App.3d 253, 162 Cal.Rptr. 857 (1980); O'Connor v. Johnson, 287 N.W.2d 400 (Minn.1979).

See Bloom, The Law Office Search: An Emerging Problem and Some Suggested Solutions, 69 Georgetown L.J. 1 (1980).

Attempts have been made to deal with the problem through legislation. California, for example, now provides for the appointment of attorneys as special masters to conduct the searches of professionals whose clients have a state law privilege. California Penal Code, § 1524. For other legislation, see 42 U.S.C. § 2000aa–11(a) and 28 C.F.R. 59.1 et seq.; Or.Rev.Stat. § 9.695.

d.   Strictly speaking, of course, the foregoing cases do not directly involve the attorney-client privilege since no attempt was made to introduce testimony at trial involving disclosure of an attorney-client communication or its fruits. Yet in each case the question can be raised whether the particular governmental intrusion transgressed the substantive rules applied under the attorney-client privilege or would fall within an exception.

Most of the cases fail explicitly to relate the attorney-client privilege rules to the constitutional issue. See, e.g., United States v. Ginsberg, 758 F.2d 823 (2d Cir.1985). Query, in which of the foregoing cases might a plausible claim have been made that, applying attorney-client privilege doctrine, there was no breach of attorney-client confidentiality? Perhaps a partial explanation for the failure to discuss the attorney-client privilege is that in most of the cases there is conduct that the court views as infringing on the attorney-client relationship, and most of the judicial attention therefore is focused on whether prejudice must be shown and the appropriate remedy.

An exception is United States v. Melvin, supra, 650 F.2d 641, 645–646 (5th Cir.1981), where the court directly related the attorney-client privilege to the constitutional issue:

> ... Appellees complain that the government's argument would reduce the Sixth Amendment to little more than a restatement of the common-law attorney-client privilege; however, it seems that the traditional sanctity of the attorney-client relationship, characterized by the confidentiality of communications between the attorney and client, is precisely what the appellees in this case have sought to vindicate as against government intrusions. The attorney-client privilege,whether or not, and to what extent, it defines or limits the Sixth Amendment right to counsel in other contexts,offers an appropriate framework of analysis in this case.... Appellees miss the mark when they argue that a finding that there is no Sixth Amendment violation here would jeopardize group defense strategy in multi-defendant cases. We do not hold that disclosures between and among several defendants and their counsel in such group defense contexts would lack confidentiality, and therefore lack Sixth Amendment protection. On the contrary, there is a respectable body of law from other courts to the effect that the attorney-client privilege applies to confidential communications among attorneys and their clients for purposes of a common defense.... However, even in the multiparty context, the disclosures must be made in circumstances which indicate that they were made in confidence.... We observe only that there is no confidentiality when disclosures are made in the presence of a person who has not joined the defense team, and with respect to whom there is no reasonable expectation of confidentiality. We hold today only that there is no governmental intrusion into the attorney-client relationship in violation of the Sixth Amendment when a confidential informant attends a meeting of other defendants and their counsel, at the request of other defendants and their attorneys, under such circumstances that the informant could not reasonably refuse to attend without jeopardizing his undercover status, and under circumstances indi-

cating that the other defendants and their counsel knew or should have known that the informant was not part of the defense team and knew or should have known that there was no reasonable expectation of confidentiality in the presence of the informant.

See also United States v. Gartner, 518 F.2d 633 (2d Cir.1975); United States v. Franklin, 598 F.2d 954 (5th Cir.), cert. denied, 444 U.S. 870 (1979); Clutchette v. Rushen, 770 F.2d 1469 (9th Cir.1985).

Sometimes in treating the Sixth Amendment issue, a court may articulate many of the same policies that underlie the privilege. For example, at one point in Weatherford, the Court cited attorney-client precedents in support of the policies under discussion. See Weatherford, 429 U.S. 545 . United States v. Levy, supra, 577 F.2d 200, 209 (3d Cir.1978), provides an even clearer illustration:

> The fundamental justification for the sixth amendment right to counsel is the presumed inability of a defendant to make informed choices about the preparation and conduct of his defense. Free two-way communication between client and attorney is essential if the professional assistance guaranteed by the sixth amendment is to be meaningful. The purpose of the attorney-client privilege is inextricably linked to the very integrity and accuracy of the fact finding process itself. Even guilty individuals are entitled to be advised of strategies for their defense. In order for the adversary system to function properly, any advice received as a result of a defendant's disclosure to counsel must be insulated from the government. . . .

Of course, there are considerations in addition to attorney-client privilege issues involved in these cases. The fact, for example, that deceit by the government may be involved in breaching the attorney-client relationship may influence judicial reactions. On the other hand, the general needs of law enforcement may also be taken into account. For example, in Weatherford the Court noted that "[o]ur cases . . . have recognized the unfortunate necessity of undercover work and the value it often is to effective law enforcement" and rejected an approach that would "require the informant to refuse to participate in attorney-client meetings, even though invited and thus for all practical purposes to unmask himself."

2.   Denial of Attorney Client Privilege as a Violation of Right to Counsel

The relationship between the attorney-client privilege and the Sixth Amendment may also be posed in connection with a contention that a particular denial of attorney-client privilege violated the constitutional rights of the criminal accused.[1]

Several cases bear on the issue. In United States ex rel. Edney v. Smith, 425 F.Supp. 1038, 1049 (E.D.N.Y.1976), aff'd 556 F.2d 556 (2d Cir.1977) a defendant whose privilege claim was rejected in the state court argued in federal habeas corpus proceedings that the state's rejection of his claim violated his rights under the Sixth Amendment counsel provision. A psychiatrist had examined the defendant at the request of his attorney. The prosecutor called the psychiatrist as its witness, and the defense objected, claiming privilege. The state court rejected the claim on the ground that by asserting the insanity defense and offering evidence to establish the claim, the defendant had waived his privilege. In the federal court, the defendant argued that unless communica-

---

1. Suppose a jurisdiction abolished the attorney-client privilege. Would that violate the Sixth Amendment? See Comment, The Attorney–Client Privilege: Fixed Rules, Balancing and Constitutional Entitlement, 91 Harv.L.Rev. 464, 485 (1977).

tions to the psychiatrist in this type of situation are held to be privileged, the accused would not be candid with the psychiatrist and this would in turn impede the defense attorney's ability to present an effective defense.

The state court had suggested that acceptance of the claim of privilege in this context would permit the defendant to shop around for a "friendly" expert and take any unfriendly experts, whom he had retained in the first instance, off the market by invoking the attorney-client privilege. Judge Weinstein noted that "it is the fact that defendants may be more cooperative with their 'own' experts" and thus "as a pragmatic matter, defendant may be prejudiced by this rule." After examining the concerns underlying the extension of the attorney-client privilege to agents and particularly to examining psychiatrists, he concluded that the issue was "whether the balance drawn by New York is so detrimental to the attorney's effective representation of his client as to be prohibited by the Sixth Amendment." In answering this question in the negative, he said, "We can only speculate that the New York rule results in substantial prejudice" particularly since "[t]he statements by the defendant to his psychiatrist were not admitted to establish the fact of his having committed the murder. . . . Given this limited use, any possible prejudice may be balanced, within limits not exceeded in this case, by the strong counterbalancing interest of the State in accurate factfinding by its courts."

A Fifth Circuit case involving an almost identical situation followed Edney. In Granviel v. Estelle, 655 F.2d 673, 682 (5th Cir.1981), the claim of attorney-client privilege had been rejected in the Texas courts, not on the ground of waiver as in Edney, but rather on the ground that the court-appointed psychiatrists were not agents of defense counsel or the prosecutor but rather "disinterested qualified experts." The Third Circuit opinion in United States v. Alvarez, 519 F.2d 1036 (3d Cir.1975) should also be mentioned. In deciding that the attorney-client privilege attached in federal criminal proceedings in a psychiatrist-defendant situation similar to that in Edney and Granviel, the court expressed concern that a contrary rule would "have the inevitable effect of depriving defendants of the effective assistance of counsel. . . . The attorney must be free to make an informed judgment with respect to the best course for the defense without the inhibition of creating a potential government witness."

Judge Weinstein in Edney noted that while the Alvarez court used language "constitutional in tone," it did not have a constitutional question before it. Indeed, it is hard to see how in the federal courts, this type of constitutional issue will be reached. Since under Rule 501 privilege issues in criminal proceedings are "governed by the principles of the common law . . . in the light of reason and experience," any concerns about whether rejection of a privilege claim would deny effective assistance of counsel would, it is assumed, be taken into account in resolving the question of whether the privilege applied. Compare, however, United States v. Nobles, 422 U.S. 225 (1975).

SECTION 4.   THE SPOUSAL PRIVILEGES

A.   THE PRIVILEGE AGAINST ADVERSE SPOUSAL TESTIMONY

Trammel v. United States

Supreme Court of the United States, 1980.
445 U.S. 40, 100 S.Ct. 906, 63 L.Ed.2d 186.

■ MR. CHIEF JUSTICE BURGER delivered the opinion of the Court.

We granted certiorari to consider whether an accused may invoke the privilege against adverse spousal testimony so as to exclude the voluntary testimony of his wife. 440 U.S. 934, 99 S.Ct. 1277, 59 L.Ed.2d 492 (1979). This calls for a re-examination of Hawkins v. United States, 358 U.S. 74, 79 S.Ct. 136, 3 L.Ed.2d 125 (1958). . . .

I

According to the indictment, petitioner and his wife flew from the Philippines to California in August 1975, carrying with them a quantity of heroin. Freeman and Roberts assisted them in its distribution. Elizabeth Trammel then travelled to Thailand where she purchased another supply of the drug. On November 3, 1975, with four ounces of heroin on her person, she boarded a plane for the United States. During a routine customs search in Hawaii, she was searched, the heroin was discovered, and she was arrested. After discussions with Drug Enforcement Administration agents, she agreed to cooperate with the Government.

Prior to trial on this indictment, petitioner moved to sever his case from that of Roberts and Freeman. He advised the court that the Government intended to call his wife as an adverse witness and asserted his claim to a privilege to prevent her from testifying against him. At a hearing on the motion, Mrs. Trammel was called as a Government witness under a grant of use immunity. She testified that she and petitioner were married in May 1975 and that they remained married.[1] She explained that her cooperation with the Government was based on assurances that she would be given lenient treatment. She then described, in considerable detail, her role and that of her husband in the heroin distribution conspiracy.

After hearing this testimony, the District Court ruled that Mrs. Trammel could testify in support of the Government's case to any act she observed during the marriage and to any communication "made in the presence of a third person"; however, confidential communications between petitioner and his wife were held to be privileged and inadmissible. The motion to sever was denied.

At trial, Elizabeth Trammel testified within the limits of the court's pretrial ruling; her testimony, as the Government concedes, constituted virtually its entire case against petitioner. He was found guilty on both the substantive and conspiracy charges and sentenced to an indeterminate term of years pursuant to the Federal Youth Corrections Act, 18 U.S.C. § 5010(b).

In the Court of Appeals petitioner's only claim of error was that the admission of the adverse testimony of his wife, over his objection, contravened this Court's teaching in Hawkins v. United States, 358 U.S. 74, 79 S.Ct. 136, 3 L.Ed.2d 125 (1958), and therefore constituted reversible error. The Court of Appeals rejected this contention. It concluded that Hawkins did not prohibit "the voluntary testimony of a spouse who appears as an unindicted co-conspirator under grant of immunity from the Government in return for her testimony." 583 F.2d 1166, 1168 (C.A.10 1978).

II

The privilege claimed by petitioner has ancient roots. Writing in 1628, Lord Coke observed that "it hath been resolved by the Justices that a wife cannot be

---

1. In response to the question whether divorce was contemplated, Mrs. Trammel testified that her husband had said that "I would go my way and he would go his." (App., at 27). [Footnotes are those of the court. Some footnotes have been omitted and others renumbered.]

produced either against or for her husband." 1 Coke, A Commentarie upon Littleton 6b (1628). See, generally, 8 J. Wigmore, Evidence § 2227, (McNaughton rev. 1961). This spousal disqualification sprang from two canons of medieval jurisprudence: first, the rule that an accused was not permitted to testify in his own behalf because of his interest in the proceeding; second, the concept that husband and wife were one, and that since the woman had no recognized separate legal existence, the husband was that one. From those two now long-abandoned doctrines, it followed that what was inadmissible from the lips of the defendant-husband was also inadmissible from his wife.

Despite its medieval origins, this rule of spousal disqualification remained intact in most common-law jurisdictions well into the 19th century. See 8 Wigmore, § 2333. It was applied by this Court in Stein v. Bowman, 13 Pet. 209, 220–223, 10 L.Ed. 129 (1839), in Graves v. United States, 150 U.S. 118, 14 S.Ct. 40, 37 L.Ed. 1021 (1893), and again in Jin Fuey Moy v. United States, 254 U.S. 189, 195, 41 S.Ct. 98, 101, 65 L.Ed. 214 (1920), where it was deemed so well established a proposition as to "hardly requir[e] mention." Indeed, it was not until 1933, in Funk v. United States, 290 U.S. 371, 54 S.Ct. 212, 78 L.Ed. 369, that this Court abolished the testimonial disqualification in the federal courts, so as to permit the spouse of a defendant to testify in the defendant's behalf. Funk, however, left undisturbed the rule that either spouse could prevent the other from giving adverse testimony. Id., at 373, 54 S.Ct., at 212. The rule thus evolved into one of privilege rather than one of absolute disqualification. See J. Maguire, Evidence, Common Sense and Common Law, at 78–92 (1947).

The modern justification for this privilege against adverse spousal testimony is its perceived role in fostering the harmony and sanctity of the marriage relationship. Notwithstanding this benign purpose, the rule was sharply criticized. Professor Wigmore termed it "the merest anachronism in legal theory and an indefensible obstruction to truth in practice." 8 Wigmore, § 2228, at 221. The Committee on the Improvement of the Law of Evidence of the American Bar Association called for its abolition. 63 American Bar Association Reports, at 594–595 (1938). In its place, Wigmore and others suggested a privilege protecting only private marital communications, modeled on the privilege between priest and penitent, attorney and client, and physician and patient. See 8 Wigmore, § 2332 et seq.

These criticisms influenced the American Law Institute, which, in its 1942 Model Code of Evidence advocated a privilege for marital confidences, but expressly rejected a rule vesting in the defendant the right to exclude all adverse testimony of his spouse. See American Law Institute, Model Code of Evidence, Rule 215 (1942). In 1953 the Uniform Rules of Evidence, drafted by the National Conference of Commissioners on Uniform State Laws, followed a similar course; it limited the privilege to confidential communications and "abolishe[d] the rule, still existing in some states, and largely a sentimental relic, of not requiring one spouse to testify against the other in a criminal action." See Rule 23(2) and comments. Several state legislatures enacted similarly patterned provisions into law.

In Hawkins v. United States, 358 U.S. 74, 79 S.Ct. 136, 3 L.Ed.2d 125 (1958), this Court considered the continued vitality of the privilege against adverse spousal testimony in the federal courts. There the District Court had permitted petitioner's wife, over his objection, to testify against him. With one questioning concurring opinion, the Court held the wife's testimony inadmissible; it took note of the critical comments that the common-law rule had engendered, id., at 76, and n. 4, 79 S.Ct., at 137, but chose not to abandon it. Also rejected was the Government's suggestion that the Court modify the privilege by vesting it in the witness spouse, with freedom to testify or not independent of the defendant's control. The Court viewed this proposed modification as antithetical to the widespread belief, evidenced in the rules then in effect in a majority of the States and in England, "that the law should not force or encourage testimony which might alienate husband and wife, or further inflame existing domestic differences." Id., at 79, 79 S.Ct., at 139.

Hawkins, then, left the federal privilege for adverse spousal testimony where it found it, continuing "a rule which bars the testimony of one spouse against the other unless both consent." Id., at 78, 79 S.Ct., at 138. Accord, Wyatt v. United States, 362 U.S. 525, 528, 80 S.Ct. 901, 903, 4 L.Ed.2d 931 (1960). However, in so doing, the Court made clear that its decision was not meant to "foreclose whatever changes in the rule may eventually be dictated by 'reason and experience.' " 358 U.S., at 79, 79 S.Ct., at 139.

III

A

The Federal Rules of Evidence acknowledge the authority of the federal courts to continue the evolutionary development of testimonial privileges in federal criminal trials "governed by the principles of the common law as they may be interpreted ... in the light of reason and experience." Fed.Rule Evid. 501. The general mandate of Rule 501 was substituted by the Congress for a set of privilege rules drafted by the Judicial Conference Advisory Committee on Rules of Evidence and approved by the Judicial Conference of the United States and by this Court. That proposal defined nine specific privileges, including a husband-wife privilege which would have codified the Hawkins rule and eliminated the privilege for confidential marital communications. See Fed.Rule of Evid., Proposed Rule 505. In rejecting the proposed rules and enacting Rule 501, Congress manifested an affirmative intention not to freeze the law of privilege. Its purpose rather was to "provide the courts with the flexibility to develop rules of privilege on a case-by-case basis," 120 Cong.Rec. 40891 (1974) (statement of Rep. Hungate), and to leave the door open to change. See also S.Rep. No. 93–1277, 93d Cong., 2d Sess., 11 (1974); H.R.Rep. No. 93–650, 93d Cong., 1st Sess., 8 (1973), U.S.Code Cong. & Admin.News 1974, p. 7051.

Although Rule 501 confirms the authority of the federal courts to reconsider the continued validity of the Hawkins rule, the long history of the privilege suggests that it ought not to be casually cast aside. That the privilege is one affecting marriage, home, and family relationships—already subject to much erosion in our day—also counsels caution. At the same time we cannot escape the reality that the law on occasion adheres to doctrinal concepts long after the reasons which gave them birth have disappeared and after experience suggest the need for change. This was recognized in Funk where the Court "decline[d] to enforce ... ancient rule[s] of the common law under conditions as they now exist." 290 U.S., at 382, 54 S.Ct., at 215.

B

Since 1958, when Hawkins was decided, support for the privilege against adverse spousal testimony has been eroded further. Thirty-one jurisdictions, including Alaska and Hawaii, then allowed an accused a privilege to prevent adverse spousal testimony. 358 U.S., at 81, n. 3, 79 S.Ct., at 140, (Stewart, J., concurring). The number has now declined to 24.[2] In 1974, the National

2. Eight states provide that one spouse is incompetent to testify against the other in a criminal proceeding: see Haw.Rev.Stat. § 621–18 (1968); Iowa Code § 622.7 (1979);

Conference on Uniform States Laws revised its Uniform Rules of Evidence, but again rejected the Hawkins rule in favor of a limited privilege for confidential communications. See Uniform Rules of Evidence, Rule 504. That proposed rule has been enacted in Arkansas, North Dakota, and Oklahoma—each of which in 1958 permitted an accused to exclude adverse spousal testimony. The trend in state law toward divesting the accused of the privilege to bar adverse spousal testimony has special relevance because the law of marriage and domestic relations are concerns traditionally reserved to the states. See Sosna v. Iowa, 419 U.S. 393, 404, 95 S.Ct. 553, 559, 42 L.Ed.2d 532 (1975). Scholarly criticism of the Hawkins rule has also continued unabated.

C

Testimonial exclusionary rules and privileges contravene the fundamental principle that "the public ... has a right to every man's evidence." United States v. Bryan, 339 U.S. 323, 331, 70 S.Ct. 724, 730, 94 L.Ed. 884 (1950). As such, they must be strictly construed and accepted "only to the very limited extent that permitting a refusal to testify or excluding relevant evidence has a public good transcending the normally predominant principle of utilizing all rational means for ascertaining truth." Elkins v. United States, 364 U.S. 206, 224, 80 S.Ct. 1437, 1449, 4 L.Ed.2d 1669 (1960) (Frankfurter, J., dissenting). Accord, United States v. Nixon, 418 U.S. 683, 709–710, 94 S.Ct. 3090, 3108–3109, 41 L.Ed.2d 1039 (1974). Here we must decide whether the privilege against adverse spousal testimony promotes sufficiently important interests to outweigh the need for probative evidence in the administration of criminal justice.

It is essential to remember that the Hawkins privilege is not needed to protect information privately disclosed between husband and wife in the confidence of the marital relationship—once described by this Court as "the best solace of human existence." Stein v. Bowman, 13 Pet., at 223. Those confidences are privileged under the independent rule protecting confidential marital communications. Blau v. United States, 340 U.S. 332, 71 S.Ct. 301, 95 L.Ed. 306 (1951); ... The Hawkins privilege is invoked, not to exclude private marital communications, but rather to exclude evidence of criminal acts and of communications made in the presence of third persons.

No other testimonial privilege sweeps so broadly. The privileges between priest and penitent, attorney and client, and physician and patient limit

---

Miss.Code Ann. § 13–1–5 (Cum.Supp.1978); N.C.Gen.Stat. § 8–57 (Cum.Supp.1977); Ohio Rev.Code Ann. § 2945.42; Pa.Stat.Ann., Tit. 42, §§ 5913, 5915 (Purdon Supp.1979); Tex. Crim.Pro.Code Ann. Art. 38.11 (Vernon 1979); Wyo.Stat. § 1–12–104 (1977).

Sixteen states provide a privilege against adverse spousal testimony and vest the privilege in both spouses or in the defendant-spouse alone: see Alaska Crim.Proc.Rules 26(b)(2) (Supp. Sept. 1968); Colo.Rev.Stat. § 13–90–107 (1974); Idaho Code § 9–203 (Cum.Supp.1978); Mich.Comp.Laws § 600.2162 (Mich.Stat.Ann. § 27A.2162 (Callaghan 1976)); Minn.Stat.Ann. § 595.02 (West Cum.Supp.1978); Mo.Ann.Stat. § 546.260 (Vernon 1953); Mont.Rev.Codes Ann. § 95–3011 (Cum.Supp.1975); Neb.Rev. Stat. § 27–505 (1975); Nev.Rev.Stat.

§ 49.295 (1977); N.J.Stat.Ann. § 2A:84A–17 (West 1976); N.M.Stat.Ann. § 20–4–505 (Cum.Supp.1975); Ore.Rev.Stat. § 44.040 (1977); Utah Code Ann. § 78–24–8 (1977); Va.Code § 19.2–271.2 (Cum.Supp.1978); Wash.Rev.Code Ann. § 5.60.060 (Supp.1979); W.Va.Code § 57–3–3 (1966).

Nine states entitle the witness-spouse alone to assert a privilege against adverse spousal testimony: see Ala.Code, Tit. 12, § 21–227 (1977); Cal.Evid.Code §§ 970–973 (West 1966); Conn.Gen.Stat.Ann. § 54–84 (West Cum.Supp.1979); Ga.Code Ann. § 38–1604 (1974); Ky.Rev.Stat. § 421.210 (Cum. Supp.1978); La.Rev.Stat.Ann. § 15:461 (West 1967); Md.Cts. and Jud.Proc.Code Ann. §§ 9–101, 9–106 (1974); Mass.Ann.Laws ch. 233, § 20 (Law.Co-op 1974); R.I.Gen.Laws § 12–17–10 (1970).

protection to private communications. These privileges are rooted in the imperative need for confidence and trust. . . .

The Hawkins rule stands in marked contrast to these three privileges. Its protection is not limited to confidential communications; rather it permits an accused to exclude all adverse spousal testimony. As Jeremy Bentham observed more than a century and a half ago, such a privilege goes far beyond making "every man's house his castle," and permits a person to convert his house into "a den of thieves." 5 Rationale of Judicial Evidence 340 (1827). It "secures, to every man, one safe and unquestionable and ever ready accomplice for every imaginable crime." Id., at 338.

The ancient foundations for so sweeping a privilege have long since disappeared. Nowhere in the common-law world,indeed in any modern society—is a woman regarded as chattel or demeaned by denial of a separate legal identity and the dignity associated with recognition as a whole human being. Chip by chip, over the years those archaic notions have been cast aside so that "[n]o longer is the female destined solely for the home and the rearing of the family, and only the male for the marketplace and the world of ideas." Stanton v. Stanton, 421 U.S. 7, 14, 15, 95 S.Ct. 1373, 1377, 1378, 43 L.Ed.2d 688 (1975).

The contemporary justification for affording an accused such a privilege is also unpersuasive. When one spouse is willing to testify against the other in a criminal proceeding—whatever the motivation—their relationship is almost certainly in disrepair; there is probably little in the way of marital harmony for the privilege to preserve. In these circumstances, a rule of evidence that permits an accused to prevent adverse spousal testimony seems far more likely to frustrate justice than to foster family peace. Indeed, there is reason to believe that vesting the privilege in the accused could actually undermine the marital relationship. For example, in a case such as this the Government is unlikely to offer a wife immunity and lenient treatment if it knows that her husband can prevent her from giving adverse testimony. If the Government is dissuaded from making such an offer, the privilege can have the untoward effect of permitting one spouse to escape justice at the expense of the other. It hardly seems conducive to the preservation of the marital relation to place a wife in jeopardy solely by virtue of her husband's control over her testimony.

IV

Our consideration of the foundations for the privilege and its history satisfy us that "reason and experience" no longer justify so sweeping a rule as that found acceptable by the Court in Hawkins. Accordingly, we conclude that the existing rule should be modified so that the witness spouse alone has a privilege to refuse to testify adversely; the witness may be neither compelled to testify nor foreclosed from testifying. This modification—vesting the privilege in the witness spouse—furthers the important public interest in marital harmony without unduly burdening legitimate law enforcement needs.

Here, petitioner's spouse chose to testify against him. That she did so after a grant of immunity and assurances of lenient treatment does not render her testimony involuntary. Cf. Bordenkircher v. Hayes, 434 U.S. 357, 98 S.Ct. 663, 54 L.Ed.2d 604 (1978). Accordingly, the District Court and the Court of Appeals were correct in rejecting petitioner's claim of privilege, and the judgment of the Court of Appeals is affirmed.

Affirmed.

■ MR. JUSTICE STEWART, concurr[ed] in the judgment.

NOTES

1. Most of the analysis in the Court's opinion in the principal case is directed against the rule that empowers the accused to prevent adverse spousal testimony. But the Court's decision approves the rule that gives the witness spouse a privilege to decline to testify adversely to the accused spouse. How adequate is the Court's treatment of the reasons for giving the privilege to the witness-spouse? The Court's assumption is that if the witness-spouse is "willing to testify ...—whatever the motivation—their relationship is almost certainly in disrepair" and that "[t]his modification ... furthers the important public interest in marital harmony...." How does the rule the Court adopts promote marital harmony? Is the particular motivation of the witness-spouse significant? Does the Court's approach oversimplify the enormous range of subtleties and motivations in marriage relationships? Consider, the following illustrations which, admittedly, are themselves oversimplified:

a) The marriage—a lengthy one—has had its ups and downs. At the time of trial, the couple are quite angry at each other. The prosecutor encourages the angry witness-spouse to cooperate and testify against the accused, and she does so.

b) The couple are newly married after a whirlwind courtship. At the time the witness-spouse agrees to testify, they have known each other barely six months.

c) Prior to the commission of the crime, the marriage relationship was good. The witness-spouse was also a participant in the criminal activity and is offered immunity by the prosecution in exchange for testifying. Note that the Court in Trammel argued that vesting the privilege in the accused could result in the government's not offering immunity to the witness-spouse, "hardly ... conducive to the preservation of the marital relation." Does vesting the privilege in the witness-spouse, however, serve to preserve the marriage, or will it encourage the government to tempt the witness-spouse by offering immunity? Consider in this connection the statement quoted by the Trammel Court from Hawkins referring to the widespread belief "that the law should not ... encourage testimony which might alienate husband and wife, or further inflame existing domestic differences."

d) At the time of trial, the couple are contemplating divorce and have been involved in an angry dispute about child custody and property. What effect is vesting the privilege in the witness-spouse likely to have in such a situation?

e) The defendants include both the witness-spouse's husband and her son.

2. The argument for retaining the witness-spouse's privilege can be cast in terms similar to that made in support of the privilege against self-incrimination—i.e. not putting the witness to the cruel trilemma of choice among self-incrimination, contempt or perjury. In place of fear of self-incrimination, the element substituted in the trilemma would be concern about giving testimony that will have the effect of alienating one's spouse and possibly destroying the marriage. Can it be argued, however, that if the witness-spouse's privilege were abolished and the witness-spouse thereby put to the trilemma, the risk that his or her testimony adverse to the accused spouse would in fact destroy the marriage would be reduced by the very fact that the accused spouse would know that the witness had been compelled to testify or face the prospect of a penalty for contempt or committing perjury with its concomitant penalties?

3. The privilege against adverse testimony by a spouse—whatever form it takes, that is, whether it may be claimed by both spouses, only by the accused-spouse or only by the witness-spouse (see footnote 2 in the principal case)—typically has a number of limitations and exceptions.

The privilege does not survive termination of the marriage, United States v. Bolzer, 556 F.2d 948 (9th Cir.1977), even where the judgment of divorce is under appeal. United States v. Fisher, 518 F.2d 836 (2d Cir.), cert. den., 423 U.S. 1033 (1975).

4. If the marriage is viewed as a sham, the ostensible spouse may be required to testify. Lutwak v. United States, 344 U.S. 604 (1953) (marriage entered into to gain admission into country); United States v. Apodaca, 522 F.2d 568 (10th Cir.1975) (marriage entered into three days before trial; accused previously had threatened witness-"spouse" and had been released on bail on condition he not contact her).

5. If a claim is made that a common law marriage existed, the federal courts look to whether the law of the domicile state recognizes such marriages. United States v. Lustig, 555 F.2d 737 (9th Cir.), cert. denied, 434 U.S. 926 (1977).

6. Changing attitudes toward the desirability of a formal marriage ceremony and the increasing incidence of stable relationships not solemnized by marriage raised questions about whether these developments might lead to extension of the privilege to non-marrieds. See People v. Delph, 94 Cal.App.3d 411, 156 Cal.Rptr. 422 (1979) (couple had lived together for four years; court ruled that it was for the legislature to determine if the privilege should apply to meretricious relationships). What result if a jurisdiction recognizes same-gender marriages? Suppose a jurisdiction does not recognize the legitimacy of same-gender marriages but does provide to long-term same-gender partners some of the traditional benefits coverage available to married persons, such as health and retirement survivor benefits?

7. Suppose that although the couple are still legally married, the marriage is no longer viable and there appears to be no desire for a reconciliation. United States v. Cameron, 556 F.2d 752 (5th Cir.1977) disallowed the privilege in such circumstances. See also United States v. Brown, 605 F.2d 389 (8th Cir.1979). Compare, however, United States v. Lilley, 581 F.2d 182 (8th Cir.1978). Per contra, suppose the marriage appears to be unusually strong, having lasted for 40 years and no specific claim is made that denial of the privilege would affect the marriage. Ryan v. Commissioner, 568 F.2d 531 (7th Cir.1977), cert. denied, 439 U.S. 820 (1978) took such facts into account in disallowing the privilege.

8. In Lutwak v. United States, supra, 344 U.S. 604, 622 (1953), three dissenting justices (Jackson, Black and Frankfurter) argued: "[T]he trial court could only conclude that the marriage was a sham from the very testimony whose admissibility is in question. The Court's position seems to be that privileged testimony may be received to destroy its own privilege. We think this is not allowable for the same reason that one cannot lift himself by his own bootstraps." The conundrum this presented is quite old. One way out, suggested by the reporter's quaere in Peat's Case, 2 Lewin Cr.Case (Eng.) 288, 289 (1838) is to treat the voir dire as an independent inquiry separate from the issues on the merits, and perhaps not subject to the exclusionary rules of evidence. Rule 104(a) of the Federal Rules indicates that the rules with respect to privileges apply to preliminary questions concerning, inter alia, the existence of a privilege, but see United States v. Zolin, supra, p. 1465, and see section 915, California Evidence Code. Consider the implications of In re Lifschutz, 2 Cal.3d 415, 429 at n. 10, 85 Cal.Rptr. 829, 838, 467 P.2d 557, 566 (1970).

9. The rules proposed by the Supreme Court withdrew the privilege as to matters occurring prior to marriage, Rule 505(c). The Court in United States v.

Van Drunen, 501 F.2d 1393 (7th Cir.), cert. denied, 419 U.S. 1091 (1974) adopted this view.

10.   The privilege applies only to testimonial or communicative evidence from the witness-spouse. It does not, for example, include the use of the witness-spouse's fingerprints where that evidence tends to incriminate the accused-spouse. United States v. Thomann, 609 F.2d 560 (1st Cir.1979). In re Rovner, 377 F.Supp. 954 (E.D.Pa.), aff'd, 500 F.2d 1400 (3d Cir.1974) (handwriting samples); In re Clark, 461 F.Supp. 1149 (S.D.N.Y.1978) (same); United States v. Scott, 784 F.2d 787 (7th Cir.1986) (handwriting samples and fingerprints).

11.   See 8 Wigmore, Evidence § 2237(2) (McNaughton rev. 1961), pointing out that confusion of the adverse spousal testimony doctrine with that covering confidential inter-spousal communications may lead lawyers astray as to whether the time when testimony is offered or the time of occurrence of the condition or event to be evidenced is the vital moment. See State v. Gyngard, 333 S.W.2d 73 (Mo.1960).

12.   In examining the precedents, one should be certain which version of the spousal privilege is being relied upon. Certain issues present different problems, depending on whether the privilege is that of the accused or the witness.

In Wyatt v. United States, 362 U.S. 525 (1960), the Supreme Court decided that in a prosecution under the Mann Act for transporting a woman in interstate commerce for the purpose of prostitution, the testimony of witness-spouse (who married the accused before trial) could be used over her objection and that of the accused. As to the husband's privilege (pre-Trammel), the majority ruled that in a Mann Act prosecution the common law exception applied—namely, that in the case of certain kinds of offenses committed against the witness-spouse, the accused may not bar the spouse's testimony. "Where a man has prostituted his own wife, he has committed an offense against both her and the marriage relation, and ... [he is disabled] from excluding her testimony against him." Id. 362 U.S. 525, 529. As to the wife's objection, the Court concluded that Congress in the Mann Act sought

> to protect women who were weak from men who were bad.... For if a defendant can induce a woman, against her 'will' to enter a life of prostitution for his benefit ... by the same token ... he can, at least as easily, persuade one who has already fallen victim to his influence that she must also protect him. To make matters turn upon ad hoc inquiries into the actual state of mind of particular women ... is hardly an acceptable solution.

The three dissenting justices (Warren, Black and Douglas) characterized the fatal defect in the majority's conclusion "in the Court's evaluation of the mental state of the wife, an evaluation which finds no support in the record and which cannot be justified by any legislative enactment." Id. 362 U.S. 525, 533. Rather than being mesmerized by the defendant, the evidence, according to the dissenters, suggested that she played a managerial role in the enterprise.

13.   California, like Trammel, gives the spousal privilege to the witness-spouse, not the accused. California Evidence Code, §§ 970–973. It also recognizes an exception to the privilege "in criminal proceedings in which one spouse is charged with ... a crime against the person or property of the other spouse or of a child of either, whether committed before or during marriage." Does the reasoning used in Wyatt, supra, justify disallowing the privilege whenever the witness-spouse is alleged to have been the victim of a crime committed by the accused spouse? Are there other sound reasons for disallowing the privilege in such cases? Compare the reasons for the "victim" exception where the privilege is held by the accused.

14. The pre-Trammel case law in the federal courts has construed the "victim" exception rather broadly. See, for example, United States v. Smith, 533 F.2d 1077 (8th Cir.1976) which ruled that defendant's conduct in planting heroin on his wife and thus subjecting her to a related, albeit unsuccessful criminal prosecution constituted an offense against her thus providing a basis for disallowing the accused husband's privilege to bar her testimony. What effect would you expect the Trammel decision to have on the use of this exception? Is it significant that in Wyatt, in dealing with the testifying spouse's privilege, the Court did not apply the standard "victim" exception? Should it make a difference whether the crime charged against the accused spouse was committed against the witness-spouse prior to their marriage? See Stevens v. Commonwealth, 150 S.E.2d 229 (Va.1966).

15. An issue sometimes arises as to whether the privilege should apply to the spouse's testimony where the accused is charged with a crime against X and in the course of committing that crime also committed a crime against the spouse. In jurisdictions where the accused has the privilege, there is authority for expansively applying the "victim" exception in such cases to permit the spouse to testify. State v. Briley, 251 A.2d 442 (N.J.1969), noted in 74 Dick.L.Rev. 499 (1969–70) (prosecution for manslaughter of X in the course of which accused assaulted his wife); People v. Ford, 60 Cal.2d 772, 785, 36 Cal.Rptr. 620, 629, 388 P.2d 892, 901 (1964) (husband prosecuted for homicide of X while kidnapping his (H's) wife). At the same time that California gave the privilege to the witness-spouse, it codified the Ford rule in section 972(e)(2) of the Evidence Code. See Fortes v. Sacramento Municipal Court District, 113 Cal.App.3d 704, 170 Cal.Rptr. 292 (1980). Is the expansion of the "victim" exception justified where the witness-spouse is the only holder of the privilege?

16. California also disallows the spouse witness privilege where the crime charged was committed against a child of either spouse. § 972(e)(1), California Evidence Code. There was a similar provision in the Federal Rules proposed by the Supreme Court. Rule 505(c). Rule 505, however, gave the privilege to the accused spouse. Prior to Trammel and relying in part on the proposed Rule, the court in United States v. Allery, 526 F.2d 1362 (8th Cir.1975) extended the victim exception to include a crime against the couple's child. Judge Henley dissenting argued: "The reason ... [for adopting this exception] is no more compelling with respect to some children than with respect to some grandchildren, cousins or social guests." Id. 526 F.2d 1362, 1368. How should the issue in Allery be decided after Trammel?

17. Tallo v. United States, 344 F.2d 467 (1st Cir.1965) (decided prior to Trammel) held that the defendant-spouse is entitled to invoke his privilege outside the presence of the jury to prevent the witness-spouse from testifying against him. See also Courtney v. United States, 390 F.2d 521 (9th Cir.), cert. denied, 393 U.S. 857 (1968) holding it error for the prosecutor to comment on defendant's failure to call his wife as a witness and to question defendant on cross-examination as to whether he had married her to prevent her from testifying. Compare United States v. Burkhart, 501 F.2d 993 (6th Cir.1974), cert. denied, 420 U.S. 946, where the court ruled that the prosecutor's comment on defendant husband's failure to call his wife to testify was not violative of the privilege where his wife's testimony would have elucidated the transaction that was the basis of his defense and where the defendant himself had first injected his wife's statements by cross-examining government witnesses regarding them.

It has been suggested, again pre-Trammel, that the privilege does not protect a spouse from being called to the stand in a grand jury investigation but must be asserted as to particular questions. In re Lochiatto, 497 F.2d 803, 805, n. 3 (1st Cir.1974). What result, post Trammel? See the Comment to § 971, California Evidence Code.

18. Does the privilege bar the use against the defendant spouse of the declarant-spouse's adverse extrajudicial statement? In a pre-Trammel case, United States v. Tsinnijinnie, 601 F.2d 1035 (9th Cir.1979) the charge was voluntary manslaughter. At trial, a witness testified as to the defendant's wife's excited utterance at the time of the event. The Ninth Circuit following the Second and Seventh Circuits and rejecting its own prior view (see United States v. Price, 577 F.2d 1356 (9th Cir.1978)), which had also been followed by the Fifth Circuit, held the privilege inapplicable to extrajudicial statements of the declarant-spouse. Post–Trammel, United States v. Archer, 733 F.2d 354, 359 (5th Cir.1984), reached a similar conclusion: "[I]t would strain ... the logic of Trammel.... Marital harmony would be enhanced minimally if at all ... by excluding the statement when offered after the fact through a third-party witness at trial...."

19. The privilege is normally limited to testimony that "disfavors the other spouse's legal interests in the very case in which the testimony is offered." In re Snoonian, 502 F.2d 110, 112 (1st Cir.1974). See 8 Wigmore, Evidence §§ 2234, 2235 (McNaughton rev. 1961). Thus where one of the spouses is called to testify in a grand jury proceeding, the applicability of the privilege may depend on whether the other spouse is a target of the inquiry.

In the Matter of Grand Jury Subpoena of Ford v. United States

United States Court of Appeals, Second Circuit, 1985.
756 F.2d 249.

■ TIMBERS, CIRCUIT JUDGE:

The essential question presented on this appeal—one of first impression in this Circuit—is whether the district court correctly held in civil contempt a grand jury witness who, relying on a claim of privilege against adverse spousal testimony, refused to testify where his wife was a target of the grand jury investigation, despite assurances by the government, which the district court found were sufficient, that the witness' testimony would not be used, directly or indirectly, against his wife. We hold that the district court correctly held the witness in contempt.

I.

On November 13, 1984 appellant was subpoenaed to testify before a Special Grand Jury sitting in the Southern District of New York. On October 29, 1984 the grand jury had returned an indictment against eight individuals, including appellant's wife, Colette Pean, charging them with conspiracy to commit armed robberies of armored trucks and banks, in violation of 18 U.S.C. § 1951 (1982).

The government sought appellant's testimony as part of its continuing investigation into these alleged conspiracies, intending to obtain a superseding indictment. On December 20, 1984 appellant filed a motion in the district court to quash the subpoena, claiming the privilege against adverse spousal testimony....

In response to the motion, and in an effort to meet the claim of privilege, the government filed an affidavit of Assistant United States Attorney Kenneth Roth, the principal prosecutor in charge of the grand jury investigation, setting forth a procedure to insulate Colette Pean from any inculpatory effect of her husband's testimony.

Essentially, the Roth affidavit stated the government's promise not to use any of appellant's testimony, either directly or indirectly, in the investigation or prosecution of Colette Pean. In order to guarantee its promise, the government proposed the erection of a so-called "Chinese Wall". Pursuant to this procedure, appellant would be questioned by an AUSA other than Roth and before a grand jury other than the one conducting the principal investigation. That AUSA then would confer with others not connected with the principal investigation to determine if appellant's testimony was of sufficient value, in the view of the government, with regard to Pean's alleged co-conspirators to warrant using it. If the government determined that it was of such value, then Pean's trial under the October 29 indictment would be severed from that of her alleged co-conspirators and would be conducted by an AUSA who had had no contact with appellant's testimony or its fruits. Any superseding indictment which might be returned against Pean would be the product of an independent grand jury assisted by an AUSA who had had no contact with the prior grand jury proceedings. If appellant's testimony were found to be of insufficient value to warrant a separate prosecution of Pean, then no further use would be made of it and no person connected with the principal investigation would have contact with appellant's testimony or its fruits.

In a memorandum opinion filed January 9, 1985, Judge Haight held that the proposed procedure set forth in the Roth affidavit was sufficient to insure that no grand jury testimony elicited from appellant would be used, either directly or indirectly, against appellant's wife. Accordingly, the court ordered appellant to comply with the subpoena.

II.

The question before us is whether the procedure proposed by the government is sufficient to meet the claim of privilege against adverse spousal testimony. Although we have never addressed the issue of what protective procedure might be sufficient to meet that claim of privilege, the question has arisen in at least three other circuits in recent years. In re Grand Jury Matter, 673 F.2d 688 (3d Cir.), cert. denied, 459 U.S. 1015 (1982); In re Grand Jury Proceedings (Hermann), 664 F.2d 423 (5th Cir.1981), cert. denied, 455 U.S. 1000 (1982); In re Snoonian, 502 F.2d 110 (1st Cir.1974).

In Snoonian, the First Circuit, recognizing that the marital privilege has never been construed as absolute, held that the government's affidavit stating that the non-witness spouse was not a target of the grand jury's investigation, coupled with the government's unequivocal and convincing promise not to use any of the witness-spouse's testimony, or its fruits, against the other, adequately met the claim of privilege. 502 F.2d at 112–113. Although in the instant case appellant's spouse is a target of the grand jury investigation, the government has promised the same "use-fruits" immunity which the court in Snoonian held was the more tangible assurance that the marital privilege would be protected. Id. at 112. See also In re Grand Jury Proceedings (Hermann), supra, 664 F.2d at 430–431.

We hold that the government's promise not to use any of the witness-spouse's testimony before the grand jury, either directly or indirectly, against the non-witness spouse, is sufficient to meet the claim of privilege by the testifying spouse.

III.

We turn next to various claims asserted by appellant. Despite the government's promise, appellant argues that the proposed Chinese Wall procedure is "unrealistic, unworkable and insufficiently protective of the marital privilege." In support of this claim, appellant attempts to analogize the instant situation to conflict of interest situations involving law firms. We are not persuaded. We have held that lawyer disqualification in the case of a law firm should be ordered where a conflict undermines the court's confidence in the vigor of the attorney's representation of his client or where the attorney is in a position to use privileged information concerning the other side through prior representation. In such cases, the policy behind the disqualification is the lawyer's duty of loyalty to his client. Courts are more likely to construe disqualification guidelines strictly in such situations since a private party always may retain another law firm. Such policy considerations do not apply to the United States Attorney's Office, since its attorneys represent only one "client". Furthermore, if the disqualification of one government attorney could serve as the predicate for the disqualification of the entire United States Attorney's Office, the administration of justice would be irreparably damaged. Indeed, federal regulations expressly provide for the substitution of another AUSA where an AUSA originally assigned to a case for some reason must recuse himself. 28 C.F.R. § 0.131 (1984). We also have recognized the propriety of screening procedures that insulate a former government attorney from particular matters being handled by the law firm which employs him where the former government attorney must disqualify himself.

[W]hile possibilities for abuse do exist, we emphasize that it will be the government's burden to show that any investigation or prosecution of Pean has not been tainted by the testimony of appellant.

Appellant also argues that the immunity granted by the government to Pean in this case is invalid since, unlike grants of immunity where claims of self-incrimination are involved, Congress has not provided any statutory authority for grants of immunity in marital privilege cases. Although appellant claims that the decision to grant immunity in these cases should be a matter of Congressional prerogative, he fails to establish that courts are without authority to sanction an executive decision to grant immunity in cases dealing with common law privileges.... That Congress has not acted in the area of marital privilege is not surprising, for at least two reasons. First, the marital privilege, unlike that against self-incrimination, is derived from the common law and has no equivalent Constitutional stature. Second, ... Rule 501 of the Federal Rules of Evidence provides that the privilege of a witness shall be governed by principles of common law as "interpreted by the courts ... in the light of reason and experience." The Supreme Court in Trammel ... recognized that rules of privilege must be developed on a case-by-case basis. 445 U.S. at 47. In view of this policy, and the Court's determination that the marital privilege must be balanced against the search for the truth, id. at 50, it is hardly incumbent on us to abstain from approving a procedure which adequately respects these competing goals merely because there is no express statutory authority for such procedure.

To summarize: Since we find that the "use-fruits" immunity granted by the government to Colette Pean is fully co-extensive with the scope of the privilege against adverse spousal testimony, and that the screening procedure proposed by the government is both appropriate and workable, the order of the district court is affirmed. The stay previously entered by a panel of this Court is dissolved. The mandate shall issue forthwith.

Affirmed.

NOTES

1. Also see In re Grand Jury Proceedings Larson, 785 F.2d 629 (8th Cir.1986).

2. Dr. Ford was released after six months confinement as a result of Second Circuit rulings that a person confined under a civil contempt order for refusing to testify is to be released if there is no realistic possibility that he might testify if his confinement is continued. Matter of Ford, 615 F.Supp. 259 (S.D.N.Y. 1985).

3. The Second and Third Circuits ruled that the adverse spousal privilege is not subject to an exception where the spouses are joint participants in criminal activity, In re Grand Jury Subpoena United States, Koecher, 755 F.2d 1022 (2d Cir.1985) (judgment vacated and remanded with instructions to dismiss as moot, 475 U.S. 133 (1986)); Appeal of Malfitano, 633 F.2d 276 (3d Cir.1980); while the Seventh and Tenth Circuits apply the exception and require the witness spouse to testify in a joint participation situation, United States v. Keck, 773 F.2d 759 (7th Cir.1985); United States v. Trammel, 583 F.2d 1166 (10th Cir.1978), aff'd on other grounds 455 U.S. 40 (1982). See Judge Friendly's opinion in In re Grand Jury Subpoena United States, Koecher, supra, for an assessment of the reasons for and against recognition of the exception after the Supreme Court's decision in Trammel. See generally Note, Partners in Crime: An Examination of the Privilege Against Adverse Spousal Testimony, 22 J.Fam.L. 713 (1984). Regarding the application of the exception to the marital confidential communication privilege, see infra pp. 1514–1515.

4. United States v. Benford, 457 F.Supp. 589 (E.D.Mich.1978): On a charge against the husband of possession of illegal firearms, the government planned to call the wife to testify as to the fact of possession of the firearms. She had earlier complained to the police that she had been beaten by her husband with a revolver. Defendant invoked the pre-Trammel marital privilege to prevent her from testifying in the prosecution's case in chief. Later in his defense, he testified that he had not been in the house during the period when the firearms were there. The court ruled that his exercise of the privilege in the prosecution's case in chief was properly sustained, but that when he testified as he did, he thereby waived his privilege to keep his wife from testifying in rebuttal insofar as his testimony covered the same ground as that which she would testify to and she was in a unique position to know the facts involved. "If the jury is not permitted to hear the wife's version of the facts, they may be misled into believing no such testimony exists." Compare Walder v. United States, 347 U.S. 62 (1954) and see Harris v. New York, 401 U.S. 222 (1971). The court in Benford went on to say: "If . . . the testimony of the wife was not voluntary, perhaps a different result should be reached." Benford, supra, 457 F.Supp. 589, 598.

5. See generally Regan, Spousal Privilege and the Meanings of Marriage, 81 Va. L.Rev. 2045 (1995); Glenn, Comment, The Deconstruction of the Marital Privilege, 12 Pepp. L.Rev. 723 (1985); Lempert, A Right to Every Woman's Evidence, 66 Ia. L.Rev. 725 (1981).

B.   THE HUSBAND–WIFE CONFIDENTIAL COMMUNICATION PRIVILEGE

United States v. Marashi

United States Court of Appeals, Ninth Circuit, 1990.
913 F.2d 724.

■ HALL, CIRCUIT JUDGE.

A jury convicted appellant S. Mohammad Marashi on four counts of a five count indictment. It convicted him of three counts of attempted tax evasion in violation of 26 U.S.C. § 7201 (1988) and one count of willful subscription to a false tax return in violation of 26 U.S.C. § 7206(1). Marashi claims on appeal that (1) the district court abused its discretion by admitting evidence of marital communications. . . .

I

A

In the late summer of 1984, Sharon Smith Marashi ("Smith") learned that her husband, Dr. S. Mohammad Marashi was having an extramarital affair with his secretary, Mrs. Sherrie Danzig. Smith also learned from the secretary's husband, Steve Danzig, that the two had flown off to Europe. In August, Smith and Danzig's brother-in-law, Earl Doering, entered Marashi's office in an attempt to obtain Marashi's travel itinerary. Because Smith did not have a key to Marashi's desk, she had a locksmith open the top drawer.

Marashi returned from Europe to discover that his wife was filing for divorce. Several months later, on December 22, 1984, he moved out of their house and into a condominium.

Filing for divorce was not enough for Smith and Danzig. They met several times to discuss how to get even with their unfaithful spouses. At one point, Smith mentioned that Marashi had under-reported his federal income tax for some years. Seeing an opportunity to exact revenge upon his rival, Danzig contacted the IRS. Later, he pressured Smith to come forward with information implicating Marashi.

In December, 1984, Smith came forward. She phoned the IRS and set up an interview with Special Agent Robert Lake. Smith, accompanied by her divorce lawyer, Carl Maxey, spoke briefly with Agent Lake on January 10, 1985. Agent Lake took notes. Smith began to relate how her husband had used her to underreport their income for several years. Upon realizing that Smith was implicating herself as a tax evader, Agent Lake terminated the interview in order to permit Smith to consult with her lawyer.

On January 16, Smith, unaccompanied by counsel, met with Agent Lake again. Agent Lake tape recorded the interview. He declined to give Smith a Miranda warning and suggested instead that if she were honest and cooperative, she would not be prosecuted.

Smith then described how Marashi had enlisted her aid to evade federal income taxes. She explained that daily her husband would bring home slips of paper indicating how much patients had paid him. Marashi would then store the slips in a desk drawer located in his study. Periodically, he would ask Smith to record the information from the slips into either a black ledger for that year or a stenographer's notebook. Marashi would highlight certain items of income and instruct Smith to enter them into the notebook for his own records; this income went unreported to the IRS. Next, he would instruct her to enter the remaining items of income into that year's black ledger, which he kept as an official record for audit purposes. Marashi would then discard the slips of paper.

Smith added that Marashi had employed this double-ledger scheme at least from 1981–84. She estimated that the unreported income contained in the stenographer's notebook ran into the thousands.

Agent Lake then asked Smith to obtain both the black ledgers and the notebook. However, Smith never made the attempt because as far as she knew, they remained in the desk which Marashi had recently moved into his condominium.

Shortly after the interview, the Marashi investigation was reassigned to Special Agent Stephen Houghton. On May 18, the IRS opened a case file on Marashi. Roughly a month later, Agent Houghton contacted Marashi and summoned him to produce corporate records. He also began an investigation of Marashi's bank transactions in an effort to reconstruct his income. That investigation revealed that Marashi had cashed, rather than deposited, numerous checks for substantial sums.

Meanwhile, the IRS cultivated its relationship with Sharon Smith. Agent Thomas Abrahamson spoke with her over the telephone on June 19 and 21, 1985. He took notes on both occasions. On the latter date, Smith produced several of Marashi's appointment books. On July 18, Smith returned to the IRS and recounted her story to Agents Abrahamson and Houghton. Agent Abrahamson did not take notes during the interview, but later jotted them down from memory. Agent Houghton tape recorded Smith's sworn statement.

Because the IRS could not get its hands on the black ledgers or the stenographer's notebook, the investigation slowed to a snail's pace. Marashi claimed that the black ledgers for 1981–83 had been stolen from his condominium and that the alleged notebook listing unreported income had never existed. Consequently, the IRS returned to the slow process of reconstructing Marashi's income by the bank deposits method.

B

On July 5, 1988, Marashi had his lawyers depose his ex-wife to find out exactly what she had told the IRS. Several days later, the IRS provided Marashi with (1) an audio tape and a transcript of Smith's January 16, 1985 interview with Special Agent Lake and (2) an audio tape of Smith's July 18, 1985 interview with Special Agent Houghton.

On July 12, Marashi moved to suppress Smith's testimony and the fruits thereof on the basis of the marital communications privilege. Ten days later, Smith testified at a pretrial conference. On July 28, the district court denied Marashi's motion.

At the outset of the trial, Marashi freely admitted that he had had an extramarital affair with Sherrie Danzig. His defense was that his ex-wife and Steve Danzig sought revenge by fabricating the double ledger story and stealing Marashi's black ledgers for the years 1981–83 from his condominium. Any under-reporting, Marashi maintained, was the product of oversight.

II

Marashi ... appeals the denial of his motion to suppress Smith's testimony regarding his instructions to have her (1) underreport income and (2) erase entries in his appointment books several weeks before an IRS audit. He claims that his statements are covered by the marital communications privilege. He also seeks to suppress all evidence derived therefrom as "fruits of the poisonous tree."

A

The ... so-called "marital communications" privilege, bars testimony concerning statements privately communicated between spouses. In re Grand Jury Investigation of Hugle, 754 F.2d 863, 864 (9th Cir.1985); United States v. Lustig, 555 F.2d 737, 747 (9th Cir.1977), cert. denied, 434 U.S. 926, 98 S.Ct. 408, 54 L.Ed.2d 285, and cert. denied, 434 U.S. 1045, 98 S.Ct. 889, 54 L.Ed.2d 795 (1978). The non-testifying spouse may invoke the privilege, Hugle, 754 F.2d at 864, even after dissolution of the marriage, Lustig, 555 F.2d at 747. Thus, Marashi may attempt to invoke it.

The confines of the marital communications privilege are easy to describe. First, the privilege extends only to words or acts intended as communication to the other spouse. Pereira v. United States, 347 U.S. 1, 6, 74 S.Ct. 358, 98 L.Ed. 435 (1954); United States v. Lefkowitz, 618 F.2d 1313, 1318 (9th Cir.), cert. denied, 449 U.S. 824, 101 S.Ct. 86, 66 L.Ed.2d 27 (1980). Second, it covers only those communications made during a valid marriage, see Hugle, 754 F.2d at 865; Lustig, 555 F.2d at 747, unless the couple had irreconcilably separated, see United States v. Roberson, 859 F.2d 1376, 1381 (9th Cir.1988). Third, the privilege applies only to those marital communications which are confidential. That is, the privilege does not extend to statements which are made before, or likely to be overheard by, third parties. See, e.g., Pereira, 347 U.S. at 6 (statements to, or in presence of, third parties); Lefkowitz, 618 F.2d at 1318 (same).

Marital communications are presumptively confidential; the government has the burden of demonstrating that they are not.

This last presumption notwithstanding, we have emphasized that we will narrowly construe the marital communications privilege because it obstructs the truth-seeking process. See Roberson, 859 F.2d at 1378. Use of the privilege in criminal proceedings requires a particularly narrow construction because of society's strong interest in the administration of justice. Id. at 1380.

Under this analysis, it is readily apparent that the privilege does not extend to Smith's testimony regarding Marashi's orders to have her erase entries in his appointment books. The presence of a third person, Marya LaSalandra, during the communications destroyed the privilege.

It is also clear that the privilege covers Smith's testimony regarding Marashi's instructions to have her underreport income. Marashi made the statements while the marriage was legally valid. Moreover, because his instructions were made in the privacy of the couple's bedroom, they were confidential.

The government concedes that the privilege extends to the latter testimony. It urges us to adopt a narrow exception to that rule. We consider this point below.

B

Every circuit addressing the issue has held that the marital communications privilege does not apply to communications having to do with present or future crimes in which both spouses are participants.

This view is consistent with our attitude toward evidentiary privileges in general. We have emphasized that the policies underlying the marital communications privilege pale in the face of public concerns about bringing criminals to justice. Roberson, 859 F.2d at 1380. Thus we join our sister circuits in holding that the marital communications privilege does not apply to statements made in furtherance of joint criminal activity.[1]

Marashi argues that in any event, the exception should not apply here because the IRS did not prosecute Smith. In rejecting a similar argument, the Fourth Circuit reasoned:

> The policies behind the joint criminal participation exception are concerned with the actual participation by both spouses in a crime, not with their joint prosecution for that crime. The exception arises out of a careful balancing of the policies behind protecting the intimacy of private marital communications and the public policy of getting at the truth and attaining justice.... Whether the spouse testifying has been indicted and is being prosecuted for his or her participation is a prosecutorial prerogative that is not material to the policies at issue here.

Parker, 834 F.2d at 412. We agree. The government may well decide, as it has in this case, to forego prosecution of one spouse in order to secure her testimony against the other. The greater public interest is to assure a criminal that if he enlists the aid of his spouse, he is creating a potential witness for the government. Accordingly, the government's decision not to prosecute Smith does not preclude application of the partnership in crime exception.

There is little question that the communications in this case were made in furtherance of a joint criminal venture. Marashi directed Smith to help him underreport income on their joint income tax returns. Smith freely did so, in violation of 26 U.S.C. § 7201. Accordingly, Marashi's statements in furtherance of these criminal acts were admissible under the partnership in crime exception to the marital communications privilege.

In sum, we hold that the district court did not abuse its discretion by admitting Smith's testimony.

NOTES

1. The Supreme Court's proposed Federal Rules of Evidence contained no provision for a husband-wife confidential communication privilege while it did grant a privilege to an accused spouse to prevent his spouse from testifying against him in a criminal proceeding. Is the rejection of the one privilege and acceptance of the other defensible? See the Advisory Committee's Note to proposed Federal Rule 505. See also Reutlinger, Policy, Privacy, and Prerogatives: A Critical Examination of the Proposed Federal Rules of Evidence as They Affect Marital Privilege, 61 Cal. L.Rev. 1353 (1973).

California has preserved a broad husband-wife confidential communication privilege. Cal.Evid.Code § 980. The original Uniform Rules of Evidence in Rule 28 provided for the privilege but restricted it to the "spouse who transmitted to the other the information which constitutes the communication," and the privilege was deemed to exist only during the marital relationship. For discussion of this rule see Note, 6 Washb.L.J. 144 (1966). Rule 504 of the Uniform Rules promulgated in 1974 gives an accused spouse in a criminal proceeding a privilege to prevent his spouse from testifying as to a confidential communication between them. These Rules contained no other provision relating to adverse spousal testimony. In Massachusetts, even if both spouses desire it, neither may testify to the substance of their private conversations. Mass.Gen.L.

---

1. However, we do not embrace the Sixth Circuit's narrower version of the exception, which would apply only to statements made in furtherance of "patently illegal activity." Sims, 755 F.2d at 1243 (emphasis added).

c. 233 § 20. This statutory disqualification is applied in the colorful case of Kaye v. Newhall, 249 N.E.2d 583, 585 (Mass.1969).

2. In the principal case, the couple was divorced in 1986, and the former wife's deposition was taken in 1988. Is that significant for the application of the confidential communication privilege? In connection with the adverse spousal privilege?

3. In United States v. Byrd, 750 F.2d 585 (7th Cir.1984), the court ruled that the marital confidential communications privilege does not apply to communications made after the couple is permanently separated. Only communications made while the couple is validly married and still cohabiting are covered. Also see United States v. Tipton, 23 M.J. 338 (C.M.A.1987).

4. Many jurisdictions refuse to recognize acts of a spouse not intended as a communication as being within the marital communications privilege, even if they were done privately and in confidence. See, for example, the rather audacious claim in United States v. Smith, 533 F.2d 1077 (8th Cir.1976) that the husband's concealing heroin on his wife's person against her will was protected by the confidential communications privilege. The court said that the communications privilege is limited to "utterances or expressions intended by one spouse to convey a message to the other." Id. at 1079. Accord: United States v. Estes, 793 F.2d 465, 467 (2d Cir.1986): "[N]ormally, the confidential communication privilege extends only to utterances and not to acts. Testimony concerning a spouse's conduct can be precluded upon the spouse's challenge only in the rare instances where the conduct was intended to convey a confidential message from the actor to the observer. The counting, hiding and laundering of the money conveyed no confidential message from appellant to Lydia. Acts do not become privileged communications simply because they are performed in the presence of the spouse." In Pereira v. United States, 347 U.S. 1, 6–7 (1954), defendant was charged with having used the mails to defraud a wealthy widow after marrying her. The Supreme Court rejected the accused's attempt to invoke the marital communications privilege to bar the widow's testimony, relying inter alia on the fact that some matters she testified to were "acts not amounting to communications." Also see United States v. Lewis, 433 F.2d 1146, 1151 (D.C.Cir.1970): In a robbery prosecution, the accused's wife was called by the prosecution to testify that the accused was at their apartment on the night in question, thereby rebutting his alibi that he was in another city; also that he had returned to their apartment at 3 or 3:30 A.M. on the morning in question carrying a sawed off shotgun. Other evidence in the case indicated that one of the robbers had carried a weapon of that type. The court stated that in particular contexts acts can be communicative: "Some acts conceivably may so convey a message and may so bespeak a trust, as to necessitate nothing more to demonstrate entitlement to the privilege." The court went on to say, however, that on the record they could not determine whether the privilege might apply since there was no way to determine from the testimony whether the accused's entry into the apartment was open or clandestine or whether he was unaware of or indifferent to the observations of his wife. Suppose the accused upon entering into the apartment and seeing his wife had said, "Shh" while pointing to his lips or uttered the words, "Don't say anything to anyone"?

4. Compare with the case law described in note 3 supra, the approach taken in People v. Daghita, 299 N.Y. 194, 86 N.E.2d 172 (1949): The term "communication" includes "knowledge derived from the observance of disclosive acts done in the presence or view of one spouse by the other because of the confidence existing between them by reason of the marital relation and which would not

have been performed except for the confidence so existing." See also **People v. Sullivan**, 42 Misc.2d 1014, 249 N.Y.S.2d 589 (1964): Defendant tossed his pants over a chair and went to sleep; his wife searched his pants pockets for money and found a gun which she delivered to her sister who handed it over to their policeman-father. Held: privileged. What of testimony by a wife that she, unperceived by her husband, saw him through the kitchen window, obviously desiring secrecy, burying in the backyard a bulky object later discovered to be a corpse? See Smith v. State, 152 N.E. 803 (Ind.1926).

5. The question of confidentiality is often disputed. In Blau v. United States, 340 U.S. 332 (1951), the Court ruled that a husband could refuse to reveal to the grand jury the whereabouts of his wife based upon his privilege against disclosing confidential marital communications. The government argued that the husband had failed to prove that the information regarding her whereabouts was communicated in confidence. The court majority disagreed, relying on a presumption of confidentiality with respect to marital communications and on the fact that the communication was "of the kind likely to be confidential." See also United States v. McCown, 711 F.2d 1441, (9th Cir.1983) (husband's request that wife write check to purchase gun at pawn shop not confidential because no indication husband intended to keep request secret from friends living in same house).

6. Note that in the principal case, the presence of a third party at the time of the communication defeated confidentiality, making the privilege inapplicable. Under what circumstances may the privilege be held applicable despite the involvement of third parties?

a) In Wolfle v. United States, 291 U.S. 7 (1934), the court held that the written communication by a husband to his wife was not privileged when the letter was prepared by his stenographer. The court also stated:

> [W]e do not think the question ... is whether the petitioner's letter to his wife was intended to be confidential. We may take it that communications between husband and wife may sometimes be made in confidence even though in the presence of a third person. ...

> Normally husband and wife may conveniently communicate without stenographic aid and the privilege ... may be reasonably ... preserved without embracing within it the testimony of third persons to whom such communications have been voluntarily revealed. The uniform ruling that communications between husband and wife, voluntarily made in the presence of their children, old enough to comprehend them, or other members of the family within the intimacy of the family circle, are not privileged ... is persuasive that communications like the present, even though made in confidence, are not to be protected. Id. 291 U.S. 7, 16–17.

Consider in light of the foregoing quotation from Wolfle, State v. Fiddler, 360 P.2d 155, 157–158 (Wash.1961): A husband wrote two incriminating letters to his wife, who was illiterate; the necessity of having the letters read to his wife by a third person was viewed as removing the letters from privileged status. Is this decision sound in light of Wolfle? In Fiddler, one letter also showed an expectation that the writer's sisters would read it. Accord: Grulkey v. United States, 394 F.2d 244, 246 (8th Cir.1968).

b) Suppose the third person present at the time of the husband-wife conversation is the attorney for one of them. See Commonwealth v. O'Brien, 388 N.E.2d 658, 661 (Mass.1979).

c) In People v. Melski, 10 N.Y.2d 78, 217 N.Y.S.2d 65, 176 N.E.2d 81 (1961), the wife was permitted to testify that when she arose at 6:00 a.m. and entered the kitchen, she observed her husband and a few of his friends and guns. Although in New York acts as well as words may be covered by the privilege, see note 4 supra, a majority of the court held the wife's observations not privileged, in part because of the presence of third parties. The minority argued: "When the presence of the third person or persons is . . . as in this case, part of the very fact confidentially communicated, the presence of these others cannot destroy confidentiality."

d) Consider also State v. Benner, 284 A.2d 91, 109–110 (Me.1971): Prosecution of husband for kidnapping and assault with intent to rape; not error to admit testimony of wife as to observations around the family camper—namely, absence of husband and his car, slamming of door at 3 a.m., and blue plaid shirt on the bed—because of presence of 8–year–old son in the camper, to the knowledge of the husband. Compare Hicks v. Hicks, 155 S.E.2d 799 (N.C.1967) where the presence of 8–year–old daughter was held not to destroy the privilege.

7. May a former spouse testify that a third person was present at an incriminating conversation between her and her then husband? Does this present the same type of boot-strapping issue involved in Lutwak v. United States, supra p. 1501. See Picciurro v. United States, 250 F.2d 585, 589 (8th Cir.1958).

8. May an eavesdropper whose presence is unknown to the spouses and who overhears a confidential conversation between them testify? See North v. Superior Court, 8 Cal.3d 301, 311, 104 Cal.Rptr. 833, 839, 502 P.2d 1305, 1312 (1972), and the Comment to California Evidence Code, § 980. Jailhouse eavesdropping cases are collected in 57 A.L.R.3d 191–195. In North, where the privilege was upheld, officers secretly tape recorded a conversation between a visiting wife and her inmate husband in a detective's private office in the facility "under circumstances which strongly indicate that [the spouses] . . . were lulled into believing that their conversation would be confidential." However, a conversation between a husband and wife that takes place during a jailhouse visit and is to their knowledge being monitored is not protected by the privilege. People v. Santos, 26 Cal.App.3d 397, 402, 102 Cal.Rptr. 678, 681 (1972). Also see People v. Baker, 88 Cal.App.3d 115, 121–122, 151 Cal.Rptr. 362, 365–366 (1978). Sometimes the issue of whether the spouses had a reasonable expectation of privacy is disputed. People v. Rodriguez, 117 Cal. App.3d 706, 173 Cal.Rptr. 82 (1981). In holding that a married jail inmate cannot generally claim the marital privilege for confidential communications with respect to oral or written communications between the inmate and the inmate's spouse, the courts have balanced the competing interests of the need for jail security and the need for privacy between spouses in favor of jail security. Id. 117 Cal.App.3d 706, 715, 173 Cal.Rptr. 82, 87.

9. Recall the rule in Massachusetts disqualifying both spouses from testifying regarding private conversations between them, supra note 1, p. 1511. May a third person who overhears their conversation testify regarding it? See Commonwealth v. O'Brien, 388 N.E.2d 658, 661 (Mass.1979). Is the statutory disqualification violated when police officers testify as to statements the wife made to them describing statements her husband, the defendant, made to her? See Commonwealth v. Black, 351 N.E.2d 859 (Mass.App.1976) which held the police officers' testimony given in a pretrial hearing to have been non-prejudicial.

10. The principal case ruled that communications in furtherance of a crime in which the spouses jointly participate are not protected by the privilege. Most of the federal circuits have similarly ruled. See, e.g., United States v. Parker, 834

F.2d 408, 411 (4th Cir.1987), cert. denied, 485 U.S. 938 (1988); United States v. Estes, 793 F.2d 465, 468 (2d Cir.1986); United States v. Picciandra, 788 F.2d 39, 43 (1st Cir.), cert. denied, 479 U.S. 847 (1986). Compare the material on the joint participants exception to the adverse spousal privilege, supra, p.

11. At what point does a spouse become a joint participant in the criminal activity so as to make the confidential communications privilege inapplicable? See United States v. Estes, 793 F.2d 465, 467 (2d Cir.1986): "[T]he communication of ... knowledge [of the theft] was a necessary precursor to her involvement and could not have been made as part of an on-going joint criminal activity."

12. Once joint participation is established, is the privilege lost for all relevant statements? Does it matter whether the communication relates to previous criminal behavior by the speaking spouse, or is in furtherance of the joint criminal activity, or is a statement of intent to commit a crime in the future? Compare the crime-fraud exception to the attorney-client privilege, supra, p. 1473. Consider the following:

> The in camera submissions ... demonstrate a prima facie showing of the crime-fraud exception. As with the discussion of this exception and its application to the attorney-client privilege, it should not be the case that there is a wholesale abrogation of the privilege surrounding the entirety of Ferris' and Dolores' marital communications. Only those involved in the perpetration of the crime or fraud should be found to overrule any assertion of privilege.

United States v. Alexander, 736 F.Supp. 968 (D.Minn.1990).

13. Assume there has been no showing of prior joint criminal activity and:

a) Suppose that in the presence of his wife a husband makes a telephone call communicating a bomb threat to a third person. Does the privilege apply? Is the reason for not applying the privilege that the involvement of third persons disallows the privilege or that the telephone call is an act and not a communication vis a vis his spouse, or is there another reason? See People v. Delph, 94 Cal.App.3d 411, 416–417, 156 Cal.Rptr. 422, 425–426 (1979).

b) Suppose an accused spouse asks his spouse to write a letter containing false statements that would serve to exonerate him: Is the conversation in which he makes that request privileged? See People v. Baker, 88 Cal.App.3d 115, 121–122, 151 Cal.Rptr. 362, 365–366 (1978). Compare State v. Pizzolotto, 25 So.2d 292, 294–296 (La.1946). May the spouse testify as to statements made by the other spouse before the alleged commission of an offense as to what he intended to do or after the commission of the offense as to what he had done? See People v. Dorsey, 46 Cal.App.3d 706, 716–720, 120 Cal.Rptr. 508, 514–516 (1975).

14. An interesting decision on waiver of the privilege is People v. Worthington, 38 Cal.App.3d 359, 113 Cal.Rptr. 322 (1974). The prosecution called the wife to testify to her husband's confession to her concerning his commission of the murder. The defendant-husband earlier had volunteered to the police the details of how the victims had been murdered by his wife, a description identical to the confession he had made to his wife but with their roles reversed. After a police officer testified outside the presence of the jury as to the husband's statement accusing the wife, the trial court ruled that the husband thereby waived his privilege and permitted the wife to testify. The court of appeals ruled that the husband himself had disclosed a significant if twisted version of the conversation with his wife and affirmed the conviction, stating: "[I]t would be the ultimate irony if one spouse can under the guise of 'squealing' on the other, silence the other's response to his charges, in this case, of murder." Id. 38 Cal.App.3d 359, 365, 113 Cal.Rptr. 322, 326. Query: Suppose the husband in his statement to the police accusing his wife had disclosed nothing of the conversation between them. Would the mere fact that he had accused his wife waive his privilege?

15.   Allen v. Lindeman, 148 N.W.2d 610 (Iowa1967) involved a husband-wife communication issue reminiscent of one of the issues in Fisher v. United States, supra, p. 1336. A sued B for alienation of the affections of A's wife. B's wife found in their house the letters written to her husband by A's wife. B's wife turned the letters over to her minister. The trial court ordered the minister to produce the letters and permitted their introduction against B. H: No error. The letters would be privileged in the minister's hands only if they were privileged in B's wife's hands, and they were not since they were not communications between husband and wife.

16.   United States v. Brown, 634 F.2d 819 (5th Cir.1981) involved the clash between the marital communications privilege and a defendant's Sixth Amendment rights. Defendant wished to impeach the principal witness against him through the testimony of the witness's former wife that while they were still married her husband had admitted that he had lied to the grand jury hearing evidence in the case. The witness invoked the marital communications privilege to keep his wife's testimony from the jury.

The reviewing court rejected the Sixth Amendment claim on the ground that the defendant had adequately impeached the witness by other evidence and thus the exclusion of the wife's testimony did not deprive him of the ability to test the truthfulness of the witness's testimony. For further treatment of the conflict between evidentiary privileges and a defendant's Sixth Amendment rights, see pp. 270–271 supra.

17.   Generally both spouses are holders of the privilege, and either spouse may claim it. People v. Dorsey, 46 Cal.App.3d 706, 717, 120 Cal.Rptr. 508, 514–515 (1975) and see the Comment to California Evidence Code, § 980. Suppose that both spouses are indicted for joint criminal activity, and one spouse seeks to exculpate himself by testifying to a confidential communication from the other. Would separate trials solve the problem? See Note, 34 U.Chi.L.Rev. 196 (1966). California Evidence Code § 987 provides for an exception to the privilege in a criminal proceeding in which a confidential spousal communication is offered in evidence by the defendant spouse. In a criminal prosecution in which the defendant calls his wife as a witness, should the prosecution be permitted to cross-examine her about acts or communications from her husband relevant to his guilt? Cf. Hanvy v. State, 385 S.W.2d 752, 754–755 (Tenn.1965) (Held: privileged).

SECTION 5.   THE PHYSICIAN–PATIENT, PSYCHOTHERAPIST–PATIENT AND SIMILAR COUNSELOR–CLIENT PRIVILEGES

Jaffee v. Redmond

Supreme Court of the United States, 1996.
—— U.S. ——, 116 S.Ct. 1923, 135 L.Ed.2d 337.

■ MR. JUSTICE STEVENS delivered the opinion of the court.

After a traumatic incident in which she shot and killed a man, a police officer received extensive counseling from a licensed clinical social worker. The question we address is whether statements the officer made to her therapist during the counseling sessions are protected from compelled disclosure in a federal civil action brought by the family of the deceased. Stated otherwise, the question is whether it is appropriate for federal courts to recognize a "psychotherapist privilege" under Rule 501 of the Federal Rules of Evidence.

I

Petitioner is the administrator of the estate of Ricky Allen. Respondents are Mary Lu Redmond, a former police officer, and the Village of Hoffman Estates, Illinois, her employer during the time that she served on the police force. Petitioner commenced this action against respondents after Redmond shot and killed Allen while on patrol duty.

Petitioner filed suit in Federal District Court alleging that Redmond had violated Allen's constitutional rights by using excessive force during the encounter. . . . The complaint sought damages under Rev. Stat. § 1979, 42 U.S.C. § 1983 and the Illinois wrongful death statute, Ill. Comp. Stat., ch. 740, § 180/1 et seq. (1994). At trial, petitioner presented testimony from members of Allen's family that conflicted with Redmond's version of the incident in several important respects.

During pretrial discovery petitioner learned that after the shooting Redmond had participated in about 50 counseling sessions with Karen Beyer, a clinical social worker licensed by the State of Illinois and employed at that time by the Village of Hoffman Estates. Petitioner sought access to Beyer's notes concerning the sessions for use in cross-examining Redmond. Respondents vigorously resisted the discovery. They asserted that the contents of the conversations between Beyer and Redmond were protected against involuntary disclosure by a psychotherapist-patient privilege. The district judge rejected this argument. Neither Beyer nor Redmond, however, complied with his order to disclose the contents of Beyer's notes. At depositions and on the witness stand both either refused to answer certain questions or professed an inability to recall details of their conversations.

In his instructions at the end of the trial, the judge advised the jury that the refusal to turn over Beyer's notes had no "legal justification" and that the jury could therefore presume that the contents of the notes would have been unfavorable to respondents. The jury awarded petitioner $45,000 on the federal claim and $500,000 on her state-law claim.

The Court of Appeals for the Seventh Circuit reversed and remanded for a new trial. Addressing the issue for the first time, the court concluded that "reason and experience," the touchstones for acceptance of a privilege under Rule 501 of the Federal Rules of Evidence, compelled recognition of a psychotherapist-patient privilege. 51 F.3d 1346, 1355 (7th Cir.1995). "Reason tells us that psychotherapists and patients share a unique relationship, in which the ability to communicate freely without the fear of public disclosure is the key to successful treatment." Id., at 1355–1356. As to experience, the court observed that all 50 States have adopted some form of the psychotherapist-patient privilege. Id., at 1356. The court attached particular significance to the fact that Illinois law expressly extends such a privilege to social workers like Karen Beyer. The court also noted that, with one exception, the federal decisions rejecting the privilege were more than five years old and that the "need and demand for counseling services has skyrocketed during the past several years." Id., at 1355–1356.

The Court of Appeals qualified its recognition of the privilege by stating that it would not apply if "in the interests of justice, the evidentiary need for the disclosure of the contents of a patient's counseling sessions outweighs that patient's privacy interests." Id., at 1357. Balancing those conflicting interests, the court observed, on the one hand, that the evidentiary need for the contents of the confidential conversations was diminished in this case because there were numerous eyewitnesses to the shooting, and, on the other hand, that Officer Redmond's privacy interests were substantial. Based on this assessment, the court concluded that the trial court had erred by refusing to afford protection to the confidential communications between Redmond and Beyer.

The United States courts of appeals do not uniformly agree that the federal courts should recognize a psychotherapist privilege under Rule 501. Compare In re Doe, 964 F.2d 1325 (C.A.2 1992) (recognizing privilege); In re Zuniga, 714 F.2d 632 (CA6), cert. denied, 464 U.S. 983, 104 S.Ct. 426, 78 L.Ed.2d 361 (1983) (same), with United States v. Burtrum, 17 F.3d 1299 (C.A.10), cert. denied, 513 U.S. (1994) (declining to recognize privilege). Because of the conflict among the courts of appeals and the importance of the question, we granted certiorari. We affirm.

II

Rule 501 of the Federal Rules of Evidence authorizes federal courts to define new privileges by interpreting "common law principles ... in the light of reason and experience." ... The Senate Report accompanying the 1975 adoption of the Rules indicates that Rule 501 "should be understood as reflecting the view that the recognition of a privilege based on a confidential relationship ... should be determined on a case-by-case basis." S. Rep. No. 93–1277, p. 13 (1974). The Rule thus did not freeze the law governing the privileges of witnesses in federal trials at a particular point in our history, but rather directed federal courts to "continue the evolutionary development of testimonial privileges." Trammel v. United States, 445 U.S. 40, 47, 100 S.Ct. 906, 63 L.Ed.2d 186 (1980).

The common-law principles underlying the recognition of testimonial privileges can be stated simply. " 'For more than three centuries it has now been recognized as a fundamental maxim that the public ... has a right to every man's evidence. When we come to examine the various claims of exemption, we start with the primary assumption that there is a general duty to give what testimony one is capable of giving, and that any exemptions which may exist are distinctly exceptional, being so many derogations from a positive general rule.' " United States v. Bryan, 339 U.S. 323, 331, 70 S.Ct. 724, 94 L.Ed. 884 (1950) (quoting 8 J. Wigmore, Evidence § 2192, p. 64 (3d ed. 1940)). Exceptions from the general rule disfavoring testimonial privileges may be justified, however, by a " 'public good transcending the normally predominant principle of utilizing all rational means for ascertaining the truth.' " Trammel, 445 U.S. at 50.

Guided by these principles, the question we address today is whether a privilege protecting confidential communications between a psychotherapist and her patient "promotes sufficiently important interests to outweigh the need for probative evidence...." 445 U.S. at 51. Both "reason and experience" persuade us that it does.

III

Like the spousal and attorney-client privileges, the psychotherapist-patient privilege is "rooted in the imperative need for confidence and trust." Trammel, 445 U.S. at 51. Treatment by a physician for physical ailments can often proceed successfully on the basis of a physical examination, objective information supplied by the patient, and the results of diagnostic tests. Effective psychotherapy, by contrast, depends upon an atmosphere of confidence and trust in which the patient is willing to make a frank and complete disclosure of facts, emotions, memories, and fears. Because of the sensitive nature of the problems for which individuals consult psychotherapists, disclosure of confidential communications made during counseling sessions may cause embarrassment or disgrace. For this reason, the mere possibility of disclosure may impede development of the confidential relationship necessary for successful treatment. As the Judicial Conference Advisory Committee observed in 1972 when it recommended that Congress recognize a psychotherapist privilege as part of the Proposed Federal Rules of Evidence, a psychiatrist's ability to help her patients

"is completely dependent upon [the patients'] willingness and ability to talk freely. This makes it difficult if not impossible for [a psychiatrist] to function without being able to assure ... patients of confidentiality and, indeed, privileged communication. Where there may be exceptions to this general rule ..., there is wide agreement that confidentiality is a sine qua non for successful psychiatric treatment." Advisory Committee's Notes to Proposed Rules, 56 F.R.D. 183, 242 (1972) (quoting Group for Advancement of Psychiatry, Report No. 45, Confidentiality and Privileged Communication in the Practice of Psychiatry 92 (June 1960)).

By protecting confidential communications between a psychotherapist and her patient from involuntary disclosure, the proposed privilege thus serves important private interests.

Our cases make clear that an asserted privilege must also "serve public ends." Upjohn Co. v. United States, 449 U.S. 383, 389, 101 S.Ct. 677, 66 L.Ed.2d 584 (1981). Thus, the purpose of the attorney-client privilege is to "encourage full and frank communication between attorneys and their clients and thereby promote broader public interests in the observance of law and administration of justice." Ibid. And the spousal privilege, as modified in Trammel, is justified because it "furthers the important public interest in marital harmony," 445 U.S. at 53. The psychotherapist privilege serves the public interest by facilitating the provision of appropriate treatment for individuals suffering the effects of a mental or emotional problem. The mental health of our citizenry, no less than its physical health, is a public good of transcendent importance.[1]

In contrast to the significant public and private interests supporting recognition of the privilege, the likely evidentiary benefit that would result from the denial of the privilege is modest. If the privilege were rejected, confidential conversations between psychotherapists and their patients would surely be chilled, particularly when it is obvious that the circumstances that give rise to the need for treatment will probably result in litigation. Without a privilege, much of the desirable evidence to which litigants such as petitioner seek access—for example, admissions against interest by a party—is unlikely to come into being. This unspoken "evidence" will therefore serve no greater truth-seeking function than if it had been spoken and privileged.

---

1. This case amply demonstrates the importance of allowing individuals to receive confidential counseling. Police officers engaged in the dangerous and difficult tasks associated with protecting the safety of our communities not only confront the risk of physical harm but also face stressful circumstances that may give rise to anxiety, depression, fear, or anger. The entire community may suffer if police officers are not able to receive effective counseling and treatment after traumatic incidents, either because trained officers leave the profession prematurely or because those in need of treatment remain on the job. [The footnotes are those of the court. Some footnotes have been omitted, and others renumbered.]

That it is appropriate for the federal courts to recognize a psychotherapist privilege under Rule 501 is confirmed by the fact that all 50 States and the District of Columbia have enacted into law some form of psychotherapist privilege. ... [G]iven the importance of the patient's understanding that her communications with her therapist will not be publicly disclosed, any State's promise of confidentiality would have little value if the patient were aware that the privilege would not be honored in a federal court. Denial of the federal privilege therefore would frustrate the purposes of the state legislation that was enacted to foster these confidential communications.

It is of no consequence that recognition of the privilege in the vast majority of States is the product of legislative action rather than judicial decision. Although common-law rulings may once have been the primary source of new developments in federal privilege law, that is no longer the case. ... The present unanimous acceptance of the privilege shows that the state lawmakers moved quickly. That the privilege may have developed faster legislatively than it would have in the courts demonstrates only that the States rapidly recognized the wisdom of the rule as the field of psychotherapy developed.[2]

The uniform judgment of the States is reinforced by the fact that a psychotherapist privilege was among the nine specific privileges recommended by the Advisory Committee in its proposed privilege rules. In United States v. Gillock, 445 U.S. 360, 367–368, 100 S.Ct. 1185, 63 L.Ed.2d 454 (1980), our holding that Rule 501 did not include a state legislative privilege relied, in part, on the fact that no such privilege was included in the Advisory Committee's draft.

Because we agree with the judgment of the state legislatures and the Advisory Committee that a psychotherapist-patient privilege will serve a "public good transcending the normally predominant principle of utilizing all rational means for ascertaining truth," Trammel, 445 U.S. at 50, we hold that confidential communications between a licensed psychotherapist and her patients in the course of diagnosis or treatment are protected from compelled disclosure under Rule 501 of the Federal Rules of Evidence.

IV

All agree that a psychotherapist privilege covers confidential communications made to licensed psychiatrists and psychologists. We have no hesitation in concluding in this case that the federal privilege should also extend to confidential communications made to licensed social workers in the course of psychotherapy. The reasons for recognizing a privilege for treatment by psychiatrists and psychologists apply with equal force to treatment by a clinical social worker

---

2. Petitioner acknowledges that all 50 state legislatures favor a psychotherapist privilege. She nevertheless discounts the relevance of the state privilege statutes by pointing to divergence among the States concerning the types of therapy relationships protected and the exceptions recognized. A small number of state statutes, for example, grant the privilege only to psychiatrists and psychologists, while most apply the protection more broadly. Compare Haw. Rules Evid. 504, 504.1 and N. D. Rule Evid. 503 (privilege extends to physicians and psychotherapists), with Ariz. Rev. Stat. Ann. § 32– 3283 (1992) (privilege covers "behavioral health professionals"); Tex. Rule Civ. Evid. 510(a)(1) (privilege extends to persons "licensed or certified by the State of Texas in the diagnosis, evaluation or treatment of any mental or emotional disorder" or "involved in the treatment or examination of drug abusers"); Utah Rule Evid. 506 (privilege protects confidential communications made to marriage and family therapists, professional counselors, and psychiatric mental health nurse specialists). The range of exceptions recognized by the States is similarly varied.

such as Karen Beyer.[3] Today, social workers provide a significant amount of mental health treatment. Their clients often include the poor and those of modest means who could not afford the assistance of a psychiatrist or psychologist, id., at 6–7 (citing authorities), but whose counseling sessions serve the same public goals. Perhaps in recognition of these circumstances, the vast majority of States explicitly extend a testimonial privilege to licensed social workers. We therefore agree with the Court of Appeals that "drawing a distinction between the counseling provided by costly psychotherapists and the counseling provided by more readily accessible social workers serves no discernible public purpose." 51 F.3d at 1358, n. 19.

We part company with the Court of Appeals on a separate point. We reject the balancing component of the privilege implemented by that court and a small number of States. Making the promise of confidentiality contingent upon a trial judge's later evaluation of the relative importance of the patient's interest in privacy and the evidentiary need for disclosure would eviscerate the effectiveness of the privilege. As we explained in Upjohn, if the purpose of the privilege is to be served, the participants in the confidential conversation "must be able to predict with some degree of certainty whether particular discussions will be protected. An uncertain privilege, or one which purports to be certain but results in widely varying applications by the courts, is little better than no privilege at all." 449 U.S. at 393.

These considerations are all that is necessary for decision of this case. A rule that authorizes the recognition of new privileges on a case-by-case basis makes it appropriate to define the details of new privileges in a like manner. Because this is the first case in which we have recognized a psychotherapist privilege, it is neither necessary nor feasible to delineate its full contours in a way that would "govern all conceivable future questions in this area."

V

The conversations between Officer Redmond and Karen Beyer and the notes taken during their counseling sessions are protected from compelled disclosure under Rule 501 of the Federal Rules of Evidence. The judgment of the Court of Appeals is affirmed.

It is so ordered.

■ MR. JUSTICE SCALIA, with whom THE CHIEF JUSTICE joins as to Part III, dissenting.

The Court has discussed at some length the benefit that will be purchased by creation of the evidentiary privilege in this case: the encouragement of psychoanalytic counseling. It has not mentioned the purchase price: occasional injustice. That is the cost of every rule which excludes reliable and probative

---

3. If petitioner had filed her complaint in an Illinois state court, respondents' claim of privilege would surely have been upheld, at least with respect to the state wrongful death action. An Illinois statute provides that conversations between a therapist and her patients are privileged from compelled disclosure in any civil or criminal proceeding. Ill. Comp. Stat., ch. 740, § 1¹⁰⁄₁₀ (1994). The term "therapist" is broadly defined to encompass a number of licensed professionals including social workers. Ch. 740, § 11½. Karen Beyer, having satisfied the strict standards for licensure, qualifies as a clinical social worker in Illinois. 51 F.3d 1346, 1358, n. 19 (C.A.7 1995).

We note that there is disagreement concerning the proper rule in cases such as this in which both federal and state claims are asserted in federal court and relevant evidence would be privileged under state law but not under federal law. See C. Wright & K. Graham, 23 Federal Practice and Procedure § 5434 (1980). Because the parties do not raise this question and our resolution of the case does not depend on it, we express no opinion on the matter.

evidence—or at least every one categorical enough to achieve its announced policy objective. In the case of some of these rules, such as the one excluding confessions that have not been properly "Mirandized," see Miranda v. Arizona, 384 U.S. 436, 86 S.Ct. 1602, 16 L.Ed.2d 694 (1966), the victim of the injustice is always the impersonal State or the faceless "public at large." For the rule proposed here, the victim is more likely to be some individual who is prevented from proving a valid claim—or (worse still) prevented from establishing a valid defense. The latter is particularly unpalatable for those who love justice, because it causes the courts of law not merely to let stand a wrong, but to become themselves the instruments of wrong.

The Court today ignores this traditional judicial preference for the truth, and ends up creating a privilege that is new, vast, and ill-defined. I respectfully dissent.

I

[T]he prototypical evidentiary privilege analogous to the one asserted here—the lawyer-client privilege—is not identified by the broad area of advice-giving practiced by the person to whom the privileged communication is given, but rather by the professional status of that person. Hence, it seems a long step from a lawyer-client privilege to a tax advisor-client or accountant-client privilege. But if one recharacterizes it as a "legal advisor" privilege, the extension seems like the most natural thing in the world. That is the illusion the Court has produced here: It first frames an overly general question ("Should there be a psychotherapist privilege?") that can be answered in the negative only by excluding from protection office consultations with professional psychiatrists (i.e., doctors) and clinical psychologists. And then, having answered that in the affirmative, it comes to the only question that the facts of this case present ("Should there be a social worker-client privilege with regard to psychotherapeutic counseling?") with the answer seemingly a foregone conclusion. At that point, to conclude against the privilege one must subscribe to the difficult proposition, "Yes, there is a psychotherapist privilege, but not if the psychotherapist is a social worker."

II

To say that the Court devotes the bulk of its opinion to the much easier question of psychotherapist-patient privilege is not to say that its answer to that question is convincing. At bottom, the Court's decision to recognize such a privilege is based on its view that "successful [psychotherapeutic] treatment" serves "important private interests" (namely those of patients undergoing psychotherapy) as well as the "public good" of "the mental health of our citizenry." Ante, at 7–9. I have no quarrel with these premises. Effective psychotherapy undoubtedly is beneficial to individuals with mental problems, and surely serves some larger social interest in maintaining a mentally stable society. But merely mentioning these values does not answer the critical question: are they of such importance, and is the contribution of psychotherapy to them so distinctive, and is the application of normal evidentiary rules so destructive to psychotherapy, as to justify making our federal courts occasional instruments of injustice? On that central question I find the Court's analysis insufficiently convincing to satisfy the high standard we have set for rules that "are in derogation of the search for truth."

When is it, one must wonder, that the psychotherapist came to play such an indispensable role in the maintenance of the citizenry's mental health? For most of history, men and women have worked out their difficulties by talking to, inter alios, parents, siblings, best friends and bartenders—none of whom was awarded a privilege against testifying in court. Ask the average citizen: Would your mental health be more significantly impaired by preventing you from seeing a psychotherapist, or by preventing you from getting advice from your mom? I have little doubt what the answer would be. Yet there is no mother-child privilege.

How likely is it that a person will be deterred from seeking psychological counseling, or from being completely truthful in the course of such counseling, because of fear of later disclosure in litigation? And even more pertinent to today's decision, to what extent will the evidentiary privilege reduce that deterrent? The Court does not try to answer the first of these questions; and it cannot possibly have any notion of what the answer is to the second, since that depends entirely upon the scope of the privilege, which the Court amazingly finds it "neither necessary nor feasible to delineate," ante, at 16.

Even where it is certain that absence of the psychotherapist privilege will inhibit disclosure of the information, it is not clear to me that that is an unacceptable state of affairs. Let us assume the very worst in the circumstances of the present case: that to be truthful about what was troubling her, the police officer who sought counseling would have to confess that she shot without reason, and wounded an innocent man. If (again to assume the worst) such an act constituted the crime of negligent wounding under Illinois law, the officer would of course have the absolute right not to admit that she shot without reason in criminal court. But I see no reason why she should be enabled both not to admit it in criminal court (as a good citizen should), and to get the benefits of psychotherapy by admitting it to a therapist who cannot tell anyone else. And even less reason why she should be enabled to deny her guilt in the criminal trial—or in a civil trial for negligence—while yet obtaining the benefits of psychotherapy by confessing guilt to a social worker who cannot testify. It seems to me entirely fair to say that if she wishes the benefits of telling the truth she must also accept the adverse consequences. To be sure, in most cases the statements to the psychotherapist will be only marginally relevant, and one of the purposes of the privilege (though not one relied upon by the Court) may be simply to spare patients needless intrusion upon their privacy, and to spare psychotherapists needless expenditure of their time in deposition and trial. But surely this can be achieved by means short of excluding even evidence that is of the most direct and conclusive effect.

The Court confidently asserts that not much truth-finding capacity would be destroyed by the privilege anyway, since "without a privilege, much of the desirable evidence to which litigants such as petitioner seek access ... is unlikely to come into being." Ante, at 10. If that is so, how come psychotherapy got to be a thriving practice before the "psychotherapist privilege" was invented? Were the patients paying money to lie to their analysts all those years? Of course the evidence-generating effect of the privilege (if any) depends entirely upon its scope, which the Court steadfastly declines to consider. And even if one assumes that scope to be the broadest possible, is it really true that most, or even many, of those who seek psychological counseling have the worry of litigation in the back of their minds? I doubt that, and the Court provides no evidence to support it.

III

Turning from the general question that was not involved in this case to the specific one that is: The Court's conclusion that a social-worker psychothera-peutic privilege deserves recognition is even less persuasive.

Of course this brief analysis—like the earlier, more extensive, discussion of the general psychotherapist privilege—contains no explanation of why the psychotherapy provided by social workers is a public good of such transcendent importance as to be purchased at the price of occasional injustice. Moreover, it considers only the respects in which social workers providing therapeutic services are similar to licensed psychiatrists and psychologists; not a word about the respects in which they are different. A licensed psychiatrist or psychologist is an expert in psychotherapy—and that may suffice (though I think it not so clear that this Court should make the judgment) to justify the use of extraordinary means to encourage counseling with him, as opposed to counseling with one's rabbi, minister, family or friends. One must presume that a social worker does not bring this greatly heightened degree of skill to bear, which is alone a reason for not encouraging that consultation as generously. Does a social worker bring to bear at least a significantly heightened degree of skill—more than a minister or rabbi, for example? I have no idea, and neither does the Court. The social worker in the present case, Karen Beyer, was a "licensed clinical social worker" in Illinois, App. 18, a job title whose training requirements consist of "master's degree in social work from an approved program," and "3,000 hours of satisfactory, supervised clinical professional experience." Ill. Comp. Stat., ch. 225, § 2% (1994). It is not clear that the degree in social work requires any training in psychotherapy. The "clinical professional experience" apparently will impart some such training, but only of the vaguest sort, judging from the Illinois Code's definition of "clinical social work practice," viz., "the providing of mental health services for the evaluation, treatment, and prevention of mental and emotional disorders in individuals, families and groups based on knowledge and theory of psychosocial development, behavior, psychopathology, unconscious motivation, interpersonal relationships, and environmental stress." Ch. 225, § 2%(5).

In its consideration of this case, the Court was the beneficiary of no fewer than 14 amicus briefs supporting respondents, most of which came from such organizations as the American Psychiatric Association, the American Psychoanalytic Association, the American Association of State Social Work Boards, the Employee Assistance Professionals Association, Inc., the American Counseling Association, and the National Association of Social Workers. Not a single amicus brief was filed in support of petitioner. That is no surprise. There is no self-interested organization out there devoted to pursuit of the truth in the federal courts. The expectation is, however, that this Court will have that interest prominently—indeed, primarily—in mind. Today we have failed that expectation, and that responsibility. It is no small matter to say that, in some cases, our federal courts will be the tools of injustice rather than unearth the truth where it is available to be found. The common law has identified a few instances where that is tolerable. Perhaps Congress may conclude that it is also tolerable for the purpose of encouraging psychotherapy by social workers. But that conclusion assuredly does not burst upon the mind with such clarity that a judgment in favor of suppressing the truth ought to be pronounced by this honorable Court. I respectfully dissent.

NOTES

1. The physician-patient privilege was discussed in United States ex rel. Edney v. Smith, 425 F.Supp. 1038, 1040 (E.D.N.Y.1976) as follows:

> The physician-patient relationship, unlike that of attorney-client, did not give rise to a testimonial privilege at common law; a physician called as a witness had a duty to disclose all information obtained from a patient. See

generally 8 Wigmore, Evidence §§ 2380–2391 (McNaughton rev. 1961). In 1828 New York became the first jurisdiction to alter the common-law rule by establishing a statutory privilege. N.Y.Rev.Stat.1828, 406 (pt. 3, ch. 7, Tit. 3, Art. 9, § 73). Since that time approximately three-quarters of the states have followed New York's lead and enacted similar statutory provisions. 8 Wigmore, Evidence § 2380 (McNaughton rev. 1961).

Legal scholars have been virtually unanimous in their condemnation of these legislative attempts to foster the doctor-patient relationship by rules of exclusion. Professor Chafee's well-known criticism is typical:

> The reasons usually advanced for extending the privilege of silence to the medical profession are not wholly satisfactory. First, it is said that if the patient knows that his confidences may be divulged in future litigation he will hesitate in many cases to get needed medical aid. But although the man who consults a lawyer usually has litigation in mind, men very rarely go to a doctor with any such thought. And even if they did, medical treatment is so valuable that few would lose it to prevent facts from coming to light in court. Indeed, it may be doubted whether, except for a small range of disgraceful or peculiarly private matters, patients worry much about having a doctor keep their private affairs concealed from the world. This whole argument that the privilege is necessary to induce persons to see a doctor sounds like a philosopher's speculation on how men may logically be expected to behave rather than the result of observation of the way men actually behave. ...

> The same a priori quality vitiates a second argument concerning the evils of compelling medical testimony, namely, that a strong sense of professional honor will prompt perversion or concealment of the truth.

> ...

Chafee, Privileged Communications: Is Justice Served or Obstructed by Closing the Doctor's Mouth on the Witness Stand?, 52 Yale L.J. 607, 609–10 (1943).

Legal practice in the states which have adopted a general medical privilege confirms the criticism of the commentators. Although no state has repealed the privilege once it has been adopted, recognition of its undesirable effects has led to judicial and legislative whittling away so that its scope has been considerably reduced. Numerous nonuniform exceptions have evolved which have rendered the privilege "substantially impotent," Comment, Federal Rules of Evidence and the Law of Privileges, 15 Wayne L.Rev. 1286, 1324 (1969), and difficult to administer.

In the federal sphere awareness of these difficulties led the Advisory Committee on the Federal Rules of Evidence to omit any provision for a general physician-patient privilege.

2. What kinds of medical personnel are within the physician-patient privilege? Issues arise with respect to nurses, attendants, dentists, chiropractors, osteopaths, podiatrists, veterinarians and similar categories of medically-related fields.

3. The physician-patient privilege covers persons whose presence is "reasonably necessary" for "the accomplishment of the purpose for which the physician is consulted." California Evidence Code § 992. An interesting application of this principle is State v. Gibson, 3476 P.2d 727, 730 (Wash.App.1970); Error to allow a police officer to testify to a statement made by the defendant patient to a treating physician, the policeman being present to protect the doctor and prevent the patient from escaping. Accord: People v. Decina, 2 N.Y.2d 133, 157 N.Y.S.2d 558, 138 N.E.2d 799 (1956). What about participants in group therapy? See Cross, Privileged Communications between Participants in Group Psychotherapy, 1970 Law and Soc.Order 191. And see J.B. Weinstein & M.A. Berger, 2 Weinstein's Evidence ¶ 504(05) suggesting that Rule 504(a)(3) of the Supreme Court's proposed Federal Rules is broad enough to cover a group therapy situation.

4. Who are patients within the privilege? The California Evidence Code § 1011 includes a person who consults a psychotherapist "for the purpose of scientific research on mental or emotional problems." There is no similar clause in § 991 of the Code which defines patient for purposes of the physician-patient privilege. Is there reason so to distinguish between the two privileges? See also Rule 504 of the Supreme Court's proposed Federal Rules.

A party to litigation who is examined by a doctor to enable him to testify regarding that person's condition does not consult the expert for treatment and is therefore not covered by the privilege. See Taylor v. United States, 222 F.2d 398 (D.C.Cir.1955). State v. Kuljis, 422 P.2d 480, 482 (Wash.1967) involved a physician taking a blood sample to make a blood alcohol test for police purposes. Held: doctor-patient privilege not violated. Compare, however, the Comment to § 991, California Evidence Code. Does it imply that consultation with a physician for purposes of diagnosis in contemplation of a legal proceeding is covered by the privilege? Of course, if the medical expert is engaged by the party's attorney, an attorney-client privilege issue is also raised. See p. 1457 supra.

5. In re Coddington's Will, 307 N.Y. 181, 120 N.E.2d 777, 783–784 (1954) applied the physician-patient privilege to privileged communications noted in a hospital record. In Blue Cross of Northern California v. Superior Court, 61 Cal.App.3d 798, 132 Cal.Rptr. 635 (1976) the court ruled that patients identities and descriptions of their ailments recorded in the claims records of a prepaid health care plan were covered by the privilege. Does the privilege apply to drug reaction reports submitted by a physician to the drug manufacturer? What test should the court apply in answering this question? See Rudnick v. Superior Court, 11 Cal.3d 924, 114 Cal.Rptr. 603, 523 P.2d 643 (1974). Suppose a physician reports to the county community health department that a patient who is a food handler has a communicable disease. Has he breached the confidentiality of the physician-patient relationship? See 58 Ops.Calif.Att.Gen. 904 (1975) and also see § 1006 and § 1026 of the California Evidence Code which makes the physician-patient and the psychotherapist-patient privileges inapplicable to information required to be reported to a public office "if such report . . . is open to public inspection."

6. The kinds of questions raised in the previous note came into sharp focus in connection with the AIDS (acquired immune deficiency syndrome) epidemic. The issues are extraordinarily difficult. Should a physician be allowed, or required, to report a positive test result to a spouse, family member or known sexual partner of the carrier? Was it desirable to adopt legislation allowing, or requiring, the disclosure of a positive test result to institutions with which the carrier is or may become involved—e.g. hospitals, funeral directors, employers, schools?

It has been argued that there is a duty to protect those who are at risk because of potential harmful contact with the carrier. Query: How specific and probable must the threat of harm be to overcome the tradition of confidentiality? On the other hand, it has been argued that breaking the traditional pattern of confidentiality will discourage people from being tested and that increased disclosure will inevitably lead to widespread discrimination against AIDS virus carriers and those who are victims of the disease. See generally, Note, The

Constitutional Rights of AIDS Carriers, 99 Harv.L.Rev. 1274 (1986); Marco, AIDS 1986: A Medical–Legal Explosion, 33 Med. Trial Technique Q. 360 (1987); Weldon–Linne, Weldon–Linne and Murphy, AIDS–Virus Antibody Testing: Issues of Informed Consent and Patient Confidentiality, 75 Ill.B.J. 206 (1986).

7. Wrongful death action. A patient is brought to a hospital unconscious following an accident; a blood sample is taken, and a blood alcohol test is done for medical reasons; the sample is later made available to the police. Held: Privileged under the physician-patient privilege. Branch v. Wilkinson, 256 N.W.2d 307, 315 (Neb.1977). Compare State v. Figueroa, 515 A.2d 242 (N.J.Super.1986). Query: Is it significant that the patient was unconscious? That there was no oral communication, merely the taking of a sample of body fluids? Suppose the "patient" is already dead when the blood sample is taken. See Hinote v. Aluminum Co. of America, 463 N.E.2d 531 (Ind.App.1984). Compare State v. Kuljis, supra note 4.

8. Are a physician's observations of a person's intoxicated state within the privilege? Compare the similar issue that arises regarding an attorney's observations of his client's mental condition, supra note 10, p. 1406. Is the person's drunken state not within the privilege because it is plainly visible and he therefore could not reasonably expect it to be confidential? Suppose, however, the doctor's observations are relevant to the treatment of the patient? See People v. Deadmond, 683 P.2d 763 (Colo.1984).

9. Some states do not apply the physician-patient privilege in criminal proceedings. See e.g. Section 998, California Evidence Code; Ore.Rev.Stat.Annot. § 40.235(2) (1981). Other states do not apply the privilege in certain types of criminal cases, for example, drunk driving, see e.g. State v. Dyal, 478 A.2d 390 (N.J.1984), and child abuse cases, see e.g. State v. Efird, 309 S.E.2d 228 (N.C.1983).

10. The federal courts have been disinclined to apply a physician-patient privilege except where the matter arises under state law, see e.g. United States v. University Hospital of State University of N.Y., 575 F.Supp. 607 (E.D.N.Y. 1983), aff'd 729 F.2d 144 (2d Cir.1984); United States v. Burzynski, 819 F.2d 1301 (5th Cir.1987) while even prior to the principal case, many of the circuits had been willing to apply a psychotherapist-patient privilege under Rule 501. Does the decision in the principal case portend a similar approach in physician-patient cases?

11. Does disclosure of the fact of psychiatric treatment involve disclosure of privileged information? See Smith v. Superior Court, 118 Cal.App.3d 136, 173 Cal.Rptr. 145 (1981): Action for spousal support. Psychologist not required to produce names, addresses and telephone numbers of patients and former patients; disclosure of patient's identity reveals confidential information, namely that the patient suffers from mental or emotional problems. Compare In re Albert Lindley Lee Memorial Hospital, 115 F.Supp. 643 (N.D.N.Y.), aff'd, 209 F.2d 122 (2d Cir.1953). (Names of patients required to check income tax returns of doctor not privileged.) Also see In re: Search Warrant (Sealed), 810 F.2d 67 (3d Cir.1987). Suppose a subpoena seeks the names and addresses of patients who have been treated for knife wounds. See In re Grand Jury Investigation, 59 N.Y.2d 130, 463 N.Y.S.2d 758, 450 N.E.2d 678 (1983). Is the appropriate principle that the identity of the patient is privileged if its disclosure also discloses the nature of the ailment treated or the nature of the treatment? Should a distinction be drawn in this connection between the physician-patient and psychotherapist-patient privileges? Query: are attorney-client privilege—identity-of-the-client cases distinguishable? See p. 1409 supra.

12. In re Lifschutz, 2 Cal.3d 415, 85 Cal.Rptr. 829 (1977), the court ruled on the defendant's claim that any communication between the plaintiff-patient and his psychotherapist had lost its privileged status because the plaintiff had filed a personal injury action in which he claimed recovery for "mental and emotional distress." The court dealt with that issue as follows:

> Defendant relies on section 1016 of the Evidence Code, the patient-litigant exception to the psychotherapist-patient privilege, which provides that: "[t]here is no privilege under this article as to a communication relevant to an issue concerning the mental or emotional condition of the patient if such issue has been tendered by: (a) the patient...."
>
> First, the courts have noted that the patient, in raising the issue of a specific ailment or condition in litigation, in effect dispenses with the confidentiality of that ailment and may no longer justifiably seek protection from the humiliation of its exposure. Second, the exception represents a judgment that, in all fairness, a patient should not be permitted to establish a claim while simultaneously foreclosing inquiry into relevant matters.... In previous physician-patient privilege cases the exception has been generally applied only to compel disclosure of medical treatment and communication concerning the very injury or impairment that was the subject matter of the litigation. There is certainly nothing to suggest that in the context of the more liberal psychotherapist-patient privilege this exception should be given a broader reading.
>
> If the provision had as broad an effect as is suggested by petitioner, it might effectively deter many psychotherapeutic patients from instituting any general claim for mental suffering and damage out of fear of opening up all past communications to discovery. This result would clearly be an intolerable and overbroad intrusion into the patient's privacy, not sufficiently limited to the legitimate state interest embodied in the provision and would create opportunities for harassment and blackmail.
>
> In light of these considerations, the "automatic" waiver of privilege contemplated by section 1016 must be construed not as a complete waiver of the privilege but only as a limited waiver concomitant with the purposes of the exception. Under section 1016 disclosure can be compelled only with respect to those mental conditions the patient-litigant has "disclose[d] ... by bringing an action in which they are in issue" (City & County of San Francisco v. Superior Court, 37 Cal.2d 227, 232, 231 P.2d 26).... Disclosure cannot be compelled with respect to other aspects of the patient-litigant's personality even though they may, in some sense, be "relevant" to the substantive issues of litigation. The patient thus is not obligated to sacrifice all privacy to seek redress for a specific mental or emotional injury; the scope of the inquiry permitted depends upon the nature of the injuries which the patient-litigant himself has brought before the court.
>
> ... [T]he determination of the specific "mental condition" in issue may present ... complex problems.
>
> Because only the patient, and not the party seeking disclosure, knows both the nature of the ailments for which recovery is sought and the general content of the psychotherapeutic communications, the burden rests upon the patient initially to submit some showing that a given confidential communication is not directly related to the issue he has tendered to the court. (Cf. Evid.Code, § 404 (person claiming privilege against incrimination bears burden of showing proffered evidence might tend to incriminate him).)

Accord: Caesar v. Mountanos, 542 F.2d 1064 (9th Cir.1976), cert. denied, 430 U.S. 954 (1977).

13.   The waiver-by-filing-a-lawsuit issue has led to a substantial number of imaginative contentions that have produced appellate court rulings in California: See, e.g., Simek v. Superior Court, 117 Cal.App.3d 169, 172 Cal.Rptr. 564 (1981) where the court ruled that in a divorce proceeding the husband had not waived his privilege by seeking "extensive" visitation rights; he had not thereby tendered an issue concerning his "mental and emotional condition"; Koshman v. Superior Court, 111 Cal.App.3d 294, 168 Cal.Rptr. 558 (1980) (father seeks custody; mother's denial responding to the father's complaint did not tender her mental condition as an issue); Huelter v. Superior Court, 87 Cal.App.3d 544, 151 Cal.Rptr. 138 (1978) (wife seeks spousal support alleging physical infirmity; she does not thereby tender the issue of her mental condition); City of Alhambra v. Superior Court, 110 Cal.App.3d 513, 518–519, 168 Cal.Rptr. 49, 51–52 (1980) involved an action against police officers for assault and battery, false imprisonment and violation of the plaintiffs' civil rights. The plaintiffs sought information about whether the defendants had received psychiatric treatment. Held: Section 999 of the California Evidence Code is not applicable, and under Section 1016, the defendants had not tendered an issue concerning their mental and emotional condition by denying liability.

14.   Where the patient is accused in a criminal case and raises the insanity defense he may have waived his privilege. Compare the materials, supra p. 1459 relating to the applicability of the attorney-client privilege to this type of situation. Of course, where the psychiatrist examined the patient only for purposes of testifying at trial, the privilege may be deemed any way inapplicable, see e.g. Corder v. Indiana, 467 N.E.2d 409 (Ind.1984), and see note 4, p. 1559 supra. Even, however, where the psychiatrist involved had treated the patient-accused the same result may be reached by implying a waiver. See People v. Carfora, 25 N.Y.2d 972, 305 N.Y.S.2d 363, 252 N.E.2d 859 (1969); People v. Edney, 39 N.Y.2d 620, 385 N.Y.S.2d 23, 350 N.E.2d 400 (1976). For an argument to the effect that the attorney-client privilege should not protect psychiatric evidence when the patient's mental condition is at issue for the same reasons that make the psychotherapist privilege inapplicable, see Saltzburg, Privileges and Professionals: Lawyers and Psychiatrists, 66 Va.L.Rev. 583, 635–42 (1980).

15.   Section 1027 of the California Evidence Code makes the psychotherapist-patient inapplicable if the patient is under 16 years of age and the psychotherapist has reasonable cause to believe the patient has been the victim of a crime and disclosure is in his or her best interest.

16.   In re Lifschutz, supra note 12, addressed constitutional issues related to the psychotherapist-patient privilege. The court: a) rejected a psychotherapist's claim of his constitutional right to maintain absolute confidentiality regarding his communications with and treatment of his patients; b) rejected the claim that the statutory creation of an absolute clergyman-penitent privilege rendered the absence of a similar psychotherapist-patient privilege a denial of equal protection; c) recognized that the confidentiality of psychotherapist-patient communications falls within a constitutional zone of privacy (as well as being supported by statute); and d) concluded that the limited (as construed by the court) waiver provided for in section 1016 of the California Evidence Code meets constitutional standards. Regarding the constitutional privacy issue, see Roe v. Ingraham, 403 F.Supp. 931, 935–936 (S.D.N.Y.1975) (recognizing the constitutional claim but reversed sub nom. Whalen v. Roe, 429 U.S. 589, 601–

603 (1977); and United States ex rel. Edney v. Smith, 425 F.Supp. 1038 (E.D.N.Y.1976).

Menendez v. Superior Court of Los Angeles County

Supreme Court of California, 1992.
3 Cal.4th 435, 11 Cal.Rptr.2d 92, 834 P.2d 786.

■ MOSK, JUSTICE.

We granted review in this matter to consider a claim of the psychotherapist-patient privilege. . . .

I

On August 20, 1989, Jose and Mary Louise Menendez were killed in their Beverly Hills residence. The incident was reported shortly after its occurrence by their sons Joseph Lyle (Lyle) and Erik Galen (Erik) Menendez (collectively sometimes the Menendezes or the brothers), who were then apparently 21 and 18 years of age, respectively.

On March 7, 1990, a magistrate in the Municipal Court of the Beverly Hills Judicial District of Los Angeles County issued a search warrant, pursuant to Penal Code section 1524, authorizing a search of the offices and residence of Leon Jerome Oziel, Ph.D., a clinical psychologist who was Lyle's and Erik's psychotherapist, and seizure of specified items if found therein, including audiotape recordings containing information relating to the killings. It seems that at or about the time of issuance, the magistrate appointed a special master pursuant to subdivision (c) of Penal Code section 1524 to accompany those who would serve the warrant.[1]

On March 8, 1990, accompanied by the special master, among others, officers of the Beverly Hills Police Department served the search warrant. The special master informed Dr. Oziel of the items sought. Dr. Oziel provided the materials. Claiming the psychotherapist-patient privilege on behalf of the Menendezes, he stated that none of the items should be disclosed because all were within the scope of the protection. The special master sealed the materials for a subsequent hearing in the superior court. Among the items in question were three audiotape cassettes (and certain copies thereof): one contains Dr. Oziel's notes relating to sessions with Lyle and Erik on October 31 and November 2, 1989; one contains Dr. Oziel's notes relating to a session with Erik on November 28, 1989; and one contains an actual session Dr. Oziel conducted with Lyle and Erik on December 11, 1989. Lyle and Erik were subsequently arrested and placed in custody.

---

1. Penal Code section 1524, subdivision (c), provides in pertinent part as follows:

"... [N]o search warrant shall issue for any documentary evidence in the possession or under the control of any person, who is ... a psychotherapist ... [,] and who is not reasonably suspected of engaging or having engaged in criminal activity related to the documentary evidence for which a warrant is requested unless the following procedure has been complied with:

"(1) At the time of the issuance of the warrant the court shall appoint a special master ... to accompany the person who will serve the warrant. . . .

"(2) If the party who has been served states that an item or items should not be disclosed, they shall be sealed by the special master and taken to court for a hearing.

"At the hearing the party searched shall be entitled to raise ... a claim that the item or items are privileged, as provided by law. Any such hearing shall be held in the superior court. ..." [Footnotes are those of the court. Some footnotes have been renumbered; others have been omitted.]

On March 12, 1990, a felony complaint was filed on behalf of the People against the Menendezes in the Municipal Court of the Beverly Hills Judicial District of Los Angeles County.

Count I charged the brothers with the murder of their father. (Pen. Code, § 187.) As to this offense, it alleged, inter alia, the special circumstances of intentional murder for financial gain and intentional murder while lying in wait.

Count II charged the brothers with the murder of their mother. As to this offense, it alleged, inter alia, the special circumstances of intentional murder for financial gain and intentional murder while lying in wait.

The complaint separately alleged the special circumstance of multiple murder.

II

On March 19, 1990, Dr. Oziel filed a motion in the Los Angeles Superior Court under Penal Code section 1524, subdivision (c), effectively claiming for the Menendezes the psychotherapist-patient privilege, as established by Evidence Code section 1014, as to the items seized pursuant to the search warrant.

The Menendezes successfully moved to intervene. They filed papers in support of the privilege.

By contrast, the People, through the Los Angeles District Attorney, filed papers in opposition. They argued, inter alia, that the privilege was not available on its own terms. They also argued that certain exceptions operated. Most prominent was the exception for a "dangerous patient," as stated in Evidence Code section 1024.[2] Also cited was the exception for a "crime or tort" under Evidence Code section 1018....

. . .

A

We first consider the portion of the audiotape containing Dr. Oziel's notes of his October 31 session with Lyle and Erik.

At the outset, the psychotherapist-patient privilege was available. The notes reflect "confidential communication[s] between patient[s]," i.e., Lyle and Erik, "and psychotherapist," i.e., Dr. Oziel. The "information" that passed among them was "transmitted ... in the course of [the psychotherapeutic] relationship and in confidence by a means which, so far as [Lyle and Erik] [were] aware, disclose[d] the information" to no "outside" third person.

The availability of the privilege is compelled under the facts found by the superior court. Such findings are reviewed for substantial evidence. The findings here are more than adequately supported. Dr. Oziel gave testimony that provided a sufficient basis in and of itself. Further, Judalon Smyth gave testimony that furnished corroboration. True, the superior court recognized—altogether soundly, in our view—that Dr. Oziel and Smyth were witnesses whose testimony could be credited only after careful scrutiny of both their words and demeanor. To quote the court's charitable description, each had

---

2. Evidence Code section 1024 provides: "There is no privilege ... if the psychotherapist has reasonable cause to believe that the patient is in such mental or emotional condi- tion as to be dangerous to himself or to the person or property of another and that disclo- sure of the communication is necessary to prevent the threatened danger."

"multiple motives, multiple motivations, multiple agendas." But it nevertheless believed them in part relevant here. We see no reason to disagree.[3]

. . .

The "dangerous patient" exception, however, was indeed applicable. Its conditions were met: Dr. Oziel had reasonable cause to believe that Lyle and Erik were dangerous to himself directly and to Laurel Oziel and Judalon Smyth collaterally, and that disclosure to the two women was necessary to prevent any harm.

The superior court made findings—which are amply supported—that establish the exception. It impliedly recognized that the "reasonableness" of the requisite "reasonable cause to believe" must be determined in light of the standards of the psychotherapeutic community. The test is objective, but takes account of all the relevant circumstances; it is based on the norms prevailing among psychotherapists as a group, but allows broad discretion to the individual psychotherapist. In certain cases, expert testimony as to the relevant standards may be necessary. Here, it was not: the evidence all but compelled the conclusion of "reasonableness." In any event, expert testimony bearing on the standards was, in fact, presented by Dr. Oziel himself.

The superior court found—with more than sufficient support in the record—that Dr. Oziel disclosed to Laurel Oziel and Judalon Smyth, in separate warnings against any collateral harm, all the communications made at this session and reflected on audiotape, having reasonable cause to believe that the Menendezes were dangerous and that disclosure of these communications was necessary.

We emphasize that the "dangerous patient" exception requires only reasonable cause for belief by the psychotherapist in the dangerousness of the patient and the necessity of disclosure. Certainly, it does not demand that the patient must be dangerous to a person other than the psychotherapist— although here the patients were. Nor does it demand that the psychotherapist must actually disclose the relevant communication or even issue a warning. . . .

If ever there was any question about the matter, it was answered, implicitly but clearly, in Tarasoff v. Regents of University of California. There, we dealt generally with the psychotherapist's duty under the common law "to use reasonable care to protect the intended victim" of a patient who "presents a serious danger of violence." Plainly, the policies of the common law are similar to those of the "dangerous patient" exception.

In Tarasoff, we held that "[w]hen a therapist determines, or pursuant to the standards of his profession should determine, that his patient presents a serious danger of violence to another, he incurs an obligation to use reasonable care to protect the intended victim against such danger. The discharge of this duty may require the therapist to take one or more of various steps, depending upon the nature of the case. Thus it may call for him to warn the intended victim or others likely to apprise the victim of the danger, to notify the police, or to take whatever other steps are reasonably necessary under the circumstances." On that basis, we concluded that the plaintiffs therein could state a cause of action in negligence against the defendant psychotherapists for their alleged failure to give a warning to their patient's intended, and actual, victim or to others.

---

3.   The superior court's finding that Judalon Smyth overheard some of the communications at the October 31 session as an eavesdropper does not negate the privilege. As noted, the superior court itself impliedly so concluded. The privilege, we have stated above, can cover a communication that was never, in fact, confidential.

In the course of our discussion in Tarasoff, we implied that the "dangerous patient" exception would be applicable to the psychotherapist-patient communications as pleaded. We noted that Evidence Code section 1024—which "established that psychotherapeutic communication is not privileged when disclosure is necessary to prevent threatened danger"—was a " 'clear expression of legislative policy concerning the balance between the confidentiality values of the patient and the safety values of his foreseeable victims[]' " Accordingly, we concluded that "the public policy favoring protection of the confidential character of patient-psychotherapist communications must yield to the extent to which disclosure is essential to avert danger to others. The protective privilege ends where the public peril begins."

To the extent that the Menendezes argue that the "dangerous patient" exception requires something more than reasonable cause for belief by the psychotherapist in the dangerousness of the patient and the necessity of disclosure, they are unpersuasive.

[The court proceeded to consider the application of the privilege to the other three sessions with the brothers. The court ruled that—

a) the privilege did not protect communications at one of the sessions: the dangerous patient exception applied;

b) the privilege claim should be sustained as to the remaining two sessions: the dangerous patient exception requirements were not met because of the trial court finding that the evidence was insufficient to establish that Dr. Oziel had reasonable cause to believe that disclosure was necessary.]

NOTES

1. Should a doctrine similar to that of Tarasoff v. Regents of the University of California, 17 Cal.3d 425, 131 Cal.Rptr. 14, 551 P.2d 334 (1976) (imposing a duty on psychotherapists to warn regarding a dangerous patient and to that extent making the privilege inapplicable) be applied in connection with other confidential communication privileges? Which ones?

2. The California Child Abuse Reporting Act, see California Penal Code, § 11166, requires a medical practitioner (and others) when he or she reasonably suspects a person to have been the victim of child abuse to report the matter to a child protective agency. This reporting obligation takes precedence over the physician-patient or psychotherapist-patient privilege. People v. Stritzinger, 34 Cal.3d 505, 194 Cal.Rptr. 431 (1983).

3. In Tarasoff the court stated:

We realize that the open and confidential character of psychotherapeutic dialogue encourages patients to express threats of violence, few of which are ever executed. Certainly a therapist should not be encouraged routinely to reveal such threats; such disclosures could seriously disrupt the patient's relationship with his therapist and with the persons threatened. To the contrary, the therapist's obligations to his patient require that he not disclose a confidence unless such disclosure is necessary to avert danger to others, and even then that he do so discreetly, and in a fashion that would preserve the privacy of his patient to the fullest extent compatible with the prevention of the threatened danger . . . .

The revelation of a communication under the above circumstances is not a breach of trust or a violation of professional ethics; as stated in the

Principles of Medical Ethics of the American Medical Association (1957), section 9: "A physician may not reveal the confidence entrusted to him in the course of medical attendance ... unless he is required to do so by law or unless it becomes necessary in order to protect the welfare of the individual or of the community." We conclude that the public policy favoring protection of the confidential character of patient-psychotherapist communications must yield to the extent to which disclosure is essential to avert danger to others. The protective privilege ends where the public peril begins. Tarasoff, supra note 1 at 17 Cal.3d at 440–442.

4. Note that the exception contained in section 1024 of the California Evidence Code in two different ways may bear on the substantive issues in a tort action involving the Tarasoff doctrine. It may be relied upon in a tort action, as the court did in Tarasoff itself to negate a defensive claim that "the needs of confidentiality are paramount" and that therefore no duty to warn arises. It may also be directly in issue where a plaintiff, after an injury has been caused, seeks to discover the psychiatric records of the injury-causing patient with a view to using them in support of a cause of action against the psychiatrist. In ruling on the claim of privilege, is the judge not making a preliminary evidentiary ruling on the very issue that constitutes the plaintiff's cause of action?

5. Grosslight v. Superior Court, 72 Cal.App.3d 502, 507–508, 140 Cal.Rptr. 278, 280–281 (1977). Plaintiffs seek in-camera order for examination of minor defendant's records at psychiatric hospital for purposes of obtaining information regarding any admissions by her parents of knowledge of her dangerous propensities. Held: Any such statements by parents are privileged, and discovery procedures seeking such privileged statements are subject to the privilege. See also People v. Hopkins, 44 Cal.App.3d 669, 673–674, 119 Cal.Rptr. 61, 63–64 (1975). See generally, Lewis, Duty to Warn Versus Duty to Maintain Confidentiality: Conflicting Demands on Mental Health Professionals, 20 Suffolk U.L.Rev. 579 (1986); Discovery of Psychotherapist–Patient Communications after Tarasoff, 15 San Diego L.Rev. 265 (1978); Where the Public Peril Begins: A Survey of Psychotherapists to Determine the Effects of Tarasoff, 31 Stan.L.Rev. 165 (1978); Untangling Tarasoff: Duty of Psychotherapists to Warn Potential Victim of Mentally Ill Patient, 29 Hastings L.J. 179 (1977); Patient or His Victim: The Therapist's Dilemma, 61 Calif.L.Rev. 1025 (1974).

SECTION 6. OTHER RELATIONSHIP PRIVILEGES

In many jurisdictions, privileges are limited to those created by statute. See e.g. Calif.Evid.Code § 911. In the federal courts, Rule 501 provides that, except in civil actions where state law provides the rule of decision, the privileges are "governed by the principles of the common law as they may be interpreted ... in the light of reason and experience." In applying this open-ended Rule, the Supreme Court's Proposed Rules relating to privileges still provide "a convenient, comprehensive guide to the federal law of privileges as they now stand ... subject to considerably more flexibility in construction than is vouchsafed to courts construing formally adopted Rules." J.B. Weinstein & M.A. Berger, 2 Weinstein's Evidence ¶ 501[03]. Not only can the federal courts further develop existing privileges under this authority but they have, when a need has been perceived created new privileges. Generally, however, the Supreme Court in providing leadership in this area has, with some exceptions, see Jaffee v Redmond, supra p. 1516, been reluctant to create new privileges. See University of Pennsylvania v. EEOC, infra p. 1540. In applying Rule 501, the federal courts also may consider state privilege law and, of course, take into account the policy justification for recognition of the particular privilege or its claimed scope. It should be mentioned, too, that under federal law, numerous specific privileges, qualified or not, exist by dint of statute or rule. See generally J.B. Weinstein & M.A. Berger, 2 Weinstein's Evidence ¶ 501[04][05].

A.   CLERGY–PENITENT

A statutory privilege covering communications between a clergy and penitent, exists in about two-thirds of the states. Rule 506 of the Supreme Court's proposed Federal Rules provides for such a privilege. Some jurisdictions limit the privilege to communications in the doctrinally required confessional. Others apply it to any confidential communication to a clergyman in his professional character.

The rationale for this privilege roughly parallels that of the attorney-client and husband-wife privileges. "The benefit of preserving these confidences inviolate overbalances the possible benefit of permitting litigation to prosper at the expense of . . . the spiritual rehabilitation of a penitent." Mullen v. United States, 263 F.2d 275, 280 (D.C.Cir.1958) (Fahey, J. concurring).

The issues that arise are therefore likely to be similar to those previously considered in connection with the other confidential communications privileges. One question, for example, is whether the privilege extends to situations in which others are present. The decision in In re Verplank, 329 F.Supp. 433, 435–436 (C.D.Cal.1971) goes very far in upholding the privilege. Relying in part on the proposed draft of Rule 506, the court held that communications to unordained counsellors working in Rev. Verplank's draft counselling center were privileged because their services were sufficiently like those performed by clergy. Compare J.B. Weinstein & M.A. Berger, 2 Weinstein's Evidence ¶ 506[02]:

> The attendance of non-clergy charged with the task of assisting the clergyman in carrying out spiritual duties should not defeat confidentiality if the clergyman himself is present . . . .

> It is considerably more questionable, whether . . . the privilege should extend to communications made in the clergyman's absence to his assistants whom the communicant does not believe to be clergymen.

See also California Evidence Code § 1032.

What kinds of communications are covered by the privilege? In People v. Edwards, 194 Cal.App.3d 430, 239 Cal.Rptr. 526 (1987), an Episcopal priest testified that he believed defendant's statements to him were "in the nature of a secular or pastoral confession seeking counselling and not absolution." The defendant had also earlier confessed to another priest on the same matter. Held: The later communication was not "a penitential communication" under section 1031 of the California Evidence Code. Is it relevant whether the individual requests confidentiality? See People v. Edwards, supra and see Lucy v. State, 443 So.2d 1335 (Ala.Crim.App.1983).

Does the privilege cover acts as well as communications? In United States v. Mohanlal, 867 F.Supp. 199 (S.D.N.Y.1994), a minister testified that in his judgment, the defendant knew the difference between right and wrong. Held: The testimony was not violative of the clergy-penitent privilege. The court stated:

> [The Minister's] . . . testimony concerning his conclusion as to defendant's mental state, although no doubt based upon communications to him by

defendant, as well as observations of defendant, did not reveal, or suggest, the content of any communication by defendant.

Determining who are clergymen for purposes of the privilege may present special problems. The statutory definition of clergymen typically is very broad (see proposed Federal Rule 506(a)(1)), and in some jurisdictions is liberalized even more by provisions extending the privilege to a person reasonably believed by the communicant to be a clergyman.

Should mail order ministers and ministers of fringe cults qualify? See J.B. Weinstein & M.A. Berger, 2 Weinstein's Evidence ¶ 506[2]. Jehovah's Witnesses where each member is designated a minister? Ibid. Does the refusal to extend the privilege to a minister of a particular sect violate the First Amendment religion clauses? See generally Stoyles, The Dilemma of the Constitutionality of the Priest–Penitent Privilege—The Application of the Religion Clauses, 29 U.Pitt.L.Rev. 27 (1967). Is there an unconstitutional discrimination if non-believers who perform analogous advisory functions without religious affiliation are excluded from the coverage of the privilege?

Statutes requiring clergy to disclose information regarding potential child abuse violations have been enacted in some states. See Mitchell, Must Clergy Tell? Child Abuse Reporting Requirements versus The Clergy Privilege and Free Exercise of Religion, 71 Minn. l.REv. 723 (1987); Yellin, The History and Current Status of the Clergy–Penitent Privilege, 23 Santa Clara L.Rev. 95 (1983).

See generally, Callahan Historical Inquiry into the Priest–Penitent Privilege, 36 Jurist 328 (1976); Catholic Sisters, Irregularly Ordained Women and the Clergy–Penitent Privilege, 9 U.C.D.L.Rev. 523 (1976); Kuhlmann, Communications to Clergymen—When Are They Privileged?, 2 Val.U.L.Rev. 265 (1968).

B. OTHER PROFESSIONAL–CLIENT RELATIONSHIPS

A claim for a confidential communications privilege can be made on behalf of numerous other professionals who perform advising, counselling or representational functions for their clients. Such other professionals include accountants, social workers, psychologists, marriage counselors, family counselors, teachers and lay advocates. Generally, in the absence of a statute creating the privilege, the courts reject such claims. See e.g. William T. Thompson Co. v. General Nutrition Corps, Inc., 671 F.2d 100 (3d Cir.1982) (federal court refused to apply a state accountant-client privilege). Also see United States v. El Paso Co., 682 F.2d 530 (5th Cir.1982), and Couch v. United States, 409 U.S. 322 (1973). And see United States v. Arthur Young and Co., 465 U.S. 805 (1984) (rejecting a qualified work product privilege for accountant's tax accrual papers). Statutes creating such privileges do exist in a minority of states. See Functional Overlap Between the Lawyer and Other Professionals: Its Implications for the Privileged Communications Doctrines, 71 Yale L.J. 1226 (1962).

A recent development is the effort to establish a privilege for communications to an ombudsperson in a corporate or institutional setting by a grievant or person complaining about misconduct. Thus far, there are only a few cases. See, e.g., Garstang v. Superior Court, 46 Cal.Rptr.2d 84 (Cal.App.1995); Kientzy v. McDonnell Douglas Corp., 133 F.R.D. 570 (E.D.Mo.1991). See generally, Thompson, Corporate Ombudsmen and Privileged Communications, 61 U.Cinn.L.Rev. 653 (1992).

Some of the counselling professionals may be covered by the psychotherapist's privilege. See the Supreme Court's decision in Jaffee v. Redmond, supra,

p. 1516, and see particularly Justice Scalia's dissent in that case, at p. 1521. See California Evidence Code, § 1010. Also see Welfare Rights Organization v. Crisan, 33 Cal.3d 766, 190 Cal.Rptr. 919, 661 P.2d 1073 (1983): A law advocate represented claimants in aid to families with dependent children (AFDC) administrative "fair hearings." Communications between the claimants and the nonattorney lay advocate were held to be privileged under a privilege "comparable to the attorney-client . . . impliedly provided by statute."

Finally mention should be made of two new privileges added by legislative action to the California Evidence Code: a Sexual Assault Victim–Counselor Privilege, California Evidence Code §§ 1035–1036.2, and a Domestic Violence Victim–Counselor Privilege, California Evidence Code, §§ 1037–1037.7.

C.   JOURNALIST'S PRIVILEGE AND SCHOLAR'S PRIVILEGE

In Branzburg v. Hayes, 408 U.S. 665 (1972) a claim was made that under the First Amendment a reporter has a privilege to refuse to disclose to a criminal grand jury his sources or other information communicated to him in confidence; that in the absence of such a privilege "confidential sources . . . will be measurably deterred from furnishing publishable information . . . to the detriment of the free flow of information protected by the First Amendment."

The reporters in the case did not argue for an absolute privilege but rather that they should not be required either to appear or testify before the grand jury unless a showing was made that they had information relevant to a crime, the information was unavailable from other sources and the need for the information was sufficiently great to overcome the First Amendment interests that would be invaded by the reporter's disclosure. By a 5–4 vote, the Supreme Court rejected the reporters' claims. The majority did indicate that the reporter should be protected from "official harassment . . . undertaken not for purposes of law enforcement but to disrupt . . . [his] relationship with his news sources. . . ."

Mr. Justice Powell who joined in the Opinion of the Court also wrote a separate concurrence in which he was somewhat more explicit about the protection that subpoenaed reporters could expect under the Constitution:

> [I]f the newsman is called upon to give information bearing only a remote and tenuous relationship to the subject of the investigation or if he has some reason to believe that his testimony implicates confidential source relationships without a legitimate need of law enforcement, he will have access to the Court on a motion to quash and an appropriate protective order may be entered. The asserted claims of privilege should be judged on its facts by a striking of a proper balance between freedom of the press and the obligation of all citizens to give relevant testimony with respect to criminal conduct. Id. 408 U.S. 665, 710.

At the time of the Branzburg decision, approximately one-third of the states provided some sort of statutory protection to a journalist's sources. In the aftermath of the decision, bills providing for either an absolute or qualified journalistic privilege were introduced in a number of state legislatures and in Congress. Some of the state legislative proposals were enacted; more than half of the states now have shield laws. The proposed federal legislation has not become law. See Newsman's Privilege After "Branzburg", The Case for a Federal Shield Law, 4 UCLA L.Rev. 160 (1976); Murasky, The Journalist's Privilege: Branzburg and Its Aftermath, 52 Tex.L.Rev. 829 (1974).

The shield laws vary in their coverage. Some apply the privilege to journalists' notes and other unpublished material while others restrict the coverage of the protection to confidential sources or information provided by confidential sources. See e.g. Knight–Ridder Broadcasting, Inc. v. Greenberg, 70

N.Y.2d 151, 518 N.Y.S.2d 595, 511 N.E.2d 1116 (1987). Compare Goodale, Back to the Drawing Board for New York's Shield Law, Nat.L.J., p. 13, July 27, 1987.

The proposed Federal Rules did not contain a journalist's privilege provision. Federal cases since Branzburg have recognized some protection for a newsman's sources, however. In Baker v. F & F Investment, 470 F.2d 778 (2d Cir.1972), in a civil rights class action directed against racially discriminatory "blockbusting" the court denied a discovery order that would have compelled a journalist to reveal his confidential source. The court first approved the fact that in reaching his decision, the trial judge "informed his judgment" concerning appropriate federal public policy in the area of the privilege by looking to the shield statutes of the two states where the litigation was taking place. The court then proceeded to distinguish Branzburg in the following terms:

> If, as Mr. Justice Powell noted ... instances will arise in which First Amendment values outweigh the duty of a journalist to testify even in the context of a criminal investigation, surely in civil cases courts must recognize that the public's interest in non-disclosure of journalists' confidential news sources will often be weightier than the private interest in compelled disclosure. Id. at 785.

See also Silkwood v. Kerr–McGee Corp., 563 F.2d 433, 436–438 (10th Cir.1977); Continental Cablevision, Inc. v. Storer; United States v. Burke, 700 F.2d 70 (2d Cir.1983).

In In re Farber, 394 A.2d 330, 335–339 (N.J.), cert. denied, 439 U.S. 997 (1978), on motion of the defendant the trial court had ordered a reporter to disclose his sources and other information relating to articles he had written on a series of homicides, which articles had led to the indictment of the defendant. The reporter refused to comply, citing inter alia the state's shield law. The state supreme court upheld the contempt convictions of the reporter and his newspaper, on the ground that the defendant's Sixth Amendment right to obtain evidence in his behalf outweighed the statutory privilege. See Journalist's Privilege: In re Farber and the New Jersey Shield Law, 32 Rutgers L.Rev. 545 (1979). Also see State v. Boiardo, 414 A.2d 14 (N.J.1980); Maressa v. New Jersey Monthly, 445 A.2d 376 (N.J.1982).

Rather than directly giving the newsmen a privilege to refuse to disclose, the California approach is to immunize the journalist from a contempt citation for refusing to disclose confidential information. Query, is this difference in approach significant? In Farr v. Superior Court, 22 Cal.App.3d 60, 99 Cal.Rptr. 342, 347–348 (1971), cert. denied, 409 U.S. 1011 (1972), the court ruled that a reporter could be held in contempt for failure to reveal the names of the attorneys and others who had, in violation of a court order, furnished him with a copy of an incriminating statement made by the defendant; that to apply the statutory immunity against contempt to prevent a citation in such a case would be an unconstitutional interference by the legislature into the power of the court to control its own proceedings.

In 1980, the California statutory immunity against contempt provision was elevated into the state constitution via the initiative process. See Division 8, Chapter 5, California Evidence Code. In Delaney v. Superior Court, 50 Cal.3d 785, 268 Cal.Rptr. 753, 789 P.2d 934 (1990), the California Supreme Court ruled that a newsperson's non-confidential, eyewitness observations in a public place are covered by the state newsperson's shield law (both the statutory and the constitutional versions); but that the newsperson's protection must yield when a criminal defendant is able to show a reasonable possibility that the information will materially assist the defense.

Claims analogous to the claim for a journalist's privilege have been made for the protection of the confidentiality of the research and sources of academic researchers—a so-called "scholar's" privilege. See e.g. In re Grand Jury Sub-poena, January 4, 1984, 750 F.2d 223 (2d Cir.1984); Wright v. Jeep Corp., 547 F.Supp. 871 (E.D.Mich.1982); Richards of Rockford, Inc. v. Pacific Gas and Electric Co., 71 F.R.D. 388 (N.D.Cal.1976). Does the difference between the work of the journalist and the academic researcher make the claim for a scholar's privilege less persuasive than the journalist's claim? Consider issues of academic freedom discussed in University of Pennsylvania v. EEOC, infra, p. 1540. Can it be argued that the academic researcher's claim for a privilege should be treated as a specific type of journalist's privilege?

See generally Kaplan and Cogan, The Case Against Recognition of A General Academic Privilege, 60 U.Det.J.Urb.L. 205 (1983); "Scholar's privilege" under Rule 501 of Federal Rules of Evidence, 81 ALR Fed 904.

D.   PARENT–CHILD AND OTHER FAMILIAL RELATIONSHIPS

Do the same kind of concerns that led to the creation of a husband-wife confidential communication privilege justify a comparable parent-child privilege? Three states have recognized a parent-child confidential communication privilege—Idaho and Minnesota by statute, Idaho Code § 9–203(7); Minn.Stat. § 595.02(9); and New York through judicial decisions. See People v. Fitzgerald, 101 Misc.2d 712, 422 N.Y.S.2d 309 (1979); People v. Harrell, 87 A.D.2d 21, 450 N.Y.S.2d 501 (1982); In re Gloria L., 124 Misc.2d 50, 475 N.Y.S.2d 1000 (1984). But see In the Matter of Harry R., 134 Misc.2d 404, 510 N.Y.S.2d 792 (1986). See also, in the Matter of Application of A and M, 61 A.D.2d 426, 403 N.Y.S.2d 375 (1978) (child-parent confidential communication possibly involving admissions of arson by 16 year old son may be constitutionally protected). Other states have rejected the notion of developing such a privilege through judicial decision. See People v. Dixon, 411 N.W.2d 760 (Mich.App.1987) which collects the authorities.

Federal courts of appeal have consistently rejected claims of a parent-child privilege or familial privileges other than the spousal privileges. See authorities collected in In re Subpoena Issued to Mary Erato, 2 F.3d 11 (2d Cir.1993). Two federal district courts have recognized a parent-child privilege, In re Agosto, 553 F.Supp. 1298 (D.Nev.1983); and In re Grand Jury Proceedings (Greenberg), 11 Fed.R. Evid. Serv. 579 (D.Conn. 1982).

Under a parent-child confidential communication privilege, should the privilege apply both to communications from the parent to child and child to parent or only to the latter? Who should be the holder of the privilege? Should it apply to emancipated adults? In In re Subpoena Issued to Mary Erato, supra, the court noted that the claim for a parent-child privilege in a case involving an adult child was weaker than in a case involving a minor child:

> At least in that situation the argument would be available that compelling a parent to inculpate a minor child risks a strain on the family relationship that might impair the mother's ability to provide parental guidance during the child's formative years.

Were a parent-child confidential communication privilege recognized, it might have an effect on decisions rejecting the application of the husband-wife privilege because the children were present when the conversation took place. See p. 1514 supra. On the other hand, even in the absence of a recognition of such a privilege, in some factual settings on occasion, either the attorney-client or physician-parent privilege might be applicable to a parent-child communication. See De Los Santos v. Superior Court, 27 Cal.3d 677, 166 Cal.Rptr. 172, 613 P.2d 233 (1980). See also, People v. Tesh, 124 A.D.2d 843, 508 N.Y.S.2d 560 (1986) (son's conversations with mother in presence of third party not covered by privilege).

Can an argument also be made for a parent-child adverse testimony privilege involving the parent as a witness against the child, or vice versa? Claims of such a privilege have generally been rejected. See De Leon v. State, 684 S.W.2d 778 (Tex.App.1984); United States v. Jones, 683 F.2d 817 (4th Cir.1982). Compare In re Agosto, supra. See L.A. Times, Sec. I, p. 2, col. 2, September 13, 1984 (reporting the surrender of parents of a teenage murder suspect in Houston to begin serving jail time for refusing to testify against their son in a grand jury proceeding); In re Luis T., Cal.App. (unpublished) (1980) reported in L.A. Times, Sec. I, p. 28, col. 3, July 27, 1980 (juvenile defendant does not have a privilege to keep his mother from testifying as a prosecution witness; mother testified that her son knew it was wrong to set fire to a school); National L.J. p. 3, col. 2, March 9, 1981 (reporting a U.S. district court ruling ordering a 16–year-old daughter to testify before a federal grand jury as to matters that tended to incriminate her mother and threatening the daughter with civil contempt if she refused to testify). Were such a privilege recognized, who should be the holder? Should it apply to emancipated adults?

Should there be a privilege for other familial relationships? What about grandchildren? Compare Judge Henley dissenting in United States v. Allery, 526 F.2d 1362 (8th Cir.1975), and see In re Ryan, 123 Misc.2d 854, 474 N.Y.S.2d 931 (Fam.Ct.1984) applying the privilege to a grandmother-child relationship where the grandmother was in fact a long-term surrogate for the mother. In re Matthews, 714 F.2d 223 (2d Cir.1983) rejected an "in-laws" privilege and affirmed a contempt citation for a witness' refusal to testify before a grand jury concerning his in-laws' business. And see In re Grand Jury Proceedings, 607 F.Supp. 1002 (S.D.N.Y.1985) where the court, relying on Matthews, rejected a claimed "sibling" privilege and ordered one brother to testify against his sibling before a grand jury.

The topic has been the subject of much law review commentary. See generally, Developments in the Law, Privileged Communications, 98 Harv. L.Rev. 1450, 1575 (1985); Note, Parent–Child Loyalty and Testimonial Privilege, 100 Harv.L.Rev. 910 (1987). Comment, Parent–Child Testimonial Privilege: An Absolute Right or an Absolute Privilege? 11 U.Dayton L.Rev. 709 (1986); Kraft, Parent–Child Testimonial Privilege; Who's Minding the Kids? 18 Fam.L.Q. 505 (1985); Kandoian, The Parent–Child Privilege and the Parent–Child Crime: Observations on State v. De Long and In re Agosto, 36 Me.L.Rev. 59 (1984); Comment, Underprivileged Communications: The Rationale for a Parent–Child Testimonial Privilege, 36 S.W.L.J. 1175 (1983); Comment, Parent–Child Testimonial Privilege: Preserving and Protecting the Fundamental Right to Family Privacy, 52 U.Cinn.L.Rev. 901 (1983).

SECTION 7. INSTITUTIONAL AND INSTITUTIONAL PROCESS PRIVILEGES

A. PEER REVIEW PRIVILEGE AND CRITICAL SELF-ANALYSIS PRIVILEGE

University of Pennsylvania v. EEOC
Supreme Court of the United States, 1990.
493 U.S. 182, 110 S.Ct. 577, 107 L.Ed.2d 571.

[Briefs of amici curiae urging reversal were filed for the American Association of University Professors; for the President and Fellows of Harvard College; for Stanford University et al.; and for the American Council on Education.

... [A] brief [was filed] for the Now Legal Defense and Education Fund et al. as amici curiae urging affirmance.]

■ MR. JUSTICE BLACKMAN delivered the opinion of the Court.

In this case we are asked to decide whether a university enjoys a special privilege, grounded in either the common law or the First Amendment, against disclosure of peer review materials that are relevant to charges of racial or sexual discrimination in tenure decisions.

I

The University of Pennsylvania, petitioner here, is a private institution. It currently operates 12 schools, including the Wharton School of Business, which collectively enroll approximately 18,000 full-time students.

In 1985, the University denied tenure to Rosalie Tung, an associate professor on the Wharton faculty. Tung then filed a sworn charge of discrimination with respondent Equal Employment Opportunity Commission (EEOC or Commission). As subsequently amended, the charge alleged that Tung was the victim of discrimination on the basis of race, sex, and national origin, in violation of § 703(a) of Title VII of the Civil Rights Act of 1964, 78 Stat. 255, as amended, 42 U.S.C. § 2000e–2(a) (1982 ed.), which makes it unlawful "to discriminate against any individual with respect to his compensation, terms, conditions, or privileges of employment, because of such individual's race, color, religion, sex, or national origin."

In her charge, Tung stated that the department chairman had sexually harassed her and that, in her belief, after she insisted that their relationship remain professional, he had submitted a negative letter to the University's Personnel Committee which possessed ultimate responsibility for tenure decisions. She also alleged that her qualifications were "equal to or better than" those of five named male faculty members who had received more favorable treatment. Tung noted that the majority of the members of her department had recommended her for tenure, and stated that she had been given no reason for the decision against her, but had discovered of her own efforts that the Personnel Committee had attempted to justify its decision "on the ground that the Wharton School is not interested in China-related research." This explanation, Tung's charge alleged, was a pretext for discrimination: "simply their way of saying they do not want a Chinese–American, Oriental, woman in their school."

The Commission undertook an investigation into Tung's charge and requested a variety of relevant information from petitioner. When the University refused to provide certain of that information, the Commission's Acting District Director issued a subpoena seeking, among other things, Tung's tenure-review file and the tenure files of the five male faculty members identified in the charge. Petitioner refused to produce a number of the tenure-file documents. It applied to the Commission for modification of the subpoena to exclude what it termed "confidential peer review information," specifically, (1) confidential letters written by Tung's evaluators; (2) the department chairman's letter of evaluation; (3) documents reflecting the internal deliberations of faculty committees considering applications for tenure, including the Department Evaluation Report summarizing the deliberations relating to Tung's application for tenure; and (4) comparable portions of the tenure-review files of the five males. The University urged the Commission to "adopt a balancing approach reflecting the constitutional and societal interest inherent in the peer review process" and to resort to "all feasible methods to minimize the intrusive effects of its investigations."

The Commission denied the University's application. It concluded that the withheld documents were needed in order to determine the merit of Tung's charges. The Commission found: "There has not been enough data supplied in order for the Commission to determine whether there is reasonable cause to believe that the allegations of sex, race and national origin discrimination is [sic] true." The Commission rejected petitioner's contention that a letter, which set forth the Personnel Committee's reasons for denying Tung tenure, was sufficient for disposition of the charge. "The Commission would fall short of its obligation" to investigate charges of discrimination, the EEOC's order stated, "if it stopped its investigation once [the employer] has ... provided the reasons for its employment decisions, without verifying whether that reason is a pretext for discrimination." The Commission also rejected petitioner's proposed balancing test, explaining that "such an approach in the instant case ... would impair the Commission's ability to fully investigate this charge of discrimination." The Commission indicated that enforcement proceedings might be necessary if a response was not forthcoming within 20 days.

The University continued to withhold the tenure-review materials. The Commission then applied to the United States District Court for the Eastern District of Pennsylvania for enforcement of its subpoena. The court entered a brief enforcement order.

The Court of Appeals for the Third Circuit affirmed the enforcement decision. 850 F.2d 969 (3d Cir.1988). Relying upon its earlier opinion in EEOC v. Franklin and Marshall College, 775 F.2d 110 (3d Cir.1985), cert. denied, 476 U.S. 1163 (1986), the court rejected petitioner's claim that policy considerations and First Amendment principles of academic freedom required the recognition of a qualified privilege or the adoption of a balancing approach that would require the Commission to demonstrate some particularized need, beyond a showing of relevance, to obtain peer review materials. Because of what might be thought of as a conflict in approach with the Seventh Circuit's decision in EEOC v. University of Notre Dame Du Lac, 715 F.2d 331, 337 (7th Cir.1983), and because of the importance of the issue, we granted certiorari limited to the compelled-disclosure question.

II

As it had done before the Commission, the District Court, and the Court of Appeals, the University raises here essentially two claims. First, it urges us to recognize a qualified common-law privilege against disclosure of confidential peer review materials. Second, it asserts a First Amendment right of "academic freedom" against wholesale disclosure of the contested documents. With respect to each of the two claims, the remedy petitioner seeks is the same: a requirement of a judicial finding of particularized necessity of access, beyond a showing of mere relevance, before peer review materials are disclosed to the Commission.

A

Petitioner's common-law privilege claim is grounded in Federal Rule of Evidence 501. This provides in relevant part:

"Except as otherwise required by the Constitution ... as provided by Act of Congress or in rules prescribed by the Supreme Court ..., the privilege of a witness ... shall be governed by the principles of the common law as they may be interpreted by the courts of the United States in the light of reason and experience."

The University asks us to invoke this provision to fashion anew privilege that it claims is necessary to protect the integrity of the peer review process, which in turn is central to the proper functioning of many colleges and universities. These institutions are special, observes petitioner, because they function as "centers of learning, innovation and discovery."

We do not create and apply an evidentiary privilege unless it "promotes sufficiently important interests to outweigh the need for probative evidence...." Trammel v. United States, 445 U.S. 40, 51 (1980). Inasmuch as "testimonial exclusionary rules and privileges contravene the fundamental principle that 'the public ... has a right to every man's evidence,'" id., at 50, quoting United States v. Bryan, 339 U.S. 323, 331 (1950), any such privilege must "be strictly construed." 445 U.S., at 50.

Moreover, although Rule 501 manifests a congressional desire "not to freeze the law of privilege" but rather to provide the courts with flexibility to develop rules of privilege on a case-by-case basis, id., at 47, we are disinclined to exercise this authority expansively. We are especially reluctant to recognize a privilege in an area where it appears that Congress has considered the relevant competing concerns but has not provided the privilege itself. Cf. Branzburg v. Hayes, 408 U.S. 665, 706 (1972). The balancing of conflicting interests of this type is particularly a legislative function.

With all this in mind, we cannot accept the University's invitation to create a new privilege against the disclosure of peer review materials. We begin by noting that Congress, in extending Title VII to educational institutional and in providing for broad EEOC subpoena powers, did not see fit to create a privilege for peer review documents.

When Title VII was enacted originally in 1964, it exempted an "educational institution with respect to the employment of individuals to perform work connected with the educational activities of such institution." § 702, 78 Stat. 255. Eight years later, Congress eliminated that specific exemption by enacting § 3 of the Equal Employment Opportunity Act of 1972, 86 Stat. 103. This extension of Title VII was Congress' considered response to the widespread and compelling problem of invidious discrimination in educational institutions. The House Report focused specifically on discrimination in higher education, including the lack of access for women and minorities to higher ranking (i. e., tenured) academic positions. See H. R. Rep. No. 92–238, pp. 19–20 (1971). Significantly, opponents of the extension claimed that enforcement of Title VII would weaken institutions of higher education by interfering with decisions to hire and promote faculty members. Petitioner therefore cannot seriously contend that Congress was oblivious to concerns of academic autonomy when it abandoned the exemption for educational institutions.

The effect of the elimination of this exemption was to expose tenure determinations to the same enforcement procedures applicable to other employment decisions. The Commission's enforcement responsibilities are triggered by the filing of a specific sworn charge of discrimination. The Act obligates the Commission to investigate a charge of discrimination to determine whether there is "reasonable cause to believe that the charge is true." 42 U.S.C. § 2000e–5(b) (1982 ed.). If it finds no such reasonable cause, the Commission is directed to dismiss the charge. If it does find reasonable cause, the Commission shall "endeavor to eliminate [the] alleged unlawful employment practice by informal methods of conference, conciliation, and persuasion." Ibid. If attempts at voluntary resolution fail, the Commission may bring an action against the employer. § 2000e–5(f)(1).

To enable the Commission to make informed decisions at each stage of the enforcement process, § 2000e–8(a) confers a broad right of access to relevant evidence:

"The Commission or its designated representative shall at all reasonable times have access to, for the purposes of examination, and the right to copy any evidence of any person being investigated ... that relates to unlawful employment practices covered by [the Act] and is relevant to the charge under investigation."

If an employer refuses to provide this information voluntarily, the Act authorizes the Commission to issue a subpoena and to seek an order enforcing it.

On their face, §§ 2000e–8(a) and 2000e–9 do not carve out any special privilege relating to peer review materials, despite the fact that Congress undoubtedly was aware, when it extended Title VII's coverage, of the potential burden that access to such material might create. Moreover, we have noted previously that when a court is asked to enforce a Commission subpoena, its responsibility is to "satisfy itself that the charge is valid and that the material requested is 'relevant' to the charge ... and [* * *19] more generally to assess any contentions by the employer that the demand for information is too indefinite or has been made for an illegitimate purpose." It is not then to determine "whether the charge of discrimination is 'well founded' or 'verifiable.' " EEOC v. Shell Oil Co., 466 U.S., at 72, n. 26.

The University concedes that the information sought by the Commission in this case passes the relevance test set forth in Shell Oil. Petitioner argues, nevertheless, that Title VII affirmatively grants courts the discretion to require more than relevance in order to protect tenure-review documents. Although petitioner recognizes that Title VII gives the Commission broad "power to seek access to all evidence that may be 'relevant to the charge under investigation,' " Brief for Petitioner 38 (emphasis added), it contends that Title VII's subpoena enforcement provisions do not give the Commission an unqualified right to acquire such evidence. Id., at 38–41. This interpretation simply cannot be reconciled with the plain language of the text of § 2000e–8(a), which states that the Commission "shall ... have access" to "relevant" evidence. The provision can be read only as giving the Commission a right to obtain that evidence, not a mere license to seek it.

Although the text of the access provisions thus provides no privilege, Congress did address situations in which an employer may have an interest in the confidentiality of its records. The same § 2000e–8 which gives the Commission access to any evidence relevant to its investigation also makes it "unlawful for any officer or employee of the Commission to make public in any manner whatever any information obtained by the Commission pursuant to its authority under this section prior to the institution of any proceeding" under the Act. A violation of this provision subjects the employee to criminal penalties. Ibid. To be sure, the protection of confidentiality that § 2000e–8(e) provides is less than complete.[1] But this, if anything, weakens petitioner's argument. Congress apparently considered the issue of confidentiality, and it provided a modicum of protection. Petitioner urges us to go further than Congress thought necessary to safeguard that value, that is, to strike the balance differently from the one Congress adopted. Petitioner, however, does not offer any persuasive justification for that suggestion.

---

1. The prohibition on Commission disclosure does not apply, for example, to the charging party. See EEOC v. Associated Dry Goods Corp., 449 U.S. 590, 598–604 (1981).

We readily agree with petitioner that universities and colleges play significant roles in American society. Nor need we question, at this point, petitioner's assertion that confidentiality is important to the proper functioning of the peer review process under which many academic institutions operate. The costs that ensue from disclosure, however, constitute only one side of the balance. As Congress has recognized, the costs associated with racial and sexual discrimination in institutions of higher learning are very substantial. Few would deny that ferreting out this kind of invidious discrimination is a great, if not compelling, governmental interest. Often, as even petitioner seems to admit, see Reply Brief for Petitioner 15, disclosure of peer review materials will be necessary in order for the Commission to determine whether illegal discrimination has taken place. Indeed, if there is a "smoking gun" to be found that demonstrates discrimination in tenure decisions, it is likely to be tucked away in peer review files. The Court of Appeals for the Third Circuit expressed it this way:

> "Clearly, an alleged perpetrator of discrimination cannot be allowed to pick and choose the evidence which may be necessary for an agency investigation. There may be evidence of discriminatory intent and of pretext in the confidential notes and memoranda which the [college] seeks to protect. Likewise, confidential material pertaining to other candidates for tenure in a similar time frame may demonstrate that persons with lesser qualifications were granted tenure or that some pattern of discrimination appears.... The peer review material itself must be investigated to determine whether the evaluations are based in discrimination and whether they are reflected in the tenure decision." EEOC v. Franklin and Marshall College, 775 F.2d, at 116 (emphasis deleted).

Moreover, we agree with the EEOC that the adoption of a requirement that the Commission demonstrate a "specific reason for disclosure," see Brief for Petitioner 46, beyond a showing of relevance, would place a substantial litigation-producing obstacle in the way of the Commission's efforts to investigate and remedy alleged discrimination. A university faced with a disclosure request might well utilize the privilege in a way that frustrates the EEOC's mission. We are reluctant to "place a potent weapon in the hands of employers who have no interest in complying voluntarily with the Act, who wish instead to delay as long as possible investigations by the EEOC." EEOC v. Shell Oil Co., 466 U.S., at 81.

Acceptance of petitioner's claim would also lead to a wave of similar privilege claims by other employers who play significant roles in furthering speech and learning in society. What of writers, publishers, musicians, lawyers? It surely is not unreasonable to believe, for example, that confidential peer reviews play an important part in partnership determinations at some law firms. We perceive no limiting principle in petitioner's argument. Accordingly, we stand behind the breakwater Congress has established: unless specifically provided otherwise in the statute, the EEOC may obtain "relevant" evidence. Congress has made the choice. If it dislikes the result, it of course may revise the statute.

Finally, we see nothing in our precedents that supports petitioner's claim. In United States v. Nixon, 418 U.S. 683 (1974), upon which petitioner relies, we recognized a qualified privilege for Presidential communications. It is true that in fashioning this privilege we noted the importance of confidentiality in certain contexts:

> "Human experience teaches that those who expect public dissemination of their remarks may well temper candor with a concern for appearances and

for their own interests to the detriment of the decisionmaking process." Id., at 705.

But the privilege we recognized in Nixon was grounded in the separation of powers between the Branches of the Federal Government. "The privilege can be said to derive from the supremacy of each branch within its own assigned area of constitutional duties. Certain powers and privileges flow from the nature of enumerated powers; the protection of the confidentiality of Presidential communications has similar constitutional underpinnings" Id., at 705–706 As we discuss below, petitioner's claim of privilege lacks similar constitutional foundation.

In Douglas Oil Co. of Cal. v. Petrol Stops Northwest, 441 U.S. 211 (1979), the Court recognized the privileged nature of grand jury proceedings. We noted there that the rule of secrecy dated back to the 17th century, was imported into our federal common law, and was eventually codified in Federal Rule of Criminal Procedure 6(e) as "an integral part of our criminal justice system." 441 U.S., at 218, n. 9. Similarly, in Clark v. United States, 289 U.S. 1, 13 (1933), the Court recognized a privilege for the votes and deliberations of a petit jury, noting that references to the privilege "bear with them the implications of an immemorial tradition." More recently, in NLRB v. Sears, Roebuck & Co., 421 U.S. 132 (1975), we construed an exception to the Freedom of Information Act in which Congress had incorporated a well-established privilege for deliberative intraagency documents. A privilege for peer review materials has no similar historical or statutory basis.

B

As noted above, petitioner characterizes its First Amendment claim as one of "academic freedom." Petitioner begins its argument by focusing our attention upon language in prior cases acknowledging the crucial role universities play in the dissemination of ideas in our society and recognizing "academic freedom" as a "special concern of the First Amendment." Keyishian v. Board of Regents of University of New York, 385 U.S. 589, 603 (1967). In that case the Court said:

> "Our Nation is deeply committed to safeguarding academic freedom, which is of transcendent value to all of us and not merely to the teachers concerned." See also Adler v. Board of Education of City of New York, 342 U.S. 485, 511 (1952) (academic freedom is central to "the pursuit of truth which the First Amendment was designed to protect" (Douglas, J., dissenting)). Petitioner places special reliance on Justice Frankfurter's opinion, concurring in the result, in Sweezy v. New Hampshire, 354 U.S. 234, 263 (1957), where the Justice recognized that one of "four essential freedoms" that a university possesses under the First Amendment is the right to "determine for itself on academic grounds who may teach."

Petitioner contends that it exercises this right of determining "on academic grounds who may teach" through the process of awarding tenure. A tenure system, asserts petitioner, determines what the university will look like over time. "In making tenure decisions, therefore, a university is doing nothing less than shaping its own identity." Brief for Petitioner 19.

Petitioner next maintains that the peer review process is the most important element in the effective operation of a tenure system. A properly functioning tenure system requires the faculty to obtain candid and detailed written evaluations of the candidate's scholarship, both from the candidate's peers at the university and from scholars at other institutions. These evaluations, says petitioner, traditionally have been provided with express or implied assurances of confidentiality. It is confidentiality that ensures candor and enables an institution to make its tenure decisions on the basis of valid academic criteria.

Building from these premises, petitioner claims that requiring the disclosure of peer review evaluations on a finding of mere relevance will undermine the existing process of awarding tenure, and therefore will result in a significant infringement of petitioner's First Amendment right of academic freedom. As more and more peer evaluations are disclosed to the EEOC and become public, a "chilling effect" on candid evaluations and discussions of candidates will result. And as the quality of peer review evaluations declines, tenure committees will no longer be able to rely on them. "This will work to the detriment of universities, as less qualified persons achieve tenure causing the quality of instruction and scholarship to decline." Id., at 35. Compelling disclosure of materials "also will result in divisiveness and tension, placing strain on faculty relations and impairing the free interchange of ideas that is a hallmark of academic freedom." Ibid. The prospect of these deleterious effects on American colleges and universities, concludes petitioner, compels recognition of a First Amendment privilege.

In our view, petitioner's reliance on the so-called academic-freedom cases is somewhat misplaced. In those cases government was attempting to control or direct the content of the speech engaged in by the university or those affiliated with it. In Sweezy, for example, the Court invalidated the conviction of a person found in contempt for refusing to answer questions about the content of a lecture he had delivered at a state university. Similarly, in Keyishian, the Court invalidated a network of state laws that required public employees, including teachers at state universities, to make certifications with respect to their membership in the Communist Party. When, in those cases, the Court spoke of "academic freedom" and the right to determine on "academic grounds who may teach" the Court was speaking in reaction to content-based regulation.

Fortunately, we need not define today the precise contours of any academic-freedom right against governmental attempts to influence the content of academic speech through the selection of faculty or by other means, because petitioner does not allege that the Commission's subpoenas are intended to or will in fact direct the content of university discourse toward or away from particular subjects or points of view. Instead, as noted above, petitioner claims that the "quality of instruction and scholarship [will] decline" as a result of the burden EEOC subpoenas place on the peer review process.

Also, the cases upon which petitioner places emphasis involved direct infringements on the asserted right to "determine for itself on academic grounds who may teach." In Keyishian, for example, government was attempting to substitute its teaching employment criteria for those already in place at the academic institutions, directly and completely usurping the discretion of each institution. In contrast, the EEOC subpoena at issue here effects no such usurpation. The Commission is not providing criteria that petitioner must use in selecting teachers. Nor is it preventing the University from using any criteria it may wish to use, except those—including race, sex, and national origin—that are proscribed under Title VII. In keeping with Title VII's [*199] preservation of employers' remaining freedom of choice, see Price Waterhouse v. Hopkins, 490 U.S. 228 (1989) (plurality opinion), courts have stressed the importance of avoiding second-guessing of legitimate academic judgments. This Court itself has cautioned that "judges ... asked to review the substance of a genuinely academic decision ... should show great respect for the faculty's professional judgment." Regents of University of Michigan v. Ewing, 474 U.S.

214, 225 (1985). Nothing we say today should be understood as a retreat from this principle of respect for legitimate academic decisionmaking.

In addition to being remote and attenuated, the injury to academic freedom claimed by petitioner is also speculative. As the EEOC points out, confidentiality is not the norm in all peer review systems. See, e. g., G. Bednash, The Relationship Between Access and Selectivity in Tenure Review Outcomes (1989) (unpublished Ph.D. dissertation, University of Maryland). Moreover, some disclosure of peer evaluations would take place even if petitioner's "special necessity" test were adopted. Thus, the "chilling effect" petitioner fears is at most only incrementally worsened by the absence of a privilege. Finally, we are not so ready as petitioner seems to be to assume the worst about those in the academic community. Although it is possible that some evaluators may become less candid as the possibility of disclosure increases, others may simply ground their evaluations in specific examples and illustrations in order to deflect potential claims of bias or unfairness. Not all academics will hesitate to stand up and be counted when they evaluate their peers.

Because we conclude that the EEOC subpoena process does not infringe any First Amendment right enjoyed by petitioner, the EEOC need not demonstrate any special justification to sustain the constitutionality of Title VII as applied to tenure peer review materials in general or to the subpoena involved in this case. Accordingly, we need not address the Commission's alternative argument that any infringement of petitioner's First Amendment rights is permissible because of the substantial relation between the Commission's request and the overriding and compelling state interest in eradicating invidious discrimination.[2]

The judgment of the Court of Appeals is affirmed.

It is so ordered.

NOTES

1. Claims that the confidentiality of communications in certain kinds of internal processes of institutions should be protected by privileges have been made in two different types of contexts—in connection with the peer evaluation process in institutional settings and in connection with the self-evaluative or self-analysis processes in which institutions engage. The two specific contexts in which a peer review privilege has been argued for are the process by which academics are evaluated for tenure or promotion in university and other school settings, and the process by which medical personnel are evaluated for hospital privileges.

2. Prior to the decision in the principal case, a number of courts had recognized a qualified privilege in the academic setting, balancing the claims for confidentiality with the need to give a plaintiff in a discrimination case "a fair opportunity to uncover evidence necessary to establishing a prima facie case of discrimination." See, e.g., Gray v. Board of Higher Education, 692 F.2d 901 (2d Cir.1982); while others rejected creation of such a privilege. See In re Dinnan, 661 F.2d 426 (5th Cir.1981). Also see EEOC v. University of Notre Dame Du Lac, 715 F.2d 331 (7th Cir.1983); Zaustinsky v. University of California, 96 F.R.D. 622 (N.D.Cal.1983), aff'd 782 F.2d 1055 (9th Cir.1985).

2. We also do not consider the question, not passed upon by the Court of Appeals, whether the District Court's enforcement of the Commission's subpoena will allow petitioner to redact information from the contested materials before disclosing them.

3. Absent a statute (see, e.g. 42 U.S.C. §§ 11101(5), 11137(b)), many courts have generally not been receptive to the claim for a peer review privilege in the hospital setting, see Robinson v. Magovern, 83 F.R.D. 79 (W.D.Pa.1979); also see Memorial Hospital v. Shadur, 664 F.2d 1058 (7th Cir.1981). But some district courts have recognized such a privilege in cases involving alleged medical malpractice. See Mewborn v. Heckler, 101 F.R.D. 691 (D.D.C.1984). Bredice v. Doctors hospital, Inc., 50 F.R.D. 249 (D.D.C.), aff'd, 156 U.S.App. D.C. 199, 479 F.2d 920 (D.C.Cir.1973). Is there a stronger basis for an academic peer view privilege than for a comparable privilege in the hospital setting? See Bredice, supra, 50 F.R.D. at 250 where it is stated that the medical peer review process "is a sine qua non of adequate hospital care." What follows from that proposition? Also see United States v. Harris Methodist Fort Worth, 970 F.2d 94 (5th Cir.1992).

4. In the absence of a privilege, the focus of an academic institution trying to protect the confidentiality of extramural evaluators of a faculty candidate for promotion is likely to be on possibility of redacting the identity of the evaluators from the documents being provided. See footnote 2 in the principal case, supra. Is redaction of the identity of the evaluators while providing their evaluations a reasonable alternative? How important is it for a reviewing agency or a court to know who said what as opposed to what was the evaluation? The University of California, for example, in the wake of the decision in the principal case adopted detailed provisions making available to candidates for promotion the materials in their files but nevertheless maintaining the confidentiality of the identity of the extramural evaluators by redacting their names and institutions from the relevant documents. See University of California, Academic Personnel Manual, sections 160–20b., c. and 220–80–d, e, h, and i. (1992)

The Supreme Court in the principal case was skeptical about the argument of the university that unless the identity of the evaluators were protected they would be unwilling to participate in the peer review process. After the decision in the principal case, what can be done to try to ensure the continuing participation of extramural evaluators in university peer review processes?

Suppose the EEOC opposes redaction and the courts support the agency position. If you represent the university, what would you do next? Consider the following excerpt from the United States v. Harris Methodist Fort Worth case, supra:

> HHS [the federal reviewing agency] has also agreed that the district court could issue an appropriate order tailoring the scope of any compliance review and establishing particular requirements to protect sensitive documents. If HHS continues to pursue this type of compliance review, its targets are always free to seek the assistance of the courts when necessary to protect restricted access materials.

5. See generally, Case Comment, An Academic Freedom Privilege in the Peer Review Context: In re Dinnan and Gray v. Board of Higher Education, 36 Rutgers L.Rev. 286 (1986); Note, The Challenge to Antidiscrimination Enforcement on Campus: Consideration of an Academic Freedom Privilege, 57 St. John's L.Rev. 546 (1983); Smith, Protecting the Confidentiality of Faculty Peer Review Records: Department of Labor v. The University of California, 8 J. Coll. & Univ. L. 20 (1981); Academic Peer Review Privilege in Federal Court, 85 ALR Fed. 691 (1987), Horowitz, The Authority of the University of California Under the State Constitution, 25 UCLA L.Rev. 23, 45, n. 59 (1977).

Also see Paulsen, Reverse Discrimination and Law School Faculty Hiring,: The Undiscovered Opinion, 71 Tex. L.Rev. 993 (1993); Pacholski, Title VII in the University: The Difference Academic Freedom Makes, 59 U. Chi. L. Rev. 1317 (1992).

6. Should internal reports prepared by an institution to evaluate its performance—so-called critical self-analysis—be protected by a privilege? Compare Bredice v. Doctors Hospital, Inc., 479 F.2d 920 (D.C.Cir.1973) with Resnick v. American Dental Association, 95 F.R.D. 372 (N.D.Ill.1982). Also see Bergman v. Kemp, 97 F.R.D. 413 (W.D.Mich.1983). And see California Evidence Code, §§ 1156–1157.7.

6. See generally, Bush, Comment: Stimulating Corporate Self–Regulation— The Corporate Self–Evaluative Privilege, 87 Nw. U. L. Rev. 597 (1993); Note, The Privilege of Self–Critical Analysis, 96 Harv.L.Rev. 1083 (1983); Flanagan, Rejecting a General Privilege for Self–Critical Analyses, 51 Geo.Wash.L.Rev. 551 (1983); Ranck, Critical Self–Analysis: When Are the Findings Privileged Material? Nat. L.J. p. 28–29, March 23, 1987.

B.   GOVERNMENT INFORMATION—EXECUTIVE PRIVILEGE

There are several different categories of information subject to treatment under this heading: state secrets—i.e., information disclosure of which would be harmful to the national defense or international relations of the country; various forms of official information—e.g., communications to the government, internal governmental memoranda, law enforcement investigatory files; and the special category of presidential conversations (which, of course, involves confidentiality needs that inhere in a relationship but is conveniently treated along with executive privilege generally). The subject is complex, and the following discussion only highlights the principal issues and some of the leading authorities.

1.   STATE SECRETS

There is general agreement that a testimonial privilege applies to certain categories of military information and diplomatic secrets. The rationale, of course, is that disclosure of certain types of governmental secrets would cause serious harm to the national interest, and the risk of that harm outweighs a litigant's need for the information. The difficult question, where the government claims executive privilege on the ground that secrets of that nature are involved, is whether the court may examine the materials in camera to determine the validity of the claim. The alternative, of course, would be that the mere statement of such a claim by the government would bar disclosure to a litigant.

Several Supreme Court cases bear on this issue. In United States v. Reynolds, 345 U.S. 1 (1953), widows of three civilians who died in a B–29 airplane crash sued the government under the Federal Tort Claims Act. During the pretrial stage they moved for production of the Air Force's accident investigation report and the official statements taken from the surviving crew members. The government moved to quash, claiming privilege, alleging inter alia that the aircraft had been engaged in "a highly secret mission of the Air Force," and that the demanded material could not be furnished "without seriously hampering national security, flying safety and the development of highly technical and secret military equipment." The district court decision ordering the Government to produce the documents for examination by the court so it could determine whether they contained privileged matter was affirmed by the Court of Appeals and then reversed by the Supreme Court, applying "the privilege against revealing military secrets, a privilege which is well established in the law of evidence."

The Court described the procedure to be applied by a trial court in connection with the claim of such a privilege. First, the Court indicated that there must be a formal claim of privilege personally passed upon by the head of the government department concerned. Second, the Court, in terms somewhat confusing, elaborated upon the question whether the trial court could examine the documents sought:

The court itself must determine whether the circumstances are appropriate for the claim of privilege, and yet do so without forcing a disclosure of the very thing the privilege is designed to protect. ... We find it helpful to draw upon judicial experience in dealing with an analogous privilege, the privilege against self-incrimination. ...

Judicial control over the evidence ... cannot be abdicated to the caprice of executive officers. Yet we will not go so far as to say that the court may automatically require a complete disclosure to the judge before the claim of privilege will be accepted. ... It may be possible to satisfy the court, from all the circumstances of the case, that there is a reasonable danger that compulsion of the evidence will expose military matters which, in the interest of national security should not be divulged. When this is the case ... the court should not jeopardize the security which the privilege is meant to protect by insisting upon an examination of the evidence, even by the judge alone in chambers.

In the instant case we cannot escape judicial notice that this is a time of vigorous preparation for national defense. ... Certainly there was a reasonable danger that the accident investigation report would contain references to the secret electronic equipment which was the primary concern of the mission.

[W]hen the formal claim of privilege was filed by the Secretary of the Air Force, under circumstances indicating a reasonable possibility that military secrets were involved, there was certainly a sufficient showing of privilege to cut off further demand for the documents on the showing of necessity for its compulsion that had then been made.

In each case, the showing of necessity which is made will determine how far the court should probe in satisfying itself that the occasion for invoking the privilege is appropriate. Where there is a strong showing of necessity, the claim of privilege should not be lightly accepted, but even the most compelling necessity cannot overcome the claim of privilege if the court is ultimately satisfied that military secrets are at stake. Id. 345 U.S. 1, 8–11.

Query: What is the significance of the Court's reference to the "analogous privilege ... against self-incrimination"? Does the clause in the very first sentence quoted above, "without forcing a disclosure of the very thing the privilege is designed to protect" mean that the court must always rule on the claim of privilege without examining the documents? If so, is it inconsistent with all of the quoted material that follows? If it does not mean this, what might it mean? In some cases, is the court supposed to decide upon the claim without regard to any showing of need for the documents by the party seeking them? If so, in what types of cases? How can the judge determine the danger to national security that disclosure might pose without knowing what might be disclosed? How can the judge decide how much necessity there is for the information contained in the documents sought without knowing what they contain? Under Reynolds, who in the final analysis has control of the determination of whether the documents contain state secrets, the court or the executive? See generally Zagel, The State Secrets Privilege, 50 Minn.L.Rev. 875

(1966); Hardin, Executive Privilege in the Federal Courts, 71 Yale L.J. 879 (1962); J.B. Weinstein & M. A. Berger, 2 Weinstein's Evidence ¶ 509[04].

Does proposed Federal Rule 509 capture the essence of the doctrine of United States v. Reynolds? How do the Mink and Nixon cases, descriptions of which follow, affect the answers to the foregoing questions?

The Supreme Court's decision in Environmental Protection Agency v. Mink, 410 U.S. 73, 81 (1973), involved a suit under the Freedom of Information Act to obtain information relating to a scheduled underground nuclear test. The Government inter alia invoked the state secret exemption under the Act. A majority of the Court interpreting the Act ruled that the exemption provided for state secrets in the Act precluded in camera examination by the court of documents classified top secret or secret.

Dicta in United States v. Nixon, 418 U.S. 683 (1974) should also be taken into account:

> Absent a claim of need to protect military, diplomatic or sensitive national security secrets, we find it difficult to accept the argument that even the very important interest in confidentiality of presidential communications is significantly diminished by production of such material for in camera inspection with all the protection that a district court will be obliged to provide.

> ... "[The President] ... does not place his claim of privilege on the ground they are military or diplomatic secrets. As to those areas of Art. II duties the Courts have traditionally shown the utmost deference to presidential responsibilities." [citing and quoting from C & S Airline v. Waterman Steamship Lines, 333 U.S. 103, 111, 68 S.Ct. 431, 436, 92 L.Ed. 568 (1948) regarding the President's role as Commander-in-Chief and in regard to foreign affairs and also from the language in United States v. Reynolds, supra, indicating that when the court is satisfied that there is "a reasonable danger" of exposure of military secrets, the court should not insist upon in chambers examination].

See also footnote 21 in the Opinion at United States v. Nixon, 418 U.S. 683, 714, 94 S.Ct. 3090, 3110–3111, 41 L.Ed.2d 1039 (1974). Does United States v. Nixon raise the state secrets privilege to constitutional status? For a case describing a procedure to be followed in dealing with state secrets claims of privilege, see In re "Agent Orange" Product Liability Litigation, 97 F.R.D. 427, 436–438 (E.D.N.Y.1983).

The Classified Information Procedures Act, P.L. 96–456, Oct. 15, 1980 (see 4 U.S.Code Cong. and Admin.News, 96th Cong., 2d Sess.1980, at p. 4294) provides inter alia, detailed procedures governing criminal defendants' attempts through discovery to obtain classified information. Provision is made for a hearing by the court to be held upon request of the government to make "determinations concerning the use, relevance, or admissibility of classified information." Such a hearing is to be held in camera "if the Attorney General certifies to the court ... that a public proceeding may result in the disclosure of classified information." The statute also authorizes as a substitute for disclosure of classified information a statement admitting facts the classified information would tend to prove or a summary of the classified information, provided that the court finds "that the statement or summary will provide the defendant with substantially the same ability to make his defense as would disclosure of the specific classified information." The statute also requires the Chief Justice of the United States in consultation with named government officials to prescribe rules establishing procedures for protection against unauthorized disclosure of classified information in the custody of the courts and requires the Attorney General to issue guidelines specifying factors governing decisions to prosecute in cases where classified information may be involved. See generally Tamanaha, A Critical Review of the Classified Information Procedures Act, 13 Am.J.Crim.L. 277 (1986).

2. PRESIDENTIAL COMMUNICATIONS

United States v. Nixon, supra, involved the question of whether a privilege based in the Constitution attaches to confidential conversations between the President and his advisors, and, if so, whether the privilege is absolute.

The issue in Nixon arose as a result of a third party subpoena duces tecum issued by the district court on motion of the Special Prosecutor in a criminal prosecution charging seven persons with various crimes growing out of the Watergate scandal and naming the President among others as an unindicted conspirator. The Court, inter alia, ruled that a constitutionally based privilege does attach to a presidential conversation derived "from the supremacy of each branch within its own assigned area of constitutional duties," but that such a privilege in the context of the kind of claim for confidentiality made is not absolute and unqualified:

> To read the Art. II powers of the President as providing an absolute privilege as against a subpoena essential to enforcement of criminal statutes on no more than a generalized claim of the public interest in confidentiality of non-military and nondiplomatic discussions would upset the constitutional balance of "a workable government" and gravely impair the role of the courts under Art. III. Nixon, supra 418 U.S. 683, 707.

The Court went on to conclude the presidential need for the confidentiality of his conversations justified a presumptive privilege for presidential communications "inextricably rooted in the separation of powers under the Constitution." The Court was at pains, however, to emphasize that the materials at issue were sought in a criminal trial:

> We are not here concerned with the balance between the President's generalized interest in confidentiality and the need for relevant evidence in civil litigation, nor with that between the confidentiality interest and congressional demands for information, nor with the President's interest in preserving state secrets. Id. 418 U.S. 683, 712 (1974).

And "[t]he right to the production of all evidence at a criminal trial similarly has constitutional dimensions. ... The generalized assertion of privilege must yield to the demonstrated, specific need for evidence in a pending criminal trial." The burden is on the party seeking the material to make a sufficient showing to rebut the presumption of privilege and to justify the district court in ordering an in camera inspection of the subpoenaed material. In connection with that in camera inspection, the district court is to take extreme care to see to it that presidential conversations not relevant or admissible are not revealed.

Relying generally on the principles articulated in United States v. Nixon, supra, the Eighth Circuit held in In re Grand Jury Subpoena Duces Tecum, 112 F.3d 910 (8th Cir.1997) that the Office of the President (in this instance in a matter involving the President's wife) may not invoke the attorney-client privilege to withhold documents sought under a federal grand jury subpoena.

3. OFFICIAL INFORMATION

Communications to and within the government are covered under this heading. The rationale for extending privileged status generally to such material is that unless confidentiality is assured, fear of disclosure will inhibit those who make such communications. Both the proposed Federal Rule 509 and the Freedom of Information Act exemption provisions, 5 U.S.C. § 552(b) deal with the subject in a tangled and inter-related fashion. Recent decisions, however, suggest that where information is sought in a litigation context, "the authorization for barring disclosure will in each instance have its origin in a source outside the Freedom of Information Act since that Act is exclusively a disclosure statute." J. B. Weinstein & M. A. Berger, 2 Weinstein's Evidence ¶ 509[06].

The approach taken in United States v. Nixon is not irrelevant to the official information topic although the constitutional basis for that decision focuses on the President's unique position. Nevertheless, one would expect a similar type of balancing of the public interest in confidentiality against the public interest in disclosure of the information sought,the approach reflected in Rule 509. "A court is authorized to admit official information if in the particular case the public's interest in the correct determination of the truth outweighs the public's interest in effective operations." Id. at ¶ 509[05].

For a detailed discussion of the various categories of official information, particularly intragovernmental recommendations and investigatory files compiled for law enforcement purposes, under both the proposed Federal Rule and the FOIA, see J. B. Weinstein and M. A. Berger, 2 Weinstein's Evidence ¶ 509[07].

The type of privilege that arises under this heading has sometimes been referred to as the deliberative process privilege. See Kinoy v. Mitchell, 67 F.R.D. 1 (S.D.N.Y.1975) and In re "Agent Orange" Product Liability Litigation, 97 F.R.D. 427 (E.D.N.Y.1983). It has been suggested that this privilege applies only to material reflecting the deliberative process—"evaluations, expressions of opinions and recommendations on policy matters," 97 F.R.D. at 434, and not to "raw data and factual findings." Ibid.

In general, a court in ruling on a claim of privilege under this heading may examine the materials sought in camera. See Black v. Sheraton Corp. of America, 564 F.2d 531 (D.C.Cir.1977); In Carl Zeiss Stiftung v. V.E.B. Carl Zeiss, Jena, 40 F.R.D. 318 (D.D.C.1966), aff'd, 384 F.2d 979 (D.C.Cir.1967).

A type of government information protected against disclosure in many jurisdictions that merits special mention relates to grand jury proceedings. See Rule 6(e) of the Federal Rules of Criminal Procedure. Rule 6(e)(3)(C)(i) and (ii) provide for disclosure "when so directed by the court preliminarily to or in connection with a judicial proceeding," and "when permitted by the court at the request of the defendant, upon a showing that grounds may exist for a motion to dismiss the indictment because of matters occurring before the grand jury." The ban against disclosure of grand jury testimony applies to the U.S. Attorney, any grand juror, court reporter or any other person who knew of the witness's testimony. See In re 1979 Grand Jury Subpoena, 478 F.Supp. 59 (D.La.1979). However, generally it does not apply to the witness with respect to his own testimony before the grand jury. See In re Investigation Before April 1975 Grand Jury, 531 F.2d 600 (D.C.Cir.1976). Suppose a state statute bars a grand jury witness from disclosing his own testimony even after the term of the grand jury has ended. Held: Such a statutory bar violates the First Amendment. Butterworth v. Smith, 494 U.S. 624 (1990).

It has been suggested that requests for disclosure are being granted more frequently than in the past. See J. B. Weinstein & M. A. Berger, Weinstein's Evidence ¶ 501[04]. Some courts have indicated that once an indictment has been handed down, disclosure may more freely be made. See State of Wisconsin v. Schaffer, 565 F.2d 961 (7th Cir.1977). However, the Supreme Court has stated, "[I]n considering the effects of disclosure on grand jury proceedings, the courts must consider not only the immediate effects upon a particular grand jury, but also the possible effect upon the function of future grand juries." Douglas Oil Co. of California v. Petrol Stops Northwest, 441 U.S. 211, 222 (1979).

In United States v. Sells Engineering, Inc., 463 U.S. 418 (1983), the Court ruled that the government must demonstrate a particularized need before it can disclose grand jury materials to Justice Department attorneys who were not involved in the grand jury proceedings. Subsequently, it ruled that government attorneys who were involved in the grand jury proceedings may continue to use the materials in a later civil matter—that such continued use is not "disclosure" within the meaning of Rule 6(e) and therefore does not require judicial approval. United States v. John Doe, Inc. I, 481 U.S. 102 (1987).

4. THE GOVERNMENT AS A PARTY–LITIGANT—SUSTAINING A CLAIM OF PRIVILEGE

A claim of executive privilege by the government where it is a litigant poses special problems. Compare the varying treatment of the consequences of a claim of privilege by a litigant in connection with the other evidentiary privileges considered in these materials. For example, in a lawsuit brought by a client against his attorney for breach of duty, the attorney-client privilege does not apply. Proposed Federal Rule 503(d)(3). Where the patient tenders an issue as to his condition in a lawsuit, there is no physician-patient privilege with respect to communications relevant to an issue concerning the patient's condition. California Evidence Code § 996. Where the accused in a criminal case raises the insanity defense, he waives his attorney-client privilege as to communications to a psychiatrist engaged by his attorney. People v. Edney, 39 N.Y.2d 620, 385 N.Y.S.2d 23, 350 N.E.2d 400 (1976).

The government may be a party in several ways—as a plaintiff in civil proceedings, as the prosecutor in criminal proceedings or as a defendant where it has consented to be sued. May the government as a litigant deprive its adversary of relevant information by claiming some form of executive privilege? The answer varies with the government's position in the litigation. Where the government is the criminal prosecutor, it would be unfair for it to institute prosecution and then deprive the defendant of material evidence, see United States v. Reynolds, 345 U.S. 1, 12 (1953), and dismissal of the prosecution may be appropriate if the government persists in its claim of privilege. Other less drastic remedies may be appropriate where the withheld information is not so crucial to the defense. Thus the new Classified Information Procedures Act, supra p. 1578, provides that where disclosure of classified information sought by a criminal defendant is barred, the court may order dismissal of the charges, or dismissal of particular counts, or a "finding against the United States on any issue as to which the excluded classified information relates" or the "striking or precluding all or part of the testimony of a witness." See J. B. Weinstein and M. A. Berger, 2 Weinstein's Evidence ¶ 509[10]. Similarly, where the Government is a civil plaintiff, the same approach may be appropriate although it has been suggested that a distinction might be drawn between cases where a civil suit is brought by the government to punish or regulate and where the government is suing in a proprietary capacity. Ibid. Where the Government is a defendant in a civil suit it will certainly not as a result of its claim of privilege automatically lose the case although the court may draw an inference adverse to the government's position on the particular fact in issue. Compare McCormick, Evidence 268 (3d ed., Cleary, 1984) with J. B. Weinstein & M. A. Berger, 2 Weinstein's Evidence ¶ 509[10]. See proposed Federal Rule 509(e) and consider California Evidence Code § 1040(b)(2): "... In determining whether disclosure of the information is against the public interest, the interest of the public entity as a party in the outcome of the proceeding may not be considered."

SECTION 8.   CONFLICTS

NOTES

1. The basic approach of the Federal Rules is to establish a uniform set of evidentiary rules for the federal courts. This is a change from the pattern of partial conformity with state practice that existed prior to enactment of the Rules. The only general exceptions to the uniformity approach are found in Rules 501 and 601 which in specified contexts (see below) provide that state doctrine relating to a privilege or competency of a witness is to be applied. State law relating to an evidentiary issue may also be applied in certain special contexts. For example: "A number of states ... have enacted product liability legislation which contains an exclusionary rule for subsequent repairs. In diversity cases, Erie concerns should require that these statutes be given effect because of their largely substantive content." J.B. Weinstein & M.A. Berger, Weinstein's Evidence ¶ 407[03]. See generally Weinstein, The Uniformity-Conformity Dilemma Facing Draftsmen of Federal Rules of Evidence, 69 Colum.L.Rev. 353 (1969).

2. The draft of the proposed Federal Rules of Evidence prepared by the Advisory Committee of the Judicial Conference contained detailed provisions covering the subject of privileges. Among the various objections made to these provisions was the concern that state evidentiary privileges would not be honored in the federal courts. See J. B. Weinstein and M. A. Berger, 2 Weinstein's Evidence ¶ 501[01] at 501–515. For a careful analysis of the reasoning underlying the Advisory Committee's approach and the implications, policies and legal issues associated with that approach see id. at ¶ 501[06].

3. Rule 501 as enacted by Congress provided that privileges "shall be governed by the principles of the common law as they may be interpreted by the courts of the United States in the light of reason and experience." But "in civil actions and proceedings, with respect to an element of a claim or defense as to which State law supplies the rule of decision" privileges are to "be determined in accordance with State law." The impact of the first clause of Rule 501 is to make existing federal privilege law applicable in criminal cases and federal question cases except those governed by the second clause of the Rule. Id. at 501–520.

4. Various questions arise in connection with the interpretation and application of the second clause of Rule 501. Although there are some contrary indications in the legislative history, the Conference Report provided:

If an item of proof tends to support or defeat a claim or defense, or an element of a claim or defense, and if state law supplies the rule of decision for that claim or defense, then state privilege law applies to that item of proof.

The Conference Report also stated:

There may be diversity cases ... where a claim or defense is based upon federal law. In such instances, federal privilege law will apply to evidence relevant to the federal claim or defense.

Finally, the Conference Report indicated that sometimes in cases where the federal court is supposed to apply federal law, "it may see fit for special reasons to give the law of a particular state highly persuasive or even controlling effect ..." [quoting from Justice Jackson's concurring opinion in D'Oench, Duhme & Co. v. FDIC, 315 U.S. 447, 471 (1942)]. The Conference Report proceeded to further characterize such situations:

When a federal court chooses to absorb state law, it is applying the state law as a matter of federal common law. Thus, state law does not supply the rule of decision (even though the federal court may apply a rule derived from state decisions), and state privilege law would not apply.

5. A federal civil proceeding may include claims based upon both state and federal law. Under Rule 501, the court may end up applying both federal and state rules of privilege to the same item of evidence, each with a different result, in the same proceeding. As Weinstein and Berger point out, this is not the ordinary situation as difficult as that may be, where evidence is admissible for one purpose and not for another. "[T]he moment privileged information is divulged the point of having the privilege is largely lost." J. B. Weinstein and M. A. Berger, 2 Weinstein's Evidence ¶ 501[02] at 501–521. How should the problem be resolved? Admit the evidence with a limiting instruction? Apply a balancing test, weighing, e.g., the need for information on the federal issue against the harm to the substantive policy underlying the state privilege? Always follow federal policy and reject the state privilege? See ibid.

6. An interesting criminal law issue involving a choice between state and federal law was presented in United States v. Pforzheimer, 826 F.2d 200 (2d Cir.1987): The question was whether a state or federal exclusionary rule should be applied in a federal court on a motion to suppress evidence where the search was conducted solely by state authorities and the state constitution provided a broader rule of protection of the individual than the federal Constitution. A dictum in a Ninth Circuit case, United States v. Henderson, 721 F.2d 662, 665 (9th Cir.1983) cert. denied 467 U.S. 1218 (1984), supported the application of the state exclusionary rule: "[T]here is much to be said for the argument that federal courts should, in the interest of comity, defer to a state's more stringent exclusionary rule with respect to evidence secured without federal involvement." But most of the other circuits have reached a contrary conclusion. See, e.g., United States v. Quinones, 758 F.2d 40 (1st Cir.1985); United States v. Montgomery, 708 F.2d 343 (8th Cir.1983). The defendant argued that if state law were not applied it would encourage forum shopping by state prosecutors. However, the court found support for its conclusion that the federal exclusionary rule should be applied in two policy considerations: the importance of uniformity of evidentiary rules among the federal courts; and the fact that if the state rule were to be applied the federal court would have to decide the breadth of the state constitutional rule.

7. Choice of law problems still arise under Rule 501 in situations where the Rule dictates that a state privilege is to be applied. The privilege of which state? A number of states may somehow be involved in the litigation—e.g., the forum state; the state whose substantive law is deemed controlling; the state where a deposition was taken invoking a claim of privilege and finally the state where the communication in question occurred. Klaxon Co. v. Stentor Electric Manufacturing Co., 313 U.S. 487 (1941) requires the application in diversity cases of the forum state's choice of law rule. Recent cases indicate that the federal courts are still applying Klaxon. For an argument that under the Federal Rules, a federal choice of laws rule should be applied, see Berger, Privileges, Presumptions and Competency of Witnesses in the Federal Court: A Federal Choice of Laws Rule, 42 Brooklyn L.Rev. 417 (1976).

The issue of whether the judge or the jury should decide the facts necessary to determine what law applies has been infrequently addressed by the courts. For a discussion of the issues and the relevant cases, see J.B. Weinstein & M.A. Berger, 1 Weinstein's Evidence ¶ 104[08]. Also see Reese, Smit & Reese, The Role of the Jury in Choice of Law, 25 Case W.L.Rev. 82 (1974).

Ghana Supply Commission v. New England Power Co.

United States District Court, District of Massachusetts, 1979.
83 F.R.D. 586.

■ GARRITY, DISTRICT JUDGE.

On October 2, 1975, plaintiff Ghana Supply Commission (hereinafter GSC), a subject of the Republic of Ghana, filed its original complaint against defendant New England Power Company (hereinafter NEPCO), a citizen of the Commonwealth of Massachusetts, to recover the unpaid portion of the sales price of fuel oil allegedly converted by NEPCO to its own use. Jurisdiction is based on diversity of citizenship, 28 U.S.C. § 1332. After nearly four years, the case, expanded to include third and fourth party defendants, is still at the discovery stage. The motions now before the court relate to a small, yet significant, segment of that discovery.

Before proceeding with the analysis of the issues, it will be helpful briefly to summarize the essential background to this litigation. On or about May, 1974, GSC entered into a contract with Trefalcon Corporation, an American oil merchant and shipper, in which GSC promised to supply residual fuel oil refined in Ghana at an agreed F.O.B. price. Trefalcon sold the oil it received to Incontrade, Inc., who in turn sold some to NEPCO. Although relations between GSC and Trefalcon began smoothly, their association gradually deteriorated over the period from August 1974 to July 1975. According to GSC, it continued to supply oil to Trefalcon, but Trefalcon failed to meet several of its obligations under the contract. In particular, GSC claims that Trefalcon did not pay for much of the oil it received.

In May 1975, Mr. J. V. Mensah assumed the position of Managing Director of GSC and, with the assistance of high level Ghanaian officials, took steps to collect on the debt owed GSC by Trefalcon. Following unsuccessful attempts to negotiate with Trefalcon for payment, GSC commenced this action against NEPCO for unlawful conversion of the fuel oil, arguing both (a) that NEPCO could not have received title to the oil because the agreed-upon procedure for transferring title from GSC to Trefalcon had not been followed and (b) that NEPCO was not a bona fide purchaser in good faith because it knew or should have known that possession of a negotiable bill of lading which Incontrade did not have, was a necessary condition to possession of title to the oil.

On August 30, 1975, the National Redemption Council of the Republic of Ghana created a Committee of Inquiry to investigate the indebtedness of Trefalcon Corporation to GSC, to explore the existence of possible fraud on the part of Ghanaians and to recommend methods for collecting the outstanding debt and sanctions against those suspected of wrongdoing. Executive Instrument 126, § 2 (August 30, 1975). The proceedings of the Committee were to be held in camera, Executive Instrument 126, § 4(3), and the Committee was expressly given power to compel attendance and testimony of witnesses. Id., at

§§ 5, 6. It appears that the testimony was recorded. Scc, Deposition of J. V. Mensah, Sept. 7, 1977, at 75. Although testimony was completed and briefs filed with the Committee by April 22, 1977, no final report has yet been issued.

NEPCO seeks to obtain by way of a request for documents, pursuant to Rule 34, Fed.R.Civ.P., by means of answers to interrogatories, and through questions on oral deposition, the content of certain documents, memoranda, reports and correspondence and the substance of testimony introduced before the Committee of Inquiry. The Republic of Ghana has asserted a limited privilege against disclosure of this information. It has produced all regular documents in its custody, possession or control which were generated in the normal course of business and which were in existence prior to the creation of the Committee of Inquiry, even though these documents may have been produced as evidence before the Committee. However, documents created solely for the Committee and all oral testimony before the Committee have been withheld pursuant to a claim of executive privilege. It is the assertion of this privilege that forms the core of the present controversy.

. . .

I.   *Choice of Law*

First there is a threshold conflicts question: whether to apply the privilege law of the United States or of Ghana. Rule 501 of the Federal Rules of Evidence guides our choice. . . .

Jurisdiction in this case is based on the diversity grant of 28 U.S.C. § 1332 since the plaintiff is "[a] foreign states or citizens or subjects thereof" and the defendant is a citizen of Massachusetts. The crux of plaintiff's claim is to recover for unlawful conversion of fuel oil, a common law tort, and there is no federal law or strong federal interest involved. Under these circumstances Erie Railroad Co. v. Tompkins, 1938, 304 U.S. 64, 58 S.Ct. 817, 82 L.Ed. 1188, mandates that state law provide the rule of decision as to claims and defenses. Fed.R.Ev., Rule 501 thus requires that we look to state law for resolution of the privilege question.

We disagree with NEPCO's arguments that United States federal law ought to apply. The cases cited to support this proposition fall into two groups. The first group includes cases like Boeing Airplane Company v. Coggeshall, D.C.Cir.1960, 108 U.S.App.D.C. 106, 280 F.2d 654, which, although based solely on diversity, were decided well before the enactment of Fed.R.Ev., Rule 501, at a time when Erie was thought not to apply to questions of privilege. In the second group are cases like Societe Internationale Etc. v. McGranery, D.D.C. 1953, 111 F.Supp. 435, mod. un oth. grds., sub nom. Societe Internationale Etc. v. Brownell, D.C.Cir.1955, 96 U.S.App.D.C. 232, 225 F.2d 532, mod. on oth. grds., sub nom., Societe Internationale v. Rogers, 1958, 357 U.S. 197, 78 S.Ct. 1087, 2 L.Ed.2d 1255, which apply federal privilege law in the context of overriding federal interests.

Having resolved the vertical conflicts problem, there remains a horizontal issue, namely, which state's law to apply. Since the purpose of Rule 501 is to create the same effect for the law of privilege as now exists for substantive law in diversity cases, H.R.Rep. No. 93–650, 93d Cong., 2d Sess., reprinted in [1974] U.S.Code Cong. & Admin.News pp. 7082–7083; H.R.Rep. No. 93–1597, 93d Cong., 2d Sess., reprinted in [1974] U.S.Code Cong. & Admin.News, pp. 7100–7101, we should follow the rule of Klaxon Co. v. Stentor Electric Manufacturing Co., Inc., 1941, 313 U.S. 487, 61 S.Ct. 1020, 85 L.Ed. 1477 and look to the conflicts law of Massachusetts, the forum state. Massachusetts applies its own law, characterizing questions of privilege as procedural. Hoadley v. Northern

Transportation Co., 1874, 115 Mass. 304, 306–307; cf., Lenn v. Riche, 1954, 331 Mass. 104, 111, 117 N.E.2d 129. See generally, K. B. Hughes, Massachusetts Practice—Evidence, § 3 (1961). Therefore, the controlling law on the subject of privilege in the instant case is that of Massachusetts, the forum state.

The choice of American as opposed to Ghanaian law comports with basic standards of fairness. GSC as plaintiff in this litigation has selected a United States forum in which to press its claims, and it is therefore only reasonable that GSC should be held to the procedural law of its chosen forum. Societe Internationale, Etc., supra, 111 F.Supp., at 444. All the more ought this to be so when the issue involves the defendant's access to highly material evidence through legitimate discovery procedures. Furthermore, Massachusetts does have substantial contacts with the transactions involved in the present litigation. See, Restatement (Second) Conflict of Laws § 139(2).

II. *Scope of the Privilege*

On April 9, 1979 we received a document entitled "Claim of Executive Privilege" dated March 9, 1979, and signed by Frederick William Kwasi Akuffo, Head of State and Chairman of the Supreme Military Council of Ghana. This document was later authenticated by Joseph Felli, Deputy Consul–General of the Republic of Ghana, on April 30, 1979. This "Claim of Executive Privilege" seems to satisfy all the requirements of a formal claim of privilege: it appears to be signed by an official having control over the relevant matters and represents a formal determination that the documents and information sought should be withheld in the public interest. United States v. Reynolds, 1953, 345 U.S. 1, 7–8, 73 S.Ct. 528, 97 L.Ed. 727; Duncan v. Cammell, Larid & Co. [1942], 1 All E.R. 587, 593 (H.L.); K. B. Hughes, Mass. Practice—Evidence, § 172; cf., Badu v. The Republic, [1974], 2 Ghana L.Rep. 361. However, the continuing validity of this formal claim is questionable after the recent coup and the execution of General Akuffo. Nevertheless we do not rest our decision on the absence of a properly executed claim since we may assume that the Ghanaian government would be prepared to cure this oversight, if it remains interested in pursuing this lawsuit.

Because the existence of a privilege depends on the reasons for preserving secrecy and the nature of the information to be kept secret, it is important at this stage to outline as precisely as possible the contours of the privilege asserted on behalf of the Republic of Ghana. The task is rendered quite difficult by the absence of any specification of the grounds for invoking the privilege in the April 9, 1979 document.

It is quite clear from the briefs submitted by GSC that the Republic of Ghana does not argue that disclosure of this sensitive information would endanger its national security or threaten its diplomatic relations. No one insists that the relevant documents contain military or diplomatic secrets, even though counsel is well aware that a claim of this type would strengthen considerably the submission supporting the existence of the privilege. Instead the Ghanaian government appears to support its position by three arguments: (1) that the command of the Ghanaian government that the Committee's sessions be held in camera creates an official privilege barring discovery of matters that occurred before the Committee, (2) that the overall "sensitivity" of the documents justifies their nondisclosure, and, most significantly, (3) that the confidentiality of the documents ought to be preserved in order to encourage open communications with and within the government. Id. The order of a foreign government that sessions be held in camera does not automatically create a privilege under American law, although it is a factor to consider before ordering disclosure, and no American privilege exists protecting "sensitive" documents in general without a more particularized showing as to the reason for their sensitivity. Therefore, the strongest basis for the privilege asserted in this case is found in the third argument, viz., encouraging unrestrained communication with and within government.

. . .

IV. *Merits of the Privilege Claim*

We turn now to the law of Massachusetts on the subject of government privilege. The mandate of Erie requires a creative search of Massachusetts and federal authority in order to predict what the Massachusetts Supreme Judicial Court would hold when presented with this issue. See, C.I.R. v. Bosch's Estate, 1967, 387 U.S. 456, 464–466, 87 S.Ct. 1776, 18 L.Ed.2d 886. Our task is complicated by the paucity of relevant Massachusetts caselaw.

Hughes's volume devoted to the Massachusetts law of evidence in the Massachusetts Practice Series recognizes the proposition that a governmental body, by commencing a civil action, waives any privilege of nondisclosure it might have had, at least regarding matters not immediately implicating military or diplomatic secrets. K. B. Hughes, Massachusetts Practice—Evidence, § 172, at 182, n. 10 (1961). As support Hughes offers only a federal case construing the discovery provisions of the Federal Rules of Civil Procedure. And federal authority is cited for the rule that military or diplomatic secrets are privileged. Hughes, supra, at 181. Moreover, Leach and Liacos in their Handbook of Massachusetts Evidence state the same waiver rule, except in the context of criminal proceedings. Leach, W. B., Liacos, P. J., Handbook of Massachusetts Evidence, 150–51 (4th ed. 1967). Significantly only federal cases are cited.

The few Massachusetts cases bearing on the privilege of a government to withhold information on grounds of public policy address the distinct, yet related, question of when and how the identity of a government informer must be revealed to a private party. E.g., Commonwealth v. Ennis, 1973, 1 Mass.App. 499, 301 N.E.2d 589, 590–592; Pihl v. Morris, 1946, 319 Mass. 577, 579–580, 66 N.E.2d 804; Wheeler v. Hager, 1936, 293 Mass. 534, 536, 200 N.E. 561; Commonwealth v. Congdon, 1928, 265 Mass. 166, 174–175, 165 N.E. 467; Attorney General v. Tufts, 1921, 239 Mass. 458, 491–492, 131 N.E. 573; Worthington v. Scribner, 1872, 109 Mass. 487. Although not entirely clear, it appears that the privilege of nondisclosure extends only to the identity of the informant and does not also include the content of his information, which almost always would be presented by the government at trial in any event. Even though the Massachusetts law on informant privilege is not particularly germane, it is significant that many of the cases cite federal precedent along with Massachusetts caselaw when discussing the nature of the privilege and the circumstances under which it is available. See, e.g., Ennis supra, 301 N.E.2d at 590–592; Wheeler, supra, 293 Mass. at 536, 200 N.E.2d 561; Congdon, supra, 265 Mass. at 174–175, 165 N.E.2d 467; Tufts, supra, 239 Mass. at 491, 131 N.E. 573. Because recognized Massachusetts treatise and case authority relies heavily on federal precedent in analyzing claims of government privilege, it is our opinion that the Massachusetts Supreme Judicial Court would look to federal law, as well as other authority, in those areas of government privilege for which there is no controlling Massachusetts law, and we adopt that approach for this case, especially since we find no indication that Massachusetts would refuse to follow the majority position.[1]

There are two different approaches to resolving the question of whether a privilege otherwise available to the government can be invoked against the defendant in civil litigation to which the government is a party-plaintiff. By far the great weight of authority holds that fairness to the defendant requires the government to make available all information relevant to the defense insofar as that information does not contain military or diplomatic secrets or involve the informant privilege. The theory is one of automatic waiver triggered by the government's instituting suit. ... Some cases appear to apply a balancing standard, weighing the defendant's need for the information against the importance of maintaining secrecy, or they at least appear to allow a wider range of exceptions to the waiver rule. ...

. . .

The plaintiff argues that even if GSC is bringing this lawsuit on behalf of the Republic of Ghana and even if a production order might be appropriate in cases involving only domestic parties, the variable of international comity at stake here should lead us at least to require that NEPCO exhaust direct discovery of the facts surrounding the Trefalcon transaction by deposition, interrogatory, or letters rogatory examination of witnesses and analysis of all available documents before ordering production of the material subject to the claim of privilege. We do not agree. International comity counsels restraint whenever a domestic court's action may cause the violation of another nation's law. Note, Foreign Nondisclosure Laws and Domestic Discovery Orders in Antitrust Litigation, 88 Yale L.J. 612, 614 (1979). The comity principle does not prevent domestic courts from issuing orders that conflict in some general sense with the rules of a foreign sovereign. If that were so, a foreign nation could bring suit against a domestic party in an American court and then unilaterally restrict the defendant's access to information and otherwise exert control over the course of the litigation.

An order to produce documents and testimony in the instant case would not necessarily cause a violation of Ghanaian law. Our order merely puts the Ghanaian government as plaintiff to a choice. If it wants to continue the litigation, it must make an exception to its nondisclosure order,the plaintiff almost certainly has the power to do so,or face sanctions for failure to comply with our discovery order. The plaintiff, of course, also has the option to dismiss the lawsuit voluntarily at any time. No party to this case is placed in the position of risking violation of foreign law by complying with a discovery order of this court.

We conclude that the Massachusetts Supreme Judicial Court, if confronted with this issue, would follow the majority position and hold that the Republic of Ghana, by instituting this civil action through the GSC, has waived any privilege it might have otherwise had to prevent disclosure of information sought by NEPCO that is material to NEPCO's defense. In so holding we have given some consideration to the impact on the Republic of Ghana resulting from disclosure. It appears to us that disclosure will not infringe seriously on any legally recognized privilege.

1. Primarily because there is a widely accepted analysis of the government privilege doctrine, because the issue is a relatively simple one, and because some analogous Massachusetts authority in the informant privilege context is available, we have chosen not to certify this question of state law to the Supreme Judicial Court of Massachusetts. See, Daigle v. Hall, 1 Cir.1977, 564 F.2d 884, 886. [The footnote is the court's. It has been renumbered.]

NOTES

1. Other cases include Samuelson v. Susen, 576 F.2d 546, 551 (3d Cir.1978); In re Westinghouse Electric Corporation Uranium Contracts Litigation, 76 F.R.D. 47 (W.D.Pa.1977); Union Planters National Bank v. ABC Records, Inc., 82 F.R.D. 472 (W.D.Tenn.1979). See Sterk, Testimonial Privileges: An Analysis of Horizontal Choice of Law Problems, 61 Minn.L.Rev. 461 (1977); Reese and Leiwant, Testimonial Privileges and Conflict of Laws, 41 L. and Contemp. Probs. 85 (1977); Seidelson, The Federal Rules of Evidence: Rule 501, Klaxon and the Constitution, 5 Hofstra L.Rev. 21 (1976).

2. It has been suggested that existing differences between state-state and state-federal rules of privilege which underlie the conflicts problems discussed in this section may begin to disappear as the states adopt new evidence rules, often under the influence of the Advisory Committee's draft of proposed Rules relating to privileges. J. B. Weinstein and M. A. Berger, 2 Weinstein's Evidence ¶ 501[06] at 501–65. In this connection it is significant also that the Uniform Rules of Evidence promulgated in 1974, with certain exceptions, follow the Advisory Committee's draft. For a listing of recent state statutes, see id. at ¶ 501[07].

3. There are times when the rules of evidence in another jurisdiction prevent witnesses and parties from freely testifying or submitting documents. Is this a practical problem in court administration or one calling for application of principles of comity? Note the approach taken in the principal case. Compare Societe Internationale v. Rogers, 357 U.S. 197 (1958) with Trade Development Bank v. The Continental Insurance Co., 469 F.2d 35 (2d Cir.1972), dealing with Swiss bank secrecy laws. See generally, Cole, The Hague Evidence Convention: Determining Its Applicability Through Comity Analysis, 38 Syracuse L.Rev. 717 (1987).

4. See In re Subpoena Issued to Mary Erato, 2 F.3d 11 (2d Cir.1993) for a case illustrating the complexities when a U.S. person is subpoenaed by a foreign jurisdiction, and her testimony is taken in United States pursuant to a Treaty arrangement. In the instant case, the witness claimed that a parent-child privilege under Dutch as well as U.S. law was applicable. The court rejected both claims as a ground for her not testifying.

*

INDEX

†